Patterns of Economic Change by State and Area

INCOME, EMPLOYMENT, AND GROSS DOMESTIC PRODUCT

Tenth Edition
2023

EDITED BY HANNAH ANDERSON KROG

Bernan Press

Lanham • Boulder • New York • London

Published by Bernan Press
An imprint of The Rowman & Littlefield Publishing Group, Inc.
4501 Forbes Boulevard, Suite 200, Lanham, Maryland 20706
www.rowman.com

86-90 Paul Street, London EC2A 4NE

ISBN 978-1-63671-417-2 (paperback) | ISBN 978-1-63671-418-9 (ebook)

Contents

PREFACE

Bernan Press is pleased to present the tenth edition of *Patterns of Economic Change by State and Area*. It is a special edition of *Business Statistics of the United States: Patterns of Economic Change*, bringing together measurements for regions, states, and metropolitan areas of some of the time trends that are displayed at the national level in *Business Statistics*.

This tenth edition of *Patterns of Economic Change* includes a new section, Part D, which includes data on consumer spending by region and state and regional price parities by MSA.

This volume also complements such titles as *State and Metropolitan Area Data Book* and *County and City Extra*. In contrast to their predominantly current and detailed cross-section data on states and metropolitan areas, this book contributes historical time-series measurements of key aggregates that show how the economies of regions, states, and metropolitan areas have responded over time to cyclical currents and long-term trends.

All these data are compiled and published by U.S. government professional statistical agencies—the Bureau of Economic Analysis and the Census Bureau. Specific references to publications and web sites, along with definitions of terms and other essential information, are detailed before each data series. With this information, the user can properly interpret and use the data and can update it, if desired, as the source agencies release new information over the course of the year.

The largest body of data included is "Part A: Personal Income and Employment by Region, State, and Metropolitan Statistical Area." These tables provide annual data, going as far back as 1960, for farm and nonfarm earnings of persons; payments to persons of dividends, interest, and rent; personal current transfer receipts, which are income sources such as Social Security; total personal income; population; per capita personal income and disposable (after income taxes) personal income (that is, total income divided by the size of the population); and the total number of jobs in the state or area. Using these data, the performance of any given state or area, whether at one moment in time or over a span of years, can be studied and compared and contrasted with that of the nation and other states or areas.

Even more comprehensive than personal income is gross domestic product (GDP), the measure of total U.S. economic activity, available and published here at the state level both in current dollar values and in the form of an index of quantities produced (that is to say, change in real output, corrected to remove the effects of inflation).

Moving from indicators of aggregate economic trends to effects on individuals and households, the third section shows data on the poverty rate and median household incomes (the income of the "typical" household in the exact middle of the income distribution), corrected for inflation.

Hannah Anderson Krog edited the past seven editions of *Patterns of Economic Change by State and Area*. Mary Meghan Ryan edited previous editions, and Cornelia J. Strawser provided assistance in planning the first edition.

PART A

PERSONAL INCOME AND EMPLOYMENT BY REGION, STATE, AND AREA

PART A: PERSONAL INCOME AND EMPLOYMENT BY REGION, STATE, AND AREA

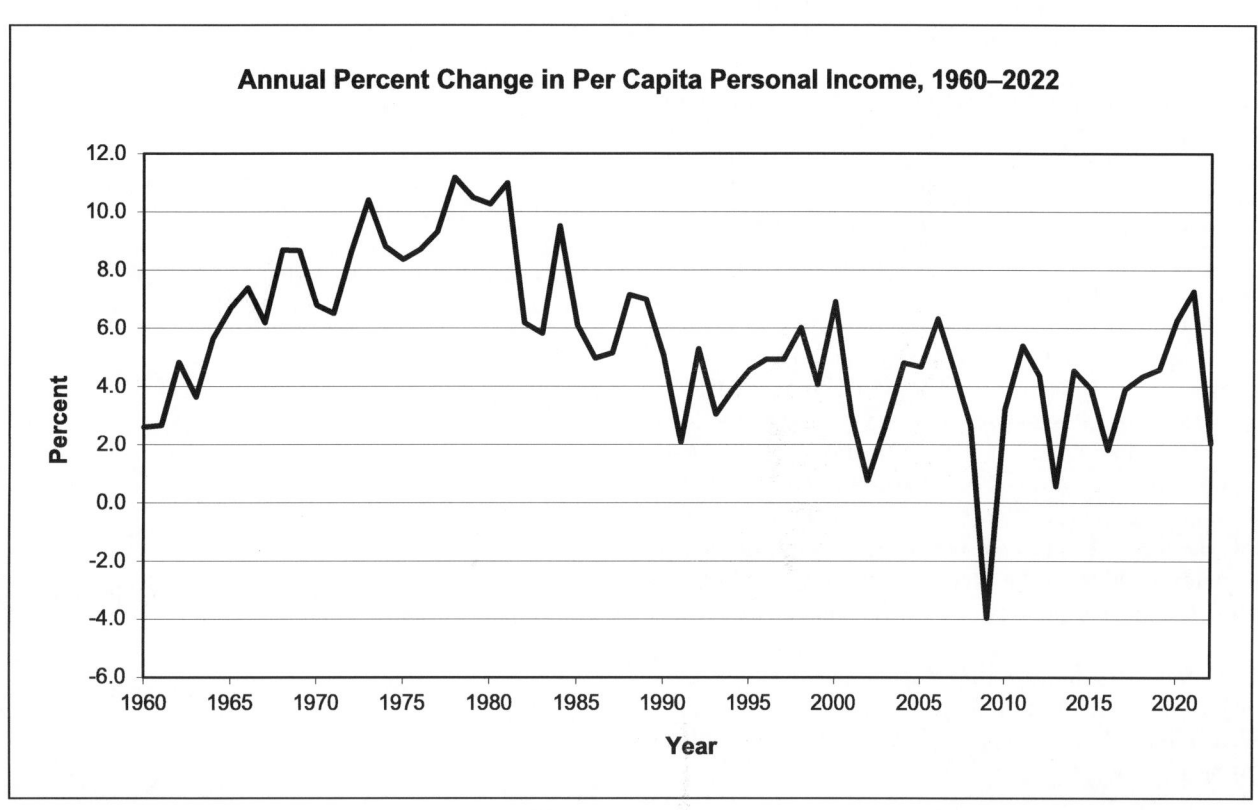

HIGHLIGHTS

- In 2022, nationwide per capita personal income increased 2.0 percent after increasing 7.3 percent in 2021 and 6.2 percent in 2020. From 1960 through 2020, per capita personal income only declined once, dropping from $40,904 in 2008 to $39,284 in 2009.

- Per capita personal income provides one measure of the affluence of the states and regions, and it varies widely. The District of Columbia had the highest per capita personal income in 2022, at $96,728, followed by Connecticut ($84,972), and Massachusetts ($84,945). Mississippi had the lowest per capita income at $46,248. The per capita personal income nationally was $65,423.

- Employment growth also differs significantly by state and metropolitan area. After a significant drop in employment during the height of the COVID-19 pandemic in 2020, total employment increased in all but 12 MSAs in 2021. The areas that saw the largest growth in employment from 2020-2021 were: Kahului-Wailuku-Lahaina, HI (9.6 percent), Elkhart-Goshen, IN (8.7 percent), Ocean City, NJ (7.9 percent), Atlantic City-Hammonton, NJ (7.4 percent), and Las Vegas-Henderson-Paradise, NV (6.6 percent). These are all popular tourist destinations that had seen large decreases in employment from 2019 to 2020. The areas with the largest drop in employment in 2021 were: Sebring-Avon Park, FL (1.6 percent), Kokomo, IN (1.5 percent), and Kankakee, IL (1.1 percent).

- The value of total earnings by place of work in the United States increased 8.1 percent in 2022, after also increasing 8.1 percent in 2021. These earnings include wages and salaries, supplements, and proprietors' income.

3

PART A NOTES AND DEFINITIONS: PERSONAL INCOME AND EMPLOYMENT BY REGION, STATE, AND METROPOLITAN AREA

Source: U.S. Department of Commerce, Bureau of Economic Analysis (BEA), https://www.bea.gov.

The personal income data set presented here provides a comprehensive, though not complete, measure of economic activity and purchasing power for individual states and smaller areas, with historical records that enable users to observe developments over extensive periods of time.

These data are stated in current-dollar terms not corrected for inflation, so that changes over time represent changes in both quantity and price. And they do not completely represent corporate economic activity: compensation of corporate employees is covered, as are corporate dividends received by individuals, but the remaining undistributed corporate profits—difficult to allocate to small geographical units—are not. See Part B that follows for measures of Gross Domestic Product by state, which provide a complete allocation to states of GDP in current dollars and include inflation-corrected indexes of growth in quantity terms.

The summary definitions of personal income and its components in the next section are taken from a BEA press release. In a following section, further detail and explanation of the concepts is provided.

BEA Definitions

Personal income is the income received by persons from all sources. Personal income is the sum of net earnings by place of residence, property income, and personal current transfer receipts. **Property income** is rental income of persons, personal dividend income, and personal interest income. **Net earnings** is earnings by place of work (the sum of wage and salary disbursements, supplements to wages and salaries, and proprietors' income) less contributions for government social insurance, plus an adjustment to convert earnings by place of work to a place-of-residence basis. Personal income is measured before the deduction of personal income taxes and other personal taxes and is reported in current dollars (no adjustment is made for price changes).

The estimate of personal income in the United States is derived as the sum of the state estimates and the estimate for the District of Columbia; it differs from the estimate of personal income in the national income and product accounts (NIPAs) because of differences in coverage, in the methodologies used to prepare the estimates, and in the timing of the availability of source data.

BEA groups all 50 states and the District of Columbia into eight distinct regions for purposes of data collecting and analyses:

New England (Connecticut, Maine, Massachusetts, New Hampshire, Rhode Island, and Vermont);

Mideast (Delaware, District of Columbia, Maryland, New Jersey, New York, and Pennsylvania);

Great Lakes (Illinois, Indiana, Michigan, Ohio, and Wisconsin);

Plains (Iowa, Kansas, Minnesota, Missouri, Nebraska, North Dakota, and South Dakota);

Southeast (Alabama, Arkansas, Florida, Georgia, Kentucky, Louisiana, Mississippi, North Carolina, South Carolina, Tennessee, Virginia, and West Virginia);

Southwest (Arizona, New Mexico, Oklahoma, and Texas);

Rocky Mountain (Colorado, Idaho, Montana, Utah, and Wyoming); and

Far West (Alaska, California, Hawaii, Nevada, Oregon, and Washington).

State personal income statistics provide a framework for analyzing current economic conditions in each state and can serve as a basis for decision-making. For example:

- Federal government agencies use the statistics as a basis for allocating funds and determining matching grants to states. The statistics are also used in forecasting models to project energy and water use.

- State governments use the statistics to project tax revenues and the need for public services.

- Academic regional economists use the statistics for applied research.

- Businesses, trade associations, and labor organizations use the statistics for market research.

BEA's national, international, regional, and industry estimates; the Survey of Current Business; and BEA news releases are available without charge at www.bea.gov.

By visiting the site, you can also subscribe to receive free e-mail summaries of BEA releases and announcements.

More about Income Concepts

For the sake of simplicity, the following definitions and clarifications are written in terms of states, but all statements about "states" apply equally to regions and metropolitan areas.

The sum of state personal incomes for the United States (50 states and the District of Columbia) is somewhat smaller than U.S. personal income as shown in the national income and product accounts (NIPAs), due to slightly different definitions. The national total of the state estimates consists only of the income earned by persons who live in the United States and of foreign residents who work in the United States. The measure of personal income in the NIPAs is broader. It includes the earnings of federal civilian and military personnel stationed abroad and of U.S. residents on foreign assignment for less than a year. It also includes the investment income received by federal retirement plans for federal workers stationed abroad. NIPA personal income includes all income earned by U.S. citizens living abroad for less than a year; state personal income excludes the portion earned while the individual lives abroad. Earnings of foreign residents are included in the NIPAs only if they live and work in the United States for a year or more; state personal income, on the other hand, includes income paid to foreign nationals working in the United States regardless of length of residency. There are also statistical differences that reflect different timing of the availability of source data.

As in the NIPAs, personal income is defined to exclude capital gains.

Earnings by place of work consists of payments, to persons who work in the state, of wages and salaries; all supplements to wages and salaries (including employer contributions for government social insurance and all other benefits); and farm and nonfarm proprietors' income. Proprietor's income includes inventory valuation and capital consumption adjustments.

Contributions for government social insurance, which is subtracted from total earnings, includes both the employer and the employee contributions, on behalf of persons working in the state, for Social Security, Medicare, unemployment insurance, and other government social insurance, but does not include contributions to government employee retirement plans. Hence, personal income is defined as net of all contributions for government social insurance, which

are commonly referred to as "Social Security taxes." Personal income is not net of other taxes on wages or other income such as Federal and state income taxes. These taxes are subtracted, however, to yield *"disposable personal income."*

Adjustment for residence. BEA adjusts earnings by place of work to a place-of-residence basis, to account for interstate and international commuting. The difference between earnings by place of residence and earnings by place of work is shown in the "Adjustment for residence" column. This adjustment is a net figure, equaling income received by state residents from employment outside the state minus income paid to persons residing outside the state but working in the state.

The effect of interstate commuting can be seen in its most extreme form in the District of Columbia. Its large negative adjustment for residence says that roughly half of total earnings by people working there are paid to persons living outside D.C. Compare with Maryland and Virginia, which have substantial positive adjustments, representing income flowing from the District of Columbia and other employment sources outside the state. There is also a large negative adjustment for New York, associated with positive adjustments for New Jersey and Connecticut.

Dividends, interest, and rent. The rental income component of personal income, like that in the NIPAs, includes imputed rent on owner-occupied homes, net of capital consumption with capital consumption adjustment.

Personal current transfer receipts are aggregates for state residents of benefits from Social Security, Medicare, Medicaid, unemployment insurance, veterans' benefits, and other government benefits including the earned income credit. It does not include payments from government employee retirement plans, which are accounted for in supplements to wages and salaries.

It should be noted that in both the personal income and the NIPA accounts, the value of Medicare and Medicaid spending, even though in practice it is usually paid directly from the government to the health care provider, is treated as if it were cash income to the consumer, which is then expended in personal consumption expenditures.

Population is the U.S. Census Bureau estimate for the *middle* of the year. Note that because Hurricane Katrina occurred in August 2005, the population decline in Louisiana caused by that event does not appear until the entry for 2006.

Total employment is the total number of jobs, full-time plus part-time; each job that any person holds is counted at full weight. The employment estimates are on a place-of-work basis. Both wage and salary employment and self-employment are included. The main source for the wage and salary employment estimates is Bureau of Labor Statistics (BLS) estimates from unemployment insurance data (the ES-202 data), which also provides benchmarks for the widely followed BLS payroll employment measures. Self-employment is estimated mainly from individual and partnership federal income tax returns. Therefore, this definition of employment is broader than BLS "total nonfarm payroll employment."

This concept of employment also differs from the concept of employment in the Current Population Survey (CPS), another BLS monthly survey, which is derived from a monthly count of persons employed; any individual will appear only once in the CPS in a given month, no matter how many different jobs he or she might hold. In addition, a self-employed individual who files more than one Schedule C income-tax filing will be counted more than once in the state figures. Finally, the state figures include members of the armed forces, who are not covered in the CPS. Due to these differences and other possible reporting inconsistencies, the BEA employment estimates are different from, and usually larger than, state employment estimates from the CPS.

The employment estimates correspond closely in coverage to the earnings estimates by place of work. However, the earnings estimates include the income of limited partnerships and of tax-exempt cooperatives, for which there are no corresponding employment estimates.

Per capita income is total income divided by the state's midyear population. This is an important tool for "scaling" income data to the size of the state, so that meaningful comparisons of economic performance among states can be made. Per capita income provides a useful gauge of economic strength, purchasing power, and fiscal capacity.

Users should not, however, assume that per capita income well represents the income of a typical state resident. Per capita incomes are averages—"means" in the technical language of statistics. Income of a typical person is better represented by the "median," which is the income of a person at the middle of the income distribution; half the population has higher income and half has lower. Where income is distributed so unequally that a relatively small number of persons have extremely high incomes, the mean will be higher than the median; and if the income distribution is becoming more unequal, the mean will rise faster than the median. Both of these conditions have been present for the U.S. economy as a whole in recent decades. Median household (not personal) incomes by state are presented in Part C.

UNITED STATES

Personal Income and Employment by Region and State: United States

(Millions of dollars, except as noted.)

Year	Personal income, total	Derivation of personal income								Per capita (dollars)		Population (thousands)	Total employment (thousands)
		Earnings by place of work			Less: Contributions for government social insurance	Plus: Adjustment for residence	Equals: Net earnings by place of residence	Plus: Dividends, interest, and rent	Plus: Personal current transfer receipts	Personal income	Disposable personal income		
		Nonfarm	Farm	Total									
1960	417,700	334,492	13,734	348,226	16,358	-260	331,608	60,352	25,740	2,321	2,066	179,972	...
1961	436,047	345,444	14,467	359,911	16,916	-250	342,745	63,852	29,450	2,383	2,126	182,976	...
1962	464,000	368,896	14,526	383,422	19,023	-202	364,197	69,411	30,392	2,498	2,221	185,739	...
1963	487,780	388,214	14,414	402,628	21,559	-173	380,896	74,675	32,209	2,589	2,300	188,434	...
1964	522,633	417,196	13,227	430,423	22,258	-170	407,995	81,134	33,504	2,735	2,463	191,085	...
1965	564,444	448,173	15,576	463,749	23,278	-111	440,360	87,906	36,178	2,918	2,620	193,460	...
1966	612,713	493,890	16,631	510,521	31,136	-99	479,286	93,810	39,617	3,134	2,796	195,499	...
1967	656,828	528,209	15,259	543,468	34,600	-96	508,772	100,042	48,014	3,328	2,959	197,375	...
1968	720,877	580,338	15,420	595,758	38,392	-119	557,247	107,536	56,094	3,617	3,183	199,312	...
1969	791,229	636,235	17,430	653,665	43,791	-107	609,767	119,140	62,322	3,931	3,415	201,298	91,053
1970	855,525	675,692	17,660	693,352	46,012	-112	647,228	133,564	74,733	4,198	3,695	203,799	91,278
1971	924,613	723,952	18,142	742,094	50,859	-122	691,113	145,252	88,248	4,471	3,981	206,818	91,581
1972	1,016,408	797,699	21,947	819,646	58,897	-145	760,604	157,674	98,130	4,857	4,269	209,275	94,312
1973	1,133,468	884,089	34,875	918,964	75,183	-153	843,628	176,992	112,848	5,363	4,739	211,349	98,428
1974	1,244,912	963,812	30,097	993,909	84,872	-163	908,874	202,399	133,639	5,836	5,130	213,334	100,112
1975	1,362,505	1,030,360	29,132	1,059,492	88,974	-199	970,319	221,762	170,424	6,324	5,641	215,457	98,901
1976	1,495,704	1,148,053	25,218	1,173,271	100,987	-211	1,072,073	238,786	184,845	6,875	6,083	217,554	101,591
1977	1,651,632	1,279,276	24,491	1,303,767	112,699	-235	1,190,833	265,688	195,111	7,516	6,618	219,761	105,042
1978	1,855,849	1,447,696	28,384	1,476,080	130,827	-257	1,344,996	300,292	210,561	8,356	7,324	222,098	109,687
1979	2,073,257	1,618,142	30,221	1,648,363	152,273	-231	1,495,859	341,022	236,376	9,232	8,038	224,569	113,147
1980	2,313,160	1,763,859	20,738	1,784,597	165,670	-255	1,618,672	413,614	280,874	10,180	8,865	227,225	113,983
1981	2,592,915	1,933,697	27,476	1,961,173	195,066	-208	1,765,899	507,254	319,762	11,300	9,797	229,466	114,914
1982	2,779,794	2,028,963	24,766	2,053,729	208,173	-255	1,845,301	578,352	356,141	11,999	10,472	231,664	114,163
1983	2,968,676	2,170,568	17,450	2,188,018	225,143	-212	1,962,663	621,342	384,671	12,698	11,192	233,792	115,646
1984	3,279,488	2,400,243	32,159	2,432,402	256,550	-254	2,175,598	702,658	401,232	13,906	12,308	235,825	120,528
1985	3,510,471	2,583,536	32,255	2,615,791	280,379	-257	2,335,155	749,555	425,761	14,755	13,003	237,924	123,797
1986	3,719,647	2,753,507	33,394	2,786,901	302,389	228	2,484,740	783,196	451,711	15,490	13,671	240,133	126,232
1987	3,946,593	2,956,412	39,588	2,996,000	322,006	259	2,674,253	804,246	468,094	16,289	14,273	242,289	129,548
1988	4,267,813	3,220,748	39,231	3,259,979	360,285	226	2,899,920	870,483	497,410	17,455	15,391	244,499	133,564
1989	4,609,667	3,420,858	46,169	3,467,027	384,001	236	3,083,262	982,219	544,186	18,676	16,381	246,819	136,178
1990	4,897,821	3,631,845	47,615	3,679,460	408,676	313	3,271,097	1,029,493	597,231	19,621	17,244	249,623	138,331
1991	5,067,291	3,746,947	42,481	3,789,428	428,555	367	3,361,240	1,038,003	668,048	20,030	17,708	252,981	137,613
1992	5,409,920	4,008,307	50,716	4,059,023	453,768	478	3,605,733	1,056,248	747,939	21,090	18,705	256,514	138,166
1993	5,648,732	4,189,837	47,600	4,237,437	476,331	493	3,761,599	1,094,227	792,906	21,733	19,240	259,919	140,774
1994	5,940,128	4,405,940	51,008	4,456,948	507,188	533	3,950,293	1,160,955	828,880	22,575	19,945	263,126	144,197
1995	6,286,143	4,635,040	39,809	4,674,849	531,874	703	4,143,678	1,259,091	883,374	23,607	20,800	266,278	147,916
1996	6,673,186	4,900,819	55,361	4,956,180	554,150	675	4,402,705	1,341,353	929,128	24,771	21,667	269,394	151,056
1997	7,086,935	5,236,736	51,311	5,288,047	586,295	672	4,702,424	1,429,714	954,797	25,993	22,559	272,647	154,541
1998	7,601,594	5,658,042	48,972	5,707,014	623,685	755	5,084,084	1,533,632	983,878	27,557	23,818	275,854	158,481
1999	8,001,563	6,048,481	49,561	6,098,042	660,310	2,515	5,440,247	1,535,172	1,026,144	28,675	24,694	279,040	161,531
2000	8,650,325	6,546,103	52,640	6,598,743	704,849	2,587	5,896,481	1,666,564	1,087,280	30,657	26,279	282,162	165,371
2001	9,001,839	6,810,126	55,165	6,865,291	732,117	2,692	6,135,866	1,673,408	1,192,565	31,589	27,245	284,969	165,522
2002	9,155,663	6,957,749	43,381	7,001,130	750,339	2,657	6,253,448	1,617,025	1,285,190	31,832	28,177	287,625	165,095
2003	9,480,901	7,184,365	59,300	7,243,665	777,956	2,679	6,468,388	1,665,285	1,347,228	32,681	29,225	290,108	165,922
2004	10,028,781	7,598,827	76,306	7,675,133	827,824	2,659	6,849,968	1,757,607	1,421,206	34,251	30,673	292,805	168,840
2005	10,593,946	7,967,309	72,339	8,039,648	871,945	2,614	7,170,317	1,906,918	1,516,711	35,849	31,750	295,517	172,338
2006	11,372,589	8,463,962	55,815	8,519,777	921,128	2,617	7,601,266	2,157,509	1,613,814	38,114	33,572	298,380	175,869
2007	12,002,204	8,798,362	68,422	8,866,784	960,003	2,596	7,909,377	2,364,762	1,728,065	39,844	34,895	301,231	179,544
2008	12,438,527	8,943,677	69,781	9,013,458	986,875	2,649	8,029,232	2,454,213	1,955,082	40,904	35,952	304,094	179,214
2009	12,051,307	8,630,392	58,054	8,688,446	962,827	3,019	7,728,638	2,175,976	2,146,693	39,284	35,533	306,772	173,637
2010	12,541,995	8,955,253	67,945	9,023,198	982,045	3,068	8,044,221	2,172,657	2,325,117	40,546	36,550	309,326	172,902
2011	13,315,478	9,349,989	93,539	9,443,528	915,062	3,201	8,531,667	2,425,157	2,358,654	42,735	38,076	311,580	176,092
2012	13,998,383	9,808,544	93,338	9,901,882	948,953	3,411	8,956,340	2,679,055	2,362,988	44,599	39,796	313,874	178,980
2013	14,175,503	10,105,775	125,703	10,231,478	1,102,460	3,651	9,132,669	2,618,537	2,424,297	44,851	39,554	316,058	182,325
2014	14,969,527	10,583,612	104,789	10,688,401	1,151,698	3,438	9,540,141	2,887,870	2,541,516	46,887	41,304	319,270	186,234
2015	15,681,233	11,024,631	90,912	11,115,543	1,202,909	3,403	9,916,037	3,079,826	2,685,370	48,725	42,705	321,829	190,326
2016	16,092,713	11,313,066	71,704	11,384,770	1,237,020	3,062	10,150,812	3,164,918	2,776,983	49,613	43,581	324,368	193,426
2017	16,837,337	11,848,453	77,008	11,925,461	1,297,292	2,980	10,631,149	3,350,543	2,855,645	51,550	45,282	326,623	196,394
2018	17,671,054	12,449,176	64,396	12,513,572	1,359,345	3,451	11,157,678	3,536,824	2,976,552	53,786	47,477	328,542	200,281
2019	18,575,467	12,971,316	66,747	13,038,063	1,422,196	3,438	11,619,305	3,811,394	3,144,768	56,250	49,599	330,233	201,648
2020	19,812,171	13,134,492	80,583	13,215,075	1,447,574	3,815	11,771,316	3,809,734	4,231,121	59,763	53,023	331,512	195,302
2021	21,288,709	14,186,669	97,905	14,284,574	1,538,417	3,952	12,750,109	3,921,286	4,617,314	64,117	56,107	332,032	201,143
2022	21,804,788	15,302,189	141,200	15,443,389	1,673,937	3,804	13,773,257	4,120,785	3,910,746	65,423	55,832	333,288	...

... = Not available.

REGION

Personal Income and Employment by Region and State: Far West

(Millions of dollars, except as noted.)

Year	Personal income, total	Derivation of personal income								Per capita (dollars)		Population (thousands)	Total employment (thousands)
		Earnings by place of work			Less: Contributions for government social insurance	Plus: Adjustment for residence	Equals: Net earnings by place of residence	Plus: Dividends, interest, and rent	Plus: Personal current transfer receipts	Personal income	Disposable personal income		
		Nonfarm	Farm	Total									
1960	61,279	48,132	1,965	50,097	2,357	-1	47,739	10,027	3,513	2,829	2,513	21,659	...
1961	64,770	50,820	1,866	52,687	2,496	-1	50,189	10,531	4,049	2,894	2,574	22,378	...
1962	69,808	55,159	1,975	57,134	2,978	-3	54,153	11,406	4,250	3,020	2,683	23,114	...
1963	74,242	58,967	1,914	60,881	3,461	-5	57,415	12,187	4,640	3,118	2,768	23,811	...
1964	80,068	63,360	2,018	65,379	3,582	-6	61,791	13,285	4,992	3,283	2,962	24,389	...
1965	85,799	67,585	2,009	69,594	3,732	-7	65,855	14,470	5,474	3,445	3,109	24,908	...
1966	93,565	74,686	2,259	76,945	4,926	-8	72,010	15,559	5,996	3,697	3,315	25,311	...
1967	100,755	80,087	2,125	82,211	5,452	-10	76,750	16,635	7,370	3,908	3,493	25,779	...
1968	110,716	88,310	2,383	90,692	6,123	-12	84,558	17,662	8,496	4,234	3,744	26,151	...
1969	121,725	96,417	2,481	98,898	6,626	-149	92,124	19,909	9,693	4,570	4,006	26,635	12,295
1970	131,576	101,828	2,440	104,267	6,894	-178	97,195	22,413	11,967	4,855	4,327	27,101	12,313
1971	140,637	107,701	2,470	110,171	7,515	-203	102,453	24,340	13,844	5,101	4,596	27,570	12,300
1972	154,353	118,742	3,114	121,855	8,729	-211	112,916	26,464	14,973	5,529	4,905	27,918	12,742
1973	170,589	131,079	4,254	135,333	11,058	-212	124,063	29,675	16,852	6,022	5,377	28,328	13,405
1974	191,194	144,766	5,389	150,155	12,600	-293	137,262	34,000	19,933	6,638	5,906	28,801	13,865
1975	212,899	159,546	4,811	164,358	13,656	-482	150,220	37,624	25,054	7,255	6,529	29,346	14,103
1976	236,675	179,946	4,813	184,759	15,727	-594	168,438	40,593	27,644	7,908	7,050	29,929	14,625
1977	262,401	201,508	4,684	206,192	17,862	-399	187,931	45,093	29,377	8,588	7,607	30,553	15,287
1978	298,986	231,858	4,757	236,615	21,059	-318	215,237	51,947	31,801	9,557	8,410	31,285	16,248
1979	339,286	263,608	5,909	269,516	25,060	-37	244,419	59,781	35,087	10,614	9,275	31,965	17,133
1980	385,032	291,682	7,355	299,037	27,354	-123	271,560	72,341	41,131	11,746	10,266	32,780	17,523
1981	430,716	320,814	5,852	326,665	32,526	-175	293,964	88,466	48,287	12,883	11,271	33,434	17,693
1982	460,617	338,206	5,929	344,136	34,875	-211	309,050	97,938	53,628	13,513	11,931	34,086	17,564
1983	496,483	364,642	5,969	370,611	38,249	-236	332,125	107,130	57,228	14,301	12,681	34,716	17,989
1984	547,058	403,662	6,614	410,276	43,877	-307	366,091	121,175	59,792	15,488	13,740	35,321	18,767
1985	588,982	437,078	6,383	443,461	48,006	-365	395,091	129,313	64,578	16,344	14,425	36,037	19,392
1986	630,292	471,785	7,290	479,075	52,251	-379	426,446	134,801	69,046	17,120	15,122	36,815	19,959
1987	675,313	513,537	8,487	522,024	56,781	-450	464,793	138,414	72,106	17,941	15,688	37,641	20,793
1988	734,929	563,551	8,996	572,547	64,107	-540	507,900	149,654	77,375	19,068	16,808	38,542	21,790
1989	796,500	602,481	9,003	611,484	69,060	-636	541,789	169,761	84,950	20,147	17,581	39,534	22,453
1990	857,643	649,865	9,490	659,355	74,731	-748	583,876	180,256	93,511	21,119	18,462	40,610	23,122
1991	894,209	677,754	8,641	686,395	78,399	-745	607,251	182,718	104,240	21,585	19,044	41,428	23,124
1992	948,870	716,768	9,397	726,165	82,247	-732	643,186	186,390	119,293	22,471	19,960	42,226	22,825
1993	980,448	735,050	10,709	745,759	84,534	-724	660,501	193,461	126,487	22,909	20,356	42,798	22,934
1994	1,018,477	762,545	10,055	772,600	88,381	-750	683,468	204,678	130,331	23,537	20,882	43,271	23,380
1995	1,073,913	797,148	9,667	806,815	91,651	-782	714,382	221,734	137,797	24,549	21,689	43,745	23,938
1996	1,143,491	846,798	11,191	857,989	95,355	-851	761,782	236,934	144,775	25,804	22,567	44,314	24,580
1997	1,218,605	910,066	11,489	921,555	101,059	-928	819,568	252,213	146,824	27,048	23,448	45,054	25,149
1998	1,322,184	995,053	11,103	1,006,155	108,701	-1,017	896,437	271,241	154,506	28,870	24,872	45,798	26,089
1999	1,413,243	1,078,866	11,608	1,090,475	116,479	-1,087	972,909	277,337	162,998	30,389	25,835	46,506	26,659
2000	1,546,581	1,193,146	11,786	1,204,932	127,413	-1,188	1,076,331	299,400	170,850	32,775	27,454	47,188	27,241
2001	1,598,370	1,230,263	11,209	1,241,472	132,590	-1,266	1,107,616	300,841	189,913	33,375	28,500	47,891	27,369
2002	1,623,162	1,254,999	11,813	1,266,813	136,542	-1,341	1,128,930	289,889	204,343	33,472	29,502	48,493	27,369
2003	1,695,736	1,308,013	13,773	1,321,786	143,078	-1,503	1,177,205	303,635	214,897	34,569	30,762	49,053	27,604
2004	1,804,870	1,396,614	16,077	1,412,691	155,412	-1,716	1,255,563	325,342	223,964	36,387	32,412	49,602	28,155
2005	1,911,241	1,471,392	15,895	1,487,288	163,406	-1,889	1,321,993	353,472	235,776	38,156	33,513	50,090	28,787
2006	2,064,708	1,566,031	13,861	1,579,893	170,460	-1,958	1,407,475	404,066	253,167	40,828	35,707	50,571	29,438
2007	2,170,692	1,618,839	16,867	1,635,707	174,771	-2,092	1,458,844	441,604	270,244	42,536	37,019	51,031	30,069
2008	2,216,349	1,614,974	15,027	1,630,002	177,537	-2,233	1,450,232	457,499	308,618	42,945	37,566	51,609	29,819
2009	2,138,293	1,551,506	16,144	1,567,650	172,567	-2,097	1,392,986	403,423	341,883	40,989	36,930	52,168	28,628
2010	2,231,422	1,612,040	17,169	1,629,209	174,538	-2,014	1,452,657	400,948	377,817	42,354	37,963	52,685	28,335
2011	2,365,274	1,689,935	20,268	1,710,203	164,053	-1,917	1,544,233	440,660	380,381	44,484	39,380	53,172	28,789
2012	2,517,584	1,791,267	22,597	1,813,865	170,690	-1,973	1,641,201	493,465	382,917	46,926	41,526	53,651	29,624
2013	2,558,464	1,855,098	25,738	1,880,836	199,269	-1,830	1,679,737	482,172	396,556	47,273	41,218	54,121	30,462
2014	2,732,124	1,953,160	27,534	1,980,694	210,379	-2,000	1,768,315	536,743	427,066	49,992	43,476	54,651	31,367
2015	2,924,970	2,075,564	28,149	2,103,713	222,552	-2,123	1,879,038	588,931	457,000	52,981	45,737	55,208	32,305
2016	3,053,983	2,169,905	24,515	2,194,420	231,825	-2,441	1,960,154	618,671	475,158	54,791	47,324	55,738	33,039
2017	3,201,003	2,291,037	25,431	2,316,469	244,852	-2,695	2,068,921	655,176	476,905	56,984	49,271	56,174	33,655
2018	3,367,660	2,422,613	20,309	2,442,922	259,093	-2,812	2,181,017	685,226	501,417	59,628	51,559	56,477	34,414
2019	3,566,195	2,547,526	20,960	2,568,486	273,398	-3,277	2,291,811	740,140	534,244	62,936	54,492	56,663	34,649
2020	3,861,509	2,610,168	22,856	2,633,024	279,159	-3,096	2,350,769	741,881	768,859	68,020	59,241	56,770	33,105
2021	4,164,036	2,864,325	18,069	2,882,394	300,621	-3,741	2,578,031	762,868	823,137	73,742	62,868	56,468	34,191
2022	4,207,381	3,025,726	24,255	3,049,981	319,986	-3,859	2,726,135	803,586	677,660	74,590	61,893	56,407	...

... = Not available.

Personal Income and Employment by Area: Great Lakes

(Millions of dollars, except as noted.)

Year	Personal income, total	Derivation of personal income									Per capita (dollars)		Population (thousands)	Total employment (thousands)
		Earnings by place of work			Less: Contributions for government social insurance	Plus: Adjustment for residence	Equals: Net earnings by place of residence	Plus: Dividends, interest, and rent	Plus: Personal current transfer receipts		Personal income	Disposable personal income		
		Nonfarm	Farm	Total										
1960	88,934	73,742	2,014	75,757	3,657	-123	71,977	11,699	5,257		2,451	2,173	36,290	...
1961	91,139	73,915	2,446	76,361	3,618	-111	72,632	12,377	6,130		2,489	2,220	36,616	...
1962	96,685	78,906	2,352	81,259	4,044	-116	77,099	13,432	6,154		2,618	2,323	36,927	...
1963	101,231	82,828	2,365	85,193	4,562	-114	80,516	14,371	6,343		2,710	2,401	37,357	...
1964	108,770	89,549	2,045	91,594	4,763	-122	86,710	15,586	6,474		2,872	2,578	37,868	...
1965	118,706	97,360	2,631	99,992	4,947	-133	94,912	16,859	6,935		3,091	2,763	38,405	...
1966	129,096	107,454	2,972	110,426	6,742	-146	103,538	18,028	7,529		3,314	2,943	38,951	...
1967	135,847	112,657	2,535	115,192	7,274	-134	107,784	19,054	9,009		3,453	3,056	39,347	...
1968	148,258	123,088	2,431	125,519	7,989	-144	117,386	20,459	10,413		3,740	3,272	39,645	...
1969	162,017	134,868	2,870	137,737	9,311	262	128,688	21,994	11,334		4,060	3,495	39,904	17,785
1970	170,705	139,623	2,518	142,141	9,503	246	132,884	24,274	13,548		4,234	3,688	40,320	17,630
1971	183,695	148,678	2,899	151,577	10,424	319	141,472	26,120	16,102		4,522	3,992	40,622	17,549
1972	200,708	163,199	3,168	166,367	12,095	366	154,638	28,097	17,972		4,916	4,279	40,824	17,933
1973	224,429	182,057	5,213	187,271	15,631	417	172,057	31,434	20,938		5,481	4,794	40,947	18,710
1974	243,766	195,283	4,661	199,944	17,400	512	183,056	35,778	24,932		5,940	5,177	41,037	18,911
1975	263,253	203,397	5,818	209,215	17,669	587	192,134	39,088	32,031		6,404	5,658	41,105	18,399
1976	289,628	228,236	4,816	233,052	20,242	719	213,529	41,851	34,248		7,032	6,149	41,187	18,891
1977	321,434	256,353	4,818	261,171	22,758	899	239,311	46,353	35,769		7,773	6,740	41,353	19,508
1978	356,578	287,356	4,506	291,861	26,286	1,105	266,680	51,456	38,442		8,590	7,432	41,510	20,190
1979	392,788	314,968	5,223	320,191	29,932	1,269	291,528	57,795	43,465		9,440	8,131	41,611	20,491
1980	425,781	327,614	3,317	330,931	30,928	1,532	301,535	69,642	54,603		10,212	8,856	41,694	19,978
1981	464,804	349,522	3,683	353,205	35,439	1,340	319,107	84,994	60,703		11,160	9,639	41,648	19,795
1982	486,801	353,935	2,926	356,861	36,377	1,215	321,698	96,990	68,113		11,732	10,270	41,492	19,248
1983	512,203	374,045	-119	373,926	38,845	1,209	336,290	103,144	72,769		12,382	10,880	41,366	19,265
1984	565,478	413,823	4,409	418,232	44,260	1,335	375,307	115,639	74,532		13,661	12,059	41,393	20,028
1985	600,324	442,954	4,964	447,918	48,192	1,397	401,123	120,947	78,253		14,494	12,746	41,418	20,492
1986	632,500	470,521	4,488	475,008	51,647	1,472	424,833	125,733	81,934		15,257	13,439	41,455	20,934
1987	664,886	500,363	5,012	505,375	54,318	1,528	452,585	128,117	84,183		15,987	13,986	41,590	21,516
1988	712,816	543,351	3,363	546,714	60,614	1,647	487,747	137,155	87,914		17,085	15,014	41,721	22,070
1989	767,370	576,171	7,032	583,202	64,605	1,665	520,262	152,796	94,311		18,326	16,028	41,873	22,556
1990	810,354	608,229	6,005	614,234	68,950	1,923	547,206	160,090	103,058		19,252	16,866	42,091	22,928
1991	830,741	625,096	3,606	628,702	72,225	1,908	558,385	160,089	112,267		19,549	17,197	42,496	22,845
1992	890,729	670,955	6,123	677,078	76,663	2,021	602,436	164,296	123,996		20,762	18,346	42,903	22,971
1993	930,988	704,234	5,204	709,438	81,158	2,094	630,373	170,302	130,313		21,513	18,930	43,275	23,359
1994	987,886	748,980	6,083	755,063	87,642	2,271	669,692	183,830	134,363		22,663	19,879	43,590	24,060
1995	1,041,549	786,952	3,336	790,289	92,242	2,430	700,477	199,416	141,656		23,713	20,743	43,924	24,713
1996	1,099,479	824,326	6,936	831,263	95,305	2,677	738,635	212,662	148,182		24,853	21,609	44,239	25,105
1997	1,161,499	872,470	6,589	879,059	99,864	2,981	782,176	226,237	153,085		26,105	22,582	44,494	25,513
1998	1,234,435	933,009	5,575	938,584	104,854	3,020	836,750	242,145	155,539		27,599	23,765	44,728	25,953
1999	1,285,398	988,745	4,553	993,298	110,196	3,449	886,550	237,189	161,659		28,584	24,617	44,969	26,333
2000	1,370,277	1,049,572	5,392	1,054,964	114,559	3,792	944,197	254,851	171,229		30,305	26,140	45,216	26,830
2001	1,411,718	1,078,110	5,655	1,083,765	116,267	4,089	971,587	252,256	187,876		31,094	26,962	45,402	26,554
2002	1,427,691	1,097,558	3,724	1,101,283	117,883	4,145	987,545	240,495	199,651		31,343	27,725	45,550	26,272
2003	1,464,134	1,121,525	6,154	1,127,679	121,240	4,423	1,010,861	244,929	208,344		32,032	28,642	45,708	26,220
2004	1,522,011	1,164,163	10,141	1,174,304	127,570	4,927	1,051,660	253,214	217,137		33,200	29,783	45,844	26,440
2005	1,573,034	1,194,815	6,817	1,201,632	132,744	5,347	1,074,234	265,282	233,517		34,234	30,484	45,949	26,682
2006	1,654,970	1,242,517	6,502	1,249,019	138,350	5,657	1,116,326	293,182	245,462		35,922	31,832	46,072	26,875
2007	1,728,248	1,275,325	9,229	1,284,554	142,423	5,774	1,147,905	314,899	265,444		37,418	32,989	46,188	27,135
2008	1,783,644	1,283,795	11,362	1,295,157	145,147	6,360	1,156,370	328,482	298,791		38,544	34,078	46,275	26,872
2009	1,716,691	1,220,625	7,590	1,228,215	138,919	5,479	1,094,774	289,434	332,483		37,033	33,630	46,356	25,773
2010	1,776,452	1,257,773	9,086	1,266,858	140,960	5,352	1,131,250	289,206	355,996		38,244	34,608	46,451	25,659
2011	1,879,160	1,317,224	16,776	1,334,000	132,004	5,314	1,207,311	318,901	352,948		40,342	36,037	46,581	26,128
2012	1,960,700	1,378,179	11,775	1,389,954	137,137	5,636	1,258,453	349,196	353,052		41,983	37,515	46,702	26,417
2013	1,991,994	1,417,512	21,762	1,439,273	157,360	5,410	1,287,324	343,243	361,427		42,511	37,666	46,858	26,732
2014	2,079,147	1,471,608	13,213	1,484,821	162,452	5,842	1,328,210	375,020	375,917		44,254	39,255	46,982	27,123
2015	2,171,984	1,533,049	6,176	1,539,225	168,304	6,351	1,377,272	399,144	395,568		46,165	40,780	47,049	27,534
2016	2,213,770	1,561,035	7,713	1,568,748	172,690	6,498	1,402,556	408,496	402,718		46,965	41,500	47,136	27,817
2017	2,285,392	1,616,065	7,605	1,623,670	180,086	6,885	1,450,470	422,737	412,185		48,384	42,937	47,234	28,025
2018	2,389,048	1,683,620	8,591	1,692,211	187,158	7,984	1,513,038	448,445	427,565		50,501	45,009	47,307	28,347
2019	2,476,684	1,736,148	6,238	1,742,385	193,704	8,571	1,557,252	470,078	449,354		52,296	46,538	47,359	28,335
2020	2,647,244	1,745,578	13,154	1,758,732	195,914	7,887	1,570,706	470,479	606,059		55,921	50,071	47,339	27,187
2021	2,825,996	1,865,269	18,839	1,884,109	205,113	8,703	1,687,699	479,961	658,336		59,896	53,014	47,182	27,894
2022	2,872,947	2,005,749	27,594	2,033,343	222,340	9,570	1,820,573	498,290	554,084		61,000	52,738	47,098	...

... = Not available.

Personal Income and Employment by Region and State: Mideast

(Millions of dollars, except as noted.)

Year	Personal income, total	Earnings by place of work			Less: Contributions for government social insurance	Plus: Adjustment for residence	Equals: Net earnings by place of residence	Plus: Dividends, interest, and rent	Plus: Personal current transfer receipts	Per capita (dollars)		Population (thousands)	Total employment (thousands)
		Nonfarm	Farm	Total						Personal income	Disposable personal income		
1960	102,030	85,593	901	86,495	4,355	-761	81,378	14,533	6,119	2,643	2,319	38,597	...
1961	106,262	88,420	906	89,326	4,582	-791	83,953	15,316	6,994	2,715	2,383	39,133	...
1962	112,437	93,612	733	94,345	5,118	-804	88,423	16,864	7,150	2,843	2,488	39,552	...
1963	117,654	97,361	799	98,160	5,644	-841	91,675	18,386	7,593	2,935	2,569	40,083	...
1964	126,000	103,790	802	104,592	5,693	-902	97,997	20,142	7,861	3,107	2,758	40,555	...
1965	134,825	110,543	896	111,439	5,940	-933	104,567	21,854	8,405	3,286	2,906	41,025	...
1966	145,317	120,725	917	121,642	7,891	-1,011	112,740	23,176	9,401	3,513	3,088	41,360	...
1967	156,524	129,069	972	130,040	8,614	-1,183	120,243	24,679	11,602	3,761	3,290	41,617	...
1968	171,747	140,938	920	141,859	9,400	-1,301	131,157	26,718	13,872	4,097	3,550	41,924	...
1969	184,917	153,081	1,105	154,186	11,072	-1,782	141,332	28,328	15,257	4,391	3,753	42,111	19,432
1970	199,975	163,311	1,063	164,374	11,658	-1,703	151,013	30,857	18,105	4,703	4,078	42,517	19,465
1971	214,652	173,493	970	174,464	12,772	-1,779	159,912	33,002	21,738	5,007	4,399	42,870	19,299
1972	232,153	188,066	966	189,032	14,535	-1,950	172,546	35,188	24,419	5,400	4,679	42,992	19,521
1973	251,007	203,906	1,387	205,293	18,195	-2,082	185,016	38,689	27,301	5,860	5,104	42,837	19,968
1974	272,562	218,491	1,292	219,783	20,160	-2,296	197,327	43,426	31,808	6,382	5,535	42,709	19,954
1975	295,272	230,686	1,198	231,884	20,837	-2,641	208,405	46,400	40,467	6,911	6,085	42,728	19,480
1976	317,632	249,080	1,278	250,359	22,890	-2,964	224,504	49,380	43,748	7,444	6,518	42,667	19,563
1977	345,171	271,848	1,097	272,946	24,858	-3,354	244,734	54,358	46,080	8,113	7,062	42,547	19,848
1978	378,978	301,100	1,311	302,412	28,208	-3,971	270,233	59,882	48,863	8,934	7,747	42,421	20,411
1979	416,696	331,582	1,523	333,105	32,254	-4,760	296,091	66,982	53,623	9,837	8,468	42,358	20,871
1980	462,775	360,298	1,140	361,438	35,164	-5,615	320,660	80,371	61,744	10,947	9,412	42,272	20,911
1981	514,658	392,584	1,499	394,083	40,993	-5,943	347,147	97,890	69,621	12,159	10,371	42,329	20,978
1982	555,921	415,170	1,458	416,628	43,999	-6,123	366,506	112,109	77,306	13,117	11,217	42,382	20,858
1983	594,414	445,111	1,092	446,202	47,849	-6,182	392,171	118,668	83,575	13,972	12,117	42,544	21,045
1984	653,790	490,129	1,904	492,033	54,383	-6,584	431,066	135,759	86,965	15,316	13,310	42,687	21,766
1985	699,171	528,536	2,016	530,552	59,564	-6,967	464,021	143,756	91,394	16,338	14,132	42,794	22,333
1986	744,959	567,698	2,200	569,898	64,798	-6,872	498,227	150,152	96,579	17,328	14,987	42,991	22,837
1987	795,876	616,451	2,286	618,737	69,479	-7,221	542,037	154,624	99,214	18,427	15,795	43,190	23,321
1988	870,727	679,111	2,187	681,298	77,653	-7,991	595,653	169,705	105,368	20,046	17,350	43,435	23,927
1989	940,367	719,726	2,579	722,305	81,572	-8,372	632,361	194,009	113,997	21,576	18,599	43,585	24,201
1990	998,459	761,626	2,519	764,145	84,116	-8,635	671,394	202,182	124,884	22,816	19,778	43,762	24,260
1991	1,017,674	767,150	2,052	769,202	86,917	-9,023	673,262	203,031	141,381	23,092	20,132	44,071	23,703
1992	1,077,695	816,603	2,646	819,250	91,293	-10,687	717,270	203,621	156,803	24,277	21,201	44,392	23,597
1993	1,113,459	842,950	2,516	845,467	94,558	-10,451	740,457	207,452	165,549	24,900	21,699	44,717	23,714
1994	1,152,220	871,502	2,305	873,807	99,384	-10,167	764,256	216,473	171,491	25,622	22,281	44,970	23,879
1995	1,211,698	908,644	1,759	910,403	102,991	-10,953	796,458	233,909	181,331	26,816	23,278	45,186	24,157
1996	1,275,883	952,756	2,698	955,454	106,056	-11,404	837,993	247,571	190,318	28,113	24,225	45,384	24,387
1997	1,347,506	1,012,597	1,845	1,014,442	110,906	-11,756	891,780	263,308	192,419	29,564	25,267	45,580	24,763
1998	1,430,853	1,079,778	2,312	1,082,090	116,433	-13,004	952,652	279,203	198,998	31,226	26,525	45,822	25,170
1999	1,507,596	1,154,584	2,304	1,156,888	122,348	-13,274	1,021,266	279,733	206,597	32,699	27,664	46,106	25,710
2000	1,630,935	1,249,144	2,767	1,251,910	130,693	-11,982	1,109,236	303,745	217,955	35,160	29,657	46,386	26,409
2001	1,696,754	1,306,543	2,840	1,309,383	136,829	-12,805	1,159,749	302,561	234,444	36,396	30,624	46,619	26,496
2002	1,715,338	1,329,037	1,955	1,330,992	140,474	-14,570	1,175,948	286,568	252,822	36,620	31,808	46,841	26,442
2003	1,759,198	1,360,983	2,893	1,363,876	144,547	-15,729	1,203,600	292,797	262,801	37,402	32,813	47,035	26,529
2004	1,850,195	1,434,166	3,660	1,437,825	152,321	-17,734	1,267,770	305,781	276,644	39,230	34,393	47,162	26,904
2005	1,926,908	1,488,293	3,439	1,491,732	159,755	-19,406	1,312,571	328,077	286,261	40,790	35,303	47,239	27,309
2006	2,056,531	1,569,368	2,970	1,572,338	168,347	-22,335	1,381,657	372,222	302,652	43,447	37,283	47,334	27,713
2007	2,190,498	1,652,887	3,554	1,656,441	177,048	-25,134	1,454,259	416,595	319,645	46,141	39,189	47,474	28,252
2008	2,254,167	1,678,568	3,916	1,682,484	183,282	-28,269	1,470,934	428,562	354,672	47,272	40,289	47,685	28,371
2009	2,207,523	1,643,572	3,003	1,646,575	179,777	-24,955	1,441,843	377,430	388,249	46,044	40,622	47,944	27,759
2010	2,297,100	1,714,487	3,856	1,718,343	184,384	-28,623	1,505,336	375,820	415,945	47,617	41,886	48,242	27,763
2011	2,417,297	1,781,875	4,699	1,786,574	170,225	-31,443	1,584,906	410,207	422,184	49,707	43,158	48,631	28,282
2012	2,519,931	1,850,360	5,232	1,855,592	174,527	-32,977	1,648,087	451,544	420,300	51,461	44,879	48,968	28,579
2013	2,544,627	1,899,800	6,139	1,905,938	203,074	-31,493	1,671,372	446,859	426,397	51,661	44,347	49,256	28,990
2014	2,652,752	1,967,030	6,309	1,973,340	211,456	-34,212	1,727,671	484,911	440,170	53,575	45,901	49,515	29,461
2015	2,769,073	2,045,100	4,352	2,049,452	220,325	-35,193	1,793,934	513,908	461,231	55,689	47,438	49,724	29,958
2016	2,857,260	2,105,894	3,110	2,109,004	225,028	-36,189	1,847,788	530,955	478,516	57,265	49,061	49,895	30,375
2017	2,986,509	2,197,104	4,634	2,201,739	236,266	-39,311	1,926,162	561,064	499,283	59,651	51,133	50,066	30,687
2018	3,103,957	2,291,802	3,106	2,294,908	245,086	-41,194	2,008,628	587,342	507,986	61,810	53,138	50,218	31,231
2019	3,231,321	2,360,720	4,540	2,365,260	254,643	-43,493	2,067,124	627,111	537,086	64,235	55,196	50,305	31,353
2020	3,417,697	2,352,962	3,563	2,356,525	253,248	-42,135	2,061,142	621,600	734,956	68,067	59,020	50,211	29,684
2021	3,626,371	2,523,088	4,814	2,527,903	269,017	-46,843	2,212,042	637,120	777,209	72,548	62,061	49,986	30,536
2022	3,674,350	2,702,134	8,163	2,710,297	291,672	-49,629	2,368,996	664,710	640,644	73,833	61,291	49,766	...

... = Not available.

Personal Income and Employment by Region and State: New England

(Millions of dollars, except as noted.)

Year	Personal income, total	Earnings by place of work			Less: Contributions for government social insurance	Plus: Adjustment for residence	Equals: Net earnings by place of residence	Plus: Dividends, interest, and rent	Plus: Personal current transfer receipts	Per capita (dollars)		Population (thousands)	Total employment (thousands)
		Nonfarm	Farm	Total						Personal income	Disposable personal income		
1960	26,543	21,356	318	21,674	1,025	27	20,676	4,106	1,761	2,520	2,219	10,532	...
1961	27,858	22,281	269	22,550	1,073	28	21,504	4,377	1,977	2,612	2,311	10,666	...
1962	29,543	23,651	259	23,910	1,216	32	22,725	4,810	2,007	2,735	2,414	10,800	...
1963	30,881	24,585	251	24,837	1,358	36	23,515	5,239	2,126	2,811	2,476	10,986	...
1964	33,063	26,134	289	26,423	1,400	42	25,064	5,792	2,207	2,956	2,646	11,186	...
1965	35,462	27,879	340	28,220	1,451	44	26,813	6,319	2,330	3,130	2,794	11,329	...
1966	38,500	30,746	345	31,090	1,937	51	29,204	6,785	2,512	3,368	2,982	11,430	...
1967	41,842	33,161	239	33,401	2,135	58	31,324	7,436	3,082	3,619	3,192	11,562	...
1968	45,291	35,993	266	36,260	2,370	71	33,961	7,649	3,682	3,892	3,382	11,637	...
1969	50,009	39,196	294	39,490	2,639	835	37,686	8,213	4,111	4,262	3,656	11,735	5,516
1970	53,915	41,706	306	42,012	2,775	842	40,080	8,932	4,903	4,539	3,961	11,878	5,518
1971	57,438	43,877	283	44,161	3,015	885	42,031	9,532	5,876	4,788	4,237	11,996	5,454
1972	62,243	47,830	288	48,118	3,456	951	45,613	10,223	6,408	5,149	4,491	12,088	5,573
1973	67,916	52,504	398	52,903	4,364	997	49,536	11,183	7,197	5,591	4,904	12,148	5,783
1974	73,639	55,983	430	56,413	4,833	1,083	52,663	12,445	8,531	6,058	5,303	12,157	5,843
1975	79,316	58,456	313	58,769	4,922	1,183	55,030	13,150	11,136	6,514	5,791	12,176	5,685
1976	86,257	64,298	428	64,727	5,524	1,286	60,488	14,078	11,690	7,066	6,227	12,207	5,811
1977	94,470	71,062	385	71,447	6,136	1,435	66,746	15,593	12,131	7,707	6,776	12,257	6,007
1978	104,955	79,969	397	80,366	7,102	1,626	74,890	17,244	12,821	8,531	7,451	12,303	6,276
1979	117,375	89,790	380	90,169	8,296	1,840	83,714	19,381	14,279	9,508	8,237	12,345	6,503
1980	132,710	99,350	368	99,718	9,177	2,158	92,700	23,571	16,439	10,727	9,260	12,372	6,623
1981	148,438	108,669	471	109,140	10,790	2,345	100,696	28,938	18,804	11,936	10,240	12,436	6,666
1982	161,734	116,202	513	116,715	11,780	2,514	107,449	33,733	20,552	12,972	11,194	12,468	6,667
1983	174,683	127,158	480	127,637	13,047	2,665	117,256	35,484	21,944	13,925	12,145	12,544	6,799
1984	195,850	143,581	568	144,149	15,176	2,859	131,832	41,025	22,992	15,492	13,575	12,642	7,159
1985	211,532	157,286	558	157,844	16,770	3,119	144,193	43,153	24,186	16,603	14,452	12,741	7,400
1986	228,359	171,426	576	172,002	18,495	3,237	156,744	46,218	25,396	17,795	15,409	12,833	7,638
1987	248,105	189,165	638	189,803	20,166	3,427	173,064	48,930	26,112	19,157	16,468	12,951	7,771
1988	273,207	208,760	653	209,413	22,629	3,693	190,477	54,645	28,085	20,880	18,157	13,085	8,018
1989	293,086	219,160	609	219,770	23,628	3,745	199,886	61,837	31,362	22,234	19,305	13,182	8,005
1990	301,735	223,211	702	223,912	24,142	3,436	203,207	63,459	35,069	22,808	19,840	13,230	7,853
1991	306,345	223,851	645	224,497	24,627	3,434	203,304	62,483	40,558	23,125	20,217	13,248	7,526
1992	323,879	236,864	794	237,658	25,840	4,688	216,507	63,392	43,980	24,405	21,318	13,271	7,566
1993	335,792	246,571	731	247,302	27,034	4,116	224,384	65,853	45,555	25,182	21,934	13,334	7,689
1994	350,230	257,843	678	258,521	28,609	3,910	233,821	68,542	47,866	26,144	22,729	13,396	7,782
1995	369,981	270,399	602	271,001	30,150	4,674	245,525	73,536	50,920	27,462	23,753	13,473	7,875
1996	390,679	285,779	688	286,468	31,550	5,430	260,348	77,905	52,426	28,822	24,642	13,555	8,004
1997	415,533	306,363	593	306,957	33,589	5,059	278,426	82,726	54,380	30,459	25,766	13,642	8,165
1998	445,365	330,053	656	330,708	35,668	6,550	301,591	88,678	55,096	32,428	27,187	13,734	8,361
1999	472,872	357,524	700	358,224	37,882	6,507	326,849	89,135	56,888	34,173	28,545	13,838	8,513
2000	521,001	396,459	774	397,233	41,129	6,760	362,864	98,091	60,046	37,349	30,758	13,950	8,740
2001	545,723	415,327	713	416,040	42,479	6,808	380,370	100,147	65,206	38,866	32,436	14,041	8,766
2002	547,767	418,659	658	419,316	43,106	6,900	383,110	94,467	70,190	38,787	33,577	14,122	8,712
2003	560,206	426,773	699	427,472	44,051	6,969	390,389	96,425	73,392	39,500	34,547	14,182	8,697
2004	590,004	450,422	798	451,221	47,107	8,000	412,114	100,557	77,332	41,530	36,341	14,207	8,809
2005	615,880	465,579	756	466,335	49,067	8,821	426,090	107,753	82,037	43,321	37,458	14,217	8,901
2006	661,557	490,664	659	491,323	51,069	9,945	450,198	124,962	86,397	46,440	39,981	14,246	8,998
2007	699,133	511,831	803	512,634	53,392	11,517	470,758	136,846	91,528	48,962	41,653	14,279	9,168
2008	730,691	526,193	910	527,103	55,036	12,570	484,636	141,622	104,433	50,954	43,764	14,340	9,173
2009	720,334	524,775	743	525,519	54,101	9,806	481,224	124,743	114,367	50,011	44,493	14,404	8,936
2010	752,443	549,291	909	550,201	55,130	11,707	506,777	125,105	120,560	51,978	46,016	14,476	8,892
2011	782,522	562,225	911	563,137	51,191	12,183	524,129	136,929	121,465	53,729	46,812	14,564	9,003
2012	809,133	574,116	1,117	575,233	52,764	13,874	536,344	150,536	122,253	55,229	48,264	14,650	9,113
2013	807,742	582,291	1,157	583,448	61,078	12,990	535,360	148,406	123,975	54,831	47,041	14,732	9,266
2014	845,796	602,172	1,013	603,185	63,561	13,406	553,031	164,144	128,622	57,084	48,875	14,817	9,411
2015	886,726	627,996	875	628,871	65,961	13,695	576,605	174,290	135,832	59,633	50,867	14,870	9,656
2016	912,818	645,822	717	646,539	67,873	13,010	591,676	180,776	140,367	61,156	52,384	14,926	9,778
2017	945,993	670,172	794	670,966	70,763	15,441	615,644	187,156	143,193	63,092	54,075	14,994	9,870
2018	989,903	698,060	619	698,679	73,829	17,155	642,006	197,136	150,761	65,760	56,650	15,053	9,992
2019	1,040,547	727,031	850	727,881	76,810	20,352	671,423	213,283	155,842	68,959	59,341	15,089	9,988
2020	1,105,999	736,524	710	737,234	77,546	19,849	679,537	211,665	214,797	73,369	63,615	15,074	9,515
2021	1,177,024	794,345	597	794,942	82,799	23,494	735,637	216,973	224,414	77,837	66,400	15,122	9,834
2022	1,200,162	847,257	888	848,145	88,996	25,262	784,411	227,078	188,673	79,326	65,755	15,130	...

... = Not available.

Personal Income and Employment by Region and State: Plains

(Millions of dollars, except as noted.)

Year	Personal income, total	Nonfarm	Farm	Total	Less: Contributions for government social insurance	Plus: Adjustment for residence	Equals: Net earnings by place of residence	Plus: Dividends, interest, and rent	Plus: Personal current transfer receipts	Personal income	Disposable personal income	Population (thousands)	Total employment (thousands)
1960	33,349	24,119	3,122	27,240	1,157	8	26,091	5,040	2,218	2,162	1,942	15,424	...
1961	34,589	25,031	3,042	28,073	1,212	6	26,867	5,257	2,464	2,221	1,996	15,570	...
1962	36,922	26,543	3,542	30,084	1,317	7	28,774	5,589	2,560	2,358	2,117	15,657	...
1963	38,403	27,780	3,487	31,267	1,493	4	29,778	5,929	2,696	2,444	2,190	15,715	...
1964	40,038	29,687	2,795	32,482	1,555	5	30,932	6,317	2,788	2,536	2,303	15,787	...
1965	43,929	31,633	4,110	35,743	1,632	4	34,114	6,794	3,021	2,777	2,515	15,819	...
1966	47,250	34,720	4,310	39,030	2,197	-0	36,833	7,154	3,263	2,974	2,673	15,888	...
1967	49,583	37,182	3,678	40,860	2,551	-5	38,304	7,385	3,894	3,110	2,788	15,942	...
1968	54,099	40,694	3,670	44,364	2,839	-14	41,510	8,084	4,505	3,371	3,000	16,047	...
1969	59,316	44,699	4,220	48,918	3,160	-402	45,356	9,020	4,940	3,661	3,210	16,202	7,506
1970	64,334	47,663	4,443	52,106	3,338	-340	48,429	10,114	5,792	3,935	3,489	16,350	7,516
1971	69,267	51,030	4,611	55,640	3,693	-338	51,610	11,004	6,653	4,204	3,772	16,475	7,544
1972	76,510	55,663	6,161	61,823	4,221	-343	57,259	11,999	7,252	4,619	4,092	16,563	7,731
1973	89,249	61,651	11,294	72,944	5,396	-379	67,169	13,630	8,450	5,367	4,789	16,628	8,065
1974	94,449	67,832	7,686	75,518	6,185	-415	68,918	15,681	9,850	5,665	4,973	16,672	8,219
1975	103,645	73,512	7,499	81,012	6,595	-411	74,006	17,517	12,122	6,191	5,505	16,743	8,181
1976	111,098	82,629	4,408	87,036	7,513	-502	79,022	18,882	13,194	6,588	5,818	16,864	8,438
1977	122,799	91,373	5,192	96,565	8,271	-634	87,659	21,197	13,943	7,245	6,385	16,950	8,657
1978	138,981	102,717	7,837	110,554	9,610	-787	100,157	23,647	15,177	8,162	7,171	17,028	8,953
1979	153,329	115,180	6,613	121,793	11,215	-974	109,604	26,729	16,996	8,968	7,813	17,097	9,232
1980	165,726	124,093	1,879	125,973	12,037	-1,126	112,809	32,596	20,321	9,631	8,386	17,208	9,227
1981	187,486	133,902	5,447	139,348	13,885	-1,299	124,164	40,165	23,157	10,860	9,435	17,264	9,180
1982	199,706	138,806	4,004	142,811	14,670	-1,295	126,846	47,064	25,797	11,549	10,053	17,292	9,050
1983	209,174	147,580	1,577	149,157	15,668	-1,380	132,109	49,321	27,745	12,073	10,663	17,325	9,163
1984	233,264	162,450	6,545	168,995	17,707	-1,544	149,743	54,614	28,906	13,420	11,963	17,382	9,470
1985	246,146	171,852	7,464	179,317	19,108	-1,660	158,549	56,988	30,609	14,145	12,585	17,402	9,612
1986	257,591	180,991	8,061	189,052	20,469	-1,784	166,799	58,702	32,090	14,810	13,214	17,393	9,701
1987	271,386	193,085	9,777	202,861	21,690	-1,894	179,277	59,097	33,012	15,572	13,807	17,428	9,949
1988	284,961	206,938	7,383	214,321	24,079	-2,057	188,184	62,118	34,659	16,253	14,421	17,533	10,156
1989	307,374	220,563	9,207	229,771	25,698	-2,138	201,935	67,836	37,604	17,469	15,442	17,595	10,357
1990	325,179	233,385	10,544	243,929	27,917	-2,413	213,599	70,926	40,655	18,374	16,225	17,698	10,544
1991	336,324	243,055	8,117	251,171	29,420	-2,433	219,319	72,214	44,792	18,849	16,721	17,843	10,597
1992	360,431	261,004	10,635	271,639	31,222	-2,549	237,868	74,034	48,529	19,995	17,776	18,026	10,708
1993	372,543	273,681	6,237	279,918	32,831	-2,645	244,443	76,616	51,484	20,459	18,140	18,210	10,934
1994	397,796	290,478	10,482	300,960	35,227	-2,806	262,928	81,090	53,778	21,642	19,175	18,381	11,230
1995	417,276	306,991	5,742	312,733	37,055	-3,038	272,640	87,600	57,037	22,495	19,845	18,550	11,537
1996	448,955	324,702	13,572	338,274	38,591	-3,300	296,383	92,878	59,694	24,002	21,075	18,705	11,761
1997	471,677	345,600	9,882	355,482	41,154	-3,691	310,637	99,426	61,614	25,021	21,839	18,851	11,980
1998	502,325	371,105	9,199	380,303	43,759	-3,930	332,615	106,144	63,566	26,455	23,030	18,988	12,240
1999	522,632	393,034	7,938	400,972	46,129	-4,237	350,607	105,514	66,511	27,319	23,820	19,131	12,411
2000	559,765	418,180	9,609	427,788	48,646	-4,537	374,605	113,990	71,169	29,040	25,277	19,275	12,604
2001	579,933	432,831	9,072	441,903	50,180	-4,637	387,085	114,602	78,246	29,932	26,141	19,375	12,601
2002	590,943	446,157	6,191	452,348	51,454	-4,689	396,205	110,572	84,167	30,355	27,030	19,468	12,519
2003	616,547	460,358	12,389	472,746	53,396	-4,853	414,497	114,760	87,291	31,506	28,370	19,569	12,521
2004	651,320	486,059	16,614	502,673	56,026	-5,119	441,527	118,384	91,409	33,082	29,895	19,688	12,674
2005	676,843	504,101	15,836	519,937	58,723	-5,409	455,805	124,101	96,937	34,179	30,592	19,803	12,863
2006	718,682	532,789	10,687	543,476	62,088	-5,672	475,716	138,049	104,917	36,012	32,045	19,957	13,061
2007	765,239	556,398	15,648	572,047	64,930	-5,689	501,428	151,061	112,750	38,061	33,684	20,106	13,280
2008	812,833	576,901	20,702	597,603	67,568	-6,129	523,906	161,548	127,379	40,142	35,594	20,249	13,298
2009	788,919	563,635	15,070	578,705	66,212	-5,252	507,241	144,042	137,636	38,687	35,172	20,393	12,991
2010	819,841	581,757	17,862	599,619	67,455	-5,108	527,056	145,486	147,299	39,915	36,191	20,540	12,918
2011	878,497	607,439	29,737	637,176	62,813	-5,333	569,030	159,827	149,640	42,520	38,163	20,661	13,099
2012	927,647	642,047	27,881	669,928	65,079	-5,908	598,941	178,740	149,966	44,630	40,050	20,785	13,262
2013	939,418	660,871		695,092	75,793	-6,335	612,964	172,937	153,517	44,905	39,924	20,920	13,446
2014	979,811	691,009	24,418	715,428	78,653	-7,066	629,708	189,523	160,580	46,549	41,359	21,049	13,614
2015	1,011,992	716,535	18,158	734,693	81,606	-7,229	645,859	198,458	167,676	47,815	42,314	21,165	13,783
2016	1,024,103	724,401	13,093	737,494	83,190	-7,074	647,229	204,021	172,853	48,141	42,597	21,273	13,866
2017	1,053,457	749,259	11,839	761,098	86,278	-7,262	667,559	208,374	177,525	49,272	43,736	21,380	13,939
2018	1,101,846	779,543	11,794	791,338	90,004	-7,737	693,597	220,733	187,516	51,311	45,762	21,474	14,074
2019	1,148,499	805,824	12,031	817,855	93,502	-8,291	716,062	235,287	197,150	53,266	47,457	21,562	14,081
2020	1,223,899	818,027	20,186	838,213	96,318	-7,468	734,427	235,917	253,555	56,604	50,730	21,622	13,664
2021	1,302,891	863,431	27,240	890,670	99,582	-7,463	783,626	240,716	278,549	60,167	53,352	21,655	13,949
2022	1,339,456	929,750	34,873	964,623	107,736	-8,091	848,796	250,357	240,303	61,755	53,642	21,690	...

... = Not available.

Personal Income and Employment by Region and State: Rocky Mountain

(Millions of dollars, except as noted.)

Year	Personal income, total	Nonfarm	Farm	Total	Less: Contributions for government social insurance	Plus: Adjustment for residence	Equals: Net earnings by place of residence	Plus: Dividends, interest, and rent	Plus: Personal current transfer receipts	Personal income	Disposable personal income	Population (thousands)	Total employment (thousands)
1960	9,819	7,372	590	7,962	354	-2	7,605	1,591	624	2,257	2,021	4,350	...
1961	10,407	7,883	536	8,420	382	-3	8,035	1,682	690	2,314	2,072	4,497	...
1962	11,218	8,366	721	9,087	412	-3	8,673	1,825	721	2,449	2,201	4,580	...
1963	11,583	8,759	636	9,395	478	-2	8,915	1,911	758	2,501	2,241	4,632	...
1964	12,120	9,267	520	9,786	491	-2	9,293	2,049	777	2,594	2,364	4,673	...
1965	13,010	9,747	736	10,483	499	-2	9,982	2,187	840	2,766	2,518	4,703	...
1966	13,792	10,506	706	11,212	646	-1	10,565	2,326	902	2,913	2,637	4,735	...
1967	14,653	11,125	717	11,842	722	-1	11,119	2,465	1,069	3,064	2,762	4,783	...
1968	15,901	12,166	754	12,920	805	-1	12,115	2,572	1,215	3,267	2,921	4,868	...
1969	17,806	13,437	889	14,326	881	18	13,463	2,998	1,345	3,602	3,177	4,943	2,216
1970	19,931	14,797	1,003	15,799	962	20	14,858	3,472	1,601	3,956	3,530	5,038	2,271
1971	22,182	16,543	966	17,510	1,102	20	16,428	3,883	1,871	4,271	3,834	5,194	2,343
1972	25,137	18,788	1,269	20,056	1,320	23	18,759	4,288	2,090	4,682	4,174	5,368	2,482
1973	28,740	21,327	1,751	23,078	1,728	22	21,372	4,926	2,442	5,200	4,630	5,527	2,646
1974	32,390	23,981	1,836	25,818	2,002	24	23,840	5,712	2,838	5,733	5,079	5,650	2,740
1975	35,793	26,573	1,385	27,958	2,179	36	25,815	6,449	3,530	6,191	5,551	5,782	2,778
1976	39,578	30,110	1,026	31,136	2,512	40	28,665	7,024	3,889	6,690	5,957	5,916	2,912
1977	44,131	34,200	685	34,885	2,870	42	32,057	7,919	4,154	7,260	6,429	6,079	3,060
1978	51,079	39,772	956	40,728	3,411	52	37,370	9,168	4,542	8,164	7,217	6,257	3,257
1979	57,686	45,355	748	46,103	4,090	45	42,058	10,471	5,157	8,959	7,860	6,439	3,402
1980	65,483	50,410	964	51,374	4,596	68	46,846	12,580	6,056	9,933	8,723	6,592	3,474
1981	74,507	56,598	1,053	57,651	5,564	51	52,138	15,295	7,074	11,050	9,651	6,743	3,559
1982	80,525	60,191	824	61,015	6,033	52	55,034	17,443	8,048	11,664	10,215	6,904	3,596
1983	86,074	63,433	1,144	64,577	6,397	54	58,234	18,995	8,845	12,235	10,905	7,035	3,642
1984	93,219	69,070	1,042	70,113	7,175	75	63,012	20,975	9,231	13,113	11,733	7,109	3,801
1985	98,385	72,878	844	73,722	7,730	92	66,084	22,512	9,789	13,726	12,257	7,168	3,861
1986	101,921	74,974	1,242	76,216	8,019	113	68,309	23,104	10,508	14,156	12,693	7,200	3,854
1987	105,381	77,291	1,578	78,869	8,209	135	70,795	23,439	11,147	14,625	13,061	7,206	3,885
1988	111,343	82,283	1,625	83,908	9,123	174	74,959	24,629	11,755	15,459	13,819	7,203	4,021
1989	120,543	87,594	2,216	89,811	9,870	209	80,150	27,416	12,976	16,663	14,809	7,234	4,114
1990	128,616	94,193	2,514	96,707	10,976	245	85,976	28,608	14,032	17,606	15,580	7,305	4,230
1991	136,495	100,831	2,466	103,297	12,004	274	91,567	29,458	15,470	18,255	16,206	7,477	4,335
1992	147,774	110,190	2,543	112,733	12,992	306	100,047	30,506	17,221	19,200	17,036	7,696	4,434
1993	159,847	119,354	3,220	122,574	14,206	341	108,709	32,599	18,539	20,135	17,838	7,939	4,626
1994	171,008	128,625	2,094	130,719	15,410	393	115,701	35,814	19,492	20,928	18,480	8,171	4,886
1995	184,801	137,320	1,995	139,315	16,397	452	123,370	39,970	21,461	22,053	19,457	8,380	5,046
1996	198,591	147,253	2,190	149,442	17,263	524	132,704	43,423	22,464	23,185	20,325	8,565	5,249
1997	212,577	158,556	2,053	160,609	18,380	601	142,829	46,716	23,032	24,306	21,175	8,746	5,440
1998	231,642	173,756	2,393	176,148	19,327	699	157,520	50,371	23,750	25,974	22,555	8,918	5,621
1999	246,465	188,205	2,740	190,945	20,642	798	171,100	50,392	24,972	27,101	23,443	9,094	5,752
2000	269,912	206,935	2,383	209,318	22,510	857	187,664	55,450	26,798	29,120	25,067	9,269	5,953
2001	282,691	215,810	3,060	218,870	23,609	843	196,104	57,051	29,536	29,975	26,052	9,431	6,007
2002	286,676	219,913	2,314	222,226	24,377	834	198,684	55,736	32,256	29,964	26,667	9,567	6,002
2003	296,150	225,148	2,367	227,515	25,131	850	203,234	58,844	34,071	30,609	27,534	9,675	6,023
2004	312,695	236,940	3,372	240,312	26,919	880	214,274	62,513	35,908	31,883	28,709	9,808	6,166
2005	336,666	252,872	3,381	256,252	28,876	884	228,260	69,644	38,763	33,761	30,013	9,972	6,371
2006	368,734	275,817	2,310	278,127	31,435	858	247,550	79,368	41,817	36,186	31,904	10,190	6,589
2007	395,225	290,970	3,414	294,384	33,418	871	261,837	88,377	45,011	37,979	33,309	10,406	6,848
2008	412,916	297,173	3,381	300,554	34,540	929	266,943	93,672	52,301	38,919	34,397	10,610	6,895
2009	393,820	283,932	2,369	286,301	33,450	1,047	253,898	82,217	57,705	36,485	33,099	10,794	6,686
2010	408,127	290,997	3,355	294,351	34,008	1,225	261,568	82,249	64,310	37,273	33,719	10,950	6,635
2011	440,398	306,509	4,793	311,302	32,096	1,628	280,834	93,851	65,713	39,715	35,555	11,089	6,761
2012	468,046	324,898	4,534	329,432	33,558	2,254	298,129	103,835	66,083	41,678	37,262	11,230	6,882
2013	486,655	345,907	5,494	351,401	39,025	2,554	314,929	103,345	68,381	42,740	37,948	11,386	7,055
2014	522,937	369,365	5,622	374,988	41,462	2,825	336,350	114,223	72,364	45,316	40,170	11,540	7,252
2015	550,867	384,524	5,621	390,145	43,321	2,653	349,476	123,570	77,820	46,995	41,491	11,722	7,456
2016	563,546	392,692	4,498	397,191	44,706	2,456	354,940	127,154	81,452	47,294	41,653	11,916	7,643
2017	598,125	419,559	3,464	423,023	47,421	2,673	378,275	135,377	84,473	49,455	43,667	12,094	7,837
2018	639,081	448,847	3,599	452,446	50,257	2,833	405,022	143,667	90,392	52,093	46,217	12,268	8,058
2019	687,391	477,212	4,522	481,734	53,057	3,115	431,791	159,325	96,274	55,312	48,930	12,427	8,157
2020	737,629	497,641	4,798	502,439	55,580	2,914	449,772	161,366	126,491	58,623	52,140	12,583	8,122
2021	800,698	540,949	4,128	545,077	59,319	3,115	488,873	168,587	143,238	62,847	55,113	12,740	8,419
2022	840,999	594,192	4,969	599,160	65,417	3,308	537,051	179,653	124,295	65,376	56,022	12,864	...

... = Not available.

Personal Income and Employment by Region and State: Southeast

(Millions of dollars, except as noted.)

Year	Personal income, total	Earnings by place of work			Less: Contributions for government social insurance	Plus: Adjustment for residence	Equals: Net earnings by place of residence	Plus: Dividends, interest, and rent	Plus: Personal current transfer receipts	Per capita (dollars)		Population (thousands)	Total employment (thousands)
		Nonfarm	Farm	Total						Personal income	Disposable personal income		
1960	66,930	51,896	3,350	55,246	2,447	589	53,388	8,939	4,603	1,721	1,565	38,885	...
1961	70,593	53,773	3,773	57,546	2,513	616	55,650	9,648	5,295	1,785	1,626	39,544	...
1962	75,390	57,877	3,533	61,410	2,806	676	59,281	10,553	5,556	1,876	1,700	40,179	...
1963	80,425	61,902	3,765	65,667	3,287	738	63,117	11,406	5,901	1,974	1,787	40,742	...
1964	86,835	67,360	3,625	70,985	3,444	801	68,343	12,335	6,157	2,100	1,920	41,349	...
1965	94,368	73,503	3,505	77,007	3,677	899	74,229	13,416	6,723	2,255	2,054	41,857	...
1966	103,487	81,959	3,714	85,673	4,914	1,000	81,759	14,388	7,340	2,449	2,214	42,257	...
1967	112,234	88,700	3,700	92,400	5,668	1,160	87,892	15,596	8,746	2,634	2,381	42,611	...
1968	124,348	98,752	3,572	102,324	6,410	1,258	97,173	17,075	10,100	2,889	2,585	43,042	...
1969	138,939	109,456	4,060	113,516	7,214	1,173	107,475	20,075	11,390	3,198	2,826	43,440	19,085
1970	152,550	117,976	4,050	122,026	7,779	1,084	115,332	23,440	13,778	3,469	3,095	43,974	19,254
1971	168,335	129,403	4,262	133,664	8,837	1,064	125,891	26,165	16,279	3,740	3,362	45,013	19,635
1972	189,159	146,065	4,964	151,029	10,454	1,127	141,702	29,037	18,420	4,110	3,653	46,019	20,523
1973	214,956	164,853	7,279	172,132	13,506	1,205	159,831	33,295	21,829	4,574	4,084	46,992	21,636
1974	239,478	181,787	6,663	188,450	15,479	1,305	174,276	38,811	26,391	4,994	4,439	47,955	22,069
1975	262,258	193,771	5,996	199,767	16,286	1,575	185,055	42,950	34,253	5,376	4,864	48,788	21,642
1976	291,460	217,654	6,366	224,020	18,675	1,779	207,124	46,883	37,453	5,886	5,281	49,514	22,351
1977	323,485	243,985	5,766	249,751	20,914	1,996	230,833	52,777	39,876	6,430	5,750	50,312	23,208
1978	367,595	278,118	6,931	285,048	24,375	2,393	263,066	60,877	43,652	7,192	6,399	51,113	24,305
1979	412,930	311,625	6,844	318,469	28,418	2,748	292,799	69,795	50,337	7,945	7,024	51,977	24,987
1980	465,434	343,617	4,173	347,790	31,420	3,314	319,685	85,651	60,098	8,802	7,771	52,881	25,324
1981	526,762	379,323	6,634	385,957	37,261	3,641	352,337	105,694	68,731	9,823	8,643	53,627	25,594
1982	564,551	399,041	6,759	405,799	39,941	3,822	369,680	118,617	76,254	10,407	9,201	54,249	25,499
1983	607,945	431,608	4,899	436,507	43,698	3,815	396,625	128,271	83,049	11,083	9,876	54,856	26,030
1984	675,543	479,757	8,400	488,156	49,934	4,070	442,293	145,742	87,508	12,169	10,910	55,515	27,280
1985	726,369	518,345	7,444	525,789	54,899	4,250	475,139	157,809	93,421	12,925	11,519	56,199	28,090
1986	773,946	555,092	6,952	562,043	59,997	4,449	506,496	167,839	99,611	13,611	12,139	56,861	28,826
1987	826,506	599,058	8,292	607,350	64,249	4,649	547,750	175,037	103,718	14,365	12,753	57,536	29,529
1988	898,850	651,929	10,868	662,797	72,102	5,120	595,815	191,737	111,298	15,465	13,800	58,120	30,527
1989	977,273	693,926	11,406	705,332	77,510	5,499	633,321	220,220	123,732	16,639	14,784	58,733	31,251
1990	1,039,866	737,578	10,875	748,453	83,396	6,148	671,205	232,836	135,825	17,472	15,561	59,516	31,840
1991	1,089,343	768,150	12,420	780,569	87,898	6,635	699,307	236,439	153,597	18,005	16,125	60,501	31,724
1992	1,169,367	829,036	13,206	842,242	94,074	7,073	755,241	240,780	173,347	19,012	17,058	61,508	32,180
1993	1,235,141	877,705	12,804	890,509	100,058	7,353	797,804	251,649	185,688	19,753	17,695	62,531	33,186
1994	1,309,965	931,123	14,006	945,129	107,408	7,255	844,975	267,727	197,262	20,605	18,410	63,574	34,135
1995	1,395,633	985,443	12,430	997,873	113,546	7,511	891,838	291,102	212,692	21,604	19,258	64,602	35,254
1996	1,481,272	1,042,682	14,181	1,056,863	118,968	7,178	945,073	310,847	225,352	22,576	20,002	65,611	36,087
1997	1,571,741	1,110,100	13,860	1,123,960	126,228	7,989	1,005,721	332,117	233,903	23,580	20,772	66,655	37,050
1998	1,688,323	1,203,741	12,928	1,216,669	135,202	8,011	1,089,478	358,255	240,590	24,965	21,901	67,627	38,014
1999	1,771,502	1,281,763	13,076	1,294,839	143,365	9,821	1,161,295	359,095	251,113	25,835	22,638	68,569	38,802
2000	1,899,856	1,371,739	14,403	1,386,143	151,844	8,281	1,242,580	389,079	268,197	27,337	23,935	69,497	39,694
2001	1,986,389	1,428,773	16,278	1,445,051	158,517	8,981	1,295,514	395,106	295,769	28,249	24,797	70,318	39,630
2002	2,040,468	1,477,937	10,337	1,488,274	163,459	10,636	1,335,451	385,801	319,216	28,678	25,705	71,152	39,667
2003	2,132,775	1,543,439	13,217	1,556,656	170,390	11,636	1,397,901	399,936	334,938	29,638	26,847	71,962	40,062
2004	2,281,487	1,648,067	16,814	1,664,882	181,838	12,366	1,495,409	427,073	359,005	31,245	28,336	73,019	41,037
2005	2,443,495	1,747,755	17,670	1,765,425	193,106	13,173	1,585,492	468,589	389,414	32,954	29,581	74,148	42,110
2006	2,622,134	1,857,901	13,150	1,871,051	206,547	15,098	1,679,602	529,080	413,453	34,931	31,212	75,066	43,151
2007	2,766,647	1,923,455	12,284	1,935,739	215,107	16,374	1,737,006	587,472	442,169	36,345	32,389	76,123	44,065
2008	2,857,799	1,939,932	11,664	1,951,595	220,562	18,547	1,749,580	606,223	501,995	37,086	33,209	77,058	43,725
2009	2,770,280	1,873,626	11,661	1,885,287	216,160	18,413	1,687,539	535,779	546,962	35,601	32,627	77,815	42,223
2010	2,889,337	1,934,702	10,695	1,945,397	220,605	20,186	1,744,978	551,235	593,124	36,774	33,641	78,570	42,066
2011	3,038,507	1,996,837	10,777	2,007,614	203,951	22,817	1,826,479	601,836	610,191	38,365	34,752	79,199	42,886
2012	3,173,916	2,086,275	14,358	2,100,633	211,144	22,825	1,912,314	649,409	612,193	39,729	36,038	79,889	43,433
2013	3,188,791	2,128,908	22,526	2,151,434	244,534	22,973	1,929,873	629,375	629,544	39,605	35,579	80,516	44,149
2014	3,366,607	2,233,482	17,297	2,250,779	255,034	25,236	2,020,980	687,573	658,053	41,459	37,205	81,204	45,199
2015	3,539,297	2,334,020	16,641	2,350,660	266,608	25,790	2,109,842	734,232	695,222	43,171	38,539	81,983	46,293
2016	3,640,705	2,403,979	11,750	2,415,729	274,475	26,899	2,168,152	754,751	717,802	43,951	39,316	82,835	47,201
2017	3,822,624	2,513,258	16,153	2,529,411	286,904	26,993	2,269,501	809,722	743,401	45,732	40,772	83,587	48,150
2018	4,010,921	2,639,636	10,751	2,650,387	301,380	27,046	2,376,053	857,425	777,443	47,617	42,784	84,233	49,282
2019	4,240,361	2,763,567	11,416	2,774,984	316,778	26,412	2,484,618	934,105	821,638	49,978	44,813	84,845	49,826
2020	4,518,896	2,820,008	9,333	2,829,341	326,272	25,790	2,528,859	937,261	1,052,777	52,904	47,712	85,417	49,065
2021	4,899,060	3,063,143	16,478	3,079,621	347,734	26,147	2,758,033	964,215	1,176,811	57,000	50,829	85,948	50,611
2022	5,061,159	3,344,979	30,715	3,375,695	383,280	26,936	3,019,351	1,017,490	1,024,318	58,300	50,765	86,812	...

... = Not available.

Personal Income and Employment by Region and State: Southwest

(Millions of dollars, except as noted.)

| Year | Personal income, total | Derivation of personal income | | | | | | | | Per capita (dollars) | | Population (thousands) | Total employment (thousands) |
| | | Earnings by place of work | | | Less: Contributions for government social insurance | Plus: Adjustment for residence | Equals: Net earnings by place of residence | Plus: Dividends, interest, and rent | Plus: Personal current transfer receipts | Personal income | Disposable personal income | | |
		Nonfarm	Farm	Total									
1960	28,817	22,282	1,474	23,756	1,006	5	22,755	4,417	1,645	2,024	1,826	14,235	...
1961	30,430	23,321	1,628	24,949	1,040	6	23,915	4,664	1,851	2,088	1,883	14,572	...
1962	31,996	24,782	1,411	26,192	1,132	9	25,069	4,932	1,995	2,143	1,928	14,930	...
1963	33,362	26,032	1,197	27,229	1,277	12	25,964	5,246	2,152	2,208	1,985	15,108	...
1964	35,741	28,050	1,132	29,182	1,330	14	27,865	5,629	2,247	2,339	2,134	15,278	...
1965	38,346	29,923	1,349	31,272	1,400	16	29,888	6,007	2,451	2,488	2,264	15,414	...
1966	41,706	33,093	1,409	34,503	1,882	17	32,638	6,394	2,674	2,679	2,420	15,567	...
1967	45,390	36,228	1,294	37,522	2,185	19	35,356	6,792	3,242	2,885	2,600	15,734	...
1968	50,518	40,397	1,423	41,820	2,456	24	39,388	7,318	3,812	3,158	2,817	15,998	...
1969	56,501	45,081	1,513	46,594	2,887	-62	43,644	8,604	4,252	3,460	3,052	16,328	7,219
1970	62,539	48,789	1,837	50,626	3,104	-84	47,438	10,062	5,038	3,763	3,356	16,621	7,311
1971	68,408	53,227	1,681	54,907	3,501	-90	51,317	11,206	5,885	4,006	3,615	17,077	7,457
1972	76,145	59,347	2,017	61,364	4,085	-107	57,171	12,379	6,594	4,350	3,884	17,503	7,807
1973	86,582	66,711	3,298	70,009	5,306	-121	64,583	14,160	7,839	4,825	4,325	17,943	8,215
1974	97,435	75,688	2,139	77,828	6,213	-82	71,532	16,546	9,357	5,309	4,712	18,354	8,511
1975	110,068	84,419	2,112	86,530	6,831	-46	79,653	18,584	11,831	5,858	5,276	18,789	8,633
1976	123,377	96,099	2,083	98,182	7,904	25	90,303	20,095	12,980	6,403	5,723	19,270	9,001
1977	137,741	108,947	1,864	110,811	9,030	-220	101,562	22,399	13,781	6,988	6,199	19,710	9,466
1978	158,697	126,806	1,689	128,496	10,776	-357	117,363	26,071	15,263	7,864	6,960	20,180	10,046
1979	183,167	146,035	2,982	149,017	13,007	-363	135,647	30,087	17,433	8,816	7,726	20,777	10,528
1980	210,220	166,795	1,542	168,336	14,995	-463	152,877	36,862	20,480	9,811	8,563	21,426	10,923
1981	245,544	192,286	2,837	195,123	18,608	-168	176,347	45,812	23,385	11,169	9,641	21,985	11,449
1982	269,939	207,412	2,353	209,765	20,499	-229	189,038	54,458	26,443	11,844	10,301	22,791	11,682
1983	287,700	216,992	2,409	219,401	21,389	-159	197,854	60,329	29,517	12,292	10,909	23,405	11,712
1984	315,288	237,772	2,677	240,449	24,038	-157	216,254	67,729	31,305	13,260	11,829	23,776	12,259
1985	339,561	254,606	2,582	257,188	26,109	-124	230,954	75,077	33,530	14,051	12,531	24,166	12,617
1986	350,080	261,020	2,586	263,606	26,713	-7	236,885	76,647	36,548	14,240	12,835	24,585	12,483
1987	359,140	267,461	3,519	270,980	27,114	84	243,951	76,587	38,602	14,512	13,014	24,748	12,785
1988	380,981	284,825	4,156	288,981	29,977	180	259,185	80,840	40,956	15,325	13,806	24,860	13,055
1989	407,156	301,237	4,117	305,354	32,059	264	273,559	88,344	45,253	16,232	14,541	25,083	13,241
1990	435,970	323,758	4,967	328,725	34,447	357	294,635	91,137	50,198	17,157	15,341	25,411	13,553
1991	456,160	341,059	4,535	345,594	37,064	316	308,845	91,570	55,744	17,601	15,816	25,917	13,759
1992	491,175	366,887	5,371	372,258	39,437	357	333,177	93,228	64,769	18,541	16,737	26,491	13,885
1993	520,514	390,291	6,179	396,470	41,953	409	354,927	96,295	69,292	19,196	17,310	27,116	14,332
1994	552,548	414,846	5,304	420,149	45,127	428	375,450	102,801	74,297	19,896	17,915	27,772	14,845
1995	591,292	442,143	4,279	446,422	47,841	408	398,988	111,824	80,480	20,806	18,706	28,420	15,396
1996	634,837	476,523	3,905	480,428	51,061	421	429,787	119,132	85,918	21,876	19,533	29,020	15,883
1997	687,796	520,983	5,000	525,984	55,115	417	471,285	126,972	89,539	23,217	20,599	29,625	16,482
1998	746,467	571,548	4,808	576,356	59,742	427	517,040	137,594	91,833	24,685	21,819	30,240	17,034
1999	786,877	605,760	6,642	612,403	63,268	537	549,671	141,800	95,406	25,525	22,564	30,827	17,353
2000	856,234	660,929	5,526	666,455	68,054	603	599,004	156,195	101,035	27,285	24,031	31,381	17,900
2001	908,263	702,469	6,338	708,808	71,645	678	637,841	158,846	111,575	28,479	25,210	31,892	18,099
2002	925,637	713,489	6,261	719,750	73,044	742	647,448	155,645	122,545	28,542	25,858	32,431	18,111
2003	966,646	738,126	7,522	745,648	76,122	887	670,412	164,740	131,494	29,360	26,849	32,924	18,266
2004	1,024,731	782,396	8,481	790,877	80,630	1,055	711,302	173,622	139,807	30,611	28,053	33,475	18,655
2005	1,115,535	842,502	8,135	850,637	86,268	1,092	765,461	196,068	154,006	32,715	29,632	34,098	19,317
2006	1,226,825	928,875	5,247	934,122	92,832	1,024	842,315	218,562	165,949	35,107	31,607	34,945	20,044
2007	1,298,425	968,656	5,990	974,646	98,913	975	876,709	240,442	181,274	36,448	32,726	35,624	20,726
2008	1,407,499	1,026,141	3,395	1,029,536	103,204	875	927,207	273,401	206,892	38,807	34,765	36,269	21,061
2009	1,337,548	968,720	1,880	970,600	101,641	578	869,538	240,601	227,408	36,249	33,476	36,899	20,640
2010	1,411,786	1,014,206	5,645	1,019,851	104,964	344	915,231	246,489	250,067	37,682	34,708	37,465	20,634
2011	1,528,781	1,087,946	6,415	1,094,361	98,730	-48	995,582	277,067	256,132	40,289	36,647	37,945	21,144
2012	1,626,388	1,161,401	6,283	1,167,684	104,055	-320	1,063,309	306,855	256,224	42,278	38,508	38,469	21,670
2013	1,671,537	1,215,389	9,287	1,224,676	122,327	-618	1,101,731	305,287	264,520	42,919	38,771	38,946	22,225
2014	1,790,353	1,295,785	9,382	1,305,168	128,701	-592	1,175,875	335,734	278,745	45,311	40,863	39,513	22,805
2015	1,826,324	1,307,844	10,939	1,318,783	134,231	-542	1,184,011	347,293	295,020	45,532	40,975	40,110	23,342
2016	1,826,528	1,309,336	6,308	1,315,644	137,232	-96	1,178,317	340,093	308,117	44,935	40,670	40,648	23,708
2017	1,944,235	1,391,998	7,087	1,399,085	144,723	256	1,254,618	370,937	318,680	47,312	42,641	41,094	24,232
2018	2,068,637	1,485,055	5,626	1,490,681	152,539	175	1,338,317	396,850	333,471	49,832	45,341	41,512	24,884
2019	2,184,469	1,553,289	6,190	1,559,479	160,304	49	1,399,224	432,065	353,180	52,033	47,209	41,982	25,260
2020	2,299,298	1,553,585	5,983	1,559,568	163,537	73	1,396,105	429,565	473,628	54,107	49,268	42,496	24,960
2021	2,492,633	1,672,120	7,740	1,679,860	174,233	540	1,506,167	450,846	535,620	58,061	52,306	42,932	25,709
2022	2,608,334	1,852,403	9,743	1,862,145	194,510	308	1,667,943	479,621	460,770	59,932	52,775	43,522	...

... = Not available.

STATE

Personal Income and Employment by Region and State: Alabama

(Millions of dollars, except as noted.)

Year	Personal income, total	Derivation of personal income								Per capita (dollars)		Population (thousands)	Total employment (thousands)
		Earnings by place of work			Less: Contributions for government social insurance	Plus: Adjustment for residence	Equals: Net earnings by place of residence	Plus: Dividends, interest, and rent	Plus: Personal current transfer receipts	Personal income	Disposable personal income		
		Nonfarm	Farm	Total									
1960	5,188	4,170	257	4,427	187	2	4,242	561	385	1,585	1,448	3,274	...
1961	5,360	4,279	247	4,526	194	3	4,335	596	429	1,616	1,484	3,316	...
1962	5,634	4,512	227	4,738	219	4	4,523	643	468	1,695	1,545	3,323	...
1963	5,984	4,779	275	5,054	260	7	4,801	687	496	1,782	1,625	3,358	...
1964	6,498	5,244	247	5,492	265	8	5,234	750	513	1,914	1,755	3,395	...
1965	7,052	5,704	257	5,961	273	11	5,699	803	551	2,048	1,874	3,443	...
1966	7,564	6,246	244	6,491	376	17	6,132	834	599	2,184	1,981	3,464	...
1967	7,992	6,613	209	6,822	429	23	6,415	886	691	2,311	2,096	3,458	...
1968	8,738	7,184	229	7,413	473	27	6,967	970	801	2,536	2,282	3,446	...
1969	9,738	7,833	280	8,112	550	130	7,692	1,154	892	2,831	2,515	3,440	1,411
1970	10,628	8,378	250	8,629	590	127	8,166	1,366	1,097	3,081	2,781	3,450	1,413
1971	11,699	9,124	279	9,403	655	133	8,881	1,534	1,285	3,345	3,032	3,497	1,423
1972	12,999	10,148	348	10,496	765	165	9,896	1,672	1,431	3,672	3,303	3,540	1,471
1973	14,639	11,327	535	11,862	983	183	11,062	1,896	1,681	4,088	3,677	3,581	1,526
1974	16,241	12,621	340	12,961	1,136	194	12,019	2,211	2,011	4,477	4,019	3,628	1,552
1975	18,100	13,631	414	14,045	1,222	200	13,024	2,476	2,601	4,918	4,460	3,681	1,543
1976	20,324	15,499	479	15,978	1,422	214	14,770	2,706	2,849	5,438	4,896	3,737	1,594
1977	22,395	17,332	383	17,716	1,596	246	16,365	3,024	3,005	5,920	5,324	3,783	1,651
1978	25,340	19,656	509	20,165	1,840	266	18,591	3,480	3,269	6,609	5,928	3,834	1,713
1979	28,151	21,682	521	22,204	2,103	291	20,392	3,951	3,809	7,275	6,491	3,869	1,736
1980	31,037	23,498	211	23,709	2,277	324	21,755	4,803	4,479	7,957	7,082	3,900	1,732
1981	34,466	25,323	490	25,813	2,644	421	23,589	5,851	5,025	8,796	7,811	3,919	1,719
1982	36,396	26,219	411	26,629	2,783	444	24,291	6,552	5,553	9,272	8,315	3,925	1,687
1983	38,971	28,289	293	28,582	3,053	436	25,965	6,994	6,012	9,906	8,884	3,934	1,717
1984	42,870	31,153	482	31,634	3,427	465	28,672	7,847	6,352	10,848	9,772	3,952	1,780
1985	46,099	33,713	467	34,180	3,739	473	30,914	8,477	6,708	11,604	10,388	3,973	1,822
1986	48,790	35,877	458	36,336	3,972	503	32,866	8,945	6,980	12,223	10,944	3,992	1,858
1987	51,652	38,286	541	38,827	4,194	513	35,145	9,373	7,133	12,864	11,454	4,015	1,912
1988	55,559	41,170	802	41,973	4,668	517	37,821	10,287	7,451	13,807	12,391	4,024	1,970
1989	60,396	43,679	941	44,619	4,970	539	40,188	11,785	8,422	14,986	13,377	4,030	2,006
1990	64,240	46,584	849	47,433	5,366	532	42,599	12,366	9,275	15,861	14,175	4,050	2,048
1991	67,930	48,981	1,124	50,105	5,681	563	44,987	12,686	10,257	16,572	14,867	4,099	2,060
1992	73,040	52,806	1,003	53,809	6,062	614	48,361	13,027	11,652	17,583	15,821	4,154	2,097
1993	76,398	55,246	1,018	56,263	6,419	665	50,509	13,522	12,366	18,129	16,294	4,214	2,159
1994	80,848	58,196	1,069	59,265	6,849	758	53,174	14,554	13,120	18,977	16,995	4,260	2,180
1995	85,474	60,931	788	61,720	7,217	839	55,342	15,938	14,194	19,892	17,772	4,297	2,242
1996	89,350	63,517	917	64,434	7,464	845	57,815	16,534	15,000	20,630	18,364	4,331	2,275
1997	93,981	66,557	954	67,511	7,830	949	60,630	17,674	15,678	21,516	19,087	4,368	2,321
1998	99,848	71,089	1,076	72,165	8,228	1,065	65,001	18,859	15,987	22,668	20,120	4,405	2,362
1999	103,369	74,185	1,244	75,429	8,593	1,131	67,968	18,749	16,653	23,333	20,685	4,430	2,378
2000	108,215	77,019	960	77,979	8,886	1,257	70,349	20,117	17,750	24,306	21,574	4,452	2,392
2001	111,947	78,918	1,391	80,309	9,189	1,315	72,435	20,306	19,207	25,057	22,255	4,468	2,376
2002	114,905	81,659	987	82,646	9,484	1,374	74,536	19,815	20,554	25,648	23,170	4,480	2,365
2003	120,123	84,600	1,307	85,907	9,831	1,455	77,532	20,780	21,812	26,673	24,304	4,503	2,371
2004	128,829	89,760	1,804	91,564	10,332	1,489	82,721	23,001	23,107	28,434	26,011	4,531	2,426
2005	136,861	95,148	1,675	96,824	10,989	1,555	87,389	24,621	24,851	29,949	27,130	4,570	2,487
2006	145,692	101,211	1,010	102,221	11,667	1,611	92,165	26,764	26,764	31,474	28,296	4,629	2,546
2007	152,984	104,734	828	105,562	12,224	1,726	95,064	29,109	28,812	32,739	29,371	4,673	2,604
2008	158,451	105,357	861	106,218	12,606	1,834	95,446	30,826	32,179	33,583	30,202	4,718	2,583
2009	155,914	103,271	915	104,186	12,336	1,804	93,654	27,583	34,677	32,769	30,155	4,758	2,480
2010	162,531	106,276	777	107,053	12,710	1,888	96,230	28,322	37,978	33,946	31,187	4,788	2,460
2011	168,474	109,425	382	109,806	11,646	2,033	100,193	29,561	38,720	35,010	31,883	4,812	2,498
2012	173,362	111,972	691	112,663	11,885	2,294	103,071	31,429	38,862	35,824	32,760	4,839	2,504
2013	175,185	113,965	2,016	115,981	13,696	2,378	104,663	30,813	39,710	36,014	32,699	4,864	2,523
2014	181,079	117,731	1,377	119,109	14,070	2,368	107,407	32,355	41,317	37,055	33,675	4,887	2,552
2015	189,115	121,351	1,545	122,896	14,541	2,352	110,707	34,148	44,261	38,531	34,872	4,908	2,587
2016	192,364	124,361	828	125,189	14,817	2,435	112,806	34,728	44,829	39,014	35,220	4,931	2,620
2017	199,192	128,779	1,238	130,017	15,394	2,393	117,016	36,541	45,635	40,223	36,418	4,952	2,649
2018	206,712	134,750	964	135,714	16,253	2,537	121,998	37,413	47,301	41,539	37,848	4,976	2,692
2019	216,588	140,271	723	140,993	16,857	2,639	126,775	40,010	49,803	43,288	39,298	5,003	2,712
2020	232,040	145,181	313	145,494	17,559	2,539	130,473	40,322	61,245	46,119	42,126	5,031	2,671
2021	250,829	154,917	1,432	156,349	18,474	2,871	140,746	41,194	68,889	49,671	45,040	5,050	2,738
2022	256,949	167,286	3,248	170,534	20,166	3,204	153,571	42,948	60,431	50,637	45,079	5,074	...

... = Not available.

Personal Income and Employment by Region and State: Alaska

(Millions of dollars, except as noted.)

Year	Personal income, total	Earnings by place of work			Less: Contributions for government social insurance	Plus: Adjustment for residence	Equals: Net earnings by place of residence	Plus: Dividends, interest, and rent	Plus: Personal current transfer receipts	Per capita (dollars)		Population (thousands)	Total employment (thousands)
		Nonfarm	Farm	Total						Personal income	Disposable personal income		
1960	806	721	2	723	28	-2	694	91	22	3,521	3,162	229	...
1961	797	707	2	709	28	-3	678	92	27	3,347	3,026	238	...
1962	831	739	1	741	29	-5	707	98	26	3,378	3,030	246	...
1963	901	804	1	805	33	-9	763	110	27	3,518	3,146	256	...
1964	1,009	903	1	904	37	-13	854	126	29	3,835	3,497	263	...
1965	1,089	980	1	981	41	-18	922	135	31	4,016	3,612	271	...
1966	1,159	1,050	1	1,051	48	-23	980	145	34	4,276	3,853	271	...
1967	1,264	1,151	1	1,152	54	-31	1,067	158	39	4,545	4,091	278	...
1968	1,365	1,256	2	1,258	67	-39	1,152	166	48	4,790	4,293	285	...
1969	1,575	1,434	1	1,436	94	-25	1,317	206	53	5,322	4,624	296	144
1970	1,799	1,622	2	1,624	105	-46	1,472	255	72	5,911	5,222	304	149
1971	1,984	1,786	2	1,787	118	-60	1,609	284	91	6,269	5,569	316	153
1972	2,167	1,955	2	1,957	134	-75	1,748	314	104	6,636	5,822	326	158
1973	2,508	2,159	2	2,161	165	-93	1,902	359	246	7,525	6,681	333	167
1974	3,043	2,863	2	2,865	241	-209	2,415	419	208	8,827	7,643	345	189
1975	4,157	4,428	4	4,432	408	-610	3,414	506	237	11,205	9,577	371	227
1976	4,893	5,490	4	5,494	526	-879	4,088	571	234	12,447	10,600	393	243
1977	5,082	5,079	5	5,084	463	-452	4,169	635	278	12,789	10,937	397	237
1978	5,236	4,964	5	4,969	435	-324	4,210	727	299	13,018	11,335	402	238
1979	5,547	5,183	4	5,186	468	-274	4,445	809	293	13,745	11,817	404	241
1980	6,285	5,857	3	5,860	511	-329	5,021	920	344	15,507	13,586	405	244
1981	7,152	6,775	2	6,777	653	-457	5,667	1,078	407	17,091	14,647	418	252
1982	8,733	7,842	3	7,844	766	-548	6,530	1,339	864	19,424	16,935	450	277
1983	9,514	8,772	2	8,774	852	-606	7,316	1,564	633	19,478	17,172	488	297
1984	10,121	9,284	2	9,287	952	-620	7,714	1,724	683	19,701	17,573	514	309
1985	10,966	9,767	2	9,769	976	-616	8,177	1,902	887	20,593	18,455	532	316
1986	11,066	9,597	7	9,603	925	-561	8,118	1,950	998	20,331	18,461	544	310
1987	10,618	9,031	9	9,040	871	-526	7,643	1,935	1,039	19,688	17,703	539	310
1988	11,068	9,443	11	9,454	949	-552	7,953	1,997	1,118	20,420	18,483	542	317
1989	12,111	10,312	6	10,318	1,048	-618	8,652	2,220	1,239	22,133	19,732	547	329
1990	12,843	10,927	8	10,936	1,169	-625	9,142	2,331	1,371	23,213	20,549	553	339
1991	13,405	11,449	9	11,458	1,239	-669	9,551	2,382	1,473	23,510	21,008	570	347
1992	14,271	12,110	9	12,119	1,307	-705	10,107	2,529	1,635	24,240	21,767	589	351
1993	15,007	12,557	11	12,569	1,387	-726	10,455	2,731	1,821	25,036	22,515	599	358
1994	15,513	12,877	12	12,889	1,442	-741	10,706	2,942	1,866	25,713	23,059	603	363
1995	15,956	13,067	13	13,080	1,455	-746	10,880	3,120	1,956	26,399	23,705	604	365
1996	16,403	13,276	14	13,290	1,459	-769	11,062	3,236	2,105	26,953	24,138	609	369
1997	17,277	13,869	16	13,885	1,505	-777	11,604	3,400	2,273	28,185	25,176	613	374
1998	18,136	14,510	17	14,527	1,548	-822	12,157	3,509	2,471	29,255	26,080	620	382
1999	18,713	14,863	19	14,882	1,570	-827	12,485	3,512	2,716	29,951	26,769	625	381
2000	20,122	15,846	21	15,867	1,644	-878	13,345	3,700	3,077	32,044	28,606	628	390
2001	21,309	17,010	20	17,030	1,738	-863	14,429	3,661	3,220	33,626	29,967	634	395
2002	22,325	18,003	20	18,023	1,828	-792	15,404	3,614	3,307	34,756	31,583	642	402
2003	23,340	18,940	12	18,952	1,891	-700	16,361	3,734	3,246	35,996	33,032	648	406
2004	24,404	19,916	15	19,930	2,015	-608	17,307	3,889	3,208	37,016	34,156	659	414
2005	26,061	21,147	14	21,161	2,156	-513	18,492	4,165	3,405	39,075	35,849	667	421
2006	27,793	22,320	10	22,330	2,363	-420	19,547	4,631	3,616	41,157	37,574	675	431
2007	29,869	23,384	9	23,393	2,462	-308	20,624	5,162	4,084	43,906	39,806	680	440
2008	32,908	24,430	0	24,430	2,543	-173	21,714	5,732	5,461	47,869	43,261	687	444
2009	33,028	25,466	5	25,471	2,587	-179	22,705	5,576	4,748	47,258	43,732	699	442
2010	35,452	26,974	6	26,980	2,677	-180	24,124	5,993	5,336	49,652	45,912	714	444
2011	37,982	28,469	6	28,475	2,546	-194	25,735	6,708	5,539	52,569	48,304	723	450
2012	39,266	29,645	11	29,656	2,698	-205	26,753	7,111	5,402	53,708	49,533	731	459
2013	38,978	29,863	10	29,873	3,120	-206	26,547	7,018	5,414	52,812	48,237	738	461
2014	41,210	30,596	11	30,608	3,116	-220	27,272	7,458	6,480	55,867	51,038	738	461
2015	42,555	31,422	11	31,433	3,164	-223	28,046	7,871	6,639	57,575	52,379	739	462
2016	41,837	30,568	15	30,583	3,057	-194	27,332	7,946	6,559	56,278	51,460	743	457
2017	42,431	30,659	11	30,670	3,082	-181	27,406	8,048	6,977	57,189	52,613	742	455
2018	43,981	31,602	12	31,615	3,153	-191	28,270	8,151	7,560	59,618	55,260	738	455
2019	45,057	32,204	12	32,216	3,275	-197	28,745	8,364	7,948	61,316	56,603	735	455
2020	45,965	31,821	9	31,831	3,271	-191	28,369	8,225	9,371	62,715	57,902	733	431
2021	48,219	33,296	19	33,315	3,447	-191	29,678	8,269	10,273	65,677	60,099	734	441
2022	50,558	35,554	14	35,567	3,774	-205	31,589	8,586	10,383	68,919	62,045	734	...

... = Not available.

Personal Income and Employment by Region and State: Arizona

(Millions of dollars, except as noted.)

Year	Personal income, total	Derivation of personal income									Per capita (dollars)		Population (thousands)	Total employment (thousands)
		Earnings by place of work			Less: Contributions for government social insurance	Plus: Adjustment for residence	Equals: Net earnings by place of residence	Plus: Dividends, interest, and rent	Plus: Personal current transfer receipts		Personal income	Disposable personal income		
		Nonfarm	Farm	Total										
1960	2,856	2,205	128	2,333	118	-2	2,213	477	166		2,162	1,940	1,321	...
1961	3,110	2,370	135	2,505	125	-2	2,378	538	194		2,210	1,994	1,407	...
1962	3,350	2,567	138	2,705	139	-2	2,564	574	212		2,277	2,046	1,471	...
1963	3,522	2,724	113	2,837	162	-1	2,675	616	231		2,315	2,082	1,521	...
1964	3,777	2,898	130	3,029	167	L	2,861	666	250		2,427	2,219	1,556	...
1965	4,004	3,060	128	3,188	174	1	3,015	707	282		2,528	2,310	1,584	...
1966	4,360	3,425	121	3,547	232	0	3,315	740	305		2,701	2,456	1,614	...
1967	4,739	3,680	149	3,829	266	0	3,564	799	377		2,879	2,604	1,646	...
1968	5,437	4,161	192	4,353	313	3	4,043	959	435		3,233	2,902	1,682	...
1969	6,327	4,775	203	4,979	322	-26	4,631	1,204	492		3,643	3,218	1,737	711
1970	7,216	5,379	180	5,559	362	-30	5,168	1,456	592		4,020	3,570	1,795	747
1971	8,256	6,140	201	6,341	430	-29	5,882	1,664	710		4,354	3,912	1,896	786
1972	9,465	7,126	205	7,332	525	-32	6,775	1,874	816		4,711	4,192	2,009	850
1973	10,934	8,273	240	8,512	695	-31	7,786	2,165	983		5,145	4,624	2,125	925
1974	12,336	9,075	384	9,458	791	-41	8,627	2,522	1,188		5,546	4,956	2,224	955
1975	13,318	9,462	217	9,680	816	-47	8,816	2,841	1,660		5,825	5,324	2,286	935
1976	14,813	10,558	330	10,888	916	-48	9,924	3,061	1,828		6,309	5,723	2,348	976
1977	16,647	12,112	267	12,378	1,061	-57	11,261	3,459	1,928		6,858	6,175	2,427	1,048
1978	19,560	14,371	318	14,689	1,292	-70	13,328	4,059	2,173		7,768	6,935	2,518	1,150
1979	22,987	17,050	399	17,449	1,606	-72	15,771	4,743	2,472		8,712	7,722	2,639	1,240
1980	26,478	19,104	477	19,580	1,822	-81	17,678	5,824	2,976		9,671	8,602	2,738	1,283
1981	30,247	21,357	414	21,771	2,191	-16	19,564	7,187	3,496		10,764	9,489	2,810	1,313
1982	32,197	22,187	396	22,583	2,315	-9	20,259	8,037	3,902		11,141	9,872	2,890	1,315
1983	35,453	24,367	328	24,695	2,580	2	22,117	9,065	4,271		11,941	10,678	2,969	1,379
1984	40,056	27,746	526	28,272	3,018	5	25,259	10,218	4,578		13,060	11,696	3,067	1,504
1985	44,570	31,023	492	31,515	3,435	18	28,098	11,504	4,968		14,000	12,479	3,184	1,622
1986	48,739	34,175	472	34,646	3,805	38	30,880	12,409	5,450		14,733	13,153	3,308	1,701
1987	52,518	36,899	634	37,533	4,075	64	33,522	13,042	5,954		15,280	13,615	3,437	1,765
1988	56,718	39,995	760	40,755	4,563	106	36,298	13,885	6,536		16,044	14,382	3,535	1,833
1989	60,863	41,532	690	42,222	4,873	164	37,513	15,770	7,580		16,803	14,990	3,622	1,865
1990	63,821	43,722	642	44,364	5,269	223	39,319	16,099	8,403		17,323	15,440	3,684	1,894
1991	67,175	46,430	739	47,169	5,627	220	41,761	16,030	9,383		17,731	15,840	3,789	1,903
1992	71,692	50,011	673	50,683	6,016	247	44,914	16,094	10,684		18,309	16,429	3,916	1,925
1993	77,041	53,898	789	54,687	6,488	264	48,463	17,054	11,525		18,950	16,974	4,065	2,011
1994	84,344	59,449	577	60,026	7,169	275	53,131	18,906	12,306		19,869	17,750	4,245	2,141
1995	91,989	64,517	824	65,341	7,483	292	58,150	20,723	13,117		20,753	18,526	4,432	2,258
1996	99,708	70,756	737	71,493	8,373	322	63,442	22,296	13,969		21,737	19,202	4,587	2,388
1997	108,023	77,028	740	77,768	8,976	358	69,150	24,296	14,578		22,804	20,080	4,737	2,497
1998	118,043	85,265	870	86,136	9,786	406	76,756	26,157	15,130		24,173	21,189	4,883	2,616
1999	125,394	91,374	847	92,222	10,488	466	82,200	27,078	16,116		24,960	21,855	5,024	2,696
2000	136,175	99,984	807	100,790	11,419	525	89,896	29,251	17,028		26,388	23,048	5,161	2,802
2001	142,424	104,198	747	104,945	11,946	638	93,637	29,474	19,313		27,008	23,731	5,273	2,829
2002	147,602	107,767	765	108,532	12,346	696	96,882	29,206	21,514		27,353	24,599	5,396	2,847
2003	156,458	113,571	724	114,295	12,824	796	102,267	30,716	23,475		28,393	25,748	5,510	2,917
2004	170,822	123,952	1,024	124,976	13,892	947	112,030	33,016	25,775		30,221	27,367	5,652	3,041
2005	188,762	136,543	986	137,529	15,248	1,058	123,339	36,936	28,487		32,327	28,904	5,839	3,220
2006	209,229	151,863	713	152,575	16,722	1,092	136,945	41,152	31,132		34,703	30,918	6,029	3,375
2007	221,245	158,413	852	159,266	17,693	1,175	142,748	44,713	33,784		35,872	31,988	6,168	3,465
2008	224,508	156,224	634	156,858	17,904	1,214	140,168	44,980	39,360		35,748	32,197	6,280	3,403
2009	212,646	145,068	490	145,558	17,068	1,224	129,714	38,921	44,011		33,524	30,950	6,343	3,228
2010	216,874	145,606	671	146,277	17,246	1,249	130,281	38,707	47,886		33,876	31,157	6,402	3,182
2011	227,700	151,127	1,167	152,294	15,979	1,248	137,563	42,314	47,823		35,321	32,052	6,447	3,239
2012	237,809	158,590	881	159,471	16,523	1,349	144,297	45,660	47,852		36,545	33,231	6,507	3,296
2013	243,752	165,559	1,290	166,849	19,314	1,345	148,881	45,333	49,539		37,139	33,502	6,563	3,371
2014	257,272	172,868	1,065	173,932	19,980	1,455	155,407	49,086	52,780		38,756	34,977	6,638	3,448
2015	270,816	181,242	1,415	182,657	21,012	1,513	163,158	52,955	54,702		40,334	36,174	6,714	3,548
2016	282,085	189,170	1,508	190,678	21,876	1,595	170,396	54,924	56,765		41,473	37,199	6,802	3,645
2017	299,249	200,385	1,416	201,801	23,183	1,668	180,287	57,890	61,073		43,497	39,047	6,880	3,741
2018	316,896	213,879	1,050	214,929	24,906	1,720	191,743	61,095	64,059		45,466	40,904	6,970	3,855
2019	340,260	226,785	1,317	228,102	26,557	1,921	203,466	68,100	68,694		48,124	43,161	7,071	3,930
2020	375,601	239,328	893	240,221	28,181	1,637	213,677	69,029	92,895		52,313	47,331	7,180	3,920
2021	403,739	258,127	814	258,941	29,882	1,911	230,971	71,419	101,350		55,574	49,633	7,265	4,056
2022	417,021	280,723	1,146	281,869	32,702	2,053	251,220	75,823	89,978		56,667	49,493	7,359	...

... = Not available.

Personal Income and Employment by Region and State: Arkansas

(Millions of dollars, except as noted.)

Year	Personal income, total	Earnings by place of work Nonfarm	Farm	Total	Less: Contributions for government social insurance	Plus: Adjustment for residence	Equals: Net earnings by place of residence	Plus: Dividends, interest, and rent	Plus: Personal current transfer receipts	Per capita (dollars) Personal income	Disposable personal income	Population (thousands)	Total employment (thousands)
1960	2,548	1,805	313	2,118	92	-2	2,025	283	240	1,424	1,314	1,789	...
1961	2,772	1,919	368	2,287	95	-2	2,190	313	269	1,535	1,418	1,806	...
1962	2,966	2,112	324	2,436	109	-3	2,324	354	288	1,600	1,464	1,853	...
1963	3,142	2,254	322	2,577	127	-4	2,446	386	310	1,676	1,533	1,875	...
1964	3,412	2,441	360	2,802	137	-4	2,661	425	326	1,799	1,668	1,897	...
1965	3,602	2,621	288	2,909	147	-6	2,756	488	357	1,902	1,755	1,894	...
1966	4,005	2,876	393	3,269	191	-4	3,074	540	391	2,109	1,925	1,899	...
1967	4,254	3,123	301	3,424	221	-5	3,198	588	468	2,238	2,043	1,901	...
1968	4,601	3,437	337	3,774	252	-7	3,516	560	525	2,419	2,184	1,902	...
1969	5,129	3,775	346	4,121	278	32	3,875	670	584	2,681	2,399	1,913	800
1970	5,627	4,026	415	4,441	296	24	4,168	775	684	2,915	2,623	1,930	805
1971	6,263	4,503	407	4,911	340	22	4,593	869	802	3,176	2,893	1,972	831
1972	7,071	5,123	482	5,605	405	22	5,222	956	893	3,504	3,178	2,018	867
1973	8,376	5,773	914	6,687	524	18	6,180	1,113	1,083	4,069	3,676	2,058	902
1974	9,354	6,468	833	7,301	609	11	6,704	1,335	1,315	4,453	3,993	2,100	927
1975	10,292	6,938	795	7,732	638	9	7,103	1,520	1,669	4,769	4,355	2,158	905
1976	11,379	7,991	641	8,632	745	-1	7,886	1,664	1,829	5,247	4,726	2,169	941
1977	12,662	8,968	725	9,693	847	-7	8,839	1,881	1,942	5,736	5,183	2,207	981
1978	14,669	10,203	1,176	11,379	987	-12	10,380	2,157	2,132	6,546	5,912	2,241	1,021
1979	16,088	11,320	995	12,315	1,134	-15	11,166	2,478	2,444	7,090	6,355	2,269	1,031
1980	17,388	12,275	372	12,647	1,220	-5	11,422	3,067	2,900	7,597	6,773	2,289	1,032
1981	19,703	13,193	851	14,044	1,422	-23	12,598	3,824	3,280	8,592	7,669	2,293	1,026
1982	20,702	13,647	642	14,289	1,498	-21	12,770	4,366	3,567	9,024	8,006	2,294	1,011
1983	21,935	14,819	417	15,237	1,638	-50	13,548	4,528	3,859	9,513	8,538	2,306	1,039
1984	24,458	16,424	883	17,307	1,869	-69	15,369	5,046	4,044	10,543	9,533	2,320	1,079
1985	25,982	17,435	865	18,300	2,005	-75	16,219	5,482	4,282	11,165	10,065	2,327	1,098
1986	27,304	18,534	805	19,338	2,141	-101	17,097	5,695	4,512	11,708	10,588	2,332	1,110
1987	28,435	19,594	935	20,529	2,251	-124	18,154	5,638	4,644	12,139	10,933	2,342	1,137
1988	30,506	20,919	1,344	22,264	2,507	-158	19,599	6,022	4,885	13,022	11,754	2,343	1,170
1989	32,721	22,240	1,238	23,477	2,675	-161	20,641	6,681	5,399	13,946	12,550	2,346	1,189
1990	34,458	23,756	1,048	24,803	2,965	-220	21,618	6,993	5,847	14,622	13,137	2,357	1,204
1991	36,459	25,240	1,128	26,368	3,149	-248	22,971	7,005	6,483	15,299	13,787	2,383	1,230
1992	39,714	27,564	1,430	28,994	3,409	-271	25,314	7,212	7,189	16,438	14,838	2,416	1,255
1993	41,648	29,115	1,336	30,450	3,619	-308	26,524	7,538	7,587	16,956	15,301	2,456	1,301
1994	44,289	31,067	1,466	32,533	3,908	-334	28,291	8,035	7,963	17,758	15,957	2,494	1,329
1995	47,165	32,823	1,481	34,305	4,110	-304	29,891	8,684	8,590	18,602	16,674	2,535	1,382
1996	50,048	34,261	1,922	36,183	4,251	-301	31,631	9,315	9,102	19,458	17,424	2,572	1,405
1997	52,508	36,076	1,811	37,887	4,460	-305	33,122	9,884	9,502	20,187	17,992	2,601	1,427
1998	55,698	38,815	1,596	40,410	4,734	-306	35,370	10,511	9,818	21,208	18,841	2,626	1,446
1999	57,999	40,849	1,807	42,655	4,962	-322	37,372	10,506	10,121	21,871	19,463	2,652	1,460
2000	61,021	43,005	1,704	44,709	5,196	-360	39,153	11,126	10,741	22,781	20,218	2,679	1,482
2001	64,255	44,768	2,010	46,778	5,350	-374	41,054	11,291	11,910	23,873	21,234	2,692	1,483
2002	65,770	46,555	1,271	47,825	5,517	-373	41,936	11,009	12,825	24,306	21,976	2,706	1,479
2003	69,742	48,609	2,403	51,012	5,719	-351	44,941	11,410	13,391	25,595	23,392	2,725	1,482
2004	74,405	51,512	2,763	54,276	6,005	-319	47,951	12,104	14,350	27,059	24,781	2,750	1,505
2005	78,501	54,262	1,866	56,128	6,357	-288	49,483	13,622	15,395	28,227	25,653	2,781	1,538
2006	83,572	56,821	1,506	58,327	6,817	-249	51,262	15,501	16,810	29,617	26,840	2,822	1,568
2007	89,171	58,692	1,900	60,592	7,102	-182	53,309	17,686	18,176	31,303	28,186	2,849	1,583
2008	92,865	59,189	1,613	60,803	7,393	-139	53,270	19,328	20,267	32,306	29,065	2,875	1,579
2009	91,171	58,443	943	59,386	7,393	-120	51,874	17,301	21,997	31,472	28,864	2,897	1,543
2010	94,576	60,514	679	61,194	7,603	-129	53,461	17,503	23,612	32,372	29,723	2,922	1,541
2011	100,739	62,848	724	63,572	7,116	-112	56,344	20,308	24,087	34,279	31,201	2,939	1,562
2012	107,877	65,849	1,127	66,976	7,258	-156	59,562	23,979	24,337	36,582	33,378	2,949	1,565
2013	108,368	67,122	2,513	69,635	8,263	-215	61,157	22,453	24,758	36,677	33,186	2,955	1,569
2014	114,743	69,339	2,044	71,383	8,600	-225	62,558	25,935	26,250	38,749	35,102	2,961	1,587
2015	118,720	71,190	1,396	72,586	8,865	-258	63,463	27,823	27,434	39,968	36,127	2,970	1,611
2016	121,826	72,425	995	73,419	8,981	-209	64,229	29,174	28,423	40,873	36,889	2,981	1,630
2017	125,286	74,838	1,632	76,470	9,311	-318	66,840	29,464	28,981	41,890	37,824	2,991	1,640
2018	130,033	77,054	1,329	78,384	9,586	-367	68,431	31,686	29,917	43,384	39,493	2,997	1,658
2019	133,161	80,292	779	81,071	10,056	-368	70,647	30,938	31,577	44,324	40,285	3,004	1,664
2020	142,039	83,252	955	84,207	10,651	-373	73,183	30,262	38,593	47,123	43,087	3,014	1,640
2021	153,186	89,125	2,144	91,269	11,146	-489	79,635	31,022	42,530	50,588	45,909	3,028	1,676
2022	157,725	96,082	4,665	100,747	12,073	-501	88,173	32,259	37,293	51,787	46,218	3,046	...

... = Not available.

Personal Income and Employment by Region and State: California

(Millions of dollars, except as noted.)

Year	Personal income, total	Earnings by place of work			Less: Contributions for government social insurance	Plus: Adjustment for residence	Equals: Net earnings by place of residence	Plus: Dividends, interest, and rent	Plus: Personal current transfer receipts	Per capita (dollars)		Population (thousands)	Total employment (thousands)
		Nonfarm	Farm	Total						Personal income	Disposable personal income		
1960	46,521	36,478	1,437	37,915	1,720	-5	36,190	7,747	2,585	2,931	2,602	15,870	...
1961	49,267	38,626	1,369	39,995	1,832	-5	38,158	8,109	2,999	2,986	2,654	16,497	...
1962	53,086	41,937	1,433	43,370	2,249	-6	41,116	8,791	3,179	3,110	2,759	17,072	...
1963	56,740	45,049	1,367	46,416	2,625	-6	43,786	9,437	3,517	3,211	2,850	17,668	...
1964	61,405	48,481	1,517	49,997	2,731	-7	47,260	10,332	3,813	3,383	3,053	18,151	...
1965	65,618	51,529	1,464	52,993	2,846	-8	50,138	11,267	4,213	3,531	3,187	18,585	...
1966	71,356	56,763	1,583	58,346	3,740	-11	54,595	12,108	4,653	3,784	3,397	18,858	...
1967	76,732	60,732	1,496	62,227	4,100	-12	58,115	12,862	5,755	4,001	3,578	19,176	...
1968	84,056	66,766	1,720	68,486	4,587	-14	63,885	13,528	6,643	4,334	3,832	19,394	...
1969	92,160	72,625	1,705	74,329	4,827	-98	69,405	15,139	7,616	4,676	4,105	19,711	9,033
1970	99,418	76,644	1,709	78,352	5,018	-94	73,241	16,876	9,301	4,965	4,430	20,023	9,057
1971	105,987	80,876	1,707	82,583	5,449	-111	77,023	18,269	10,696	5,209	4,701	20,346	9,036
1972	116,351	89,229	2,173	91,402	6,333	-118	84,951	19,878	11,522	5,652	5,013	20,585	9,368
1973	127,777	97,953	2,931	100,884	7,973	-103	92,808	22,211	12,758	6,123	5,477	20,868	9,844
1974	142,507	107,472	3,645	111,117	9,013	-100	102,004	25,386	15,118	6,731	5,998	21,173	10,163
1975	157,640	117,020	3,273	120,293	9,600	17	110,710	27,936	18,994	7,320	6,602	21,537	10,286
1976	174,925	131,249	3,477	134,726	10,978	120	123,868	30,045	21,012	7,975	7,121	21,935	10,633
1977	194,033	147,538	3,543	151,081	12,560	-21	138,500	33,226	22,307	8,681	7,699	22,350	11,119
1978	220,640	169,787	3,489	173,277	14,806	-22	158,449	38,085	24,106	9,661	8,509	22,839	11,816
1979	250,174	192,947	4,573	197,520	17,663	62	179,919	43,770	26,486	10,758	9,410	23,255	12,461
1980	284,308	214,018	5,582	219,600	19,262	7	200,344	53,180	30,784	11,945	10,434	23,801	12,762
1981	319,557	236,420	4,354	240,774	23,093	286	217,967	65,379	36,211	13,158	11,518	24,286	12,935
1982	342,343	250,604	4,600	255,203	24,994	296	230,504	72,151	39,688	13,793	12,165	24,820	12,863
1983	369,809	271,683	4,235	275,917	27,641	300	248,577	78,857	42,376	14,582	12,896	25,360	13,182
1984	410,796	303,540	4,910	308,450	32,061	245	276,634	89,947	44,216	15,895	14,046	25,844	13,797
1985	444,067	330,520	4,950	335,470	35,323	195	300,342	95,922	47,803	16,795	14,755	26,441	14,285
1986	476,682	358,456	5,390	363,846	38,688	154	325,313	100,017	51,353	17,588	15,467	27,102	14,710
1987	513,377	392,750	6,591	399,341	42,355	76	357,062	102,736	53,579	18,482	16,073	27,777	15,300
1988	558,041	430,149	6,936	437,086	47,729	38	389,394	111,296	57,351	19,605	17,205	28,464	16,022
1989	600,755	456,298	6,839	463,137	51,065	25	412,098	125,843	62,814	20,561	17,869	29,218	16,426
1990	643,685	488,244	7,216	495,460	54,273	-47	441,140	133,372	69,173	21,485	18,711	29,960	16,835
1991	665,993	505,398	6,316	511,714	56,411	-38	455,264	134,003	76,725	21,857	19,253	30,471	16,750
1992	702,449	529,964	6,825	536,789	58,517	-43	478,229	135,584	88,636	22,678	20,135	30,975	16,391
1993	719,731	538,594	7,769	546,363	59,531	25	486,856	139,271	93,604	23,013	20,437	31,275	16,367
1994	742,429	554,983	7,547	562,530	61,692	36	500,874	145,732	95,824	23,581	20,913	31,484	16,541
1995	780,643	579,282	7,227	586,509	63,539	25	522,995	157,304	100,343	24,629	21,714	31,697	16,940
1996	829,667	614,255	8,129	622,384	65,645	14	556,752	167,650	105,264	25,912	22,592	32,019	17,342
1997	882,677	659,334	8,693	668,027	69,728	-68	598,231	178,621	105,825	27,171	23,454	32,486	17,667
1998	959,694	721,879	8,186	730,065	75,085	-74	654,906	193,062	111,725	29,092	24,955	32,988	18,433
1999	1,030,885	785,504	8,940	794,444	81,356	-79	713,009	200,491	117,386	30,773	26,014	33,499	18,852
2000	1,135,543	878,689	8,860	887,549	90,070	-254	797,226	216,140	122,178	33,410	27,660	33,988	19,229
2001	1,173,879	906,336	8,429	914,765	94,915	-314	819,536	218,658	135,685	34,046	28,808	34,479	19,341
2002	1,190,224	923,182	8,965	932,148	97,840	-428	833,879	210,300	146,045	34,131	29,928	34,872	19,358
2003	1,243,466	963,387	10,102	973,489	102,893	-594	870,002	219,221	154,242	35,272	31,229	35,253	19,479
2004	1,318,744	1,029,140	12,298	1,041,438	112,470	-788	928,180	229,112	161,452	37,070	32,832	35,575	19,784
2005	1,394,855	1,078,900	12,380	1,091,281	117,547	-977	972,757	252,797	169,301	38,932	33,966	35,828	20,127
2006	1,503,754	1,144,294	10,330	1,154,624	120,870	-1,232	1,032,522	289,379	181,853	41,746	36,259	36,021	20,505
2007	1,572,721	1,176,705	12,902	1,189,607	122,701	-1,504	1,065,402	314,524	192,795	43,385	37,446	36,250	20,888
2008	1,594,743	1,168,747	11,119	1,179,866	125,000	-1,754	1,053,112	323,563	218,067	43,567	37,777	36,604	20,654
2009	1,540,873	1,124,230	12,363	1,136,593	121,063	-1,514	1,014,015	285,807	241,051	41,689	37,319	36,961	19,838
2010	1,614,041	1,172,948	13,171	1,186,119	121,824	-1,453	1,062,843	284,291	266,907	43,246	38,472	37,322	19,642
2011	1,715,227	1,233,632	15,225	1,248,857	114,605	-1,400	1,132,852	313,871	268,504	45,557	40,011	37,651	19,986
2012	1,827,167	1,308,356	17,370	1,325,726	119,274	-1,306	1,205,146	350,920	271,101	48,121	42,215	37,970	20,667
2013	1,857,201	1,354,086	20,066	1,374,152	139,628	-1,160	1,233,363	341,830	282,008	48,502	41,878	38,291	21,320
2014	1,980,737	1,426,952	22,120	1,449,072	147,564	-1,250	1,300,259	379,127	301,351	51,266	44,115	38,636	21,997
2015	2,125,430	1,520,153	21,168	1,541,321	156,315	-1,457	1,383,548	416,148	325,735	54,546	46,585	38,966	22,687
2016	2,218,458	1,588,891	18,505	1,607,396	162,945	-1,624	1,442,827	437,469	338,162	56,560	48,417	39,223	23,178
2017	2,318,281	1,673,390	19,958	1,693,348	171,572	-1,849	1,519,927	463,265	335,089	58,804	50,341	39,424	23,549
2018	2,431,774	1,761,836	15,863	1,777,700	181,953	-1,903	1,593,844	485,742	352,188	61,508	52,565	39,536	24,078
2019	2,567,426	1,850,457	15,858	1,866,315	192,290	-2,079	1,671,946	519,850	375,630	64,919	55,602	39,548	24,228
2020	2,790,524	1,899,441	16,999	1,916,441	196,085	-2,216	1,718,140	521,103	551,281	70,643	60,853	39,502	23,155
2021	3,006,184	2,089,644	13,001	2,102,645	211,918	-2,622	1,888,105	534,935	583,144	76,800	64,579	39,143	23,906
2022	3,018,471	2,190,763	17,991	2,208,754	223,613	-2,523	1,982,619	562,060	473,792	77,339	63,219	39,029	...

... = Not available.

Personal Income and Employment by Region and State: Colorado

(Millions of dollars, except as noted.)

Year	Personal income, total	Earnings by place of work — Nonfarm	Earnings by place of work — Farm	Earnings by place of work — Total	Less: Contributions for government social insurance	Plus: Adjustment for residence	Equals: Net earnings by place of residence	Plus: Dividends, interest, and rent	Plus: Personal current transfer receipts	Per capita (dollars) — Personal income	Per capita (dollars) — Disposable personal income	Population (thousands)	Total employment (thousands)
1960	4,353	3,287	174	3,461	133	1	3,330	748	276	2,461	2,184	1,769	...
1961	4,684	3,557	176	3,733	150	1	3,584	799	302	2,540	2,255	1,844	...
1962	4,942	3,755	156	3,911	163	1	3,748	875	319	2,602	2,314	1,899	...
1963	5,174	3,960	140	4,100	191	0	3,909	926	339	2,673	2,377	1,936	...
1964	5,474	4,206	137	4,343	197	L	4,146	985	344	2,779	2,520	1,970	...
1965	5,841	4,408	213	4,621	198	-0	4,423	1,043	375	2,942	2,664	1,985	...
1966	6,276	4,831	192	5,023	263	-1	4,759	1,110	407	3,127	2,812	2,007	...
1967	6,764	5,189	186	5,375	295	-1	5,079	1,201	483	3,294	2,951	2,053	...
1968	7,503	5,768	244	6,012	334	-2	5,676	1,278	549	3,539	3,137	2,120	...
1969	8,439	6,455	251	6,706	387	1	6,319	1,514	605	3,896	3,409	2,166	1,001
1970	9,540	7,184	289	7,473	427	3	7,049	1,761	730	4,290	3,800	2,224	1,032
1971	10,760	8,147	301	8,449	499	4	7,954	1,956	850	4,671	4,160	2,304	1,072
1972	12,176	9,340	333	9,673	606	5	9,072	2,162	943	5,064	4,452	2,405	1,149
1973	13,923	10,680	440	11,120	798	3	10,326	2,490	1,108	5,579	4,923	2,496	1,243
1974	15,609	11,815	535	12,350	905	4	11,449	2,877	1,283	6,142	5,396	2,541	1,276
1975	17,250	12,904	464	13,368	967	9	12,409	3,230	1,610	6,670	5,939	2,586	1,285
1976	18,981	14,483	336	14,820	1,105	9	13,723	3,496	1,762	7,211	6,385	2,632	1,340
1977	21,174	16,379	266	16,645	1,261	11	15,395	3,911	1,869	7,854	6,904	2,696	1,411
1978	24,414	19,130	209	19,339	1,507	19	17,852	4,529	2,033	8,824	7,733	2,767	1,506
1979	27,979	22,126	218	22,343	1,839	13	20,518	5,178	2,284	9,820	8,549	2,849	1,593
1980	32,051	24,945	290	25,235	2,106	20	23,149	6,250	2,653	11,019	9,589	2,909	1,651
1981	36,883	28,429	306	28,735	2,598	3	26,140	7,629	3,114	12,386	10,714	2,978	1,717
1982	40,506	31,059	185	31,244	2,908	0	28,336	8,641	3,529	13,230	11,429	3,062	1,760
1983	43,694	32,980	361	33,341	3,130	-2	30,209	9,582	3,903	13,944	12,353	3,134	1,788
1984	47,645	36,070	426	36,496	3,539	7	32,964	10,567	4,113	15,030	13,361	3,170	1,883
1985	50,484	38,164	396	38,559	3,835	16	34,741	11,438	4,305	15,733	13,954	3,209	1,915
1986	52,446	39,583	398	39,981	4,021	21	35,981	11,844	4,621	16,200	14,421	3,237	1,914
1987	54,400	40,935	477	41,413	4,121	32	37,323	12,096	4,981	16,685	14,800	3,260	1,903
1988	57,557	43,443	578	44,020	4,530	46	39,536	12,771	5,249	17,643	15,693	3,262	1,968
1989	62,010	45,962	621	46,582	4,888	63	41,757	14,403	5,850	18,930	16,715	3,276	2,003
1990	65,667	49,007	713	49,719	5,334	86	44,471	14,928	6,269	19,853	17,471	3,308	2,040
1991	69,602	52,468	640	53,107	5,856	97	47,348	15,291	6,963	20,549	18,121	3,387	2,087
1992	75,599	57,556	679	58,235	6,359	112	51,989	15,791	7,819	21,625	19,077	3,496	2,135
1993	81,812	62,492	815	63,307	6,987	124	56,444	16,986	8,382	22,639	19,922	3,614	2,234
1994	87,984	67,131	584	67,714	7,557	142	60,299	18,792	8,893	23,625	20,733	3,724	2,345
1995	95,649	72,072	544	72,616	8,075	163	64,704	20,970	9,975	24,995	21,930	3,827	2,425
1996	103,236	77,860	671	78,531	8,626	182	70,088	22,814	10,335	26,336	22,924	3,920	2,519
1997	111,208	84,530	676	85,206	9,300	205	76,111	24,597	10,501	27,675	23,881	4,018	2,629
1998	123,090	94,416	806	95,222	9,710	231	85,743	26,629	10,719	29,901	25,664	4,117	2,732
1999	132,294	103,813	937	104,750	10,549	261	94,462	26,429	11,404	31,305	26,747	4,226	2,808
2000	147,242	116,473	777	117,250	11,704	288	105,835	29,359	12,049	34,029	28,897	4,327	2,918
2001	154,445	121,840	1,074	122,915	12,314	309	110,910	30,180	13,355	34,897	30,030	4,426	2,942
2002	154,640	122,448	714	123,162	12,725	339	110,776	29,023	14,841	34,438	30,355	4,490	2,917
2003	157,852	123,990	754	124,744	12,955	363	112,153	30,116	15,583	34,856	31,113	4,529	2,909
2004	163,873	128,797	957	129,755	13,827	398	116,326	31,306	16,241	35,819	31,975	4,575	2,958
2005	175,069	136,332	1,115	137,448	14,684	429	123,193	34,328	17,549	37,797	33,364	4,632	3,037
2006	189,466	145,616	811	146,428	15,587	476	131,316	39,296	18,853	40,137	35,139	4,720	3,109
2007	202,116	152,466	1,106	153,572	16,420	505	137,657	44,267	20,193	42,074	36,588	4,804	3,218
2008	210,029	155,239	907	156,146	17,113	523	139,556	46,949	23,524	42,953	37,572	4,890	3,251
2009	199,352	146,735	766	147,501	16,490	563	131,574	41,648	26,130	40,093	36,072	4,972	3,164
2010	205,866	150,240	1,017	151,258	16,668	663	135,253	41,020	29,593	40,790	36,484	5,047	3,144
2011	223,493	159,116	1,326	160,442	15,796	827	145,473	47,469	30,551	43,658	38,570	5,119	3,204
2012	236,759	168,505	1,250	169,756	16,572	1,027	154,211	51,848	30,701	45,630	40,386	5,189	3,263
2013	249,513	182,350	1,339	183,689	19,223	1,183	165,649	52,001	31,862	47,404	41,677	5,264	3,356
2014	271,410	197,495	1,415	198,910	20,676	1,232	179,466	57,750	34,195	50,797	44,581	5,343	3,468
2015	284,837	203,744	1,620	205,364	21,820	1,232	184,776	62,643	37,418	52,339	45,711	5,442	3,574
2016	289,673	206,332	1,307	207,639	22,566	1,204	186,277	64,417	38,979	52,390	45,598	5,529	3,667
2017	309,417	223,011	967	223,978	23,930	1,319	201,367	68,073	39,978	55,251	48,265	5,600	3,761
2018	331,851	238,798	880	239,678	25,512	1,346	215,512	72,987	43,352	58,453	51,382	5,677	3,858
2019	356,341	253,549	1,059	254,607	26,948	1,386	229,046	81,652	45,644	62,124	54,511	5,736	3,895
2020	378,051	259,851	847	260,699	27,640	1,378	234,437	82,104	61,511	65,352	57,647	5,785	3,822
2021	410,948	283,044	1,272	284,315	29,440	1,552	256,427	85,564	68,957	70,715	61,514	5,811	3,946
2022	433,128	310,555	1,486	312,041	32,397	1,661	281,304	91,340	60,484	74,167	62,984	5,840	...

... = Not available.

Personal Income and Employment by Region and State: Connecticut

(Millions of dollars, except as noted.)

Year	Personal income, total	Derivation of personal income									Per capita (dollars)		Population (thousands)	Total employment (thousands)
		Earnings by place of work			Less: Contributions for government social insurance	Plus: Adjustment for residence	Equals: Net earnings by place of residence	Plus: Dividends, interest, and rent	Plus: Personal current transfer receipts		Personal income	Disposable personal income		
		Nonfarm	Farm	Total										
1960	7,276	5,829	63	5,892	278	3	5,617	1,270	389		2,860	2,499	2,544	...
1961	7,702	6,094	58	6,152	290	3	5,864	1,389	448		2,978	2,612	2,586	...
1962	8,227	6,517	59	6,576	320	3	6,259	1,528	441		3,108	2,722	2,647	...
1963	8,691	6,865	64	6,929	369	4	6,564	1,658	469		3,187	2,777	2,727	...
1964	9,335	7,337	62	7,399	379	5	7,025	1,815	495		3,336	2,963	2,798	...
1965	10,039	7,858	71	7,929	395	2	7,535	1,980	523		3,514	3,100	2,857	...
1966	11,024	8,795	73	8,868	553	-1	8,315	2,145	564		3,797	3,323	2,903	...
1967	12,086	9,505	58	9,562	602	1	8,961	2,424	702		4,118	3,575	2,935	...
1968	12,829	10,213	68	10,281	671	7	9,617	2,358	854		4,328	3,689	2,964	...
1969	14,693	11,149	67	11,216	753	723	11,187	2,559	948		4,898	4,144	3,000	1,417
1970	15,674	11,734	72	11,805	784	717	11,738	2,790	1,146		5,158	4,485	3,039	1,414
1971	16,514	12,145	69	12,215	841	749	12,122	2,968	1,424		5,394	4,764	3,061	1,388
1972	17,805	13,216	68	13,284	969	793	13,108	3,191	1,505		5,800	5,050	3,070	1,416
1973	19,393	14,633	81	14,714	1,236	804	14,283	3,481	1,630		6,319	5,537	3,069	1,480
1974	21,157	15,832	84	15,916	1,397	838	15,357	3,882	1,918		6,879	6,024	3,076	1,511
1975	22,726	16,487	75	16,563	1,424	929	16,068	4,112	2,546		7,367	6,547	3,085	1,468
1976	24,536	17,946	83	18,028	1,578	1,000	17,450	4,373	2,714		7,951	6,974	3,086	1,493
1977	27,033	19,979	84	20,062	1,779	1,105	19,389	4,807	2,837		8,752	7,678	3,089	1,546
1978	30,081	22,509	80	22,590	2,061	1,264	21,793	5,364	2,924		9,720	8,441	3,095	1,615
1979	33,814	25,390	79	25,469	2,421	1,439	24,487	6,073	3,254		10,908	9,397	3,100	1,673
1980	38,494	28,231	84	28,315	2,680	1,689	27,324	7,425	3,745		12,365	10,593	3,113	1,705
1981	43,243	30,953	82	31,035	3,155	1,893	29,772	9,151	4,320		13,821	11,788	3,129	1,727
1982	46,701	33,014	108	33,122	3,431	2,040	31,732	10,167	4,802		14,878	12,672	3,139	1,726
1983	49,958	35,629	106	35,735	3,737	2,178	34,176	10,598	5,185		15,798	13,799	3,162	1,743
1984	55,881	40,098	129	40,228	4,306	2,339	38,261	12,199	5,421		17,572	15,436	3,180	1,823
1985	60,000	43,677	128	43,805	4,742	2,577	41,640	12,612	5,748		18,743	16,319	3,201	1,879
1986	64,553	47,450	140	47,590	5,165	2,674	45,098	13,375	6,080		20,024	17,335	3,224	1,937
1987	70,443	52,742	142	52,884	5,653	2,823	50,054	14,105	6,284		21,693	18,593	3,247	1,984
1988	77,668	58,304	155	58,459	6,356	3,072	55,175	15,712	6,781		23,738	20,612	3,272	2,039
1989	84,249	61,502	141	61,642	6,676	3,087	58,053	18,594	7,602		25,659	22,300	3,283	2,032
1990	86,889	63,319	186	63,504	6,798	2,745	59,451	18,938	8,500		26,394	23,007	3,292	2,003
1991	87,816	64,201	165	64,366	7,011	2,709	60,065	18,230	9,521		26,588	23,198	3,303	1,923
1992	94,269	67,580	188	67,768	7,251	3,939	64,456	18,614	11,200		28,560	24,665	3,301	1,904
1993	97,348	70,246	210	70,456	7,515	3,346	66,286	19,379	11,683		29,417	25,298	3,309	1,925
1994	100,108	72,569	186	72,755	7,873	3,102	67,984	20,026	12,099		30,188	25,958	3,316	1,906
1995	105,643	75,853	173	76,026	8,269	3,827	71,584	21,105	12,954		31,780	27,144	3,324	1,944
1996	110,746	79,352	161	79,513	8,622	4,537	75,428	22,016	13,303		33,191	27,863	3,337	1,975
1997	117,992	86,018	158	86,175	9,146	4,072	81,102	23,222	13,668		35,228	29,192	3,349	2,000
1998	127,302	92,714	179	92,893	9,592	5,482	88,782	24,680	13,840		37,827	31,058	3,365	2,037
1999	134,439	99,841	192	100,033	10,054	5,362	95,341	24,927	14,171		39,700	32,506	3,386	2,070
2000	146,946	109,656	225	109,881	10,680	5,526	104,728	27,299	14,920		43,070	34,980	3,412	2,118
2001	155,003	116,759	200	116,959	11,047	5,563	111,474	27,692	15,836		45,153	36,781	3,433	2,125
2002	154,596	117,549	189	117,738	11,506	5,728	111,961	25,656	16,980		44,697	37,991	3,459	2,118
2003	156,785	118,824	189	119,013	11,752	5,830	113,091	26,369	17,325		44,997	38,667	3,484	2,112
2004	165,149	123,788	199	123,987	12,345	6,843	118,485	28,289	18,376		47,238	40,493	3,496	2,144
2005	174,430	129,022	189	129,211	12,768	7,652	124,095	31,377	18,958		49,738	41,950	3,507	2,172
2006	188,873	135,627	174	135,801	13,240	8,814	131,375	37,267	20,231		53,696	45,093	3,517	2,202
2007	203,467	143,090	200	143,291	13,837	10,336	139,790	42,211	21,466		57,684	47,878	3,527	2,246
2008	216,175	150,694	210	150,904	14,286	11,467	148,084	43,528	24,563		60,970	51,372	3,546	2,256
2009	212,583	152,772	204	152,976	13,919	8,859	147,915	37,424	27,244		59,684	52,436	3,562	2,196
2010	221,059	157,166	207	157,373	14,026	10,852	154,199	37,794	29,066		61,743	53,964	3,580	2,172
2011	226,907	158,628	192	158,820	12,981	11,364	157,204	40,551	29,153		63,132	54,252	3,594	2,206
2012	231,171	156,966	252	157,218	13,324	13,194	157,088	44,584	29,499		64,121	55,025	3,605	2,223
2013	226,176	155,691	260	155,951	15,441	12,508	153,019	43,328	29,829		62,647	52,494	3,610	2,247
2014	236,757	160,188	189	160,377	15,917	12,952	157,412	48,606	30,739		65,498	54,983	3,615	2,266
2015	243,165	163,676	195	163,871	16,409	13,275	160,737	50,681	31,746		67,321	56,384	3,612	2,288
2016	247,777	166,770	170	166,940	16,710	12,657	162,886	52,210	32,681		68,680	58,105	3,608	2,301
2017	252,571	168,818	184	169,002	17,157	15,097	166,942	52,454	33,176		70,011	59,101	3,608	2,300
2018	263,358	172,273	157	172,429	17,598	16,843	171,674	56,249	35,435		72,926	61,964	3,611	2,314
2019	272,459	174,610	192	174,802	18,108	20,160	176,854	59,272	36,333		75,533	64,298	3,607	2,298
2020	282,486	174,684	153	174,837	18,160	19,771	176,447	58,333	47,706		78,526	67,090	3,597	2,217
2021	300,324	185,090	149	185,240	18,870	23,599	189,969	59,296	51,059		82,885	69,692	3,623	2,283
2022	308,126	198,018	208	198,227	20,334	25,354	203,246	61,503	43,377		84,972	69,247	3,626	...

... = Not available.

Personal Income and Employment by Region and State: Delaware

(Millions of dollars, except as noted.)

Year	Personal income, total	Earnings by place of work			Less: Contributions for government social insurance	Plus: Adjustment for residence	Equals: Net earnings by place of residence	Plus: Dividends, interest, and rent	Plus: Personal current transfer receipts	Per capita (dollars)		Population (thousands)	Total employment (thousands)
		Nonfarm	Farm	Total						Personal income	Disposable personal income		
1960	1,290	1,035	34	1,069	53	-51	966	270	54	2,873	2,414	449	...
1961	1,331	1,062	30	1,092	51	-51	990	277	65	2,888	2,441	461	...
1962	1,414	1,127	33	1,160	58	-52	1,050	297	67	3,014	2,518	469	...
1963	1,517	1,223	26	1,249	69	-56	1,124	323	70	3,140	2,647	483	...
1964	1,641	1,322	26	1,348	68	-58	1,221	346	74	3,302	2,789	497	...
1965	1,806	1,459	35	1,494	69	-65	1,360	366	80	3,561	3,004	507	...
1966	1,903	1,599	26	1,625	99	-69	1,457	357	88	3,687	3,122	516	...
1967	2,031	1,701	32	1,733	117	-68	1,548	374	108	3,868	3,289	525	...
1968	2,215	1,860	29	1,889	119	-70	1,700	388	127	4,148	3,503	534	...
1969	2,441	2,000	55	2,055	139	-29	1,887	415	139	4,521	3,753	540	271
1970	2,600	2,136	35	2,171	147	-31	1,993	443	165	4,724	3,949	550	275
1971	2,844	2,360	38	2,398	168	-46	2,184	466	194	5,032	4,248	565	280
1972	3,125	2,616	49	2,665	196	-54	2,415	495	215	5,446	4,584	574	293
1973	3,462	2,912	96	3,007	253	-76	2,679	535	248	5,979	5,020	579	305
1974	3,747	3,129	82	3,211	282	-80	2,850	594	303	6,426	5,412	583	302
1975	4,029	3,316	92	3,408	293	-90	3,025	596	408	6,844	5,848	589	292
1976	4,404	3,643	84	3,727	325	-99	3,303	662	439	7,430	6,258	593	296
1977	4,741	3,934	56	3,990	351	-114	3,525	739	478	7,971	6,721	595	296
1978	5,202	4,368	61	4,429	401	-138	3,890	812	500	8,696	7,335	598	304
1979	5,717	4,798	54	4,853	460	-156	4,236	907	573	9,547	7,983	599	312
1980	6,431	5,318	13	5,331	510	-193	4,627	1,108	695	10,809	9,028	595	312
1981	7,094	5,714	43	5,756	591	-211	4,955	1,357	782	11,903	9,868	596	314
1982	7,634	6,145	65	6,211	647	-243	5,320	1,483	831	12,742	10,710	599	317
1983	8,132	6,622	79	6,700	703	-289	5,707	1,539	886	13,431	11,430	605	325
1984	8,973	7,280	96	7,376	779	-328	6,268	1,755	949	14,671	12,569	612	340
1985	9,734	7,963	104	8,068	865	-370	6,833	1,903	998	15,743	13,489	618	357
1986	10,357	8,434	144	8,578	933	-398	7,247	2,030	1,080	16,503	14,113	628	370
1987	11,194	9,270	114	9,384	1,016	-466	7,901	2,168	1,125	17,575	15,106	637	387
1988	12,256	10,126	181	10,307	1,149	-525	8,633	2,386	1,237	18,925	16,359	648	403
1989	13,631	11,092	192	11,284	1,262	-618	9,404	2,885	1,342	20,707	17,869	658	415
1990	14,367	11,762	141	11,903	1,312	-688	9,903	3,023	1,441	21,457	18,503	670	420
1991	15,196	12,294	133	12,427	1,378	-681	10,367	3,155	1,674	22,247	19,373	683	414
1992	15,854	12,884	117	13,001	1,421	-725	10,855	3,177	1,822	22,814	19,905	695	413
1993	16,467	13,255	108	13,363	1,476	-681	11,207	3,312	1,948	23,312	20,310	706	421
1994	17,165	13,863	121	13,985	1,571	-722	11,692	3,404	2,070	23,922	20,726	718	424
1995	18,172	14,617	87	14,704	1,656	-848	12,200	3,710	2,262	24,902	21,585	730	442
1996	19,434	15,554	120	15,675	1,735	-1,049	12,891	4,036	2,507	26,227	22,555	741	453
1997	20,342	16,633	95	16,728	1,843	-1,346	13,540	4,268	2,535	27,069	23,004	751	464
1998	22,497	18,456	142	18,597	1,997	-1,456	15,145	4,653	2,700	29,472	25,137	763	476
1999	24,165	20,474	140	20,613	2,134	-1,696	16,784	4,567	2,814	31,181	26,733	775	491
2000	26,645	22,371	147	22,519	2,237	-1,790	18,492	5,083	3,071	33,884	29,292	786	503
2001	29,379	24,863	212	25,074	2,295	-1,809	20,970	5,041	3,368	36,922	32,117	796	503
2002	30,359	25,689	88	25,776	2,399	-1,761	21,617	5,114	3,628	37,658	33,511	806	501
2003	31,137	26,094	175	26,269	2,500	-1,800	21,969	5,273	3,896	38,065	34,140	818	504
2004	32,380	26,896	254	27,151	2,690	-1,940	22,521	5,665	4,194	38,974	34,840	831	518
2005	33,274	27,494	291	27,785	2,820	-2,089	22,877	5,875	4,522	39,370	34,643	845	529
2006	35,275	28,903	207	29,111	3,001	-2,321	23,789	6,590	4,896	41,053	36,111	859	537
2007	36,380	29,161	210	29,371	3,084	-2,166	24,121	6,952	5,307	41,733	36,647	872	545
2008	36,145	27,996	229	28,225	3,192	-2,216	22,817	7,211	6,118	40,894	35,919	884	545
2009	36,433	27,669	295	27,964	3,122	-1,541	23,301	6,500	6,632	40,856	36,991	892	526
2010	36,838	27,994	262	28,257	3,144	-1,734	23,378	6,301	7,158	40,942	36,987	900	522
2011	39,925	30,298	231	30,529	2,847	-2,154	25,528	6,924	7,473	43,962	39,222	908	530
2012	40,393	30,312	290	30,603	2,981	-2,165	25,457	7,289	7,648	44,070	39,402	917	534
2013	41,100	30,783	440	31,223	3,483	-2,101	25,639	7,424	8,038	44,404	39,457	926	545
2014	43,032	32,146	508	32,653	3,676	-2,469	26,508	8,030	8,494	46,015	40,953	935	557
2015	45,216	33,694	388	34,082	3,826	-2,442	27,814	8,350	9,053	47,868	42,406	945	563
2016	46,445	33,921	309	34,230	3,864	-2,138	28,228	8,787	9,430	48,734	43,244	953	579
2017	48,476	35,187	500	35,687	4,018	-2,515	29,155	9,319	10,003	50,417	44,601	961	585
2018	51,191	37,224	397	37,621	4,220	-2,565	30,837	9,853	10,502	52,716	46,746	971	597
2019	53,203	37,976	411	38,387	4,375	-2,615	31,397	10,677	11,129	54,217	47,771	981	603
2020	55,867	38,132	203	38,335	4,487	-2,437	31,412	10,690	13,764	56,311	49,809	992	592
2021	60,134	40,593	329	40,921	4,769	-2,108	34,045	10,948	15,141	59,846	52,407	1,005	609
2022	62,516	43,871	792	44,663	5,234	-2,362	37,067	11,592	13,857	61,387	52,591	1,018	...

... = Not available.

Personal Income and Employment by Region and State: District of Columbia

(Millions of dollars, except as noted.)

Year	Personal income, total	Derivation of personal income								Per capita (dollars)		Population (thousands)	Total employment (thousands)
		Earnings by place of work			Less: Contributions for government social insurance	Plus: Adjustment for residence	Equals: Net earnings by place of residence	Plus: Dividends, interest, and rent	Plus: Personal current transfer receipts	Personal income	Disposable personal income		
		Nonfarm	Farm	Total									
1960	2,390	3,255	0	3,255	102	-1,391	1,762	516	112	3,125	2,702	765	...
1961	2,517	3,454	0	3,454	108	-1,483	1,863	531	123	3,236	2,838	778	...
1962	2,709	3,718	0	3,718	115	-1,578	2,026	557	127	3,438	3,003	788	...
1963	2,877	4,005	0	4,005	139	-1,704	2,163	580	135	3,605	3,174	798	...
1964	3,054	4,294	0	4,294	136	-1,848	2,311	603	140	3,827	3,417	798	...
1965	3,291	4,631	0	4,631	141	-1,992	2,499	641	151	4,129	3,706	797	...
1966	3,436	4,995	0	4,995	186	-2,188	2,621	655	160	4,344	3,860	791	...
1967	3,682	5,651	0	5,651	215	-2,617	2,819	671	192	4,655	4,159	791	...
1968	3,865	6,079	0	6,079	237	-2,891	2,951	685	230	4,968	4,429	778	...
1969	3,764	6,459	0	6,459	254	-3,366	2,839	690	235	4,939	4,289	762	676
1970	4,174	7,066	0	7,066	276	-3,707	3,083	790	302	5,528	4,832	755	672
1971	4,647	7,747	0	7,747	301	-4,082	3,364	909	375	6,191	5,482	751	666
1972	5,044	8,391	0	8,391	346	-4,441	3,605	992	447	6,781	5,973	744	668
1973	5,316	8,916	0	8,916	417	-4,744	3,755	1,049	512	7,246	6,362	734	662
1974	5,769	9,625	0	9,625	475	-5,119	4,031	1,142	595	8,004	7,040	721	673
1975	6,275	10,598	0	10,598	524	-5,737	4,337	1,197	741	8,834	7,803	710	677
1976	6,648	11,463	0	11,463	576	-6,286	4,601	1,277	771	9,548	8,307	696	674
1977	7,138	12,407	0	12,407	612	-6,843	4,952	1,396	790	10,469	9,191	682	680
1978	7,604	13,579	0	13,579	674	-7,700	5,205	1,588	812	11,349	9,880	670	693
1979	8,003	14,711	0	14,711	777	-8,592	5,342	1,755	906	12,207	10,481	656	704
1980	8,447	16,000	0	16,000	866	-9,709	5,425	1,991	1,031	13,235	11,389	638	701
1981	9,094	17,115	0	17,115	1,010	-10,406	5,699	2,256	1,139	14,279	12,103	637	689
1982	9,694	18,049	0	18,049	1,077	-10,935	6,037	2,386	1,271	15,286	12,987	634	673
1983	10,193	18,929	0	18,929	1,298	-11,234	6,396	2,468	1,328	16,117	13,829	632	667
1984	11,126	20,642	0	20,642	1,472	-12,165	7,005	2,705	1,416	17,566	15,063	633	689
1985	11,782	22,068	0	22,068	1,687	-12,899	7,481	2,882	1,418	18,567	15,891	635	703
1986	12,399	23,269	0	23,269	1,867	-13,474	7,927	3,000	1,472	19,426	16,657	638	721
1987	13,079	24,768	0	24,768	2,031	-14,246	8,491	3,072	1,516	20,534	17,459	637	733
1988	14,310	27,404	0	27,404	2,320	-15,744	9,339	3,340	1,630	22,698	19,483	630	756
1989	15,153	29,005	0	29,005	2,556	-16,821	9,629	3,890	1,634	24,276	20,805	624	763
1990	15,818	30,998	0	30,998	2,759	-17,983	10,256	3,819	1,744	26,132	22,509	605	773
1991	16,537	32,678	0	32,678	2,940	-18,918	10,820	3,771	1,945	27,521	23,972	601	759
1992	17,369	34,522	0	34,522	3,124	-20,092	11,306	3,879	2,184	29,067	25,455	598	752
1993	18,067	35,643	0	35,643	3,273	-20,649	11,720	3,949	2,398	30,349	26,699	595	750
1994	18,485	36,434	0	36,434	3,414	-21,021	11,998	4,048	2,439	31,370	27,398	589	730
1995	18,621	36,700	0	36,700	3,484	-21,063	12,152	4,100	2,368	32,077	28,033	581	718
1996	19,387	37,294	0	37,294	3,521	-21,057	12,716	4,096	2,576	33,872	29,338	572	704
1997	20,291	38,590	0	38,590	3,666	-21,682	13,242	4,479	2,570	35,739	30,608	568	699
1998	21,548	40,635	0	40,635	3,742	-22,791	14,102	4,707	2,739	38,122	32,327	565	698
1999	22,693	44,067	0	44,067	4,084	-24,874	15,109	4,849	2,736	39,798	33,512	570	711
2000	24,898	46,750	0	46,750	4,310	-25,486	16,954	5,127	2,817	43,524	36,488	572	735
2001	25,778	50,026	0	50,026	4,922	-27,225	17,879	4,984	2,915	44,871	37,711	575	742
2002	25,876	52,652	0	52,652	5,233	-29,486	17,933	4,735	3,209	45,147	39,028	573	757
2003	26,158	55,165	0	55,165	5,453	-31,609	18,103	4,791	3,263	46,011	39,869	569	755
2004	28,438	59,956	0	59,956	5,836	-34,103	20,017	5,125	3,296	50,088	43,367	568	763
2005	30,028	63,302	0	63,302	6,161	-36,176	20,966	5,494	3,569	52,947	45,252	567	770
2006	31,847	65,685	0	65,685	6,524	-37,315	21,847	6,378	3,622	55,805	47,572	571	778
2007	34,363	69,568	0	69,568	6,877	-39,186	23,506	6,978	3,879	59,824	50,377	574	788
2008	35,329	71,891	0	71,891	7,403	-40,872	23,616	7,439	4,274	60,887	51,654	580	795
2009	35,619	73,246	0	73,246	7,631	-41,095	24,520	6,353	4,746	60,143	52,440	592	796
2010	38,324	78,016	0	78,016	8,047	-43,311	26,658	6,245	5,421	63,368	55,622	605	809
2011	41,395	81,593	0	81,593	7,369	-45,567	28,657	6,974	5,765	67,005	57,971	618	827
2012	43,011	82,524	0	82,524	7,611	-45,344	29,569	7,784	5,658	68,148	58,518	631	834
2013	43,697	83,741	0	83,741	8,863	-44,926	29,951	7,769	5,977	67,774	57,654	645	848
2014	46,780	87,976	0	87,976	9,282	-46,273	32,421	8,477	5,883	71,469	60,788	655	861
2015	50,337	92,240	0	92,240	9,655	-47,333	35,253	8,959	6,126	75,623	63,870	666	873
2016	52,685	96,206	0	96,206	9,950	-49,334	36,923	9,203	6,558	78,186	66,435	674	893
2017	54,465	99,066	0	99,066	10,369	-50,578	38,119	9,696	6,650	79,984	67,959	681	903
2018	56,708	102,984	0	102,984	10,870	-52,598	39,517	10,403	6,788	82,708	70,031	686	914
2019	58,203	104,659	0	104,659	11,137	-53,738	39,785	11,240	7,179	84,671	71,186	687	915
2020	61,926	106,615	0	106,616	11,296	-54,812	40,508	10,928	10,489	92,307	78,272	671	866
2021	64,645	112,487	0	112,487	11,592	-58,154	42,741	11,215	10,689	96,659	80,479	669	869
2022	64,982	118,011	0	118,011	12,253	-61,023	44,735	11,776	8,471	96,728	77,937	672	...

... = Not available.

Personal Income and Employment by Region and State: Florida

(Millions of dollars, except as noted.)

Year	Personal income, total	Earnings by place of work			Less: Contributions for government social insurance	Plus: Adjustment for residence	Equals: Net earnings by place of residence	Plus: Dividends, interest, and rent	Plus: Personal current transfer receipts	Per capita (dollars)		Population (thousands)	Total employment (thousands)
		Nonfarm	Farm	Total						Personal income	Disposable personal income		
1960	10,532	7,667	381	8,048	329	-1	7,718	2,099	715	2,105	1,911	5,004	...
1961	11,165	7,958	440	8,398	344	-1	8,053	2,284	829	2,130	1,934	5,243	...
1962	12,056	8,583	454	9,037	389	-1	8,647	2,481	929	2,209	2,004	5,458	...
1963	12,939	9,261	436	9,697	449	-1	9,247	2,681	1,011	2,299	2,087	5,628	...
1964	14,155	10,196	492	10,689	481	-1	10,206	2,895	1,055	2,449	2,238	5,781	...
1965	15,473	11,173	466	11,639	516	-1	11,122	3,180	1,171	2,599	2,369	5,954	...
1966	16,976	12,423	476	12,899	680	-2	12,217	3,453	1,306	2,781	2,530	6,104	...
1967	18,772	13,625	515	14,140	809	-3	13,327	3,816	1,628	3,007	2,711	6,242	...
1968	21,581	15,533	528	16,061	966	-5	15,091	4,555	1,936	3,355	2,989	6,433	...
1969	25,005	17,876	636	18,513	1,132	-19	17,361	5,450	2,195	3,765	3,326	6,641	2,857
1970	28,276	19,936	546	20,482	1,272	-22	19,188	6,443	2,646	4,131	3,692	6,845	2,966
1971	31,756	22,121	639	22,759	1,473	-17	21,270	7,299	3,188	4,433	3,987	7,163	3,082
1972	36,550	25,645	738	26,384	1,798	-14	24,572	8,223	3,755	4,860	4,302	7,520	3,338
1973	42,578	30,022	837	30,859	2,422	-12	28,425	9,593	4,561	5,371	4,778	7,927	3,666
1974	47,883	32,994	908	33,902	2,782	-3	31,117	11,268	5,498	5,757	5,139	8,317	3,766
1975	52,168	34,450	998	35,448	2,860	-11	32,577	12,408	7,183	6,107	5,558	8,542	3,676
1976	57,012	37,531	1,035	38,566	3,170	8	35,405	13,630	7,978	6,557	5,924	8,695	3,730
1977	63,844	42,079	1,033	43,112	3,572	19	39,560	15,555	8,730	7,182	6,471	8,889	3,929
1978	73,633	48,719	1,234	49,952	4,251	22	45,723	18,212	9,698	8,064	7,216	9,132	4,239
1979	84,660	55,770	1,312	57,082	5,112	13	51,982	21,441	11,237	8,939	7,942	9,471	4,454
1980	99,827	63,915	1,667	65,583	5,909	6	59,680	26,768	13,379	10,145	8,972	9,840	4,688
1981	115,731	72,211	1,402	73,613	7,183	117	66,547	33,555	15,630	11,354	10,023	10,193	4,865
1982	125,053	77,085	1,777	78,862	7,887	140	71,116	36,249	17,689	11,942	10,461	10,471	4,954
1983	138,093	85,333	2,465	87,798	8,778	166	79,187	39,565	19,341	12,846	11,520	10,750	5,167
1984	153,888	95,966	1,828	97,794	10,141	208	87,861	45,430	20,597	13,939	12,610	11,040	5,502
1985	168,327	105,471	1,835	107,306	11,348	254	96,212	49,892	22,224	14,829	13,259	11,351	5,772
1986	182,124	114,881	1,972	116,853	12,681	317	104,489	53,690	23,945	15,610	13,909	11,668	6,015
1987	197,185	126,439	2,135	128,573	13,789	378	115,162	56,637	25,387	16,436	14,620	11,997	6,094
1988	216,605	138,988	2,687	141,675	15,631	454	126,498	62,302	27,805	17,601	15,724	12,306	6,390
1989	241,143	148,914	2,484	151,397	16,945	534	134,986	74,787	31,370	19,081	17,028	12,638	6,596
1990	257,571	159,051	2,084	161,136	17,936	633	143,832	79,357	34,382	19,763	17,714	13,033	6,740
1991	268,375	165,646	2,458	168,104	18,806	677	149,975	79,765	38,635	20,073	18,125	13,370	6,718
1992	284,266	177,651	2,460	180,111	20,071	743	160,783	79,138	44,345	20,825	18,808	13,651	6,763
1993	301,393	189,871	2,535	192,406	21,337	793	171,862	82,049	47,482	21,641	19,522	13,927	7,002
1994	317,675	200,976	2,165	203,141	22,867	854	181,129	85,928	50,619	22,310	20,082	14,239	7,234
1995	341,584	214,077	2,211	216,287	24,235	922	192,974	93,937	54,673	23,496	21,107	14,538	7,494
1996	363,907	228,542	1,953	230,496	25,571	994	205,919	100,141	57,847	24,500	21,784	14,853	7,740
1997	385,402	242,218	2,167	244,384	27,135	1,095	218,344	107,053	60,005	25,378	22,365	15,186	8,005
1998	416,328	263,272	2,644	265,915	29,130	1,221	238,007	116,952	61,369	26,883	23,600	15,487	8,317
1999	436,361	282,203	2,703	284,906	30,996	1,353	255,264	117,300	63,797	27,689	24,283	15,759	8,578
2000	472,852	306,169	2,582	308,752	33,262	1,516	277,006	127,836	68,010	29,466	25,759	16,048	8,881
2001	497,539	324,422	2,582	327,004	35,634	1,618	292,988	130,412	74,139	30,418	26,738	16,357	8,939
2002	514,203	340,530	2,515	343,045	37,184	1,676	307,537	126,798	79,868	30,810	27,680	16,689	9,056
2003	540,474	359,791	2,200	361,991	39,193	1,773	324,571	130,638	85,265	31,785	28,974	17,004	9,283
2004	588,257	389,697	2,275	391,972	42,579	1,918	351,310	145,235	91,712	33,778	30,606	17,415	9,644
2005	642,291	422,431	2,689	425,120	46,457	2,080	380,743	163,062	98,486	35,999	32,102	17,842	10,067
2006	697,350	449,862	2,640	452,502	50,370	2,298	404,430	187,842	105,077	38,386	34,207	18,167	10,384
2007	727,261	457,268	2,266	459,535	51,861	2,597	410,270	205,184	111,807	39,594	35,295	18,368	10,531
2008	729,994	443,315	2,064	445,379	51,692	2,786	396,473	206,532	126,989	39,401	35,423	18,527	10,269
2009	686,756	418,121	2,186	420,307	49,961	2,644	372,990	175,283	138,483	36,818	33,921	18,653	9,842
2010	732,458	436,509	2,475	438,984	50,688	2,726	391,022	189,749	151,686	38,872	35,766	18,843	9,805
2011	771,410	448,314	2,184	450,499	46,682	2,932	406,748	206,904	157,758	40,517	36,851	19,039	10,037
2012	800,552	465,630	2,780	468,411	48,814	3,017	422,614	221,825	156,113	41,540	37,719	19,272	10,249
2013	802,976	480,064	2,834	482,898	56,726	3,052	429,225	212,831	160,920	41,162	36,956	19,508	10,539
2014	861,412	509,540	2,836	512,375	59,770	3,211	455,816	235,889	169,708	43,516	38,937	19,795	10,937
2015	919,835	540,806	3,603	544,409	62,910	3,344	484,842	256,148	178,845	45,659	40,565	20,146	11,367
2016	954,070	567,031	2,739	569,769	65,678	3,375	507,466	260,397	186,207	46,454	41,733	20,538	11,682
2017	1,023,855	600,562	3,068	603,630	69,201	3,460	537,889	290,385	195,581	49,055	43,265	20,872	12,098
2018	1,088,795	636,986	2,317	639,303	73,839	3,522	568,987	314,641	205,167	51,520	46,134	21,134	12,556
2019	1,165,093	670,139	2,489	672,627	78,903	3,594	597,318	349,699	218,076	54,560	48,825	21,355	12,762
2020	1,235,793	683,921	2,322	686,244	81,066	3,553	608,731	352,209	274,853	57,240	51,473	21,590	12,720
2021	1,356,319	762,089	2,394	764,483	87,829	3,716	680,370	364,846	311,103	62,136	54,955	21,828	13,221
2022	1,414,698	844,193	2,868	847,061	98,118	3,954	752,897	389,586	272,215	63,597	54,596	22,245	...

... = Not available.

Personal Income and Employment by Region and State: Georgia

(Millions of dollars, except as noted.)

Year	Personal income, total	Earnings by place of work			Less: Contributions for government social insurance	Plus: Adjustment for residence	Equals: Net earnings by place of residence	Plus: Dividends, interest, and rent	Plus: Personal current transfer receipts	Per capita (dollars)		Population (thousands)	Total employment (thousands)
		Nonfarm	Farm	Total						Personal income	Disposable personal income		
1960	6,918	5,602	326	5,928	262	-15	5,651	849	418	1,749	1,587	3,956	...
1961	7,221	5,764	347	6,111	266	-17	5,828	920	473	1,799	1,636	4,015	...
1962	7,768	6,279	312	6,591	298	-21	6,272	1,008	488	1,901	1,719	4,086	...
1963	8,445	6,797	400	7,196	349	-25	6,822	1,101	522	2,024	1,829	4,172	...
1964	9,145	7,457	334	7,791	377	-30	7,385	1,213	547	2,148	1,954	4,258	...
1965	10,099	8,214	377	8,591	408	-36	8,148	1,351	601	2,331	2,116	4,332	...
1966	11,144	9,210	389	9,599	546	-45	9,008	1,479	656	2,545	2,296	4,379	...
1967	12,120	10,017	386	10,403	626	-54	9,723	1,616	781	2,750	2,490	4,408	...
1968	13,381	11,201	343	11,544	684	-64	10,796	1,655	930	2,986	2,671	4,482	...
1969	14,980	12,475	420	12,895	786	-93	12,015	1,902	1,063	3,292	2,889	4,551	2,119
1970	16,310	13,324	398	13,722	837	-78	12,807	2,204	1,299	3,542	3,153	4,605	2,121
1971	18,010	14,590	456	15,047	952	-78	14,017	2,447	1,546	3,823	3,439	4,710	2,167
1972	20,206	16,489	471	16,960	1,128	-71	15,761	2,705	1,741	4,203	3,730	4,807	2,253
1973	22,848	18,461	788	19,249	1,445	-70	17,734	3,104	2,010	4,656	4,159	4,907	2,356
1974	25,068	20,011	672	20,684	1,628	-70	18,986	3,570	2,511	5,019	4,479	4,995	2,374
1975	27,084	20,982	638	21,620	1,680	-58	19,883	3,874	3,327	5,354	4,869	5,059	2,313
1976	30,147	23,786	629	24,415	1,946	-88	22,381	4,204	3,562	5,881	5,297	5,126	2,400
1977	33,332	26,898	365	27,263	2,190	-105	24,968	4,670	3,694	6,396	5,726	5,212	2,503
1978	37,819	30,533	568	31,101	2,552	-86	28,463	5,343	4,013	7,154	6,365	5,286	2,621
1979	42,321	34,176	598	34,774	2,974	-106	31,693	6,057	4,571	7,850	6,900	5,391	2,700
1980	47,193	37,709	40	37,749	3,302	-115	34,332	7,380	5,481	8,602	7,587	5,486	2,741
1981	53,459	41,622	523	42,145	3,919	-36	38,190	9,025	6,243	9,600	8,432	5,568	2,776
1982	57,867	44,454	683	45,137	4,272	-77	40,788	10,262	6,817	10,242	9,051	5,650	2,793
1983	63,380	49,088	476	49,563	4,793	-120	44,651	11,331	7,398	11,064	9,761	5,728	2,877
1984	71,863	55,825	956	56,782	5,611	-155	51,015	12,947	7,901	12,316	10,918	5,835	3,068
1985	78,686	61,833	787	62,620	6,361	-169	56,090	14,124	8,472	13,196	11,617	5,963	3,207
1986	85,846	68,004	828	68,832	7,085	-218	61,529	15,291	9,026	14,109	12,440	6,085	3,335
1987	92,434	73,645	895	74,540	7,617	-227	66,696	16,271	9,467	14,888	13,059	6,208	3,433
1988	100,797	80,114	1,151	81,266	8,521	-229	72,516	18,063	10,218	15,959	14,076	6,316	3,545
1989	108,619	84,605	1,357	85,961	9,070	-192	76,699	20,566	11,354	16,942	14,881	6,411	3,608
1990	116,150	90,194	1,261	91,455	9,696	-113	81,646	21,873	12,631	17,835	15,686	6,513	3,664
1991	121,895	93,591	1,565	95,156	10,179	-132	84,845	22,424	14,626	18,322	16,225	6,653	3,622
1992	131,979	102,091	1,640	103,731	10,960	-178	92,594	23,062	16,323	19,360	17,182	6,817	3,698
1993	140,173	108,698	1,475	110,172	11,712	-182	98,279	24,435	17,460	20,087	17,759	6,978	3,866
1994	150,942	116,328	1,941	118,269	12,670	-237	105,362	26,758	18,823	21,090	18,618	7,157	4,020
1995	162,948	125,360	1,764	127,125	13,607	-340	113,178	29,427	20,344	22,235	19,580	7,328	4,188
1996	176,086	135,472	1,857	137,329	14,539	-375	122,415	32,016	21,655	23,475	20,535	7,501	4,333
1997	187,548	144,937	1,813	146,750	15,463	-448	130,839	34,551	22,158	24,404	21,213	7,685	4,449
1998	205,650	161,028	1,803	162,832	16,839	-585	145,408	37,581	22,661	26,152	22,643	7,864	4,608
1999	219,284	174,671	1,945	176,616	18,151	-600	157,865	37,510	23,909	27,254	23,571	8,046	4,729
2000	237,370	188,470	1,845	190,315	19,382	-732	170,201	41,245	25,924	28,851	24,907	8,227	4,861
2001	249,321	196,991	2,218	199,209	20,151	-777	178,282	42,541	28,499	29,762	25,814	8,377	4,872
2002	256,380	201,889	1,644	203,534	20,555	-821	182,158	41,972	32,250	30,133	26,793	8,508	4,858
2003	266,411	209,005	2,047	211,053	21,154	-840	189,059	44,511	32,841	30,896	27,762	8,623	4,895
2004	280,917	221,459	2,159	223,618	23,015	-799	199,805	45,719	35,393	32,034	28,864	8,769	5,022
2005	298,526	231,981	2,472	234,454	23,999	-782	209,673	50,230	38,622	33,445	29,857	8,926	5,196
2006	318,544	245,752	1,575	247,327	25,478	-786	221,063	56,000	41,480	34,791	30,859	9,156	5,358
2007	333,612	252,085	1,873	253,958	26,200	-777	226,982	61,976	44,654	35,680	31,540	9,350	5,491
2008	336,828	247,721	2,187	249,908	27,303	-697	221,908	63,493	51,427	35,438	31,494	9,505	5,451
2009	329,745	241,418	1,935	243,353	26,537	-925	215,891	57,323	56,531	34,274	31,221	9,621	5,247
2010	338,276	245,949	1,386	247,335	27,011	-948	219,376	56,924	61,975	34,829	31,624	9,713	5,211
2011	361,251	256,199	1,618	257,817	24,828	-1,183	231,805	64,531	64,914	36,842	33,174	9,805	5,326
2012	371,457	264,003	2,463	266,466	25,731	-1,339	239,396	67,770	64,291	37,495	33,802	9,907	5,385
2013	377,202	273,354	2,614	275,968	30,209	-1,514	244,245	66,328	66,630	37,794	33,722	9,981	5,497
2014	402,791	290,893	2,007	292,900	31,724	-1,608	259,568	73,351	69,872	39,969	35,651	10,078	5,671
2015	427,437	308,016	2,696	310,712	33,355	-1,629	275,729	78,652	73,057	41,941	37,252	10,191	5,833
2016	444,024	321,141	1,953	323,093	34,605	-1,833	286,656	81,821	75,547	43,033	38,292	10,318	5,974
2017	469,214	337,612	2,451	340,063	36,144	-1,704	302,215	89,004	77,995	44,993	39,935	10,428	6,128
2018	493,507	356,027	1,680	357,707	38,317	-1,610	317,780	93,766	81,961	46,855	41,890	10,533	6,287
2019	522,393	374,632	1,873	376,505	40,333	-1,452	334,721	101,270	86,403	49,083	43,798	10,643	6,399
2020	557,601	378,062	1,272	379,333	41,102	-1,481	336,751	102,078	118,772	51,967	46,664	10,730	6,327
2021	602,464	411,584	1,845	413,429	44,412	-1,787	367,231	105,180	130,053	55,846	49,607	10,788	6,542
2022	623,447	449,546	4,162	453,708	49,500	-2,053	402,155	111,184	110,108	57,129	49,538	10,913	...

... = Not available.

Personal Income and Employment by Region and State: Hawaii

(Millions of dollars, except as noted.)

Year	Personal income, total	Earnings by place of work			Less: Contributions for government social insurance	Plus: Adjustment for residence	Equals: Net earnings by place of residence	Plus: Dividends, interest, and rent	Plus: Personal current transfer receipts	Per capita (dollars)		Population (thousands)	Total employment (thousands)
		Nonfarm	Farm	Total						Personal income	Disposable personal income		
1960	1,615	1,278	82	1,360	52	0	1,307	260	48	2,516	2,191	642	...
1961	1,754	1,383	75	1,458	57	0	1,401	294	59	2,661	2,316	659	...
1962	1,881	1,471	79	1,550	61	0	1,489	325	67	2,750	2,434	684	...
1963	2,011	1,579	88	1,667	76	0	1,591	350	70	2,949	2,614	682	...
1964	2,188	1,725	89	1,814	82	0	1,731	386	70	3,125	2,805	700	...
1965	2,402	1,887	91	1,978	85	0	1,893	428	81	3,412	3,076	704	...
1966	2,608	2,077	95	2,172	114	0	2,058	455	95	3,674	3,262	710	...
1967	2,831	2,239	98	2,338	131	0	2,206	504	121	3,915	3,468	723	...
1968	3,184	2,540	117	2,658	153	0	2,505	539	140	4,338	3,814	734	...
1969	3,643	2,922	119	3,041	182	0	2,859	624	160	4,903	4,254	743	416
1970	4,225	3,338	133	3,471	211	0	3,260	759	207	5,538	4,833	763	434
1971	4,584	3,579	131	3,709	236	0	3,474	840	270	5,791	5,131	792	437
1972	5,048	3,944	131	4,076	274	0	3,802	923	323	6,170	5,401	818	453
1973	5,593	4,378	138	4,517	348	0	4,168	1,055	370	6,643	5,828	842	473
1974	6,361	4,783	340	5,123	400	0	4,723	1,194	444	7,412	6,525	858	485
1975	6,919	5,288	202	5,489	442	0	5,047	1,295	577	7,907	7,111	875	499
1976	7,466	5,731	173	5,904	484	0	5,420	1,371	675	8,367	7,465	892	505
1977	8,084	6,219	184	6,403	522	0	5,881	1,495	708	8,828	7,840	916	509
1978	8,954	6,897	168	7,065	597	0	6,467	1,726	761	9,640	8,501	929	528
1979	10,043	7,752	193	7,945	700	0	7,245	1,958	840	10,571	9,281	950	556
1980	11,484	8,624	374	8,998	777	0	8,221	2,298	965	11,867	10,429	968	575
1981	12,434	9,318	199	9,517	896	0	8,620	2,680	1,134	12,711	11,174	978	568
1982	13,166	9,913	234	10,147	946	0	9,201	2,736	1,229	13,249	11,860	994	567
1983	14,443	10,665	338	11,003	1,036	0	9,967	3,125	1,351	14,262	12,762	1,013	577
1984	15,473	11,448	239	11,687	1,135	0	10,552	3,496	1,425	15,052	13,490	1,028	582
1985	16,453	12,245	222	12,467	1,237	0	11,230	3,712	1,511	15,824	14,124	1,040	598
1986	17,458	13,099	256	13,355	1,351	0	12,004	3,880	1,574	16,599	14,788	1,052	612
1987	18,619	14,206	239	14,445	1,477	0	12,969	4,021	1,629	17,435	15,321	1,068	643
1988	20,478	15,815	262	16,077	1,696	0	14,381	4,350	1,746	18,964	16,647	1,080	669
1989	22,874	17,595	248	17,843	1,887	0	15,956	4,981	1,937	20,897	18,160	1,095	696
1990	24,979	19,526	260	19,786	2,178	0	17,608	5,273	2,098	22,433	19,510	1,113	724
1991	26,433	20,771	232	21,003	2,345	0	18,658	5,471	2,304	23,253	20,119	1,137	745
1992	28,435	22,194	219	22,412	2,494	0	19,918	5,841	2,676	24,542	21,669	1,159	746
1993	29,477	22,716	216	22,932	2,543	0	20,389	6,157	2,930	25,133	22,226	1,173	742
1994	30,164	22,921	210	23,131	2,588	0	20,543	6,449	3,172	25,400	22,485	1,188	737
1995	30,864	22,936	199	23,136	2,586	0	20,550	6,727	3,587	25,788	22,962	1,197	734
1996	30,895	22,905	195	23,100	2,590	0	20,511	6,705	3,680	25,665	22,714	1,204	733
1997	31,908	23,537	205	23,742	2,630	0	21,112	7,102	3,694	26,334	23,298	1,212	734
1998	32,515	23,901	218	24,119	2,671	0	21,448	7,301	3,766	26,756	23,576	1,215	738
1999	33,608	24,831	245	25,076	2,740	0	22,336	7,350	3,922	27,768	24,434	1,210	738
2000	35,579	26,352	240	26,593	2,889	0	23,704	7,745	4,130	29,319	25,738	1,214	749
2001	37,059	27,826	237	28,063	3,048	0	25,015	7,593	4,450	30,229	26,583	1,226	753
2002	38,747	29,586	251	29,837	3,244	0	26,593	7,347	4,807	31,257	27,993	1,240	758
2003	40,621	31,511	250	31,761	3,491	0	28,269	7,389	4,963	32,467	29,269	1,251	774
2004	43,655	33,798	251	34,049	3,667	0	30,381	7,982	5,292	34,277	30,888	1,274	797
2005	47,023	36,263	260	36,523	3,934	0	32,588	8,707	5,727	36,375	32,416	1,293	820
2006	50,399	38,330	260	38,590	4,247	0	34,343	10,015	6,042	38,480	34,225	1,310	842
2007	53,272	39,641	247	39,888	4,443	0	35,445	11,190	6,637	40,490	35,999	1,316	865
2008	55,911	40,428	253	40,681	4,532	0	36,149	12,035	7,727	41,969	37,522	1,332	858
2009	55,326	39,873	294	40,167	4,476	0	35,691	11,341	8,294	41,082	37,537	1,347	830
2010	56,751	40,674	279	40,953	4,707	0	36,246	11,218	9,287	41,574	38,080	1,365	824
2011	59,288	42,147	306	42,454	4,477	0	37,977	11,659	9,653	42,809	38,880	1,385	835
2012	61,557	44,150	345	44,496	4,633	0	39,863	12,180	9,515	43,812	39,774	1,405	849
2013	62,521	45,503	319	45,821	5,413	0	40,409	12,249	9,864	43,931	39,457	1,423	868
2014	66,037	47,344	291	47,635	5,452	0	42,183	13,225	10,629	46,044	41,327	1,434	883
2015	69,109	49,697	316	50,012	5,699	0	44,313	13,785	11,011	47,777	42,535	1,446	901
2016	71,572	51,339	284	51,623	5,830	0	45,794	14,339	11,440	49,122	43,680	1,457	915
2017	74,543	53,545	265	53,810	6,074	0	47,736	14,869	11,937	51,114	45,480	1,458	921
2018	76,168	55,265	218	55,482	6,284	0	49,198	14,819	12,152	52,164	46,598	1,460	924
2019	79,700	57,067	200	57,267	6,539	0	50,727	16,268	12,705	54,700	48,717	1,457	914
2020	83,110	53,734	206	53,939	6,237	0	47,702	16,078	19,330	57,276	51,095	1,451	818
2021	87,858	57,716	205	57,921	6,624	0	51,297	16,367	20,193	60,711	53,393	1,447	851
2022	88,104	61,411	220	61,631	7,150	0	54,481	17,136	16,487	61,175	52,515	1,440	...

... = Not available.

Personal Income and Employment by Region and State: Idaho

(Millions of dollars, except as noted.)

Year	Personal income, total	Earnings by place of work			Less: Contributions for government social insurance	Plus: Adjustment for residence	Equals: Net earnings by place of residence	Plus: Dividends, interest, and rent	Plus: Personal current transfer receipts	Per capita (dollars)		Population (thousands)	Total employment (thousands)
		Nonfarm	Farm	Total						Personal income	Disposable personal income		
1960	1,316	925	159	1,084	50	-3	1,031	195	90	1,961	1,762	671	...
1961	1,392	984	159	1,143	56	-3	1,084	206	102	2,035	1,841	684	...
1962	1,488	1,059	167	1,226	62	-3	1,161	221	106	2,150	1,949	692	...
1963	1,523	1,076	175	1,251	69	-2	1,180	234	109	2,230	2,013	683	...
1964	1,575	1,155	135	1,290	70	-2	1,218	245	112	2,316	2,117	680	...
1965	1,794	1,259	232	1,491	76	-2	1,414	260	120	2,615	2,392	686	...
1966	1,817	1,331	180	1,511	93	-1	1,417	271	129	2,638	2,401	689	...
1967	1,932	1,395	207	1,601	107	-1	1,494	283	155	2,808	2,547	688	...
1968	2,065	1,522	186	1,707	122	-0	1,586	305	174	2,971	2,682	695	...
1969	2,391	1,688	253	1,941	126	14	1,828	369	194	3,382	3,030	707	315
1970	2,648	1,843	267	2,110	136	15	1,988	431	229	3,691	3,336	717	324
1971	2,894	2,021	249	2,270	154	16	2,132	493	269	3,918	3,541	739	332
1972	3,304	2,302	320	2,622	182	17	2,457	541	306	4,329	3,938	763	347
1973	3,821	2,602	453	3,055	239	19	2,835	635	351	4,885	4,408	782	365
1974	4,497	2,966	628	3,594	281	23	3,336	740	422	5,566	4,983	808	381
1975	4,867	3,369	387	3,756	314	28	3,469	874	524	5,850	5,288	832	393
1976	5,436	3,895	343	4,237	368	35	3,904	940	593	6,343	5,719	857	419
1977	5,942	4,381	240	4,621	416	35	4,240	1,074	628	6,726	6,048	883	435
1978	6,830	5,069	308	5,377	485	42	4,935	1,225	670	7,497	6,722	911	460
1979	7,469	5,595	233	5,828	564	47	5,311	1,376	783	8,009	7,161	933	469
1980	8,395	5,969	408	6,376	606	60	5,830	1,627	937	8,856	7,924	948	464
1981	9,238	6,435	427	6,862	703	53	6,212	1,951	1,074	9,600	8,508	962	462
1982	9,700	6,450	393	6,844	720	62	6,186	2,282	1,233	9,961	8,928	974	452
1983	10,600	6,960	584	7,543	779	63	6,827	2,469	1,304	10,795	9,755	982	463
1984	11,294	7,546	501	8,046	870	76	7,253	2,692	1,349	11,399	10,324	991	472
1985	11,933	7,931	458	8,389	929	85	7,545	2,943	1,445	12,004	10,851	994	474
1986	12,177	8,066	479	8,545	955	100	7,690	2,962	1,525	12,297	11,172	990	474
1987	12,724	8,509	594	9,103	988	108	8,223	2,932	1,570	12,918	11,709	985	487
1988	13,766	9,340	670	10,010	1,128	126	9,008	3,072	1,686	13,966	12,640	986	508
1989	15,147	10,122	881	11,003	1,243	142	9,902	3,411	1,834	15,232	13,637	994	525
1990	16,352	11,071	1,000	12,071	1,435	157	10,794	3,580	1,979	16,152	14,407	1,012	548
1991	17,191	11,836	829	12,664	1,564	178	11,278	3,698	2,214	16,509	14,748	1,041	566
1992	18,905	13,141	875	14,016	1,701	196	12,510	3,917	2,478	17,640	15,673	1,072	586
1993	20,721	14,340	1,085	15,424	1,863	217	13,778	4,276	2,667	18,688	16,641	1,109	612
1994	22,179	15,699	779	16,478	2,051	246	14,673	4,678	2,829	19,368	17,244	1,145	647
1995	23,843	16,559	844	17,403	2,180	285	15,508	5,221	3,114	20,252	18,013	1,177	667
1996	25,335	17,375	952	18,327	2,242	331	16,416	5,590	3,330	21,058	18,687	1,203	689
1997	26,420	18,242	756	18,998	2,337	378	17,039	5,926	3,455	21,506	19,009	1,229	708
1998	28,531	19,713	956	20,669	2,483	446	18,632	6,301	3,599	22,783	20,166	1,252	733
1999	30,219	21,302	1,006	22,307	2,616	510	20,202	6,194	3,823	23,688	20,873	1,276	747
2000	32,724	23,290	1,013	24,304	2,847	524	21,981	6,598	4,145	25,183	22,059	1,299	777
2001	34,054	23,893	1,126	25,020	2,894	516	22,642	6,781	4,631	25,799	22,735	1,320	783
2002	35,162	24,863	1,100	25,963	2,979	501	23,485	6,652	5,026	26,233	23,749	1,340	791
2003	36,441	25,599	860	26,459	3,101	512	23,870	7,234	5,337	26,728	24,364	1,363	801
2004	39,412	27,142	1,372	28,514	3,310	520	25,724	7,971	5,718	28,317	25,821	1,392	825
2005	41,979	28,963	1,182	30,145	3,589	513	27,069	8,732	6,178	29,392	26,365	1,428	862
2006	46,228	32,014	1,092	33,106	3,998	489	29,597	9,924	6,707	31,476	28,017	1,469	900
2007	49,227	33,280	1,646	34,926	4,194	511	31,243	10,702	7,282	32,707	29,102	1,505	929
2008	50,389	33,026	1,652	34,678	4,226	562	31,014	10,897	8,477	32,841	29,499	1,534	921
2009	48,625	32,166	1,009	33,175	4,135	655	29,695	9,606	9,324	31,281	28,794	1,554	880
2010	50,433	32,618	1,432	34,050	4,317	724	30,458	9,726	10,249	32,097	29,552	1,571	869
2011	53,274	33,126	2,057	35,183	3,946	870	32,107	10,873	10,294	33,579	30,635	1,587	879
2012	56,177	34,321	2,066	36,387	4,045	1,098	33,440	12,307	10,431	35,110	32,022	1,600	883
2013	58,404	36,600	2,365	38,965	4,668	1,131	35,428	12,202	10,774	36,095	32,706	1,618	903
2014	61,801	38,421	2,452	40,873	4,856	1,233	37,250	13,209	11,343	37,680	34,121	1,640	926
2015	65,476	40,650	2,306	42,956	5,073	1,222	39,106	14,350	12,020	39,386	35,481	1,662	950
2016	68,009	42,355	2,071	44,426	5,327	1,285	40,383	15,076	12,551	40,098	35,990	1,696	977
2017	71,888	45,443	1,655	47,098	5,695	1,338	42,741	15,961	13,186	41,457	37,251	1,734	1,008
2018	76,435	48,617	1,660	50,277	6,057	1,384	45,605	16,797	14,033	43,217	39,026	1,769	1,041
2019	83,032	51,922	2,135	54,057	6,394	1,625	49,287	18,614	15,131	45,924	41,318	1,808	1,064
2020	91,449	56,143	2,354	58,498	6,972	1,621	53,146	19,096	19,207	49,453	44,758	1,849	1,078
2021	99,550	61,512	1,699	63,210	7,480	1,790	57,521	19,900	22,129	52,276	46,770	1,904	1,125
2022	105,748	68,621	2,503	71,124	8,327	1,906	64,703	21,322	19,724	54,537	47,859	1,939	...

... = Not available.

Personal Income and Employment by Region and State: Illinois

(Millions of dollars, except as noted.)

Year	Personal income, total	Nonfarm	Farm	Total	Less: Contributions for government social insurance	Plus: Adjustment for residence	Equals: Net earnings by place of residence	Plus: Dividends, interest, and rent	Plus: Personal current transfer receipts	Personal income	Disposable personal income	Population (thousands)	Total employment (thousands)
1960	27,210	22,630	647	23,277	1,073	-133	22,071	3,666	1,472	2,698	2,378	10,086	...
1961	28,282	23,063	814	23,877	1,089	-138	22,650	3,933	1,699	2,792	2,470	10,130	...
1962	29,885	24,344	798	25,142	1,196	-154	23,792	4,330	1,763	2,907	2,563	10,280	...
1963	31,096	25,257	821	26,078	1,329	-159	24,590	4,690	1,816	2,989	2,642	10,402	...
1964	33,241	27,105	665	27,770	1,337	-175	26,259	5,136	1,847	3,142	2,816	10,580	...
1965	36,068	29,103	903	30,006	1,356	-194	28,456	5,631	1,981	3,373	3,015	10,693	...
1966	39,099	32,041	976	33,017	1,821	-222	30,975	5,979	2,145	3,608	3,200	10,836	...
1967	41,606	34,021	936	34,957	1,988	-239	32,731	6,320	2,555	3,801	3,358	10,947	...
1968	44,582	36,706	691	37,397	2,193	-264	34,939	6,649	2,993	4,055	3,542	10,995	...
1969	48,485	40,069	913	40,982	2,715	64	38,330	6,918	3,236	4,392	3,765	11,039	5,179
1970	51,524	42,215	723	42,937	2,810	-16	40,111	7,576	3,837	4,632	3,992	11,125	5,144
1971	55,317	44,907	885	45,792	3,074	-59	42,659	8,068	4,590	4,936	4,321	11,206	5,104
1972	60,030	48,752	1,000	49,752	3,517	-83	46,152	8,711	5,167	5,332	4,608	11,258	5,155
1973	66,968	53,736	1,841	55,577	4,490	-100	50,987	9,833	6,147	5,947	5,172	11,260	5,351
1974	73,216	58,539	1,673	60,212	5,078	-117	55,016	11,192	7,009	6,494	5,622	11,274	5,441
1975	79,866	61,631	2,463	64,093	5,194	-141	58,758	12,125	8,984	7,064	6,202	11,306	5,342
1976	86,832	68,269	1,713	69,981	5,881	-132	63,969	12,936	9,927	7,644	6,642	11,360	5,458
1977	95,460	75,690	1,716	77,406	6,516	-70	70,819	14,256	10,384	8,369	7,252	11,406	5,587
1978	105,342	84,402	1,510	85,912	7,466	7	78,453	15,841	11,048	9,213	7,958	11,434	5,748
1979	115,570	92,288	1,838	94,126	8,484	74	85,716	17,822	12,032	10,117	8,674	11,423	5,803
1980	125,211	97,471	381	97,852	8,931	177	89,097	21,504	14,610	10,950	9,407	11,435	5,675
1981	138,877	104,307	1,522	105,829	10,249	116	95,696	26,399	16,782	12,136	10,408	11,443	5,664
1982	147,012	107,173	914	108,087	10,690	32	97,429	31,156	18,426	12,869	11,230	11,423	5,563
1983	153,020	112,268	-485	111,782	11,259	17	100,540	32,755	19,725	13,412	11,781	11,409	5,520
1984	168,717	123,383	1,227	124,610	12,810	-47	111,754	36,872	20,091	14,784	13,059	11,412	5,718
1985	177,210	130,498	1,718	132,215	13,763	-92	118,361	37,884	20,965	15,545	13,684	11,400	5,780
1986	186,406	138,918	1,426	140,344	14,681	-131	125,533	39,146	21,727	16,370	14,431	11,387	5,892
1987	197,183	149,490	1,431	150,921	15,562	-202	135,157	39,851	22,175	17,310	15,107	11,391	6,031
1988	212,643	163,793	856	164,649	17,396	-303	146,950	42,739	22,953	18,669	16,399	11,390	6,187
1989	226,917	172,648	2,174	174,822	18,513	-324	155,985	46,547	24,385	19,888	17,360	11,410	6,294
1990	240,801	183,408	1,763	185,172	19,273	-272	165,627	48,552	26,622	21,025	18,363	11,453	6,390
1991	245,872	187,719	977	188,696	20,215	-322	168,159	49,029	28,684	21,253	18,665	11,569	6,369
1992	265,737	201,962	2,056	204,018	21,320	-410	182,289	50,624	32,824	22,724	20,072	11,694	6,351
1993	275,363	210,352	1,712	212,063	22,492	-591	188,980	51,959	34,424	23,317	20,511	11,810	6,441
1994	290,055	221,487	2,306	223,794	24,002	-685	199,107	55,272	35,676	24,349	21,336	11,913	6,611
1995	307,809	234,255	604	234,860	25,277	-928	208,654	61,101	38,054	25,633	22,416	12,008	6,773
1996	327,553	246,538	2,501	249,039	26,332	-935	221,773	65,756	40,024	27,066	23,527	12,102	6,875
1997	346,339	261,993	2,135	264,128	27,787	-952	235,389	70,183	40,768	28,422	24,525	12,186	6,981
1998	367,299	279,080	1,537	280,617	29,384	-1,034	250,199	75,541	41,559	29,930	25,673	12,272	7,139
1999	383,973	297,355	1,083	298,437	30,782	-1,146	266,510	75,253	42,210	31,068	26,607	12,359	7,219
2000	412,966	317,609	1,810	319,419	32,338	-1,380	285,701	82,375	44,890	33,212	28,440	12,434	7,357
2001	428,339	331,258	1,691	332,949	33,140	-1,562	298,248	81,655	48,436	34,299	29,602	12,488	7,310
2002	433,315	337,841	981	338,822	33,648	-1,669	303,505	77,711	52,099	34,594	30,525	12,526	7,218
2003	442,126	343,273	1,860	345,133	34,518	-1,593	309,022	78,806	54,298	35,212	31,459	12,556	7,191
2004	459,762	356,072	3,626	359,698	36,574	-1,632	321,493	82,010	56,259	36,519	32,709	12,590	7,245
2005	478,866	368,408	1,730	370,138	38,658	-1,770	329,709	87,389	61,767	37,975	33,666	12,610	7,335
2006	510,377	388,814	1,923	390,737	40,457	-1,833	348,448	99,117	62,812	40,365	35,533	12,644	7,449
2007	539,737	404,621	3,145	407,766	42,265	-2,307	363,194	107,192	69,351	42,513	37,143	12,696	7,578
2008	553,984	406,969	4,568	411,537	43,040	-1,771	366,726	110,972	76,286	43,460	38,029	12,747	7,553
2009	526,968	386,056	2,625	388,681	41,145	-2,093	345,444	95,817	85,707	41,180	37,159	12,797	7,304
2010	543,084	396,181	2,652	398,833	41,808	-2,140	354,885	94,945	93,254	42,278	37,988	12,846	7,251
2011	569,776	412,361	5,490	417,851	39,296	-2,570	375,985	104,521	89,270	44,194	38,993	12,893	7,376
2012	595,074	431,195	3,122	434,317	41,008	-2,412	390,897	114,807	89,370	46,029	40,555	12,928	7,435
2013	609,779	445,747	8,048	453,795	47,040	-2,678	404,078	112,514	93,187	47,047	41,065	12,961	7,503
2014	638,640	465,933	3,695	469,628	48,529	-2,343	418,755	125,236	94,650	49,238	43,014	12,970	7,613
2015	666,944	485,080	392	485,472	49,987	-2,578	432,907	132,835	101,202	51,443	44,779	12,965	7,749
2016	673,691	488,327	2,699	491,026	50,996	-2,699	437,342	134,550	101,800	52,036	45,533	12,947	7,805
2017	692,896	501,634	2,310	503,944	52,655	-3,168	448,121	139,688	105,087	53,611	47,119	12,925	7,823
2018	728,667	524,698	2,991	527,689	55,079	-3,023	469,587	150,934	108,146	56,536	49,739	12,889	7,881
2019	750,936	540,665	1,922	542,588	56,747	-3,259	482,582	155,809	112,545	58,438	51,407	12,850	7,860
2020	794,460	539,149	3,824	542,973	56,876	-3,843	482,255	155,237	156,968	62,132	54,892	12,787	7,520
2021	852,082	578,424	7,313	585,737	59,496	-4,547	521,694	157,970	172,418	67,165	58,597	12,686	7,685
2022	865,923	621,718	9,846	631,563	64,520	-4,865	562,179	163,869	139,875	68,822	58,437	12,582	...

... = Not available.

Personal Income and Employment by Region and State: Indiana

(Millions of dollars, except as noted.)

Year	Personal income, total	Earnings by place of work			Less: Contributions for government social insurance	Plus: Adjustment for residence	Equals: Net earnings by place of residence	Plus: Dividends, interest, and rent	Plus: Personal current transfer receipts	Per capita (dollars)		Population (thousands)	Total employment (thousands)
		Nonfarm	Farm	Total						Personal income	Disposable personal income		
1960	10,390	8,573	366	8,939	415	41	8,564	1,222	604	2,223	1,986	4,674	...
1961	10,707	8,628	464	9,092	411	44	8,724	1,291	693	2,264	2,035	4,730	...
1962	11,464	9,328	452	9,779	461	49	9,367	1,400	697	2,421	2,163	4,736	...
1963	12,043	9,814	470	10,284	526	49	9,807	1,512	724	2,509	2,229	4,799	...
1964	12,817	10,637	301	10,938	545	47	10,440	1,629	749	2,639	2,368	4,856	...
1965	14,162	11,587	553	12,140	581	49	11,608	1,748	806	2,877	2,578	4,922	...
1966	15,288	12,835	480	13,315	818	56	12,553	1,869	866	3,058	2,715	4,999	...
1967	16,017	13,443	431	13,874	916	59	13,017	1,989	1,011	3,170	2,806	5,053	...
1968	17,413	14,645	379	15,024	993	69	14,100	2,133	1,180	3,419	3,001	5,093	...
1969	19,238	16,009	550	16,559	1,097	43	15,506	2,453	1,280	3,741	3,241	5,143	2,327
1970	20,029	16,441	381	16,821	1,115	78	15,785	2,744	1,501	3,849	3,377	5,204	2,291
1971	21,794	17,475	596	18,071	1,227	139	16,984	3,020	1,790	4,151	3,681	5,250	2,290
1972	23,847	19,381	507	19,888	1,440	178	18,625	3,252	1,970	4,503	3,950	5,296	2,367
1973	27,368	21,745	1,228	22,973	1,863	220	21,330	3,704	2,335	5,136	4,547	5,329	2,483
1974	29,274	23,332	735	24,066	2,089	280	22,258	4,260	2,757	5,472	4,769	5,350	2,493
1975	31,608	24,024	1,097	25,121	2,120	328	23,329	4,767	3,512	5,907	5,245	5,351	2,405
1976	35,132	27,285	1,076	28,362	2,438	385	26,309	5,149	3,674	6,540	5,742	5,372	2,489
1977	38,901	30,856	724	31,579	2,754	443	29,269	5,775	3,857	7,197	6,295	5,405	2,578
1978	43,398	34,726	731	35,457	3,190	498	32,765	6,392	4,242	7,968	6,938	5,446	2,670
1979	47,806	38,177	672	38,849	3,630	570	35,788	7,146	4,872	8,732	7,568	5,475	2,708
1980	51,419	39,292	379	39,671	3,714	682	36,639	8,680	6,099	9,365	8,176	5,491	2,626
1981	56,407	42,198	306	42,504	4,296	748	38,956	10,638	6,813	10,292	8,944	5,480	2,603
1982	58,429	42,247	307	42,555	4,390	811	38,975	11,863	7,592	10,686	9,370	5,468	2,522
1983	61,277	44,685	-260	44,425	4,660	839	40,603	12,501	8,172	11,243	9,928	5,450	2,542
1984	68,009	49,217	753	49,970	5,258	984	45,696	13,744	8,569	12,460	11,050	5,458	2,642
1985	71,813	52,223	682	52,905	5,686	1,058	48,277	14,517	9,019	13,154	11,625	5,459	2,695
1986	75,637	55,367	578	55,945	6,056	1,135	51,024	15,088	9,525	13,868	12,288	5,454	2,755
1987	80,258	59,677	763	60,440	6,434	1,185	55,191	15,358	9,709	14,664	12,945	5,473	2,849
1988	85,926	64,771	284	65,055	7,215	1,283	59,123	16,513	10,290	15,646	13,824	5,492	2,935
1989	93,581	69,194	965	70,158	7,737	1,349	63,770	18,623	11,188	16,942	14,897	5,524	3,010
1990	98,749	73,007	863	73,870	8,408	1,487	66,949	19,642	12,158	17,768	15,638	5,558	3,070
1991	101,775	76,121	242	76,363	8,884	1,495	68,973	19,423	13,378	18,121	15,996	5,616	3,072
1992	110,148	81,916	849	82,766	9,455	1,646	74,957	19,905	15,287	19,411	17,210	5,675	3,121
1993	116,112	86,578	866	87,444	10,062	1,866	79,247	20,727	16,138	20,232	17,892	5,739	3,197
1994	123,384	92,445	828	93,273	10,900	1,997	84,369	22,178	16,837	21,297	18,753	5,794	3,287
1995	129,006	96,459	349	96,808	11,416	2,278	87,671	24,184	17,151	22,047	19,381	5,851	3,379
1996	136,364	100,767	1,196	101,962	11,792	2,418	92,588	25,667	18,108	23,089	20,232	5,906	3,418
1997	143,496	106,429	1,161	107,590	12,409	2,547	97,728	27,178	18,590	24,096	21,018	5,955	3,476
1998	154,708	115,626	769	116,395	13,176	2,574	105,793	29,610	19,305	25,790	22,451	5,999	3,543
1999	160,798	122,398	473	122,871	13,815	2,826	111,882	28,713	20,202	26,600	23,179	6,045	3,597
2000	171,502	129,173	873	130,046	14,397	3,115	118,764	31,002	21,736	28,153	24,664	6,092	3,648
2001	175,494	130,784	1,068	131,852	14,582	3,360	120,629	30,837	24,028	28,639	25,108	6,128	3,589
2002	178,021	133,914	466	134,380	14,954	3,431	122,857	29,661	25,503	28,918	25,757	6,156	3,553
2003	182,929	136,958	1,242	138,199	15,463	3,515	126,252	30,164	26,513	29,521	26,543	6,197	3,552
2004	191,919	143,308	2,049	145,357	16,260	3,801	132,898	30,947	28,073	30,791	27,800	6,233	3,593
2005	198,189	147,892	1,321	149,213	16,990	4,105	136,328	31,293	30,568	31,566	28,316	6,279	3,635
2006	209,756	154,967	1,113	156,080	17,854	4,322	142,549	34,211	32,997	33,123	29,589	6,333	3,674
2007	217,254	158,183	1,550	159,733	18,368	4,696	146,061	36,581	34,612	34,055	30,238	6,380	3,720
2008	227,487	160,723	2,311	163,034	18,787	4,686	148,932	38,512	40,042	35,408	31,616	6,425	3,683
2009	221,343	154,097	1,564	155,661	18,024	4,601	142,238	34,854	44,251	34,267	31,309	6,459	3,523
2010	231,707	161,921	1,633	163,554	18,441	4,465	149,578	34,814	47,315	35,695	32,532	6,491	3,525
2011	246,494	170,806	2,816	173,622	17,084	4,722	161,260	37,875	47,359	37,799	34,112	6,521	3,590
2012	258,136	179,196	2,291	181,488	17,787	4,729	168,430	40,849	48,858	39,433	35,752	6,546	3,642
2013	261,702	182,049	5,354	187,403	20,662	5,231	171,972	40,494	49,237	39,766	35,796	6,581	3,684
2014	272,245	189,466	3,060	192,526	21,415	5,178	176,290	43,365	52,590	41,188	37,113	6,610	3,740
2015	282,821	197,460	1,324	198,784	22,311	5,760	182,234	45,901	54,687	42,667	38,244	6,629	3,796
2016	290,604	203,235	1,613	204,847	22,790	5,887	187,944	46,653	56,007	43,645	39,064	6,658	3,848
2017	300,965	210,693	1,555	212,249	23,706	6,285	194,827	48,619	57,519	45,015	40,510	6,686	3,903
2018	315,740	221,356	1,571	222,927	24,814	6,539	204,652	51,169	59,919	46,945	42,557	6,726	3,963
2019	329,625	229,896	1,125	231,021	25,922	7,225	212,324	53,731	63,570	48,749	43,941	6,762	3,970
2020	354,338	235,290	2,627	237,917	27,031	7,549	218,435	54,220	81,683	52,194	47,118	6,789	3,844
2021	384,520	252,673	3,731	256,404	28,500	7,783	235,687	55,209	93,625	56,435	50,501	6,814	3,950
2022	395,839	274,045	5,732	279,777	31,282	8,341	256,835	57,301	81,703	57,930	50,796	6,833	...

... = Not available.

Personal Income and Employment by Region and State: Iowa

(Millions of dollars, except as noted.)

Year	Personal income, total	Derivation of personal income									Per capita (dollars)		Population (thousands)	Total employment (thousands)
		Earnings by place of work			Less: Contributions for government social insurance	Plus: Adjustment for residence	Equals: Net earnings by place of residence	Plus: Dividends, interest, and rent	Plus: Personal current transfer receipts		Personal income	Disposable personal income		
		Nonfarm	Farm	Total										
1960	5,745	3,908	732	4,640	186	35	4,489	872	385		2,085	1,876	2,756	...
1961	6,084	4,022	852	4,874	189	38	4,723	937	424		2,207	1,997	2,756	...
1962	6,345	4,203	883	5,086	203	41	4,924	977	444		2,307	2,086	2,750	...
1963	6,744	4,425	1,001	5,425	233	43	5,236	1,044	464		2,455	2,222	2,747	...
1964	7,059	4,742	921	5,663	247	47	5,463	1,117	479		2,571	2,346	2,746	...
1965	7,818	5,070	1,247	6,318	261	50	6,108	1,189	522		2,851	2,596	2,742	...
1966	8,513	5,640	1,346	6,986	352	55	6,689	1,258	566		3,082	2,777	2,762	...
1967	8,672	6,028	1,080	7,109	418	59	6,750	1,247	675		3,105	2,790	2,793	...
1968	9,347	6,490	1,021	7,511	457	63	7,117	1,448	782		3,335	2,974	2,803	...
1969	10,374	7,116	1,238	8,354	543	89	7,900	1,619	856		3,698	3,267	2,805	1,289
1970	11,095	7,540	1,215	8,756	567	97	8,285	1,818	992		3,923	3,493	2,829	1,295
1971	11,642	8,048	1,012	9,060	626	97	8,531	1,984	1,127		4,082	3,676	2,852	1,297
1972	13,040	8,770	1,485	10,255	719	103	9,640	2,185	1,216		4,559	4,039	2,861	1,316
1973	15,655	9,825	2,732	12,557	930	98	11,725	2,526	1,404		5,466	4,881	2,864	1,374
1974	16,225	11,001	1,721	12,722	1,092	91	11,721	2,878	1,626		5,657	4,920	2,868	1,407
1975	18,134	11,982	1,970	13,951	1,167	107	12,892	3,225	2,017		6,293	5,562	2,881	1,407
1976	19,280	13,552	1,227	14,779	1,322	100	13,557	3,504	2,219		6,640	5,815	2,904	1,455
1977	21,275	15,107	1,226	16,333	1,459	74	14,948	3,982	2,345		7,300	6,395	2,914	1,488
1978	24,537	16,681	2,441	19,122	1,671	73	17,524	4,430	2,584		8,406	7,387	2,919	1,513
1979	26,298	18,685	1,575	20,260	1,955	79	18,384	5,020	2,895		9,016	7,842	2,917	1,554
1980	27,994	19,755	717	20,473	2,058	98	18,513	6,068	3,412		9,607	8,340	2,914	1,537
1981	31,681	20,927	1,639	22,566	2,315	127	20,378	7,420	3,882		10,894	9,466	2,908	1,507
1982	32,544	20,949	816	21,765	2,344	200	19,621	8,497	4,426		11,268	9,892	2,888	1,471
1983	33,150	21,840	6	21,846	2,426	213	19,633	8,773	4,743		11,548	10,223	2,871	1,474
1984	36,944	23,534	1,463	24,997	2,684	242	22,555	9,530	4,859		12,924	11,616	2,859	1,499
1985	38,216	24,197	1,752	25,949	2,810	279	23,418	9,642	5,156		13,505	12,137	2,830	1,495
1986	39,480	24,982	2,128	27,110	2,966	274	24,418	9,711	5,351		14,141	12,738	2,792	1,494
1987	41,377	26,817	2,459	29,277	3,174	268	26,371	9,541	5,466		14,954	13,344	2,767	1,514
1988	42,760	28,845	1,646	30,491	3,527	311	27,276	9,771	5,714		15,446	13,756	2,768	1,557
1989	46,555	30,867	2,400	33,267	3,765	321	29,823	10,631	6,101		16,803	14,909	2,771	1,600
1990	49,023	32,666	2,504	35,170	4,079	319	31,410	10,983	6,630		17,628	15,602	2,781	1,635
1991	50,145	34,141	1,780	35,921	4,285	373	32,009	11,008	7,127		17,924	15,897	2,798	1,654
1992	53,792	36,441	2,700	39,141	4,529	411	35,023	11,070	7,698		19,086	17,013	2,818	1,669
1993	54,053	38,235	889	39,124	4,773	401	34,752	11,243	8,058		19,053	16,919	2,837	1,692
1994	58,946	40,747	2,861	43,608	5,142	423	38,889	11,682	8,376		20,677	18,410	2,851	1,725
1995	61,329	42,772	1,818	44,589	5,400	484	39,673	12,832	8,824		21,388	19,004	2,867	1,785
1996	66,841	44,925	3,724	48,649	5,382	529	43,796	13,776	9,269		23,209	20,634	2,880	1,815
1997	69,956	47,570	3,397	50,966	5,908	604	45,663	14,763	9,530		24,197	21,351	2,891	1,841
1998	73,172	51,278	2,161	53,438	6,289	695	47,844	15,559	9,769		25,207	22,215	2,903	1,877
1999	75,099	54,018	1,601	55,619	6,558	796	49,857	15,109	10,133		25,740	22,685	2,918	1,896
2000	80,229	56,758	2,462	59,219	6,806	881	53,295	16,082	10,853		27,390	24,223	2,929	1,915
2001	82,571	58,305	2,273	60,578	6,967	905	54,516	16,309	11,746		28,162	24,960	2,932	1,902
2002	84,424	59,792	2,128	61,919	7,118	943	55,744	15,748	12,932		28,772	25,969	2,934	1,880
2003	86,444	61,937	2,253	64,190	7,442	972	57,720	15,847	12,877		29,383	26,721	2,942	1,873
2004	93,643	65,916	4,787	70,703	7,833	989	63,859	16,443	13,341		31,704	28,961	2,954	1,902
2005	96,705	69,147	3,871	73,018	8,243	907	65,682	16,769	14,254		32,621	29,563	2,964	1,934
2006	102,747	73,669	2,848	76,517	8,684	841	68,674	18,353	15,720		34,448	31,042	2,983	1,966
2007	110,011	77,112	3,899	81,011	9,120	1,079	72,970	20,316	16,726		36,680	32,807	2,999	1,994
2008	116,757	79,752	4,807	84,559	9,546	1,149	76,163	21,540	19,054		38,703	34,725	3,017	1,998
2009	113,085	77,744	3,234	80,978	9,426	1,150	72,702	19,999	20,384		37,286	34,077	3,033	1,959
2010	116,906	80,001	3,653	83,654	9,739	1,187	75,102	20,083	21,721		38,312	34,933	3,051	1,950
2011	125,978	81,967	7,397	89,364	9,092	1,306	81,578	22,340	22,060		41,036	37,052	3,070	1,976
2012	132,159	87,000	6,739	93,739	9,384	1,230	85,584	24,591	21,984		42,873	38,636	3,083	1,993
2013	134,758	89,457	8,567	98,024	10,787	1,211	88,447	23,841	22,469		43,439	38,947	3,102	2,019
2014	139,531	94,509	5,839	100,349	11,114	1,048	90,283	25,600	23,649		44,699	40,100	3,122	2,039
2015	144,588	97,843	5,175	103,018	11,382	1,001	92,637	27,045	24,905		46,104	41,209	3,136	2,060
2016	145,790	100,058	2,747	102,805	11,877	1,049	91,977	28,300	25,513		46,291	41,344	3,149	2,067
2017	149,420	102,043	3,401	105,445	12,201	1,365	94,609	29,363	25,448		47,246	42,266	3,163	2,062
2018	155,916	105,901	3,848	109,748	12,725	1,358	98,381	29,890	27,646		49,163	44,281	3,171	2,076
2019	160,361	108,173	3,280	111,452	13,151	1,402	99,703	31,402	29,255		50,367	45,261	3,184	2,071
2020	169,994	110,095	2,991	113,086	13,711	1,652	101,027	31,605	37,362		53,280	48,210	3,191	2,010
2021	182,525	115,859	6,744	122,604	14,192	1,761	110,172	32,024	40,329		57,080	51,353	3,198	2,049
2022	188,526	125,352	9,184	134,536	15,403	1,897	121,030	33,062	34,433		58,905	52,071	3,201	...

... = Not available.

Personal Income and Employment by Region and State: Kansas

(Millions of dollars, except as noted.)

Year	Personal income, total	Earnings by place of work			Less: Contributions for government social insurance	Plus: Adjustment for residence	Equals: Net earnings by place of residence	Plus: Dividends, interest, and rent	Plus: Personal current transfer receipts	Per capita (dollars)		Population (thousands)	Total employment (thousands)
		Nonfarm	Farm	Total						Personal income	Disposable personal income		
1960	4,827	3,295	443	3,737	161	175	3,752	773	302	2,211	1,991	2,183	...
1961	5,039	3,453	451	3,904	177	178	3,906	799	335	2,275	2,051	2,215	...
1962	5,244	3,635	422	4,057	183	194	4,068	831	345	2,351	2,110	2,231	...
1963	5,364	3,735	404	4,138	206	214	4,147	852	366	2,420	2,162	2,217	...
1964	5,650	3,980	368	4,349	213	236	4,371	900	379	2,558	2,330	2,209	...
1965	6,024	4,155	462	4,617	222	259	4,655	957	413	2,731	2,486	2,206	...
1966	6,452	4,550	478	5,029	293	294	5,030	979	444	2,933	2,633	2,200	...
1967	6,756	4,840	407	5,247	340	325	5,232	992	532	3,075	2,755	2,197	...
1968	7,360	5,311	400	5,711	377	355	5,689	1,055	616	3,321	2,948	2,216	...
1969	8,195	5,780	465	6,245	421	445	6,269	1,237	689	3,665	3,226	2,236	1,029
1970	8,893	6,084	606	6,690	442	445	6,693	1,396	803	3,956	3,510	2,248	1,017
1971	9,654	6,558	706	7,264	492	439	7,211	1,527	916	4,298	3,867	2,246	1,022
1972	10,763	7,252	963	8,215	573	458	8,101	1,678	985	4,772	4,252	2,256	1,048
1973	12,266	8,095	1,386	9,480	734	472	9,218	1,897	1,151	5,417	4,814	2,264	1,090
1974	13,262	9,028	1,060	10,088	853	485	9,720	2,219	1,324	5,848	5,138	2,268	1,122
1975	14,488	10,011	807	10,817	936	500	10,381	2,494	1,613	6,358	5,656	2,279	1,133
1976	15,746	11,265	584	11,848	1,069	510	11,290	2,673	1,784	6,850	6,082	2,299	1,169
1977	17,182	12,400	498	12,898	1,175	553	12,276	2,977	1,930	7,413	6,537	2,318	1,208
1978	19,014	14,055	285	14,340	1,374	599	13,565	3,345	2,104	8,151	7,161	2,333	1,252
1979	21,715	15,868	706	16,574	1,615	642	15,601	3,794	2,321	9,251	8,047	2,347	1,296
1980	23,869	17,382	101	17,483	1,757	716	16,442	4,666	2,761	10,075	8,750	2,369	1,309
1981	27,049	19,035	345	19,380	2,055	742	18,066	5,802	3,181	11,342	9,756	2,385	1,322
1982	29,327	19,733	577	20,310	2,180	764	18,893	6,865	3,569	12,213	10,552	2,401	1,306
1983	30,540	20,767	384	21,151	2,288	741	19,604	7,131	3,804	12,643	11,148	2,416	1,323
1984	33,518	22,750	751	23,500	2,567	800	21,734	7,862	3,922	13,827	12,314	2,424	1,365
1985	35,255	23,846	811	24,657	2,732	853	22,778	8,342	4,136	14,524	12,882	2,427	1,368
1986	36,959	25,183	938	26,121	2,885	843	24,079	8,540	4,340	15,193	13,586	2,433	1,368
1987	38,648	26,490	1,173	27,663	3,003	914	25,574	8,612	4,462	15,805	14,021	2,445	1,421
1988	40,704	28,096	1,141	29,237	3,318	918	26,838	9,184	4,682	16,533	14,675	2,462	1,432
1989	43,110	29,937	831	30,768	3,510	975	28,233	9,736	5,142	17,433	15,368	2,473	1,454
1990	45,751	31,587	1,383	32,970	3,887	968	30,051	10,119	5,582	18,438	16,317	2,481	1,474
1991	47,310	32,967	1,035	34,001	4,119	947	30,829	10,417	6,064	18,934	16,817	2,499	1,489
1992	50,940	35,562	1,408	36,970	4,382	1,027	33,614	10,603	6,723	20,115	17,970	2,532	1,502
1993	53,312	37,361	1,346	38,707	4,591	1,115	35,231	10,959	7,122	20,853	18,584	2,557	1,525
1994	55,736	39,217	1,436	40,653	4,897	1,066	36,822	11,558	7,357	21,599	19,210	2,581	1,551
1995	58,129	41,202	794	41,996	5,091	1,157	38,063	12,314	7,752	22,349	19,771	2,601	1,600
1996	61,934	43,512	1,508	45,020	5,327	1,147	40,840	13,080	8,015	23,688	20,863	2,615	1,632
1997	65,771	46,643	1,421	48,064	5,697	1,044	43,411	13,950	8,410	24,958	21,823	2,635	1,677
1998	69,763	49,938	1,309	51,248	6,069	1,065	46,244	14,975	8,544	26,221	22,893	2,661	1,724
1999	72,121	52,375	1,403	53,778	6,343	1,018	48,453	14,765	8,902	26,927	23,495	2,678	1,740
2000	76,105	55,059	1,014	56,073	6,656	1,121	50,538	15,916	9,651	28,253	24,606	2,694	1,760
2001	78,665	56,918	1,164	58,081	6,870	1,133	52,345	15,771	10,549	29,112	25,463	2,702	1,768
2002	79,365	58,363	493	58,855	7,008	1,198	53,045	15,112	11,209	29,248	26,101	2,714	1,746
2003	81,890	59,165	1,649	60,814	7,173	1,169	54,811	15,371	11,709	30,074	27,127	2,723	1,734
2004	84,336	61,348	1,566	62,913	7,557	1,118	56,475	15,821	12,041	30,843	27,860	2,734	1,751
2005	89,346	64,190	1,963	66,154	7,911	1,260	59,502	17,147	12,697	32,545	29,113	2,745	1,766
2006	98,610	70,755	1,133	71,888	8,407	1,368	64,850	20,118	13,643	35,690	31,763	2,763	1,796
2007	105,943	74,901	1,640	76,541	8,807	1,254	68,987	22,269	14,687	38,057	33,643	2,784	1,844
2008	115,853	80,038	2,083	82,121	9,207	1,414	74,328	24,973	16,553	41,257	36,669	2,808	1,858
2009	111,697	77,530	1,996	79,527	9,003	1,694	72,218	21,454	18,026	39,431	35,925	2,833	1,813
2010	114,240	79,213	2,537	81,750	9,236	1,674	74,189	20,861	19,190	39,960	36,274	2,859	1,802
2011	123,559	84,164	3,659	87,823	8,516	1,239	80,545	23,388	19,626	43,015	38,731	2,872	1,819
2012	130,948	90,029	3,052	93,080	8,816	1,640	85,904	25,689	19,355	45,294	40,922	2,891	1,841
2013	133,980	93,431	4,936	98,367	10,225	1,367	89,508	24,832	19,639	46,174	41,461	2,902	1,869
2014	136,879	95,719	2,788	98,507	10,610	1,188	89,085	27,413	20,381	47,013	42,224	2,912	1,896
2015	138,337	98,044	1,804	99,848	11,028	1,156	89,976	27,244	21,117	47,332	42,455	2,923	1,911
2016	138,534	96,838	2,159	98,997	10,916	1,275	89,356	27,293	21,885	47,326	42,473	2,927	1,916
2017	142,422	100,052	1,373	101,426	11,220	1,541	91,746	28,126	22,550	48,651	43,691	2,927	1,913
2018	148,523	103,938	1,565	105,503	11,750	1,553	95,307	29,587	23,630	50,663	45,490	2,932	1,926
2019	155,126	108,222	1,524	109,746	12,247	1,651	99,150	30,916	25,059	52,876	47,424	2,934	1,925
2020	164,334	109,892	2,807	112,699	12,588	1,442	101,553	30,791	31,990	55,935	50,395	2,938	1,879
2021	172,918	114,733	3,132	117,865	12,997	1,589	106,457	31,472	34,989	58,857	52,429	2,938	1,912
2022	176,676	123,101	3,567	126,668	14,075	1,762	114,356	32,472	29,848	60,152	52,484	2,937	...

... = Not available.

Personal Income and Employment by Region and State: Kentucky

(Millions of dollars, except as noted.)

Year	Personal income, total	Earnings by place of work Nonfarm	Farm	Total	Less: Contributions for government social insurance	Plus: Adjustment for residence	Equals: Net earnings by place of residence	Plus: Dividends, interest, and rent	Plus: Personal current transfer receipts	Per capita (dollars) Personal income	Disposable personal income	Population (thousands)	Total employment (thousands)
1960	5,022	3,739	323	4,062	184	89	3,967	626	429	1,651	1,494	3,041	...
1961	5,346	3,838	396	4,234	185	81	4,131	661	555	1,750	1,593	3,054	...
1962	5,678	4,177	396	4,573	209	84	4,448	726	504	1,844	1,666	3,079	...
1963	5,968	4,445	405	4,850	240	84	4,693	771	504	1,928	1,745	3,096	...
1964	6,226	4,735	297	5,033	245	91	4,879	817	530	1,990	1,811	3,129	...
1965	6,750	5,119	366	5,485	258	96	5,323	848	579	2,150	1,953	3,140	...
1966	7,379	5,706	382	6,088	339	104	5,853	899	627	2,345	2,107	3,147	...
1967	7,988	6,206	383	6,589	400	79	6,268	974	746	2,518	2,274	3,172	...
1968	8,731	6,858	372	7,231	446	86	6,871	1,018	843	2,733	2,444	3,195	...
1969	9,712	7,494	428	7,922	509	162	7,575	1,193	944	3,037	2,669	3,198	1,332
1970	10,535	8,058	393	8,451	547	153	8,057	1,373	1,105	3,261	2,896	3,231	1,336
1971	11,466	8,773	408	9,180	615	97	8,662	1,506	1,298	3,476	3,116	3,298	1,360
1972	12,680	9,708	507	10,215	713	90	9,591	1,647	1,441	3,801	3,361	3,336	1,392
1973	14,253	10,966	579	11,545	919	45	10,670	1,863	1,720	4,227	3,780	3,372	1,461
1974	16,052	12,203	665	12,868	1,060	17	11,825	2,176	2,051	4,698	4,121	3,417	1,496
1975	17,479	13,107	482	13,589	1,122	10	12,478	2,418	2,584	5,039	4,517	3,469	1,465
1976	19,544	14,815	557	15,372	1,291	-18	14,063	2,650	2,831	5,536	4,938	3,530	1,523
1977	21,934	16,748	683	17,430	1,451	6	15,985	2,982	2,968	6,135	5,425	3,575	1,579
1978	24,444	18,942	605	19,547	1,686	28	17,890	3,377	3,178	6,769	5,962	3,611	1,645
1979	27,455	21,161	679	21,839	1,944	21	19,916	3,835	3,704	7,535	6,631	3,644	1,665
1980	29,872	22,189	561	22,750	2,059	52	20,743	4,661	4,469	8,152	7,209	3,664	1,642
1981	33,238	23,920	939	24,858	2,392	16	22,483	5,716	5,039	9,056	7,961	3,670	1,634
1982	35,402	24,786	902	25,689	2,526	10	23,173	6,730	5,499	9,611	8,475	3,683	1,616
1983	36,755	26,062	232	26,294	2,653	33	23,674	7,128	5,953	9,949	8,827	3,694	1,624
1984	41,062	28,742	1,121	29,863	3,000	3	26,866	7,968	6,229	11,111	9,954	3,695	1,676
1985	42,816	30,249	876	31,125	3,218	-4	27,903	8,396	6,517	11,588	10,334	3,695	1,698
1986	44,019	31,229	648	31,877	3,453	21	28,445	8,750	6,824	11,936	10,644	3,688	1,733
1987	46,497	33,475	731	34,207	3,682	4	30,529	8,911	7,057	12,624	11,202	3,683	1,765
1988	50,573	36,827	778	37,605	4,098	-7	33,500	9,578	7,495	13,743	12,246	3,680	1,816
1989	54,364	38,940	1,142	40,082	4,407	-43	35,632	10,497	8,235	14,784	13,084	3,677	1,865
1990	57,673	41,267	1,123	42,390	4,818	-32	37,540	11,124	9,010	15,613	13,788	3,694	1,906
1991	60,843	43,165	1,123	44,288	5,093	-38	39,157	11,441	10,245	16,345	14,521	3,722	1,903
1992	65,547	46,962	1,309	48,271	5,520	-255	42,496	11,803	11,248	17,407	15,474	3,765	1,949
1993	68,128	49,271	1,115	50,386	5,886	-245	44,255	12,170	11,702	17,871	15,868	3,812	1,993
1994	71,608	51,944	1,166	53,111	6,331	-328	46,452	12,883	12,274	18,604	16,478	3,849	2,035
1995	75,054	54,219	708	54,927	6,635	-330	47,963	13,890	13,202	19,307	17,035	3,887	2,110
1996	79,621	56,870	1,138	58,008	6,898	-314	50,796	14,843	13,982	20,314	17,882	3,920	2,141
1997	84,542	60,547	1,139	61,687	7,299	-315	54,073	15,693	14,777	21,388	18,729	3,953	2,189
1998	89,452	64,414	1,011	65,425	7,748	-188	57,490	16,791	15,171	22,445	19,599	3,985	2,224
1999	93,315	68,675	784	69,459	8,257	-272	60,930	16,649	15,736	23,224	20,278	4,018	2,264
2000	100,691	72,859	1,493	74,352	8,525	-295	65,533	18,251	16,908	24,868	21,792	4,049	2,306
2001	104,127	75,371	1,082	76,453	8,743	-444	67,267	18,434	18,427	25,596	22,411	4,068	2,284
2002	106,568	77,861	678	78,538	9,022	-510	69,006	17,829	19,733	26,057	23,228	4,090	2,263
2003	109,877	80,896	705	81,601	9,278	-736	71,587	17,943	20,347	26,687	23,965	4,117	2,273
2004	116,453	85,576	1,249	86,825	9,669	-928	76,228	18,325	21,900	28,087	25,377	4,146	2,301
2005	122,306	89,680	1,551	91,231	10,147	-1,313	79,771	19,327	23,207	29,241	26,247	4,183	2,338
2006	129,361	93,656	1,267	94,923	10,681	-1,360	82,882	21,478	25,001	30,660	27,500	4,219	2,375
2007	135,057	96,954	817	97,772	11,164	-1,502	85,106	23,054	26,897	31,728	28,310	4,257	2,415
2008	141,573	99,663	352	100,015	11,636	-1,793	86,587	24,657	30,329	33,002	29,480	4,290	2,403
2009	139,862	96,533	677	97,209	11,506	-1,855	83,848	22,547	33,466	32,397	29,560	4,317	2,325
2010	145,301	100,897	349	101,246	11,822	-2,141	87,284	22,563	35,454	33,409	30,430	4,349	2,326
2011	152,219	104,479	848	105,327	10,929	-2,344	92,054	24,234	35,930	34,799	31,435	4,374	2,368
2012	157,636	107,969	928	108,898	11,284	-2,397	95,216	26,444	35,976	35,875	32,500	4,394	2,389
2013	159,225	109,091	2,719	111,810	12,899	-2,041	96,870	25,512	36,843	36,058	32,428	4,416	2,408
2014	166,717	112,990	1,736	114,726	13,455	-1,974	99,297	27,233	40,187	37,645	33,826	4,429	2,440
2015	174,33:	117,754	1,442	119,196	14,040	-2,053	103,102	28,789	42,440	39,232	35,077	4,444	2,474
2016	177,191	119,847	900	120,747	14,380	-2,010	104,357	30,137	42,697	39,750	35,491	4,458	2,499
2017	182,392	123,074	1,372	124,446	14,764	-2,140	107,542	30,902	43,948	40,751	36,497	4,476	2,520
2018	188,348	127,718	957	128,675	15,296	-2,421	110,959	32,124	45,266	41,974	37,754	4,487	2,546
2019	197,356	133,140	1,260	134,400	15,819	-2,718	115,864	34,264	47,229	43,875	39,427	4,498	2,550
2020	214,053	135,652	1,061	136,713	16,420	-3,004	117,288	34,371	62,393	47,489	43,043	4,507	2,472
2021	231,180	145,387	1,918	147,305	17,412	-3,789	126,105	35,227	69,848	51,298	46,211	4,507	2,548
2022	235,132	158,291	2,676	160,967	19,117	-4,260	137,590	36,605	60,937	52,109	46,016	4,512	...

... = Not available.

Personal Income and Employment by Region and State: Louisiana

(Millions of dollars, except as noted.)

Year	Personal income, total	Earnings by place of work			Less: Contributions for government social insurance	Plus: Adjustment for residence	Equals: Net earnings by place of residence	Plus: Dividends, interest, and rent	Plus: Personal current transfer receipts	Per capita (dollars)		Population (thousands)	Total employment (thousands)
		Nonfarm	Farm	Total						Personal income	Disposable personal income		
1960	5,591	4,382	186	4,567	185	-1	4,381	775	436	1,715	1,566	3,260	...
1961	5,819	4,499	218	4,717	187	-1	4,529	804	486	1,770	1,616	3,287	...
1962	6,158	4,790	204	4,994	208	-0	4,786	867	504	1,841	1,677	3,345	...
1963	6,564	5,086	261	5,347	246	-0	5,101	928	535	1,944	1,762	3,377	...
1964	7,016	5,530	226	5,756	262	-1	5,494	968	554	2,036	1,865	3,446	...
1965	7,602	6,052	198	6,250	286	-0	5,964	1,039	598	2,174	1,994	3,496	...
1966	8,410	6,812	239	7,051	389	3	6,665	1,103	642	2,369	2,140	3,550	...
1967	9,225	7,454	267	7,721	432	5	7,294	1,179	752	2,576	2,334	3,581	...
1968	10,106	8,199	299	8,498	489	4	8,012	1,243	850	2,805	2,521	3,603	...
1969	10,766	8,703	241	8,944	569	8	8,384	1,421	961	2,975	2,655	3,619	1,440
1970	11,663	9,199	283	9,482	592	6	8,897	1,612	1,154	3,195	2,893	3,650	1,429
1971	12,715	9,970	320	10,290	658	-7	9,625	1,772	1,318	3,427	3,107	3,711	1,445
1972	13,912	10,959	349	11,308	757	-20	10,531	1,931	1,450	3,698	3,330	3,762	1,488
1973	15,529	12,105	579	12,684	960	-37	11,687	2,156	1,686	4,098	3,701	3,789	1,550
1974	17,652	13,654	614	14,268	1,118	-54	13,096	2,581	1,975	4,620	4,135	3,821	1,598
1975	19,875	15,433	419	15,852	1,243	-83	14,526	2,909	2,440	5,113	4,627	3,887	1,641
1976	22,416	17,701	455	18,157	1,454	-112	16,591	3,126	2,698	5,672	5,077	3,952	1,702
1977	25,031	19,962	454	20,416	1,627	-138	18,651	3,477	2,903	6,234	5,563	4,016	1,756
1978	28,631	23,191	373	23,565	1,933	-184	21,448	4,026	3,157	7,029	6,227	4,073	1,849
1979	32,478	26,312	503	26,815	2,277	-234	24,304	4,582	3,592	7,846	6,896	4,139	1,897
1980	37,369	30,111	175	30,286	2,594	-337	27,356	5,721	4,292	8,849	7,747	4,223	1,964
1981	43,084	34,383	266	34,650	3,177	-352	31,121	7,173	4,790	10,059	8,735	4,283	2,030
1982	46,380	35,925	263	36,188	3,376	-331	32,481	8,374	5,525	10,656	9,399	4,353	2,023
1983	48,423	36,383	232	36,614	3,378	-312	32,924	9,213	6,285	11,017	9,834	4,395	1,984
1984	51,505	38,469	323	38,792	3,663	-302	34,827	10,133	6,544	11,704	10,499	4,400	2,023
1985	53,630	39,411	231	39,642	3,775	-273	35,594	10,988	7,048	12,166	10,902	4,408	2,009
1986	53,695	38,636	235	38,871	3,646	-219	35,006	10,953	7,737	12,184	11,063	4,407	1,928
1987	53,932	38,778	396	39,174	3,609	-185	35,380	10,717	7,834	12,415	11,253	4,344	1,904
1988	56,881	41,049	629	41,678	4,014	-166	37,498	11,162	8,221	13,263	12,068	4,289	1,935
1989	60,326	43,148	469	43,616	4,273	-133	39,210	12,125	8,991	14,185	12,821	4,253	1,953
1990	64,881	46,811	404	47,216	4,760	-111	42,345	12,630	9,905	15,369	13,875	4,222	2,005
1991	68,408	49,195	469	49,664	5,135	-127	44,403	12,680	11,325	16,084	14,554	4,253	2,030
1992	73,264	52,243	577	52,821	5,381	-125	47,315	12,954	12,995	17,066	15,517	4,293	2,038
1993	76,873	54,349	590	54,939	5,634	-129	49,176	13,389	14,307	17,809	16,174	4,316	2,086
1994	81,906	57,537	679	58,216	6,083	-148	51,984	14,097	15,824	18,840	17,083	4,347	2,126
1995	85,953	60,393	673	61,066	6,384	-176	54,505	15,443	16,005	19,630	17,758	4,379	2,194
1996	89,777	63,217	884	64,101	6,696	-204	57,202	16,283	16,292	20,409	18,287	4,399	2,239
1997	94,401	67,211	643	67,855	7,088	-219	60,549	17,265	16,587	21,352	19,017	4,421	2,290
1998	99,071	71,061	464	71,525	7,530	-236	63,759	18,499	16,813	22,312	19,901	4,440	2,336
1999	101,468	73,312	636	73,948	7,651	-217	66,080	18,137	17,251	22,746	20,362	4,461	2,353
2000	107,311	77,536	622	78,158	7,906	-230	70,022	19,600	17,688	23,997	21,482	4,472	2,389
2001	114,917	82,970	659	83,630	8,345	-272	75,013	19,621	20,284	25,663	22,967	4,478	2,398
2002	118,229	86,236	427	86,663	8,644	-299	77,720	19,137	21,373	26,289	23,936	4,497	2,399
2003	122,170	89,330	789	90,119	8,885	-349	80,885	19,863	21,422	27,022	24,853	4,521	2,419
2004	127,758	92,217	788	93,004	9,167	-383	83,455	20,654	23,650	28,065	25,917	4,552	2,434
2005	137,935	96,408	670	97,078	9,387	-361	87,330	22,886	27,720	30,139	27,776	4,577	2,397
2006	145,646	103,301	722	104,024	10,064	-424	93,535	26,550	25,560	33,850	30,793	4,303	2,414
2007	159,411	108,992	755	109,748	10,739	-452	98,557	34,261	26,594	36,432	32,840	4,376	2,501
2008	170,869	117,282	546	117,829	11,405	-497	105,927	34,655	30,287	38,522	34,633	4,436	2,551
2009	165,876	114,980	744	115,725	11,366	-484	103,875	29,890	32,111	36,930	33,994	4,492	2,530
2010	173,801	120,783	805	121,589	11,721	-514	109,354	29,957	34,490	38,242	35,295	4,545	2,537
2011	179,073	122,618	853	123,471	10,832	-414	112,225	31,902	34,947	39,124	35,896	4,577	2,565
2012	188,761	127,520	1,186	128,705	11,164	-348	117,194	35,854	35,713	41,003	37,436	4,604	2,601
2013	191,497	131,984	1,510	133,494	13,014	-411	120,070	34,469	36,959	41,376	37,520	4,628	2,642
2014	200,294	140,434	882	141,317	13,559	-561	127,196	36,441	36,657	43,085	39,055	4,649	2,685
2015	201,364	138,314	628	138,942	13,806	-579	124,556	36,340	40,467	43,113	39,185	4,671	2,697
2016	200,191	134,634	620	135,254	13,760	-734	120,759	36,600	42,832	42,725	38,748	4,686	2,691
2017	206,122	138,256	782	139,038	14,118	-953	123,968	37,787	44,366	44,056	40,157	4,679	2,693
2018	215,086	144,873	653	145,526	14,847	-897	129,782	39,076	46,229	46,057	42,202	4,670	2,725
2019	222,349	148,274	707	148,981	15,109	-720	133,152	40,646	48,551	47,668	43,527	4,665	2,718
2020	236,324	146,562	924	147,486	15,243	-564	131,679	40,657	63,989	50,804	46,659	4,652	2,593
2021	250,701	153,346	868	154,215	15,785	-772	137,658	41,850	71,194	54,181	49,461	4,627	2,639
2022	250,728	162,716	1,252	163,968	17,115	-774	146,079	43,405	61,243	54,622	48,882	4,590	...

... = Not available.

Personal Income and Employment by Region and State: Maine

(Millions of dollars, except as noted.)

Year	Personal income, total	Earnings by place of work			Less: Contributions for government social insurance	Plus: Adjustment for residence	Equals: Net earnings by place of residence	Plus: Dividends, interest, and rent	Plus: Personal current transfer receipts	Per capita (dollars)		Population (thousands)	Total employment (thousands)
		Nonfarm	Farm	Total						Personal income	Disposable personal income		
1960	1,952	1,507	103	1,610	70	-32	1,508	292	152	2,002	1,825	975	...
1961	1,977	1,548	67	1,615	73	-33	1,509	301	167	1,987	1,812	995	...
1962	2,054	1,609	66	1,675	78	-34	1,563	319	172	2,067	1,878	994	...
1963	2,122	1,660	59	1,719	87	-34	1,598	344	181	2,137	1,952	993	...
1964	2,293	1,766	90	1,856	92	-34	1,730	379	184	2,309	2,125	993	...
1965	2,474	1,864	126	1,989	93	-32	1,865	417	192	2,482	2,286	997	...
1966	2,630	2,031	107	2,138	119	-36	1,984	436	210	2,632	2,420	999	...
1967	2,761	2,175	55	2,230	138	-38	2,055	458	248	2,750	2,515	1,004	...
1968	2,940	2,352	55	2,407	157	-41	2,209	452	279	2,958	2,673	994	...
1969	3,236	2,534	74	2,608	181	-25	2,402	522	312	3,262	2,913	992	443
1970	3,557	2,733	78	2,810	193	-20	2,596	590	371	3,569	3,225	997	446
1971	3,823	2,903	66	2,969	211	-19	2,739	645	438	3,764	3,450	1,016	443
1972	4,188	3,190	65	3,255	242	-22	2,992	706	490	4,047	3,690	1,035	453
1973	4,707	3,513	148	3,661	302	-13	3,347	776	584	4,498	4,064	1,046	470
1974	5,229	3,795	195	3,991	338	-8	3,645	881	703	4,933	4,462	1,060	478
1975	5,652	4,076	82	4,157	357	-21	3,779	974	899	5,266	4,815	1,073	475
1976	6,447	4,705	163	4,869	422	-24	4,422	1,048	977	5,915	5,381	1,090	498
1977	7,008	5,144	129	5,273	461	-26	4,786	1,181	1,041	6,340	5,773	1,105	513
1978	7,741	5,772	90	5,862	531	-25	5,306	1,318	1,117	6,939	6,282	1,115	531
1979	8,590	6,412	76	6,488	607	-18	5,863	1,465	1,262	7,636	6,870	1,125	545
1980	9,654	7,073	49	7,122	668	-15	6,439	1,739	1,475	8,567	7,680	1,127	553
1981	10,652	7,583	118	7,701	771	-48	6,882	2,089	1,681	9,401	8,359	1,133	551
1982	11,581	8,044	104	8,148	831	-46	7,271	2,467	1,843	10,188	9,000	1,137	553
1983	12,473	8,737	72	8,809	910	-33	7,866	2,614	1,992	10,896	9,749	1,145	565
1984	13,787	9,668	118	9,786	1,043	-26	8,717	2,969	2,101	11,930	10,722	1,156	587
1985	14,893	10,525	103	10,628	1,132	-5	9,492	3,179	2,223	12,807	11,458	1,163	606
1986	16,123	11,477	93	11,570	1,239	35	10,366	3,450	2,306	13,779	12,259	1,170	630
1987	17,491	12,596	135	12,731	1,356	59	11,434	3,697	2,360	14,766	13,007	1,185	653
1988	19,277	14,036	117	14,153	1,543	73	12,683	4,088	2,507	16,013	14,150	1,204	686
1989	21,011	15,133	126	15,258	1,650	72	13,681	4,631	2,700	17,223	15,240	1,220	702
1990	21,870	15,631	173	15,804	1,788	71	14,086	4,770	3,014	17,756	15,759	1,232	701
1991	22,250	15,598	127	15,725	1,803	88	14,010	4,769	3,470	17,986	16,077	1,237	678
1992	23,325	16,247	178	16,424	1,905	132	14,651	4,841	3,832	18,833	16,914	1,239	681
1993	24,095	16,785	156	16,942	2,016	191	15,117	4,936	4,042	19,395	17,435	1,242	692
1994	25,086	17,450	148	17,598	2,130	251	15,719	5,137	4,229	20,187	18,081	1,243	703
1995	26,179	17,924	123	18,047	2,208	318	16,157	5,561	4,461	21,053	18,859	1,243	705
1996	27,653	18,705	151	18,856	2,273	371	16,954	5,927	4,772	22,139	19,716	1,249	714
1997	29,170	19,794	105	19,898	2,399	445	17,945	6,232	4,993	23,247	20,555	1,255	727
1998	31,233	21,291	178	21,468	2,544	519	19,443	6,649	5,141	24,805	21,764	1,259	749
1999	32,657	22,861	194	23,055	2,684	584	20,956	6,410	5,291	25,779	22,621	1,267	763
2000	35,107	24,454	207	24,662	2,815	701	22,548	6,938	5,622	27,491	24,005	1,277	784
2001	37,058	25,921	193	26,115	2,949	712	23,878	7,125	6,056	28,824	25,275	1,286	788
2002	38,324	27,010	157	27,167	2,974	677	24,870	6,993	6,461	29,572	26,473	1,296	791
2003	40,248	28,099	162	28,262	3,059	657	25,859	7,359	7,029	30,805	27,877	1,307	795
2004	42,316	29,560	178	29,738	3,218	682	27,202	7,624	7,489	32,211	29,213	1,314	808
2005	43,421	30,128	172	30,300	3,322	689	27,667	7,611	8,143	32,925	29,603	1,319	809
2006	45,600	31,683	170	31,853	3,540	723	29,035	8,225	8,339	34,451	30,878	1,324	818
2007	47,357	32,332	184	32,516	3,697	723	29,542	8,867	8,949	35,686	31,885	1,327	828
2008	49,445	32,799	192	32,992	3,803	706	29,895	9,227	10,324	37,163	33,275	1,331	824
2009	49,403	32,493	184	32,677	3,724	688	29,641	8,552	11,209	37,157	33,966	1,330	801
2010	50,604	33,486	264	33,750	3,831	729	30,649	8,624	11,331	38,106	34,823	1,328	791
2011	52,789	33,952	220	34,172	3,510	796	31,458	9,514	11,817	39,690	35,934	1,330	794
2012	53,783	34,643	268	34,911	3,610	832	32,132	9,897	11,753	40,411	36,632	1,331	797
2013	53,742	35,093	275	35,368	4,183	870	32,056	9,690	11,996	40,329	36,264	1,333	804
2014	55,864	36,244	235	36,479	4,271	928	33,136	10,388	12,340	41,797	37,647	1,337	811
2015	58,331	37,705	244	37,949	4,495	986	34,440	11,048	12,843	43,672	39,137	1,336	817
2016	59,959	38,780	180	38,960	4,619	1,003	35,344	11,464	13,151	44,740	39,946	1,340	827
2017	62,372	40,309	205	40,514	4,788	1,020	36,746	12,022	13,604	46,378	41,616	1,345	834
2018	65,015	42,096	166	42,262	5,056	1,069	38,276	12,349	14,390	48,141	43,427	1,351	844
2019	68,863	43,916	228	44,144	5,268	1,126	40,002	13,718	15,143	50,728	45,503	1,357	842
2020	74,806	45,750	204	45,955	5,508	1,136	41,583	13,744	19,479	54,861	49,574	1,364	813
2021	80,254	49,615	155	49,771	5,914	1,337	45,193	14,055	21,006	58,272	52,161	1,377	842
2022	82,377	53,331	228	53,559	6,404	1,384	48,539	14,758	19,080	59,463	52,236	1,385	...

... = Not available.

Personal Income and Employment by Region and State: Maryland

(Millions of dollars, except as noted.)

Year	Personal income, total	Earnings by place of work			Less: Contributions for government social insurance	Plus: Adjustment for residence	Equals: Net earnings by place of residence	Plus: Dividends, interest, and rent	Plus: Personal current transfer receipts	Per capita (dollars)		Population (thousands)	Total employment (thousands)
		Nonfarm	Farm	Total						Personal income	Disposable personal income		
1960	7,739	5,743	94	5,837	289	627	6,176	1,222	341	2,486	2,178	3,113	...
1961	8,234	6,077	90	6,167	312	690	6,545	1,298	392	2,593	2,287	3,176	...
1962	8,897	6,552	85	6,638	351	774	7,061	1,420	416	2,727	2,377	3,263	...
1963	9,532	6,995	67	7,062	381	865	7,547	1,550	436	2,815	2,445	3,386	...
1964	10,386	7,593	86	7,679	397	953	8,235	1,692	460	2,974	2,622	3,492	...
1965	11,317	8,199	98	8,297	399	1,066	8,964	1,849	504	3,144	2,762	3,600	...
1966	12,477	9,210	79	9,289	526	1,187	9,950	1,970	557	3,377	2,926	3,695	...
1967	13,580	9,797	95	9,891	587	1,451	10,756	2,133	691	3,615	3,125	3,757	...
1968	15,000	10,868	87	10,955	643	1,619	11,930	2,244	826	3,932	3,310	3,815	...
1969	17,236	12,123	133	12,256	751	2,321	13,827	2,465	944	4,456	3,742	3,868	1,679
1970	19,167	13,216	122	13,338	815	2,717	15,240	2,801	1,126	4,867	4,165	3,938	1,702
1971	21,126	14,414	94	14,508	917	3,028	16,620	3,133	1,373	5,252	4,559	4,023	1,729
1972	23,176	15,835	128	15,964	1,060	3,285	18,189	3,414	1,574	5,679	4,854	4,081	1,781
1973	25,561	17,561	209	17,770	1,354	3,485	19,901	3,844	1,816	6,221	5,343	4,109	1,846
1974	27,903	19,131	165	19,295	1,533	3,687	21,450	4,348	2,105	6,751	5,749	4,133	1,868
1975	30,204	20,257	204	20,461	1,624	4,065	22,903	4,655	2,647	7,265	6,290	4,157	1,846
1976	32,907	22,268	175	22,443	1,808	4,359	24,995	5,057	2,855	7,887	6,823	4,172	1,866
1977	35,676	24,203	130	24,332	1,974	4,701	27,059	5,574	3,042	8,505	7,290	4,195	1,919
1978	39,617	26,948	184	27,132	2,262	5,074	29,944	6,319	3,354	9,407	8,050	4,212	2,004
1979	43,546	29,721	160	29,881	2,611	5,401	32,671	7,070	3,805	10,311	8,762	4,223	2,059
1980	48,503	32,476	58	32,534	2,866	5,863	35,531	8,437	4,535	11,473	9,794	4,228	2,070
1981	54,043	35,670	129	35,800	3,381	6,253	38,671	10,177	5,195	12,680	10,706	4,262	2,095
1982	58,611	37,520	144	37,664	3,617	6,771	40,819	12,009	5,783	13,685	11,633	4,283	2,084
1983	62,787	40,823	90	40,913	4,071	7,143	43,986	12,498	6,303	14,557	12,531	4,313	2,151
1984	69,665	45,375	266	45,641	4,672	7,820	48,789	14,233	6,644	15,959	13,712	4,365	2,243
1985	75,503	49,797	278	50,075	5,284	8,423	53,213	15,267	7,023	17,109	14,759	4,413	2,342
1986	81,545	54,136	288	54,424	5,837	9,033	57,620	16,431	7,494	18,174	15,697	4,487	2,428
1987	88,008	59,251	300	59,550	6,331	9,663	62,883	17,345	7,780	19,276	16,446	4,566	2,553
1988	96,740	65,472	365	65,837	7,214	10,709	69,331	19,104	8,304	20,769	17,948	4,658	2,647
1989	104,601	69,951	366	70,316	7,758	11,515	74,073	21,482	9,046	22,127	18,945	4,727	2,704
1990	110,894	74,155	357	74,512	8,395	12,115	78,232	22,753	9,910	23,104	19,835	4,800	2,737
1991	114,899	75,897	310	76,207	8,671	12,660	80,196	23,541	11,162	23,605	20,428	4,868	2,662
1992	120,637	79,300	343	79,643	9,016	13,419	84,045	24,078	12,514	24,503	21,306	4,923	2,636
1993	125,486	82,522	320	82,842	9,364	13,639	87,117	25,314	13,056	25,239	21,916	4,972	2,659
1994	131,410	86,487	308	86,796	9,916	14,036	90,915	26,853	13,642	26,161	22,650	5,023	2,706
1995	137,245	90,139	215	90,354	10,287	14,003	94,069	28,874	14,302	27,070	23,337	5,070	2,765
1996	143,742	93,888	395	94,283	10,645	14,376	98,014	30,433	15,296	28,119	24,104	5,112	2,806
1997	151,792	100,296	280	100,576	11,307	14,308	103,577	32,605	15,610	29,432	24,837	5,157	2,870
1998	163,854	108,959	325	109,284	11,980	15,668	112,972	34,595	16,288	31,483	26,758	5,204	2,935
1999	173,589	116,908	350	117,258	12,721	16,747	121,284	35,043	17,262	33,036	28,039	5,255	3,008
2000	189,024	126,761	416	127,177	13,591	18,990	132,576	38,202	18,246	35,591	30,130	5,311	3,092
2001	199,273	134,797	417	135,214	14,646	19,868	140,436	38,961	19,877	37,076	31,453	5,375	3,120
2002	206,925	142,124	225	142,349	15,367	20,233	147,216	38,360	21,350	38,035	32,996	5,440	3,157
2003	216,522	148,946	310	149,256	16,068	21,098	154,286	39,253	22,983	39,394	34,498	5,496	3,191
2004	230,980	159,351	444	159,794	17,263	22,546	165,077	41,908	23,995	41,641	36,529	5,547	3,248
2005	243,352	167,942	384	168,326	18,189	23,607	173,744	43,623	25,984	43,515	37,809	5,592	3,311
2006	256,472	176,191	315	176,506	19,379	22,949	180,076	49,358	27,037	45,576	39,384	5,627	3,378
2007	267,561	181,199	308	181,507	20,236	23,615	184,885	53,322	29,354	47,327	40,595	5,653	3,441
2008	279,623	188,007	429	188,436	21,009	23,077	190,503	55,688	33,432	49,186	42,553	5,685	3,431
2009	277,628	188,565	438	189,003	20,985	23,232	191,251	50,361	36,016	48,448	42,895	5,730	3,359
2010	287,652	196,115	387	196,502	21,768	23,631	198,365	50,093	39,194	49,668	43,985	5,792	3,345
2011	303,518	205,473	480	205,952	20,183	23,278	209,047	54,116	40,355	51,845	45,377	5,854	3,395
2012	312,176	211,641	628	212,269	20,764	22,941	214,446	56,962	40,768	52,787	46,283	5,914	3,439
2013	311,524	213,421	787	214,208	23,557	22,903	213,553	55,756	42,215	52,249	45,301	5,962	3,494
2014	322,438	219,465	626	220,091	24,139	22,088	218,040	59,580	44,818	53,659	46,486	6,009	3,538
2015	337,703	230,755	480	231,236	25,378	22,417	228,275	62,853	46,575	55,825	48,186	6,049	3,603
2016	350,384	241,214	378	241,592	25,960	22,489	238,121	63,299	48,965	57,632	49,780	6,080	3,659
2017	361,606	248,045	593	248,639	26,787	23,039	244,891	66,765	49,951	59,155	51,221	6,113	3,697
2018	371,870	253,454	358	253,812	28,083	24,572	250,301	69,048	52,521	60,577	52,541	6,139	3,751
2019	384,074	257,167	542	257,709	29,030	26,560	255,240	73,774	55,061	62,313	53,625	6,164	3,744
2020	405,455	258,847	267	259,114	29,242	28,013	257,885	73,464	74,105	65,680	57,032	6,173	3,621
2021	430,429	275,488	611	276,099	31,130	30,066	275,034	75,266	80,130	69,710	59,931	6,175	3,714
2022	436,028	290,315	1,199	291,514	33,294	31,926	290,146	78,234	67,648	70,730	59,307	6,165	...

... = Not available.

Personal Income and Employment by Region and State: Massachusetts

(Millions of dollars, except as noted.)

Year	Personal income, total	Earnings by place of work Nonfarm	Farm	Total	Less: Contributions for government social insurance	Plus: Adjustment for residence	Equals: Net earnings by place of residence	Plus: Dividends, interest, and rent	Plus: Personal current transfer receipts	Per capita (dollars) Personal income	Disposable personal income	Population (thousands)	Total employment (thousands)
1960	13,147	10,795	68	10,864	499	-75	10,290	1,937	921	2,548	2,229	5,160	...
1961	13,814	11,303	60	11,363	528	-82	10,753	2,035	1,027	2,647	2,335	5,219	...
1962	14,597	11,957	61	12,017	617	-92	11,309	2,237	1,051	2,773	2,435	5,263	...
1963	15,203	12,363	61	12,424	680	-98	11,646	2,448	1,110	2,845	2,498	5,344	...
1964	16,233	13,084	63	13,147	698	-108	12,341	2,742	1,151	2,980	2,658	5,448	...
1965	17,320	13,887	69	13,956	714	-122	13,121	2,987	1,212	3,148	2,804	5,502	...
1966	18,650	15,162	72	15,234	942	-141	14,151	3,199	1,301	3,369	2,974	5,535	...
1967	20,261	16,325	56	16,381	1,033	-157	15,191	3,465	1,605	3,622	3,190	5,594	...
1968	22,127	17,783	65	17,847	1,139	-175	16,534	3,657	1,936	3,938	3,416	5,618	...
1969	24,042	19,391	66	19,458	1,262	-133	18,062	3,823	2,157	4,255	3,627	5,650	2,679
1970	25,961	20,692	69	20,761	1,327	-111	19,323	4,088	2,551	4,552	3,941	5,704	2,679
1971	27,742	21,885	63	21,948	1,448	-108	20,393	4,329	3,020	4,834	4,243	5,739	2,644
1972	29,978	23,764	63	23,826	1,651	-105	22,071	4,593	3,314	5,203	4,492	5,762	2,697
1973	32,574	25,968	71	26,039	2,075	-124	23,840	5,018	3,716	5,632	4,897	5,784	2,787
1974	35,182	27,560	70	27,630	2,275	-141	25,213	5,564	4,405	6,090	5,279	5,777	2,811
1975	37,802	28,677	69	28,746	2,295	-152	26,298	5,772	5,732	6,560	5,779	5,762	2,728
1976	40,689	31,218	76	31,295	2,556	-172	28,567	6,176	5,946	7,078	6,185	5,749	2,756
1977	44,298	34,335	79	34,414	2,817	-218	31,379	6,811	6,108	7,712	6,710	5,744	2,833
1978	48,939	38,438	104	38,542	3,248	-278	35,016	7,447	6,476	8,522	7,388	5,743	2,958
1979	54,481	43,061	91	43,152	3,796	-373	38,983	8,330	7,169	9,481	8,146	5,746	3,074
1980	61,389	47,684	106	47,789	4,215	-493	43,082	10,119	8,189	10,684	9,133	5,746	3,134
1981	68,493	52,262	116	52,378	4,981	-621	46,776	12,413	9,304	11,873	10,061	5,769	3,142
1982	75,099	56,170	132	56,301	5,484	-747	50,070	14,972	10,056	13,013	11,153	5,771	3,143
1983	81,446	61,918	164	62,082	6,141	-918	55,023	15,768	10,655	14,044	12,090	5,799	3,215
1984	91,928	70,529	183	70,711	7,225	-1,176	62,311	18,413	11,204	15,739	13,618	5,841	3,402
1985	99,342	77,403	160	77,564	8,002	-1,371	68,191	19,429	11,722	16,893	14,526	5,881	3,510
1986	107,147	84,175	175	84,350	8,883	-1,494	73,973	20,841	12,332	18,152	15,535	5,903	3,605
1987	116,044	92,452	153	92,605	9,651	-1,665	81,290	22,076	12,679	19,552	16,636	5,935	3,632
1988	127,723	101,838	172	102,010	10,787	-1,881	89,342	24,721	13,661	21,358	18,427	5,980	3,739
1989	135,209	106,030	153	106,183	11,166	-2,031	92,987	26,817	15,406	22,477	19,309	6,015	3,710
1990	139,233	107,297	153	107,450	11,186	-2,074	94,190	27,779	17,264	23,118	19,865	6,023	3,615
1991	141,352	107,264	173	107,436	11,384	-2,237	93,815	27,741	19,796	23,486	20,321	6,018	3,451
1992	148,478	113,789	171	113,960	11,985	-2,346	99,630	28,190	20,658	24,628	21,367	6,029	3,482
1993	154,367	118,617	164	118,781	12,586	-2,561	103,634	29,477	21,256	25,471	22,035	6,061	3,548
1994	162,175	124,844	150	124,994	13,379	-2,764	108,850	30,839	22,486	26,607	22,937	6,095	3,616
1995	171,742	131,467	146	131,613	14,168	-2,826	114,619	33,299	23,824	27,964	23,955	6,141	3,649
1996	182,580	140,289	166	140,455	14,935	-3,094	122,427	35,587	24,567	29,545	25,041	6,180	3,713
1997	194,131	149,916	168	150,084	15,992	-3,402	130,690	38,013	25,428	31,180	26,170	6,226	3,802
1998	206,431	160,461	108	160,568	17,060	-3,602	139,907	40,972	25,552	32,914	27,290	6,272	3,896
1999	220,901	175,059	108	175,167	18,309	-4,185	152,673	41,770	26,458	34,967	28,856	6,317	3,962
2000	245,503	196,523	131	196,654	20,253	-5,050	171,351	46,267	27,884	38,594	31,160	6,361	4,070
2001	255,087	203,031	110	203,141	20,769	-5,197	177,175	47,429	30,483	39,872	32,916	6,398	4,076
2002	253,739	201,858	131	201,989	20,729	-5,088	176,172	44,485	33,082	39,540	33,983	6,417	4,022
2003	258,617	204,748	130	204,878	20,951	-5,091	178,836	44,833	34,948	40,267	34,931	6,423	3,992
2004	271,927	217,930	146	218,076	22,741	-5,588	189,746	45,816	36,364	42,407	36,826	6,412	4,029
2005	284,123	224,359	124	224,483	23,801	-5,426	195,255	49,807	39,060	44,371	38,113	6,403	4,071
2006	306,082	236,941	131	237,072	24,663	-5,697	206,712	58,437	40,933	47,750	40,851	6,410	4,110
2007	322,126	248,480	132	248,612	25,846	-6,111	216,655	62,844	42,627	50,085	42,193	6,432	4,203
2008	335,157	254,266	193	254,459	26,684	-6,078	221,698	64,788	48,671	51,810	44,082	6,469	4,216
2009	330,910	252,246	165	252,410	26,302	-5,472	220,636	56,957	53,318	50,772	44,822	6,518	4,116
2010	347,492	267,013	166	267,179	26,859	-5,997	234,323	57,025	56,145	52,894	46,399	6,570	4,116
2011	363,396	275,703	165	275,869	25,046	-6,649	244,174	62,816	56,406	54,812	47,225	6,630	4,175
2012	379,268	285,713	231	285,944	25,914	-7,380	252,650	69,847	56,771	56,669	49,080	6,693	4,253
2013	382,611	293,084	208	293,293	30,058	-7,342	255,893	69,391	57,327	56,628	48,075	6,757	4,354
2014	401,833	304,069	152	304,221	31,528	-6,940	265,753	76,964	59,116	58,924	49,801	6,819	4,448
2015	428,229	321,761	134	321,894	32,706	-7,751	281,438	83,167	63,625	62,376	52,507	6,865	4,631
2016	444,184	332,801	124	332,926	33,828	-8,306	290,792	87,271	66,121	64,295	54,376	6,909	4,710
2017	463,981	349,548	117	349,665	35,535	-8,838	305,292	91,582	67,107	66,679	56,416	6,958	4,778
2018	487,437	367,642	93	367,736	37,412	-9,665	320,659	96,421	70,357	69,693	59,207	6,994	4,855
2019	513,710	387,634	130	387,764	39,235	-11,777	336,752	104,593	72,366	73,213	62,085	7,017	4,873
2020	550,460	392,336	110	392,447	39,393	-11,771	341,283	104,045	105,132	78,685	67,426	6,996	4,600
2021	584,291	423,957	101	424,058	42,629	-12,130	369,299	107,217	107,775	83,593	70,392	6,990	4,761
2022	593,083	450,830	127	450,956	45,778	-12,875	392,303	112,768	88,012	84,945	69,316	6,982	...

... = Not available.

Personal Income and Employment by Region and State: Michigan

(Millions of dollars, except as noted.)

Year	Personal income, total	Earnings by place of work			Less: Contributions for government social insurance	Plus: Adjustment for residence	Equals: Net earnings by place of residence	Plus: Dividends, interest, and rent	Plus: Personal current transfer receipts	Per capita (dollars)		Population (thousands)	Total employment (thousands)
		Nonfarm	Farm	Total						Personal income	Disposable personal income		
1960	18,884	15,838	240	16,078	824	37	15,290	2,482	1,112	2,411	2,148	7,834	...
1961	18,957	15,471	300	15,771	786	38	15,023	2,602	1,332	2,402	2,158	7,893	...
1962	20,319	16,771	275	17,047	888	42	16,200	2,815	1,304	2,561	2,280	7,933	...
1963	21,692	18,060	300	18,360	1,038	44	17,366	2,998	1,327	2,692	2,388	8,058	...
1964	23,774	19,843	295	20,138	1,077	49	19,111	3,298	1,366	2,904	2,608	8,187	...
1965	26,375	22,126	274	22,399	1,122	54	21,332	3,568	1,476	3,156	2,823	8,357	...
1966	28,764	24,429	349	24,778	1,572	63	23,270	3,877	1,617	3,379	3,006	8,512	...
1967	29,992	25,177	276	25,453	1,652	68	23,869	4,122	2,002	3,475	3,086	8,630	...
1968	33,161	27,965	304	28,269	1,854	76	26,491	4,357	2,312	3,813	3,325	8,696	...
1969	36,068	30,702	351	31,054	2,206	105	28,952	4,557	2,559	4,107	3,519	8,781	3,640
1970	37,362	30,875	341	31,216	2,196	113	29,132	5,014	3,216	4,200	3,656	8,897	3,558
1971	40,644	33,471	310	33,781	2,450	106	31,437	5,369	3,838	4,530	3,982	8,972	3,571
1972	45,132	37,389	427	37,816	2,905	114	35,024	5,790	4,318	5,001	4,319	9,025	3,687
1973	50,383	42,183	561	42,745	3,800	140	39,085	6,373	4,925	5,554	4,828	9,072	3,858
1974	53,913	43,801	649	44,450	4,082	140	40,507	7,253	6,153	5,918	5,170	9,109	3,854
1975	57,745	45,051	578	45,629	4,091	149	41,687	7,983	8,075	6,340	5,629	9,108	3,695
1976	64,458	51,691	478	52,169	4,794	191	47,566	8,569	8,323	7,070	6,176	9,117	3,844
1977	72,466	59,122	559	59,681	5,491	217	54,406	9,514	8,545	7,913	6,848	9,157	4,016
1978	80,773	66,736	510	67,245	6,391	260	61,115	10,575	9,083	8,778	7,527	9,202	4,186
1979	88,479	72,515	545	73,060	7,194	292	66,158	11,848	10,473	9,566	8,200	9,249	4,228
1980	94,684	73,189	536	73,725	7,174	337	66,888	13,970	13,826	10,230	8,898	9,256	4,030
1981	101,254	77,169	515	77,684	8,186	378	69,876	16,733	14,646	10,995	9,528	9,209	3,978
1982	104,817	76,677	410	77,087	8,241	381	69,227	19,241	16,349	11,499	10,105	9,115	3,823
1983	111,577	81,930	222	82,152	8,954	413	73,612	20,665	17,300	12,332	10,808	9,048	3,866
1984	123,177	91,555	551	92,106	10,356	479	82,229	23,458	17,491	13,612	11,958	9,049	4,040
1985	133,599	100,998	663	101,661	11,666	501	90,497	25,052	18,051	14,720	12,841	9,076	4,233
1986	142,048	108,387	493	108,879	12,551	488	96,817	26,301	18,930	15,562	13,596	9,128	4,349
1987	147,561	112,807	665	113,472	12,896	507	101,083	27,015	19,464	16,061	13,991	9,187	4,483
1988	157,523	121,619	585	122,204	14,305	515	108,413	28,808	20,302	17,089	14,959	9,218	4,582
1989	169,629	128,976	981	129,956	15,142	512	115,326	32,337	21,966	18,332	15,981	9,253	4,709
1990	177,393	134,521	776	135,297	16,053	458	119,702	33,888	23,803	19,051	16,695	9,311	4,791
1991	181,414	136,787	667	137,453	16,559	488	121,382	33,551	26,481	19,298	16,996	9,400	4,721
1992	192,235	146,116	757	146,873	17,547	552	129,879	34,306	28,051	20,280	17,975	9,479	4,751
1993	202,433	154,077	737	154,813	18,603	628	136,837	35,613	29,982	21,219	18,650	9,540	4,812
1994	217,745	165,969	563	166,532	20,421	754	146,865	40,605	30,276	22,687	19,874	9,598	4,985
1995	230,306	175,290	695	175,985	21,539	797	155,242	43,108	31,955	23,801	20,768	9,676	5,142
1996	242,219	183,671	618	184,289	22,020	823	163,092	45,570	33,557	24,821	21,542	9,759	5,247
1997	254,939	192,907	608	193,515	23,099	909	171,326	48,128	35,486	25,990	22,466	9,809	5,330
1998	270,130	206,810	628	207,438	24,260	993	184,171	50,713	35,247	27,430	23,573	9,848	5,384
1999	283,340	219,980	821	220,801	25,631	1,081	196,250	49,318	37,772	28,629	24,620	9,897	5,486
2000	302,001	235,341	607	235,949	26,849	1,098	210,197	52,760	39,043	30,344	26,225	9,952	5,621
2001	307,221	237,231	564	237,795	26,634	1,189	212,350	51,396	43,475	30,749	26,755	9,991	5,526
2002	306,503	237,599	601	238,200	26,922	1,217	212,495	48,945	45,063	30,602	27,180	10,016	5,466
2003	314,078	241,419	710	242,129	27,308	1,272	216,093	50,684	47,301	31,279	28,066	10,041	5,442
2004	323,457	246,940	1,152	248,092	28,277	1,369	221,184	52,956	49,317	32,168	29,015	10,055	5,468
2005	331,143	250,130	1,044	251,174	29,162	1,445	223,457	55,237	52,449	32,946	29,562	10,051	5,492
2006	339,338	252,219	1,144	253,363	29,854	1,631	225,139	58,207	55,993	33,812	30,260	10,036	5,457
2007	349,332	253,634	1,236	254,870	30,219	1,677	226,328	61,762	61,242	34,929	31,098	10,001	5,457
2008	357,780	250,525	1,383	251,908	30,253	1,682	223,338	64,730	69,712	35,969	32,086	9,947	5,338
2009	339,695	231,825	868	232,692	28,274	1,517	205,936	56,338	77,422	34,307	31,448	9,902	5,047
2010	353,316	239,307	1,421	240,728	28,641	1,579	213,667	56,965	82,685	35,760	32,623	9,880	5,038
2011	373,861	250,209	2,646	252,855	26,598	1,727	227,985	63,335	82,542	37,781	34,054	9,895	5,165
2012	389,544	262,301	1,653	263,953	27,730	1,911	238,135	69,281	82,129	39,266	35,326	9,921	5,234
2013	393,577	269,036	2,188	271,224	32,215	1,919	240,928	69,263	83,385	39,566	35,249	9,947	5,324
2014	411,020	278,754	1,383	280,137	33,286	2,075	248,926	75,661	86,433	41,207	36,731	9,975	5,412
2015	433,689	292,705	1,130	293,835	34,703	2,130	261,262	80,951	91,476	43,425	38,525	9,987	5,502
2016	446,030	301,848	935	302,783	35,679	2,265	269,369	83,029	93,632	44,527	39,329	10,017	5,576
2017	459,438	315,699	1,046	316,745	37,104	2,320	281,962	83,764	93,712	45,716	40,548	10,050	5,631
2018	477,925	327,226	964	328,190	39,015	2,531	291,706	88,068	98,152	47,457	42,326	10,071	5,715
2019	495,269	335,997	909	336,906	39,909	2,650	299,647	91,821	103,800	49,142	43,870	10,078	5,714
2020	537,494	334,409	1,888	336,297	39,714	2,637	299,220	92,111	146,163	53,378	48,136	10,070	5,388
2021	567,807	359,221	2,098	361,320	41,840	3,289	322,769	93,905	151,132	56,569	50,280	10,038	5,580
2022	570,065	386,798	3,255	390,052	45,411	3,574	348,215	96,965	124,885	56,813	49,256	10,034	...

... = Not available.

Personal Income and Employment by Region and State: Minnesota

(Millions of dollars, except as noted.)

Year	Personal income, total	Earnings by place of work — Nonfarm	Earnings by place of work — Farm	Earnings by place of work — Total	Less: Contributions for government social insurance	Plus: Adjustment for residence	Equals: Net earnings by place of residence	Plus: Dividends, interest, and rent	Plus: Personal current transfer receipts	Per capita (dollars) — Personal income	Per capita (dollars) — Disposable personal income	Population (thousands)	Total employment (thousands)
1960	7,472	5,596	514	6,111	260	-1	5,849	1,116	507	2,182	1,948	3,425	...
1961	7,853	5,842	540	6,382	269	-3	6,110	1,172	571	2,263	2,023	3,470	...
1962	8,278	6,282	467	6,748	303	-3	6,443	1,245	590	2,356	2,096	3,513	...
1963	8,779	6,540	621	7,162	339	-4	6,819	1,336	625	2,486	2,220	3,531	...
1964	9,132	6,997	402	7,399	348	-4	7,048	1,433	651	2,566	2,317	3,558	...
1965	10,088	7,547	652	8,199	372	-7	7,821	1,559	708	2,808	2,526	3,592	...
1966	10,934	8,323	733	9,056	522	-13	8,521	1,652	761	3,023	2,701	3,617	...
1967	11,750	9,035	643	9,678	602	-17	9,059	1,766	925	3,211	2,859	3,659	...
1968	12,934	9,982	680	10,662	683	-24	9,955	1,921	1,058	3,493	3,092	3,703	...
1969	14,388	11,172	720	11,892	781	-33	11,079	2,147	1,162	3,829	3,331	3,758	1,691
1970	15,709	11,935	876	12,811	825	-26	11,959	2,376	1,373	4,117	3,632	3,815	1,699
1971	16,766	12,725	796	13,521	910	-27	12,585	2,588	1,594	4,353	3,880	3,852	1,706
1972	18,229	13,797	959	14,756	1,036	-29	13,691	2,776	1,762	4,714	4,139	3,867	1,780
1973	21,370	15,357	2,179	17,536	1,333	-35	16,168	3,137	2,066	5,500	4,891	3,885	1,878
1974	23,012	16,889	1,644	18,533	1,525	-31	16,977	3,611	2,424	5,903	5,146	3,898	1,921
1975	24,891	18,306	1,264	19,571	1,613	-32	17,925	4,042	2,924	6,340	5,571	3,926	1,920
1976	26,907	20,452	782	21,235	1,845	-40	19,350	4,343	3,214	6,801	5,936	3,957	1,977
1977	30,293	22,648	1,501	24,150	2,043	-54	22,052	4,860	3,380	7,612	6,630	3,980	2,034
1978	33,989	25,807	1,625	27,432	2,409	-69	24,954	5,407	3,628	8,487	7,354	4,005	2,122
1979	37,795	29,364	1,245	30,609	2,855	-94	27,661	6,079	4,056	9,360	8,030	4,038	2,218
1980	42,002	32,001	959	32,960	3,107	-101	29,752	7,384	4,866	10,282	8,862	4,085	2,248
1981	46,548	34,622	1,040	35,662	3,604	-132	31,926	9,039	5,583	11,321	9,725	4,112	2,233
1982	49,868	36,143	819	36,962	3,838	-155	32,969	10,622	6,277	12,070	10,433	4,131	2,192
1983	52,578	38,691	119	38,810	4,161	-183	34,465	11,347	6,766	12,696	11,020	4,141	2,219
1984	59,667	43,444	1,444	44,889	4,796	-240	39,852	12,719	7,097	14,351	12,586	4,158	2,324
1985	63,361	46,561	1,343	47,903	5,234	-288	42,382	13,439	7,540	15,143	13,282	4,184	2,385
1986	67,018	49,447	1,641	51,088	5,701	-326	45,061	14,078	7,879	15,937	14,026	4,205	2,417
1987	71,480	53,311	2,138	55,450	6,107	-376	48,967	14,385	8,128	16,878	14,728	4,235	2,509
1988	75,425	57,661	1,253	58,914	6,828	-452	51,633	15,204	8,588	17,556	15,353	4,296	2,580
1989	82,388	61,745	2,051	63,796	7,303	-439	56,054	16,984	9,351	18,992	16,584	4,338	2,634
1990	87,514	65,807	1,956	67,763	7,829	-471	59,463	18,001	10,051	19,935	17,342	4,390	2,692
1991	90,246	68,763	1,207	69,970	8,278	-476	61,216	18,225	10,805	20,322	17,777	4,441	2,717
1992	97,019	74,587	1,401	75,987	8,869	-509	66,609	18,661	11,748	21,581	18,838	4,496	2,762
1993	99,990	77,969	187	78,156	9,313	-515	68,328	19,267	12,395	21,947	19,094	4,556	2,817
1994	107,155	82,615	1,340	83,954	9,990	-561	73,403	20,715	13,037	23,242	20,214	4,610	2,904
1995	113,338	87,329	519	87,848	10,530	-610	76,708	22,812	13,817	24,320	21,044	4,660	2,995
1996	122,211	93,303	1,921	95,224	11,136	-685	83,403	24,343	14,464	25,932	22,188	4,713	3,056
1997	129,028	99,731	898	100,629	11,836	-767	88,026	26,310	14,692	27,087	23,114	4,763	3,109
1998	140,369	108,801	1,397	110,198	12,712	-847	96,639	28,523	15,206	29,162	24,804	4,813	3,189
1999	147,681	115,841	1,261	117,103	13,570	-951	102,582	29,112	15,988	30,303	25,969	4,873	3,257
2000	160,089	125,396	1,453	126,849	14,525	-1,037	111,288	31,673	17,128	32,448	27,620	4,934	3,331
2001	166,872	130,650	1,029	131,679	15,034	-1,084	115,561	32,089	19,222	33,490	28,708	4,983	3,347
2002	170,419	134,110	1,010	135,120	15,409	-1,112	118,599	30,950	20,870	33,955	29,630	5,019	3,338
2003	178,356	139,299	1,827	141,126	16,100	-1,180	123,846	32,627	21,884	35,293	31,181	5,054	3,347
2004	189,321	148,517	2,445	150,962	17,010	-1,258	132,694	33,618	23,009	37,211	33,029	5,088	3,390
2005	194,877	152,028	2,903	154,931	17,755	-1,321	135,856	34,909	24,112	38,065	33,389	5,120	3,448
2006	204,824	157,035	2,520	159,555	18,564	-1,276	139,716	38,555	26,553	39,667	34,626	5,164	3,496
2007	216,907	164,544	2,579	167,122	19,330	-1,393	146,399	41,430	29,078	41,655	36,197	5,207	3,540
2008	226,467	167,952	4,015	171,967	19,934	-1,422	150,612	42,896	32,960	43,161	37,519	5,247	3,526
2009	216,946	160,670	2,155	162,825	19,269	-1,148	142,408	38,355	36,183	41,079	36,757	5,281	3,424
2010	226,957	166,543	3,187	169,730	19,580	-1,106	149,044	38,887	39,027	42,724	38,071	5,312	3,409
2011	242,593	175,384	4,370	179,754	18,318	-1,143	160,293	42,960	39,340	45,323	39,884	5,353	3,469
2012	257,164	184,204	6,012	190,216	19,060	-928	170,228	47,580	39,356	47,726	42,037	5,388	3,506
2013	259,782	189,648	5,666	195,313	22,415	-890	172,009	47,006	40,768	47,838	41,523	5,430	3,556
2014	273,488	198,997	3,715	202,712	23,114	-921	178,677	51,579	43,232	49,967	43,365	5,473	3,604
2015	286,423	208,123	3,257	211,380	23,931	-1,024	186,425	55,396	44,602	51,985	44,797	5,510	3,663
2016	292,235	213,237	1,429	214,666	24,615	-1,197	188,853	57,305	46,077	52,596	45,298	5,556	3,698
2017	304,180	222,356	1,980	224,336	25,691	-1,336	197,308	59,091	47,781	54,266	46,958	5,605	3,736
2018	319,453	232,535	1,524	234,059	26,967	-1,320	205,773	62,843	50,837	56,539	49,198	5,650	3,777
2019	332,916	240,143	1,043	241,186	27,940	-1,495	211,751	67,891	53,275	58,543	50,932	5,687	3,784
2020	355,211	241,940	3,410	245,350	28,293	-1,438	215,619	68,254	71,339	62,210	54,482	5,710	3,608
2021	378,285	257,494	4,077	261,571	29,362	-1,591	230,618	69,678	77,989	66,232	57,193	5,711	3,695
2022	388,828	276,420	5,801	282,221	31,610	-1,693	248,918	72,833	67,077	68,010	57,359	5,717	...

... = Not available.

Personal Income and Employment by Region and State: Mississippi

(Millions of dollars, except as noted.)

Year	Personal income, total	Earnings by place of work			Less: Contributions for government social insurance	Plus: Adjustment for residence	Equals: Net earnings by place of residence	Plus: Dividends, interest, and rent	Plus: Personal current transfer receipts	Per capita (dollars)		Population (thousands)	Total employment (thousands)
		Nonfarm	Farm	Total						Personal income	Disposable personal income		
1960	2,764	2,031	281	2,312	101	12	2,224	308	233	1,267	1,174	2,182	...
1961	2,997	2,122	353	2,475	104	13	2,384	351	262	1,359	1,270	2,206	...
1962	3,133	2,277	297	2,574	115	15	2,474	385	273	1,397	1,294	2,243	...
1963	3,442	2,422	432	2,854	136	17	2,735	418	290	1,534	1,419	2,244	...
1964	3,563	2,588	370	2,958	143	20	2,834	427	303	1,590	1,482	2,241	...
1965	3,869	2,874	352	3,226	152	22	3,096	445	328	1,722	1,601	2,246	...
1966	4,217	3,219	347	3,566	197	23	3,392	465	360	1,879	1,732	2,245	...
1967	4,563	3,441	386	3,826	226	25	3,625	507	432	2,048	1,890	2,228	...
1968	4,993	3,823	364	4,187	253	31	3,966	539	489	2,250	2,065	2,219	...
1969	5,541	4,222	349	4,571	291	36	4,316	673	552	2,496	2,279	2,220	909
1970	6,077	4,487	394	4,881	310	37	4,608	780	689	2,736	2,488	2,221	917
1971	6,737	4,918	436	5,354	351	59	5,062	861	814	2,974	2,746	2,266	939
1972	7,677	5,655	494	6,148	421	74	5,801	958	918	3,327	3,029	2,307	979
1973	8,779	6,358	692	7,050	538	94	6,606	1,109	1,065	3,736	3,421	2,350	1,019
1974	9,648	7,017	515	7,532	615	123	7,039	1,297	1,312	4,056	3,677	2,379	1,031
1975	10,463	7,519	377	7,895	653	149	7,391	1,441	1,631	4,360	4,015	2,400	1,001
1976	11,878	8,537	576	9,112	757	179	8,535	1,557	1,786	4,887	4,461	2,430	1,039
1977	13,222	9,598	609	10,208	850	218	9,575	1,738	1,910	5,375	4,919	2,460	1,071
1978	14,722	10,879	455	11,334	982	272	10,624	1,998	2,100	5,917	5,355	2,488	1,101
1979	16,637	12,059	704	12,763	1,129	325	11,960	2,280	2,396	6,633	5,981	2,508	1,114
1980	18,098	13,012	185	13,198	1,210	410	12,398	2,821	2,879	7,166	6,458	2,525	1,111
1981	20,332	14,215	334	14,548	1,421	440	13,566	3,502	3,263	8,008	7,164	2,539	1,107
1982	21,465	14,610	425	15,035	1,497	457	13,995	3,883	3,588	8,395	7,645	2,557	1,079
1983	22,452	15,392	102	15,494	1,594	513	14,413	4,088	3,951	8,744	7,931	2,568	1,088
1984	24,528	16,655	480	17,135	1,773	572	15,934	4,509	4,086	9,514	8,673	2,578	1,117
1985	25,819	17,582	438	18,020	1,914	603	16,709	4,830	4,280	9,976	9,089	2,588	1,124
1986	26,781	18,498	204	18,702	2,032	592	17,261	4,985	4,535	10,326	9,450	2,594	1,131
1987	28,324	19,421	587	20,008	2,125	630	18,512	5,091	4,721	10,942	9,982	2,589	1,141
1988	30,303	20,790	733	21,523	2,374	672	19,821	5,453	5,029	11,744	10,753	2,580	1,169
1989	32,736	22,229	569	22,798	2,542	715	20,971	6,269	5,495	12,717	11,587	2,574	1,189
1990	34,443	23,665	493	24,157	2,803	749	22,103	6,377	5,962	13,356	12,165	2,579	1,203
1991	36,288	24,732	588	25,320	2,989	804	23,136	6,444	6,708	13,964	12,773	2,599	1,211
1992	39,063	26,698	671	27,369	3,192	823	25,000	6,548	7,515	14,888	13,634	2,624	1,234
1993	41,597	28,775	584	29,359	3,453	840	26,746	6,839	8,012	15,667	14,304	2,655	1,287
1994	45,005	31,222	844	32,066	3,779	838	29,125	7,381	8,500	16,737	15,231	2,689	1,335
1995	47,613	32,721	679	33,400	3,946	920	30,374	7,949	9,291	17,488	15,888	2,723	1,365
1996	50,526	34,139	1,078	35,217	4,069	962	32,110	8,457	9,959	18,386	16,655	2,748	1,389
1997	53,378	36,134	991	37,125	4,284	1,112	33,954	9,090	10,334	19,221	17,369	2,777	1,415
1998	56,585	38,719	967	39,686	4,579	1,188	36,294	9,871	10,419	20,174	18,196	2,805	1,445
1999	58,573	40,448	946	41,394	4,783	1,287	37,898	9,944	10,731	20,709	18,670	2,828	1,470
2000	61,755	42,172	792	42,964	4,926	1,478	39,516	10,713	11,526	21,681	19,594	2,848	1,476
2001	65,176	43,147	1,583	44,730	5,013	1,541	41,258	11,051	12,867	22,845	20,664	2,853	1,456
2002	66,375	44,724	639	45,363	5,214	1,583	41,733	10,827	13,815	23,219	21,321	2,859	1,455
2003	69,022	46,392	1,182	47,574	5,375	1,667	43,865	10,717	14,440	24,064	22,226	2,868	1,453
2004	73,110	48,860	1,801	50,661	5,698	1,778	46,740	10,847	15,523	25,306	23,580	2,889	1,464
2005	77,982	51,006	1,754	52,759	5,914	1,895	48,740	11,782	17,460	26,835	24,848	2,906	1,474
2006	81,284	53,796	816	54,612	6,399	2,113	50,326	13,375	17,583	27,981	25,654	2,905	1,508
2007	86,544	55,411	1,151	56,563	6,671	2,268	52,160	16,017	18,368	29,554	27,126	2,928	1,539
2008	90,748	57,604	742	58,346	6,889	2,409	53,866	16,091	20,791	30,785	28,148	2,948	1,537
2009	89,227	55,446	847	56,293	6,799	2,366	51,860	15,139	22,228	30,157	28,090	2,959	1,492
2010	92,933	57,481	892	58,373	6,891	2,428	53,910	14,933	24,090	31,287	28,975	2,970	1,491
2011	96,918	59,114	581	59,694	6,404	2,649	55,940	16,044	24,935	32,546	30,160	2,978	1,510
2012	100,377	61,595	815	62,410	6,617	2,850	58,643	16,820	24,915	33,657	31,140	2,982	1,520
2013	102,317	62,706	2,308	65,014	7,551	2,990	60,453	16,397	25,468	34,259	31,523	2,987	1,533
2014	104,256	64,352	1,361	65,713	7,739	3,049	61,022	17,023	26,211	34,896	32,125	2,988	1,557
2015	106,064	64,866	948	65,814	7,944	3,177	61,048	17,710	27,307	35,533	32,600	2,985	1,568
2016	107,500	65,616	733	66,349	8,125	3,218	61,442	17,847	28,211	36,021	33,002	2,984	1,581
2017	110,093	66,901	1,505	68,407	8,382	3,316	63,341	18,356	28,396	36,902	33,964	2,983	1,592
2018	112,739	68,873	1,167	70,041	8,584	3,512	64,969	18,420	29,351	37,900	35,055	2,975	1,603
2019	117,113	70,963	1,051	72,014	8,926	3,758	66,847	19,523	30,743	39,445	36,402	2,969	1,608
2020	126,307	72,886	734	73,620	9,306	3,689	68,003	19,552	38,752	42,698	39,572	2,958	1,574
2021	135,347	77,550	1,557	79,106	9,660	3,950	73,396	19,895	42,057	45,887	42,239	2,950	1,609
2022	135,972	82,732	2,860	85,592	10,435	4,385	79,542	20,505	35,925	46,248	41,887	2,940	...

... = Not available.

Personal Income and Employment by Region and State: Missouri

(Millions of dollars, except as noted.)

Year	Personal income, total	Earnings by place of work			Less: Contributions for government social insurance	Plus: Adjustment for residence	Equals: Net earnings by place of residence	Plus: Dividends, interest, and rent	Plus: Personal current transfer receipts	Per capita (dollars)		Population (thousands)	Total employment (thousands)
		Nonfarm	Farm	Total						Personal income	Disposable personal income		
1960	9,630	7,698	443	8,141	358	-180	7,603	1,356	671	2,226	1,984	4,326	...
1961	9,955	7,877	484	8,361	375	-185	7,801	1,409	745	2,289	2,040	4,349	...
1962	10,489	8,346	486	8,832	408	-202	8,222	1,496	771	2,407	2,138	4,357	...
1963	11,002	8,855	440	9,295	469	-227	8,599	1,595	808	2,505	2,219	4,392	...
1964	11,620	9,486	335	9,820	491	-250	9,079	1,710	830	2,616	2,354	4,442	...
1965	12,635	10,171	533	10,704	517	-275	9,911	1,835	888	2,828	2,528	4,467	...
1966	13,536	11,194	417	11,611	695	-314	10,602	1,974	960	2,993	2,666	4,523	...
1967	14,407	11,953	404	12,356	797	-351	11,209	2,078	1,120	3,174	2,825	4,539	...
1968	15,950	13,133	478	13,612	898	-387	12,326	2,310	1,313	3,492	3,086	4,568	...
1969	16,913	14,263	450	14,713	954	-752	13,006	2,478	1,428	3,645	3,163	4,640	2,216
1970	18,480	15,173	525	15,698	1,005	-694	13,999	2,788	1,692	3,945	3,471	4,685	2,203
1971	19,939	16,187	571	16,758	1,109	-680	14,970	3,018	1,951	4,222	3,750	4,723	2,200
1972	21,682	17,549	714	18,263	1,261	-698	16,304	3,266	2,112	4,562	4,003	4,753	2,242
1973	24,090	19,085	1,215	20,301	1,584	-729	17,987	3,653	2,450	5,045	4,473	4,775	2,325
1974	25,775	20,574	640	21,214	1,767	-756	18,691	4,192	2,892	5,386	4,737	4,785	2,341
1975	28,213	21,854	698	22,552	1,842	-771	19,939	4,618	3,655	5,883	5,248	4,795	2,291
1976	30,912	24,496	471	24,967	2,097	-839	22,032	4,976	3,904	6,409	5,667	4,824	2,365
1977	34,252	27,206	717	27,924	2,332	-969	24,623	5,555	4,075	7,070	6,250	4,845	2,424
1978	38,130	30,397	920	31,317	2,697	-1,121	27,499	6,202	4,428	7,828	6,869	4,871	2,512
1979	42,514	33,687	1,179	34,866	3,090	-1,287	30,489	7,016	5,008	8,695	7,592	4,889	2,576
1980	46,120	35,990	242	36,232	3,279	-1,495	31,458	8,564	6,099	9,370	8,186	4,922	2,549
1981	51,517	38,771	773	39,543	3,789	-1,629	34,125	10,539	6,852	10,445	9,083	4,932	2,540
1982	55,084	40,570	347	40,917	4,044	-1,685	35,189	12,425	7,470	11,174	9,672	4,929	2,516
1983	58,758	43,678	-103	43,575	4,389	-1,709	37,477	13,259	8,022	11,885	10,511	4,944	2,562
1984	65,189	48,321	426	48,746	4,997	-1,858	41,892	14,926	8,372	13,103	11,645	4,975	2,667
1985	69,744	51,821	798	52,619	5,479	-1,988	45,153	15,762	8,830	13,948	12,348	5,000	2,738
1986	73,417	55,042	584	55,626	5,879	-2,053	47,694	16,424	9,298	14,616	12,956	5,023	2,801
1987	77,346	58,668	739	59,407	6,196	-2,170	51,042	16,730	9,574	15,296	13,520	5,057	2,836
1988	82,132	62,711	658	63,368	6,836	-2,253	54,280	17,742	10,109	16,162	14,331	5,082	2,885
1989	88,040	66,534	912	67,446	7,299	-2,386	57,761	19,307	10,972	17,277	15,257	5,096	2,938
1990	91,909	69,600	708	70,308	7,872	-2,600	59,837	20,182	11,890	17,920	15,821	5,129	2,972
1991	95,964	71,629	589	72,218	8,214	-2,592	61,413	20,656	13,895	18,559	16,509	5,171	2,942
1992	102,139	76,312	862	77,173	8,666	-2,716	65,792	21,511	14,836	19,578	17,460	5,217	2,957
1993	106,821	79,824	500	80,324	9,093	-2,834	68,397	22,496	15,928	20,265	18,048	5,271	3,041
1994	113,391	84,809	725	85,534	9,774	-2,860	72,900	23,791	16,701	21,296	18,904	5,324	3,113
1995	119,590	90,015	219	90,234	10,357	-3,110	76,766	25,021	17,803	22,236	19,673	5,378	3,196
1996	126,668	94,801	1,052	95,854	10,779	-3,210	81,865	26,198	18,605	23,321	20,531	5,432	3,255
1997	134,328	100,826	1,059	101,886	11,410	-3,388	87,087	27,933	19,308	24,507	21,472	5,481	3,328
1998	141,027	106,686	545	107,230	12,010	-3,551	91,670	29,420	19,937	25,540	22,281	5,522	3,385
1999	146,511	113,122	241	113,363	12,637	-3,680	97,046	28,590	20,875	26,342	22,974	5,562	3,423
2000	156,676	120,047	788	120,835	13,301	-3,964	103,571	30,808	22,298	27,941	24,373	5,607	3,471
2001	161,842	123,503	836	124,340	13,689	-4,019	106,632	30,612	24,598	28,690	25,035	5,641	3,452
2002	165,526	127,628	401	128,029	14,020	-4,131	109,878	29,391	26,257	29,168	26,032	5,675	3,437
2003	171,767	131,172	1,038	132,210	14,448	-4,182	113,580	30,771	27,416	30,085	27,156	5,709	3,445
2004	181,112	137,267	2,270	139,536	14,984	-4,282	120,271	31,917	28,924	31,510	28,579	5,748	3,479
2005	187,996	142,569	1,429	143,997	15,738	-4,572	123,687	33,383	30,926	32,467	29,167	5,790	3,533
2006	199,348	149,820	1,254	151,074	16,725	-4,974	129,376	37,099	32,873	34,119	30,484	5,843	3,586
2007	209,021	154,567	1,401	155,968	17,499	-4,838	133,632	40,264	35,125	35,502	31,526	5,888	3,636
2008	221,034	160,269	2,045	162,314	18,254	-5,426	138,634	42,920	39,479	37,312	33,151	5,924	3,626
2009	216,894	157,486	1,637	159,124	17,721	-5,119	136,283	37,798	42,812	36,385	33,206	5,961	3,523
2010	222,564	160,003	1,481	161,484	17,701	-4,927	138,856	38,136	45,572	37,118	33,854	5,996	3,475
2011	231,646	163,161	2,185	165,346	16,304	-4,337	144,705	40,539	46,402	38,533	34,770	6,012	3,507
2012	242,981	169,903	1,401	171,304	16,747	-4,878	149,679	46,382	46,921	40,317	36,436	6,027	3,528
2013	245,200	175,077	2,900	177,977	19,443	-4,723	153,810	43,546	47,845	40,569	36,337	6,044	3,566
2014	254,318	178,792	3,144	181,935	20,009	-4,788	157,138	47,876	49,304	41,963	37,532	6,060	3,597
2015	263,271	186,044	810	186,854	21,081	-4,946	160,827	50,573	51,872	43,322	38,514	6,077	3,656
2016	270,604	189,876	1,064	190,940	21,468	-5,111	164,360	52,958	53,285	44,410	39,494	6,093	3,701
2017	276,574	196,408	1,057	197,464	22,209	-5,470	169,786	52,210	54,579	45,239	40,377	6,114	3,736
2018	288,565	203,471	528	203,999	23,160	-5,798	175,041	56,904	56,620	47,085	42,210	6,129	3,777
2019	301,031	210,961	1,015	211,975	24,150	-6,200	181,625	60,277	59,129	49,001	43,904	6,143	3,780
2020	320,698	215,592	1,667	217,259	25,013	-5,758	186,488	60,363	73,848	52,112	46,960	6,154	3,693
2021	341,254	227,760	2,121	229,881	25,729	-5,729	198,423	61,146	81,685	55,310	49,316	6,170	3,773
2022	349,370	245,804	3,154	248,957	27,871	-6,259	214,828	63,440	71,102	56,551	49,367	6,178	...

... = Not available.

Personal Income and Employment by Region and State: Montana

(Millions of dollars, except as noted.)

Year	Personal income, total	Earnings by place of work			Less: Contributions for government social insurance	Plus: Adjustment for residence	Equals: Net earnings by place of residence	Plus: Dividends, interest, and rent	Plus: Personal current transfer receipts	Per capita (dollars)		Population (thousands)	Total employment (thousands)
		Nonfarm	Farm	Total						Personal income	Disposable personal income		
1960	1,451	1,011	162	1,173	62	0	1,111	233	108	2,137	1,933	679	...
1961	1,455	1,059	110	1,169	63	L	1,106	231	117	2,090	1,878	696	...
1962	1,701	1,121	277	1,398	64	-0	1,334	248	119	2,437	2,223	698	...
1963	1,692	1,172	213	1,385	72	-0	1,313	258	121	2,406	2,181	703	...
1964	1,728	1,226	169	1,395	74	-0	1,321	281	126	2,447	2,245	706	...
1965	1,856	1,303	190	1,493	76	-0	1,417	305	134	2,629	2,398	706	...
1966	1,990	1,390	227	1,616	99	-0	1,517	330	143	2,814	2,556	707	...
1967	2,029	1,429	191	1,620	108	-0	1,511	349	169	2,895	2,620	701	...
1968	2,128	1,505	196	1,701	115	-1	1,585	352	191	3,040	2,750	700	...
1969	2,351	1,632	242	1,874	127	-1	1,747	394	210	3,387	2,980	694	298
1970	2,604	1,754	291	2,046	137	-1	1,908	455	241	3,735	3,339	697	301
1971	2,787	1,919	251	2,170	151	-1	2,018	489	280	3,920	3,549	711	307
1972	3,230	2,156	401	2,557	177	-0	2,380	541	310	4,492	4,022	719	319
1973	3,745	2,404	575	2,980	227	0	2,753	632	360	5,149	4,594	727	333
1974	4,070	2,705	466	3,171	262	1	2,909	738	423	5,521	4,909	737	344
1975	4,479	3,010	400	3,410	283	2	3,129	836	514	5,978	5,365	749	344
1976	4,807	3,419	225	3,644	324	3	3,323	913	570	6,337	5,639	759	359
1977	5,198	3,839	71	3,910	369	4	3,545	1,038	615	6,739	5,956	771	372
1978	6,091	4,361	303	4,664	433	3	4,235	1,182	675	7,768	6,908	784	390
1979	6,549	4,806	119	4,925	496	6	4,434	1,355	760	8,298	7,275	789	396
1980	7,211	5,108	120	5,228	542	13	4,699	1,617	895	9,142	8,037	789	393
1981	8,194	5,562	227	5,789	632	25	5,181	1,979	1,034	10,303	9,093	795	395
1982	8,636	5,714	172	5,886	664	17	5,239	2,239	1,158	10,741	9,586	804	391
1983	9,077	6,039	127	6,166	700	9	5,476	2,333	1,268	11,151	9,993	814	398
1984	9,603	6,392	44	6,436	758	6	5,684	2,566	1,353	11,698	10,519	821	408
1985	9,738	6,525	-84	6,441	790	3	5,655	2,653	1,431	11,843	10,650	822	406
1986	10,126	6,529	238	6,767	805	-2	5,960	2,638	1,528	12,443	11,302	814	402
1987	10,398	6,713	317	7,030	827	-3	6,200	2,598	1,601	12,916	11,635	805	406
1988	10,688	7,148	110	7,258	927	-1	6,331	2,664	1,693	13,356	11,972	800	416
1989	11,776	7,565	420	7,985	997	-3	6,985	2,935	1,856	14,726	13,121	800	424
1990	12,378	8,033	396	8,429	1,118	-4	7,306	3,040	2,033	15,469	13,806	800	433
1991	13,196	8,627	551	9,179	1,219	-11	7,948	3,109	2,140	16,298	14,625	810	444
1992	14,014	9,338	489	9,827	1,324	-2	8,501	3,192	2,321	16,971	15,208	826	456
1993	15,163	10,048	773	10,821	1,462	1	9,360	3,311	2,493	17,950	16,108	845	470
1994	15,585	10,634	390	11,024	1,547	5	9,482	3,515	2,589	18,095	16,162	861	494
1995	16,416	11,009	339	11,347	1,564	9	9,792	3,851	2,774	18,728	16,760	877	504
1996	17,203	11,496	310	11,806	1,563	11	10,255	4,069	2,880	19,411	17,326	886	519
1997	17,939	11,963	239	12,202	1,585	13	10,630	4,369	2,940	20,159	17,918	890	526
1998	19,152	12,772	299	13,071	1,643	18	11,446	4,654	3,052	21,461	19,048	892	536
1999	19,561	13,180	389	13,570	1,692	21	11,898	4,631	3,031	21,794	19,278	898	543
2000	20,860	13,996	261	14,256	1,793	26	12,490	4,981	3,390	23,081	20,376	904	553
2001	21,764	14,472	350	14,823	1,908	28	12,943	5,150	3,671	23,996	21,194	907	560
2002	22,385	15,313	198	15,510	2,019	26	13,517	5,059	3,808	24,554	22,090	912	565
2003	24,025	16,259	358	16,617	2,121	24	14,520	5,525	3,981	26,125	23,729	920	571
2004	26,162	17,548	555	18,103	2,257	23	15,869	6,049	4,243	28,131	25,623	930	586
2005	28,273	19,029	588	19,618	2,455	20	17,183	6,548	4,542	30,074	27,127	940	601
2006	30,670	20,729	162	20,891	2,655	15	18,251	7,503	4,917	32,193	28,874	953	617
2007	32,976	21,869	427	22,296	2,858	17	19,455	8,274	5,247	34,183	30,428	965	636
2008	34,948	22,476	522	22,998	2,930	27	20,095	8,887	5,965	35,792	32,034	976	636
2009	34,134	22,189	395	22,584	2,876	37	19,745	7,923	6,465	34,689	31,685	984	619
2010	36,060	23,195	565	23,760	2,943	74	20,891	8,111	7,059	36,393	33,340	991	616
2011	38,488	24,452	678	25,129	2,789	180	22,521	8,977	6,990	38,558	34,961	998	623
2012	40,920	25,717	750	26,467	2,871	358	23,954	9,779	7,187	40,701	36,776	1,005	633
2013	41,323	26,227	1,006	27,233	3,337	447	24,344	9,609	7,370	40,674	36,484	1,016	642
2014	43,556	27,300	759	28,058	3,486	548	25,120	10,681	7,754	42,494	37,948	1,025	649
2015	45,454	28,357	777	29,134	3,589	428	25,974	11,359	8,121	43,941	39,179	1,034	661
2016	46,074	28,672	579	29,251	3,556	269	25,965	11,354	8,755	44,063	39,342	1,046	668
2017	48,705	30,093	287	30,380	3,826	312	26,865	12,341	9,499	46,036	41,198	1,058	674
2018	50,780	31,133	508	31,641	4,045	381	27,977	12,945	9,857	47,612	42,769	1,067	684
2019	54,084	32,635	705	33,340	4,182	415	29,573	14,036	10,475	50,289	44,927	1,075	686
2020	58,770	34,328	902	35,230	4,480	295	31,044	14,278	13,447	54,062	48,576	1,087	684
2021	62,887	37,597	438	38,035	4,761	267	33,541	14,794	14,552	56,848	50,347	1,106	709
2022	64,811	41,398	198	41,596	5,240	289	36,644	15,527	12,640	57,719	49,936	1,123	...

... = Not available.

Personal Income and Employment by Region and State: Nebraska

(Millions of dollars, except as noted.)

| Year | Personal income, total | Earnings by place of work | | | Less: Contributions for government social insurance | Plus: Adjustment for residence | Equals: Net earnings by place of residence | Plus: Dividends, interest, and rent | Plus: Personal current transfer receipts | Per capita (dollars) | | Population (thousands) | Total employment (thousands) |
		Nonfarm	Farm	Total						Personal income	Disposable personal income		
1960	3,140	2,154	392	2,546	116	-11	2,419	536	185	2,216	2,005	1,417	...
1961	3,214	2,263	319	2,583	119	-11	2,452	557	205	2,223	1,996	1,446	...
1962	3,494	2,388	437	2,825	128	-10	2,687	591	216	2,386	2,165	1,464	...
1963	3,591	2,471	394	2,865	140	-10	2,716	646	229	2,433	2,201	1,476	...
1964	3,691	2,618	312	2,930	146	-9	2,775	680	236	2,491	2,282	1,482	...
1965	4,061	2,732	497	3,229	148	-8	3,074	730	258	2,761	2,537	1,471	...
1966	4,360	2,935	592	3,527	196	-8	3,323	757	280	2,995	2,729	1,456	...
1967	4,513	3,166	488	3,654	228	-8	3,418	754	341	3,097	2,809	1,457	...
1968	4,815	3,457	444	3,901	245	-8	3,648	774	394	3,282	2,952	1,467	...
1969	5,379	3,830	604	4,434	269	-103	4,062	888	429	3,649	3,220	1,474	704
1970	5,798	4,151	542	4,693	289	-110	4,294	1,007	498	3,897	3,468	1,488	715
1971	6,369	4,468	688	5,156	321	-113	4,722	1,084	562	4,234	3,833	1,504	728
1972	7,053	4,905	808	5,713	364	-122	5,227	1,206	620	4,645	4,131	1,518	748
1973	8,226	5,471	1,227	6,698	468	-125	6,105	1,379	741	5,382	4,798	1,529	775
1974	8,565	6,061	771	6,832	541	-133	6,158	1,561	847	5,570	4,906	1,538	793
1975	9,766	6,605	1,109	7,713	580	-142	6,992	1,739	1,036	6,336	5,693	1,541	790
1976	10,217	7,468	588	8,056	662	-149	7,246	1,867	1,105	6,597	5,901	1,549	811
1977	11,073	8,140	532	8,672	722	-148	7,801	2,095	1,177	7,123	6,291	1,554	831
1978	12,811	9,100	1,085	10,185	831	-171	9,184	2,323	1,305	8,208	7,287	1,561	854
1979	13,834	10,164	754	10,919	966	-199	9,753	2,628	1,453	8,843	7,750	1,564	876
1980	14,758	11,014	107	11,121	1,044	-216	9,861	3,200	1,697	9,386	8,239	1,572	877
1981	17,141	11,868	834	12,702	1,201	-254	11,247	3,938	1,956	10,859	9,615	1,579	871
1982	18,421	12,340	767	13,107	1,279	-262	11,566	4,700	2,154	11,646	10,162	1,582	861
1983	19,047	12,961	550	13,511	1,351	-276	11,884	4,832	2,331	12,022	10,760	1,584	867
1984	21,215	14,166	1,161	15,327	1,520	-316	13,491	5,279	2,444	13,354	12,089	1,589	886
1985	22,348	14,896	1,450	16,346	1,645	-342	14,359	5,393	2,596	14,103	12,759	1,585	898
1986	23,000	15,506	1,414	16,920	1,766	-344	14,810	5,475	2,715	14,609	13,216	1,574	898
1987	24,066	16,415	1,636	18,051	1,867	-343	15,841	5,448	2,777	15,362	13,848	1,567	925
1988	25,727	17,530	2,031	19,560	2,086	-379	17,095	5,736	2,896	16,371	14,753	1,571	947
1989	27,306	18,699	1,847	20,546	2,231	-392	17,924	6,262	3,119	17,338	15,529	1,575	965
1990	29,240	19,999	2,199	22,198	2,466	-391	19,341	6,516	3,383	18,487	16,527	1,582	988
1991	30,305	20,980	1,997	22,977	2,606	-427	19,945	6,720	3,640	18,989	17,022	1,596	992
1992	32,208	22,441	2,117	24,558	2,735	-471	21,352	6,905	3,952	19,984	17,956	1,612	999
1993	33,289	23,559	1,746	25,305	2,880	-487	21,938	7,131	4,220	20,478	18,375	1,626	1,021
1994	35,431	25,213	1,851	27,064	3,086	-502	23,476	7,554	4,401	21,617	19,372	1,639	1,061
1995	37,436	26,903	1,324	28,227	3,235	-548	24,444	8,304	4,688	22,593	20,137	1,657	1,071
1996	40,790	28,434	2,596	31,030	3,415	-599	27,016	8,787	4,988	24,371	21,703	1,674	1,097
1997	42,018	30,040	1,757	31,797	3,637	-677	27,484	9,363	5,171	24,915	21,968	1,686	1,111
1998	44,805	32,115	1,647	33,762	3,856	-714	29,192	10,102	5,511	26,421	23,254	1,696	1,138
1999	46,958	34,145	1,575	35,721	4,061	-800	30,860	10,272	5,826	27,545	24,242	1,705	1,157
2000	49,768	36,088	1,450	37,538	4,242	-868	32,428	11,229	6,110	29,039	25,500	1,714	1,174
2001	52,069	37,631	1,815	39,446	4,412	-875	34,159	11,190	6,720	30,275	26,748	1,720	1,175
2002	52,885	39,231	1,062	40,292	4,574	-902	34,816	10,923	7,146	30,599	27,557	1,728	1,166
2003	56,241	40,432	2,672	43,104	4,742	-938	37,424	11,364	7,454	32,348	29,477	1,739	1,169
2004	58,826	42,734	2,759	45,494	4,957	-944	39,593	11,424	7,810	33,627	30,658	1,749	1,180
2005	61,064	43,939	2,980	46,919	5,221	-941	40,757	12,039	8,268	34,666	31,349	1,761	1,192
2006	63,851	46,712	1,589	48,301	5,617	-856	41,828	13,089	8,933	36,019	32,290	1,773	1,208
2007	68,718	48,745	2,742	51,487	5,847	-947	44,693	14,604	9,421	38,531	34,387	1,783	1,231
2008	72,816	50,482	3,051	53,533	6,044	-980	46,510	15,724	10,582	40,535	36,339	1,796	1,237
2009	71,664	50,873	2,707	53,580	6,055	-957	46,567	14,044	11,053	39,535	36,236	1,813	1,223
2010	75,490	53,303	3,151	56,454	6,269	-898	49,287	14,334	11,868	41,248	37,682	1,830	1,220
2011	84,212	56,725	6,447	63,173	5,733	-963	56,477	15,643	12,093	45,674	41,559	1,844	1,232
2012	86,754	59,515	4,593	64,108	5,899	-999	57,211	17,360	12,184	46,670	42,237	1,859	1,251
2013	87,399	59,509	6,782	66,291	6,761	-969	58,561	16,504	12,334	46,653	41,922	1,873	1,266
2014	92,524	64,125	5,693	69,819	7,098	-937	61,784	17,830	12,909	48,957	43,912	1,890	1,283
2015	96,282	66,973	5,215	72,188	7,388	-1,020	63,781	18,940	13,561	50,556	45,386	1,904	1,303
2016	94,838	66,518	3,866	70,383	7,589	-1,067	61,727	19,051	14,060	49,360	44,206	1,921	1,311
2017	96,996	69,437	2,143	71,579	7,940	-1,167	62,473	19,781	14,743	50,144	45,031	1,934	1,318
2018	100,995	72,188	1,850	74,038	8,218	-1,122	64,698	20,694	15,603	51,916	46,873	1,945	1,330
2019	105,922	73,482	2,743	76,224	8,544	-1,137	66,543	22,885	16,495	54,182	48,778	1,955	1,329
2020	112,630	74,677	4,076	78,753	8,948	-1,170	68,634	23,130	20,865	57,387	51,904	1,963	1,306
2021	120,189	78,480	4,887	83,368	9,288	-1,284	72,796	23,689	23,704	61,210	54,860	1,964	1,330
2022	124,611	84,636	6,035	90,670	10,060	-1,388	79,222	24,792	20,597	63,321	55,766	1,968	...

... = Not available.

Personal Income and Employment by Region and State: Nevada

(Millions of dollars, except as noted.)

Year	Personal income, total	Earnings by place of work			Less: Contributions for government social insurance	Plus: Adjustment for residence	Equals: Net earnings by place of residence	Plus: Dividends, interest, and rent	Plus: Personal current transfer receipts	Per capita (dollars)		Population (thousands)	Total employment (thousands)
		Nonfarm	Farm	Total						Personal income	Disposable personal income		
1960	896	746	15	760	36	-2	722	134	41	3,079	2,730	291	...
1961	993	822	13	835	40	-3	792	152	49	3,153	2,771	315	...
1962	1,186	1,002	19	1,021	50	-4	966	168	51	3,369	2,975	352	...
1963	1,330	1,146	20	1,166	66	-6	1,094	178	58	3,350	2,941	397	...
1964	1,443	1,241	12	1,252	67	-6	1,180	198	65	3,388	3,040	426	...
1965	1,545	1,306	14	1,319	66	-5	1,249	225	72	3,480	3,130	444	...
1966	1,630	1,381	18	1,399	80	-4	1,316	237	78	3,656	3,279	446	...
1967	1,732	1,452	17	1,469	87	-3	1,379	258	95	3,857	3,451	449	...
1968	2,014	1,670	20	1,689	101	-4	1,585	316	113	4,340	3,802	464	...
1969	2,279	1,924	32	1,956	132	-33	1,791	363	125	4,747	4,068	480	244
1970	2,560	2,135	34	2,169	144	-39	1,986	427	148	5,191	4,615	493	256
1971	2,860	2,366	35	2,401	165	-41	2,195	481	184	5,501	4,945	520	267
1972	3,197	2,634	42	2,677	194	-44	2,439	540	218	5,847	5,225	547	280
1973	3,630	3,010	56	3,066	256	-54	2,756	621	254	6,381	5,703	569	304
1974	4,025	3,300	35	3,335	288	-56	2,992	718	315	6,746	6,006	597	317
1975	4,544	3,646	33	3,679	313	-58	3,308	798	438	7,331	6,692	620	326
1976	5,171	4,178	36	4,214	368	-68	3,778	902	490	7,994	7,184	647	349
1977	5,978	4,909	27	4,936	439	-84	4,413	1,030	535	8,815	7,873	678	384
1978	7,226	5,994	23	6,017	555	-116	5,346	1,276	604	10,045	8,883	719	432
1979	8,375	6,950	9	6,959	681	-132	6,147	1,516	713	10,945	9,597	765	468
1980	9,683	7,877	57	7,934	778	-160	6,996	1,822	866	11,951	10,547	810	489
1981	11,012	8,829	28	8,857	931	-167	7,759	2,197	1,055	12,991	11,428	848	500
1982	11,762	9,116	33	9,148	953	-168	8,027	2,560	1,175	13,343	11,839	882	494
1983	12,530	9,656	26	9,683	1,049	-177	8,457	2,788	1,285	13,892	12,425	902	499
1984	13,652	10,514	36	10,549	1,191	-190	9,168	3,107	1,376	14,760	13,219	925	523
1985	14,799	11,352	29	11,381	1,313	-200	9,868	3,420	1,512	15,561	13,853	951	545
1986	15,989	12,283	28	12,311	1,452	-217	10,642	3,661	1,685	16,305	14,478	981	570
1987	17,474	13,601	48	13,649	1,615	-240	11,794	3,881	1,798	17,075	15,087	1,023	616
1988	19,843	15,637	65	15,701	1,873	-281	13,547	4,321	1,975	18,458	16,250	1,075	662
1989	22,353	17,406	79	17,485	2,119	-326	15,040	5,032	2,280	19,653	17,297	1,137	710
1990	25,043	19,593	82	19,675	2,497	-377	16,802	5,633	2,609	20,516	18,027	1,221	756
1991	27,515	21,109	76	21,185	2,660	-346	18,179	6,116	3,221	21,228	18,841	1,296	769
1992	30,479	23,280	73	23,353	2,890	-305	20,158	6,677	3,645	22,554	19,987	1,351	776
1993	32,966	25,264	119	25,383	3,163	-344	21,876	7,241	3,849	23,360	20,627	1,411	819
1994	36,486	27,991	82	28,073	3,534	-354	24,186	8,263	4,037	24,335	21,570	1,499	898
1995	40,138	30,668	70	30,738	3,879	-349	26,510	9,249	4,379	25,379	22,487	1,582	953
1996	44,435	33,947	70	34,017	4,196	-368	29,453	10,267	4,714	26,667	23,367	1,666	1,024
1997	48,573	37,158	70	37,228	4,477	-328	32,423	11,124	5,025	27,534	24,183	1,764	1,089
1998	54,324	41,713	93	41,806	4,785	-350	36,671	12,302	5,352	29,314	25,613	1,853	1,131
1999	58,825	45,777	85	45,862	5,086	-382	40,395	12,848	5,583	30,405	26,557	1,935	1,189
2000	64,572	49,569	104	49,673	4,986	-338	44,348	14,222	6,001	31,986	27,871	2,019	1,254
2001	68,117	52,424	118	52,542	5,292	-354	46,896	14,431	6,789	32,461	28,484	2,098	1,285
2002	69,843	53,742	90	53,832	5,482	-364	47,987	14,205	7,651	32,130	28,707	2,174	1,300
2003	74,483	56,548	93	56,641	5,568	-410	50,664	15,601	8,219	33,121	29,837	2,249	1,353
2004	82,663	62,741	127	62,868	6,093	-494	56,281	17,506	8,876	35,232	31,545	2,346	1,441
2005	92,687	69,646	135	69,781	6,696	-549	62,536	20,574	9,577	38,109	33,742	2,432	1,534
2006	100,318	75,438	129	75,566	7,751	-474	67,341	22,628	10,349	39,767	35,271	2,523	1,604
2007	104,596	77,497	98	77,595	8,179	-400	69,015	24,266	11,314	40,212	35,704	2,601	1,644
2008	103,056	73,626	150	73,776	7,699	-321	65,757	23,938	13,362	38,836	34,880	2,654	1,619
2009	97,267	68,983	126	69,109	7,419	-308	61,383	20,619	15,265	36,231	33,198	2,685	1,513
2010	101,307	71,373	145	71,518	7,311	-252	63,955	20,526	16,827	37,494	34,399	2,702	1,478
2011	105,105	72,853	206	73,059	6,915	-145	65,998	22,056	17,051	38,777	35,366	2,711	1,502
2012	109,347	74,011	114	74,126	7,274	-157	66,695	25,458	17,195	39,909	36,286	2,740	1,519
2013	109,871	75,970	118	76,088	8,006	-136	67,946	24,349	17,575	39,664	35,556	2,770	1,561
2014	117,372	79,438	213	79,651	8,812	-177	70,663	27,447	19,263	41,773	37,647	2,810	1,608
2015	127,117	84,579	147	84,726	9,393	-128	75,206	30,876	21,035	44,493	39,934	2,857	1,665
2016	132,058	87,588	84	87,672	9,842	-204	77,626	32,215	22,217	45,450	40,427	2,906	1,725
2017	140,348	93,192	118	93,309	10,188	-195	82,927	34,100	23,321	47,485	42,530	2,956	1,781
2018	149,612	99,525	112	99,637	10,876	-207	88,554	36,278	24,780	49,678	44,528	3,012	1,849
2019	161,434	106,693	176	106,869	11,961	-282	94,626	40,267	26,540	52,602	47,408	3,069	1,884
2020	172,539	104,126	177	104,303	11,627	71	92,747	40,612	39,180	55,378	50,210	3,116	1,771
2021	189,308	116,971	183	117,154	12,752	-103	104,299	42,435	42,574	60,167	53,673	3,146	1,876
2022	194,741	129,946	209	130,155	14,368	-241	115,546	45,306	33,889	61,282	53,076	3,178	...

... = Not available.

Personal Income and Employment by Region and State: New Hampshire

(Millions of dollars, except as noted.)

Year	Personal income, total	Earnings by place of work Nonfarm	Farm	Total	Less: Contributions for government social insurance	Plus: Adjustment for residence	Equals: Net earnings by place of residence	Plus: Dividends, interest, and rent	Plus: Personal current transfer receipts	Per capita (dollars) Personal income	Disposable personal income	Population (thousands)	Total employment (thousands)
1960	1,383	1,037	20	1,056	55	82	1,083	210	90	2,271	2,036	609	...
1961	1,456	1,081	21	1,101	56	89	1,134	221	102	2,356	2,119	618	...
1962	1,557	1,153	19	1,172	62	98	1,208	244	105	2,464	2,210	632	...
1963	1,625	1,197	18	1,215	68	103	1,250	262	113	2,503	2,235	649	...
1964	1,747	1,283	18	1,301	71	112	1,342	290	116	2,635	2,401	663	...
1965	1,884	1,377	21	1,399	75	122	1,446	315	123	2,787	2,527	676	...
1966	2,064	1,528	24	1,552	103	142	1,591	341	132	3,031	2,716	681	...
1967	2,255	1,677	17	1,695	116	157	1,735	365	155	3,235	2,897	697	...
1968	2,491	1,846	20	1,866	128	175	1,913	399	180	3,513	3,124	709	...
1969	2,781	2,003	21	2,024	129	234	2,129	450	203	3,842	3,401	724	334
1970	2,966	2,125	17	2,141	136	220	2,226	499	241	3,997	3,520	742	334
1971	3,220	2,283	15	2,297	151	229	2,376	552	292	4,225	3,789	762	336
1972	3,562	2,536	16	2,552	177	252	2,628	611	322	4,557	4,025	782	350
1973	4,013	2,882	21	2,903	230	280	2,954	679	380	5,005	4,475	802	374
1974	4,417	3,114	14	3,128	258	323	3,193	769	456	5,406	4,812	817	381
1975	4,802	3,278	17	3,295	267	356	3,384	833	586	5,786	5,227	830	370
1976	5,436	3,779	19	3,798	310	400	3,888	922	626	6,418	5,748	847	394
1977	6,146	4,295	18	4,313	354	473	4,431	1,054	661	7,050	6,284	872	418
1978	7,091	5,008	19	5,027	421	564	5,170	1,196	725	7,932	7,008	894	446
1979	8,112	5,725	22	5,746	504	678	5,921	1,363	829	8,896	7,848	912	468
1980	9,278	6,347	14	6,361	559	840	6,642	1,664	972	10,039	8,884	924	482
1981	10,517	7,018	23	7,041	667	950	7,324	2,055	1,138	11,229	9,909	937	492
1982	11,580	7,573	19	7,592	740	1,036	7,889	2,443	1,248	12,219	10,904	948	498
1983	12,713	8,496	17	8,514	841	1,153	8,826	2,555	1,333	13,269	11,834	958	518
1984	14,376	9,593	22	9,614	977	1,362	9,999	2,967	1,410	14,717	13,166	977	553
1985	15,842	10,764	24	10,788	1,126	1,496	11,159	3,208	1,476	15,894	14,096	997	586
1986	17,509	12,099	25	12,124	1,276	1,571	12,419	3,541	1,548	17,081	15,055	1,025	617
1987	19,362	13,663	43	13,706	1,420	1,683	13,968	3,813	1,581	18,365	16,169	1,054	635
1988	21,322	15,081	45	15,126	1,606	1,823	15,343	4,266	1,713	19,696	17,464	1,083	660
1989	22,847	15,717	35	15,752	1,677	1,941	16,016	4,912	1,919	20,685	18,361	1,105	660
1990	23,007	15,582	44	15,626	1,710	1,972	15,889	4,968	2,150	20,682	18,456	1,112	643
1991	23,792	15,565	45	15,610	1,730	2,118	15,998	4,913	2,882	21,436	19,271	1,110	616
1992	24,968	16,677	51	16,728	1,839	2,177	17,067	4,832	3,070	22,337	20,105	1,118	629
1993	25,787	17,425	42	17,467	1,919	2,303	17,851	4,963	2,973	22,831	20,463	1,129	642
1994	27,522	18,583	40	18,623	2,074	2,399	18,947	5,199	3,376	24,088	21,614	1,143	666
1995	29,203	19,714	35	19,749	2,224	2,391	19,916	5,645	3,641	25,228	22,560	1,158	679
1996	30,942	21,039	41	21,079	2,347	2,566	21,298	6,044	3,599	26,339	23,331	1,175	696
1997	33,274	22,802	38	22,840	2,521	2,803	23,121	6,412	3,741	27,975	24,472	1,189	717
1998	36,563	25,535	40	25,575	2,734	2,904	25,745	6,938	3,880	30,319	26,559	1,206	743
1999	38,924	27,627	44	27,672	2,904	3,376	28,143	6,823	3,958	31,852	27,738	1,222	761
2000	43,811	31,066	44	31,111	3,190	4,021	31,941	7,609	4,261	35,335	30,508	1,240	784
2001	46,137	33,033	42	33,075	3,324	4,064	33,815	7,669	4,654	36,747	32,230	1,256	788
2002	46,923	33,922	43	33,965	3,385	3,935	34,515	7,341	5,067	36,974	33,274	1,269	788
2003	47,829	34,887	49	34,936	3,550	3,949	35,335	7,299	5,196	37,371	33,966	1,280	798
2004	50,874	36,828	58	36,886	3,809	4,229	37,306	7,886	5,682	39,434	35,978	1,290	813
2005	52,744	38,492	49	38,541	3,977	4,220	38,784	8,033	5,927	40,619	36,743	1,298	826
2006	56,460	40,909	41	40,950	4,150	4,375	41,175	8,957	6,329	43,153	38,863	1,308	836
2007	58,663	41,470	43	41,513	4,321	4,747	41,939	9,855	6,869	44,695	39,995	1,313	848
2008	60,381	41,580	60	41,639	4,460	4,878	42,058	10,371	7,953	45,886	41,200	1,316	845
2009	59,358	41,571	37	41,608	4,432	4,162	41,338	9,445	8,575	45,101	41,575	1,316	821
2010	62,032	43,425	53	43,478	4,558	4,768	43,688	9,208	9,136	47,098	43,254	1,317	814
2011	64,945	44,428	48	44,477	4,225	5,086	45,338	10,534	9,074	49,131	44,612	1,322	819
2012	67,855	45,470	85	45,554	4,330	5,493	46,718	11,922	9,216	51,123	46,653	1,327	824
2013	67,704	46,030	91	46,121	4,954	5,202	46,370	11,937	9,398	50,865	45,940	1,331	835
2014	70,501	47,760	64	47,825	5,128	4,943	47,639	12,851	10,012	52,643	47,363	1,339	844
2015	73,475	49,151	66	49,217	5,334	5,474	49,357	13,333	10,784	54,684	48,910	1,344	861
2016	76,092	50,867	46	50,914	5,520	5,854	51,248	13,430	11,415	56,321	50,208	1,351	873
2017	79,313	53,057	50	53,108	5,827	6,085	53,366	14,115	11,832	58,362	52,255	1,359	882
2018	83,026	55,625	37	55,662	6,074	6,411	55,999	14,502	12,525	60,831	54,821	1,365	893
2019	88,823	58,452	41	58,493	6,321	7,304	59,476	16,295	13,052	64,747	58,226	1,372	890
2020	94,441	60,787	26	60,813	6,548	6,820	61,085	16,179	17,178	68,505	61,901	1,379	859
2021	101,675	68,383	-7	68,376	7,070	5,748	67,054	16,547	18,073	73,279	64,912	1,388	889
2022	104,173	72,142	11	72,153	7,407	6,318	71,065	17,320	15,788	74,663	64,826	1,395	...

... = Not available.

Personal Income and Employment by Region and State: New Jersey

(Millions of dollars, except as noted.)

Year	Personal income, total	Derivation of personal income								Per capita (dollars)		Population (thousands)	Total employment (thousands)
		Earnings by place of work			Less: Contributions for government social insurance	Plus: Adjustment for residence	Equals: Net earnings by place of residence	Plus: Dividends, interest, and rent	Plus: Personal current transfer receipts	Personal income	Disposable personal income		
		Nonfarm	Farm	Total									
1960	16,553	13,148	121	13,269	660	863	13,472	2,185	896	2,712	2,400	6,103	...
1961	17,396	13,698	120	13,818	695	920	14,044	2,328	1,024	2,777	2,457	6,265	...
1962	18,719	14,646	110	14,755	771	1,021	15,006	2,634	1,079	2,936	2,594	6,376	...
1963	19,647	15,280	108	15,388	869	1,097	15,615	2,873	1,159	3,008	2,655	6,531	...
1964	21,064	16,215	103	16,319	881	1,213	16,651	3,208	1,205	3,163	2,843	6,660	...
1965	22,629	17,351	119	17,471	935	1,324	17,860	3,484	1,286	3,344	2,983	6,767	...
1966	24,503	18,937	120	19,056	1,212	1,522	19,366	3,752	1,385	3,577	3,188	6,851	...
1967	26,394	20,281	105	20,386	1,346	1,687	20,726	4,025	1,642	3,810	3,372	6,928	...
1968	28,967	22,134	102	22,236	1,535	1,894	22,595	4,408	1,964	4,135	3,627	7,005	...
1969	32,504	24,069	105	24,174	1,829	3,165	25,510	4,782	2,213	4,581	3,982	7,095	3,061
1970	35,295	26,002	100	26,102	1,958	3,117	27,261	5,344	2,689	4,909	4,313	7,190	3,125
1971	38,078	27,808	93	27,902	2,170	3,213	28,944	5,857	3,277	5,229	4,658	7,282	3,119
1972	41,395	30,359	89	30,448	2,484	3,418	31,381	6,351	3,663	5,642	4,959	7,337	3,184
1973	45,063	33,412	127	33,538	3,131	3,513	33,921	7,011	4,131	6,143	5,442	7,335	3,288
1974	48,945	35,871	138	36,009	3,461	3,683	36,231	7,867	4,848	6,673	5,886	7,335	3,301
1975	52,878	37,649	97	37,746	3,544	3,887	38,090	8,451	6,338	7,203	6,445	7,341	3,191
1976	57,409	41,278	102	41,380	3,933	4,061	41,509	9,047	6,853	7,817	6,921	7,344	3,248
1977	62,802	45,429	112	45,541	4,316	4,420	45,645	9,929	7,229	8,554	7,490	7,342	3,325
1978	69,699	50,935	127	51,062	4,987	4,992	51,067	10,944	7,689	9,475	8,274	7,356	3,465
1979	77,363	56,448	127	56,575	5,748	5,707	56,534	12,279	8,550	10,493	9,068	7,373	3,552
1980	87,047	61,774	116	61,890	6,317	6,658	62,230	15,035	9,782	11,801	10,176	7,376	3,601
1981	97,265	67,613	150	67,763	7,368	7,275	67,669	18,615	10,980	13,131	11,292	7,407	3,631
1982	105,090	72,175	166	72,341	7,997	7,760	72,104	20,951	12,035	14,142	12,173	7,431	3,639
1983	113,439	78,787	192	78,979	8,983	8,101	78,097	22,350	12,992	15,190	13,221	7,468	3,739
1984	125,567	87,803	200	88,003	10,427	8,526	86,102	25,918	13,548	16,708	14,609	7,515	3,914
1985	134,574	95,257	227	95,484	11,395	8,952	93,040	27,334	14,199	17,788	15,407	7,566	4,026
1986	144,070	103,092	229	103,321	12,408	9,537	100,450	28,753	14,868	18,902	16,349	7,622	4,122
1987	155,341	113,024	258	113,281	13,525	10,071	109,828	30,154	15,360	20,251	17,353	7,671	4,220
1988	170,598	125,277	253	125,530	15,224	10,488	120,795	33,448	16,355	22,120	19,170	7,712	4,317
1989	183,043	132,044	246	132,290	15,871	10,338	126,757	38,759	17,527	23,692	20,554	7,726	4,351
1990	192,164	137,883	243	138,126	16,024	10,354	132,456	40,376	19,331	24,754	21,556	7,763	4,310
1991	195,933	139,450	228	139,678	16,533	10,312	133,457	40,228	22,249	25,072	21,919	7,815	4,172
1992	210,510	149,174	237	149,411	17,491	12,066	143,986	40,760	25,764	26,713	23,410	7,881	4,170
1993	217,596	155,154	265	155,419	18,116	12,251	149,554	41,120	26,922	27,374	23,904	7,949	4,197
1994	225,285	161,704	282	161,986	19,138	12,234	155,082	42,899	27,303	28,110	24,445	8,014	4,232
1995	239,165	169,469	277	169,746	19,894	13,366	163,218	46,776	29,170	29,588	25,794	8,083	4,296
1996	253,062	178,047	297	178,344	20,745	15,322	172,921	50,039	30,102	31,052	26,870	8,150	4,352
1997	269,606	188,565	247	188,812	21,524	18,082	185,369	53,372	30,865	32,804	28,153	8,219	4,412
1998	287,265	201,534	264	201,798	22,686	19,596	198,709	56,841	31,715	34,663	29,448	8,287	4,501
1999	300,654	213,127	230	213,357	23,766	21,496	211,088	56,527	33,039	35,965	30,341	8,360	4,571
2000	330,614	233,831	322	234,154	25,555	24,547	233,146	62,206	35,262	39,216	32,872	8,431	4,749
2001	341,788	241,842	269	242,111	26,593	25,181	240,700	61,890	39,198	40,245	33,864	8,493	4,777
2002	346,164	249,498	289	249,787	27,299	22,806	245,294	58,467	42,402	40,474	35,131	8,553	4,792
2003	354,362	256,930	307	257,237	27,736	23,053	252,554	58,930	42,878	41,198	36,177	8,601	4,825
2004	370,215	267,971	330	268,301	29,106	26,123	265,317	61,443	43,455	42,876	37,718	8,635	4,910
2005	384,731	276,971	337	277,309	30,543	28,566	275,331	63,640	45,760	44,467	38,576	8,652	4,991
2006	413,115	289,727	383	290,110	31,792	33,853	292,172	71,256	49,687	47,695	41,233	8,662	5,057
2007	438,001	300,007	397	300,404	33,660	40,276	307,020	78,927	52,055	50,473	43,114	8,678	5,130
2008	451,052	305,139	351	305,490	34,557	39,545	310,478	81,846	58,728	51,779	44,338	8,711	5,124
2009	436,504	300,446	358	300,804	33,747	31,111	298,168	73,072	65,264	49,854	44,237	8,756	4,992
2010	449,927	306,593	337	306,930	34,243	35,034	307,721	71,488	70,718	51,076	45,207	8,809	4,961
2011	470,008	312,683	358	313,042	31,436	39,097	320,702	77,852	71,454	52,947	46,200	8,877	5,019
2012	487,528	324,625	433	325,058	32,108	39,742	332,692	84,513	70,323	54,574	47,906	8,933	5,054
2013	492,488	334,895	406	335,301	37,384	40,740	338,657	82,853	70,978	54,813	47,345	8,985	5,133
2014	515,515	346,661	335	346,995	38,484	43,679	352,191	89,399	73,925	57,065	49,332	9,034	5,207
2015	537,106	359,156	407	359,564	39,788	45,674	365,450	95,171	76,484	59,175	50,846	9,077	5,303
2016	552,051	366,849	371	367,220	40,434	47,417	374,203	98,653	79,196	60,533	52,090	9,120	5,391
2017	573,106	380,320	370	380,690	42,190	50,580	389,081	103,180	80,845	62,465	53,894	9,175	5,449
2018	598,429	396,337	305	396,642	43,437	55,140	408,344	105,958	84,127	64,914	56,325	9,219	5,550
2019	633,651	411,477	478	411,956	45,015	61,754	428,695	116,751	88,205	68,438	59,386	9,259	5,571
2020	663,544	411,278	413	411,691	45,125	60,149	426,715	116,129	120,701	71,567	62,500	9,272	5,320
2021	713,721	440,069	400	440,469	48,463	70,886	462,892	119,366	131,463	77,009	66,426	9,268	5,537
2022	728,900	475,341	513	475,854	53,058	75,812	498,608	124,880	105,412	78,700	65,844	9,262	...

... = Not available.

Personal Income and Employment by Region and State: New Mexico

(Millions of dollars, except as noted.)

Year	Personal income, total	Earnings by place of work			Less: Contributions for government social insurance	Plus: Adjustment for residence	Equals: Net earnings by place of residence	Plus: Dividends, interest, and rent	Plus: Personal current transfer receipts	Per capita (dollars)		Population (thousands)	Total employment (thousands)
		Nonfarm	Farm	Total						Personal income	Disposable personal income		
1960	1,912	1,535	86	1,622	61	-16	1,545	264	102	2,004	1,829	954	...
1961	2,000	1,573	102	1,675	61	-16	1,598	284	118	2,073	1,892	965	...
1962	2,079	1,662	83	1,745	66	-17	1,662	297	120	2,124	1,932	979	...
1963	2,150	1,714	87	1,801	74	-18	1,708	313	129	2,174	1,979	989	...
1964	2,273	1,828	66	1,894	78	-19	1,797	342	135	2,260	2,083	1,006	...
1965	2,412	1,924	78	2,002	81	-21	1,901	366	145	2,383	2,180	1,012	...
1966	2,535	2,014	100	2,114	104	-21	1,990	388	156	2,517	2,302	1,007	...
1967	2,620	2,084	90	2,174	121	-21	2,032	393	195	2,620	2,395	1,000	...
1968	2,837	2,228	102	2,330	125	-23	2,183	426	228	2,854	2,597	994	...
1969	3,144	2,456	107	2,563	152	-21	2,391	493	261	3,109	2,787	1,011	395
1970	3,500	2,653	131	2,784	163	-23	2,598	576	325	3,420	3,081	1,023	399
1971	3,872	2,926	130	3,055	188	-24	2,844	651	378	3,677	3,363	1,053	416
1972	4,353	3,302	137	3,439	220	-22	3,197	734	422	4,039	3,668	1,078	440
1973	4,882	3,673	180	3,853	282	-19	3,552	830	500	4,421	4,016	1,104	461
1974	5,487	4,119	147	4,266	328	-17	3,921	965	601	4,858	4,391	1,130	478
1975	6,268	4,626	177	4,803	366	-14	4,423	1,107	738	5,391	4,955	1,163	491
1976	6,987	5,255	124	5,379	420	-14	4,944	1,215	828	5,846	5,323	1,195	512
1977	7,820	5,942	135	6,076	481	-12	5,583	1,364	872	6,382	5,802	1,225	539
1978	8,948	6,813	168	6,980	565	-12	6,403	1,589	956	7,148	6,435	1,252	568
1979	10,088	7,655	207	7,862	667	-11	7,184	1,801	1,103	7,878	7,078	1,281	592
1980	11,323	8,418	180	8,598	736	-6	7,856	2,153	1,315	8,647	7,779	1,309	597
1981	12,800	9,461	129	9,590	888	-16	8,686	2,612	1,502	9,604	8,540	1,333	611
1982	14,023	10,094	116	10,210	966	-19	9,225	3,146	1,651	10,282	9,125	1,364	619
1983	15,086	10,729	127	10,856	1,035	-14	9,808	3,475	1,804	10,819	9,825	1,394	631
1984	16,471	11,720	147	11,867	1,164	-6	10,697	3,847	1,927	11,626	10,594	1,417	655
1985	17,824	12,558	208	12,766	1,271	1	11,496	4,263	2,064	12,392	11,266	1,438	674
1986	18,525	12,962	194	13,156	1,327	8	11,837	4,466	2,223	12,665	11,572	1,463	680
1987	19,309	13,505	241	13,746	1,371	22	12,398	4,561	2,350	13,059	11,805	1,479	699
1988	20,402	14,296	319	14,616	1,530	33	13,119	4,763	2,520	13,689	12,383	1,490	733
1989	21,855	15,180	383	15,563	1,648	42	13,956	5,104	2,796	14,532	13,082	1,504	749
1990	23,301	16,339	417	16,756	1,872	49	14,934	5,320	3,048	15,314	13,793	1,522	761
1991	24,937	17,558	403	17,961	2,032	61	15,990	5,530	3,417	16,034	14,484	1,555	784
1992	26,803	18,875	484	19,359	2,166	77	17,271	5,733	3,799	16,800	15,202	1,595	797
1993	28,827	20,373	530	20,903	2,341	96	18,658	6,051	4,118	17,616	15,899	1,636	825
1994	30,772	21,761	457	22,218	2,547	111	19,782	6,560	4,430	18,291	16,479	1,682	857
1995	33,071	23,209	391	23,600	2,718	122	21,004	7,188	4,878	19,223	17,341	1,720	898
1996	34,741	23,984	402	24,386	2,808	142	21,720	7,699	5,323	19,826	17,805	1,752	909
1997	36,520	25,169	543	25,713	2,931	163	22,945	8,138	5,437	20,576	18,381	1,775	923
1998	38,344	26,412	585	26,996	3,083	187	24,099	8,526	5,719	21,380	19,083	1,793	938
1999	39,031	27,183	679	27,862	3,203	215	24,874	8,107	6,051	21,587	19,207	1,808	942
2000	42,074	29,687	542	30,229	3,386	240	27,083	8,568	6,423	23,102	20,618	1,821	965
2001	45,062	31,502	789	32,291	3,624	212	28,878	9,015	7,169	24,601	21,888	1,832	977
2002	46,856	33,268	548	33,817	3,806	194	30,205	8,778	7,873	25,255	22,911	1,855	984
2003	48,999	34,975	570	35,545	3,994	182	31,734	8,835	8,430	26,097	23,872	1,878	1,003
2004	52,163	37,042	876	37,918	4,205	136	33,849	9,322	8,992	27,399	25,124	1,904	1,027
2005	55,762	39,326	878	40,204	4,469	70	35,805	10,253	9,704	28,858	26,232	1,932	1,050
2006	60,036	42,281	607	42,888	4,874	82	38,097	11,354	10,585	30,597	27,614	1,962	1,079
2007	63,583	43,892	872	44,764	5,136	73	39,702	12,361	11,521	31,950	28,749	1,990	1,103
2008	67,657	45,812	732	46,545	5,414	58	41,189	13,223	13,245	33,649	30,528	2,011	1,105
2009	67,034	45,121	413	45,534	5,359	69	40,243	12,124	14,667	32,911	30,306	2,037	1,072
2010	69,607	46,229	889	47,118	5,452	8	41,674	12,054	15,879	33,710	31,185	2,065	1,060
2011	72,968	47,679	1,133	48,812	5,032	-21	43,759	13,146	16,063	35,045	32,152	2,082	1,064
2012	74,725	48,413	1,024	49,437	5,142	-16	44,279	14,429	16,018	35,749	32,861	2,090	1,067
2013	73,562	48,446	997	49,444	5,919	-41	43,484	13,899	16,179	35,088	31,928	2,097	1,075
2014	77,975	49,917	1,258	51,175	6,120	-48	45,007	15,244	17,724	37,219	33,898	2,095	1,084
2015	79,864	51,037	882	51,920	6,446	-41	45,433	15,283	19,148	38,103	34,657	2,096	1,092
2016	81,414	51,568	930	52,499	6,456	1	46,044	15,768	19,603	38,775	35,311	2,100	1,093
2017	82,904	52,746	932	53,678	6,563	35	47,150	16,132	19,622	39,458	36,002	2,101	1,095
2018	86,686	55,357	781	56,138	6,864	-28	49,246	16,676	20,764	41,218	37,766	2,103	1,111
2019	91,854	58,342	850	59,192	7,160	40	52,073	18,083	21,698	43,530	39,726	2,110	1,117
2020	99,018	58,527	891	59,419	7,325	119	52,212	17,966	28,840	46,742	43,038	2,118	1,070
2021	106,451	61,982	722	62,704	7,707	157	55,155	18,561	32,735	50,292	46,034	2,117	1,087
2022	108,836	67,736	972	68,708	8,471	199	60,436	19,391	29,010	51,500	46,270	2,113	...

... = Not available.

Personal Income and Employment by Region and State: New York

(Millions of dollars, except as noted.)

Year	Personal income, total	Earnings by place of work			Less: Contributions for government social insurance	Plus: Adjustment for residence	Equals: Net earnings by place of residence	Plus: Dividends, interest, and rent	Plus: Personal current transfer receipts	Per capita (dollars)		Population (thousands)	Total employment (thousands)
		Nonfarm	Farm	Total						Personal income	Disposable personal income		
1960	47,939	40,466	353	40,819	2,041	-729	38,050	7,096	2,794	2,847	2,478	16,838	...
1961	50,098	41,996	364	42,360	2,191	-781	39,387	7,504	3,207	2,936	2,543	17,061	...
1962	52,853	44,321	287	44,607	2,490	-866	41,251	8,307	3,295	3,055	2,649	17,301	...
1963	55,174	45,815	336	46,152	2,712	-930	42,509	9,116	3,549	3,160	2,742	17,461	...
1964	58,939	48,567	318	48,885	2,681	-1,026	45,177	10,039	3,723	3,351	2,948	17,589	...
1965	62,625	51,252	366	51,618	2,803	-1,110	47,705	10,904	4,016	3,531	3,097	17,734	...
1966	67,240	55,598	427	56,025	3,720	-1,263	51,042	11,563	4,636	3,768	3,284	17,843	...
1967	72,538	59,464	380	59,844	4,032	-1,404	54,407	12,231	5,900	4,044	3,496	17,935	...
1968	80,062	65,209	388	65,597	4,446	-1,584	59,568	13,281	7,213	4,435	3,807	18,051	...
1969	83,626	70,364	440	70,804	5,291	-3,437	62,076	13,815	7,735	4,619	3,896	18,105	8,494
1970	89,895	74,760	420	75,179	5,534	-3,395	66,251	14,736	8,909	4,920	4,228	18,272	8,466
1971	96,121	79,088	410	79,497	6,030	-3,518	69,949	15,428	10,744	5,234	4,564	18,365	8,345
1972	102,834	84,861	353	85,214	6,796	-3,786	74,633	16,208	11,994	5,603	4,833	18,352	8,348
1973	109,572	90,472	470	90,943	8,413	-3,919	78,611	17,672	13,289	6,022	5,217	18,195	8,465
1974	118,065	95,731	444	96,175	9,188	-4,120	82,867	19,780	15,418	6,533	5,640	18,073	8,392
1975	127,414	100,445	379	100,824	9,452	-4,406	86,966	20,942	19,506	7,066	6,194	18,032	8,172
1976	134,981	106,699	401	107,100	10,248	-4,663	92,189	21,992	20,800	7,510	6,550	17,975	8,125
1977	145,640	115,644	331	115,975	11,010	-5,198	99,767	24,115	21,759	8,158	7,088	17,852	8,199
1978	158,584	127,304	433	127,737	12,375	-5,879	109,483	26,314	22,786	8,949	7,741	17,720	8,384
1979	173,362	139,951	539	140,490	14,082	-6,758	119,649	29,376	24,337	9,831	8,442	17,634	8,581
1980	193,259	153,334	530	153,864	15,430	-7,854	130,580	34,688	27,991	11,001	9,409	17,567	8,602
1981	215,681	168,282	543	168,825	18,083	-8,521	142,221	41,872	31,588	12,277	10,400	17,568	8,666
1982	234,418	180,684	518	181,203	19,681	-9,315	152,207	47,656	34,555	13,327	11,268	17,590	8,673
1983	252,683	195,069	371	195,440	21,224	-9,879	164,337	50,969	37,377	14,286	12,290	17,687	8,730
1984	279,484	215,022	494	215,517	23,937	-10,582	180,997	58,927	39,559	15,749	13,587	17,746	9,003
1985	299,164	232,681	561	233,242	26,272	-11,352	195,618	61,790	41,755	16,815	14,409	17,792	9,227
1986	319,479	251,553	654	252,207	28,844	-11,969	211,394	63,839	44,246	17,915	15,338	17,833	9,424
1987	340,643	272,882	732	273,613	30,680	-12,771	230,163	65,093	45,387	19,064	16,160	17,869	9,472
1988	373,665	300,763	645	301,408	34,031	-13,698	253,679	71,692	48,295	20,827	17,865	17,941	9,684
1989	403,910	317,544	777	318,320	35,481	-13,758	269,082	81,805	53,023	22,461	19,156	17,983	9,752
1990	432,318	337,820	775	338,594	35,787	-13,471	289,337	84,816	58,165	23,990	20,644	18,021	9,727
1991	432,543	332,725	647	333,372	36,733	-13,448	283,190	84,609	64,744	23,868	20,645	18,123	9,483
1992	457,271	355,360	749	356,109	38,353	-16,580	301,176	83,732	72,364	25,061	21,711	18,247	9,410
1993	470,054	363,633	793	364,427	39,223	-16,351	308,852	84,348	76,854	25,581	22,080	18,375	9,431
1994	484,731	372,726	672	373,398	40,889	-16,345	316,164	87,966	80,601	26,259	22,662	18,459	9,465
1995	510,818	390,103	538	390,641	42,381	-18,578	329,683	95,361	85,775	27,576	23,746	18,524	9,511
1996	537,882	412,086	767	412,853	43,658	-21,430	347,765	100,682	89,435	28,936	24,705	18,588	9,595
1997	567,956	440,716	456	441,172	45,606	-23,990	371,576	107,042	89,338	30,443	25,810	18,657	9,732
1998	600,947	469,005	688	469,693	47,880	-27,293	394,521	113,099	93,328	32,040	26,922	18,756	9,901
1999	637,109	504,751	769	505,520	50,242	-28,503	426,775	114,167	96,167	33,740	28,199	18,883	10,165
2000	685,783	547,861	778	548,639	54,137	-32,299	462,203	122,934	100,646	36,090	30,065	19,002	10,425
2001	711,466	571,260	930	572,191	56,439	-33,137	482,615	121,639	107,213	37,283	30,705	19,083	10,439
2002	709,785	568,084	712	568,796	57,356	-30,952	480,488	112,711	116,586	37,088	31,820	19,138	10,348
2003	720,549	573,248	874	574,122	59,158	-31,551	483,413	115,633	121,503	37,576	32,556	19,176	10,378
2004	754,007	599,326	1,087	600,413	62,073	-36,228	502,113	121,021	130,874	39,329	33,899	19,172	10,513
2005	782,225	619,185	1,059	620,244	64,894	-40,207	515,143	136,756	130,326	40,884	34,712	19,133	10,655
2006	843,048	663,219	923	664,142	68,629	-46,842	548,671	156,883	137,493	44,128	36,957	19,105	10,810
2007	907,403	711,219	1,312	712,531	72,626	-55,898	584,008	179,712	143,683	47,428	39,227	19,132	11,083
2008	925,728	717,130	1,528	718,658	75,327	-56,378	586,954	181,703	157,071	48,184	39,951	19,212	11,198
2009	907,953	695,374	953	696,327	73,029	-43,993	579,304	156,587	172,062	47,027	40,753	19,307	10,984
2010	947,077	731,563	1,520	733,083	74,823	-50,246	608,014	156,591	182,471	48,768	42,053	19,420	11,006
2011	997,756	761,148	1,835	762,984	68,971	-53,964	640,049	172,074	185,633	50,904	43,266	19,601	11,294
2012	1,049,158	796,498	1,821	798,319	70,738	-56,380	671,202	193,668	184,288	53,102	45,415	19,757	11,433
2013	1,062,135	817,167	2,195	819,362	83,125	-56,260	679,977	196,286	185,872	53,395	44,695	19,892	11,619
2014	1,105,908	846,884	2,213	849,097	87,657	-60,207	701,233	214,755	189,920	55,290	46,088	20,002	11,866
2015	1,154,723	877,971	1,385	879,356	91,564	-62,459	725,333	229,153	200,236	57,481	47,603	20,089	12,099
2016	1,194,535	906,896	1,189	908,085	93,800	-64,052	750,233	239,075	205,227	59,280	49,668	20,151	12,259
2017	1,270,252	960,169	1,551	961,720	99,218	-69,832	792,670	255,958	221,624	62,913	52,678	20,190	12,391
2018	1,311,428	1,008,171	1,055	1,009,226	102,942	-76,617	829,668	267,132	214,628	64,849	54,278	20,223	12,655
2019	1,362,299	1,042,442	1,641	1,044,084	107,452	-87,090	849,542	282,223	230,533	67,366	56,549	20,222	12,747
2020	1,442,625	1,034,153	1,614	1,035,767	106,014	-85,199	844,554	278,557	319,514	71,743	60,956	20,108	11,872
2021	1,524,129	1,119,603	1,738	1,121,341	113,618	-100,893	906,831	285,408	331,890	76,753	64,216	19,857	12,187
2022	1,536,577	1,196,780	2,645	1,199,425	123,164	-108,266	967,996	297,640	270,941	78,089	63,118	19,677	...

... = Not available.

Personal Income and Employment by Region and State: North Carolina

(Millions of dollars, except as noted.)

Year	Personal income, total	Earnings by place of work			Less: Contributions for government social insurance	Plus: Adjustment for residence	Equals: Net earnings by place of residence	Plus: Dividends, interest, and rent	Plus: Personal current transfer receipts	Per capita (dollars)		Population (thousands)	Total employment (thousands)
		Nonfarm	Farm	Total						Personal income	Disposable personal income		
1960	7,618	5,979	604	6,583	307	10	6,287	874	457	1,666	1,517	4,573	...
1961	8,064	6,250	645	6,895	314	10	6,591	950	524	1,729	1,576	4,663	...
1962	8,661	6,763	627	7,391	347	11	7,055	1,054	552	1,840	1,668	4,707	...
1963	9,110	7,182	606	7,788	412	11	7,387	1,128	595	1,921	1,737	4,742	...
1964	9,868	7,796	634	8,431	435	12	8,007	1,238	623	2,055	1,880	4,802	...
1965	10,671	8,580	532	9,113	467	11	8,656	1,336	679	2,194	1,989	4,863	...
1966	11,855	9,662	618	10,280	617	11	9,673	1,444	738	2,421	2,182	4,896	...
1967	12,817	10,510	607	11,117	716	10	10,412	1,546	859	2,588	2,335	4,952	...
1968	14,136	11,783	518	12,301	826	13	11,487	1,667	981	2,825	2,516	5,004	...
1969	15,858	13,023	673	13,695	900	19	12,814	1,937	1,107	3,152	2,772	5,031	2,458
1970	17,320	13,993	672	14,665	971	20	13,713	2,270	1,338	3,397	3,008	5,099	2,469
1971	18,857	15,279	627	15,906	1,102	15	14,819	2,469	1,569	3,626	3,238	5,201	2,490
1972	21,319	17,367	750	18,117	1,309	9	16,817	2,745	1,757	4,025	3,550	5,296	2,602
1973	24,175	19,497	1,162	20,658	1,678	7	18,988	3,148	2,038	4,491	3,986	5,382	2,720
1974	26,654	21,242	1,110	22,351	1,901	13	20,463	3,658	2,533	4,881	4,306	5,461	2,743
1975	28,943	22,287	1,066	23,353	1,978	15	21,390	4,030	3,523	5,229	4,723	5,535	2,647
1976	32,132	25,041	1,148	26,189	2,272	14	23,931	4,403	3,798	5,745	5,128	5,593	2,754
1977	35,208	27,878	857	28,734	2,513	19	26,240	4,961	4,007	6,211	5,520	5,668	2,851
1978	39,736	31,523	1,142	32,665	2,920	18	29,763	5,659	4,315	6,922	6,125	5,740	2,946
1979	43,908	35,226	757	35,982	3,390	8	32,601	6,375	4,933	7,568	6,638	5,802	3,046
1980	49,247	38,582	651	39,233	3,717	11	35,528	7,822	5,898	8,348	7,320	5,899	3,052
1981	55,497	42,422	1,049	43,472	4,380	-29	39,062	9,637	6,798	9,317	8,154	5,957	3,072
1982	59,420	44,527	1,064	45,591	4,635	-41	40,916	10,936	7,568	9,872	8,762	6,019	3,042
1983	64,645	49,212	635	49,847	5,173	-59	44,615	11,875	8,155	10,637	9,411	6,077	3,129
1984	73,126	55,475	1,292	56,767	5,969	-95	50,703	13,808	8,615	11,863	10,535	6,164	3,292
1985	79,020	60,390	1,161	61,550	6,589	-157	54,804	14,979	9,237	12,635	11,179	6,254	3,392
1986	85,195	65,521	1,145	66,666	7,294	-219	59,153	16,214	9,827	13,477	11,920	6,322	3,494
1987	91,885	71,603	1,141	72,744	7,869	-301	64,574	17,091	10,220	14,349	12,591	6,404	3,610
1988	100,590	78,140	1,477	79,617	8,838	-363	70,416	19,097	11,077	15,522	13,707	6,481	3,751
1989	109,693	83,798	1,722	85,519	9,490	-418	75,611	21,715	12,367	16,708	14,661	6,565	3,838
1990	116,523	88,317	2,135	90,452	10,257	-458	79,738	23,111	13,674	17,485	15,425	6,664	3,902
1991	121,893	91,320	2,394	93,715	10,747	-440	82,527	23,642	15,724	17,967	15,926	6,784	3,866
1992	132,675	100,252	2,340	102,592	11,649	-465	90,479	24,787	17,409	19,236	17,103	6,897	3,964
1993	141,458	106,326	2,613	108,939	12,435	-481	96,022	26,302	19,134	20,085	17,824	7,043	4,087
1994	150,583	113,462	2,826	116,288	13,399	-546	102,343	28,332	19,908	20,951	18,521	7,187	4,201
1995	161,487	120,481	2,710	123,191	14,228	-618	108,345	30,837	22,305	21,987	19,386	7,345	4,355
1996	172,817	127,553	2,996	130,549	14,926	-682	114,941	33,660	24,216	23,040	20,244	7,501	4,459
1997	185,688	137,434	3,064	140,498	15,978	-760	123,760	36,510	25,418	24,251	21,205	7,657	4,603
1998	198,667	148,217	2,409	150,625	17,207	-738	132,681	39,561	26,425	25,440	22,077	7,809	4,708
1999	208,586	157,709	2,240	159,949	18,335	-807	140,807	39,718	28,062	26,239	22,798	7,949	4,802
2000	222,326	167,496	2,965	170,462	19,428	-921	150,113	42,187	30,026	27,510	23,834	8,082	4,892
2001	228,556	170,991	3,122	174,113	20,100	-930	153,083	41,969	33,504	27,838	24,168	8,210	4,855
2002	231,900	174,692	1,513	176,205	20,369	-899	154,937	40,700	36,264	27,852	24,685	8,326	4,842
2003	241,851	181,782	1,592	183,374	21,376	-756	161,242	42,471	38,139	28,715	25,727	8,423	4,852
2004	262,024	195,607	2,371	197,977	22,463	-757	174,758	46,149	41,117	30,635	27,583	8,553	4,962
2005	281,572	208,311	3,206	211,517	24,022	-826	186,669	50,273	44,631	32,345	28,859	8,705	5,093
2006	306,618	226,964	2,607	229,571	25,771	-1,010	202,790	55,170	48,659	34,385	30,551	8,917	5,252
2007	330,170	243,046	2,296	245,343	27,518	-1,240	216,585	61,242	52,344	36,211	32,027	9,118	5,431
2008	352,222	255,263	2,239	257,501	28,279	-1,272	227,951	64,821	59,450	37,835	33,776	9,309	5,414
2009	339,556	240,899	2,268	243,167	27,493	-1,046	214,628	58,429	66,498	35,933	32,800	9,450	5,216
2010	343,348	241,363	2,399	243,762	27,813	-962	214,988	57,716	70,644	35,872	32,634	9,571	5,178
2011	355,827	245,402	2,066	247,468	25,927	-891	220,651	62,798	72,378	36,902	33,158	9,643	5,293
2012	380,161	264,182	2,892	267,074	26,956	-939	239,179	67,005	73,977	39,103	35,316	9,722	5,356
2013	376,392	263,347	3,417	266,764	31,308	-847	234,609	66,392	75,391	38,394	34,277	9,803	5,437
2014	398,100	276,942	3,696	280,638	32,936	-919	246,783	72,973	78,343	40,293	35,986	9,880	5,569
2015	419,334	290,529	3,277	293,806	34,571	-1,162	258,074	78,585	82,676	42,076	37,280	9,966	5,695
2016	432,626	301,027	2,553	303,581	35,460	-1,294	266,827	80,730	85,070	42,936	37,967	10,076	5,825
2017	453,729	315,836	3,221	319,057	36,887	-1,365	280,804	84,588	88,337	44,591	39,595	10,175	5,920
2018	476,309	333,026	1,592	334,617	38,396	-1,564	294,657	88,889	92,763	46,352	41,320	10,276	6,056
2019	505,470	351,062	1,980	353,042	40,562	-1,600	310,880	96,537	98,053	48,741	43,362	10,371	6,150
2020	542,727	363,905	1,567	365,473	42,278	-2,103	321,092	97,172	124,463	51,938	46,515	10,449	6,055
2021	592,695	396,541	2,744	399,285	45,332	-2,495	351,459	99,262	141,974	56,095	49,718	10,566	6,276
2022	614,297	435,476	5,583	441,058	50,110	-2,841	388,108	103,760	122,430	57,416	49,728	10,699	...

... = Not available.

Personal Income and Employment by Region and State: North Dakota

(Millions of dollars, except as noted.)

| | | Derivation of personal income | | | | | | | | Per capita (dollars) | | | |
| | | Earnings by place of work | | | Less: Contributions for government social insurance | Plus: Adjustment for residence | Equals: Net earnings by place of residence | Plus: Dividends, interest, and rent | Plus: Personal current transfer receipts | | | | |
Year	Personal income, total	Nonfarm	Farm	Total						Personal income	Disposable personal income	Population (thousands)	Total employment (thousands)
1960	1,210	716	273	989	41	-12	937	190	83	1,909	1,764	634	...
1961	1,109	750	145	894	43	-12	840	179	90	1,730	1,593	641	...
1962	1,555	812	478	1,290	47	-14	1,229	232	94	2,441	2,268	637	...
1963	1,448	865	328	1,193	56	-14	1,123	228	98	2,249	2,072	644	...
1964	1,441	932	241	1,173	59	-17	1,097	239	104	2,220	2,051	649	...
1965	1,677	995	382	1,377	62	-17	1,298	265	114	2,584	2,402	649	...
1966	1,697	1,048	349	1,397	74	-16	1,307	267	123	2,623	2,422	647	...
1967	1,699	1,077	310	1,388	89	-16	1,282	270	147	2,714	2,489	626	...
1968	1,778	1,147	285	1,431	95	-16	1,320	294	164	2,864	2,624	621	...
1969	1,991	1,251	385	1,635	102	-55	1,478	330	183	3,205	2,889	621	274
1970	2,102	1,392	306	1,698	115	-58	1,525	365	212	3,397	3,088	619	281
1971	2,424	1,526	434	1,959	129	-60	1,770	406	248	3,868	3,573	627	284
1972	2,887	1,706	668	2,373	147	-64	2,162	449	276	4,576	4,215	631	288
1973	4,037	1,921	1,529	3,449	189	-68	3,193	534	310	6,383	5,880	632	300
1974	3,998	2,163	1,164	3,327	224	-79	3,024	619	356	6,304	5,635	634	308
1975	4,182	2,439	945	3,384	256	-83	3,045	716	420	6,549	5,881	638	314
1976	4,102	2,773	478	3,250	294	-97	2,860	777	465	6,357	5,704	645	326
1977	4,261	3,004	274	3,278	303	-103	2,873	882	507	6,564	5,918	649	331
1978	5,358	3,419	865	4,284	354	-113	3,818	987	553	8,235	7,398	651	345
1979	5,507	3,822	502	4,324	412	-130	3,783	1,112	613	8,445	7,565	652	353
1980	5,270	4,149	-383	3,766	450	-145	3,170	1,375	725	8,053	7,077	654	355
1981	6,899	4,637	372	5,009	533	-166	4,310	1,758	831	10,462	9,218	660	359
1982	7,453	4,903	306	5,209	576	-168	4,465	2,057	932	11,141	10,032	669	360
1983	7,831	5,163	366	5,529	613	-171	4,745	2,050	1,036	11,573	10,503	677	365
1984	8,458	5,361	612	5,973	652	-170	5,151	2,197	1,111	12,429	11,322	680	366
1985	8,741	5,453	699	6,152	678	-170	5,304	2,256	1,180	12,912	11,775	677	364
1986	8,870	5,510	693	6,203	698	-168	5,337	2,246	1,287	13,248	12,141	670	357
1987	9,133	5,736	789	6,525	727	-168	5,629	2,158	1,346	13,814	12,601	661	363
1988	8,467	5,984	-61	5,924	794	-175	4,954	2,159	1,353	12,920	11,669	655	366
1989	9,483	6,233	442	6,675	840	-180	5,655	2,353	1,474	14,671	13,292	646	370
1990	10,257	6,591	773	7,363	933	-184	6,246	2,432	1,578	16,084	14,590	638	374
1991	10,388	6,936	614	7,550	1,002	-191	6,357	2,426	1,605	16,340	14,795	636	382
1992	11,392	7,373	1,074	8,447	1,064	-206	7,176	2,444	1,772	17,849	16,256	638	388
1993	11,548	7,876	624	8,500	1,146	-225	7,129	2,552	1,867	18,009	16,303	641	397
1994	12,548	8,363	1,059	9,422	1,221	-241	7,961	2,686	1,901	19,460	17,688	645	411
1995	12,571	8,787	429	9,215	1,270	-262	7,684	2,877	2,010	19,404	17,530	648	418
1996	14,066	9,280	1,308	10,588	1,327	-294	8,967	3,006	2,093	21,627	19,626	650	426
1997	13,771	9,766	304	10,070	1,374	-321	8,375	3,215	2,182	21,196	19,052	650	430
1998	15,078	10,323	972	11,295	1,439	-344	9,513	3,356	2,209	23,285	21,015	648	435
1999	15,272	10,862	692	11,554	1,479	-370	9,705	3,263	2,304	23,705	21,375	644	436
2000	16,623	11,500	1,100	12,600	1,550	-404	10,646	3,505	2,472	25,892	23,379	642	441
2001	16,961	12,056	801	12,857	1,591	-432	10,833	3,591	2,537	26,541	23,872	639	445
2002	17,370	12,614	597	13,211	1,648	-447	11,116	3,565	2,689	27,218	24,902	638	443
2003	18,959	13,273	1,468	14,741	1,737	-469	12,534	3,637	2,788	29,678	27,425	639	444
2004	19,410	14,153	943	15,096	1,840	-522	12,735	3,728	2,948	30,107	27,807	645	453
2005	20,653	14,896	1,138	16,035	1,919	-570	13,546	4,001	3,107	31,967	29,336	646	462
2006	21,663	15,947	731	16,678	2,011	-635	14,033	4,317	3,314	33,357	30,323	649	471
2007	23,965	16,792	1,648	18,440	2,114	-704	15,623	4,790	3,552	36,709	33,184	653	483
2008	27,009	18,012	2,412	20,424	2,262	-762	17,400	5,591	4,018	41,075	36,953	658	492
2009	26,740	18,946	1,548	20,494	2,420	-803	17,272	5,269	4,200	40,212	36,904	665	492
2010	29,881	20,841	2,123	22,963	2,504	-967	19,493	5,845	4,543	44,264	40,443	675	504
2011	33,666	23,830	1,998	25,828	2,625	-1,322	21,881	7,135	4,650	49,000	44,002	687	530
2012	39,796	27,822	3,560	31,382	2,844	-1,901	26,637	8,468	4,692	56,443	50,512	705	567
2013	39,934	29,961	1,929	31,890	3,477	-2,292	26,121	8,956	4,857	54,900	48,586	727	587
2014	42,820	33,191	888	34,079	3,867	-2,635	27,578	10,072	5,170	57,523	50,966	744	607
2015	41,179	32,390	270	32,660	3,849	-2,385	26,426	9,397	5,356	53,991	48,215	763	598
2016	39,766	30,277	776	31,053	3,694	-1,969	25,390	8,861	5,515	52,005	46,861	765	577
2017	40,266	30,560	897	31,457	3,856	-2,083	25,518	9,127	5,621	52,521	47,478	767	573
2018	42,733	31,906	950	32,857	3,895	-2,281	26,681	10,016	6,036	55,396	50,481	771	578
2019	44,347	33,202	1,002	34,204	3,963	-2,372	27,869	10,119	6,359	57,110	51,800	777	582
2020	47,411	32,531	2,543	35,074	3,997	-2,028	29,048	9,851	8,512	60,821	55,457	780	561
2021	50,003	33,663	2,800	36,463	4,057	-1,998	30,409	10,508	9,086	64,276	58,123	778	566
2022	51,575	36,341	3,079	39,420	4,411	-2,182	32,828	10,996	7,751	66,184	58,659	779	...

... = Not available.

Personal Income and Employment by Region and State: Ohio

(Millions of dollars, except as noted.)

Year	Personal income, total	Earnings by place of work			Less: Contributions for government social insurance	Plus: Adjustment for residence	Equals: Net earnings by place of residence	Plus: Dividends, interest, and rent	Plus: Personal current transfer receipts	Per capita (dollars)		Population (thousands)	Total employment (thousands)
		Nonfarm	Farm	Total						Personal income	Disposable personal income		
1960	23,455	19,684	334	20,018	1,003	-131	18,884	3,060	1,512	2,410	2,139	9,734	...
1961	23,910	19,655	373	20,028	984	-122	18,922	3,227	1,760	2,426	2,167	9,854	...
1962	25,207	20,898	336	21,234	1,125	-126	19,983	3,493	1,731	2,539	2,258	9,929	...
1963	26,265	21,806	334	22,140	1,236	-129	20,775	3,708	1,782	2,630	2,336	9,986	...
1964	28,028	23,456	305	23,761	1,355	-134	22,272	3,967	1,789	2,781	2,505	10,080	...
1965	30,302	25,392	358	25,750	1,409	-147	24,195	4,214	1,893	2,970	2,659	10,201	...
1966	33,057	28,058	496	28,554	1,864	-166	26,524	4,495	2,039	3,200	2,850	10,330	...
1967	34,630	29,319	329	29,648	1,958	-160	27,529	4,722	2,379	3,325	2,959	10,414	...
1968	38,207	32,237	412	32,649	2,134	-183	30,332	5,186	2,690	3,633	3,194	10,516	...
1969	41,801	35,425	417	35,843	2,360	-200	33,284	5,617	2,900	3,957	3,432	10,563	4,695
1970	44,142	36,735	435	37,170	2,408	-183	34,579	6,168	3,396	4,137	3,640	10,669	4,683
1971	46,980	38,635	415	39,050	2,603	-134	36,313	6,654	4,014	4,376	3,911	10,735	4,627
1972	50,968	42,041	506	42,547	2,985	-133	39,429	7,101	4,438	4,743	4,173	10,747	4,710
1973	56,552	46,849	667	47,516	3,864	-158	43,494	7,893	5,166	5,252	4,626	10,767	4,902
1974	61,925	50,430	798	51,228	4,310	-134	46,784	8,939	6,203	5,752	5,051	10,766	4,964
1975	66,162	52,187	814	53,001	4,336	-93	48,572	9,658	7,933	6,143	5,444	10,770	4,809
1976	72,598	58,033	787	58,820	4,942	-108	53,770	10,325	8,502	6,752	5,945	10,753	4,889
1977	80,397	65,044	675	65,718	5,554	-114	60,050	11,417	8,930	7,464	6,530	10,771	5,034
1978	88,855	72,503	628	73,130	6,397	-136	66,598	12,662	9,594	8,231	7,180	10,795	5,206
1979	98,136	79,674	762	80,435	7,322	-172	72,942	14,241	10,953	9,088	7,871	10,799	5,291
1980	107,185	83,320	575	83,895	7,612	-194	76,089	17,285	13,811	9,924	8,646	10,801	5,204
1981	116,652	89,154	167	89,321	8,708	-483	80,130	21,175	15,348	10,813	9,365	10,788	5,135
1982	122,082	90,048	270	90,318	8,900	-609	80,810	23,462	17,810	11,349	9,952	10,757	4,967
1983	129,133	95,299	-69	95,230	9,613	-711	84,906	25,181	19,045	12,026	10,560	10,738	4,960
1984	142,661	105,804	874	106,678	10,932	-842	94,904	28,108	19,649	13,286	11,737	10,738	5,160
1985	151,426	113,033	870	113,904	11,870	-919	101,115	29,366	20,944	14,106	12,423	10,735	5,287
1986	158,493	118,945	684	119,629	12,856	-952	105,821	30,487	22,185	14,771	13,034	10,730	5,401
1987	166,090	125,890	734	126,624	13,614	-995	112,015	31,024	23,052	15,436	13,511	10,760	5,548
1988	178,268	136,113	783	136,896	15,149	-1,042	120,705	33,330	24,233	16,508	14,519	10,799	5,682
1989	191,708	144,483	1,171	145,654	16,209	-1,105	128,340	37,537	25,831	17,703	15,494	10,829	5,803
1990	202,980	152,071	1,205	153,276	17,415	-1,093	134,767	39,473	28,740	18,683	16,380	10,864	5,863
1991	207,677	156,084	702	156,786	18,308	-1,115	137,363	39,326	30,988	18,973	16,690	10,946	5,842
1992	221,201	166,674	1,184	167,858	19,470	-1,230	147,158	40,009	34,034	20,056	17,695	11,029	5,854
1993	230,366	174,334	933	175,267	20,592	-1,327	153,348	41,629	35,389	20,752	18,259	11,101	5,960
1994	243,307	185,104	1,162	186,265	22,172	-1,450	162,643	43,920	36,744	21,816	19,163	11,152	6,136
1995	255,101	192,988	891	193,879	23,353	-1,491	169,036	47,291	38,774	22,771	19,937	11,203	6,300
1996	267,147	201,099	1,250	202,348	24,062	-1,546	176,741	50,197	40,209	23,762	20,641	11,243	6,395
1997	282,809	212,537	1,684	214,221	24,790	-1,644	187,788	53,598	41,423	25,078	21,713	11,277	6,500
1998	299,096	226,220	1,270	227,491	25,558	-1,819	200,113	56,800	42,183	26,442	22,813	11,312	6,599
1999	308,329	237,388	851	238,238	26,717	-1,789	209,733	55,076	43,521	27,200	23,492	11,335	6,681
2000	324,978	248,750	1,208	249,958	27,014	-1,749	221,135	57,576	46,267	28,598	24,649	11,364	6,789
2001	333,912	254,539	1,139	255,679	27,710	-1,737	226,232	57,273	50,407	29,323	25,352	11,387	6,726
2002	338,738	259,456	581	260,036	27,770	-1,758	230,508	54,410	53,820	29,693	26,135	11,408	6,640
2003	348,859	267,397	786	268,184	28,880	-1,771	237,533	54,945	56,380	30,509	27,153	11,435	6,621
2004	362,573	278,685	1,412	280,097	30,585	-1,716	247,796	55,842	58,934	31,660	28,232	11,452	6,667
2005	373,789	284,831	1,066	285,897	31,413	-1,731	252,752	58,613	62,424	32,607	28,899	11,463	6,709
2006	392,817	296,182	932	297,114	32,780	-1,885	262,449	64,619	65,749	34,214	30,218	11,481	6,747
2007	409,746	304,152	1,181	305,333	33,588	-1,974	269,771	69,978	69,998	35,629	31,371	11,500	6,795
2008	424,082	307,648	1,282	308,931	34,516	-1,965	272,450	72,747	78,885	36,827	32,604	11,515	6,725
2009	412,219	295,081	1,591	296,672	33,450	-1,837	261,385	64,907	85,927	35,755	32,444	11,529	6,455
2010	425,362	303,736	1,604	305,341	33,656	-1,795	269,889	64,780	90,693	36,854	33,316	11,542	6,418
2011	453,595	319,958	2,890	322,849	31,792	-1,923	289,135	71,336	93,125	39,245	35,121	11,558	6,522
2012	471,704	334,603	1,941	336,544	32,846	-1,888	301,810	78,616	91,277	40,759	36,520	11,573	6,606
2013	479,089	345,355	3,063	348,418	36,901	-2,316	309,201	76,641	93,247	41,259	36,748	11,612	6,681
2014	498,895	356,407	1,942	358,349	38,048	-2,555	317,746	83,218	97,930	42,829	38,198	11,648	6,771
2015	518,827	369,571	612	370,183	39,397	-2,592	328,194	88,667	101,966	44,442	39,532	11,674	6,862
2016	529,070	375,804	597	376,400	40,913	-2,690	332,797	91,867	104,406	45,212	40,237	11,702	6,931
2017	547,517	389,679	939	390,618	43,319	-2,463	344,836	95,931	106,750	46,646	41,627	11,738	6,988
2018	568,458	402,708	1,463	404,171	44,168	-2,003	358,000	100,964	109,495	48,327	43,362	11,763	7,067
2019	589,836	415,098	522	415,620	46,073	-2,250	367,297	107,528	115,012	50,035	44,825	11,789	7,072
2020	631,331	418,691	1,925	420,616	46,683	-2,412	371,521	107,243	152,567	53,514	48,260	11,798	6,854
2021	670,036	443,833	2,948	446,781	48,637	-2,073	396,071	109,541	164,424	56,955	50,821	11,764	7,010
2022	680,435	475,660	4,397	480,057	52,474	-2,103	425,480	114,135	140,821	57,880	50,577	11,756	...

... = Not available.

Personal Income and Employment by Region and State: Oklahoma

(Millions of dollars, except as noted.)

		Earnings by place of work			Less: Contributions for government social insurance	Plus: Adjustment for residence	Equals: Net earnings by place of residence	Plus: Dividends, interest, and rent	Plus: Personal current transfer receipts	Per capita (dollars)			
Year	Personal income, total	Nonfarm	Farm	Total						Personal income	Disposable personal income	Population (thousands)	Total employment (thousands)
1960	4,612	3,359	335	3,694	150	7	3,550	684	378	1,974	1,789	2,336	...
1961	4,774	3,492	301	3,793	159	9	3,643	715	416	2,006	1,811	2,380	...
1962	4,985	3,723	240	3,963	178	11	3,796	749	441	2,054	1,853	2,427	...
1963	5,151	3,889	214	4,104	208	12	3,908	773	471	2,112	1,907	2,439	...
1964	5,519	4,180	208	4,388	208	14	4,195	833	491	2,256	2,056	2,446	...
1965	5,913	4,415	278	4,693	216	17	4,494	894	526	2,424	2,209	2,440	...
1966	6,343	4,812	267	5,079	286	21	4,814	946	584	2,585	2,343	2,454	...
1967	6,929	5,274	276	5,550	337	25	5,239	991	700	2,784	2,519	2,489	...
1968	7,589	5,856	219	6,076	385	31	5,721	1,080	789	3,032	2,726	2,503	...
1969	8,455	6,400	275	6,676	401	64	6,338	1,261	856	3,335	2,954	2,535	1,107
1970	9,326	6,897	359	7,256	431	65	6,890	1,454	981	3,634	3,257	2,566	1,120
1971	10,164	7,484	335	7,819	484	64	7,400	1,633	1,131	3,882	3,522	2,618	1,132
1972	11,153	8,246	417	8,664	558	73	8,179	1,735	1,240	4,197	3,754	2,657	1,183
1973	12,653	9,142	734	9,875	720	83	9,238	2,009	1,406	4,696	4,237	2,694	1,221
1974	14,080	10,379	452	10,831	845	106	10,092	2,324	1,664	5,153	4,576	2,732	1,256
1975	15,736	11,485	404	11,889	928	142	11,103	2,581	2,052	5,677	5,116	2,772	1,269
1976	17,349	12,810	338	13,148	1,054	177	12,270	2,828	2,251	6,145	5,503	2,823	1,305
1977	19,296	14,590	183	14,773	1,198	152	13,728	3,176	2,393	6,733	5,993	2,866	1,359
1978	21,896	16,739	174	16,913	1,418	149	15,644	3,678	2,575	7,517	6,623	2,913	1,428
1979	25,415	19,128	634	19,762	1,688	162	18,236	4,224	2,955	8,557	7,517	2,970	1,481
1980	29,279	22,149	265	22,413	1,971	170	20,612	5,248	3,419	9,629	8,399	3,041	1,547
1981	34,204	25,621	330	25,952	2,450	198	23,699	6,623	3,882	11,047	9,492	3,096	1,625
1982	38,176	28,022	487	28,509	2,748	204	25,965	7,835	4,376	11,907	10,157	3,206	1,673
1983	39,077	28,143	214	28,357	2,739	241	25,858	8,417	4,801	11,876	10,470	3,290	1,638
1984	41,927	29,974	376	30,351	2,969	289	27,671	9,275	4,982	12,761	11,354	3,286	1,665
1985	43,606	30,826	382	31,208	3,109	331	28,430	9,854	5,322	13,330	11,869	3,271	1,648
1986	43,882	30,715	645	31,360	3,161	382	28,580	9,644	5,658	13,491	12,279	3,253	1,588
1987	43,754	30,681	564	31,245	3,181	429	28,493	9,375	5,886	13,630	12,241	3,210	1,599
1988	45,620	31,950	765	32,715	3,498	478	29,694	9,695	6,231	14,405	12,936	3,167	1,608
1989	48,521	33,778	802	34,580	3,731	505	31,354	10,539	6,629	15,402	13,754	3,150	1,623
1990	51,121	35,735	862	36,597	4,066	568	33,099	10,889	7,133	16,235	14,319	3,149	1,655
1991	52,678	37,115	623	37,738	4,324	597	34,011	10,862	7,804	16,589	14,774	3,175	1,668
1992	56,034	39,331	844	40,175	4,550	618	36,244	11,060	8,730	17,399	15,567	3,221	1,680
1993	58,247	41,115	867	41,982	4,798	657	37,841	11,226	9,180	17,910	16,032	3,252	1,716
1994	60,818	42,739	826	43,565	5,058	714	39,221	11,845	9,753	18,537	16,561	3,281	1,748
1995	63,427	44,418	286	44,704	5,276	747	40,175	12,719	10,533	19,173	17,118	3,308	1,800
1996	67,223	47,018	359	47,377	5,474	780	42,682	13,486	11,055	20,126	17,883	3,340	1,850
1997	71,075	49,951	662	50,613	5,734	859	45,738	13,978	11,359	21,072	18,590	3,373	1,897
1998	74,934	52,879	518	53,397	6,033	893	48,257	15,088	11,589	22,006	19,379	3,405	1,939
1999	77,034	54,004	839	54,843	6,218	939	49,564	15,366	12,105	22,412	19,713	3,437	1,953
2000	83,519	58,212	831	59,044	6,600	1,019	53,463	17,260	12,797	24,178	21,278	3,454	1,994
2001	88,786	62,083	815	62,899	7,047	1,014	56,865	17,789	14,132	25,608	22,552	3,467	2,009
2002	90,798	63,593	977	64,570	7,256	987	58,300	17,400	15,098	26,023	23,424	3,489	1,987
2003	95,328	66,895	956	67,851	7,473	968	61,346	17,891	16,091	27,198	24,727	3,505	1,971
2004	103,162	72,789	1,260	74,049	7,998	950	67,001	19,162	16,999	29,264	26,693	3,525	1,998
2005	113,043	79,876	1,300	81,177	8,476	912	73,612	21,170	18,261	31,856	28,823	3,549	2,043
2006	125,269	88,925	681	89,606	9,116	884	81,374	23,891	20,004	34,854	31,355	3,594	2,096
2007	129,787	89,778	664	90,442	9,593	848	81,697	26,643	21,447	35,711	31,956	3,634	2,150
2008	144,283	99,901	800	100,701	10,044	793	91,450	28,775	24,058	39,325	35,341	3,669	2,187
2009	133,524	91,165	56	91,220	9,852	682	82,050	25,529	25,945	35,917	33,064	3,718	2,137
2010	140,140	94,771	815	95,586	10,092	615	86,108	26,345	27,688	37,276	34,329	3,760	2,130
2011	150,710	101,109	1,351	102,460	9,730	564	93,294	29,392	28,023	39,800	36,171	3,787	2,159
2012	161,128	108,510	1,760	110,271	10,320	555	100,505	31,981	28,642	42,232	38,439	3,815	2,212
2013	169,383	118,040	1,790	119,830	11,897	475	108,407	31,717	29,259	44,017	39,956	3,848	2,248
2014	180,469	125,064	2,593	127,657	12,224	465	115,898	34,398	30,173	46,614	42,345	3,872	2,273
2015	175,134	120,357	1,890	122,247	12,304	437	110,381	33,567	31,186	44,894	40,628	3,901	2,288
2016	166,548	112,398	951	113,349	12,059	458	101,748	32,648	32,151	42,521	38,526	3,917	2,287
2017	174,160	117,848	1,035	118,884	12,541	443	106,786	34,089	33,284	44,423	40,324	3,920	2,292
2018	182,341	123,823	860	124,683	13,264	476	111,895	36,091	34,355	46,415	42,377	3,928	2,311
2019	191,852	129,514	964	130,478	13,750	482	117,210	38,023	36,619	48,646	44,438	3,944	2,310
2020	200,153	128,821	707	129,528	13,950	491	116,069	37,917	46,167	50,481	46,292	3,965	2,263
2021	214,761	135,604	1,230	136,834	14,473	646	123,007	39,565	52,189	53,808	49,099	3,991	2,290
2022	221,081	147,188	1,211	148,399	15,718	729	133,410	41,282	46,388	54,998	49,398	4,020	...

... = Not available.

Personal Income and Employment by Region and State: Oregon

(Millions of dollars, except as noted.)

Year	Personal income, total	Earnings by place of work			Less: Contributions for government social insurance	Plus: Adjustment for residence	Equals: Net earnings by place of residence	Plus: Dividends, interest, and rent	Plus: Personal current transfer receipts	Per capita (dollars)		Population (thousands)	Total employment (thousands)
		Nonfarm	Farm	Total						Personal income	Disposable personal income		
1960	4,192	3,290	174	3,463	207	-18	3,238	650	304	2,366	2,083	1,772	...
1961	4,351	3,378	161	3,539	211	-19	3,309	690	352	2,435	2,163	1,787	...
1962	4,622	3,606	172	3,778	232	-23	3,524	739	359	2,542	2,249	1,818	...
1963	4,867	3,849	163	4,012	266	-27	3,718	778	371	2,626	2,304	1,853	...
1964	5,236	4,178	150	4,328	271	-33	4,025	828	384	2,773	2,451	1,888	...
1965	5,681	4,540	168	4,708	276	-39	4,394	872	414	2,933	2,610	1,937	...
1966	6,118	4,942	195	5,137	352	-42	4,742	929	447	3,107	2,747	1,969	...
1967	6,487	5,198	185	5,383	392	-47	4,945	1,010	533	3,278	2,899	1,979	...
1968	7,063	5,693	183	5,876	444	-54	5,378	1,085	601	3,524	3,085	2,004	...
1969	7,832	6,225	226	6,451	482	-82	5,887	1,283	662	3,798	3,273	2,062	920
1970	8,537	6,605	216	6,821	505	-63	6,254	1,479	805	4,065	3,564	2,100	926
1971	9,383	7,232	204	7,437	569	-52	6,817	1,634	932	4,364	3,861	2,150	951
1972	10,511	8,165	259	8,424	679	-45	7,700	1,789	1,022	4,788	4,197	2,195	1,001
1973	11,845	9,177	371	9,548	880	-50	8,618	2,015	1,213	5,291	4,653	2,239	1,058
1974	13,432	10,174	477	10,651	1,002	-58	9,590	2,346	1,496	5,889	5,144	2,281	1,089
1975	14,920	11,053	394	11,447	1,056	-31	10,359	2,660	1,901	6,418	5,699	2,325	1,105
1976	16,822	12,730	370	13,099	1,234	-15	11,850	2,901	2,071	7,091	6,233	2,372	1,156
1977	18,812	14,459	320	14,778	1,420	-74	13,284	3,290	2,239	7,712	6,683	2,439	1,223
1978	21,563	16,791	317	17,108	1,693	-128	15,288	3,831	2,444	8,592	7,418	2,510	1,296
1979	24,392	18,994	390	19,384	1,987	-178	17,220	4,432	2,740	9,461	8,135	2,578	1,350
1980	27,030	20,316	477	20,793	2,127	-218	18,449	5,326	3,256	10,234	8,850	2,641	1,350
1981	29,170	21,172	406	21,578	2,369	-269	18,941	6,461	3,767	10,933	9,494	2,668	1,319
1982	30,006	21,075	293	21,369	2,403	-258	18,708	7,052	4,247	11,260	9,809	2,665	1,270
1983	31,906	22,242	301	22,543	2,558	-246	19,739	7,603	4,564	12,026	10,585	2,653	1,295
1984	34,585	24,305	402	24,707	2,890	-286	21,532	8,340	4,713	12,970	11,467	2,667	1,342
1985	36,321	25,609	428	26,037	3,070	-315	22,652	8,737	4,931	13,590	11,967	2,673	1,370
1986	38,222	27,194	550	27,744	3,251	-371	24,123	9,079	5,020	14,243	12,479	2,684	1,406
1987	40,195	29,134	515	29,649	3,438	-433	25,778	9,220	5,197	14,881	13,036	2,701	1,455
1988	43,776	32,115	702	32,817	3,931	-501	28,385	9,859	5,531	15,969	14,160	2,741	1,522
1989	48,095	34,896	675	35,571	4,272	-562	30,738	11,274	6,083	17,235	15,011	2,791	1,574
1990	51,941	38,183	713	38,896	4,791	-618	33,487	11,839	6,615	18,159	15,965	2,860	1,626
1991	54,674	40,258	727	40,985	5,106	-683	35,196	12,153	7,325	18,670	16,349	2,929	1,636
1992	58,477	43,359	730	44,089	5,459	-780	37,850	12,476	8,151	19,546	17,116	2,992	1,654
1993	62,591	46,361	850	47,211	5,830	-875	40,506	13,381	8,704	20,452	17,869	3,060	1,698
1994	67,030	49,956	776	50,732	6,322	-941	43,469	14,525	9,037	21,475	18,691	3,121	1,781
1995	72,166	53,273	688	53,961	6,789	-1,119	46,053	16,102	10,011	22,663	19,747	3,184	1,845
1996	77,845	57,824	840	58,665	7,452	-1,355	49,858	17,335	10,652	23,974	20,791	3,247	1,920
1997	82,657	62,090	956	63,046	7,910	-1,540	53,596	18,099	10,963	25,015	21,514	3,304	1,986
1998	87,241	66,141	859	67,000	8,366	-1,664	56,971	18,871	11,399	26,023	22,415	3,352	2,022
1999	90,337	69,695	821	70,516	8,726	-1,757	60,033	17,898	12,406	26,617	22,779	3,394	2,051
2000	97,355	75,653	823	76,476	9,417	-1,999	65,060	19,245	13,049	28,386	24,189	3,430	2,092
2001	99,976	77,069	833	77,902	9,449	-2,111	66,342	18,982	14,652	28,829	24,885	3,468	2,079
2002	101,009	78,057	836	78,893	9,605	-2,190	67,098	18,090	15,821	28,749	25,317	3,513	2,062
2003	104,741	80,639	1,115	81,754	9,914	-2,368	69,472	19,010	16,259	29,526	26,206	3,547	2,077
2004	110,639	85,573	1,254	86,826	10,617	-2,594	73,616	20,294	16,730	30,996	27,522	3,569	2,133
2005	116,692	90,281	1,236	91,517	11,208	-2,885	77,423	21,600	17,669	32,296	28,263	3,613	2,197
2006	127,440	97,409	1,333	98,741	12,042	-3,274	83,425	25,011	19,004	34,716	30,302	3,671	2,256
2007	133,556	100,946	1,334	102,280	12,549	-3,546	86,186	26,949	20,421	35,879	31,500	3,722	2,307
2008	139,412	101,918	1,312	103,230	12,717	-3,667	86,847	28,855	23,711	36,992	32,421	3,769	2,289
2009	134,493	96,519	1,119	97,638	12,204	-3,490	81,945	25,468	27,081	35,313	31,811	3,809	2,189
2010	138,292	98,505	1,051	99,556	12,551	-3,371	83,634	25,376	29,282	36,036	32,347	3,838	2,174
2011	145,596	102,331	1,277	103,608	11,569	-3,703	88,336	27,574	29,687	37,596	33,311	3,873	2,202
2012	153,548	108,492	1,405	109,897	12,112	-3,914	93,871	30,018	29,659	39,371	34,966	3,900	2,220
2013	156,130	112,129	1,646	113,775	14,201	-3,909	95,664	29,716	30,750	39,788	34,831	3,924	2,260
2014	167,077	118,111	1,593	119,704	15,043	-3,890	100,771	32,635	33,672	42,134	36,874	3,965	2,323
2015	179,600	126,398	1,806	128,204	15,900	-4,145	108,159	35,598	35,843	44,694	38,816	4,018	2,391
2016	188,283	133,327	1,746	135,074	16,633	-4,527	113,914	37,488	36,882	45,999	39,828	4,093	2,450
2017	198,958	141,916	1,303	143,219	17,835	-4,750	120,634	40,326	37,998	47,974	41,669	4,147	2,516
2018	211,542	150,982	1,369	152,351	18,597	-5,130	128,624	42,639	40,278	50,567	44,126	4,183	2,570
2019	222,257	158,475	1,286	159,762	19,584	-5,479	134,698	44,866	42,692	52,718	45,881	4,216	2,578
2020	241,790	163,956	1,425	165,381	20,111	-5,721	139,549	45,417	56,824	56,962	50,133	4,245	2,494
2021	261,547	177,316	1,462	178,778	21,477	-5,992	151,309	46,810	63,427	61,449	53,445	4,256	2,559
2022	266,139	189,618	1,802	191,420	23,142	-6,398	161,880	49,425	54,834	62,767	53,361	4,240	...

... = Not available.

Personal Income and Employment by Region and State: Pennsylvania

(Millions of dollars, except as noted.)

Year	Personal income, total	Earnings by place of work			Less: Contributions for government social insurance	Plus: Adjustment for residence	Equals: Net earnings by place of residence	Plus: Dividends, interest, and rent	Plus: Personal current transfer receipts	Per capita (dollars)		Population (thousands)	Total employment (thousands)
		Nonfarm	Farm	Total						Personal income	Disposable personal income		
1960	26,119	21,947	298	22,245	1,211	-81	20,954	3,243	1,922	2,305	2,049	11,329	...
1961	26,686	22,134	302	22,436	1,225	-86	21,125	3,378	2,183	2,342	2,095	11,392	...
1962	27,845	23,248	219	23,467	1,334	-104	22,029	3,650	2,167	2,452	2,180	11,355	...
1963	28,908	24,044	261	24,305	1,474	-113	22,719	3,945	2,245	2,530	2,246	11,424	...
1964	30,915	25,799	269	26,068	1,530	-136	24,401	4,255	2,259	2,684	2,412	11,519	...
1965	33,159	27,650	278	27,928	1,594	-155	26,180	4,609	2,370	2,854	2,556	11,620	...
1966	35,757	30,386	266	30,652	2,148	-201	28,303	4,879	2,575	3,066	2,726	11,664	...
1967	38,299	32,176	359	32,535	2,317	-231	29,987	5,244	3,068	3,279	2,918	11,681	...
1968	41,638	34,789	314	35,102	2,421	-268	32,413	5,713	3,512	3,546	3,132	11,741	...
1969	45,346	38,065	372	38,437	2,809	-436	35,192	6,162	3,992	3,862	3,364	11,741	5,250
1970	48,844	40,132	387	40,519	2,928	-405	37,187	6,743	4,914	4,135	3,630	11,812	5,226
1971	51,836	42,076	335	42,411	3,186	-373	38,851	7,209	5,775	4,362	3,872	11,884	5,159
1972	56,580	46,003	347	46,350	3,654	-373	42,323	7,730	6,527	4,753	4,132	11,905	5,247
1973	62,033	50,635	485	51,119	4,627	-342	46,150	8,578	7,305	5,219	4,565	11,885	5,402
1974	68,133	55,005	463	55,468	5,222	-348	49,898	9,695	8,539	5,743	4,996	11,864	5,419
1975	74,473	58,422	425	58,847	5,400	-361	53,085	10,560	10,828	6,259	5,535	11,898	5,302
1976	81,283	63,729	517	64,245	6,000	-337	57,908	11,345	12,030	6,838	6,021	11,887	5,353
1977	89,174	70,233	469	70,701	6,595	-321	63,786	12,606	12,783	7,505	6,571	11,882	5,429
1978	98,272	77,966	506	78,472	7,508	-320	70,644	13,906	13,722	8,283	7,224	11,865	5,562
1979	108,706	85,953	642	86,595	8,576	-360	77,659	15,595	15,452	9,155	7,942	11,874	5,664
1980	119,088	91,396	424	91,820	9,175	-380	82,266	19,112	17,711	10,034	8,717	11,868	5,624
1981	131,482	98,190	635	98,825	10,559	-333	87,932	23,613	19,937	11,088	9,566	11,859	5,584
1982	140,474	100,597	564	101,160	10,980	-162	90,019	27,624	22,831	11,859	10,323	11,845	5,474
1983	147,181	104,882	361	105,242	11,570	-23	93,648	28,844	24,688	12,433	10,957	11,838	5,433
1984	158,975	114,007	848	114,855	13,095	145	101,905	32,221	24,849	13,455	11,861	11,815	5,577
1985	168,416	120,770	846	121,616	14,060	280	107,836	34,579	26,001	14,308	12,598	11,771	5,679
1986	177,108	127,213	886	128,098	14,908	399	113,589	36,100	27,420	15,031	13,261	11,783	5,772
1987	187,611	137,257	883	138,140	15,896	528	122,772	36,793	28,046	15,885	13,928	11,811	5,957
1988	203,158	150,069	743	150,812	17,715	779	133,876	39,734	29,547	17,150	15,089	11,846	6,120
1989	220,030	160,091	998	161,089	18,645	971	143,415	45,188	31,426	18,543	16,269	11,866	6,216
1990	232,899	169,009	1,002	170,011	19,839	1,039	151,211	47,395	34,293	19,566	17,218	11,903	6,293
1991	242,566	174,106	734	174,841	20,662	1,053	155,231	47,728	39,607	20,244	17,920	11,982	6,212
1992	256,052	185,362	1,202	186,565	21,889	1,226	165,902	47,995	42,155	21,250	18,804	12,049	6,216
1993	265,789	192,744	1,030	193,773	23,105	1,340	172,008	49,410	44,371	21,930	19,421	12,120	6,256
1994	275,145	200,288	921	201,209	24,456	1,652	178,405	51,304	45,436	22,616	19,970	12,166	6,323
1995	287,676	207,617	642	208,259	25,290	2,167	185,136	55,087	47,453	23,583	20,751	12,198	6,423
1996	302,376	215,888	1,118	217,006	25,752	2,433	193,687	58,286	50,402	24,743	21,643	12,220	6,477
1997	317,520	227,798	767	228,564	26,960	2,873	204,477	61,543	51,501	25,967	22,571	12,228	6,585
1998	334,743	241,189	893	242,082	28,148	3,271	217,204	65,309	52,229	27,336	23,659	12,246	6,658
1999	349,385	255,257	815	256,072	29,402	3,556	230,227	64,580	54,579	28,489	24,641	12,264	6,764
2000	373,972	271,569	1,103	272,672	30,864	4,056	245,865	70,193	57,914	30,443	26,321	12,284	6,905
2001	389,070	283,756	1,011	284,767	31,934	4,317	257,150	70,046	61,874	31,634	27,471	12,299	6,915
2002	396,229	290,990	641	291,631	32,821	4,591	263,401	67,181	65,647	32,133	28,512	12,331	6,887
2003	410,471	300,600	1,227	301,827	33,631	5,080	273,276	68,917	68,278	33,170	29,714	12,375	6,876
2004	434,176	320,665	1,545	322,211	35,353	5,869	292,726	70,619	70,831	34,984	31,446	12,411	6,952
2005	453,298	333,399	1,367	334,766	37,149	6,892	304,509	72,688	76,101	36,410	32,403	12,450	7,054
2006	476,775	345,643	1,142	346,784	39,023	7,341	315,102	81,757	79,916	38,109	33,712	12,511	7,153
2007	506,790	361,732	1,327	363,060	40,566	8,225	330,719	90,704	85,367	40,337	35,453	12,564	7,265
2008	526,290	368,405	1,380	369,784	41,794	8,576	336,566	94,675	95,049	41,728	36,771	12,612	7,279
2009	513,386	358,271	960	359,231	41,263	7,332	325,300	84,558	103,529	40,530	36,598	12,667	7,102
2010	537,282	374,206	1,351	375,556	42,359	8,003	341,200	85,101	110,982	42,251	38,068	12,717	7,120
2011	564,695	390,681	1,794	392,475	39,419	7,867	360,923	92,267	111,506	44,211	39,424	12,773	7,217
2012	587,666	404,760	2,059	406,820	40,325	8,229	374,723	101,329	111,615	45,855	41,014	12,816	7,285
2013	593,682	419,793	2,311	422,104	46,661	8,151	383,594	96,772	113,316	46,213	40,953	12,847	7,351
2014	619,079	433,899	2,627	436,527	48,218	8,970	397,279	104,669	117,131	48,063	42,537	12,880	7,434
2015	643,988	451,284	1,691	452,975	50,115	8,949	411,809	109,422	122,757	49,927	43,954	12,899	7,510
2016	661,160	460,808	862	461,670	51,019	9,430	420,081	111,939	129,140	51,181	45,161	12,918	7,594
2017	678,605	474,317	1,620	475,937	53,684	9,995	432,247	116,147	130,211	52,421	46,326	12,945	7,662
2018	714,332	493,632	991	494,624	55,536	10,875	449,963	124,949	139,420	55,030	48,966	12,981	7,763
2019	739,892	506,999	1,466	508,466	57,635	11,636	462,467	132,446	144,979	56,952	50,563	12,991	7,773
2020	788,282	503,937	1,066	505,002	57,084	12,150	460,068	131,832	196,382	60,663	54,195	12,994	7,413
2021	833,315	534,849	1,736	536,585	59,445	13,360	490,500	134,917	207,898	64,042	56,475	13,012	7,619
2022	845,347	577,817	3,014	580,831	64,670	14,284	530,445	140,587	174,315	65,167	56,034	12,972	...

... = Not available.

Personal Income and Employment by Region and State: Rhode Island

(Millions of dollars, except as noted.)

Year	Personal income, total	Earnings by place of work			Less: Contributions for government social insurance	Plus: Adjustment for residence	Equals: Net earnings by place of residence	Plus: Dividends, interest, and rent	Plus: Personal current transfer receipts	Per capita (dollars)		Population (thousands)	Total employment (thousands)
		Nonfarm	Farm	Total						Personal income	Disposable personal income		
1960	2,016	1,615	8	1,622	96	54	1,580	285	151	2,358	2,107	855	...
1961	2,108	1,669	7	1,676	98	57	1,635	307	166	2,457	2,189	858	...
1962	2,267	1,788	7	1,796	108	62	1,750	348	169	2,603	2,328	871	...
1963	2,368	1,845	7	1,852	118	67	1,801	388	179	2,703	2,416	876	...
1964	2,522	1,969	8	1,977	122	73	1,928	410	184	2,849	2,580	885	...
1965	2,723	2,122	8	2,130	133	82	2,079	446	198	3,049	2,755	893	...
1966	2,973	2,344	9	2,353	162	95	2,286	469	218	3,307	2,966	899	...
1967	3,223	2,516	7	2,523	175	105	2,452	506	265	3,546	3,193	909	...
1968	3,522	2,748	8	2,757	200	115	2,672	543	308	3,820	3,403	922	...
1969	3,742	2,949	8	2,957	231	62	2,789	606	347	4,015	3,554	932	440
1970	4,093	3,164	9	3,174	245	63	2,992	678	423	4,306	3,854	951	440
1971	4,337	3,323	8	3,331	267	58	3,123	718	497	4,499	4,030	964	436
1972	4,722	3,656	8	3,664	307	53	3,410	766	546	4,836	4,283	976	447
1973	5,045	3,888	6	3,895	381	69	3,582	838	625	5,158	4,569	978	452
1974	5,289	3,956	9	3,965	410	88	3,642	913	734	5,547	4,898	954	439
1975	5,742	4,115	9	4,124	416	82	3,790	980	972	6,068	5,468	946	424
1976	6,272	4,606	9	4,615	473	88	4,229	1,049	995	6,600	5,890	950	442
1977	6,865	5,066	8	5,074	521	103	4,656	1,167	1,042	7,187	6,427	955	459
1978	7,531	5,628	9	5,637	597	101	5,141	1,278	1,112	7,868	6,937	957	474
1979	8,363	6,268	8	6,276	685	108	5,699	1,428	1,236	8,742	7,633	957	483
1980	9,391	6,823	8	6,831	745	122	6,208	1,752	1,431	9,898	8,696	949	484
1981	10,464	7,350	9	7,359	851	153	6,661	2,167	1,636	10,980	9,650	953	484
1982	11,271	7,701	27	7,728	902	207	7,034	2,442	1,796	11,812	10,441	954	475
1983	12,185	8,339	37	8,376	988	263	7,651	2,620	1,914	12,741	11,306	956	480
1984	13,381	9,223	32	9,256	1,136	331	8,451	2,963	1,967	13,911	12,388	962	504
1985	14,414	10,012	42	10,054	1,220	391	9,225	3,101	2,088	14,876	13,228	969	519
1986	15,453	10,873	43	10,917	1,330	417	10,003	3,277	2,172	15,811	13,981	977	537
1987	16,547	11,788	41	11,829	1,430	484	10,883	3,427	2,237	16,721	14,631	990	546
1988	18,239	12,997	42	13,039	1,595	559	12,003	3,838	2,398	18,305	16,122	996	560
1989	19,853	13,734	32	13,766	1,661	625	12,730	4,510	2,613	19,839	17,474	1,001	560
1990	20,438	14,076	31	14,107	1,790	671	12,987	4,561	2,890	20,316	17,943	1,006	550
1991	20,636	13,825	32	13,857	1,809	697	12,745	4,381	3,511	20,419	18,105	1,011	524
1992	21,597	14,684	29	14,713	1,923	718	13,508	4,428	3,661	21,329	18,997	1,013	529
1993	22,515	15,214	30	15,244	2,011	761	13,993	4,548	3,973	22,180	19,728	1,015	533
1994	23,091	15,747	25	15,772	2,109	830	14,492	4,648	3,951	22,728	20,177	1,016	533
1995	24,324	16,467	25	16,492	2,182	859	15,168	4,986	4,170	23,918	21,224	1,017	536
1996	25,172	16,958	23	16,981	2,229	929	15,681	5,238	4,253	24,657	21,751	1,021	540
1997	26,634	17,884	16	17,899	2,334	995	16,560	5,557	4,516	25,975	22,700	1,025	546
1998	28,410	19,354	15	19,370	2,472	1,074	17,971	5,873	4,566	27,552	23,978	1,031	555
1999	29,647	20,593	15	20,608	2,589	1,175	19,194	5,708	4,746	28,496	24,782	1,040	567
2000	31,947	22,225	16	22,241	2,756	1,335	20,820	6,204	4,922	30,417	26,260	1,050	583
2001	33,633	23,226	18	23,244	2,866	1,429	21,807	6,322	5,505	31,815	27,518	1,057	585
2002	34,973	24,464	22	24,486	2,961	1,414	22,939	6,289	5,744	32,807	29,066	1,066	588
2003	36,748	25,891	23	25,914	3,119	1,373	24,168	6,675	5,905	34,301	30,682	1,071	594
2004	38,606	27,193	25	27,218	3,286	1,598	25,530	6,778	6,298	35,927	32,182	1,075	602
2005	39,496	27,985	24	28,009	3,403	1,437	26,043	6,904	6,549	36,984	32,912	1,068	606
2006	41,491	29,346	23	29,369	3,592	1,449	27,226	7,479	6,786	39,028	34,584	1,063	611
2007	43,238	29,848	24	29,871	3,700	1,530	27,701	8,101	7,436	40,894	36,070	1,057	618
2008	43,929	29,720	27	29,747	3,750	1,311	27,308	8,359	8,262	41,638	36,862	1,055	609
2009	42,789	28,686	27	28,713	3,692	1,239	26,261	7,565	8,963	40,610	36,879	1,054	588
2010	45,116	30,577	27	30,604	3,791	1,024	27,836	7,746	9,534	42,766	38,786	1,055	586
2011	46,794	31,170	22	31,193	3,498	1,280	28,975	8,201	9,618	44,201	39,518	1,059	592
2012	48,502	32,469	26	32,495	3,581	1,423	30,337	8,675	9,490	45,601	40,987	1,064	593
2013	48,545	33,157	26	33,183	4,116	1,413	30,481	8,435	9,630	45,447	40,340	1,068	602
2014	50,646	34,427	21	34,447	4,290	1,154	31,311	8,977	10,358	47,199	41,846	1,073	613
2015	52,448	35,594	26	35,620	4,494	1,341	32,467	9,399	10,581	48,682	43,054	1,077	627
2016	53,230	36,139	19	36,157	4,616	1,424	32,966	9,640	10,623	49,184	43,411	1,082	634
2017	55,311	37,288	29	37,317	4,769	1,658	34,207	10,093	11,011	50,982	45,125	1,085	639
2018	57,491	38,508	22	38,530	4,933	2,066	35,664	10,515	11,312	52,659	46,888	1,092	649
2019	61,107	39,788	19	39,807	5,086	3,046	37,768	11,447	11,892	55,830	49,627	1,095	651
2020	65,709	40,066	18	40,084	5,089	3,350	38,345	11,474	15,890	59,935	53,569	1,096	616
2021	70,532	42,941	16	42,957	5,405	4,282	41,834	11,757	16,940	64,296	56,767	1,097	639
2022	71,505	46,520	18	46,538	5,921	4,425	45,042	12,262	14,201	65,377	56,289	1,094	...

... = Not available.

Personal Income and Employment by Region and State: South Carolina

(Millions of dollars, except as noted.)

Year	Personal income, total	Earnings by place of work			Less: Contributions for government social insurance	Plus: Adjustment for residence	Equals: Net earnings by place of residence	Plus: Dividends, interest, and rent	Plus: Personal current transfer receipts	Per capita (dollars)		Population (thousands)	Total employment (thousands)
		Nonfarm	Farm	Total						Personal income	Disposable personal income		
1960	3,570	2,898	169	3,068	135	18	2,950	410	210	1,493	1,371	2,392	...
1961	3,748	2,990	196	3,186	138	19	3,067	443	238	1,556	1,427	2,409	...
1962	4,018	3,227	185	3,412	153	23	3,282	484	253	1,658	1,512	2,423	...
1963	4,252	3,433	189	3,621	189	26	3,458	522	272	1,728	1,577	2,460	...
1964	4,567	3,721	180	3,902	203	30	3,729	554	284	1,845	1,697	2,475	...
1965	5,048	4,125	182	4,307	221	35	4,122	616	310	2,024	1,853	2,494	...
1966	5,672	4,720	196	4,916	290	44	4,670	660	342	2,251	2,043	2,520	...
1967	6,121	5,099	197	5,296	342	50	5,004	715	401	2,416	2,193	2,533	...
1968	6,796	5,728	155	5,884	387	58	5,554	771	471	2,656	2,391	2,559	...
1969	7,604	6,260	188	6,448	417	128	6,159	909	537	2,959	2,641	2,570	1,170
1970	8,380	6,753	189	6,942	449	128	6,621	1,090	669	3,225	2,912	2,598	1,196
1971	9,181	7,360	204	7,564	509	138	7,193	1,209	779	3,449	3,120	2,662	1,215
1972	10,309	8,311	214	8,525	600	154	8,080	1,353	876	3,792	3,368	2,718	1,262
1973	11,692	9,405	303	9,708	773	167	9,101	1,547	1,044	4,213	3,758	2,775	1,328
1974	13,235	10,506	342	10,849	898	180	10,131	1,786	1,318	4,655	4,144	2,843	1,365
1975	14,394	11,040	277	11,317	928	191	10,580	2,000	1,814	4,963	4,529	2,900	1,326
1976	16,096	12,610	234	12,844	1,089	225	11,980	2,189	1,927	5,472	4,926	2,941	1,376
1977	17,593	13,900	188	14,088	1,199	247	13,135	2,444	2,013	5,886	5,280	2,989	1,411
1978	19,879	15,746	246	15,993	1,389	264	14,868	2,801	2,210	6,537	5,848	3,041	1,466
1979	22,284	17,625	260	17,885	1,608	286	16,563	3,171	2,549	7,219	6,387	3,087	1,507
1980	24,967	19,452	36	19,488	1,774	318	18,032	3,833	3,103	7,965	7,064	3,135	1,523
1981	28,120	21,429	172	21,601	2,091	348	19,857	4,679	3,584	8,845	7,805	3,179	1,536
1982	29,894	22,212	195	22,406	2,196	381	20,591	5,368	3,935	9,320	8,307	3,208	1,514
1983	32,447	24,358	51	24,408	2,470	392	22,330	5,921	4,196	10,033	8,940	3,234	1,547
1984	36,183	27,185	270	27,455	2,850	425	25,030	6,728	4,425	11,059	9,900	3,272	1,625
1985	38,710	29,037	197	29,233	3,096	477	26,614	7,301	4,794	11,719	10,457	3,303	1,655
1986	41,372	31,238	91	31,329	3,425	543	28,446	7,868	5,058	12,377	11,053	3,343	1,697
1987	44,372	33,735	250	33,985	3,665	586	30,906	8,267	5,199	13,126	11,672	3,381	1,738
1988	48,237	36,871	348	37,219	4,151	610	33,678	9,010	5,549	14,137	12,646	3,412	1,809
1989	52,509	39,458	367	39,825	4,513	571	35,883	10,204	6,423	15,190	13,489	3,457	1,858
1990	56,400	42,562	300	42,862	4,974	507	38,395	10,888	7,116	16,109	14,299	3,501	1,913
1991	58,893	43,801	399	44,200	5,192	494	39,502	11,232	8,159	16,495	14,764	3,570	1,886
1992	62,694	46,512	377	46,889	5,480	504	41,913	11,604	9,177	17,316	15,538	3,620	1,897
1993	65,908	48,866	337	49,203	5,824	520	43,900	12,174	9,835	17,991	16,130	3,663	1,931
1994	69,909	51,258	491	51,749	6,195	636	46,190	13,032	10,688	18,867	16,874	3,705	1,979
1995	74,092	54,047	384	54,431	6,555	767	48,644	14,019	11,430	19,765	17,600	3,749	2,038
1996	78,792	56,777	463	57,241	6,771	878	51,347	15,141	12,303	20,755	18,396	3,796	2,080
1997	83,865	60,342	472	60,814	7,187	1,036	54,663	16,315	12,888	21,728	19,187	3,860	2,141
1998	89,932	65,002	334	65,336	7,734	1,115	58,717	17,667	13,548	22,946	20,203	3,919	2,191
1999	94,454	69,147	403	69,550	8,169	1,203	62,585	17,495	14,374	23,764	20,908	3,975	2,241
2000	101,139	73,288	526	73,814	8,623	1,429	66,621	19,066	15,452	25,133	22,199	4,024	2,280
2001	104,621	74,810	650	75,460	8,877	1,519	68,102	19,274	17,245	25,737	22,782	4,065	2,257
2002	107,552	77,106	230	77,336	9,138	1,557	69,756	19,071	18,726	26,182	23,624	4,108	2,248
2003	111,360	80,021	524	80,545	9,524	1,592	72,612	19,065	19,682	26,832	24,399	4,150	2,264
2004	117,847	83,865	643	84,509	10,011	1,675	76,173	20,388	21,287	27,986	25,488	4,211	2,306
2005	125,050	88,065	639	88,704	10,495	1,869	80,079	22,086	22,885	29,285	26,419	4,270	2,356
2006	135,022	93,883	463	94,346	11,432	2,143	85,057	25,208	24,758	30,984	27,815	4,358	2,419
2007	143,997	98,715	306	99,021	11,953	2,515	89,582	28,061	26,354	32,402	29,017	4,444	2,482
2008	150,518	100,154	445	100,599	12,282	2,598	90,915	29,220	30,383	33,234	30,002	4,529	2,472
2009	146,920	95,769	490	96,259	11,923	2,586	86,921	26,421	33,578	32,010	29,497	4,590	2,368
2010	152,231	98,689	488	99,177	12,136	2,527	89,568	26,305	36,357	32,852	30,235	4,634	2,358
2011	160,767	103,574	367	103,941	11,406	2,564	95,099	28,920	36,749	34,479	31,434	4,663	2,427
2012	169,185	109,874	477	110,351	11,739	2,853	101,464	30,804	36,917	35,989	32,854	4,701	2,453
2013	171,617	112,968	743	113,711	13,581	2,956	103,087	30,604	37,927	36,204	32,727	4,740	2,501
2014	182,833	119,549	240	119,789	14,249	3,112	108,652	33,861	40,320	38,152	34,564	4,792	2,564
2015	194,364	126,360	219	126,578	15,017	3,487	115,048	36,397	42,919	40,053	36,051	4,853	2,637
2016	202,215	130,981	188	131,169	15,557	3,900	119,512	38,424	44,279	41,178	36,944	4,911	2,700
2017	212,325	138,029	296	138,325	16,422	4,079	125,982	40,655	45,688	42,758	38,448	4,966	2,759
2018	221,707	144,180	156	144,336	17,246	4,253	131,343	42,234	48,130	44,155	39,844	5,021	2,843
2019	237,025	151,938	127	152,065	18,261	4,494	138,299	47,496	51,230	46,681	41,917	5,078	2,882
2020	251,946	152,962	103	153,065	18,436	5,149	139,778	47,988	64,180	49,095	44,334	5,132	2,825
2021	272,340	164,567	425	164,992	19,570	5,848	151,270	49,463	71,606	52,441	46,971	5,193	2,905
2022	281,668	179,804	997	180,800	21,668	6,476	165,609	52,406	63,654	53,320	46,720	5,283	...

... = Not available.

Personal Income and Employment by Region and State: South Dakota

(Millions of dollars, except as noted.)

Year	Personal income, total	Derivation of personal income									Per capita (dollars)		Population (thousands)	Total employment (thousands)
		Earnings by place of work			Less: Contributions for government social insurance	Plus: Adjustment for residence	Equals: Net earnings by place of residence	Plus: Dividends, interest, and rent	Plus: Personal current transfer receipts		Personal income	Disposable personal income		
		Nonfarm	Farm	Total										
1960	1,325	752	324	1,076	35	1	1,042	198	86		1,940	1,803	683	...
1961	1,333	823	251	1,074	39	0	1,035	203	94		1,924	1,774	693	...
1962	1,519	877	368	1,246	45	1	1,201	218	100		2,154	1,993	705	...
1963	1,473	889	299	1,188	51	1	1,138	229	106		2,081	1,916	708	...
1964	1,445	932	216	1,148	50	1	1,099	238	109		2,062	1,922	701	...
1965	1,626	963	334	1,298	51	2	1,248	259	119		2,350	2,198	692	...
1966	1,758	1,030	393	1,424	64	2	1,362	267	129		2,574	2,394	683	...
1967	1,786	1,084	344	1,429	77	3	1,354	278	154		2,662	2,472	671	...
1968	1,914	1,174	362	1,536	84	3	1,456	281	177		2,861	2,633	669	...
1969	2,076	1,288	357	1,645	90	6	1,561	321	194		3,108	2,838	668	303
1970	2,257	1,388	373	1,762	95	6	1,672	363	222		3,386	3,126	667	305
1971	2,473	1,518	404	1,921	106	6	1,821	396	255		3,684	3,441	671	306
1972	2,855	1,684	564	2,248	121	7	2,134	439	282		4,215	3,940	677	309
1973	3,605	1,897	1,027	2,924	158	7	2,773	505	327		5,310	4,928	679	323
1974	3,612	2,115	688	2,803	183	8	2,628	602	383		5,313	4,861	680	326
1975	3,972	2,315	707	3,022	200	10	2,832	684	456		5,829	5,411	681	326
1976	3,933	2,624	277	2,901	225	12	2,688	742	503		5,726	5,246	687	336
1977	4,463	2,867	445	3,312	238	13	3,087	846	530		6,477	6,011	689	342
1978	5,143	3,258	616	3,874	274	14	3,614	953	575		7,460	6,880	689	355
1979	5,665	3,590	652	4,242	322	15	3,935	1,081	649		8,222	7,560	689	359
1980	5,713	3,801	137	3,938	342	16	3,612	1,340	761		8,269	7,511	691	353
1981	6,652	4,042	444	4,486	388	13	4,111	1,669	872		9,646	8,789	690	348
1982	7,010	4,167	373	4,540	408	10	4,143	1,899	969		10,151	9,198	691	344
1983	7,271	4,480	255	4,736	440	4	4,299	1,930	1,042		10,491	9,670	693	353
1984	8,272	4,874	689	5,563	491	-2	5,069	2,101	1,102		11,864	11,048	697	362
1985	8,481	5,078	612	5,690	530	-5	5,155	2,154	1,171		12,143	11,284	698	365
1986	8,848	5,322	663	5,985	574	-12	5,400	2,228	1,220		12,711	11,822	696	366
1987	9,336	5,646	843	6,489	618	-19	5,852	2,224	1,260		13,413	12,410	696	381
1988	9,748	6,112	715	6,826	692	-27	6,108	2,322	1,318		13,962	12,909	698	388
1989	10,492	6,549	724	7,273	750	-37	6,485	2,563	1,445		15,060	13,863	697	396
1990	11,485	7,136	1,021	8,157	851	-54	7,252	2,693	1,540		16,475	15,115	697	409
1991	11,967	7,639	894	8,533	916	-68	7,549	2,761	1,656		17,006	15,618	704	420
1992	12,942	8,289	1,074	9,363	976	-85	8,301	2,840	1,800		18,156	16,676	713	431
1993	13,531	8,858	945	9,803	1,035	-100	8,668	2,969	1,895		18,737	17,120	722	442
1994	14,588	9,514	1,211	10,725	1,117	-130	9,477	3,106	2,005		19,962	18,334	731	464
1995	14,884	9,983	640	10,623	1,171	-150	9,302	3,440	2,142		20,169	18,426	738	472
1996	16,445	10,446	1,462	11,908	1,224	-189	10,494	3,689	2,262		22,157	20,310	742	479
1997	16,806	11,025	1,046	12,070	1,292	-186	10,593	3,892	2,321		22,582	20,460	744	485
1998	18,112	11,964	1,167	13,132	1,385	-233	11,514	4,209	2,389		24,277	22,021	746	491
1999	18,990	12,670	1,165	13,835	1,482	-249	12,104	4,403	2,483		25,306	22,834	750	502
2000	20,276	13,332	1,342	14,674	1,568	-267	12,840	4,778	2,658		26,825	24,265	756	512
2001	20,954	13,768	1,153	14,922	1,617	-265	13,040	5,040	2,874		27,645	25,015	758	512
2002	20,955	14,420	501	14,921	1,678	-237	13,006	4,884	3,065		27,572	25,312	760	510
2003	22,890	15,079	1,483	16,562	1,754	-225	14,583	5,143	3,165		29,972	27,908	764	510
2004	24,672	16,124	1,844	17,969	1,847	-221	15,900	5,434	3,338		32,025	29,826	770	518
2005	26,202	17,332	1,552	18,884	1,937	-171	16,775	5,854	3,573		33,788	31,256	775	528
2006	27,640	18,851	611	19,463	2,081	-141	17,240	6,519	3,882		35,299	32,362	783	539
2007	30,674	19,738	1,740	21,478	2,214	-140	19,125	7,388	4,161		38,748	35,492	792	552
2008	32,899	20,397	2,288	22,685	2,322	-104	20,260	7,904	4,735		41,168	37,772	799	561
2009	31,894	20,386	1,792	22,178	2,318	-69	19,792	7,124	4,978		39,518	36,968	807	556
2010	33,804	21,853	1,730	23,584	2,427	-71	21,085	7,341	5,378		41,423	38,681	816	558
2011	36,843	22,209	3,680	25,888	2,225	-113	23,550	7,822	5,470		44,758	41,413	823	566
2012	37,844	23,574	2,524	26,099	2,328	-72	23,699	8,670	5,476		45,442	41,814	833	575
2013	38,366	23,789	3,441	27,230	2,685	-39	24,507	8,253	5,606		45,608	41,737	841	581
2014	40,252	25,676	2,351	28,028	2,843	-22	25,164	9,153	5,936		47,488	43,309	848	589
2015	41,913	27,119	1,627	28,746	2,948	-12	25,787	9,862	6,263		49,186	44,783	852	593
2016	42,337	27,598	1,052	28,650	3,031	-53	25,566	10,254	6,518		49,192	44,765	861	597
2017	43,599	28,403	989	29,392	3,161	-112	26,119	10,676	6,804		50,104	45,896	870	601
2018	45,661	29,604	1,529	31,133	3,289	-126	27,718	10,799	7,145		52,166	48,112	875	610
2019	48,797	31,642	1,426	33,068	3,507	-140	29,421	11,798	7,578		55,294	51,083	883	611
2020	53,622	33,300	2,693	35,993	3,768	-167	32,058	11,923	9,640		60,398	56,154	888	607
2021	57,718	35,440	3,479	38,919	3,957	-210	34,752	12,199	10,767		64,405	59,379	896	622
2022	59,872	38,096	4,054	42,150	4,305	-229	37,616	12,762	9,493		65,806	59,688	910	...

... = Not available.

Personal Income and Employment by Region and State: Tennessee

(Millions of dollars, except as noted.)

Year	Personal income, total	Earnings by place of work			Less: Contributions for government social insurance	Plus: Adjustment for residence	Equals: Net earnings by place of residence	Plus: Dividends, interest, and rent	Plus: Personal current transfer receipts	Per capita (dollars)		Population (thousands)	Total employment (thousands)
		Nonfarm	Farm	Total						Personal income	Disposable personal income		
1960	5,931	4,826	246	5,072	243	31	4,861	666	404	1,659	1,512	3,575	...
1961	6,278	5,025	294	5,319	247	31	5,103	716	459	1,733	1,584	3,622	...
1962	6,668	5,395	254	5,649	273	31	5,406	784	477	1,815	1,633	3,673	...
1963	7,072	5,748	278	6,026	323	31	5,733	836	502	1,902	1,730	3,718	...
1964	7,604	6,251	238	6,490	339	30	6,181	899	525	2,016	1,853	3,771	...
1965	8,287	6,821	254	7,075	363	32	6,744	965	578	2,182	1,996	3,798	...
1966	9,123	7,675	258	7,933	502	34	7,465	1,023	636	2,387	2,164	3,822	...
1967	9,770	8,209	219	8,428	564	51	7,914	1,093	763	2,532	2,302	3,859	...
1968	10,894	9,124	225	9,349	635	50	8,764	1,255	875	2,809	2,523	3,878	...
1969	11,816	9,978	256	10,233	659	-146	9,428	1,410	978	3,032	2,692	3,897	1,789
1970	12,849	10,605	269	10,875	696	-144	10,035	1,618	1,197	3,264	2,920	3,937	1,785
1971	14,188	11,668	267	11,935	789	-155	10,990	1,801	1,397	3,538	3,190	4,010	1,817
1972	15,971	13,224	326	13,550	938	-183	12,429	2,003	1,539	3,906	3,518	4,088	1,924
1973	18,142	14,917	493	15,409	1,211	-166	14,032	2,293	1,817	4,384	3,946	4,138	2,025
1974	20,074	16,415	318	16,733	1,384	-176	15,173	2,680	2,221	4,778	4,299	4,202	2,055
1975	21,894	17,316	250	17,566	1,431	-180	15,955	3,005	2,934	5,138	4,671	4,261	1,983
1976	24,520	19,499	371	19,871	1,640	-173	18,057	3,256	3,207	5,664	5,123	4,329	2,052
1977	27,176	21,943	300	22,242	1,847	-230	20,165	3,644	3,367	6,174	5,586	4,402	2,135
1978	30,979	25,254	319	25,573	2,152	-294	23,127	4,179	3,673	6,943	6,248	4,462	2,227
1979	34,544	27,996	342	28,337	2,482	-348	25,508	4,761	4,276	7,620	6,843	4,533	2,279
1980	38,078	30,027	197	30,224	2,668	-416	27,139	5,780	5,159	8,277	7,420	4,600	2,259
1981	42,383	32,695	360	33,055	3,136	-446	29,473	7,064	5,846	9,159	8,207	4,628	2,255
1982	45,046	33,928	302	34,230	3,331	-404	30,495	8,137	6,415	9,696	8,732	4,646	2,217
1983	48,057	36,658	-33	36,625	3,652	-417	32,555	8,614	6,888	10,313	9,312	4,660	2,239
1984	53,481	40,665	412	41,078	4,190	-443	36,444	9,826	7,211	11,411	10,362	4,687	2,344
1985	57,208	43,854	335	44,190	4,589	-469	39,132	10,412	7,664	12,132	10,972	4,715	2,399
1986	61,216	47,325	241	47,567	5,066	-505	41,996	10,992	8,228	12,918	11,699	4,739	2,477
1987	65,941	51,556	305	51,861	5,474	-534	45,853	11,420	8,667	13,787	12,430	4,783	2,578
1988	71,646	56,016	389	56,405	6,108	-546	49,751	12,578	9,317	14,857	13,460	4,822	2,663
1989	76,928	59,415	443	59,858	6,569	-571	52,719	13,952	10,257	15,847	14,304	4,854	2,735
1990	81,784	62,856	443	63,299	7,002	-629	55,668	14,762	11,354	16,709	15,129	4,894	2,777
1991	86,009	65,826	510	66,336	7,455	-622	58,258	14,837	12,914	17,318	15,736	4,967	2,778
1992	94,053	72,205	665	72,871	8,067	-483	64,321	15,202	14,529	18,625	16,930	5,050	2,837
1993	100,092	77,302	593	77,895	8,654	-596	68,646	15,864	15,582	19,482	17,691	5,138	2,943
1994	106,497	82,665	655	83,320	9,401	-687	73,232	16,917	16,348	20,357	18,430	5,231	3,061
1995	114,365	88,262	441	88,703	10,015	-767	77,920	18,518	17,926	21,469	19,406	5,327	3,145
1996	120,799	93,021	393	93,414	10,377	-785	82,252	19,671	18,876	22,301	20,051	5,417	3,195
1997	127,953	99,351	381	99,732	11,008	-1,031	87,694	20,636	19,624	23,267	20,856	5,499	3,269
1998	139,897	110,098	205	110,304	11,708	-1,175	97,421	21,984	20,492	25,116	22,556	5,570	3,340
1999	145,517	115,549	57	115,607	12,361	-1,359	101,887	22,253	21,377	25,807	23,182	5,639	3,397
2000	154,379	121,594	328	121,922	12,928	-1,550	107,445	23,739	23,195	27,066	24,367	5,704	3,459
2001	158,385	123,577	461	124,038	13,337	-1,563	109,138	23,956	25,290	27,541	24,772	5,751	3,421
2002	162,942	128,463	89	128,552	13,952	-1,548	113,052	22,765	27,126	28,113	25,758	5,796	3,409
2003	170,160	133,344	198	133,541	14,456	-1,555	117,531	23,838	28,791	29,098	26,867	5,848	3,433
2004	180,115	141,709	383	142,092	15,257	-1,639	125,196	24,296	30,624	30,472	28,219	5,911	3,508
2005	189,004	147,085	545	147,630	15,889	-1,454	130,287	25,952	32,764	31,548	29,027	5,991	3,572
2006	201,325	155,875	276	156,151	16,748	-1,382	138,021	28,706	34,598	33,065	30,184	6,089	3,644
2007	210,987	160,680	-110	160,570	17,529	-1,482	141,559	31,388	38,040	34,164	31,101	6,176	3,702
2008	219,027	161,821	245	162,066	17,986	-1,383	142,697	33,558	42,772	35,059	32,127	6,247	3,677
2009	217,219	158,807	319	159,126	17,639	-968	140,519	30,679	46,020	34,446	32,261	6,306	3,524
2010	227,883	164,455	117	164,572	17,983	-747	145,842	31,631	50,411	35,851	33,498	6,356	3,516
2011	241,618	173,088	520	173,608	16,678	-760	156,171	34,060	51,386	37,727	34,963	6,404	3,589
2012	254,471	183,524	343	183,867	17,199	-1,073	165,595	36,987	51,889	39,373	36,518	6,463	3,635
2013	256,754	187,617	1,026	188,643	19,853	-1,241	167,549	35,777	53,429	39,454	36,320	6,508	3,689
2014	267,289	196,478	402	196,880	20,600	-1,197	175,083	38,137	54,069	40,753	37,421	6,559	3,772
2015	281,281	206,717	359	207,076	21,642	-1,318	184,117	40,314	56,850	42,535	38,879	6,613	3,860
2016	290,240	214,333	-13	214,320	22,455	-1,591	190,274	41,882	58,084	43,499	39,636	6,672	3,952
2017	302,462	223,664	44	223,708	23,726	-1,753	198,229	44,455	59,778	44,879	41,076	6,739	4,033
2018	319,022	235,480	-312	235,168	24,856	-1,960	208,353	47,849	62,821	46,870	43,141	6,807	4,119
2019	338,609	246,844	34	246,878	26,162	-2,315	218,401	53,518	66,690	49,343	45,418	6,862	4,169
2020	362,278	254,857	-49	254,807	27,307	-2,281	225,220	53,479	83,580	52,310	48,356	6,926	4,121
2021	394,520	278,801	597	279,398	28,769	-2,557	248,072	54,568	91,880	56,616	51,767	6,968	4,249
2022	410,945	306,835	1,032	307,867	31,537	-2,898	273,432	58,216	79,297	58,279	52,262	7,051	...

... = Not available.

Personal Income and Employment by Region and State: Texas

(Millions of dollars, except as noted.)

Year	Personal income, total	Earnings by place of work — Nonfarm	Earnings by place of work — Farm	Earnings by place of work — Total	Less: Contributions for government social insurance	Plus: Adjustment for residence	Equals: Net earnings by place of residence	Plus: Dividends, interest, and rent	Plus: Personal current transfer receipts	Per capita (dollars) — Personal income	Per capita (dollars) — Disposable personal income	Population (thousands)	Total employment (thousands)
1960	19,438	15,184	924	16,108	677	16	15,447	2,993	998	2,020	1,819	9,624	...
1961	20,546	15,886	1,090	16,976	696	16	16,296	3,127	1,122	2,092	1,884	9,820	...
1962	21,582	16,829	950	17,779	749	17	17,047	3,314	1,222	2,147	1,928	10,053	...
1963	22,539	17,705	783	18,488	832	18	17,674	3,544	1,321	2,219	1,990	10,159	...
1964	24,171	19,143	728	19,871	877	18	19,012	3,788	1,371	2,354	2,144	10,270	...
1965	26,017	20,524	865	21,389	930	19	20,478	4,040	1,498	2,507	2,278	10,378	...
1966	28,469	22,842	920	23,762	1,259	17	22,519	4,320	1,630	2,713	2,444	10,492	...
1967	31,101	25,190	778	25,969	1,461	15	24,522	4,610	1,969	2,934	2,637	10,599	...
1968	34,654	28,151	910	29,061	1,634	14	27,441	4,853	2,360	3,203	2,845	10,819	...
1969	38,575	31,449	927	32,376	2,012	-79	30,285	5,646	2,644	3,493	3,073	11,045	5,005
1970	42,497	33,860	1,168	35,027	2,149	-96	32,782	6,575	3,139	3,782	3,370	11,237	5,045
1971	46,116	36,677	1,015	37,692	2,399	-101	35,192	7,258	3,667	4,007	3,611	11,510	5,123
1972	51,173	40,672	1,257	41,929	2,783	-126	39,020	8,037	4,116	4,352	3,880	11,759	5,334
1973	58,113	45,624	2,145	47,768	3,608	-154	44,007	9,156	4,950	4,835	4,320	12,019	5,608
1974	65,532	52,116	1,157	53,272	4,249	-131	48,893	10,735	5,904	5,342	4,728	12,268	5,822
1975	74,747	58,845	1,314	60,159	4,721	-127	55,311	12,055	7,380	5,947	5,332	12,568	5,938
1976	84,228	67,476	1,292	68,768	5,513	-91	63,164	12,991	8,073	6,528	5,809	12,903	6,207
1977	93,979	76,304	1,280	77,583	6,290	-303	70,990	14,401	8,588	7,124	6,285	13,192	6,521
1978	108,293	88,884	1,030	89,914	7,501	-424	81,989	16,745	9,560	8,023	7,086	13,498	6,900
1979	124,678	102,202	1,741	103,943	9,047	-442	94,455	19,319	10,903	8,978	7,831	13,887	7,215
1980	143,140	117,125	620	117,744	10,466	-546	106,732	23,638	12,770	9,983	8,662	14,338	7,496
1981	168,292	135,846	1,963	137,810	13,078	-334	124,398	29,390	14,505	11,413	9,800	14,746	7,900
1982	185,543	147,110	1,354	148,463	14,470	-405	133,589	35,441	16,514	12,102	10,517	15,331	8,074
1983	198,084	153,753	1,741	155,493	15,035	-388	140,071	39,372	18,640	12,575	11,141	15,752	8,064
1984	216,834	168,331	1,628	169,959	16,887	-445	152,627	44,389	19,818	13,546	12,061	16,007	8,434
1985	233,562	180,199	1,500	181,698	18,295	-474	162,930	49,456	21,176	14,353	12,786	16,273	8,674
1986	238,934	183,168	1,275	184,443	18,420	-435	165,588	50,129	23,217	14,427	12,993	16,561	8,514
1987	243,559	186,375	2,081	188,456	18,487	-431	169,538	49,609	24,412	14,653	13,146	16,622	8,723
1988	258,240	198,583	2,312	200,896	20,385	-437	180,074	52,497	25,669	15,494	13,976	16,667	8,880
1989	275,917	210,747	2,242	212,989	21,806	-446	190,737	56,931	28,248	16,417	14,722	16,807	9,005
1990	297,726	227,961	3,047	231,008	23,239	-485	207,284	58,829	31,613	17,455	15,646	17,057	9,243
1991	311,370	239,956	2,770	242,726	25,081	-563	217,083	59,148	35,140	17,897	16,120	17,398	9,404
1992	336,646	258,670	3,370	262,040	26,705	-586	234,749	60,341	41,556	18,956	17,156	17,760	9,483
1993	356,399	274,904	3,993	278,898	28,325	-607	249,966	61,965	44,468	19,624	17,741	18,162	9,781
1994	376,614	290,896	3,444	294,340	30,353	-671	263,316	65,490	47,808	20,287	18,322	18,564	10,098
1995	402,805	309,999	2,778	312,777	32,365	-753	279,659	71,194	51,952	21,246	19,149	18,959	10,440
1996	433,165	334,765	2,408	337,172	34,406	-823	301,943	75,651	55,571	22,397	20,052	19,340	10,738
1997	472,178	368,835	3,055	371,890	37,474	-963	333,453	80,560	58,166	23,919	21,266	19,740	11,165
1998	515,147	406,992	2,835	409,827	40,840	-1,058	367,928	87,823	59,396	25,556	22,627	20,158	11,542
1999	545,418	433,199	4,277	437,477	43,360	-1,083	393,034	91,250	61,135	26,530	23,509	20,558	11,761
2000	594,466	473,046	3,347	476,393	46,650	-1,180	428,562	101,117	64,787	28,383	25,024	20,944	12,139
2001	631,991	504,687	3,987	508,674	49,028	-1,185	458,461	102,569	70,962	29,644	26,294	21,320	12,285
2002	640,382	508,861	3,970	512,831	49,636	-1,135	462,061	100,261	78,060	29,524	26,815	21,690	12,292
2003	665,861	522,686	5,272	527,957	51,832	-1,060	475,066	107,298	83,498	30,224	27,715	22,031	12,375
2004	698,584	548,613	5,321	553,935	54,535	-978	498,422	112,122	88,041	31,195	28,690	22,394	12,588
2005	757,969	586,757	4,971	591,728	58,075	-948	532,705	127,709	97,554	33,276	30,233	22,778	13,004
2006	832,292	645,806	3,246	649,053	62,120	-1,034	585,899	142,165	104,228	35,630	32,160	23,360	13,493
2007	883,810	676,574	3,601	680,175	66,492	-1,121	612,562	156,726	114,522	37,085	33,367	23,832	14,008
2008	971,051	724,203	1,229	725,432	69,843	-1,190	654,399	186,424	130,228	39,946	35,692	24,309	14,366
2009	924,344	687,367	922	688,288	69,361	-1,396	617,532	164,026	142,786	37,269	34,445	24,802	14,203
2010	985,165	727,600	3,270	730,870	72,174	-1,528	657,168	169,383	158,615	39,034	35,953	25,239	14,263
2011	1,077,403	788,031	2,764	790,795	67,989	-1,840	720,966	192,215	164,222	42,037	38,238	25,630	14,681
2012	1,152,725	845,888	2,618	848,506	72,070	-2,208	774,228	214,785	163,712	44,241	40,288	26,056	15,096
2013	1,184,841	883,344	5,210	888,554	85,197	-2,397	800,959	214,339	169,542	44,816	40,449	26,438	15,530
2014	1,274,637	947,937	4,466	952,404	90,377	-2,463	859,563	237,006	178,068	47,370	42,644	26,908	16,001
2015	1,300,510	955,208	6,752	961,960	94,470	-2,452	865,038	245,488	189,984	47,465	42,685	27,399	16,415
2016	1,296,481	956,200	2,919	959,119	96,841	-2,150	860,128	236,753	199,599	46,586	42,224	27,830	16,683
2017	1,387,923	1,021,018	3,705	1,024,723	102,437	-1,890	920,395	262,827	204,701	49,231	44,335	28,192	17,105
2018	1,482,714	1,091,995	2,936	1,094,932	107,506	-1,993	985,433	282,988	214,293	52,005	47,393	28,511	17,607
2019	1,560,504	1,138,647	3,059	1,141,706	112,838	-2,394	1,026,475	307,860	226,169	54,076	49,127	28,858	17,903
2020	1,624,526	1,126,909	3,491	1,130,401	114,081	-2,174	1,014,146	304,654	305,726	55,573	50,599	29,232	17,707
2021	1,767,682	1,216,407	4,974	1,221,381	122,172	-2,174	1,097,035	321,300	349,346	59,802	53,846	29,559	18,276
2022	1,861,396	1,356,756	6,414	1,363,170	137,620	-2,673	1,222,877	343,125	295,394	61,985	54,488	30,030	...

... = Not available.

Personal Income and Employment by Region and State: Utah

(Millions of dollars, except as noted.)

Year	Personal income, total	Earnings by place of work			Less: Contributions for government social insurance	Plus: Adjustment for residence	Equals: Net earnings by place of residence	Plus: Dividends, interest, and rent	Plus: Personal current transfer receipts	Per capita (dollars)		Population (thousands)	Total employment (thousands)
		Nonfarm	Farm	Total						Personal income	Disposable personal income		
1960	1,910	1,545	44	1,589	75	1	1,515	289	105	2,122	1,917	900	...
1961	2,047	1,665	35	1,700	79	1	1,621	309	117	2,187	1,972	936	...
1962	2,228	1,805	54	1,858	87	1	1,772	334	122	2,326	2,103	958	...
1963	2,315	1,904	41	1,945	105	1	1,841	343	132	2,377	2,146	974	...
1964	2,437	1,990	30	2,020	106	1	1,915	382	141	2,492	2,280	978	...
1965	2,583	2,079	47	2,127	109	1	2,019	412	152	2,599	2,381	994	...
1966	2,751	2,241	49	2,290	144	1	2,147	442	162	2,727	2,487	1,009	...
1967	2,904	2,356	63	2,419	159	1	2,262	451	191	2,849	2,592	1,019	...
1968	3,112	2,541	67	2,608	175	1	2,434	457	220	3,024	2,720	1,029	...
1969	3,407	2,751	74	2,825	175	4	2,654	505	248	3,254	2,895	1,047	444
1970	3,791	3,024	78	3,101	190	2	2,913	580	299	3,558	3,201	1,066	455
1971	4,243	3,363	77	3,440	218	2	3,224	666	352	3,855	3,495	1,101	467
1972	4,741	3,764	88	3,852	260	4	3,597	743	402	4,179	3,768	1,135	494
1973	5,283	4,198	130	4,328	338	7	3,997	814	472	4,520	4,070	1,169	523
1974	5,910	4,724	97	4,820	395	10	4,435	937	538	4,930	4,430	1,199	545
1975	6,591	5,232	67	5,299	432	13	4,880	1,037	673	5,341	4,854	1,234	553
1976	7,464	5,992	74	6,066	502	16	5,580	1,152	732	5,866	5,262	1,272	580
1977	8,441	6,842	64	6,906	575	21	6,351	1,301	788	6,412	5,733	1,316	613
1978	9,712	7,880	72	7,952	678	25	7,299	1,535	878	7,119	6,354	1,364	651
1979	10,972	8,911	82	8,993	810	33	8,216	1,757	999	7,748	6,877	1,416	678
1980	12,319	9,851	60	9,911	902	49	9,059	2,082	1,179	8,366	7,446	1,473	687
1981	13,893	11,026	42	11,067	1,088	53	10,032	2,480	1,381	9,167	8,116	1,515	697
1982	15,067	11,725	46	11,771	1,176	53	10,648	2,833	1,587	9,669	8,545	1,558	707
1983	16,135	12,479	36	12,515	1,267	43	11,291	3,115	1,729	10,116	9,048	1,595	719
1984	17,820	13,871	57	13,928	1,448	39	12,519	3,519	1,783	10,984	9,875	1,622	761
1985	19,070	14,844	57	14,901	1,578	41	13,364	3,771	1,936	11,607	10,406	1,643	789
1986	20,042	15,517	87	15,604	1,658	35	13,982	3,966	2,094	12,053	10,800	1,663	801
1987	20,995	16,182	130	16,313	1,723	26	14,616	4,135	2,244	12,511	11,172	1,678	830
1988	22,330	17,307	208	17,516	1,936	24	15,604	4,382	2,344	13,218	11,824	1,689	865
1989	23,967	18,536	205	18,741	2,115	22	16,648	4,731	2,588	14,050	12,584	1,706	897
1990	25,985	20,280	252	20,533	2,390	17	18,160	4,985	2,840	15,010	13,286	1,731	938
1991	27,864	21,905	233	22,138	2,619	12	19,530	5,197	3,137	15,656	13,941	1,780	961
1992	30,126	23,826	279	24,106	2,832	7	21,281	5,365	3,480	16,401	14,609	1,837	979
1993	32,491	25,763	300	26,063	3,077	7	22,993	5,723	3,775	17,115	15,208	1,898	1,026
1994	35,157	28,088	219	28,307	3,388	7	24,927	6,341	3,889	17,933	15,841	1,960	1,102
1995	38,308	30,417	166	30,583	3,687	0	26,896	7,193	4,219	19,019	16,738	2,014	1,150
1996	41,739	32,992	173	33,164	3,920	0	29,245	8,028	4,467	20,183	17,724	2,068	1,218
1997	45,125	35,831	198	36,029	4,202	-0	31,827	8,655	4,644	21,288	18,649	2,120	1,270
1998	48,228	38,426	232	38,658	4,484	-4	34,170	9,211	4,847	22,266	19,481	2,166	1,310
1999	50,859	40,937	240	41,177	4,730	-1	36,445	9,295	5,119	23,081	20,164	2,203	1,338
2000	54,451	43,537	207	43,744	5,046	5	38,703	10,249	5,499	24,260	21,186	2,245	1,381
2001	56,923	45,270	317	45,587	5,292	-0	40,295	10,596	6,031	24,925	21,900	2,284	1,392
2002	58,563	46,406	201	46,607	5,427	-2	41,177	10,785	6,601	25,190	22,598	2,325	1,395
2003	60,873	47,944	214	48,157	5,651	1	42,507	11,340	7,025	25,792	23,317	2,360	1,406
2004	64,887	51,568	307	51,875	6,128	2	45,748	11,700	7,439	27,018	24,468	2,402	1,453
2005	71,095	55,763	268	56,031	6,639	15	49,408	13,578	8,110	28,927	25,807	2,458	1,518
2006	79,116	62,511	147	62,658	7,282	19	55,396	14,910	8,811	31,327	27,752	2,526	1,593
2007	86,153	67,087	186	67,273	7,829	16	59,459	17,092	9,602	33,165	29,258	2,598	1,676
2008	90,387	68,359	193	68,551	8,022	33	60,563	18,610	11,214	33,941	30,297	2,663	1,688
2009	86,762	65,471	109	65,580	7,768	7	57,818	16,534	12,410	31,858	29,018	2,723	1,634
2010	89,439	66,726	218	66,943	7,863	1	59,081	16,591	13,767	32,218	29,399	2,776	1,621
2011	96,357	70,697	364	71,061	7,464	-1	63,596	18,541	14,220	34,190	30,931	2,818	1,664
2012	102,991	76,135	330	76,465	7,854	16	68,627	20,253	14,111	36,005	32,465	2,860	1,706
2013	106,176	79,862	536	80,398	9,302	27	71,124	20,462	14,591	36,511	32,639	2,908	1,753
2014	112,620	84,204	617	84,822	9,791	34	75,064	22,453	15,103	38,168	34,072	2,951	1,804
2015	121,339	89,814	610	90,424	10,232	8	80,200	25,083	16,057	40,459	35,953	2,999	1,866
2016	127,881	94,755	365	95,121	10,759	-28	84,334	26,769	16,779	41,750	36,965	3,063	1,933
2017	135,162	100,101	369	100,469	11,412	-34	89,024	28,899	17,239	43,241	38,397	3,126	1,995
2018	145,256	107,915	348	108,263	12,016	-31	96,217	30,705	18,334	45,665	40,587	3,181	2,070
2019	157,045	116,028	401	116,429	12,781	-49	103,599	33,496	19,950	48,580	43,013	3,233	2,103
2020	171,385	124,484	435	124,919	13,747	-101	111,070	34,494	25,821	52,191	46,489	3,284	2,135
2021	186,991	134,810	433	135,243	14,769	-143	120,331	36,162	30,498	56,000	49,084	3,339	2,229
2022	195,834	147,774	559	148,333	16,318	-169	131,846	38,674	25,314	57,925	49,632	3,381	...

... = Not available.

Personal Income and Employment by Region and State: Vermont

(Millions of dollars, except as noted.)

Year	Personal income, total	Earnings by place of work			Less: Contributions for government social insurance	Plus: Adjustment for residence	Equals: Net earnings by place of residence	Plus: Dividends, interest, and rent	Plus: Personal current transfer receipts	Per capita (dollars)		Population (thousands)	Total employment (thousands)
		Nonfarm	Farm	Total						Personal income	Disposable personal income		
1960	768	574	56	630	27	-6	597	112	59	1,975	1,781	389	...
1961	801	587	56	643	28	-5	609	124	67	2,053	1,855	390	...
1962	841	627	46	673	31	-5	637	134	70	2,139	1,933	393	...
1963	871	655	43	698	36	-5	657	140	75	2,195	1,963	397	...
1964	934	694	49	744	38	-5	700	156	77	2,340	2,110	399	...
1965	1,022	771	45	816	41	-8	767	174	81	2,530	2,297	404	...
1966	1,160	886	59	945	58	-10	877	196	87	2,808	2,513	413	...
1967	1,256	964	46	1,010	71	-10	929	219	107	2,969	2,654	423	...
1968	1,382	1,050	51	1,101	74	-11	1,016	240	126	3,215	2,844	430	...
1969	1,515	1,170	58	1,228	83	-27	1,118	254	144	3,468	3,019	437	203
1970	1,664	1,259	62	1,321	89	-26	1,205	287	172	3,728	3,265	446	205
1971	1,802	1,339	61	1,400	98	-24	1,278	319	205	3,967	3,570	454	206
1972	1,989	1,467	68	1,536	111	-21	1,404	355	230	4,294	3,797	463	211
1973	2,184	1,619	72	1,691	141	-20	1,531	391	262	4,661	4,168	469	220
1974	2,364	1,725	59	1,784	155	-16	1,613	436	315	4,996	4,469	473	222
1975	2,592	1,823	61	1,884	162	-11	1,711	479	401	5,401	4,857	480	220
1976	2,876	2,044	78	2,122	184	-5	1,933	511	432	5,928	5,356	485	228
1977	3,120	2,244	66	2,310	203	-1	2,105	572	442	6,339	5,679	492	236
1978	3,573	2,614	95	2,709	244	-1	2,464	642	467	7,171	6,417	498	252
1979	4,015	2,934	105	3,039	284	6	2,761	724	530	7,940	7,057	506	261
1980	4,505	3,191	108	3,299	309	15	3,005	872	629	8,790	7,782	513	266
1981	5,069	3,503	123	3,627	364	18	3,281	1,064	725	9,832	8,670	516	270
1982	5,502	3,699	123	3,822	392	24	3,454	1,242	807	10,600	9,448	519	271
1983	5,908	4,039	83	4,122	430	23	3,714	1,329	864	11,289	10,092	523	277
1984	6,496	4,469	84	4,553	489	29	4,092	1,514	890	12,335	11,053	527	289
1985	7,041	4,905	101	5,006	548	30	4,488	1,625	929	13,284	11,842	530	300
1986	7,574	5,352	99	5,452	602	34	4,884	1,733	957	14,182	12,584	534	311
1987	8,218	5,924	124	6,048	656	42	5,434	1,812	971	15,210	13,386	540	320
1988	8,977	6,505	121	6,626	742	47	5,931	2,021	1,025	16,328	14,441	550	334
1989	9,917	7,045	123	7,168	798	51	6,420	2,375	1,121	17,782	15,677	558	341
1990	10,298	7,306	115	7,421	870	52	6,603	2,444	1,251	18,233	16,108	565	341
1991	10,499	7,399	104	7,503	890	60	6,672	2,449	1,379	18,465	16,422	569	334
1992	11,242	7,887	177	8,064	937	68	7,195	2,487	1,560	19,627	17,517	573	342
1993	11,681	8,284	128	8,412	986	78	7,503	2,549	1,629	20,218	18,034	578	349
1994	12,247	8,650	129	8,780	1,043	93	7,829	2,693	1,725	20,977	18,739	584	359
1995	12,890	8,974	100	9,074	1,100	106	8,081	2,940	1,870	21,885	19,561	589	362
1996	13,586	9,436	147	9,583	1,144	122	8,561	3,093	1,932	22,883	20,318	594	367
1997	14,333	9,950	110	10,060	1,197	146	9,009	3,290	2,034	23,999	21,136	597	373
1998	15,427	10,699	136	10,835	1,266	174	9,743	3,567	2,117	25,693	22,559	600	381
1999	16,304	11,544	146	11,690	1,343	196	10,542	3,498	2,264	26,963	23,642	605	390
2000	17,688	12,534	150	12,685	1,435	227	11,477	3,774	2,437	29,014	25,338	610	401
2001	18,805	13,357	149	13,507	1,523	237	12,221	3,911	2,673	30,716	27,015	612	404
2002	19,212	13,856	115	13,971	1,552	235	12,654	3,703	2,856	31,217	27,941	615	406
2003	19,980	14,323	146	14,469	1,620	251	13,100	3,891	2,989	32,338	29,331	618	406
2004	21,131	15,123	194	15,317	1,709	238	13,845	4,163	3,123	34,087	30,987	620	413
2005	21,667	15,593	198	15,791	1,795	250	14,246	4,020	3,401	34,878	31,350	621	417
2006	23,052	16,157	121	16,278	1,884	281	14,675	4,598	3,780	37,008	33,076	623	421
2007	24,281	16,611	221	16,831	1,991	291	15,132	4,969	4,181	38,944	34,623	623	425
2008	25,604	17,133	229	17,362	2,054	286	15,593	5,350	4,661	41,022	36,682	624	424
2009	25,292	17,008	125	17,134	2,032	332	15,433	4,800	5,058	40,479	37,161	625	414
2010	26,140	17,625	193	17,818	2,065	330	16,083	4,709	5,348	41,733	38,284	626	413
2011	27,691	18,343	263	18,607	1,931	305	16,981	5,313	5,397	43,982	39,858	630	417
2012	28,554	18,856	255	19,111	2,005	313	17,419	5,611	5,525	45,277	41,167	631	422
2013	28,964	19,236	295	19,531	2,326	338	17,543	5,625	5,796	45,770	41,223	633	425
2014	30,196	19,485	352	19,837	2,427	371	17,780	6,359	6,057	47,641	42,849	634	429
2015	31,079	20,109	210	20,319	2,523	371	18,166	6,660	6,253	48,876	43,824	636	433
2016	31,576	20,465	178	20,643	2,581	378	18,440	6,761	6,375	49,621	44,406	636	434
2017	32,446	21,152	208	21,360	2,688	419	19,091	6,891	6,463	50,771	45,495	639	436
2018	33,577	21,916	143	22,060	2,755	431	19,735	7,100	6,742	52,409	47,182	641	438
2019	35,585	22,631	240	22,871	2,793	494	20,572	7,957	7,056	55,442	49,718	642	434
2020	38,098	22,900	199	23,099	2,848	544	20,794	7,890	9,413	59,260	53,290	643	409
2021	39,949	24,358	182	24,540	2,910	658	22,288	8,101	9,561	61,748	54,658	647	420
2022	40,898	26,416	296	26,712	3,152	657	24,216	8,467	8,215	63,206	54,714	647	...

... = Not available.

Personal Income and Employment by Region and State: Virginia

(Millions of dollars, except as noted.)

Year	Personal income, total	Earnings by place of work			Less: Contributions for government social insurance	Plus: Adjustment for residence	Equals: Net earnings by place of residence	Plus: Dividends, interest, and rent	Plus: Personal current transfer receipts	Per capita (dollars)		Population (thousands)	Total employment (thousands)
		Nonfarm	Farm	Total						Personal income	Disposable personal income		
1960	8,173	6,217	214	6,432	268	467	6,631	1,170	373	2,050	1,837	3,986	...
1961	8,706	6,557	225	6,782	284	500	6,998	1,280	428	2,126	1,911	4,095	...
1962	9,396	7,075	222	7,297	318	553	7,532	1,411	452	2,248	2,010	4,180	...
1963	10,107	7,687	136	7,823	370	611	8,064	1,558	485	2,364	2,097	4,276	...
1964	11,151	8,410	222	8,632	384	664	8,912	1,728	512	2,559	2,312	4,357	...
1965	12,038	9,029	208	9,237	403	748	9,581	1,896	560	2,729	2,453	4,411	...
1966	13,027	9,948	156	10,104	544	827	10,387	2,029	610	2,923	2,608	4,456	...
1967	14,251	10,760	201	10,961	633	988	11,316	2,201	734	3,161	2,815	4,508	...
1968	15,768	12,027	178	12,205	700	1,064	12,569	2,344	855	3,459	3,057	4,558	...
1969	17,848	13,676	213	13,889	799	991	14,080	2,789	979	3,868	3,361	4,614	2,148
1970	19,372	14,675	213	14,889	869	909	14,928	3,264	1,180	4,157	3,633	4,660	2,158
1971	21,411	16,168	193	16,362	999	947	16,310	3,688	1,413	4,505	3,975	4,753	2,196
1972	23,764	17,994	254	18,248	1,166	1,003	18,085	4,058	1,622	4,922	4,286	4,828	2,263
1973	26,613	20,139	355	20,494	1,483	1,081	20,092	4,584	1,938	5,424	4,752	4,907	2,384
1974	29,490	22,172	316	22,488	1,701	1,189	21,976	5,212	2,302	5,924	5,150	4,978	2,451
1975	32,380	23,842	266	24,108	1,822	1,457	23,743	5,689	2,948	6,404	5,688	5,056	2,425
1976	35,771	26,494	237	26,731	2,071	1,684	26,344	6,198	3,229	6,969	6,147	5,133	2,501
1977	39,631	29,463	169	29,633	2,302	1,907	29,238	6,931	3,463	7,613	6,675	5,206	2,585
1978	44,990	33,182	291	33,473	2,624	2,313	33,162	8,005	3,824	8,514	7,427	5,284	2,698
1979	50,182	36,945	157	37,102	3,054	2,734	36,783	9,012	4,388	9,425	8,203	5,325	2,767
1980	56,727	40,771	69	40,840	3,380	3,317	40,776	10,726	5,224	10,567	9,189	5,368	2,797
1981	63,698	45,128	271	45,399	4,013	3,413	44,799	12,870	6,029	11,700	10,106	5,444	2,812
1982	68,855	48,523	122	48,645	4,369	3,433	47,709	14,559	6,586	12,535	10,900	5,493	2,824
1983	74,239	53,033	45	53,078	4,945	3,378	51,511	15,607	7,120	13,341	11,712	5,565	2,897
1984	82,638	59,187	328	59,515	5,702	3,575	57,388	17,719	7,531	14,642	12,932	5,644	3,041
1985	89,308	64,824	231	65,055	6,436	3,698	62,316	18,945	8,048	15,627	13,717	5,715	3,181
1986	96,342	70,638	277	70,915	7,279	3,821	67,457	20,353	8,531	16,577	14,558	5,812	3,316
1987	104,064	77,372	371	77,743	7,981	3,935	73,697	21,507	8,860	17,542	15,282	5,932	3,480
1988	113,917	84,771	523	85,293	9,002	4,328	80,620	23,823	9,474	18,870	16,542	6,037	3,558
1989	123,237	90,578	643	91,221	9,746	4,562	86,037	26,824	10,376	20,136	17,574	6,120	3,655
1990	129,558	94,416	687	95,103	10,317	5,196	89,982	28,313	11,263	20,840	18,255	6,217	3,700
1991	135,042	97,909	622	98,531	10,808	5,629	93,352	29,248	12,442	21,431	18,873	6,301	3,642
1992	143,669	104,131	672	104,803	11,444	6,032	99,391	30,284	13,994	22,398	19,780	6,414	3,657
1993	150,973	109,183	544	109,727	12,027	6,344	104,045	32,129	14,800	23,192	20,440	6,510	3,730
1994	158,883	114,674	644	115,318	12,719	6,269	108,867	34,343	15,673	24,098	21,173	6,593	3,813
1995	167,003	119,719	567	120,286	13,264	6,376	113,398	36,631	16,975	25,035	21,972	6,671	3,903
1996	175,342	126,233	570	126,802	13,952	5,925	118,776	38,627	17,940	25,973	22,684	6,751	3,983
1997	186,846	135,316	425	135,742	14,948	6,482	127,276	41,006	18,564	27,360	23,782	6,829	4,082
1998	200,073	147,092	419	147,511	16,045	6,211	137,677	43,182	19,213	28,992	24,857	6,901	4,168
1999	214,461	159,093	326	159,419	17,282	7,922	150,058	44,154	20,249	30,637	26,061	7,000	4,261
2000	232,470	174,742	568	175,310	18,641	6,063	162,731	48,048	21,690	32,715	27,844	7,106	4,399
2001	244,754	184,178	488	184,667	19,664	6,575	171,577	49,039	24,137	34,001	29,006	7,198	4,417
2002	251,380	188,769	377	189,146	20,320	8,079	176,906	48,878	25,596	34,498	30,202	7,287	4,422
2003	266,598	199,635	284	199,919	21,347	8,775	187,348	51,803	27,447	36,188	31,997	7,367	4,467
2004	285,113	216,281	548	216,829	23,262	9,241	202,808	53,322	28,983	38,139	33,810	7,476	4,587
2005	304,350	230,067	591	230,658	24,881	9,508	215,286	57,465	31,599	40,167	35,240	7,577	4,701
2006	325,252	241,488	293	241,780	26,494	10,809	226,095	64,595	34,561	42,385	37,023	7,674	4,782
2007	342,963	251,271	258	251,529	27,640	11,417	235,306	70,863	36,794	44,248	38,557	7,751	4,869
2008	356,536	255,377	400	255,777	28,546	13,258	240,489	73,714	42,334	45,514	39,698	7,833	4,870
2009	349,429	252,926	372	253,298	28,610	13,084	237,771	66,248	45,409	44,087	39,463	7,926	4,758
2010	365,246	263,616	356	263,972	29,525	14,598	249,045	66,617	49,584	45,513	40,631	8,025	4,743
2011	385,985	271,491	626	272,117	27,123	16,876	261,870	72,699	51,416	47,608	41,982	8,108	4,803
2012	404,180	282,615	661	283,275	27,998	16,848	272,126	80,147	51,906	49,309	43,716	8,197	4,857
2013	401,684	285,074	796	285,869	32,386	16,612	270,095	77,718	53,872	48,513	42,579	8,270	4,899
2014	419,330	293,036	699	293,735	33,131	18,512	279,116	83,665	56,549	50,318	44,083	8,334	4,953
2015	438,273	305,714	531	306,245	34,658	18,960	290,547	88,219	59,507	52,238	45,516	8,390	5,060
2016	449,830	311,282	284	311,567	35,376	19,929	296,120	91,993	61,717	53,268	46,416	8,445	5,157
2017	466,611	322,376	538	322,914	37,043	20,359	306,229	96,192	64,190	54,879	47,874	8,503	5,228
2018	483,922	334,028	305	334,333	38,322	20,808	316,819	99,561	67,542	56,619	49,552	8,547	5,298
2019	507,874	348,888	423	349,311	39,949	19,373	328,735	107,485	71,654	59,073	51,474	8,597	5,330
2020	536,817	357,017	203	357,220	41,022	18,576	334,774	106,670	95,374	62,157	54,529	8,636	5,225
2021	573,028	381,086	605	381,691	43,248	19,307	357,750	108,891	106,387	66,190	57,432	8,657	5,351
2022	592,315	410,406	1,318	411,724	46,848	19,728	384,605	113,277	94,434	68,211	57,789	8,684	...

... = Not available.

Personal Income and Employment by Region and State: Washington

(Millions of dollars, except as noted.)

| Year | Personal income, total | Earnings by place of work | | | Less: Contributions for government social insurance | Plus: Adjustment for residence | Equals: Net earnings by place of residence | Plus: Dividends, interest, and rent | Plus: Personal current transfer receipts | Per capita (dollars) | | Population (thousands) | Total employment (thousands) |
		Nonfarm	Farm	Total						Personal income	Disposable personal income		
1960	7,248	5,620	256	5,876	313	26	5,588	1,146	514	2,539	2,285	2,855	...
1961	7,609	5,904	247	6,150	327	29	5,852	1,194	563	2,640	2,374	2,882	...
1962	8,203	6,404	271	6,675	358	35	6,352	1,285	567	2,788	2,501	2,942	...
1963	8,394	6,541	275	6,815	395	42	6,463	1,333	598	2,841	2,544	2,955	...
1964	8,787	6,833	251	7,084	394	52	6,742	1,415	631	2,968	2,711	2,961	...
1965	9,465	7,343	271	7,614	418	63	7,259	1,543	663	3,190	2,905	2,967	...
1966	10,693	8,475	366	8,840	593	72	8,319	1,686	689	3,498	3,149	3,057	...
1967	11,710	9,314	327	9,642	688	83	9,037	1,845	829	3,689	3,307	3,174	...
1968	13,035	10,385	341	10,725	770	99	10,054	2,030	951	3,986	3,549	3,270	...
1969	14,236	11,287	398	11,685	909	89	10,865	2,294	1,077	4,258	3,755	3,343	1,539
1970	15,037	11,485	346	11,831	911	63	10,983	2,618	1,435	4,400	3,957	3,417	1,491
1971	15,839	11,863	391	12,254	979	61	11,336	2,831	1,671	4,595	4,171	3,447	1,457
1972	17,079	12,813	507	13,320	1,115	71	12,276	3,019	1,785	4,955	4,452	3,447	1,481
1973	19,236	14,402	756	15,158	1,435	87	13,810	3,415	2,011	5,532	4,953	3,477	1,558
1974	21,827	16,174	891	17,064	1,656	130	15,539	3,936	2,352	6,152	5,512	3,548	1,622
1975	24,720	18,112	906	19,018	1,837	200	17,381	4,431	2,907	6,831	6,145	3,619	1,659
1976	27,399	20,569	754	21,322	2,137	249	19,434	4,803	3,162	7,424	6,655	3,691	1,739
1977	30,412	23,305	604	23,909	2,457	232	21,684	5,418	3,310	8,062	7,206	3,772	1,815
1978	35,367	27,425	754	28,179	2,973	272	25,477	6,302	3,588	9,101	8,052	3,886	1,939
1979	40,756	31,782	740	32,521	3,561	484	29,444	7,296	4,015	10,156	8,909	4,013	2,058
1980	46,242	34,990	861	35,851	3,898	577	32,530	8,796	4,917	11,130	9,782	4,155	2,105
1981	51,391	38,301	863	39,163	4,585	431	35,009	10,670	5,712	12,133	10,630	4,236	2,119
1982	54,606	39,658	767	40,424	4,812	468	36,080	12,101	6,425	12,769	11,403	4,277	2,094
1983	58,282	41,624	1,066	42,690	5,114	494	38,070	13,193	7,019	13,553	12,233	4,300	2,140
1984	62,431	44,571	1,024	45,595	5,647	544	40,492	14,561	7,378	14,373	13,028	4,344	2,214
1985	66,376	47,585	753	48,337	6,087	572	42,823	15,619	7,935	15,085	13,645	4,400	2,277
1986	70,876	51,156	1,060	52,216	6,585	616	46,247	16,213	8,416	15,917	14,426	4,453	2,351
1987	75,031	54,816	1,084	55,899	7,025	672	49,547	16,622	8,862	16,556	14,890	4,532	2,470
1988	81,724	60,393	1,020	61,412	7,929	757	54,240	17,830	9,654	17,613	15,906	4,640	2,600
1989	90,313	65,974	1,156	67,129	8,669	845	59,305	20,412	10,596	19,028	17,006	4,746	2,718
1990	99,151	73,392	1,210	74,602	9,823	918	65,698	21,808	11,646	20,222	18,027	4,903	2,842
1991	106,189	78,770	1,281	80,051	10,637	990	70,404	22,593	13,192	21,129	18,935	5,026	2,877
1992	114,759	85,861	1,542	87,403	11,580	1,101	76,924	23,284	14,552	22,237	19,962	5,161	2,907
1993	120,677	89,558	1,744	91,302	12,079	1,196	80,419	24,680	15,578	22,860	20,585	5,279	2,951
1994	126,855	93,816	1,429	95,245	12,804	1,250	83,691	26,768	16,396	23,600	21,183	5,375	3,060
1995	134,146	97,921	1,468	99,389	13,404	1,407	87,393	29,232	17,521	24,475	21,935	5,481	3,101
1996	144,246	104,590	1,943	106,533	14,014	1,627	94,146	31,741	18,360	25,898	23,014	5,570	3,192
1997	155,514	114,078	1,549	115,627	14,810	1,786	102,602	33,867	19,044	27,405	24,160	5,675	3,298
1998	170,275	126,908	1,730	128,638	16,245	1,892	114,285	36,196	19,794	29,513	25,728	5,770	3,383
1999	180,876	138,196	1,498	139,694	17,002	1,958	124,651	35,239	20,986	30,958	26,537	5,843	3,447
2000	193,410	147,036	1,737	148,774	18,407	2,281	132,648	38,348	22,415	32,723	28,257	5,911	3,527
2001	198,031	149,599	1,573	151,171	18,149	2,376	135,399	37,516	25,117	33,084	29,060	5,986	3,516
2002	201,014	152,429	1,651	154,080	18,543	2,432	137,970	36,332	26,712	33,212	29,852	6,052	3,489
2003	209,085	156,988	2,201	159,189	19,320	2,568	142,437	38,680	27,968	34,253	31,116	6,104	3,516
2004	224,765	165,447	2,133	167,581	20,550	2,767	149,798	46,560	28,407	36,378	33,274	6,179	3,585
2005	233,923	175,155	1,871	177,026	21,864	3,035	158,196	45,630	30,097	37,384	33,834	6,257	3,688
2006	255,003	188,241	1,800	190,041	23,187	3,442	170,296	52,404	32,303	40,027	35,984	6,371	3,798
2007	276,678	200,667	2,278	202,944	24,438	3,665	182,172	59,513	34,994	42,819	38,250	6,462	3,925
2008	290,319	205,825	2,193	208,018	25,047	3,682	186,653	63,376	40,291	44,241	39,846	6,562	3,955
2009	277,305	196,435	2,237	198,672	24,818	3,394	177,248	54,613	45,445	41,591	38,370	6,667	3,816
2010	285,580	201,566	2,517	204,083	25,468	3,241	181,856	53,545	50,179	42,348	38,908	6,744	3,771
2011	302,076	210,503	3,248	213,751	23,941	3,525	193,335	58,793	49,948	44,225	40,089	6,830	3,814
2012	326,699	226,613	3,351	229,965	24,700	3,609	208,874	67,779	50,046	47,320	43,030	6,904	3,909
2013	333,764	237,548	3,580	241,127	28,901	3,582	215,807	67,010	50,946	47,857	43,055	6,974	3,992
2014	359,691	250,719	3,305	254,024	30,392	3,536	227,168	76,853	55,670	50,890	45,652	7,068	4,094
2015	381,158	263,316	4,702	268,018	32,081	3,830	239,767	84,655	56,737	53,083	47,279	7,180	4,199
2016	401,774	278,192	3,880	282,071	33,518	4,108	252,661	89,215	59,899	54,918	48,708	7,316	4,314
2017	426,443	298,335	3,777	302,112	36,101	4,280	270,291	94,569	61,583	57,265	50,926	7,447	4,432
2018	454,584	323,403	2,734	326,137	38,229	4,619	292,526	97,597	64,460	60,221	53,813	7,549	4,538
2019	490,322	342,629	3,429	346,058	39,749	4,759	311,068	110,526	68,729	64,189	57,247	7,639	4,590
2020	527,582	357,089	4,040	361,129	41,828	4,961	324,262	110,446	92,874	68,304	61,302	7,724	4,436
2021	570,921	389,382	3,200	392,581	44,403	5,166	353,344	114,052	103,525	73,755	65,165	7,741	4,558
2022	589,368	418,434	4,019	422,453	47,941	5,508	380,020	121,073	88,275	75,698	65,210	7,786	...

... = Not available.

Personal Income and Employment by Region and State: West Virginia

(Millions of dollars, except as noted.)

Year	Personal income, total	Earnings by place of work			Less: Contributions for government social insurance	Plus: Adjustment for residence	Equals: Net earnings by place of residence	Plus: Dividends, interest, and rent	Plus: Personal current transfer receipts	Per capita (dollars)		Population (thousands)	Total employment (thousands)
		Nonfarm	Farm	Total						Personal income	Disposable personal income		
1960	3,076	2,579	50	2,629	155	-20	2,454	318	304	1,660	1,491	1,853	...
1961	3,117	2,572	43	2,615	153	-20	2,442	331	344	1,705	1,533	1,828	...
1962	3,256	2,687	32	2,719	168	-19	2,532	357	368	1,800	1,619	1,809	...
1963	3,400	2,809	25	2,834	186	-18	2,630	391	379	1,893	1,697	1,796	...
1964	3,628	2,988	23	3,011	173	-17	2,821	422	385	2,019	1,831	1,797	...
1965	3,878	3,190	25	3,215	184	-13	3,018	449	411	2,171	1,973	1,786	...
1966	4,115	3,463	15	3,477	244	-10	3,223	459	434	2,318	2,092	1,775	...
1967	4,361	3,642	29	3,671	268	-8	3,395	473	492	2,465	2,227	1,769	...
1968	4,623	3,855	23	3,877	298	2	3,581	498	544	2,622	2,344	1,763	...
1969	4,944	4,142	31	4,173	323	-73	3,777	569	599	2,832	2,487	1,746	652
1970	5,512	4,542	26	4,568	350	-75	4,143	647	722	3,156	2,800	1,747	660
1971	6,052	4,929	26	4,954	395	-90	4,469	712	871	3,418	3,049	1,770	670
1972	6,701	5,443	31	5,474	455	-103	4,917	786	998	3,729	3,312	1,797	684
1973	7,333	5,883	45	5,928	568	-105	5,255	892	1,186	4,062	3,631	1,805	700
1974	8,129	6,485	29	6,514	648	-120	5,747	1,038	1,344	4,481	3,959	1,814	711
1975	9,186	7,226	15	7,240	711	-124	6,405	1,180	1,601	4,991	4,423	1,841	717
1976	10,241	8,150	4	8,154	819	-153	7,183	1,300	1,758	5,455	4,805	1,877	739
1977	11,457	9,217	-1	9,215	918	-185	8,113	1,469	1,875	6,012	5,306	1,906	758
1978	12,753	10,288	13	10,301	1,058	-215	9,029	1,641	2,083	6,641	5,879	1,920	781
1979	14,223	11,352	18	11,370	1,212	-227	9,931	1,853	2,438	7,335	6,450	1,939	790
1980	15,633	12,076	9	12,085	1,311	-250	10,525	2,272	2,836	8,011	7,019	1,951	782
1981	17,051	12,783	-22	12,761	1,484	-227	11,051	2,798	3,203	8,726	7,661	1,954	762
1982	18,069	13,126	-28	13,098	1,572	-170	11,357	3,201	3,512	9,268	8,184	1,950	740
1983	18,550	12,983	-15	12,968	1,571	-145	11,252	3,407	3,891	9,537	8,475	1,945	722
1984	19,941	14,010	24	14,034	1,737	-112	12,185	3,781	3,975	10,344	9,237	1,928	732
1985	20,766	14,546	22	14,569	1,828	-107	12,633	3,984	4,149	10,890	9,721	1,907	732
1986	21,261	14,710	48	14,758	1,921	-86	12,751	4,104	4,406	11,295	10,122	1,882	731
1987	21,785	15,153	7	15,160	1,992	-26	13,142	4,114	4,528	11,728	10,500	1,858	738
1988	23,238	16,273	6	16,278	2,190	8	14,096	4,362	4,779	12,697	11,451	1,830	751
1989	24,601	16,923	34	16,957	2,310	95	14,743	4,815	5,043	13,618	12,191	1,807	757
1990	26,186	18,101	47	18,148	2,502	92	15,738	5,042	5,407	14,608	13,073	1,793	778
1991	27,308	18,745	37	18,782	2,663	74	16,194	5,035	6,079	15,182	13,632	1,799	779
1992	29,404	19,919	62	19,982	2,840	134	17,276	5,159	6,970	16,277	14,701	1,806	789
1993	30,499	20,703	65	20,767	3,059	132	17,840	5,238	7,420	16,780	15,160	1,818	801
1994	31,821	21,792	61	21,853	3,205	181	18,829	5,468	7,524	17,480	15,740	1,820	822
1995	32,895	22,410	24	22,434	3,352	224	19,306	5,829	7,759	18,037	16,219	1,824	838
1996	34,209	23,081	9	23,090	3,454	234	19,870	6,158	8,182	18,767	16,844	1,823	847
1997	35,630	23,976	-0	23,976	3,548	393	20,820	6,442	8,368	19,587	17,524	1,819	858
1998	37,123	24,934	1	24,935	3,721	439	21,653	6,798	8,673	20,447	18,272	1,816	868
1999	38,114	25,920	-13	25,907	3,826	501	22,582	6,680	8,853	21,037	18,802	1,812	868
2000	40,328	27,387	19	27,406	4,141	625	23,891	7,150	9,287	22,317	19,945	1,807	876
2001	42,792	28,630	30	28,660	4,115	772	25,317	7,214	10,261	23,754	21,205	1,801	873
2002	44,263	29,453	-33	29,420	4,061	817	26,176	7,001	11,087	24,517	22,265	1,805	871
2003	44,987	30,035	-14	30,021	4,253	961	26,729	6,897	11,361	24,823	22,700	1,812	868
2004	46,658	31,525	30	31,555	4,381	1,090	28,264	7,035	11,359	25,687	23,581	1,816	879
2005	49,119	33,311	11	33,323	4,571	1,289	30,041	7,283	11,795	26,981	24,552	1,820	891
2006	52,468	35,291	-24	35,267	4,627	1,336	31,977	7,890	12,601	28,704	26,067	1,828	903
2007	54,491	35,606	-57	35,549	4,508	1,486	32,526	8,634	13,331	29,711	26,848	1,834	916
2008	58,167	37,186	-30	37,156	4,546	1,441	34,051	9,328	14,789	31,607	28,418	1,840	918
2009	58,609	37,014	-35	36,979	4,598	1,328	33,709	8,935	15,965	31,718	29,058	1,848	899
2010	60,754	38,170	-29	38,141	4,702	1,459	34,898	9,015	16,841	32,762	30,011	1,854	899
2011	64,227	40,287	7	40,294	4,381	1,468	37,380	9,875	16,972	34,581	31,313	1,857	909
2012	65,899	41,543	-4	41,538	4,499	1,215	38,254	10,346	17,299	35,453	32,323	1,859	919
2013	65,573	41,616	30	41,646	5,049	1,256	37,853	10,082	17,638	35,318	31,994	1,857	914
2014	67,764	42,198	17	42,215	5,203	1,470	38,482	10,711	18,572	36,570	33,080	1,853	912
2015	69,179	42,404	-2	42,401	5,259	1,469	38,611	11,108	19,459	37,468	33,859	1,846	904
2016	68,630	41,302	-30	41,272	5,280	1,712	37,704	11,020	19,907	37,380	33,889	1,836	890
2017	71,345	43,332	5	43,337	5,511	1,619	39,445	11,395	20,505	39,140	35,560	1,823	889
2018	74,740	46,640	-57	46,583	5,838	1,233	41,978	11,766	20,996	41,279	37,723	1,811	898
2019	77,330	47,124	-27	47,097	5,843	1,725	42,979	12,719	21,632	42,951	39,161	1,800	882
2020	80,971	45,751	-71	45,680	5,883	2,091	41,888	12,500	26,583	45,199	41,372	1,791	841
2021	86,452	48,149	-51	48,099	6,098	2,343	44,344	12,818	29,290	48,418	44,022	1,786	858
2022	87,282	51,613	55	51,668	6,593	2,515	47,591	13,340	26,352	49,169	43,972	1,775	...

... = Not available.

Personal Income and Employment by Region and State: Wisconsin

(Millions of dollars, except as noted.)

Year	Personal income, total	Earnings by place of work			Less: Contributions for government social insurance	Plus: Adjustment for residence	Equals: Net earnings by place of residence	Plus: Dividends, interest, and rent	Plus: Personal current transfer receipts	Per capita (dollars)		Population (thousands)	Total employment (thousands)
		Nonfarm	Farm	Total						Personal income	Disposable personal income		
1960	8,994	7,017	428	7,445	341	64	7,167	1,269	558	2,270	2,003	3,962	...
1961	9,282	7,098	496	7,593	348	67	7,312	1,324	646	2,315	2,061	4,009	...
1962	9,810	7,565	492	8,056	374	75	7,757	1,395	658	2,423	2,146	4,049	...
1963	10,135	7,890	439	8,329	433	81	7,978	1,462	695	2,465	2,174	4,112	...
1964	10,909	8,508	478	8,986	449	92	8,628	1,557	724	2,619	2,336	4,165	...
1965	11,798	9,151	545	9,696	479	104	9,321	1,698	779	2,788	2,477	4,232	...
1966	12,888	10,092	670	10,762	668	124	10,217	1,809	863	3,016	2,654	4,274	...
1967	13,602	10,696	564	11,260	760	137	10,637	1,902	1,063	3,161	2,759	4,303	...
1968	14,896	11,536	645	12,181	815	158	11,524	2,135	1,237	3,428	2,991	4,345	...
1969	16,425	12,662	638	13,300	934	250	12,616	2,450	1,359	3,752	3,218	4,378	1,944
1970	17,649	13,357	639	13,997	974	255	13,277	2,773	1,599	3,988	3,469	4,426	1,954
1971	18,959	14,190	693	14,883	1,070	267	14,080	3,010	1,870	4,251	3,748	4,460	1,957
1972	20,732	15,635	729	16,365	1,248	291	15,408	3,244	2,079	4,609	4,019	4,498	2,014
1973	23,158	17,544	916	18,460	1,614	316	17,162	3,631	2,365	5,125	4,478	4,518	2,116
1974	25,437	19,183	806	19,988	1,840	343	18,491	4,135	2,811	5,605	4,870	4,538	2,159
1975	27,872	20,504	867	21,371	1,927	345	19,789	4,556	3,528	6,099	5,358	4,570	2,148
1976	30,609	22,957	762	23,720	2,188	383	21,915	4,872	3,823	6,676	5,828	4,585	2,211
1977	34,210	25,642	1,144	26,787	2,443	423	24,767	5,390	4,054	7,416	6,452	4,613	2,293
1978	38,210	28,989	1,128	30,117	2,843	475	27,749	5,986	4,475	8,249	7,117	4,632	2,380
1979	42,798	32,314	1,407	33,721	3,302	506	30,925	6,740	5,134	9,172	7,931	4,666	2,460
1980	47,282	34,342	1,446	35,788	3,497	530	32,822	8,203	6,257	10,034	8,712	4,712	2,443
1981	51,613	36,695	1,172	37,867	3,999	581	34,449	10,050	7,115	10,920	9,424	4,726	2,415
1982	54,462	37,789	1,024	38,814	4,156	601	35,258	11,268	7,936	11,517	10,034	4,729	2,373
1983	57,197	39,863	473	40,336	4,359	651	36,628	12,041	8,527	12,114	10,671	4,721	2,376
1984	62,913	43,864	1,003	44,868	4,904	761	40,725	13,457	8,732	13,285	11,739	4,736	2,467
1985	66,277	46,202	1,031	47,233	5,208	849	42,874	14,128	9,275	13,960	12,337	4,748	2,495
1986	69,917	48,904	1,307	50,211	5,503	930	45,638	14,711	9,568	14,702	12,995	4,756	2,537
1987	73,794	52,499	1,418	53,917	5,811	1,033	49,139	14,871	9,784	15,445	13,569	4,778	2,605
1988	78,456	57,055	855	57,910	6,549	1,194	52,555	15,766	10,136	16,269	14,312	4,822	2,684
1989	85,534	60,870	1,741	62,611	7,004	1,233	56,840	17,752	10,942	17,612	15,464	4,857	2,740
1990	90,431	65,223	1,397	66,620	7,801	1,343	60,161	18,535	11,735	18,438	16,162	4,905	2,814
1991	94,002	68,386	1,018	69,404	8,259	1,363	62,507	18,760	12,735	18,936	16,632	4,964	2,840
1992	101,408	74,287	1,276	75,563	8,872	1,462	68,153	19,453	13,802	20,179	17,742	5,025	2,894
1993	106,714	78,894	956	79,850	9,408	1,519	71,961	20,373	14,381	20,986	18,418	5,085	2,950
1994	113,394	83,975	1,224	85,199	10,146	1,656	76,709	21,855	14,830	22,088	19,334	5,134	3,040
1995	119,327	87,960	797	88,757	10,657	1,775	79,875	23,731	15,722	23,015	20,097	5,185	3,120
1996	126,197	92,251	1,372	93,623	11,100	1,918	84,442	25,472	16,283	24,129	20,934	5,230	3,171
1997	133,915	98,605	1,000	99,605	11,780	2,121	89,946	27,151	16,818	25,429	21,934	5,266	3,226
1998	143,202	105,273	1,370	106,643	12,476	2,306	96,473	29,482	17,247	27,031	23,223	5,298	3,288
1999	148,959	111,625	1,325	112,950	13,251	2,477	102,176	28,829	17,954	27,933	24,023	5,333	3,350
2000	158,832	118,698	894	119,592	13,901	2,707	108,399	31,139	19,294	29,556	25,484	5,374	3,414
2001	166,752	124,298	1,192	125,491	14,202	2,839	114,128	31,095	21,529	30,841	26,741	5,407	3,404
2002	171,113	128,749	1,095	129,845	14,589	2,924	118,180	29,768	23,166	31,425	27,841	5,445	3,395
2003	176,143	132,479	1,555	134,034	15,072	2,999	121,961	30,329	23,853	32,148	28,723	5,479	3,413
2004	184,302	139,157	1,903	141,059	15,875	3,105	128,289	31,459	24,554	33,424	29,968	5,514	3,468
2005	191,047	143,554	1,657	145,211	16,520	3,299	131,989	32,749	26,309	34,447	30,648	5,546	3,511
2006	202,681	150,336	1,389	151,725	17,406	3,423	137,742	37,028	27,912	36,338	32,139	5,578	3,547
2007	212,179	154,734	2,117	156,851	17,984	3,683	142,551	39,387	30,241	37,816	33,400	5,611	3,585
2008	220,312	157,930	1,818	159,748	18,552	3,728	144,924	41,521	33,867	39,055	34,479	5,641	3,573
2009	216,466	153,566	942	154,508	18,027	3,291	139,772	37,518	39,176	38,182	34,530	5,669	3,445
2010	222,983	156,627	1,775	158,402	18,413	3,243	143,232	37,702	42,049	39,175	35,413	5,692	3,426
2011	235,434	163,890	2,934	166,823	17,234	3,357	152,946	41,834	40,653	41,209	36,855	5,713	3,474
2012	246,242	170,884	2,767	173,652	17,766	3,296	159,182	45,643	41,418	42,944	38,468	5,734	3,499
2013	247,847	175,325	3,108	178,433	20,543	3,254	161,145	44,331	42,372	43,050	38,175	5,757	3,540
2014	258,348	181,048	3,132	184,180	21,174	3,487	166,494	47,540	44,314	44,709	39,755	5,778	3,586
2015	269,704	188,232	2,719	190,951	21,905	3,630	172,676	50,790	46,238	46,548	41,134	5,794	3,625
2016	274,375	191,821	1,870	193,691	22,322	3,735	175,103	52,398	46,873	47,205	41,595	5,812	3,658
2017	284,577	198,360	1,754	200,114	23,301	3,911	180,724	54,735	49,117	48,758	43,202	5,836	3,679
2018	298,257	207,633	1,603	209,236	24,082	3,940	189,094	57,310	51,853	50,908	45,339	5,859	3,721
2019	311,019	214,491	1,760	216,251	25,053	4,205	195,402	61,189	54,427	52,893	46,894	5,880	3,719
2020	329,623	218,039	2,890	220,929	25,609	3,956	199,275	61,669	68,679	55,904	49,940	5,896	3,583
2021	351,551	231,118	2,748	233,867	26,640	4,251	211,477	63,337	76,738	59,787	52,933	5,880	3,669
2022	360,684	247,529	4,365	251,894	28,653	4,623	227,864	66,021	66,800	61,210	53,062	5,893	...

... = Not available.

Personal Income and Employment by Region and State: Wyoming

(Millions of dollars, except as noted.)

Year	Personal income, total	Derivation of personal income								Per capita (dollars)		Population (thousands)	Total employment (thousands)
		Earnings by place of work			Less: Contributions for government social insurance	Plus: Adjustment for residence	Equals: Net earnings by place of residence	Plus: Dividends, interest, and rent	Plus: Personal current transfer receipts	Personal income	Disposable personal income		
		Nonfarm	Farm	Total									
1960	789	603	51	654	34	-2	618	125	45	2,382	2,138	331	...
1961	829	618	57	675	34	-1	640	137	53	2,461	2,223	337	...
1962	859	627	67	694	35	-1	658	147	55	2,580	2,319	333	...
1963	879	646	67	713	40	-1	672	151	56	2,616	2,327	336	...
1964	906	690	47	738	43	-1	694	158	55	2,673	2,445	339	...
1965	936	698	53	751	41	-1	710	168	58	2,818	2,574	332	...
1966	958	714	58	772	48	-0	724	173	62	2,967	2,692	323	...
1967	1,025	756	70	827	53	-0	773	181	72	3,184	2,871	322	...
1968	1,094	830	62	892	59	0	833	180	81	3,375	3,030	324	...
1969	1,219	911	70	981	66	L	915	215	89	3,704	3,285	329	158
1970	1,348	991	79	1,070	71	0	999	246	103	4,038	3,600	334	159
1971	1,498	1,093	88	1,181	81	-1	1,100	279	119	4,404	3,954	340	165
1972	1,685	1,226	126	1,352	95	-3	1,254	301	129	4,856	4,408	347	172
1973	1,969	1,443	153	1,596	127	-7	1,461	355	152	5,571	4,987	353	182
1974	2,303	1,771	111	1,882	158	-14	1,710	421	172	6,317	5,554	365	194
1975	2,607	2,058	67	2,125	181	-16	1,928	472	208	6,853	6,118	380	203
1976	2,890	2,322	48	2,369	213	-22	2,135	524	232	7,309	6,466	395	214
1977	3,376	2,759	45	2,804	249	-29	2,526	595	254	8,203	7,254	412	231
1978	4,034	3,331	65	3,396	309	-38	3,050	698	286	9,361	8,254	431	250
1979	4,716	3,917	96	4,014	380	-54	3,579	806	331	10,437	9,055	452	266
1980	5,506	4,538	86	4,623	441	-74	4,109	1,005	393	11,612	10,109	474	279
1981	6,300	5,146	51	5,197	541	-83	4,573	1,256	471	12,812	11,087	492	289
1982	6,617	5,242	29	5,271	565	-80	4,626	1,449	542	13,066	11,479	506	287
1983	6,568	4,976	36	5,012	522	-59	4,431	1,496	641	12,870	11,486	510	274
1984	6,857	5,193	14	5,207	560	-53	4,593	1,631	633	13,581	12,212	505	276
1985	7,160	5,414	18	5,432	599	-52	4,780	1,708	672	14,330	12,882	500	277
1986	7,131	5,279	40	5,319	581	-42	4,696	1,694	741	14,387	13,075	496	264
1987	6,864	4,951	59	5,010	550	-27	4,434	1,679	752	14,392	13,014	477	258
1988	7,003	5,045	59	5,104	602	-22	4,480	1,740	783	15,056	13,597	465	264
1989	7,643	5,410	90	5,500	628	-15	4,858	1,936	849	16,673	14,956	458	265
1990	8,233	5,802	153	5,955	699	-11	5,246	2,075	913	18,147	16,286	454	271
1991	8,642	5,996	213	6,209	745	-1	5,463	2,164	1,015	18,818	16,945	459	277
1992	9,131	6,328	221	6,549	777	-6	5,766	2,242	1,123	19,583	17,659	466	280
1993	9,660	6,712	247	6,959	817	-8	6,134	2,303	1,223	20,419	18,359	473	285
1994	10,103	7,073	122	7,195	866	-8	6,321	2,488	1,293	21,034	18,891	480	298
1995	10,585	7,263	102	7,365	891	-5	6,469	2,736	1,380	21,818	19,611	485	301
1996	11,078	7,530	83	7,614	913	0	6,702	2,923	1,453	22,693	19,960	488	304
1997	11,885	7,990	184	8,174	957	5	7,223	3,170	1,492	24,282	21,265	489	307
1998	12,640	8,429	99	8,528	1,007	8	7,529	3,577	1,534	25,755	22,514	491	310
1999	13,533	8,974	168	9,142	1,055	7	8,093	3,843	1,596	27,518	24,012	492	315
2000	14,635	9,639	124	9,764	1,121	14	8,656	4,262	1,716	29,607	25,645	494	325
2001	15,506	10,334	192	10,526	1,202	-9	9,315	4,343	1,849	31,347	27,384	495	330
2002	15,928	10,884	102	10,986	1,227	-29	9,729	4,219	1,980	31,854	28,622	500	334
2003	16,959	11,357	181	11,538	1,303	-50	10,185	4,629	2,145	33,686	30,636	503	337
2004	18,361	11,885	181	12,066	1,397	-63	10,606	5,488	2,267	36,065	32,888	509	344
2005	20,250	12,784	227	13,011	1,510	-93	11,408	6,458	2,385	39,385	35,337	514	354
2006	23,255	14,947	98	15,045	1,914	-141	12,990	7,735	2,530	44,492	39,194	523	370
2007	24,753	16,269	49	16,317	2,117	-177	14,023	8,042	2,687	46,278	40,569	535	388
2008	27,163	18,073	107	18,180	2,250	-216	15,714	8,328	3,121	49,746	43,947	546	399
2009	24,949	17,371	91	17,462	2,181	-216	15,065	6,507	3,377	44,564	40,979	560	387
2010	26,329	18,218	122	18,340	2,218	-238	15,885	6,802	3,642	46,649	42,508	564	385
2011	28,787	19,118	369	19,487	2,102	-247	17,137	7,991	3,658	50,783	46,125	567	390
2012	31,200	20,220	137	20,358	2,215	-246	17,897	9,649	3,654	54,213	48,368	575	397
2013	31,240	20,868	248	21,116	2,496	-235	18,385	9,071	3,784	53,776	47,898	581	400
2014	33,549	21,946	380	22,326	2,653	-222	19,451	10,130	3,969	57,749	51,573	581	406
2015	33,762	21,959	308	22,267	2,608	-237	19,421	10,136	4,205	57,846	51,811	584	406
2016	31,909	20,578	176	20,754	2,499	-275	17,981	9,539	4,389	54,827	49,499	582	398
2017	32,952	20,912	186	21,098	2,558	-263	18,278	10,103	4,571	57,184	51,411	576	399
2018	34,760	22,383	203	22,587	2,628	-247	19,711	10,233	4,815	60,472	54,886	575	405
2019	36,889	23,078	222	23,301	2,753	-262	20,286	11,528	5,075	64,117	57,948	575	408
2020	37,974	22,834	260	23,094	2,740	-279	20,075	11,393	6,506	65,744	59,462	578	402
2021	40,323	23,986	288	24,274	2,870	-350	21,054	12,168	7,101	69,584	62,175	579	409
2022	41,477	25,845	222	26,067	3,134	-379	22,554	12,789	6,134	71,342	62,227	581	...

... = Not available.

METROPOLITAN STATISTICAL AREA

Personal Income and Employment by Area: Abilene, TX

(Thousands of dollars, except as noted.)

Year	Personal income, total	Derivation of personal income								Per capita personal income (dollars)	Population (persons)	Total employment
		Earnings by place of work			Less: Contributions for government social insurance	Plus: Adjustment for residence	Equals: Net earnings by place of residence	Plus: Dividends, interest, and rent	Plus: Personal current transfer receipts			
		Nonfarm	Farm	Total								
1970	445,225	322,395	23,059	345,454	19,934	1,887	327,407	76,169	41,649	3,634	122,505	56,215
1971	476,061	346,964	20,798	367,762	22,303	2,011	347,470	81,400	47,191	3,813	124,841	56,614
1972	541,293	392,737	28,946	421,683	26,147	2,370	397,906	91,107	52,280	4,212	128,517	59,092
1973	581,519	418,998	27,728	446,726	31,846	2,456	417,336	101,206	62,977	4,560	127,533	60,359
1974	655,804	487,544	8,813	496,357	38,282	1,621	459,696	122,291	73,817	5,099	128,625	63,366
1975	771,668	561,861	21,367	583,228	44,278	1,693	540,643	142,335	88,690	5,889	131,031	65,822
1976	852,803	632,663	17,641	650,304	50,603	2,088	601,789	154,059	96,955	6,394	133,379	68,298
1977	926,754	695,027	12,946	707,973	55,793	2,168	654,348	169,472	102,934	6,965	133,052	69,994
1978	1,062,407	805,455	9,999	815,454	65,480	1,508	751,482	196,762	114,163	7,901	134,462	72,932
1979	1,210,051	915,614	20,602	936,216	78,599	1,030	858,647	224,550	126,854	8,858	136,601	75,773
1980	1,396,724	1,053,472	10,764	1,064,236	91,347	350	973,239	278,688	144,797	9,970	140,098	78,280
1981	1,681,889	1,246,899	46,280	1,293,179	116,795	-3,110	1,173,274	345,886	162,729	11,736	143,310	84,737
1982	1,805,340	1,317,942	23,155	1,341,097	125,452	-1,682	1,213,963	410,323	181,054	12,125	148,899	86,685
1983	1,890,446	1,371,204	8,428	1,379,632	129,737	-2,173	1,247,722	445,261	197,463	12,361	152,939	86,693
1984	2,010,700	1,447,398	10,327	1,457,725	140,379	-2,598	1,314,748	485,357	210,595	13,092	153,587	87,720
1985	2,138,884	1,530,638	308	1,530,946	150,084	-2,406	1,378,456	535,274	225,154	13,937	153,470	88,722
1986	2,128,927	1,495,841	10,951	1,506,792	144,782	-323	1,361,687	520,671	246,569	13,732	155,031	83,720
1987	2,097,573	1,429,973	28,279	1,458,252	138,648	1,501	1,321,105	516,185	260,283	13,651	153,655	82,965
1988	2,189,009	1,520,668	15,165	1,535,833	152,195	3,296	1,386,934	530,510	271,565	14,589	150,042	83,645
1989	2,274,917	1,521,562	18,571	1,540,133	154,717	7,412	1,392,828	591,738	290,351	15,235	149,324	82,367
1990	2,324,820	1,556,932	38,433	1,595,365	156,668	10,185	1,448,882	554,967	320,971	15,726	147,834	80,942
1991	2,382,790	1,624,567	14,310	1,638,877	168,263	4,971	1,475,585	549,345	357,860	16,165	147,400	82,259
1992	2,541,971	1,720,134	36,748	1,756,882	176,728	6,095	1,586,249	547,480	408,242	16,956	149,917	82,277
1993	2,668,070	1,800,905	30,802	1,831,707	184,214	6,165	1,653,658	585,307	429,105	17,449	152,909	84,362
1994	2,724,394	1,872,355	19,614	1,891,969	193,362	4,548	1,703,155	561,550	459,689	17,716	153,779	85,682
1995	2,915,506	1,974,194	17,649	1,991,843	203,788	3,487	1,791,542	622,815	501,149	18,678	156,097	88,181
1996	3,105,725	2,120,190	6,377	2,126,567	214,106	3,104	1,915,565	654,785	535,375	19,864	156,351	89,587
1997	3,322,907	2,298,130	22,943	2,321,073	227,051	4,368	2,098,390	663,437	561,080	21,111	157,405	91,934
1998	3,469,198	2,405,758	8,463	2,414,221	232,366	6,340	2,188,195	714,271	566,732	21,920	158,264	92,577
1999	3,611,700	2,511,768	30,364	2,542,132	240,232	7,570	2,309,470	716,248	585,982	22,608	159,755	91,417
2000	3,706,538	2,540,158	7,822	2,547,980	244,234	10,116	2,313,862	785,457	607,219	23,124	160,288	91,027
2001	3,790,618	2,555,473	37,105	2,592,578	251,060	10,981	2,352,499	781,933	656,186	23,853	158,917	89,511
2002	3,945,616	2,715,045	15,591	2,730,636	266,877	5,496	2,469,255	769,446	706,915	24,813	159,012	90,338
2003	4,192,472	2,874,746	32,464	2,907,210	283,998	3,834	2,627,046	811,918	753,508	26,399	158,810	91,132
2004	4,386,531	3,045,136	36,681	3,081,817	301,298	2,716	2,783,235	808,881	794,415	27,389	160,156	91,998
2005	4,626,050	3,188,812	30,714	3,219,526	315,039	1,887	2,906,374	856,970	862,706	28,776	160,761	92,937
2006	4,922,468	3,456,489	8,247	3,464,736	334,553	358	3,130,541	883,751	908,176	30,501	161,389	94,097
2007	5,185,518	3,543,192	30,011	3,573,203	355,078	-4,346	3,213,779	980,663	991,076	32,005	162,023	96,484
2008	5,734,957	3,864,811	-15,144	3,849,667	377,471	-4,085	3,468,111	1,181,231	1,085,615	35,290	162,508	99,264
2009	5,487,739	3,675,427	-12,614	3,662,813	377,132	-6,820	3,278,861	1,043,767	1,165,111	33,485	163,888	97,269
2010	5,804,497	3,836,098	22,493	3,858,591	386,173	-2,870	3,469,548	1,063,693	1,271,256	35,053	165,590	96,809
2011	6,161,538	3,993,859	11,209	4,005,068	357,559	5,658	3,653,167	1,205,473	1,302,898	36,973	166,651	98,193
2012	6,462,295	4,231,415	-7,152	4,224,263	376,026	16,274	3,864,511	1,296,369	1,301,415	38,585	167,483	99,843
2013	6,654,742	4,434,433	25,509	4,459,942	434,726	21,002	4,046,218	1,258,690	1,349,834	39,726	167,515	101,199
2014	7,129,665	4,768,923	-1,276	4,767,647	457,906	28,615	4,338,356	1,379,950	1,411,359	41,974	169,859	102,316
2015	6,948,394	4,483,886	3,186	4,487,072	455,607	20,587	4,052,052	1,391,012	1,505,330	40,497	171,579	102,611
2016	6,852,464	4,373,559	-25,127	4,348,432	458,028	6,733	3,897,137	1,372,881	1,582,446	39,784	172,242	102,467
2017	7,057,059	4,452,828	-26,588	4,426,240	479,426	17,793	3,964,607	1,470,528	1,621,924	40,812	172,915	102,799
2018	7,530,739	4,799,857	-22,008	4,777,849	512,306	34,382	4,299,925	1,534,779	1,696,035	43,279	174,005	104,568
2019	8,001,810	5,155,133	-12,945	5,142,188	546,892	41,848	4,637,144	1,588,460	1,776,206	45,676	175,187	106,629
2020	8,700,850	5,262,414	-8,699	5,253,715	563,286	10,487	4,700,916	1,774,739	2,225,195	49,210	176,809	105,872
2021	9,850,903	5,516,621	-2,098	5,514,523	584,574	9,500	4,939,449	2,294,349	2,617,105	55,556	177,314	107,895

Personal Income and Employment by Metropolitan Statistical Area: Akron, OH

(Thousands of dollars, except as noted.)

Year	Personal income, total	Earnings by place of work			Less: Contributions for government social insurance	Plus: Adjustment for residence	Equals: Net earnings by place of residence	Plus: Dividends, interest, and rent	Plus: Personal current transfer receipts	Per capita personal income (dollars)	Population (persons)	Total employment
		Nonfarm	Farm	Total								
1970	2,838,776	2,326,281	6,504	2,332,785	158,576	98,246	2,272,455	358,765	207,556	4,180	679,077	279,931
1971	2,990,538	2,419,744	8,998	2,428,742	169,666	102,133	2,361,209	386,161	243,168	4,403	679,231	274,958
1972	3,263,561	2,662,679	9,046	2,671,725	197,372	105,272	2,579,625	412,531	271,405	4,820	677,046	283,207
1973	3,568,727	2,911,961	11,556	2,923,517	250,765	126,857	2,799,609	450,759	318,359	5,278	676,196	292,971
1974	3,882,656	3,113,113	14,191	3,127,304	276,803	144,555	2,995,056	508,902	378,698	5,793	670,284	296,332
1975	4,114,360	3,167,018	12,512	3,179,530	270,258	165,235	3,074,507	544,606	495,247	6,115	672,844	285,325
1976	4,425,010	3,391,701	11,154	3,402,855	295,638	209,112	3,316,329	578,749	529,932	6,625	667,910	284,907
1977	4,944,761	3,856,406	8,387	3,864,793	337,775	239,996	3,767,014	633,699	544,048	7,467	662,233	297,537
1978	5,471,768	4,283,010	2,354	4,285,364	387,518	290,804	4,188,650	702,735	580,383	8,309	658,517	305,459
1979	6,012,395	4,663,360	2,036	4,665,396	438,962	339,628	4,566,062	788,014	658,319	9,105	660,364	307,763
1980	6,607,832	4,904,761	136	4,904,897	458,075	379,799	4,826,621	954,523	826,688	10,007	660,334	300,754
1981	7,243,539	5,261,838	885	5,262,723	526,076	407,217	5,143,864	1,180,459	919,216	10,994	658,870	297,681
1982	7,575,849	5,343,818	3,026	5,346,844	538,767	396,010	5,204,087	1,327,335	1,044,427	11,546	656,126	289,691
1983	7,987,788	5,627,447	608	5,628,055	579,166	394,467	5,443,356	1,420,927	1,123,505	12,214	653,968	285,981
1984	8,702,211	6,154,095	10,113	6,164,208	647,822	435,915	5,952,301	1,593,526	1,156,384	13,349	651,917	296,150
1985	9,210,231	6,512,011	5,841	6,517,852	693,342	464,893	6,289,403	1,683,929	1,236,899	14,203	648,457	303,855
1986	9,636,333	6,863,252	5,499	6,868,751	748,895	462,711	6,582,567	1,746,516	1,307,250	14,902	646,647	308,919
1987	10,095,804	7,236,430	5,481	7,241,911	787,366	485,340	6,939,885	1,781,192	1,374,727	15,585	647,810	316,920
1988	10,770,981	7,723,140	3,746	7,726,886	868,903	530,037	7,388,020	1,929,623	1,453,338	16,499	652,814	325,266
1989	11,738,137	8,307,340	6,396	8,313,736	941,016	566,540	7,939,260	2,230,918	1,567,959	17,904	655,626	333,052
1990	12,392,974	8,699,694	5,510	8,705,204	1,005,923	627,937	8,327,218	2,303,426	1,762,330	18,816	658,654	337,124
1991	12,698,519	8,976,304	4,478	8,980,782	1,062,749	614,157	8,532,190	2,298,720	1,867,609	19,111	664,478	337,813
1992	13,573,246	9,637,314	9,294	9,646,608	1,140,106	644,341	9,150,843	2,374,952	2,047,451	20,266	669,752	341,070
1993	14,178,987	10,194,639	9,975	10,204,614	1,217,357	600,562	9,587,819	2,433,830	2,157,338	21,034	674,114	350,680
1994	15,065,195	10,847,749	12,657	10,860,406	1,316,336	662,179	10,206,249	2,593,450	2,265,496	22,218	678,063	364,299
1995	15,997,336	11,348,459	8,600	11,357,059	1,390,837	687,325	10,653,547	2,930,695	2,413,094	23,451	682,146	374,193
1996	16,821,909	11,972,235	14,035	11,986,270	1,454,194	734,339	11,266,415	3,056,427	2,499,067	24,477	687,264	380,965
1997	17,779,727	12,528,610	15,526	12,544,136	1,480,989	883,240	11,946,387	3,249,541	2,583,799	25,788	689,461	387,561
1998	18,928,138	13,369,513	11,111	13,380,624	1,527,802	973,513	12,826,335	3,506,658	2,595,145	27,391	691,039	385,717
1999	19,547,530	13,807,667	9,566	13,817,233	1,567,162	1,245,555	13,495,626	3,383,264	2,668,640	28,202	693,125	393,612
2000	20,722,983	14,486,445	7,362	14,493,807	1,585,455	1,355,831	14,264,183	3,607,450	2,851,350	29,777	695,946	397,340
2001	21,096,103	14,807,041	7,183	14,814,224	1,592,013	1,329,140	14,551,351	3,465,810	3,078,942	30,219	698,108	396,954
2002	21,391,814	15,333,043	6,875	15,339,918	1,622,718	1,142,381	14,859,581	3,232,709	3,299,524	30,580	699,533	396,663
2003	22,238,213	16,021,843	6,513	16,028,356	1,709,171	1,056,407	15,375,592	3,402,545	3,460,076	31,717	701,139	396,391
2004	23,105,169	16,886,806	7,470	16,894,276	1,839,142	1,133,274	16,188,408	3,317,147	3,599,614	32,922	701,811	404,591
2005	23,771,959	17,421,590	8,741	17,430,331	1,911,879	895,639	16,414,091	3,588,390	3,769,478	33,839	702,498	412,097
2006	24,716,672	17,967,925	5,465	17,973,390	1,988,461	826,992	16,811,921	3,946,990	3,957,761	35,187	702,433	417,595
2007	26,022,232	18,817,678	8,793	18,826,471	2,068,324	688,328	17,446,475	4,374,958	4,200,799	36,994	703,423	424,012
2008	27,184,842	19,588,143	5,314	19,593,457	2,166,590	445,820	17,872,687	4,565,496	4,746,659	38,653	703,300	424,079
2009	26,373,017	18,662,479	8,002	18,670,481	2,077,838	508,311	17,100,954	4,083,373	5,188,690	37,496	703,361	404,521
2010	27,146,196	19,109,700	6,774	19,116,474	2,090,236	512,733	17,538,971	4,096,246	5,510,979	38,612	703,056	402,554
2011	28,219,626	19,537,969	18,060	19,556,029	1,931,753	596,466	18,220,742	4,387,057	5,611,827	40,127	703,262	407,811
2012	29,059,109	19,935,528	12,463	19,947,991	1,979,829	801,551	18,769,713	4,830,555	5,458,841	41,382	702,224	412,049
2013	29,711,470	20,545,913	13,413	20,559,326	2,204,963	984,006	19,338,369	4,812,742	5,560,359	42,217	703,778	414,502
2014	31,064,986	21,464,753	5,147	21,469,900	2,292,515	856,131	20,033,516	5,205,733	5,825,737	44,055	705,134	421,225
2015	31,951,292	22,197,530	446	22,197,976	2,380,984	647,742	20,464,734	5,428,016	6,058,542	45,343	704,664	426,047
2016	32,371,034	22,380,853	-3,767	22,377,086	2,458,901	636,326	20,554,511	5,654,888	6,161,635	45,991	703,862	427,371
2017	33,614,139	23,052,130	-4,659	23,047,471	2,583,254	902,216	21,366,433	5,952,640	6,295,066	47,732	704,229	427,997
2018	34,936,203	23,779,471	-3,406	23,776,065	2,619,675	962,721	22,119,111	6,340,755	6,476,337	49,631	703,925	430,286
2019	36,453,022	24,656,840	-7,570	24,649,270	2,727,381	1,112,433	23,034,322	6,617,121	6,801,579	51,827	703,361	428,462
2020	38,734,676	24,779,995	-688	24,779,307	2,739,062	1,069,537	23,109,782	6,594,263	9,030,631	55,232	701,305	415,505
2021	41,115,423	26,424,360	1,936	26,426,296	2,874,188	1,171,955	24,724,063	6,703,583	9,687,777	58,735	700,015	422,869

Personal Income and Employment by Metropolitan Statistical Area: Albany, GA

(Thousands of dollars, except as noted.)

Year	Personal income, total	Earnings by place of work			Less: Contributions for government social insurance	Plus: Adjustment for residence	Equals: Net earnings by place of residence	Plus: Dividends, interest, and rent	Plus: Personal current transfer receipts	Per capita personal income (dollars)	Population (persons)	Total employment
		Nonfarm	Farm	Total								
1970	380,798	300,020	19,201	319,221	18,064	-11,335	289,822	55,539	35,437	2,989	127,420	55,527
1971	434,484	336,405	25,573	361,978	21,332	-11,882	328,764	63,147	42,573	3,315	131,064	57,139
1972	490,511	390,164	22,936	413,100	26,092	-14,535	372,473	69,852	48,186	3,621	135,481	60,656
1973	568,382	444,423	40,135	484,558	33,919	-17,256	433,383	80,797	54,202	4,126	137,763	64,136
1974	589,429	451,538	40,403	491,941	36,260	-17,412	438,269	83,856	67,304	4,395	134,109	61,360
1975	618,246	468,861	30,736	499,597	37,272	-18,414	443,911	88,420	85,915	4,560	135,587	59,212
1976	686,380	528,528	30,246	558,774	42,341	-20,655	495,778	96,473	94,129	4,969	138,131	59,886
1977	747,257	600,450	15,785	616,235	47,827	-24,558	543,850	107,874	95,533	5,288	141,309	61,621
1978	862,964	696,783	24,946	721,729	57,001	-29,480	635,248	123,715	104,001	6,074	142,070	64,454
1979	968,065	795,922	20,042	815,964	68,376	-34,591	712,997	138,273	116,795	6,700	144,480	66,510
1980	1,074,212	876,912	-8,766	868,146	75,763	-30,405	761,978	170,529	141,705	7,318	146,793	66,284
1981	1,230,188	962,046	28,242	990,288	89,744	-37,381	863,163	205,009	162,016	8,280	148,567	67,040
1982	1,300,003	1,002,000	24,404	1,026,404	94,880	-39,758	891,766	232,639	175,598	8,686	149,660	66,060
1983	1,383,439	1,066,869	20,128	1,086,997	102,460	-42,004	942,533	249,140	191,766	9,240	149,716	66,278
1984	1,550,524	1,171,682	61,678	1,233,360	115,267	-45,720	1,072,373	275,110	203,041	10,315	150,313	69,522
1985	1,625,321	1,246,634	44,877	1,291,511	125,679	-46,971	1,118,861	290,475	215,985	10,759	151,062	71,096
1986	1,694,029	1,280,578	45,601	1,326,179	130,292	-44,523	1,151,364	309,313	233,352	11,263	150,405	70,814
1987	1,752,164	1,312,476	49,300	1,361,776	132,851	-43,934	1,184,991	323,042	244,131	11,711	149,611	71,010
1988	1,883,454	1,400,869	67,038	1,467,907	146,217	-44,332	1,277,358	342,532	263,564	12,670	148,651	70,486
1989	2,012,897	1,472,070	53,026	1,525,096	155,229	-44,279	1,325,588	395,706	291,603	13,628	147,705	70,955
1990	2,141,335	1,579,018	49,756	1,628,774	166,216	-47,881	1,414,677	406,102	320,556	14,602	146,642	72,212
1991	2,285,168	1,658,907	72,623	1,731,530	177,460	-57,610	1,496,460	420,482	368,226	15,450	147,910	71,684
1992	2,398,393	1,727,307	78,943	1,806,250	183,592	-57,739	1,564,919	422,257	411,217	15,982	150,065	71,406
1993	2,511,560	1,820,880	65,440	1,886,320	195,110	-61,413	1,629,797	443,699	438,064	16,524	151,993	73,056
1994	2,747,228	1,984,527	106,393	2,090,920	214,939	-71,193	1,804,788	473,465	468,975	17,929	153,232	76,059
1995	2,901,057	2,111,421	99,771	2,211,192	227,328	-75,204	1,908,660	499,624	492,773	18,827	154,087	78,366
1996	3,082,004	2,255,348	91,318	2,346,666	240,644	-83,905	2,022,117	537,657	522,230	19,810	155,576	80,407
1997	3,171,774	2,310,699	89,293	2,399,992	245,035	-85,876	2,069,081	562,936	539,757	20,235	156,748	80,915
1998	3,216,466	2,400,126	65,585	2,465,711	249,706	-109,947	2,106,058	575,196	535,212	20,961	153,449	79,360
1999	3,302,988	2,464,269	73,900	2,538,169	253,470	-109,693	2,175,006	566,347	561,635	21,510	153,555	78,769
2000	3,434,771	2,553,705	76,284	2,629,989	261,329	-119,936	2,248,724	578,814	607,233	22,364	153,585	79,557
2001	3,524,676	2,568,979	82,171	2,651,150	268,699	-117,191	2,265,260	602,204	657,212	22,928	153,730	78,011
2002	3,671,978	2,643,583	85,606	2,729,189	276,427	-115,408	2,337,354	599,630	734,994	23,996	153,024	77,100
2003	3,809,952	2,742,928	92,069	2,834,997	285,448	-116,786	2,432,763	638,200	738,989	24,936	152,790	78,282
2004	3,899,347	2,832,337	69,070	2,901,407	304,214	-116,691	2,480,502	630,024	788,821	25,505	152,887	78,126
2005	4,035,833	2,936,348	91,348	3,027,696	314,374	-117,876	2,595,446	610,456	829,931	26,392	152,919	80,177
2006	4,130,270	2,981,651	77,513	3,059,164	322,558	-113,077	2,623,529	628,982	877,759	26,901	153,535	80,621
2007	4,306,086	3,012,184	76,992	3,089,176	325,687	-111,401	2,652,088	729,483	924,515	28,023	153,661	81,153
2008	4,481,946	3,051,384	80,597	3,131,981	347,247	-107,018	2,677,716	765,694	1,038,536	29,137	153,823	80,663
2009	4,567,668	3,086,596	78,904	3,165,500	347,072	-106,022	2,712,406	716,436	1,138,826	29,582	154,409	78,714
2010	4,706,821	3,146,637	51,189	3,197,826	354,266	-108,244	2,735,316	737,620	1,233,885	30,533	154,155	77,793
2011	5,033,320	3,185,592	99,389	3,284,981	317,799	-103,417	2,863,765	878,554	1,291,001	32,563	154,571	79,189
2012	5,057,703	3,257,660	109,306	3,366,966	324,410	-88,053	2,954,503	842,925	1,260,275	32,839	154,015	79,388
2013	4,996,966	3,298,266	95,319	3,393,585	370,890	-94,545	2,928,150	777,524	1,291,292	32,720	152,721	79,694
2014	5,092,197	3,345,836	20,169	3,366,005	374,317	-80,131	2,911,557	829,577	1,351,063	33,225	153,263	80,577
2015	5,190,635	3,334,618	62,576	3,397,194	375,552	-67,583	2,954,059	854,565	1,382,011	34,145	152,018	81,418
2016	5,231,088	3,398,872	67,950	3,466,822	384,825	-91,917	2,990,080	846,491	1,394,517	34,633	151,044	81,655
2017	5,341,918	3,477,017	67,853	3,544,870	395,657	-100,840	3,048,373	854,113	1,439,432	35,521	150,387	81,911
2018	5,459,864	3,591,242	39,585	3,630,827	417,297	-112,075	3,101,455	873,870	1,484,539	36,293	150,440	82,473
2019	5,699,835	3,671,962	93,430	3,765,392	430,506	-112,339	3,222,547	920,900	1,556,388	38,118	149,530	82,670
2020	6,234,457	3,755,403	88,090	3,843,493	441,870	-111,095	3,290,528	915,381	2,028,548	42,006	148,417	81,176
2021	6,741,302	4,071,817	65,318	4,137,135	473,644	-118,530	3,544,961	932,515	2,263,826	45,619	147,773	82,150

Personal Income and Employment by Metropolitan Statistical Area: Albany-Lebanon, OR

(Thousands of dollars, except as noted.)

Year	Personal income, total	Earnings by place of work			Less: Contributions for government social insurance	Plus: Adjustment for residence	Equals: Net earnings by place of residence	Plus: Dividends, interest, and rent	Plus: Personal current transfer receipts	Per capita personal income (dollars)	Population (persons)	Total employment
		Nonfarm	Farm	Total								
1970	242,957	197,621	9,156	206,777	16,044	-10,338	180,395	37,828	24,734	3,347	72,587	29,190
1971	268,934	219,603	9,305	228,908	18,472	-12,424	198,012	41,960	28,962	3,560	75,547	30,345
1972	298,356	246,218	9,966	256,184	21,770	-14,580	219,834	46,454	32,068	3,902	76,467	31,600
1973	345,781	279,172	20,904	300,076	28,275	-18,157	253,644	52,795	39,342	4,425	78,150	33,577
1974	396,139	315,326	24,904	340,230	32,806	-22,752	284,672	61,574	49,893	5,014	79,006	34,924
1975	430,189	345,304	10,517	355,821	34,806	-26,928	294,087	71,346	64,756	5,315	80,942	35,650
1976	496,928	405,812	18,081	423,893	41,288	-33,236	349,369	78,143	69,416	6,029	82,420	37,031
1977	561,977	464,701	17,381	482,082	47,606	-38,499	395,977	90,402	75,598	6,633	84,723	38,988
1978	626,200	530,514	8,533	539,047	55,649	-43,790	439,608	104,119	82,473	7,253	86,334	40,485
1979	692,242	580,794	7,402	588,196	62,649	-48,051	477,496	121,851	92,895	7,778	88,999	41,045
1980	763,418	621,534	8,106	629,640	67,047	-55,267	507,326	145,813	110,279	8,514	89,668	40,737
1981	833,933	639,605	21,633	661,238	73,921	-54,930	532,387	173,251	128,295	9,248	90,173	39,457
1982	858,057	626,513	17,560	644,073	73,527	-47,246	523,300	190,338	144,419	9,561	89,748	37,614
1983	904,395	665,038	11,243	676,281	79,247	-47,055	549,979	200,561	153,855	10,115	89,415	38,353
1984	971,595	712,679	13,701	726,380	88,384	-46,157	591,839	218,467	161,289	10,886	89,253	39,132
1985	1,012,785	732,336	20,176	752,512	91,647	-44,134	616,731	224,687	171,367	11,506	88,019	39,314
1986	1,055,672	749,081	27,446	776,527	93,033	-35,988	647,506	231,464	176,702	11,993	88,026	39,908
1987	1,120,327	801,795	35,590	837,385	98,036	-33,211	706,138	231,740	182,449	12,721	88,069	40,842
1988	1,247,940	886,310	65,344	951,654	111,697	-32,172	807,785	246,678	193,477	13,987	89,223	42,853
1989	1,344,041	949,388	46,701	996,089	119,410	-25,567	851,112	280,232	212,697	14,952	89,890	44,288
1990	1,415,677	994,709	47,858	1,042,567	128,354	-18,516	895,697	289,975	230,005	15,440	91,690	44,792
1991	1,493,662	1,040,462	49,302	1,089,764	136,171	-21,853	931,740	299,834	262,088	16,036	93,145	44,656
1992	1,589,035	1,103,699	56,730	1,160,429	143,269	-21,005	996,155	299,124	293,756	16,885	94,112	44,762
1993	1,700,272	1,169,018	60,085	1,229,103	153,941	-12,765	1,062,397	321,360	316,515	17,805	95,496	46,076
1994	1,799,553	1,277,105	57,032	1,334,137	168,314	-13,676	1,152,147	330,041	317,365	18,568	96,919	48,997
1995	1,920,465	1,381,992	31,183	1,413,175	183,023	-17,804	1,212,348	360,770	347,347	19,427	98,853	51,874
1996	2,092,053	1,494,822	60,586	1,555,408	200,735	-17,113	1,337,560	390,223	364,270	20,799	100,582	54,263
1997	2,163,857	1,583,734	35,554	1,619,288	209,543	-12,888	1,396,857	393,465	373,535	21,203	102,054	55,265
1998	2,217,651	1,609,166	28,929	1,638,095	212,715	-8,802	1,416,578	396,180	404,893	21,579	102,770	54,813
1999	2,264,611	1,633,202	35,709	1,668,911	214,179	-2,896	1,451,836	364,508	448,267	21,888	103,462	53,186
2000	2,353,572	1,678,360	24,495	1,702,855	218,515	14,037	1,498,377	387,044	468,151	22,846	103,020	52,649
2001	2,567,006	1,802,278	45,245	1,847,523	228,218	22,171	1,641,476	401,946	523,584	24,791	103,544	54,749
2002	2,641,126	1,838,219	56,978	1,895,197	231,758	37,475	1,700,914	382,279	557,933	25,259	104,561	54,136
2003	2,704,906	1,859,988	62,667	1,922,655	234,705	55,212	1,743,162	387,649	574,095	25,510	106,035	53,710
2004	2,888,624	1,951,478	85,826	2,037,304	248,687	77,753	1,866,370	417,683	604,571	27,047	106,799	54,697
2005	3,009,212	2,045,418	72,036	2,117,454	264,965	88,471	1,940,960	419,045	649,207	27,829	108,132	57,088
2006	3,279,740	2,188,736	92,766	2,281,502	284,227	103,791	2,101,066	475,489	703,185	29,610	110,764	58,162
2007	3,438,887	2,273,114	72,006	2,345,120	296,296	116,852	2,165,676	520,756	752,455	30,451	112,932	59,546
2008	3,568,970	2,293,938	45,560	2,339,498	303,652	100,844	2,136,690	588,685	843,595	31,043	114,967	59,473
2009	3,553,980	2,148,749	40,347	2,189,096	284,153	112,394	2,017,337	551,602	985,041	30,637	116,001	56,122
2010	3,697,658	2,203,879	35,238	2,239,117	291,232	120,856	2,068,741	556,198	1,072,719	31,634	116,887	55,562
2011	3,818,109	2,238,941	32,688	2,271,629	264,515	127,094	2,134,208	584,797	1,099,104	32,309	118,175	55,341
2012	3,947,158	2,362,091	42,145	2,404,236	276,312	129,160	2,257,084	585,054	1,105,020	33,368	118,293	55,676
2013	4,006,682	2,366,949	55,505	2,422,454	316,208	151,478	2,257,724	605,002	1,143,956	33,829	118,439	56,161
2014	4,287,895	2,444,786	62,492	2,507,278	332,266	150,218	2,325,230	695,772	1,266,893	36,251	118,285	57,670
2015	4,578,379	2,598,568	80,424	2,678,992	348,582	155,608	2,486,018	727,244	1,365,117	38,379	119,295	58,997
2016	4,789,469	2,775,767	74,474	2,850,241	370,164	176,420	2,656,497	727,441	1,405,531	39,372	121,648	59,658
2017	5,067,439	2,924,743	52,409	2,977,152	392,163	259,851	2,844,840	777,825	1,444,774	40,980	123,657	61,769
2018	5,457,809	3,183,347	62,882	3,246,229	418,384	264,622	3,092,467	824,351	1,540,991	43,389	125,788	63,407
2019	5,682,784	3,274,888	54,644	3,329,532	438,230	289,379	3,180,681	864,943	1,637,160	44,501	127,700	63,361
2020	6,235,005	3,318,030	54,945	3,372,975	448,023	348,530	3,273,482	882,146	2,079,377	48,357	128,936	61,891
2021	6,841,839	3,500,367	64,779	3,565,146	471,693	465,548	3,559,001	905,494	2,377,344	52,695	129,839	64,271

Personal Income and Employment by Metropolitan Statistical Area: Albany-Schenectady-Troy, NY

(Thousands of dollars, except as noted.)

Year	Personal income, total	Earnings by place of work			Less: Contributions for government social insurance	Plus: Adjustment for residence	Equals: Net earnings by place of residence	Plus: Dividends, interest, and rent	Plus: Personal current transfer receipts	Per capita personal income (dollars)	Population (persons)	Total employment
		Nonfarm	Farm	Total								
1970	3,299,252	2,800,707	18,008	2,818,715	218,154	-99,150	2,501,411	499,322	298,519	4,401	749,695	338,712
1971	3,648,157	3,097,958	17,331	3,115,289	248,053	-110,976	2,756,260	540,963	350,934	4,792	761,289	347,216
1972	3,926,002	3,331,968	16,643	3,348,611	278,178	-112,208	2,958,225	581,267	386,510	5,082	772,468	350,334
1973	4,229,899	3,586,099	19,914	3,606,013	345,098	-118,024	3,142,891	645,339	441,669	5,462	774,486	358,789
1974	4,588,365	3,834,657	18,043	3,852,700	380,223	-134,734	3,337,743	731,934	518,688	5,938	772,691	359,694
1975	4,962,911	3,999,876	16,565	4,016,441	390,931	-146,276	3,479,234	798,212	685,465	6,409	774,345	354,340
1976	5,302,714	4,294,760	19,204	4,313,964	432,721	-179,480	3,701,763	843,484	757,467	6,861	772,927	357,485
1977	5,731,221	4,641,126	14,406	4,655,532	466,785	-208,916	3,979,831	929,932	821,458	7,399	774,635	366,349
1978	6,268,119	5,157,580	17,638	5,175,218	532,454	-244,120	4,398,644	1,002,078	867,397	8,071	776,648	378,544
1979	6,893,883	5,657,652	22,512	5,680,164	604,006	-272,498	4,803,660	1,139,504	950,719	8,882	776,196	385,189
1980	7,704,596	6,118,178	22,965	6,141,143	639,168	-301,060	5,200,915	1,383,816	1,119,865	9,982	771,823	385,427
1981	8,548,119	6,637,413	22,763	6,660,176	733,697	-309,278	5,617,201	1,675,633	1,255,285	11,065	772,505	383,685
1982	9,367,569	7,134,458	22,347	7,156,805	787,805	-323,217	6,045,783	1,946,226	1,375,560	12,108	773,678	384,637
1983	10,089,285	7,659,313	17,273	7,676,586	848,981	-329,004	6,498,601	2,111,501	1,479,183	12,974	777,649	387,575
1984	11,168,909	8,560,738	20,518	8,581,256	966,547	-347,090	7,267,619	2,383,836	1,517,454	14,323	779,804	404,423
1985	11,991,143	9,303,284	21,973	9,325,257	1,069,592	-365,545	7,890,120	2,493,139	1,607,884	15,300	783,736	419,617
1986	12,906,310	10,094,951	26,337	10,121,288	1,174,343	-372,515	8,574,430	2,656,461	1,675,419	16,363	788,761	435,382
1987	13,699,039	10,838,435	26,652	10,865,087	1,244,257	-377,748	9,243,082	2,756,466	1,699,491	17,308	791,466	442,103
1988	14,869,767	11,884,885	23,341	11,908,226	1,399,086	-390,105	10,119,035	2,949,809	1,800,923	18,631	798,121	457,684
1989	16,410,897	12,842,634	28,838	12,871,472	1,481,657	-419,754	10,970,061	3,498,994	1,941,842	20,414	803,919	468,296
1990	17,345,125	13,640,429	27,860	13,668,289	1,509,964	-436,492	11,721,833	3,525,352	2,097,940	21,378	811,352	477,904
1991	17,921,053	14,006,763	22,539	14,029,302	1,595,895	-439,648	11,993,759	3,584,296	2,342,998	21,901	818,272	474,065
1992	18,991,395	14,855,342	27,212	14,882,554	1,662,870	-476,352	12,743,332	3,588,601	2,659,462	23,040	824,285	476,931
1993	19,596,837	15,378,083	27,362	15,405,445	1,725,843	-515,846	13,163,756	3,629,321	2,803,760	23,673	827,812	483,377
1994	20,238,686	15,887,306	22,765	15,910,071	1,809,582	-528,409	13,572,080	3,756,949	2,909,657	24,360	830,817	491,282
1995	20,895,200	16,098,700	19,459	16,118,159	1,830,759	-528,421	13,758,979	4,060,792	3,075,429	25,162	830,439	484,903
1996	21,549,433	16,572,119	27,042	16,599,161	1,844,696	-576,687	14,177,778	4,171,237	3,200,418	26,026	828,007	482,555
1997	22,681,039	17,552,800	6,249	17,559,049	1,923,586	-624,309	15,011,154	4,421,576	3,248,309	27,502	824,711	487,706
1998	23,792,054	18,413,682	21,201	18,434,883	2,013,354	-689,778	15,731,751	4,584,413	3,475,890	28,884	823,712	500,443
1999	24,995,537	19,682,457	25,279	19,707,736	2,098,294	-719,347	16,890,095	4,519,459	3,585,983	30,330	824,119	512,344
2000	26,837,786	21,461,551	28,751	21,490,302	2,271,840	-852,548	18,365,914	4,814,242	3,657,630	32,436	827,399	524,195
2001	28,174,147	22,599,727	33,873	22,633,600	2,404,546	-906,198	19,322,856	4,893,039	3,958,252	33,903	831,034	516,432
2002	28,445,224	23,179,258	25,165	23,204,423	2,489,727	-895,883	19,818,813	4,365,350	4,261,061	33,995	836,753	514,437
2003	29,483,413	23,932,420	30,860	23,963,280	2,599,227	-914,138	20,449,915	4,636,162	4,397,336	34,907	844,619	518,106
2004	30,830,928	24,796,920	35,046	24,831,966	2,695,080	-901,596	21,235,290	4,963,786	4,631,852	36,255	850,384	524,002
2005	31,713,253	25,256,370	31,046	25,287,416	2,780,069	-864,883	21,642,464	5,247,853	4,822,936	37,109	854,604	530,740
2006	33,457,949	26,455,175	25,125	26,480,300	2,900,003	-927,565	22,652,732	5,701,246	5,103,971	38,888	860,365	534,257
2007	34,968,131	27,195,447	33,202	27,228,649	2,963,700	-816,364	23,448,585	6,227,718	5,291,828	40,516	863,068	540,904
2008	36,913,180	28,219,064	48,821	28,267,885	3,113,054	-772,146	24,382,685	6,538,916	5,991,579	42,611	866,282	543,929
2009	37,132,647	28,736,891	36,220	28,773,111	3,127,237	-850,233	24,795,641	5,752,595	6,584,411	42,713	869,361	535,314
2010	38,682,101	29,562,584	60,332	29,622,916	3,155,582	-776,609	25,690,725	5,954,675	7,036,701	44,406	871,101	528,095
2011	40,070,328	30,075,638	72,245	30,147,883	2,895,080	-805,798	26,447,005	6,268,998	7,354,325	45,906	872,870	531,541
2012	41,457,094	30,941,184	80,507	31,021,691	2,957,624	-763,928	27,300,139	6,921,733	7,235,222	47,388	874,851	537,634
2013	42,289,493	32,225,263	95,542	32,320,805	3,476,985	-923,316	27,920,504	7,019,829	7,349,160	48,205	877,282	543,162
2014	43,822,909	32,869,319	91,708	32,961,027	3,621,309	-832,100	28,507,618	7,796,938	7,518,353	49,407	886,981	548,362
2015	46,106,193	34,187,480	61,111	34,248,591	3,791,818	-832,624	29,624,149	8,440,261	8,041,783	51,809	889,918	556,276
2016	46,921,640	35,037,705	49,747	35,087,452	3,886,169	-910,740	30,290,543	8,455,164	8,175,933	52,558	892,762	563,746
2017	49,379,492	36,344,419	69,667	36,414,086	4,059,637	-990,585	31,363,864	9,169,619	8,846,009	55,039	897,172	570,656
2018	50,828,850	37,499,570	50,416	37,549,986	4,132,527	-1,039,905	32,377,554	9,754,025	8,697,271	56,501	899,605	575,619
2019	53,457,161	39,073,123	82,134	39,155,257	4,278,885	-1,221,769	33,654,603	10,469,967	9,332,591	59,477	898,791	574,665
2020	57,464,262	39,918,074	65,329	39,983,403	4,348,378	-1,355,411	34,279,614	10,445,321	12,739,327	63,951	898,561	545,052
2021	60,961,078	43,014,715	70,347	43,085,062	4,696,466	-1,486,499	36,902,097	11,007,757	13,051,224	67,788	899,286	556,944

Personal Income and Employment by Metropolitan Statistical Area: Albuquerque, NM

(Thousands of dollars, except as noted.)

Year	Personal income, total	Earnings by place of work			Less: Contributions for government social insurance	Plus: Adjustment for residence	Equals: Net earnings by place of residence	Plus: Dividends, interest, and rent	Plus: Personal current transfer receipts	Per capita personal income (dollars)	Population (persons)	Total employment
		Nonfarm	Farm	Total								
1970	1,414,627	1,099,938	8,526	1,108,464	69,248	14,663	1,053,879	237,800	122,948	3,702	382,076	152,994
1971	1,598,397	1,239,222	7,925	1,247,147	81,837	16,932	1,182,242	273,730	142,425	4,021	397,496	164,049
1972	1,834,590	1,433,302	9,518	1,442,820	98,796	19,045	1,363,069	311,896	159,625	4,499	407,732	177,980
1973	2,045,489	1,598,491	10,994	1,609,485	126,791	22,122	1,504,816	350,520	190,153	4,795	426,583	187,854
1974	2,292,455	1,754,689	11,608	1,766,297	142,552	32,265	1,656,010	408,348	228,097	5,203	440,633	193,502
1975	2,593,217	1,939,587	10,450	1,950,037	156,325	48,104	1,841,816	466,004	285,397	5,754	450,712	198,943
1976	2,935,369	2,205,178	8,613	2,213,791	180,604	66,231	2,099,418	514,117	321,834	6,318	464,570	210,271
1977	3,288,372	2,489,152	10,504	2,499,656	206,193	85,768	2,379,231	572,801	336,340	6,832	481,349	221,559
1978	3,809,512	2,895,245	16,512	2,911,757	247,261	107,888	2,772,384	672,595	364,533	7,729	492,914	237,762
1979	4,332,145	3,290,949	22,012	3,312,961	295,139	129,817	3,147,639	762,190	422,316	8,518	508,581	247,977
1980	4,859,365	3,607,732	25,181	3,632,913	322,760	127,562	3,437,715	908,977	512,673	9,245	525,593	248,765
1981	5,413,999	3,960,840	23,779	3,984,619	378,663	119,337	3,725,293	1,099,964	588,742	10,131	534,415	250,776
1982	5,724,635	4,126,812	21,598	4,148,410	400,925	60,614	3,808,099	1,299,080	617,456	11,199	511,169	248,041
1983	6,289,945	4,597,074	16,765	4,613,839	454,754	32,285	4,191,370	1,434,540	664,035	12,041	522,356	259,621
1984	6,990,630	5,122,781	22,804	5,145,585	522,520	33,113	4,656,178	1,609,844	724,608	13,102	533,544	275,851
1985	7,673,240	5,622,921	19,816	5,642,737	585,624	26,631	5,083,744	1,808,321	781,175	14,090	544,603	290,100
1986	8,175,036	5,990,074	17,588	6,007,662	631,203	27,506	5,403,965	1,930,577	840,494	14,628	558,859	300,497
1987	8,672,045	6,388,377	16,156	6,404,533	667,865	31,985	5,768,653	2,001,942	901,450	15,100	574,324	314,235
1988	9,220,626	6,832,863	22,915	6,855,778	739,904	31,959	6,147,833	2,100,605	972,188	15,789	583,976	330,259
1989	9,794,205	7,222,455	32,012	7,254,467	790,733	40,280	6,504,014	2,201,248	1,088,943	16,488	594,036	336,572
1990	10,482,512	7,735,466	31,253	7,766,719	899,468	49,046	6,916,297	2,371,975	1,194,240	17,396	602,588	341,067
1991	11,204,303	8,293,771	33,167	8,326,938	973,861	46,750	7,399,827	2,458,050	1,346,426	18,179	616,345	348,198
1992	12,036,684	8,977,563	26,268	9,003,831	1,045,197	41,967	8,000,601	2,548,515	1,487,568	19,014	633,032	355,488
1993	13,000,443	9,777,523	29,723	9,807,246	1,138,606	30,337	8,698,977	2,689,433	1,612,033	20,001	649,987	370,109
1994	14,131,170	10,695,020	23,835	10,718,855	1,270,717	30,222	9,478,360	2,953,717	1,699,093	21,100	669,734	389,822
1995	15,220,016	11,492,294	18,021	11,510,315	1,369,032	23,339	10,164,622	3,180,458	1,874,936	22,125	687,901	411,302
1996	16,044,180	11,983,379	24,087	12,007,466	1,425,874	9,135	10,590,727	3,413,153	2,040,300	22,915	700,161	418,022
1997	16,881,644	12,610,490	27,038	12,637,528	1,494,644	233	11,143,117	3,640,701	2,097,826	23,788	709,661	425,091
1998	17,665,363	13,235,479	27,424	13,262,903	1,568,638	3,629	11,697,894	3,824,459	2,143,010	24,624	717,406	431,253
1999	18,031,319	13,715,891	31,829	13,747,720	1,634,401	-6,493	12,106,826	3,636,166	2,288,327	24,950	722,692	433,808
2000	19,569,699	15,025,978	27,248	15,053,226	1,742,775	-16,452	13,293,999	3,827,861	2,447,839	26,727	732,220	446,700
2001	20,569,010	15,702,720	37,056	15,739,776	1,838,468	-27,041	13,874,267	3,942,570	2,752,173	27,724	741,932	448,753
2002	21,351,783	16,331,479	22,199	16,353,678	1,904,883	78	14,448,873	3,877,619	3,025,291	28,179	757,716	448,871
2003	22,366,283	17,161,008	35,287	17,196,295	1,992,807	24,911	15,228,399	3,876,296	3,261,588	28,967	772,128	454,370
2004	23,847,822	18,242,070	53,047	18,295,117	2,091,917	100,091	16,303,291	4,044,930	3,499,601	30,216	789,237	466,415
2005	25,413,565	19,200,183	43,282	19,243,465	2,207,354	174,409	17,210,520	4,414,795	3,788,250	31,392	809,551	476,212
2006	27,515,738	20,627,767	26,070	20,653,837	2,393,414	153,967	18,414,390	4,933,823	4,167,525	33,102	831,252	494,456
2007	28,849,578	21,244,419	46,252	21,290,671	2,491,506	194,118	18,993,283	5,323,307	4,532,988	33,955	849,641	503,901
2008	30,367,135	21,774,235	39,703	21,813,938	2,584,071	221,492	19,451,359	5,649,008	5,266,768	35,172	863,383	503,242
2009	30,272,517	21,634,214	16,833	21,651,047	2,572,182	168,099	19,246,964	5,212,130	5,813,423	34,540	876,448	486,519
2010	30,782,149	21,637,703	25,056	21,662,759	2,581,414	165,554	19,246,899	5,180,539	6,354,711	34,603	889,581	477,820
2011	32,072,865	22,105,548	49,909	22,155,457	2,361,015	173,240	19,967,682	5,652,637	6,452,546	35,711	898,123	476,883
2012	32,448,367	22,246,380	43,476	22,289,856	2,407,248	134,592	20,017,200	5,966,505	6,464,662	35,970	902,091	476,646
2013	32,072,019	22,079,236	38,830	22,118,066	2,763,231	150,124	19,504,959	5,989,913	6,577,147	35,433	905,143	479,148
2014	22,948,512	56,990	23,005,502	2,852,738	115,987	20,268,751	6,447,850	7,192,125	37,585	902,178	33,908,726	483,204
2015	23,746,770	45,431	23,792,201	3,053,434	135,676	20,874,443	6,554,885	7,752,813	38,958	903,085	35,182,141	489,372
2016	24,852,197	47,160	24,899,357	3,135,751	2,943	21,766,549	6,785,132	7,955,949	40,305	905,774	36,507,630	497,097
2017	25,376,685	39,513	25,416,198	3,158,345	5,487	22,263,340	7,012,927	7,973,144	41,014	908,217	37,249,411	502,357
2018	26,329,319	40,118	26,369,437	3,261,861	-25,407	23,082,169	7,102,136	8,424,724	42,414	910,284	38,609,029	508,990
2019	27,673,266	38,054	27,711,320	3,400,244	42,418	24,353,494	7,802,710	8,833,362	44,884	913,231	40,989,566	511,694
2020	28,296,638	44,320	28,340,958	3,535,018	16,803	24,822,743	7,818,148	11,855,090	48,514	917,179	44,495,981	493,283
2021	30,165,880	37,556	30,203,436	3,746,897	33,378	26,489,917	8,117,996	13,382,767	52,263	918,259	47,990,680	506,910

Personal Income and Employment by Metropolitan Statistical Area: Alexandria, LA

(Thousands of dollars, except as noted.)

Year	Personal income, total	Earnings by place of work			Less: Contributions for government social insurance	Plus: Adjustment for residence	Equals: Net earnings by place of residence	Plus: Dividends, interest, and rent	Plus: Personal current transfer receipts	Per capita personal income (dollars)	Population (persons)	Total employment
		Nonfarm	Farm	Total								
1970	398,474	293,678	7,270	300,948	17,442	2,398	285,904	62,613	49,957	3,012	132,287	50,427
1971	452,673	332,276	9,715	341,991	20,344	2,819	324,466	72,441	55,766	3,310	136,756	52,411
1972	494,074	363,553	10,548	374,101	22,986	2,898	354,013	79,113	60,948	3,595	137,425	52,809
1973	549,564	400,679	13,353	414,032	28,429	5,206	390,809	88,749	70,006	3,926	139,971	55,643
1974	596,522	430,241	9,874	440,115	31,787	4,381	412,709	100,669	83,144	4,256	140,176	55,277
1975	667,030	469,271	7,520	476,791	34,510	5,242	447,523	112,767	106,740	4,726	141,141	55,321
1976	750,300	526,745	15,920	542,665	39,761	7,174	510,078	122,768	117,454	5,218	143,786	57,332
1977	821,170	579,625	10,656	590,281	43,249	10,160	557,192	137,858	126,120	5,614	146,270	58,249
1978	932,091	654,535	14,608	669,143	49,095	15,216	635,264	159,792	137,035	6,314	147,614	60,432
1979	1,032,092	713,720	16,103	729,823	55,037	20,727	695,513	179,210	157,369	6,886	149,880	60,097
1980	1,177,286	809,564	3,030	812,594	62,753	24,091	773,932	217,606	185,748	7,735	152,197	61,010
1981	1,310,750	887,640	3,317	890,957	73,153	30,391	848,195	260,169	202,386	8,580	152,773	61,163
1982	1,410,470	926,121	2,289	928,410	76,196	25,654	877,868	295,086	237,516	9,226	152,877	61,401
1983	1,522,769	991,698	16,209	1,007,907	82,131	23,013	948,789	318,767	255,213	9,887	154,017	62,122
1984	1,614,010	1,059,657	8,389	1,068,046	90,312	19,160	996,894	343,864	273,252	10,446	154,515	63,636
1985	1,711,522	1,102,838	9,225	1,112,063	95,519	16,072	1,032,616	378,282	300,624	11,115	153,989	63,606
1986	1,775,833	1,144,184	8,769	1,152,953	99,624	7,976	1,061,305	391,871	322,657	11,506	154,335	63,566
1987	1,832,036	1,189,757	14,161	1,203,918	102,962	3,153	1,104,109	395,216	332,711	11,959	153,188	64,188
1988	1,932,716	1,257,149	22,823	1,279,972	113,970	1,237	1,167,239	415,464	350,013	12,768	151,377	64,413
1989	2,080,986	1,349,066	14,966	1,364,032	126,114	-8,031	1,229,887	464,875	386,224	13,857	150,180	65,261
1990	2,207,846	1,442,368	14,302	1,456,670	137,338	-8,714	1,310,618	465,430	431,798	14,820	148,982	65,706
1991	2,285,734	1,494,613	6,633	1,501,246	147,455	-7,307	1,346,484	457,961	481,289	15,336	149,046	65,863
1992	2,374,547	1,529,044	20,480	1,549,524	149,629	-3,450	1,396,445	445,039	533,063	16,085	147,621	64,337
1993	2,509,158	1,582,398	20,678	1,603,076	156,108	-5,674	1,441,294	454,154	613,710	17,642	142,225	65,441
1994	2,692,139	1,654,611	24,939	1,679,550	167,106	-6,194	1,506,250	486,405	699,484	18,815	143,086	66,500
1995	2,790,875	1,733,426	22,071	1,755,497	176,030	-5,574	1,573,893	529,209	687,773	19,359	144,162	69,293
1996	2,868,955	1,796,210	26,878	1,823,088	184,216	-5,173	1,633,699	553,232	682,024	19,927	143,970	69,670
1997	2,972,718	1,839,380	19,408	1,858,788	190,137	-3,261	1,665,390	596,833	710,495	20,646	143,986	70,362
1998	3,145,349	1,980,148	13,743	1,993,891	206,167	-7,698	1,780,026	638,480	726,843	21,793	144,330	72,287
1999	3,260,268	2,115,717	22,035	2,137,752	216,492	-12,790	1,908,470	626,487	725,311	22,515	144,803	74,507
2000	3,400,066	2,200,674	23,985	2,224,659	222,383	-12,528	1,989,748	669,472	740,846	23,420	145,179	75,003
2001	3,712,780	2,358,499	21,860	2,380,359	232,946	-16,286	2,131,127	680,904	900,749	25,587	145,102	74,686
2002	3,845,010	2,494,642	16,287	2,510,929	245,216	-25,238	2,240,475	672,776	931,759	26,441	145,416	75,251
2003	3,906,470	2,558,818	28,616	2,587,434	251,283	-30,182	2,305,969	695,390	905,111	26,754	146,017	75,320
2004	4,197,276	2,709,789	21,344	2,731,133	267,943	-45,428	2,417,762	740,164	1,039,350	28,558	146,973	77,127
2005	4,596,706	2,928,839	21,263	2,950,102	284,521	-53,959	2,611,622	842,483	1,142,601	31,074	147,930	79,635
2006	4,825,839	3,189,155	28,488	3,217,643	312,783	-73,189	2,831,671	821,540	1,172,628	31,929	151,142	83,038
2007	5,054,135	3,294,064	31,584	3,325,648	329,214	-79,586	2,916,848	910,693	1,226,594	33,359	151,506	84,415
2008	5,372,766	3,401,233	23,974	3,425,207	343,634	-87,858	2,993,715	1,039,388	1,339,663	35,245	152,442	84,931
2009	5,305,778	3,394,914	38,473	3,433,387	344,861	-96,874	2,991,652	912,769	1,401,357	34,641	153,164	82,896
2010	5,409,858	3,489,606	47,920	3,537,526	348,434	-90,891	3,098,201	859,074	1,452,583	35,109	154,088	81,419
2011	5,691,867	3,576,356	55,356	3,631,712	323,078	-94,742	3,213,892	1,004,422	1,473,553	36,861	154,416	81,795
2012	5,972,060	3,688,071	69,018	3,757,089	329,425	-102,455	3,325,209	1,113,170	1,533,681	38,673	154,424	81,062
2013	5,990,723	3,783,896	51,091	3,834,987	377,807	-116,325	3,340,855	1,047,677	1,602,191	38,736	154,654	80,884
2014	6,095,124	3,951,805	29,732	3,981,537	385,821	-112,777	3,482,939	1,066,760	1,545,425	39,318	155,021	81,642
2015	6,178,447	3,939,956	24,644	3,964,600	393,176	-114,484	3,456,940	1,043,032	1,678,475	39,949	154,658	81,926
2016	6,268,931	4,005,664	22,625	4,028,289	405,988	-129,437	3,492,864	1,050,289	1,725,778	40,507	154,763	81,668
2017	6,309,012	4,033,347	35,911	4,069,258	406,717	-131,316	3,531,225	1,017,169	1,760,618	40,890	154,292	80,945
2018	6,529,351	4,166,954	43,618	4,210,572	422,809	-130,964	3,656,799	1,057,889	1,814,663	42,505	153,614	80,907
2019	6,741,618	4,263,399	59,800	4,323,199	430,433	-131,808	3,760,958	1,083,983	1,896,677	44,057	153,019	80,071
2020	7,332,785	4,429,145	67,304	4,496,449	454,657	-148,041	3,893,751	1,077,004	2,362,030	48,326	151,736	78,948
2021	7,806,684	4,641,056	56,429	4,697,485	471,133	-160,906	4,065,446	1,092,855	2,648,383	51,738	150,890	80,638

Personal Income and Employment by Metropolitan Statistical Area: Allentown-Bethlehem-Easton, PA-NJ

(Thousands of dollars, except as noted.)

Year	Personal income, total	Earnings by place of work			Less: Contributions for government social insurance	Plus: Adjustment for residence	Equals: Net earnings by place of residence	Plus: Dividends, interest, and rent	Plus: Personal current transfer receipts	Per capita personal income (dollars)	Population (persons)	Total employment
		Nonfarm	Farm	Total								
1970	2,470,715	2,045,622	15,931	2,061,553	156,077	22,192	1,927,668	326,336	216,711	4,148	595,577	272,973
1971	2,634,493	2,150,247	12,596	2,162,843	170,660	31,656	2,023,839	356,311	254,343	4,377	601,892	271,090
1972	2,921,986	2,392,436	13,758	2,406,194	199,397	39,217	2,246,014	388,667	287,305	4,828	605,156	277,879
1973	3,293,107	2,712,131	19,656	2,731,787	260,516	49,597	2,520,868	447,230	325,009	5,390	610,947	292,047
1974	3,695,845	3,016,404	21,975	3,038,379	300,799	56,673	2,794,253	517,312	384,280	5,983	617,690	297,119
1975	4,063,395	3,204,702	19,496	3,224,198	312,338	67,694	2,979,554	574,912	508,929	6,532	622,114	290,754
1976	4,421,259	3,450,069	21,927	3,471,996	339,840	92,278	3,224,434	615,702	581,123	7,076	624,814	291,781
1977	4,886,917	3,822,661	21,206	3,843,867	371,422	120,689	3,593,134	686,515	607,268	7,787	627,598	296,393
1978	5,432,118	4,270,480	23,713	4,294,193	426,495	152,251	4,019,949	756,715	655,454	8,626	629,719	304,849
1979	6,060,391	4,755,921	31,467	4,787,388	490,392	183,177	4,480,173	851,049	729,169	9,573	633,073	310,781
1980	6,686,058	5,061,136	16,665	5,077,801	527,711	227,997	4,778,087	1,054,915	853,056	10,506	636,389	310,670
1981	7,404,955	5,420,311	23,287	5,443,598	604,656	272,717	5,111,659	1,311,487	981,809	11,593	638,748	310,155
1982	7,937,732	5,533,041	20,473	5,553,514	626,695	325,890	5,252,709	1,548,087	1,136,936	12,387	640,790	302,259
1983	8,299,386	5,696,938	3,954	5,700,892	651,169	392,006	5,441,729	1,609,685	1,247,972	12,935	641,637	298,035
1984	9,105,802	6,311,417	26,639	6,338,056	750,312	454,017	6,041,761	1,815,859	1,248,182	14,121	644,843	309,576
1985	9,740,893	6,687,998	27,471	6,715,469	801,788	527,228	6,440,909	1,976,079	1,323,905	15,026	648,256	314,763
1986	10,260,641	6,957,755	22,123	6,979,878	829,533	614,509	6,764,854	2,077,696	1,418,091	15,680	654,365	317,329
1987	10,969,909	7,548,433	21,949	7,570,382	889,895	690,163	7,370,650	2,149,521	1,449,738	16,536	663,413	329,686
1988	11,895,780	8,212,969	26,781	8,239,750	988,633	800,418	8,051,535	2,299,876	1,544,369	17,629	674,767	339,830
1989	12,979,588	8,760,090	36,413	8,796,503	1,042,536	889,927	8,643,894	2,681,958	1,653,736	19,013	682,657	345,404
1990	13,678,791	9,185,091	33,673	9,218,764	1,088,667	984,129	9,114,226	2,731,010	1,833,555	19,859	688,801	349,846
1991	14,337,995	9,461,336	20,150	9,481,486	1,135,891	998,553	9,344,148	2,859,111	2,134,736	20,596	696,168	345,339
1992	15,192,704	10,179,798	35,527	10,215,325	1,211,040	1,077,087	10,081,372	2,821,100	2,290,232	21,613	702,948	345,658
1993	15,755,236	10,631,079	26,975	10,658,054	1,286,552	1,162,902	10,534,404	2,823,488	2,397,344	22,229	708,776	347,081
1994	16,334,381	11,053,320	21,304	11,074,624	1,360,581	1,207,430	10,921,473	2,948,811	2,464,097	22,877	714,019	351,274
1995	17,021,853	11,459,478	15,864	11,475,342	1,405,503	1,271,053	11,340,892	3,088,119	2,592,842	23,718	717,685	355,394
1996	17,945,703	11,906,128	33,545	11,939,673	1,420,267	1,395,872	11,915,278	3,262,070	2,768,355	24,853	722,063	357,386
1997	18,899,145	12,476,805	14,314	12,491,119	1,481,970	1,533,501	12,542,650	3,492,511	2,863,984	26,015	726,464	365,995
1998	19,832,960	13,062,238	16,069	13,078,307	1,539,031	1,712,513	13,251,789	3,669,414	2,911,757	27,139	730,779	369,703
1999	20,960,406	14,065,385	7,909	14,073,294	1,626,634	1,827,739	14,274,399	3,612,681	3,073,326	28,466	736,327	377,848
2000	22,603,250	14,900,759	27,725	14,928,484	1,702,769	2,172,147	15,397,862	3,930,919	3,274,469	30,470	741,817	388,803
2001	24,300,177	16,368,345	17,931	16,386,276	1,828,447	2,231,074	16,788,903	3,938,897	3,572,377	32,456	748,705	396,203
2002	25,052,772	16,928,003	11,046	16,939,049	1,889,748	2,304,666	17,353,967	3,857,764	3,841,041	33,111	756,628	395,667
2003	25,988,799	17,474,757	28,491	17,503,248	1,935,981	2,435,514	18,002,781	4,042,948	3,943,070	33,886	766,938	400,604
2004	27,430,360	18,568,532	38,700	18,607,232	2,031,865	2,808,519	19,383,886	3,940,245	4,106,229	35,290	777,277	408,168
2005	29,363,798	20,008,951	25,108	20,034,059	2,177,665	3,077,685	20,934,079	3,977,331	4,452,388	37,276	787,738	418,886
2006	30,833,117	20,590,733	22,710	20,613,443	2,294,300	3,432,685	21,751,828	4,361,086	4,720,203	38,610	798,586	428,104
2007	33,389,669	21,926,785	37,101	21,963,886	2,395,702	3,869,608	23,437,792	4,882,739	5,069,138	41,345	807,578	435,473
2008	34,630,212	22,241,740	36,429	22,278,169	2,443,427	3,716,281	23,551,023	5,337,335	5,741,854	42,541	814,050	435,265
2009	33,407,120	21,359,312	27,328	21,386,640	2,397,558	3,158,722	22,147,804	4,944,166	6,315,150	40,851	817,779	424,470
2010	34,750,711	22,072,425	33,408	22,105,833	2,457,007	3,423,484	23,072,310	4,863,733	6,814,668	42,288	821,768	425,825
2011	35,946,602	22,812,197	43,971	22,856,168	2,293,351	3,311,032	23,873,849	5,245,878	6,826,875	43,579	824,860	432,726
2012	36,566,423	23,329,145	56,842	23,385,987	2,343,780	3,078,446	24,120,653	5,577,474	6,868,296	44,261	826,157	438,772
2013	37,065,336	24,023,037	58,722	24,081,759	2,718,682	3,143,603	24,506,680	5,617,681	6,940,975	44,883	825,817	445,553
2014	38,612,541	24,936,746	47,396	24,984,142	2,820,023	3,175,295	25,339,414	6,074,653	7,198,474	46,238	835,077	452,876
2015	40,422,983	26,198,395	52,858	26,251,253	2,941,729	3,228,123	26,537,647	6,303,369	7,581,967	48,209	838,490	459,142
2016	41,717,926	26,904,629	26,502	26,931,131	3,036,954	3,328,353	27,222,530	6,475,496	8,019,900	49,477	843,181	466,967
2017	42,994,431	27,794,164	43,149	27,837,313	3,187,876	3,320,342	27,969,779	6,815,347	8,209,305	50,599	849,703	472,692
2018	45,081,246	28,588,226	29,821	28,618,047	3,272,471	3,739,753	29,085,329	7,213,550	8,782,367	52,666	855,983	480,491
2019	47,457,363	29,816,845	54,581	29,871,426	3,440,250	4,144,925	30,576,101	7,689,714	9,191,548	55,269	858,656	484,177
2020	50,370,106	29,262,723	45,284	29,308,007	3,415,484	4,224,984	30,117,507	7,632,796	12,619,803	58,454	861,705	462,653
2021	54,184,376	31,704,493	59,072	31,763,565	3,647,851	4,874,650	32,990,364	7,770,291	13,423,721	62,618	865,310	483,466

Personal Income and Employment by Metropolitan Statistical Area: Altoona, PA

(Thousands of dollars, except as noted.)

Year	Personal income, total	Earnings by place of work			Less: Contributions for government social insurance	Plus: Adjustment for residence	Equals: Net earnings by place of residence	Plus: Dividends, interest, and rent	Plus: Personal current transfer receipts	Per capita personal income (dollars)	Population (persons)	Total employment
		Nonfarm	Farm	Total								
1970	470,275	399,460	5,984	405,444	34,429	-18,697	352,318	49,266	68,691	3,470	135,538	57,438
1971	499,206	420,062	4,239	424,301	37,056	-19,261	367,984	52,867	78,355	3,644	136,999	56,621
1972	535,727	450,677	4,049	454,726	41,151	-21,087	392,488	56,584	86,655	3,891	137,687	57,144
1973	589,763	500,165	4,690	504,855	50,902	-24,338	429,615	63,530	96,618	4,319	136,556	59,254
1974	647,183	542,510	3,915	546,425	57,822	-26,668	461,935	72,020	113,228	4,725	136,956	58,969
1975	713,117	575,826	4,079	579,905	59,813	-27,735	492,357	79,630	141,130	5,220	136,611	57,981
1976	795,308	653,745	5,067	658,812	69,525	-33,229	556,058	86,372	152,878	5,847	136,023	59,523
1977	877,132	733,477	4,591	738,068	79,292	-39,330	619,446	96,830	160,856	6,402	137,015	60,379
1978	965,705	810,012	5,878	815,890	87,981	-45,210	682,699	106,910	176,096	7,013	137,705	61,616
1979	1,066,392	890,750	7,240	897,990	99,294	-50,634	748,062	119,180	199,150	7,729	137,966	61,945
1980	1,139,914	910,505	4,455	914,960	100,441	-53,620	760,899	151,205	227,810	8,355	136,443	60,840
1981	1,230,999	946,422	5,475	951,897	111,386	-53,458	787,053	187,643	256,303	9,088	135,457	59,371
1982	1,283,897	925,693	5,733	931,426	110,192	-46,927	774,307	219,944	289,646	9,468	135,600	56,566
1983	1,331,897	934,576	4,292	938,868	109,361	-44,964	784,543	231,797	315,557	9,910	134,397	55,220
1984	1,414,118	1,006,311	9,577	1,015,888	123,518	-48,291	844,079	257,706	312,333	10,638	132,925	56,874
1985	1,511,644	1,090,909	10,326	1,101,235	137,017	-57,124	907,094	276,574	327,976	11,430	132,253	58,346
1986	1,597,220	1,165,110	10,854	1,175,964	148,647	-62,355	964,962	293,776	338,482	12,141	131,556	59,616
1987	1,658,933	1,227,636	12,261	1,239,897	154,461	-63,570	1,021,866	295,697	341,370	12,595	131,712	60,857
1988	1,743,086	1,285,413	11,739	1,297,152	166,697	-60,752	1,069,703	314,600	358,783	13,265	131,408	62,323
1989	1,888,384	1,372,373	13,450	1,385,823	174,681	-61,465	1,149,677	362,271	376,436	14,465	130,546	63,201
1990	1,999,299	1,456,984	10,361	1,467,345	183,815	-65,532	1,217,998	364,998	416,303	15,309	130,593	64,824
1991	2,092,950	1,498,771	8,733	1,507,504	190,791	-68,366	1,248,347	370,500	474,103	15,957	131,160	63,975
1992	2,237,068	1,640,139	12,423	1,652,562	207,353	-80,663	1,364,546	374,825	497,697	17,042	131,270	65,472
1993	2,350,285	1,751,662	8,334	1,759,996	223,632	-91,553	1,444,811	386,003	519,471	17,851	131,661	67,208
1994	2,456,062	1,845,493	10,107	1,855,600	238,564	-99,031	1,518,005	405,807	532,250	18,589	132,124	68,011
1995	2,549,386	1,901,075	10,105	1,911,180	242,941	-103,166	1,565,073	433,097	551,216	19,343	131,802	69,263
1996	2,689,142	2,004,060	12,725	2,016,785	246,893	-112,103	1,657,789	447,730	583,623	20,515	131,080	70,018
1997	2,832,129	2,123,957	12,656	2,136,613	257,659	-118,624	1,760,330	473,618	598,181	21,631	130,931	70,970
1998	2,973,338	2,238,940	23,528	2,262,468	268,336	-132,051	1,862,081	491,503	619,754	22,783	130,509	71,039
1999	3,086,478	2,361,790	23,487	2,385,277	281,060	-144,847	1,959,370	483,341	643,767	23,787	129,757	72,406
2000	3,215,690	2,434,056	19,218	2,453,274	284,690	-151,027	2,017,557	516,381	681,752	24,932	128,981	72,331
2001	3,259,007	2,441,574	22,366	2,463,940	291,311	-152,562	2,020,067	507,967	730,973	25,368	128,471	72,750
2002	3,348,867	2,505,730	14,113	2,519,843	296,054	-154,328	2,069,461	503,477	775,929	26,239	127,631	72,974
2003	3,479,545	2,613,251	19,762	2,633,013	303,436	-165,657	2,163,920	514,294	801,331	27,322	127,353	73,403
2004	3,647,106	2,766,849	35,645	2,802,494	318,006	-175,153	2,309,335	496,738	841,033	28,674	127,194	74,357
2005	3,780,807	2,857,792	32,274	2,890,066	338,114	-186,337	2,365,615	521,097	894,095	29,834	126,730	75,271
2006	3,903,106	2,914,333	21,610	2,935,943	348,162	-179,555	2,408,226	555,886	938,994	30,733	127,002	75,417
2007	4,099,495	2,999,297	35,962	3,035,259	360,554	-189,511	2,485,194	618,197	996,104	32,267	127,048	76,076
2008	4,250,268	3,018,725	30,690	3,049,415	367,348	-183,925	2,498,142	653,715	1,098,411	33,437	127,112	75,332
2009	4,303,724	3,030,605	17,802	3,048,407	371,060	-186,218	2,491,129	637,029	1,175,566	33,845	127,161	74,055
2010	4,457,638	3,135,125	33,220	3,168,345	379,559	-179,120	2,609,666	631,935	1,216,037	35,086	127,049	73,707
2011	4,722,568	3,261,317	41,468	3,302,785	356,819	-186,725	2,759,241	721,246	1,242,081	37,189	126,990	74,408
2012	4,804,848	3,294,228	35,572	3,329,800	358,199	-192,466	2,779,135	765,822	1,259,891	37,962	126,569	74,542
2013	4,780,079	3,385,298	36,186	3,421,484	409,877	-196,610	2,814,997	693,005	1,272,077	37,977	125,869	75,183
2014	4,967,059	3,494,197	47,027	3,541,224	423,210	-200,265	2,917,749	740,000	1,309,310	39,425	125,986	75,206
2015	5,210,224	3,663,736	21,954	3,685,690	439,936	-209,616	3,036,138	792,577	1,381,509	41,526	125,469	75,538
2016	5,274,704	3,675,294	18,164	3,693,458	441,495	-202,205	3,049,758	782,377	1,442,569	42,277	124,764	75,256
2017	5,403,887	3,788,929	31,570	3,820,499	462,891	-213,094	3,144,514	799,614	1,459,759	43,471	124,310	75,498
2018	5,644,514	3,904,697	15,392	3,920,089	475,106	-217,691	3,227,292	868,822	1,548,400	45,574	123,854	75,515
2019	5,802,876	3,972,702	28,817	4,001,519	487,960	-228,797	3,284,762	907,145	1,610,969	47,034	123,376	75,097
2020	6,249,262	3,942,070	26,047	3,968,117	481,534	-230,337	3,256,246	896,964	2,096,052	51,007	122,518	71,779
2021	6,632,617	4,164,169	31,314	4,195,483	500,333	-243,544	3,451,606	907,524	2,273,487	54,470	121,767	73,915

Personal Income and Employment by Metropolitan Statistical Area: Amarillo, TX

(Thousands of dollars, except as noted.)

| Year | Personal income, total | Derivation of personal income | | | | | | | | Per capita personal income (dollars) | Population (persons) | Total employment |
| | | Earnings by place of work | | | Less: Contributions for government social insurance | Plus: Adjustment for residence | Equals: Net earnings by place of residence | Plus: Dividends, interest, and rent | Plus: Personal current transfer receipts | | | |
		Nonfarm	Farm	Total								
1970	603,484	462,240	34,855	497,095	30,161	-4,164	462,770	98,008	42,706	3,887	155,258	73,776
1971	657,441	503,098	35,705	538,803	33,600	-3,889	501,314	107,091	49,036	4,156	158,182	74,731
1972	702,455	545,465	26,606	572,071	38,300	-3,550	530,221	116,881	55,353	4,375	160,557	76,674
1973	819,510	610,516	61,278	671,794	49,703	-608	621,483	132,086	65,941	5,070	161,637	80,252
1974	891,605	718,026	5,605	723,631	60,173	-3,125	660,333	156,031	75,241	5,457	163,395	85,601
1975	1,100,596	847,704	57,335	905,039	69,359	-1,596	834,084	175,231	91,281	6,633	165,916	89,728
1976	1,204,978	969,914	30,894	1,000,808	80,048	-4,906	915,854	190,633	98,491	7,115	169,368	92,626
1977	1,330,264	1,072,517	33,243	1,105,760	89,765	-6,346	1,009,649	214,116	106,499	7,688	173,027	95,339
1978	1,505,057	1,221,268	28,581	1,249,849	104,114	-2,644	1,143,091	243,353	118,613	8,568	175,670	98,271
1979	1,692,963	1,366,620	38,566	1,405,186	122,572	-1,899	1,280,715	276,162	136,086	9,347	181,120	101,304
1980	1,855,393	1,501,915	-2,565	1,499,350	135,124	-1,471	1,362,755	335,400	157,238	10,000	185,546	102,188
1981	2,142,554	1,667,196	34,200	1,701,396	162,641	-795	1,537,960	424,110	180,484	11,360	188,598	104,700
1982	2,356,454	1,794,509	28,833	1,823,342	178,863	5,419	1,649,898	504,219	202,337	12,238	192,559	106,682
1983	2,628,888	1,943,123	113,847	2,056,970	192,822	-1,697	1,862,451	541,268	225,169	13,432	195,720	109,796
1984	2,792,319	2,083,090	74,321	2,157,411	213,771	2,274	1,945,914	602,063	244,342	14,038	198,910	113,248
1985	2,926,895	2,177,776	54,116	2,231,892	227,019	2,440	2,007,313	654,295	265,287	14,678	199,407	115,109
1986	2,961,570	2,192,953	62,145	2,255,098	226,562	-1,186	2,027,350	644,687	289,533	14,762	200,618	111,050
1987	3,012,867	2,248,365	39,110	2,287,475	227,335	-1,011	2,059,129	644,258	309,480	15,037	200,360	113,749
1988	3,054,730	2,216,356	49,748	2,266,104	234,504	27,341	2,058,941	661,353	334,436	15,192	201,069	112,617
1989	3,201,986	2,284,958	53,257	2,338,215	242,026	12,809	2,108,998	733,911	359,077	16,032	199,721	109,387
1990	3,338,739	2,388,468	81,987	2,470,455	246,417	17,061	2,241,099	706,847	390,793	16,821	198,488	110,406
1991	3,419,313	2,438,745	84,189	2,522,934	259,945	14,419	2,277,408	706,587	435,318	17,043	200,626	112,231
1992	3,678,063	2,650,568	90,477	2,741,045	277,660	7,537	2,470,922	701,062	506,079	18,085	203,371	113,046
1993	3,920,092	2,860,015	100,772	2,960,787	298,737	3,461	2,665,511	719,208	535,373	18,912	207,282	117,950
1994	4,150,926	3,078,651	58,101	3,136,752	325,510	-2,381	2,808,861	773,082	568,983	19,644	211,306	122,956
1995	4,399,764	3,289,609	49,618	3,339,227	346,914	-3,259	2,989,054	794,151	616,559	20,238	217,400	126,957
1996	4,598,530	3,421,890	49,137	3,471,027	355,720	-2,258	3,113,049	828,542	656,939	20,921	219,808	128,079
1997	4,902,690	3,644,809	63,534	3,708,343	374,066	-146	3,334,131	881,598	686,961	22,079	222,054	130,252
1998	5,137,865	3,803,670	67,524	3,871,194	390,246	2,469	3,483,417	959,398	695,050	22,984	223,545	141,013
1999	5,293,371	3,936,421	88,984	4,025,405	406,433	-3,044	3,615,928	961,496	715,947	23,358	226,621	141,705
2000	5,549,165	4,095,874	72,046	4,167,920	418,071	-4,561	3,745,288	1,050,441	753,436	24,209	229,215	144,574
2001	6,108,166	4,571,814	101,522	4,673,336	448,820	-9,830	4,214,686	1,069,767	823,713	26,517	230,351	136,232
2002	6,308,358	4,794,380	85,158	4,879,538	468,321	-15,321	4,395,896	1,029,006	883,456	27,153	232,326	137,018
2003	6,576,882	4,928,967	111,901	5,040,868	496,339	-21,125	4,523,404	1,112,829	940,649	27,970	235,138	139,781
2004	6,688,393	5,024,425	100,726	5,125,151	517,784	-18,600	4,588,767	1,106,677	992,949	28,154	237,566	142,937
2005	7,131,130	5,250,911	96,284	5,347,195	538,059	-9,760	4,799,376	1,255,487	1,076,267	29,666	240,380	144,955
2006	7,625,580	5,697,638	77,494	5,775,132	571,200	-6,598	5,197,334	1,286,083	1,142,163	31,425	242,656	148,345
2007	8,119,578	5,929,745	115,621	6,045,366	602,197	9,419	5,452,588	1,421,044	1,245,946	33,194	244,608	151,879
2008	9,060,734	6,507,325	78,728	6,586,053	642,427	49,315	5,992,941	1,673,677	1,394,116	36,764	246,458	154,926
2009	8,794,080	6,463,357	65,404	6,528,761	656,650	69,474	5,941,585	1,368,603	1,483,892	35,265	249,373	154,258
2010	9,637,796	6,918,446	158,831	7,077,277	679,257	90,795	6,488,815	1,511,406	1,637,575	38,144	252,666	152,820
2011	10,295,132	7,275,009	172,164	7,447,173	620,720	98,302	6,924,755	1,671,000	1,699,377	40,216	255,996	155,100
2012	10,604,532	7,530,122	125,437	7,655,559	638,544	112,456	7,129,471	1,795,069	1,679,992	41,128	257,842	156,747
2013	10,799,173	7,744,271	124,919	7,869,190	740,764	103,585	7,232,011	1,839,556	1,727,606	41,705	258,939	159,559
2014	11,410,513	8,063,065	179,842	8,242,907	766,009	118,692	7,595,590	2,005,505	1,809,418	43,529	262,135	160,727
2015	11,495,829	8,004,249	285,536	8,289,785	794,318	142,484	7,637,951	1,953,001	1,904,877	43,672	263,232	162,593
2016	11,501,531	8,068,743	161,352	8,230,095	821,886	145,906	7,554,115	1,952,777	1,994,639	43,437	264,785	164,586
2017	11,916,012	8,280,836	175,705	8,456,541	845,098	144,025	7,755,468	2,135,632	2,024,912	44,745	266,308	164,440
2018	12,366,183	8,609,745	151,714	8,761,459	877,648	124,828	8,008,639	2,231,661	2,125,883	46,403	266,497	165,408
2019	13,120,533	9,051,136	155,290	9,206,426	916,287	114,320	8,404,459	2,467,928	2,248,146	49,109	267,174	165,556
2020	14,144,505	9,551,933	138,027	9,689,960	959,113	103,223	8,834,070	2,436,530	2,873,905	52,617	268,820	164,152
2021	15,170,292	10,019,825	178,119	10,197,944	1,018,177	95,711	9,275,478	2,582,430	3,312,384	56,248	269,703	168,109

Personal Income and Employment by Metropolitan Statistical Area: Ames, IA

(Thousands of dollars, except as noted.)

Year	Personal income, total	Earnings by place of work			Less: Contributions for government social insurance	Plus: Adjustment for residence	Equals: Net earnings by place of residence	Plus: Dividends, interest, and rent	Plus: Personal current transfer receipts	Per capita personal income (dollars)	Population (persons)	Total employment
		Nonfarm	Farm	Total								
1970	222,847	160,836	15,700	176,536	11,447	-78	165,011	42,638	15,198	3,544	62,885	28,559
1971	240,660	178,348	10,914	189,262	13,161	-383	175,718	47,764	17,178	3,781	63,651	29,140
1972	266,529	194,310	16,979	211,289	15,190	-1,578	194,521	53,319	18,689	4,125	64,612	30,331
1973	315,555	221,386	34,059	255,445	20,092	-3,109	232,244	61,477	21,834	4,754	66,375	32,103
1974	337,848	248,923	20,755	269,678	23,826	-4,195	241,657	70,808	25,383	4,993	67,669	33,140
1975	377,054	277,968	19,247	297,215	26,318	-5,693	265,204	80,496	31,354	5,544	68,014	33,849
1976	415,960	318,241	12,761	331,002	30,197	-8,081	292,724	88,585	34,651	6,022	69,071	35,772
1977	458,102	368,955	-3,110	365,845	34,371	-11,734	319,740	101,714	36,648	6,554	69,899	37,579
1978	542,013	418,642	24,041	442,683	40,785	-14,675	387,223	113,384	41,406	7,601	71,311	39,155
1979	592,743	466,761	13,252	480,013	47,392	-16,408	416,213	129,302	47,228	8,297	71,442	40,186
1980	655,592	499,319	15,415	514,734	50,488	-19,523	444,723	155,010	55,859	9,047	72,468	40,763
1981	722,576	527,073	20,826	547,899	56,844	-17,461	473,594	185,621	63,361	9,917	72,864	39,295
1982	769,717	550,255	14,919	565,174	59,804	-18,135	487,235	213,072	69,410	10,647	72,292	39,073
1983	817,399	583,464	11,120	594,584	62,991	-18,784	512,809	226,180	78,410	11,149	73,316	39,812
1984	901,569	646,359	20,908	667,267	71,024	-20,358	575,885	244,812	80,872	12,282	73,408	41,501
1985	958,563	691,232	22,178	713,410	77,553	-21,203	614,654	255,317	88,592	12,945	74,050	42,726
1986	993,869	715,035	28,768	743,803	82,313	-18,780	642,710	260,135	91,024	13,427	74,022	42,744
1987	1,042,047	757,142	30,112	787,254	87,119	-17,124	683,011	262,423	96,613	14,214	73,312	43,166
1988	1,082,342	813,510	13,091	826,601	98,163	-17,702	710,736	271,757	99,849	14,650	73,881	45,013
1989	1,189,917	885,539	31,276	916,815	105,469	-18,839	792,507	288,187	109,223	16,143	73,711	46,420
1990	1,257,769	937,448	22,564	960,012	113,310	-17,861	828,841	310,601	118,327	16,910	74,382	47,526
1991	1,316,042	981,271	19,915	1,001,186	117,896	-19,022	864,268	326,228	125,546	17,666	74,497	47,846
1992	1,385,475	1,039,401	32,604	1,072,005	123,238	-21,111	927,656	325,681	132,138	18,441	75,130	47,929
1993	1,431,363	1,104,388	6,480	1,110,868	129,803	-26,970	954,095	334,552	142,716	18,832	76,008	48,460
1994	1,544,758	1,166,301	33,163	1,199,464	138,000	-30,198	1,031,266	365,308	148,184	20,353	75,899	48,857
1995	1,628,002	1,214,911	30,095	1,245,006	143,315	-32,996	1,068,695	403,214	156,093	21,347	76,265	50,377
1996	1,746,967	1,288,223	42,044	1,330,267	146,287	-37,015	1,146,965	434,074	165,928	22,706	76,937	50,625
1997	1,858,513	1,380,235	40,002	1,420,237	161,806	-42,097	1,216,334	467,157	175,022	23,878	77,833	51,103
1998	2,616,193	1,805,306	43,084	1,848,390	215,453	53,670	1,686,607	628,271	301,315	25,119	104,151	65,058
1999	2,711,014	1,921,798	31,087	1,952,885	227,888	56,108	1,781,105	619,371	310,538	25,688	105,536	66,585
2000	2,862,828	2,016,484	39,500	2,055,984	236,987	56,121	1,875,118	653,085	334,625	26,906	106,403	67,065
2001	2,932,174	2,070,111	33,238	2,103,349	239,914	59,687	1,923,122	644,633	364,419	27,530	106,509	69,062
2002	3,038,805	2,146,870	45,536	2,192,406	248,270	59,133	2,003,269	626,827	408,709	28,145	107,971	69,334
2003	3,166,969	2,261,054	47,606	2,308,660	262,456	50,897	2,097,101	671,157	398,711	29,243	108,300	69,908
2004	3,350,088	2,379,196	91,343	2,470,539	273,983	30,080	2,226,636	712,289	411,163	30,699	109,126	71,202
2005	3,448,830	2,480,575	78,588	2,559,163	284,707	19,101	2,293,557	731,272	424,001	31,530	109,384	71,916
2006	3,722,039	2,652,001	59,565	2,711,566	301,139	-5,519	2,404,908	824,714	492,417	33,469	111,210	72,886
2007	3,956,967	2,776,638	95,368	2,872,006	316,272	1,683	2,557,417	874,371	525,179	34,989	113,093	73,697
2008	4,200,932	3,003,831	76,286	3,080,117	338,716	-18,445	2,722,956	876,882	601,094	36,758	114,285	73,810
2009	4,020,328	2,886,052	76,301	2,962,353	330,167	-81,730	2,550,456	834,815	635,057	34,764	115,645	72,907
2010	4,013,386	2,894,154	53,732	2,947,886	334,485	-148,405	2,464,996	856,543	691,847	34,618	115,932	72,318
2011	4,327,442	2,957,493	123,382	3,080,875	306,759	-104,519	2,669,597	953,583	704,262	36,845	117,451	73,103
2012	4,774,502	3,369,774	125,644	3,495,418	331,853	-78,989	3,084,576	1,005,993	683,933	40,399	118,184	73,379
2013	4,658,707	3,354,658	158,930	3,513,588	376,501	-185,794	2,951,293	993,465	713,949	38,748	120,232	75,036
2014	4,842,726	3,551,051	109,076	3,660,127	396,508	-223,607	3,040,012	1,069,269	733,445	39,516	122,552	75,869
2015	4,992,267	3,734,283	73,076	3,807,359	409,601	-272,805	3,124,953	1,100,496	766,818	40,373	123,653	77,350
2016	5,018,968	3,749,327	32,490	3,781,817	415,017	-251,417	3,115,383	1,135,742	767,843	40,485	123,972	77,076
2017	5,130,989	3,874,172	23,075	3,897,247	432,664	-295,198	3,169,385	1,203,698	757,906	41,231	124,446	77,537
2018	5,357,899	4,019,578	31,186	4,050,764	451,218	-293,735	3,305,811	1,222,079	830,009	43,279	123,798	77,929
2019	5,558,989	4,127,874	33,880	4,161,754	468,118	-293,728	3,399,908	1,283,252	875,829	44,630	124,556	77,330
2020	5,862,650	4,109,881	52,246	4,162,127	482,931	-244,911	3,434,285	1,298,146	1,130,219	46,787	125,306	74,381
2021	6,223,934	4,393,701	113,589	4,507,290	508,362	-288,241	3,710,687	1,307,948	1,205,299	49,320	126,195	76,273

Personal Income and Employment by Area: Anchorage, AK

(Thousands of dollars, except as noted.)

Year	Personal income, total	Earnings by place of work			Less: Contributions for government social insurance	Plus: Adjustment for residence	Equals: Net earnings by place of residence	Plus: Dividends, interest, and rent	Plus: Personal current transfer receipts	Per capita personal income (dollars)	Population (persons)	Total employment
		Nonfarm	Farm	Total								
1970	910,435	782,862	1,403	784,265	49,609	14,764	749,420	136,228	24,787	6,783	134,230	70,329
1971	1,004,489	870,955	1,236	872,191	56,795	4,983	820,379	152,187	31,923	7,080	141,875	73,124
1972	1,110,361	966,339	1,442	967,781	65,427	-3,500	898,854	172,734	38,773	7,353	151,010	77,502
1973	1,225,781	1,055,467	1,218	1,056,685	79,061	-10,972	966,652	199,536	59,593	7,871	155,729	81,822
1974	1,510,511	1,340,109	1,222	1,341,331	108,671	-16,019	1,216,641	232,101	61,769	9,361	161,355	92,715
1975	2,016,802	1,801,557	2,448	1,804,005	156,755	22,151	1,669,401	274,147	73,254	11,509	175,236	106,942
1976	2,407,760	2,155,068	2,892	2,157,960	195,289	55,863	2,018,534	306,719	82,507	12,936	186,127	113,300
1977	2,679,418	2,420,912	3,230	2,424,142	219,220	20,708	2,225,630	347,935	105,853	14,126	189,680	117,650
1978	2,727,115	2,416,737	3,226	2,419,963	213,574	4,834	2,211,223	400,681	115,211	14,052	194,074	119,090
1979	2,861,807	2,506,877	3,340	2,510,217	228,100	45,162	2,327,279	421,011	113,517	14,674	195,031	119,439
1980	3,211,582	2,795,046	3,111	2,798,157	246,621	54,739	2,606,275	471,532	133,775	16,568	193,839	119,735
1981	3,723,866	3,235,962	1,537	3,237,499	313,005	85,836	3,010,330	549,503	164,033	18,635	199,831	123,606
1982	4,632,735	3,836,987	2,413	3,839,400	380,164	94,389	3,553,625	683,393	395,717	21,363	216,861	139,054
1983	5,128,428	4,342,077	2,824	4,344,901	440,388	135,723	4,040,236	808,410	279,782	21,611	237,309	150,798
1984	5,583,720	4,781,737	4,136	4,785,873	510,278	107,272	4,382,867	897,154	303,699	22,134	252,265	158,830
1985	5,961,447	5,032,259	5,421	5,037,680	527,826	58,487	4,568,341	998,867	394,239	22,570	264,128	163,306
1986	5,979,180	5,009,371	8,802	5,018,173	505,305	-8,021	4,504,847	1,023,134	451,199	22,139	270,074	158,789
1987	5,660,841	4,688,726	10,913	4,699,639	466,304	-45,950	4,187,385	994,833	478,623	21,345	265,211	157,016
1988	5,718,140	4,714,736	11,517	4,726,253	486,333	-57,780	4,182,140	1,015,875	520,125	21,689	263,645	156,200
1989	6,221,162	5,048,301	8,453	5,056,754	524,312	-1,616	4,530,826	1,114,987	575,349	23,569	263,958	159,968
1990	6,668,663	5,512,466	8,855	5,521,321	605,982	-94,744	4,820,595	1,198,847	649,221	24,905	267,762	166,968
1991	7,008,195	5,826,891	8,567	5,835,458	646,249	-110,827	5,078,382	1,230,365	699,448	25,263	277,407	172,470
1992	7,527,293	6,197,631	6,855	6,204,486	680,640	-106,026	5,417,820	1,330,013	779,460	25,929	290,307	173,979
1993	7,962,980	6,507,768	8,900	6,516,668	728,971	-123,144	5,664,553	1,434,413	864,014	26,855	296,514	177,780
1994	8,283,282	6,707,187	10,960	6,718,147	763,899	-121,120	5,833,128	1,566,387	883,767	27,594	300,188	181,242
1995	8,443,275	6,718,610	11,250	6,729,860	759,813	-113,140	5,856,907	1,647,212	939,156	27,969	301,878	182,105
1996	8,710,468	6,836,109	11,873	6,847,982	762,965	-111,168	5,973,849	1,724,079	1,012,540	28,785	302,606	183,521
1997	9,293,914	7,278,480	13,771	7,292,251	801,936	-119,187	6,371,128	1,820,748	1,102,038	30,325	306,480	187,454
1998	9,869,517	7,698,396	11,040	7,709,436	834,620	-108,225	6,766,591	1,898,401	1,204,525	31,543	312,895	193,548
1999	10,233,797	7,952,096	11,946	7,964,042	855,896	-123,196	6,984,950	1,915,632	1,333,215	32,266	317,172	193,959
2000	10,952,722	8,402,434	11,862	8,414,296	890,910	-117,364	7,406,022	2,025,702	1,520,998	34,161	320,618	197,879
2001	11,826,499	9,201,434	11,047	9,212,481	962,532	-53,594	8,196,355	2,028,626	1,601,518	36,269	326,081	203,258
2002	12,506,020	9,830,668	11,631	9,842,299	1,024,380	-6,052	8,811,867	2,053,052	1,641,101	37,603	332,582	207,654
2003	13,061,196	10,384,677	8,859	10,393,536	1,065,156	26,397	9,354,777	2,100,647	1,605,772	38,673	337,730	211,659
2004	13,785,083	11,036,263	10,456	11,046,719	1,142,603	89,738	9,993,854	2,189,651	1,601,578	39,928	345,245	215,930
2005	14,759,944	11,718,482	9,865	11,728,347	1,218,735	170,283	10,679,895	2,386,418	1,693,631	42,063	350,903	220,731
2006	15,854,673	12,318,498	8,335	12,326,833	1,324,071	334,211	11,336,973	2,705,042	1,812,658	44,198	358,718	226,471
2007	17,150,319	12,937,145	7,453	12,944,598	1,378,202	524,844	12,091,240	2,992,572	2,066,507	47,614	360,194	231,097
2008	18,988,778	13,526,519	5,089	13,531,608	1,426,081	738,650	12,844,177	3,312,716	2,831,885	51,934	365,633	233,394
2009	18,989,149	14,130,539	6,633	14,137,172	1,451,533	725,155	13,410,794	3,157,449	2,420,906	50,697	374,562	233,589
2010	20,307,816	14,902,944	5,465	14,908,409	1,500,924	692,240	14,099,725	3,479,108	2,728,983	52,955	383,491	233,963
2011	21,465,330	15,565,246	4,099	15,569,345	1,412,652	725,344	14,882,037	3,754,221	2,829,072	55,261	388,434	236,733
2012	22,023,910	16,060,987	6,030	16,067,017	1,500,542	723,087	15,289,562	3,996,870	2,737,478	56,108	392,524	242,955
2013	21,725,063	16,099,987	6,278	16,106,265	1,734,283	683,777	15,055,759	3,905,180	2,764,124	54,621	397,741	244,406
2014	22,953,064	16,422,587	8,245	16,430,832	1,730,759	783,416	15,483,489	4,139,416	3,330,159	57,484	399,295	244,034
2015	23,840,060	16,968,966	8,418	16,977,384	1,758,427	776,372	15,995,329	4,410,783	3,433,948	59,595	400,037	245,111
2016	23,373,908	16,568,310	7,801	16,576,111	1,707,615	667,037	15,535,533	4,491,593	3,346,782	58,006	402,960	243,475
2017	23,624,289	16,626,013	9,060	16,635,073	1,724,638	623,072	15,533,507	4,505,769	3,585,013	58,734	402,227	242,955
2018	24,479,371	17,031,928	8,160	17,040,088	1,763,820	627,673	15,903,941	4,682,972	3,892,458	61,288	399,416	242,591
2019	25,012,258	17,265,337	7,951	17,273,288	1,821,511	668,493	16,120,270	4,781,112	4,110,876	62,824	398,135	242,291
2020	25,624,192	17,288,863	7,599	17,296,462	1,839,727	599,526	16,056,261	4,679,896	4,888,035	64,367	398,097	232,127
2021	26,753,998	18,100,818	10,068	18,110,886	1,938,948	560,970	16,732,908	4,706,094	5,314,996	67,085	398,807	238,319

Personal Income and Employment by Area: Ann Arbor, MI

(Thousands of dollars, except as noted.)

Year	Personal income, total	Earnings by place of work			Less: Contributions for government social insurance	Plus: Adjustment for residence	Equals: Net earnings by place of residence	Plus: Dividends, interest, and rent	Plus: Personal current transfer receipts	Per capita personal income (dollars)	Population (persons)	Total employment
		Nonfarm	Farm	Total								
1970	1,095,725	933,143	6,117	939,260	64,093	3,652	878,819	157,250	59,656	4,678	234,226	105,059
1971	1,212,039	1,060,056	5,067	1,065,123	74,950	-20,983	969,190	172,550	70,299	5,131	236,222	109,389
1972	1,349,916	1,186,555	9,904	1,196,459	89,223	-28,705	1,078,531	191,146	80,239	5,590	241,470	114,647
1973	1,518,740	1,373,322	12,572	1,385,894	120,110	-53,405	1,212,379	211,846	94,515	6,154	246,780	124,307
1974	1,638,400	1,431,938	6,577	1,438,515	129,203	-37,088	1,272,224	242,031	124,145	6,389	256,447	128,003
1975	1,805,963	1,518,701	12,638	1,531,339	133,228	-37,224	1,360,887	272,102	172,974	7,194	251,024	126,982
1976	2,038,347	1,835,426	7,804	1,843,230	164,904	-113,380	1,564,946	298,801	174,600	8,027	253,934	136,907
1977	2,297,921	2,151,919	9,577	2,161,496	192,960	-181,580	1,786,956	334,914	176,051	8,927	257,407	146,330
1978	2,616,066	2,545,115	4,964	2,550,079	236,617	-258,238	2,055,224	376,997	183,845	10,071	259,775	157,722
1979	2,903,669	2,852,435	5,136	2,857,571	272,261	-324,480	2,260,830	426,173	216,666	11,046	262,859	165,863
1980	3,191,960	2,989,418	3,921	2,993,339	277,809	-332,044	2,383,486	503,045	305,429	12,072	264,400	164,425
1981	3,436,150	3,203,486	7,135	3,210,621	322,787	-362,705	2,525,129	604,278	306,743	13,092	262,466	165,139
1982	3,640,222	3,267,964	3,102	3,271,066	334,386	-343,456	2,593,224	708,419	338,579	13,988	260,239	163,116
1983	3,925,847	3,567,477	-339	3,567,138	373,401	-397,982	2,795,755	772,537	357,555	15,087	260,212	167,452
1984	4,311,669	4,027,371	4,921	4,032,292	438,596	-498,030	3,095,666	863,011	352,992	16,536	260,737	174,759
1985	4,700,285	4,458,840	9,576	4,468,416	495,653	-567,117	3,405,646	932,851	361,788	17,901	262,568	181,371
1986	5,019,182	4,719,198	4,022	4,723,220	525,235	-543,793	3,654,192	995,962	369,028	18,863	266,087	187,119
1987	5,279,965	4,931,560	4,932	4,936,492	543,160	-546,194	3,847,138	1,052,271	380,556	19,576	269,717	195,094
1988	5,775,220	5,459,398	3,421	5,462,819	622,017	-627,286	4,213,516	1,164,577	397,127	21,128	273,346	202,667
1989	6,274,868	5,801,327	8,223	5,809,550	658,594	-659,477	4,491,479	1,347,625	435,764	22,464	279,329	207,606
1990	6,667,023	6,199,718	7,757	6,207,475	713,841	-697,952	4,795,682	1,393,647	477,694	23,477	283,987	213,654
1991	6,758,413	6,232,810	3,050	6,235,860	726,643	-689,658	4,819,559	1,408,849	530,005	23,538	287,126	210,795
1992	7,223,539	6,661,953	6,866	6,668,819	768,751	-707,095	5,192,973	1,468,894	561,672	24,881	290,323	213,642
1993	7,623,930	6,912,845	3,227	6,916,072	800,545	-663,691	5,451,836	1,568,472	603,622	26,144	291,617	217,534
1994	8,170,770	7,310,896	2,302	7,313,198	865,568	-667,420	5,780,210	1,771,894	618,666	27,823	293,671	220,460
1995	8,731,492	7,458,630	1,933	7,460,563	883,360	-439,452	6,137,751	1,895,789	697,952	29,308	297,926	221,177
1996	9,139,407	7,797,612	1,301	7,798,913	903,407	-457,241	6,438,265	1,945,605	755,537	30,150	303,133	224,214
1997	9,635,229	8,432,516	1,284	8,433,800	975,250	-659,409	6,799,141	2,088,637	747,451	31,243	308,398	228,650
1998	10,242,886	9,071,528	3,088	9,074,616	1,042,070	-730,986	7,301,560	2,199,049	742,277	32,767	312,601	230,049
1999	10,946,325	10,052,448	6,636	10,059,084	1,141,127	-1,008,574	7,909,383	2,204,735	832,207	34,393	318,270	238,824
2000	11,776,425	10,778,116	1,878	10,779,994	1,201,623	-1,027,237	8,551,134	2,355,101	870,190	36,305	324,372	244,514
2001	12,288,891	11,159,108	853	11,159,961	1,208,371	-967,782	8,983,808	2,341,579	963,504	37,381	328,749	244,933
2002	12,730,052	11,651,753	1,481	11,653,234	1,265,834	-1,022,842	9,364,558	2,341,224	1,024,270	38,256	332,763	245,437
2003	13,325,699	11,860,308	6,190	11,866,498	1,279,997	-890,242	9,696,259	2,529,970	1,099,470	39,642	336,154	243,666
2004	13,506,829	12,031,394	12,728	12,044,122	1,317,704	-1,095,059	9,631,359	2,734,845	1,140,625	39,794	339,422	245,401
2005	13,799,026	12,256,129	11,001	12,267,130	1,350,284	-1,095,072	9,821,774	2,752,418	1,224,834	40,320	342,234	247,846
2006	14,304,031	12,455,279	12,057	12,467,336	1,382,634	-1,171,097	9,913,605	3,074,895	1,315,531	41,579	344,018	247,735
2007	14,737,620	12,764,942	11,577	12,776,519	1,417,960	-1,160,970	10,197,589	3,090,835	1,449,196	42,679	345,310	247,748
2008	15,293,344	12,535,687	8,179	12,543,866	1,402,995	-695,399	10,445,472	3,131,585	1,716,287	44,770	341,595	242,983
2009	14,330,929	12,077,070	8,988	12,086,058	1,358,983	-1,028,420	9,698,655	2,757,194	1,875,080	41,718	343,520	238,387
2010	15,869,987	12,569,194	13,486	12,582,680	1,381,305	-310,579	10,890,796	2,921,108	2,058,083	45,870	345,980	241,984
2011	15,865,909	12,812,297	36,747	12,849,044	1,235,317	-938,146	10,675,581	3,106,126	2,084,202	45,322	350,072	245,292
2012	16,999,507	13,444,530	12,455	13,456,985	1,287,629	-827,407	11,341,949	3,596,508	2,061,050	48,200	352,685	246,785
2013	17,138,025	13,780,552	10,775	13,791,327	1,506,425	-959,422	11,325,480	3,666,149	2,146,396	48,077	356,474	250,522
2014	17,982,020	14,013,088	-3,437	14,009,651	1,551,067	-729,441	11,729,143	4,009,055	2,243,822	49,584	362,657	252,686
2015	19,086,775	14,956,967	2,178	14,959,145	1,635,562	-938,557	12,385,026	4,314,920	2,386,829	52,119	366,217	258,276
2016	19,921,507	15,404,397	-861	15,403,536	1,681,875	-759,824	12,961,837	4,499,987	2,459,683	53,818	370,164	261,979
2017	20,914,027	16,248,355	1,675	16,250,030	1,775,282	-830,201	13,644,547	4,777,616	2,491,864	56,002	373,451	266,434
2018	21,817,464	17,023,668	2,042	17,025,710	1,878,349	-928,636	14,218,725	4,968,929	2,629,810	58,207	374,825	272,078
2019	22,920,571	17,807,315	4,981	17,812,296	1,963,582	-1,206,072	14,642,642	5,484,830	2,793,099	61,447	373,011	274,917
2020	24,022,427	18,059,869	12,915	18,072,784	1,990,676	-1,569,000	14,513,108	5,525,696	3,983,623	64,636	371,656	258,964
2021	25,372,530	19,234,776	17,448	19,252,224	2,075,822	-1,560,929	15,615,473	5,664,436	4,092,621	68,688	369,390	265,544

Personal Income and Employment by Area: Anniston-Oxford, AL

(Thousands of dollars, except as noted.)

Year	Personal income, total	Earnings by place of work			Less: Contributions for government social insurance	Plus: Adjustment for residence	Equals: Net earnings by place of residence	Plus: Dividends, interest, and rent	Plus: Personal current transfer receipts	Per capita personal income (dollars)	Population (persons)	Total employment
		Nonfarm	Farm	Total								
1970	313,931	278,760	2,076	280,836	17,144	-27,477	236,215	46,648	31,068	3,044	103,125	46,650
1971	353,608	313,482	2,099	315,581	19,851	-31,130	264,600	52,488	36,520	3,412	103,622	47,036
1972	396,486	351,388	2,782	354,170	23,011	-33,457	297,702	58,462	40,322	3,818	103,846	48,347
1973	433,646	376,675	5,683	382,358	28,220	-33,219	320,919	65,440	47,287	4,129	105,027	49,305
1974	485,455	413,937	2,398	416,335	32,063	-35,241	349,031	78,368	58,056	4,583	105,917	50,224
1975	557,197	458,904	5,713	464,617	35,225	-39,070	390,322	90,919	75,956	5,207	107,005	50,663
1976	624,434	522,276	4,806	527,082	42,063	-41,648	443,371	100,489	80,574	5,537	112,768	53,001
1977	702,104	589,344	4,940	594,284	47,028	-45,335	501,921	115,115	85,068	6,224	112,801	55,396
1978	776,570	642,831	5,394	648,225	51,477	-44,892	551,856	132,970	91,744	6,667	116,474	56,359
1979	849,706	693,419	5,118	698,537	58,357	-43,210	596,970	147,289	105,447	7,278	116,742	56,639
1980	972,898	786,063	4,448	790,511	64,801	-52,911	672,799	174,878	125,221	8,106	120,016	57,453
1981	1,069,632	854,152	3,916	858,068	75,747	-58,267	724,054	204,053	141,525	8,854	120,814	55,980
1982	1,144,879	899,287	4,605	903,892	78,953	-66,489	758,450	230,256	156,173	9,376	122,109	55,531
1983	1,219,116	960,897	2,359	963,256	90,000	-70,040	803,216	247,822	168,078	10,055	121,249	56,216
1984	1,341,222	1,066,173	2,759	1,068,932	101,985	-78,926	888,021	276,290	176,911	11,017	121,739	58,552
1985	1,403,278	1,118,946	2,982	1,121,928	109,495	-86,890	925,543	290,218	187,517	11,828	118,644	58,483
1986	1,470,316	1,170,716	3,899	1,174,615	114,975	-90,548	969,092	306,800	194,424	12,492	117,700	59,039
1987	1,525,463	1,223,249	360	1,223,609	120,758	-93,560	1,009,291	318,469	197,703	12,918	118,092	59,851
1988	1,607,503	1,290,433	3,502	1,293,935	133,515	-97,178	1,063,242	337,277	206,984	13,709	117,260	61,561
1989	1,703,924	1,326,583	14,589	1,341,172	139,597	-102,966	1,098,609	369,331	235,984	14,641	116,381	61,654
1990	1,759,063	1,356,847	17,407	1,374,254	146,927	-103,935	1,123,392	377,465	258,206	15,149	116,118	61,400
1991	1,851,118	1,425,250	22,715	1,447,965	155,902	-112,350	1,179,713	383,174	288,231	16,062	115,247	60,775
1992	1,951,649	1,489,528	12,187	1,501,715	163,387	-108,720	1,229,608	397,322	324,719	16,853	115,804	61,360
1993	2,005,237	1,510,253	15,986	1,526,239	170,059	-105,947	1,250,233	410,768	344,236	17,238	116,324	61,935
1994	2,073,014	1,546,583	12,121	1,558,704	175,668	-98,566	1,284,470	427,452	361,092	17,846	116,161	60,986
1995	2,183,521	1,597,298	12,631	1,609,929	183,008	-99,088	1,327,833	463,964	391,724	18,696	116,790	61,993
1996	2,248,460	1,609,612	15,864	1,625,476	185,003	-92,483	1,347,990	483,621	416,849	19,270	116,684	62,273
1997	2,324,902	1,677,526	17,029	1,694,555	193,510	-90,749	1,410,296	480,632	433,974	19,828	117,254	63,984
1998	2,460,397	1,765,235	14,078	1,779,313	201,956	-98,262	1,479,095	530,147	451,155	20,997	117,179	64,336
1999	2,467,100	1,782,332	7,744	1,790,076	205,216	-93,841	1,491,019	502,107	473,974	21,470	114,910	63,078
2000	2,453,535	1,709,381	4,909	1,714,290	198,768	-68,390	1,447,132	500,384	506,019	22,088	111,081	60,846
2001	2,576,061	1,770,120	10,174	1,780,294	206,787	-77,911	1,495,596	527,529	552,936	23,152	111,266	59,639
2002	2,689,343	1,871,325	5,881	1,877,206	217,398	-88,491	1,571,317	521,472	596,554	24,093	111,625	60,124
2003	2,832,888	1,977,208	7,453	1,984,661	229,871	-106,783	1,648,007	551,223	633,658	25,135	112,705	60,521
2004	3,016,269	2,136,035	10,806	2,146,841	245,599	-132,143	1,769,099	592,386	654,784	26,584	113,462	62,604
2005	3,156,868	2,251,084	16,128	2,267,212	260,128	-142,634	1,864,450	593,310	699,108	27,576	114,477	63,108
2006	3,308,983	2,368,483	7,336	2,375,819	273,744	-169,138	1,932,937	630,679	745,367	28,677	115,388	63,816
2007	3,513,133	2,544,497	7,301	2,551,798	297,131	-220,981	2,033,686	686,565	792,882	30,231	116,211	65,674
2008	3,634,409	2,591,948	8,281	2,600,229	308,810	-254,694	2,036,725	714,279	883,405	30,991	117,274	64,696
2009	3,578,268	2,529,596	13,361	2,542,957	300,767	-257,600	1,984,590	636,167	957,511	30,231	118,363	61,551
2010	3,672,478	2,539,537	13,283	2,552,820	305,756	-237,625	2,009,439	629,459	1,033,580	31,012	118,420	60,194
2011	3,743,496	2,560,128	5,201	2,565,329	277,251	-232,474	2,055,604	643,491	1,044,401	31,787	117,767	60,613
2012	3,784,756	2,493,885	13,665	2,507,550	270,995	-178,078	2,058,477	675,872	1,050,407	32,286	117,227	59,998
2013	3,734,209	2,382,847	25,396	2,408,243	293,613	-107,880	2,006,750	667,168	1,060,291	32,046	116,528	58,414
2014	3,818,636	2,429,608	18,973	2,448,581	295,352	-91,027	2,062,202	679,882	1,076,552	32,580	117,209	58,092
2015	3,957,946	2,417,853	24,380	2,442,233	294,451	-63,668	2,084,114	713,653	1,160,179	33,815	117,048	58,062
2016	3,994,209	2,470,768	9,818	2,480,586	300,359	-68,700	2,111,527	712,125	1,170,557	34,194	116,810	57,697
2017	4,070,579	2,543,992	14,321	2,558,313	313,354	-84,035	2,160,924	724,734	1,184,921	34,852	116,796	58,550
2018	4,162,915	2,614,548	10,303	2,624,851	324,803	-78,305	2,221,743	725,735	1,215,437	35,696	116,622	58,800
2019	4,301,429	2,725,172	6,457	2,731,629	336,112	-96,336	2,299,181	742,713	1,259,535	36,869	116,669	58,468
2020	4,597,862	2,774,585	-23	2,774,562	347,854	-95,812	2,330,896	730,246	1,536,720	39,546	116,266	57,303
2021	4,942,877	2,938,799	12,005	2,950,804	363,533	-98,013	2,489,258	730,346	1,723,273	42,621	115,972	58,474

Personal Income and Employment by Area: Appleton, WI

(Thousands of dollars, except as noted.)

Year	Personal income, total	Nonfarm	Farm	Total	Less: Contributions for government social insurance	Plus: Adjustment for residence	Equals: Net earnings by place of residence	Plus: Dividends, interest, and rent	Plus: Personal current transfer receipts	Per capita personal income (dollars)	Population (persons)	Total employment
1970	550,635	431,402	21,585	452,987	31,605	3,446	424,828	85,862	39,945	3,738	147,307	65,092
1971	581,862	450,163	24,127	474,290	34,056	2,602	442,836	92,757	46,269	3,923	148,324	64,945
1972	638,012	497,053	27,064	524,117	39,697	1,950	486,370	99,714	51,928	4,275	149,228	66,928
1973	723,046	573,426	31,917	605,343	53,011	-2,312	550,020	111,983	61,043	4,853	148,989	71,600
1974	800,861	642,544	27,607	670,151	61,582	-8,097	600,472	127,717	72,672	5,319	150,556	74,056
1975	877,279	676,090	32,698	708,788	63,425	-6,324	639,039	142,515	95,725	5,715	153,496	72,298
1976	977,626	777,488	30,329	807,817	74,164	-10,485	723,168	152,292	102,166	6,419	152,296	74,840
1977	1,092,940	865,519	48,117	913,636	82,671	-13,759	817,206	168,805	106,929	7,084	154,282	77,570
1978	1,211,224	975,152	42,134	1,017,286	95,932	-19,606	901,748	190,094	119,382	7,785	155,590	80,387
1979	1,398,104	1,146,008	59,161	1,205,169	117,583	-40,430	1,047,156	214,968	135,980	8,917	156,784	86,376
1980	1,543,317	1,232,348	57,885	1,290,233	126,106	-48,489	1,115,638	260,883	166,796	9,652	159,892	86,329
1981	1,685,126	1,325,034	40,137	1,365,171	144,820	-43,284	1,177,067	322,032	186,027	10,487	160,685	86,079
1982	1,781,003	1,377,941	30,510	1,408,451	152,278	-38,845	1,217,328	350,668	213,007	11,031	161,454	84,927
1983	1,907,996	1,471,855	19,134	1,490,989	162,367	-33,729	1,294,893	385,223	227,880	11,771	162,093	85,443
1984	2,132,295	1,646,098	36,915	1,683,013	185,940	-28,565	1,468,508	433,796	229,991	13,058	163,293	89,336
1985	2,283,300	1,768,288	39,811	1,808,099	201,469	-23,510	1,583,120	457,301	242,879	13,866	164,668	91,393
1986	2,448,636	1,899,329	50,700	1,950,029	215,930	-17,527	1,716,572	476,486	255,578	14,710	166,459	94,148
1987	2,607,322	2,063,562	57,328	2,120,890	230,837	-20,938	1,869,115	477,243	260,964	15,471	168,530	98,260
1988	2,776,949	2,246,891	33,449	2,280,340	259,451	-20,411	2,000,478	506,808	269,663	16,198	171,443	100,937
1989	3,026,601	2,393,085	64,510	2,457,595	274,877	-16,439	2,166,279	567,434	292,888	17,467	173,276	102,137
1990	3,206,585	2,533,011	51,740	2,584,751	303,945	10,546	2,291,352	600,674	314,559	18,289	175,333	105,276
1991	3,368,949	2,700,986	41,255	2,742,241	328,248	11,114	2,425,107	606,307	337,535	19,029	177,039	107,722
1992	3,694,968	2,957,411	62,295	3,019,706	354,871	18,120	2,682,955	648,170	363,843	20,581	179,533	109,626
1993	3,897,358	3,128,853	45,837	3,174,690	374,975	57,290	2,857,005	665,113	375,240	21,377	182,315	112,232
1994	4,188,266	3,361,225	66,530	3,427,755	407,322	62,392	3,082,825	716,003	389,438	22,540	185,813	116,611
1995	4,432,852	3,503,484	42,794	3,546,278	424,531	101,396	3,223,143	789,455	420,254	23,497	188,656	120,299
1996	4,715,137	3,725,578	61,312	3,786,890	448,721	87,188	3,425,357	847,473	442,307	24,611	191,586	124,832
1997	4,937,783	3,877,099	43,848	3,920,947	465,284	121,879	3,577,542	899,513	460,728	25,446	194,050	126,560
1998	5,224,251	3,988,543	64,275	4,052,818	475,235	188,751	3,766,334	982,829	475,088	26,549	196,776	125,341
1999	5,592,695	4,308,500	64,876	4,373,376	513,024	259,060	4,119,412	969,850	503,433	28,034	199,495	128,535
2000	6,053,028	4,637,123	43,974	4,681,097	545,383	303,560	4,439,274	1,067,682	546,072	29,874	202,618	132,249
2001	6,446,834	5,032,357	48,602	5,080,959	582,870	286,140	4,784,229	1,064,403	598,202	31,345	205,676	135,693
2002	6,694,151	5,193,223	43,894	5,237,117	592,111	347,645	4,992,651	1,036,764	664,736	32,068	208,747	136,552
2003	6,885,381	5,335,924	71,702	5,407,626	613,675	356,143	5,150,094	1,046,184	689,103	32,578	211,350	138,629
2004	7,149,651	5,667,843	73,694	5,741,537	654,962	285,842	5,372,417	1,062,531	714,703	33,473	213,592	142,535
2005	7,443,509	5,831,115	74,306	5,905,421	682,436	310,092	5,533,077	1,138,507	771,925	34,473	215,925	143,877
2006	7,832,967	6,037,098	55,441	6,092,539	712,776	325,748	5,705,511	1,289,200	838,256	35,859	218,441	145,286
2007	8,240,126	6,296,769	92,709	6,389,478	742,746	344,374	5,991,106	1,330,868	918,152	37,393	220,368	147,868
2008	8,613,142	6,381,609	80,625	6,462,234	760,132	402,322	6,104,424	1,450,786	1,057,932	38,728	222,402	146,873
2009	8,445,772	6,222,410	25,936	6,248,346	741,643	436,427	5,943,130	1,301,745	1,200,897	37,598	224,632	142,760
2010	8,714,612	6,325,323	59,999	6,385,322	759,551	469,005	6,094,776	1,319,948	1,299,888	38,580	225,884	141,901
2011	9,293,171	6,668,449	112,095	6,780,544	717,105	537,182	6,600,621	1,419,033	1,273,517	40,849	227,500	144,429
2012	9,690,932	6,985,940	120,226	7,106,166	743,427	526,978	6,889,717	1,527,566	1,273,649	42,390	228,613	146,010
2013	9,837,011	7,060,208	137,770	7,197,978	847,075	644,553	6,995,456	1,538,620	1,302,935	42,779	229,950	147,007
2014	10,361,192	7,379,872	162,819	7,542,691	879,080	621,601	7,285,212	1,693,116	1,382,864	44,394	233,393	150,010
2015	10,816,576	7,744,824	140,547	7,885,371	913,551	610,847	7,582,667	1,782,745	1,451,164	45,958	235,357	151,907
2016	11,176,590	8,022,767	96,362	8,119,129	943,661	646,723	7,822,191	1,863,597	1,490,802	47,186	236,862	154,721
2017	11,598,264	8,269,718	91,807	8,361,525	977,265	677,268	8,061,528	1,971,252	1,565,484	48,545	238,918	154,892
2018	12,108,934	8,631,391	78,366	8,709,757	1,008,597	652,975	8,354,135	2,077,990	1,676,809	50,316	240,660	157,204
2019	12,709,567	8,999,241	98,145	9,097,386	1,056,875	641,129	8,681,640	2,247,455	1,780,472	52,516	242,015	158,328
2020	13,424,989	9,166,792	138,506	9,305,298	1,077,974	593,180	8,820,504	2,269,987	2,334,498	55,177	243,308	153,440
2021	14,232,954	9,705,490	127,021	9,832,511	1,124,671	579,247	9,287,087	2,332,985	2,612,882	58,312	244,084	156,850

Personal Income and Employment by Area: Asheville, NC

(Thousands of dollars, except as noted.)

Year	Personal income, total	Earnings by place of work			Less: Contributions for government social insurance	Plus: Adjustment for residence	Equals: Net earnings by place of residence	Plus: Dividends, interest, and rent	Plus: Personal current transfer receipts	Per capita personal income (dollars)	Population (persons)	Total employment
		Nonfarm	Farm	Total								
1970	785,483	604,225	19,802	624,027	41,768	1,294	583,553	122,752	79,178	3,190	246,263	107,391
1971	861,652	664,748	17,192	681,940	47,442	916	635,414	135,111	91,127	3,431	251,104	108,988
1972	973,755	757,294	21,447	778,741	56,878	2,319	724,182	148,794	100,779	3,844	253,306	115,239
1973	1,111,269	875,051	20,034	895,085	75,821	2,068	821,332	171,493	118,444	4,319	257,291	122,493
1974	1,218,978	934,189	18,913	953,102	84,149	4,569	873,522	199,581	145,875	4,671	260,984	121,406
1975	1,318,910	950,469	23,361	973,830	84,222	8,332	897,940	219,298	201,672	4,981	264,807	115,701
1976	1,474,607	1,077,829	26,738	1,104,567	96,895	12,349	1,020,021	240,976	213,610	5,523	266,999	120,996
1977	1,653,861	1,210,375	37,511	1,247,886	108,165	15,775	1,155,496	273,240	225,125	6,108	270,770	126,497
1978	1,859,539	1,376,336	38,342	1,414,678	126,742	19,089	1,307,025	309,450	243,064	6,746	275,655	131,939
1979	2,064,325	1,516,845	38,992	1,555,837	144,801	25,828	1,436,864	350,370	277,091	7,382	279,654	134,546
1980	2,349,553	1,668,929	33,427	1,702,356	160,220	34,717	1,576,853	443,387	329,313	8,284	283,635	135,100
1981	2,649,227	1,810,736	49,471	1,860,207	186,898	38,174	1,711,483	553,853	383,891	9,263	285,988	136,135
1982	2,822,797	1,881,821	46,631	1,928,452	198,322	40,233	1,770,363	627,060	425,374	9,765	289,085	134,442
1983	3,096,007	2,063,902	54,479	2,118,381	219,368	41,075	1,940,088	692,203	463,716	10,682	289,822	138,779
1984	3,450,320	2,319,438	50,544	2,369,982	251,548	42,564	2,160,998	794,410	494,912	11,756	293,506	145,445
1985	3,685,999	2,486,906	41,163	2,528,069	274,382	39,411	2,293,098	861,067	531,834	12,428	296,586	149,776
1986	3,931,739	2,656,077	27,646	2,683,723	239,078	35,552	2,420,197	940,204	571,338	13,147	299,050	153,313
1987	4,225,639	2,873,920	36,167	2,910,087	319,888	37,108	2,627,307	995,122	603,210	14,075	300,229	156,232
1988	4,605,228	3,141,647	51,225	3,192,872	360,711	35,881	2,868,042	1,094,120	643,066	15,212	302,741	163,112
1989	5,040,778	3,339,472	38,993	3,378,465	386,395	34,969	3,027,039	1,298,345	715,394	16,501	305,480	167,964
1990	5,377,067	3,538,322	71,916	3,610,238	417,886	35,576	3,227,928	1,359,290	789,849	17,373	309,502	171,956
1991	5,661,789	3,714,616	70,075	3,784,691	443,852	32,881	3,373,720	1,385,991	902,078	17,965	315,160	172,486
1992	6,102,912	4,031,916	94,323	4,126,239	475,354	30,054	3,680,939	1,429,106	992,867	18,998	321,240	176,331
1993	6,523,774	4,299,374	112,821	4,412,195	510,769	22,600	3,924,026	1,511,364	1,088,384	19,876	328,220	181,752
1994	6,861,121	4,535,966	119,581	4,655,547	545,982	18,892	4,128,457	1,607,169	1,125,495	20,488	334,878	186,248
1995	7,389,530	4,772,356	123,208	4,895,564	576,466	16,742	4,335,840	1,795,521	1,258,169	21,623	341,739	191,577
1996	7,799,315	5,021,019	99,626	5,120,645	600,150	15,536	4,536,031	1,907,124	1,356,160	22,417	347,921	196,267
1997	8,430,196	5,440,362	96,290	5,536,652	642,957	14,820	4,908,515	2,098,868	1,422,813	23,811	354,052	203,879
1998	8,973,363	5,790,643	109,394	5,900,037	682,594	17,644	5,235,087	2,269,264	1,469,012	24,932	359,909	208,191
1999	9,285,699	6,081,178	129,993	6,211,171	718,055	15,146	5,508,262	2,213,032	1,564,405	25,429	365,159	211,901
2000	9,789,426	6,333,301	117,976	6,451,277	748,289	13,182	5,716,170	2,396,236	1,677,020	26,414	370,615	215,601
2001	10,198,705	6,709,701	94,007	6,803,708	782,811	-1,833	6,019,064	2,329,041	1,850,600	27,204	374,904	214,044
2002	10,320,437	6,842,908	57,881	6,900,789	795,106	-13,505	6,092,178	2,246,353	1,981,906	27,172	379,818	214,661
2003	10,593,378	7,102,009	66,597	7,168,606	840,127	-42,995	6,285,484	2,238,125	2,069,769	27,503	385,178	218,080
2004	11,428,673	7,526,612	75,212	7,601,824	880,685	-62,604	6,658,535	2,530,552	2,239,586	29,251	390,713	223,209
2005	12,117,490	7,890,658	116,491	8,007,149	935,048	-79,898	6,992,203	2,722,981	2,402,306	30,568	396,408	229,213
2006	13,209,535	8,514,868	113,002	8,627,870	1,000,668	-94,532	7,532,670	3,061,986	2,614,879	32,653	404,546	236,531
2007	14,034,797	8,922,819	56,473	8,979,292	1,060,696	-110,655	7,807,941	3,439,976	2,786,880	34,078	411,842	246,173
2008	14,490,759	8,991,775	71,048	9,062,823	1,071,356	-123,570	7,867,897	3,521,532	3,101,330	34,712	417,457	244,313
2009	14,058,396	8,543,399	76,567	8,619,966	1,040,010	-106,742	7,473,214	3,148,631	3,436,551	33,313	422,014	234,371
2010	14,392,166	8,777,903	65,223	8,843,126	1,056,950	-98,497	7,687,679	3,095,469	3,609,018	33,835	425,365	233,877
2011	14,993,048	8,897,799	65,555	8,963,354	986,200	-99,301	7,877,853	3,401,261	3,713,934	35,012	428,220	238,793
2012	15,866,833	9,411,895	59,512	9,471,407	1,019,399	-82,220	8,369,788	3,677,394	3,819,651	36,801	431,151	241,450
2013	15,922,993	9,651,852	61,862	9,713,714	1,194,773	-62,204	8,456,737	3,577,771	3,888,485	36,514	436,078	246,183
2014	17,041,705	10,288,088	66,143	10,354,231	1,265,113	-71,041	9,018,077	3,965,843	4,057,785	38,626	441,196	252,658
2015	18,099,884	10,843,242	70,348	10,913,590	1,335,369	-76,946	9,501,275	4,350,417	4,248,192	40,541	446,457	260,028
2016	18,941,396	11,481,291	61,902	11,543,193	1,398,101	-82,946	10,062,146	4,534,302	4,344,948	41,856	452,542	267,692
2017	19,846,037	11,963,144	67,102	12,030,246	1,446,781	-82,103	10,501,362	4,822,311	4,522,364	43,373	457,567	273,406
2018	21,024,621	12,739,744	39,426	12,779,170	1,525,835	-88,325	11,165,010	5,133,118	4,726,493	45,476	462,324	281,339
2019	22,483,378	13,448,289	47,080	13,495,369	1,614,506	-79,524	11,801,339	5,662,386	5,019,653	48,247	466,006	284,616
2020	23,891,106	13,503,995	53,352	13,557,347	1,642,071	-42,557	11,872,719	5,683,185	6,335,202	50,891	469,454	272,226
2021	25,896,806	14,836,105	44,307	14,880,412	1,772,519	-61,458	13,046,435	5,822,599	7,027,772	54,827	472,341	284,290

Personal Income and Employment by Area: Athens-Clarke County, GA

(Thousands of dollars, except as noted.)

Year	Personal income, total	Earnings by place of work			Less: Contributions for government social insurance	Plus: Adjustment for residence	Equals: Net earnings by place of residence	Plus: Dividends, interest, and rent	Plus: Personal current transfer receipts	Per capita personal income (dollars)	Population (persons)	Total employment
		Nonfarm	Farm	Total								
1970	287,152	243,816	4,596	248,412	14,503	-10,546	223,363	42,106	21,683	3,033	94,672	42,435
1971	321,923	274,050	3,976	278,026	16,774	-11,825	249,427	47,055	25,441	3,311	97,214	44,721
1972	363,661	310,458	4,906	315,364	20,077	-13,930	281,357	53,011	29,293	3,601	100,987	47,189
1973	415,511	349,981	11,328	361,309	25,915	-16,563	318,831	61,879	34,801	3,936	105,560	48,552
1974	470,958	399,911	6,262	406,173	30,536	-20,689	354,948	72,985	43,025	4,374	107,666	50,427
1975	520,622	417,929	13,538	431,467	31,436	-18,723	381,308	81,556	57,758	4,811	108,211	49,988
1976	579,382	475,100	12,846	487,946	36,710	-23,136	428,100	89,810	61,472	5,460	106,120	51,555
1977	641,865	532,485	14,142	546,627	41,017	-28,419	477,191	100,468	64,206	5,981	107,309	54,049
1978	719,753	603,796	16,686	620,482	47,935	-35,789	536,758	112,296	70,699	6,637	108,452	56,422
1979	790,245	658,558	18,183	676,741	54,760	-36,548	585,433	124,390	80,422	7,240	109,148	57,722
1980	871,547	714,172	2,511	716,683	59,414	-38,926	618,343	155,667	97,537	7,623	114,324	57,313
1981	998,482	792,156	12,091	804,247	70,904	-39,355	693,988	193,001	111,493	8,533	117,011	58,812
1982	1,081,243	825,577	22,803	848,380	75,119	-38,765	734,496	223,636	123,111	9,141	118,289	58,163
1983	1,209,146	930,147	22,242	952,389	85,981	-42,326	824,082	249,831	135,233	10,046	120,365	60,122
1984	1,326,414	1,004,553	37,211	1,041,764	95,629	-41,377	904,758	276,775	144,881	10,830	122,473	63,350
1985	1,435,020	1,095,499	30,358	1,125,857	107,113	-42,511	976,233	301,187	157,600	11,542	124,327	65,645
1986	1,576,707	1,200,748	44,593	1,245,341	118,968	-44,402	1,081,971	325,516	169,220	12,570	125,434	68,018
1987	1,680,289	1,300,064	28,113	1,328,177	127,801	-44,317	1,156,059	345,018	179,212	13,127	128,002	70,290
1988	1,845,495	1,426,064	43,576	1,469,640	146,013	-44,020	1,279,607	375,189	190,699	14,132	130,586	72,042
1989	2,051,027	1,539,424	61,980	1,601,404	158,330	-45,100	1,397,974	442,681	210,372	15,318	133,894	73,601
1990	2,202,783	1,659,584	57,138	1,716,722	170,741	-46,416	1,499,565	465,377	237,841	16,089	136,914	74,955
1991	2,289,739	1,700,838	59,358	1,760,196	177,351	-45,552	1,537,293	479,297	273,149	16,431	139,359	73,882
1992	2,414,496	1,794,059	59,742	1,853,801	186,659	-38,696	1,628,446	482,763	303,287	17,016	141,899	74,262
1993	2,575,471	1,906,970	61,475	1,968,445	198,815	-32,637	1,736,993	517,037	321,441	17,772	144,916	78,030
1994	2,747,204	2,038,143	66,849	2,104,992	213,691	-39,481	1,851,820	555,623	339,761	18,443	148,953	80,774
1995	2,968,596	2,191,628	58,360	2,249,988	229,113	-37,209	1,983,666	615,268	369,662	19,567	151,718	85,085
1996	3,188,396	2,348,219	66,352	2,414,571	242,468	-38,754	2,133,349	661,575	393,472	20,573	154,977	88,923
1997	3,347,496	2,470,050	68,759	2,538,809	250,368	-49,553	2,238,888	712,505	396,103	21,148	158,291	90,120
1998	3,581,252	2,668,278	82,975	2,751,253	267,867	-49,059	2,434,327	744,630	402,295	22,337	160,330	92,124
1999	3,743,447	2,827,933	82,917	2,910,850	281,958	-58,411	2,570,481	743,861	429,105	22,902	163,456	93,748
2000	3,936,118	2,940,142	74,919	3,015,061	291,795	-62,125	2,661,141	800,231	474,746	23,603	166,763	95,550
2001	4,159,150	3,107,434	102,078	3,209,512	310,959	-81,430	2,817,123	821,531	520,496	24,614	168,973	95,547
2002	4,302,729	3,254,463	62,571	3,317,034	324,936	-97,788	2,894,310	825,313	583,106	25,186	170,838	96,128
2003	4,547,270	3,464,118	65,878	3,529,996	341,405	-139,016	3,049,575	909,315	588,380	26,157	173,847	97,807
2004	4,743,446	3,620,825	96,916	3,717,741	366,561	-142,074	3,209,106	901,278	633,062	26,633	178,106	99,793
2005	4,992,407	3,802,279	103,185	3,905,464	380,914	-171,113	3,353,437	942,287	696,683	27,895	178,974	103,703
2006	5,231,528	4,023,488	48,384	4,071,872	408,052	-225,718	3,438,102	1,056,032	737,394	28,561	183,171	107,249
2007	5,522,005	4,147,524	74,964	4,222,488	410,986	-286,005	3,525,497	1,196,072	800,436	29,564	186,781	111,049
2008	5,682,997	4,282,145	114,855	4,397,000	455,761	-398,848	3,542,391	1,209,053	931,553	29,919	189,948	111,948
2009	5,616,021	4,232,033	100,378	4,332,411	443,561	-463,858	3,424,992	1,177,519	1,013,510	29,247	192,021	109,067
2010	5,727,515	4,326,879	74,184	4,401,063	447,925	-516,735	3,436,403	1,169,622	1,121,490	29,609	193,436	108,282
2011	5,995,183	4,409,883	63,644	4,473,527	403,613	-516,773	3,553,141	1,246,024	1,196,018	30,842	194,384	108,818
2012	6,286,925	4,571,656	148,152	4,719,808	416,226	-517,869	3,785,713	1,322,336	1,178,876	32,073	196,017	110,126
2013	6,411,938	4,730,720	148,112	4,878,832	484,583	-502,916	3,891,333	1,301,146	1,219,459	32,443	197,639	112,559
2014	6,888,906	4,945,931	161,294	5,107,225	507,015	-420,342	4,179,868	1,439,201	1,269,837	34,662	198,748	114,078
2015	7,421,252	5,314,660	175,431	5,490,091	539,524	-477,237	4,473,330	1,606,990	1,340,932	36,549	203,049	117,371
2016	7,675,005	5,544,866	111,985	5,656,851	565,996	-488,334	4,602,521	1,694,903	1,377,581	37,284	205,850	121,920
2017	8,153,063	5,820,116	143,067	5,963,183	590,823	-519,012	4,853,348	1,880,631	1,419,084	38,915	209,508	125,941
2018	8,518,868	6,103,753	114,148	6,217,901	636,858	-496,568	5,084,475	1,940,418	1,493,975	40,169	212,076	128,905
2019	9,172,485	6,407,813	91,556	6,499,369	662,889	-252,693	5,583,787	2,009,224	1,579,474	42,765	214,486	129,827
2020	9,713,654	6,500,049	21,320	6,521,369	678,170	-271,385	5,571,814	2,005,775	2,136,065	45,046	215,638	125,846
2021	10,522,716	6,991,577	82,659	7,074,236	728,562	-195,813	6,149,861	2,052,117	2,320,738	48,323	217,759	130,611

Personal Income and Employment by Area: Atlanta-Sandy Springs-Alpharetta, GA

(Thousands of dollars, except as noted.)

Year	Personal income, total	Earnings by place of work			Less: Contributions for government social insurance	Plus: Adjustment for residence	Equals: Net earnings by place of residence	Plus: Dividends, interest, and rent	Plus: Personal current transfer receipts	Per capita personal income (dollars)	Population (persons)	Total employment
		Nonfarm	Farm	Total								
1970	7,695,760	6,697,987	32,676	6,730,663	424,490	-79,274	6,226,899	997,013	471,848	4,133	1,862,083	924,492
1971	8,534,310	7,385,975	28,231	7,414,206	485,358	-85,378	6,843,470	1,125,779	565,061	4,436	1,923,687	956,707
1972	9,754,566	8,498,897	36,008	8,534,905	587,731	-103,187	7,843,987	1,268,080	642,499	4,910	1,986,477	1,013,051
1973	11,042,213	9,652,707	67,946	9,720,653	767,896	-122,909	8,829,848	1,460,906	751,459	5,373	2,055,233	1,078,478
1974	12,157,534	10,475,353	33,695	10,509,048	862,290	-133,408	9,513,350	1,696,160	948,024	5,764	2,109,395	1,089,091
1975	13,096,935	10,934,479	63,265	10,997,744	880,136	-138,055	9,979,553	1,801,246	1,316,136	6,155	2,127,779	1,049,087
1976	14,504,859	12,264,616	71,420	12,336,036	1,009,289	-149,629	11,177,118	1,931,061	1,396,680	6,737	2,152,893	1,087,337
1977	16,314,364	14,013,062	63,099	14,076,161	1,148,484	-164,028	12,763,649	2,115,323	1,435,392	7,435	2,194,331	1,147,650
1978	18,510,403	16,006,272	68,900	16,075,172	1,351,575	-177,354	14,546,243	2,410,476	1,553,684	8,282	2,234,980	1,217,960
1979	20,856,158	18,059,329	72,610	18,131,939	1,586,598	-212,299	16,333,042	2,751,871	1,771,245	9,085	2,295,738	1,273,760
1980	23,755,858	20,259,773	27,771	20,287,544	1,788,440	-247,838	18,251,266	3,381,544	2,123,048	10,100	2,352,155	1,312,418
1981	26,827,948	22,567,671	57,878	22,625,549	2,148,708	-277,588	20,199,253	4,224,701	2,403,994	11,162	2,403,406	1,337,201
1982	29,069,283	24,236,859	95,879	24,332,738	2,366,061	-297,200	21,669,477	4,769,841	2,629,965	11,848	2,453,618	1,357,118
1983	32,382,541	27,101,118	69,657	27,170,775	2,681,241	-334,130	24,155,404	5,364,658	2,862,479	12,868	2,516,569	1,418,357
1984	37,264,505	31,372,930	106,421	31,479,351	3,192,267	-374,976	27,912,108	6,292,401	3,059,996	14,366	2,593,856	1,541,244
1985	41,718,654	35,461,380	84,875	35,546,255	3,691,992	-410,793	31,443,470	6,998,262	3,276,922	15,512	2,689,442	1,644,282
1986	46,111,602	39,467,364	101,677	39,569,041	4,155,215	-429,017	34,984,809	7,626,337	3,500,456	16,558	2,784,902	1,737,089
1987	50,350,752	43,416,808	57,437	43,474,245	4,528,976	-500,831	38,444,438	8,250,662	3,655,652	17,472	2,881,787	1,799,907
1988	55,371,110	47,539,042	100,323	47,639,365	5,075,484	-518,129	42,045,752	9,373,447	3,951,911	18,673	2,965,367	1,869,917
1989	59,512,828	50,102,768	153,761	50,256,529	5,379,911	-511,292	44,365,326	10,726,546	4,420,956	19,621	3,033,139	1,902,034
1990	64,033,797	53,655,678	144,832	53,800,510	5,790,472	-526,809	47,483,229	11,563,196	4,987,372	20,628	3,104,221	1,936,224
1991	66,969,658	55,810,627	160,299	55,970,926	6,085,729	-540,550	49,344,647	11,804,654	5,820,357	20,958	3,195,398	1,917,337
1992	72,962,981	61,307,423	172,661	61,480,084	6,580,558	-607,507	54,292,019	12,106,935	6,564,027	22,164	3,291,991	1,962,091
1993	78,347,953	65,856,736	167,381	66,024,117	7,086,996	-663,795	58,273,326	12,987,330	7,087,297	23,028	3,402,250	2,072,915
1994	84,778,242	70,877,072	192,293	71,069,365	7,724,387	-723,448	62,621,530	14,431,218	7,725,494	24,059	3,523,718	2,172,516
1995	92,783,942	77,202,240	156,150	77,358,390	8,385,323	-802,384	68,170,683	16,153,984	8,459,275	25,457	3,644,699	2,273,047
1996	101,611,806	84,644,509	175,481	84,819,990	9,078,334	-914,641	74,827,015	17,774,560	9,010,231	26,983	3,765,817	2,380,579
1997	109,575,090	91,523,953	178,862	91,702,815	9,784,315	-1,025,407	80,893,093	19,474,418	9,207,579	28,180	3,888,398	2,460,237
1998	122,679,761	103,542,136	213,859	103,755,995	10,810,080	-1,198,021	91,747,894	21,492,745	9,439,122	30,507	4,021,410	2,584,632
1999	132,469,030	113,892,335	203,708	114,096,043	11,840,565	-1,358,877	100,896,601	21,633,464	9,938,965	31,860	4,157,862	2,676,550
2000	146,051,653	125,267,913	164,511	125,432,424	12,836,545	-1,554,455	111,041,424	24,120,580	10,889,649	34,017	4,293,475	2,770,951
2001	154,078,100	131,982,805	228,703	132,211,508	13,367,097	-1,524,749	117,319,662	24,612,577	12,145,861	34,998	4,402,455	2,809,261
2002	157,408,271	134,031,669	135,124	134,166,793	13,489,090	-1,412,092	119,265,611	24,328,321	13,814,339	35,063	4,489,288	2,795,141
2003	162,817,542	137,548,536	146,064	137,694,600	13,785,907	-1,268,535	122,640,158	25,925,347	14,252,037	35,608	4,572,541	2,813,569
2004	172,414,934	146,174,959	228,425	146,403,384	14,994,851	-1,237,973	130,170,560	26,859,011	15,385,363	37,002	4,659,574	2,896,329
2005	184,510,966	153,303,562	233,096	153,536,658	15,640,385	-1,002,389	136,893,884	30,482,100	17,134,982	38,674	4,770,870	3,014,860
2006	199,065,515	163,145,705	111,702	163,257,407	16,619,894	-846,088	145,791,425	34,753,501	18,520,589	40,363	4,931,848	3,134,434
2007	208,227,838	167,969,314	167,294	168,136,608	17,218,155	-850,098	150,068,355	38,031,146	20,128,337	41,100	5,066,356	3,232,964
2008	207,251,556	162,656,494	225,698	162,882,192	17,708,073	-107,513	145,066,606	38,502,903	23,682,047	40,087	5,170,099	3,206,861
2009	201,128,460	157,520,889	193,247	157,714,136	17,109,971	279,788	140,883,953	33,937,385	26,307,122	38,377	5,240,828	3,087,160
2010	205,618,971	159,566,734	145,144	159,711,878	17,338,719	417,145	142,790,304	33,649,357	29,179,310	38,776	5,302,733	3,070,701
2011	221,053,599	167,473,923	107,999	167,581,922	15,945,728	321,380	151,957,574	38,451,507	30,644,518	41,187	5,367,069	3,151,193
2012	228,766,278	172,627,394	274,580	172,901,974	16,562,510	287,225	156,626,689	41,789,312	30,350,277	42,010	5,445,543	3,199,601
2013	232,742,020	179,660,888	265,227	179,926,115	19,666,589	277,928	160,537,454	40,599,266	31,605,300	42,224	5,512,111	3,285,219
2014	252,324,699	193,365,163	277,010	193,642,173	20,820,810	70,393	172,891,756	46,053,688	33,379,255	45,051	5,600,845	3,420,843
2015	268,518,657	205,758,688	289,802	206,048,490	21,988,465	85,931	184,145,956	49,241,099	35,131,602	47,145	5,695,632	3,540,278
2016	281,844,991	216,999,757	152,356	217,152,113	23,011,133	-408,337	193,732,643	51,609,735	36,502,613	48,591	5,800,316	3,653,479
2017	300,029,739	229,365,178	208,061	229,573,239	24,130,185	-218,017	205,225,037	57,098,972	37,705,730	50,968	5,886,680	3,762,132
2018	317,811,690	242,945,592	135,793	243,081,385	25,582,721	-300,668	217,197,996	60,835,439	39,778,255	53,300	5,962,727	3,879,761
2019	338,957,566	257,972,084	107,434	258,079,518	27,064,146	-671,458	230,343,914	66,502,532	42,111,120	56,120	6,039,848	3,962,831
2020	359,744,528	259,052,510	23,831	259,076,341	27,442,233	-465,409	231,168,699	67,319,416	61,256,413	58,963	6,101,146	3,911,821
2021	388,423,431	283,607,263	113,442	283,720,705	29,803,916	-1,102,853	252,813,936	69,815,103	65,794,392	63,219	6,144,050	4,059,726

Personal Income and Employment by Area: Atlantic City-Hammonton, NJ

(Thousands of dollars, except as noted.)

Year	Personal income, total	Earnings by place of work Nonfarm	Farm	Total	Less: Contributions for government social insurance	Plus: Adjustment for residence	Equals: Net earnings by place of residence	Plus: Dividends, interest, and rent	Plus: Personal current transfer receipts	Per capita personal income (dollars)	Population (persons)	Total employment
1970	782,866	555,691	6,342	562,033	39,518	35,867	558,382	124,240	100,244	4,450	175,908	79,885
1971	871,879	593,872	6,399	600,271	43,642	57,677	614,306	137,345	120,228	4,849	179,824	79,392
1972	964,555	651,292	5,316	656,608	50,285	74,206	680,529	149,736	134,290	5,214	184,987	82,297
1973	1,081,593	728,853	8,073	736,926	63,329	88,957	762,554	166,721	152,318	5,778	187,199	85,385
1974	1,173,626	763,744	8,991	772,735	68,812	104,358	808,281	186,919	178,426	6,206	189,113	84,867
1975	1,283,784	803,960	8,100	812,060	70,323	117,849	859,586	200,118	224,080	6,773	189,544	82,280
1976	1,421,862	901,015	8,936	909,951	77,981	129,498	961,468	213,516	246,878	7,499	189,613	84,161
1977	1,575,347	1,008,725	11,534	1,020,259	85,279	144,519	1,079,499	235,029	260,819	8,321	189,311	85,095
1978	1,779,776	1,180,610	11,718	1,192,328	103,083	149,616	1,238,861	265,544	275,371	9,312	191,121	90,253
1979	2,069,787	1,486,929	9,673	1,496,602	143,412	114,209	1,467,399	300,119	302,269	10,720	193,082	99,716
1980	2,386,106	1,792,440	11,740	1,804,180	180,700	65,015	1,688,495	366,979	330,632	12,264	194,566	109,410
1981	2,735,574	2,159,658	10,799	2,170,457	239,169	-2,231	1,929,057	450,004	356,513	13,958	195,984	118,656
1982	2,921,164	2,304,397	14,457	2,318,854	256,363	-34,785	2,027,706	517,231	376,227	14,862	196,548	119,783
1983	3,177,478	2,599,353	20,497	2,619,850	296,657	-86,287	2,236,906	540,568	400,004	15,954	199,168	124,824
1984	3,586,003	3,022,968	15,085	3,038,053	354,970	-143,070	2,540,013	633,745	412,245	17,687	202,752	133,475
1985	3,831,249	3,295,773	20,107	3,315,880	392,565	-198,372	2,724,943	669,942	436,364	18,594	206,045	139,336
1986	4,099,040	3,608,819	21,519	3,630,338	429,653	-269,689	2,930,996	708,854	459,190	19,576	209,388	141,884
1987	4,343,758	3,925,341	18,435	3,943,776	469,836	-349,855	3,124,085	743,494	476,179	20,433	212,581	148,142
1988	4,747,699	4,365,864	18,427	4,384,291	525,747	-450,998	3,407,546	827,597	512,556	21,834	217,445	152,703
1989	4,945,472	4,511,522	18,262	4,529,784	544,251	-548,976	3,436,557	955,801	553,114	22,318	221,589	155,641
1990	5,065,020	4,701,103	17,135	4,718,238	553,501	-679,996	3,484,741	973,839	606,440	22,468	225,431	159,479
1991	4,796,490	4,302,985	20,486	4,323,471	531,003	-647,708	3,144,760	938,737	712,993	20,967	228,763	152,342
1992	5,394,249	4,845,531	22,501	4,868,032	576,430	-672,976	3,618,626	934,693	840,930	23,290	231,612	152,205
1993	5,662,193	5,126,534	26,421	5,152,955	598,218	-705,633	3,849,104	929,720	883,369	24,168	234,288	153,047
1994	5,805,053	5,262,155	26,756	5,288,911	629,876	-704,206	3,954,829	972,187	878,037	24,536	236,589	154,444
1995	6,268,051	5,617,638	28,932	5,646,570	659,802	-708,400	4,278,368	1,043,188	946,495	26,203	239,212	157,855
1996	6,682,656	5,976,437	31,538	6,007,975	692,844	-713,318	4,601,813	1,103,413	977,430	27,597	242,152	159,704
1997	7,028,062	6,292,371	30,222	6,322,593	707,823	-746,039	4,868,731	1,157,117	1,002,214	28,713	244,771	162,668
1998	7,331,652	6,588,140	26,903	6,615,043	729,056	-780,184	5,105,803	1,198,712	1,027,137	29,579	247,863	167,700
1999	7,551,014	6,820,454	22,442	6,842,896	739,954	-781,138	5,321,804	1,178,835	1,050,375	30,152	250,432	170,052
2000	8,003,271	7,148,384	31,255	7,179,639	765,413	-793,178	5,621,048	1,258,149	1,124,074	31,549	253,674	173,765
2001	7,465,854	6,476,388	29,657	6,506,045	759,301	-839,103	4,907,641	1,297,556	1,260,657	29,193	255,737	171,600
2002	7,739,659	6,701,016	36,863	6,737,879	785,707	-811,716	5,140,456	1,217,749	1,381,454	29,853	259,263	171,667
2003	8,035,328	6,946,922	35,156	6,982,078	812,256	-789,408	5,380,414	1,224,433	1,430,481	30,520	263,285	174,184
2004	8,560,614	7,436,315	34,839	7,471,154	854,218	-784,864	5,832,072	1,303,851	1,424,691	31,976	267,723	177,412
2005	9,047,863	7,907,787	45,697	7,953,484	918,806	-792,152	6,242,526	1,246,387	1,558,950	33,469	270,332	183,113
2006	9,912,276	8,584,788	67,264	8,652,052	969,782	-740,365	6,941,905	1,263,783	1,706,588	36,475	271,759	184,525
2007	10,393,984	8,766,567	71,830	8,838,397	1,006,112	-697,377	7,134,908	1,445,739	1,813,337	38,171	272,303	183,099
2008	10,707,304	8,657,435	58,847	8,716,282	1,022,528	-692,251	7,001,503	1,651,657	2,054,144	39,219	273,014	181,292
2009	10,456,060	8,056,167	60,447	8,116,614	963,570	-592,771	6,560,273	1,600,454	2,295,333	38,154	274,049	172,715
2010	10,643,725	8,131,673	50,624	8,182,297	972,952	-631,937	6,577,408	1,575,263	2,491,054	38,753	274,654	171,005
2011	11,092,222	8,234,494	60,035	8,294,529	895,568	-537,587	6,861,374	1,698,320	2,532,528	40,389	274,635	170,762
2012	11,344,374	8,490,418	71,358	8,561,776	905,782	-585,813	7,070,181	1,776,087	2,498,106	41,304	274,657	171,854
2013	11,508,671	8,699,261	55,660	8,754,921	1,025,543	-528,536	7,200,842	1,770,441	2,537,388	41,947	274,360	171,401
2014	11,773,482	8,805,312	58,566	8,863,878	1,033,337	-595,007	7,235,534	1,887,176	2,650,772	42,419	277,553	168,468
2015	11,889,267	8,648,311	61,771	8,710,082	1,025,443	-505,024	7,179,615	1,970,922	2,738,730	43,040	276,237	164,855
2016	11,961,892	8,654,388	60,820	8,715,208	1,027,757	-457,842	7,229,609	1,916,453	2,815,830	43,605	274,324	165,303
2017	12,305,784	8,763,184	67,878	8,831,062	1,051,061	-350,205	7,429,796	1,996,574	2,879,414	44,969	273,651	163,865
2018	12,731,517	9,246,672	45,979	9,292,651	1,100,018	-455,639	7,736,994	2,009,178	2,985,345	46,585	273,295	168,120
2019	13,757,969	9,958,172	57,211	10,015,383	1,174,175	-386,899	8,454,309	2,142,133	3,161,527	50,196	274,085	169,864
2020	15,155,351	9,549,819	52,691	9,602,510	1,123,142	-9,018	8,470,350	2,113,064	4,571,937	55,273	274,191	150,996
2021	16,033,351	10,595,427	41,080	10,636,507	1,245,304	-266,857	9,124,346	2,117,346	4,791,659	58,310	274,966	162,122

Personal Income and Employment by Area: Auburn-Opelika, AL

(Thousands of dollars, except as noted.)

Year	Personal income, total	Earnings by place of work			Less: Contributions for government social insurance	Plus: Adjustment for residence	Equals: Net earnings by place of residence	Plus: Dividends, interest, and rent	Plus: Personal current transfer receipts	Per capita personal income (dollars)	Population (persons)	Total employment
		Nonfarm	Farm	Total								
1970	169,722	135,029	2,208	137,237	10,502	7,656	134,391	22,021	13,310	2,770	61,262	25,031
1971	189,457	147,579	2,833	150,412	11,785	10,370	148,997	25,207	15,253	3,061	61,896	24,952
1972	214,225	168,266	3,307	171,573	14,043	11,540	169,070	28,048	17,107	3,446	62,158	26,173
1973	243,444	191,905	4,206	196,111	18,356	13,257	191,012	32,093	20,339	3,769	64,588	27,551
1974	273,005	212,386	1,937	214,323	20,983	16,472	209,812	37,967	25,226	3,967	68,823	27,763
1975	303,672	227,786	1,641	229,427	22,485	19,230	226,172	43,349	34,151	4,377	69,373	27,700
1976	344,275	257,209	3,543	260,752	25,931	23,778	258,599	49,023	36,653	4,920	69,980	28,875
1977	397,165	301,124	4,294	305,418	30,201	25,493	300,710	56,963	39,492	5,527	71,861	30,460
1978	457,487	346,744	6,677	353,421	35,224	29,437	347,634	66,941	42,912	6,176	74,069	32,087
1979	505,368	377,118	7,184	384,302	39,536	34,245	379,011	75,520	50,837	6,650	75,990	32,315
1980	571,438	421,296	6,441	427,737	44,769	36,674	419,642	90,078	61,718	7,459	76,610	32,917
1981	627,182	458,987	6,436	465,423	52,590	37,801	450,634	109,037	67,511	8,064	77,777	32,811
1982	665,335	473,717	6,100	479,817	54,906	41,196	466,107	125,400	73,828	8,422	79,001	32,816
1983	737,201	536,226	4,844	541,070	61,814	41,271	520,527	136,379	80,295	9,317	79,121	34,028
1984	818,528	609,253	3,601	612,854	71,016	41,928	583,766	151,300	83,462	10,195	80,289	36,719
1985	879,390	646,777	4,710	651,487	74,525	48,195	625,157	164,147	90,086	10,833	81,176	37,024
1986	932,599	678,665	3,796	682,461	77,162	54,313	659,612	177,517	95,470	11,267	82,776	37,444
1987	993,407	725,045	4,876	729,921	81,299	58,920	707,542	187,571	98,294	12,015	82,681	38,845
1988	1,074,858	794,060	5,176	799,236	92,555	58,536	765,217	205,417	104,224	12,705	84,601	40,675
1989	1,199,799	881,891	5,290	887,181	101,734	54,220	839,667	239,541	120,591	13,975	85,851	43,158
1990	1,263,716	923,878	6,036	929,914	107,168	61,294	884,040	244,449	135,227	14,404	87,735	43,140
1991	1,337,279	945,484	9,466	954,950	109,328	80,735	926,357	258,654	152,268	14,940	89,508	43,300
1992	1,461,242	1,031,334	6,649	1,037,983	117,463	98,903	1,019,423	270,048	171,771	15,957	91,572	44,434
1993	1,552,650	1,070,623	17,090	1,087,713	122,334	120,990	1,086,369	281,609	184,672	16,466	94,295	45,513
1994	1,657,056	1,133,461	8,893	1,142,354	130,330	143,858	1,155,882	301,330	199,844	17,251	96,057	46,095
1995	1,784,325	1,188,482	8,524	1,197,006	137,146	167,338	1,227,198	340,558	216,569	17,953	99,386	48,314
1996	1,872,181	1,225,957	5,676	1,231,633	140,354	196,688	1,287,967	354,190	230,024	18,321	102,185	49,880
1997	2,018,792	1,304,017	6,079	1,310,096	149,463	228,032	1,388,665	383,494	246,633	18,942	106,578	51,253
1998	2,160,909	1,383,142	5,148	1,388,290	154,724	266,300	1,499,866	404,311	256,732	19,656	109,936	51,944
1999	2,294,540	1,471,067	4,228	1,475,295	163,671	294,251	1,605,875	414,470	274,195	20,324	112,898	52,880
2000	2,418,320	1,515,212	3,701	1,518,913	169,746	322,128	1,671,295	450,287	296,738	20,951	115,430	54,697
2001	2,492,079	1,507,898	5,273	1,513,171	174,007	343,829	1,682,993	471,499	337,587	21,333	116,819	54,497
2002	2,619,814	1,604,699	7,272	1,611,971	184,752	350,472	1,777,691	483,368	358,755	22,128	118,392	56,381
2003	2,806,043	1,724,439	7,303	1,731,742	197,842	355,150	1,889,050	533,483	383,510	23,370	120,071	57,402
2004	3,074,824	1,937,175	9,592	1,946,767	218,977	344,791	2,072,581	590,653	411,590	25,147	122,274	61,407
2005	3,291,119	2,058,127	6,605	2,064,732	232,622	364,839	2,196,949	645,696	448,474	26,092	126,133	63,934
2006	3,545,170	2,207,729	8,005	2,215,734	250,336	375,641	2,341,039	713,242	490,889	27,429	129,247	67,109
2007	3,777,164	2,312,488	7,892	2,320,380	265,002	409,105	2,464,483	763,292	549,389	28,629	131,934	69,314
2008	4,056,164	2,334,832	4,350	2,339,182	274,996	464,420	2,528,606	891,433	636,125	30,152	134,524	68,626
2009	4,047,307	2,307,070	5,922	2,312,992	269,746	463,872	2,507,118	860,483	679,706	29,209	138,566	66,847
2010	4,238,735	2,331,483	4,142	2,335,625	273,748	527,730	2,589,607	877,906	771,222	30,101	140,815	66,719
2011	4,493,791	2,434,279	4,766	2,439,045	254,037	596,185	2,781,193	907,539	805,059	31,165	144,194	69,655
2012	4,815,002	2,563,562	14,316	2,577,878	264,422	675,895	2,989,351	1,008,476	817,175	32,387	148,670	71,770
2013	4,898,132	2,686,060	6,482	2,692,542	311,297	696,869	3,078,114	976,433	843,585	32,237	151,943	73,932
2014	5,197,077	2,862,907	2,776	2,865,683	330,373	694,619	3,229,929	1,066,527	900,621	32,959	157,684	76,547
2015	5,481,025	3,017,362	4,226	3,021,588	347,768	700,749	3,374,569	1,108,295	998,161	34,058	160,934	78,204
2016	5,746,170	3,175,694	7,946	3,183,640	363,680	770,525	3,590,485	1,126,989	1,028,696	35,036	164,008	80,756
2017	6,003,899	3,395,953	11,418	3,407,371	391,903	691,305	3,706,773	1,248,488	1,048,638	35,912	167,184	83,725
2018	6,256,187	3,496,055	9,259	3,505,314	409,307	800,087	3,896,094	1,255,356	1,104,737	36,710	170,423	85,741
2019	6,770,191	3,689,452	9,427	3,698,879	432,536	877,605	4,143,948	1,439,643	1,186,600	39,355	172,030	87,126
2020	7,291,278	3,858,118	9,018	3,867,136	459,423	841,799	4,249,512	1,509,571	1,532,195	41,760	174,601	86,006
2021	7,975,201	4,145,850	6,111	4,151,961	488,491	1,011,075	4,674,545	1,564,555	1,736,101	45,002	177,218	88,602

Personal Income and Employment by Area: Augusta-Richmond County, GA-SC

(Thousands of dollars, except as noted.)

Year	Personal income, total	Earnings by place of work			Less: Contributions for government social insurance	Plus: Adjustment for residence	Equals: Net earnings by place of residence	Plus: Dividends, interest, and rent	Plus: Personal current transfer receipts	Per capita personal income (dollars)	Population (persons)	Total employment
		Nonfarm	Farm	Total								
1970	1,151,713	947,281	12,844	960,125	59,380	-17,736	883,009	176,536	92,168	3,489	330,105	149,954
1971	1,243,591	1,019,335	17,231	1,036,566	67,016	-28,026	941,524	188,779	113,288	3,765	330,340	149,885
1972	1,347,080	1,104,590	16,681	1,121,271	75,514	-27,996	1,017,761	199,876	129,443	4,102	328,410	151,635
1973	1,500,532	1,213,557	34,737	1,248,294	94,054	-27,946	1,126,294	224,582	149,656	4,513	332,508	157,074
1974	1,683,378	1,353,556	22,469	1,376,025	109,140	-30,503	1,236,382	260,168	186,828	4,940	340,794	160,613
1975	1,813,963	1,419,381	20,486	1,439,867	114,385	-30,688	1,294,794	281,439	237,730	5,199	348,901	157,238
1976	2,080,859	1,663,727	24,825	1,688,552	136,281	-43,537	1,508,734	314,989	257,136	5,795	359,074	165,293
1977	2,283,948	1,844,119	22,400	1,866,519	150,578	-47,837	1,668,104	348,734	267,110	6,261	364,786	172,285
1978	2,550,572	2,059,940	20,102	2,080,042	171,732	-53,344	1,854,966	402,686	292,920	6,815	374,244	178,197
1979	2,884,567	2,309,983	41,217	2,351,200	199,677	-63,263	2,088,260	461,793	334,514	7,524	383,370	184,512
1980	3,191,499	2,534,164	5,825	2,539,989	219,943	-72,927	2,247,119	543,920	400,460	8,173	390,476	186,358
1981	3,573,855	2,777,968	25,099	2,803,067	259,245	-64,820	2,479,002	631,300	463,553	9,084	393,411	187,332
1982	3,989,271	3,126,131	22,811	3,148,942	297,024	-82,576	2,769,342	717,542	502,387	10,020	398,117	191,980
1983	4,319,593	3,400,961	-1,782	3,399,179	330,052	-85,013	2,984,114	791,994	543,485	10,716	403,081	192,244
1984	4,897,233	3,880,023	26,619	3,906,642	388,635	-91,864	3,426,143	892,625	578,465	11,948	409,893	205,007
1985	5,387,174	4,315,114	28,328	4,343,442	440,626	-102,968	3,799,848	961,956	625,370	12,865	418,761	214,148
1986	5,841,699	4,686,708	21,646	4,708,354	487,627	-102,569	4,118,158	1,052,806	670,735	13,661	427,630	221,104
1987	6,047,138	4,809,401	28,808	4,838,209	495,899	-95,359	4,246,951	1,085,084	715,103	14,083	429,399	221,744
1988	6,491,268	5,143,292	44,131	5,187,423	549,924	-97,053	4,540,446	1,176,105	774,717	15,024	432,054	227,226
1989	7,142,251	5,608,818	47,243	5,656,061	608,662	-111,217	4,936,182	1,332,848	873,221	16,372	436,235	235,072
1990	7,801,627	6,210,727	28,140	6,238,867	683,729	-133,955	5,421,183	1,414,940	965,504	17,485	446,200	247,348
1991	8,156,486	6,372,144	45,798	6,417,942	712,568	-122,362	5,583,012	1,454,063	1,119,411	17,740	459,773	243,584
1992	8,750,900	6,823,478	43,057	6,866,535	756,502	-117,741	5,992,292	1,524,473	1,234,135	18,446	474,398	243,360
1993	9,017,776	6,996,807	26,637	7,023,444	782,284	-111,450	6,129,710	1,565,621	1,322,445	18,912	476,818	247,474
1994	9,417,837	7,172,991	46,644	7,219,635	810,718	-93,362	6,315,555	1,707,522	1,394,760	19,485	483,333	251,197
1995	9,798,542	7,347,772	38,406	7,386,178	828,559	-75,545	6,482,074	1,807,134	1,509,334	20,034	489,089	253,558
1996	10,231,097	7,471,391	36,765	7,508,156	830,913	-46,035	6,631,208	1,983,943	1,615,946	20,846	490,788	254,613
1997	10,683,901	7,773,394	37,575	7,810,969	857,519	-25,107	6,928,343	2,092,689	1,662,869	21,539	496,030	260,000
1998	11,409,235	8,313,140	34,545	8,347,685	908,746	5,770	7,444,709	2,253,029	1,711,497	22,789	500,636	264,879
1999	11,894,873	8,768,146	38,979	8,807,125	957,095	8,189	7,858,219	2,226,624	1,810,030	23,559	504,895	270,712
2000	12,536,546	9,120,444	48,318	9,168,762	993,415	15,467	8,190,814	2,399,632	1,946,100	24,635	508,896	274,209
2001	12,920,916	9,277,824	72,270	9,350,094	1,021,886	-10,958	8,317,250	2,471,273	2,132,393	25,205	512,626	269,418
2002	13,498,240	9,668,968	54,668	9,723,636	1,069,564	-24,470	8,629,602	2,480,693	2,387,945	26,118	516,818	269,277
2003	14,155,121	10,288,488	62,390	10,350,878	1,117,525	-32,767	9,200,586	2,504,017	2,450,518	27,215	520,120	273,401
2004	14,911,812	10,903,716	86,622	10,990,338	1,200,423	-31,334	9,758,581	2,537,872	2,615,359	28,307	526,789	279,068
2005	15,517,103	11,249,179	97,180	11,346,359	1,234,223	-35,729	10,076,407	2,648,732	2,791,964	29,206	531,294	282,917
2006	16,357,904	11,671,736	71,227	11,742,963	1,295,240	-28,788	10,418,935	2,940,944	2,998,025	30,369	538,643	284,058
2007	17,162,708	12,025,847	56,295	12,082,142	1,324,056	-39,411	10,718,675	3,250,169	3,193,864	31,461	545,524	289,914
2008	17,932,477	12,438,401	54,757	12,493,158	1,423,640	-44,945	11,024,573	3,272,484	3,635,420	32,450	552,627	289,736
2009	18,111,183	12,510,474	64,287	12,574,761	1,426,701	-103,165	11,044,895	3,110,715	3,955,573	32,452	558,096	284,308
2010	18,853,789	13,043,462	59,403	13,102,865	1,481,910	-153,910	11,467,045	3,108,820	4,277,924	33,269	566,712	284,786
2011	19,976,611	13,545,499	37,705	13,583,204	1,376,175	-207,820	11,999,209	3,486,818	4,490,584	34,987	570,971	288,575
2012	20,206,144	13,863,773	54,142	13,917,915	1,408,379	-232,340	12,277,196	3,473,098	4,455,850	35,054	576,421	289,106
2013	20,398,492	13,985,059	106,713	14,091,772	1,591,151	-253,084	12,247,537	3,561,883	4,589,072	35,162	580,123	292,212
2014	21,359,296	14,633,031	61,893	14,694,924	1,656,990	-256,864	12,781,070	3,784,650	4,793,576	36,662	582,602	299,609
2015	22,680,135	15,495,218	73,319	15,568,537	1,746,360	-279,590	13,542,587	4,089,391	5,048,157	38,509	588,955	307,278
2016	23,257,172	15,887,474	54,757	15,942,231	1,783,586	-280,276	13,878,369	4,140,865	5,237,938	39,130	594,350	311,160
2017	24,340,641	16,648,745	65,993	16,714,738	1,861,925	-287,890	14,564,923	4,354,346	5,421,372	40,615	599,308	318,670
2018	25,205,279	17,294,372	25,702	17,320,074	1,952,772	-291,319	15,075,983	4,430,334	5,698,962	41,782	603,251	326,109
2019	26,688,992	18,250,842	44,582	18,295,424	2,074,154	-324,701	15,896,569	4,764,186	6,028,237	43,905	607,877	331,229
2020	28,674,382	18,635,269	51,299	18,686,568	2,132,568	-347,897	16,206,103	4,771,434	7,696,845	46,875	611,720	328,165
2021	30,447,049	19,520,096	64,001	19,584,097	2,228,628	-344,540	17,010,929	4,825,704	8,610,416	49,432	615,933	334,259

Personal Income and Employment by Area: Austin-Round Rock-Georgetown, TX

(Thousands of dollars, except as noted.)

Year	Personal income, total	Derivation of personal income									Per capita personal income (dollars)	Population (persons)	Total employment
		Earnings by place of work			Less: Contributions for government social insurance	Plus: Adjustment for residence	Equals: Net earnings by place of residence	Plus: Dividends, interest, and rent	Plus: Personal current transfer receipts				
		Nonfarm	Farm	Total									
1970	1,475,763	1,154,458	13,108	1,167,566	69,396	-1,049	1,097,121	273,548	105,094		3,672	401,871	184,371
1971	1,672,669	1,310,024	11,680	1,321,704	82,025	-126	1,239,553	311,934	121,182		3,990	419,249	195,537
1972	1,931,675	1,508,104	25,787	1,533,891	98,461	834	1,436,264	359,114	136,297		4,312	447,971	210,710
1973	2,213,246	1,716,806	45,885	1,762,691	128,968	1,944	1,635,667	408,966	168,613		4,676	473,351	226,304
1974	2,498,475	1,932,352	25,287	1,957,639	149,877	1,682	1,809,444	482,501	206,530		5,141	485,969	235,030
1975	2,874,184	2,192,861	18,666	2,211,527	167,560	3,940	2,047,907	560,196	266,081		5,779	497,356	240,694
1976	3,295,435	2,548,061	30,898	2,578,959	195,426	2,245	2,385,778	616,244	293,413		6,366	517,680	255,068
1977	3,657,562	2,880,709	6,674	2,887,383	224,831	-462	2,662,090	689,610	305,862		6,874	532,052	272,296
1978	4,258,129	3,352,895	15,778	3,368,673	269,208	-4,328	3,095,137	820,471	342,521		7,905	538,668	290,687
1979	4,928,128	3,869,012	28,186	3,897,198	326,104	-2,239	3,568,855	964,007	395,266		8,623	571,520	308,207
1980	5,676,806	4,419,614	2,256	4,421,870	373,621	382	4,048,631	1,160,715	467,460		9,629	589,582	322,221
1981	6,636,769	5,102,203	25,653	5,127,856	467,038	5,812	4,666,630	1,433,286	536,853		10,952	605,961	342,388
1982	7,620,658	5,760,113	28,665	5,788,778	532,851	6,331	5,262,258	1,753,626	604,774		12,030	633,452	362,756
1983	8,803,015	6,731,140	12,928	6,744,068	616,451	-8,127	6,119,490	2,016,247	667,278		13,172	668,303	388,622
1984	10,311,423	8,030,625	13,370	8,043,995	758,728	-23,084	7,262,183	2,328,810	720,430		14,571	707,646	431,932
1985	11,666,538	9,146,128	-6,662	9,139,466	877,555	-34,193	8,227,718	2,647,563	791,257		15,381	758,510	468,315
1986	12,187,544	9,532,708	-2,221	9,530,487	911,319	-34,431	8,584,737	2,717,941	884,866		15,367	793,109	471,436
1987	12,383,763	9,653,165	2,914	9,656,079	901,106	-22,248	8,732,725	2,695,303	955,735		15,338	807,392	481,326
1988	13,117,712	10,178,244	807	10,179,051	988,494	-11,237	9,179,320	2,914,725	1,023,667		16,053	817,153	484,629
1989	14,083,859	10,667,283	11,448	10,678,731	1,052,806	-1,386	9,624,539	3,316,151	1,143,169		16,931	831,848	490,138
1990	15,544,953	11,869,880	7,443	11,877,323	1,162,435	2,892	10,717,780	3,555,155	1,272,018		18,247	851,898	512,913
1991	16,505,681	12,992,033	12,737	13,004,770	1,301,884	-19,991	11,682,895	3,407,472	1,415,314		18,742	880,678	536,269
1992	18,131,918	14,340,745	19,923	14,360,668	1,432,140	-42,128	12,886,400	3,585,686	1,659,832		19,863	912,833	554,727
1993	19,850,908	15,873,548	30,278	15,903,826	1,589,251	-76,034	14,238,541	3,844,612	1,767,755		20,900	949,788	591,053
1994	21,711,558	17,465,266	20,938	17,486,204	1,777,162	-109,402	15,599,640	4,214,335	1,897,583		21,955	988,925	624,671
1995	23,996,690	19,454,834	21,924	19,476,758	1,994,940	-157,841	17,323,977	4,616,188	2,056,525		23,263	1,031,557	663,975
1996	26,309,157	21,522,017	-12,971	21,509,046	2,197,103	-212,794	19,099,149	5,000,228	2,209,780		24,518	1,073,037	692,327
1997	29,242,714	24,084,404	15,227	24,099,631	2,457,286	-280,329	21,362,016	5,538,089	2,342,609		26,315	1,111,264	725,886
1998	34,105,307	28,738,440	-5,486	28,732,954	2,734,186	-410,722	25,438,046	6,229,106	2,438,155		29,514	1,155,579	766,659
1999	38,540,390	32,838,693	28,249	32,866,942	3,276,563	-561,025	29,029,354	6,884,242	2,626,794		31,960	1,205,898	805,105
2000	42,271,727	36,152,559	13,534	36,166,093	3,638,499	-666,685	31,860,909	7,586,407	2,824,411		33,418	1,264,950	849,746
2001	46,821,765	40,358,290	14,131	40,372,421	3,785,399	-613,349	35,973,673	7,681,634	3,166,458		35,436	1,321,316	863,762
2002	46,554,229	39,585,787	15,431	39,601,218	3,686,463	-514,239	35,400,516	7,608,802	3,544,911		34,540	1,347,822	856,715
2003	47,418,251	39,768,561	42,553	39,811,114	3,826,655	-491,258	35,493,201	8,111,546	3,813,504		34,460	1,376,030	864,159
2004	48,557,629	39,965,238	67,393	40,032,631	3,965,472	-481,908	35,585,251	8,896,961	4,075,417		34,437	1,410,058	886,034
2005	53,276,858	43,095,008	48,994	43,144,002	4,256,605	-494,209	38,393,188	10,380,080	4,503,590		36,658	1,453,358	934,981
2006	59,526,630	47,795,297	43,351	47,838,648	4,565,360	-484,969	42,788,319	11,868,351	4,869,960		39,279	1,515,485	981,793
2007	63,336,435	50,582,289	43,868	50,626,157	4,905,324	-478,074	45,242,759	12,689,281	5,404,395		40,141	1,577,856	1,042,215
2008	68,997,143	52,205,817	-10,258	52,195,559	5,043,718	-416,707	46,735,134	15,847,999	6,414,010		42,229	1,633,870	1,072,058
2009	67,133,803	51,025,814	-12,453	51,013,361	5,068,719	-306,014	45,638,628	14,312,439	7,182,736		39,905	1,682,338	1,068,447
2010	71,847,849	54,517,840	561	54,518,401	5,340,082	-232,944	48,945,375	14,705,796	8,196,678		41,590	1,727,514	1,082,191
2011	79,592,592	59,487,729	-8,696	59,479,033	5,074,987	-117,203	54,286,843	16,714,806	8,590,943		44,698	1,780,679	1,116,595
2012	87,541,859	63,792,917	11,786	63,804,703	5,399,512	6,821	58,412,012	20,477,936	8,651,911		47,710	1,834,861	1,154,689
2013	91,483,349	68,163,151	46,644	68,209,795	6,507,476	114,367	61,816,686	20,547,726	9,118,937		48,565	1,883,749	1,211,228
2014	99,810,005	74,125,469	14,405	74,139,874	6,980,441	194,034	67,353,467	22,721,759	9,734,779		51,333	1,944,376	1,264,086
2015	105,452,591	78,561,244	49,304	78,610,548	7,612,287	157,277	71,155,538	23,786,932	10,510,121		52,607	2,004,539	1,324,618
2016	110,167,569	82,752,461	-1,433	82,751,028	8,173,507	63,777	74,641,298	24,456,135	11,070,136		53,352	2,064,915	1,382,302
2017	120,974,412	92,086,422	-3,899	92,082,523	8,947,132	6,480	83,141,871	26,347,988	11,484,553		57,103	2,118,521	1,441,842
2018	131,553,640	99,737,845	-18,487	99,719,358	9,538,898	-51,458	90,129,002	29,227,443	12,197,195		60,631	2,169,743	1,509,740
2019	141,617,720	106,115,418	-20,250	106,095,168	10,314,843	-129,131	95,651,194	32,801,504	13,165,022		63,466	2,231,398	1,557,157
2020	149,250,080	108,994,399	-14,438	108,979,961	10,921,612	-278,404	97,779,945	32,656,936	18,813,199		64,916	2,299,125	1,555,342
2021	167,896,493	125,148,950	-11,253	125,137,697	12,429,901	-432,578	112,275,218	34,710,977	20,910,298		71,372	2,352,426	1,648,626

Personal Income and Employment by Area: Bakersfield, CA

(Thousands of dollars, except as noted.)

Year	Personal income, total	Earnings by place of work			Less: Contributions for government social insurance	Plus: Adjustment for residence	Equals: Net earnings by place of residence	Plus: Dividends, interest, and rent	Plus: Personal current transfer receipts	Per capita personal income (dollars)	Population (persons)	Total employment
		Nonfarm	Farm	Total								
1970	1,357,079	1,005,293	118,613	1,123,906	62,497	-43,180	1,018,229	188,910	149,940	4,102	330,868	138,871
1971	1,464,866	1,078,629	130,600	1,209,229	69,145	-46,629	1,093,455	205,956	165,455	4,357	336,227	142,153
1972	1,593,327	1,166,044	149,304	1,315,348	77,970	-49,631	1,187,747	226,230	179,350	4,730	336,833	145,354
1973	1,818,667	1,307,130	203,198	1,510,328	99,741	-54,822	1,355,765	262,251	200,651	5,302	343,007	153,762
1974	2,156,400	1,485,631	316,347	1,801,978	118,147	-66,163	1,617,668	297,492	241,240	6,253	344,840	163,320
1975	2,343,300	1,671,625	255,472	1,927,097	130,242	-85,738	1,711,117	335,080	297,103	6,566	356,866	170,339
1976	2,763,966	1,890,159	418,562	2,308,721	150,213	-94,369	2,064,139	358,999	340,828	7,533	366,932	173,782
1977	2,921,259	2,097,594	334,713	2,432,307	170,352	-103,900	2,158,055	398,684	364,520	7,848	372,217	179,070
1978	3,216,417	2,384,974	276,117	2,661,091	196,120	-109,405	2,355,566	462,091	398,760	8,509	377,990	185,586
1979	3,830,294	2,728,872	473,541	3,202,413	233,331	-121,331	2,847,751	537,921	444,622	9,741	393,198	197,044
1980	4,498,790	3,072,783	641,573	3,714,356	260,094	-142,610	3,311,652	663,895	523,243	11,070	406,407	202,903
1981	4,819,966	3,457,147	398,604	3,855,751	321,575	-140,209	3,393,967	806,282	619,717	11,507	418,877	207,514
1982	5,253,132	3,730,040	447,822	4,177,862	358,328	-145,264	3,674,270	899,249	679,613	12,112	433,698	205,351
1983	5,467,802	3,922,694	346,178	4,268,872	388,348	-141,093	3,739,431	982,457	745,914	12,233	446,961	211,093
1984	6,028,100	4,347,523	367,679	4,715,202	447,857	-151,227	4,116,118	1,113,135	798,847	13,121	459,411	217,562
1985	6,466,455	4,731,854	335,570	5,067,424	495,995	-152,613	4,418,816	1,185,385	862,254	13,635	474,243	223,569
1986	6,902,908	4,975,803	428,057	5,403,860	528,616	-145,814	4,729,430	1,233,419	940,059	14,197	486,217	227,198
1987	7,159,440	5,140,302	464,962	5,605,264	547,258	-125,235	4,932,771	1,244,219	982,450	14,379	497,910	231,475
1988	7,851,244	5,707,273	503,156	6,210,429	629,888	-133,969	5,446,572	1,338,760	1,065,912	15,365	510,980	243,334
1989	8,365,507	5,987,471	483,707	6,471,178	667,124	-129,372	5,674,682	1,507,975	1,182,850	15,846	527,922	245,816
1990	9,089,058	6,519,468	567,906	7,087,374	724,774	-146,082	6,216,518	1,566,242	1,306,298	16,540	549,535	253,759
1991	9,706,159	7,128,741	440,670	7,569,411	796,668	-167,838	6,604,905	1,620,493	1,480,761	17,048	569,346	267,697
1992	10,190,092	7,301,971	502,880	7,804,851	810,003	-150,334	6,844,514	1,610,723	1,734,855	17,274	589,897	262,789
1993	10,682,018	7,465,810	695,604	8,161,414	832,911	-147,121	7,181,382	1,644,384	1,856,252	17,808	599,843	262,890
1994	10,926,342	7,607,304	650,492	8,257,796	846,041	-138,549	7,273,206	1,747,976	1,905,160	17,775	614,707	266,806
1995	11,322,808	7,931,250	566,500	8,497,750	871,572	-141,365	7,484,813	1,828,497	2,009,498	18,257	620,201	278,216
1996	11,936,703	8,247,029	647,960	8,894,989	875,197	-129,687	7,890,105	1,932,286	2,114,312	19,046	626,719	288,670
1997	12,276,732	8,594,613	560,139	9,154,752	900,356	-124,296	8,130,000	2,037,629	2,109,103	19,343	634,695	289,487
1998	12,994,011	9,332,739	425,385	9,758,124	958,485	-122,151	8,677,488	2,116,394	2,200,129	20,208	643,016	303,568
1999	13,407,973	9,554,119	402,941	9,957,060	980,461	-92,364	8,884,235	2,185,413	2,338,325	20,457	655,428	309,279
2000	14,211,992	10,219,431	503,584	10,723,015	1,049,406	-82,897	9,590,712	2,217,431	2,403,849	21,410	663,803	310,380
2001	15,170,250	10,919,007	510,950	11,429,957	1,194,181	-78,422	10,157,354	2,350,762	2,662,134	22,422	676,574	308,719
2002	16,077,655	11,533,511	725,680	12,259,191	1,280,172	-64,580	10,914,439	2,287,920	2,875,296	23,165	694,059	314,541
2003	17,151,814	12,405,001	633,535	13,038,536	1,387,820	-71,276	11,579,440	2,468,982	3,103,392	24,013	714,272	321,579
2004	18,423,467	13,167,709	1,076,137	14,243,846	1,518,863	-45,992	12,678,991	2,457,587	3,286,889	25,022	736,296	325,067
2005	19,842,944	14,393,242	1,166,554	15,559,796	1,653,897	-38,334	13,867,565	2,514,160	3,461,219	26,084	760,726	341,791
2006	21,461,861	15,966,371	887,209	16,853,580	1,756,593	-29,780	15,067,207	2,653,336	3,741,318	27,357	784,511	354,866
2007	23,254,646	16,716,607	1,260,787	17,977,394	1,812,222	-13,017	16,152,155	3,071,514	4,030,977	28,950	803,281	363,988
2008	23,941,459	17,273,406	772,349	18,045,755	1,895,186	-3,705	16,146,864	3,242,824	4,551,771	29,257	818,327	364,533
2009	23,714,483	16,748,027	900,474	17,648,501	1,866,619	-86,512	15,695,370	3,010,934	5,008,179	28,567	830,137	349,093
2010	25,788,759	18,088,817	1,244,522	19,333,339	1,904,122	-151,754	17,277,463	3,006,548	5,504,748	30,651	841,365	348,449
2011	27,316,563	19,230,642	1,354,080	20,584,722	1,846,502	-219,839	18,518,381	3,279,135	5,519,047	32,188	848,651	361,933
2012	29,004,846	20,465,160	1,601,504	22,066,664	1,960,969	-304,834	19,800,861	3,659,155	5,544,830	33,948	854,392	381,650
2013	29,769,366	21,117,965	1,912,297	23,030,262	2,258,026	-339,326	20,432,910	3,574,038	5,762,418	34,506	862,727	393,903
2014	31,726,727	22,251,449	1,984,884	24,236,333	2,362,063	-355,636	21,518,634	4,114,448	6,093,645	36,335	873,177	404,213
2015	32,431,855	22,156,260	1,918,946	24,075,206	2,342,579	-323,479	21,409,148	4,431,340	6,591,367	36,825	880,708	404,831
2016	32,240,783	21,908,112	1,791,944	23,700,056	2,356,894	-318,539	21,024,623	4,342,594	6,873,566	36,386	886,081	406,705
2017	32,852,879	22,411,209	2,031,813	24,443,022	2,429,659	-365,654	21,647,709	4,418,384	6,786,786	36,783	893,150	411,621
2018	33,980,966	23,751,043	1,636,159	25,387,202	2,582,320	-394,840	22,410,042	4,486,082	7,084,842	37,743	900,315	422,760
2019	35,784,162	24,951,580	1,649,361	26,600,941	2,748,008	-431,542	23,421,391	4,797,328	7,565,443	39,477	906,453	429,837
2020	40,097,301	25,559,262	1,751,779	27,311,041	2,814,883	-475,558	24,020,600	4,786,370	11,290,331	44,063	909,997	418,395
2021	42,177,029	27,070,415	1,219,463	28,289,878	2,984,537	-457,787	24,847,554	4,856,293	12,473,182	45,961	917,673	431,960

Personal Income and Employment by Area: Baltimore-Columbia-Towson, MD

(Thousands of dollars, except as noted.)

Year	Personal income, total	Earnings by place of work			Less: Contributions for government social insurance	Plus: Adjustment for residence	Equals: Net earnings by place of residence	Plus: Dividends, interest, and rent	Plus: Personal current transfer receipts	Per capita personal income (dollars)	Population (persons)	Total employment
		Nonfarm	Farm	Total								
1970	9,420,898	7,783,621	31,091	7,814,712	496,727	65,121	7,383,106	1,329,181	708,611	4,497	2,094,838	991,821
1971	10,314,326	8,380,680	23,419	8,404,099	552,062	144,280	7,996,317	1,454,228	863,781	4,838	2,132,113	994,410
1972	11,336,168	9,114,000	32,179	9,146,179	629,686	236,439	8,752,932	1,586,680	996,556	5,267	2,152,232	1,011,325
1973	12,535,270	10,041,060	47,689	10,088,749	797,680	318,125	9,609,194	1,784,358	1,141,718	5,782	2,167,899	1,041,876
1974	13,835,894	10,987,901	44,100	11,032,001	907,009	393,552	10,518,544	2,014,321	1,303,029	6,349	2,179,392	1,056,134
1975	14,987,764	11,626,158	50,531	11,676,689	956,010	485,063	11,205,742	2,149,559	1,632,463	6,861	2,184,332	1,038,096
1976	16,344,005	12,660,144	42,381	12,702,525	1,058,328	611,567	12,255,764	2,329,451	1,758,790	7,467	2,188,964	1,040,323
1977	17,827,450	13,748,804	32,102	13,780,906	1,154,071	753,890	13,380,725	2,571,031	1,875,694	8,096	2,201,877	1,068,371
1978	19,889,912	15,288,294	47,166	15,335,460	1,319,784	910,339	14,926,015	2,895,953	2,067,944	9,023	2,204,362	1,108,082
1979	21,951,910	16,746,277	44,409	16,790,686	1,515,579	1,103,496	16,378,603	3,235,802	2,337,505	9,937	2,209,160	1,139,209
1980	24,628,751	18,238,156	25,118	18,263,274	1,651,213	1,320,361	17,932,422	3,896,476	2,799,853	11,178	2,203,385	1,139,485
1981	27,264,037	19,959,348	36,098	19,995,446	1,938,378	1,310,455	19,367,523	4,737,286	3,159,228	12,312	2,214,413	1,146,005
1982	29,340,768	20,849,242	36,616	20,885,858	2,050,386	1,384,754	20,220,226	5,620,302	3,500,240	13,212	2,220,748	1,137,050
1983	31,328,742	22,518,185	29,743	22,547,928	2,279,282	1,452,291	21,720,937	5,811,316	3,796,489	14,059	2,228,439	1,164,025
1984	34,416,475	24,765,818	69,673	24,835,491	2,588,034	1,613,921	23,861,378	6,590,357	3,964,740	15,332	2,244,735	1,202,935
1985	37,069,457	26,919,116	68,515	26,987,631	2,895,298	1,773,196	25,865,529	7,032,713	4,171,215	16,432	2,255,970	1,243,523
1986	39,775,035	28,898,196	55,037	28,953,233	3,148,149	1,927,138	27,732,222	7,537,656	4,505,157	17,402	2,285,633	1,276,452
1987	42,482,919	31,231,004	67,075	31,298,079	3,371,142	2,092,435	30,019,372	7,894,530	4,569,017	18,393	2,309,719	1,332,191
1988	46,438,466	34,334,191	78,740	34,412,931	3,819,265	2,264,376	32,858,042	8,731,007	4,849,417	19,838	2,340,870	1,366,737
1989	49,698,479	36,436,528	78,618	36,515,146	4,076,345	2,397,515	34,836,316	9,618,980	5,243,183	21,053	2,360,610	1,393,176
1990	52,649,611	38,575,462	90,099	38,665,561	4,397,515	2,495,792	36,763,838	10,182,738	5,703,035	22,024	2,390,543	1,404,128
1991	54,612,636	39,562,706	77,117	39,639,823	4,548,857	2,581,863	37,672,829	10,524,209	6,415,598	22,585	2,418,136	1,358,484
1992	57,198,936	41,152,714	94,402	41,247,116	4,706,278	2,767,040	39,307,878	10,735,526	7,155,532	23,441	2,440,078	1,339,950
1993	59,178,785	42,528,842	96,257	42,625,099	4,858,716	2,908,926	40,675,309	11,081,488	7,421,988	24,076	2,458,038	1,347,488
1994	61,769,826	44,198,785	88,186	44,286,971	5,092,663	3,072,885	42,267,193	11,739,173	7,763,460	24,954	2,475,364	1,371,332
1995	64,703,504	46,019,964	78,522	46,098,486	5,271,529	3,169,341	43,996,298	12,636,306	8,070,900	25,981	2,490,370	1,394,314
1996	67,881,395	47,942,214	112,173	48,054,387	5,437,437	3,334,711	45,951,661	13,271,534	8,658,200	27,137	2,501,453	1,409,343
1997	71,926,659	50,712,845	91,119	50,803,964	5,714,623	3,594,943	48,684,284	14,448,920	8,793,455	28,616	2,513,492	1,436,116
1998	77,238,782	54,763,917	106,533	54,870,450	6,024,788	3,866,286	52,711,948	15,461,491	9,065,343	30,586	2,525,266	1,466,512
1999	82,063,320	59,216,255	106,605	59,322,860	6,433,162	4,204,385	57,094,083	15,403,475	9,565,762	32,304	2,540,307	1,509,853
2000	88,401,166	63,612,480	131,510	63,743,990	6,818,698	4,661,709	61,587,001	16,793,880	10,020,285	34,559	2,557,958	1,543,762
2001	92,334,957	66,769,920	110,311	66,880,231	7,351,630	4,695,480	64,224,081	17,307,494	10,803,382	35,852	2,575,471	1,547,690
2002	95,821,431	70,335,292	89,626	70,424,918	7,720,452	4,606,875	67,311,341	17,007,901	11,502,189	36,904	2,596,501	1,558,796
2003	99,686,317	73,070,163	74,370	73,144,533	8,021,749	4,767,419	69,890,203	17,474,575	12,321,539	38,132	2,614,232	1,566,963
2004	105,352,345	77,482,066	94,317	77,576,383	8,593,992	4,842,740	73,825,131	18,693,843	12,833,371	40,044	2,630,946	1,593,882
2005	111,168,193	82,198,090	77,069	82,275,159	9,076,807	5,117,153	78,315,505	18,954,260	13,898,428	42,042	2,644,231	1,623,895
2006	118,228,437	87,173,388	66,005	87,239,393	9,727,534	4,634,214	82,146,073	21,677,797	14,404,567	44,478	2,658,162	1,658,564
2007	124,181,890	90,476,473	60,414	90,536,887	10,183,135	4,680,071	85,033,823	23,542,430	15,605,637	46,552	2,667,619	1,689,183
2008	128,715,446	93,095,897	92,861	93,188,758	10,541,624	3,971,803	86,618,937	24,538,575	17,557,934	48,031	2,679,819	1,686,091
2009	127,149,857	92,928,614	123,247	93,051,861	10,480,108	3,533,102	86,104,855	22,074,165	18,970,837	47,162	2,696,018	1,649,432
2010	131,152,089	96,126,711	108,238	96,234,949	10,865,805	3,507,335	88,876,479	21,830,568	20,445,042	48,292	2,715,794	1,645,096
2011	137,797,460	100,185,082	117,209	100,302,291	10,081,866	2,879,000	93,099,425	23,702,640	20,995,395	50,400	2,734,058	1,677,182
2012	141,955,861	104,457,121	159,357	104,616,478	10,495,986	1,794,723	95,915,215	24,813,758	21,226,888	51,524	2,755,152	1,707,280
2013	142,981,471	106,895,319	163,566	107,058,885	12,007,281	1,471,075	96,522,679	24,561,116	21,897,676	51,636	2,769,005	1,734,251
2014	148,791,101	110,569,660	118,039	110,687,699	12,331,564	943,838	99,299,973	26,266,030	23,225,098	53,164	2,798,729	1,755,256
2015	154,813,354	115,350,369	76,366	115,426,735	12,956,733	542,777	103,012,779	27,741,408	24,059,167	55,035	2,812,978	1,788,444
2016	159,582,151	119,808,410	75,043	119,883,453	13,232,760	48,764	106,699,457	27,661,276	25,221,418	56,561	2,821,424	1,814,635
2017	164,845,548	123,233,080	117,859	123,350,939	13,635,324	80,372	109,795,987	29,430,762	25,618,799	58,244	2,830,275	1,834,614
2018	170,101,926	127,362,893	66,723	127,429,616	14,357,202	9,580	113,081,994	30,231,355	26,788,577	59,946	2,837,598	1,863,452
2019	177,337,368	131,178,500	126,705	131,305,205	14,933,910	566,029	116,937,324	32,485,915	27,914,129	62,379	2,842,883	1,861,518
2020	188,482,699	133,657,033	95,118	133,752,151	15,117,327	757,657	119,392,481	32,431,196	36,659,022	66,328	2,841,691	1,797,975
2021	200,073,844	141,427,609	144,809	141,572,418	16,028,667	1,677,824	127,221,575	33,214,976	39,637,293	70,490	2,838,327	1,841,907

Personal Income and Employment by Area: Bangor, ME

(Thousands of dollars, except as noted.)

Year	Personal income, total	Earnings by place of work			Less: Contributions for government social insurance	Plus: Adjustment for residence	Equals: Net earnings by place of residence	Plus: Dividends, interest, and rent	Plus: Personal current transfer receipts	Per capita personal income (dollars)	Population (persons)	Total employment
		Nonfarm	Farm	Total								
1970	412,911	334,644	4,999	339,643	24,136	-2,996	312,511	57,990	42,410	3,282	125,812	53,058
1971	446,233	360,661	4,725	365,386	26,637	-5,384	333,365	62,468	50,400	3,488	127,935	53,213
1972	493,117	403,087	5,027	408,114	31,014	-8,233	368,867	67,583	56,667	3,822	129,035	54,697
1973	547,346	443,745	9,235	452,980	38,652	-9,060	405,268	75,253	66,825	4,185	130,797	57,117
1974	609,213	479,220	10,276	489,496	43,214	-4,829	441,453	86,528	81,232	4,614	132,038	58,222
1975	676,072	526,793	5,129	531,922	47,314	-8,272	476,336	96,199	103,537	5,067	133,434	59,000
1976	768,008	607,507	12,834	620,341	56,185	-10,571	553,585	102,596	111,827	5,666	135,542	61,770
1977	825,136	661,538	5,670	667,208	60,903	-14,938	591,367	114,349	119,420	6,061	136,134	63,665
1978	906,943	731,169	6,218	737,387	68,841	-18,780	649,766	128,697	128,480	6,624	136,912	65,596
1979	1,012,641	823,157	4,827	827,984	79,837	-23,430	724,717	143,154	144,770	7,383	137,157	67,939
1980	1,130,404	900,280	2,486	902,766	86,748	-27,548	788,470	170,437	171,497	8,237	137,228	68,884
1981	1,233,592	961,500	8,985	970,485	99,796	-34,106	836,583	202,560	194,449	8,942	137,952	68,180
1982	1,318,547	1,004,640	7,172	1,011,812	106,957	-35,775	869,080	237,689	211,778	9,553	138,020	67,853
1983	1,423,485	1,097,490	5,266	1,102,756	117,253	-41,548	943,955	251,046	228,484	10,308	138,101	69,290
1984	1,571,009	1,217,415	8,837	1,226,252	134,109	-45,212	1,046,931	282,832	241,246	11,344	138,488	71,880
1985	1,663,854	1,291,851	6,847	1,298,698	142,720	-46,503	1,109,475	300,757	253,622	12,000	138,654	73,522
1986	1,763,093	1,363,505	7,908	1,371,413	149,155	-46,070	1,176,188	323,722	263,183	12,669	139,169	74,368
1987	1,924,212	1,511,111	9,727	1,520,838	162,172	-53,500	1,305,166	348,930	270,116	13,724	140,207	76,675
1988	2,126,846	1,686,494	8,582	1,695,076	184,350	-61,776	1,448,950	390,771	287,125	14,911	142,639	80,867
1989	2,296,550	1,840,411	8,983	1,849,394	197,205	-66,925	1,585,264	400,874	310,412	15,794	145,402	82,915
1990	2,369,319	1,868,941	11,056	1,879,997	210,934	-62,442	1,606,621	413,943	348,755	16,113	147,046	82,886
1991	2,427,871	1,860,744	7,187	1,867,931	211,944	-65,701	1,590,286	438,679	398,906	16,481	147,315	80,019
1992	2,537,917	1,951,744	10,722	1,962,466	224,740	-70,779	1,666,947	433,708	437,262	17,331	146,435	80,228
1993	2,641,980	2,034,549	9,406	2,043,955	240,364	-74,733	1,728,858	442,826	470,296	18,003	146,752	82,174
1994	2,748,288	2,103,393	7,486	2,110,879	251,418	-77,337	1,782,124	474,259	491,905	18,696	147,000	82,635
1995	2,813,406	2,136,625	6,318	2,142,943	257,778	-79,564	1,805,601	489,826	517,979	19,306	145,724	82,741
1996	2,933,552	2,196,852	8,227	2,205,079	261,809	-79,117	1,864,153	516,616	552,783	20,182	145,356	83,203
1997	3,069,151	2,301,036	4,537	2,305,573	273,134	-83,599	1,948,840	541,360	578,951	21,180	144,910	83,642
1998	3,242,944	2,457,212	7,392	2,464,604	288,033	-92,875	2,083,696	559,838	599,410	22,431	144,574	85,931
1999	3,365,690	2,606,726	8,026	2,614,752	301,186	-101,797	2,211,769	535,685	618,236	23,227	144,902	86,803
2000	3,605,630	2,773,485	7,803	2,781,288	313,688	-107,485	2,360,115	592,391	653,124	24,877	144,937	89,410
2001	3,756,522	2,920,462	6,979	2,927,441	331,092	-127,140	2,469,209	589,875	697,438	25,710	146,110	90,067
2002	3,924,658	3,033,876	4,219	3,038,095	333,046	-134,626	2,570,423	611,475	742,760	26,644	147,298	90,467
2003	4,058,692	3,059,633	4,881	3,064,514	332,860	-128,404	2,603,250	639,342	816,100	27,284	148,759	89,799
2004	4,214,436	3,193,533	7,769	3,201,302	347,899	-139,083	2,714,320	621,178	878,938	28,320	148,814	90,971
2005	4,390,973	3,334,782	6,332	3,341,114	367,549	-151,206	2,822,359	616,418	952,196	29,327	149,726	92,341
2006	4,559,001	3,470,098	3,322	3,473,420	387,431	-160,563	2,925,426	654,838	978,737	30,103	151,446	93,316
2007	4,749,035	3,522,488	6,682	3,529,170	402,648	-167,580	2,958,942	734,688	1,055,405	31,196	152,232	94,140
2008	4,993,265	3,577,604	6,933	3,584,537	415,280	-172,471	2,996,786	781,057	1,215,422	32,557	153,372	93,709
2009	5,130,833	3,663,166	5,565	3,668,731	414,430	-178,119	3,076,182	739,464	1,315,187	33,367	153,770	91,487
2010	5,159,464	3,649,197	18,774	3,667,971	417,860	-162,207	3,087,904	743,275	1,328,285	33,533	153,864	89,458
2011	5,363,665	3,684,463	10,822	3,695,285	380,232	-158,162	3,156,891	820,078	1,386,696	34,879	153,781	89,529
2012	5,406,649	3,727,743	15,166	3,742,909	388,407	-152,396	3,202,106	825,709	1,378,834	35,247	153,392	89,690
2013	5,417,537	3,790,969	14,062	3,805,031	448,950	-142,263	3,213,818	797,586	1,406,133	35,342	153,289	90,222
2014	5,585,152	3,882,085	14,219	3,896,304	453,666	-140,955	3,301,683	851,290	1,432,179	36,388	153,487	90,518
2015	5,778,018	4,015,676	6,946	4,022,622	476,420	-154,013	3,392,189	894,480	1,491,349	37,946	152,271	90,454
2016	5,885,687	4,068,903	5,072	4,073,975	481,290	-156,886	3,435,799	918,313	1,531,575	38,797	151,703	90,403
2017	6,080,489	4,200,176	5,681	4,205,857	498,192	-159,165	3,548,500	964,795	1,567,194	39,974	152,112	90,589
2018	6,296,977	4,404,694	3,095	4,407,789	528,376	-178,992	3,700,421	951,668	1,644,888	41,382	152,166	91,885
2019	6,559,119	4,562,599	8,708	4,571,307	547,603	-201,915	3,821,789	1,015,444	1,721,886	43,086	152,234	92,417
2020	7,231,595	4,792,069	4,635	4,796,704	575,070	-212,269	4,009,365	1,019,884	2,202,346	47,574	152,007	89,207
2021	7,711,591	5,106,324	4,348	5,110,672	602,681	-194,422	4,313,569	1,023,688	2,374,334	50,480	152,765	91,748

Personal Income and Employment by Area: Barnstable Town, MA

(Thousands of dollars, except as noted.)

				Derivation of personal income								
		Earnings by place of work			Less: Contributions for government social insurance	Plus: Adjustment for residence	Equals: Net earnings by place of residence	Plus: Dividends, interest, and rent	Plus: Personal current transfer receipts	Per capita personal income (dollars)	Population (persons)	Total employment
Year	Personal income, total	Nonfarm	Farm	Total								
1970	467,126	295,491	1,016	296,507	17,483	-10,716	268,308	143,900	54,918	4,785	97,632	47,104
1971	537,720	331,593	942	332,535	20,635	-4,014	307,886	160,261	69,573	5,418	99,244	49,746
1972	614,361	371,515	1,042	372,557	24,040	3,759	352,276	178,694	83,391	6,191	99,237	52,776
1973	686,560	409,426	1,303	410,729	30,244	17,073	397,558	190,705	98,297	6,180	111,093	57,102
1974	756,444	429,015	1,271	430,286	32,765	29,222	426,743	210,591	119,110	6,109	123,816	57,828
1975	852,195	459,968	1,063	461,031	34,194	42,233	469,070	225,775	157,350	6,584	129,437	58,475
1976	966,532	529,904	1,205	531,109	39,344	54,757	546,522	251,143	168,867	7,259	133,142	61,244
1977	1,092,583	597,808	1,215	599,023	44,795	70,656	624,884	285,392	182,307	7,913	138,071	65,095
1978	1,240,807	685,664	1,853	687,517	52,316	90,647	725,848	315,846	199,113	8,802	140,966	69,572
1979	1,423,153	766,689	1,531	768,220	61,720	116,878	823,378	367,301	232,474	9,730	146,265	73,652
1980	1,650,105	846,968	2,161	849,129	69,045	147,756	927,840	448,494	273,771	11,086	148,847	76,419
1981	1,884,653	932,662	2,144	934,806	82,871	154,505	1,006,440	556,074	322,139	12,384	152,189	78,745
1982	2,110,736	996,095	2,902	998,997	91,500	165,848	1,073,345	680,874	356,517	13,665	154,460	81,237
1983	2,322,750	1,131,883	5,211	1,137,094	105,359	180,737	1,212,472	730,700	379,578	14,764	157,320	86,481
1984	2,673,043	1,334,972	4,481	1,339,453	128,140	202,418	1,413,731	849,937	409,375	16,487	162,135	92,174
1985	2,952,928	1,530,626	4,296	1,534,922	150,310	225,312	1,609,924	900,287	442,717	17,727	166,578	96,878
1986	3,250,014	1,718,921	4,405	1,723,326	174,084	248,003	1,797,245	975,310	477,459	18,936	171,633	101,045
1987	3,609,563	1,978,263	3,632	1,981,895	198,958	288,392	2,071,329	1,032,887	505,347	20,484	176,215	100,196
1988	3,929,722	2,162,931	4,838	2,167,769	221,023	321,312	2,268,058	1,127,201	534,463	21,695	181,137	104,357
1989	4,047,024	2,188,168	4,793	2,192,961	224,702	335,110	2,303,369	1,156,722	586,933	21,918	184,642	102,008
1990	4,324,877	2,167,716	4,460	2,172,176	219,873	390,739	2,343,042	1,314,076	667,759	23,086	187,335	100,006
1991	4,390,932	2,169,782	6,354	2,176,136	224,243	399,445	2,351,338	1,289,663	749,931	23,212	189,165	96,477
1992	4,695,441	2,324,864	6,365	2,331,229	237,615	424,900	2,518,514	1,365,042	811,885	24,507	191,595	99,683
1993	5,029,717	2,469,225	6,266	2,475,491	253,387	474,134	2,696,238	1,472,894	860,585	25,816	194,830	103,453
1994	5,348,810	2,641,858	5,500	2,647,358	273,854	528,302	2,901,806	1,543,369	903,635	26,942	198,533	107,427
1995	5,724,396	2,807,648	5,627	2,813,275	294,442	588,562	3,107,395	1,650,756	966,245	28,217	202,874	109,482
1996	6,153,648	2,998,292	9,896	3,008,188	308,868	625,068	3,324,388	1,802,918	1,026,342	29,749	206,852	112,108
1997	6,543,178	3,144,317	12,317	3,156,634	327,633	718,551	3,547,552	1,922,336	1,073,290	31,102	210,380	116,668
1998	7,111,913	3,452,014	3,014	3,455,028	355,236	806,527	3,906,319	2,102,725	1,102,869	33,156	214,497	121,308
1999	7,714,947	3,917,060	2,184	3,919,244	392,936	888,760	4,415,068	2,143,564	1,156,315	35,235	218,960	126,407
2000	8,133,042	4,058,090	3,581	4,061,671	408,383	1,011,313	4,664,601	2,237,438	1,231,003	36,466	223,031	131,099
2001	8,915,461	4,679,467	2,317	4,681,784	455,093	1,008,118	5,234,809	2,330,766	1,349,886	39,786	224,087	131,337
2002	8,948,940	4,955,001	3,135	4,958,136	486,791	963,643	5,434,988	2,084,437	1,429,515	39,699	225,421	133,340
2003	9,190,831	5,209,559	3,236	5,212,795	512,783	915,424	5,615,436	2,072,967	1,502,428	40,665	226,011	135,968
2004	9,833,545	5,561,252	4,216	5,565,468	563,635	930,044	5,931,877	2,339,725	1,561,943	43,848	224,264	138,761
2005	9,857,621	5,613,309	4,402	5,617,711	591,811	909,422	5,935,322	2,279,240	1,643,059	44,405	221,995	139,159
2006	10,279,408	5,727,897	4,621	5,732,518	601,490	900,600	6,031,628	2,497,318	1,750,462	46,717	220,037	138,664
2007	10,583,268	5,722,367	6,395	5,728,762	617,215	943,627	6,055,174	2,697,053	1,831,041	48,463	218,380	141,003
2008	10,874,857	5,694,363	8,762	5,703,125	621,997	861,288	5,942,416	2,900,394	2,032,047	50,099	217,066	139,828
2009	10,776,135	5,627,470	5,917	5,633,387	611,471	902,713	5,924,629	2,625,362	2,226,144	49,891	215,994	136,753
2010	11,175,999	5,857,906	7,074	5,864,980	613,201	893,863	6,145,642	2,698,342	2,332,015	51,763	215,909	136,163
2011	11,679,826	6,020,425	6,667	6,027,092	580,869	1,014,905	6,461,128	2,877,478	2,341,220	54,227	215,389	136,699
2012	12,205,789	6,339,662	8,464	6,348,126	603,006	1,043,356	6,788,476	3,046,616	2,370,697	56,810	214,854	139,344
2013	12,375,203	6,535,965	6,293	6,542,258	683,728	970,001	6,828,531	3,121,527	2,425,145	57,664	214,609	142,566
2014	12,994,256	6,771,042	2,283	6,773,325	715,981	866,225	6,923,569	3,570,965	2,499,722	58,814	220,938	145,002
2015	13,637,650	7,040,363	2,572	7,042,935	735,200	908,554	7,216,289	3,743,506	2,677,855	61,401	222,109	150,132
2016	14,194,286	7,256,848	1,290	7,258,138	766,346	1,042,125	7,533,917	3,874,296	2,786,073	63,517	223,471	151,450
2017	14,690,999	7,490,515	2,165	7,492,680	796,706	1,131,338	7,827,312	3,998,203	2,865,484	65,261	225,110	152,559
2018	15,398,336	7,844,601	3,164	7,847,765	841,860	1,128,141	8,134,046	4,248,473	3,015,817	67,947	226,622	153,918
2019	16,845,412	8,252,398	4,328	8,256,726	879,383	1,548,193	8,925,536	4,734,796	3,185,080	74,107	227,312	151,526
2020	18,119,802	8,078,379	4,435	8,082,814	864,257	1,838,249	9,056,806	4,719,190	4,343,806	79,136	228,969	141,669
2021	19,334,595	8,832,811	2,584	8,835,395	954,117	2,108,242	9,989,520	4,860,589	4,484,486	83,191	232,411	148,827

Personal Income and Employment by Area: Baton Rouge, LA

(Thousands of dollars, except as noted.)

Year	Personal income, total	Earnings by place of work Nonfarm	Farm	Total	Less: Contributions for government social insurance	Plus: Adjustment for residence	Equals: Net earnings by place of residence	Plus: Dividends, interest, and rent	Plus: Personal current transfer receipts	Per capita personal income (dollars)	Population (persons)	Total employment
1970	1,530,009	1,231,543	27,926	1,259,469	77,644	20,555	1,202,380	199,176	128,453	3,275	467,187	175,083
1971	1,672,394	1,339,322	29,516	1,368,838	86,480	22,044	1,304,402	221,700	146,292	3,511	476,302	179,120
1972	1,848,151	1,478,494	34,997	1,513,491	100,089	27,326	1,440,728	244,817	162,606	3,780	488,967	187,519
1973	2,056,364	1,641,385	51,347	1,692,732	128,175	25,441	1,589,998	274,215	192,151	4,133	497,516	197,959
1974	2,415,768	1,930,598	58,585	1,989,183	156,257	26,961	1,859,887	329,288	226,593	4,758	507,687	210,762
1975	2,769,705	2,219,675	32,065	2,251,740	175,628	31,374	2,107,486	377,418	284,801	5,347	517,996	221,963
1976	3,258,211	2,667,239	50,527	2,717,766	216,961	27,664	2,528,469	414,341	315,401	6,116	532,769	238,072
1977	3,675,283	3,037,902	39,029	3,076,931	242,233	30,162	2,864,860	461,872	348,551	6,693	549,090	244,790
1978	4,179,496	3,482,653	34,979	3,517,632	285,513	36,322	3,268,441	534,731	376,324	7,448	561,187	260,518
1979	4,750,479	3,945,844	37,084	3,982,928	333,758	52,376	3,701,546	615,267	433,666	8,224	577,630	268,260
1980	5,619,785	4,631,816	20,204	4,652,020	389,604	44,655	4,307,071	796,375	516,339	9,450	594,659	281,511
1981	6,337,334	5,162,258	24,461	5,186,719	465,610	39,707	4,760,816	995,163	581,355	10,445	606,705	289,146
1982	6,802,548	5,429,538	22,044	5,451,582	492,704	14,966	4,973,844	1,162,688	666,016	11,000	618,386	291,462
1983	7,195,140	5,588,938	26,311	5,615,249	498,738	25,987	5,142,498	1,285,403	767,239	11,451	628,340	291,172
1984	7,708,483	5,969,320	13,358	5,982,678	545,584	20,074	5,457,168	1,444,748	806,567	12,169	633,436	302,207
1985	8,077,467	6,171,344	18,578	6,189,922	564,852	7,824	5,632,894	1,574,817	869,756	12,681	636,971	302,128
1986	8,056,846	6,050,010	27,665	6,077,675	542,967	-4,534	5,530,174	1,565,439	961,233	12,653	636,761	295,628
1987	8,135,858	6,159,239	20,017	6,179,256	545,242	-17,458	5,616,556	1,544,544	974,758	12,934	629,017	296,915
1988	8,717,878	6,722,630	46,644	6,769,274	631,749	-33,134	6,104,391	1,584,689	1,028,798	13,946	625,135	303,980
1989	9,435,874	7,192,807	31,248	7,224,055	688,189	-29,593	6,506,273	1,815,615	1,113,986	15,137	623,372	309,087
1990	10,229,877	7,901,442	32,403	7,933,845	779,814	-27,732	7,126,299	1,868,401	1,235,177	16,360	625,305	321,133
1991	10,877,066	8,460,602	19,804	8,480,406	857,415	-62,896	7,560,095	1,908,690	1,408,281	17,124	635,197	329,966
1992	11,924,123	9,312,910	42,460	9,355,370	935,409	-98,133	8,321,828	1,973,116	1,629,179	18,425	647,179	340,665
1993	12,405,170	9,600,844	35,260	9,636,104	971,506	-90,162	8,574,436	2,040,200	1,790,534	18,875	657,226	347,916
1994	13,307,240	10,177,906	33,531	10,211,437	1,057,987	-101,278	9,052,172	2,242,024	2,013,044	20,027	664,462	356,542
1995	13,976,531	10,652,950	39,919	10,692,869	1,108,555	-99,635	9,484,679	2,430,704	2,061,148	20,822	671,247	368,168
1996	14,649,770	11,213,890	53,083	11,266,973	1,179,826	-109,332	9,977,815	2,566,908	2,105,047	21,591	678,500	377,415
1997	15,210,031	11,707,567	48,323	11,755,890	1,226,628	-102,504	10,426,758	2,645,670	2,137,603	22,171	686,021	381,499
1998	16,637,814	12,753,768	42,150	12,795,918	1,351,094	-16,896	11,427,928	2,963,098	2,246,788	23,229	716,245	402,809
1999	17,234,622	13,391,961	59,778	13,451,739	1,398,847	-39,359	12,013,533	2,923,334	2,297,755	23,800	724,139	412,481
2000	18,287,703	14,199,277	60,411	14,259,688	1,453,728	-48,147	12,757,813	3,141,904	2,387,986	25,020	730,913	422,692
2001	19,150,754	14,784,415	58,899	14,843,314	1,477,134	-59,232	13,306,948	3,108,487	2,735,319	26,094	733,925	419,933
2002	19,799,599	15,385,592	48,922	15,434,514	1,536,061	-81,125	13,817,328	3,054,010	2,928,261	26,807	738,589	421,115
2003	20,658,861	16,120,963	53,694	16,174,657	1,585,887	-102,705	14,486,065	3,207,979	2,964,817	27,710	745,536	427,177
2004	22,288,750	17,111,277	56,090	17,167,367	1,641,823	-70,558	15,454,986	3,509,251	3,324,513	29,596	753,093	430,922
2005	24,403,082	18,032,499	50,038	18,082,537	1,709,487	-93,958	16,279,092	3,832,708	4,291,282	32,164	758,706	447,001
2006	26,726,231	19,680,981	68,930	19,749,911	1,890,592	392,832	18,252,151	4,338,007	4,136,073	33,600	795,417	468,436
2007	28,949,113	21,068,400	60,271	21,128,671	2,039,503	448,761	19,537,929	5,134,868	4,276,316	36,036	803,339	479,796
2008	31,045,048	22,401,941	50,733	22,452,674	2,159,389	455,345	20,748,630	5,362,280	4,934,138	38,266	811,301	487,178
2009	30,769,822	22,743,486	54,682	22,798,168	2,192,837	46,751	20,652,082	4,937,556	5,180,184	37,551	819,405	486,007
2010	31,875,137	23,069,320	66,105	23,135,425	2,203,943	259,906	21,191,388	5,121,218	5,562,531	38,512	827,673	481,646
2011	33,660,792	23,802,038	72,925	23,874,963	2,049,278	472,707	22,298,392	5,697,836	5,664,564	40,477	831,605	486,911
2012	34,967,423	25,110,446	89,687	25,200,133	2,150,924	134,960	23,184,169	5,994,781	5,788,473	41,807	836,394	494,149
2013	35,669,783	26,311,513	106,776	26,418,289	2,567,946	-211,327	23,639,016	6,057,048	5,973,719	42,350	842,270	506,666
2014	37,047,753	27,432,810	57,359	27,490,169	2,661,623	-285,773	24,542,773	6,541,101	5,963,879	43,475	852,164	518,841
2015	37,686,521	28,207,761	44,312	28,252,073	2,799,318	-663,548	24,789,207	6,289,185	6,608,129	43,936	857,755	523,501
2016	38,517,291	28,362,770	20,762	28,383,532	2,856,515	-784,337	24,742,680	6,822,088	6,952,523	44,542	864,743	525,841
2017	39,557,238	29,262,401	27,272	29,289,673	2,946,248	-926,273	25,417,152	6,962,459	7,177,627	45,814	863,436	529,322
2018	41,499,159	30,876,528	26,245	30,902,773	3,120,270	-1,163,478	26,619,025	7,383,705	7,496,429	47,973	865,057	539,311
2019	43,091,025	31,553,730	42,996	31,596,726	3,173,505	-1,077,986	27,345,235	7,830,922	7,914,868	49,639	868,080	538,139
2020	46,208,214	31,658,181	52,446	31,710,627	3,200,498	-888,269	27,621,860	7,873,228	10,713,126	53,102	870,178	517,644
2021	49,171,959	33,136,845	46,647	33,183,492	3,322,516	-872,983	28,987,993	8,154,648	12,029,318	56,396	871,905	530,892

Personal Income and Employment by Area: Battle Creek, MI

(Thousands of dollars, except as noted.)

Year	Personal income, total	Earnings by place of work			Less: Contributions for government social insurance	Plus: Adjustment for residence	Equals: Net earnings by place of residence	Plus: Dividends, interest, and rent	Plus: Personal current transfer receipts	Per capita personal income (dollars)	Population (persons)	Total employment
		Nonfarm	Farm	Total								
1970	576,982	500,248	7,173	507,421	36,214	-26,553	444,654	74,283	58,045	4,076	141,561	62,407
1971	628,950	546,341	6,267	552,608	40,854	-33,271	478,483	81,254	69,213	4,472	140,647	63,123
1972	692,203	604,719	9,419	614,138	47,211	-40,066	526,861	88,679	76,663	4,876	141,963	64,437
1973	761,421	672,120	15,821	687,941	60,903	-47,757	579,281	95,994	86,146	5,349	142,349	66,077
1974	806,447	708,617	7,321	715,938	66,185	-53,975	595,778	107,386	103,283	5,639	143,021	66,005
1975	895,883	762,360	12,747	775,107	69,442	-64,100	641,565	118,972	135,346	6,281	142,640	64,320
1976	980,447	857,529	9,566	867,095	80,024	-77,455	709,616	128,389	142,442	6,887	142,359	66,464
1977	1,061,283	943,955	8,157	952,112	88,510	-89,130	774,472	143,440	143,371	7,433	142,772	67,485
1978	1,163,902	1,047,678	6,575	1,054,253	100,211	-103,802	850,240	157,899	155,763	8,113	143,463	68,846
1979	1,263,112	1,130,988	6,581	1,137,569	112,584	-117,738	907,247	177,802	178,063	8,874	142,341	69,077
1980	1,339,901	1,142,470	4,081	1,146,551	112,244	-124,667	909,640	207,655	222,606	9,456	141,701	65,129
1981	1,452,074	1,202,812	10,190	1,213,002	127,255	-126,719	959,028	247,021	246,025	10,235	141,880	62,898
1982	1,516,735	1,199,419	2,563	1,201,982	127,081	-125,214	949,687	286,898	280,150	10,843	139,886	59,788
1983	1,553,984	1,221,002	-5,022	1,215,980	133,201	-121,649	961,130	300,344	292,510	11,291	137,629	59,063
1984	1,638,441	1,275,636	7,011	1,282,647	143,995	-122,003	1,016,649	330,076	291,716	12,076	135,682	59,859
1985	1,757,818	1,399,947	7,368	1,407,315	162,003	-134,740	1,110,572	348,784	298,462	13,067	134,523	61,694
1986	1,850,392	1,473,452	8,658	1,482,110	172,267	-139,362	1,170,481	366,901	313,010	13,776	134,316	62,869
1987	1,979,736	1,620,896	9,943	1,630,839	186,783	-159,302	1,284,754	374,848	320,134	14,681	134,849	66,233
1988	2,065,989	1,731,766	6,745	1,738,511	207,464	-169,553	1,361,494	372,780	331,715	15,365	134,459	66,844
1989	2,213,983	1,821,811	16,229	1,838,040	216,946	-171,425	1,449,669	409,717	354,597	16,345	135,457	67,838
1990	2,323,434	1,932,491	13,863	1,946,354	232,873	-180,538	1,532,943	412,890	377,601	17,056	136,226	69,258
1991	2,438,165	2,039,389	9,803	2,049,192	248,912	-197,954	1,602,326	419,162	416,677	17,821	136,814	71,364
1992	2,590,929	2,199,098	10,524	2,209,622	266,635	-221,296	1,721,691	429,004	440,234	18,871	137,298	72,964
1993	2,677,654	2,253,999	11,144	2,265,143	276,241	-221,768	1,767,134	440,602	469,918	19,435	137,775	73,362
1994	2,839,825	2,400,182	10,077	2,410,259	299,050	-238,393	1,872,816	489,993	477,016	20,592	137,910	75,666
1995	2,937,277	2,506,336	8,068	2,514,404	313,032	-250,736	1,950,636	487,756	498,885	21,379	137,393	78,757
1996	3,039,351	2,577,393	7,857	2,585,250	314,813	-252,279	2,018,158	502,976	518,217	22,245	136,630	77,972
1997	3,245,454	2,766,412	10,019	2,776,431	334,717	-274,919	2,166,795	526,252	552,407	23,718	136,834	80,495
1998	3,344,799	2,873,916	9,059	2,882,975	340,302	-278,926	2,263,747	536,479	544,573	24,276	137,783	78,310
1999	3,400,229	2,861,055	8,029	2,869,084	337,500	-259,013	2,272,571	545,239	582,419	24,636	138,021	75,611
2000	3,469,055	2,898,094	10,171	2,908,265	340,899	-265,474	2,301,892	563,157	604,006	25,136	138,014	75,174
2001	3,553,372	2,890,670	14,323	2,904,993	341,903	-257,764	2,305,326	570,760	677,286	25,720	138,158	77,978
2002	3,677,694	3,049,584	7,463	3,057,047	360,308	-285,682	2,411,057	566,892	699,745	26,538	138,580	77,978
2003	3,760,315	3,067,704	9,505	3,077,209	361,260	-270,404	2,445,545	576,278	738,492	27,060	138,962	76,411
2004	3,862,879	3,172,498	22,202	3,194,700	375,721	-306,826	2,512,153	583,827	766,899	27,702	139,443	76,704
2005	3,960,724	3,214,968	15,279	3,230,247	383,032	-317,470	2,529,745	619,694	811,285	28,505	138,946	75,646
2006	4,018,000	3,267,488	7,206	3,274,694	395,553	-325,781	2,553,360	593,686	870,954	29,055	138,291	74,704
2007	4,148,403	3,313,062	12,687	3,325,749	400,063	-347,056	2,578,630	624,329	945,444	30,152	137,582	74,215
2008	4,330,535	3,390,532	8,993	3,399,525	414,113	-402,884	2,582,528	685,372	1,062,635	31,538	137,313	72,227
2009	4,244,268	3,295,694	15,712	3,311,406	406,088	-439,641	2,465,677	622,288	1,156,303	31,139	136,301	68,941
2010	4,376,648	3,377,731	27,811	3,405,542	411,884	-495,236	2,498,422	634,491	1,243,735	32,192	135,953	68,650
2011	4,468,042	3,365,365	49,872	3,415,237	369,765	-487,982	2,557,490	674,792	1,235,760	33,069	135,111	69,084
2012	4,606,751	3,536,915	12,862	3,549,777	387,164	-529,015	2,633,598	748,724	1,224,429	34,186	134,755	68,495
2013	4,646,972	3,603,863	22,291	3,626,154	444,623	-539,069	2,642,462	757,873	1,246,637	34,478	134,782	69,546
2014	4,763,100	3,712,010	1,557	3,713,567	456,774	-583,957	2,672,836	797,449	1,292,815	35,262	135,079	70,343
2015	5,005,889	3,857,973	-187	3,857,786	472,837	-610,582	2,774,367	853,629	1,377,893	37,173	134,665	71,329
2016	5,084,995	3,974,638	-331	3,974,307	482,753	-650,233	2,841,321	837,901	1,405,773	37,754	134,688	71,222
2017	5,144,150	4,019,244	6,545	4,025,789	489,193	-633,720	2,902,876	848,949	1,392,325	38,239	134,526	70,753
2018	5,253,603	4,065,340	5,873	4,071,213	503,368	-635,567	2,932,278	867,499	1,453,826	39,115	134,311	69,916
2019	5,439,319	4,035,821	3,688	4,039,509	501,514	-532,304	3,005,691	898,894	1,534,734	40,497	134,314	68,706
2020	6,007,726	4,049,279	24,333	4,073,612	504,689	-563,746	3,005,177	904,927	2,097,622	44,796	134,113	64,856
2021	6,395,035	4,288,913	24,755	4,313,668	524,497	-546,336	3,242,835	929,194	2,223,006	47,789	133,819	66,226

Personal Income and Employment by Area: Bay City, MI

(Thousands of dollars, except as noted.)

Year	Personal income, total	Earnings by place of work Nonfarm	Earnings by place of work Farm	Earnings by place of work Total	Less: Contributions for government social insurance	Plus: Adjustment for residence	Equals: Net earnings by place of residence	Plus: Dividends, interest, and rent	Plus: Personal current transfer receipts	Per capita personal income (dollars)	Population (persons)	Total employment
1970	420,933	293,171	5,220	298,391	20,928	44,339	321,802	58,218	40,913	3,582	117,502	39,729
1971	464,555	319,945	4,167	324,112	23,426	52,885	353,571	62,993	47,991	3,920	118,513	39,422
1972	499,669	342,221	4,894	347,115	26,568	58,462	379,009	68,296	52,364	4,196	119,094	39,885
1973	561,721	385,948	11,092	397,040	34,621	65,470	427,889	75,372	58,460	4,688	119,824	41,851
1974	621,936	413,451	23,624	437,075	38,401	64,229	462,903	85,811	73,222	5,159	120,548	41,896
1975	662,994	428,891	10,222	439,113	39,024	70,387	470,476	97,405	95,113	5,505	120,441	40,211
1976	755,195	490,642	10,673	501,315	45,513	98,700	554,502	103,975	96,718	6,264	120,560	41,485
1977	862,681	562,104	10,968	573,072	52,335	124,738	645,475	116,510	100,696	7,100	121,500	43,222
1978	949,558	611,899	13,745	625,644	58,492	148,382	715,534	126,272	107,752	7,780	122,057	43,662
1979	1,037,742	653,386	17,957	671,343	64,790	164,777	771,330	141,809	124,603	8,571	121,074	43,509
1980	1,133,350	665,840	26,055	691,895	65,510	157,780	784,165	173,209	175,976	9,442	120,037	41,737
1981	1,220,646	734,563	4,991	739,554	78,205	170,925	832,274	210,158	178,214	10,138	120,401	42,279
1982	1,263,933	727,939	6,508	734,447	78,800	160,042	815,689	244,618	203,626	10,639	118,804	40,466
1983	1,328,915	753,758	5,011	758,769	82,139	174,651	851,281	259,663	217,971	11,326	117,330	40,371
1984	1,423,673	804,884	7,458	812,342	90,753	189,716	911,305	288,686	223,682	12,202	116,677	40,939
1985	1,499,357	847,921	13,314	861,235	98,160	207,748	970,823	299,657	228,877	13,036	115,017	41,442
1986	1,564,800	906,430	1,131	907,561	103,782	210,496	1,014,275	310,784	239,741	13,694	114,267	42,479
1987	1,621,964	935,297	10,654	945,951	105,920	220,599	1,060,630	311,138	250,196	14,233	113,959	43,197
1988	1,719,331	1,009,826	8,551	1,018,377	119,000	235,241	1,134,618	325,479	259,234	15,229	112,898	44,027
1989	1,800,018	1,028,296	16,004	1,044,300	121,084	252,792	1,176,008	340,953	283,057	16,063	112,061	44,282
1990	1,911,834	1,100,123	13,106	1,113,229	131,061	253,075	1,235,243	368,622	307,969	17,100	111,804	45,908
1991	1,975,535	1,132,904	11,929	1,144,833	137,290	264,235	1,271,778	368,833	334,924	17,670	111,803	45,846
1992	2,096,904	1,202,448	17,461	1,219,909	144,951	286,599	1,361,557	378,973	356,374	18,692	112,182	46,227
1993	2,183,299	1,280,894	14,293	1,295,187	155,429	273,025	1,412,783	390,230	380,286	19,425	112,397	46,432
1994	2,305,243	1,354,690	6,640	1,361,330	167,355	289,541	1,483,516	431,311	390,416	20,578	112,025	47,608
1995	2,388,194	1,432,599	17,518	1,450,117	177,855	274,341	1,546,603	436,858	404,733	21,384	111,680	49,673
1996	2,481,873	1,545,725	5,539	1,551,264	187,407	242,475	1,606,332	459,100	416,441	22,313	111,231	51,133
1997	2,598,926	1,608,401	7,438	1,615,839	194,336	249,806	1,671,309	488,747	438,870	23,405	111,040	52,171
1998	2,663,591	1,684,544	2,486	1,687,030	199,719	230,193	1,717,504	506,586	439,501	24,060	110,704	51,665
1999	2,768,336	1,741,541	8,506	1,750,047	204,049	270,226	1,816,224	478,859	473,253	25,099	110,295	52,077
2000	2,916,279	1,813,676	938	1,814,614	211,997	303,785	1,906,402	514,060	495,817	26,465	110,192	53,512
2001	2,975,726	1,812,489	-7,251	1,805,238	209,834	320,334	1,915,738	509,448	550,540	27,092	109,836	52,307
2002	2,963,820	1,823,264	8,389	1,831,653	212,588	292,773	1,911,838	483,796	568,186	26,978	109,861	51,737
2003	3,033,850	1,834,155	4,284	1,838,439	213,637	300,729	1,925,531	506,731	601,588	27,691	109,559	51,158
2004	3,103,979	1,855,888	12,238	1,868,126	219,614	326,478	1,974,990	498,113	630,876	28,359	109,453	51,482
2005	3,144,488	1,875,900	12,900	1,888,800	225,469	308,508	1,971,839	508,840	663,809	28,805	109,165	50,662
2006	3,254,007	1,940,076	15,321	1,955,397	236,407	315,391	2,034,381	507,591	712,035	29,933	108,711	50,201
2007	3,352,534	1,959,538	12,411	1,971,949	241,864	294,677	2,024,762	549,670	778,102	31,004	108,132	50,347
2008	3,508,060	1,983,745	21,254	2,004,999	248,127	259,395	2,016,267	615,180	876,613	32,386	108,320	49,858
2009	3,490,053	1,953,248	5,385	1,958,633	245,488	238,237	1,951,382	579,974	958,697	32,341	107,913	47,922
2010	3,634,680	1,978,754	12,849	1,991,603	244,673	273,825	2,020,755	573,210	1,040,715	33,755	107,678	47,473
2011	3,754,847	2,011,635	26,775	2,038,410	222,666	290,970	2,106,714	604,615	1,043,518	34,954	107,423	47,644
2012	3,803,280	2,066,829	18,956	2,085,785	229,709	277,163	2,133,239	636,507	1,033,534	35,551	106,980	48,000
2013	3,816,791	2,108,233	27,520	2,135,753	264,332	257,399	2,128,820	624,671	1,063,300	35,732	106,817	48,195
2014	3,903,699	2,113,487	4,013	2,117,500	266,688	281,072	2,131,884	660,546	1,111,269	36,620	106,599	48,039
2015	4,060,968	2,166,665	2,648	2,169,313	271,130	291,690	2,189,873	696,513	1,174,582	38,341	105,916	47,387
2016	4,138,758	2,175,263	-986	2,174,277	272,697	331,228	2,232,808	708,811	1,197,139	39,348	105,184	47,534
2017	4,184,796	2,170,333	1,646	2,171,979	273,442	363,695	2,262,232	720,588	1,201,976	39,868	104,967	46,700
2018	4,393,322	2,214,624	-2,858	2,211,766	285,452	490,774	2,417,088	715,732	1,260,502	41,971	104,674	46,556
2019	4,499,337	2,250,048	-4,139	2,245,909	290,442	482,079	2,437,546	721,769	1,340,022	43,230	104,079	46,801
2020	4,913,457	2,372,754	22,320	2,395,074	304,318	346,378	2,437,134	716,799	1,759,524	47,430	103,594	44,545
2021	5,190,073	2,552,315	33,335	2,585,650	320,141	348,121	2,613,630	716,549	1,859,894	50,396	102,985	45,956

Personal Income and Employment by Area: Beaumont-Port Arthur, TX

(Thousands of dollars, except as noted.)

Year	Personal income, total	Earnings by place of work			Less: Contributions for government social insurance	Plus: Adjustment for residence	Equals: Net earnings by place of residence	Plus: Dividends, interest, and rent	Plus: Personal current transfer receipts	Per capita personal income (dollars)	Population (persons)	Total employment
		Nonfarm	Farm	Total								
1970	1,295,373	1,109,643	2,176	1,111,819	72,923	-13,221	1,025,675	164,327	105,371	3,605	359,291	139,079
1971	1,390,512	1,176,508	3,751	1,180,259	79,889	-11,883	1,088,487	178,747	123,278	3,849	361,233	140,072
1972	1,499,073	1,262,933	4,717	1,267,650	90,461	-11,049	1,166,140	194,382	138,551	4,133	362,681	141,566
1973	1,632,850	1,372,941	6,352	1,379,293	114,895	-10,271	1,254,127	214,685	164,038	4,567	357,512	146,460
1974	1,911,191	1,614,597	12,000	1,626,597	139,034	-17,393	1,470,170	250,169	190,852	5,331	358,506	153,311
1975	2,150,975	1,776,184	15,416	1,791,600	147,808	-12,083	1,631,709	282,382	236,884	5,916	363,590	153,637
1976	2,490,332	2,144,103	3,153	2,147,256	182,614	-36,485	1,928,157	307,191	254,984	6,744	369,268	163,590
1977	2,795,101	2,425,989	10,809	2,436,798	206,723	-47,854	2,182,221	341,543	271,337	7,446	375,363	169,957
1978	3,100,074	2,687,181	2,880	2,690,061	234,638	-47,528	2,407,895	390,325	301,854	8,217	377,286	173,977
1979	3,478,948	2,997,474	9,394	3,006,868	271,907	-49,393	2,685,568	449,425	343,955	9,064	383,832	179,197
1980	3,894,545	3,274,630	6,220	3,280,850	298,249	-43,981	2,938,620	556,039	399,886	10,036	388,072	177,396
1981	4,448,323	3,723,642	-1,830	3,721,812	363,444	-52,809	3,305,559	691,883	450,881	11,309	393,359	186,607
1982	4,709,723	3,795,119	-2,306	3,792,813	383,646	-56,376	3,352,791	829,860	527,072	11,795	399,300	179,648
1983	4,894,733	3,821,755	-21	3,821,734	380,754	-62,559	3,378,421	899,839	616,473	12,217	400,634	172,840
1984	5,073,713	3,868,056	-3,947	3,864,109	395,358	-61,382	3,407,369	1,010,339	656,005	12,732	398,516	172,570
1985	5,155,380	3,808,963	3,305	3,812,268	392,355	-57,437	3,362,476	1,108,820	684,084	13,092	393,786	168,736
1986	5,096,859	3,691,691	751	3,692,442	375,743	-54,775	3,261,924	1,092,988	741,947	13,363	381,420	160,923
1987	5,072,629	3,670,374	-2,137	3,668,237	371,899	-53,310	3,243,028	1,056,990	772,611	13,380	379,118	165,149
1988	5,358,455	3,920,221	13,434	3,933,655	414,438	-58,823	3,460,394	1,099,590	798,471	14,280	375,245	167,774
1989	5,682,550	4,050,356	11,139	4,061,495	432,120	-67,347	3,562,028	1,249,517	871,005	15,193	374,021	168,178
1990	5,985,015	4,388,768	10,633	4,399,401	460,790	-85,841	3,852,770	1,171,337	960,908	15,958	375,055	174,023
1991	6,464,237	4,853,887	15,972	4,869,859	519,315	-112,614	4,237,930	1,181,618	1,044,689	17,008	380,069	183,546
1992	6,947,521	5,180,624	12,654	5,193,278	550,141	-123,194	4,519,943	1,204,819	1,222,759	18,055	384,799	183,011
1993	6,959,068	5,175,625	12,148	5,187,773	549,863	-104,160	4,533,750	1,136,938	1,288,380	17,847	389,937	183,297
1994	7,248,211	5,371,328	8,869	5,380,197	579,146	-97,227	4,703,824	1,165,321	1,379,066	18,498	391,836	183,107
1995	7,566,027	5,489,225	8,961	5,498,186	599,028	-98,486	4,800,672	1,273,432	1,491,923	19,120	395,704	186,653
1996	7,764,317	5,576,851	4,727	5,581,578	603,707	-109,484	4,868,387	1,309,393	1,586,537	19,649	395,151	187,334
1997	8,425,327	6,207,265	6,022	6,213,287	661,351	-140,293	5,411,643	1,363,251	1,650,433	21,242	396,639	194,273
1998	8,699,970	6,645,111	6,272	6,651,383	697,109	-257,440	5,696,834	1,415,523	1,587,613	22,726	382,827	194,777
1999	8,703,782	6,630,003	6,005	6,636,008	691,860	-227,038	5,717,110	1,398,631	1,588,041	22,605	385,034	193,452
2000	9,189,725	6,980,261	3,477	6,983,738	708,536	-239,082	6,036,120	1,502,091	1,651,514	23,884	384,759	196,236
2001	9,572,194	7,233,341	2,348	7,235,689	725,149	-247,506	6,263,034	1,525,176	1,783,984	25,012	382,708	193,752
2002	9,737,141	7,346,889	2,482	7,349,371	741,983	-244,968	6,362,420	1,458,797	1,915,924	25,423	383,004	192,762
2003	10,145,532	7,614,302	13,464	7,627,766	782,714	-267,148	6,577,904	1,535,949	2,031,679	26,475	383,208	193,921
2004	10,317,241	7,769,273	20,567	7,789,840	797,522	-255,575	6,736,743	1,475,093	2,105,405	26,837	384,438	191,526
2005	10,949,090	8,122,087	27,771	8,149,858	845,529	-272,240	7,032,089	1,469,741	2,447,260	28,403	385,490	195,198
2006	11,701,084	8,962,750	33,601	8,996,351	922,842	-340,540	7,732,969	1,590,439	2,377,676	30,864	379,119	203,221
2007	12,288,665	9,300,009	33,168	9,333,177	975,871	-373,928	7,983,378	1,742,011	2,563,276	32,142	382,330	206,608
2008	13,290,923	9,926,461	577	9,927,038	1,031,780	-486,315	8,408,943	2,058,129	2,823,851	34,500	385,248	209,036
2009	13,139,254	9,731,862	861	9,732,723	1,022,477	-476,903	8,233,343	1,872,617	3,033,294	33,939	387,146	204,734
2010	13,876,426	10,131,513	-3,593	10,127,920	1,072,062	-522,305	8,533,553	2,049,626	3,293,247	35,648	389,257	203,230
2011	14,495,902	10,562,497	-8,617	10,553,880	996,824	-593,962	8,963,094	2,155,484	3,377,324	37,081	390,924	207,905
2012	15,222,177	11,035,319	-9,011	11,026,308	1,030,370	-617,914	9,378,024	2,487,813	3,356,340	39,066	389,654	207,797
2013	14,895,563	10,915,445	-4,188	10,911,257	1,150,454	-599,182	9,161,621	2,269,379	3,464,563	38,071	391,255	204,946
2014	16,105,319	11,829,369	-7,221	11,822,148	1,230,686	-524,073	10,067,389	2,446,138	3,591,792	40,864	394,119	210,516
2015	16,599,217	12,267,619	-6,394	12,261,225	1,283,514	-504,076	10,473,635	2,348,649	3,776,933	41,716	397,910	212,293
2016	16,585,574	12,167,232	-9,603	12,157,629	1,297,307	-395,076	10,465,246	2,190,263	3,930,065	41,439	400,237	208,882
2017	17,079,053	12,314,958	-12,898	12,302,060	1,331,058	-314,547	10,656,455	2,459,731	3,962,867	42,456	402,279	209,691
2018	17,363,796	12,657,456	-12,498	12,644,958	1,365,328	-325,857	10,953,773	2,359,228	4,050,795	43,665	397,657	213,502
2019	17,806,471	12,903,005	-11,481	12,891,524	1,393,449	-472,934	11,025,141	2,594,080	4,187,250	44,816	397,323	213,634
2020	18,542,205	12,313,387	-11,138	12,302,249	1,338,379	-444,681	10,519,189	2,561,072	5,461,944	46,711	396,958	206,108
2021	19,377,903	12,335,591	-13,397	12,322,194	1,335,624	-344,779	10,641,791	2,633,105	6,103,007	49,006	395,419	205,149

Personal Income and Employment by Area: Beckley, WV

(Thousands of dollars, except as noted.)

Year	Personal income, total	Earnings by place of work			Less: Contributions for government social insurance	Plus: Adjustment for residence	Equals: Net earnings by place of residence	Plus: Dividends, interest, and rent	Plus: Personal current transfer receipts	Per capita personal income (dollars)	Population (persons)	Total employment
		Nonfarm	Farm	Total								
1970	342,410	251,677	140	251,817	18,662	10,841	243,996	35,075	63,339	2,858	119,794	34,722
1971	383,565	272,329	278	272,607	21,177	11,565	262,995	39,343	81,227	3,134	122,399	35,712
1972	443,014	313,974	381	314,355	25,404	13,130	302,081	44,455	96,478	3,502	126,518	38,148
1973	494,158	337,210	651	337,861	31,511	13,764	320,114	51,802	122,242	3,839	128,707	39,217
1974	546,723	375,669	526	376,195	36,347	13,024	352,872	60,924	132,927	4,226	129,362	40,310
1975	645,359	451,517	488	452,005	43,395	16,415	425,025	70,688	149,646	4,867	132,602	43,351
1976	746,571	542,705	276	542,981	54,034	14,793	503,740	79,183	163,648	5,395	138,390	46,063
1977	810,403	592,080	288	592,368	57,770	15,216	549,814	88,826	171,763	5,697	142,246	46,317
1978	912,215	667,242	372	667,614	66,952	13,628	614,290	98,920	199,005	6,329	144,129	47,908
1979	1,002,767	695,943	837	696,780	72,995	23,404	647,189	112,357	243,221	6,913	145,047	46,987
1980	1,093,976	732,080	789	732,869	78,397	26,479	680,951	137,728	275,297	7,563	144,639	46,598
1981	1,191,482	790,176	-344	789,832	91,020	25,742	724,554	168,960	297,968	8,256	144,324	46,263
1982	1,276,557	820,539	-259	820,280	97,721	36,213	758,772	195,998	321,787	8,844	144,345	45,744
1983	1,281,513	781,388	-333	781,055	93,195	32,657	720,517	205,124	355,872	8,894	144,081	43,320
1984	1,375,395	862,166	100	862,266	105,675	36,121	792,712	228,573	354,110	9,674	142,180	44,190
1985	1,419,473	897,714	-292	897,422	112,018	35,997	821,401	239,733	358,339	10,123	140,228	44,214
1986	1,440,289	891,188	-411	890,777	114,608	44,867	821,036	239,565	379,688	10,450	137,822	43,044
1987	1,461,495	904,011	-346	903,665	117,441	54,278	840,502	237,663	383,330	10,929	133,725	42,517
1988	1,512,726	935,417	-553	934,864	124,629	52,249	862,484	248,310	401,932	11,658	129,757	42,630
1989	1,579,755	946,290	274	946,564	129,105	61,442	878,901	276,777	424,077	12,552	125,854	42,806
1990	1,664,276	999,207	-85	999,122	138,156	77,382	938,348	275,876	450,052	13,348	124,685	43,965
1991	1,766,203	1,051,158	-406	1,050,752	150,790	79,169	979,131	282,902	504,170	14,134	124,959	44,633
1992	1,881,320	1,101,416	53	1,101,469	160,399	86,581	1,027,651	283,448	570,221	15,024	125,222	45,282
1993	1,958,201	1,163,043	-51	1,162,992	176,515	71,683	1,058,160	291,049	608,992	15,499	126,345	46,344
1994	2,069,106	1,236,678	-316	1,236,362	187,441	83,729	1,132,650	307,723	628,733	16,347	126,577	48,415
1995	2,183,086	1,327,110	-576	1,326,534	205,287	86,741	1,207,988	331,913	643,185	17,113	127,571	50,747
1996	2,290,661	1,394,318	-958	1,393,360	215,541	89,176	1,266,995	350,680	672,986	17,837	128,425	52,378
1997	2,377,498	1,446,899	-635	1,446,264	220,495	93,424	1,319,193	372,604	685,701	18,534	128,275	53,304
1998	2,496,419	1,515,487	-917	1,514,570	232,045	96,184	1,378,709	394,664	723,046	19,520	127,892	54,760
1999	2,534,251	1,557,327	-1,396	1,555,931	236,771	99,162	1,418,322	386,193	729,736	19,887	127,431	54,481
2000	2,632,223	1,605,364	-978	1,604,386	250,295	107,593	1,461,684	415,069	755,470	20,804	126,525	54,322
2001	2,817,916	1,735,352	-1,087	1,734,265	253,180	95,904	1,576,989	418,920	822,007	22,486	125,318	54,716
2002	2,919,916	1,795,878	-1,843	1,794,035	251,145	85,016	1,627,906	409,567	882,443	23,234	125,672	54,883
2003	2,927,236	1,790,233	-1,970	1,788,263	257,247	79,065	1,610,081	404,498	912,657	23,321	125,519	54,029
2004	3,008,745	1,884,686	-1,467	1,883,219	267,977	67,772	1,683,014	405,669	920,062	24,042	125,145	55,171
2005	3,162,913	2,036,995	-1,955	2,035,040	285,315	57,103	1,806,828	406,135	949,950	25,391	124,570	56,027
2006	3,361,965	2,157,406	-2,080	2,155,326	290,006	56,066	1,921,386	434,983	1,005,596	27,030	124,378	56,871
2007	3,350,052	2,036,829	-2,583	2,034,246	283,284	41,224	1,792,186	490,904	1,066,962	26,894	124,566	57,277
2008	3,605,683	2,159,720	-1,433	2,158,287	287,698	27,809	1,898,398	549,155	1,158,130	28,950	124,550	57,762
2009	3,697,262	2,177,831	-1,371	2,176,460	297,863	33,791	1,912,388	554,702	1,230,172	29,622	124,816	56,337
2010	3,865,402	2,337,523	-1,196	2,336,327	305,862	43,252	2,073,717	513,084	1,278,601	30,936	124,950	56,736
2011	4,254,692	2,608,972	-907	2,608,065	291,637	72,517	2,388,945	586,099	1,279,648	33,959	125,290	58,011
2012	4,311,701	2,547,687	-563	2,547,124	294,292	86,839	2,339,671	658,519	1,313,511	34,450	125,157	58,220
2013	4,199,595	2,528,415	-483	2,527,932	318,237	87,018	2,296,713	578,004	1,324,878	33,755	124,413	56,917
2014	4,282,888	2,492,651	-729	2,491,922	318,632	86,716	2,260,006	613,023	1,409,859	34,739	123,289	56,258
2015	4,343,732	2,432,337	-363	2,431,974	313,012	89,615	2,208,577	653,980	1,481,175	35,605	121,997	55,280
2016	4,176,471	2,281,800	-726	2,281,074	305,045	67,829	2,043,858	623,341	1,509,272	34,707	120,335	53,373
2017	4,394,896	2,463,075	-286	2,462,789	324,863	54,149	2,192,075	644,427	1,558,394	37,076	118,537	53,656
2018	4,599,762	2,652,269	-804	2,651,465	342,639	67,674	2,376,500	634,465	1,588,797	39,275	117,118	53,888
2019	4,792,430	2,782,697	-160	2,782,537	354,851	51,160	2,478,846	679,277	1,634,307	41,334	115,943	53,802
2020	4,907,456	2,582,512	-465	2,582,047	349,131	44,310	2,277,226	667,594	1,962,636	42,783	114,707	51,215
2021	5,249,011	2,713,885	-1,138	2,712,747	362,089	45,465	2,396,123	676,844	2,176,044	46,166	113,698	51,947

Personal Income and Employment by Area: Bellingham, WA

(Thousands of dollars, except as noted.)

Year	Personal income, total	Earnings by place of work			Less: Contributions for government social insurance	Plus: Adjustment for residence	Equals: Net earnings by place of residence	Plus: Dividends, interest, and rent	Plus: Personal current transfer receipts	Per capita personal income (dollars)	Population (persons)	Total employment
		Nonfarm	Farm	Total								
1970	321,153	236,478	15,801	252,279	19,139	-308	232,832	54,573	33,748	3,888	82,606	34,551
1971	369,028	278,308	17,662	295,970	23,859	-2,177	269,934	60,405	38,689	4,307	85,688	37,206
1972	389,183	287,246	20,011	307,257	25,342	-1,094	280,821	64,962	43,400	4,351	89,443	36,628
1973	434,564	318,446	24,205	342,651	32,310	-335	310,006	74,733	49,825	4,845	89,700	38,054
1974	490,746	355,963	25,038	381,001	37,079	-809	343,113	86,801	60,832	5,390	91,043	39,342
1975	557,944	402,445	25,466	427,911	41,778	-1,713	384,420	98,390	75,134	5,978	93,332	41,368
1976	635,961	464,202	32,419	496,621	48,448	-1,343	446,830	109,080	80,051	6,620	96,070	44,257
1977	703,824	522,154	29,485	551,639	55,259	-2,917	493,463	126,738	83,623	7,149	98,453	46,132
1978	799,446	603,850	26,584	630,434	65,007	-3,348	562,079	146,787	90,580	7,878	101,482	48,497
1979	911,802	683,912	32,817	716,729	76,119	-1,289	639,321	169,702	102,779	8,735	104,380	50,544
1980	996,713	722,336	24,518	746,854	80,749	312	666,417	204,118	126,178	9,296	107,222	50,074
1981	1,078,348	751,920	28,200	780,120	91,221	45	688,944	245,248	144,156	9,884	109,096	50,010
1982	1,133,041	773,910	26,531	800,441	96,332	951	705,060	267,887	160,094	10,311	109,885	49,658
1983	1,242,287	831,766	36,157	867,923	103,961	2,039	766,001	300,287	175,999	11,229	110,630	51,784
1984	1,327,116	881,058	35,699	916,757	113,542	2,930	806,145	333,471	187,500	11,924	111,294	52,881
1985	1,418,833	932,529	42,527	975,056	120,523	5,457	859,990	358,377	200,466	12,618	112,441	53,901
1986	1,522,449	1,013,620	53,521	1,067,141	131,482	6,433	942,092	369,034	211,323	13,442	113,262	56,022
1987	1,620,055	1,091,865	60,023	1,151,888	142,081	5,644	1,015,451	380,760	223,844	14,043	115,361	58,864
1988	1,754,371	1,186,058	57,470	1,243,528	157,061	11,123	1,097,590	415,969	240,812	14,742	119,002	62,798
1989	1,979,145	1,343,093	66,655	1,409,748	178,574	14,233	1,245,407	475,803	257,935	16,052	123,294	67,307
1990	2,262,361	1,591,920	75,914	1,667,834	213,535	14,172	1,468,471	508,597	285,293	17,523	129,111	73,036
1991	2,452,464	1,702,544	69,168	1,771,712	231,296	21,865	1,562,281	564,118	326,065	18,326	133,823	74,567
1992	2,607,648	1,815,695	89,406	1,905,101	246,567	29,336	1,687,870	564,799	354,979	18,766	138,957	77,046
1993	2,718,753	1,892,642	76,300	1,968,942	259,140	35,131	1,744,933	591,482	382,338	18,924	143,669	78,697
1994	2,901,284	2,013,979	75,184	2,089,163	277,226	41,244	1,853,181	635,651	412,452	19,657	147,593	82,327
1995	3,067,945	2,116,062	67,442	2,183,504	290,765	49,817	1,942,556	675,917	449,472	20,268	151,369	83,655
1996	3,318,052	2,241,436	95,281	2,336,717	300,369	57,166	2,093,514	745,932	478,606	21,388	155,134	86,113
1997	3,505,782	2,363,529	77,362	2,440,891	303,396	70,900	2,208,395	793,098	504,289	22,170	158,133	88,181
1998	3,764,002	2,520,536	104,978	2,625,514	320,373	85,804	2,390,945	843,014	530,043	23,381	160,988	89,503
1999	3,923,839	2,642,184	108,236	2,750,420	327,986	105,017	2,527,451	820,700	575,688	23,844	164,566	91,585
2000	4,150,206	2,751,660	89,497	2,841,157	347,087	122,266	2,616,336	903,635	630,235	24,748	167,696	93,409
2001	4,473,800	2,998,977	109,552	3,108,529	373,447	107,673	2,842,755	914,708	716,337	26,136	171,172	94,252
2002	4,543,671	3,152,746	91,078	3,243,824	392,261	108,943	2,960,506	824,988	758,177	25,978	174,904	96,470
2003	4,896,223	3,375,375	119,116	3,494,491	422,875	105,460	3,177,076	916,118	803,029	27,530	177,851	99,418
2004	5,313,673	3,677,652	124,623	3,802,275	459,408	102,545	3,445,412	1,032,888	835,373	29,235	181,756	102,987
2005	5,660,645	3,992,107	123,938	4,116,045	505,863	104,645	3,714,827	1,061,032	884,786	30,524	185,450	107,985
2006	6,143,150	4,236,005	85,639	4,321,644	528,570	124,971	3,918,045	1,274,114	950,991	32,516	188,926	110,385
2007	6,727,407	4,454,241	113,555	4,567,796	555,608	145,733	4,157,921	1,534,934	1,034,552	34,886	192,837	114,493
2008	7,188,087	4,644,222	86,351	4,730,573	579,312	151,152	4,302,413	1,685,005	1,200,669	36,542	196,708	114,978
2009	7,079,611	4,615,824	66,144	4,681,968	590,504	144,137	4,235,601	1,499,126	1,344,884	35,422	199,865	110,709
2010	7,364,364	4,760,000	104,339	4,864,339	602,292	141,244	4,403,291	1,469,630	1,491,443	36,539	201,549	109,057
2011	7,757,550	4,885,951	150,391	5,036,342	566,004	153,604	4,623,942	1,642,058	1,491,550	38,120	203,503	110,303
2012	8,278,672	5,241,209	145,548	5,386,757	582,202	161,948	4,966,503	1,820,497	1,491,672	40,403	204,902	112,790
2013	8,242,933	5,390,629	154,502	5,545,131	667,333	153,756	5,031,554	1,687,318	1,524,061	39,987	206,139	115,116
2014	8,724,792	5,449,186	196,766	5,645,952	681,888	175,581	5,139,645	1,915,400	1,669,747	42,175	206,873	117,166
2015	9,201,343	5,730,152	186,100	5,916,252	721,110	185,757	5,380,899	2,092,553	1,727,891	43,769	210,224	119,694
2016	9,576,953	6,004,190	161,887	6,166,077	751,511	201,867	5,616,433	2,129,396	1,831,124	44,669	214,400	123,377
2017	10,062,596	6,423,578	159,215	6,582,793	812,878	199,739	5,969,654	2,197,876	1,895,066	45,959	218,946	126,255
2018	10,802,154	6,958,844	121,279	7,080,123	859,979	237,549	6,457,693	2,339,296	2,005,165	48,605	222,242	129,113
2019	11,650,371	7,234,477	166,992	7,401,469	872,276	257,912	6,787,105	2,713,430	2,149,836	51,683	225,421	129,697
2020	12,485,186	7,303,269	191,906	7,495,175	895,269	246,351	6,846,257	2,728,358	2,910,571	54,927	227,304	123,878
2021	13,303,658	7,793,458	149,397	7,942,855	950,514	281,346	7,273,687	2,839,977	3,189,994	58,137	228,831	127,225

Personal Income and Employment by Area: Bend, OR

(Thousands of dollars, except as noted.)

Year	Personal income, total	Earnings by place of work			Less: Contributions for government social insurance	Plus: Adjustment for residence	Equals: Net earnings by place of residence	Plus: Dividends, interest, and rent	Plus: Personal current transfer receipts	Per capita personal income (dollars)	Population (persons)	Total employment
		Nonfarm	Farm	Total								
1970	124,676	90,412	1,419	91,831	6,623	2,318	87,526	24,821	12,329	4,037	30,882	13,667
1971	143,502	104,384	1,428	105,812	7,921	2,597	100,488	28,617	14,397	4,370	32,835	15,106
1972	168,880	123,271	3,740	127,011	9,891	2,933	120,053	32,392	16,435	4,852	34,804	16,767
1973	196,159	143,736	4,286	148,022	13,282	3,074	137,814	38,445	19,900	5,206	37,682	18,403
1974	221,209	156,821	3,468	160,289	14,878	3,635	149,046	46,476	25,687	5,509	40,155	18,902
1975	256,795	176,577	3,663	180,240	16,127	5,689	169,802	53,575	33,418	6,053	42,422	19,706
1976	308,998	221,349	3,277	224,626	20,214	4,372	208,784	62,484	37,730	6,915	44,686	22,354
1977	369,658	269,303	2,384	271,687	25,185	4,443	250,945	75,067	43,646	7,706	47,969	25,288
1978	443,826	328,928	132	329,060	31,690	4,307	301,677	92,920	49,229	8,319	53,349	28,444
1979	525,431	390,196	894	391,090	39,375	3,542	355,257	111,315	58,859	8,989	58,452	30,620
1980	573,952	402,570	1,159	403,729	40,276	4,173	367,626	132,643	73,683	9,203	62,365	30,066
1981	618,235	406,905	1,658	408,563	43,436	6,080	371,207	158,554	88,474	9,793	63,130	29,334
1982	640,723	400,660	901	401,561	43,503	6,727	364,785	173,134	102,804	10,165	63,031	27,771
1983	709,259	447,402	6,098	453,500	49,112	7,800	412,188	187,773	109,298	11,345	62,516	29,659
1984	791,075	508,790	6,702	515,492	57,380	9,011	467,123	208,760	115,192	12,392	63,839	31,566
1985	857,434	555,920	5,061	560,981	63,842	10,390	507,529	225,691	124,214	13,200	64,959	33,037
1986	914,324	596,503	1,660	598,163	68,210	12,448	542,401	244,005	127,918	13,820	66,160	34,685
1987	978,932	643,989	373	644,362	72,643	14,371	586,090	260,317	132,525	14,641	66,862	35,621
1988	1,091,408	728,980	2,340	731,320	85,024	17,310	663,606	281,964	145,838	15,845	68,882	38,234
1989	1,226,870	795,948	3,178	799,126	95,276	18,830	722,680	343,589	160,601	17,179	71,415	41,660
1990	1,392,418	940,480	1,483	941,963	114,536	17,956	845,383	372,005	175,030	18,309	76,053	45,455
1991	1,539,726	1,052,685	743	1,053,428	128,482	18,193	943,139	398,612	197,975	19,137	80,456	46,995
1992	1,680,779	1,145,013	-1,148	1,143,865	137,688	24,217	1,030,394	424,820	225,565	19,962	84,199	48,397
1993	1,848,330	1,264,066	-2,400	1,261,666	150,783	23,328	1,134,211	470,506	243,613	20,989	88,061	51,071
1994	1,982,640	1,359,337	-2,878	1,356,459	164,055	25,445	1,217,849	502,631	262,160	21,694	91,393	54,760
1995	2,150,396	1,426,925	-2,694	1,424,231	174,057	25,928	1,276,102	579,271	295,023	22,519	95,491	57,626
1996	2,353,833	1,555,263	-2,979	1,552,284	190,652	26,913	1,388,545	643,641	321,647	23,689	99,362	60,831
1997	2,516,282	1,653,885	-2,219	1,651,666	201,419	27,687	1,477,934	694,318	344,030	24,530	102,581	64,237
1998	2,759,459	1,807,304	176	1,807,480	219,272	27,725	1,615,933	782,919	360,607	25,833	106,820	66,592
1999	2,932,324	1,990,949	-4,365	1,986,584	240,501	26,447	1,772,530	756,683	403,111	26,197	111,933	70,590
2000	3,222,454	2,202,270	-5,976	2,196,294	266,207	26,246	1,956,333	832,605	433,516	27,645	116,566	74,782
2001	3,502,790	2,434,227	-4,569	2,429,658	284,014	19,196	2,164,840	842,551	495,399	29,063	120,526	76,099
2002	3,622,928	2,570,256	-4,726	2,565,530	301,903	13,600	2,277,227	792,100	553,601	28,926	125,247	77,415
2003	3,852,722	2,751,150	-3,137	2,748,013	324,572	3,942	2,427,383	844,908	580,431	29,844	129,094	80,405
2004	4,160,923	2,956,642	1,228	2,957,870	359,270	6,595	2,605,195	954,075	601,653	31,108	133,756	86,200
2005	4,654,531	3,325,222	-3,886	3,321,336	407,288	-796	2,913,252	1,089,534	651,745	33,113	140,567	92,848
2006	5,336,025	3,804,561	-5,093	3,799,468	462,651	-21,732	3,315,085	1,301,851	719,089	36,018	148,149	98,924
2007	5,655,946	3,915,527	-11,928	3,903,599	480,300	-18,993	3,404,306	1,460,958	790,682	37,056	152,633	102,267
2008	5,903,707	3,774,769	-13,685	3,761,084	467,725	-9,916	3,283,443	1,644,125	976,139	37,646	156,820	98,956
2009	5,452,070	3,332,177	-13,087	3,319,090	426,762	22,555	2,914,883	1,365,566	1,171,621	34,650	157,345	92,268
2010	5,511,958	3,261,827	-12,533	3,249,294	425,807	41,279	2,864,766	1,362,156	1,285,036	34,942	157,744	90,538
2011	5,897,282	3,373,770	-10,844	3,362,926	393,165	64,026	3,033,787	1,546,938	1,316,557	36,931	159,683	91,525
2012	6,364,028	3,717,463	-8,879	3,708,584	417,901	101,454	3,392,137	1,647,253	1,324,638	39,428	161,408	92,973
2013	6,839,354	4,077,638	-4,306	4,073,332	510,191	110,668	3,673,809	1,775,852	1,389,693	41,354	165,385	96,988
2014	7,391,622	4,605,303	-6,892	4,598,411	573,527	64,182	4,089,066	1,773,165	1,529,391	43,796	168,775	103,030
2015	8,302,221	5,147,921	-6,086	5,141,835	631,657	55,189	4,565,367	2,080,183	1,656,671	47,904	173,308	109,469
2016	9,093,771	5,660,537	-5,660	5,654,877	681,282	68,768	5,042,363	2,323,246	1,728,162	50,666	179,485	114,986
2017	9,881,017	6,208,529	-12,789	6,195,740	750,047	56,352	5,502,045	2,573,554	1,805,418	53,303	185,374	119,789
2018	10,667,029	6,678,895	-11,491	6,667,404	789,926	48,957	5,926,435	2,813,469	1,927,125	56,169	189,910	124,418
2019	11,455,993	7,182,734	-11,254	7,171,480	848,448	32,825	6,355,857	3,038,917	2,061,219	58,666	195,275	126,288
2020	12,733,152	7,697,998	-12,477	7,685,521	899,065	32,594	6,819,050	3,107,404	2,806,698	63,872	199,355	125,237
2021	13,873,903	8,484,765	-14,522	8,470,243	982,013	66,294	7,554,524	3,257,421	3,061,958	67,743	204,801	130,681

Personal Income and Employment by Area: Billings, MT

(Thousands of dollars, except as noted.)

Year	Personal income, total	Earnings by place of work			Less: Contributions for government social insurance	Plus: Adjustment for residence	Equals: Net earnings by place of residence	Plus: Dividends, interest, and rent	Plus: Personal current transfer receipts	Per capita personal income (dollars)	Population (persons)	Total employment
		Nonfarm	Farm	Total								
1970	372,929	278,723	21,119	299,842	21,611	-574	277,657	64,402	30,870	3,892	95,810	43,329
1971	411,959	310,999	19,473	330,472	24,478	-419	305,575	70,217	36,167	4,193	98,257	44,885
1972	474,208	351,753	33,796	385,549	29,206	-414	355,929	77,702	40,577	4,730	100,254	47,205
1973	526,066	394,204	32,842	427,046	37,863	-563	388,620	89,991	47,455	5,158	101,991	50,349
1974	597,877	450,760	29,474	480,234	44,203	-445	435,586	106,032	56,259	5,683	105,198	52,867
1975	668,970	509,450	13,919	523,369	48,184	1,845	477,030	123,217	68,723	6,214	107,654	53,779
1976	753,100	594,302	4,887	599,189	57,135	919	542,973	134,754	75,373	6,824	110,368	57,467
1977	856,148	682,848	3,628	686,476	66,290	1,292	621,478	153,049	81,621	7,592	112,764	60,302
1978	976,887	781,896	8,724	790,620	78,780	1,316	713,156	173,031	90,700	8,402	116,271	64,090
1979	1,090,579	877,427	3,293	880,720	92,405	949	789,264	199,825	101,490	9,290	117,391	65,442
1980	1,210,179	931,516	5,962	937,478	99,612	10,690	848,556	240,654	120,969	10,279	117,733	64,651
1981	1,372,329	1,033,149	3,939	1,037,088	118,482	8,037	926,643	306,367	139,319	11,470	119,645	66,183
1982	1,488,457	1,100,423	4,625	1,105,048	129,309	7,948	983,687	347,540	157,230	12,153	122,475	67,078
1983	1,577,691	1,170,300	5,439	1,175,739	137,993	4,800	1,042,546	359,987	175,158	12,558	125,635	68,542
1984	1,696,577	1,245,484	9,641	1,255,125	151,242	-948	1,102,935	404,143	189,499	13,223	128,301	70,868
1985	1,747,917	1,276,336	10,451	1,286,787	157,990	-1,828	1,126,969	418,539	202,409	13,550	128,999	70,516
1986	1,751,728	1,273,186	10,786	1,283,972	160,248	-2,254	1,121,470	412,806	217,452	13,681	128,041	69,709
1987	1,786,188	1,282,402	20,444	1,302,846	159,795	53	1,143,104	412,192	230,892	14,216	125,649	69,468
1988	1,850,342	1,338,384	18,826	1,357,210	174,565	1,287	1,183,932	417,785	248,625	14,973	123,581	71,737
1989	2,003,884	1,417,718	23,378	1,441,096	186,021	3,059	1,258,134	472,928	272,822	16,323	122,761	73,107
1990	2,102,123	1,503,603	22,084	1,525,687	209,623	4,817	1,320,881	477,649	303,593	17,154	122,545	73,868
1991	2,244,596	1,637,179	28,195	1,665,374	232,241	5,818	1,438,951	485,610	320,035	18,059	124,295	75,939
1992	2,396,044	1,768,367	33,817	1,802,184	252,659	2,620	1,552,145	499,808	344,091	18,782	127,568	78,363
1993	2,545,266	1,904,867	37,464	1,942,331	278,600	1,372	1,665,103	507,792	372,371	19,468	130,744	80,093
1994	2,688,980	2,015,001	25,776	2,040,777	295,285	1,610	1,747,102	549,453	392,425	20,182	133,239	83,702
1995	2,829,423	2,086,990	13,238	2,100,228	298,040	1,732	1,803,920	605,949	419,554	20,909	135,318	84,768
1996	2,954,768	2,165,649	14,053	2,179,702	296,114	1,188	1,884,776	636,064	433,928	21,596	136,818	87,037
1997	3,101,003	2,259,630	10,961	2,270,591	299,256	1,415	1,972,750	683,307	444,946	22,524	137,674	87,651
1998	3,459,754	2,509,925	14,690	2,524,615	325,010	-703	2,198,902	776,084	484,768	23,878	144,892	94,168
1999	3,566,579	2,640,436	20,498	2,660,934	340,573	-3,032	2,317,329	767,799	481,451	24,373	146,331	96,026
2000	3,835,325	2,836,738	19,656	2,856,394	365,032	-6,217	2,485,145	814,708	535,472	26,024	147,378	97,833
2001	3,987,579	2,941,863	33,283	2,975,146	389,390	-6,671	2,579,085	827,104	581,390	26,788	148,858	99,701
2002	4,086,734	3,089,024	14,982	3,104,006	412,826	-9,752	2,681,428	803,988	601,318	27,187	150,320	100,724
2003	4,324,783	3,253,980	30,508	3,284,488	431,185	-10,988	2,842,315	854,261	628,207	28,469	151,913	101,673
2004	4,722,304	3,521,484	51,749	3,573,233	461,785	-14,027	3,097,421	949,819	675,064	30,730	153,672	104,544
2005	5,085,431	3,798,369	49,221	3,847,590	497,556	-15,336	3,334,698	1,026,571	724,162	32,594	156,025	106,966
2006	5,476,447	4,071,354	6,936	4,078,290	530,009	-18,920	3,529,361	1,153,215	793,871	34,627	158,157	108,832
2007	5,945,950	4,384,389	9,355	4,393,744	578,524	-22,796	3,792,424	1,301,160	852,366	37,079	160,358	112,638
2008	6,363,306	4,539,396	6,733	4,546,129	592,532	-23,988	3,929,609	1,462,589	971,108	38,999	163,165	113,507
2009	6,223,375	4,530,828	7,570	4,538,398	587,876	-5,274	3,945,248	1,243,237	1,034,890	37,586	165,575	111,282
2010	6,548,868	4,670,911	17,942	4,688,853	597,996	10,159	4,101,016	1,307,966	1,139,886	39,079	167,580	110,687
2011	7,023,353	4,942,736	41,469	4,984,205	567,956	47,377	4,463,626	1,434,163	1,125,564	41,547	169,047	112,650
2012	7,662,521	5,317,069	38,851	5,355,920	593,284	115,833	4,878,469	1,623,896	1,160,156	44,812	170,993	114,730
2013	7,757,799	5,561,016	68,042	5,629,058	696,063	154,155	5,087,150	1,486,371	1,184,278	44,728	173,445	115,007
2014	8,290,106	5,836,494	69,241	5,905,735	727,257	189,836	5,368,314	1,671,375	1,250,417	47,276	175,356	116,397
2015	8,552,091	6,058,202	84,754	6,142,956	754,579	146,454	5,534,831	1,714,405	1,302,855	48,354	176,865	119,090
2016	8,556,479	5,990,378	77,045	6,067,423	731,956	86,932	5,422,399	1,719,424	1,414,656	47,970	178,373	119,832
2017	9,039,714	6,294,219	38,259	6,332,478	782,801	92,008	5,641,685	1,867,151	1,530,878	50,196	180,087	120,253
2018	9,412,640	6,438,983	47,009	6,485,992	822,927	109,681	5,772,746	2,048,343	1,591,551	52,026	180,923	121,324
2019	9,750,428	6,676,402	61,345	6,737,747	845,860	111,557	6,003,444	2,059,704	1,687,280	53,437	182,465	121,377
2020	10,430,717	6,931,789	70,104	7,001,893	897,873	68,991	6,173,011	2,082,883	2,174,823	56,515	184,567	121,473
2021	11,165,820	7,517,091	22,220	7,539,311	940,846	45,341	6,643,806	2,157,076	2,364,938	59,698	187,037	125,516

Personal Income and Employment by Area: Binghamton, NY

(Thousands of dollars, except as noted.)

Year	Personal income, total	Earnings by place of work Nonfarm	Farm	Total	Less: Contributions for government social insurance	Plus: Adjustment for residence	Equals: Net earnings by place of residence	Plus: Dividends, interest, and rent	Plus: Personal current transfer receipts	Per capita personal income (dollars)	Population (persons)	Total employment
1970	1,096,008	947,976	8,644	956,620	71,901	-32,537	852,182	139,431	104,395	4,077	268,851	117,119
1971	1,169,453	995,597	8,709	1,004,306	78,160	-35,921	890,225	150,584	128,644	4,319	270,746	116,349
1972	1,235,754	1,053,517	8,840	1,062,357	87,343	-36,472	938,542	162,556	134,656	4,619	267,509	117,444
1973	1,332,843	1,135,541	10,063	1,145,604	108,690	-37,418	999,496	181,261	152,086	4,982	267,518	120,927
1974	1,441,396	1,210,104	7,005	1,217,109	119,004	-38,143	1,059,962	204,081	177,353	5,426	265,630	121,541
1975	1,582,300	1,290,938	6,632	1,297,570	124,685	-44,596	1,128,289	224,056	229,955	5,890	268,656	119,091
1976	1,693,251	1,388,506	8,396	1,396,902	137,684	-48,956	1,210,262	238,667	244,322	6,293	269,063	120,675
1977	1,846,831	1,529,082	4,869	1,533,951	151,332	-59,543	1,323,076	263,691	260,064	6,874	268,668	124,414
1978	2,028,177	1,699,925	7,722	1,707,647	172,170	-67,866	1,467,611	280,747	279,819	7,576	267,705	128,940
1979	2,224,229	1,866,116	9,421	1,875,537	194,532	-76,784	1,604,221	317,638	302,370	8,331	266,989	130,555
1980	2,454,074	2,015,721	9,728	2,025,449	209,227	-85,762	1,730,460	378,136	345,478	9,308	263,639	129,633
1981	2,732,896	2,209,511	7,811	2,217,322	243,390	-96,836	1,877,096	460,720	395,080	10,357	263,859	129,925
1982	3,013,449	2,397,588	14,097	2,411,685	266,749	-110,602	2,034,334	535,359	443,756	11,414	264,005	129,662
1983	3,222,929	2,554,158	7,900	2,562,058	287,485	-113,789	2,160,784	587,019	475,126	12,232	263,473	128,801
1984	3,580,021	2,855,913	8,857	2,864,770	328,436	-125,157	2,411,177	674,795	494,049	13,603	263,182	135,188
1985	3,788,498	3,064,351	9,830	3,074,181	355,797	-136,692	2,581,692	689,421	517,385	14,311	264,719	139,580
1986	3,961,533	3,177,263	10,358	3,187,621	375,398	-133,264	2,678,959	730,908	551,666	15,026	263,651	140,401
1987	4,170,309	3,382,819	10,639	3,393,458	390,613	-136,720	2,866,125	740,626	563,558	15,901	262,266	140,900
1988	4,420,720	3,597,159	7,672	3,604,831	424,415	-138,516	3,041,900	781,024	597,796	16,758	263,797	145,553
1989	4,747,737	3,753,003	12,087	3,765,090	437,573	-135,423	3,192,094	908,290	647,353	17,957	264,388	143,469
1990	4,923,618	3,842,113	13,620	3,855,733	429,025	-137,304	3,289,404	929,666	704,548	18,599	264,731	142,457
1991	5,086,610	3,964,362	9,602	3,973,964	452,179	-142,050	3,379,735	938,328	768,547	19,149	265,632	139,936
1992	5,278,830	4,071,105	13,779	4,084,884	457,065	-148,880	3,478,939	936,282	863,609	19,803	266,571	138,396
1993	5,271,085	4,067,779	14,745	4,082,524	463,676	-152,952	3,465,896	889,898	915,291	19,817	265,993	137,687
1994	5,307,142	4,047,652	13,015	4,060,667	464,806	-145,663	3,450,198	903,330	953,614	20,097	264,082	136,661
1995	5,426,728	4,075,874	9,727	4,085,601	463,522	-145,195	3,476,884	946,333	1,003,511	20,866	260,079	134,001
1996	5,583,950	4,161,812	16,315	4,178,127	465,062	-139,323	3,573,742	968,095	1,042,113	21,753	256,702	132,577
1997	5,785,985	4,325,356	5,366	4,330,722	479,294	-135,514	3,715,914	1,032,736	1,037,335	22,760	254,213	134,726
1998	5,897,030	4,402,992	8,881	4,411,873	486,807	-141,432	3,783,634	1,036,094	1,077,302	23,287	253,235	134,427
1999	6,178,171	4,697,560	6,443	4,704,003	505,997	-152,591	4,045,415	1,027,382	1,105,374	24,442	252,773	138,052
2000	6,552,614	5,044,966	4,267	5,049,233	540,277	-172,029	4,336,927	1,081,727	1,133,960	25,983	252,189	141,139
2001	6,653,612	5,069,982	4,485	5,074,467	558,884	-153,972	4,361,611	1,077,505	1,214,496	26,343	252,580	139,580
2002	6,768,903	5,117,374	254	5,117,628	565,640	-137,345	4,414,643	1,033,892	1,320,368	26,709	253,430	136,479
2003	6,815,779	5,073,915	7,120	5,081,035	560,893	-109,166	4,410,976	1,038,433	1,366,370	26,947	252,932	134,838
2004	7,111,026	5,221,159	15,341	5,236,500	577,492	-99,309	4,559,699	1,119,199	1,432,128	28,151	252,605	134,828
2005	7,177,813	5,388,745	18,890	5,407,635	606,328	-100,057	4,701,250	977,796	1,498,767	28,473	252,088	135,172
2006	7,628,846	5,726,703	17,447	5,744,150	643,237	-100,481	5,000,432	1,034,892	1,593,522	30,220	252,441	136,660
2007	8,105,852	5,996,956	16,589	6,013,545	665,459	-97,136	5,250,950	1,169,551	1,685,351	32,110	252,442	139,310
2008	8,581,155	6,184,028	15,172	6,199,200	695,629	-84,883	5,418,688	1,286,138	1,876,329	33,981	252,527	139,391
2009	8,692,957	6,162,102	6,957	6,169,059	685,578	-72,346	5,411,135	1,195,619	2,086,203	34,472	252,171	135,666
2010	8,952,263	6,225,391	12,630	6,238,021	683,220	-11,531	5,543,270	1,183,525	2,225,468	35,597	251,486	133,187
2011	9,150,929	6,222,093	17,527	6,239,620	619,363	39,591	5,659,848	1,242,471	2,248,610	36,566	250,256	132,381
2012	9,396,191	6,347,743	13,571	6,361,314	619,900	87,899	5,829,313	1,333,036	2,233,842	37,738	248,986	131,868
2013	9,435,526	6,398,006	22,584	6,420,590	701,720	115,498	5,834,368	1,345,862	2,255,296	38,034	248,081	130,482
2014	9,584,011	6,427,262	23,254	6,450,516	715,566	132,589	5,867,539	1,417,186	2,299,286	38,154	251,193	129,528
2015	9,804,470	6,467,301	10,596	6,477,897	727,467	145,451	5,895,881	1,484,708	2,423,881	39,166	250,330	128,347
2016	9,848,438	6,523,015	9,564	6,532,579	739,316	118,391	5,911,654	1,487,800	2,448,984	39,504	249,300	128,162
2017	10,323,347	6,786,956	16,118	6,803,074	773,884	131,498	6,160,688	1,565,531	2,597,128	41,511	248,689	126,879
2018	10,518,381	6,994,011	10,286	7,004,297	793,733	131,556	6,342,120	1,621,782	2,554,479	42,340	248,426	127,506
2019	10,970,121	7,139,051	21,981	7,161,032	817,749	132,326	6,475,609	1,774,762	2,719,750	44,318	247,533	126,286
2020	11,912,953	7,174,767	18,322	7,193,089	826,366	119,169	6,485,892	1,780,439	3,646,622	48,318	246,554	117,723
2021	12,578,671	7,640,111	22,506	7,662,617	874,984	129,563	6,917,196	1,832,323	3,829,152	51,295	245,220	120,249

Personal Income and Employment by Area: Birmingham-Hoover, AL

(Thousands of dollars, except as noted.)

Year	Personal income, total	Earnings by place of work			Less: Contributions for government social insurance	Plus: Adjustment for residence	Equals: Net earnings by place of residence	Plus: Dividends, interest, and rent	Plus: Personal current transfer receipts	Per capita personal income (dollars)	Population (persons)	Total employment
		Nonfarm	Farm	Total								
1970	2,851,440	2,379,405	17,346	2,396,751	173,881	-7,814	2,215,056	345,407	290,977	3,418	834,280	356,195
1971	3,131,911	2,588,676	19,381	2,608,057	192,855	-18,466	2,396,736	383,812	351,363	3,704	845,548	360,430
1972	3,483,840	2,902,582	25,868	2,928,450	227,028	-33,633	2,667,789	419,336	396,715	4,086	852,711	373,689
1973	3,921,783	3,259,867	43,422	3,303,289	294,270	-39,533	2,969,486	473,734	478,563	4,539	864,085	388,783
1974	4,415,944	3,681,181	18,811	3,699,992	342,915	-44,767	3,312,310	551,487	552,147	5,074	870,341	398,688
1975	4,949,600	4,022,722	36,095	4,058,817	369,872	-47,010	3,641,935	614,471	693,194	5,604	883,172	399,287
1976	5,502,353	4,491,330	36,100	4,527,430	421,711	-43,119	4,062,600	669,101	770,652	6,144	895,598	407,393
1977	6,076,351	5,001,680	40,289	5,041,969	470,750	-43,865	4,527,354	740,870	808,127	6,687	908,642	421,750
1978	6,835,177	5,662,734	35,593	5,698,327	543,275	-42,711	5,112,341	839,834	883,002	7,436	919,252	435,995
1979	7,643,332	6,287,066	42,940	6,330,006	624,929	-43,845	5,661,232	956,529	1,025,571	8,239	927,712	445,633
1980	8,400,830	6,705,487	28,813	6,734,300	664,678	-37,030	6,032,592	1,164,174	1,204,064	9,027	930,680	438,371
1981	9,130,207	7,120,792	29,113	7,149,905	761,575	-50,109	6,338,221	1,449,101	1,342,885	9,815	930,227	430,843
1982	9,656,392	7,392,455	33,312	7,425,767	805,577	-50,958	6,569,232	1,619,688	1,467,472	10,426	926,197	423,068
1983	10,253,529	7,844,071	28,481	7,872,552	863,791	-59,130	6,949,631	1,719,865	1,584,033	11,060	927,062	425,578
1984	11,255,663	8,632,338	36,137	8,668,475	968,769	-58,180	7,641,526	1,946,000	1,668,137	12,085	931,399	442,199
1985	12,146,097	9,392,640	40,217	9,432,857	1,063,034	-67,817	8,302,006	2,115,559	1,728,532	12,964	936,926	457,464
1986	12,842,801	9,999,584	25,798	10,025,382	1,130,344	-76,208	8,818,830	2,235,552	1,788,419	13,641	941,503	471,914
1987	13,619,661	10,640,407	37,999	10,678,406	1,188,957	-89,757	9,399,692	2,388,498	1,831,471	14,360	948,471	485,505
1988	14,769,020	11,548,036	62,445	11,610,481	1,327,575	-113,454	10,169,452	2,711,701	1,887,867	15,529	951,042	500,481
1989	16,089,171	12,264,688	88,893	12,353,581	1,408,117	-121,245	10,824,219	3,144,970	2,119,982	16,858	954,416	507,055
1990	17,264,731	13,205,865	86,432	13,292,297	1,532,421	-129,295	11,630,581	3,322,939	2,311,211	18,008	958,709	518,079
1991	18,149,374	13,837,557	109,684	13,947,241	1,617,459	-137,408	12,192,374	3,434,545	2,522,455	18,721	969,491	519,983
1992	19,417,458	14,888,185	96,330	14,984,515	1,717,648	-150,989	13,115,878	3,452,047	2,849,533	19,813	980,037	528,501
1993	20,328,105	15,528,498	111,156	15,639,654	1,809,070	-146,386	13,684,198	3,645,006	2,998,901	20,494	991,884	542,304
1994	21,673,590	16,500,447	84,611	16,585,058	1,947,552	-153,763	14,483,743	4,021,275	3,168,572	21,605	1,003,186	549,975
1995	23,137,991	17,528,347	83,420	17,611,767	2,080,194	-162,430	15,369,143	4,354,069	3,414,779	22,827	1,013,634	566,345
1996	24,409,346	18,593,810	76,686	18,670,496	2,182,003	-174,643	16,313,850	4,501,961	3,593,535	23,874	1,022,434	578,023
1997	25,743,326	19,460,501	88,902	19,549,403	2,287,543	-179,664	17,082,196	4,932,116	3,729,014	24,983	1,030,425	590,779
1998	26,028,906	20,292,537	83,508	20,376,045	2,338,478	-472,270	17,565,297	5,067,538	3,396,071	26,865	968,885	576,169
1999	27,202,588	21,531,704	79,306	21,611,010	2,477,863	-502,877	18,630,270	5,051,085	3,521,233	27,853	976,656	584,344
2000	29,086,960	22,948,891	57,090	23,005,981	2,605,907	-521,380	19,878,694	5,463,131	3,745,135	29,599	982,704	590,606
2001	29,839,216	23,573,428	84,818	23,658,246	2,704,349	-542,293	20,411,604	5,476,979	3,950,633	30,180	988,718	591,371
2002	30,748,093	24,474,520	60,210	24,534,730	2,805,303	-549,688	21,179,739	5,339,416	4,228,938	30,959	993,201	589,367
2003	32,009,711	25,146,925	81,107	25,228,032	2,885,975	-525,681	21,816,376	5,714,668	4,478,667	31,953	1,001,781	589,756
2004	34,648,938	26,656,418	98,160	26,754,578	3,016,779	-570,345	23,167,454	6,761,515	4,719,969	34,320	1,009,575	600,389
2005	36,825,246	27,990,660	76,883	28,067,543	3,165,020	-515,206	24,387,317	7,381,401	5,056,528	36,181	1,017,818	613,937
2006	39,334,319	29,453,874	36,910	29,490,784	3,312,618	-449,923	25,728,243	8,143,245	5,462,831	38,167	1,030,584	626,827
2007	41,021,619	30,598,611	31,421	30,630,032	3,477,773	-437,803	26,714,456	8,448,175	5,858,988	39,461	1,039,561	640,584
2008	42,124,192	30,646,233	26,230	30,672,463	3,571,736	-369,546	26,731,181	8,766,894	6,626,117	40,146	1,049,266	634,784
2009	40,338,997	29,671,905	39,210	29,711,115	3,441,179	-335,859	25,934,077	7,370,244	7,034,676	38,130	1,057,924	606,607
2010	41,972,662	30,261,110	35,482	30,296,592	3,487,666	-269,045	26,539,881	7,713,167	7,719,614	39,532	1,061,728	600,850
2011	43,626,635	31,269,790	2,707	31,272,497	3,186,497	-322,836	27,763,164	7,844,547	8,018,924	40,998	1,064,114	608,220
2012	45,896,274	32,786,706	22,992	32,809,698	3,324,243	-364,999	29,120,456	8,742,771	8,033,047	42,985	1,067,725	616,845
2013	45,842,549	33,315,954	96,795	33,412,749	3,843,499	-354,311	29,214,939	8,381,311	8,246,299	42,719	1,073,110	622,895
2014	47,761,771	34,432,863	70,971	34,503,834	3,954,499	-292,628	30,256,707	8,906,326	8,598,738	43,975	1,086,106	631,022
2015	50,097,042	35,563,706	83,690	35,647,396	4,106,332	-242,184	31,298,880	9,652,329	9,145,833	45,870	1,092,150	639,514
2016	50,918,364	36,164,635	34,414	36,199,049	4,152,884	-293,520	31,752,645	9,890,192	9,275,527	46,389	1,097,647	649,463
2017	53,405,244	37,906,290	62,992	37,969,282	4,330,368	-313,021	33,325,893	10,602,843	9,476,508	48,428	1,102,770	656,440
2018	55,799,175	39,950,434	53,106	40,003,540	4,589,253	-430,976	34,983,311	11,042,291	9,773,573	50,385	1,107,463	671,271
2019	58,175,164	41,326,164	30,250	41,356,414	4,737,758	-453,615	36,165,041	11,772,947	10,237,176	52,310	1,112,118	676,786
2020	61,405,118	42,243,664	5,327	42,248,991	4,856,022	-537,780	36,855,189	11,842,444	12,707,485	55,086	1,114,710	663,709
2021	65,860,284	45,232,974	74,431	45,307,405	5,118,987	-733,307	39,455,111	12,165,884	14,239,289	59,107	1,114,262	683,080

Personal Income and Employment by Area: Bismarck, ND

(Thousands of dollars, except as noted.)

Year	Personal income, total	Earnings by place of work			Less: Contributions for government social insurance	Plus: Adjustment for residence	Equals: Net earnings by place of residence	Plus: Dividends, interest, and rent	Plus: Personal current transfer receipts	Per capita personal income (dollars)	Population (persons)	Total employment
		Nonfarm	Farm	Total								
1970	236,408	174,435	19,530	193,965	14,005	-1,542	178,418	37,303	20,687	3,522	67,114	30,677
1971	266,948	190,710	26,517	217,227	15,628	-1,292	200,307	41,748	24,893	3,924	68,027	30,842
1972	310,645	214,880	40,442	255,322	18,163	-941	236,218	46,426	28,001	4,499	69,047	31,964
1973	371,001	246,597	63,093	309,690	24,380	-769	284,541	54,474	31,986	5,210	71,215	33,892
1974	403,772	286,062	43,830	329,892	29,821	1,920	301,991	64,548	37,233	5,525	73,082	35,517
1975	455,966	332,615	35,926	368,541	34,764	4,453	338,230	72,743	44,993	6,027	75,660	37,555
1976	508,456	397,230	21,483	418,713	41,802	-215	376,696	81,538	50,222	6,510	78,103	40,157
1977	572,017	446,356	17,503	463,859	44,847	3,982	422,994	94,217	54,806	7,140	80,117	42,079
1978	671,227	499,758	39,405	539,163	51,417	13,120	500,866	109,709	60,652	8,216	81,696	44,053
1979	749,997	572,610	26,722	599,332	61,512	16,516	554,336	127,350	68,311	8,904	84,232	46,483
1980	805,123	630,631	-12,474	618,157	68,504	16,519	566,172	155,553	83,398	9,326	86,328	46,997
1981	945,350	672,320	37,449	709,769	76,741	18,749	651,777	197,062	96,511	10,861	87,039	46,555
1982	1,023,070	714,573	21,043	735,616	82,943	29,921	682,594	233,319	107,157	11,596	88,228	46,654
1983	1,090,262	754,093	15,437	769,530	87,850	55,557	737,237	231,691	121,334	12,119	89,961	47,560
1984	1,138,657	797,672	20,450	818,122	95,770	35,064	757,416	246,891	134,350	12,462	91,367	48,441
1985	1,163,848	825,104	18,564	843,668	102,064	20,797	762,401	257,469	143,978	12,702	91,624	48,697
1986	1,210,015	845,821	34,382	880,203	106,830	14,198	787,571	261,379	161,065	13,239	91,397	48,760
1987	1,260,964	890,215	42,197	932,412	112,261	15,470	835,621	255,658	169,685	13,949	90,400	50,050
1988	1,257,530	937,002	362	937,364	123,481	12,612	826,495	257,147	173,888	13,971	90,011	50,981
1989	1,372,266	992,200	18,557	1,010,757	132,065	11,856	890,548	285,693	196,025	15,249	89,992	52,751
1990	1,457,206	1,064,500	18,746	1,083,246	149,758	11,621	945,109	300,366	211,731	16,172	90,106	54,138
1991	1,515,753	1,128,410	18,326	1,146,736	161,543	9,946	995,139	302,090	218,524	16,675	90,902	55,794
1992	1,660,810	1,222,249	39,129	1,261,378	174,664	10,021	1,096,735	316,566	247,509	17,962	92,461	57,107
1993	1,766,425	1,311,011	38,413	1,349,424	188,636	9,615	1,170,403	333,195	262,827	18,791	94,002	58,940
1994	1,850,810	1,397,572	24,811	1,422,383	203,405	8,960	1,227,938	356,222	266,650	19,484	94,993	61,673
1995	1,942,568	1,469,915	5,617	1,475,532	213,375	10,650	1,272,807	384,702	285,059	20,161	96,355	62,530
1996	2,063,310	1,529,007	23,807	1,552,814	220,010	16,211	1,349,015	410,551	303,744	21,107	97,755	63,482
1997	2,143,129	1,614,210	-12,555	1,601,655	229,789	9,150	1,381,016	439,759	322,354	21,721	98,667	64,878
1998	2,258,646	1,679,740	26,304	1,706,044	237,727	20,078	1,488,395	455,481	314,770	23,581	95,784	64,969
1999	2,350,341	1,779,370	23,233	1,802,603	246,108	21,807	1,578,302	446,182	325,857	24,401	96,321	66,643
2000	2,544,971	1,892,666	48,741	1,941,407	259,464	21,156	1,703,099	485,849	356,023	26,259	96,917	67,825
2001	2,738,598	2,078,714	40,254	2,118,968	273,230	26,153	1,871,891	496,509	370,198	28,160	97,253	68,045
2002	2,803,987	2,169,571	8,595	2,178,166	282,618	29,330	1,924,878	487,952	391,157	28,538	98,254	68,452
2003	3,003,951	2,299,489	41,288	2,340,777	301,948	31,300	2,070,129	522,337	411,485	30,304	99,128	69,556
2004	3,201,613	2,421,697	43,529	2,465,226	316,883	38,812	2,187,155	571,802	442,656	31,973	100,134	71,510
2005	3,419,003	2,566,269	61,741	2,628,010	331,407	41,618	2,338,221	608,471	472,311	33,566	101,858	73,520
2006	3,645,322	2,734,501	23,548	2,758,049	347,908	51,731	2,461,872	676,471	506,979	35,148	103,713	76,118
2007	3,944,862	2,897,627	55,224	2,952,851	365,199	58,474	2,646,126	748,388	550,348	37,340	105,648	78,226
2008	4,264,200	3,050,681	57,342	3,108,023	382,517	72,286	2,797,792	836,096	630,312	39,774	107,210	79,890
2009	4,442,921	3,246,754	51,951	3,298,705	415,772	98,918	2,981,851	801,529	659,541	40,757	109,009	80,758
2010	4,859,072	3,497,659	59,926	3,557,585	421,212	112,934	3,249,307	881,399	728,366	43,729	111,119	82,274
2011	5,418,751	3,779,916	58,103	3,838,019	418,749	154,866	3,574,136	1,093,213	751,402	48,001	112,889	84,543
2012	6,140,998	4,100,466	157,162	4,257,628	424,074	220,813	4,054,367	1,322,399	764,232	53,064	115,728	88,020
2013	6,450,891	4,412,186	73,988	4,486,174	519,936	281,975	4,248,213	1,406,961	795,717	54,072	119,302	91,075
2014	7,059,980	4,802,860	50,759	4,853,619	569,675	332,302	4,616,246	1,587,536	856,198	57,004	123,850	93,393
2015	7,148,398	5,013,920	25,527	5,039,447	604,324	304,910	4,740,033	1,517,881	890,484	56,083	127,462	95,082
2016	7,079,103	4,997,670	20,899	5,018,569	609,750	264,767	4,673,586	1,485,592	919,925	54,545	129,785	94,914
2017	7,111,157	4,991,425	35,748	5,027,173	630,768	268,834	4,665,239	1,503,992	941,926	54,226	131,140	93,885
2018	7,424,596	5,102,996	25,160	5,128,156	626,435	281,521	4,783,242	1,628,493	1,012,861	56,328	131,811	93,404
2019	7,734,424	5,235,944	20,681	5,256,625	632,120	306,660	4,931,165	1,725,784	1,077,475	58,252	132,775	93,675
2020	8,122,410	5,343,654	79,630	5,423,284	665,351	263,122	5,021,055	1,686,884	1,414,471	60,766	133,666	92,067
2021	8,620,683	5,602,809	142,135	5,744,944	680,265	248,439	5,313,118	1,774,416	1,533,149	64,134	134,417	94,022

Personal Income and Employment by Area: Blacksburg-Christiansburg, VA

(Thousands of dollars, except as noted.)

Year	Personal income, total	Earnings by place of work			Less: Contributions for government social insurance	Plus: Adjustment for residence	Equals: Net earnings by place of residence	Plus: Dividends, interest, and rent	Plus: Personal current transfer receipts	Per capita personal income (dollars)	Population (persons)	Total employment
		Nonfarm	Farm	Total								
1970	335,464	291,005	3,517	294,522	18,674	-9,625	266,223	39,245	29,996	2,916	115,045	49,602
1971	359,393	303,774	3,480	307,254	20,368	-7,283	279,603	43,842	35,948	3,045	118,015	49,332
1972	405,115	342,380	5,497	347,877	24,187	-7,696	315,994	48,764	40,357	3,348	120,995	51,367
1973	463,509	389,006	5,989	394,995	31,566	-6,493	356,936	57,254	49,319	3,719	124,637	54,208
1974	513,456	423,545	3,673	427,218	35,812	-4,008	387,398	66,691	59,367	3,969	129,374	55,589
1975	566,031	445,318	2,466	447,784	36,957	-778	410,049	75,832	80,150	4,270	132,569	54,664
1976	632,223	497,462	4,474	501,936	41,894	265	460,307	83,946	87,970	4,704	134,388	56,066
1977	708,570	564,943	3,143	568,086	47,710	48	520,424	94,772	93,374	5,168	137,116	58,455
1978	808,838	646,087	5,140	651,227	55,965	671	595,933	109,632	103,273	5,779	139,973	61,737
1979	906,550	715,446	7,963	723,409	64,393	-520	658,496	127,474	120,580	6,413	141,368	63,660
1980	1,017,435	773,887	7,021	780,908	70,302	3,425	714,031	159,380	144,024	7,174	141,822	64,487
1981	1,118,359	832,596	4,556	837,152	81,279	4,407	760,280	191,801	166,278	7,794	143,481	63,247
1982	1,205,480	880,845	2,145	882,990	87,722	2,377	797,645	226,947	180,888	8,379	143,876	62,976
1983	1,319,131	975,062	5,436	980,498	98,504	-4,187	877,807	245,167	196,157	9,164	143,941	64,508
1984	1,473,420	1,111,926	6,653	1,118,579	115,917	-11,647	991,015	277,943	204,462	10,148	145,187	68,180
1985	1,575,086	1,198,865	5,447	1,204,312	126,974	-15,989	1,061,349	296,623	217,114	10,794	145,916	70,289
1986	1,674,747	1,280,380	7,149	1,287,529	139,607	-20,034	1,127,888	318,316	228,543	11,389	147,046	71,382
1987	1,788,695	1,388,395	16,600	1,404,995	149,787	-26,304	1,228,904	327,677	232,114	12,076	148,117	73,880
1988	1,932,312	1,519,525	18,940	1,538,465	168,842	-36,753	1,332,870	353,035	246,407	12,852	150,354	76,291
1989	2,070,289	1,599,220	21,935	1,621,155	177,761	-42,234	1,401,160	402,513	266,616	13,666	151,489	77,183
1990	2,149,409	1,649,935	22,893	1,672,828	183,297	-41,182	1,448,349	408,743	292,317	14,033	153,166	77,391
1991	2,180,806	1,634,178	18,421	1,652,599	183,662	-32,522	1,436,415	427,883	316,508	14,167	153,932	75,259
1992	2,298,730	1,725,405	16,396	1,741,801	192,718	-33,564	1,515,519	433,065	350,146	14,813	155,188	75,068
1993	2,390,952	1,795,786	13,579	1,809,365	200,436	-31,574	1,577,355	446,600	366,997	15,317	156,096	76,456
1994	2,529,809	1,911,175	13,357	1,924,532	211,220	-32,275	1,681,037	464,067	384,705	16,051	157,612	78,109
1995	2,662,916	1,972,832	11,046	1,983,878	217,257	-26,548	1,740,073	508,267	414,576	16,813	158,380	80,647
1996	2,754,298	2,029,878	9,239	2,039,117	221,187	-24,673	1,793,257	526,125	434,916	17,305	159,164	81,325
1997	2,948,493	2,180,732	7,357	2,188,089	235,847	-27,568	1,924,674	572,699	451,120	18,403	160,219	82,437
1998	2,844,344	2,228,590	5,012	2,233,602	236,411	-103,390	1,893,801	524,629	425,914	19,081	149,066	77,742
1999	3,021,178	2,422,161	3,918	2,426,079	255,810	-120,780	2,049,489	529,696	441,993	20,044	150,727	81,341
2000	3,193,060	2,517,489	10,937	2,528,426	264,386	-119,052	2,144,988	578,060	470,012	21,069	151,553	82,109
2001	3,342,172	2,600,273	9,104	2,609,377	285,975	-120,142	2,203,260	616,100	522,812	21,795	153,348	81,027
2002	3,460,034	2,729,085	7,908	2,736,993	300,396	-125,201	2,311,396	604,666	543,972	22,567	153,326	81,473
2003	3,637,378	2,866,300	4,220	2,870,520	312,167	-139,583	2,418,770	627,649	590,959	23,618	154,009	82,185
2004	3,817,097	3,011,528	8,789	3,020,317	330,954	-152,268	2,537,095	653,248	626,754	24,683	154,647	82,917
2005	4,018,021	3,165,423	9,418	3,174,841	355,337	-165,591	2,653,913	683,395	680,713	25,690	156,402	84,239
2006	4,253,600	3,299,917	2,115	3,302,032	375,123	-175,542	2,751,367	761,184	741,049	26,874	158,277	84,962
2007	4,511,579	3,415,476	-1,795	3,413,681	387,592	-172,040	2,854,049	864,665	792,865	28,182	160,085	85,719
2008	4,648,263	3,388,300	-1,242	3,387,058	391,572	-153,366	2,842,120	904,658	901,485	28,827	161,247	85,816
2009	4,666,627	3,307,204	79	3,307,283	383,792	-136,791	2,786,700	917,426	962,501	28,738	162,385	83,111
2010	4,696,167	3,321,017	953	3,321,970	384,426	-138,534	2,799,010	861,468	1,035,689	28,786	163,139	81,285
2011	4,892,255	3,413,156	6,585	3,419,741	355,487	-155,013	2,909,241	934,179	1,048,835	29,927	163,471	82,747
2012	5,095,615	3,591,045	8,303	3,599,348	371,534	-168,562	3,059,252	984,849	1,051,514	31,038	164,176	84,061
2013	5,160,021	3,717,051	9,473	3,726,524	429,089	-175,809	3,121,626	962,137	1,076,258	31,211	165,325	85,064
2014	5,433,270	3,889,000	11,712	3,900,712	447,093	-195,876	3,257,743	1,054,258	1,121,269	32,859	165,353	85,953
2015	5,673,141	4,074,727	9,304	4,084,031	466,039	-193,260	3,424,732	1,095,985	1,152,424	34,313	165,333	87,449
2016	5,808,161	4,132,721	1,013	4,133,734	471,649	-207,932	3,454,153	1,157,252	1,196,756	34,960	166,139	87,663
2017	5,996,830	4,245,466	5,500	4,250,966	489,657	-212,623	3,548,686	1,211,773	1,236,371	36,124	166,007	87,743
2018	6,299,824	4,491,362	2,070	4,493,432	518,170	-248,762	3,726,500	1,282,632	1,290,692	37,773	166,780	88,899
2019	6,487,253	4,591,469	4,559	4,596,028	537,475	-264,223	3,794,330	1,332,775	1,360,148	38,907	166,737	89,521
2020	6,864,032	4,590,433	3,144	4,593,577	544,663	-253,249	3,795,665	1,313,989	1,754,378	41,322	166,111	85,777
2021	7,422,393	5,089,637	3,812	5,093,449	595,223	-320,346	4,177,880	1,326,616	1,917,897	44,904	165,293	89,483

Personal Income and Employment by Area: Bloomington, IL

(Thousands of dollars, except as noted.)

Year	Personal income, total	Earnings by place of work Nonfarm	Earnings by place of work Farm	Earnings by place of work Total	Less: Contributions for government social insurance	Plus: Adjustment for residence	Equals: Net earnings by place of residence	Plus: Dividends, interest, and rent	Plus: Personal current transfer receipts	Per capita personal income (dollars)	Population (persons)	Total employment
1970	490,812	365,452	29,630	395,082	23,520	5,779	377,341	77,444	36,027	4,022	122,030	55,784
1971	546,799	403,982	39,221	443,203	26,753	5,818	422,268	83,591	40,940	4,376	124,949	57,171
1972	592,522	448,834	28,618	477,452	31,363	5,640	451,729	94,830	45,963	4,544	130,387	59,551
1973	703,300	497,947	71,492	569,439	40,161	6,581	535,859	113,892	53,549	5,336	131,804	62,641
1974	783,554	552,977	79,086	632,063	46,806	8,346	593,603	128,182	61,769	5,921	132,331	64,356
1975	917,951	617,865	115,397	733,262	50,512	9,068	691,818	146,152	79,981	6,973	131,642	64,245
1976	980,657	693,636	92,531	786,167	57,886	7,121	735,402	157,438	87,817	7,366	133,130	65,859
1977	1,075,006	785,019	85,863	870,882	66,262	651	805,271	177,414	92,321	7,977	134,758	68,361
1978	1,146,883	877,551	50,209	927,760	75,943	1,522	853,339	194,106	99,438	8,453	135,673	71,369
1979	1,288,875	990,143	67,792	1,057,935	90,113	-9,409	958,413	220,170	110,292	9,459	136,266	73,714
1980	1,369,395	1,064,989	13,240	1,078,229	96,731	-10,836	970,662	261,852	136,881	9,961	137,480	72,290
1981	1,567,817	1,175,991	53,382	1,229,373	115,975	-19,426	1,093,972	315,649	158,196	11,350	138,131	73,541
1982	1,676,607	1,239,559	31,970	1,271,529	123,132	-31,853	1,116,544	384,083	175,980	12,128	138,240	73,521
1983	1,711,983	1,338,115	-28,814	1,309,301	133,345	-52,032	1,123,924	398,659	189,400	12,290	139,295	74,776
1984	1,930,840	1,517,486	48,744	1,566,230	158,542	-111,947	1,295,741	440,778	194,321	13,804	139,879	77,336
1985	2,015,095	1,616,241	63,185	1,679,426	171,195	-137,555	1,370,676	437,083	207,336	14,357	140,360	76,738
1986	2,041,708	1,506,603	56,875	1,563,478	156,364	-36,109	1,371,005	455,741	214,962	14,607	139,774	74,708
1987	2,125,397	1,596,971	44,850	1,641,821	163,611	-20,234	1,457,976	445,108	222,313	15,068	141,058	76,745
1988	2,270,890	1,799,682	21,887	1,821,569	188,934	-53,085	1,579,550	456,768	234,572	15,920	142,641	81,146
1989	2,556,281	2,005,130	60,313	2,065,443	213,136	-78,657	1,773,650	535,988	246,643	17,731	144,167	85,475
1990	2,733,280	2,225,880	58,264	2,284,144	231,699	-100,422	1,952,023	514,462	266,795	18,687	146,269	87,860
1991	2,805,644	2,332,476	19,548	2,352,024	249,665	-110,159	1,992,200	528,180	285,264	18,853	148,813	89,538
1992	3,085,816	2,565,217	55,349	2,620,566	270,416	-129,074	2,221,076	546,041	318,699	20,453	150,875	92,071
1993	3,195,007	2,686,839	33,397	2,720,236	284,835	-135,751	2,299,650	561,296	334,061	20,807	153,557	93,063
1994	3,465,374	2,938,231	74,024	3,012,255	313,951	-155,033	2,543,271	580,502	341,601	22,290	155,467	96,956
1995	3,635,438	3,137,017	-3,723	3,133,294	332,327	-175,429	2,625,538	642,522	367,378	23,043	157,769	99,502
1996	3,912,016	3,266,741	91,253	3,357,994	340,464	-182,512	2,835,018	686,924	390,074	24,589	159,099	101,224
1997	4,118,727	3,441,494	77,821	3,519,315	354,331	-191,447	2,973,537	741,837	403,353	25,566	161,099	104,868
1998	3,942,365	3,441,991	19,716	3,461,707	346,448	-226,302	2,888,957	698,314	355,094	26,906	146,526	100,753
1999	4,265,113	3,830,848	24,808	3,855,656	377,888	-277,500	3,200,268	699,504	365,341	28,599	149,135	106,179
2000	4,534,227	4,060,709	55,570	4,116,279	396,157	-314,850	3,405,272	742,611	386,344	30,059	150,844	108,052
2001	4,903,592	4,461,950	58,547	4,520,497	442,049	-343,258	3,735,190	751,863	416,539	32,110	152,713	109,029
2002	5,051,363	4,746,267	47,167	4,793,434	469,806	-384,441	3,939,187	667,073	445,103	32,405	155,882	110,523
2003	5,238,481	4,904,666	57,310	4,961,976	486,478	-413,067	4,062,431	709,932	466,118	33,198	157,795	110,088
2004	5,413,528	4,969,388	104,248	5,073,636	504,363	-422,271	4,147,002	772,651	493,875	34,027	159,096	109,225
2005	5,497,950	5,084,670	52,634	5,137,304	514,298	-416,689	4,206,317	744,218	547,415	34,298	160,299	109,996
2006	5,973,715	5,426,775	70,791	5,497,566	545,516	-435,825	4,516,225	882,699	574,791	36,665	162,925	110,931
2007	6,241,272	5,535,654	126,666	5,662,320	560,534	-422,315	4,679,471	932,175	629,626	37,775	165,223	112,603
2008	6,599,839	5,758,696	172,186	5,930,882	587,797	-436,776	4,906,309	975,916	717,614	39,561	166,825	113,546
2009	6,599,555	5,791,413	97,262	5,888,675	589,026	-455,568	4,844,081	960,046	795,428	39,114	168,727	111,824
2010	6,855,885	6,003,759	99,954	6,103,713	602,389	-501,021	5,000,303	970,976	884,606	40,373	169,815	111,398
2011	7,243,433	6,169,947	197,499	6,367,446	552,815	-487,713	5,326,918	1,042,630	873,885	42,374	170,939	112,002
2012	7,400,151	6,359,593	122,624	6,482,217	574,902	-525,123	5,382,192	1,147,989	869,970	42,834	172,762	113,158
2013	7,643,206	6,565,268	291,243	6,856,511	667,501	-584,407	5,604,603	1,137,397	901,206	43,654	175,087	111,461
2014	7,618,046	6,496,432	141,741	6,638,173	657,165	-512,652	5,468,356	1,228,141	921,549	43,774	174,031	110,664
2015	7,987,415	6,696,589	30,475	6,727,064	665,668	-362,484	5,698,912	1,298,934	989,569	46,155	173,055	112,393
2016	8,120,297	6,699,774	118,736	6,818,510	672,210	-375,977	5,770,323	1,337,313	1,012,661	46,950	172,957	111,454
2017	8,174,361	6,707,416	78,944	6,786,360	673,306	-362,098	5,750,956	1,371,853	1,051,552	47,378	172,536	111,863
2018	8,499,246	6,941,503	106,832	7,048,335	694,585	-379,309	5,974,441	1,422,942	1,101,863	49,385	172,103	111,520
2019	8,574,798	6,889,148	63,019	6,952,167	693,056	-366,345	5,892,766	1,514,007	1,168,025	50,152	170,976	110,651
2020	9,432,566	7,414,650	125,645	7,540,295	753,167	-483,951	6,303,177	1,516,622	1,612,767	55,203	170,870	107,144
2021	9,997,479	7,686,321	244,538	7,930,859	771,592	-484,864	6,674,403	1,528,624	1,794,452	58,503	170,889	109,584

Personal Income and Employment by Area: Bloomington, IN

(Thousands of dollars, except as noted.)

Year	Personal income, total	Earnings by place of work			Less: Contributions for government social insurance	Plus: Adjustment for residence	Equals: Net earnings by place of residence	Plus: Dividends, interest, and rent	Plus: Personal current transfer receipts	Per capita personal income (dollars)	Population (persons)	Total employment
		Nonfarm	Farm	Total								
1970	295,962	245,530	1,772	247,302	16,732	-2,338	228,232	46,647	21,083	3,031	97,656	40,115
1971	339,662	284,719	2,718	287,437	20,166	-4,207	263,064	52,579	24,019	3,406	99,712	43,719
1972	372,513	307,737	3,263	311,000	23,115	-682	287,203	57,952	27,358	3,597	103,553	45,422
1973	417,304	339,642	6,908	346,550	29,379	1,126	318,297	65,496	33,511	4,001	104,311	47,027
1974	449,449	357,808	4,027	361,835	32,425	4,273	333,683	75,322	40,444	4,231	106,218	46,825
1975	486,091	360,750	3,663	364,413	32,416	12,169	344,166	86,349	55,576	4,676	103,965	44,564
1976	551,508	419,148	5,377	424,525	37,758	13,308	400,075	95,585	55,848	5,206	105,944	47,509
1977	620,179	471,357	3,593	474,950	42,021	18,067	450,996	108,966	60,217	5,647	109,821	48,817
1978	707,249	535,610	3,150	538,760	49,020	24,014	513,754	125,161	68,334	6,302	112,226	50,475
1979	778,383	578,870	2,958	581,828	54,893	33,960	560,895	138,787	78,701	6,886	113,041	51,520
1980	875,590	634,954	-424	634,530	59,704	37,379	612,205	171,123	92,262	7,610	115,057	53,462
1981	983,597	700,631	3	700,634	71,211	38,864	668,287	210,018	105,292	8,440	116,537	54,013
1982	1,049,632	737,043	27	737,070	76,225	36,206	697,051	235,380	117,201	8,932	117,520	54,716
1983	1,124,867	802,262	-6,533	795,729	82,352	31,933	745,310	253,534	126,023	9,530	118,037	55,528
1984	1,235,117	880,014	-150	879,864	91,264	36,295	824,895	277,300	132,922	10,472	117,945	57,620
1985	1,322,254	947,634	-1,712	945,922	99,460	38,674	885,136	295,799	141,319	11,192	118,146	59,678
1986	1,432,339	1,045,555	-2,662	1,042,893	110,086	35,283	968,090	317,806	146,443	12,032	119,043	61,907
1987	1,539,923	1,151,256	-1,707	1,149,549	118,969	28,128	1,058,708	326,946	154,269	12,780	120,497	65,078
1988	1,662,395	1,251,405	-4,104	1,247,301	135,487	25,857	1,137,671	358,003	166,721	13,614	122,111	67,474
1989	1,831,845	1,353,762	1,960	1,355,722	146,849	26,440	1,235,313	412,209	184,323	14,672	124,856	68,835
1990	1,963,426	1,450,795	6	1,450,801	161,910	28,689	1,317,580	443,718	202,128	15,488	126,773	70,276
1991	2,070,731	1,543,240	-1,831	1,541,409	173,933	27,578	1,395,054	450,575	225,102	16,180	127,983	70,628
1992	2,233,800	1,674,679	2,602	1,677,281	187,554	19,265	1,508,992	472,388	252,420	17,166	130,131	72,264
1993	2,333,948	1,762,577	2,007	1,764,584	198,452	7,109	1,573,241	492,607	268,100	17,629	132,395	74,141
1994	2,448,178	1,856,263	2,090	1,858,353	213,630	-9,161	1,635,562	534,252	278,364	18,178	134,678	75,988
1995	2,579,856	1,950,252	50	1,950,302	224,497	-13,051	1,712,754	578,573	288,529	18,931	136,275	78,167
1996	2,741,973	2,061,017	2,885	2,063,902	235,628	-23,395	1,804,879	621,432	315,662	19,899	137,794	80,732
1997	2,919,063	2,208,500	2,638	2,211,138	251,722	-36,313	1,923,103	666,265	329,695	20,960	139,271	82,095
1998	3,108,752	2,343,880	-566	2,343,314	262,697	-43,185	2,037,432	709,306	362,014	22,122	140,527	82,583
1999	3,251,905	2,480,930	-1,511	2,479,419	275,245	-51,496	2,152,678	710,961	388,266	22,938	141,770	84,309
2000	3,463,734	2,633,042	792	2,633,834	289,429	-61,788	2,282,617	764,074	417,043	24,271	142,709	85,477
2001	3,530,281	2,639,104	1,579	2,640,683	285,517	-67,074	2,288,092	784,175	458,014	24,576	143,650	86,472
2002	3,589,925	2,744,548	-356	2,744,192	296,646	-73,285	2,374,261	732,041	483,623	24,808	144,707	86,455
2003	3,774,514	2,890,934	3,461	2,894,395	314,116	-90,637	2,489,642	779,603	505,269	25,706	146,835	88,861
2004	4,003,726	3,004,633	7,656	3,012,289	327,716	-98,686	2,585,887	883,402	534,437	26,952	148,549	90,050
2005	4,142,036	3,113,808	5,211	3,119,019	345,004	-100,176	2,673,839	883,129	585,068	27,596	150,096	90,907
2006	4,395,962	3,230,539	2,643	3,233,182	361,448	-103,980	2,767,754	990,857	637,351	28,817	152,548	92,092
2007	4,558,023	3,339,134	4,539	3,343,673	377,803	-113,037	2,852,833	1,032,473	672,717	29,530	154,352	94,409
2008	4,879,581	3,445,614	7,899	3,453,513	391,779	-121,911	2,939,823	1,153,265	786,493	31,247	156,164	94,475
2009	4,838,905	3,470,103	8,256	3,478,359	395,412	-116,596	2,966,351	1,022,893	849,661	30,657	157,840	94,200
2010	4,965,941	3,514,359	10,533	3,524,892	395,372	-104,375	3,025,145	1,011,580	929,216	31,010	160,140	93,020
2011	5,250,474	3,648,620	13,108	3,661,728	358,388	-93,581	3,209,759	1,107,902	932,813	32,457	161,769	93,309
2012	5,488,466	3,807,294	3,075	3,810,369	370,821	-77,599	3,361,949	1,164,714	961,803	33,684	162,938	92,926
2013	5,494,001	3,818,366	19,608	3,837,974	428,201	-74,066	3,335,707	1,194,950	963,344	33,636	163,337	92,762
2014	5,773,122	3,971,413	3,378	3,974,791	443,341	-80,698	3,450,752	1,275,267	1,047,103	35,803	161,248	93,841
2015	6,066,095	4,205,150	-1,839	4,203,311	467,071	-96,185	3,640,055	1,334,418	1,091,622	37,645	161,138	94,441
2016	6,375,132	4,412,599	7,139	4,419,738	481,448	-88,223	3,850,067	1,387,978	1,137,087	39,379	161,893	95,314
2017	6,718,810	4,676,937	1,710	4,678,647	509,137	-92,694	4,076,816	1,480,493	1,161,501	41,509	161,864	97,286
2018	7,020,043	4,880,016	2,359	4,882,375	526,113	-82,602	4,273,660	1,529,593	1,216,790	43,405	161,733	99,297
2019	7,344,856	5,101,104	103	5,101,207	555,426	-105,133	4,440,648	1,610,298	1,293,910	45,426	161,687	100,288
2020	7,781,173	5,255,558	9,031	5,264,589	591,782	-147,726	4,525,081	1,610,102	1,645,990	48,386	160,815	97,534
2021	8,372,366	5,683,310	14,564	5,697,874	626,230	-202,211	4,869,433	1,630,460	1,872,473	51,899	161,321	100,111

Personal Income and Employment by Area: Bloomsberg-Berwick, PA

(Thousands of dollars, except as noted.)

Year	Personal income, total	Earnings by place of work			Less: Contributions for government social insurance	Plus: Adjustment for residence	Equals: Net earnings by place of residence	Plus: Dividends, interest, and rent	Plus: Personal current transfer receipts	Per capita personal income (dollars)	Population (persons)	Total employment
		Nonfarm	Farm	Total								
1970	250,744	206,101	6,163	212,264	15,627	-11,192	185,445	30,231	35,068	3,488	71,882	33,766
1971	267,673	218,976	4,975	223,951	17,361	-8,829	197,761	32,696	37,216	3,655	73,233	33,943
1972	303,979	249,270	4,873	254,143	20,463	-9,182	224,498	36,461	43,020	4,080	74,511	35,339
1973	344,214	282,155	7,632	289,787	26,299	-9,585	253,903	42,002	48,309	4,577	75,213	37,183
1974	382,390	313,792	7,241	321,033	30,729	-14,991	275,313	48,051	59,026	5,021	76,162	37,830
1975	412,614	309,436	7,075	316,511	28,978	-5,749	281,784	52,710	78,120	5,364	76,926	35,596
1976	450,624	332,725	8,236	340,961	31,763	-3,376	305,822	56,924	87,878	5,847	77,069	35,569
1977	489,756	369,040	7,012	376,052	35,346	-5,216	335,490	64,086	90,180	6,323	77,452	36,182
1978	546,098	421,502	7,769	429,271	41,398	-8,244	379,629	70,805	95,664	7,020	77,789	37,911
1979	611,134	476,008	10,442	486,450	48,245	-14,956	423,249	78,668	109,217	7,796	78,394	38,953
1980	659,398	502,503	5,215	507,718	51,415	-19,705	436,598	96,977	125,823	8,369	78,787	38,905
1981	734,265	542,114	9,826	551,940	59,321	-20,012	472,607	118,682	142,976	9,270	79,211	38,916
1982	785,807	559,300	8,196	567,496	61,708	-20,217	485,571	138,316	161,920	9,919	79,223	37,763
1983	836,923	607,619	-1,411	606,208	67,718	-28,282	510,208	153,426	173,289	10,504	79,674	38,203
1984	902,402	663,927	7,281	671,208	76,996	-37,327	556,885	169,843	175,674	11,403	79,135	39,057
1985	965,954	725,646	8,420	734,066	85,560	-48,209	600,297	183,880	181,777	12,277	78,679	40,396
1986	1,015,938	758,597	6,188	764,785	89,567	-46,058	629,160	195,094	191,684	12,904	78,729	40,797
1987	1,072,407	814,135	7,788	821,923	94,966	-49,643	677,314	200,317	194,776	13,623	78,718	41,605
1988	1,156,290	887,567	9,295	896,862	106,285	-51,226	739,351	211,158	205,781	14,554	79,446	43,282
1989	1,262,724	952,530	12,390	964,920	112,265	-57,291	795,364	241,108	226,252	15,740	80,226	44,433
1990	1,318,551	1,018,861	11,032	1,029,893	120,234	-68,356	841,303	242,909	234,339	16,256	81,113	45,090
1991	1,386,457	1,063,339	3,361	1,066,700	126,958	-77,757	861,985	251,012	273,460	16,977	81,669	44,976
1992	1,474,922	1,154,012	18,069	1,172,081	137,573	-100,202	934,306	253,821	286,795	17,904	82,381	45,346
1993	1,527,400	1,211,594	15,083	1,226,677	146,651	-111,035	968,991	261,758	296,651	18,446	82,802	45,742
1994	1,566,890	1,291,421	15,604	1,307,025	159,541	-134,793	1,012,691	264,464	289,735	18,924	82,801	46,889
1995	1,618,697	1,256,991	5,784	1,262,775	154,393	-83,180	1,025,202	290,669	302,826	19,500	83,012	46,421
1996	1,676,366	1,263,296	15,878	1,279,174	151,946	-66,384	1,060,844	294,246	321,276	20,194	83,013	45,448
1997	1,731,032	1,347,040	14,226	1,361,266	161,202	-108,159	1,091,905	311,796	327,331	20,877	82,914	45,712
1998	1,804,833	1,480,203	12,366	1,492,569	173,093	-163,352	1,156,124	323,429	325,280	21,844	82,623	47,654
1999	1,849,167	1,546,587	8,392	1,554,979	177,329	-174,267	1,203,383	307,930	337,854	22,428	82,449	47,905
2000	1,974,418	1,593,669	15,455	1,609,124	180,255	-141,578	1,287,291	325,916	361,211	24,016	82,211	48,593
2001	2,054,192	1,596,968	10,948	1,607,916	180,680	-102,868	1,324,368	341,087	388,737	24,872	82,592	46,782
2002	2,176,574	1,707,785	5,975	1,713,760	190,816	-105,420	1,417,524	340,524	418,526	26,275	82,838	47,456
2003	2,272,358	1,743,993	15,517	1,759,510	192,731	-76,591	1,490,188	341,359	440,811	27,299	83,240	47,107
2004	2,350,046	1,865,083	23,544	1,888,627	205,739	-124,750	1,558,138	331,988	459,920	28,141	83,511	48,150
2005	2,420,121	1,955,460	17,722	1,973,182	218,402	-147,109	1,607,671	317,690	494,760	28,908	83,718	49,459
2006	2,538,518	2,065,598	16,258	2,081,856	230,710	-167,148	1,683,998	338,978	515,542	30,222	83,996	50,639
2007	2,717,872	2,206,108	14,849	2,220,957	247,073	-193,478	1,780,406	383,736	553,730	32,239	84,303	51,636
2008	2,862,154	2,280,346	10,492	2,290,838	258,398	-230,911	1,801,529	437,284	623,341	33,778	84,735	52,004
2009	2,833,927	2,285,844	8,421	2,294,265	261,015	-302,000	1,731,250	416,028	686,649	33,190	85,385	51,230
2010	2,987,652	2,401,698	16,403	2,418,101	271,973	-288,590	1,857,538	422,516	707,598	34,881	85,653	51,591
2011	3,134,855	2,540,737	14,811	2,555,548	254,857	-335,772	1,964,919	448,002	721,934	36,687	85,448	52,582
2012	3,213,581	2,623,778	22,117	2,645,895	260,633	-354,612	2,030,650	465,214	717,717	37,597	85,474	53,550
2013	3,291,793	2,781,205	27,601	2,808,806	307,652	-418,331	2,082,823	479,052	729,918	38,455	85,601	54,477
2014	3,354,781	2,728,813	24,063	2,752,876	308,641	-354,992	2,089,243	504,068	761,470	39,223	85,531	53,086
2015	3,466,422	2,830,818	16,734	2,847,552	319,199	-371,706	2,156,647	518,627	791,148	40,794	84,973	52,723
2016	3,558,213	2,901,939	4,747	2,906,686	325,655	-350,727	2,230,304	513,503	814,406	42,169	84,379	52,694
2017	3,677,455	3,000,135	14,154	3,014,289	344,199	-366,493	2,303,597	551,321	822,537	43,855	83,855	52,892
2018	3,790,888	3,066,676	8,165	3,074,841	348,689	-374,870	2,351,282	564,940	874,666	45,452	83,405	52,813
2019	3,873,813	3,139,300	15,662	3,154,962	359,674	-425,335	2,369,953	587,301	916,559	46,588	83,150	53,058
2020	4,175,226	3,157,804	12,206	3,170,010	362,164	-435,010	2,372,836	588,298	1,214,092	50,436	82,782	51,249
2021	4,422,467	3,315,310	26,723	3,342,033	375,583	-447,430	2,519,020	592,759	1,310,688	53,309	82,959	52,193

Personal Income and Employment by Area: Boise City, ID

(Thousands of dollars, except as noted.)

					Derivation of personal income							
		Earnings by place of work			Less: Contributions for government social insurance	Plus: Adjustment for residence	Equals: Net earnings by place of residence	Plus: Dividends, interest, and rent	Plus: Personal current transfer receipts	Per capita personal income (dollars)	Population (persons)	Total employment
Year	Personal income, total	Nonfarm	Farm	Total								
1970	779,735	574,503	42,703	617,206	40,945	4,147	580,408	133,624	65,703	4,042	192,885	93,530
1971	875,459	645,302	42,222	687,524	47,174	4,019	644,369	153,300	77,790	4,322	202,549	97,869
1972	996,230	744,039	49,919	793,958	57,213	3,496	740,241	167,099	88,890	4,709	211,579	103,513
1973	1,146,673	849,734	74,955	924,689	76,192	3,112	851,609	192,729	102,335	5,214	219,916	110,066
1974	1,319,146	965,328	87,151	1,052,479	88,942	3,533	967,070	226,367	125,709	5,733	230,081	114,790
1975	1,511,201	1,118,116	64,001	1,182,117	101,179	6,646	1,087,584	269,165	154,452	6,382	236,798	119,885
1976	1,703,255	1,302,391	52,111	1,354,502	120,033	7,997	1,242,466	292,150	168,639	6,915	246,322	128,647
1977	1,919,604	1,490,477	39,297	1,529,774	138,147	10,256	1,401,883	337,244	180,477	7,499	255,984	136,175
1978	2,225,440	1,746,071	47,195	1,793,266	163,952	12,028	1,641,342	384,840	199,258	8,330	267,147	146,795
1979	2,448,845	1,913,838	42,590	1,956,428	190,026	15,110	1,781,512	430,112	237,221	8,874	275,953	150,083
1980	2,715,190	2,045,709	62,521	2,108,230	205,087	15,438	1,918,581	508,015	288,594	9,650	281,376	148,453
1981	2,992,865	2,207,009	64,806	2,271,815	239,179	18,793	2,051,429	611,326	330,110	10,468	285,918	146,355
1982	3,202,197	2,280,504	66,400	2,346,904	252,351	15,708	2,110,261	716,249	375,687	11,066	289,363	145,330
1983	3,471,725	2,449,761	93,734	2,543,495	271,882	16,562	2,288,175	781,503	402,047	11,874	292,391	148,415
1984	3,767,611	2,701,653	84,064	2,785,717	307,614	14,476	2,492,579	859,873	415,159	12,683	297,051	154,103
1985	4,037,683	2,886,607	76,445	2,963,052	334,317	12,063	2,640,798	950,209	446,676	13,408	301,145	156,609
1986	4,163,993	2,979,838	77,450	3,057,288	347,902	12,836	2,722,222	969,845	471,926	13,754	302,755	158,446
1987	4,380,898	3,175,513	89,486	3,264,999	361,845	12,405	2,915,559	977,973	487,366	14,424	303,727	163,218
1988	4,809,880	3,561,184	100,905	3,662,089	422,204	9,423	3,249,308	1,039,163	521,409	15,695	306,455	172,597
1989	5,292,858	3,897,915	135,821	4,033,736	468,796	6,977	3,571,917	1,155,656	565,285	16,912	312,962	181,032
1990	5,757,151	4,272,798	145,370	4,418,168	543,905	11,592	3,885,855	1,263,559	607,737	17,862	322,316	190,433
1991	6,186,865	4,654,453	149,546	4,803,999	605,818	9,628	4,207,809	1,294,068	684,988	18,447	335,378	198,902
1992	6,934,761	5,296,795	143,780	5,440,575	674,563	9,581	4,775,593	1,390,227	768,941	19,948	347,646	207,984
1993	7,750,940	5,953,007	192,678	6,145,685	758,923	5,427	5,392,189	1,530,575	828,176	21,287	364,123	220,250
1994	8,604,211	6,676,807	134,865	6,811,672	855,552	10,394	5,966,514	1,756,729	880,968	22,633	380,160	236,337
1995	9,363,965	7,217,877	132,566	7,350,443	931,138	15,141	6,434,446	1,956,699	972,820	23,683	395,382	245,882
1996	9,900,474	7,562,474	135,754	7,698,228	957,172	15,618	6,756,674	2,095,081	1,048,719	24,179	409,471	255,743
1997	10,425,733	7,949,378	121,237	8,070,615	999,287	19,051	7,090,379	2,245,210	1,090,144	24,659	422,797	266,539
1998	11,444,764	8,679,243	155,169	8,834,412	1,075,034	20,059	7,779,437	2,487,584	1,177,743	26,105	438,421	279,851
1999	12,420,883	9,626,878	150,283	9,777,161	1,159,224	23,671	8,641,608	2,517,106	1,262,169	27,429	452,837	287,846
2000	13,907,878	10,991,436	147,349	11,138,785	1,317,635	25,516	9,846,666	2,693,155	1,368,057	29,653	469,017	304,508
2001	14,193,813	11,030,879	181,107	11,211,986	1,326,071	30,618	9,916,533	2,751,589	1,525,691	29,201	486,078	311,229
2002	14,774,324	11,404,835	168,084	11,572,919	1,343,255	42,516	10,272,180	2,811,425	1,690,719	29,549	499,994	313,222
2003	15,310,987	11,692,889	139,377	11,832,266	1,388,577	45,796	10,489,485	3,010,967	1,810,535	29,876	512,491	317,239
2004	16,516,058	12,452,373	214,950	12,667,323	1,490,680	46,305	11,222,948	3,356,149	1,936,961	31,401	525,975	328,238
2005	17,693,873	13,348,298	190,427	13,538,725	1,626,095	64,235	11,976,865	3,592,220	2,124,788	32,348	546,980	346,498
2006	19,884,957	14,889,873	164,888	15,054,761	1,833,479	33,384	13,254,666	4,322,209	2,308,082	34,850	570,583	367,714
2007	20,864,663	15,367,463	241,629	15,609,092	1,897,889	57,237	13,768,440	4,549,897	2,546,326	35,344	590,330	379,138
2008	20,932,163	15,057,639	228,444	15,286,083	1,876,568	84,701	13,494,216	4,380,396	3,057,551	34,701	603,218	373,367
2009	20,241,149	14,589,960	103,544	14,693,504	1,820,750	159,454	13,032,208	3,761,028	3,447,913	33,109	611,341	353,830
2010	20,855,803	14,672,680	222,399	14,895,079	1,898,951	193,696	13,189,824	3,841,551	3,824,428	33,753	617,899	350,361
2011	21,971,435	15,069,427	299,623	15,369,050	1,746,172	238,752	13,861,630	4,277,012	3,832,793	34,997	627,804	356,775
2012	23,330,950	15,599,652	318,282	15,917,934	1,794,041	290,823	14,414,716	4,991,979	3,924,255	36,589	637,657	361,944
2013	24,481,275	16,948,481	331,992	17,280,473	2,106,846	326,069	15,499,696	4,887,673	4,093,906	37,690	649,541	372,414
2014	26,239,685	18,120,877	359,230	18,480,107	2,218,684	343,563	16,604,986	5,321,890	4,312,809	39,583	662,904	383,129
2015	27,858,704	19,171,041	326,637	19,497,678	2,334,423	314,069	17,477,324	5,807,752	4,573,628	41,273	674,981	395,866
2016	29,174,046	20,071,664	293,925	20,365,589	2,463,903	332,286	18,233,972	6,142,475	4,797,599	42,178	691,695	411,070
2017	31,179,596	21,717,357	234,080	21,951,437	2,650,018	335,264	19,636,683	6,492,673	5,050,240	43,912	710,044	427,320
2018	33,613,762	23,474,019	236,550	23,710,569	2,863,113	332,633	21,180,089	7,034,229	5,399,444	46,092	729,282	448,880
2019	36,277,012	24,979,517	298,077	25,277,594	3,045,933	320,232	22,551,893	7,905,296	5,819,823	48,396	749,581	463,999
2020	40,152,284	27,102,059	327,301	27,429,360	3,334,695	327,502	24,422,167	8,147,303	7,582,814	52,174	769,581	472,504
2021	44,127,185	30,040,986	240,153	30,281,139	3,601,293	280,495	26,960,341	8,526,945	8,639,899	55,487	795,268	497,804

Personal Income and Employment by Area: Boston-Cambridge-Newton, MA-NH

(Thousands of dollars, except as noted.)

Year	Personal income, total	Earnings by place of work			Less: Contributions for government social insurance	Plus: Adjustment for residence	Equals: Net earnings by place of residence	Plus: Dividends, interest, and rent	Plus: Personal current transfer receipts	Per capita personal income (dollars)	Population (persons)	Total employment
		Nonfarm	Farm	Total								
1970	18,740,176	15,238,914	28,963	15,267,877	969,109	-250,943	14,047,825	2,956,834	1,735,517	4,770	3,928,508	1,906,572
1971	20,020,412	16,180,918	27,487	16,208,405	1,061,528	-306,074	14,840,803	3,132,887	2,046,722	5,064	3,953,760	1,880,515
1972	21,594,282	17,579,606	29,773	17,609,379	1,211,526	-373,090	16,024,763	3,322,375	2,247,144	5,425	3,980,347	1,918,584
1973	23,369,418	19,146,754	32,016	19,178,770	1,515,854	-461,314	17,201,602	3,645,133	2,522,683	5,867	3,982,918	1,976,758
1974	25,216,971	20,325,075	30,843	20,355,918	1,663,210	-547,831	18,144,877	4,065,765	3,006,329	6,352	3,969,705	1,995,376
1975	26,958,682	21,255,778	32,501	21,288,279	1,692,392	-632,845	18,963,042	4,199,728	3,795,912	6,819	3,953,504	1,943,843
1976	28,988,024	23,089,919	36,941	23,126,860	1,878,742	-743,612	20,504,506	4,507,373	3,976,145	7,345	3,946,719	1,961,507
1977	31,575,637	25,498,977	39,821	25,538,798	2,078,220	-930,894	22,529,684	4,980,850	4,065,103	7,999	3,947,472	2,021,580
1978	34,874,102	28,644,337	50,711	28,695,048	2,404,024	-1,179,412	25,111,612	5,467,860	4,294,630	8,842	3,944,294	2,118,025
1979	38,842,908	32,274,276	49,871	32,324,147	2,826,669	-1,457,149	28,040,329	6,105,362	4,697,217	9,852	3,942,625	2,213,716
1980	43,921,452	36,087,528	59,301	36,146,829	3,172,323	-1,787,547	31,186,959	7,390,134	5,344,359	11,130	3,946,114	2,271,006
1981	49,271,786	39,821,372	61,881	39,883,253	3,786,086	-1,980,790	34,116,377	9,085,353	6,070,056	12,421	3,966,836	2,288,684
1982	54,290,274	43,175,506	71,846	43,247,352	4,217,874	-2,182,492	36,846,986	10,939,512	6,503,776	13,650	3,977,211	2,304,308
1983	59,199,900	47,930,787	93,378	48,024,165	4,762,616	-2,450,105	40,811,444	11,498,679	6,889,777	14,775	4,006,648	2,364,109
1984	67,016,058	54,621,754	96,576	54,718,330	5,601,867	-2,806,856	46,309,607	13,457,036	7,249,415	16,594	4,038,686	2,509,018
1985	72,686,413	60,146,142	83,269	60,229,411	6,241,202	-3,102,538	50,885,671	14,253,445	7,547,297	17,851	4,071,845	2,591,649
1986	78,488,998	65,421,072	88,426	65,509,498	6,932,105	-3,314,520	55,262,873	15,327,121	7,899,004	19,197	4,088,650	2,660,368
1987	85,049,895	71,704,507	79,340	71,783,847	7,518,153	-3,591,271	60,674,423	16,304,135	8,071,337	20,720	4,104,797	2,682,717
1988	93,972,761	79,054,496	94,044	79,148,540	8,407,372	-3,948,663	66,792,505	18,450,528	8,729,728	22,780	4,125,293	2,758,108
1989	99,301,380	82,231,809	80,238	82,312,047	8,689,863	-4,062,384	69,559,800	19,918,697	9,822,883	23,989	4,139,484	2,735,161
1990	102,262,812	83,295,942	78,374	83,374,316	8,743,141	-4,220,117	70,411,058	20,838,524	11,013,230	24,717	4,137,302	2,665,144
1991	103,975,559	83,460,145	95,748	83,555,893	8,918,557	-4,176,836	70,460,500	20,862,492	12,652,567	25,187	4,128,150	2,541,026
1992	109,710,065	88,716,165	97,012	88,813,177	9,416,088	-4,306,428	75,090,661	21,379,516	13,239,888	26,515	4,137,692	2,555,157
1993	114,095,209	92,389,532	96,751	92,486,283	9,866,980	-4,450,400	78,168,903	22,325,382	13,600,924	27,402	4,163,698	2,603,207
1994	119,824,758	97,285,822	85,358	97,371,180	10,519,475	-4,828,291	82,023,414	23,388,679	14,412,665	28,603	4,189,180	2,655,650
1995	127,433,681	103,307,414	89,064	103,396,478	11,225,962	-5,320,083	86,850,433	25,264,463	15,318,785	30,121	4,230,795	2,685,848
1996	135,889,771	110,564,610	93,865	110,658,475	11,888,420	-5,660,085	93,109,970	27,008,492	15,771,309	31,857	4,265,564	2,740,663
1997	144,739,232	118,842,425	91,918	118,934,343	12,809,869	-6,630,096	99,494,378	28,930,630	16,314,224	33,639	4,302,696	2,813,151
1998	154,955,005	128,057,917	60,552	128,118,469	13,741,716	-7,301,778	107,074,975	31,490,496	16,389,534	35,722	4,337,751	2,889,492
1999	166,600,539	140,634,220	53,847	140,688,067	14,842,772	-8,453,737	117,391,558	32,274,522	16,934,459	38,126	4,369,743	2,941,149
2000	187,340,509	159,789,607	64,743	159,854,350	16,565,380	-10,018,985	133,269,985	36,215,767	17,854,757	42,565	4,401,256	3,027,183
2001	193,251,714	163,740,905	54,833	163,795,738	16,817,846	-10,386,385	136,591,507	37,139,451	19,520,756	43,602	4,432,132	3,031,090
2002	191,085,395	161,255,578	69,146	161,324,724	16,637,668	-10,070,715	134,616,341	35,320,592	21,148,462	43,037	4,440,034	2,977,857
2003	193,927,420	162,754,544	72,388	162,826,932	16,743,174	-10,033,899	136,049,859	35,630,084	22,247,477	43,729	4,434,723	2,947,152
2004	204,311,368	173,999,551	78,518	174,078,069	18,186,655	-11,009,869	144,881,545	36,238,834	23,190,989	46,173	4,424,956	2,973,111
2005	214,410,947	179,531,093	63,246	179,594,339	18,995,745	-11,303,716	149,294,878	40,321,050	24,795,019	48,531	4,418,046	3,013,744
2006	232,453,100	190,564,613	75,782	190,640,395	19,749,913	-12,122,554	158,767,928	47,701,736	25,983,436	52,504	4,427,356	3,051,211
2007	245,076,259	200,660,820	78,306	200,739,126	20,798,237	-12,797,170	167,143,719	50,784,345	27,148,195	55,100	4,447,838	3,131,667
2008	254,305,370	204,951,342	122,812	205,074,154	21,500,151	-12,582,828	170,991,175	52,171,816	31,142,379	56,725	4,483,141	3,150,417
2009	250,823,803	204,527,338	100,632	204,627,970	21,258,788	-11,843,658	171,525,524	45,311,687	33,986,592	55,403	4,527,220	3,081,345
2010	264,820,177	217,480,223	98,707	217,578,930	21,814,477	-12,445,003	183,319,450	45,629,629	35,871,098	57,993	4,566,448	3,085,620
2011	277,269,108	224,057,599	121,090	224,178,689	20,238,088	-13,025,749	190,914,852	50,341,517	36,012,739	60,142	4,610,267	3,132,923
2012	289,512,591	231,788,634	174,808	231,963,442	20,969,245	-14,120,513	196,873,684	56,537,869	36,101,038	62,160	4,657,545	3,190,639
2013	292,115,726	238,021,621	154,767	238,176,388	24,425,192	-13,883,852	199,867,344	55,771,431	36,476,951	62,096	4,704,297	3,268,018
2014	307,960,766	247,530,731	130,913	247,661,644	25,657,152	-13,814,628	208,189,864	62,075,053	37,695,849	64,507	4,774,046	3,344,569
2015	329,417,797	262,802,603	118,720	262,921,323	26,747,608	-14,732,073	221,441,642	67,479,302	40,496,853	68,453	4,812,312	3,490,822
2016	342,700,021	272,657,373	132,154	272,789,527	27,683,877	-15,794,464	229,311,186	71,240,933	42,147,902	70,664	4,849,741	3,557,001
2017	359,730,194	287,093,486	112,735	287,206,221	29,147,408	-16,330,946	241,727,867	75,114,065	42,888,262	73,576	4,889,220	3,611,263
2018	378,960,462	302,728,224	89,925	302,818,149	30,724,566	-17,297,645	254,795,938	79,147,789	45,016,735	77,141	4,912,542	3,673,582
2019	400,174,114	320,606,400	96,557	320,702,957	32,324,538	-20,340,293	268,038,126	85,791,354	46,344,634	81,126	4,932,771	3,695,712
2020	425,717,529	325,719,650	91,304	325,810,954	32,506,173	-21,039,014	272,265,767	85,309,400	68,142,362	86,239	4,936,511	3,494,368
2021	452,212,436	354,356,978	66,980	354,423,958	35,261,926	-24,191,107	294,970,925	88,077,704	69,163,807	92,290	4,899,932	3,612,213

Personal Income and Employment by Area: Boulder, CO

(Thousands of dollars, except as noted.)

Year	Personal income, total	Earnings by place of work			Less: Contributions for government social insurance	Plus: Adjustment for residence	Equals: Net earnings by place of residence	Plus: Dividends, interest, and rent	Plus: Personal current transfer receipts	Per capita personal income (dollars)	Population (persons)	Total employment
		Nonfarm	Farm	Total								
1970	600,343	394,155	5,052	399,207	21,172	78,885	456,920	110,838	32,585	4,502	133,342	55,395
1971	680,907	452,090	474	452,564	24,881	88,777	516,460	125,725	38,722	4,836	140,808	59,121
1972	768,819	512,284	4,041	516,325	30,157	100,009	586,177	138,854	43,788	5,081	151,309	64,116
1973	864,808	574,054	2,914	576,968	39,837	115,077	652,208	157,983	54,617	5,422	159,509	69,942
1974	979,831	660,914	2,695	663,609	46,970	115,564	732,203	184,486	63,142	5,887	166,449	75,635
1975	1,109,846	749,498	6,510	756,008	52,425	114,065	817,648	211,485	80,713	6,659	166,670	78,961
1976	1,245,164	859,746	7,921	867,667	61,907	116,065	921,825	234,964	88,375	7,363	169,117	85,236
1977	1,434,420	1,020,741	7,292	1,028,033	74,657	119,529	1,072,905	265,788	95,727	8,053	178,121	92,627
1978	1,683,852	1,223,210	6,797	1,230,007	92,236	130,401	1,268,172	310,863	104,817	9,180	183,432	102,720
1979	1,959,091	1,429,615	5,149	1,434,764	114,316	162,073	1,482,521	357,574	118,996	10,469	187,125	110,002
1980	2,217,801	1,557,263	9,224	1,566,487	127,270	209,267	1,648,484	432,280	137,037	11,615	190,935	112,861
1981	2,556,325	1,774,431	12,943	1,787,374	156,444	227,322	1,858,252	537,969	160,104	13,062	195,705	117,528
1982	2,822,610	1,988,313	8,662	1,996,975	181,654	226,234	2,041,555	603,751	177,304	14,055	200,827	121,300
1983	3,095,368	2,223,219	9,338	2,232,557	208,132	212,014	2,236,439	665,206	193,723	14,994	206,440	128,223
1984	3,452,403	2,530,218	10,185	2,540,403	247,455	202,813	2,495,761	755,428	201,214	16,346	211,206	141,199
1985	3,621,559	2,597,339	5,064	2,602,403	258,111	241,883	2,586,175	821,066	214,318	16,928	213,942	140,650
1986	3,793,647	2,725,919	4,846	2,730,765	273,381	244,942	2,702,326	858,542	232,779	17,566	215,971	141,908
1987	4,022,785	2,957,351	5,572	2,962,923	294,035	210,790	2,879,678	891,281	251,826	18,451	218,024	143,586
1988	4,339,346	3,217,085	8,427	3,225,512	332,840	224,968	3,117,640	955,442	266,264	19,732	219,915	152,086
1989	4,740,937	3,423,711	10,222	3,433,933	361,914	224,851	3,296,870	1,136,975	307,092	21,212	223,507	155,495
1990	5,074,432	3,724,890	11,309	3,736,199	403,647	217,693	3,550,245	1,199,966	324,221	22,416	226,374	160,076
1991	5,390,167	4,074,399	12,648	4,087,047	452,876	166,419	3,800,590	1,237,454	352,123	23,149	232,846	164,862
1992	5,960,244	4,587,347	7,319	4,594,666	503,546	142,533	4,233,653	1,336,427	390,164	24,790	240,430	169,291
1993	6,429,321	5,016,126	9,237	5,025,363	555,170	93,209	4,563,402	1,448,771	417,148	25,987	247,405	178,775
1994	6,968,605	5,446,358	9,281	5,455,639	609,705	-20,036	4,825,898	1,701,357	441,350	27,401	254,324	186,270
1995	7,546,846	5,868,502	9,403	5,877,905	658,239	-72,238	5,147,428	1,915,835	483,583	29,080	259,520	192,888
1996	8,159,812	6,352,059	11,385	6,363,444	707,621	-78,666	5,577,157	2,074,447	508,208	30,835	264,630	198,754
1997	8,878,042	6,998,726	11,363	7,010,089	779,674	-133,779	6,096,636	2,271,159	510,247	32,791	270,744	207,295
1998	9,779,597	8,176,368	10,361	8,186,729	867,531	-516,243	6,802,955	2,468,408	508,234	35,234	277,562	213,453
1999	10,647,732	8,983,948	9,179	8,993,127	944,613	-451,240	7,597,274	2,513,008	537,450	37,243	285,901	221,120
2000	12,219,618	11,068,542	8,218	11,076,760	1,144,858	-1,144,908	8,786,994	2,856,315	576,309	41,654	293,358	237,310
2001	12,677,543	11,318,053	10,105	11,328,158	1,165,776	-992,797	9,169,585	2,853,263	654,695	42,239	300,137	243,644
2002	11,557,324	9,853,922	9,449	9,863,371	1,020,608	-556,997	8,285,766	2,595,045	676,513	41,355	279,468	215,538
2003	11,795,789	9,891,866	6,004	9,897,870	1,027,830	-476,215	8,393,825	2,669,924	732,040	42,314	278,768	210,519
2004	12,111,744	10,279,616	10,390	10,290,006	1,096,365	-693,131	8,500,510	2,863,575	747,659	43,298	279,728	214,515
2005	12,963,891	10,654,708	8,622	10,663,330	1,134,702	-756,806	8,771,822	3,348,605	843,464	46,260	280,241	218,044
2006	13,962,986	11,187,758	7,018	11,194,776	1,187,091	-757,229	9,250,456	3,868,290	844,240	49,123	284,243	221,750
2007	14,628,219	11,695,477	7,082	11,702,559	1,250,510	-931,009	9,521,040	4,178,931	928,248	50,894	287,428	228,962
2008	15,268,220	11,926,862	6,911	11,933,773	1,285,109	-908,099	9,740,565	4,367,504	1,160,151	52,494	290,859	235,192
2009	13,822,780	11,344,781	10,396	11,355,177	1,218,922	-1,325,961	8,810,294	3,760,630	1,251,856	47,146	293,190	228,871
2010	14,943,624	11,719,225	9,111	11,728,336	1,243,235	-787,287	9,697,814	3,815,174	1,430,636	50,647	295,056	227,803
2011	15,781,304	12,225,111	16,679	12,241,790	1,177,083	-940,549	10,124,158	4,192,721	1,464,425	52,596	300,045	234,434
2012	16,760,622	12,961,278	9,944	12,971,222	1,233,999	-986,009	10,751,214	4,542,771	1,466,637	55,004	304,717	239,480
2013	17,598,739	13,612,955	12,565	13,625,520	1,438,949	-953,003	11,233,568	4,824,334	1,540,837	56,855	309,538	245,013
2014	18,963,795	14,489,604	10,754	14,500,358	1,530,477	-1,002,828	11,967,053	5,349,498	1,647,244	60,411	313,911	252,707
2015	20,519,882	15,203,847	12,805	15,216,652	1,620,065	-824,554	12,772,033	5,947,388	1,800,461	64,094	320,154	258,598
2016	20,987,868	15,550,154	10,993	15,561,147	1,671,960	-940,240	12,948,947	6,158,469	1,880,452	64,804	323,865	263,946
2017	22,410,849	16,486,996	10,480	16,497,476	1,760,979	-837,686	13,898,811	6,570,423	1,941,615	68,856	325,475	269,042
2018	23,625,957	17,470,166	10,503	17,480,669	1,875,497	-1,190,205	14,414,967	7,093,965	2,117,025	71,974	328,259	274,079
2019	26,236,032	19,386,017	8,928	19,394,945	2,038,984	-1,475,706	15,880,255	8,089,369	2,266,408	79,698	329,194	275,800
2020	27,514,385	19,695,893	9,751	19,705,644	2,077,259	-1,341,281	16,287,104	8,120,927	3,106,354	83,173	330,811	269,173
2021	29,524,725	21,699,275	9,943	21,709,218	2,237,674	-1,846,138	17,625,406	8,518,100	3,381,219	89,593	329,543	277,978

Personal Income and Employment by Area: Bowling Green, KY

(Thousands of dollars, except as noted.)

Year	Personal income, total	Earnings by place of work			Less: Contributions for government social insurance	Plus: Adjustment for residence	Equals: Net earnings by place of residence	Plus: Dividends, interest, and rent	Plus: Personal current transfer receipts	Per capita personal income (dollars)	Population (persons)	Total employment
		Nonfarm	Farm	Total								
1970	238,044	175,431	15,726	191,157	11,945	710	179,922	29,864	28,258	2,655	89,652	37,297
1971	265,227	195,047	17,127	212,174	13,712	744	199,206	33,690	32,331	2,836	93,520	38,393
1972	303,342	224,576	21,037	245,613	16,575	766	229,804	38,107	35,431	3,183	95,307	40,228
1973	350,258	259,340	25,936	285,276	21,794	2,357	265,839	42,966	41,453	3,669	95,464	42,648
1974	387,810	286,550	22,853	309,403	25,070	3,170	287,503	50,095	50,212	4,002	96,904	43,625
1975	427,934	311,056	15,600	326,656	26,799	3,162	303,019	58,089	66,826	4,351	98,351	43,179
1976	485,803	358,953	14,572	373,525	31,446	5,009	347,088	64,516	74,199	4,832	100,546	45,371
1977	541,776	397,195	22,342	419,537	34,784	7,967	392,720	73,739	75,317	5,294	102,335	46,883
1978	620,309	465,232	21,200	486,432	41,834	8,768	453,366	85,380	81,563	5,953	104,207	50,148
1979	707,127	522,879	26,878	549,757	48,699	12,358	513,416	98,483	95,228	6,694	105,640	50,732
1980	776,348	551,391	16,764	568,155	51,615	13,489	530,029	125,350	120,969	7,218	107,557	49,865
1981	902,933	629,693	27,548	657,241	63,699	15,670	609,212	156,278	137,443	8,239	109,593	50,960
1982	963,143	649,035	23,333	672,368	66,817	23,721	629,272	180,851	153,020	8,384	114,875	50,359
1983	999,561	696,520	-5,907	690,613	71,491	21,752	640,874	194,702	163,985	8,554	116,854	51,861
1984	1,135,188	780,102	26,201	806,303	81,520	19,740	744,523	219,855	170,810	9,975	113,805	53,904
1985	1,195,288	847,991	13,813	861,804	90,459	20,072	791,417	225,528	178,343	10,562	113,170	54,825
1986	1,207,908	846,391	13,792	860,183	93,862	22,487	788,808	230,222	188,878	10,735	112,523	55,198
1987	1,275,438	894,216	21,528	915,744	98,646	25,649	842,747	235,002	197,689	11,365	112,227	55,910
1988	1,404,839	995,269	24,017	1,019,286	110,514	23,971	932,743	260,010	212,086	12,507	112,325	57,594
1989	1,536,005	1,069,756	36,531	1,106,287	121,280	19,333	1,004,340	296,062	235,603	13,632	112,679	59,974
1990	1,608,506	1,114,048	36,270	1,150,318	129,977	20,252	1,040,593	304,727	263,186	14,076	114,270	61,201
1991	1,723,952	1,197,080	37,618	1,234,698	141,901	18,917	1,111,714	314,046	298,192	14,915	115,583	62,846
1992	1,881,486	1,338,490	43,313	1,381,803	158,802	16,766	1,239,767	318,876	322,843	16,012	117,502	65,051
1993	1,992,916	1,430,073	37,730	1,467,803	172,045	20,304	1,316,062	336,443	340,411	16,563	120,327	66,995
1994	2,138,330	1,573,545	34,123	1,607,668	192,986	16,269	1,430,951	350,451	356,928	17,429	122,686	69,464
1995	2,249,560	1,669,832	14,256	1,684,088	205,612	13,615	1,492,091	373,529	383,940	17,947	125,345	72,461
1996	2,414,904	1,767,588	31,371	1,798,959	215,456	9,334	1,592,837	405,232	416,835	18,904	127,749	73,893
1997	2,591,321	1,903,766	32,931	1,936,697	229,465	10,223	1,717,455	430,857	443,009	19,919	130,090	75,666
1998	2,704,466	2,010,486	12,190	2,022,676	240,271	13,702	1,796,107	451,140	457,219	20,452	132,238	75,648
1999	2,843,480	2,165,497	3,828	2,169,325	257,540	12,565	1,924,350	445,540	473,590	21,260	133,747	77,333
2000	3,082,818	2,293,106	34,044	2,327,150	263,296	14,898	2,078,752	496,151	507,915	22,774	135,367	78,805
2001	3,208,981	2,364,156	31,734	2,395,890	267,659	18,233	2,146,464	500,649	561,868	23,440	136,901	79,048
2002	3,316,119	2,480,671	22,188	2,502,859	279,955	23,278	2,246,182	462,117	607,820	23,941	138,510	78,927
2003	3,453,369	2,598,906	24,321	2,623,227	290,813	30,275	2,362,689	464,391	626,289	24,506	140,921	80,185
2004	3,703,714	2,744,151	46,468	2,790,619	303,789	24,894	2,511,724	514,713	677,277	25,892	143,044	82,086
2005	3,937,376	2,925,981	60,734	2,986,715	327,754	24,464	2,683,425	533,582	720,369	26,983	145,918	84,829
2006	4,126,071	3,040,998	55,565	3,096,563	344,983	19,985	2,771,565	572,658	781,848	27,632	149,324	86,880
2007	4,344,443	3,176,551	25,799	3,202,350	361,929	13,310	2,853,731	638,982	851,730	28,636	151,710	89,670
2008	4,599,705	3,275,586	16,672	3,292,258	379,143	15,328	2,928,443	694,441	976,821	29,769	154,513	89,166
2009	4,509,409	3,080,716	24,190	3,104,906	367,218	-4,361	2,733,327	673,280	1,102,802	28,726	156,978	85,556
2010	4,781,173	3,266,380	28,177	3,294,557	378,583	-1,076	2,914,898	689,526	1,176,749	30,004	159,352	86,256
2011	5,009,044	3,408,552	53,020	3,461,572	351,015	-19,283	3,091,274	718,220	1,199,550	31,107	161,024	89,444
2012	5,195,474	3,585,357	56,821	3,642,178	366,459	-20,007	3,255,712	743,588	1,196,174	31,971	162,507	90,993
2013	5,306,489	3,686,970	104,412	3,791,382	426,784	-43,640	3,320,958	762,289	1,223,242	32,213	164,733	92,293
2014	5,579,586	3,856,508	74,134	3,930,642	451,853	-55,920	3,422,869	803,135	1,353,582	33,528	166,417	94,218
2015	5,889,510	4,078,239	58,118	4,136,357	476,111	-60,168	3,600,078	857,068	1,432,364	34,797	169,252	96,195
2016	6,037,860	4,218,015	38,878	4,256,893	501,467	-71,825	3,683,601	916,087	1,438,172	35,144	171,804	99,933
2017	6,279,806	4,357,557	51,438	4,408,995	516,782	-59,952	3,832,261	951,763	1,495,782	35,956	174,654	101,374
2018	6,395,939	4,486,368	26,884	4,513,252	533,255	-55,986	3,924,011	918,560	1,553,368	36,251	176,436	102,881
2019	6,740,418	4,647,716	38,664	4,686,380	549,977	-51,815	4,084,588	1,011,366	1,644,464	37,772	178,450	103,207
2020	7,308,818	4,693,427	37,199	4,730,626	570,161	-81,743	4,078,722	1,015,548	2,214,548	40,610	179,978	100,416
2021	7,902,962	4,998,566	78,251	5,076,817	607,568	-78,145	4,391,104	1,025,585	2,486,273	43,282	182,594	103,943

Personal Income and Employment by Area: Bremerton-Silverdale-Port Orchard, WA

(Thousands of dollars, except as noted.)

Year	Personal income, total	Earnings by place of work			Less: Contributions for government social insurance	Plus: Adjustment for residence	Equals: Net earnings by place of residence	Plus: Dividends, interest, and rent	Plus: Personal current transfer receipts	Per capita personal income (dollars)	Population (persons)	Total employment
		Nonfarm	Farm	Total								
1970	486,434	391,738	1,502	393,240	17,268	-42,165	333,807	117,933	34,694	4,787	101,617	45,195
1971	507,925	401,290	1,060	402,350	18,254	-46,638	337,458	128,587	41,880	4,999	101,606	41,911
1972	550,509	432,237	1,156	433,393	20,733	-47,840	364,820	138,859	46,830	5,385	102,225	41,798
1973	629,457	489,297	2,012	491,309	26,640	-49,714	414,955	160,827	53,675	5,607	112,257	45,114
1974	742,964	582,283	1,568	583,851	32,475	-59,689	491,687	189,692	61,585	6,636	111,965	49,047
1975	858,418	673,210	1,237	674,447	40,020	-65,973	568,454	213,532	76,432	7,207	119,117	51,652
1976	955,374	751,785	1,182	752,967	47,753	-66,976	638,238	231,812	85,324	7,897	120,976	54,063
1977	1,101,571	868,973	1,259	870,232	56,003	-73,202	741,027	267,355	93,189	8,749	125,902	58,694
1978	1,260,302	970,341	1,744	972,085	63,907	-65,994	842,184	316,688	101,430	9,502	132,640	61,793
1979	1,449,681	1,098,866	1,980	1,100,846	74,979	-53,386	972,481	364,338	112,862	10,301	140,733	65,222
1980	1,625,238	1,180,646	1,577	1,182,223	82,672	-31,881	1,067,670	415,982	141,586	10,925	148,762	67,650
1981	1,785,897	1,275,129	1,644	1,276,773	97,426	-40,319	1,139,028	478,356	168,513	11,529	154,907	68,860
1982	1,981,503	1,411,352	1,663	1,413,015	105,653	-59,487	1,247,875	548,595	185,033	12,779	155,059	70,104
1983	2,208,199	1,600,922	1,159	1,602,081	131,219	-65,729	1,405,133	606,663	196,403	13,757	160,515	73,806
1984	2,323,081	1,658,720	406	1,659,126	141,762	-54,598	1,462,766	648,266	212,049	14,363	161,742	75,920
1985	2,450,140	1,708,620	133	1,708,753	155,676	-30,562	1,522,515	698,109	229,516	14,981	163,546	77,990
1986	2,521,180	1,708,605	-354	1,708,251	162,310	3,016	1,548,957	726,235	245,988	15,346	164,293	77,909
1987	2,709,242	1,844,068	1,287	1,845,355	179,383	27,602	1,693,574	753,507	262,161	15,959	169,760	83,191
1988	2,998,253	2,085,596	577	2,086,173	211,614	24,680	1,899,239	819,661	279,353	16,757	178,929	90,373
1989	3,260,819	2,206,752	3,607	2,210,359	231,970	55,871	2,034,260	916,407	310,152	17,871	182,461	92,716
1990	3,784,198	2,518,561	2,237	2,520,798	274,093	217,275	2,463,980	975,648	344,570	19,722	191,879	99,487
1991	4,157,382	2,789,438	3,826	2,793,264	308,907	220,130	2,704,487	1,051,366	401,529	20,825	199,636	103,816
1992	4,501,517	3,008,567	3,536	3,012,103	340,130	266,715	2,938,688	1,111,377	451,452	21,481	209,562	105,396
1993	4,743,043	3,010,174	3,068	3,013,242	347,167	391,393	3,057,468	1,185,134	500,441	22,451	211,262	103,073
1994	4,957,911	3,104,821	3,211	3,108,032	362,329	418,926	3,164,629	1,262,156	531,126	23,122	214,422	106,538
1995	5,229,188	3,220,839	1,691	3,222,530	377,135	430,611	3,276,006	1,377,463	575,719	23,408	223,391	108,268
1996	5,495,060	3,332,704	1,399	3,334,103	385,052	420,946	3,369,997	1,517,192	607,871	24,252	226,584	112,627
1997	5,942,242	3,493,289	2,134	3,495,423	396,145	598,614	3,697,892	1,600,463	643,887	25,903	229,403	111,977
1998	6,188,347	3,537,432	720	3,538,152	401,458	746,110	3,882,804	1,634,575	670,968	27,038	228,878	110,034
1999	6,449,419	3,699,802	918	3,700,720	414,137	834,946	4,121,529	1,619,884	708,006	28,115	229,393	110,431
2000	7,060,260	3,943,478	1,281	3,944,759	444,603	1,068,776	4,568,932	1,711,666	779,662	30,338	232,720	112,566
2001	7,308,867	4,138,066	890	4,138,956	467,175	1,047,814	4,719,595	1,714,354	874,918	31,166	234,513	113,167
2002	7,627,847	4,617,413	1,080	4,618,493	526,058	961,616	5,054,051	1,636,178	937,618	32,032	238,129	117,072
2003	8,041,905	4,926,815	2,693	4,929,508	562,593	917,830	5,284,745	1,766,425	990,735	33,542	239,758	119,293
2004	8,594,772	5,292,128	1,914	5,294,042	609,263	925,073	5,609,852	1,960,466	1,024,454	35,521	241,960	121,918
2005	9,037,625	5,598,099	810	5,598,909	647,190	919,949	5,871,668	2,062,874	1,103,083	37,687	239,806	124,980
2006	9,513,394	5,847,290	2,126	5,849,416	682,502	874,922	6,041,836	2,274,124	1,197,434	38,822	245,054	127,063
2007	9,957,891	5,964,686	1,580	5,966,266	700,185	926,488	6,192,569	2,474,154	1,291,168	40,793	244,105	127,595
2008	10,503,242	6,164,839	-709	6,164,130	723,862	873,451	6,313,719	2,696,249	1,493,274	42,538	246,912	127,474
2009	10,287,984	6,176,304	424	6,176,728	746,258	805,379	6,235,849	2,389,374	1,662,761	41,350	248,800	123,188
2010	10,608,195	6,394,586	-1,235	6,393,351	764,443	766,892	6,395,800	2,367,197	1,845,198	42,147	251,696	120,811
2011	10,912,185	6,451,873	339	6,452,212	707,421	713,183	6,457,974	2,599,785	1,854,426	42,902	254,351	120,718
2012	11,336,136	6,608,066	-462	6,607,604	712,656	738,189	6,633,137	2,830,464	1,872,535	44,558	254,414	121,380
2013	11,352,250	6,587,546	-768	6,586,778	795,463	862,625	6,653,940	2,793,769	1,904,541	44,953	252,538	121,564
2014	12,011,744	6,846,367	-372	6,845,995	829,682	963,897	6,980,210	2,961,983	2,069,551	47,159	254,705	124,396
2015	12,571,216	7,188,488	2,937	7,191,425	877,206	978,006	7,292,225	3,150,177	2,128,814	48,183	260,904	127,315
2016	13,205,819	7,572,996	-115	7,572,881	910,192	1,033,468	7,696,157	3,266,868	2,242,794	49,803	265,159	131,345
2017	13,876,050	7,828,316	646	7,828,962	948,761	1,237,769	8,117,970	3,435,259	2,322,821	51,645	268,681	132,154
2018	14,738,705	8,031,318	-832	8,030,486	968,161	1,640,547	8,702,872	3,581,340	2,454,493	54,199	271,938	131,593
2019	16,027,659	8,351,857	1,086	8,352,943	993,550	2,048,253	9,407,646	4,000,336	2,619,677	58,290	274,963	131,591
2020	17,175,888	8,862,516	5,005	8,867,521	1,062,107	1,995,305	9,800,719	3,969,193	3,405,976	62,308	275,660	127,976
2021	18,610,871	9,265,291	5,361	9,270,652	1,098,144	2,579,356	10,751,864	4,076,843	3,782,164	67,845	274,314	130,260

Personal Income and Employment by Area: Bridgeport-Stamford-Norwalk, CT

(Thousands of dollars, except as noted.)

Year	Personal income, total	Earnings by place of work			Less: Contributions for government social insurance	Plus: Adjustment for residence	Equals: Net earnings by place of residence	Plus: Dividends, interest, and rent	Plus: Personal current transfer receipts	Per capita personal income (dollars)	Population (persons)	Total employment
		Nonfarm	Farm	Total								
1970	4,860,504	3,147,197	3,681	3,150,878	208,962	665,217	3,607,133	969,894	283,477	6,130	792,934	366,252
1971	5,101,426	3,251,071	3,673	3,254,744	223,363	679,467	3,710,848	1,039,763	350,815	6,435	792,758	358,267
1972	5,483,660	3,537,389	3,649	3,541,038	258,000	702,508	3,985,546	1,124,024	374,090	6,959	788,034	364,054
1973	5,883,424	3,911,903	4,252	3,916,155	330,354	698,151	4,283,952	1,192,810	406,662	7,480	786,524	379,191
1974	6,352,715	4,229,786	4,041	4,233,827	374,258	717,665	4,577,234	1,300,388	475,093	8,059	788,324	383,909
1975	6,814,123	4,464,601	3,695	4,468,296	386,283	775,075	4,857,088	1,334,125	622,910	8,576	794,554	374,936
1976	7,449,088	4,970,834	3,072	4,973,906	437,127	811,283	5,348,062	1,430,568	670,458	9,341	797,444	385,892
1977	8,289,329	5,643,127	3,313	5,646,440	498,579	872,536	6,020,397	1,566,193	702,739	10,228	810,423	403,360
1978	9,308,626	6,427,273	3,316	6,430,589	585,428	966,337	6,811,498	1,758,611	738,517	11,597	802,642	425,460
1979	10,522,084	7,296,754	2,917	7,299,671	692,806	1,082,157	7,689,022	2,012,196	820,866	13,109	802,656	442,700
1980	12,114,690	8,285,890	2,688	8,288,578	789,350	1,234,151	8,733,379	2,431,320	949,991	14,980	808,703	455,859
1981	13,778,176	9,249,786	2,181	9,251,967	949,492	1,354,594	9,657,069	3,047,512	1,073,595	16,943	813,186	470,540
1982	14,892,004	9,924,754	3,067	9,927,821	1,048,044	1,444,001	10,323,778	3,374,846	1,193,380	18,207	817,943	474,803
1983	15,790,894	10,612,277	2,425	10,614,702	1,128,848	1,557,939	11,043,793	3,460,588	1,286,513	19,214	821,854	476,184
1984	17,748,238	12,032,503	2,881	12,035,384	1,308,932	1,661,584	12,388,036	4,015,430	1,344,772	21,510	825,107	495,194
1985	19,125,106	13,146,476	2,624	13,149,100	1,448,341	1,845,563	13,546,322	4,148,942	1,429,842	23,031	830,396	509,468
1986	20,490,336	14,290,306	2,965	14,293,271	1,579,604	1,884,766	14,598,433	4,376,546	1,515,357	24,634	831,797	519,808
1987	22,322,461	15,825,783	3,085	15,828,868	1,717,306	2,004,167	16,115,729	4,640,769	1,565,963	26,950	828,277	525,397
1988	24,980,133	17,752,236	2,656	17,754,892	1,932,958	2,175,903	17,997,837	5,291,854	1,690,442	30,220	826,605	537,634
1989	27,114,309	18,556,240	2,065	18,558,305	2,015,062	2,193,847	18,737,090	6,491,874	1,885,345	32,766	827,517	532,086
1990	27,933,582	19,191,242	3,099	19,194,341	2,057,938	1,815,410	18,951,813	6,873,370	2,108,399	33,701	828,860	521,951
1991	28,246,727	19,492,459	3,962	19,496,421	2,126,970	1,795,318	19,164,769	6,726,335	2,355,623	33,906	833,094	503,321
1992	31,689,819	21,065,940	5,910	21,071,850	2,232,533	2,923,827	21,763,144	7,151,225	2,775,450	37,980	834,372	501,927
1993	32,629,970	22,181,213	8,461	22,189,674	2,333,814	2,285,973	22,141,833	7,581,865	2,906,272	38,894	838,945	512,679
1994	33,471,898	22,923,375	9,607	22,932,982	2,452,079	2,033,100	22,514,003	7,954,305	3,003,590	39,730	842,482	508,287
1995	36,425,112	24,736,400	10,395	24,746,795	2,636,559	2,592,670	24,702,906	8,497,768	3,224,438	42,951	848,057	518,746
1996	39,005,828	26,343,803	5,162	26,348,965	2,785,707	3,161,417	26,724,675	8,971,062	3,310,091	45,652	854,421	528,175
1997	41,990,761	29,305,153	4,646	29,309,799	3,007,275	2,478,555	28,781,079	9,806,739	3,402,943	48,769	861,020	537,529
1998	46,647,794	32,008,342	6,901	32,015,243	3,184,139	3,677,052	32,508,156	10,727,073	3,412,565	53,701	868,651	551,305
1999	49,689,093	34,919,382	10,098	34,929,480	3,371,946	3,364,443	34,921,977	11,267,635	3,499,481	56,655	877,043	563,031
2000	55,126,558	39,248,422	11,380	39,259,802	3,622,577	3,214,954	38,852,179	12,574,811	3,699,568	62,335	884,364	577,741
2001	59,034,357	42,880,869	11,820	42,892,689	3,734,864	3,100,931	42,258,756	12,853,897	3,921,704	66,401	889,063	576,192
2002	57,784,980	41,948,341	11,781	41,960,122	3,798,008	3,486,105	41,648,219	11,947,116	4,189,645	64,716	892,900	574,103
2003	57,947,816	42,139,530	11,379	42,150,909	3,886,095	3,517,429	41,782,243	11,914,028	4,251,545	64,649	896,342	575,380
2004	61,493,041	42,614,889	12,626	42,627,515	4,027,408	4,418,506	43,018,613	13,911,396	4,563,032	68,518	897,472	583,542
2005	66,714,459	44,840,627	14,839	44,855,466	4,175,830	4,857,027	45,536,663	16,558,524	4,619,272	74,321	897,653	591,253
2006	73,860,592	47,270,420	16,258	47,286,678	4,359,447	5,573,534	48,500,765	20,464,373	4,895,454	82,410	896,254	600,698
2007	81,800,722	51,799,497	19,327	51,818,824	4,656,868	6,848,105	54,010,061	22,637,955	5,152,706	91,143	897,498	617,956
2008	90,495,008	58,529,955	17,853	58,547,808	4,892,936	8,207,554	61,862,426	22,748,438	5,884,144	100,125	903,824	621,959
2009	89,586,996	62,472,700	18,613	62,491,313	4,713,627	6,574,007	64,351,693	18,732,068	6,503,235	98,402	910,421	608,209
2010	95,416,974	64,789,280	17,608	64,806,888	4,772,230	8,447,019	68,481,677	20,020,096	6,915,201	103,785	919,371	605,628
2011	96,341,946	63,667,897	14,288	63,682,185	4,356,656	8,686,351	68,011,880	21,413,741	6,916,325	103,806	928,099	621,735
2012	96,709,567	60,000,645	19,784	60,020,429	4,414,138	10,502,419	66,108,710	23,599,989	7,000,868	103,400	935,293	628,379
2013	91,249,002	56,951,229	26,074	56,977,303	5,099,406	9,853,566	61,731,463	22,436,013	7,081,526	97,054	940,189	639,193
2014	96,793,056	58,532,768	17,662	58,550,430	5,266,379	10,043,795	63,327,846	26,137,461	7,327,749	101,851	950,338	646,561
2015	98,842,169	58,583,806	20,184	58,603,990	5,417,754	10,666,132	63,852,368	27,412,120	7,577,681	103,769	952,518	657,033
2016	101,347,852	59,922,032	17,127	59,939,159	5,497,094	10,063,871	64,505,936	28,989,057	7,852,859	106,272	953,669	663,781
2017	103,905,405	59,996,531	23,909	60,020,440	5,560,651	12,618,746	67,078,535	28,890,409	7,936,461	108,910	954,050	658,195
2018	109,774,739	60,374,179	19,022	60,393,201	5,643,143	13,758,973	68,509,031	32,781,086	8,484,622	114,725	956,852	663,339
2019	111,976,677	59,912,173	25,567	59,937,740	5,728,717	15,732,977	69,942,000	33,391,491	8,643,186	116,996	957,097	653,830
2020	114,101,074	59,618,994	15,964	59,634,958	5,686,907	15,895,829	69,843,880	32,791,266	11,465,928	119,366	955,895	633,875
2021	122,265,576	64,390,513	13,168	64,403,681	6,007,615	18,212,684	76,608,750	33,494,293	12,162,533	127,391	959,768	656,093

Personal Income and Employment by Area: Brownsville-Harlingen, TX

(Thousands of dollars, except as noted.)

Year	Personal income, total	Earnings by place of work			Less: Contributions for government social insurance	Plus: Adjustment for residence	Equals: Net earnings by place of residence	Plus: Dividends, interest, and rent	Plus: Personal current transfer receipts	Per capita personal income (dollars)	Population (persons)	Total employment
		Nonfarm	Farm	Total								
1970	313,753	235,891	12,535	248,426	15,000	-8,878	224,548	50,419	38,786	2,222	141,196	48,384
1971	365,169	265,273	24,210	289,483	17,408	-9,731	262,344	57,081	45,744	2,471	147,753	50,443
1972	413,943	311,343	20,676	332,019	21,566	-12,223	298,230	64,453	51,260	2,628	157,489	54,936
1973	485,003	367,116	15,921	383,037	29,725	-15,229	338,083	75,667	71,253	2,905	166,939	59,244
1974	571,166	422,375	25,565	447,940	35,323	-17,547	395,070	90,871	85,225	3,317	172,211	62,830
1975	653,609	486,103	17,041	503,144	40,246	-21,223	441,675	106,211	105,723	3,575	182,806	64,977
1976	729,412	547,870	16,964	564,834	45,664	-23,177	495,993	115,036	118,383	3,851	189,415	67,457
1977	800,019	593,551	25,495	619,046	49,589	-24,873	544,584	129,059	126,376	4,109	194,722	69,508
1978	943,986	707,392	33,308	740,700	60,254	-27,499	652,947	150,912	140,127	4,745	198,941	74,442
1979	1,075,955	816,103	13,414	829,517	72,680	-27,998	728,839	179,309	167,807	5,235	205,544	77,871
1980	1,235,507	921,222	3,944	925,166	82,787	-27,631	814,748	218,291	202,468	5,829	211,944	81,655
1981	1,455,488	1,048,635	39,017	1,087,652	101,802	-22,495	963,355	266,447	225,686	6,610	220,184	84,935
1982	1,561,377	1,108,240	15,480	1,123,720	108,940	-23,753	991,027	318,927	251,423	6,767	230,718	85,599
1983	1,672,892	1,122,637	30,554	1,153,191	107,925	-22,308	1,022,958	355,239	294,695	7,003	238,878	83,585
1984	1,774,807	1,170,093	28,770	1,198,863	114,124	-22,305	1,062,434	391,208	321,165	7,323	242,355	83,931
1985	1,926,454	1,251,313	43,113	1,294,426	122,365	-22,590	1,149,471	431,440	345,543	7,834	245,894	85,022
1986	1,983,233	1,295,455	15,734	1,311,189	124,438	-22,434	1,164,317	443,972	374,944	7,901	250,996	83,543
1987	2,043,684	1,318,754	41,152	1,359,906	125,588	-22,625	1,211,693	441,640	390,351	8,055	253,714	85,358
1988	2,205,592	1,436,577	50,888	1,487,465	143,188	-21,344	1,322,933	467,138	415,521	8,669	254,410	88,741
1989	2,380,309	1,558,053	28,628	1,586,681	160,254	-22,753	1,403,674	511,734	464,901	9,280	256,512	93,483
1990	2,650,173	1,756,567	39,592	1,796,159	177,535	-26,635	1,591,989	516,989	541,195	10,126	261,728	98,639
1991	2,857,614	1,881,741	30,741	1,912,482	194,117	-26,856	1,691,509	535,712	630,393	10,613	269,261	101,267
1992	3,203,167	2,065,785	38,156	2,103,941	211,567	-30,382	1,861,992	565,295	775,880	11,550	277,322	104,646
1993	3,476,116	2,254,178	57,997	2,312,175	232,090	-32,174	2,047,911	575,123	853,082	12,057	288,297	109,851
1994	3,700,012	2,405,663	51,942	2,457,605	251,640	-33,139	2,172,826	597,991	929,195	12,445	297,316	115,588
1995	3,869,868	2,480,523	25,422	2,505,945	260,821	-31,483	2,213,641	653,237	1,002,990	12,691	304,928	117,889
1996	4,086,295	2,583,709	48,255	2,631,964	269,176	-27,407	2,335,381	662,672	1,088,242	13,093	312,086	121,253
1997	4,365,735	2,811,319	44,581	2,855,900	289,749	-26,725	2,539,426	686,635	1,139,674	13,717	318,281	124,620
1998	4,656,163	3,039,491	69,786	3,109,277	308,587	-27,514	2,773,176	735,471	1,147,516	14,346	324,556	127,625
1999	4,836,666	3,183,321	73,284	3,256,605	320,998	-22,899	2,912,708	748,319	1,175,639	14,644	330,277	132,109
2000	5,211,517	3,417,713	67,296	3,485,009	342,345	-21,320	3,121,344	823,454	1,266,719	15,505	336,123	139,353
2001	5,753,886	3,871,867	62,748	3,934,615	370,866	-69,123	3,494,626	868,357	1,390,903	16,806	342,368	142,995
2002	6,152,788	4,143,338	55,222	4,198,560	397,227	-76,743	3,724,590	869,403	1,558,795	17,570	350,194	148,213
2003	6,487,175	4,272,540	93,272	4,365,812	418,315	-70,064	3,877,433	946,849	1,662,893	18,096	358,492	150,342
2004	6,694,992	4,440,793	81,499	4,522,292	437,404	-62,384	4,022,504	927,072	1,745,416	18,277	366,299	154,155
2005	7,066,182	4,566,777	80,994	4,647,771	459,399	-42,931	4,145,441	972,197	1,948,544	18,922	373,429	156,329
2006	7,573,947	4,921,344	65,117	4,986,461	490,192	-34,922	4,461,347	1,040,522	2,072,078	19,923	380,169	162,680
2007	8,076,996	5,109,869	63,096	5,172,965	522,876	-19,399	4,630,690	1,129,488	2,316,818	20,908	386,306	167,167
2008	8,673,165	5,311,560	41,071	5,352,631	544,268	-3,384	4,804,979	1,283,936	2,584,250	22,069	393,000	169,857
2009	8,992,818	5,471,975	32,798	5,504,773	562,517	-13,130	4,929,126	1,199,314	2,864,378	22,465	400,303	170,020
2010	9,655,488	5,848,917	47,639	5,896,556	597,145	-23,918	5,275,493	1,228,363	3,151,632	23,688	407,608	171,929
2011	10,118,922	6,093,006	42,559	6,135,565	550,462	-31,058	5,554,045	1,339,529	3,225,348	24,494	413,116	178,631
2012	10,370,463	6,330,028	36,614	6,366,642	571,957	-30,975	5,763,710	1,430,653	3,176,100	24,945	415,729	181,256
2013	10,599,551	6,464,960	73,257	6,538,217	655,974	-25,088	5,857,155	1,476,553	3,265,843	25,411	417,129	185,556
2014	11,007,562	6,701,812	32,827	6,734,639	679,309	-17,407	6,037,923	1,586,715	3,382,924	26,366	417,498	187,720
2015	11,261,161	6,863,128	45,526	6,908,654	706,769	-26,473	6,175,412	1,521,829	3,563,920	26,968	417,572	188,752
2016	11,581,945	7,010,523	33,940	7,044,463	735,441	-47,242	6,261,780	1,564,757	3,755,408	27,635	419,104	191,134
2017	11,742,422	7,062,062	43,938	7,106,000	752,447	-38,793	6,314,760	1,630,089	3,797,573	27,997	419,418	192,454
2018	12,205,997	7,347,819	37,141	7,384,960	784,428	-28,536	6,571,996	1,675,319	3,958,682	29,127	419,064	196,293
2019	12,750,515	7,704,140	29,894	7,734,034	822,974	-24,488	6,886,572	1,770,909	4,093,034	30,361	419,958	197,889
2020	14,337,302	8,031,279	45,595	8,076,874	880,510	-9,935	7,186,429	1,751,587	5,399,286	34,040	421,191	196,895
2021	16,016,476	8,735,265	70,612	8,805,877	952,412	-26,584	7,826,881	1,809,626	6,379,969	37,861	423,029	204,834

Personal Income and Employment by Area: Brunswick, GA

(Thousands of dollars, except as noted.)

Year	Personal income, total	Derivation of personal income									Per capita personal income (dollars)	Population (persons)	Total employment
		Earnings by place of work			Less: Contributions for government social insurance	Plus: Adjustment for residence	Equals: Net earnings by place of residence	Plus: Dividends, interest, and rent	Plus: Personal current transfer receipts				
		Nonfarm	Farm	Total									
1970	217,294	170,827	2,545	173,372	10,952	2,535	164,955	34,841	17,498		3,390	64,102	27,191
1971	248,873	196,850	2,304	199,154	13,264	2,749	188,639	39,534	20,700		3,782	65,809	28,897
1972	275,680	217,472	2,732	220,204	15,250	3,828	208,782	43,607	23,291		4,082	67,537	29,346
1973	297,353	229,832	4,341	234,173	18,125	4,829	220,877	48,693	27,783		4,344	68,446	29,715
1974	314,290	235,988	4,817	240,805	19,641	6,201	227,365	52,381	34,544		4,638	67,760	29,309
1975	320,878	227,190	5,782	232,972	18,695	7,249	221,526	52,935	46,417		4,840	66,301	27,827
1976	367,868	266,859	5,543	272,402	22,053	7,772	258,121	59,975	49,772		5,504	66,832	29,663
1977	412,371	302,830	4,017	306,847	24,900	8,840	290,787	68,329	53,255		6,041	68,260	31,063
1978	469,980	342,739	5,484	348,223	28,580	10,391	330,034	81,261	58,685		6,865	68,464	32,995
1979	531,687	385,094	3,838	388,932	33,403	12,738	368,267	96,225	67,195		7,564	70,289	33,871
1980	600,992	425,002	2,186	427,188	37,008	16,925	407,105	113,949	79,938		8,353	71,952	34,773
1981	667,188	454,115	3,723	457,838	42,747	19,961	435,052	140,276	91,860		9,175	72,718	34,166
1982	706,194	464,925	4,853	469,778	44,653	21,601	446,726	158,128	101,340		9,592	73,627	33,888
1983	756,277	497,565	3,778	501,343	48,038	22,239	475,544	170,970	109,763		10,162	74,420	34,276
1984	839,210	552,992	5,345	558,337	54,688	25,732	529,381	190,643	119,186		11,113	75,513	35,831
1985	920,227	618,061	4,013	622,074	62,484	24,486	584,076	208,724	127,427		12,026	76,517	37,907
1986	993,481	666,243	4,978	671,221	68,210	27,883	630,894	226,041	136,546		12,757	77,877	38,823
1987	1,054,558	707,612	3,121	710,733	72,101	29,283	667,915	241,538	145,105		13,341	79,049	39,594
1988	1,150,821	772,898	5,119	778,017	81,220	28,963	725,760	265,763	159,298		14,337	80,269	41,522
1989	1,271,085	823,750	8,088	831,838	87,379	30,895	775,354	324,164	171,567		15,613	81,414	42,364
1990	1,356,242	871,336	6,950	878,286	91,814	33,871	820,343	345,886	190,013		16,452	82,437	42,569
1991	1,426,502	900,538	7,553	908,091	96,001	43,029	855,119	350,195	221,188		17,124	83,303	42,130
1992	1,538,624	973,310	8,274	981,584	102,507	43,025	922,102	371,247	245,275		18,261	84,259	42,703
1993	1,625,010	1,026,748	7,183	1,033,931	109,033	42,316	967,214	392,853	264,943		18,978	85,624	44,165
1994	1,731,405	1,079,618	6,499	1,086,117	116,267	47,788	1,017,638	425,255	288,512		20,019	86,487	45,056
1995	1,871,148	1,160,986	5,703	1,166,689	124,503	50,984	1,093,170	466,961	311,017		21,379	87,522	47,089
1996	2,025,088	1,241,338	5,420	1,246,758	131,581	53,320	1,168,497	521,602	334,989		22,872	88,541	48,188
1997	2,138,358	1,304,075	4,864	1,308,939	135,852	58,135	1,231,222	560,559	346,577		23,752	90,027	48,883
1998	2,281,938	1,408,496	5,060	1,413,556	143,870	68,851	1,338,537	590,608	352,793		25,032	91,160	50,359
1999	2,355,178	1,468,638	5,340	1,473,978	148,574	73,638	1,399,042	589,829	366,307		25,483	92,420	50,905
2000	2,495,274	1,544,424	4,867	1,549,291	155,640	65,682	1,459,333	646,266	389,675		26,732	93,344	52,025
2001	2,581,398	1,596,451	5,619	1,602,070	164,136	59,104	1,497,038	668,531	415,829		27,158	95,052	52,363
2002	2,680,079	1,681,416	3,544	1,684,960	172,591	54,306	1,566,675	648,422	464,982		27,741	96,612	52,596
2003	2,847,102	1,821,422	3,677	1,825,099	185,578	45,728	1,685,249	687,216	474,637		28,999	98,180	52,535
2004	3,099,762	1,983,838	3,910	1,987,748	207,193	33,457	1,814,012	767,074	518,676		31,035	99,879	54,370
2005	3,308,131	2,123,203	3,707	2,126,910	216,392	30,503	1,941,021	824,927	542,183		32,582	101,532	56,363
2006	3,585,893	2,312,205	1,129	2,313,334	239,006	18,453	2,092,781	914,226	578,886		34,244	104,715	58,121
2007	3,699,634	2,327,124	1,674	2,328,798	239,320	9,656	2,099,134	981,225	619,275		34,468	107,334	59,407
2008	3,662,070	2,254,007	1,282	2,255,289	252,584	-5,620	1,997,085	964,853	700,132		33,419	109,579	59,054
2009	3,512,195	2,149,672	1,218	2,150,890	240,785	862	1,910,967	841,843	759,385		31,544	111,343	55,728
2010	3,660,581	2,249,219	1,244	2,250,463	243,940	7,122	2,013,645	824,727	822,209		32,532	112,524	53,860
2011	3,812,676	2,226,378	1,299	2,227,677	217,481	8,125	2,018,321	933,532	860,823		33,771	112,898	53,751
2012	3,842,899	2,224,266	2,956	2,227,222	222,403	4,104	2,008,923	972,203	861,773		33,919	113,298	54,206
2013	3,900,201	2,268,331	3,004	2,271,335	255,852	4,293	2,019,776	990,183	890,242		34,268	113,816	54,753
2014	4,088,528	2,319,579	1,122	2,320,701	259,293	11,837	2,073,245	1,072,870	942,413		36,420	112,260	55,998
2015	4,382,095	2,483,789	2,580	2,486,369	275,496	9,747	2,220,620	1,160,004	1,001,471		38,809	112,915	57,153
2016	4,443,169	2,513,170	1,904	2,515,074	284,983	22,811	2,252,902	1,156,793	1,033,474		39,240	113,230	57,862
2017	4,667,588	2,595,490	2,689	2,598,179	294,884	19,448	2,322,743	1,262,587	1,082,258		41,033	113,753	59,067
2018	4,933,686	2,764,341	-647	2,763,694	318,532	10,846	2,456,008	1,347,780	1,129,898		43,361	113,781	60,421
2019	5,087,803	2,806,803	-453	2,806,350	326,690	17,447	2,497,107	1,416,714	1,173,982		44,776	113,629	60,595
2020	5,482,952	2,859,901	349	2,860,250	332,637	16,618	2,544,231	1,413,023	1,525,698		48,311	113,492	59,534
2021	5,857,721	3,090,280	-468	3,089,812	358,845	19,984	2,750,951	1,439,996	1,666,774		51,400	113,963	61,918

Personal Income and Employment by Area: Buffalo-Cheektowaga, NY

(Thousands of dollars, except as noted.)

Year	Personal income, total	Earnings by place of work			Less: Contributions for government social insurance	Plus: Adjustment for residence	Equals: Net earnings by place of residence	Plus: Dividends, interest, and rent	Plus: Personal current transfer receipts	Per capita personal income (dollars)	Population (persons)	Total employment
		Nonfarm	Farm	Total								
1970	5,668,577	4,726,169	22,870	4,749,039	357,861	-65,438	4,325,740	793,271	549,566	4,194	1,351,513	568,934
1971	6,108,318	5,045,253	22,715	5,067,968	392,449	-72,100	4,603,419	831,633	673,266	4,509	1,354,743	567,469
1972	6,463,718	5,358,152	18,241	5,376,393	439,976	-75,416	4,861,001	869,349	733,368	4,796	1,347,603	566,533
1973	7,018,358	5,874,983	26,612	5,901,595	559,600	-79,245	5,262,750	956,667	798,941	5,262	1,333,861	585,656
1974	7,575,057	6,237,591	25,992	6,263,583	613,643	-78,942	5,570,998	1,082,439	921,620	5,744	1,318,687	586,402
1975	8,181,205	6,467,022	23,307	6,490,329	623,846	-79,680	5,786,803	1,181,521	1,212,881	6,231	1,312,980	568,364
1976	8,816,270	7,026,697	23,390	7,050,087	691,508	-87,641	6,270,938	1,242,949	1,302,383	6,766	1,303,095	569,298
1977	9,606,553	7,699,188	22,196	7,721,384	753,883	-97,786	6,869,715	1,365,810	1,371,028	7,448	1,289,794	577,315
1978	10,367,645	8,389,444	27,648	8,417,092	840,374	-104,683	7,472,035	1,469,604	1,426,006	8,125	1,276,092	585,744
1979	11,384,785	9,203,500	31,775	9,235,275	949,644	-111,376	8,174,255	1,656,334	1,554,196	9,010	1,263,570	597,758
1980	12,362,259	9,593,044	31,575	9,624,619	985,941	-110,055	8,528,623	1,985,543	1,848,093	9,959	1,241,275	583,672
1981	13,489,641	10,277,495	34,392	10,311,887	1,125,826	-112,834	9,073,227	2,373,960	2,042,454	10,943	1,232,720	575,313
1982	14,206,810	10,360,665	32,821	10,393,486	1,144,119	-104,891	9,144,476	2,716,537	2,345,797	11,611	1,223,579	552,973
1983	14,899,860	10,730,086	24,781	10,754,867	1,191,178	-101,940	9,461,749	2,900,392	2,537,719	12,309	1,210,449	542,712
1984	16,286,109	11,788,276	31,688	11,819,964	1,329,736	-103,711	10,386,517	3,258,826	2,640,766	13,600	1,197,531	560,459
1985	17,216,569	12,622,536	34,497	12,657,033	1,447,002	-108,043	11,101,988	3,382,270	2,732,311	14,445	1,191,856	572,233
1986	18,118,687	13,354,940	39,283	13,394,223	1,548,370	-106,435	11,739,418	3,490,408	2,888,861	15,296	1,184,555	585,218
1987	18,859,407	14,049,820	45,235	14,095,055	1,606,660	-101,381	12,387,014	3,514,490	2,957,903	15,986	1,179,756	593,226
1988	20,208,866	15,274,567	39,417	15,313,984	1,777,758	-105,557	13,430,669	3,631,944	3,146,253	17,109	1,181,174	611,066
1989	21,653,398	16,189,409	43,670	16,233,079	1,869,984	-104,205	14,258,890	4,033,217	3,361,291	18,258	1,185,954	623,408
1990	23,061,417	17,086,455	42,119	17,128,574	1,890,005	-107,287	15,131,282	4,277,274	3,652,861	19,364	1,190,943	630,513
1991	23,541,813	17,404,398	35,470	17,439,868	1,994,519	-109,638	15,335,711	4,222,687	3,983,415	19,700	1,194,992	622,358
1992	24,696,198	18,336,720	36,249	18,372,969	2,068,492	-114,500	16,189,977	4,132,941	4,373,280	20,606	1,198,490	619,834
1993	25,198,310	18,683,220	37,038	18,720,258	2,125,441	-117,044	16,477,773	4,142,234	4,578,303	20,986	1,200,744	620,260
1994	26,119,373	19,353,292	31,806	19,385,098	2,223,142	-120,362	17,041,594	4,251,776	4,826,003	21,757	1,200,479	633,711
1995	27,236,237	19,965,145	26,445	19,991,590	2,294,800	-129,294	17,567,496	4,612,390	5,056,351	22,737	1,197,885	626,083
1996	28,053,194	20,504,777	31,638	20,536,415	2,313,895	-144,685	18,077,835	4,728,256	5,247,103	23,492	1,194,167	626,699
1997	29,053,334	21,277,274	26,443	21,303,717	2,362,260	-150,298	18,791,159	4,970,851	5,291,324	24,493	1,186,175	631,833
1998	29,999,740	21,995,986	33,540	22,029,526	2,421,097	-171,229	19,437,200	5,097,799	5,464,741	25,457	1,178,462	627,096
1999	31,213,551	23,311,324	43,617	23,354,941	2,509,677	-186,096	20,659,168	4,974,762	5,579,621	26,608	1,173,102	638,318
2000	32,858,975	24,628,699	47,912	24,676,611	2,628,277	-204,560	21,843,774	5,270,073	5,745,128	28,107	1,169,060	646,437
2001	33,028,168	24,366,486	52,046	24,418,532	2,695,014	-184,030	21,539,488	5,369,416	6,119,264	28,349	1,165,067	634,355
2002	33,577,910	24,952,207	46,347	24,998,554	2,795,662	-180,011	22,022,881	5,092,849	6,462,180	28,905	1,161,678	630,515
2003	34,696,497	25,753,527	52,594	25,806,121	2,893,911	-174,710	22,737,500	5,320,222	6,638,775	29,913	1,159,918	631,286
2004	36,068,535	27,112,512	57,583	27,170,095	3,043,193	-184,928	23,941,974	5,113,139	7,013,422	31,199	1,156,070	635,979
2005	36,397,809	27,329,722	52,883	27,382,605	3,119,545	-164,255	24,098,805	5,010,002	7,289,002	31,690	1,148,563	636,763
2006	38,217,123	28,599,384	49,363	28,648,747	3,243,924	-162,920	25,241,903	5,273,517	7,701,703	33,474	1,141,712	636,520
2007	40,170,894	29,614,169	71,477	29,685,646	3,328,662	-139,052	26,217,932	5,905,043	8,047,919	35,310	1,137,678	643,412
2008	41,972,949	30,314,871	91,581	30,406,452	3,449,906	-108,762	26,847,784	6,217,304	8,907,861	36,936	1,136,364	648,214
2009	42,267,646	30,270,211	62,131	30,332,342	3,419,092	-106,444	26,806,806	5,766,127	9,694,713	37,228	1,135,377	635,320
2010	43,738,567	31,350,082	88,967	31,439,049	3,487,809	-139,987	27,811,253	5,697,526	10,229,788	38,515	1,135,634	634,444
2011	45,454,211	32,382,808	96,969	32,479,777	3,254,462	-213,535	29,011,780	6,084,174	10,358,257	40,026	1,135,627	642,219
2012	46,983,454	33,526,206	102,078	33,628,284	3,317,178	-297,012	30,014,094	6,630,651	10,338,709	41,405	1,134,722	646,715
2013	47,395,038	34,356,457	110,441	34,466,898	3,826,998	-361,831	30,278,069	6,616,177	10,500,792	41,753	1,135,140	651,226
2014	48,710,230	35,033,402	91,681	35,125,083	3,982,800	-399,003	30,743,280	7,216,400	10,750,550	42,275	1,152,225	656,943
2015	50,777,383	36,418,935	58,900	36,477,835	4,137,043	-426,204	31,914,588	7,570,787	11,292,008	43,995	1,154,153	663,501
2016	51,745,119	37,164,111	43,526	37,207,637	4,236,724	-451,716	32,519,197	7,727,989	11,497,933	44,786	1,155,397	667,539
2017	54,334,649	38,776,762	54,693	38,831,455	4,409,544	-480,698	33,941,213	8,143,382	12,250,054	46,874	1,159,165	670,082
2018	55,657,008	40,302,943	34,827	40,337,770	4,517,549	-510,224	35,309,997	8,263,613	12,083,398	47,849	1,163,185	678,061
2019	58,221,488	41,644,683	57,634	41,702,317	4,669,050	-547,772	36,485,495	8,802,195	12,933,798	49,961	1,165,340	679,055
2020	63,475,770	41,780,076	61,914	41,841,990	4,648,912	-491,169	36,701,909	8,697,302	18,076,559	54,462	1,165,506	631,877
2021	66,029,955	44,227,617	64,478	44,292,095	4,951,693	-462,790	38,877,612	8,866,921	18,285,422	56,808	1,162,336	648,659

Personal Income and Employment by Area: Burlington, NC

(Thousands of dollars, except as noted.)

Year	Personal income, total	Earnings by place of work Nonfarm	Earnings by place of work Farm	Earnings by place of work Total	Less: Contributions for government social insurance	Plus: Adjustment for residence	Equals: Net earnings by place of residence	Plus: Dividends, interest, and rent	Plus: Personal current transfer receipts	Per capita personal income (dollars)	Population (persons)	Total employment
1970	350,273	292,866	6,208	299,074	21,451	8,984	286,607	40,056	23,610	3,617	96,843	51,242
1971	381,007	314,564	5,430	319,994	24,016	12,575	308,553	43,718	28,736	3,868	98,499	51,105
1972	424,017	348,621	6,033	354,654	27,936	17,226	343,944	47,873	32,200	4,251	99,740	52,100
1973	469,926	383,222	9,782	393,004	35,009	21,217	379,212	53,137	37,577	4,702	99,940	53,563
1974	504,551	397,986	9,484	407,470	37,926	27,630	397,174	60,448	46,929	5,083	99,272	52,836
1975	536,960	402,929	6,373	409,302	37,596	32,948	404,654	66,561	65,745	5,466	98,243	49,823
1976	590,057	433,619	11,436	445,055	41,198	40,692	444,549	72,477	73,031	5,977	98,721	49,923
1977	628,721	453,265	9,621	462,886	42,848	52,776	472,814	80,789	75,118	6,383	98,505	49,601
1978	697,983	496,298	8,532	504,830	48,507	72,615	528,938	90,053	78,992	7,083	98,540	50,016
1979	781,945	552,483	6,792	559,275	55,701	88,374	591,948	100,174	89,823	7,895	99,048	53,068
1980	871,795	592,943	4,996	597,939	60,008	101,791	639,722	124,940	107,133	8,759	99,532	52,664
1981	979,962	662,094	9,242	671,336	71,609	100,131	699,858	156,363	123,741	9,791	100,083	53,335
1982	1,050,004	686,110	9,436	695,546	74,489	99,631	720,688	186,295	143,021	10,396	101,000	52,891
1983	1,133,432	760,024	4,830	764,854	82,845	100,760	782,769	200,420	150,243	11,160	101,559	53,988
1984	1,254,093	848,649	10,577	859,226	94,675	103,009	867,560	232,009	154,524	12,331	101,706	56,603
1985	1,334,700	908,102	6,762	914,864	102,634	104,358	916,588	250,858	167,254	13,018	102,524	57,844
1986	1,448,617	1,004,694	7,089	1,011,783	116,026	98,867	994,624	275,628	178,365	13,994	103,515	59,960
1987	1,548,484	1,104,383	5,294	1,109,677	125,289	95,262	1,079,650	280,705	188,129	14,737	105,072	62,866
1988	1,682,733	1,215,900	8,774	1,224,674	140,611	89,085	1,173,148	304,999	204,586	15,826	106,327	66,241
1989	1,829,543	1,295,831	14,869	1,310,700	150,086	82,898	1,243,512	359,610	226,421	17,031	107,425	67,397
1990	1,901,481	1,351,755	19,328	1,371,083	160,375	74,882	1,285,590	370,697	245,194	17,494	108,695	68,152
1991	1,981,909	1,408,424	18,350	1,426,774	170,158	70,134	1,326,750	375,255	279,904	17,893	110,762	66,347
1992	2,111,525	1,499,798	18,130	1,517,928	178,542	80,636	1,420,022	384,995	306,508	18,715	112,825	67,347
1993	2,245,397	1,600,013	16,625	1,616,638	192,222	80,759	1,505,175	411,205	329,017	19,580	114,678	68,752
1994	2,379,702	1,696,634	15,536	1,712,170	206,111	87,961	1,594,020	438,081	347,601	20,376	116,788	69,706
1995	2,545,725	1,780,465	10,378	1,790,843	216,596	100,358	1,674,605	485,286	385,834	21,429	118,796	71,463
1996	2,695,792	1,871,189	10,954	1,882,143	226,641	103,465	1,758,967	522,115	414,710	22,231	121,263	73,122
1997	2,900,497	2,031,817	10,023	2,041,840	242,913	107,055	1,905,982	561,083	433,432	23,414	123,877	74,821
1998	3,111,318	2,178,210	9,317	2,187,527	260,532	134,533	2,061,528	603,372	446,418	24,648	126,232	78,580
1999	3,276,134	2,361,889	12,115	2,374,004	282,326	126,220	2,217,898	589,392	468,844	25,447	128,743	80,175
2000	3,449,727	2,447,515	16,135	2,463,650	292,749	140,918	2,311,819	635,557	502,351	26,249	131,423	81,244
2001	3,593,947	2,482,777	16,481	2,499,258	296,194	182,235	2,385,299	641,913	566,735	26,952	133,346	77,847
2002	3,665,037	2,502,125	5,156	2,507,281	293,838	216,186	2,429,629	628,566	606,842	27,100	135,239	76,384
2003	3,798,799	2,498,106	10,705	2,508,811	299,426	288,394	2,497,779	660,396	640,624	27,930	136,009	75,173
2004	3,883,968	2,623,545	11,166	2,634,711	311,194	212,403	2,535,920	658,941	689,107	28,223	137,619	75,967
2005	4,046,903	2,695,913	14,689	2,710,602	325,522	238,814	2,623,894	682,206	740,803	29,049	139,311	76,703
2006	4,403,150	2,847,193	12,569	2,859,762	342,219	279,891	2,797,434	777,274	828,442	31,126	141,462	77,138
2007	4,704,481	2,938,128	11,613	2,949,741	354,728	345,637	2,940,650	886,284	877,547	32,509	144,712	80,082
2008	4,889,345	2,987,076	5,653	2,992,729	361,101	380,557	3,012,185	873,852	1,003,308	33,102	147,704	78,758
2009	4,750,311	2,749,568	2,957	2,752,525	336,694	441,618	2,857,449	792,285	1,100,577	31,678	149,954	74,921
2010	4,864,367	2,846,114	2,642	2,848,756	342,402	441,402	2,947,756	760,650	1,155,961	32,121	151,437	74,330
2011	5,074,254	2,943,838	-486	2,943,352	324,302	439,783	3,058,833	851,375	1,164,046	33,228	152,712	76,422
2012	5,248,013	3,130,221	5,722	3,135,943	336,892	404,739	3,203,790	849,238	1,194,985	34,234	153,299	77,711
2013	5,328,813	3,144,992	7,560	3,152,552	390,015	451,886	3,214,423	900,977	1,213,413	34,556	154,209	77,884
2014	5,582,707	3,221,485	9,380	3,230,865	399,610	532,668	3,363,923	976,999	1,241,785	35,865	155,658	78,970
2015	5,759,612	3,284,031	6,338	3,290,369	409,126	594,275	3,475,518	968,341	1,315,753	36,600	157,367	79,319
2016	5,994,355	3,472,869	646	3,473,515	430,352	598,873	3,642,036	997,480	1,354,839	37,310	160,663	81,194
2017	6,253,563	3,586,655	1,216	3,587,871	442,848	653,275	3,798,298	1,046,644	1,408,621	38,208	163,671	82,386
2018	6,606,297	3,744,714	-5,508	3,739,206	457,059	751,168	4,033,315	1,093,648	1,479,334	39,582	166,901	84,194
2019	7,036,830	3,980,578	-3,836	3,976,742	485,485	788,222	4,279,479	1,185,897	1,571,454	41,493	169,590	85,914
2020	7,632,800	4,204,995	-5,300	4,199,695	516,592	745,735	4,428,838	1,206,374	1,997,588	44,418	171,842	83,916
2021	8,366,592	4,618,024	-1,656	4,616,368	558,668	773,500	4,831,200	1,235,263	2,300,129	48,118	173,877	87,667

Personal Income and Employment by Area: Burlington-South Burlington, VT

(Thousands of dollars, except as noted.)

Year	Personal income, total	Earnings by place of work			Less: Contributions for government social insurance	Plus: Adjustment for residence	Equals: Net earnings by place of residence	Plus: Dividends, interest, and rent	Plus: Personal current transfer receipts	Per capita personal income (dollars)	Population (persons)	Total employment
		Nonfarm	Farm	Total								
1970	516,335	422,616	17,722	440,338	29,444	-13,527	397,367	72,287	46,681	3,834	134,673	62,022
1971	556,777	447,386	17,720	465,106	31,994	-12,818	420,294	80,023	56,460	4,048	137,553	62,103
1972	606,443	484,457	19,304	503,761	36,122	-13,220	454,419	87,894	64,130	4,314	140,585	62,800
1973	654,967	521,330	20,573	541,903	44,911	-12,976	484,016	97,541	73,410	4,650	140,865	64,201
1974	706,184	553,004	16,913	569,917	49,146	-12,374	508,397	109,757	88,030	4,985	141,657	64,786
1975	791,194	604,097	17,982	622,079	52,565	-13,623	555,891	125,097	110,206	5,509	143,608	64,467
1976	880,961	681,928	22,301	704,229	60,602	-15,170	628,457	134,176	118,328	6,067	145,209	67,585
1977	960,758	755,626	18,942	774,568	67,583	-16,735	690,250	150,250	120,258	6,513	147,509	70,446
1978	1,114,324	893,339	27,525	920,864	82,639	-21,653	816,572	171,296	126,456	7,478	149,023	76,185
1979	1,265,516	1,023,961	29,838	1,053,799	98,499	-26,303	928,997	192,999	143,520	8,350	151,554	80,057
1980	1,428,519	1,134,802	30,079	1,164,881	109,727	-29,188	1,025,966	233,625	168,928	9,191	155,430	82,463
1981	1,622,347	1,283,722	32,918	1,316,640	133,162	-36,152	1,147,326	283,346	191,675	10,332	157,017	85,578
1982	1,768,338	1,389,929	31,780	1,421,709	147,354	-42,601	1,231,754	328,992	207,592	11,145	158,663	87,158
1983	1,913,244	1,523,752	21,355	1,545,107	163,393	-49,561	1,332,153	360,259	220,832	11,936	160,287	89,680
1984	2,106,272	1,687,829	22,047	1,709,876	186,031	-56,226	1,467,619	411,747	226,906	13,024	161,724	94,035
1985	2,313,562	1,866,984	27,639	1,894,623	209,699	-64,958	1,619,966	455,093	238,503	14,129	163,751	98,992
1986	2,495,723	2,029,452	27,935	2,057,387	228,907	-71,776	1,756,704	493,329	245,690	15,050	165,834	103,108
1987	2,708,768	2,233,000	36,515	2,269,515	247,883	-80,470	1,941,162	516,264	251,342	16,147	167,755	107,321
1988	2,991,002	2,490,757	34,060	2,524,817	284,100	-97,568	2,143,149	580,640	267,213	17,443	171,477	113,250
1989	3,346,857	2,739,025	35,548	2,774,573	309,471	-108,811	2,356,291	694,040	296,526	19,127	174,979	117,499
1990	3,521,968	2,895,469	33,930	2,929,399	346,095	-117,385	2,465,919	726,502	329,547	19,813	177,757	117,930
1991	3,614,329	2,964,492	28,614	2,993,106	357,372	-118,632	2,517,102	734,489	362,738	20,141	179,447	115,960
1992	3,852,004	3,133,575	49,875	3,183,450	373,108	-123,622	2,686,720	755,307	409,977	21,261	181,178	117,796
1993	4,023,183	3,296,137	39,987	3,336,124	394,254	-129,512	2,812,358	777,683	433,142	21,876	183,909	120,276
1994	4,184,528	3,388,569	40,336	3,428,905	409,134	-129,998	2,889,773	840,583	454,172	22,355	187,186	123,280
1995	4,461,385	3,560,273	31,957	3,592,230	434,510	-142,111	3,015,609	950,454	495,322	23,568	189,300	125,287
1996	4,741,595	3,810,527	46,011	3,856,538	460,096	-159,377	3,237,065	991,872	512,658	24,820	191,043	128,300
1997	5,001,261	4,007,208	34,235	4,041,443	480,696	-169,545	3,391,202	1,067,106	542,953	25,908	193,040	130,011
1998	5,405,166	4,352,659	44,123	4,396,782	513,716	-185,351	3,697,715	1,144,084	563,367	27,763	194,691	133,049
1999	5,784,707	4,757,783	47,902	4,805,685	552,638	-201,416	4,051,631	1,126,745	606,331	29,360	197,026	136,879
2000	6,317,905	5,207,839	51,158	5,258,997	595,562	-223,176	4,440,259	1,215,914	661,732	31,653	199,600	142,039
2001	6,636,374	5,460,384	52,174	5,512,558	630,201	-231,906	4,650,451	1,259,762	726,161	32,958	201,361	144,163
2002	6,797,675	5,606,012	39,718	5,645,730	634,572	-230,736	4,780,422	1,239,344	777,909	33,478	203,052	143,707
2003	7,134,439	5,817,168	48,319	5,865,487	660,647	-235,735	4,969,105	1,350,068	815,266	34,938	204,201	144,044
2004	7,516,339	6,132,343	65,327	6,197,670	695,390	-241,367	5,260,913	1,407,887	847,539	36,549	205,652	147,053
2005	7,731,154	6,311,090	66,593	6,377,683	724,231	-247,779	5,405,673	1,400,540	924,941	37,414	206,637	147,964
2006	8,208,148	6,536,953	41,219	6,578,172	758,595	-240,416	5,579,161	1,611,579	1,017,408	39,571	207,426	149,069
2007	8,636,564	6,758,765	72,418	6,831,183	800,297	-251,526	5,779,360	1,717,107	1,140,097	41,476	208,232	151,286
2008	9,193,802	7,057,271	71,475	7,128,746	833,866	-254,021	6,040,859	1,862,827	1,290,116	43,920	209,332	151,588
2009	9,073,387	7,059,412	40,120	7,099,532	833,051	-245,536	6,020,945	1,655,918	1,396,524	43,117	210,435	149,147
2010	9,342,137	7,298,604	62,146	7,360,750	852,794	-256,331	6,251,625	1,600,945	1,489,567	44,162	211,543	150,311
2011	10,051,515	7,614,009	84,549	7,698,558	796,124	-241,024	6,661,410	1,870,257	1,519,848	47,126	213,291	153,443
2012	10,404,787	7,892,529	79,629	7,972,158	834,949	-266,780	6,870,429	1,980,532	1,553,826	48,604	214,074	156,025
2013	10,649,920	8,149,744	99,055	8,248,799	975,939	-264,870	7,007,990	2,017,123	1,624,807	49,538	214,984	157,592
2014	11,192,236	8,294,518	118,350	8,412,868	1,017,254	-244,513	7,151,101	2,334,201	1,706,934	51,408	217,712	159,899
2015	11,494,038	8,601,132	74,054	8,675,186	1,061,701	-249,940	7,363,545	2,382,652	1,747,841	52,317	219,701	162,217
2016	11,779,845	8,806,354	65,281	8,871,635	1,088,803	-248,993	7,533,839	2,464,535	1,781,471	53,425	220,494	163,808
2017	12,138,521	9,064,847	74,220	9,139,067	1,127,829	-223,875	7,787,363	2,538,548	1,812,610	54,572	222,432	164,701
2018	12,545,943	9,446,664	54,130	9,500,794	1,158,671	-231,485	8,110,638	2,535,066	1,900,239	56,048	223,841	165,592
2019	13,260,315	9,794,906	86,335	9,881,241	1,176,237	-231,427	8,473,577	2,854,378	1,932,360	59,027	224,648	165,455
2020	14,070,317	9,951,889	74,569	10,026,458	1,203,264	-248,717	8,574,477	2,806,849	2,688,991	62,379	225,563	156,953
2021	14,748,604	10,625,921	69,312	10,695,233	1,235,032	-280,022	9,180,179	2,849,884	2,718,541	65,083	226,611	161,636

Personal Income and Employment by Area: California-Lexington Park, MD

(Thousands of dollars, except as noted.)

Year	Personal income, total	Earnings by place of work			Less: Contributions for government social insurance	Plus: Adjustment for residence	Equals: Net earnings by place of residence	Plus: Dividends, interest, and rent	Plus: Personal current transfer receipts	Per capita personal income (dollars)	Population (persons)	Total employment
		Nonfarm	Farm	Total								
1970	205,033	147,579	5,694	153,273	7,478	9,180	154,975	40,708	9,350	4,286	47,840	19,164
1971	230,307	162,424	4,453	166,877	8,459	16,464	174,882	44,176	11,249	4,594	50,127	19,026
1972	259,542	180,400	5,240	185,640	9,625	21,320	197,335	49,277	12,930	5,109	50,805	19,653
1973	278,652	184,440	8,012	192,452	10,637	28,303	210,118	53,378	15,156	5,581	49,928	19,221
1974	314,963	206,087	7,933	214,020	12,701	34,066	235,385	61,333	18,245	6,096	51,667	20,064
1975	313,494	194,757	6,410	201,167	12,572	40,585	229,180	61,405	22,909	5,944	52,738	18,610
1976	347,827	213,201	7,717	220,918	14,073	48,689	255,534	67,077	25,216	6,474	53,724	18,852
1977	383,723	229,288	7,698	236,986	15,214	58,547	280,319	75,729	27,675	7,038	54,522	19,582
1978	429,820	247,819	10,702	258,521	16,768	70,747	312,500	86,780	30,540	7,575	56,744	20,556
1979	464,968	265,540	7,430	272,970	19,870	83,876	336,976	92,906	35,086	7,943	58,541	20,935
1980	527,810	299,399	3,785	303,184	22,922	97,923	378,185	107,048	42,577	8,771	60,176	21,211
1981	637,140	360,097	11,537	371,634	26,509	114,503	459,628	127,687	49,825	10,414	61,182	22,032
1982	695,208	388,632	18,623	407,255	29,106	116,780	494,929	144,883	55,396	11,268	61,697	22,268
1983	736,046	422,493	9,533	432,026	34,543	123,654	521,137	154,754	60,155	11,786	62,450	23,501
1984	807,286	465,867	8,430	474,297	39,891	133,613	568,019	173,738	65,529	12,764	63,245	24,650
1985	880,016	508,956	12,874	521,830	45,530	146,604	622,904	186,830	70,282	13,619	64,618	25,721
1986	950,696	563,958	4,446	568,404	52,568	159,571	675,407	201,441	73,848	14,281	66,570	27,230
1987	1,042,225	628,687	5,201	633,888	59,506	169,875	744,257	215,780	82,188	15,087	69,083	29,457
1988	1,178,101	736,180	6,935	743,115	73,916	182,863	852,062	236,792	89,247	16,412	71,785	32,351
1989	1,293,795	809,524	3,530	813,054	83,119	195,682	925,617	266,060	102,118	17,453	74,130	34,042
1990	1,395,218	882,991	5,634	888,625	93,090	206,199	1,001,734	279,085	114,399	18,271	76,361	35,990
1991	1,475,771	946,457	6,380	952,837	101,081	194,623	1,046,379	297,347	132,045	18,932	77,952	36,785
1992	1,554,785	994,877	4,799	999,676	106,975	195,047	1,087,748	312,585	154,452	19,727	78,815	36,686
1993	1,585,392	1,004,048	4,259	1,008,307	108,684	201,152	1,100,775	322,931	161,686	20,327	77,994	35,928
1994	1,638,346	1,039,231	5,236	1,044,467	114,623	200,746	1,130,590	341,066	166,690	20,808	78,737	36,940
1995	1,713,367	1,091,329	-5,492	1,085,837	119,644	196,155	1,162,348	372,544	178,475	21,627	79,222	38,098
1996	1,842,676	1,192,243	14,510	1,206,753	130,378	184,227	1,260,602	393,490	188,584	22,853	80,633	40,147
1997	2,113,630	1,460,019	7,330	1,467,349	159,123	149,108	1,457,334	459,194	197,102	25,415	83,165	44,464
1998	2,356,873	1,709,910	1,114	1,711,024	183,865	116,209	1,643,368	510,750	202,755	27,739	84,967	47,377
1999	2,441,709	1,772,182	2,619	1,774,801	190,597	120,945	1,705,149	520,032	216,528	28,516	85,627	48,147
2000	2,635,434	1,941,485	10,795	1,952,280	206,222	105,661	1,851,719	550,017	233,698	30,468	86,498	49,501
2001	2,683,900	1,957,713	10,929	1,968,642	210,328	135,972	1,894,286	528,530	261,084	30,689	87,455	47,090
2002	2,914,676	2,175,502	-4,722	2,170,780	232,318	142,907	2,081,369	542,125	291,182	32,451	89,819	49,310
2003	3,172,352	2,402,817	6,115	2,408,932	256,921	139,447	2,291,458	571,285	309,609	34,358	92,333	51,659
2004	3,414,534	2,582,730	8,146	2,590,876	280,805	190,741	2,500,812	579,020	334,702	35,980	94,900	52,800
2005	3,639,998	2,685,268	5,064	2,690,332	290,721	274,106	2,673,717	597,546	368,735	37,576	96,871	53,234
2006	3,906,209	2,898,916	3,289	2,902,205	318,660	272,546	2,856,091	657,892	392,226	39,517	98,849	54,953
2007	4,196,315	3,052,797	2,443	3,055,240	339,933	295,570	3,010,877	752,740	432,698	41,713	100,599	56,573
2008	4,498,567	3,116,763	3,087	3,119,850	352,595	367,348	3,134,603	856,944	507,020	44,138	101,921	56,063
2009	4,682,612	3,372,049	3,069	3,375,118	379,999	310,046	3,305,165	836,488	540,959	45,342	103,273	56,276
2010	4,960,797	3,721,687	-278	3,721,409	422,440	217,945	3,516,914	846,128	597,755	46,901	105,772	57,614
2011	5,267,373	3,996,247	2,846	3,999,093	402,889	118,793	3,714,997	922,310	630,066	48,958	107,589	58,334
2012	5,367,756	4,035,182	102	4,035,284	408,618	127,299	3,753,965	962,895	650,896	49,315	108,847	58,503
2013	5,380,529	4,049,610	-454	4,049,156	463,363	120,803	3,706,596	998,371	675,562	49,234	109,284	59,093
2014	5,554,775	4,155,159	-3,017	4,152,142	473,433	130,169	3,808,878	1,028,862	717,035	50,615	109,745	59,496
2015	5,811,132	4,288,493	-4,678	4,283,815	490,348	178,292	3,971,759	1,082,255	757,118	52,460	110,772	60,303
2016	5,978,975	4,437,792	-3,384	4,434,408	499,630	166,135	4,100,913	1,080,708	797,354	53,623	111,500	61,226
2017	6,119,942	4,583,568	735	4,584,303	518,262	150,836	4,216,877	1,084,365	818,700	54,558	112,174	62,069
2018	6,361,488	4,694,276	-2,285	4,691,991	535,416	222,301	4,378,876	1,116,367	866,245	56,583	112,427	62,582
2019	6,660,477	4,926,619	4,360	4,930,979	564,785	184,885	4,551,079	1,191,822	917,576	58,853	113,172	63,541
2020	7,050,778	5,293,895	1,943	5,295,838	605,365	-28,469	4,662,004	1,173,720	1,215,054	61,874	113,953	64,019
2021	7,527,632	5,488,840	6,193	5,495,033	628,221	125,351	4,992,163	1,187,317	1,348,152	65,762	114,468	65,835

Personal Income and Employment by Area: Canton-Massillon, OH

(Thousands of dollars, except as noted.)

Year	Personal income, total	Earnings by place of work			Less: Contributions for government social insurance	Plus: Adjustment for residence	Equals: Net earnings by place of residence	Plus: Dividends, interest, and rent	Plus: Personal current transfer receipts	Per capita personal income (dollars)	Population (persons)	Total employment
		Nonfarm	Farm	Total								
1970	1,539,014	1,257,308	6,263	1,263,571	86,403	32,588	1,209,756	204,466	124,792	3,902	394,389	166,024
1971	1,594,880	1,266,119	7,849	1,273,968	89,495	43,474	1,227,947	218,615	148,318	4,019	396,830	160,591
1972	1,767,736	1,416,355	7,807	1,424,162	105,412	52,319	1,371,069	232,722	163,945	4,480	394,589	163,820
1973	1,991,029	1,613,297	9,499	1,622,796	139,857	59,081	1,542,020	258,597	190,412	4,919	404,798	173,392
1974	2,228,143	1,791,284	10,639	1,801,923	161,136	65,845	1,706,632	296,003	225,508	5,483	406,348	179,109
1975	2,393,365	1,852,965	14,869	1,867,834	162,465	73,265	1,778,634	320,367	294,364	5,947	402,470	173,184
1976	2,607,650	2,026,060	15,741	2,041,801	180,923	82,159	1,943,037	342,940	321,673	6,510	400,573	173,726
1977	2,889,951	2,249,265	13,768	2,263,033	200,669	112,452	2,174,816	380,708	334,427	7,201	401,304	177,260
1978	3,219,758	2,529,202	8,722	2,537,924	233,670	133,927	2,438,181	425,251	356,326	7,967	404,117	184,559
1979	3,618,783	2,836,297	7,293	2,843,590	272,784	154,282	2,725,088	484,643	409,052	8,982	402,887	189,646
1980	3,960,435	2,948,295	297	2,948,592	282,431	174,671	2,840,832	597,744	521,859	9,794	404,365	186,051
1981	4,377,425	3,211,721	2,760	3,214,481	329,515	176,999	3,061,965	736,985	578,475	10,856	403,233	184,686
1982	4,520,150	3,144,256	4,582	3,148,838	326,647	188,297	3,010,488	818,427	691,235	11,255	401,616	177,193
1983	4,673,058	3,194,008	-311	3,193,697	334,666	204,919	3,063,950	868,682	740,426	11,691	399,727	172,450
1984	5,082,542	3,513,085	10,183	3,523,268	378,965	220,889	3,365,192	962,772	754,578	12,734	399,131	179,713
1985	5,308,867	3,659,949	12,457	3,672,406	400,955	235,901	3,507,352	1,001,813	799,702	13,388	396,527	183,119
1986	5,454,943	3,703,347	12,327	3,715,674	417,024	263,292	3,561,942	1,033,654	859,347	13,860	393,569	185,112
1987	5,716,044	3,940,389	14,925	3,955,314	443,742	265,131	3,776,703	1,041,977	897,364	14,577	392,135	191,292
1988	6,115,930	4,259,918	14,230	4,274,148	494,459	278,247	4,057,936	1,118,347	939,647	15,532	393,752	194,561
1989	6,556,918	4,483,325	19,738	4,503,063	522,312	303,825	4,284,576	1,270,035	1,002,307	16,622	394,481	198,003
1990	6,931,864	4,723,907	17,440	4,741,347	560,477	311,808	4,492,678	1,313,115	1,126,071	17,567	394,606	201,081
1991	7,042,221	4,813,851	9,328	4,823,179	582,378	322,021	4,562,822	1,287,546	1,191,853	17,737	397,025	200,722
1992	7,530,403	5,160,203	20,514	5,180,717	617,528	340,888	4,904,077	1,317,828	1,308,498	18,854	399,399	199,451
1993	7,861,478	5,424,606	16,229	5,440,835	661,054	364,750	5,144,531	1,365,318	1,351,629	19,551	402,098	202,448
1994	8,293,385	5,766,366	25,708	5,792,074	711,120	391,221	5,472,175	1,456,998	1,364,212	20,548	403,612	207,012
1995	8,681,847	5,995,431	27,036	6,022,467	749,400	416,943	5,690,010	1,558,783	1,433,054	21,441	404,924	212,418
1996	9,048,955	6,186,992	26,678	6,213,670	762,440	452,524	5,903,754	1,643,588	1,501,613	22,293	405,915	215,591
1997	9,423,245	6,412,641	27,659	6,440,300	772,726	476,334	6,143,908	1,739,802	1,539,535	23,197	406,235	218,984
1998	10,115,178	6,956,008	54,885	7,010,893	807,271	500,235	6,703,857	1,813,315	1,598,006	24,903	406,189	224,798
1999	10,387,636	7,180,885	46,529	7,227,414	824,802	532,880	6,935,492	1,797,595	1,654,549	25,524	406,983	226,886
2000	10,965,249	7,560,069	35,204	7,595,273	837,972	560,094	7,317,395	1,880,518	1,767,336	26,949	406,887	232,230
2001	11,080,545	7,564,434	33,110	7,597,544	853,492	606,301	7,350,353	1,819,616	1,910,576	27,275	406,256	225,330
2002	11,230,099	7,629,000	26,076	7,655,076	843,586	676,437	7,487,927	1,700,610	2,041,562	27,658	406,039	221,364
2003	11,564,627	7,763,278	25,282	7,788,560	868,856	768,246	7,687,950	1,733,873	2,142,804	28,481	406,046	217,698
2004	11,940,111	8,094,418	29,738	8,124,156	916,589	818,160	8,025,727	1,722,204	2,192,180	29,412	405,960	218,617
2005	12,329,275	8,253,621	31,614	8,285,235	948,774	912,148	8,248,609	1,746,730	2,333,936	30,430	405,168	220,170
2006	12,846,085	8,319,521	25,162	8,344,683	962,325	1,081,278	8,463,636	1,915,442	2,467,007	31,692	405,343	216,097
2007	13,529,760	8,516,401	31,855	8,548,256	983,455	1,164,629	8,729,430	2,165,949	2,634,381	33,330	405,939	217,378
2008	14,007,322	8,686,058	33,555	8,719,613	1,016,361	1,132,431	8,835,683	2,221,368	2,950,271	34,489	406,140	215,543
2009	13,468,282	8,160,398	39,978	8,200,376	973,870	1,021,740	8,248,246	1,990,713	3,229,323	33,245	405,127	205,924
2010	13,840,877	8,265,656	44,704	8,310,360	969,438	1,100,755	8,441,677	1,993,070	3,406,130	34,242	404,207	203,967
2011	14,739,349	8,801,349	58,998	8,860,347	935,786	1,127,463	9,052,024	2,205,580	3,481,745	36,543	403,344	209,428
2012	15,348,126	9,193,126	47,596	9,240,722	964,807	1,207,115	9,483,030	2,440,815	3,424,281	38,041	403,465	213,719
2013	15,529,017	9,622,396	51,259	9,673,655	1,088,758	1,074,697	9,659,594	2,326,060	3,543,363	38,493	403,424	217,118
2014	16,144,219	9,994,052	41,546	10,035,598	1,119,958	1,070,556	9,986,196	2,522,241	3,635,782	39,799	405,644	220,086
2015	16,699,598	10,046,881	16,924	10,063,805	1,129,017	1,272,024	10,206,812	2,707,374	3,785,412	41,248	404,863	219,327
2016	16,671,110	9,963,191	10,002	9,973,193	1,148,945	1,269,170	10,093,418	2,718,623	3,859,069	41,269	403,961	220,200
2017	17,183,521	10,402,406	9,774	10,412,180	1,232,336	1,244,389	10,424,233	2,829,804	3,929,484	42,674	402,666	221,474
2018	17,714,512	10,649,002	15,686	10,664,688	1,246,694	1,326,786	10,744,780	2,941,005	4,028,727	44,044	402,202	222,207
2019	18,318,532	10,898,104	1,182	10,899,286	1,286,958	1,356,938	10,969,266	3,145,642	4,203,624	45,591	401,805	220,305
2020	19,624,021	10,921,384	18,206	10,939,590	1,300,065	1,361,705	11,001,230	3,127,070	5,495,721	48,932	401,046	214,405
2021	20,888,378	11,555,759	33,471	11,589,230	1,354,919	1,528,420	11,762,731	3,178,427	5,947,220	52,152	400,525	218,874

Personal Income and Employment by Area: Cape Coral-Fort Myers, FL

(Thousands of dollars, except as noted.)

Year	Personal income, total	Earnings by place of work			Less: Contributions for government social insurance	Plus: Adjustment for residence	Equals: Net earnings by place of residence	Plus: Dividends, interest, and rent	Plus: Personal current transfer receipts	Per capita personal income (dollars)	Population (persons)	Total employment
		Nonfarm	Farm	Total								
1970	424,777	255,307	7,788	263,095	16,301	5,688	252,482	122,719	49,576	3,954	107,430	42,485
1971	481,303	281,710	8,448	290,158	18,792	5,892	277,258	141,942	62,103	4,116	116,946	44,589
1972	566,888	337,228	9,099	346,327	23,700	6,875	329,502	161,431	75,955	4,440	127,672	49,836
1973	700,122	418,684	10,076	428,760	33,844	9,862	404,778	199,141	96,203	5,100	137,276	58,032
1974	822,773	483,494	9,569	493,063	41,155	10,583	462,491	243,677	116,605	5,604	146,825	61,830
1975	916,640	503,421	15,192	518,613	42,100	8,456	484,969	277,494	154,177	5,917	154,905	61,397
1976	1,045,610	577,994	17,346	595,340	48,458	8,386	555,268	316,668	173,674	6,550	159,632	65,373
1977	1,224,202	680,308	18,233	698,541	57,763	10,705	651,483	376,352	196,367	7,036	173,998	73,310
1978	1,483,214	833,626	23,175	856,801	72,566	14,151	798,386	456,106	228,722	8,109	182,920	83,121
1979	1,761,290	986,198	24,644	1,010,842	90,397	14,876	935,321	553,556	272,413	9,145	192,597	90,770
1980	2,149,997	1,146,092	25,998	1,172,090	106,373	17,288	1,083,005	733,490	333,502	10,334	208,050	96,755
1981	2,569,819	1,313,646	22,103	1,335,749	131,787	18,978	1,222,940	943,339	403,540	11,745	218,795	103,581
1982	2,744,856	1,363,942	27,149	1,391,091	142,832	16,969	1,265,228	1,006,855	472,773	11,886	230,932	106,186
1983	3,093,013	1,542,321	39,899	1,582,220	160,655	14,593	1,436,158	1,133,657	523,198	12,805	241,554	113,430
1984	3,531,951	1,774,399	39,545	1,813,944	189,367	16,479	1,641,056	1,321,244	569,651	13,835	255,299	121,575
1985	3,987,867	2,003,597	43,315	2,046,912	218,359	18,900	1,847,453	1,502,095	638,319	14,930	267,107	129,854
1986	4,441,540	2,253,269	50,847	2,304,116	252,185	18,722	2,070,653	1,664,855	706,032	15,835	280,483	136,443
1987	4,920,677	2,556,640	58,630	2,615,270	282,950	19,805	2,352,125	1,803,634	764,918	16,665	295,262	138,260
1988	5,486,734	2,881,768	58,449	2,940,217	329,695	23,554	2,634,076	2,011,611	841,047	17,881	306,842	149,455
1989	6,386,328	3,197,310	61,650	3,258,960	372,326	24,713	2,911,347	2,518,329	956,652	19,818	322,253	159,512
1990	6,807,498	3,426,826	41,827	3,468,653	394,898	30,003	3,103,758	2,651,395	1,052,345	20,080	339,012	164,024
1991	6,933,177	3,616,892	48,490	3,665,382	417,708	-93,352	3,154,322	2,606,869	1,171,986	19,749	351,069	163,361
1992	7,308,276	3,871,763	46,252	3,918,015	445,103	-147,040	3,325,872	2,645,164	1,337,240	20,319	359,679	162,757
1993	7,782,306	4,134,713	49,101	4,183,814	472,610	-79,233	3,631,971	2,720,752	1,429,583	21,094	368,938	170,194
1994	8,330,303	4,468,729	39,826	4,508,555	518,294	-69,540	3,920,721	2,878,991	1,530,591	21,868	380,928	178,317
1995	9,093,151	4,768,774	41,282	4,810,056	549,600	-75,801	4,184,655	3,253,328	1,655,168	23,207	391,823	186,043
1996	9,535,549	5,136,363	30,688	5,167,051	582,228	-150,179	4,434,644	3,338,998	1,761,907	23,796	400,723	191,718
1997	10,162,884	5,292,558	33,445	5,326,003	604,113	-57,310	4,664,580	3,657,513	1,840,791	24,737	410,841	196,507
1998	10,978,685	5,885,618	43,275	5,928,893	656,736	-145,508	5,126,649	3,991,201	1,860,835	26,023	421,889	205,733
1999	11,554,742	6,446,621	45,651	6,492,272	710,017	-147,080	5,635,175	3,968,732	1,950,835	26,748	431,981	211,109
2000	12,779,956	6,961,704	43,776	7,005,480	764,422	-7,656	6,233,402	4,447,904	2,098,650	28,764	444,311	219,932
2001	14,404,506	8,167,560	42,924	8,210,484	886,105	-9,902	7,314,477	4,807,551	2,282,478	31,244	461,037	232,767
2002	14,933,731	8,748,005	45,612	8,793,617	943,875	-21,899	7,827,843	4,642,875	2,463,013	31,184	478,889	240,323
2003	16,180,454	9,739,725	43,847	9,783,572	1,049,738	-22,867	8,710,967	4,824,463	2,645,024	32,513	497,662	258,600
2004	18,758,720	11,282,868	42,380	11,325,248	1,210,610	-74,365	10,040,273	5,846,241	2,872,206	35,907	522,431	276,146
2005	20,970,488	12,523,544	45,660	12,569,204	1,361,579	-52,907	11,154,718	6,719,402	3,096,368	37,783	555,029	300,554
2006	24,210,220	14,475,819	35,410	14,511,229	1,548,833	-91,054	12,871,342	7,964,722	3,374,156	41,550	582,678	316,326
2007	24,905,810	14,264,308	25,761	14,290,069	1,563,192	37,587	12,764,464	8,466,800	3,674,546	41,186	604,716	315,773
2008	25,409,577	13,424,417	25,750	13,450,167	1,514,409	-16,034	11,919,724	9,238,854	4,250,999	41,588	610,984	298,689
2009	24,560,064	12,542,672	30,718	12,573,390	1,449,151	9,058	11,133,297	8,716,639	4,710,128	40,111	612,297	284,886
2010	24,629,058	12,753,521	41,158	12,794,679	1,432,490	-148,347	11,213,842	8,231,414	5,183,802	39,693	620,481	284,625
2011	26,487,133	13,053,824	41,120	13,094,944	1,331,097	-21,680	11,742,167	9,285,563	5,459,403	41,963	631,198	292,596
2012	27,325,128	13,517,932	56,641	13,574,573	1,395,604	-209,241	11,969,728	9,783,549	5,571,851	42,401	644,451	301,974
2013	27,819,048	13,865,747	50,120	13,915,867	1,630,182	-113,886	12,171,799	9,825,310	5,821,939	42,137	660,197	314,675
2014	30,579,176	15,104,058	40,702	15,144,760	1,762,713	-291,945	13,090,102	11,270,464	6,218,610	45,747	668,448	334,635
2015	33,018,323	16,463,632	52,346	16,515,978	1,903,562	-505,501	14,106,915	12,247,604	6,663,804	47,961	688,440	353,157
2016	35,429,171	17,628,590	48,071	17,676,661	2,026,380	-604,614	15,045,667	13,352,970	7,030,534	49,973	708,970	364,210
2017	37,512,569	18,678,534	48,734	18,727,268	2,140,529	-733,438	15,853,301	14,193,333	7,465,935	51,814	723,989	378,114
2018	39,466,839	19,406,220	53,734	19,459,954	2,276,044	-751,154	16,432,756	15,101,087	7,932,996	53,678	735,249	391,944
2019	42,383,795	19,818,294	52,635	19,870,929	2,402,016	-764,228	16,704,685	17,171,974	8,507,136	56,549	749,512	398,572
2020	45,345,499	20,715,045	52,115	20,767,160	2,515,884	-743,957	17,507,319	17,293,036	10,545,144	59,300	764,679	403,030
2021	49,552,254	22,957,460	49,234	23,006,694	2,739,921	-658,536	19,608,237	18,018,039	11,925,978	62,885	787,976	423,452

Personal Income and Employment by Area: Cape Girardeau, MO-IL

(Thousands of dollars, except as noted.)

Year	Personal income, total	Earnings by place of work			Less: Contributions for government social insurance	Plus: Adjustment for residence	Equals: Net earnings by place of residence	Plus: Dividends, interest, and rent	Plus: Personal current transfer receipts	Per capita personal income (dollars)	Population (persons)	Total employment
		Nonfarm	Farm	Total								
1970	222,083	169,627	9,171	178,798	11,405	-6,509	160,884	33,039	28,160	3,153	70,436	30,842
1971	242,481	185,875	8,250	194,125	12,963	-7,055	174,107	36,531	31,843	3,373	71,899	31,125
1972	262,465	198,524	10,466	208,990	14,450	-6,576	187,964	40,310	34,191	3,564	73,647	31,770
1973	296,723	217,718	18,539	236,257	18,254	-6,082	211,921	45,786	39,016	4,048	73,297	33,247
1974	330,521	250,830	10,119	260,949	21,944	-7,705	231,300	52,907	46,314	4,431	74,588	34,420
1975	379,546	274,221	17,405	291,626	23,478	-8,765	259,383	60,443	59,720	5,087	74,605	34,141
1976	422,961	317,320	15,432	332,752	27,451	-10,990	294,311	66,143	62,507	5,506	76,817	36,445
1977	463,456	349,977	14,501	364,478	30,208	-11,215	323,055	75,134	65,267	5,973	77,598	37,517
1978	526,451	401,003	19,953	420,956	35,866	-12,988	372,102	83,560	70,789	6,678	78,829	39,115
1979	589,997	444,672	24,964	469,636	41,160	-14,618	413,858	95,695	80,444	7,380	79,941	39,912
1980	632,790	466,106	2,883	468,989	43,073	-11,193	414,723	120,146	97,921	7,758	81,562	39,014
1981	720,486	496,981	16,547	513,528	49,323	-11,267	452,938	147,219	120,329	8,782	82,038	39,055
1982	755,887	513,919	10,882	524,801	51,882	-12,557	460,362	176,084	119,441	9,266	81,576	39,480
1983	802,466	561,348	-1,820	559,528	56,354	-16,825	486,349	187,345	128,772	9,841	81,546	40,586
1984	892,923	616,270	13,170	629,440	63,602	-17,580	548,258	210,896	133,769	10,925	81,732	41,905
1985	948,768	656,136	16,431	672,567	68,883	-18,391	585,293	221,826	141,649	11,541	82,211	43,356
1986	996,935	714,065	2,341	716,406	75,566	-22,000	618,840	230,111	147,984	12,103	82,368	44,845
1987	1,063,917	775,813	9,625	785,438	81,133	-23,305	681,000	231,063	151,854	12,892	82,524	46,098
1988	1,115,402	826,657	4,319	830,976	89,028	-23,958	717,990	237,809	159,603	13,475	82,775	46,557
1989	1,204,185	877,513	12,982	890,495	95,487	-25,682	769,326	258,739	176,120	14,555	82,734	47,610
1990	1,238,100	911,743	9,411	921,154	102,290	-30,307	788,557	259,892	189,651	14,910	83,037	49,146
1991	1,301,814	947,215	6,612	953,827	108,025	-33,450	812,352	274,223	215,239	15,518	83,892	48,247
1992	1,403,424	1,030,767	14,305	1,045,072	116,490	-44,219	884,363	285,820	233,241	16,488	85,118	49,450
1993	1,474,699	1,084,704	10,172	1,094,876	123,263	-49,132	922,481	304,338	247,880	17,187	85,803	50,713
1994	1,560,150	1,165,094	8,418	1,173,512	133,147	-53,235	987,130	314,072	258,948	18,085	86,267	52,387
1995	1,662,831	1,248,750	3,121	1,251,871	142,368	-62,958	1,046,545	338,814	277,472	19,095	87,084	54,098
1996	1,736,429	1,286,209	9,210	1,295,419	144,810	-67,070	1,083,539	360,114	292,776	19,738	87,975	54,280
1997	1,828,121	1,351,047	8,961	1,360,008	150,825	-71,907	1,137,276	383,562	307,283	20,711	88,270	54,484
1998	1,926,111	1,449,492	3,270	1,452,762	161,180	-81,892	1,209,690	393,641	322,780	21,719	88,682	56,838
1999	2,028,754	1,586,002	2,332	1,588,334	175,468	-100,140	1,312,726	386,400	329,628	22,538	90,016	58,769
2000	2,169,420	1,670,686	10,129	1,680,815	181,444	-107,855	1,391,516	422,158	355,746	23,964	90,527	59,512
2001	2,255,621	1,715,256	13,124	1,728,380	186,856	-110,703	1,430,821	428,972	395,828	24,726	91,226	57,816
2002	2,343,588	1,803,446	7,252	1,810,698	195,024	-118,160	1,497,514	414,433	431,641	25,559	91,694	57,787
2003	2,452,204	1,871,087	21,867	1,892,954	201,823	-120,353	1,570,778	428,697	452,729	26,701	91,840	58,156
2004	2,628,045	1,984,976	37,677	2,022,653	210,578	-115,199	1,696,876	448,759	482,410	28,340	92,734	58,289
2005	2,717,938	2,094,001	19,044	2,113,045	223,291	-119,045	1,770,709	426,548	520,681	29,171	93,173	59,727
2006	2,866,288	2,211,379	11,786	2,223,165	238,399	-131,728	1,853,038	463,011	550,239	30,438	94,167	61,015
2007	3,065,286	2,326,385	5,856	2,332,241	255,213	-144,093	1,932,935	540,283	592,068	32,397	94,616	62,379
2008	3,142,462	2,273,926	30,233	2,304,159	255,109	-137,335	1,911,715	575,194	655,553	33,068	95,031	61,857
2009	3,121,881	2,277,226	13,566	2,290,792	255,777	-144,297	1,890,718	524,004	707,159	32,644	95,634	60,395
2010	3,211,514	2,327,552	20,351	2,347,903	256,053	-140,841	1,951,009	506,909	753,596	33,294	96,459	59,229
2011	3,352,012	2,367,987	23,889	2,391,876	234,207	-121,762	2,035,907	552,307	763,798	34,556	97,002	59,171
2012	3,574,091	2,494,947	17,970	2,512,917	242,173	-108,906	2,161,838	640,555	771,698	36,754	97,244	59,680
2013	3,614,185	2,572,261	45,358	2,617,619	279,783	-108,293	2,229,543	595,717	788,925	37,174	97,224	60,567
2014	3,678,431	2,576,161	46,519	2,622,680	283,140	-92,803	2,246,737	628,152	803,542	37,727	97,502	60,057
2015	3,841,857	2,697,779	3,298	2,701,077	295,195	-75,078	2,330,804	656,100	854,953	39,416	97,470	60,159
2016	3,923,516	2,720,953	19,633	2,740,586	299,467	-81,225	2,359,894	690,096	873,526	40,311	97,330	60,494
2017	4,024,710	2,791,107	17,306	2,808,413	306,847	-79,001	2,422,565	703,912	898,233	41,467	97,058	60,474
2018	4,143,381	2,880,728	1,305	2,882,033	322,523	-88,687	2,470,823	740,194	932,364	42,606	97,249	61,480
2019	4,179,100	2,886,688	11,452	2,898,140	330,492	-91,820	2,475,828	731,394	971,878	42,998	97,193	61,620
2020	4,483,501	2,959,004	23,053	2,982,057	344,356	-93,345	2,544,356	730,408	1,208,737	45,994	97,481	60,685
2021	4,733,269	3,076,095	31,235	3,107,330	349,763	-69,937	2,687,630	724,830	1,320,809	48,447	97,699	61,405

Personal Income and Employment by Area: Carbondale-Marion, IL

(Thousands of dollars, except as noted.)

Year	Personal income, total	Earnings by place of work			Less: Contributions for government social insurance	Plus: Adjustment for residence	Equals: Net earnings by place of residence	Plus: Dividends, interest, and rent	Plus: Personal current transfer receipts	Per capita personal income (dollars)	Population (persons)	Total employment
		Nonfarm	Farm	Total								
1970	324,924	258,599	2,145	260,744	15,052	-2,209	243,483	42,515	38,926	3,112	104,404	40,154
1971	364,863	286,980	2,871	289,851	17,188	-2,617	270,046	46,932	47,885	3,415	106,828	41,453
1972	401,416	312,025	3,009	315,034	19,471	-1,349	294,214	52,115	55,087	3,705	108,334	42,454
1973	456,578	342,541	9,466	352,007	24,400	-1,292	326,315	60,142	70,121	4,271	106,903	43,396
1974	495,243	364,480	9,510	373,990	27,065	1,189	348,114	69,309	77,820	4,615	107,320	44,408
1975	587,924	417,458	12,813	430,271	29,669	2,761	403,363	81,695	102,866	5,329	110,316	44,949
1976	660,254	484,980	8,797	493,777	36,115	1,508	459,170	89,371	111,713	5,790	114,039	47,991
1977	720,975	530,488	11,370	541,858	40,062	4,761	506,557	100,353	114,065	6,229	115,743	49,432
1978	786,172	585,648	8,304	593,952	45,110	4,783	553,625	111,423	121,124	6,748	116,505	50,217
1979	884,913	641,961	11,013	652,974	51,396	15,846	617,424	128,234	139,255	7,505	117,908	51,476
1980	972,624	683,292	2,196	685,488	54,271	19,040	650,257	157,300	165,067	8,195	118,692	51,285
1981	1,075,070	727,487	7,504	734,991	61,069	17,946	691,868	193,438	189,764	8,921	120,509	51,216
1982	1,181,923	778,860	3,490	782,350	66,357	24,409	740,402	241,355	200,166	9,823	120,316	51,051
1983	1,254,280	836,669	-520	836,149	71,714	15,516	779,951	257,279	217,050	10,396	120,650	52,036
1984	1,359,665	912,161	2,643	914,804	80,827	14,991	848,968	287,902	222,795	11,343	119,864	53,250
1985	1,414,180	928,017	11,698	939,715	83,347	25,275	881,643	302,305	230,232	11,785	119,997	53,361
1986	1,448,925	962,489	-4,184	958,305	86,303	25,458	897,460	317,460	234,005	12,113	119,619	54,938
1987	1,514,826	1,011,748	6,915	1,018,663	89,066	20,023	949,620	320,595	244,611	12,632	119,923	55,376
1988	1,569,041	1,049,891	8,316	1,058,207	96,661	23,924	985,470	325,656	257,915	13,157	119,255	55,452
1989	1,690,108	1,102,139	21,601	1,123,740	103,011	27,381	1,048,110	366,563	275,435	14,211	118,928	56,439
1990	1,756,374	1,187,537	9,269	1,196,806	109,136	23,847	1,111,517	353,680	291,177	14,788	118,770	58,256
1991	1,818,343	1,246,499	6,273	1,252,772	119,032	9,367	1,143,107	364,592	310,644	15,335	118,578	58,784
1992	1,963,415	1,340,694	12,146	1,352,840	126,134	5,121	1,231,827	373,646	357,942	16,396	119,749	59,722
1993	2,007,125	1,370,579	13,889	1,384,468	130,850	-1,659	1,251,959	382,558	372,608	16,600	120,909	60,133
1994	2,121,111	1,469,618	16,030	1,485,648	143,723	919	1,342,844	400,297	377,970	17,467	121,436	62,968
1995	2,235,413	1,533,939	8,874	1,542,813	150,424	-4,602	1,387,787	444,498	403,128	18,394	121,529	63,549
1996	2,324,611	1,573,953	14,467	1,588,420	152,865	-6,679	1,428,876	471,986	423,749	19,132	121,503	63,587
1997	2,419,295	1,633,675	14,443	1,648,118	156,971	-9,627	1,481,520	499,138	438,637	19,863	121,801	64,237
1998	2,720,532	1,790,486	17,908	1,808,394	171,964	27,870	1,664,300	560,274	495,958	20,211	134,607	69,232
1999	2,839,002	1,935,175	9,825	1,945,000	181,240	20,873	1,784,633	553,228	501,141	21,142	134,280	71,824
2000	2,976,883	2,035,732	13,587	2,049,319	187,218	19,808	1,881,909	568,403	526,571	22,257	133,748	73,462
2001	3,222,576	2,233,162	8,894	2,242,056	199,667	9,261	2,051,650	609,082	561,844	24,038	134,061	73,611
2002	3,352,899	2,398,635	197	2,398,832	215,119	-5,413	2,178,300	573,572	601,027	25,108	133,540	73,596
2003	3,443,407	2,428,495	10,695	2,439,190	221,183	-8,084	2,209,923	608,304	625,180	25,552	134,761	73,383
2004	3,552,947	2,498,192	25,894	2,524,086	229,988	-14,371	2,279,727	610,572	662,648	26,174	135,744	73,641
2005	3,693,245	2,641,544	11,930	2,653,474	252,751	-32,778	2,367,945	593,553	731,747	27,018	136,697	75,320
2006	3,854,951	2,789,187	12,508	2,801,695	265,681	-48,675	2,487,339	621,377	746,235	28,039	137,483	76,453
2007	4,003,818	2,864,172	7,046	2,871,218	275,205	-55,630	2,540,383	644,222	819,213	29,116	137,511	76,746
2008	4,221,396	2,948,483	18,765	2,967,248	284,780	-78,877	2,603,591	723,946	893,859	30,601	137,950	76,316
2009	4,382,474	3,024,022	2,051	3,026,073	290,392	-86,340	2,649,341	743,242	989,891	31,643	138,497	75,989
2010	4,663,546	3,244,456	10,302	3,254,758	306,363	-85,511	2,862,884	726,895	1,073,767	33,452	139,409	76,016
2011	4,824,700	3,332,336	21,449	3,353,785	286,832	-85,321	2,981,632	796,489	1,046,579	34,469	139,972	76,746
2012	4,899,146	3,380,156	9,689	3,389,845	294,109	-77,000	3,018,736	837,226	1,043,184	35,316	138,725	76,453
2013	4,951,592	3,409,039	21,691	3,430,730	328,507	-88,413	3,013,810	844,931	1,092,851	35,340	140,112	75,323
2014	5,013,583	3,427,377	-1,228	3,426,149	333,024	-72,985	3,020,140	883,470	1,109,973	36,137	138,740	75,609
2015	5,213,533	3,526,364	-11,795	3,514,569	340,550	-83,810	3,090,209	912,899	1,210,425	37,700	138,289	76,612
2016	5,234,436	3,532,564	9,481	3,542,045	348,324	-100,011	3,093,710	932,430	1,208,296	38,119	137,319	76,751
2017	5,343,949	3,596,350	5,467	3,601,817	358,795	-109,392	3,133,630	950,607	1,259,712	39,332	135,866	76,471
2018	5,494,323	3,785,453	11,704	3,797,157	377,977	-141,487	3,277,693	920,707	1,295,923	40,706	134,976	76,594
2019	5,651,919	3,842,213	3,388	3,845,601	389,155	-126,987	3,329,459	983,316	1,339,144	42,199	133,935	76,592
2020	6,060,032	3,864,397	10,351	3,874,748	397,349	-149,294	3,328,105	966,009	1,765,918	45,463	133,297	73,519
2021	6,481,782	4,089,096	45,899	4,134,995	413,640	-163,461	3,557,894	961,613	1,962,275	48,769	132,907	74,835

Personal Income and Employment by Area: Carson City, NV

(Thousands of dollars, except as noted.)

Year	Personal income, total	Earnings by place of work			Less: Contributions for government social insurance	Plus: Adjustment for residence	Equals: Net earnings by place of residence	Plus: Dividends, interest, and rent	Plus: Personal current transfer receipts	Per capita personal income (dollars)	Population (persons)	Total employment
		Nonfarm	Farm	Total								
1970	86,094	65,872	47	65,919	2,301	842	64,460	16,519	5,115	5,367	16,041	8,194
1971	104,264	78,136	305	78,441	2,907	2,438	77,972	19,716	6,576	5,655	18,439	9,095
1972	122,082	90,520	155	90,675	3,824	4,421	91,272	22,899	7,911	6,107	19,991	9,860
1973	142,199	105,907	460	106,367	5,579	6,513	107,301	25,575	9,323	6,418	22,158	11,152
1974	163,239	121,672	96	121,768	6,755	7,175	122,188	29,322	11,729	6,856	23,808	12,036
1975	189,435	138,032	137	138,169	7,117	7,685	138,737	33,800	16,898	7,433	25,484	12,528
1976	220,730	162,807	143	162,950	8,899	7,350	161,401	40,294	19,035	8,459	26,094	13,820
1977	256,190	190,877	134	191,011	11,001	6,348	186,358	47,840	21,992	9,374	27,331	15,384
1978	311,643	237,818	116	237,934	14,851	2,251	225,334	60,625	25,684	10,398	29,972	17,838
1979	352,566	271,089	122	271,211	18,744	-2,476	249,991	72,998	29,577	11,093	31,782	19,081
1980	397,895	295,960	234	296,194	20,592	4	275,606	85,528	36,761	12,310	32,323	19,360
1981	452,262	338,030	153	338,183	24,862	-7,787	305,534	102,505	44,223	13,510	33,475	19,536
1982	475,708	341,380	164	341,544	25,085	-6,997	309,462	119,063	47,183	13,859	34,324	18,960
1983	503,576	362,389	163	362,552	29,896	-12,149	320,507	129,624	53,445	14,532	34,654	19,392
1984	552,520	397,542	274	397,816	35,190	-13,078	349,548	146,102	56,870	15,670	35,260	20,535
1985	601,045	438,202	115	438,317	41,267	-21,131	375,919	162,230	62,896	16,517	36,389	21,622
1986	646,402	470,487	104	470,591	45,552	-26,442	398,597	178,467	69,338	17,430	37,086	22,495
1987	672,934	509,136	221	509,357	49,982	-35,743	423,632	175,029	74,273	17,991	37,403	24,244
1988	736,821	564,654	116	564,770	57,172	-41,237	466,361	190,478	79,982	19,199	38,379	25,165
1989	808,735	606,056	153	606,209	62,183	-49,839	494,187	221,764	92,784	20,393	39,657	25,785
1990	872,217	658,267	190	658,457	69,064	-41,374	548,019	221,937	102,261	21,423	40,714	26,766
1991	941,474	705,768	152	705,920	73,328	-50,234	582,358	236,183	122,933	22,456	41,926	27,173
1992	1,025,626	777,146	140	777,286	79,210	-58,763	639,313	251,337	134,976	23,724	43,231	27,073
1993	1,080,695	834,535	176	834,711	86,047	-80,502	668,162	271,130	141,403	24,246	44,572	28,566
1994	1,163,386	916,896	79	916,975	96,962	-99,375	720,638	299,546	143,202	25,232	46,108	30,498
1995	1,260,239	1,002,315	-8	1,002,307	106,936	-119,214	776,157	327,565	156,517	26,382	47,768	32,941
1996	1,338,679	1,076,306	-105	1,076,201	110,691	-146,982	818,528	357,054	163,097	27,159	49,290	34,369
1997	1,431,386	1,171,737	-179	1,171,558	116,711	-172,289	882,558	377,557	171,271	28,365	50,463	35,519
1998	1,520,273	1,274,413	-6	1,274,407	122,451	-183,328	968,628	372,329	179,316	29,889	50,864	36,263
1999	1,587,105	1,369,872	117	1,369,989	128,616	-211,838	1,029,535	376,490	181,080	30,549	51,953	37,564
2000	1,749,562	1,484,649	139	1,484,788	122,044	-220,960	1,141,784	412,525	195,253	33,282	52,568	39,240
2001	1,254,182	997,010	315	997,325	127,172	-231,773	638,380	399,700	216,102	23,455	53,472	41,635
2002	1,095,415	882,445	564	883,009	131,364	-257,767	493,878	362,090	239,447	20,098	54,503	41,771
2003	1,169,772	920,810	302	921,112	134,489	-282,172	504,451	412,419	252,902	21,178	55,234	41,908
2004	1,183,088	938,014	300	938,314	138,796	-322,089	477,429	442,003	263,656	21,128	55,995	43,058
2005	1,379,667	1,158,762	297	1,159,059	146,934	-365,798	646,327	453,388	279,952	24,645	55,982	43,878
2006	1,692,006	1,493,084	320	1,493,404	156,129	-392,100	945,175	456,367	290,464	30,536	55,410	43,921
2007	1,626,289	1,452,036	193	1,452,229	177,871	-450,252	824,106	493,181	309,002	29,415	55,288	42,266
2008	1,665,151	1,509,886	1,167	1,511,053	181,826	-488,368	840,859	476,795	347,497	29,975	55,552	41,157
2009	2,291,005	2,117,882	1,442	2,119,324	167,012	-510,821	1,441,491	458,283	391,231	41,353	55,401	39,407
2010	2,462,574	2,299,171	2,439	2,301,610	165,668	-533,699	1,602,243	433,331	427,000	44,788	54,983	38,440
2011	2,369,543	2,149,681	3,390	2,153,071	151,544	-532,168	1,469,359	467,641	432,543	43,329	54,687	38,076
2012	2,156,063	1,945,635	3,584	1,949,219	159,178	-524,803	1,265,238	449,907	440,918	39,685	54,330	37,406
2013	2,202,043	2,004,365	2,001	2,006,366	171,349	-539,457	1,295,560	458,984	447,499	40,971	53,746	37,531
2014	2,314,927	2,030,733	2,490	2,033,223	174,989	-553,945	1,304,289	505,254	505,384	41,975	55,150	37,521
2015	2,454,469	2,162,878	1,471	2,164,349	183,090	-589,404	1,391,855	519,486	543,128	44,273	55,439	37,670
2016	2,461,281	2,119,007	1,388	2,120,395	185,796	-573,517	1,361,082	538,666	561,533	44,057	55,866	38,255
2017	2,623,999	2,306,882	1,382	2,308,264	203,221	-629,066	1,475,977	568,272	579,750	46,450	56,491	39,442
2018	2,789,811	2,388,758	1,322	2,390,080	209,624	-593,444	1,587,012	587,698	615,101	48,628	57,370	39,504
2019	2,969,713	2,557,792	1,038	2,558,830	226,983	-649,733	1,682,114	629,112	658,487	50,973	58,260	39,692
2020	3,241,259	2,631,501	1,523	2,633,024	235,629	-629,628	1,767,767	642,939	830,553	55,239	58,677	39,171
2021	3,565,831	2,770,887	1,617	2,772,504	245,167	-577,318	1,950,019	673,621	942,191	60,445	58,993	40,350

Personal Income and Employment by Area: Casper, WY

(Thousands of dollars, except as noted.)

					Derivation of personal income							
		Earnings by place of work			Less: Contributions for government social insurance	Plus: Adjustment for residence	Equals: Net earnings by place of residence	Plus: Dividends, interest, and rent	Plus: Personal current transfer receipts	Per capita personal income (dollars)	Population (persons)	Total employment
Year	Personal income, total	Nonfarm	Farm	Total								
1970	241,410	188,187	4,641	192,828	12,904	6,633	186,557	39,276	15,577	4,698	51,381	25,733
1971	259,416	201,896	2,614	204,510	14,304	7,402	197,608	44,035	17,773	4,977	52,121	26,453
1972	276,780	215,571	4,135	219,706	16,194	7,371	210,883	46,949	18,948	5,212	53,106	27,009
1973	317,814	247,875	7,885	255,760	21,425	6,133	240,468	55,207	22,139	6,018	52,814	28,431
1974	389,544	312,607	5,375	317,982	26,848	6,833	297,967	66,489	25,088	7,281	53,504	30,410
1975	468,746	389,022	2,302	391,324	32,946	7,283	365,661	72,880	30,205	8,357	56,088	33,334
1976	517,903	434,447	1,994	436,441	39,067	5,594	402,968	82,115	32,820	8,843	58,567	35,183
1977	632,083	544,927	1,847	546,774	47,380	3,957	503,351	93,416	35,316	10,273	61,526	39,229
1978	769,151	678,521	1,662	680,183	61,393	-603	618,187	111,199	39,765	11,740	65,515	44,060
1979	883,607	786,350	2,593	788,943	75,562	-5,854	707,527	129,485	46,595	12,927	68,354	46,821
1980	1,016,095	896,573	1,898	898,471	86,058	-13,176	799,237	161,742	55,116	14,011	72,523	48,294
1981	1,180,992	1,026,343	1,174	1,027,517	106,676	-10,562	910,279	205,009	65,704	15,738	75,042	51,043
1982	1,206,850	1,003,390	3,855	1,007,245	107,639	-7,792	891,814	238,202	76,834	15,654	77,094	49,117
1983	1,122,025	878,412	7,597	886,009	92,206	-3,794	790,009	240,988	91,028	14,707	76,292	44,001
1984	1,149,274	899,112	3,260	902,372	97,199	-1,058	804,115	255,788	89,371	15,708	73,166	44,094
1985	1,135,127	864,391	2,436	866,827	95,245	2,316	773,898	262,493	98,736	15,861	71,569	42,169
1986	1,032,877	748,539	839	749,378	83,057	5,496	671,817	253,385	107,675	14,931	69,177	37,710
1987	1,037,545	752,602	1,434	754,036	80,841	6,040	679,235	248,885	109,425	16,073	64,552	36,574
1988	1,049,271	750,229	988	751,217	87,737	8,298	671,778	262,786	114,707	16,786	62,507	37,519
1989	1,177,887	844,153	-123	844,030	91,643	11,744	764,131	287,172	126,584	19,084	61,722	37,111
1990	1,300,666	934,077	-415	933,662	105,507	13,547	841,702	319,015	139,949	21,219	61,296	38,058
1991	1,307,580	883,181	3,403	886,584	107,684	12,180	791,080	363,490	153,010	20,984	62,312	38,809
1992	1,385,029	924,194	2,646	926,840	110,741	12,014	828,113	384,754	172,162	21,954	63,087	38,045
1993	1,459,222	972,736	2,716	975,452	115,007	11,615	872,060	396,854	190,308	22,807	63,981	38,759
1994	1,500,533	1,000,710	1,633	1,002,343	119,060	11,880	895,163	413,021	192,349	22,973	65,316	39,738
1995	1,525,891	1,024,082	1,098	1,025,180	121,354	10,863	914,689	404,629	206,573	23,230	65,687	40,383
1996	1,589,804	1,070,284	782	1,071,066	123,361	10,381	958,086	414,874	216,844	24,140	65,859	40,551
1997	1,730,814	1,194,660	2,625	1,197,285	131,861	10,045	1,075,469	433,477	221,868	26,101	66,311	41,280
1998	1,804,109	1,230,220	1,420	1,231,640	137,166	8,824	1,103,298	471,209	229,602	27,275	66,146	41,582
1999	1,912,295	1,323,556	2,592	1,326,148	144,108	7,132	1,189,172	487,136	235,987	28,851	66,282	42,325
2000	2,173,767	1,535,293	2,137	1,537,430	164,005	2,549	1,375,974	542,847	254,946	32,638	66,603	43,624
2001	2,138,896	1,489,692	3,642	1,493,334	169,590	3,509	1,327,253	541,707	269,936	31,934	66,978	44,539
2002	2,184,413	1,548,525	3,261	1,551,786	171,609	2,946	1,383,123	509,547	291,743	32,336	67,554	44,730
2003	2,327,477	1,652,444	5,489	1,657,933	183,913	293	1,474,313	535,488	317,676	34,104	68,246	45,554
2004	2,493,170	1,770,214	4,539	1,774,753	204,198	-3,291	1,567,264	593,487	332,419	36,115	69,035	47,196
2005	2,841,147	1,982,354	7,469	1,989,823	225,303	-6,200	1,758,320	737,884	344,943	40,633	69,922	48,826
2006	3,317,238	2,397,724	1,245	2,398,969	287,633	-9,988	2,101,348	863,247	352,643	46,850	70,806	50,902
2007	3,425,087	2,526,219	-431	2,525,788	312,679	-6,076	2,207,033	844,606	373,448	47,331	72,365	52,732
2008	3,988,615	2,994,274	-1,029	2,993,245	340,285	54	2,653,014	895,326	440,275	54,133	73,682	53,987
2009	3,446,325	2,601,280	336	2,601,616	314,443	-2,058	2,285,115	686,131	475,079	45,806	75,238	51,712
2010	3,814,303	2,866,167	1,321	2,867,488	327,771	-13,480	2,526,237	778,744	509,322	50,536	75,477	51,833
2011	4,149,314	3,100,951	8,998	3,109,949	320,922	-32,173	2,756,854	885,696	506,764	54,288	76,431	53,356
2012	4,806,500	3,641,539	1,463	3,643,002	356,996	-42,913	3,243,093	1,064,387	499,020	61,136	78,620	55,493
2013	5,159,817	3,882,898	4,123	3,887,021	408,056	-45,315	3,433,650	1,204,147	522,020	63,564	81,175	56,643
2014	5,826,652	4,313,712	7,522	4,321,234	446,470	-50,294	3,824,470	1,456,991	545,191	71,761	81,195	57,785
2015	6,068,254	4,300,934	4,759	4,305,693	429,951	-28,382	3,847,360	1,630,309	590,585	74,099	81,894	57,144
2016	5,184,929	3,774,765	943	3,775,708	382,724	-2,975	3,390,009	1,189,968	604,952	64,295	80,643	53,916
2017	5,026,314	3,781,972	377	3,782,349	395,392	-6,751	3,380,206	1,021,482	624,626	63,472	79,190	53,763
2018	5,634,456	4,352,286	1,231	4,353,517	415,072	-8,641	3,929,804	1,051,778	652,874	71,637	78,653	54,091
2019	5,526,261	4,279,941	1,933	4,281,874	430,836	14,933	3,865,971	966,897	693,393	69,791	79,183	54,318
2020	5,393,722	3,912,390	3,750	3,916,140	405,487	19,929	3,530,582	942,102	921,038	67,229	80,229	52,315
2021	5,582,770	3,977,896	3,753	3,981,649	411,455	21,483	3,591,677	1,005,943	985,150	70,175	79,555	52,883

Personal Income and Employment by Area: Cedar Rapids, IA

(Thousands of dollars, except as noted.)

Year	Personal income, total	Earnings by place of work			Less: Contributions for government social insurance	Plus: Adjustment for residence	Equals: Net earnings by place of residence	Plus: Dividends, interest, and rent	Plus: Personal current transfer receipts	Per capita personal income (dollars)	Population (persons)	Total employment
		Nonfarm	Farm	Total								
1970	867,743	679,218	45,908	725,126	51,334	-2,882	670,910	134,314	62,519	4,209	206,165	96,649
1971	907,248	707,397	41,325	748,722	55,651	-4,373	688,698	145,349	73,201	4,372	207,532	94,803
1972	981,866	759,844	52,935	812,779	63,501	-5,226	744,052	157,433	80,381	4,721	207,990	96,324
1973	1,117,635	853,889	84,216	938,105	82,738	-7,020	848,347	177,093	92,195	5,400	206,982	100,990
1974	1,220,471	954,387	61,195	1,015,582	95,619	-8,229	911,734	201,519	107,218	5,871	207,881	104,894
1975	1,361,320	1,043,807	68,297	1,112,104	102,083	-8,965	1,001,056	226,327	133,937	6,481	210,055	105,550
1976	1,485,204	1,178,599	42,148	1,220,747	116,619	-11,145	1,092,983	244,575	147,646	7,023	211,491	108,639
1977	1,624,848	1,297,383	39,153	1,336,536	127,413	-13,161	1,195,962	274,570	154,316	7,706	210,846	110,943
1978	1,842,812	1,460,396	77,545	1,537,941	148,920	-18,597	1,370,424	305,064	167,324	8,732	211,033	114,026
1979	2,051,499	1,679,912	40,486	1,720,398	178,273	-26,118	1,516,007	346,999	188,493	9,680	211,937	121,050
1980	2,207,069	1,766,082	4,504	1,770,586	185,620	-26,026	1,558,940	418,960	229,169	10,330	213,666	119,634
1981	2,434,346	1,850,059	45,517	1,895,576	206,607	-29,124	1,659,845	516,285	258,216	11,454	212,534	116,231
1982	2,520,131	1,832,522	14,324	1,846,846	206,424	-30,294	1,610,128	608,216	301,787	11,979	210,374	111,314
1983	2,570,471	1,895,554	-19,506	1,876,048	213,291	-26,154	1,636,603	613,294	320,574	12,344	208,238	110,835
1984	2,827,567	2,036,395	51,007	2,087,402	234,825	-24,354	1,828,223	677,907	321,437	13,596	207,969	113,084
1985	2,966,502	2,185,531	35,174	2,220,705	255,289	-32,133	1,933,283	694,984	338,235	14,331	206,995	115,476
1986	3,118,213	2,311,408	59,524	2,370,932	274,778	-35,343	2,060,811	702,978	354,424	15,147	205,865	117,488
1987	3,313,101	2,507,122	71,887	2,579,009	296,097	-38,284	2,244,628	706,440	362,033	16,116	205,577	119,721
1988	3,484,804	2,712,436	22,352	2,734,788	329,956	-40,599	2,364,233	739,203	381,368	16,801	207,415	125,116
1989	3,856,667	2,934,587	81,773	3,016,360	354,020	-42,079	2,620,261	828,473	407,933	18,406	209,528	129,901
1990	4,039,220	3,113,667	83,721	3,197,388	386,919	-47,345	2,763,124	826,293	449,803	19,125	211,200	131,540
1991	4,162,304	3,237,493	48,500	3,285,993	405,898	-46,218	2,833,877	846,707	481,720	19,500	213,453	132,831
1992	4,412,071	3,433,228	87,268	3,520,496	427,000	-50,178	3,043,318	844,925	523,828	20,349	216,818	133,978
1993	4,585,152	3,646,243	35,798	3,682,041	457,550	-56,146	3,168,345	871,470	545,337	20,847	219,948	136,563
1994	4,933,129	3,927,887	85,138	4,013,025	498,316	-63,500	3,451,209	908,317	573,603	22,150	222,711	140,427
1995	5,223,835	4,165,021	44,740	4,209,761	528,393	-77,691	3,603,677	1,009,905	610,253	23,078	226,357	146,630
1996	5,586,117	4,352,447	115,314	4,467,761	532,629	-87,329	3,847,803	1,092,874	645,440	24,507	227,938	149,382
1997	5,912,525	4,620,115	100,181	4,720,296	580,125	-99,070	4,041,101	1,201,894	669,530	25,652	230,490	152,680
1998	6,453,537	5,216,993	67,573	5,284,566	645,874	-133,066	4,505,626	1,258,903	689,008	27,769	232,402	157,170
1999	6,794,573	5,607,686	60,402	5,668,088	684,543	-150,861	4,832,684	1,236,965	724,924	28,868	235,365	161,738
2000	7,258,897	5,972,706	78,402	6,051,108	721,437	-181,137	5,148,534	1,333,287	777,076	30,506	237,950	164,865
2001	7,408,617	5,981,819	93,973	6,075,792	720,710	-156,157	5,198,925	1,348,081	861,611	30,851	240,145	163,779
2002	7,529,451	5,947,686	87,246	6,034,932	713,594	-127,157	5,194,181	1,366,496	968,774	31,101	242,099	160,448
2003	7,696,934	6,103,847	84,190	6,188,037	738,934	-115,796	5,333,307	1,384,526	979,101	31,639	243,272	159,065
2004	8,110,644	6,447,451	138,449	6,585,900	771,074	-96,036	5,718,790	1,376,979	1,014,875	33,090	245,108	161,774
2005	8,450,527	6,732,390	91,743	6,824,133	809,927	-90,573	5,923,633	1,427,294	1,099,600	34,176	247,265	164,717
2006	8,962,710	7,047,904	69,435	7,117,339	847,858	-93,786	6,175,695	1,582,495	1,204,520	35,919	249,524	168,369
2007	9,657,103	7,542,681	103,605	7,646,286	907,831	-104,875	6,633,580	1,734,527	1,288,996	38,214	252,709	172,462
2008	10,311,943	7,926,142	112,525	8,038,667	962,583	-128,252	6,947,832	1,882,554	1,481,557	40,359	255,503	174,581
2009	10,223,482	7,822,135	78,051	7,900,186	953,304	-91,746	6,855,136	1,765,826	1,602,520	39,796	256,896	172,876
2010	10,660,420	8,120,697	86,928	8,207,625	991,674	-57,518	7,158,433	1,790,366	1,711,621	41,248	258,449	173,011
2011	11,219,793	8,387,198	192,983	8,580,181	926,521	-127,562	7,526,098	1,949,203	1,744,492	42,977	261,064	175,478
2012	11,811,975	8,762,733	140,962	8,903,695	944,189	-113,346	7,846,160	2,216,409	1,749,406	45,089	261,973	176,557
2013	11,870,561	8,923,242	193,809	9,117,051	1,077,564	-30,561	8,008,926	2,081,545	1,780,090	45,172	262,787	177,257
2014	12,437,633	9,363,607	86,616	9,450,223	1,111,439	-88,384	8,250,400	2,285,587	1,901,646	46,850	265,477	178,979
2015	12,935,867	9,611,405	91,495	9,702,900	1,136,688	-51,261	8,514,951	2,386,994	2,033,922	48,307	267,786	181,126
2016	13,250,207	9,787,787	56,785	9,844,572	1,177,300	-38,618	8,628,654	2,527,758	2,093,795	49,086	269,939	181,354
2017	13,600,538	10,050,437	71,225	10,121,662	1,213,610	-32,349	8,875,703	2,618,092	2,106,743	49,871	272,715	181,236
2018	14,143,289	10,544,581	71,112	10,615,693	1,276,953	-231,036	9,107,704	2,733,210	2,302,375	51,541	274,409	182,255
2019	14,537,548	10,509,867	75,234	10,585,101	1,294,887	-120,130	9,170,084	2,914,769	2,452,695	52,697	275,868	182,819
2020	15,443,762	10,568,431	119,146	10,687,577	1,334,057	-102,428	9,251,092	2,989,351	3,203,319	55,865	276,446	175,757
2021	16,268,026	11,006,084	267,258	11,273,342	1,366,690	-132,218	9,774,434	3,094,464	3,399,128	59,063	275,435	178,953

Personal Income and Employment by Area: Chambersburg-Waynesboro, PA

(Thousands of dollars, except as noted.)

Year	Personal income, total	Earnings by place of work			Less: Contributions for government social insurance	Plus: Adjustment for residence	Equals: Net earnings by place of residence	Plus: Dividends, interest, and rent	Plus: Personal current transfer receipts	Per capita personal income (dollars)	Population (persons)	Total employment
		Nonfarm	Farm	Total								
1970	402,056	309,060	16,046	325,106	18,784	5,766	312,088	56,053	33,915	3,976	101,127	45,763
1971	425,498	324,248	13,591	337,839	20,346	5,906	323,399	62,672	39,427	4,128	103,082	44,890
1972	477,416	365,265	15,581	380,846	24,028	6,773	363,591	69,487	44,338	4,630	103,103	46,239
1973	536,494	412,697	17,730	430,427	31,392	7,042	406,077	81,097	49,320	5,144	104,285	48,655
1974	598,323	454,468	20,778	475,246	36,378	8,300	447,168	92,240	58,915	5,611	106,640	50,542
1975	657,255	498,091	13,610	511,701	38,922	5,461	478,240	102,310	76,705	6,083	108,052	50,373
1976	715,956	534,221	17,185	551,406	42,775	8,489	517,120	111,164	87,672	6,498	110,183	50,555
1977	779,494	572,139	15,349	587,488	45,380	18,131	560,239	125,589	93,666	7,072	110,218	50,537
1978	878,988	646,979	19,434	666,413	52,338	21,139	635,214	144,298	99,476	7,907	111,166	51,634
1979	963,986	698,445	23,399	721,844	59,353	30,962	693,453	160,694	109,839	8,594	112,172	52,438
1980	1,059,936	768,492	15,522	784,014	66,285	20,079	737,808	196,440	125,688	9,313	113,810	53,620
1981	1,180,283	829,800	24,183	853,983	76,659	21,831	799,155	235,591	145,537	10,326	114,302	53,452
1982	1,245,982	812,820	25,195	838,015	75,731	28,294	790,578	276,179	179,225	10,864	114,688	52,664
1983	1,300,079	826,574	21,758	848,332	79,810	37,685	806,207	293,795	200,077	11,276	115,293	51,891
1984	1,415,951	899,524	40,751	940,275	91,648	54,666	903,293	323,083	189,575	12,156	116,482	52,342
1985	1,524,474	969,709	43,945	1,013,654	100,315	59,405	972,744	352,817	198,913	13,043	116,882	53,479
1986	1,607,610	1,003,965	52,853	1,056,818	106,556	71,896	1,022,158	373,769	211,683	13,686	117,464	54,682
1987	1,701,619	1,085,071	40,582	1,125,653	114,902	83,772	1,094,523	390,407	216,689	14,443	117,819	56,100
1988	1,820,976	1,170,801	40,010	1,210,811	128,795	99,761	1,181,777	410,274	228,925	15,308	118,953	58,222
1989	1,963,437	1,267,849	46,972	1,314,821	139,385	113,546	1,288,982	430,003	244,452	16,392	119,780	60,503
1990	2,106,171	1,337,049	39,001	1,376,050	148,842	130,521	1,357,729	476,726	271,716	17,334	121,503	62,343
1991	2,195,668	1,381,189	29,346	1,410,535	156,037	134,849	1,389,347	487,051	319,270	17,845	123,039	61,587
1992	2,314,959	1,445,747	53,088	1,498,835	165,136	151,350	1,485,049	494,420	335,490	18,655	124,095	61,679
1993	2,414,863	1,508,199	44,271	1,552,470	176,823	163,469	1,539,116	523,157	352,590	19,310	125,056	62,013
1994	2,507,603	1,584,387	39,805	1,624,192	188,917	181,351	1,616,626	529,021	361,956	19,901	126,002	62,399
1995	2,595,338	1,633,690	27,916	1,661,606	194,707	202,646	1,669,545	548,017	377,776	20,520	126,479	63,732
1996	2,775,625	1,723,243	47,791	1,771,034	200,937	217,740	1,787,837	583,275	404,513	21,873	126,897	65,054
1997	2,881,522	1,775,823	42,297	1,818,120	207,474	241,628	1,852,274	608,506	420,742	22,565	127,696	66,252
1998	3,054,393	1,874,924	54,958	1,929,882	215,656	267,058	1,981,284	633,580	439,529	23,771	128,492	65,520
1999	3,156,086	1,905,835	57,776	1,963,611	217,466	305,872	2,052,017	633,184	470,885	24,490	128,875	64,503
2000	3,338,658	1,982,095	61,459	2,043,554	224,819	335,075	2,153,810	682,252	502,596	25,732	129,745	65,163
2001	3,533,739	2,060,147	71,433	2,131,580	232,527	390,571	2,289,624	689,786	554,329	27,057	130,604	64,999
2002	3,637,447	2,152,137	32,176	2,184,313	243,423	424,741	2,365,631	684,192	587,624	27,557	131,998	65,382
2003	3,864,979	2,271,187	64,983	2,336,170	255,349	468,447	2,549,268	700,668	615,043	28,933	133,583	66,732
2004	4,221,230	2,512,914	95,718	2,608,632	280,557	534,891	2,862,966	702,640	655,624	31,097	135,742	69,437
2005	4,580,258	2,740,864	93,513	2,834,377	310,316	631,558	3,155,619	712,337	712,302	32,969	138,927	72,375
2006	4,893,960	2,909,751	72,431	2,982,182	334,002	689,558	3,337,738	781,871	774,351	34,363	142,421	74,675
2007	5,216,965	3,032,124	107,444	3,139,568	349,669	702,207	3,492,106	893,623	831,236	36,019	144,840	76,580
2008	5,380,694	3,073,170	113,352	3,186,522	356,339	679,569	3,509,752	951,255	919,687	36,595	147,032	77,395
2009	5,267,420	2,939,870	70,584	3,010,454	351,199	641,259	3,300,514	900,283	1,066,623	35,432	148,662	73,881
2010	5,460,472	3,040,427	91,830	3,132,257	362,491	680,490	3,450,256	883,405	1,126,811	36,421	149,925	73,831
2011	5,756,548	3,142,058	123,906	3,265,964	340,136	762,720	3,688,548	925,230	1,142,770	38,136	150,949	74,708
2012	5,872,816	3,232,541	124,666	3,357,207	347,155	764,370	3,774,422	942,814	1,155,580	38,760	151,518	75,353
2013	5,974,307	3,341,763	129,982	3,471,745	400,032	748,372	3,820,085	953,688	1,200,534	39,303	152,005	76,282
2014	6,259,418	3,453,460	161,659	3,615,119	414,061	771,837	3,972,895	1,024,373	1,262,150	40,960	152,819	77,148
2015	6,467,987	3,632,948	98,346	3,731,294	433,002	744,179	4,042,471	1,086,135	1,339,381	42,193	153,297	78,835
2016	6,567,092	3,697,793	44,175	3,741,968	442,858	788,269	4,087,379	1,061,268	1,418,445	42,606	154,136	79,391
2017	6,846,022	3,839,039	95,638	3,934,677	464,277	828,475	4,298,875	1,097,940	1,449,207	44,179	154,962	79,408
2018	7,190,550	4,039,523	57,000	4,096,523	486,099	862,932	4,473,356	1,162,288	1,554,906	46,329	155,205	80,989
2019	7,481,769	4,159,013	87,163	4,246,176	506,004	915,246	4,655,418	1,201,156	1,625,195	48,017	155,814	80,799
2020	8,053,226	4,163,626	59,625	4,223,251	503,794	975,730	4,695,187	1,192,464	2,165,575	51,665	155,874	77,920
2021	8,617,580	4,334,045	104,051	4,438,096	517,353	1,124,066	5,044,809	1,206,630	2,366,141	55,139	156,289	79,463

Personal Income and Employment by Area: Champaign-Urbana, IL

(Thousands of dollars, except as noted.)

Year	Personal income, total	Earnings by place of work			Less: Contributions for government social insurance	Plus: Adjustment for residence	Equals: Net earnings by place of residence	Plus: Dividends, interest, and rent	Plus: Personal current transfer receipts	Per capita personal income (dollars)	Population (persons)	Total employment
		Nonfarm	Farm	Total								
1970	798,136	604,676	38,946	643,622	32,629	-6,309	604,684	148,450	45,002	4,093	195,003	92,168
1971	892,758	663,881	59,975	723,856	37,394	-6,483	679,979	159,560	53,219	4,564	195,599	94,618
1972	948,496	711,012	47,080	758,092	41,835	-5,245	711,012	176,661	60,823	4,868	194,839	95,753
1973	1,095,132	769,489	103,088	872,577	51,561	-4,257	816,759	206,273	72,100	5,508	198,829	99,841
1974	1,177,786	832,723	98,889	931,612	59,138	-4,248	868,226	226,601	82,959	5,906	199,411	101,332
1975	1,386,487	951,798	146,278	1,098,076	66,143	-6,546	1,025,387	255,680	105,420	7,008	197,848	103,387
1976	1,459,308	1,036,596	116,436	1,153,032	74,742	-3,591	1,074,699	270,833	113,776	7,266	200,853	104,608
1977	1,559,213	1,107,687	116,575	1,224,262	80,335	1,079	1,145,006	296,176	118,031	7,710	202,220	106,004
1978	1,664,757	1,212,826	85,953	1,298,779	90,163	2,422	1,211,038	326,724	126,995	8,192	203,216	107,412
1979	1,835,510	1,312,709	112,465	1,425,174	102,411	5,704	1,328,467	367,572	139,471	9,190	199,739	109,443
1980	1,922,947	1,382,678	39,793	1,422,471	106,373	12,124	1,328,222	426,202	168,523	9,576	200,808	108,626
1981	2,170,414	1,494,721	82,765	1,577,486	123,365	14,156	1,468,277	502,651	199,486	10,706	202,737	108,357
1982	2,322,548	1,581,468	54,692	1,636,160	131,302	9,112	1,513,970	592,133	216,445	11,419	203,390	108,510
1983	2,393,816	1,681,030	-10,191	1,670,839	141,172	6,904	1,536,571	617,561	239,684	11,854	201,935	107,989
1984	2,696,969	1,823,441	85,634	1,909,075	158,361	16,041	1,766,755	680,880	249,334	13,341	202,158	110,746
1985	2,834,224	1,933,532	108,823	2,042,355	171,638	8,716	1,879,433	697,967	256,824	13,998	202,468	113,254
1986	2,969,832	2,093,305	90,222	2,183,527	186,822	-20,147	1,976,558	730,069	263,205	14,555	204,047	118,091
1987	3,111,488	2,248,864	70,748	2,319,612	198,396	-32,873	2,088,343	749,828	273,317	15,228	204,329	120,675
1988	3,278,349	2,430,877	47,518	2,478,395	225,642	-37,256	2,215,497	780,276	282,576	16,009	204,777	123,729
1989	3,535,412	2,523,637	99,706	2,623,343	237,274	-42,407	2,343,662	886,790	304,960	17,406	203,114	123,578
1990	3,716,621	2,749,546	97,719	2,847,265	257,135	-56,283	2,533,847	855,167	327,607	18,298	203,117	125,903
1991	3,751,030	2,812,559	44,233	2,856,792	270,875	-55,607	2,530,310	865,282	355,438	18,286	205,133	124,402
1992	4,026,525	2,998,252	90,344	3,088,596	285,716	-64,284	2,738,596	888,398	399,531	19,370	207,870	124,588
1993	4,046,830	2,964,511	103,642	3,068,153	285,674	-57,003	2,725,476	897,634	423,720	19,788	204,513	120,796
1994	4,187,478	3,070,580	134,730	3,205,310	301,781	-58,358	2,845,171	911,457	430,850	20,664	202,646	123,137
1995	4,339,292	3,213,985	32,677	3,246,662	317,013	-63,094	2,866,555	1,012,806	459,931	21,362	203,128	125,336
1996	4,633,206	3,335,484	127,332	3,462,816	327,309	-63,227	3,072,280	1,074,596	486,330	22,557	205,401	126,882
1997	4,874,557	3,485,619	107,009	3,592,628	339,176	-69,717	3,183,735	1,186,207	504,615	23,525	207,211	128,334
1998	4,707,203	3,528,494	40,226	3,568,720	339,068	-139,354	3,090,298	1,150,505	466,400	24,360	193,235	123,316
1999	4,952,015	3,806,203	32,532	3,838,735	358,735	-157,042	3,322,958	1,141,694	487,363	25,390	195,040	126,090
2000	5,351,144	4,095,238	63,767	4,159,005	377,806	-182,344	3,598,855	1,241,430	510,859	27,242	196,428	128,979
2001	5,703,387	4,456,259	66,335	4,522,594	398,790	-225,801	3,898,003	1,248,650	556,734	28,760	198,313	129,448
2002	5,858,890	4,742,458	51,853	4,794,311	423,409	-282,232	4,088,670	1,169,495	600,725	29,234	200,414	128,925
2003	6,069,981	4,847,386	66,278	4,913,664	437,321	-302,899	4,173,444	1,265,946	630,591	29,844	203,388	128,853
2004	6,358,002	5,015,713	133,361	5,149,074	452,079	-341,551	4,355,444	1,338,806	663,752	31,003	205,080	130,064
2005	6,444,591	5,139,104	55,760	5,194,864	472,216	-346,382	4,376,266	1,334,872	733,453	31,087	207,308	129,866
2006	6,775,075	5,369,739	83,509	5,453,248	487,153	-376,004	4,590,091	1,425,897	759,087	32,182	210,526	130,940
2007	7,197,810	5,628,858	141,521	5,770,379	513,780	-397,754	4,858,845	1,510,350	828,615	33,747	213,285	133,070
2008	7,649,842	5,882,353	212,858	6,095,211	540,236	-449,993	5,104,982	1,599,801	945,059	35,699	214,286	134,046
2009	8,073,144	6,011,528	122,065	6,133,593	541,133	-375,243	5,217,217	1,804,670	1,051,257	37,248	216,742	131,717
2010	8,412,269	6,416,390	130,467	6,546,857	560,829	-375,367	5,610,661	1,641,251	1,160,357	38,541	218,268	130,045
2011	8,754,059	6,501,676	233,362	6,735,038	514,214	-322,569	5,898,255	1,731,487	1,124,317	39,805	219,922	129,488
2012	8,941,819	6,752,091	123,939	6,876,030	534,973	-305,592	6,035,465	1,793,242	1,113,112	40,424	221,202	129,617
2013	9,385,959	7,111,769	302,743	7,414,512	611,029	-320,081	6,483,402	1,737,287	1,165,270	42,096	222,964	130,365
2014	9,711,047	7,439,229	160,406	7,599,635	634,905	-305,769	6,658,961	1,832,937	1,219,149	43,528	223,099	131,733
2015	10,023,544	7,667,438	25,287	7,692,725	650,726	-292,848	6,749,151	1,968,238	1,306,155	44,715	224,166	133,586
2016	9,901,180	7,421,064	106,382	7,527,446	649,633	-281,539	6,596,274	1,966,820	1,338,086	44,037	224,840	133,426
2017	10,001,231	7,378,839	100,734	7,479,573	661,492	-292,089	6,525,992	2,110,343	1,364,896	44,516	224,667	134,686
2018	10,192,072	7,539,663	138,912	7,678,575	683,824	-295,575	6,699,176	2,069,589	1,423,307	45,527	223,868	135,213
2019	10,526,764	7,756,819	75,874	7,832,693	710,246	-307,507	6,814,940	2,217,898	1,493,926	47,211	222,972	135,930
2020	11,408,693	8,087,153	164,992	8,252,145	750,312	-378,412	7,123,421	2,212,181	2,073,091	51,362	222,123	132,798
2021	12,322,902	8,635,221	309,267	8,944,488	789,171	-392,832	7,762,485	2,218,717	2,341,700	55,335	222,696	136,240

Personal Income and Employment by Area: Charleston, WV

(Thousands of dollars, except as noted.)

Year	Personal income, total	Earnings by place of work			Less: Contributions for government social insurance	Plus: Adjustment for residence	Equals: Net earnings by place of residence	Plus: Dividends, interest, and rent	Plus: Personal current transfer receipts	Per capita personal income (dollars)	Population (persons)	Total employment
		Nonfarm	Farm	Total								
1970	993,837	873,810	234	874,044	65,362	-36,987	771,695	120,420	101,722	3,765	263,984	112,925
1971	1,071,943	933,887	192	934,079	72,695	-42,079	819,305	131,103	121,535	4,042	265,194	113,601
1972	1,171,846	1,032,731	240	1,032,971	84,627	-58,908	889,436	142,658	139,752	4,423	264,953	116,423
1973	1,279,952	1,138,833	262	1,139,095	108,477	-76,255	954,363	160,684	164,905	4,868	262,931	119,946
1974	1,413,891	1,265,509	139	1,265,648	124,719	-101,014	1,039,915	188,040	185,936	5,406	261,523	123,324
1975	1,587,047	1,419,875	164	1,420,039	138,115	-124,406	1,157,518	210,944	218,585	5,983	265,278	125,757
1976	1,759,365	1,592,240	195	1,592,435	158,063	-147,225	1,287,147	230,787	241,431	6,597	266,697	129,397
1977	1,952,255	1,786,995	292	1,787,287	175,948	-172,848	1,438,491	257,857	255,907	7,250	269,295	132,961
1978	2,167,029	2,018,647	335	2,018,982	204,935	-213,731	1,600,316	284,610	282,103	7,971	271,875	138,957
1979	2,418,669	2,270,984	448	2,271,432	240,654	-262,931	1,767,847	319,768	331,054	8,870	272,681	142,342
1980	2,605,697	2,396,460	356	2,396,816	259,227	-292,278	1,845,311	381,288	379,098	9,538	273,195	138,180
1981	2,840,831	2,509,715	133	2,509,848	290,164	-295,652	1,924,032	469,478	447,321	10,403	273,065	131,513
1982	3,046,381	2,664,954	284	2,665,238	317,090	-326,453	2,021,695	534,338	490,348	11,207	271,826	128,902
1983	3,111,775	2,629,830	447	2,630,277	315,041	-317,382	1,997,854	564,301	549,620	11,540	269,657	124,483
1984	3,318,347	2,786,090	1,038	2,787,128	339,576	-326,912	2,120,640	624,699	573,008	12,427	267,030	125,051
1985	3,463,300	2,910,274	701	2,910,975	357,693	-341,596	2,211,686	656,502	595,112	13,181	262,742	125,298
1986	3,512,860	2,943,246	819	2,944,065	377,669	-359,756	2,206,640	671,978	634,242	13,574	258,796	125,037
1987	3,534,260	2,945,756	12	2,945,768	381,504	-358,393	2,205,871	674,313	654,076	13,801	256,091	124,011
1988	3,825,349	3,161,494	134	3,161,628	412,899	-339,137	2,409,592	721,446	694,311	15,275	250,433	125,278
1989	4,034,982	3,287,816	221	3,288,037	435,334	-353,568	2,499,135	807,073	728,774	16,379	246,351	125,964
1990	4,296,318	3,540,261	677	3,540,938	477,024	-401,959	2,661,955	856,780	777,583	17,671	243,124	129,747
1991	4,477,881	3,714,592	622	3,715,214	514,962	-432,609	2,767,643	829,532	880,706	18,418	243,125	130,517
1992	4,768,059	3,929,614	928	3,930,542	548,653	-482,870	2,899,019	856,355	1,012,685	19,535	244,084	132,244
1993	4,957,134	4,083,410	450	4,083,860	588,138	-493,996	3,001,726	873,475	1,081,933	20,316	244,001	134,391
1994	5,191,393	4,315,915	338	4,316,253	618,857	-534,192	3,163,204	932,303	1,095,886	21,356	243,093	138,091
1995	5,347,220	4,489,501	70	4,489,571	653,956	-582,872	3,252,743	976,176	1,118,301	22,021	242,822	140,818
1996	5,532,883	4,651,499	-819	4,650,680	678,621	-639,379	3,332,680	1,028,389	1,171,814	22,837	242,282	142,338
1997	5,691,420	4,824,347	-1,130	4,823,217	697,090	-685,132	3,440,995	1,055,285	1,195,140	23,610	241,059	144,325
1998	6,849,497	5,534,265	-3,919	5,530,346	804,457	-572,673	4,153,216	1,259,054	1,437,227	23,726	288,693	162,819
1999	7,007,498	5,775,376	-4,522	5,770,854	831,439	-600,769	4,338,646	1,209,833	1,459,019	24,397	287,226	164,269
2000	7,405,879	6,080,645	-1,440	6,079,205	895,804	-635,534	4,547,867	1,321,379	1,536,633	25,922	285,694	165,406
2001	7,628,584	6,159,076	-944	6,158,132	873,693	-664,936	4,619,503	1,315,197	1,693,884	26,900	283,588	163,753
2002	7,831,142	6,241,982	-3,383	6,238,599	847,741	-688,956	4,701,902	1,284,792	1,844,448	27,723	282,476	162,135
2003	7,909,654	6,296,229	-4,507	6,291,722	878,435	-693,556	4,719,731	1,305,365	1,884,558	28,034	282,146	160,497
2004	7,981,306	6,523,922	-1,360	6,522,562	894,356	-742,536	4,885,670	1,235,131	1,860,505	28,331	281,718	160,428
2005	8,415,430	6,925,302	-2,473	6,922,829	929,809	-839,284	5,153,736	1,333,776	1,927,918	30,074	279,823	161,220
2006	8,926,668	7,295,008	-6,469	7,288,539	935,937	-951,804	5,400,798	1,473,780	2,052,090	32,031	278,691	162,759
2007	9,263,852	7,410,996	-8,398	7,402,598	909,950	-960,678	5,531,970	1,558,760	2,173,122	33,298	278,207	164,092
2008	9,855,881	7,719,568	-5,326	7,714,242	909,929	-983,076	5,821,237	1,630,812	2,403,832	35,479	277,793	163,921
2009	9,865,883	7,737,204	-4,377	7,732,827	922,660	-1,060,682	5,749,485	1,518,889	2,597,509	35,442	278,370	160,817
2010	10,097,029	7,865,992	-4,301	7,861,691	930,900	-1,093,278	5,837,513	1,547,767	2,711,749	36,344	277,821	159,715
2011	10,598,208	8,188,890	-1,573	8,187,317	856,257	-1,089,838	6,241,222	1,658,496	2,698,490	38,280	276,860	160,242
2012	10,824,093	8,321,036	1,077	8,322,113	865,580	-1,116,636	6,339,897	1,723,498	2,760,698	39,109	276,770	160,455
2013	10,639,598	8,184,017	-605	8,183,412	956,481	-1,062,273	6,164,658	1,650,719	2,824,221	38,616	275,520	158,512
2014	10,929,193	8,226,057	-3,272	8,222,785	978,289	-1,027,690	6,216,806	1,722,407	2,989,980	39,681	275,423	156,904
2015	11,018,373	8,200,534	-3,779	8,196,755	984,303	-1,066,213	6,146,239	1,763,592	3,108,542	40,350	273,071	154,423
2016	10,840,348	7,967,687	-6,857	7,960,830	984,657	-1,064,827	5,911,346	1,775,624	3,153,378	40,033	270,787	151,237
2017	11,039,268	8,105,850	-7,804	8,098,046	1,001,729	-1,127,322	5,968,995	1,817,926	3,252,347	41,314	267,206	148,794
2018	11,530,401	9,017,306	-8,737	9,008,569	1,094,648	-1,552,237	6,361,684	1,854,788	3,313,929	43,764	263,466	152,477
2019	11,788,186	8,633,389	-6,666	8,626,723	1,041,513	-1,191,987	6,393,223	1,982,196	3,412,767	45,195	260,828	145,341
2020	12,435,457	8,428,365	-7,983	8,420,382	1,049,599	-1,060,330	6,310,453	1,958,595	4,166,409	48,229	257,840	137,318
2021	13,168,698	8,795,386	-9,485	8,785,901	1,080,361	-1,109,426	6,596,114	1,993,088	4,579,496	51,638	255,020	139,420

Personal Income and Employment by Area: Charleston-North Charleston, SC

(Thousands of dollars, except as noted.)

Year	Personal income, total	Derivation of personal income									Per capita personal income (dollars)	Population (persons)	Total employment
		Earnings by place of work			Less: Contributions for government social insurance	Plus: Adjustment for residence	Equals: Net earnings by place of residence	Plus: Dividends, interest, and rent	Plus: Personal current transfer receipts				
		Nonfarm	Farm	Total									
1970	1,279,669	1,056,968	7,639	1,064,607	59,898	-11,367	993,342	216,524	69,803	3,801	336,669	152,101
1971	1,383,879	1,130,473	7,446	1,137,919	66,798	-11,343	1,059,778	238,548	85,553	4,011	345,034	151,142
1972	1,517,813	1,232,701	9,813	1,242,514	75,438	-10,819	1,156,257	263,516	98,040	4,286	354,123	153,558
1973	1,680,008	1,364,230	10,318	1,374,548	94,055	-12,543	1,267,950	294,968	117,090	4,634	362,524	162,266
1974	1,959,389	1,576,872	15,077	1,591,949	113,060	-14,022	1,464,867	346,905	147,617	5,189	377,614	172,300
1975	2,213,586	1,756,358	19,661	1,776,019	128,328	-16,947	1,630,744	388,448	194,394	5,691	388,945	176,227
1976	2,459,268	1,977,834	12,311	1,990,145	148,863	-21,212	1,820,070	424,015	215,183	6,111	402,464	183,691
1977	2,651,205	2,136,753	8,786	2,145,539	159,554	-24,348	1,961,637	463,506	226,062	6,511	407,216	188,099
1978	3,009,689	2,408,891	15,418	2,424,309	181,834	-28,414	2,214,061	545,654	249,974	7,209	417,483	197,797
1979	3,372,609	2,698,623	20,159	2,718,782	212,054	-34,732	2,471,996	612,965	287,648	7,933	425,158	204,605
1980	3,809,937	3,020,853	6,976	3,027,829	237,871	-41,007	2,748,951	707,666	353,320	8,786	433,615	209,543
1981	4,325,681	3,408,083	10,642	3,418,725	287,607	-45,365	3,085,753	832,985	406,943	9,715	445,278	217,214
1982	4,676,711	3,626,698	23,524	3,650,222	308,623	-46,431	3,295,168	937,168	444,375	10,317	453,298	217,116
1983	5,039,496	3,909,629	10,127	3,919,756	349,967	-40,132	3,529,657	1,033,966	475,873	10,934	460,906	222,685
1984	5,573,828	4,339,955	19,015	4,358,970	403,264	-50,105	3,905,601	1,158,709	509,518	11,927	467,325	236,807
1985	5,934,775	4,635,729	8,199	4,643,928	444,899	-56,914	4,142,115	1,246,149	546,511	12,645	469,353	246,759
1986	6,361,315	4,964,353	7,302	4,971,655	493,245	-59,917	4,418,493	1,359,572	583,250	13,227	480,947	255,473
1987	6,797,770	5,323,389	11,954	5,335,343	528,764	-62,639	4,743,940	1,451,630	602,200	13,862	490,378	263,378
1988	7,329,506	5,787,906	17,965	5,805,871	601,080	-69,612	5,135,179	1,551,970	642,357	14,874	492,783	270,818
1989	7,956,613	6,149,175	13,890	6,163,065	653,838	-75,414	5,433,813	1,723,378	799,422	15,824	502,823	275,672
1990	8,658,930	6,731,605	12,967	6,744,572	739,637	-85,291	5,919,644	1,864,973	874,313	17,017	508,851	289,036
1991	9,034,156	6,961,780	19,060	6,980,840	777,915	-77,665	6,125,260	1,954,240	954,656	17,246	523,852	287,878
1992	9,495,342	7,237,437	16,418	7,253,855	813,485	-64,278	6,376,092	2,019,035	1,100,215	17,903	530,382	283,152
1993	9,860,162	7,402,313	23,960	7,426,273	843,836	-58,346	6,524,091	2,137,955	1,198,116	18,537	531,913	282,830
1994	10,089,234	7,417,182	34,106	7,451,288	861,532	-42,789	6,546,967	2,240,729	1,301,538	19,059	529,376	280,828
1995	10,310,767	7,435,391	31,774	7,467,165	869,583	-27,616	6,569,966	2,330,876	1,409,925	19,745	522,192	281,375
1996	10,813,743	7,691,660	27,846	7,719,506	889,684	-19,559	6,810,263	2,484,964	1,518,516	20,877	517,970	282,824
1997	11,576,341	8,250,086	28,077	8,278,163	958,508	-16,237	7,303,418	2,676,616	1,596,307	21,910	528,354	293,859
1998	12,610,199	9,068,067	20,573	9,088,640	1,053,237	-12,938	8,022,465	2,918,978	1,668,756	23,541	535,674	304,992
1999	13,487,782	9,889,082	24,118	9,913,200	1,142,910	-10,635	8,759,655	2,963,171	1,764,956	24,695	546,169	316,969
2000	14,611,931	10,713,020	25,266	10,738,286	1,227,919	-1,877	9,508,490	3,210,681	1,892,760	26,523	550,916	323,851
2001	14,979,640	10,896,374	26,859	10,923,233	1,271,569	-8,593	9,643,071	3,236,961	2,099,608	26,898	556,901	327,147
2002	15,695,772	11,566,180	16,070	11,582,250	1,353,488	-18,219	10,210,543	3,206,167	2,279,062	27,771	565,179	333,500
2003	16,486,558	12,252,126	25,889	12,278,015	1,440,587	-26,183	10,811,245	3,269,853	2,405,460	28,753	573,376	341,030
2004	17,886,660	13,231,252	21,899	13,253,151	1,548,462	-33,531	11,671,158	3,619,229	2,596,273	30,459	587,231	353,803
2005	19,551,830	14,313,955	23,744	14,337,699	1,659,581	-45,995	12,632,123	4,113,313	2,806,394	32,678	598,313	364,423
2006	21,258,700	15,397,210	15,704	15,412,914	1,819,614	-48,102	13,545,198	4,708,032	3,005,470	34,597	614,463	374,776
2007	23,027,799	16,690,687	15,356	16,706,043	1,957,941	-61,154	14,686,948	5,158,750	3,182,101	36,646	628,384	391,799
2008	23,635,504	16,703,046	10,193	16,713,239	2,017,422	-62,455	14,633,362	5,281,703	3,720,439	36,723	643,613	394,806
2009	22,936,450	16,082,697	16,333	16,099,030	1,973,274	-41,180	14,084,576	4,728,143	4,123,731	34,994	655,447	381,979
2010	24,722,643	17,202,262	17,848	17,220,110	2,050,295	-28,344	15,141,471	5,068,114	4,513,058	37,038	667,495	384,824
2011	26,839,152	18,667,465	15,018	18,682,483	1,952,530	-19,534	16,710,419	5,504,370	4,624,363	39,385	681,449	399,885
2012	29,421,434	20,747,454	18,576	20,766,030	2,053,143	-8,038	18,704,849	6,043,752	4,672,833	42,196	697,254	408,522
2013	29,295,950	20,713,789	25,968	20,739,757	2,365,833	-7,873	18,366,051	6,075,429	4,854,470	41,155	711,850	418,733
2014	31,727,355	22,205,982	10,563	22,216,545	2,517,167	2,828	19,702,206	6,835,608	5,189,541	43,994	721,173	432,505
2015	34,095,331	23,777,413	7,198	23,784,611	2,684,779	-13,974	21,085,858	7,436,514	5,572,959	46,196	738,057	448,927
2016	36,003,842	24,978,173	7,337	24,985,510	2,815,630	-40,589	22,129,291	8,078,022	5,796,529	47,824	752,834	468,522
2017	37,983,716	26,314,943	8,013	26,322,956	2,979,563	-48,498	23,294,895	8,669,760	6,019,061	49,611	765,626	480,397
2018	39,873,855	27,522,330	4,822	27,527,152	3,141,983	-66,865	24,318,304	9,205,708	6,349,843	51,333	776,775	497,800
2019	43,519,895	29,670,269	5,477	29,675,746	3,384,175	-82,031	26,209,540	10,532,754	6,777,601	55,099	789,852	505,329
2020	45,677,752	29,770,246	9,757	29,780,003	3,398,308	-81,215	26,300,480	10,619,495	8,757,777	56,887	802,961	494,342
2021	49,396,282	32,467,295	12,682	32,479,977	3,648,464	-101,546	28,729,967	11,011,883	9,654,432	60,754	813,052	512,301

Personal Income and Employment by Area: Charlotte-Concord-Gastonia, NC-SC

(Thousands of dollars, except as noted.)

Year	Personal income, total	Earnings by place of work			Less: Contributions for government social insurance	Plus: Adjustment for residence	Equals: Net earnings by place of residence	Plus: Dividends, interest, and rent	Plus: Personal current transfer receipts	Per capita personal income (dollars)	Population (persons)	Total employment
		Nonfarm	Farm	Total								
1970	3,570,757	3,182,109	23,102	3,205,211	225,700	-51,022	2,928,489	397,045	245,223	3,613	988,444	503,563
1971	3,904,425	3,458,387	27,218	3,485,605	254,522	-55,099	3,175,984	439,309	289,132	3,875	1,007,583	511,003
1972	4,403,475	3,924,723	32,679	3,957,402	303,176	-64,005	3,590,221	487,622	325,632	4,284	1,027,951	534,518
1973	4,912,458	4,369,985	64,193	4,434,178	387,915	-69,663	3,976,600	550,750	385,108	4,710	1,042,990	557,073
1974	5,344,543	4,677,751	51,734	4,729,485	429,910	-72,566	4,227,009	634,981	482,553	5,071	1,054,007	556,610
1975	5,752,816	4,834,237	43,467	4,877,704	434,093	-78,175	4,365,436	696,736	690,644	5,435	1,058,573	531,234
1976	6,427,283	5,484,004	48,150	5,532,154	504,519	-87,701	4,939,934	762,400	724,949	6,031	1,065,660	552,899
1977	7,124,675	6,140,199	44,271	6,184,470	562,819	-101,503	5,520,148	852,106	752,421	6,619	1,076,317	576,425
1978	8,074,560	7,015,507	58,283	7,073,790	662,281	-120,818	6,290,691	973,865	810,004	7,374	1,095,051	604,651
1979	9,125,808	7,957,450	66,030	8,023,480	778,268	-147,938	7,097,274	1,112,460	916,074	8,182	1,115,330	631,747
1980	10,266,424	8,787,537	33,877	8,821,414	859,393	-175,236	7,786,785	1,388,427	1,091,212	8,984	1,142,703	636,966
1981	11,555,367	9,741,341	40,927	9,782,268	1,021,767	-208,766	8,551,735	1,745,865	1,257,767	9,963	1,159,800	644,468
1982	12,379,107	10,197,544	58,007	10,255,551	1,081,665	-223,361	8,950,525	2,012,197	1,416,385	10,520	1,176,768	634,435
1983	13,563,373	11,250,363	47,855	11,298,218	1,203,729	-244,188	9,850,301	2,188,033	1,525,039	11,430	1,186,619	648,334
1984	15,390,998	12,767,309	134,902	12,902,211	1,399,933	-274,575	11,227,703	2,561,987	1,601,308	12,755	1,206,699	687,850
1985	16,698,309	13,855,878	155,607	14,011,485	1,538,805	-300,085	12,172,595	2,794,495	1,731,219	13,577	1,229,877	711,901
1986	18,098,776	15,137,698	144,780	15,282,478	1,717,076	-331,024	13,234,378	3,029,630	1,834,768	14,506	1,247,714	738,057
1987	19,784,206	16,822,651	85,527	16,908,178	1,881,794	-379,226	14,647,158	3,232,579	1,904,469	15,551	1,272,213	768,719
1988	21,875,684	18,554,858	124,151	18,679,009	2,116,214	-420,953	16,141,842	3,669,664	2,064,178	16,865	1,297,129	803,761
1989	23,890,954	20,072,039	161,528	20,233,567	2,287,189	-461,682	17,484,696	4,094,975	2,311,283	18,091	1,320,598	826,270
1990	25,648,599	21,567,003	206,836	21,773,839	2,521,599	-507,093	18,745,147	4,346,334	2,557,118	19,001	1,349,847	844,984
1991	26,613,112	22,040,075	237,338	22,277,413	2,611,399	-496,537	19,169,477	4,485,207	2,958,428	19,272	1,380,932	830,828
1992	28,830,767	23,923,406	233,381	24,156,787	2,794,437	-520,667	20,841,683	4,707,698	3,281,386	20,516	1,405,306	844,448
1993	30,863,992	25,528,199	246,803	25,775,002	2,995,693	-541,191	22,238,118	5,049,808	3,576,066	21,497	1,435,716	873,760
1994	33,368,371	27,661,930	245,601	27,907,531	3,279,929	-584,722	24,042,880	5,577,332	3,748,159	22,694	1,470,366	909,458
1995	36,286,667	29,931,378	275,626	30,207,004	3,542,791	-636,842	26,027,371	6,126,134	4,133,162	24,046	1,509,023	948,911
1996	39,213,260	32,078,331	258,514	32,336,845	3,751,922	-664,292	27,920,631	6,803,150	4,489,479	25,288	1,550,697	975,193
1997	42,249,833	34,750,688	237,600	34,988,288	4,042,307	-721,183	30,224,798	7,333,232	4,691,803	26,492	1,594,838	1,014,492
1998	46,939,936	38,543,631	315,066	38,858,697	4,459,525	-759,400	33,639,772	8,264,664	5,035,500	28,187	1,665,276	1,056,196
1999	50,062,950	41,531,700	356,253	41,887,953	4,812,048	-838,212	36,237,693	8,491,673	5,333,584	29,244	1,711,905	1,094,733
2000	53,705,949	44,492,894	348,315	44,841,209	5,133,767	-901,601	38,805,841	9,138,006	5,762,102	30,620	1,753,958	1,126,455
2001	52,755,216	43,146,367	380,186	43,526,553	5,352,451	-967,272	37,206,830	9,063,745	6,484,641	29,390	1,795,029	1,131,782
2002	54,259,516	44,700,228	223,713	44,923,941	5,500,613	-1,004,096	38,419,232	8,754,463	7,085,821	29,612	1,832,361	1,134,667
2003	57,635,651	47,500,112	258,723	47,758,835	5,752,681	-1,000,921	41,005,233	9,129,527	7,500,891	30,867	1,867,238	1,137,783
2004	64,162,309	52,856,261	304,480	53,160,741	6,063,848	-1,087,689	46,009,204	10,071,306	8,081,799	33,656	1,906,396	1,166,374
2005	70,935,665	58,401,486	339,661	58,741,147	6,600,549	-1,164,311	50,976,287	11,212,772	8,746,606	36,178	1,960,753	1,209,673
2006	80,265,078	66,361,168	312,105	66,673,273	7,246,355	-1,184,001	58,242,917	12,423,239	9,598,922	39,426	2,035,838	1,263,361
2007	89,949,600	74,633,739	261,299	74,895,038	7,893,384	-1,177,855	65,823,799	13,711,611	10,414,190	42,573	2,112,817	1,320,238
2008	100,556,106	82,591,571	176,347	82,767,918	8,192,522	-1,136,409	73,438,987	15,028,022	12,089,097	46,156	2,178,593	1,322,580
2009	92,650,289	73,994,199	183,818	74,178,017	7,772,409	-874,600	65,531,008	13,282,341	13,836,940	41,682	2,222,773	1,269,767
2010	87,638,856	67,743,652	191,051	67,934,703	7,606,518	-727,542	59,600,643	13,106,989	14,931,224	38,947	2,250,187	1,263,077
2011	92,503,012	70,626,599	195,311	70,821,910	7,210,697	-608,132	63,003,081	14,365,674	15,134,257	40,543	2,281,611	1,318,012
2012	104,404,396	81,287,738	313,623	81,601,361	7,720,584	-495,535	73,385,242	15,653,114	15,366,040	45,016	2,319,298	1,347,262
2013	100,105,902	77,942,332	356,328	78,298,660	8,989,001	-322,048	68,987,611	15,432,918	15,685,373	42,425	2,359,584	1,383,036
2014	106,648,113	82,668,482	388,850	83,057,332	9,568,254	-461,766	73,027,312	17,144,437	16,476,364	44,498	2,396,711	1,437,676
2015	114,567,872	88,437,009	468,814	88,905,823	10,226,945	-527,309	78,151,569	18,815,218	17,601,085	46,896	2,443,016	1,490,981
2016	120,320,313	93,538,561	337,880	93,876,441	10,672,755	-547,129	82,656,557	19,528,949	18,134,807	48,249	2,493,738	1,541,256
2017	128,403,383	99,711,966	414,089	100,126,055	11,207,577	-609,910	88,308,568	21,221,850	18,872,965	50,495	2,542,910	1,589,355
2018	135,569,510	105,649,285	244,409	105,893,694	11,706,353	-703,197	93,484,144	22,220,426	19,864,940	52,452	2,584,646	1,637,161
2019	143,966,000	111,673,924	267,887	111,941,811	12,422,364	-788,160	98,731,287	24,296,496	20,938,217	54,809	2,626,694	1,675,754
2020	154,075,451	115,477,825	232,318	115,710,143	12,947,689	-999,546	101,762,908	24,628,136	27,684,407	57,713	2,669,665	1,668,797
2021	167,617,407	125,799,657	351,258	126,150,915	13,901,547	-1,229,343	111,020,025	25,251,840	31,345,542	62,056	2,701,046	1,735,271

Personal Income and Employment by Area: Charlottesville, VA

(Thousands of dollars, except as noted.)

Year	Personal income, total	Earnings by place of work			Less: Contributions for government social insurance	Plus: Adjustment for residence	Equals: Net earnings by place of residence	Plus: Dividends, interest, and rent	Plus: Personal current transfer receipts	Per capita personal income (dollars)	Population (persons)	Total employment
		Nonfarm	Farm	Total								
1970	382,009	306,035	7,606	313,641	19,212	-19,465	274,964	77,462	29,583	3,415	111,846	51,870
1971	418,835	332,208	7,062	339,270	21,688	-18,976	298,606	85,070	35,159	3,684	113,689	52,468
1972	479,147	366,133	7,473	373,606	25,221	-3,395	344,990	94,025	40,132	4,031	118,870	54,890
1973	552,697	420,065	11,906	431,971	32,841	-3,687	395,443	109,148	48,106	4,519	122,296	58,728
1974	617,706	463,653	11,765	475,418	37,815	-3,840	433,763	125,306	58,637	4,923	125,476	60,912
1975	682,296	499,850	7,047	506,897	39,984	2,629	469,542	134,944	77,810	5,219	130,734	60,189
1976	762,356	555,719	5,038	560,757	44,944	10,489	526,302	150,331	85,723	5,755	132,458	62,508
1977	837,372	611,855	4,325	616,180	50,026	10,983	577,137	168,612	91,623	6,273	133,491	64,427
1978	957,134	707,233	10,296	717,529	58,754	5,344	664,119	193,906	99,109	7,090	135,000	68,132
1979	1,062,765	809,740	9,895	819,635	70,191	-9,646	739,798	209,791	113,176	7,764	136,881	71,979
1980	1,208,283	908,115	5,051	913,166	79,955	-17,691	815,520	258,036	134,727	8,753	138,046	74,348
1981	1,372,332	989,058	3,310	992,368	93,685	-11,935	886,748	329,759	155,825	9,810	139,886	74,591
1982	1,505,033	1,064,286	1,726	1,066,012	102,224	-14,597	949,191	384,760	171,082	10,686	140,835	75,162
1983	1,639,061	1,184,304	308	1,184,612	116,121	-21,679	1,046,812	405,538	186,711	11,516	142,328	77,404
1984	1,824,054	1,310,255	4,960	1,315,215	132,138	-21,569	1,161,508	464,016	198,530	12,697	143,655	80,110
1985	1,974,578	1,425,294	3,726	1,429,020	146,738	-23,996	1,258,286	505,588	210,704	13,519	146,056	82,356
1986	2,132,538	1,551,877	4,783	1,556,660	165,238	-23,794	1,367,628	544,802	220,108	14,601	146,055	86,235
1987	2,305,118	1,685,215	9,041	1,694,256	178,297	-21,543	1,494,416	582,920	227,782	15,508	148,641	90,858
1988	2,610,003	1,919,924	9,720	1,929,644	206,942	-23,492	1,699,210	668,532	242,261	17,250	151,301	91,623
1989	2,861,492	2,061,740	14,215	2,075,955	223,857	-21,609	1,830,489	760,593	270,410	18,532	154,409	94,636
1990	3,075,262	2,191,381	16,958	2,208,339	240,899	-20,628	1,946,812	837,636	290,814	19,476	157,899	95,934
1991	3,251,634	2,297,763	16,746	2,314,509	253,534	-19,591	2,041,384	887,839	322,411	20,252	160,559	95,320
1992	3,497,935	2,435,807	15,763	2,451,570	267,841	-20,334	2,163,395	962,261	372,279	21,439	163,154	96,170
1993	3,752,715	2,612,224	13,869	2,626,093	284,848	-26,502	2,314,743	1,038,022	399,950	22,512	166,695	99,792
1994	3,956,587	2,750,452	14,130	2,764,582	299,974	-30,125	2,434,483	1,106,125	415,979	23,242	170,234	101,956
1995	4,234,263	2,870,389	15,150	2,885,539	311,424	-34,392	2,539,723	1,237,075	457,465	24,439	173,261	104,722
1996	4,482,129	3,050,323	15,355	3,065,678	329,990	-44,071	2,691,617	1,303,849	486,663	25,397	176,481	107,633
1997	4,819,459	3,293,134	9,436	3,302,570	352,469	-47,354	2,902,747	1,406,135	510,577	26,803	179,813	110,980
1998	4,957,984	3,486,975	6,382	3,493,357	369,879	-108,672	3,014,806	1,474,109	469,069	29,527	167,916	110,257
1999	5,230,261	3,715,652	6,658	3,722,310	393,824	-118,560	3,209,926	1,525,315	495,020	30,468	171,662	113,129
2000	5,696,359	4,063,842	10,249	4,074,091	423,552	-138,277	3,512,262	1,643,251	540,846	32,555	174,979	116,535
2001	5,995,357	4,273,600	4,581	4,278,181	451,927	-150,070	3,676,184	1,722,357	596,816	33,728	177,754	117,073
2002	6,131,946	4,475,313	4,594	4,479,907	473,655	-169,175	3,837,077	1,668,820	626,049	33,983	180,442	118,132
2003	6,549,097	4,679,124	-509	4,678,615	493,685	-183,410	4,001,520	1,879,416	668,161	35,877	182,545	118,620
2004	7,013,109	5,032,930	1,473	5,034,403	532,291	-202,936	4,299,176	2,013,818	700,115	37,946	184,817	122,148
2005	7,555,762	5,390,480	-1,892	5,388,588	575,589	-236,667	4,576,332	2,210,567	768,863	40,068	188,574	126,006
2006	8,303,954	5,743,656	-11,897	5,731,759	617,504	-265,648	4,848,607	2,612,098	843,249	43,256	191,972	130,624
2007	8,827,859	6,059,783	-14,081	6,045,702	657,472	-297,628	5,090,602	2,841,541	895,716	45,353	194,646	134,180
2008	9,214,870	6,298,734	1,078	6,299,812	687,303	-330,162	5,282,347	2,915,054	1,017,469	46,574	197,853	135,572
2009	8,857,642	6,285,899	3,895	6,289,794	689,617	-316,511	5,283,666	2,483,947	1,090,029	44,282	200,028	133,004
2010	9,350,101	6,584,709	2,700	6,587,409	706,376	-287,644	5,593,389	2,575,096	1,181,616	46,308	201,913	132,313
2011	9,835,193	6,676,477	5,072	6,681,549	641,229	-283,279	5,757,041	2,862,548	1,215,604	48,287	203,683	134,038
2012	10,689,669	7,093,874	14,912	7,108,786	665,172	-270,606	6,173,008	3,276,917	1,239,744	51,983	205,636	135,970
2013	10,633,906	7,151,882	5,177	7,157,059	775,893	-252,192	6,128,974	3,212,839	1,292,093	51,400	206,887	137,587
2014	11,258,181	7,485,534	-1,993	7,483,541	813,138	-270,492	6,399,911	3,492,492	1,365,778	53,608	210,010	141,037
2015	11,986,056	7,989,906	-3,974	7,985,932	872,637	-311,618	6,801,677	3,741,212	1,443,167	56,401	212,514	145,782
2016	12,680,678	8,287,114	-5,702	8,281,412	901,091	-324,644	7,055,677	4,125,908	1,499,093	58,987	214,974	149,406
2017	13,700,729	8,796,164	5,099	8,801,263	965,400	-367,684	7,468,179	4,666,761	1,565,789	62,945	217,661	152,778
2018	14,472,984	9,175,422	-6,727	9,168,695	1,007,805	-398,252	7,762,638	5,004,254	1,706,092	66,061	219,086	155,635
2019	15,317,653	9,362,657	1,429	9,364,086	1,033,717	-404,845	7,925,524	5,593,125	1,799,004	69,409	220,686	157,819
2020	15,955,174	9,440,255	-3,662	9,436,593	1,053,076	-412,656	7,970,861	5,577,869	2,406,444	72,025	221,522	151,119
2021	17,162,532	10,320,063	-5,686	10,314,377	1,142,048	-474,233	8,698,096	5,759,778	2,704,658	77,070	222,688	155,530

Personal Income and Employment by Area: Chattanooga, TN-GA

(Thousands of dollars, except as noted.)

Year	Personal income, total	Derivation of personal income									Per capita personal income (dollars)	Population (persons)	Total employment
		Earnings by place of work			Less: Contributions for government social insurance	Plus: Adjustment for residence	Equals: Net earnings by place of residence	Plus: Dividends, interest, and rent	Plus: Personal current transfer receipts				
		Nonfarm	Farm	Total									
1970	1,330,318	1,169,675	4,311	1,173,986	76,760	-43,113	1,054,113	163,961	112,244		3,575	372,113	172,095
1971	1,474,581	1,286,539	3,807	1,290,346	86,418	-46,757	1,157,171	185,424	131,986		3,876	380,419	174,934
1972	1,674,323	1,471,219	5,289	1,476,508	103,374	-52,526	1,320,608	206,648	147,067		4,326	387,034	186,173
1973	1,872,144	1,645,219	9,097	1,654,316	133,722	-55,932	1,464,662	232,672	174,810		4,739	395,063	196,966
1974	2,054,698	1,779,157	4,370	1,783,527	149,824	-59,310	1,574,393	269,803	210,502		5,154	398,683	197,405
1975	2,230,144	1,866,010	7,212	1,873,222	152,748	-54,890	1,665,584	291,987	272,573		5,554	401,552	190,016
1976	2,492,020	2,092,790	9,431	2,102,221	174,051	-51,873	1,876,297	317,315	298,408		6,140	405,890	196,745
1977	2,755,079	2,327,332	6,532	2,333,864	191,994	-62,047	2,079,823	356,215	319,041		6,703	411,025	201,417
1978	3,145,986	2,683,708	5,564	2,689,272	222,836	-75,066	2,391,370	408,219	346,397		7,563	415,992	211,442
1979	3,430,114	2,893,475	7,112	2,900,587	250,372	-80,228	2,569,987	458,947	401,180		8,096	423,664	214,637
1980	3,723,675	3,037,880	5,674	3,043,554	263,229	-80,633	2,699,692	539,426	484,557		8,712	427,429	208,292
1981	4,085,895	3,251,775	8,296	3,260,071	304,253	-83,778	2,872,040	661,753	552,102		9,491	430,519	206,190
1982	4,329,526	3,351,053	9,992	3,361,045	319,349	-79,210	2,962,486	768,457	598,583		10,135	427,203	199,884
1983	4,557,833	3,516,322	4,627	3,520,949	343,115	-71,071	3,106,763	810,737	640,333		10,769	423,243	199,125
1984	4,953,151	3,815,634	10,868	3,826,502	385,049	-72,288	3,369,165	911,372	672,614		11,678	424,137	206,887
1985	5,276,069	4,064,629	9,024	4,073,653	420,743	-69,584	3,583,326	976,474	716,269		12,428	424,535	211,855
1986	5,638,776	4,383,968	9,036	4,393,004	464,410	-85,131	3,843,463	1,033,810	761,503		13,273	424,816	218,811
1987	6,115,956	4,829,699	6,719	4,836,418	507,109	-89,610	4,239,699	1,079,405	796,852		14,245	429,335	229,011
1988	6,668,836	5,256,800	9,993	5,266,793	566,692	-94,921	4,605,180	1,211,172	852,484		15,394	433,218	235,200
1989	7,076,123	5,448,067	15,959	5,464,026	598,981	-98,410	4,766,635	1,367,059	942,429		16,304	434,018	240,365
1990	7,498,710	5,750,245	15,581	5,765,826	637,022	-89,725	5,039,079	1,434,336	1,025,295		17,289	433,718	243,572
1991	7,747,533	5,893,734	18,198	5,911,932	664,466	-91,520	5,155,946	1,423,444	1,168,143		17,692	437,902	243,018
1992	8,336,210	6,284,235	19,817	6,304,052	701,306	-64,594	5,538,152	1,476,252	1,321,806		18,878	441,576	245,510
1993	8,920,828	6,763,107	20,399	6,783,506	757,314	-68,373	5,957,819	1,548,877	1,414,132		19,939	447,416	254,759
1994	9,341,819	7,123,340	22,557	7,145,897	810,876	-92,961	6,242,060	1,612,442	1,487,317		20,629	452,845	261,969
1995	9,921,900	7,519,582	14,640	7,534,222	857,439	-105,977	6,570,806	1,745,503	1,605,591		21,659	458,090	266,963
1996	10,504,425	7,945,480	16,684	7,962,164	893,109	-93,577	6,975,478	1,849,956	1,678,991		22,732	462,090	273,762
1997	11,056,648	8,511,578	17,224	8,528,802	943,645	-113,277	7,471,880	1,840,884	1,743,884		23,688	466,756	276,491
1998	11,824,483	9,153,506	21,914	9,175,420	983,559	-101,354	8,090,507	1,977,539	1,756,437		25,151	470,131	282,947
1999	12,551,728	9,860,405	19,584	9,879,989	1,058,967	-118,792	8,702,230	2,008,543	1,840,955		26,490	473,820	291,583
2000	13,300,923	10,430,505	16,622	10,447,127	1,113,624	-134,478	9,199,025	2,122,912	1,978,986		27,848	477,630	298,758
2001	13,367,099	10,321,957	30,395	10,352,352	1,129,226	-135,925	9,087,201	2,126,676	2,153,222		27,744	481,798	295,485
2002	13,656,138	10,560,237	12,803	10,573,040	1,160,547	-120,526	9,291,967	2,039,178	2,324,993		28,102	485,957	293,159
2003	14,287,440	11,067,607	12,475	11,080,082	1,211,925	-125,631	9,742,526	2,122,777	2,422,137		29,153	490,089	295,067
2004	14,975,575	11,585,114	24,814	11,609,928	1,258,412	-89,697	10,261,819	2,133,360	2,580,396		30,271	494,709	297,575
2005	15,675,210	12,049,676	29,597	12,079,273	1,313,554	-105,337	10,660,382	2,262,806	2,752,022		31,378	499,564	302,725
2006	16,706,167	12,677,865	8,312	12,686,177	1,381,430	-134,447	11,170,300	2,592,869	2,942,998		32,985	506,473	308,555
2007	17,491,027	13,039,024	11,383	13,050,407	1,437,626	-122,934	11,489,847	2,786,389	3,214,791		34,089	513,100	313,955
2008	18,202,130	13,430,273	29,530	13,459,803	1,499,277	-201,798	11,758,728	2,848,900	3,594,502		35,087	518,778	309,896
2009	17,936,505	13,073,106	26,637	13,099,743	1,457,864	-142,288	11,499,591	2,621,294	3,815,620		34,225	524,082	291,690
2010	18,962,903	13,781,876	16,387	13,798,263	1,515,959	-198,457	12,083,847	2,722,170	4,156,886		35,835	529,167	290,655
2011	19,999,079	14,500,414	7,528	14,507,942	1,402,888	-216,560	12,888,494	2,850,866	4,259,719		37,468	533,759	297,413
2012	21,237,128	15,387,589	44,714	15,432,303	1,447,672	-258,930	13,725,701	3,224,873	4,286,554		39,451	538,322	300,036
2013	21,178,516	15,486,507	58,118	15,544,625	1,654,814	-267,062	13,622,749	3,119,727	4,436,040		39,041	542,475	303,347
2014	21,825,319	15,763,089	62,094	15,825,183	1,686,364	-114,450	14,024,369	3,266,833	4,534,117		40,257	542,153	303,571
2015	22,987,576	16,558,491	66,925	16,625,416	1,768,567	-182,725	14,674,124	3,560,430	4,753,022		42,206	544,658	310,802
2016	23,571,214	17,051,137	34,684	17,085,821	1,824,957	-140,195	15,120,669	3,589,158	4,861,387		42,952	548,785	318,233
2017	24,592,653	17,886,739	50,588	17,937,327	1,933,775	-296,040	15,707,512	3,861,489	5,023,652		44,532	552,242	326,596
2018	25,729,604	18,704,134	36,148	18,740,282	2,023,081	-422,978	16,294,223	4,167,423	5,267,958		46,242	556,415	335,354
2019	26,981,700	19,417,872	26,728	19,444,600	2,119,963	-491,891	16,832,746	4,590,129	5,558,825		48,210	559,673	339,125
2020	28,499,082	19,737,136	-6,048	19,731,088	2,209,833	-531,881	16,989,374	4,570,010	6,939,698		50,566	563,599	334,329
2021	30,599,485	21,205,731	35,093	21,240,824	2,311,883	-649,273	18,279,668	4,641,292	7,678,525		53,906	567,641	342,348

Personal Income and Employment by Area: Cheyenne, WY

(Thousands of dollars, except as noted.)

		Derivation of personal income										
		Earnings by place of work			Less: Contributions for government social insurance	Plus: Adjustment for residence	Equals: Net earnings by place of residence	Plus: Dividends, interest, and rent	Plus: Personal current transfer receipts	Per capita personal income (dollars)	Population (persons)	Total employment
Year	Personal income, total	Nonfarm	Farm	Total								
1970	252,643	194,127	4,016	198,143	14,212	-933	182,998	50,776	18,869	4,462	56,619	28,563
1971	278,822	214,779	3,692	218,471	16,164	-1,574	200,733	56,613	21,476	4,812	57,944	29,358
1972	316,308	248,403	5,405	253,808	19,435	-2,894	231,479	61,832	22,997	5,272	59,997	31,164
1973	368,918	299,024	2,699	301,723	26,358	-4,924	270,441	71,862	26,615	5,907	62,458	33,858
1974	421,372	339,216	5,972	345,188	30,392	-6,058	308,738	82,317	30,317	6,504	64,789	34,558
1975	460,198	369,276	3,179	372,455	32,738	-7,183	332,534	91,017	36,647	7,118	64,656	34,715
1976	499,110	401,915	2,462	404,377	37,177	-8,805	358,395	99,945	40,770	7,608	65,603	35,707
1977	545,964	439,633	1,956	441,589	40,521	-10,254	390,814	110,483	44,667	8,233	66,313	36,652
1978	633,865	513,924	3,702	517,626	48,371	-13,259	455,996	128,116	49,753	9,461	67,001	39,071
1979	714,130	582,650	3,925	586,575	57,616	-16,372	512,587	143,894	57,649	10,325	69,168	41,258
1980	815,794	654,505	5,503	660,008	63,994	-19,446	576,568	172,098	67,128	11,824	68,994	42,593
1981	913,139	720,837	4,130	724,967	75,197	-19,777	629,993	203,850	79,296	13,012	70,176	42,834
1982	986,599	763,875	2,479	766,354	80,704	-20,797	664,853	233,079	88,667	13,871	71,129	43,159
1983	1,017,431	770,854	3,502	774,356	80,500	-20,521	673,335	242,078	102,018	13,955	72,907	41,915
1984	1,079,459	819,217	1,091	820,308	87,568	-21,390	711,350	263,043	105,066	14,718	73,345	42,415
1985	1,127,157	852,893	828	853,721	92,828	-22,115	738,778	277,475	110,904	15,419	73,102	42,570
1986	1,172,405	878,550	4,623	883,173	96,753	-21,676	764,744	287,554	120,107	15,756	74,411	42,461
1987	1,189,497	881,608	8,265	889,873	98,059	-20,752	771,062	293,943	124,492	15,839	75,101	43,181
1988	1,223,589	907,476	7,579	915,055	107,833	-21,294	785,928	307,074	130,587	16,419	74,523	43,939
1989	1,308,019	954,078	8,791	962,869	112,896	-21,744	828,229	336,722	143,068	17,756	73,667	44,287
1990	1,400,438	997,700	14,182	1,011,882	122,599	-22,116	867,167	379,246	154,025	19,138	73,175	44,257
1991	1,463,370	1,053,903	14,714	1,068,617	130,928	-21,637	916,052	376,522	170,796	19,781	73,978	45,286
1992	1,549,319	1,129,599	16,041	1,145,640	139,826	-22,010	983,804	375,946	189,569	20,433	75,826	46,097
1993	1,631,027	1,199,571	19,740	1,219,311	147,894	-20,663	1,050,754	375,384	204,889	21,047	77,495	47,556
1994	1,721,747	1,259,646	9,595	1,269,241	155,020	-17,720	1,096,501	405,913	219,333	21,826	78,885	48,911
1995	1,806,934	1,286,473	15,818	1,302,291	157,386	-14,328	1,130,577	447,087	229,270	22,725	79,513	49,370
1996	1,868,181	1,305,018	12,029	1,317,047	159,500	-11,386	1,146,161	482,603	239,417	23,298	80,186	49,791
1997	1,962,802	1,337,613	24,662	1,362,275	165,561	-9,471	1,187,243	528,670	246,889	24,435	80,328	50,275
1998	2,110,868	1,442,052	16,567	1,458,619	176,008	-8,275	1,274,336	585,168	251,364	26,215	80,522	50,884
1999	2,233,570	1,536,445	13,621	1,550,066	186,812	-6,981	1,356,273	614,397	262,900	27,572	81,009	51,821
2000	2,396,728	1,635,750	15,282	1,651,032	195,864	-2,791	1,452,377	658,200	286,151	29,291	81,825	53,509
2001	2,511,537	1,737,212	19,801	1,757,013	207,338	-7,773	1,541,902	655,160	314,475	30,423	82,554	52,757
2002	2,668,640	1,889,208	5,629	1,894,837	218,963	-17,577	1,658,297	669,384	340,959	32,065	83,226	54,629
2003	2,856,196	2,012,166	12,995	2,025,161	236,407	-24,978	1,763,776	721,788	370,632	33,968	84,084	55,774
2004	3,046,520	2,132,226	13,465	2,145,691	252,873	-31,234	1,861,584	784,449	400,487	35,662	85,427	56,596
2005	3,210,063	2,239,784	18,228	2,258,012	263,575	-37,310	1,957,127	827,178	425,758	37,443	85,732	57,722
2006	3,483,094	2,500,343	13,013	2,513,356	323,956	-47,317	2,142,083	881,847	459,164	40,119	86,819	58,704
2007	3,660,650	2,603,796	19,309	2,623,105	341,251	-51,025	2,230,829	938,842	490,979	41,762	87,654	61,107
2008	4,047,841	2,786,630	30,373	2,817,003	353,669	-58,583	2,404,751	1,070,087	573,003	45,442	89,077	62,254
2009	3,813,588	2,750,685	25,317	2,776,002	357,519	-77,264	2,341,219	848,626	623,743	42,172	90,430	61,625
2010	3,997,384	2,838,972	32,978	2,871,950	362,183	-89,780	2,419,987	898,247	679,150	43,334	92,246	61,441
2011	4,453,966	3,024,727	70,644	3,095,371	344,661	-109,548	2,641,162	1,122,581	690,223	48,094	92,610	62,826
2012	4,597,599	3,226,485	38,397	3,264,882	369,815	-133,614	2,761,453	1,145,415	690,731	48,523	94,751	63,565
2013	4,646,282	3,397,663	32,884	3,430,547	424,333	-153,790	2,852,424	1,088,857	705,001	48,507	95,786	65,591
2014	4,787,400	3,459,563	38,070	3,497,633	442,769	-155,439	2,899,425	1,146,153	741,822	49,794	96,145	66,331
2015	4,861,385	3,527,121	16,771	3,543,892	445,653	-157,966	2,940,273	1,141,050	780,062	50,058	97,116	67,107
2016	4,736,057	3,498,495	13,747	3,512,242	444,842	-159,747	2,907,653	1,021,071	807,333	48,294	98,067	67,489
2017	4,894,308	3,610,239	13,419	3,623,658	458,496	-163,578	3,001,584	1,048,430	844,294	49,620	98,636	68,811
2018	5,175,230	3,795,215	11,134	3,806,349	467,417	-172,713	3,166,219	1,126,435	882,576	52,113	99,308	70,820
2019	5,313,563	3,966,349	15,927	3,982,276	496,127	-185,610	3,300,539	1,087,715	925,309	53,181	99,914	72,218
2020	5,533,843	4,012,543	8,181	4,020,724	510,253	-190,150	3,320,321	1,063,877	1,149,645	54,959	100,690	73,401
2021	5,915,191	4,236,563	29,628	4,266,191	535,437	-210,886	3,519,868	1,122,082	1,273,241	58,646	100,863	75,024

Personal Income and Employment by Area: Chicago-Naperville-Elgin, IL-IN-WI

(Thousands of dollars, except as noted.)

Year	Personal income, total	Earnings by place of work Nonfarm	Farm	Total	Less: Contributions for government social insurance	Plus: Adjustment for residence	Equals: Net earnings by place of residence	Plus: Dividends, interest, and rent	Plus: Personal current transfer receipts	Per capita personal income (dollars)	Population (persons)	Total employment
1970	39,042,067	33,236,351	86,734	33,323,085	2,242,085	-220,877	30,860,123	5,547,563	2,634,381	4,945	7,895,845	3,748,330
1971	41,693,277	35,164,992	126,592	35,291,584	2,443,040	-244,656	32,603,888	5,907,509	3,181,880	5,241	7,955,398	3,702,932
1972	45,123,683	38,201,968	88,392	38,290,360	2,799,518	-282,518	35,208,324	6,315,266	3,600,093	5,660	7,972,491	3,731,149
1973	49,732,970	42,130,409	182,890	42,313,299	3,579,992	-323,899	38,409,408	7,039,001	4,284,561	6,243	7,966,188	3,874,673
1974	54,553,129	45,828,588	148,968	45,977,556	4,034,979	-355,799	41,586,778	8,058,457	4,907,894	6,842	7,973,418	3,934,993
1975	58,433,668	47,799,792	229,126	48,028,918	4,091,563	-373,026	43,564,329	8,592,841	6,276,498	7,315	7,988,641	3,831,128
1976	64,192,731	52,906,047	158,417	53,064,464	4,622,553	-385,479	48,056,432	9,175,117	6,961,182	8,009	8,014,978	3,918,359
1977	71,017,879	59,068,433	161,840	59,230,273	5,147,532	-420,169	53,662,572	10,062,019	7,293,288	8,825	8,047,518	4,032,483
1978	78,718,037	65,965,004	168,100	66,133,104	5,908,887	-471,484	59,752,733	11,183,394	7,781,910	9,757	8,067,880	4,165,078
1979	86,307,014	72,420,326	198,815	72,619,141	6,739,277	-549,764	65,330,100	12,548,879	8,428,035	10,714	8,055,256	4,212,288
1980	94,171,212	76,333,919	73,393	76,407,312	7,075,545	-549,110	68,782,657	15,125,229	10,263,326	11,694	8,052,943	4,122,105
1981	103,627,947	81,715,572	171,801	81,887,373	8,119,333	-532,929	73,235,111	18,680,720	11,712,116	12,892	8,038,127	4,108,351
1982	109,546,668	83,822,464	126,959	83,949,423	8,481,571	-536,551	74,931,301	21,833,292	12,782,075	13,613	8,047,477	4,025,482
1983	115,032,419	87,965,256	-55,778	87,909,478	8,964,223	-522,985	78,422,270	22,966,534	13,643,615	14,299	8,044,580	3,992,825
1984	126,082,430	96,611,498	128,843	96,740,341	10,162,988	-549,846	86,027,507	26,055,572	13,999,351	15,628	8,067,923	4,150,208
1985	132,939,813	102,665,752	184,891	102,850,643	10,958,616	-559,835	91,332,192	27,022,489	14,585,132	16,469	8,072,070	4,206,304
1986	140,682,691	109,791,496	169,806	109,961,302	11,741,284	-592,810	97,627,208	27,920,476	15,135,007	17,415	8,078,098	4,297,096
1987	150,034,541	118,922,940	208,759	119,131,699	12,511,093	-687,125	105,933,481	28,736,589	15,364,471	18,525	8,099,059	4,429,471
1988	163,636,534	130,986,934	127,766	131,114,700	14,014,942	-769,460	116,330,298	31,423,977	15,882,259	20,160	8,116,756	4,560,934
1989	173,570,066	138,222,041	323,630	138,545,671	14,916,130	-824,615	122,804,926	33,859,973	16,905,167	21,289	8,153,134	4,646,403
1990	185,617,214	146,689,250	253,715	146,942,965	15,585,480	-888,115	130,469,370	36,622,105	18,525,739	22,627	8,203,210	4,719,223
1991	190,171,343	150,385,797	96,837	150,482,634	16,335,975	-929,968	133,216,691	36,970,400	19,984,252	22,900	8,304,560	4,690,670
1992	205,137,770	162,159,225	181,171	162,340,396	17,251,406	-1,051,239	144,037,751	38,151,586	22,948,433	24,384	8,412,788	4,668,331
1993	213,324,335	168,909,187	167,898	169,077,085	18,167,401	-1,147,986	149,761,698	39,370,681	24,191,956	25,059	8,512,911	4,745,984
1994	224,768,787	177,411,966	258,907	177,670,873	19,346,697	-1,259,920	157,064,256	42,397,641	25,306,890	26,118	8,605,735	4,860,416
1995	240,472,614	188,258,913	115,890	188,374,803	20,441,215	-1,377,373	166,556,215	47,059,038	26,857,361	27,662	8,693,383	4,989,418
1996	255,530,533	199,112,850	251,170	199,364,020	21,398,761	-1,524,040	176,441,219	50,779,417	28,309,897	29,096	8,782,253	5,072,565
1997	271,320,981	212,456,555	226,612	212,683,167	22,676,284	-1,679,736	188,327,147	54,227,302	28,766,532	30,614	8,862,719	5,159,787
1998	290,079,543	227,396,945	164,548	227,561,493	24,078,958	-1,891,667	201,590,868	59,240,008	29,248,667	32,414	8,949,190	5,291,308
1999	304,707,566	242,852,778	137,640	242,990,418	25,310,222	-2,081,340	215,598,856	59,343,657	29,765,053	33,723	9,035,654	5,357,397
2000	329,263,847	260,611,635	171,115	260,782,750	26,717,579	-2,294,321	231,770,850	65,629,657	31,863,340	36,130	9,113,234	5,462,648
2001	339,603,680	269,996,256	186,933	270,183,189	27,152,182	-2,482,647	240,548,360	64,563,342	34,491,978	37,036	9,169,580	5,450,274
2002	343,034,866	273,760,755	138,948	273,899,703	27,430,645	-2,610,018	243,859,040	62,009,289	37,166,537	37,262	9,206,032	5,386,960
2003	348,999,439	278,568,893	186,129	278,755,022	28,186,417	-2,713,809	247,854,796	62,488,063	38,656,580	37,798	9,233,303	5,387,028
2004	362,365,604	289,207,298	381,473	289,588,771	29,883,372	-2,899,830	256,805,569	65,602,198	39,957,837	39,129	9,260,676	5,446,229
2005	380,240,440	298,975,560	233,194	299,208,754	31,491,180	-3,150,194	264,567,380	71,751,469	43,921,591	40,991	9,276,302	5,528,261
2006	406,369,066	315,442,397	228,649	315,671,046	32,960,486	-3,408,058	279,302,502	82,544,267	44,522,297	43,706	9,297,749	5,627,599
2007	430,477,088	329,019,542	435,723	329,455,265	34,449,849	-3,547,516	291,457,900	89,866,375	49,152,813	46,104	9,337,140	5,733,881
2008	438,057,264	329,697,565	448,599	330,146,164	34,986,401	-3,551,570	291,608,193	92,045,527	54,403,544	46,679	9,384,555	5,715,056
2009	410,548,266	308,745,517	209,246	308,954,763	33,126,963	-2,998,139	272,829,661	76,343,260	61,375,345	43,539	9,429,498	5,515,227
2010	421,551,636	315,159,842	241,443	315,401,285	33,512,140	-3,000,880	278,888,265	75,689,538	66,973,833	44,511	9,470,661	5,470,609
2011	441,879,521	327,925,371	535,711	328,461,082	31,420,766	-3,130,112	293,910,204	83,833,205	64,136,112	46,509	9,500,919	5,581,826
2012	467,171,875	345,987,639	352,541	346,340,180	32,998,829	-3,273,757	310,067,594	92,706,612	64,397,669	49,031	9,528,134	5,643,024
2013	477,318,470	360,248,682	879,288	361,127,970	38,155,633	-3,291,076	319,681,261	90,694,499	66,942,710	49,980	9,550,227	5,730,430
2014	506,321,629	378,254,586	476,083	378,730,669	39,436,999	-3,274,589	336,019,081	102,123,604	68,178,944	52,501	9,643,982	5,831,728
2015	532,704,911	395,379,069	99,394	395,478,463	40,798,199	-3,580,907	351,099,357	108,930,384	72,675,170	55,170	9,655,619	5,963,729
2016	538,828,443	400,493,389	248,024	400,741,413	41,781,963	-3,669,659	355,289,791	110,375,400	73,163,252	55,800	9,656,432	6,043,935
2017	556,044,433	412,681,119	154,499	412,835,618	43,269,098	-3,915,060	365,651,460	114,945,595	75,447,378	57,586	9,655,887	6,077,001
2018	587,827,113	432,924,861	174,688	433,099,549	45,319,632	-4,112,730	383,667,187	126,482,536	77,677,390	60,938	9,646,352	6,136,292
2019	607,175,706	447,074,227	143,510	447,217,737	46,807,017	-4,249,987	396,160,733	130,068,543	80,946,430	63,024	9,634,076	6,136,056
2020	638,254,959	444,445,551	342,197	444,787,748	46,789,267	-4,068,855	393,929,626	129,752,972	114,572,361	66,474	9,601,605	5,861,932
2021	684,641,078	479,674,193	616,625	480,290,818	49,122,398	-4,665,030	426,503,390	132,390,619	125,747,069	71,992	9,509,934	6,000,711

Personal Income and Employment by Area: Chico, CA

(Thousands of dollars, except as noted.)

Year	Personal income, total	Earnings by place of work Nonfarm	Farm	Total	Less: Contributions for government social insurance	Plus: Adjustment for residence	Equals: Net earnings by place of residence	Plus: Dividends, interest, and rent	Plus: Personal current transfer receipts	Per capita personal income (dollars)	Population (persons)	Total employment
1970	381,579	226,169	24,434	250,603	14,475	6,603	242,731	75,745	63,103	3,716	102,682	36,830
1971	415,603	245,668	24,962	270,630	16,360	7,415	261,685	83,366	70,552	3,924	105,916	38,010
1972	461,533	273,571	28,920	302,491	19,113	8,632	292,010	92,503	77,020	4,093	112,775	40,361
1973	536,861	308,483	46,152	354,635	24,717	10,218	340,136	107,837	88,888	4,742	113,223	42,508
1974	630,119	341,944	70,657	412,601	28,409	12,178	396,370	125,323	108,426	5,372	117,295	44,300
1975	699,800	385,750	52,089	437,839	31,333	15,044	421,550	144,403	133,847	5,754	121,626	45,985
1976	766,349	448,738	29,862	478,600	36,886	17,894	459,608	157,418	149,323	6,112	125,377	48,998
1977	861,046	504,728	38,057	542,785	42,231	21,127	521,681	179,095	160,270	6,651	129,470	51,665
1978	974,489	579,081	31,548	610,629	49,225	25,708	587,112	210,537	176,840	7,394	131,797	54,807
1979	1,130,636	653,895	56,369	710,264	58,625	29,538	681,177	247,487	201,972	8,162	138,531	58,299
1980	1,320,695	741,991	61,407	803,398	65,175	32,436	770,659	309,880	240,156	9,119	144,828	60,482
1981	1,467,413	789,069	56,521	845,590	75,524	33,286	803,352	376,235	287,826	9,885	148,451	61,097
1982	1,532,666	803,809	42,256	846,065	78,860	34,777	801,982	408,439	322,245	10,089	151,913	59,921
1983	1,647,030	875,651	16,628	892,279	87,126	34,913	840,066	456,215	350,749	10,677	154,263	62,688
1984	1,803,653	965,397	31,211	996,608	99,960	37,453	934,101	496,849	372,703	11,504	156,791	64,197
1985	1,946,271	1,056,120	33,846	1,089,966	111,319	39,682	1,018,329	526,799	401,143	12,113	160,680	66,863
1986	2,079,377	1,150,414	27,616	1,178,030	122,664	44,484	1,099,850	546,773	432,754	12,739	163,233	68,099
1987	2,257,359	1,271,158	64,147	1,335,305	137,044	47,262	1,245,523	555,159	456,677	13,520	166,970	71,391
1988	2,468,501	1,411,174	80,281	1,491,455	157,578	51,066	1,384,943	591,651	491,907	14,359	171,909	76,545
1989	2,663,869	1,525,321	43,753	1,569,074	174,453	54,397	1,449,018	671,924	542,927	15,086	176,583	79,880
1990	2,872,915	1,672,337	63,550	1,735,887	187,601	59,937	1,608,223	683,454	581,238	15,643	183,652	84,276
1991	3,052,820	1,774,585	64,187	1,838,772	200,253	63,722	1,702,241	700,923	649,656	16,266	187,678	85,153
1992	3,239,403	1,859,396	80,716	1,940,112	209,022	67,796	1,798,886	706,903	733,614	17,013	190,409	84,849
1993	3,340,767	1,905,387	83,170	1,988,557	214,257	71,090	1,845,390	727,466	767,911	17,325	192,831	84,708
1994	3,480,305	2,041,969	64,102	2,106,071	228,399	73,431	1,951,103	740,294	788,908	17,880	194,648	88,262
1995	3,589,571	2,075,376	46,513	2,121,889	230,371	81,829	1,973,347	790,745	825,479	18,306	196,083	89,235
1996	3,798,320	2,194,163	58,420	2,252,583	234,610	86,177	2,104,150	833,892	860,278	19,347	196,327	91,583
1997	4,034,871	2,353,526	75,495	2,429,021	245,932	93,018	2,276,107	894,242	864,522	20,379	197,994	93,148
1998	4,195,618	2,499,915	14,212	2,514,127	256,909	101,508	2,358,726	926,585	910,307	20,979	199,993	94,625
1999	4,394,584	2,658,288	44,542	2,702,830	272,895	110,869	2,540,804	915,111	938,669	21,833	201,282	97,199
2000	4,713,452	2,890,524	59,537	2,950,061	292,111	123,407	2,781,357	956,086	976,009	23,127	203,807	98,639
2001	5,117,621	3,214,580	59,442	3,274,022	333,459	132,905	3,073,468	974,804	1,069,349	24,820	206,193	99,172
2002	5,252,568	3,426,545	65,900	3,492,445	360,959	134,194	3,265,680	863,246	1,123,642	25,117	209,120	101,094
2003	5,487,431	3,552,921	91,099	3,644,020	376,812	143,785	3,410,993	889,393	1,187,045	25,948	211,481	100,790
2004	5,839,462	3,752,384	101,965	3,854,349	414,246	151,353	3,591,456	988,530	1,259,476	27,407	213,065	101,812
2005	6,047,256	3,900,127	115,424	4,015,551	437,978	158,527	3,736,100	989,256	1,321,900	28,159	214,752	103,948
2006	6,489,127	4,105,830	77,841	4,183,671	447,064	167,978	3,904,585	1,152,551	1,431,991	29,928	216,824	105,268
2007	6,843,262	4,203,643	104,705	4,308,348	452,326	178,600	4,034,622	1,289,911	1,518,729	31,468	217,469	106,781
2008	6,986,308	4,105,166	151,539	4,256,705	455,815	186,852	3,987,742	1,303,805	1,694,761	31,896	219,034	103,874
2009	6,996,743	4,042,429	212,293	4,254,722	454,280	157,224	3,957,666	1,192,334	1,846,743	31,836	219,777	99,078
2010	7,232,516	4,176,259	201,860	4,378,119	451,222	146,891	4,073,788	1,153,617	2,005,111	32,882	219,951	97,799
2011	7,416,138	4,272,003	217,258	4,489,261	422,856	130,661	4,197,066	1,208,487	2,010,585	33,712	219,983	97,756
2012	7,649,670	4,366,644	236,478	4,603,122	434,148	118,931	4,287,905	1,314,586	2,047,179	34,633	220,877	100,633
2013	7,855,622	4,545,099	282,607	4,827,706	502,890	110,260	4,435,076	1,293,841	2,126,705	35,442	221,649	104,335
2014	8,226,406	4,725,565	185,879	4,911,444	524,068	113,260	4,500,636	1,444,749	2,281,021	37,000	222,335	107,441
2015	8,872,869	5,038,388	182,998	5,221,386	552,719	117,106	4,785,773	1,618,906	2,468,190	39,759	223,167	110,044
2016	9,253,840	5,263,707	202,055	5,465,762	582,128	116,167	4,999,801	1,705,860	2,548,179	41,228	224,454	112,493
2017	9,488,984	5,550,320	205,247	5,755,567	616,623	122,257	5,261,201	1,685,867	2,541,916	41,870	226,630	114,438
2018	9,781,656	5,839,947	184,916	6,024,863	657,264	114,658	5,482,257	1,654,521	2,644,878	42,909	227,962	114,453
2019	9,983,194	5,982,558	149,996	6,132,554	671,688	135,850	5,596,716	1,743,429	2,643,049	46,174	216,206	111,195
2020	10,798,585	6,000,860	174,630	6,175,490	676,419	159,950	5,659,021	1,719,330	3,420,234	51,402	210,083	105,056
2021	11,393,205	6,373,769	122,010	6,495,779	711,924	178,556	5,962,411	1,724,353	3,706,441	54,694	208,309	107,818

Personal Income and Employment by Area: Cincinnati, OH-KY-IN

(Thousands of dollars, except as noted.)

Year	Personal income, total	Earnings by place of work			Less: Contributions for government social insurance	Plus: Adjustment for residence	Equals: Net earnings by place of residence	Plus: Dividends, interest, and rent	Plus: Personal current transfer receipts	Per capita personal income (dollars)	Population (persons)	Total employment
		Nonfarm	Farm	Total								
1970	6,912,576	5,628,139	40,395	5,668,534	375,829	49,721	5,342,426	1,041,278	528,872	4,106	1,683,357	717,838
1971	7,226,566	5,806,640	34,064	5,840,704	398,814	44,196	5,486,086	1,114,606	625,874	4,274	1,690,881	706,103
1972	7,855,798	6,338,865	41,085	6,379,950	459,114	55,070	5,975,906	1,186,085	693,807	4,650	1,689,419	719,327
1973	8,699,916	7,058,616	51,828	7,110,444	590,318	59,107	6,579,233	1,312,659	808,024	5,119	1,699,443	749,255
1974	9,555,877	7,636,619	68,025	7,704,644	662,115	55,402	7,097,931	1,489,821	968,125	5,629	1,697,582	757,725
1975	10,288,933	8,034,595	68,008	8,102,603	679,411	52,718	7,475,910	1,607,125	1,205,898	6,070	1,695,118	742,023
1976	11,375,486	8,976,233	67,242	9,043,475	776,392	63,428	8,330,511	1,727,135	1,317,840	6,673	1,704,762	759,472
1977	12,649,315	10,075,974	63,076	10,139,050	873,120	72,973	9,338,903	1,914,756	1,395,656	7,377	1,714,809	787,208
1978	14,123,449	11,412,646	46,675	11,459,321	1,020,929	74,983	10,513,375	2,122,602	1,487,472	8,172	1,728,350	824,603
1979	15,721,207	12,696,209	42,197	12,738,406	1,186,960	75,274	11,626,720	2,394,649	1,699,838	9,057	1,735,736	843,934
1980	17,422,886	13,549,956	39,232	13,589,188	1,260,328	68,775	12,397,635	2,924,217	2,101,034	9,996	1,743,032	840,256
1981	19,152,012	14,468,567	40,325	14,508,892	1,436,896	79,607	13,151,603	3,655,538	2,344,871	10,963	1,747,031	829,486
1982	20,264,386	14,886,162	70,631	14,956,793	1,504,010	89,687	13,542,470	4,036,971	2,684,945	11,573	1,751,052	812,056
1983	21,541,896	15,839,233	654	15,839,887	1,628,333	100,805	14,312,359	4,342,005	2,887,532	12,297	1,751,730	815,951
1984	23,731,687	17,497,225	58,149	17,555,374	1,833,247	126,428	15,848,555	4,852,781	3,030,351	13,486	1,759,676	850,061
1985	25,388,148	18,879,228	56,936	18,936,164	2,009,271	148,210	17,075,103	5,078,283	3,234,762	14,347	1,769,618	880,814
1986	26,950,995	20,254,515	18,728	20,273,243	2,225,351	155,931	18,203,823	5,348,965	3,398,207	15,117	1,782,790	909,075
1987	28,668,980	21,833,787	21,856	21,855,643	2,400,246	155,884	19,611,281	5,533,608	3,524,091	15,923	1,800,487	939,655
1988	30,872,030	23,459,811	28,797	23,488,608	2,651,022	190,136	21,027,722	6,106,358	3,737,950	17,042	1,811,516	970,621
1989	33,434,666	25,098,557	55,762	25,154,319	2,852,722	202,168	22,503,765	6,951,882	3,979,019	18,362	1,820,832	995,454
1990	36,029,560	27,006,672	52,890	27,059,562	3,132,668	202,046	24,128,940	7,492,678	4,407,942	19,611	1,837,214	1,015,267
1991	37,089,143	28,025,896	47,051	28,072,947	3,329,567	222,057	24,965,437	7,314,940	4,808,766	19,952	1,858,915	1,016,454
1992	39,852,332	30,262,851	69,950	30,332,801	3,576,150	221,079	26,977,730	7,595,174	5,279,428	21,214	1,878,558	1,026,671
1993	41,614,861	31,580,115	49,054	31,629,169	3,756,467	249,331	28,122,033	7,968,268	5,524,560	21,901	1,900,124	1,043,171
1994	43,800,294	33,285,961	60,742	33,346,703	4,029,069	279,279	29,596,913	8,467,047	5,736,334	22,891	1,913,442	1,071,538
1995	46,188,097	34,954,790	15,287	34,970,077	4,268,072	299,525	31,001,530	9,097,871	6,088,696	23,971	1,926,822	1,101,936
1996	49,149,374	37,076,603	40,972	37,117,575	4,476,519	293,047	32,934,103	9,882,239	6,333,032	25,338	1,939,779	1,131,097
1997	52,501,626	39,792,873	65,864	39,858,737	4,708,798	303,418	35,453,357	10,516,355	6,531,914	26,838	1,956,236	1,158,927
1998	57,055,946	43,304,226	47,151	43,351,377	4,984,849	490,273	38,856,801	11,521,691	6,677,454	28,631	1,992,781	1,201,335
1999	59,326,612	46,046,251	19,700	46,065,951	5,301,303	506,938	41,271,586	11,159,082	6,895,944	29,568	2,006,474	1,221,846
2000	62,734,109	48,369,062	87,037	48,456,099	5,424,065	527,228	43,559,262	11,793,087	7,381,760	31,029	2,021,806	1,242,902
2001	65,466,486	50,511,601	71,377	50,582,978	5,577,960	532,370	45,537,388	11,827,902	8,101,196	32,177	2,034,543	1,235,548
2002	66,943,498	51,887,956	15,309	51,903,265	5,669,737	540,640	46,774,168	11,487,475	8,681,855	32,769	2,042,871	1,226,574
2003	69,043,509	53,542,773	37,207	53,579,980	5,888,063	524,836	48,216,753	11,806,122	9,020,634	33,610	2,054,229	1,233,732
2004	72,773,556	56,144,331	94,396	56,238,727	6,218,591	497,302	50,517,438	12,754,109	9,502,009	35,231	2,065,605	1,249,101
2005	75,862,917	58,219,385	66,169	58,285,554	6,446,326	473,302	52,312,530	13,431,334	10,119,053	36,509	2,077,928	1,266,491
2006	80,249,612	60,230,823	52,988	60,283,811	6,692,059	586,451	54,178,203	15,320,238	10,751,171	38,340	2,093,082	1,276,660
2007	82,900,986	62,147,497	33,811	62,181,308	6,924,086	535,405	55,792,627	15,639,969	11,468,390	39,340	2,107,318	1,291,887
2008	85,759,588	62,953,081	30,060	62,983,141	7,154,776	523,098	56,351,463	16,314,791	13,093,334	40,484	2,118,370	1,287,371
2009	83,322,712	61,786,714	60,710	61,847,424	7,052,795	434,381	55,229,010	13,870,979	14,222,723	39,103	2,130,844	1,246,446
2010	87,233,159	64,829,965	39,339	64,869,304	7,172,316	403,042	58,100,030	13,981,526	15,151,603	40,745	2,140,963	1,236,429
2011	93,627,828	68,608,055	84,802	68,692,857	6,700,131	424,841	62,417,567	15,696,594	15,513,667	43,611	2,146,885	1,251,397
2012	97,148,234	71,131,559	58,895	71,190,454	6,898,280	433,632	64,725,806	17,157,602	15,264,826	45,112	2,153,475	1,262,590
2013	98,239,973	72,535,117	119,621	72,654,738	7,826,233	462,306	65,290,811	17,270,719	15,678,443	45,415	2,163,183	1,276,941
2014	101,961,975	74,145,063	20,085	74,165,148	8,088,036	464,217	66,541,329	18,846,298	16,574,348	46,690	2,183,787	1,298,614
2015	106,754,965	76,833,720	-21,671	76,812,049	8,402,415	460,609	68,870,243	20,497,892	17,386,830	48,618	2,195,796	1,322,762
2016	110,315,041	79,498,204	-127	79,498,077	8,811,919	419,293	71,105,451	21,370,295	17,839,295	49,940	2,208,942	1,345,164
2017	114,733,220	82,687,929	4,372	82,692,301	9,303,787	455,557	73,844,071	22,617,800	18,271,349	51,613	2,222,957	1,367,654
2018	119,537,218	86,210,570	8,834	86,219,404	9,560,203	489,845	77,149,046	23,569,659	18,818,513	53,489	2,234,793	1,392,290
2019	126,246,404	90,738,952	-6,161	90,732,791	10,097,075	456,712	81,092,428	25,270,651	19,883,325	56,152	2,248,317	1,401,014
2020	134,334,777	92,235,500	61,056	92,296,556	10,296,218	490,162	82,490,500	25,202,558	26,641,719	59,502	2,257,667	1,359,562
2021	142,639,155	98,084,661	100,328	98,184,989	10,784,778	463,447	87,863,658	25,889,394	28,886,103	63,116	2,259,935	1,403,290

Personal Income and Employment by Area: Clarksville, TN-KY

(Thousands of dollars, except as noted.)

Year	Personal income, total	Earnings by place of work			Less: Contributions for government social insurance	Plus: Adjustment for residence	Equals: Net earnings by place of residence	Plus: Dividends, interest, and rent	Plus: Personal current transfer receipts	Per capita personal income (dollars)	Population (persons)	Total employment
		Nonfarm	Farm	Total								
1970	463,454	354,164	15,890	370,054	21,775	1,699	349,978	79,015	34,461	3,612	128,304	62,242
1971	521,409	397,658	20,030	417,688	25,845	1,828	393,671	87,377	40,361	3,946	132,120	63,181
1972	558,891	428,780	23,281	452,061	28,838	-1,493	421,730	92,497	44,664	4,282	130,523	62,873
1973	734,687	570,281	31,550	601,831	41,057	-7,140	553,634	128,267	52,786	5,059	145,221	74,314
1974	820,430	637,109	26,176	663,285	48,129	-7,921	607,235	149,850	63,345	5,451	150,507	75,527
1975	857,553	658,768	17,110	675,878	52,597	-6,413	616,868	161,113	79,572	5,789	148,128	73,152
1976	995,464	772,477	21,803	794,280	63,869	-7,878	722,533	187,008	85,923	6,562	151,709	79,719
1977	1,067,383	811,457	36,406	847,863	65,767	-4,161	777,935	197,880	91,568	6,817	156,582	78,755
1978	1,172,444	893,432	27,245	920,677	71,696	-6,391	842,590	229,976	99,878	7,455	157,269	80,086
1979	1,303,823	979,508	41,820	1,021,328	81,232	-4,999	935,097	253,116	115,610	8,158	159,822	80,031
1980	1,371,628	1,013,595	17,832	1,031,427	85,368	1,375	947,434	283,816	140,378	8,573	159,999	78,851
1981	1,546,004	1,141,440	34,486	1,175,926	101,188	-15,706	1,059,032	327,068	159,904	9,589	161,222	79,659
1982	1,658,087	1,203,100	28,822	1,231,922	104,253	-13,723	1,113,946	366,238	177,903	9,984	166,069	78,823
1983	1,719,478	1,288,028	-14,518	1,273,510	115,463	-13,274	1,144,773	386,258	188,447	10,327	166,510	79,185
1984	1,882,074	1,369,288	31,278	1,400,566	127,470	-6,408	1,266,688	416,898	198,488	11,257	167,189	81,128
1985	2,010,419	1,460,435	28,672	1,489,107	137,774	1,373	1,352,706	446,654	211,059	11,725	171,467	82,547
1986	2,119,127	1,546,539	21,627	1,568,166	149,810	6,081	1,424,437	471,853	222,837	12,397	170,942	83,901
1987	2,272,627	1,660,836	25,809	1,686,645	161,872	14,575	1,539,348	500,585	232,694	13,213	171,998	86,982
1988	2,432,753	1,782,209	24,288	1,806,497	181,357	21,803	1,646,943	533,621	252,189	13,979	174,027	88,495
1989	2,588,368	1,839,899	37,711	1,877,610	192,354	29,761	1,715,017	591,417	281,934	14,662	176,531	90,093
1990	2,588,750	1,822,845	32,107	1,854,952	196,307	40,777	1,699,422	573,002	316,326	14,314	180,857	87,447
1991	2,777,276	1,960,370	28,318	1,988,688	214,457	41,896	1,816,127	597,132	364,017	15,421	180,093	87,685
1992	3,306,544	2,394,728	43,760	2,438,488	265,243	35,295	2,208,540	692,561	405,443	17,406	189,963	97,180
1993	3,437,595	2,484,904	33,852	2,518,756	280,040	36,279	2,274,995	738,208	424,392	17,940	191,616	99,926
1994	3,617,678	2,587,409	43,322	2,630,731	290,403	42,022	2,382,350	787,486	447,842	18,391	196,709	102,624
1995	3,895,693	2,770,909	30,410	2,801,319	306,003	40,951	2,536,267	861,197	498,229	19,378	201,040	107,625
1996	4,136,965	2,922,443	49,821	2,972,264	320,710	42,979	2,694,533	915,815	526,617	19,860	208,307	109,895
1997	4,290,274	3,057,319	43,952	3,101,271	335,237	52,683	2,818,717	910,986	560,571	20,187	212,526	112,425
1998	4,769,426	3,311,998	23,236	3,335,234	357,207	105,281	3,083,308	1,050,190	635,928	21,032	226,773	116,885
1999	5,063,569	3,577,627	3,879	3,581,506	386,471	108,128	3,303,163	1,085,608	674,798	22,076	229,368	121,792
2000	5,574,501	3,931,621	49,123	3,980,744	416,483	114,900	3,679,161	1,156,266	739,074	23,887	233,367	124,843
2001	5,628,382	3,959,206	46,793	4,005,999	433,231	96,449	3,669,217	1,138,217	820,948	23,895	235,549	125,242
2002	5,972,473	4,276,941	29,266	4,306,207	467,675	82,466	3,920,998	1,160,568	890,907	25,226	236,758	126,533
2003	6,390,540	4,623,604	39,321	4,662,925	496,906	67,254	4,233,273	1,200,213	957,054	27,013	236,569	127,599
2004	6,880,185	5,068,704	70,898	5,139,602	538,577	56,049	4,657,074	1,190,852	1,032,259	28,484	241,543	131,322
2005	7,737,820	5,864,486	92,639	5,957,125	614,785	3,946	5,346,286	1,275,628	1,115,906	30,892	250,476	138,270
2006	8,314,105	6,330,715	69,334	6,400,049	667,309	-14,495	5,718,245	1,385,845	1,210,015	33,218	250,292	141,076
2007	8,631,120	6,501,637	30,986	6,532,623	690,305	-16,367	5,825,951	1,487,534	1,317,635	33,089	260,846	143,438
2008	9,272,694	6,873,913	46,219	6,920,132	739,122	-52,125	6,128,885	1,616,368	1,527,441	35,456	261,530	143,785
2009	9,431,994	6,945,445	53,175	6,998,620	761,488	-33,095	6,204,037	1,568,687	1,659,270	34,959	269,798	141,667
2010	9,984,642	7,345,847	22,542	7,368,389	803,647	-53,734	6,511,008	1,639,948	1,833,686	36,309	274,994	143,636
2011	10,857,326	7,885,888	68,051	7,953,939	778,657	-72,767	7,102,515	1,820,716	1,934,095	39,117	277,558	147,219
2012	11,045,493	7,976,739	72,698	8,049,437	785,202	-44,898	7,219,337	1,868,426	1,957,730	38,400	287,642	147,359
2013	10,931,483	7,730,572	146,841	7,877,413	848,895	-15,955	7,012,563	1,883,708	2,035,212	38,250	285,789	147,236
2014	11,038,912	7,763,949	63,986	7,827,935	862,152	-5,615	6,960,168	1,931,283	2,147,461	37,700	292,807	148,713
2015	11,412,587	7,933,882	52,018	7,985,900	884,669	19,757	7,120,988	1,956,471	2,335,128	38,447	296,839	151,142
2016	11,549,235	7,890,760	30,628	7,921,388	872,259	40,573	7,089,702	2,005,842	2,453,691	38,703	298,403	150,231
2017	11,984,257	8,195,951	56,745	8,252,696	910,887	60,512	7,402,321	1,978,823	2,603,113	39,388	304,258	154,803
2018	12,449,998	8,552,422	21,537	8,573,959	943,017	57,088	7,688,030	2,028,163	2,733,805	40,052	310,842	157,919
2019	13,125,992	8,948,810	47,522	8,996,332	976,913	62,863	8,082,282	2,115,720	2,927,990	41,503	316,267	160,929
2020	14,334,775	9,395,985	57,970	9,453,955	1,024,610	69,412	8,498,757	2,100,059	3,735,959	44,572	321,607	163,004
2021	15,600,689	10,072,351	117,858	10,190,209	1,075,916	101,802	9,216,095	2,089,574	4,295,020	47,519	328,304	167,663

Personal Income and Employment by Area: Cleveland, TN

(Thousands of dollars, except as noted.)

Year	Personal income, total	Earnings by place of work			Less: Contributions for government social insurance	Plus: Adjustment for residence	Equals: Net earnings by place of residence	Plus: Dividends, interest, and rent	Plus: Personal current transfer receipts	Per capita personal income (dollars)	Population (persons)	Total employment
		Nonfarm	Farm	Total								
1970	194,832	162,070	1,834	163,904	10,907	2,891	155,888	21,776	17,168	3,100	62,840	28,344
1971	219,046	182,333	1,642	183,975	12,691	3,605	174,889	24,270	19,887	3,352	65,350	29,244
1972	250,052	209,708	2,478	212,186	15,388	4,579	201,377	26,910	21,765	3,719	67,241	31,705
1973	289,286	241,832	4,671	246,503	20,176	5,569	231,896	31,443	25,947	4,154	69,648	34,135
1974	306,477	248,205	1,718	249,923	21,519	7,385	235,789	36,749	33,939	4,275	71,692	32,962
1975	328,845	256,727	1,754	258,481	21,615	5,185	242,051	42,087	44,707	4,542	72,406	30,714
1976	373,202	293,661	2,363	296,024	25,427	10,653	281,250	44,653	47,299	5,048	73,937	32,387
1977	405,364	307,285	3,381	310,666	26,937	20,899	304,628	49,130	51,606	5,342	75,881	33,401
1978	463,234	361,237	1,083	362,320	32,219	21,888	351,989	55,502	55,743	5,966	77,652	35,414
1979	524,542	404,388	2,423	406,811	37,619	26,497	395,689	62,875	65,978	6,587	79,631	36,135
1980	600,426	451,872	4,438	456,310	41,941	26,364	440,733	77,040	82,653	7,380	81,363	36,047
1981	679,756	507,718	7,806	515,524	50,809	27,805	492,520	95,686	91,550	8,284	82,061	36,618
1982	724,715	528,431	7,029	535,460	53,899	29,804	511,365	112,099	101,251	8,823	82,139	36,932
1983	798,079	594,647	3,427	598,074	60,906	29,205	566,373	123,442	108,264	9,680	82,449	37,384
1984	885,383	654,245	11,349	665,594	69,126	33,524	629,992	140,243	115,148	10,584	83,652	39,385
1985	947,214	704,741	7,979	712,720	75,125	35,663	673,258	151,555	122,401	11,211	84,486	39,808
1986	1,011,521	736,719	12,234	748,953	80,203	47,574	716,324	163,397	131,800	11,919	84,865	40,542
1987	1,098,514	809,196	6,728	815,924	86,928	54,090	783,086	177,599	137,829	12,872	85,340	42,402
1988	1,183,209	859,208	7,790	866,998	94,423	71,293	843,868	189,668	149,673	13,678	86,505	43,780
1989	1,296,710	916,032	18,674	934,706	100,873	80,223	914,056	217,094	165,560	14,922	86,902	44,308
1990	1,361,760	962,812	16,411	979,223	106,456	81,257	954,024	222,660	185,076	15,530	87,684	43,815
1991	1,435,420	1,013,578	20,118	1,033,696	114,229	77,395	996,862	222,775	215,783	16,137	88,954	43,128
1992	1,585,623	1,123,040	19,717	1,142,757	124,999	82,863	1,100,621	231,327	253,675	17,556	90,317	44,380
1993	1,646,763	1,150,811	20,987	1,171,798	129,003	97,991	1,140,786	234,923	271,054	17,904	91,979	45,808
1994	1,756,417	1,238,505	17,079	1,255,584	140,271	98,985	1,214,298	261,179	280,940	18,854	93,161	46,481
1995	1,852,505	1,300,093	10,124	1,310,217	146,305	101,286	1,265,198	280,141	307,166	19,473	95,133	48,418
1996	1,993,616	1,406,596	13,214	1,419,810	154,757	100,678	1,365,731	300,297	327,588	20,585	96,848	50,123
1997	2,155,431	1,557,220	5,690	1,562,910	166,490	97,664	1,494,084	316,826	344,521	21,550	100,019	51,829
1998	2,322,517	1,688,769	10,176	1,698,945	173,033	107,919	1,633,831	334,283	354,403	22,825	101,755	51,846
1999	2,388,715	1,740,269	8,715	1,748,984	182,631	111,191	1,677,544	341,232	369,939	23,195	102,982	52,450
2000	2,437,251	1,722,547	6,423	1,728,970	182,997	128,758	1,674,731	363,689	398,831	23,359	104,338	52,528
2001	2,460,472	1,655,376	25,895	1,681,271	185,478	140,352	1,636,145	378,682	445,645	23,367	105,295	53,704
2002	2,518,104	1,720,649	4,486	1,725,135	193,616	155,759	1,687,278	354,449	476,377	23,760	105,979	53,647
2003	2,668,817	1,790,500	6,119	1,796,619	201,000	186,850	1,782,469	377,138	509,210	25,000	106,754	54,086
2004	2,844,553	1,937,543	19,793	1,957,336	216,022	177,443	1,918,757	377,026	548,770	26,314	108,099	55,465
2005	2,957,418	1,962,492	21,960	1,984,452	219,303	205,704	1,970,853	395,879	590,686	27,031	109,410	55,733
2006	3,160,091	2,043,266	6,323	2,049,589	226,658	273,500	2,096,431	422,181	641,479	28,424	111,177	56,345
2007	3,353,571	2,106,790	3,833	2,110,623	234,833	297,162	2,172,952	472,981	707,638	29,695	112,935	56,070
2008	3,542,273	2,113,583	12,530	2,126,113	239,447	331,413	2,218,079	524,137	800,057	30,989	114,306	55,208
2009	3,456,621	2,014,254	19,158	2,033,412	236,865	298,917	2,095,464	499,915	861,242	30,034	115,090	53,667
2010	3,588,608	2,097,077	26,812	2,123,889	241,480	300,603	2,183,012	450,885	954,711	30,963	115,899	53,265
2011	3,808,216	2,228,325	25,800	2,254,125	230,357	302,238	2,326,006	515,985	966,225	32,665	116,585	54,831
2012	4,034,273	2,474,230	27,371	2,501,601	245,511	256,575	2,512,665	547,397	974,211	34,275	117,703	56,876
2013	4,063,839	2,543,444	49,117	2,592,561	287,633	201,781	2,506,709	563,557	993,573	34,307	118,455	60,379
2014	4,197,388	2,660,420	48,873	2,709,293	298,112	170,489	2,581,670	590,493	1,025,225	35,059	119,723	62,276
2015	4,369,051	2,692,861	34,839	2,727,700	303,803	231,430	2,655,327	638,540	1,075,184	36,147	120,870	61,954
2016	4,422,645	2,725,431	16,140	2,741,571	311,452	252,926	2,683,045	621,536	1,118,064	36,387	121,546	62,665
2017	4,537,028	2,750,269	16,894	2,767,163	317,659	293,725	2,743,229	634,094	1,159,705	36,984	122,674	62,338
2018	4,764,509	2,892,682	13,511	2,906,193	331,930	323,272	2,897,535	638,868	1,228,106	38,262	124,524	62,651
2019	4,932,087	3,028,892	5,171	3,034,063	352,127	277,954	2,959,890	673,943	1,298,254	39,329	125,405	64,464
2020	5,340,313	3,240,217	-9,340	3,230,877	379,861	236,039	3,087,055	667,304	1,585,954	42,279	126,310	65,245
2021	5,808,942	3,345,694	33,963	3,379,657	380,112	375,626	3,375,171	663,292	1,770,479	45,404	127,938	64,612

Personal Income and Employment by Area: Cleveland-Elyria, OH

(Thousands of dollars, except as noted.)

Year	Personal income, total	Derivation of personal income								Per capita personal income (dollars)	Population (persons)	Total employment
		Earnings by place of work			Less: Contributions for government social insurance	Plus: Adjustment for residence	Equals: Net earnings by place of residence	Plus: Dividends, interest, and rent	Plus: Personal current transfer receipts			
		Nonfarm	Farm	Total								
1970	10,739,310	9,265,524	19,843	9,285,367	615,025	-286,840	8,383,502	1,563,124	792,684	4,631	2,318,811	1,076,814
1971	11,259,149	9,579,995	26,837	9,606,832	653,378	-305,674	8,647,780	1,662,229	949,140	4,869	2,312,528	1,044,149
1972	12,122,234	10,377,214	28,586	10,405,800	747,243	-333,289	9,325,268	1,751,339	1,045,627	5,322	2,277,630	1,053,824
1973	13,319,112	11,511,398	20,630	11,532,028	964,373	-386,076	10,181,579	1,933,610	1,203,923	5,878	2,266,062	1,095,299
1974	14,613,538	12,493,333	27,215	12,520,548	1,082,844	-437,928	10,999,776	2,199,298	1,414,464	6,502	2,247,641	1,114,246
1975	15,457,357	12,922,717	37,515	12,960,232	1,088,512	-478,207	11,393,513	2,321,621	1,742,223	6,908	2,237,565	1,077,447
1976	16,767,087	14,216,214	39,604	14,255,818	1,227,678	-556,120	12,472,020	2,447,461	1,847,606	7,553	2,219,936	1,088,064
1977	18,581,102	15,973,198	35,760	16,008,958	1,377,706	-655,152	13,976,100	2,664,318	1,940,684	8,394	2,213,651	1,114,106
1978	20,527,552	17,785,247	35,968	17,821,215	1,585,566	-765,894	15,469,755	2,964,130	2,093,667	9,302	2,206,866	1,148,501
1979	22,408,647	19,369,101	28,215	19,397,316	1,799,238	-879,608	16,718,470	3,322,545	2,367,632	10,257	2,184,615	1,159,618
1980	24,310,668	20,080,895	27,342	20,108,237	1,851,713	-945,404	17,311,120	3,974,859	3,024,689	11,191	2,172,438	1,133,733
1981	26,500,199	21,402,715	31,574	21,434,289	2,110,018	-1,026,226	18,298,045	4,881,341	3,320,813	12,257	2,162,129	1,112,891
1982	27,714,318	21,587,658	29,419	21,617,077	2,157,804	-1,021,570	18,437,703	5,418,939	3,857,676	12,886	2,150,690	1,072,341
1983	29,110,176	22,541,029	29,722	22,570,751	2,293,980	-1,053,273	19,223,498	5,736,053	4,150,625	13,561	2,146,550	1,058,826
1984	31,917,925	24,857,262	34,010	24,891,272	2,586,673	-1,156,170	21,148,429	6,449,386	4,320,110	14,906	2,141,290	1,090,297
1985	33,862,734	26,504,152	30,694	26,534,846	2,793,441	-1,228,522	22,512,883	6,768,987	4,580,864	15,889	2,131,240	1,106,952
1986	35,188,992	27,642,351	28,348	27,670,699	2,998,393	-1,261,039	23,411,267	6,905,934	4,871,791	16,594	2,120,606	1,123,074
1987	36,909,884	29,256,843	43,283	29,300,126	3,175,125	-1,319,711	24,805,290	7,056,260	5,048,334	17,461	2,113,892	1,145,205
1988	39,873,290	31,881,886	72,163	31,954,049	3,540,963	-1,427,920	26,985,166	7,609,770	5,278,354	18,969	2,102,075	1,171,445
1989	42,411,894	33,661,202	92,851	33,754,053	3,777,616	-1,526,393	28,450,044	8,334,778	5,627,072	20,161	2,103,702	1,194,435
1990	45,294,907	35,534,500	91,401	35,625,901	4,077,758	-1,658,953	29,889,190	9,210,505	6,195,212	21,525	2,104,288	1,206,598
1991	45,865,297	35,967,900	64,799	36,032,699	4,222,480	-1,660,691	30,149,528	9,056,318	6,659,451	21,660	2,117,512	1,192,489
1992	48,108,841	37,974,810	120,349	38,095,159	4,431,334	-1,781,332	31,882,493	8,995,635	7,230,713	22,575	2,131,036	1,181,133
1993	49,991,115	39,298,637	115,739	39,414,376	4,636,173	-1,807,043	32,971,160	9,464,338	7,555,617	23,356	2,140,398	1,195,585
1994	52,498,143	41,807,523	110,591	41,918,114	4,994,766	-1,965,583	34,957,765	9,738,409	7,801,969	24,460	2,146,303	1,223,705
1995	55,073,147	43,425,785	111,046	43,536,831	5,246,490	-2,075,032	36,215,309	10,612,654	8,245,184	25,613	2,150,203	1,251,048
1996	57,314,432	44,919,621	110,572	45,030,193	5,370,277	-2,208,654	37,451,262	11,365,209	8,497,961	26,613	2,153,598	1,268,542
1997	60,274,826	47,458,441	111,744	47,570,185	5,550,527	-2,497,579	39,522,079	11,996,623	8,756,124	28,000	2,152,676	1,290,060
1998	63,624,674	49,987,166	118,657	50,105,823	5,695,634	-2,704,627	41,705,562	13,137,443	8,781,669	29,571	2,151,568	1,305,773
1999	65,257,917	52,420,534	123,577	52,544,111	5,938,787	-3,063,285	43,542,039	12,698,746	9,017,132	30,353	2,149,943	1,324,094
2000	68,562,997	54,993,962	97,698	55,091,660	6,021,111	-3,318,379	45,752,170	13,274,882	9,535,945	31,926	2,147,532	1,341,671
2001	68,458,235	54,501,337	103,652	54,604,989	6,010,848	-3,400,755	45,193,386	13,038,237	10,226,612	31,963	2,141,787	1,322,201
2002	68,518,006	54,453,608	94,179	54,547,787	5,906,187	-3,327,372	45,314,228	12,397,384	10,806,394	32,075	2,136,201	1,294,109
2003	69,956,554	56,290,876	71,326	56,362,202	6,154,488	-3,414,902	46,792,812	11,819,749	11,343,993	32,826	2,131,150	1,291,744
2004	72,725,597	58,593,854	116,004	58,709,858	6,508,595	-3,629,648	48,571,615	12,359,765	11,794,217	34,257	2,122,934	1,296,299
2005	75,131,312	59,553,495	125,297	59,678,792	6,651,173	-3,620,776	49,406,843	13,377,070	12,347,399	35,579	2,111,699	1,299,430
2006	79,426,916	62,410,685	85,721	62,496,406	6,960,253	-3,845,196	51,690,957	14,887,360	12,848,599	37,833	2,099,415	1,309,383
2007	83,078,078	64,290,494	101,949	64,392,443	7,126,159	-3,865,797	53,400,487	16,074,376	13,603,215	39,720	2,091,596	1,316,266
2008	85,771,494	65,019,022	92,038	65,111,060	7,288,676	-3,620,444	54,201,940	16,453,541	15,116,013	41,135	2,085,110	1,302,283
2009	81,508,160	61,284,667	102,605	61,387,272	6,977,213	-3,327,934	51,082,125	14,280,698	16,145,337	39,167	2,081,063	1,251,077
2010	82,866,533	62,087,605	103,667	62,191,272	6,994,678	-3,380,035	51,816,559	14,104,865	16,945,109	39,927	2,075,476	1,243,015
2011	87,982,947	65,271,102	115,500	65,386,602	6,604,575	-3,615,335	55,166,692	15,488,702	17,327,553	42,522	2,069,115	1,260,014
2012	92,165,799	68,475,584	129,544	68,605,128	6,856,993	-3,915,499	57,832,636	17,291,587	17,041,576	44,632	2,065,018	1,277,714
2013	93,170,732	70,783,580	119,321	70,902,901	7,732,642	-3,988,864	59,181,395	16,563,710	17,425,627	45,065	2,067,461	1,290,652
2014	97,627,009	72,790,528	91,877	72,882,405	7,899,195	-3,901,151	61,082,059	18,269,464	18,275,486	46,811	2,085,571	1,299,826
2015	100,906,513	74,876,069	90,703	74,966,772	8,113,272	-3,847,943	63,005,557	19,017,140	18,883,816	48,361	2,086,509	1,313,549
2016	103,273,041	76,136,012	100,244	76,236,256	8,395,897	-3,797,456	64,042,903	19,910,287	19,319,851	49,473	2,087,456	1,324,002
2017	106,522,950	78,966,264	76,547	79,042,811	8,864,389	-3,951,407	66,227,015	20,533,057	19,762,878	51,020	2,087,871	1,329,849
2018	110,340,774	81,154,869	77,122	81,231,991	9,022,683	-4,284,440	67,924,868	22,171,954	20,243,952	52,841	2,088,149	1,349,027
2019	114,529,385	83,294,939	74,704	83,369,643	9,414,541	-4,534,567	69,420,535	23,923,410	21,185,440	54,867	2,087,392	1,351,498
2020	121,398,073	83,074,110	81,139	83,155,249	9,435,979	-4,546,705	69,172,565	23,811,515	28,413,993	58,215	2,085,357	1,300,712
2021	128,582,329	88,769,832	92,178	88,862,010	9,880,840	-4,914,686	74,066,484	24,350,687	30,165,158	61,948	2,075,662	1,327,726

Personal Income and Employment by Area: Coeur d'Alene, ID

(Thousands of dollars, except as noted.)

Year	Personal income, total	Earnings by place of work			Less: Contributions for government social insurance	Plus: Adjustment for residence	Equals: Net earnings by place of residence	Plus: Dividends, interest, and rent	Plus: Personal current transfer receipts	Per capita personal income (dollars)	Population (persons)	Total employment
		Nonfarm	Farm	Total								
1970	128,305	73,697	2,621	76,318	5,381	19,416	90,353	23,733	14,219	3,606	35,579	12,625
1971	144,854	83,293	2,309	85,602	6,311	21,534	100,825	27,061	16,968	3,953	36,644	13,312
1972	167,854	99,844	3,474	103,318	7,992	23,533	118,859	29,712	19,283	4,283	39,195	14,772
1973	189,600	119,658	-2,546	117,112	11,145	26,406	132,373	34,293	22,934	4,459	42,519	16,223
1974	226,270	132,897	5,892	138,789	12,506	31,147	157,430	40,687	28,153	5,073	44,600	17,126
1975	258,825	146,483	4,059	150,542	13,391	36,093	173,244	49,070	36,511	5,464	47,365	17,382
1976	299,824	175,897	4,336	180,233	16,255	41,164	205,142	54,520	40,162	6,140	48,828	19,043
1977	345,686	209,355	2,752	212,107	19,534	45,764	238,337	64,401	42,948	6,704	51,565	20,572
1978	414,419	253,716	4,235	257,951	23,770	55,165	289,346	77,393	47,680	7,482	55,386	22,466
1979	475,380	289,101	3,523	292,624	28,596	64,247	328,275	90,284	56,821	8,095	58,728	24,047
1980	527,870	302,354	3,992	306,346	29,744	73,117	349,719	108,860	69,291	8,798	59,996	23,469
1981	575,842	315,204	2,922	318,126	33,338	79,541	364,329	131,478	80,035	9,467	60,827	23,099
1982	600,503	310,392	2,918	313,310	33,498	71,656	351,468	152,863	96,172	9,618	62,436	22,576
1983	679,298	362,177	5,631	367,808	39,518	76,449	404,739	173,466	101,093	10,785	62,987	24,041
1984	748,375	407,933	4,995	412,928	46,351	83,776	450,353	194,261	103,761	11,427	65,494	26,144
1985	793,754	426,584	3,827	430,411	49,274	85,468	466,605	214,916	112,233	11,886	66,783	26,831
1986	827,347	446,205	3,458	449,663	52,293	87,858	485,228	222,841	119,278	12,393	66,761	27,960
1987	856,137	475,753	147	475,900	54,613	94,272	515,559	216,961	123,617	12,940	66,160	29,674
1988	941,881	527,218	3,150	530,368	63,210	106,935	574,093	233,216	134,572	14,088	66,859	31,474
1989	1,049,203	591,079	3,829	594,908	72,137	117,228	639,999	260,978	148,226	15,489	67,738	33,071
1990	1,150,054	667,785	5,524	673,309	85,508	127,284	715,085	272,166	162,803	16,326	70,443	35,431
1991	1,247,483	737,398	2,405	739,803	96,752	127,420	770,471	291,255	185,757	16,870	73,946	38,117
1992	1,421,786	860,885	4,753	865,638	110,936	138,587	893,289	320,329	208,168	18,327	77,577	41,164
1993	1,577,666	968,572	5,297	973,869	125,377	143,321	991,813	356,770	229,083	19,088	82,654	44,016
1994	1,737,402	1,088,379	570	1,088,949	141,171	157,630	1,105,408	388,517	243,477	19,733	88,046	48,249
1995	1,867,673	1,132,332	339	1,132,671	148,654	170,330	1,154,347	442,958	270,368	20,152	92,677	50,172
1996	2,010,419	1,206,336	1,380	1,207,716	154,829	192,665	1,245,552	471,112	293,755	20,814	96,590	51,999
1997	2,132,629	1,275,589	-898	1,274,691	163,795	214,740	1,325,636	496,981	310,012	21,303	100,108	54,341
1998	2,316,914	1,401,944	1,090	1,403,034	175,767	244,964	1,472,231	517,936	326,747	22,556	102,717	55,676
1999	2,440,138	1,507,297	1,902	1,509,199	183,862	267,873	1,593,210	495,398	351,530	22,945	106,346	57,772
2000	2,631,729	1,659,765	2,872	1,662,637	198,607	240,520	1,704,550	540,951	386,228	24,037	109,487	59,995
2001	2,815,185	1,796,108	3,530	1,799,638	210,469	227,309	1,816,478	553,384	445,323	25,239	111,542	61,217
2002	2,906,010	1,891,994	4,042	1,896,036	222,605	222,242	1,895,673	527,030	483,307	25,566	113,667	62,919
2003	3,077,533	1,975,205	3,167	1,978,372	237,222	230,974	1,972,124	590,855	514,554	26,414	116,512	64,164
2004	3,363,465	2,158,926	4,144	2,163,070	262,863	239,348	2,139,555	665,445	558,465	27,797	121,002	68,866
2005	3,718,515	2,373,789	3,240	2,377,029	294,548	228,299	2,310,780	798,202	609,533	29,519	125,972	73,502
2006	4,040,727	2,653,411	1,703	2,655,114	332,799	208,325	2,530,640	856,098	653,989	31,200	129,510	77,152
2007	4,319,688	2,774,358	2,008	2,776,366	352,942	227,027	2,650,451	958,172	711,065	32,525	132,811	80,534
2008	4,453,980	2,725,601	-1,491	2,724,110	353,834	264,239	2,634,515	990,206	829,259	32,840	135,627	80,340
2009	4,358,113	2,558,152	314	2,558,466	341,867	313,622	2,530,221	913,350	914,542	31,717	137,407	76,284
2010	4,504,758	2,602,289	-2,182	2,600,107	359,998	336,164	2,576,273	919,492	1,008,993	32,441	138,860	75,121
2011	4,791,220	2,638,930	3,463	2,642,393	329,602	414,788	2,727,579	1,040,899	1,022,742	33,984	140,986	75,818
2012	5,076,926	2,687,913	4,160	2,692,073	333,041	547,081	2,906,113	1,124,509	1,046,304	35,709	142,173	75,139
2013	5,328,098	2,893,628	2,633	2,896,261	386,891	532,951	3,042,321	1,205,687	1,080,090	36,996	144,019	77,725
2014	5,703,244	3,026,292	2,054	3,028,346	401,467	563,333	3,190,212	1,348,273	1,164,759	38,684	147,432	80,329
2015	6,095,554	3,238,648	2,321	3,240,969	425,088	571,771	3,387,652	1,469,184	1,238,718	40,501	150,504	82,699
2016	6,366,835	3,426,565	2,496	3,429,061	450,551	608,588	3,587,098	1,479,978	1,299,759	41,248	154,354	85,109
2017	6,810,186	3,707,079	725	3,707,804	485,018	613,146	3,835,932	1,593,808	1,380,446	42,846	158,944	88,109
2018	7,287,461	3,995,568	57	3,995,625	521,260	672,664	4,147,029	1,668,223	1,472,209	44,747	162,860	91,565
2019	7,995,798	4,301,128	-29	4,301,099	553,661	785,505	4,532,943	1,860,851	1,602,004	47,745	167,469	93,486
2020	8,823,814	4,731,179	2,390	4,733,569	610,013	749,604	4,873,160	1,922,116	2,028,538	51,109	172,646	95,362
2021	9,781,680	5,260,502	430	5,260,932	661,292	849,794	5,449,434	2,037,060	2,295,186	54,406	179,789	99,794

Personal Income and Employment by Area: College Station-Bryan, TX

(Thousands of dollars, except as noted.)

Year	Personal income, total	Earnings by place of work			Less: Contributions for government social insurance	Plus: Adjustment for residence	Equals: Net earnings by place of residence	Plus: Dividends, interest, and rent	Plus: Personal current transfer receipts	Per capita personal income (dollars)	Population (persons)	Total employment
		Nonfarm	Farm	Total								
1970	239,328	175,727	9,198	184,925	11,227	67	173,765	40,225	25,338	2,901	82,495	33,470
1971	273,855	204,457	8,439	212,896	13,554	-418	198,924	45,721	29,210	3,229	84,820	35,764
1972	313,756	228,045	17,136	245,181	15,656	-159	229,366	52,246	32,144	3,483	90,094	37,801
1973	349,995	253,478	14,939	268,417	19,832	889	249,474	62,083	38,438	3,687	94,934	39,127
1974	384,608	276,825	7,244	284,069	22,472	2,363	263,960	74,108	46,540	3,861	99,612	39,846
1975	439,121	317,036	-2,657	314,379	25,202	3,532	292,709	87,888	58,524	4,449	98,699	41,325
1976	508,891	370,375	3,632	374,007	29,612	4,330	348,725	96,480	63,686	4,983	102,118	44,451
1977	579,396	424,639	6,122	430,761	34,291	5,755	402,225	109,327	67,844	5,486	105,615	48,208
1978	671,254	496,345	7,202	503,547	40,972	6,793	469,368	126,102	75,784	5,992	112,021	51,286
1979	763,510	565,527	7,896	573,423	48,901	9,181	533,703	144,082	85,725	6,521	117,089	53,353
1980	902,991	667,756	194	667,950	57,432	11,575	622,093	181,082	99,816	7,360	122,685	57,181
1981	1,143,205	871,905	14,397	886,302	81,533	-5,411	799,358	230,816	113,031	8,737	130,852	63,834
1982	1,296,359	957,990	9,929	967,919	90,480	-3,472	873,967	294,018	128,374	9,099	142,471	66,877
1983	1,410,044	1,031,014	5,877	1,036,891	94,658	-5,074	937,159	332,196	140,689	9,591	147,011	68,500
1984	1,551,996	1,123,356	4,258	1,127,614	103,557	-795	1,023,262	378,565	150,169	10,364	149,749	70,778
1985	1,621,915	1,149,608	2,369	1,151,977	105,487	2,815	1,049,305	412,410	160,200	10,620	152,724	71,201
1986	1,625,456	1,154,713	-8,884	1,145,829	104,172	4,815	1,046,472	405,573	173,411	10,560	153,931	69,985
1987	1,666,036	1,171,910	5,750	1,177,660	103,761	6,139	1,080,038	403,496	182,502	10,942	152,259	71,753
1988	1,768,139	1,272,115	3,305	1,275,420	119,754	2,524	1,158,190	417,952	191,997	11,719	150,882	74,831
1989	1,927,466	1,374,458	11,017	1,385,475	131,463	-3,105	1,250,907	462,613	213,946	12,818	150,375	77,282
1990	2,043,366	1,480,269	13,272	1,493,541	139,619	-1,242	1,352,680	454,739	235,947	13,488	151,495	79,083
1991	2,163,816	1,570,220	14,666	1,584,886	152,142	1,780	1,434,524	471,125	258,167	14,045	154,062	81,933
1992	2,317,612	1,691,121	20,737	1,711,858	163,031	147	1,548,974	471,794	296,844	14,640	158,308	83,359
1993	2,486,992	1,819,336	18,552	1,837,888	175,008	-4,050	1,658,830	516,959	311,203	15,096	164,742	87,560
1994	2,601,084	1,925,310	18,169	1,943,479	188,508	-6,590	1,748,381	526,806	325,897	15,491	167,911	90,558
1995	2,741,565	1,990,436	11,857	2,002,293	195,985	-7,923	1,798,385	580,984	362,196	16,069	170,608	92,132
1996	2,888,041	2,093,838	-883	2,092,955	204,183	-9,269	1,879,503	620,335	388,203	16,758	172,341	93,646
1997	3,161,697	2,321,249	8,985	2,330,234	224,079	-10,138	2,096,017	656,621	409,059	17,954	176,098	97,342
1998	3,346,587	2,503,138	-1,658	2,501,480	240,604	-14,063	2,246,813	675,694	424,080	18,644	179,498	100,944
1999	3,529,293	2,652,241	27,165	2,679,406	252,813	-16,569	2,410,024	683,767	435,502	19,357	182,327	100,840
2000	3,802,160	2,847,417	11,517	2,858,934	269,367	-19,758	2,569,809	767,483	464,868	20,468	185,760	104,085
2001	4,083,693	3,086,973	26,826	3,113,799	284,046	-24,635	2,805,118	771,940	506,635	21,685	188,315	107,288
2002	4,235,903	3,184,108	45,586	3,229,694	291,673	-31,934	2,906,087	774,900	554,916	22,060	192,016	108,148
2003	4,596,528	3,401,210	62,901	3,464,111	317,190	-49,382	3,097,539	892,225	606,764	23,424	196,234	109,810
2004	4,811,361	3,572,589	60,344	3,632,933	333,919	-41,012	3,258,002	916,479	636,880	24,132	199,374	111,780
2005	5,138,317	3,793,927	48,937	3,842,864	354,367	-33,275	3,455,222	985,416	697,679	25,250	203,500	115,746
2006	5,579,031	4,119,815	29,259	4,149,074	376,630	-41,280	3,731,164	1,105,206	742,661	26,692	209,014	119,940
2007	5,908,162	4,289,701	26,720	4,316,421	399,549	-40,195	3,876,677	1,212,227	819,258	27,738	213,000	120,087
2008	6,579,583	4,564,243	-12,605	4,551,638	421,316	-25,489	4,104,833	1,529,583	945,167	30,091	218,658	123,029
2009	6,651,894	4,771,046	-9,713	4,761,333	443,978	-44,862	4,272,493	1,348,583	1,030,818	29,549	225,114	127,108
2010	7,148,787	5,027,625	14,327	5,041,952	461,514	-28,942	4,551,496	1,447,553	1,149,738	31,155	229,460	128,073
2011	7,460,603	5,144,394	-3,774	5,140,620	422,387	11,367	4,729,600	1,547,127	1,183,876	32,232	231,463	128,362
2012	7,944,320	5,426,142	986	5,427,128	441,606	36,055	5,021,577	1,737,187	1,185,556	33,923	234,188	131,867
2013	8,316,842	5,739,793	54,190	5,793,983	519,470	35,631	5,310,144	1,779,254	1,227,444	34,966	237,856	137,253
2014	8,929,018	6,151,024	41,640	6,192,664	554,884	60,310	5,698,090	1,943,349	1,287,579	36,729	243,106	141,744
2015	9,235,278	6,387,710	78,728	6,466,438	584,391	39,465	5,921,512	1,928,420	1,385,346	36,804	250,932	146,060
2016	9,347,666	6,493,506	25,944	6,519,450	599,924	7,416	5,926,942	1,964,372	1,456,352	36,669	254,919	149,632
2017	9,962,557	6,886,965	18,704	6,905,669	640,180	-19,020	6,246,469	2,206,695	1,509,393	38,375	259,613	152,744
2018	10,743,058	7,317,701	14,698	7,332,399	681,592	-18,397	6,632,410	2,532,212	1,578,436	40,995	262,055	158,608
2019	11,211,619	7,548,396	8,638	7,557,034	712,493	-21,635	6,822,906	2,684,598	1,704,115	42,228	265,501	161,656
2020	11,926,300	7,782,447	8,268	7,790,715	749,046	-38,206	7,003,463	2,635,455	2,287,382	44,358	268,864	159,584
2021	13,004,370	8,427,584	30,216	8,457,800	814,804	-65,042	7,577,954	2,803,148	2,623,268	47,803	272,041	165,359

Personal Income and Employment by Area: Colorado Springs, CO

(Thousands of dollars, except as noted.)

Year	Personal income, total	Earnings by place of work			Less: Contributions for government social insurance	Plus: Adjustment for residence	Equals: Net earnings by place of residence	Plus: Dividends, interest, and rent	Plus: Personal current transfer receipts	Per capita personal income (dollars)	Population (persons)	Total employment
		Nonfarm	Farm	Total								
1970	1,072,245	797,479	2,787	800,266	44,176	-1,431	754,659	256,190	61,396	4,439	241,543	116,502
1971	1,171,605	873,849	2,542	876,391	50,659	720	826,452	270,050	75,103	4,614	253,897	117,553
1972	1,372,920	1,036,652	2,983	1,039,635	63,176	3,817	980,276	304,806	87,838	5,020	273,474	128,822
1973	1,580,510	1,192,341	5,401	1,197,742	80,698	10,160	1,127,204	348,639	104,667	5,358	294,996	140,951
1974	1,736,052	1,294,218	3,687	1,297,905	91,168	15,798	1,222,535	393,970	119,547	5,793	299,705	142,577
1975	1,868,907	1,357,894	4,571	1,362,465	97,001	21,608	1,287,072	430,007	151,828	6,234	299,777	139,515
1976	2,016,953	1,464,140	5,370	1,469,510	106,204	29,776	1,393,082	460,611	163,260	6,777	297,633	143,093
1977	2,188,790	1,573,271	5,306	1,578,577	114,467	39,738	1,503,848	512,179	172,763	7,119	307,449	147,428
1978	2,528,015	1,809,887	4,390	1,814,277	132,674	50,253	1,731,856	606,473	189,686	8,101	312,072	154,227
1979	2,888,059	2,083,521	1,307	2,084,828	161,856	63,743	1,986,715	687,031	214,313	9,107	317,132	164,283
1980	3,281,712	2,336,633	2,454	2,339,087	185,717	81,271	2,234,641	793,160	253,911	10,250	320,180	170,287
1981	3,848,756	2,738,309	471	2,738,780	233,888	85,164	2,590,056	955,362	303,338	11,653	330,278	178,535
1982	4,259,676	3,016,989	2,944	3,019,933	259,813	88,409	2,848,529	1,069,367	341,780	12,476	341,418	185,178
1983	4,674,710	3,317,823	2,039	3,319,862	295,714	87,858	3,112,006	1,181,120	381,584	13,222	353,551	192,322
1984	5,294,525	3,804,454	1,309	3,805,763	353,241	86,829	3,539,351	1,336,311	418,863	14,516	364,735	209,639
1985	5,822,397	4,205,563	70	4,205,633	402,736	86,991	3,889,888	1,482,220	450,289	15,277	381,127	220,895
1986	6,273,129	4,557,466	-280	4,557,186	442,102	85,509	4,200,593	1,584,557	487,979	15,913	394,224	226,673
1987	6,658,876	4,838,504	1,600	4,840,104	467,635	85,321	4,457,790	1,667,196	533,890	16,369	406,810	229,718
1988	7,052,499	5,185,712	289	5,186,001	520,170	87,236	4,753,067	1,729,632	569,800	17,273	408,302	236,180
1989	7,409,205	5,327,103	467	5,327,570	551,517	90,538	4,866,591	1,904,595	638,019	18,082	409,747	238,697
1990	7,608,768	5,437,106	-297	5,436,809	578,739	104,702	4,962,772	1,949,153	696,843	18,557	410,017	235,412
1991	8,091,293	5,851,287	380	5,851,667	637,897	106,627	5,320,397	1,982,929	787,967	19,393	417,227	241,791
1992	8,833,091	6,426,039	2,367	6,428,406	703,765	108,413	5,833,054	2,111,089	888,948	20,274	435,686	250,936
1993	9,392,302	6,838,459	1,656	6,840,115	760,643	111,913	6,191,385	2,249,493	951,424	20,786	451,855	262,001
1994	10,176,944	7,428,476	-983	7,427,493	830,835	109,639	6,706,297	2,452,867	1,017,780	21,517	472,965	279,017
1995	11,140,692	8,038,681	-1,140	8,037,541	890,427	109,933	7,257,047	2,738,880	1,144,765	22,882	486,869	291,270
1996	12,002,210	8,705,752	-1,053	8,704,699	958,233	112,962	7,859,428	2,951,757	1,191,025	24,172	496,543	303,895
1997	12,719,484	9,328,054	-285	9,327,769	1,023,592	123,854	8,428,031	3,059,898	1,231,555	25,132	506,107	315,465
1998	14,162,366	10,509,130	301	10,509,431	1,084,615	136,164	9,560,980	3,324,027	1,277,359	27,351	517,799	326,466
1999	15,211,328	11,521,836	1,521	11,523,357	1,170,527	156,118	10,508,948	3,328,726	1,373,654	28,737	529,338	334,576
2000	16,640,005	12,695,641	3,994	12,699,635	1,280,838	177,419	11,596,216	3,586,502	1,457,287	30,781	540,593	345,217
2001	17,342,919	13,233,676	5,866	13,239,542	1,350,375	184,267	12,073,434	3,640,701	1,628,784	31,133	557,057	349,511
2002	17,688,357	13,553,324	3,869	13,557,193	1,415,819	175,949	12,317,323	3,540,581	1,830,453	31,269	565,688	347,088
2003	18,165,414	13,850,516	1,052	13,851,568	1,455,412	183,430	12,579,586	3,637,585	1,948,243	31,912	569,231	347,795
2004	18,920,155	14,465,867	8,390	14,474,257	1,562,530	194,033	13,105,760	3,766,870	2,047,525	32,714	578,345	353,744
2005	20,124,319	15,430,176	4,803	15,434,979	1,674,176	204,677	13,965,480	3,921,849	2,236,990	34,238	587,778	365,026
2006	21,333,183	16,066,939	1,045	16,067,984	1,752,455	229,881	14,545,410	4,354,639	2,433,134	35,406	602,532	371,136
2007	22,552,974	16,555,032	-2,044	16,552,988	1,805,208	260,042	15,007,822	4,899,739	2,645,413	37,003	609,490	378,789
2008	23,519,004	16,775,664	-3,627	16,772,037	1,855,722	280,320	15,196,635	5,143,730	3,178,639	37,895	620,644	378,125
2009	23,773,871	17,022,066	-1,198	17,020,868	1,886,211	309,946	15,444,603	4,725,321	3,603,947	37,677	630,998	371,574
2010	24,889,440	17,673,790	-769	17,673,021	1,958,299	358,191	16,072,913	4,652,428	4,164,099	38,258	650,562	372,146
2011	26,550,199	18,408,382	3,867	18,412,249	1,861,762	424,969	16,975,456	5,221,347	4,353,396	40,182	660,754	378,167
2012	27,530,228	18,922,418	1,810	18,924,228	1,912,978	673,067	17,684,317	5,441,132	4,404,779	41,129	669,356	379,506
2013	27,992,442	19,369,755	4,055	19,373,810	2,145,874	559,820	17,787,756	5,652,925	4,551,761	41,253	678,550	386,396
2014	29,690,074	20,285,249	3,594	20,288,843	2,252,602	667,664	18,703,905	6,116,974	4,869,195	43,196	687,337	394,852
2015	31,183,253	21,056,030	4,601	21,060,631	2,358,250	700,515	19,402,896	6,364,613	5,415,744	44,632	698,671	404,632
2016	32,050,551	21,680,903	3,940	21,684,843	2,427,298	622,780	19,880,325	6,473,562	5,696,664	44,877	714,179	412,279
2017	33,821,448	22,943,309	779	22,944,088	2,556,432	717,195	21,104,851	6,798,561	5,918,036	46,508	727,221	426,157
2018	35,783,153	24,217,452	-638	24,216,814	2,687,934	693,912	22,222,792	7,124,163	6,436,198	48,366	739,845	437,437
2019	38,312,368	25,764,017	-2,647	25,761,370	2,838,525	857,199	23,780,044	7,735,415	6,796,909	51,113	749,558	444,808
2020	41,473,183	27,221,878	-1,378	27,220,500	2,989,426	740,314	24,971,388	7,659,256	8,842,539	54,817	756,573	446,468
2021	44,803,161	29,214,073	-2,993	29,211,080	3,152,120	787,792	26,846,752	7,829,614	10,126,795	58,736	762,793	461,513

Personal Income and Employment by Area: Columbia, MO

(Thousands of dollars, except as noted.)

Year	Personal income, total	Earnings by place of work			Less: Contributions for government social insurance	Plus: Adjustment for residence	Equals: Net earnings by place of residence	Plus: Dividends, interest, and rent	Plus: Personal current transfer receipts	Per capita personal income (dollars)	Population (persons)	Total employment
		Nonfarm	Farm	Total								
1970	285,184	240,607	3,792	244,399	14,721	-7,685	221,993	45,819	17,372	3,518	81,073	39,470
1971	316,338	264,748	4,649	269,397	16,668	-7,452	245,277	51,041	20,020	3,831	82,578	40,284
1972	351,410	293,659	4,267	297,926	18,832	-7,579	271,515	57,606	22,289	4,181	84,046	41,917
1973	400,911	327,026	11,501	338,527	24,222	-7,418	306,887	66,862	27,162	4,525	88,593	44,491
1974	452,747	367,822	8,518	376,340	28,234	-7,460	340,646	79,342	32,759	4,978	90,958	45,535
1975	513,216	414,633	2,514	417,147	31,481	-7,702	377,964	92,329	42,923	5,781	88,769	46,649
1976	586,161	474,602	3,918	478,520	36,313	-6,847	435,360	102,606	48,195	6,335	92,528	49,134
1977	654,451	527,709	6,431	534,140	40,445	-4,546	489,149	114,481	50,821	6,952	94,134	51,203
1978	739,584	598,491	5,950	604,441	47,635	-1,584	555,222	128,587	55,775	7,634	96,886	53,672
1979	838,394	673,322	10,408	683,730	55,730	-594	627,406	146,693	64,295	8,586	97,649	56,890
1980	942,492	743,655	758	744,413	60,654	989	684,748	179,313	78,431	9,352	100,776	57,601
1981	1,033,646	785,110	6,557	791,667	68,617	2,285	725,335	217,099	91,212	10,118	102,163	56,917
1982	1,121,500	828,243	3,079	831,322	73,046	1,063	759,339	262,496	99,665	10,886	103,024	56,723
1983	1,238,841	928,372	-574	927,798	82,481	-4,973	840,344	286,862	111,635	11,962	103,564	59,821
1984	1,335,217	1,000,234	1,682	1,001,916	91,460	-10,936	899,520	317,904	117,793	12,773	104,531	62,097
1985	1,428,310	1,081,368	9,767	1,091,135	101,030	-20,248	969,857	333,943	124,510	13,629	104,800	64,693
1986	1,522,601	1,168,848	608	1,169,456	110,932	-24,193	1,034,331	355,938	132,332	14,358	106,045	67,855
1987	1,628,955	1,265,547	1,953	1,267,500	119,102	-29,962	1,118,436	370,345	140,174	15,170	107,382	69,530
1988	1,732,743	1,368,761	1,682	1,370,443	136,520	-38,361	1,195,562	387,917	149,264	15,849	109,331	72,316
1989	1,862,641	1,472,229	6,610	1,478,839	148,002	-42,897	1,287,940	406,639	168,062	16,755	111,171	73,951
1990	2,009,729	1,600,279	4,558	1,604,837	165,780	-53,702	1,385,355	439,595	184,779	17,812	112,827	76,763
1991	2,169,259	1,728,180	4,930	1,733,110	181,303	-62,908	1,488,899	464,463	215,897	18,835	115,171	78,338
1992	2,354,002	1,902,649	2,660	1,905,309	197,728	-72,560	1,635,021	487,627	231,354	20,008	117,651	80,387
1993	2,513,059	1,997,235	5,222	2,002,457	208,164	-78,994	1,715,299	537,595	260,165	20,885	120,329	83,169
1994	2,687,395	2,160,567	1,758	2,162,325	226,726	-97,936	1,837,663	576,773	272,959	21,881	122,817	86,022
1995	2,855,792	2,271,998	-1,921	2,270,077	237,823	-105,748	1,926,506	631,423	297,863	22,752	125,520	89,182
1996	3,057,214	2,437,075	5,949	2,443,024	251,607	-119,976	2,071,441	673,041	312,732	23,816	128,366	92,799
1997	3,272,038	2,557,729	3,168	2,560,897	262,942	-127,487	2,170,468	775,864	325,706	24,981	130,981	94,940
1998	3,958,074	2,990,932	12,278	3,003,210	307,797	-47,091	2,648,322	869,412	440,340	24,870	159,149	109,260
1999	4,114,805	3,183,320	-7,019	3,176,301	322,969	-49,699	2,803,633	849,695	461,477	25,593	160,778	110,017
2000	4,401,664	3,374,216	17,740	3,391,956	339,597	-58,341	2,994,018	902,939	504,707	27,023	162,886	113,660
2001	4,626,633	3,562,806	16,631	3,579,437	359,748	-59,023	3,160,666	898,450	567,517	28,032	165,050	114,547
2002	4,768,988	3,762,406	9,533	3,771,939	376,633	-73,201	3,322,105	842,131	604,752	28,426	167,766	115,747
2003	4,983,470	3,869,828	20,842	3,890,670	387,009	-67,240	3,436,421	912,657	634,392	29,301	170,077	116,248
2004	5,391,931	4,089,984	63,520	4,153,504	408,812	-75,746	3,668,946	1,051,680	671,305	31,246	172,563	118,996
2005	5,591,624	4,278,231	16,253	4,294,484	434,381	-79,181	3,780,922	1,083,172	727,530	31,724	176,257	122,431
2006	5,952,472	4,490,930	18,588	4,509,518	462,157	-83,025	3,964,336	1,207,430	780,706	32,992	180,420	124,978
2007	6,255,530	4,601,479	32,422	4,633,901	480,868	-66,810	4,086,223	1,330,290	839,017	34,102	183,438	126,699
2008	6,736,324	4,738,672	45,304	4,783,976	498,628	-30,354	4,254,994	1,495,701	985,629	36,270	185,729	126,583
2009	6,992,394	4,846,674	40,284	4,886,958	500,480	-33,427	4,353,051	1,569,379	1,069,964	37,134	188,301	124,038
2010	7,018,337	5,057,366	40,010	5,097,376	512,500	-54,255	4,530,621	1,312,580	1,175,136	36,755	190,950	125,030
2011	7,374,978	5,282,556	53,728	5,336,284	480,722	-61,434	4,794,128	1,359,781	1,221,069	38,004	194,057	128,180
2012	7,794,943	5,609,279	25,589	5,634,868	505,563	-91,910	5,037,395	1,515,995	1,241,553	39,648	196,604	131,554
2013	8,058,805	5,929,723	52,312	5,982,035	597,871	-101,304	5,282,860	1,507,718	1,268,227	40,514	198,912	134,754
2014	8,310,432	6,064,924	62,531	6,127,455	617,756	-106,442	5,403,257	1,598,420	1,308,755	41,335	201,050	136,034
2015	8,686,516	6,301,579	9,225	6,310,804	650,718	-101,661	5,558,425	1,749,493	1,378,598	42,823	202,849	138,311
2016	8,871,965	6,439,193	24,982	6,464,175	667,179	-111,121	5,685,875	1,741,188	1,444,902	43,289	204,946	139,920
2017	9,214,394	6,616,665	30,823	6,647,488	691,584	-136,770	5,819,134	1,906,488	1,488,772	44,568	206,747	142,234
2018	9,406,342	6,789,479	13,137	6,802,616	712,827	-141,830	5,947,959	1,907,062	1,551,321	45,214	208,039	143,663
2019	10,073,662	7,211,468	30,811	7,242,279	761,793	-169,528	6,310,958	2,125,116	1,637,588	48,068	209,569	143,855
2020	10,718,365	7,439,568	49,454	7,489,022	815,619	-197,061	6,476,342	2,175,198	2,066,825	50,767	211,127	141,295
2021	11,419,709	7,959,666	64,912	8,024,578	852,889	-248,943	6,922,746	2,234,592	2,262,371	53,583	213,123	146,022

Personal Income and Employment by Area: Columbia, SC

(Thousands of dollars, except as noted.)

Year	Personal income, total	Earnings by place of work Nonfarm	Farm	Total	Less: Contributions for government social insurance	Plus: Adjustment for residence	Equals: Net earnings by place of residence	Plus: Dividends, interest, and rent	Plus: Personal current transfer receipts	Per capita personal income (dollars)	Population (persons)	Total employment
1970	1,458,229	1,201,538	16,335	1,217,873	75,700	3,781	1,145,954	214,869	97,406	3,598	405,343	198,370
1971	1,616,213	1,329,307	18,059	1,347,366	87,312	59	1,260,113	241,138	114,962	3,842	420,632	204,042
1972	1,823,762	1,504,783	19,471	1,524,254	102,692	-2,007	1,419,555	271,112	133,095	4,265	427,654	213,386
1973	2,066,739	1,709,134	30,056	1,739,190	133,028	-7,773	1,598,389	307,624	160,726	4,713	438,518	225,415
1974	2,366,539	1,953,031	27,300	1,980,331	157,478	-17,789	1,805,064	360,780	200,695	5,198	455,302	237,022
1975	2,609,730	2,107,240	20,220	2,127,460	168,366	-23,138	1,935,956	401,503	272,271	5,651	461,809	235,356
1976	2,864,484	2,340,665	22,657	2,363,322	192,250	-31,126	2,139,946	431,774	292,764	6,131	467,203	240,094
1977	3,126,547	2,575,393	17,681	2,593,074	210,735	-37,931	2,344,408	477,280	304,859	6,547	477,566	247,405
1978	3,486,845	2,881,165	22,598	2,903,763	240,838	-46,195	2,616,730	535,739	334,376	7,215	483,307	255,079
1979	3,918,442	3,234,514	38,056	3,272,570	280,476	-59,818	2,932,276	601,479	384,687	7,968	491,796	263,946
1980	4,364,480	3,550,356	11,064	3,561,420	308,873	-68,581	3,183,966	714,638	465,876	8,733	499,796	267,308
1981	4,884,473	3,892,115	20,223	3,912,338	362,580	-67,307	3,482,451	864,101	537,921	9,667	505,283	268,434
1982	5,230,157	4,104,020	23,009	4,127,029	389,853	-66,546	3,670,630	980,864	578,663	10,303	507,615	268,213
1983	5,719,181	4,536,553	5,736	4,542,289	445,301	-72,302	4,024,686	1,072,990	621,505	11,141	513,337	276,269
1984	6,348,484	5,050,832	39,351	5,090,183	513,530	-75,959	4,500,694	1,192,313	655,477	12,239	518,709	289,340
1985	6,844,835	5,465,683	24,303	5,489,986	567,218	-75,135	4,847,633	1,291,023	706,179	13,130	521,313	298,320
1986	7,369,987	5,921,990	22,745	5,944,735	633,376	-77,944	5,233,415	1,392,933	743,639	13,949	528,371	308,968
1987	7,889,174	6,391,718	22,246	6,413,964	679,178	-76,109	5,658,677	1,464,565	765,932	14,806	532,846	314,930
1988	8,530,135	6,944,769	30,612	6,975,381	773,397	-82,102	6,119,882	1,590,593	819,660	15,870	537,516	327,808
1989	9,243,178	7,403,954	36,732	7,440,686	833,624	-75,081	6,531,981	1,771,070	940,127	16,994	543,917	335,359
1990	9,824,889	7,847,709	30,645	7,878,354	906,993	-101,390	6,869,971	1,905,495	1,049,423	17,811	551,633	341,316
1991	10,307,314	8,091,255	49,811	8,141,066	945,457	-75,699	7,119,910	1,969,747	1,217,657	18,300	563,238	336,460
1992	10,910,866	8,577,220	44,069	8,621,289	995,843	-92,263	7,533,183	2,021,627	1,356,056	19,064	572,323	340,420
1993	11,428,631	8,933,708	34,259	8,967,967	1,046,068	-55,597	7,866,302	2,111,091	1,451,238	19,638	581,956	344,577
1994	12,159,886	9,459,480	53,843	9,513,323	1,124,681	-77,629	8,311,013	2,280,325	1,568,548	20,614	589,879	356,921
1995	12,971,726	10,040,859	48,331	10,089,190	1,195,160	-73,669	8,820,361	2,478,015	1,673,350	21,650	599,158	369,402
1996	13,929,763	10,742,757	60,899	10,803,656	1,257,023	-85,793	9,460,840	2,671,134	1,797,789	22,875	608,946	382,266
1997	14,776,849	11,442,836	64,606	11,507,442	1,338,110	-84,631	10,084,701	2,815,955	1,876,193	23,843	619,752	393,077
1998	16,088,477	12,490,556	78,087	12,568,643	1,454,543	-87,387	11,026,713	3,087,398	1,974,366	25,498	630,966	405,382
1999	16,844,723	13,268,852	73,988	13,342,840	1,534,020	-115,584	11,693,236	3,056,543	2,094,944	26,315	640,126	413,431
2000	18,056,470	14,149,775	69,282	14,219,057	1,623,335	-99,471	12,496,251	3,301,601	2,258,618	27,798	649,567	422,563
2001	18,479,240	14,375,388	86,135	14,461,523	1,663,788	-125,806	12,671,929	3,271,157	2,536,154	28,036	659,125	416,234
2002	19,070,939	14,875,691	48,429	14,924,120	1,716,542	-153,666	13,053,912	3,254,529	2,762,498	28,631	666,087	415,110
2003	19,809,876	15,517,714	83,983	15,601,697	1,799,123	-189,905	13,612,669	3,285,981	2,911,226	29,301	676,083	418,233
2004	20,950,160	16,383,540	115,669	16,499,209	1,904,529	-236,574	14,358,106	3,445,543	3,146,511	30,344	690,421	424,587
2005	22,086,670	17,212,058	100,267	17,312,325	1,990,070	-292,613	15,029,642	3,666,700	3,390,328	31,590	699,160	433,120
2006	23,910,172	18,541,208	86,184	18,627,392	2,177,546	-359,446	16,090,400	4,148,631	3,671,141	33,437	715,091	446,637
2007	25,314,358	19,439,853	56,893	19,496,746	2,270,778	-389,221	16,836,747	4,555,742	3,921,869	34,651	730,546	459,367
2008	26,589,352	20,106,862	59,578	20,166,440	2,364,142	-397,121	17,405,177	4,625,109	4,559,066	35,655	745,740	459,041
2009	26,151,470	19,512,768	72,524	19,585,292	2,321,070	-356,113	16,908,109	4,307,211	4,936,150	34,437	759,400	443,153
2010	26,795,766	19,612,487	85,498	19,697,985	2,320,156	-339,557	17,038,272	4,320,143	5,437,351	34,814	769,682	438,955
2011	27,965,604	20,278,150	42,992	20,321,142	2,142,986	-364,595	17,813,561	4,645,892	5,506,151	36,022	776,353	446,229
2012	29,134,652	21,208,495	77,538	21,286,033	2,196,535	-363,413	18,726,085	4,916,015	5,492,552	37,184	783,524	453,369
2013	29,926,079	22,092,194	146,855	22,239,049	2,567,004	-402,679	19,269,366	4,984,241	5,672,472	37,822	791,238	463,133
2014	31,611,752	23,407,804	48,757	23,456,561	2,704,020	-492,926	20,259,615	5,273,312	6,078,825	39,881	792,645	473,864
2015	33,623,251	24,770,226	87,831	24,858,057	2,859,974	-559,630	21,438,453	5,672,889	6,511,909	41,957	801,380	489,446
2016	34,580,444	25,619,113	57,799	25,676,912	2,945,728	-603,164	22,128,020	5,769,923	6,682,501	42,802	807,908	498,389
2017	36,128,620	26,606,500	80,902	26,687,402	3,059,852	-523,609	23,103,941	6,123,874	6,900,805	44,385	813,987	504,530
2018	37,121,760	27,238,677	69,994	27,308,671	3,133,847	-430,420	23,744,404	6,085,228	7,292,128	45,297	819,515	511,430
2019	39,135,575	28,390,615	42,134	28,432,749	3,299,118	-464,145	24,669,486	6,658,133	7,807,956	47,430	825,129	513,672
2020	41,476,548	28,742,200	22,539	28,764,739	3,345,634	-447,610	24,971,495	6,705,114	9,799,939	49,926	830,767	504,791
2021	44,666,614	30,645,733	97,810	30,743,543	3,522,545	-471,909	26,749,089	6,823,928	11,093,597	53,286	838,250	516,108

Personal Income and Employment by Area: Columbus, GA-AL

(Thousands of dollars, except as noted.)

Year	Personal income, total	Earnings by place of work			Less: Contributions for government social insurance	Plus: Adjustment for residence	Equals: Net earnings by place of residence	Plus: Dividends, interest, and rent	Plus: Personal current transfer receipts	Per capita personal income (dollars)	Population (persons)	Total employment
		Nonfarm	Farm	Total								
1970	967,543	776,328	3,997	780,325	48,135	-9,177	723,013	175,263	69,267	3,799	254,664	122,623
1971	1,021,290	820,138	4,129	824,267	53,641	-10,832	759,794	179,939	81,557	4,026	253,660	120,026
1972	1,060,253	848,124	4,756	852,880	57,423	-11,271	784,186	182,951	93,116	4,294	246,940	115,160
1973	1,147,277	911,466	6,869	918,335	68,631	-12,801	836,903	201,389	108,985	4,829	237,599	116,481
1974	1,257,757	983,462	5,792	989,254	77,488	-16,961	894,805	227,772	135,180	5,148	244,309	117,043
1975	1,343,420	1,037,990	4,544	1,042,534	82,792	-23,824	935,918	240,156	167,346	5,384	249,515	114,971
1976	1,485,062	1,161,899	7,064	1,168,963	95,139	-33,629	1,040,195	262,229	182,638	5,823	255,031	119,819
1977	1,625,200	1,292,253	3,966	1,296,219	105,274	-44,260	1,146,685	288,881	189,634	6,410	253,528	124,514
1978	1,808,318	1,431,563	6,433	1,437,996	117,541	-55,195	1,265,260	336,183	206,875	6,964	259,685	127,399
1979	1,931,077	1,513,396	8,641	1,522,037	130,139	-57,951	1,333,947	361,754	235,376	7,424	260,109	126,043
1980	2,118,690	1,625,606	5,831	1,631,437	140,572	-59,755	1,431,110	412,719	274,861	8,151	259,921	125,648
1981	2,362,778	1,760,596	11,671	1,772,267	161,373	-34,081	1,576,813	472,872	313,093	9,112	259,295	123,547
1982	2,581,586	1,900,790	10,761	1,911,551	172,386	-39,894	1,699,271	543,502	338,813	9,804	263,318	126,188
1983	2,732,469	2,025,101	6,895	2,031,996	190,739	-44,393	1,796,864	572,860	362,745	10,436	261,838	126,279
1984	3,040,241	2,277,241	8,984	2,286,225	220,617	-54,542	2,011,066	646,139	383,036	11,561	262,983	133,890
1985	3,265,662	2,459,460	5,799	2,465,259	242,463	-65,966	2,156,830	700,715	408,117	12,344	264,556	136,899
1986	3,491,651	2,646,520	4,482	2,651,002	264,403	-72,866	2,313,733	751,839	426,079	13,106	266,407	139,494
1987	3,699,763	2,834,227	7,097	2,841,324	283,897	-81,802	2,475,625	786,296	437,842	13,827	267,567	141,956
1988	3,937,472	3,000,047	9,422	3,009,469	312,128	-85,665	2,611,676	864,431	461,365	14,770	266,586	144,303
1989	4,075,458	3,072,703	9,688	3,082,391	325,525	-92,864	2,664,002	898,156	513,300	15,342	265,634	142,868
1990	4,304,282	3,238,224	7,902	3,246,126	345,930	-94,610	2,805,586	933,423	565,273	16,125	266,931	142,037
1991	4,502,606	3,361,678	11,981	3,373,659	363,117	-108,763	2,901,779	969,035	631,792	16,907	266,314	138,678
1992	4,895,487	3,653,209	11,533	3,664,742	395,434	-134,678	3,134,630	1,059,157	701,700	17,756	275,715	142,086
1993	5,044,598	3,754,066	12,340	3,766,406	409,945	-153,830	3,202,631	1,104,818	737,149	18,169	277,655	144,549
1994	5,270,251	3,898,302	15,542	3,913,844	426,661	-172,482	3,314,701	1,163,995	791,555	18,763	280,889	145,839
1995	5,491,266	4,043,618	10,178	4,053,796	439,992	-185,058	3,428,746	1,212,453	850,067	19,635	279,663	147,697
1996	5,698,929	4,236,806	14,706	4,251,512	458,775	-215,707	3,577,030	1,227,986	893,913	20,373	279,725	152,880
1997	6,060,075	4,561,830	13,875	4,575,705	490,039	-257,252	3,828,414	1,309,965	921,696	21,574	280,896	157,278
1998	6,719,611	4,991,538	18,908	5,010,446	529,087	-237,111	4,244,248	1,481,805	993,558	22,969	292,548	165,506
1999	6,989,555	5,261,308	26,325	5,287,633	556,450	-261,779	4,469,404	1,475,895	1,044,256	23,884	292,647	166,756
2000	7,347,884	5,499,529	19,386	5,518,915	577,251	-286,901	4,654,763	1,584,812	1,108,309	24,969	294,278	169,412
2001	7,711,627	5,750,451	25,487	5,775,938	602,745	-327,785	4,845,408	1,649,686	1,216,533	26,081	295,679	166,770
2002	8,009,644	5,946,853	22,852	5,969,705	619,180	-370,976	4,979,549	1,696,858	1,333,237	26,917	297,571	164,750
2003	8,257,044	6,169,666	25,919	6,195,585	638,571	-443,779	5,113,235	1,774,115	1,369,694	28,361	291,137	163,793
2004	8,577,787	6,376,918	23,704	6,400,622	677,670	-518,248	5,204,704	1,907,330	1,465,753	28,862	297,196	165,954
2005	9,002,925	6,707,482	25,059	6,732,541	712,753	-695,223	5,324,565	2,097,834	1,580,526	30,124	298,859	168,743
2006	9,418,130	7,008,085	18,276	7,026,361	752,293	-839,196	5,434,872	2,311,385	1,671,873	31,215	301,715	171,426
2007	9,587,078	7,197,526	13,254	7,210,780	773,800	-995,293	5,441,687	2,347,944	1,797,447	32,065	298,991	171,822
2008	9,834,053	7,530,240	19,286	7,549,526	836,370	-1,267,440	5,445,716	2,357,564	2,030,773	32,813	299,698	175,500
2009	9,643,006	7,639,985	17,882	7,657,867	853,624	-1,448,992	5,355,251	2,106,219	2,181,536	31,533	305,809	175,492
2010	10,144,411	7,987,150	13,409	8,000,559	892,436	-1,453,348	5,654,775	2,105,739	2,383,897	32,776	309,504	177,570
2011	10,916,232	8,310,982	12,134	8,323,116	832,771	-1,439,420	6,050,925	2,348,131	2,517,176	34,609	315,415	182,910
2012	11,188,435	8,646,978	21,665	8,668,643	867,734	-1,569,579	6,231,330	2,440,805	2,516,300	34,649	322,904	183,610
2013	11,173,437	8,631,094	31,994	8,663,088	975,138	-1,649,498	6,038,452	2,522,982	2,612,003	34,057	328,084	184,172
2014	11,441,410	8,661,359	14,258	8,675,617	978,250	-1,606,723	6,090,644	2,632,646	2,718,120	34,848	328,321	182,964
2015	11,949,155	8,868,240	16,861	8,885,101	1,001,552	-1,599,852	6,283,697	2,825,408	2,840,050	36,597	326,506	182,260
2016	12,132,385	8,817,388	11,061	8,828,449	989,677	-1,492,094	6,346,678	2,891,949	2,893,758	37,525	323,312	180,272
2017	12,427,204	9,093,137	11,073	9,104,210	1,020,207	-1,558,181	6,525,822	2,920,292	2,981,090	38,751	320,695	181,453
2018	12,808,926	9,386,491	5,480	9,391,971	1,063,770	-1,621,821	6,706,380	2,987,616	3,114,930	39,573	323,682	184,192
2019	13,291,888	9,697,958	7,265	9,705,223	1,105,822	-1,673,812	6,925,589	3,086,503	3,279,796	40,594	327,435	186,287
2020	14,330,626	9,916,883	6,540	9,923,423	1,131,092	-1,732,937	7,059,394	3,070,501	4,200,731	43,539	329,141	184,188
2021	15,508,368	10,562,218	10,412	10,572,630	1,190,175	-1,693,774	7,688,681	3,128,413	4,691,274	47,349	327,536	186,591

Personal Income and Employment by Area: Columbus, IN

(Thousands of dollars, except as noted.)

Year	Personal income, total	Earnings by place of work			Less: Contributions for government social insurance	Plus: Adjustment for residence	Equals: Net earnings by place of residence	Plus: Dividends, interest, and rent	Plus: Personal current transfer receipts	Per capita personal income (dollars)	Population (persons)	Total employment
		Nonfarm	Farm	Total								
1970	238,843	265,039	3,416	268,455	17,850	-58,896	191,709	33,176	13,958	4,184	57,080	32,082
1971	261,594	282,359	5,698	288,057	19,784	-60,499	207,774	37,204	16,616	4,537	57,662	32,179
1972	285,134	307,801	4,624	312,425	22,947	-63,887	225,591	40,728	18,815	4,845	58,851	32,600
1973	332,282	356,150	12,215	368,365	30,828	-73,882	263,655	46,444	22,183	5,564	59,716	35,298
1974	373,571	403,896	10,806	414,702	36,163	-84,379	294,160	53,609	25,802	6,200	60,249	36,323
1975	380,739	390,507	7,833	398,340	34,116	-76,970	287,254	58,974	34,511	6,258	60,844	33,996
1976	437,420	462,798	12,561	475,359	41,400	-96,326	337,633	64,082	35,705	7,134	61,316	35,623
1977	495,850	539,452	7,900	547,352	47,605	-113,660	386,087	71,939	37,824	7,950	62,371	37,582
1978	550,984	609,589	7,443	617,032	55,638	-130,820	430,574	78,504	41,906	8,711	63,254	39,086
1979	608,115	687,200	4,795	691,995	65,182	-152,334	474,479	86,162	47,474	9,485	64,113	40,753
1980	623,160	658,768	1,774	660,542	62,493	-143,579	454,470	108,231	60,459	9,593	64,960	37,946
1981	703,651	728,834	4,143	732,977	74,793	-159,201	498,983	136,912	67,756	10,943	64,301	38,067
1982	712,995	695,270	3,942	699,212	72,517	-141,961	484,734	148,009	80,252	11,142	63,992	35,323
1983	759,805	743,070	-1,617	741,453	78,199	-145,820	517,434	157,624	84,747	11,916	63,765	35,344
1984	917,429	911,817	13,083	924,900	98,989	-182,858	643,053	187,036	87,340	14,432	63,567	37,712
1985	932,749	898,158	9,932	908,090	98,711	-163,978	645,401	194,419	92,929	14,713	63,398	37,442
1986	923,800	879,346	6,887	886,233	97,528	-150,726	637,979	188,125	97,696	14,677	62,940	37,657
1987	1,019,865	1,002,494	5,872	1,008,366	108,090	-171,116	729,160	191,035	99,670	16,079	63,427	38,972
1988	1,078,724	1,051,930	1,467	1,053,397	115,962	-166,340	771,095	201,664	105,965	17,016	63,395	40,195
1989	1,150,473	1,060,263	8,580	1,068,843	116,697	-148,862	803,284	232,067	115,122	18,153	63,375	40,871
1990	1,204,019	1,095,690	7,761	1,103,451	124,521	-140,685	838,245	241,295	124,479	18,856	63,855	42,137
1991	1,223,379	1,128,809	400	1,129,209	131,024	-151,044	847,141	240,892	135,346	18,867	64,843	42,105
1992	1,359,185	1,276,994	8,547	1,285,541	147,202	-184,484	953,855	248,611	156,719	20,761	65,467	44,050
1993	1,472,526	1,420,880	7,836	1,428,716	165,337	-223,872	1,039,507	267,589	165,430	22,191	66,357	46,277
1994	1,570,771	1,524,128	4,260	1,528,388	178,444	-238,573	1,111,371	287,691	171,709	23,349	67,273	48,419
1995	1,696,662	1,614,573	2,103	1,616,676	189,198	-252,260	1,175,218	341,717	179,727	24,801	68,410	49,868
1996	1,771,766	1,656,196	15,960	1,672,156	191,464	-267,226	1,213,466	363,246	195,054	25,666	69,031	50,171
1997	1,861,557	1,753,770	9,042	1,762,812	201,100	-285,052	1,276,660	385,782	199,115	26,759	69,568	51,045
1998	2,019,194	1,909,550	4,959	1,914,509	213,218	-312,028	1,389,263	419,102	210,829	28,733	70,275	52,869
1999	2,089,883	2,009,145	720	2,009,865	223,325	-318,862	1,467,678	403,603	218,602	29,585	70,639	52,944
2000	2,234,342	2,126,433	10,554	2,136,987	231,664	-342,622	1,562,701	436,225	235,416	31,135	71,763	52,846
2001	2,155,108	1,952,872	11,863	1,964,735	218,591	-283,116	1,463,028	426,825	265,255	29,886	72,110	50,295
2002	2,199,897	1,975,423	1,348	1,976,771	221,526	-257,611	1,497,634	417,973	284,290	30,601	71,890	49,158
2003	2,292,497	2,032,215	12,906	2,045,121	231,597	-257,668	1,555,856	438,249	298,392	31,709	72,299	48,777
2004	2,417,389	2,177,306	22,170	2,199,476	250,193	-289,936	1,659,347	439,419	318,623	33,169	72,882	50,421
2005	2,474,349	2,273,213	12,674	2,285,887	261,213	-323,289	1,701,385	424,891	348,073	33,591	73,660	51,636
2006	2,668,558	2,423,695	9,967	2,433,662	281,630	-346,170	1,805,862	486,516	376,180	35,816	74,508	52,453
2007	2,770,867	2,527,229	10,714	2,537,943	294,244	-383,939	1,859,760	513,338	397,769	36,815	75,265	53,859
2008	2,925,539	2,654,424	21,859	2,676,283	308,877	-436,097	1,931,309	533,780	460,450	38,453	76,080	54,442
2009	2,770,257	2,410,766	28,414	2,439,180	285,740	-367,706	1,785,734	473,698	510,825	36,181	76,566	50,963
2010	2,921,860	2,551,553	7,584	2,559,137	297,775	-354,828	1,906,534	472,705	542,621	38,034	76,823	50,843
2011	3,156,787	2,825,410	22,543	2,847,953	294,199	-456,148	2,097,606	516,791	542,390	40,660	77,639	54,100
2012	3,441,550	3,179,278	25,052	3,204,330	326,437	-591,251	2,286,642	591,399	563,509	43,547	79,031	57,396
2013	3,412,188	3,154,148	47,716	3,201,864	368,950	-564,358	2,268,556	573,894	569,738	42,817	79,692	57,346
2014	3,629,436	3,361,228	20,906	3,382,134	389,173	-591,831	2,401,130	627,174	601,132	45,565	79,654	59,040
2015	3,756,097	3,563,108	3,516	3,566,624	413,387	-671,525	2,481,712	639,062	635,323	46,716	80,403	60,064
2016	3,815,918	3,610,572	17,408	3,627,980	409,732	-694,376	2,523,872	638,346	653,700	47,090	81,035	60,665
2017	3,952,247	3,735,478	18,640	3,754,118	420,365	-713,652	2,620,101	665,204	666,942	48,852	80,902	61,245
2018	4,256,143	4,025,721	18,194	4,043,915	453,789	-790,835	2,799,291	766,331	690,521	52,363	81,282	61,978
2019	4,438,762	4,184,557	18,793	4,203,350	477,893	-805,051	2,920,406	787,331	731,025	54,102	82,045	61,916
2020	4,726,875	4,046,659	34,930	4,081,589	474,464	-610,002	2,997,123	786,297	943,455	57,535	82,157	58,407
2021	5,042,172	4,230,773	43,386	4,274,159	489,760	-615,224	3,169,175	801,103	1,071,894	61,136	82,475	58,961

Personal Income and Employment by Area: Columbus, OH

(Thousands of dollars, except as noted.)

Year	Personal income, total	Earnings by place of work			Less: Contributions for government social insurance	Plus: Adjustment for residence	Equals: Net earnings by place of residence	Plus: Dividends, interest, and rent	Plus: Personal current transfer receipts	Per capita personal income (dollars)	Population (persons)	Total employment
		Nonfarm	Farm	Total								
1970	4,968,990	4,158,986	53,117	4,212,103	255,499	-13,377	3,943,227	676,637	349,126	4,061	1,223,517	547,892
1971	5,458,636	4,557,086	45,568	4,602,654	286,905	-18,713	4,297,036	750,203	411,397	4,378	1,246,879	559,807
1972	5,989,818	5,012,476	58,579	5,071,055	332,507	-23,089	4,715,459	814,676	459,683	4,759	1,258,508	585,094
1973	6,652,006	5,574,927	69,628	5,644,555	427,157	-25,458	5,191,940	914,853	545,213	5,232	1,271,417	610,863
1974	7,312,298	6,007,561	100,605	6,108,166	477,150	-26,863	5,604,153	1,042,202	665,943	5,682	1,286,905	619,395
1975	7,847,629	6,277,019	95,947	6,372,966	487,253	-30,747	5,854,966	1,128,666	863,997	6,038	1,299,613	608,330
1976	8,620,957	6,961,090	91,912	7,053,002	554,547	-33,276	6,465,179	1,215,221	940,557	6,619	1,302,532	620,404
1977	9,594,795	7,827,893	90,878	7,918,771	625,734	-39,334	7,253,703	1,350,317	990,775	7,292	1,315,830	642,252
1978	10,614,320	8,728,771	85,091	8,813,862	721,267	-45,812	8,046,783	1,507,739	1,059,798	8,018	1,323,883	669,335
1979	11,803,035	9,686,036	123,960	9,809,996	837,183	-52,602	8,920,211	1,686,556	1,196,268	8,872	1,330,412	687,708
1980	12,975,478	10,378,815	66,247	10,445,062	900,504	-63,572	9,480,986	2,034,954	1,459,538	9,762	1,329,236	695,825
1981	14,232,984	11,194,518	6,487	11,201,005	1,037,963	-67,261	10,095,781	2,464,091	1,673,112	10,617	1,340,612	689,230
1982	15,251,563	11,726,956	25,071	11,752,027	1,093,306	-88,359	10,570,362	2,767,405	1,913,796	11,348	1,343,981	680,904
1983	16,477,889	12,727,787	-10,765	12,717,022	1,220,698	-109,713	11,386,611	3,022,501	2,068,777	12,188	1,351,988	690,537
1984	18,347,133	14,248,862	107,378	14,356,240	1,398,990	-140,536	12,816,714	3,379,878	2,150,541	13,470	1,362,111	726,332
1985	19,845,598	15,606,512	114,542	15,721,054	1,565,680	-184,658	13,970,716	3,568,676	2,306,206	14,439	1,374,432	760,496
1986	21,096,622	16,780,235	93,278	16,873,513	1,734,416	-224,227	14,914,870	3,748,760	2,432,992	15,199	1,388,054	787,782
1987	22,393,952	18,059,786	71,251	18,131,037	1,872,917	-262,106	15,996,014	3,866,577	2,531,361	15,932	1,405,633	823,595
1988	24,329,289	19,774,678	86,205	19,860,883	2,098,442	-331,281	17,431,160	4,203,521	2,694,608	17,012	1,430,091	848,911
1989	26,596,663	21,362,530	99,899	21,462,429	2,280,710	-399,247	18,782,472	4,921,333	2,892,858	18,369	1,447,914	876,674
1990	28,251,968	22,788,408	104,717	22,893,125	2,493,677	-450,009	19,949,439	5,105,579	3,196,950	19,242	1,468,263	894,479
1991	29,386,946	23,755,872	42,654	23,798,526	2,670,032	-462,922	20,665,572	5,174,862	3,546,512	19,689	1,492,559	898,033
1992	31,746,301	25,693,055	118,915	25,811,970	2,899,512	-507,699	22,404,759	5,406,788	3,934,754	20,919	1,517,612	909,049
1993	33,518,973	27,102,667	111,147	27,213,814	3,083,895	-536,334	23,593,585	5,802,609	4,122,779	21,757	1,540,611	930,524
1994	35,813,171	28,958,344	141,493	29,099,837	3,359,274	-576,201	25,164,362	6,344,121	4,304,688	22,954	1,560,222	964,490
1995	37,589,154	30,531,351	104,343	30,635,694	3,583,732	-629,522	26,422,440	6,585,178	4,581,536	23,799	1,579,412	1,001,985
1996	39,460,101	32,171,506	147,669	32,319,175	3,743,954	-677,696	27,897,525	6,873,435	4,689,141	24,769	1,593,111	1,023,195
1997	42,456,133	34,509,309	204,551	34,713,860	3,916,245	-763,713	30,033,902	7,588,234	4,833,997	26,319	1,613,135	1,044,212
1998	45,674,587	37,692,726	142,351	37,835,077	4,130,792	-861,347	32,842,938	7,849,950	4,981,699	27,907	1,636,690	1,074,387
1999	48,106,814	40,285,312	106,766	40,392,078	4,419,902	-940,715	35,031,461	7,813,909	5,261,444	29,012	1,658,194	1,096,790
2000	52,108,152	43,775,730	156,430	43,932,160	4,623,523	-1,045,656	38,262,981	8,191,122	5,654,049	30,979	1,682,068	1,132,103
2001	53,095,115	44,279,579	150,075	44,429,654	4,741,456	-1,121,142	38,567,056	8,275,048	6,253,011	31,108	1,706,779	1,142,117
2002	54,603,492	45,642,469	79,958	45,722,427	4,808,282	-1,163,370	39,750,775	8,037,146	6,815,571	31,629	1,726,352	1,136,086
2003	56,570,530	47,114,805	100,258	47,215,063	4,983,428	-1,214,113	41,017,522	8,338,509	7,214,499	32,340	1,749,262	1,137,227
2004	59,333,902	49,665,498	178,725	49,844,223	5,315,215	-1,332,615	43,196,393	8,479,782	7,657,727	33,530	1,769,572	1,151,480
2005	61,996,861	51,369,868	95,230	51,465,098	5,481,189	-1,397,536	44,586,373	9,137,882	8,272,606	34,613	1,791,126	1,166,767
2006	65,607,480	53,800,779	91,746	53,892,525	5,762,738	-1,457,117	46,672,670	10,090,402	8,844,408	36,108	1,816,992	1,181,275
2007	69,278,556	56,317,498	130,466	56,447,964	5,992,663	-1,476,843	48,978,458	10,803,355	9,496,743	37,620	1,841,539	1,205,643
2008	72,147,022	57,421,007	131,413	57,552,420	6,209,516	-1,446,888	49,896,016	11,317,085	10,933,921	38,671	1,865,647	1,204,031
2009	71,197,105	56,166,335	193,242	56,359,577	6,138,319	-1,367,045	48,854,213	10,423,166	11,919,726	37,719	1,887,548	1,174,285
2010	74,023,369	58,101,193	193,378	58,294,571	6,180,839	-1,393,636	50,720,096	10,490,222	12,813,051	38,829	1,906,408	1,173,163
2011	79,845,206	61,687,384	348,744	62,036,128	5,866,488	-1,472,125	54,697,515	11,787,180	13,360,511	41,445	1,926,556	1,200,586
2012	85,441,741	66,166,937	222,633	66,389,570	6,142,786	-1,669,381	58,577,403	13,800,635	13,063,703	43,870	1,947,602	1,228,248
2013	87,303,834	69,093,962	353,388	69,447,350	6,996,415	-1,753,731	60,697,204	13,227,509	13,379,121	44,212	1,974,649	1,256,858
2014	91,505,512	71,681,426	182,523	71,863,949	7,260,997	-1,823,761	62,779,191	14,579,820	14,146,501	45,676	2,003,354	1,285,655
2015	96,420,710	74,991,808	24,999	75,016,807	7,605,318	-1,887,101	65,524,388	16,066,358	14,829,964	47,504	2,029,729	1,314,371
2016	99,396,167	77,180,705	32,023	77,212,728	7,954,458	-2,007,670	67,250,600	16,899,266	15,246,301	48,367	2,055,047	1,343,684
2017	103,392,956	80,802,888	92,211	80,895,099	8,507,165	-2,199,525	70,188,409	17,549,966	15,654,581	49,566	2,085,945	1,369,731
2018	107,556,367	83,654,136	146,845	83,800,981	8,694,965	-2,348,922	72,757,094	18,696,268	16,103,005	51,026	2,107,893	1,395,404
2019	111,993,459	86,612,165	22,794	86,634,959	9,119,042	-2,446,294	75,069,623	19,875,447	17,048,389	52,627	2,128,071	1,407,701
2020	121,049,023	89,396,481	245,465	89,641,946	9,422,545	-2,588,254	77,631,147	19,960,153	23,457,723	56,537	2,141,042	1,383,169
2021	128,774,408	95,111,014	361,367	95,472,381	9,872,882	-2,853,840	82,745,659	20,442,591	25,586,158	59,867	2,151,017	1,424,878

Personal Income and Employment by Area: Corpus Christi, TX

(Thousands of dollars, except as noted.)

Year	Personal income, total	Earnings by place of work			Less: Contributions for government social insurance	Plus: Adjustment for residence	Equals: Net earnings by place of residence	Plus: Dividends, interest, and rent	Plus: Personal current transfer receipts	Per capita personal income (dollars)	Population (persons)	Total employment
		Nonfarm	Farm	Total								
1970	1,072,943	885,238	14,784	900,022	51,642	-14,011	834,369	165,509	73,065	3,636	295,082	126,000
1971	1,174,065	965,963	14,510	980,473	58,101	-14,803	907,569	179,767	86,729	3,865	303,749	128,721
1972	1,276,672	1,042,115	20,263	1,062,378	65,233	-16,171	980,974	195,117	100,581	4,086	312,437	129,292
1973	1,422,778	1,144,257	40,995	1,185,252	82,891	-18,263	1,084,098	215,842	122,838	4,563	311,819	134,114
1974	1,619,615	1,296,369	40,590	1,336,959	96,621	-21,415	1,218,923	250,973	149,719	5,210	310,879	137,156
1975	1,834,018	1,473,831	29,555	1,503,386	107,771	-25,320	1,370,295	279,495	184,228	5,787	316,939	138,280
1976	2,095,395	1,713,890	33,517	1,747,407	125,053	-30,660	1,591,694	300,713	202,988	6,487	323,036	142,172
1977	2,217,943	1,813,094	21,713	1,834,807	134,752	-29,861	1,670,194	331,068	216,681	6,825	324,964	145,244
1978	2,560,177	2,122,210	18,406	2,140,616	161,523	-39,385	1,939,708	383,081	237,388	7,814	327,620	154,230
1979	2,945,208	2,461,309	21,507	2,482,816	198,186	-49,272	2,235,358	438,865	270,985	8,797	334,805	162,460
1980	3,294,818	2,749,986	-14,783	2,735,203	225,898	-52,945	2,456,360	522,863	315,595	9,628	342,213	166,236
1981	3,828,183	3,111,272	44,999	3,156,271	280,185	-49,788	2,826,298	652,005	349,880	10,997	348,104	175,453
1982	4,123,312	3,313,585	12,212	3,325,797	309,970	-64,722	2,951,105	778,841	393,366	11,454	359,988	180,014
1983	4,285,205	3,310,589	18,277	3,328,866	308,004	-57,774	2,963,088	860,662	461,455	11,654	367,695	176,099
1984	4,532,470	3,461,613	24,334	3,485,947	331,130	-54,536	3,100,281	943,878	488,311	12,254	369,879	178,794
1985	4,784,425	3,600,449	32,145	3,632,594	349,986	-49,544	3,233,064	1,040,620	510,741	12,911	370,569	180,370
1986	4,746,523	3,482,442	13,963	3,496,405	333,115	-43,439	3,119,851	1,054,516	572,156	12,676	374,442	170,111
1987	4,710,517	3,392,641	40,530	3,433,171	320,232	-32,258	3,080,681	1,021,279	608,557	12,742	369,672	171,076
1988	4,929,074	3,573,510	36,296	3,609,806	352,965	-34,841	3,222,000	1,070,103	636,971	13,432	366,973	172,794
1989	5,187,667	3,697,931	-1,111	3,696,820	372,376	-33,143	3,291,301	1,199,326	697,040	14,161	366,328	173,076
1990	5,603,771	4,093,068	2,719	4,095,787	407,484	-31,174	3,657,129	1,179,264	767,378	15,217	368,255	178,082
1991	5,969,118	4,335,047	43,331	4,378,378	443,257	-38,427	3,896,694	1,200,524	871,900	15,992	373,245	181,527
1992	6,457,746	4,629,666	30,655	4,660,321	470,390	-43,873	4,146,058	1,281,556	1,030,132	17,081	378,071	182,760
1993	6,753,977	4,931,511	39,245	4,970,756	502,521	-45,653	4,422,582	1,256,798	1,074,597	17,508	385,768	188,525
1994	7,143,164	5,194,116	53,812	5,247,928	534,800	-51,760	4,661,368	1,320,695	1,161,101	18,220	392,050	193,248
1995	7,469,196	5,329,797	72,122	5,401,919	552,531	-58,843	4,790,545	1,416,095	1,262,556	18,924	394,701	197,179
1996	7,964,093	5,768,821	5,115	5,773,936	591,130	-67,386	5,115,420	1,496,350	1,352,323	19,984	398,529	203,672
1997	8,454,758	6,129,857	41,118	6,170,975	622,733	-69,876	5,478,366	1,568,119	1,408,273	21,005	402,504	209,271
1998	8,431,967	6,309,961	34,458	6,344,419	636,963	-177,118	5,530,338	1,544,987	1,356,642	22,092	381,683	204,098
1999	8,704,871	6,537,649	103,570	6,641,219	651,074	-180,490	5,809,655	1,532,510	1,362,706	22,803	381,738	203,469
2000	9,056,064	6,767,338	72,949	6,840,287	674,582	-201,054	5,964,651	1,667,827	1,423,586	23,769	381,006	206,855
2001	9,781,343	7,463,876	16,287	7,480,163	720,713	-235,902	6,523,548	1,719,871	1,537,924	25,716	380,360	209,256
2002	10,081,503	7,725,140	17,780	7,742,920	751,178	-271,835	6,719,907	1,687,851	1,673,745	26,317	383,076	210,084
2003	10,648,427	8,131,689	98,256	8,229,945	800,923	-319,882	7,109,140	1,756,560	1,782,727	27,725	384,072	212,756
2004	11,159,588	8,607,997	122,759	8,730,756	839,556	-382,158	7,509,042	1,770,172	1,880,374	28,698	388,869	213,608
2005	11,997,516	9,184,659	52,311	9,236,970	895,108	-392,103	7,949,759	1,988,467	2,059,290	30,548	392,747	217,363
2006	12,807,841	10,037,139	2,285	10,039,424	958,124	-554,148	8,527,152	2,090,526	2,190,163	32,332	396,135	221,335
2007	13,252,063	10,175,947	64,469	10,240,416	1,010,563	-657,393	8,572,460	2,274,036	2,405,567	33,361	397,235	228,301
2008	14,683,938	11,330,384	27,584	11,357,968	1,086,878	-824,372	9,446,718	2,566,495	2,670,725	36,715	399,943	233,317
2009	13,922,591	10,451,794	27,718	10,479,512	1,056,536	-682,262	8,740,714	2,293,652	2,888,225	34,464	403,971	229,560
2010	14,926,127	10,830,649	174,475	11,005,124	1,095,604	-573,330	9,336,190	2,400,349	3,189,588	36,884	404,675	228,466
2011	16,169,227	11,481,430	217,966	11,699,396	1,021,283	-435,048	10,243,065	2,651,343	3,274,819	39,656	407,733	231,628
2012	16,998,179	12,212,081	42,911	12,254,992	1,090,611	-372,632	10,791,749	2,967,507	3,238,923	41,135	413,227	238,395
2013	17,753,991	12,807,505	180,455	12,987,960	1,273,225	-297,813	11,416,922	3,007,325	3,329,744	42,360	419,119	243,432
2014	18,603,591	13,483,988	-4,915	13,479,073	1,340,789	-325,290	11,812,994	3,313,594	3,477,003	44,298	419,964	248,375
2015	18,363,761	13,211,191	26,060	13,237,251	1,350,900	-358,080	11,528,271	3,149,573	3,685,917	43,367	423,451	248,922
2016	17,471,905	12,622,276	4,658	12,626,934	1,343,841	-456,574	10,826,519	2,789,076	3,856,310	41,208	423,993	246,842
2017	18,311,883	13,080,933	44,089	13,125,022	1,395,950	-476,281	11,252,791	3,111,354	3,947,738	43,325	422,659	250,841
2018	18,691,522	13,167,203	35,335	13,202,538	1,409,490	-423,671	11,369,377	3,240,975	4,081,170	44,290	422,025	252,102
2019	19,818,326	14,060,087	41,605	14,101,692	1,456,980	-367,943	12,276,769	3,281,112	4,260,445	47,023	421,457	250,549
2020	20,618,709	13,713,493	-22,464	13,691,029	1,435,075	-456,987	11,798,967	3,233,822	5,585,920	48,875	421,862	240,371
2021	22,243,036	14,366,843	119,980	14,486,823	1,490,118	-500,351	12,496,354	3,425,450	6,321,232	52,612	422,778	243,747

Personal Income and Employment by Area: Corvallis, OR

(Thousands of dollars, except as noted.)

Year	Personal income, total	Earnings by place of work			Less: Contributions for government social insurance	Plus: Adjustment for residence	Equals: Net earnings by place of residence	Plus: Dividends, interest, and rent	Plus: Personal current transfer receipts	Per capita personal income (dollars)	Population (persons)	Total employment
		Nonfarm	Farm	Total								
1970	183,578	134,535	3,433	137,968	9,350	3,667	132,285	38,670	12,623	3,403	53,943	19,498
1971	205,429	149,891	3,253	153,144	10,653	4,572	147,063	43,658	14,708	3,740	54,929	20,207
1972	232,456	169,342	4,151	173,493	12,614	6,328	167,207	48,778	16,471	3,866	60,135	21,016
1973	263,806	188,695	7,172	195,867	16,164	8,837	188,540	55,152	20,114	4,448	59,313	22,257
1974	299,249	208,349	8,217	216,566	18,409	11,940	210,097	64,254	24,898	4,887	61,230	23,381
1975	338,181	234,630	4,033	238,663	20,124	14,727	233,266	73,162	31,753	5,488	61,618	24,344
1976	389,271	272,697	5,906	278,603	23,621	18,516	273,498	80,894	34,879	6,248	62,299	25,929
1977	446,823	319,660	5,389	325,049	28,481	20,496	317,064	91,855	37,904	6,815	65,569	28,314
1978	514,888	372,914	5,090	378,004	34,732	23,441	366,713	106,666	41,509	7,690	66,955	30,807
1979	569,961	407,035	6,139	413,174	39,681	28,321	401,814	120,739	47,408	8,361	68,171	30,922
1980	629,806	436,130	6,890	443,020	43,078	32,430	432,372	141,987	55,447	9,198	68,471	30,495
1981	706,844	480,849	9,536	490,385	51,101	33,438	472,722	172,195	61,927	10,190	69,369	30,876
1982	745,397	510,570	8,591	519,161	55,909	26,470	489,722	185,338	70,337	10,731	69,461	31,071
1983	798,385	542,406	10,905	553,311	60,004	26,286	519,593	202,819	75,973	11,699	68,245	31,395
1984	858,862	580,422	14,585	595,007	65,980	27,920	556,947	221,983	79,932	12,729	67,474	32,566
1985	888,296	590,442	15,656	606,098	66,999	30,460	569,559	233,502	85,235	13,204	67,275	33,707
1986	937,245	635,723	19,477	655,200	72,524	26,593	609,269	244,719	83,257	14,001	66,940	35,204
1987	990,373	684,582	16,704	701,286	76,909	26,063	650,440	251,543	88,390	14,653	67,590	36,280
1988	1,063,347	752,431	23,404	775,835	89,034	25,898	712,699	258,209	92,439	15,666	67,876	37,645
1989	1,170,796	820,494	18,932	839,426	96,679	23,954	766,701	304,831	99,264	16,755	69,879	38,457
1990	1,226,515	868,393	17,570	885,963	104,845	25,074	806,192	311,674	108,649	17,261	71,059	39,188
1991	1,279,973	909,801	15,276	925,077	110,006	25,743	840,814	323,167	115,992	17,900	71,507	39,115
1992	1,368,381	987,886	12,485	1,000,371	118,561	22,193	904,003	337,386	126,992	18,844	72,618	39,372
1993	1,479,727	1,093,560	17,297	1,110,857	131,750	8,954	988,061	358,683	132,983	19,997	73,997	41,016
1994	1,591,629	1,200,624	21,742	1,222,366	146,441	1,459	1,077,384	370,614	143,631	21,086	75,481	42,864
1995	1,744,720	1,299,198	18,212	1,317,410	159,999	-7,508	1,149,903	433,576	161,241	22,802	76,517	44,979
1996	1,929,118	1,442,262	25,420	1,467,682	180,491	-21,546	1,265,645	491,568	171,905	24,804	77,776	48,096
1997	2,074,710	1,577,311	25,086	1,602,397	194,761	-34,854	1,372,782	525,100	176,828	26,409	78,560	49,568
1998	2,166,313	1,644,178	24,245	1,668,423	201,579	-33,501	1,433,343	545,889	187,081	27,441	78,943	50,743
1999	2,172,694	1,652,069	30,850	1,682,919	199,773	-29,732	1,453,414	514,353	204,927	27,765	78,254	50,485
2000	2,282,112	1,745,987	28,512	1,774,499	212,636	-45,008	1,516,855	552,279	212,978	29,170	78,236	51,408
2001	2,369,154	1,822,814	38,241	1,861,055	210,891	-45,090	1,605,074	530,295	233,785	30,184	78,491	48,298
2002	2,404,354	1,849,796	38,259	1,888,055	213,697	-35,190	1,639,168	515,898	249,288	29,978	80,203	45,836
2003	2,543,577	1,909,748	42,869	1,952,617	220,301	-40,056	1,692,260	587,930	263,387	31,667	80,322	45,891
2004	2,596,419	1,973,614	45,092	2,018,706	228,537	-83,706	1,706,463	621,241	268,715	32,395	80,149	47,624
2005	2,663,375	2,058,759	35,430	2,094,189	240,166	-84,847	1,769,176	601,850	292,349	32,904	80,943	48,107
2006	2,812,644	2,143,796	37,796	2,181,592	252,430	-81,606	1,847,556	648,499	316,589	34,319	81,957	48,815
2007	2,925,620	2,188,415	29,138	2,217,553	260,660	-66,124	1,890,769	696,248	338,603	34,946	83,718	48,386
2008	3,092,647	2,212,583	25,614	2,238,197	265,582	-48,864	1,923,751	771,862	397,034	36,752	84,150	48,213
2009	2,952,473	2,207,420	24,383	2,231,803	263,245	-137,821	1,830,737	681,949	439,787	34,576	85,390	47,494
2010	3,068,758	2,279,643	21,208	2,300,851	271,759	-140,326	1,888,766	700,226	479,766	35,860	85,577	47,457
2011	3,242,400	2,316,366	27,747	2,344,113	244,850	-151,098	1,948,165	813,659	480,576	37,580	86,281	48,590
2012	3,281,101	2,410,269	32,455	2,442,724	253,838	-171,590	2,017,296	794,441	469,364	37,841	86,708	48,486
2013	3,272,729	2,425,676	30,073	2,455,749	290,380	-158,364	2,007,005	776,641	489,083	37,954	86,228	48,185
2014	3,477,264	2,491,259	23,744	2,515,003	301,938	-131,301	2,081,764	879,264	516,236	39,499	88,034	49,282
2015	3,640,560	2,603,039	25,523	2,628,562	312,860	-155,461	2,160,241	933,198	547,121	40,737	89,368	50,429
2016	3,840,665	2,715,089	26,712	2,741,801	327,069	-119,320	2,295,412	976,963	568,290	42,123	91,178	50,748
2017	3,995,270	2,866,849	22,427	2,889,276	346,783	-154,383	2,388,110	1,023,478	583,682	42,842	93,257	52,222
2018	4,245,863	3,033,068	23,068	3,056,136	361,140	-161,798	2,533,198	1,096,335	616,330	45,149	94,042	52,771
2019	4,485,136	3,140,002	19,198	3,159,200	372,662	-150,770	2,635,768	1,192,416	656,952	47,290	94,844	52,518
2020	4,818,137	3,261,930	24,238	3,286,168	381,294	-161,237	2,743,637	1,204,637	869,863	50,628	95,167	50,798
2021	5,201,650	3,502,636	23,535	3,526,171	405,528	-128,841	2,991,802	1,247,448	962,400	54,174	96,017	51,943

Personal Income and Employment by Area: Crestview-Fort Walton Beach-Destin, FL

(Thousands of dollars, except as noted.)

Year	Personal income, total	Earnings by place of work			Less: Contributions for government social insurance	Plus: Adjustment for residence	Equals: Net earnings by place of residence	Plus: Dividends, interest, and rent	Plus: Personal current transfer receipts	Per capita personal income (dollars)	Population (persons)	Total employment
		Nonfarm	Farm	Total								
1970	397,526	320,410	1,010	321,420	17,638	-22,403	281,379	92,961	23,186	3,797	104,708	43,341
1971	451,674	365,524	2,955	368,479	21,210	-25,032	322,237	102,043	27,394	4,194	107,706	45,369
1972	512,479	413,090	3,357	416,447	24,411	-27,783	364,253	115,408	32,818	4,547	112,702	46,894
1973	559,571	440,551	7,473	448,024	28,184	-27,264	392,576	127,077	39,918	4,872	114,864	49,238
1974	617,777	478,596	9,103	487,699	32,799	-26,278	428,622	141,985	47,170	5,302	116,509	51,718
1975	691,636	520,856	9,441	530,297	36,987	-27,385	465,925	161,890	63,821	5,583	123,878	51,954
1976	757,512	573,751	5,722	579,473	41,822	-31,306	506,345	180,898	70,269	6,100	124,190	53,408
1977	830,796	626,811	2,592	629,403	45,680	-32,180	551,543	203,270	75,983	6,522	127,380	55,208
1978	949,826	702,757	6,354	709,111	51,189	-33,630	624,292	242,590	82,944	7,374	128,807	58,497
1979	1,042,862	762,910	8,298	771,208	58,529	-35,615	677,064	268,535	97,263	7,920	131,677	60,253
1980	1,158,307	827,984	3,131	831,115	62,925	-36,598	731,592	310,371	116,344	8,768	132,104	60,453
1981	1,355,782	974,409	1,404	975,813	79,429	-43,819	852,565	365,094	138,123	10,014	135,394	63,432
1982	1,483,117	1,060,369	2,488	1,062,857	87,829	-46,562	928,466	395,833	158,818	10,649	139,276	65,789
1983	1,632,927	1,164,725	1,356	1,166,081	102,149	-46,609	1,017,323	439,044	176,560	11,298	144,536	69,831
1984	1,834,874	1,305,357	3,932	1,309,289	118,650	-50,444	1,140,195	501,841	192,838	12,279	149,428	75,701
1985	1,987,754	1,400,002	2,645	1,402,647	131,934	-47,872	1,222,841	551,186	213,727	12,848	154,718	79,525
1986	2,163,609	1,531,459	3,898	1,535,357	149,316	-51,256	1,334,785	598,054	230,770	13,569	159,450	84,261
1987	2,353,072	1,673,457	3,871	1,677,328	163,337	-53,044	1,460,947	646,622	245,503	14,345	164,034	86,072
1988	2,557,660	1,802,928	7,717	1,810,645	183,804	-65,426	1,561,415	726,626	269,619	15,310	167,059	88,777
1989	2,800,987	1,931,770	8,849	1,940,619	200,434	-62,308	1,677,877	818,689	304,421	16,493	169,832	91,122
1990	3,048,476	2,047,442	7,352	2,054,794	216,146	-14,630	1,824,018	887,741	336,717	17,694	172,290	91,622
1991	3,258,442	2,191,957	7,569	2,199,526	234,359	-33,655	1,931,512	942,659	384,271	18,325	177,811	94,263
1992	3,553,894	2,359,319	8,806	2,368,125	254,874	-3,601	2,109,650	1,007,803	436,441	19,389	183,299	96,788
1993	3,791,859	2,505,998	7,412	2,513,410	272,059	-31,395	2,209,956	1,110,731	471,172	20,090	188,744	100,240
1994	3,981,554	2,605,404	7,325	2,612,729	285,679	-31,456	2,295,594	1,182,242	503,718	20,561	193,649	105,827
1995	4,309,037	2,817,684	7,071	2,824,755	304,730	-99,185	2,420,840	1,313,402	574,795	21,820	197,484	109,725
1996	4,587,952	3,040,468	10,114	3,050,582	327,754	-133,987	2,588,841	1,409,360	589,751	22,806	201,172	114,103
1997	4,877,442	3,197,909	9,292	3,207,201	347,886	-120,858	2,738,457	1,511,785	627,200	23,814	204,814	118,905
1998	5,182,771	3,395,559	4,895	3,400,454	368,075	-163,154	2,869,225	1,666,112	647,434	25,073	206,708	122,256
1999	5,512,128	3,590,191	7,235	3,597,426	386,769	-158,668	3,051,989	1,763,581	696,558	26,384	208,918	124,906
2000	5,829,151	3,855,011	3,353	3,858,364	413,892	-215,937	3,228,535	1,835,980	764,636	27,502	211,955	129,035
2001	6,173,652	4,150,979	3,174	4,154,153	439,687	-229,929	3,484,537	1,831,288	857,827	28,721	214,955	123,262
2002	6,631,526	4,622,763	-4,639	4,618,124	486,859	-285,554	3,845,711	1,848,663	937,152	30,117	220,192	128,008
2003	7,274,920	5,205,623	488	5,206,111	542,287	-343,061	4,320,763	1,942,747	1,011,410	32,590	223,227	134,491
2004	7,929,056	5,850,618	2,231	5,852,849	610,719	-396,745	4,845,385	1,995,262	1,088,409	34,471	230,024	145,298
2005	8,537,709	6,356,687	2,257	6,358,944	665,704	-447,163	5,246,077	2,147,096	1,144,536	36,574	233,437	150,544
2006	9,086,066	6,619,892	4,349	6,624,241	718,273	-481,458	5,424,510	2,446,569	1,214,987	38,629	235,216	155,241
2007	9,331,808	6,593,403	3,564	6,596,967	727,009	-516,367	5,353,591	2,695,660	1,282,557	39,704	235,032	155,616
2008	9,379,893	6,396,600	2,423	6,399,023	720,548	-532,892	5,145,583	2,764,690	1,469,620	39,861	235,315	150,985
2009	9,081,695	6,241,552	1,181	6,242,733	728,251	-548,546	4,965,936	2,508,932	1,606,827	38,533	235,687	146,856
2010	9,627,474	6,458,983	2,569	6,461,552	742,749	-571,295	5,147,508	2,655,493	1,824,473	40,805	235,939	144,422
2011	9,983,691	6,672,860	4,056	6,676,916	699,477	-618,628	5,358,811	2,728,090	1,896,790	41,805	238,818	148,422
2012	10,777,988	7,284,628	6,668	7,291,296	761,321	-704,352	5,825,623	3,094,787	1,857,578	43,605	247,172	151,356
2013	10,932,050	7,489,604	9,243	7,498,847	868,799	-731,748	5,898,300	3,090,688	1,943,062	43,347	252,201	155,637
2014	11,564,078	7,713,576	16,850	7,730,426	895,583	-732,348	6,102,495	3,401,336	2,060,247	45,224	255,707	158,392
2015	12,208,288	8,070,838	24,034	8,094,872	931,674	-743,489	6,419,709	3,609,895	2,178,684	46,832	260,683	163,188
2016	12,836,170	8,522,023	11,939	8,533,962	968,861	-782,443	6,782,658	3,765,745	2,287,767	48,354	265,460	167,595
2017	13,714,909	9,023,623	15,709	9,039,332	1,019,091	-817,640	7,202,601	4,053,568	2,458,740	50,559	271,267	173,642
2018	14,685,305	9,488,650	10,545	9,499,195	1,076,929	-847,434	7,574,832	4,497,700	2,612,773	52,959	277,296	179,233
2019	16,149,603	10,391,249	9,375	10,400,624	1,185,368	-951,949	8,263,307	5,088,400	2,797,896	56,856	284,042	183,057
2020	17,318,908	11,027,759	8,965	11,036,724	1,258,470	-1,053,001	8,725,253	5,114,506	3,479,149	60,205	287,664	186,859
2021	18,966,449	12,217,505	18,924	12,236,429	1,358,900	-1,153,665	9,723,864	5,261,587	3,980,998	64,660	293,324	195,162

Personal Income and Employment by Area: Cumberland, MD-WV

(Thousands of dollars, except as noted.)

Year	Personal income, total	Derivation of personal income								Per capita personal income (dollars)	Population (persons)	Total employment
		Earnings by place of work			Less: Contributions for government social insurance	Plus: Adjustment for residence	Equals: Net earnings by place of residence	Plus: Dividends, interest, and rent	Plus: Personal current transfer receipts			
		Nonfarm	Farm	Total								
1970	356,715	312,900	927	313,827	24,342	-16,997	272,488	37,925	46,302	3,329	107,140	42,280
1971	385,369	330,253	911	331,164	26,475	-15,047	289,642	40,826	54,901	3,577	107,735	41,720
1972	416,815	352,062	1,034	353,096	29,385	-13,265	310,446	43,942	62,427	3,807	109,483	41,890
1973	454,127	382,041	1,507	383,548	36,229	-13,120	334,199	49,681	70,247	4,186	108,476	42,897
1974	492,609	408,275	1,269	409,544	40,100	-16,764	352,680	57,331	82,598	4,516	109,091	42,044
1975	530,985	412,802	1,056	413,858	39,740	-14,308	359,810	63,995	107,180	4,903	108,304	40,012
1976	572,138	448,160	568	448,728	43,766	-15,627	389,335	70,221	112,582	5,290	108,148	39,976
1977	635,602	506,203	561	506,764	49,281	-18,480	439,003	78,999	117,600	5,892	107,873	40,722
1978	698,318	560,358	1,506	561,864	56,213	-19,548	486,103	86,768	125,447	6,518	107,138	42,694
1979	773,257	612,568	1,558	614,126	63,670	-17,884	532,572	96,270	144,415	7,163	107,955	42,382
1980	861,065	654,571	1,299	655,870	68,487	-16,712	570,671	120,694	169,700	7,983	107,868	42,213
1981	939,893	687,247	590	687,837	77,975	-11,664	598,198	147,334	194,361	8,701	108,027	41,782
1982	998,653	693,114	703	693,817	80,802	-7,662	605,353	176,683	216,617	9,307	107,298	40,498
1983	1,053,386	718,611	2,040	720,651	84,752	-4,970	630,929	186,810	235,647	9,924	106,147	40,484
1984	1,116,190	759,600	2,909	762,509	93,196	-5,439	663,874	207,213	245,103	10,682	104,497	40,688
1985	1,173,066	794,867	2,419	797,286	99,367	-4,048	693,871	220,027	259,168	11,345	103,396	41,264
1986	1,198,124	802,512	2,684	805,196	103,360	-143	701,693	231,871	264,560	11,670	102,668	40,906
1987	1,266,928	854,754	1,439	856,193	108,253	-78	747,862	233,333	285,733	12,388	102,270	42,300
1988	1,343,924	928,205	1,185	929,390	123,070	-1,823	804,497	238,536	300,891	13,152	102,187	43,808
1989	1,435,674	967,968	1,388	969,356	128,927	-1,033	839,396	275,001	321,277	14,063	102,086	44,253
1990	1,509,208	1,007,002	1,622	1,008,624	132,333	8,436	884,727	279,638	344,843	14,849	101,634	44,793
1991	1,560,142	1,016,568	967	1,017,535	133,761	10,177	893,951	286,586	379,605	15,280	102,101	44,400
1992	1,609,264	1,024,395	1,954	1,026,349	134,115	13,211	905,445	280,577	423,242	15,729	102,312	43,742
1993	1,661,886	1,066,450	2,083	1,068,533	139,819	11,659	940,373	284,516	436,997	16,236	102,359	43,705
1994	1,726,488	1,107,793	2,166	1,109,959	144,814	9,941	975,086	303,506	447,896	16,842	102,508	44,034
1995	1,781,012	1,132,264	823	1,133,087	148,127	9,550	994,510	316,216	470,286	17,341	102,704	44,466
1996	1,846,848	1,172,719	992	1,173,711	153,051	7,442	1,028,102	331,525	487,221	18,031	102,424	45,200
1997	1,930,600	1,228,414	-525	1,227,889	158,815	3,270	1,072,344	361,152	497,104	18,843	102,457	45,957
1998	1,983,323	1,266,304	108	1,266,412	160,072	3,955	1,110,295	369,564	503,464	19,308	102,718	46,271
1999	2,046,412	1,320,591	126	1,320,717	165,147	5,968	1,161,538	357,095	527,779	19,973	102,458	46,460
2000	2,149,453	1,386,992	1,054	1,388,046	172,771	7,132	1,222,407	380,015	547,031	21,102	101,858	47,376
2001	2,518,065	1,717,190	273	1,717,463	195,246	14,263	1,536,480	389,732	591,853	24,785	101,596	47,090
2002	2,629,906	1,836,441	319	1,836,760	203,551	9,258	1,642,467	360,831	626,608	25,920	101,462	46,958
2003	2,724,221	1,901,216	1,987	1,903,203	210,813	10,307	1,702,697	356,356	665,168	26,851	101,457	46,793
2004	2,811,773	1,969,359	3,929	1,973,288	218,087	8,139	1,763,340	370,702	677,731	27,659	101,658	47,694
2005	2,761,082	1,887,675	3,214	1,890,889	222,972	13,369	1,681,286	355,652	724,144	27,291	101,172	48,486
2006	2,744,740	1,842,098	1,060	1,843,158	228,490	16,027	1,630,695	363,298	750,747	27,094	101,304	48,721
2007	2,826,845	1,809,793	-783	1,809,010	228,499	26,027	1,606,538	421,692	798,615	27,719	101,981	48,389
2008	3,024,294	1,875,905	16	1,875,921	235,024	24,961	1,665,858	473,487	884,949	29,516	102,462	48,378
2009	3,116,338	1,931,752	-143	1,931,609	241,388	6,096	1,696,317	462,049	957,972	30,203	103,181	48,072
2010	3,239,093	2,027,046	-184	2,026,862	252,207	-12,245	1,762,410	456,015	1,020,668	31,394	103,176	48,285
2011	3,332,365	2,075,308	98	2,075,406	230,949	-24,964	1,819,493	480,663	1,032,209	32,465	102,646	48,584
2012	3,376,008	2,086,365	-2,143	2,084,222	231,033	-31,163	1,822,026	505,735	1,048,247	33,143	101,861	48,372
2013	3,380,128	2,119,001	9	2,119,010	262,121	-37,397	1,819,492	479,724	1,080,912	33,367	101,302	48,052
2014	3,486,074	2,132,528	-905	2,131,623	266,219	-33,236	1,832,168	516,297	1,137,609	34,929	99,805	47,977
2015	3,580,055	2,207,694	-1,875	2,205,819	278,504	-37,613	1,889,702	531,877	1,158,476	36,191	98,920	48,361
2016	3,722,112	2,270,073	-2,212	2,267,861	286,168	-39,628	1,942,065	575,443	1,204,604	37,869	98,290	48,297
2017	3,788,301	2,340,206	-1,145	2,339,061	294,494	-37,256	2,007,311	559,357	1,221,633	38,967	97,217	48,087
2018	3,900,660	2,412,158	-2,467	2,409,691	306,414	-39,238	2,064,039	567,493	1,269,128	40,462	96,403	48,310
2019	4,016,637	2,471,238	-1,093	2,470,145	315,529	-38,348	2,116,268	587,605	1,312,764	41,971	95,701	47,992
2020	4,282,558	2,453,558	-3,267	2,450,291	319,325	-31,025	2,099,941	578,625	1,603,992	45,163	94,824	45,360
2021	4,500,036	2,531,638	-1,078	2,530,560	329,830	-27,376	2,173,354	571,558	1,755,124	47,576	94,586	45,971

Personal Income and Employment by Area: Dallas-Fort Worth-Arlington, TX

(Thousands of dollars, except as noted.)

Year	Personal income, total	Earnings by place of work			Less: Contributions for government social insurance	Plus: Adjustment for residence	Equals: Net earnings by place of residence	Plus: Dividends, interest, and rent	Plus: Personal current transfer receipts	Per capita personal income (dollars)	Population (persons)	Total employment
		Nonfarm	Farm	Total								
1970	10,545,542	8,981,425	39,410	9,020,835	588,164	-19,523	8,413,148	1,514,566	617,828	4,332	2,434,181	1,192,710
1971	11,277,664	9,452,237	34,789	9,487,026	634,413	11,163	8,863,776	1,674,374	739,514	4,550	2,478,739	1,193,666
1972	12,497,876	10,484,822	47,357	10,532,179	739,267	30,378	9,823,290	1,844,371	830,215	5,010	2,494,430	1,251,641
1973	14,020,526	11,780,249	81,724	11,861,973	960,442	40,291	10,941,822	2,093,376	985,328	5,500	2,549,156	1,329,267
1974	15,872,127	13,242,064	30,445	13,272,509	1,104,244	57,862	12,226,127	2,473,606	1,172,394	6,055	2,621,429	1,373,955
1975	17,701,993	14,554,019	33,749	14,587,768	1,183,094	75,648	13,480,322	2,709,412	1,512,259	6,634	2,668,519	1,372,695
1976	19,776,572	16,538,704	57,461	16,596,165	1,377,182	56,301	15,275,284	2,878,646	1,622,642	7,221	2,738,645	1,432,668
1977	22,134,245	18,929,201	16,900	18,946,101	1,595,697	-66,381	17,284,023	3,149,322	1,700,900	7,927	2,792,291	1,514,786
1978	25,721,166	22,152,524	38,316	22,190,840	1,912,937	-141,898	20,136,005	3,688,265	1,896,896	8,993	2,860,247	1,621,566
1979	29,835,185	25,888,747	41,806	25,930,553	2,339,737	-179,998	23,410,818	4,288,730	2,135,637	10,132	2,944,580	1,722,152
1980	34,682,915	29,899,406	-1,690	29,897,716	2,720,561	-223,281	26,953,874	5,239,358	2,489,683	11,344	3,057,465	1,795,112
1981	40,009,203	34,198,647	49,945	34,248,592	3,347,388	-231,232	30,669,972	6,492,834	2,846,397	12,737	3,141,226	1,877,705
1982	44,545,589	37,397,808	51,598	37,449,406	3,739,342	-287,777	33,422,287	7,874,844	3,248,458	13,685	3,255,044	1,927,039
1983	49,396,186	41,481,125	51,241	41,532,366	4,156,712	-354,822	37,020,832	8,822,543	3,552,811	14,672	3,366,597	1,997,325
1984	56,277,143	47,617,966	46,326	47,664,292	4,904,822	-419,496	42,339,974	10,168,711	3,768,458	16,154	3,483,781	2,168,499
1985	62,493,040	52,831,984	25,465	52,857,449	5,523,559	-497,485	46,836,405	11,579,502	4,077,133	17,240	3,624,952	2,297,002
1986	66,122,416	55,970,190	-844	55,969,346	5,798,886	-554,993	49,615,467	12,057,619	4,449,330	17,576	3,762,028	2,325,559
1987	68,490,940	58,166,909	10,756	58,177,665	5,929,767	-599,226	51,648,672	12,133,200	4,709,068	17,806	3,846,478	2,400,673
1988	72,428,887	61,561,518	13,230	61,574,748	6,426,900	-633,100	54,514,748	12,918,884	4,995,255	18,604	3,893,126	2,433,185
1989	77,232,775	65,389,882	43,067	65,432,949	6,835,300	-703,446	57,894,203	13,824,177	5,514,395	19,537	3,953,105	2,465,294
1990	83,386,617	70,343,790	53,108	70,396,898	7,245,131	-758,136	62,393,631	14,833,249	6,159,737	20,621	4,043,744	2,522,308
1991	86,498,849	73,112,738	48,648	73,161,386	7,719,174	-822,793	64,619,419	14,977,848	6,901,582	20,869	4,144,813	2,546,010
1992	92,983,781	78,418,699	72,152	78,490,851	8,201,798	-897,199	69,391,854	15,428,066	8,163,861	21,976	4,231,065	2,558,964
1993	98,716,611	83,765,367	65,492	83,830,859	8,733,904	-949,600	74,147,355	15,786,457	8,782,799	22,842	4,321,701	2,631,521
1994	105,315,356	89,317,557	76,248	89,393,805	9,447,713	-1,031,161	78,914,931	16,932,416	9,468,009	23,794	4,426,050	2,723,712
1995	113,303,501	95,941,456	33,318	95,974,774	10,164,002	-1,138,505	84,672,267	18,357,783	10,273,451	24,978	4,536,179	2,830,895
1996	123,505,879	104,839,585	25,250	104,864,835	10,969,460	-1,275,518	92,619,857	19,893,805	10,992,217	26,479	4,664,290	2,940,089
1997	135,440,045	116,084,529	67,224	116,151,753	12,087,897	-1,497,919	102,565,937	21,351,954	11,522,154	28,167	4,808,429	3,074,940
1998	149,349,755	129,370,634	36,899	129,407,533	13,297,916	-1,953,563	114,156,054	23,430,675	11,763,026	30,400	4,912,807	3,176,906
1999	159,238,429	139,008,780	91,109	139,099,889	14,342,833	-2,192,533	122,564,523	24,622,073	12,051,833	31,503	5,054,705	3,284,237
2000	176,477,456	154,028,523	38,113	154,066,636	15,627,779	-2,534,723	135,904,134	27,651,439	12,921,883	34,022	5,187,122	3,417,830
2001	184,303,643	160,954,791	63,369	161,018,160	16,143,727	-2,571,751	142,302,682	27,687,666	14,313,295	34,598	5,326,971	3,463,068
2002	185,988,226	161,755,324	58,533	161,813,857	16,157,514	-2,491,473	143,164,870	26,901,281	15,922,075	34,237	5,432,371	3,424,897
2003	190,184,214	163,170,710	120,715	163,291,425	16,662,065	-2,391,183	144,238,177	29,027,310	16,918,727	34,429	5,523,937	3,432,695
2004	198,074,894	169,556,197	129,416	169,685,613	17,465,946	-2,480,993	149,738,674	30,482,147	17,854,073	35,286	5,613,420	3,499,362
2005	215,735,437	181,252,764	111,779	181,364,543	18,485,046	-2,504,296	160,375,201	35,478,806	19,881,430	37,700	5,722,444	3,621,905
2006	237,636,584	198,483,210	107,228	198,590,438	19,567,869	-2,680,185	176,342,384	39,780,868	21,513,332	40,367	5,886,950	3,766,949
2007	251,420,813	206,148,406	96,587	206,244,993	20,664,759	-2,645,344	182,934,890	44,769,817	23,716,106	41,729	6,025,041	3,913,910
2008	271,400,104	214,416,180	24,902	214,441,082	21,309,269	-2,471,859	190,659,954	53,050,005	27,690,145	44,110	6,152,770	3,993,545
2009	253,050,120	200,468,584	8,048	200,476,632	20,884,280	-2,215,233	177,377,119	45,075,700	30,597,301	40,279	6,282,484	3,914,429
2010	267,155,382	210,141,419	25,952	210,167,371	21,613,786	-2,093,595	186,459,990	46,468,028	34,227,364	41,795	6,392,097	3,929,790
2011	297,532,347	228,358,211	11,643	228,369,854	20,178,522	-2,072,338	206,118,994	55,901,775	35,511,578	45,700	6,510,550	4,068,890
2012	315,014,126	244,167,122	88,241	244,255,363	21,302,419	-2,145,123	220,807,821	58,576,157	35,630,148	47,410	6,644,519	4,191,061
2013	324,239,897	257,069,184	61,739	257,130,923	25,309,369	-2,075,291	229,746,263	57,522,396	36,971,238	48,008	6,753,804	4,318,879
2014	349,820,139	275,108,856	-1,574	275,107,282	26,780,160	-2,196,316	246,130,806	64,630,515	39,058,818	50,866	6,877,353	4,464,293
2015	362,498,137	284,546,649	58,547	284,605,196	28,626,543	-2,591,429	253,387,224	67,315,188	41,795,725	51,588	7,026,835	4,634,221
2016	375,008,965	293,557,249	-77,303	293,479,946	30,111,937	-3,103,518	260,264,491	70,828,391	43,916,083	52,254	7,176,620	4,794,739
2017	400,076,019	315,693,873	-141,634	315,552,239	32,064,684	-3,493,915	279,993,640	75,318,516	44,763,863	54,689	7,315,457	4,930,512
2018	429,106,358	336,120,921	-177,434	335,943,487	33,425,147	-3,588,317	298,930,023	83,070,362	47,105,973	57,737	7,432,101	5,085,372
2019	453,135,721	353,910,822	-162,485	353,748,337	35,298,963	-4,188,629	314,260,745	88,892,386	49,982,590	60,053	7,545,583	5,186,048
2020	473,715,898	356,173,047	-152,489	356,020,558	36,248,900	-4,444,049	315,327,609	88,400,057	69,988,232	61,824	7,662,325	5,172,124
2021	517,778,595	389,953,137	-164,866	389,788,271	39,385,833	-5,431,375	344,971,063	93,128,257	79,679,275	66,727	7,759,615	5,392,753

Personal Income and Employment by Area: Dalton, GA

(Thousands of dollars, except as noted.)

Year	Personal income, total	Earnings by place of work			Less: Contributions for government social insurance	Plus: Adjustment for residence	Equals: Net earnings by place of residence	Plus: Dividends, interest, and rent	Plus: Personal current transfer receipts	Per capita personal income (dollars)	Population (persons)	Total employment
		Nonfarm	Farm	Total								
1970	226,414	216,086	1,961	218,047	14,777	-17,244	186,026	23,412	16,976	3,302	68,569	35,168
1971	261,434	250,526	1,661	252,187	17,866	-19,826	214,495	27,731	19,208	3,668	71,282	37,695
1972	308,176	298,195	2,312	300,507	22,166	-23,763	254,578	32,270	21,328	4,181	73,703	41,452
1973	352,394	338,969	6,935	345,904	28,752	-26,394	290,758	36,323	25,313	4,572	77,080	43,738
1974	368,916	350,741	2,108	352,849	30,881	-27,036	294,932	41,509	32,475	4,641	79,491	42,486
1975	390,877	345,986	7,050	353,036	29,680	-25,210	298,146	45,394	47,337	4,936	79,193	39,069
1976	449,453	413,024	6,373	419,397	36,331	-30,444	352,622	49,729	47,102	5,630	79,835	42,562
1977	507,878	477,596	5,544	483,140	41,985	-36,857	404,298	55,433	48,147	6,203	81,872	45,560
1978	569,576	535,049	7,840	542,889	48,285	-40,370	454,234	63,446	51,896	6,826	83,444	47,923
1979	637,591	597,910	6,303	604,213	55,821	-44,599	503,793	73,639	60,159	7,512	84,874	49,185
1980	687,094	633,071	1,856	634,927	59,510	-49,270	526,147	87,986	72,961	8,012	85,754	48,891
1981	753,069	683,023	3,224	686,247	68,680	-56,357	561,210	107,843	84,016	8,679	86,771	48,672
1982	787,997	698,261	4,025	702,286	70,769	-61,810	569,707	125,232	93,058	9,039	87,177	46,909
1983	893,820	817,804	3,407	821,211	84,276	-78,978	657,957	136,877	98,986	10,198	87,649	50,744
1984	999,164	928,458	6,665	935,123	98,633	-94,550	741,940	151,416	105,808	11,188	89,307	54,398
1985	1,076,073	1,005,792	5,828	1,011,620	108,630	-108,117	794,873	167,440	113,760	11,869	90,663	56,119
1986	1,182,219	1,125,642	7,744	1,133,386	123,034	-128,881	881,471	179,902	120,846	12,826	92,171	58,945
1987	1,298,855	1,263,199	4,010	1,267,209	136,072	-153,868	977,269	196,135	125,451	13,766	94,353	62,232
1988	1,406,602	1,369,835	8,831	1,378,666	150,179	-172,975	1,055,512	217,200	133,890	14,606	96,302	65,112
1989	1,523,230	1,447,870	13,693	1,461,563	159,680	-189,612	1,112,271	260,337	150,622	15,570	97,831	66,708
1990	1,594,884	1,517,577	12,135	1,529,712	167,188	-205,558	1,156,966	269,356	168,562	16,117	98,957	67,995
1991	1,652,362	1,551,461	13,775	1,565,236	173,148	-216,677	1,175,411	281,057	195,894	16,460	100,385	66,329
1992	1,809,155	1,739,010	13,431	1,752,441	190,828	-254,775	1,306,838	281,818	220,499	17,769	101,814	69,845
1993	1,941,850	1,898,056	15,688	1,913,744	209,087	-289,727	1,414,930	292,431	234,489	18,755	103,540	73,741
1994	2,082,676	2,027,206	18,282	2,045,488	224,844	-318,611	1,502,033	323,708	256,935	19,615	106,177	76,724
1995	2,188,957	2,099,390	16,696	2,116,086	231,754	-334,129	1,550,203	356,828	281,926	20,124	108,771	78,552
1996	2,344,575	2,229,592	21,771	2,251,363	243,654	-363,782	1,643,927	394,117	306,531	21,109	111,071	80,144
1997	2,455,130	2,355,967	21,618	2,377,585	254,299	-389,889	1,733,397	409,313	312,420	21,600	113,661	81,060
1998	2,629,188	2,544,839	28,777	2,573,616	272,825	-426,690	1,874,101	436,746	318,341	22,780	115,417	82,126
1999	2,710,483	2,652,304	28,180	2,680,484	283,031	-447,055	1,950,398	419,416	340,669	22,970	118,000	83,196
2000	2,892,636	2,859,875	23,481	2,883,356	305,756	-506,969	2,070,631	452,411	369,594	23,914	120,959	87,006
2001	3,213,319	3,134,462	32,936	3,167,398	324,501	-533,712	2,309,185	488,885	415,249	25,911	124,015	85,876
2002	3,311,714	3,220,564	22,658	3,243,222	332,181	-566,386	2,344,655	491,240	475,819	26,240	126,208	86,500
2003	3,453,244	3,369,082	19,089	3,388,171	347,956	-612,609	2,427,606	539,365	486,273	26,879	128,476	86,673
2004	3,568,109	3,517,515	24,635	3,542,150	386,133	-647,205	2,508,812	538,227	521,070	27,174	131,307	88,308
2005	3,567,774	3,535,019	22,486	3,557,505	389,894	-676,733	2,490,878	516,407	560,489	26,648	133,885	89,189
2006	3,656,472	3,595,683	-555	3,595,128	394,120	-711,155	2,489,853	554,041	612,578	26,771	136,581	90,340
2007	3,769,420	3,612,654	8,193	3,620,847	394,960	-741,219	2,484,668	617,917	666,835	27,159	138,792	89,950
2008	3,779,480	3,407,563	19,527	3,427,090	388,889	-695,803	2,342,398	668,788	768,294	26,916	140,415	84,979
2009	3,574,680	3,175,897	15,620	3,191,517	364,657	-674,540	2,152,320	569,118	853,242	25,371	140,897	77,658
2010	3,688,815	3,206,025	9,855	3,215,880	365,007	-657,936	2,192,937	566,351	929,527	25,928	142,272	76,810
2011	3,820,337	3,246,346	3,114	3,249,460	339,828	-698,968	2,210,664	650,032	959,641	26,852	142,272	77,683
2012	3,958,608	3,378,819	34,770	3,413,589	350,837	-678,669	2,384,083	628,122	946,403	27,831	142,237	76,671
2013	4,145,170	3,560,907	45,478	3,606,385	409,424	-697,220	2,499,741	672,143	973,286	29,219	141,864	76,813
2014	4,454,154	3,885,031	53,427	3,938,458	439,833	-806,728	2,691,897	753,592	1,008,665	31,418	141,769	80,170
2015	4,790,243	4,088,154	69,497	4,157,651	458,112	-820,849	2,878,690	880,710	1,030,843	33,628	142,446	81,980
2016	4,908,980	4,231,645	39,115	4,270,760	474,084	-875,707	2,920,969	930,501	1,057,510	34,349	142,913	81,885
2017	5,019,478	4,187,252	55,718	4,242,970	468,044	-773,476	3,001,450	925,060	1,092,968	35,099	143,008	79,926
2018	5,293,413	4,288,054	42,909	4,330,963	478,238	-748,549	3,104,176	1,047,539	1,141,698	37,020	142,988	81,613
2019	5,481,386	4,308,495	28,493	4,336,988	481,357	-666,175	3,189,456	1,119,790	1,172,140	38,282	143,183	79,983
2020	5,940,048	4,315,805	-6,498	4,309,307	485,338	-618,917	3,205,052	1,139,881	1,595,115	41,636	142,665	78,005
2021	6,378,615	4,607,626	27,875	4,635,501	518,550	-704,572	3,412,379	1,185,656	1,780,580	44,668	142,799	80,320

Personal Income and Employment by Area: Danville, IL

(Thousands of dollars, except as noted.)

Year	Personal income, total	Earnings by place of work			Less: Contributions for government social insurance	Plus: Adjustment for residence	Equals: Net earnings by place of residence	Plus: Dividends, interest, and rent	Plus: Personal current transfer receipts	Per capita personal income (dollars)	Population (persons)	Total employment
		Nonfarm	Farm	Total								
1970	373,467	304,412	13,951	318,363	20,397	-10,243	287,723	48,330	37,414	3,846	97,100	43,790
1971	414,577	333,407	21,318	354,725	22,802	-14,798	317,125	52,163	45,289	4,255	97,441	43,260
1972	449,098	370,566	17,581	388,147	26,546	-19,719	341,882	57,540	49,676	4,591	97,815	44,707
1973	529,893	426,433	39,440	465,873	35,525	-26,151	404,197	67,439	58,257	5,404	98,058	46,897
1974	558,284	445,175	38,951	484,126	38,523	-29,029	416,574	75,557	66,153	5,713	97,719	46,993
1975	623,023	472,955	54,161	527,116	39,974	-32,495	454,647	82,867	85,509	6,382	97,623	45,416
1976	674,821	537,858	44,156	582,014	46,452	-40,496	495,066	88,503	91,252	6,874	98,166	46,632
1977	720,640	584,000	41,993	625,993	50,321	-47,384	528,288	98,484	93,868	7,365	97,842	46,973
1978	779,928	650,821	31,194	682,015	57,774	-56,369	567,872	112,597	99,459	7,977	97,772	47,926
1979	841,483	681,808	48,559	730,367	62,548	-62,406	605,413	126,392	109,678	8,682	96,928	47,142
1980	865,521	687,293	14,957	702,250	62,509	-65,522	574,219	155,531	135,771	9,098	95,130	44,925
1981	964,702	726,477	30,391	756,868	71,108	-69,179	616,581	189,404	158,717	10,198	94,596	44,283
1982	1,001,723	724,682	18,848	743,530	72,098	-62,866	608,566	220,820	172,337	10,771	92,998	42,605
1983	1,008,751	753,304	-1,949	751,355	75,918	-61,656	613,781	214,760	180,210	10,875	92,758	42,368
1984	1,131,583	828,630	34,545	863,175	87,063	-66,032	710,080	240,827	180,676	12,281	92,141	42,881
1985	1,161,226	841,809	39,563	881,372	89,976	-63,658	727,738	244,219	189,269	12,679	91,584	42,021
1986	1,186,410	858,317	33,487	891,804	92,516	-59,737	739,551	249,579	197,280	12,959	91,551	42,054
1987	1,223,209	903,088	21,977	925,065	95,654	-58,103	771,308	248,491	203,410	13,455	90,909	42,017
1988	1,269,663	941,167	16,305	957,472	102,026	-53,168	802,278	255,469	211,916	14,134	89,831	42,051
1989	1,359,427	960,779	44,448	1,005,227	105,252	-48,630	851,345	287,066	221,016	15,319	88,740	41,546
1990	1,380,611	968,231	39,532	1,007,763	103,486	-36,920	867,357	270,864	242,390	15,661	88,155	41,527
1991	1,404,343	1,000,442	18,429	1,018,871	109,806	-37,298	871,767	271,671	260,905	15,961	87,986	41,296
1992	1,523,911	1,062,372	42,431	1,104,803	114,270	-39,303	951,230	276,814	295,867	17,328	87,944	41,311
1993	1,554,597	1,077,925	48,604	1,126,529	118,952	-37,074	970,503	278,195	305,899	17,719	87,738	40,834
1994	1,647,161	1,151,333	60,617	1,211,950	128,418	-39,610	1,043,922	290,906	312,333	18,734	87,922	42,042
1995	1,621,843	1,128,310	18,415	1,146,725	126,039	-30,257	990,429	303,657	327,757	18,734	86,570	41,796
1996	1,706,235	1,147,025	47,654	1,194,679	127,040	-27,277	1,040,362	324,652	341,221	20,003	85,298	42,425
1997	1,726,506	1,170,655	32,364	1,203,019	129,080	-23,568	1,050,371	330,870	345,265	20,247	85,274	42,515
1998	1,772,520	1,219,685	15,118	1,234,803	133,571	-25,432	1,075,800	342,825	353,895	20,854	84,996	42,324
1999	1,805,826	1,260,848	10,270	1,271,118	134,904	-19,156	1,117,058	331,548	357,220	21,428	84,276	42,214
2000	1,875,388	1,275,179	29,716	1,304,895	133,817	-9,630	1,161,448	341,114	372,826	22,374	83,821	42,344
2001	1,969,602	1,320,447	30,901	1,351,348	137,411	-2,108	1,211,829	360,413	397,360	23,547	83,646	40,683
2002	2,005,247	1,354,969	18,824	1,373,793	139,447	4,056	1,238,402	342,484	424,361	24,073	83,299	40,062
2003	2,134,731	1,443,235	35,520	1,478,755	149,072	-146	1,329,537	356,758	448,436	25,721	82,996	40,636
2004	2,192,939	1,487,897	60,329	1,548,226	156,192	2,572	1,394,606	330,765	467,568	26,435	82,955	40,029
2005	2,190,817	1,519,771	21,046	1,540,817	166,762	5,600	1,379,655	307,464	503,698	26,482	82,728	40,190
2006	2,278,139	1,572,013	39,951	1,611,964	171,034	9,670	1,450,600	304,205	523,334	27,542	82,715	39,863
2007	2,358,364	1,565,097	59,759	1,624,856	171,456	23,689	1,477,089	314,880	566,395	28,670	82,258	39,718
2008	2,524,780	1,587,287	101,924	1,689,211	175,866	31,123	1,544,468	375,539	604,773	30,816	81,930	39,183
2009	2,514,221	1,561,953	61,794	1,623,747	172,795	23,051	1,474,003	360,476	679,742	30,770	81,710	37,825
2010	2,630,848	1,638,120	78,361	1,716,481	178,474	22,610	1,560,617	347,409	722,822	32,224	81,642	37,284
2011	2,763,271	1,720,222	127,600	1,847,822	169,333	12,707	1,691,196	368,853	703,222	33,936	81,427	38,010
2012	2,753,785	1,751,191	84,428	1,835,619	173,878	12,590	1,674,331	385,654	693,800	34,047	80,881	38,165
2013	2,842,672	1,743,652	156,943	1,900,595	192,010	7,980	1,716,565	399,708	726,399	35,265	80,608	37,345
2014	2,815,524	1,781,113	79,344	1,860,457	196,592	10,082	1,673,947	399,400	742,177	35,463	79,393	37,667
2015	2,858,492	1,819,948	15,585	1,835,533	198,800	11,233	1,647,966	420,777	789,749	36,323	78,696	37,770
2016	2,819,439	1,780,174	41,642	1,821,816	198,057	11,815	1,635,574	395,981	787,884	36,194	77,897	36,637
2017	2,900,331	1,784,546	43,514	1,828,060	199,958	20,567	1,648,669	433,578	818,084	37,654	77,026	35,991
2018	2,948,681	1,809,873	61,972	1,871,845	204,291	25,361	1,692,915	418,467	837,299	38,839	75,921	35,434
2019	2,998,893	1,857,763	37,371	1,895,134	209,900	27,912	1,713,146	432,627	853,120	40,054	74,871	35,082
2020	3,322,909	1,874,518	84,392	1,958,910	213,339	39,149	1,784,720	436,300	1,101,889	44,975	73,883	33,964
2021	3,601,015	1,943,732	143,144	2,086,876	217,399	58,189	1,927,666	431,710	1,241,639	49,265	73,095	34,091

Personal Income and Employment by Area: Daphne-Fairhope-Foley, AL

(Thousands of dollars, except as noted.)

Year	Personal income, total	Earnings by place of work			Less: Contributions for government social insurance	Plus: Adjustment for residence	Equals: Net earnings by place of residence	Plus: Dividends, interest, and rent	Plus: Personal current transfer receipts	Per capita personal income (dollars)	Population (persons)	Total employment
		Nonfarm	Farm	Total								
1970	172,745	79,248	5,789	85,037	6,071	47,185	126,151	28,828	17,766	2,905	59,474	19,749
1971	196,684	89,196	8,786	97,982	6,919	51,482	142,545	33,364	20,775	3,270	60,142	20,505
1972	223,797	104,139	9,606	113,745	8,432	57,438	162,751	37,514	23,532	3,584	62,435	21,727
1973	268,069	121,106	20,473	141,579	11,236	63,826	194,169	45,617	28,283	4,176	64,196	23,015
1974	305,794	137,576	17,877	155,453	13,293	73,014	215,174	55,843	34,777	4,628	66,072	23,738
1975	345,248	151,882	16,280	168,162	14,678	83,503	236,987	63,422	44,839	5,088	67,861	24,458
1976	406,080	180,248	27,854	208,102	17,557	94,603	285,148	71,220	49,712	5,781	70,244	25,750
1977	435,048	202,296	9,603	211,899	19,860	107,108	299,147	82,483	53,418	6,009	72,399	26,965
1978	496,475	218,663	20,914	239,577	21,592	124,081	342,066	95,253	59,156	6,660	74,550	27,291
1979	542,296	244,352	4,309	248,661	24,913	138,082	361,830	109,267	71,199	7,080	76,594	27,875
1980	615,733	263,431	1,749	265,180	26,777	159,044	397,447	134,553	83,733	7,801	78,931	27,777
1981	717,874	291,361	10,495	301,856	32,333	184,421	453,944	168,087	95,843	8,941	80,287	28,722
1982	759,626	306,308	438	306,746	34,707	192,619	464,658	188,246	106,722	9,226	82,331	29,388
1983	844,438	349,814	6,907	356,721	39,188	203,122	520,655	205,632	118,151	10,055	83,978	31,306
1984	940,987	395,399	4,842	400,241	45,369	224,335	579,207	233,008	128,772	10,847	86,752	33,057
1985	1,048,339	437,883	14,040	451,923	49,964	250,708	652,667	255,836	139,836	11,726	89,401	33,969
1986	1,115,365	469,386	9,187	478,573	53,058	270,666	696,181	271,500	147,684	12,215	91,311	34,674
1987	1,182,205	499,048	14,112	513,160	56,032	289,608	746,736	283,649	151,820	12,683	93,214	36,081
1988	1,281,576	528,899	14,640	543,539	61,784	315,329	797,084	316,101	168,391	13,540	94,649	37,654
1989	1,436,895	568,898	18,028	586,926	67,236	347,393	867,083	377,268	192,544	14,937	96,198	38,889
1990	1,566,530	631,608	11,511	643,119	74,864	390,110	958,365	397,921	210,244	15,831	98,955	40,545
1991	1,736,418	697,625	17,516	715,141	82,626	448,657	1,081,172	414,972	240,274	16,954	102,420	42,388
1992	1,930,098	773,910	20,742	794,652	90,355	506,108	1,210,405	441,852	277,841	18,107	106,595	44,246
1993	2,128,721	860,852	26,233	887,085	101,563	564,261	1,349,783	478,258	300,680	19,106	111,416	47,280
1994	2,346,375	965,130	21,661	986,791	116,178	601,469	1,472,082	538,851	335,442	20,129	116,565	50,770
1995	2,557,326	1,073,129	22,922	1,096,051	129,352	621,992	1,588,691	600,128	368,507	21,153	120,896	54,511
1996	2,801,985	1,194,516	23,839	1,218,355	140,649	669,688	1,747,394	652,671	401,920	22,342	125,412	56,932
1997	3,050,203	1,299,527	23,367	1,322,894	154,451	740,059	1,908,502	714,133	427,568	23,434	130,164	60,806
1998	3,313,871	1,498,614	4,949	1,503,563	171,529	745,606	2,077,640	786,855	449,376	24,649	134,444	64,758
1999	3,500,710	1,625,770	20,689	1,646,459	187,352	760,813	2,219,920	809,273	471,517	25,450	137,555	67,472
2000	3,792,123	1,746,938	15,186	1,762,124	199,875	816,514	2,378,763	892,376	520,984	26,829	141,342	69,423
2001	3,942,661	1,808,269	10,662	1,818,931	211,491	828,822	2,436,262	915,814	590,585	27,214	144,875	70,661
2002	4,077,725	1,922,298	3,454	1,925,752	224,876	823,431	2,524,307	902,848	650,570	27,560	147,957	71,892
2003	4,287,483	2,047,201	16,655	2,063,856	240,077	846,720	2,670,499	906,915	710,069	28,299	151,509	73,844
2004	4,801,448	2,264,675	19,135	2,283,810	263,116	884,707	2,905,401	1,113,564	782,483	30,726	156,266	77,691
2005	5,314,389	2,575,798	9,487	2,585,285	298,743	927,632	3,214,174	1,251,830	848,385	32,768	162,183	82,612
2006	5,940,548	2,887,750	17,331	2,905,081	333,566	976,514	3,548,029	1,463,903	928,616	35,335	168,121	87,768
2007	6,311,686	2,994,484	15,845	3,010,329	355,021	1,049,847	3,705,155	1,598,750	1,007,781	36,610	172,404	92,728
2008	6,411,800	2,861,480	10,238	2,871,718	360,128	1,151,309	3,662,899	1,606,947	1,141,954	36,467	175,827	92,684
2009	6,364,898	2,705,574	15,567	2,721,141	344,003	1,248,139	3,625,277	1,483,633	1,255,988	35,478	179,406	89,324
2010	6,768,269	2,794,361	5,419	2,799,780	353,166	1,367,980	3,814,594	1,512,497	1,441,178	36,961	183,121	89,246
2011	7,184,451	2,899,092	8,153	2,907,245	328,267	1,530,395	4,109,373	1,590,251	1,484,827	38,506	186,579	92,000
2012	7,375,651	3,002,939	14,452	3,017,391	337,507	1,568,206	4,248,090	1,624,114	1,503,447	38,778	190,203	93,226
2013	7,612,912	3,197,592	27,060	3,224,652	401,285	1,552,679	4,376,046	1,664,145	1,572,721	39,045	194,978	96,469
2014	8,065,302	3,418,697	8,048	3,426,745	425,022	1,596,350	4,598,073	1,794,080	1,673,149	40,174	200,759	99,807
2015	8,634,950	3,648,986	10,634	3,659,620	452,052	1,690,775	4,898,343	1,928,862	1,807,745	42,137	204,925	103,917
2016	9,161,041	3,879,865	10,776	3,890,641	477,759	1,853,164	5,266,046	2,009,224	1,885,771	43,623	210,004	107,829
2017	9,663,394	4,045,886	15,023	4,060,909	504,607	1,945,053	5,501,355	2,185,499	1,976,540	44,870	215,365	111,624
2018	10,226,651	4,340,497	15,441	4,355,938	548,376	2,044,526	5,852,088	2,253,466	2,121,097	46,247	221,132	115,697
2019	10,986,182	4,592,540	12,740	4,605,280	579,123	2,107,010	6,133,167	2,535,588	2,317,427	48,380	227,079	117,000
2020	11,971,269	4,878,740	18,789	4,897,529	617,791	2,207,909	6,487,647	2,618,212	2,865,410	51,348	233,140	117,257
2021	13,079,505	5,370,893	22,110	5,393,003	672,976	2,425,083	7,145,110	2,738,909	3,195,486	54,659	239,294	122,061

Personal Income and Employment by Area: Davenport-Moline-Rock Island, IA-IL

(Thousands of dollars, except as noted.)

Year	Personal income, total	Earnings by place of work			Less: Contributions for government social insurance	Plus: Adjustment for residence	Equals: Net earnings by place of residence	Plus: Dividends, interest, and rent	Plus: Personal current transfer receipts	Per capita personal income (dollars)	Population (persons)	Total employment
		Nonfarm	Farm	Total								
1970	1,622,020	1,314,949	48,364	1,363,313	86,009	-23,965	1,253,339	247,937	120,744	4,271	379,817	169,173
1971	1,717,581	1,386,972	39,893	1,426,865	93,458	-24,620	1,308,787	267,879	140,915	4,505	381,302	167,145
1972	1,887,827	1,523,131	59,947	1,583,078	108,874	-27,326	1,446,878	288,283	152,666	4,942	382,010	171,157
1973	2,171,907	1,743,142	100,802	1,843,944	145,158	-34,572	1,664,214	329,699	177,994	5,648	384,562	183,158
1974	2,433,004	1,994,591	80,378	2,074,969	173,786	-45,473	1,855,710	376,985	200,309	6,229	390,568	193,442
1975	2,697,281	2,135,977	126,030	2,262,007	182,626	-50,025	2,029,356	417,038	250,887	6,809	396,120	192,380
1976	2,898,322	2,358,686	83,964	2,442,650	206,986	-61,919	2,173,745	443,408	281,169	7,267	398,850	194,882
1977	3,188,957	2,644,316	69,582	2,713,898	233,113	-79,809	2,400,976	489,416	298,565	7,967	400,292	199,126
1978	3,503,443	2,903,381	91,583	2,994,964	265,345	-93,679	2,635,940	544,638	322,865	8,709	402,294	202,184
1979	3,914,573	3,293,948	77,154	3,371,102	315,315	-111,632	2,944,155	610,723	359,695	9,699	403,603	207,010
1980	4,256,874	3,540,230	-3,913	3,536,317	335,077	-124,393	3,076,847	746,302	433,725	10,526	404,420	202,488
1981	4,741,795	3,758,083	68,794	3,826,877	380,316	-124,569	3,321,992	911,027	508,776	11,703	405,162	201,299
1982	4,903,774	3,642,553	38,353	3,680,906	362,166	-108,850	3,209,890	1,088,275	605,609	12,198	402,024	190,760
1983	4,879,252	3,610,918	-51,993	3,558,925	361,772	-102,481	3,094,672	1,118,034	666,546	12,291	396,986	186,120
1984	5,377,191	3,914,382	80,114	3,994,496	403,808	-110,539	3,480,149	1,239,019	658,023	13,686	392,904	190,977
1985	5,568,600	4,057,419	106,178	4,163,597	426,120	-111,729	3,625,748	1,257,944	684,908	14,396	386,807	191,204
1986	5,575,402	4,037,613	73,382	4,110,995	428,583	-101,697	3,580,715	1,285,377	709,310	14,671	380,036	188,955
1987	5,849,134	4,329,220	95,775	4,424,995	455,506	-108,218	3,861,271	1,270,606	717,257	15,625	374,353	191,033
1988	6,030,020	4,507,399	53,648	4,561,047	489,638	-103,667	3,967,742	1,311,630	750,648	16,277	370,464	194,882
1989	6,473,546	4,767,320	78,925	4,846,245	524,236	-105,354	4,216,655	1,463,879	793,012	17,550	368,854	199,096
1990	6,794,051	5,089,042	80,068	5,169,110	563,270	-110,837	4,495,003	1,442,286	856,762	18,446	368,316	203,953
1991	6,970,971	5,230,028	66,233	5,296,261	591,533	-114,757	4,589,971	1,461,014	919,986	18,791	370,975	207,790
1992	7,418,850	5,539,152	105,292	5,644,444	618,884	-119,908	4,905,652	1,486,175	1,027,023	19,860	373,565	207,908
1993	7,521,401	5,620,413	65,738	5,686,151	641,015	-114,245	4,930,891	1,520,586	1,069,924	20,100	374,198	206,295
1994	7,848,215	5,932,866	92,223	6,025,089	686,342	-124,994	5,213,753	1,550,447	1,084,015	20,961	374,425	209,569
1995	8,271,770	6,231,860	16,812	6,248,672	720,540	-130,454	5,397,678	1,712,562	1,161,530	22,059	374,979	214,131
1996	8,843,950	6,549,229	117,691	6,666,920	739,237	-128,012	5,799,671	1,844,775	1,199,504	23,602	374,708	218,500
1997	9,321,653	6,968,091	96,402	7,064,493	794,612	-147,431	6,122,450	1,990,561	1,208,642	24,857	375,006	223,429
1998	9,826,755	7,364,741	70,613	7,435,354	836,377	-148,741	6,450,236	2,114,981	1,261,538	26,166	375,549	229,670
1999	9,931,673	7,513,258	36,182	7,549,440	844,388	-140,449	6,564,603	2,051,921	1,315,149	26,366	376,678	229,932
2000	10,440,393	7,836,990	69,660	7,906,650	871,865	-141,403	6,893,382	2,149,907	1,397,104	27,785	375,763	231,704
2001	10,808,140	8,135,379	59,323	8,194,702	894,376	-153,147	7,147,179	2,146,064	1,514,897	28,855	374,561	228,307
2002	10,989,805	8,343,105	45,070	8,388,175	912,969	-168,561	7,306,645	2,041,135	1,642,025	29,405	373,740	224,701
2003	11,398,626	8,628,909	123,781	8,752,690	945,226	-176,239	7,631,225	2,089,913	1,677,488	30,561	372,975	223,492
2004	12,338,105	9,443,973	166,503	9,610,476	1,021,118	-189,513	8,399,845	2,188,191	1,750,069	33,101	372,740	226,886
2005	12,728,376	9,870,961	71,519	9,942,480	1,085,932	-204,505	8,652,043	2,181,885	1,894,448	34,136	372,876	231,269
2006	13,432,281	10,336,218	68,135	10,404,353	1,127,018	-212,555	9,064,780	2,340,819	2,026,682	35,938	373,762	231,766
2007	14,203,852	10,739,782	136,289	10,876,071	1,181,192	-162,027	9,532,852	2,480,648	2,190,352	37,865	375,121	233,972
2008	15,123,426	11,149,108	196,389	11,345,497	1,237,781	-155,311	9,952,405	2,698,222	2,472,799	40,172	376,467	234,372
2009	14,714,556	10,856,711	88,303	10,945,014	1,212,592	-179,334	9,553,088	2,395,610	2,765,858	38,916	378,108	225,854
2010	15,240,556	11,170,602	70,053	11,240,655	1,253,207	-226,874	9,760,574	2,433,712	3,046,270	40,131	379,773	223,989
2011	16,227,414	11,701,135	249,864	11,950,999	1,185,374	-261,252	10,504,373	2,750,808	2,972,233	42,617	380,773	227,447
2012	16,607,270	12,089,570	157,208	12,246,778	1,213,528	-279,868	10,753,382	2,933,729	2,920,159	43,411	382,560	228,828
2013	16,830,214	12,097,863	408,715	12,506,578	1,367,776	-282,506	10,856,296	2,957,661	3,016,257	43,827	384,016	228,832
2014	16,984,347	12,114,417	214,058	12,328,475	1,363,725	-253,652	10,711,098	3,150,705	3,122,544	43,908	386,816	230,123
2015	17,274,963	12,285,003	31,847	12,316,850	1,378,408	-242,778	10,695,664	3,280,627	3,298,672	44,668	386,743	229,912
2016	17,548,883	12,368,044	95,709	12,463,753	1,407,089	-198,449	10,858,215	3,359,126	3,331,542	45,446	386,144	228,280
2017	18,097,393	12,846,751	77,622	12,924,373	1,468,758	-253,786	11,201,829	3,520,485	3,375,079	46,932	385,612	229,926
2018	18,515,134	13,160,606	102,835	13,263,441	1,514,613	-270,462	11,478,366	3,491,881	3,544,887	48,089	385,016	230,157
2019	18,866,017	13,344,550	71,188	13,415,738	1,553,253	-328,070	11,534,415	3,687,804	3,643,798	49,005	384,985	229,710
2020	20,210,665	13,511,643	159,801	13,671,444	1,591,023	-356,838	11,723,583	3,703,902	4,783,180	52,697	383,526	219,093
2021	21,436,850	14,162,692	344,768	14,507,460	1,639,802	-405,135	12,462,523	3,777,860	5,196,467	56,181	381,568	224,055

Personal Income and Employment by Area: Dayton-Kettering, OH

(Thousands of dollars, except as noted.)

Year	Personal income, total	Earnings by place of work			Less: Contributions for government social insurance	Plus: Adjustment for residence	Equals: Net earnings by place of residence	Plus: Dividends, interest, and rent	Plus: Personal current transfer receipts	Per capita personal income (dollars)	Population (persons)	Total employment
		Nonfarm	Farm	Total								
1970	3,724,442	3,390,457	19,936	3,410,393	206,990	-242,805	2,960,598	543,195	220,649	4,556	817,533	388,647
1971	3,850,553	3,424,747	18,705	3,443,452	213,624	-233,979	2,995,849	585,702	269,002	4,717	816,329	370,912
1972	4,198,442	3,763,377	22,439	3,785,816	249,182	-252,601	3,284,033	616,987	297,422	5,158	813,964	380,981
1973	4,556,792	4,086,845	38,039	4,124,884	313,612	-271,616	3,539,656	671,252	345,884	5,652	806,273	389,418
1974	4,879,893	4,261,889	41,241	4,303,130	335,862	-267,085	3,700,183	748,201	431,509	6,109	798,827	389,620
1975	5,259,095	4,445,463	35,020	4,480,483	342,172	-252,970	3,885,341	818,851	554,903	6,593	797,720	377,791
1976	5,777,472	4,971,522	30,386	5,001,908	397,541	-287,581	4,316,786	876,501	584,185	7,276	794,070	386,876
1977	6,352,071	5,511,820	24,938	5,536,758	443,501	-321,804	4,771,453	971,897	608,721	8,056	788,517	399,513
1978	6,966,972	6,061,433	24,825	6,086,258	502,416	-354,280	5,229,562	1,082,236	655,174	8,835	788,528	414,200
1979	7,679,484	6,636,020	42,521	6,678,541	573,379	-397,072	5,708,090	1,207,651	763,743	9,705	791,260	421,805
1980	8,298,078	6,896,544	27,641	6,924,185	592,645	-405,543	5,925,997	1,424,698	947,383	10,477	792,002	412,506
1981	8,924,098	7,464,360	2,936	7,467,296	684,596	-624,734	6,157,966	1,712,568	1,053,564	11,284	790,829	408,425
1982	9,320,916	7,536,479	14,243	7,550,722	698,140	-622,600	6,229,982	1,868,202	1,222,732	11,856	786,167	394,889
1983	9,944,010	8,060,817	-10,541	8,050,276	778,279	-648,339	6,623,658	2,023,471	1,296,881	12,694	783,366	397,786
1984	11,015,219	9,009,710	36,095	9,045,805	897,233	-720,736	7,427,836	2,248,614	1,338,769	14,018	785,813	418,017
1985	11,794,419	9,735,177	49,998	9,785,175	998,701	-773,045	8,013,429	2,353,247	1,427,743	14,951	788,847	431,975
1986	12,433,030	10,281,818	35,647	10,317,465	1,092,539	-796,345	8,428,581	2,483,916	1,520,533	15,717	791,049	443,823
1987	12,913,874	10,672,036	29,137	10,701,173	1,134,955	-798,189	8,768,029	2,561,987	1,583,858	16,220	796,181	455,751
1988	13,950,371	11,648,723	35,824	11,684,547	1,283,792	-867,320	9,533,435	2,743,295	1,673,641	17,381	802,640	464,150
1989	14,961,083	12,273,783	47,404	12,321,187	1,363,771	-887,701	10,069,715	3,127,133	1,764,235	18,646	802,358	471,695
1990	15,592,863	12,712,259	45,026	12,757,285	1,450,064	-914,708	10,392,513	3,213,970	1,986,380	19,386	804,335	473,295
1991	16,195,814	13,084,446	27,917	13,112,363	1,529,416	-940,617	10,642,330	3,431,142	2,122,342	20,000	809,809	470,098
1992	16,894,463	13,721,775	53,109	13,774,884	1,603,407	-951,356	11,220,121	3,339,092	2,335,250	20,743	814,480	464,432
1993	17,556,271	14,359,306	41,646	14,400,952	1,695,609	-1,043,833	11,661,510	3,491,063	2,403,698	21,491	816,922	469,215
1994	18,396,461	15,117,514	45,918	15,163,432	1,812,080	-1,139,751	12,211,601	3,676,109	2,508,751	22,576	814,885	481,730
1995	19,494,409	15,864,914	30,974	15,895,888	1,915,624	-1,230,619	12,749,645	4,095,089	2,649,675	23,902	815,608	491,268
1996	20,222,281	16,405,037	44,535	16,449,572	1,962,614	-1,282,642	13,204,316	4,276,224	2,741,741	24,837	814,188	492,909
1997	21,220,106	17,230,660	66,260	17,296,920	2,022,001	-1,395,764	13,879,155	4,507,135	2,833,816	26,157	811,250	499,170
1998	22,078,689	17,840,225	46,723	17,886,948	2,030,387	-1,355,259	14,501,302	4,694,587	2,882,800	27,218	811,168	502,538
1999	22,513,807	18,413,785	26,549	18,440,334	2,092,884	-1,391,137	14,956,313	4,590,184	2,967,310	27,863	808,010	497,259
2000	23,657,111	19,185,952	42,182	19,228,134	2,113,710	-1,480,499	15,633,925	4,844,481	3,178,705	29,354	805,938	503,030
2001	24,246,941	19,566,553	48,764	19,615,317	2,150,185	-1,478,645	15,986,487	4,755,223	3,505,231	30,140	804,479	497,721
2002	24,516,363	19,841,703	25,474	19,867,177	2,149,017	-1,479,150	16,239,010	4,530,811	3,746,542	30,482	804,286	488,980
2003	25,014,610	20,321,200	38,325	20,359,525	2,222,736	-1,493,598	16,643,191	4,451,434	3,919,985	31,077	804,926	484,370
2004	25,665,771	21,126,077	53,633	21,179,710	2,333,908	-1,544,812	17,300,990	4,265,089	4,099,692	31,846	805,930	484,036
2005	26,187,589	21,334,814	40,938	21,375,752	2,372,460	-1,579,348	17,423,944	4,423,407	4,340,238	32,541	804,766	482,766
2006	27,604,662	22,097,126	39,182	22,136,308	2,472,685	-1,589,078	18,074,545	4,904,178	4,625,939	34,356	803,498	481,807
2007	28,402,664	22,087,806	45,898	22,133,704	2,471,427	-1,515,255	18,147,022	5,306,401	4,949,241	35,421	801,852	481,030
2008	29,069,279	21,906,106	31,044	21,937,150	2,497,925	-1,426,051	18,013,174	5,441,211	5,614,894	36,327	800,209	471,122
2009	28,431,194	21,007,014	53,882	21,060,896	2,413,732	-1,334,085	17,313,079	4,994,749	6,123,366	35,588	798,895	450,129
2010	29,197,926	21,482,383	44,596	21,526,979	2,433,199	-1,455,977	17,637,803	5,027,856	6,532,267	36,511	799,706	447,825
2011	30,917,378	22,507,133	67,986	22,575,119	2,292,497	-1,540,561	18,742,061	5,490,257	6,685,060	38,599	800,980	454,622
2012	31,762,349	23,291,906	46,807	23,338,713	2,352,969	-1,538,192	19,447,552	5,767,432	6,547,365	39,613	801,814	457,498
2013	32,107,478	23,801,912	82,795	23,884,707	2,607,835	-1,454,647	19,822,225	5,635,089	6,650,164	40,050	801,680	457,954
2014	33,381,806	24,475,179	21,142	24,496,321	2,679,014	-1,450,293	20,367,014	6,055,233	6,959,559	41,558	803,249	463,441
2015	34,617,758	25,206,009	-11,051	25,194,958	2,775,193	-1,405,346	21,014,419	6,357,711	7,245,628	43,116	802,897	470,131
2016	35,449,082	25,779,253	7,371	25,786,624	2,887,651	-1,408,903	21,490,070	6,527,568	7,431,444	44,031	805,086	474,324
2017	36,951,188	26,811,873	26,408	26,838,281	3,056,902	-1,450,516	22,330,863	7,038,915	7,581,410	45,782	807,112	481,866
2018	38,311,115	28,018,887	31,379	28,050,266	3,138,423	-1,476,799	23,435,044	7,095,055	7,781,016	47,336	809,348	487,394
2019	39,746,624	29,022,678	331	29,023,009	3,285,744	-1,590,033	24,147,232	7,472,528	8,126,864	48,913	812,591	488,594
2020	42,788,204	29,759,608	68,554	29,828,162	3,365,303	-1,714,955	24,747,904	7,423,831	10,616,469	52,599	813,475	475,236
2021	45,208,430	31,205,428	96,843	31,302,271	3,470,002	-1,693,207	26,139,062	7,563,830	11,505,538	55,572	813,516	482,216

Personal Income and Employment by Area: Decatur, AL

(Thousands of dollars, except as noted.)

Year	Personal income, total	Earnings by place of work — Nonfarm	Earnings by place of work — Farm	Earnings by place of work — Total	Less: Contributions for government social insurance	Plus: Adjustment for residence	Equals: Net earnings by place of residence	Plus: Dividends, interest, and rent	Plus: Personal current transfer receipts	Per capita personal income (dollars)	Population (persons)	Total employment
1970	350,823	250,850	13,280	264,130	18,331	38,890	284,689	34,748	31,386	3,341	105,018	41,444
1971	375,836	259,423	13,605	273,028	19,308	44,382	298,102	39,856	37,878	3,491	107,661	41,034
1972	407,614	285,521	15,993	301,514	22,367	43,641	322,788	43,186	41,640	3,716	109,678	42,354
1973	453,561	322,270	25,527	347,797	29,339	39,651	358,109	48,194	47,258	4,106	110,455	44,291
1974	492,008	371,689	10,504	382,193	35,236	34,359	381,316	55,450	55,242	4,359	112,864	46,325
1975	564,046	417,398	22,106	439,504	39,305	28,271	428,470	61,781	73,795	4,943	114,103	46,956
1976	623,154	457,488	28,380	485,868	43,614	31,851	474,105	67,845	81,204	5,387	115,667	47,493
1977	691,124	514,088	27,274	541,362	48,987	38,188	530,563	76,445	84,116	5,901	117,115	49,637
1978	781,117	600,536	21,239	621,775	58,622	39,714	602,867	88,721	89,529	6,548	119,287	52,721
1979	892,073	681,679	26,101	707,780	68,697	48,524	687,607	101,203	103,263	7,383	120,822	53,931
1980	957,906	694,627	10,421	705,048	69,838	69,996	705,206	125,596	127,104	7,954	120,435	51,505
1981	1,074,370	752,569	20,057	772,626	81,113	85,280	776,793	154,511	143,066	8,927	120,351	51,147
1982	1,132,143	771,157	14,944	786,101	85,213	92,499	793,387	177,439	161,317	9,350	121,091	49,815
1983	1,222,667	831,192	5,425	836,617	92,272	114,380	858,725	189,193	174,749	10,028	121,928	50,679
1984	1,397,534	927,618	26,803	954,421	104,560	144,518	994,379	215,966	187,189	11,314	123,522	53,337
1985	1,529,018	999,951	19,773	1,019,724	112,814	185,141	1,092,051	237,135	199,832	12,225	125,076	54,919
1986	1,630,068	1,054,073	25,274	1,079,347	118,461	207,277	1,168,163	251,635	210,270	12,883	126,532	56,295
1987	1,721,944	1,131,996	27,374	1,159,370	125,489	211,141	1,245,022	262,010	214,912	13,437	128,146	58,491
1988	1,876,472	1,209,923	41,230	1,251,153	138,353	249,350	1,362,150	289,046	225,276	14,544	129,017	60,490
1989	2,037,815	1,300,380	45,530	1,345,910	149,201	254,361	1,451,070	325,644	261,101	15,656	130,162	62,258
1990	2,174,460	1,404,547	33,469	1,438,016	163,235	260,888	1,535,669	348,035	290,756	16,458	132,118	65,211
1991	2,304,469	1,504,415	46,433	1,550,848	176,515	245,307	1,619,640	361,778	323,051	17,170	134,218	65,427
1992	2,473,319	1,597,818	43,713	1,641,531	184,643	293,168	1,750,056	358,389	364,874	18,192	135,959	65,640
1993	2,564,676	1,682,309	36,775	1,719,084	197,412	288,543	1,810,215	369,975	384,486	18,583	138,014	67,205
1994	2,729,151	1,741,331	51,368	1,792,699	205,850	323,328	1,910,177	409,215	409,759	19,642	138,947	67,605
1995	2,856,699	1,823,949	25,330	1,849,279	217,009	334,812	1,967,082	446,785	442,832	20,346	140,404	69,872
1996	2,969,447	1,911,547	40,469	1,952,016	224,534	300,111	2,027,593	473,629	468,225	20,973	141,587	71,005
1997	3,091,715	2,018,406	42,605	2,061,011	235,839	274,345	2,099,517	498,067	494,131	21,627	142,959	72,474
1998	3,297,266	2,178,344	57,964	2,236,308	251,529	275,818	2,260,597	527,806	508,863	22,867	144,192	74,066
1999	3,406,507	2,286,978	61,927	2,348,905	265,258	259,700	2,343,347	525,032	538,128	23,460	145,207	75,040
2000	3,499,045	2,318,222	43,601	2,361,823	269,729	265,431	2,357,525	560,997	580,523	23,950	146,095	75,786
2001	3,594,818	2,383,860	64,564	2,448,424	281,825	267,944	2,434,543	561,537	598,738	24,529	146,552	75,846
2002	3,598,534	2,328,583	33,728	2,362,311	274,587	316,905	2,404,629	557,029	636,876	24,569	146,464	73,525
2003	3,791,951	2,388,843	53,739	2,442,582	281,069	353,086	2,514,599	597,528	679,824	25,728	147,386	72,553
2004	4,020,793	2,566,223	87,416	2,653,639	298,093	337,421	2,692,967	621,178	706,648	27,292	147,324	74,234
2005	4,193,982	2,645,592	71,149	2,716,741	310,273	371,980	2,778,448	650,830	764,704	28,262	148,399	74,947
2006	4,400,689	2,749,465	17,581	2,767,046	323,724	421,658	2,864,980	698,355	837,354	29,432	149,519	75,300
2007	4,614,571	2,858,385	33,770	2,892,155	340,627	405,916	2,957,444	750,992	906,135	30,623	150,690	77,096
2008	4,777,881	2,873,383	45,725	2,919,108	347,875	370,196	2,941,429	825,221	1,011,231	31,456	151,890	76,549
2009	4,692,235	2,744,270	41,498	2,785,768	332,728	392,252	2,845,292	733,814	1,113,129	30,614	153,269	72,444
2010	4,843,526	2,838,224	29,352	2,867,576	348,004	365,041	2,884,613	756,761	1,202,152	31,460	153,956	71,651
2011	4,935,343	2,928,802	-3,104	2,925,698	321,786	359,850	2,963,762	762,929	1,208,652	32,030	154,084	73,429
2012	5,063,613	3,010,926	14,827	3,025,753	328,454	362,337	3,059,636	780,405	1,223,572	32,896	153,930	73,498
2013	5,165,110	3,047,560	77,532	3,125,092	375,728	366,582	3,115,946	791,919	1,257,245	33,720	153,178	73,771
2014	5,365,704	3,136,405	41,926	3,178,331	380,347	402,190	3,200,174	868,094	1,297,436	34,735	154,475	73,321
2015	5,437,548	3,109,510	40,405	3,149,915	382,314	421,717	3,189,318	854,246	1,393,984	35,229	154,349	72,990
2016	5,444,362	3,188,433	-5,487	3,182,946	391,683	399,882	3,191,145	831,304	1,421,913	35,224	154,563	73,266
2017	5,625,989	3,255,516	14,061	3,269,577	402,451	432,155	3,299,281	886,493	1,440,215	36,388	154,610	73,930
2018	5,869,038	3,466,521	-326	3,466,195	432,205	410,613	3,444,603	933,146	1,491,289	37,834	155,126	75,682
2019	6,192,449	3,734,495	-13,108	3,721,387	460,990	363,928	3,624,325	1,020,800	1,547,324	39,731	155,859	77,102
2020	6,715,815	3,960,837	-32,190	3,928,647	491,195	353,524	3,790,976	1,043,334	1,881,505	42,940	156,399	76,608
2021	7,294,383	4,187,933	46,411	4,234,344	511,607	357,054	4,079,791	1,071,846	2,142,746	46,533	156,758	77,668

Personal Income and Employment by Area: Decatur, IL

(Thousands of dollars, except as noted.)

Year	Personal income, total	Earnings by place of work			Less: Contributions for government social insurance	Plus: Adjustment for residence	Equals: Net earnings by place of residence	Plus: Dividends, interest, and rent	Plus: Personal current transfer receipts	Per capita personal income (dollars)	Population (persons)	Total employment
		Nonfarm	Farm	Total								
1970	534,200	488,789	10,288	499,077	34,906	-46,430	417,741	72,420	44,039	4,277	124,905	61,590
1971	572,760	516,740	12,685	529,425	37,852	-49,155	442,418	77,520	52,822	4,572	125,278	60,980
1972	620,388	568,459	10,017	578,476	43,869	-56,878	477,729	84,808	57,851	4,954	125,241	62,469
1973	694,282	625,380	23,435	648,815	55,686	-63,795	529,334	95,765	69,183	5,471	126,910	65,047
1974	769,313	698,627	25,338	723,965	64,811	-74,750	584,404	107,382	77,527	6,022	127,752	66,355
1975	841,296	730,642	37,107	767,749	66,126	-78,732	622,891	118,966	99,439	6,511	129,218	65,268
1976	919,355	820,774	28,793	849,567	75,820	-90,491	683,256	126,297	109,802	7,088	129,701	66,311
1977	1,002,082	904,795	28,199	932,994	83,754	-101,449	747,791	139,167	115,124	7,628	131,366	68,395
1978	1,101,786	1,018,082	21,022	1,039,104	96,485	-117,748	824,871	155,806	121,109	8,321	132,404	69,932
1979	1,176,523	1,073,949	26,143	1,100,092	105,044	-122,398	872,650	171,192	132,681	8,889	132,364	69,000
1980	1,292,317	1,153,101	7,733	1,160,834	112,300	-137,072	911,462	217,420	163,435	9,850	131,205	67,250
1981	1,445,131	1,231,812	25,701	1,257,513	128,901	-143,184	985,428	271,043	188,660	11,091	130,295	67,071
1982	1,488,283	1,199,761	17,011	1,216,772	126,890	-127,184	962,698	310,319	215,266	11,583	128,485	63,475
1983	1,479,684	1,195,349	-9,713	1,185,636	127,257	-116,645	941,734	310,069	227,881	11,657	126,932	60,376
1984	1,647,591	1,339,794	19,603	1,359,397	148,894	-127,377	1,083,126	343,648	220,817	13,073	126,033	62,722
1985	1,723,662	1,400,256	24,463	1,424,719	158,147	-130,489	1,136,083	355,470	232,109	13,793	124,970	62,271
1986	1,765,939	1,440,701	21,468	1,462,169	163,100	-147,547	1,151,522	367,872	246,545	14,384	122,775	62,625
1987	1,839,902	1,523,430	18,364	1,541,794	169,262	-158,174	1,214,358	373,331	252,213	15,265	120,527	62,642
1988	1,918,551	1,601,787	11,177	1,612,964	183,047	-152,525	1,277,392	379,486	261,673	16,119	119,024	63,093
1989	2,079,085	1,680,742	25,595	1,706,337	192,223	-159,311	1,354,803	443,696	280,586	17,661	117,723	64,147
1990	2,151,903	1,773,585	18,461	1,792,046	197,032	-159,738	1,435,276	412,249	304,378	18,350	117,271	64,900
1991	2,189,750	1,806,697	10,554	1,817,251	206,416	-158,589	1,452,246	408,214	329,290	18,560	117,984	65,857
1992	2,351,131	1,879,588	30,313	1,909,901	209,510	-161,039	1,539,352	441,003	370,776	19,875	118,297	65,119
1993	2,396,054	1,943,611	21,164	1,964,775	220,566	-169,068	1,575,141	430,571	390,342	20,317	117,933	65,228
1994	2,467,381	2,005,041	35,406	2,040,447	229,876	-175,665	1,634,906	437,672	394,803	21,001	117,490	65,479
1995	2,543,005	2,032,617	4,948	2,037,565	232,692	-173,821	1,631,052	494,258	417,695	21,682	117,289	65,836
1996	2,719,215	2,195,898	35,233	2,231,131	248,948	-199,862	1,782,321	498,177	438,717	23,326	116,573	68,553
1997	2,784,270	2,245,218	30,525	2,275,743	253,983	-206,579	1,815,181	519,520	449,569	24,063	115,706	68,850
1998	2,929,888	2,386,526	12,501	2,399,027	267,200	-221,328	1,910,499	556,805	462,584	25,377	115,453	68,933
1999	3,107,355	2,614,091	13,372	2,627,463	285,856	-247,578	2,094,029	541,666	471,660	26,987	115,142	71,554
2000	3,188,681	2,631,495	22,768	2,654,263	285,957	-251,727	2,116,579	579,270	492,832	27,849	114,499	71,803
2001	3,438,979	2,814,876	24,597	2,839,473	294,524	-223,745	2,321,204	586,433	531,342	30,272	113,604	68,070
2002	3,440,047	2,819,463	17,532	2,836,995	287,827	-192,312	2,356,856	503,095	580,096	30,561	112,564	65,473
2003	3,401,497	2,766,736	20,436	2,787,172	293,082	-195,778	2,298,312	504,078	599,107	30,487	111,572	64,829
2004	3,550,126	2,836,818	49,960	2,886,778	312,426	-192,341	2,382,011	551,997	616,118	31,931	111,181	65,063
2005	3,634,551	2,962,110	23,611	2,985,721	332,328	-216,240	2,437,153	535,784	661,614	32,719	111,083	65,139
2006	3,832,697	3,098,243	30,660	3,128,903	342,451	-200,649	2,585,803	566,924	679,970	34,589	110,808	65,741
2007	4,078,571	3,264,086	51,210	3,315,296	363,188	-213,932	2,738,176	596,019	744,376	36,826	110,751	66,941
2008	4,304,123	3,328,281	69,384	3,397,665	372,411	-190,324	2,834,930	666,048	803,145	38,920	110,588	66,551
2009	4,290,563	3,222,605	49,791	3,272,396	359,957	-170,022	2,742,417	650,589	897,557	38,747	110,732	64,187
2010	4,347,860	3,268,988	47,053	3,316,041	361,653	-190,080	2,764,308	618,896	964,656	39,246	110,786	63,818
2011	4,585,960	3,422,130	84,198	3,506,328	341,987	-196,861	2,967,480	691,201	927,279	41,427	110,699	65,204
2012	4,567,477	3,463,655	36,223	3,499,878	347,002	-257,607	2,895,269	731,779	940,429	41,461	110,162	64,625
2013	4,683,322	3,447,799	128,119	3,575,918	385,338	-224,454	2,966,126	733,180	984,016	42,733	109,596	63,050
2014	4,793,189	3,700,426	47,960	3,748,386	405,199	-283,230	3,059,957	735,756	997,476	44,033	108,855	63,088
2015	4,744,109	3,781,403	12,306	3,793,709	414,250	-438,634	2,940,825	753,796	1,049,488	44,027	107,755	63,016
2016	4,758,752	3,687,506	71,280	3,758,786	411,908	-429,229	2,917,649	783,503	1,057,600	44,544	106,832	62,579
2017	4,770,081	3,715,513	31,844	3,747,357	417,829	-441,544	2,887,984	788,899	1,093,198	45,019	105,958	62,135
2018	4,985,862	3,896,810	42,681	3,939,491	438,946	-462,929	3,037,616	824,650	1,123,596	47,451	105,075	62,219
2019	4,968,610	3,863,263	21,926	3,885,189	435,401	-437,067	3,012,721	792,552	1,163,337	47,492	104,620	60,486
2020	5,369,381	3,830,514	47,886	3,878,400	430,628	-393,707	3,054,065	789,852	1,525,464	51,804	103,647	57,277
2021	5,792,317	4,086,252	88,522	4,174,774	449,398	-438,916	3,286,460	797,513	1,708,344	56,548	102,432	57,552

Personal Income and Employment by Area: Deltona-Daytona Beach-Ormond Beach, FL

(Thousands of dollars, except as noted.)

| | | Derivation of personal income | | | | | | | | | | |
| | | Earnings by place of work | | | Less: Contributions for government social insurance | Plus: Adjustment for residence | Equals: Net earnings by place of residence | Plus: Dividends, interest, and rent | Plus: Personal current transfer receipts | Per capita personal income (dollars) | Population (persons) | Total employment |
Year	Personal income, total	Nonfarm	Farm	Total								
1970	639,900	359,669	9,803	369,472	23,287	19,725	365,910	176,934	97,056	3,659	174,894	64,013
1971	714,677	399,988	11,223	411,211	27,196	20,456	404,471	196,772	113,434	3,928	181,923	67,875
1972	817,755	468,530	13,503	482,033	33,731	21,860	470,162	217,774	129,819	4,311	189,672	74,167
1973	968,502	563,638	17,467	581,105	46,286	24,516	559,335	252,842	156,325	4,748	203,993	82,359
1974	1,098,055	630,594	16,556	647,150	54,411	24,871	617,610	296,592	183,853	5,058	217,106	86,169
1975	1,220,491	667,839	21,824	689,663	56,789	26,874	659,748	328,800	231,943	5,424	225,008	85,659
1976	1,339,947	731,492	21,117	752,609	62,502	29,616	719,723	364,031	256,193	5,820	230,241	86,843
1977	1,500,427	811,580	19,171	830,751	69,862	33,186	794,075	420,703	285,649	6,309	237,833	91,275
1978	1,738,599	949,251	21,542	970,793	83,901	41,409	928,301	494,354	315,944	7,044	246,836	98,192
1979	2,025,975	1,099,207	20,979	1,120,186	102,201	48,652	1,066,637	590,349	368,989	7,767	260,852	104,567
1980	2,428,260	1,247,869	27,051	1,274,920	117,822	57,387	1,214,485	768,251	445,524	8,906	272,648	110,011
1981	2,857,102	1,397,086	27,496	1,424,582	142,423	77,320	1,359,479	972,134	525,489	10,059	284,026	114,209
1982	3,113,811	1,482,872	40,034	1,522,906	156,730	98,522	1,464,698	1,052,862	596,251	10,557	294,958	117,353
1983	3,493,310	1,657,339	44,242	1,701,581	174,334	122,416	1,649,663	1,181,022	662,625	11,440	305,348	123,065
1984	3,914,893	1,897,103	42,595	1,939,698	204,642	151,886	1,886,942	1,328,747	699,204	12,390	315,969	131,569
1985	4,327,149	2,124,848	40,643	2,165,491	233,859	180,917	2,112,549	1,455,460	759,140	13,198	327,855	140,900
1986	4,727,208	2,333,911	44,216	2,378,127	263,237	216,896	2,331,786	1,572,591	822,831	13,892	340,285	148,201
1987	5,121,555	2,596,306	41,088	2,637,394	288,771	257,582	2,606,205	1,637,436	877,914	14,445	354,554	149,553
1988	5,660,854	2,839,151	48,483	2,887,634	327,682	305,066	2,865,018	1,810,956	984,880	15,312	369,706	156,611
1989	6,229,772	2,983,452	47,893	3,031,345	355,332	356,069	3,032,082	2,109,174	1,088,516	16,207	384,379	156,972
1990	6,652,633	3,154,811	47,618	3,202,429	369,846	415,168	3,247,751	2,209,852	1,195,030	16,480	403,674	155,591
1991	6,874,294	3,272,734	56,995	3,329,729	387,560	429,510	3,371,679	2,166,372	1,336,243	16,541	415,595	155,691
1992	7,283,319	3,494,452	64,726	3,559,178	412,271	472,100	3,619,007	2,149,206	1,515,106	17,108	425,733	156,162
1993	7,705,254	3,738,673	61,361	3,800,034	440,756	509,667	3,868,945	2,202,018	1,634,291	17,693	435,486	162,045
1994	8,171,784	3,947,259	62,090	4,009,349	474,971	547,248	4,081,626	2,337,286	1,752,872	18,350	445,335	166,426
1995	8,781,837	4,221,394	59,703	4,281,097	508,047	583,368	4,356,418	2,531,935	1,893,484	19,367	453,432	173,778
1996	9,356,269	4,469,265	59,170	4,528,435	529,476	643,166	4,642,125	2,710,889	2,003,255	20,315	460,565	177,992
1997	9,917,969	4,680,035	67,347	4,747,382	554,799	724,253	4,916,836	2,904,405	2,096,728	21,062	470,889	180,114
1998	10,488,885	4,883,458	64,760	4,948,218	575,459	819,196	5,191,955	3,131,916	2,165,014	21,898	478,995	183,443
1999	10,975,597	5,256,778	67,523	5,324,301	610,568	906,693	5,620,426	3,107,933	2,247,238	22,551	486,692	187,376
2000	11,826,743	5,592,601	65,783	5,658,384	646,447	1,018,547	6,030,484	3,417,991	2,378,268	23,868	495,514	192,200
2001	12,992,119	6,385,296	66,948	6,452,244	718,318	1,152,404	6,886,330	3,490,315	2,615,474	25,725	505,047	214,468
2002	13,661,997	6,868,317	61,795	6,930,112	767,907	1,267,241	7,429,446	3,432,479	2,800,072	26,469	516,153	220,863
2003	14,600,507	7,427,610	56,442	7,484,052	830,139	1,402,101	8,056,014	3,565,384	2,979,109	27,599	529,021	229,419
2004	15,968,202	8,046,828	62,350	8,109,178	911,750	1,589,305	8,786,733	3,926,132	3,255,337	29,233	546,232	239,566
2005	17,299,602	8,583,049	75,173	8,658,222	991,792	1,948,377	9,614,807	4,128,023	3,556,772	30,711	563,305	253,529
2006	18,725,849	9,191,135	66,248	9,257,383	1,086,550	2,186,277	10,357,110	4,509,960	3,858,779	32,337	579,087	263,121
2007	19,776,475	9,231,634	69,172	9,300,806	1,114,930	2,390,241	10,576,117	5,105,003	4,095,355	33,551	589,451	265,560
2008	20,078,673	8,903,733	62,592	8,966,325	1,109,375	2,467,273	10,324,223	5,175,111	4,579,339	33,979	590,912	256,904
2009	18,915,645	8,300,641	67,032	8,367,673	1,062,645	2,251,835	9,556,863	4,370,089	4,988,693	32,094	589,388	244,590
2010	19,901,729	8,613,124	66,529	8,679,653	1,084,782	2,231,923	9,826,794	4,670,547	5,404,388	33,702	590,527	241,576
2011	20,542,528	8,759,670	58,183	8,817,853	997,861	2,196,722	10,016,714	4,939,203	5,586,611	34,698	592,031	245,674
2012	21,363,467	9,239,490	71,384	9,310,874	1,051,010	2,333,144	10,593,008	5,154,917	5,615,542	35,895	595,172	249,416
2013	21,537,186	9,377,363	54,447	9,431,810	1,199,113	2,377,465	10,610,162	5,098,926	5,828,098	35,863	600,547	254,046
2014	22,827,216	9,820,246	55,773	9,876,019	1,256,747	2,467,589	11,086,861	5,588,879	6,151,476	37,685	605,730	261,476
2015	24,062,439	10,318,596	82,428	10,401,024	1,314,586	2,642,812	11,729,250	5,790,158	6,543,031	38,965	617,539	269,031
2016	25,504,540	10,917,067	76,722	10,993,789	1,394,128	2,967,512	12,567,173	6,054,765	6,882,602	40,377	631,664	278,026
2017	27,146,429	11,482,102	95,177	11,577,279	1,468,787	3,203,600	13,312,092	6,575,012	7,259,325	42,211	643,106	287,061
2018	28,720,440	12,134,500	87,326	12,221,826	1,571,152	3,440,275	14,090,949	7,018,235	7,611,256	44,007	652,635	296,317
2019	31,307,208	12,701,211	85,764	12,786,975	1,671,340	3,900,942	15,016,577	8,191,498	8,099,133	47,312	661,722	299,786
2020	33,080,822	12,953,463	78,138	13,031,601	1,730,562	3,612,596	14,913,635	8,272,157	9,895,030	49,310	670,869	300,281
2021	36,706,507	14,320,584	69,963	14,390,547	1,868,092	4,480,039	17,002,494	8,545,981	11,158,032	53,559	685,344	312,746

Personal Income and Employment by Area: Denver-Aurora-Lakewood, CO

(Thousands of dollars, except as noted.)

Year	Personal income, total	Earnings by place of work			Less: Contributions for government social insurance	Plus: Adjustment for residence	Equals: Net earnings by place of residence	Plus: Dividends, interest, and rent	Plus: Personal current transfer receipts	Per capita personal income (dollars)	Population (persons)	Total employment
		Nonfarm	Farm	Total								
1970	5,351,690	4,403,071	26,626	4,429,697	270,949	-109,466	4,049,282	932,879	369,529	4,756	1,125,162	567,136
1971	6,094,357	5,053,265	23,366	5,076,631	320,688	-131,908	4,624,035	1,042,520	427,802	5,241	1,162,772	597,433
1972	6,853,290	5,762,156	25,378	5,787,534	387,316	-157,136	5,243,082	1,139,174	471,034	5,684	1,205,736	638,174
1973	7,737,318	6,568,662	24,903	6,593,565	508,353	-191,006	5,894,206	1,294,503	548,609	6,200	1,247,871	688,969
1974	8,578,515	7,183,300	32,259	7,215,559	566,765	-208,214	6,440,580	1,498,373	639,562	6,793	1,262,795	697,029
1975	9,496,789	7,791,838	37,955	7,829,793	597,161	-223,994	7,008,638	1,672,380	815,771	7,387	1,285,565	696,348
1976	10,499,533	8,708,263	20,824	8,729,087	680,395	-253,921	7,794,771	1,810,821	893,941	7,975	1,316,528	721,876
1977	11,794,472	9,896,069	23,133	9,919,202	779,024	-298,472	8,841,706	2,012,975	939,791	8,778	1,343,631	763,237
1978	13,650,331	11,591,379	23,197	11,614,576	936,019	-357,878	10,320,679	2,313,138	1,016,514	9,819	1,390,221	821,600
1979	15,561,186	13,377,621	13,171	13,390,792	1,137,696	-454,110	11,798,986	2,628,492	1,133,708	10,866	1,432,057	870,090
1980	17,850,113	15,219,049	25,601	15,244,650	1,310,693	-561,062	13,372,895	3,178,064	1,299,154	12,218	1,460,960	901,316
1981	20,573,043	17,376,595	11,188	17,387,783	1,620,340	-624,457	15,142,986	3,907,120	1,522,937	13,734	1,497,985	939,574
1982	22,833,423	19,151,580	6,212	19,157,792	1,831,815	-650,748	16,675,229	4,438,741	1,719,453	14,815	1,541,261	968,403
1983	24,592,766	20,348,236	26,176	20,374,412	1,974,064	-642,135	17,758,213	4,945,791	1,888,762	15,578	1,578,689	980,047
1984	26,831,886	22,248,352	14,552	22,262,904	2,229,228	-642,135	19,391,541	5,453,548	1,986,797	16,768	1,600,224	1,034,156
1985	28,530,685	23,602,827	19,681	23,622,508	2,418,292	-672,310	20,531,906	5,920,363	2,078,416	17,578	1,623,121	1,054,857
1986	29,500,834	24,316,255	19,923	24,336,178	2,515,287	-662,969	21,157,922	6,110,522	2,232,390	18,018	1,637,259	1,047,201
1987	30,299,202	24,797,776	29,466	24,827,242	2,545,953	-614,437	21,666,852	6,212,106	2,420,244	18,424	1,644,586	1,033,523
1988	31,823,983	26,000,447	28,334	26,028,781	2,755,193	-606,011	22,667,577	6,597,220	2,559,186	19,425	1,638,280	1,053,281
1989	34,369,476	27,507,728	22,435	27,530,163	2,951,815	-592,139	23,986,209	7,529,017	2,854,250	20,965	1,639,407	1,065,789
1990	36,448,193	29,346,793	14,816	29,361,609	3,221,649	-583,435	25,556,525	7,824,039	3,067,629	21,983	1,658,024	1,084,091
1991	38,680,251	31,355,518	10,303	31,365,821	3,524,055	-567,243	27,274,523	8,020,708	3,385,020	22,722	1,702,298	1,108,061
1992	41,775,503	34,248,653	29,343	34,277,996	3,808,347	-593,442	29,876,207	8,103,078	3,796,218	23,723	1,760,945	1,129,013
1993	45,261,221	37,206,046	43,203	37,249,249	4,179,058	-586,670	32,483,521	8,696,584	4,081,116	24,878	1,819,298	1,174,291
1994	48,525,423	39,521,899	16,130	39,538,029	4,464,304	-495,940	34,577,785	9,619,306	4,328,332	26,048	1,862,948	1,223,582
1995	52,734,135	42,410,544	30,701	42,441,245	4,763,892	-484,530	37,192,823	10,696,646	4,844,666	27,600	1,910,680	1,259,599
1996	56,935,003	45,859,517	20,003	45,879,520	5,092,702	-533,473	40,253,345	11,656,008	5,025,650	29,055	1,959,552	1,304,522
1997	61,360,455	49,757,078	27,672	49,784,750	5,494,671	-566,941	43,723,138	12,573,481	5,063,836	30,494	2,012,227	1,362,615
1998	68,316,730	55,481,178	24,582	55,505,760	5,730,471	-321,911	49,453,378	13,762,074	5,101,278	33,146	2,061,091	1,421,735
1999	73,638,655	61,510,032	28,850	61,538,882	6,276,909	-523,419	54,738,554	13,510,977	5,389,124	34,759	2,118,555	1,465,962
2000	82,670,387	68,859,102	24,780	68,883,882	6,951,624	-58,794	61,873,464	15,104,120	5,692,803	38,080	2,170,977	1,523,011
2001	86,017,423	71,556,760	36,317	71,593,077	7,264,826	-212,803	64,115,448	15,587,121	6,314,854	38,768	2,218,759	1,518,724
2002	86,527,862	72,209,192	32,856	72,242,048	7,553,325	-468,830	64,219,893	15,207,621	7,100,348	38,172	2,266,781	1,521,825
2003	87,732,173	72,917,388	19,829	72,937,217	7,660,597	-577,409	64,699,211	15,587,235	7,445,727	38,397	2,284,876	1,510,967
2004	90,688,100	75,630,328	49,809	75,680,137	8,141,576	-543,554	66,995,007	15,972,691	7,720,402	39,347	2,304,818	1,533,283
2005	96,755,545	80,100,444	51,162	80,151,606	8,620,198	-599,239	70,932,169	17,561,251	8,262,125	41,477	2,332,749	1,571,107
2006	105,268,755	85,712,069	39,026	85,751,095	9,141,048	-744,474	75,865,573	20,499,524	8,903,658	44,339	2,374,194	1,607,028
2007	111,377,576	89,279,766	56,272	89,336,038	9,577,780	-728,483	79,029,775	22,811,630	9,536,171	46,049	2,418,686	1,664,565
2008	115,107,640	90,970,030	42,545	91,012,575	10,039,912	-856,210	80,116,453	23,647,806	11,343,381	46,716	2,463,971	1,683,596
2009	108,013,503	84,735,263	52,534	84,787,797	9,653,356	-545,651	74,588,790	20,772,450	12,652,263	43,043	2,509,417	1,643,661
2010	111,610,909	87,355,388	46,177	87,401,565	9,763,596	-1,000,570	76,637,399	20,591,285	14,382,225	43,690	2,554,588	1,637,488
2011	123,297,104	93,772,072	83,325	93,855,397	9,232,256	-858,639	83,764,502	24,712,338	14,820,264	47,363	2,603,261	1,672,982
2012	131,697,083	100,065,475	55,855	100,121,330	9,746,788	-999,438	89,375,104	27,462,861	14,859,118	49,680	2,650,895	1,715,507
2013	139,868,643	110,111,704	50,019	110,161,723	11,438,220	-935,029	97,788,474	26,643,466	15,436,703	51,775	2,701,454	1,776,516
2014	153,166,428	120,305,792	44,865	120,350,657	12,365,706	-936,535	107,048,416	29,586,281	16,531,731	55,771	2,746,356	1,843,962
2015	159,472,464	123,552,119	52,891	123,605,010	13,099,799	-1,328,924	109,176,287	32,275,103	18,021,074	56,888	2,803,288	1,917,066
2016	161,690,505	124,491,193	30,512	124,521,705	13,590,775	-1,523,458	109,407,472	33,633,794	18,649,239	56,832	2,845,074	1,981,837
2017	174,497,172	136,458,765	19,549	136,478,314	14,468,916	-1,732,124	120,277,274	35,242,303	18,977,595	60,632	2,877,961	2,030,495
2018	188,007,218	146,708,683	19,177	146,727,860	15,439,263	-1,677,749	129,610,848	37,910,934	20,485,436	64,477	2,915,881	2,088,812
2019	201,953,560	156,003,504	24,284	156,027,788	16,320,450	-1,964,733	137,742,605	42,732,959	21,477,996	68,591	2,944,333	2,114,572
2020	212,982,610	159,402,681	18,884	159,421,565	16,691,217	-2,493,393	140,236,955	43,014,558	29,731,097	71,728	2,969,289	2,065,836
2021	232,306,241	175,246,078	40,697	175,286,775	17,865,632	-2,975,365	154,445,778	44,808,343	33,052,120	78,150	2,972,566	2,136,923

Personal Income and Employment by Area: Des Moines-West Des Moines, IA

(Thousands of dollars, except as noted.)

		Derivation of personal income										
		Earnings by place of work			Less: Contributions for government social insurance	Plus: Adjustment for residence	Equals: Net earnings by place of residence	Plus: Dividends, interest, and rent	Plus: Personal current transfer receipts	Per capita personal income (dollars)	Population (persons)	Total employment
Year	Personal income, total	Nonfarm	Farm	Total								
1970	1,603,428	1,319,167	51,333	1,370,500	96,859	-41,294	1,232,347	244,005	127,076	4,399	364,467	187,011
1971	1,728,848	1,425,631	40,576	1,466,207	108,259	-44,687	1,313,261	269,095	146,492	4,675	369,809	189,174
1972	1,914,734	1,578,983	58,300	1,637,283	126,616	-50,454	1,460,213	294,837	159,684	5,130	373,239	195,315
1973	2,163,689	1,751,335	112,447	1,863,782	162,979	-55,698	1,645,105	331,931	186,653	5,706	379,164	203,486
1974	2,366,096	1,954,339	64,587	2,018,926	189,351	-62,567	1,767,008	380,750	218,338	6,173	383,309	207,989
1975	2,651,254	2,154,655	73,588	2,228,243	203,688	-68,675	1,955,880	419,829	275,545	6,864	386,229	211,349
1976	2,913,692	2,387,712	65,152	2,452,864	226,760	-73,641	2,152,463	455,013	306,216	7,493	388,848	218,073
1977	3,212,935	2,686,172	31,862	2,718,034	252,881	-83,121	2,382,032	510,565	320,338	8,276	388,226	226,273
1978	3,615,525	2,991,778	80,810	3,072,588	291,525	-91,193	2,689,870	572,962	352,693	9,267	390,158	234,444
1979	4,038,288	3,388,301	49,838	3,438,139	344,884	-101,732	2,991,523	653,053	393,712	10,344	390,395	241,384
1980	4,371,573	3,576,978	15,720	3,592,698	361,661	-108,243	3,122,794	782,119	466,660	11,133	392,658	241,141
1981	4,841,822	3,822,173	53,719	3,875,892	411,680	-115,397	3,348,815	957,537	535,470	12,303	393,561	236,774
1982	5,152,143	3,949,405	32,174	3,981,579	427,680	-117,920	3,435,979	1,108,870	607,294	13,122	392,625	233,881
1983	5,397,524	4,196,729	-8,792	4,187,937	454,509	-126,404	3,607,024	1,140,814	649,686	13,712	393,623	236,788
1984	5,880,834	4,583,650	28,443	4,612,093	510,009	-137,872	3,964,212	1,256,609	660,013	14,893	394,875	244,988
1985	6,164,620	4,820,407	41,488	4,861,895	544,317	-146,572	4,171,006	1,292,471	701,143	15,567	395,994	249,172
1986	6,445,693	5,073,675	59,709	5,133,384	586,402	-156,769	4,390,213	1,328,168	727,312	16,236	397,004	252,303
1987	6,840,440	5,467,207	79,243	5,546,450	629,331	-171,959	4,745,160	1,357,226	738,054	17,101	399,998	259,847
1988	7,390,708	6,023,074	39,021	6,062,095	711,416	-193,561	5,157,118	1,454,443	779,147	18,256	404,844	270,261
1989	8,040,434	6,483,734	93,387	6,577,121	762,743	-208,431	5,605,947	1,611,329	823,158	19,575	410,759	279,484
1990	8,678,919	6,982,320	72,630	7,054,950	847,489	-230,319	5,977,142	1,797,621	904,156	20,760	418,062	290,422
1991	8,965,868	7,350,899	55,449	7,406,348	899,799	-240,933	6,265,616	1,718,744	981,508	21,128	424,368	295,382
1992	9,599,392	7,923,998	87,279	8,011,277	964,092	-262,604	6,784,581	1,750,979	1,063,832	22,220	432,014	300,284
1993	9,975,691	8,327,881	17,551	8,345,432	1,014,808	-274,985	7,055,639	1,802,789	1,117,263	22,718	439,105	305,489
1994	10,677,069	8,864,871	97,543	8,962,414	1,094,395	-289,750	7,578,269	1,938,233	1,160,567	24,011	444,671	313,372
1995	11,391,115	9,424,764	56,275	9,481,039	1,161,305	-309,984	8,009,750	2,154,902	1,226,463	25,237	451,372	326,428
1996	12,178,313	9,978,493	132,079	10,110,572	1,190,682	-327,656	8,592,234	2,286,510	1,299,569	26,631	457,294	333,775
1997	12,887,104	10,611,962	107,054	10,719,016	1,290,994	-349,871	9,078,151	2,478,993	1,329,960	27,878	462,263	338,246
1998	14,854,769	12,077,511	102,190	12,179,701	1,449,079	-292,358	10,438,264	2,911,416	1,505,089	29,411	505,070	366,381
1999	15,582,087	12,982,788	69,901	13,052,689	1,550,281	-315,768	11,186,640	2,841,484	1,553,963	30,373	513,020	373,463
2000	16,540,909	13,651,157	95,291	13,746,448	1,607,242	-325,510	11,813,696	3,051,976	1,675,237	31,779	520,495	378,721
2001	17,368,876	14,430,966	80,993	14,511,959	1,691,234	-348,081	12,472,644	3,061,900	1,834,332	32,949	527,138	380,712
2002	17,908,430	14,941,636	93,468	15,035,104	1,754,261	-361,084	12,919,759	2,972,561	2,016,110	33,547	533,828	379,700
2003	18,544,349	15,609,846	98,773	15,708,619	1,846,647	-365,559	13,496,413	3,035,037	2,012,899	34,271	541,109	381,332
2004	20,101,383	16,743,494	241,380	16,984,874	1,956,075	-367,555	14,661,244	3,360,651	2,079,488	36,621	548,902	391,738
2005	21,126,583	17,571,797	188,906	17,760,703	2,050,009	-366,083	15,344,611	3,538,169	2,243,803	37,789	559,060	399,647
2006	22,705,607	18,640,586	145,407	18,785,993	2,160,684	-364,328	16,260,981	3,961,431	2,483,195	39,833	570,026	410,353
2007	23,960,302	19,396,086	241,482	19,637,568	2,274,882	-387,082	16,975,604	4,310,948	2,673,750	41,257	580,757	421,384
2008	25,147,747	20,003,098	278,449	20,281,547	2,369,376	-365,485	17,546,686	4,446,610	3,154,451	42,569	590,747	424,043
2009	24,677,942	19,763,566	202,913	19,966,479	2,372,675	-304,638	17,289,166	4,006,827	3,381,949	41,166	599,480	419,245
2010	25,765,345	20,449,508	130,956	20,580,464	2,443,526	-240,694	17,896,244	4,178,177	3,690,924	42,312	608,942	417,404
2011	26,982,720	20,749,540	342,773	21,092,313	2,257,262	-298,068	18,536,983	4,667,426	3,778,311	43,636	618,362	423,430
2012	28,852,685	22,127,954	280,528	22,408,482	2,344,605	-340,200	19,723,677	5,320,164	3,808,844	46,025	626,897	431,268
2013	29,351,120	22,917,913	328,789	23,246,702	2,739,189	-237,365	20,270,148	5,144,395	3,936,577	46,004	638,013	441,164
2014	31,414,973	24,483,538	197,429	24,680,967	2,852,593	-239,750	21,588,624	5,635,194	4,191,155	48,258	650,974	451,435
2015	33,211,313	25,605,031	155,860	25,760,891	2,948,411	-197,329	22,615,151	6,152,667	4,443,495	50,228	661,212	459,052
2016	34,482,290	26,653,948	79,624	26,733,572	3,130,663	-238,302	23,364,607	6,533,456	4,584,227	51,222	673,194	470,091
2017	35,759,801	27,681,908	101,559	27,783,467	3,262,249	-223,348	24,297,870	6,840,970	4,620,961	52,278	684,038	477,097
2018	37,128,794	28,710,192	125,689	28,835,881	3,410,130	-247,071	25,178,680	6,871,053	5,079,061	53,520	693,742	484,420
2019	38,810,054	29,655,192	108,600	29,763,792	3,548,086	-254,347	25,961,359	7,386,557	5,462,138	55,183	703,296	487,345
2020	41,743,978	30,944,758	140,029	31,084,787	3,760,338	-319,722	27,004,727	7,405,811	7,333,440	58,725	710,843	477,083
2021	44,466,630	32,957,675	323,338	33,281,013	3,923,461	-336,457	29,021,095	7,494,362	7,951,173	61,833	719,146	491,869

Personal Income and Employment by Area: Detroit-Warren-Dearborn, MI

(Thousands of dollars, except as noted.)

| Year | Personal income, total | Derivation of personal income | | | | | | | | Per capita personal income (dollars) | Population (persons) | Total employment |
| | | Earnings by place of work | | | Less: Contributions for government social insurance | Plus: Adjustment for residence | Equals: Net earnings by place of residence | Plus: Dividends, interest, and rent | Plus: Personal current transfer receipts | | | |
		Nonfarm	Farm	Total								
1970	20,473,778	17,605,595	34,095	17,639,690	1,256,732	-159,525	16,223,433	2,652,970	1,597,375	4,612	4,439,498	1,819,813
1971	22,059,058	18,836,787	31,718	18,868,505	1,384,176	-163,954	17,320,375	2,817,309	1,921,374	4,946	4,459,793	1,803,088
1972	24,440,594	21,041,099	41,104	21,082,203	1,647,001	-194,485	19,240,717	3,002,171	2,197,706	5,488	4,453,517	1,854,501
1973	27,254,747	23,795,186	46,739	23,841,925	2,162,977	-205,465	21,473,483	3,271,605	2,509,659	6,144	4,435,796	1,939,903
1974	28,883,744	24,572,344	46,143	24,618,487	2,307,355	-272,983	22,038,149	3,724,458	3,121,137	6,532	4,422,090	1,926,974
1975	30,323,450	24,691,187	48,695	24,739,882	2,257,459	-276,919	22,205,504	4,022,648	4,095,298	6,900	4,394,458	1,808,270
1976	33,800,030	28,193,834	46,030	28,239,864	2,634,598	-247,928	25,357,338	4,297,514	4,145,178	7,750	4,361,574	1,876,295
1977	38,051,495	32,337,048	54,020	32,391,068	3,025,529	-259,649	29,105,890	4,714,191	4,231,414	8,744	4,351,973	1,960,763
1978	42,389,221	36,367,129	37,866	36,404,995	3,511,594	-272,371	32,621,030	5,251,067	4,517,124	9,730	4,356,619	2,043,005
1979	46,120,599	39,215,984	42,807	39,258,791	3,917,301	-295,693	35,045,797	5,840,040	5,234,762	10,586	4,356,811	2,045,908
1980	48,824,209	39,109,989	42,303	39,152,292	3,863,007	-295,440	34,993,845	6,825,800	7,004,564	11,250	4,339,778	1,921,891
1981	51,395,115	40,433,542	42,368	40,475,910	4,317,843	-219,346	35,938,721	8,154,598	7,301,796	12,020	4,275,732	1,876,138
1982	52,922,315	40,006,836	38,997	40,045,833	4,330,097	-214,096	35,501,640	9,336,076	8,084,599	12,532	4,223,098	1,789,482
1983	56,201,073	42,406,862	28,272	42,435,134	4,666,625	-160,427	37,608,082	10,009,789	8,583,202	13,429	4,185,050	1,798,974
1984	62,456,215	47,915,976	43,472	47,959,448	5,454,814	-172,234	42,332,400	11,467,499	8,656,316	14,932	4,182,763	1,897,635
1985	68,591,338	53,790,970	47,716	53,838,686	6,254,816	-203,195	47,380,675	12,354,345	8,856,318	16,347	4,195,986	2,012,186
1986	73,127,376	57,955,880	32,547	57,988,427	6,757,969	-269,732	50,960,726	12,906,970	9,259,680	17,330	4,219,771	2,067,378
1987	75,541,248	60,063,155	43,870	60,107,025	6,922,493	-322,849	52,861,683	13,235,783	9,443,782	17,810	4,241,494	2,118,647
1988	80,991,059	64,885,558	43,872	64,929,430	7,645,413	-370,301	56,913,716	14,245,785	9,831,558	19,128	4,234,083	2,168,474
1989	86,947,955	68,592,022	58,979	68,651,001	8,080,678	-361,934	60,208,389	16,187,839	10,551,727	20,517	4,237,904	2,227,089
1990	90,544,457	71,050,389	53,028	71,103,417	8,530,456	-373,478	62,199,483	16,984,466	11,360,508	21,300	4,250,986	2,244,909
1991	91,197,557	71,286,205	52,748	71,338,953	8,683,405	-387,980	62,267,568	16,403,285	12,526,704	21,280	4,285,663	2,181,991
1992	96,314,198	76,355,416	50,528	76,405,944	9,228,885	-555,608	66,621,451	16,432,536	13,260,211	22,296	4,319,806	2,182,305
1993	101,454,753	80,702,199	49,252	80,751,451	9,788,207	-775,673	70,187,571	17,097,700	14,169,482	23,351	4,344,712	2,209,546
1994	109,115,048	86,839,370	47,119	86,886,489	10,725,780	-938,142	75,222,567	19,607,988	14,284,493	24,995	4,365,423	2,279,342
1995	115,768,562	92,219,112	50,486	92,269,598	11,339,603	-1,317,006	79,612,989	21,095,523	15,060,050	26,313	4,399,746	2,339,032
1996	121,857,583	96,737,305	44,670	96,781,975	11,578,418	-1,524,152	83,679,405	22,392,749	15,785,429	27,488	4,433,102	2,391,801
1997	128,129,940	101,384,059	46,255	101,430,314	12,118,956	-1,579,550	87,731,808	23,518,061	16,880,071	28,855	4,440,400	2,425,583
1998	137,112,081	109,829,810	45,202	109,875,012	12,817,546	-1,894,327	95,163,139	25,334,559	16,614,383	30,869	4,441,717	2,463,358
1999	143,464,226	116,860,796	55,365	116,916,161	13,571,475	-1,982,089	101,362,597	24,518,116	17,583,513	32,256	4,447,649	2,511,959
2000	154,532,353	126,766,959	36,107	126,803,066	14,321,259	-2,449,788	110,032,019	26,523,587	17,976,747	34,683	4,455,503	2,580,828
2001	155,929,821	127,540,579	32,098	127,572,677	14,283,779	-2,502,466	110,786,432	25,274,329	19,869,060	34,947	4,461,855	2,536,678
2002	153,806,274	125,716,370	32,990	125,749,360	14,271,465	-2,402,026	109,075,869	24,254,019	20,476,386	34,513	4,456,433	2,500,131
2003	156,868,603	127,849,091	40,208	127,889,299	14,474,485	-2,674,803	110,740,011	24,760,979	21,367,613	35,225	4,453,371	2,486,062
2004	160,066,107	130,460,339	64,133	130,524,472	14,917,357	-2,716,213	112,890,902	24,982,002	22,193,203	36,003	4,445,887	2,487,090
2005	163,684,874	132,083,879	64,360	132,148,239	15,358,581	-3,039,316	113,750,342	26,325,656	23,608,876	36,940	4,431,048	2,503,800
2006	165,629,834	131,045,041	78,586	131,123,627	15,478,851	-2,804,443	112,840,333	27,778,847	25,010,654	37,560	4,409,697	2,474,998
2007	170,112,119	131,778,100	66,479	131,844,579	15,637,977	-2,791,512	113,415,090	29,405,828	27,291,201	38,864	4,377,116	2,470,996
2008	170,872,060	128,760,349	71,795	128,832,144	15,513,105	-3,013,310	110,305,729	29,541,002	31,025,329	39,376	4,339,504	2,413,765
2009	160,283,198	115,922,844	50,253	115,973,097	14,141,218	-1,878,189	99,953,690	25,563,501	34,766,007	37,174	4,311,728	2,255,835
2010	164,671,091	119,038,448	61,595	119,100,043	14,283,013	-2,418,748	102,398,282	25,283,923	36,988,886	38,373	4,291,281	2,258,061
2011	175,954,582	126,667,778	109,795	126,777,573	13,404,715	-2,111,404	111,261,454	27,830,997	36,862,131	41,000	4,291,613	2,329,607
2012	184,197,649	133,549,883	96,388	133,646,271	14,022,911	-2,433,483	117,189,877	30,346,659	36,661,113	42,827	4,300,923	2,372,902
2013	185,606,992	136,827,229	100,972	136,928,201	16,308,667	-2,209,366	118,410,168	30,430,654	36,766,170	43,106	4,305,782	2,415,196
2014	195,052,471	142,707,714	56,264	142,763,978	16,830,973	-2,558,189	123,374,816	33,701,344	37,976,311	44,884	4,345,692	2,458,060
2015	206,622,428	150,328,721	69,451	150,398,172	17,604,007	-2,582,573	130,211,592	36,330,096	40,080,740	47,473	4,352,394	2,508,369
2016	212,279,414	155,037,358	57,826	155,095,184	18,109,071	-2,986,096	134,000,017	37,345,717	40,933,680	48,605	4,367,436	2,547,293
2017	218,218,576	162,108,102	58,608	162,166,710	18,852,962	-3,282,730	140,031,018	37,428,692	40,758,866	49,809	4,381,076	2,581,905
2018	227,532,657	167,527,343	57,701	167,585,044	19,738,485	-3,423,435	144,423,124	40,472,021	42,637,512	51,823	4,390,557	2,628,760
2019	234,769,732	171,901,501	67,355	171,968,856	20,150,129	-3,416,789	148,401,938	41,437,643	44,930,151	53,428	4,394,145	2,637,343
2020	253,299,113	169,399,471	99,565	169,499,036	19,839,661	-3,109,807	146,549,568	41,575,467	65,174,078	57,755	4,385,748	2,480,532
2021	266,123,984	182,480,667	109,271	182,589,938	20,892,529	-3,645,336	158,052,073	42,449,182	65,622,729	60,965	4,365,205	2,577,343

Personal Income and Employment by Area: Dothan, AL

(Thousands of dollars, except as noted.)

Year	Personal income, total	Earnings by place of work			Less: Contributions for government social insurance	Plus: Adjustment for residence	Equals: Net earnings by place of residence	Plus: Dividends, interest, and rent	Plus: Personal current transfer receipts	Per capita personal income (dollars)	Population (persons)	Total employment
		Nonfarm	Farm	Total								
1970	278,801	176,422	18,077	194,499	13,404	33,743	214,838	34,597	29,366	3,026	92,122	41,593
1971	309,458	202,576	18,535	221,111	15,620	30,304	235,795	39,747	33,916	3,287	94,147	43,039
1972	349,141	236,764	26,184	262,948	19,290	24,201	267,859	43,535	37,747	3,567	97,881	45,497
1973	427,476	299,282	42,225	341,507	28,113	18,936	332,330	51,235	43,911	4,257	100,409	49,519
1974	477,002	343,152	34,200	377,352	33,309	18,523	362,566	61,501	52,935	4,526	105,391	51,163
1975	519,787	350,060	40,273	390,333	33,496	21,286	378,123	71,999	69,665	4,811	108,046	49,593
1976	598,322	425,514	38,312	463,826	41,836	21,820	443,810	78,332	76,180	5,450	109,777	51,727
1977	642,890	473,313	24,878	498,191	46,582	22,871	474,480	87,443	80,967	5,794	110,966	53,046
1978	728,189	537,027	33,225	570,252	53,830	22,535	538,957	100,998	88,234	6,457	112,772	54,447
1979	792,719	572,646	31,322	603,968	59,219	30,298	575,047	114,813	102,859	6,976	113,631	54,259
1980	870,374	655,750	-14,240	641,510	68,002	32,645	606,153	143,581	120,640	7,601	114,505	55,050
1981	1,038,673	691,486	44,870	736,356	77,054	64,388	723,690	176,978	138,005	8,987	115,576	54,328
1982	1,064,555	700,654	24,051	724,705	79,005	73,451	719,151	192,579	152,825	9,172	116,060	52,319
1983	1,121,096	749,082	9,441	758,523	84,617	76,092	749,998	204,776	166,322	9,667	115,974	52,832
1984	1,267,023	820,164	55,594	875,758	94,794	78,841	859,805	231,273	175,945	10,876	116,501	54,538
1985	1,329,945	883,993	28,328	912,321	102,348	81,062	891,035	249,691	189,219	11,336	117,318	55,398
1986	1,416,153	956,258	22,117	978,375	109,452	82,499	951,422	265,170	199,561	12,039	117,628	56,956
1987	1,517,449	1,037,794	35,133	1,072,927	117,653	82,672	1,037,946	271,967	207,536	12,754	118,980	59,215
1988	1,656,851	1,127,224	59,962	1,187,186	131,995	80,068	1,135,259	298,867	222,725	13,888	119,302	61,390
1989	1,839,932	1,234,438	75,457	1,309,895	144,223	71,898	1,237,570	351,214	251,148	15,403	119,455	64,645
1990	1,887,410	1,319,482	53,615	1,373,097	155,000	29,317	1,247,414	372,117	267,879	15,621	120,826	66,534
1991	1,983,201	1,376,551	82,868	1,459,419	163,317	19,532	1,315,634	378,193	289,374	16,188	122,507	67,078
1992	2,155,078	1,506,764	76,357	1,583,121	176,485	35,014	1,441,650	384,526	328,902	17,431	123,636	68,384
1993	2,195,197	1,555,054	62,167	1,617,221	184,224	23,562	1,456,559	393,337	345,301	17,565	124,976	69,447
1994	2,328,710	1,623,796	79,605	1,703,401	194,602	20,669	1,529,468	428,959	370,283	18,624	125,036	69,704
1995	2,477,812	1,718,817	76,707	1,795,524	207,125	19,157	1,607,556	466,407	403,849	19,685	125,872	71,949
1996	2,547,319	1,777,315	63,168	1,840,483	211,223	11,889	1,641,149	476,995	429,175	20,048	127,060	72,959
1997	2,664,477	1,855,721	46,335	1,902,056	220,356	26,823	1,708,523	505,529	450,425	20,806	128,062	74,932
1998	2,839,892	1,983,475	55,439	2,038,914	231,918	41,493	1,848,489	538,287	453,116	22,027	128,927	75,252
1999	2,966,910	2,045,876	78,733	2,124,609	239,342	64,556	1,949,823	538,930	478,157	22,828	129,970	75,357
2000	3,051,238	2,103,806	38,648	2,142,454	247,014	70,657	1,966,097	574,109	511,032	23,288	131,024	75,270
2001	3,310,442	2,212,312	94,751	2,307,063	256,021	79,644	2,130,686	600,009	579,747	25,191	131,413	74,332
2002	3,415,407	2,283,023	94,590	2,377,613	264,630	102,809	2,215,792	576,529	623,086	25,881	131,967	73,972
2003	3,536,370	2,369,435	85,700	2,455,135	275,618	118,749	2,298,266	571,274	666,830	26,473	133,586	74,707
2004	3,803,973	2,523,057	85,842	2,608,899	292,749	132,455	2,448,605	627,891	727,477	28,166	135,057	77,191
2005	4,067,241	2,660,101	89,104	2,749,205	308,847	148,281	2,588,639	695,659	782,943	29,765	136,643	78,855
2006	4,327,397	2,812,336	57,596	2,869,932	329,989	195,293	2,735,236	740,016	852,145	31,117	139,070	80,328
2007	4,602,609	2,879,297	55,870	2,935,167	342,318	226,038	2,818,887	858,966	924,756	32,606	141,157	82,333
2008	4,710,375	2,830,732	58,018	2,888,750	344,538	247,750	2,791,962	892,076	1,026,337	32,949	142,958	80,560
2009	4,682,831	2,770,934	39,023	2,809,957	338,722	304,914	2,776,149	791,095	1,115,587	32,430	144,396	77,260
2010	4,928,761	2,840,735	35,949	2,876,684	349,017	343,739	2,871,406	831,196	1,226,159	33,788	145,871	76,393
2011	5,114,864	2,887,104	31,276	2,918,380	316,458	349,892	2,951,814	903,883	1,259,167	34,879	146,644	76,925
2012	5,181,265	2,949,305	25,505	2,974,810	320,460	364,774	3,019,124	889,740	1,272,401	35,130	147,490	76,750
2013	5,244,474	3,027,157	105,029	3,132,186	370,058	309,659	3,071,787	870,795	1,301,892	35,554	147,507	76,941
2014	5,380,942	3,092,428	62,840	3,155,268	375,937	291,750	3,071,081	930,853	1,379,008	36,289	148,281	77,257
2015	5,599,384	3,184,373	79,925	3,264,298	388,391	282,574	3,158,481	965,311	1,475,592	37,696	148,542	77,970
2016	5,693,929	3,257,728	69,683	3,327,411	395,914	290,900	3,222,397	990,068	1,481,464	38,350	148,472	77,732
2017	5,862,413	3,341,463	90,575	3,432,038	410,280	319,975	3,341,733	1,011,539	1,509,141	39,445	148,624	78,397
2018	6,093,609	3,518,874	70,811	3,589,685	436,449	304,310	3,457,546	1,050,300	1,585,763	40,878	149,067	79,719
2019	6,451,311	3,678,353	82,857	3,761,210	452,468	299,103	3,607,845	1,152,994	1,690,472	42,868	150,494	80,621
2020	6,923,178	3,846,144	50,405	3,896,549	477,480	324,737	3,743,806	1,150,960	2,028,412	45,839	151,032	80,405
2021	7,481,323	4,081,352	96,419	4,177,771	501,157	329,762	4,006,376	1,169,196	2,305,751	49,343	151,618	81,859

Personal Income and Employment by Area: Dover, DE

(Thousands of dollars, except as noted.)

Year	Personal income, total	Earnings by place of work			Less: Contributions for government social insurance	Plus: Adjustment for residence	Equals: Net earnings by place of residence	Plus: Dividends, interest, and rent	Plus: Personal current transfer receipts	Per capita personal income (dollars)	Population (persons)	Total employment
		Nonfarm	Farm	Total								
1970	329,298	278,854	9,441	288,295	18,575	-15,601	254,119	53,737	21,442	3,985	82,633	42,223
1971	366,988	310,011	9,377	319,388	21,322	-15,923	282,143	59,234	25,611	4,236	86,628	43,110
1972	408,579	343,571	11,098	354,669	24,323	-15,582	314,764	65,369	28,446	4,565	89,512	45,268
1973	456,659	370,705	24,117	394,822	29,554	-14,087	351,181	72,425	33,053	5,058	90,286	46,076
1974	510,034	406,440	29,191	435,631	33,776	-14,561	387,294	82,590	40,150	5,603	91,026	45,692
1975	562,531	442,630	21,485	464,115	37,052	-14,248	412,815	92,126	57,590	6,080	92,521	44,751
1976	607,527	477,290	20,993	498,283	41,024	-12,981	444,278	100,515	62,734	6,431	94,465	44,883
1977	649,026	515,906	11,058	526,964	43,991	-13,072	469,901	111,225	67,900	6,742	96,264	45,851
1978	716,082	553,939	18,542	572,481	48,484	-7,114	516,883	125,887	73,312	7,288	98,251	45,902
1979	771,030	587,704	14,983	602,687	53,413	-2,193	547,081	139,724	84,225	7,775	99,166	46,424
1980	842,712	631,423	-63	631,360	58,556	4,109	576,913	165,643	100,156	8,575	98,280	46,321
1981	949,603	696,007	10,271	706,278	69,248	7,624	644,654	191,535	113,414	9,659	98,317	46,451
1982	1,026,420	747,928	9,497	757,425	74,883	11,834	694,376	210,139	121,905	10,344	99,225	47,096
1983	1,090,616	785,065	10,206	795,271	79,384	20,652	736,539	222,848	131,229	10,803	100,953	47,036
1984	1,193,297	859,394	15,794	875,188	87,901	24,726	812,013	245,469	135,815	11,784	101,261	48,525
1985	1,286,780	931,003	12,394	943,397	95,516	31,182	879,063	263,717	144,000	12,515	102,818	51,069
1986	1,388,580	1,010,584	12,461	1,023,045	105,128	32,184	950,101	283,927	154,552	13,261	104,713	52,893
1987	1,495,350	1,093,487	9,590	1,103,077	112,217	38,754	1,029,614	304,024	161,712	14,072	106,263	54,198
1988	1,638,237	1,185,429	26,827	1,212,256	128,408	45,280	1,129,128	330,319	178,790	15,316	106,965	55,677
1989	1,799,718	1,291,494	25,551	1,317,045	140,250	48,822	1,225,617	379,140	194,961	16,503	109,052	57,099
1990	1,913,129	1,403,891	21,541	1,425,432	150,359	50,540	1,325,613	374,591	212,925	17,137	111,638	58,224
1991	2,032,361	1,467,999	24,819	1,492,818	159,055	42,593	1,376,356	407,548	248,457	17,783	114,288	59,918
1992	2,143,911	1,559,597	28,902	1,588,499	168,611	33,120	1,453,008	414,969	275,934	18,533	115,682	61,604
1993	2,209,117	1,625,135	20,250	1,645,385	177,808	22,458	1,490,035	419,506	299,576	18,723	117,987	62,713
1994	2,313,151	1,709,259	24,506	1,733,765	188,586	14,551	1,559,730	452,778	300,643	19,432	119,039	63,944
1995	2,466,683	1,821,555	13,066	1,834,621	202,186	256	1,632,691	492,776	341,216	20,434	120,715	65,999
1996	2,644,216	1,914,314	25,237	1,939,551	209,957	-5,152	1,724,442	530,416	389,358	21,773	121,447	67,066
1997	2,705,802	1,941,933	15,958	1,957,891	211,276	6,399	1,753,014	554,981	397,807	22,103	122,419	66,499
1998	2,932,809	2,136,507	25,618	2,162,125	224,793	3,728	1,941,060	558,621	433,128	23,641	124,056	67,593
1999	3,149,164	2,357,061	25,467	2,382,528	236,636	-1,564	2,144,328	564,732	440,104	25,071	125,611	70,155
2000	3,452,392	2,602,664	30,733	2,633,397	245,923	-3,311	2,384,163	590,935	477,294	27,135	127,229	71,832
2001	3,480,979	2,577,598	33,580	2,611,178	247,663	-7,454	2,356,061	604,784	520,134	26,937	129,228	72,004
2002	3,700,111	2,814,479	12,677	2,827,156	284,854	-30,570	2,511,732	621,788	566,591	28,069	131,824	73,663
2003	3,958,153	2,971,093	24,081	2,995,174	299,736	-25,412	2,670,026	668,575	619,552	29,406	134,605	75,124
2004	4,299,235	3,249,185	45,504	3,294,689	328,424	-33,726	2,932,539	689,579	677,117	30,854	139,342	78,240
2005	4,507,299	3,383,451	52,868	3,436,319	350,949	-29,524	3,055,846	702,570	748,883	31,174	144,585	81,729
2006	4,873,075	3,585,733	45,961	3,631,694	374,340	27,006	3,284,360	767,597	821,118	32,551	149,704	83,361
2007	5,119,257	3,664,695	52,145	3,716,840	394,204	34,468	3,357,104	857,883	904,270	33,249	153,969	84,923
2008	5,283,482	3,558,297	49,073	3,607,370	405,184	64,867	3,267,053	958,030	1,058,399	33,456	157,925	84,602
2009	5,530,466	3,630,143	72,627	3,702,770	405,581	120,123	3,417,312	948,780	1,164,374	34,548	160,081	81,628
2010	5,564,431	3,672,197	67,804	3,740,001	407,573	32,469	3,364,897	931,950	1,267,584	34,143	162,972	81,669
2011	5,899,797	3,802,343	79,915	3,882,258	370,879	28,946	3,540,325	1,023,531	1,335,941	35,721	165,161	83,855
2012	5,984,915	3,869,478	97,398	3,966,876	391,044	15,796	3,591,628	1,018,439	1,374,848	35,759	167,370	84,764
2013	6,186,209	3,953,878	127,088	4,080,966	454,133	47,040	3,673,873	1,064,836	1,447,500	36,574	169,144	86,585
2014	6,420,914	4,093,893	141,344	4,235,237	478,950	11,732	3,768,019	1,093,771	1,559,124	37,542	171,031	87,627
2015	6,565,954	4,142,354	95,260	4,237,614	490,504	60,899	3,808,009	1,115,943	1,642,002	38,040	172,605	88,488
2016	6,875,705	4,349,523	81,702	4,431,225	505,771	39,967	3,965,421	1,189,695	1,720,589	39,529	173,940	90,378
2017	7,187,186	4,482,177	136,160	4,618,337	523,874	47,606	4,142,069	1,227,566	1,817,551	40,886	175,786	91,846
2018	7,528,005	4,732,831	114,122	4,846,953	546,872	7,550	4,307,631	1,309,233	1,911,141	42,327	177,853	94,116
2019	8,019,553	5,072,235	126,139	5,198,374	578,096	2,860	4,623,138	1,377,595	2,018,820	44,490	180,255	95,292
2020	8,482,532	5,221,991	70,420	5,292,411	613,589	-112,772	4,566,050	1,420,729	2,495,753	46,542	182,256	95,049
2021	9,287,020	5,579,744	103,790	5,683,534	647,840	-41,947	4,993,747	1,495,710	2,797,563	50,432	184,149	97,789

Personal Income and Employment by Area: Dubuque, IA

(Thousands of dollars, except as noted.)

					Derivation of personal income							
		Earnings by place of work			Less: Contributions for government social insurance	Plus: Adjustment for residence	Equals: Net earnings by place of residence	Plus: Dividends, interest, and rent	Plus: Personal current transfer receipts	Per capita personal income (dollars)	Population (persons)	Total employment
Year	Personal income, total	Nonfarm	Farm	Total								
1970	337,786	307,536	17,404	324,940	23,291	-44,302	257,347	53,394	27,045	3,721	90,790	43,244
1971	359,129	331,103	14,793	345,896	26,066	-49,402	270,428	57,715	30,986	3,915	91,739	42,981
1972	395,076	371,627	15,811	387,438	30,892	-57,756	298,790	62,315	33,971	4,260	92,731	44,134
1973	447,182	422,366	22,897	445,263	40,709	-67,567	336,987	70,607	39,588	4,772	93,700	47,239
1974	496,919	486,881	13,798	500,679	48,829	-83,056	368,794	81,629	46,496	5,299	93,779	48,892
1975	546,504	516,800	20,357	537,157	50,614	-88,482	398,061	88,916	59,527	5,774	94,655	48,652
1976	595,507	573,928	13,839	587,767	57,048	-99,337	431,382	97,669	66,456	6,223	95,687	49,568
1977	672,610	665,079	12,712	677,791	65,783	-121,728	490,280	111,401	70,929	7,135	94,270	51,642
1978	748,022	731,010	27,794	758,804	74,826	-137,240	546,738	123,429	77,855	7,982	93,716	52,499
1979	807,693	808,131	15,871	824,002	85,847	-156,094	582,061	138,694	86,938	8,645	93,425	53,560
1980	856,714	846,784	-3,233	843,551	89,565	-169,579	584,407	167,324	104,983	9,143	93,701	52,948
1981	944,822	862,351	16,276	878,627	96,839	-161,420	620,368	205,592	118,862	10,126	93,307	50,728
1982	955,294	794,332	5,392	799,724	90,003	-131,970	577,751	234,822	142,721	10,385	91,992	47,472
1983	981,524	817,102	-12,104	804,998	92,792	-127,843	584,363	245,724	151,437	10,870	90,296	47,693
1984	1,104,426	898,295	30,820	929,115	105,242	-138,338	685,535	269,773	149,118	12,324	89,616	49,513
1985	1,144,351	932,711	27,501	960,212	110,615	-139,541	710,056	280,084	154,211	12,844	89,096	49,643
1986	1,170,040	924,084	38,284	962,368	111,192	-127,164	724,012	288,907	157,121	13,331	87,771	49,358
1987	1,265,517	1,040,545	46,379	1,086,924	123,784	-144,570	818,570	288,527	158,420	14,525	87,125	51,309
1988	1,304,156	1,082,791	29,898	1,112,689	132,632	-144,506	835,551	302,703	165,902	14,930	87,351	52,579
1989	1,405,943	1,130,826	50,926	1,181,752	137,134	-144,691	899,927	326,610	179,406	16,227	86,644	53,836
1990	1,467,082	1,189,145	49,245	1,238,390	148,355	-151,890	938,145	334,986	193,951	16,968	86,462	55,086
1991	1,514,201	1,245,508	35,645	1,281,153	156,991	-156,853	967,309	339,980	206,912	17,407	86,988	56,048
1992	1,642,851	1,353,425	55,414	1,408,839	169,294	-169,792	1,069,753	349,670	223,428	18,739	87,672	56,773
1993	1,695,548	1,418,303	36,742	1,455,045	178,349	-171,571	1,105,125	354,321	236,102	19,211	88,261	57,566
1994	1,818,686	1,543,263	48,326	1,591,589	196,176	-182,267	1,213,146	360,996	244,544	20,514	88,654	58,805
1995	1,923,481	1,634,454	29,762	1,664,216	207,539	-195,227	1,261,450	404,483	257,548	21,627	88,938	60,614
1996	2,007,121	1,622,889	58,676	1,681,565	198,749	-197,429	1,285,387	444,763	276,971	22,527	89,097	60,234
1997	2,081,386	1,703,508	48,299	1,751,807	214,751	-209,668	1,327,388	469,013	284,985	23,387	88,996	61,363
1998	2,206,899	1,779,884	41,126	1,821,010	223,409	-217,955	1,379,646	522,341	304,912	24,859	88,775	61,304
1999	2,222,353	1,829,015	29,371	1,858,386	227,345	-218,595	1,412,446	494,439	315,468	24,989	88,934	61,845
2000	2,353,401	1,896,204	48,391	1,944,595	232,991	-225,429	1,486,175	532,923	334,303	26,383	89,201	62,242
2001	2,397,101	1,900,513	43,056	1,943,569	231,545	-216,138	1,495,886	537,329	363,886	26,954	88,932	61,990
2002	2,452,880	1,969,498	31,449	2,000,947	239,481	-212,718	1,548,748	509,229	394,903	27,520	89,132	61,804
2003	2,535,914	2,064,672	35,101	2,099,773	254,800	-217,498	1,627,475	511,360	397,079	28,173	90,012	62,344
2004	2,630,222	2,142,236	56,407	2,198,643	268,985	-242,459	1,687,199	530,214	412,809	29,075	90,462	63,647
2005	2,735,770	2,233,959	44,572	2,278,531	283,573	-252,747	1,742,211	555,870	437,689	30,140	90,769	65,285
2006	2,988,244	2,389,117	29,150	2,418,267	296,355	-258,143	1,863,769	636,222	488,253	32,745	91,258	67,149
2007	3,259,119	2,523,323	40,805	2,564,128	305,928	-257,905	2,000,295	727,302	531,522	35,375	92,130	67,770
2008	3,398,009	2,608,543	32,078	2,640,621	320,286	-251,745	2,068,590	730,722	598,697	36,728	92,519	67,401
2009	3,314,307	2,589,579	7,288	2,596,867	321,010	-247,823	2,028,034	671,189	615,084	35,658	92,948	66,382
2010	3,483,318	2,770,242	25,960	2,796,202	349,020	-282,320	2,164,862	659,848	658,608	37,083	93,933	67,896
2011	3,720,285	2,907,201	62,115	2,969,316	331,794	-317,660	2,319,862	738,097	662,326	39,303	94,656	69,906
2012	3,934,993	3,126,009	69,918	3,195,927	346,497	-375,643	2,473,787	799,067	662,139	41,341	95,183	71,133
2013	3,988,966	3,158,797	86,325	3,245,122	392,217	-364,974	2,487,931	807,634	693,401	41,556	95,990	71,678
2014	4,164,933	3,290,169	71,120	3,361,289	397,771	-387,436	2,576,082	858,271	730,580	42,833	97,237	72,511
2015	4,359,261	3,368,014	103,732	3,471,746	402,689	-410,311	2,658,746	920,868	779,647	44,576	97,794	73,525
2016	4,426,660	3,401,025	54,138	3,455,163	414,241	-411,351	2,629,571	993,030	804,059	45,242	97,843	72,787
2017	4,543,304	3,516,281	63,993	3,580,274	432,149	-430,852	2,717,273	1,020,929	805,102	46,193	98,355	72,835
2018	4,812,334	3,695,224	56,197	3,751,421	456,185	-457,372	2,837,864	1,101,155	873,315	48,948	98,316	73,462
2019	4,984,576	3,850,376	47,498	3,897,874	477,607	-495,418	2,924,849	1,141,864	917,863	50,370	98,959	73,351
2020	5,326,982	3,898,913	62,183	3,961,096	492,446	-483,827	2,984,823	1,137,761	1,204,398	53,684	99,229	70,887
2021	5,605,450	4,135,946	87,920	4,223,866	512,626	-506,667	3,204,573	1,142,909	1,257,968	56,782	98,718	72,335

Personal Income and Employment by Area: Duluth, MN-WI

(Thousands of dollars, except as noted.)

Year	Personal income, total	Earnings by place of work			Less: Contributions for government social insurance	Plus: Adjustment for residence	Equals: Net earnings by place of residence	Plus: Dividends, interest, and rent	Plus: Personal current transfer receipts	Per capita personal income (dollars)	Population (persons)	Total employment
		Nonfarm	Farm	Total								
1970	1,049,497	828,978	3,931	832,909	60,088	-6,895	765,926	156,091	127,480	3,570	293,960	115,741
1971	1,132,812	890,539	3,502	894,041	66,901	-7,548	819,592	167,388	145,832	3,824	296,224	116,412
1972	1,224,210	963,080	3,989	967,069	76,060	-8,217	882,792	177,287	164,131	4,142	295,529	118,378
1973	1,339,703	1,052,051	6,388	1,058,439	94,972	-8,284	955,183	198,412	186,108	4,584	292,286	121,637
1974	1,471,299	1,136,578	4,775	1,141,353	107,630	-7,288	1,026,435	228,212	216,652	5,095	288,748	123,186
1975	1,713,412	1,326,197	3,549	1,329,746	124,602	-2,570	1,202,574	255,139	255,699	5,896	290,582	126,320
1976	1,928,015	1,506,276	4,370	1,510,646	142,497	2,238	1,370,387	273,230	284,398	6,536	294,985	130,460
1977	1,996,351	1,527,893	6,518	1,534,411	144,800	-5,759	1,383,852	301,289	311,210	6,765	295,109	128,310
1978	2,290,895	1,798,715	7,071	1,805,786	173,075	-1,661	1,631,050	328,989	330,856	7,777	294,586	133,882
1979	2,530,495	1,984,698	7,888	1,992,586	197,885	3,946	1,798,647	364,790	367,058	8,543	296,193	137,174
1980	2,769,373	2,085,219	7,481	2,092,700	206,539	-10,992	1,875,169	444,462	449,742	9,343	296,407	135,992
1981	3,056,061	2,259,939	8,649	2,268,588	242,547	-17,106	2,008,935	545,982	501,144	10,359	295,015	133,167
1982	3,037,474	2,065,951	6,837	2,072,788	227,149	-18,607	1,827,032	609,784	600,658	10,395	292,192	122,580
1983	3,061,711	2,002,974	4,722	2,007,696	221,818	-14,251	1,771,627	644,937	645,147	10,684	286,582	117,782
1984	3,267,436	2,162,574	4,884	2,167,458	247,187	-13,731	1,906,540	708,869	652,027	11,627	281,016	120,193
1985	3,362,193	2,205,443	6,222	2,211,665	256,484	-14,727	1,940,454	737,897	683,842	12,182	275,987	120,332
1986	3,472,524	2,277,552	11,792	2,289,344	270,970	-19,262	1,999,112	770,889	702,523	12,793	271,434	121,403
1987	3,588,068	2,407,989	3,552	2,411,541	283,103	-23,760	2,104,678	768,562	714,828	13,335	269,076	123,967
1988	3,769,511	2,598,808	2,386	2,601,194	320,562	-23,526	2,257,106	789,365	723,040	14,093	267,468	127,214
1989	4,134,686	2,841,717	5,961	2,847,678	352,729	-22,922	2,472,027	889,902	772,757	15,413	268,268	131,705
1990	4,403,781	3,043,512	3,747	3,047,259	376,401	25,628	2,696,486	891,749	815,546	16,326	269,746	134,052
1991	4,576,088	3,234,527	1,700	3,236,227	403,328	-27,641	2,805,258	904,302	866,528	16,870	271,256	137,205
1992	4,850,559	3,456,422	4,799	3,461,221	423,798	-33,287	3,004,136	906,591	939,832	17,772	272,939	139,402
1993	4,959,750	3,541,162	4,697	3,545,859	438,076	-37,872	3,069,911	919,273	970,566	18,139	273,424	139,020
1994	5,189,680	3,715,358	5,411	3,720,769	464,395	-43,893	3,212,481	966,285	1,010,914	18,952	273,834	141,956
1995	5,511,765	3,912,526	2,895	3,915,421	487,298	-43,870	3,384,253	1,070,203	1,057,309	20,280	271,777	145,458
1996	5,805,483	4,110,844	2,958	4,113,802	506,276	-47,815	3,559,711	1,146,934	1,098,838	21,310	272,433	148,086
1997	6,019,195	4,293,547	2,008	4,295,555	530,306	-53,517	3,711,732	1,191,279	1,116,184	21,999	273,609	150,364
1998	6,703,674	4,802,703	3,394	4,806,097	584,617	-61,516	4,159,964	1,337,431	1,206,279	23,561	284,526	159,178
1999	6,974,435	5,084,830	3,181	5,088,011	617,074	-67,573	4,403,364	1,329,030	1,242,041	24,410	285,719	162,282
2000	7,430,825	5,407,240	2,252	5,409,492	647,086	-71,594	4,690,812	1,429,271	1,310,742	25,904	286,858	165,422
2001	7,581,057	5,365,702	2,628	5,368,330	647,895	-65,682	4,654,753	1,449,030	1,477,274	26,315	288,091	163,056
2002	7,879,690	5,593,672	1,718	5,595,390	670,566	-66,932	4,857,892	1,427,761	1,594,037	27,362	287,980	162,994
2003	8,121,713	5,709,794	4,189	5,713,983	687,231	-64,612	4,962,140	1,506,936	1,652,637	28,164	288,371	162,557
2004	8,424,602	6,000,645	4,470	6,005,115	716,829	-64,681	5,223,605	1,464,954	1,736,043	29,233	288,187	163,221
2005	8,474,810	6,078,444	3,088	6,081,532	745,162	-64,551	5,271,819	1,393,990	1,809,001	29,458	287,696	165,001
2006	8,894,145	6,312,074	4,118	6,316,192	782,020	-64,933	5,469,239	1,475,900	1,949,006	30,918	287,672	166,991
2007	9,438,494	6,604,181	5,330	6,609,511	815,575	-67,337	5,726,599	1,610,919	2,100,976	32,756	288,147	169,341
2008	10,067,988	7,018,132	505	7,018,637	862,994	-71,932	6,083,711	1,687,656	2,296,621	34,785	289,433	169,040
2009	9,969,451	6,770,141	-1,599	6,768,542	837,501	-77,111	5,853,930	1,570,774	2,544,747	34,338	290,337	163,400
2010	10,623,794	7,308,012	3,709	7,311,721	876,169	-85,618	6,349,934	1,598,290	2,675,570	36,565	290,547	163,278
2011	11,189,782	7,722,508	4,031	7,726,539	829,490	-103,013	6,794,036	1,718,674	2,677,072	38,503	290,620	164,463
2012	11,393,069	7,835,655	1,989	7,837,644	835,868	-107,329	6,894,447	1,818,876	2,679,746	39,256	290,223	165,114
2013	11,391,577	7,867,337	4,029	7,871,366	965,677	-119,619	6,786,070	1,831,021	2,774,486	39,245	290,266	167,118
2014	11,821,767	8,059,849	5,906	8,065,755	984,611	-124,270	6,956,874	1,956,842	2,908,051	40,555	291,503	168,563
2015	12,171,982	8,178,272	6,753	8,185,025	999,114	-122,652	7,063,259	2,089,782	3,018,941	41,788	291,279	169,240
2016	12,143,146	8,080,724	3,531	8,084,255	995,038	-129,776	6,959,441	2,104,919	3,078,786	41,699	291,213	168,550
2017	12,542,694	8,382,668	180	8,382,848	1,044,289	-137,263	7,201,296	2,167,896	3,173,502	43,067	291,236	170,315
2018	13,246,979	8,867,252	-1,360	8,865,892	1,109,707	-145,712	7,610,473	2,273,302	3,363,204	45,392	291,834	170,719
2019	13,712,853	9,131,851	-1,855	9,129,996	1,153,873	-149,129	7,826,994	2,322,893	3,562,966	47,006	291,727	169,620
2020	14,581,835	9,037,052	1,677	9,038,729	1,149,546	-147,691	7,741,492	2,328,496	4,511,847	50,062	291,278	158,897
2021	15,624,703	9,740,514	-2,116	9,738,398	1,206,150	-160,081	8,372,167	2,359,049	4,893,487	53,734	290,780	162,680

Personal Income and Employment by Area: Durham-Chapel Hill, NC

(Thousands of dollars, except as noted.)

Year	Personal income, total	Earnings by place of work Nonfarm	Farm	Total	Less: Contributions for government social insurance	Plus: Adjustment for residence	Equals: Net earnings by place of residence	Plus: Dividends, interest, and rent	Plus: Personal current transfer receipts	Per capita personal income (dollars)	Population (persons)	Total employment
1970	896,581	757,721	22,672	780,393	50,259	-21,428	708,706	118,834	69,041	3,637	246,517	120,512
1971	1,010,661	862,391	24,128	886,519	59,151	-31,986	795,382	133,342	81,937	4,000	252,666	125,379
1972	1,118,503	958,548	26,764	985,312	68,592	-39,393	877,327	149,408	91,768	4,282	261,180	130,456
1973	1,233,761	1,046,288	45,351	1,091,639	86,838	-46,040	958,761	169,736	105,264	4,625	266,750	133,616
1974	1,363,250	1,157,774	36,434	1,194,208	99,818	-57,753	1,036,637	197,200	129,413	5,020	271,564	136,334
1975	1,527,220	1,278,443	42,026	1,320,469	109,791	-75,803	1,134,875	222,253	170,092	5,640	270,769	134,827
1976	1,690,429	1,422,098	47,767	1,469,865	124,369	-87,822	1,257,674	244,678	188,077	6,143	275,162	139,310
1977	1,875,322	1,600,483	46,880	1,647,363	138,761	-110,435	1,398,167	275,896	201,259	6,670	281,149	145,598
1978	2,108,943	1,836,976	45,608	1,882,584	165,451	-136,434	1,580,699	313,146	215,098	7,420	284,208	152,779
1979	2,340,659	2,060,026	33,060	2,093,086	193,578	-159,879	1,739,629	356,628	244,402	8,089	289,360	159,411
1980	2,642,356	2,283,907	29,054	2,312,961	215,340	-185,895	1,911,726	441,354	289,276	9,023	292,831	161,496
1981	2,996,125	2,548,198	49,217	2,597,415	259,568	-220,612	2,117,235	550,180	328,710	10,129	295,796	164,424
1982	3,271,417	2,789,460	46,400	2,835,860	285,480	-265,038	2,285,342	632,778	353,297	10,951	298,730	165,394
1983	3,549,486	3,082,842	29,439	3,112,281	319,465	-308,992	2,483,824	683,769	381,893	11,742	302,298	169,000
1984	4,055,512	3,555,700	57,383	3,613,083	375,208	-389,444	2,848,431	803,508	403,573	13,212	306,946	181,343
1985	4,483,187	4,037,273	39,559	4,076,832	433,856	-478,133	3,164,843	889,894	428,450	14,331	312,842	194,306
1986	4,850,330	4,401,453	45,407	4,446,860	484,101	-538,987	3,423,772	976,809	449,749	15,113	320,939	202,479
1987	5,241,180	4,834,783	41,562	4,876,345	523,175	-626,201	3,726,969	1,041,383	472,828	16,011	327,345	210,424
1988	5,745,334	5,306,392	50,485	5,356,877	593,447	-700,672	4,062,758	1,167,837	514,739	17,239	333,279	219,599
1989	6,407,741	5,836,526	73,992	5,910,518	652,385	-826,920	4,431,213	1,406,073	570,455	18,860	339,747	227,827
1990	6,889,138	6,379,292	76,802	6,456,094	732,505	-940,086	4,783,503	1,471,143	634,492	19,859	346,907	234,238
1991	7,303,956	6,937,599	81,031	7,018,630	806,872	-1,153,298	5,058,460	1,515,289	730,207	20,596	354,625	240,084
1992	7,966,650	7,666,502	70,716	7,737,218	877,736	-1,329,660	5,529,822	1,630,580	806,248	21,962	362,754	246,553
1993	8,482,748	8,134,028	82,794	8,216,822	932,898	-1,430,448	5,853,476	1,736,975	892,297	22,793	372,169	253,905
1994	8,941,962	8,585,093	75,492	8,660,585	1,002,171	-1,534,853	6,123,561	1,884,946	933,455	23,527	380,071	259,586
1995	9,509,941	9,219,347	77,519	9,296,866	1,078,060	-1,746,463	6,472,343	2,000,286	1,037,312	24,498	388,187	269,469
1996	10,159,357	9,870,034	78,209	9,948,243	1,149,885	-1,926,881	6,871,477	2,171,756	1,116,124	25,657	395,974	279,035
1997	10,825,403	10,713,078	74,928	10,788,006	1,241,276	-2,267,901	7,278,829	2,376,644	1,169,930	26,724	405,085	288,450
1998	12,555,238	12,323,937	97,087	12,421,024	1,423,321	-2,508,066	8,489,637	2,727,196	1,338,405	27,333	459,340	323,476
1999	13,309,949	13,508,901	93,206	13,602,107	1,555,195	-2,887,562	9,159,350	2,755,603	1,394,996	28,457	467,724	332,170
2000	14,289,599	15,042,125	99,737	15,141,862	1,712,365	-3,560,578	9,868,919	2,913,770	1,506,910	30,087	474,940	339,445
2001	14,808,947	15,464,420	115,865	15,580,285	1,761,358	-3,577,117	10,241,810	2,892,757	1,674,380	30,511	485,366	335,490
2002	14,890,239	15,537,447	48,339	15,585,786	1,754,849	-3,584,375	10,246,562	2,819,418	1,824,259	30,157	493,757	335,512
2003	15,397,873	15,974,286	58,336	16,032,622	1,825,908	-3,641,244	10,565,470	2,918,240	1,914,163	30,843	499,238	335,976
2004	17,208,329	17,230,555	85,956	17,316,511	1,923,330	-3,602,399	11,790,782	3,365,772	2,051,775	34,102	504,619	344,725
2005	18,403,837	17,948,957	87,170	18,036,127	2,005,070	-3,560,612	12,470,445	3,689,960	2,243,432	35,917	512,402	349,831
2006	19,985,680	19,504,619	86,063	19,590,682	2,166,613	-3,921,877	13,502,192	4,073,713	2,409,775	38,184	523,405	361,753
2007	21,641,565	21,035,766	72,480	21,108,246	2,350,480	-4,266,565	14,491,201	4,527,456	2,622,908	40,372	536,055	375,705
2008	22,723,334	21,694,585	67,968	21,762,553	2,438,267	-4,313,758	15,010,528	4,696,569	3,016,237	41,445	548,275	377,788
2009	22,363,265	21,540,500	65,924	21,606,424	2,440,100	-4,381,691	14,784,633	4,239,471	3,339,161	39,994	559,164	372,046
2010	23,269,960	22,592,221	67,617	22,659,838	2,496,471	-4,624,587	15,538,780	4,141,075	3,590,105	41,092	566,291	370,041
2011	24,281,376	22,195,969	37,129	22,233,098	2,214,484	-4,101,661	15,916,953	4,645,490	3,718,933	42,404	572,619	372,166
2012	25,569,595	23,452,607	71,983	23,524,590	2,302,260	-4,493,202	16,729,128	5,030,767	3,809,700	43,939	581,939	380,080
2013	25,647,468	24,025,170	78,325	24,103,495	2,729,882	-4,710,596	16,663,017	5,075,646	3,908,805	43,423	590,648	385,957
2014	27,420,292	25,476,975	99,895	25,576,870	2,907,250	-5,100,283	17,569,337	5,754,075	4,096,880	45,760	599,215	401,226
2015	28,868,203	25,940,837	103,998	26,044,835	2,963,764	-4,791,416	18,289,655	6,299,225	4,279,323	47,509	607,634	407,881
2016	30,284,384	26,790,548	73,640	26,864,188	3,045,013	-4,728,221	19,090,954	6,746,627	4,446,803	49,008	617,947	426,376
2017	31,820,648	27,951,598	82,939	28,034,537	3,171,666	-4,830,482	20,032,389	7,164,784	4,623,475	50,888	625,313	434,195
2018	33,291,988	29,540,106	33,542	29,573,648	3,313,511	-5,270,901	20,989,236	7,426,262	4,876,490	52,245	637,232	446,162
2019	35,787,242	31,337,629	38,251	31,375,880	3,522,470	-5,551,271	22,302,139	8,330,673	5,154,430	55,548	644,257	453,896
2020	38,088,584	33,750,267	39,551	33,789,818	3,795,591	-6,939,580	23,054,647	8,403,033	6,630,904	58,491	651,192	452,506
2021	41,447,871	36,839,774	47,915	36,887,689	4,092,473	-7,551,826	25,243,390	8,702,479	7,502,002	63,375	654,012	470,308

Personal Income and Employment by Area: East Stroudsburg, PA

(Thousands of dollars, except as noted.)

Year	Personal income, total	Earnings by place of work			Less: Contributions for government social insurance	Plus: Adjustment for residence	Equals: Net earnings by place of residence	Plus: Dividends, interest, and rent	Plus: Personal current transfer receipts	Per capita personal income (dollars)	Population (persons)	Total employment
		Nonfarm	Farm	Total								
1970	194,209	182,295	827	183,122	10,715	-31,752	140,655	35,461	18,093	4,274	45,441	25,965
1971	213,335	196,699	428	197,127	12,257	-32,102	152,768	39,287	21,280	4,607	46,302	26,505
1972	248,897	225,488	371	225,859	14,780	-30,103	180,976	43,302	24,619	5,088	48,917	27,900
1973	288,633	255,839	1,253	257,092	19,290	-27,452	210,350	49,387	28,896	5,582	51,711	30,353
1974	332,565	284,289	444	284,733	22,923	-21,738	240,072	57,013	35,480	6,060	54,877	31,305
1975	376,892	310,120	1,209	311,329	24,286	-21,927	265,116	63,225	48,551	6,539	57,637	31,147
1976	419,438	340,807	1,441	342,248	27,013	-20,304	294,931	69,090	55,417	6,948	60,370	31,868
1977	466,232	374,938	1,261	376,199	29,933	-18,455	327,811	78,578	59,843	7,418	62,848	33,116
1978	527,126	428,874	605	429,479	34,743	-20,408	374,328	87,436	65,362	8,043	65,535	34,888
1979	594,040	464,086	1,693	465,779	39,493	-7,479	418,807	100,718	74,515	8,747	67,911	35,265
1980	671,280	502,881	847	503,728	43,763	-1,091	458,874	123,937	88,469	9,638	69,649	35,960
1981	748,267	543,688	1,354	545,042	50,517	-2,152	492,373	153,781	102,113	10,618	70,470	36,945
1982	820,383	575,935	628	576,563	53,316	-3,409	519,838	183,750	116,795	11,444	71,688	37,363
1983	886,219	621,275	-703	620,572	60,457	3,873	563,988	192,646	129,585	12,231	72,455	38,614
1984	996,821	705,394	127	705,521	71,441	12,221	646,301	215,952	134,568	13,552	73,556	41,607
1985	1,101,908	772,694	490	773,184	80,655	20,504	713,033	243,869	145,006	14,643	75,250	43,899
1986	1,225,161	858,957	-310	858,647	91,421	34,923	802,149	266,866	156,146	15,682	78,127	46,679
1987	1,358,778	975,575	-184	975,391	104,863	38,173	908,701	287,301	162,776	16,642	81,647	49,932
1988	1,520,404	1,077,847	258	1,078,105	119,941	64,965	1,023,129	319,368	177,907	17,442	87,169	52,588
1989	1,661,775	1,172,745	307	1,173,052	129,279	80,753	1,124,526	344,087	193,162	17,974	92,452	54,322
1990	1,753,086	1,198,259	1,230	1,199,489	134,266	91,776	1,156,999	374,386	221,701	18,094	96,889	54,242
1991	1,824,976	1,191,145	805	1,191,950	134,807	142,673	1,199,816	362,986	262,174	17,986	101,469	51,670
1992	1,954,018	1,223,833	652	1,224,485	139,601	219,505	1,304,389	359,511	290,118	18,495	105,649	51,456
1993	2,099,128	1,272,615	376	1,272,991	148,043	274,122	1,399,070	390,352	309,706	19,072	110,062	52,129
1994	2,241,252	1,342,685	813	1,343,498	159,585	308,249	1,492,162	410,471	338,619	19,531	114,752	54,504
1995	2,387,172	1,412,106	221	1,412,327	167,964	333,079	1,577,442	448,581	361,149	20,048	119,070	55,406
1996	2,553,234	1,485,514	874	1,486,388	172,585	377,439	1,691,242	470,421	391,571	20,706	123,307	56,753
1997	2,745,753	1,556,759	300	1,557,059	179,586	449,521	1,826,994	504,257	414,502	21,540	127,470	58,180
1998	2,981,064	1,664,753	67	1,664,820	189,520	514,905	1,990,205	550,263	440,596	22,755	131,007	59,561
1999	3,195,152	1,795,717	-421	1,795,296	202,208	590,379	2,183,467	544,688	466,997	23,679	134,936	61,565
2000	3,567,449	2,006,772	945	2,007,717	222,797	677,943	2,462,863	597,692	506,894	25,535	139,710	65,634
2001	3,814,532	2,176,915	-112	2,176,803	239,633	695,600	2,632,770	626,085	555,677	26,531	143,775	67,036
2002	4,011,713	2,343,141	-558	2,342,583	259,696	704,460	2,787,347	611,079	613,287	26,954	148,833	68,786
2003	4,236,917	2,492,342	826	2,493,168	274,943	732,387	2,950,612	631,046	655,259	27,508	154,027	70,438
2004	4,534,821	2,745,961	2,174	2,748,135	300,564	763,525	3,211,096	615,810	707,915	28,669	158,181	72,677
2005	4,802,690	2,913,729	1,270	2,914,999	324,017	818,830	3,409,812	644,165	748,713	29,638	162,045	74,896
2006	5,074,251	3,109,251	1,121	3,110,372	347,584	852,622	3,615,410	661,370	797,471	30,719	165,185	77,436
2007	5,401,544	3,246,699	-592	3,246,107	366,335	908,481	3,788,253	751,140	862,151	32,277	167,352	79,621
2008	5,639,407	3,337,135	1,380	3,338,515	380,165	827,629	3,785,979	840,778	1,012,650	33,453	168,576	80,002
2009	5,509,355	3,244,682	2,346	3,247,028	375,063	709,276	3,581,241	820,211	1,107,903	32,525	169,390	77,120
2010	5,512,283	3,364,629	2,746	3,367,375	386,051	525,387	3,506,711	806,761	1,198,811	32,453	169,852	76,353
2011	5,784,442	3,390,590	2,454	3,393,044	353,271	619,104	3,658,877	902,309	1,223,256	34,042	169,921	75,724
2012	5,720,936	3,396,615	4,018	3,400,633	351,987	561,528	3,610,174	896,845	1,213,917	33,917	168,675	75,092
2013	5,995,776	3,381,459	3,672	3,385,131	391,240	827,030	3,820,921	921,296	1,253,559	35,810	167,435	74,392
2014	6,255,460	3,400,978	3,531	3,404,509	392,790	929,691	3,941,410	1,000,889	1,313,161	37,537	166,649	73,902
2015	6,518,581	3,599,021	2,060	3,601,081	411,673	912,118	4,101,526	1,036,422	1,380,633	39,341	165,695	75,418
2016	6,663,172	3,705,909	1,201	3,707,110	424,734	930,934	4,213,310	968,182	1,481,680	40,323	165,244	76,876
2017	6,903,699	3,822,245	1,923	3,824,168	445,220	945,795	4,324,743	1,043,347	1,535,609	41,397	166,769	77,757
2018	7,228,009	3,893,600	676	3,894,276	453,278	1,066,540	4,507,538	1,066,845	1,653,626	43,005	168,072	78,493
2019	7,613,060	4,024,954	1,984	4,026,938	477,555	1,167,076	4,716,459	1,171,224	1,725,377	45,196	168,447	79,506
2020	8,323,052	4,026,105	1,167	4,027,272	475,088	1,175,239	4,727,423	1,216,255	2,379,374	49,469	168,248	74,802
2021	8,991,360	4,269,197	1,430	4,270,627	498,901	1,423,463	5,195,189	1,273,360	2,522,811	53,118	169,273	77,752

Personal Income and Employment by Area: Eau Claire, WI

(Thousands of dollars, except as noted.)

Year	Personal income, total	Earnings by place of work			Less: Contributions for government social insurance	Plus: Adjustment for residence	Equals: Net earnings by place of residence	Plus: Dividends, interest, and rent	Plus: Personal current transfer receipts	Per capita personal income (dollars)	Population (persons)	Total employment
		Nonfarm	Farm	Total								
1970	419,956	338,337	18,916	357,253	24,606	-15,205	317,442	60,574	41,940	3,634	115,555	51,672
1971	458,788	366,348	19,437	385,785	27,578	-15,059	343,148	66,738	48,902	3,868	118,617	52,507
1972	498,973	396,468	21,232	417,700	31,497	-14,966	371,237	72,549	55,187	4,117	121,204	53,066
1973	544,971	421,461	27,307	448,768	38,435	-13,749	396,584	82,783	65,604	4,532	120,238	53,548
1974	593,854	448,670	23,743	472,413	42,635	-12,378	417,400	95,445	81,009	4,900	121,193	53,903
1975	654,586	478,280	23,005	501,285	44,802	-10,849	445,634	105,868	103,084	5,278	124,012	54,581
1976	718,124	522,433	22,471	544,904	49,332	-8,453	487,119	114,646	116,359	5,768	124,496	55,598
1977	809,882	591,713	33,334	625,047	55,755	-8,927	560,365	128,716	120,801	6,376	127,012	58,235
1978	903,140	663,937	32,358	696,295	64,252	-8,085	623,958	145,308	133,874	7,006	128,912	60,913
1979	1,001,516	721,254	39,869	761,123	73,061	-5,310	682,752	163,382	155,382	7,746	129,293	62,962
1980	1,134,990	788,012	38,953	826,965	80,069	-3,752	743,144	203,928	187,918	8,637	131,405	63,315
1981	1,258,094	867,406	28,946	896,352	94,693	-6,369	795,290	253,342	209,462	9,460	132,986	63,776
1982	1,335,786	897,855	31,085	928,940	98,771	-5,587	824,582	284,237	226,967	9,988	133,738	63,651
1983	1,418,059	962,471	17,044	979,515	104,736	-6,070	868,709	303,807	245,543	10,620	133,527	63,838
1984	1,540,874	1,036,771	36,546	1,073,317	114,793	-6,756	951,768	333,284	255,822	11,483	134,188	65,777
1985	1,624,946	1,091,947	38,545	1,130,492	121,819	-6,865	1,001,808	348,985	274,153	12,116	134,120	66,855
1986	1,738,763	1,188,545	46,202	1,234,747	132,621	-9,456	1,092,670	365,859	280,234	12,951	134,252	69,351
1987	1,836,251	1,280,738	46,161	1,326,899	140,459	-8,519	1,177,921	367,429	290,901	13,578	135,233	71,536
1988	1,932,390	1,382,778	35,469	1,418,247	158,022	-8,101	1,252,124	379,880	300,386	14,196	136,125	73,958
1989	2,103,205	1,458,885	58,235	1,517,120	168,017	-6,236	1,342,867	438,623	321,715	15,331	137,187	74,933
1990	2,210,384	1,549,512	45,879	1,595,391	184,659	-3,909	1,406,823	457,352	346,209	16,044	137,771	75,588
1991	2,291,073	1,634,203	29,109	1,663,312	196,411	-5,928	1,460,973	457,717	372,383	16,444	139,325	77,150
1992	2,473,941	1,770,557	39,166	1,809,723	210,432	-6,098	1,593,193	478,354	402,394	17,594	140,614	78,688
1993	2,556,898	1,849,389	28,959	1,878,348	219,142	-4,464	1,654,742	496,495	405,661	18,008	141,985	79,787
1994	2,731,707	1,993,723	39,188	2,032,911	238,979	-8,667	1,785,265	531,646	414,796	19,103	142,998	83,136
1995	2,890,743	2,122,856	23,168	2,146,024	256,322	-13,876	1,875,826	578,603	436,314	20,082	143,950	87,319
1996	3,073,447	2,260,603	48,049	2,308,652	271,154	-19,616	2,017,882	604,820	450,745	21,219	144,842	90,392
1997	3,291,681	2,463,325	27,624	2,490,949	293,360	-29,143	2,168,446	659,539	463,696	22,571	145,834	92,863
1998	3,557,521	2,683,325	41,695	2,725,020	316,442	-34,822	2,373,756	704,998	478,767	24,288	146,470	95,170
1999	3,719,700	2,878,236	40,283	2,918,519	339,429	-36,658	2,542,432	685,574	491,694	25,239	147,378	98,899
2000	3,982,422	3,086,019	23,291	3,109,310	358,894	-42,184	2,708,232	743,629	530,561	26,790	148,656	99,914
2001	4,124,483	3,097,389	30,283	3,127,672	349,893	-40,232	2,737,547	792,641	594,295	27,560	149,655	95,828
2002	4,252,717	3,247,083	26,906	3,273,989	363,063	-46,614	2,864,312	750,152	638,253	28,192	150,846	95,806
2003	4,382,504	3,349,585	39,142	3,388,727	375,660	-45,407	2,967,660	756,849	657,995	28,867	151,816	96,732
2004	4,558,285	3,516,014	56,976	3,572,990	396,051	-28,359	3,148,580	730,416	679,289	29,711	153,419	98,739
2005	4,744,718	3,643,923	43,810	3,687,733	419,561	-31,023	3,237,149	774,572	732,997	30,649	154,809	100,615
2006	5,075,585	3,903,679	31,468	3,935,147	450,264	-43,341	3,441,542	865,839	768,204	32,501	156,167	103,409
2007	5,426,510	4,123,968	50,974	4,174,942	473,842	-54,827	3,646,273	941,977	838,260	34,420	157,654	105,103
2008	5,680,754	4,218,685	54,337	4,273,022	489,409	-61,422	3,722,191	1,020,917	937,646	35,796	158,700	104,841
2009	5,786,710	4,257,365	17,745	4,275,110	490,112	-50,536	3,734,462	977,953	1,074,295	36,106	160,271	101,939
2010	6,012,246	4,429,002	54,944	4,483,946	507,210	-57,029	3,919,707	935,909	1,156,630	37,191	161,658	102,785
2011	6,356,838	4,576,027	96,764	4,672,791	468,984	-58,524	4,145,283	1,077,253	1,134,302	39,021	162,910	104,747
2012	6,629,824	4,762,943	81,167	4,844,110	485,896	-71,067	4,287,147	1,180,922	1,161,755	40,444	163,925	106,085
2013	6,678,050	4,797,992	101,601	4,899,593	552,230	-72,303	4,275,060	1,200,148	1,202,842	40,503	164,877	106,196
2014	6,996,748	4,996,835	91,059	5,087,894	577,362	-60,596	4,449,936	1,292,317	1,254,495	42,156	165,972	107,727
2015	7,151,789	5,120,020	79,414	5,199,434	593,442	-83,920	4,522,072	1,313,391	1,316,326	42,910	166,668	108,525
2016	7,184,360	5,134,902	50,600	5,185,502	598,509	-90,251	4,496,742	1,355,379	1,332,239	42,798	167,865	109,144
2017	7,549,560	5,418,514	37,816	5,456,330	637,296	-111,222	4,707,812	1,455,017	1,386,731	44,684	168,956	110,396
2018	7,988,313	5,764,038	41,322	5,805,360	665,041	-122,751	5,017,568	1,509,531	1,461,214	46,963	170,097	111,740
2019	8,314,829	5,941,989	39,300	5,981,289	691,749	-156,280	5,133,260	1,619,796	1,561,773	48,595	171,106	111,727
2020	8,884,594	6,078,916	77,960	6,156,876	715,326	-164,295	5,277,255	1,651,272	1,956,067	51,626	172,097	107,922
2021	9,500,197	6,438,300	84,513	6,522,813	745,785	-174,072	5,602,956	1,706,516	2,190,725	54,814	173,317	111,175

Personal Income and Employment by Area: El Centro, CA

(Thousands of dollars, except as noted.)

Year	Personal income, total	Earnings by place of work			Less: Contributions for government social insurance	Plus: Adjustment for residence	Equals: Net earnings by place of residence	Plus: Dividends, interest, and rent	Plus: Personal current transfer receipts	Per capita personal income (dollars)	Population (persons)	Total employment
		Nonfarm	Farm	Total								
1970	299,115	175,395	102,809	278,204	12,340	-39,358	226,506	35,112	37,497	3,999	74,795	34,273
1971	301,362	187,379	88,107	275,486	13,656	-38,450	223,380	37,989	39,993	4,022	74,931	34,377
1972	384,220	203,216	148,542	351,758	15,533	-37,939	298,286	42,324	43,610	5,064	75,869	35,499
1973	425,947	232,410	155,052	387,462	20,286	-39,142	328,034	50,959	46,954	5,348	79,648	37,260
1974	488,692	268,810	177,654	446,464	24,223	-47,271	374,970	57,885	55,837	5,994	81,526	39,718
1975	523,162	305,287	168,146	473,433	26,376	-57,783	389,274	65,016	68,872	6,304	82,989	42,553
1976	581,199	343,522	181,160	524,682	30,301	-65,269	429,112	67,212	84,875	6,816	85,264	44,782
1977	603,258	373,672	166,362	540,034	32,857	-71,274	435,903	73,034	94,321	6,936	86,981	44,503
1978	656,466	414,805	168,076	582,881	36,740	-77,911	468,230	84,373	103,863	7,420	88,474	44,679
1979	929,275	466,456	371,339	837,795	43,714	-76,661	717,420	97,418	114,437	10,315	90,086	46,745
1980	892,604	501,697	271,261	772,958	46,460	-87,007	639,491	119,747	133,366	9,641	92,584	45,523
1981	937,766	534,114	203,896	738,010	52,687	-53,920	631,403	147,688	158,675	9,944	94,301	43,663
1982	1,039,053	549,167	267,565	816,732	54,739	-61,416	700,577	164,268	174,208	10,859	95,688	43,260
1983	1,100,336	550,956	290,123	841,079	56,053	-60,135	724,891	184,073	191,372	11,357	96,890	42,970
1984	1,127,019	600,390	255,088	855,478	63,262	-65,130	727,086	188,991	210,942	11,562	97,475	42,308
1985	1,123,270	635,816	200,804	836,620	66,587	-64,735	705,298	190,390	227,582	11,323	99,199	41,051
1986	1,161,225	700,264	174,015	874,279	74,683	-63,037	736,559	194,658	230,008	11,743	98,885	42,325
1987	1,363,167	768,105	303,976	1,072,081	81,927	-62,779	927,375	197,166	238,626	13,621	100,077	43,579
1988	1,568,327	881,931	393,506	1,275,437	98,187	-65,519	1,111,731	204,377	252,219	15,394	101,881	47,530
1989	1,688,937	966,360	385,739	1,352,099	110,979	-67,273	1,173,847	234,710	280,380	16,060	105,166	52,145
1990	1,789,097	1,045,624	369,225	1,414,849	118,763	-64,759	1,231,327	241,450	316,320	16,141	110,839	52,121
1991	1,874,590	1,094,401	359,154	1,453,555	123,658	-57,914	1,271,983	244,914	357,693	16,003	117,143	51,265
1992	2,015,111	1,232,205	297,403	1,529,608	135,611	-63,856	1,330,141	249,669	435,301	16,274	123,823	52,634
1993	2,262,259	1,315,565	431,050	1,746,615	144,367	-62,945	1,539,303	262,817	460,139	17,040	132,758	55,335
1994	2,284,882	1,371,806	382,693	1,754,499	150,955	-65,039	1,538,505	282,712	463,665	17,011	134,315	56,933
1995	2,360,428	1,372,800	396,911	1,769,711	149,162	-60,419	1,560,130	307,361	492,937	17,231	136,986	58,101
1996	2,345,878	1,406,497	306,694	1,713,191	146,736	-56,152	1,510,303	316,234	519,341	17,001	137,987	58,050
1997	2,440,859	1,492,990	312,060	1,805,050	151,731	-53,773	1,599,546	331,269	510,044	17,608	138,624	59,914
1998	2,611,388	1,601,412	352,679	1,954,091	159,715	-49,135	1,745,241	327,044	539,103	18,704	139,615	61,395
1999	2,705,995	1,679,382	336,057	2,015,439	169,696	-42,253	1,803,490	335,593	566,912	19,184	141,056	63,093
2000	2,712,646	1,760,164	256,305	2,016,469	176,722	-33,083	1,806,664	333,111	572,871	19,048	142,410	60,311
2001	2,984,655	1,940,927	263,770	2,204,697	201,616	-1,292	2,001,789	360,561	622,305	20,769	143,707	59,479
2002	3,361,559	2,116,860	420,879	2,537,739	224,188	-13,561	2,299,990	368,942	692,627	23,081	145,640	63,149
2003	3,495,156	2,291,170	330,729	2,621,899	246,737	-24,601	2,350,561	409,724	734,871	23,460	148,984	65,353
2004	3,594,395	2,399,849	337,700	2,737,549	264,132	-30,088	2,443,329	396,241	754,825	23,607	152,259	65,534
2005	3,773,375	2,550,118	359,551	2,909,669	281,823	-48,341	2,579,505	396,202	797,668	24,171	156,113	67,019
2006	4,081,732	2,763,435	359,157	3,122,592	297,424	-66,805	2,758,363	435,014	888,355	25,431	160,505	71,933
2007	4,340,537	2,920,499	367,927	3,288,426	306,836	-100,968	2,880,622	481,464	978,451	26,371	164,596	74,210
2008	4,732,242	3,018,166	570,993	3,589,159	323,826	-139,253	3,126,080	521,139	1,085,023	28,182	167,917	74,053
2009	4,796,535	3,031,927	488,178	3,520,105	328,891	-144,503	3,046,711	519,722	1,230,102	27,886	172,008	72,584
2010	5,087,722	3,176,001	468,740	3,644,741	327,185	-147,385	3,170,171	539,577	1,377,974	29,122	174,704	72,573
2011	5,490,146	3,312,875	693,343	4,006,218	310,398	-151,912	3,543,908	569,598	1,376,640	31,242	175,731	73,804
2012	5,566,933	3,398,162	636,806	4,034,968	319,759	-157,064	3,558,145	623,784	1,385,004	31,543	176,487	75,293
2013	5,769,757	3,453,971	797,545	4,251,516	359,238	-164,632	3,727,646	610,471	1,431,640	32,727	176,301	77,672
2014	6,065,862	3,531,686	945,439	4,477,125	374,038	-168,656	3,934,431	618,164	1,513,267	34,184	177,447	80,244
2015	6,507,966	3,683,997	1,120,288	4,804,285	384,248	-180,340	4,239,697	627,831	1,640,438	36,504	178,280	81,488
2016	6,378,864	3,736,371	845,318	4,581,689	395,925	-173,260	4,012,504	658,701	1,707,659	35,561	179,377	79,771
2017	6,512,842	3,856,611	855,144	4,711,755	414,765	-183,980	4,113,010	692,052	1,707,780	36,050	180,662	80,091
2018	6,459,533	3,980,999	576,907	4,557,906	431,225	-180,036	3,946,645	707,894	1,804,994	35,808	180,396	80,995
2019	6,811,102	4,151,387	621,384	4,772,771	457,039	-184,673	4,131,059	743,146	1,936,897	37,904	179,694	81,032
2020	8,080,812	4,373,129	620,246	4,993,375	481,059	-188,917	4,323,399	744,505	3,012,908	45,021	179,489	78,469
2021	8,570,390	4,705,141	432,636	5,137,777	520,371	-201,535	4,415,871	757,983	3,396,536	47,653	179,851	82,115

Personal Income and Employment by Area: Elizabethtown-Fort Knox, KY

(Thousands of dollars, except as noted.)

| Year | Personal income, total | Derivation of personal income | | | | | | | | | Per capita personal income (dollars) | Population (persons) | Total employment |
| | | Earnings by place of work | | | Less: Contributions for government social insurance | Plus: Adjustment for residence | Equals: Net earnings by place of residence | Plus: Dividends, interest, and rent | Plus: Personal current transfer receipts | | | |
		Nonfarm	Farm	Total								
1970	491,984	398,423	12,529	410,952	23,039	-14,461	373,452	98,882	19,650	4,570	107,652	63,118
1971	506,089	410,110	12,972	423,082	25,386	-13,153	384,543	98,997	22,549	4,693	107,830	58,437
1972	542,596	436,669	15,160	451,829	27,167	-11,239	413,423	104,010	25,163	5,120	105,967	55,176
1973	560,221	437,445	20,332	457,777	28,728	-7,041	422,008	107,957	30,256	5,651	99,133	53,229
1974	652,568	507,481	21,922	529,403	35,205	-8,168	486,030	128,841	37,697	6,222	104,885	56,273
1975	671,920	527,785	8,542	536,327	39,119	-9,799	487,409	135,350	49,161	6,085	110,417	55,211
1976	706,293	550,417	11,074	561,491	41,609	-7,908	511,974	139,162	55,157	5,984	118,037	54,863
1977	813,909	630,775	15,044	645,819	47,522	-5,233	593,064	164,089	56,756	6,840	118,999	58,950
1978	870,028	663,260	13,202	676,462	49,187	-891	626,384	183,007	60,637	7,440	116,940	58,530
1979	963,407	726,754	18,573	745,327	55,912	1,808	691,223	200,731	71,453	8,099	118,949	58,857
1980	1,043,585	774,609	12,994	787,603	60,353	6,490	733,740	222,770	87,075	8,467	123,258	59,302
1981	1,120,007	824,555	23,285	847,840	67,596	-1,735	778,509	238,939	102,559	9,239	121,230	55,951
1982	1,224,859	902,266	19,247	921,513	73,092	-6,467	841,954	270,514	112,391	10,139	120,805	57,731
1983	1,301,661	970,267	-4,977	965,290	82,238	-4,472	878,580	301,075	122,006	10,686	121,809	59,250
1984	1,419,848	1,040,392	20,621	1,061,013	89,965	-6,182	964,866	323,023	131,959	11,617	122,225	59,602
1985	1,507,158	1,115,054	13,121	1,128,175	98,762	-7,492	1,021,921	343,728	141,509	12,271	122,818	61,588
1986	1,570,448	1,159,048	10,639	1,169,687	107,212	-4,045	1,058,430	360,946	151,072	12,745	123,219	62,886
1987	1,646,379	1,216,479	15,614	1,232,093	114,431	-1,060	1,116,602	372,470	157,307	13,379	123,053	63,165
1988	1,740,487	1,287,933	13,949	1,301,882	127,116	3,614	1,178,380	389,243	172,864	13,939	124,869	64,064
1989	1,867,718	1,356,676	27,634	1,384,310	137,220	1,961	1,249,051	421,558	197,109	15,005	124,472	65,539
1990	1,952,934	1,417,728	27,448	1,445,176	149,829	-1,596	1,293,751	441,466	217,717	15,565	125,466	66,277
1991	2,026,159	1,465,668	26,767	1,492,435	157,434	3,573	1,338,574	437,630	249,955	16,677	121,495	63,642
1992	2,221,243	1,601,058	31,941	1,632,999	174,927	12,968	1,471,040	469,946	280,257	18,501	120,059	64,628
1993	2,261,877	1,616,181	28,089	1,644,270	179,628	26,923	1,491,565	480,250	290,062	17,880	126,505	64,846
1994	2,353,163	1,650,695	29,606	1,680,301	185,251	42,886	1,537,936	512,089	303,138	18,338	128,321	65,357
1995	2,427,074	1,676,822	12,002	1,688,824	187,469	58,150	1,559,505	537,840	329,729	18,753	129,423	66,847
1996	2,551,053	1,737,716	25,435	1,763,151	193,965	70,444	1,639,630	558,547	352,876	19,792	128,895	67,246
1997	2,657,710	1,821,853	13,987	1,835,840	203,643	87,851	1,720,048	558,277	379,385	20,415	130,182	67,884
1998	2,842,869	1,918,497	2,078	1,920,575	213,770	112,510	1,819,315	625,174	398,380	21,631	131,428	69,443
1999	2,970,423	2,028,470	-17,686	2,010,784	226,410	138,522	1,922,896	633,660	413,867	22,408	132,558	70,620
2000	3,287,456	2,218,645	10,401	2,229,046	241,336	158,738	2,146,448	689,164	451,844	24,441	134,506	72,649
2001	3,417,136	2,316,789	12,327	2,329,116	253,373	150,293	2,226,036	690,122	500,978	25,190	135,657	73,306
2002	3,484,457	2,403,553	-8,285	2,395,268	263,545	134,731	2,266,454	668,108	549,895	25,510	136,591	72,023
2003	3,644,264	2,583,778	-395	2,583,383	281,482	95,338	2,397,239	674,473	572,552	26,731	136,333	73,739
2004	3,835,040	2,742,619	12,133	2,754,752	296,701	79,623	2,537,674	671,739	625,627	27,744	138,230	74,797
2005	3,990,078	2,840,721	28,565	2,869,286	306,621	68,515	2,631,180	689,533	669,365	28,465	140,177	73,784
2006	4,190,987	3,056,116	19,473	3,075,589	333,357	-5,567	2,736,665	720,998	733,324	29,751	140,870	76,298
2007	4,383,848	3,126,494	7,363	3,133,857	342,919	-13,447	2,777,491	809,572	796,785	30,906	141,844	76,947
2008	4,636,525	3,324,964	-2,310	3,322,654	367,072	-114,141	2,841,441	879,933	915,151	32,426	142,988	76,798
2009	4,837,767	3,451,678	3,851	3,455,529	387,612	-121,719	2,946,198	867,779	1,023,790	33,636	143,829	75,095
2010	5,114,173	3,905,188	-5,024	3,900,164	430,212	-368,992	3,100,960	903,960	1,109,253	34,128	149,852	78,858
2011	5,377,314	4,215,031	13,722	4,228,753	420,164	-581,445	3,227,144	1,020,610	1,129,560	35,524	151,370	80,821
2012	5,469,102	4,047,365	15,997	4,063,362	408,705	-346,262	3,308,395	1,019,002	1,141,705	36,077	151,594	78,596
2013	5,417,539	3,962,025	72,901	4,034,926	449,434	-346,323	3,239,169	1,002,634	1,175,736	35,561	152,346	78,173
2014	5,659,474	3,948,047	23,128	3,971,175	446,692	-160,667	3,363,816	1,031,125	1,264,533	37,146	152,356	76,912
2015	5,764,756	3,869,821	6,678	3,876,499	446,689	-16,202	3,413,608	1,010,700	1,340,448	38,715	148,904	76,571
2016	5,968,124	3,930,875	-6,043	3,924,832	453,201	75,454	3,547,085	1,050,348	1,370,691	39,830	149,841	77,452
2017	6,143,318	4,002,182	-8,216	3,993,966	460,722	137,339	3,670,583	1,039,801	1,432,934	40,563	151,451	77,460
2018	6,354,979	4,076,565	-23,805	4,052,760	470,114	223,561	3,806,207	1,057,696	1,491,076	41,158	154,405	78,123
2019	6,687,821	4,236,662	-481	4,236,181	483,956	237,373	3,989,598	1,124,485	1,573,738	43,113	155,123	78,432
2020	7,240,275	4,335,540	9,687	4,345,227	505,688	206,515	4,046,054	1,110,412	2,083,809	46,540	155,570	76,142
2021	7,840,828	4,640,464	30,120	4,670,584	540,708	269,730	4,399,606	1,100,745	2,340,477	50,016	156,766	77,505

Personal Income and Employment by Area: Elkhart-Goshen, IN

(Thousands of dollars, except as noted.)

Year	Personal income, total	Earnings by place of work			Less: Contributions for government social insurance	Plus: Adjustment for residence	Equals: Net earnings by place of residence	Plus: Dividends, interest, and rent	Plus: Personal current transfer receipts	Per capita personal income (dollars)	Population (persons)	Total employment
		Nonfarm	Farm	Total								
1970	552,330	558,921	6,678	565,599	39,107	-84,845	441,647	75,883	34,800	4,362	126,624	71,287
1971	601,971	610,634	8,364	618,998	44,415	-97,279	477,304	83,731	40,936	4,739	127,025	73,110
1972	683,157	714,024	8,090	722,114	55,043	-119,974	547,097	90,643	45,417	5,271	129,596	80,429
1973	759,373	796,745	15,797	812,542	70,119	-137,515	604,908	101,066	53,399	5,740	132,290	84,783
1974	749,526	758,336	8,299	766,635	69,608	-128,774	568,253	114,582	66,691	5,656	132,510	77,343
1975	785,862	762,915	14,151	777,066	68,709	-132,132	576,225	122,928	86,709	5,977	131,484	73,077
1976	908,745	942,599	15,240	957,839	86,525	-176,615	694,699	132,572	81,474	6,916	131,402	82,175
1977	1,021,030	1,088,803	10,433	1,099,236	101,518	-211,138	786,580	147,905	86,545	7,644	133,567	87,444
1978	1,141,941	1,247,694	4,913	1,252,607	119,592	-251,937	881,078	166,552	94,311	8,428	135,493	93,129
1979	1,203,224	1,286,651	3,826	1,290,477	126,331	-260,684	903,462	186,875	112,887	8,803	136,687	89,398
1980	1,226,176	1,224,092	8,290	1,232,382	118,426	-245,510	868,446	216,102	141,628	8,931	137,292	80,021
1981	1,353,592	1,332,543	6,274	1,338,817	137,810	-264,066	936,941	261,466	155,185	9,892	136,836	81,375
1982	1,443,216	1,403,536	2,142	1,405,678	148,234	-281,887	975,557	295,620	172,039	10,445	138,179	82,288
1983	1,645,532	1,695,142	-736	1,694,406	179,196	-355,256	1,159,954	311,213	174,365	11,730	140,286	91,798
1984	1,885,250	1,950,161	14,866	1,965,027	212,635	-409,292	1,343,100	357,397	184,753	13,029	144,701	100,401
1985	1,993,676	2,050,682	14,229	2,064,911	228,276	-427,103	1,409,532	381,274	202,870	13,536	147,287	101,827
1986	2,160,033	2,242,074	14,300	2,256,374	250,771	-465,717	1,539,886	402,986	217,161	14,498	148,990	106,079
1987	2,354,303	2,476,699	17,339	2,494,038	273,523	-514,418	1,706,097	425,584	222,622	15,574	151,167	112,993
1988	2,542,726	2,706,767	9,082	2,715,849	306,591	-562,980	1,846,278	457,778	238,670	16,520	153,917	118,921
1989	2,732,709	2,807,367	24,021	2,831,388	319,493	-572,219	1,939,676	539,416	253,617	17,538	155,813	119,871
1990	2,803,794	2,822,729	20,457	2,843,186	330,838	-558,262	1,954,086	569,489	280,219	17,914	156,517	117,792
1991	2,854,501	2,854,635	11,015	2,865,650	336,297	-557,371	1,971,982	567,403	315,116	18,050	158,141	113,810
1992	3,141,154	3,178,927	18,894	3,197,821	369,889	-627,461	2,200,471	577,726	362,957	19,577	160,454	117,964
1993	3,350,572	3,431,207	18,421	3,449,628	399,069	-673,830	2,376,729	593,909	379,934	20,492	163,510	123,339
1994	3,619,981	3,765,878	16,011	3,781,889	444,647	-743,793	2,593,449	629,615	396,917	21,742	166,498	129,440
1995	3,812,383	3,942,977	10,087	3,953,064	468,165	-765,387	2,719,512	681,485	411,386	22,443	169,869	134,046
1996	3,977,379	4,047,205	21,687	4,068,892	480,126	-779,650	2,809,116	724,322	443,941	23,046	172,582	133,328
1997	4,141,940	4,180,777	26,012	4,206,789	495,175	-799,408	2,912,206	773,276	456,458	23,631	175,274	134,160
1998	4,491,783	4,584,103	25,812	4,609,915	534,681	-880,246	3,194,988	808,796	487,999	25,251	177,885	140,573
1999	4,784,689	5,000,052	12,762	5,012,814	576,084	-968,374	3,468,356	803,041	513,292	26,487	180,645	146,242
2000	5,036,713	5,215,659	16,832	5,232,491	593,743	-1,011,425	3,627,323	856,621	552,769	27,461	183,412	147,774
2001	4,940,677	4,933,784	27,500	4,961,284	558,095	-953,677	3,449,512	865,848	625,317	26,749	184,708	137,494
2002	5,125,933	5,237,871	21,523	5,259,394	592,996	-1,033,099	3,633,299	833,550	659,084	27,776	184,543	137,557
2003	5,341,984	5,483,030	37,248	5,520,278	625,035	-1,117,229	3,778,014	879,427	684,543	28,544	187,149	140,017
2004	5,664,572	6,079,768	50,735	6,130,503	691,342	-1,353,370	4,085,791	851,459	727,322	29,921	189,316	148,000
2005	5,939,471	6,396,016	35,677	6,431,693	732,632	-1,459,080	4,239,981	898,872	800,618	30,896	192,242	150,926
2006	6,178,363	6,633,219	25,931	6,659,150	761,053	-1,589,518	4,308,579	997,835	871,949	31,676	195,047	153,411
2007	6,341,670	6,624,585	36,147	6,660,732	760,667	-1,572,003	4,328,062	1,094,293	919,315	32,305	196,304	152,211
2008	6,196,381	6,005,156	37,192	6,042,348	702,700	-1,359,553	3,980,095	1,117,798	1,098,488	31,333	197,762	140,901
2009	5,653,479	4,914,416	11,965	4,926,381	594,486	-917,944	3,413,951	950,608	1,288,920	28,623	197,514	120,605
2010	6,049,330	5,451,546	36,227	5,487,773	652,006	-1,083,490	3,752,277	980,492	1,316,561	30,637	197,453	126,843
2011	6,440,280	5,711,253	66,753	5,778,006	614,706	-1,120,021	4,043,279	1,086,742	1,310,259	32,479	198,292	130,784
2012	6,955,673	6,444,020	63,695	6,507,715	673,007	-1,311,378	4,523,330	1,089,250	1,343,093	34,955	198,988	136,452
2013	7,221,058	6,870,601	111,674	6,982,275	815,693	-1,454,665	4,711,917	1,167,078	1,342,063	36,065	200,225	142,375
2014	7,803,468	7,553,871	115,646	7,669,517	877,982	-1,649,933	5,141,602	1,228,206	1,433,660	38,674	201,774	148,051
2015	8,196,076	8,061,154	100,288	8,161,442	933,860	-1,777,138	5,450,444	1,282,799	1,462,833	40,289	203,430	151,732
2016	8,566,765	8,690,923	64,537	8,755,460	986,412	-1,974,822	5,794,226	1,283,839	1,488,700	41,970	204,114	154,723
2017	9,257,924	9,771,511	81,470	9,852,981	1,094,012	-2,430,815	6,328,154	1,405,441	1,524,329	45,195	204,843	162,377
2018	9,531,649	10,035,990	74,846	10,110,836	1,115,705	-2,564,821	6,430,310	1,524,562	1,576,777	46,219	206,230	166,155
2019	9,495,118	9,575,853	51,489	9,627,342	1,086,805	-2,350,771	6,189,766	1,626,259	1,679,093	45,873	206,985	161,303
2020	10,201,740	9,780,147	92,258	9,872,405	1,158,047	-2,483,694	6,230,664	1,693,541	2,277,535	49,321	206,842	153,508
2021	11,382,003	11,949,798	127,285	12,077,083	1,408,581	-3,733,563	6,934,939	1,834,526	2,612,538	55,007	206,921	166,861

Personal Income and Employment by Area: Elmira, NY

(Thousands of dollars, except as noted.)

Year	Personal income, total	Earnings by place of work			Less: Contributions for government social insurance	Plus: Adjustment for residence	Equals: Net earnings by place of residence	Plus: Dividends, interest, and rent	Plus: Personal current transfer receipts	Per capita personal income (dollars)	Population (persons)	Total employment
		Nonfarm	Farm	Total								
1970	396,780	335,313	2,368	337,681	25,373	-12,399	299,909	53,299	43,572	3,911	101,457	45,446
1971	417,926	347,540	2,230	349,770	27,192	-12,258	310,320	55,746	51,860	4,135	101,080	44,720
1972	450,654	375,041	2,196	377,237	30,787	-12,053	334,397	60,356	55,901	4,433	101,665	44,763
1973	493,677	413,405	2,892	416,297	39,391	-11,728	365,178	66,953	61,546	4,915	100,452	47,207
1974	534,102	431,076	2,210	433,286	42,454	-7,486	383,346	76,704	74,052	5,344	99,936	46,263
1975	573,579	441,164	1,974	443,138	42,399	-4,851	395,888	82,717	94,974	5,707	100,497	44,186
1976	619,058	479,784	2,702	482,486	47,320	-5,821	429,345	87,803	101,910	6,190	100,008	44,018
1977	663,650	500,579	2,167	502,746	49,351	695	454,090	96,318	113,242	6,681	99,335	43,206
1978	714,037	546,455	2,186	548,641	55,145	3,982	497,478	101,245	115,314	7,235	98,689	43,898
1979	774,162	585,742	2,967	588,709	60,779	8,535	536,465	110,354	127,343	7,793	99,339	44,018
1980	866,444	638,179	3,316	641,495	65,977	11,908	587,426	132,748	146,270	8,892	97,443	43,155
1981	949,566	687,973	3,108	691,081	75,556	7,810	623,335	160,268	165,963	9,850	96,406	43,073
1982	998,061	684,350	3,010	687,360	75,753	10,379	621,986	187,261	188,814	10,393	96,032	40,676
1983	1,045,639	706,479	2,736	709,215	78,723	11,496	641,988	195,761	207,890	11,046	94,659	39,693
1984	1,129,476	766,289	3,740	770,029	86,977	11,202	694,254	214,628	220,594	12,120	93,190	40,900
1985	1,159,337	778,630	4,238	782,868	89,739	18,782	711,911	221,603	225,823	12,574	92,200	41,191
1986	1,220,687	820,878	5,105	825,983	96,525	21,794	751,252	234,062	235,373	13,388	91,179	42,328
1987	1,299,640	913,947	5,771	919,718	105,457	10,338	824,599	237,949	237,092	14,154	91,819	44,422
1988	1,395,009	1,001,625	4,398	1,006,023	118,303	11,924	899,644	246,879	248,486	14,977	93,142	46,262
1989	1,535,913	1,094,119	4,544	1,098,663	127,681	9,090	980,072	294,302	261,539	16,219	94,701	47,884
1990	1,612,204	1,147,490	4,132	1,151,622	127,221	10,605	1,035,006	296,903	280,295	16,919	95,292	48,188
1991	1,665,578	1,178,931	3,035	1,181,966	133,598	8,796	1,057,164	301,178	307,236	17,532	95,001	47,118
1992	1,728,476	1,225,409	3,014	1,228,423	136,941	-230	1,091,252	297,012	340,212	18,203	94,954	46,818
1993	1,757,154	1,252,064	3,197	1,255,261	142,315	-8,945	1,104,001	300,272	352,881	18,553	94,711	46,964
1994	1,820,741	1,307,149	2,784	1,309,933	150,604	-19,537	1,139,792	310,120	370,829	19,342	94,132	47,823
1995	1,890,135	1,356,925	2,175	1,359,100	156,193	-23,720	1,179,187	324,623	386,325	20,178	93,675	47,762
1996	1,957,988	1,405,460	3,161	1,408,621	160,241	-27,928	1,220,452	334,964	402,572	21,060	92,972	48,771
1997	2,022,561	1,474,302	1,506	1,475,808	165,208	-41,805	1,268,795	343,788	409,978	21,946	92,162	49,516
1998	2,091,797	1,547,533	2,626	1,550,159	172,207	-50,812	1,327,140	345,343	419,314	22,789	91,791	50,968
1999	2,177,775	1,618,285	2,624	1,620,909	175,117	-45,224	1,400,568	338,208	438,999	23,857	91,284	51,569
2000	2,306,929	1,672,978	2,705	1,675,683	180,729	8,745	1,503,699	359,874	443,356	25,325	91,094	51,377
2001	2,323,950	1,668,533	3,073	1,671,606	185,828	-3,329	1,482,449	365,440	476,061	25,600	90,780	49,776
2002	2,312,373	1,668,132	1,242	1,669,374	187,974	-16,560	1,464,840	326,279	521,254	25,519	90,613	48,141
2003	2,358,268	1,701,103	2,124	1,703,227	192,036	-21,127	1,490,064	329,121	539,083	26,158	90,154	47,038
2004	2,441,456	1,750,990	2,754	1,753,744	198,673	-29,364	1,525,707	342,033	573,716	27,195	89,777	46,333
2005	2,528,078	1,839,560	2,304	1,841,864	214,037	-31,036	1,596,791	334,482	596,805	28,450	88,860	46,498
2006	2,656,872	1,914,719	1,410	1,916,129	223,712	5,605	1,698,022	333,356	625,494	29,943	88,732	47,090
2007	2,776,661	1,989,116	1,961	1,991,077	229,744	-14,274	1,747,059	374,169	655,433	31,327	88,634	47,911
2008	2,979,322	2,096,938	1,900	2,098,838	243,955	-21,377	1,833,506	424,140	721,676	33,664	88,503	47,835
2009	2,991,144	2,054,454	103	2,054,557	235,740	-15,137	1,803,680	396,567	790,897	33,665	88,849	45,895
2010	3,126,423	2,211,111	1,726	2,212,837	249,700	-42,309	1,920,828	373,003	832,592	35,170	88,895	45,941
2011	3,271,729	2,289,437	2,756	2,292,193	234,526	-27,361	2,030,306	411,907	829,516	36,796	88,916	46,425
2012	3,338,095	2,347,191	2,871	2,350,062	235,926	-32,618	2,081,518	427,968	828,609	37,439	89,162	45,982
2013	3,353,842	2,360,273	5,016	2,365,289	267,866	-21,078	2,076,345	429,276	848,221	38,012	88,230	45,276
2014	3,430,082	2,387,834	4,186	2,392,020	276,393	-12,503	2,103,124	460,611	866,347	39,055	87,826	45,283
2015	3,462,055	2,387,451	1,581	2,389,032	276,158	-21,809	2,091,065	464,819	906,171	39,571	87,489	45,076
2016	3,451,653	2,338,849	1,907	2,340,756	274,189	-6,488	2,060,079	466,939	924,635	39,887	86,535	44,004
2017	3,590,685	2,365,478	3,380	2,368,858	279,508	25,460	2,114,810	489,434	986,441	41,853	85,793	43,540
2018	3,687,087	2,456,854	2,316	2,459,170	286,472	40,569	2,213,267	508,278	965,542	43,313	85,126	43,681
2019	3,841,977	2,488,642	3,947	2,492,589	291,941	62,025	2,262,673	547,842	1,031,462	45,402	84,622	43,375
2020	4,119,306	2,484,609	4,124	2,488,733	291,444	10,987	2,208,276	550,767	1,360,263	49,108	83,882	41,188
2021	4,348,209	2,669,603	6,565	2,676,168	312,722	7,588	2,371,034	568,678	1,408,497	52,360	83,045	41,484

Personal Income and Employment by Area: El Paso, TX

(Thousands of dollars, except as noted.)

Year	Personal income, total	Earnings by place of work			Less: Contributions for government social insurance	Plus: Adjustment for residence	Equals: Net earnings by place of residence	Plus: Dividends, interest, and rent	Plus: Personal current transfer receipts	Per capita personal income (dollars)	Population (persons)	Total employment
		Nonfarm	Farm	Total								
1970	1,203,259	973,527	9,345	982,872	62,026	-22,756	898,090	218,760	86,409	3,316	362,854	150,442
1971	1,316,139	1,072,835	7,844	1,080,679	71,639	-32,199	976,841	236,278	103,020	3,542	371,562	155,024
1972	1,427,111	1,168,213	13,411	1,181,624	81,214	-48,817	1,051,593	255,821	119,697	3,748	380,771	158,645
1973	1,630,778	1,347,813	10,984	1,358,797	105,969	-63,759	1,189,069	298,364	143,345	4,069	400,736	172,265
1974	1,831,322	1,504,699	11,675	1,516,374	122,106	-76,391	1,317,877	344,888	168,557	4,422	414,149	178,186
1975	1,939,079	1,650,839	11,999	1,662,838	135,057	-180,306	1,347,475	376,772	214,832	4,509	430,008	183,213
1976	2,161,399	1,845,061	16,226	1,861,287	153,446	-198,826	1,509,015	408,068	244,316	4,879	443,031	189,986
1977	2,380,879	2,036,842	20,615	2,057,457	168,057	-224,304	1,665,096	452,808	262,975	5,260	452,639	194,248
1978	2,668,601	2,290,265	12,779	2,303,044	192,179	-249,540	1,861,325	514,473	292,803	5,762	463,126	200,883
1979	3,036,740	2,583,433	10,812	2,594,245	227,863	-248,753	2,117,629	576,343	342,768	6,394	474,925	208,458
1980	3,371,958	2,851,352	6,588	2,857,940	253,028	-311,008	2,293,904	671,261	406,793	6,931	486,485	214,832
1981	4,064,006	3,239,015	20,461	3,259,476	308,726	-128,327	2,822,423	790,063	451,520	8,120	500,476	223,237
1982	4,390,171	3,442,956	6,794	3,449,750	326,341	-157,921	2,965,488	919,803	504,880	8,525	514,949	222,683
1983	4,728,022	3,635,297	17,879	3,653,176	343,899	-152,590	3,156,687	1,003,255	568,080	9,023	523,973	219,571
1984	5,096,456	3,935,097	15,534	3,950,631	383,119	-181,848	3,385,664	1,095,811	614,981	9,573	532,385	227,764
1985	5,502,556	4,238,111	17,161	4,255,272	416,452	-198,636	3,640,184	1,205,685	656,687	10,161	541,534	232,617
1986	5,806,357	4,470,682	8,031	4,478,713	438,314	-195,351	3,845,048	1,248,068	713,241	10,513	552,279	235,285
1987	6,029,678	4,645,236	19,333	4,664,569	453,731	-214,745	3,996,093	1,276,536	757,049	10,725	562,186	245,513
1988	6,454,997	5,017,373	18,127	5,035,500	508,260	-231,511	4,295,729	1,348,297	810,971	11,292	571,624	254,501
1989	7,067,940	5,375,779	16,492	5,392,271	554,062	-242,817	4,595,392	1,537,271	935,277	12,106	583,850	264,114
1990	7,634,080	5,714,230	12,285	5,726,515	581,941	-267,853	4,876,721	1,694,930	1,062,429	12,761	598,255	269,064
1991	7,942,059	6,040,646	7,748	6,048,394	624,970	-296,909	5,126,515	1,598,686	1,216,858	12,997	611,092	271,145
1992	8,771,712	6,659,925	26,917	6,686,842	688,724	-318,195	5,679,923	1,621,602	1,470,187	14,102	622,040	281,367
1993	9,242,850	7,005,752	23,325	7,029,077	731,023	-330,787	5,967,267	1,682,845	1,592,738	14,511	636,952	288,491
1994	9,749,666	7,426,708	31,411	7,458,119	774,093	-367,066	6,316,960	1,729,969	1,702,737	15,021	649,075	295,015
1995	10,234,554	7,715,170	27,551	7,742,721	802,130	-381,764	6,558,827	1,823,720	1,852,007	15,569	657,359	299,334
1996	10,632,063	7,885,941	25,758	7,911,699	813,916	-393,012	6,704,771	1,894,071	2,033,221	16,118	659,655	298,829
1997	11,373,629	8,455,018	31,215	8,486,233	865,889	-433,301	7,187,043	2,049,941	2,136,645	17,019	668,300	307,305
1998	12,019,247	8,983,520	37,465	9,020,985	913,758	-461,794	7,645,433	2,247,872	2,125,942	17,820	674,484	313,506
1999	12,339,887	9,318,037	32,288	9,350,325	942,936	-476,669	7,930,720	2,243,351	2,165,816	18,181	678,720	317,940
2000	13,149,062	9,963,918	28,706	9,992,624	984,600	-497,230	8,510,794	2,355,256	2,283,012	19,193	685,086	325,078
2001	13,749,629	10,347,298	29,458	10,376,756	1,019,086	-367,751	8,989,919	2,278,773	2,480,937	19,853	692,568	324,108
2002	14,509,859	10,837,513	31,405	10,868,918	1,064,814	-376,248	9,427,856	2,337,149	2,744,854	20,733	699,844	331,527
2003	15,065,022	11,314,505	41,980	11,356,485	1,124,126	-370,521	9,861,838	2,268,919	2,934,265	21,262	708,545	336,122
2004	15,904,628	11,966,213	36,514	12,002,727	1,187,470	-337,792	10,477,465	2,397,580	3,029,583	22,059	720,997	342,434
2005	16,907,396	12,521,173	36,324	12,557,497	1,250,725	-286,786	11,019,986	2,555,748	3,331,662	23,113	731,511	351,148
2006	17,941,104	13,191,529	20,194	13,211,723	1,313,759	-311,214	11,586,750	2,817,074	3,537,280	23,977	748,254	363,333
2007	19,049,849	13,716,866	23,047	13,739,913	1,396,064	-335,955	12,007,894	3,142,393	3,899,562	25,097	759,040	375,521
2008	20,123,842	14,068,657	12,211	14,080,868	1,450,836	-344,337	12,285,695	3,432,290	4,405,857	26,023	773,304	381,999
2009	21,098,884	14,701,719	9,959	14,711,678	1,526,138	-381,621	12,803,919	3,427,426	4,867,539	26,701	790,182	382,242
2010	23,214,670	16,161,701	18,344	16,180,045	1,657,124	-347,639	14,175,282	3,600,740	5,438,648	28,766	807,020	389,852
2011	24,755,066	17,026,028	13,030	17,039,058	1,563,687	-306,918	15,168,453	3,953,960	5,632,653	30,072	823,205	402,636
2012	25,971,644	17,739,970	7,487	17,747,457	1,639,491	-270,008	15,837,958	4,554,429	5,579,257	31,086	835,471	406,476
2013	25,594,493	17,588,135	17,401	17,605,536	1,838,180	-193,169	15,574,187	4,280,463	5,739,843	30,692	833,918	411,095
2014	26,902,225	18,212,451	19,134	18,231,585	1,898,509	-164,068	16,169,008	4,714,085	6,019,132	31,789	846,285	415,532
2015	27,711,000	18,872,774	22,786	18,895,560	1,989,160	-205,564	16,700,836	4,650,114	6,360,050	32,727	846,733	424,007
2016	28,274,056	19,295,874	17,568	19,313,442	2,037,509	-259,383	17,016,550	4,647,928	6,609,578	33,172	852,347	431,484
2017	29,300,258	20,023,445	16,751	20,040,196	2,120,487	-249,194	17,670,515	4,843,686	6,786,057	34,194	856,887	438,396
2018	30,609,997	20,887,121	12,831	20,899,952	2,194,871	-125,337	18,579,744	4,931,272	7,098,981	35,644	858,769	450,437
2019	32,694,880	22,572,590	12,196	22,584,786	2,324,062	-160,952	20,099,772	5,178,227	7,416,881	37,883	863,056	459,303
2020	35,434,497	23,075,427	14,618	23,090,045	2,414,802	-183,727	20,491,516	5,104,786	9,838,195	40,763	869,289	452,940
2021	38,384,749	24,364,909	15,428	24,380,337	2,543,550	-259,031	21,577,756	5,237,839	11,569,154	44,058	871,234	463,544

Personal Income and Employment by Area: Enid, OK

(Thousands of dollars, except as noted.)

Year	Personal income, total	Earnings by place of work			Less: Contributions for government social insurance	Plus: Adjustment for residence	Equals: Net earnings by place of residence	Plus: Dividends, interest, and rent	Plus: Personal current transfer receipts	Per capita personal income (dollars)	Population (persons)	Total employment
		Nonfarm	Farm	Total								
1970	220,525	166,678	8,631	175,309	11,088	-2,899	161,322	39,804	19,399	3,901	56,532	27,435
1971	240,055	178,534	10,934	189,468	12,299	-3,212	173,957	43,734	22,364	4,166	57,616	27,233
1972	259,831	196,276	11,158	207,434	13,972	-3,625	189,837	45,394	24,600	4,511	57,604	27,881
1973	289,212	214,464	16,047	230,511	17,570	-3,914	209,027	51,890	28,295	5,115	56,540	28,388
1974	320,536	240,903	12,184	253,087	20,314	-4,312	228,461	58,966	33,109	5,568	57,571	29,130
1975	359,151	270,396	9,176	279,572	22,654	-4,663	252,255	66,454	40,442	6,115	58,729	29,368
1976	398,849	300,179	11,996	312,175	25,466	-5,485	281,224	72,464	45,161	6,633	60,129	29,733
1977	451,706	346,053	10,672	356,725	29,242	-5,644	321,839	81,213	48,654	7,393	61,098	31,156
1978	505,892	397,053	2,592	399,645	34,472	-6,976	358,197	94,515	53,180	8,169	61,926	32,482
1979	594,705	454,123	19,567	473,690	40,859	-7,145	425,686	108,030	60,989	9,551	62,264	33,792
1980	694,855	529,905	12,190	542,095	47,952	-7,285	486,858	137,626	70,371	10,998	63,179	35,874
1981	825,882	634,097	-2,412	631,685	61,671	-5,745	564,269	180,440	81,173	12,804	64,500	38,599
1982	908,798	658,696	20,290	678,986	65,953	-5,431	607,602	206,109	95,087	13,444	67,597	38,596
1983	889,002	641,599	-1,483	640,116	63,240	-9,440	567,436	216,796	104,770	13,224	67,225	36,727
1984	951,281	660,272	25,158	685,430	66,602	-10,526	608,302	232,914	110,065	14,466	65,759	36,862
1985	937,021	643,775	12,083	655,858	66,345	-8,527	580,986	236,027	120,008	14,606	64,151	35,121
1986	912,366	613,712	21,029	634,741	64,342	-6,325	564,074	217,857	130,435	14,586	62,550	32,271
1987	881,225	587,530	18,944	606,474	62,250	-3,540	540,684	209,302	131,239	14,722	59,858	31,523
1988	918,649	599,302	33,457	632,759	67,383	-3,391	561,985	217,828	138,836	15,924	57,691	31,608
1989	954,368	613,127	35,200	648,327	69,388	-686	578,253	228,402	147,713	16,691	57,178	31,302
1990	982,357	639,771	30,832	670,603	74,187	-783	595,633	226,728	159,996	17,330	56,686	31,722
1991	988,747	658,766	7,459	666,225	78,644	-4,160	583,421	226,918	178,408	17,504	56,486	32,187
1992	1,050,094	682,126	18,974	701,100	81,154	-6,919	613,027	242,506	194,561	18,494	56,780	31,861
1993	1,081,363	717,264	19,081	736,345	86,160	-7,870	642,315	230,425	208,623	19,012	56,879	32,707
1994	1,133,191	748,281	20,343	768,624	90,287	-8,893	669,444	247,220	216,527	19,778	57,296	33,416
1995	1,151,110	760,362	3,273	763,635	91,903	-8,459	663,273	255,901	231,936	19,868	57,939	33,519
1996	1,194,696	775,439	7,042	782,481	92,905	-9,612	679,964	274,242	240,490	20,672	57,794	33,499
1997	1,293,667	844,995	23,345	868,340	98,343	-11,154	758,843	283,655	251,169	22,370	57,831	34,343
1998	1,337,706	860,952	21,705	882,657	99,713	-11,914	771,030	306,357	260,319	23,015	58,122	34,609
1999	1,330,457	862,383	18,653	881,036	100,653	-13,548	766,835	308,779	254,843	22,861	58,197	34,232
2000	1,401,741	891,784	24,460	916,244	102,943	-13,372	799,929	337,840	263,972	24,285	57,721	34,319
2001	1,465,618	948,756	15,557	964,313	109,627	-14,280	840,406	339,093	286,119	25,587	57,279	33,369
2002	1,518,611	995,385	20,046	1,015,431	115,844	-18,453	881,134	331,981	305,496	26,526	57,249	33,265
2003	1,618,433	1,051,517	43,860	1,095,377	121,019	-20,358	954,000	345,273	319,160	28,279	57,230	33,999
2004	1,739,708	1,124,567	52,558	1,177,125	129,510	-21,797	1,025,818	367,001	346,889	30,277	57,459	34,452
2005	1,830,098	1,216,666	39,461	1,256,127	136,455	-21,715	1,097,957	378,129	354,012	31,907	57,358	34,825
2006	2,042,318	1,314,996	43,894	1,358,890	145,352	-20,179	1,193,359	460,210	388,749	35,381	57,723	35,569
2007	2,127,250	1,350,898	17,589	1,368,487	154,300	-25,084	1,189,103	523,844	414,303	36,580	58,153	36,830
2008	2,284,732	1,465,186	22,127	1,487,313	161,364	-31,649	1,294,300	537,232	453,200	38,826	58,845	38,102
2009	2,201,724	1,457,551	2,670	1,460,221	164,783	-39,589	1,255,849	469,653	476,222	36,702	59,989	37,704
2010	2,415,274	1,598,600	10,005	1,608,605	173,085	-46,291	1,389,229	526,960	499,085	39,744	60,771	38,004
2011	2,564,249	1,658,838	30,321	1,689,159	165,616	-46,362	1,477,181	585,467	501,601	42,197	60,768	38,074
2012	2,774,012	1,796,085	48,532	1,844,617	180,102	-60,540	1,603,975	661,450	508,587	45,205	61,365	39,161
2013	2,722,644	1,890,788	16,487	1,907,275	209,941	-63,610	1,633,724	583,292	505,628	43,655	62,368	39,620
2014	2,938,492	2,022,929	36,347	2,059,276	221,108	-69,090	1,769,078	664,788	504,626	46,230	63,563	40,232
2015	2,822,350	1,987,021	15,886	2,002,907	220,288	-72,974	1,709,645	597,182	515,523	43,968	64,191	39,839
2016	2,767,561	1,967,969	3,473	1,971,442	223,109	-85,643	1,662,690	574,712	530,159	43,450	63,696	39,662
2017	2,668,180	1,765,049	7,567	1,772,616	201,083	-34,346	1,537,187	583,781	547,212	42,359	62,990	37,553
2018	2,709,767	1,760,414	1,006	1,761,420	204,529	-25,234	1,531,657	623,467	554,643	43,216	62,703	37,255
2019	2,750,370	1,760,921	13,168	1,774,089	206,336	-21,707	1,546,046	627,578	576,746	43,701	62,936	36,802
2020	2,808,927	1,705,398	18,687	1,724,085	205,585	-38,392	1,480,108	615,678	713,141	44,850	62,629	36,102
2021	3,025,775	1,776,281	35,945	1,812,226	212,501	-38,643	1,561,082	645,517	819,176	48,861	61,926	35,964

Personal Income and Employment by Area: Erie, PA

(Thousands of dollars, except as noted.)

Year	Personal income, total	Earnings by place of work			Less: Contributions for government social insurance	Plus: Adjustment for residence	Equals: Net earnings by place of residence	Plus: Dividends, interest, and rent	Plus: Personal current transfer receipts	Per capita personal income (dollars)	Population (persons)	Total employment
		Nonfarm	Farm	Total								
1970	1,032,554	874,070	9,693	883,763	65,451	-14,813	803,499	129,382	99,673	3,907	264,315	117,410
1971	1,114,365	945,500	7,669	953,169	73,696	-17,222	862,251	137,096	115,018	4,148	268,634	118,885
1972	1,215,863	1,040,511	6,961	1,047,472	85,357	-19,558	942,557	144,961	128,345	4,464	272,384	121,771
1973	1,356,689	1,172,171	13,611	1,185,782	110,177	-22,308	1,053,297	161,374	142,018	4,942	274,509	128,972
1974	1,518,598	1,310,640	13,040	1,323,680	128,119	-26,417	1,169,144	182,506	166,948	5,516	275,306	133,424
1975	1,650,464	1,377,633	12,089	1,389,722	130,633	-28,723	1,230,366	199,742	220,356	5,910	279,275	131,019
1976	1,762,065	1,452,937	13,712	1,466,649	140,390	-28,375	1,297,884	212,574	251,607	6,262	281,390	128,968
1977	1,926,260	1,603,342	15,839	1,619,181	157,429	-31,394	1,430,358	234,711	261,191	6,879	280,019	131,617
1978	2,133,750	1,794,375	19,266	1,813,641	181,303	-35,723	1,596,615	257,994	279,141	7,664	278,420	136,329
1979	2,351,026	1,976,366	15,477	1,991,843	205,530	-39,030	1,747,283	290,632	313,111	8,433	278,792	137,775
1980	2,572,414	2,091,398	10,104	2,101,502	214,290	-41,132	1,846,080	357,630	368,704	9,186	280,043	134,200
1981	2,827,865	2,239,417	16,432	2,255,849	244,875	-45,621	1,965,353	442,663	419,849	10,080	280,529	131,270
1982	2,984,718	2,289,517	10,085	2,299,602	254,517	-49,390	1,995,695	506,723	482,300	10,610	281,320	128,148
1983	3,080,333	2,318,991	7,358	2,326,349	260,836	-49,879	2,015,634	532,148	532,551	10,935	281,683	124,998
1984	3,310,930	2,537,766	10,711	2,548,477	298,687	-56,030	2,193,760	595,051	522,119	11,786	280,928	128,793
1985	3,479,883	2,668,220	13,588	2,681,808	317,654	-61,846	2,302,308	632,345	545,230	12,536	277,584	130,880
1986	3,607,065	2,741,417	15,076	2,756,493	325,801	-66,196	2,364,496	661,235	581,334	13,016	277,123	131,407
1987	3,757,515	2,878,186	21,354	2,899,540	336,665	-70,451	2,492,424	671,633	593,458	13,626	275,759	133,889
1988	4,019,275	3,129,085	14,988	3,144,073	373,075	-78,674	2,692,324	704,058	622,893	14,630	274,732	138,424
1989	4,404,653	3,379,005	21,128	3,400,133	393,719	-87,655	2,918,759	822,705	663,189	15,989	275,474	141,704
1990	4,658,382	3,605,066	23,708	3,628,774	423,356	-97,078	3,108,340	821,766	728,276	16,884	275,911	145,501
1991	4,911,352	3,779,019	23,928	3,802,947	449,018	-104,717	3,249,212	829,896	832,244	17,668	277,973	145,836
1992	5,231,718	4,031,863	36,226	4,068,089	477,472	-115,153	3,475,464	865,161	891,093	18,715	279,548	146,388
1993	5,483,858	4,230,493	25,935	4,256,428	508,745	-122,734	3,624,949	918,448	940,461	19,530	280,796	148,918
1994	5,711,514	4,369,077	21,488	4,390,565	537,160	-125,821	3,727,584	1,021,164	962,766	20,279	281,649	149,803
1995	5,876,065	4,527,431	15,063	4,542,494	557,374	-133,657	3,851,463	1,015,469	1,009,133	20,828	282,127	153,226
1996	6,178,960	4,639,289	28,540	4,667,829	562,161	-138,863	3,966,805	1,135,309	1,076,846	21,866	282,582	154,003
1997	6,465,592	4,845,324	19,469	4,864,793	582,948	-146,456	4,135,389	1,228,703	1,101,500	22,878	282,609	155,708
1998	6,618,774	4,991,938	23,396	5,015,334	594,444	-152,531	4,268,359	1,237,601	1,112,814	23,490	281,764	156,304
1999	6,819,997	5,268,700	31,915	5,300,615	617,585	-165,525	4,517,505	1,145,573	1,156,919	24,245	281,294	160,400
2000	7,122,715	5,426,173	29,401	5,455,574	629,898	-174,993	4,650,683	1,247,779	1,224,253	25,366	280,803	163,440
2001	7,301,311	5,548,634	25,505	5,574,139	635,251	-186,510	4,752,378	1,221,903	1,327,030	26,016	280,647	161,055
2002	7,454,912	5,607,113	17,123	5,624,236	639,111	-190,808	4,794,317	1,231,914	1,428,681	26,589	280,379	158,749
2003	7,571,300	5,645,700	26,202	5,671,902	638,942	-196,820	4,836,140	1,226,892	1,508,268	27,026	280,153	157,208
2004	7,896,182	5,961,389	19,706	5,981,095	671,673	-201,811	5,107,611	1,231,579	1,556,992	28,417	277,864	159,170
2005	8,151,740	6,197,481	19,089	6,216,570	715,798	-210,621	5,290,151	1,196,339	1,665,250	29,406	277,211	161,240
2006	8,593,683	6,426,262	16,815	6,443,077	744,207	-216,551	5,482,319	1,357,633	1,753,731	30,869	278,389	161,898
2007	9,114,561	6,641,399	16,094	6,657,493	767,540	-225,800	5,664,153	1,572,413	1,877,995	32,719	278,573	163,256
2008	9,510,023	6,760,807	13,437	6,774,244	781,656	-218,375	5,774,213	1,608,574	2,127,236	34,125	278,686	162,487
2009	9,368,405	6,464,082	7,830	6,471,912	760,584	-189,409	5,521,919	1,416,707	2,429,779	33,478	279,838	156,498
2010	9,772,310	6,673,579	11,334	6,684,913	779,809	-188,816	5,716,288	1,463,182	2,592,840	34,801	280,809	156,247
2011	10,398,446	7,178,301	18,709	7,197,010	751,002	-213,599	6,232,409	1,568,639	2,597,398	36,973	281,244	159,178
2012	10,699,351	7,307,149	27,111	7,334,260	758,146	-212,942	6,363,172	1,833,487	2,502,692	38,020	281,416	160,356
2013	10,678,048	7,444,015	26,010	7,470,025	861,107	-199,788	6,409,130	1,635,901	2,633,017	38,013	280,905	160,538
2014	10,947,648	7,550,769	24,890	7,575,659	872,912	-198,494	6,504,253	1,774,603	2,668,792	39,016	280,592	161,041
2015	11,272,600	7,813,871	20,413	7,834,284	904,710	-191,727	6,737,847	1,765,080	2,769,673	40,317	279,599	161,264
2016	11,371,469	7,691,531	13,482	7,705,013	900,301	-188,842	6,615,870	1,846,845	2,908,754	40,905	277,995	158,751
2017	11,516,472	7,714,797	23,753	7,738,550	918,040	-157,692	6,662,818	1,936,820	2,916,834	41,816	275,410	157,829
2018	12,105,353	7,950,574	11,834	7,962,408	943,905	-172,795	6,845,708	2,146,022	3,113,623	44,255	273,535	158,383
2019	12,456,039	8,146,514	19,755	8,166,269	972,472	-183,373	7,010,424	2,226,453	3,219,162	45,883	271,476	157,519
2020	13,512,886	8,092,553	17,590	8,110,143	962,675	-197,121	6,950,347	2,207,742	4,354,797	49,969	270,427	148,944
2021	14,189,543	8,403,792	20,683	8,424,475	980,101	-186,338	7,258,036	2,253,635	4,677,872	52,747	269,011	152,481

Personal Income and Employment by Area: Eugene-Springfield, OR

(Thousands of dollars, except as noted.)

Year	Personal income, total	Earnings by place of work			Less: Contributions for government social insurance	Plus: Adjustment for residence	Equals: Net earnings by place of residence	Plus: Dividends, interest, and rent	Plus: Personal current transfer receipts	Per capita personal income (dollars)	Population (persons)	Total employment
		Nonfarm	Farm	Total								
1970	790,124	621,254	6,452	627,706	49,259	8,542	586,989	131,403	71,732	3,651	216,409	85,936
1971	879,451	692,758	5,215	697,973	56,290	9,497	651,180	145,222	83,049	3,983	220,797	90,186
1972	997,847	798,153	6,534	804,687	68,255	10,105	746,537	158,553	92,757	4,395	227,016	96,964
1973	1,130,280	906,120	11,626	917,746	88,722	10,947	839,971	179,716	110,593	4,898	230,743	103,424
1974	1,260,360	978,382	15,718	994,100	98,024	12,657	908,733	210,351	141,276	5,328	236,565	105,876
1975	1,401,281	1,053,462	9,081	1,062,543	101,333	14,525	975,735	241,064	184,482	5,831	240,324	106,648
1976	1,623,286	1,251,885	12,309	1,264,194	122,087	16,756	1,158,863	267,512	196,911	6,601	245,932	114,312
1977	1,861,298	1,455,925	9,812	1,465,737	144,512	18,971	1,340,196	305,464	215,638	7,388	251,925	122,378
1978	2,139,948	1,684,533	7,703	1,692,236	170,596	21,750	1,543,390	360,246	236,312	8,223	260,240	130,003
1979	2,403,456	1,874,776	10,665	1,885,441	195,854	27,639	1,717,226	419,670	266,560	8,974	267,827	133,161
1980	2,602,364	1,946,630	5,590	1,952,220	203,446	33,881	1,782,655	498,487	321,222	9,439	275,708	131,154
1981	2,775,658	1,983,381	13,181	1,996,562	222,567	24,719	1,798,714	603,863	373,081	10,018	277,068	126,204
1982	2,775,517	1,900,988	9,777	1,910,765	217,298	24,260	1,717,727	641,577	416,213	10,191	272,346	118,130
1983	2,958,424	2,028,661	4,847	2,033,508	233,172	26,017	1,826,353	688,188	443,883	11,020	268,453	121,237
1984	3,199,434	2,220,843	14,399	2,235,242	263,752	25,668	1,997,158	745,244	457,032	11,944	267,878	127,016
1985	3,346,049	2,325,967	15,078	2,341,045	278,457	25,767	2,088,355	775,026	482,668	12,530	267,051	129,177
1986	3,494,361	2,442,536	20,513	2,463,049	292,120	25,690	2,196,619	805,608	492,134	13,125	266,239	132,737
1987	3,728,839	2,662,080	18,942	2,681,022	315,104	25,038	2,390,956	826,734	511,149	13,881	268,636	139,567
1988	4,091,201	2,933,454	31,426	2,964,880	361,121	26,120	2,629,879	916,291	545,031	14,985	273,014	146,319
1989	4,497,330	3,159,084	30,636	3,189,720	390,738	24,929	2,823,911	1,076,608	596,811	16,139	278,665	151,322
1990	4,749,152	3,362,480	33,135	3,395,615	422,888	27,283	3,000,010	1,099,093	650,049	16,707	284,261	154,526
1991	4,942,665	3,475,986	25,783	3,501,769	440,054	29,390	3,091,105	1,131,324	720,236	17,133	288,490	152,184
1992	5,252,388	3,704,663	26,624	3,731,287	466,027	29,869	3,295,129	1,150,375	806,884	17,958	292,482	153,541
1993	5,624,250	3,950,642	39,806	3,990,448	494,180	28,868	3,525,136	1,233,175	865,939	18,919	297,281	156,357
1994	6,036,094	4,293,508	35,161	4,328,669	538,188	29,209	3,819,690	1,309,361	907,043	19,999	301,819	164,297
1995	6,452,420	4,466,458	27,241	4,493,699	562,765	34,489	3,965,423	1,475,944	1,011,053	21,038	306,704	167,644
1996	6,870,127	4,733,782	25,572	4,759,354	605,433	37,165	4,191,086	1,609,536	1,069,505	22,090	311,004	173,379
1997	7,276,385	5,078,260	25,440	5,103,700	640,341	37,429	4,500,788	1,672,374	1,103,223	22,984	316,579	177,912
1998	7,704,636	5,397,826	15,137	5,412,963	677,272	32,764	4,768,455	1,735,840	1,200,341	24,104	319,646	181,115
1999	7,874,023	5,606,560	15,656	5,622,216	697,280	30,168	4,955,104	1,620,302	1,298,617	24,470	321,778	184,549
2000	8,348,123	5,934,551	15,178	5,949,729	732,125	29,534	5,247,138	1,736,834	1,364,151	25,806	323,492	186,789
2001	8,730,677	6,166,390	18,503	6,184,893	748,825	14,083	5,450,151	1,760,225	1,520,301	26,876	324,855	185,129
2002	8,788,692	6,315,116	18,066	6,333,182	773,283	652	5,560,551	1,655,482	1,572,659	26,835	327,506	184,589
2003	9,004,028	6,546,399	29,257	6,575,656	800,740	-14,491	5,760,425	1,609,285	1,634,318	27,215	330,845	185,159
2004	9,572,081	6,965,168	31,849	6,997,017	860,691	-32,895	6,103,431	1,763,755	1,704,895	28,803	332,327	191,076
2005	10,244,384	7,442,951	29,145	7,472,096	924,078	-54,346	6,493,672	1,948,211	1,802,501	30,505	335,831	196,415
2006	11,228,421	7,975,035	39,288	8,014,323	983,895	-72,022	6,958,406	2,332,763	1,937,252	33,032	339,926	201,138
2007	11,521,037	8,102,580	38,442	8,141,022	1,012,384	-89,076	7,039,562	2,416,489	2,064,986	33,409	344,844	205,433
2008	11,820,171	8,067,221	40,618	8,107,839	1,018,065	-99,797	6,989,977	2,500,628	2,329,566	33,949	348,176	201,514
2009	11,472,933	7,535,530	38,477	7,574,007	959,310	-75,269	6,539,428	2,227,460	2,706,045	32,700	350,850	189,685
2010	11,855,216	7,715,151	33,545	7,748,696	983,761	-70,908	6,694,027	2,278,003	2,883,186	33,685	351,948	187,126
2011	12,225,196	7,878,802	39,236	7,918,038	897,421	-70,076	6,950,541	2,359,500	2,915,155	34,523	354,119	189,044
2012	12,795,633	8,289,561	46,270	8,335,831	932,867	-68,791	7,334,173	2,548,083	2,913,377	36,022	355,217	189,457
2013	12,849,433	8,431,273	58,535	8,489,808	1,079,550	-65,486	7,344,772	2,492,260	3,012,401	36,129	355,654	191,198
2014	13,698,558	8,815,246	55,153	8,870,399	1,138,610	-67,678	7,664,111	2,714,414	3,320,033	38,240	358,230	195,852
2015	14,670,562	9,433,948	65,817	9,499,765	1,203,050	-75,495	8,221,220	2,931,071	3,518,271	40,503	362,208	201,100
2016	15,346,493	9,907,306	70,256	9,977,562	1,252,451	-68,662	8,656,449	3,048,638	3,641,406	41,573	369,149	204,867
2017	16,276,989	10,484,834	57,950	10,542,784	1,332,783	-71,745	9,138,256	3,351,657	3,787,076	43,332	375,633	209,429
2018	17,050,394	11,001,089	54,868	11,055,957	1,380,071	-66,707	9,609,179	3,411,974	4,029,241	45,018	378,749	213,466
2019	17,859,486	11,383,920	50,086	11,434,006	1,438,972	-66,330	9,928,704	3,682,216	4,248,566	46,752	382,003	213,071
2020	19,634,078	11,873,990	56,855	11,930,845	1,493,806	-70,279	10,366,760	3,721,155	5,546,163	51,272	382,940	205,449
2021	21,131,525	12,712,429	57,482	12,769,911	1,581,988	-65,527	11,122,396	3,801,563	6,207,566	55,146	383,189	210,053

Personal Income and Employment by Area: Evansville, IN-KY

(Thousands of dollars, except as noted.)

Year	Personal income, total	Earnings by place of work			Less: Contributions for government social insurance	Plus: Adjustment for residence	Equals: Net earnings by place of residence	Plus: Dividends, interest, and rent	Plus: Personal current transfer receipts	Per capita personal income (dollars)	Population (persons)	Total employment
		Nonfarm	Farm	Total								
1970	949,474	831,356	6,874	838,230	57,264	-57,900	723,066	140,278	86,130	3,725	254,890	118,647
1971	1,042,382	897,264	16,810	914,074	64,130	-61,476	788,468	154,108	99,806	4,044	257,776	121,245
1972	1,131,669	983,940	15,568	999,508	74,477	-69,189	855,842	165,904	109,923	4,384	258,125	124,254
1973	1,292,367	1,108,139	33,292	1,141,431	96,499	-73,780	971,152	188,286	132,929	4,969	260,065	130,416
1974	1,415,870	1,200,170	25,662	1,225,832	108,186	-77,528	1,040,118	218,779	156,973	5,434	260,547	129,898
1975	1,557,836	1,281,996	24,500	1,306,496	113,155	-72,907	1,120,434	241,653	195,749	5,970	260,965	127,384
1976	1,744,746	1,460,432	29,192	1,489,624	131,133	-86,889	1,271,602	265,907	207,237	6,647	262,498	133,259
1977	2,012,432	1,713,916	26,138	1,740,054	151,081	-100,161	1,488,812	302,808	220,812	7,564	266,046	139,775
1978	2,252,233	1,949,581	16,816	1,966,397	177,541	-118,834	1,670,022	342,175	240,036	8,331	270,348	146,579
1979	2,500,776	2,152,238	26,957	2,179,195	203,196	-132,555	1,843,444	382,697	274,635	9,165	272,865	148,866
1980	2,733,336	2,266,959	18,288	2,285,247	215,759	-140,803	1,928,685	478,485	326,166	9,887	276,466	146,600
1981	3,016,477	2,417,357	14,470	2,431,827	248,251	-140,233	2,043,343	597,766	375,368	10,902	276,701	145,853
1982	3,199,760	2,500,387	11,966	2,512,353	263,673	-136,868	2,111,812	674,025	413,923	11,519	277,792	144,080
1983	3,337,875	2,622,082	-24,714	2,597,368	275,498	-139,789	2,182,081	709,488	446,306	11,993	278,314	143,145
1984	3,733,480	2,924,062	22,230	2,946,292	315,667	-155,717	2,474,908	787,188	471,384	13,360	279,451	148,687
1985	3,922,567	3,058,474	15,490	3,073,964	337,196	-156,070	2,580,698	842,919	498,950	13,998	280,221	149,820
1986	4,064,600	3,153,899	16,298	3,170,197	352,470	-153,517	2,664,210	870,089	530,301	14,528	279,786	150,742
1987	4,196,686	3,281,954	11,856	3,293,810	360,659	-147,745	2,785,406	868,065	543,215	15,023	279,347	152,301
1988	4,500,810	3,535,865	10,569	3,546,434	398,862	-160,263	2,987,309	938,361	575,140	16,136	278,923	155,991
1989	4,827,390	3,687,445	33,366	3,720,811	419,194	-160,296	3,141,321	1,056,979	629,090	17,307	278,930	158,985
1990	5,114,966	3,922,661	10,152	3,932,813	457,802	-168,193	3,306,818	1,119,470	688,678	18,308	279,384	161,461
1991	5,268,274	4,105,751	-6,760	4,098,991	484,657	-174,894	3,439,440	1,073,855	754,979	18,730	281,270	161,774
1992	5,694,486	4,427,157	28,439	4,455,596	515,557	-198,143	3,741,896	1,104,806	847,784	20,038	284,179	164,642
1993	5,979,454	4,674,717	16,998	4,691,715	550,692	-217,135	3,923,888	1,157,092	898,474	20,854	286,723	169,312
1994	6,242,059	4,878,218	18,122	4,896,340	584,389	-238,672	4,073,279	1,237,132	931,648	21,623	288,681	174,356
1995	6,449,760	5,010,893	6,702	5,017,595	602,783	-245,369	4,169,443	1,318,836	961,481	22,244	289,950	177,218
1996	6,867,883	5,313,183	52,924	5,366,107	633,377	-278,699	4,454,031	1,398,060	1,015,792	23,509	292,136	179,775
1997	7,194,717	5,657,704	23,574	5,681,278	670,544	-310,124	4,700,610	1,460,445	1,033,662	24,481	293,894	182,816
1998	7,752,594	6,091,662	12,250	6,103,912	710,749	-299,669	5,093,494	1,589,083	1,070,017	26,323	294,517	183,227
1999	7,935,818	6,346,737	4,679	6,351,416	741,752	-315,197	5,294,467	1,529,193	1,112,158	26,846	295,610	185,640
2000	8,416,984	6,635,421	41,242	6,676,663	763,431	-314,978	5,598,254	1,630,717	1,188,013	28,390	296,480	188,367
2001	8,776,387	6,947,248	45,299	6,992,547	781,347	-346,605	5,864,595	1,617,156	1,294,636	29,547	297,027	189,688
2002	8,976,513	7,196,859	14,821	7,211,680	808,749	-360,653	6,042,278	1,560,137	1,374,098	30,084	298,383	188,934
2003	9,235,547	7,346,603	48,576	7,395,179	831,116	-356,782	6,207,281	1,608,745	1,419,521	30,721	300,628	188,816
2004	9,576,662	7,548,546	78,217	7,626,763	855,288	-339,747	6,431,728	1,640,337	1,504,597	31,678	302,310	187,460
2005	9,983,408	7,862,355	76,614	7,938,969	899,799	-360,133	6,679,037	1,684,685	1,619,686	32,857	303,844	188,590
2006	10,610,360	8,311,760	62,663	8,374,423	950,741	-380,093	7,043,589	1,809,931	1,756,840	34,726	305,549	189,353
2007	10,713,171	8,256,188	53,200	8,309,388	954,062	-390,085	6,965,241	1,900,960	1,846,970	34,843	307,468	189,398
2008	11,343,188	8,552,450	93,838	8,646,288	998,876	-426,264	7,221,148	2,017,839	2,104,201	36,755	308,614	189,148
2009	11,158,473	8,342,401	88,101	8,430,502	974,487	-349,282	7,106,733	1,798,603	2,253,137	35,975	310,170	183,626
2010	11,890,954	8,912,119	35,594	8,947,713	1,006,035	-312,022	7,629,656	1,866,499	2,394,799	38,135	311,809	184,471
2011	12,674,688	9,371,692	114,636	9,486,328	921,319	-278,618	8,286,391	1,996,579	2,391,718	40,528	312,741	188,291
2012	13,151,258	9,454,217	54,226	9,508,443	926,991	-190,238	8,391,214	2,293,539	2,466,505	41,951	313,494	188,271
2013	12,711,484	9,115,372	192,717	9,308,089	1,047,265	-116,794	8,144,030	2,070,804	2,496,650	40,426	314,437	186,855
2014	13,265,573	9,441,398	58,929	9,500,327	1,093,881	-117,357	8,289,089	2,278,589	2,697,895	42,205	314,315	189,261
2015	13,672,665	9,683,170	20,039	9,703,209	1,134,645	-131,287	8,437,277	2,389,149	2,846,239	43,499	314,320	191,199
2016	13,809,697	9,716,758	52,937	9,769,695	1,133,803	-115,126	8,520,766	2,380,271	2,908,660	43,914	314,468	191,986
2017	14,292,987	10,033,093	50,625	10,083,718	1,177,947	-145,238	8,760,533	2,522,108	3,010,346	45,549	313,795	193,477
2018	14,724,493	10,400,300	33,383	10,433,683	1,224,377	-160,030	9,049,276	2,550,882	3,124,335	46,984	313,392	195,560
2019	15,519,767	10,869,684	49,165	10,918,849	1,281,895	-153,584	9,483,370	2,727,777	3,308,620	49,485	313,624	194,824
2020	16,619,152	10,965,840	89,223	11,055,063	1,305,535	-125,566	9,623,962	2,794,865	4,200,325	52,939	313,930	186,821
2021	17,785,111	11,475,015	128,272	11,603,287	1,344,229	-125,669	10,133,389	2,878,585	4,773,137	56,650	313,946	190,726

Personal Income and Employment by Area: Fairbanks, AK

(Thousands of dollars, except as noted.)

Year	Personal income, total	Derivation of personal income									Per capita personal income (dollars)	Population (persons)	Total employment
		Earnings by place of work			Less: Contributions for government social insurance	Plus: Adjustment for residence	Equals: Net earnings by place of residence	Plus: Dividends, interest, and rent	Plus: Personal current transfer receipts				
		Nonfarm	Farm	Total									
1970	278,000	251,770	204	251,974	16,197	-10,816	224,961	45,117	7,922		6,051	45,940	23,571
1971	290,765	270,347	203	270,550	17,661	-20,842	232,047	48,301	10,417		6,152	47,260	23,042
1972	310,392	296,147	334	296,481	19,878	-30,049	246,554	51,911	11,927		6,509	47,690	23,612
1973	328,225	312,778	325	313,103	23,188	-35,913	254,002	56,336	17,887		6,888	47,654	23,221
1974	453,568	509,522	560	510,082	45,652	-94,118	370,312	66,370	16,886		9,356	48,480	28,366
1975	808,224	934,522	905	935,427	92,818	-136,400	706,209	81,971	20,044		15,613	51,765	38,163
1976	853,100	945,688	943	946,631	95,099	-114,199	737,333	91,765	24,002		15,239	55,983	36,768
1977	765,561	819,917	704	820,621	77,007	-117,926	625,688	102,826	37,047		13,811	55,433	34,246
1978	737,979	707,912	884	708,796	62,669	-65,693	580,434	116,434	41,111		13,339	55,325	31,953
1979	756,770	729,717	438	730,155	66,245	-65,855	598,055	122,151	36,564		13,782	54,910	32,015
1980	826,592	788,250	272	788,522	67,972	-72,008	648,542	138,686	39,364		15,161	54,520	31,780
1981	941,399	895,633	30	895,663	82,597	-81,623	731,443	160,729	49,227		16,640	56,576	33,124
1982	1,194,321	1,070,101	5	1,070,106	99,139	-91,359	879,608	200,102	114,611		19,937	59,905	36,850
1983	1,271,568	1,170,511	-237	1,170,274	108,703	-102,343	959,228	227,223	85,117		19,356	65,695	38,748
1984	1,328,195	1,247,388	-879	1,246,509	122,340	-135,328	988,841	248,402	90,952		19,446	68,300	41,113
1985	1,425,756	1,323,381	-1,903	1,321,478	129,256	-152,881	1,039,341	273,658	112,757		19,959	71,433	42,878
1986	1,398,719	1,245,323	-943	1,244,380	115,724	-139,393	989,263	279,585	129,871		19,025	73,520	41,269
1987	1,368,064	1,185,755	527	1,186,282	109,801	-129,908	946,573	285,869	135,622		18,606	73,528	42,080
1988	1,406,800	1,200,925	848	1,201,773	117,071	-128,112	956,590	303,531	146,679		18,667	75,364	42,911
1989	1,535,059	1,253,789	-338	1,253,451	122,923	-88,941	1,041,587	330,440	163,032		19,905	77,121	43,488
1990	1,586,890	1,318,497	777	1,319,274	134,191	-123,168	1,061,915	339,442	185,533		20,327	78,067	43,739
1991	1,653,668	1,379,678	1,557	1,381,235	142,481	-132,571	1,106,183	349,799	197,686		20,548	80,479	44,917
1992	1,784,644	1,493,547	2,452	1,495,999	156,612	-149,132	1,190,255	373,847	220,542		21,630	82,506	45,630
1993	1,863,705	1,524,482	1,486	1,525,968	161,877	-151,533	1,212,558	408,003	243,144		22,460	82,979	46,493
1994	1,879,554	1,527,702	312	1,528,014	164,413	-145,660	1,217,941	414,489	247,124		22,506	83,512	46,423
1995	1,959,578	1,585,299	1,216	1,586,515	170,479	-156,030	1,260,006	443,451	256,121		23,914	81,941	46,681
1996	2,011,923	1,620,618	111	1,620,729	173,795	-164,431	1,282,503	455,741	273,679		24,275	82,880	47,330
1997	2,105,279	1,696,642	271	1,696,913	182,291	-177,090	1,337,532	472,507	295,240		25,524	82,483	48,611
1998	2,220,032	1,780,539	641	1,781,180	189,355	-181,737	1,410,088	488,338	321,606		26,651	83,299	49,469
1999	2,295,368	1,828,744	567	1,829,311	191,633	-190,440	1,447,238	500,928	347,202		27,526	83,390	49,335
2000	2,465,145	1,951,993	399	1,952,392	201,949	-207,277	1,543,166	531,072	390,907		29,699	83,005	50,450
2001	2,547,983	2,021,037	2,036	2,023,073	208,023	-183,774	1,631,276	504,330	412,377		30,042	84,814	51,232
2002	2,714,756	2,188,990	2,280	2,191,270	224,781	-167,072	1,799,417	496,289	419,050		31,532	86,095	52,613
2003	2,887,253	2,346,977	3,946	2,350,923	238,105	-147,783	1,965,035	515,292	406,926		33,231	86,885	52,971
2004	3,040,217	2,479,650	3,971	2,483,621	255,847	-119,413	2,108,361	534,147	397,709		34,143	89,043	54,102
2005	3,335,514	2,691,677	5,617	2,697,294	278,753	-84,752	2,333,789	578,383	423,342		36,885	90,431	55,121
2006	3,657,464	2,919,276	4,800	2,924,076	312,163	-36,583	2,575,330	631,771	450,363		40,394	90,545	56,731
2007	3,935,767	2,998,798	4,937	3,003,735	317,033	23,629	2,710,331	715,190	510,246		42,074	93,545	57,967
2008	4,347,893	3,100,915	1,281	3,102,196	328,694	88,490	2,861,992	790,182	695,719		45,984	94,552	58,040
2009	4,329,576	3,192,774	3,425	3,196,199	336,199	86,588	2,946,588	783,694	599,294		45,461	95,238	57,509
2010	4,558,918	3,335,241	3,642	3,338,883	343,881	79,192	3,074,194	808,157	676,567		46,391	98,272	57,318
2011	5,029,620	3,635,293	3,369	3,638,662	335,975	77,550	3,380,237	946,521	702,862		51,244	98,151	58,909
2012	5,125,487	3,733,503	5,794	3,739,297	349,590	67,096	3,456,803	991,176	677,508		51,057	100,388	59,373
2013	5,000,990	3,652,722	1,792	3,654,514	382,233	64,716	3,336,997	993,509	670,484		49,492	101,046	58,147
2014	5,193,285	3,685,079	3,550	3,688,629	377,276	74,386	3,385,739	1,003,945	803,601		52,333	99,236	57,188
2015	5,378,774	3,806,871	1,948	3,808,819	389,598	78,541	3,497,762	1,053,742	827,270		54,000	99,607	58,111
2016	5,320,345	3,760,180	3,553	3,763,733	381,501	70,583	3,452,815	1,055,687	811,843		52,866	100,639	57,738
2017	5,371,369	3,752,673	2,186	3,754,859	387,265	69,971	3,437,565	1,065,258	868,546		53,907	99,641	58,013
2018	5,600,132	3,904,975	3,393	3,908,368	400,973	70,603	3,577,998	1,068,425	953,709		56,887	98,443	58,188
2019	5,709,591	3,956,673	3,494	3,960,167	410,371	72,783	3,622,579	1,091,798	995,214		59,011	96,755	57,845
2020	5,894,026	4,029,790	1,384	4,031,174	420,647	60,752	3,671,279	1,079,992	1,142,755		61,856	95,286	56,481
2021	6,243,530	4,257,171	2,405	4,259,576	445,192	67,627	3,882,011	1,084,186	1,277,333		65,314	95,593	57,996

Personal Income and Employment by Area: Fargo, ND-MN

(Thousands of dollars, except as noted.)

Year	Personal income, total	Derivation of personal income									Per capita personal income (dollars)	Population (persons)	Total employment
		Earnings by place of work			Less: Contributions for government social insurance	Plus: Adjustment for residence	Equals: Net earnings by place of residence	Plus: Dividends, interest, and rent	Plus: Personal current transfer receipts				
		Nonfarm	Farm	Total									
1970	462,348	361,915	26,901	388,816	28,348	-5,513	354,955	71,315	36,078		3,831	120,690	57,963
1971	509,069	392,060	32,997	425,057	31,523	-6,368	387,166	78,783	43,120		4,123	123,471	58,638
1972	565,942	432,614	43,016	475,630	36,305	-7,404	431,921	85,331	48,690		4,511	125,464	60,388
1973	740,158	493,239	148,456	641,695	47,657	-8,724	585,314	98,645	56,199		5,863	126,247	64,939
1974	775,821	552,470	107,712	660,182	55,300	-10,016	594,866	115,532	65,423		6,084	127,527	66,730
1975	804,871	613,867	53,703	667,570	60,545	-11,089	595,936	131,978	76,957		6,242	128,935	68,868
1976	954,422	711,829	100,034	811,863	71,960	-13,660	726,243	143,295	84,884		7,244	131,761	72,986
1977	966,351	792,758	13,485	806,243	78,082	-16,702	711,459	162,641	92,251		7,239	133,484	75,490
1978	1,164,667	899,988	90,175	990,163	91,267	-20,479	878,417	183,566	102,684		8,549	136,239	78,760
1979	1,241,704	996,539	47,748	1,044,287	105,121	-23,809	915,357	209,604	116,743		9,063	137,013	80,905
1980	1,282,880	1,031,439	-10,742	1,020,697	108,371	-25,814	886,512	257,728	138,640		9,298	137,979	78,475
1981	1,480,087	1,110,942	34,643	1,145,585	123,868	-27,913	993,804	327,889	158,394		10,637	139,144	77,415
1982	1,590,659	1,159,755	29,562	1,189,317	131,226	-27,365	1,030,726	383,351	176,582		11,344	140,221	76,983
1983	1,688,887	1,240,660	37,578	1,278,238	142,297	-27,895	1,108,046	385,339	195,502		11,861	142,387	79,004
1984	1,845,072	1,354,008	55,770	1,409,778	160,412	-29,543	1,219,823	415,563	209,686		12,797	144,178	82,450
1985	1,926,305	1,433,338	39,665	1,473,003	174,605	-30,232	1,268,166	434,406	223,733		13,182	146,132	84,299
1986	2,052,916	1,525,323	65,203	1,590,526	190,012	-29,970	1,370,544	442,794	239,578		13,941	147,258	85,952
1987	2,174,116	1,624,747	87,881	1,712,628	202,064	-30,064	1,480,500	436,799	256,817		14,633	148,578	89,329
1988	2,237,854	1,727,719	43,833	1,771,552	222,884	-30,925	1,517,743	452,765	267,346		14,872	150,478	92,213
1989	2,417,863	1,843,034	40,085	1,883,119	240,368	-31,437	1,611,314	509,405	297,144		15,925	151,829	94,155
1990	2,609,655	1,981,888	80,174	2,062,062	271,881	-32,461	1,757,720	525,149	326,786		16,973	153,752	96,333
1991	2,710,777	2,100,563	64,604	2,165,167	294,377	-36,981	1,833,809	543,756	333,212		17,429	155,533	100,109
1992	2,944,037	2,252,448	97,922	2,350,370	313,892	-40,252	1,996,226	579,564	368,247		18,612	158,182	102,535
1993	3,046,222	2,393,887	30,961	2,424,848	336,103	-43,728	2,045,017	607,823	393,382		18,983	160,472	104,841
1994	3,298,751	2,572,735	91,129	2,663,864	362,866	-48,204	2,252,794	645,449	400,508		20,248	162,919	109,730
1995	3,473,885	2,706,890	51,556	2,758,446	378,920	-53,013	2,326,513	724,958	422,414		21,044	165,081	113,090
1996	3,770,530	2,890,201	136,773	3,026,974	400,545	-57,562	2,568,867	760,764	440,899		22,620	166,691	115,991
1997	3,951,158	3,087,997	65,393	3,153,390	421,829	-64,461	2,667,100	827,250	456,808		23,415	168,747	118,867
1998	4,287,276	3,376,136	71,915	3,448,051	453,932	-74,523	2,919,596	885,781	481,899		25,087	170,893	121,710
1999	4,538,651	3,606,690	96,598	3,703,288	476,985	-81,307	3,144,996	880,408	513,247		26,251	172,892	123,691
2000	4,971,092	3,946,395	98,584	4,044,979	512,075	-89,308	3,443,596	973,959	553,537		28,411	174,970	126,440
2001	5,012,461	3,982,345	90,341	4,072,686	516,223	-94,605	3,461,858	971,185	579,418		28,314	177,033	128,846
2002	5,263,492	4,186,896	89,618	4,276,514	540,080	-96,855	3,639,579	1,001,903	622,010		29,423	178,891	129,742
2003	5,563,238	4,417,522	138,790	4,556,312	571,971	-103,024	3,881,317	1,027,538	654,383		30,645	181,539	131,637
2004	5,935,515	4,780,845	118,423	4,899,268	610,954	-111,504	4,176,810	1,062,481	696,224		31,835	186,448	135,324
2005	6,301,176	5,045,765	111,989	5,157,754	639,237	-120,046	4,398,471	1,167,557	735,148		33,286	189,303	139,308
2006	6,841,706	5,428,348	122,112	5,550,460	674,123	-134,329	4,742,008	1,302,046	797,652		35,374	193,412	144,064
2007	7,331,864	5,740,605	143,259	5,883,864	708,965	-140,480	5,034,419	1,427,167	870,278		37,195	197,121	148,966
2008	8,074,660	6,089,259	181,519	6,270,778	747,598	-146,117	5,377,063	1,681,613	1,015,984		40,103	201,346	151,713
2009	7,972,418	6,225,223	54,265	6,279,488	783,789	-162,930	5,332,769	1,547,534	1,092,115		38,659	206,223	151,422
2010	8,504,703	6,384,631	137,681	6,522,312	771,123	-169,230	5,581,959	1,727,374	1,195,370		40,602	209,465	152,299
2011	9,260,724	6,871,979	136,193	7,008,172	758,644	-195,099	6,054,429	1,973,835	1,232,460		43,416	213,300	156,425
2012	10,348,842	7,544,095	268,088	7,812,183	775,446	-209,092	6,827,645	2,272,036	1,249,161		47,523	217,763	161,529
2013	10,590,141	8,045,955	104,732	8,150,687	928,779	-231,712	6,990,196	2,292,322	1,307,623		47,363	223,594	166,066
2014	11,422,668	8,812,612	18,786	8,831,398	1,009,851	-251,931	7,569,616	2,458,978	1,394,074		49,924	228,801	171,340
2015	11,807,797	9,129,005	3,831	9,132,836	1,071,201	-278,242	7,783,393	2,577,310	1,447,094		50,429	234,149	174,366
2016	11,913,502	9,271,743	42,519	9,314,262	1,111,014	-281,276	7,921,972	2,485,461	1,506,069		49,904	238,729	176,288
2017	12,335,580	9,451,279	52,424	9,503,703	1,158,116	-305,534	8,040,053	2,732,644	1,562,883		50,714	243,239	177,982
2018	13,151,783	9,850,881	34,117	9,884,998	1,183,518	-308,358	8,393,122	3,079,037	1,679,624		53,379	246,383	180,095
2019	13,488,363	10,267,514	64,258	10,331,772	1,218,344	-316,318	8,797,110	2,922,442	1,768,811		54,323	248,298	182,265
2020	14,513,246	10,611,886	197,775	10,809,661	1,295,273	-328,299	9,186,089	2,926,040	2,401,117		58,002	250,219	178,530
2021	15,637,671	11,363,506	222,608	11,586,114	1,361,048	-345,961	9,879,105	3,096,541	2,662,025		62,021	252,136	184,113

Personal Income and Employment by Area: Farmington, NM

(Thousands of dollars, except as noted.)

Year	Personal income, total	Earnings by place of work			Less: Contributions for government social insurance	Plus: Adjustment for residence	Equals: Net earnings by place of residence	Plus: Dividends, interest, and rent	Plus: Personal current transfer receipts	Per capita personal income (dollars)	Population (persons)	Total employment
		Nonfarm	Farm	Total								
1970	142,881	114,267	1,940	116,207	7,015	1,483	110,675	16,931	15,275	2,707	52,779	16,564
1971	169,166	138,014	1,434	139,448	8,874	1,095	131,669	19,602	17,895	3,138	53,916	17,929
1972	196,092	159,271	1,861	161,132	10,557	1,102	151,677	22,671	21,744	3,517	55,756	18,919
1973	231,880	190,934	2,493	193,427	14,961	625	179,091	26,211	26,578	3,949	58,722	21,634
1974	281,735	231,832	2,617	234,449	18,932	-95	215,422	31,952	34,361	4,609	61,123	24,337
1975	330,766	269,538	2,067	271,605	21,833	-476	249,296	39,869	41,601	5,117	64,638	26,037
1976	388,734	322,765	1,509	324,274	26,842	-1,819	295,613	45,593	47,528	5,703	68,161	27,389
1977	464,962	398,173	2,605	400,778	33,905	-6,503	360,370	53,296	51,296	6,514	71,376	30,699
1978	547,021	484,735	-835	483,900	42,910	-11,789	429,201	61,858	55,962	7,281	75,134	33,028
1979	603,458	534,884	-1,030	533,854	48,919	-17,273	467,662	70,772	65,024	7,647	78,915	34,065
1980	705,424	633,084	-2,554	630,530	57,992	-27,037	545,501	86,254	73,669	8,569	82,318	36,207
1981	827,140	744,103	-277	743,826	73,413	-33,574	636,839	109,148	81,153	9,641	85,794	38,634
1982	864,389	756,826	-2,089	754,737	75,962	-33,125	645,650	133,644	85,095	9,730	88,833	37,760
1983	852,747	706,122	2,322	708,444	70,334	-27,335	610,775	143,820	98,152	9,401	90,708	35,488
1984	888,571	727,078	2,359	729,437	74,216	-24,925	630,296	155,670	102,605	9,728	91,339	35,364
1985	944,181	767,645	4,056	771,701	79,346	-26,175	666,180	170,749	107,252	10,303	91,644	36,677
1986	949,129	753,247	5,969	759,216	78,176	-24,865	656,175	175,019	117,935	10,143	93,577	35,730
1987	927,185	716,349	13,662	730,011	72,747	-21,284	635,980	170,662	120,543	10,047	92,289	34,608
1988	977,868	759,373	23,430	782,803	81,894	-22,870	678,039	173,633	126,196	10,625	92,031	36,149
1989	1,078,673	834,745	29,476	864,221	91,184	-25,552	747,485	189,075	142,113	11,672	92,413	37,919
1990	1,194,625	961,062	29,246	990,308	111,589	-29,917	848,802	194,758	151,065	13,046	91,567	40,164
1991	1,294,574	1,036,456	25,319	1,061,775	121,371	-31,740	908,664	211,915	173,995	13,808	93,755	42,648
1992	1,382,774	1,101,192	31,061	1,132,253	127,329	-32,119	972,805	217,081	192,888	14,520	95,233	43,061
1993	1,497,682	1,188,491	38,632	1,227,123	137,673	-34,399	1,055,051	231,407	211,224	15,310	97,821	44,491
1994	1,609,242	1,269,470	38,871	1,308,341	148,593	-36,437	1,123,311	249,276	236,655	16,075	100,106	46,604
1995	1,726,308	1,354,505	42,618	1,397,123	157,750	-38,218	1,201,155	270,082	255,071	17,026	101,390	49,846
1996	1,803,323	1,380,975	37,394	1,418,369	159,973	-35,828	1,222,568	290,117	290,638	17,354	103,911	50,807
1997	1,914,781	1,438,097	70,613	1,508,710	165,344	-36,747	1,306,619	314,238	293,924	18,149	105,501	52,569
1998	1,991,274	1,507,873	54,905	1,562,778	173,867	-37,617	1,351,294	318,736	321,244	18,342	108,565	53,560
1999	2,037,414	1,568,884	44,525	1,613,409	181,862	-35,726	1,395,821	297,802	343,791	18,098	112,574	54,235
2000	2,175,296	1,696,172	31,985	1,728,157	188,995	-33,991	1,505,171	306,219	363,906	19,060	114,131	54,446
2001	2,370,430	1,856,583	18,884	1,875,467	214,303	-34,674	1,626,490	339,368	404,572	20,480	115,745	56,802
2002	2,459,001	1,910,674	9,185	1,919,859	219,937	-27,039	1,672,883	342,349	443,769	20,589	119,430	57,347
2003	2,592,232	2,001,762	7,736	2,009,498	228,879	-20,209	1,760,410	357,190	474,632	21,326	121,553	58,042
2004	2,819,193	2,193,855	7,212	2,201,067	248,775	-15,601	1,936,691	385,895	496,607	22,887	123,179	60,223
2005	3,110,083	2,390,818	6,696	2,397,514	267,181	-7,315	2,123,018	448,403	538,662	24,919	124,809	62,057
2006	3,435,761	2,663,972	175	2,664,147	299,538	3,768	2,368,377	492,010	575,374	27,480	125,028	64,092
2007	3,743,871	2,845,190	10,473	2,855,663	324,538	23,464	2,554,589	566,766	622,516	29,678	126,149	65,736
2008	4,165,716	3,133,898	13,133	3,147,031	358,156	31,660	2,820,535	629,362	715,819	32,825	126,905	67,365
2009	3,937,462	2,888,646	16,555	2,905,201	335,826	11,377	2,580,752	563,722	792,988	30,438	129,359	64,351
2010	4,005,472	2,909,561	14,186	2,923,747	334,004	-8,977	2,580,766	559,873	864,833	30,762	130,209	62,510
2011	4,233,615	3,101,532	31,601	3,133,133	317,885	-34,802	2,780,446	579,809	873,360	32,634	129,732	63,442
2012	4,311,086	3,164,437	25,119	3,189,556	325,120	-58,462	2,805,974	641,382	863,730	33,215	129,792	64,476
2013	4,195,983	3,143,200	22,339	3,165,539	372,185	-76,208	2,717,146	617,877	860,960	32,399	129,509	64,535
2014	4,419,381	3,216,575	35,262	3,251,837	385,153	-76,144	2,790,540	689,580	939,261	34,436	128,335	65,451
2015	4,423,985	3,201,509	26,846	3,228,355	395,494	-81,367	2,751,494	657,623	1,014,868	34,744	127,330	65,143
2016	4,260,475	2,988,438	25,199	3,013,637	369,986	-67,819	2,575,832	639,178	1,045,465	33,591	126,832	62,575
2017	4,323,896	3,039,019	18,956	3,057,975	378,984	-73,543	2,605,448	665,618	1,052,830	34,402	125,687	62,156
2018	4,448,324	3,096,101	18,587	3,114,688	386,909	-73,090	2,654,689	682,638	1,110,997	35,836	124,131	61,228
2019	4,477,477	3,079,648	19,019	3,098,667	380,462	-73,875	2,644,330	674,148	1,158,999	36,599	122,339	60,236
2020	4,715,660	2,883,169	24,298	2,907,467	362,222	-57,763	2,487,482	662,038	1,566,140	38,835	121,429	55,806
2021	5,049,661	3,022,279	21,930	3,044,209	377,697	-64,379	2,602,133	669,070	1,778,458	41,735	120,993	55,858

Personal Income and Employment by Area: Fayetteville, NC

(Thousands of dollars, except as noted.)

		Derivation of personal income										
		Earnings by place of work			Less: Contributions for government social insurance	Plus: Adjustment for residence	Equals: Net earnings by place of residence	Plus: Dividends, interest, and rent	Plus: Personal current transfer receipts	Per capita personal income (dollars)	Population (persons)	Total employment
Year	Personal income, total	Nonfarm	Farm	Total								
1970	895,508	756,061	12,471	768,532	46,776	-44,509	677,247	176,742	41,519	3,920	228,446	112,945
1971	943,591	802,118	12,250	814,368	53,127	-46,677	714,564	178,763	50,264	4,081	231,237	109,455
1972	1,079,144	923,693	14,413	938,106	62,149	-55,238	820,719	199,575	58,850	4,635	232,815	113,149
1973	1,217,676	1,041,004	16,664	1,057,668	75,642	-61,609	920,417	229,333	67,926	5,100	238,764	119,544
1974	1,405,028	1,189,674	17,555	1,207,229	90,462	-67,085	1,049,682	271,240	84,106	5,601	250,874	124,799
1975	1,514,949	1,258,022	13,314	1,271,336	100,659	-66,055	1,104,622	295,511	114,816	5,988	252,984	123,017
1976	1,618,849	1,336,989	17,565	1,354,554	110,252	-69,067	1,175,235	311,763	131,851	6,282	257,713	123,376
1977	1,725,916	1,410,413	14,753	1,425,166	114,407	-67,226	1,243,533	342,258	140,125	6,577	262,434	123,810
1978	1,891,547	1,518,122	13,994	1,532,116	122,616	-65,395	1,344,105	396,691	150,751	7,134	265,132	123,934
1979	2,033,223	1,640,744	9,296	1,650,040	138,588	-70,511	1,440,941	423,243	169,039	7,708	263,783	126,562
1980	2,347,916	1,874,637	6,546	1,881,183	156,816	-73,040	1,651,327	493,607	202,982	8,749	268,372	132,509
1981	2,600,610	2,073,528	11,003	2,084,531	182,868	-75,443	1,826,220	543,232	231,158	9,601	270,877	131,023
1982	2,806,231	2,222,490	16,299	2,238,789	192,186	-81,353	1,965,250	588,911	252,070	10,299	272,471	130,296
1983	3,073,279	2,443,763	7,674	2,451,437	220,950	-87,676	2,142,811	653,920	276,548	11,126	276,236	134,692
1984	3,375,291	2,680,611	15,688	2,696,299	248,824	-96,353	2,351,122	727,528	296,641	12,035	280,454	140,886
1985	3,582,929	2,842,152	12,212	2,854,364	268,890	-100,270	2,485,204	778,919	318,806	12,648	283,286	143,770
1986	3,808,289	3,008,205	18,349	3,026,554	291,300	-103,773	2,631,481	843,074	333,734	13,406	284,080	145,243
1987	4,013,967	3,188,939	17,097	3,206,036	311,027	-111,062	2,783,947	886,199	343,821	13,937	288,001	149,275
1988	4,262,191	3,416,052	22,814	3,438,866	350,797	-120,553	2,967,516	917,637	377,038	14,854	286,942	151,677
1989	4,539,251	3,574,701	26,197	3,600,898	372,502	-119,180	3,109,216	1,002,280	427,755	15,393	294,889	155,228
1990	4,681,857	3,680,857	38,352	3,719,209	397,072	-136,705	3,185,432	1,019,251	477,174	15,670	298,784	153,724
1991	4,915,528	3,869,784	30,448	3,900,232	423,656	-155,835	3,320,741	1,053,244	541,543	16,225	302,956	152,205
1992	5,884,299	4,735,632	28,091	4,763,723	523,865	-218,392	4,021,466	1,262,397	600,436	19,282	305,176	169,016
1993	6,131,748	4,862,968	28,512	4,891,480	549,440	-226,130	4,115,910	1,347,924	667,914	19,471	314,917	172,380
1994	6,273,478	4,937,656	29,614	4,967,270	550,402	-233,412	4,183,456	1,392,714	697,308	19,685	318,691	174,463
1995	6,599,849	5,107,865	18,412	5,126,277	560,183	-249,327	4,316,767	1,498,273	784,809	20,462	322,543	178,702
1996	6,871,863	5,243,121	35,109	5,278,230	573,485	-259,793	4,444,952	1,568,917	857,994	21,153	324,870	179,262
1997	7,114,105	5,492,371	41,694	5,534,065	598,707	-278,229	4,657,129	1,543,836	913,140	21,580	329,662	181,817
1998	9,279,395	6,545,363	48,987	6,594,350	718,439	175,085	6,050,996	2,009,621	1,218,778	22,221	417,599	220,834
1999	9,692,454	6,815,755	46,389	6,862,144	750,233	207,757	6,319,668	2,054,812	1,317,974	22,883	423,568	223,872
2000	10,236,445	7,135,895	99,232	7,235,127	785,625	235,411	6,684,913	2,138,538	1,412,994	23,857	429,071	226,368
2001	10,454,092	7,283,152	98,094	7,381,246	806,105	190,580	6,765,721	2,101,078	1,587,293	24,188	432,206	215,091
2002	10,951,770	7,897,938	31,228	7,929,166	870,797	13,958	7,072,327	2,138,485	1,740,958	25,050	437,190	219,277
2003	11,427,288	8,547,440	18,576	8,566,016	944,999	-248,376	7,372,641	2,200,259	1,854,388	26,173	436,610	223,180
2004	12,056,380	9,134,719	83,012	9,217,731	1,007,295	-416,589	7,793,847	2,240,636	2,021,897	27,136	444,293	228,124
2005	12,771,723	10,017,433	123,327	10,140,760	1,100,674	-861,796	8,178,290	2,351,449	2,241,984	28,751	444,221	234,800
2006	13,336,778	10,665,012	128,911	10,793,923	1,172,477	-1,179,630	8,441,816	2,459,438	2,435,524	29,522	451,761	239,259
2007	13,836,282	11,424,914	58,276	11,483,190	1,258,987	-1,775,641	8,448,562	2,738,798	2,648,922	30,306	456,550	246,441
2008	14,687,330	12,189,213	93,711	12,282,924	1,344,352	-2,168,666	8,769,906	2,899,263	3,018,161	31,622	464,464	249,482
2009	14,825,849	12,564,441	77,538	12,641,979	1,408,438	-2,612,083	8,621,458	2,899,662	3,304,729	31,244	474,524	248,677
2010	15,553,541	13,212,685	74,749	13,287,434	1,480,950	-2,814,745	8,991,739	2,982,505	3,579,297	31,709	490,502	248,905
2011	16,137,310	13,491,131	57,560	13,548,691	1,395,298	-2,998,292	9,155,101	3,207,608	3,774,601	32,320	499,299	250,818
2012	16,578,152	13,632,680	89,105	13,721,785	1,404,861	-2,887,768	9,429,156	3,257,572	3,891,424	32,964	502,910	249,550
2013	16,597,489	13,399,647	114,174	13,513,821	1,553,788	-2,628,875	9,331,158	3,289,369	3,976,962	32,574	509,536	248,769
2014	17,059,847	13,322,458	120,909	13,443,367	1,557,465	-2,380,879	9,505,023	3,406,586	4,148,238	33,603	507,688	248,248
2015	17,519,807	13,564,168	94,457	13,658,625	1,600,329	-2,459,041	9,599,255	3,444,858	4,475,694	34,469	508,274	249,094
2016	17,650,816	13,578,061	83,588	13,661,649	1,583,837	-2,500,517	9,577,295	3,449,070	4,624,451	34,444	512,445	252,103
2017	18,144,901	13,978,212	112,078	14,090,290	1,628,620	-2,614,232	9,847,438	3,435,956	4,861,507	35,414	512,370	255,728
2018	18,960,578	14,451,080	71,588	14,522,668	1,669,388	-2,562,402	10,290,878	3,523,342	5,146,358	36,694	516,726	260,287
2019	19,941,677	15,110,341	77,589	15,187,930	1,744,205	-2,695,967	10,747,758	3,692,661	5,501,258	38,364	519,801	264,085
2020	21,627,474	15,581,732	59,772	15,641,504	1,797,897	-2,767,165	11,076,442	3,643,125	6,907,907	41,563	520,354	262,748
2021	23,890,639	16,651,882	103,325	16,755,207	1,891,112	-2,638,896	12,225,199	3,631,019	8,034,421	45,542	524,588	270,057

Personal Income and Employment by Area: Fayetteville-Springdale-Rogers, AR

(Thousands of dollars, except as noted.)

Year	Personal income, total	Derivation of personal income									Per capita personal income (dollars)	Population (persons)	Total employment
		Earnings by place of work			Less: Contributions for government social insurance	Plus: Adjustment for residence	Equals: Net earnings by place of residence	Plus: Dividends, interest, and rent	Plus: Personal current transfer receipts			
		Nonfarm	Farm	Total								
1970	412,591	315,125	11,894	327,019	22,812	-10,792	293,415	68,372	50,804	2,742	150,488	70,807
1971	468,205	348,047	18,310	366,357	25,755	-10,367	330,235	78,002	59,968	3,008	155,659	71,683
1972	553,810	400,938	39,992	440,930	31,077	-10,377	399,476	87,464	66,870	3,365	164,587	75,556
1973	663,756	456,983	72,183	529,166	40,696	-10,478	477,992	105,917	79,847	3,914	169,595	78,403
1974	704,052	510,139	23,347	533,486	47,146	-10,577	475,763	129,865	98,424	4,012	175,478	80,412
1975	834,946	540,622	75,475	616,097	48,945	-10,832	556,320	150,501	128,125	4,683	178,301	78,703
1976	942,247	642,039	61,328	703,367	58,721	-12,264	632,382	168,312	141,553	5,135	183,484	83,760
1977	1,056,713	739,566	51,710	791,276	68,496	-13,649	709,131	195,819	151,763	5,543	190,629	88,950
1978	1,224,928	852,691	73,510	926,201	81,127	-16,091	828,983	228,264	167,681	6,265	195,519	93,869
1979	1,368,526	962,084	59,363	1,021,447	94,495	-19,580	907,372	268,628	192,526	6,813	200,858	97,375
1980	1,542,368	1,056,612	42,790	1,099,402	103,799	-22,786	972,817	338,947	230,604	7,510	205,371	99,074
1981	1,766,790	1,170,397	60,434	1,230,831	125,196	-30,143	1,075,492	424,026	267,272	8,543	206,809	101,476
1982	1,884,290	1,214,692	61,102	1,275,794	131,870	-32,426	1,111,498	480,480	292,312	9,053	208,135	101,411
1983	2,068,897	1,353,619	67,759	1,421,378	148,333	-38,382	1,234,663	514,095	320,139	9,805	211,010	104,781
1984	2,375,253	1,549,935	137,228	1,687,163	174,083	-46,545	1,466,535	570,414	338,304	11,052	214,918	110,511
1985	2,591,283	1,683,659	163,140	1,846,799	190,645	-52,753	1,603,401	627,320	360,562	11,864	218,411	114,621
1986	2,864,747	1,860,110	230,081	2,090,191	211,461	-60,740	1,817,990	666,028	380,729	12,914	221,825	119,025
1987	3,011,835	2,066,897	169,772	2,236,669	233,366	-68,045	1,935,258	677,422	399,155	13,265	227,055	125,866
1988	3,278,023	2,297,924	163,036	2,460,960	269,759	-82,574	2,108,627	747,739	421,657	14,196	230,907	132,435
1989	3,612,924	2,507,900	205,230	2,713,130	294,318	-94,504	2,324,308	824,431	464,185	15,404	234,537	136,787
1990	3,852,885	2,714,888	161,597	2,876,485	332,716	-115,946	2,427,823	919,567	505,495	15,955	241,478	139,593
1991	4,159,396	2,934,727	154,255	3,088,982	360,900	-116,161	2,611,921	987,661	559,814	16,593	250,665	146,715
1992	4,654,255	3,300,099	178,397	3,478,496	403,544	-115,004	2,959,948	1,074,025	620,282	17,891	260,143	153,194
1993	5,045,330	3,592,067	163,215	3,755,282	440,864	-124,150	3,190,268	1,192,157	662,905	18,476	273,070	163,449
1994	5,548,566	3,974,636	180,065	4,154,701	493,471	-146,682	3,514,548	1,324,361	709,657	19,430	285,563	172,371
1995	6,096,510	4,323,668	180,164	4,503,832	533,319	-156,741	3,813,772	1,509,413	773,325	20,345	299,657	183,452
1996	6,592,046	4,566,174	223,540	4,789,714	559,345	-171,345	4,059,024	1,704,612	828,410	21,127	312,015	189,353
1997	7,105,019	4,882,456	234,173	5,116,629	598,209	-196,551	4,321,869	1,900,744	882,406	22,089	321,648	193,813
1998	7,427,331	5,204,145	216,424	5,420,569	634,212	-266,596	4,519,761	2,038,944	868,626	24,096	308,242	187,561
1999	8,004,814	5,714,097	249,331	5,963,428	696,033	-288,728	4,978,667	2,121,342	904,805	25,231	317,266	193,627
2000	8,682,479	6,215,188	206,038	6,421,226	753,958	-313,891	5,353,377	2,355,761	973,341	26,482	327,867	200,211
2001	9,334,216	6,688,601	246,378	6,934,979	792,881	-333,507	5,808,591	2,434,064	1,091,561	27,726	336,662	208,886
2002	9,901,153	7,291,574	174,386	7,465,960	859,875	-343,346	6,262,739	2,464,507	1,173,907	28,623	345,922	216,346
2003	10,670,418	7,808,386	189,913	7,998,299	914,125	-341,798	6,742,376	2,689,844	1,238,198	29,860	357,352	222,187
2004	12,065,882	8,601,924	304,531	8,906,455	988,852	-337,272	7,580,331	3,154,281	1,331,270	32,585	370,284	230,625
2005	13,428,120	9,312,694	223,685	9,536,379	1,074,336	-327,903	8,134,140	3,839,758	1,454,222	34,854	385,269	244,037
2006	15,010,711	9,931,273	114,561	10,045,834	1,169,675	-301,967	8,574,192	4,811,946	1,624,573	37,430	401,039	253,470
2007	16,365,010	10,187,270	170,469	10,357,739	1,212,792	-262,315	8,882,632	5,691,657	1,790,721	39,573	413,543	257,530
2008	17,437,168	10,336,473	146,580	10,483,053	1,273,521	-226,409	8,983,123	6,379,897	2,074,148	41,159	423,649	256,032
2009	16,490,139	10,205,863	23,657	10,229,520	1,268,299	-204,763	8,756,458	5,428,101	2,305,580	38,166	432,067	248,545
2010	17,441,151	10,744,943	16,730	10,761,673	1,322,091	-191,404	9,248,178	5,644,096	2,548,877	39,432	442,308	249,946
2011	19,854,045	11,327,353	-39,025	11,288,328	1,257,263	-196,632	9,834,433	7,378,134	2,641,478	43,832	452,961	256,840
2012	23,247,071	12,247,815	83,101	12,330,916	1,309,485	-222,533	10,798,898	9,748,747	2,699,426	50,271	462,438	263,197
2013	23,330,651	13,227,666	195,642	13,423,308	1,574,502	-263,173	11,585,633	8,933,827	2,811,191	49,497	471,356	269,951
2014	26,805,050	14,096,030	300,498	14,396,528	1,682,523	-283,247	12,430,758	11,357,820	3,016,472	55,704	481,205	281,203
2015	29,191,269	15,026,789	230,779	15,257,568	1,789,879	-314,454	13,153,235	12,834,537	3,203,497	59,260	492,594	292,329
2016	31,087,736	15,737,327	116,571	15,853,898	1,864,351	-325,229	13,664,318	14,066,917	3,356,501	61,580	504,839	304,625
2017	32,269,251	16,779,917	196,939	16,976,856	1,987,695	-369,683	14,619,478	14,191,379	3,458,394	62,442	516,787	312,742
2018	34,966,595	17,384,484	192,741	17,577,225	2,054,023	-387,751	15,135,451	16,202,629	3,628,515	66,407	526,546	321,479
2019	34,636,869	18,538,662	27,950	18,566,612	2,211,665	-422,688	15,932,259	14,813,107	3,891,503	64,552	536,574	327,215
2020	36,388,302	19,898,082	-83,219	19,814,863	2,421,971	-464,886	16,928,006	14,424,795	5,035,501	66,213	549,566	330,625
2021	39,582,672	21,805,762	233,703	22,039,465	2,592,478	-534,452	18,912,535	15,000,371	5,669,766	70,594	560,709	342,927

Personal Income and Employment by Area: Flagstaff, AZ

(Thousands of dollars, except as noted.)

Year	Personal income, total	Earnings by place of work			Less: Contributions for government social insurance	Plus: Adjustment for residence	Equals: Net earnings by place of residence	Plus: Dividends, interest, and rent	Plus: Personal current transfer receipts	Per capita personal income (dollars)	Population (persons)	Total employment
		Nonfarm	Farm	Total								
1970	161,686	132,931	2,083	135,014	7,929	-8,930	118,155	27,929	15,602	3,288	49,180	20,148
1971	191,445	162,410	2,268	164,678	10,419	-13,511	140,748	31,211	19,486	3,590	53,330	21,705
1972	232,114	207,239	3,051	210,290	14,192	-21,420	174,678	35,213	22,223	3,988	58,203	24,041
1973	274,482	248,659	4,013	252,672	19,668	-25,647	207,357	41,102	26,023	4,452	61,654	26,189
1974	296,520	262,069	150	262,219	21,044	-21,542	219,633	46,865	30,022	4,574	64,831	26,719
1975	335,707	276,024	5,866	281,890	21,637	-16,201	244,052	51,260	40,395	4,808	69,825	26,902
1976	361,820	292,722	1,493	294,215	22,768	-10,177	261,270	55,485	45,065	5,449	66,403	27,565
1977	397,913	321,980	1,148	323,128	25,138	-5,960	292,030	63,450	42,433	5,772	68,939	29,570
1978	470,375	379,802	6,516	386,318	30,620	-6,757	348,941	74,313	47,121	6,642	70,815	32,397
1979	520,701	420,865	646	421,511	35,957	-6,140	379,414	86,365	54,922	7,098	73,357	33,879
1980	600,418	474,627	2,285	476,912	41,461	-5,742	429,709	104,306	66,403	7,944	75,579	35,165
1981	665,849	513,603	666	514,269	48,110	-2,137	464,022	127,641	74,186	8,559	77,794	35,739
1982	713,246	530,367	3,444	533,811	50,961	169	483,019	149,521	80,706	9,011	79,156	35,849
1983	783,166	573,780	3,431	577,211	57,080	-871	519,260	173,080	90,826	9,655	81,118	37,242
1984	872,848	642,102	5,768	647,870	64,982	-4,049	578,839	196,345	97,664	10,436	83,640	39,790
1985	956,449	707,414	935	708,349	73,183	-5,919	629,247	219,122	108,080	11,328	84,431	41,603
1986	1,054,836	788,879	3,307	792,186	82,627	-8,346	701,213	239,127	114,496	12,045	87,575	43,483
1987	1,124,707	844,065	1,538	845,603	88,022	-9,829	747,752	251,087	125,868	12,444	90,380	45,220
1988	1,207,907	911,094	678	911,772	99,815	-14,652	797,305	273,192	137,410	12,939	93,355	46,586
1989	1,281,478	928,295	-305	927,990	104,398	-15,740	807,852	309,757	163,869	13,462	95,194	47,115
1990	1,388,541	1,006,709	775	1,007,484	116,587	-20,241	870,656	335,403	182,482	14,299	97,106	48,543
1991	1,485,117	1,078,998	1,751	1,080,749	126,058	-22,486	932,205	349,910	203,002	14,904	99,647	49,766
1992	1,629,994	1,184,719	2,163	1,186,882	138,436	-25,497	1,022,949	375,294	231,751	15,903	102,498	51,643
1993	1,723,819	1,252,786	107	1,252,893	147,040	-24,798	1,081,055	396,156	246,608	16,329	105,570	53,787
1994	1,872,310	1,347,781	-1,110	1,346,671	157,844	-23,859	1,164,968	446,444	260,898	17,228	108,680	56,507
1995	2,001,700	1,416,351	-1,248	1,415,103	158,661	-23,422	1,233,020	504,281	264,399	18,041	110,954	58,867
1996	2,149,711	1,522,068	899	1,522,967	174,577	-23,145	1,325,245	539,953	284,513	19,077	112,686	61,574
1997	2,303,810	1,618,796	734	1,619,530	181,721	-18,896	1,418,913	590,411	294,486	20,130	114,444	62,567
1998	2,455,852	1,718,819	4,577	1,723,396	190,811	-15,932	1,516,653	628,858	310,341	21,379	114,874	65,405
1999	2,591,717	1,813,712	9,544	1,823,256	200,315	-13,820	1,609,121	651,457	331,139	22,477	115,307	66,761
2000	2,781,601	1,944,066	4,261	1,948,327	213,779	-11,272	1,723,276	709,350	348,975	23,821	116,773	69,832
2001	2,950,839	2,038,508	9,119	2,047,627	226,594	-4,873	1,816,160	724,169	410,510	24,947	118,283	66,819
2002	3,090,314	2,153,906	424	2,154,330	239,810	2,277	1,916,797	717,282	456,235	25,475	121,308	67,698
2003	3,240,698	2,288,713	-120	2,288,593	250,755	9,125	2,046,963	690,726	503,009	26,372	122,882	69,161
2004	3,494,610	2,465,444	1,732	2,467,176	268,694	17,403	2,215,885	756,325	522,400	27,931	125,117	72,523
2005	3,749,167	2,613,239	29	2,613,268	288,079	32,195	2,357,384	817,726	574,057	29,515	127,025	74,562
2006	4,119,876	2,836,261	-18	2,836,243	307,268	43,340	2,572,315	935,079	612,482	32,013	128,695	76,556
2007	4,427,336	3,076,489	18,019	3,094,508	336,655	43,759	2,801,612	962,015	663,709	33,941	130,442	79,194
2008	4,741,621	3,187,844	9,916	3,197,760	350,892	42,819	2,889,687	1,078,847	773,087	35,961	131,853	78,696
2009	4,542,224	3,028,485	5,392	3,033,877	341,473	51,875	2,744,279	935,223	862,722	34,030	133,477	76,109
2010	4,675,714	3,132,093	5,765	3,137,858	350,340	63,229	2,850,747	876,656	948,311	34,732	134,624	76,341
2011	5,013,142	3,317,502	6,708	3,324,210	324,541	86,414	3,086,083	985,175	941,884	37,325	134,309	76,961
2012	5,089,649	3,256,347	1,005	3,257,352	322,951	108,991	3,043,392	1,125,722	920,535	37,368	136,204	78,072
2013	5,312,248	3,456,554	3,803	3,460,357	382,960	128,961	3,206,358	1,161,776	944,114	38,836	136,788	80,096
2014	5,608,907	3,610,234	5,213	3,615,447	399,625	125,786	3,341,608	1,237,205	1,030,094	40,452	138,656	81,613
2015	5,992,731	3,828,143	8,830	3,836,973	423,271	130,932	3,544,634	1,369,755	1,078,342	42,706	140,326	83,442
2016	6,202,954	3,971,420	7,125	3,978,545	433,805	141,933	3,686,673	1,394,681	1,121,600	43,655	142,091	84,993
2017	6,648,800	4,227,828	11,533	4,239,361	459,422	148,658	3,928,597	1,512,468	1,207,735	46,483	143,036	86,597
2018	6,955,736	4,423,885	22,539	4,446,424	481,907	155,748	4,120,265	1,576,699	1,258,772	47,997	144,921	87,178
2019	7,232,353	4,414,389	7,644	4,422,033	488,803	172,367	4,105,597	1,793,124	1,333,632	49,454	146,244	86,405
2020	7,837,473	4,377,769	23,260	4,401,029	491,842	202,931	4,112,118	1,829,961	1,895,394	54,008	145,116	81,636
2021	8,255,426	4,600,506	32,540	4,633,046	510,840	242,727	4,364,933	1,892,472	1,998,021	56,914	145,052	84,555

Personal Income and Employment by Area: Flint, MI

(Thousands of dollars, except as noted.)

Year	Personal income, total	Earnings by place of work			Less: Contributions for government social insurance	Plus: Adjustment for residence	Equals: Net earnings by place of residence	Plus: Dividends, interest, and rent	Plus: Personal current transfer receipts	Per capita personal income (dollars)	Population (persons)	Total employment
		Nonfarm	Farm	Total								
1970	1,771,022	1,618,255	3,749	1,622,004	113,439	-119,282	1,389,283	218,119	163,620	3,970	446,058	169,418
1971	2,050,637	1,926,510	3,188	1,929,698	138,409	-154,672	1,636,617	232,021	181,999	4,574	448,310	180,597
1972	2,232,036	2,115,753	5,044	2,120,797	164,610	-174,935	1,781,252	246,822	203,962	4,975	448,656	181,540
1973	2,452,316	2,368,810	6,331	2,375,141	213,069	-199,956	1,962,116	263,227	226,973	5,428	451,762	190,536
1974	2,474,702	2,265,756	6,992	2,272,748	211,254	-185,181	1,876,313	291,930	306,459	5,497	450,155	181,085
1975	2,695,600	2,418,511	7,264	2,425,775	222,103	-204,701	1,998,971	311,066	385,563	6,032	446,850	172,646
1976	3,205,305	3,025,601	6,365	3,031,966	283,603	-283,283	2,465,080	346,210	394,015	7,205	444,880	184,610
1977	3,692,290	3,590,047	5,861	3,595,908	336,765	-356,096	2,903,047	391,656	397,587	8,269	446,546	197,459
1978	4,042,108	3,975,603	1,933	3,977,536	387,416	-396,187	3,193,933	431,999	416,176	8,990	449,607	205,560
1979	4,414,030	4,291,343	4,071	4,295,414	427,340	-427,461	3,440,613	485,648	487,769	9,785	451,082	209,373
1980	4,644,626	4,176,568	3,704	4,180,272	408,258	-413,108	3,358,906	563,140	722,580	10,341	449,131	193,291
1981	5,064,084	4,628,517	4,682	4,633,199	493,230	-463,852	3,676,117	674,951	713,016	11,434	442,878	196,257
1982	5,039,827	4,339,488	-159	4,339,329	468,809	-408,904	3,461,616	776,863	801,348	11,530	437,115	180,848
1983	5,492,110	4,828,984	2,642	4,831,626	531,404	-466,921	3,833,301	830,625	828,184	12,696	432,600	184,486
1984	6,109,702	5,469,115	5,904	5,475,019	624,808	-524,443	4,325,768	947,380	836,554	14,200	430,254	194,055
1985	6,637,303	6,008,042	4,895	6,012,937	705,066	-561,600	4,746,271	1,020,657	870,375	15,390	431,268	202,416
1986	6,962,585	6,236,728	3,838	6,240,566	732,763	-554,803	4,953,000	1,090,954	918,631	16,078	433,037	205,863
1987	6,661,000	5,698,352	4,050	5,702,402	661,344	-421,645	4,619,413	1,075,417	966,170	15,371	433,335	202,507
1988	6,894,660	5,769,787	3,977	5,773,764	685,436	-378,341	4,709,987	1,146,076	1,038,597	16,031	430,096	194,226
1989	7,224,829	5,982,754	6,405	5,989,159	714,198	-370,688	4,904,273	1,184,987	1,135,569	16,843	428,946	198,317
1990	7,558,747	6,128,473	5,372	6,133,845	741,866	-353,885	5,038,094	1,299,104	1,221,549	17,540	430,938	201,117
1991	7,929,183	6,395,000	1,817	6,396,817	786,256	-356,856	5,253,705	1,285,177	1,390,301	18,389	431,184	196,856
1992	8,182,401	6,499,758	1,331	6,501,089	789,813	-291,065	5,420,211	1,296,746	1,465,444	18,987	430,944	195,695
1993	8,539,785	6,717,044	1,467	6,718,511	823,066	-248,481	5,646,964	1,337,384	1,555,437	19,828	430,702	195,165
1994	9,421,322	7,556,622	-1,445	7,555,177	930,484	-287,550	6,337,143	1,521,565	1,562,614	21,872	430,742	205,760
1995	9,932,124	7,821,296	1,510	7,822,806	957,530	-235,380	6,629,896	1,618,088	1,684,140	22,977	432,261	214,744
1996	10,362,715	7,855,211	-1,952	7,853,259	933,462	-128,532	6,791,265	1,690,559	1,880,891	23,916	433,302	218,418
1997	10,527,497	7,909,096	-2,213	7,906,883	937,396	-17,786	6,951,701	1,789,657	1,786,139	24,314	432,978	218,542
1998	10,846,647	8,131,759	-2,760	8,128,999	942,670	120,122	7,306,451	1,798,300	1,741,896	25,041	433,160	217,360
1999	11,154,392	8,222,323	2,631	8,224,954	956,751	248,024	7,516,227	1,769,028	1,869,137	25,677	434,409	214,621
2000	11,709,317	8,496,090	-2,081	8,494,009	970,839	391,559	7,914,729	1,837,614	1,956,974	26,797	436,965	215,500
2001	11,669,950	8,213,631	-5,569	8,208,062	953,701	505,479	7,759,840	1,753,987	2,156,123	26,608	438,584	208,522
2002	11,747,269	8,255,490	-899	8,254,591	963,434	511,326	7,802,483	1,703,663	2,241,123	26,695	440,062	206,216
2003	12,115,065	8,312,599	2,261	8,314,860	965,243	612,741	7,962,358	1,774,225	2,378,482	27,429	441,689	204,035
2004	12,351,589	8,490,076	6,580	8,496,656	1,003,440	721,729	8,214,945	1,668,071	2,468,573	27,911	442,534	205,076
2005	12,558,914	8,208,000	7,689	8,215,689	980,365	978,901	8,214,225	1,727,231	2,617,458	28,381	442,508	199,141
2006	12,951,147	8,413,025	8,496	8,421,521	1,027,454	970,398	8,364,465	1,815,886	2,770,796	29,357	441,164	199,333
2007	13,091,464	8,167,142	8,310	8,175,452	1,005,866	971,150	8,140,736	1,902,821	3,047,907	29,882	438,109	197,347
2008	13,226,344	7,734,411	12,062	7,746,473	969,629	1,011,757	7,788,601	1,948,308	3,489,435	30,540	433,082	189,381
2009	12,705,196	7,296,062	5,203	7,301,265	924,427	688,279	7,065,117	1,751,763	3,888,316	29,686	427,989	181,507
2010	13,035,018	7,425,432	10,107	7,435,539	918,996	541,625	7,058,168	1,768,726	4,208,124	30,674	424,959	179,309
2011	13,590,692	7,730,570	22,279	7,752,849	852,305	632,653	7,533,197	1,884,865	4,172,630	32,201	422,062	182,703
2012	13,961,925	7,925,397	22,228	7,947,625	871,551	790,020	7,866,094	1,979,425	4,116,406	33,382	418,243	182,470
2013	14,178,021	8,048,586	24,054	8,072,640	1,004,991	809,667	7,877,316	2,040,706	4,259,999	34,105	415,713	185,571
2014	14,579,396	8,228,281	10,710	8,238,991	1,024,225	817,976	8,032,742	2,178,988	4,367,666	35,272	413,344	187,614
2015	15,252,202	8,605,665	16,777	8,622,442	1,062,493	853,710	8,413,659	2,250,698	4,587,845	37,105	411,060	187,291
2016	15,603,033	8,672,750	14,284	8,687,034	1,076,175	979,050	8,589,909	2,383,129	4,629,995	38,090	409,634	186,025
2017	15,959,689	8,944,933	9,901	8,954,834	1,111,715	1,117,025	8,960,144	2,411,648	4,587,897	39,084	408,345	187,281
2018	16,478,474	9,210,668	9,010	9,219,678	1,167,826	1,195,800	9,247,652	2,460,206	4,770,616	40,449	407,386	188,349
2019	17,132,439	9,485,180	11,214	9,496,394	1,199,733	1,232,363	9,529,024	2,617,767	4,985,648	42,141	406,554	188,204
2020	18,810,409	9,150,998	17,599	9,168,597	1,170,196	1,404,904	9,403,305	2,647,157	6,759,947	46,371	405,648	175,062
2021	19,967,292	9,728,638	20,109	9,748,747	1,217,503	1,613,753	10,144,997	2,690,936	7,131,359	49,399	404,208	180,865

Personal Income and Employment by Area: Florence, SC

(Thousands of dollars, except as noted.)

Year	Personal income, total	Earnings by place of work			Less: Contributions for government social insurance	Plus: Adjustment for residence	Equals: Net earnings by place of residence	Plus: Dividends, interest, and rent	Plus: Personal current transfer receipts	Per capita personal income (dollars)	Population (persons)	Total employment
		Nonfarm	Farm	Total								
1970	406,157	335,541	23,087	358,628	23,637	-14,584	320,407	44,564	41,186	2,838	143,122	68,218
1971	445,235	367,395	23,811	391,206	26,699	-15,648	348,859	49,311	47,065	3,058	145,616	69,457
1972	501,497	419,930	24,895	444,825	31,941	-18,444	394,440	54,827	52,230	3,411	147,002	72,381
1973	576,880	485,934	30,377	516,311	42,491	-22,080	451,740	63,233	61,907	3,797	151,937	76,728
1974	674,759	556,988	43,467	600,455	50,584	-27,202	522,669	71,430	80,660	4,281	157,632	78,964
1975	713,992	562,197	31,022	593,219	49,699	-24,181	519,339	81,545	113,108	4,438	160,899	74,439
1976	792,398	647,423	23,012	670,435	58,461	-27,504	584,470	88,827	119,101	4,881	162,337	76,550
1977	870,486	719,410	20,706	740,116	65,020	-29,942	645,154	99,658	125,674	5,230	166,445	77,460
1978	994,242	816,651	32,603	849,254	75,495	-32,210	741,549	111,762	140,931	5,879	169,123	79,149
1979	1,099,503	915,714	21,030	936,744	87,479	-37,987	811,278	125,807	162,418	6,400	171,805	80,572
1980	1,223,173	1,014,044	1,734	1,015,778	96,820	-44,287	874,671	155,996	192,506	7,061	173,231	81,883
1981	1,400,222	1,127,787	25,746	1,153,533	115,644	-52,448	985,441	195,872	218,909	8,044	174,072	82,700
1982	1,462,646	1,133,795	33,593	1,167,388	119,110	-48,188	1,000,090	225,773	236,783	8,387	174,401	79,678
1983	1,557,357	1,220,378	11,315	1,231,693	130,065	-45,508	1,056,120	248,956	252,281	8,959	173,824	80,119
1984	1,737,405	1,371,216	23,390	1,394,606	151,219	-53,936	1,189,451	282,357	265,597	9,934	174,898	83,677
1985	1,832,209	1,422,115	22,453	1,444,568	158,687	-51,826	1,234,055	306,751	291,403	10,444	175,430	82,212
1986	1,928,084	1,527,243	-3,836	1,523,407	174,548	-49,323	1,299,536	323,624	304,924	11,004	175,210	83,463
1987	2,067,273	1,621,557	28,369	1,649,926	182,753	-46,687	1,420,486	334,820	311,967	11,826	174,806	84,803
1988	2,254,760	1,773,409	39,132	1,812,541	207,128	-50,803	1,554,610	367,572	332,578	12,904	174,734	88,568
1989	2,481,749	1,897,413	37,198	1,934,611	225,135	-51,146	1,658,330	438,539	384,880	14,128	175,658	91,566
1990	2,655,971	2,058,136	23,238	2,081,374	247,476	-52,701	1,781,197	446,632	428,142	15,030	176,706	93,814
1991	2,829,845	2,166,822	33,573	2,200,395	262,966	-60,015	1,877,414	458,678	493,753	15,763	179,519	94,063
1992	3,024,174	2,304,152	36,008	2,340,160	277,060	-61,101	2,001,999	463,520	558,655	16,612	182,044	95,003
1993	3,186,980	2,439,147	29,036	2,468,183	296,509	-64,948	2,106,726	483,562	596,692	17,303	184,186	96,466
1994	3,365,240	2,541,304	43,427	2,584,731	312,172	-64,294	2,208,265	521,236	635,739	18,118	185,744	98,121
1995	3,530,073	2,689,484	23,097	2,712,581	329,940	-72,024	2,310,617	546,847	672,609	18,799	187,778	100,459
1996	3,778,617	2,857,197	44,991	2,902,188	344,323	-82,434	2,475,431	584,273	718,913	20,000	188,929	102,855
1997	3,956,507	3,005,831	40,799	3,046,630	360,923	-88,509	2,597,198	614,862	744,447	20,750	190,674	106,126
1998	4,182,079	3,210,444	17,350	3,227,794	384,709	-94,785	2,748,300	655,933	777,846	21,818	191,680	107,187
1999	4,324,016	3,333,481	20,786	3,354,267	395,262	-94,334	2,864,671	635,463	823,882	22,446	192,641	107,966
2000	4,609,070	3,521,866	50,162	3,572,028	416,543	-101,366	3,054,119	689,797	865,154	23,845	193,290	108,664
2001	4,791,243	3,591,338	67,434	3,658,772	427,543	-106,652	3,124,577	716,293	950,373	24,667	194,240	106,048
2002	4,923,207	3,727,652	-7,340	3,720,312	441,809	-110,648	3,167,855	715,495	1,039,857	25,171	195,590	106,518
2003	5,091,533	3,802,498	47,197	3,849,695	451,545	-106,893	3,291,257	717,433	1,082,843	25,838	197,053	105,208
2004	5,350,993	3,950,385	37,849	3,988,234	470,779	-107,883	3,409,572	767,940	1,173,481	27,024	198,010	105,332
2005	5,537,062	4,041,258	24,231	4,065,489	482,259	-105,234	3,477,996	806,947	1,252,119	27,801	199,167	105,676
2006	5,926,910	4,282,967	22,526	4,305,493	521,617	-116,161	3,667,715	926,280	1,332,915	29,500	200,913	107,464
2007	6,215,219	4,455,872	8,266	4,464,138	540,977	-121,821	3,801,340	1,010,967	1,402,912	30,731	202,246	109,510
2008	6,453,006	4,502,363	14,546	4,516,909	550,831	-128,412	3,837,666	1,021,869	1,593,471	31,663	203,805	109,121
2009	6,313,244	4,333,832	11,300	4,345,132	538,097	-149,826	3,657,209	930,611	1,725,424	30,823	204,825	104,986
2010	6,448,391	4,408,284	8,744	4,417,028	543,286	-167,749	3,705,993	893,726	1,848,672	31,352	205,674	104,404
2011	6,724,236	4,558,156	17,989	4,576,145	503,161	-189,317	3,883,667	990,937	1,849,632	32,669	205,832	106,929
2012	6,855,201	4,730,567	24,809	4,755,376	513,945	-218,780	4,022,651	987,187	1,845,363	33,264	206,084	107,460
2013	6,980,910	4,925,104	34,242	4,959,346	599,189	-254,279	4,105,878	1,010,753	1,864,279	33,881	206,039	108,522
2014	7,238,937	5,058,608	162	5,058,770	611,069	-264,881	4,182,820	1,088,572	1,967,545	35,392	204,537	109,069
2015	7,496,279	5,243,008	-16,390	5,226,618	636,548	-277,331	4,312,739	1,106,866	2,076,674	36,762	203,913	110,732
2016	7,712,176	5,295,653	9,173	5,304,826	644,015	-269,557	4,391,254	1,210,660	2,110,262	37,967	203,128	111,475
2017	7,912,620	5,495,430	12,933	5,508,363	670,548	-274,259	4,563,556	1,215,055	2,134,009	39,122	202,254	112,386
2018	8,212,070	5,746,573	498	5,747,071	702,660	-283,367	4,761,044	1,228,927	2,222,099	40,779	201,378	116,279
2019	8,733,781	6,026,237	21,800	6,048,037	739,177	-296,921	5,011,939	1,418,333	2,303,509	43,528	200,647	116,524
2020	9,292,393	6,066,391	24,365	6,090,756	744,060	-288,443	5,058,253	1,428,294	2,805,846	46,546	199,638	113,704
2021	10,039,856	6,458,701	41,432	6,500,133	779,139	-303,045	5,417,949	1,466,984	3,154,923	50,386	199,259	115,632

Personal Income and Employment by Area: Florence-Muscle Shoals, AL

(Thousands of dollars, except as noted.)

Year	Personal income, total	Earnings by place of work Nonfarm	Earnings by place of work Farm	Earnings by place of work Total	Less: Contributions for government social insurance	Plus: Adjustment for residence	Equals: Net earnings by place of residence	Plus: Dividends, interest, and rent	Plus: Personal current transfer receipts	Per capita personal income (dollars)	Population (persons)	Total employment
1970	364,774	287,164	11,269	298,433	19,076	2,687	282,044	46,066	36,664	3,089	118,093	45,574
1971	407,840	318,621	13,503	332,124	21,253	1,580	312,451	52,655	42,734	3,383	120,545	46,466
1972	445,489	358,547	14,600	373,147	25,604	-4,397	343,146	55,976	46,367	3,664	121,579	48,921
1973	491,305	395,681	19,485	415,166	33,191	-7,031	374,944	62,878	53,483	3,976	123,562	50,449
1974	546,775	444,839	13,243	458,082	38,994	-9,088	410,000	72,785	63,990	4,405	124,134	51,771
1975	599,466	470,334	11,781	482,115	40,917	-9,315	431,883	82,063	85,520	4,741	126,431	50,742
1976	692,149	554,355	23,631	577,986	48,689	-22,388	506,909	91,098	94,142	5,413	127,873	53,503
1977	763,431	630,581	17,434	648,015	55,060	-32,363	560,592	104,147	98,692	5,863	130,206	55,877
1978	875,787	733,682	18,412	752,094	64,530	-39,858	647,706	121,832	106,249	6,641	131,868	59,286
1979	975,515	791,588	28,891	820,479	72,305	-34,423	713,751	139,753	122,011	7,250	134,560	59,603
1980	1,078,322	855,949	12,059	868,008	77,974	-37,922	752,112	175,164	151,046	7,969	135,322	58,791
1981	1,195,164	902,580	22,282	924,862	89,305	-20,524	815,033	212,734	167,397	8,781	136,104	57,118
1982	1,241,658	911,897	22,328	934,225	92,173	-18,223	823,829	231,877	185,952	9,188	135,139	55,778
1983	1,289,950	943,668	1,285	944,953	98,913	-6,182	839,858	243,868	206,224	9,623	134,050	56,395
1984	1,395,554	993,222	13,187	1,006,409	106,894	4,489	904,004	271,514	220,036	10,455	133,488	57,561
1985	1,475,173	1,029,173	12,687	1,041,860	112,866	24,358	953,352	289,951	231,870	11,062	133,350	57,338
1986	1,554,521	1,077,852	7,737	1,085,589	118,286	40,267	1,007,570	304,641	242,310	11,719	132,653	57,115
1987	1,635,178	1,124,151	13,778	1,137,929	122,477	57,339	1,072,791	313,560	248,827	12,403	131,839	58,321
1988	1,777,323	1,216,672	18,618	1,235,290	137,899	80,045	1,177,436	343,336	256,551	13,554	131,132	60,565
1989	1,893,865	1,276,150	14,515	1,290,665	147,401	82,228	1,225,492	380,964	287,409	14,483	130,762	62,347
1990	2,078,612	1,396,662	9,946	1,406,608	161,988	111,392	1,356,012	408,367	314,233	15,766	131,838	64,761
1991	2,173,766	1,460,542	19,772	1,480,314	170,877	107,923	1,417,360	407,649	348,757	16,255	133,733	66,343
1992	2,321,763	1,565,121	23,991	1,589,112	180,401	112,866	1,521,577	410,469	389,717	17,176	135,174	67,141
1993	2,414,084	1,633,439	16,628	1,650,067	192,102	120,224	1,578,189	425,201	410,694	17,625	136,971	68,977
1994	2,555,253	1,724,956	32,016	1,756,972	204,809	117,419	1,669,582	448,898	436,773	18,545	137,786	69,508
1995	2,702,119	1,806,876	3,344	1,810,220	217,006	129,057	1,722,271	506,908	472,940	19,445	138,962	72,519
1996	2,819,101	1,865,923	25,920	1,891,843	221,563	124,747	1,795,027	523,975	500,099	20,091	140,318	73,172
1997	2,909,428	1,912,989	15,974	1,928,963	226,908	129,863	1,831,918	550,852	526,658	20,585	141,339	73,294
1998	2,966,475	1,894,596	15,560	1,910,156	222,525	147,908	1,835,539	581,649	549,287	20,885	142,041	71,742
1999	3,034,656	1,950,726	11,379	1,962,105	229,243	157,117	1,889,979	575,005	569,672	21,325	142,305	71,492
2000	3,147,818	1,979,834	18,250	1,998,084	231,976	163,177	1,929,285	615,750	602,783	22,007	143,036	71,922
2001	3,242,327	1,998,908	20,577	2,019,485	237,371	171,354	1,953,468	619,305	669,554	22,740	142,584	70,339
2002	3,271,591	2,006,045	6,630	2,012,675	236,329	173,100	1,949,446	605,475	716,670	23,013	142,163	67,794
2003	3,430,806	2,086,850	32,598	2,119,448	245,314	191,443	2,065,577	609,770	755,459	24,096	142,382	67,531
2004	3,654,924	2,233,813	49,806	2,283,619	260,371	201,117	2,224,365	618,370	812,189	25,539	143,112	68,949
2005	3,885,356	2,363,160	48,392	2,411,552	279,324	217,446	2,349,674	670,574	865,108	27,035	143,717	71,142
2006	4,099,827	2,515,973	38,672	2,554,645	298,490	232,950	2,489,105	677,792	932,930	28,332	144,707	73,600
2007	4,334,451	2,563,441	30,004	2,593,445	310,370	243,345	2,526,420	813,450	994,581	29,771	145,593	74,996
2008	4,441,478	2,536,000	32,597	2,568,597	318,338	252,182	2,502,441	847,116	1,091,921	30,281	146,675	74,033
2009	4,398,618	2,533,895	26,418	2,560,313	316,607	221,315	2,465,021	759,029	1,174,568	29,932	146,952	72,415
2010	4,617,499	2,683,486	1,427	2,684,913	335,193	220,421	2,570,141	775,441	1,271,917	31,355	147,265	72,486
2011	4,743,885	2,736,640	1,541	2,738,181	307,986	219,599	2,649,794	827,111	1,266,980	32,236	147,160	73,883
2012	4,815,077	2,766,116	4,175	2,770,291	309,254	225,850	2,686,887	856,773	1,271,417	32,697	147,265	73,577
2013	4,834,908	2,827,024	47,331	2,874,355	354,023	204,406	2,724,738	819,325	1,290,845	32,828	147,282	73,903
2014	5,043,514	2,948,289	17,242	2,965,531	366,025	203,332	2,802,838	903,686	1,336,990	33,981	148,422	74,883
2015	5,168,756	3,022,693	2,120	3,024,813	374,915	187,209	2,837,107	908,202	1,423,447	34,910	148,058	75,152
2016	5,230,686	3,044,261	-7,198	3,037,063	379,905	198,037	2,855,195	946,694	1,428,797	35,270	148,304	75,447
2017	5,308,901	3,086,128	-64	3,086,064	390,151	206,868	2,902,781	959,735	1,446,385	35,655	148,895	75,472
2018	5,463,267	3,166,899	-11,034	3,155,865	406,818	234,951	2,983,998	979,895	1,499,374	36,561	149,427	76,474
2019	5,766,498	3,256,933	-8,935	3,247,998	414,853	256,387	3,089,532	1,096,472	1,580,494	38,390	150,210	76,822
2020	6,262,592	3,368,817	-5,273	3,363,544	433,372	281,743	3,211,915	1,124,082	1,926,595	41,516	150,846	75,215
2021	6,758,402	3,583,224	28,281	3,611,505	454,362	292,343	3,449,486	1,163,503	2,145,413	44,605	151,517	76,617

Personal Income and Employment by Area: Fond du Lac, WI

(Thousands of dollars, except as noted.)

Year	Personal income, total	Earnings by place of work			Less: Contributions for government social insurance	Plus: Adjustment for residence	Equals: Net earnings by place of residence	Plus: Dividends, interest, and rent	Plus: Personal current transfer receipts	Per capita personal income (dollars)	Population (persons)	Total employment
		Nonfarm	Farm	Total								
1970	322,337	245,447	18,456	263,903	18,807	-2,948	242,148	51,698	28,491	3,820	84,380	39,020
1971	344,029	256,193	21,497	277,690	20,238	-439	257,013	54,692	32,324	4,117	83,569	38,765
1972	375,685	283,304	20,008	303,312	23,510	2,230	282,032	57,881	35,772	4,406	85,264	40,118
1973	423,011	320,486	21,909	342,395	30,581	4,070	315,884	65,629	41,498	4,889	86,518	41,920
1974	463,052	342,328	21,018	363,346	33,885	9,154	338,615	74,774	49,663	5,349	86,561	42,694
1975	510,326	358,433	25,368	383,801	34,687	14,014	363,128	82,665	64,533	5,857	87,138	41,961
1976	565,686	406,292	22,955	429,247	39,852	17,934	407,329	88,011	70,346	6,515	86,830	42,917
1977	637,421	447,527	39,691	487,218	44,127	23,397	466,488	97,760	73,173	7,271	87,670	44,071
1978	702,220	499,994	32,151	532,145	50,575	32,239	513,809	107,829	80,582	8,005	87,720	44,857
1979	794,391	561,380	40,505	601,885	59,087	40,462	583,260	119,385	91,746	9,010	88,172	46,299
1980	864,166	584,669	35,167	619,836	61,496	45,419	603,759	147,047	113,360	9,718	88,924	45,661
1981	949,353	648,281	24,762	673,043	73,081	43,431	643,393	181,025	124,935	10,720	88,556	46,334
1982	1,000,826	663,058	21,333	684,391	75,710	43,957	652,638	205,956	142,232	11,327	88,361	45,665
1983	1,041,471	698,402	6,129	704,531	79,161	49,116	674,486	217,047	149,938	11,796	88,289	45,170
1984	1,161,467	779,539	23,085	802,624	90,274	52,567	764,917	245,159	151,391	13,116	88,552	46,517
1985	1,215,461	812,202	25,336	837,538	94,159	55,589	798,968	254,242	162,251	13,666	88,942	46,739
1986	1,277,850	847,996	33,960	881,956	98,070	65,577	849,463	261,565	166,822	14,373	88,909	45,908
1987	1,365,050	929,495	41,385	970,880	105,180	70,435	936,135	260,461	168,454	15,331	89,038	46,598
1988	1,428,705	1,005,506	20,739	1,026,245	117,347	76,933	985,831	268,031	174,843	15,912	89,787	47,180
1989	1,607,235	1,142,789	45,809	1,188,598	132,902	66,671	1,122,367	293,847	191,021	17,908	89,748	50,119
1990	1,688,612	1,205,476	39,054	1,244,530	145,119	81,364	1,180,775	301,987	205,850	18,701	90,296	51,402
1991	1,725,333	1,235,946	34,829	1,270,775	151,298	80,649	1,200,126	305,500	219,707	18,905	91,265	51,910
1992	1,855,836	1,348,197	37,534	1,385,731	163,385	84,970	1,307,316	309,439	239,081	20,161	92,049	52,863
1993	1,959,430	1,441,595	27,400	1,468,995	175,227	86,871	1,380,639	329,843	248,948	21,097	92,876	54,466
1994	2,103,886	1,549,146	42,564	1,591,710	189,851	93,629	1,495,488	351,107	257,291	22,449	93,717	55,863
1995	2,197,751	1,599,473	26,664	1,626,137	196,601	100,715	1,530,251	396,440	271,060	23,254	94,509	56,839
1996	2,317,192	1,659,296	43,435	1,702,731	202,376	106,941	1,607,296	425,486	284,410	24,256	95,529	57,633
1997	2,426,645	1,733,499	27,387	1,760,886	211,527	111,298	1,660,657	472,352	293,636	25,278	95,998	57,950
1998	2,565,865	1,847,042	41,761	1,888,803	224,813	115,714	1,779,704	481,130	305,031	26,586	96,512	59,514
1999	2,627,134	1,903,914	36,959	1,940,873	232,476	126,455	1,834,852	478,868	313,414	27,088	96,985	59,881
2000	2,783,060	2,020,475	22,116	2,042,591	241,625	133,365	1,934,331	506,667	342,062	28,576	97,390	60,814
2001	2,826,489	1,994,474	29,469	2,023,943	235,571	160,123	1,948,495	496,801	381,193	28,884	97,856	58,683
2002	2,930,596	2,082,438	23,906	2,106,344	242,588	161,076	2,024,832	493,983	411,781	29,874	98,097	58,998
2003	3,002,558	2,102,689	42,383	2,145,072	247,994	176,898	2,073,976	503,086	425,496	30,492	98,470	58,352
2004	3,106,476	2,193,977	48,949	2,242,926	260,099	196,056	2,178,883	494,983	432,610	31,401	98,929	58,529
2005	3,204,165	2,257,130	45,457	2,302,587	270,870	207,974	2,239,691	501,151	463,323	32,268	99,297	58,968
2006	3,338,872	2,327,685	34,752	2,362,437	281,068	222,048	2,303,417	543,618	491,837	33,415	99,920	59,304
2007	3,545,948	2,402,597	66,217	2,468,814	291,601	242,390	2,419,603	593,197	533,148	35,276	100,520	59,937
2008	3,737,015	2,491,794	64,676	2,556,470	305,265	249,489	2,500,694	641,892	594,429	36,956	101,122	59,767
2009	3,611,144	2,371,627	19,752	2,391,379	292,019	231,050	2,330,410	581,037	699,697	35,623	101,370	56,808
2010	3,755,171	2,435,894	63,761	2,499,655	298,106	229,456	2,431,005	570,969	753,197	36,968	101,579	56,460
2011	3,907,067	2,505,054	109,318	2,614,372	279,847	231,005	2,565,530	623,449	718,088	38,372	101,822	57,214
2012	4,076,184	2,646,654	104,692	2,751,346	292,631	210,122	2,668,837	679,559	727,788	40,040	101,802	57,437
2013	4,093,879	2,701,397	110,838	2,812,235	334,806	188,453	2,665,882	677,417	750,580	40,212	101,808	58,967
2014	4,305,091	2,818,794	131,700	2,950,494	346,362	195,956	2,800,088	718,079	786,924	42,003	102,495	59,845
2015	4,471,300	2,950,313	94,323	3,044,636	358,609	199,054	2,885,081	767,594	818,625	43,584	102,590	60,013
2016	4,519,367	3,015,937	66,532	3,082,469	364,107	194,675	2,913,037	767,337	838,993	43,908	102,927	60,071
2017	4,713,419	3,125,837	74,857	3,200,694	380,250	212,929	3,033,373	797,262	882,784	45,682	103,180	59,986
2018	4,962,840	3,319,829	59,939	3,379,768	399,962	199,209	3,179,015	848,967	934,858	47,833	103,754	61,270
2019	5,208,301	3,437,347	74,619	3,511,966	416,537	206,355	3,301,784	927,641	978,876	49,996	104,175	61,604
2020	5,528,983	3,443,769	112,079	3,555,848	421,201	224,668	3,359,315	939,657	1,230,011	53,124	104,076	58,502
2021	5,883,749	3,655,595	104,696	3,760,291	438,617	240,505	3,562,179	956,405	1,365,165	56,378	104,362	59,863

Personal Income and Employment by Area: Fort Collins, CO

(Thousands of dollars, except as noted.)

Year	Personal income, total	Earnings by place of work			Less: Contributions for government social insurance	Plus: Adjustment for residence	Equals: Net earnings by place of residence	Plus: Dividends, interest, and rent	Plus: Personal current transfer receipts	Per capita personal income (dollars)	Population (persons)	Total employment
		Nonfarm	Farm	Total								
1970	313,677	208,982	6,352	215,334	10,780	10,531	215,085	71,132	27,460	3,443	91,095	35,982
1971	368,477	241,027	11,168	252,195	12,652	15,147	254,690	81,986	31,801	3,794	97,125	37,219
1972	428,182	287,685	8,067	295,752	16,568	20,953	300,137	92,060	35,985	4,002	106,999	41,926
1973	500,034	333,401	9,374	342,775	22,325	28,122	348,572	108,156	43,306	4,447	112,441	45,809
1974	577,813	378,997	8,603	387,600	26,294	37,079	398,385	128,229	51,199	4,817	119,945	48,576
1975	676,045	432,904	12,393	445,297	29,156	45,535	461,676	149,076	65,293	5,606	120,593	51,021
1976	782,016	513,053	9,461	522,514	35,067	57,830	545,277	165,255	71,484	6,348	123,187	55,630
1977	898,522	601,869	5,331	607,200	42,418	68,661	633,443	188,208	76,871	6,808	131,973	60,594
1978	1,065,075	723,405	6,673	730,078	52,744	84,224	761,558	218,268	85,249	7,730	137,780	66,489
1979	1,255,180	864,441	399	864,840	66,507	101,647	899,980	258,248	96,952	8,628	145,474	71,512
1980	1,436,880	958,536	127	958,663	75,088	119,479	1,003,054	317,500	116,326	9,573	150,091	73,957
1981	1,631,363	1,054,111	7,402	1,061,513	88,905	131,876	1,104,484	386,013	140,866	10,638	153,347	74,913
1982	1,786,871	1,136,352	5,147	1,141,499	97,245	151,874	1,196,128	429,889	160,854	11,352	157,410	76,547
1983	1,976,418	1,249,884	10,291	1,260,175	109,134	166,883	1,317,924	481,841	176,653	12,214	161,816	80,642
1984	2,171,404	1,394,294	8,358	1,402,652	126,427	181,030	1,457,255	527,366	186,783	13,154	165,073	86,194
1985	2,336,369	1,495,821	6,159	1,501,980	139,172	194,165	1,556,973	578,781	200,615	13,769	169,687	88,750
1986	2,500,223	1,618,044	5,133	1,623,177	153,186	201,889	1,671,880	609,959	218,384	14,347	174,271	91,424
1987	2,672,269	1,739,402	4,839	1,744,241	162,522	213,223	1,794,942	637,240	240,087	15,046	177,612	92,603
1988	2,856,494	1,875,881	8,116	1,883,997	184,099	232,046	1,931,944	671,281	253,269	15,816	180,610	98,006
1989	3,133,629	2,036,601	13,274	2,049,875	205,906	249,525	2,093,494	755,653	284,482	17,076	183,507	101,762
1990	3,367,283	2,227,547	13,687	2,241,234	232,183	267,881	2,276,932	784,245	306,106	17,978	187,299	105,353
1991	3,589,411	2,397,691	13,097	2,410,788	256,406	291,957	2,446,339	804,572	338,500	18,583	193,154	110,094
1992	3,920,444	2,653,828	17,321	2,671,149	280,347	307,507	2,698,309	840,109	382,026	19,581	200,212	113,837
1993	4,289,008	2,924,534	21,225	2,945,759	314,947	321,978	2,952,790	927,215	409,003	20,606	208,143	121,231
1994	4,650,188	3,224,557	16,963	3,241,520	352,302	333,719	3,222,937	993,311	433,940	21,442	216,868	128,209
1995	5,068,498	3,464,978	13,973	3,478,951	378,997	352,543	3,452,497	1,129,324	486,677	22,754	222,750	134,280
1996	5,554,984	3,858,405	22,078	3,880,483	417,305	363,199	3,826,377	1,220,444	508,163	24,327	228,350	143,321
1997	6,019,839	4,170,154	22,625	4,192,779	445,415	395,887	4,143,251	1,358,690	517,898	25,754	233,746	148,781
1998	6,520,607	4,538,775	21,216	4,559,991	454,298	452,499	4,558,192	1,428,865	533,550	27,083	240,765	154,951
1999	6,938,667	4,888,876	17,691	4,906,567	485,220	503,442	4,924,789	1,443,372	570,506	28,105	246,884	159,167
2000	7,819,437	5,546,268	13,743	5,560,011	547,163	592,449	5,605,297	1,605,620	608,520	30,898	253,072	166,868
2001	8,371,684	6,052,944	17,855	6,070,799	592,762	592,491	6,070,528	1,618,084	683,072	32,132	260,541	170,194
2002	8,460,625	6,274,352	7,465	6,281,817	634,158	514,182	6,161,841	1,538,011	760,773	31,882	265,372	171,113
2003	8,555,530	6,333,366	2,445	6,335,811	645,201	517,085	6,207,695	1,552,933	794,902	31,870	268,448	171,677
2004	8,903,054	6,522,130	18,501	6,540,631	686,674	531,583	6,385,540	1,685,745	831,769	32,791	271,510	176,191
2005	9,393,876	6,815,658	19,771	6,835,429	726,883	537,424	6,645,970	1,833,164	914,742	34,145	275,116	180,859
2006	10,103,666	7,175,125	14,420	7,189,545	764,783	563,136	6,987,898	2,111,099	1,004,669	35,993	280,713	184,627
2007	10,855,874	7,505,817	25,068	7,530,885	802,051	588,808	7,317,642	2,445,824	1,092,408	37,943	286,112	190,983
2008	11,233,037	7,508,917	21,425	7,530,342	817,909	613,206	7,325,639	2,584,340	1,323,058	38,515	291,650	192,586
2009	10,997,354	7,400,649	19,362	7,420,011	803,660	551,696	7,168,047	2,339,556	1,489,751	37,066	296,696	188,924
2010	11,317,042	7,576,807	27,770	7,604,577	822,054	540,145	7,322,668	2,320,950	1,673,424	37,667	300,453	189,251
2011	11,962,115	7,842,605	30,474	7,873,079	783,034	569,242	7,659,287	2,573,033	1,729,795	39,179	305,320	193,349
2012	12,751,190	8,377,921	33,180	8,411,101	827,258	600,391	8,184,234	2,823,787	1,743,169	41,003	310,983	196,967
2013	13,490,021	8,889,599	33,317	8,922,916	933,156	637,281	8,627,041	3,035,674	1,827,306	42,632	316,426	203,389
2014	14,667,914	9,544,983	36,946	9,581,929	1,010,670	703,083	9,274,342	3,421,994	1,971,578	45,279	323,942	210,458
2015	15,689,539	10,158,186	36,406	10,194,592	1,083,319	710,060	9,821,333	3,714,319	2,153,887	47,085	333,219	217,249
2016	16,377,606	10,705,971	25,491	10,731,462	1,151,501	658,348	10,238,309	3,861,269	2,278,028	48,327	338,891	226,367
2017	17,701,753	11,591,030	23,195	11,614,225	1,230,295	710,636	11,094,566	4,226,551	2,380,636	51,471	343,920	233,037
2018	18,897,143	12,287,294	25,754	12,313,048	1,314,271	781,387	11,780,164	4,525,208	2,591,771	53,935	350,367	240,134
2019	20,265,801	13,032,865	31,339	13,064,204	1,388,015	868,206	12,544,395	4,970,782	2,750,624	56,851	356,472	241,744
2020	21,659,942	13,530,473	26,555	13,557,028	1,440,898	833,350	12,949,480	5,029,869	3,680,593	60,219	359,686	238,132
2021	23,295,659	14,565,819	33,305	14,599,124	1,528,892	844,858	13,915,090	5,296,394	4,084,175	64,258	362,533	246,878

Personal Income and Employment by Area: Fort Smith, AR-OK

(Thousands of dollars, except as noted.)

Year	Personal income, total	Nonfarm	Farm	Total	Less: Contributions for government social insurance	Plus: Adjustment for residence	Equals: Net earnings by place of residence	Plus: Dividends, interest, and rent	Plus: Personal current transfer receipts	Per capita personal income (dollars)	Population (persons)	Total employment
1970	466,259	358,754	10,804	369,558	26,257	-5,275	338,026	64,117	64,116	2,891	161,302	63,978
1971	523,088	396,392	12,403	408,795	29,933	-3,034	375,828	71,696	75,564	3,139	166,652	66,079
1972	585,188	446,382	16,324	462,706	35,379	-4,926	422,401	78,211	84,576	3,429	170,641	69,301
1973	668,147	504,024	25,669	529,693	46,121	-6,001	477,571	91,186	99,390	3,861	173,030	72,952
1974	765,079	581,384	19,627	601,011	54,915	-7,339	538,757	108,817	117,505	4,277	178,875	76,608
1975	854,776	632,230	19,367	651,597	58,104	-7,886	585,607	121,081	148,088	4,115	207,746	76,082
1976	962,779	725,125	18,936	744,061	68,361	-7,735	667,965	132,522	162,292	5,115	188,214	79,870
1977	1,087,611	838,612	16,361	854,973	79,970	-9,847	765,156	150,787	171,668	5,596	194,364	84,651
1978	1,229,277	960,522	11,478	972,000	94,147	-12,559	865,294	176,471	187,512	6,199	198,313	89,078
1979	1,377,579	1,054,483	21,150	1,075,633	106,792	-13,335	955,506	203,775	218,298	6,826	201,812	89,789
1980	1,546,557	1,148,928	9,011	1,157,939	114,137	-12,606	1,031,196	254,551	260,810	7,594	203,668	89,678
1981	1,755,949	1,276,023	22,295	1,298,318	136,486	-18,783	1,143,049	317,951	294,949	8,613	203,878	92,299
1982	1,836,866	1,296,325	12,381	1,308,706	141,865	-19,330	1,147,511	364,595	324,760	9,001	204,078	89,608
1983	1,973,228	1,418,773	11,829	1,430,602	157,205	-24,369	1,249,028	377,587	346,613	9,520	207,278	93,043
1984	2,191,936	1,605,453	13,707	1,619,160	182,941	-29,670	1,406,549	426,369	359,018	10,416	210,446	98,057
1985	2,344,884	1,717,087	16,340	1,733,427	197,098	-32,890	1,503,439	460,335	381,110	11,049	212,229	100,810
1986	2,494,394	1,849,920	24,613	1,874,533	212,533	-37,116	1,624,884	471,856	397,654	11,635	214,383	103,742
1987	2,648,495	2,014,925	20,187	2,035,112	228,643	-43,491	1,762,978	473,604	411,913	12,201	217,078	108,679
1988	2,821,071	2,150,044	24,423	2,174,467	253,138	-48,234	1,873,095	509,356	438,620	12,938	218,039	112,329
1989	2,989,752	2,245,833	37,611	2,283,444	263,533	-58,504	1,961,407	546,251	482,094	13,653	218,975	113,097
1990	3,131,696	2,371,934	24,139	2,396,073	289,452	-66,738	2,039,883	564,595	527,218	14,248	219,804	114,149
1991	3,285,532	2,478,247	26,621	2,504,868	303,297	-55,264	2,146,307	554,151	585,074	14,744	222,842	116,211
1992	3,607,601	2,731,862	35,627	2,767,489	331,416	-60,066	2,376,007	569,943	661,651	15,941	226,308	118,602
1993	3,752,811	2,852,884	45,470	2,898,354	350,115	-63,079	2,485,160	572,904	694,747	16,238	231,118	124,499
1994	4,051,154	3,093,319	60,742	3,154,061	384,468	-71,001	2,698,592	617,918	734,644	17,310	234,032	128,786
1995	4,281,397	3,251,524	39,525	3,291,049	401,122	-74,709	2,815,218	671,241	794,938	17,879	239,471	133,767
1996	4,496,824	3,377,518	53,384	3,430,902	411,636	-71,317	2,947,949	709,055	839,820	18,466	243,520	136,556
1997	4,732,813	3,561,080	60,439	3,621,519	430,819	-71,885	3,118,815	751,068	862,930	19,173	246,842	138,117
1998	4,526,828	3,595,756	53,280	3,649,036	430,791	-187,829	3,030,416	732,489	763,923	20,624	219,494	129,066
1999	4,710,599	3,769,537	64,028	3,833,565	452,252	-187,529	3,193,784	721,478	795,337	21,176	222,450	131,182
2000	5,040,189	4,053,396	59,895	4,113,291	480,186	-202,464	3,430,641	768,233	841,315	22,326	225,759	133,529
2001	5,109,791	4,000,545	67,259	4,067,804	481,031	-209,223	3,377,550	792,491	939,750	22,421	227,899	133,586
2002	5,200,811	4,052,059	53,278	4,105,337	483,831	-206,910	3,414,596	764,879	1,021,336	22,646	229,652	132,476
2003	5,473,378	4,268,292	56,891	4,325,183	502,202	-210,365	3,612,616	783,169	1,077,593	23,655	231,379	132,613
2004	5,923,712	4,613,779	87,841	4,701,620	531,189	-213,792	3,956,639	797,091	1,169,982	25,384	233,367	134,158
2005	6,232,218	4,832,678	72,484	4,905,162	561,828	-221,174	4,122,160	863,585	1,246,473	26,418	235,912	137,292
2006	6,690,573	5,156,519	46,027	5,202,546	610,269	-235,823	4,356,454	961,776	1,372,343	27,875	240,017	140,454
2007	6,977,290	5,203,719	51,206	5,254,925	622,192	-230,838	4,401,895	1,097,493	1,477,902	28,719	242,953	142,476
2008	7,361,631	5,270,193	34,525	5,304,718	646,774	-218,146	4,439,798	1,253,240	1,668,593	30,078	244,749	141,877
2009	7,255,341	5,016,033	10,877	5,026,910	625,680	-178,281	4,222,949	1,197,832	1,834,560	29,366	247,064	136,486
2010	7,498,446	5,196,553	5,828	5,202,381	650,023	-153,327	4,399,031	1,137,415	1,962,000	30,188	248,393	134,599
2011	7,997,083	5,428,987	-4,691	5,424,296	602,571	-124,706	4,697,019	1,289,613	2,010,451	32,076	249,317	132,397
2012	8,298,640	5,564,086	32,786	5,596,872	603,456	-105,641	4,887,775	1,373,811	2,037,054	33,247	249,607	132,219
2013	8,293,839	5,535,647	50,339	5,585,986	671,439	-62,470	4,852,077	1,350,855	2,090,907	33,345	248,729	130,884
2014	8,653,768	5,665,221	79,728	5,744,949	693,262	-41,466	5,010,221	1,447,850	2,195,697	35,200	245,849	131,677
2015	8,869,671	5,754,639	54,169	5,808,808	709,239	-35,038	5,064,531	1,517,041	2,288,099	36,075	245,866	133,291
2016	8,934,724	5,836,543	15,243	5,851,786	716,360	-48,131	5,087,295	1,487,335	2,360,094	36,369	245,667	134,880
2017	9,114,697	5,922,568	32,195	5,954,763	731,441	-58,771	5,164,551	1,542,169	2,407,977	37,040	246,078	134,163
2018	9,277,591	6,045,864	28,008	6,073,872	746,298	-62,931	5,264,643	1,533,033	2,479,915	37,796	245,468	134,739
2019	9,681,755	6,316,221	-9,036	6,307,185	788,508	-67,298	5,451,379	1,602,777	2,627,599	39,548	244,808	134,198
2020	10,224,213	6,364,211	-30,596	6,333,615	820,745	-83,918	5,428,952	1,582,629	3,212,632	41,864	244,223	130,814
2021	11,078,663	6,799,188	54,702	6,853,890	855,537	-120,384	5,877,969	1,611,143	3,589,551	45,134	245,459	133,190

Personal Income and Employment by Area: Fort Wayne, IN

(Thousands of dollars, except as noted.)

Year	Personal income, total	Derivation of personal income								Per capita personal income (dollars)	Population (persons)	Total employment
		Earnings by place of work			Less: Contributions for government social insurance	Plus: Adjustment for residence	Equals: Net earnings by place of residence	Plus: Dividends, interest, and rent	Plus: Personal current transfer receipts			
		Nonfarm	Farm	Total								
1970	1,344,891	1,230,094	16,694	1,246,788	84,534	-105,879	1,056,375	201,647	86,869	4,092	328,656	161,511
1971	1,457,060	1,312,822	25,182	1,338,004	93,298	-111,303	1,133,403	219,528	104,129	4,373	333,164	161,889
1972	1,609,556	1,473,598	20,761	1,494,359	111,541	-124,201	1,258,617	235,121	115,818	4,787	336,249	169,353
1973	1,815,005	1,640,355	48,325	1,688,680	143,480	-134,565	1,410,635	266,483	137,887	5,364	338,398	177,766
1974	1,971,311	1,785,961	29,248	1,815,209	162,478	-146,510	1,506,221	307,298	157,792	5,801	339,819	181,183
1975	2,068,003	1,789,601	37,895	1,827,496	160,154	-140,224	1,527,118	336,444	204,441	6,090	339,555	171,717
1976	2,314,529	2,043,139	37,029	2,080,168	185,573	-156,908	1,737,687	364,284	212,558	6,833	338,719	178,522
1977	2,598,589	2,327,244	33,271	2,360,515	211,259	-178,429	1,970,827	407,929	219,833	7,653	339,540	186,924
1978	2,904,203	2,637,023	21,395	2,658,418	246,446	-199,154	2,212,818	449,791	241,594	8,451	343,658	194,996
1979	3,226,819	2,921,962	27,928	2,949,890	282,399	-218,504	2,448,987	501,573	276,259	9,337	345,596	198,262
1980	3,432,417	2,964,538	24,654	2,989,192	284,910	-210,035	2,494,247	596,460	341,710	9,935	345,480	188,701
1981	3,742,757	3,156,732	3,073	3,159,805	326,300	-219,470	2,614,035	733,546	395,176	10,917	342,832	187,540
1982	3,828,809	3,090,414	9,876	3,100,290	324,805	-204,648	2,570,837	815,205	442,767	11,240	340,642	179,724
1983	3,962,692	3,210,181	-10,192	3,199,989	339,241	-199,324	2,661,424	827,246	474,022	11,718	338,181	179,245
1984	4,413,032	3,581,712	22,941	3,604,653	388,068	-210,979	3,005,606	916,343	491,083	13,069	337,671	188,092
1985	4,763,564	3,918,659	11,685	3,930,344	432,651	-232,020	3,265,673	982,924	514,967	13,968	341,030	196,048
1986	5,206,052	4,339,874	18,399	4,358,273	481,318	-259,967	3,616,988	1,045,539	543,525	15,066	345,561	205,357
1987	5,600,519	4,745,331	23,661	4,768,992	519,846	-283,544	3,965,602	1,084,472	550,445	15,953	351,063	214,510
1988	6,135,115	5,181,971	13,141	5,195,112	582,586	-309,862	4,302,664	1,227,837	604,614	17,381	352,986	222,312
1989	6,677,700	5,571,054	20,838	5,591,892	626,465	-325,756	4,639,671	1,389,248	648,781	18,856	354,134	229,759
1990	6,971,492	5,801,951	34,492	5,836,443	672,046	-342,486	4,821,911	1,452,573	697,008	19,618	355,358	230,671
1991	7,029,692	5,876,709	15,755	5,892,464	693,978	-360,359	4,838,127	1,415,321	776,244	19,606	358,547	229,542
1992	7,646,379	6,356,537	25,215	6,381,752	740,403	-377,351	5,263,998	1,471,311	911,070	21,139	361,726	233,513
1993	7,947,234	6,684,705	30,087	6,714,792	782,068	-397,047	5,535,677	1,471,638	939,919	21,770	365,059	237,212
1994	8,425,690	7,074,314	27,727	7,102,041	838,448	-402,559	5,861,034	1,569,872	994,784	22,913	367,729	242,100
1995	8,894,037	7,412,385	15,027	7,427,412	877,663	-391,327	6,158,422	1,717,022	1,018,593	23,977	370,934	247,340
1996	9,334,281	7,702,715	40,260	7,742,975	900,962	-411,392	6,430,621	1,838,640	1,065,020	24,902	374,837	249,925
1997	9,802,772	8,111,499	59,087	8,170,586	945,142	-456,325	6,769,119	1,950,236	1,083,417	25,888	378,663	255,042
1998	9,885,498	8,330,216	17,345	8,347,561	950,813	-549,857	6,846,891	1,976,363	1,062,244	27,791	355,706	244,426
1999	10,255,523	8,812,920	-3,065	8,809,855	994,717	-574,017	7,241,121	1,911,702	1,102,700	28,543	359,306	244,700
2000	10,799,822	9,174,804	6,689	9,181,493	1,024,677	-632,835	7,523,981	2,058,308	1,217,533	29,717	363,420	247,124
2001	10,784,938	9,032,200	13,199	9,045,399	1,028,352	-600,065	7,416,982	2,018,236	1,349,720	29,471	365,954	243,280
2002	11,007,720	9,168,413	23	9,168,436	1,047,418	-564,316	7,556,702	2,018,110	1,432,908	29,880	368,402	240,687
2003	11,035,594	9,144,023	26,499	9,170,522	1,059,633	-498,037	7,612,852	1,935,322	1,487,420	29,730	371,190	237,013
2004	11,523,482	9,392,222	42,245	9,434,467	1,097,468	-468,967	7,868,032	2,077,091	1,578,359	30,914	372,757	239,512
2005	11,926,922	9,730,045	21,543	9,751,588	1,145,621	-457,161	8,148,806	2,047,151	1,730,965	31,770	375,420	242,116
2006	12,825,680	10,334,705	24,687	10,359,392	1,208,507	-488,384	8,662,501	2,295,371	1,867,808	33,849	378,911	246,947
2007	13,336,770	10,634,246	30,204	10,664,450	1,246,112	-496,039	8,922,299	2,460,253	1,954,218	34,878	382,387	250,309
2008	13,614,115	10,572,168	47,443	10,619,611	1,249,381	-489,918	8,880,312	2,451,032	2,282,771	35,425	384,311	247,713
2009	13,054,319	9,945,750	49,892	9,995,642	1,198,808	-455,772	8,341,062	2,182,210	2,531,047	33,748	386,818	236,234
2010	13,493,546	10,286,802	22,073	10,308,875	1,221,320	-461,304	8,626,251	2,153,787	2,713,508	34,660	389,307	235,585
2011	14,409,252	10,840,831	47,827	10,888,658	1,134,411	-476,254	9,277,993	2,404,749	2,726,510	36,724	392,370	240,881
2012	15,185,604	11,299,111	77,824	11,376,935	1,162,224	-463,726	9,750,985	2,607,184	2,827,435	38,515	394,282	243,327
2013	15,252,614	11,409,685	154,849	11,564,534	1,330,408	-390,372	9,843,754	2,555,700	2,853,160	38,447	396,719	243,321
2014	16,162,338	12,005,132	85,315	12,090,447	1,385,053	-362,759	10,342,635	2,767,243	3,052,460	40,381	400,246	247,271
2015	17,007,305	12,634,386	27,892	12,662,278	1,457,783	-339,482	10,865,013	2,941,717	3,200,575	42,215	402,877	252,459
2016	17,410,892	12,946,106	57,919	13,004,025	1,478,532	-416,858	11,108,635	3,016,258	3,285,999	42,958	405,304	254,711
2017	17,919,601	13,394,748	43,557	13,438,305	1,532,887	-461,514	11,443,904	3,085,351	3,390,346	43,898	408,212	258,279
2018	18,972,757	14,198,290	45,031	14,243,321	1,622,855	-459,726	12,160,740	3,280,207	3,531,810	46,031	412,177	264,021
2019	19,731,290	14,769,249	33,662	14,802,911	1,708,774	-507,391	12,586,746	3,411,979	3,732,565	47,392	416,338	266,468
2020	21,263,388	15,214,391	65,015	15,279,406	1,783,549	-567,859	12,927,998	3,441,042	4,894,348	50,602	420,208	258,694
2021	23,107,730	16,312,224	103,195	16,415,419	1,874,986	-554,454	13,985,979	3,500,759	5,620,992	54,623	423,038	266,252

Personal Income and Employment by Area: Fresno, CA

(Thousands of dollars, except as noted.)

Year	Personal income, total	Derivation of personal income								Per capita personal income (dollars)	Population (persons)	Total employment
		Earnings by place of work			Less: Contributions for government social insurance	Plus: Adjustment for residence	Equals: Net earnings by place of residence	Plus: Dividends, interest, and rent	Plus: Personal current transfer receipts			
		Nonfarm	Farm	Total								
1970	1,653,102	1,109,998	163,187	1,273,185	75,618	-4,476	1,193,091	232,777	227,234	3,984	414,886	180,330
1971	1,799,992	1,225,503	164,215	1,389,718	85,514	-7,487	1,296,717	255,099	248,176	4,238	424,697	185,808
1972	2,036,193	1,390,133	213,278	1,603,411	100,608	-11,442	1,491,361	285,236	259,596	4,714	431,918	198,065
1973	2,339,957	1,570,947	293,372	1,864,319	129,483	-16,508	1,718,328	336,201	285,428	5,320	439,865	206,954
1974	2,740,807	1,763,526	430,003	2,193,529	149,994	-23,959	2,019,576	389,487	331,744	6,092	449,886	216,106
1975	2,963,789	1,964,177	335,593	2,299,770	162,430	-33,144	2,104,196	445,799	413,794	6,385	464,183	222,296
1976	3,397,744	2,227,009	456,376	2,683,385	187,712	-43,594	2,452,079	485,010	460,655	7,121	477,162	231,059
1977	3,628,639	2,495,762	367,290	2,863,052	214,584	-54,572	2,593,896	546,221	488,522	7,420	489,016	239,078
1978	4,040,140	2,864,223	324,389	3,188,612	250,027	-68,567	2,870,018	632,586	537,536	8,120	497,564	249,946
1979	4,792,511	3,311,998	539,229	3,851,227	303,647	-88,968	3,458,612	740,893	593,006	9,465	506,332	267,295
1980	5,540,745	3,628,152	717,272	4,345,424	326,936	-107,200	3,911,288	926,504	702,953	10,703	517,679	275,120
1981	5,809,316	3,879,272	444,440	4,323,712	379,992	-93,593	3,850,127	1,120,000	839,189	10,984	528,891	275,530
1982	6,125,148	4,010,237	471,836	4,482,073	401,117	-100,053	3,980,903	1,207,863	936,382	11,311	541,500	277,400
1983	6,443,188	4,302,610	347,771	4,650,381	437,230	-102,263	4,110,888	1,306,445	1,025,855	11,591	555,873	284,985
1984	7,119,275	4,687,867	487,089	5,174,956	495,426	-109,563	4,569,967	1,444,314	1,104,994	12,444	572,091	289,156
1985	7,644,924	4,986,147	583,227	5,569,374	532,729	-114,982	4,921,663	1,513,971	1,209,290	13,089	584,070	292,647
1986	8,160,310	5,335,201	634,627	5,969,828	579,005	-117,592	5,273,231	1,576,115	1,310,964	13,747	593,621	296,092
1987	8,910,556	5,873,438	806,603	6,680,041	641,395	-126,559	5,912,087	1,628,426	1,370,043	14,636	608,831	308,325
1988	9,572,858	6,374,272	855,872	7,230,144	718,300	-138,381	6,373,463	1,713,876	1,485,519	15,252	627,658	320,730
1989	10,378,753	6,867,247	832,276	7,699,523	785,036	-157,434	6,757,053	1,983,393	1,638,307	15,949	650,755	328,682
1990	11,305,019	7,597,429	880,645	8,478,074	861,373	-181,107	7,435,594	2,012,808	1,856,617	16,815	672,302	342,583
1991	11,853,761	8,138,502	690,165	8,828,667	924,760	-184,097	7,719,810	2,044,894	2,089,057	17,140	691,569	351,296
1992	12,614,523	8,519,837	743,824	9,263,661	961,799	-178,295	8,123,567	2,044,048	2,446,908	17,760	710,263	347,643
1993	13,359,184	8,957,593	890,254	9,847,847	1,007,233	-189,181	8,651,433	2,116,418	2,591,333	18,379	726,859	356,938
1994	13,672,905	9,296,839	828,600	10,125,439	1,043,404	-190,868	8,891,167	2,203,064	2,578,674	18,481	739,835	364,559
1995	14,222,713	9,619,847	725,940	10,345,787	1,062,270	-189,176	9,094,341	2,437,970	2,690,402	18,975	749,534	377,757
1996	14,865,185	9,940,951	834,813	10,775,764	1,063,581	-186,490	9,525,693	2,517,410	2,822,082	19,523	761,409	384,048
1997	15,268,932	10,297,980	829,925	11,127,905	1,082,842	-168,788	9,876,275	2,590,427	2,802,230	19,794	771,391	379,588
1998	16,150,808	11,076,614	705,103	11,781,717	1,136,945	-164,956	10,479,816	2,647,174	3,023,818	20,743	778,615	392,386
1999	17,122,168	11,660,991	897,326	12,558,317	1,195,780	-159,393	11,203,144	2,735,557	3,183,467	21,690	789,405	395,669
2000	18,468,337	13,044,566	807,023	13,851,589	1,302,738	-151,134	12,397,717	2,797,440	3,273,180	23,048	801,288	400,136
2001	19,156,823	13,553,352	610,836	14,164,188	1,459,012	-170,559	12,534,617	2,929,811	3,692,395	23,563	813,021	399,740
2002	20,487,249	14,607,061	823,323	15,430,384	1,595,778	-204,057	13,630,549	2,912,408	3,944,292	24,691	829,762	410,513
2003	21,972,350	15,463,196	1,178,666	16,641,862	1,706,215	-205,959	14,729,688	3,022,062	4,220,600	25,935	847,193	411,423
2004	23,242,215	16,604,990	1,363,578	17,968,568	1,886,991	-232,098	15,849,479	2,949,656	4,443,080	26,993	861,035	416,389
2005	24,166,137	17,364,903	1,282,863	18,647,766	1,983,101	-237,363	16,427,302	3,075,762	4,663,073	27,699	872,470	424,613
2006	25,850,536	18,641,556	1,196,373	19,837,929	2,046,598	-213,424	17,577,907	3,280,151	4,992,478	29,247	883,862	435,397
2007	27,263,143	19,244,174	1,227,121	20,471,295	2,079,998	-231,384	18,159,913	3,734,626	5,368,604	30,430	895,933	445,265
2008	27,788,298	19,159,318	844,354	20,003,672	2,125,391	-212,406	17,665,875	4,108,415	6,014,008	30,549	909,630	441,468
2009	27,798,393	18,450,463	1,294,767	19,745,230	2,075,859	-227,758	17,441,613	3,701,415	6,655,365	30,167	921,478	424,077
2010	29,073,705	18,941,164	1,404,630	20,345,794	2,056,735	-246,042	18,043,017	3,629,820	7,400,868	31,195	932,011	420,791
2011	30,768,390	19,736,471	1,760,759	21,497,230	1,935,985	-254,809	19,306,436	4,017,434	7,444,520	32,758	939,251	426,268
2012	31,695,916	20,249,572	1,687,727	21,937,299	1,984,469	-206,536	19,746,294	4,359,887	7,589,735	33,548	944,779	439,605
2013	32,998,669	20,991,319	2,170,494	23,161,813	2,306,361	-207,769	20,647,683	4,401,014	7,949,972	34,694	951,143	455,451
2014	35,251,689	22,025,456	2,319,400	24,344,856	2,408,856	-209,710	21,726,290	5,009,526	8,515,873	36,600	963,149	465,023
2015	37,630,893	23,339,307	2,276,983	25,616,290	2,532,014	-283,189	22,801,087	5,542,582	9,287,224	38,686	972,726	475,905
2016	38,671,647	24,458,209	1,928,548	26,386,757	2,673,063	-283,385	23,430,309	5,608,274	9,633,064	39,427	980,843	486,870
2017	39,544,598	25,577,683	2,013,451	27,591,134	2,792,173	-292,128	24,506,833	5,660,260	9,377,505	39,939	990,130	496,698
2018	40,860,228	26,906,579	1,614,158	28,520,737	2,950,278	-327,084	25,243,375	5,773,997	9,842,856	40,963	997,501	508,801
2019	43,195,403	28,590,798	1,405,308	29,996,106	3,152,096	-395,492	26,448,518	6,239,914	10,506,971	42,987	1,004,849	520,083
2020	48,744,997	29,731,715	1,510,922	31,242,637	3,265,700	-327,184	27,649,753	6,239,203	14,856,041	48,312	1,008,966	506,047
2021	52,120,107	31,972,663	1,044,683	33,017,346	3,496,488	-447,000	29,073,858	6,399,809	16,646,440	51,422	1,013,581	522,348

Personal Income and Employment by Area: Gadsden, AL

(Thousands of dollars, except as noted.)

Year	Personal income, total	Derivation of personal income									Per capita personal income (dollars)	Population (persons)	Total employment
		Earnings by place of work			Less: Contributions for government social insurance	Plus: Adjustment for residence	Equals: Net earnings by place of residence	Plus: Dividends, interest, and rent	Plus: Personal current transfer receipts				
		Nonfarm	Farm	Total									
1970	283,339	229,243	2,232	231,475	16,770	6,374	221,079	29,382	32,878	3,010	94,134	35,044
1971	311,494	242,333	2,771	245,104	18,185	11,363	238,282	32,903	40,309	3,283	94,887	35,388
1972	349,727	274,756	3,487	278,243	21,681	13,044	269,606	36,166	43,955	3,652	95,758	36,119
1973	387,651	304,307	5,490	309,797	27,982	14,122	295,937	41,468	50,246	4,035	96,072	37,400
1974	425,798	329,803	2,314	332,117	31,337	16,052	316,832	49,118	59,848	4,409	96,579	37,366
1975	471,815	346,616	5,355	351,971	32,685	19,206	338,492	56,235	77,088	4,818	97,936	36,837
1976	515,075	378,681	5,050	383,731	36,323	23,586	370,994	61,110	82,971	5,204	98,984	36,805
1977	589,445	448,970	5,004	453,974	43,210	23,590	434,354	68,414	86,677	5,884	100,171	39,116
1978	670,912	519,574	6,142	525,716	51,079	25,699	500,336	78,024	92,552	6,595	101,731	41,070
1979	752,567	584,238	5,449	589,687	59,354	27,393	557,726	88,366	106,475	7,311	102,937	42,239
1980	821,916	614,799	-41	614,758	62,117	35,288	587,929	107,562	126,425	7,971	103,112	41,418
1981	915,406	664,594	8,550	673,144	72,394	40,580	641,330	130,223	143,853	8,875	103,143	40,735
1982	928,164	638,288	4,786	643,074	71,414	46,895	618,555	146,207	163,402	9,053	102,524	38,726
1983	986,146	677,930	5,322	683,252	77,162	46,113	652,203	157,702	176,241	9,602	102,707	38,722
1984	1,078,216	744,516	4,324	748,840	86,808	50,694	712,726	179,019	186,471	10,539	102,307	40,376
1985	1,130,889	771,669	6,044	777,713	90,103	57,510	745,120	191,196	194,573	11,056	102,291	40,925
1986	1,177,473	789,320	8,419	797,739	91,110	62,145	768,774	204,701	203,998	11,582	101,664	40,944
1987	1,249,587	866,238	3,147	869,385	98,401	64,708	835,692	206,093	207,802	12,334	101,314	41,863
1988	1,329,676	920,953	8,917	929,870	107,870	73,322	895,322	219,977	214,377	13,201	100,728	42,754
1989	1,412,547	934,795	13,807	948,602	109,714	82,360	921,248	247,157	244,142	14,079	100,327	43,434
1990	1,458,035	947,542	12,087	959,629	111,742	86,859	934,746	257,877	265,412	14,608	99,809	43,565
1991	1,499,998	962,533	12,656	975,189	114,402	91,643	952,430	251,349	296,219	14,945	100,365	43,913
1992	1,614,531	1,050,939	13,248	1,064,187	123,013	92,086	1,033,260	251,444	329,827	15,993	100,950	44,463
1993	1,692,700	1,101,830	13,949	1,115,779	131,091	99,478	1,084,166	263,503	345,031	16,708	101,310	46,081
1994	1,793,727	1,182,869	17,652	1,200,521	141,431	87,771	1,146,861	274,616	372,250	17,549	102,213	46,709
1995	1,856,191	1,232,100	9,837	1,241,937	149,036	81,420	1,174,321	290,878	390,992	18,137	102,342	47,735
1996	1,944,422	1,229,260	16,302	1,245,562	147,524	128,938	1,226,976	300,631	416,815	18,866	103,063	48,513
1997	2,041,488	1,280,513	20,697	1,301,210	153,033	138,860	1,287,037	321,507	432,944	19,605	104,129	49,701
1998	2,120,491	1,334,617	20,001	1,354,618	157,471	141,853	1,339,000	332,478	449,013	20,318	104,367	49,727
1999	2,166,545	1,344,520	21,306	1,365,826	157,854	161,326	1,369,298	329,278	467,969	20,832	104,002	49,023
2000	2,244,941	1,377,546	17,878	1,395,424	160,962	167,009	1,401,471	347,639	495,831	21,735	103,286	49,443
2001	2,296,429	1,356,832	23,460	1,380,292	162,238	172,714	1,390,768	362,047	543,614	22,301	102,976	48,338
2002	2,370,461	1,412,155	16,869	1,429,024	169,540	175,431	1,434,915	356,635	578,911	23,017	102,988	49,064
2003	2,455,565	1,436,301	20,140	1,456,441	173,156	189,074	1,472,359	378,236	604,970	23,835	103,025	48,002
2004	2,592,943	1,526,427	31,030	1,557,457	183,166	204,238	1,578,529	387,213	627,201	25,155	103,080	49,327
2005	2,690,168	1,589,152	12,341	1,601,493	192,031	217,959	1,627,421	391,508	671,239	26,074	103,174	50,115
2006	2,780,125	1,638,182	-4,338	1,633,844	198,733	231,052	1,666,163	394,533	719,429	26,854	103,528	49,828
2007	2,958,090	1,674,162	2,942	1,677,104	205,144	249,022	1,720,982	461,493	775,615	28,472	103,893	49,838
2008	3,054,340	1,676,379	4,786	1,681,165	211,569	251,964	1,721,560	484,619	848,161	29,311	104,206	49,618
2009	3,043,242	1,650,623	4,698	1,655,321	207,513	225,109	1,672,917	451,737	918,588	29,195	104,239	46,996
2010	3,170,357	1,715,204	4,231	1,719,435	216,826	216,942	1,719,551	460,603	990,203	30,356	104,440	46,792
2011	3,219,524	1,752,751	-7,976	1,744,775	198,801	209,508	1,755,482	477,834	986,208	30,851	104,356	48,421
2012	3,262,663	1,777,916	-3,004	1,774,912	200,879	211,572	1,785,605	483,049	994,009	31,290	104,271	48,495
2013	3,271,110	1,785,220	18,046	1,803,266	227,218	208,199	1,784,247	466,835	1,020,028	31,486	103,891	48,599
2014	3,383,736	1,844,916	15,493	1,860,409	232,769	215,947	1,843,587	485,036	1,055,113	32,574	103,880	49,566
2015	3,519,018	1,891,849	19,652	1,911,501	239,686	221,250	1,893,065	519,201	1,106,752	33,967	103,601	49,740
2016	3,572,945	1,939,683	5,578	1,945,261	244,864	231,531	1,931,928	509,828	1,131,189	34,487	103,603	50,610
2017	3,670,350	1,980,163	13,477	1,993,640	251,921	240,716	1,982,435	523,738	1,164,177	35,341	103,854	50,443
2018	3,760,475	2,031,223	11,012	2,042,235	262,602	253,990	2,033,623	517,167	1,209,685	36,282	103,646	50,722
2019	3,869,418	2,061,200	4,721	2,065,921	263,422	276,675	2,079,174	530,330	1,259,914	37,407	103,440	49,726
2020	4,114,541	2,051,777	-4,099	2,047,678	270,445	293,422	2,070,655	532,996	1,510,890	39,795	103,393	46,505
2021	4,390,379	2,082,739	18,105	2,100,844	269,375	338,462	2,169,931	538,441	1,682,007	42,558	103,162	46,403

Personal Income and Employment by Area: Gainesville, FL

(Thousands of dollars, except as noted.)

Year	Personal income, total	Earnings by place of work			Less: Contributions for government social insurance	Plus: Adjustment for residence	Equals: Net earnings by place of residence	Plus: Dividends, interest, and rent	Plus: Personal current transfer receipts	Per capita personal income (dollars)	Population (persons)	Total employment
		Nonfarm	Farm	Total								
1970	357,683	293,873	7,286	301,159	16,834	-12,638	271,687	59,490	26,506	3,289	108,745	50,213
1971	411,352	335,053	9,489	344,542	20,266	-15,492	308,784	69,083	33,485	3,651	112,666	52,801
1972	489,251	405,125	10,011	415,136	25,691	-20,574	368,871	81,372	39,008	3,949	123,894	58,353
1973	577,199	480,081	14,785	494,866	35,519	-25,260	434,087	96,986	46,126	4,429	130,322	63,584
1974	649,392	536,739	12,339	549,078	41,868	-27,995	479,215	114,305	55,872	4,776	135,976	66,040
1975	724,464	583,393	12,518	595,911	45,622	-28,950	521,339	129,336	73,789	5,268	137,514	66,766
1976	786,807	631,390	12,808	644,198	51,462	-31,533	561,203	140,834	84,770	5,711	137,769	66,895
1977	864,086	700,045	7,984	708,029	57,914	-35,166	614,949	156,497	92,640	6,058	142,625	70,025
1978	988,750	799,121	12,297	811,418	69,143	-39,829	702,446	181,862	104,442	6,676	148,102	74,708
1979	1,117,094	892,236	19,483	911,719	81,590	-43,192	786,937	206,493	123,664	7,363	151,718	78,191
1980	1,289,205	1,007,536	17,545	1,025,081	90,425	-49,663	884,993	256,428	147,784	8,154	158,113	81,820
1981	1,472,713	1,124,259	16,891	1,141,150	109,255	-48,359	983,536	317,128	172,049	9,106	161,727	83,589
1982	1,626,496	1,230,772	24,066	1,254,838	122,497	-55,691	1,076,650	360,178	189,668	9,801	165,951	86,074
1983	1,805,152	1,371,360	22,341	1,393,701	136,448	-65,504	1,191,749	401,443	211,960	10,688	168,900	88,731
1984	2,033,459	1,563,482	19,767	1,583,249	158,498	-79,480	1,345,271	459,630	228,558	11,764	172,859	94,216
1985	2,246,516	1,746,180	17,559	1,763,739	179,980	-91,384	1,492,375	504,400	249,741	12,675	177,239	99,763
1986	2,404,582	1,866,024	16,930	1,882,954	195,812	-99,118	1,588,024	547,422	269,136	13,385	179,646	104,449
1987	2,585,939	2,009,862	15,531	2,025,393	206,174	-107,818	1,711,401	586,235	288,303	14,158	182,650	105,549
1988	2,823,524	2,205,604	20,755	2,226,359	236,123	-122,169	1,868,067	640,845	314,612	15,210	185,638	109,865
1989	3,117,916	2,389,807	24,108	2,413,915	256,282	-137,157	2,020,476	734,220	363,220	16,521	188,728	112,555
1990	3,338,016	2,568,285	23,443	2,591,728	272,992	-152,794	2,165,942	771,756	400,318	17,343	192,474	116,385
1991	3,517,630	2,707,499	26,863	2,734,362	289,668	-163,338	2,281,356	785,491	450,783	17,713	198,591	117,284
1992	3,726,564	2,880,388	39,066	2,919,454	308,246	-179,308	2,431,900	783,278	511,386	18,269	203,980	117,689
1993	3,948,578	3,065,625	38,006	3,103,631	325,364	-193,303	2,584,964	815,059	548,555	18,929	208,594	122,951
1994	4,150,834	3,242,901	34,269	3,277,170	347,643	-219,934	2,709,593	862,948	578,293	19,679	210,925	126,720
1995	4,427,468	3,394,994	28,505	3,423,499	363,962	-231,923	2,827,614	973,367	626,487	20,489	216,093	130,710
1996	4,637,667	3,566,515	29,770	3,596,285	380,520	-261,211	2,954,554	1,021,996	661,117	21,114	219,654	134,282
1997	4,904,857	3,760,862	36,206	3,797,068	402,714	-288,217	3,106,137	1,116,668	682,052	21,952	223,439	135,691
1998	5,808,006	4,297,882	70,920	4,368,802	460,320	-236,830	3,671,652	1,307,842	828,512	22,371	259,624	152,389
1999	6,052,312	4,526,172	77,583	4,603,755	482,434	-212,167	3,909,154	1,286,968	856,190	22,943	263,802	155,906
2000	6,428,611	4,791,405	67,219	4,858,624	508,786	-237,074	4,112,764	1,376,646	939,201	24,014	267,698	160,520
2001	6,863,279	5,112,522	79,957	5,192,479	543,138	-251,381	4,397,960	1,421,637	1,043,682	25,315	271,119	165,423
2002	7,059,894	5,378,871	51,395	5,430,266	568,393	-262,227	4,599,646	1,331,255	1,128,993	25,665	275,080	167,142
2003	7,335,276	5,538,234	52,119	5,590,353	587,072	-248,746	4,754,535	1,367,714	1,213,027	26,333	278,563	168,457
2004	8,124,861	6,224,387	65,174	6,289,561	660,760	-313,383	5,315,418	1,587,598	1,221,845	28,746	282,648	173,010
2005	8,751,414	6,634,803	65,680	6,700,483	709,206	-320,188	5,671,089	1,719,514	1,360,811	30,396	287,912	176,134
2006	9,404,847	7,040,723	54,540	7,095,263	762,857	-333,066	5,999,340	1,986,020	1,419,487	31,862	295,176	179,880
2007	9,885,066	7,302,552	33,717	7,336,269	798,762	-338,930	6,198,577	2,174,112	1,512,377	33,005	299,499	182,003
2008	10,239,191	7,347,346	30,139	7,377,485	815,947	-347,665	6,213,873	2,281,109	1,744,209	33,849	302,494	179,848
2009	9,936,137	7,201,613	23,995	7,225,608	810,659	-349,877	6,065,072	1,994,234	1,876,831	32,645	304,366	172,835
2010	10,420,488	7,390,753	53,291	7,444,044	819,086	-376,971	6,247,987	2,100,932	2,071,569	34,126	305,357	170,971
2011	10,816,959	7,410,139	49,181	7,459,320	736,258	-398,463	6,324,599	2,317,606	2,174,754	35,229	307,046	171,780
2012	10,877,080	7,597,910	95,515	7,693,425	763,853	-439,881	6,489,691	2,255,400	2,131,989	35,276	308,339	172,951
2013	10,955,553	7,776,580	101,363	7,877,943	885,673	-467,028	6,525,242	2,220,606	2,209,705	35,454	309,006	174,944
2014	11,589,090	8,080,279	141,562	8,221,841	921,881	-457,438	6,842,522	2,414,494	2,332,074	36,811	314,827	179,714
2015	12,090,127	8,442,242	155,694	8,597,936	954,931	-473,068	7,169,937	2,475,242	2,444,948	37,797	319,868	184,354
2016	12,541,278	8,783,526	122,879	8,906,405	993,059	-499,252	7,414,094	2,577,297	2,549,887	38,467	326,030	187,752
2017	13,366,561	9,273,460	160,177	9,433,637	1,048,663	-559,167	7,825,807	2,842,957	2,697,797	40,516	329,906	193,894
2018	14,096,992	9,865,942	115,184	9,981,126	1,123,042	-598,065	8,260,019	3,008,679	2,828,294	42,177	334,234	198,874
2019	14,909,169	10,286,607	123,693	10,410,300	1,187,828	-623,538	8,598,934	3,286,279	3,023,956	44,323	336,378	202,155
2020	16,049,561	10,770,164	116,546	10,886,710	1,254,816	-692,259	8,939,635	3,353,377	3,756,549	47,251	339,663	200,144
2021	17,300,562	11,571,559	124,325	11,695,884	1,321,476	-788,659	9,585,749	3,460,506	4,254,307	50,623	341,756	205,276

Personal Income and Employment by Area: Gainesville, GA

(Thousands of dollars, except as noted.)

Year	Personal income, total	Derivation of personal income								Per capita personal income (dollars)	Population (persons)	Total employment
		Earnings by place of work			Less: Contributions for government social insurance	Plus: Adjustment for residence	Equals: Net earnings by place of residence	Plus: Dividends, interest, and rent	Plus: Personal current transfer receipts			
		Nonfarm	Farm	Total								
1970	196,115	166,060	3,899	169,959	10,560	-984	158,415	22,573	15,127	3,279	59,814	29,685
1971	211,988	176,451	3,140	179,591	11,564	239	168,266	25,655	18,067	3,419	62,007	30,211
1972	241,760	199,657	4,894	204,551	13,765	1,616	192,402	28,815	20,543	3,813	63,406	30,977
1973	275,604	217,549	12,623	230,172	17,172	3,451	216,451	34,675	24,478	4,187	65,831	31,482
1974	300,115	237,747	5,711	243,458	19,557	3,811	227,712	41,882	30,521	4,494	66,786	32,098
1975	337,306	245,702	15,535	261,237	19,800	5,242	246,679	47,460	43,167	4,884	69,063	31,241
1976	381,368	286,568	16,659	303,227	23,544	6,513	286,196	50,643	44,529	5,477	69,626	33,292
1977	431,665	331,720	15,914	347,634	27,087	8,017	328,564	55,649	47,452	6,064	71,185	35,486
1978	497,468	386,312	17,534	403,846	32,505	9,659	381,000	64,226	52,242	6,858	72,534	37,509
1979	559,831	444,692	9,311	454,003	39,116	11,140	426,027	74,510	59,294	7,537	74,275	39,816
1980	637,061	487,502	2,974	490,476	42,989	19,235	466,722	96,914	73,425	8,374	76,074	39,846
1981	716,441	533,787	5,942	539,729	50,546	20,331	509,514	123,313	83,614	9,229	77,629	40,631
1982	769,971	557,933	10,285	568,218	53,837	24,027	538,408	137,704	93,859	9,767	78,832	40,711
1983	844,841	614,201	9,698	623,899	59,650	26,538	590,787	152,728	101,326	10,524	80,278	42,095
1984	986,980	711,590	29,324	740,914	71,046	28,735	698,603	181,249	107,128	12,033	82,024	45,932
1985	1,085,046	799,866	24,107	823,973	81,984	29,615	771,604	199,983	113,459	12,891	84,174	48,216
1986	1,204,312	880,117	40,447	920,564	91,438	30,729	859,855	223,891	120,566	13,834	87,054	49,668
1987	1,279,647	974,783	25,526	1,000,309	101,462	25,453	924,300	229,255	126,092	14,363	89,092	51,538
1988	1,397,799	1,058,771	35,774	1,094,545	113,502	23,561	1,004,604	254,040	139,155	15,263	91,583	53,765
1989	1,522,304	1,123,222	49,850	1,173,072	121,110	17,584	1,069,546	299,121	153,637	16,218	93,865	55,176
1990	1,613,754	1,199,398	41,786	1,241,184	129,249	9,654	1,121,589	319,047	173,118	16,772	96,215	55,485
1991	1,692,195	1,239,543	41,418	1,280,961	135,421	16,961	1,162,501	327,637	202,057	17,003	99,525	55,068
1992	1,838,303	1,357,096	38,613	1,395,709	145,832	21,789	1,271,666	333,972	232,665	17,990	102,186	56,420
1993	1,992,980	1,497,728	40,924	1,538,652	161,353	10,821	1,388,120	354,753	250,107	18,819	105,903	60,311
1994	2,185,594	1,650,342	37,617	1,687,959	178,913	6,591	1,515,637	396,313	273,644	19,864	110,029	64,802
1995	2,337,505	1,761,205	33,533	1,794,738	190,092	13,408	1,618,054	417,690	301,761	20,421	114,464	67,737
1996	2,542,486	1,882,168	39,090	1,921,258	200,645	29,986	1,750,599	466,498	325,389	21,339	119,147	69,621
1997	2,699,384	2,016,335	34,976	2,051,311	212,011	30,223	1,869,523	495,240	334,621	21,731	124,219	71,817
1998	3,006,937	2,245,116	48,776	2,293,892	230,680	42,724	2,105,936	556,508	344,493	23,277	129,182	74,904
1999	3,300,669	2,510,516	46,581	2,557,097	254,113	50,162	2,353,146	583,335	364,188	24,489	134,781	77,324
2000	3,589,725	2,711,986	37,046	2,749,032	274,545	47,380	2,521,867	660,085	407,773	25,460	140,993	81,590
2001	3,786,216	2,812,035	53,698	2,865,733	290,758	72,104	2,647,079	687,408	451,729	25,907	146,148	81,018
2002	3,974,877	2,950,927	32,710	2,983,637	303,385	75,605	2,755,857	700,897	518,123	26,459	150,229	81,381
2003	4,279,597	3,190,145	32,565	3,222,710	320,759	84,179	2,986,130	763,025	530,442	27,869	153,561	83,278
2004	4,612,834	3,375,356	49,591	3,424,947	350,878	190,507	3,264,576	756,893	591,365	29,497	156,385	85,877
2005	4,992,506	3,610,590	46,660	3,657,250	372,970	150,995	3,435,275	898,311	658,920	31,013	160,979	89,023
2006	5,310,918	3,795,261	16,373	3,811,634	399,417	200,742	3,612,959	975,419	722,540	31,893	166,524	92,744
2007	5,602,303	3,914,410	15,469	3,929,879	413,818	265,155	3,781,216	1,038,666	782,421	32,487	172,446	97,240
2008	5,599,086	3,927,608	20,042	3,947,650	439,757	62,677	3,570,570	1,118,526	909,990	31,584	177,277	97,443
2009	5,471,384	3,726,029	12,360	3,738,389	413,604	63,916	3,388,701	1,063,636	1,019,047	30,651	178,503	91,963
2010	5,582,980	3,824,005	4,380	3,828,385	423,458	58,923	3,463,850	992,489	1,126,641	31,004	180,070	92,717
2011	6,047,646	4,184,770	-7,150	4,177,620	403,048	-45,486	3,729,086	1,134,739	1,183,821	33,174	182,299	95,786
2012	6,260,153	4,256,896	18,172	4,275,068	411,050	64,142	3,928,160	1,146,616	1,185,377	33,997	184,136	96,011
2013	6,473,906	4,527,825	20,719	4,548,544	493,630	46,766	4,101,680	1,130,142	1,242,084	34,720	186,459	99,650
2014	6,954,061	4,869,629	24,150	4,893,779	523,663	48,655	4,418,771	1,258,051	1,277,239	36,984	188,031	102,052
2015	7,584,512	5,339,498	32,564	5,372,062	568,676	-8,780	4,794,606	1,411,232	1,378,674	39,744	190,834	107,240
2016	7,955,942	5,597,562	11,904	5,609,466	596,087	51,001	5,064,380	1,458,580	1,432,982	40,915	194,452	111,548
2017	8,505,646	6,062,729	16,488	6,079,217	639,387	-33,179	5,406,651	1,618,275	1,480,720	43,214	196,827	116,274
2018	9,059,807	6,439,345	9,592	6,448,937	687,554	-60,648	5,700,735	1,784,861	1,574,211	45,513	199,059	119,646
2019	9,530,371	6,703,887	2,160	6,706,047	732,693	18,368	5,991,722	1,877,083	1,661,566	47,263	201,647	121,190
2020	10,164,280	6,954,643	-15,206	6,939,437	758,937	-131,747	6,048,753	1,912,657	2,202,870	49,925	203,589	121,926
2021	11,181,330	7,653,785	3,691	7,657,476	832,702	-101,596	6,723,178	1,975,046	2,483,106	53,920	207,369	126,650

Personal Income and Employment by Area: Gettysburg, PA

(Thousands of dollars, except as noted.)

Year	Personal income, total	Earnings by place of work			Less: Contributions for government social insurance	Plus: Adjustment for residence	Equals: Net earnings by place of residence	Plus: Dividends, interest, and rent	Plus: Personal current transfer receipts	Per capita personal income (dollars)	Population (persons)	Total employment
		Nonfarm	Farm	Total								
1970	220,477	127,784	8,495	136,279	9,340	45,619	172,558	30,080	17,839	3,857	57,165	24,009
1971	237,257	135,820	6,958	142,778	10,344	51,401	183,835	32,904	20,518	4,047	58,628	23,992
1972	267,285	148,867	7,988	156,855	11,787	61,140	206,208	36,362	24,715	4,395	60,815	24,380
1973	301,015	164,296	11,039	175,335	14,854	70,682	231,163	42,540	27,312	4,806	62,627	25,256
1974	335,085	175,629	15,221	190,850	16,536	80,121	254,435	48,094	32,556	5,275	63,523	24,999
1975	363,640	184,376	9,788	194,164	16,850	87,465	264,779	55,566	43,295	5,697	63,834	24,443
1976	414,886	211,826	16,688	228,514	19,568	98,477	307,423	59,358	48,105	6,439	64,435	25,654
1977	458,548	230,076	18,720	248,796	21,206	114,087	341,677	66,439	50,432	7,012	65,398	26,298
1978	511,846	264,210	10,236	274,446	24,871	133,925	383,500	74,873	53,473	7,728	66,235	27,477
1979	574,470	289,874	10,133	300,007	28,216	155,522	427,313	87,782	59,375	8,522	67,409	28,152
1980	643,770	316,371	5,865	322,236	31,259	173,845	464,822	109,956	68,992	9,396	68,513	28,790
1981	710,744	345,427	6,185	351,612	36,658	182,038	496,992	133,857	79,895	10,226	69,506	28,581
1982	767,808	361,305	15,662	376,967	38,529	181,085	519,523	154,994	93,291	10,903	70,422	28,659
1983	804,716	394,083	8,998	403,081	42,342	185,341	546,080	157,149	101,487	11,386	70,679	29,204
1984	886,368	436,075	18,378	454,453	48,502	203,780	609,731	176,805	99,832	12,610	70,290	30,229
1985	950,348	472,516	17,063	489,579	53,468	217,442	653,553	190,050	106,745	13,377	71,043	31,718
1986	1,026,278	511,426	27,130	538,556	58,291	228,438	708,703	203,880	113,695	14,157	72,492	32,650
1987	1,097,423	567,064	21,028	588,092	64,203	246,419	770,308	209,055	118,060	14,835	73,976	34,638
1988	1,201,940	630,820	22,895	653,715	72,596	266,978	848,097	224,757	129,086	15,957	75,326	35,985
1989	1,307,944	691,461	19,197	710,658	78,200	279,016	911,474	256,011	140,459	17,073	76,609	36,964
1990	1,397,840	737,450	29,588	767,038	83,836	295,928	979,130	261,659	157,051	17,740	78,797	37,551
1991	1,449,162	753,256	31,501	784,757	87,711	297,569	994,615	271,356	183,191	17,995	80,531	37,987
1992	1,541,070	816,671	40,966	857,637	94,768	298,829	1,061,698	278,002	201,370	18,846	81,771	38,543
1993	1,590,800	860,235	33,922	894,157	101,617	302,232	1,094,772	284,243	211,785	19,163	83,013	38,395
1994	1,630,088	896,407	19,829	916,236	108,842	302,310	1,109,704	295,550	224,834	19,363	84,186	39,636
1995	1,728,939	918,521	29,863	948,384	112,176	311,242	1,147,450	343,791	237,698	20,325	85,063	40,120
1996	1,837,041	941,005	41,584	982,589	112,157	334,327	1,204,759	374,568	257,714	21,299	86,252	40,211
1997	1,967,209	977,396	33,758	1,011,154	114,458	394,644	1,291,340	409,281	266,588	22,418	87,751	40,491
1998	2,072,593	1,057,905	25,231	1,083,136	120,725	397,152	1,359,563	435,717	277,313	23,268	89,074	43,308
1999	2,217,415	1,173,198	32,651	1,205,849	129,700	411,820	1,487,969	433,677	295,769	24,539	90,363	44,773
2000	2,401,063	1,249,309	19,880	1,269,189	137,388	469,514	1,601,315	477,287	322,461	26,253	91,457	46,362
2001	2,606,150	1,331,603	32,258	1,363,861	146,441	523,107	1,740,527	506,458	359,165	28,147	92,591	42,614
2002	2,712,085	1,406,502	19,216	1,425,718	153,904	564,013	1,835,827	494,604	381,654	28,872	93,934	43,293
2003	2,895,158	1,495,200	32,800	1,528,000	161,750	623,818	1,990,068	505,249	399,841	30,315	95,503	43,866
2004	3,031,247	1,588,908	22,265	1,611,173	172,377	675,208	2,114,004	487,975	429,268	31,154	97,300	44,833
2005	3,195,692	1,686,829	18,730	1,705,559	185,542	736,568	2,256,585	472,626	466,481	32,409	98,606	46,439
2006	3,346,998	1,747,351	8,824	1,756,175	199,633	773,744	2,330,286	514,144	502,568	33,504	99,899	47,899
2007	3,546,944	1,776,563	30,566	1,807,129	205,116	820,587	2,422,600	579,394	544,950	35,292	100,502	48,286
2008	3,745,127	1,732,356	66,495	1,798,851	206,023	894,293	2,487,121	635,945	622,061	37,060	101,056	47,539
2009	3,729,888	1,656,842	59,537	1,716,379	201,833	873,585	2,388,131	573,772	767,985	36,838	101,252	45,689
2010	3,821,068	1,721,556	56,894	1,778,450	205,143	900,878	2,474,185	585,712	761,171	37,656	101,472	45,039
2011	3,982,195	1,776,467	57,158	1,833,625	191,147	941,158	2,583,636	651,313	747,246	39,243	101,476	44,677
2012	4,076,529	1,822,563	78,927	1,901,490	195,499	945,379	2,651,370	674,647	750,512	40,256	101,265	45,139
2013	4,155,359	1,923,056	69,665	1,992,721	230,446	932,303	2,694,578	691,631	769,150	41,079	101,156	47,117
2014	4,371,735	1,993,861	67,437	2,061,298	238,892	1,007,786	2,830,192	733,573	807,970	42,932	101,830	47,507
2015	4,579,257	2,060,990	46,558	2,107,548	244,940	1,033,429	2,896,037	812,859	870,361	44,715	102,411	47,602
2016	4,646,222	2,118,591	27,798	2,146,389	252,900	992,084	2,885,573	847,434	913,215	45,274	102,625	48,547
2017	4,809,239	2,223,980	56,775	2,280,755	269,975	1,000,974	3,011,754	865,324	932,161	46,505	103,414	48,900
2018	5,030,235	2,301,833	22,352	2,324,185	278,260	1,060,590	3,106,515	917,617	1,006,103	48,399	103,932	49,103
2019	5,124,600	2,386,149	34,856	2,421,005	290,429	1,070,945	3,201,521	866,107	1,056,972	49,380	103,778	48,729
2020	5,480,483	2,371,522	26,254	2,397,776	286,033	1,083,169	3,194,912	863,808	1,421,763	52,801	103,795	46,427
2021	5,805,329	2,503,635	49,884	2,553,519	299,091	1,155,125	3,409,553	884,743	1,511,033	55,752	104,127	47,860

Personal Income and Employment by Area: Glens Falls, NY

(Thousands of dollars, except as noted.)

Year	Personal income, total	Earnings by place of work			Less: Contributions for government social insurance	Plus: Adjustment for residence	Equals: Net earnings by place of residence	Plus: Dividends, interest, and rent	Plus: Personal current transfer receipts	Per capita personal income (dollars)	Population (persons)	Total employment
		Nonfarm	Farm	Total								
1970	370,853	296,401	9,468	305,869	22,577	-2,946	280,346	49,620	40,887	3,614	102,612	43,236
1971	398,502	313,681	9,831	323,512	24,786	-5,209	293,517	55,570	49,415	3,807	104,666	43,913
1972	426,819	335,677	10,127	345,804	27,754	-7,268	310,782	62,395	53,642	4,030	105,917	44,230
1973	465,658	365,632	11,125	376,757	34,816	-8,843	333,098	71,137	61,423	4,378	106,354	45,768
1974	507,356	392,985	9,488	402,473	38,663	-10,694	353,116	80,230	74,010	4,753	106,739	46,106
1975	550,664	405,548	7,154	412,702	39,089	-10,840	362,773	88,338	99,553	5,081	108,378	44,892
1976	600,360	451,064	9,186	460,250	44,431	-12,579	403,240	93,763	103,357	5,513	108,894	46,339
1977	647,233	492,063	6,145	498,208	48,256	-17,165	432,787	104,268	110,178	5,893	109,831	47,327
1978	711,564	551,820	10,298	562,118	55,170	-24,050	482,898	110,443	118,223	6,449	110,335	48,379
1979	779,711	605,743	14,680	620,423	62,393	-31,440	526,590	125,346	127,775	7,059	110,464	49,743
1980	869,768	652,921	15,690	668,611	67,336	-36,254	565,021	154,125	150,622	7,927	109,725	49,896
1981	965,096	705,103	15,255	720,358	77,390	-37,415	605,553	187,679	171,864	8,787	109,830	50,090
1982	1,048,683	746,098	16,038	762,136	82,735	-35,763	643,638	212,418	192,627	9,554	109,768	50,097
1983	1,128,992	797,043	14,578	811,621	88,645	-33,967	689,009	236,482	203,501	10,259	110,046	50,967
1984	1,263,830	906,295	14,725	921,020	102,388	-35,462	783,170	268,855	211,805	11,434	110,536	52,557
1985	1,353,577	965,146	15,939	981,085	110,118	-28,379	842,588	287,305	223,684	12,147	111,433	53,905
1986	1,472,546	1,070,654	17,836	1,088,490	123,438	-30,789	934,263	306,118	232,165	13,118	112,257	56,468
1987	1,601,833	1,183,461	18,413	1,201,874	134,970	-30,310	1,036,594	328,281	236,958	14,045	114,046	57,673
1988	1,756,523	1,317,205	14,952	1,332,157	153,030	-29,409	1,149,718	352,710	254,095	15,188	115,651	60,396
1989	1,906,821	1,370,907	19,982	1,390,889	158,086	-16,979	1,215,824	420,276	270,721	16,295	117,016	60,320
1990	1,998,011	1,418,909	22,262	1,441,171	157,428	-8,934	1,274,809	426,033	297,169	16,786	119,027	60,604
1991	2,054,214	1,447,568	16,786	1,464,354	164,915	-41	1,299,398	423,335	331,481	17,078	120,286	59,605
1992	2,214,533	1,551,649	22,557	1,574,206	172,985	6,686	1,407,907	427,850	378,776	18,258	121,290	59,655
1993	2,268,337	1,589,942	22,127	1,612,069	178,490	15,201	1,448,780	426,575	392,982	18,506	122,572	60,889
1994	2,353,423	1,654,966	17,571	1,672,537	188,805	17,416	1,501,148	434,087	418,188	19,167	122,783	63,236
1995	2,472,394	1,714,967	13,731	1,728,698	193,808	25,277	1,560,167	469,228	442,999	20,020	123,496	64,371
1996	2,570,081	1,754,698	23,186	1,777,884	194,754	37,117	1,620,247	484,409	465,425	20,791	123,615	63,799
1997	2,679,720	1,838,420	9,380	1,847,800	199,577	53,437	1,701,660	507,249	470,811	21,714	123,410	63,862
1998	2,805,491	1,890,558	24,182	1,914,740	204,778	70,462	1,780,424	529,071	495,996	22,728	123,436	62,144
1999	2,913,678	1,966,985	23,760	1,990,745	206,746	93,592	1,877,591	520,268	515,819	23,483	124,074	63,464
2000	3,144,914	2,150,218	20,324	2,170,542	222,553	114,458	2,062,447	546,981	535,486	25,311	124,250	64,595
2001	3,178,719	2,089,308	25,354	2,114,662	228,593	147,006	2,033,075	568,475	577,169	25,522	124,548	65,139
2002	3,245,154	2,158,186	16,178	2,174,364	240,909	150,412	2,083,867	537,483	623,804	25,977	124,926	65,403
2003	3,412,889	2,287,046	20,441	2,307,487	254,547	159,151	2,212,091	546,175	654,623	27,098	125,944	66,490
2004	3,683,266	2,468,469	29,186	2,497,655	273,301	191,757	2,416,111	567,423	699,732	29,035	126,854	68,542
2005	3,765,844	2,561,320	28,434	2,589,754	290,462	181,258	2,480,550	549,018	736,276	29,496	127,674	69,447
2006	3,924,381	2,656,976	17,700	2,674,676	303,119	218,750	2,590,307	542,209	791,865	30,582	128,325	70,191
2007	4,063,686	2,711,498	20,908	2,732,406	307,285	229,400	2,654,521	570,910	838,255	31,552	128,794	71,096
2008	4,368,033	2,829,919	21,644	2,851,563	325,242	188,029	2,714,350	717,419	936,264	33,834	129,100	72,890
2009	4,487,014	2,865,154	12,948	2,878,102	325,611	208,706	2,761,197	684,021	1,041,796	34,845	128,771	71,224
2010	4,689,562	2,991,598	31,564	3,023,162	333,816	187,249	2,876,595	700,803	1,112,164	36,346	129,027	70,234
2011	4,856,307	3,030,326	47,273	3,077,599	310,064	214,260	2,981,795	744,622	1,129,890	37,690	128,850	70,770
2012	4,997,782	3,152,898	47,229	3,200,127	318,724	175,536	3,056,939	807,709	1,133,134	38,907	128,454	70,839
2013	5,054,658	3,166,376	58,710	3,225,086	361,540	256,648	3,120,194	794,393	1,140,071	39,522	127,896	70,568
2014	5,126,626	3,242,128	65,529	3,307,657	378,856	180,733	3,109,534	822,026	1,195,066	39,906	128,468	71,307
2015	5,277,978	3,349,252	31,272	3,380,524	391,503	149,624	3,138,645	895,456	1,243,877	41,222	128,038	71,747
2016	5,398,067	3,402,894	25,030	3,427,924	399,063	186,837	3,215,698	907,121	1,275,248	42,207	127,895	71,316
2017	5,704,147	3,557,928	32,237	3,590,165	417,239	208,517	3,381,443	973,640	1,349,064	44,629	127,812	71,626
2018	5,824,978	3,643,592	20,634	3,664,226	421,466	250,675	3,493,435	991,665	1,339,878	45,630	127,658	71,729
2019	6,141,959	3,740,481	37,150	3,777,631	433,719	286,018	3,629,930	1,066,874	1,445,155	48,193	127,446	70,939
2020	6,711,884	3,758,463	34,905	3,793,368	433,472	357,194	3,717,090	1,062,775	1,932,019	52,941	126,781	66,508
2021	7,093,199	4,055,479	33,542	4,089,021	471,580	369,941	3,987,382	1,079,652	2,026,165	56,040	126,574	68,467

Personal Income and Employment by Area: Goldsboro, NC

(Thousands of dollars, except as noted.)

Year	Personal income, total	Earnings by place of work			Less: Contributions for government social insurance	Plus: Adjustment for residence	Equals: Net earnings by place of residence	Plus: Dividends, interest, and rent	Plus: Personal current transfer receipts	Per capita personal income (dollars)	Population (persons)	Total employment
		Nonfarm	Farm	Total								
1970	287,524	231,276	16,522	247,798	15,680	-13,255	218,863	45,911	22,750	3,353	85,747	42,648
1971	314,929	253,442	17,910	271,352	17,999	-14,972	238,381	49,683	26,865	3,581	87,943	43,039
1972	355,430	282,502	23,683	306,185	20,513	-15,628	270,044	54,623	30,763	3,943	90,151	43,682
1973	393,421	303,687	35,177	338,864	24,689	-14,463	299,712	59,977	33,732	4,355	90,338	44,400
1974	446,433	340,317	40,079	380,396	28,817	-16,734	334,845	70,375	41,213	4,863	91,807	45,687
1975	479,207	357,004	36,633	393,637	31,216	-14,561	347,860	77,419	53,928	5,181	92,498	44,628
1976	521,085	390,154	35,703	425,857	35,037	-13,861	376,959	84,659	59,467	5,582	93,352	45,876
1977	551,523	421,116	21,812	442,928	37,333	-12,618	392,977	95,911	62,635	5,825	94,674	46,344
1978	618,738	464,609	33,578	498,187	41,876	-12,063	444,248	107,345	67,145	6,393	96,788	46,994
1979	671,208	519,193	18,240	537,433	48,700	-11,014	477,719	117,333	76,156	6,910	97,135	48,534
1980	739,544	561,213	13,743	574,956	52,559	-10,891	511,506	136,787	91,251	7,600	97,314	48,041
1981	815,058	600,252	26,141	626,393	60,103	-14,058	552,232	157,208	105,618	8,311	98,066	47,291
1982	875,938	635,369	28,662	664,031	63,595	-17,091	583,345	177,153	115,440	8,883	98,603	46,959
1983	935,715	690,958	16,564	707,522	70,066	-17,294	620,162	190,574	124,979	9,414	99,391	47,490
1984	1,062,173	751,523	61,483	813,006	78,344	-16,233	718,429	211,997	131,747	10,580	100,393	48,551
1985	1,107,760	786,648	55,857	842,505	83,299	-13,452	745,754	220,788	141,218	10,947	101,193	48,845
1986	1,154,436	821,094	53,196	874,290	88,997	-11,929	773,364	230,970	150,102	11,521	100,205	48,493
1987	1,201,745	882,543	28,753	911,296	95,038	-10,412	805,846	240,608	155,291	11,864	101,296	49,782
1988	1,301,456	960,115	30,270	990,385	107,845	-15,596	866,944	265,736	168,776	12,726	102,269	52,540
1989	1,428,127	1,018,678	46,259	1,064,937	114,807	-12,413	937,717	304,473	185,937	13,740	103,938	52,694
1990	1,542,500	1,074,164	56,241	1,130,405	123,204	17,181	1,024,382	309,966	208,152	14,705	104,896	53,244
1991	1,628,725	1,105,557	73,633	1,179,190	128,107	20,249	1,071,332	317,899	239,494	15,287	106,545	51,973
1992	1,768,834	1,186,551	69,324	1,255,875	136,880	50,575	1,169,570	334,572	264,692	16,437	107,614	52,502
1993	1,866,996	1,256,753	73,468	1,330,221	146,115	45,901	1,230,007	342,855	294,134	17,227	108,374	53,661
1994	1,982,989	1,309,248	79,421	1,388,669	152,634	71,720	1,307,755	367,738	307,496	18,116	109,459	55,617
1995	2,102,483	1,385,452	73,618	1,459,070	161,288	60,401	1,358,183	400,455	343,845	18,843	111,578	57,476
1996	2,212,889	1,437,978	82,389	1,520,367	165,815	62,704	1,417,256	423,731	371,902	19,601	112,898	57,498
1997	2,322,481	1,511,699	82,324	1,594,023	173,536	49,655	1,470,142	457,017	395,322	20,487	113,366	59,127
1998	2,387,483	1,584,247	59,431	1,643,678	182,322	35,955	1,497,311	484,914	405,258	21,048	113,429	58,373
1999	2,473,534	1,642,987	43,209	1,686,196	190,142	63,705	1,559,759	482,399	431,376	21,856	113,176	58,682
2000	2,606,783	1,717,943	50,595	1,768,538	198,294	72,444	1,642,688	508,448	455,647	22,937	113,648	59,844
2001	2,752,331	1,828,022	56,717	1,884,739	209,699	75,818	1,750,858	507,217	494,256	24,157	113,934	59,739
2002	2,830,141	1,905,838	36,652	1,942,490	218,422	72,107	1,796,175	501,040	532,926	24,760	114,305	59,786
2003	2,884,785	1,923,770	16,009	1,939,779	223,402	83,671	1,800,048	517,256	567,481	25,174	114,595	58,552
2004	3,076,523	2,050,306	34,089	2,084,395	236,175	88,848	1,937,068	531,337	608,118	26,412	116,484	58,827
2005	3,221,245	2,113,889	56,634	2,170,523	245,602	96,217	2,021,138	541,248	658,859	27,530	117,009	58,868
2006	3,392,264	2,221,475	37,197	2,258,672	259,380	97,942	2,097,234	573,261	721,769	28,862	117,534	59,751
2007	3,637,965	2,303,274	69,665	2,372,939	272,745	117,046	2,217,240	652,761	767,964	30,586	118,942	61,543
2008	3,761,492	2,326,995	107,066	2,434,061	276,384	115,560	2,273,237	639,046	849,209	31,369	119,910	60,722
2009	3,767,052	2,323,882	94,156	2,418,038	279,591	86,704	2,225,151	609,798	932,103	31,077	121,217	59,757
2010	3,891,704	2,391,115	111,696	2,502,811	283,111	77,272	2,296,972	616,265	978,467	31,668	122,891	58,747
2011	4,016,029	2,472,332	102,442	2,574,774	269,417	59,565	2,364,922	643,032	1,008,075	32,373	124,055	60,034
2012	4,209,035	2,582,681	141,308	2,723,989	276,031	39,949	2,487,907	688,545	1,032,583	33,784	124,587	59,949
2013	4,154,349	2,551,097	171,199	2,722,296	309,384	34,839	2,447,751	651,352	1,055,246	33,335	124,625	59,387
2014	4,287,335	2,567,802	183,527	2,751,329	311,321	67,117	2,507,125	692,199	1,088,011	35,198	121,805	59,124
2015	4,370,598	2,586,409	144,841	2,731,250	316,854	76,967	2,491,363	753,190	1,126,045	36,147	120,912	58,965
2016	4,394,368	2,630,130	101,602	2,731,732	318,724	84,778	2,497,786	747,753	1,148,829	36,554	120,215	58,742
2017	4,558,206	2,696,148	130,483	2,826,631	325,340	92,646	2,593,937	773,292	1,190,977	38,488	118,432	59,157
2018	4,691,818	2,792,124	68,204	2,860,328	333,330	115,427	2,642,425	814,023	1,235,370	39,745	118,048	59,782
2019	4,969,279	2,996,822	82,065	3,078,887	354,262	127,945	2,852,570	827,454	1,289,255	42,187	117,792	59,815
2020	5,323,777	3,122,222	50,364	3,172,586	371,148	124,007	2,925,445	826,631	1,571,701	45,415	117,226	58,884
2021	5,827,845	3,265,316	132,161	3,397,477	382,870	140,601	3,155,208	825,628	1,847,009	49,881	116,835	59,463

Personal Income and Employment by Area: Grand Forks, ND-MN

(Thousands of dollars, except as noted.)

Year	Personal income, total	Earnings by place of work			Less: Contributions for government social insurance	Plus: Adjustment for residence	Equals: Net earnings by place of residence	Plus: Dividends, interest, and rent	Plus: Personal current transfer receipts	Per capita personal income (dollars)	Population (persons)	Total employment
		Nonfarm	Farm	Total								
1970	358,608	247,966	33,965	281,931	18,853	4,879	267,957	61,147	29,504	3,738	95,935	43,052
1971	392,498	269,553	34,767	304,320	21,288	7,785	290,817	67,120	34,561	4,010	97,885	43,405
1972	442,727	300,299	47,267	347,566	24,388	7,675	330,853	73,963	37,911	4,490	98,607	44,636
1973	580,655	339,134	142,350	481,484	30,746	1,052	451,790	86,188	42,677	5,818	99,795	46,958
1974	604,087	376,816	119,775	496,591	36,013	-4,430	456,148	97,751	50,188	6,035	100,100	48,256
1975	644,297	414,932	102,682	517,614	40,614	-4,337	472,663	111,422	60,212	6,561	98,203	48,980
1976	683,917	485,209	67,380	552,589	48,357	-7,470	496,762	121,311	65,844	6,797	100,617	51,544
1977	679,040	500,791	29,499	530,290	48,635	-7,202	474,453	133,621	70,966	6,661	101,935	51,571
1978	819,219	549,210	105,612	654,822	54,218	-8,021	592,583	147,963	78,673	8,093	101,225	52,678
1979	851,678	599,987	72,976	672,963	61,546	-9,252	602,165	162,500	87,013	8,401	101,383	52,989
1980	885,826	643,622	19,371	662,993	66,540	-10,034	586,419	195,762	103,645	8,764	101,074	53,483
1981	1,002,265	698,397	30,374	728,771	75,838	-9,498	643,435	239,878	118,952	9,887	101,367	52,972
1982	1,095,948	741,001	37,012	778,013	80,770	-9,023	688,220	275,959	131,769	10,760	101,851	53,099
1983	1,168,682	783,530	47,597	831,127	86,799	-7,839	736,489	283,591	148,602	11,335	103,104	54,018
1984	1,303,531	830,392	111,083	941,475	94,693	-8,065	838,717	304,682	160,132	12,565	103,741	54,465
1985	1,317,111	875,412	62,395	937,807	102,024	-8,259	827,524	318,005	171,582	12,700	103,712	55,684
1986	1,419,084	920,225	110,567	1,030,792	110,241	-8,929	911,622	327,769	179,693	13,731	103,349	55,969
1987	1,471,031	975,157	110,250	1,085,407	117,601	-9,350	958,456	322,733	189,842	14,224	103,422	57,658
1988	1,474,407	1,018,897	63,615	1,082,512	128,680	-8,138	945,694	332,242	196,471	14,131	104,341	58,645
1989	1,561,546	1,074,278	56,876	1,131,154	137,303	-7,758	986,093	362,592	212,861	15,001	104,094	59,627
1990	1,654,164	1,119,893	89,844	1,209,737	148,093	-7,858	1,053,786	371,963	228,415	16,032	103,177	59,698
1991	1,686,811	1,184,404	64,659	1,249,063	159,621	-10,696	1,078,746	375,201	232,864	16,371	103,034	61,249
1992	1,824,367	1,252,808	121,728	1,374,536	169,609	-14,019	1,190,908	374,235	259,224	17,512	104,181	61,836
1993	1,823,335	1,326,213	29,754	1,355,967	181,395	-17,530	1,157,042	395,427	270,866	17,458	104,443	63,139
1994	1,950,802	1,399,164	63,520	1,462,684	191,770	-20,806	1,250,108	427,994	272,700	18,473	105,601	65,108
1995	2,025,516	1,467,099	42,450	1,509,549	199,214	-25,651	1,284,684	453,021	287,811	19,172	105,650	66,896
1996	2,177,493	1,526,145	129,960	1,656,105	206,135	-28,969	1,421,001	459,374	297,118	20,651	105,443	67,548
1997	2,147,195	1,586,608	31,905	1,618,513	212,440	-33,015	1,373,058	475,814	298,323	20,717	103,643	65,519
1998	2,263,466	1,643,083	96,213	1,739,296	219,425	-36,686	1,483,185	485,254	295,027	22,649	99,938	65,303
1999	2,258,027	1,678,306	61,419	1,739,725	222,496	-38,384	1,478,845	468,027	311,155	23,060	97,919	64,607
2000	2,386,078	1,724,420	107,074	1,831,494	228,382	-41,347	1,561,765	488,732	335,581	24,496	97,405	64,457
2001	2,421,118	1,794,739	60,123	1,854,862	230,233	-44,746	1,579,883	484,356	356,879	25,047	96,663	65,352
2002	2,533,687	1,897,052	56,463	1,953,515	240,278	-49,791	1,663,446	488,042	382,199	26,292	96,367	65,622
2003	2,738,819	2,012,883	144,655	2,157,538	253,892	-57,343	1,846,303	492,816	399,700	28,450	96,267	66,495
2004	2,803,218	2,137,147	62,141	2,199,288	267,546	-63,269	1,868,473	512,364	422,381	28,556	98,164	67,733
2005	2,929,648	2,226,870	76,934	2,303,804	278,755	-68,010	1,957,039	523,120	449,489	29,963	97,777	69,046
2006	3,109,771	2,329,903	107,748	2,437,651	288,254	-73,252	2,076,145	554,669	478,957	31,646	98,266	69,872
2007	3,326,061	2,424,853	146,083	2,570,936	299,272	-78,429	2,193,235	618,012	514,814	34,076	97,606	70,645
2008	3,627,346	2,499,977	240,135	2,740,112	307,913	-82,198	2,350,001	697,460	579,885	36,979	98,092	69,995
2009	3,537,775	2,566,130	103,553	2,669,683	323,477	-83,537	2,262,669	657,062	618,044	36,121	97,941	69,557
2010	3,738,327	2,662,216	152,261	2,814,477	318,656	-82,637	2,413,184	661,880	663,263	37,901	98,633	69,234
2011	4,013,480	2,762,425	146,504	2,908,929	306,320	-69,067	2,533,542	798,830	681,108	40,872	98,196	69,292
2012	4,437,571	2,944,168	283,644	3,227,812	310,444	-46,733	2,870,635	882,250	684,686	44,745	99,175	71,410
2013	4,507,336	3,049,128	244,073	3,293,201	362,873	-39,330	2,890,998	911,129	705,209	44,693	100,850	71,782
2014	4,610,983	3,216,839	92,370	3,309,209	386,494	-42,757	2,879,958	980,968	750,057	44,788	102,951	72,223
2015	4,724,890	3,353,760	42,418	3,396,178	407,937	-40,657	2,947,584	1,001,757	775,549	45,464	103,926	72,811
2016	4,761,048	3,466,870	59,541	3,526,411	421,283	-50,749	3,054,379	914,069	792,600	45,471	104,705	72,533
2017	4,882,851	3,535,888	71,522	3,607,410	435,743	-50,796	3,120,871	946,806	815,174	46,464	105,090	72,401
2018	5,044,932	3,625,973	13,462	3,639,435	439,200	-55,025	3,145,210	1,027,872	871,850	47,982	105,143	72,222
2019	5,203,901	3,691,634	43,829	3,735,463	446,062	-57,054	3,232,347	1,059,740	911,814	49,829	104,436	71,693
2020	5,701,817	3,725,156	237,589	3,962,745	460,700	-49,708	3,452,337	1,056,333	1,193,147	54,766	104,113	69,218
2021	6,031,344	3,880,781	240,143	4,120,924	470,065	-10,811	3,640,048	1,093,619	1,297,677	58,295	103,462	70,064

Personal Income and Employment by Area: Grand Island, NE

(Thousands of dollars, except as noted.)

Year	Personal income, total	Earnings by place of work			Less: Contributions for government social insurance	Plus: Adjustment for residence	Equals: Net earnings by place of residence	Plus: Dividends, interest, and rent	Plus: Personal current transfer receipts	Per capita personal income (dollars)	Population (persons)	Total employment
		Nonfarm	Farm	Total								
1970	257,019	170,309	36,916	207,225	11,911	-5,111	190,203	44,110	22,706	3,824	67,211	31,910
1971	271,900	179,178	37,327	216,505	12,841	-4,888	198,776	47,803	25,321	4,034	67,395	31,655
1972	300,622	199,281	39,107	238,388	14,654	-5,343	218,391	54,303	27,928	4,428	67,890	33,218
1973	351,679	226,718	54,970	281,688	19,273	-6,081	256,334	62,144	33,201	5,121	68,678	35,148
1974	376,782	246,664	49,501	296,165	21,797	-6,204	268,164	70,233	38,385	5,483	68,715	35,595
1975	437,270	269,390	72,115	341,505	23,314	-6,868	311,323	80,412	45,535	6,253	69,925	35,293
1976	447,374	307,060	40,153	347,213	26,855	-7,306	313,052	86,103	48,219	6,388	70,033	36,625
1977	459,313	338,885	8,055	346,940	29,475	-8,263	309,202	97,742	52,369	6,449	71,220	37,764
1978	563,425	376,710	63,368	440,078	33,695	-9,079	397,304	108,389	57,732	7,884	71,462	39,141
1979	588,735	423,392	27,977	451,369	39,400	-10,638	401,331	122,475	64,929	8,132	72,400	39,560
1980	602,738	465,096	-33,537	431,559	43,359	-13,003	375,197	151,159	76,382	8,262	72,954	40,087
1981	758,159	505,234	39,462	544,696	50,049	-12,520	482,127	186,795	89,237	10,277	73,771	40,254
1982	776,854	507,440	10,899	518,339	51,424	-11,602	455,313	221,409	100,132	10,453	74,317	38,976
1983	803,797	522,489	11,381	533,870	53,185	-10,919	469,766	225,160	108,871	10,853	74,064	39,138
1984	927,062	558,584	81,854	640,438	58,537	-10,171	571,730	240,568	114,764	12,500	74,167	39,328
1985	932,677	567,298	71,892	639,190	61,318	-9,468	568,404	243,596	120,677	12,659	73,677	38,879
1986	975,902	592,097	91,630	683,727	65,846	-9,997	607,884	241,256	126,762	13,477	72,410	38,811
1987	1,012,470	619,051	106,083	725,134	68,955	-8,988	647,191	235,446	129,833	14,071	71,955	39,539
1988	1,081,672	653,541	133,897	787,438	75,952	-7,152	704,334	240,742	136,596	15,060	71,826	40,534
1989	1,154,190	692,075	127,812	819,887	80,722	-6,345	732,820	275,795	145,575	16,089	71,740	41,448
1990	1,209,581	748,261	134,690	882,951	89,958	-6,380	786,613	266,465	156,503	16,783	72,071	42,489
1991	1,280,768	793,710	142,669	936,379	96,197	-8,050	832,132	280,173	168,463	17,605	72,752	43,359
1992	1,334,544	849,171	127,794	976,965	101,326	-8,272	867,367	282,857	184,320	18,162	73,479	44,308
1993	1,363,086	908,934	85,512	994,446	108,969	-9,303	876,174	293,396	193,516	18,302	74,477	45,175
1994	1,481,224	987,461	111,096	1,098,557	118,562	-9,890	970,105	305,931	205,188	19,727	75,088	47,719
1995	1,545,879	1,034,258	94,093	1,128,351	122,434	-9,572	996,345	333,576	215,958	20,349	75,970	47,414
1996	1,688,168	1,081,746	155,638	1,237,384	127,485	-10,110	1,099,789	357,367	231,012	22,058	76,534	48,688
1997	1,710,751	1,139,982	102,854	1,242,836	135,455	-10,668	1,096,713	373,008	241,030	22,206	77,040	49,347
1998	1,574,839	1,105,471	62,388	1,167,859	130,199	-37,197	1,000,463	347,089	227,287	23,101	68,171	45,183
1999	1,631,364	1,158,878	52,503	1,211,381	135,135	-39,283	1,036,963	351,059	243,342	23,840	68,430	45,980
2000	1,712,044	1,202,665	56,105	1,258,770	139,264	-41,044	1,078,462	380,658	252,924	25,087	68,244	46,005
2001	1,816,244	1,278,677	59,050	1,337,727	146,404	-44,022	1,147,301	388,602	280,341	26,709	68,001	45,317
2002	1,848,868	1,337,174	38,373	1,375,547	152,054	-50,550	1,172,943	374,666	301,259	27,108	68,203	44,652
2003	1,967,482	1,375,294	89,046	1,464,340	157,327	-59,002	1,248,011	401,045	318,426	28,684	68,592	44,908
2004	1,977,373	1,420,483	80,871	1,501,354	162,219	-64,826	1,274,309	369,679	333,385	28,701	68,896	45,228
2005	2,062,139	1,484,485	104,380	1,588,865	173,843	-71,154	1,343,868	366,640	351,631	29,942	68,871	46,165
2006	2,153,405	1,585,315	60,978	1,646,293	189,295	-78,524	1,378,474	400,832	374,099	31,047	69,360	47,288
2007	2,337,365	1,690,234	95,317	1,785,551	201,445	-90,328	1,493,778	450,075	393,512	33,494	69,784	48,150
2008	2,499,613	1,719,748	85,787	1,805,535	205,873	-88,220	1,511,442	547,136	441,035	35,310	70,790	48,903
2009	2,445,489	1,734,499	97,002	1,831,501	208,391	-109,313	1,513,797	472,205	459,487	33,939	72,056	48,927
2010	2,532,749	1,799,539	98,370	1,897,909	219,012	-114,127	1,564,770	476,153	491,826	34,722	72,944	48,642
2011	2,777,542	1,867,444	197,633	2,065,077	198,979	-127,968	1,738,130	545,497	493,915	37,756	73,565	49,680
2012	2,874,139	1,983,785	163,075	2,146,860	204,583	-144,103	1,798,174	576,846	499,119	38,709	74,249	50,685
2013	2,940,922	2,022,899	255,297	2,278,196	235,599	-152,377	1,890,220	548,293	502,409	39,387	74,667	51,313
2014	3,034,808	2,160,458	196,407	2,356,865	248,143	-162,875	1,945,847	560,072	528,889	39,981	75,906	51,589
2015	3,173,879	2,217,771	192,484	2,410,255	250,420	-144,802	2,015,033	604,134	554,712	41,687	76,136	51,138
2016	3,162,278	2,242,733	152,959	2,395,692	257,768	-143,829	1,994,095	601,329	566,854	41,267	76,629	51,377
2017	3,226,800	2,348,782	81,296	2,430,078	271,294	-152,833	2,005,951	628,025	592,824	42,073	76,696	51,511
2018	3,264,923	2,396,213	59,670	2,455,883	276,874	-154,371	2,024,638	620,024	620,261	42,387	77,026	51,696
2019	3,426,594	2,432,308	105,642	2,537,950	286,230	-161,960	2,089,760	685,495	651,339	44,417	77,146	51,006
2020	3,699,901	2,499,103	138,357	2,637,460	305,474	-159,183	2,172,803	691,287	835,811	48,123	76,885	49,775
2021	3,997,032	2,706,874	136,721	2,843,595	328,654	-181,631	2,333,310	704,563	959,159	52,472	76,175	51,327

Personal Income and Employment by Area: Grand Junction, CO

(Thousands of dollars, except as noted.)

Year	Personal income, total	Earnings by place of work			Less: Contributions for government social insurance	Plus: Adjustment for residence	Equals: Net earnings by place of residence	Plus: Dividends, interest, and rent	Plus: Personal current transfer receipts	Per capita personal income (dollars)	Population (persons)	Total employment
		Nonfarm	Farm	Total								
1970	193,533	138,826	3,993	142,819	8,195	121	134,745	35,603	23,185	3,552	54,479	23,121
1971	214,485	149,183	7,157	156,340	8,932	453	147,861	39,596	27,028	3,878	55,311	23,077
1972	236,705	168,812	4,600	173,412	10,758	1,085	163,739	43,570	29,396	4,159	56,912	24,258
1973	275,667	193,357	8,130	201,487	14,205	2,062	189,344	51,947	34,376	4,756	57,962	26,242
1974	326,263	232,044	6,702	238,746	17,459	3,077	224,364	62,191	39,708	5,532	58,973	28,069
1975	383,882	275,267	7,304	282,571	20,538	3,683	265,716	70,980	47,186	6,068	63,261	30,541
1976	429,725	311,045	5,577	316,622	23,291	5,450	298,781	79,703	51,241	6,450	66,628	32,111
1977	516,171	386,961	3,986	390,947	28,908	6,548	368,587	92,818	54,766	7,526	68,585	35,299
1978	600,883	456,683	827	457,510	35,274	8,449	430,685	110,150	60,048	8,320	72,223	37,820
1979	693,452	524,270	4,395	528,665	43,288	10,824	496,201	128,941	68,310	9,012	76,946	40,671
1980	815,643	609,596	2,580	612,176	51,893	13,732	574,015	160,526	81,102	9,851	82,796	43,710
1981	987,643	743,970	2,350	746,320	69,526	15,786	692,580	199,535	95,528	11,267	87,659	48,937
1982	1,093,557	798,516	-1,789	796,727	76,842	21,073	740,958	238,686	113,913	11,615	94,152	50,531
1983	1,108,483	768,535	1,206	769,741	73,346	23,077	719,472	255,218	133,793	11,545	96,012	48,319
1984	1,105,881	749,044	1,610	750,654	72,847	21,440	699,247	265,029	141,605	11,703	94,496	46,669
1985	1,102,098	730,827	-854	729,973	73,140	21,662	678,495	275,756	147,847	12,332	89,368	44,600
1986	1,082,075	688,008	-4,408	683,600	71,250	22,458	634,808	284,196	163,071	12,383	87,386	42,603
1987	1,168,654	752,858	-1,131	751,727	75,766	22,254	698,215	291,344	179,095	13,365	87,443	42,211
1988	1,277,022	839,702	433	840,135	87,270	22,207	775,072	312,100	189,850	14,369	88,872	45,112
1989	1,370,073	881,899	2,537	884,436	96,136	23,659	811,959	346,945	211,169	15,018	91,231	47,556
1990	1,470,377	958,419	2,293	960,712	107,105	28,304	881,911	361,624	226,842	15,683	93,757	49,479
1991	1,568,876	1,034,550	4,680	1,039,230	119,169	26,522	946,583	369,072	253,221	16,283	96,348	50,610
1992	1,709,903	1,131,597	8,463	1,140,060	128,847	23,770	1,034,983	391,717	283,203	17,452	97,977	51,414
1993	1,825,477	1,211,686	10,155	1,221,841	139,318	25,404	1,107,927	409,862	307,688	18,150	100,579	53,284
1994	1,940,144	1,286,510	7,041	1,293,551	149,380	30,782	1,174,953	439,289	325,902	18,768	103,373	55,648
1995	2,114,524	1,365,684	6,204	1,371,888	158,716	32,017	1,245,189	503,788	365,547	19,954	105,968	58,004
1996	2,245,219	1,462,006	8,137	1,470,143	167,445	33,633	1,336,331	529,494	379,394	20,764	108,131	61,078
1997	2,442,397	1,613,502	8,572	1,622,074	181,526	36,097	1,476,645	576,333	389,419	22,090	110,566	63,850
1998	2,667,228	1,764,478	12,211	1,776,689	183,059	39,817	1,633,447	603,645	430,136	23,670	112,686	66,443
1999	2,787,404	1,884,287	8,016	1,892,303	193,575	42,442	1,741,170	589,062	457,172	24,275	114,827	68,110
2000	3,016,503	2,033,166	8,630	2,041,796	204,229	47,355	1,884,922	652,970	478,611	25,644	117,631	69,890
2001	3,267,860	2,239,100	12,979	2,252,079	225,828	51,528	2,077,779	666,234	523,847	27,347	119,496	71,083
2002	3,384,441	2,379,679	13,499	2,393,178	250,205	53,855	2,196,828	610,450	577,163	27,642	122,440	72,725
2003	3,495,301	2,444,409	9,124	2,453,533	260,211	60,165	2,253,487	646,557	595,257	27,964	124,994	73,953
2004	3,671,166	2,541,330	14,581	2,555,911	282,780	71,125	2,344,256	693,863	633,047	28,753	127,678	76,252
2005	3,984,462	2,749,334	17,844	2,767,178	310,413	98,234	2,554,999	742,142	687,321	30,604	130,194	79,069
2006	4,431,343	3,051,552	11,871	3,063,423	342,096	144,929	2,866,256	825,838	739,249	32,906	134,665	82,251
2007	4,971,748	3,406,313	10,886	3,417,199	382,902	186,706	3,221,003	970,617	780,128	35,657	139,434	87,490
2008	5,565,975	3,716,675	7,862	3,724,537	424,450	222,995	3,523,082	1,167,345	875,548	38,881	143,155	90,899
2009	5,166,519	3,470,543	6,523	3,477,066	396,099	177,414	3,258,381	997,447	910,691	34,944	147,851	86,309
2010	5,043,048	3,277,432	7,441	3,284,873	374,119	186,511	3,097,265	943,366	1,002,417	34,479	146,266	83,210
2011	5,255,517	3,341,833	14,250	3,356,083	352,844	218,517	3,221,756	1,015,448	1,018,313	35,702	147,205	83,893
2012	5,467,595	3,474,464	14,188	3,488,652	363,340	254,447	3,379,759	1,069,269	1,018,567	37,104	147,360	84,751
2013	5,568,824	3,573,731	9,473	3,583,204	403,793	281,981	3,461,392	1,058,043	1,049,389	37,819	147,249	84,914
2014	5,890,377	3,703,775	21,141	3,724,916	420,178	308,937	3,613,675	1,149,561	1,127,141	39,983	147,323	86,731
2015	6,035,265	3,728,303	20,300	3,748,603	428,823	270,548	3,590,328	1,163,593	1,281,344	40,698	148,294	86,504
2016	6,015,888	3,676,250	10,069	3,686,319	428,608	226,253	3,483,964	1,166,775	1,365,149	40,094	150,045	86,751
2017	6,429,128	3,987,130	4,626	3,991,756	460,068	232,003	3,763,691	1,259,491	1,405,946	42,401	151,628	88,778
2018	6,860,139	4,271,215	9,220	4,280,435	495,569	249,897	4,034,763	1,284,844	1,540,532	44,673	153,563	90,768
2019	7,170,335	4,399,168	9,556	4,408,724	512,078	257,566	4,154,212	1,397,429	1,618,694	46,318	154,807	90,926
2020	7,622,988	4,450,137	9,738	4,459,875	520,611	229,787	4,169,051	1,401,572	2,052,365	48,884	155,939	89,425
2021	8,200,469	4,737,157	14,278	4,751,435	549,710	224,828	4,426,553	1,450,815	2,323,101	52,121	157,335	92,746

Personal Income and Employment by Area: Grand Rapids-Kentwood, MI

(Thousands of dollars, except as noted.)

Year	Personal income, total	Earnings by place of work			Less: Contributions for government social insurance	Plus: Adjustment for residence	Equals: Net earnings by place of residence	Plus: Dividends, interest, and rent	Plus: Personal current transfer receipts	Per capita personal income (dollars)	Population (persons)	Total employment
		Nonfarm	Farm	Total								
1970	2,418,757	1,995,172	34,693	2,029,865	144,453	-19,801	1,865,611	340,079	213,067	3,916	617,650	260,078
1971	2,614,403	2,144,596	31,639	2,176,235	160,305	-19,674	1,996,256	365,097	253,050	4,211	620,779	264,236
1972	2,911,575	2,406,416	39,810	2,446,226	189,300	-19,529	2,237,397	395,001	279,177	4,644	626,892	276,468
1973	3,253,585	2,725,480	50,705	2,776,185	248,822	-22,981	2,504,382	432,221	316,982	5,099	638,073	292,681
1974	3,562,594	2,933,280	55,816	2,989,096	277,431	-25,952	2,685,713	490,557	386,324	5,539	643,154	298,385
1975	3,854,169	3,036,890	50,408	3,087,298	277,745	-20,311	2,789,242	553,894	511,033	5,945	648,334	289,665
1976	4,302,756	3,483,005	48,437	3,531,442	327,765	-23,930	3,179,747	591,122	531,887	6,577	654,247	305,252
1977	4,853,772	4,004,902	64,106	4,069,008	378,367	-34,851	3,655,790	656,805	541,177	7,323	662,779	323,181
1978	5,537,622	4,657,898	74,469	4,732,367	453,517	-48,157	4,230,693	736,118	570,811	8,238	672,225	345,133
1979	6,195,436	5,251,728	76,263	5,327,991	535,810	-69,424	4,722,757	831,020	641,659	9,043	685,105	356,907
1980	6,758,881	5,504,029	80,761	5,584,790	559,568	-69,024	4,956,198	1,001,936	800,747	9,695	697,163	349,556
1981	7,399,160	5,927,038	77,555	6,004,593	648,341	-80,415	5,275,837	1,227,350	895,973	10,507	704,228	350,029
1982	7,844,634	6,053,208	92,839	6,146,047	670,446	-92,153	5,383,448	1,440,882	1,020,304	11,106	706,354	344,069
1983	8,454,528	6,624,570	60,933	6,685,503	747,007	-121,327	5,817,169	1,561,002	1,076,357	11,918	709,384	356,659
1984	9,482,044	7,558,586	97,112	7,655,698	882,329	-165,514	6,607,855	1,791,389	1,082,800	13,176	719,650	378,005
1985	10,274,630	8,248,273	125,919	8,374,192	973,045	-190,916	7,210,231	1,916,781	1,147,618	14,060	730,764	396,691
1986	10,956,729	8,838,909	94,631	8,933,540	1,040,299	-178,311	7,714,930	2,027,931	1,213,868	14,788	740,945	405,607
1987	11,763,944	9,578,448	110,195	9,688,643	1,105,433	-214,571	8,368,639	2,133,636	1,261,669	15,604	753,914	423,569
1988	12,752,234	10,534,633	98,368	10,633,001	1,256,808	-265,862	9,110,331	2,320,225	1,321,678	16,569	769,644	441,855
1989	13,863,932	11,378,744	149,788	11,528,532	1,341,168	-303,157	9,884,207	2,513,548	1,466,177	17,729	782,004	458,586
1990	14,854,523	12,081,321	133,568	12,214,889	1,451,923	-335,861	10,427,105	2,813,241	1,614,177	18,675	795,411	473,830
1991	15,479,383	12,410,455	141,032	12,551,487	1,510,578	-329,917	10,710,992	2,937,928	1,830,463	19,096	810,613	472,642
1992	16,758,325	13,410,128	138,874	13,549,002	1,619,270	-382,758	11,546,974	3,252,790	1,958,561	20,355	823,316	479,549
1993	17,645,753	14,373,687	127,202	14,500,889	1,748,982	-447,585	12,304,322	3,250,454	2,090,977	21,115	835,716	492,605
1994	19,234,448	15,785,277	112,139	15,897,416	1,964,860	-557,955	13,374,601	3,750,336	2,109,511	22,642	849,497	519,290
1995	20,532,133	17,002,467	117,484	17,119,951	2,121,869	-676,006	14,322,076	4,024,245	2,185,812	23,744	864,714	546,139
1996	21,845,200	18,044,525	123,971	18,168,496	2,213,624	-756,397	15,198,475	4,351,317	2,295,408	24,823	880,047	559,946
1997	23,294,662	19,194,666	127,828	19,322,494	2,363,732	-866,338	16,092,424	4,719,533	2,482,705	26,057	893,999	575,693
1998	24,733,337	20,894,136	135,664	21,029,800	2,525,095	-1,142,604	17,362,101	4,853,197	2,518,039	27,108	912,389	583,457
1999	25,924,942	22,197,283	156,719	22,354,002	2,662,582	-1,293,595	18,397,825	4,813,823	2,713,294	27,997	926,004	594,828
2000	27,789,742	23,896,814	128,484	24,025,298	2,803,105	-1,461,189	19,761,004	5,148,144	2,880,594	29,597	938,933	613,988
2001	28,501,459	24,141,237	135,027	24,276,264	2,715,861	-1,462,557	20,097,846	5,159,891	3,243,722	30,031	949,059	611,718
2002	28,549,598	24,443,904	142,447	24,586,351	2,754,772	-1,395,276	20,436,303	4,681,661	3,431,634	29,820	957,389	603,724
2003	29,475,787	24,729,643	156,053	24,885,696	2,791,721	-1,373,958	20,720,017	5,135,876	3,619,894	30,565	964,358	602,504
2004	31,306,087	25,397,873	206,052	25,603,925	2,921,559	-1,473,597	21,208,769	6,309,780	3,787,538	32,253	970,646	613,650
2005	32,359,578	26,181,710	183,108	26,364,818	3,055,523	-1,585,812	21,723,483	6,603,667	4,032,428	33,161	975,837	622,729
2006	34,133,153	26,871,640	212,394	27,084,034	3,171,188	-1,580,202	22,332,644	7,414,842	4,385,667	34,753	982,157	621,166
2007	35,258,811	26,999,407	233,789	27,233,196	3,206,668	-1,485,011	22,541,517	7,910,725	4,806,569	35,728	986,863	622,413
2008	37,162,727	27,117,754	261,942	27,379,696	3,243,971	-1,285,950	22,849,775	8,745,308	5,567,644	37,540	989,942	612,240
2009	34,232,303	25,470,340	210,720	25,681,060	3,066,469	-1,039,172	21,575,419	6,494,773	6,162,111	34,520	991,670	578,845
2010	36,361,609	26,378,830	289,953	26,668,783	3,122,183	-905,735	22,640,865	7,057,049	6,663,695	36,571	994,270	580,527
2011	39,470,842	27,608,111	433,504	28,041,615	2,914,202	-940,774	24,186,639	8,614,925	6,669,278	39,369	1,002,590	605,097
2012	42,478,380	29,516,770	297,424	29,814,194	3,094,675	-964,543	25,754,976	10,097,615	6,625,789	41,903	1,013,729	623,491
2013	42,862,648	30,725,083	391,205	31,116,288	3,630,494	-1,007,651	26,478,143	9,643,716	6,740,789	41,793	1,025,605	642,098
2014	45,194,894	32,611,368	289,874	32,901,242	3,818,656	-1,134,282	27,948,304	10,255,303	6,991,287	43,488	1,039,241	661,192
2015	48,114,619	34,674,414	255,563	34,929,977	4,025,611	-1,230,943	29,673,423	11,016,680	7,424,516	45,885	1,048,602	681,556
2016	49,542,706	36,044,799	210,562	36,255,361	4,180,626	-1,531,179	30,543,556	11,398,316	7,600,834	46,768	1,059,323	703,076
2017	50,732,134	37,992,794	208,271	38,201,065	4,367,670	-1,652,242	32,181,153	10,896,829	7,654,152	47,460	1,068,952	715,847
2018	52,738,641	39,832,619	211,501	40,044,120	4,641,704	-1,761,276	33,641,140	11,054,796	8,042,705	48,968	1,077,003	732,853
2019	54,973,791	41,215,115	164,435	41,379,550	4,790,127	-2,020,565	34,568,858	11,804,974	8,599,959	50,762	1,082,982	735,768
2020	59,626,921	41,699,845	289,465	41,989,310	4,816,714	-2,073,323	35,099,273	11,837,489	12,690,159	54,794	1,088,203	692,266
2021	62,950,668	44,705,129	292,238	44,997,367	5,091,489	-2,350,145	37,555,733	12,111,053	13,283,882	57,667	1,091,620	718,837

Personal Income and Employment by Area: Grants Pass, OR

(Thousands of dollars, except as noted.)

Year	Personal income, total	Earnings by place of work			Less: Contributions for government social insurance	Plus: Adjustment for residence	Equals: Net earnings by place of residence	Plus: Dividends, interest, and rent	Plus: Personal current transfer receipts	Per capita personal income (dollars)	Population (persons)	Total employment
		Nonfarm	Farm	Total								
1970	127,591	84,708	1,526	86,234	6,304	439	80,369	27,610	19,612	3,515	36,304	12,674
1971	145,879	97,541	756	98,297	7,507	763	91,553	31,251	23,075	3,755	38,848	13,786
1972	164,653	112,117	246	112,363	9,217	1,163	104,309	34,611	25,733	4,085	40,305	14,944
1973	189,515	128,229	688	128,917	11,930	1,500	118,487	39,534	31,494	4,392	43,151	16,085
1974	210,775	131,836	2,143	133,979	12,576	2,481	123,884	46,312	40,579	4,603	45,787	15,850
1975	244,329	148,887	2,164	151,051	13,613	2,464	139,902	53,550	50,877	5,087	48,032	16,628
1976	288,436	184,198	2,857	187,055	17,001	2,488	172,542	60,980	54,914	5,688	50,710	18,506
1977	328,896	211,863	2,509	214,372	20,079	2,836	197,129	71,580	60,187	6,259	52,549	19,980
1978	378,846	247,264	1,869	249,133	23,949	3,295	228,479	84,367	66,000	6,794	55,762	21,235
1979	422,703	269,795	2,398	272,193	27,102	4,392	249,483	98,518	74,702	7,301	57,893	22,222
1980	470,230	277,918	3,929	281,847	28,014	5,255	259,088	120,942	90,200	7,977	58,948	22,300
1981	509,163	281,703	2,732	284,435	30,389	4,082	258,128	146,508	104,527	8,600	59,202	21,755
1982	526,423	273,541	2,478	276,019	30,290	3,901	249,630	161,151	115,642	9,052	58,154	21,089
1983	585,847	302,726	2,473	305,199	33,996	5,462	276,665	185,485	123,697	10,180	57,548	21,796
1984	637,966	332,766	2,819	335,585	38,447	7,612	304,750	203,389	129,827	10,798	59,083	22,691
1985	682,639	354,174	2,161	356,335	41,573	7,614	322,376	222,737	137,526	11,252	60,666	23,251
1986	717,762	373,838	1,591	375,429	43,644	9,298	341,083	234,385	142,294	11,824	60,702	23,778
1987	747,132	404,470	1,206	405,676	47,005	10,745	369,416	229,258	148,458	12,200	61,238	24,388
1988	804,406	448,091	1,426	449,517	54,412	11,923	407,028	236,760	160,618	13,033	61,721	25,684
1989	890,844	482,737	2,335	485,072	59,498	11,803	437,377	273,318	180,149	14,400	61,865	26,508
1990	936,461	511,815	2,100	513,915	63,479	14,406	464,842	272,989	198,630	14,868	62,985	26,838
1991	980,341	516,620	2,494	519,114	65,289	16,434	470,259	286,686	223,396	15,181	64,575	26,716
1992	1,037,962	544,658	1,564	546,222	68,861	20,249	497,610	293,900	246,452	15,845	65,507	27,206
1993	1,117,044	586,946	4,314	591,260	73,697	22,483	540,046	311,642	265,356	16,549	67,500	27,970
1994	1,195,664	626,934	5,559	632,493	79,320	27,199	580,372	326,398	288,894	17,227	69,406	29,344
1995	1,286,063	645,406	5,102	650,508	83,051	30,847	598,304	358,998	328,761	18,034	71,313	29,760
1996	1,369,702	692,375	3,890	696,265	88,809	35,021	642,477	378,112	349,113	18,942	72,310	30,589
1997	1,448,015	741,202	3,505	744,707	93,532	39,940	691,115	392,400	364,500	19,716	73,442	31,808
1998	1,529,685	797,896	4,311	802,207	99,068	45,096	748,235	393,074	388,376	20,545	74,455	32,339
1999	1,581,720	845,805	1,351	847,156	104,471	50,794	793,479	363,710	424,531	21,031	75,209	33,340
2000	1,669,233	878,821	684	879,505	108,782	60,684	831,407	393,780	444,046	22,007	75,851	33,734
2001	1,758,376	920,955	1,903	922,858	111,719	68,112	879,251	382,860	496,265	23,000	76,452	33,417
2002	1,799,784	976,260	954	977,214	120,061	73,697	930,850	349,960	518,974	23,160	77,712	33,916
2003	1,895,241	1,061,180	2,635	1,063,815	130,071	77,918	1,011,662	356,309	527,270	24,058	78,779	35,230
2004	2,053,906	1,174,394	4,667	1,179,061	144,774	84,734	1,119,021	395,213	539,672	25,761	79,729	36,699
2005	2,186,350	1,254,032	4,323	1,258,355	158,279	90,566	1,190,642	433,360	562,348	27,106	80,660	37,991
2006	2,325,363	1,319,637	2,315	1,321,952	167,348	90,290	1,244,894	481,682	598,787	28,497	81,601	38,788
2007	2,426,701	1,293,615	-138	1,293,477	169,037	110,455	1,234,895	553,561	638,245	29,686	81,746	38,856
2008	2,423,821	1,232,736	-2,363	1,230,373	165,925	96,250	1,160,698	550,702	712,421	29,419	82,389	37,739
2009	2,412,853	1,187,042	-1,139	1,185,903	163,172	89,751	1,112,482	487,433	812,938	29,312	82,315	35,858
2010	2,487,305	1,215,925	-682	1,215,243	166,894	86,831	1,135,180	471,397	880,728	30,011	82,880	34,891
2011	2,550,180	1,228,546	1,847	1,230,393	152,957	79,111	1,156,547	491,423	902,210	30,828	82,722	35,008
2012	2,659,500	1,278,244	4,073	1,282,317	156,457	103,120	1,228,980	522,410	908,110	32,124	82,789	34,959
2013	2,718,819	1,273,705	5,076	1,278,781	176,371	134,173	1,236,583	538,092	944,144	32,688	83,175	35,030
2014	2,882,532	1,360,153	4,565	1,364,718	189,160	110,036	1,285,594	563,809	1,033,129	34,542	83,449	36,111
2015	3,084,191	1,470,608	3,823	1,474,431	200,806	100,460	1,374,085	601,825	1,108,281	36,445	84,626	37,117
2016	3,179,622	1,558,232	4,351	1,562,583	209,882	103,728	1,456,429	595,728	1,127,465	37,135	85,624	37,763
2017	3,370,335	1,686,414	2,689	1,689,103	226,346	109,021	1,571,778	633,883	1,164,674	38,846	86,762	38,764
2018	3,588,710	1,842,071	2,715	1,844,786	241,740	110,615	1,713,661	644,772	1,230,277	41,035	87,455	39,777
2019	3,863,970	2,028,401	1,420	2,029,821	261,543	85,339	1,853,617	708,994	1,301,359	44,048	87,721	40,184
2020	4,322,610	2,201,259	3,218	2,204,477	281,497	71,069	1,994,049	739,252	1,589,309	49,062	88,105	40,263
2021	4,811,881	2,409,842	2,521	2,412,363	301,067	86,544	2,197,840	781,191	1,832,850	54,466	88,346	41,718

Personal Income and Employment by Area: Great Falls, MT

(Thousands of dollars, except as noted.)

Year	Personal income, total	Earnings by place of work			Less: Contributions for government social insurance	Plus: Adjustment for residence	Equals: Net earnings by place of residence	Plus: Dividends, interest, and rent	Plus: Personal current transfer receipts	Per capita personal income (dollars)	Population (persons)	Total employment
		Nonfarm	Farm	Total								
1970	357,739	274,671	13,037	287,708	20,138	-2,111	265,459	65,329	26,951	4,349	82,258	37,297
1971	384,731	293,892	13,295	307,187	21,982	-2,088	283,117	69,545	32,069	4,556	84,453	37,626
1972	429,950	328,497	17,116	345,613	25,407	-2,093	318,113	75,876	35,961	5,068	84,842	38,689
1973	468,382	355,573	17,888	373,461	30,802	-1,945	340,714	86,205	41,463	5,528	84,728	39,742
1974	516,168	389,822	17,376	407,198	34,694	-1,442	371,062	97,763	47,343	6,064	85,126	40,285
1975	558,424	417,570	16,120	433,690	37,319	420	396,791	105,311	56,322	6,594	84,693	39,860
1976	619,187	476,800	10,105	486,905	43,737	1,464	444,632	113,283	61,272	7,296	84,869	42,084
1977	670,908	523,517	3,862	527,379	48,578	3,160	481,961	124,099	64,848	7,779	86,247	43,274
1978	740,513	571,385	7,251	578,636	54,438	6,830	531,028	137,934	71,551	8,550	86,611	44,429
1979	798,576	609,316	5,506	614,822	60,509	10,180	564,493	152,585	81,498	9,453	84,475	44,026
1980	847,771	620,563	6,544	627,107	62,439	16,247	580,915	173,132	93,724	10,515	80,627	42,836
1981	911,044	654,362	4,250	658,612	70,056	9,533	598,089	205,865	107,090	11,362	80,183	42,087
1982	956,506	670,222	4,248	674,470	72,419	8,405	610,456	228,024	118,026	11,988	79,791	41,059
1983	1,019,329	710,399	10,537	720,936	77,767	7,234	650,403	238,315	130,611	12,643	80,621	41,553
1984	1,075,396	741,781	8,905	750,686	84,046	6,851	673,491	262,350	139,555	13,389	80,318	41,719
1985	1,084,569	742,958	1,261	744,219	85,621	6,025	664,623	273,396	146,550	13,627	79,591	40,524
1986	1,118,501	757,102	9,147	766,249	89,223	4,320	681,346	279,348	157,807	14,307	78,179	40,276
1987	1,150,773	777,522	9,394	786,916	91,849	3,831	698,898	284,027	167,848	14,804	77,733	40,260
1988	1,215,641	830,277	5,527	835,804	103,647	2,181	734,338	303,252	178,051	15,649	77,681	42,046
1989	1,303,500	875,469	20,390	895,859	109,806	2,000	788,053	326,201	189,246	16,691	78,098	42,690
1990	1,352,856	920,421	12,318	932,739	122,123	2,415	813,031	334,319	205,506	17,392	77,788	43,160
1991	1,421,630	978,542	18,455	996,997	132,082	948	865,863	337,959	217,808	18,075	78,651	44,293
1992	1,479,441	1,029,610	16,016	1,045,626	141,655	291	904,262	343,061	232,118	18,556	79,727	44,595
1993	1,572,673	1,079,972	35,116	1,115,088	151,703	-738	962,647	360,736	249,290	19,409	81,028	44,940
1994	1,594,870	1,107,873	12,336	1,120,209	155,313	-1,055	963,841	374,031	256,998	19,418	82,134	46,791
1995	1,676,640	1,142,382	15,472	1,157,854	156,308	-2,638	998,908	404,670	273,062	20,397	82,201	47,358
1996	1,730,378	1,183,971	7,935	1,191,906	156,317	-3,493	1,032,096	416,224	282,058	20,992	82,429	47,981
1997	1,780,473	1,199,096	9,215	1,208,311	154,218	-4,108	1,049,985	440,509	289,979	22,019	80,861	47,438
1998	1,873,173	1,265,147	8,516	1,273,663	159,070	-6,373	1,108,220	465,105	299,848	23,209	80,709	48,102
1999	1,891,563	1,291,078	9,690	1,300,768	161,459	-7,906	1,131,403	464,139	296,021	23,470	80,596	47,682
2000	1,976,458	1,331,049	2,228	1,333,277	166,538	-9,304	1,157,435	488,254	330,769	24,608	80,318	47,944
2001	2,058,344	1,395,999	4,962	1,400,961	175,485	-10,347	1,215,129	490,241	352,974	25,712	80,055	47,844
2002	2,138,335	1,484,453	1,753	1,486,206	185,822	-11,928	1,288,456	487,577	362,302	26,780	79,848	47,693
2003	2,225,408	1,560,008	4,941	1,564,949	194,437	-12,113	1,358,399	490,895	376,114	27,946	79,633	47,643
2004	2,365,612	1,651,711	16,473	1,668,184	206,069	-14,084	1,448,031	518,959	398,622	29,497	80,198	48,326
2005	2,470,875	1,725,949	18,073	1,744,022	216,694	-16,083	1,511,245	530,250	429,380	30,870	80,041	48,759
2006	2,676,742	1,840,334	9,947	1,850,281	232,648	-19,363	1,598,270	618,667	459,805	33,466	79,984	49,919
2007	2,810,376	1,904,173	14,720	1,918,893	243,637	-21,269	1,653,987	673,653	482,736	35,086	80,099	50,132
2008	2,933,954	1,974,944	16,526	1,991,470	253,308	-20,894	1,717,268	669,963	546,723	36,434	80,529	50,810
2009	2,961,860	2,032,147	10,339	2,042,486	259,110	-22,514	1,760,862	609,493	591,505	36,711	80,680	50,231
2010	3,128,471	2,131,006	15,840	2,146,846	267,307	-20,799	1,858,740	631,701	638,030	38,380	81,513	49,971
2011	3,221,572	2,162,386	21,592	2,183,978	247,202	-11,934	1,924,842	666,375	630,355	39,415	81,734	49,736
2012	3,304,685	2,178,466	19,353	2,197,819	247,452	5,033	1,955,400	712,967	636,318	40,470	81,657	49,761
2013	3,291,830	2,162,526	26,768	2,189,294	277,157	11,015	1,923,152	719,443	649,235	40,027	82,241	50,030
2014	3,435,423	2,258,048	20,876	2,278,924	290,678	14,300	2,002,546	753,928	678,949	41,212	83,359	50,082
2015	3,537,502	2,325,922	18,591	2,344,513	296,924	7,091	2,054,680	774,688	708,134	42,370	83,491	50,307
2016	3,596,195	2,353,981	12,397	2,366,378	292,995	-2,033	2,071,350	774,632	750,213	43,080	83,478	50,074
2017	3,732,448	2,439,307	3,396	2,442,703	311,814	799	2,131,688	799,834	800,926	44,512	83,852	50,333
2018	3,873,297	2,499,528	17,228	2,516,756	325,931	6,335	2,197,160	854,150	821,987	46,014	84,177	50,624
2019	3,978,270	2,574,298	28,611	2,602,909	332,722	7,739	2,277,926	837,746	862,598	47,303	84,102	50,637
2020	4,264,931	2,667,214	33,873	2,701,087	350,521	-252	2,350,314	836,729	1,077,888	50,576	84,328	49,473
2021	4,543,743	2,865,789	8,205	2,873,994	365,462	-2,843	2,505,689	849,370	1,188,684	53,765	84,511	50,706

Personal Income and Employment by Area: Greeley, CO

(Thousands of dollars, except as noted.)

Year	Personal income, total	Derivation of personal income									Per capita personal income (dollars)	Population (persons)	Total employment
		Earnings by place of work			Less: Contributions for government social insurance	Plus: Adjustment for residence	Equals: Net earnings by place of residence	Plus: Dividends, interest, and rent	Plus: Personal current transfer receipts				
		Nonfarm	Farm	Total									
1970	331,691	170,975	74,032	245,007	10,272	17,255	251,990	50,900	28,801		3,685	90,012	34,611
1971	368,062	197,135	70,784	267,919	12,225	21,518	277,212	57,097	33,753		3,925	93,779	35,647
1972	431,460	244,014	77,292	321,306	16,200	24,968	330,074	64,144	37,242		4,332	99,597	39,546
1973	513,873	293,321	93,932	387,253	22,619	28,633	393,267	76,129	44,477		4,922	104,411	44,129
1974	613,721	344,588	127,349	471,937	27,829	30,523	474,631	87,798	51,292		5,679	108,059	47,670
1975	670,486	376,142	120,928	497,070	29,231	38,025	505,864	102,237	62,385		6,181	108,479	47,671
1976	726,285	439,870	100,074	539,944	34,841	43,656	548,759	109,805	67,721		6,599	110,052	49,788
1977	745,537	478,520	49,520	528,040	38,072	58,979	548,947	123,442	73,148		6,624	112,555	51,346
1978	871,664	536,035	72,424	608,459	42,909	80,550	646,100	142,967	82,597		7,585	114,919	52,739
1979	978,249	604,891	59,800	664,691	50,846	102,936	716,781	168,738	92,730		8,139	120,194	53,520
1980	1,065,290	655,293	16,013	671,306	55,380	129,636	745,562	206,871	112,857		8,607	123,767	54,564
1981	1,232,706	709,558	68,999	778,557	63,899	140,449	855,107	247,066	130,533		9,879	124,780	55,002
1982	1,295,207	769,127	33,936	803,063	70,895	140,138	872,306	276,728	146,173		10,301	125,733	55,718
1983	1,405,402	845,887	40,986	886,873	78,878	131,316	939,311	305,177	160,914		10,849	129,542	58,126
1984	1,549,866	916,915	85,385	1,002,300	88,737	134,174	1,047,737	331,457	170,672		11,852	130,764	59,839
1985	1,605,619	996,896	56,504	1,053,400	99,499	117,776	1,071,677	355,279	178,663		12,219	131,402	60,864
1986	1,643,095	1,036,242	69,237	1,105,479	106,056	107,015	1,106,438	346,348	190,309		12,475	131,715	60,862
1987	1,715,610	1,075,134	93,869	1,169,003	108,873	96,737	1,156,867	356,958	201,785		13,025	131,713	61,351
1988	1,817,102	1,162,629	119,612	1,282,241	123,424	73,192	1,232,009	369,991	215,102		13,782	131,842	65,219
1989	1,980,673	1,260,501	150,496	1,410,997	136,556	61,342	1,335,783	411,360	233,530		14,982	132,202	66,292
1990	2,052,824	1,332,867	158,672	1,491,539	146,974	58,020	1,402,585	401,996	248,243		15,533	132,161	66,690
1991	2,158,526	1,427,706	140,126	1,567,832	163,701	70,484	1,474,615	411,318	272,593		16,077	134,262	68,491
1992	2,336,869	1,540,781	133,374	1,674,155	173,718	108,144	1,608,581	421,424	306,864		16,988	137,560	69,676
1993	2,590,543	1,688,187	180,102	1,868,289	193,207	133,523	1,808,605	453,427	328,511		18,168	142,586	73,905
1994	2,767,862	1,836,512	142,257	1,978,769	211,562	157,873	1,925,080	492,375	350,407		18,787	147,328	77,289
1995	2,939,796	1,942,759	114,611	2,057,370	221,986	184,968	2,020,352	521,489	397,955		19,323	152,140	79,705
1996	3,208,174	2,076,067	152,216	2,228,283	231,869	228,382	2,224,796	573,652	409,726		20,547	156,140	82,605
1997	3,467,474	2,218,265	188,080	2,406,345	243,969	280,704	2,443,080	605,679	418,715		21,467	161,525	86,239
1998	3,842,403	2,479,772	185,670	2,665,442	247,932	348,822	2,766,332	648,813	427,258		23,071	166,547	89,357
1999	4,211,687	2,749,869	208,377	2,958,246	271,280	415,698	3,102,664	647,499	461,524		24,158	174,342	92,082
2000	4,648,440	3,025,098	176,691	3,201,789	294,496	526,439	3,433,732	722,321	492,387		25,421	182,861	95,735
2001	5,012,509	3,201,258	270,794	3,472,052	325,591	555,525	3,701,986	760,763	549,760		26,058	192,360	103,132
2002	5,024,248	3,388,536	146,890	3,535,426	357,227	524,563	3,702,762	715,169	606,317		24,844	202,234	104,924
2003	5,287,179	3,505,388	145,363	3,650,751	371,907	586,260	3,865,074	779,297	642,808		25,315	208,858	108,331
2004	5,828,479	3,726,321	190,522	3,916,843	405,901	799,692	4,310,634	835,357	682,488		27,069	215,322	112,357
2005	6,408,917	3,957,480	235,805	4,193,285	432,469	963,199	4,724,015	935,915	748,987		28,755	222,879	116,668
2006	6,938,571	4,281,676	179,281	4,460,957	466,128	1,146,785	5,141,614	987,056	809,901		30,076	230,703	121,484
2007	7,698,541	4,572,964	243,474	4,816,438	502,028	1,335,699	5,650,109	1,178,681	869,751		32,389	237,692	126,301
2008	8,324,002	4,749,475	238,183	4,987,658	526,843	1,465,975	5,926,790	1,368,404	1,028,808		34,193	243,442	125,730
2009	8,148,522	4,469,462	184,903	4,654,365	496,841	1,587,297	5,744,821	1,233,986	1,169,715		32,831	248,193	122,003
2010	8,517,152	4,629,190	271,746	4,900,936	512,342	1,510,426	5,899,020	1,266,179	1,351,953		33,503	254,224	121,409
2011	9,197,260	5,060,056	289,748	5,349,804	504,479	1,529,199	6,374,524	1,415,367	1,407,369		35,529	258,867	126,413
2012	9,843,410	5,613,721	340,657	5,954,378	549,915	1,535,893	6,940,356	1,480,555	1,422,499		37,282	264,025	129,876
2013	10,558,536	6,235,534	371,912	6,607,446	660,631	1,607,264	7,554,079	1,526,918	1,477,539		39,090	270,105	136,789
2014	11,844,469	7,227,168	451,506	7,678,674	757,140	1,519,176	8,440,710	1,808,471	1,595,288		42,833	276,529	146,116
2015	12,690,713	7,550,574	580,190	8,130,764	796,168	1,712,330	9,046,926	1,903,928	1,739,859		44,485	285,282	150,061
2016	12,994,119	7,405,325	490,188	7,895,513	791,223	2,163,441	9,267,731	1,894,119	1,832,269		44,072	294,841	148,524
2017	13,643,399	7,890,030	445,537	8,335,567	861,287	2,190,202	9,664,482	2,081,692	1,897,225		44,764	304,788	156,093
2018	15,077,894	8,758,118	393,545	9,151,663	947,103	2,488,227	10,692,787	2,315,156	2,069,951		48,129	313,278	162,377
2019	16,152,882	9,184,889	439,454	9,624,343	1,004,660	2,844,536	11,464,219	2,489,982	2,198,681		50,117	322,305	166,365
2020	17,348,019	8,991,837	391,672	9,383,509	987,412	3,414,058	11,810,155	2,506,098	3,031,766		52,354	331,358	163,078
2021	19,230,197	9,180,047	390,340	9,570,387	1,004,629	4,505,743	13,071,501	2,622,857	3,535,839		56,553	340,036	164,157

Personal Income and Employment by Area: Green Bay, WI

(Thousands of dollars, except as noted.)

Year	Personal income, total	Earnings by place of work			Less: Contributions for government social insurance	Plus: Adjustment for residence	Equals: Net earnings by place of residence	Plus: Dividends, interest, and rent	Plus: Personal current transfer receipts	Per capita personal income (dollars)	Population (persons)	Total employment
		Nonfarm	Farm	Total								
1970	723,595	568,772	26,951	595,723	42,146	-2,902	550,675	113,239	59,681	3,554	203,616	84,132
1971	787,959	616,445	28,725	645,170	47,141	-3,678	594,351	124,304	69,304	3,814	206,593	84,910
1972	872,204	690,828	29,312	720,140	55,645	-4,683	659,812	135,357	77,035	4,184	208,479	89,459
1973	972,298	770,852	33,593	804,445	71,346	-3,882	729,217	153,938	89,143	4,609	210,941	94,338
1974	1,097,809	868,232	31,139	899,371	83,458	-4,612	811,301	177,764	108,744	5,172	212,277	98,309
1975	1,222,330	950,818	32,090	982,908	89,570	-4,320	889,018	196,751	136,561	5,675	215,386	100,255
1976	1,361,715	1,063,775	36,830	1,100,605	101,874	-2,297	996,434	211,575	153,706	6,257	217,622	103,497
1977	1,542,093	1,207,214	52,286	1,259,500	114,792	-859	1,143,849	236,141	162,103	7,053	218,655	107,283
1978	1,736,528	1,372,594	48,825	1,421,419	133,934	1,719	1,289,204	266,289	181,035	7,884	220,260	112,205
1979	1,942,531	1,508,557	67,284	1,575,841	153,374	8,535	1,431,002	299,291	212,238	8,798	220,801	114,982
1980	2,165,761	1,624,828	70,215	1,695,043	165,303	9,919	1,539,659	370,327	255,775	9,654	224,345	115,673
1981	2,369,968	1,751,084	53,614	1,804,698	190,829	7,175	1,621,044	456,285	292,639	10,481	226,129	114,829
1982	2,532,151	1,851,639	49,943	1,901,582	204,176	-1,303	1,696,103	512,388	323,660	11,142	227,271	115,900
1983	2,706,237	2,013,353	28,352	2,041,705	221,114	-11,241	1,809,350	546,656	350,231	11,857	228,249	117,407
1984	3,006,969	2,253,006	46,873	2,299,879	254,312	-18,931	2,026,636	619,045	361,288	13,020	230,950	122,659
1985	3,229,540	2,435,652	56,057	2,491,709	277,836	-26,487	2,187,386	661,959	380,195	13,903	232,292	126,109
1986	3,431,905	2,633,306	55,903	2,689,209	299,488	-33,444	2,356,277	683,684	391,944	14,622	234,712	131,147
1987	3,591,445	2,796,453	62,502	2,858,955	312,667	-40,046	2,506,242	679,599	405,604	15,156	236,959	132,768
1988	3,792,400	2,988,209	38,158	3,026,367	344,451	-50,500	2,631,416	739,637	421,347	15,837	239,462	136,000
1989	4,176,682	3,187,002	96,220	3,283,222	364,293	-58,638	2,860,291	861,849	454,542	17,314	241,229	138,858
1990	4,473,948	3,530,005	76,628	3,606,633	420,243	-79,617	3,106,773	879,423	487,752	18,282	244,716	145,741
1991	4,692,872	3,718,119	56,536	3,774,655	447,195	-62,196	3,265,264	891,510	536,098	18,845	249,019	147,990
1992	5,080,648	4,062,741	73,858	4,136,599	482,357	-65,812	3,588,430	913,343	578,875	20,076	253,077	152,470
1993	5,401,186	4,373,207	57,581	4,430,788	517,199	-91,534	3,822,055	971,521	607,610	20,943	257,897	157,686
1994	5,770,787	4,716,105	72,490	4,788,595	565,259	-128,942	4,094,394	1,047,494	628,899	22,021	262,056	164,348
1995	6,120,445	4,979,922	46,735	5,026,657	601,021	-160,361	4,265,275	1,186,000	669,170	22,943	266,765	170,096
1996	6,546,122	5,271,944	72,413	5,344,357	631,804	-179,216	4,533,337	1,312,818	699,967	24,166	270,879	174,894
1997	7,059,587	5,758,015	54,416	5,812,431	685,183	-220,022	4,907,226	1,428,288	724,073	25,748	274,177	179,143
1998	7,545,175	6,143,632	90,304	6,233,936	725,345	-238,480	5,270,111	1,530,230	744,834	27,246	276,931	183,607
1999	7,884,435	6,634,854	94,194	6,729,048	784,256	-323,117	5,621,675	1,490,820	771,940	28,149	280,100	190,780
2000	8,438,491	7,138,862	68,234	7,207,096	833,331	-400,819	5,972,946	1,637,789	827,756	29,788	283,282	196,203
2001	8,636,769	7,176,226	87,080	7,263,306	822,957	-392,524	6,047,825	1,665,417	923,527	30,221	285,783	195,881
2002	8,954,908	7,481,396	80,052	7,561,448	855,591	-394,352	6,311,505	1,633,833	1,009,570	31,017	288,713	195,984
2003	9,327,690	7,834,797	119,140	7,953,937	892,015	-393,271	6,668,651	1,610,321	1,048,718	32,035	291,169	199,248
2004	9,816,531	8,282,921	138,742	8,421,663	942,950	-429,356	7,049,357	1,678,913	1,088,261	33,325	294,570	204,045
2005	10,154,316	8,514,521	121,586	8,636,107	979,182	-411,017	7,245,908	1,724,692	1,183,716	34,213	296,800	205,762
2006	10,742,690	8,849,909	99,627	8,949,536	1,025,801	-429,885	7,493,850	1,967,229	1,281,611	35,965	298,702	206,832
2007	11,274,525	9,125,987	162,106	9,288,093	1,059,617	-429,426	7,799,050	2,079,116	1,396,359	37,433	301,190	209,193
2008	11,806,761	9,379,838	162,297	9,542,135	1,099,837	-424,746	8,017,552	2,197,908	1,591,301	39,035	302,468	207,798
2009	11,604,119	9,238,113	67,467	9,305,580	1,084,496	-416,336	7,804,748	1,967,713	1,831,658	38,086	304,686	202,060
2010	12,123,129	9,452,526	142,518	9,595,044	1,111,826	-437,306	8,045,912	2,090,548	1,986,669	39,521	306,749	201,974
2011	12,843,807	9,933,265	225,229	10,158,494	1,036,846	-465,489	8,656,159	2,241,670	1,945,978	41,616	308,623	204,703
2012	13,538,967	10,411,654	243,197	10,654,851	1,073,272	-458,087	9,123,492	2,449,131	1,966,344	43,587	310,622	206,579
2013	13,711,989	10,760,901	252,061	11,012,962	1,244,283	-501,316	9,267,363	2,425,215	2,019,411	43,951	311,987	208,640
2014	14,247,493	11,031,165	318,518	11,349,683	1,275,206	-465,899	9,608,578	2,538,324	2,100,591	45,072	316,105	210,992
2015	14,823,169	11,525,798	260,960	11,786,758	1,326,604	-522,147	9,938,007	2,692,033	2,193,129	46,576	318,259	213,901
2016	15,030,048	11,675,240	186,559	11,861,799	1,344,409	-524,952	9,992,438	2,767,981	2,269,629	46,898	320,483	215,854
2017	15,647,482	12,094,191	183,511	12,277,702	1,406,563	-538,664	10,332,475	2,939,316	2,375,691	48,415	323,196	218,173
2018	16,550,371	12,776,075	151,879	12,927,954	1,463,457	-604,683	10,859,814	3,132,671	2,557,886	50,876	325,306	221,634
2019	17,132,283	13,040,463	186,646	13,227,109	1,511,638	-617,534	11,097,937	3,364,238	2,670,108	52,398	326,962	220,781
2020	18,177,539	13,303,386	247,727	13,551,113	1,548,124	-641,155	11,361,834	3,372,870	3,442,835	55,365	328,323	213,026
2021	19,189,367	13,869,784	221,028	14,090,812	1,590,233	-644,660	11,855,919	3,457,475	3,875,973	58,240	329,490	217,682

Personal Income and Employment by Area: Greensboro-High Point, NC

(Thousands of dollars, except as noted.)

Year	Personal income, total	Derivation of personal income									Per capita personal income (dollars)	Population (persons)	Total employment
		Earnings by place of work			Less: Contributions for government social insurance	Plus: Adjustment for residence	Equals: Net earnings by place of residence	Plus: Dividends, interest, and rent	Plus: Personal current transfer receipts			
		Nonfarm	Farm	Total								
1970	1,732,134	1,582,881	25,267	1,608,148	112,594	-84,167	1,411,387	208,940	111,807	3,948	438,730	247,290
1971	1,898,502	1,735,432	29,467	1,764,899	128,225	-98,959	1,537,715	228,812	131,975	4,237	448,079	251,788
1972	2,112,332	1,951,088	29,637	1,980,725	151,619	-114,907	1,714,199	251,481	146,652	4,637	455,577	262,903
1973	2,343,880	2,161,142	48,538	2,209,680	192,675	-128,401	1,888,604	283,978	171,298	5,087	460,732	272,867
1974	2,552,770	2,331,214	42,217	2,373,431	215,681	-143,080	2,014,670	327,723	210,377	5,501	464,097	272,067
1975	2,729,702	2,391,914	46,541	2,438,455	216,506	-149,287	2,072,662	356,806	300,234	5,851	466,520	258,218
1976	2,998,783	2,651,047	47,890	2,698,937	245,749	-166,917	2,286,271	390,453	322,059	6,362	471,352	268,292
1977	3,321,180	2,960,163	46,006	3,006,169	273,013	-188,910	2,544,246	438,513	338,421	6,959	477,233	278,421
1978	3,780,639	3,433,254	49,194	3,482,448	326,691	-237,130	2,918,627	494,830	367,182	7,836	482,440	291,685
1979	4,169,668	3,803,078	32,284	3,835,362	375,104	-268,693	3,191,565	560,256	417,847	8,558	487,216	298,117
1980	4,619,368	4,112,067	23,149	4,135,216	406,218	-298,967	3,430,031	688,846	500,491	9,366	493,196	296,162
1981	5,168,724	4,491,894	43,888	4,535,782	475,054	-334,560	3,726,168	865,537	577,019	10,400	496,975	298,011
1982	5,488,160	4,688,531	47,363	4,735,894	500,111	-354,412	3,881,371	964,100	642,689	10,962	500,656	295,265
1983	5,969,097	5,146,874	33,403	5,180,277	552,305	-395,415	4,232,557	1,050,816	685,724	11,838	504,241	302,975
1984	6,705,371	5,798,995	32,881	5,831,876	639,045	-448,454	4,744,377	1,241,849	719,145	13,189	508,397	320,355
1985	7,178,836	6,206,659	32,460	6,239,119	692,214	-476,702	5,070,203	1,340,831	767,802	14,014	512,256	327,294
1986	7,697,781	6,666,345	37,953	6,704,298	757,438	-511,721	5,435,139	1,447,623	815,019	14,896	516,765	338,297
1987	8,375,056	7,387,134	34,186	7,421,320	825,923	-575,556	6,019,841	1,504,676	850,539	16,007	523,217	351,897
1988	9,145,853	7,991,259	51,903	8,043,162	914,104	-624,503	6,504,555	1,719,580	921,718	17,256	530,011	364,650
1989	9,812,259	8,471,197	81,424	8,552,621	967,586	-658,708	6,926,327	1,862,159	1,023,773	18,329	535,336	368,711
1990	10,460,806	8,869,060	94,276	8,963,336	1,040,295	-689,531	7,233,510	2,111,550	1,115,746	19,279	542,612	373,827
1991	10,758,443	8,986,075	100,492	9,086,567	1,067,433	-654,972	7,364,162	2,130,009	1,264,272	19,462	552,787	365,866
1992	11,581,973	9,750,456	100,651	9,851,107	1,141,837	-696,522	8,012,748	2,183,002	1,386,223	20,624	561,591	368,982
1993	12,276,239	10,302,681	113,315	10,415,996	1,216,308	-775,697	8,423,991	2,341,727	1,510,521	21,489	571,281	381,473
1994	13,049,753	11,015,725	120,599	11,136,324	1,313,291	-825,774	8,997,259	2,476,745	1,575,749	22,426	581,897	391,593
1995	13,841,711	11,705,459	118,868	11,824,327	1,397,498	-940,721	9,486,108	2,597,711	1,757,892	23,287	594,390	405,535
1996	14,759,901	12,350,650	137,178	12,487,828	1,458,882	-1,023,858	10,005,088	2,842,477	1,912,336	24,389	605,175	414,861
1997	15,812,360	13,136,041	139,871	13,275,912	1,537,512	-1,056,843	10,681,557	3,127,490	2,003,313	25,689	615,526	423,430
1998	16,921,254	14,084,198	140,740	14,224,938	1,645,589	-1,099,608	11,479,741	3,353,309	2,088,204	26,992	626,891	427,270
1999	17,492,591	14,897,603	146,895	15,044,498	1,741,108	-1,192,187	12,111,203	3,192,965	2,188,423	27,460	637,026	434,398
2000	18,302,100	15,419,731	129,924	15,549,655	1,798,470	-1,183,164	12,568,021	3,391,191	2,342,888	28,357	645,409	437,861
2001	18,770,112	15,792,348	136,387	15,928,735	1,838,663	-1,224,241	12,865,831	3,296,388	2,607,893	28,756	652,741	436,712
2002	18,879,077	15,911,488	63,891	15,975,379	1,833,412	-1,259,081	12,882,886	3,186,875	2,809,316	28,698	657,855	431,446
2003	19,303,021	16,307,230	72,375	16,379,605	1,920,276	-1,338,785	13,120,544	3,258,476	2,924,001	29,109	663,140	430,127
2004	20,524,745	17,043,809	99,600	17,143,409	1,984,880	-1,295,527	13,863,002	3,499,829	3,161,914	30,739	667,711	437,752
2005	21,647,008	17,787,730	113,918	17,901,648	2,090,740	-1,369,302	14,441,606	3,803,670	3,401,732	31,971	677,080	445,612
2006	23,296,637	18,883,597	109,869	18,993,466	2,199,028	-1,425,998	15,368,440	4,234,611	3,693,586	33,781	689,637	455,391
2007	24,334,505	19,493,276	79,181	19,572,457	2,287,384	-1,529,783	15,755,290	4,627,364	3,951,851	34,740	700,485	464,629
2008	25,142,666	19,749,475	59,885	19,809,360	2,318,767	-1,535,470	15,955,123	4,664,988	4,522,555	35,342	711,405	460,767
2009	24,170,346	18,540,323	70,294	18,610,617	2,207,020	-1,376,184	15,027,413	4,040,386	5,102,547	33,621	718,902	437,294
2010	24,909,690	19,025,521	75,894	19,101,415	2,235,859	-1,375,932	15,489,624	3,996,092	5,423,974	34,344	725,292	434,446
2011	25,715,529	19,306,641	36,301	19,342,942	2,079,809	-1,356,298	15,906,835	4,270,206	5,538,488	35,217	730,192	443,003
2012	27,114,397	20,343,631	77,218	20,420,849	2,146,666	-1,399,568	16,874,615	4,623,671	5,616,111	36,860	735,614	445,779
2013	27,022,157	20,774,610	93,901	20,868,511	2,513,294	-1,465,717	16,889,500	4,433,996	5,698,661	36,478	740,780	450,699
2014	28,620,319	21,680,892	122,372	21,803,264	2,611,066	-1,394,143	17,798,055	4,902,955	5,919,309	38,313	747,011	457,315
2015	30,133,379	22,681,484	123,694	22,805,178	2,725,885	-1,421,330	18,657,963	5,219,314	6,256,102	40,078	751,869	466,161
2016	30,516,033	22,907,316	87,596	22,994,912	2,730,007	-1,474,638	18,790,267	5,353,369	6,372,397	40,192	759,247	470,826
2017	31,585,852	23,730,336	100,526	23,830,862	2,804,470	-1,563,915	19,462,477	5,538,395	6,584,980	41,408	762,787	472,718
2018	32,814,143	24,499,773	48,390	24,548,163	2,855,412	-1,550,766	20,141,985	5,756,433	6,915,725	42,760	767,401	478,611
2019	34,617,596	25,562,003	52,554	25,614,557	2,993,321	-1,571,308	21,049,928	6,243,061	7,324,607	44,799	772,730	483,289
2020	37,106,168	25,942,505	47,862	25,990,367	3,062,625	-1,470,762	21,456,980	6,283,540	9,365,648	47,770	776,761	468,408
2021	40,400,066	27,862,835	74,215	27,937,050	3,237,252	-1,455,950	23,243,848	6,441,771	10,714,447	51,872	778,848	481,205

Personal Income and Employment by Area: Greenville, NC

(Thousands of dollars, except as noted.)

Year	Personal income, total	Earnings by place of work			Less: Contributions for government social insurance	Plus: Adjustment for residence	Equals: Net earnings by place of residence	Plus: Dividends, interest, and rent	Plus: Personal current transfer receipts	Per capita personal income (dollars)	Population (persons)	Total employment
		Nonfarm	Farm	Total								
1970	217,915	137,288	31,833	169,121	9,442	7,107	166,786	30,911	20,218	2,941	74,101	32,746
1971	236,862	158,056	25,375	183,431	11,293	7,848	179,986	33,751	23,125	3,145	75,306	33,622
1972	265,316	177,025	28,590	205,615	13,155	10,292	202,752	37,703	24,861	3,539	74,977	34,854
1973	310,619	199,898	42,623	242,521	17,074	12,152	237,599	44,363	28,657	4,099	75,787	36,126
1974	352,192	224,206	44,966	269,172	19,969	15,769	264,972	51,862	35,358	4,636	75,977	37,100
1975	405,664	258,569	47,129	305,698	23,147	17,238	299,789	59,383	46,492	5,142	78,887	37,475
1976	462,176	296,537	51,297	347,834	27,161	21,331	342,004	66,428	53,744	5,767	80,147	39,729
1977	486,896	334,443	24,155	358,598	30,283	24,331	352,646	75,954	58,296	6,015	80,948	40,727
1978	566,804	379,836	47,162	426,998	35,460	27,257	418,795	84,327	63,682	6,915	81,969	41,601
1979	604,576	426,208	20,821	447,029	41,457	30,469	436,041	94,692	73,843	7,300	82,819	43,563
1980	700,605	475,032	28,325	503,357	46,473	35,653	492,537	118,435	89,633	7,735	90,580	43,433
1981	794,865	525,309	35,185	560,494	55,352	38,079	543,221	148,753	102,891	8,635	92,047	44,149
1982	867,221	566,857	41,688	608,545	60,823	37,344	585,066	169,323	112,832	9,285	93,400	44,824
1983	927,663	629,339	21,149	650,488	67,871	40,284	622,901	182,216	122,546	9,791	94,750	46,159
1984	1,059,713	730,122	35,167	765,289	80,509	40,104	724,884	206,255	128,574	11,020	96,164	48,581
1985	1,128,984	781,517	34,765	816,282	86,971	43,464	772,775	219,160	137,049	11,552	97,730	49,206
1986	1,219,372	861,438	31,169	892,607	97,342	43,334	838,599	235,758	145,015	12,239	99,626	51,663
1987	1,324,700	952,467	32,498	984,965	105,837	46,019	925,147	249,518	150,035	12,987	102,001	53,714
1988	1,474,065	1,063,172	43,205	1,106,377	122,968	48,572	1,031,981	281,088	160,996	14,132	104,306	57,254
1989	1,664,409	1,195,880	47,865	1,243,745	137,500	43,883	1,150,128	331,931	182,350	15,632	106,474	59,652
1990	1,816,345	1,322,371	54,999	1,377,370	153,437	34,813	1,258,746	345,113	212,486	16,655	109,054	62,264
1991	1,926,099	1,371,088	56,497	1,427,585	160,932	53,890	1,320,543	358,433	247,123	17,203	111,965	61,864
1992	2,066,552	1,500,945	42,116	1,543,061	173,496	48,821	1,418,386	371,921	276,245	18,077	114,318	62,509
1993	2,218,000	1,618,738	41,781	1,660,519	186,632	42,996	1,516,883	393,826	307,291	19,001	116,728	64,747
1994	2,349,434	1,739,749	43,301	1,783,050	202,221	13,487	1,594,316	433,862	321,256	19,629	119,694	67,248
1995	2,535,983	1,847,686	28,171	1,875,857	214,195	31,276	1,692,938	475,285	367,760	20,698	122,525	71,899
1996	2,683,537	1,951,259	51,852	2,003,111	223,116	-18,914	1,761,081	520,682	401,774	21,492	124,861	72,840
1997	2,921,499	2,099,700	61,051	2,160,751	238,592	-1,329	1,920,830	579,581	421,088	22,858	127,812	73,994
1998	3,007,564	2,207,378	25,190	2,232,568	252,510	6,117	1,986,175	610,727	410,662	23,043	130,519	74,574
1999	3,133,911	2,373,472	16,643	2,390,115	272,347	-43,849	2,073,919	602,507	457,485	23,643	132,554	77,601
2000	3,365,244	2,577,602	36,589	2,614,191	293,428	-62,513	2,258,250	629,870	477,124	25,058	134,298	79,638
2001	3,460,467	2,669,431	29,737	2,699,168	298,481	-73,790	2,326,897	614,605	518,965	25,332	136,605	80,176
2002	3,567,421	2,752,134	16,506	2,768,640	306,392	-93,400	2,368,848	627,747	570,826	25,641	139,128	80,735
2003	3,711,107	2,839,435	20,720	2,860,155	322,909	-110,582	2,426,664	676,845	607,598	26,207	141,610	81,225
2004	3,947,865	2,979,827	27,675	3,007,502	336,570	-108,263	2,562,669	727,042	658,154	27,324	144,486	83,747
2005	4,267,848	3,194,471	25,556	3,220,027	364,464	-101,364	2,754,199	784,860	728,789	28,851	147,929	86,281
2006	4,656,597	3,452,674	26,138	3,478,812	389,295	-115,212	2,974,305	864,933	817,359	30,448	152,934	89,256
2007	5,019,963	3,687,424	33,386	3,720,810	420,416	-114,369	3,186,025	940,161	893,777	31,877	157,479	93,882
2008	5,342,694	3,800,688	41,971	3,842,659	431,506	-108,133	3,303,020	1,017,449	1,022,225	32,956	162,116	94,593
2009	5,296,028	3,733,572	45,397	3,778,969	427,942	-104,795	3,246,232	944,047	1,105,749	31,985	165,581	91,737
2010	5,494,494	3,917,900	41,051	3,958,951	441,882	-123,268	3,393,801	921,945	1,178,748	32,538	168,865	91,866
2011	5,655,267	3,953,412	43,241	3,996,653	404,923	-109,858	3,481,872	953,474	1,219,921	33,108	170,813	93,859
2012	6,104,131	4,274,293	64,312	4,338,605	429,421	-136,325	3,772,859	1,066,995	1,264,277	35,280	173,021	95,599
2013	6,129,601	4,358,197	61,850	4,420,047	500,389	-134,263	3,785,395	1,048,494	1,295,712	35,138	174,443	96,312
2014	6,373,223	4,535,794	63,148	4,598,942	522,547	-156,892	3,919,503	1,120,376	1,333,344	37,470	170,087	97,888
2015	6,584,472	4,698,190	43,000	4,741,190	539,522	-181,475	4,020,193	1,195,875	1,368,404	38,729	170,015	98,466
2016	6,754,901	4,838,080	40,939	4,879,019	554,009	-183,195	4,141,815	1,192,918	1,420,168	39,755	169,913	99,318
2017	7,007,465	5,055,214	51,683	5,106,897	572,610	-193,105	4,341,182	1,196,052	1,470,231	41,208	170,051	100,298
2018	7,394,650	5,337,131	20,894	5,358,025	595,614	-218,642	4,543,769	1,298,100	1,552,781	43,539	169,839	102,520
2019	7,818,556	5,640,999	28,793	5,669,792	627,538	-254,188	4,788,066	1,385,840	1,644,650	45,951	170,150	103,811
2020	8,417,591	5,821,853	20,193	5,842,046	654,287	-225,004	4,962,755	1,385,081	2,069,755	49,350	170,570	101,689
2021	9,159,356	6,253,785	41,402	6,295,187	694,048	-245,104	5,356,035	1,418,712	2,384,609	53,200	172,169	104,699

Personal Income and Employment by Area: Greenville-Anderson, SC

(Thousands of dollars, except as noted.)

Year	Personal income, total	Earnings by place of work			Less: Contributions for government social insurance	Plus: Adjustment for residence	Equals: Net earnings by place of residence	Plus: Dividends, interest, and rent	Plus: Personal current transfer receipts	Per capita personal income (dollars)	Population (persons)	Total employment
		Nonfarm	Farm	Total								
1970	1,517,638	1,293,717	8,982	1,302,699	91,249	15,671	1,227,121	173,462	117,055	3,326	456,342	218,306
1971	1,662,943	1,412,959	11,057	1,424,016	103,491	14,053	1,334,578	192,023	136,342	3,556	467,592	222,013
1972	1,881,594	1,623,546	9,444	1,632,990	124,784	8,914	1,517,120	212,529	151,945	3,918	480,222	236,053
1973	2,156,975	1,876,081	15,114	1,891,195	165,193	3,580	1,729,582	245,943	181,450	4,389	491,446	252,272
1974	2,430,522	2,103,600	12,242	2,115,842	191,998	-5,886	1,917,958	285,791	226,773	4,811	505,159	260,780
1975	2,583,672	2,127,910	10,248	2,138,158	188,404	-2,358	1,947,396	315,266	321,010	5,048	511,828	245,959
1976	2,908,608	2,441,789	11,286	2,453,075	222,212	-1,082	2,229,781	343,912	334,915	5,683	511,833	258,160
1977	3,222,013	2,729,079	11,405	2,740,484	248,827	-8,633	2,483,024	386,767	352,222	6,135	525,157	267,903
1978	3,629,476	3,102,405	14,667	3,117,072	290,594	-15,926	2,810,552	434,931	383,993	6,795	534,157	279,956
1979	4,091,614	3,497,367	18,593	3,515,960	338,065	-24,405	3,153,490	494,864	443,260	7,533	543,173	288,304
1980	4,630,336	3,866,445	4,404	3,870,849	372,658	-26,156	3,472,035	619,322	538,979	8,338	555,331	291,377
1981	5,165,797	4,219,502	5,059	4,224,561	436,152	-29,495	3,758,914	775,871	631,012	9,156	564,171	292,183
1982	5,457,774	4,304,405	10,036	4,314,441	451,197	-26,750	3,836,494	916,959	704,321	9,596	568,779	286,688
1983	5,915,924	4,670,057	4,206	4,674,263	497,912	-27,013	4,149,338	1,014,889	751,697	10,349	571,626	291,548
1984	6,549,474	5,179,946	11,794	5,191,740	569,765	-26,911	4,595,064	1,164,789	789,621	11,373	575,900	304,398
1985	7,031,242	5,553,548	8,695	5,562,243	618,437	-28,007	4,915,799	1,254,248	861,195	12,092	581,502	310,248
1986	7,550,259	6,009,604	6,087	6,015,691	686,336	-35,717	5,293,638	1,343,779	912,842	12,873	586,510	318,643
1987	8,151,912	6,568,268	13,879	6,582,147	739,784	-36,905	5,805,458	1,404,849	941,605	13,755	592,638	328,469
1988	8,993,265	7,308,389	18,862	7,327,251	844,693	-50,015	6,432,543	1,555,172	1,005,550	14,944	601,817	345,744
1989	9,724,120	7,810,300	21,905	7,832,205	913,491	-63,625	6,855,089	1,739,230	1,129,801	15,928	610,505	356,698
1990	10,501,838	8,415,151	22,059	8,437,210	1,001,801	-87,539	7,347,870	1,896,301	1,257,667	16,931	620,288	364,023
1991	10,853,994	8,599,197	21,967	8,621,164	1,038,668	-79,447	7,503,049	1,908,866	1,442,059	17,268	628,575	358,319
1992	11,553,662	9,021,057	28,135	9,049,192	1,079,692	10,735	7,980,235	1,965,660	1,607,767	18,127	637,366	358,466
1993	12,294,952	9,686,658	31,473	9,718,131	1,169,456	-29,883	8,518,792	2,061,308	1,714,852	18,997	647,208	372,522
1994	13,164,535	10,332,964	33,321	10,366,285	1,262,494	-5,713	9,098,078	2,205,878	1,860,579	20,030	657,228	383,788
1995	14,225,499	11,116,545	22,907	11,139,452	1,364,194	13,361	9,788,619	2,466,719	1,970,161	21,278	668,549	398,851
1996	15,145,702	11,779,574	10,759	11,790,333	1,420,055	-7,333	10,362,945	2,673,983	2,108,774	22,232	681,257	409,377
1997	16,052,932	12,433,582	18,703	12,452,285	1,498,581	20,076	10,973,780	2,880,415	2,198,737	23,146	693,566	418,744
1998	17,329,617	13,357,101	19,993	13,377,094	1,608,087	72,280	11,841,287	3,172,151	2,316,179	24,536	706,300	427,192
1999	18,038,122	14,157,217	27,821	14,185,038	1,692,276	15,120	12,507,882	3,078,816	2,451,424	25,140	717,514	437,552
2000	19,351,222	15,124,937	31,760	15,156,697	1,796,844	-46,857	13,312,996	3,383,988	2,654,238	26,591	727,743	448,598
2001	20,196,585	15,713,625	29,280	15,742,905	1,859,079	-43,509	13,840,317	3,375,499	2,980,769	27,453	735,668	440,664
2002	20,444,662	15,722,938	20,991	15,743,929	1,854,726	-21,328	13,867,875	3,338,342	3,238,445	27,586	741,131	428,775
2003	20,784,107	16,040,080	14,418	16,054,498	1,909,853	-43,112	14,101,533	3,301,898	3,380,676	27,813	747,276	430,601
2004	21,392,062	16,172,728	26,281	16,199,009	1,950,341	43,127	14,291,795	3,423,620	3,676,647	28,364	754,196	435,716
2005	22,456,093	16,862,170	32,847	16,895,017	2,038,974	20,692	14,876,735	3,616,945	3,962,413	29,429	763,048	446,423
2006	24,212,485	17,830,724	10,949	17,841,673	2,208,205	71,551	15,705,019	4,193,022	4,314,444	31,142	777,494	457,273
2007	26,009,345	18,836,805	4,977	18,841,782	2,317,166	146,834	16,671,450	4,748,083	4,589,812	32,778	793,500	470,173
2008	27,127,103	19,232,450	-1,745	19,230,705	2,391,973	135,656	16,974,388	4,857,074	5,295,641	33,541	808,765	470,312
2009	26,118,977	18,136,234	16,319	18,152,553	2,288,166	147,472	16,011,859	4,204,621	5,902,497	31,880	819,279	445,295
2010	27,373,666	18,898,879	23,126	18,922,005	2,348,512	187,106	16,760,599	4,243,824	6,369,243	33,154	825,646	444,311
2011	28,831,609	20,049,308	6,327	20,055,635	2,240,299	103,277	17,918,613	4,521,867	6,391,129	34,597	833,352	462,592
2012	30,476,768	21,380,900	15,121	21,396,021	2,302,258	184,702	19,278,465	4,775,307	6,422,996	36,233	841,134	466,221
2013	31,027,846	22,067,891	37,141	22,105,032	2,677,304	270,048	19,697,776	4,779,839	6,550,231	36,556	848,776	476,285
2014	33,177,586	23,456,595	17,376	23,473,971	2,808,527	313,106	20,978,550	5,247,540	6,951,496	38,597	859,587	491,119
2015	35,221,642	24,878,856	16,449	24,895,305	2,961,000	281,108	22,215,413	5,681,040	7,325,189	40,407	871,665	507,362
2016	36,345,326	25,602,153	-261	25,601,892	3,056,380	269,774	22,815,286	6,011,945	7,518,095	41,144	883,360	516,705
2017	38,291,681	26,908,289	5,844	26,914,133	3,215,533	273,759	23,972,359	6,562,924	7,756,398	42,825	894,137	528,416
2018	39,930,644	28,098,727	-1,105	28,097,622	3,377,159	240,240	24,960,703	6,841,958	8,127,983	44,100	905,447	545,637
2019	42,285,894	29,303,165	-6,054	29,297,111	3,535,763	340,139	26,101,487	7,582,086	8,602,321	46,017	918,912	552,765
2020	44,577,291	29,292,537	-7,893	29,284,644	3,552,710	351,151	26,083,085	7,667,963	10,826,243	47,924	930,165	540,221
2021	47,893,301	31,593,253	4,404	31,597,657	3,771,433	134,816	27,961,040	7,866,742	12,065,519	50,908	940,774	558,712

Personal Income and Employment by Area: Gulfport-Biloxi, MS

(Thousands of dollars, except as noted.)

Year	Personal income, total	Earnings by place of work			Less: Contributions for government social insurance	Plus: Adjustment for residence	Equals: Net earnings by place of residence	Plus: Dividends, interest, and rent	Plus: Personal current transfer receipts	Per capita personal income (dollars)	Population (persons)	Total employment
		Nonfarm	Farm	Total								
1970	843,647	747,906	1,991	749,897	48,020	-56,548	645,329	143,140	55,178	3,493	241,495	109,735
1971	906,576	789,913	2,199	792,112	52,602	-51,346	688,164	152,543	65,869	3,607	251,347	111,651
1972	1,068,122	950,858	1,906	952,764	66,088	-63,543	823,133	169,776	75,213	4,128	258,728	120,441
1973	1,214,035	1,074,743	2,790	1,077,533	82,592	-67,901	927,040	196,689	90,306	4,473	271,384	128,013
1974	1,328,702	1,154,594	2,334	1,156,928	92,019	-69,835	995,074	221,529	112,099	4,823	275,483	128,526
1975	1,500,557	1,306,351	1,712	1,308,063	106,258	-82,745	1,119,060	242,722	138,775	5,418	276,941	131,617
1976	1,673,786	1,466,834	2,093	1,468,927	121,873	-91,365	1,255,689	262,183	155,914	5,869	285,195	137,857
1977	1,831,149	1,613,407	2,950	1,616,357	138,001	-104,224	1,374,132	286,658	170,359	6,283	291,439	142,534
1978	2,016,600	1,753,428	2,607	1,756,035	151,565	-108,322	1,496,148	329,372	191,080	6,797	296,689	142,259
1979	2,174,351	1,833,025	3,426	1,836,451	163,127	-94,951	1,578,373	366,086	229,892	7,280	298,661	138,800
1980	2,469,858	2,030,046	595	2,030,641	176,151	-94,953	1,759,537	438,319	272,002	8,202	301,117	142,303
1981	2,844,488	2,326,090	525	2,326,615	215,889	-114,387	1,996,339	531,624	316,525	9,347	304,337	144,575
1982	3,127,220	2,595,914	2,706	2,598,620	246,833	-156,171	2,195,616	580,277	351,327	10,056	310,986	148,783
1983	3,174,155	2,525,746	491	2,526,237	243,657	-125,318	2,157,262	613,263	403,630	10,064	315,399	141,240
1984	3,334,443	2,622,416	671	2,623,087	258,966	-123,555	2,240,566	672,823	421,054	10,610	314,280	143,148
1985	3,544,459	2,798,942	764	2,799,706	283,269	-144,841	2,371,596	726,841	446,022	11,147	317,972	147,352
1986	3,786,236	3,008,817	-564	3,008,253	308,351	-169,097	2,530,805	781,021	474,410	11,721	323,031	153,422
1987	3,893,055	3,091,395	837	3,092,232	316,701	-182,238	2,593,293	800,516	499,246	12,105	321,614	152,171
1988	4,112,745	3,256,542	1,467	3,258,009	349,138	-195,049	2,713,822	864,006	534,917	12,936	317,926	153,728
1989	4,361,896	3,365,596	1,603	3,367,199	362,300	-194,709	2,810,190	955,281	596,425	13,874	314,383	153,676
1990	4,567,144	3,542,930	1,563	3,544,493	399,762	-207,213	2,937,518	973,469	656,157	14,616	312,471	154,152
1991	4,840,436	3,780,762	1,477	3,782,239	434,237	-224,169	3,123,833	977,550	739,053	15,366	315,015	157,723
1992	5,251,445	4,113,710	2,913	4,116,623	471,416	-245,312	3,399,895	1,013,420	838,130	16,240	323,357	162,663
1993	5,829,635	4,646,759	1,236	4,647,995	536,147	-287,771	3,824,077	1,107,549	898,009	17,561	331,962	177,618
1994	6,298,442	5,039,080	26	5,039,106	596,904	-296,148	4,146,054	1,205,427	946,961	18,477	340,882	187,042
1995	6,589,498	5,146,581	-531	5,146,050	607,070	-294,883	4,244,097	1,294,127	1,051,274	19,046	345,981	185,900
1996	6,858,054	5,227,467	-2,101	5,225,366	617,575	-279,820	4,327,971	1,384,323	1,145,760	19,767	346,950	188,184
1997	7,240,813	5,521,496	-1,918	5,519,578	655,547	-299,495	4,564,536	1,469,708	1,206,569	20,625	351,065	194,086
1998	8,256,847	6,426,347	-1,093	6,425,254	767,772	-342,831	5,314,651	1,673,533	1,268,663	22,390	368,769	209,623
1999	8,668,331	6,807,360	639	6,807,999	813,073	-348,738	5,646,188	1,706,233	1,315,910	23,145	374,519	216,805
2000	9,204,464	7,120,464	1,503	7,121,967	837,826	-352,587	5,931,554	1,841,531	1,431,379	24,282	379,061	215,671
2001	9,331,215	7,025,913	3,944	7,029,857	800,869	-378,292	5,850,696	1,885,819	1,594,700	24,409	382,293	213,234
2002	9,545,233	7,181,502	1,695	7,183,197	822,450	-407,001	5,953,746	1,886,843	1,704,644	24,789	385,054	212,995
2003	9,954,621	7,601,326	2,537	7,603,863	866,496	-481,901	6,255,466	1,891,353	1,807,802	25,807	385,735	215,168
2004	10,331,144	7,953,572	4,017	7,957,589	908,976	-537,658	6,510,955	1,854,920	1,965,269	26,225	393,947	215,075
2005	11,369,937	8,234,743	2,507	8,237,250	943,865	-637,841	6,655,544	1,763,171	2,951,222	28,525	398,601	205,255
2006	10,951,434	8,400,966	3,592	8,404,558	985,022	-684,944	6,734,592	1,990,087	2,226,755	30,151	363,221	201,743
2007	12,926,273	9,052,628	-3,958	9,048,670	1,073,319	-795,005	7,180,346	3,620,577	2,125,350	34,650	373,053	214,728
2008	12,854,244	9,589,423	-5,457	9,583,966	1,124,092	-925,500	7,534,374	2,889,989	2,429,881	33,794	380,374	217,791
2009	12,882,324	9,540,903	-4,438	9,536,465	1,135,042	-922,776	7,478,647	2,802,648	2,601,029	33,462	384,985	213,003
2010	13,380,478	9,853,285	-7,472	9,845,813	1,147,651	-920,648	7,777,514	2,699,367	2,903,597	34,366	389,356	213,877
2011	13,458,449	9,716,494	-5,200	9,711,294	1,029,200	-863,276	7,818,818	2,593,242	3,046,389	34,171	393,855	212,487
2012	13,617,094	9,823,466	-3,899	9,819,567	1,047,240	-815,823	7,956,504	2,622,238	3,038,352	34,302	396,980	212,589
2013	13,638,975	9,928,653	1,909	9,930,562	1,200,036	-820,110	7,910,416	2,596,945	3,131,614	34,082	400,176	214,894
2014	14,010,350	10,120,251	-992	10,119,259	1,214,179	-790,474	8,114,606	2,647,271	3,248,473	34,758	403,078	215,158
2015	14,205,644	10,133,315	-1,328	10,131,987	1,234,010	-811,870	8,086,107	2,703,968	3,415,569	35,021	405,634	214,586
2016	14,534,687	10,360,775	-3,007	10,357,768	1,270,341	-838,524	8,248,903	2,722,472	3,563,312	35,649	407,720	217,120
2017	14,867,524	10,545,142	-233	10,544,909	1,304,491	-823,872	8,416,546	2,790,762	3,660,216	36,155	411,212	219,249
2018	15,204,961	10,794,843	-4,940	10,789,903	1,331,558	-863,195	8,595,150	2,780,158	3,829,653	36,851	412,609	221,038
2019	15,938,308	11,115,057	-3,486	11,111,571	1,378,068	-861,391	8,872,112	2,990,631	4,075,565	38,424	414,800	222,788
2020	17,423,326	11,454,167	-669	11,453,498	1,428,935	-908,585	9,115,978	3,025,790	5,281,558	41,852	416,312	218,935
2021	18,599,821	12,308,542	-3,319	12,305,223	1,501,146	-1,008,809	9,795,268	3,115,639	5,688,914	44,488	418,082	226,990

Personal Income and Employment by Area: Hagerstown-Martinsburg, MD-WV

(Thousands of dollars, except as noted.)

Year	Personal income, total	Earnings by place of work			Less: Contributions for government social insurance	Plus: Adjustment for residence	Equals: Net earnings by place of residence	Plus: Dividends, interest, and rent	Plus: Personal current transfer receipts	Per capita personal income (dollars)	Population (persons)	Total employment
		Nonfarm	Farm	Total								
1970	529,615	416,554	11,573	428,127	30,006	21,607	419,728	63,383	46,504	3,773	140,356	61,187
1971	579,295	441,017	10,561	451,578	32,550	31,297	450,325	69,962	59,008	4,072	142,270	60,568
1972	642,962	495,442	12,910	508,352	38,553	34,977	504,776	77,166	61,020	4,443	144,718	62,605
1973	712,792	550,756	15,830	566,586	48,918	39,066	556,734	87,914	68,144	4,847	147,060	65,091
1974	799,667	614,376	17,050	631,426	56,559	42,362	617,229	102,360	80,078	5,347	149,552	66,441
1975	881,803	661,091	13,828	674,919	59,782	47,549	662,686	114,294	104,823	5,815	151,655	65,786
1976	960,251	717,182	10,573	727,755	65,495	58,299	720,559	124,046	115,646	6,244	153,782	66,479
1977	1,066,638	814,076	9,073	823,149	75,148	59,319	807,320	138,761	120,557	6,883	154,974	68,660
1978	1,202,992	918,234	18,477	936,711	85,635	67,200	918,276	156,987	127,729	7,674	156,758	71,340
1979	1,345,129	1,034,800	17,323	1,052,123	100,560	68,021	1,019,584	179,383	146,162	8,467	158,863	73,750
1980	1,449,053	1,062,953	10,237	1,073,190	103,211	86,518	1,056,497	215,204	177,352	9,057	159,999	71,741
1981	1,589,205	1,141,098	9,391	1,150,489	118,001	93,328	1,125,816	260,101	203,288	9,915	160,281	71,196
1982	1,691,793	1,149,118	9,169	1,158,287	120,861	102,656	1,140,082	313,139	238,572	10,523	160,772	69,372
1983	1,777,698	1,214,042	9,288	1,223,330	131,440	97,126	1,189,016	328,998	259,684	10,918	162,823	70,800
1984	1,990,476	1,380,275	17,047	1,397,322	154,420	102,113	1,345,015	377,033	268,428	12,075	164,837	73,953
1985	2,119,446	1,467,960	18,508	1,486,468	166,993	112,032	1,431,507	400,475	287,464	12,709	166,763	75,989
1986	2,255,665	1,548,910	24,866	1,573,776	178,749	135,407	1,530,434	426,287	298,944	13,360	168,834	78,736
1987	2,425,713	1,682,980	22,279	1,705,259	192,889	151,257	1,663,627	441,029	321,057	14,153	171,398	82,899
1988	2,620,163	1,819,763	22,460	1,842,223	214,711	177,666	1,805,178	470,073	344,912	15,077	173,783	86,869
1989	2,853,045	1,954,309	19,599	1,973,908	231,566	196,916	1,939,258	539,763	374,024	16,113	177,068	89,711
1990	2,981,526	2,078,559	23,169	2,101,728	250,305	173,217	2,024,640	552,925	403,961	16,401	181,790	91,971
1991	3,071,235	2,184,028	21,715	2,205,743	268,834	108,808	2,045,717	565,686	459,832	16,541	185,679	92,208
1992	3,232,194	2,298,187	31,988	2,330,175	283,423	92,847	2,139,599	569,048	523,547	17,095	189,071	91,949
1993	3,360,762	2,380,033	20,418	2,400,451	296,787	105,011	2,208,675	597,855	554,232	17,575	191,225	93,693
1994	3,582,059	2,532,846	17,635	2,550,481	317,112	124,771	2,358,140	646,548	577,371	18,517	193,451	95,211
1995	3,741,579	2,677,223	8,978	2,686,201	335,630	110,924	2,461,495	686,736	593,348	19,105	195,846	99,247
1996	3,974,297	2,798,848	14,789	2,813,637	348,519	141,603	2,606,721	730,783	636,793	20,067	198,049	101,073
1997	4,319,515	3,003,168	10,476	3,013,644	368,868	229,964	2,874,740	795,957	648,818	21,603	199,951	103,427
1998	4,797,471	3,293,045	14,994	3,308,039	401,042	256,981	3,163,978	889,525	743,968	22,091	217,168	109,543
1999	5,010,122	3,537,500	15,490	3,552,990	425,463	222,529	3,350,056	873,978	786,088	22,753	220,200	111,434
2000	5,484,355	3,753,385	16,001	3,769,386	452,027	392,475	3,709,834	942,241	832,280	24,546	223,429	113,751
2001	5,996,080	4,050,167	19,277	4,069,444	485,079	481,751	4,066,116	995,541	934,423	26,439	226,791	118,685
2002	6,273,260	4,168,899	8,650	4,177,549	495,250	568,866	4,251,165	988,929	1,033,166	27,137	231,167	118,963
2003	6,645,070	4,385,562	21,456	4,407,018	524,460	696,392	4,578,950	964,723	1,101,397	28,018	237,168	120,742
2004	7,181,223	4,698,661	31,689	4,730,350	558,997	848,603	5,019,956	1,036,986	1,124,281	29,456	243,798	123,473
2005	7,723,051	4,989,808	30,224	5,020,032	595,141	1,051,605	5,476,496	1,041,731	1,204,824	30,811	250,660	127,898
2006	8,316,619	5,276,942	26,042	5,302,984	626,428	1,193,833	5,870,389	1,155,435	1,290,795	32,280	257,642	130,836
2007	8,814,759	5,340,060	26,538	5,366,598	630,542	1,343,338	6,079,394	1,328,705	1,406,660	33,553	262,715	132,391
2008	9,158,780	5,323,967	29,769	5,353,736	633,486	1,397,145	6,117,395	1,413,516	1,627,869	34,454	265,823	131,015
2009	9,109,050	5,197,835	25,807	5,223,642	620,411	1,368,242	5,971,473	1,362,803	1,774,774	34,070	267,363	127,113
2010	9,446,735	5,357,214	27,948	5,385,162	643,100	1,431,843	6,173,905	1,334,728	1,938,102	35,006	269,857	126,562
2011	9,896,298	5,637,303	45,913	5,683,216	603,062	1,393,553	6,473,707	1,427,627	1,994,964	36,376	272,056	129,309
2012	10,247,641	5,911,515	60,437	5,971,952	631,435	1,363,168	6,703,685	1,515,439	2,028,517	37,462	273,548	132,926
2013	10,313,951	6,032,233	56,971	6,089,204	713,870	1,326,835	6,702,169	1,488,835	2,122,947	37,492	275,095	134,166
2014	10,702,850	6,204,115	58,395	6,262,510	730,974	1,355,786	6,887,322	1,584,210	2,231,318	38,459	278,295	135,347
2015	11,119,037	6,390,775	24,875	6,415,650	756,685	1,462,760	7,121,725	1,657,317	2,339,995	39,692	280,131	136,190
2016	11,572,010	6,511,826	22,365	6,534,191	771,059	1,638,609	7,401,741	1,716,913	2,453,356	40,897	282,952	137,003
2017	11,938,908	6,717,568	38,373	6,755,941	797,752	1,713,723	7,671,912	1,739,981	2,527,015	41,817	285,504	138,452
2018	12,456,742	7,012,610	38,206	7,050,816	844,749	1,809,398	8,015,465	1,782,845	2,658,432	43,157	288,635	140,342
2019	13,073,049	7,082,602	67,307	7,149,909	864,729	2,117,277	8,402,457	1,874,312	2,796,280	44,846	291,510	139,220
2020	14,090,438	7,162,376	47,680	7,210,056	888,196	2,284,273	8,606,133	1,853,394	3,630,911	47,882	294,277	134,734
2021	15,239,999	7,732,851	53,950	7,786,801	955,141	2,467,354	9,299,014	1,901,891	4,039,094	51,102	298,227	139,258

Personal Income and Employment by Area: Hammond, LA

(Thousands of dollars, except as noted.)

Year	Personal income, total	Earnings by place of work			Less: Contributions for government social insurance	Plus: Adjustment for residence	Equals: Net earnings by place of residence	Plus: Dividends, interest, and rent	Plus: Personal current transfer receipts	Per capita personal income (dollars)	Population (persons)	Total employment
		Nonfarm	Farm	Total								
1970	155,386	92,684	9,962	102,646	5,808	12,770	109,608	19,447	26,331	2,346	66,244	20,955
1971	172,304	99,361	12,708	112,069	6,320	14,793	120,542	21,298	30,464	2,518	68,421	21,042
1972	191,624	111,771	13,297	125,068	7,388	17,725	135,405	23,458	32,761	2,803	68,368	22,132
1973	221,073	127,091	17,087	144,178	9,546	20,763	155,395	27,758	37,920	3,207	68,944	23,356
1974	246,895	139,869	12,603	152,472	10,737	26,110	167,845	34,186	44,864	3,527	70,000	23,840
1975	287,159	151,486	16,710	168,196	11,233	34,234	191,197	39,119	56,843	3,987	72,031	23,535
1976	326,518	171,822	15,038	186,860	12,930	45,232	219,162	43,822	63,534	4,400	74,202	24,397
1977	368,182	193,437	15,626	209,063	14,430	53,638	248,271	50,386	69,525	4,826	76,299	24,835
1978	417,571	225,679	11,984	237,663	17,242	64,465	284,886	57,144	75,541	5,349	78,065	26,739
1979	476,084	251,175	9,122	260,297	19,426	83,092	323,963	64,789	87,332	5,968	79,771	26,121
1980	550,410	275,442	7,470	282,912	21,049	100,702	362,565	80,636	107,209	6,793	81,026	27,010
1981	623,041	306,832	7,413	314,245	24,519	114,797	404,523	98,855	119,663	7,580	82,194	27,882
1982	688,997	325,855	6,516	332,371	25,612	119,746	426,505	118,070	144,422	8,138	84,663	28,300
1983	746,838	349,457	7,721	357,178	26,796	116,784	447,166	138,009	161,663	8,628	86,562	28,974
1984	797,869	384,254	8,146	392,400	30,162	117,027	479,265	149,218	169,386	9,063	88,037	29,761
1985	844,941	407,758	13,146	420,904	32,175	111,116	499,845	162,228	182,868	9,507	88,876	30,136
1986	866,835	423,075	16,492	439,567	33,353	103,401	509,615	165,513	191,707	9,714	89,239	30,240
1987	870,683	424,920	20,654	445,574	33,584	100,001	511,991	159,468	199,224	9,897	87,971	29,887
1988	903,581	435,394	20,048	455,442	37,054	111,084	529,472	165,154	208,955	10,384	87,019	30,165
1989	965,358	462,187	22,992	485,179	41,367	115,890	559,702	174,180	231,476	11,169	86,429	30,880
1990	1,038,985	504,404	18,542	522,946	45,965	128,229	605,210	174,921	258,854	12,116	85,754	31,266
1991	1,134,263	565,490	15,416	580,906	52,909	133,241	661,238	180,896	292,129	13,115	86,485	32,005
1992	1,257,041	635,286	21,559	656,845	58,929	141,865	739,781	182,972	334,288	14,264	88,124	33,722
1993	1,369,982	696,338	21,192	717,530	64,390	143,434	796,574	193,917	379,491	15,241	89,885	35,685
1994	1,490,974	752,348	23,940	776,288	71,411	155,376	860,253	212,248	418,473	16,255	91,726	37,632
1995	1,564,101	800,723	25,547	826,270	76,855	165,856	915,271	225,687	423,143	16,679	93,775	39,337
1996	1,630,230	842,588	28,427	871,015	81,835	175,604	964,784	238,102	427,344	17,187	94,851	40,716
1997	1,724,504	896,674	20,373	917,047	86,394	194,278	1,024,931	253,893	445,680	17,868	96,515	41,476
1998	1,810,083	946,882	24,539	971,421	90,979	218,644	1,099,086	268,131	442,866	18,424	98,246	41,204
1999	1,873,187	1,014,851	25,309	1,040,160	96,629	222,633	1,166,164	266,651	440,372	18,799	99,643	42,758
2000	1,993,185	1,101,390	21,034	1,122,424	102,926	231,556	1,251,054	280,538	461,593	19,790	100,716	44,352
2001	2,165,555	1,166,515	21,916	1,188,431	110,355	244,223	1,322,299	284,968	558,288	21,303	101,657	46,530
2002	2,245,688	1,226,381	13,545	1,239,926	116,284	260,478	1,384,120	289,555	572,013	21,907	102,511	46,879
2003	2,351,692	1,324,890	11,619	1,336,509	124,029	263,123	1,475,603	310,316	565,773	22,660	103,782	48,697
2004	2,561,663	1,465,534	19,015	1,484,549	134,381	253,860	1,604,028	314,460	643,175	24,319	105,335	50,294
2005	2,837,620	1,620,955	12,275	1,633,230	146,162	267,489	1,754,557	341,223	741,840	26,523	106,987	52,420
2006	3,301,993	1,907,766	16,267	1,924,033	174,219	350,717	2,100,531	424,757	776,705	28,939	114,102	57,421
2007	3,599,114	1,991,608	15,740	2,007,348	183,589	383,861	2,207,620	572,317	819,177	30,816	116,792	59,683
2008	3,866,327	2,112,130	12,106	2,124,236	195,852	425,265	2,353,649	590,531	922,147	32,594	118,621	60,137
2009	3,842,824	2,079,951	6,592	2,086,543	192,291	384,253	2,278,505	581,642	982,677	32,021	120,009	59,761
2010	4,097,162	2,386,208	11,153	2,397,361	214,601	302,084	2,484,844	563,462	1,048,856	33,732	121,463	60,129
2011	4,261,112	2,509,209	13,354	2,522,563	206,187	288,331	2,604,707	582,087	1,074,318	34,730	122,694	60,288
2012	4,377,614	2,458,021	14,000	2,472,021	199,908	396,326	2,668,439	597,478	1,111,697	35,402	123,656	60,275
2013	4,388,653	2,372,300	10,525	2,382,825	222,294	467,854	2,628,385	606,338	1,153,930	34,955	125,550	60,198
2014	4,517,754	2,456,906	9,135	2,466,041	229,429	500,419	2,737,031	632,361	1,148,362	35,903	125,831	60,853
2015	4,584,187	2,336,210	6,389	2,342,599	225,496	671,037	2,788,140	590,452	1,205,595	36,028	127,239	60,782
2016	4,755,177	2,408,888	2,749	2,411,637	236,753	655,563	2,830,447	656,435	1,268,295	36,890	128,900	62,733
2017	4,923,791	2,536,570	4,491	2,541,061	246,569	614,572	2,909,064	692,810	1,321,917	37,800	130,259	64,747
2018	5,079,271	2,577,302	3,690	2,580,992	253,438	669,014	2,996,568	697,134	1,385,569	38,644	131,438	65,207
2019	5,400,692	2,677,230	5,123	2,682,353	263,243	775,308	3,194,418	732,767	1,473,507	40,912	132,009	66,055
2020	5,907,444	2,827,953	9,180	2,837,133	291,047	667,592	3,213,678	738,388	1,955,378	44,234	133,549	65,510
2021	6,365,448	3,050,264	6,617	3,056,881	308,610	672,959	3,421,230	755,987	2,188,231	47,076	135,217	67,298

Personal Income and Employment by Area: Hanford-Corcoran, CA

(Thousands of dollars, except as noted.)

Year	Personal income, total	Earnings by place of work			Less: Contributions for government social insurance	Plus: Adjustment for residence	Equals: Net earnings by place of residence	Plus: Dividends, interest, and rent	Plus: Personal current transfer receipts	Per capita personal income (dollars)	Population (persons)	Total employment
		Nonfarm	Farm	Total								
1970	265,191	175,825	37,589	213,414	11,865	-8,679	192,870	43,833	28,488	3,984	66,570	28,533
1971	278,879	191,990	32,327	224,317	13,714	-8,561	202,042	46,309	30,528	4,197	66,450	29,151
1972	314,305	208,843	45,745	254,588	15,460	-8,092	231,036	50,634	32,635	4,611	68,161	29,839
1973	345,342	229,881	49,406	279,287	18,610	-7,992	252,685	58,022	34,635	5,056	68,308	30,582
1974	437,143	254,002	108,358	362,360	21,533	-7,783	333,044	63,756	40,343	6,329	69,067	31,905
1975	445,741	273,562	83,520	357,082	23,364	-8,100	325,618	69,573	50,550	6,315	70,590	32,738
1976	532,959	285,581	150,747	436,328	25,188	-6,386	404,754	71,307	56,898	7,432	71,708	32,207
1977	531,403	315,464	110,503	425,967	28,226	-6,872	390,869	79,788	60,746	7,333	72,467	33,077
1978	525,109	351,796	48,869	400,665	31,315	-6,554	362,796	93,740	68,573	7,139	73,556	33,605
1979	684,421	394,720	147,861	542,581	36,572	-5,747	500,262	107,816	76,343	9,304	73,562	35,517
1980	846,922	419,904	246,478	666,382	37,787	-4,077	624,518	129,044	93,360	11,404	74,265	35,016
1981	828,510	486,981	126,860	613,841	46,727	-3,357	563,757	156,148	108,605	10,869	76,229	35,983
1982	892,113	519,191	139,665	658,856	49,548	-2,700	606,608	170,100	115,405	11,406	78,213	34,679
1983	858,897	550,976	51,580	602,556	53,930	-3,003	545,623	191,537	121,737	10,586	81,138	35,641
1984	999,413	608,023	125,454	733,477	62,251	-6,245	664,981	206,783	127,649	12,041	83,004	36,754
1985	1,006,438	622,559	107,477	730,036	64,022	-5,716	660,298	208,851	137,289	11,812	85,205	36,258
1986	1,007,552	632,734	82,972	715,706	66,238	-4,883	644,585	212,718	150,249	11,665	86,372	36,047
1987	1,157,771	691,427	170,505	861,932	72,961	-12,208	776,763	224,355	156,653	13,152	88,032	36,612
1988	1,243,853	800,009	149,802	949,811	87,444	-24,926	837,441	237,436	168,976	13,161	94,510	39,367
1989	1,382,176	917,990	150,800	1,068,790	99,417	-40,996	928,377	268,562	185,237	13,843	99,850	41,267
1990	1,393,565	938,368	117,547	1,055,915	102,318	-37,194	916,403	271,235	205,927	13,678	101,885	40,087
1991	1,495,923	995,724	157,140	1,152,864	111,478	-44,469	996,917	266,312	232,694	14,338	104,334	41,203
1992	1,630,271	1,035,715	207,796	1,243,511	116,239	-42,021	1,085,251	269,205	275,815	15,177	107,414	41,535
1993	1,719,615	1,098,392	208,763	1,307,155	124,648	-42,907	1,139,600	285,508	294,507	15,753	109,161	43,577
1994	1,782,529	1,149,491	201,742	1,351,233	128,725	-44,300	1,178,208	310,646	293,675	15,977	111,565	44,229
1995	1,802,543	1,187,253	165,464	1,352,717	130,220	-44,008	1,178,489	317,052	307,002	15,834	113,840	45,163
1996	1,929,607	1,228,973	219,171	1,448,144	131,371	-40,775	1,275,998	331,163	322,446	16,719	115,411	47,583
1997	1,972,942	1,303,109	173,915	1,477,024	136,100	-40,667	1,300,257	351,562	321,123	16,896	116,769	48,573
1998	1,998,252	1,333,866	119,950	1,453,816	135,158	-24,769	1,293,889	353,961	350,402	16,452	121,457	47,999
1999	2,135,835	1,412,665	157,289	1,569,954	143,528	-23,215	1,403,211	362,965	369,659	16,897	126,402	48,316
2000	2,253,273	1,516,274	153,947	1,670,221	153,816	-24,455	1,491,950	380,003	381,320	17,355	129,835	49,518
2001	2,465,233	1,610,764	207,143	1,817,907	171,804	-8,638	1,637,465	400,097	427,671	18,552	132,881	48,875
2002	2,719,851	1,903,255	183,324	2,086,579	200,190	-51,166	1,835,223	422,652	461,976	20,092	135,369	53,293
2003	3,062,578	2,118,089	298,467	2,416,556	224,736	-90,746	2,101,074	456,500	505,004	21,971	139,393	55,626
2004	3,309,645	2,280,691	417,367	2,698,058	249,996	-119,388	2,328,674	443,788	537,183	23,048	143,601	56,222
2005	3,412,644	2,376,094	390,554	2,766,648	259,066	-117,082	2,390,500	452,746	569,398	23,512	145,147	57,079
2006	3,452,184	2,550,289	191,888	2,742,177	271,456	-108,764	2,361,957	480,721	609,506	23,371	147,712	57,125
2007	3,975,375	2,678,836	507,796	3,186,632	276,396	-131,465	2,778,771	538,333	658,271	26,429	150,420	58,761
2008	3,860,335	2,781,593	237,676	3,019,269	292,229	-175,078	2,551,962	560,907	747,466	25,392	152,027	58,713
2009	3,705,122	2,714,114	95,858	2,809,972	291,777	-176,322	2,341,873	550,477	812,772	24,331	152,278	56,878
2010	3,987,408	2,799,327	224,793	3,024,120	291,865	-214,507	2,517,748	563,297	906,363	26,174	152,342	56,175
2011	4,427,949	2,867,364	575,377	3,442,741	275,058	-243,946	2,923,737	593,237	910,975	29,174	151,779	56,158
2012	4,309,648	2,864,136	445,838	3,309,974	275,956	-250,097	2,783,921	604,731	920,996	28,563	150,884	56,739
2013	4,418,084	2,914,012	486,089	3,400,101	306,387	-235,559	2,858,155	596,115	963,814	29,407	150,237	57,519
2014	4,782,762	3,079,123	612,096	3,691,219	320,497	-258,859	3,111,863	653,146	1,017,753	32,028	149,329	59,723
2015	4,933,486	3,171,827	517,151	3,688,978	332,667	-211,539	3,144,772	689,148	1,099,566	32,911	149,905	60,559
2016	5,118,040	3,389,686	443,298	3,832,984	358,738	-262,160	3,212,086	771,067	1,134,887	34,302	149,205	63,263
2017	5,320,411	3,571,245	547,817	4,119,062	384,708	-328,306	3,406,048	802,994	1,111,369	35,596	149,468	65,247
2018	5,324,507	3,608,039	424,406	4,032,445	389,091	-281,225	3,362,129	800,128	1,162,250	35,229	151,138	65,247
2019	5,586,182	3,811,072	449,248	4,260,320	416,615	-332,775	3,510,930	826,871	1,248,381	36,599	152,633	66,542
2020	6,318,254	3,991,201	517,434	4,508,635	435,143	-378,644	3,694,848	828,392	1,795,014	41,397	152,627	65,289
2021	6,625,114	4,204,203	363,073	4,567,276	459,768	-362,000	3,745,508	851,120	2,028,486	43,176	153,443	66,518

Personal Income and Employment by Area: Harrisburg-Carlisle, PA

(Thousands of dollars, except as noted.)

Year	Personal income, total	Earnings by place of work			Less: Contributions for government social insurance	Plus: Adjustment for residence	Equals: Net earnings by place of residence	Plus: Dividends, interest, and rent	Plus: Personal current transfer receipts	Per capita personal income (dollars)	Population (persons)	Total employment
		Nonfarm	Farm	Total								
1970	1,758,789	1,560,954	20,955	1,581,909	110,101	-106,855	1,364,953	245,001	148,835	4,275	411,421	212,257
1971	1,917,418	1,706,275	14,838	1,721,113	124,668	-126,574	1,469,871	272,500	175,047	4,599	416,883	214,199
1972	2,121,103	1,910,446	14,822	1,925,268	145,631	-157,035	1,622,602	301,387	197,114	5,030	421,671	223,174
1973	2,356,228	2,156,395	22,403	2,178,798	187,977	-190,961	1,799,860	339,716	216,652	5,519	426,925	233,699
1974	2,599,131	2,383,862	22,150	2,406,012	215,859	-234,788	1,955,365	388,242	255,524	6,067	428,390	239,598
1975	2,821,295	2,521,931	17,999	2,539,930	222,482	-256,242	2,061,206	432,620	327,469	6,575	429,067	235,721
1976	3,088,512	2,789,215	22,334	2,811,549	253,182	-301,773	2,256,594	472,452	359,466	7,174	430,488	239,343
1977	3,368,794	3,083,367	15,433	3,098,800	281,710	-358,783	2,458,307	530,428	380,059	7,746	434,923	244,658
1978	3,691,961	3,419,471	16,109	3,435,580	320,415	-420,237	2,694,928	589,596	407,437	8,454	436,716	251,930
1979	4,054,250	3,787,793	21,438	3,809,231	368,646	-502,307	2,938,278	657,051	458,921	9,178	441,734	257,914
1980	4,473,051	4,119,103	3,739	4,122,842	400,551	-589,267	3,133,024	809,261	530,766	9,969	448,717	260,074
1981	4,961,310	4,448,631	13,774	4,462,405	462,945	-625,109	3,374,351	982,956	604,003	10,975	452,040	259,996
1982	5,432,382	4,709,298	18,666	4,727,964	493,249	-649,964	3,584,751	1,160,145	687,486	12,047	450,941	259,191
1983	5,795,021	5,028,179	10,726	5,038,905	535,159	-678,339	3,825,407	1,231,002	738,612	12,790	453,087	260,817
1984	6,339,855	5,541,161	39,001	5,580,162	615,633	-737,641	4,226,888	1,366,611	746,356	13,926	455,244	271,598
1985	6,807,984	5,932,606	38,270	5,970,876	670,934	-761,516	4,538,426	1,469,261	800,297	14,915	456,461	279,915
1986	7,316,877	6,410,164	39,315	6,449,479	733,678	-821,765	4,894,036	1,566,770	856,071	15,914	459,787	288,050
1987	7,794,042	6,906,025	35,700	6,941,725	783,928	-859,359	5,298,438	1,616,214	879,390	16,850	462,555	299,738
1988	8,438,709	7,552,283	22,946	7,575,229	887,071	-912,004	5,776,154	1,724,195	938,360	18,099	466,243	310,881
1989	9,279,115	8,155,649	40,703	8,196,352	941,695	-962,377	6,292,280	1,980,825	1,006,010	19,716	470,638	320,922
1990	9,905,094	8,739,119	38,935	8,778,054	1,015,958	-994,629	6,767,467	2,012,124	1,125,503	20,815	475,860	327,398
1991	10,438,253	9,218,616	23,514	9,242,130	1,082,773	-1,092,637	7,066,720	2,078,327	1,293,206	21,657	481,975	329,899
1992	11,022,202	9,848,115	49,123	9,897,238	1,150,845	-1,201,056	7,545,337	2,105,579	1,371,286	22,657	486,480	332,619
1993	11,464,584	10,313,123	42,620	10,355,743	1,220,846	-1,293,108	7,841,789	2,183,443	1,439,352	23,309	491,859	336,584
1994	11,938,573	10,821,713	44,246	10,865,959	1,306,071	-1,383,393	8,176,495	2,281,460	1,480,618	24,062	496,159	345,672
1995	12,490,168	11,282,037	26,713	11,308,750	1,359,786	-1,502,117	8,446,847	2,487,118	1,556,203	25,040	498,803	353,789
1996	13,192,157	11,873,357	53,202	11,926,559	1,401,137	-1,638,746	8,886,676	2,647,207	1,658,274	26,280	501,990	360,378
1997	13,845,272	12,531,392	27,454	12,558,846	1,467,197	-1,732,115	9,359,534	2,777,010	1,708,728	27,491	503,624	364,360
1998	14,563,894	13,347,757	37,548	13,385,305	1,541,738	-1,899,027	9,944,540	2,862,536	1,756,818	28,754	506,506	370,887
1999	15,125,248	13,979,510	34,938	14,014,448	1,600,680	-1,986,138	10,427,630	2,840,543	1,857,075	29,764	508,176	373,847
2000	15,839,404	14,514,089	51,106	14,565,195	1,639,948	-2,042,311	10,882,936	2,990,848	1,965,620	31,091	509,451	377,751
2001	16,684,271	15,323,664	49,032	15,372,696	1,720,160	-2,113,951	11,538,585	2,996,189	2,149,497	32,625	511,391	374,212
2002	17,261,502	15,990,748	23,148	16,013,896	1,801,381	-2,222,639	11,989,876	2,966,730	2,304,896	33,482	515,553	376,379
2003	17,926,569	16,544,346	57,227	16,601,573	1,853,338	-2,288,727	12,459,508	3,061,950	2,405,111	34,530	519,152	377,860
2004	18,632,702	17,523,366	87,520	17,610,886	1,951,285	-2,530,803	13,128,798	3,009,504	2,494,400	35,703	521,882	382,824
2005	19,314,063	18,068,097	76,729	18,144,826	2,022,863	-2,586,780	13,535,183	3,053,357	2,725,523	36,734	525,775	386,116
2006	20,032,470	18,714,964	61,130	18,776,094	2,104,067	-2,772,613	13,899,414	3,233,537	2,899,519	37,636	532,268	393,455
2007	21,167,764	19,410,618	100,779	19,511,397	2,169,880	-2,857,076	14,484,441	3,625,931	3,057,392	39,399	537,268	397,219
2008	21,970,993	19,681,763	111,837	19,793,600	2,216,871	-2,941,554	14,635,175	3,848,032	3,487,786	40,514	542,301	397,581
2009	21,712,053	19,395,947	69,282	19,465,229	2,214,584	-2,999,982	14,250,663	3,567,358	3,894,032	39,702	546,874	389,711
2010	22,468,359	19,858,178	82,934	19,941,112	2,260,581	-3,048,866	14,631,665	3,599,821	4,236,873	40,843	550,112	387,050
2011	23,549,382	20,565,251	128,334	20,693,585	2,090,176	-3,227,808	15,375,601	3,864,475	4,309,306	42,635	552,353	391,078
2012	24,408,600	21,146,222	135,250	21,281,472	2,133,960	-3,262,604	15,884,908	4,162,505	4,361,187	43,965	555,180	393,306
2013	24,762,150	22,106,883	140,077	22,246,960	2,498,589	-3,542,438	16,205,933	4,076,573	4,479,644	44,353	558,303	398,120
2014	25,845,787	22,876,844	168,820	23,045,664	2,586,239	-3,665,138	16,794,287	4,415,765	4,635,735	45,692	565,650	402,870
2015	27,040,057	24,026,259	99,118	24,125,377	2,710,619	-3,843,265	17,571,493	4,559,762	4,908,802	47,417	570,255	409,325
2016	27,450,610	24,292,113	38,613	24,330,726	2,742,311	-3,891,803	17,696,612	4,579,517	5,174,481	47,803	574,247	412,503
2017	28,544,329	25,253,441	91,552	25,344,993	2,899,690	-3,991,026	18,454,277	4,806,039	5,284,013	49,333	578,608	416,808
2018	29,960,836	26,342,622	53,838	26,396,460	2,999,346	-4,148,885	19,248,229	5,057,977	5,654,630	51,381	583,108	423,369
2019	31,516,297	27,625,210	91,815	27,717,025	3,153,948	-4,361,149	20,201,928	5,362,743	5,951,626	53,645	587,497	427,290
2020	34,143,909	28,221,735	58,182	28,279,917	3,187,910	-4,432,251	20,659,756	5,339,913	8,144,240	57,640	592,361	410,976
2021	36,086,493	29,593,905	117,762	29,711,667	3,307,688	-4,522,771	21,881,208	5,429,179	8,776,106	60,517	596,305	423,481

Personal Income and Employment by Area: Harrisonburg, VA

(Thousands of dollars, except as noted.)

Year	Personal income, total	Earnings by place of work			Less: Contributions for government social insurance	Plus: Adjustment for residence	Equals: Net earnings by place of residence	Plus: Dividends, interest, and rent	Plus: Personal current transfer receipts	Per capita personal income (dollars)	Population (persons)	Total employment
		Nonfarm	Farm	Total								
1970	210,184	159,308	12,492	171,800	10,339	8,817	170,278	25,491	14,415	3,347	62,807	31,524
1971	229,751	176,658	12,350	189,008	11,932	7,283	184,359	28,595	16,797	3,529	65,099	32,660
1972	253,679	193,377	15,843	209,220	13,760	7,118	202,578	31,893	19,208	3,721	68,174	33,531
1973	294,399	222,196	23,025	245,221	18,182	6,335	233,374	38,404	22,621	4,248	69,311	35,796
1974	303,767	236,044	7,781	243,825	20,082	6,971	230,714	45,086	27,967	4,237	71,687	35,967
1975	333,756	249,944	11,408	261,352	20,724	2,530	243,158	49,898	40,700	4,543	73,459	35,112
1976	372,627	287,316	10,015	297,331	24,226	2,083	275,188	55,956	41,483	5,023	74,179	36,872
1977	413,003	319,000	11,996	330,996	26,990	544	304,550	64,616	43,837	5,498	75,123	37,960
1978	462,426	359,285	14,429	373,714	30,889	-1,674	341,151	72,758	48,517	6,038	76,581	38,530
1979	520,307	409,958	12,404	422,362	36,745	-7,855	377,762	87,727	54,818	6,769	76,866	40,432
1980	589,540	456,943	6,669	463,612	41,118	-9,633	412,861	111,088	65,591	7,647	77,093	41,367
1981	652,992	488,353	9,645	497,998	47,159	-12,103	438,736	135,909	78,347	8,320	78,483	40,603
1982	707,705	534,390	6,509	540,899	52,748	-16,796	471,355	152,807	83,543	8,949	79,086	41,535
1983	767,527	582,123	7,545	589,668	57,810	-18,349	513,509	162,394	91,624	9,645	79,575	43,301
1984	878,856	644,472	39,436	683,908	65,629	-18,823	599,456	182,142	97,258	11,024	79,725	44,841
1985	950,585	698,847	45,043	743,890	72,863	-22,617	648,410	195,349	106,826	11,821	80,416	46,105
1986	1,070,477	804,368	62,602	866,970	86,474	-32,815	747,681	211,386	111,410	13,146	81,428	48,414
1987	1,122,254	880,142	33,168	913,310	94,127	-33,757	785,426	221,245	115,583	13,543	82,868	49,974
1988	1,252,258	967,379	47,932	1,015,311	106,028	-38,916	870,367	251,798	130,093	14,745	84,927	51,531
1989	1,380,963	1,040,573	73,416	1,113,989	115,263	-43,427	955,299	287,395	138,269	15,957	86,545	52,875
1990	1,445,744	1,102,078	71,671	1,173,749	122,934	-50,622	1,000,193	290,135	155,416	16,270	88,857	54,138
1991	1,515,686	1,157,523	72,910	1,230,433	130,379	-60,434	1,039,620	304,149	171,917	16,670	90,921	54,601
1992	1,642,250	1,266,277	91,635	1,357,912	141,737	-73,959	1,142,216	308,897	191,137	17,642	93,087	56,747
1993	1,744,362	1,359,286	93,859	1,453,145	151,741	-85,787	1,215,617	326,995	201,750	18,298	95,333	58,861
1994	1,836,663	1,454,191	91,837	1,546,028	161,951	-96,375	1,287,702	340,232	208,729	18,812	97,631	60,901
1995	1,908,047	1,512,773	85,100	1,597,873	168,027	-106,463	1,323,383	357,725	226,939	19,078	100,011	62,815
1996	1,985,399	1,563,057	82,479	1,645,536	171,045	-109,937	1,364,554	380,638	240,207	19,341	102,652	63,643
1997	2,094,973	1,687,792	67,985	1,755,777	182,829	-123,374	1,449,574	398,832	246,567	20,102	104,218	65,073
1998	2,230,795	1,798,793	85,944	1,884,737	191,849	-136,888	1,556,000	418,031	256,764	21,143	105,512	65,511
1999	2,334,741	1,928,816	81,427	2,010,243	205,633	-157,027	1,647,583	416,097	271,061	21,757	107,311	68,004
2000	2,507,243	2,053,095	95,406	2,148,501	215,833	-173,068	1,759,600	456,314	291,329	23,127	108,414	69,394
2001	2,743,527	2,229,623	153,535	2,383,158	240,341	-198,151	1,944,666	475,300	323,561	24,869	110,317	71,676
2002	2,692,132	2,301,909	51,649	2,353,558	249,133	-220,057	1,884,368	459,509	348,255	24,004	112,152	72,157
2003	2,876,454	2,438,935	64,765	2,503,700	261,725	-254,856	1,987,119	519,766	369,569	25,421	113,151	72,919
2004	3,042,761	2,542,505	113,527	2,656,032	275,389	-247,978	2,132,665	505,952	404,144	26,565	114,542	74,115
2005	3,209,981	2,657,973	144,880	2,802,853	290,146	-265,027	2,247,680	515,444	446,857	27,529	116,602	74,983
2006	3,349,182	2,832,426	76,352	2,908,778	316,211	-311,429	2,281,138	577,468	490,576	28,178	118,858	77,390
2007	3,541,443	2,932,318	106,407	3,038,725	328,432	-342,676	2,367,617	651,964	521,862	29,311	120,825	79,009
2008	3,723,314	3,014,238	104,520	3,118,758	341,769	-355,431	2,421,558	709,237	592,519	30,429	122,361	79,039
2009	3,648,987	2,989,926	67,017	3,056,943	340,462	-365,037	2,351,444	664,306	633,237	29,393	124,144	77,220
2010	3,839,206	3,075,477	115,375	3,190,852	346,798	-353,819	2,490,235	665,920	683,051	30,613	125,412	77,309
2011	4,039,819	3,138,247	132,712	3,270,959	317,574	-367,987	2,585,398	737,025	717,396	31,855	126,818	78,824
2012	4,229,279	3,293,688	112,110	3,405,798	329,161	-372,843	2,703,794	793,967	731,518	32,917	128,485	79,301
2013	4,331,077	3,360,052	189,741	3,549,793	380,953	-358,055	2,810,785	781,907	738,385	33,572	129,009	79,920
2014	4,571,578	3,458,558	236,506	3,695,064	390,236	-346,252	2,958,576	823,842	789,160	35,049	130,433	80,908
2015	4,796,782	3,656,639	215,978	3,872,617	411,234	-341,764	3,119,619	852,618	824,545	36,576	131,145	82,108
2016	4,848,169	3,744,895	146,125	3,891,020	423,871	-365,642	3,101,507	894,868	851,794	36,450	133,007	84,320
2017	5,108,353	3,895,102	173,656	4,068,758	443,832	-364,762	3,260,164	950,599	897,590	38,071	134,178	85,179
2018	5,336,046	4,090,563	131,253	4,221,816	463,198	-379,752	3,378,866	993,211	963,969	39,527	134,997	86,300
2019	5,522,681	4,265,048	113,725	4,378,773	488,280	-450,115	3,440,378	1,069,470	1,012,833	40,770	135,460	87,268
2020	5,881,147	4,438,302	32,808	4,471,110	514,817	-500,156	3,456,137	1,087,516	1,337,494	43,425	135,433	84,091
2021	6,413,266	4,665,186	184,040	4,849,226	538,371	-511,867	3,798,988	1,110,337	1,503,941	47,217	135,824	86,488

Personal Income and Employment by Area: Hartford-East Hartford-Middletown, CT

(Thousands of dollars, except as noted.)

Year	Personal income, total	Earnings by place of work			Less: Contributions for government social insurance	Plus: Adjustment for residence	Equals: Net earnings by place of residence	Plus: Dividends, interest, and rent	Plus: Personal current transfer receipts	Per capita personal income (dollars)	Population (persons)	Total employment
		Nonfarm	Farm	Total								
1970	5,171,164	4,382,190	37,659	4,419,849	293,222	-178,390	3,948,237	837,241	385,686	4,983	1,037,762	515,814
1971	5,395,535	4,476,209	34,903	4,511,112	309,310	-172,558	4,029,244	879,270	487,021	5,155	1,046,710	504,925
1972	5,783,030	4,851,833	32,162	4,883,995	356,062	-185,231	4,342,702	930,871	509,457	5,503	1,050,940	514,795
1973	6,343,191	5,387,507	38,187	5,425,694	455,426	-210,705	4,759,563	1,037,071	546,557	6,031	1,051,711	538,925
1974	6,962,111	5,840,648	53,090	5,893,738	515,034	-238,519	5,140,185	1,178,313	643,613	6,602	1,054,609	551,581
1975	7,500,799	6,140,389	40,568	6,180,957	528,872	-267,332	5,384,753	1,267,437	848,609	7,139	1,050,706	539,442
1976	8,014,376	6,582,807	43,958	6,626,765	579,288	-286,404	5,761,073	1,344,305	908,998	7,649	1,047,780	544,412
1977	8,754,771	7,252,770	43,950	7,296,720	650,126	-315,200	6,331,394	1,477,326	946,051	8,409	1,041,160	560,291
1978	9,761,716	8,269,703	39,082	8,308,785	764,832	-378,481	7,165,472	1,636,876	959,368	9,325	1,046,844	589,554
1979	11,040,256	9,452,555	39,097	9,491,652	909,025	-476,857	8,105,770	1,853,752	1,080,734	10,531	1,048,331	614,832
1980	12,564,493	10,559,925	46,358	10,606,283	1,004,620	-574,712	9,026,951	2,289,381	1,248,161	11,927	1,053,458	629,793
1981	13,960,708	11,475,731	41,916	11,517,647	1,172,453	-633,163	9,712,031	2,808,227	1,440,450	13,188	1,058,562	632,664
1982	15,089,526	12,238,619	47,685	12,286,304	1,267,473	-688,284	10,330,547	3,158,677	1,600,302	14,234	1,060,120	629,064
1983	16,156,298	13,197,026	50,346	13,247,372	1,378,411	-757,302	11,111,659	3,311,366	1,733,273	15,126	1,068,101	636,326
1984	17,990,270	14,777,920	53,766	14,831,686	1,579,981	-880,412	12,371,293	3,799,160	1,819,817	16,747	1,074,268	666,698
1985	19,348,449	16,206,894	58,141	16,265,035	1,750,056	-1,026,210	13,488,769	3,922,535	1,937,145	17,889	1,081,595	692,320
1986	21,041,995	17,892,877	64,897	17,957,774	1,939,613	-1,198,652	14,819,509	4,171,009	2,051,477	19,263	1,092,348	723,469
1987	23,023,590	19,938,607	66,046	20,004,653	2,126,561	-1,376,167	16,501,925	4,395,130	2,126,535	20,809	1,106,430	745,697
1988	25,234,539	21,868,359	84,760	21,953,119	2,387,606	-1,530,090	18,035,423	4,899,576	2,299,540	22,507	1,121,183	767,174
1989	27,418,784	23,219,803	77,794	23,297,597	2,517,746	-1,692,058	19,087,793	5,739,061	2,591,930	24,409	1,123,307	766,227
1990	28,313,207	24,047,525	102,455	24,149,980	2,579,643	-1,913,925	19,656,412	5,760,408	2,896,387	25,166	1,125,047	758,360
1991	28,578,741	24,265,381	88,972	24,354,353	2,641,821	-1,872,015	19,840,517	5,486,089	3,252,135	25,347	1,127,479	724,845
1992	29,840,621	25,028,753	93,327	25,122,080	2,694,450	-1,886,543	20,541,087	5,485,098	3,814,436	26,523	1,125,083	709,988
1993	30,699,193	25,702,048	97,715	25,799,763	2,765,965	-1,903,408	21,130,390	5,597,582	3,971,221	27,273	1,125,634	710,405
1994	31,403,791	26,294,783	79,656	26,374,439	2,867,030	-1,891,772	21,615,637	5,679,678	4,108,476	27,891	1,125,949	698,042
1995	32,409,889	26,836,961	81,929	26,918,890	2,952,749	-1,781,485	22,184,656	5,827,236	4,397,997	28,821	1,124,531	708,359
1996	33,649,580	27,697,988	68,047	27,766,035	3,044,154	-1,619,123	23,102,758	6,035,793	4,511,029	29,874	1,126,396	715,650
1997	35,686,266	29,605,234	62,968	29,668,202	3,199,897	-1,608,984	24,859,321	6,195,985	4,630,960	31,609	1,128,992	722,220
1998	38,098,466	31,962,098	71,910	32,034,008	3,362,301	-1,723,468	26,948,239	6,441,762	4,708,465	33,586	1,134,353	733,474
1999	40,042,729	34,401,456	72,652	34,474,108	3,536,467	-1,950,035	28,987,606	6,248,355	4,806,768	35,085	1,141,318	745,821
2000	43,680,848	37,524,738	88,871	37,613,609	3,753,931	-1,947,231	31,912,447	6,716,335	5,052,066	37,955	1,150,872	762,284
2001	45,111,001	38,692,120	81,841	38,773,961	3,855,347	-1,993,367	32,925,247	6,831,798	5,353,956	38,939	1,158,513	765,606
2002	45,314,597	39,188,330	73,389	39,261,719	4,025,568	-1,866,608	33,369,543	6,204,124	5,740,930	38,764	1,169,000	757,708
2003	46,328,633	39,652,134	73,070	39,725,204	4,089,061	-1,752,993	33,883,150	6,581,303	5,864,180	39,282	1,179,394	752,250
2004	48,978,873	42,473,824	74,132	42,547,956	4,355,010	-1,934,681	36,258,265	6,552,319	6,168,289	41,416	1,182,605	763,538
2005	51,093,019	44,368,030	66,197	44,434,227	4,530,285	-1,973,328	37,930,614	6,766,800	6,395,605	43,010	1,187,929	775,261
2006	54,805,344	46,775,490	63,720	46,839,210	4,693,398	-1,920,368	40,225,444	7,726,635	6,853,265	45,911	1,193,725	786,925
2007	58,145,136	48,744,446	79,869	48,824,315	4,878,964	-2,112,346	41,833,005	9,014,746	7,297,385	48,519	1,198,395	801,933
2008	60,372,934	49,213,021	76,596	49,289,617	4,988,521	-1,903,031	42,398,065	9,616,427	8,358,442	50,125	1,204,436	807,415
2009	59,495,128	48,223,561	74,868	48,298,429	4,882,075	-1,755,606	41,660,748	8,556,331	9,278,049	49,186	1,209,604	785,190
2010	60,919,181	49,460,554	80,738	49,541,292	4,915,727	-1,739,375	42,886,190	8,127,035	9,905,956	50,177	1,214,080	774,625
2011	63,386,209	51,231,781	75,931	51,307,712	4,593,817	-1,943,610	44,770,285	8,686,791	9,929,133	52,120	1,216,165	786,151
2012	65,318,749	52,344,755	95,190	52,439,945	4,751,954	-2,009,194	45,678,797	9,597,818	10,042,134	53,739	1,215,477	791,456
2013	65,697,386	53,555,620	91,662	53,647,282	5,552,855	-2,139,732	45,954,695	9,563,325	10,179,366	54,069	1,215,058	798,573
2014	68,491,326	55,590,233	75,650	55,665,883	5,750,282	-2,359,180	47,556,421	10,457,933	10,476,972	56,198	1,218,741	806,900
2015	70,603,216	57,567,783	62,345	57,630,128	5,943,282	-2,514,236	49,172,610	10,656,114	10,774,492	57,979	1,217,737	813,765
2016	71,619,427	58,131,943	63,414	58,195,357	6,032,811	-2,339,905	49,822,641	10,746,740	11,050,046	58,922	1,215,505	816,196
2017	72,748,419	59,086,188	55,575	59,141,763	6,228,435	-2,388,452	50,524,876	10,969,932	11,253,611	59,876	1,214,984	818,365
2018	75,201,063	61,130,424	45,716	61,176,140	6,440,418	-2,469,487	52,266,235	10,907,468	12,027,360	61,871	1,215,440	824,033
2019	77,822,892	62,740,132	58,035	62,798,167	6,675,548	-2,678,646	53,443,973	12,035,370	12,343,549	64,078	1,214,503	821,532
2020	81,184,200	62,367,773	44,671	62,412,444	6,656,343	-2,674,469	53,081,632	11,937,480	16,165,088	67,011	1,211,505	789,972
2021	84,774,218	64,434,670	49,860	64,484,530	6,777,703	-2,331,252	55,375,575	12,068,607	17,330,036	69,951	1,211,906	807,095

Personal Income and Employment by Area: Hattiesburg, MS

(Thousands of dollars, except as noted.)

Year	Personal income, total	Earnings by place of work			Less: Contributions for government social insurance	Plus: Adjustment for residence	Equals: Net earnings by place of residence	Plus: Dividends, interest, and rent	Plus: Personal current transfer receipts	Per capita personal income (dollars)	Population (persons)	Total employment
		Nonfarm	Farm	Total								
1970	225,607	177,307	4,196	181,503	12,383	-74	169,046	29,620	26,941	2,742	82,290	33,601
1971	250,584	195,461	4,164	199,625	13,978	73	185,720	33,697	31,167	2,984	83,983	35,050
1972	283,106	221,480	4,590	226,070	16,506	193	209,757	37,896	35,453	3,243	87,298	37,235
1973	320,040	245,733	8,399	254,132	20,913	850	234,069	44,309	41,662	3,588	89,186	38,607
1974	362,770	275,395	6,110	281,505	24,295	944	258,154	53,038	51,578	3,988	90,966	39,612
1975	402,726	300,874	5,691	306,565	26,179	1,789	282,175	57,176	63,375	4,375	92,048	39,716
1976	458,073	346,316	6,391	352,707	30,522	2,364	324,549	62,824	70,700	4,902	93,441	41,341
1977	518,117	395,522	7,741	403,263	34,591	3,255	371,927	70,182	76,008	5,432	95,376	43,243
1978	578,619	440,281	8,334	448,615	39,365	4,936	414,186	79,743	84,690	5,977	96,810	44,696
1979	644,162	482,697	11,511	494,208	44,782	7,272	456,698	89,612	97,852	6,551	98,328	45,088
1980	724,251	530,030	5,523	535,553	49,257	8,043	494,339	113,988	115,924	7,222	100,284	45,403
1981	812,820	582,062	5,230	587,292	58,512	6,118	534,898	145,405	132,517	7,935	102,434	45,484
1982	858,873	603,365	9,239	612,604	62,413	4,047	554,238	160,002	144,633	8,247	104,145	45,036
1983	929,035	682,770	4,944	687,714	71,411	-17,468	598,835	170,160	160,040	8,694	106,863	47,090
1984	999,766	720,180	6,410	726,590	76,966	-10,844	638,780	192,340	168,646	9,285	107,674	47,377
1985	1,045,549	728,112	7,722	735,834	79,176	4,718	661,376	209,260	174,913	9,702	107,761	47,057
1986	1,096,216	775,583	7,520	783,103	85,344	-1,062	696,697	219,177	180,342	10,124	108,276	47,970
1987	1,164,035	834,398	8,302	842,700	91,608	-5,214	745,878	226,030	192,127	10,738	108,400	49,468
1988	1,237,918	893,336	10,026	903,362	102,495	-6,468	794,399	237,121	206,398	11,461	108,015	50,464
1989	1,362,173	974,158	11,126	985,284	111,165	-10,074	864,045	270,786	227,342	12,469	109,245	51,867
1990	1,446,152	1,058,033	5,456	1,063,489	124,938	-13,389	925,162	271,904	249,086	13,195	109,601	52,390
1991	1,502,120	1,081,069	6,003	1,087,072	130,549	-10,966	945,557	277,988	278,575	13,593	110,509	52,773
1992	1,622,547	1,162,732	9,012	1,171,744	138,705	-15,706	1,017,333	293,584	311,630	14,587	111,229	53,563
1993	1,733,867	1,241,861	9,715	1,251,576	147,626	-15,152	1,088,798	314,674	330,395	15,421	112,437	55,796
1994	1,875,606	1,358,433	14,191	1,372,624	162,289	-19,228	1,191,107	336,744	347,755	16,461	113,942	58,389
1995	2,018,606	1,449,442	12,874	1,462,316	172,288	-24,438	1,265,590	371,582	381,434	17,367	116,231	61,030
1996	2,135,047	1,528,976	14,408	1,543,384	179,153	-23,981	1,340,250	388,933	405,864	18,070	118,152	62,103
1997	2,296,720	1,642,024	16,490	1,658,514	191,108	-23,486	1,443,920	429,742	423,058	19,200	119,618	64,061
1998	2,732,138	1,879,848	37,276	1,917,124	217,896	24,419	1,723,647	513,572	494,919	19,499	140,118	73,886
1999	2,847,492	1,976,248	38,139	2,014,387	228,785	21,799	1,807,401	525,901	514,190	20,092	141,723	76,332
2000	2,983,577	2,026,629	35,748	2,062,377	232,737	23,459	1,853,099	578,573	551,905	20,753	143,768	77,033
2001	3,201,418	2,167,927	51,780	2,219,707	246,714	16,392	1,989,385	586,539	625,494	22,165	144,434	76,420
2002	3,341,606	2,284,704	39,827	2,324,531	259,961	10,295	2,074,865	582,669	684,072	22,943	145,651	77,225
2003	3,417,461	2,377,159	39,205	2,416,364	269,755	8,441	2,155,050	548,959	713,452	23,243	147,031	78,100
2004	3,665,691	2,536,724	74,125	2,610,849	289,800	2,841	2,323,890	575,548	766,253	24,670	148,587	78,713
2005	3,934,720	2,693,612	74,294	2,767,906	304,621	3,896	2,467,181	600,211	867,328	26,180	150,295	80,555
2006	4,249,066	2,997,680	37,078	3,034,758	345,525	-1,154	2,688,079	691,519	869,468	27,641	153,722	85,805
2007	4,490,520	3,101,868	43,101	3,144,969	362,096	-8,174	2,774,699	798,160	917,661	28,638	156,803	88,479
2008	4,758,614	3,151,688	31,630	3,183,318	367,034	19,294	2,835,578	879,495	1,043,541	29,947	158,899	87,815
2009	4,808,221	3,159,588	32,834	3,192,422	372,743	24,586	2,844,265	840,552	1,123,404	29,905	160,782	86,219
2010	5,037,963	3,268,544	25,440	3,293,984	376,619	52,348	2,969,713	839,678	1,228,572	30,933	162,866	86,345
2011	5,256,973	3,326,988	-4,499	3,322,489	345,832	86,743	3,063,400	909,252	1,284,321	31,893	164,829	87,325
2012	5,559,935	3,502,232	16,631	3,518,863	361,501	109,933	3,267,295	1,014,288	1,278,352	33,483	166,050	88,382
2013	5,682,986	3,550,103	93,988	3,644,091	411,789	148,440	3,380,742	1,000,173	1,302,071	34,018	167,057	89,260
2014	5,921,939	3,722,134	99,924	3,822,058	429,884	153,830	3,546,004	1,032,197	1,343,738	35,162	168,418	91,546
2015	6,122,876	3,862,433	77,076	3,939,509	452,885	131,886	3,618,510	1,099,462	1,404,904	36,146	169,393	93,160
2016	6,141,355	3,911,180	40,414	3,951,594	464,305	107,189	3,594,478	1,093,938	1,452,939	36,137	169,946	93,472
2017	6,312,904	4,018,324	98,945	4,117,269	484,163	94,411	3,727,517	1,118,145	1,467,242	37,181	169,789	95,408
2018	6,457,237	4,092,921	86,710	4,179,631	493,043	110,121	3,796,709	1,135,712	1,524,816	37,847	170,615	96,149
2019	6,632,320	4,157,452	65,081	4,222,533	508,126	115,158	3,829,565	1,194,804	1,607,951	38,676	171,485	96,367
2020	7,141,091	4,315,088	9,985	4,325,073	535,585	99,872	3,889,360	1,212,617	2,039,114	41,449	172,287	94,984
2021	7,708,499	4,641,662	82,325	4,723,987	564,670	82,590	4,241,907	1,243,362	2,223,230	44,538	173,078	97,163

Personal Income and Employment by Area: Hickory-Lenoir-Morganton, NC

(Thousands of dollars, except as noted.)

Year	Personal income, total	Earnings by place of work			Less: Contributions for government social insurance	Plus: Adjustment for residence	Equals: Net earnings by place of residence	Plus: Dividends, interest, and rent	Plus: Personal current transfer receipts	Per capita personal income (dollars)	Population (persons)	Total employment
		Nonfarm	Farm	Total								
1970	784,523	713,459	5,822	719,281	51,357	-23,029	644,895	86,257	53,371	3,436	228,324	123,300
1971	866,297	785,457	7,418	792,875	58,880	-25,108	708,887	95,199	62,211	3,695	234,432	126,489
1972	980,621	901,560	4,440	906,000	70,924	-28,007	807,069	105,342	68,210	4,078	240,460	133,573
1973	1,106,372	1,008,941	17,369	1,026,310	90,692	-30,299	905,319	119,939	81,114	4,476	247,184	139,492
1974	1,187,079	1,063,524	12,392	1,075,916	99,690	-30,382	945,844	139,272	101,963	4,722	251,418	138,142
1975	1,257,076	1,056,724	12,323	1,069,047	97,494	-26,341	945,212	151,529	160,335	4,962	253,359	129,718
1976	1,414,855	1,225,822	15,129	1,240,951	116,385	-32,821	1,091,745	165,410	157,700	5,553	254,783	137,473
1977	1,593,399	1,395,622	18,542	1,414,164	132,099	-37,335	1,244,730	185,145	163,524	6,187	257,538	143,921
1978	1,760,066	1,551,002	15,989	1,566,991	151,127	-39,311	1,376,553	208,652	174,861	6,710	262,291	148,852
1979	1,936,487	1,693,762	15,718	1,709,480	170,929	-40,681	1,497,870	237,047	201,570	7,288	265,722	150,985
1980	2,158,080	1,830,125	11,711	1,841,836	183,352	-41,466	1,617,018	294,605	246,457	7,961	271,068	151,175
1981	2,430,415	2,028,459	20,220	2,048,679	217,563	-48,764	1,782,352	367,170	280,893	8,912	272,705	153,144
1982	2,574,701	2,089,696	17,859	2,107,555	224,665	-50,410	1,832,480	416,490	325,731	9,364	274,966	150,999
1983	2,852,208	2,354,136	16,805	2,370,941	255,634	-59,225	2,056,082	452,170	343,956	10,347	275,660	156,262
1984	3,196,501	2,641,839	30,453	2,672,292	295,026	-68,055	2,309,211	526,525	360,765	11,459	278,940	164,550
1985	3,388,460	2,794,099	29,010	2,823,109	315,256	-68,794	2,439,059	561,908	387,493	11,981	282,830	167,043
1986	3,686,292	3,051,532	33,545	3,085,077	350,071	-75,541	2,659,465	612,262	414,565	12,977	284,074	172,324
1987	3,980,000	3,348,547	22,195	3,370,742	377,613	-82,637	2,910,492	640,851	428,657	13,905	286,235	178,889
1988	4,359,547	3,653,979	23,866	3,677,845	420,871	-90,229	3,166,745	726,791	466,011	15,060	289,487	185,685
1989	4,742,121	3,861,043	44,579	3,905,622	443,266	-92,308	3,370,048	852,415	519,658	16,289	291,125	189,029
1990	4,965,260	4,031,894	54,256	4,086,150	474,202	-93,216	3,518,732	875,337	571,191	16,918	293,489	191,322
1991	5,122,563	4,081,079	64,011	4,145,090	485,908	-90,920	3,568,262	889,428	664,873	17,246	297,026	187,870
1992	5,557,612	4,492,475	71,782	4,564,257	526,798	-104,012	3,933,447	904,690	719,475	18,465	300,989	193,366
1993	5,911,871	4,780,030	77,439	4,857,469	566,701	-109,425	4,181,343	941,459	789,069	19,332	305,812	198,101
1994	6,295,271	5,096,740	78,139	5,174,879	610,972	-113,116	4,450,791	1,025,383	819,097	20,242	310,993	201,756
1995	6,615,773	5,225,176	75,032	5,300,208	628,501	-100,268	4,571,439	1,119,264	925,070	20,899	316,556	206,522
1996	6,986,474	5,437,075	80,034	5,517,109	648,959	-101,226	4,766,924	1,211,226	1,008,324	21,704	321,905	208,510
1997	7,436,275	5,766,804	83,910	5,850,714	681,434	-97,363	5,071,917	1,298,986	1,065,372	22,705	327,516	211,062
1998	7,920,801	6,149,800	92,049	6,241,849	730,047	-99,149	5,412,653	1,394,886	1,113,262	23,796	332,861	213,060
1999	8,310,949	6,504,145	96,133	6,600,278	768,441	-96,545	5,735,292	1,403,414	1,172,243	24,592	337,955	216,340
2000	8,715,752	6,803,751	89,654	6,893,405	802,122	-99,426	5,991,857	1,467,632	1,256,263	25,392	343,247	221,379
2001	8,965,984	6,829,102	92,276	6,921,378	808,511	-74,891	6,037,976	1,501,549	1,426,459	25,842	346,952	215,026
2002	8,936,826	6,746,980	54,215	6,801,195	785,700	-58,428	5,957,067	1,431,675	1,548,084	25,658	348,299	206,898
2003	9,062,557	6,692,166	56,295	6,748,461	797,555	-35,409	5,915,497	1,520,365	1,626,695	25,932	349,472	201,090
2004	9,500,373	7,039,404	65,434	7,104,838	828,509	-19,954	6,256,375	1,507,419	1,736,579	27,049	351,224	203,385
2005	9,984,157	7,170,171	100,228	7,270,399	860,725	19,824	6,429,498	1,662,495	1,892,164	28,191	354,159	203,025
2006	10,530,160	7,552,721	89,036	7,641,757	901,190	-9,944	6,730,623	1,728,409	2,071,128	29,456	357,492	205,211
2007	10,932,380	7,665,897	58,143	7,724,040	920,673	11,128	6,814,495	1,896,480	2,221,405	30,301	360,791	205,462
2008	11,167,234	7,604,883	24,294	7,629,177	915,375	39,770	6,753,572	1,908,372	2,505,290	30,679	364,003	200,169
2009	10,884,543	6,954,106	48,914	7,003,020	847,907	73,589	6,228,702	1,763,521	2,892,320	29,769	365,639	185,648
2010	11,125,736	7,158,782	52,056	7,210,838	864,134	72,385	6,419,089	1,702,917	3,003,730	30,433	365,582	182,847
2011	11,330,682	7,246,417	20,299	7,266,716	815,299	70,062	6,521,479	1,801,283	3,007,920	31,084	364,523	185,630
2012	11,762,457	7,501,254	41,165	7,542,419	822,972	91,197	6,810,644	1,893,923	3,057,890	32,339	363,724	185,886
2013	11,674,775	7,559,557	61,412	7,620,969	950,102	87,867	6,758,734	1,842,547	3,073,494	32,122	363,455	187,066
2014	12,223,533	7,867,191	92,110	7,959,301	986,217	128,386	7,101,470	1,967,597	3,154,466	33,848	361,130	188,549
2015	12,880,766	8,228,837	121,827	8,350,664	1,033,414	137,320	7,454,570	2,083,150	3,343,046	35,685	360,956	191,540
2016	13,275,947	8,484,341	82,957	8,567,298	1,057,553	148,439	7,658,184	2,199,080	3,418,683	36,685	361,895	194,855
2017	13,967,704	8,988,041	94,710	9,082,751	1,107,070	136,104	8,111,785	2,328,558	3,527,361	38,427	363,490	198,232
2018	14,438,563	9,360,573	58,971	9,419,544	1,135,795	157,832	8,441,581	2,331,819	3,665,163	39,650	364,152	199,680
2019	15,162,640	9,676,439	56,652	9,733,091	1,184,164	174,450	8,723,377	2,525,467	3,913,796	41,556	364,876	200,544
2020	16,318,013	9,864,300	43,962	9,908,262	1,215,862	206,233	8,898,633	2,544,373	4,875,007	44,678	365,235	194,758
2021	17,783,141	10,658,546	96,273	10,754,819	1,288,067	199,790	9,666,542	2,577,487	5,539,112	48,529	366,441	199,561

Personal Income and Employment by Area: Hilton Head Island-Bluffton, SC

(Thousands of dollars, except as noted.)

Year	Personal income, total	Earnings by place of work			Less: Contributions for government social insurance	Plus: Adjustment for residence	Equals: Net earnings by place of residence	Plus: Dividends, interest, and rent	Plus: Personal current transfer receipts	Per capita personal income (dollars)	Population (persons)	Total employment
		Nonfarm	Farm	Total								
1970	266,573	199,240	4,221	203,461	12,006	4,872	196,327	56,914	13,332	4,224	63,110	34,783
1971	270,191	202,275	4,282	206,557	13,002	4,711	198,266	56,195	15,730	4,179	64,658	32,961
1972	326,122	248,954	4,614	253,568	16,252	3,954	241,270	66,636	18,216	4,743	68,755	35,347
1973	365,162	280,043	3,754	283,797	20,026	2,965	266,736	76,815	21,611	5,321	68,623	37,134
1974	393,386	293,067	5,248	298,315	22,034	3,859	280,140	85,961	27,285	5,933	66,303	36,514
1975	434,814	312,863	6,507	319,370	24,645	5,268	299,993	96,610	38,211	5,791	75,090	36,956
1976	512,916	369,939	4,328	374,267	29,810	6,623	351,080	117,781	44,055	6,570	78,071	40,575
1977	557,655	401,628	3,417	405,045	32,099	6,390	379,336	132,675	45,644	7,274	76,668	41,908
1978	620,329	440,125	2,761	442,886	35,133	5,554	413,307	155,924	51,098	7,899	78,535	43,150
1979	698,738	495,328	3,202	498,530	41,307	3,591	460,814	176,334	61,590	8,764	79,724	44,712
1980	795,986	557,774	396	558,170	46,426	2,366	514,110	206,145	75,731	9,884	80,532	46,210
1981	957,453	663,141	579	663,720	58,587	6,585	611,718	257,181	88,554	11,546	82,926	46,448
1982	1,013,318	690,976	3,044	694,020	61,621	7,778	640,177	277,863	95,278	11,848	85,527	46,606
1983	1,068,526	729,606	6	729,612	67,731	8,013	669,894	294,895	103,737	12,229	87,375	47,483
1984	1,233,893	851,902	-714	851,188	82,141	4,762	773,809	345,918	114,166	13,670	90,263	51,207
1985	1,353,277	937,203	-1,446	935,757	93,582	2,551	844,726	384,712	123,839	14,697	92,077	54,742
1986	1,475,579	1,018,037	508	1,018,545	104,259	4,790	919,076	423,452	133,051	15,666	94,192	56,562
1987	1,560,551	1,055,800	2,219	1,058,019	108,382	9,401	959,038	461,507	140,006	16,219	96,218	57,567
1988	1,676,998	1,119,053	3,149	1,122,202	119,791	15,898	1,018,309	509,133	149,556	17,039	98,423	58,897
1989	1,838,580	1,181,398	3,522	1,184,920	128,926	18,814	1,074,808	590,521	173,251	18,359	100,147	60,252
1990	2,031,884	1,279,139	3,677	1,282,816	143,710	16,965	1,156,071	682,051	193,762	19,774	102,754	61,850
1991	2,119,190	1,309,073	5,364	1,314,437	149,813	18,060	1,182,684	711,537	224,969	19,999	105,964	60,325
1992	2,336,051	1,425,795	3,751	1,429,546	163,687	17,969	1,283,828	794,313	257,910	21,340	109,469	61,579
1993	2,494,089	1,498,321	13,358	1,511,679	174,901	19,813	1,356,591	854,040	283,458	21,958	113,587	63,720
1994	2,743,540	1,642,656	9,740	1,652,396	194,233	18,933	1,477,096	949,902	316,542	23,253	117,989	66,792
1995	2,944,891	1,804,789	8,815	1,813,604	213,245	8,319	1,608,678	990,104	346,109	24,096	122,214	71,135
1996	3,238,165	1,948,874	5,183	1,954,057	227,817	17,956	1,744,196	1,111,831	382,138	25,481	127,083	74,453
1997	3,576,440	2,116,373	5,582	2,121,955	247,887	8,334	1,882,402	1,281,613	412,425	27,095	131,994	78,311
1998	3,946,739	2,316,514	6,592	2,323,106	271,066	3,717	2,055,757	1,444,804	446,178	29,013	136,035	81,074
1999	4,217,564	2,545,248	9,812	2,555,060	294,660	-12,247	2,248,153	1,488,541	480,870	30,469	138,422	84,993
2000	4,524,502	2,706,826	8,601	2,715,427	314,195	-18,944	2,382,288	1,614,749	527,465	31,634	143,027	88,583
2001	4,790,328	2,926,818	9,910	2,936,728	335,758	-19,084	2,581,886	1,607,269	601,173	32,682	146,574	92,982
2002	4,912,039	3,024,449	10,842	3,035,291	349,161	-15,691	2,670,439	1,581,975	659,625	32,662	150,392	94,863
2003	5,200,957	3,241,118	21,298	3,262,416	377,504	-15,542	2,869,370	1,614,822	716,765	34,164	152,234	97,376
2004	5,767,784	3,500,374	28,207	3,528,581	410,841	-12,053	3,105,687	1,887,616	774,481	36,554	157,787	101,288
2005	6,309,014	3,773,408	24,890	3,798,298	440,990	-8,224	3,349,084	2,110,409	849,521	38,624	163,343	105,260
2006	7,079,170	4,096,116	28,605	4,124,721	492,784	2,980	3,634,917	2,500,392	943,861	41,736	169,619	109,635
2007	7,565,159	4,329,805	12,892	4,342,697	519,885	21,242	3,844,054	2,692,816	1,028,289	43,383	174,382	112,983
2008	7,735,907	4,276,908	23,387	4,300,295	520,680	38,468	3,818,083	2,726,074	1,191,750	42,973	180,019	110,918
2009	7,527,191	3,993,588	22,119	4,015,707	497,123	43,922	3,562,506	2,621,151	1,343,534	40,915	183,971	105,838
2010	7,377,778	3,951,855	26,044	3,977,899	488,729	49,751	3,538,921	2,374,891	1,463,966	39,287	187,792	103,807
2011	7,843,569	4,049,783	22,190	4,071,973	451,948	62,585	3,682,610	2,630,131	1,530,828	41,464	189,167	104,363
2012	8,310,258	4,298,950	16,132	4,315,082	470,593	64,276	3,908,765	2,828,594	1,572,899	43,021	193,166	106,089
2013	8,596,344	4,493,210	13,253	4,506,463	542,076	65,757	4,030,144	2,901,627	1,664,573	43,538	197,443	108,037
2014	9,389,191	4,786,496	6,230	4,792,726	572,454	72,329	4,292,601	3,310,674	1,785,916	47,401	198,078	111,523
2015	10,095,236	5,097,519	8,788	5,106,307	611,444	66,506	4,561,369	3,600,456	1,933,411	49,838	202,563	115,580
2016	10,491,047	5,139,200	6,407	5,145,607	618,907	68,244	4,594,944	3,860,558	2,035,545	50,959	205,872	118,540
2017	11,023,980	5,397,910	7,563	5,405,473	662,050	68,515	4,811,938	4,085,563	2,126,479	52,892	208,425	122,680
2018	11,623,292	5,603,289	6,496	5,609,785	696,381	84,478	4,997,882	4,366,327	2,259,083	55,198	210,576	127,452
2019	12,783,360	6,010,077	3,854	6,013,931	747,565	69,514	5,335,880	4,996,478	2,451,002	59,860	213,556	129,500
2020	13,587,151	6,245,817	4,613	6,250,430	773,094	59,265	5,536,601	5,059,330	2,991,220	62,682	216,764	127,541
2021	14,713,566	6,815,236	7,585	6,822,821	830,920	75,562	6,067,463	5,332,715	3,313,388	66,256	222,072	131,804

Personal Income and Employment by Area: Hinesville, GA

(Thousands of dollars, except as noted.)

Year	Personal income, total	Earnings by place of work			Less: Contributions for government social insurance	Plus: Adjustment for residence	Equals: Net earnings by place of residence	Plus: Dividends, interest, and rent	Plus: Personal current transfer receipts	Per capita personal income (dollars)	Population (persons)	Total employment
		Nonfarm	Farm	Total								
1970	76,182	69,871	971	70,842	3,612	-15,192	52,038	18,977	5,167	3,576	21,303	9,248
1971	81,026	73,877	1,172	75,049	4,095	-15,067	55,887	18,749	6,390	3,753	21,587	9,029
1972	88,560	79,395	1,184	80,579	4,411	-14,059	62,109	19,458	6,993	4,045	21,894	8,729
1973	95,721	83,692	1,648	85,340	4,854	-14,302	66,184	21,462	8,075	4,516	21,198	8,747
1974	106,241	92,488	1,473	93,961	5,503	-15,517	72,941	23,150	10,150	5,014	21,188	9,148
1975	124,820	103,795	1,017	104,812	6,553	-12,661	85,598	26,095	13,127	5,005	24,937	9,529
1976	172,775	188,499	734	189,233	13,903	-64,524	110,806	47,879	14,090	5,980	28,894	15,280
1977	228,210	266,272	-512	265,760	19,864	-102,625	143,271	70,274	14,665	6,787	33,625	20,349
1978	267,881	304,939	1,463	306,402	21,728	-120,805	163,869	87,554	16,458	7,042	38,038	21,446
1979	309,234	352,061	1,416	353,477	25,705	-138,622	189,150	101,054	19,030	7,856	39,364	22,895
1980	356,727	398,492	986	399,478	29,189	-148,494	221,795	111,886	23,046	8,298	42,989	24,553
1981	398,316	443,478	940	444,418	33,385	-155,526	255,507	116,158	26,651	8,576	46,444	26,045
1982	449,527	490,269	1,455	491,724	36,015	-161,725	293,984	125,961	29,582	9,257	48,561	26,948
1983	454,769	487,866	1,604	489,470	38,682	-156,903	293,885	128,505	32,379	9,545	47,647	25,701
1984	488,877	517,505	1,431	518,936	41,864	-160,001	317,071	135,712	36,094	9,771	50,034	25,809
1985	528,780	557,970	599	558,569	46,189	-168,505	343,875	145,931	38,974	10,314	51,268	26,658
1986	558,583	584,465	770	585,235	49,627	-176,841	358,767	158,273	41,543	10,765	51,890	27,196
1987	593,298	612,650	366	613,016	53,134	-178,405	381,477	168,156	43,665	10,941	54,228	28,028
1988	616,917	642,680	800	643,480	59,925	-188,242	395,313	174,163	47,441	11,060	55,780	27,945
1989	658,073	666,133	1,200	667,333	63,613	-186,668	417,052	187,714	53,307	11,429	57,578	28,135
1990	661,699	596,900	743	597,643	58,718	-109,372	429,553	169,575	62,571	11,168	59,247	24,410
1991	722,835	688,479	1,200	689,679	69,660	-161,302	458,717	191,740	72,378	12,016	60,158	25,608
1992	864,430	871,334	1,504	872,838	92,266	-243,358	537,214	241,742	85,474	13,284	65,072	29,828
1993	907,488	849,496	1,405	850,901	91,634	-193,799	565,468	248,538	93,482	14,006	64,792	29,680
1994	954,332	876,294	1,744	878,038	91,285	-198,157	588,596	264,264	101,472	14,074	67,809	30,543
1995	1,026,812	930,826	1,482	932,308	93,857	-211,560	626,891	288,071	111,850	14,997	68,468	32,025
1996	1,080,060	953,228	1,722	954,950	95,815	-201,751	657,384	300,189	122,487	15,481	69,766	32,488
1997	1,122,243	1,009,225	1,817	1,011,042	100,400	-203,774	706,868	286,903	128,472	15,701	71,477	32,627
1998	1,162,413	1,036,761	2,480	1,039,241	102,701	-223,067	713,473	316,368	132,572	16,364	71,035	32,828
1999	1,234,479	1,068,254	3,138	1,071,392	105,026	-192,882	773,484	318,381	142,614	17,123	72,095	32,807
2000	1,298,189	1,159,678	3,118	1,162,796	114,134	-239,751	808,911	332,177	157,101	17,985	72,181	34,607
2001	1,371,877	1,233,903	4,471	1,238,374	123,958	-256,574	857,842	335,788	178,247	19,070	71,939	34,716
2002	1,461,551	1,321,527	3,432	1,324,959	132,020	-287,216	905,723	351,091	204,737	19,912	73,399	34,713
2003	1,615,161	1,528,123	3,827	1,531,950	150,519	-358,032	1,023,399	381,637	210,125	22,668	71,252	35,794
2004	1,705,739	1,641,711	4,236	1,645,947	166,570	-396,429	1,082,948	386,529	236,262	22,862	74,609	37,376
2005	1,776,700	1,848,759	3,889	1,852,648	183,338	-572,588	1,096,722	415,016	264,962	23,257	76,395	37,293
2006	1,890,656	1,949,051	2,419	1,951,470	195,037	-566,928	1,189,505	418,493	282,658	25,142	75,199	37,608
2007	1,937,266	2,075,984	2,989	2,078,973	205,465	-705,323	1,168,185	462,200	306,881	25,461	76,089	38,874
2008	2,060,920	2,345,922	3,629	2,349,551	239,914	-894,016	1,215,621	494,552	350,747	27,341	75,379	41,570
2009	2,140,764	2,363,803	2,892	2,366,695	246,337	-841,975	1,278,383	483,114	379,267	26,479	80,848	41,165
2010	2,225,262	2,564,604	2,757	2,567,361	271,739	-1,015,178	1,280,444	518,481	426,337	28,770	77,347	42,508
2011	2,421,170	2,704,016	3,018	2,707,034	263,363	-1,055,023	1,388,648	570,540	461,982	30,149	80,307	44,250
2012	2,398,615	2,657,993	4,264	2,662,257	262,510	-995,996	1,403,751	546,642	448,222	29,798	80,495	43,430
2013	2,411,485	2,618,488	6,480	2,624,968	284,880	-941,955	1,398,133	540,036	473,316	30,545	78,948	43,178
2014	2,483,050	2,549,367	5,185	2,554,552	278,663	-834,048	1,441,841	537,793	503,416	30,745	80,764	42,013
2015	2,537,232	2,549,570	5,139	2,554,709	280,901	-806,818	1,466,990	533,364	536,878	32,225	78,734	41,526
2016	2,536,722	2,464,805	4,476	2,469,281	266,741	-752,181	1,450,359	520,139	566,224	32,055	79,137	40,497
2017	2,631,042	2,526,296	3,538	2,529,834	274,016	-763,546	1,492,272	539,225	599,545	33,079	79,538	42,119
2018	2,758,043	2,604,179	2,587	2,606,766	283,305	-743,953	1,579,508	542,901	635,634	35,030	78,734	43,067
2019	2,852,109	2,683,747	2,452	2,686,199	292,300	-780,293	1,613,606	558,563	679,940	35,207	81,009	43,902
2020	3,107,689	2,729,465	1,764	2,731,229	297,253	-808,750	1,625,226	558,149	924,314	38,128	81,507	43,976
2021	3,398,352	2,968,649	3,018	2,971,667	319,526	-868,936	1,783,205	542,589	1,072,558	41,012	82,863	45,812

Personal Income and Employment by Area: Homosassa Springs, FL

(Thousands of dollars, except as noted.)

Year	Personal income, total	Earnings by place of work			Less: Contributions for government social insurance	Plus: Adjustment for residence	Equals: Net earnings by place of residence	Plus: Dividends, interest, and rent	Plus: Personal current transfer receipts	Per capita personal income (dollars)	Population (persons)	Total employment
		Nonfarm	Farm	Total								
1970	63,421	35,041	678	35,719	2,186	-1,249	32,284	19,180	11,957	3,203	19,799	6,020
1971	76,322	40,929	795	41,724	2,741	-1,234	37,749	23,066	15,507	3,365	22,680	6,864
1972	95,300	53,382	1,015	54,397	3,804	-2,118	48,475	26,951	19,874	3,542	26,906	8,318
1973	128,831	77,449	1,403	78,852	6,375	-4,742	67,735	35,003	26,093	3,829	33,646	10,406
1974	143,423	73,420	1,064	74,484	6,439	-1,982	66,063	43,948	33,412	3,851	37,239	10,038
1975	166,390	75,222	1,144	76,366	6,531	-1,571	68,264	49,888	48,238	4,175	39,855	9,797
1976	184,511	85,307	1,259	86,566	7,386	-1,648	77,532	56,670	50,309	4,472	41,261	10,225
1977	214,481	96,935	1,277	98,212	8,587	-737	88,888	67,976	57,617	4,721	45,432	11,298
1978	259,922	116,001	1,533	117,534	10,487	324	107,371	85,459	67,092	5,375	48,361	12,617
1979	317,379	140,283	1,520	141,803	13,412	-16	128,375	107,129	81,875	6,152	51,586	14,045
1980	395,705	171,115	1,412	172,527	16,575	-1,208	154,744	140,461	100,500	7,102	55,719	15,605
1981	485,018	208,787	669	209,456	21,753	-1,676	186,027	177,098	121,893	8,127	59,678	17,682
1982	546,771	239,393	1,306	240,699	26,216	-4,893	209,590	192,545	144,636	8,687	62,938	18,878
1983	618,839	255,254	743	255,997	27,762	1,709	229,944	220,110	168,785	9,257	66,850	19,846
1984	759,551	304,519	901	305,420	33,645	3,346	275,121	292,126	192,304	10,690	71,051	21,909
1985	891,898	381,495	223	381,718	43,101	-1,079	337,538	342,218	212,142	11,936	74,724	24,290
1986	964,889	377,798	266	378,064	44,255	10,193	344,002	387,113	233,774	12,198	79,104	25,542
1987	1,062,137	443,599	-472	443,127	50,824	13,832	406,135	403,483	252,519	12,780	83,112	26,811
1988	1,175,099	467,778	39	467,817	56,724	23,189	434,282	452,999	287,818	13,661	86,021	27,981
1989	1,332,866	519,534	242	519,776	65,527	27,136	481,385	535,673	315,808	14,875	89,607	29,039
1990	1,429,401	547,819	129	547,948	68,280	30,514	510,182	569,145	350,074	15,103	94,645	29,942
1991	1,513,828	606,784	692	607,476	75,406	32,426	564,496	551,122	398,210	15,515	97,569	30,207
1992	1,609,740	663,014	1,314	664,328	81,939	36,770	619,159	536,089	454,492	16,064	100,210	30,105
1993	1,698,253	711,859	999	712,858	87,648	43,854	669,064	545,347	483,842	16,653	101,978	31,764
1994	1,818,061	755,961	977	756,938	95,342	51,934	713,530	584,757	519,774	17,410	104,429	33,496
1995	1,899,323	778,770	617	779,387	99,307	62,224	742,304	590,925	566,094	17,655	107,581	34,117
1996	2,019,182	818,976	626	819,602	102,910	72,172	788,864	625,849	604,469	18,364	109,954	35,859
1997	2,177,620	889,315	1,288	890,603	111,376	77,935	857,162	688,249	632,209	19,448	111,972	36,610
1998	2,310,124	935,509	1,638	937,147	116,114	90,667	911,700	745,532	652,892	20,203	114,344	38,580
1999	2,463,630	1,024,157	2,957	1,027,114	123,987	99,394	1,002,521	784,161	676,948	21,123	116,634	40,133
2000	2,670,638	1,079,942	2,660	1,082,602	130,395	110,746	1,062,953	882,598	725,087	22,509	118,649	41,747
2001	2,829,263	1,189,915	2,970	1,192,885	141,404	118,580	1,170,061	873,353	785,849	23,344	121,197	41,251
2002	2,928,480	1,233,417	2,375	1,235,792	146,150	132,335	1,221,977	868,332	838,171	23,714	123,491	41,905
2003	3,101,793	1,324,854	1,744	1,326,598	157,304	151,121	1,320,415	889,618	891,760	24,575	126,215	42,829
2004	3,296,820	1,409,693	1,723	1,411,416	170,865	170,447	1,410,998	908,554	977,268	25,391	129,840	44,819
2005	3,645,556	1,588,999	1,673	1,590,672	195,407	193,727	1,588,992	979,192	1,077,372	27,248	133,791	47,674
2006	3,976,757	1,751,467	2,162	1,753,629	222,376	212,931	1,744,184	1,051,377	1,181,196	28,853	137,826	50,648
2007	4,245,877	1,758,328	1,752	1,760,080	230,168	224,562	1,754,474	1,220,504	1,270,899	30,118	140,974	51,287
2008	4,333,875	1,682,618	1,642	1,684,260	228,552	232,933	1,688,641	1,229,768	1,415,466	30,494	142,122	49,583
2009	4,257,870	1,664,128	1,803	1,665,931	231,258	207,061	1,641,734	1,092,990	1,523,146	30,116	141,381	47,289
2010	4,459,819	1,738,168	1,626	1,739,794	239,108	196,563	1,697,249	1,140,652	1,621,918	31,590	141,177	46,761
2011	4,532,023	1,729,685	1,137	1,730,822	219,658	203,719	1,714,883	1,141,717	1,675,423	32,422	139,782	46,578
2012	4,589,955	1,788,193	2,628	1,790,821	228,286	214,962	1,777,497	1,126,143	1,686,315	32,970	139,215	46,871
2013	4,683,400	1,777,534	2,234	1,779,768	253,311	220,623	1,747,080	1,214,064	1,722,256	33,721	138,888	46,808
2014	4,822,799	1,783,606	3,544	1,787,150	255,013	244,791	1,776,928	1,227,976	1,817,895	34,584	139,450	47,078
2015	5,047,158	1,855,921	1,972	1,857,893	262,981	271,030	1,865,942	1,288,047	1,893,169	35,776	141,075	47,834
2016	5,227,042	1,888,562	1,881	1,890,443	271,358	293,572	1,912,657	1,351,690	1,962,695	36,347	143,811	48,738
2017	5,411,622	1,948,397	1,751	1,950,148	283,906	315,022	1,981,264	1,372,204	2,058,154	36,916	146,591	49,671
2018	5,654,987	2,002,928	50	2,002,978	301,181	339,642	2,041,439	1,447,022	2,166,526	37,942	149,044	50,956
2019	6,055,302	2,061,971	400	2,062,371	318,422	364,506	2,108,455	1,619,000	2,327,847	39,985	151,440	51,015
2020	6,529,959	2,105,250	-655	2,104,595	331,828	392,330	2,165,097	1,628,690	2,736,172	42,292	154,403	50,939
2021	7,121,669	2,296,031	-2,287	2,293,744	353,385	437,922	2,378,281	1,686,258	3,057,130	45,050	158,083	52,537

Personal Income and Employment by Area: Hot Springs, AR

(Thousands of dollars, except as noted.)

Year	Personal income, total	Earnings by place of work			Less: Contributions for government social insurance	Plus: Adjustment for residence	Equals: Net earnings by place of residence	Plus: Dividends, interest, and rent	Plus: Personal current transfer receipts	Per capita personal income (dollars)	Population (persons)	Total employment
		Nonfarm	Farm	Total								
1970	173,467	119,289	641	119,930	8,762	-1,571	109,597	37,543	26,327	3,176	54,620	23,344
1971	200,806	139,363	719	140,082	10,589	-1,719	127,774	42,337	30,695	3,510	57,207	25,542
1972	227,659	159,222	1,156	160,378	12,631	-1,443	146,304	46,817	34,538	3,845	59,206	26,849
1973	260,759	180,998	2,534	183,532	16,531	-1,700	165,301	53,861	41,597	4,251	61,347	28,786
1974	298,775	204,407	1,321	205,728	19,377	-938	185,413	63,626	49,736	4,691	63,691	29,920
1975	325,437	209,333	2,726	212,059	19,256	-2,398	190,405	71,302	63,730	5,080	64,058	27,808
1976	370,291	242,384	2,507	244,891	22,333	-949	221,609	80,088	68,594	5,634	65,728	29,099
1977	417,981	275,434	1,754	277,188	25,723	-280	251,185	92,960	73,836	6,190	67,520	30,813
1978	470,699	307,926	2,692	310,618	29,330	545	281,833	107,601	81,265	6,872	68,495	31,529
1979	525,701	337,778	2,588	340,366	33,365	714	307,715	124,754	93,232	7,507	70,026	31,939
1980	603,823	369,045	2,229	371,274	36,186	2,563	337,651	157,200	108,972	8,559	70,545	31,739
1981	681,007	391,403	2,699	394,102	41,789	1,359	353,672	199,633	127,702	9,667	70,445	31,654
1982	732,189	413,381	2,682	416,063	45,082	-3,473	367,508	224,427	140,254	10,381	70,534	31,979
1983	765,712	438,565	1,524	440,089	48,177	-277	391,635	222,344	151,733	10,716	71,455	32,719
1984	837,059	473,557	1,806	475,363	53,759	2,854	424,458	252,442	160,159	11,598	72,172	33,519
1985	891,564	497,825	1,429	499,254	57,652	2,247	443,849	277,151	170,564	12,347	72,209	34,063
1986	937,601	519,566	2,412	521,978	60,434	1,635	463,179	291,075	183,347	12,935	72,487	34,160
1987	974,954	546,713	863	547,576	63,590	1,967	485,953	295,014	193,987	13,311	73,244	34,459
1988	1,028,191	571,580	1,125	572,705	69,363	4,117	507,459	312,355	208,377	14,119	72,821	34,781
1989	1,137,699	604,959	2,193	607,152	74,204	6,208	539,156	369,341	229,202	15,543	73,195	35,525
1990	1,202,719	638,633	1,272	639,905	81,091	9,261	568,075	384,870	249,774	16,350	73,563	35,662
1991	1,271,051	682,663	1,532	684,195	86,841	6,726	604,080	384,381	282,590	16,983	74,844	36,928
1992	1,383,018	745,386	1,842	747,228	94,627	6,072	658,673	407,581	316,764	18,066	76,553	38,245
1993	1,488,981	809,422	4,640	814,062	103,034	3,742	714,770	437,976	336,235	18,951	78,568	40,364
1994	1,577,635	871,695	5,867	877,562	113,501	2,184	766,245	461,584	349,806	19,556	80,673	41,171
1995	1,680,736	937,569	7,341	944,910	121,724	420	823,606	480,916	376,214	20,493	82,015	43,164
1996	1,765,555	972,955	7,369	980,324	125,848	786	855,262	514,027	396,266	21,115	83,615	43,870
1997	1,863,919	1,019,293	8,089	1,027,382	132,076	-500	894,806	549,223	419,890	21,923	85,021	45,357
1998	1,973,673	1,099,347	7,695	1,107,042	140,574	-1,689	964,779	571,983	436,911	22,904	86,172	45,848
1999	2,009,223	1,152,918	6,924	1,159,842	147,049	-3,476	1,009,317	554,122	445,784	23,048	87,177	46,295
2000	2,099,618	1,208,787	3,928	1,212,715	153,070	-3,617	1,056,028	572,976	470,614	23,775	88,311	47,186
2001	2,177,312	1,259,323	3,438	1,262,761	156,158	7,077	1,113,680	544,557	519,075	24,455	89,032	48,005
2002	2,217,309	1,305,901	1,613	1,307,514	161,008	19,251	1,165,757	505,273	546,279	24,738	89,630	47,862
2003	2,321,413	1,379,705	2,413	1,382,118	169,390	30,622	1,243,350	510,454	567,609	25,656	90,483	48,612
2004	2,457,836	1,446,524	3,586	1,450,110	177,333	32,730	1,305,507	552,995	599,334	26,984	91,084	49,727
2005	2,639,667	1,519,912	3,740	1,523,652	188,749	42,784	1,377,687	618,460	643,520	28,662	92,096	51,052
2006	2,867,576	1,599,181	4,435	1,603,616	202,247	67,415	1,468,784	690,321	708,471	30,481	94,077	52,168
2007	3,001,360	1,626,971	7,444	1,634,415	209,643	87,704	1,512,476	733,809	755,075	31,676	94,753	52,990
2008	3,033,486	1,620,097	6,108	1,626,205	214,860	95,614	1,506,959	693,293	833,234	31,719	95,636	52,336
2009	3,032,858	1,608,168	3,208	1,611,376	216,082	85,353	1,480,647	643,099	909,112	31,645	95,840	51,467
2010	3,111,008	1,665,153	2,321	1,667,474	220,796	69,331	1,516,009	637,542	957,457	32,379	96,080	50,918
2011	3,263,355	1,745,502	1,353	1,746,855	208,967	67,460	1,605,348	682,072	975,935	33,683	96,884	51,177
2012	3,409,250	1,841,173	2,291	1,843,464	213,512	51,523	1,681,475	738,972	988,803	35,131	97,043	51,561
2013	3,361,206	1,851,718	3,385	1,855,103	239,897	21,627	1,636,833	715,151	1,009,222	34,391	97,734	51,638
2014	3,553,133	1,888,314	2,855	1,891,169	247,560	25,444	1,669,053	811,803	1,072,277	36,253	98,008	52,148
2015	3,644,454	1,941,530	2,069	1,943,599	255,075	33,503	1,722,027	796,290	1,126,137	37,142	98,121	52,089
2016	3,736,474	1,990,862	1,595	1,992,457	259,837	37,221	1,769,841	798,992	1,167,641	37,902	98,582	52,157
2017	3,839,488	2,095,060	1,959	2,097,019	274,135	33,301	1,856,185	783,541	1,199,762	38,886	98,737	52,343
2018	3,950,037	2,149,262	1,141	2,150,403	283,569	22,610	1,889,444	820,885	1,239,708	39,732	99,417	53,316
2019	4,142,767	2,240,553	1,158	2,241,711	295,924	24,062	1,969,849	852,057	1,320,861	41,510	99,802	53,693
2020	4,454,403	2,320,233	1,800	2,322,033	321,918	28,616	2,028,731	839,727	1,585,945	44,472	100,162	52,175
2021	4,705,205	2,434,385	1,929	2,436,314	332,088	25,888	2,130,114	858,386	1,716,705	46,897	100,330	53,519

Personal Income and Employment by Area: Houma-Thibodaux, LA

(Thousands of dollars, except as noted.)

Year	Personal income, total	Earnings by place of work			Less: Contributions for government social insurance	Plus: Adjustment for residence	Equals: Net earnings by place of residence	Plus: Dividends, interest, and rent	Plus: Personal current transfer receipts	Per capita personal income (dollars)	Population (persons)	Total employment
		Nonfarm	Farm	Total								
1970	423,303	328,870	9,719	338,589	21,274	29,133	346,448	47,657	29,198	2,910	145,445	50,412
1971	468,085	363,406	10,296	373,702	24,071	30,669	380,300	53,522	34,263	3,163	147,993	51,619
1972	516,657	402,699	11,561	414,260	28,022	32,663	418,901	59,174	38,582	3,413	151,395	53,708
1973	583,587	456,134	20,999	477,133	36,898	31,238	471,473	66,501	45,613	3,816	152,931	56,711
1974	685,979	525,971	34,047	560,018	43,757	35,480	551,741	80,827	53,411	4,432	154,770	59,281
1975	791,965	624,045	15,974	640,019	51,256	41,742	630,505	96,568	64,892	4,984	158,910	62,632
1976	922,987	735,221	24,000	759,221	61,058	44,598	742,761	106,845	73,381	5,671	162,751	66,030
1977	1,044,855	840,102	26,866	866,968	70,733	47,446	843,681	120,779	80,395	6,283	166,289	69,860
1978	1,229,617	1,022,063	11,096	1,033,159	88,373	57,282	1,002,068	137,090	90,459	7,248	169,656	75,915
1979	1,417,748	1,194,781	10,196	1,204,977	107,246	60,569	1,158,300	155,954	103,494	8,148	173,998	79,997
1980	1,686,588	1,402,591	7,637	1,410,228	124,425	69,867	1,355,670	205,089	125,829	9,458	178,317	84,311
1981	1,982,295	1,621,737	12,222	1,633,959	154,750	91,968	1,571,177	264,898	146,220	10,787	183,763	88,068
1982	2,100,905	1,648,024	12,443	1,660,467	160,941	101,437	1,600,963	325,181	174,761	11,153	188,371	87,004
1983	2,026,473	1,477,704	7,082	1,484,786	140,742	104,600	1,448,644	355,846	221,983	10,674	189,850	78,980
1984	2,112,315	1,528,496	1,389	1,529,885	150,224	114,505	1,494,166	391,839	226,310	11,145	189,525	79,729
1985	2,161,592	1,541,748	1,402	1,543,150	151,877	120,042	1,511,315	407,687	242,590	11,397	189,669	79,101
1986	2,043,388	1,372,901	2,912	1,375,813	131,002	112,971	1,357,782	396,592	289,014	10,831	188,665	71,653
1987	1,982,983	1,319,396	5,552	1,324,948	124,085	108,649	1,309,512	381,935	291,536	10,723	184,936	70,421
1988	2,106,898	1,405,752	8,702	1,414,454	140,681	126,961	1,400,734	406,929	299,235	11,456	183,916	71,686
1989	2,245,153	1,459,834	9,953	1,469,787	147,345	140,830	1,463,272	452,594	329,287	12,253	183,230	71,631
1990	2,449,660	1,638,318	5,470	1,643,788	170,148	161,035	1,634,675	452,468	362,517	13,397	182,852	75,007
1991	2,591,535	1,719,511	6,979	1,726,490	182,082	166,839	1,711,247	456,314	423,974	14,049	184,458	75,913
1992	2,708,122	1,742,531	9,646	1,752,177	180,380	164,456	1,736,253	470,802	501,067	14,594	185,561	73,772
1993	2,859,910	1,861,746	11,240	1,872,986	196,269	154,328	1,831,045	476,975	551,890	15,369	186,083	77,661
1994	3,063,879	1,995,190	9,383	2,004,573	215,175	158,227	1,947,625	501,883	614,371	16,378	187,077	79,935
1995	3,209,393	2,074,168	10,704	2,084,872	223,948	166,285	2,027,209	557,169	625,015	17,074	187,973	82,540
1996	3,436,755	2,261,051	8,758	2,269,809	243,694	166,024	2,192,139	603,804	640,812	18,157	189,283	86,114
1997	3,819,586	2,606,894	9,871	2,616,765	278,714	165,980	2,504,031	665,850	649,705	19,962	191,339	92,368
1998	4,045,628	2,819,076	8,663	2,827,739	301,210	169,977	2,696,506	710,404	638,718	20,890	193,664	97,205
1999	3,985,448	2,766,418	10,281	2,776,699	291,840	153,362	2,638,221	689,962	657,265	20,483	194,569	95,887
2000	4,329,918	3,039,474	9,093	3,048,567	311,883	138,158	2,874,842	772,369	682,707	22,258	194,531	98,985
2001	4,763,663	3,407,810	9,210	3,417,020	358,268	141,195	3,199,947	777,053	786,663	24,384	195,360	99,867
2002	4,927,127	3,556,404	8,204	3,564,608	374,120	141,422	3,331,910	771,169	824,048	25,050	196,692	102,116
2003	5,086,458	3,677,295	8,064	3,685,359	386,143	147,099	3,446,315	792,976	847,167	25,669	198,156	103,898
2004	5,256,944	3,754,583	8,740	3,763,323	391,040	151,577	3,523,860	793,992	939,092	26,369	199,363	104,125
2005	5,917,807	4,194,455	10,967	4,205,422	422,028	118,387	3,901,781	970,477	1,045,549	29,520	200,467	108,049
2006	7,031,353	5,199,614	28,266	5,227,880	515,947	61,646	4,773,579	1,172,599	1,085,175	34,404	204,379	115,415
2007	7,877,866	5,921,219	12,657	5,933,876	586,578	3,740	5,351,038	1,382,856	1,143,972	38,354	205,401	120,804
2008	8,550,633	6,264,134	30,281	6,294,415	622,315	-21,726	5,650,374	1,605,538	1,294,721	41,296	207,056	123,100
2009	8,181,859	5,995,116	30,116	6,025,232	605,212	-88,445	5,331,575	1,497,075	1,353,209	39,380	207,769	119,739
2010	8,354,679	6,344,661	40,244	6,384,905	626,591	-165,252	5,593,062	1,290,863	1,470,754	40,119	208,245	119,412
2011	8,342,436	6,329,070	40,638	6,369,708	565,649	-229,068	5,574,991	1,293,922	1,473,523	39,969	208,721	118,227
2012	8,866,567	6,768,924	37,365	6,806,289	602,401	-390,484	5,813,404	1,569,038	1,484,125	42,445	208,893	121,800
2013	9,150,434	7,299,930	34,282	7,334,212	748,656	-624,578	5,960,978	1,638,207	1,551,249	43,572	210,008	126,517
2014	9,706,859	7,754,549	25,900	7,780,449	781,634	-678,836	6,319,979	1,854,812	1,532,068	45,969	211,162	129,181
2015	9,389,445	7,119,210	31,129	7,150,339	736,534	-585,299	5,828,506	1,881,057	1,679,882	44,316	211,874	124,487
2016	8,707,271	6,172,418	22,078	6,194,496	649,769	-403,498	5,141,229	1,761,168	1,804,874	41,227	211,203	116,728
2017	8,813,466	6,192,733	20,284	6,213,017	642,002	-360,683	5,210,332	1,701,324	1,901,810	42,062	209,536	113,713
2018	8,955,759	6,369,282	21,688	6,390,970	675,422	-425,518	5,290,030	1,662,112	2,003,617	42,913	208,698	115,344
2019	9,240,137	6,486,671	31,688	6,518,359	686,942	-446,326	5,385,091	1,741,146	2,113,900	44,489	207,696	114,690
2020	9,699,198	6,338,476	31,793	6,370,269	690,305	-431,105	5,248,859	1,720,805	2,729,534	46,898	206,814	109,903
2021	10,230,754	6,467,209	27,984	6,495,193	699,283	-424,268	5,371,642	1,755,452	3,103,660	49,613	206,212	109,770

Personal Income and Employment by Area: Houston-The Woodlands-Sugar Land, TX

(Thousands of dollars, except as noted.)

Year	Personal income, total	Earnings by place of work			Less: Contributions for government social insurance	Plus: Adjustment for residence	Equals: Net earnings by place of residence	Plus: Dividends, interest, and rent	Plus: Personal current transfer receipts	Per capita personal income (dollars)	Population (persons)	Total employment
		Nonfarm	Farm	Total								
1970	9,359,224	8,128,677	28,654	8,157,331	527,413	-74,349	7,555,569	1,305,406	498,249	4,240	2,207,116	1,022,725
1971	10,267,131	8,894,756	28,463	8,923,219	594,467	-117,671	8,211,081	1,458,027	598,023	4,513	2,275,020	1,053,329
1972	11,387,434	9,901,050	32,560	9,933,610	697,119	-153,914	9,082,577	1,620,638	684,219	4,881	2,333,148	1,105,219
1973	12,901,143	11,326,510	64,053	11,390,563	931,233	-205,257	10,254,073	1,831,342	815,728	5,371	2,401,849	1,187,670
1974	15,333,368	13,502,750	60,173	13,562,923	1,140,478	-216,332	12,206,113	2,164,938	962,317	6,183	2,479,921	1,264,423
1975	18,149,058	15,962,486	60,526	16,023,012	1,320,396	-165,827	14,536,789	2,416,939	1,195,330	7,014	2,587,627	1,336,396
1976	20,806,358	18,545,698	27,670	18,573,368	1,570,081	-118,601	16,884,686	2,594,763	1,326,909	7,717	2,696,239	1,417,454
1977	23,738,842	21,411,387	67,965	21,479,352	1,816,811	-185,043	19,477,498	2,848,120	1,413,224	8,477	2,800,536	1,511,549
1978	28,053,834	25,502,679	32,374	25,535,053	2,223,125	-231,447	23,080,481	3,386,542	1,586,811	9,622	2,915,493	1,631,614
1979	32,753,401	29,880,688	67,348	29,948,036	2,726,076	-285,482	26,936,478	4,007,910	1,809,013	10,800	3,032,641	1,734,505
1980	38,342,568	34,806,575	44,589	34,851,164	3,205,119	-344,911	31,301,134	4,901,945	2,139,489	12,085	3,172,859	1,823,264
1981	45,604,291	41,379,084	37,608	41,416,692	4,104,376	-364,642	36,947,674	6,196,987	2,459,630	13,780	3,309,381	1,961,475
1982	50,603,018	45,112,034	17,728	45,129,762	4,584,155	-387,445	40,158,162	7,537,275	2,907,581	14,438	3,504,930	2,009,330
1983	51,615,508	44,694,129	43,932	44,738,061	4,497,421	-366,729	39,873,911	8,279,561	3,462,036	14,316	3,605,388	1,927,450
1984	54,984,610	47,258,042	21,480	47,279,522	4,858,734	-382,208	42,038,580	9,309,380	3,636,650	15,178	3,622,633	1,979,788
1985	57,793,830	48,932,715	91,236	49,023,951	5,058,357	-308,419	43,657,175	10,270,837	3,865,818	15,927	3,628,588	1,979,670
1986	57,624,679	48,113,481	49,160	48,162,641	4,916,134	-272,658	42,973,849	10,283,816	4,367,014	15,710	3,668,133	1,894,904
1987	58,410,772	48,745,125	42,192	48,787,317	4,881,212	-224,470	43,681,635	10,177,848	4,551,289	16,109	3,626,052	1,925,079
1988	63,013,300	52,787,551	112,518	52,900,069	5,486,529	-289,877	47,123,663	11,162,352	4,727,285	17,430	3,615,294	2,000,883
1989	68,672,225	57,955,088	87,195	58,042,283	6,026,368	-345,623	51,670,292	11,855,555	5,146,378	18,711	3,670,089	2,075,840
1990	75,811,049	64,229,024	70,910	64,299,934	6,578,646	-431,247	57,290,041	12,763,722	5,757,286	20,079	3,775,620	2,171,989
1991	80,189,049	68,217,795	95,407	68,313,202	7,166,962	-488,862	60,657,378	13,058,815	6,472,856	20,641	3,884,885	2,231,824
1992	86,984,024	73,858,873	86,891	73,945,764	7,594,953	-517,876	65,832,935	13,343,092	7,807,997	21,802	3,989,770	2,228,085
1993	91,238,366	77,380,665	80,701	77,461,366	7,899,739	-540,777	69,020,850	13,666,607	8,550,909	22,387	4,075,564	2,271,445
1994	95,209,292	80,350,595	100,474	80,451,069	8,337,138	-572,265	71,541,666	14,431,027	9,236,599	22,923	4,153,355	2,333,616
1995	102,555,928	85,862,865	109,662	85,972,527	8,851,912	-622,251	76,498,364	15,981,616	10,075,948	24,259	4,227,574	2,402,453
1996	111,691,346	94,023,956	86,489	94,110,445	9,450,817	-699,915	83,959,713	17,042,104	10,689,529	25,887	4,314,589	2,471,047
1997	123,473,024	105,106,474	103,190	105,209,664	10,346,003	-813,227	94,050,434	18,264,916	11,157,674	28,016	4,407,210	2,579,858
1998	135,954,069	116,187,125	96,728	116,283,853	11,307,087	-915,769	104,060,997	20,493,454	11,399,618	30,119	4,513,913	2,704,046
1999	143,311,526	122,882,811	119,355	123,002,166	11,887,878	-966,359	110,147,929	21,303,515	11,860,082	31,001	4,622,857	2,735,747
2000	157,576,705	134,785,426	86,633	134,872,059	12,816,910	-1,116,483	120,938,666	24,035,859	12,602,180	33,403	4,717,507	2,817,971
2001	166,408,766	143,046,975	91,011	143,137,986	13,603,411	-1,277,626	128,256,949	24,290,971	13,860,846	34,540	4,817,815	2,877,532
2002	165,772,223	141,227,640	98,344	141,325,984	13,726,085	-1,304,586	126,295,313	24,112,738	15,364,172	33,577	4,937,081	2,901,048
2003	172,952,292	145,782,848	142,427	145,925,275	14,246,884	-1,312,866	130,365,525	26,183,942	16,402,825	34,341	5,036,393	2,921,541
2004	186,228,877	157,582,145	158,762	157,740,907	15,097,326	-1,491,241	141,152,340	27,767,142	17,309,395	36,284	5,132,602	2,974,098
2005	203,752,784	169,551,763	149,901	169,701,664	16,153,198	-1,736,719	151,811,747	32,511,712	19,429,325	38,931	5,233,729	3,078,388
2006	228,501,623	189,306,211	154,987	189,461,198	17,472,182	-2,084,706	169,904,310	37,856,145	20,741,168	42,131	5,423,615	3,209,343
2007	244,218,854	201,894,405	115,097	202,009,502	19,068,874	-2,517,084	180,423,544	41,028,668	22,766,642	44,076	5,540,882	3,331,799
2008	272,609,293	219,569,956	95,073	219,665,029	20,213,918	-2,735,468	196,715,643	49,600,386	26,293,264	48,025	5,676,381	3,456,148
2009	256,264,156	206,067,421	69,618	206,137,039	19,990,690	-2,496,857	183,649,492	43,693,651	28,921,013	43,985	5,826,108	3,431,276
2010	272,323,857	217,718,918	56,872	217,775,790	20,546,425	-2,417,936	194,811,429	44,761,491	32,750,937	45,790	5,947,185	3,435,171
2011	295,639,668	235,971,237	35,702	236,006,939	19,425,557	-2,806,666	213,774,716	47,709,192	34,155,760	48,818	6,056,008	3,546,818
2012	326,338,142	258,966,085	77,881	259,043,966	20,883,791	-3,262,915	234,897,260	57,452,848	33,988,034	52,779	6,183,119	3,675,499
2013	332,017,267	267,753,821	78,031	267,831,852	25,025,010	-3,500,509	239,306,333	57,460,160	35,250,774	52,471	6,327,622	3,809,180
2014	360,312,797	290,407,089	25,612	290,432,701	26,755,411	-3,881,861	259,795,429	63,335,200	37,182,168	55,485	6,493,835	3,950,496
2015	367,009,212	289,988,916	74,678	290,063,594	27,701,851	-3,873,743	258,488,000	68,590,053	39,931,159	55,077	6,663,596	4,049,921
2016	351,069,749	281,333,060	28,091	281,361,151	27,619,756	-3,676,531	250,064,864	58,685,229	42,319,656	51,648	6,797,324	4,043,183
2017	378,069,999	294,874,390	34,709	294,909,099	28,669,741	-3,310,278	262,929,080	71,174,826	43,966,093	54,888	6,888,064	4,165,289
2018	403,712,321	316,478,096	6,143	316,484,239	30,021,505	-3,587,894	282,874,840	74,998,456	45,839,025	57,986	6,962,207	4,297,373
2019	424,133,763	325,150,160	-3,063	325,147,097	31,200,173	-3,869,779	290,077,145	85,426,195	48,630,423	60,173	7,048,589	4,384,581
2020	436,352,682	317,338,355	23,205	317,361,560	30,844,010	-3,477,506	283,040,044	84,677,452	68,635,186	61,133	7,137,747	4,328,344
2021	467,267,288	336,197,423	37,951	336,235,374	32,273,303	-3,453,156	300,508,915	88,711,500	78,046,873	64,837	7,206,841	4,436,737

Personal Income and Employment by Area: Huntington-Ashland, WV-KY-OH

(Thousands of dollars, except as noted.)

Year	Personal income, total	Nonfarm	Farm	Total	Less: Contributions for government social insurance	Plus: Adjustment for residence	Equals: Net earnings by place of residence	Plus: Dividends, interest, and rent	Plus: Personal current transfer receipts	Per capita personal income (dollars)	Population (persons)	Total employment
1970	1,061,462	857,286	4,535	861,821	66,999	9,325	804,147	126,820	130,495	3,175	334,330	119,730
1971	1,160,546	923,446	3,869	927,315	73,953	14,265	867,627	139,138	153,781	3,412	340,145	121,125
1972	1,246,078	978,721	5,675	984,396	81,687	22,351	925,060	150,575	170,443	3,628	343,475	120,225
1973	1,377,893	1,080,280	7,086	1,087,366	102,949	27,085	1,011,502	169,962	196,429	4,017	342,989	123,834
1974	1,552,031	1,193,458	6,952	1,200,410	117,003	41,787	1,125,194	198,127	228,710	4,507	344,384	126,438
1975	1,733,898	1,297,338	7,304	1,304,642	125,815	53,081	1,231,908	222,855	279,135	4,995	347,122	126,903
1976	1,959,834	1,492,663	6,858	1,499,521	147,512	57,738	1,409,747	246,611	303,476	5,516	355,311	131,120
1977	2,196,243	1,685,871	5,480	1,691,351	165,477	69,580	1,595,454	280,731	320,058	6,085	360,951	136,556
1978	2,467,240	1,919,632	4,395	1,924,027	194,916	81,807	1,810,918	307,691	348,631	6,766	364,651	141,485
1979	2,773,857	2,157,547	2,983	2,160,530	226,166	96,091	2,030,455	344,191	399,211	7,497	370,018	143,365
1980	3,049,638	2,268,394	1,439	2,269,833	238,617	110,021	2,141,237	419,254	489,147	8,171	373,228	141,228
1981	3,299,515	2,400,698	2,632	2,403,330	271,413	103,947	2,235,864	512,416	551,235	8,852	372,735	138,629
1982	3,444,302	2,402,798	4,214	2,407,012	280,021	122,566	2,249,557	585,926	608,819	9,287	370,867	132,782
1983	3,548,829	2,409,359	-247	2,409,112	283,358	129,416	2,255,170	620,604	673,055	9,541	371,942	129,173
1984	3,822,421	2,586,737	6,685	2,593,422	311,280	150,405	2,432,547	693,126	696,748	10,361	368,941	131,431
1985	4,024,213	2,719,706	3,597	2,723,303	331,973	166,246	2,557,576	723,641	742,996	11,008	365,559	132,535
1986	4,143,169	2,787,128	1,026	2,788,154	353,825	176,771	2,611,100	750,755	781,314	11,473	361,118	133,493
1987	4,313,934	2,948,968	-1,505	2,947,463	371,417	177,330	2,753,376	746,120	814,438	12,049	358,041	135,685
1988	4,573,525	3,169,933	-1,587	3,168,346	414,365	179,757	2,933,738	783,506	856,281	12,885	354,959	139,421
1989	4,879,764	3,345,023	447	3,345,470	441,148	186,775	3,091,097	874,051	914,616	13,805	353,470	142,984
1990	5,197,872	3,589,578	3,579	3,593,157	481,096	204,166	3,316,227	888,590	993,055	14,744	352,539	148,238
1991	5,426,046	3,698,340	5,010	3,703,350	503,022	217,675	3,418,003	900,025	1,108,018	15,291	354,853	148,269
1992	5,883,409	4,018,230	6,060	4,024,290	538,780	238,521	3,724,031	916,932	1,242,446	16,481	356,976	151,101
1993	6,088,680	4,129,321	3,146	4,132,467	571,443	262,601	3,823,625	947,059	1,317,996	16,901	360,258	152,539
1994	6,338,896	4,321,992	5,192	4,327,184	599,514	265,036	3,992,706	983,590	1,362,600	17,527	361,659	156,273
1995	6,551,783	4,362,824	1,321	4,364,145	614,520	312,979	4,062,604	1,048,263	1,440,916	18,064	362,701	159,781
1996	6,808,380	4,457,383	-24	4,457,359	631,305	350,363	4,176,417	1,117,236	1,514,727	18,755	363,025	161,222
1997	7,169,614	4,687,313	2,050	4,689,363	655,381	375,208	4,409,190	1,187,730	1,572,694	19,738	363,240	163,757
1998	7,507,145	4,905,959	2,222	4,908,181	686,548	382,341	4,603,974	1,259,971	1,643,200	20,421	367,621	171,051
1999	7,672,573	5,056,626	-3,163	5,053,463	706,841	404,423	4,751,045	1,219,288	1,702,240	20,896	367,182	172,069
2000	8,057,423	5,275,115	3,479	5,278,594	745,464	419,546	4,952,676	1,301,156	1,803,591	21,958	366,942	172,735
2001	8,493,002	5,496,742	-1,508	5,495,234	751,470	434,541	5,178,305	1,324,543	1,990,154	23,218	365,792	170,396
2002	8,802,265	5,690,985	-4,827	5,686,158	761,600	441,576	5,366,134	1,294,844	2,141,287	24,066	365,758	169,975
2003	9,032,897	5,904,831	-1,507	5,903,324	798,864	425,923	5,530,383	1,292,161	2,210,353	24,599	367,208	171,333
2004	9,238,899	6,159,946	543	6,160,489	824,917	393,443	5,729,015	1,237,577	2,272,307	25,165	367,134	173,535
2005	9,594,758	6,364,069	-1,591	6,362,478	853,413	420,049	5,929,114	1,268,570	2,397,074	26,110	367,471	174,516
2006	10,216,091	6,717,832	-4,507	6,713,325	873,590	453,437	6,293,172	1,375,593	2,547,326	27,707	368,725	176,397
2007	10,787,349	7,035,447	-8,215	7,027,232	888,756	414,706	6,553,182	1,528,126	2,706,041	29,213	369,267	180,405
2008	11,532,409	7,396,125	-9,612	7,386,513	914,290	370,854	6,843,077	1,680,826	3,008,506	31,188	369,769	180,445
2009	11,722,190	7,333,650	-6,008	7,327,642	916,770	445,913	6,856,785	1,612,222	3,253,183	31,620	370,722	174,367
2010	12,052,439	7,561,061	-7,958	7,553,103	935,788	469,589	7,086,904	1,562,558	3,402,977	32,481	371,061	173,771
2011	12,551,937	7,791,408	-6,107	7,785,301	854,609	417,329	7,348,021	1,754,197	3,449,719	33,817	371,168	174,018
2012	12,787,414	7,954,760	-3,806	7,950,954	877,637	418,432	7,491,749	1,814,560	3,481,105	34,462	371,060	174,889
2013	12,690,202	7,982,042	-2,121	7,979,921	982,376	400,356	7,397,901	1,748,637	3,543,664	34,267	370,333	173,872
2014	13,131,180	8,194,547	-6,512	8,188,035	1,021,072	382,764	7,549,727	1,825,109	3,756,344	35,364	371,320	174,352
2015	13,528,464	8,319,651	-3,779	8,315,872	1,036,367	453,613	7,733,118	1,894,006	3,901,340	36,546	370,178	173,640
2016	13,438,619	8,109,926	-6,522	8,103,404	1,038,740	531,295	7,595,959	1,880,318	3,962,342	36,463	368,557	171,957
2017	13,814,299	8,353,351	-8,521	8,344,830	1,062,926	535,896	7,817,800	1,915,263	4,081,236	37,741	366,030	172,720
2018	14,483,600	8,810,745	-8,967	8,801,778	1,107,754	628,888	8,322,912	1,979,130	4,181,558	39,838	363,565	172,742
2019	14,875,730	9,068,769	-6,857	9,061,912	1,131,235	466,691	8,397,368	2,144,810	4,333,552	41,213	360,946	172,308
2020	15,893,124	9,083,048	-6,054	9,076,994	1,162,947	421,674	8,335,721	2,144,731	5,412,672	44,258	359,100	166,073
2021	16,939,356	9,466,862	-6,178	9,460,684	1,198,533	529,912	8,792,063	2,203,224	5,944,069	47,505	356,581	169,239

Personal Income and Employment by Area: Huntsville, AL

(Thousands of dollars, except as noted.)

Year	Personal income, total	Earnings by place of work			Less: Contributions for government social insurance	Plus: Adjustment for residence	Equals: Net earnings by place of residence	Plus: Dividends, interest, and rent	Plus: Personal current transfer receipts	Per capita personal income (dollars)	Population (persons)	Total employment
		Nonfarm	Farm	Total								
1970	904,666	873,867	19,625	893,492	43,750	-126,294	723,448	133,007	48,211	3,962	228,314	107,133
1971	999,215	955,338	26,234	981,572	48,042	-144,472	789,058	154,603	55,554	4,335	230,509	106,235
1972	1,083,376	1,029,043	26,466	1,055,509	55,275	-147,449	852,785	168,389	62,202	4,663	232,339	109,439
1973	1,167,328	1,086,939	35,145	1,122,084	68,262	-147,250	906,572	186,355	74,401	5,005	233,247	111,439
1974	1,257,789	1,154,541	29,060	1,183,601	76,269	-150,845	956,487	209,969	91,333	5,424	231,872	112,513
1975	1,339,700	1,205,924	21,649	1,227,573	81,776	-154,615	991,182	226,889	121,629	5,770	232,194	110,559
1976	1,487,058	1,332,981	31,163	1,364,144	95,385	-159,128	1,109,631	245,271	132,156	6,337	234,646	113,836
1977	1,626,884	1,482,801	18,543	1,501,344	109,274	-172,591	1,219,479	271,369	136,036	6,866	236,952	119,368
1978	1,830,708	1,662,427	24,866	1,687,293	126,390	-187,817	1,373,086	311,502	146,120	7,689	238,094	125,751
1979	2,019,757	1,831,386	33,993	1,865,379	145,226	-216,300	1,503,853	345,885	170,019	8,417	239,958	126,654
1980	2,232,060	2,012,098	6,819	2,018,917	157,763	-251,689	1,609,465	412,593	210,002	9,162	243,620	126,604
1981	2,507,130	2,237,668	29,027	2,266,695	190,810	-291,987	1,783,898	490,528	232,704	10,201	245,771	128,803
1982	2,743,765	2,442,661	28,965	2,471,626	213,585	-323,357	1,934,684	551,924	257,157	11,012	249,166	131,353
1983	3,024,815	2,809,057	-7,338	2,801,719	263,464	-384,785	2,153,470	591,960	279,385	11,915	253,867	139,295
1984	3,462,975	3,244,000	23,922	3,267,922	312,351	-460,090	2,495,481	672,356	295,138	13,401	258,407	149,177
1985	3,844,542	3,677,065	18,660	3,695,725	365,035	-545,450	2,785,240	740,936	318,366	14,530	264,588	158,683
1986	4,172,807	4,038,312	10,465	4,048,777	407,722	-603,322	3,037,733	797,364	337,710	15,441	270,237	166,030
1987	4,552,696	4,420,443	13,831	4,434,274	445,998	-646,247	3,342,029	865,399	345,268	16,454	276,697	174,660
1988	4,987,694	4,878,755	28,462	4,907,217	508,593	-740,551	3,658,073	963,425	366,196	17,577	283,769	182,016
1989	5,414,253	5,178,900	20,431	5,199,331	546,312	-765,364	3,887,655	1,105,746	420,852	18,696	289,588	186,585
1990	5,788,609	5,560,434	14,241	5,574,675	604,328	-829,780	4,140,567	1,181,084	466,958	19,666	294,353	191,461
1991	6,154,316	5,840,931	30,927	5,871,858	640,791	-832,534	4,398,533	1,221,703	534,080	20,375	302,052	192,008
1992	6,694,265	6,378,932	32,797	6,411,729	699,801	-918,549	4,793,379	1,293,851	607,035	21,513	311,170	195,615
1993	6,873,823	6,538,408	18,591	6,556,999	726,486	-941,644	4,888,869	1,334,485	650,469	21,414	320,998	200,042
1994	7,106,675	6,691,189	42,729	6,733,918	762,922	-985,929	4,985,067	1,441,410	680,198	21,825	325,620	196,887
1995	7,446,835	6,941,009	6,460	6,947,469	796,018	-1,037,016	5,114,435	1,589,373	743,027	22,873	325,571	200,903
1996	7,759,869	7,047,168	37,511	7,084,679	811,714	-989,520	5,283,445	1,679,751	796,673	23,692	327,532	204,454
1997	8,269,832	7,431,943	8,422	7,440,365	861,785	-949,176	5,629,404	1,801,077	839,351	25,039	330,281	209,852
1998	8,860,948	7,954,029	24,699	7,978,728	917,217	-988,959	6,072,552	1,922,638	865,758	26,331	336,527	216,761
1999	9,085,323	8,172,540	27,566	8,200,106	952,310	-999,169	6,248,627	1,916,053	920,643	26,755	339,572	218,936
2000	9,775,967	8,740,684	31,325	8,772,009	1,015,421	-1,059,724	6,696,864	2,073,635	1,005,468	28,421	343,972	224,393
2001	10,042,730	8,995,422	26,206	9,021,628	1,034,389	-1,099,829	6,887,410	2,023,079	1,132,241	28,821	348,453	226,046
2002	10,387,539	9,419,376	-4,581	9,414,795	1,082,576	-1,164,233	7,167,986	1,981,849	1,237,704	29,334	354,116	225,574
2003	11,037,524	10,008,306	55,126	10,063,432	1,151,578	-1,250,196	7,661,658	2,036,414	1,339,452	30,667	359,920	230,523
2004	11,818,781	10,541,192	78,134	10,619,326	1,203,659	-1,268,339	8,147,328	2,233,484	1,437,969	32,358	365,248	237,472
2005	12,737,602	11,252,033	61,034	11,313,067	1,288,577	-1,349,335	8,675,155	2,488,926	1,573,521	34,169	372,777	244,689
2006	13,782,532	12,121,847	54,221	12,176,068	1,388,149	-1,475,261	9,312,658	2,737,861	1,732,013	36,003	382,821	252,344
2007	14,819,108	12,825,620	35,478	12,861,098	1,478,082	-1,491,648	9,891,368	3,021,648	1,906,092	37,811	391,922	263,130
2008	15,958,149	13,400,036	56,103	13,456,139	1,566,758	-1,475,356	10,414,025	3,349,746	2,194,378	39,661	402,361	267,107
2009	16,094,944	13,748,559	35,274	13,783,833	1,601,339	-1,511,384	10,671,110	3,031,466	2,392,368	39,048	412,182	262,881
2010	16,973,698	14,210,953	1,112	14,212,065	1,670,117	-1,471,486	11,070,462	3,214,718	2,688,518	40,483	419,282	262,764
2011	17,935,177	14,662,082	34,234	14,696,316	1,525,538	-1,485,955	11,684,823	3,438,752	2,811,602	42,183	425,176	266,691
2012	18,465,534	14,923,818	39,038	14,962,856	1,558,473	-1,456,825	11,947,558	3,668,248	2,849,728	42,927	430,159	267,871
2013	18,654,253	15,220,288	92,305	15,312,593	1,814,591	-1,437,922	12,060,080	3,635,315	2,958,858	42,815	435,695	271,685
2014	19,301,903	15,734,373	31,400	15,765,773	1,871,456	-1,500,253	12,394,064	3,787,349	3,120,490	43,336	445,402	274,586
2015	20,186,182	16,302,087	18,141	16,320,228	1,945,000	-1,530,200	12,845,028	3,976,599	3,364,555	44,780	450,781	280,653
2016	20,958,416	16,861,369	3,712	16,865,081	1,989,946	-1,507,812	13,367,323	4,118,519	3,472,574	45,852	457,090	287,070
2017	21,886,301	17,621,093	14,762	17,635,855	2,082,834	-1,549,555	14,003,466	4,282,016	3,600,819	47,100	464,678	294,036
2018	23,165,217	18,682,399	3,514	18,685,913	2,217,574	-1,581,808	14,886,531	4,460,977	3,817,709	48,936	473,379	302,005
2019	24,810,646	19,945,435	10,289	19,955,724	2,360,075	-1,617,123	15,978,526	4,739,780	4,092,340	51,384	482,846	309,020
2020	26,962,074	21,382,444	15,281	21,397,725	2,531,621	-1,769,950	17,096,154	4,741,436	5,124,484	54,577	494,018	309,955
2021	29,065,186	22,816,132	56,147	22,872,279	2,674,120	-1,768,959	18,429,200	4,844,588	5,791,398	57,815	502,728	322,289

Personal Income and Employment by Area: Idaho Falls, ID

(Thousands of dollars, except as noted.)

Year	Personal income, total	Earnings by place of work Nonfarm	Earnings by place of work Farm	Earnings by place of work Total	Less: Contributions for government social insurance	Plus: Adjustment for residence	Equals: Net earnings by place of residence	Plus: Dividends, interest, and rent	Plus: Personal current transfer receipts	Per capita personal income (dollars)	Population (persons)	Total employment
1970	249,121	198,596	24,705	223,301	14,927	-10,811	197,563	34,689	16,869	3,705	67,248	31,286
1971	269,269	212,764	23,431	236,195	16,559	-10,097	209,539	39,780	19,950	4,001	67,297	31,832
1972	304,063	241,079	26,886	267,965	19,582	-10,943	237,440	43,715	22,908	4,370	69,575	33,559
1973	351,493	266,228	44,126	310,354	24,925	-11,685	273,744	51,777	25,972	5,006	70,208	34,784
1974	410,130	302,807	57,679	360,486	29,228	-11,978	319,280	60,750	30,100	5,605	73,174	36,116
1975	444,191	347,607	34,227	381,834	33,247	-13,891	334,696	71,791	37,704	5,906	75,210	37,509
1976	500,212	408,781	27,596	436,377	39,932	-18,324	378,121	77,337	44,754	6,487	77,106	40,884
1977	553,282	469,082	20,883	489,965	46,295	-23,854	419,816	87,235	46,231	6,943	79,685	43,056
1978	616,679	536,043	21,740	557,783	53,797	-32,363	471,623	97,935	47,121	7,444	82,839	45,361
1979	664,981	583,963	15,097	599,060	61,177	-37,303	500,580	108,652	55,749	7,902	84,150	44,826
1980	748,365	627,866	31,508	659,374	65,989	-37,807	555,578	126,756	66,031	8,808	84,969	44,180
1981	819,037	667,660	40,290	707,950	74,874	-41,904	591,172	151,485	76,380	9,496	86,247	42,968
1982	861,468	687,115	38,654	725,769	78,757	-45,064	601,948	176,989	82,531	10,023	85,951	42,575
1983	934,549	741,751	50,722	792,473	85,383	-53,762	653,328	191,574	89,647	10,764	86,820	43,606
1984	1,013,489	817,070	41,824	858,894	96,249	-53,399	709,246	210,053	94,190	11,556	87,700	44,662
1985	1,104,973	897,409	41,031	938,440	107,543	-58,347	772,550	230,968	101,455	12,538	88,130	46,059
1986	1,148,805	949,246	40,198	989,444	114,285	-67,189	807,970	232,031	108,804	12,948	88,724	46,656
1987	1,206,166	1,003,024	46,630	1,049,654	118,797	-71,136	859,721	232,376	114,069	13,419	89,885	47,643
1988	1,284,775	1,066,947	41,180	1,108,127	125,814	-66,438	915,875	244,333	124,567	14,226	90,313	49,146
1989	1,411,362	1,139,087	62,426	1,201,513	136,728	-67,336	997,449	278,162	135,751	15,569	90,651	50,522
1990	1,526,182	1,256,424	76,906	1,333,330	162,007	-79,336	1,091,987	284,342	149,853	16,569	92,109	53,055
1991	1,594,702	1,345,490	56,415	1,401,905	176,974	-94,526	1,130,405	296,781	167,516	16,827	94,772	55,402
1992	1,730,733	1,444,051	65,525	1,509,576	187,529	-98,697	1,223,350	316,630	190,753	17,770	97,397	56,340
1993	1,832,141	1,520,859	76,074	1,596,933	197,824	-106,344	1,292,765	331,296	208,080	18,514	98,961	58,099
1994	1,897,700	1,576,824	49,431	1,626,255	209,700	-100,477	1,316,078	359,809	221,813	18,914	100,332	59,318
1995	1,977,785	1,601,801	59,956	1,661,757	217,304	-99,172	1,345,281	388,224	244,280	19,623	100,789	58,985
1996	2,036,575	1,661,754	64,420	1,726,174	224,566	-139,057	1,362,551	413,029	260,995	20,202	100,809	60,883
1997	2,124,714	1,743,803	48,598	1,792,401	234,734	-143,215	1,414,452	437,547	272,715	20,932	101,505	62,038
1998	2,251,788	1,859,080	62,680	1,921,760	248,314	-151,122	1,522,324	452,134	277,330	21,985	102,425	63,214
1999	2,371,014	1,954,862	72,803	2,027,665	258,050	-146,309	1,623,306	449,099	298,609	22,919	103,450	64,963
2000	2,534,579	2,080,952	80,240	2,161,192	274,220	-158,336	1,728,636	476,850	329,093	24,126	105,055	66,613
2001	2,725,497	2,239,280	76,805	2,316,085	267,143	-193,621	1,855,321	505,941	364,235	25,692	106,082	67,441
2002	2,851,800	2,341,230	110,099	2,451,329	279,253	-194,554	1,977,522	484,013	390,265	26,462	107,768	68,159
2003	2,992,359	2,446,016	62,030	2,508,046	294,923	-195,111	2,018,012	558,536	415,811	27,219	109,937	70,441
2004	3,263,528	2,581,460	102,479	2,683,939	311,420	-179,185	2,193,334	615,223	454,971	28,838	113,168	72,823
2005	3,545,825	2,752,800	71,676	2,824,476	333,388	-184,490	2,306,598	742,353	496,874	30,513	116,208	76,232
2006	3,945,651	3,066,014	90,193	3,156,207	368,773	-195,770	2,591,664	803,809	550,178	32,886	119,981	79,150
2007	4,238,031	3,207,009	134,896	3,341,905	390,283	-199,333	2,752,289	901,220	584,522	34,122	124,203	82,923
2008	4,373,909	3,180,720	137,574	3,318,294	401,827	-172,303	2,744,164	954,162	675,583	34,077	128,353	82,656
2009	4,247,176	3,269,615	98,234	3,367,849	410,042	-163,250	2,794,557	729,014	723,605	32,268	131,621	80,095
2010	4,412,663	3,395,392	89,471	3,484,863	435,459	-193,223	2,856,181	764,398	792,084	32,975	133,818	80,052
2011	4,594,392	3,340,142	125,101	3,465,243	388,488	-198,645	2,878,110	916,565	799,717	34,038	134,980	80,140
2012	4,885,503	3,443,475	102,153	3,545,628	391,065	-160,012	2,994,551	1,067,217	823,735	35,873	136,188	79,832
2013	4,929,559	3,591,116	125,433	3,716,549	441,543	-153,295	3,121,711	954,739	853,109	36,013	136,881	81,086
2014	5,116,149	3,736,209	108,870	3,845,079	452,719	-142,882	3,249,478	985,490	881,181	36,815	138,970	82,824
2015	5,596,854	4,030,037	120,123	4,150,160	481,170	-175,851	3,493,139	1,154,500	949,215	39,702	140,971	85,576
2016	5,972,481	4,192,580	110,129	4,302,709	505,248	-195,499	3,601,962	1,376,878	993,641	41,418	144,201	88,726
2017	6,345,829	4,551,507	58,237	4,609,744	543,996	-238,328	3,827,420	1,481,189	1,037,220	42,999	147,582	91,228
2018	6,710,681	4,915,148	76,438	4,991,586	580,046	-266,576	4,144,964	1,458,272	1,107,445	44,460	150,939	94,340
2019	7,443,996	5,642,747	106,723	5,749,470	630,285	-319,936	4,799,249	1,450,384	1,194,363	48,207	154,417	96,643
2020	8,227,029	6,174,409	122,314	6,296,723	691,721	-355,580	5,249,422	1,478,537	1,499,070	51,985	158,258	99,439
2021	8,966,946	6,684,399	64,729	6,749,128	731,275	-381,735	5,636,118	1,528,505	1,802,323	55,084	162,786	104,151

Personal Income and Employment by Area: Indianapolis-Carmel-Anderson, IN

(Thousands of dollars, except as noted.)

Year	Personal income, total	Earnings by place of work			Less: Contributions for government social insurance	Plus: Adjustment for residence	Equals: Net earnings by place of residence	Plus: Dividends, interest, and rent	Plus: Personal current transfer receipts	Per capita personal income (dollars)	Population (persons)	Total employment
		Nonfarm	Farm	Total								
1970	5,360,907	4,622,519	39,661	4,662,180	310,573	-84,768	4,266,839	739,463	354,605	4,164	1,287,512	599,216
1971	5,839,732	4,978,349	70,109	5,048,458	346,518	-95,670	4,606,270	812,287	421,175	4,506	1,295,884	600,061
1972	6,365,329	5,482,566	56,661	5,539,227	404,591	-106,019	5,028,617	870,883	465,829	4,872	1,306,519	616,990
1973	7,184,781	6,138,364	152,176	6,290,540	522,040	-121,213	5,647,287	979,685	557,809	5,478	1,311,545	646,904
1974	7,780,405	6,615,844	91,430	6,707,274	584,815	-131,081	5,991,378	1,125,819	663,208	5,892	1,320,524	656,064
1975	8,387,294	6,899,935	137,348	7,037,283	599,376	-139,061	6,298,846	1,243,125	845,323	6,362	1,318,435	637,432
1976	9,268,165	7,728,948	139,556	7,868,504	683,115	-153,850	7,031,539	1,336,461	900,165	7,010	1,322,178	654,608
1977	10,288,075	8,706,575	91,621	8,798,196	771,125	-171,716	7,855,355	1,484,625	948,095	7,749	1,327,653	676,374
1978	11,464,111	9,736,240	100,568	9,836,808	887,910	-191,630	8,757,268	1,664,203	1,042,640	8,574	1,337,003	701,877
1979	12,664,452	10,755,794	91,570	10,847,364	1,017,331	-212,498	9,617,535	1,852,067	1,194,850	9,435	1,342,252	718,694
1980	13,863,701	11,281,584	71,980	11,353,564	1,059,244	-217,028	10,077,292	2,260,333	1,526,076	10,279	1,348,738	706,615
1981	15,190,610	12,131,363	55,427	12,186,790	1,227,322	-225,997	10,733,471	2,783,736	1,673,403	11,247	1,350,644	699,352
1982	15,720,656	12,254,495	47,358	12,301,853	1,262,594	-208,770	10,830,489	3,047,390	1,842,777	11,633	1,351,396	681,888
1983	16,745,780	13,091,688	-12,281	13,079,407	1,354,195	-201,043	11,524,169	3,230,212	1,991,399	12,381	1,352,538	690,577
1984	18,595,927	14,633,969	91,586	14,725,555	1,547,881	-260,579	12,917,095	3,588,011	2,090,821	13,664	1,360,966	724,435
1985	19,978,591	15,837,763	91,139	15,928,902	1,707,527	-284,544	13,936,831	3,833,871	2,207,889	14,612	1,367,229	748,013
1986	21,288,267	17,030,091	52,965	17,083,056	1,846,264	-312,443	14,924,349	4,023,180	2,340,738	15,479	1,375,291	774,534
1987	22,729,803	18,361,542	78,028	18,439,570	1,969,893	-321,382	16,148,295	4,191,441	2,390,067	16,370	1,388,481	801,322
1988	24,601,442	19,975,913	34,077	20,009,990	2,210,822	-334,944	17,464,224	4,588,349	2,548,869	17,595	1,398,243	826,484
1989	26,893,524	21,482,143	107,608	21,589,751	2,383,415	-369,621	18,836,715	5,279,662	2,777,147	19,048	1,411,888	856,717
1990	28,818,108	22,980,471	102,593	23,083,064	2,636,267	-397,893	20,048,904	5,747,817	3,021,387	20,134	1,431,307	881,268
1991	30,124,193	24,337,484	23,006	24,360,490	2,823,491	-409,169	21,127,830	5,637,070	3,359,293	20,669	1,457,442	887,840
1992	32,604,860	26,165,767	93,135	26,258,902	3,012,842	-360,895	22,885,165	5,855,270	3,864,425	22,015	1,481,005	898,464
1993	34,567,038	27,711,309	120,286	27,831,595	3,201,070	-359,879	24,270,646	6,195,997	4,100,395	22,961	1,505,485	922,306
1994	36,964,595	29,621,276	94,716	29,715,992	3,476,896	-356,744	25,882,352	6,785,940	4,296,303	24,169	1,529,405	948,056
1995	38,684,993	30,873,402	43,899	30,917,301	3,642,370	-346,062	26,928,869	7,394,706	4,361,418	24,934	1,551,504	975,060
1996	40,957,147	32,614,207	137,691	32,751,898	3,801,785	-371,019	28,579,094	7,841,308	4,536,745	26,027	1,573,626	992,151
1997	43,291,995	34,702,931	135,600	34,838,531	4,032,517	-395,362	30,410,652	8,183,773	4,697,570	27,145	1,594,815	1,015,309
1998	47,723,363	38,270,405	82,284	38,352,689	4,339,653	-478,054	33,534,982	9,351,396	4,836,985	29,542	1,615,438	1,044,041
1999	50,130,126	40,931,923	52,781	40,984,704	4,606,376	-510,985	35,867,343	9,162,900	5,099,883	30,576	1,639,509	1,070,835
2000	54,675,471	44,493,137	99,289	44,592,426	4,924,340	-560,648	39,107,438	10,018,078	5,549,955	32,858	1,663,995	1,099,383
2001	56,490,132	45,999,363	116,763	46,116,126	5,039,789	-644,793	40,431,544	9,913,370	6,145,218	33,481	1,687,209	1,095,475
2002	57,278,128	46,824,827	55,033	46,879,860	5,147,929	-667,603	41,064,328	9,634,568	6,579,232	33,535	1,708,018	1,089,132
2003	58,548,187	47,640,695	139,141	47,779,836	5,310,240	-686,371	41,783,225	9,868,850	6,896,112	33,857	1,729,297	1,096,058
2004	61,499,021	50,084,514	233,312	50,317,826	5,612,409	-766,909	43,938,508	10,265,300	7,295,213	35,129	1,750,639	1,114,589
2005	63,964,885	51,987,105	145,905	52,133,010	5,887,014	-805,520	45,440,476	10,575,049	7,949,360	36,078	1,772,959	1,133,886
2006	68,360,752	55,021,414	125,043	55,146,457	6,242,263	-835,701	48,068,493	11,723,232	8,569,027	37,963	1,800,724	1,153,305
2007	70,434,313	56,357,800	165,386	56,523,186	6,437,311	-811,353	49,274,522	12,099,491	9,060,300	38,562	1,826,515	1,176,677
2008	74,527,950	58,461,554	268,002	58,729,556	6,674,876	-767,475	51,287,205	12,590,409	10,650,336	40,278	1,850,321	1,180,108
2009	74,501,729	58,378,065	294,493	58,672,558	6,540,780	-813,877	51,317,901	11,333,979	11,849,849	39,767	1,873,460	1,141,299
2010	78,884,140	61,761,057	215,787	61,976,844	6,650,553	-856,638	54,469,653	11,484,697	12,929,790	41,679	1,892,663	1,141,412
2011	84,516,339	65,525,318	322,770	65,848,088	6,138,130	-756,793	58,953,165	12,507,869	13,055,305	44,229	1,910,895	1,165,477
2012	88,643,748	68,666,381	183,066	68,849,447	6,426,397	-626,210	61,796,840	13,507,222	13,339,686	45,929	1,930,010	1,190,492
2013	89,951,268	70,389,473	559,495	70,948,968	7,554,321	-603,946	62,790,701	13,589,643	13,570,924	46,032	1,954,103	1,214,285
2014	93,705,932	72,841,810	180,841	73,022,651	7,816,483	-587,557	64,618,611	14,583,351	14,503,970	47,305	1,980,873	1,239,086
2015	98,473,894	76,527,799	-10,297	76,517,502	8,197,184	-534,073	67,786,245	15,652,431	15,035,218	49,275	1,998,456	1,269,276
2016	102,561,594	79,968,022	93,394	80,061,416	8,479,534	-584,523	70,997,359	16,204,367	15,359,868	50,729	2,021,771	1,299,022
2017	105,972,823	82,742,113	85,028	82,827,141	8,840,397	-597,826	73,388,918	16,877,645	15,706,260	51,813	2,045,301	1,328,759
2018	112,303,934	87,408,961	92,307	87,501,268	9,268,292	-566,008	77,666,968	18,191,320	16,445,646	54,193	2,072,279	1,355,116
2019	119,720,576	93,297,753	64,301	93,362,054	9,830,585	-690,105	82,841,364	19,373,115	17,506,097	57,156	2,094,610	1,369,664
2020	129,263,715	97,815,199	207,037	98,022,236	10,376,350	-941,093	86,704,793	19,729,148	22,829,774	61,155	2,113,700	1,337,920
2021	139,954,077	105,153,566	279,484	105,433,050	10,933,402	-1,221,420	93,278,228	20,347,728	26,328,121	65,805	2,126,804	1,384,606

Personal Income and Employment by Area: Iowa City, IA

(Thousands of dollars, except as noted.)

Year	Personal income, total	Earnings by place of work			Less: Contributions for government social insurance	Plus: Adjustment for residence	Equals: Net earnings by place of residence	Plus: Dividends, interest, and rent	Plus: Personal current transfer receipts	Per capita personal income (dollars)	Population (persons)	Total employment
		Nonfarm	Farm	Total								
1970	344,368	252,377	28,880	281,257	18,405	-4,060	258,792	63,584	21,992	3,774	91,237	44,389
1971	373,977	278,994	25,278	304,272	21,175	-4,434	278,663	69,347	25,967	4,039	92,581	45,252
1972	408,804	295,816	35,247	331,063	23,487	-1,627	305,949	75,610	27,245	4,417	92,551	45,759
1973	475,914	331,842	55,593	387,435	30,370	-63	357,002	87,063	31,849	5,049	94,258	48,094
1974	510,072	374,099	33,921	408,020	36,076	699	372,643	100,138	37,291	5,339	95,544	50,462
1975	603,951	420,639	61,549	482,188	40,020	2,621	444,789	113,544	45,618	6,293	95,973	52,099
1976	658,636	482,778	39,319	522,097	45,784	4,516	480,829	127,411	50,396	6,667	98,784	54,408
1977	742,509	555,447	33,628	589,075	51,730	3,831	541,176	147,932	53,401	7,485	99,194	56,853
1978	857,185	628,384	60,378	688,762	61,179	4,806	632,389	165,812	58,984	8,604	99,624	59,367
1979	939,303	696,009	47,130	743,139	70,908	9,314	681,545	190,988	66,770	9,233	101,738	60,040
1980	1,025,778	762,195	19,130	781,325	77,533	12,160	715,952	231,024	78,802	10,026	102,308	61,267
1981	1,171,524	819,717	52,002	871,719	88,949	17,524	800,294	280,061	91,169	11,278	103,873	60,386
1982	1,252,508	871,463	39,792	911,255	95,657	13,743	829,341	321,514	101,653	11,963	104,697	61,469
1983	1,329,515	955,722	15,720	971,442	104,077	8,346	875,711	343,776	110,028	12,558	105,874	62,017
1984	1,483,287	1,034,760	63,644	1,098,404	115,033	5,829	989,200	380,251	113,836	13,845	107,132	64,839
1985	1,546,071	1,089,623	53,494	1,143,117	123,179	7,948	1,027,886	393,844	124,341	14,275	108,304	65,524
1986	1,625,031	1,159,225	51,982	1,211,207	134,748	6,884	1,083,343	411,646	130,042	14,905	109,024	66,717
1987	1,712,764	1,240,814	58,387	1,299,201	143,026	8,453	1,164,628	411,722	136,414	15,569	110,013	67,957
1988	1,812,251	1,366,548	28,662	1,395,210	163,850	6,309	1,237,669	428,799	145,783	16,152	112,201	70,554
1989	2,039,035	1,513,547	54,196	1,567,743	179,342	-75	1,388,326	491,220	159,489	17,892	113,962	73,114
1990	2,156,494	1,618,888	58,582	1,677,470	194,937	-1,045	1,481,488	501,287	173,719	18,557	116,212	75,272
1991	2,262,137	1,722,505	43,157	1,765,662	206,707	-5,743	1,553,212	522,342	186,583	19,283	117,311	77,243
1992	2,422,145	1,841,677	58,207	1,899,884	217,347	-5,799	1,676,738	545,129	200,278	20,280	119,436	78,669
1993	2,544,162	1,944,021	32,319	1,976,340	227,463	-10,078	1,738,799	591,467	213,896	21,020	121,037	81,316
1994	2,760,047	2,106,782	63,227	2,170,009	249,094	-19,265	1,901,650	632,641	225,756	22,424	123,084	84,043
1995	2,884,690	2,212,381	27,996	2,240,377	260,281	-23,981	1,956,115	687,306	241,269	23,127	124,733	87,281
1996	3,089,305	2,321,242	72,285	2,393,527	263,873	-27,391	2,102,263	729,215	257,827	24,576	125,704	88,742
1997	3,261,362	2,448,788	77,451	2,526,239	285,923	-28,400	2,211,916	779,280	270,166	25,670	127,050	90,147
1998	3,463,103	2,660,824	38,181	2,699,005	308,010	-26,951	2,364,044	821,704	277,355	26,987	128,325	93,857
1999	3,668,662	2,896,256	24,210	2,920,466	331,844	-35,371	2,553,251	820,872	294,539	28,136	130,392	95,422
2000	4,019,986	3,211,957	43,068	3,255,025	361,484	-51,433	2,842,108	853,368	324,510	30,415	132,173	97,843
2001	4,172,267	3,365,797	46,197	3,411,994	376,231	-98,373	2,937,390	881,697	353,180	30,995	134,610	101,247
2002	4,319,685	3,543,834	34,653	3,578,487	393,484	-137,253	3,047,750	880,153	391,782	31,749	136,056	103,321
2003	4,467,076	3,710,064	36,487	3,746,551	414,172	-168,232	3,164,147	912,488	390,441	32,402	137,863	105,134
2004	4,743,572	3,909,479	91,080	4,000,559	433,211	-215,143	3,352,205	977,581	413,786	33,847	140,149	107,207
2005	4,882,173	4,066,088	66,314	4,132,402	450,949	-252,358	3,429,095	1,001,151	451,927	34,466	141,650	109,151
2006	5,227,649	4,285,480	71,060	4,356,540	474,417	-285,462	3,596,661	1,133,336	497,652	36,379	143,698	111,747
2007	5,599,071	4,562,302	81,684	4,643,986	508,041	-323,209	3,812,736	1,235,019	551,316	38,316	146,129	114,856
2008	6,005,377	4,794,306	95,498	4,889,804	538,039	-323,218	4,028,547	1,316,999	659,831	40,359	148,799	116,152
2009	6,005,860	4,886,018	60,456	4,946,474	545,022	-361,993	4,039,459	1,278,650	687,751	39,628	151,556	116,043
2010	6,181,990	5,041,477	64,427	5,105,904	561,769	-388,363	4,155,772	1,277,290	748,928	40,397	153,031	115,917
2011	6,756,886	5,211,325	168,758	5,380,083	520,783	-338,494	4,520,806	1,456,998	779,082	43,327	155,950	119,002
2012	7,132,906	5,505,368	154,627	5,659,995	542,425	-348,676	4,768,894	1,573,451	790,561	44,836	159,090	121,282
2013	7,424,869	5,833,154	225,651	6,058,805	636,841	-422,074	4,999,890	1,604,324	820,655	45,770	162,220	123,987
2014	7,885,783	6,164,467	191,417	6,355,884	659,668	-391,173	5,305,043	1,709,958	870,782	47,829	164,876	124,923
2015	8,119,021	6,371,817	134,019	6,505,836	679,043	-436,751	5,390,042	1,790,859	938,120	48,551	167,226	126,641
2016	8,385,665	6,586,398	85,259	6,671,657	706,239	-463,047	5,502,371	1,903,119	980,175	49,546	169,251	129,619
2017	8,835,371	6,835,253	138,439	6,973,692	737,987	-483,847	5,751,858	2,082,145	1,001,368	51,410	171,862	130,915
2018	9,387,264	7,094,941	151,092	7,246,033	761,076	-340,138	6,144,819	2,145,366	1,097,079	54,261	173,002	131,045
2019	9,681,989	7,318,701	131,001	7,449,702	786,347	-434,973	6,228,382	2,265,024	1,188,583	55,518	174,394	130,727
2020	10,063,781	7,395,101	76,029	7,471,130	818,575	-470,408	6,182,147	2,289,932	1,591,702	57,345	175,495	126,183
2021	10,690,422	7,797,092	173,235	7,970,327	847,304	-465,538	6,657,485	2,333,819	1,699,118	60,316	177,239	128,187

Personal Income and Employment by Area: Ithaca, NY

(Thousands of dollars, except as noted.)

Year	Personal income, total	Earnings by place of work			Less: Contributions for government social insurance	Plus: Adjustment for residence	Equals: Net earnings by place of residence	Plus: Dividends, interest, and rent	Plus: Personal current transfer receipts	Per capita personal income (dollars)	Population (persons)	Total employment
		Nonfarm	Farm	Total								
1970	271,269	236,134	4,196	240,330	16,309	-20,643	203,378	45,649	22,242	3,523	77,008	31,858
1971	294,050	251,453	4,118	255,571	17,878	-20,846	216,847	49,515	27,688	3,805	77,277	32,074
1972	322,700	277,365	4,935	282,300	20,756	-23,888	237,656	54,134	30,910	4,029	80,102	33,322
1973	362,411	313,742	9,405	323,147	27,404	-28,274	267,469	60,705	34,237	4,349	83,324	35,318
1974	403,237	352,450	6,680	359,130	32,015	-33,404	293,711	68,707	40,819	4,712	85,580	37,573
1975	431,758	362,864	7,334	370,198	33,070	-34,553	302,575	74,270	54,913	5,052	85,471	36,913
1976	455,987	383,542	7,249	390,791	35,377	-35,343	320,071	78,517	57,399	5,298	86,067	37,712
1977	473,732	390,126	6,288	396,414	36,238	-34,468	325,708	86,784	61,240	5,490	86,287	38,255
1978	518,008	433,202	7,527	440,729	42,019	-38,273	360,437	92,078	65,493	5,992	86,457	39,942
1979	567,246	475,124	9,980	485,104	47,948	-43,727	393,429	102,542	71,275	6,508	87,161	41,218
1980	652,170	540,195	8,416	548,611	54,902	-51,772	441,937	126,423	83,810	7,468	87,331	41,835
1981	754,540	616,279	9,996	626,275	66,918	-57,250	502,107	157,550	94,883	8,560	88,150	43,881
1982	840,569	695,191	9,818	705,009	73,620	-66,837	564,552	171,732	104,285	9,502	88,458	45,648
1983	950,308	795,641	8,255	803,896	83,920	-78,166	641,810	194,399	114,099	10,698	88,828	48,064
1984	1,062,926	900,504	10,705	911,209	95,917	-86,543	728,749	214,348	119,829	11,932	89,080	50,756
1985	1,137,413	973,550	13,415	986,965	105,424	-96,482	785,059	225,062	127,292	12,667	89,791	52,407
1986	1,217,340	1,048,076	12,947	1,061,023	115,514	-102,515	842,994	240,826	133,520	13,573	89,687	54,502
1987	1,296,586	1,136,011	10,312	1,146,323	123,762	-111,024	911,537	249,146	135,903	14,364	90,264	55,893
1988	1,389,244	1,226,604	11,747	1,238,351	138,425	-121,893	978,033	266,659	144,552	15,119	91,888	58,258
1989	1,556,344	1,346,359	15,043	1,361,402	150,636	-133,080	1,077,686	323,696	154,962	16,688	93,262	60,237
1990	1,618,413	1,395,401	16,417	1,411,818	149,888	-141,085	1,120,845	328,713	168,855	17,173	94,241	60,340
1991	1,662,267	1,435,577	16,652	1,452,229	158,268	-150,020	1,143,941	330,577	187,749	17,446	95,283	60,526
1992	1,744,481	1,488,179	25,689	1,513,868	160,008	-156,245	1,197,615	335,859	211,007	18,231	95,685	59,647
1993	1,775,998	1,502,659	33,802	1,536,461	162,169	-164,510	1,209,782	346,869	219,347	18,476	96,122	59,660
1994	1,844,869	1,586,272	24,187	1,610,459	175,117	-181,222	1,254,120	363,436	227,313	19,136	96,409	60,253
1995	1,928,260	1,635,949	23,837	1,659,786	181,551	-193,555	1,284,680	393,760	249,820	19,906	96,870	60,082
1996	1,954,698	1,634,953	25,893	1,660,846	181,412	-196,039	1,283,395	414,988	256,315	20,298	96,298	58,651
1997	2,022,092	1,737,912	10,029	1,747,941	192,824	-215,993	1,339,124	422,092	260,876	21,016	96,216	58,558
1998	2,104,788	1,797,884	13,350	1,811,234	200,197	-235,942	1,375,095	452,976	276,717	21,917	96,036	57,896
1999	2,243,630	1,984,828	13,566	1,998,394	216,490	-275,376	1,506,528	451,784	285,318	23,213	96,656	61,479
2000	2,367,777	2,077,015	17,245	2,094,260	226,797	-290,858	1,576,605	491,615	299,557	24,509	96,608	62,504
2001	2,509,905	2,203,643	18,594	2,222,237	244,051	-304,997	1,673,189	510,651	326,065	25,754	97,458	64,225
2002	2,576,894	2,331,511	10,079	2,341,590	263,058	-332,238	1,746,294	475,648	354,952	26,234	98,227	64,594
2003	2,710,666	2,481,982	12,503	2,494,485	283,560	-363,920	1,847,005	495,220	368,441	27,367	99,049	66,031
2004	2,869,862	2,605,296	16,096	2,621,392	293,714	-373,781	1,953,897	524,079	391,886	28,834	99,531	67,459
2005	2,868,155	2,644,289	14,527	2,658,816	302,597	-388,852	1,967,367	494,196	406,592	28,845	99,433	68,246
2006	3,023,350	2,775,914	10,279	2,786,193	315,944	-406,968	2,063,281	530,770	429,299	30,339	99,651	68,278
2007	3,197,907	2,888,470	18,706	2,907,176	324,405	-413,071	2,169,700	575,347	452,860	32,008	99,910	69,485
2008	3,447,438	3,057,871	20,050	3,077,921	351,023	-434,682	2,292,216	645,038	510,184	34,343	100,383	70,253
2009	3,482,281	3,131,083	10,729	3,141,812	355,236	-466,427	2,320,149	601,978	560,154	34,309	101,497	68,613
2010	3,577,734	3,195,235	18,477	3,213,712	356,135	-476,489	2,381,088	592,169	604,477	35,164	101,743	67,611
2011	3,736,227	3,261,890	22,896	3,284,786	327,659	-489,171	2,467,956	654,247	614,024	36,680	101,861	67,421
2012	3,921,402	3,437,821	20,940	3,458,761	339,277	-530,999	2,588,485	731,942	600,975	38,146	102,800	68,184
2013	3,921,837	3,479,093	26,262	3,505,355	386,096	-523,990	2,595,269	712,401	614,167	37,831	103,668	68,898
2014	4,014,231	3,508,305	28,631	3,536,936	395,606	-528,928	2,612,402	770,288	631,541	38,086	105,398	67,815
2015	4,233,005	3,668,116	14,520	3,682,636	418,002	-532,267	2,732,367	831,246	669,392	40,128	105,487	69,690
2016	4,226,296	3,723,914	12,843	3,736,757	422,990	-605,475	2,708,292	840,262	677,742	39,954	105,780	69,915
2017	4,443,345	3,857,133	18,252	3,875,385	438,246	-602,479	2,834,660	876,919	731,766	41,957	105,903	69,889
2018	4,565,035	4,004,926	11,852	4,016,778	457,602	-622,965	2,936,211	895,465	733,359	43,071	105,989	70,095
2019	4,794,901	3,991,867	21,820	4,013,687	455,209	-587,708	2,970,770	1,024,693	799,438	45,232	106,008	68,213
2020	5,116,408	3,990,427	18,714	4,009,141	459,453	-585,846	2,963,842	1,026,179	1,126,387	48,541	105,404	64,971
2021	5,402,874	4,271,958	20,524	4,292,482	488,297	-622,041	3,182,144	1,070,953	1,149,777	51,377	105,162	65,628

Personal Income and Employment by Area: Jackson, MI

(Thousands of dollars, except as noted.)

Year	Personal income, total	Earnings by place of work			Less: Contributions for government social insurance	Plus: Adjustment for residence	Equals: Net earnings by place of residence	Plus: Dividends, interest, and rent	Plus: Personal current transfer receipts	Per capita personal income (dollars)	Population (persons)	Total employment
		Nonfarm	Farm	Total								
1970	584,669	480,910	6,320	487,230	34,559	7,225	459,896	74,513	50,260	4,082	143,227	58,293
1971	610,313	488,957	5,032	493,989	36,270	12,886	470,605	78,483	61,225	4,250	143,589	56,632
1972	686,460	560,197	6,598	566,795	44,160	15,317	537,952	84,046	64,462	4,755	144,372	59,352
1973	772,999	634,747	9,711	644,458	58,182	20,765	607,041	93,496	72,462	5,313	145,481	62,549
1974	828,625	672,318	3,531	675,849	63,956	21,257	633,150	106,901	88,574	5,641	146,903	62,188
1975	907,391	703,745	8,532	712,277	65,210	22,433	669,500	119,346	118,545	6,135	147,902	60,080
1976	981,361	750,851	6,588	757,439	70,800	38,279	724,918	127,665	128,778	6,609	148,498	60,290
1977	1,091,243	841,405	6,622	848,027	79,826	51,413	819,614	142,471	129,158	7,260	150,313	62,569
1978	1,229,816	962,270	4,487	966,757	93,660	64,487	937,584	155,861	136,371	8,117	151,502	65,436
1979	1,348,062	1,042,928	3,241	1,046,169	105,633	77,711	1,018,247	174,074	155,741	8,881	151,789	65,967
1980	1,436,360	1,058,381	1,934	1,060,315	105,607	81,281	1,035,989	206,111	194,260	9,478	151,554	62,760
1981	1,549,914	1,119,591	5,662	1,125,253	120,698	80,832	1,085,387	247,413	217,114	10,233	151,459	62,048
1982	1,589,960	1,099,663	3,562	1,103,225	120,194	76,595	1,059,626	282,552	247,782	10,586	150,195	58,972
1983	1,650,938	1,119,695	-6,602	1,113,093	123,429	85,070	1,074,734	310,668	265,536	11,160	147,930	57,854
1984	1,764,489	1,182,823	5,205	1,188,028	135,043	99,092	1,152,077	347,669	264,743	12,138	145,374	58,403
1985	1,843,509	1,223,763	7,805	1,231,568	142,157	113,853	1,203,264	364,371	275,874	12,749	144,602	59,140
1986	1,944,221	1,296,592	5,415	1,302,007	150,672	113,037	1,264,372	386,001	293,848	13,376	145,355	60,642
1987	2,087,854	1,437,206	11,410	1,448,616	164,651	102,930	1,386,895	397,110	303,849	14,130	147,758	62,691
1988	2,196,361	1,513,779	7,773	1,521,552	180,075	116,534	1,458,011	416,832	321,518	14,805	148,357	63,018
1989	2,380,392	1,625,741	15,571	1,641,312	191,220	112,710	1,562,802	472,062	345,528	15,996	148,816	65,309
1990	2,456,766	1,686,143	9,843	1,695,986	200,410	113,644	1,609,220	473,175	374,371	16,364	150,128	65,679
1991	2,508,078	1,699,562	5,075	1,704,637	204,988	118,715	1,618,364	469,119	420,595	16,605	151,039	64,640
1992	2,652,804	1,795,129	4,868	1,799,997	214,691	136,774	1,722,080	479,883	450,841	17,514	151,465	65,537
1993	2,801,739	1,895,789	2,106	1,897,895	228,257	142,608	1,812,246	506,327	483,166	18,379	152,445	66,378
1994	2,976,825	2,019,463	1,032	2,020,495	248,591	161,288	1,933,192	557,626	486,007	19,547	152,288	68,008
1995	3,155,630	2,136,255	1,839	2,138,094	264,250	166,847	2,040,691	606,829	508,110	20,583	153,313	70,813
1996	3,296,485	2,231,711	1,558	2,233,269	269,764	181,293	2,144,798	622,740	528,947	21,366	154,289	72,489
1997	3,468,826	2,330,312	471	2,330,783	282,425	205,748	2,254,106	658,162	556,558	22,332	155,331	73,186
1998	3,598,261	2,424,176	1,044	2,425,220	290,915	238,333	2,372,638	665,395	560,228	23,067	155,991	72,741
1999	3,834,521	2,643,432	4,576	2,648,008	314,985	260,178	2,593,201	635,727	605,593	24,410	157,085	75,602
2000	4,040,111	2,765,447	4,304	2,769,751	326,581	289,834	2,733,004	682,819	624,288	25,461	158,679	77,800
2001	4,126,354	2,793,374	880	2,794,254	320,100	282,016	2,756,170	673,249	696,935	25,827	159,772	76,959
2002	4,158,962	2,821,238	136	2,821,374	325,126	295,178	2,791,426	640,283	727,253	25,849	160,893	76,539
2003	4,231,638	2,817,119	-1,025	2,816,094	323,332	309,466	2,802,228	661,901	767,509	26,102	162,119	75,903
2004	4,374,729	2,989,153	7,247	2,996,400	343,809	288,830	2,941,421	641,450	791,858	26,981	162,140	77,085
2005	4,486,495	3,062,990	5,796	3,068,786	359,845	277,155	2,986,096	658,247	842,152	27,517	163,047	77,179
2006	4,581,809	3,089,314	8,168	3,097,482	366,161	272,065	3,003,386	671,368	907,055	28,043	163,387	75,802
2007	4,700,665	3,103,132	7,334	3,110,466	371,721	264,630	3,003,375	707,249	990,041	28,783	163,316	75,170
2008	4,857,313	3,105,599	-768	3,104,831	376,203	241,667	2,970,295	769,222	1,117,796	30,202	160,825	74,162
2009	4,742,905	2,937,190	1,440	2,938,630	358,440	186,206	2,766,396	727,507	1,249,002	29,622	160,114	70,410
2010	4,890,871	3,048,735	12,935	3,061,670	363,255	160,568	2,858,983	694,686	1,337,202	30,547	160,109	69,182
2011	5,065,610	3,165,410	25,804	3,191,214	344,025	126,376	2,973,565	757,277	1,334,768	31,726	159,666	72,195
2012	5,197,240	3,300,655	4,676	3,305,331	356,683	95,884	3,044,532	811,290	1,341,418	32,485	159,988	72,243
2013	5,263,483	3,457,268	11,331	3,468,599	420,803	28,222	3,076,018	816,395	1,371,070	32,964	159,672	73,846
2014	5,450,315	3,529,842	-5,896	3,523,946	428,327	44,991	3,140,610	881,241	1,428,464	33,884	160,850	74,190
2015	5,698,567	3,654,066	-6,140	3,647,926	440,919	54,806	3,261,813	935,594	1,501,160	35,386	161,039	74,819
2016	5,912,626	3,811,277	-8,083	3,803,194	458,262	46,562	3,391,494	973,380	1,547,752	36,867	160,376	75,586
2017	6,009,918	3,922,590	-1,473	3,921,117	471,377	52,338	3,502,078	964,321	1,543,519	37,325	161,016	75,241
2018	6,257,626	4,065,811	-2,079	4,063,732	496,271	57,742	3,625,203	1,020,057	1,612,366	38,799	161,284	76,061
2019	6,418,551	4,148,212	-2,781	4,145,431	505,214	58,092	3,698,309	1,014,746	1,705,496	39,775	161,372	74,770
2020	7,073,091	4,162,271	7,666	4,169,937	505,108	43,493	3,708,322	1,042,744	2,322,025	44,152	160,200	70,832
2021	7,602,801	4,510,567	12,149	4,522,716	537,260	36,220	4,021,676	1,130,765	2,450,360	47,503	160,050	74,093

Personal Income and Employment by Area: Jackson, MS

(Thousands of dollars, except as noted.)

Year	Personal income, total	Earnings by place of work			Less: Contributions for government social insurance	Plus: Adjustment for residence	Equals: Net earnings by place of residence	Plus: Dividends, interest, and rent	Plus: Personal current transfer receipts	Per capita personal income (dollars)	Population (persons)	Total employment
		Nonfarm	Farm	Total								
1970	1,169,060	940,224	50,369	990,593	63,915	-12,406	914,272	149,918	104,870	3,234	361,473	170,261
1971	1,301,693	1,039,078	57,412	1,096,490	73,056	-13,500	1,009,934	167,182	124,577	3,521	369,687	175,421
1972	1,466,101	1,176,282	64,881	1,241,163	86,602	-15,638	1,138,923	184,746	142,432	3,876	378,229	182,347
1973	1,686,270	1,349,531	90,830	1,440,361	114,495	-20,045	1,305,821	213,825	166,624	4,378	385,151	194,536
1974	1,912,388	1,526,913	76,358	1,603,271	133,895	-16,478	1,452,898	253,652	205,838	4,818	396,911	200,851
1975	2,056,099	1,612,632	44,671	1,657,303	139,323	-5,091	1,512,889	284,363	258,847	5,082	404,561	194,047
1976	2,319,273	1,803,225	74,095	1,877,320	159,022	2,298	1,720,596	308,141	290,536	5,641	411,149	198,388
1977	2,605,251	2,062,144	61,160	2,123,304	180,875	6,074	1,948,503	344,230	312,518	6,238	417,649	207,091
1978	2,985,707	2,379,007	62,119	2,441,126	214,810	17,222	2,243,538	398,397	343,772	6,990	427,123	219,759
1979	3,417,328	2,694,498	87,364	2,781,862	253,438	38,374	2,566,798	463,429	387,101	7,871	434,186	226,855
1980	3,735,115	2,929,599	26,842	2,956,441	274,623	15,216	2,697,034	576,277	461,804	8,478	440,574	225,694
1981	4,153,650	3,158,574	34,497	3,193,071	318,814	28,295	2,902,552	721,236	529,862	9,344	444,541	224,409
1982	4,374,546	3,253,427	62,076	3,315,503	335,421	20,213	3,000,295	802,452	571,799	9,760	448,195	219,440
1983	4,646,101	3,490,000	20,107	3,510,107	362,829	27,183	3,174,461	842,933	628,707	10,274	452,220	222,590
1984	5,098,415	3,831,054	86,329	3,917,383	409,134	11,198	3,519,447	930,162	648,806	11,161	456,787	230,375
1985	5,371,781	4,087,570	46,240	4,133,810	446,933	-3,023	3,683,854	1,004,283	683,644	11,553	464,955	234,972
1986	5,625,605	4,311,667	39,452	4,351,119	476,306	-17,947	3,856,866	1,040,800	727,939	12,027	467,741	238,293
1987	5,973,414	4,570,773	70,985	4,641,758	501,189	-25,690	4,114,879	1,085,588	772,947	12,731	469,189	241,648
1988	6,405,601	4,900,131	85,723	4,985,854	557,801	-25,250	4,402,803	1,173,291	829,507	13,667	468,678	248,098
1989	7,028,472	5,263,982	77,521	5,341,503	595,516	-31,878	4,714,109	1,408,467	905,896	14,956	469,951	253,316
1990	7,386,961	5,593,677	67,312	5,660,989	657,579	-32,766	4,970,644	1,423,278	993,039	15,597	473,615	255,177
1991	7,777,023	5,872,557	74,803	5,947,360	704,996	-39,717	5,202,647	1,457,532	1,116,844	16,287	477,502	257,780
1992	8,354,284	6,317,067	74,220	6,391,287	749,201	-42,015	5,600,071	1,500,485	1,253,728	17,317	482,440	262,586
1993	8,877,636	6,734,864	73,656	6,808,520	797,752	-49,914	5,960,854	1,564,390	1,352,392	18,230	486,974	272,370
1994	9,589,368	7,253,366	102,556	7,355,922	865,582	-57,237	6,433,103	1,701,355	1,454,910	19,455	492,911	281,002
1995	10,302,550	7,789,564	73,314	7,862,878	923,054	-69,124	6,870,700	1,849,372	1,582,478	20,682	498,145	289,786
1996	10,912,754	8,168,427	120,867	8,289,294	955,556	-79,752	7,253,986	1,976,927	1,681,841	21,598	505,267	295,891
1997	11,622,486	8,691,909	104,279	8,796,188	1,011,505	-96,715	7,687,968	2,191,986	1,742,532	22,744	511,024	302,489
1998	12,681,192	9,491,240	125,251	9,616,491	1,096,164	-91,682	8,428,645	2,393,655	1,858,892	23,512	539,345	316,636
1999	13,090,250	9,914,428	118,142	10,032,570	1,147,161	-101,359	8,784,050	2,397,074	1,909,126	24,100	543,159	319,753
2000	13,880,238	10,434,923	86,941	10,521,864	1,192,489	-115,367	9,214,008	2,609,508	2,056,722	25,333	547,903	322,368
2001	14,634,474	10,882,728	151,534	11,034,262	1,232,812	-119,336	9,682,114	2,631,333	2,321,027	26,638	549,383	324,028
2002	14,977,810	11,220,166	43,004	11,263,170	1,276,099	-108,415	9,878,656	2,594,556	2,504,598	27,145	551,767	324,326
2003	15,657,335	11,759,730	128,416	11,888,146	1,330,221	-129,019	10,428,906	2,612,435	2,615,994	28,161	555,999	329,226
2004	16,663,543	12,502,071	214,015	12,716,086	1,423,548	-165,420	11,127,118	2,737,284	2,799,141	29,629	562,401	334,948
2005	17,849,528	13,131,398	212,159	13,343,557	1,468,918	-176,338	11,698,301	3,169,451	2,981,776	31,453	567,496	340,095
2006	19,210,674	13,992,230	96,970	14,089,200	1,603,311	-204,870	12,281,019	3,762,750	3,166,905	33,305	576,809	350,993
2007	19,814,496	14,258,291	129,754	14,388,045	1,657,208	-217,784	12,513,053	3,945,250	3,356,193	34,230	578,863	357,696
2008	21,296,449	15,251,742	78,433	15,330,175	1,743,795	-192,638	13,393,742	4,066,618	3,836,089	36,619	581,567	359,792
2009	20,445,506	14,440,267	102,306	14,542,573	1,706,165	-220,065	12,616,343	3,702,620	4,126,543	35,019	583,837	354,325
2010	21,400,531	14,996,497	110,950	15,107,447	1,724,868	-225,966	13,156,613	3,750,379	4,493,539	36,378	588,285	353,866
2011	22,775,469	15,681,221	72,567	15,753,788	1,601,584	-279,092	13,873,112	4,235,268	4,667,089	38,378	593,450	359,843
2012	23,554,168	16,295,251	68,140	16,363,391	1,648,751	-282,878	14,431,762	4,471,264	4,651,142	39,541	595,691	361,090
2013	23,957,657	16,969,485	228,299	17,197,784	1,923,116	-395,259	14,879,409	4,316,260	4,761,988	40,165	596,483	366,115
2014	24,774,025	17,604,216	93,333	17,697,549	1,994,535	-402,879	15,300,135	4,549,980	4,923,910	41,424	598,060	373,048
2015	25,154,977	17,576,498	85,929	17,662,427	2,051,335	-420,584	15,190,508	4,822,494	5,141,975	42,007	598,827	378,458
2016	25,246,535	17,592,289	57,483	17,649,772	2,080,394	-407,066	15,162,312	4,778,591	5,305,632	42,025	600,752	381,142
2017	25,444,208	17,643,292	122,554	17,765,846	2,123,026	-385,682	15,257,138	4,867,308	5,319,762	42,371	600,507	382,210
2018	25,932,753	17,995,085	84,763	18,079,848	2,153,926	-374,960	15,550,962	4,885,444	5,496,347	43,313	598,726	383,049
2019	26,858,780	18,393,710	94,701	18,488,411	2,228,795	-376,755	15,882,861	5,226,066	5,749,853	45,026	596,513	383,789
2020	28,864,955	18,854,522	40,799	18,895,321	2,308,715	-311,059	16,275,547	5,213,835	7,375,573	48,872	590,626	371,257
2021	30,523,762	19,874,948	112,485	19,987,433	2,382,458	-336,290	17,268,685	5,307,065	7,948,012	51,982	587,202	377,379

Personal Income and Employment by Area: Jackson, TN

(Thousands of dollars, except as noted.)

Year	Personal income, total	Earnings by place of work			Less: Contributions for government social insurance	Plus: Adjustment for residence	Equals: Net earnings by place of residence	Plus: Dividends, interest, and rent	Plus: Personal current transfer receipts	Per capita personal income (dollars)	Population (persons)	Total employment
		Nonfarm	Farm	Total								
1970	269,815	209,180	13,008	222,188	14,425	1,472	209,235	30,516	30,064	2,983	90,439	41,609
1971	301,085	231,735	17,810	249,545	16,233	-863	232,449	34,537	34,099	3,261	92,319	42,190
1972	334,930	267,310	14,517	281,827	19,475	-3,617	258,735	38,699	37,496	3,531	94,860	45,340
1973	380,494	300,088	22,036	322,124	24,814	-6,314	290,996	44,476	45,022	3,980	95,609	47,469
1974	418,028	345,677	8,372	354,049	30,102	-12,328	311,619	51,799	54,610	4,330	96,538	48,962
1975	462,505	371,145	8,638	379,783	31,703	-15,578	332,502	59,284	70,719	4,737	97,641	47,350
1976	512,759	418,531	9,335	427,866	36,392	-20,509	370,965	64,264	77,530	5,202	98,570	48,158
1977	569,044	477,073	8,000	485,073	41,703	-28,027	415,343	72,430	81,271	5,715	99,563	49,487
1978	628,988	527,432	10,746	538,178	46,912	-32,004	459,262	81,774	87,952	6,317	99,563	49,960
1979	684,079	578,689	5,172	583,861	53,566	-39,386	490,909	92,378	100,792	6,762	101,162	50,542
1980	738,104	605,500	-3,475	602,025	56,056	-45,962	500,007	114,993	123,104	7,210	102,369	49,086
1981	811,291	636,123	4,408	640,531	62,639	-44,656	533,236	140,665	137,390	7,893	102,788	47,615
1982	859,434	644,333	4,601	648,934	64,169	-44,699	540,066	168,732	150,636	8,366	102,728	46,149
1983	923,100	710,964	-7,837	703,127	71,432	-47,468	584,227	177,885	160,988	9,026	102,276	47,546
1984	1,046,698	802,617	12,393	815,010	84,022	-52,537	678,451	202,410	165,837	10,180	102,820	51,276
1985	1,099,909	850,048	1,621	851,669	90,239	-53,854	707,576	215,275	177,058	10,594	103,826	51,084
1986	1,176,843	919,726	4,848	924,574	99,596	-59,625	765,353	220,978	190,512	11,355	103,639	52,206
1987	1,277,256	985,644	30,992	1,016,636	105,690	-60,767	850,179	226,068	201,009	12,345	103,462	53,337
1988	1,375,379	1,071,694	24,912	1,096,606	118,914	-60,364	917,328	243,284	214,767	13,264	103,695	55,784
1989	1,474,301	1,171,024	19,309	1,190,333	131,705	-71,021	987,607	253,934	232,760	14,186	103,923	58,447
1990	1,600,587	1,271,312	16,924	1,288,236	143,303	-81,279	1,063,654	284,128	252,805	15,305	104,582	59,632
1991	1,680,920	1,332,275	27,594	1,359,869	152,484	-86,219	1,121,166	278,640	281,114	15,839	106,123	60,230
1992	1,866,010	1,498,727	40,605	1,539,332	168,540	-101,609	1,269,183	282,101	314,726	17,301	107,853	63,184
1993	1,964,131	1,596,524	27,732	1,624,256	180,258	-112,908	1,331,090	291,245	341,796	17,891	109,784	65,375
1994	2,134,214	1,752,362	45,076	1,797,438	200,519	-130,766	1,466,153	309,409	358,652	19,139	111,509	69,405
1995	2,260,006	1,863,506	29,647	1,893,153	213,596	-144,740	1,534,817	327,715	397,474	19,898	113,582	71,076
1996	2,389,569	1,967,373	37,090	2,004,463	221,727	-159,876	1,622,860	352,015	414,694	20,725	115,301	71,865
1997	2,559,871	2,163,147	25,704	2,188,851	242,154	-189,250	1,757,447	371,620	430,804	21,887	116,961	75,450
1998	3,807,763	3,073,768	19,498	3,093,266	331,532	-171,798	2,589,936	541,457	676,370	22,774	167,199	102,040
1999	3,936,227	3,222,909	1,492	3,224,401	348,793	-187,182	2,688,426	547,720	700,081	23,288	169,023	103,784
2000	4,177,426	3,373,283	33,123	3,406,406	361,878	-200,785	2,843,743	575,753	757,930	24,535	170,267	105,147
2001	4,043,575	3,139,400	35,344	3,174,744	354,886	-191,515	2,628,343	592,986	822,246	23,597	171,360	101,082
2002	4,133,173	3,214,354	10,792	3,225,146	366,798	-180,184	2,678,164	568,916	886,093	24,060	171,787	99,407
2003	4,404,943	3,345,937	46,997	3,392,934	377,585	-177,004	2,838,345	593,465	973,133	25,669	171,605	99,396
2004	4,652,459	3,593,458	52,261	3,645,719	399,057	-194,010	3,052,652	569,122	1,030,685	26,864	173,185	100,986
2005	4,824,337	3,677,102	74,083	3,751,185	411,771	-194,353	3,145,061	581,003	1,098,273	27,708	174,116	100,977
2006	4,989,047	3,794,950	73,294	3,868,244	426,169	-200,791	3,241,284	599,561	1,148,202	28,395	175,703	102,274
2007	5,262,664	3,958,167	28,417	3,986,584	444,823	-214,425	3,327,336	667,898	1,267,430	29,799	176,608	103,593
2008	5,471,396	3,957,359	61,517	4,018,876	454,846	-218,895	3,345,135	732,864	1,393,397	30,798	177,654	103,293
2009	5,554,444	3,861,395	70,490	3,931,885	448,472	-163,437	3,319,976	737,430	1,497,038	31,076	178,739	98,665
2010	5,779,001	4,044,296	24,353	4,068,649	457,877	-175,181	3,435,591	707,659	1,635,751	32,147	179,767	98,869
2011	6,235,917	4,312,550	112,709	4,425,259	424,311	-203,513	3,797,435	775,549	1,662,933	34,701	179,704	101,112
2012	6,323,029	4,513,454	-3,749	4,509,705	432,852	-223,602	3,853,251	803,301	1,666,477	35,149	179,892	102,026
2013	6,338,117	4,513,226	93,413	4,606,639	489,206	-253,687	3,863,746	773,870	1,700,501	35,236	179,874	102,093
2014	6,321,729	4,600,862	-36,909	4,563,953	497,537	-266,241	3,800,175	823,023	1,698,531	35,127	179,967	103,037
2015	6,554,064	4,729,276	-13,865	4,715,411	512,376	-263,167	3,939,868	845,121	1,769,075	36,544	179,345	103,824
2016	6,629,704	4,849,865	-20,576	4,829,289	532,289	-284,918	4,012,082	851,066	1,766,556	36,997	179,197	105,746
2017	6,861,343	5,025,184	-19,708	5,005,476	557,906	-307,842	4,139,728	894,335	1,827,280	38,260	179,335	106,343
2018	7,059,915	5,198,084	-53,583	5,144,501	577,407	-322,767	4,244,327	900,151	1,915,437	39,329	179,507	107,671
2019	7,494,496	5,388,035	10,724	5,398,759	599,272	-336,725	4,462,762	993,010	2,038,724	41,672	179,846	108,433
2020	8,103,910	5,654,116	8,358	5,662,474	638,558	-361,018	4,662,898	987,267	2,453,745	44,926	180,383	106,956
2021	8,808,250	6,060,308	67,936	6,128,244	663,195	-381,077	5,083,972	999,960	2,724,318	48,718	180,799	109,762

Personal Income and Employment by Area: Jacksonville, FL

(Thousands of dollars, except as noted.)

				Derivation of personal income								
		Earnings by place of work			Less: Contributions for government social insurance	Plus: Adjustment for residence	Equals: Net earnings by place of residence	Plus: Dividends, interest, and rent	Plus: Personal current transfer receipts	Per capita personal income (dollars)	Population (persons)	Total employment
Year	Personal income, total	Nonfarm	Farm	Total								
1970	2,567,000	2,114,878	13,021	2,127,899	135,388	-12,090	1,980,421	409,149	177,430	4,118	623,388	295,684
1971	2,840,266	2,332,698	15,481	2,348,179	155,780	-13,747	2,178,652	452,843	208,771	4,475	634,713	301,891
1972	3,189,179	2,625,387	17,939	2,643,326	183,196	-15,387	2,444,743	498,579	245,857	4,935	646,275	313,941
1973	3,576,714	2,951,238	22,872	2,974,110	235,105	-17,600	2,721,405	560,453	294,856	5,421	659,829	332,075
1974	4,037,450	3,303,980	26,398	3,330,378	272,986	-20,804	3,036,588	657,261	343,601	5,871	687,746	345,616
1975	4,422,511	3,540,411	33,133	3,573,544	290,668	-22,670	3,260,206	721,995	440,310	6,403	690,714	341,634
1976	4,737,665	3,786,512	32,329	3,818,841	319,292	-25,046	3,474,503	767,905	495,257	6,782	698,553	340,298
1977	5,172,586	4,145,695	25,448	4,171,143	350,583	-29,579	3,790,981	846,601	535,004	7,338	704,888	349,448
1978	5,780,316	4,638,128	17,301	4,655,429	401,184	-31,398	4,222,847	972,313	585,156	8,076	715,770	368,161
1979	6,356,757	5,078,857	14,875	5,093,732	460,712	-32,343	4,600,677	1,088,595	667,485	8,807	721,782	371,167
1980	7,255,473	5,688,556	20,702	5,709,258	517,785	-33,196	5,158,277	1,312,363	784,833	9,786	741,394	381,950
1981	8,275,617	6,405,018	34,314	6,439,332	624,302	-36,377	5,778,653	1,591,677	905,287	10,955	755,420	390,199
1982	9,061,807	6,947,284	53,584	7,000,868	690,891	-24,581	6,285,396	1,764,248	1,012,163	11,793	768,427	397,586
1983	9,888,233	7,612,807	48,983	7,661,790	769,182	-31,186	6,861,422	1,920,117	1,106,694	12,623	783,354	411,897
1984	11,143,991	8,642,815	45,034	8,687,849	897,080	-35,688	7,755,081	2,219,827	1,169,083	13,858	804,178	442,276
1985	12,241,386	9,543,628	41,498	9,585,126	1,005,112	-37,216	8,542,798	2,449,373	1,249,215	14,789	827,746	470,849
1986	13,305,113	10,427,117	46,883	10,474,000	1,129,350	-32,231	9,312,419	2,665,830	1,326,864	15,594	853,211	493,439
1987	14,366,224	11,296,748	48,872	11,345,620	1,211,438	-10,755	10,123,427	2,848,491	1,394,306	16,423	874,757	503,658
1988	15,543,633	12,191,677	55,776	12,247,453	1,355,028	-4,925	10,887,500	3,128,457	1,527,676	17,340	896,417	519,933
1989	17,005,492	12,973,452	51,174	13,024,626	1,448,341	10,052	11,586,337	3,687,497	1,731,658	18,805	904,284	536,809
1990	18,327,614	13,916,376	59,205	13,975,581	1,553,282	32,226	12,454,525	3,971,597	1,901,492	19,661	932,169	555,661
1991	19,025,780	14,449,029	60,202	14,509,231	1,627,259	36,270	12,918,242	3,964,947	2,142,591	19,910	955,572	555,630
1992	20,155,442	15,363,270	56,741	15,420,011	1,733,723	44,234	13,730,522	3,960,395	2,464,525	20,615	977,699	555,070
1993	21,337,411	16,253,606	55,119	16,308,725	1,823,866	43,100	14,527,959	4,159,628	2,649,824	21,542	990,520	568,743
1994	22,511,450	17,124,875	51,594	17,176,469	1,928,864	41,921	15,289,526	4,446,291	2,775,633	22,411	1,004,478	582,196
1995	24,212,435	18,259,675	48,373	18,308,048	2,042,844	34,463	16,299,667	4,910,671	3,002,097	23,723	1,020,631	603,371
1996	26,014,364	19,617,974	54,202	19,672,176	2,176,148	20,583	17,516,611	5,323,778	3,173,975	24,720	1,052,363	630,841
1997	27,676,463	20,976,000	61,165	21,037,165	2,327,388	5,447	18,715,224	5,662,142	3,299,097	25,696	1,077,069	648,513
1998	30,100,946	22,790,872	69,420	22,860,292	2,491,426	-5,807	20,363,059	6,396,869	3,341,018	27,492	1,094,889	671,238
1999	31,380,633	23,841,114	71,207	23,912,321	2,602,713	-655	21,308,953	6,585,948	3,485,732	28,272	1,109,951	687,819
2000	34,265,912	26,097,668	71,479	26,169,147	2,809,077	-19,811	23,340,259	7,164,202	3,761,451	30,424	1,126,282	715,920
2001	35,377,996	26,796,632	85,413	26,882,045	2,938,300	-38,467	23,905,278	7,331,491	4,141,227	30,815	1,148,091	682,257
2002	36,695,503	28,001,791	72,630	28,074,421	3,062,951	-68,456	24,943,014	7,196,140	4,556,349	31,327	1,171,363	685,898
2003	39,053,569	30,014,986	62,836	30,077,822	3,269,761	-82,790	26,725,271	7,435,582	4,892,716	32,734	1,193,042	706,052
2004	41,920,826	31,993,812	71,382	32,065,194	3,495,589	-145,695	28,423,910	8,207,811	5,289,105	34,281	1,222,866	728,218
2005	45,458,135	34,246,197	71,668	34,317,865	3,747,900	-171,880	30,398,085	9,316,029	5,744,021	36,394	1,249,072	752,286
2006	49,574,815	36,796,169	61,328	36,857,497	4,128,642	-217,784	32,511,071	10,806,223	6,257,521	38,661	1,282,311	781,243
2007	51,903,643	37,917,238	63,886	37,981,124	4,264,951	-231,680	33,484,493	11,674,868	6,744,282	39,718	1,306,788	794,744
2008	52,626,361	37,052,349	52,185	37,104,534	4,249,651	-187,749	32,667,134	12,130,583	7,828,644	39,786	1,322,728	783,542
2009	49,908,579	35,137,191	43,098	35,180,289	4,104,344	-76,866	30,999,079	10,216,685	8,692,815	37,385	1,334,972	750,560
2010	52,639,050	36,477,233	48,657	36,525,890	4,197,699	7,447	32,335,638	10,587,430	9,715,982	39,022	1,348,967	746,907
2011	55,333,348	37,030,940	30,783	37,061,723	3,856,076	64,674	33,270,321	11,921,110	10,141,917	40,620	1,362,204	762,037
2012	57,682,381	38,740,061	32,677	38,772,738	4,062,478	72,413	34,782,673	12,852,067	10,047,641	41,859	1,378,027	771,167
2013	58,456,176	39,895,290	36,698	39,931,988	4,689,475	106,416	35,348,929	12,676,690	10,430,557	41,933	1,394,024	787,571
2014	61,400,749	41,920,828	34,481	41,955,309	4,917,583	53,136	37,090,862	13,230,901	11,078,986	43,043	1,426,514	810,712
2015	65,132,528	44,107,696	48,174	44,155,870	5,131,912	45,298	39,069,256	14,367,333	11,695,939	44,695	1,457,278	839,215
2016	68,108,189	46,444,358	35,120	46,479,478	5,374,762	24,528	41,129,244	14,813,879	12,165,066	45,654	1,491,834	869,041
2017	73,266,458	49,957,573	36,600	49,994,173	5,744,622	-11,139	44,238,412	16,125,640	12,902,406	48,091	1,523,486	912,936
2018	77,177,148	52,961,049	31,356	52,992,405	6,089,183	-102,330	46,800,892	16,822,609	13,553,647	49,671	1,553,781	941,775
2019	82,476,598	55,896,289	30,509	55,926,798	6,503,787	-163,245	49,259,766	18,711,982	14,504,850	52,086	1,583,466	960,189
2020	88,880,224	58,371,078	33,358	58,404,436	6,790,242	-123,923	51,490,271	18,880,266	18,509,687	55,158	1,611,388	965,365
2021	97,066,568	63,687,425	41,107	63,728,532	7,221,672	-154,602	56,352,258	19,498,010	21,216,300	59,271	1,637,666	1,002,118

Personal Income and Employment by Area: Jacksonville, NC

(Thousands of dollars, except as noted.)

Year	Personal income, total	Earnings by place of work — Nonfarm	Earnings by place of work — Farm	Earnings by place of work — Total	Less: Contributions for government social insurance	Plus: Adjustment for residence	Equals: Net earnings by place of residence	Plus: Dividends, interest, and rent	Plus: Personal current transfer receipts	Per capita personal income (dollars)	Population (persons)	Total employment
1970	469,455	387,871	6,832	394,703	23,178	-10,622	360,903	96,734	11,818	4,576	102,582	63,781
1971	454,696	381,011	5,501	386,512	24,401	-11,196	350,915	89,706	14,075	4,509	100,831	56,615
1972	504,609	422,174	6,898	429,072	27,138	-11,986	389,948	98,491	16,170	5,330	94,669	55,778
1973	548,029	451,825	12,176	464,001	30,157	-12,840	421,004	108,671	18,354	5,881	93,193	55,913
1974	638,970	525,931	11,996	537,927	37,150	-14,725	486,052	130,787	22,131	6,631	96,362	59,332
1975	717,056	586,542	14,622	601,164	45,481	-15,531	540,152	146,977	29,927	6,361	112,734	62,166
1976	758,046	619,248	11,994	631,242	49,730	-15,706	565,806	157,783	34,457	6,576	115,272	62,032
1977	800,311	651,778	6,364	658,142	51,230	-16,926	589,986	173,609	36,716	6,877	116,382	62,822
1978	882,656	703,220	8,889	712,109	54,031	-18,155	639,923	203,192	39,541	7,451	118,455	63,952
1979	906,526	724,563	4,673	729,236	57,850	-18,387	652,999	207,492	46,035	8,011	113,156	61,681
1980	956,728	757,109	7,614	764,723	60,076	-18,985	685,662	214,721	56,345	8,428	113,515	60,235
1981	1,231,227	987,034	7,606	994,640	81,794	-17,691	895,155	270,536	65,536	10,605	116,100	62,778
1982	1,333,970	1,059,261	11,799	1,071,060	85,350	-16,697	969,013	290,497	74,460	11,221	118,881	62,899
1983	1,434,585	1,145,114	4,867	1,149,981	97,164	-17,228	1,035,589	317,304	81,692	11,549	124,216	66,943
1984	1,606,763	1,283,199	3,660	1,286,859	112,447	-16,632	1,157,780	359,610	89,373	12,524	128,297	69,653
1985	1,771,396	1,418,385	1,713	1,420,098	125,829	-17,746	1,276,523	397,627	97,246	13,295	133,240	72,992
1986	1,858,766	1,474,006	2,639	1,476,645	134,088	-15,520	1,327,037	426,376	105,353	13,455	138,143	73,307
1987	1,988,812	1,570,567	7,133	1,577,700	144,848	-15,119	1,417,733	460,863	110,216	14,088	141,166	77,154
1988	2,075,055	1,643,768	4,219	1,647,987	161,757	-12,476	1,473,754	479,324	121,977	14,542	142,695	77,449
1989	2,237,858	1,751,909	4,745	1,756,654	175,342	-11,933	1,569,379	529,997	138,482	15,002	149,174	80,413
1990	2,108,899	1,624,641	18,608	1,643,249	169,454	-16,633	1,457,162	498,626	153,111	14,050	150,098	73,735
1991	2,159,313	1,642,416	27,745	1,670,161	174,542	-11,292	1,484,327	499,214	175,772	14,268	151,342	71,053
1992	2,543,504	1,963,168	24,415	1,987,583	214,925	-21,223	1,751,435	597,639	194,430	17,377	146,370	78,921
1993	2,544,441	1,912,752	32,473	1,945,225	214,636	-15,069	1,715,520	611,732	217,189	17,217	147,789	79,122
1994	2,736,073	2,041,898	32,768	2,074,666	222,585	-14,988	1,837,093	666,213	232,767	18,643	146,760	80,724
1995	2,866,410	2,101,260	31,653	2,132,913	222,558	-11,550	1,898,805	700,909	266,696	19,465	147,258	83,029
1996	2,994,879	2,164,203	35,414	2,199,617	229,257	-5,315	1,965,045	733,849	295,985	20,146	148,658	84,330
1997	3,201,094	2,298,137	35,197	2,333,334	243,953	-4,131	2,085,250	803,519	312,325	21,636	147,955	86,093
1998	3,331,648	2,411,819	13,744	2,425,563	255,504	1,376	2,171,435	827,218	332,995	22,097	150,773	86,108
1999	3,499,119	2,527,615	16,338	2,543,953	268,261	4,483	2,280,175	860,005	358,939	23,385	149,628	87,777
2000	3,616,675	2,581,409	33,097	2,614,506	275,415	9,829	2,348,920	884,130	383,625	24,003	150,678	87,507
2001	3,766,416	2,736,528	35,247	2,771,775	291,416	2,089	2,482,448	854,471	429,497	24,932	151,068	88,590
2002	3,800,127	2,776,774	12,960	2,789,734	294,301	-3,047	2,492,386	840,030	467,711	24,773	153,397	90,613
2003	4,158,839	3,117,344	6,944	3,124,288	329,509	-25,163	2,769,616	887,696	501,527	27,637	150,481	92,408
2004	4,643,074	3,561,554	11,407	3,572,961	378,179	-48,619	3,146,163	938,931	557,980	29,232	158,837	95,728
2005	5,078,647	3,915,158	27,341	3,942,499	414,080	-68,037	3,460,382	999,680	618,585	32,306	157,205	99,289
2006	5,380,266	4,181,771	8,505	4,190,276	452,126	-83,672	3,654,478	1,043,093	682,695	33,379	161,185	102,152
2007	5,987,235	4,670,767	22,758	4,693,525	502,503	-116,376	4,074,646	1,173,270	739,319	36,674	163,256	104,594
2008	6,723,689	5,253,674	38,732	5,292,406	561,674	-164,745	4,565,987	1,304,987	852,715	39,771	169,059	109,708
2009	7,273,537	5,781,798	34,911	5,816,709	632,060	-215,196	4,969,453	1,368,020	936,064	42,028	173,064	113,560
2010	7,837,683	6,226,878	56,883	6,283,761	675,364	-247,420	5,360,977	1,438,848	1,037,858	41,931	186,918	114,629
2011	8,120,805	6,303,439	49,944	6,353,383	634,304	-257,564	5,461,515	1,568,006	1,091,284	43,880	185,068	114,456
2012	8,168,616	6,299,064	67,433	6,366,497	643,493	-254,165	5,468,839	1,567,897	1,131,880	42,810	190,813	113,433
2013	8,044,243	6,157,883	74,157	6,232,040	691,145	-244,125	5,296,770	1,569,733	1,177,740	41,784	192,522	113,476
2014	8,134,143	6,139,882	78,280	6,218,162	692,317	-235,236	5,290,609	1,598,879	1,244,655	42,275	192,411	112,789
2015	8,264,308	6,098,358	62,872	6,161,230	698,876	-219,083	5,243,271	1,618,426	1,402,611	42,638	193,823	110,289
2016	7,653,008	5,444,833	51,497	5,496,330	615,596	-176,225	4,704,509	1,474,463	1,474,036	39,606	193,227	109,293
2017	8,250,656	5,961,232	63,005	6,024,237	672,948	-199,867	5,151,422	1,530,742	1,568,492	42,121	195,881	110,876
2018	8,624,490	6,259,562	42,273	6,301,835	699,130	-205,835	5,396,870	1,562,096	1,665,524	43,628	197,682	110,614
2019	9,015,341	6,494,972	45,912	6,540,884	722,931	-207,023	5,610,930	1,620,414	1,783,997	44,307	203,475	111,795
2020	9,616,799	6,743,241	39,694	6,782,935	747,336	-218,197	5,817,402	1,572,527	2,226,870	46,972	204,735	110,351
2021	10,487,249	7,294,122	56,671	7,350,793	794,942	-240,368	6,315,483	1,551,625	2,620,141	50,869	206,160	114,004

Personal Income and Employment by Area: Janesville-Beloit, WI

(Thousands of dollars, except as noted.)

Year	Personal income, total	Earnings by place of work			Less: Contributions for government social insurance	Plus: Adjustment for residence	Equals: Net earnings by place of residence	Plus: Dividends, interest, and rent	Plus: Personal current transfer receipts	Per capita personal income (dollars)	Population (persons)	Total employment
		Nonfarm	Farm	Total								
1970	508,949	375,550	15,862	391,412	27,547	26,750	390,615	73,909	44,425	3,859	131,872	53,249
1971	554,306	405,743	18,858	424,601	30,633	26,140	420,108	80,143	54,055	4,191	132,257	53,167
1972	597,945	438,445	18,644	457,089	35,424	29,198	450,863	86,080	61,002	4,487	133,253	53,902
1973	675,634	502,648	27,163	529,811	46,955	30,845	513,701	95,047	66,886	5,019	134,603	57,505
1974	732,589	543,377	20,932	564,309	52,883	31,782	543,208	106,539	82,842	5,387	135,984	59,092
1975	789,143	564,013	24,949	588,962	53,851	29,997	565,108	116,622	107,413	5,732	137,680	58,336
1976	886,974	673,086	11,494	684,580	64,971	26,211	645,820	125,638	115,516	6,455	137,402	60,119
1977	1,002,959	776,744	22,736	799,480	74,572	24,746	749,654	139,568	113,737	7,275	137,859	62,999
1978	1,113,290	868,548	21,388	889,936	86,392	32,246	835,790	153,315	124,185	8,064	138,065	64,619
1979	1,234,630	955,810	28,106	983,916	98,137	33,792	919,571	168,707	146,352	8,831	139,809	66,458
1980	1,320,334	932,825	28,814	961,639	94,885	41,361	908,115	202,935	209,284	9,480	139,269	63,602
1981	1,469,057	1,042,565	26,676	1,069,241	113,731	40,377	995,887	248,224	224,946	10,619	138,336	64,284
1982	1,485,534	1,014,534	13,209	1,027,743	112,561	41,601	956,783	284,140	244,611	10,773	137,893	61,023
1983	1,605,844	1,144,744	-1,542	1,143,202	126,634	39,358	1,055,926	305,664	244,254	11,675	137,549	62,519
1984	1,789,236	1,280,520	12,983	1,293,503	145,659	52,690	1,200,534	338,855	249,847	13,010	137,523	65,192
1985	1,888,355	1,350,155	18,198	1,368,353	156,866	62,931	1,274,418	349,038	264,899	13,712	137,713	65,868
1986	1,958,185	1,359,842	23,452	1,383,294	156,925	85,072	1,311,441	369,088	277,656	14,236	137,555	66,699
1987	2,033,381	1,400,451	36,795	1,437,246	158,400	99,535	1,378,381	366,737	288,263	14,991	135,641	68,104
1988	2,206,337	1,582,383	16,307	1,598,690	184,087	115,125	1,529,728	383,285	293,324	16,153	136,588	70,857
1989	2,355,648	1,649,706	35,354	1,685,060	193,402	130,629	1,622,287	420,559	312,802	17,050	138,161	71,522
1990	2,494,373	1,764,660	30,483	1,795,143	214,277	140,084	1,720,950	436,876	336,547	17,835	139,859	73,269
1991	2,550,011	1,760,612	22,044	1,782,656	215,679	145,160	1,712,137	454,662	383,212	18,057	141,219	71,991
1992	2,818,423	2,027,663	31,349	2,059,012	245,807	128,273	1,941,478	471,619	405,326	19,722	142,904	75,226
1993	2,943,921	2,132,308	19,344	2,151,652	258,685	135,774	2,028,741	498,985	416,195	20,391	144,372	76,394
1994	3,124,299	2,286,242	29,048	2,315,290	277,868	151,810	2,189,232	515,144	419,923	21,402	145,982	78,980
1995	3,315,600	2,435,468	23,590	2,459,058	295,923	152,581	2,315,716	556,072	443,812	22,376	148,179	82,349
1996	3,444,607	2,501,199	34,925	2,536,124	299,102	159,787	2,396,809	588,570	459,228	22,974	149,937	82,642
1997	3,624,936	2,656,207	22,985	2,679,192	313,931	166,044	2,531,305	625,320	468,311	24,143	150,145	84,076
1998	3,802,603	2,763,896	27,031	2,790,927	323,369	184,816	2,652,374	673,500	476,729	25,212	150,827	83,619
1999	3,896,755	2,857,959	28,459	2,886,418	334,925	202,514	2,754,007	645,467	497,281	25,714	151,541	84,649
2000	4,071,746	2,937,423	21,376	2,958,799	340,681	225,805	2,843,923	682,831	544,992	26,706	152,464	84,977
2001	4,203,882	2,979,790	27,152	3,006,942	350,877	231,875	2,887,940	706,381	609,561	27,445	153,174	83,958
2002	4,337,720	3,104,837	19,682	3,124,519	361,346	231,054	2,994,227	688,504	654,989	28,235	153,628	83,122
2003	4,497,215	3,240,077	33,732	3,273,809	376,851	229,391	3,126,349	695,274	675,592	29,152	154,268	83,550
2004	4,660,492	3,313,045	49,064	3,362,109	386,508	287,926	3,263,527	699,205	697,760	29,935	155,685	84,840
2005	4,811,866	3,389,575	37,510	3,427,085	401,677	320,082	3,345,490	715,695	750,681	30,696	156,761	85,936
2006	5,144,580	3,673,931	32,317	3,706,248	439,899	311,739	3,578,088	775,557	790,935	32,450	158,538	87,118
2007	5,308,483	3,644,309	44,589	3,688,898	438,700	333,670	3,583,868	871,601	853,014	33,196	159,912	87,009
2008	5,422,881	3,559,317	31,103	3,590,420	433,989	354,366	3,510,797	928,393	983,691	33,757	160,647	84,580
2009	5,308,870	3,272,405	26,474	3,298,879	398,873	398,580	3,298,586	864,978	1,145,306	33,095	160,411	78,107
2010	5,450,145	3,264,949	39,383	3,304,332	399,323	374,604	3,279,613	958,556	1,211,976	34,008	160,261	77,420
2011	5,721,237	3,430,403	72,364	3,502,767	375,072	453,625	3,581,320	977,849	1,162,068	35,780	159,899	77,870
2012	5,987,243	3,662,872	37,395	3,700,267	396,364	392,366	3,696,269	1,101,505	1,189,469	37,394	160,113	79,446
2013	6,125,557	3,965,537	49,957	4,015,494	474,815	285,758	3,826,437	1,079,088	1,220,032	38,189	160,402	80,890
2014	6,222,366	3,885,161	20,616	3,905,777	473,288	360,152	3,792,641	1,154,139	1,275,586	38,586	161,261	82,038
2015	6,450,417	4,073,354	26,762	4,100,116	491,985	351,782	3,959,913	1,159,955	1,330,549	39,961	161,417	83,322
2016	6,590,784	4,180,698	25,232	4,205,930	505,802	363,080	4,063,208	1,184,545	1,343,031	40,748	161,746	84,038
2017	6,796,377	4,320,460	21,316	4,341,776	530,038	339,957	4,151,695	1,249,967	1,394,715	41,767	162,721	85,173
2018	7,134,598	4,608,171	24,573	4,632,744	557,954	319,886	4,394,676	1,281,788	1,458,134	43,685	163,319	86,317
2019	7,510,105	4,814,395	17,755	4,832,150	589,260	386,731	4,629,621	1,343,414	1,537,070	45,883	163,681	86,916
2020	8,039,652	4,874,440	47,567	4,922,007	599,288	421,333	4,744,052	1,352,653	1,942,947	49,129	163,643	83,480
2021	8,677,198	5,120,307	56,862	5,177,169	617,937	537,243	5,096,475	1,383,406	2,197,317	52,787	164,381	85,465

Personal Income and Employment by Area: Jefferson City, MO

(Thousands of dollars, except as noted.)

Year	Personal income, total	Derivation of personal income								Per capita personal income (dollars)	Population (persons)	Total employment
		Earnings by place of work			Less: Contributions for government social insurance	Plus: Adjustment for residence	Equals: Net earnings by place of residence	Plus: Dividends, interest, and rent	Plus: Personal current transfer receipts			
		Nonfarm	Farm	Total								
1970	342,121	265,871	17,635	283,506	16,832	-8,684	257,990	52,799	31,332	3,639	94,027	47,791
1971	371,341	291,732	14,825	306,557	19,137	-10,723	276,697	58,903	35,741	3,926	94,588	48,879
1972	406,798	316,119	19,926	336,045	21,652	-11,969	302,424	65,672	38,702	4,166	97,637	50,046
1973	465,525	350,251	35,029	385,280	27,702	-13,646	343,932	76,362	45,231	4,726	98,495	52,912
1974	514,010	393,519	25,828	419,347	32,363	-15,738	371,246	89,718	53,046	5,143	99,942	54,087
1975	560,744	421,875	19,171	441,046	33,845	-17,562	389,639	102,264	68,841	5,495	102,037	53,159
1976	628,573	491,201	14,904	506,105	39,834	-24,515	441,756	112,340	74,477	6,060	103,718	55,939
1977	702,792	560,481	19,949	580,430	45,955	-35,386	499,089	126,394	77,309	6,689	105,067	59,122
1978	809,163	664,645	27,687	692,332	57,196	-50,724	584,412	140,490	84,261	7,477	108,217	63,595
1979	896,624	738,510	30,741	769,251	66,049	-60,044	643,158	158,025	95,441	8,172	109,714	64,788
1980	992,623	815,622	3,830	819,452	71,753	-71,472	676,227	200,054	116,342	8,759	113,330	65,774
1981	1,130,066	897,104	16,658	913,762	85,063	-77,297	751,402	245,406	133,258	9,876	114,422	66,216
1982	1,235,960	966,390	12,608	978,998	93,981	-86,028	798,989	288,751	148,220	10,728	115,211	65,896
1983	1,326,342	1,032,427	3,568	1,035,995	100,137	-84,266	851,592	313,954	160,796	11,389	116,456	67,159
1984	1,441,180	1,085,083	19,960	1,105,043	106,525	-74,361	924,157	348,874	168,149	12,282	117,342	68,046
1985	1,495,213	1,094,732	22,559	1,117,291	107,857	-61,483	947,951	369,649	177,613	12,780	117,000	67,660
1986	1,608,769	1,196,428	21,281	1,217,709	119,473	-67,254	1,030,982	390,649	187,138	13,592	118,360	69,180
1987	1,678,323	1,260,239	23,077	1,283,316	124,791	-69,140	1,089,385	399,225	189,713	14,076	119,231	69,132
1988	1,753,421	1,341,431	15,683	1,357,114	140,418	-67,557	1,149,139	406,545	197,737	14,655	119,646	70,870
1989	1,920,764	1,446,941	23,913	1,470,854	152,246	-72,008	1,246,600	457,000	217,164	15,973	120,250	73,463
1990	2,018,562	1,559,467	21,113	1,580,580	167,205	-83,079	1,330,296	449,889	238,377	16,668	121,107	75,568
1991	2,144,345	1,644,181	18,083	1,662,264	178,156	-88,557	1,395,551	472,036	276,758	17,420	123,100	76,650
1992	2,289,461	1,773,417	17,008	1,790,425	190,254	-95,943	1,504,228	481,859	303,374	18,345	124,802	77,896
1993	2,405,852	1,856,797	16,679	1,873,476	199,701	-100,530	1,573,245	509,405	323,202	18,994	126,662	79,861
1994	2,548,476	1,983,027	4,921	1,987,948	214,580	-106,865	1,666,503	537,300	344,673	19,834	128,490	82,641
1995	2,708,402	2,118,785	-4,155	2,114,630	229,148	-118,395	1,767,087	573,486	367,829	20,651	131,148	85,679
1996	2,899,119	2,259,849	19,850	2,279,699	240,978	-130,198	1,908,523	610,075	380,521	21,700	133,601	88,188
1997	3,101,355	2,425,120	21,067	2,446,187	256,540	-144,513	2,045,134	658,905	397,316	22,853	135,707	90,574
1998	3,226,050	2,548,816	8,891	2,557,707	268,657	-152,478	2,136,572	675,224	414,254	23,502	137,268	92,096
1999	3,391,465	2,763,728	-4,584	2,759,144	287,921	-173,270	2,297,953	659,998	433,514	24,445	138,736	93,723
2000	3,593,337	2,903,311	10,394	2,913,705	301,096	-184,985	2,427,624	706,558	459,155	25,615	140,285	95,500
2001	3,733,013	3,015,686	13,394	3,029,080	313,499	-201,145	2,514,436	707,546	511,031	26,477	140,991	96,794
2002	3,790,455	3,093,238	4,397	3,097,635	319,957	-203,963	2,573,715	671,456	545,284	26,658	142,190	95,941
2003	3,987,328	3,257,233	16,797	3,274,030	335,366	-230,067	2,708,597	707,970	570,761	27,850	143,171	97,932
2004	4,270,092	3,443,767	80,498	3,524,265	350,871	-235,883	2,937,511	720,348	612,233	29,937	142,637	98,610
2005	4,413,647	3,565,422	57,036	3,622,458	367,770	-242,833	3,011,855	742,756	659,036	30,555	144,450	99,222
2006	4,651,274	3,757,045	48,847	3,805,892	386,093	-241,183	3,178,616	771,263	701,395	31,934	145,654	99,545
2007	4,893,557	3,854,611	52,135	3,906,746	401,578	-252,042	3,253,126	882,601	757,830	33,413	146,455	100,715
2008	5,212,684	4,018,085	80,010	4,098,095	421,323	-273,927	3,402,845	950,000	859,839	35,270	147,792	101,618
2009	5,147,129	3,976,565	48,558	4,025,123	414,925	-295,229	3,314,969	900,013	932,147	34,572	148,880	100,049
2010	5,263,622	4,069,481	65,599	4,135,080	421,323	-312,570	3,401,187	858,505	1,003,930	35,092	149,994	99,159
2011	5,389,954	4,095,764	80,020	4,175,784	381,216	-323,241	3,471,327	900,761	1,017,866	35,832	150,421	98,429
2012	5,592,528	4,161,391	52,219	4,213,610	382,567	-316,915	3,514,128	1,043,422	1,034,978	37,181	150,415	97,656
2013	5,699,131	4,395,629	67,759	4,463,388	446,898	-346,250	3,670,240	964,210	1,064,681	37,816	150,705	98,070
2014	5,873,585	4,462,481	116,795	4,579,276	458,174	-348,812	3,772,290	1,009,479	1,091,816	38,954	150,782	98,203
2015	6,029,547	4,578,497	50,956	4,629,453	477,033	-362,197	3,790,223	1,076,929	1,162,395	39,931	151,000	98,979
2016	6,079,904	4,627,130	11,764	4,638,894	489,331	-369,638	3,779,925	1,090,671	1,209,308	40,145	151,449	100,789
2017	6,275,680	4,742,313	4,736	4,747,049	504,311	-373,082	3,869,656	1,165,889	1,240,135	41,449	151,408	101,350
2018	6,356,219	4,827,521	1,009	4,828,530	515,737	-389,137	3,923,656	1,146,573	1,285,990	41,957	151,493	101,583
2019	6,744,391	5,038,889	5,768	5,044,657	542,639	-406,300	4,095,718	1,276,478	1,372,195	44,668	150,990	102,064
2020	7,292,384	5,270,523	22,405	5,292,928	576,012	-425,311	4,291,605	1,308,885	1,691,894	48,551	150,199	101,146
2021	7,729,173	5,404,295	30,717	5,435,012	580,322	-387,713	4,466,977	1,376,325	1,885,871	51,286	150,706	101,781

Personal Income and Employment by Area: Johnson City, TN

(Thousands of dollars, except as noted.)

Year	Personal income, total	Earnings by place of work			Less: Contributions for government social insurance	Plus: Adjustment for residence	Equals: Net earnings by place of residence	Plus: Dividends, interest, and rent	Plus: Personal current transfer receipts	Per capita personal income (dollars)	Population (persons)	Total employment
		Nonfarm	Farm	Total								
1970	399,260	283,219	7,417	290,636	18,568	36,480	308,548	46,788	43,924	3,002	132,997	51,412
1971	442,056	317,167	6,578	323,745	21,424	36,652	338,973	52,757	50,326	3,241	136,401	53,402
1972	494,553	355,301	10,656	365,957	25,215	39,926	380,668	58,854	55,031	3,529	140,121	56,559
1973	561,016	409,661	13,635	423,296	33,261	40,407	430,442	66,783	63,791	3,980	140,947	60,518
1974	618,936	445,610	10,492	456,102	37,493	44,492	463,101	77,246	78,589	4,320	143,257	60,850
1975	656,423	437,761	7,022	444,783	35,459	51,423	460,747	87,020	108,656	4,511	145,524	55,431
1976	728,393	491,869	11,555	503,424	40,948	59,464	521,940	92,739	113,714	4,867	149,645	57,109
1977	802,321	546,191	9,283	555,474	45,671	71,439	581,242	103,325	117,754	5,371	149,374	59,709
1978	918,853	629,814	9,013	638,827	53,515	88,273	673,585	118,985	126,283	6,094	150,780	62,719
1979	1,033,038	707,064	4,474	711,538	63,248	101,892	750,182	137,525	145,331	6,727	153,562	64,552
1980	1,172,305	783,979	7,798	791,777	70,751	109,669	830,695	169,912	171,698	7,518	155,925	66,128
1981	1,316,291	858,016	14,605	872,621	83,424	121,557	910,754	206,690	198,847	8,330	158,024	65,685
1982	1,377,633	878,357	13,403	891,760	86,848	118,993	923,905	232,024	221,704	8,696	158,424	64,173
1983	1,471,834	945,994	4,682	950,676	94,516	124,980	981,140	251,350	239,344	9,257	158,995	64,560
1984	1,603,935	1,036,645	10,254	1,046,899	107,358	127,354	1,066,895	285,595	251,445	10,041	159,742	67,109
1985	1,689,743	1,089,982	10,028	1,100,010	114,429	142,887	1,128,468	296,850	264,425	10,599	159,422	67,936
1986	1,808,207	1,176,558	5,215	1,181,773	126,535	152,564	1,207,802	318,647	281,758	11,349	159,326	69,445
1987	1,918,038	1,271,104	7,170	1,278,274	136,009	155,758	1,298,023	323,608	296,407	12,038	159,337	72,376
1988	2,059,479	1,361,853	10,211	1,372,064	152,084	169,513	1,389,493	352,003	317,983	12,938	159,181	75,181
1989	2,227,164	1,436,197	11,320	1,447,517	162,954	193,774	1,478,337	396,477	352,350	13,970	159,430	77,238
1990	2,402,074	1,567,238	17,634	1,584,872	178,343	207,179	1,613,708	400,346	388,020	14,925	160,942	80,870
1991	2,531,865	1,646,317	19,679	1,665,996	190,435	208,654	1,684,215	410,076	437,574	15,525	163,079	80,820
1992	2,744,462	1,819,474	22,254	1,841,728	208,268	207,427	1,840,887	414,114	489,461	16,650	164,834	83,910
1993	2,869,754	1,883,846	22,440	1,906,286	215,761	230,210	1,920,735	422,685	526,334	17,174	167,100	85,376
1994	2,977,181	1,995,543	21,143	2,016,686	233,661	194,648	1,977,673	448,397	551,111	17,583	169,319	88,631
1995	3,170,334	2,104,697	14,908	2,119,605	248,129	206,493	2,077,969	489,331	603,034	18,469	171,654	91,968
1996	3,354,781	2,208,066	7,894	2,215,960	257,747	230,464	2,188,677	526,984	639,120	19,248	174,296	93,587
1997	3,555,236	2,376,632	12,082	2,388,714	273,736	219,192	2,334,170	549,909	671,157	20,103	176,853	95,673
1998	3,764,200	2,547,861	10,984	2,558,845	287,385	213,403	2,484,863	567,657	711,680	21,078	178,581	96,099
1999	3,826,142	2,651,017	7,567	2,658,584	298,780	155,243	2,515,047	571,293	739,802	21,239	180,145	97,479
2000	4,079,583	2,856,665	13,316	2,869,981	318,515	106,503	2,657,969	606,274	815,340	22,422	181,944	99,329
2001	4,238,087	2,916,257	7,002	2,923,259	327,879	127,902	2,723,282	633,308	881,497	23,262	182,187	98,166
2002	4,356,361	2,987,733	3,079	2,990,812	338,198	135,335	2,787,949	600,287	968,125	23,679	183,973	96,239
2003	4,547,231	3,105,074	3,843	3,108,917	348,931	144,509	2,904,495	629,926	1,012,810	24,442	186,040	97,295
2004	4,924,853	3,391,794	5,198	3,396,992	376,733	147,731	3,167,990	667,710	1,089,153	26,292	187,317	100,015
2005	5,099,599	3,519,750	6,785	3,526,535	394,839	131,605	3,263,301	673,209	1,163,089	26,956	189,182	102,263
2006	5,409,685	3,677,951	2,550	3,680,501	414,490	177,785	3,443,796	730,460	1,235,429	28,184	191,943	103,414
2007	5,765,719	3,846,536	-2,994	3,843,542	437,566	173,133	3,579,109	828,023	1,358,587	29,748	193,819	106,084
2008	6,066,492	3,929,452	-2,409	3,927,043	455,147	179,211	3,651,107	901,490	1,513,895	30,913	196,242	105,554
2009	6,082,977	3,900,494	5,962	3,906,456	456,342	143,864	3,593,978	870,839	1,618,160	30,769	197,698	101,327
2010	6,366,510	3,962,948	887	3,963,835	459,179	205,104	3,709,760	886,843	1,769,907	31,989	199,019	100,747
2011	6,758,717	4,178,552	-852	4,177,700	429,051	257,584	4,006,233	939,955	1,812,529	33,861	199,600	103,422
2012	6,974,687	4,373,787	2,848	4,376,635	435,044	234,750	4,176,341	976,797	1,821,549	34,782	200,525	103,604
2013	6,943,582	4,342,817	5,869	4,348,686	488,256	267,481	4,127,911	964,653	1,851,018	34,624	200,541	101,646
2014	7,105,793	4,393,685	7,920	4,401,605	493,615	280,854	4,188,844	1,024,013	1,892,936	35,308	201,252	102,054
2015	7,405,715	4,608,192	8,216	4,616,408	515,333	273,774	4,374,849	1,065,316	1,965,550	36,688	201,857	103,382
2016	7,509,190	4,671,093	25	4,671,118	525,973	264,581	4,409,726	1,100,571	1,998,893	36,930	203,338	104,222
2017	7,770,890	4,895,523	611	4,896,134	557,413	249,437	4,588,158	1,127,619	2,055,113	38,059	204,179	106,082
2018	8,104,453	5,088,950	-2,640	5,086,310	579,284	255,846	4,762,872	1,179,446	2,162,135	39,425	205,565	106,812
2019	8,613,447	5,298,459	-1,621	5,296,838	596,684	233,799	4,933,953	1,362,724	2,316,770	41,712	206,496	106,647
2020	9,278,432	5,579,323	-2,345	5,576,978	627,081	162,687	5,112,584	1,402,359	2,763,489	44,767	207,262	106,006
2021	10,040,810	6,021,867	1,761	6,023,628	659,391	160,383	5,524,620	1,480,972	3,035,218	48,257	208,068	109,932

Personal Income and Employment by Area: Johnstown, PA

(Thousands of dollars, except as noted.)

Year	Personal income, total	Earnings by place of work			Less: Contributions for government social insurance	Plus: Adjustment for residence	Equals: Net earnings by place of residence	Plus: Dividends, interest, and rent	Plus: Personal current transfer receipts	Per capita personal income (dollars)	Population (persons)	Total employment
		Nonfarm	Farm	Total								
1970	607,109	520,299	2,913	523,212	39,131	-33,390	450,691	64,614	91,804	3,246	187,061	70,524
1971	652,058	546,212	2,272	548,484	42,709	-35,117	470,658	68,879	112,521	3,453	188,837	70,619
1972	729,191	618,943	1,235	620,178	50,029	-41,017	529,132	73,513	126,546	3,848	189,521	71,565
1973	810,449	686,485	4,001	690,486	63,793	-45,292	581,401	83,154	145,894	4,282	189,286	73,454
1974	915,701	781,170	3,920	785,090	75,704	-54,371	655,015	96,054	164,632	4,858	188,475	74,173
1975	1,052,072	887,051	3,081	890,132	83,580	-63,706	742,846	111,633	197,593	5,572	188,819	76,041
1976	1,149,286	958,304	3,689	961,993	91,481	-65,987	804,525	120,748	224,013	6,046	190,087	76,121
1977	1,262,593	1,041,240	3,134	1,044,374	98,398	-69,171	876,805	135,930	249,858	6,635	190,302	76,013
1978	1,361,707	1,099,172	6,242	1,105,414	105,791	-68,354	931,269	153,374	277,064	7,237	188,155	74,653
1979	1,521,037	1,239,482	7,715	1,247,197	122,559	-85,132	1,039,506	176,438	305,093	8,161	186,373	76,327
1980	1,594,958	1,210,659	9,740	1,220,399	120,236	-78,987	1,021,176	222,144	351,638	8,716	182,986	71,866
1981	1,716,391	1,246,443	13,143	1,259,586	133,237	-73,017	1,053,332	273,077	389,982	9,456	181,509	69,018
1982	1,764,176	1,189,815	4,771	1,194,586	129,013	-53,757	1,011,816	310,815	441,545	9,878	178,601	65,149
1983	1,796,066	1,146,506	2,825	1,149,331	124,334	-42,414	982,583	338,630	474,853	10,147	176,996	62,516
1984	1,901,340	1,229,874	6,383	1,236,257	140,633	-40,069	1,055,555	376,530	469,255	10,820	175,730	63,475
1985	1,937,778	1,244,431	4,915	1,249,346	144,362	-35,815	1,069,169	390,713	477,896	11,214	172,797	64,019
1986	1,957,248	1,226,039	4,333	1,230,372	145,986	-31,281	1,053,105	404,341	499,802	11,486	170,400	64,855
1987	2,019,148	1,288,327	3,779	1,292,106	151,505	-24,581	1,116,020	395,776	507,352	11,981	168,535	66,371
1988	2,209,157	1,482,240	574	1,482,814	173,230	-27,356	1,282,228	404,130	522,799	13,308	166,006	68,288
1989	2,360,720	1,570,265	3,398	1,573,663	183,133	-31,027	1,359,503	457,059	544,158	14,397	163,970	69,263
1990	2,485,662	1,655,592	5,587	1,661,179	193,552	-26,802	1,440,825	453,256	591,581	15,255	162,938	71,269
1991	2,630,127	1,717,959	5,359	1,723,318	202,554	-22,261	1,498,503	449,496	682,128	16,188	162,473	70,635
1992	2,729,538	1,778,494	8,837	1,787,331	209,030	-6,225	1,572,076	447,468	709,994	16,823	162,247	70,141
1993	2,799,978	1,814,365	8,520	1,822,885	218,475	5,337	1,609,747	449,740	740,491	17,308	161,770	70,383
1994	2,887,963	1,883,497	7,006	1,890,503	232,805	12,598	1,670,296	467,425	750,242	17,964	160,766	71,846
1995	2,995,364	1,939,322	5,389	1,944,711	240,731	10,014	1,713,994	510,982	770,388	18,734	159,892	73,380
1996	3,073,460	1,940,042	8,967	1,949,009	237,144	20,471	1,732,336	528,742	812,382	19,380	158,588	73,457
1997	3,166,958	1,992,758	2,679	1,995,437	243,537	26,392	1,778,292	561,272	827,394	20,121	157,396	73,397
1998	3,300,407	2,118,843	2,245	2,121,088	251,288	27,903	1,897,703	572,760	829,944	21,200	155,677	74,169
1999	3,429,608	2,235,900	625	2,236,525	262,887	29,888	2,003,526	561,660	864,422	22,283	153,911	75,076
2000	3,522,289	2,232,539	3,120	2,235,659	260,881	46,805	2,021,583	595,271	905,435	23,157	152,107	75,088
2001	3,723,765	2,327,849	-1,257	2,326,592	267,609	60,928	2,119,911	632,302	971,552	24,677	150,902	72,951
2002	3,781,469	2,362,918	-2,518	2,360,400	271,738	74,643	2,163,305	592,099	1,026,065	25,238	149,831	71,797
2003	3,906,683	2,445,189	4,066	2,449,255	278,920	83,911	2,254,246	601,616	1,050,821	26,248	148,836	71,477
2004	4,017,819	2,556,723	2,501	2,559,224	291,415	88,986	2,356,795	564,606	1,096,418	27,168	147,886	72,180
2005	4,138,628	2,635,215	5,314	2,640,529	311,725	95,680	2,424,484	553,103	1,161,041	28,159	146,975	72,655
2006	4,276,506	2,724,360	7,126	2,731,486	324,573	77,782	2,484,695	580,030	1,211,781	29,272	146,093	74,221
2007	4,510,289	2,795,398	8,234	2,803,632	336,402	81,176	2,548,406	671,232	1,290,651	31,045	145,283	74,950
2008	4,731,067	2,868,385	12,687	2,881,072	347,884	87,045	2,620,233	705,969	1,404,865	32,708	144,646	75,025
2009	4,708,617	2,817,606	6,770	2,824,376	347,349	101,100	2,578,127	686,250	1,444,240	32,657	144,186	72,738
2010	4,710,033	2,917,948	5,866	2,923,814	356,545	-20,831	2,546,438	657,016	1,506,579	32,832	143,458	72,287
2011	5,027,999	2,979,699	16,006	2,995,705	328,453	147,921	2,815,173	700,054	1,512,772	35,262	142,590	72,198
2012	5,067,659	2,974,401	17,106	2,991,507	325,523	179,166	2,845,150	724,370	1,498,139	35,798	141,563	71,679
2013	5,051,561	2,977,152	12,492	2,989,644	362,494	206,495	2,833,645	692,648	1,525,268	36,379	138,858	70,678
2014	5,170,656	2,992,735	10,235	3,002,970	375,216	225,344	2,853,098	747,642	1,569,916	37,065	139,503	69,876
2015	5,278,964	3,031,212	4,627	3,035,839	374,151	232,926	2,894,614	748,202	1,636,148	38,135	138,427	69,157
2016	5,291,172	2,992,609	1,763	2,994,372	373,750	224,144	2,844,766	751,541	1,694,865	38,543	137,280	68,017
2017	5,367,732	3,023,204	4,920	3,028,124	384,308	242,197	2,886,013	787,404	1,694,315	39,408	136,209	66,667
2018	5,645,339	3,121,057	1,341	3,122,398	395,787	276,190	3,002,801	828,973	1,813,565	41,801	135,052	66,025
2019	5,781,409	3,193,920	6,254	3,200,174	406,226	277,839	3,071,787	826,314	1,883,308	43,120	134,077	65,095
2020	6,196,994	3,103,860	5,301	3,109,161	399,987	269,855	2,979,029	823,365	2,394,600	46,609	132,957	61,339
2021	6,538,569	3,174,917	9,578	3,184,495	400,949	311,616	3,095,162	822,418	2,620,989	49,472	132,167	62,261

Personal Income and Employment by Area: Jonesboro, AR

(Thousands of dollars, except as noted.)

Year	Personal income, total	Earnings by place of work			Less: Contributions for government social insurance	Plus: Adjustment for residence	Equals: Net earnings by place of residence	Plus: Dividends, interest, and rent	Plus: Personal current transfer receipts	Per capita personal income (dollars)	Population (persons)	Total employment
		Nonfarm	Farm	Total								
1970	232,177	146,372	43,150	189,522	11,136	3,789	182,175	25,548	24,454	2,919	79,540	34,569
1971	251,604	164,558	38,960	203,518	12,866	3,752	194,404	28,764	28,436	3,050	82,495	35,576
1972	278,732	188,955	37,116	226,071	15,373	3,709	214,407	31,858	32,467	3,330	83,698	36,928
1973	340,701	207,580	72,099	279,679	19,394	3,969	264,254	37,607	38,840	4,010	84,953	37,486
1974	382,837	227,529	78,869	306,398	21,956	4,146	288,588	46,024	48,225	4,465	85,734	37,982
1975	408,780	257,744	54,099	311,843	24,362	3,836	291,317	55,182	62,281	4,735	86,332	38,045
1976	438,467	300,452	36,526	336,978	28,746	3,042	311,274	59,555	67,638	4,971	88,200	39,374
1977	491,063	337,792	44,679	382,471	32,614	1,791	351,648	66,348	73,067	5,478	89,644	41,014
1978	630,210	386,681	126,999	513,680	38,343	1,378	476,715	74,094	79,401	6,981	90,272	42,812
1979	629,548	431,483	67,534	499,017	44,209	280	455,088	84,795	89,665	6,931	90,835	42,949
1980	650,383	455,975	28,711	484,686	46,459	148	438,375	103,206	108,802	7,205	90,274	42,267
1981	738,967	474,473	67,706	542,179	52,321	-315	489,543	128,440	120,984	8,202	90,094	40,797
1982	768,278	490,565	51,517	542,082	54,932	183	487,333	149,963	130,982	8,603	89,303	40,231
1983	787,400	527,441	25,220	552,661	59,214	93	493,540	150,691	143,169	8,841	89,065	40,737
1984	907,637	594,052	64,617	658,669	68,381	223	590,511	166,019	151,107	10,151	89,417	42,557
1985	948,682	630,009	51,211	681,220	73,061	512	608,671	180,280	159,731	10,571	89,745	43,490
1986	967,408	677,597	17,228	694,825	78,652	135	616,308	186,098	165,002	10,769	89,832	44,766
1987	1,060,016	745,089	50,416	795,505	85,954	-737	708,814	181,335	169,867	11,642	91,051	46,963
1988	1,159,019	805,294	78,456	883,750	96,410	580	787,920	192,991	178,108	12,606	91,939	48,776
1989	1,221,318	863,127	46,661	909,788	103,622	1,084	807,250	214,972	199,096	13,173	92,714	49,447
1990	1,288,921	906,721	43,599	950,320	112,976	4,871	842,215	228,126	218,580	13,712	93,999	49,752
1991	1,378,040	951,822	67,661	1,019,483	118,918	7,372	907,937	225,712	244,391	14,627	94,210	49,788
1992	1,514,843	1,048,408	89,017	1,137,425	130,022	6,749	1,014,152	231,475	269,216	15,781	95,994	51,479
1993	1,577,750	1,115,099	74,143	1,189,242	138,930	5,848	1,056,160	240,164	281,426	16,110	97,939	52,981
1994	1,656,838	1,182,789	81,584	1,264,373	148,863	6,386	1,121,896	247,693	287,249	16,757	98,872	53,314
1995	1,795,999	1,263,900	98,035	1,361,935	158,288	4,583	1,208,230	276,768	311,001	17,812	100,831	56,015
1996	1,902,309	1,321,408	113,473	1,434,881	164,198	5,299	1,275,982	298,024	328,303	18,532	102,652	56,986
1997	1,992,389	1,398,162	108,787	1,506,949	172,907	5,343	1,339,385	310,812	342,192	19,134	104,130	57,997
1998	2,101,631	1,508,926	90,009	1,598,935	182,681	5,668	1,421,922	322,443	357,266	19,900	105,607	59,098
1999	2,211,846	1,625,636	79,814	1,705,450	194,296	2,149	1,513,303	324,669	373,874	20,756	106,563	60,455
2000	2,331,730	1,701,763	90,537	1,792,300	202,406	2,084	1,591,978	343,846	395,906	21,563	108,136	61,241
2001	2,397,039	1,695,634	93,165	1,788,799	201,817	-2,814	1,584,168	360,957	451,914	22,037	108,774	61,014
2002	2,460,967	1,775,898	43,622	1,819,520	209,111	-13,894	1,596,515	359,525	504,927	22,538	109,191	61,139
2003	2,703,301	1,863,458	184,100	2,047,558	218,204	-24,578	1,804,776	370,037	528,488	24,536	110,177	61,586
2004	2,799,502	1,994,517	165,866	2,160,383	231,097	-35,313	1,893,973	330,421	575,108	25,137	111,370	62,829
2005	2,892,663	2,089,201	102,011	2,191,212	244,733	-38,572	1,907,907	363,047	621,709	25,697	112,570	63,514
2006	3,030,555	2,153,942	113,817	2,267,759	259,162	-44,734	1,963,863	391,940	674,752	26,438	114,629	64,964
2007	3,203,540	2,208,325	108,634	2,316,959	268,241	-41,248	2,007,470	461,998	734,072	27,578	116,163	64,741
2008	3,376,976	2,292,084	109,956	2,402,040	286,437	-64,406	2,051,197	493,142	832,637	28,639	117,915	64,977
2009	3,431,232	2,295,941	100,470	2,396,411	290,642	-60,180	2,045,589	469,536	916,107	28,566	120,114	64,443
2010	3,634,968	2,462,350	95,189	2,557,539	305,297	-60,891	2,191,351	459,608	984,009	29,976	121,261	65,208
2011	3,889,264	2,584,049	123,647	2,707,696	289,073	-48,206	2,370,417	503,456	1,015,391	31,655	122,865	67,910
2012	4,084,618	2,743,593	79,988	2,823,581	297,068	-30,808	2,495,705	557,001	1,031,912	32,858	124,312	68,060
2013	4,195,465	2,818,110	178,977	2,997,087	339,301	-32,986	2,624,800	520,976	1,049,689	33,333	125,866	69,158
2014	4,273,574	2,923,281	34,916	2,958,197	355,696	-30,980	2,571,521	584,379	1,117,674	33,799	126,442	70,423
2015	4,404,709	3,034,031	21,252	3,055,283	370,670	-39,543	2,645,070	587,275	1,172,364	34,414	127,992	72,438
2016	4,513,825	3,112,770	21,384	3,134,154	379,337	-61,494	2,693,323	600,484	1,220,018	34,882	129,403	74,463
2017	4,668,349	3,226,089	68,855	3,294,944	396,745	-89,122	2,809,077	621,849	1,237,423	35,740	130,618	76,748
2018	4,806,249	3,376,282	37,751	3,414,033	412,346	-105,665	2,896,022	629,801	1,280,426	36,383	132,103	78,206
2019	5,077,529	3,549,711	67,929	3,617,640	437,911	-119,603	3,060,126	667,332	1,350,071	38,086	133,316	79,706
2020	5,572,287	3,800,241	107,074	3,907,315	477,168	-158,716	3,271,431	659,565	1,641,291	41,439	134,469	79,181
2021	6,009,338	4,102,250	97,922	4,200,172	502,681	-181,867	3,515,624	672,215	1,821,499	44,554	134,878	81,363

Personal Income and Employment by Area: Joplin, MO

(Thousands of dollars, except as noted.)

Year	Personal income, total	Earnings by place of work			Less: Contributions for government social insurance	Plus: Adjustment for residence	Equals: Net earnings by place of residence	Plus: Dividends, interest, and rent	Plus: Personal current transfer receipts	Per capita personal income (dollars)	Population (persons)	Total employment
		Nonfarm	Farm	Total								
1970	354,813	273,450	10,341	283,791	18,399	-6,324	259,068	50,657	45,088	3,139	113,028	48,807
1971	379,110	291,191	9,671	300,862	20,308	-8,264	272,290	55,148	51,672	3,314	114,407	49,252
1972	428,365	331,460	15,571	347,031	24,322	-9,849	312,860	60,360	55,145	3,650	117,364	52,210
1973	485,292	368,637	26,756	395,393	31,341	-10,957	353,095	68,326	63,871	4,064	119,399	55,584
1974	523,487	407,601	9,893	417,494	35,911	-12,970	368,613	79,832	75,042	4,328	120,962	55,905
1975	568,447	423,422	10,444	433,866	36,445	-12,682	384,739	88,212	95,496	4,693	121,126	53,422
1976	632,272	474,540	14,454	488,994	41,337	-14,227	433,430	97,416	101,426	5,192	121,777	55,436
1977	702,099	534,084	13,728	547,812	46,634	-15,924	485,254	111,778	105,067	5,675	123,716	57,532
1978	786,186	607,725	14,860	622,585	54,953	-19,920	547,712	124,480	113,994	6,294	124,905	59,753
1979	879,690	678,401	16,617	695,018	63,378	-21,304	610,336	141,139	128,215	6,940	126,753	61,872
1980	979,951	724,351	17,943	742,294	67,466	-23,754	651,074	174,134	154,743	7,665	127,845	61,478
1981	1,100,055	801,562	15,893	817,455	79,874	-27,315	710,266	212,948	176,841	8,535	128,894	62,909
1982	1,178,246	838,831	6,326	845,157	84,985	-32,243	727,929	251,660	198,657	9,118	129,226	62,312
1983	1,269,131	905,250	6,240	911,490	91,712	-35,713	784,065	273,355	211,711	9,790	129,634	64,321
1984	1,403,816	1,013,969	5,248	1,019,217	105,788	-41,985	871,444	312,544	219,828	10,743	130,678	67,177
1985	1,493,928	1,092,186	7,212	1,099,398	116,190	-47,730	935,478	325,524	232,926	11,360	131,504	69,624
1986	1,590,326	1,169,757	14,388	1,184,145	124,873	-55,234	1,004,038	339,450	246,838	12,033	132,165	71,862
1987	1,671,774	1,263,879	7,274	1,271,153	132,982	-61,637	1,076,534	338,141	257,099	12,543	133,284	73,545
1988	1,783,976	1,340,886	12,251	1,353,137	145,718	-64,608	1,142,811	362,215	278,950	13,346	133,670	74,700
1989	1,898,391	1,415,771	20,801	1,436,572	155,491	-66,999	1,214,082	389,996	294,313	14,125	134,404	75,726
1990	2,000,160	1,499,680	14,731	1,514,411	169,119	-74,123	1,271,169	410,139	318,852	14,792	135,219	77,595
1991	2,115,915	1,589,294	12,284	1,601,578	181,051	-79,848	1,340,679	405,465	369,771	15,478	136,705	78,870
1992	2,312,996	1,731,192	14,248	1,745,440	195,106	-87,409	1,462,925	449,168	400,903	16,656	138,865	81,177
1993	2,456,286	1,845,759	13,136	1,858,895	209,232	-95,612	1,554,051	468,117	434,118	17,352	141,558	84,247
1994	2,645,707	2,014,517	11,926	2,026,443	230,112	-109,248	1,687,083	503,273	455,351	18,346	144,212	88,024
1995	2,801,857	2,142,519	7,933	2,150,452	245,997	-116,625	1,787,830	523,310	490,717	19,092	146,755	90,789
1996	2,965,766	2,258,581	21,944	2,280,525	256,494	-123,538	1,900,493	539,381	525,892	19,844	149,456	93,362
1997	3,157,183	2,414,215	22,213	2,436,428	274,230	-136,764	2,025,434	574,147	557,602	20,791	151,852	95,844
1998	3,309,461	2,548,530	22,394	2,570,924	289,694	-144,713	2,136,517	596,627	576,317	21,481	154,066	98,516
1999	3,452,969	2,691,431	15,778	2,707,209	303,575	-148,092	2,255,542	588,745	608,682	22,160	155,822	99,452
2000	3,647,014	2,814,860	8,374	2,823,234	313,644	-151,922	2,357,668	638,343	651,003	23,131	157,665	100,269
2001	3,873,543	2,990,232	21,161	3,011,393	329,644	-159,064	2,522,685	618,733	732,125	24,428	158,567	99,129
2002	3,954,725	3,091,631	15,217	3,106,848	335,678	-171,294	2,599,876	567,765	787,084	24,703	160,092	97,883
2003	4,081,419	3,182,840	29,189	3,212,029	347,507	-185,691	2,678,831	575,522	827,066	25,188	162,037	97,823
2004	4,370,421	3,332,363	67,733	3,400,096	363,436	-192,359	2,844,301	661,312	864,808	26,649	163,997	98,482
2005	4,472,233	3,388,473	64,671	3,453,144	376,618	-194,260	2,882,266	657,815	932,152	26,915	166,160	99,546
2006	4,713,254	3,582,006	41,478	3,623,484	404,196	-211,602	3,007,686	728,646	976,922	27,939	168,701	102,126
2007	4,949,512	3,698,859	40,873	3,739,732	425,543	-209,940	3,104,249	792,878	1,052,385	28,907	171,224	105,104
2008	5,300,088	3,822,556	84,755	3,907,311	448,293	-203,112	3,255,906	869,167	1,175,015	30,682	172,744	105,170
2009	5,307,077	3,799,232	49,960	3,849,192	441,888	-186,564	3,220,740	810,543	1,275,794	30,432	174,394	101,990
2010	5,417,617	3,856,626	62,301	3,918,927	442,524	-181,811	3,294,592	773,196	1,349,829	30,811	175,834	100,016
2011	5,747,375	4,010,695	56,888	4,067,583	414,457	-181,418	3,471,708	890,420	1,385,247	33,054	173,877	101,070
2012	6,045,795	4,216,297	59,075	4,275,372	422,457	-173,067	3,679,848	1,022,570	1,343,377	34,654	174,464	102,073
2013	5,973,176	4,290,230	75,782	4,366,012	482,860	-171,227	3,711,925	899,983	1,361,268	34,092	175,210	101,935
2014	6,213,166	4,349,872	114,180	4,464,052	490,095	-134,879	3,839,078	967,983	1,406,105	35,204	176,489	101,446
2015	6,494,565	4,577,829	85,896	4,663,725	516,924	-124,789	4,022,012	997,288	1,475,265	36,599	177,452	101,634
2016	6,636,874	4,647,542	42,754	4,690,296	523,496	-101,737	4,065,063	1,040,528	1,531,283	37,220	178,314	101,833
2017	6,839,597	4,827,900	31,830	4,859,730	542,761	-112,430	4,204,539	1,064,210	1,570,848	38,160	179,235	102,397
2018	7,189,446	4,998,653	39,094	5,037,747	562,591	-115,789	4,359,367	1,199,878	1,630,201	40,026	179,620	103,608
2019	7,192,698	5,004,390	30,785	5,035,175	581,599	-102,857	4,350,719	1,138,969	1,703,010	39,800	180,723	104,008
2020	7,553,632	4,933,966	48,645	4,982,611	593,579	-78,299	4,310,733	1,129,162	2,113,737	41,646	181,379	100,884
2021	8,085,095	5,242,036	72,150	5,314,186	611,546	-105,782	4,596,858	1,119,827	2,368,410	44,292	182,541	103,915

Personal Income and Employment by Area: Kahului-Wailuku-Lahaina, HI

(Thousands of dollars, except as noted.)

Year	Personal income, total	Earnings by place of work			Less: Contributions for government social insurance	Plus: Adjustment for residence	Equals: Net earnings by place of residence	Plus: Dividends, interest, and rent	Plus: Personal current transfer receipts	Per capita personal income (dollars)	Population (persons)	Total employment
		Nonfarm	Farm	Total								
1970	199,508	124,379	37,343	161,722	9,259	33	152,496	31,550	15,462	4,338	45,995	22,016
1971	220,100	135,780	37,904	173,684	10,635	-55	162,994	36,754	20,352	4,250	51,784	22,664
1972	242,138	148,307	39,733	188,040	12,183	-104	175,753	41,218	25,167	4,703	51,488	23,264
1973	268,541	165,033	38,686	203,719	15,878	-219	187,622	50,240	30,679	5,096	52,693	24,568
1974	357,443	191,969	89,294	281,263	19,580	-722	260,961	58,908	37,574	6,661	53,661	26,464
1975	379,559	233,660	54,923	288,583	21,968	-2,371	264,244	66,618	48,697	6,698	56,669	29,157
1976	423,121	269,325	54,157	323,482	25,324	-3,083	295,075	72,317	55,729	7,032	60,173	31,192
1977	475,251	315,645	55,733	371,378	29,810	-4,017	337,551	81,038	56,662	7,572	62,763	33,058
1978	529,548	365,868	47,483	413,351	36,293	-4,767	372,291	95,966	61,291	8,030	65,950	35,880
1979	612,079	424,955	53,938	478,893	43,393	-5,641	429,859	114,786	67,434	8,802	69,537	37,847
1980	733,508	469,621	97,238	566,859	47,270	-6,073	513,516	138,903	81,089	10,241	71,624	39,255
1981	769,699	515,529	51,457	566,986	55,584	-4,128	507,274	166,686	95,739	10,395	74,043	38,790
1982	838,061	569,940	58,659	628,599	62,351	-4,242	562,006	169,266	106,789	10,869	77,103	40,711
1983	979,608	634,055	103,443	737,498	68,462	-3,693	665,343	196,377	117,888	12,236	80,060	43,194
1984	1,038,831	705,774	69,577	775,351	77,922	-3,750	693,679	222,365	122,787	12,521	82,969	44,749
1985	1,127,368	788,252	63,316	851,568	88,160	-4,534	758,874	239,058	129,436	13,240	85,147	48,048
1986	1,228,301	865,151	73,511	938,662	97,650	-4,753	836,259	257,201	134,841	14,056	87,389	50,149
1987	1,329,873	961,975	73,277	1,035,252	108,359	-4,900	921,993	268,924	138,956	14,690	90,532	53,953
1988	1,500,439	1,124,023	66,870	1,190,893	128,164	-5,472	1,057,257	295,268	147,914	16,002	93,767	58,381
1989	1,748,023	1,324,148	60,850	1,384,998	149,806	-8,235	1,226,957	357,131	163,935	18,055	96,819	62,829
1990	1,953,686	1,503,118	67,682	1,570,800	177,004	-9,771	1,384,025	389,246	180,415	19,209	101,709	66,255
1991	2,080,622	1,618,460	67,274	1,685,734	192,438	-10,153	1,483,143	394,395	203,084	19,703	105,599	69,643
1992	2,302,938	1,760,085	97,223	1,857,308	208,876	-9,965	1,638,467	418,835	245,636	21,209	108,585	72,764
1993	2,441,170	1,861,638	57,066	1,918,704	215,201	-9,403	1,694,100	484,897	262,173	21,807	111,944	72,912
1994	2,539,146	1,942,678	58,477	2,001,155	228,246	-10,547	1,762,362	495,926	280,858	22,127	114,754	73,468
1995	2,620,030	1,972,859	59,511	2,032,370	229,713	-9,454	1,793,203	505,445	321,382	22,223	117,895	73,984
1996	2,652,637	1,988,076	56,091	2,044,167	233,397	-10,586	1,800,184	510,737	341,716	21,979	120,689	74,645
1997	2,744,581	2,043,023	57,536	2,100,559	238,101	-10,989	1,851,469	555,363	337,749	22,355	122,772	75,979
1998	2,866,660	2,124,904	65,049	2,189,953	245,746	-12,084	1,932,123	581,281	353,256	22,998	124,648	78,154
1999	3,085,912	2,318,242	70,622	2,388,864	264,067	-14,833	2,109,964	597,781	378,167	24,460	126,160	80,371
2000	3,298,238	2,481,256	62,275	2,543,531	281,362	-16,679	2,245,490	654,178	398,570	25,552	129,078	82,260
2001	3,509,708	2,675,614	66,466	2,742,080	298,538	-14,901	2,428,641	660,008	421,059	26,503	132,428	85,069
2002	3,706,856	2,850,122	72,148	2,922,270	318,036	-12,850	2,591,384	656,487	458,985	27,543	134,583	85,815
2003	3,948,734	3,092,773	73,624	3,166,397	345,829	-10,435	2,810,133	659,395	479,206	28,698	137,596	87,997
2004	4,296,647	3,332,273	78,711	3,410,984	362,204	-8,327	3,040,453	735,656	520,538	30,554	140,625	91,839
2005	4,662,694	3,617,779	85,014	3,702,793	395,208	-7,140	3,300,445	797,557	564,692	32,504	143,448	96,095
2006	5,022,966	3,818,015	95,124	3,913,139	430,575	-4,681	3,477,883	951,836	593,247	34,457	145,776	98,710
2007	5,354,750	3,985,578	94,225	4,079,803	455,502	-2,703	3,621,598	1,075,439	657,713	36,152	148,117	102,898
2008	5,603,863	3,981,217	77,585	4,058,802	454,037	2,030	3,606,795	1,215,634	781,434	37,008	151,424	101,182
2009	5,285,618	3,722,263	76,734	3,798,997	423,252	8,213	3,383,958	1,035,278	866,382	34,458	153,393	94,943
2010	5,506,302	3,745,763	78,758	3,824,521	441,206	13,074	3,396,389	1,127,786	982,127	35,498	155,115	93,935
2011	5,774,970	3,914,963	84,141	3,999,104	423,108	17,772	3,593,768	1,159,556	1,021,646	36,770	157,057	95,096
2012	6,209,315	4,243,652	103,187	4,346,839	444,975	20,958	3,922,822	1,286,962	999,531	39,046	159,025	97,164
2013	6,255,282	4,352,033	98,636	4,450,669	525,287	25,606	3,950,988	1,273,391	1,030,903	38,816	161,154	100,042
2014	6,653,306	4,580,170	91,634	4,671,804	528,764	27,128	4,170,168	1,365,241	1,117,897	41,098	161,887	102,722
2015	7,031,111	4,889,961	76,245	4,966,206	557,218	28,210	4,437,198	1,446,846	1,147,067	43,282	162,447	104,666
2016	7,337,330	5,066,361	77,546	5,143,907	575,661	30,160	4,598,406	1,525,198	1,213,726	44,813	163,731	106,856
2017	7,712,376	5,380,458	39,829	5,420,287	609,656	30,024	4,840,655	1,600,012	1,271,709	46,943	164,291	108,601
2018	7,997,206	5,680,960	25,377	5,706,337	648,090	30,743	5,088,990	1,617,164	1,291,052	48,496	164,904	110,305
2019	8,624,269	6,097,600	20,353	6,117,953	694,968	30,299	5,453,284	1,781,876	1,389,109	52,301	164,897	112,686
2020	8,827,651	5,174,094	18,200	5,192,294	600,080	30,314	4,622,528	1,752,158	2,452,965	53,586	164,737	93,378
2021	9,615,088	6,045,140	19,150	6,064,290	631,184	28,763	5,461,869	1,799,781	2,353,438	58,520	164,303	102,358

Personal Income and Employment by Area: Kalamazoo-Portage, MI

(Thousands of dollars, except as noted.)

Year	Personal income, total	Derivation of personal income									Per capita personal income (dollars)	Population (persons)	Total employment
		Earnings by place of work			Less: Contributions for government social insurance	Plus: Adjustment for residence	Equals: Net earnings by place of residence	Plus: Dividends, interest, and rent	Plus: Personal current transfer receipts				
		Nonfarm	Farm	Total									
1970	1,024,094	834,532	18,026	852,558	59,929	-3,231	789,398	149,462	85,234	3,971	257,900	108,004
1971	1,083,816	873,031	17,465	890,496	64,642	-1,949	823,905	157,410	102,501	4,173	259,747	106,654
1972	1,187,917	961,313	20,557	981,870	74,874	-652	906,344	168,247	113,326	4,515	263,099	110,715
1973	1,330,915	1,079,201	29,593	1,108,794	97,611	-2,783	1,008,400	190,740	131,775	5,076	262,173	115,785
1974	1,471,063	1,178,093	27,751	1,205,844	110,553	-9,137	1,086,154	221,445	163,464	5,564	264,388	118,408
1975	1,618,247	1,258,389	28,432	1,286,821	114,779	-12,593	1,159,449	240,637	218,161	6,062	266,969	117,797
1976	1,775,166	1,413,221	20,303	1,433,524	131,604	-17,193	1,284,727	259,005	231,434	6,584	269,631	121,403
1977	1,985,399	1,598,931	29,010	1,627,941	147,877	-21,208	1,458,856	289,184	237,359	7,298	272,051	126,334
1978	2,213,477	1,798,316	30,743	1,829,059	170,622	-25,045	1,633,392	321,308	258,777	8,073	274,191	131,628
1979	2,447,355	2,017,573	21,330	2,038,903	200,012	-42,898	1,795,993	358,432	292,930	8,858	276,290	134,464
1980	2,672,972	2,138,880	12,626	2,151,506	211,258	-57,678	1,882,570	427,968	362,434	9,559	279,626	132,685
1981	2,955,316	2,316,453	21,181	2,337,634	246,051	-56,063	2,035,520	524,096	395,700	10,526	280,754	132,264
1982	3,092,685	2,348,534	20,089	2,368,623	253,826	-50,003	2,064,794	590,864	437,027	11,019	280,662	129,119
1983	3,300,427	2,500,724	15,861	2,516,585	274,339	-48,809	2,193,437	638,325	468,665	11,818	279,280	129,086
1984	3,591,333	2,716,635	28,677	2,745,312	308,601	-46,801	2,389,910	719,873	481,550	12,849	279,510	132,514
1985	3,847,126	2,934,373	43,510	2,977,883	338,590	-54,157	2,585,136	752,427	509,563	13,707	280,675	136,989
1986	4,129,760	3,160,197	35,216	3,195,413	365,172	-39,247	2,790,994	802,182	536,584	14,587	283,122	141,796
1987	4,420,491	3,402,637	51,943	3,454,580	386,888	-35,723	3,031,969	838,276	550,246	15,439	286,324	148,346
1988	4,759,164	3,740,676	44,055	3,784,731	436,953	-37,860	3,309,918	877,089	572,157	16,418	289,882	153,749
1989	5,204,218	3,980,662	60,902	4,041,564	461,156	-35,942	3,544,466	1,034,786	624,966	17,816	292,105	159,164
1990	5,381,969	4,121,475	51,771	4,173,246	487,081	-27,914	3,658,251	1,043,560	680,158	18,290	294,251	161,538
1991	5,655,166	4,331,163	57,279	4,388,442	517,848	-23,630	3,846,964	1,051,342	756,860	19,095	296,165	163,402
1992	5,969,442	4,582,609	57,236	4,639,845	544,711	-8,790	4,086,344	1,076,295	806,803	19,937	299,414	164,582
1993	6,308,395	4,823,755	50,729	4,874,484	576,255	2,937	4,301,166	1,135,754	871,475	20,843	302,658	167,830
1994	6,684,124	5,041,778	47,794	5,089,572	614,936	31,658	4,506,294	1,304,394	873,436	21,962	304,355	170,650
1995	7,021,344	5,300,857	54,012	5,354,869	648,377	38,271	4,744,763	1,329,059	947,522	22,908	306,504	175,650
1996	7,380,403	5,588,009	49,406	5,637,415	669,041	38,474	5,006,848	1,408,014	965,541	23,880	309,056	177,475
1997	7,659,961	5,739,872	55,568	5,795,440	688,364	77,067	5,184,143	1,451,857	1,023,961	24,676	310,425	178,617
1998	6,448,785	5,243,335	30,258	5,273,593	619,032	-244,441	4,410,120	1,295,383	743,282	27,289	236,312	148,671
1999	6,581,875	5,396,176	33,010	5,429,186	632,509	-242,094	4,554,583	1,213,482	813,810	27,704	237,581	149,974
2000	6,846,101	5,546,696	36,657	5,583,353	644,803	-244,327	4,694,223	1,308,229	843,649	28,644	239,008	151,273
2001	7,276,494	5,954,478	37,022	5,991,500	649,242	-270,333	5,071,925	1,256,316	948,253	30,309	240,080	148,422
2002	7,406,625	6,124,612	41,508	6,166,120	673,473	-314,670	5,177,977	1,245,228	983,420	30,614	241,937	147,622
2003	7,580,164	6,335,710	33,477	6,369,187	697,473	-400,956	5,270,758	1,275,946	1,033,460	31,087	243,834	146,659
2004	7,722,668	6,253,598	43,318	6,296,916	707,053	-349,370	5,240,493	1,386,537	1,095,638	31,845	242,505	147,672
2005	7,898,782	6,277,857	37,580	6,315,437	724,166	-350,144	5,241,127	1,490,548	1,167,107	32,471	243,259	148,848
2006	8,322,664	6,460,660	44,379	6,505,039	754,263	-277,079	5,473,697	1,595,036	1,253,931	34,084	244,178	149,364
2007	8,591,885	6,623,617	43,330	6,666,947	779,194	-277,641	5,610,112	1,607,893	1,373,880	35,007	245,431	151,002
2008	9,137,450	6,822,931	43,986	6,866,917	809,874	-208,111	5,848,932	1,715,387	1,573,131	37,014	246,862	148,550
2009	8,955,457	6,575,234	47,091	6,622,325	784,021	-212,905	5,625,399	1,606,772	1,723,286	35,962	249,023	143,338
2010	9,212,733	6,695,370	62,691	6,758,061	782,628	-188,435	5,786,998	1,565,194	1,860,541	36,740	250,754	140,779
2011	9,803,414	6,894,747	81,583	6,976,330	715,889	-189,320	6,071,121	1,850,551	1,881,742	38,805	252,634	141,490
2012	10,216,183	7,216,484	61,980	7,278,464	747,083	-206,910	6,324,471	2,042,807	1,848,905	39,999	255,413	143,342
2013	10,469,509	7,471,869	62,719	7,534,588	878,574	-202,177	6,453,837	2,125,190	1,890,482	40,674	257,399	145,786
2014	10,807,598	7,598,359	46,393	7,644,752	895,123	-171,603	6,578,026	2,272,854	1,956,718	42,001	257,316	147,914
2015	11,502,288	8,057,821	51,449	8,109,270	940,506	-195,967	6,972,797	2,436,524	2,092,967	44,642	257,654	150,360
2016	11,882,573	8,370,473	52,991	8,423,464	973,305	-151,162	7,298,997	2,433,206	2,150,370	45,879	258,996	153,179
2017	12,201,065	8,825,033	61,115	8,886,148	1,018,559	-252,495	7,615,094	2,431,649	2,154,322	46,861	260,368	155,478
2018	12,747,075	9,212,468	54,257	9,266,725	1,075,366	-283,587	7,907,772	2,574,400	2,264,903	48,716	261,663	158,145
2019	13,301,075	9,602,949	59,553	9,662,502	1,115,750	-443,449	8,103,303	2,800,364	2,397,408	50,835	261,653	158,236
2020	14,377,431	9,637,187	78,553	9,715,740	1,110,346	-337,760	8,267,634	2,764,196	3,345,601	54,954	261,629	150,795
2021	15,281,103	10,416,024	68,402	10,484,426	1,181,704	-398,345	8,904,377	2,834,196	3,542,530	58,524	261,108	154,941

Personal Income and Employment by Area: Kankakee, IL

(Thousands of dollars, except as noted.)

Year	Personal income, total	Earnings by place of work			Less: Contributions for government social insurance	Plus: Adjustment for residence	Equals: Net earnings by place of residence	Plus: Dividends, interest, and rent	Plus: Personal current transfer receipts	Per capita personal income (dollars)	Population (persons)	Total employment
		Nonfarm	Farm	Total								
1970	374,165	287,108	11,263	298,371	19,044	13,017	292,344	50,444	31,377	3,844	97,342	39,706
1971	414,326	310,688	18,119	328,807	21,318	14,675	322,164	54,359	37,803	4,200	98,659	40,376
1972	449,044	341,706	12,309	354,015	24,795	16,894	346,114	60,005	42,925	4,504	99,695	40,906
1973	513,219	373,462	30,151	403,613	31,456	19,694	391,851	68,386	52,982	5,166	99,351	42,692
1974	553,924	405,097	23,455	428,552	35,238	22,246	415,560	77,069	61,295	5,551	99,787	43,581
1975	607,935	412,224	36,404	448,628	34,949	26,458	440,137	87,154	80,644	6,080	99,990	42,589
1976	653,633	445,681	30,555	476,236	38,528	32,936	470,644	92,157	90,832	6,507	100,458	42,763
1977	719,099	491,423	30,958	522,381	42,611	39,799	519,569	101,895	97,635	7,076	101,619	44,000
1978	791,542	545,425	27,246	572,671	48,497	49,309	573,483	112,909	105,150	7,683	103,025	45,063
1979	865,021	584,871	33,924	618,795	54,028	58,966	623,733	125,840	115,448	8,299	104,238	44,868
1980	924,442	607,234	10,574	617,808	55,847	64,991	626,952	157,531	139,959	8,985	102,886	43,027
1981	1,038,412	651,774	27,418	679,192	64,401	66,403	681,194	194,539	162,679	10,127	102,544	43,280
1982	1,082,227	654,843	18,876	673,719	65,026	67,399	676,092	225,023	181,112	10,692	101,218	41,632
1983	1,092,859	667,295	-1,245	666,050	66,316	68,982	668,716	225,791	198,352	10,977	99,560	40,857
1984	1,182,279	698,087	24,129	722,216	71,530	79,457	730,143	251,827	200,309	12,001	98,513	41,023
1985	1,219,117	723,948	29,777	753,725	75,637	83,448	761,536	252,085	205,496	12,563	97,039	41,045
1986	1,266,413	758,244	28,807	787,051	79,429	87,192	794,814	259,591	212,008	13,202	95,926	41,221
1987	1,327,206	815,370	25,452	840,822	84,303	91,790	848,309	262,516	216,381	13,870	95,692	42,154
1988	1,406,788	867,158	33,595	900,753	92,654	99,526	907,625	271,061	228,102	14,734	95,481	42,337
1989	1,508,945	911,043	43,751	954,794	98,324	105,489	961,959	304,229	242,757	15,782	95,611	42,756
1990	1,641,340	1,012,318	60,016	1,072,334	106,983	103,992	1,069,343	306,962	265,035	16,998	96,560	45,566
1991	1,664,898	1,055,434	38,170	1,093,604	114,440	107,255	1,086,419	293,510	284,969	17,059	97,598	47,700
1992	1,789,950	1,122,429	42,895	1,165,324	119,928	115,052	1,160,448	304,449	325,053	18,041	99,215	45,999
1993	1,896,814	1,215,709	50,451	1,266,160	131,719	114,605	1,249,046	309,956	337,812	18,824	100,766	47,610
1994	1,996,534	1,294,961	53,546	1,348,507	142,625	120,356	1,326,238	324,035	346,261	19,625	101,736	50,134
1995	2,128,529	1,387,561	35,545	1,423,106	153,522	120,890	1,390,474	364,426	373,629	20,884	101,923	52,190
1996	2,228,451	1,418,261	52,412	1,470,673	154,895	133,964	1,449,742	387,111	391,598	21,784	102,296	51,612
1997	2,294,289	1,465,262	30,408	1,495,670	159,395	148,634	1,484,909	407,927	401,453	22,285	102,951	52,245
1998	2,368,746	1,512,696	21,850	1,534,546	163,146	169,291	1,540,691	418,924	409,131	22,948	103,222	53,006
1999	2,452,606	1,592,738	18,531	1,611,269	168,868	189,759	1,632,160	404,808	415,638	23,657	103,675	53,241
2000	2,619,089	1,687,502	28,639	1,716,141	175,943	208,469	1,748,667	434,609	435,813	25,222	103,842	54,118
2001	2,744,680	1,751,718	23,880	1,775,598	182,946	237,350	1,830,002	446,216	468,462	26,267	104,490	53,784
2002	2,820,366	1,820,547	15,438	1,835,985	189,306	247,941	1,894,620	419,037	506,709	26,878	104,932	52,857
2003	2,899,272	1,826,008	15,862	1,841,870	191,356	268,490	1,919,004	445,889	534,379	27,405	105,794	52,113
2004	2,986,748	1,876,667	49,132	1,925,799	200,805	295,659	2,020,653	409,400	556,695	27,980	106,744	52,379
2005	3,116,679	1,945,204	34,536	1,979,740	214,232	337,573	2,103,081	395,076	618,522	28,880	107,917	53,554
2006	3,304,281	2,045,268	37,872	2,083,140	225,240	366,876	2,224,776	436,363	643,142	30,111	109,735	54,878
2007	3,509,390	2,106,024	75,198	2,181,222	234,685	384,713	2,331,250	472,800	705,340	31,475	111,499	55,452
2008	3,692,490	2,150,696	102,822	2,253,518	240,596	373,908	2,386,830	532,525	773,135	32,776	112,658	55,182
2009	3,638,802	2,136,240	69,549	2,205,789	236,176	293,165	2,262,778	504,240	871,784	32,171	113,107	54,090
2010	3,720,589	2,168,962	55,745	2,224,707	238,501	319,991	2,306,197	476,709	937,683	32,804	113,420	53,693
2011	3,836,017	2,238,044	88,672	2,326,716	223,521	322,875	2,426,070	506,780	903,167	33,788	113,532	53,599
2012	3,887,047	2,358,967	53,342	2,412,309	236,832	268,857	2,444,334	540,601	902,112	34,400	112,995	54,818
2013	4,026,125	2,435,043	116,681	2,551,724	269,508	275,392	2,557,608	541,139	927,378	35,704	112,764	55,123
2014	4,054,209	2,510,285	64,389	2,574,674	277,837	252,889	2,549,726	565,775	938,708	36,409	111,352	55,371
2015	4,186,168	2,596,393	28,104	2,624,497	284,355	265,479	2,605,621	574,836	1,005,711	37,683	111,089	55,582
2016	4,265,177	2,614,977	57,277	2,672,254	289,942	261,996	2,644,308	612,937	1,007,932	38,690	110,241	55,166
2017	4,359,923	2,731,631	26,025	2,757,656	305,174	257,756	2,710,238	602,361	1,047,324	39,788	109,578	56,551
2018	4,521,383	2,821,564	36,556	2,858,120	316,010	281,062	2,823,172	625,071	1,073,140	41,562	108,787	56,312
2019	4,715,509	2,955,096	33,472	2,988,568	330,980	259,240	2,916,828	681,470	1,117,211	43,515	108,365	56,410
2020	5,130,821	2,994,476	52,099	3,046,575	335,420	212,917	2,924,072	714,206	1,492,543	47,846	107,236	54,481
2021	5,667,456	3,082,357	99,428	3,181,785	338,914	364,869	3,207,740	785,946	1,673,770	53,165	106,601	53,870

Personal Income and Employment by Area: Kansas City, MO-KS

(Thousands of dollars, except as noted.)

Year	Personal income, total	Earnings by place of work			Less: Contributions for government social insurance	Plus: Adjustment for residence	Equals: Net earnings by place of residence	Plus: Dividends, interest, and rent	Plus: Personal current transfer receipts	Per capita personal income (dollars)	Population (persons)	Total employment
		Nonfarm	Farm	Total								
1970	6,169,809	5,158,197	69,514	5,227,711	347,962	-33,526	4,846,223	879,775	443,811	4,346	1,419,593	674,424
1971	6,725,331	5,595,335	73,673	5,669,008	390,806	-34,424	5,243,778	965,919	515,634	4,695	1,432,356	679,124
1972	7,371,520	6,140,083	96,596	6,236,679	452,442	-35,334	5,748,903	1,054,654	567,963	5,120	1,439,848	697,223
1973	8,099,191	6,738,317	139,328	6,877,645	574,782	-36,305	6,266,558	1,168,589	664,044	5,568	1,454,634	727,985
1974	8,769,756	7,240,121	70,030	7,310,151	637,906	-33,670	6,638,575	1,352,257	778,924	6,044	1,450,974	734,327
1975	9,649,950	7,825,073	73,351	7,898,424	677,428	-37,882	7,183,114	1,474,431	992,405	6,684	1,443,816	727,345
1976	10,609,345	8,742,798	50,836	8,793,634	772,971	-44,874	7,975,789	1,575,007	1,058,549	7,306	1,452,126	751,366
1977	11,816,254	9,797,017	83,989	9,881,006	861,914	-55,016	8,964,076	1,738,988	1,113,190	8,120	1,455,117	776,160
1978	13,124,062	10,954,612	94,470	11,049,082	996,230	-61,952	9,990,900	1,941,426	1,191,736	8,935	1,468,792	807,453
1979	14,672,460	12,193,464	153,550	12,347,014	1,149,435	-70,298	11,127,281	2,198,680	1,346,499	9,943	1,475,676	828,859
1980	16,045,353	13,021,290	7,307	13,028,597	1,224,137	-76,412	11,728,048	2,680,720	1,636,585	10,811	1,484,234	821,393
1981	17,650,245	13,876,092	99,884	13,975,976	1,399,849	-83,329	12,492,798	3,279,326	1,878,121	11,848	1,489,775	814,405
1982	18,927,613	14,519,770	34,995	14,554,765	1,495,497	-87,283	12,971,985	3,892,099	2,063,529	12,664	1,494,551	808,137
1983	20,011,290	15,482,528	-19,609	15,462,919	1,612,417	-92,196	13,758,306	4,090,884	2,162,100	13,317	1,502,652	812,620
1984	22,231,657	17,270,105	12,963	17,283,068	1,846,369	-93,130	15,343,569	4,630,012	2,258,076	14,638	1,518,797	856,338
1985	24,066,925	18,816,530	107,515	18,924,045	2,056,544	-137,357	16,730,144	4,939,970	2,396,811	15,665	1,536,347	889,683
1986	25,602,564	20,192,538	68,334	20,260,872	2,220,942	-159,229	17,880,701	5,169,878	2,551,985	16,470	1,554,473	916,814
1987	27,190,369	21,620,669	75,366	21,696,035	2,345,522	-174,089	19,176,424	5,350,169	2,663,776	17,246	1,576,591	941,024
1988	28,922,680	22,922,233	69,250	22,991,483	2,566,560	-181,644	20,243,279	5,813,532	2,865,869	18,145	1,593,958	960,486
1989	30,773,818	24,223,330	103,879	24,327,209	2,711,475	-182,651	21,433,083	6,254,247	3,086,488	19,201	1,602,744	975,387
1990	32,210,378	25,380,669	55,057	25,435,726	2,964,632	-225,927	22,245,167	6,614,119	3,351,092	19,896	1,618,905	985,056
1991	33,743,201	26,428,389	23,415	26,451,804	3,126,474	-242,345	23,082,985	6,855,956	3,804,260	20,619	1,636,516	981,595
1992	36,232,652	28,549,610	103,864	28,653,474	3,342,084	-286,900	25,024,490	7,052,005	4,156,157	21,915	1,653,327	988,989
1993	38,073,218	30,125,270	34,715	30,159,985	3,523,700	-308,698	26,327,587	7,295,096	4,450,535	22,744	1,673,964	1,013,149
1994	40,341,404	31,940,776	89,670	32,030,446	3,772,849	-361,296	27,896,301	7,765,910	4,679,193	23,815	1,693,952	1,037,813
1995	42,675,082	33,740,224	7,622	33,747,846	3,955,817	-392,203	29,399,826	8,264,963	5,010,293	24,948	1,710,587	1,069,637
1996	45,301,736	35,806,521	121,449	35,927,970	4,151,627	-442,821	31,333,522	8,701,114	5,267,100	26,135	1,733,398	1,093,386
1997	48,052,227	38,174,909	111,615	38,286,524	4,413,127	-498,104	33,375,293	9,295,661	5,381,273	27,356	1,756,537	1,131,838
1998	51,634,104	41,143,594	64,375	41,207,969	4,716,704	-557,056	35,934,209	10,160,622	5,539,273	29,057	1,776,976	1,162,276
1999	54,437,960	44,255,862	36,660	44,292,522	5,060,339	-635,431	38,596,752	10,044,929	5,796,279	30,299	1,796,711	1,182,542
2000	58,466,684	47,485,220	61,218	47,546,438	5,395,456	-719,949	41,431,033	10,822,166	6,213,485	32,161	1,817,929	1,202,207
2001	58,696,980	47,439,060	91,953	47,531,013	5,572,852	-733,621	41,224,540	10,633,939	6,838,501	31,943	1,837,551	1,208,113
2002	60,093,574	48,909,845	20,077	48,929,922	5,691,860	-742,014	42,496,048	10,314,570	7,282,956	32,330	1,858,778	1,200,000
2003	61,485,369	49,804,556	75,208	49,879,764	5,842,597	-755,625	43,281,542	10,586,453	7,617,374	32,790	1,875,142	1,198,497
2004	63,409,237	51,316,717	240,333	51,557,050	6,098,930	-743,409	44,714,711	10,718,354	7,976,172	33,513	1,892,097	1,214,807
2005	66,673,707	53,855,622	134,124	53,989,746	6,359,755	-768,809	46,861,182	11,316,069	8,496,456	34,918	1,909,428	1,233,735
2006	73,398,359	58,763,633	80,356	58,843,989	6,759,037	-788,246	51,296,706	12,968,146	9,133,507	37,996	1,931,764	1,255,225
2007	78,736,704	62,346,144	117,115	62,463,259	7,110,877	-829,499	54,522,883	14,351,201	9,862,620	40,281	1,954,688	1,286,659
2008	84,514,860	65,177,023	167,668	65,344,691	7,411,498	-839,786	57,093,407	16,076,717	11,344,736	42,816	1,973,888	1,288,893
2009	82,785,312	64,479,852	172,830	64,652,682	7,277,844	-644,660	56,730,178	13,766,363	12,288,771	41,500	1,994,834	1,254,465
2010	83,642,829	64,177,849	121,846	64,299,695	7,304,873	-568,358	56,426,464	13,964,965	13,251,400	41,543	2,013,423	1,237,277
2011	88,120,388	66,295,338	205,163	66,500,501	6,705,668	-488,066	59,306,767	15,334,733	13,478,888	43,498	2,025,864	1,254,941
2012	93,925,817	71,447,898	119,286	71,567,184	6,979,678	-393,226	64,194,280	16,190,226	13,541,311	46,060	2,039,210	1,269,552
2013	95,664,688	74,151,380	242,922	74,394,302	8,133,854	-285,619	65,974,829	15,811,938	13,877,921	46,558	2,054,764	1,288,943
2014	99,255,862	76,235,772	202,569	76,438,341	8,452,617	-310,849	67,674,875	17,131,753	14,449,234	47,748	2,078,737	1,313,862
2015	104,336,497	79,979,812	-6,079	79,973,733	8,982,630	-373,455	70,617,648	18,487,039	15,231,810	49,737	2,097,773	1,342,598
2016	106,225,100	80,531,915	67,047	80,598,962	9,055,124	-295,090	71,248,748	19,149,869	15,826,483	50,077	2,121,223	1,367,845
2017	110,052,215	83,814,046	98,870	83,912,916	9,380,102	-332,879	74,199,935	19,545,094	16,307,186	51,330	2,143,999	1,386,138
2018	114,939,971	87,422,665	45,078	87,467,743	9,822,099	-408,587	77,237,057	20,655,162	17,047,752	53,108	2,164,286	1,406,642
2019	120,578,905	91,451,022	113,862	91,564,884	10,261,907	-466,166	80,836,811	21,800,268	17,941,826	55,300	2,180,431	1,411,505
2020	127,545,882	93,326,642	220,800	93,547,442	10,592,586	-403,620	82,551,236	21,860,566	23,134,080	58,145	2,193,578	1,379,015
2021	135,071,125	98,319,187	260,965	98,580,152	10,931,664	-485,278	87,163,210	22,337,315	25,570,600	61,410	2,199,490	1,409,910

Personal Income and Employment by Area: Kennewick-Richland, WA

(Thousands of dollars, except as noted.)

Year	Personal income, total	Earnings by place of work			Less: Contributions for government social insurance	Plus: Adjustment for residence	Equals: Net earnings by place of residence	Plus: Dividends, interest, and rent	Plus: Personal current transfer receipts	Per capita personal income (dollars)	Population (persons)	Total employment
		Nonfarm	Farm	Total								
1970	382,393	297,502	25,178	322,680	24,115	553	299,118	49,341	33,934	4,090	93,499	40,817
1971	403,538	308,377	26,738	335,115	26,085	119	309,149	54,984	39,405	4,289	94,080	40,315
1972	451,875	341,910	38,957	380,867	30,826	-1,475	348,566	61,045	42,264	4,753	95,067	41,832
1973	523,780	392,533	57,633	450,166	41,352	-4,858	403,956	73,021	46,803	5,501	95,211	44,867
1974	634,502	471,785	84,601	556,386	51,670	-8,891	495,825	84,289	54,388	6,431	98,666	49,005
1975	764,899	594,964	84,272	679,236	65,038	-16,353	597,845	100,652	66,402	7,282	105,045	54,232
1976	857,709	684,978	79,488	764,466	75,583	-18,344	670,539	112,492	74,678	7,601	112,838	58,982
1977	1,001,877	868,960	50,060	919,020	96,883	-33,539	788,598	134,023	79,256	8,375	119,629	64,042
1978	1,228,865	1,084,451	72,695	1,157,146	124,589	-49,876	982,681	160,140	86,044	9,510	129,214	71,236
1979	1,418,757	1,281,988	58,472	1,340,460	152,526	-59,727	1,128,207	191,426	99,124	10,286	137,929	77,504
1980	1,594,474	1,349,092	107,312	1,456,404	159,895	-62,359	1,234,150	232,040	128,284	10,957	145,515	78,001
1981	1,881,536	1,675,968	95,127	1,771,095	217,248	-104,700	1,449,147	283,518	148,871	12,592	149,418	82,905
1982	1,950,930	1,663,589	87,982	1,751,571	216,889	-89,311	1,445,371	322,781	182,778	12,745	153,079	77,676
1983	1,989,897	1,632,158	93,703	1,725,861	210,908	-68,500	1,446,453	342,487	200,957	13,322	149,371	74,772
1984	1,978,250	1,513,389	126,040	1,639,429	199,586	-45,382	1,394,461	370,960	212,829	13,418	147,429	71,264
1985	2,006,634	1,578,698	71,484	1,650,182	210,827	-47,764	1,391,591	391,053	223,990	13,707	146,400	72,013
1986	2,102,949	1,629,793	98,519	1,728,312	218,866	-45,946	1,463,500	401,749	237,700	14,350	146,551	72,890
1987	2,176,813	1,681,752	105,728	1,787,480	225,286	-45,205	1,516,989	409,301	250,523	14,753	147,547	76,282
1988	2,242,461	1,711,011	123,261	1,834,272	236,351	-44,705	1,553,216	412,757	276,488	15,281	146,750	76,763
1989	2,396,892	1,785,798	123,374	1,909,172	246,957	-40,653	1,621,562	476,529	298,801	16,404	146,117	78,677
1990	2,633,067	2,030,622	127,930	2,158,552	286,225	-48,263	1,824,064	480,404	328,599	17,399	151,331	84,264
1991	2,879,090	2,210,477	116,961	2,327,438	315,115	-22,007	1,990,316	507,401	381,373	18,457	155,993	86,871
1992	3,205,242	2,469,799	144,861	2,614,660	349,838	-23,399	2,241,423	543,360	420,459	19,825	161,680	89,400
1993	3,558,964	2,714,808	217,013	2,931,821	377,536	-24,295	2,529,990	578,588	450,386	21,175	168,075	93,769
1994	3,827,224	3,008,774	186,200	3,194,974	429,446	-30,291	2,735,237	616,785	475,202	21,875	174,957	100,015
1995	3,909,404	2,971,296	215,708	3,187,004	428,019	-22,365	2,736,620	656,606	516,178	21,659	180,501	97,934
1996	4,052,626	2,948,025	281,136	3,229,161	416,240	-14,156	2,798,765	698,422	555,439	22,316	181,605	97,910
1997	4,150,810	3,025,474	226,829	3,252,303	411,766	-10,146	2,830,391	741,158	579,261	22,570	183,909	98,810
1998	4,347,375	3,185,984	244,470	3,430,454	433,364	870	2,997,960	742,945	606,470	23,337	186,290	98,097
1999	4,543,221	3,392,668	221,052	3,613,720	446,774	8,716	3,175,662	712,819	654,740	24,035	189,025	101,094
2000	4,887,244	3,585,883	263,398	3,849,281	481,824	15,860	3,383,317	767,246	736,681	25,362	192,696	102,447
2001	5,293,965	3,919,513	252,573	4,172,086	509,989	16,490	3,678,587	790,146	825,232	26,952	196,420	106,138
2002	5,584,796	4,261,726	279,452	4,541,178	563,442	17,012	3,994,748	737,860	852,188	27,554	202,688	109,060
2003	5,986,232	4,514,714	358,271	4,872,985	595,000	24,481	4,302,466	765,031	918,735	28,636	209,043	111,933
2004	6,332,688	4,864,248	313,785	5,178,033	642,401	26,228	4,561,860	826,276	944,552	29,612	213,854	113,664
2005	6,583,543	5,048,348	319,340	5,367,688	670,151	29,383	4,726,920	835,066	1,021,557	30,050	219,086	116,263
2006	6,820,969	5,096,609	352,451	5,449,060	671,382	46,621	4,824,299	895,211	1,101,459	30,431	224,149	117,441
2007	7,548,623	5,529,584	403,746	5,933,330	728,330	46,575	5,251,575	1,091,620	1,205,428	32,927	229,255	123,032
2008	8,274,220	5,947,072	330,036	6,277,108	778,985	51,473	5,549,596	1,311,610	1,413,014	34,861	237,348	127,067
2009	8,769,782	6,378,850	359,206	6,738,056	847,427	43,622	5,934,251	1,269,019	1,566,512	35,708	245,600	129,446
2010	9,618,699	7,115,608	384,500	7,500,108	912,509	34,357	6,621,956	1,263,457	1,733,286	37,640	255,543	134,755
2011	10,271,649	7,359,411	494,505	7,853,916	855,345	29,589	7,028,160	1,476,136	1,767,353	38,982	263,497	137,296
2012	10,224,633	7,070,797	510,503	7,581,300	809,514	72,392	6,844,178	1,556,286	1,824,169	38,139	268,091	138637
2013	10,236,227	7,104,337	602,220	7,706,557	923,698	83,071	6,865,930	1,517,296	1,853,001	37,800	270,803	139,039
2014	10,669,792	7,328,322	532,498	7,860,820	962,783	91,245	6,989,282	1,630,162	2,050,348	38,868	274,511	141,356
2015	11,516,896	7,857,195	790,581	8,647,776	1,018,992	75,658	7,704,442	1,717,957	2,094,497	41,222	279,386	145,217
2016	11,878,712	8,160,843	655,996	8,816,839	1,056,344	83,294	7,843,789	1,816,669	2,218,254	41,794	284,221	148,488
2017	12,312,621	8,543,650	599,842	9,143,492	1,123,294	68,890	8,089,088	1,925,140	2,298,393	42,363	290,646	152,043
2018	12,713,094	9,024,102	405,373	9,429,475	1,168,038	77,558	8,338,995	1,958,765	2,415,334	42,974	295,833	156,333
2019	13,698,979	9,542,217	536,450	10,078,667	1,202,233	69,391	8,945,825	2,168,639	2,584,515	45,599	300,422	159,765
2020	14,904,735	9,933,728	540,503	10,474,231	1,264,996	84,988	9,294,223	2,194,707	3,415,805	48,979	304,306	155,535
2021	16,056,627	10,566,224	405,587	10,971,811	1,339,966	84,604	9,716,449	2,250,691	4,089,487	52,082	308,293	160,959

Personal Income and Employment by Area: Killeen-Temple, TX

(Thousands of dollars, except as noted.)

Year	Personal income, total	Earnings by place of work			Less: Contributions for government social insurance	Plus: Adjustment for residence	Equals: Net earnings by place of residence	Plus: Dividends, interest, and rent	Plus: Personal current transfer receipts	Per capita personal income (dollars)	Population (persons)	Total employment
		Nonfarm	Farm	Total								
1970	748,345	597,282	6,948	604,230	36,662	-13,348	554,220	153,901	40,224	4,410	169,695	89,828
1971	809,895	650,281	5,616	655,897	42,553	-12,151	601,193	161,896	46,806	4,644	174,387	90,083
1972	983,904	790,808	10,687	801,495	51,897	-13,039	736,559	193,728	53,617	5,081	193,630	97,294
1973	1,137,414	888,878	26,109	914,987	62,086	-3,559	849,342	224,455	63,617	5,248	216,716	102,623
1974	1,257,555	989,954	5,656	995,610	72,599	819	923,830	259,042	74,683	5,669	221,833	106,605
1975	1,410,652	1,101,052	6,746	1,107,798	85,600	-2,353	1,019,845	297,248	93,559	6,380	221,119	110,740
1976	1,567,438	1,225,124	4,861	1,229,985	97,634	4,614	1,136,965	326,238	104,235	6,819	229,880	115,223
1977	1,669,358	1,299,360	-4,065	1,295,295	102,590	5,241	1,197,946	358,650	112,762	7,180	232,517	117,302
1978	1,862,386	1,427,039	2,093	1,429,132	111,551	-204	1,317,377	419,298	125,711	7,859	236,961	120,403
1979	1,899,568	1,442,481	2,644	1,445,125	118,080	3,477	1,330,522	422,093	146,953	8,163	232,714	114,795
1980	2,156,912	1,621,366	-3,352	1,618,014	132,995	8,282	1,493,301	488,849	174,762	9,462	227,951	117,723
1981	2,450,680	1,858,642	8,900	1,867,542	159,975	-13,481	1,694,086	558,168	198,426	10,531	232,715	121,283
1982	2,677,896	2,018,611	6,046	2,024,657	170,762	-14,745	1,839,150	620,066	218,680	11,202	239,048	121,716
1983	2,887,904	2,163,268	-2,144	2,161,124	188,938	-13,979	1,958,207	688,741	240,956	11,921	242,252	122,761
1984	3,123,342	2,335,619	439	2,336,058	209,963	-11,974	2,114,121	750,892	258,329	12,764	244,697	126,897
1985	3,359,414	2,498,086	-5,052	2,493,034	228,543	-12,639	2,251,852	824,242	283,320	13,297	252,645	131,716
1986	3,539,987	2,633,785	-6,190	2,627,595	243,038	-18,992	2,365,565	866,900	307,522	13,971	253,385	133,296
1987	3,661,865	2,713,229	2,846	2,716,075	250,254	-23,820	2,442,001	890,434	329,430	14,100	259,706	137,444
1988	3,890,447	2,903,587	442	2,904,029	283,667	-28,334	2,592,028	940,935	357,484	14,828	262,373	139,949
1989	4,051,729	2,965,417	7,253	2,972,670	296,528	-28,094	2,648,048	1,007,107	396,574	15,206	266,463	140,155
1990	4,170,021	3,070,759	4,510	3,075,269	310,506	-32,843	2,731,920	990,857	447,244	15,472	269,515	139,118
1991	4,065,537	2,944,663	9,484	2,954,147	303,482	-21,645	2,629,020	947,984	488,533	15,304	265,657	128,838
1992	4,718,136	3,450,897	9,043	3,459,940	361,663	-27,040	3,071,237	1,062,426	584,473	17,428	270,722	139,350
1993	5,248,592	3,874,091	9,453	3,883,544	411,515	-31,496	3,440,533	1,185,690	622,369	18,314	286,593	151,294
1994	5,705,706	4,238,387	7,485	4,245,872	444,099	-32,735	3,769,038	1,291,633	645,035	18,532	307,884	162,733
1995	6,039,084	4,453,068	-73	4,452,995	458,481	-26,274	3,968,240	1,369,480	701,364	19,281	313,222	169,153
1996	6,316,799	4,600,007	2,812	4,602,819	473,084	-10,976	4,118,759	1,445,765	752,275	19,826	318,613	170,885
1997	6,480,237	4,776,377	2,363	4,778,740	487,424	13,395	4,304,711	1,378,402	797,124	20,136	321,821	172,991
1998	6,942,795	5,016,445	-5,193	5,011,252	506,799	47,122	4,551,575	1,552,671	838,549	21,340	325,335	176,092
1999	7,445,703	5,343,100	10,188	5,353,288	535,396	90,303	4,908,195	1,653,630	883,878	22,877	325,473	179,581
2000	7,871,881	5,625,492	5,480	5,630,972	561,098	117,911	5,187,785	1,707,347	976,749	23,640	332,989	182,507
2001	8,386,265	6,092,130	4,920	6,097,050	602,166	95,123	5,590,007	1,708,631	1,087,627	24,929	336,409	181,905
2002	8,876,576	6,533,244	8,839	6,542,083	644,568	49,990	5,947,505	1,737,298	1,191,773	26,013	341,231	184,092
2003	9,509,772	7,082,753	24,499	7,107,252	701,512	28,816	6,434,556	1,746,078	1,329,138	27,736	342,865	185,268
2004	10,028,932	7,465,559	27,503	7,493,062	746,261	20,081	6,766,882	1,850,359	1,411,691	28,675	349,745	187,498
2005	10,989,705	8,247,402	23,348	8,270,750	818,661	4,066	7,456,155	1,983,717	1,549,833	30,738	357,533	194,934
2006	12,126,612	9,232,496	20,136	9,252,632	906,031	-22,240	8,324,361	2,133,359	1,668,892	33,182	365,460	203,763
2007	13,325,886	10,067,447	2,717	10,070,164	991,951	-38,500	9,039,713	2,427,767	1,858,406	34,994	380,804	214,008
2008	14,589,914	10,919,265	-33,981	10,885,284	1,085,261	-82,450	9,717,573	2,727,660	2,144,681	37,197	392,237	222,216
2009	14,955,156	11,289,291	-41,034	11,248,257	1,153,538	-127,983	9,966,736	2,722,245	2,266,175	37,825	395,375	220,670
2010	15,361,893	11,355,474	-26,490	11,328,984	1,173,156	-140,882	10,014,946	2,732,102	2,614,845	37,624	408,299	216,539
2011	16,177,017	11,685,336	-29,472	11,655,864	1,099,683	-174,280	10,381,901	3,009,599	2,785,517	39,218	412,491	219,858
2012	16,415,125	11,700,040	-5,852	11,694,188	1,104,926	-176,664	10,412,598	3,166,152	2,836,375	38,742	423,703	219,547
2013	16,194,348	11,494,731	4,372	11,499,103	1,207,467	-202,936	10,088,700	3,109,258	2,996,390	38,174	424,219	218,810
2014	16,648,075	11,665,835	-9,495	11,656,340	1,224,259	-211,935	10,220,146	3,243,686	3,184,243	38,708	430,099	219,238
2015	17,395,591	12,141,186	6,584	12,147,770	1,294,812	-221,678	10,631,280	3,263,875	3,500,436	39,793	437,152	224,802
2016	17,516,714	12,173,546	-20,479	12,153,067	1,303,128	-206,431	10,643,508	3,188,665	3,684,541	39,649	441,790	225,403
2017	18,413,631	12,705,086	-32,024	12,673,062	1,362,853	-202,491	11,107,718	3,401,615	3,904,298	41,001	449,098	230,621
2018	19,002,099	13,073,670	-34,855	13,038,815	1,391,892	-183,196	11,463,727	3,380,373	4,157,999	41,476	458,143	232,767
2019	19,826,868	13,554,892	-32,866	13,522,026	1,436,305	-164,412	11,921,309	3,464,942	4,440,617	42,265	469,109	235,572
2020	21,403,605	14,046,286	-23,684	14,022,602	1,494,754	-160,096	12,367,752	3,426,109	5,609,744	44,892	476,784	238,050
2021	23,213,690	14,892,864	-27,723	14,865,141	1,572,066	-158,101	13,134,974	3,481,245	6,597,471	47,755	486,101	243,492

Personal Income and Employment by Area: Kingsport-Bristol, TN-VA

(Thousands of dollars, except as noted.)

Year	Personal income, total	Earnings by place of work			Less: Contributions for government social insurance	Plus: Adjustment for residence	Equals: Net earnings by place of residence	Plus: Dividends, interest, and rent	Plus: Personal current transfer receipts	Per capita personal income (dollars)	Population (persons)	Total employment
		Nonfarm	Farm	Total								
1970	756,289	657,355	19,281	676,636	43,978	-29,013	603,645	83,145	69,499	3,128	241,800	103,480
1971	815,430	699,806	16,521	716,327	48,661	-25,377	642,289	92,330	80,811	3,301	247,013	103,817
1972	905,205	769,693	23,320	793,013	56,042	-24,552	712,419	102,083	90,703	3,625	249,683	106,749
1973	1,020,110	863,873	27,630	891,503	72,613	-23,459	795,431	116,176	108,503	4,028	253,233	112,348
1974	1,142,412	967,469	21,652	989,121	84,923	-27,950	876,248	134,502	131,662	4,439	257,350	115,905
1975	1,245,816	1,037,484	12,733	1,050,217	88,947	-41,942	919,328	154,390	172,098	4,779	260,702	114,222
1976	1,397,018	1,171,544	19,217	1,190,761	101,998	-48,104	1,040,659	169,393	186,966	5,282	264,479	119,484
1977	1,556,484	1,329,485	13,402	1,342,887	115,508	-60,005	1,167,374	192,127	196,983	5,819	267,499	124,891
1978	1,765,212	1,532,092	16,489	1,548,581	133,630	-86,041	1,328,910	219,250	217,052	6,497	271,688	131,666
1979	1,942,752	1,692,646	6,596	1,699,242	151,086	-110,267	1,437,889	251,023	253,840	7,064	275,007	133,425
1980	2,124,978	1,779,746	9,212	1,788,958	159,005	-117,623	1,512,330	311,848	300,800	7,623	278,763	130,586
1981	2,418,900	1,986,809	23,148	2,009,957	191,421	-133,767	1,684,769	385,645	348,486	8,639	279,993	131,108
1982	2,564,038	2,035,633	19,381	2,055,014	206,451	-100,961	1,747,602	434,168	382,268	9,144	280,418	128,310
1983	2,707,146	2,131,874	7,064	2,138,938	218,001	-98,156	1,822,781	471,004	413,361	9,699	279,113	127,756
1984	2,913,286	2,246,681	13,856	2,260,537	235,450	-87,676	1,937,411	537,104	438,771	10,461	278,485	129,086
1985	3,139,534	2,456,970	14,105	2,471,075	261,926	-97,035	2,112,114	561,798	465,622	11,298	277,884	132,126
1986	3,316,776	2,604,902	4,864	2,609,766	285,255	-97,743	2,226,768	593,278	496,730	11,979	276,878	133,598
1987	3,488,475	2,745,119	14,931	2,760,050	298,286	-93,670	2,368,094	598,835	521,546	12,584	277,217	136,288
1988	3,763,391	2,961,603	18,197	2,979,800	330,066	-104,253	2,545,481	658,955	558,955	13,644	275,824	139,584
1989	4,039,813	3,176,435	21,918	3,198,353	358,458	-117,313	2,722,582	701,860	615,371	14,655	275,656	143,467
1990	4,356,278	3,379,242	28,262	3,407,504	383,983	-117,090	2,906,431	775,503	674,344	15,772	276,205	147,539
1991	4,605,142	3,565,438	29,767	3,595,205	410,767	-125,344	3,059,094	791,712	754,336	16,515	278,847	148,554
1992	4,907,001	3,789,679	39,437	3,829,116	431,847	-120,006	3,277,263	783,452	846,286	17,383	282,292	151,184
1993	5,062,326	3,910,474	31,123	3,941,597	448,578	-132,514	3,360,505	799,940	901,881	17,754	285,142	153,439
1994	5,221,189	3,959,881	27,311	3,987,192	458,289	-95,866	3,433,037	839,507	948,645	18,216	286,625	153,499
1995	5,554,474	4,183,207	15,043	4,198,250	483,661	-110,917	3,603,672	917,637	1,033,165	19,169	289,762	158,102
1996	5,857,460	4,414,634	2,027	4,416,661	500,828	-139,533	3,776,300	996,313	1,084,847	20,049	292,153	158,808
1997	6,085,311	4,505,090	6,655	4,511,745	505,902	-111,564	3,894,279	1,048,570	1,142,462	20,681	294,250	160,258
1998	6,354,566	4,650,940	8,213	4,659,153	512,556	-92,894	4,053,703	1,112,543	1,188,320	21,444	296,333	158,389
1999	6,646,911	4,825,182	9,366	4,834,548	527,387	-21,954	4,285,207	1,128,958	1,232,746	22,315	297,863	159,345
2000	7,017,857	4,927,108	24,280	4,951,388	537,426	28,269	4,442,231	1,245,568	1,330,058	23,508	298,534	158,601
2001	7,221,125	5,074,232	17,871	5,092,103	575,413	-8,782	4,507,908	1,259,356	1,453,861	24,179	298,648	158,986
2002	7,393,506	5,193,069	10,985	5,204,054	594,505	-11,039	4,598,510	1,231,558	1,563,438	24,705	299,267	158,930
2003	7,698,978	5,437,319	-2,085	5,435,234	619,789	-31,075	4,784,370	1,279,392	1,635,216	25,632	300,370	158,839
2004	8,071,823	5,725,664	8,338	5,734,002	646,429	-27,037	5,060,536	1,263,341	1,747,946	26,846	300,668	157,418
2005	8,391,046	5,900,428	8,378	5,908,806	670,806	-16,772	5,221,228	1,279,339	1,890,479	27,737	302,519	159,083
2006	9,034,709	6,288,996	-9,449	6,279,547	722,081	-80,437	5,477,029	1,507,700	2,049,980	29,667	304,535	161,822
2007	9,554,388	6,524,342	-18,293	6,506,049	750,932	-86,091	5,669,026	1,661,423	2,223,939	31,142	306,805	162,848
2008	10,138,301	6,791,719	-14,110	6,777,609	786,456	-108,386	5,882,767	1,772,816	2,482,718	32,909	308,069	163,301
2009	9,911,201	6,533,639	-11,400	6,522,239	766,996	-73,269	5,681,974	1,549,705	2,679,522	32,045	309,293	157,034
2010	10,101,713	6,680,859	-10,641	6,670,218	782,445	-115,689	5,772,084	1,462,200	2,867,429	32,640	309,488	154,844
2011	10,726,845	7,113,443	-6,611	7,106,832	739,785	-174,862	6,192,185	1,612,682	2,921,978	34,698	309,145	158,091
2012	11,191,732	7,400,001	-8,483	7,391,518	747,437	-156,646	6,487,435	1,766,918	2,937,379	36,253	308,713	157,063
2013	10,939,029	7,289,113	1,028	7,290,141	833,853	-170,172	6,286,116	1,647,685	3,005,228	35,521	307,957	156,849
2014	10,987,291	7,163,206	14,315	7,177,521	833,276	-176,235	6,168,010	1,761,238	3,058,043	35,771	307,154	157,324
2015	11,195,078	7,228,728	9,056	7,237,784	852,789	-160,792	6,224,203	1,788,070	3,182,805	36,559	306,220	156,738
2016	11,256,990	7,182,292	-12,070	7,170,222	862,573	-143,973	6,163,676	1,843,809	3,249,505	36,789	305,989	157,800
2017	11,654,247	7,486,207	-7,424	7,478,783	897,258	-132,129	6,449,396	1,880,047	3,324,804	38,031	306,443	158,080
2018	12,149,293	7,837,033	-17,676	7,819,357	932,584	-145,800	6,740,973	1,940,885	3,467,435	39,624	306,618	158,568
2019	12,585,754	7,907,329	-15,581	7,891,748	945,945	-125,221	6,820,582	2,120,688	3,644,484	40,968	307,208	156,892
2020	13,475,294	8,032,859	-17,234	8,015,625	966,584	-54,239	6,994,802	2,100,472	4,380,020	43,835	307,406	153,827
2021	14,595,741	8,679,987	-13,576	8,666,411	1,019,277	-49,959	7,597,175	2,136,907	4,861,659	47,287	308,661	156,223

Personal Income and Employment by Area: Kingston, NY

(Thousands of dollars, except as noted.)

Year	Personal income, total	Derivation of personal income									Per capita personal income (dollars)	Population (persons)	Total employment
		Earnings by place of work			Less: Contributions for government social insurance	Plus: Adjustment for residence	Equals: Net earnings by place of residence	Plus: Dividends, interest, and rent	Plus: Personal current transfer receipts				
		Nonfarm	Farm	Total									
1970	574,715	408,659	6,869	415,528	31,226	42,656	426,958	92,490	55,267	4,040	142,242	52,414
1971	623,694	434,425	6,704	441,129	34,452	51,529	458,206	99,732	65,756	4,251	146,705	53,640
1972	675,172	463,921	4,043	467,964	38,536	62,140	491,568	107,667	75,937	4,498	150,111	54,890
1973	754,760	514,178	7,123	521,301	49,347	70,847	542,801	123,627	88,332	4,934	152,980	57,237
1974	828,152	543,464	8,995	552,459	53,684	81,243	580,018	142,095	106,039	5,376	154,057	57,453
1975	913,241	564,474	9,644	574,118	54,755	92,992	612,355	156,217	144,669	5,853	156,022	55,738
1976	967,361	593,541	8,456	601,997	58,960	103,865	646,902	162,711	157,748	6,131	157,793	55,635
1977	1,038,576	634,078	9,387	643,465	62,659	120,240	701,046	176,929	160,601	6,592	157,559	56,665
1978	1,143,405	708,103	10,910	719,013	71,437	139,471	787,047	188,084	168,274	7,209	158,617	58,794
1979	1,271,278	792,499	13,556	806,055	82,280	160,972	884,747	204,431	182,100	7,965	159,606	61,376
1980	1,420,810	855,033	12,069	867,102	89,455	185,478	963,125	244,954	212,731	8,986	158,111	61,668
1981	1,575,049	924,422	10,227	934,649	102,508	203,748	1,035,889	296,028	243,132	9,992	157,625	61,536
1982	1,769,422	1,045,447	12,650	1,058,097	116,493	219,266	1,160,870	342,018	266,534	11,215	157,770	63,222
1983	1,943,945	1,193,234	6,514	1,199,748	134,108	222,073	1,287,713	373,463	282,769	12,271	158,414	66,330
1984	2,185,698	1,365,290	8,563	1,373,853	156,527	242,039	1,459,365	431,737	294,596	13,699	159,557	69,296
1985	2,348,100	1,468,029	11,961	1,479,990	170,522	266,506	1,575,974	462,489	309,637	14,687	159,880	71,174
1986	2,526,813	1,627,393	12,194	1,639,587	191,321	275,582	1,723,848	482,628	320,337	15,816	159,760	74,612
1987	2,650,981	1,704,139	15,992	1,720,131	196,061	300,025	1,824,095	500,151	326,735	16,378	161,865	73,866
1988	2,825,364	1,795,549	18,746	1,814,295	211,745	333,553	1,936,103	538,794	350,467	17,345	162,889	76,380
1989	3,082,747	1,904,405	19,024	1,923,429	220,621	354,067	2,056,875	641,057	384,815	18,756	164,359	76,774
1990	3,207,655	1,978,148	18,161	1,996,309	219,512	376,801	2,153,598	630,270	423,787	19,318	166,049	77,348
1991	3,378,129	2,098,553	23,424	2,121,977	238,891	376,771	2,259,857	645,881	472,391	20,004	168,869	77,826
1992	3,584,672	2,192,767	18,949	2,211,716	244,835	403,842	2,370,723	673,237	540,712	20,979	170,872	78,504
1993	3,519,350	2,073,378	18,762	2,092,140	232,371	443,940	2,303,709	644,944	570,697	20,391	172,594	76,404
1994	3,528,255	2,006,115	16,512	2,022,627	226,596	466,460	2,262,491	652,226	613,538	20,483	172,252	76,405
1995	3,605,143	1,944,036	16,993	1,961,029	219,587	518,840	2,260,282	698,706	646,155	20,916	172,362	74,331
1996	3,707,142	1,942,217	14,804	1,957,021	215,026	573,216	2,315,211	713,199	678,732	21,403	173,205	74,388
1997	3,881,535	2,051,499	13,923	2,065,422	222,365	606,784	2,449,841	739,463	692,231	22,289	174,148	75,635
1998	4,180,648	2,212,794	12,085	2,224,879	238,236	673,725	2,660,368	780,918	739,362	23,878	175,085	77,766
1999	4,422,626	2,388,061	19,247	2,407,308	250,908	745,784	2,902,184	766,417	754,025	25,054	176,526	80,901
2000	4,742,606	2,551,539	18,365	2,569,904	268,289	827,780	3,129,395	819,291	793,920	26,672	177,810	83,102
2001	4,909,024	2,576,336	19,102	2,595,438	275,273	886,434	3,206,599	846,617	855,808	27,511	178,440	84,862
2002	4,957,908	2,682,874	7,966	2,690,840	290,988	887,495	3,287,347	757,792	912,769	27,524	180,128	85,462
2003	5,139,380	2,809,730	15,130	2,824,860	304,573	899,628	3,419,915	768,115	951,350	28,403	180,942	86,617
2004	5,625,228	2,981,808	12,611	2,994,419	320,172	1,095,122	3,769,369	853,977	1,001,882	30,934	181,847	86,991
2005	5,864,971	3,076,880	8,175	3,085,055	337,282	1,168,314	3,916,087	901,271	1,047,613	32,148	182,438	87,641
2006	6,216,713	3,360,208	13,307	3,373,515	372,788	1,151,941	4,152,668	950,641	1,113,404	34,000	182,845	88,732
2007	6,524,864	3,463,090	26,234	3,489,324	384,211	1,221,246	4,326,359	1,017,872	1,180,633	35,690	182,818	89,799
2008	6,839,898	3,512,311	28,594	3,540,905	395,887	1,172,870	4,317,888	1,206,401	1,315,609	37,341	183,174	89,273
2009	6,811,781	3,512,775	23,538	3,536,313	390,153	1,039,557	4,185,717	1,170,748	1,455,316	37,297	182,638	87,247
2010	7,037,454	3,666,760	27,335	3,694,095	395,474	1,040,170	4,338,791	1,136,949	1,561,714	38,578	182,422	86,535
2011	7,282,559	3,681,235	22,657	3,703,892	360,738	1,098,911	4,442,065	1,235,524	1,604,970	39,914	182,458	86,146
2012	7,492,756	3,800,008	24,454	3,824,462	364,992	1,062,439	4,521,909	1,333,259	1,637,588	41,270	181,555	85,986
2013	7,518,186	3,866,930	27,391	3,894,321	417,952	1,058,662	4,535,031	1,324,098	1,659,057	41,601	180,722	86,820
2014	7,774,170	3,922,006	20,306	3,942,312	434,841	1,092,622	4,600,093	1,436,720	1,737,357	42,675	182,173	88,656
2015	8,055,356	4,055,591	19,433	4,075,024	452,744	1,118,444	4,740,724	1,476,057	1,838,575	44,302	181,830	89,297
2016	8,287,526	4,155,321	19,503	4,174,824	466,688	1,184,986	4,893,122	1,528,339	1,866,065	45,643	181,574	90,304
2017	8,659,005	4,303,166	27,429	4,330,595	485,969	1,215,184	5,059,810	1,597,622	2,001,573	47,687	181,579	90,943
2018	8,975,938	4,509,431	11,470	4,520,901	504,167	1,290,951	5,307,685	1,696,937	1,971,316	49,360	181,848	92,072
2019	9,705,800	4,604,314	17,404	4,621,718	518,430	1,624,500	5,727,788	1,873,593	2,104,419	53,426	181,669	91,162
2020	10,366,436	4,563,734	17,705	4,581,439	521,349	1,645,426	5,705,516	1,858,135	2,802,785	57,057	181,687	86,524
2021	11,078,945	4,917,789	16,773	4,934,562	562,572	1,922,537	6,294,527	1,903,744	2,880,674	60,557	182,951	88,467

Personal Income and Employment by Area: Knoxville, TN

(Thousands of dollars, except as noted.)

Year	Personal income, total	Earnings by place of work			Less: Contributions for government social insurance	Plus: Adjustment for residence	Equals: Net earnings by place of residence	Plus: Dividends, interest, and rent	Plus: Personal current transfer receipts	Per capita personal income (dollars)	Population (persons)	Total employment
		Nonfarm	Farm	Total								
1970	1,680,029	1,386,721	10,161	1,396,882	89,115	-11,835	1,295,932	212,269	171,828	3,179	528,426	214,863
1971	1,852,013	1,516,930	9,787	1,526,717	100,676	-11,161	1,414,880	235,236	201,897	3,422	541,129	218,824
1972	2,050,991	1,681,597	14,737	1,696,334	117,150	-8,761	1,570,423	258,268	222,300	3,737	548,773	227,791
1973	2,308,986	1,884,751	21,507	1,906,258	150,269	-11,029	1,744,960	297,651	266,375	4,170	553,697	239,669
1974	2,592,488	2,093,078	17,094	2,110,172	172,065	-13,735	1,924,372	350,601	317,515	4,626	560,437	243,085
1975	2,914,956	2,284,083	11,946	2,296,029	184,289	-12,055	2,099,685	409,641	405,630	5,106	570,915	242,890
1976	3,299,657	2,603,859	24,786	2,628,645	213,154	-13,196	2,402,295	450,660	446,702	5,655	583,484	255,754
1977	3,697,468	2,962,892	17,342	2,980,234	241,560	-18,588	2,720,086	509,185	468,197	6,221	594,330	266,898
1978	4,226,526	3,409,806	16,052	3,425,858	280,965	-15,947	3,128,946	581,128	516,452	7,023	601,788	279,856
1979	4,746,730	3,813,980	13,358	3,827,338	327,653	-21,823	3,477,862	663,148	605,720	7,751	612,421	290,671
1980	5,280,415	4,113,604	20,384	4,133,988	353,824	-29,585	3,750,579	812,551	717,285	8,466	623,731	291,449
1981	5,902,130	4,504,518	28,817	4,533,335	420,463	-21,549	4,091,323	993,926	816,881	9,364	630,304	295,737
1982	6,341,916	4,784,834	25,314	4,810,148	461,203	-30,721	4,318,224	1,138,247	885,445	9,964	636,499	299,009
1983	6,694,130	5,032,922	12,007	5,044,929	493,333	-23,414	4,528,182	1,200,232	965,716	10,487	638,326	291,743
1984	7,312,091	5,485,558	23,314	5,508,872	560,310	-27,183	4,921,379	1,379,158	1,011,554	11,486	636,588	301,274
1985	7,730,785	5,823,193	16,093	5,839,286	607,134	-26,043	5,206,109	1,453,396	1,071,280	12,139	636,844	306,615
1986	8,164,676	6,175,165	13,926	6,189,091	661,427	-36,821	5,490,843	1,519,250	1,154,583	12,884	633,710	314,957
1987	8,822,278	6,759,068	14,322	6,773,390	714,866	-39,597	6,018,927	1,582,590	1,220,761	13,857	636,657	327,828
1988	9,686,119	7,502,996	13,375	7,516,371	815,405	-54,274	6,646,692	1,735,486	1,303,941	15,079	642,344	344,316
1989	10,243,893	7,894,761	20,362	7,915,123	874,218	-51,370	6,989,535	1,808,441	1,445,917	15,815	647,744	351,772
1990	11,022,808	8,363,701	22,419	8,386,120	933,748	-35,455	7,416,917	2,011,612	1,594,279	16,866	653,537	358,570
1991	11,609,330	8,800,752	24,568	8,825,320	1,002,648	-72,966	7,749,706	2,055,216	1,804,408	17,454	665,146	360,963
1992	12,578,914	9,652,786	30,375	9,683,161	1,086,651	-104,972	8,491,538	2,061,560	2,025,816	18,555	677,924	371,887
1993	13,413,355	10,335,383	30,355	10,365,738	1,167,112	-119,225	9,079,401	2,166,017	2,167,937	19,468	688,984	385,921
1994	14,075,225	10,837,851	24,992	10,862,843	1,256,249	-127,853	9,478,741	2,324,540	2,271,944	20,064	701,511	398,164
1995	14,971,059	11,412,913	21,094	11,434,007	1,327,501	-148,408	9,958,098	2,545,011	2,467,950	20,958	714,347	407,652
1996	15,659,428	11,900,196	10,497	11,910,693	1,364,047	-168,746	10,377,900	2,696,483	2,585,045	21,607	724,741	411,103
1997	16,518,900	12,559,459	15,120	12,574,579	1,431,113	-205,679	10,937,787	2,895,457	2,685,656	22,562	732,158	415,188
1998	17,586,712	13,682,890	12,666	13,695,556	1,507,663	-325,525	11,862,368	3,021,118	2,703,226	24,515	717,379	417,918
1999	18,033,180	14,055,207	19,363	14,074,570	1,566,871	-302,253	12,205,446	3,006,999	2,820,735	24,940	723,054	423,353
2000	19,455,516	15,080,288	22,683	15,102,971	1,658,686	-327,567	13,116,718	3,240,931	3,097,867	26,681	729,194	433,435
2001	19,706,407	15,072,548	34,613	15,107,161	1,676,524	-347,722	13,082,915	3,286,433	3,337,059	26,784	735,744	429,902
2002	20,482,659	15,888,454	33,815	15,922,269	1,780,732	-377,869	13,763,668	3,135,401	3,583,590	27,589	742,420	433,333
2003	21,387,300	16,579,056	20,380	16,599,436	1,857,575	-386,057	14,355,804	3,300,688	3,730,808	28,484	750,863	438,809
2004	22,635,435	17,737,563	17,138	17,754,701	1,968,952	-415,876	15,369,873	3,309,761	3,955,801	29,838	758,622	452,211
2005	23,831,494	18,605,790	13,939	18,619,729	2,055,128	-463,619	16,100,982	3,513,269	4,217,243	30,998	768,798	460,971
2006	25,363,429	19,679,233	3,768	19,683,001	2,169,220	-517,999	16,995,782	3,863,939	4,503,708	32,406	782,685	471,865
2007	26,640,587	20,399,165	-6,350	20,392,815	2,275,502	-571,861	17,545,452	4,186,807	4,908,328	33,545	794,171	480,558
2008	27,839,626	20,690,462	-5,514	20,684,948	2,354,287	-625,669	17,704,992	4,624,989	5,509,645	34,595	804,719	483,283
2009	27,267,964	20,149,439	833	20,150,272	2,323,311	-662,604	17,164,357	4,178,807	5,924,800	33,608	811,349	463,595
2010	28,543,694	20,929,471	3,794	20,933,265	2,388,936	-633,046	17,911,283	4,216,735	6,415,676	34,979	816,021	462,463
2011	30,298,372	21,966,688	1,393	21,968,081	2,222,393	-771,151	18,974,537	4,792,003	6,531,832	36,912	820,819	470,931
2012	31,988,212	22,976,181	13,469	22,989,650	2,249,039	-644,114	20,096,497	5,250,804	6,640,911	38,763	825,215	470,540
2013	32,009,246	23,494,617	25,603	23,520,220	2,593,966	-666,077	20,260,177	4,914,426	6,834,643	38,597	829,313	473,535
2014	33,340,847	24,432,267	22,654	24,454,921	2,675,174	-667,302	21,112,445	5,309,761	6,918,641	39,934	834,896	482,039
2015	35,008,711	25,583,061	22,934	25,605,995	2,794,396	-683,223	22,128,376	5,521,467	7,358,868	41,665	840,236	491,065
2016	36,088,290	26,410,957	2,846	26,413,803	2,895,187	-677,444	22,841,172	5,643,718	7,603,400	42,565	847,835	500,805
2017	37,580,418	27,421,281	7,965	27,429,246	3,042,600	-652,133	23,734,513	6,036,736	7,809,169	43,851	857,009	507,625
2018	39,847,421	28,930,790	-2,352	28,928,438	3,179,855	-684,305	25,064,278	6,523,397	8,259,746	46,054	865,239	516,198
2019	42,592,235	30,194,032	750	30,194,782	3,306,376	-636,768	26,251,638	7,598,449	8,742,148	48,813	872,567	520,082
2020	45,917,952	31,876,123	344	31,876,467	3,507,219	-760,899	27,608,349	7,605,845	10,703,758	52,083	881,628	519,568
2021	49,809,217	34,711,464	6,681	34,718,145	3,703,245	-760,919	30,253,981	7,788,351	11,766,885	55,752	893,412	537,202

Personal Income and Employment by Area: Kokomo, IN

(Thousands of dollars, except as noted.)

Year	Personal income, total	Derivation of personal income								Per capita personal income (dollars)	Population (persons)	Total employment
		Earnings by place of work			Less: Contributions for government social insurance	Plus: Adjustment for residence	Equals: Net earnings by place of residence	Plus: Dividends, interest, and rent	Plus: Personal current transfer receipts			
		Nonfarm	Farm	Total								
1970	331,938	339,172	5,101	344,273	22,733	-52,896	268,644	41,170	22,124	3,982	83,353	42,282
1971	384,616	400,068	7,664	407,732	27,903	-65,921	313,908	45,197	25,511	4,584	83,904	44,735
1972	429,095	460,468	5,807	466,275	34,537	-78,852	352,886	48,118	28,091	5,058	84,832	46,840
1973	498,639	535,902	17,916	553,818	46,926	-94,878	412,014	54,917	31,708	5,815	85,745	50,105
1974	506,802	533,449	9,731	543,180	48,464	-94,141	400,575	62,950	43,277	5,811	87,215	47,441
1975	529,985	520,790	17,570	538,360	46,757	-92,491	399,112	70,449	60,424	6,098	86,906	43,959
1976	603,238	646,150	10,822	656,972	58,907	-124,706	473,359	77,332	52,547	6,958	86,700	47,377
1977	672,470	746,027	5,793	751,820	67,991	-152,531	531,298	87,137	54,035	7,719	87,123	49,509
1978	739,370	827,340	9,483	836,823	77,815	-174,283	584,725	94,161	60,484	8,474	87,248	50,886
1979	782,962	868,097	7,452	875,549	84,319	-185,636	605,594	102,436	74,932	8,968	87,305	49,709
1980	839,617	862,252	1,444	863,696	83,180	-187,632	592,884	123,519	123,214	9,676	86,774	45,809
1981	887,944	921,843	85	921,928	95,940	-197,215	628,773	149,943	109,228	10,313	86,098	46,275
1982	883,200	865,791	2,790	868,581	91,592	-176,894	600,095	161,716	121,389	10,390	85,004	42,641
1983	974,632	993,201	-1,920	991,281	106,423	-208,022	676,836	172,420	125,376	11,530	84,532	43,455
1984	1,114,265	1,164,886	7,157	1,172,043	128,577	-250,029	793,437	192,841	127,987	13,160	84,671	47,020
1985	1,209,975	1,285,017	8,624	1,293,641	143,969	-278,525	871,147	205,765	133,063	14,326	84,459	47,707
1986	1,233,883	1,289,057	6,711	1,295,768	143,515	-271,605	880,648	212,780	140,455	14,730	83,768	47,674
1987	1,256,526	1,302,142	9,828	1,311,970	143,223	-267,045	901,702	209,759	145,065	15,266	82,308	48,068
1988	1,367,182	1,450,340	5,576	1,455,916	163,395	-302,451	990,070	221,496	155,616	16,880	80,994	48,902
1989	1,472,569	1,534,112	10,431	1,544,543	173,296	-317,319	1,053,928	247,436	171,205	18,236	80,751	49,968
1990	1,515,935	1,541,538	13,107	1,554,645	180,308	-304,114	1,070,223	255,881	189,831	18,721	80,976	50,562
1991	1,551,343	1,587,854	8,786	1,596,640	187,804	-319,740	1,089,096	252,272	209,975	18,936	81,924	50,375
1992	1,662,725	1,715,362	12,379	1,727,741	199,092	-359,591	1,169,058	252,889	240,778	20,145	82,537	52,015
1993	1,770,673	1,857,559	15,884	1,873,443	218,365	-404,640	1,250,438	268,474	251,761	21,264	83,271	53,683
1994	1,884,528	2,043,334	16,630	2,059,964	240,029	-467,548	1,352,387	274,408	257,733	22,547	83,584	53,788
1995	1,979,095	2,129,197	8,025	2,137,222	236,695	-505,926	1,394,601	320,316	264,178	23,587	83,905	56,546
1996	2,042,827	2,162,744	21,936	2,184,680	229,036	-525,716	1,429,928	331,109	281,790	24,131	84,656	56,874
1997	2,080,986	2,175,566	20,605	2,196,171	227,438	-528,344	1,440,389	351,374	289,223	24,578	84,669	56,082
1998	2,206,190	2,327,553	11,951	2,339,504	232,284	-568,732	1,538,488	370,471	297,231	26,152	84,361	56,595
1999	2,311,971	2,500,430	7,155	2,507,585	245,559	-627,794	1,634,232	361,834	315,905	27,273	84,772	57,213
2000	2,405,253	2,558,018	13,580	2,571,598	248,837	-648,040	1,674,721	390,097	340,435	28,317	84,940	57,398
2001	2,352,872	2,448,629	15,228	2,463,857	281,622	-594,994	1,587,241	380,977	384,654	27,711	84,909	54,466
2002	2,393,558	2,506,249	9,637	2,515,886	287,595	-600,244	1,628,047	362,268	403,243	28,305	84,563	53,920
2003	2,454,586	2,531,807	14,733	2,546,540	291,765	-597,455	1,657,320	375,220	422,046	29,035	84,538	52,448
2004	2,530,083	2,629,356	24,688	2,654,044	300,112	-620,624	1,733,308	345,288	451,487	30,016	84,291	52,038
2005	2,572,055	2,617,770	15,350	2,633,120	300,181	-605,810	1,727,129	352,286	492,640	30,481	84,382	51,636
2006	2,652,776	2,665,025	10,263	2,675,288	310,452	-615,261	1,749,575	365,143	538,058	31,602	83,943	51,247
2007	2,771,585	2,687,272	11,820	2,699,092	314,196	-595,188	1,789,708	416,388	565,489	33,096	83,743	50,656
2008	2,718,493	2,393,985	25,075	2,419,060	285,908	-469,668	1,663,484	411,840	643,169	32,568	83,472	48,220
2009	2,532,829	2,000,794	10,866	2,011,660	246,460	-325,463	1,439,737	385,898	707,194	30,626	82,701	43,224
2010	2,592,678	2,029,463	3,774	2,033,237	246,312	-323,821	1,463,104	389,142	740,432	31,330	82,753	44,555
2011	2,739,653	2,162,099	20,913	2,183,012	233,900	-364,208	1,584,904	410,280	744,469	33,086	82,805	45,557
2012	2,865,087	2,263,219	26,260	2,289,479	241,939	-382,668	1,664,872	431,300	768,915	34,580	82,853	46,485
2013	2,916,649	2,354,032	63,575	2,417,607	291,083	-423,453	1,703,071	428,010	785,568	35,242	82,761	47,655
2014	3,041,987	2,474,723	36,100	2,510,823	303,163	-433,848	1,773,812	440,520	827,655	36,642	83,020	48,392
2015	3,135,380	2,543,513	3,043	2,546,556	313,023	-428,246	1,805,287	469,723	860,370	37,842	82,855	48,492
2016	3,185,346	2,590,075	13,599	2,603,674	314,833	-439,918	1,848,923	462,886	873,537	38,394	82,965	49,708
2017	3,273,754	2,642,312	10,085	2,652,397	314,775	-444,987	1,892,635	481,540	899,579	39,462	82,960	49,760
2018	3,421,963	2,676,017	13,643	2,689,660	321,861	-360,140	2,007,659	481,501	932,803	41,185	83,087	48,915
2019	3,495,598	2,714,726	6,277	2,721,003	336,789	-375,748	2,008,466	512,777	974,355	41,863	83,500	47,873
2020	3,701,513	2,536,578	21,492	2,558,070	333,256	-270,690	1,954,124	513,812	1,233,577	44,266	83,619	45,867
2021	3,935,876	2,567,918	31,783	2,599,701	331,913	-227,486	2,040,302	503,104	1,392,470	47,031	83,687	45,192

Personal Income and Employment by Area: La Crosse-Onalaska, WI-MN

(Thousands of dollars, except as noted.)

Year	Personal income, total	Earnings by place of work			Less: Contributions for government social insurance	Plus: Adjustment for residence	Equals: Net earnings by place of residence	Plus: Dividends, interest, and rent	Plus: Personal current transfer receipts	Per capita personal income (dollars)	Population (persons)	Total employment
		Nonfarm	Farm	Total								
1970	351,917	265,134	18,975	284,109	19,719	-6,989	257,401	58,922	35,594	3,581	98,260	42,995
1971	379,780	284,348	19,289	303,637	21,845	-7,215	274,577	63,301	41,902	3,825	99,301	43,907
1972	413,433	312,253	21,855	334,108	25,281	-8,400	300,427	67,254	45,752	4,187	98,738	45,533
1973	468,010	352,671	31,478	384,149	32,705	-9,942	341,502	73,946	52,562	4,672	100,165	48,430
1974	514,132	391,540	24,873	416,413	37,822	-11,753	366,838	83,326	63,968	5,050	101,810	49,921
1975	566,448	428,642	19,890	448,532	40,610	-13,097	394,825	93,088	78,535	5,414	104,618	50,747
1976	637,150	492,901	19,442	512,343	47,636	-16,096	448,611	103,081	85,458	6,143	103,720	53,331
1977	718,376	552,252	30,107	582,359	53,355	-19,477	509,527	117,690	91,159	6,757	106,314	55,192
1978	803,419	632,290	28,734	661,024	62,648	-24,020	574,356	128,712	100,351	7,337	109,509	57,889
1979	898,823	712,223	27,666	739,889	73,651	-26,480	639,758	141,662	117,403	8,072	111,346	60,200
1980	1,021,439	791,881	25,165	817,046	81,539	-31,203	704,304	177,119	140,016	9,312	109,696	61,582
1981	1,139,565	868,894	25,271	894,165	95,804	-38,062	760,299	219,989	159,277	10,315	110,473	62,428
1982	1,218,145	903,873	24,697	928,570	100,726	-38,787	789,057	253,596	175,492	10,974	111,000	61,655
1983	1,293,441	972,405	9,211	981,616	107,946	-42,044	831,626	270,392	191,423	11,640	111,122	62,200
1984	1,416,499	1,059,573	25,696	1,085,269	120,446	-45,464	919,359	299,460	197,680	12,622	112,222	64,086
1985	1,492,240	1,110,621	30,350	1,140,971	127,277	-47,789	965,905	313,127	213,208	13,213	112,937	64,642
1986	1,569,389	1,161,748	41,491	1,203,239	133,262	-49,390	1,020,587	330,597	218,205	13,875	113,108	65,626
1987	1,674,088	1,254,420	46,390	1,300,810	141,399	-53,645	1,105,766	343,930	224,392	14,662	114,178	67,341
1988	1,771,034	1,375,472	26,650	1,402,122	161,277	-60,672	1,180,173	357,121	233,740	15,403	114,981	70,751
1989	1,943,296	1,479,517	45,117	1,524,634	174,225	-64,302	1,286,107	403,642	253,547	16,797	115,693	70,706
1990	2,092,451	1,562,487	47,337	1,609,824	190,348	-65,650	1,353,826	467,936	270,689	17,920	116,769	72,019
1991	2,141,819	1,634,282	34,342	1,668,624	201,250	-69,287	1,398,087	456,374	287,358	18,197	117,700	73,440
1992	2,281,479	1,761,316	33,911	1,795,227	213,581	-74,424	1,507,222	461,929	312,328	19,139	119,207	75,248
1993	2,420,515	1,878,634	23,131	1,901,765	226,964	-79,069	1,595,732	502,357	322,426	20,071	120,597	77,177
1994	2,563,583	2,004,817	25,708	2,030,525	244,263	-83,919	1,702,343	532,033	329,207	21,038	121,856	79,874
1995	2,640,060	2,052,175	12,051	2,064,226	251,076	-83,820	1,729,330	558,719	352,011	21,480	122,910	81,628
1996	2,792,695	2,193,133	26,283	2,219,416	266,816	-90,450	1,862,150	571,145	359,400	22,536	123,920	83,209
1997	2,947,156	2,350,771	19,722	2,370,493	283,334	-98,561	1,988,598	587,783	370,775	23,668	124,521	85,030
1998	3,164,542	2,514,344	29,424	2,543,768	300,088	-103,770	2,139,910	646,601	378,031	25,241	125,371	86,896
1999	3,270,400	2,617,847	24,211	2,642,058	311,887	-97,344	2,232,827	639,904	397,669	25,947	126,041	87,257
2000	3,449,527	2,732,021	14,949	2,746,970	322,952	-99,162	2,324,856	691,041	433,630	27,157	127,021	88,620
2001	3,600,693	2,834,617	17,959	2,852,576	331,754	-113,360	2,407,462	707,101	486,130	28,213	127,624	88,333
2002	3,690,924	2,922,021	14,382	2,936,403	339,715	-105,986	2,490,702	665,953	534,269	28,777	128,261	87,533
2003	3,849,231	3,050,196	26,484	3,076,680	353,386	-110,875	2,612,419	687,469	549,343	29,890	128,780	88,472
2004	4,006,941	3,174,819	38,063	3,212,882	365,231	-125,167	2,722,484	718,802	565,655	31,063	128,992	88,138
2005	4,170,868	3,293,899	36,430	3,330,329	382,385	-131,369	2,816,575	753,241	601,052	32,195	129,549	89,432
2006	4,402,981	3,457,759	27,261	3,485,020	404,670	-144,487	2,935,863	831,546	635,572	33,831	130,147	91,459
2007	4,639,972	3,573,578	27,117	3,600,695	421,718	-154,799	3,024,178	926,332	689,462	35,368	131,190	92,487
2008	4,937,304	3,718,281	32,204	3,750,485	440,932	-171,457	3,138,096	1,028,419	770,789	37,427	131,920	92,633
2009	4,986,676	3,777,476	13,682	3,791,158	444,713	-189,439	3,157,006	946,746	882,924	37,474	133,072	90,829
2010	5,099,300	3,900,569	28,986	3,929,555	462,045	-207,216	3,260,294	879,924	959,082	38,081	133,906	91,117
2011	5,392,466	4,028,212	53,718	4,081,930	428,269	-228,052	3,425,609	1,039,486	927,371	40,203	134,132	92,209
2012	5,705,971	4,223,468	57,914	4,281,382	442,636	-255,502	3,583,244	1,171,718	951,009	42,158	135,347	93,979
2013	5,661,496	4,341,667	56,142	4,397,809	513,989	-276,427	3,607,393	1,074,526	979,577	41,715	135,718	95,064
2014	6,007,284	4,561,471	55,857	4,617,328	535,137	-287,990	3,794,201	1,168,605	1,044,478	43,760	137,279	95,398
2015	6,231,003	4,703,663	42,154	4,745,817	548,997	-290,363	3,906,457	1,249,836	1,074,710	45,219	137,795	95,859
2016	6,328,293	4,816,636	24,971	4,841,607	560,459	-325,074	3,956,074	1,273,473	1,098,746	45,819	138,115	96,690
2017	6,557,888	4,945,304	29,881	4,975,185	584,797	-332,516	4,057,872	1,342,576	1,157,440	47,283	138,693	97,116
2018	6,839,385	5,185,657	24,217	5,209,874	606,289	-347,007	4,256,578	1,358,842	1,223,965	49,238	138,904	97,913
2019	7,165,663	5,420,641	22,355	5,442,996	634,646	-374,016	4,434,334	1,451,306	1,280,023	51,497	139,146	97,343
2020	7,640,135	5,540,543	51,094	5,591,637	648,881	-378,977	4,563,779	1,469,210	1,607,146	54,701	139,670	93,449
2021	8,131,912	5,884,340	46,563	5,930,903	679,532	-419,989	4,831,382	1,514,556	1,785,974	58,414	139,211	96,283

Personal Income and Employment by Area: Lafayette, LA

(Thousands of dollars, except as noted.)

Year	Personal income, total	Earnings by place of work			Less: Contributions for government social insurance	Plus: Adjustment for residence	Equals: Net earnings by place of residence	Plus: Dividends, interest, and rent	Plus: Personal current transfer receipts	Per capita personal income (dollars)	Population (persons)	Total employment
		Nonfarm	Farm	Total								
1970	805,165	584,621	39,652	624,273	36,957	24,925	612,241	109,467	83,457	2,707	297,437	106,400
1971	884,670	645,894	38,897	684,791	41,721	23,475	666,545	122,172	95,953	2,932	301,678	108,662
1972	985,311	729,548	45,181	774,729	49,714	21,077	746,092	134,920	104,299	3,201	307,819	113,843
1973	1,152,474	825,043	101,536	926,579	65,085	17,213	878,707	152,911	120,856	3,689	312,430	119,859
1974	1,347,267	952,477	122,915	1,075,392	77,644	17,866	1,015,614	187,384	144,269	4,248	317,134	124,542
1975	1,562,706	1,128,221	105,665	1,233,886	91,074	18,513	1,161,325	224,040	177,341	4,844	322,597	130,569
1976	1,724,255	1,333,387	42,940	1,376,327	109,380	13,869	1,280,816	246,297	197,142	5,211	330,873	137,893
1977	1,992,514	1,574,370	50,850	1,625,220	128,516	6,313	1,503,017	279,570	209,927	5,899	337,770	147,120
1978	2,381,562	1,960,774	35,423	1,996,197	164,968	-2,722	1,828,507	324,157	228,898	6,917	344,306	161,185
1979	2,787,799	2,320,543	53,177	2,373,720	204,852	-15,882	2,152,986	374,480	260,333	7,925	351,776	170,540
1980	3,334,622	2,773,721	27,202	2,800,923	244,515	-32,872	2,523,536	501,041	310,045	9,226	361,450	181,105
1981	4,095,563	3,456,825	16,031	3,472,856	329,428	-61,617	3,081,811	670,453	343,299	11,035	371,133	199,253
1982	4,572,504	3,752,185	42,429	3,794,614	370,924	-77,237	3,346,453	823,010	403,041	11,855	385,710	205,964
1983	4,550,157	3,528,606	27,416	3,556,022	341,351	-63,472	3,151,199	895,901	503,057	11,556	393,737	193,845
1984	4,700,343	3,651,637	12,044	3,663,681	364,278	-57,348	3,242,055	953,725	504,563	11,961	392,956	193,564
1985	4,913,527	3,748,245	28,171	3,776,416	379,562	-57,444	3,339,410	1,040,782	533,335	12,423	395,505	192,643
1986	4,645,752	3,370,084	16,568	3,386,652	334,428	-35,476	3,016,748	994,395	634,609	11,700	397,056	174,850
1987	4,402,044	3,143,569	22,222	3,165,791	306,254	-15,162	2,844,375	925,071	632,598	11,313	389,109	164,848
1988	4,756,912	3,434,996	79,750	3,514,746	352,178	-16,763	3,145,805	964,861	646,246	12,393	383,841	171,932
1989	5,111,895	3,646,308	65,716	3,712,024	376,285	-11,263	3,324,476	1,075,130	712,289	13,319	383,800	177,407
1990	5,550,876	4,079,953	36,132	4,116,085	432,146	-18,684	3,665,255	1,105,216	780,405	14,478	383,397	186,879
1991	5,837,167	4,272,778	43,202	4,315,980	464,821	-21,801	3,829,358	1,111,155	896,654	15,033	388,299	191,220
1992	6,136,561	4,406,144	61,344	4,467,488	470,247	-2,034	3,995,207	1,112,651	1,028,703	15,633	392,531	188,119
1993	6,524,512	4,676,688	72,349	4,749,037	503,980	-5,552	4,239,505	1,163,828	1,121,179	16,396	397,922	195,210
1994	7,013,882	5,037,096	54,811	5,091,907	554,587	-24,162	4,513,158	1,241,963	1,258,761	17,431	402,385	201,325
1995	7,421,515	5,295,005	89,238	5,384,243	582,134	-47,360	4,754,749	1,367,119	1,299,647	18,250	406,658	208,746
1996	8,010,673	5,806,145	99,344	5,905,489	636,479	-76,643	5,192,367	1,492,500	1,325,806	19,480	411,228	217,292
1997	8,806,045	6,521,408	85,973	6,607,381	707,931	-100,298	5,799,152	1,644,060	1,362,833	21,140	416,562	228,667
1998	9,356,438	6,991,300	78,049	7,069,349	751,691	-126,093	6,191,565	1,762,700	1,402,173	22,220	421,081	237,170
1999	9,327,120	6,831,560	72,812	6,904,372	723,676	-93,214	6,087,482	1,767,797	1,471,841	21,992	424,114	232,472
2000	9,953,226	7,309,973	71,407	7,381,380	761,358	-116,591	6,503,431	1,933,549	1,516,246	23,411	425,158	236,014
2001	10,860,314	8,058,627	76,068	8,134,695	861,628	-154,234	7,118,833	1,988,173	1,753,308	25,449	426,750	241,219
2002	11,050,013	8,263,055	44,949	8,308,004	879,517	-148,809	7,279,678	1,912,310	1,858,025	25,676	430,358	241,717
2003	11,500,347	8,594,489	89,341	8,683,830	898,686	-129,827	7,655,317	1,985,768	1,859,262	26,566	432,900	243,521
2004	11,937,637	8,903,213	75,309	8,978,522	927,099	-171,060	7,880,363	2,014,035	2,043,239	27,379	436,018	244,291
2005	13,457,149	9,904,598	54,594	9,959,192	999,165	-238,892	8,721,135	2,461,809	2,274,205	30,589	439,936	252,865
2006	15,393,978	11,407,239	65,584	11,472,823	1,141,128	-301,433	10,030,262	2,980,247	2,383,469	34,153	450,740	266,576
2007	16,397,532	12,112,623	68,047	12,180,670	1,229,186	-361,561	10,589,923	3,312,088	2,495,521	36,093	454,315	274,647
2008	18,394,263	13,133,252	134,199	13,267,451	1,313,846	-407,875	11,545,730	3,976,327	2,872,206	40,065	459,111	281,721
2009	17,249,640	12,476,093	126,464	12,602,557	1,273,471	-322,983	11,006,103	3,232,301	3,011,236	37,176	463,998	277,490
2010	18,300,287	13,076,439	139,306	13,215,745	1,308,472	-256,005	11,651,268	3,436,772	3,212,247	39,135	467,617	278,005
2011	18,999,611	13,614,753	115,166	13,729,919	1,226,981	-196,938	12,306,000	3,421,764	3,271,847	40,340	470,988	284,493
2012	20,933,892	14,719,390	145,813	14,865,203	1,305,208	-154,378	13,405,617	4,206,571	3,321,704	44,136	474,308	292,872
2013	21,407,740	15,773,472	153,577	15,927,049	1,552,322	-22,363	14,352,364	3,606,926	3,448,450	44,606	479,931	299,500
2014	22,605,761	16,629,654	106,839	16,736,493	1,605,568	34,612	15,165,537	3,986,761	3,453,463	47,067	480,285	303,431
2015	21,386,214	15,047,682	75,207	15,122,889	1,518,782	137,765	13,741,872	3,809,723	3,834,619	44,205	483,798	295,375
2016	20,029,882	13,136,492	68,798	13,205,290	1,369,199	294,655	12,130,746	3,779,652	4,119,484	41,379	484,056	286,647
2017	20,689,352	13,325,892	101,619	13,427,511	1,388,322	300,494	12,339,683	4,021,406	4,328,263	42,900	482,268	285,251
2018	21,384,869	13,807,038	88,041	13,895,079	1,462,639	323,428	12,755,868	4,095,258	4,533,743	44,491	480,655	289,347
2019	21,847,769	13,992,270	95,665	14,087,935	1,485,574	307,625	12,909,986	4,182,692	4,755,091	45,588	479,248	288,781
2020	23,584,672	14,139,628	167,399	14,307,027	1,511,454	313,069	13,108,642	4,184,302	6,291,728	49,332	478,077	280,602
2021	25,034,409	14,732,003	114,013	14,846,016	1,556,925	335,054	13,624,145	4,308,701	7,101,563	52,241	479,212	286,396

Personal Income and Employment by Area: Lafayette-West Lafayette, IN

(Thousands of dollars, except as noted.)

Year	Personal income, total	Earnings by place of work			Less: Contributions for government social insurance	Plus: Adjustment for residence	Equals: Net earnings by place of residence	Plus: Dividends, interest, and rent	Plus: Personal current transfer receipts	Per capita personal income (dollars)	Population (persons)	Total employment
		Nonfarm	Farm	Total								
1970	507,331	412,779	20,631	433,410	28,045	-14,774	390,591	83,303	33,437	3,660	138,617	62,709
1971	562,517	439,001	35,303	474,304	30,892	-13,844	429,568	92,990	39,959	3,995	140,794	63,225
1972	604,019	479,613	27,485	507,098	35,671	-14,346	457,081	101,326	45,612	4,184	144,368	64,982
1973	716,411	531,175	75,074	606,249	45,500	-15,013	545,736	116,880	53,795	5,009	143,014	67,510
1974	755,819	581,705	49,767	631,472	52,537	-18,171	560,764	133,882	61,173	5,205	145,206	68,865
1975	853,224	611,047	87,733	698,780	54,672	-18,540	625,568	149,874	77,782	5,883	145,041	68,001
1976	907,714	679,066	62,857	741,923	61,149	-17,271	663,503	162,371	81,840	6,179	146,905	70,142
1977	987,994	770,336	37,801	808,137	68,649	-21,066	718,422	183,537	86,035	6,650	148,579	72,763
1978	1,120,873	879,573	47,200	926,773	80,449	-25,245	821,079	203,944	95,850	7,456	150,334	75,536
1979	1,245,382	974,236	53,338	1,027,574	92,420	-28,212	906,942	229,571	108,869	8,209	151,718	75,825
1980	1,335,883	1,035,609	19,870	1,055,479	97,674	-30,111	927,694	278,477	129,712	8,794	151,907	76,075
1981	1,499,152	1,108,911	41,251	1,150,162	113,096	-28,849	1,008,217	341,048	149,887	9,822	152,637	75,590
1982	1,576,984	1,139,611	38,427	1,178,038	118,701	-31,409	1,027,928	380,814	168,242	10,258	153,738	74,541
1983	1,620,823	1,188,320	-2,527	1,185,793	123,193	-29,644	1,032,956	404,239	183,628	10,529	153,944	74,681
1984	1,800,695	1,299,011	48,005	1,347,016	137,269	-31,101	1,178,646	429,164	192,885	11,727	153,552	77,450
1985	1,903,656	1,372,142	52,368	1,424,510	147,204	-34,398	1,242,908	456,939	203,809	12,343	154,225	78,778
1986	1,996,757	1,470,444	36,502	1,506,946	158,406	-41,227	1,307,313	474,395	215,049	12,944	154,265	80,336
1987	2,110,956	1,583,438	45,674	1,629,112	167,220	-50,073	1,411,819	480,781	218,356	13,634	154,829	82,628
1988	2,214,919	1,718,330	11,447	1,729,777	189,751	-51,313	1,488,713	495,832	230,374	14,157	156,458	85,370
1989	2,472,054	1,875,447	55,990	1,931,437	207,583	-61,024	1,662,830	559,334	249,890	15,555	158,926	87,860
1990	2,625,434	2,034,920	50,175	2,085,095	231,032	-76,281	1,777,782	578,459	269,193	16,504	159,075	90,758
1991	2,707,383	2,178,241	-3,015	2,175,226	250,304	-89,610	1,835,312	581,789	290,282	16,751	161,622	92,258
1992	2,927,312	2,328,803	38,090	2,366,893	264,547	-101,193	2,001,153	599,127	327,032	17,856	163,942	93,614
1993	3,073,903	2,440,601	41,225	2,481,826	278,886	-105,298	2,097,642	632,196	344,065	18,424	166,846	95,426
1994	3,264,594	2,596,669	52,280	2,648,949	299,855	-117,383	2,231,711	674,355	358,528	19,342	168,780	97,690
1995	3,446,261	2,778,689	3,352	2,782,041	320,351	-139,157	2,322,533	756,343	367,385	20,132	171,187	101,510
1996	3,644,275	2,894,448	77,639	2,972,087	328,711	-156,796	2,486,580	770,623	387,072	21,024	173,337	103,302
1997	3,871,340	3,094,530	69,596	3,164,126	350,340	-183,586	2,630,200	839,283	401,857	22,188	174,481	105,842
1998	4,299,310	3,414,183	39,039	3,453,222	375,728	-147,738	2,929,756	909,293	460,261	23,351	184,114	112,548
1999	4,435,356	3,580,025	30,716	3,610,741	390,929	-151,121	3,068,691	882,064	484,601	23,886	185,692	115,035
2000	4,776,584	3,843,493	39,265	3,882,758	411,728	-168,618	3,302,412	948,514	525,658	25,495	187,356	116,546
2001	4,818,034	3,847,952	54,025	3,901,977	424,143	-181,181	3,296,653	948,764	572,617	25,457	189,259	112,123
2002	4,867,012	3,914,500	39,750	3,954,250	429,467	-193,759	3,331,024	923,712	612,276	25,565	190,379	111,411
2003	4,921,912	3,955,689	59,337	4,015,026	437,847	-198,595	3,378,584	903,045	640,283	25,607	192,210	108,782
2004	5,208,329	4,140,834	113,389	4,254,223	461,121	-188,718	3,604,384	921,955	681,990	26,902	193,605	109,760
2005	5,427,715	4,359,224	76,506	4,435,730	489,484	-206,503	3,739,743	942,139	745,833	27,601	196,649	111,853
2006	5,694,546	4,483,984	71,699	4,555,683	508,304	-188,877	3,858,502	1,027,175	808,869	28,376	200,685	114,338
2007	5,996,510	4,663,065	114,728	4,777,793	529,125	-205,106	4,043,562	1,096,179	856,769	29,438	203,703	116,329
2008	6,479,679	4,852,671	185,614	5,038,285	552,893	-196,267	4,289,125	1,183,585	1,006,969	31,370	206,556	116,405
2009	6,327,852	4,709,853	111,734	4,821,587	539,684	-199,334	4,082,569	1,143,600	1,101,683	30,232	209,308	112,440
2010	6,597,267	4,861,654	123,479	4,985,133	548,327	-193,896	4,242,910	1,144,172	1,210,185	31,313	210,689	112,302
2011	7,063,000	5,156,799	227,709	5,384,508	513,470	-216,724	4,654,314	1,218,691	1,189,995	33,118	213,265	116,157
2012	7,404,778	5,471,356	147,724	5,619,080	537,785	-239,399	4,841,896	1,344,511	1,218,371	34,201	216,510	119,327
2013	7,554,646	5,482,682	400,102	5,882,784	616,618	-228,676	5,037,490	1,289,689	1,227,467	34,452	219,282	119,791
2014	7,809,204	5,800,725	199,267	5,999,992	648,083	-230,536	5,121,373	1,378,676	1,309,155	35,851	217,825	122,078
2015	7,954,477	6,013,845	33,056	6,046,901	676,899	-248,052	5,121,950	1,472,147	1,360,380	36,313	219,051	123,159
2016	8,227,521	6,190,040	102,677	6,292,717	688,925	-268,278	5,335,514	1,494,485	1,397,522	37,126	221,610	125,220
2017	8,542,778	6,446,714	72,062	6,518,776	719,094	-284,159	5,515,523	1,591,697	1,435,558	38,538	221,673	127,509
2018	9,072,100	6,967,428	78,157	7,045,585	771,970	-334,707	5,938,908	1,633,020	1,500,172	40,628	223,295	130,313
2019	9,295,286	7,034,307	55,561	7,089,868	796,097	-337,328	5,956,443	1,744,048	1,594,795	41,571	223,602	131,673
2020	9,831,809	6,926,087	153,812	7,079,899	814,803	-284,619	5,980,477	1,745,982	2,105,350	43,955	223,679	126,220
2021	10,554,142	7,273,691	230,104	7,503,795	837,614	-278,332	6,387,849	1,761,344	2,404,949	46,968	224,709	130,455

Personal Income and Employment by Area: Lake Charles, LA

(Thousands of dollars, except as noted.)

Year	Personal income, total	Earnings by place of work			Less: Contributions for government social insurance	Plus: Adjustment for residence	Equals: Net earnings by place of residence	Plus: Dividends, interest, and rent	Plus: Personal current transfer receipts	Per capita personal income (dollars)	Population (persons)	Total employment
		Nonfarm	Farm	Total								
1970	491,476	408,068	8,433	416,501	26,515	-3,039	386,947	59,370	45,159	3,200	153,590	57,589
1971	529,251	439,671	8,758	448,429	29,222	-5,714	413,493	65,351	50,407	3,422	154,666	57,881
1972	556,300	457,816	8,903	466,719	31,780	-5,935	429,004	70,912	56,384	3,540	157,151	57,794
1973	626,807	515,599	18,047	533,646	41,616	-10,313	481,717	78,029	67,061	3,945	158,870	60,991
1974	712,607	590,165	16,504	606,669	49,209	-15,434	542,026	93,025	77,556	4,472	159,343	62,986
1975	811,538	669,467	15,228	684,695	54,433	-21,300	608,962	106,385	96,191	5,060	160,391	65,067
1976	919,711	790,080	2,070	792,150	65,168	-28,884	698,098	115,252	106,361	5,652	162,731	68,125
1977	1,036,821	894,285	8,560	902,845	73,112	-36,865	792,868	127,998	115,955	6,263	165,539	71,271
1978	1,224,395	1,090,022	10,762	1,100,784	91,950	-59,417	949,417	151,283	123,695	7,304	167,630	78,314
1979	1,407,862	1,283,800	11,753	1,295,553	112,962	-85,509	1,097,082	174,199	136,581	8,189	171,913	82,909
1980	1,641,103	1,492,938	8,637	1,501,575	130,913	-112,164	1,258,498	215,691	166,914	9,248	177,456	86,336
1981	1,898,005	1,722,383	3,871	1,726,254	162,348	-127,778	1,436,128	276,345	185,532	10,502	180,724	89,401
1982	1,942,542	1,644,337	5,670	1,650,007	157,870	-105,339	1,386,798	326,660	229,084	10,565	183,865	82,812
1983	2,038,162	1,661,668	4,750	1,666,418	157,302	-108,239	1,400,877	364,576	272,709	11,036	184,681	80,277
1984	2,058,711	1,630,558	2,356	1,632,914	156,757	-94,455	1,381,702	402,166	274,843	11,171	184,287	78,899
1985	2,122,274	1,659,056	4,615	1,663,671	160,808	-95,607	1,407,256	433,837	281,181	11,595	183,031	78,558
1986	2,129,263	1,643,559	61	1,643,620	158,069	-95,019	1,390,532	429,743	308,988	11,745	181,297	76,259
1987	2,193,774	1,712,486	1,930	1,714,416	162,760	-95,225	1,456,431	423,178	314,165	12,173	180,214	77,853
1988	2,327,620	1,796,623	13,651	1,810,274	179,495	-95,490	1,535,289	465,706	326,625	13,007	178,955	79,865
1989	2,467,738	1,920,278	2,519	1,922,797	195,459	-106,515	1,620,823	479,152	367,763	13,881	177,773	82,655
1990	2,749,054	2,170,146	4,960	2,175,106	227,865	-125,659	1,821,582	519,860	407,612	15,486	177,524	87,736
1991	2,908,113	2,306,447	2,286	2,308,733	247,094	-131,832	1,929,807	523,967	454,339	16,207	179,439	89,353
1992	3,055,947	2,404,060	4,581	2,408,641	254,461	-133,887	2,020,293	529,334	506,320	16,908	180,736	88,809
1993	3,204,424	2,483,285	5,344	2,488,629	264,065	-143,262	2,081,302	566,643	556,479	17,598	182,093	89,641
1994	3,455,815	2,665,015	1,629	2,666,644	287,657	-157,124	2,221,863	611,965	621,987	18,763	184,181	93,804
1995	3,674,810	2,832,378	6,465	2,838,843	305,109	-169,093	2,364,641	667,761	642,408	19,693	186,607	97,914
1996	3,897,417	3,061,153	2,306	3,063,459	330,253	-187,238	2,545,968	698,284	653,165	20,585	189,335	102,120
1997	4,109,314	3,286,609	3,640	3,290,249	353,288	-199,666	2,737,295	699,461	672,558	21,506	191,076	105,423
1998	4,241,178	3,377,266	6,882	3,384,148	369,902	-214,006	2,800,240	765,056	675,882	22,036	192,470	107,839
1999	4,312,480	3,432,825	6,198	3,439,023	370,431	-216,882	2,851,710	749,205	711,565	22,297	193,408	107,766
2000	4,485,434	3,547,016	5,291	3,552,307	374,473	-217,516	2,960,318	792,802	732,314	23,182	193,491	108,617
2001	4,715,428	3,671,268	11,315	3,682,583	382,945	-238,312	3,061,326	823,201	830,901	24,411	193,171	108,198
2002	4,804,110	3,751,561	5,371	3,756,932	394,247	-236,560	3,126,125	810,121	867,864	24,850	193,321	108,036
2003	4,859,491	3,792,365	10,549	3,802,914	395,209	-228,971	3,178,734	793,531	887,226	24,978	194,552	107,586
2004	5,118,516	4,005,443	11,106	4,016,549	410,074	-253,921	3,352,554	797,475	968,487	26,189	195,444	106,568
2005	5,614,207	4,310,694	4,233	4,314,927	431,046	-292,334	3,591,547	872,498	1,150,162	28,606	196,263	108,680
2006	6,066,956	4,635,513	13,460	4,648,973	460,006	-305,236	3,883,731	1,099,675	1,083,550	31,424	193,069	110,930
2007	6,717,190	4,892,002	3,261	4,895,263	489,501	-327,641	4,078,121	1,517,344	1,121,725	34,518	194,598	113,094
2008	7,177,505	5,261,541	2,405	5,263,946	522,330	-377,730	4,363,886	1,527,912	1,285,707	36,552	196,362	115,652
2009	6,809,163	5,069,188	6,188	5,075,376	507,067	-315,749	4,252,560	1,204,963	1,351,640	34,388	198,010	112,613
2010	7,014,079	5,138,247	8,721	5,146,968	505,242	-288,013	4,353,713	1,206,336	1,454,030	35,081	199,938	110,785
2011	7,332,599	5,313,807	8,284	5,322,091	475,308	-305,922	4,540,861	1,310,161	1,481,577	36,562	200,553	112,346
2012	7,752,872	5,604,168	16,021	5,620,189	495,004	-315,707	4,809,478	1,412,824	1,530,570	38,544	201,146	114,545
2013	7,878,106	5,907,800	22,175	5,929,975	586,735	-368,841	4,974,399	1,322,384	1,581,323	38,950	202,261	117,150
2014	8,457,472	6,801,793	14,599	6,816,392	667,541	-634,872	5,513,979	1,380,250	1,563,243	40,667	207,970	123,692
2015	9,012,597	7,298,556	1,212	7,299,768	728,489	-760,001	5,811,278	1,473,157	1,728,162	42,688	211,129	129,076
2016	9,240,342	7,880,917	-2,998	7,877,919	805,869	-1,054,924	6,017,126	1,397,047	1,826,169	43,050	214,640	135,688
2017	9,747,124	8,500,091	52	8,500,143	877,834	-1,306,585	6,315,724	1,528,875	1,902,525	44,756	217,783	143,036
2018	10,212,736	9,033,157	-5,713	9,027,444	941,189	-1,397,623	6,688,632	1,538,758	1,985,346	46,439	219,916	145,899
2019	10,221,381	8,900,621	-6,571	8,894,050	923,207	-1,260,213	6,710,630	1,421,709	2,089,042	46,117	221,639	141,978
2020	10,504,942	8,042,638	627	8,043,265	845,516	-977,113	6,220,636	1,416,894	2,867,412	47,312	222,035	124,239
2021	10,745,275	8,319,580	-7,036	8,312,544	868,626	-1,121,652	6,322,266	1,424,069	2,998,940	51,080	210,362	124,716

Personal Income and Employment by Area: Lake Havasu City-Kingman, AZ

(Thousands of dollars, except as noted.)

Year	Personal income, total	Earnings by place of work			Less: Contributions for government social insurance	Plus: Adjustment for residence	Equals: Net earnings by place of residence	Plus: Dividends, interest, and rent	Plus: Personal current transfer receipts	Per capita personal income (dollars)	Population (persons)	Total employment
		Nonfarm	Farm	Total								
1970	102,490	66,091	1,274	67,365	4,225	11,209	74,349	18,445	9,696	3,891	26,338	9,297
1971	118,683	73,925	2,040	75,965	4,937	13,553	84,581	21,589	12,513	4,130	28,736	9,969
1972	135,971	83,329	3,489	86,818	5,873	14,746	95,691	24,804	15,476	4,374	31,084	10,832
1973	163,490	97,737	5,483	103,220	7,882	18,447	113,785	30,171	19,534	4,804	34,030	11,853
1974	182,255	115,194	686	115,880	9,800	16,123	122,203	36,302	23,750	4,983	36,572	13,269
1975	211,573	125,660	9,382	135,042	10,576	15,944	140,410	42,053	29,110	5,372	39,388	13,882
1976	230,847	141,398	54	141,452	11,874	18,049	147,627	47,091	36,129	5,437	42,458	14,593
1977	269,381	160,553	2,912	163,465	13,812	21,870	171,523	55,967	41,891	6,220	43,312	15,773
1978	328,934	196,295	3,876	200,171	17,289	26,737	209,619	69,182	50,133	7,148	46,017	17,606
1979	397,496	247,144	1,930	249,074	23,306	27,618	253,386	83,844	60,266	7,676	51,783	20,022
1980	460,917	268,553	4,924	273,477	25,668	31,928	279,737	105,262	75,918	8,169	56,423	21,285
1981	515,652	282,505	3,578	286,083	29,311	36,741	293,513	128,316	93,823	8,798	58,607	21,566
1982	548,776	270,741	4,562	275,303	28,949	42,111	288,465	149,880	110,431	8,775	62,539	20,609
1983	614,716	289,999	7,597	297,596	31,045	49,929	316,480	174,940	123,296	9,604	64,005	21,081
1984	716,005	341,804	5,857	347,661	37,252	56,842	367,251	211,921	136,833	10,629	67,364	23,340
1985	815,304	389,168	2,387	391,555	43,430	66,435	414,560	244,637	156,107	11,521	70,769	25,423
1986	910,427	432,044	1,266	433,310	48,416	77,985	462,879	273,129	174,419	12,080	75,366	26,881
1987	1,001,345	485,900	1,456	487,356	54,319	92,319	525,356	280,404	195,585	12,952	77,314	29,243
1988	1,120,161	536,321	3,910	540,231	62,328	112,478	590,381	308,988	220,792	13,597	82,381	31,315
1989	1,258,408	595,501	6,951	602,452	72,849	136,044	665,647	343,048	249,713	14,458	87,040	33,410
1990	1,445,167	702,053	8,192	710,245	86,995	164,857	788,107	374,259	282,801	15,134	95,491	36,930
1991	1,546,282	759,732	7,829	767,561	94,310	170,535	843,786	379,424	323,072	15,121	102,263	38,893
1992	1,653,450	811,377	7,696	819,073	100,658	182,942	901,357	385,755	366,338	15,219	108,644	39,206
1993	1,797,994	875,755	6,157	881,912	109,043	198,515	971,384	425,138	401,472	15,539	115,706	40,507
1994	1,988,757	957,454	5,223	962,677	120,219	216,911	1,059,369	486,091	443,297	16,181	122,906	43,326
1995	2,041,225	982,316	1,863	984,179	120,797	234,062	1,097,444	459,983	483,798	15,669	130,274	43,977
1996	2,196,237	1,046,698	3,450	1,050,148	131,001	255,698	1,174,845	494,357	527,035	16,097	136,436	46,030
1997	2,382,431	1,158,289	2,951	1,161,240	139,999	277,141	1,298,482	524,153	559,796	16,906	140,922	47,793
1998	2,571,475	1,250,558	4,018	1,254,576	149,045	302,842	1,408,373	551,589	611,513	17,715	145,155	49,316
1999	2,749,788	1,351,280	6,174	1,357,454	160,454	332,622	1,529,622	568,160	652,006	18,289	150,351	51,247
2000	2,974,573	1,472,338	7,868	1,480,206	174,489	355,097	1,660,814	611,284	702,475	19,042	156,215	54,312
2001	3,268,134	1,630,318	7,331	1,637,649	193,606	389,455	1,833,498	651,231	783,405	20,386	160,312	57,796
2002	3,480,429	1,777,994	5,176	1,783,170	211,404	418,687	1,990,453	626,995	862,981	20,947	166,155	59,875
2003	3,743,837	1,905,194	8,565	1,913,759	226,657	472,110	2,159,212	645,058	939,567	21,687	172,633	63,760
2004	4,145,861	2,093,064	11,858	2,104,922	249,049	563,921	2,419,794	702,599	1,023,468	22,966	180,521	67,457
2005	4,540,194	2,281,505	11,241	2,292,746	278,894	621,982	2,635,834	780,321	1,124,039	24,051	188,773	72,539
2006	4,829,713	2,490,628	9,552	2,500,180	305,773	601,381	2,795,788	794,101	1,239,824	24,620	196,168	75,359
2007	5,023,874	2,472,704	6,371	2,479,075	313,332	593,428	2,759,171	921,346	1,343,357	25,150	199,760	74,677
2008	5,140,527	2,439,089	5,703	2,444,792	316,552	547,036	2,675,276	957,060	1,508,191	25,693	200,078	70,529
2009	5,129,291	2,279,732	3,936	2,283,668	302,516	571,976	2,553,128	893,905	1,682,258	25,685	199,696	65,562
2010	5,193,370	2,284,675	3,493	2,288,168	308,727	562,784	2,542,225	870,225	1,780,920	25,923	200,336	64,092
2011	5,256,949	2,271,687	17,789	2,289,476	283,958	496,448	2,501,966	943,753	1,811,230	25,911	202,888	64,077
2012	5,359,199	2,309,146	2,792	2,311,938	286,607	520,994	2,546,325	961,646	1,851,228	26,337	203,484	63,231
2013	5,533,132	2,438,730	20,709	2,459,439	330,224	492,806	2,622,021	987,219	1,923,892	27,214	203,322	64,003
2014	5,851,991	2,550,690	21,612	2,572,302	341,431	538,382	2,769,253	1,050,556	2,032,182	28,921	202,345	65,380
2015	6,033,286	2,644,273	26,549	2,670,822	355,316	537,451	2,852,957	1,062,000	2,118,329	29,685	203,247	66,864
2016	6,287,403	2,703,997	22,739	2,726,736	369,705	605,885	2,962,916	1,118,916	2,205,571	30,830	203,940	67,873
2017	6,668,387	2,869,046	26,918	2,895,964	396,152	630,318	3,130,130	1,164,285	2,373,972	32,467	205,389	69,882
2018	7,017,179	3,016,925	26,659	3,043,584	427,592	642,839	3,258,831	1,242,514	2,515,834	33,776	207,757	71,847
2019	7,517,261	3,156,867	26,017	3,182,884	451,727	767,904	3,499,061	1,321,434	2,696,766	35,647	210,880	72,860
2020	8,288,070	3,450,681	33,927	3,484,608	492,814	499,919	3,491,713	1,335,382	3,460,975	38,717	214,070	73,795
2021	8,997,444	3,775,894	31,137	3,807,031	531,267	658,320	3,934,084	1,364,926	3,698,434	41,331	217,692	78,406

Personal Income and Employment by Area: Lakeland-Winter Haven, FL

(Thousands of dollars, except as noted.)

Year	Personal income, total	Earnings by place of work			Less: Contributions for government social insurance	Plus: Adjustment for residence	Equals: Net earnings by place of residence	Plus: Dividends, interest, and rent	Plus: Personal current transfer receipts	Per capita personal income (dollars)	Population (persons)	Total employment
		Nonfarm	Farm	Total								
1970	804,411	584,104	54,769	638,873	38,981	-22,544	577,348	145,461	81,602	3,492	230,334	97,281
1971	895,766	644,399	62,637	707,036	44,615	-23,517	638,904	159,356	97,506	3,709	241,479	100,888
1972	1,029,634	746,353	76,593	822,946	54,268	-27,489	741,189	175,690	112,755	4,079	252,394	107,814
1973	1,199,202	891,703	73,763	965,466	74,503	-34,508	856,455	208,355	134,392	4,576	262,049	118,069
1974	1,383,145	1,044,138	75,436	1,119,574	91,301	-44,243	984,030	244,445	154,670	5,047	274,042	125,364
1975	1,564,674	1,170,262	79,911	1,250,173	100,928	-56,828	1,092,417	273,124	199,133	5,501	284,417	128,059
1976	1,690,740	1,244,502	91,047	1,335,549	108,871	-57,797	1,168,881	297,710	224,149	5,839	289,562	128,195
1977	1,904,825	1,395,553	116,831	1,512,384	122,456	-68,148	1,321,780	337,426	245,619	6,434	296,048	134,567
1978	2,198,857	1,599,310	156,694	1,756,004	143,986	-80,311	1,531,707	396,279	270,871	7,301	301,183	142,680
1979	2,511,872	1,842,204	154,007	1,996,211	173,781	-98,243	1,724,187	469,946	317,739	8,032	312,723	149,427
1980	2,985,678	2,132,894	203,370	2,336,264	202,950	-117,504	2,015,810	592,688	377,180	9,214	324,038	156,846
1981	3,308,242	2,358,635	135,209	2,493,844	241,458	-125,421	2,126,965	738,586	442,691	9,935	332,973	160,268
1982	3,452,120	2,358,083	132,440	2,490,523	247,168	-111,860	2,131,495	808,479	512,146	10,155	339,930	155,026
1983	3,752,174	2,508,403	171,774	2,680,177	263,157	-99,305	2,317,715	878,123	556,336	10,842	346,080	157,947
1984	4,110,432	2,805,097	122,032	2,927,129	301,586	-90,952	2,534,591	996,704	579,137	11,598	354,414	165,687
1985	4,441,065	3,010,169	127,755	3,137,924	329,542	-83,599	2,724,783	1,084,720	631,562	12,207	363,802	173,302
1986	4,743,098	3,178,503	117,296	3,295,799	356,930	-68,405	2,870,464	1,182,613	690,021	12,748	372,057	176,446
1987	5,144,012	3,483,511	136,969	3,620,480	383,942	-65,200	3,171,338	1,245,250	727,424	13,533	380,106	178,789
1988	5,688,370	3,820,099	190,740	4,010,839	434,129	-59,470	3,517,240	1,349,844	821,286	14,617	389,160	188,505
1989	6,252,503	4,131,686	148,850	4,280,536	475,193	-61,495	3,743,848	1,601,237	907,418	15,701	398,231	195,457
1990	6,556,679	4,303,229	120,957	4,424,186	489,615	-25,670	3,908,901	1,642,391	1,005,387	16,080	407,756	194,693
1991	6,815,714	4,398,968	134,981	4,533,949	504,114	61,879	4,091,714	1,599,215	1,124,785	16,418	415,136	191,941
1992	7,203,889	4,648,776	78,279	4,727,055	530,097	99,681	4,296,639	1,612,433	1,294,817	17,024	423,171	188,240
1993	7,598,387	4,888,768	84,171	4,972,939	553,994	183,094	4,602,039	1,591,359	1,404,989	17,703	429,224	192,484
1994	8,221,179	5,279,642	87,382	5,367,024	604,922	234,620	4,996,722	1,716,141	1,508,316	18,749	438,480	199,641
1995	8,853,107	5,584,518	96,626	5,681,144	636,279	339,012	5,383,877	1,849,748	1,619,482	19,798	447,182	205,287
1996	9,396,345	5,976,920	80,402	6,057,322	670,561	338,439	5,725,200	1,949,323	1,721,822	20,673	454,512	210,699
1997	9,746,932	6,128,069	89,533	6,217,602	692,674	440,210	5,965,138	1,987,083	1,794,711	21,028	463,519	214,741
1998	10,645,419	6,693,894	132,364	6,826,258	746,304	506,341	6,586,295	2,186,900	1,872,224	22,580	471,450	223,190
1999	11,174,894	7,116,170	115,792	7,231,962	781,582	674,472	7,124,852	2,116,102	1,933,940	23,376	478,047	227,091
2000	11,708,270	7,269,959	120,892	7,390,851	808,731	760,536	7,342,656	2,311,970	2,053,644	24,115	485,515	234,576
2001	12,672,035	8,098,941	102,568	8,201,509	886,154	710,179	8,025,534	2,415,565	2,230,936	25,708	492,917	232,840
2002	12,944,176	8,346,928	118,585	8,465,513	908,615	725,143	8,282,041	2,247,126	2,415,009	25,813	501,469	235,387
2003	13,646,294	8,791,254	94,544	8,885,798	956,143	713,200	8,642,855	2,394,496	2,608,943	26,598	513,058	238,688
2004	14,734,852	9,349,574	92,689	9,442,263	1,028,382	726,585	9,140,466	2,727,806	2,866,580	27,924	527,685	249,751
2005	16,095,306	10,205,860	134,776	10,340,636	1,138,913	716,856	9,918,579	3,093,073	3,083,654	29,405	547,373	266,193
2006	16,857,753	10,539,449	150,622	10,690,071	1,227,149	695,547	10,158,469	3,357,372	3,341,912	29,662	568,324	275,020
2007	17,648,497	10,688,255	90,920	10,779,175	1,253,064	686,555	10,212,666	3,763,562	3,672,269	30,118	585,982	276,628
2008	18,176,582	10,594,989	80,768	10,675,757	1,265,064	617,218	10,027,911	3,953,960	4,194,711	30,559	594,801	268,495
2009	17,447,041	10,210,169	106,799	10,316,968	1,250,578	485,581	9,551,971	3,376,950	4,518,120	29,142	598,683	258,199
2010	18,650,683	10,461,764	125,789	10,587,553	1,250,476	437,820	9,774,897	3,969,198	4,906,588	30,924	603,119	255,704
2011	19,666,336	10,620,827	132,974	10,753,801	1,144,245	416,173	10,025,729	4,510,716	5,129,891	32,239	610,026	258,249
2012	19,815,333	11,122,917	147,101	11,270,018	1,197,353	398,293	10,470,958	4,200,462	5,143,913	32,190	615,581	261,791
2013	19,915,841	11,524,415	146,769	11,671,184	1,392,944	325,783	10,604,023	3,980,993	5,330,825	31,977	622,808	266,990
2014	20,916,503	11,898,642	130,747	12,029,389	1,440,937	402,237	10,990,689	4,309,295	5,616,519	33,239	629,269	273,845
2015	21,904,119	12,370,795	150,119	12,520,914	1,489,830	450,880	11,481,964	4,510,178	5,911,977	34,115	642,067	281,071
2016	22,444,145	12,790,863	111,484	12,902,347	1,551,129	484,128	11,835,346	4,469,759	6,139,040	34,109	658,019	287,241
2017	24,087,049	13,540,362	119,942	13,660,304	1,637,976	488,881	12,511,209	5,085,977	6,489,863	35,634	675,948	300,222
2018	25,360,562	14,401,114	77,717	14,478,831	1,755,896	498,233	13,221,168	5,350,036	6,789,358	36,461	695,556	312,786
2019	27,185,956	15,282,728	96,718	15,379,446	1,903,410	543,053	14,019,089	5,935,773	7,231,094	38,196	711,750	323,580
2020	29,876,967	16,335,184	71,075	16,406,259	2,051,627	282,728	14,637,360	6,001,591	9,238,016	40,970	729,233	336,118
2021	32,820,004	17,744,154	47,523	17,791,677	2,174,057	376,694	15,994,314	6,184,081	10,641,609	43,556	753,520	352,402

Personal Income and Employment by Area: Lancaster, PA

(Thousands of dollars, except as noted.)

Year	Personal income, total	Earnings by place of work Nonfarm	Farm	Total	Less: Contributions for government social insurance	Plus: Adjustment for residence	Equals: Net earnings by place of residence	Plus: Dividends, interest, and rent	Plus: Personal current transfer receipts	Per capita personal income (dollars)	Population (persons)	Total employment
1970	1,391,393	1,059,372	84,767	1,144,139	78,563	42,606	1,108,182	182,577	100,634	4,331	321,290	156,017
1971	1,454,953	1,116,689	66,208	1,182,897	86,287	48,751	1,145,361	193,890	115,702	4,447	327,155	156,834
1972	1,616,518	1,258,627	65,432	1,324,059	102,540	56,771	1,278,290	208,956	129,272	4,867	332,160	163,540
1973	1,831,295	1,428,735	87,805	1,516,540	134,168	65,280	1,447,652	240,102	143,541	5,437	336,819	172,896
1974	1,976,296	1,532,955	68,078	1,601,033	149,336	78,236	1,529,933	271,772	174,591	5,810	340,170	173,356
1975	2,128,090	1,595,007	62,793	1,657,800	150,550	88,929	1,596,179	300,811	231,100	6,172	344,814	168,983
1976	2,345,672	1,790,272	51,857	1,842,129	172,580	101,587	1,771,136	326,352	248,184	6,752	347,407	173,386
1977	2,594,683	2,012,731	28,510	2,041,241	193,513	116,154	1,963,882	368,503	262,298	7,390	351,084	179,617
1978	2,972,383	2,299,560	70,842	2,370,402	226,062	133,832	2,278,172	410,765	283,446	8,381	354,667	187,604
1979	3,337,881	2,563,110	90,470	2,653,580	261,659	155,987	2,547,908	464,992	324,981	9,289	359,329	192,732
1980	3,610,692	2,707,502	46,456	2,753,958	279,918	181,615	2,655,655	576,941	378,096	9,935	363,420	194,330
1981	4,000,474	2,902,309	83,261	2,985,570	320,438	195,278	2,860,410	706,863	433,201	10,901	366,979	193,300
1982	4,303,177	3,025,906	69,015	3,094,921	338,229	198,595	2,955,287	842,032	505,858	11,599	370,992	191,675
1983	4,603,334	3,282,674	52,440	3,335,114	370,797	199,558	3,163,875	895,905	543,554	12,235	376,234	194,960
1984	5,154,347	3,662,780	147,665	3,810,445	431,253	211,263	3,590,455	1,011,721	552,171	13,532	380,892	203,704
1985	5,546,988	3,975,471	116,493	4,091,964	472,106	216,995	3,836,853	1,111,415	598,720	14,399	385,245	210,863
1986	6,046,419	4,345,460	167,565	4,513,025	516,025	219,696	4,216,696	1,188,332	641,391	15,411	392,339	218,827
1987	6,531,002	4,774,976	168,649	4,943,625	560,536	231,498	4,614,587	1,244,960	671,455	16,255	401,773	228,379
1988	7,052,177	5,282,181	81,846	5,364,027	627,239	244,879	4,981,667	1,341,012	729,498	17,194	410,152	237,036
1989	7,887,990	5,727,587	178,115	5,905,702	666,534	259,862	5,499,030	1,593,151	795,809	18,890	417,585	244,037
1990	8,253,673	6,099,780	110,193	6,209,973	717,200	264,732	5,757,505	1,632,441	863,727	19,423	424,947	250,269
1991	8,493,752	6,235,028	83,396	6,318,424	740,612	275,491	5,853,303	1,644,646	995,803	19,697	431,229	247,396
1992	9,083,365	6,670,842	146,879	6,817,721	787,280	288,418	6,318,859	1,699,463	1,065,043	20,839	435,886	249,064
1993	9,652,801	7,049,622	148,174	7,197,796	845,373	288,318	6,640,741	1,891,525	1,120,535	21,886	441,056	251,472
1994	9,876,689	7,343,425	123,479	7,466,904	895,352	298,940	6,870,492	1,837,180	1,169,017	22,132	446,254	255,573
1995	10,275,090	7,668,162	77,836	7,745,998	929,798	306,171	7,122,371	1,913,774	1,238,945	22,742	451,817	263,269
1996	10,916,661	7,994,597	183,834	8,178,431	946,195	320,010	7,552,246	2,031,523	1,332,892	23,951	455,783	266,835
1997	11,584,904	8,547,278	149,084	8,696,362	996,179	337,155	8,037,338	2,167,264	1,380,302	25,180	460,085	273,421
1998	12,102,286	8,929,601	140,947	9,070,548	1,035,042	359,356	8,394,862	2,258,169	1,449,255	26,067	464,272	272,593
1999	12,632,736	9,426,029	114,586	9,540,615	1,078,043	376,553	8,839,125	2,255,211	1,538,400	27,000	467,879	276,989
2000	13,714,728	10,188,376	167,337	10,355,713	1,146,931	393,303	9,602,085	2,461,276	1,651,367	29,059	471,955	282,826
2001	14,520,868	10,846,497	179,171	11,025,668	1,201,685	422,900	10,246,883	2,451,841	1,822,144	30,539	475,483	287,532
2002	14,690,788	11,222,436	97,545	11,319,981	1,240,880	425,803	10,504,904	2,221,614	1,964,270	30,598	480,118	287,524
2003	15,364,753	11,594,430	177,982	11,772,412	1,276,445	434,314	10,930,281	2,341,362	2,093,110	31,672	485,119	287,563
2004	16,432,640	12,358,303	265,552	12,623,855	1,342,907	464,120	11,745,068	2,498,587	2,188,985	33,538	489,977	294,482
2005	17,254,989	12,965,009	262,121	13,227,130	1,412,188	478,030	12,292,972	2,542,942	2,419,075	34,878	494,722	300,350
2006	17,835,949	13,297,550	205,690	13,503,240	1,469,461	533,394	12,567,173	2,679,107	2,589,669	35,606	500,922	303,188
2007	18,671,889	13,415,607	308,081	13,723,688	1,481,733	573,452	12,815,407	3,076,736	2,779,746	36,854	506,639	307,737
2008	19,420,963	13,516,689	229,957	13,746,646	1,513,079	572,415	12,805,982	3,431,548	3,183,433	37,935	511,957	308,123
2009	18,964,433	12,980,030	126,220	13,106,250	1,478,431	646,318	12,274,137	3,142,108	3,548,188	36,712	516,577	299,341
2010	19,927,942	13,512,785	265,399	13,778,184	1,514,004	751,975	13,016,155	3,103,396	3,808,391	38,299	520,325	298,774
2011	20,920,557	13,834,991	324,736	14,159,727	1,395,397	893,140	13,657,470	3,412,404	3,850,683	39,925	523,996	300,897
2012	21,722,057	14,276,402	331,176	14,607,578	1,424,267	961,920	14,145,231	3,681,297	3,895,529	41,222	526,949	305,697
2013	22,379,442	14,887,009	427,964	15,314,973	1,644,672	1,044,647	14,714,948	3,674,205	3,990,289	42,217	530,109	309,716
2014	23,662,087	15,737,785	517,371	16,255,156	1,723,135	1,049,483	15,581,504	3,945,200	4,135,383	44,135	536,132	316,744
2015	25,037,037	16,989,952	341,770	17,331,722	1,832,446	1,046,279	16,545,555	4,147,140	4,344,342	46,422	539,334	323,991
2016	25,785,278	17,661,804	119,571	17,781,375	1,900,932	1,056,098	16,936,541	4,317,646	4,531,091	47,545	542,338	330,633
2017	27,155,951	18,591,415	266,417	18,857,832	2,013,928	1,103,651	17,947,555	4,590,059	4,618,337	49,731	546,058	334,589
2018	28,586,084	19,644,753	211,137	19,855,890	2,100,924	1,093,090	18,848,056	4,789,888	4,948,140	52,037	549,342	341,647
2019	29,814,037	20,380,028	223,485	20,603,513	2,201,058	1,119,460	19,521,915	5,090,757	5,201,365	54,061	551,484	342,522
2020	32,168,792	20,805,258	134,908	20,940,166	2,221,638	1,113,233	19,831,761	5,053,499	7,283,532	58,214	552,597	328,959
2021	34,075,719	22,128,783	309,336	22,438,119	2,338,001	1,170,401	21,270,519	5,125,612	7,679,588	61,547	553,652	340,679

Personal Income and Employment by Area: Lansing-East Lansing, MI

(Thousands of dollars, except as noted.)

Year	Personal income, total	Derivation of personal income									Per capita personal income (dollars)	Population (persons)	Total employment
		Earnings by place of work			Less: Contributions for government social insurance	Plus: Adjustment for residence	Equals: Net earnings by place of residence	Plus: Dividends, interest, and rent	Plus: Personal current transfer receipts				
		Nonfarm	Farm	Total									
1970	1,495,784	1,269,779	22,940	1,292,719	86,343	-34,127	1,172,249	208,840	114,695	3,946	379,047	158,585
1971	1,693,566	1,466,952	20,531	1,487,483	102,438	-55,360	1,329,685	228,673	135,208	4,428	382,476	163,734
1972	1,873,250	1,630,931	27,688	1,658,619	121,231	-66,858	1,470,530	252,296	150,424	4,848	386,369	169,358
1973	2,077,275	1,835,573	31,672	1,867,245	157,845	-79,880	1,629,520	279,352	168,403	5,286	392,980	176,554
1974	2,188,334	1,834,643	35,555	1,870,198	162,471	-57,794	1,649,933	317,646	220,755	5,509	397,253	176,321
1975	2,437,112	2,005,650	33,314	2,038,964	174,693	-71,622	1,792,649	361,131	283,332	6,114	398,619	177,812
1976	2,731,051	2,331,656	24,793	2,356,449	207,138	-104,706	2,044,605	392,211	294,235	6,818	400,590	184,014
1977	3,072,820	2,644,562	29,327	2,673,889	234,369	-130,469	2,309,051	439,136	324,633	7,599	404,394	190,769
1978	3,392,620	2,996,173	20,992	3,017,165	274,162	-157,516	2,585,487	489,279	317,854	8,276	409,950	200,143
1979	3,786,474	3,343,526	28,336	3,371,862	315,533	-181,459	2,874,870	552,577	359,027	9,154	413,652	206,975
1980	4,145,242	3,505,631	25,126	3,530,757	322,550	-189,799	3,018,408	655,281	471,553	9,867	420,109	204,514
1981	4,547,576	3,855,771	33,643	3,889,414	387,823	-227,371	3,274,220	770,494	502,862	10,811	420,637	203,789
1982	4,722,294	3,885,629	14,054	3,899,683	393,485	-224,824	3,281,374	885,996	554,924	11,382	414,906	196,333
1983	5,143,867	4,309,729	6,816	4,316,545	446,673	-274,619	3,595,253	966,893	581,721	12,466	412,647	200,932
1984	5,566,408	4,627,712	24,922	4,652,634	492,443	-280,964	3,879,227	1,079,975	607,206	13,482	412,862	204,494
1985	5,997,322	5,072,485	28,171	5,100,656	559,288	-311,486	4,229,882	1,142,980	624,460	14,430	415,612	215,819
1986	6,389,365	5,399,117	22,605	5,421,722	598,253	-314,381	4,509,088	1,216,686	663,591	15,131	422,282	222,907
1987	6,594,284	5,494,743	31,248	5,525,991	602,002	-284,229	4,639,760	1,254,436	700,088	15,456	426,652	232,298
1988	6,996,185	5,897,770	23,640	5,921,410	672,780	-301,297	4,947,333	1,322,333	726,519	16,283	429,673	237,230
1989	7,555,816	6,295,076	51,818	6,346,894	714,993	-311,669	5,320,232	1,442,452	793,132	17,550	430,527	243,788
1990	7,902,111	6,563,813	40,127	6,603,940	754,900	-316,225	5,532,815	1,506,976	862,320	18,232	433,414	248,011
1991	8,266,911	6,883,101	25,930	6,909,031	803,645	-334,601	5,770,785	1,531,918	964,208	18,918	436,979	248,866
1992	8,711,034	7,279,076	29,953	7,309,029	842,607	-348,433	6,117,989	1,588,039	1,005,006	19,837	439,128	249,680
1993	8,975,449	7,394,457	28,731	7,423,188	857,338	-323,545	6,242,305	1,642,703	1,090,441	20,342	441,234	249,094
1994	9,590,301	7,910,601	25,464	7,936,065	934,929	-346,912	6,654,224	1,828,361	1,107,716	21,665	442,671	256,015
1995	10,011,131	8,278,822	27,552	8,306,374	980,290	-357,121	6,968,963	1,888,925	1,153,243	22,578	443,395	268,156
1996	10,508,406	8,642,327	33,210	8,675,537	997,635	-367,182	7,310,720	1,990,963	1,206,723	23,506	447,043	272,297
1997	11,001,409	8,951,631	31,741	8,983,372	1,033,672	-366,324	7,583,376	2,123,013	1,295,020	24,562	447,895	271,236
1998	12,878,984	9,945,998	35,490	9,981,488	1,137,314	140,947	8,985,121	2,342,213	1,551,650	24,802	519,274	297,865
1999	13,591,921	10,683,129	56,482	10,739,611	1,218,168	145,480	9,666,923	2,265,781	1,659,217	26,199	518,786	302,774
2000	14,252,539	11,221,512	27,636	11,249,148	1,264,231	165,347	10,150,264	2,371,953	1,730,322	27,385	520,449	306,462
2001	14,728,527	11,555,547	26,688	11,582,235	1,277,633	133,992	10,438,594	2,360,499	1,929,434	28,104	524,067	305,758
2002	14,799,820	11,801,606	25,238	11,826,844	1,315,900	107,648	10,618,592	2,178,425	2,002,803	28,052	527,582	303,963
2003	15,107,868	11,908,635	38,900	11,947,535	1,327,206	89,735	10,710,064	2,286,742	2,111,062	28,461	530,834	304,316
2004	15,468,125	12,055,602	80,556	12,136,158	1,349,749	115,287	10,901,696	2,357,384	2,209,045	28,925	534,758	302,526
2005	15,739,003	12,147,358	58,217	12,205,575	1,383,075	95,428	10,917,928	2,454,437	2,366,638	29,391	535,500	299,192
2006	16,254,286	12,513,470	66,816	12,580,286	1,447,541	43,624	11,176,369	2,530,865	2,547,052	30,315	536,188	300,257
2007	16,768,259	12,613,232	77,706	12,690,938	1,473,313	-1,836	11,215,789	2,750,156	2,802,314	31,271	536,230	301,650
2008	17,397,716	12,714,988	88,954	12,803,942	1,503,284	-68,373	11,232,285	2,932,848	3,232,583	32,509	535,161	296,431
2009	17,000,995	12,174,901	43,613	12,218,514	1,439,500	-106,845	10,672,169	2,735,340	3,593,486	31,846	533,857	282,692
2010	17,846,833	12,817,398	92,807	12,910,205	1,485,804	-177,793	11,246,608	2,749,050	3,851,175	33,365	534,902	282,885
2011	18,375,245	12,872,160	215,964	13,088,124	1,326,874	-144,384	11,616,866	2,908,689	3,849,690	34,240	536,663	285,895
2012	18,667,345	13,003,904	134,426	13,138,330	1,347,538	-138,562	11,652,230	3,177,914	3,837,201	34,754	537,121	284,715
2013	18,852,135	13,350,285	158,212	13,508,497	1,569,346	-169,550	11,769,601	3,145,190	3,937,344	35,024	538,262	286,930
2014	19,579,213	13,698,175	90,221	13,788,396	1,612,688	-168,539	12,007,169	3,446,843	4,125,201	36,446	537,214	290,480
2015	20,446,254	14,317,312	44,783	14,362,095	1,669,323	-134,788	12,557,984	3,517,918	4,370,352	38,020	537,777	293,688
2016	21,130,180	14,850,475	25,057	14,875,532	1,731,934	-147,765	12,995,833	3,640,315	4,494,032	39,088	540,583	296,895
2017	21,802,785	15,373,460	32,670	15,406,130	1,795,098	-134,489	13,476,543	3,785,599	4,540,643	40,161	542,883	299,461
2018	22,618,501	15,928,538	33,449	15,961,987	1,885,731	-129,315	13,946,941	3,911,446	4,760,114	41,710	542,279	300,869
2019	23,425,523	16,339,099	55,483	16,394,582	1,934,043	-135,063	14,325,476	4,077,600	5,022,447	43,178	542,535	298,756
2020	25,663,120	16,551,724	115,797	16,667,521	1,966,271	-162,241	14,539,009	4,102,643	7,021,468	47,460	540,737	283,457
2021	27,190,424	17,676,313	142,343	17,818,656	2,062,387	-183,273	15,572,996	4,165,610	7,451,818	50,326	540,281	290,963

Personal Income and Employment by Area: Laredo, TX

(Thousands of dollars, except as noted.)

Year	Personal income, total	Earnings by place of work			Less: Contributions for government social insurance	Plus: Adjustment for residence	Equals: Net earnings by place of residence	Plus: Dividends, interest, and rent	Plus: Personal current transfer receipts	Per capita personal income (dollars)	Population (persons)	Total employment
		Nonfarm	Farm	Total								
1970	182,339	148,940	3,057	151,997	9,355	-6,614	136,028	26,908	19,403	2,480	73,536	27,042
1971	197,620	160,158	4,055	164,213	10,408	-7,881	145,924	29,265	22,431	2,548	77,556	26,710
1972	220,806	180,117	3,804	183,921	12,054	-9,644	162,223	33,058	25,525	2,725	81,025	27,421
1973	236,894	193,246	4,793	198,039	14,681	-11,745	171,613	34,890	30,391	2,851	83,080	28,534
1974	242,858	195,468	3,075	198,543	16,009	-13,392	169,142	31,894	41,822	3,141	77,327	28,206
1975	280,802	225,483	2,604	228,087	18,440	-16,652	192,995	34,875	52,932	3,383	83,006	29,172
1976	315,306	257,838	1,274	259,112	21,264	-18,238	219,610	37,659	58,037	3,564	88,481	30,810
1977	353,652	293,594	895	294,489	24,151	-20,362	249,976	41,780	61,896	3,864	91,535	32,558
1978	404,598	335,136	753	335,889	27,980	-21,926	285,983	50,368	68,247	4,315	93,776	34,251
1979	471,397	385,312	4,058	389,370	33,811	-23,487	332,072	60,384	78,941	4,868	96,844	36,084
1980	558,776	461,411	-189	461,222	41,358	-29,385	390,479	74,428	93,869	5,561	100,481	38,920
1981	673,332	549,253	82	549,335	53,540	-21,138	474,657	94,852	103,823	6,408	105,077	42,261
1982	727,949	571,934	3,387	575,321	56,014	-23,214	496,093	112,443	119,413	6,552	111,106	42,033
1983	722,900	527,107	-2,178	524,929	49,979	-21,025	453,925	121,967	147,008	6,263	115,419	37,681
1984	780,395	578,509	-2,660	575,849	56,077	-24,618	495,154	136,318	148,923	6,695	116,566	39,429
1985	846,527	644,650	-6,055	638,595	63,528	-28,700	546,367	146,960	153,200	7,164	118,164	42,213
1986	883,094	662,819	-5,409	657,410	64,312	-27,396	565,702	149,927	167,465	7,238	122,011	41,857
1987	928,656	700,009	-1,422	698,587	66,954	-28,954	602,679	150,937	175,040	7,457	124,528	43,947
1988	1,031,112	792,458	-1,595	790,863	78,923	-30,282	681,658	164,029	185,425	8,146	126,575	46,882
1989	1,165,152	886,758	-482	886,276	89,321	-32,409	764,546	183,427	217,179	8,967	129,943	50,230
1990	1,314,914	1,011,975	1,399	1,013,374	99,842	-35,655	877,877	187,912	249,125	9,781	134,430	53,910
1991	1,481,511	1,147,790	1,924	1,149,714	116,074	-40,331	993,309	200,509	287,693	10,576	140,082	57,729
1992	1,712,818	1,304,340	1,666	1,306,006	130,193	-44,505	1,131,308	229,520	351,990	11,650	147,026	60,857
1993	1,885,877	1,455,104	-406	1,454,698	144,729	-49,309	1,260,660	251,245	373,972	12,203	154,536	65,418
1994	2,070,719	1,614,502	-1,622	1,612,880	162,665	-54,234	1,395,981	257,766	416,972	12,853	161,107	69,329
1995	2,162,955	1,616,084	-803	1,615,281	162,391	-51,570	1,401,320	293,578	468,057	12,916	167,466	68,700
1996	2,332,538	1,730,822	-2,648	1,728,174	172,940	-54,560	1,500,674	314,325	517,539	13,594	171,583	70,431
1997	2,556,556	1,924,038	-390	1,923,648	193,219	-60,237	1,670,192	341,739	544,625	14,432	177,140	75,384
1998	2,711,666	2,049,169	2,566	2,051,735	206,035	-60,021	1,785,679	378,518	547,469	14,818	182,994	78,704
1999	2,836,359	2,151,340	8,200	2,159,540	218,126	-62,139	1,879,275	398,863	558,221	15,006	189,014	81,214
2000	3,103,489	2,347,214	9,208	2,356,422	235,889	-67,012	2,053,521	456,926	593,042	15,950	194,576	85,583
2001	3,802,285	2,965,545	14,027	2,979,572	265,924	-83,565	2,630,083	521,104	651,098	18,978	200,347	90,442
2002	4,029,129	3,159,452	14,802	3,174,254	285,143	-92,312	2,796,799	495,473	736,857	19,559	206,001	95,631
2003	4,261,095	3,267,602	23,183	3,290,785	305,192	-96,490	2,889,103	577,852	794,140	20,120	211,786	98,782
2004	4,369,928	3,369,094	20,699	3,389,793	321,688	-101,475	2,966,630	575,031	828,267	20,059	217,858	103,893
2005	4,879,238	3,714,846	9,998	3,724,844	351,724	-108,319	3,264,801	675,680	938,757	21,811	223,703	108,658
2006	5,302,539	3,990,964	12,563	4,003,527	368,244	-108,902	3,526,381	772,441	1,003,717	23,124	229,307	113,275
2007	5,529,318	4,084,367	2,388	4,086,755	388,575	-111,162	3,587,018	816,866	1,125,434	23,570	234,594	117,861
2008	6,350,504	4,568,467	-1,971	4,566,496	410,677	-108,212	4,047,607	1,008,643	1,294,254	26,429	240,287	119,894
2009	6,121,385	4,270,727	-4,221	4,266,506	404,822	-105,374	3,756,310	907,026	1,458,049	24,893	245,908	118,445
2010	6,633,786	4,660,857	-5,409	4,655,448	435,005	-106,069	4,114,374	900,737	1,618,675	26,392	251,358	119,888
2011	7,231,314	5,080,036	1,639	5,081,675	416,876	-104,187	4,560,612	1,013,013	1,657,689	28,261	255,877	126,846
2012	7,536,057	5,287,755	1,733	5,289,488	437,279	-97,012	4,755,197	1,132,787	1,648,073	28,931	260,487	128,758
2013	7,708,851	5,351,493	16,139	5,367,632	501,131	-78,350	4,788,151	1,228,578	1,692,122	29,169	264,280	132,181
2014	7,985,534	5,565,542	17,896	5,583,438	519,901	-71,864	4,991,673	1,233,700	1,760,161	30,356	263,059	135,967
2015	8,089,639	5,600,326	21,225	5,621,551	541,230	-97,727	4,982,594	1,236,653	1,870,392	30,599	264,372	139,279
2016	8,185,993	5,617,244	1,598	5,618,842	553,360	-125,612	4,939,870	1,284,120	1,962,003	30,800	265,778	140,052
2017	8,394,768	5,811,355	440	5,811,795	573,436	-111,311	5,127,048	1,288,253	1,979,467	31,551	266,072	141,349
2018	8,759,698	6,059,529	3,497	6,063,026	597,862	-92,200	5,372,964	1,342,015	2,044,719	32,883	266,391	144,037
2019	9,279,652	6,433,963	2,584	6,436,547	627,423	-106,256	5,702,868	1,462,620	2,114,164	34,757	266,986	147,705
2020	9,960,505	6,404,732	1,300	6,406,032	635,251	-138,748	5,632,033	1,431,210	2,897,262	37,273	267,234	142,789
2021	10,945,472	6,720,323	2,319	6,722,642	672,979	-156,718	5,892,945	1,513,794	3,538,733	40,850	267,945	145,963

Personal Income and Employment by Area: Las Cruces, NM

(Thousands of dollars, except as noted.)

Year	Personal income, total	Earnings by place of work			Less: Contributions for government social insurance	Plus: Adjustment for residence	Equals: Net earnings by place of residence	Plus: Dividends, interest, and rent	Plus: Personal current transfer receipts	Per capita personal income (dollars)	Population (persons)	Total employment
		Nonfarm	Farm	Total								
1970	228,654	179,992	12,396	192,388	8,393	-7,128	176,867	33,883	17,904	3,255	70,254	27,080
1971	258,499	201,793	14,117	215,910	9,841	-9,006	197,063	39,537	21,899	3,554	72,726	28,316
1972	282,005	216,482	15,179	231,661	11,044	-7,422	213,195	44,161	24,649	3,684	76,553	29,477
1973	311,428	236,988	16,334	253,322	14,266	-6,964	232,092	50,351	28,985	4,049	76,909	30,621
1974	358,809	258,971	28,036	287,007	16,312	-6,599	264,096	59,152	35,561	4,548	78,888	31,045
1975	392,408	277,990	16,500	294,490	17,752	1,175	277,913	70,047	44,448	4,787	81,979	31,211
1976	444,278	315,981	22,899	338,880	20,374	-1,548	316,958	77,039	50,281	5,211	85,259	32,448
1977	494,883	362,914	20,042	382,956	24,369	-3,966	354,621	86,662	53,600	5,604	88,302	35,175
1978	568,285	414,060	24,856	438,916	28,803	-4,403	405,710	102,735	59,840	6,164	92,193	37,771
1979	621,528	455,273	14,132	469,405	33,333	-3,067	433,005	117,998	70,525	6,630	93,741	39,643
1980	702,558	486,953	21,677	508,630	35,824	1,380	474,186	142,026	86,346	7,242	97,012	39,628
1981	811,807	544,423	35,568	579,991	43,145	4,760	541,606	171,615	98,586	8,149	99,623	40,165
1982	904,449	596,421	32,691	629,112	48,468	8,417	589,061	204,893	110,495	8,743	103,448	41,829
1983	1,026,637	673,980	46,103	720,083	57,163	9,322	672,242	230,893	123,502	9,539	107,627	44,305
1984	1,126,676	740,969	41,180	782,149	64,306	12,808	730,651	258,915	137,110	10,017	112,474	46,879
1985	1,233,770	798,558	49,585	848,143	71,816	18,442	794,769	291,491	147,510	10,607	116,321	48,564
1986	1,332,333	846,845	67,614	914,459	78,524	26,879	862,814	311,866	157,653	11,059	120,474	49,986
1987	1,423,598	903,131	65,169	968,300	84,078	35,159	919,381	332,044	172,173	11,386	125,032	52,506
1988	1,499,691	946,044	66,638	1,012,682	94,931	44,420	962,171	349,847	187,673	11,535	130,016	55,774
1989	1,663,014	1,021,714	93,269	1,114,983	104,886	45,867	1,055,964	394,996	212,054	12,508	132,957	57,095
1990	1,784,665	1,098,787	103,630	1,202,417	118,717	54,573	1,138,273	404,520	241,872	13,066	136,593	57,771
1991	1,911,004	1,189,970	87,239	1,277,209	130,352	66,502	1,213,359	422,096	275,549	13,531	141,228	59,961
1992	2,099,588	1,301,388	102,692	1,404,080	141,765	81,056	1,343,371	443,799	312,418	14,283	146,995	60,744
1993	2,239,522	1,384,856	86,376	1,471,232	151,673	95,860	1,415,419	476,111	347,992	14,633	153,049	61,738
1994	2,330,012	1,415,925	75,878	1,491,803	159,767	110,897	1,442,933	505,306	381,773	14,791	157,530	62,238
1995	2,539,316	1,511,295	100,397	1,611,692	170,318	120,042	1,561,416	546,851	431,049	15,771	161,014	65,557
1996	2,654,863	1,568,447	76,986	1,645,433	177,394	129,003	1,597,042	588,315	469,506	16,030	165,618	67,010
1997	2,794,236	1,632,149	104,121	1,736,270	185,515	144,038	1,694,793	616,330	483,113	16,526	169,081	68,290
1998	2,980,826	1,760,777	112,492	1,873,269	201,388	156,247	1,828,128	635,800	516,898	17,325	172,057	69,944
1999	3,047,916	1,829,059	112,265	1,941,324	213,429	174,051	1,901,946	595,885	550,085	17,528	173,889	72,267
2000	3,224,956	1,975,603	80,172	2,055,775	223,570	188,888	2,021,093	611,360	592,503	18,418	175,098	74,836
2001	3,618,702	2,221,309	112,816	2,334,125	243,433	169,986	2,260,678	677,937	680,087	20,503	176,496	78,825
2002	3,842,339	2,436,766	94,733	2,531,499	264,739	154,891	2,421,651	659,599	761,089	21,530	178,464	80,989
2003	4,089,072	2,645,829	115,943	2,761,772	286,991	141,966	2,616,747	655,731	816,594	22,462	182,045	83,352
2004	4,354,229	2,829,251	152,375	2,981,626	306,367	100,674	2,775,933	704,732	873,564	23,544	184,939	86,099
2005	4,709,110	3,097,431	172,058	3,269,489	336,910	38,868	2,971,447	787,828	949,835	24,890	189,199	89,628
2006	5,017,521	3,313,584	123,121	3,436,705	366,469	45,532	3,115,768	861,874	1,039,879	25,903	193,701	91,995
2007	5,378,745	3,442,702	177,270	3,619,972	389,990	37,157	3,267,139	962,457	1,149,149	27,186	197,853	94,725
2008	5,654,380	3,572,065	108,784	3,680,849	413,616	26,239	3,293,472	1,033,591	1,327,317	28,152	200,855	95,890
2009	5,982,692	3,728,021	127,540	3,855,561	429,207	81,625	3,507,979	975,625	1,499,088	29,127	205,401	94,906
2010	6,408,745	3,912,498	222,335	4,134,833	443,131	87,010	3,778,712	1,002,617	1,627,416	30,504	210,096	95,627
2011	6,609,738	3,953,595	197,008	4,150,603	403,185	111,841	3,859,259	1,097,696	1,652,783	31,014	213,123	97,248
2012	6,719,697	3,959,092	129,693	4,088,785	407,245	171,835	3,853,375	1,225,832	1,640,490	31,334	214,452	97,093
2013	6,542,627	3,956,438	133,252	4,089,690	468,585	168,822	3,789,927	1,107,872	1,644,828	30,532	214,285	98,950
2014	6,831,530	4,040,695	139,226	4,179,921	482,970	163,940	3,860,891	1,159,790	1,810,849	32,011	213,413	99,350
2015	7,146,468	4,183,350	144,429	4,327,779	516,760	173,003	3,984,022	1,188,997	1,973,449	33,493	213,373	99,925
2016	7,388,435	4,323,108	157,184	4,480,292	529,311	174,045	4,125,026	1,243,884	2,019,525	34,544	213,885	100,748
2017	7,576,803	4,426,138	158,355	4,584,493	536,634	197,872	4,245,731	1,291,658	2,039,414	35,189	215,315	100,115
2018	7,805,306	4,665,368	113,191	4,778,559	565,465	145,388	4,358,482	1,267,186	2,179,638	36,063	216,434	102,572
2019	8,303,074	4,893,233	115,963	5,009,196	587,471	223,661	4,645,386	1,361,760	2,295,928	38,142	217,687	103,223
2020	9,147,189	5,001,972	100,468	5,102,440	616,671	261,243	4,747,012	1,345,003	3,055,174	41,597	219,899	100,335
2021	9,977,874	5,330,083	101,627	5,431,710	649,420	306,030	5,088,320	1,368,974	3,520,580	45,045	221,508	102,222

Personal Income and Employment by Area: Las Vegas-Henderson-Paradise, NV

(Thousands of dollars, except as noted.)

Year	Personal income, total	Earnings by place of work			Less: Contributions for government social insurance	Plus: Adjustment for residence	Equals: Net earnings by place of residence	Plus: Dividends, interest, and rent	Plus: Personal current transfer receipts	Per capita personal income (dollars)	Population (persons)	Total employment
		Nonfarm	Farm	Total								
1970	1,429,017	1,180,655	1,732	1,182,387	82,314	41,419	1,141,492	211,557	75,968	5,176	276,079	134,095
1971	1,582,762	1,301,670	1,334	1,303,004	93,505	37,347	1,246,846	238,405	97,511	5,402	293,008	138,801
1972	1,747,451	1,447,250	1,318	1,448,568	109,842	26,181	1,364,907	265,291	117,253	5,684	307,426	145,742
1973	1,984,224	1,677,474	1,418	1,678,892	146,925	12,703	1,544,670	302,171	137,383	6,212	319,399	160,282
1974	2,221,573	1,845,898	2,006	1,847,904	164,868	13,850	1,696,886	350,892	173,795	6,594	336,930	168,726
1975	2,515,704	2,038,508	2,074	2,040,582	180,969	15,006	1,874,619	398,951	242,134	7,160	351,339	174,218
1976	2,863,774	2,335,534	2,783	2,338,317	213,203	9,012	2,134,126	454,439	275,209	7,750	369,529	186,546
1977	3,296,192	2,723,422	2,580	2,726,002	251,966	931	2,474,967	517,855	303,370	8,453	389,965	204,806
1978	3,959,777	3,293,521	2,496	3,296,017	314,392	-2,960	2,978,665	642,527	338,585	9,590	412,913	228,609
1979	4,631,857	3,856,001	1,518	3,857,519	388,226	-10,567	3,458,726	765,266	407,865	10,495	441,358	251,535
1980	5,359,706	4,367,073	3,213	4,370,286	443,251	-3,508	3,923,527	933,019	503,160	11,423	469,185	265,076
1981	6,162,457	4,920,769	1,887	4,922,656	530,878	19,508	4,411,286	1,128,864	622,307	12,506	492,747	272,538
1982	6,629,060	5,103,473	2,477	5,105,950	541,265	40,724	4,605,409	1,326,890	696,761	12,904	513,708	269,949
1983	7,092,525	5,443,056	926	5,443,982	597,931	43,564	4,889,615	1,446,134	756,776	13,377	530,195	274,043
1984	7,685,375	5,869,268	2,951	5,872,219	670,344	52,388	5,254,263	1,613,093	818,019	14,104	544,893	286,101
1985	8,375,859	6,356,946	2,478	6,359,424	739,665	69,681	5,689,440	1,779,991	906,428	14,928	561,081	300,096
1986	9,142,842	6,937,323	1,535	6,938,858	825,195	64,130	6,177,793	1,941,284	1,023,765	15,742	580,775	316,982
1987	10,067,109	7,766,744	2,128	7,768,872	930,044	46,213	6,885,041	2,078,122	1,103,946	16,456	611,763	345,999
1988	11,504,022	8,971,169	2,161	8,973,330	1,086,946	42,522	7,928,906	2,343,693	1,231,423	17,769	647,410	375,496
1989	13,196,124	10,218,492	2,945	10,221,437	1,263,165	13,806	8,972,078	2,796,324	1,427,722	19,084	691,467	412,843
1990	15,093,525	11,841,257	3,280	11,844,537	1,541,960	-15,835	10,286,742	3,147,173	1,659,610	19,960	756,170	452,016
1991	16,727,113	12,877,528	3,501	12,881,029	1,653,818	-2,894	11,224,317	3,433,258	2,069,538	20,497	816,085	465,549
1992	18,671,191	14,327,433	4,769	14,332,202	1,812,173	-11,810	12,508,219	3,797,102	2,365,870	21,778	857,357	472,519
1993	20,550,154	15,885,082	5,733	15,890,815	2,021,746	-83,001	13,786,068	4,235,704	2,528,382	22,774	902,338	504,060
1994	23,043,214	17,922,081	5,450	17,927,531	2,295,749	-143,308	15,488,474	4,857,758	2,696,982	23,692	972,624	567,840
1995	25,587,458	19,882,711	5,574	19,888,285	2,551,332	-189,245	17,147,708	5,518,262	2,921,488	24,702	1,035,847	606,312
1996	28,648,985	22,357,483	6,320	22,363,803	2,809,592	-279,104	19,275,107	6,204,871	3,169,007	26,047	1,099,894	662,190
1997	31,677,828	24,752,452	6,527	24,758,979	3,033,850	-302,979	21,422,150	6,853,726	3,401,952	26,909	1,177,230	713,369
1998	35,983,324	28,188,695	6,871	28,195,566	3,280,705	-317,567	24,597,294	7,738,544	3,647,486	28,758	1,251,258	749,408
1999	39,344,173	31,281,166	6,434	31,287,600	3,531,451	-350,779	27,405,370	8,112,001	3,826,802	29,778	1,321,254	803,146
2000	43,367,422	34,131,998	5,112	34,137,110	3,489,358	-371,878	30,275,874	8,970,516	4,121,032	31,112	1,393,909	853,137
2001	46,460,056	36,905,547	5,103	36,910,650	3,741,988	-414,649	32,754,013	9,018,645	4,687,398	31,811	1,460,500	882,073
2002	48,235,667	38,223,367	3,951	38,227,318	3,908,978	-423,369	33,894,971	9,033,446	5,307,250	31,672	1,522,962	896,528
2003	51,556,991	40,220,622	3,434	40,224,056	3,964,985	-461,398	35,797,673	10,044,637	5,714,681	32,545	1,584,166	941,654
2004	57,614,171	45,189,560	3,455	45,193,015	4,393,181	-555,331	40,244,503	11,219,105	6,150,563	34,649	1,662,773	1,011,906
2005	65,484,528	50,641,606	3,115	50,644,721	4,878,488	-616,635	45,149,598	13,688,110	6,646,820	37,863	1,729,522	1,087,078
2006	71,206,581	54,943,632	3,874	54,947,506	5,710,201	-578,268	48,659,037	15,367,379	7,180,165	39,476	1,803,774	1,145,464
2007	74,679,221	56,921,694	2,609	56,924,303	6,034,265	-547,282	50,342,756	16,468,666	7,867,799	39,982	1,867,817	1,174,103
2008	73,503,271	54,067,867	4,288	54,072,155	5,658,995	-484,852	47,928,308	16,208,848	9,366,115	38,436	1,912,349	1,160,263
2009	67,889,554	49,279,252	4,333	49,283,585	5,419,677	-449,997	43,413,911	13,755,124	10,720,519	35,005	1,939,407	1,081,892
2010	70,047,316	50,038,582	3,738	50,042,320	5,289,625	-377,701	44,374,994	13,806,359	11,865,963	35,873	1,952,640	1,056,986
2011	72,788,770	51,746,037	4,291	51,750,328	5,001,060	-278,599	46,470,669	14,326,349	11,991,752	37,096	1,962,162	1,076,766
2012	77,731,488	53,527,489	1,881	53,529,370	5,288,759	-316,612	47,923,999	17,719,022	12,088,467	39,068	1,989,644	1,092,996
2013	77,807,956	55,285,799	1,513	55,287,312	5,810,936	-327,309	49,149,067	16,324,251	12,334,638	38,561	2,017,798	1,125,627
2014	83,488,842	58,096,786	1,727	58,098,513	6,449,694	-363,351	51,285,468	18,686,140	13,517,234	40,967	2,037,960	1,168,811
2015	90,220,176	61,548,848	1,326	61,550,174	6,902,417	-364,707	54,283,050	21,137,112	14,800,014	43,421	2,077,790	1,216,015
2016	93,775,241	63,776,425	142	63,776,567	7,227,197	-462,504	56,086,866	21,977,359	15,711,016	44,318	2,115,963	1,263,381
2017	99,056,863	67,239,793	852	67,240,645	7,390,033	-483,313	59,367,299	23,137,797	16,551,767	45,974	2,154,616	1,303,282
2018	104,985,712	71,519,213	-90	71,519,123	7,875,782	-509,904	63,133,437	24,263,008	17,589,267	47,814	2,195,698	1,355,083
2019	114,155,310	77,175,029	1,484	77,176,513	8,718,003	-625,674	67,832,836	27,472,472	18,850,002	51,012	2,237,815	1,387,818
2020	121,767,470	73,603,986	517	73,604,503	8,273,300	-246,269	65,084,934	27,656,080	29,026,456	53,562	2,273,386	1,283,826
2021	133,596,955	83,181,591	570	83,182,161	9,118,651	-494,761	73,568,749	28,847,704	31,180,502	58,276	2,292,476	1,368,492

Personal Income and Employment by Area: Lawrence, KS

(Thousands of dollars, except as noted.)

Year	Personal income, total	Earnings by place of work Nonfarm	Earnings by place of work Farm	Earnings by place of work Total	Less: Contributions for government social insurance	Plus: Adjustment for residence	Equals: Net earnings by place of residence	Plus: Dividends, interest, and rent	Plus: Personal current transfer receipts	Per capita personal income (dollars)	Population (persons)	Total employment
1970	189,361	142,025	2,913	144,938	10,193	8,576	143,321	32,485	13,555	3,252	58,233	23,010
1971	213,246	161,457	4,306	165,763	12,103	7,864	161,524	36,144	15,578	3,577	59,621	24,197
1972	229,915	168,765	5,104	173,869	13,315	11,364	171,918	39,849	18,148	3,784	60,767	24,524
1973	254,888	186,789	6,280	193,069	17,182	12,738	188,625	44,338	21,925	4,121	61,848	25,994
1974	284,949	214,048	2,360	216,408	20,658	11,429	207,179	51,485	26,285	4,534	62,844	27,633
1975	323,561	237,196	4,435	241,631	22,712	12,337	231,256	60,123	32,182	5,341	60,580	27,762
1976	364,929	274,812	3,491	278,303	26,556	12,679	264,426	64,704	35,799	5,934	61,498	29,598
1977	418,143	316,234	7,089	323,323	30,394	13,500	306,429	71,205	40,509	6,644	62,932	31,544
1978	465,468	355,024	4,192	359,216	35,431	16,802	340,587	80,154	44,727	7,086	65,685	33,135
1979	518,678	396,388	4,206	400,594	41,165	19,444	378,873	92,052	47,753	7,775	66,710	34,211
1980	571,918	419,356	-20	419,336	43,725	23,859	399,470	114,536	57,912	8,405	68,045	34,501
1981	643,120	451,328	2,407	453,735	50,291	30,125	433,569	142,623	66,928	9,244	69,569	33,622
1982	674,394	460,947	353	461,300	51,836	35,502	444,966	160,011	69,417	9,641	69,948	33,433
1983	724,190	492,959	-3,135	489,824	54,363	40,770	476,231	172,916	75,043	10,353	69,947	33,914
1984	799,122	537,198	1,966	539,164	59,561	48,678	528,281	194,114	76,727	11,316	70,618	35,192
1985	864,981	569,561	7,741	577,302	63,298	56,939	570,943	211,225	82,813	11,988	72,151	36,131
1986	934,057	626,540	5,794	632,334	69,329	62,871	625,876	225,279	82,902	12,531	74,538	37,149
1987	983,375	657,993	8,028	666,021	72,255	69,053	662,819	231,915	88,641	12,914	76,148	39,566
1988	1,068,926	721,227	10,187	731,414	83,155	76,146	724,405	247,165	97,356	13,569	78,779	42,190
1989	1,181,331	794,481	8,100	802,581	90,618	82,085	794,048	278,529	108,754	14,750	80,092	43,552
1990	1,242,686	849,239	5,626	854,865	102,000	88,542	841,407	278,856	122,423	15,113	82,229	44,906
1991	1,319,533	900,019	4,465	904,484	109,468	98,469	893,485	288,268	137,780	15,768	83,683	46,550
1992	1,437,674	974,359	11,483	985,842	117,094	110,528	979,276	303,259	155,139	16,839	85,379	47,328
1993	1,528,457	1,038,426	2,834	1,041,260	124,409	124,739	1,041,590	319,477	167,390	17,383	87,926	48,723
1994	1,648,908	1,109,372	5,717	1,115,089	135,054	137,113	1,117,148	359,051	172,709	18,386	89,683	49,946
1995	1,750,526	1,173,731	1,989	1,175,720	141,405	151,082	1,185,397	381,558	183,571	19,151	91,408	53,006
1996	1,860,095	1,232,841	9,201	1,242,042	146,670	168,413	1,263,785	405,773	190,537	19,919	93,381	54,732
1997	2,036,292	1,355,899	8,054	1,363,953	161,080	182,491	1,385,364	448,292	202,636	21,277	95,706	57,637
1998	2,210,085	1,478,444	504	1,478,948	173,287	206,192	1,511,853	483,378	214,854	22,652	97,566	59,943
1999	2,307,771	1,556,298	-2,401	1,553,897	182,295	234,450	1,606,052	475,974	225,745	23,196	99,490	62,118
2000	2,496,349	1,671,754	-5,718	1,666,036	196,728	260,619	1,729,927	517,817	248,605	24,902	100,247	63,729
2001	2,696,313	1,861,995	-3,140	1,858,855	214,525	257,261	1,901,591	520,635	274,087	26,625	101,269	67,353
2002	2,772,665	1,911,803	-7,119	1,904,684	219,043	263,175	1,948,816	531,254	292,595	27,037	102,552	65,803
2003	2,858,900	1,941,453	-1,972	1,939,481	224,232	263,653	1,978,902	572,700	307,298	27,604	103,570	66,165
2004	2,923,978	2,021,920	7,815	2,029,735	234,594	249,150	2,044,291	559,793	319,894	27,894	104,826	67,337
2005	3,077,290	2,088,059	1,779	2,089,838	243,740	274,094	2,120,192	619,529	337,569	29,119	105,681	67,579
2006	3,306,914	2,176,057	-3,085	2,172,972	253,544	296,941	2,216,369	731,928	358,617	30,852	107,187	68,153
2007	3,470,635	2,223,437	1,667	2,225,104	256,662	336,988	2,305,430	770,248	394,957	32,168	107,892	69,124
2008	3,705,342	2,363,317	4,311	2,367,628	266,391	348,189	2,449,426	783,645	472,271	33,991	109,010	67,975
2009	3,755,074	2,369,330	13,378	2,382,708	270,322	345,737	2,458,123	784,649	512,302	34,125	110,039	67,419
2010	3,817,833	2,386,088	6,269	2,392,357	273,069	391,712	2,511,000	743,941	562,892	34,332	111,204	66,702
2011	4,010,662	2,428,594	14,881	2,443,475	242,698	396,412	2,597,189	830,053	583,420	35,650	112,500	66,327
2012	4,126,876	2,467,583	9,825	2,477,408	246,711	474,050	2,704,747	844,508	577,621	36,405	113,360	66,197
2013	4,228,652	2,581,031	11,656	2,592,687	289,447	469,362	2,772,602	859,336	596,714	36,842	114,779	67,805
2014	4,430,822	2,706,596	2,595	2,709,191	303,511	482,776	2,888,456	923,195	619,171	38,504	115,075	69,520
2015	4,674,017	2,865,252	1,779	2,867,031	319,266	517,350	3,065,115	967,627	641,275	40,144	116,431	70,431
2016	4,814,294	2,965,092	3,821	2,968,913	327,043	477,150	3,119,020	1,019,369	675,905	40,914	117,670	71,529
2017	5,053,085	3,082,421	6,206	3,088,627	341,159	527,241	3,274,709	1,075,785	702,591	42,841	117,950	73,546
2018	5,309,641	3,184,700	11,422	3,196,122	353,393	590,654	3,433,383	1,127,910	748,348	44,846	118,398	74,338
2019	5,545,320	3,317,796	11,734	3,329,530	370,910	603,003	3,561,623	1,183,154	800,543	46,612	118,968	74,667
2020	5,856,305	3,342,125	20,937	3,363,062	380,521	630,671	3,613,212	1,178,411	1,064,682	49,290	118,814	70,970
2021	6,171,456	3,519,766	27,474	3,547,240	397,450	685,781	3,835,571	1,203,038	1,132,847	51,703	119,363	72,157

Personal Income and Employment by Area: Lawton, OK

(Thousands of dollars, except as noted.)

Year	Personal income, total	Earnings by place of work			Less: Contributions for government social insurance	Plus: Adjustment for residence	Equals: Net earnings by place of residence	Plus: Dividends, interest, and rent	Plus: Personal current transfer receipts	Per capita personal income (dollars)	Population (persons)	Total employment
		Nonfarm	Farm	Total								
1970	474,227	374,178	6,559	380,737	21,692	-8,085	350,960	98,035	25,232	4,130	114,835	57,235
1971	477,877	376,915	5,259	382,174	23,342	-8,435	350,397	98,092	29,388	4,166	114,717	53,368
1972	488,467	382,516	7,874	390,390	23,936	-8,844	357,610	98,147	32,710	4,561	107,106	50,475
1973	547,261	417,401	18,630	436,031	28,238	-9,675	398,118	111,374	37,769	5,005	109,334	51,921
1974	601,813	461,535	11,260	472,795	32,850	-10,389	429,556	126,662	45,595	5,431	110,808	53,070
1975	644,183	489,898	9,177	499,075	37,042	-10,527	451,506	136,542	56,135	5,721	112,591	53,108
1976	746,867	571,485	10,070	581,555	44,720	-10,773	526,062	158,260	62,545	6,164	121,157	56,963
1977	793,076	611,743	1,099	612,842	47,460	-11,188	554,194	172,660	66,222	6,476	122,462	57,631
1978	877,968	678,582	1,598	680,180	53,308	-15,422	611,450	196,142	70,376	7,057	124,413	58,416
1979	974,090	729,988	18,862	748,850	59,447	-11,862	677,541	214,574	81,975	7,971	122,200	58,783
1980	1,063,769	793,776	5,723	799,499	64,973	-8,850	725,676	242,471	95,622	8,847	120,234	59,943
1981	1,226,622	905,657	13,931	919,588	77,698	-6,092	835,798	282,984	107,840	10,073	121,777	60,159
1982	1,388,372	1,035,816	9,655	1,045,471	87,837	-10,703	946,931	321,085	120,356	10,982	126,418	63,838
1983	1,461,836	1,075,200	8,504	1,083,704	93,866	-10,191	979,647	351,286	130,903	11,325	129,084	63,134
1984	1,554,491	1,149,242	4,486	1,153,728	102,427	-11,491	1,039,810	376,771	137,910	12,140	128,046	64,339
1985	1,658,380	1,224,058	12,685	1,236,743	111,421	-13,857	1,111,465	399,995	146,920	13,031	127,261	65,425
1986	1,722,616	1,272,786	24,740	1,297,526	118,538	-16,188	1,162,800	406,251	153,565	13,683	125,897	64,430
1987	1,777,007	1,331,655	12,310	1,343,965	125,431	-19,141	1,199,393	414,582	163,032	14,182	125,301	65,717
1988	1,794,611	1,334,787	22,196	1,356,983	134,684	-16,025	1,206,274	411,833	176,504	14,556	123,289	64,438
1989	1,829,424	1,343,760	17,241	1,361,001	138,495	-14,968	1,207,538	430,977	190,909	15,368	119,044	63,133
1990	1,900,927	1,386,326	27,272	1,413,598	147,994	-14,148	1,251,456	438,808	210,663	16,094	118,112	62,529
1991	1,952,710	1,436,876	13,199	1,450,075	157,106	-15,065	1,277,904	442,271	232,535	16,563	117,896	60,909
1992	2,205,964	1,641,892	20,012	1,661,904	181,848	-22,261	1,457,795	486,173	261,996	17,313	127,413	65,370
1993	2,197,770	1,611,894	19,351	1,631,245	182,537	-18,488	1,430,220	495,129	272,421	17,514	125,485	64,545
1994	2,225,033	1,623,666	11,813	1,635,479	183,414	-16,913	1,435,152	499,667	290,214	17,754	125,323	63,353
1995	2,300,015	1,646,448	2,162	1,648,610	185,112	-16,592	1,446,906	536,210	316,899	18,637	123,412	64,135
1996	2,360,609	1,664,511	9,673	1,674,184	185,858	-13,949	1,474,377	553,557	332,675	19,136	123,357	64,864
1997	2,392,990	1,702,736	12,275	1,715,011	189,191	-10,752	1,515,068	537,519	340,403	19,535	122,497	64,740
1998	2,500,407	1,766,176	11,404	1,777,580	195,291	-11,733	1,570,556	582,864	346,987	20,482	122,076	64,171
1999	2,568,124	1,794,498	17,240	1,811,738	199,703	-11,159	1,600,876	594,502	372,746	20,957	122,542	64,417
2000	2,691,246	1,865,730	19,278	1,885,008	206,075	-8,451	1,670,482	626,305	394,459	22,115	121,695	64,749
2001	2,898,390	2,039,629	10,597	2,050,226	221,370	-17,673	1,811,183	645,687	441,520	24,162	119,955	64,488
2002	3,021,131	2,156,654	18,577	2,175,231	234,076	-28,518	1,912,637	636,275	472,219	25,199	119,889	64,635
2003	3,205,427	2,327,355	19,711	2,347,066	250,550	-43,943	2,052,573	636,313	516,541	27,284	117,484	64,923
2004	3,316,694	2,438,817	31,667	2,470,484	267,170	-57,120	2,146,194	631,711	538,789	27,110	122,341	66,046
2005	3,476,194	2,548,270	35,723	2,583,993	274,270	-67,939	2,241,784	647,292	587,118	28,617	121,475	64,462
2006	3,798,881	2,835,082	13,925	2,849,007	302,852	-87,941	2,458,214	705,614	635,053	30,890	122,980	67,139
2007	3,988,427	2,927,956	3,469	2,931,425	315,554	-99,072	2,516,799	783,310	688,318	31,701	125,814	68,756
2008	4,285,572	3,103,150	21,320	3,124,470	333,294	-114,718	2,676,458	836,109	773,005	34,515	124,166	69,391
2009	4,375,559	3,228,907	-12,102	3,216,805	355,353	-120,833	2,740,619	803,712	831,228	34,691	126,131	69,558
2010	4,736,011	3,520,607	-5,428	3,515,179	384,202	-130,445	3,000,532	837,423	898,056	35,997	131,568	71,532
2011	4,891,873	3,509,519	10,691	3,520,210	352,280	-113,376	3,054,554	909,452	927,867	36,977	132,294	69,613
2012	4,869,630	3,435,341	26,003	3,461,344	346,864	-92,973	3,021,507	893,884	954,239	36,728	132,586	68,302
2013	4,930,764	3,454,933	33,071	3,488,004	389,770	-84,673	3,013,561	939,225	977,978	37,694	130,812	68,861
2014	5,014,148	3,459,658	67,284	3,526,942	389,015	-80,045	3,057,882	941,715	1,014,551	38,351	130,742	68,608
2015	5,095,940	3,551,797	42,719	3,594,516	399,400	-87,168	3,107,948	932,180	1,055,812	39,299	129,671	68,984
2016	5,017,761	3,483,338	20,162	3,503,500	387,268	-98,583	3,017,649	908,963	1,091,149	39,374	127,438	68,421
2017	5,135,947	3,537,421	11,887	3,549,308	399,176	-95,106	3,055,026	947,461	1,133,460	40,185	127,809	68,937
2018	5,227,751	3,610,351	5,154	3,615,505	412,037	-95,334	3,108,134	944,998	1,174,619	41,250	126,734	68,750
2019	5,404,228	3,717,838	8,007	3,725,845	423,347	-96,160	3,206,338	936,839	1,261,051	42,622	126,793	69,665
2020	5,765,490	3,811,224	10,890	3,822,114	436,317	-93,831	3,291,966	911,610	1,561,914	45,515	126,672	68,460
2021	6,097,408	3,967,329	4,576	3,971,905	449,262	-97,279	3,425,364	901,623	1,770,421	47,807	127,543	68,261

Personal Income and Employment by Area: Lebanon, PA

(Thousands of dollars, except as noted.)

Year	Personal income, total	Derivation of personal income									Per capita personal income (dollars)	Population (persons)	Total employment
		Earnings by place of work			Less: Contributions for government social insurance	Plus: Adjustment for residence	Equals: Net earnings by place of residence	Plus: Dividends, interest, and rent	Plus: Personal current transfer receipts				
		Nonfarm	Farm	Total									
1970	391,453	298,815	11,617	310,432	20,759	19,833	309,506	47,907	34,040	3,907	100,193	44,662
1971	404,211	306,448	9,638	316,086	21,967	18,236	312,355	52,181	39,675	3,928	102,907	43,469
1972	447,121	342,576	9,890	352,466	25,787	19,329	346,008	56,886	44,227	4,324	103,414	44,721
1973	496,917	379,209	12,642	391,851	33,035	23,374	382,190	65,090	49,637	4,729	105,069	45,978
1974	552,795	420,008	10,251	430,259	38,229	26,580	418,610	74,675	59,510	5,249	105,311	46,696
1975	608,263	453,233	8,655	461,888	39,642	20,145	442,391	83,740	82,132	4,894	124,289	46,734
1976	663,856	494,491	9,602	504,093	43,853	26,255	486,495	90,724	86,637	6,135	108,206	46,955
1977	736,809	549,915	8,027	557,942	48,559	33,321	542,704	102,161	91,944	6,819	108,055	47,783
1978	815,150	603,635	10,665	614,300	54,533	42,959	602,726	115,077	97,347	7,457	109,308	48,272
1979	917,852	671,491	14,272	685,763	62,616	56,864	680,011	129,274	108,567	8,337	110,096	49,036
1980	1,003,263	704,701	8,178	712,879	66,213	70,289	716,955	161,714	124,594	9,218	108,839	48,871
1981	1,108,773	739,817	12,109	751,926	74,753	90,543	767,716	197,012	144,045	10,112	109,645	48,150
1982	1,173,241	727,547	10,790	738,337	74,059	110,562	774,840	229,964	168,437	10,610	110,574	46,129
1983	1,240,662	757,908	10,838	768,746	79,392	123,749	813,103	245,855	181,704	11,258	110,199	45,813
1984	1,345,183	802,345	24,989	827,334	88,124	152,585	891,795	272,683	180,705	12,201	110,250	46,912
1985	1,425,678	840,161	25,334	865,495	93,751	167,294	939,038	293,958	192,682	12,916	110,382	47,415
1986	1,515,240	874,113	32,066	906,179	97,923	191,796	1,000,052	308,833	206,355	13,680	110,764	47,688
1987	1,612,240	950,214	28,399	978,613	106,467	215,662	1,087,808	315,363	209,069	14,441	111,646	50,000
1988	1,749,890	1,055,604	14,420	1,070,024	120,929	241,298	1,190,393	333,402	226,095	15,535	112,643	52,423
1989	1,925,481	1,129,960	23,680	1,153,640	127,606	275,678	1,301,712	380,312	243,457	17,038	113,009	52,792
1990	2,027,721	1,170,877	31,606	1,202,483	133,393	289,932	1,359,022	397,729	270,970	17,770	114,109	52,552
1991	2,129,806	1,195,964	26,362	1,222,326	138,596	323,655	1,407,385	406,958	315,463	18,480	115,248	52,326
1992	2,247,926	1,277,068	28,901	1,305,969	147,783	351,273	1,509,459	407,349	331,118	19,368	116,066	52,293
1993	2,342,535	1,314,541	24,837	1,339,378	155,620	387,085	1,570,843	418,798	352,894	20,062	116,764	51,088
1994	2,453,208	1,400,028	23,340	1,423,368	166,279	409,686	1,666,775	427,021	359,412	20,893	117,415	51,472
1995	2,530,553	1,381,406	16,045	1,397,451	166,169	469,945	1,701,227	448,651	380,675	21,480	117,809	52,277
1996	2,664,623	1,398,455	28,451	1,426,906	164,900	525,979	1,787,985	468,698	407,940	22,507	118,391	52,193
1997	2,801,704	1,473,706	26,696	1,500,402	172,786	556,098	1,883,714	497,463	420,527	23,593	118,753	53,347
1998	2,968,290	1,544,604	29,248	1,573,852	179,237	609,017	2,003,632	527,975	436,683	24,821	119,590	51,923
1999	3,080,412	1,641,066	20,649	1,661,715	187,998	613,924	2,087,641	525,587	467,184	25,682	119,944	52,886
2000	3,237,393	1,737,945	38,391	1,776,336	198,705	605,962	2,183,593	558,997	494,803	26,909	120,309	54,561
2001	3,468,638	1,928,060	40,987	1,969,047	215,421	623,154	2,376,780	557,122	534,736	28,677	120,954	58,544
2002	3,551,033	1,992,970	21,049	2,014,019	221,538	659,939	2,452,420	523,893	574,720	29,179	121,698	58,829
2003	3,684,642	2,083,577	47,453	2,131,030	230,400	665,950	2,566,580	518,661	599,401	29,919	123,154	59,506
2004	3,997,216	2,224,449	73,684	2,298,133	245,325	724,106	2,776,914	581,257	639,045	32,069	124,644	60,913
2005	4,191,238	2,322,361	67,623	2,389,984	259,682	776,053	2,906,355	582,593	702,290	33,212	126,197	62,302
2006	4,386,738	2,470,225	44,494	2,514,719	280,114	784,010	3,018,615	627,096	741,027	34,191	128,302	64,150
2007	4,612,136	2,535,641	64,630	2,600,271	287,742	793,001	3,105,530	720,280	786,326	35,428	130,182	65,328
2008	4,822,354	2,557,543	66,717	2,624,260	294,976	806,237	3,135,521	785,357	901,476	36,651	131,574	64,936
2009	4,764,125	2,520,242	52,255	2,572,497	295,988	735,100	3,011,609	739,422	1,013,094	35,832	132,959	64,003
2010	4,963,334	2,674,360	60,280	2,734,640	311,430	742,869	3,166,079	724,527	1,072,728	37,132	133,667	64,608
2011	5,191,005	2,802,588	87,827	2,890,415	294,583	728,149	3,323,981	779,021	1,088,003	38,586	134,530	66,020
2012	5,299,194	2,902,837	93,524	2,996,361	302,554	680,831	3,374,638	827,565	1,096,991	39,099	135,531	67,515
2013	5,383,510	2,954,056	105,574	3,059,630	341,424	717,373	3,435,579	815,898	1,132,033	39,642	135,803	67,426
2014	5,587,226	2,991,603	121,055	3,112,658	346,741	773,009	3,538,926	876,269	1,172,031	40,723	137,201	67,167
2015	5,894,376	3,114,862	77,147	3,192,009	357,649	855,014	3,689,374	962,024	1,242,978	42,615	138,317	66,946
2016	6,108,797	3,220,172	19,545	3,239,717	370,745	904,924	3,773,896	1,015,104	1,319,797	43,800	139,470	67,314
2017	6,398,377	3,378,793	50,032	3,428,825	392,201	958,097	3,994,721	1,055,937	1,347,719	45,498	140,629	67,358
2018	6,723,226	3,530,251	40,422	3,570,673	408,392	993,102	4,155,383	1,125,368	1,442,475	47,198	142,446	68,442
2019	6,985,072	3,700,722	40,594	3,741,316	434,135	984,115	4,291,296	1,189,484	1,504,292	48,912	142,809	69,197
2020	7,505,803	3,709,836	20,270	3,730,106	435,561	979,298	4,273,843	1,188,284	2,043,676	52,399	143,242	66,507
2021	8,007,372	4,004,256	71,969	4,076,225	462,190	971,873	4,585,908	1,218,050	2,203,414	55,803	143,493	68,861

Personal Income and Employment by Area: Lewiston, ID-WA

(Thousands of dollars, except as noted.)

Year	Personal income, total	Earnings by place of work			Less: Contributions for government social insurance	Plus: Adjustment for residence	Equals: Net earnings by place of residence	Plus: Dividends, interest, and rent	Plus: Personal current transfer receipts	Per capita personal income (dollars)	Population (persons)	Total employment
		Nonfarm	Farm	Total								
1970	166,225	115,690	8,313	124,003	9,095	4,896	119,804	28,181	18,240	3,760	44,211	17,980
1971	181,691	127,026	8,214	135,240	10,329	4,341	129,252	31,868	20,571	4,056	44,792	18,651
1972	203,450	142,757	11,849	154,606	12,020	3,283	145,869	34,459	23,122	4,384	46,404	18,905
1973	228,028	161,996	15,283	177,279	15,830	877	162,326	39,323	26,379	4,909	46,454	20,121
1974	264,950	182,986	25,104	208,090	18,365	-1,615	188,110	45,392	31,448	5,679	46,658	20,911
1975	290,248	206,659	13,662	220,321	20,154	-1,031	199,136	52,835	38,277	6,209	46,744	21,367
1976	317,152	232,783	12,210	244,993	23,000	-1,725	220,268	55,180	41,704	6,660	47,617	22,040
1977	345,508	259,594	10,087	269,681	25,749	-4,144	239,788	61,530	44,190	7,213	47,898	22,824
1978	387,945	295,864	10,330	306,194	29,545	-5,900	270,749	68,503	48,693	7,992	48,543	23,861
1979	428,688	333,801	8,658	342,459	35,020	-11,042	296,397	76,522	55,769	8,744	49,026	24,620
1980	480,292	358,439	15,518	373,957	37,639	-13,004	323,314	91,021	65,957	9,590	50,082	24,405
1981	520,159	372,463	18,414	390,877	42,011	-12,380	336,486	109,169	74,504	10,368	50,169	23,670
1982	546,709	368,653	19,741	388,394	42,465	-10,409	335,520	127,544	83,645	10,966	49,856	22,989
1983	601,076	399,246	27,815	427,061	46,124	-9,347	371,590	141,109	88,377	12,101	49,673	23,660
1984	626,335	419,818	16,212	436,030	50,195	-8,228	377,607	155,853	92,875	12,461	50,264	23,775
1985	639,323	423,522	4,636	428,158	51,026	-6,531	370,601	167,807	100,915	12,721	50,257	23,403
1986	662,296	434,370	11,266	445,636	52,988	-4,807	387,841	168,726	105,729	13,275	49,891	23,465
1987	681,648	457,146	8,254	465,400	55,791	-4,977	404,632	165,890	111,126	13,616	50,063	24,138
1988	729,895	494,108	12,478	506,586	62,664	-2,210	441,712	169,262	118,921	14,599	49,995	25,462
1989	795,736	529,533	18,246	547,779	67,867	-393	479,519	189,659	126,558	15,614	50,964	26,044
1990	853,804	578,610	21,540	600,150	77,582	1,310	523,878	192,184	137,742	16,570	51,526	26,983
1991	901,816	616,733	10,877	627,610	83,610	364	544,364	199,620	157,832	17,182	52,487	27,518
1992	985,763	689,699	9,824	699,523	92,283	-1,673	605,567	208,553	171,643	18,381	53,629	28,639
1993	1,067,086	742,210	23,147	765,357	99,583	-2,502	663,272	220,782	183,032	19,490	54,750	29,620
1994	1,117,613	796,689	7,128	803,817	107,177	-3,639	693,001	229,392	195,220	19,962	55,987	31,132
1995	1,162,691	796,278	10,704	806,982	107,804	-2,827	696,351	254,768	211,572	20,500	56,718	31,384
1996	1,232,323	838,195	13,468	851,663	111,092	-5,414	735,157	273,500	223,666	21,495	57,332	32,113
1997	1,290,985	894,615	426	895,041	116,075	-7,940	771,026	288,742	231,217	22,307	57,874	33,058
1998	1,365,963	954,521	6,457	960,978	121,624	-9,839	829,515	291,824	244,624	23,504	58,116	33,458
1999	1,415,037	1,012,036	8,571	1,020,607	124,741	-11,683	884,183	276,823	254,031	24,380	58,042	33,588
2000	1,478,608	1,041,145	19,696	1,060,841	129,407	-12,685	918,749	286,541	273,318	25,518	57,944	34,320
2001	1,526,846	1,062,263	19,933	1,082,196	132,703	-13,731	935,762	291,291	299,793	26,579	57,446	33,539
2002	1,537,521	1,090,821	16,574	1,107,395	136,005	-12,675	958,715	264,710	314,096	26,693	57,601	33,446
2003	1,600,475	1,125,622	18,567	1,144,189	141,174	-13,277	989,738	280,419	330,318	27,508	58,183	33,600
2004	1,675,909	1,161,869	23,439	1,185,308	145,310	-12,410	1,027,588	297,969	350,352	28,608	58,581	33,585
2005	1,710,712	1,181,917	21,822	1,203,739	150,957	-13,545	1,039,237	303,894	367,581	29,005	58,979	33,984
2006	1,827,262	1,262,437	16,318	1,278,755	161,548	-12,486	1,104,721	325,219	397,322	30,635	59,646	34,467
2007	1,961,921	1,322,009	21,217	1,343,226	169,787	-10,974	1,162,465	368,894	430,562	32,749	59,908	35,176
2008	2,066,692	1,349,073	24,405	1,373,478	174,135	-12,335	1,187,008	407,312	472,372	34,329	60,203	34,975
2009	2,039,964	1,322,441	17,931	1,340,372	173,102	-11,575	1,155,695	376,951	507,318	33,738	60,464	33,927
2010	2,140,901	1,384,231	22,622	1,406,853	182,320	-12,420	1,212,113	382,753	546,035	35,073	61,042	33,982
2011	2,202,291	1,386,738	25,248	1,411,986	164,252	-13,571	1,234,163	421,062	547,066	35,852	61,428	33,980
2012	2,249,335	1,417,211	22,302	1,439,513	165,131	-12,418	1,261,964	443,614	543,757	36,606	61,447	33,494
2013	2,319,079	1,498,662	34,241	1,532,903	190,921	-18,757	1,323,225	433,304	562,550	37,413	61,986	34,437
2014	2,400,725	1,530,597	10,012	1,540,609	197,379	-18,596	1,324,634	472,785	603,306	38,449	62,439	34,882
2015	2,489,909	1,597,880	23,256	1,621,136	205,620	-19,096	1,396,420	484,892	608,597	39,763	62,618	35,302
2016	2,564,531	1,663,797	11,427	1,675,224	214,806	-19,964	1,440,454	488,036	636,041	40,673	63,053	35,922
2017	2,693,803	1,753,227	4,596	1,757,823	226,435	-22,188	1,509,200	519,566	665,037	42,383	63,559	36,457
2018	2,797,739	1,791,691	6,184	1,797,875	229,793	-19,185	1,548,897	550,952	697,890	43,879	63,760	36,157
2019	2,929,341	1,845,114	14,555	1,859,669	237,563	-17,730	1,604,376	584,652	740,313	45,752	64,026	36,098
2020	3,178,857	1,954,273	23,510	1,977,783	256,577	-21,638	1,699,568	591,920	887,369	49,378	64,378	35,631
2021	3,409,316	2,045,597	24,948	2,070,545	260,586	-20,995	1,788,964	606,144	1,014,208	52,572	64,851	36,424

Personal Income and Employment by Area: Lewiston-Auburn, ME

(Thousands of dollars, except as noted.)

Year	Personal income, total	Earnings by place of work			Less: Contributions for government social insurance	Plus: Adjustment for residence	Equals: Net earnings by place of residence	Plus: Dividends, interest, and rent	Plus: Personal current transfer receipts	Per capita personal income (dollars)	Population (persons)	Total employment
		Nonfarm	Farm	Total								
1970	339,559	245,390	6,907	252,297	19,291	21,803	254,809	46,393	38,357	3,713	91,463	42,844
1971	350,474	240,860	7,099	247,959	19,477	25,854	254,336	49,865	46,273	3,773	92,881	40,634
1972	373,641	255,844	9,495	265,339	21,738	27,410	271,011	53,438	49,192	3,985	93,756	40,343
1973	423,220	288,072	18,096	306,168	27,820	29,065	307,413	58,582	57,225	4,451	95,076	42,562
1974	459,977	308,823	13,975	322,798	30,844	32,348	324,302	67,275	68,400	4,798	95,870	43,143
1975	506,117	329,092	14,041	343,133	32,268	35,036	345,901	74,436	85,780	5,298	95,535	42,320
1976	579,076	381,103	23,386	404,489	38,489	43,097	409,097	78,590	91,389	5,962	97,130	44,591
1977	622,266	416,443	18,291	434,734	42,096	46,293	438,931	87,384	95,951	6,338	98,181	46,014
1978	683,401	465,446	15,016	480,462	48,555	54,180	486,087	95,442	101,872	6,914	98,837	47,120
1979	750,882	509,826	12,901	522,727	54,493	63,221	531,455	103,342	116,085	7,535	99,656	47,810
1980	843,510	553,477	11,128	564,605	59,010	77,759	583,354	123,770	136,386	8,475	99,531	47,774
1981	920,680	583,782	13,423	597,205	66,270	85,622	616,557	147,758	156,365	9,251	99,522	47,298
1982	994,172	600,158	15,140	615,298	68,408	100,216	647,106	176,253	170,813	10,056	98,860	45,953
1983	1,075,398	655,243	13,366	668,609	74,858	107,146	700,897	189,208	185,293	10,834	99,262	46,577
1984	1,180,324	729,743	20,067	749,810	85,417	111,488	775,881	210,700	193,743	11,801	100,018	48,103
1985	1,242,315	773,236	17,568	790,804	90,215	112,663	813,252	224,272	204,791	12,409	100,114	48,570
1986	1,336,704	837,104	14,671	851,775	97,136	127,450	882,089	242,490	212,125	13,340	100,204	50,078
1987	1,455,273	939,048	14,137	953,185	107,058	138,865	984,992	254,351	215,930	14,355	101,378	51,603
1988	1,595,764	1,028,427	12,437	1,040,864	119,791	163,975	1,085,048	280,150	230,566	15,409	103,559	53,611
1989	1,733,855	1,097,709	10,731	1,108,440	126,141	184,319	1,166,618	321,098	246,139	16,470	105,276	54,122
1990	1,785,505	1,113,528	17,088	1,130,616	134,139	195,162	1,191,639	315,952	277,914	16,938	105,412	53,181
1991	1,788,322	1,115,132	16,841	1,131,973	136,424	167,018	1,162,567	306,877	318,878	17,036	104,973	50,918
1992	1,861,172	1,155,416	16,732	1,172,148	142,774	180,542	1,209,916	298,742	352,514	17,838	104,335	50,835
1993	1,925,212	1,217,047	22,212	1,239,259	154,004	172,019	1,257,274	298,868	369,070	18,429	104,464	52,166
1994	2,015,499	1,287,349	27,361	1,314,710	164,818	168,189	1,318,081	310,208	387,210	19,359	104,112	53,466
1995	2,070,025	1,327,018	10,621	1,337,639	171,013	162,335	1,328,961	336,455	404,609	19,948	103,769	53,265
1996	2,165,578	1,378,531	21,502	1,400,033	174,536	153,081	1,378,578	354,899	432,101	21,032	102,966	53,134
1997	2,270,628	1,448,483	14,203	1,462,686	182,904	174,217	1,453,999	367,510	449,119	22,149	102,518	53,271
1998	2,374,116	1,557,054	13,637	1,570,691	194,455	161,145	1,537,381	376,987	459,748	23,023	103,120	55,697
1999	2,486,006	1,702,606	23,816	1,726,422	208,786	145,825	1,663,461	356,723	465,822	24,042	103,403	58,684
2000	2,639,071	1,828,505	23,546	1,852,051	220,048	130,307	1,762,310	386,627	490,134	25,412	103,852	60,420
2001	2,733,591	1,874,917	24,369	1,899,286	226,267	138,779	1,811,798	394,236	527,557	26,219	104,260	59,480
2002	2,882,918	2,012,772	23,319	2,036,091	235,756	113,608	1,913,943	405,692	563,283	27,440	105,063	60,214
2003	3,036,708	2,087,279	30,885	2,118,164	242,031	123,088	1,999,221	419,367	618,120	28,610	106,140	60,114
2004	3,119,113	2,162,790	23,172	2,185,962	248,568	145,535	2,082,929	384,466	651,718	29,187	106,867	60,631
2005	3,192,262	2,202,154	8,922	2,211,076	255,619	137,193	2,092,650	382,130	717,482	29,736	107,352	60,554
2006	3,328,239	2,344,001	10,657	2,354,658	274,258	123,283	2,203,683	402,408	722,148	30,836	107,932	61,323
2007	3,487,452	2,427,109	17,514	2,444,623	288,397	103,570	2,259,796	458,466	769,190	32,369	107,739	62,993
2008	3,641,916	2,472,240	29,372	2,501,612	296,394	78,538	2,283,756	470,255	887,905	33,633	108,284	62,500
2009	3,630,901	2,419,408	21,321	2,440,729	289,614	61,988	2,213,103	444,281	973,517	33,672	107,830	60,515
2010	3,674,598	2,472,053	21,029	2,493,082	298,760	28,178	2,222,500	483,346	968,752	34,115	107,712	60,259
2011	3,764,486	2,496,413	22,896	2,519,309	272,561	6,080	2,252,828	497,988	1,013,670	35,032	107,458	60,362
2012	3,835,281	2,562,892	37,614	2,600,506	280,756	-3,136	2,316,614	518,630	1,000,037	35,671	107,517	60,347
2013	3,793,094	2,584,105	46,080	2,630,185	323,972	-6,123	2,300,090	483,701	1,009,303	35,361	107,267	60,395
2014	3,892,638	2,701,291	32,024	2,733,315	333,563	-46,309	2,353,443	514,230	1,024,965	35,889	108,463	61,256
2015	4,063,997	2,792,883	57,660	2,850,543	348,502	-34,423	2,467,618	533,228	1,063,151	37,461	108,485	61,710
2016	4,109,375	2,860,843	25,097	2,885,940	354,001	-63,291	2,468,648	557,865	1,082,862	37,723	108,936	62,432
2017	4,245,029	2,946,692	27,438	2,974,130	363,694	-58,781	2,551,655	581,824	1,111,550	38,837	109,303	62,616
2018	4,395,956	3,073,810	21,773	3,095,583	381,970	-55,328	2,658,285	571,847	1,165,824	39,949	110,040	63,258
2019	4,656,425	3,234,450	25,241	3,259,691	401,224	-80,745	2,777,722	659,278	1,219,425	42,075	110,670	63,269
2020	5,123,802	3,382,014	25,442	3,407,456	420,826	-102,359	2,884,271	658,684	1,580,847	46,144	111,039	61,620
2021	5,525,754	3,612,311	19,909	3,632,220	446,954	-51,370	3,133,896	666,942	1,724,916	49,766	111,034	62,632

Personal Income and Employment by Area: Lexington-Fayette, KY

(Thousands of dollars, except as noted.)

Year	Personal income, total	Earnings by place of work			Less: Contributions for government social insurance	Plus: Adjustment for residence	Equals: Net earnings by place of residence	Plus: Dividends, interest, and rent	Plus: Personal current transfer receipts	Per capita personal income (dollars)	Population (persons)	Total employment
		Nonfarm	Farm	Total								
1970	1,017,530	857,895	42,124	900,019	54,163	-49,882	795,974	147,327	74,229	3,804	267,481	140,584
1971	1,127,053	949,712	39,006	988,718	61,436	-52,159	875,123	165,006	86,924	4,118	273,697	143,669
1972	1,251,564	1,055,175	51,243	1,106,418	72,088	-61,923	972,407	182,977	96,180	4,440	281,894	148,727
1973	1,400,290	1,196,803	54,506	1,251,309	94,851	-71,630	1,084,828	204,737	110,725	4,868	287,662	158,535
1974	1,560,999	1,325,589	56,972	1,382,561	108,738	-83,358	1,190,465	236,865	133,669	5,270	296,218	162,910
1975	1,710,621	1,417,655	60,952	1,478,607	115,190	-84,944	1,278,473	257,114	175,034	5,747	297,670	157,519
1976	1,934,689	1,627,457	71,845	1,699,302	135,761	-104,743	1,458,798	285,649	190,242	6,377	303,393	166,412
1977	2,150,870	1,802,950	94,260	1,897,210	150,367	-118,230	1,628,613	318,572	203,685	6,973	308,473	170,538
1978	2,444,284	2,029,243	148,323	2,177,566	175,832	-139,295	1,862,439	362,713	219,132	7,841	311,728	180,152
1979	2,731,660	2,297,636	141,902	2,439,538	206,600	-166,088	2,066,850	417,484	247,326	8,622	316,817	184,649
1980	3,034,438	2,437,328	193,405	2,630,733	221,253	-173,540	2,235,940	501,868	296,630	9,537	318,175	183,059
1981	3,438,971	2,664,961	258,179	2,923,140	260,843	-186,483	2,475,814	626,296	336,861	10,751	319,884	183,889
1982	3,696,393	2,822,928	231,382	3,054,310	281,232	-195,340	2,577,738	755,718	362,937	11,469	322,286	185,181
1983	4,024,789	3,083,752	280,225	3,363,977	310,274	-218,600	2,835,103	795,589	394,097	12,413	324,231	191,185
1984	4,557,690	3,502,078	364,345	3,866,423	359,216	-258,001	3,249,206	893,314	415,170	14,018	325,133	200,185
1985	4,852,230	3,792,516	341,328	4,133,844	396,859	-285,048	3,451,937	955,883	444,410	14,682	330,485	205,232
1986	4,992,158	3,988,198	253,497	4,241,695	433,192	-295,642	3,512,861	1,012,278	467,019	14,894	335,169	212,210
1987	5,285,964	4,279,590	238,901	4,518,491	463,752	-322,510	3,732,229	1,062,367	491,368	15,592	339,008	216,098
1988	5,881,666	4,827,944	245,711	5,073,655	520,277	-352,113	4,201,265	1,147,142	533,259	17,138	343,186	223,962
1989	6,321,218	5,208,599	233,857	5,442,456	570,760	-400,890	4,470,806	1,253,762	596,650	18,328	344,891	230,602
1990	6,893,882	5,737,963	242,676	5,980,639	652,399	-465,640	4,862,600	1,374,410	656,872	19,688	350,161	235,619
1991	7,320,865	6,058,058	248,903	6,306,961	692,106	-469,386	5,145,469	1,429,296	746,100	20,572	355,861	237,345
1992	7,837,414	6,483,642	314,329	6,797,971	739,905	-507,662	5,550,404	1,463,270	823,740	21,579	363,195	242,428
1993	8,150,083	6,757,974	281,970	7,039,944	778,884	-510,742	5,750,318	1,523,419	876,346	22,037	369,839	248,440
1994	8,471,303	6,998,601	278,514	7,277,115	825,454	-546,720	5,904,941	1,653,252	913,110	22,561	375,478	251,588
1995	9,028,358	7,412,527	279,784	7,692,311	878,581	-602,243	6,211,487	1,832,808	984,063	23,753	380,096	264,124
1996	9,661,628	7,992,998	321,845	8,314,843	937,877	-698,997	6,677,969	1,935,190	1,048,469	25,023	386,117	272,024
1997	10,316,250	8,544,408	387,127	8,931,535	999,011	-776,624	7,155,900	2,051,339	1,109,011	26,380	391,065	279,832
1998	11,084,024	9,158,863	448,361	9,607,224	1,069,447	-811,958	7,725,819	2,217,174	1,141,031	27,865	397,775	286,606
1999	11,751,612	9,783,837	547,130	10,330,967	1,148,367	-846,332	8,336,268	2,240,809	1,174,535	29,060	404,393	293,947
2000	12,680,903	10,402,017	643,031	11,045,048	1,192,481	-920,499	8,932,068	2,455,023	1,293,812	30,935	409,924	300,557
2001	12,753,744	10,585,664	402,456	10,988,120	1,215,144	-956,318	8,816,658	2,487,301	1,449,785	30,767	414,520	297,666
2002	12,995,754	10,941,938	390,176	11,332,114	1,256,338	-993,258	9,082,518	2,337,507	1,575,729	31,057	418,448	293,692
2003	13,398,801	11,396,697	285,935	11,682,632	1,292,944	-1,039,267	9,350,421	2,417,946	1,630,434	31,530	424,953	296,949
2004	14,250,683	12,050,187	340,598	12,390,785	1,340,919	-1,079,548	9,970,318	2,531,864	1,748,501	33,123	430,229	301,335
2005	15,011,069	12,610,352	292,086	12,902,438	1,393,135	-1,154,514	10,354,789	2,793,380	1,862,900	34,358	436,898	307,901
2006	16,148,413	13,301,421	301,621	13,603,042	1,476,249	-1,219,607	10,907,186	3,228,141	2,013,086	36,233	445,685	316,801
2007	16,970,574	13,979,046	243,639	14,222,685	1,556,041	-1,288,165	11,378,479	3,407,544	2,184,551	37,534	452,138	324,498
2008	17,540,889	14,389,110	-43,634	14,345,476	1,618,946	-1,252,460	11,474,070	3,514,055	2,552,764	38,123	460,112	322,909
2009	17,084,413	13,687,273	5,743	13,693,016	1,573,437	-1,130,416	10,989,163	3,261,452	2,833,798	36,558	467,328	312,564
2010	17,693,447	14,039,628	41,189	14,080,817	1,589,355	-1,056,986	11,434,476	3,125,458	3,133,513	37,373	473,425	312,898
2011	18,718,091	14,518,441	57,893	14,576,334	1,456,059	-1,083,991	12,036,284	3,495,822	3,185,985	39,077	479,004	317,157
2012	19,636,899	15,169,412	146,800	15,316,212	1,514,020	-1,117,592	12,684,600	3,764,678	3,187,621	40,458	485,365	321,742
2013	20,308,642	15,589,618	616,737	16,206,355	1,770,036	-1,126,481	13,309,838	3,703,484	3,295,320	41,354	491,089	327,542
2014	21,308,792	16,277,263	517,865	16,795,128	1,855,461	-1,208,343	13,731,324	4,032,852	3,544,616	43,123	494,144	335,671
2015	22,491,855	17,206,803	566,939	17,773,742	1,974,427	-1,284,804	14,514,511	4,255,346	3,721,998	44,963	500,235	345,937
2016	22,999,429	17,478,469	505,517	17,983,986	2,032,397	-1,437,918	14,513,671	4,791,143	3,694,615	45,617	504,186	352,153
2017	23,768,193	17,904,099	613,870	18,517,969	2,079,254	-1,557,473	14,881,242	5,143,996	3,742,955	46,616	509,867	356,610
2018	24,622,698	18,332,446	576,342	18,908,788	2,104,596	-1,502,486	15,301,706	5,433,111	3,887,881	48,030	512,657	357,796
2019	26,109,414	19,286,495	620,189	19,906,684	2,189,803	-1,622,254	16,094,627	5,903,751	4,111,036	50,708	514,901	358,020
2020	27,940,617	19,788,696	453,026	20,241,722	2,278,696	-1,680,689	16,282,337	5,931,204	5,727,076	54,041	517,028	346,871
2021	29,786,050	21,092,494	507,621	21,600,115	2,400,314	-1,808,419	17,391,382	6,141,090	6,253,578	57,519	517,846	355,177

Personal Income and Employment by Area: Lima, OH

(Thousands of dollars, except as noted.)

Year	Personal income, total	Earnings by place of work			Less: Contributions for government social insurance	Plus: Adjustment for residence	Equals: Net earnings by place of residence	Plus: Dividends, interest, and rent	Plus: Personal current transfer receipts	Per capita personal income (dollars)	Population (persons)	Total employment
		Nonfarm	Farm	Total								
1970	439,385	419,832	4,748	424,580	28,588	-51,050	344,942	59,351	35,092	3,955	111,084	56,153
1971	465,872	433,323	4,889	438,212	30,076	-47,402	360,734	62,791	42,347	4,181	111,437	54,945
1972	489,289	452,316	6,580	458,896	33,227	-47,821	377,848	66,074	45,367	4,422	110,643	54,610
1973	554,243	523,367	9,359	532,726	44,576	-59,143	429,007	73,044	52,192	5,027	110,245	57,847
1974	607,835	571,175	10,743	581,918	50,375	-67,191	464,352	81,822	61,661	5,494	110,637	58,786
1975	647,153	592,884	8,751	601,635	50,985	-71,164	479,486	88,010	79,657	5,840	110,806	56,340
1976	699,455	642,001	10,327	652,328	56,239	-76,457	519,632	94,956	84,867	6,367	109,853	56,613
1977	775,298	733,388	6,671	740,059	64,248	-95,838	579,973	106,674	88,651	7,018	110,465	58,352
1978	861,705	837,741	6,315	844,056	76,299	-116,955	650,802	117,121	93,782	7,846	109,828	60,165
1979	953,492	931,402	7,214	938,616	88,075	-137,447	713,094	131,439	108,959	8,571	111,247	61,611
1980	1,034,998	954,363	7,039	961,402	88,646	-145,698	727,058	163,769	144,171	9,226	112,188	58,688
1981	1,098,158	980,401	-194	980,207	97,348	-146,869	735,990	200,889	161,279	9,829	111,726	57,444
1982	1,147,388	1,007,272	-1,951	1,005,321	101,638	-155,678	748,005	219,439	179,944	10,447	109,826	55,345
1983	1,223,736	1,080,158	-5,489	1,074,669	110,331	-169,124	795,214	235,444	193,078	11,234	108,936	55,927
1984	1,385,983	1,237,251	14,176	1,251,427	129,461	-199,519	922,447	265,217	198,319	12,641	109,642	58,993
1985	1,466,696	1,341,397	12,473	1,353,870	142,609	-222,020	989,241	273,412	204,043	13,382	109,601	61,057
1986	1,548,122	1,449,376	10,201	1,459,577	158,698	-246,519	1,054,360	281,631	212,131	14,105	109,755	62,105
1987	1,585,393	1,494,184	10,926	1,505,110	164,129	-250,705	1,090,276	281,175	213,942	14,397	110,123	62,506
1988	1,667,335	1,563,857	12,609	1,576,466	176,828	-258,948	1,140,690	294,753	231,892	15,087	110,518	64,316
1989	1,750,403	1,597,140	22,643	1,619,783	182,532	-261,467	1,175,784	326,731	247,888	15,874	110,270	65,527
1990	1,815,379	1,635,960	26,710	1,662,670	190,919	-265,352	1,206,399	332,341	276,639	16,527	109,841	65,107
1991	1,852,229	1,676,769	16,968	1,693,737	199,575	-269,672	1,224,490	331,839	295,900	16,851	109,916	64,909
1992	1,979,850	1,750,331	18,530	1,768,861	207,498	-263,603	1,297,760	340,737	341,353	17,959	110,242	63,879
1993	1,994,037	1,790,955	12,010	1,802,965	213,805	-273,608	1,315,552	344,317	334,168	18,085	110,262	64,648
1994	2,113,276	1,883,849	14,207	1,898,056	227,168	-285,339	1,385,549	372,297	355,430	19,188	110,138	65,381
1995	2,167,849	1,877,951	4,325	1,882,276	227,671	-263,976	1,390,629	402,144	375,076	19,736	109,841	66,147
1996	2,224,976	1,895,983	6,756	1,902,739	226,168	-259,872	1,416,699	422,463	385,814	20,306	109,573	66,212
1997	2,296,398	1,933,167	20,069	1,953,236	224,798	-269,304	1,459,134	442,080	395,184	21,039	109,150	66,563
1998	2,437,028	2,057,428	7,448	2,064,876	230,519	-287,615	1,546,742	480,050	410,236	22,441	108,599	67,726
1999	2,552,132	2,250,359	875	2,251,234	249,302	-350,157	1,651,775	476,051	424,306	23,589	108,192	71,158
2000	2,682,204	2,375,739	13,401	2,389,140	252,349	-379,848	1,756,943	478,544	446,717	24,701	108,589	72,973
2001	2,726,187	2,382,326	12,328	2,394,654	259,990	-369,227	1,765,437	475,825	484,925	25,121	108,523	69,825
2002	2,781,076	2,434,841	-2,090	2,432,751	261,682	-359,597	1,811,472	461,746	507,858	25,628	108,518	69,133
2003	2,863,193	2,508,788	3,641	2,512,429	272,397	-352,164	1,887,868	443,063	532,262	26,655	107,418	68,371
2004	2,933,385	2,605,735	19,221	2,624,956	289,405	-374,212	1,961,339	415,354	556,692	27,459	106,826	68,615
2005	3,008,218	2,655,186	12,819	2,668,005	299,329	-366,918	2,001,758	412,045	594,415	28,151	106,861	68,553
2006	3,161,205	2,736,630	14,500	2,751,130	307,081	-354,541	2,089,508	437,317	634,380	29,623	106,716	67,907
2007	3,318,961	2,772,376	14,487	2,786,863	310,142	-323,940	2,152,781	488,710	677,470	31,101	106,717	66,745
2008	3,409,679	2,744,274	14,733	2,759,007	311,433	-296,703	2,150,871	511,765	747,043	31,934	106,773	65,417
2009	3,419,058	2,744,411	20,182	2,764,593	312,192	-339,020	2,113,381	479,692	825,985	32,098	106,518	62,898
2010	3,518,436	2,812,047	32,733	2,844,780	312,278	-367,742	2,164,760	481,533	872,143	33,086	106,342	62,432
2011	3,644,189	2,881,227	47,431	2,928,658	290,059	-399,785	2,238,814	506,179	899,196	34,385	105,981	62,950
2012	3,751,296	2,949,246	27,851	2,977,097	298,528	-393,136	2,285,433	578,983	886,880	35,641	105,251	63,339
2013	3,736,101	3,008,671	45,253	3,053,924	330,996	-406,447	2,316,481	514,732	904,888	35,558	105,071	63,598
2014	3,882,218	3,071,742	20,995	3,092,737	335,425	-388,900	2,368,412	574,804	939,002	36,996	104,935	63,375
2015	3,997,983	3,123,109	-1,172	3,121,937	339,984	-352,227	2,429,726	582,909	985,348	38,368	104,201	63,572
2016	4,069,554	3,216,876	-23	3,216,853	359,228	-388,824	2,468,801	598,448	1,002,305	39,220	103,763	63,436
2017	4,191,659	3,340,571	9,986	3,350,557	381,098	-418,421	2,551,038	612,484	1,028,137	40,594	103,258	63,905
2018	4,350,939	3,437,619	16,015	3,453,634	386,562	-412,426	2,654,646	647,019	1,049,274	42,307	102,843	63,641
2019	4,473,356	3,458,670	4,915	3,463,585	393,857	-379,284	2,690,444	685,279	1,097,633	43,618	102,558	62,953
2020	4,828,783	3,520,267	25,432	3,545,699	404,812	-424,934	2,715,953	683,959	1,428,871	47,314	102,059	61,135
2021	5,119,426	3,684,967	46,842	3,731,809	415,604	-436,636	2,879,569	697,864	1,541,993	50,353	101,670	62,103

Personal Income and Employment by Area: Lincoln, NE

(Thousands of dollars, except as noted.)

Year	Personal income, total	Earnings by place of work			Less: Contributions for government social insurance	Plus: Adjustment for residence	Equals: Net earnings by place of residence	Plus: Dividends, interest, and rent	Plus: Personal current transfer receipts	Per capita personal income (dollars)	Population (persons)	Total employment
		Nonfarm	Farm	Total								
1970	761,119	608,314	15,182	623,496	40,790	-6,171	576,535	129,698	54,886	4,153	183,265	94,866
1971	834,654	664,518	18,341	682,859	45,895	-7,420	629,544	142,287	62,823	4,446	187,741	98,445
1972	918,081	733,434	19,078	752,512	52,849	-8,983	690,680	157,073	70,328	4,705	195,133	102,842
1973	1,035,680	824,266	30,980	855,246	69,063	-11,138	775,045	176,253	84,382	5,280	196,134	107,748
1974	1,148,954	925,745	21,704	947,449	81,359	-14,011	852,079	200,984	95,891	5,756	199,608	111,765
1975	1,303,224	1,018,528	45,582	1,064,110	87,628	-16,032	960,450	223,085	119,689	6,552	198,905	112,328
1976	1,421,987	1,151,154	19,752	1,170,906	100,169	-18,503	1,052,234	241,615	128,138	7,145	199,025	116,047
1977	1,554,224	1,264,079	14,912	1,278,991	110,723	-19,926	1,148,342	270,128	135,754	7,743	200,719	119,912
1978	1,768,411	1,415,813	55,099	1,470,912	128,277	-23,080	1,319,555	297,763	151,093	8,711	203,010	123,341
1979	1,931,967	1,570,522	26,032	1,596,554	147,910	-26,869	1,421,775	341,196	168,996	9,453	204,382	127,203
1980	2,095,217	1,689,474	-10,358	1,679,116	158,154	-29,388	1,491,574	404,293	199,350	10,007	209,378	127,424
1981	2,368,019	1,830,003	23,553	1,853,556	184,336	-33,852	1,635,368	500,104	232,547	11,185	211,713	125,565
1982	2,573,068	1,908,397	44,769	1,953,166	196,722	-35,309	1,721,135	596,349	255,584	12,089	212,839	123,845
1983	2,687,403	2,025,454	18,131	2,043,585	209,412	-38,474	1,795,699	614,565	277,139	12,546	214,209	124,320
1984	2,924,125	2,223,999	22,541	2,246,540	236,591	-43,916	1,966,033	671,779	286,313	13,523	216,231	128,322
1985	3,123,414	2,375,135	36,630	2,411,765	259,391	-46,389	2,105,985	705,601	311,828	14,351	217,648	132,780
1986	3,261,137	2,504,488	45,520	2,550,008	283,776	-51,466	2,214,766	722,603	323,768	14,896	218,934	134,997
1987	3,451,673	2,703,200	41,939	2,745,139	306,228	-57,545	2,381,366	736,620	333,687	15,660	220,410	140,194
1988	3,724,621	2,900,111	61,759	2,961,870	343,753	-62,871	2,555,246	814,992	354,383	16,693	223,119	146,113
1989	3,991,872	3,121,506	59,010	3,180,516	368,854	-69,400	2,742,262	863,997	385,613	17,630	226,420	149,477
1990	4,302,681	3,379,562	63,057	3,442,619	412,491	-77,428	2,952,700	929,241	420,740	18,696	230,144	155,589
1991	4,513,709	3,547,152	45,534	3,592,686	434,956	-83,056	3,074,674	982,679	456,356	19,337	233,419	156,858
1992	4,836,798	3,802,221	59,416	3,861,637	456,948	-92,375	3,312,314	1,025,903	498,581	20,337	237,827	158,269
1993	5,081,565	4,029,718	31,059	4,060,777	484,027	-102,357	3,474,393	1,067,686	539,486	20,931	242,779	162,253
1994	5,480,020	4,314,357	58,159	4,372,516	520,710	-112,431	3,739,375	1,180,727	559,918	22,283	245,933	169,247
1995	5,879,906	4,613,025	17,899	4,630,924	546,447	-119,231	3,965,246	1,312,771	601,889	23,473	250,498	172,577
1996	6,286,324	4,851,905	94,383	4,946,288	577,489	-128,618	4,240,181	1,400,887	645,256	24,759	253,904	177,454
1997	6,575,773	5,122,993	53,369	5,176,362	615,519	-139,184	4,421,659	1,484,973	669,141	25,547	257,404	180,195
1998	7,142,044	5,579,685	54,298	5,633,983	663,623	-157,927	4,812,433	1,595,174	734,437	27,362	261,021	184,836
1999	7,531,960	5,927,873	47,648	5,975,521	698,063	-170,234	5,107,224	1,652,248	772,488	28,543	263,880	189,577
2000	8,192,390	6,436,624	43,775	6,480,399	741,392	-186,868	5,552,139	1,821,085	819,166	30,564	268,042	193,410
2001	8,384,109	6,681,116	45,303	6,726,419	767,732	-202,813	5,755,874	1,709,727	918,508	30,911	271,237	196,992
2002	8,744,096	7,055,273	14,274	7,069,547	805,752	-213,177	6,050,618	1,700,661	992,817	31,800	274,972	198,177
2003	9,121,689	7,249,100	61,202	7,310,302	831,581	-221,382	6,257,339	1,817,675	1,046,675	32,672	279,194	200,972
2004	9,486,088	7,574,216	87,739	7,661,955	865,452	-220,550	6,575,953	1,802,308	1,107,827	33,666	281,768	203,838
2005	9,865,876	7,887,230	57,738	7,944,968	911,890	-229,699	6,803,379	1,879,456	1,183,041	34,560	285,469	206,855
2006	10,422,642	8,247,573	28,707	8,276,280	970,086	-227,710	7,078,484	2,081,079	1,263,079	36,072	288,940	209,583
2007	11,016,241	8,569,546	68,362	8,637,908	1,002,094	-210,286	7,425,528	2,241,082	1,349,631	37,662	292,502	213,477
2008	11,572,414	8,767,611	99,012	8,866,623	1,023,671	-220,792	7,622,160	2,413,959	1,536,295	39,062	296,258	212,954
2009	11,374,963	8,761,289	88,005	8,849,294	1,019,574	-233,048	7,596,672	2,165,168	1,613,123	37,963	299,633	209,775
2010	11,781,973	9,018,280	92,296	9,110,576	1,056,439	-258,511	7,795,626	2,233,257	1,753,090	38,888	302,975	208,789
2011	12,450,082	9,228,795	183,203	9,411,998	958,711	-307,597	8,145,690	2,515,320	1,789,072	40,598	306,670	210,610
2012	13,191,966	9,837,686	94,030	9,931,716	989,942	-341,735	8,600,039	2,775,200	1,816,727	42,498	310,414	215,151
2013	13,274,809	10,059,502	144,743	10,204,245	1,152,330	-369,782	8,682,133	2,738,267	1,854,409	42,246	314,229	218,788
2014	13,934,194	10,595,474	90,182	10,685,656	1,206,231	-386,563	9,092,862	2,894,129	1,947,203	43,419	320,926	222,010
2015	14,662,117	11,084,468	79,783	11,164,251	1,258,282	-400,993	9,504,976	3,096,693	2,060,448	45,155	324,704	226,752
2016	14,962,042	11,356,595	37,709	11,394,304	1,303,628	-399,987	9,690,689	3,107,737	2,163,616	45,428	329,359	229,362
2017	15,673,844	11,832,414	45,894	11,878,308	1,365,186	-434,665	10,078,457	3,324,600	2,270,787	47,056	333,088	230,630
2018	16,451,904	12,426,369	47,061	12,473,430	1,430,929	-473,247	10,569,254	3,466,704	2,415,946	48,975	335,926	235,630
2019	17,263,841	12,737,323	65,305	12,802,628	1,490,880	-503,018	10,808,730	3,888,057	2,567,054	51,034	338,279	236,426
2020	18,359,712	12,999,943	103,633	13,103,576	1,554,638	-470,254	11,078,684	3,962,407	3,318,621	53,917	340,515	230,924
2021	19,462,058	13,639,698	142,421	13,782,119	1,610,879	-523,831	11,647,409	4,073,383	3,741,266	56,887	342,117	234,605

Personal Income and Employment by Area: Little Rock-North Little Rock-Conway, AR

(Thousands of dollars, except as noted.)

Year	Personal income, total	Earnings by place of work			Less: Contributions for government social insurance	Plus: Adjustment for residence	Equals: Net earnings by place of residence	Plus: Dividends, interest, and rent	Plus: Personal current transfer receipts	Per capita personal income (dollars)	Population (persons)	Total employment
		Nonfarm	Farm	Total								
1970	1,450,105	1,195,466	28,284	1,223,750	85,462	-22,602	1,115,686	212,105	122,314	3,635	398,923	189,395
1971	1,637,474	1,351,485	29,033	1,380,518	99,363	-27,327	1,253,828	238,788	144,858	3,989	410,511	196,544
1972	1,855,105	1,542,392	36,863	1,579,255	119,038	-29,083	1,431,134	261,792	162,179	4,397	421,948	209,206
1973	2,127,721	1,751,201	68,368	1,819,569	155,333	-35,216	1,629,020	295,990	202,711	4,901	434,101	221,631
1974	2,415,090	1,963,866	72,021	2,035,887	180,073	-35,516	1,820,298	346,681	248,111	5,364	450,208	229,229
1975	2,686,035	2,144,029	53,257	2,197,286	192,768	-35,115	1,969,403	396,535	320,097	5,906	454,800	226,577
1976	2,986,826	2,424,519	40,363	2,464,882	221,591	-36,549	2,206,742	429,553	350,531	6,451	463,036	234,682
1977	3,296,427	2,702,565	41,072	2,743,637	249,469	-37,769	2,456,399	473,904	366,124	7,000	470,916	243,509
1978	3,760,823	3,065,938	70,406	3,136,344	290,242	-36,380	2,809,722	544,482	406,619	7,845	479,418	254,644
1979	4,186,018	3,405,122	49,201	3,454,323	334,368	-14,005	3,105,950	614,411	465,657	8,623	485,427	260,249
1980	4,659,808	3,718,187	28,470	3,746,657	364,058	-20,345	3,362,254	742,492	555,062	9,400	495,743	259,470
1981	5,129,744	4,005,442	38,154	4,043,596	423,958	-34,267	3,585,371	914,702	629,671	10,291	498,489	257,023
1982	5,490,849	4,248,231	21,921	4,270,152	457,671	-47,239	3,765,242	1,040,629	684,978	10,953	501,306	256,891
1983	5,923,152	4,626,428	18,750	4,645,178	504,405	-54,245	4,086,528	1,089,248	747,376	11,724	505,195	264,519
1984	6,479,257	5,064,971	35,275	5,100,246	567,820	-60,883	4,471,543	1,222,768	784,946	12,688	510,658	275,936
1985	7,004,721	5,492,804	35,424	5,528,228	623,358	-72,796	4,832,074	1,332,626	840,021	13,567	516,324	284,898
1986	7,454,320	5,854,297	26,615	5,880,912	669,379	-72,437	5,139,096	1,420,197	895,027	14,277	522,119	289,743
1987	7,761,114	6,149,972	45,518	6,195,490	700,160	-87,015	5,408,315	1,426,652	926,147	14,710	527,622	295,390
1988	8,218,799	6,494,406	75,779	6,570,185	770,332	-94,651	5,705,202	1,538,431	975,166	15,544	528,733	304,689
1989	8,878,036	6,900,422	63,311	6,963,733	818,996	-105,848	6,038,889	1,746,313	1,092,834	16,674	532,436	312,014
1990	9,435,305	7,417,202	50,965	7,468,167	917,204	-122,068	6,428,895	1,819,351	1,187,059	17,589	536,444	317,357
1991	10,012,498	7,934,088	49,661	7,983,749	980,039	-148,948	6,854,762	1,832,357	1,325,379	18,442	542,913	324,532
1992	10,859,711	8,656,144	64,548	8,720,692	1,060,472	-173,689	7,486,531	1,908,491	1,464,689	19,662	552,311	331,121
1993	11,386,531	9,096,830	57,578	9,154,408	1,111,552	-194,986	7,847,870	1,988,771	1,549,890	20,265	561,887	341,004
1994	12,005,290	9,606,281	63,673	9,669,954	1,191,713	-221,502	8,256,739	2,124,406	1,624,145	21,103	568,889	347,270
1995	12,797,950	10,202,122	59,899	10,262,021	1,260,003	-252,130	8,749,888	2,288,683	1,759,379	22,205	576,345	361,633
1996	13,625,516	10,773,247	83,088	10,856,335	1,319,934	-281,281	9,255,120	2,453,610	1,916,786	23,297	584,861	370,043
1997	14,280,904	11,358,757	73,912	11,432,669	1,388,622	-310,118	9,733,929	2,572,610	1,974,365	24,135	591,707	376,359
1998	15,272,878	12,223,870	60,985	12,284,855	1,476,276	-347,229	10,461,350	2,800,236	2,011,292	25,547	597,826	382,432
1999	15,911,150	12,838,448	66,956	12,905,404	1,542,730	-383,706	10,978,968	2,828,520	2,103,662	26,287	605,291	387,438
2000	16,815,108	13,541,813	71,602	13,613,415	1,612,187	-418,570	11,582,658	2,946,397	2,286,053	27,462	612,313	392,022
2001	17,849,485	14,445,131	76,119	14,521,250	1,680,385	-465,424	12,375,441	2,927,960	2,546,084	28,877	618,126	395,201
2002	18,435,819	14,881,788	50,667	14,932,455	1,718,383	-487,639	12,726,433	2,957,802	2,751,584	29,537	624,166	393,400
2003	19,510,154	15,707,138	104,485	15,811,623	1,799,892	-519,191	13,492,540	3,114,094	2,903,520	30,918	631,032	397,411
2004	20,578,034	16,547,239	108,773	16,656,012	1,878,183	-555,657	14,222,172	3,228,975	3,126,887	32,175	639,558	403,985
2005	22,087,815	17,564,439	56,773	17,621,212	1,976,408	-580,833	15,063,971	3,643,008	3,380,836	34,045	648,784	412,763
2006	23,367,423	18,306,852	66,688	18,373,540	2,117,583	-631,790	15,624,167	4,056,551	3,686,705	35,313	661,719	423,919
2007	25,028,619	19,493,198	77,627	19,570,825	2,249,437	-769,468	16,551,920	4,453,793	4,022,906	37,276	671,441	432,635
2008	25,672,890	19,187,355	61,938	19,249,293	2,306,297	-698,290	16,244,706	4,900,973	4,527,211	37,650	681,888	433,707
2009	25,639,611	19,303,231	39,321	19,342,552	2,330,859	-649,035	16,362,658	4,375,462	4,901,491	37,057	691,903	426,980
2010	26,311,436	19,415,687	25,888	19,441,575	2,346,504	-612,094	16,482,977	4,494,783	5,333,676	37,463	702,326	427,388
2011	27,567,837	19,955,858	15,403	19,971,261	2,183,635	-644,412	17,143,214	4,947,217	5,477,406	38,784	710,813	435,010
2012	29,394,300	20,943,259	34,414	20,977,673	2,236,908	-592,594	18,148,171	5,659,513	5,586,616	40,944	717,916	435,672
2013	29,074,211	21,242,099	100,118	21,342,217	2,549,866	-672,782	18,119,569	5,232,161	5,722,481	40,184	723,532	438,755
2014	30,350,009	21,918,983	56,833	21,975,816	2,641,004	-690,959	18,643,853	5,591,225	6,114,931	41,605	729,485	441,889
2015	31,425,262	22,497,016	23,994	22,521,010	2,725,348	-736,240	19,059,422	5,942,731	6,423,109	42,906	732,417	448,764
2016	32,128,942	22,903,648	13,308	22,916,956	2,746,121	-743,759	19,427,076	6,028,348	6,673,518	43,674	735,662	453,730
2017	32,764,109	23,332,840	33,311	23,366,151	2,812,827	-802,682	19,750,642	6,190,134	6,823,333	44,303	739,545	458,932
2018	33,577,292	23,951,677	17,592	23,969,269	2,898,401	-841,519	20,229,349	6,273,572	7,074,371	45,234	742,305	463,888
2019	35,132,804	24,876,117	7,795	24,883,912	3,019,774	-843,001	21,021,137	6,615,490	7,496,177	47,177	744,708	463,629
2020	37,606,546	25,713,006	45,164	25,758,170	3,161,743	-810,701	21,785,726	6,477,382	9,343,438	50,247	748,434	453,882
2021	39,918,210	27,316,458	44,322	27,360,780	3,289,686	-871,102	23,199,992	6,550,958	10,167,260	53,158	750,936	464,951

Personal Income and Employment by Area: Logan, UT-ID

(Thousands of dollars, except as noted.)

Year	Personal income, total	Earnings by place of work			Less: Contributions for government social insurance	Plus: Adjustment for residence	Equals: Net earnings by place of residence	Plus: Dividends, interest, and rent	Plus: Personal current transfer receipts	Per capita personal income (dollars)	Population (persons)	Total employment
		Nonfarm	Farm	Total								
1970	142,719	86,078	14,685	100,763	5,819	10,307	105,251	24,791	12,677	2,865	49,811	19,220
1971	159,132	94,999	15,313	110,312	6,628	11,930	115,614	28,571	14,947	3,133	50,796	19,811
1972	180,672	108,052	18,233	126,285	7,903	13,271	131,653	32,203	16,816	3,416	52,893	20,828
1973	202,208	122,470	21,084	143,554	10,481	13,859	146,932	35,522	19,754	3,716	54,413	22,111
1974	227,739	137,895	23,551	161,446	12,370	15,826	164,902	40,522	22,315	4,082	55,792	23,183
1975	252,002	156,895	17,379	174,274	13,729	18,489	179,034	45,642	27,326	4,384	57,480	23,664
1976	289,615	186,124	17,899	204,023	16,419	20,959	208,563	50,696	30,356	4,911	58,974	25,332
1977	318,071	207,964	13,463	221,427	18,121	24,211	227,517	57,793	32,761	5,228	60,841	26,351
1978	363,517	239,975	14,333	254,308	21,308	28,234	261,234	66,372	35,911	5,823	62,424	27,771
1979	412,925	275,882	11,630	287,512	25,753	33,639	295,398	76,626	40,901	6,439	64,124	29,228
1980	467,845	304,979	12,162	317,141	29,480	39,020	326,681	92,695	48,469	7,011	66,734	30,090
1981	517,200	331,033	7,358	338,391	34,407	44,931	348,915	110,204	58,081	7,469	69,244	29,973
1982	556,313	340,354	11,617	351,971	35,436	49,524	366,059	126,075	64,179	7,783	71,482	29,880
1983	608,451	376,033	9,287	385,320	38,861	54,243	400,702	138,642	69,107	8,265	73,620	30,808
1984	667,326	413,702	12,819	426,521	43,782	59,899	442,638	151,118	73,570	8,925	74,772	31,754
1985	716,586	440,197	15,646	455,843	47,165	67,155	475,833	160,483	80,270	9,521	75,261	32,227
1986	777,944	485,805	21,073	506,878	52,725	71,217	525,370	169,448	83,126	10,283	75,651	33,320
1987	846,227	522,209	33,077	555,286	56,726	78,944	577,504	177,152	91,571	11,068	76,454	34,995
1988	897,416	567,102	34,688	601,790	65,303	83,469	619,956	183,173	94,287	11,558	77,643	36,896
1989	985,686	625,543	40,451	665,994	73,152	87,105	679,947	200,319	105,420	12,496	78,881	39,229
1990	1,049,954	684,099	45,831	729,930	81,411	89,104	737,623	197,489	114,842	13,171	79,719	40,769
1991	1,118,403	743,145	42,607	785,752	89,444	91,446	787,754	205,630	125,019	13,579	82,362	41,907
1992	1,212,930	813,171	50,395	863,566	96,617	96,825	863,774	208,967	140,189	14,220	85,299	42,939
1993	1,312,112	884,289	51,483	935,772	105,471	98,462	928,763	230,158	153,191	14,881	88,175	44,894
1994	1,396,025	970,935	44,482	1,015,417	116,911	99,594	998,100	241,895	156,030	15,307	91,202	48,049
1995	1,490,544	1,022,994	39,471	1,062,465	123,620	104,255	1,043,100	275,362	172,082	15,824	94,198	50,269
1996	1,604,257	1,092,675	47,950	1,140,625	128,601	108,655	1,120,679	303,879	179,699	16,572	96,807	52,531
1997	1,730,781	1,185,898	46,597	1,232,495	137,296	116,770	1,211,969	332,724	186,088	17,523	98,774	54,389
1998	1,839,910	1,250,095	65,862	1,315,957	145,350	125,130	1,295,737	348,900	195,273	18,232	100,916	55,955
1999	1,906,909	1,313,066	64,843	1,377,909	152,513	122,288	1,347,684	351,506	207,719	18,781	101,532	57,125
2000	1,981,337	1,355,812	43,170	1,398,982	157,431	131,273	1,372,824	381,967	226,546	19,197	103,211	58,582
2001	2,135,963	1,453,528	68,348	1,521,876	167,909	128,528	1,482,495	402,273	251,195	20,480	104,294	59,183
2002	2,188,265	1,541,845	35,024	1,576,869	177,743	123,920	1,523,046	394,347	270,872	20,417	107,180	60,144
2003	2,336,324	1,676,378	34,787	1,711,165	193,853	121,265	1,638,577	412,647	285,100	21,470	108,819	62,064
2004	2,530,219	1,802,585	59,977	1,862,562	211,458	122,539	1,773,643	448,817	307,759	22,833	110,813	64,377
2005	2,610,483	1,864,540	38,242	1,902,782	220,531	130,576	1,812,827	464,021	333,635	23,188	112,580	65,734
2006	2,764,692	1,988,335	23,506	2,011,841	232,571	141,642	1,920,912	482,435	361,345	24,397	113,321	68,179
2007	3,013,799	2,118,745	46,521	2,165,266	249,013	146,207	2,062,460	551,686	399,653	26,003	115,901	71,644
2008	3,330,027	2,290,621	51,542	2,342,163	266,422	148,930	2,224,671	633,498	471,858	27,891	119,394	72,983
2009	3,336,015	2,311,351	28,659	2,340,010	265,798	140,800	2,215,012	604,409	516,594	27,111	123,048	71,800
2010	3,552,246	2,464,090	48,922	2,513,012	279,986	134,641	2,367,667	608,764	575,815	28,154	126,170	71,850
2011	3,805,517	2,605,352	65,825	2,671,177	260,617	135,864	2,546,424	667,918	591,175	29,821	127,613	73,553
2012	3,989,223	2,653,354	65,847	2,719,201	260,010	149,923	2,609,114	798,885	581,224	30,990	128,726	74,294
2013	4,009,918	2,747,810	85,575	2,833,385	306,775	171,811	2,698,421	717,753	593,744	30,874	129,879	75,291
2014	4,244,716	2,845,558	95,962	2,941,520	322,654	182,777	2,801,643	810,744	632,329	32,100	132,234	77,432
2015	4,570,431	3,021,819	96,857	3,118,676	332,544	193,412	2,979,544	911,688	679,199	33,993	134,451	79,605
2016	4,774,405	3,235,195	64,685	3,299,880	351,607	202,491	3,150,764	910,279	713,362	34,658	137,759	81,220
2017	5,092,113	3,473,108	61,273	3,534,381	374,002	214,531	3,374,910	977,452	739,751	36,271	140,390	83,593
2018	5,476,474	3,739,835	60,869	3,800,704	390,666	236,494	3,646,532	1,041,701	788,241	38,264	143,123	85,707
2019	5,914,132	4,037,586	70,185	4,107,771	415,537	254,230	3,946,464	1,113,142	854,526	40,666	145,431	87,481
2020	6,346,760	4,247,993	77,339	4,325,332	454,189	256,359	4,127,502	1,139,345	1,079,913	42,943	147,796	90,550
2021	7,133,139	4,787,968	69,822	4,857,790	510,257	283,823	4,631,356	1,180,831	1,320,952	46,903	152,083	94,694

Personal Income and Employment by Area: Longview, TX

(Thousands of dollars, except as noted.)

Year	Personal income, total	Earnings by place of work			Less: Contributions for government social insurance	Plus: Adjustment for residence	Equals: Net earnings by place of residence	Plus: Dividends, interest, and rent	Plus: Personal current transfer receipts	Per capita personal income (dollars)	Population (persons)	Total employment
		Nonfarm	Farm	Total								
1970	432,135	308,328	3,621	311,949	19,889	24,579	316,639	66,311	49,185	3,297	131,055	53,026
1971	473,200	340,009	2,366	342,375	22,565	25,076	344,886	72,336	55,978	3,541	133,616	54,346
1972	526,660	376,422	7,382	383,804	26,067	27,418	385,155	79,211	62,294	3,825	137,697	56,603
1973	596,152	426,223	12,755	438,978	34,476	28,926	433,428	89,010	73,714	4,254	140,153	59,291
1974	694,824	501,511	12,161	513,672	41,875	30,466	502,263	105,193	87,368	4,857	143,059	62,300
1975	795,160	568,982	3,785	572,767	46,219	35,547	562,095	125,425	107,640	5,407	147,050	64,378
1976	922,874	685,315	4,128	689,443	56,627	34,208	667,024	137,912	117,938	6,143	150,221	68,830
1977	1,025,983	762,977	2,988	765,965	63,446	40,004	742,523	156,505	126,955	6,603	155,386	71,742
1978	1,187,253	890,733	5,108	895,841	75,591	45,900	866,150	180,046	141,057	7,429	159,818	76,038
1979	1,358,644	1,035,803	4,321	1,040,124	92,299	43,777	991,602	207,229	159,813	8,199	165,709	79,930
1980	1,570,275	1,171,201	-372	1,170,829	105,502	51,300	1,116,627	267,433	186,215	9,199	170,696	82,526
1981	1,867,981	1,388,593	797	1,389,390	135,515	53,727	1,307,602	346,788	213,591	10,668	175,096	89,406
1982	2,081,883	1,480,783	12,637	1,493,420	148,512	52,525	1,397,433	434,644	249,806	11,308	184,111	91,268
1983	2,161,571	1,490,039	4,438	1,494,477	147,543	40,314	1,387,248	491,439	282,884	11,556	187,045	88,609
1984	2,311,503	1,584,937	5,936	1,590,873	160,976	53,320	1,483,217	534,573	293,713	12,401	186,400	90,541
1985	2,463,271	1,651,178	4,222	1,655,400	169,884	67,090	1,552,606	600,221	310,444	13,284	185,436	91,871
1986	2,481,459	1,643,533	4,911	1,648,444	167,096	58,607	1,539,955	599,374	342,130	13,493	183,911	88,573
1987	2,476,045	1,650,892	-138	1,650,754	165,730	61,546	1,546,570	572,551	356,924	13,624	181,744	91,065
1988	2,614,944	1,759,714	200	1,759,914	183,535	66,355	1,642,734	601,851	370,359	14,475	180,657	92,809
1989	2,771,835	1,804,317	13,548	1,817,865	190,398	68,022	1,695,489	677,017	399,329	15,459	179,308	91,708
1990	2,917,207	1,932,355	16,475	1,948,830	199,402	79,128	1,828,556	648,581	440,070	16,188	180,206	94,053
1991	3,037,707	2,022,799	18,908	2,041,707	214,382	77,478	1,904,803	650,826	482,078	16,640	182,550	95,739
1992	3,242,022	2,181,380	28,511	2,209,891	228,364	63,371	2,044,898	642,157	554,967	17,643	183,757	96,484
1993	3,318,827	2,216,722	25,190	2,241,912	232,014	83,765	2,093,663	633,500	591,664	17,942	184,979	98,115
1994	3,479,568	2,348,524	23,536	2,372,060	248,598	58,504	2,181,966	669,447	628,155	18,683	186,238	100,672
1995	3,678,091	2,449,490	11,758	2,461,248	261,970	68,253	2,267,531	728,398	682,162	19,497	188,646	102,590
1996	3,913,247	2,632,141	10,242	2,642,383	277,748	68,560	2,433,195	757,394	722,658	20,536	190,556	105,595
1997	4,168,805	2,866,432	20,789	2,887,221	298,681	42,766	2,631,306	781,153	756,346	21,697	192,139	109,323
1998	5,629,978	3,913,548	26,650	3,940,198	404,423	82,949	3,618,724	1,023,834	987,420	22,094	254,823	140,025
1999	5,803,157	4,031,555	42,491	4,074,046	414,217	89,532	3,749,361	1,053,789	1,000,007	22,654	256,162	140,452
2000	6,231,034	4,291,395	31,814	4,323,209	432,635	103,191	3,993,765	1,188,071	1,049,198	24,325	256,153	143,195
2001	6,571,442	4,497,331	49,045	4,546,376	454,452	93,669	4,185,593	1,242,754	1,143,095	25,507	257,630	143,402
2002	6,693,058	4,577,463	54,394	4,631,857	461,344	78,182	4,248,695	1,200,249	1,244,114	25,761	259,812	142,651
2003	7,010,931	4,782,901	57,250	4,840,151	490,799	61,882	4,411,234	1,285,895	1,313,802	26,804	261,565	143,488
2004	7,228,900	4,991,309	49,735	5,041,044	517,070	55,146	4,579,120	1,264,982	1,384,798	27,402	263,814	144,629
2005	7,894,788	5,513,599	36,298	5,549,897	566,021	31,983	5,015,859	1,378,681	1,500,248	29,694	265,873	149,152
2006	8,771,770	6,270,644	17,040	6,287,684	617,516	-11,768	5,658,400	1,522,819	1,590,551	32,580	269,236	153,906
2007	9,311,270	6,581,183	18,265	6,599,448	665,412	-57,759	5,876,277	1,712,637	1,722,356	34,299	271,474	160,757
2008	10,743,126	7,559,513	-9,843	7,549,670	725,170	-124,333	6,700,167	2,128,475	1,914,484	39,185	274,165	165,638
2009	10,040,855	6,888,968	-12,391	6,876,577	705,237	-152,677	6,018,663	1,932,341	2,089,851	36,078	278,306	161,784
2010	10,460,137	7,405,458	4,594	7,410,052	756,731	-184,437	6,468,884	1,726,994	2,264,259	37,292	280,493	163,902
2011	11,459,417	7,951,845	-3,396	7,948,449	720,684	-245,724	6,982,041	2,163,519	2,313,857	40,573	282,441	166,676
2012	11,633,043	8,417,363	21,635	8,438,998	769,118	-322,117	7,347,763	1,983,793	2,301,487	41,094	283,083	172,032
2013	11,563,813	8,512,847	46,698	8,559,545	885,922	-357,478	7,316,145	1,875,859	2,371,809	40,914	282,638	174,027
2014	12,145,567	8,810,068	43,521	8,853,589	905,864	-352,767	7,594,958	2,083,822	2,466,787	42,929	282,920	175,411
2015	11,704,361	8,260,055	60,601	8,320,656	882,668	-330,272	7,107,716	1,983,440	2,613,205	41,300	283,400	174,384
2016	11,263,595	7,715,691	9,619	7,725,310	853,549	-272,236	6,599,525	1,922,006	2,742,064	39,763	283,267	171,379
2017	11,489,935	7,770,131	8,714	7,778,845	878,236	-269,955	6,630,654	2,074,711	2,784,570	40,444	284,096	170,232
2018	12,056,162	8,239,981	15,864	8,255,845	922,628	-293,726	7,039,491	2,112,998	2,903,673	42,345	284,711	172,803
2019	12,595,244	8,578,197	-1,983	8,576,214	947,297	-321,411	7,307,506	2,260,600	3,027,138	44,068	285,815	173,426
2020	13,133,143	8,236,532	-843	8,235,689	910,381	-244,769	7,080,539	2,208,206	3,844,398	45,896	286,153	168,669
2021	14,067,567	8,529,395	15,100	8,544,495	939,960	-215,396	7,389,139	2,301,505	4,376,923	48,868	287,868	170,456

Personal Income and Employment by Area: Longview, WA

(Thousands of dollars, except as noted.)

Year	Personal income, total	Earnings by place of work			Less: Contributions for government social insurance	Plus: Adjustment for residence	Equals: Net earnings by place of residence	Plus: Dividends, interest, and rent	Plus: Personal current transfer receipts	Per capita personal income (dollars)	Population (persons)	Total employment
		Nonfarm	Farm	Total								
1970	274,017	243,870	2,108	245,978	22,330	-12,156	211,492	35,172	27,353	3,983	68,799	29,467
1971	285,111	247,004	2,301	249,305	23,414	-11,683	214,208	38,153	32,750	4,083	69,830	28,695
1972	322,011	286,469	3,030	289,499	28,573	-14,451	246,475	41,290	34,246	4,660	69,102	30,465
1973	364,830	325,522	6,572	332,094	37,278	-17,067	277,749	47,421	39,660	5,126	71,174	32,414
1974	415,761	370,547	6,439	376,986	43,530	-21,077	312,379	56,157	47,225	5,774	72,006	33,292
1975	476,003	422,291	5,023	427,314	48,366	-24,976	353,972	63,974	58,057	6,394	74,445	34,143
1976	538,891	498,857	5,355	504,212	58,514	-39,452	406,246	69,345	63,300	7,249	74,340	35,416
1977	579,382	529,984	3,537	533,521	61,768	-39,331	432,422	77,622	69,338	7,760	74,659	35,411
1978	641,679	581,592	6,920	588,512	69,021	-42,967	476,524	88,945	76,210	8,495	75,532	35,985
1979	715,480	639,634	8,125	647,759	77,342	-47,517	522,900	103,283	89,297	9,159	78,118	36,487
1980	801,254	706,760	4,568	711,328	85,927	-58,814	566,587	123,681	110,986	10,066	79,601	37,129
1981	855,922	731,944	6,468	738,412	95,066	-56,299	587,047	147,122	121,753	10,745	79,657	36,029
1982	877,213	706,263	7,424	713,687	93,703	-49,030	570,954	165,096	141,163	11,103	79,006	34,093
1983	947,460	758,964	7,525	766,489	102,389	-53,278	610,822	184,686	151,952	12,007	78,908	34,630
1984	999,166	795,732	7,438	803,170	111,335	-49,979	641,856	197,453	159,857	12,626	79,138	35,602
1985	1,020,930	788,948	8,431	797,379	110,318	-43,725	643,336	208,127	169,467	12,984	78,627	35,058
1986	1,063,558	817,574	8,571	826,145	114,439	-40,562	671,144	215,333	177,081	13,700	77,632	35,534
1987	1,110,951	872,300	5,495	877,795	121,803	-43,108	712,884	213,377	184,690	14,165	78,428	37,670
1988	1,197,856	955,100	6,574	961,674	136,437	-43,348	781,889	226,639	189,328	15,061	79,531	39,451
1989	1,312,840	1,026,077	9,732	1,035,809	145,867	-43,866	846,076	261,453	205,311	16,212	80,982	40,985
1990	1,410,879	1,118,843	10,582	1,129,425	161,250	-44,735	923,440	261,613	225,826	17,106	82,478	42,731
1991	1,530,092	1,210,750	12,040	1,222,790	176,574	-56,409	989,807	282,082	258,203	18,171	84,207	43,637
1992	1,574,445	1,204,947	13,060	1,218,007	172,426	-41,090	1,004,491	285,103	284,851	18,454	85,316	42,176
1993	1,640,894	1,251,714	13,214	1,264,928	181,554	-43,207	1,040,167	289,725	311,002	18,969	86,506	42,678
1994	1,724,984	1,328,882	11,345	1,340,227	192,804	-54,152	1,093,271	303,729	327,984	19,649	87,791	44,279
1995	1,795,948	1,372,206	10,264	1,382,470	198,976	-52,115	1,131,379	319,435	345,134	20,115	89,284	45,260
1996	1,869,179	1,411,803	8,959	1,420,762	197,846	-47,190	1,175,726	341,377	352,076	20,694	90,325	46,179
1997	1,941,944	1,438,446	7,117	1,445,563	192,889	-40,751	1,211,923	365,224	364,797	21,254	91,367	46,315
1998	2,037,797	1,507,223	7,488	1,514,711	200,348	-38,655	1,275,708	375,246	386,843	22,078	92,301	46,458
1999	2,118,611	1,589,674	7,662	1,597,336	205,288	-42,231	1,349,817	358,443	410,351	22,825	92,820	47,768
2000	2,206,449	1,645,205	4,851	1,650,056	218,063	-38,015	1,393,978	378,506	433,965	23,729	92,984	48,330
2001	2,326,477	1,691,118	4,953	1,696,071	226,888	-21,765	1,447,418	385,546	493,513	24,853	93,608	47,910
2002	2,330,528	1,676,647	3,632	1,680,279	222,756	4,955	1,462,478	344,601	523,449	24,707	94,325	46,430
2003	2,410,384	1,704,175	7,748	1,711,923	227,401	37,318	1,521,840	344,683	543,861	25,502	94,516	46,147
2004	2,541,903	1,771,010	7,277	1,778,287	239,378	86,596	1,625,505	357,144	559,254	26,605	95,541	46,412
2005	2,728,668	1,884,685	2,038	1,886,723	256,892	142,509	1,772,340	361,821	594,507	28,266	96,536	47,467
2006	2,925,169	1,961,359	-50	1,961,309	264,259	207,787	1,904,837	371,020	649,312	29,499	99,162	48,319
2007	3,237,238	2,119,911	-616	2,119,295	278,573	213,841	2,054,563	476,807	705,868	32,133	100,744	49,380
2008	3,402,325	2,135,266	1,225	2,136,491	278,159	206,246	2,064,578	528,249	809,498	33,458	101,688	48,587
2009	3,380,012	2,037,018	2,831	2,039,849	275,260	173,877	1,938,466	516,974	924,572	33,096	102,126	46,239
2010	3,582,639	2,299,669	4,348	2,304,017	298,240	89,271	2,095,048	490,387	997,204	35,001	102,358	45,873
2011	3,619,700	2,254,114	7,530	2,261,644	272,455	113,883	2,103,072	536,057	980,571	35,379	102,313	45,880
2012	3,804,772	2,436,240	6,924	2,443,164	279,672	90,206	2,253,698	555,316	995,758	37,423	101,669	45,861
2013	3,840,399	2,541,525	6,995	2,548,520	324,477	51,031	2,275,074	549,518	1,015,807	37,838	101,497	46,455
2014	4,009,926	2,635,047	7,437	2,642,484	340,400	9,917	2,312,001	605,958	1,091,967	39,447	101,654	48,210
2015	4,145,768	2,710,721	16,228	2,726,949	349,901	42,886	2,419,934	611,051	1,114,783	40,315	102,835	48,551
2016	4,284,492	2,690,911	16,893	2,707,804	352,995	128,069	2,482,878	633,142	1,168,472	40,991	104,523	48,786
2017	4,466,131	2,795,438	24,140	2,819,578	372,862	166,182	2,612,898	651,285	1,201,948	41,927	106,522	50,047
2018	4,716,913	2,931,017	23,913	2,954,930	387,111	211,238	2,779,057	678,686	1,259,170	43,534	108,351	50,658
2019	5,072,786	3,109,355	19,316	3,128,671	399,697	249,877	2,978,851	751,629	1,342,306	46,108	110,020	51,401
2020	5,533,068	3,291,620	26,287	3,317,907	428,328	225,900	3,115,479	755,568	1,662,021	49,882	110,924	50,360
2021	6,083,588	3,518,158	24,644	3,542,802	451,081	292,549	3,384,270	776,770	1,922,548	54,550	111,524	51,886

Personal Income and Employment by Area: Los Angeles-Long Beach-Anaheim, CA

(Thousands of dollars, except as noted.)

Year	Personal income, total	Earnings by place of work			Less: Contributions for government social insurance	Plus: Adjustment for residence	Equals: Net earnings by place of residence	Plus: Dividends, interest, and rent	Plus: Personal current transfer receipts	Per capita personal income (dollars)	Population (persons)	Total employment
		Nonfarm	Farm	Total								
1970	42,898,309	35,477,189	66,565	35,543,754	2,395,587	-780,077	32,368,090	6,588,317	3,941,902	5,062	8,475,377	3,938,904
1971	44,962,023	36,759,101	64,606	36,823,707	2,548,382	-971,593	33,303,732	7,066,371	4,591,920	5,236	8,587,868	3,890,306
1972	48,982,924	40,567,852	78,966	40,646,818	2,973,135	-1,207,361	36,466,322	7,597,646	4,918,956	5,700	8,593,421	4,034,431
1973	53,179,424	44,483,547	94,016	44,577,563	3,757,828	-1,409,001	39,410,734	8,379,692	5,388,998	6,150	8,647,592	4,258,523
1974	58,755,856	48,584,652	111,613	48,696,265	4,214,122	-1,628,292	42,853,851	9,556,937	6,345,068	6,711	8,754,864	4,372,383
1975	64,589,683	52,389,382	102,827	52,492,209	4,418,812	-1,799,274	46,274,123	10,404,577	7,910,983	7,304	8,842,499	4,367,984
1976	71,531,619	58,791,328	124,366	58,915,694	5,066,226	-2,010,333	51,839,135	11,024,916	8,667,568	7,962	8,984,368	4,520,496
1977	79,408,612	66,386,922	139,889	66,526,811	5,818,748	-2,417,011	58,291,052	11,993,009	9,124,551	8,761	9,063,784	4,733,736
1978	90,398,475	76,611,969	133,347	76,745,316	6,892,751	-2,864,364	66,988,201	13,620,952	9,789,322	9,821	9,204,893	5,044,872
1979	102,138,575	87,340,061	187,217	87,527,278	8,234,187	-3,332,339	75,960,752	15,658,137	10,519,686	10,991	9,292,983	5,314,599
1980	115,300,613	96,965,793	267,554	97,233,347	8,975,819	-4,027,096	84,230,432	19,049,691	12,020,490	12,195	9,454,611	5,404,030
1981	129,996,980	107,551,171	228,530	107,779,701	10,795,659	-4,596,711	92,387,331	23,579,797	14,029,852	13,522	9,613,602	5,490,043
1982	138,320,599	112,998,736	253,341	113,252,077	11,580,792	-5,010,937	96,660,348	26,247,365	15,412,886	14,095	9,813,347	5,398,676
1983	148,472,241	121,526,229	310,139	121,836,368	12,641,973	-5,613,165	103,581,230	28,493,676	16,397,335	14,833	10,009,841	5,496,333
1984	164,224,282	135,345,465	318,906	135,664,371	14,595,207	-6,471,654	114,597,510	32,723,808	16,902,964	16,156	10,165,047	5,772,337
1985	177,250,747	147,249,103	316,614	147,565,717	16,037,576	-7,382,219	124,145,922	34,894,148	18,210,677	17,118	10,354,836	5,967,933
1986	189,742,328	159,613,704	301,198	159,914,902	17,526,767	-8,322,840	134,065,295	36,240,181	19,436,852	17,862	10,622,535	6,154,066
1987	204,800,735	176,172,958	299,373	176,472,331	19,283,345	-9,568,987	147,619,999	37,072,534	20,108,202	18,901	10,835,330	6,389,935
1988	220,419,002	191,114,270	325,423	191,439,693	21,470,922	-10,671,083	159,297,688	39,962,807	21,158,507	20,037	11,000,781	6,660,585
1989	233,985,898	200,934,238	345,310	201,279,548	22,709,207	-11,806,804	166,763,537	44,314,768	22,907,593	20,933	11,177,630	6,773,734
1990	251,230,793	214,141,690	377,725	214,519,415	23,982,890	-13,665,422	176,871,103	49,194,448	25,165,242	22,238	11,297,143	6,881,721
1991	255,593,617	216,050,544	310,597	216,361,141	24,281,688	-13,199,420	178,880,033	48,882,605	27,830,979	22,419	11,400,816	6,700,497
1992	267,793,738	223,782,190	277,269	224,059,459	24,789,754	-12,911,995	186,357,710	49,089,593	32,346,435	23,181	11,552,438	6,471,123
1993	270,571,376	224,582,107	282,541	224,864,648	24,834,589	-13,017,954	187,012,105	49,409,586	34,149,685	23,259	11,632,798	6,397,429
1994	277,469,993	228,868,687	274,942	229,143,629	25,480,488	-12,819,200	190,843,941	51,274,895	35,351,157	23,790	11,663,207	6,402,534
1995	289,416,398	235,778,197	319,223	236,097,420	25,913,590	-12,865,864	197,317,966	55,263,926	36,834,506	24,752	11,692,693	6,550,063
1996	306,055,522	247,567,022	323,988	247,891,010	26,499,315	-12,764,236	208,627,459	58,771,742	38,656,321	26,001	11,771,038	6,656,417
1997	323,174,030	262,890,272	364,919	263,255,191	27,831,330	-13,905,135	221,518,726	62,887,055	38,768,249	27,121	11,915,815	6,736,278
1998	351,619,452	285,689,526	411,870	286,101,396	29,795,724	-14,126,996	242,178,676	68,432,363	41,008,413	29,091	12,086,776	7,020,536
1999	371,299,872	303,490,236	441,804	303,932,040	31,532,370	-14,210,576	258,189,094	69,907,780	43,202,998	30,302	12,253,223	7,121,223
2000	395,968,325	324,205,955	463,293	324,669,248	33,580,848	-14,915,022	276,173,378	74,855,516	44,939,431	31,952	12,392,704	7,216,670
2001	410,867,760	335,106,592	393,286	335,499,878	35,406,470	-15,732,824	284,360,584	76,301,071	50,206,105	32,839	12,511,491	7,247,391
2002	420,861,285	345,691,801	410,577	346,102,378	36,949,442	-16,231,687	292,921,249	74,061,269	53,878,767	33,364	12,614,158	7,236,765
2003	442,277,059	363,596,204	459,063	364,055,267	39,073,582	-16,786,986	308,194,699	77,261,936	56,820,424	34,835	12,696,521	7,270,628
2004	468,615,009	391,538,637	418,822	391,957,459	42,807,245	-17,817,967	331,332,247	77,858,477	59,424,285	36,797	12,734,974	7,374,051
2005	498,906,751	409,449,610	420,968	409,870,578	44,577,221	-18,363,897	346,929,460	90,065,797	61,911,494	39,202	12,726,428	7,475,717
2006	539,348,506	433,798,266	461,376	434,259,642	45,773,250	-19,663,003	368,823,389	104,687,969	65,837,148	42,568	12,670,216	7,603,489
2007	558,278,018	442,605,230	389,914	442,995,144	46,280,539	-20,201,192	376,513,413	112,636,046	69,128,559	44,196	12,631,988	7,727,181
2008	565,344,462	437,980,026	382,575	438,362,601	46,930,801	-19,722,303	371,709,497	116,008,904	77,626,061	44,541	12,692,740	7,623,443
2009	543,359,346	417,950,448	355,882	418,306,330	45,012,876	-18,360,708	354,932,746	102,969,853	85,456,747	42,534	12,774,577	7,303,651
2010	571,360,427	437,376,022	304,223	437,680,245	45,346,180	-17,791,763	374,542,302	102,273,315	94,544,810	44,505	12,838,023	7,244,649
2011	605,823,344	460,760,318	259,327	461,019,645	42,582,559	-18,623,846	399,813,240	110,864,589	95,145,515	46,876	12,923,899	7,398,718
2012	651,126,932	490,250,757	312,300	490,563,057	44,145,559	-19,146,220	427,271,278	127,782,378	96,073,276	50,048	13,010,104	7,684,611
2013	648,727,818	500,355,905	262,912	500,618,817	51,140,635	-19,091,168	430,387,014	118,520,237	99,820,567	49,550	13,092,451	7,926,250
2014	687,038,909	521,421,651	244,705	521,666,356	53,633,642	-19,249,757	448,782,957	131,604,041	106,651,911	52,109	13,184,705	8,163,879
2015	734,219,371	548,218,224	272,242	548,490,466	56,283,291	-19,143,825	473,063,350	145,587,830	115,568,191	55,384	13,256,931	8,403,138
2016	759,668,115	566,859,426	255,948	567,115,374	58,193,214	-21,117,881	487,804,279	151,618,286	120,245,550	57,135	13,295,906	8,564,060
2017	785,246,971	588,754,921	312,318	589,067,239	60,534,399	-21,298,240	507,234,600	159,355,398	118,656,973	59,000	13,309,287	8,656,055
2018	814,754,882	610,734,357	190,103	610,924,460	63,652,111	-22,929,702	524,342,647	165,577,216	124,835,019	61,325	13,285,814	8,851,057
2019	860,475,721	639,419,333	232,409	639,651,742	66,880,105	-24,841,642	547,929,995	179,351,282	133,194,444	65,006	13,236,839	8,889,656
2020	925,816,257	636,945,121	249,951	637,195,072	66,474,782	-21,962,858	548,757,432	179,346,377	197,712,448	70,280	13,173,266	8,404,731
2021	985,473,353	691,631,815	247,405	691,879,220	71,277,152	-26,579,528	594,022,540	184,020,206	207,430,607	75,821	12,997,353	8,681,229

Personal Income and Employment by Area: Louisville/Jefferson County, KY-IN

(Thousands of dollars, except as noted.)

Year	Personal income, total	Earnings by place of work			Less: Contributions for government social insurance	Plus: Adjustment for residence	Equals: Net earnings by place of residence	Plus: Dividends, interest, and rent	Plus: Personal current transfer receipts	Per capita personal income (dollars)	Population (persons)	Total employment
		Nonfarm	Farm	Total								
1970	3,820,968	3,210,852	41,471	3,252,323	223,314	-15,020	3,013,989	514,798	292,181	3,952	966,908	446,276
1971	4,099,843	3,407,887	43,840	3,451,727	244,722	-19,594	3,187,411	561,297	351,135	4,179	981,174	447,479
1972	4,508,151	3,780,800	48,027	3,828,827	287,478	-28,832	3,512,517	604,240	391,394	4,581	983,998	459,721
1973	5,033,586	4,243,437	60,149	4,303,586	371,632	-39,444	3,892,510	676,659	464,417	5,051	996,523	481,524
1974	5,517,618	4,565,353	68,263	4,633,616	413,747	-42,322	4,177,547	781,863	558,208	5,488	1,005,432	489,621
1975	5,890,816	4,716,300	54,950	4,771,250	417,596	-40,599	4,313,055	851,949	725,812	5,839	1,008,789	470,167
1976	6,474,476	5,228,719	60,122	5,288,841	471,191	-42,715	4,774,935	918,284	781,257	6,387	1,013,771	477,680
1977	7,202,842	5,887,979	63,950	5,951,929	529,935	-46,334	5,375,660	1,023,914	803,268	7,092	1,015,639	494,112
1978	8,026,281	6,636,639	50,516	6,687,155	611,688	-47,391	6,028,076	1,139,236	858,969	7,848	1,022,668	516,166
1979	8,847,180	7,265,633	50,623	7,316,256	693,242	-53,509	6,569,505	1,289,908	987,767	8,615	1,026,904	521,237
1980	9,692,544	7,656,435	48,608	7,705,043	729,738	-56,205	6,919,100	1,564,468	1,208,976	9,463	1,024,218	512,145
1981	10,739,846	8,252,131	76,117	8,328,248	846,518	-56,407	7,425,323	1,948,854	1,365,669	10,494	1,023,428	508,363
1982	11,361,296	8,384,560	89,059	8,473,619	875,073	-39,711	7,558,835	2,288,755	1,513,706	11,081	1,025,301	492,030
1983	12,019,904	8,933,007	33,528	8,966,535	938,500	-43,763	7,984,272	2,421,827	1,613,805	11,732	1,024,512	493,381
1984	13,210,185	9,817,215	118,551	9,935,766	1,055,205	-66,247	8,814,314	2,714,697	1,681,174	12,917	1,022,721	509,674
1985	13,909,034	10,346,913	112,848	10,459,761	1,128,342	-74,391	9,257,028	2,874,790	1,777,216	13,623	1,020,967	518,551
1986	14,572,810	10,854,795	103,562	10,958,357	1,220,063	-78,143	9,660,151	3,036,733	1,875,926	14,288	1,019,913	531,916
1987	15,387,719	11,580,569	117,671	11,698,240	1,295,341	-85,145	10,317,754	3,134,253	1,935,712	15,080	1,020,403	543,749
1988	16,822,610	12,740,405	119,520	12,859,925	1,441,135	-95,761	11,323,029	3,442,498	2,057,083	16,498	1,019,654	564,610
1989	18,142,144	13,542,935	196,800	13,739,735	1,537,577	-94,984	12,107,174	3,774,370	2,260,600	17,770	1,020,953	577,251
1990	19,238,493	14,310,534	172,686	14,483,220	1,677,135	-77,982	12,728,103	4,052,750	2,457,640	18,761	1,025,448	592,058
1991	20,031,421	14,856,420	156,551	15,012,971	1,766,056	-91,107	13,155,808	4,140,587	2,735,026	19,343	1,035,577	589,956
1992	21,577,444	16,145,247	113,191	16,258,438	1,907,344	-115,525	14,235,569	4,339,547	3,002,328	20,630	1,045,950	600,441
1993	22,572,958	17,042,715	98,241	17,140,956	2,032,341	-149,039	14,959,576	4,482,863	3,130,519	21,357	1,056,941	616,676
1994	23,772,055	18,049,131	87,372	18,136,503	2,192,088	-183,399	15,761,016	4,733,291	3,277,748	22,287	1,066,643	634,530
1995	25,110,941	18,961,179	45,519	19,006,698	2,305,462	-198,180	16,503,056	5,124,932	3,482,953	23,323	1,076,646	655,893
1996	26,485,862	19,820,478	74,027	19,894,505	2,389,301	-222,010	17,283,194	5,516,437	3,686,231	24,406	1,085,228	665,467
1997	27,924,269	20,962,239	58,311	21,020,550	2,516,575	-244,469	18,259,506	5,788,166	3,876,597	25,525	1,094,013	681,426
1998	29,631,514	22,580,603	56,772	22,637,375	2,685,645	-449,097	19,502,633	6,267,290	3,861,591	27,624	1,072,659	684,771
1999	30,939,263	24,159,266	25,682	24,184,948	2,875,422	-524,368	20,785,158	6,204,157	3,949,948	28,564	1,083,137	698,297
2000	33,194,992	25,745,719	81,159	25,826,878	2,979,378	-588,667	22,258,833	6,698,245	4,237,914	30,376	1,092,810	712,388
2001	34,128,847	26,574,134	65,900	26,640,034	3,075,407	-625,778	22,938,849	6,573,362	4,616,636	31,014	1,100,423	705,441
2002	34,753,760	27,028,670	27,188	27,055,858	3,140,101	-631,089	23,284,668	6,514,855	4,954,237	31,357	1,108,339	696,603
2003	35,745,098	27,866,479	53,506	27,919,985	3,209,664	-629,661	24,080,660	6,541,501	5,122,937	31,931	1,119,435	695,620
2004	37,795,066	29,590,860	75,671	29,666,531	3,357,057	-667,508	25,641,966	6,687,864	5,465,236	33,463	1,129,452	703,467
2005	39,280,164	30,454,338	43,579	30,497,917	3,462,042	-693,470	26,342,405	7,101,662	5,836,097	34,458	1,139,934	715,555
2006	41,950,213	31,803,158	43,732	31,846,890	3,646,139	-672,343	27,528,408	8,163,947	6,257,858	36,341	1,154,352	729,842
2007	43,696,670	33,001,171	41,247	33,042,418	3,820,882	-694,745	28,526,791	8,448,829	6,721,050	37,358	1,169,680	744,101
2008	44,975,686	32,959,609	38,193	32,997,802	3,897,058	-566,246	28,534,498	8,808,347	7,632,841	37,992	1,183,814	739,848
2009	43,963,735	32,029,657	29,292	32,058,949	3,830,640	-459,614	27,768,695	7,750,631	8,444,409	36,791	1,194,945	715,565
2010	45,959,327	33,290,078	23,940	33,314,018	3,911,691	-361,678	29,040,649	7,890,642	9,028,036	38,151	1,204,684	713,517
2011	48,413,432	34,869,041	59,792	34,928,833	3,605,300	-231,454	31,092,079	8,165,197	9,156,156	39,945	1,212,009	723,731
2012	51,717,742	36,949,069	58,958	37,008,027	3,798,986	-475,347	32,733,694	9,767,587	9,216,461	42,376	1,220,448	738,035
2013	51,380,019	37,782,086	170,398	37,952,484	4,424,220	-518,009	33,010,255	8,987,279	9,382,485	41,686	1,232,541	752,554
2014	53,972,147	39,389,912	94,131	39,484,043	4,646,318	-650,713	34,187,012	9,626,231	10,158,904	43,296	1,246,579	769,694
2015	57,091,141	41,801,890	89,846	41,891,736	4,945,053	-864,003	36,082,680	10,337,556	10,670,905	45,483	1,255,214	788,122
2016	58,609,092	43,327,469	57,157	43,384,626	5,117,462	-1,061,091	37,206,073	10,609,567	10,793,452	46,399	1,263,150	805,255
2017	60,703,653	44,968,652	60,443	45,029,095	5,289,392	-1,104,371	38,635,332	10,955,996	11,112,325	47,720	1,272,088	816,779
2018	63,479,641	46,905,608	48,195	46,953,803	5,501,029	-1,198,553	40,254,221	11,716,192	11,509,228	49,742	1,276,167	828,825
2019	66,339,376	49,017,228	43,508	49,060,736	5,741,902	-1,277,965	42,040,869	12,259,487	12,039,020	51,779	1,281,193	830,103
2020	71,135,156	49,673,549	84,491	49,758,040	5,946,528	-1,211,853	42,599,659	12,314,340	16,221,157	55,356	1,285,058	802,929
2021	76,335,024	53,257,211	133,642	53,390,853	6,293,516	-1,365,500	45,731,837	12,642,085	17,961,102	59,425	1,284,566	829,600

Personal Income and Employment by Area: Lubbock, TX

(Thousands of dollars, except as noted.)

Year	Personal income, total	Earnings by place of work			Less: Contributions for government social insurance	Plus: Adjustment for residence	Equals: Net earnings by place of residence	Plus: Dividends, interest, and rent	Plus: Personal current transfer receipts	Per capita personal income (dollars)	Population (persons)	Total employment
		Nonfarm	Farm	Total								
1970	727,087	533,818	72,755	606,573	32,937	-1,711	571,925	109,849	45,313	3,665	198,372	89,704
1971	744,276	572,888	36,994	609,882	36,625	-1,626	571,631	119,421	53,224	3,657	203,502	90,946
1972	836,301	646,093	42,473	688,566	43,026	-2,402	643,138	132,929	60,234	3,980	210,117	96,524
1973	1,017,162	726,950	128,140	855,090	56,164	-3,917	795,009	149,038	73,115	4,840	210,167	102,204
1974	1,062,522	835,745	39,322	875,067	66,753	-5,234	803,080	174,571	84,871	4,970	213,786	106,461
1975	1,163,883	919,912	16,898	936,810	72,294	-5,652	858,864	200,995	104,024	5,385	216,123	107,353
1976	1,353,581	1,049,798	64,733	1,114,531	84,120	-6,996	1,023,415	217,755	112,411	6,204	218,179	112,458
1977	1,533,010	1,183,170	91,656	1,274,826	95,619	-9,115	1,170,092	243,382	119,536	6,923	221,434	118,015
1978	1,686,400	1,336,251	61,042	1,397,293	110,060	-10,588	1,276,645	275,371	134,384	7,496	224,976	121,963
1979	1,900,130	1,497,212	76,650	1,573,862	129,659	-13,776	1,430,427	313,220	156,483	8,366	227,137	122,321
1980	2,085,251	1,661,255	23,238	1,684,493	145,428	-13,303	1,525,762	377,589	181,900	9,084	229,562	124,241
1981	2,415,914	1,793,157	128,361	1,921,518	168,020	-12,483	1,741,015	467,131	207,768	10,473	230,672	124,379
1982	2,574,425	1,919,228	53,595	1,972,823	181,998	-9,493	1,781,332	559,917	233,176	11,073	232,493	125,658
1983	2,844,144	2,101,300	79,715	2,181,015	197,026	-13,552	1,970,437	611,971	261,736	12,059	235,862	126,896
1984	2,965,254	2,170,234	66,769	2,237,003	205,249	-7,688	2,024,066	655,748	285,440	12,496	237,294	126,165
1985	3,141,737	2,295,354	59,799	2,355,153	219,087	-7,907	2,128,159	703,964	309,614	13,341	235,499	127,720
1986	3,189,005	2,348,151	34,368	2,382,519	222,947	-12,273	2,147,299	703,746	337,960	13,517	235,917	125,110
1987	3,321,960	2,343,976	142,163	2,486,139	222,187	-1,761	2,262,191	694,152	365,617	14,110	235,440	129,492
1988	3,511,268	2,519,661	145,844	2,665,505	247,887	-3,960	2,413,658	707,229	390,381	14,854	236,385	131,935
1989	3,645,095	2,625,134	79,322	2,704,456	262,524	-9,791	2,432,141	780,941	432,013	15,368	237,184	131,633
1990	3,912,018	2,825,466	131,118	2,956,584	277,252	-2,107	2,677,225	751,537	483,256	16,493	237,193	134,323
1991	3,987,165	2,957,733	47,069	3,004,802	296,464	-2,744	2,705,594	747,148	534,423	16,642	239,584	135,650
1992	4,275,318	3,105,408	115,664	3,221,072	308,706	-13,049	2,899,317	741,036	634,965	17,727	241,180	134,968
1993	4,545,047	3,288,856	169,934	3,458,790	326,178	-15,083	3,117,529	757,158	670,360	18,543	245,109	139,393
1994	4,781,209	3,489,819	134,153	3,623,972	349,420	-19,007	3,255,545	796,812	728,852	19,162	249,516	141,802
1995	4,980,851	3,614,435	91,851	3,706,286	364,715	-24,753	3,316,818	876,686	787,347	19,750	252,199	146,373
1996	5,289,323	3,790,123	139,585	3,929,708	378,064	-29,956	3,521,688	920,233	847,402	20,861	253,555	147,374
1997	5,495,428	3,981,279	128,863	4,110,142	393,844	-32,856	3,683,442	926,176	885,810	21,620	254,178	150,419
1998	5,738,830	4,295,901	74,900	4,370,801	416,963	-41,369	3,912,469	991,480	834,881	22,638	253,502	151,104
1999	5,902,186	4,421,911	90,276	4,512,187	423,366	-45,919	4,042,902	990,944	868,340	23,191	254,507	151,946
2000	6,262,690	4,727,713	41,836	4,769,549	448,345	-55,290	4,265,914	1,077,411	919,365	24,402	256,651	155,675
2001	6,437,156	4,786,222	56,871	4,843,093	462,169	-55,594	4,325,330	1,115,521	996,305	24,757	260,015	157,772
2002	6,670,114	5,005,602	54,829	5,060,431	483,543	-70,120	4,506,768	1,089,452	1,073,894	25,393	262,680	157,232
2003	7,061,097	5,102,812	122,437	5,225,249	503,852	-70,375	4,651,022	1,259,698	1,150,377	26,512	266,338	156,117
2004	7,244,969	5,299,307	188,658	5,487,965	524,237	-68,313	4,895,415	1,152,818	1,196,736	26,987	268,466	158,613
2005	7,686,852	5,530,920	207,998	5,738,918	549,042	-81,516	5,108,360	1,268,965	1,309,527	28,420	270,478	161,147
2006	8,089,593	5,951,019	74,540	6,025,559	579,446	-81,696	5,364,417	1,313,338	1,411,838	29,479	274,419	164,127
2007	8,601,321	6,037,602	174,709	6,212,311	597,360	-73,564	5,541,387	1,529,050	1,530,884	31,000	277,466	166,211
2008	9,164,248	6,334,375	20,262	6,354,637	626,444	-34,914	5,693,279	1,773,725	1,697,244	32,692	280,321	170,038
2009	9,323,917	6,463,646	62,804	6,526,450	646,478	-24,654	5,855,318	1,635,796	1,832,803	32,574	286,236	170,816
2010	10,019,680	6,811,601	168,660	6,980,261	671,532	17,525	6,326,254	1,690,549	2,002,877	34,282	292,269	170,484
2011	10,426,001	7,005,551	-10,755	6,994,796	611,302	96,098	6,479,592	1,866,395	2,080,014	35,295	295,400	174,057
2012	11,070,882	7,362,736	-31,631	7,331,105	639,497	191,690	6,883,298	2,135,090	2,052,494	37,165	297,888	176,461
2013	11,459,781	7,722,698	165,273	7,887,971	752,799	235,402	7,370,574	1,977,426	2,111,781	38,035	301,295	181,118
2014	11,957,697	8,153,372	-48,750	8,104,622	792,260	277,828	7,590,190	2,173,697	2,193,810	39,264	304,548	184,474
2015	12,336,253	8,441,489	-7,631	8,433,858	834,260	227,951	7,827,549	2,192,017	2,316,687	40,041	308,090	188,340
2016	12,582,925	8,627,982	-43,583	8,584,399	867,901	146,666	7,863,164	2,296,442	2,423,319	40,395	311,496	194,046
2017	13,037,192	8,909,366	29,704	8,939,070	908,338	183,136	8,213,868	2,343,397	2,479,927	41,463	314,428	198,590
2018	13,785,876	9,330,226	8,886	9,339,112	944,217	245,338	8,640,233	2,550,412	2,595,231	43,583	316,314	200,911
2019	14,555,620	9,762,636	35,541	9,798,177	985,156	266,322	9,079,343	2,743,838	2,732,439	45,637	318,941	203,063
2020	15,404,541	10,062,455	-6,528	10,055,927	1,025,326	132,771	9,163,372	2,695,119	3,546,050	47,822	322,123	201,350
2021	16,602,246	10,524,276	128,350	10,652,626	1,070,257	126,313	9,708,682	2,836,574	4,056,990	51,045	325,245	207,472

Personal Income and Employment by Area: Lynchburg, VA

(Thousands of dollars, except as noted.)

Year	Personal income, total	Earnings by place of work Nonfarm	Earnings by place of work Farm	Earnings by place of work Total	Less: Contributions for government social insurance	Plus: Adjustment for residence	Equals: Net earnings by place of residence	Plus: Dividends, interest, and rent	Plus: Personal current transfer receipts	Per capita personal income (dollars)	Population (persons)	Total employment
1970	547,509	472,206	9,319	481,525	31,116	-26,330	424,079	75,244	48,186	3,289	166,469	79,441
1971	587,464	504,460	8,535	512,995	34,589	-30,739	447,667	82,670	57,127	3,428	171,359	79,326
1972	657,724	575,398	9,656	585,054	41,585	-40,432	503,037	90,628	64,059	3,764	174,732	82,093
1973	737,153	644,213	13,386	657,599	53,726	-45,041	558,832	103,314	75,007	4,177	176,483	86,237
1974	823,007	714,378	13,987	728,365	61,975	-51,373	615,017	119,232	88,758	4,617	178,257	88,455
1975	894,903	745,675	7,790	753,465	62,991	-42,580	647,894	128,750	118,259	4,856	184,275	85,436
1976	1,004,788	846,797	6,035	852,832	72,634	-45,667	734,531	141,546	128,711	5,418	185,470	89,082
1977	1,121,386	945,660	3,417	949,077	81,181	-47,207	820,689	159,905	140,792	6,006	186,723	91,298
1978	1,275,770	1,083,347	4,841	1,088,188	95,045	-55,066	938,077	180,566	157,127	6,672	191,211	95,509
1979	1,443,773	1,223,282	5,991	1,229,273	111,791	-61,112	1,056,370	207,533	179,870	7,448	193,855	99,044
1980	1,607,090	1,308,883	1,023	1,309,906	119,808	-63,517	1,126,581	260,030	220,479	8,257	194,636	97,473
1981	1,782,308	1,400,922	3,913	1,404,835	138,455	-64,800	1,201,580	323,711	257,017	9,089	196,102	96,671
1982	1,900,788	1,440,062	-3,295	1,436,767	144,672	-54,140	1,237,955	375,113	287,720	9,641	197,158	95,302
1983	2,070,894	1,552,528	953	1,553,481	158,174	-45,584	1,349,723	407,473	313,698	10,506	197,122	95,745
1984	2,297,990	1,720,334	3,257	1,723,591	180,864	-38,718	1,504,009	464,211	329,770	11,591	198,260	99,984
1985	2,455,570	1,816,934	803	1,817,737	194,439	-22,129	1,601,169	492,838	361,563	12,335	199,074	102,302
1986	2,622,256	1,938,447	916	1,939,363	213,488	-9,377	1,716,498	514,591	391,167	13,086	200,383	103,804
1987	2,843,193	2,088,859	7,842	2,096,701	227,523	5,716	1,874,894	551,001	417,298	14,111	201,487	108,094
1988	3,061,488	2,221,508	8,971	2,230,479	248,829	20,049	2,001,699	612,306	447,483	15,069	203,166	109,641
1989	3,347,570	2,371,309	13,715	2,385,024	268,223	37,284	2,154,085	715,677	477,808	16,345	204,803	112,967
1990	3,502,166	2,499,655	14,603	2,514,258	284,313	57,530	2,287,475	703,874	510,817	16,926	206,913	115,259
1991	3,607,438	2,569,006	11,071	2,580,077	295,244	62,796	2,347,629	715,862	543,947	17,263	208,971	114,238
1992	3,827,638	2,704,000	12,641	2,716,641	306,734	77,106	2,487,013	732,444	608,181	17,980	212,888	114,404
1993	4,051,149	2,899,911	5,357	2,905,268	329,660	87,355	2,662,963	764,715	623,471	18,852	214,890	117,353
1994	4,257,699	3,049,551	9,034	3,058,585	346,479	98,953	2,811,059	791,578	655,062	19,555	217,728	120,192
1995	4,443,256	3,134,649	4,530	3,139,179	355,677	115,837	2,899,339	839,154	704,763	20,232	219,612	122,217
1996	4,638,387	3,237,784	3,755	3,241,539	365,273	128,260	3,004,526	893,201	740,660	20,906	221,872	123,775
1997	4,863,143	3,419,938	685	3,420,623	382,495	141,842	3,179,970	917,232	765,941	21,695	224,156	125,140
1998	5,170,129	3,632,268	3,828	3,636,096	400,557	164,647	3,400,186	967,109	802,834	22,910	225,675	125,567
1999	5,446,604	3,888,300	-1,754	3,886,546	426,803	178,118	3,637,861	954,434	854,309	23,958	227,337	128,961
2000	5,805,132	4,082,567	10,769	4,093,336	440,851	201,019	3,853,504	1,036,955	914,673	25,366	228,855	131,133
2001	5,950,826	4,076,674	2,414	4,079,088	459,821	205,875	3,825,142	1,099,996	1,025,688	25,930	229,499	127,137
2002	6,030,404	4,093,841	-775	4,093,066	464,589	213,318	3,841,795	1,100,476	1,088,133	26,179	230,356	124,534
2003	6,265,093	4,247,204	-9,238	4,237,966	479,313	210,407	3,969,060	1,130,787	1,165,246	26,931	232,634	124,264
2004	6,562,530	4,461,839	-3,194	4,458,645	511,258	216,780	4,164,167	1,175,276	1,223,087	27,976	234,574	126,419
2005	6,883,938	4,722,203	-3,950	4,718,253	549,814	220,808	4,389,247	1,184,492	1,310,199	28,862	238,515	129,811
2006	7,375,927	4,982,359	-22,519	4,959,840	586,604	221,873	4,595,109	1,322,668	1,458,150	30,327	243,213	132,755
2007	7,774,422	5,196,334	-24,613	5,171,721	612,007	226,100	4,785,814	1,437,009	1,551,599	31,497	246,827	135,949
2008	8,210,971	5,324,766	-18,538	5,306,228	633,480	228,366	4,901,114	1,532,466	1,777,391	32,936	249,299	137,054
2009	8,083,563	5,231,608	-13,979	5,217,629	626,489	225,774	4,816,914	1,343,676	1,922,973	32,149	251,441	133,014
2010	8,328,418	5,341,561	-12,744	5,328,817	639,615	223,559	4,912,761	1,324,906	2,090,751	32,922	252,975	131,504
2011	8,633,171	5,385,589	-5,263	5,380,326	581,406	242,927	5,041,847	1,388,289	2,203,035	33,958	254,232	131,578
2012	8,972,745	5,551,968	121	5,552,089	592,346	257,466	5,217,209	1,573,680	2,181,856	35,077	255,804	132,229
2013	8,965,507	5,641,137	-3,045	5,638,092	685,063	258,755	5,211,784	1,495,427	2,258,296	34,893	256,943	132,789
2014	9,348,555	5,817,688	-2,785	5,814,903	704,060	260,276	5,371,119	1,637,499	2,339,937	36,382	256,953	134,231
2015	9,625,733	5,937,804	-6,436	5,931,368	721,291	286,114	5,496,191	1,702,580	2,426,962	37,280	258,199	135,058
2016	9,703,595	5,934,448	-14,871	5,919,577	727,973	283,985	5,475,589	1,703,383	2,524,623	37,464	259,012	135,126
2017	10,030,665	6,136,832	-9,019	6,127,813	761,153	277,247	5,643,907	1,775,815	2,610,943	38,571	260,059	136,725
2018	10,435,135	6,368,813	-16,511	6,352,302	791,545	288,842	5,849,599	1,865,257	2,720,279	39,966	261,098	138,885
2019	10,819,022	6,511,343	-9,172	6,502,171	813,981	296,935	5,985,125	1,984,964	2,848,933	41,365	261,549	138,675
2020	11,658,388	6,650,216	-11,473	6,638,743	831,459	302,283	6,109,567	1,967,021	3,581,800	44,598	261,408	135,779
2021	12,424,165	6,927,945	-10,042	6,917,903	858,606	323,882	6,383,179	1,982,206	4,058,780	47,374	262,258	137,571

Personal Income and Employment by Area: Macon-Bibb County, GA

(Thousands of dollars, except as noted.)

Year	Personal income, total	Earnings by place of work Nonfarm	Farm	Total	Less: Contributions for government social insurance	Plus: Adjustment for residence	Equals: Net earnings by place of residence	Plus: Dividends, interest, and rent	Plus: Personal current transfer receipts	Per capita personal income (dollars)	Population (persons)	Total employment
1970	664,522	453,972	5,480	459,452	29,751	92,391	522,092	84,817	57,613	3,667	181,228	78,317
1971	732,150	495,189	6,314	501,503	33,500	98,912	566,915	96,346	68,889	3,940	185,839	79,907
1972	795,018	545,837	6,403	552,240	38,739	98,209	611,710	104,987	78,321	4,219	188,436	81,664
1973	856,424	596,161	9,270	605,431	48,637	95,145	651,939	116,182	88,303	4,539	188,667	83,070
1974	945,818	663,483	6,565	670,048	56,266	92,922	706,704	131,618	107,496	4,996	189,318	85,187
1975	1,047,179	726,728	6,406	733,134	60,628	92,610	765,116	146,321	135,742	5,458	191,852	85,941
1976	1,138,426	803,285	7,557	810,842	68,332	90,120	832,630	157,814	147,982	5,921	192,268	87,195
1977	1,231,221	870,916	5,885	876,801	73,582	98,538	901,757	175,529	153,935	6,292	195,693	87,585
1978	1,341,220	959,621	7,626	967,247	83,090	95,486	979,643	195,696	165,881	6,790	197,518	88,125
1979	1,488,345	1,082,640	8,213	1,090,853	97,897	89,177	1,082,133	218,651	187,561	7,497	198,531	89,341
1980	1,660,351	1,211,020	3,215	1,214,235	109,783	73,345	1,177,797	261,796	220,758	8,351	198,810	91,031
1981	1,876,514	1,335,345	4,189	1,339,534	130,634	97,210	1,306,110	319,994	250,410	9,395	199,746	91,575
1982	2,012,774	1,414,743	6,712	1,421,455	140,826	100,751	1,381,380	360,862	270,532	10,020	200,885	91,762
1983	2,165,903	1,528,127	4,380	1,532,507	152,985	94,033	1,473,555	396,771	295,577	10,699	202,440	92,018
1984	2,377,497	1,699,389	7,142	1,706,531	175,195	89,478	1,620,814	443,478	313,205	11,684	203,490	95,941
1985	2,528,505	1,826,714	7,939	1,834,653	192,199	82,643	1,725,097	466,087	337,321	12,376	204,300	97,593
1986	2,694,161	1,981,740	8,443	1,990,183	210,655	58,584	1,838,112	497,780	358,269	13,182	204,377	99,644
1987	2,875,064	2,151,765	11,064	2,162,829	226,332	24,200	1,960,697	536,591	377,776	14,022	205,043	101,989
1988	3,106,124	2,330,908	15,057	2,345,965	253,819	10,072	2,102,218	588,240	415,666	15,071	206,097	105,223
1989	3,343,748	2,457,819	17,966	2,475,785	268,615	7,373	2,214,543	680,778	448,427	16,169	206,803	106,740
1990	3,482,850	2,596,757	19,002	2,615,759	282,424	-43,720	2,289,615	702,885	490,350	16,810	207,190	108,636
1991	3,654,861	2,687,702	20,952	2,708,654	296,447	-50,100	2,362,107	725,171	567,583	17,457	209,358	106,541
1992	3,890,153	2,877,444	20,696	2,898,140	313,038	-39,517	2,545,585	718,749	625,819	18,462	210,716	107,456
1993	4,057,527	2,987,869	23,445	3,011,314	326,647	-48,346	2,636,321	752,831	668,375	19,005	213,497	111,132
1994	4,297,360	3,162,059	24,655	3,186,714	347,432	-63,202	2,776,080	803,057	718,223	19,949	215,416	113,744
1995	4,600,725	3,375,736	19,344	3,395,080	370,203	-54,567	2,970,310	877,075	753,340	21,204	216,979	118,082
1996	4,920,854	3,544,448	16,840	3,561,288	389,881	21,561	3,192,968	928,317	799,569	22,500	218,702	121,131
1997	5,077,295	3,728,143	17,764	3,745,907	408,023	-41,540	3,296,344	958,307	822,644	22,989	220,860	122,871
1998	5,384,922	3,943,828	20,479	3,964,307	424,429	-15,330	3,524,548	1,033,497	826,877	24,285	221,736	123,933
1999	5,558,969	4,124,315	26,541	4,150,856	439,740	-5,875	3,705,241	991,680	862,048	25,036	222,038	125,300
2000	5,821,887	4,202,019	23,909	4,225,928	446,287	39,601	3,819,242	1,086,174	916,471	26,177	222,407	126,496
2001	5,946,881	4,254,559	30,298	4,284,857	453,101	31,819	3,863,575	1,103,886	979,420	26,683	222,869	123,568
2002	6,216,860	4,383,081	21,422	4,404,503	467,972	44,320	3,980,851	1,109,080	1,126,929	27,672	224,661	123,274
2003	6,320,116	4,499,838	23,439	4,523,277	476,836	50,319	4,096,760	1,089,767	1,133,589	27,967	225,987	124,397
2004	6,533,332	4,731,513	26,604	4,758,117	512,874	691	4,245,934	1,093,569	1,193,829	28,731	227,394	126,769
2005	6,761,056	4,819,841	29,042	4,848,883	521,900	16,815	4,343,798	1,117,943	1,299,315	29,638	228,125	127,960
2006	7,046,244	4,989,215	14,187	5,003,402	541,999	-12,653	4,448,750	1,214,158	1,383,336	30,682	229,655	128,869
2007	7,286,308	4,922,460	18,177	4,940,637	535,592	43,722	4,448,767	1,351,928	1,485,613	31,617	230,452	129,865
2008	7,522,638	5,063,461	23,873	5,087,334	577,014	-27,403	4,482,917	1,378,759	1,660,962	32,521	231,314	131,938
2009	7,398,330	5,010,777	22,394	5,033,171	569,045	-89,449	4,374,677	1,241,242	1,782,411	31,880	232,065	126,729
2010	7,581,063	5,106,356	22,651	5,129,007	576,797	-108,725	4,443,485	1,200,382	1,937,196	32,649	232,199	126,182
2011	7,960,582	5,242,544	30,189	5,272,733	523,424	-152,787	4,596,522	1,365,400	1,998,660	34,205	232,734	128,211
2012	7,923,560	5,363,273	40,591	5,403,864	535,248	-242,067	4,626,549	1,325,794	1,971,217	34,040	232,774	129,506
2013	7,952,677	5,561,492	42,045	5,603,537	628,231	-325,217	4,650,089	1,300,350	2,002,238	34,385	231,282	130,173
2014	8,297,609	5,811,294	39,966	5,851,260	649,363	-382,363	4,819,534	1,397,800	2,080,275	35,754	232,076	132,995
2015	8,582,850	6,054,623	45,886	6,100,509	673,132	-467,861	4,959,516	1,483,984	2,139,350	37,026	231,805	134,807
2016	8,654,493	6,054,864	30,253	6,085,117	674,157	-426,952	4,984,008	1,473,873	2,196,612	37,394	231,443	134,406
2017	8,958,878	6,219,989	34,224	6,254,213	693,753	-467,321	5,093,139	1,607,987	2,257,752	38,672	231,664	136,521
2018	9,221,913	6,440,396	22,276	6,462,672	730,850	-492,463	5,239,359	1,631,628	2,350,926	39,640	232,641	137,960
2019	9,494,766	6,517,085	18,992	6,536,077	748,824	-485,010	5,302,243	1,736,136	2,456,387	40,676	233,424	139,441
2020	10,213,810	6,547,404	7,203	6,554,607	756,560	-493,885	5,304,162	1,735,385	3,174,263	43,725	233,592	137,041
2021	10,963,263	7,045,752	20,110	7,065,862	807,262	-580,375	5,678,225	1,777,687	3,507,351	46,875	233,883	139,679

Personal Income and Employment by Area: Madera, CA

(Thousands of dollars, except as noted.)

		Earnings by place of work			Less: Contributions for government social insurance	Plus: Adjustment for residence	Equals: Net earnings by place of residence	Plus: Dividends, interest, and rent	Plus: Personal current transfer receipts	Per capita personal income (dollars)	Population (persons)	Total employment
Year	Personal income, total	Nonfarm	Farm	Total								
1970	157,504	77,600	31,793	109,393	5,536	4,117	107,974	24,016	25,514	3,776	41,707	16,486
1971	172,911	87,734	31,328	119,062	6,478	5,925	118,509	26,382	28,020	4,044	42,754	17,136
1972	203,344	101,333	42,466	143,799	7,799	8,456	144,456	30,122	28,766	4,705	43,223	18,531
1973	252,612	114,738	67,670	182,408	10,095	11,556	183,869	36,730	32,013	5,682	44,458	19,251
1974	288,523	129,786	76,193	205,979	11,862	14,683	208,800	41,798	37,925	6,263	46,071	20,413
1975	303,984	147,138	57,037	204,175	13,043	16,991	208,123	48,018	47,843	6,344	47,917	21,108
1976	351,479	169,492	69,799	239,291	15,238	21,020	245,073	52,088	54,318	7,072	49,699	22,320
1977	404,651	192,466	84,098	276,564	17,549	26,612	285,627	59,394	59,630	7,667	52,777	23,161
1978	443,859	224,422	68,117	292,539	20,658	34,823	306,704	71,974	65,181	7,963	55,741	24,123
1979	599,802	271,185	149,895	421,080	25,567	43,401	438,914	88,157	72,731	9,969	60,169	26,794
1980	679,239	296,759	158,035	454,794	27,387	51,617	479,024	112,352	87,863	10,620	63,961	27,854
1981	665,972	318,383	81,551	399,934	31,941	56,724	424,717	135,973	105,282	9,908	67,214	28,249
1982	687,423	324,111	77,066	401,177	33,232	59,124	427,069	147,097	113,257	9,928	69,240	28,791
1983	699,323	351,466	40,329	391,795	36,685	63,411	418,521	156,285	124,517	9,780	71,504	30,018
1984	780,203	394,232	59,288	453,520	42,339	69,856	481,037	169,759	129,407	10,688	72,996	29,837
1985	830,324	423,961	53,885	477,846	46,061	74,742	506,527	175,251	148,546	11,054	75,118	30,233
1986	922,147	471,010	78,828	549,838	51,630	78,322	576,530	183,283	162,334	11,982	76,960	30,149
1987	1,049,058	540,669	125,140	665,809	59,764	81,084	687,129	193,015	168,914	13,279	79,003	32,257
1988	1,133,911	585,973	120,682	706,655	67,278	89,250	728,627	212,196	193,088	13,868	81,762	33,655
1989	1,222,046	615,483	111,293	726,776	71,317	109,158	764,617	247,460	209,969	14,411	84,797	34,542
1990	1,330,613	679,841	111,716	791,557	77,542	121,671	835,686	263,111	231,816	14,930	89,125	35,423
1991	1,418,479	762,409	90,776	853,185	87,066	120,407	886,526	265,164	266,789	14,936	94,973	38,461
1992	1,602,982	826,780	164,280	991,060	94,001	121,154	1,018,213	270,847	313,922	16,105	99,536	38,949
1993	1,665,036	886,417	129,811	1,016,228	99,760	124,899	1,041,367	284,026	339,643	16,004	104,039	39,682
1994	1,700,029	940,685	94,313	1,034,998	105,318	125,166	1,054,846	300,134	345,049	15,830	107,396	41,256
1995	1,729,154	955,518	66,891	1,022,409	108,669	124,663	1,038,403	323,595	367,156	15,820	109,300	44,780
1996	1,886,968	998,930	136,248	1,135,178	109,957	122,880	1,148,101	344,145	394,722	16,678	113,143	46,793
1997	2,030,119	1,091,316	176,901	1,268,217	116,813	116,193	1,267,597	362,920	399,602	17,435	116,442	48,055
1998	2,107,353	1,240,423	91,598	1,332,021	128,752	109,005	1,312,274	368,949	426,130	17,688	119,143	52,112
1999	2,236,441	1,303,914	131,265	1,435,179	137,399	113,086	1,410,866	373,538	452,037	18,349	121,883	52,404
2000	2,338,943	1,344,791	151,869	1,496,660	142,081	129,054	1,483,633	390,455	464,855	18,925	123,587	51,446
2001	2,534,808	1,550,605	105,360	1,655,965	165,852	138,005	1,628,118	393,037	513,653	20,185	125,581	50,566
2002	2,738,233	1,672,768	149,658	1,822,426	182,266	157,491	1,797,651	389,253	551,329	21,331	128,369	51,998
2003	2,931,937	1,822,057	150,365	1,972,422	201,227	147,578	1,918,773	426,272	586,892	22,088	132,738	54,041
2004	3,251,384	1,945,894	353,971	2,299,865	222,441	156,689	2,234,113	409,081	608,190	23,714	137,106	56,155
2005	3,396,327	2,080,092	345,183	2,425,275	238,778	149,124	2,335,621	420,131	640,575	24,205	140,313	57,801
2006	3,590,433	2,315,048	249,120	2,564,168	253,507	110,787	2,421,448	473,734	695,251	24,999	143,622	60,055
2007	3,933,440	2,408,923	360,829	2,769,752	258,740	116,823	2,627,835	559,429	746,176	26,929	146,067	60,959
2008	3,938,796	2,395,321	298,020	2,693,341	262,155	90,010	2,521,196	575,660	841,940	26,549	148,359	59,936
2009	3,813,538	2,373,468	138,299	2,511,767	265,121	96,438	2,343,084	541,960	928,494	25,554	149,234	58,448
2010	4,237,224	2,434,268	382,501	2,816,769	258,826	114,710	2,672,653	542,582	1,021,989	28,060	151,006	57,484
2011	4,465,373	2,505,485	492,059	2,997,544	244,299	108,021	2,861,266	574,015	1,030,092	29,438	151,685	57,253
2012	4,703,565	2,616,924	677,327	3,294,251	256,460	40,129	3,077,920	579,718	1,045,927	31,043	151,520	59,606
2013	4,856,514	2,702,160	755,193	3,457,353	295,919	22,200	3,183,634	599,333	1,073,547	32,100	151,295	61,063
2014	5,201,678	2,805,192	861,531	3,666,723	306,702	17,261	3,377,282	689,518	1,134,878	34,025	152,878	62,799
2015	5,290,126	2,873,402	643,118	3,516,520	312,640	93,650	3,297,530	756,409	1,236,187	34,609	152,856	61,468
2016	5,531,698	3,083,479	614,938	3,698,417	335,903	74,074	3,436,588	823,524	1,271,586	36,157	152,989	63,717
2017	5,707,515	3,229,319	640,621	3,869,940	356,081	78,467	3,592,326	867,604	1,247,585	37,000	154,256	64,549
2018	5,839,577	3,392,429	594,689	3,987,118	371,356	101,432	3,717,194	821,669	1,300,714	37,570	155,430	66,067
2019	6,131,113	3,592,954	545,295	4,138,249	396,121	152,290	3,894,418	847,135	1,389,560	39,388	155,658	67,100
2020	6,902,603	3,866,323	578,518	4,444,841	424,561	60,286	4,080,566	855,979	1,966,058	44,072	156,620	66,529
2021	7,294,182	4,095,038	412,571	4,507,609	449,545	158,927	4,216,991	866,613	2,210,578	45,757	159,410	68,862

Personal Income and Employment by Area: Madison, WI

(Thousands of dollars, except as noted.)

Year	Personal income, total	Derivation of personal income									Per capita personal income (dollars)	Population (persons)	Total employment
		Earnings by place of work			Less: Contributions for government social insurance	Plus: Adjustment for residence	Equals: Net earnings by place of residence	Plus: Dividends, interest, and rent	Plus: Personal current transfer receipts				
		Nonfarm	Farm	Total									
1970	1,708,448	1,316,440	87,386	1,403,826	90,597	-18,928	1,294,301	293,796	120,351		4,524	377,631	191,581
1971	1,854,242	1,421,354	91,918	1,513,272	101,500	-19,685	1,392,087	323,086	139,069		4,846	382,627	194,234
1972	1,997,037	1,529,585	94,778	1,624,363	115,366	-18,198	1,490,799	351,273	154,965		5,219	382,656	200,459
1973	2,225,349	1,693,667	119,509	1,813,176	147,243	-16,418	1,649,515	394,456	181,378		5,766	385,942	208,252
1974	2,423,637	1,852,574	97,909	1,950,483	169,979	-16,747	1,763,757	446,644	213,236		6,172	392,653	212,493
1975	2,710,063	2,030,435	115,196	2,145,631	184,359	-17,051	1,944,221	497,860	267,982		6,920	391,644	216,816
1976	2,970,088	2,279,797	90,258	2,370,055	209,710	-13,796	2,146,549	541,772	281,767		7,488	396,665	227,364
1977	3,305,419	2,525,419	116,541	2,641,960	232,485	-8,929	2,400,546	604,477	300,396		8,234	401,437	235,127
1978	3,713,483	2,855,398	123,377	2,978,775	270,539	-5,121	2,703,115	681,225	329,143		9,141	406,224	243,149
1979	4,110,390	3,132,711	146,018	3,278,729	311,040	1,637	2,969,326	760,594	380,470		10,037	409,524	250,720
1980	4,584,488	3,413,658	147,235	3,560,893	341,201	-2,230	3,217,462	912,629	454,397		10,977	417,638	255,057
1981	4,992,447	3,646,271	135,612	3,781,883	391,202	-6	3,390,675	1,096,387	505,385		11,862	420,874	253,625
1982	5,385,057	3,897,883	109,991	4,007,874	417,110	-11,063	3,579,701	1,254,049	551,307		12,739	422,726	253,833
1983	5,716,609	4,168,577	31,920	4,200,497	438,106	-12,197	3,750,194	1,360,663	605,752		13,438	425,420	257,282
1984	6,261,877	4,558,053	92,057	4,650,110	482,639	-13,984	4,153,487	1,485,193	623,197		14,568	429,829	267,580
1985	6,721,761	4,938,119	104,018	5,042,137	525,882	-26,352	4,489,903	1,564,283	667,575		15,472	434,452	276,651
1986	7,189,445	5,312,413	144,315	5,456,728	565,268	-39,449	4,852,011	1,640,936	696,498		16,365	439,308	283,663
1987	7,715,532	5,801,217	168,547	5,969,764	607,559	-53,341	5,308,864	1,688,572	718,096		17,347	444,766	295,146
1988	8,084,248	6,250,324	76,938	6,327,262	688,813	-61,951	5,576,498	1,756,712	751,038		17,889	451,906	305,036
1989	8,980,302	6,802,542	178,065	6,980,607	753,182	-76,401	6,151,024	2,008,138	821,140		19,676	456,408	315,061
1990	9,637,953	7,421,863	140,059	7,561,922	855,604	-93,280	6,613,038	2,135,393	889,522		20,763	464,185	326,175
1991	10,158,404	7,921,260	105,479	8,026,739	923,289	-119,696	6,983,754	2,200,953	973,697		21,426	474,124	332,549
1992	11,084,296	8,657,116	140,284	8,797,400	996,869	-141,416	7,659,115	2,351,514	1,073,667		22,916	483,693	340,984
1993	11,743,501	9,279,813	94,381	9,374,194	1,061,193	-162,896	8,150,105	2,465,140	1,128,256		23,753	494,411	349,725
1994	12,505,071	9,895,627	121,567	10,017,194	1,149,866	-183,307	8,684,021	2,657,535	1,163,515		24,892	502,367	359,601
1995	13,272,015	10,407,456	76,177	10,483,633	1,211,728	-200,827	9,071,078	2,952,607	1,248,330		26,039	509,694	367,663
1996	13,998,192	10,859,504	133,845	10,993,349	1,263,846	-224,362	9,505,141	3,176,373	1,316,678		27,116	516,235	374,687
1997	14,914,973	11,677,144	87,598	11,764,742	1,351,134	-259,272	10,154,336	3,381,758	1,378,879		28,475	523,795	381,856
1998	16,030,483	12,554,806	127,719	12,682,525	1,441,825	-299,083	10,941,617	3,716,475	1,372,391		30,414	527,073	390,131
1999	16,768,672	13,430,633	141,874	13,572,507	1,549,306	-350,075	11,673,126	3,656,438	1,439,108		31,557	531,380	399,716
2000	18,187,304	14,628,035	99,766	14,727,801	1,664,914	-412,186	12,650,701	3,973,662	1,562,941		33,838	537,485	409,450
2001	19,350,427	15,837,257	138,054	15,975,311	1,745,886	-483,566	13,745,859	3,876,101	1,728,467		35,520	544,773	414,371
2002	20,119,467	16,778,587	118,414	16,897,001	1,840,633	-563,987	14,492,381	3,765,439	1,861,647		36,428	552,305	417,989
2003	20,860,726	17,365,295	159,734	17,525,029	1,914,370	-611,071	14,999,588	3,922,826	1,938,312		37,309	559,138	422,526
2004	21,819,214	18,290,810	221,076	18,511,886	2,021,862	-720,164	15,769,860	4,040,599	2,008,755		38,525	566,363	432,853
2005	22,785,495	19,028,305	191,367	19,219,672	2,109,803	-798,422	16,311,447	4,299,978	2,174,070		39,763	573,036	442,110
2006	24,338,159	19,918,208	169,774	20,087,982	2,223,323	-840,448	17,024,211	4,988,666	2,325,282		41,941	580,296	447,330
2007	25,477,146	20,571,322	238,490	20,809,812	2,307,957	-907,126	17,594,729	5,276,867	2,605,550		43,350	587,711	454,846
2008	26,196,477	20,927,531	190,210	21,117,741	2,374,933	-922,554	17,820,254	5,433,487	2,942,736		44,068	594,452	454,618
2009	25,729,984	20,573,694	124,733	20,698,427	2,328,257	-963,861	17,406,309	5,059,457	3,264,218		42,761	601,715	444,144
2010	26,499,448	20,939,396	205,613	21,145,009	2,377,965	-972,607	17,794,437	5,121,089	3,583,922		43,681	606,653	444,555
2011	28,427,286	22,289,544	326,363	22,615,907	2,242,907	-1,114,215	19,258,785	5,660,062	3,508,439		46,353	613,272	454,166
2012	29,805,380	23,298,067	245,420	23,543,487	2,322,223	-1,095,237	20,126,027	6,090,023	3,589,330		48,080	619,908	462,205
2013	30,691,115	24,593,495	242,923	24,836,418	2,779,728	-1,164,049	20,892,641	6,093,482	3,704,992		48,941	627,101	468,445
2014	32,122,695	25,548,075	223,827	25,771,902	2,868,809	-1,254,276	21,648,817	6,614,213	3,859,665		50,340	638,114	477,959
2015	34,132,616	27,100,497	179,922	27,280,419	3,025,860	-1,325,239	22,929,320	7,130,586	4,072,710		52,827	646,126	488,703
2016	35,447,175	28,178,930	129,476	28,308,406	3,139,518	-1,468,911	23,699,977	7,583,000	4,164,198		54,068	655,599	501,925
2017	36,935,581	29,320,067	133,718	29,453,785	3,299,648	-1,527,359	24,626,778	7,949,056	4,359,747		55,667	663,510	505,713
2018	39,148,335	30,939,602	127,547	31,067,149	3,423,760	-1,614,408	26,028,981	8,500,409	4,618,945		58,497	669,240	512,141
2019	41,672,119	32,770,280	126,591	32,896,871	3,646,201	-1,754,286	27,496,384	9,286,026	4,889,709		61,665	675,780	516,572
2020	44,159,680	33,805,654	268,004	34,073,658	3,775,829	-1,927,305	28,370,524	9,364,060	6,425,096		64,799	681,484	499,184
2021	47,218,781	36,354,560	267,111	36,621,671	3,968,131	-2,171,715	30,481,825	9,657,038	7,079,918		69,116	683,183	512,632

Personal Income and Employment by Area: Manchester-Nashua, NH

(Thousands of dollars, except as noted.)

Year	Personal income, total	Earnings by place of work			Less: Contributions for government social insurance	Plus: Adjustment for residence	Equals: Net earnings by place of residence	Plus: Dividends, interest, and rent	Plus: Personal current transfer receipts	Per capita personal income (dollars)	Population (persons)	Total employment
		Nonfarm	Farm	Total								
1970	961,049	790,738	3,474	794,212	51,606	679	743,285	144,957	72,807	4,245	226,390	115,787
1971	1,027,801	829,329	3,064	832,393	56,139	5,277	781,531	158,168	88,102	4,328	237,461	114,427
1972	1,119,971	899,311	3,113	902,424	64,221	13,875	852,078	172,363	95,530	4,748	235,887	115,341
1973	1,257,989	1,015,714	4,381	1,020,095	83,627	20,612	957,080	188,675	112,234	5,251	239,589	122,872
1974	1,385,255	1,097,185	2,685	1,099,870	93,381	31,323	1,037,812	212,725	134,718	5,686	243,605	125,196
1975	1,509,213	1,158,130	3,301	1,161,431	96,173	38,495	1,103,753	231,058	174,402	6,080	248,215	121,735
1976	1,718,541	1,330,041	3,868	1,333,909	111,678	55,789	1,278,020	254,812	185,709	6,718	255,826	129,826
1977	1,965,431	1,514,419	4,452	1,518,871	127,409	89,041	1,480,503	290,200	194,728	7,475	262,922	137,799
1978	2,299,436	1,760,599	5,581	1,766,180	151,020	141,574	1,756,734	329,780	212,922	8,559	268,671	147,386
1979	2,640,750	2,027,604	4,870	2,032,474	181,677	172,350	2,023,147	375,983	241,620	9,595	275,208	155,080
1980	3,041,125	2,277,113	2,559	2,279,672	204,182	217,796	2,293,286	465,114	282,725	10,932	278,189	159,785
1981	3,437,093	2,529,616	3,425	2,533,041	243,930	241,265	2,530,376	577,071	329,646	12,110	283,833	162,816
1982	3,802,574	2,774,331	4,012	2,778,343	274,341	252,767	2,756,769	688,393	357,412	13,234	287,334	166,065
1983	4,212,238	3,161,244	3,488	3,164,732	317,734	261,831	3,108,829	722,370	381,039	14,484	290,819	174,012
1984	4,819,673	3,665,172	3,817	3,668,989	380,778	286,526	3,574,737	845,704	399,232	16,169	298,089	189,171
1985	5,314,856	4,092,400	5,022	4,097,422	435,028	309,996	3,972,390	923,778	418,688	17,285	307,490	199,943
1986	5,860,757	4,567,324	5,080	4,572,404	489,177	310,582	4,393,809	1,025,236	441,712	18,531	316,260	208,594
1987	6,431,102	5,123,463	9,013	5,132,476	541,236	296,319	4,887,559	1,093,359	450,184	19,836	324,218	214,561
1988	6,980,236	5,554,163	10,442	5,564,605	600,714	323,415	5,287,306	1,202,776	490,154	21,196	329,319	220,131
1989	7,366,468	5,697,606	6,849	5,704,455	617,690	353,846	5,440,611	1,370,572	555,285	21,986	335,057	215,952
1990	7,348,699	5,663,611	7,989	5,671,600	631,768	303,373	5,343,205	1,381,334	624,160	21,821	336,768	208,783
1991	7,627,991	5,685,850	8,088	5,693,938	642,201	341,752	5,393,489	1,395,773	838,729	22,631	337,066	199,944
1992	7,969,910	6,104,347	7,564	6,111,911	684,290	295,866	5,723,487	1,355,420	891,003	23,367	341,078	202,042
1993	8,210,679	6,220,447	6,256	6,226,703	696,541	410,964	5,941,126	1,405,352	864,201	23,803	344,944	204,282
1994	8,759,634	6,532,366	5,723	6,538,089	740,156	500,159	6,298,092	1,502,657	958,885	25,086	349,190	209,544
1995	9,340,234	6,898,603	5,160	6,903,763	785,395	557,951	6,676,319	1,629,126	1,034,789	26,411	353,651	212,713
1996	10,041,720	7,486,169	5,126	7,491,295	841,908	585,806	7,235,193	1,775,995	1,030,532	28,001	358,624	218,719
1997	10,916,779	8,125,875	4,700	8,130,575	903,787	679,363	7,906,151	1,939,932	1,070,696	29,970	364,261	225,406
1998	12,039,679	9,069,530	3,949	9,073,479	978,970	699,800	8,794,309	2,129,525	1,115,845	32,487	370,595	233,399
1999	12,990,065	9,891,345	6,394	9,897,739	1,049,913	873,650	9,721,476	2,126,884	1,141,705	34,511	376,407	238,338
2000	14,722,238	11,130,903	6,002	11,136,905	1,162,891	1,135,191	11,109,205	2,394,309	1,218,724	38,524	382,162	246,068
2001	14,750,715	10,965,049	5,176	10,970,225	1,162,758	1,190,780	10,998,247	2,423,776	1,328,692	38,075	387,414	245,028
2002	14,813,931	11,095,646	5,735	11,101,381	1,163,039	1,113,805	11,052,147	2,316,662	1,445,122	38,017	389,665	242,388
2003	15,212,979	11,650,098	5,873	11,655,971	1,235,530	999,703	11,420,144	2,316,144	1,476,691	38,862	391,461	246,090
2004	16,251,880	12,344,680	5,880	12,350,560	1,324,295	1,064,676	12,090,941	2,562,656	1,598,283	41,204	394,428	250,596
2005	16,661,781	12,917,452	3,269	12,920,721	1,378,334	955,282	12,497,669	2,500,218	1,663,894	42,035	396,381	255,100
2006	17,800,289	13,526,473	2,847	13,529,320	1,424,652	1,104,642	13,209,310	2,818,127	1,772,852	44,705	398,169	256,756
2007	18,682,792	14,090,457	774	14,091,231	1,501,604	1,013,247	13,602,874	3,153,523	1,926,395	46,842	398,843	260,416
2008	19,288,146	14,289,445	1,201	14,290,646	1,549,496	986,503	13,727,653	3,318,019	2,242,474	48,274	399,556	258,229
2009	18,684,796	13,869,344	-975	13,868,369	1,514,567	774,076	13,127,878	3,120,580	2,436,338	46,695	400,148	250,764
2010	19,112,097	14,198,391	-1,067	14,197,324	1,543,834	1,106,501	13,759,991	2,738,101	2,614,005	47,653	401,064	247,058
2011	20,142,018	14,845,106	-2,744	14,842,362	1,441,909	941,328	14,341,781	3,230,307	2,569,930	50,001	402,832	249,484
2012	21,055,988	15,168,391	1,140	15,169,531	1,473,945	1,034,456	14,730,042	3,718,272	2,607,674	52,062	404,439	250,653
2013	20,935,208	15,417,219	7,980	15,425,199	1,692,853	980,841	14,713,187	3,568,727	2,653,294	51,639	405,417	254,365
2014	21,708,787	16,352,238	1,983	16,354,221	1,771,291	746,074	15,329,004	3,554,988	2,824,795	53,058	409,149	258,584
2015	22,441,176	16,841,399	2,793	16,844,192	1,831,711	879,839	15,892,320	3,516,196	3,032,660	54,558	411,330	264,868
2016	23,179,068	17,486,516	1,976	17,488,492	1,895,888	934,854	16,527,458	3,449,248	3,202,362	55,974	414,107	269,070
2017	24,092,150	18,158,408	3,475	18,161,883	1,992,420	1,043,057	17,212,520	3,564,131	3,315,499	57,847	416,477	271,987
2018	25,170,557	19,025,825	1,242	19,027,067	2,077,635	1,054,095	18,003,527	3,674,229	3,492,801	60,179	418,261	276,104
2019	26,666,042	19,837,842	4,416	19,842,258	2,161,345	1,309,516	18,990,429	4,071,022	3,604,591	63,263	421,513	276,437
2020	28,374,864	20,830,491	-1,402	20,829,089	2,250,068	860,735	19,439,756	4,098,906	4,836,202	67,127	422,705	266,897
2021	30,469,772	23,405,856	-6,359	23,399,497	2,430,437	205,713	21,174,773	4,203,286	5,091,713	71,849	424,079	275,513

Personal Income and Employment by Area: Manhattan, KS

(Thousands of dollars, except as noted.)

| Year | Personal income, total | Derivation of personal income | | | | | | | | | Per capita personal income (dollars) | Population (persons) | Total employment |
| | | Earnings by place of work | | | Less: Contributions for government social insurance | Plus: Adjustment for residence | Equals: Net earnings by place of residence | Plus: Dividends, interest, and rent | Plus: Personal current transfer receipts | | | |
		Nonfarm	Farm	Total								
1970	289,990	119,461	6,205	125,666	7,980	111,367	229,053	47,236	13,701	4,214	68,809	21,881
1971	318,404	138,350	5,617	143,967	9,592	116,135	250,510	52,300	15,594	4,540	70,127	23,477
1972	339,912	149,388	8,926	158,314	10,975	119,274	266,613	55,676	17,623	4,879	69,674	23,827
1973	368,583	159,355	12,980	172,335	13,580	125,947	284,702	63,102	20,779	5,065	72,765	24,363
1974	407,550	178,938	11,472	190,410	16,209	135,125	309,326	73,615	24,609	5,495	74,161	25,624
1975	446,565	203,994	10,758	214,752	18,551	140,027	336,228	80,249	30,088	5,962	74,899	26,460
1976	482,402	230,629	7,675	238,304	21,194	145,417	362,527	85,854	34,021	6,233	77,389	27,641
1977	526,936	261,338	3,182	264,520	23,924	151,968	392,564	96,910	37,462	6,983	75,461	29,291
1978	582,620	295,073	7,468	302,541	28,062	156,424	430,903	110,272	41,445	7,568	76,980	30,448
1979	632,536	315,107	5,094	320,201	31,057	173,885	463,029	123,736	45,771	8,182	77,305	30,601
1980	709,697	340,426	-3,482	336,944	33,768	206,668	509,844	144,802	55,051	9,024	78,646	30,601
1981	807,205	374,612	10,916	385,528	39,956	227,881	573,453	171,430	62,322	10,093	79,976	30,908
1982	870,898	397,055	9,603	406,658	42,754	242,079	605,983	197,832	67,083	10,788	80,726	31,468
1983	914,083	416,171	7,266	423,437	43,923	250,332	629,846	209,388	74,849	11,056	82,675	31,585
1984	972,971	453,944	8,182	462,126	48,262	251,803	665,667	229,203	78,101	11,894	81,804	32,746
1985	1,048,034	480,988	17,971	498,959	51,750	270,391	717,600	244,328	86,106	13,018	80,504	33,518
1986	1,086,125	505,915	13,479	519,394	54,185	277,770	742,979	257,964	85,182	13,543	80,200	33,800
1987	1,124,768	536,920	15,618	552,538	57,329	277,500	772,709	262,476	89,583	13,925	80,773	35,862
1988	1,171,817	571,988	14,442	586,430	64,382	283,219	805,267	272,667	93,883	14,349	81,667	37,095
1989	1,253,745	619,302	9,033	628,335	68,951	287,419	846,803	302,688	104,254	15,146	82,780	37,881
1990	1,261,579	647,831	13,690	661,521	75,231	271,510	857,800	292,288	111,491	15,137	83,343	38,985
1991	1,290,981	692,056	8,561	700,617	81,733	247,194	866,078	302,129	122,774	15,877	81,311	40,004
1992	1,466,960	763,646	17,072	780,718	89,294	305,628	997,052	333,696	136,212	17,304	84,774	40,430
1993	1,465,052	774,305	12,293	786,598	89,952	290,594	987,240	335,520	142,292	17,381	84,291	41,564
1994	1,556,099	832,644	15,603	848,247	98,486	304,562	1,054,323	357,859	143,917	18,204	85,482	42,235
1995	1,578,362	873,973	3,304	877,277	102,753	287,836	1,062,360	362,557	153,445	18,407	85,748	43,743
1996	1,583,264	920,749	17,937	938,686	107,215	224,339	1,055,810	368,985	158,469	19,107	82,862	44,143
1997	1,625,675	956,368	10,659	967,027	112,128	222,814	1,077,713	381,343	166,619	19,912	81,644	44,564
1998	2,312,069	1,725,061	10,064	1,735,125	194,511	-55,871	1,484,743	584,993	242,333	21,156	109,287	69,961
1999	2,429,234	1,829,494	13,389	1,842,883	205,316	-58,977	1,578,590	594,619	256,025	22,261	109,123	70,983
2000	2,605,779	1,963,909	13,000	1,976,909	221,809	-64,491	1,690,609	637,885	277,285	23,822	109,384	72,177
2001	2,750,166	2,132,191	18,443	2,150,634	237,055	-84,994	1,828,585	617,750	303,831	25,186	109,195	72,131
2002	2,813,586	2,230,009	5,867	2,235,876	246,979	-107,529	1,881,368	608,012	324,206	25,840	108,884	70,552
2003	2,987,583	2,396,292	18,563	2,414,855	264,183	-150,739	1,999,933	643,903	343,747	27,314	109,379	71,515
2004	3,146,759	2,569,498	26,616	2,596,114	284,838	-172,414	2,138,862	651,654	356,243	28,462	110,560	73,407
2005	3,275,769	2,702,353	21,992	2,724,345	299,166	-207,937	2,217,242	681,164	377,363	29,433	111,294	73,636
2006	3,683,708	3,079,305	8,602	3,087,907	339,027	-267,144	2,481,736	800,173	401,799	32,213	114,356	77,822
2007	4,118,298	3,501,345	12,958	3,514,303	380,408	-362,677	2,771,218	911,794	435,286	35,602	115,675	83,397
2008	4,579,388	3,920,382	10,429	3,930,811	423,260	-441,573	3,065,978	1,002,426	510,984	37,970	120,604	86,711
2009	4,714,800	3,999,679	20,836	4,020,515	437,741	-407,464	3,175,310	987,873	551,617	38,414	122,738	87,487
2010	5,129,291	4,330,800	15,079	4,345,879	477,610	-399,742	3,468,527	1,046,335	614,429	39,908	128,527	89,283
2011	5,471,711	4,480,724	40,775	4,521,499	443,097	-361,703	3,716,699	1,112,376	642,636	41,836	130,791	88,981
2012	5,616,924	4,527,660	33,056	4,560,716	450,096	-311,334	3,799,286	1,179,258	638,380	40,753	137,830	89,097
2013	5,535,769	4,404,614	54,659	4,459,273	485,567	-251,000	3,722,706	1,158,615	654,448	40,573	136,439	88,198
2014	5,677,296	4,498,921	26,640	4,525,561	498,655	-252,406	3,774,500	1,221,190	681,606	41,245	137,647	88,924
2015	5,812,933	4,635,582	11,954	4,647,536	517,663	-263,161	3,866,712	1,241,408	704,813	41,679	139,468	89,211
2016	5,826,111	4,607,321	12,276	4,619,597	504,516	-266,749	3,848,332	1,243,201	734,578	42,516	137,034	87,752
2017	5,900,621	4,656,111	9,656	4,665,767	512,333	-268,622	3,884,812	1,258,931	756,878	43,729	134,937	90,141
2018	6,030,036	4,761,512	22,090	4,783,602	523,448	-272,870	3,987,284	1,248,540	794,212	44,557	135,332	90,786
2019	6,137,609	4,759,897	20,180	4,780,077	528,744	-279,000	3,972,333	1,313,884	851,392	46,208	132,825	91,357
2020	6,557,208	4,941,322	37,358	4,978,680	549,847	-292,150	4,136,683	1,300,703	1,119,822	48,885	134,135	89,120
2021	6,852,329	5,120,158	35,504	5,155,662	562,386	-299,452	4,293,824	1,300,899	1,257,606	51,163	133,932	89,935

Personal Income and Employment by Area: Mankato, MN

(Thousands of dollars, except as noted.)

Year	Personal income, total	Earnings by place of work			Less: Contributions for government social insurance	Plus: Adjustment for residence	Equals: Net earnings by place of residence	Plus: Dividends, interest, and rent	Plus: Personal current transfer receipts	Per capita personal income (dollars)	Population (persons)	Total employment
		Nonfarm	Farm	Total								
1970	264,523	181,093	29,959	211,052	12,252	-954	197,846	45,102	21,575	3,434	77,037	32,324
1971	280,227	199,226	23,124	222,350	14,015	-2,141	206,194	49,222	24,811	3,592	78,012	32,665
1972	305,079	213,266	29,059	242,325	15,686	-2,016	224,623	52,926	27,530	3,937	77,494	34,258
1973	379,991	240,844	69,116	309,960	20,598	-3,140	286,222	61,588	32,181	4,944	76,854	36,352
1974	406,071	271,570	53,774	325,344	24,431	-4,673	296,240	71,574	38,257	5,240	77,488	37,064
1975	438,278	298,401	44,128	342,529	26,495	-6,458	309,576	81,837	46,865	5,668	77,328	37,194
1976	452,057	330,594	19,745	350,339	29,938	-8,012	312,389	87,667	52,001	5,809	77,818	37,739
1977	538,793	364,602	62,841	427,443	33,056	-9,703	384,684	98,636	55,473	6,901	78,073	39,224
1978	598,122	414,191	65,510	479,701	38,944	-12,069	428,688	109,183	60,251	7,677	77,906	40,917
1979	639,361	461,106	47,155	508,261	45,017	-14,614	448,630	122,661	68,070	8,148	78,471	42,687
1980	689,137	489,996	32,905	522,901	47,553	-16,386	458,962	148,308	81,867	8,681	79,381	42,871
1981	764,949	529,639	34,659	564,298	55,025	-16,468	492,805	179,740	92,404	9,591	79,753	43,218
1982	810,490	552,547	19,326	571,873	58,109	-16,479	497,285	210,242	102,963	10,136	79,958	43,012
1983	839,592	589,845	-6,280	583,565	62,631	-16,743	504,191	224,045	111,356	10,522	79,795	43,112
1984	960,800	636,944	42,219	679,163	69,110	-13,609	596,444	248,193	116,163	12,043	79,784	43,684
1985	1,000,129	657,324	47,123	704,447	72,838	-10,972	620,637	254,889	124,603	12,471	80,198	44,449
1986	1,041,753	690,146	45,184	735,330	78,541	-9,726	647,063	263,869	130,821	12,975	80,288	44,537
1987	1,144,918	748,250	80,606	828,856	84,844	-10,632	733,380	273,365	138,173	14,244	80,379	45,846
1988	1,159,810	809,357	42,856	852,213	95,148	-9,481	747,584	267,913	144,313	14,254	81,366	47,128
1989	1,288,175	864,863	73,909	938,772	101,569	-6,927	830,276	304,351	153,548	15,795	81,555	47,596
1990	1,355,221	931,697	59,515	991,212	109,677	-4,752	876,783	314,401	164,037	16,470	82,283	48,587
1991	1,389,310	989,991	29,459	1,019,450	118,050	-11,133	890,267	325,278	173,765	16,788	82,758	49,463
1992	1,504,342	1,095,190	44,590	1,139,780	128,820	-16,600	994,360	323,887	186,095	18,135	82,954	51,307
1993	1,541,598	1,158,705	-331	1,158,374	136,851	-22,569	998,954	347,445	195,199	18,510	83,283	52,620
1994	1,679,712	1,239,692	51,008	1,290,700	148,154	-26,556	1,115,990	359,065	204,657	20,064	83,717	54,719
1995	1,746,853	1,295,081	22,553	1,317,634	154,359	-29,089	1,134,186	395,310	217,357	20,662	84,545	55,982
1996	1,883,239	1,360,297	81,129	1,441,426	160,183	-31,249	1,249,994	408,995	224,250	22,179	84,912	56,419
1997	1,924,793	1,414,337	51,682	1,466,019	166,294	-34,530	1,265,195	431,587	228,011	22,672	84,897	56,660
1998	2,100,327	1,582,272	53,040	1,635,312	182,558	-47,075	1,405,679	463,037	231,611	24,776	84,771	60,139
1999	2,172,852	1,652,269	43,173	1,695,442	192,115	-52,584	1,450,743	478,169	243,940	25,531	85,105	61,312
2000	2,277,243	1,739,647	59,137	1,798,784	200,945	-58,597	1,539,242	475,608	262,393	26,513	85,892	61,984
2001	2,492,204	1,915,843	48,419	1,964,262	214,998	-65,880	1,683,384	509,008	299,812	28,611	87,105	61,726
2002	2,576,573	2,042,286	41,512	2,083,798	226,585	-76,087	1,781,126	471,453	323,994	29,244	88,107	62,351
2003	2,710,281	2,108,077	60,311	2,168,388	237,200	-86,977	1,844,211	520,855	345,215	30,338	89,336	62,587
2004	2,851,578	2,212,074	125,001	2,337,075	248,187	-93,668	1,995,220	495,467	360,891	31,631	90,152	63,325
2005	2,941,806	2,320,041	145,096	2,465,137	265,780	-114,752	2,084,605	479,336	377,865	32,288	91,111	65,189
2006	3,173,937	2,514,438	130,816	2,645,254	289,662	-133,449	2,222,143	530,648	421,146	34,173	92,879	67,013
2007	3,252,996	2,532,140	96,520	2,628,660	293,160	-139,048	2,196,452	596,564	459,980	34,620	93,963	67,773
2008	3,362,163	2,484,904	165,377	2,650,281	295,701	-147,859	2,206,721	628,783	526,659	35,346	95,121	67,301
2009	3,221,076	2,403,424	104,142	2,507,566	288,583	-144,662	2,074,321	561,725	585,030	33,514	96,111	65,739
2010	3,379,683	2,456,161	147,540	2,603,701	290,729	-157,467	2,155,505	580,879	643,299	34,896	96,849	65,596
2011	3,668,969	2,596,646	223,978	2,820,624	275,133	-177,472	2,368,019	662,921	638,029	37,694	97,335	66,932
2012	3,925,997	2,760,100	263,404	3,023,504	287,787	-191,127	2,544,590	742,629	638,778	40,058	98,009	67,085
2013	3,935,076	2,848,560	213,634	3,062,194	338,106	-177,600	2,546,488	730,010	658,578	40,259	97,745	68,260
2014	4,139,946	3,025,493	182,414	3,207,907	352,012	-190,500	2,665,395	769,632	704,919	41,776	99,098	68,719
2015	4,293,978	3,159,762	113,676	3,273,438	363,376	-189,168	2,720,894	854,424	718,660	43,058	99,726	70,068
2016	4,291,077	3,227,580	37,356	3,264,936	375,032	-200,303	2,689,601	853,324	748,152	42,595	100,742	70,620
2017	4,470,366	3,361,006	100,161	3,461,167	396,455	-223,913	2,840,799	843,773	785,794	43,961	101,689	71,533
2018	4,676,454	3,514,476	79,926	3,594,402	415,449	-231,765	2,947,188	897,922	831,344	45,665	102,407	72,207
2019	4,856,288	3,649,652	54,862	3,704,514	433,480	-242,597	3,028,437	961,189	866,662	47,120	103,062	72,673
2020	5,248,711	3,680,361	111,715	3,792,076	438,710	-250,786	3,102,580	967,624	1,178,507	50,632	103,663	69,089
2021	5,547,724	3,871,882	139,079	4,010,961	449,072	-275,117	3,286,772	974,980	1,285,972	53,543	103,612	70,302

Personal Income and Employment by Area: Mansfield, OH

(Thousands of dollars, except as noted.)

Year	Personal income, total	Earnings by place of work — Nonfarm	Earnings by place of work — Farm	Earnings by place of work — Total	Less: Contributions for government social insurance	Plus: Adjustment for residence	Equals: Net earnings by place of residence	Plus: Dividends, interest, and rent	Plus: Personal current transfer receipts	Per capita personal income (dollars)	Population (persons)	Total employment
1970	516,298	469,915	2,941	472,856	31,347	-27,267	414,242	65,513	36,543	3,976	129,838	60,931
1971	567,752	518,416	1,989	520,405	36,010	-30,507	453,888	70,589	43,275	4,387	129,411	63,089
1972	606,042	554,492	3,572	558,064	40,680	-33,389	483,995	74,974	47,073	4,632	130,847	63,607
1973	670,311	618,207	4,793	623,000	53,147	-37,425	532,428	83,357	54,526	5,120	130,923	66,236
1974	707,235	629,762	5,918	635,680	56,036	-34,472	545,172	94,271	67,792	5,425	130,356	64,297
1975	746,455	636,939	7,033	643,972	55,070	-33,286	555,616	100,804	90,035	5,703	130,887	60,904
1976	822,879	716,878	8,277	725,155	63,706	-39,105	622,344	107,710	92,825	6,274	131,160	61,493
1977	924,472	823,791	6,640	830,431	74,107	-48,160	708,164	119,352	96,956	7,083	130,524	64,527
1978	1,002,098	893,232	4,947	898,179	82,483	-49,941	765,755	131,348	104,995	7,657	130,866	65,594
1979	1,097,045	969,585	4,548	974,133	92,464	-52,503	829,166	148,581	119,298	8,427	130,178	65,972
1980	1,190,148	1,009,230	153	1,009,383	95,333	-55,893	858,157	183,705	148,286	9,077	131,116	65,230
1981	1,326,930	1,113,393	327	1,113,720	112,650	-69,082	931,988	226,779	168,163	10,171	130,465	65,158
1982	1,348,026	1,066,001	3,203	1,069,204	107,859	-64,687	896,658	248,107	203,261	10,438	129,141	61,624
1983	1,481,979	1,208,763	-2,432	1,206,331	126,327	-83,038	996,966	270,494	214,519	11,572	128,066	63,435
1984	1,615,110	1,320,629	6,262	1,326,891	141,117	-89,481	1,096,293	300,940	217,877	12,570	128,485	66,715
1985	1,715,525	1,421,297	7,323	1,428,620	154,326	-101,702	1,172,592	309,786	233,147	13,384	128,181	67,043
1986	1,788,723	1,476,521	5,310	1,481,831	164,713	-104,322	1,212,796	322,524	253,403	14,038	127,418	68,043
1987	1,841,310	1,531,199	6,927	1,538,126	170,131	-105,948	1,262,047	321,937	257,326	14,459	127,345	69,183
1988	1,938,842	1,636,096	6,640	1,642,736	187,832	-113,146	1,341,758	330,262	266,822	15,246	127,167	70,397
1989	2,050,664	1,702,809	10,767	1,713,576	196,549	-118,077	1,398,950	364,327	287,387	16,199	126,590	71,654
1990	2,110,444	1,720,229	9,376	1,729,605	201,886	-114,084	1,413,635	374,360	322,449	16,728	126,160	70,803
1991	2,112,274	1,704,297	1,482	1,705,779	202,509	-103,217	1,400,053	363,928	348,293	16,627	127,040	68,169
1992	2,212,074	1,751,265	14,244	1,765,509	204,693	-95,621	1,465,195	368,405	378,474	17,353	127,475	68,884
1993	2,338,330	1,886,585	5,787	1,892,372	225,177	-101,956	1,565,239	378,323	394,768	18,298	127,792	71,627
1994	2,451,765	1,960,444	11,829	1,972,273	236,861	-88,755	1,646,657	392,408	412,700	19,112	128,281	72,358
1995	2,530,497	2,024,062	14,140	2,038,202	246,504	-93,381	1,698,317	398,479	433,701	19,736	128,217	74,128
1996	2,651,396	2,110,894	16,478	2,127,372	253,674	-99,849	1,773,849	422,556	454,991	20,570	128,894	74,963
1997	2,790,263	2,214,945	17,427	2,232,372	258,857	-102,710	1,870,805	451,309	468,149	21,652	128,868	75,038
1998	2,870,592	2,254,415	14,627	2,269,042	256,895	-93,857	1,918,290	472,041	480,261	22,332	128,540	72,778
1999	2,951,333	2,347,402	9,902	2,357,304	264,069	-96,541	1,996,694	452,769	501,870	22,837	129,233	73,336
2000	3,080,740	2,430,549	10,520	2,441,069	264,559	-95,106	2,081,404	475,065	524,271	23,909	128,853	73,985
2001	3,235,244	2,532,755	11,061	2,543,816	277,173	-91,688	2,174,955	475,860	584,429	25,238	128,187	74,473
2002	3,344,910	2,627,282	3,760	2,631,042	280,966	-85,796	2,264,280	457,592	623,038	26,058	128,363	73,890
2003	3,451,551	2,684,865	4,142	2,689,007	290,301	-80,077	2,318,629	470,742	662,180	26,900	128,312	72,842
2004	3,498,576	2,749,543	9,653	2,759,196	304,770	-104,117	2,350,309	456,111	692,156	27,313	128,094	72,726
2005	3,530,126	2,741,300	6,593	2,747,893	306,017	-100,719	2,341,157	464,230	724,739	27,639	127,724	72,383
2006	3,629,780	2,809,844	6,689	2,816,533	317,216	-117,986	2,381,331	478,829	769,620	28,515	127,292	72,402
2007	3,733,762	2,750,732	7,645	2,758,377	308,912	-88,223	2,361,242	552,254	820,266	29,401	126,995	71,443
2008	3,881,970	2,749,561	8,643	2,758,204	317,476	-74,681	2,366,047	603,903	912,020	30,778	126,128	70,018
2009	3,743,311	2,537,465	9,876	2,547,341	297,904	-63,969	2,185,468	554,963	1,002,880	29,873	125,308	65,881
2010	3,780,365	2,535,692	21,584	2,557,276	293,057	-61,257	2,202,962	537,403	1,040,000	30,449	124,156	64,781
2011	3,973,375	2,614,726	35,021	2,649,747	274,293	-59,820	2,315,634	589,943	1,067,798	32,264	123,151	66,089
2012	4,040,838	2,656,747	22,173	2,678,920	276,441	-30,794	2,371,685	609,697	1,059,456	32,947	122,645	64,818
2013	4,094,829	2,684,501	41,173	2,725,674	301,289	17,397	2,441,782	583,462	1,069,585	33,471	122,339	64,761
2014	4,292,697	2,774,299	37,183	2,811,482	311,117	19,201	2,519,566	644,699	1,128,432	34,707	123,685	65,561
2015	4,434,938	2,810,901	7,799	2,818,700	313,147	55,541	2,561,094	695,631	1,178,213	35,834	123,763	65,097
2016	4,425,219	2,822,423	3,793	2,826,216	322,368	46,895	2,550,743	674,827	1,199,649	35,758	123,753	65,016
2017	4,558,095	2,935,186	14,092	2,949,278	342,818	58,921	2,665,381	679,286	1,213,428	36,966	123,305	64,556
2018	4,742,257	3,063,029	19,369	3,082,398	353,060	23,563	2,752,901	744,608	1,244,748	38,142	124,330	65,420
2019	4,987,849	3,097,953	5,945	3,103,898	360,830	171,338	2,914,406	756,982	1,316,461	39,903	125,000	64,788
2020	5,438,154	3,100,381	21,197	3,121,578	363,997	200,108	2,957,689	768,145	1,712,320	43,561	124,840	61,979
2021	5,804,846	3,279,929	42,481	3,322,410	378,900	204,962	3,148,472	796,400	1,859,974	46,366	125,195	63,492

Personal Income and Employment by Area: McAllen-Edinburg-Mission, TX

(Thousands of dollars, except as noted.)

Year	Personal income, total	Earnings by place of work			Less: Contributions for government social insurance	Plus: Adjustment for residence	Equals: Net earnings by place of residence	Plus: Dividends, interest, and rent	Plus: Personal current transfer receipts	Per capita personal income (dollars)	Population (persons)	Total employment
		Nonfarm	Farm	Total								
1970	364,139	260,864	22,601	283,465	15,860	-9,141	258,464	59,886	45,789	1,989	183,040	55,167
1971	428,483	296,938	37,595	334,533	18,581	-8,638	307,314	67,788	53,381	2,216	193,397	58,147
1972	479,788	346,602	25,965	372,567	22,664	-8,990	340,913	77,030	61,845	2,342	204,904	64,427
1973	571,221	405,838	26,895	432,733	31,119	-9,421	392,193	91,716	87,312	2,632	217,004	69,841
1974	671,642	475,413	30,438	505,851	37,482	-11,518	456,851	110,674	104,117	3,001	223,800	74,338
1975	791,763	555,034	34,284	589,318	42,731	-12,780	533,807	130,410	127,546	3,316	238,746	77,588
1976	903,307	658,565	22,947	681,512	51,002	-14,133	616,377	145,074	141,856	3,628	249,003	82,908
1977	1,051,173	734,940	70,547	805,487	57,494	-15,582	732,411	166,181	152,581	4,063	258,732	87,780
1978	1,185,172	831,701	64,062	895,763	66,294	-14,859	814,610	194,956	175,606	4,454	266,103	90,869
1979	1,326,959	934,978	39,547	974,525	78,510	-13,656	882,359	227,993	216,607	4,817	275,488	93,698
1980	1,550,674	1,078,146	28,323	1,106,469	92,606	-14,859	999,004	283,521	268,149	5,412	286,540	99,240
1981	1,848,512	1,234,897	86,461	1,321,358	116,678	-8,014	1,196,666	351,133	300,713	6,191	298,559	106,048
1982	2,023,439	1,336,876	67,723	1,404,599	128,049	-9,088	1,267,462	421,021	334,956	6,459	313,256	110,680
1983	2,160,148	1,387,666	48,611	1,436,277	129,299	-9,757	1,297,221	462,487	400,440	6,617	326,453	108,973
1984	2,354,671	1,502,659	52,377	1,555,036	142,003	-9,061	1,403,972	511,545	439,154	7,038	334,571	110,090
1985	2,587,303	1,648,875	44,532	1,693,407	156,625	-8,546	1,528,236	570,943	488,124	7,584	341,145	113,109
1986	2,685,917	1,714,213	30,958	1,745,171	160,769	-8,836	1,575,566	586,222	524,129	7,663	350,514	112,319
1987	2,795,855	1,781,761	53,465	1,835,226	166,031	-9,065	1,660,130	589,005	546,720	7,803	358,307	117,858
1988	3,074,496	2,001,417	65,415	2,066,832	193,315	-8,300	1,865,217	613,521	595,758	8,412	365,499	124,638
1989	3,369,972	2,152,316	46,903	2,199,219	214,557	-5,100	1,979,562	704,448	685,962	8,936	377,106	131,460
1990	3,685,707	2,343,101	60,723	2,403,824	229,546	-3,836	2,170,442	713,232	802,033	9,519	387,200	134,822
1991	4,066,060	2,564,273	81,093	2,645,366	256,872	-4,084	2,384,410	760,187	921,463	10,075	403,571	138,175
1992	4,512,124	2,788,544	83,404	2,871,948	276,611	-1,656	2,593,681	766,739	1,151,704	10,634	424,312	142,423
1993	4,890,266	3,055,318	113,222	3,168,540	304,283	-2,325	2,861,932	786,619	1,241,715	10,928	447,508	148,166
1994	5,313,250	3,335,923	100,392	3,436,315	337,829	-6,002	3,092,484	836,523	1,384,243	11,331	468,906	155,816
1995	5,645,401	3,494,633	83,306	3,577,939	355,901	-6,263	3,215,775	898,866	1,530,760	11,578	487,593	163,571
1996	6,085,455	3,771,188	60,367	3,831,555	378,066	-8,099	3,445,390	951,870	1,688,195	12,088	503,411	171,626
1997	6,588,265	4,186,474	60,429	4,246,903	413,115	-11,486	3,822,302	992,814	1,773,149	12,672	519,903	182,919
1998	7,093,144	4,558,472	111,074	4,669,546	443,519	-11,719	4,214,308	1,044,295	1,834,541	13,186	537,929	188,244
1999	7,455,655	4,857,744	122,054	4,979,798	472,252	-16,449	4,491,097	1,080,894	1,883,664	13,412	555,875	199,684
2000	8,165,949	5,393,201	111,147	5,504,348	512,439	-18,981	4,972,928	1,188,320	2,004,701	14,246	573,216	212,033
2001	8,824,448	5,883,660	126,783	6,010,443	552,375	-96,632	5,361,436	1,258,651	2,204,361	14,955	590,067	220,968
2002	9,562,620	6,350,748	110,823	6,461,571	596,009	-90,806	5,774,756	1,273,344	2,514,520	15,663	610,520	230,567
2003	10,351,336	6,874,129	154,823	7,028,952	654,808	-82,502	6,291,642	1,320,323	2,739,371	16,366	632,475	242,793
2004	11,245,114	7,592,041	140,307	7,732,348	717,097	-69,603	6,945,648	1,411,062	2,888,404	17,200	653,779	256,668
2005	12,241,379	8,095,657	158,625	8,254,282	782,345	-59,886	7,412,051	1,550,368	3,278,960	18,136	674,982	270,969
2006	13,214,521	8,807,383	105,987	8,913,370	841,074	-21,467	8,050,829	1,629,001	3,534,691	19,004	695,352	282,999
2007	14,086,716	9,178,517	93,461	9,271,978	905,229	-4,975	8,361,774	1,764,813	3,960,129	19,694	715,264	302,755
2008	15,365,964	9,563,376	39,810	9,603,186	946,296	29,028	8,685,918	2,180,516	4,499,530	20,858	736,694	308,229
2009	16,202,286	10,046,419	33,713	10,080,132	997,710	67,161	9,149,583	2,051,166	5,001,537	21,390	757,468	310,579
2010	17,355,116	10,711,782	66,942	10,778,724	1,049,164	93,841	9,823,401	2,071,649	5,460,066	22,276	779,091	316,440
2011	18,336,596	11,300,163	36,628	11,336,791	980,105	157,562	10,514,248	2,234,990	5,587,358	23,056	795,305	329,907
2012	18,999,050	11,781,758	54,914	11,836,672	1,013,455	248,708	11,071,925	2,457,664	5,469,461	23,516	807,930	335,365
2013	19,688,480	12,290,492	175,901	12,466,393	1,175,876	323,611	11,614,128	2,485,583	5,588,769	24,068	818,047	342,957
2014	20,541,899	12,945,023	111,280	13,056,303	1,233,876	364,673	12,187,100	2,574,022	5,780,777	24,811	827,938	354,052
2015	21,289,111	13,301,864	161,788	13,463,652	1,291,891	335,042	12,506,803	2,659,960	6,122,348	25,425	837,320	361,838
2016	21,652,455	13,576,439	139,385	13,715,824	1,342,907	255,317	12,628,234	2,644,068	6,380,153	25,593	846,030	368,345
2017	22,214,659	14,030,281	160,947	14,191,228	1,399,805	244,801	13,036,224	2,738,911	6,439,524	26,052	852,699	374,851
2018	23,228,255	14,657,710	123,427	14,781,137	1,461,081	273,274	13,593,330	2,941,491	6,693,434	27,060	858,413	387,890
2019	24,428,598	15,501,287	87,303	15,588,590	1,533,434	292,969	14,348,125	3,066,220	7,014,253	28,256	864,536	393,996
2020	27,336,762	15,779,688	123,682	15,903,370	1,599,476	220,372	14,524,266	3,046,852	9,765,644	31,342	872,204	394,032
2021	30,374,915	16,846,904	247,413	17,094,317	1,703,480	174,960	15,565,797	3,182,582	11,626,536	34,503	880,356	406,589

Personal Income and Employment by Area: Medford, OR

(Thousands of dollars, except as noted.)

Year	Personal income, total	Earnings by place of work			Less: Contributions for government social insurance	Plus: Adjustment for residence	Equals: Net earnings by place of residence	Plus: Dividends, interest, and rent	Plus: Personal current transfer receipts	Per capita personal income (dollars)	Population (persons)	Total employment
		Nonfarm	Farm	Total								
1970	332,495	235,360	5,186	240,546	18,016	4,488	227,018	66,784	38,693	3,486	95,374	36,133
1971	380,955	270,822	8,211	279,033	21,443	4,906	262,496	74,284	44,175	3,829	99,487	39,058
1972	431,925	315,140	6,464	321,604	26,338	5,515	300,781	81,932	49,212	4,260	101,396	41,785
1973	493,284	357,936	9,492	367,428	34,228	5,701	338,901	94,253	60,130	4,600	107,245	44,421
1974	558,936	392,826	10,847	403,673	38,393	5,140	370,420	110,978	77,538	5,039	110,926	45,606
1975	631,982	431,477	9,193	440,670	40,680	5,661	405,651	126,796	99,535	5,499	114,924	46,756
1976	720,268	503,909	10,334	514,243	47,733	7,192	473,702	137,426	109,140	6,120	117,683	49,250
1977	821,643	585,794	8,841	594,635	56,268	8,152	546,519	155,328	119,796	6,717	122,329	52,964
1978	954,398	685,593	11,085	696,678	67,432	8,997	638,243	185,293	130,862	7,549	126,435	57,334
1979	1,073,460	761,390	16,388	777,778	77,611	9,066	709,233	216,461	147,766	8,263	129,918	58,937
1980	1,196,911	810,659	20,498	831,157	83,028	9,296	757,425	263,115	176,371	9,004	132,929	58,583
1981	1,282,978	824,827	12,612	837,439	90,124	11,231	758,546	320,775	203,657	9,536	134,546	57,391
1982	1,317,243	808,493	10,891	819,384	90,009	11,801	741,176	348,092	227,975	9,841	133,847	54,859
1983	1,432,497	890,677	5,080	895,757	100,092	12,197	807,862	384,272	240,363	10,760	133,130	57,463
1984	1,596,051	1,018,091	11,081	1,029,172	117,621	11,714	923,265	424,232	248,554	11,838	134,830	60,553
1985	1,687,489	1,075,541	12,473	1,088,014	125,208	12,434	975,240	446,002	266,247	12,368	136,444	61,517
1986	1,781,914	1,149,334	13,786	1,163,120	133,867	11,846	1,041,099	470,866	269,949	12,969	137,397	63,925
1987	1,899,744	1,263,653	6,955	1,270,608	146,275	11,682	1,136,015	480,402	283,327	13,606	139,626	67,656
1988	2,075,750	1,380,746	9,246	1,389,992	165,594	12,519	1,236,917	533,806	305,027	14,736	140,860	71,400
1989	2,280,964	1,473,649	13,546	1,487,195	176,766	14,277	1,324,706	616,745	339,513	15,890	143,549	72,786
1990	2,431,840	1,597,449	10,885	1,608,334	195,763	13,899	1,426,470	634,381	370,989	16,499	147,392	75,872
1991	2,570,550	1,654,405	16,701	1,671,106	205,922	13,418	1,478,602	672,587	419,361	17,028	150,956	76,214
1992	2,761,971	1,808,225	16,851	1,825,076	224,257	11,803	1,612,622	691,816	457,533	17,822	154,975	78,291
1993	2,976,728	1,957,182	19,986	1,977,168	240,025	11,393	1,748,536	738,357	489,835	18,715	159,054	80,714
1994	3,236,236	2,155,409	15,642	2,171,051	264,507	9,377	1,915,921	798,127	522,188	19,790	163,527	85,896
1995	3,443,551	2,225,294	14,502	2,239,796	276,436	9,649	1,973,009	889,500	581,042	20,573	167,378	88,260
1996	3,667,830	2,348,369	20,101	2,368,470	295,222	9,815	2,083,063	961,991	622,776	21,485	170,715	91,601
1997	3,832,637	2,470,427	19,388	2,489,815	309,399	9,581	2,189,997	1,002,639	640,001	22,087	173,523	95,490
1998	4,070,988	2,657,190	14,939	2,672,129	329,882	9,032	2,351,279	1,031,125	688,584	23,046	176,645	97,290
1999	4,305,487	2,896,065	14,277	2,910,342	352,882	8,565	2,566,025	986,379	753,083	24,018	179,264	100,050
2000	4,588,797	3,068,911	10,209	3,079,120	376,502	7,217	2,709,835	1,078,521	800,441	25,244	181,775	103,307
2001	4,923,725	3,314,083	12,986	3,327,069	393,415	1,141	2,934,795	1,090,037	898,893	26,783	183,835	103,859
2002	5,038,795	3,481,959	11,090	3,493,049	416,721	-4,308	3,072,020	1,012,876	953,899	26,988	186,704	103,968
2003	5,393,469	3,684,355	16,230	3,700,585	442,468	-7,553	3,250,564	1,134,509	1,008,396	28,411	189,838	107,562
2004	5,705,153	3,936,469	18,338	3,954,807	479,127	-11,098	3,464,582	1,197,940	1,042,631	29,686	192,185	111,967
2005	6,003,776	4,068,291	17,670	4,085,961	506,726	-14,044	3,565,191	1,327,592	1,110,993	30,836	194,701	115,395
2006	6,522,383	4,309,632	17,075	4,326,707	534,109	-9,501	3,783,097	1,542,994	1,196,292	33,132	196,858	117,401
2007	6,751,784	4,389,655	18,232	4,407,887	553,438	-26,326	3,828,123	1,645,725	1,277,936	33,903	199,152	119,400
2008	6,890,264	4,316,063	16,557	4,332,620	548,924	-13,126	3,770,570	1,672,644	1,447,050	34,252	201,162	116,112
2009	6,635,577	4,073,813	20,225	4,094,038	528,825	-25,284	3,539,929	1,448,834	1,646,814	32,801	202,301	110,154
2010	6,845,452	4,121,719	17,809	4,139,528	539,501	-32,057	3,567,970	1,501,117	1,776,365	33,662	203,357	109,131
2011	7,174,675	4,224,602	21,150	4,245,752	491,550	-32,154	3,722,048	1,633,869	1,818,758	35,033	204,798	109,021
2012	7,431,772	4,469,476	23,136	4,492,612	513,256	-65,709	3,913,647	1,668,223	1,849,902	36,087	205,939	109,916
2013	7,622,968	4,665,314	26,419	4,691,733	605,565	-107,970	3,978,198	1,716,535	1,928,235	36,770	207,313	112,518
2014	8,229,425	4,907,593	24,304	4,931,897	642,028	-82,767	4,207,102	1,886,507	2,135,816	39,199	209,941	114,835
2015	8,769,510	5,248,336	20,923	5,269,259	675,906	-70,225	4,523,128	1,967,360	2,279,022	41,302	212,327	117,913
2016	9,212,901	5,543,500	22,584	5,566,084	707,772	-73,026	4,785,286	2,083,385	2,344,230	42,752	215,498	120,464
2017	9,657,327	5,851,109	19,067	5,870,176	755,398	-77,328	5,037,450	2,178,319	2,441,558	44,282	218,087	122,923
2018	10,095,949	6,170,830	10,593	6,181,423	786,156	-78,815	5,316,452	2,192,537	2,586,960	45,717	220,838	126,171
2019	10,615,059	6,457,304	7,705	6,465,009	827,388	-57,346	5,580,275	2,303,146	2,731,638	47,774	222,195	125,156
2020	11,708,142	6,800,740	11,001	6,811,741	866,082	-41,305	5,904,354	2,311,001	3,492,787	52,410	223,394	123,857
2021	12,717,430	7,385,296	8,140	7,393,436	929,386	-59,000	6,405,050	2,344,487	3,967,893	56,842	223,734	127,209

Personal Income and Employment by Area: Memphis, TN-MS-AR

(Thousands of dollars, except as noted.)

Year	Personal income, total	Earnings by place of work			Less: Contributions for government social insurance	Plus: Adjustment for residence	Equals: Net earnings by place of residence	Plus: Dividends, interest, and rent	Plus: Personal current transfer receipts	Per capita personal income (dollars)	Population (persons)	Total employment
		Nonfarm	Farm	Total								
1970	3,229,613	2,679,114	62,006	2,741,120	175,962	-18,809	2,546,349	425,768	257,496	3,510	920,140	414,524
1971	3,624,452	3,015,320	62,028	3,077,348	205,060	-26,376	2,845,912	471,932	306,608	3,898	929,937	429,167
1972	4,111,964	3,455,097	65,820	3,520,917	244,395	-34,025	3,242,497	526,139	343,328	4,354	944,488	455,373
1973	4,578,628	3,846,863	95,319	3,942,182	312,264	-40,872	3,589,046	586,740	402,842	4,829	948,225	472,452
1974	5,070,704	4,222,041	62,031	4,284,072	354,055	-44,368	3,885,649	684,763	500,292	5,279	960,477	479,924
1975	5,499,540	4,441,414	57,072	4,498,486	367,248	-46,943	4,084,295	748,835	666,410	5,707	963,646	463,926
1976	5,986,228	4,830,102	74,410	4,904,512	409,053	-45,638	4,449,821	789,075	747,332	6,175	969,411	466,956
1977	6,574,703	5,357,506	87,727	5,445,233	455,179	-47,728	4,942,326	856,322	776,055	6,742	975,249	481,178
1978	7,425,542	6,093,997	87,774	6,181,771	526,033	-47,431	5,608,307	970,350	846,885	7,550	983,532	500,999
1979	8,302,175	6,801,353	95,662	6,897,015	612,009	-57,224	6,227,782	1,098,387	976,006	8,332	996,459	513,957
1980	9,186,803	7,431,885	13,508	7,445,393	667,951	-67,021	6,710,421	1,312,527	1,163,855	9,135	1,005,686	514,719
1981	10,051,415	7,945,322	53,659	7,998,981	768,297	-75,513	7,155,171	1,587,546	1,308,698	10,030	1,002,176	503,394
1982	10,607,099	8,244,044	43,806	8,287,850	812,081	-99,911	7,375,858	1,829,973	1,401,268	10,551	1,005,293	491,268
1983	11,380,242	8,927,920	-600	8,927,320	889,537	-116,241	7,921,542	1,940,558	1,518,142	11,270	1,009,767	501,064
1984	12,619,130	9,921,053	55,925	9,976,978	1,019,561	-129,361	8,828,056	2,209,482	1,581,592	12,453	1,013,317	522,360
1985	13,491,104	10,691,672	56,140	10,747,812	1,115,344	-140,658	9,491,810	2,334,629	1,664,665	13,172	1,024,191	533,858
1986	14,343,210	11,474,106	18,234	11,492,340	1,222,958	-151,471	10,117,911	2,449,485	1,775,814	13,870	1,034,093	551,772
1987	15,508,814	12,491,033	79,696	12,570,729	1,324,233	-148,350	11,098,146	2,556,316	1,854,352	14,811	1,047,141	573,250
1988	16,788,787	13,495,440	103,910	13,599,350	1,475,289	-137,576	11,986,485	2,828,789	1,973,513	15,815	1,061,590	595,468
1989	18,248,432	14,508,060	65,713	14,573,773	1,597,346	-171,666	12,804,761	3,308,474	2,135,197	17,037	1,071,132	616,435
1990	19,329,117	15,476,334	68,692	15,545,026	1,725,528	-203,334	13,616,164	3,394,277	2,318,676	17,921	1,078,598	623,835
1991	20,169,832	16,175,300	73,987	16,249,287	1,829,252	-219,218	14,200,817	3,382,847	2,586,168	18,475	1,091,735	618,879
1992	21,774,865	17,538,461	102,131	17,640,592	1,954,502	-243,593	15,442,497	3,457,263	2,875,105	19,716	1,104,416	620,945
1993	23,154,570	18,720,852	73,792	18,794,644	2,081,818	-275,221	16,437,605	3,604,062	3,112,903	20,724	1,117,303	638,087
1994	24,935,746	20,287,342	116,421	20,403,763	2,283,519	-325,473	17,794,771	3,861,754	3,279,221	22,009	1,132,959	671,106
1995	26,801,668	21,719,247	75,325	21,794,572	2,433,562	-369,735	18,991,275	4,194,999	3,615,394	23,342	1,148,208	688,368
1996	28,445,916	22,998,929	140,308	23,139,237	2,537,179	-416,237	20,185,821	4,444,003	3,816,092	24,488	1,161,613	702,296
1997	30,008,135	24,447,377	94,099	24,541,476	2,691,289	-468,111	21,382,076	4,718,983	3,907,076	25,593	1,172,495	721,454
1998	33,379,214	27,716,139	47,931	27,764,070	2,923,313	-569,128	24,271,629	5,034,423	4,073,162	28,314	1,178,903	738,335
1999	34,423,544	28,832,831	53,015	28,885,846	3,074,465	-622,913	25,188,468	5,031,552	4,203,524	28,812	1,194,756	748,678
2000	35,743,788	29,743,496	47,476	29,790,972	3,167,245	-675,105	25,948,622	5,322,891	4,472,275	29,584	1,208,223	761,155
2001	37,850,735	31,584,290	144,786	31,729,076	3,373,708	-708,576	27,646,792	5,325,640	4,878,303	31,111	1,216,621	758,173
2002	38,751,461	32,595,438	33,675	32,629,113	3,522,007	-730,170	28,376,936	5,144,711	5,229,814	31,579	1,227,121	754,664
2003	40,138,710	33,443,861	157,954	33,601,815	3,613,291	-757,349	29,231,175	5,353,894	5,553,641	32,387	1,239,341	756,930
2004	41,894,922	35,056,600	177,338	35,233,938	3,768,557	-806,539	30,658,842	5,438,017	5,798,063	33,494	1,250,802	765,700
2005	43,513,040	35,974,542	148,771	36,123,313	3,858,187	-826,915	31,438,211	5,872,574	6,202,255	34,434	1,263,658	777,265
2006	46,337,143	38,060,301	122,462	38,182,763	4,077,042	-863,616	33,242,105	6,612,292	6,482,746	36,105	1,283,389	796,326
2007	48,234,284	39,235,074	112,513	39,347,587	4,260,111	-910,993	34,176,483	6,976,367	7,081,434	37,285	1,293,670	811,693
2008	48,673,832	38,593,093	105,947	38,699,040	4,278,628	-903,997	33,516,415	7,163,580	7,993,837	37,382	1,302,060	808,339
2009	47,092,310	36,868,319	108,868	36,977,187	4,150,346	-820,493	32,006,348	6,522,445	8,563,517	35,975	1,309,030	780,007
2010	48,871,327	37,643,078	38,877	37,681,955	4,173,365	-803,757	32,704,833	6,686,427	9,480,067	37,093	1,317,533	778,121
2011	51,303,022	39,006,686	117,232	39,123,918	3,820,808	-832,887	34,470,223	7,138,622	9,694,177	38,750	1,323,952	792,172
2012	53,783,828	40,968,515	44,847	41,013,362	3,897,018	-869,079	36,247,265	7,727,218	9,809,345	40,386	1,331,735	797,051
2013	53,647,046	41,229,319	275,640	41,504,959	4,465,000	-842,401	36,197,558	7,381,377	10,068,111	40,258	1,332,578	801,075
2014	54,903,293	42,287,219	38,812	42,326,031	4,570,472	-852,967	36,902,592	7,849,632	10,151,069	41,290	1,329,687	813,992
2015	56,759,087	43,670,439	17,843	43,688,282	4,704,544	-880,041	38,103,697	8,003,343	10,652,047	42,673	1,330,099	826,663
2016	58,064,938	44,725,136	21,209	44,746,345	4,844,665	-923,292	38,978,388	8,249,822	10,836,728	43,637	1,330,625	841,516
2017	59,959,916	46,049,095	58,647	46,107,742	5,055,520	-943,553	40,108,669	8,805,469	11,045,778	45,013	1,332,047	849,398
2018	62,280,133	47,752,027	10,687	47,762,714	5,243,855	-973,107	41,545,752	9,207,475	11,526,906	46,647	1,335,134	863,212
2019	65,059,364	49,139,027	76,661	49,215,688	5,517,156	-1,005,933	42,692,599	10,169,804	12,196,961	48,680	1,336,471	868,994
2020	69,570,906	50,474,720	106,767	50,581,487	5,768,486	-1,056,264	43,756,737	10,096,978	15,717,191	52,023	1,337,311	853,607
2021	75,580,090	54,802,961	140,112	54,943,073	5,961,708	-1,195,289	47,786,076	10,255,754	17,538,260	56,568	1,336,103	873,393

Personal Income and Employment by Area: Merced, CA

(Thousands of dollars, except as noted.)

Year	Personal income, total	Earnings by place of work			Less: Contributions for government social insurance	Plus: Adjustment for residence	Equals: Net earnings by place of residence	Plus: Dividends, interest, and rent	Plus: Personal current transfer receipts	Per capita personal income (dollars)	Population (persons)	Total employment
		Nonfarm	Farm	Total								
1970	434,859	250,899	78,531	329,430	17,297	3,889	316,022	69,432	49,405	4,131	105,275	45,456
1971	460,187	276,214	69,534	345,748	20,013	4,009	329,744	75,213	55,230	4,260	108,032	47,188
1972	517,524	305,479	88,135	393,614	22,997	4,804	375,421	83,926	58,177	4,681	110,548	49,741
1973	612,840	341,807	130,956	472,763	28,522	4,907	449,148	99,070	64,622	5,355	114,436	51,449
1974	685,840	385,206	137,450	522,656	33,496	5,443	494,603	113,996	77,241	5,815	117,949	54,411
1975	783,346	426,877	167,674	594,551	37,128	4,103	561,526	126,213	95,607	6,450	121,456	56,336
1976	878,577	486,963	186,623	673,586	43,470	3,221	633,337	135,638	109,602	6,953	126,358	58,502
1977	964,456	545,897	191,997	737,894	49,215	3,848	692,527	151,964	119,965	7,619	126,591	60,515
1978	1,017,192	620,943	134,596	755,539	55,799	5,790	705,530	177,983	133,679	7,920	128,435	61,473
1979	1,170,290	693,339	179,664	873,003	63,665	9,295	818,633	202,344	149,313	8,881	131,775	64,328
1980	1,331,927	747,337	223,498	970,835	67,547	10,589	913,877	239,657	178,393	9,821	135,625	64,044
1981	1,362,937	802,049	127,573	929,622	77,661	16,004	867,965	282,867	212,105	9,761	139,632	62,729
1982	1,461,800	861,647	118,986	980,633	84,178	18,868	915,323	310,042	236,435	10,239	142,766	62,096
1983	1,528,943	916,685	83,605	1,000,290	91,329	22,110	931,071	335,859	262,013	10,355	147,657	62,975
1984	1,773,556	1,030,951	167,318	1,198,269	106,646	26,559	1,118,182	370,819	284,555	11,718	151,357	64,798
1985	1,911,489	1,118,344	171,155	1,289,499	116,771	32,444	1,205,172	387,791	318,526	12,258	155,939	66,196
1986	2,060,070	1,194,808	202,346	1,397,154	126,063	40,180	1,311,271	404,857	343,942	12,957	158,988	67,501
1987	2,285,290	1,318,563	271,136	1,589,699	137,528	53,453	1,505,624	421,915	357,751	14,024	162,956	70,309
1988	2,395,633	1,409,767	258,992	1,668,759	154,488	66,018	1,580,289	430,496	384,848	14,281	167,749	73,220
1989	2,610,501	1,497,751	283,848	1,781,599	166,916	76,733	1,691,416	494,799	424,286	15,091	172,988	74,815
1990	2,786,599	1,607,353	285,166	1,892,519	178,913	90,856	1,804,462	510,953	471,184	15,485	179,953	76,728
1991	2,911,291	1,679,683	275,569	1,955,252	190,027	96,776	1,862,001	517,874	531,416	15,644	186,091	78,038
1992	3,108,931	1,751,785	298,703	2,050,488	197,766	106,911	1,959,633	517,970	631,328	16,407	189,489	76,943
1993	3,207,165	1,796,353	308,550	2,104,903	204,979	117,898	2,017,822	523,982	665,361	16,606	193,137	78,232
1994	3,284,026	1,819,611	326,879	2,146,490	206,089	132,272	2,072,673	532,480	678,873	16,603	197,798	77,678
1995	3,171,229	1,752,652	218,588	1,971,240	197,363	157,534	1,931,411	527,945	711,873	16,238	195,291	77,043
1996	3,484,054	1,799,133	399,358	2,198,491	194,827	184,826	2,188,490	547,927	747,637	17,884	194,819	77,229
1997	3,595,354	1,922,956	358,554	2,281,510	203,569	219,706	2,297,647	561,183	736,524	18,130	198,312	77,931
1998	3,788,007	2,098,350	299,252	2,397,602	215,286	255,929	2,438,245	573,367	776,395	18,728	202,264	82,507
1999	3,992,325	2,211,430	291,519	2,502,949	229,183	304,963	2,578,729	593,931	819,665	19,311	206,734	83,851
2000	4,212,595	2,352,118	246,546	2,598,664	243,538	385,739	2,740,865	625,826	845,904	19,847	212,258	83,061
2001	4,567,828	2,523,778	298,821	2,822,599	269,346	394,953	2,948,206	661,956	957,666	20,875	218,816	82,590
2002	4,861,686	2,789,249	315,235	3,104,484	303,314	375,403	3,176,573	650,022	1,035,091	21,574	225,351	87,067
2003	5,315,905	3,036,090	432,323	3,468,413	332,958	395,344	3,530,799	682,532	1,102,574	22,940	231,735	87,520
2004	5,808,967	3,222,920	682,612	3,905,532	363,568	435,934	3,977,898	663,500	1,167,569	24,492	237,180	87,874
2005	6,035,083	3,419,519	612,096	4,031,615	381,609	497,065	4,147,071	661,224	1,226,788	24,881	242,554	87,573
2006	6,211,082	3,656,372	400,706	4,057,078	393,059	497,928	4,161,947	721,480	1,327,655	25,316	245,338	90,187
2007	6,949,306	3,665,731	873,753	4,539,484	395,284	535,143	4,679,343	843,063	1,426,900	27,961	248,540	92,968
2008	6,748,518	3,581,620	562,672	4,144,292	401,957	530,070	4,272,405	866,678	1,609,435	26,936	250,538	90,756
2009	6,814,285	3,673,337	464,268	4,137,605	410,772	470,290	4,197,123	829,092	1,788,070	27,008	252,302	88,875
2010	7,205,819	3,741,625	588,624	4,330,249	399,376	455,391	4,386,264	828,709	1,990,846	28,070	256,709	88,611
2011	7,758,558	3,787,343	962,118	4,749,461	371,663	521,266	4,899,064	864,873	1,994,621	29,927	259,249	88,469
2012	7,939,819	3,954,101	915,348	4,869,449	390,387	470,065	4,949,127	957,816	2,032,876	30,447	260,776	92,113
2013	8,278,545	4,078,919	1,042,511	5,121,430	446,485	477,924	5,152,869	996,601	2,129,075	31,611	261,888	94,681
2014	9,085,921	4,270,819	1,397,764	5,668,583	462,795	510,128	5,715,916	1,082,273	2,287,732	34,264	265,177	97,907
2015	9,482,446	4,532,587	1,141,237	5,673,824	484,126	553,741	5,743,439	1,246,333	2,492,674	35,475	267,299	100,019
2016	9,633,119	4,727,051	924,500	5,651,551	518,393	630,297	5,763,455	1,290,190	2,579,474	35,842	268,766	100,910
2017	9,962,542	4,976,407	1,090,247	6,066,654	551,330	643,912	6,159,236	1,280,210	2,523,096	36,562	272,480	103,851
2018	10,216,183	5,121,570	851,541	5,973,111	575,322	866,175	6,263,964	1,303,021	2,649,198	37,065	275,626	106,189
2019	10,786,869	5,406,745	763,654	6,170,399	615,841	972,933	6,527,491	1,437,337	2,822,041	38,626	279,263	106,759
2020	12,390,335	5,566,251	948,060	6,514,311	637,077	1,056,298	6,933,532	1,431,577	4,025,226	43,980	281,726	105,330
2021	13,343,412	5,891,547	762,483	6,654,030	678,754	1,324,915	7,300,191	1,452,845	4,590,376	46,580	286,461	108,476

Personal Income and Employment by Area: Miami-Fort Lauderdale-Pompano Beach, FL

(Thousands of dollars, except as noted.)

Year	Personal income, total	Earnings by place of work			Less: Contributions for government social insurance	Plus: Adjustment for residence	Equals: Net earnings by place of residence	Plus: Dividends, interest, and rent	Plus: Personal current transfer receipts	Per capita personal income (dollars)	Population (persons)	Total employment
		Nonfarm	Farm	Total								
1970	10,723,332	7,570,402	105,059	7,675,461	490,761	-12,205	7,172,495	2,659,151	891,686	4,755	2,255,202	1,054,067
1971	11,973,429	8,308,995	122,138	8,431,133	560,807	-16,498	7,853,828	3,031,972	1,087,629	5,063	2,364,750	1,087,984
1972	13,740,830	9,599,126	131,527	9,730,653	685,284	-20,550	9,024,819	3,421,480	1,294,531	5,543	2,478,824	1,178,470
1973	16,065,434	11,326,691	139,634	11,466,325	933,948	-29,219	10,503,158	3,990,093	1,572,183	6,168	2,604,637	1,304,027
1974	18,109,416	12,365,697	201,117	12,566,814	1,064,125	-29,226	11,473,463	4,697,119	1,938,834	6,595	2,745,960	1,330,500
1975	19,421,822	12,579,507	226,346	12,805,853	1,059,036	-29,180	11,717,637	5,107,965	2,596,220	6,845	2,837,578	1,275,484
1976	21,171,455	13,680,499	233,926	13,914,425	1,168,205	-26,213	12,720,007	5,586,433	2,865,015	7,341	2,884,080	1,292,596
1977	23,699,865	15,373,859	208,539	15,582,398	1,322,007	-32,310	14,228,081	6,362,645	3,109,139	8,068	2,937,632	1,367,587
1978	27,264,542	17,882,167	195,555	18,077,722	1,585,493	-48,109	16,444,120	7,376,673	3,443,749	9,079	3,002,966	1,485,993
1979	31,531,438	20,620,971	210,600	20,831,571	1,919,378	-69,043	18,843,150	8,734,555	3,953,733	10,100	3,121,950	1,567,870
1980	37,275,817	23,914,041	291,109	24,205,150	2,247,862	-92,270	21,865,018	10,748,744	4,662,055	11,452	3,254,936	1,663,461
1981	43,322,662	26,903,058	323,739	27,226,797	2,720,704	-39,422	24,466,671	13,463,775	5,392,216	12,793	3,386,317	1,715,798
1982	46,093,564	28,320,823	422,817	28,743,640	2,943,142	-48,518	25,751,980	14,309,555	6,032,029	13,361	3,449,745	1,720,145
1983	50,351,579	31,038,118	715,874	31,753,992	3,233,549	-70,133	28,450,310	15,348,907	6,552,362	14,359	3,506,541	1,771,008
1984	55,603,387	34,386,680	450,907	34,837,587	3,677,992	-90,906	31,068,689	17,516,809	7,017,889	15,618	3,560,292	1,862,036
1985	60,295,902	37,502,274	454,282	37,956,556	4,075,773	-111,884	33,768,899	19,063,328	7,463,675	16,597	3,632,834	1,921,376
1986	64,607,910	40,538,030	537,808	41,075,838	4,520,079	-120,123	36,435,636	20,203,433	7,968,841	17,418	3,709,283	1,976,279
1987	70,039,163	44,844,978	590,313	45,435,291	4,932,983	-140,525	40,361,783	21,299,216	8,378,164	18,445	3,797,118	1,983,981
1988	76,339,041	49,129,398	621,712	49,751,110	5,554,394	-157,717	44,038,999	23,211,834	9,088,208	19,616	3,891,758	2,077,107
1989	84,613,056	51,724,493	555,191	52,279,684	5,905,326	-157,569	46,216,789	28,163,578	10,232,689	21,238	3,984,047	2,124,442
1990	90,431,751	54,865,738	431,771	55,297,509	6,200,007	-183,751	48,913,751	30,376,230	11,141,770	22,172	4,078,578	2,151,815
1991	94,407,722	56,931,782	512,637	57,444,419	6,462,509	-177,290	50,804,620	31,004,997	12,598,105	22,603	4,176,731	2,129,237
1992	99,527,890	60,974,711	600,067	61,574,778	6,856,548	-166,722	54,551,508	30,384,500	14,591,882	23,347	4,262,995	2,133,944
1993	105,628,246	65,856,904	661,304	66,518,208	7,360,272	-169,949	58,987,987	31,179,397	15,460,862	24,337	4,340,175	2,221,343
1994	110,638,688	69,319,487	484,294	69,803,781	7,836,300	-175,188	61,792,293	32,481,126	16,365,269	24,890	4,445,162	2,289,282
1995	118,870,020	73,641,770	516,285	74,158,055	8,275,297	-174,552	65,708,206	35,410,789	17,751,025	26,141	4,547,191	2,367,458
1996	126,518,278	78,465,201	417,206	78,882,407	8,695,324	-179,933	70,007,150	37,705,770	18,805,358	27,194	4,652,414	2,423,829
1997	132,453,908	82,220,890	450,641	82,671,531	9,113,267	-167,907	73,390,357	39,760,131	19,303,420	27,884	4,750,249	2,495,838
1998	143,392,359	89,430,354	548,389	89,978,743	9,749,850	-173,540	80,055,353	43,686,635	19,650,371	29,646	4,836,853	2,580,377
1999	149,809,613	95,628,247	630,980	96,259,227	10,377,349	-177,720	85,704,158	43,743,260	20,362,195	30,375	4,932,004	2,668,615
2000	163,223,089	104,880,353	574,363	105,454,716	11,201,074	-196,716	94,056,926	47,499,134	21,667,029	32,476	5,025,895	2,759,068
2001	171,743,336	112,291,613	629,770	112,921,383	12,206,605	-427,793	100,286,985	47,981,505	23,474,846	33,604	5,110,780	2,854,679
2002	176,805,837	117,288,340	617,713	117,906,053	12,636,163	-641,576	104,628,314	47,086,599	25,090,924	34,019	5,197,205	2,884,746
2003	182,787,732	122,046,832	549,922	122,596,754	13,120,081	-857,475	108,619,198	47,435,002	26,733,532	34,739	5,261,713	2,947,087
2004	198,048,892	131,242,940	521,933	131,764,873	14,090,209	-1,038,087	116,636,577	52,871,749	28,540,566	37,113	5,336,368	3,033,206
2005	216,553,343	141,896,971	594,370	142,491,341	15,338,875	-1,491,277	125,661,189	60,325,588	30,566,566	40,020	5,411,148	3,153,331
2006	234,861,563	150,301,515	593,433	150,894,948	16,485,417	-1,720,866	132,688,665	70,340,131	31,832,767	43,255	5,429,748	3,234,598
2007	244,645,726	152,605,444	560,854	153,166,298	17,001,437	-1,758,335	134,406,526	77,006,585	33,232,615	45,113	5,422,987	3,292,421
2008	241,343,778	146,317,418	504,245	146,821,663	16,900,674	-1,863,514	128,057,475	75,777,098	37,509,205	44,246	5,454,633	3,238,672
2009	221,436,193	135,501,338	550,899	136,052,237	16,192,828	-1,692,151	118,167,258	62,605,265	40,663,670	40,227	5,504,624	3,113,043
2010	241,182,797	145,411,180	552,414	145,963,594	16,566,177	-1,214,351	128,183,066	68,720,552	44,279,179	43,196	5,583,460	3,125,007
2011	253,030,481	150,484,885	456,952	150,941,837	15,284,203	-1,409,564	134,248,070	73,121,315	45,661,096	44,638	5,668,482	3,232,075
2012	266,191,150	154,693,534	529,460	155,222,994	15,843,184	-2,011,976	137,367,834	84,331,620	44,491,696	46,326	5,746,090	3,317,113
2013	264,484,758	160,559,625	611,321	161,170,946	18,581,183	-2,231,975	140,357,788	78,622,843	45,504,127	45,419	5,823,221	3,435,024
2014	286,176,757	172,637,992	520,511	173,158,503	19,701,880	-2,285,178	151,171,445	87,447,143	47,558,169	48,696	5,876,841	3,586,387
2015	307,594,596	183,120,577	720,594	183,841,171	20,751,332	-2,430,699	160,659,140	97,410,000	49,525,456	51,716	5,947,797	3,752,366
2016	313,632,460	191,115,727	647,638	191,763,365	21,481,660	-3,118,056	167,163,649	95,163,660	51,305,151	52,024	6,028,626	3,836,773
2017	340,918,931	203,688,709	668,955	204,357,664	22,637,320	-3,180,641	178,539,703	109,284,739	53,094,489	56,030	6,084,581	3,948,830
2018	365,403,790	216,034,581	551,745	216,586,326	24,094,902	-3,472,070	189,019,354	120,936,733	55,447,703	59,853	6,105,049	4,109,368
2019	389,619,830	225,324,714	596,854	225,921,568	25,545,108	-3,775,650	196,600,810	134,382,114	58,636,906	63,610	6,125,139	4,152,826
2020	406,223,306	225,073,384	556,619	225,630,003	25,772,915	-3,713,547	196,143,541	134,959,972	75,119,793	66,307	6,126,441	4,140,874
2021	447,874,596	255,092,936	525,136	255,618,072	28,228,569	-5,179,808	222,209,695	140,141,841	85,523,060	73,522	6,091,747	4,295,285

Personal Income and Employment by Area: Michigan City-La Porte, IN

(Thousands of dollars, except as noted.)

Year	Personal income, total	Earnings by place of work Nonfarm	Farm	Total	Less: Contributions for government social insurance	Plus: Adjustment for residence	Equals: Net earnings by place of residence	Plus: Dividends, interest, and rent	Plus: Personal current transfer receipts	Per capita personal income (dollars)	Population (persons)	Total employment
1970	405,753	319,798	5,729	325,527	22,456	20,794	323,865	52,362	29,526	3,847	105,461	45,672
1971	430,233	326,695	10,528	337,223	23,782	24,105	337,546	57,107	35,580	4,047	106,310	44,103
1972	472,811	362,812	7,144	369,956	27,838	31,250	373,368	61,092	38,351	4,429	106,744	45,366
1973	539,615	403,999	16,325	420,324	35,558	40,068	424,834	70,270	44,511	5,037	107,134	47,958
1974	588,706	436,701	8,392	445,093	40,261	50,675	455,507	81,867	51,332	5,493	107,180	48,730
1975	640,124	444,936	17,067	462,003	40,208	59,369	481,164	91,172	67,788	5,963	107,353	46,388
1976	706,083	493,075	16,159	509,234	45,038	71,727	535,923	98,545	71,615	6,562	107,604	47,203
1977	783,754	551,728	8,926	560,654	50,054	88,834	599,434	110,281	74,039	7,224	108,496	48,332
1978	889,401	624,138	13,976	638,114	58,176	106,904	686,842	121,496	81,063	8,174	108,807	50,502
1979	980,714	678,623	9,852	688,475	65,577	128,351	751,249	135,872	93,593	8,986	109,142	50,703
1980	1,062,542	718,909	4,803	723,712	69,332	126,985	781,365	166,472	114,705	9,779	108,657	49,332
1981	1,153,658	751,346	5,889	757,235	77,837	135,856	815,254	204,356	134,048	10,631	108,515	48,011
1982	1,165,620	748,457	886	749,343	79,295	125,490	795,538	216,731	153,351	10,779	108,140	46,152
1983	1,181,177	766,599	-8,369	758,230	81,529	108,903	785,604	226,069	169,504	11,015	107,230	45,219
1984	1,277,160	820,235	10,149	830,384	89,348	111,613	852,649	252,554	171,957	11,939	106,976	46,096
1985	1,335,047	870,773	8,641	879,414	96,368	111,823	894,869	261,048	179,130	12,515	106,680	47,280
1986	1,388,792	917,291	7,760	925,051	102,005	103,385	926,431	270,192	192,169	13,139	105,696	48,106
1987	1,467,077	981,898	14,118	996,016	107,304	108,724	997,436	272,452	197,189	13,866	105,806	49,835
1988	1,565,711	1,074,771	4,993	1,079,764	123,643	113,211	1,069,332	291,099	205,280	14,779	105,941	51,945
1989	1,707,099	1,139,715	22,362	1,162,077	131,127	119,488	1,150,438	335,279	221,382	16,029	106,502	53,294
1990	1,778,907	1,193,902	20,991	1,214,893	139,609	119,409	1,194,693	345,706	238,508	16,585	107,257	53,683
1991	1,816,875	1,236,959	2,954	1,239,913	146,180	118,611	1,212,344	345,889	258,642	16,799	108,151	53,728
1992	1,957,682	1,319,951	19,383	1,339,334	154,983	126,091	1,310,442	350,506	296,734	17,972	108,928	53,920
1993	2,030,568	1,374,752	14,238	1,388,990	162,404	128,006	1,354,592	360,172	315,804	18,551	109,461	54,837
1994	2,135,740	1,446,160	19,164	1,465,324	172,869	142,006	1,434,461	376,263	325,016	19,483	109,620	55,637
1995	2,228,727	1,493,922	13,892	1,507,814	179,301	144,695	1,473,208	424,648	330,871	20,340	109,571	57,043
1996	2,332,475	1,532,927	22,259	1,555,186	182,094	154,641	1,527,733	453,571	351,171	21,246	109,783	56,722
1997	2,470,404	1,632,939	23,965	1,656,904	192,651	154,283	1,618,536	490,359	361,509	22,504	109,774	57,371
1998	2,595,518	1,740,085	18,884	1,758,969	200,631	164,043	1,722,381	502,474	370,663	23,605	109,954	58,248
1999	2,624,616	1,789,742	9,345	1,799,087	206,167	163,766	1,756,686	483,557	384,373	23,854	110,028	58,957
2000	2,782,585	1,896,580	13,320	1,909,900	216,581	156,338	1,849,657	527,041	405,887	25,268	110,121	59,904
2001	2,849,730	1,921,488	19,422	1,940,910	220,586	171,118	1,891,442	513,682	444,606	25,889	110,077	58,597
2002	2,890,779	1,947,200	10,653	1,957,853	224,665	191,509	1,924,697	494,112	471,970	26,387	109,555	57,869
2003	2,978,892	1,945,097	23,002	1,968,099	226,092	225,750	1,967,757	520,779	490,356	27,323	109,027	56,932
2004	3,050,008	2,009,860	41,129	2,050,989	235,273	225,381	2,041,097	490,859	518,052	28,004	108,914	56,935
2005	3,161,522	2,083,178	22,117	2,105,295	247,471	260,453	2,118,277	480,444	562,801	28,862	109,541	57,591
2006	3,326,622	2,149,383	25,759	2,175,142	256,234	296,071	2,214,979	509,910	601,733	30,341	109,641	57,497
2007	3,475,677	2,217,598	26,060	2,243,658	266,546	316,480	2,293,592	550,896	631,189	31,356	110,846	57,996
2008	3,664,712	2,246,625	30,643	2,277,268	271,945	340,169	2,345,492	597,493	721,727	32,936	111,267	57,091
2009	3,457,779	2,133,135	15,076	2,148,211	260,167	241,945	2,129,989	524,562	803,228	31,021	111,465	54,442
2010	3,592,846	2,160,112	32,698	2,192,810	259,881	294,297	2,227,226	509,566	856,054	32,235	111,458	53,238
2011	3,811,155	2,239,615	50,965	2,290,580	238,793	347,500	2,399,287	564,411	847,457	34,234	111,328	53,913
2012	4,023,728	2,315,329	54,660	2,369,989	243,121	383,772	2,510,640	641,069	872,019	36,145	111,321	53,668
2013	4,060,629	2,336,067	119,184	2,455,251	279,622	388,754	2,564,383	612,276	883,970	36,434	111,452	53,431
2014	4,145,020	2,402,965	72,834	2,475,799	286,330	379,294	2,568,763	635,158	941,099	36,722	112,877	53,503
2015	4,204,583	2,410,639	19,241	2,429,880	288,706	444,160	2,585,334	644,455	974,794	37,462	112,237	53,302
2016	4,328,420	2,436,228	33,993	2,470,221	290,783	476,269	2,655,707	673,049	999,664	38,668	111,937	53,132
2017	4,450,657	2,477,533	28,494	2,506,027	298,765	512,709	2,719,971	701,136	1,029,550	39,804	111,815	53,209
2018	4,639,072	2,575,054	24,431	2,599,485	311,539	522,604	2,810,550	754,500	1,074,022	41,328	112,250	53,327
2019	4,729,971	2,557,559	20,025	2,577,584	318,934	586,879	2,845,529	737,103	1,147,339	42,076	112,414	53,240
2020	5,086,230	2,606,208	50,564	2,656,772	332,321	565,547	2,889,998	732,156	1,464,076	45,323	112,222	51,428
2021	5,564,165	2,793,380	63,691	2,857,071	348,150	647,687	3,156,608	736,425	1,671,132	49,508	112,390	52,276

Personal Income and Employment by Area: Midland, MI

(Thousands of dollars, except as noted.)

Year	Personal income, total	Earnings by place of work			Less: Contributions for government social insurance	Plus: Adjustment for residence	Equals: Net earnings by place of residence	Plus: Dividends, interest, and rent	Plus: Personal current transfer receipts	Per capita personal income (dollars)	Population (persons)	Total employment
		Nonfarm	Farm	Total								
1970	277,325	285,670	1,613	287,283	20,219	-51,018	216,046	46,103	15,176	4,336	63,956	28,920
1971	299,208	301,232	1,394	302,626	22,121	-49,458	231,047	48,866	19,295	4,600	65,050	27,915
1972	321,559	317,665	2,621	320,286	24,578	-48,235	247,473	52,486	21,600	4,925	65,286	27,970
1973	352,547	350,732	3,187	353,919	31,828	-50,754	271,337	56,352	24,858	5,310	66,390	29,341
1974	410,969	406,363	7,733	414,096	38,416	-61,308	314,372	62,574	34,023	6,119	67,168	28,737
1975	449,291	438,157	4,214	442,371	40,362	-64,940	337,069	70,659	41,563	6,547	68,626	30,639
1976	511,778	508,866	2,797	511,663	47,602	-73,031	391,030	77,753	42,995	7,382	69,324	32,404
1977	594,681	603,469	4,500	607,969	56,695	-89,582	461,692	87,179	45,810	8,389	70,888	35,226
1978	663,859	672,619	3,989	676,608	64,444	-92,878	519,286	95,591	48,982	9,233	71,900	35,972
1979	730,776	738,168	3,508	741,676	74,550	-99,421	567,705	108,066	55,005	9,989	73,158	36,279
1980	773,486	735,259	2,014	737,273	73,494	-89,820	573,959	126,860	72,667	10,469	73,882	34,846
1981	854,851	791,988	2,026	794,014	85,842	-91,281	616,891	160,902	77,058	11,408	74,936	34,356
1982	904,532	823,353	1,165	824,518	92,225	-99,958	632,335	185,238	86,959	12,095	74,784	33,960
1983	953,477	841,331	-235	841,096	94,247	-89,066	657,783	200,940	94,754	12,680	75,198	33,798
1984	1,022,239	851,133	2,194	853,327	96,306	-62,394	694,627	225,008	102,604	13,480	75,835	33,330
1985	1,093,068	881,598	2,030	883,628	100,225	-41,815	741,588	243,691	107,789	15,078	72,492	33,734
1986	1,174,550	959,534	1,050	960,584	108,944	-43,366	808,274	250,469	115,807	16,179	72,598	34,691
1987	1,271,864	1,036,999	2,758	1,039,757	115,912	-47,231	876,614	273,798	121,452	17,410	73,054	36,329
1988	1,400,428	1,154,807	4,046	1,158,853	132,013	-48,428	978,412	295,422	126,594	18,908	74,065	37,224
1989	1,551,684	1,231,158	7,238	1,238,396	141,271	-52,154	1,044,971	366,182	140,531	20,754	74,767	39,737
1990	1,644,668	1,306,722	2,919	1,309,641	153,520	-48,783	1,107,338	383,173	154,157	21,640	76,002	41,424
1991	1,698,467	1,330,532	2,997	1,333,529	157,915	-28,573	1,147,041	379,751	171,675	22,135	76,733	41,784
1992	1,826,089	1,469,540	3,582	1,473,122	173,186	-49,563	1,250,373	391,414	184,302	23,456	77,853	43,653
1993	1,912,487	1,505,679	4,413	1,510,092	178,711	-25,394	1,305,987	404,280	202,220	24,328	78,614	43,354
1994	1,993,816	1,525,778	1,693	1,527,471	185,902	-4,758	1,336,811	450,098	206,907	25,126	79,352	43,013
1995	2,111,747	1,629,057	2,723	1,631,780	197,828	-12,731	1,421,221	474,534	215,992	26,449	79,841	43,166
1996	2,251,232	1,736,784	1,452	1,738,236	206,769	10,999	1,542,466	485,918	222,848	27,828	80,897	44,035
1997	2,316,023	1,798,138	1,115	1,799,253	212,924	-6,371	1,579,958	489,726	246,339	28,366	81,648	44,500
1998	2,483,853	1,879,423	859	1,880,282	219,695	31,880	1,692,467	539,875	251,511	30,261	82,081	44,439
1999	2,518,181	1,904,508	2,739	1,907,247	222,736	43,789	1,728,300	514,812	275,069	30,487	82,599	45,798
2000	2,636,208	2,088,256	2,099	2,090,355	244,437	-31,238	1,814,680	526,949	294,579	31,795	82,913	47,165
2001	2,801,089	2,236,470	1,332	2,237,802	233,432	-46,886	1,957,484	515,184	328,421	33,515	83,576	45,811
2002	2,786,911	2,190,300	1,639	2,191,939	231,501	-17,522	1,942,916	499,072	344,923	33,311	83,664	45,388
2003	2,894,864	2,269,834	1,391	2,271,225	236,073	-6,349	2,028,803	504,263	361,798	34,458	84,012	44,687
2004	3,132,036	2,433,534	4,465	2,437,999	258,827	-48,218	2,130,954	619,706	381,376	37,260	84,058	44,371
2005	3,128,519	2,376,273	5,552	2,381,825	258,627	6,768	2,129,966	588,510	410,043	37,275	83,930	44,863
2006	3,262,720	2,425,465	2,930	2,428,395	269,858	21,187	2,179,724	648,950	434,046	38,984	83,693	45,446
2007	3,359,555	2,491,025	5,395	2,496,420	282,154	21,866	2,236,132	646,012	477,411	40,186	83,600	46,416
2008	3,637,394	2,669,677	9,319	2,678,996	302,324	-16,887	2,359,785	732,324	545,285	43,507	83,605	46,547
2009	3,515,401	2,571,054	2,673	2,573,727	294,528	55,340	2,334,539	590,619	590,243	42,031	83,639	45,169
2010	3,605,283	2,693,922	6,734	2,700,656	298,866	14,120	2,415,910	557,909	631,464	43,094	83,660	45,043
2011	3,825,855	2,804,658	18,655	2,823,313	278,813	42,574	2,587,074	607,442	631,339	45,641	83,825	45,974
2012	3,818,463	2,685,462	13,756	2,699,218	280,205	68,485	2,487,498	696,540	634,425	45,597	83,743	45,863
2013	3,743,593	2,644,190	17,943	2,662,133	324,141	65,382	2,403,374	691,448	648,771	44,735	83,683	46,562
2014	3,431,765	2,219,671	8,152	2,227,823	364,009	98,192	1,962,006	788,975	680,784	41,071	83,556	47,548
2015	3,363,374	2,093,004	4,388	2,097,392	384,336	76,785	1,789,841	849,263	724,270	40,168	83,733	47,793
2016	3,921,930	2,596,920	-450	2,596,470	359,346	61,767	2,298,891	874,097	748,942	46,960	83,517	47,557
2017	4,801,948	3,394,977	645	3,395,622	372,858	104,773	3,127,537	915,044	759,367	57,522	83,480	47,231
2018	4,517,850	3,371,248	658	3,371,906	387,862	-146,986	2,837,058	882,959	797,833	54,113	83,489	47,756
2019	4,586,226	3,288,996	-161	3,288,835	382,150	-171,264	2,735,421	998,207	852,598	54,951	83,460	47,699
2020	4,886,998	3,192,730	7,904	3,200,634	372,921	-81,818	2,745,895	991,454	1,149,649	58,544	83,476	45,715
2021	5,178,900	3,400,465	7,196	3,407,661	387,790	-70,672	2,949,199	1,014,532	1,215,169	62,055	83,457	47,863

Personal Income and Employment by Area: Midland, TX

(Thousands of dollars, except as noted.)

Year	Personal income, total	Derivation of personal income									Per capita personal income (dollars)	Population (persons)	Total employment
		Earnings by place of work			Less: Contributions for government social insurance	Plus: Adjustment for residence	Equals: Net earnings by place of residence	Plus: Dividends, interest, and rent	Plus: Personal current transfer receipts				
		Nonfarm	Farm	Total									
1970	328,929	277,558	8,502	286,060	16,115	-7,782	262,163	53,050	13,716	4,679	70,297	34,454
1971	355,615	301,824	7,968	309,792	17,843	-8,549	283,400	56,237	15,978	4,987	71,302	35,324
1972	384,016	326,266	7,542	333,808	19,843	-8,860	305,105	60,738	18,173	5,373	71,477	35,958
1973	437,833	360,467	20,683	381,150	25,760	-10,138	345,252	70,440	22,141	6,144	71,259	37,635
1974	491,237	417,190	2,960	420,150	30,516	-11,597	378,037	86,365	26,835	6,701	73,313	39,497
1975	595,384	522,571	-1,933	520,638	37,720	-17,134	465,784	97,785	31,815	7,872	75,637	43,247
1976	688,235	593,053	13,799	606,852	42,464	-18,467	545,921	106,781	35,533	8,830	77,943	43,997
1977	776,522	677,281	17,684	694,965	50,590	-25,750	618,625	120,021	37,876	9,803	79,216	48,808
1978	928,623	828,981	7,603	836,584	62,781	-34,602	739,201	146,086	43,336	11,474	80,934	52,831
1979	1,084,219	941,549	32,756	974,305	74,353	-39,898	860,054	174,651	49,514	12,978	83,546	54,875
1980	1,286,647	1,177,604	-11,224	1,166,380	96,272	-59,704	1,010,404	218,600	57,643	14,506	88,700	61,483
1981	1,656,134	1,453,620	33,403	1,487,023	131,837	-69,448	1,285,738	305,806	64,590	17,625	93,964	71,676
1982	1,868,698	1,634,787	21,385	1,656,172	157,802	-75,718	1,422,652	372,033	74,013	17,975	103,959	77,759
1983	1,813,014	1,526,316	3,763	1,530,079	148,806	-64,716	1,316,557	403,577	92,880	16,159	112,195	73,906
1984	1,891,028	1,562,175	-6,629	1,555,546	157,124	-57,698	1,340,724	449,202	101,102	16,896	111,919	74,561
1985	2,054,538	1,660,032	1,141	1,661,173	171,287	-54,549	1,435,337	508,277	110,924	18,023	113,997	76,826
1986	1,965,416	1,537,951	6,383	1,544,334	154,851	-49,153	1,340,330	492,584	132,502	16,760	117,265	68,942
1987	1,906,573	1,456,826	30,395	1,487,221	145,530	-37,450	1,304,241	463,420	138,912	16,979	112,287	69,786
1988	2,099,675	1,600,115	26,466	1,626,581	164,594	-37,719	1,424,268	530,163	145,244	18,841	111,439	71,380
1989	2,215,008	1,667,737	4,013	1,671,750	167,598	-27,531	1,476,621	574,966	163,421	19,867	111,494	68,991
1990	2,417,622	1,732,693	20,527	1,753,220	170,704	-18,709	1,563,807	673,960	179,855	21,659	111,624	68,901
1991	2,405,765	1,704,105	2,682	1,706,787	178,546	-15,811	1,512,430	688,934	204,401	21,210	113,427	70,299
1992	2,584,971	1,824,349	20,668	1,845,017	185,283	-14,069	1,645,665	692,332	246,974	22,415	115,325	68,743
1993	2,755,869	1,951,608	28,854	1,980,462	195,575	-9,093	1,775,794	714,251	265,824	23,664	116,456	71,541
1994	2,817,180	1,942,231	11,153	1,953,384	195,530	4	1,757,858	767,421	291,901	23,930	117,728	72,932
1995	2,887,389	2,043,332	8,911	2,052,243	202,016	3,397	1,853,624	719,229	314,536	24,368	118,493	73,505
1996	3,142,235	2,253,914	170	2,254,084	212,205	5,456	2,047,335	757,104	337,796	26,363	119,192	74,051
1997	3,571,682	2,641,052	21,220	2,662,272	237,930	1,291	2,425,633	792,718	353,331	29,350	121,691	78,960
1998	3,648,276	2,679,311	-6,554	2,672,757	238,763	15,913	2,449,907	841,657	356,712	29,613	123,197	79,647
1999	3,553,690	2,493,359	19,973	2,513,332	223,788	17,602	2,307,146	874,978	371,566	29,024	122,440	76,928
2000	3,932,669	2,719,902	-1,135	2,718,767	237,610	30,912	2,512,069	1,029,292	391,308	32,696	120,280	77,716
2001	5,882,528	4,749,730	5,752	4,755,482	326,231	23,940	4,453,191	1,009,921	419,416	48,665	120,877	78,340
2002	5,914,618	4,824,942	593	4,825,535	329,212	30,738	4,527,061	929,175	458,382	48,333	122,371	78,309
2003	6,507,108	5,293,014	34,926	5,327,940	358,015	25,928	4,995,853	1,025,844	485,411	52,597	123,717	81,345
2004	6,752,939	5,437,986	23,788	5,461,774	381,819	20,970	5,100,925	1,141,170	510,844	53,961	125,144	82,457
2005	7,732,392	6,205,245	34,166	6,239,411	435,994	-16,617	5,786,800	1,398,154	547,438	60,903	126,963	86,823
2006	8,420,606	6,668,786	13,318	6,682,104	473,655	-22,745	6,185,704	1,649,468	585,434	64,631	130,287	92,598
2007	8,243,517	6,314,746	45,437	6,360,183	504,770	12,953	5,868,366	1,716,152	658,999	61,773	133,448	97,097
2008	11,980,585	9,792,700	-24,563	9,768,137	650,648	-44,751	9,072,738	2,184,926	722,921	87,411	137,060	105,642
2009	8,858,700	6,975,945	7,841	6,983,786	559,596	-11,171	6,413,019	1,676,045	769,636	62,851	140,948	102,364
2010	10,561,435	8,533,062	40,577	8,573,639	637,193	-118,492	7,817,954	1,904,626	838,855	74,483	141,796	107,924
2011	14,516,541	12,430,779	4,220	12,434,999	708,769	-173,991	11,552,239	2,113,660	850,642	100,023	145,132	113,311
2012	16,636,063	14,187,906	472	14,188,378	800,471	-338,755	13,049,152	2,751,524	835,387	109,203	152,341	126,039
2013	17,899,678	15,792,816	31,546	15,824,362	994,477	-438,602	14,391,283	2,656,907	851,488	113,537	157,655	133,198
2014	19,619,254	17,384,937	-8,926	17,376,011	1,122,682	-658,850	15,594,479	3,141,199	883,576	123,254	159,178	141,796
2015	15,309,164	13,025,242	2,675	13,027,917	1,003,392	-544,744	11,479,781	2,898,550	930,833	93,275	164,130	142,616
2016	13,032,489	10,646,527	1,891	10,648,418	904,174	-474,517	9,269,727	2,780,576	982,186	79,037	164,890	141,686
2017	19,018,523	16,366,013	18,851	16,384,864	1,161,718	-696,790	14,526,356	3,494,074	998,093	114,913	165,504	147,263
2018	23,328,211	20,721,624	29,731	20,751,355	1,424,748	-1,039,857	18,286,750	4,020,511	1,020,950	135,811	171,770	159,216
2019	24,823,887	22,347,664	-6,494	22,341,170	1,542,224	-1,173,605	19,625,341	4,135,531	1,063,015	141,994	174,824	160,926
2020	19,172,407	15,906,758	16,318	15,923,076	1,216,324	-1,073,643	13,633,109	3,961,745	1,577,553	109,263	175,471	145,773
2021	21,726,357	18,049,575	13,568	18,063,143	1,316,453	-1,297,238	15,449,452	4,541,622	1,735,283	125,455	173,180	149,536

Personal Income and Employment by Area: Milwaukee-Waukesha, WI

(Thousands of dollars, except as noted.)

Year	Personal income, total	Earnings by place of work			Less: Contributions for government social insurance	Plus: Adjustment for residence	Equals: Net earnings by place of residence	Plus: Dividends, interest, and rent	Plus: Personal current transfer receipts	Per capita personal income (dollars)	Population (persons)	Total employment
		Nonfarm	Farm	Total								
1970	6,418,920	5,365,616	22,593	5,388,209	393,284	-108,182	4,886,743	995,361	536,816	4,570	1,404,488	659,946
1971	6,824,581	5,640,215	26,072	5,666,287	428,350	-119,326	5,118,611	1,071,160	634,810	4,857	1,405,231	655,077
1972	7,440,734	6,206,286	23,554	6,229,840	499,766	-138,434	5,591,640	1,143,239	705,855	5,255	1,416,024	671,565
1973	8,211,703	6,947,193	28,048	6,975,241	648,379	-162,233	6,164,629	1,256,193	790,881	5,827	1,409,344	707,070
1974	9,017,395	7,565,349	23,235	7,588,584	731,201	-187,190	6,670,193	1,432,008	915,194	6,398	1,409,473	721,019
1975	9,729,832	7,980,681	29,193	8,009,874	752,534	-201,553	7,055,787	1,540,515	1,133,530	6,974	1,395,236	705,141
1976	10,579,079	8,789,971	27,862	8,817,833	844,519	-233,015	7,740,299	1,628,018	1,210,762	7,558	1,399,726	718,806
1977	11,669,454	9,793,781	40,202	9,833,983	940,487	-273,294	8,620,202	1,770,268	1,278,984	8,371	1,394,089	744,641
1978	12,981,107	10,993,424	39,093	11,032,517	1,087,913	-319,901	9,624,703	1,933,345	1,423,059	9,344	1,389,196	773,376
1979	14,416,450	12,205,380	47,736	12,253,116	1,256,825	-375,138	10,621,153	2,179,056	1,616,241	10,333	1,395,212	794,684
1980	15,861,064	12,943,741	52,592	12,996,333	1,324,228	-414,992	11,257,113	2,650,173	1,953,778	11,356	1,396,659	783,371
1981	17,381,143	13,753,251	46,335	13,799,586	1,504,611	-441,360	11,853,615	3,277,777	2,249,751	12,489	1,391,672	769,054
1982	18,377,569	14,150,386	39,592	14,189,978	1,561,049	-441,702	12,187,227	3,656,421	2,533,921	13,206	1,391,628	746,855
1983	19,055,332	14,536,177	21,344	14,557,521	1,603,592	-437,376	12,516,553	3,804,391	2,734,388	13,735	1,387,307	735,233
1984	20,876,909	16,058,439	30,560	16,088,999	1,816,823	-480,804	13,791,372	4,311,077	2,774,460	15,075	1,384,897	771,524
1985	21,969,014	16,913,597	34,538	16,948,135	1,928,278	-502,368	14,517,489	4,518,740	2,932,785	15,812	1,389,361	782,599
1986	23,061,724	17,833,942	38,849	17,872,791	2,031,939	-524,424	15,316,428	4,681,961	3,063,335	16,575	1,391,362	794,602
1987	24,372,842	19,082,113	40,547	19,122,660	2,134,088	-545,886	16,442,686	4,797,324	3,132,832	17,433	1,398,088	815,518
1988	26,338,127	20,805,707	28,981	20,834,688	2,401,141	-585,526	17,848,021	5,228,810	3,261,296	18,685	1,409,602	847,896
1989	28,499,063	22,180,765	54,825	22,235,590	2,557,497	-617,951	19,060,142	5,946,265	3,492,656	20,047	1,421,621	867,258
1990	30,025,107	23,538,894	38,823	23,577,717	2,830,199	-638,247	20,109,271	6,174,167	3,741,669	20,919	1,435,303	881,288
1991	31,020,343	24,344,100	35,545	24,379,645	2,955,609	-672,422	20,751,614	6,215,462	4,053,267	21,397	1,449,760	874,176
1992	33,195,783	26,240,001	47,706	26,287,707	3,155,661	-765,859	22,366,187	6,430,529	4,399,067	22,694	1,462,728	882,783
1993	34,793,728	27,630,930	37,627	27,668,557	3,318,792	-851,404	23,498,361	6,689,006	4,606,361	23,657	1,470,728	893,226
1994	36,651,180	29,114,093	38,932	29,153,025	3,551,456	-951,836	24,649,733	7,216,733	4,784,714	24,827	1,476,272	915,146
1995	38,531,916	30,465,172	30,041	30,495,213	3,723,666	-1,047,814	25,723,733	7,773,329	5,034,854	26,011	1,481,347	932,863
1996	40,506,865	31,983,353	36,415	32,019,768	3,875,309	-1,127,016	27,017,443	8,347,530	5,141,892	27,258	1,486,045	942,951
1997	42,916,031	34,110,390	26,294	34,136,684	4,114,381	-1,253,473	28,768,830	8,837,796	5,309,405	28,852	1,487,435	959,068
1998	46,005,644	36,523,291	34,555	36,557,846	4,363,496	-1,362,762	30,831,588	9,740,038	5,434,018	30,857	1,490,926	978,150
1999	47,781,070	38,551,066	35,752	38,586,818	4,618,169	-1,376,654	32,591,995	9,517,892	5,671,183	31,934	1,496,255	989,784
2000	50,670,340	40,621,551	30,404	40,651,955	4,803,281	-1,558,219	34,290,455	10,312,709	6,067,176	33,726	1,502,420	1,004,465
2001	53,311,185	43,113,840	42,544	43,156,384	4,923,487	-1,737,109	36,495,788	10,023,088	6,792,309	35,370	1,507,257	1,007,270
2002	53,977,469	43,957,240	43,783	44,001,023	4,994,475	-1,847,969	37,158,579	9,560,192	7,258,698	35,646	1,514,251	993,676
2003	54,700,093	44,741,398	61,459	44,802,857	5,107,747	-1,970,784	37,724,326	9,551,209	7,424,558	35,993	1,519,746	991,375
2004	56,912,087	46,637,605	66,699	46,704,304	5,335,988	-1,994,725	39,373,591	9,988,555	7,549,941	37,386	1,522,302	1,000,338
2005	59,201,507	48,103,070	51,351	48,154,421	5,526,656	-2,159,125	40,468,640	10,731,690	8,001,177	38,887	1,522,391	1,008,163
2006	63,675,835	51,053,618	47,340	51,100,958	5,866,764	-2,371,248	42,862,946	12,436,467	8,376,422	41,785	1,523,907	1,019,482
2007	66,030,875	52,639,033	57,899	52,696,932	6,052,072	-2,508,163	44,136,697	12,914,954	8,979,224	43,144	1,530,492	1,032,273
2008	67,964,318	53,805,908	53,122	53,859,030	6,238,800	-2,628,678	44,991,552	13,041,673	9,931,093	44,183	1,538,232	1,031,665
2009	66,461,043	51,762,274	43,712	51,805,986	6,009,265	-2,421,660	43,375,061	11,399,052	11,686,930	42,889	1,549,613	990,276
2010	67,982,222	52,384,645	59,617	52,444,262	6,107,049	-2,299,527	44,037,686	11,373,148	12,571,388	43,671	1,556,708	981,214
2011	71,649,388	54,916,103	78,562	54,994,665	5,713,115	-2,446,568	46,834,982	12,791,521	12,022,885	45,887	1,561,423	994,345
2012	75,091,272	56,824,775	77,505	56,902,280	5,845,449	-2,291,362	48,765,469	14,070,683	12,255,120	47,907	1,567,445	1,000,506
2013	74,863,518	58,018,805	71,605	58,090,410	6,738,265	-2,366,489	48,985,656	13,402,875	12,474,987	47,623	1,572,002	1,014,559
2014	77,576,420	59,368,505	66,102	59,434,607	6,906,412	-2,303,858	50,224,337	14,362,446	12,989,637	49,288	1,573,940	1,025,449
2015	80,947,249	61,411,707	63,818	61,475,525	7,116,328	-2,407,679	51,951,518	15,519,823	13,475,908	51,392	1,575,104	1,037,385
2016	82,278,423	62,353,476	42,647	62,396,123	7,215,090	-2,489,692	52,691,341	16,105,855	13,481,227	52,260	1,574,396	1,044,296
2017	84,691,793	64,079,214	41,063	64,120,277	7,472,645	-2,577,516	54,070,116	16,488,446	14,133,231	53,842	1,572,978	1,051,068
2018	88,691,562	66,779,063	34,995	66,814,058	7,681,586	-2,644,251	56,488,221	17,400,415	14,802,926	56,394	1,572,723	1,063,999
2019	91,611,803	68,596,091	40,321	68,636,412	7,929,213	-2,821,522	57,885,677	18,334,800	15,391,326	58,192	1,574,296	1,063,374
2020	96,584,530	69,120,615	63,206	69,183,821	8,030,835	-2,580,303	58,572,683	18,482,730	19,529,117	61,378	1,573,598	1,017,716
2021	103,079,113	73,188,978	63,737	73,252,715	8,311,244	-2,677,925	62,263,546	19,110,366	21,705,201	65,803	1,566,487	1,038,503

Personal Income and Employment by Area: Minneapolis-St. Paul-Bloomington, MN-WI

(Thousands of dollars, except as noted.)

Year	Personal income, total	Nonfarm	Farm	Total	Less: Contributions for government social insurance	Plus: Adjustment for residence	Equals: Net earnings by place of residence	Plus: Dividends, interest, and rent	Plus: Personal current transfer receipts	Per capita personal income (dollars)	Population (persons)	Total employment
1970	9,799,885	8,116,302	119,802	8,236,104	562,908	-54,519	7,618,677	1,439,880	741,328	4,701	2,084,574	1,001,143
1971	10,461,635	8,584,788	110,803	8,695,591	615,651	-52,664	8,027,276	1,565,973	868,386	4,972	2,104,296	997,890
1972	11,265,064	9,257,248	126,846	9,384,094	698,206	-55,524	8,630,364	1,676,116	958,584	5,344	2,107,895	1,038,036
1973	12,562,725	10,313,609	220,351	10,533,960	901,524	-62,315	9,570,121	1,857,463	1,135,141	5,909	2,125,921	1,097,783
1974	13,833,383	11,301,724	176,524	11,478,248	1,021,370	-65,745	10,391,133	2,127,763	1,314,487	6,449	2,145,063	1,123,468
1975	15,036,015	12,079,658	156,192	12,235,850	1,062,096	-70,917	11,102,837	2,333,013	1,600,165	6,980	2,154,275	1,115,829
1976	16,465,168	13,427,432	93,501	13,520,933	1,213,136	-81,602	12,226,195	2,488,950	1,750,023	7,595	2,167,976	1,147,906
1977	18,421,847	15,115,585	220,262	15,335,847	1,364,717	-100,752	13,870,378	2,752,591	1,798,878	8,453	2,179,319	1,198,787
1978	20,682,175	17,189,476	203,531	17,393,007	1,605,920	-117,304	15,669,783	3,086,065	1,926,327	9,400	2,200,167	1,259,054
1979	23,463,609	19,755,166	179,973	19,935,139	1,922,843	-146,912	17,865,384	3,461,122	2,137,103	10,547	2,224,748	1,330,627
1980	26,383,863	21,825,635	134,141	21,959,776	2,123,744	-162,636	19,673,396	4,175,078	2,535,389	11,654	2,263,881	1,360,454
1981	29,275,599	23,712,312	143,873	23,856,185	2,470,430	-181,003	21,204,752	5,158,076	2,912,771	12,773	2,291,962	1,357,542
1982	31,686,609	25,071,403	128,051	25,199,454	2,663,778	-187,176	22,348,500	6,093,051	3,245,058	13,674	2,317,206	1,336,848
1983	33,952,221	27,097,156	22,122	27,119,278	2,917,886	-203,902	23,997,490	6,466,146	3,488,585	14,560	2,331,850	1,356,281
1984	38,258,350	30,721,539	164,108	30,885,647	3,395,249	-242,524	27,247,874	7,364,992	3,645,484	16,246	2,354,976	1,445,106
1985	41,345,856	33,361,839	166,120	33,527,959	3,745,159	-272,482	29,510,318	7,914,734	3,920,804	17,293	2,390,959	1,497,630
1986	44,051,911	35,701,423	183,657	35,885,080	4,109,624	-289,928	31,485,528	8,436,890	4,129,493	18,142	2,428,147	1,533,116
1987	47,336,517	38,733,501	235,882	38,969,383	4,420,030	-314,109	34,235,244	8,810,626	4,290,647	19,173	2,468,889	1,602,851
1988	50,999,930	41,953,711	130,610	42,084,321	4,930,661	-344,757	36,808,903	9,592,717	4,598,310	20,210	2,523,553	1,654,072
1989	55,220,512	44,779,239	271,369	45,050,608	5,246,246	-343,566	39,460,796	10,749,278	5,010,438	21,550	2,562,410	1,689,977
1990	58,785,816	47,429,087	229,560	47,658,647	5,611,922	-333,678	41,713,047	11,636,272	5,436,497	22,557	2,606,156	1,721,797
1991	61,009,424	49,453,164	159,429	49,612,593	5,917,282	-356,073	43,339,238	11,767,787	5,902,399	23,054	2,646,336	1,728,757
1992	65,669,362	53,722,932	174,768	53,897,700	6,352,891	-411,862	47,132,947	12,102,044	6,434,371	24,424	2,688,729	1,756,753
1993	68,499,181	56,133,953	86,016	56,219,969	6,662,201	-445,363	49,112,405	12,555,145	6,831,631	25,052	2,734,239	1,794,801
1994	72,979,163	59,528,904	168,202	59,697,106	7,156,731	-507,471	52,032,904	13,755,460	7,190,799	26,283	2,776,675	1,853,150
1995	77,995,652	63,200,827	90,313	63,291,140	7,570,558	-566,829	55,153,753	15,194,444	7,647,455	27,666	2,819,211	1,911,772
1996	83,339,377	67,541,915	187,685	67,729,600	8,021,382	-645,523	59,062,695	16,251,189	8,025,493	29,124	2,861,505	1,951,582
1997	89,333,015	72,555,017	119,595	72,674,612	8,562,965	-726,606	63,385,041	17,794,927	8,153,047	30,772	2,903,107	1,989,738
1998	97,266,782	79,294,748	171,529	79,466,277	9,213,741	-911,319	69,341,217	19,520,278	8,405,287	33,181	2,931,378	2,041,242
1999	102,889,779	84,821,069	157,645	84,978,714	9,883,330	-1,078,680	74,016,704	20,031,916	8,841,159	34,534	2,979,405	2,089,976
2000	112,424,938	92,710,053	149,363	92,859,416	10,672,159	-1,267,089	80,920,168	21,965,191	9,539,579	37,115	3,029,064	2,145,458
2001	116,659,781	96,326,968	131,836	96,458,804	11,021,946	-1,387,037	84,049,821	21,920,270	10,689,690	37,984	3,071,250	2,160,572
2002	118,473,606	97,940,694	143,819	98,084,513	11,205,607	-1,417,270	85,461,636	21,351,879	11,660,091	38,207	3,100,852	2,149,673
2003	123,477,184	101,657,718	198,543	101,856,261	11,705,282	-1,488,911	88,662,068	22,631,985	12,183,131	39,473	3,128,159	2,159,233
2004	131,482,992	108,562,859	264,579	108,827,438	12,380,639	-1,657,362	94,789,437	23,903,268	12,790,287	41,652	3,156,700	2,193,049
2005	136,208,564	111,533,022	265,440	111,798,462	12,940,235	-1,750,546	97,107,681	25,628,277	13,472,606	42,780	3,183,920	2,236,087
2006	143,737,264	115,308,806	239,050	115,547,856	13,504,611	-1,771,537	100,271,708	28,616,588	14,848,968	44,650	3,219,203	2,271,775
2007	152,421,225	121,493,684	242,350	121,736,034	14,075,257	-1,840,424	105,820,353	30,203,248	16,397,624	46,836	3,254,350	2,303,992
2008	156,992,534	123,397,376	309,470	123,706,846	14,443,707	-1,801,086	107,462,053	30,701,643	18,828,838	47,777	3,285,969	2,295,814
2009	148,968,960	116,609,455	215,595	116,825,050	13,813,274	-1,404,938	101,606,838	26,785,919	20,576,203	44,933	3,315,368	2,220,758
2010	155,080,228	120,458,977	271,843	120,730,820	14,025,201	-1,387,315	105,318,304	27,387,210	22,374,714	46,430	3,340,070	2,213,817
2011	165,934,842	127,525,085	359,656	127,884,741	13,154,845	-1,490,454	113,239,442	30,152,844	22,542,556	49,184	3,373,773	2,265,061
2012	176,072,710	134,414,833	462,725	134,877,558	13,741,018	-1,467,125	119,669,415	33,770,790	22,632,505	51,686	3,406,567	2,294,188
2013	178,345,250	138,926,130	447,739	139,373,869	16,238,832	-1,465,428	121,669,609	33,171,795	23,503,846	51,819	3,441,688	2,335,231
2014	189,975,474	146,222,738	356,299	146,579,037	16,811,965	-1,516,020	128,251,052	36,748,553	24,975,869	54,409	3,491,595	2,376,165
2015	199,806,959	153,161,616	263,205	153,424,821	17,427,199	-1,526,802	134,470,820	39,550,817	25,785,322	56,717	3,522,901	2,424,287
2016	205,891,952	157,352,793	162,224	157,515,017	17,932,722	-1,545,959	138,036,336	41,186,501	26,669,115	57,806	3,561,786	2,460,228
2017	214,569,552	164,656,961	189,160	164,846,121	18,733,752	-1,669,599	144,442,770	42,494,000	27,632,782	59,555	3,602,878	2,495,861
2018	226,292,650	172,182,343	133,532	172,315,875	19,633,873	-1,737,131	150,944,871	45,905,108	29,442,671	62,161	3,640,447	2,533,484
2019	236,857,011	177,827,686	108,650	177,936,336	20,345,670	-1,797,644	155,793,022	50,127,504	30,936,485	64,496	3,672,456	2,540,664
2020	249,932,032	179,006,922	290,096	179,297,018	20,539,322	-1,690,452	157,067,244	50,430,386	42,434,402	67,688	3,692,421	2,416,743
2021	265,391,686	190,516,160	342,193	190,858,353	21,325,003	-1,897,226	167,636,124	51,686,263	46,069,299	71,912	3,690,512	2,478,903

Personal Income and Employment by Area: Missoula, MT

(Thousands of dollars, except as noted.)

Year	Personal income, total	Earnings by place of work			Less: Contributions for government social insurance	Plus: Adjustment for residence	Equals: Net earnings by place of residence	Plus: Dividends, interest, and rent	Plus: Personal current transfer receipts	Per capita personal income (dollars)	Population (persons)	Total employment
		Nonfarm	Farm	Total								
1970	208,980	173,995	696	174,691	13,535	-5,092	156,064	34,810	18,106	3,574	58,472	25,139
1971	233,708	194,017	977	194,994	15,269	-5,764	173,961	38,324	21,423	3,896	59,990	26,508
1972	263,307	221,506	1,412	222,918	18,329	-8,015	196,574	42,382	24,351	4,253	61,918	28,195
1973	290,502	243,366	2,012	245,378	23,012	-9,280	213,086	48,531	28,885	4,509	64,424	29,798
1974	329,287	272,000	1,830	273,830	26,113	-10,928	236,789	57,230	35,268	4,914	67,007	30,952
1975	367,339	295,014	1,130	296,144	26,809	-11,672	257,663	66,425	43,251	5,478	67,056	31,090
1976	421,544	346,931	1,104	348,035	32,426	-14,908	300,701	73,432	47,411	6,062	69,539	33,780
1977	491,819	415,461	176	415,637	39,930	-20,077	355,630	84,894	51,295	6,930	70,970	36,648
1978	572,589	490,751	1,716	492,467	48,972	-25,212	418,283	98,461	55,845	7,928	72,226	40,008
1979	639,139	544,983	1,559	546,542	56,986	-30,859	458,697	114,584	65,858	8,627	74,088	40,389
1980	694,462	572,923	1,393	574,316	61,324	-33,542	479,450	135,570	79,442	9,124	76,115	39,442
1981	736,988	576,096	435	576,531	65,004	-22,824	488,703	156,594	91,691	9,653	76,352	37,592
1982	771,101	586,216	309	586,525	67,402	-25,984	493,139	179,891	98,071	10,248	75,242	36,696
1983	827,333	645,419	1,154	646,573	75,130	-29,372	542,071	179,948	105,314	10,948	75,571	38,399
1984	908,109	710,418	155	710,573	84,485	-31,930	594,158	202,346	111,605	11,813	76,875	40,726
1985	952,215	743,286	-522	742,764	89,956	-32,139	620,669	211,090	120,456	12,243	77,774	41,567
1986	985,599	766,659	955	767,614	94,262	-31,563	641,789	213,464	130,346	12,644	77,949	41,942
1987	1,025,302	797,419	-243	797,176	97,936	-31,731	667,509	218,322	139,471	13,199	77,680	43,048
1988	1,085,840	844,354	-516	843,838	109,213	-33,722	700,903	235,109	149,828	13,999	77,564	44,555
1989	1,162,487	902,230	369	902,599	118,659	-36,861	747,079	248,296	167,112	14,905	77,995	45,814
1990	1,254,609	980,021	197	980,218	137,269	-40,329	802,620	266,717	185,272	15,865	79,080	47,616
1991	1,333,097	1,045,332	284	1,045,616	148,125	-43,356	854,135	284,037	194,925	16,438	81,098	49,299
1992	1,463,872	1,168,467	293	1,168,760	165,648	-51,008	952,104	300,187	211,581	17,521	83,549	51,852
1993	1,571,964	1,268,176	700	1,268,876	184,306	-56,127	1,028,443	319,590	223,931	18,227	86,243	54,021
1994	1,665,826	1,332,212	-1,778	1,330,434	191,727	-58,399	1,080,308	355,025	230,493	18,922	88,037	56,003
1995	1,779,791	1,400,291	-2,871	1,397,420	196,342	-64,169	1,136,909	393,170	249,712	19,685	90,413	58,094
1996	1,886,245	1,480,167	-4,343	1,475,824	198,806	-71,175	1,205,843	421,187	259,215	20,514	91,947	60,152
1997	1,993,492	1,551,695	-4,406	1,547,289	202,649	-75,323	1,269,317	460,870	263,305	21,401	93,151	61,250
1998	2,134,009	1,655,481	-2,582	1,652,899	210,240	-83,013	1,359,646	501,832	272,531	22,739	93,847	62,905
1999	2,206,163	1,745,093	-1,462	1,743,631	220,943	-92,443	1,430,245	509,042	266,876	23,274	94,791	64,766
2000	2,405,073	1,880,192	-1,758	1,878,434	238,255	-103,029	1,537,150	565,198	302,725	25,006	96,178	66,193
2001	2,454,479	1,923,211	632	1,923,843	251,331	-114,615	1,557,897	557,538	339,044	25,191	97,435	68,296
2002	2,590,141	2,056,624	3,088	2,059,712	270,125	-128,147	1,661,440	576,812	351,889	26,171	98,968	69,240
2003	2,755,900	2,189,698	158	2,189,856	284,812	-141,374	1,763,670	625,537	366,693	27,566	99,976	70,828
2004	2,948,577	2,326,354	753	2,327,107	297,659	-162,085	1,867,363	696,858	384,356	29,213	100,934	72,124
2005	3,112,706	2,429,596	390	2,429,986	314,779	-183,077	1,932,130	765,800	414,776	30,428	102,298	73,462
2006	3,407,201	2,574,273	-1,640	2,572,633	333,570	-195,989	2,043,074	915,049	449,078	32,645	104,372	75,245
2007	3,619,168	2,714,004	-772	2,713,232	356,513	-216,358	2,140,361	997,781	481,026	34,108	106,110	77,712
2008	3,861,545	2,798,281	-4,177	2,794,104	365,800	-233,539	2,194,765	1,100,620	566,160	35,839	107,747	76,966
2009	3,924,118	2,795,478	-1,517	2,793,961	363,686	-235,697	2,194,578	1,109,359	620,181	36,095	108,717	75,735
2010	3,827,266	2,817,404	-1,676	2,815,728	363,416	-218,700	2,233,612	903,967	689,687	34,961	109,471	75,059
2011	4,089,699	2,931,222	5,518	2,936,740	339,388	-233,008	2,364,344	1,040,651	684,704	37,088	110,270	76,137
2012	4,381,105	3,022,127	-3,286	3,018,841	344,103	-216,674	2,458,064	1,219,297	703,744	39,432	111,104	76,750
2013	4,375,065	3,114,758	214	3,114,972	400,399	-201,974	2,512,599	1,140,818	721,648	39,067	111,988	77,713
2014	4,704,613	3,258,973	-1,496	3,257,477	419,190	-196,717	2,641,570	1,297,546	765,497	42,150	111,616	78,866
2015	5,222,672	3,463,674	582	3,464,256	438,303	-207,644	2,818,309	1,597,895	806,468	46,363	112,647	80,155
2016	5,275,310	3,590,787	2,648	3,593,435	442,716	-248,948	2,901,771	1,500,873	872,666	46,029	114,608	82,177
2017	5,703,926	3,826,890	2,324	3,829,214	483,182	-268,858	3,077,174	1,682,388	944,364	49,278	115,750	83,752
2018	5,877,119	4,012,858	1,309	4,014,167	515,328	-276,124	3,222,715	1,666,608	987,796	50,531	116,307	85,947
2019	6,320,989	4,245,727	1,705	4,247,432	537,103	-314,952	3,395,377	1,890,581	1,035,031	53,992	117,072	86,834
2020	6,845,372	4,424,153	4,510	4,428,663	572,884	-328,786	3,526,993	1,944,396	1,373,983	57,895	118,238	85,616
2021	7,396,782	4,927,167	2,304	4,929,471	613,991	-392,869	3,922,611	2,016,692	1,457,479	61,881	119,533	89,008

Personal Income and Employment by Area: Mobile, AL

(Thousands of dollars, except as noted.)

Year	Personal income, total	Earnings by place of work			Less: Contributions for government social insurance	Plus: Adjustment for residence	Equals: Net earnings by place of residence	Plus: Dividends, interest, and rent	Plus: Personal current transfer receipts	Per capita personal income (dollars)	Population (persons)	Total employment
		Nonfarm	Farm	Total								
1970	950,622	776,889	6,544	783,433	58,025	-2,326	723,082	131,975	95,565	2,986	318,311	121,223
1971	1,027,930	825,238	7,528	832,766	62,798	-2,940	767,028	148,212	112,690	3,180	323,278	121,416
1972	1,136,937	914,253	8,338	922,591	72,892	13	849,712	162,187	125,038	3,506	324,325	126,180
1973	1,275,686	1,035,877	11,743	1,047,620	94,645	-2,850	950,125	181,105	144,456	3,931	324,541	133,484
1974	1,457,868	1,178,172	13,415	1,191,587	110,620	-7,644	1,073,323	210,522	174,023	4,426	329,414	137,961
1975	1,668,401	1,327,852	12,485	1,340,337	123,512	-5,359	1,211,466	235,975	220,960	4,977	335,235	141,132
1976	1,892,953	1,529,252	12,637	1,541,889	145,266	-8,544	1,388,079	257,268	247,606	5,489	344,892	147,159
1977	2,107,884	1,714,100	12,734	1,726,834	163,618	-3,680	1,559,536	285,762	262,586	5,969	353,134	153,854
1978	2,377,508	1,963,194	17,104	1,980,298	189,999	-26,781	1,763,518	327,592	286,398	6,603	360,079	162,577
1979	2,621,543	2,145,330	9,494	2,154,824	214,504	-40,682	1,899,638	375,142	346,763	7,247	361,747	163,160
1980	2,985,727	2,422,449	17,588	2,440,037	240,700	-58,168	2,141,169	459,181	385,377	8,153	366,205	167,983
1981	3,309,347	2,642,091	22,705	2,664,796	283,445	-65,288	2,316,063	554,080	439,204	8,934	370,432	168,136
1982	3,464,998	2,669,532	29,045	2,698,577	292,805	-48,945	2,356,827	615,456	492,715	9,245	374,782	161,111
1983	3,598,230	2,764,785	31,713	2,796,498	305,718	-71,221	2,419,559	631,990	546,681	9,548	376,842	159,696
1984	3,867,076	2,975,399	20,464	2,995,863	334,876	-87,751	2,573,236	709,040	584,800	10,279	376,211	164,970
1985	4,167,354	3,238,122	23,788	3,261,910	365,657	-110,365	2,785,888	761,056	620,410	11,000	378,847	169,061
1986	4,356,691	3,378,798	23,981	3,402,779	379,534	-117,993	2,905,252	802,493	648,946	11,413	381,729	169,068
1987	4,519,065	3,523,388	25,781	3,549,169	390,640	-132,906	3,025,623	826,089	667,353	11,778	383,696	171,067
1988	4,787,229	3,743,181	33,858	3,777,039	429,411	-143,719	3,203,909	889,364	693,956	12,548	381,501	175,349
1989	5,192,778	3,989,561	36,765	4,026,326	457,726	-172,421	3,396,179	1,008,188	788,411	13,706	378,869	177,801
1990	5,526,649	4,259,829	36,842	4,296,671	496,091	-191,639	3,608,941	1,053,403	864,305	14,576	379,167	181,716
1991	5,916,282	4,639,982	43,056	4,683,038	543,551	-254,753	3,884,734	1,068,649	962,899	15,448	382,978	188,154
1992	6,354,170	4,981,720	33,632	5,015,352	577,618	-304,668	4,133,066	1,119,027	1,102,077	16,373	388,097	191,637
1993	6,636,961	5,252,583	26,390	5,278,973	612,971	-355,009	4,310,993	1,159,320	1,166,648	16,856	393,740	199,587
1994	6,941,100	5,517,191	18,733	5,535,924	652,873	-395,694	4,487,357	1,217,367	1,236,376	17,542	395,685	201,086
1995	7,256,961	5,651,910	19,287	5,671,197	674,469	-420,269	4,576,459	1,337,737	1,342,765	18,341	395,664	204,219
1996	7,559,744	5,947,096	19,882	5,966,978	706,195	-474,123	4,786,660	1,362,392	1,410,692	19,082	396,163	208,206
1997	7,894,324	6,276,111	25,674	6,301,785	745,207	-550,518	5,006,060	1,423,783	1,464,481	19,839	397,917	213,334
1998	8,803,123	6,984,341	22,673	7,007,014	811,231	-537,889	5,657,894	1,584,721	1,560,508	21,142	416,387	223,312
1999	8,866,739	7,052,684	28,569	7,081,253	823,909	-556,309	5,701,035	1,559,030	1,606,674	21,247	417,326	222,875
2000	9,155,311	7,196,261	33,321	7,229,582	838,498	-607,604	5,783,480	1,660,911	1,710,920	21,894	418,174	223,778
2001	9,598,631	7,594,648	30,688	7,625,336	872,722	-596,383	6,156,231	1,567,276	1,875,124	22,960	418,062	221,613
2002	9,732,961	7,697,930	28,272	7,726,202	887,425	-575,541	6,263,236	1,523,068	1,946,657	23,372	416,444	219,084
2003	9,986,378	7,751,098	36,629	7,787,727	897,173	-554,447	6,336,107	1,609,974	2,040,297	24,006	415,992	217,261
2004	10,452,286	7,990,444	50,466	8,040,910	923,416	-544,846	6,572,648	1,715,250	2,164,388	25,140	415,760	218,847
2005	11,286,925	8,643,611	31,481	8,675,092	1,004,622	-555,476	7,114,994	1,734,197	2,437,734	27,091	416,632	225,206
2006	12,478,473	9,624,350	39,711	9,664,061	1,093,868	-577,184	7,993,009	1,980,298	2,505,166	29,667	420,621	232,657
2007	12,911,585	9,884,316	40,596	9,924,912	1,148,133	-578,788	8,197,991	2,108,099	2,605,495	30,509	423,206	239,469
2008	13,450,536	10,002,484	32,138	10,034,622	1,190,160	-596,458	8,248,004	2,246,388	2,956,144	31,523	426,692	240,257
2009	13,146,602	9,783,829	46,117	9,829,946	1,164,473	-687,774	7,977,699	2,066,314	3,102,589	30,610	429,487	231,767
2010	13,755,960	10,157,998	33,633	10,191,631	1,209,917	-800,275	8,181,439	2,130,389	3,444,132	31,920	430,955	232,814
2011	14,496,767	10,804,933	30,590	10,835,523	1,135,630	-976,613	8,723,280	2,260,734	3,512,753	33,676	430,482	239,023
2012	14,422,703	10,699,459	46,666	10,746,125	1,128,324	-982,492	8,635,309	2,280,504	3,506,890	33,460	431,040	235,118
2013	14,624,616	10,792,998	43,456	10,836,454	1,292,290	-913,369	8,630,795	2,431,680	3,562,141	33,938	430,923	234,461
2014	14,939,920	11,082,431	31,625	11,114,056	1,321,453	-944,754	8,847,849	2,356,986	3,735,085	34,611	431,655	236,756
2015	15,568,029	11,489,218	35,157	11,524,375	1,369,421	-1,050,792	9,104,162	2,476,084	3,987,783	36,030	432,080	239,814
2016	15,651,960	11,736,696	35,432	11,772,128	1,395,823	-1,235,484	9,140,821	2,496,636	4,014,503	36,192	432,476	241,886
2017	15,922,832	11,980,221	45,193	12,025,414	1,436,883	-1,338,455	9,250,076	2,587,473	4,085,283	36,902	431,494	242,360
2018	16,400,210	12,441,674	39,703	12,481,377	1,501,120	-1,417,538	9,562,719	2,622,043	4,215,448	38,006	431,516	243,618
2019	16,980,082	12,843,066	36,346	12,879,412	1,537,465	-1,472,583	9,869,364	2,687,487	4,423,231	39,416	430,797	243,672
2020	18,382,296	13,244,321	37,252	13,281,573	1,594,470	-1,579,466	10,107,637	2,690,222	5,584,437	42,795	429,546	240,960
2021	19,870,121	14,364,728	35,609	14,400,337	1,696,069	-1,777,855	10,926,413	2,735,814	6,207,894	46,402	428,220	248,410

Personal Income and Employment by Area: Modesto, CA

(Thousands of dollars, except as noted.)

Year	Personal income, total	Earnings by place of work			Less: Contributions for government social insurance	Plus: Adjustment for residence	Equals: Net earnings by place of residence	Plus: Dividends, interest, and rent	Plus: Personal current transfer receipts	Per capita personal income (dollars)	Population (persons)	Total employment
		Nonfarm	Farm	Total								
1970	790,180	502,478	62,878	565,356	35,779	30,049	559,626	116,867	113,687	4,040	195,578	83,872
1971	854,198	549,964	59,022	608,986	40,386	32,435	601,035	128,315	124,848	4,277	199,698	85,423
1972	963,489	622,412	78,807	701,219	48,113	34,458	687,564	142,323	133,602	4,778	201,644	90,511
1973	1,102,270	693,587	121,303	814,890	61,200	38,011	791,701	165,623	144,946	5,123	215,178	93,856
1974	1,255,143	782,516	136,115	918,631	70,941	43,049	890,739	191,301	173,103	5,641	222,484	98,381
1975	1,389,427	876,020	98,255	974,275	76,874	48,513	945,914	221,512	222,001	6,054	229,518	100,774
1976	1,557,694	999,983	91,410	1,091,393	88,930	54,876	1,057,339	245,322	255,033	6,592	236,293	104,388
1977	1,806,559	1,149,766	146,629	1,296,395	104,000	61,534	1,253,929	280,185	272,445	7,314	246,995	110,136
1978	2,021,879	1,317,105	136,991	1,454,096	121,266	69,710	1,402,540	324,101	295,238	8,176	247,280	116,129
1979	2,301,197	1,504,583	154,380	1,658,963	145,834	79,472	1,592,601	378,986	329,610	8,819	260,933	122,698
1980	2,594,554	1,634,898	157,655	1,792,553	155,561	88,897	1,725,889	474,097	394,568	9,687	267,852	123,136
1981	2,876,552	1,783,228	117,691	1,900,919	183,803	104,759	1,821,875	587,111	467,566	10,455	275,137	124,323
1982	3,101,512	1,886,216	120,912	2,007,128	196,831	123,528	1,933,825	649,713	517,974	11,048	280,737	124,463
1983	3,292,851	2,002,223	95,376	2,097,599	211,373	145,592	2,031,818	705,151	555,882	11,414	288,504	125,566
1984	3,676,102	2,229,810	136,281	2,366,091	242,741	182,877	2,306,227	779,153	590,722	12,509	293,879	128,705
1985	4,024,487	2,428,184	189,065	2,617,249	267,479	216,522	2,566,292	815,334	642,861	13,358	301,285	134,089
1986	4,345,529	2,649,850	188,103	2,837,953	293,716	248,773	2,793,010	855,573	696,946	13,966	311,154	137,844
1987	4,773,624	2,958,354	259,365	3,217,719	328,670	277,828	3,166,877	875,250	731,497	14,762	323,380	146,944
1988	5,207,829	3,258,154	256,249	3,514,403	372,344	320,571	3,462,630	950,133	795,066	15,497	336,063	156,458
1989	5,750,412	3,575,663	246,647	3,822,310	412,036	362,129	3,772,403	1,114,348	863,661	16,289	353,017	165,120
1990	6,278,916	3,912,080	288,259	4,200,339	448,542	405,019	4,156,816	1,157,251	964,849	16,730	375,312	171,839
1991	6,621,270	4,079,862	301,706	4,381,568	469,969	435,102	4,346,701	1,187,042	1,087,527	17,146	386,163	174,223
1992	6,985,482	4,299,538	292,584	4,592,122	492,696	455,548	4,554,974	1,167,096	1,263,412	17,697	394,725	173,045
1993	7,278,578	4,493,899	279,017	4,772,916	515,383	471,133	4,728,666	1,199,212	1,350,700	18,115	401,805	174,101
1994	7,461,839	4,628,972	252,861	4,881,833	528,258	504,910	4,858,485	1,240,801	1,362,553	18,367	406,274	174,328
1995	7,689,849	4,717,530	192,942	4,910,472	529,377	548,792	4,929,887	1,328,925	1,431,037	18,740	410,337	177,970
1996	8,220,856	4,947,496	332,517	5,280,013	538,160	584,730	5,326,583	1,395,068	1,499,205	19,802	415,159	183,775
1997	8,792,202	5,411,414	362,751	5,774,165	577,438	642,604	5,839,331	1,460,578	1,492,293	20,871	421,264	187,933
1998	9,507,374	5,969,107	384,758	6,353,865	622,773	689,947	6,421,039	1,511,942	1,574,393	22,174	428,754	198,000
1999	10,011,568	6,415,743	256,341	6,672,084	668,282	785,114	6,788,916	1,553,216	1,669,436	22,826	438,609	202,754
2000	10,904,210	7,077,587	216,298	7,293,885	720,998	948,763	7,521,650	1,612,122	1,770,438	24,260	449,471	205,267
2001	11,557,561	7,446,690	316,254	7,762,944	811,672	935,258	7,886,530	1,673,782	1,997,249	24,921	463,761	211,128
2002	12,154,126	7,931,068	322,059	8,253,127	880,235	930,869	8,303,761	1,666,468	2,183,897	25,455	477,469	215,168
2003	12,776,796	8,427,177	363,854	8,791,031	945,549	960,448	8,805,930	1,677,055	2,293,811	26,217	487,357	217,369
2004	13,689,671	8,964,597	644,938	9,609,535	1,037,635	1,016,330	9,588,230	1,723,562	2,377,879	27,790	492,613	219,983
2005	14,228,421	9,389,360	597,724	9,987,084	1,099,156	1,034,728	9,922,656	1,843,511	2,462,254	28,456	500,020	224,867
2006	14,865,192	9,649,721	559,851	10,209,572	1,089,142	1,159,125	10,279,555	1,960,737	2,624,900	29,456	504,651	225,192
2007	15,706,619	9,830,508	633,058	10,463,566	1,087,183	1,249,772	10,626,155	2,264,255	2,816,209	30,929	507,834	228,447
2008	15,839,650	9,737,804	483,657	10,221,461	1,101,500	1,272,671	10,392,632	2,235,837	3,211,181	31,117	509,032	223,665
2009	15,620,894	9,496,330	501,575	9,997,905	1,088,156	1,149,192	10,058,941	2,017,528	3,544,425	30,537	511,536	212,934
2010	16,388,842	9,815,997	554,264	10,370,261	1,081,650	1,140,368	10,428,979	2,057,390	3,902,473	31,815	515,137	210,904
2011	17,046,112	10,112,823	691,695	10,804,518	1,011,028	1,163,803	10,957,293	2,203,452	3,885,367	32,938	517,515	212,134
2012	17,695,226	10,358,808	790,552	11,149,360	1,039,227	1,276,296	11,386,429	2,355,714	3,953,083	34,007	520,336	218,345
2013	18,119,224	10,646,186	856,040	11,502,226	1,196,711	1,342,242	11,647,757	2,348,500	4,122,967	34,624	523,313	224,470
2014	19,601,062	11,185,339	1,192,194	12,377,533	1,252,824	1,437,165	12,561,874	2,612,566	4,426,622	37,067	528,795	230,538
2015	21,027,520	12,056,877	999,265	13,056,142	1,338,151	1,587,379	13,305,370	2,953,238	4,768,912	39,364	534,178	237,560
2016	21,681,457	12,605,492	845,775	13,451,267	1,409,311	1,662,272	13,704,228	3,083,248	4,893,981	40,116	540,463	242,441
2017	22,352,648	13,129,644	1,000,915	14,130,559	1,472,306	1,831,859	14,490,112	3,078,270	4,784,266	40,922	546,229	246,763
2018	22,944,298	13,785,158	793,619	14,578,777	1,560,643	1,740,981	14,759,115	3,153,058	5,032,125	41,729	549,847	252,924
2019	24,138,747	14,375,079	761,916	15,136,995	1,651,814	1,785,679	15,270,860	3,521,671	5,346,216	43,729	552,003	255,680
2020	27,153,448	14,890,963	879,659	15,770,622	1,710,909	1,862,462	15,922,175	3,560,311	7,670,962	49,128	552,710	249,833
2021	28,952,717	16,039,683	657,489	16,697,172	1,831,713	1,975,206	16,840,665	3,674,088	8,437,964	52,356	552,999	256,489

Personal Income and Employment by Area: Monroe, LA

(Thousands of dollars, except as noted.)

Year	Personal income, total	Earnings by place of work Nonfarm	Earnings by place of work Farm	Earnings by place of work Total	Less: Contributions for government social insurance	Plus: Adjustment for residence	Equals: Net earnings by place of residence	Plus: Dividends, interest, and rent	Plus: Personal current transfer receipts	Per capita personal income (dollars)	Population (persons)	Total employment
1970	369,753	287,206	5,537	292,743	18,552	-4,210	269,981	53,828	45,944	2,758	134,052	49,954
1971	417,790	324,448	7,137	331,585	21,650	-4,055	305,880	59,898	52,012	3,059	136,572	52,109
1972	465,499	364,509	6,923	371,432	25,623	-3,419	342,390	65,754	57,355	3,316	140,389	54,220
1973	521,184	409,294	9,969	419,263	33,180	-3,230	382,853	72,666	65,665	3,660	142,397	58,132
1974	581,313	450,820	4,903	455,723	37,586	-1,335	416,802	86,536	77,975	4,020	144,601	58,242
1975	657,201	493,959	6,719	500,678	40,178	-160	460,340	98,496	98,365	4,424	148,558	57,979
1976	766,408	592,253	10,866	603,119	49,545	-1,045	552,529	106,562	107,317	5,021	152,634	61,479
1977	854,758	662,495	13,048	675,543	54,637	3,128	624,034	118,430	112,294	5,534	154,446	63,178
1978	994,605	781,335	11,131	792,466	66,187	6,941	733,220	137,988	123,397	6,392	155,598	66,282
1979	1,107,073	855,644	14,055	869,699	74,866	13,789	808,622	157,856	140,595	7,023	157,646	66,963
1980	1,231,775	917,390	5,210	922,600	79,986	23,292	865,906	194,743	171,126	7,658	160,840	67,917
1981	1,380,792	1,014,942	7,587	1,022,529	93,632	19,856	948,753	241,539	190,500	8,509	162,278	68,401
1982	1,478,864	1,051,668	7,714	1,059,382	98,181	17,131	978,332	282,062	218,470	9,082	162,833	68,211
1983	1,599,046	1,135,902	7,129	1,143,031	105,205	14,469	1,052,295	306,448	240,303	9,712	164,650	69,765
1984	1,728,582	1,230,593	16,330	1,246,923	116,967	9,814	1,139,770	338,326	250,486	10,415	165,968	71,694
1985	1,842,497	1,311,773	10,285	1,322,058	126,095	3,632	1,199,595	372,365	270,537	11,040	166,887	73,963
1986	1,929,440	1,366,511	17,834	1,384,345	130,745	-1,941	1,251,659	384,753	293,028	11,416	169,012	73,356
1987	1,950,862	1,393,407	20,690	1,414,097	131,335	-3,924	1,278,838	372,631	299,393	11,646	167,513	73,825
1988	2,051,909	1,473,267	23,833	1,497,100	144,227	-6,814	1,346,059	387,439	318,411	12,373	165,842	73,947
1989	2,203,002	1,559,135	27,526	1,586,661	154,608	-8,685	1,423,368	432,645	346,989	13,424	164,107	74,432
1990	2,339,961	1,678,577	21,941	1,700,518	169,683	-10,137	1,520,698	436,570	382,693	14,361	162,944	75,648
1991	2,467,514	1,758,354	24,938	1,783,292	182,439	-11,004	1,589,849	443,444	434,221	15,035	164,119	76,682
1992	2,666,479	1,900,621	34,992	1,935,613	194,168	-13,954	1,727,491	446,372	492,616	16,036	166,280	78,203
1993	2,812,901	1,984,673	45,266	2,029,939	204,446	-17,178	1,808,315	463,005	541,581	16,812	167,314	81,017
1994	2,994,076	2,097,381	52,565	2,149,946	220,475	-23,087	1,906,384	489,088	598,604	17,841	167,822	81,542
1995	3,180,418	2,245,192	47,290	2,292,482	236,940	-32,022	2,023,520	554,796	602,102	18,841	168,806	84,945
1996	3,350,197	2,338,849	60,329	2,399,178	247,955	-38,165	2,113,058	572,111	665,028	19,792	169,266	86,982
1997	3,367,914	2,397,377	42,549	2,439,926	253,919	-40,647	2,145,360	590,439	632,115	19,819	169,934	87,893
1998	4,085,698	2,784,792	48,210	2,833,002	298,445	-1,990	2,532,567	743,679	809,452	20,277	201,490	101,616
1999	4,266,434	2,975,509	60,276	3,035,785	314,394	-10,765	2,710,626	735,995	819,813	21,221	201,049	103,785
2000	4,573,151	3,220,712	62,602	3,283,314	328,347	-13,361	2,941,606	782,845	848,700	22,753	200,994	106,383
2001	4,694,043	3,226,855	69,909	3,296,764	336,075	-18,848	2,941,841	775,194	977,008	23,449	200,177	109,919
2002	4,877,135	3,427,460	45,272	3,472,732	355,337	-24,418	3,092,977	751,712	1,032,446	24,304	200,671	111,467
2003	4,979,136	3,453,083	91,592	3,544,675	355,002	-24,723	3,164,950	776,192	1,037,994	24,707	201,530	111,044
2004	5,206,484	3,562,703	100,454	3,663,157	361,046	-18,306	3,283,805	773,545	1,149,134	25,793	201,860	110,911
2005	5,498,834	3,667,882	88,098	3,755,980	367,557	-8,338	3,380,085	889,401	1,229,348	27,277	201,596	110,477
2006	5,840,746	3,841,075	61,489	3,902,564	387,021	2,517	3,518,060	1,005,162	1,317,524	28,747	203,181	111,767
2007	6,134,001	3,978,257	77,943	4,056,200	399,562	-11,047	3,645,591	1,096,115	1,392,295	30,306	202,405	112,767
2008	6,431,805	4,041,740	47,548	4,089,288	408,188	6,077	3,687,177	1,189,096	1,555,532	31,725	202,736	112,693
2009	6,567,684	4,120,936	85,087	4,206,023	414,995	17,625	3,808,653	1,107,596	1,651,435	32,224	203,814	110,885
2010	6,705,243	4,256,969	84,567	4,341,536	423,678	23,321	3,941,179	1,023,771	1,740,293	32,759	204,681	110,563
2011	6,966,014	4,303,763	86,191	4,389,954	387,967	41,744	4,043,731	1,148,346	1,773,937	33,997	204,902	113,128
2012	7,161,874	4,418,976	131,623	4,550,599	400,054	28,325	4,178,870	1,169,370	1,813,634	34,907	205,171	114,107
2013	7,319,540	4,489,954	199,848	4,689,802	462,365	44,633	4,272,070	1,183,091	1,864,379	35,623	205,473	115,358
2014	7,316,623	4,617,660	124,970	4,742,630	471,079	16,899	4,288,450	1,201,298	1,826,875	35,025	208,895	116,549
2015	7,576,212	4,723,583	97,705	4,821,288	489,033	5,735	4,337,990	1,208,134	2,030,088	36,111	209,803	116,783
2016	7,789,951	4,813,451	106,032	4,919,483	504,787	-25,553	4,389,143	1,217,445	2,183,363	37,053	210,240	117,277
2017	7,910,595	4,900,507	104,717	5,005,224	516,334	-34,808	4,454,082	1,263,920	2,192,593	37,744	209,583	116,243
2018	8,210,154	5,078,156	86,231	5,164,387	539,887	-9,155	4,615,345	1,313,419	2,281,390	39,366	208,559	116,352
2019	8,285,859	5,080,050	89,960	5,170,010	539,994	6,458	4,636,474	1,243,651	2,405,734	39,956	207,372	114,282
2020	9,007,044	5,193,600	91,936	5,285,536	561,624	-9,393	4,714,519	1,232,422	3,060,103	43,606	206,557	110,719
2021	9,600,711	5,375,867	118,623	5,494,490	574,918	6,824	4,926,396	1,243,459	3,430,856	46,859	204,884	112,346

Personal Income and Employment by Area: Monroe, MI

(Thousands of dollars, except as noted.)

Year	Personal income, total	Earnings by place of work — Nonfarm	Earnings by place of work — Farm	Earnings by place of work — Total	Less: Contributions for government social insurance	Plus: Adjustment for residence	Equals: Net earnings by place of residence	Plus: Dividends, interest, and rent	Plus: Personal current transfer receipts	Per capita personal income (dollars)	Population (persons)	Total employment
1970	447,425	210,184	9,339	219,523	14,721	156,788	361,590	54,347	31,488	3,740	119,640	28,386
1971	490,338	233,671	7,299	240,970	16,779	168,702	392,893	59,701	37,744	4,033	121,589	29,043
1972	560,418	273,988	12,706	286,694	20,988	186,524	452,230	66,454	41,734	4,541	123,422	30,768
1973	637,123	316,224	13,417	329,641	28,072	212,547	514,116	75,001	48,006	5,126	124,301	32,201
1974	680,892	330,847	8,861	339,708	30,754	224,401	533,355	85,267	62,270	5,451	124,906	32,581
1975	732,876	339,486	16,178	355,664	30,582	224,995	550,077	94,322	88,477	5,803	126,297	31,334
1976	829,067	388,015	9,801	397,816	35,212	274,987	637,591	100,511	90,965	6,520	127,148	32,540
1977	944,403	449,249	12,484	461,733	40,796	318,843	739,780	112,584	92,039	7,265	129,995	33,950
1978	1,057,320	501,580	10,288	511,868	46,921	369,199	834,146	123,282	99,892	7,983	132,450	34,920
1979	1,172,775	533,031	16,792	549,823	51,719	415,932	914,036	139,946	118,793	8,733	134,285	34,884
1980	1,273,733	544,803	20,439	565,242	52,494	425,214	937,962	166,768	169,003	9,454	134,732	33,246
1981	1,377,975	639,071	13,626	652,697	68,849	413,014	996,862	202,710	178,403	10,228	134,729	34,698
1982	1,442,527	685,282	6,945	692,227	75,038	388,160	1,005,349	231,776	205,402	10,901	132,334	34,361
1983	1,548,486	755,372	3,366	758,738	82,542	405,904	1,082,100	252,695	213,691	11,831	130,888	35,020
1984	1,659,148	707,857	18,996	726,853	78,043	510,498	1,159,308	286,509	213,331	12,680	130,851	33,976
1985	1,757,755	728,921	15,385	744,306	81,723	576,156	1,238,739	302,273	216,743	13,481	130,386	35,020
1986	1,920,452	883,092	13,375	896,467	99,617	574,345	1,371,195	321,000	228,257	14,643	131,150	37,893
1987	1,991,738	941,070	13,857	954,927	105,040	579,138	1,429,025	327,313	235,400	15,106	131,852	39,715
1988	2,155,014	1,054,616	14,276	1,068,892	121,542	618,135	1,565,485	344,976	244,553	16,321	132,040	40,868
1989	2,281,017	1,148,509	16,162	1,164,671	134,626	622,803	1,652,848	361,940	266,229	17,189	132,700	43,343
1990	2,351,795	1,209,003	17,769	1,226,772	143,891	592,864	1,675,745	382,498	293,552	17,565	133,892	45,406
1991	2,399,561	1,245,617	8,131	1,253,748	150,623	581,136	1,684,261	381,203	334,097	17,819	134,664	46,113
1992	2,595,382	1,359,545	12,379	1,371,924	162,837	644,336	1,853,423	389,604	352,355	19,186	135,277	46,355
1993	2,762,164	1,417,824	11,056	1,428,880	171,030	721,994	1,979,844	406,328	375,992	20,366	135,623	46,938
1994	3,079,088	1,540,762	12,100	1,552,862	187,904	837,851	2,202,809	489,666	386,613	22,511	136,783	48,731
1995	3,240,237	1,618,691	17,231	1,635,922	196,616	880,604	2,319,910	519,448	400,879	23,373	138,631	50,033
1996	3,391,007	1,679,288	14,046	1,693,334	199,212	931,258	2,425,380	548,666	416,961	24,200	140,123	50,605
1997	3,587,984	1,784,394	19,730	1,804,124	210,010	975,871	2,569,985	570,622	447,377	25,317	141,725	52,094
1998	3,818,448	1,919,961	20,743	1,940,704	221,259	1,067,969	2,787,414	583,545	447,489	26,701	143,009	53,783
1999	4,106,811	2,120,045	21,704	2,141,749	243,204	1,162,904	3,061,449	565,715	479,647	28,416	144,525	56,396
2000	4,339,711	2,238,418	20,262	2,258,680	253,597	1,205,851	3,210,934	618,084	510,693	29,650	146,364	58,727
2001	4,475,368	2,323,708	14,945	2,338,653	260,999	1,229,040	3,306,694	599,629	569,045	30,320	147,605	59,030
2002	4,492,812	2,417,519	18,784	2,436,303	276,938	1,168,740	3,328,105	578,097	586,610	30,242	148,561	58,898
2003	4,648,086	2,488,186	18,567	2,506,753	282,536	1,198,861	3,423,078	606,761	618,247	31,040	149,747	58,696
2004	4,857,131	2,543,853	23,510	2,567,363	291,324	1,335,757	3,611,796	599,948	645,387	32,142	151,117	58,876
2005	5,010,888	2,513,361	20,851	2,534,212	295,452	1,436,291	3,675,051	639,845	695,992	32,885	152,374	59,054
2006	5,179,685	2,626,584	26,923	2,653,507	313,614	1,427,096	3,766,989	655,207	757,489	33,753	153,460	59,603
2007	5,323,015	2,578,552	27,040	2,605,592	311,455	1,496,141	3,790,278	705,815	826,922	34,695	153,424	59,132
2008	5,412,471	2,507,635	17,182	2,524,817	307,500	1,434,150	3,651,467	791,082	969,922	35,421	152,806	57,260
2009	5,130,224	2,287,783	22,887	2,310,670	284,745	1,291,925	3,317,850	729,483	1,082,891	33,686	152,296	53,469
2010	5,279,166	2,337,182	27,271	2,364,453	285,087	1,321,312	3,400,678	727,123	1,151,365	34,746	151,936	52,532
2011	5,548,535	2,381,311	52,016	2,433,327	258,950	1,467,462	3,641,839	757,653	1,149,043	36,621	151,511	53,377
2012	5,715,103	2,536,242	26,691	2,562,933	276,087	1,500,791	3,787,637	785,819	1,141,647	37,890	150,835	54,458
2013	5,770,146	2,629,046	28,013	2,657,059	324,878	1,469,270	3,801,451	791,490	1,177,205	38,418	150,193	56,252
2014	6,042,107	2,717,357	3,799	2,721,156	335,158	1,548,759	3,934,757	871,256	1,236,094	39,839	151,662	57,525
2015	6,376,592	2,834,892	15,199	2,850,091	345,097	1,646,430	4,151,424	925,993	1,299,175	42,065	151,589	57,934
2016	6,523,731	2,885,890	12,841	2,898,731	350,278	1,711,074	4,259,527	935,952	1,328,252	42,965	151,840	57,985
2017	6,810,534	3,022,419	15,453	3,037,872	362,061	1,795,780	4,471,591	992,449	1,346,494	44,658	152,505	57,640
2018	7,082,081	3,093,896	15,209	3,109,105	377,680	1,924,815	4,656,240	1,011,186	1,414,655	46,098	153,630	57,994
2019	7,361,611	3,151,609	23,129	3,174,738	383,031	2,027,807	4,819,514	1,024,587	1,517,510	47,726	154,248	56,868
2020	7,812,877	2,994,809	37,108	3,031,917	373,211	2,004,411	4,663,117	1,027,293	2,122,467	50,472	154,796	54,075
2021	8,308,581	3,148,101	45,506	3,193,607	388,224	2,248,375	5,053,758	1,032,714	2,222,109	53,509	155,274	55,235

Personal Income and Employment by Area: Montgomery, AL

(Thousands of dollars, except as noted.)

Year	Personal income, total	Earnings by place of work			Less: Contributions for government social insurance	Plus: Adjustment for residence	Equals: Net earnings by place of residence	Plus: Dividends, interest, and rent	Plus: Personal current transfer receipts	Per capita personal income (dollars)	Population (persons)	Total employment
		Nonfarm	Farm	Total								
1970	821,743	648,601	20,376	668,977	45,411	-2,883	620,683	129,782	71,278	3,435	239,239	109,720
1971	932,728	734,677	23,155	757,832	52,137	-3,781	701,914	147,823	82,991	3,846	242,500	112,842
1972	1,082,001	854,494	32,191	886,685	63,004	-4,927	818,754	170,200	93,047	4,288	252,309	119,422
1973	1,224,140	962,843	42,950	1,005,793	80,874	-6,957	917,962	195,847	110,331	4,744	258,064	124,450
1974	1,359,239	1,072,465	25,326	1,097,791	93,246	-10,014	994,531	228,732	135,976	5,151	263,893	126,242
1975	1,469,402	1,137,036	21,515	1,158,551	100,379	-11,539	1,046,633	248,750	174,019	5,524	265,984	124,938
1976	1,646,376	1,271,461	42,584	1,314,045	115,289	-15,561	1,183,195	269,571	193,610	6,094	270,156	127,870
1977	1,792,684	1,413,534	19,548	1,433,082	128,629	-21,154	1,283,299	300,436	208,949	6,570	272,860	132,672
1978	2,041,480	1,606,309	33,859	1,640,168	148,010	-29,809	1,462,349	347,640	231,491	7,376	276,789	139,055
1979	2,270,352	1,785,676	40,331	1,826,007	171,725	-41,172	1,613,110	387,081	270,161	8,056	281,831	142,495
1980	2,507,508	1,946,081	18,150	1,964,231	188,418	-43,970	1,731,843	458,664	317,001	8,751	286,531	142,176
1981	2,761,064	2,074,007	17,490	2,091,497	215,256	-29,463	1,846,778	556,811	357,475	9,574	288,378	139,589
1982	2,945,695	2,165,214	27,443	2,192,657	227,512	-31,417	1,933,728	613,204	398,763	10,183	289,284	137,511
1983	3,217,601	2,402,691	19,706	2,422,397	256,127	-42,377	2,123,893	665,759	427,949	11,105	289,744	141,881
1984	3,537,963	2,661,352	21,969	2,683,321	287,780	-51,895	2,343,646	740,936	453,381	12,100	292,394	147,345
1985	3,823,104	2,899,209	29,648	2,928,857	315,600	-62,721	2,550,536	795,894	476,674	12,985	294,421	150,916
1986	4,084,174	3,135,792	23,556	3,159,348	339,756	-71,924	2,747,668	839,756	496,750	13,709	297,919	156,125
1987	4,372,989	3,366,284	43,316	3,409,600	359,967	-83,824	2,965,809	898,158	509,022	14,510	301,371	160,694
1988	4,701,889	3,611,645	53,144	3,664,789	403,537	-95,245	3,166,007	996,910	538,972	15,532	302,729	166,464
1989	5,103,772	3,807,685	49,481	3,857,166	426,323	-104,099	3,326,744	1,164,083	612,945	16,734	305,003	169,489
1990	5,364,632	4,003,332	50,701	4,054,033	455,455	-111,635	3,486,943	1,191,565	686,124	17,529	306,042	170,900
1991	5,655,230	4,207,688	63,503	4,271,191	481,977	-116,986	3,672,228	1,226,560	756,442	18,176	311,129	171,043
1992	6,083,594	4,523,547	43,101	4,566,648	513,121	-126,539	3,926,988	1,297,482	859,124	19,192	316,981	175,249
1993	6,370,097	4,760,072	29,227	4,789,299	541,797	-134,807	4,112,695	1,334,993	922,409	19,740	322,707	179,984
1994	6,792,001	5,091,592	29,287	5,120,879	583,257	-144,367	4,393,255	1,427,138	971,608	20,729	327,654	183,466
1995	7,188,896	5,302,616	13,297	5,315,913	609,465	-153,064	4,553,384	1,579,601	1,055,911	21,676	331,647	189,986
1996	7,524,350	5,554,393	23,807	5,578,200	634,896	-165,318	4,777,986	1,632,649	1,113,715	22,460	335,014	194,046
1997	7,937,695	5,816,476	38,983	5,855,459	667,339	-179,617	5,008,503	1,761,694	1,167,498	23,422	338,906	197,762
1998	8,403,753	6,239,652	34,635	6,274,287	703,270	-197,355	5,373,662	1,836,101	1,193,990	24,564	342,120	201,452
1999	8,766,509	6,596,901	50,102	6,647,003	741,330	-217,042	5,688,631	1,832,474	1,245,404	25,444	344,540	205,388
2000	9,211,768	6,875,011	42,499	6,917,510	770,641	-230,656	5,916,213	1,973,527	1,322,028	26,541	347,080	206,869
2001	9,303,878	6,941,495	53,726	6,995,221	798,430	-258,064	5,938,727	1,967,704	1,397,447	26,680	348,725	209,312
2002	9,713,818	7,308,363	34,755	7,343,118	841,093	-284,212	6,217,813	1,966,876	1,529,129	27,676	350,984	210,012
2003	10,215,163	7,648,606	61,396	7,710,002	878,499	-309,575	6,521,928	2,055,029	1,638,206	28,987	352,411	212,969
2004	10,932,248	8,076,540	103,205	8,179,745	917,383	-322,500	6,939,862	2,270,716	1,721,670	30,794	355,009	216,880
2005	11,484,843	8,490,466	106,550	8,597,016	965,286	-350,143	7,281,587	2,350,750	1,852,506	32,022	358,659	222,859
2006	12,175,831	8,992,695	95,825	9,088,520	1,025,720	-388,006	7,674,794	2,495,974	2,005,063	33,268	365,989	227,676
2007	12,612,409	9,255,158	60,871	9,316,029	1,065,298	-422,537	7,828,194	2,612,261	2,171,954	34,144	369,390	234,199
2008	12,894,674	9,300,404	54,070	9,354,474	1,110,327	-453,299	7,790,848	2,678,895	2,424,931	34,827	370,249	231,517
2009	12,778,523	9,251,823	64,171	9,315,994	1,098,806	-466,928	7,750,260	2,427,019	2,601,244	34,364	371,860	223,844
2010	13,150,864	9,405,184	61,030	9,466,214	1,116,396	-482,005	7,867,813	2,402,606	2,880,445	35,059	375,111	220,603
2011	13,703,006	9,585,782	55,030	9,640,812	1,010,916	-515,218	8,114,678	2,618,204	2,970,124	36,483	375,596	221,792
2012	13,855,215	9,577,108	81,004	9,658,112	1,012,549	-528,406	8,117,157	2,789,736	2,948,322	36,951	374,961	218,631
2013	13,923,854	9,775,119	123,621	9,898,740	1,161,847	-539,406	8,197,487	2,706,584	3,019,783	37,207	374,231	219,385
2014	14,284,414	9,968,319	89,370	10,057,689	1,179,140	-546,172	8,332,377	2,827,412	3,124,625	37,679	379,109	221,207
2015	14,926,178	10,299,028	69,274	10,368,302	1,215,346	-568,760	8,584,196	2,952,276	3,389,706	39,242	380,358	222,803
2016	15,343,162	10,752,507	45,554	10,798,061	1,254,247	-597,490	8,946,324	2,978,536	3,418,302	40,133	382,309	225,530
2017	15,767,089	10,976,831	67,856	11,044,687	1,287,069	-593,506	9,164,112	3,110,833	3,492,144	41,067	383,935	228,041
2018	16,082,259	11,219,567	57,247	11,276,814	1,329,160	-598,348	9,349,306	3,103,073	3,629,880	41,878	384,025	228,021
2019	16,595,012	11,502,878	46,434	11,549,312	1,368,887	-627,698	9,552,727	3,236,020	3,806,265	43,084	385,174	227,398
2020	17,797,552	11,818,543	41,324	11,859,867	1,414,949	-643,507	9,801,411	3,229,414	4,766,727	46,139	385,738	222,914
2021	19,023,534	12,500,854	56,865	12,557,719	1,475,879	-683,171	10,398,669	3,247,867	5,376,998	49,310	385,798	227,966

Personal Income and Employment by Area: Morgantown, WV

(Thousands of dollars, except as noted.)

Year	Personal income, total	Earnings by place of work			Less: Contributions for government social insurance	Plus: Adjustment for residence	Equals: Net earnings by place of residence	Plus: Dividends, interest, and rent	Plus: Personal current transfer receipts	Per capita personal income (dollars)	Population (persons)	Total employment
		Nonfarm	Farm	Total								
1970	266,124	213,095	847	213,942	14,864	4,512	203,590	34,199	28,335	2,983	89,219	34,394
1971	296,621	236,461	952	237,413	17,315	3,306	223,404	38,242	34,975	3,271	90,684	35,273
1972	340,664	276,990	870	277,860	21,296	-358	256,206	43,192	41,266	3,622	94,067	37,872
1973	364,176	293,102	1,016	294,118	25,961	-3,432	264,725	49,168	50,283	3,791	96,069	38,107
1974	403,584	326,114	47	326,161	29,918	-7,206	289,037	57,364	57,183	4,106	98,296	38,804
1975	458,241	370,883	-100	370,783	33,555	-11,189	326,039	64,298	67,904	4,685	97,808	40,252
1976	511,329	419,851	-102	419,749	38,650	-18,190	362,909	72,906	75,514	5,135	99,573	42,073
1977	574,724	472,629	-184	472,445	42,227	-19,927	410,291	83,603	80,830	5,659	101,553	43,083
1978	645,097	532,986	905	533,891	48,968	-27,495	457,428	95,938	91,731	6,255	103,131	44,710
1979	695,822	570,263	312	570,575	55,473	-32,905	482,197	106,847	106,778	6,669	104,338	43,728
1980	775,551	623,361	32	623,393	63,757	-41,419	518,217	134,231	123,103	7,328	105,829	43,877
1981	872,076	679,195	-2,339	676,856	73,808	-38,063	564,985	165,406	141,685	8,141	107,115	43,092
1982	953,020	754,738	-2,007	752,731	85,550	-49,347	617,834	185,814	149,372	8,878	107,348	43,856
1983	1,018,515	786,567	-461	786,106	90,595	-51,575	643,936	207,955	166,624	9,436	107,934	44,249
1984	1,097,543	854,460	1,748	856,208	100,426	-54,576	701,206	223,035	173,302	10,141	108,233	45,127
1985	1,154,420	899,735	1,867	901,602	107,846	-58,776	734,980	236,524	182,916	10,811	106,785	46,436
1986	1,194,627	927,208	2,476	929,684	117,075	-66,016	746,593	250,818	197,216	11,254	106,152	47,850
1987	1,249,857	985,257	-576	984,681	125,455	-71,385	787,841	257,750	204,266	11,812	105,816	49,184
1988	1,391,272	1,097,171	-372	1,096,799	140,715	-64,059	892,025	278,488	220,759	13,195	105,441	50,388
1989	1,461,720	1,129,622	1,329	1,130,951	148,822	-56,605	925,524	298,985	237,211	13,922	104,993	51,305
1990	1,573,196	1,221,234	178	1,221,412	162,961	-58,103	1,000,348	317,898	254,950	15,026	104,696	53,460
1991	1,668,693	1,287,530	-1,523	1,286,007	175,060	-59,758	1,051,189	326,704	290,800	15,708	106,229	54,423
1992	1,825,250	1,384,288	638	1,384,926	191,376	-69,566	1,123,984	354,641	346,625	16,984	107,468	56,208
1993	1,880,315	1,421,435	814	1,422,249	202,955	-71,936	1,147,358	363,494	369,463	17,317	108,582	56,446
1994	1,978,030	1,522,433	1,007	1,523,440	217,818	-80,263	1,225,359	379,950	372,721	18,065	109,494	58,961
1995	2,038,247	1,532,728	-1,598	1,531,130	223,573	-76,227	1,231,330	421,262	385,655	18,488	110,247	59,587
1996	2,111,787	1,553,855	48	1,553,903	224,494	-73,527	1,255,882	444,792	411,113	19,102	110,553	59,610
1997	2,166,258	1,566,618	-2,136	1,564,482	223,570	-63,502	1,277,410	464,642	424,206	19,554	110,781	59,184
1998	2,255,764	1,651,870	-2,359	1,649,511	238,968	-78,661	1,331,882	489,254	434,628	20,337	110,918	59,873
1999	2,349,460	1,761,749	-3,454	1,758,295	252,997	-88,580	1,416,718	489,547	443,195	21,188	110,888	60,730
2000	2,546,157	1,952,745	-603	1,952,142	285,711	-106,902	1,559,529	517,332	469,296	22,869	111,338	62,298
2001	2,714,209	2,071,511	-1,146	2,070,365	287,987	-120,849	1,661,529	525,784	526,896	24,070	112,764	63,393
2002	2,870,430	2,196,233	-4,384	2,191,849	285,618	-133,694	1,772,537	522,205	575,688	25,104	114,343	64,332
2003	2,932,423	2,279,211	-6,934	2,272,277	308,883	-145,885	1,817,509	526,840	588,074	25,178	116,466	64,987
2004	3,158,959	2,508,951	-4,109	2,504,842	325,070	-142,106	2,037,666	539,797	581,496	26,757	118,062	67,260
2005	3,421,172	2,713,676	-4,824	2,708,852	344,938	-145,149	2,218,765	596,866	605,541	28,525	119,937	69,278
2006	3,613,351	2,822,442	-5,411	2,817,031	352,998	-158,943	2,305,090	664,938	643,323	29,643	121,894	70,374
2007	3,749,422	2,894,750	-6,700	2,888,050	348,316	-177,858	2,361,876	701,730	685,816	30,358	123,507	73,433
2008	4,014,573	3,090,124	-4,954	3,085,170	358,801	-211,544	2,514,825	737,790	761,958	32,048	125,267	75,367
2009	4,176,943	3,316,977	-6,421	3,310,556	385,374	-259,782	2,665,400	695,355	816,188	32,761	127,498	76,187
2010	4,584,549	3,587,356	-7,469	3,579,887	414,131	-285,986	2,879,770	807,238	897,541	35,181	130,314	77,855
2011	4,807,312	3,654,621	-4,577	3,650,044	373,535	-240,869	3,035,640	860,833	910,839	36,219	132,730	78,369
2012	4,969,751	3,831,431	-5,681	3,825,750	388,851	-277,836	3,159,063	889,855	920,833	36,836	134,914	80,642
2013	5,044,048	3,949,764	-2,647	3,947,117	453,935	-315,853	3,177,329	922,500	944,219	37,065	136,085	81,746
2014	5,322,262	4,136,383	-3,370	4,133,013	477,142	-313,473	3,342,398	967,906	1,011,958	38,696	137,542	82,932
2015	5,600,981	4,378,270	-3,086	4,375,184	504,268	-381,653	3,489,263	1,049,886	1,061,832	40,381	138,703	84,305
2016	5,556,059	4,343,096	-4,031	4,339,065	513,201	-419,942	3,405,922	1,047,158	1,102,979	39,789	139,638	84,204
2017	5,824,145	4,625,277	-2,988	4,622,289	550,122	-477,898	3,594,269	1,086,759	1,143,117	41,630	139,902	85,903
2018	6,110,862	4,765,372	-4,333	4,761,039	556,061	-453,594	3,751,384	1,177,862	1,181,616	43,826	139,436	86,936
2019	6,352,244	4,959,229	-1,072	4,958,157	572,757	-463,526	3,921,874	1,211,322	1,219,048	45,465	139,717	86,332
2020	6,649,694	5,055,120	-2,452	5,052,668	595,822	-545,741	3,911,105	1,185,276	1,553,313	47,467	140,092	83,338
2021	7,039,535	5,329,925	-4,662	5,325,263	620,070	-575,247	4,129,946	1,213,550	1,696,039	50,016	140,745	86,348

Personal Income and Employment by Area: Morristown, TN

(Thousands of dollars, except as noted.)

Year	Personal income, total	Derivation of personal income								Per capita personal income (dollars)	Population (persons)	Total employment
		Earnings by place of work			Less: Contributions for government social insurance	Plus: Adjustment for residence	Equals: Net earnings by place of residence	Plus: Dividends, interest, and rent	Plus: Personal current transfer receipts			
		Nonfarm	Farm	Total								
1970	179,394	173,340	5,207	178,547	11,370	-25,057	142,120	19,569	17,705	2,800	64,065	33,308
1971	204,490	200,430	4,924	205,354	13,742	-29,404	162,208	22,375	19,907	3,074	66,514	34,956
1972	238,260	234,131	7,545	241,676	16,982	-34,378	190,316	25,517	22,427	3,468	68,704	38,430
1973	271,360	261,617	10,577	272,194	21,721	-36,315	214,158	29,398	27,804	3,849	70,499	39,656
1974	294,122	280,304	7,171	287,475	24,229	-37,751	225,495	34,201	34,426	4,055	72,527	38,744
1975	310,344	276,401	3,538	279,939	23,614	-33,885	222,440	37,700	50,204	4,256	72,914	34,813
1976	351,199	317,460	8,141	325,601	27,710	-38,339	259,552	41,127	50,520	4,708	74,589	37,232
1977	392,143	364,842	4,401	369,243	32,177	-45,333	291,733	46,623	53,787	5,109	76,762	39,929
1978	449,752	420,011	5,354	425,365	37,669	-50,493	337,203	54,155	58,394	5,706	78,827	42,110
1979	502,123	461,486	4,013	465,499	42,794	-51,864	370,841	62,358	68,924	6,309	79,591	42,332
1980	547,966	472,209	2,456	474,665	43,459	-47,996	383,210	78,554	86,202	6,774	80,893	40,018
1981	604,583	500,382	5,204	505,586	49,754	-45,185	410,647	97,104	96,832	7,376	81,970	38,986
1982	645,973	523,790	3,537	527,327	52,848	-49,789	424,690	113,394	107,889	7,737	83,487	38,391
1983	700,057	576,930	-2,351	574,579	58,734	-55,455	460,390	122,642	117,025	8,090	86,535	39,955
1984	781,134	650,446	2,817	653,263	68,632	-62,947	521,684	136,730	122,720	9,049	86,327	41,739
1985	817,891	669,169	4,029	673,198	71,304	-58,449	543,445	144,072	130,374	9,790	83,544	41,597
1986	868,226	708,951	2,150	711,101	77,163	-57,073	576,865	149,531	141,830	10,440	83,162	42,533
1987	936,639	770,994	2,867	773,861	83,417	-59,066	631,378	155,473	149,788	11,350	82,524	43,935
1988	1,028,950	846,857	2,661	849,518	94,372	-59,232	695,914	170,426	162,610	12,367	83,204	45,919
1989	1,140,557	939,395	4,338	943,733	105,373	-72,215	766,145	196,708	177,704	13,729	83,074	48,607
1990	1,235,957	1,016,828	5,154	1,021,982	114,538	-67,968	839,476	197,760	198,721	14,750	83,791	50,379
1991	1,295,635	1,049,126	5,660	1,054,786	119,909	-75,624	859,253	200,584	235,798	15,284	84,770	49,816
1992	1,427,387	1,156,195	7,254	1,163,449	130,645	-76,896	955,908	199,488	271,991	16,533	86,338	51,670
1993	1,522,301	1,235,762	6,078	1,241,840	141,173	-80,510	1,020,157	209,017	293,127	17,203	88,492	53,277
1994	1,591,202	1,278,431	5,285	1,283,716	149,203	-72,662	1,061,851	224,145	305,206	17,640	90,206	53,805
1995	1,707,904	1,347,071	1,844	1,348,915	157,114	-62,742	1,129,059	249,665	329,180	18,428	92,682	54,986
1996	1,803,777	1,413,407	-2,300	1,411,107	163,214	-62,827	1,185,066	268,698	350,013	18,951	95,181	55,998
1997	1,955,568	1,517,534	2,026	1,519,560	172,478	-50,659	1,296,423	286,942	372,203	20,036	97,602	56,824
1998	2,493,799	1,800,181	10,166	1,810,347	197,918	84,491	1,696,920	331,955	464,924	20,872	119,479	65,468
1999	2,588,786	1,911,802	8,525	1,920,327	210,847	54,635	1,764,115	337,338	487,333	21,247	121,840	67,470
2000	2,712,799	1,973,460	16,320	1,989,780	219,574	43,177	1,813,383	360,707	538,709	21,975	123,449	68,923
2001	2,774,618	1,952,667	14,734	1,967,401	221,882	53,891	1,799,410	380,612	594,596	22,280	124,536	64,956
2002	2,867,986	2,003,985	12,782	2,016,767	228,571	62,419	1,850,615	363,749	653,622	22,971	124,851	63,886
2003	2,988,539	2,102,507	12,126	2,114,633	239,930	56,743	1,931,446	379,571	677,522	23,618	126,539	64,462
2004	3,147,336	2,270,263	11,054	2,281,317	256,163	48,569	2,073,723	363,372	710,241	24,624	127,816	66,066
2005	3,249,595	2,263,640	11,945	2,275,585	257,114	92,286	2,110,757	370,217	768,621	25,079	129,574	65,691
2006	3,393,020	2,311,468	6,501	2,317,969	263,112	126,803	2,181,660	391,133	820,227	25,728	131,883	66,402
2007	3,562,714	2,342,147	-3,148	2,338,999	271,517	132,894	2,200,376	456,438	905,900	26,571	134,085	66,741
2008	3,739,416	2,343,618	-5,609	2,338,009	276,999	135,232	2,196,242	515,989	1,027,185	27,598	135,495	65,924
2009	3,726,752	2,181,904	-1,282	2,180,622	263,708	183,489	2,100,403	505,924	1,120,425	27,376	136,131	61,248
2010	3,871,311	2,295,166	4,101	2,299,267	274,516	153,025	2,177,776	488,383	1,205,152	28,269	136,946	60,947
2011	4,134,367	2,360,607	-359	2,360,248	252,734	251,757	2,359,271	548,660	1,226,436	30,054	137,566	61,382
2012	4,209,971	2,512,606	2,095	2,514,701	259,118	179,542	2,435,125	541,419	1,233,427	30,557	137,773	61,631
2013	4,252,329	2,540,720	9,244	2,549,964	293,553	206,137	2,462,548	525,045	1,264,736	30,823	137,958	62,084
2014	4,403,715	2,647,432	10,371	2,657,803	301,894	203,526	2,559,435	557,887	1,286,393	31,933	137,903	63,096
2015	4,639,644	2,780,299	7,684	2,787,983	313,941	214,329	2,688,371	593,473	1,357,800	33,440	138,745	64,151
2016	4,723,776	2,834,884	-937	2,833,947	325,186	211,224	2,719,985	597,614	1,406,177	33,906	139,319	65,334
2017	4,894,190	2,962,318	-1,155	2,961,163	344,558	194,271	2,810,876	639,697	1,443,617	34,906	140,211	66,813
2018	5,154,565	3,086,372	-6,391	3,079,981	359,543	240,777	2,961,215	669,912	1,523,438	36,574	140,937	67,478
2019	5,405,385	3,214,130	-6,008	3,208,122	376,540	219,083	3,050,665	751,376	1,603,344	38,103	141,861	68,397
2020	5,861,133	3,328,681	-4,282	3,324,399	397,464	245,687	3,172,622	755,688	1,932,823	41,036	142,830	68,432
2021	6,369,754	3,564,846	-588	3,564,258	407,989	318,393	3,474,662	762,203	2,132,889	44,279	143,855	69,936

Personal Income and Employment by Area: Mount Vernon-Anacortes, WA

(Thousands of dollars, except as noted.)

Year	Personal income, total	Earnings by place of work			Less: Contributions for government social insurance	Plus: Adjustment for residence	Equals: Net earnings by place of residence	Plus: Dividends, interest, and rent	Plus: Personal current transfer receipts	Per capita personal income (dollars)	Population (persons)	Total employment
		Nonfarm	Farm	Total								
1970	210,795	141,229	11,282	152,511	11,412	7,281	148,380	37,494	24,921	4,021	52,419	21,242
1971	230,211	153,460	13,347	166,807	12,966	6,666	160,507	41,403	28,301	4,369	52,694	21,537
1972	252,938	172,325	14,626	186,951	15,490	5,487	176,948	45,513	30,477	4,759	53,145	22,736
1973	295,178	204,667	21,565	226,232	21,484	3,742	208,490	51,704	34,984	5,544	53,244	24,711
1974	326,194	215,809	26,573	242,382	22,871	4,979	224,490	58,799	42,905	6,024	54,151	24,990
1975	364,169	238,472	25,179	263,651	24,749	4,920	243,822	68,001	52,346	6,816	53,431	25,161
1976	415,084	288,481	23,491	311,972	30,573	1,063	282,462	75,232	57,390	7,351	56,468	26,771
1977	445,393	303,666	20,725	324,391	32,150	4,190	296,431	87,078	61,884	7,716	57,722	26,893
1978	506,036	352,263	18,807	371,070	37,624	5,526	338,972	100,852	66,212	8,503	59,516	28,633
1979	584,006	399,018	26,152	425,170	43,649	8,588	390,109	118,432	75,465	9,505	61,443	29,681
1980	659,107	429,456	24,671	454,127	47,239	8,273	415,161	148,103	95,843	10,220	64,491	29,998
1981	729,974	465,388	21,994	487,382	56,258	7,366	438,490	180,668	110,816	11,097	65,779	30,968
1982	784,219	482,315	22,382	504,697	59,947	7,341	452,091	206,539	125,589	11,738	66,812	30,991
1983	861,793	528,545	31,270	559,815	66,188	4,978	498,605	225,055	138,133	12,656	68,094	32,337
1984	905,850	538,015	28,703	566,718	69,957	8,803	505,564	252,966	147,320	13,167	68,795	32,176
1985	959,680	564,778	28,368	593,146	72,868	12,611	532,889	271,950	154,841	13,880	69,139	32,600
1986	1,019,315	601,228	35,546	636,774	78,055	18,410	577,129	279,166	163,020	14,489	70,353	33,374
1987	1,049,750	606,607	47,568	654,175	78,676	26,374	601,873	277,060	170,817	14,742	71,206	34,918
1988	1,167,720	688,936	53,987	742,923	91,067	30,689	682,545	301,348	183,827	15,892	73,477	37,811
1989	1,338,342	791,395	55,908	847,303	106,387	33,532	774,448	364,984	198,910	17,597	76,054	40,078
1990	1,462,704	895,756	55,632	951,388	122,256	39,460	868,592	378,142	215,970	18,180	80,457	42,865
1991	1,583,606	984,040	55,087	1,039,127	135,814	38,954	942,267	398,168	243,171	18,906	83,761	44,137
1992	1,712,498	1,056,331	66,374	1,122,705	145,824	45,697	1,022,578	410,718	279,202	19,810	86,445	44,728
1993	1,815,703	1,111,181	76,876	1,188,057	152,711	51,776	1,087,122	426,824	301,757	20,280	89,530	45,889
1994	1,941,787	1,196,398	74,805	1,271,203	166,432	45,221	1,149,992	466,941	324,854	21,146	91,829	48,619
1995	2,080,172	1,260,151	81,677	1,341,828	176,352	45,561	1,211,037	517,318	351,817	22,117	94,053	49,832
1996	2,227,233	1,301,820	84,985	1,386,805	175,792	57,486	1,268,499	582,036	376,698	23,263	95,743	51,671
1997	2,361,174	1,400,126	82,817	1,482,943	180,821	72,963	1,375,085	600,283	385,806	24,207	97,539	52,910
1998	2,572,559	1,540,170	87,614	1,627,784	193,760	89,126	1,523,150	644,696	404,713	25,749	99,909	53,846
1999	2,723,632	1,715,720	92,672	1,808,392	210,679	78,617	1,676,330	616,644	430,658	26,781	101,701	56,204
2000	2,905,581	1,853,748	83,347	1,937,095	231,506	69,827	1,775,416	668,235	461,930	28,095	103,420	58,486
2001	2,969,349	1,847,470	93,837	1,941,307	235,388	81,016	1,786,935	668,725	513,689	28,406	104,534	58,680
2002	3,041,037	1,936,308	80,226	2,016,534	247,162	108,207	1,877,579	619,953	543,505	28,808	105,563	58,710
2003	3,214,305	2,030,660	101,100	2,131,760	260,227	135,967	2,007,500	641,371	565,434	29,937	107,369	59,854
2004	3,380,218	2,162,028	84,017	2,246,045	275,001	118,681	2,089,725	703,812	586,681	31,003	109,030	60,779
2005	3,588,800	2,347,227	87,206	2,434,433	303,119	122,288	2,253,602	710,056	625,142	32,424	110,683	63,202
2006	3,946,789	2,484,993	90,102	2,575,095	317,718	152,267	2,409,644	868,536	668,609	35,045	112,621	64,921
2007	4,254,984	2,584,479	94,380	2,678,859	334,215	205,681	2,550,325	986,020	718,639	37,303	114,066	66,686
2008	4,507,429	2,668,249	107,503	2,775,752	343,325	175,980	2,608,407	1,075,075	823,947	38,922	115,808	66,360
2009	4,423,419	2,524,300	125,239	2,649,539	335,780	183,629	2,497,388	997,676	928,355	37,951	116,557	63,177
2010	4,461,685	2,589,829	114,000	2,703,829	341,268	154,212	2,516,773	925,107	1,019,805	38,154	116,939	62,291
2011	4,659,705	2,623,368	113,082	2,736,450	316,638	200,693	2,620,505	1,014,431	1,024,769	39,631	117,578	62,388
2012	4,948,702	2,795,539	115,916	2,911,455	325,476	194,154	2,780,133	1,138,500	1,030,069	42,039	117,716	62,620
2013	5,038,633	2,963,529	124,615	3,088,144	383,258	164,395	2,869,281	1,116,673	1,052,679	42,603	118,270	64,896
2014	5,274,466	3,110,808	127,790	3,238,598	402,337	127,127	2,963,388	1,166,327	1,144,751	44,083	119,648	66,269
2015	5,556,524	3,238,114	158,457	3,396,571	420,189	121,167	3,097,549	1,273,762	1,185,213	45,861	121,161	66,731
2016	5,809,972	3,358,145	131,971	3,490,116	430,940	169,196	3,228,372	1,331,951	1,249,649	47,180	123,144	67,697
2017	6,149,166	3,620,076	136,409	3,756,485	469,003	137,743	3,425,225	1,432,490	1,291,451	49,098	125,243	69,105
2018	6,486,837	3,934,554	111,701	4,046,255	500,257	64,918	3,610,916	1,513,494	1,362,427	51,067	127,025	70,905
2019	7,040,944	4,149,788	145,786	4,295,574	518,227	89,738	3,867,085	1,710,762	1,463,097	54,843	128,383	71,201
2020	7,660,712	4,088,988	152,024	4,241,012	521,768	339,518	4,058,762	1,698,826	1,903,124	58,996	129,852	67,810
2021	8,376,697	4,374,833	141,899	4,516,732	554,378	504,828	4,467,182	1,757,764	2,151,751	64,093	130,696	69,378

Personal Income and Employment by Area: Muncie, IN

(Thousands of dollars, except as noted.)

Year	Personal income, total	Earnings by place of work			Less: Contributions for government social insurance	Plus: Adjustment for residence	Equals: Net earnings by place of residence	Plus: Dividends, interest, and rent	Plus: Personal current transfer receipts	Per capita personal income (dollars)	Population (persons)	Total employment
		Nonfarm	Farm	Total								
1970	453,679	398,132	4,642	402,774	26,965	-19,063	356,746	64,129	32,804	3,506	129,415	54,161
1971	495,858	422,022	8,306	430,328	29,576	-15,021	385,731	70,305	39,822	3,799	130,524	53,900
1972	525,032	444,527	5,567	450,094	33,280	-11,531	405,283	75,122	44,627	3,937	133,342	54,086
1973	596,151	496,955	14,805	511,760	42,844	-8,954	459,962	83,914	52,275	4,482	133,005	55,918
1974	647,781	541,518	7,282	548,800	48,890	-9,909	490,001	95,856	61,924	4,935	131,273	56,276
1975	686,269	538,737	12,836	551,573	48,237	-6,185	497,151	106,361	82,757	5,266	130,324	53,413
1976	752,516	598,265	9,773	608,038	53,908	-1,661	552,469	115,032	85,015	5,766	130,508	54,644
1977	841,773	678,215	6,761	684,976	60,869	-1,438	622,669	128,705	90,399	6,467	130,160	57,114
1978	930,089	745,110	8,060	753,170	68,838	2,496	686,828	143,156	100,105	7,170	129,712	57,799
1979	1,026,345	822,227	6,886	829,113	78,526	-370	750,217	161,478	114,650	7,980	128,611	59,035
1980	1,125,163	858,189	2,578	860,767	81,171	-3,111	776,485	197,858	150,820	8,763	128,394	57,729
1981	1,218,563	900,763	1,571	902,334	92,243	540	810,631	244,599	163,333	9,570	127,338	56,902
1982	1,233,758	874,294	4,049	878,343	91,568	5,878	792,653	260,455	180,650	9,801	125,887	54,123
1983	1,310,010	938,943	-4,074	934,869	98,405	9,087	845,551	271,654	192,805	10,559	124,068	54,000
1984	1,430,165	1,025,955	8,332	1,034,287	109,770	15,135	939,652	289,966	200,547	11,574	123,569	55,565
1985	1,493,179	1,072,384	5,784	1,078,168	116,765	18,346	979,749	305,723	207,707	12,235	122,044	56,476
1986	1,572,043	1,145,382	5,656	1,151,038	125,155	13,460	1,039,343	315,527	217,173	13,017	120,770	57,543
1987	1,636,580	1,208,244	9,926	1,218,170	130,697	11,162	1,098,635	316,063	221,882	13,516	121,082	58,948
1988	1,749,526	1,306,406	4,447	1,310,853	145,694	16,740	1,181,899	333,956	233,671	14,499	120,662	60,820
1989	1,884,434	1,373,438	9,547	1,382,985	154,616	23,517	1,251,886	377,393	255,155	15,709	119,962	61,574
1990	2,003,361	1,461,454	9,279	1,470,733	168,665	21,441	1,323,509	397,497	282,355	16,726	119,774	62,976
1991	2,074,910	1,537,656	4,990	1,542,646	179,242	10,114	1,373,518	395,267	306,125	17,295	119,973	62,840
1992	2,169,482	1,664,256	8,886	1,673,142	191,084	-47,599	1,434,459	392,655	342,368	18,026	120,352	65,363
1993	2,241,264	1,721,570	11,760	1,733,330	199,661	-52,524	1,481,145	397,827	362,292	18,533	120,935	65,781
1994	2,365,872	1,837,554	15,737	1,853,291	215,603	-72,259	1,565,429	422,564	377,879	19,632	120,514	67,867
1995	2,462,428	1,914,997	8,157	1,923,154	224,657	-83,797	1,614,700	467,799	379,929	20,400	120,707	69,973
1996	2,536,454	1,918,513	11,212	1,929,725	222,557	-58,073	1,649,095	486,653	400,706	21,035	120,582	68,253
1997	2,613,740	2,008,351	16,568	2,024,919	232,241	-71,144	1,721,534	484,507	407,699	21,684	120,539	68,126
1998	2,755,031	2,051,152	13,413	2,064,565	232,569	-31,882	1,800,114	529,302	425,615	23,056	119,495	68,306
1999	2,828,116	2,097,870	10,358	2,108,228	236,184	-9,952	1,862,092	512,482	453,542	23,811	118,772	68,754
2000	2,992,421	2,201,452	12,916	2,214,368	245,065	-5,754	1,963,549	545,491	483,381	25,194	118,776	69,098
2001	3,059,569	2,208,034	14,706	2,222,740	250,885	-14,889	1,956,966	564,880	537,723	25,437	120,281	68,548
2002	3,053,252	2,209,891	4,624	2,214,515	250,859	-6,250	1,957,406	535,960	559,886	25,455	119,949	65,882
2003	3,125,647	2,249,641	12,752	2,262,393	256,666	-17,353	1,988,374	560,430	576,843	26,061	119,935	64,632
2004	3,154,980	2,282,392	22,948	2,305,340	260,189	6,480	2,051,631	497,935	605,414	26,526	118,938	63,457
2005	3,190,987	2,285,023	14,533	2,299,556	266,334	22,166	2,055,388	476,964	658,635	27,003	118,170	62,542
2006	3,199,311	2,295,400	10,442	2,305,842	271,068	-28,098	2,006,676	485,781	706,854	27,269	117,326	63,302
2007	3,231,623	2,310,820	9,084	2,319,904	275,480	-68,980	1,975,444	528,329	727,850	27,567	117,229	63,379
2008	3,335,734	2,307,920	18,025	2,325,945	277,978	-111,888	1,936,079	569,540	830,115	28,509	117,007	62,103
2009	3,270,663	2,200,346	12,223	2,212,569	269,990	-121,284	1,821,295	530,298	919,070	27,838	117,490	59,146
2010	3,324,124	2,187,357	10,256	2,197,613	264,906	-107,974	1,824,733	515,269	984,122	28,249	117,671	57,777
2011	3,482,380	2,272,279	24,472	2,296,751	243,454	-119,181	1,934,116	568,559	979,705	29,533	117,914	58,559
2012	3,625,509	2,398,828	20,694	2,419,522	254,452	-143,723	2,021,347	585,440	1,018,722	30,973	117,053	58,940
2013	3,676,449	2,439,399	56,357	2,495,756	294,856	-155,201	2,045,699	604,538	1,026,212	31,458	116,867	58,993
2014	3,805,175	2,514,605	26,135	2,540,740	302,581	-148,212	2,089,947	617,695	1,097,533	32,862	115,794	58,583
2015	3,902,765	2,614,787	2,161	2,616,948	314,868	-171,990	2,130,090	630,516	1,142,159	33,962	114,914	59,592
2016	3,966,784	2,636,648	9,084	2,645,732	314,419	-154,661	2,176,652	620,418	1,169,714	34,606	114,627	60,291
2017	4,104,835	2,713,608	7,586	2,721,194	325,061	-175,529	2,220,604	673,158	1,211,073	35,998	114,031	60,390
2018	4,177,702	2,758,421	8,965	2,767,386	333,001	-169,430	2,264,955	665,600	1,247,147	37,062	112,723	60,241
2019	4,349,369	2,868,418	7,152	2,875,570	350,868	-167,812	2,356,890	685,902	1,306,577	38,762	112,208	60,071
2020	4,690,081	2,947,374	18,248	2,965,622	366,839	-206,899	2,391,884	687,670	1,610,527	42,000	111,669	57,872
2021	5,070,606	3,056,395	27,106	3,083,501	373,947	-147,304	2,562,250	664,419	1,843,937	45,325	111,871	58,201

Personal Income and Employment by Area: Muskegon, MI

(Thousands of dollars, except as noted.)

Year	Personal income, total	Earnings by place of work			Less: Contributions for government social insurance	Plus: Adjustment for residence	Equals: Net earnings by place of residence	Plus: Dividends, interest, and rent	Plus: Personal current transfer receipts	Per capita personal income (dollars)	Population (persons)	Total employment
		Nonfarm	Farm	Total								
1970	580,833	502,485	3,319	505,804	36,139	-23,834	445,831	67,863	67,139	3,686	157,595	61,851
1971	601,588	499,296	3,304	502,600	37,037	-19,104	446,459	72,066	83,063	3,799	158,338	59,280
1972	668,217	562,195	3,743	565,938	44,138	-22,281	499,519	77,269	91,429	4,226	158,137	61,124
1973	727,752	621,504	3,694	625,198	56,776	-26,740	541,682	84,338	101,732	4,631	157,135	63,037
1974	805,200	679,210	5,755	684,965	63,978	-31,455	589,532	96,443	119,225	5,151	156,315	64,536
1975	880,409	712,195	4,593	716,788	65,004	-33,296	618,488	107,755	154,166	5,634	156,266	63,935
1976	959,264	787,449	4,627	792,076	73,762	-34,110	684,204	113,032	162,028	6,095	157,395	65,187
1977	1,051,818	872,209	5,573	877,782	81,465	-33,802	762,515	123,098	166,205	6,678	157,496	66,515
1978	1,179,804	982,422	7,285	989,707	95,122	-35,263	859,322	138,824	181,658	7,502	157,258	68,481
1979	1,295,276	1,072,957	5,242	1,078,199	108,592	-35,326	934,281	157,027	203,968	8,194	158,067	68,649
1980	1,395,210	1,108,549	5,379	1,113,928	110,521	-38,716	964,691	187,799	242,720	8,839	157,850	66,135
1981	1,505,262	1,162,622	7,758	1,170,380	125,075	-41,412	1,003,893	225,800	275,569	9,494	158,550	64,362
1982	1,575,139	1,154,252	9,653	1,163,905	125,615	-34,949	1,003,341	260,890	310,908	10,090	156,114	61,143
1983	1,639,741	1,192,327	7,477	1,199,804	131,908	-27,090	1,040,806	269,668	329,267	10,613	154,496	60,591
1984	1,809,110	1,335,798	8,729	1,344,527	154,387	-25,795	1,164,345	312,480	332,285	11,683	154,844	64,284
1985	1,916,564	1,420,334	12,683	1,433,017	166,241	-23,985	1,242,791	324,979	348,794	12,313	155,654	66,520
1986	1,984,921	1,474,821	8,086	1,482,907	172,581	-30,062	1,280,264	338,761	365,896	12,739	155,812	67,445
1987	2,075,511	1,511,736	8,319	1,520,055	173,494	-14,652	1,331,909	368,113	375,489	13,275	156,345	67,252
1988	2,165,811	1,587,473	7,751	1,595,224	188,961	-586	1,405,677	369,914	390,220	13,739	157,643	68,222
1989	2,313,446	1,669,433	10,877	1,680,310	197,412	6,304	1,489,202	403,140	421,104	14,608	158,365	69,448
1990	2,431,375	1,738,463	7,588	1,746,051	208,189	8,270	1,546,132	425,737	459,506	15,255	159,384	70,361
1991	2,499,662	1,746,604	9,589	1,756,193	211,795	17,735	1,562,133	427,202	510,327	15,537	160,885	68,332
1992	2,640,606	1,856,422	10,002	1,866,424	223,688	36,027	1,678,763	432,168	529,675	16,286	162,135	68,157
1993	2,751,922	1,917,508	8,785	1,926,293	233,846	54,267	1,746,714	450,380	554,828	16,874	163,082	67,576
1994	2,938,274	2,033,507	8,135	2,041,642	254,701	86,535	1,873,476	509,412	555,386	17,952	163,678	69,480
1995	3,082,029	2,131,597	9,654	2,141,251	270,894	98,905	1,969,262	532,146	580,621	18,741	164,457	71,863
1996	3,246,918	2,230,168	8,884	2,239,052	279,187	121,891	2,081,756	553,967	611,195	19,588	165,763	73,599
1997	3,463,258	2,378,999	9,540	2,388,539	297,185	144,462	2,235,816	585,282	642,160	20,729	167,077	75,236
1998	3,663,676	2,570,631	11,277	2,581,908	317,126	159,168	2,423,950	593,133	646,593	21,789	168,147	77,667
1999	3,881,361	2,744,430	11,905	2,756,335	335,486	171,223	2,592,072	582,604	706,685	22,922	169,331	81,008
2000	4,082,664	2,872,463	7,757	2,880,220	350,599	198,559	2,728,180	619,855	734,629	23,960	170,396	83,059
2001	4,153,982	2,824,957	8,372	2,833,329	329,755	206,920	2,710,494	615,502	827,986	24,284	171,055	79,334
2002	4,180,374	2,838,399	6,190	2,844,589	332,029	208,243	2,720,803	592,180	867,391	24,366	171,563	78,856
2003	4,283,110	2,877,411	9,459	2,886,870	338,038	198,414	2,747,246	622,820	913,044	24,863	172,269	79,851
2004	4,382,321	2,975,734	13,939	2,989,673	356,069	196,620	2,830,224	612,827	939,270	25,365	172,771	81,907
2005	4,529,871	3,038,062	13,668	3,051,730	373,747	234,846	2,912,829	619,184	997,858	26,093	173,608	82,256
2006	4,707,009	3,133,500	14,776	3,148,276	390,076	238,015	2,996,215	641,281	1,069,513	27,097	173,710	82,617
2007	4,876,222	3,143,484	19,646	3,163,130	393,949	247,799	3,016,980	690,837	1,168,405	28,067	173,738	81,964
2008	4,966,172	3,152,085	20,407	3,172,492	398,910	153,832	2,927,414	724,281	1,314,477	28,567	173,846	80,353
2009	4,811,539	2,934,018	14,753	2,948,771	372,728	109,638	2,685,681	665,117	1,460,741	27,852	172,755	75,602
2010	5,006,886	3,040,949	24,015	3,064,964	380,354	90,075	2,774,685	675,392	1,556,809	29,123	171,923	74,814
2011	5,261,858	3,155,642	40,214	3,195,856	354,811	99,127	2,940,172	787,225	1,534,461	30,942	170,056	76,745
2012	5,452,456	3,320,569	20,708	3,341,277	371,161	113,007	3,083,123	839,434	1,529,899	32,037	170,191	77,708
2013	5,510,123	3,369,522	36,892	3,406,414	424,411	132,959	3,114,962	825,539	1,569,622	31,978	172,312	78,231
2014	5,803,582	3,507,411	27,171	3,534,582	439,605	190,040	3,285,017	891,492	1,627,073	33,525	173,110	79,806
2015	6,091,855	3,657,335	20,515	3,677,850	453,019	203,775	3,428,606	942,224	1,721,025	35,111	173,504	80,448
2016	6,234,249	3,684,902	22,244	3,707,146	457,200	300,036	3,549,982	920,162	1,764,105	35,719	174,538	79,882
2017	6,426,435	3,842,137	18,150	3,860,287	474,875	301,085	3,686,497	967,310	1,772,628	36,681	175,196	81,177
2018	6,639,891	3,943,843	15,996	3,959,839	496,944	335,133	3,798,028	984,126	1,857,737	37,877	175,302	81,415
2019	6,954,757	3,984,667	14,771	3,999,438	500,194	442,721	3,941,965	1,049,531	1,963,261	39,646	175,421	80,307
2020	7,763,881	3,883,416	22,804	3,906,220	489,308	543,116	3,960,028	1,055,859	2,747,994	44,159	175,817	75,008
2021	8,243,256	4,223,553	18,397	4,241,950	521,546	547,187	4,267,591	1,070,856	2,904,809	46,701	176,511	78,476

Personal Income and Employment by Area: Myrtle Beach-Conway-North Myrtle Beach, SC-NC

(Thousands of dollars, except as noted.)

Year	Personal income, total	Earnings by place of work			Less: Contributions for government social insurance	Plus: Adjustment for residence	Equals: Net earnings by place of residence	Plus: Dividends, interest, and rent	Plus: Personal current transfer receipts	Per capita personal income (dollars)	Population (persons)	Total employment
		Nonfarm	Farm	Total								
1970	285,259	204,494	19,298	223,792	13,478	6,039	216,353	42,169	26,737	2,993	95,303	42,155
1971	335,024	240,583	18,453	259,036	16,402	9,073	251,707	52,169	31,148	3,312	101,165	45,218
1972	391,975	288,747	22,502	311,249	20,303	6,150	297,096	59,818	35,061	3,652	107,339	48,709
1973	450,877	333,232	27,197	360,429	26,458	5,982	339,953	69,526	41,398	3,977	113,376	52,009
1974	513,110	372,614	36,788	409,402	31,109	2,325	380,618	79,473	53,019	4,337	118,307	53,860
1975	578,653	422,534	28,498	451,032	35,517	-2,511	413,004	91,816	73,833	4,743	121,997	55,574
1976	641,890	479,653	22,519	502,172	40,806	-4,428	456,938	101,264	83,688	5,035	127,490	58,366
1977	708,269	540,277	17,141	557,418	45,663	-8,564	503,191	117,371	87,707	5,532	128,032	62,138
1978	829,350	619,934	36,238	656,172	53,200	-11,309	591,663	140,742	96,945	6,277	132,125	66,349
1979	914,703	697,988	15,134	713,122	62,065	-15,805	635,252	164,883	114,568	6,798	134,546	68,739
1980	1,042,425	771,768	12,589	784,357	68,908	-20,136	695,313	204,648	142,464	7,524	138,543	70,280
1981	1,207,439	864,210	27,210	891,420	83,236	-22,806	785,378	252,684	169,377	8,415	143,488	72,021
1982	1,335,999	945,094	17,925	963,019	93,370	-24,540	845,109	296,735	194,155	9,028	147,977	75,532
1983	1,541,279	1,102,138	14,018	1,116,156	109,956	-18,355	987,845	340,251	213,183	9,926	155,270	80,547
1984	1,759,761	1,266,857	10,611	1,277,468	131,306	-20,986	1,125,176	404,284	230,301	10,757	163,585	88,239
1985	1,956,690	1,391,938	18,514	1,410,452	147,079	-21,673	1,241,700	458,698	256,292	11,420	171,336	91,199
1986	2,114,823	1,487,991	-2,657	1,485,334	161,192	1,164	1,325,306	508,918	280,599	11,911	177,546	93,765
1987	2,317,270	1,621,672	21,732	1,643,404	173,473	11,217	1,481,148	539,388	296,734	12,638	183,363	95,855
1988	2,540,020	1,762,174	24,547	1,786,721	195,414	24,720	1,616,027	600,109	323,884	13,576	187,091	100,892
1989	2,812,270	1,887,664	27,082	1,914,746	213,944	39,742	1,740,544	685,199	386,527	14,744	190,746	103,297
1990	3,025,598	2,031,032	28,366	2,059,398	235,653	56,799	1,880,544	708,634	436,420	15,402	196,448	107,397
1991	3,210,173	2,168,175	37,160	2,205,335	256,757	31,685	1,980,263	734,531	495,379	15,846	202,583	108,714
1992	3,425,074	2,282,384	39,524	2,321,908	268,812	46,847	2,099,943	754,392	570,739	16,443	208,302	109,888
1993	3,584,083	2,359,916	36,261	2,396,177	281,331	45,682	2,160,528	798,071	625,484	17,197	208,415	111,547
1994	3,914,430	2,577,562	35,349	2,612,911	313,926	41,679	2,340,664	872,083	701,683	18,150	215,675	118,839
1995	4,349,220	2,872,774	23,808	2,896,582	349,625	37,615	2,584,572	987,844	776,804	19,350	224,765	128,781
1996	4,806,958	3,147,288	33,975	3,181,263	373,954	52,001	2,859,310	1,096,336	851,312	20,452	235,041	135,319
1997	5,287,584	3,469,655	39,667	3,509,322	411,646	63,604	3,161,280	1,215,559	910,745	21,574	245,090	144,171
1998	5,733,233	3,803,526	1,544	3,805,070	451,428	84,939	3,438,581	1,311,158	983,494	22,516	254,627	149,824
1999	6,136,480	4,155,680	13,674	4,169,354	490,065	94,428	3,773,717	1,311,598	1,051,165	23,315	263,200	155,162
2000	6,585,343	4,364,716	42,355	4,407,071	518,334	100,589	3,989,326	1,452,315	1,143,702	24,234	271,736	158,299
2001	6,865,901	4,480,149	60,989	4,541,138	537,167	69,926	4,073,897	1,507,718	1,284,286	24,699	277,987	161,326
2002	7,035,723	4,630,612	-10,734	4,619,878	556,979	75,498	4,138,397	1,483,585	1,413,741	24,699	284,862	163,517
2003	7,493,076	4,988,183	22,314	5,010,497	606,460	25,778	4,429,815	1,529,548	1,533,713	25,634	292,309	168,876
2004	8,292,900	5,522,004	24,121	5,546,125	666,223	21,874	4,901,776	1,679,221	1,711,903	27,422	302,421	178,122
2005	9,150,804	6,058,704	22,870	6,081,574	728,854	46,964	5,399,684	1,858,562	1,892,558	28,799	317,745	189,671
2006	10,129,772	6,635,200	12,016	6,647,216	822,288	87,903	5,912,831	2,109,921	2,107,020	30,136	336,132	202,101
2007	10,866,558	6,785,274	7,315	6,792,589	847,290	187,110	6,132,409	2,443,994	2,290,155	30,917	351,472	208,184
2008	11,350,061	6,584,502	30,314	6,614,816	836,634	212,783	5,990,965	2,685,753	2,673,343	31,193	363,866	204,744
2009	11,316,797	6,140,380	35,989	6,176,369	802,381	345,904	5,719,892	2,540,268	3,056,637	30,469	371,417	194,533
2010	11,585,215	6,205,609	37,005	6,242,614	813,277	382,603	5,811,940	2,428,160	3,345,115	30,619	378,365	192,085
2011	12,140,200	6,365,617	30,169	6,395,786	762,394	382,092	6,015,484	2,657,951	3,466,765	31,472	385,741	197,161
2012	12,758,066	6,669,963	39,186	6,709,149	784,706	376,319	6,300,762	2,858,211	3,599,093	32,424	393,480	200,115
2013	13,339,533	7,104,306	46,286	7,150,592	923,330	425,951	6,653,213	2,865,542	3,820,778	33,020	403,982	205,939
2014	14,398,168	7,560,619	30,265	7,590,884	976,038	422,419	7,037,265	3,192,593	4,168,310	35,238	408,600	211,151
2015	15,665,102	8,055,218	5,567	8,060,785	1,034,118	474,614	7,501,281	3,596,583	4,567,238	37,148	421,689	216,873
2016	16,792,516	8,499,240	9,907	8,509,147	1,094,466	620,028	8,034,709	3,877,097	4,880,710	38,544	435,666	224,552
2017	17,901,174	9,152,137	14,599	9,166,736	1,185,803	609,130	8,590,063	4,088,671	5,222,440	39,825	449,494	231,020
2018	19,197,051	9,707,868	-2,517	9,705,351	1,265,069	695,269	9,135,551	4,361,608	5,699,892	41,343	464,335	240,747
2019	20,891,989	10,304,490	-3,068	10,301,422	1,349,369	796,812	9,748,865	4,930,143	6,212,981	43,777	477,232	245,374
2020	22,916,831	10,466,692	-3,950	10,462,742	1,389,527	1,096,633	10,169,848	5,007,088	7,739,895	46,619	491,582	238,826
2021	25,099,342	11,787,646	8,019	11,795,665	1,548,358	1,184,389	11,431,696	5,149,459	8,518,187	49,234	509,794	251,603

Personal Income and Employment by Area: Napa, CA

(Thousands of dollars, except as noted.)

Year	Personal income, total	Earnings by place of work			Less: Contributions for government social insurance	Plus: Adjustment for residence	Equals: Net earnings by place of residence	Plus: Dividends, interest, and rent	Plus: Personal current transfer receipts	Per capita personal income (dollars)	Population (persons)	Total employment
		Nonfarm	Farm	Total								
1970	381,497	200,291	6,511	206,802	11,903	65,775	260,674	82,224	38,599	4,795	79,562	27,680
1971	416,801	217,607	6,258	223,865	13,468	70,994	281,391	92,646	42,764	5,097	81,771	28,531
1972	448,277	232,249	7,762	240,011	15,010	75,874	300,875	101,594	45,808	5,387	83,208	29,297
1973	508,478	267,159	13,400	280,559	19,876	80,542	341,225	114,786	52,467	5,797	87,718	31,552
1974	578,763	302,113	9,589	311,702	23,560	95,826	383,968	132,347	62,448	6,377	90,759	33,495
1975	674,732	346,569	15,444	362,013	26,750	111,299	446,562	149,514	78,656	7,207	93,627	35,667
1976	745,064	379,543	16,148	395,691	29,226	126,868	493,333	162,843	88,888	7,846	94,964	36,033
1977	827,296	412,087	21,533	433,620	32,188	144,783	546,215	183,287	97,794	8,571	96,521	36,858
1978	943,170	471,624	26,011	497,635	37,931	166,309	626,013	212,576	104,581	9,780	96,437	38,852
1979	1,055,709	542,121	20,588	562,709	46,332	175,840	692,217	242,296	121,196	10,687	98,789	41,207
1980	1,166,017	582,073	20,909	602,982	49,794	187,810	740,998	286,374	138,645	11,739	99,331	43,047
1981	1,326,710	662,298	22,664	684,962	62,311	197,520	820,171	346,476	160,063	13,312	99,662	44,376
1982	1,427,348	690,523	37,653	728,176	66,593	215,123	876,706	376,406	174,236	14,107	101,178	44,528
1983	1,519,183	733,184	19,871	753,055	72,031	235,458	916,482	413,993	188,708	14,960	101,549	45,542
1984	1,658,126	829,270	19,956	849,226	84,904	245,371	1,009,693	453,931	194,502	16,272	101,902	47,379
1985	1,788,105	900,721	21,142	921,863	93,809	261,734	1,089,788	487,774	210,543	17,358	103,014	49,000
1986	1,920,241	995,525	30,221	1,025,746	105,436	270,878	1,191,188	505,749	223,304	18,422	104,237	51,024
1987	2,007,907	1,069,171	23,722	1,092,893	113,218	281,208	1,260,883	516,964	230,060	19,121	105,010	52,434
1988	2,184,268	1,195,782	28,504	1,224,286	132,032	293,245	1,385,499	553,574	245,195	20,581	106,130	54,863
1989	2,416,052	1,265,289	59,217	1,324,506	141,886	308,321	1,490,941	654,841	270,270	22,235	108,662	56,480
1990	2,568,559	1,390,694	45,325	1,436,019	155,675	339,481	1,619,825	659,425	289,309	23,081	111,284	59,343
1991	2,715,890	1,488,245	54,906	1,543,151	167,013	345,002	1,721,140	675,745	319,005	24,199	112,233	60,173
1992	2,842,249	1,594,834	44,668	1,639,502	177,659	326,086	1,787,929	691,221	363,099	24,862	114,322	60,221
1993	2,959,035	1,665,021	33,636	1,698,657	185,461	320,854	1,834,050	741,264	383,721	25,737	114,972	60,849
1994	3,089,928	1,755,620	35,649	1,791,269	194,629	333,985	1,930,625	769,558	389,745	26,620	116,077	62,499
1995	3,225,147	1,863,604	40,338	1,903,942	205,052	301,113	2,000,003	818,442	406,702	27,637	116,697	64,022
1996	3,460,698	2,010,971	53,432	2,064,403	214,396	289,237	2,139,244	893,629	427,825	29,329	117,996	67,250
1997	3,717,064	2,194,095	98,409	2,292,504	233,144	253,070	2,312,430	966,959	437,675	31,025	119,808	70,898
1998	3,977,695	2,440,831	63,703	2,504,534	254,403	249,485	2,499,616	1,012,958	465,121	32,716	121,583	77,036
1999	4,355,769	2,803,319	76,809	2,880,128	289,604	229,023	2,819,547	1,071,628	464,594	35,405	123,026	81,319
2000	4,796,165	3,084,190	139,774	3,223,964	318,179	232,753	3,138,538	1,170,378	487,249	38,503	124,565	82,348
2001	5,205,625	3,660,354	136,466	3,796,820	378,150	132,526	3,551,196	1,131,238	523,191	41,048	126,818	83,462
2002	5,288,779	3,865,271	149,310	4,014,581	404,704	53,834	3,663,711	1,069,625	555,443	41,080	128,744	85,105
2003	5,353,383	3,964,656	116,944	4,081,600	427,803	-30,482	3,623,315	1,144,136	585,932	41,136	130,138	85,767
2004	5,427,080	4,049,495	95,311	4,144,806	463,163	-95,571	3,586,072	1,224,625	616,383	41,623	130,387	87,004
2005	5,745,111	4,174,010	151,742	4,325,752	475,505	-74,076	3,776,171	1,317,478	651,462	44,064	130,381	87,728
2006	6,098,894	4,391,241	88,488	4,479,729	480,276	-80,967	3,918,486	1,476,252	704,156	46,401	131,440	88,027
2007	6,344,502	4,606,215	67,019	4,673,234	499,580	-159,611	4,014,043	1,584,380	746,079	47,853	132,583	91,173
2008	6,384,619	4,652,354	44,965	4,697,319	514,604	-269,148	3,913,567	1,631,963	839,089	47,613	134,093	91,679
2009	6,225,337	4,504,042	107,686	4,611,728	499,292	-230,628	3,881,808	1,437,772	905,757	46,018	135,280	88,602
2010	6,393,827	4,626,054	85,620	4,711,674	490,105	-259,215	3,962,354	1,441,985	989,488	46,755	136,752	87,944
2011	6,671,541	4,698,049	60,221	4,758,270	452,371	-244,356	4,061,543	1,603,840	1,006,158	48,461	137,668	89,319
2012	7,388,952	5,094,743	206,573	5,301,316	477,361	-279,752	4,544,203	1,829,979	1,014,770	53,348	138,504	92,257
2013	7,691,668	5,538,092	229,472	5,767,564	572,909	-295,194	4,899,461	1,747,836	1,044,371	55,129	139,522	96,123
2014	8,346,524	6,058,818	210,133	6,268,951	616,049	-403,910	5,248,992	1,999,638	1,097,894	59,189	141,014	99,871
2015	9,013,122	6,596,347	167,613	6,763,960	662,149	-377,379	5,724,432	2,121,248	1,167,442	63,646	141,613	103,116
2016	9,530,051	6,933,839	174,280	7,108,119	692,464	-278,810	6,136,845	2,186,450	1,206,756	67,213	141,789	103,104
2017	9,720,839	7,074,707	193,124	7,267,831	717,596	-425,459	6,124,776	2,393,710	1,202,353	68,950	140,984	104,707
2018	9,727,067	7,043,829	156,565	7,200,394	745,659	-476,782	5,977,953	2,490,479	1,258,635	69,510	139,937	107,611
2019	10,349,607	7,311,148	140,461	7,451,609	782,606	-410,511	6,258,492	2,740,532	1,350,583	74,379	139,146	106,669
2020	11,372,288	7,139,366	153,500	7,292,866	750,791	90,901	6,632,976	2,755,742	1,983,570	82,643	137,608	98,299
2021	12,341,466	7,658,276	124,926	7,783,202	806,490	496,366	7,473,078	2,856,645	2,011,743	90,608	136,207	100,970

Personal Income and Employment by Area: Naples-Marco Island, FL

(Thousands of dollars, except as noted.)

Year	Personal income, total	Earnings by place of work			Less: Contributions for government social insurance	Plus: Adjustment for residence	Equals: Net earnings by place of residence	Plus: Dividends, interest, and rent	Plus: Personal current transfer receipts	Per capita personal income (dollars)	Population (persons)	Total employment
		Nonfarm	Farm	Total								
1970	208,518	126,251	9,560	135,811	7,829	-11,869	116,113	77,669	14,736	5,364	38,874	19,784
1971	248,158	142,417	12,446	154,863	9,157	-11,225	134,481	93,439	20,238	5,814	42,683	21,385
1972	290,752	162,864	15,182	178,046	11,053	-11,510	155,483	110,868	24,401	5,916	49,144	22,959
1973	368,203	214,688	16,135	230,823	16,968	-14,942	198,913	138,061	31,229	6,724	54,757	28,113
1974	426,924	236,006	18,908	254,914	19,697	-15,257	219,960	168,112	38,852	7,311	58,396	30,121
1975	456,499	232,806	21,777	254,583	18,884	-10,919	224,780	178,930	52,789	7,177	63,602	28,974
1976	523,920	264,984	22,891	287,875	20,883	-9,240	257,752	206,728	59,440	7,923	66,125	29,334
1977	620,590	324,165	21,698	345,863	26,089	-10,612	309,162	243,861	67,567	8,942	69,404	34,304
1978	756,148	404,583	25,432	430,015	33,747	-13,342	382,926	294,875	78,347	10,103	74,844	40,053
1979	892,743	476,453	35,609	512,062	41,994	-13,099	456,969	342,120	93,654	10,902	81,890	44,215
1980	1,082,132	555,386	37,864	593,250	49,835	-13,171	530,244	437,362	114,526	12,367	87,504	46,868
1981	1,341,559	645,952	37,397	683,349	63,122	-13,292	606,935	595,549	139,075	14,352	93,473	50,278
1982	1,446,414	657,479	49,704	707,183	67,559	-8,947	630,677	648,171	167,566	14,478	99,902	51,225
1983	1,647,968	722,358	84,208	806,566	73,794	-6,628	726,144	733,883	187,941	15,806	104,265	55,623
1984	1,904,028	832,272	78,778	911,050	87,495	-9,320	814,235	882,167	207,626	17,293	110,105	61,169
1985	2,119,244	948,845	88,742	1,037,587	102,725	-11,856	923,006	966,155	230,083	18,335	115,584	65,543
1986	2,397,468	1,069,544	104,993	1,174,537	119,764	-11,800	1,042,973	1,097,283	257,212	19,763	121,311	71,756
1987	2,773,825	1,285,247	122,892	1,408,139	141,862	-15,835	1,250,442	1,242,720	280,663	21,684	127,921	74,893
1988	3,383,296	1,491,305	142,264	1,633,569	169,085	-21,502	1,442,982	1,617,650	322,664	24,985	135,413	83,812
1989	3,859,997	1,697,170	177,436	1,874,606	196,272	-25,905	1,652,429	1,844,790	362,778	26,659	144,790	89,342
1990	4,151,199	1,835,917	114,906	1,950,823	211,501	-29,203	1,710,119	2,026,528	414,552	26,857	154,568	92,101
1991	4,642,765	1,966,306	163,669	2,129,975	226,354	100,981	2,004,602	2,161,104	477,059	28,312	163,988	94,434
1992	5,238,715	2,135,932	207,357	2,343,289	243,320	161,865	2,261,834	2,413,706	563,175	30,444	172,077	96,093
1993	5,674,400	2,337,418	204,490	2,541,908	264,512	97,714	2,375,110	2,685,233	614,057	31,300	181,288	101,102
1994	6,243,328	2,583,059	154,108	2,737,167	295,029	92,194	2,534,332	3,035,261	673,735	32,665	191,132	104,131
1995	6,792,820	2,821,678	147,719	2,969,397	316,757	106,301	2,758,941	3,301,497	732,382	34,026	199,639	107,407
1996	7,500,818	3,092,576	134,526	3,227,102	342,643	184,819	3,069,278	3,642,239	789,301	35,854	209,205	113,188
1997	8,363,682	3,500,077	142,932	3,643,009	386,804	100,338	3,356,543	4,167,984	839,155	37,858	220,923	119,660
1998	9,365,765	3,821,332	164,529	3,985,861	417,181	195,648	3,764,328	4,724,321	877,116	40,133	233,371	128,002
1999	10,075,360	4,252,919	154,215	4,407,134	457,397	202,008	4,151,745	4,979,431	944,184	41,108	245,094	133,485
2000	10,910,775	4,724,567	156,123	4,880,690	507,357	67,461	4,440,794	5,432,673	1,037,308	42,953	254,015	143,309
2001	12,268,216	5,621,460	147,768	5,769,228	592,234	80,670	5,257,664	5,861,167	1,149,385	46,428	264,240	151,622
2002	12,798,087	5,999,728	164,406	6,164,134	631,310	108,032	5,640,856	5,918,076	1,239,155	46,456	275,490	157,775
2003	13,634,233	6,526,796	142,773	6,669,569	692,883	110,527	6,087,213	6,212,147	1,334,873	47,786	285,321	168,142
2004	15,735,422	6,913,798	144,726	7,058,524	756,929	176,567	6,478,162	7,808,729	1,448,531	53,156	296,021	177,642
2005	18,098,154	7,760,561	178,014	7,938,575	843,319	166,181	7,261,437	9,230,041	1,606,676	58,865	307,452	182,757
2006	20,819,746	8,392,260	166,763	8,559,023	927,494	231,092	7,862,621	11,223,558	1,733,567	66,597	312,621	190,179
2007	21,756,961	8,285,943	155,976	8,441,919	933,083	163,909	7,672,745	12,224,542	1,859,674	69,193	314,437	186,380
2008	21,620,791	7,409,466	143,480	7,552,946	881,691	299,380	6,970,635	12,520,087	2,130,069	68,282	316,641	178,682
2009	18,419,047	6,763,865	150,231	6,914,096	833,442	311,284	6,391,938	9,655,624	2,371,485	57,833	318,485	169,935
2010	20,428,537	7,378,019	137,359	7,515,378	854,699	515,545	7,176,224	10,654,874	2,597,439	63,329	322,576	170,283
2011	21,371,445	7,634,405	116,608	7,751,013	790,943	445,361	7,405,431	11,257,438	2,708,576	65,222	327,670	176,891
2012	24,142,507	7,786,197	132,663	7,918,860	824,244	689,663	7,784,279	13,633,236	2,724,992	72,646	332,330	183,066
2013	23,834,645	7,986,856	141,180	8,128,036	956,974	641,005	7,812,067	13,207,678	2,814,900	70,281	339,133	190,509
2014	27,082,008	8,979,611	106,323	9,085,934	1,051,365	825,402	8,859,971	15,258,271	2,963,766	79,290	341,555	200,950
2015	29,889,525	9,712,122	113,475	9,825,597	1,123,300	1,058,994	9,761,291	16,968,849	3,159,385	85,669	348,897	210,279
2016	31,512,180	10,339,154	95,557	10,434,711	1,187,570	1,161,644	10,408,785	17,790,418	3,312,977	88,301	356,874	217,147
2017	33,958,713	10,706,952	100,370	10,807,322	1,230,429	1,307,758	10,884,651	19,549,637	3,524,425	93,645	362,634	222,526
2018	38,058,323	11,502,108	86,105	11,588,213	1,341,028	1,349,089	11,596,274	22,700,794	3,761,255	103,875	366,385	231,693
2019	41,014,314	12,377,429	78,580	12,456,009	1,454,526	1,381,899	12,383,382	24,533,967	4,096,965	110,272	371,939	234,791
2020	42,413,331	12,845,645	84,303	12,929,948	1,513,505	1,352,932	12,769,375	24,573,129	5,070,827	112,479	377,079	236,517
2021	45,539,558	14,505,409	86,424	14,591,833	1,674,028	1,318,765	14,236,570	25,643,025	5,659,963	117,984	385,980	245,890

Personal Income and Employment by Area: Nashville-Davidson—Murfreesboro—Franklin, TN

(Thousands of dollars, except as noted.)

Year	Personal income, total	Earnings by place of work			Less: Contributions for government social insurance	Plus: Adjustment for residence	Equals: Net earnings by place of residence	Plus: Dividends, interest, and rent	Plus: Personal current transfer receipts	Per capita personal income (dollars)	Population (persons)	Total employment
		Nonfarm	Farm	Total								
1970	2,872,703	2,378,911	54,080	2,432,991	155,235	-4,047	2,273,709	377,994	221,000	3,614	794,960	388,326
1971	3,127,554	2,578,373	49,397	2,627,770	173,003	-2,692	2,452,075	415,766	259,713	3,877	806,661	390,781
1972	3,518,921	2,928,581	59,226	2,987,807	207,389	-7,469	2,772,949	459,890	286,082	4,235	831,002	414,671
1973	4,015,481	3,348,960	84,658	3,433,618	272,313	-10,030	3,151,275	526,552	337,654	4,768	842,119	441,535
1974	4,475,688	3,717,199	62,857	3,780,056	315,214	-13,497	3,451,345	615,312	409,031	5,205	859,921	454,143
1975	4,839,952	3,917,438	37,484	3,954,922	325,367	-13,857	3,615,698	681,491	542,763	5,504	879,430	437,309
1976	5,466,439	4,468,518	62,377	4,530,895	377,132	-21,419	4,132,344	740,503	593,592	6,134	891,221	457,484
1977	6,150,674	5,084,056	65,171	5,149,227	427,494	-30,362	4,691,371	836,500	622,803	6,759	909,992	481,268
1978	7,046,834	5,884,783	67,651	5,952,434	502,365	-45,738	5,404,331	959,994	682,509	7,574	930,403	503,047
1979	7,912,979	6,593,672	63,285	6,656,957	587,718	-50,306	6,018,933	1,099,383	794,663	8,339	948,910	520,756
1980	8,740,913	7,073,328	45,449	7,118,777	632,400	-54,846	6,431,531	1,331,103	978,279	9,045	966,369	516,142
1981	9,856,746	7,874,030	72,860	7,946,890	761,086	-86,645	7,099,159	1,644,062	1,113,525	10,111	974,846	523,293
1982	10,546,452	8,244,805	71,894	8,316,699	818,066	-65,467	7,433,166	1,876,293	1,236,993	10,752	980,868	519,035
1983	11,368,590	9,052,629	-3,235	9,049,394	911,747	-66,384	8,071,263	1,978,561	1,318,766	11,480	990,291	530,629
1984	12,865,634	10,262,939	72,091	10,335,030	1,064,235	-88,792	9,182,003	2,295,194	1,388,437	12,799	1,005,226	566,641
1985	14,113,608	11,428,448	53,779	11,482,227	1,201,456	-123,065	10,157,706	2,470,487	1,485,415	13,828	1,020,620	597,123
1986	15,434,061	12,671,885	15,911	12,687,796	1,359,711	-155,373	11,172,712	2,663,261	1,598,088	14,823	1,041,249	628,746
1987	16,734,170	13,876,218	14,390	13,890,608	1,475,492	-197,297	12,217,819	2,822,395	1,693,956	15,701	1,065,808	657,288
1988	18,117,640	14,957,303	18,111	14,975,414	1,621,148	-215,445	13,138,821	3,137,078	1,841,741	16,764	1,080,719	672,526
1989	19,312,897	15,864,193	31,653	15,895,846	1,740,006	-260,339	13,895,501	3,386,182	2,031,214	17,653	1,094,048	684,522
1990	20,498,382	16,621,308	37,556	16,658,864	1,841,007	-303,771	14,514,086	3,709,124	2,275,172	18,492	1,108,523	692,179
1991	21,745,132	17,714,414	51,092	17,765,506	1,990,439	-364,496	15,410,571	3,733,051	2,601,510	19,230	1,130,775	699,011
1992	24,080,861	19,823,983	67,458	19,891,441	2,191,637	-429,337	17,270,467	3,892,151	2,918,243	20,834	1,155,871	715,870
1993	25,949,147	21,516,392	64,248	21,580,640	2,376,204	-482,392	18,722,044	4,115,926	3,111,177	21,878	1,186,057	752,674
1994	28,050,027	23,455,860	60,778	23,516,638	2,629,669	-538,212	20,348,757	4,438,414	3,262,856	23,008	1,219,138	796,197
1995	30,648,767	25,530,111	43,113	25,573,224	2,847,785	-608,130	22,117,309	4,942,804	3,588,654	24,501	1,250,936	825,158
1996	32,586,978	27,193,917	-13,087	27,180,830	2,977,182	-647,541	23,556,107	5,255,880	3,774,991	25,415	1,282,177	849,563
1997	34,792,349	29,239,931	26,655	29,266,586	3,201,904	-710,360	25,354,322	5,511,880	3,926,147	26,498	1,313,031	879,964
1998	38,346,017	32,559,548	-3,291	32,556,257	3,403,433	-871,895	28,280,929	6,005,114	4,059,974	29,098	1,317,819	904,136
1999	40,430,986	34,634,384	-35,714	34,598,670	3,629,424	-959,337	30,009,909	6,177,983	4,243,094	30,156	1,340,742	924,626
2000	43,807,751	37,422,175	24,620	37,446,795	3,872,844	-1,053,375	32,520,576	6,661,369	4,625,806	32,095	1,364,950	947,537
2001	44,743,148	38,111,079	5,204	38,116,283	3,992,997	-1,026,571	33,096,715	6,544,965	5,101,468	32,273	1,386,403	943,611
2002	46,203,278	39,758,233	-37,459	39,720,774	4,170,674	-1,025,769	34,524,331	6,196,243	5,482,704	32,893	1,404,664	942,326
2003	48,385,434	41,379,923	-45,278	41,334,645	4,331,656	-1,046,048	35,956,941	6,571,766	5,856,727	33,914	1,426,723	953,159
2004	51,487,366	44,039,994	-6,826	44,033,168	4,598,849	-1,080,409	38,353,910	6,861,766	6,271,690	35,392	1,454,773	985,139
2005	54,456,385	46,134,367	-4,481	46,129,886	4,840,995	-1,098,452	40,190,439	7,516,618	6,749,328	36,613	1,487,370	1,017,222
2006	59,242,696	50,053,645	-29,171	50,024,474	5,175,748	-1,182,078	43,666,648	8,434,223	7,141,825	38,740	1,529,238	1,047,270
2007	62,195,240	51,689,042	-74,789	51,614,253	5,452,357	-1,166,055	44,995,841	9,313,704	7,885,695	39,668	1,567,875	1,072,095
2008	65,150,017	52,772,077	-10,778	52,761,299	5,650,349	-1,147,566	45,963,384	10,145,094	9,041,539	40,660	1,602,302	1,066,093
2009	65,522,266	53,566,430	-31,377	53,535,053	5,577,413	-978,117	46,979,523	8,806,068	9,736,675	40,206	1,629,646	1,027,675
2010	69,431,797	55,757,190	-34,238	55,722,952	5,689,158	-932,963	49,100,831	9,502,854	10,828,112	42,057	1,650,887	1,028,788
2011	74,087,421	59,199,087	-8,695	59,190,392	5,289,302	-954,716	52,946,374	10,092,804	11,048,243	44,236	1,674,830	1,056,969
2012	79,504,033	63,703,215	69,157	63,772,372	5,590,189	-1,090,255	57,091,928	11,294,489	11,117,616	46,653	1,704,175	1,090,660
2013	81,400,709	66,597,519	78,984	66,676,503	6,585,576	-1,154,026	58,936,901	10,940,517	11,523,291	46,895	1,735,823	1,126,503
2014	87,397,366	72,005,402	48,360	72,053,762	7,004,323	-1,260,378	63,789,061	11,833,480	11,774,825	49,021	1,782,857	1,173,932
2015	94,166,449	77,564,520	46,383	77,610,903	7,563,530	-1,369,542	68,677,831	12,993,586	12,495,032	51,658	1,822,874	1,222,355
2016	99,320,248	81,909,538	-32,725	81,876,813	7,927,350	-1,547,093	72,402,370	14,003,948	12,913,930	53,300	1,863,407	1,273,086
2017	104,669,036	86,538,246	-16,434	86,521,812	8,485,880	-1,708,139	76,327,793	15,032,092	13,309,151	55,078	1,900,375	1,323,807
2018	112,298,144	92,308,119	-65,533	92,242,586	8,985,230	-1,812,985	81,444,371	16,835,172	14,018,601	58,056	1,934,319	1,370,081
2019	120,558,808	98,284,044	-41,490	98,242,554	9,595,018	-1,955,589	86,691,947	18,870,734	14,996,127	61,366	1,964,602	1,402,190
2020	128,436,092	101,358,637	-43,931	101,314,706	9,944,787	-1,915,608	89,454,311	18,857,557	20,124,224	64,368	1,995,343	1,384,860
2021	140,925,821	112,916,293	11,474	112,927,767	10,697,011	-2,277,280	99,953,476	19,383,294	21,589,051	70,026	2,012,476	1,443,724

Personal Income and Employment by Area: New Bern, NC

(Thousands of dollars, except as noted.)

Year	Personal income, total	Earnings by place of work Nonfarm	Farm	Total	Less: Contributions for government social insurance	Plus: Adjustment for residence	Equals: Net earnings by place of residence	Plus: Dividends, interest, and rent	Plus: Personal current transfer receipts	Per capita personal income (dollars)	Population (persons)	Total employment
1970	286,284	229,469	15,138	244,607	12,390	-13,232	218,985	47,616	19,683	3,488	82,081	40,058
1971	300,887	247,778	11,597	259,375	13,749	-16,696	228,930	49,119	22,838	3,587	83,889	38,574
1972	334,128	269,626	18,626	288,252	15,358	-18,796	254,098	53,366	26,664	3,925	85,129	38,318
1973	394,009	312,781	26,311	339,092	19,658	-21,141	298,293	65,748	29,968	4,502	87,526	40,884
1974	434,747	344,290	26,683	370,973	23,207	-22,831	324,935	73,667	36,145	5,020	86,605	41,460
1975	474,739	370,115	25,448	395,563	26,471	-23,745	345,347	82,400	46,992	5,344	88,837	41,185
1976	463,825	357,054	24,001	381,055	25,898	-21,912	333,245	77,350	53,230	5,094	91,051	37,864
1977	517,429	404,858	14,147	419,005	29,647	-22,907	366,451	93,006	57,972	5,685	91,010	40,592
1978	617,906	479,328	24,300	503,628	35,161	-29,375	439,092	115,841	62,973	6,751	91,529	43,032
1979	674,689	533,663	10,629	544,292	41,013	-30,258	473,021	130,400	71,268	7,443	90,650	44,787
1980	786,728	604,323	16,815	621,138	46,284	-32,283	542,571	158,627	85,530	8,603	91,445	46,872
1981	838,031	644,322	16,948	661,270	51,043	-49,501	560,726	179,291	98,014	9,073	92,365	43,576
1982	942,033	717,127	26,122	743,249	56,875	-56,953	629,421	202,965	109,647	10,009	94,122	45,190
1983	989,594	770,861	6,322	777,183	65,449	-58,565	653,169	218,452	117,973	10,381	95,328	46,894
1984	1,136,252	878,967	20,643	899,610	76,938	-63,452	759,220	250,529	126,503	11,683	97,256	49,839
1985	1,226,427	958,230	13,553	971,783	86,660	-70,552	814,571	274,052	137,804	12,281	99,860	51,285
1986	1,314,841	1,021,827	15,701	1,037,528	95,177	-74,935	867,416	299,284	148,141	13,108	100,306	52,168
1987	1,374,376	1,052,231	23,782	1,076,013	100,713	-70,135	905,165	311,661	157,550	13,744	99,999	52,819
1988	1,470,965	1,127,392	25,509	1,152,901	113,405	-77,603	961,893	335,801	173,271	14,522	101,292	53,217
1989	1,599,622	1,190,726	25,672	1,216,398	122,442	-81,110	1,012,846	391,507	195,269	15,720	101,757	54,451
1990	1,650,899	1,212,698	26,557	1,239,255	129,664	-73,156	1,036,435	398,392	216,072	16,041	102,918	54,413
1991	1,744,002	1,260,166	35,313	1,295,479	136,845	-80,120	1,078,514	413,505	251,983	16,728	104,258	53,677
1992	1,928,283	1,414,134	29,937	1,444,071	154,766	-91,728	1,197,577	452,590	278,116	18,251	105,655	55,701
1993	1,984,678	1,415,588	31,525	1,447,113	157,550	-86,760	1,202,803	473,388	308,487	18,746	105,871	55,763
1994	2,087,530	1,484,901	31,139	1,516,040	165,790	-92,204	1,258,046	506,784	322,700	19,612	106,443	56,340
1995	2,224,058	1,557,251	29,094	1,586,345	173,313	-96,514	1,316,518	544,561	362,979	20,565	108,147	58,223
1996	2,398,467	1,658,302	44,778	1,703,080	184,524	-102,302	1,416,254	590,662	391,551	21,834	109,848	60,554
1997	2,561,587	1,744,128	52,150	1,796,278	193,807	-97,973	1,504,498	647,480	409,609	22,977	111,484	62,242
1998	2,677,697	1,872,841	21,825	1,894,666	208,638	-106,051	1,579,977	672,243	425,477	23,783	112,591	64,020
1999	2,797,384	1,963,534	20,620	1,984,154	219,899	-108,319	1,655,936	680,757	460,691	24,519	114,091	64,804
2000	2,991,868	2,078,516	66,499	2,145,015	232,725	-113,909	1,798,381	705,651	487,836	25,981	115,156	65,818
2001	3,062,929	2,104,473	80,082	2,184,555	235,425	-121,240	1,827,890	696,821	538,218	26,317	116,388	64,919
2002	3,051,693	2,132,717	28,698	2,161,415	239,096	-117,553	1,804,766	674,211	572,716	26,384	115,664	64,573
2003	3,242,247	2,303,741	28,660	2,332,401	260,728	-138,826	1,932,847	704,836	604,564	28,004	115,776	65,373
2004	3,498,802	2,491,071	55,605	2,546,676	280,508	-154,739	2,111,429	737,323	650,050	30,027	116,520	67,058
2005	3,758,902	2,653,337	92,384	2,745,721	300,060	-171,183	2,274,478	782,330	702,094	31,913	117,787	68,387
2006	3,961,271	2,789,532	63,994	2,853,526	317,728	-173,072	2,362,726	840,515	758,030	33,034	119,915	69,504
2007	4,244,668	2,967,207	41,454	3,008,661	339,712	-197,846	2,471,103	956,801	816,764	35,117	120,873	70,196
2008	4,436,749	3,019,489	43,438	3,062,927	346,540	-186,868	2,529,519	993,336	913,894	36,221	122,491	69,705
2009	4,445,003	3,041,343	42,654	3,083,997	354,304	-232,701	2,496,992	947,214	1,000,797	35,503	125,202	67,944
2010	4,600,128	3,151,331	53,481	3,204,812	363,932	-251,803	2,589,077	945,712	1,065,339	36,100	127,427	67,088
2011	4,726,761	3,173,171	57,369	3,230,540	337,791	-281,588	2,611,161	1,017,578	1,098,022	36,881	128,164	66,549
2012	4,890,384	3,270,826	78,607	3,349,433	348,280	-304,788	2,696,365	1,063,489	1,130,530	38,069	128,462	66,858
2013	4,820,625	3,196,494	81,214	3,277,708	384,783	-288,544	2,604,381	1,059,129	1,157,115	37,885	127,243	66,965
2014	4,962,027	3,267,982	73,777	3,341,759	394,942	-300,922	2,645,895	1,122,112	1,194,020	39,260	126,389	67,107
2015	5,067,247	3,345,799	33,781	3,379,580	406,266	-304,957	2,668,357	1,155,511	1,243,379	40,574	124,890	67,414
2016	4,992,114	3,242,444	34,970	3,277,414	391,427	-275,288	2,610,699	1,105,285	1,276,130	40,131	124,394	68,053
2017	5,193,170	3,360,306	54,988	3,415,294	403,786	-260,261	2,751,247	1,118,774	1,323,149	41,858	124,065	67,326
2018	5,336,678	3,475,901	16,251	3,492,152	415,462	-264,675	2,812,015	1,135,512	1,389,151	43,095	123,836	67,294
2019	5,676,093	3,627,566	43,015	3,670,581	432,633	-279,480	2,958,468	1,238,892	1,478,733	46,182	122,906	67,695
2020	6,076,794	3,780,230	24,610	3,804,840	450,336	-295,062	3,059,442	1,236,759	1,780,593	49,815	121,988	66,683
2021	6,573,623	3,959,305	66,497	4,025,802	465,936	-282,062	3,277,804	1,260,944	2,034,875	53,762	122,273	68,047

Personal Income and Employment by Area: New Haven-Milford, CT

(Thousands of dollars, except as noted.)

					Derivation of personal income							
		Earnings by place of work			Less: Contributions for government social insurance	Plus: Adjustment for residence	Equals: Net earnings by place of residence	Plus: Dividends, interest, and rent	Plus: Personal current transfer receipts	Per capita personal income (dollars)	Population (persons)	Total employment
Year	Personal income, total	Nonfarm	Farm	Total								
1970	3,590,216	2,760,353	7,183	2,767,536	188,141	96,473	2,675,868	594,547	319,801	4,803	747,435	341,697
1971	3,810,156	2,882,319	7,292	2,889,611	203,266	99,169	2,785,514	629,329	395,313	5,033	757,031	335,504
1972	4,112,415	3,138,423	7,069	3,145,492	234,151	114,248	3,025,589	670,534	416,292	5,424	758,131	342,677
1973	4,482,966	3,443,164	8,267	3,451,431	296,384	134,906	3,289,953	742,518	450,495	5,924	756,777	357,175
1974	4,889,082	3,684,913	7,802	3,692,715	330,304	158,023	3,520,434	839,886	528,762	6,439	759,277	364,298
1975	5,244,296	3,764,841	8,099	3,772,940	329,632	190,058	3,633,366	900,869	710,061	6,904	759,648	349,425
1976	5,615,847	4,039,411	7,787	4,047,198	359,127	222,825	3,910,896	954,001	750,950	7,406	758,263	351,258
1977	6,151,807	4,438,053	9,735	4,447,788	396,063	264,928	4,316,653	1,049,528	785,626	8,117	757,917	361,753
1978	6,799,915	4,939,406	11,701	4,951,107	452,783	327,551	4,825,875	1,168,388	805,652	8,981	757,121	374,218
1979	7,571,868	5,478,014	10,419	5,488,433	524,191	404,746	5,368,988	1,313,599	889,281	9,960	760,219	385,300
1980	8,484,836	5,890,414	11,139	5,901,553	563,729	519,787	5,857,611	1,623,467	1,003,758	11,134	762,066	386,193
1981	9,468,123	6,318,965	8,176	6,327,141	648,154	622,376	6,301,363	1,984,139	1,182,621	12,403	763,373	385,348
1982	10,143,334	6,640,676	12,366	6,653,042	692,012	696,675	6,657,705	2,171,674	1,313,955	13,261	764,877	381,104
1983	10,920,825	7,217,360	12,025	7,229,385	757,949	742,720	7,214,156	2,289,546	1,417,123	14,165	770,970	385,388
1984	12,214,612	8,147,769	12,890	8,160,659	877,892	835,865	8,118,632	2,624,324	1,471,656	15,735	776,264	406,456
1985	13,068,809	8,816,021	12,253	8,828,274	961,245	935,065	8,802,094	2,716,377	1,550,338	16,689	783,092	416,819
1986	14,067,275	9,534,083	13,458	9,547,541	1,042,786	1,038,690	9,543,445	2,890,314	1,633,516	17,817	789,528	428,205
1987	15,334,181	10,654,077	12,641	10,666,718	1,151,944	1,120,314	10,635,088	3,015,372	1,683,721	19,252	796,486	441,230
1988	16,920,792	11,854,486	13,924	11,868,410	1,306,442	1,229,962	11,791,930	3,316,171	1,812,691	21,116	801,339	455,617
1989	18,240,437	12,455,333	11,670	12,467,003	1,368,849	1,329,074	12,427,228	3,780,281	2,032,928	22,687	804,000	453,175
1990	18,766,936	12,731,771	13,039	12,744,810	1,381,440	1,382,171	12,745,541	3,750,794	2,270,601	23,302	805,366	445,131
1991	18,977,915	12,984,378	11,418	12,995,796	1,436,140	1,335,227	12,894,883	3,546,826	2,536,206	23,502	807,490	426,841
1992	19,968,736	13,639,580	13,825	13,653,405	1,486,998	1,314,011	13,480,418	3,490,682	2,997,636	24,694	808,659	424,565
1993	20,740,836	14,144,222	17,019	14,161,241	1,540,077	1,374,035	13,995,199	3,619,489	3,126,148	25,638	808,977	429,976
1994	21,360,761	14,527,521	15,310	14,542,831	1,597,601	1,453,729	14,398,959	3,701,968	3,259,834	26,398	809,178	425,475
1995	22,321,221	14,995,960	16,502	15,012,462	1,665,622	1,549,737	14,896,577	3,941,078	3,483,566	27,586	809,157	432,879
1996	23,026,714	15,670,023	13,890	15,683,913	1,738,809	1,467,156	15,412,260	4,050,468	3,563,986	28,393	811,000	442,172
1997	24,263,555	16,725,898	13,178	16,739,076	1,831,397	1,524,483	16,432,162	4,171,838	3,659,555	29,826	813,505	446,766
1998	25,623,948	17,945,626	15,391	17,961,017	1,916,099	1,593,836	17,638,754	4,284,441	3,700,753	31,351	817,313	455,111
1999	26,939,870	18,998,882	17,509	19,016,391	1,982,874	1,873,298	18,906,815	4,245,150	3,787,905	32,838	820,396	460,583
2000	29,145,162	20,724,489	20,168	20,744,657	2,098,394	1,876,552	20,522,815	4,625,469	3,996,878	35,331	824,911	470,567
2001	30,571,163	21,989,599	20,368	22,009,967	2,192,188	1,982,639	21,800,418	4,535,339	4,235,406	36,838	829,875	474,576
2002	30,875,646	22,731,892	23,687	22,755,579	2,334,919	1,706,135	22,126,795	4,205,038	4,543,813	36,972	835,099	474,530
2003	31,224,106	22,920,017	23,333	22,943,350	2,388,535	1,668,745	22,223,560	4,378,183	4,622,363	37,086	841,939	472,083
2004	32,310,580	23,894,575	25,708	23,920,283	2,507,983	1,694,307	23,106,607	4,286,430	4,917,543	38,260	844,505	482,152
2005	33,501,839	24,504,213	27,769	24,531,982	2,561,576	1,983,582	23,953,988	4,451,879	5,095,972	39,546	847,162	485,556
2006	35,717,887	25,641,142	27,519	25,668,661	2,637,124	2,198,945	25,230,482	5,072,439	5,414,966	42,011	850,207	491,429
2007	37,690,880	26,347,244	31,163	26,378,407	2,716,429	2,313,280	25,975,258	5,992,772	5,722,850	44,155	853,598	498,327
2008	38,699,800	26,647,618	32,957	26,680,575	2,784,242	2,064,191	25,960,524	6,205,286	6,533,990	45,177	856,622	496,820
2009	37,546,406	25,998,913	34,749	26,033,662	2,725,994	1,366,066	24,673,734	5,637,570	7,235,102	43,657	860,025	483,308
2010	38,338,596	26,542,041	34,577	26,576,618	2,743,089	1,437,846	25,271,375	5,366,689	7,700,532	44,404	863,398	477,548
2011	39,783,861	27,014,561	26,503	27,041,064	2,547,834	1,709,674	26,202,904	5,840,727	7,740,230	46,048	863,974	482,732
2012	40,901,286	27,695,617	34,008	27,729,625	2,639,652	1,635,559	26,725,532	6,324,694	7,851,060	47,299	864,732	487,938
2013	41,159,261	28,238,838	35,778	28,274,616	3,056,332	1,611,613	26,829,897	6,437,063	7,892,301	47,691	863,035	492,770
2014	42,649,900	28,946,735	28,599	28,975,334	3,131,547	1,905,512	27,749,299	6,789,681	8,110,920	49,124	868,202	496,755
2015	43,850,793	29,927,375	33,238	29,960,613	3,229,044	1,626,308	28,357,877	7,123,029	8,369,887	50,593	866,734	501,018
2016	44,430,443	30,550,769	31,383	30,582,152	3,302,139	1,480,632	28,760,645	7,058,820	8,610,978	51,331	865,560	504,364
2017	45,013,700	31,207,888	29,689	31,237,577	3,422,110	1,404,877	29,220,344	7,075,438	8,717,918	51,953	866,435	506,198
2018	46,851,128	31,961,279	26,401	31,987,680	3,524,178	1,932,325	30,395,827	7,138,638	9,316,663	54,059	866,667	510,917
2019	49,193,763	32,813,861	28,033	32,841,894	3,647,433	2,779,376	31,973,837	7,727,887	9,492,039	56,888	864,743	511,030
2020	51,920,470	33,558,977	25,949	33,584,926	3,745,837	2,136,907	31,975,996	7,620,760	12,323,714	60,128	863,498	499,410
2021	55,832,141	35,739,147	26,752	35,765,899	3,911,775	2,991,780	34,845,904	7,681,370	13,304,867	64,643	863,700	514,751

Personal Income and Employment by Area: New Orleans-Metairie, LA

(Thousands of dollars, except as noted.)

Year	Personal income, total	Earnings by place of work			Less: Contributions for government social insurance	Plus: Adjustment for residence	Equals: Net earnings by place of residence	Plus: Dividends, interest, and rent	Plus: Personal current transfer receipts	Per capita personal income (dollars)	Population (persons)	Total employment
		Nonfarm	Farm	Total								
1970	4,300,405	3,687,179	10,681	3,697,860	241,315	-111,456	3,345,089	600,296	355,020	3,750	1,146,894	504,994
1971	4,646,375	3,963,952	11,797	3,975,749	266,323	-132,441	3,576,985	658,144	411,246	3,983	1,166,467	508,631
1972	5,077,018	4,355,333	14,514	4,369,847	307,439	-154,871	3,907,537	711,210	458,271	4,276	1,187,285	526,614
1973	5,591,596	4,802,185	22,938	4,825,123	390,737	-172,319	4,262,067	789,363	540,166	4,670	1,197,218	548,458
1974	6,302,891	5,347,613	31,416	5,379,029	446,765	-203,708	4,728,556	943,799	630,536	5,240	1,202,899	563,281
1975	7,101,589	6,018,452	13,862	6,032,314	493,477	-243,251	5,295,586	1,033,246	772,757	5,835	1,217,164	581,071
1976	7,969,835	6,848,418	15,927	6,864,345	572,554	-289,431	6,002,360	1,108,962	858,513	6,427	1,239,970	600,729
1977	8,844,129	7,649,764	14,610	7,664,374	636,449	-329,431	6,698,494	1,217,885	927,750	7,045	1,255,289	617,879
1978	10,030,800	8,731,336	11,747	8,743,083	740,630	-387,270	7,615,183	1,404,702	1,010,915	7,897	1,270,252	640,835
1979	11,305,254	9,895,502	11,342	9,906,844	872,300	-472,185	8,562,359	1,597,616	1,145,279	8,794	1,285,635	657,374
1980	12,972,514	11,253,188	9,160	11,262,348	985,674	-587,254	9,689,420	1,927,135	1,355,959	9,915	1,308,411	679,099
1981	14,871,507	12,772,706	12,294	12,785,000	1,201,115	-622,317	10,961,568	2,389,249	1,520,690	11,244	1,322,669	695,393
1982	16,023,828	13,467,443	13,603	13,481,046	1,291,861	-645,369	11,543,816	2,757,061	1,722,951	11,950	1,340,939	692,756
1983	16,765,831	13,745,419	14,467	13,759,886	1,312,453	-659,576	11,787,857	3,037,307	1,940,667	12,407	1,351,273	679,426
1984	17,875,664	14,545,801	8,367	14,554,168	1,420,914	-676,923	12,456,331	3,386,572	2,032,761	13,237	1,350,467	693,125
1985	18,574,004	14,744,956	11,223	14,756,179	1,445,102	-638,592	12,672,485	3,703,040	2,198,479	13,760	1,349,897	681,199
1986	18,892,004	14,771,492	12,490	14,783,982	1,430,585	-577,817	12,775,580	3,734,619	2,381,805	14,022	1,347,337	660,295
1987	19,076,986	14,919,564	11,818	14,931,382	1,421,105	-560,103	12,950,174	3,706,418	2,420,394	14,372	1,327,369	650,890
1988	19,960,654	15,641,137	17,881	15,659,018	1,557,720	-571,016	13,530,282	3,862,733	2,567,639	15,233	1,310,318	664,408
1989	21,099,327	16,364,374	17,963	16,382,337	1,638,471	-581,261	14,162,605	4,141,853	2,794,869	16,269	1,296,918	668,800
1990	22,547,350	17,560,423	8,413	17,568,836	1,807,204	-640,125	15,121,507	4,351,908	3,073,935	17,546	1,285,014	681,627
1991	23,666,685	18,369,775	9,733	18,379,508	1,937,658	-646,168	15,795,682	4,333,496	3,537,507	18,276	1,294,966	685,564
1992	25,301,998	19,390,972	14,708	19,405,680	2,014,170	-647,112	16,744,398	4,483,503	4,074,097	19,358	1,307,069	683,945
1993	26,422,766	20,052,448	19,104	20,071,552	2,088,595	-639,201	17,343,756	4,624,312	4,454,698	20,089	1,315,265	695,199
1994	27,922,811	21,172,538	14,246	21,186,784	2,243,430	-664,756	18,278,598	4,773,581	4,870,632	21,099	1,323,418	705,084
1995	29,487,214	22,293,618	15,692	22,309,310	2,357,522	-705,890	19,245,898	5,294,513	4,946,803	22,168	1,330,188	724,157
1996	30,461,203	22,974,303	13,828	22,988,131	2,427,218	-725,063	19,835,850	5,592,430	5,032,923	22,884	1,331,131	732,972
1997	32,129,269	24,329,973	15,079	24,345,052	2,564,260	-766,006	21,014,786	6,000,616	5,113,867	24,093	1,333,525	747,596
1998	33,741,818	25,711,172	16,509	25,727,681	2,723,496	-802,998	22,201,187	6,415,530	5,125,101	25,265	1,335,520	756,651
1999	34,531,458	26,588,208	17,049	26,605,257	2,776,012	-780,058	23,049,187	6,245,344	5,236,927	25,801	1,338,370	760,569
2000	36,540,378	27,958,350	15,318	27,973,668	2,840,824	-785,920	24,346,924	6,824,730	5,368,724	27,284	1,339,280	770,060
2001	39,050,785	30,083,144	15,637	30,098,781	2,979,655	-843,767	26,275,359	6,683,357	6,092,069	29,044	1,344,528	775,759
2002	40,239,993	31,238,515	14,848	31,253,363	3,078,836	-898,749	27,275,778	6,602,757	6,361,458	29,705	1,354,638	774,909
2003	41,400,068	32,358,859	16,072	32,374,931	3,169,408	-948,118	28,257,405	6,835,839	6,306,824	30,326	1,365,146	779,325
2004	42,255,476	32,626,848	16,519	32,643,367	3,241,327	-1,051,758	28,350,282	7,025,868	6,879,326	30,671	1,377,699	783,035
2005	44,078,627	32,349,981	17,098	32,367,079	3,140,974	-1,012,713	28,213,392	7,246,823	8,618,412	31,793	1,386,429	699,855
2006	42,717,337	32,418,464	36,775	32,455,239	3,130,020	-1,664,615	27,660,604	8,968,878	6,087,855	41,067	1,040,195	648,243
2007	49,282,715	34,213,305	21,606	34,234,911	3,344,570	-1,839,599	29,050,742	14,015,493	6,216,480	44,951	1,096,365	691,840
2008	50,936,558	37,204,815	27,333	37,232,148	3,556,440	-2,015,445	31,660,263	12,030,323	7,245,972	44,845	1,135,831	715,249
2009	48,762,403	36,229,532	28,524	36,258,056	3,558,117	-1,495,895	31,204,044	9,775,171	7,783,188	41,754	1,167,842	715,352
2010	51,602,238	38,433,218	36,758	38,469,976	3,694,010	-1,615,520	33,160,446	9,741,671	8,700,121	43,168	1,195,368	725,378
2011	52,189,967	38,733,342	37,012	38,770,354	3,385,702	-1,808,049	33,576,603	9,761,898	8,851,466	42,983	1,214,209	730,928
2012	55,879,924	39,999,775	31,002	40,030,777	3,449,396	-1,516,462	35,064,919	11,799,072	9,015,933	45,532	1,227,264	745,943
2013	56,255,686	40,586,559	29,590	40,616,149	3,982,190	-1,244,634	35,389,325	11,489,737	9,376,624	45,364	1,240,094	762,258
2014	59,665,082	43,698,258	15,268	43,713,526	4,162,651	-1,255,976	38,294,899	11,974,265	9,395,918	47,770	1,248,997	776,588
2015	61,018,970	43,814,170	17,845	43,832,015	4,327,420	-1,140,814	38,363,781	12,219,360	10,435,829	48,415	1,260,322	791,515
2016	61,211,088	43,213,358	7,521	43,220,879	4,379,431	-1,071,681	37,769,767	12,364,935	11,076,386	48,285	1,267,717	797,211
2017	63,670,120	44,721,729	7,411	44,729,140	4,502,226	-1,012,475	39,214,439	12,896,678	11,559,003	50,119	1,270,372	798,025
2018	66,875,353	47,154,692	4,507	47,159,199	4,709,116	-815,707	41,634,376	13,176,078	12,064,899	52,630	1,270,659	809,661
2019	70,052,730	49,080,639	12,199	49,092,838	4,854,455	-1,030,797	43,207,586	14,151,888	12,693,256	55,050	1,272,533	813,999
2020	73,086,513	47,364,966	11,672	47,376,638	4,844,142	-930,586	41,601,910	14,171,490	17,313,113	57,532	1,270,366	761,736
2021	77,377,871	49,868,241	6,784	49,875,025	5,040,393	-1,042,116	43,792,516	14,606,546	18,978,809	61,327	1,261,726	775,863

Personal Income and Employment by Area: New York-Newark-Jersey City, NY-NJ-PA

(Thousands of dollars, except as noted.)

Year	Personal income, total	Earnings by place of work			Less: Contributions for government social insurance	Plus: Adjustment for residence	Equals: Net earnings by place of residence	Plus: Dividends, interest, and rent	Plus: Personal current transfer receipts	Per capita personal income (dollars)	Population (persons)	Total employment
		Nonfarm	Farm	Total								
1970	90,396,327	90,340,705	55,622	73,488,033	5,439,016	-1,021,953	67,027,064	15,042,767	8,326,496	5,290	17,089,280	8,073,922
1971	96,410,189	96,358,821	51,368	77,548,455	5,921,565	-1,137,523	70,489,367	15,854,269	10,066,553	5,617	17,162,560	7,922,322
1972	103,427,115	103,382,954	44,161	83,459,004	6,692,402	-1,346,955	75,419,647	16,706,039	11,301,429	6,039	17,125,818	7,943,751
1973	110,001,431	109,933,449	67,982	89,161,002	8,282,485	-1,555,808	79,322,709	18,149,572	12,529,150	6,480	16,974,851	8,045,221
1974	118,338,536	118,266,144	72,392	94,284,596	9,026,239	-1,764,662	83,493,695	20,294,458	14,550,383	7,020	16,857,193	7,950,778
1975	127,505,633	127,445,152	60,481	99,151,203	9,286,653	-2,019,246	87,845,304	21,405,185	18,255,144	7,599	16,778,386	7,718,680
1976	135,572,917	135,514,037	58,880	105,814,046	10,084,830	-2,291,086	93,438,130	22,595,218	19,539,569	8,112	16,712,756	7,696,630
1977	146,764,176	146,692,379	71,797	115,092,008	10,869,973	-2,664,934	101,557,101	24,774,428	20,432,647	8,850	16,584,115	7,778,853
1978	160,679,003	160,592,836	86,167	127,330,660	12,303,380	-3,054,267	111,973,013	27,284,928	21,421,062	9,757	16,468,444	7,991,342
1979	175,867,875	175,773,380	94,495	140,047,685	14,032,271	-3,513,876	122,501,538	30,387,610	22,978,727	10,724	16,400,125	8,177,740
1980	196,782,794	196,668,273	114,521	154,018,033	15,480,830	-4,025,024	134,512,179	36,085,460	26,185,155	12,015	16,377,893	8,250,921
1981	220,230,388	220,102,393	127,995	169,273,836	18,179,113	-4,312,846	146,781,877	43,930,884	29,517,627	13,426	16,403,191	8,336,160
1982	239,087,400	238,958,562	128,838	182,138,826	19,905,658	-4,729,503	157,503,665	49,587,444	31,996,291	14,544	16,439,430	8,370,456
1983	258,892,128	258,756,651	135,477	198,279,909	21,808,259	-5,088,414	171,383,236	52,870,737	34,638,155	15,629	16,564,621	8,492,281
1984	286,792,373	286,639,841	152,532	218,857,702	24,806,010	-5,574,227	188,477,465	61,654,128	36,660,780	17,216	16,658,685	8,785,468
1985	307,455,061	307,300,289	154,772	237,240,394	27,207,944	-6,105,132	203,927,318	64,810,866	38,716,877	18,376	16,730,929	8,994,880
1986	329,302,718	329,145,209	157,509	257,707,513	29,941,921	-6,338,617	221,426,975	66,977,068	40,898,675	19,590	16,810,158	9,183,635
1987	354,272,209	354,087,459	184,750	282,391,802	32,261,772	-6,817,359	243,312,671	68,855,640	42,103,898	21,015	16,858,269	9,264,870
1988	391,092,698	390,908,105	184,593	312,683,187	35,900,009	-7,473,120	269,310,058	77,017,624	44,765,016	23,146	16,896,865	9,423,421
1989	420,552,012	420,376,837	175,175	328,755,966	37,268,626	-7,664,727	283,822,613	87,659,722	49,069,677	24,914	16,880,387	9,446,416
1990	449,446,258	449,281,467	164,791	348,924,459	37,600,715	-7,607,723	303,716,021	91,663,464	54,066,773	26,612	16,888,902	9,344,755
1991	448,688,350	448,546,521	141,829	342,787,208	38,386,930	-7,747,481	296,652,797	91,206,963	60,828,590	26,426	16,979,004	9,029,995
1992	477,406,170	477,260,006	146,164	367,737,037	40,355,169	-9,414,298	317,967,570	90,867,626	68,570,974	27,894	17,114,713	8,955,065
1993	492,838,676	492,690,346	148,330	378,821,666	41,431,938	-9,285,921	328,103,807	91,929,579	72,805,290	28,532	17,273,224	8,981,162
1994	509,563,177	509,419,840	143,337	390,430,947	43,437,061	-9,389,853	337,604,033	96,391,419	75,567,725	29,273	17,407,324	8,987,008
1995	541,587,941	541,443,782	144,159	411,458,090	45,240,843	-10,585,115	355,632,132	105,210,376	80,745,433	30,869	17,544,499	9,117,756
1996	574,778,359	574,634,949	143,410	437,597,532	47,073,060	-12,098,296	378,426,176	112,332,828	84,019,355	32,507	17,681,708	9,249,305
1997	611,686,455	611,559,919	126,536	469,440,839	49,278,444	-12,652,655	407,509,740	119,983,271	84,193,444	34,296	17,835,528	9,400,699
1998	652,041,483	503,497,594	151,684	503,649,278	52,101,921	-14,956,723	436,590,634	128,123,495	87,327,354	36,209	18,007,924	9,607,048
1999	690,734,663	540,521,144	153,448	540,674,592	54,860,805	-14,900,907	470,912,880	129,369,084	90,452,699	37,968	18,192,429	9,842,948
2000	753,372,850	592,734,249	191,148	592,925,397	59,450,226	-16,700,995	516,774,176	141,221,943	95,376,731	41,042	18,356,204	10,175,147
2001	782,362,499	619,780,455	166,952	619,947,407	61,773,537	-17,299,870	540,874,000	138,835,986	102,652,513	42,343	18,476,764	10,250,875
2002	779,525,792	618,373,090	191,528	618,564,618	62,592,980	-17,544,438	538,427,200	129,480,986	111,617,606	42,013	18,554,586	10,187,653
2003	788,604,678	623,531,839	195,409	623,727,248	64,018,552	-18,198,133	541,510,563	131,433,923	115,660,192	42,401	18,598,803	10,217,610
2004	824,893,750	650,776,211	195,131	650,971,342	67,179,410	-20,435,820	563,356,112	138,168,076	123,369,562	44,354	18,597,871	10,371,671
2005	859,808,462	673,444,362	196,409	673,640,771	70,323,124	-22,422,383	580,895,264	156,208,352	122,704,846	46,304	18,568,830	10,533,708
2006	932,088,454	719,476,400	216,700	719,693,100	74,166,717	-25,146,205	620,380,178	181,492,575	130,215,701	50,278	18,538,752	10,720,893
2007	1,005,066,187	769,974,801	213,432	770,188,233	79,135,159	-29,078,877	661,974,197	207,122,577	135,969,413	54,116	18,572,325	11,017,676
2008	1,019,897,481	774,763,603	292,993	775,056,596	81,671,048	-29,714,571	663,670,977	207,327,742	148,898,762	54,621	18,672,355	11,117,086
2009	987,780,567	749,374,948	304,726	749,679,674	78,915,782	-24,002,702	646,761,190	177,464,564	163,554,813	52,541	18,800,157	10,893,447
2010	1,028,238,964	784,018,223	280,972	784,299,195	80,697,953	-25,883,751	677,717,491	176,271,961	174,249,512	54,337	18,923,437	10,924,348
2011	1,085,067,799	815,197,544	250,063	815,447,607	74,269,556	-26,940,069	714,237,982	194,036,897	176,792,920	56,950	19,053,124	11,240,143
2012	1,141,789,621	854,134,773	299,798	854,434,571	76,223,064	-28,610,839	749,600,668	217,712,992	174,475,961	59,622	19,150,453	11,396,724
2013	1,156,892,804	879,062,167	280,687	879,342,854	89,884,962	-27,451,751	762,006,141	219,372,405	175,514,258	60,169	19,227,457	11,634,909
2014	1,211,973,045	916,064,276	211,723	916,275,999	94,547,821	-28,916,411	792,811,767	239,318,742	179,842,536	61,547	19,691,851	11,919,980
2015	1,266,963,636	950,388,977	218,323	950,607,300	98,651,932	-29,701,532	822,253,836	256,214,953	188,494,847	63,890	19,830,288	12,210,602
2016	1,314,901,920	982,184,928	197,071	982,381,999	100,936,970	-29,233,429	852,211,600	268,276,938	194,413,382	65,932	19,943,198	12,417,904
2017	1,392,792,185	1,038,546,867	197,052	1,038,743,919	106,754,644	-32,407,918	899,581,357	285,921,643	207,289,185	69,536	20,029,850	12,579,049
2018	1,446,753,539	1,091,278,100	174,077	1,091,452,177	110,842,016	-35,155,350	945,454,811	297,455,464	203,843,264	72,008	20,091,554	12,888,517
2019	1,509,184,339	1,128,979,374	252,243	1,129,231,617	115,643,316	-39,563,649	974,024,652	317,803,192	217,356,495	74,968	20,131,062	12,996,812
2020	1,582,130,942	1,117,606,791	216,304	1,117,823,095	114,012,530	-38,573,118	965,237,447	314,249,722	302,643,773	78,727	20,096,413	12,168,582
2021	1,683,010,967	1,208,402,032	205,039	1,208,607,071	122,208,452	-45,372,573	1,041,026,046	322,481,865	319,503,056	85,136	19,768,458	12,554,161

Personal Income and Employment by Area: Niles, MI

(Thousands of dollars, except as noted.)

		Derivation of personal income										
		Earnings by place of work			Less: Contributions for government social insurance	Plus: Adjustment for residence	Equals: Net earnings by place of residence	Plus: Dividends, interest, and rent	Plus: Personal current transfer receipts	Per capita personal income (dollars)	Population (persons)	Total employment
Year	Personal income, total	Nonfarm	Farm	Total								
1970	666,696	546,019	13,052	559,071	39,687	-10,848	508,536	93,336	64,824	4,066	163,981	74,168
1971	717,542	586,702	12,290	598,992	43,922	-12,948	542,122	98,540	76,880	4,343	165,230	73,938
1972	808,588	679,053	11,695	690,748	53,707	-17,187	619,854	105,678	83,056	4,810	168,102	78,406
1973	895,502	754,205	15,564	769,769	69,060	-17,940	682,769	116,362	96,371	5,248	170,653	81,115
1974	974,624	796,330	22,494	818,824	75,629	-18,182	725,013	132,310	117,301	5,666	172,002	80,618
1975	1,031,937	804,883	15,667	820,550	74,539	-15,095	730,916	143,838	157,183	5,951	173,395	76,020
1976	1,102,463	859,801	13,170	872,971	80,940	-9,851	782,180	153,215	167,068	6,304	174,881	77,131
1977	1,228,915	973,031	20,099	993,130	91,954	-12,492	888,684	170,555	169,676	7,028	174,870	80,061
1978	1,344,483	1,062,997	22,766	1,085,763	103,327	-8,030	974,406	186,530	183,547	7,752	173,427	81,369
1979	1,434,755	1,121,221	10,930	1,132,151	113,332	-3,241	1,015,578	207,295	211,882	8,263	173,635	80,344
1980	1,525,164	1,127,396	10,910	1,138,306	113,486	-540	1,024,280	246,919	253,965	8,904	171,288	75,636
1981	1,659,127	1,191,069	14,545	1,205,614	129,067	574	1,077,121	299,537	282,469	9,705	170,961	73,651
1982	1,725,497	1,189,713	16,173	1,205,886	130,946	2,382	1,077,322	340,255	307,920	10,342	166,840	70,908
1983	1,789,859	1,232,584	10,889	1,243,473	137,640	5,089	1,110,922	352,433	326,504	10,892	164,326	70,184
1984	1,934,226	1,342,440	15,670	1,358,110	155,332	8,530	1,211,308	393,883	329,035	11,844	163,308	71,984
1985	2,036,097	1,415,625	24,911	1,440,536	165,932	8,940	1,283,544	408,086	344,467	12,496	162,945	73,946
1986	2,158,762	1,536,716	16,730	1,553,446	180,070	4,415	1,377,791	419,981	360,990	13,292	162,415	75,938
1987	2,309,300	1,666,538	28,463	1,695,001	191,830	5,731	1,508,902	428,538	371,860	14,170	162,973	78,673
1988	2,429,013	1,754,125	20,933	1,775,058	208,736	13,657	1,579,979	462,170	386,864	14,902	163,001	80,352
1989	2,592,513	1,845,320	30,772	1,876,092	218,200	14,224	1,672,116	511,803	408,594	15,989	162,143	81,954
1990	2,678,822	1,923,656	18,952	1,942,608	231,038	13,325	1,724,895	511,466	442,461	16,596	161,415	82,670
1991	2,756,531	1,962,365	22,914	1,985,279	238,957	16,890	1,763,212	505,325	487,994	17,055	161,622	81,364
1992	2,961,887	2,120,627	24,690	2,145,317	255,654	18,768	1,908,431	532,796	520,660	18,285	161,982	81,260
1993	3,139,298	2,284,249	19,862	2,304,111	278,217	19,983	2,045,877	537,014	556,407	19,347	162,266	81,681
1994	3,317,067	2,402,562	20,202	2,422,764	300,932	25,096	2,146,928	610,879	559,260	20,431	162,353	85,310
1995	3,490,921	2,516,923	22,834	2,539,757	314,856	34,909	2,259,810	655,828	575,283	21,414	163,022	88,048
1996	3,606,947	2,578,165	19,748	2,597,913	316,430	42,537	2,324,020	688,492	594,435	22,146	162,873	88,373
1997	3,840,424	2,734,934	24,180	2,759,114	334,147	42,472	2,467,439	727,772	645,213	23,647	162,407	88,512
1998	3,974,373	2,845,060	24,055	2,869,115	340,598	61,709	2,590,226	749,954	634,193	24,526	162,046	90,479
1999	4,195,088	3,063,067	29,509	3,092,576	360,311	63,699	2,795,964	711,413	687,711	25,891	162,028	89,527
2000	4,388,398	3,195,502	25,938	3,221,440	370,470	73,171	2,924,141	751,476	712,781	27,010	162,471	90,418
2001	4,546,335	3,218,339	33,411	3,251,750	355,894	91,834	2,987,690	750,175	808,470	28,211	161,153	87,082
2002	4,580,264	3,304,278	26,109	3,330,387	364,947	78,828	3,044,268	712,013	823,983	28,519	160,604	85,403
2003	4,677,911	3,297,676	34,574	3,332,250	365,744	97,937	3,064,443	746,321	867,147	29,180	160,314	84,103
2004	4,877,281	3,444,498	47,016	3,491,514	383,639	104,581	3,212,456	769,220	895,605	30,532	159,742	84,376
2005	4,895,862	3,428,495	39,220	3,467,715	394,397	111,771	3,185,089	769,011	941,762	30,887	158,510	84,908
2006	5,148,999	3,539,616	48,234	3,587,850	409,497	159,486	3,337,839	803,477	1,007,683	32,684	157,537	84,495
2007	5,407,036	3,665,644	59,075	3,724,719	428,288	137,878	3,434,309	878,607	1,094,120	34,357	157,378	86,793
2008	5,686,896	3,656,805	46,475	3,703,280	437,410	178,727	3,444,597	1,004,384	1,237,915	36,135	157,380	85,422
2009	5,415,350	3,483,369	36,397	3,519,766	418,191	98,683	3,200,258	873,012	1,342,080	34,480	157,059	80,366
2010	5,705,942	3,651,816	45,704	3,697,520	427,925	101,984	3,371,579	899,610	1,434,753	36,404	156,740	80,301
2011	5,928,587	3,603,676	69,657	3,673,333	382,846	135,204	3,425,691	1,073,713	1,429,183	37,783	156,911	80,616
2012	5,934,610	3,624,587	56,371	3,680,958	387,452	200,169	3,493,675	1,020,247	1,420,688	37,880	156,669	80,626
2013	6,031,149	3,809,063	64,317	3,873,380	457,248	147,037	3,563,169	1,033,916	1,434,064	38,610	156,205	80,941
2014	6,278,993	3,925,962	41,685	3,967,647	474,813	174,383	3,667,217	1,124,539	1,487,237	40,112	156,538	82,471
2015	6,640,936	4,112,176	45,072	4,157,248	493,054	139,694	3,803,888	1,268,474	1,568,574	42,650	155,706	83,445
2016	6,837,084	4,179,426	56,307	4,235,733	504,694	231,293	3,962,332	1,264,201	1,610,551	44,074	155,129	82,720
2017	6,993,480	4,327,583	55,448	4,383,031	520,818	220,302	4,082,515	1,323,358	1,587,607	45,105	155,050	83,565
2018	7,307,596	4,430,905	44,212	4,475,117	540,182	324,607	4,259,542	1,389,036	1,659,018	47,212	154,784	83,447
2019	7,676,620	4,487,879	50,113	4,537,992	546,725	449,392	4,440,659	1,483,547	1,752,414	49,735	154,349	82,754
2020	8,367,859	4,533,772	80,570	4,614,342	551,468	483,445	4,546,319	1,476,951	2,344,589	54,303	154,095	77,692
2021	9,133,397	4,753,859	73,357	4,827,216	568,740	851,743	5,110,219	1,506,055	2,517,123	59,656	153,101	79,502

Personal Income and Employment by Area: North Port-Sarasota-Bradenton, FL

(Thousands of dollars, except as noted.)

Year	Personal income, total	Earnings by place of work			Less: Contributions for government social insurance	Plus: Adjustment for residence	Equals: Net earnings by place of residence	Plus: Dividends, interest, and rent	Plus: Personal current transfer receipts	Per capita personal income (dollars)	Population (persons)	Total employment
		Nonfarm	Farm	Total								
1970	980,330	504,474	18,012	522,486	33,169	-5,753	483,564	363,853	132,913	4,457	219,936	86,898
1971	1,112,894	566,278	21,641	587,919	38,956	-5,054	543,909	407,924	161,061	4,786	232,523	91,869
1972	1,283,455	666,653	25,314	691,967	48,314	-4,779	638,874	454,839	189,742	5,245	244,710	99,827
1973	1,532,026	813,255	27,042	840,297	67,612	-7,418	765,267	533,683	233,076	5,787	264,738	113,242
1974	1,747,243	902,560	28,319	930,879	79,394	-8,017	843,468	628,415	275,360	6,192	282,181	117,686
1975	1,907,301	924,571	30,883	955,454	79,931	-6,189	869,334	690,820	347,147	6,602	288,894	114,242
1976	2,152,544	1,047,108	33,441	1,080,549	89,893	-5,415	985,241	784,879	382,424	7,256	296,666	119,612
1977	2,489,070	1,214,865	32,209	1,247,074	105,433	-6,511	1,135,130	926,606	427,334	8,116	306,701	130,788
1978	2,950,698	1,466,006	37,440	1,503,446	130,343	-8,201	1,364,902	1,103,473	482,323	9,161	322,092	144,674
1979	3,450,344	1,690,972	51,405	1,742,377	157,614	-11,360	1,573,403	1,311,766	565,175	10,190	338,608	153,849
1980	4,137,609	1,916,918	71,451	1,988,369	180,928	-12,157	1,795,284	1,666,869	675,456	11,664	354,724	160,146
1981	4,935,749	2,152,201	62,577	2,214,778	218,919	8,750	2,004,609	2,134,104	797,036	13,334	370,172	166,835
1982	5,291,219	2,263,193	91,159	2,354,352	241,096	28,554	2,141,810	2,241,201	908,208	13,753	384,723	172,913
1983	5,970,132	2,567,549	140,496	2,708,045	272,030	53,104	2,489,119	2,482,003	999,010	14,942	399,556	183,463
1984	6,696,326	2,927,954	94,846	3,022,800	319,317	85,995	2,789,478	2,848,549	1,058,299	16,191	413,582	196,895
1985	7,368,070	3,167,307	94,367	3,261,674	353,652	126,462	3,034,484	3,178,932	1,154,654	17,270	426,636	204,184
1986	8,018,025	3,455,183	102,700	3,557,883	396,180	171,110	3,332,813	3,430,705	1,254,507	18,283	438,539	213,336
1987	8,724,069	3,904,690	111,600	4,016,290	441,934	221,358	3,795,714	3,587,610	1,340,745	19,376	450,241	215,825
1988	9,579,370	4,250,039	129,257	4,379,296	499,472	285,029	4,164,853	3,944,639	1,469,878	20,697	462,830	227,771
1989	11,182,418	4,620,544	127,372	4,747,916	554,788	348,031	4,541,159	5,036,045	1,605,214	23,481	476,235	237,209
1990	11,916,349	5,020,773	100,338	5,121,111	589,888	408,588	4,939,811	5,237,795	1,738,743	24,156	493,311	246,876
1991	12,152,170	5,334,006	120,688	5,454,694	630,499	337,313	5,161,508	5,097,744	1,892,918	24,059	505,103	251,512
1992	12,898,651	5,820,568	136,436	5,957,004	680,413	381,087	5,657,678	5,141,488	2,099,485	25,232	511,201	257,502
1993	13,435,528	6,273,631	139,204	6,412,835	728,539	295,151	5,979,447	5,226,947	2,229,134	25,793	520,892	269,675
1994	14,401,508	6,790,615	117,265	6,907,880	802,290	285,672	6,391,262	5,632,936	2,377,310	27,058	532,241	286,866
1995	15,347,839	7,581,935	117,902	7,699,837	892,232	122,623	6,930,228	5,890,843	2,526,768	28,330	541,758	309,665
1996	16,304,836	7,767,724	107,746	7,875,470	898,128	410,581	7,387,923	6,253,832	2,663,081	29,591	551,004	304,542
1997	17,386,400	8,308,507	132,073	8,440,580	962,960	450,745	7,928,365	6,698,474	2,759,561	30,975	561,309	317,015
1998	19,014,481	8,954,953	158,915	9,113,868	1,025,255	652,933	8,741,516	7,407,948	2,865,017	33,184	573,004	321,983
1999	19,841,616	9,631,197	159,969	9,791,166	1,085,400	880,898	9,586,664	7,292,652	2,962,300	34,098	581,892	329,161
2000	21,512,025	10,627,431	163,214	10,790,645	1,180,689	700,840	10,310,796	8,080,773	3,120,456	36,288	592,809	353,692
2001	21,541,911	10,391,700	169,717	10,561,417	1,184,832	709,952	10,086,537	8,097,920	3,357,454	35,548	605,988	324,277
2002	22,192,904	11,426,412	178,801	11,605,213	1,292,899	589,354	10,901,668	7,726,842	3,564,394	35,764	620,540	343,092
2003	23,327,362	12,194,551	162,456	12,357,007	1,359,226	516,247	11,514,028	8,064,178	3,749,156	36,744	634,862	348,500
2004	25,963,602	13,755,348	166,924	13,922,272	1,527,604	499,843	12,894,511	9,085,865	3,983,226	39,704	653,934	367,129
2005	28,713,280	15,342,949	216,194	15,559,143	1,711,537	378,323	14,225,929	10,231,999	4,255,352	42,554	674,757	387,813
2006	31,116,013	16,370,758	203,900	16,574,658	1,857,585	313,859	15,030,932	11,485,440	4,599,641	45,416	685,132	399,382
2007	31,701,108	15,736,378	187,784	15,924,162	1,843,734	295,068	14,375,496	12,424,462	4,901,150	45,828	691,735	397,906
2008	30,869,625	14,258,217	162,607	14,420,824	1,738,466	343,830	13,026,188	12,326,613	5,516,824	44,356	695,944	372,080
2009	28,375,875	13,142,110	169,870	13,311,980	1,659,161	376,040	12,028,859	10,312,717	6,034,299	40,655	697,973	355,547
2010	29,804,332	13,396,399	174,680	13,571,079	1,651,603	472,362	12,391,838	10,941,017	6,471,477	42,373	703,384	346,051
2011	31,653,664	13,861,001	139,498	14,000,499	1,533,793	547,095	13,013,801	11,926,529	6,713,334	44,588	709,917	352,488
2012	32,414,837	14,156,361	153,986	14,310,347	1,590,327	565,985	13,286,005	12,367,589	6,761,243	44,986	720,550	361,757
2013	33,427,224	14,849,782	165,705	15,015,487	1,866,695	576,485	13,725,277	12,680,170	7,021,777	45,655	732,177	375,452
2014	36,839,064	16,217,558	148,425	16,365,983	2,004,577	576,528	14,937,934	14,459,397	7,441,733	49,686	741,432	394,090
2015	39,979,733	17,771,334	175,221	17,946,555	2,152,859	592,786	16,386,482	15,646,831	7,946,420	52,609	759,948	411,471
2016	41,741,705	18,706,578	154,858	18,861,436	2,256,116	585,793	17,191,113	16,200,613	8,349,979	53,571	779,181	419,612
2017	44,920,569	19,816,162	170,138	19,986,300	2,387,339	655,382	18,254,343	17,876,913	8,789,313	56,576	793,984	434,300
2018	47,674,714	21,228,392	147,103	21,375,495	2,584,572	609,240	19,400,163	18,973,546	9,301,005	59,036	807,547	449,982
2019	52,060,220	22,265,104	149,453	22,414,557	2,764,682	624,566	20,274,441	21,716,850	10,068,929	63,279	822,713	456,400
2020	55,005,481	22,878,981	121,864	23,000,845	2,865,681	696,550	20,831,714	21,968,227	12,205,540	65,709	837,107	457,729
2021	59,646,775	25,518,268	100,438	25,618,706	3,127,536	718,094	23,209,264	22,854,818	13,582,693	69,376	859,760	478,112

Personal Income and Employment by Area: Norwich-New London, CT

(Thousands of dollars, except as noted.)

Year	Personal income, total	Earnings by place of work			Less: Contributions for government social insurance	Plus: Adjustment for residence	Equals: Net earnings by place of residence	Plus: Dividends, interest, and rent	Plus: Personal current transfer receipts	Per capita personal income (dollars)	Population (persons)	Total employment
		Nonfarm	Farm	Total								
1970	1,008,957	824,578	8,094	832,672	52,910	-39,085	740,677	196,971	71,309	4,360	231,405	102,499
1971	1,089,406	889,425	8,046	897,471	60,164	-44,709	792,598	211,530	85,278	4,656	233,975	103,331
1972	1,198,510	975,833	8,926	984,759	69,019	-48,262	867,478	235,528	95,504	5,018	238,857	104,979
1973	1,323,721	1,094,458	11,330	1,105,788	86,485	-57,752	961,551	257,823	104,347	5,559	238,138	109,925
1974	1,476,722	1,237,671	6,002	1,243,673	102,790	-73,596	1,067,287	286,834	122,601	6,195	238,362	115,819
1975	1,577,780	1,272,595	10,476	1,283,071	105,536	-71,607	1,105,928	312,521	159,331	6,530	241,627	112,930
1976	1,709,395	1,394,392	11,625	1,406,017	118,516	-77,840	1,209,661	326,218	173,516	7,065	241,968	116,012
1977	1,896,632	1,569,033	13,141	1,582,174	138,790	-91,808	1,351,576	362,075	182,981	7,861	241,265	122,050
1978	2,049,957	1,656,323	8,360	1,664,683	147,775	-81,593	1,435,315	415,903	198,739	8,445	242,732	121,499
1979	2,260,639	1,826,902	9,990	1,836,892	168,617	-83,669	1,584,606	460,340	215,693	9,388	240,812	123,476
1980	2,566,067	2,032,729	11,647	2,044,376	183,291	-90,734	1,770,351	547,964	247,752	10,726	239,228	126,114
1981	2,926,267	2,309,541	18,060	2,327,601	223,217	-115,386	1,988,998	651,469	285,800	12,093	241,985	129,103
1982	3,212,936	2,549,499	22,255	2,571,754	251,097	-141,363	2,179,294	719,228	314,414	13,219	243,051	131,160
1983	3,530,809	2,856,192	24,081	2,880,273	288,556	-163,766	2,427,951	764,395	338,463	14,306	246,802	135,782
1984	3,922,341	3,145,076	38,287	3,183,363	326,082	-166,590	2,690,691	870,807	360,843	15,753	248,990	140,610
1985	4,157,101	3,332,122	37,036	3,369,158	348,267	-155,280	2,865,611	906,252	385,238	16,749	248,201	143,521
1986	4,304,251	3,353,329	38,619	3,391,948	346,231	-110,581	2,935,136	958,571	410,544	17,302	248,765	144,825
1987	4,655,438	3,636,935	43,265	3,680,200	372,044	-92,885	3,215,271	1,014,594	425,573	18,581	250,549	149,270
1988	4,944,654	3,860,267	38,843	3,899,110	407,836	-77,896	3,413,378	1,072,245	459,031	19,552	252,893	151,325
1989	5,375,950	4,107,397	36,125	4,143,522	433,533	-86,475	3,623,514	1,235,481	516,955	21,181	253,805	152,415
1990	5,597,212	4,123,638	44,215	4,167,853	433,970	52,655	3,786,538	1,229,126	581,548	21,909	255,474	149,439
1991	5,689,125	4,242,618	40,538	4,283,156	454,987	10,904	3,839,073	1,196,133	653,919	22,244	255,761	143,950
1992	6,036,794	4,411,978	42,499	4,454,477	470,077	83,420	4,067,820	1,200,577	768,397	23,926	252,306	141,923
1993	6,266,538	4,614,692	54,397	4,669,089	491,002	28,971	4,207,058	1,253,977	805,503	24,682	253,886	143,783
1994	6,585,322	5,002,731	48,516	5,051,247	542,941	-77,498	4,430,808	1,326,630	827,884	25,762	255,618	145,989
1995	6,881,678	5,321,951	34,773	5,356,724	581,631	-195,648	4,579,445	1,415,788	886,445	26,691	257,828	151,338
1996	7,127,062	5,534,907	37,243	5,572,150	604,401	-236,645	4,731,104	1,478,557	917,401	27,545	258,741	153,594
1997	7,571,275	5,964,492	35,484	5,999,976	636,423	-277,513	5,086,040	1,538,945	946,290	29,271	258,662	157,056
1998	7,996,758	6,219,907	37,409	6,257,316	649,285	-199,519	5,408,512	1,611,941	976,305	31,161	256,626	157,246
1999	8,344,645	6,587,785	38,018	6,625,803	664,632	-203,273	5,757,898	1,585,356	1,001,391	32,398	257,568	158,947
2000	8,814,683	6,884,984	41,753	6,926,737	682,769	-131,672	6,112,296	1,654,816	1,047,571	33,922	259,848	162,098
2001	9,199,661	7,194,670	45,596	7,240,266	704,213	-125,311	6,410,742	1,668,469	1,120,450	35,194	261,396	163,919
2002	9,492,956	7,528,663	51,616	7,580,279	760,615	-175,962	6,643,702	1,642,370	1,206,884	35,863	264,698	167,600
2003	9,922,029	7,885,662	48,376	7,934,038	786,535	-236,670	6,910,833	1,767,542	1,243,654	37,219	266,584	168,575
2004	10,602,761	8,479,603	46,252	8,525,855	831,955	-175,761	7,518,139	1,772,790	1,311,832	39,475	268,595	169,467
2005	10,926,310	8,802,997	41,486	8,844,483	858,496	-206,216	7,779,771	1,778,227	1,368,312	40,518	269,664	172,255
2006	11,460,195	9,080,418	38,138	9,118,556	882,400	-195,358	8,040,798	1,944,775	1,474,622	42,318	270,814	172,895
2007	12,123,111	9,309,821	42,884	9,352,705	908,889	-75,001	8,368,815	2,167,270	1,587,026	44,789	270,669	174,716
2008	12,589,353	9,508,526	54,051	9,562,577	942,977	-199,238	8,420,362	2,346,071	1,822,920	46,177	272,634	176,181
2009	12,462,184	9,453,576	53,552	9,507,128	941,026	-295,401	8,270,701	2,157,359	2,034,124	45,544	273,630	171,178
2010	12,596,581	9,522,294	46,920	9,569,214	936,267	-307,092	8,325,855	2,072,543	2,198,183	45,970	274,019	168,288
2011	13,050,716	9,593,739	45,294	9,639,033	858,369	-197,653	8,583,011	2,254,110	2,213,595	47,790	273,086	168,024
2012	13,352,322	9,591,433	62,626	9,654,059	871,161	-144,129	8,638,769	2,484,243	2,229,310	48,700	274,173	166,652
2013	13,285,151	9,561,018	71,623	9,632,641	987,752	21,597	8,666,486	2,352,016	2,266,649	48,647	273,093	165,954
2014	13,679,599	9,663,193	51,028	9,714,221	1,004,608	141,703	8,851,316	2,489,405	2,338,878	50,101	273,038	164,518
2015	14,299,759	9,902,659	71,574	9,974,233	1,029,777	260,848	9,205,304	2,666,042	2,428,413	52,651	271,593	164,722
2016	14,584,130	10,415,645	55,375	10,471,020	1,077,905	84,817	9,477,932	2,610,365	2,495,833	53,867	270,745	166,949
2017	14,860,769	10,696,916	63,887	10,760,803	1,122,594	53,355	9,691,564	2,633,901	2,535,304	54,986	270,266	168,382
2018	15,082,110	10,790,707	59,280	10,849,987	1,133,053	118,141	9,835,075	2,543,739	2,703,296	55,889	269,857	166,338
2019	15,692,023	10,803,644	62,132	10,865,776	1,159,185	344,530	10,051,121	2,825,833	2,815,069	58,362	268,874	163,548
2020	16,422,645	10,536,493	57,166	10,593,659	1,148,382	487,857	9,933,134	2,729,570	3,759,941	61,222	268,248	150,880
2021	17,170,447	11,321,178	50,595	11,371,773	1,207,852	261,475	10,425,396	2,768,161	3,976,890	63,877	268,805	156,348

Personal Income and Employment by Area: Ocala, FL

(Thousands of dollars, except as noted.)

Year	Personal income, total	Earnings by place of work			Less: Contributions for government social insurance	Plus: Adjustment for residence	Equals: Net earnings by place of residence	Plus: Dividends, interest, and rent	Plus: Personal current transfer receipts	Per capita personal income (dollars)	Population (persons)	Total employment
		Nonfarm	Farm	Total								
1970	228,020	151,527	10,838	162,365	9,942	5,163	157,586	43,619	26,815	3,243	70,320	28,119
1971	264,761	174,869	11,581	186,450	12,020	6,115	180,545	51,201	33,015	3,452	76,690	30,308
1972	314,537	208,462	13,638	222,100	15,029	8,338	215,409	59,517	39,611	3,880	81,072	32,968
1973	382,637	252,427	15,795	268,222	20,854	10,472	257,840	74,699	50,098	4,265	89,718	36,754
1974	424,854	271,214	9,833	281,047	23,546	11,828	269,329	90,753	64,772	4,361	97,426	37,392
1975	463,166	280,611	8,011	288,622	24,147	14,187	278,662	101,142	83,362	4,644	99,728	36,675
1976	514,585	308,808	6,790	315,598	27,176	16,915	305,337	110,296	98,952	4,889	105,252	37,671
1977	576,504	344,768	6,406	351,174	30,542	19,304	339,936	125,714	110,854	5,252	109,765	39,712
1978	668,831	401,363	6,772	408,135	36,357	21,981	393,759	150,969	124,103	5,938	112,629	43,276
1979	785,914	472,472	5,470	477,942	44,930	23,639	456,651	182,100	147,163	6,672	117,793	46,365
1980	958,921	547,299	9,789	557,088	52,422	27,503	532,169	244,884	181,868	7,720	124,218	50,295
1981	1,133,868	623,975	1,985	625,960	64,198	39,039	600,801	315,396	217,671	8,662	130,907	52,796
1982	1,277,019	676,871	14,606	691,477	71,612	50,664	670,529	352,289	254,201	9,295	137,381	54,974
1983	1,444,615	767,700	17,815	785,515	80,556	58,896	763,855	398,212	282,548	9,958	145,069	58,774
1984	1,640,913	886,544	20,324	906,868	95,426	72,250	883,692	457,569	299,652	10,830	151,521	63,433
1985	1,865,116	998,809	25,105	1,023,914	109,924	89,753	1,003,743	521,537	339,836	11,696	159,464	68,511
1986	2,080,906	1,122,175	30,358	1,152,533	126,021	102,930	1,129,442	573,041	378,423	12,448	167,170	73,388
1987	2,286,904	1,247,957	27,728	1,275,685	138,434	121,210	1,258,461	613,405	415,038	13,115	174,370	74,876
1988	2,536,349	1,373,285	33,223	1,406,508	157,498	144,799	1,393,809	677,810	464,730	14,069	180,277	77,900
1989	2,842,484	1,487,741	32,666	1,520,407	174,992	169,026	1,514,441	791,519	536,524	15,155	187,560	79,822
1990	3,089,135	1,584,235	33,303	1,617,538	184,262	199,936	1,633,212	851,576	604,347	15,673	197,095	81,784
1991	3,178,850	1,651,947	32,379	1,684,326	193,640	133,289	1,623,975	859,278	695,597	15,600	203,775	81,874
1992	3,408,460	1,771,490	45,330	1,816,820	207,277	139,488	1,749,031	864,420	795,009	16,278	209,388	82,420
1993	3,665,782	1,926,896	53,045	1,979,941	225,314	154,397	1,909,024	900,159	856,599	17,065	214,818	86,980
1994	3,959,387	2,068,885	54,190	2,123,075	245,865	182,789	2,059,999	966,263	933,125	17,714	223,523	89,626
1995	4,277,453	2,218,703	55,084	2,273,787	261,688	173,431	2,185,530	1,082,102	1,009,821	18,548	230,611	92,766
1996	4,617,111	2,429,561	55,140	2,484,701	280,098	156,461	2,361,064	1,180,440	1,075,607	19,511	236,637	98,351
1997	4,917,850	2,554,042	66,722	2,620,764	295,990	198,880	2,523,654	1,256,733	1,137,463	20,216	243,264	102,369
1998	5,348,755	2,771,134	63,007	2,834,141	317,260	245,523	2,762,404	1,369,831	1,216,520	21,388	250,086	107,202
1999	5,645,857	2,974,559	56,858	3,031,417	336,418	284,985	2,979,984	1,388,075	1,277,798	22,144	254,964	110,338
2000	6,072,681	3,110,302	32,989	3,143,291	350,230	387,444	3,180,505	1,529,675	1,362,501	23,337	260,221	113,425
2001	6,420,080	3,337,243	36,351	3,373,594	381,846	370,412	3,362,160	1,566,341	1,491,579	24,268	264,553	111,456
2002	6,587,318	3,552,051	37,325	3,589,376	403,859	345,995	3,531,512	1,450,749	1,605,057	24,243	271,716	114,392
2003	7,013,176	3,851,926	21,145	3,873,071	439,516	326,838	3,760,393	1,533,179	1,719,604	25,039	280,091	119,807
2004	7,639,698	4,139,888	23,586	4,163,474	483,475	324,793	4,004,792	1,739,589	1,895,317	26,238	291,164	126,037
2005	8,525,104	4,576,528	13,061	4,589,589	540,148	318,363	4,367,804	2,039,847	2,117,453	28,084	303,558	134,595
2006	9,454,229	5,044,239	17,654	5,061,893	614,820	287,005	4,734,078	2,389,806	2,330,345	29,889	316,310	143,125
2007	9,917,261	5,077,022	-17,309	5,059,713	627,976	266,575	4,698,312	2,701,767	2,517,182	30,455	325,634	145,863
2008	10,053,018	4,919,679	-41,146	4,878,533	624,601	219,969	4,473,901	2,730,614	2,848,503	30,459	330,052	140,813
2009	9,771,482	4,520,718	-39,506	4,481,212	594,417	236,945	4,123,740	2,513,210	3,134,532	29,532	330,880	131,466
2010	10,136,453	4,568,133	-21,974	4,546,159	594,042	250,310	4,202,427	2,557,427	3,376,599	30,592	331,341	128,566
2011	10,588,623	4,610,450	-59,778	4,550,672	548,945	265,191	4,266,918	2,819,503	3,502,202	31,862	332,325	129,797
2012	10,752,899	4,792,198	26,967	4,819,165	572,253	252,404	4,499,316	2,718,633	3,534,950	32,200	333,945	132,017
2013	10,618,959	4,892,614	1,572	4,894,186	653,461	250,041	4,490,766	2,505,864	3,622,329	31,680	335,196	134,612
2014	11,100,744	5,089,248	19,357	5,108,605	679,197	261,567	4,690,975	2,643,517	3,766,252	32,682	339,657	138,693
2015	11,556,877	5,308,283	22,601	5,330,884	702,304	285,892	4,914,472	2,711,381	3,931,024	33,571	344,255	141,993
2016	12,151,980	5,671,047	15,901	5,686,948	744,867	295,369	5,237,450	2,827,049	4,087,481	34,698	350,220	146,350
2017	12,877,190	5,831,866	29,580	5,861,446	772,238	341,930	5,431,138	3,121,737	4,324,315	36,109	356,623	150,202
2018	13,460,077	6,113,034	8,309	6,121,343	826,762	373,031	5,667,612	3,266,326	4,526,139	37,109	362,717	155,512
2019	14,468,661	6,419,091	6,174	6,425,265	886,697	406,603	5,945,171	3,689,450	4,834,040	39,153	369,537	157,613
2020	15,834,332	6,827,122	-2,966	6,824,156	935,957	423,811	6,312,010	3,732,399	5,789,923	41,960	377,370	162,245
2021	17,424,672	7,474,141	41,291	7,515,432	1,001,813	488,313	7,001,932	3,843,179	6,579,561	45,152	385,915	167,540

Personal Income and Employment by Area: Ocean City, NJ

(Thousands of dollars, except as noted.)

Year	Personal income, total	Earnings by place of work			Less: Contributions for government social insurance	Plus: Adjustment for residence	Equals: Net earnings by place of residence	Plus: Dividends, interest, and rent	Plus: Personal current transfer receipts	Per capita personal income (dollars)	Population (persons)	Total employment
		Nonfarm	Farm	Total								
1970	261,323	151,397	1,101	152,498	11,075	25,634	167,057	60,153	34,113	4,337	60,259	25,672
1971	292,415	168,190	962	169,152	12,787	26,784	183,149	67,702	41,564	4,606	63,485	26,985
1972	333,999	190,401	1,019	191,420	15,084	33,244	209,580	75,505	48,914	5,036	66,321	28,236
1973	393,430	227,699	1,460	229,159	20,299	39,212	248,072	87,912	57,446	5,769	68,194	30,935
1974	441,926	246,154	1,582	247,736	22,708	46,879	271,907	101,901	68,118	6,144	71,929	30,751
1975	503,624	270,699	1,387	272,086	24,926	55,495	302,655	113,843	87,126	6,804	74,014	31,385
1976	568,484	305,685	1,313	306,998	27,963	65,176	344,211	124,376	99,897	7,398	76,838	32,553
1977	631,487	338,815	883	339,698	31,255	75,048	383,491	140,519	107,477	8,070	78,248	34,569
1978	710,744	383,200	1,093	384,293	35,993	89,114	437,414	156,072	117,258	8,900	79,862	36,393
1979	790,161	413,999	981	414,980	40,783	111,040	485,237	173,819	131,105	9,669	81,725	37,189
1980	915,302	453,260	557	453,817	44,694	137,946	547,069	217,899	150,334	11,061	82,754	38,264
1981	1,037,390	485,257	1,037	486,294	51,461	167,294	602,127	264,065	171,198	12,270	84,550	39,013
1982	1,122,061	509,761	1,647	511,408	54,472	178,275	635,211	296,327	190,523	13,185	85,104	39,669
1983	1,215,357	565,725	2,287	568,012	62,140	191,757	697,629	311,838	205,890	14,187	85,665	42,138
1984	1,335,103	626,495	2,308	628,803	71,701	208,607	765,709	354,959	214,435	15,330	87,092	43,146
1985	1,438,733	689,826	2,381	692,207	79,433	222,972	835,746	382,978	220,009	16,230	88,647	43,532
1986	1,549,740	755,144	2,461	757,605	88,217	234,715	904,103	415,132	230,505	17,194	90,130	44,391
1987	1,655,731	826,555	1,996	828,551	97,329	250,322	981,544	434,631	239,556	17,990	92,038	44,431
1988	1,805,903	928,587	2,216	930,803	112,132	267,562	1,086,233	464,162	255,508	19,426	92,961	46,515
1989	1,943,603	980,201	2,274	982,475	118,262	279,156	1,143,369	525,925	274,309	20,496	94,830	47,087
1990	2,040,511	1,015,630	2,425	1,018,055	118,685	309,461	1,208,831	531,847	299,833	21,396	95,368	47,010
1991	2,090,885	1,031,464	2,088	1,033,552	123,706	313,807	1,223,653	519,378	347,854	21,554	97,006	46,586
1992	2,240,070	1,106,230	2,240	1,108,470	131,728	328,195	1,304,937	524,227	410,906	22,830	98,121	47,721
1993	2,346,534	1,147,829	2,833	1,150,662	135,222	358,326	1,373,766	536,709	436,059	23,822	98,504	47,462
1994	2,417,588	1,195,960	3,379	1,199,339	143,375	360,307	1,416,271	553,331	447,986	24,282	99,561	47,835
1995	2,553,398	1,243,912	2,923	1,246,835	148,403	376,241	1,474,673	599,263	479,462	25,431	100,405	48,319
1996	2,674,570	1,293,094	2,485	1,295,579	154,359	390,421	1,531,641	640,105	502,824	26,517	100,861	49,078
1997	2,888,597	1,397,775	2,297	1,400,072	160,756	441,200	1,680,516	685,952	522,129	28,493	101,380	50,322
1998	3,039,729	1,449,669	3,604	1,453,273	165,875	497,999	1,785,397	717,863	536,469	29,835	101,883	51,329
1999	3,155,176	1,548,811	4,309	1,553,120	173,335	510,252	1,890,037	712,057	553,082	30,892	102,135	52,030
2000	3,369,077	1,641,421	5,603	1,647,024	181,897	542,592	2,007,719	780,132	581,226	32,929	102,314	54,163
2001	3,602,102	1,825,266	5,651	1,830,917	198,948	539,637	2,171,606	800,796	629,700	35,307	102,023	55,135
2002	3,706,979	1,945,189	6,236	1,951,425	212,463	518,215	2,257,177	740,700	709,102	36,452	101,694	55,661
2003	3,746,781	2,062,560	6,032	2,068,592	222,014	484,429	2,331,007	730,707	685,067	36,838	101,710	56,471
2004	3,921,471	2,223,110	6,109	2,229,219	240,873	459,034	2,447,380	790,459	683,632	39,027	100,482	58,373
2005	4,017,420	2,354,232	6,379	2,360,611	264,609	417,028	2,513,030	774,700	729,690	40,470	99,269	60,454
2006	4,110,084	2,382,678	7,135	2,389,813	270,288	398,432	2,517,957	793,323	798,804	41,644	98,695	60,128
2007	4,156,495	2,285,626	7,419	2,293,045	272,714	412,114	2,432,445	879,436	844,614	42,550	97,686	59,741
2008	4,171,900	2,242,894	7,057	2,249,951	275,609	307,067	2,281,409	966,306	924,185	42,767	97,550	59,281
2009	4,131,065	2,202,163	6,355	2,208,518	273,228	249,286	2,184,576	919,251	1,027,238	42,484	97,238	58,521
2010	4,325,360	2,259,469	5,770	2,265,239	278,254	249,142	2,236,127	997,817	1,091,416	44,490	97,222	58,088
2011	4,485,526	2,251,075	4,883	2,255,958	255,771	292,563	2,292,750	1,085,439	1,107,337	46,472	96,522	58,106
2012	4,598,783	2,340,686	5,486	2,346,172	259,893	322,178	2,408,457	1,089,005	1,101,321	47,771	96,267	58,053
2013	4,655,080	2,437,473	5,827	2,443,300	297,411	289,898	2,435,787	1,110,221	1,109,072	48,724	95,540	58,719
2014	4,830,338	2,564,624	5,104	2,569,728	309,602	235,722	2,495,848	1,189,756	1,144,734	50,049	96,513	59,771
2015	4,994,668	2,670,397	5,192	2,675,589	320,885	223,906	2,578,610	1,226,673	1,189,385	51,900	96,236	60,315
2016	5,144,513	2,751,606	5,682	2,757,288	328,002	276,032	2,705,318	1,219,424	1,219,771	53,541	96,085	60,593
2017	5,371,718	2,849,956	6,112	2,856,068	341,133	285,175	2,800,110	1,321,005	1,250,603	56,018	95,893	61,554
2018	5,596,973	2,988,815	5,873	2,994,688	352,734	297,121	2,939,075	1,359,257	1,298,641	58,573	95,556	62,093
2019	6,048,337	3,221,811	7,500	3,229,311	375,214	386,584	3,240,681	1,436,800	1,370,856	63,302	95,548	62,102
2020	6,496,246	3,219,662	8,446	3,228,108	374,005	412,514	3,266,617	1,432,177	1,797,452	68,326	95,077	58,221
2021	6,888,548	3,599,485	8,067	3,607,552	421,379	333,630	3,519,803	1,429,936	1,938,809	72,010	95,661	62,836

Personal Income and Employment by Area: Odessa, TX

(Thousands of dollars, except as noted.)

Year	Personal income, total	Earnings by place of work			Less: Contributions for government social insurance	Plus: Adjustment for residence	Equals: Net earnings by place of residence	Plus: Dividends, interest, and rent	Plus: Personal current transfer receipts	Per capita personal income (dollars)	Population (persons)	Total employment
		Nonfarm	Farm	Total								
1970	342,782	301,150	460	301,610	18,409	7,072	290,273	35,455	17,054	3,698	92,704	38,555
1971	367,519	321,697	99	321,796	20,093	7,271	308,974	38,512	20,033	3,926	93,609	39,295
1972	405,464	356,961	-680	356,281	23,239	7,691	340,733	42,015	22,716	4,291	94,500	40,684
1973	451,399	397,916	225	398,141	30,713	8,140	375,568	48,411	27,420	4,840	93,264	43,432
1974	542,855	479,145	610	479,755	37,996	9,519	451,278	58,976	32,601	5,616	96,667	46,851
1975	653,641	571,871	55	571,926	44,309	15,237	542,854	71,025	39,762	6,562	99,614	49,230
1976	795,881	709,582	298	709,880	52,843	16,327	673,364	78,591	43,926	7,773	102,392	51,191
1977	897,303	801,150	74	801,224	61,468	21,501	761,257	88,971	47,075	8,570	104,702	54,572
1978	1,031,873	920,635	743	921,378	73,925	29,019	876,472	102,072	53,329	9,538	108,189	58,659
1979	1,126,926	998,173	221	998,394	85,385	34,562	947,571	117,137	62,218	10,114	111,422	59,768
1980	1,349,255	1,174,121	72	1,174,193	102,391	54,480	1,126,282	150,639	72,334	11,527	117,052	64,450
1981	1,751,450	1,546,000	1,095	1,547,095	144,618	59,842	1,462,319	206,623	82,508	14,191	123,418	73,670
1982	1,890,841	1,620,139	1,234	1,621,373	158,107	64,563	1,527,829	266,375	96,637	13,954	135,501	74,922
1983	1,754,371	1,431,154	383	1,431,537	139,207	52,217	1,344,547	286,986	122,838	12,709	138,041	67,260
1984	1,759,958	1,407,125	475	1,407,600	142,278	51,889	1,317,211	314,051	128,696	13,133	134,006	66,031
1985	1,812,286	1,444,681	696	1,445,377	150,025	46,565	1,341,917	334,562	135,807	13,603	133,225	67,259
1986	1,616,613	1,215,730	509	1,216,239	123,137	44,198	1,137,300	314,542	164,771	12,101	133,588	57,894
1987	1,545,593	1,154,249	598	1,154,847	116,067	33,551	1,072,331	306,355	166,907	12,347	125,180	55,809
1988	1,601,855	1,200,397	232	1,200,629	126,055	33,441	1,108,015	323,821	170,019	13,123	122,067	57,518
1989	1,664,648	1,221,551	127	1,221,678	127,452	27,279	1,121,505	346,788	196,355	13,904	119,722	55,919
1990	1,708,198	1,268,409	-158	1,268,251	131,684	23,840	1,160,407	329,234	218,557	14,397	118,652	57,211
1991	1,810,723	1,357,487	-590	1,356,897	143,785	17,958	1,231,070	326,327	253,326	15,095	119,955	58,006
1992	1,861,672	1,364,858	-233	1,364,625	142,361	15,820	1,238,084	321,258	302,330	15,382	121,027	56,475
1993	1,930,173	1,424,822	-532	1,424,290	149,040	9,580	1,284,830	318,666	326,677	15,949	121,018	56,906
1994	1,993,286	1,473,181	-185	1,472,996	155,738	667	1,317,925	324,020	351,341	16,438	121,258	58,224
1995	2,055,845	1,499,812	-1,185	1,498,627	158,991	-1,990	1,337,646	343,962	374,237	16,988	121,017	58,734
1996	2,142,612	1,565,046	-2,232	1,562,814	163,408	-6,811	1,392,595	355,801	394,216	17,632	121,519	59,531
1997	2,341,644	1,753,101	-1,810	1,751,291	179,062	-9,729	1,562,500	372,236	406,908	19,233	121,749	61,867
1998	2,513,812	1,945,227	-1,614	1,943,613	196,917	-30,423	1,716,273	392,144	405,395	20,348	123,544	64,989
1999	2,392,656	1,795,910	-1,469	1,794,441	177,728	-24,985	1,591,728	375,743	425,185	19,540	122,450	60,926
2000	2,582,969	1,965,182	-852	1,964,330	190,295	-38,711	1,735,324	408,885	438,760	21,401	120,694	62,662
2001	2,812,383	2,164,186	-575	2,163,611	215,174	-38,117	1,910,320	429,714	472,349	23,281	120,802	64,327
2002	2,881,522	2,195,815	443	2,196,258	218,109	-47,003	1,931,146	427,371	523,005	23,581	122,199	64,267
2003	2,948,034	2,201,603	1,001	2,202,604	226,611	-42,566	1,933,427	456,806	557,801	24,019	122,739	64,158
2004	3,034,723	2,292,716	988	2,293,704	238,204	-36,078	2,019,422	440,407	574,894	24,441	124,163	65,340
2005	3,380,731	2,534,399	837	2,535,236	266,432	-5,935	2,262,869	493,872	623,990	26,964	125,378	67,933
2006	3,923,567	3,052,978	550	3,053,528	308,696	-7,333	2,737,499	538,372	647,696	30,779	127,476	72,744
2007	4,348,078	3,469,661	835	3,470,496	351,128	-53,035	3,066,333	586,772	694,973	33,329	130,459	76,549
2008	5,041,710	3,981,037	-1,809	3,979,228	394,560	-7,471	3,577,197	707,848	756,665	37,889	133,064	81,181
2009	4,553,531	3,563,001	-2,006	3,560,995	361,089	-110,681	3,089,225	644,933	819,373	33,254	136,930	77,006
2010	4,868,439	3,832,553	-2,397	3,830,156	387,840	-118,030	3,324,286	633,595	910,558	35,520	137,060	78,317
2011	5,619,730	4,640,990	-2,337	4,638,653	420,322	-272,935	3,945,396	775,829	898,505	40,247	139,631	85,207
2012	6,576,994	5,655,202	-2,294	5,652,908	489,178	-379,786	4,783,944	920,230	872,820	45,524	144,472	91,845
2013	6,732,381	6,093,039	411	6,093,450	589,948	-491,951	5,011,551	842,560	878,270	44,994	149,629	94,473
2014	7,530,400	6,764,724	414	6,765,138	653,314	-441,488	5,670,336	952,908	907,156	48,993	153,705	100,580
2015	6,872,617	5,941,897	5,293	5,947,190	594,053	-410,519	4,942,618	957,939	972,060	43,286	158,774	97,158
2016	6,054,790	5,036,293	139	5,036,432	524,783	-366,842	4,144,807	870,699	1,039,284	38,696	156,471	90,236
2017	6,809,471	5,829,155	1,027	5,830,182	604,882	-356,176	4,869,124	898,806	1,041,541	43,834	155,348	95,519
2018	7,995,785	6,996,847	907	6,997,754	719,958	-328,764	5,949,032	978,100	1,068,653	49,934	160,126	104,351
2019	8,694,234	7,612,534	-438	7,612,096	762,802	-276,857	6,572,437	1,017,858	1,103,939	52,948	164,204	107,057
2020	8,166,011	6,159,872	-841	6,159,031	625,114	-34,057	5,499,860	1,006,231	1,659,920	49,351	165,467	95,369
2021	8,636,134	6,222,837	592	6,223,429	629,134	117,836	5,712,131	1,071,271	1,852,732	53,610	161,091	94,915

Personal Income and Employment by Area: Ogden-Clearfield, UT

(Thousands of dollars, except as noted.)

Year	Personal income, total	Earnings by place of work			Less: Contributions for government social insurance	Plus: Adjustment for residence	Equals: Net earnings by place of residence	Plus: Dividends, interest, and rent	Plus: Personal current transfer receipts	Per capita personal income (dollars)	Population (persons)	Total employment
		Nonfarm	Farm	Total								
1970	969,165	736,060	19,328	755,388	36,595	24,125	742,918	161,646	64,601	3,747	258,652	101,375
1971	1,105,674	848,798	18,875	867,673	42,032	9,697	835,338	194,041	76,295	4,165	265,466	102,505
1972	1,187,967	897,136	21,518	918,654	49,285	22,305	891,674	210,639	85,654	4,379	271,286	106,947
1973	1,288,341	956,805	29,967	986,772	61,191	32,578	958,159	228,315	101,867	4,675	275,564	109,681
1974	1,428,952	1,058,738	25,577	1,084,315	71,464	41,988	1,054,839	258,192	115,921	5,109	279,691	112,270
1975	1,572,838	1,167,556	15,280	1,182,836	79,865	45,407	1,148,378	282,220	142,240	5,487	286,672	114,043
1976	1,763,256	1,318,691	15,401	1,334,092	92,699	54,155	1,295,548	313,031	154,677	6,012	293,292	118,620
1977	1,955,618	1,458,309	10,038	1,468,347	104,226	72,824	1,436,945	351,641	167,032	6,489	301,368	123,292
1978	2,244,010	1,656,985	13,471	1,670,456	121,620	93,536	1,642,372	415,834	185,804	7,217	310,926	130,121
1979	2,523,051	1,853,976	15,558	1,869,534	145,163	115,748	1,840,119	470,656	212,276	7,866	320,746	136,040
1980	2,833,369	2,032,680	12,117	2,044,797	159,248	149,395	2,034,944	548,746	249,679	8,543	331,666	137,885
1981	3,179,999	2,273,345	6,066	2,279,411	190,343	157,393	2,246,461	640,494	293,044	9,342	340,400	140,230
1982	3,466,831	2,433,209	7,952	2,441,161	206,927	178,716	2,412,950	720,311	333,570	9,940	348,770	141,296
1983	3,740,197	2,596,199	5,019	2,601,218	232,532	221,385	2,590,071	788,429	361,697	10,511	355,842	143,806
1984	4,131,769	2,895,050	7,831	2,902,881	269,072	240,057	2,873,866	883,293	374,610	11,429	361,527	152,784
1985	4,505,025	3,193,429	5,909	3,199,338	310,562	253,156	3,141,932	951,540	411,553	12,272	367,103	161,151
1986	4,766,979	3,374,296	12,637	3,386,933	334,104	267,333	3,320,162	1,007,262	439,555	12,792	372,647	166,082
1987	4,965,969	3,452,378	35,064	3,487,442	343,673	317,093	3,460,862	1,045,851	459,256	13,093	379,274	171,824
1988	5,262,010	3,664,639	52,004	3,716,643	384,819	346,550	3,678,374	1,097,135	486,501	13,803	381,216	178,142
1989	5,636,414	3,922,772	47,140	3,969,912	421,983	374,148	3,922,077	1,179,405	534,932	14,635	385,120	184,178
1990	6,111,853	4,215,190	60,135	4,275,325	471,422	497,683	4,301,586	1,220,435	589,832	15,679	389,815	190,389
1991	6,477,232	4,497,255	54,339	4,551,594	511,109	521,926	4,562,411	1,272,190	642,631	16,257	398,436	192,203
1992	6,957,437	4,779,187	73,622	4,852,809	544,894	629,575	4,937,490	1,307,141	712,806	17,021	408,757	193,998
1993	7,421,599	5,055,433	75,662	5,131,095	583,898	719,306	5,266,503	1,374,831	780,265	17,675	419,888	199,000
1994	7,913,976	5,360,880	55,777	5,416,657	630,691	810,357	5,596,323	1,511,590	806,063	18,362	430,988	213,802
1995	8,562,691	5,749,554	44,342	5,793,896	679,335	886,761	6,001,322	1,690,396	870,973	19,428	440,732	220,335
1996	9,253,574	6,161,854	49,938	6,211,792	723,711	993,911	6,481,992	1,845,281	926,301	20,530	450,737	233,975
1997	9,971,026	6,597,480	53,417	6,650,897	766,366	1,157,574	7,042,105	1,960,702	968,219	21,643	460,703	244,207
1998	10,632,892	6,951,991	54,154	7,006,145	806,334	1,316,458	7,516,269	2,100,662	1,015,961	22,613	470,206	248,177
1999	11,123,061	7,234,177	48,133	7,282,310	836,286	1,494,242	7,940,266	2,108,552	1,074,243	23,222	478,978	251,600
2000	11,865,028	7,645,893	34,947	7,680,840	884,895	1,614,349	8,410,294	2,306,651	1,148,083	24,318	487,906	257,400
2001	12,661,919	8,219,151	46,865	8,266,016	946,366	1,697,407	9,017,057	2,375,610	1,269,252	25,556	495,459	259,182
2002	13,105,641	8,645,331	23,662	8,668,993	995,204	1,702,840	9,376,629	2,342,143	1,386,869	25,991	504,247	263,457
2003	13,725,546	9,084,871	28,708	9,113,579	1,056,444	1,701,102	9,758,237	2,482,596	1,484,713	26,754	513,021	266,987
2004	14,398,665	9,585,977	41,873	9,627,850	1,133,092	1,846,177	10,340,935	2,504,340	1,553,390	27,564	522,374	276,026
2005	15,434,650	10,082,373	38,599	10,120,972	1,194,259	2,032,680	10,959,393	2,795,466	1,679,791	28,989	532,425	283,624
2006	16,960,470	11,133,567	30,917	11,164,484	1,298,207	2,306,463	12,172,740	2,967,230	1,820,500	31,078	545,746	294,833
2007	18,592,760	11,725,488	39,780	11,765,268	1,369,526	2,653,831	13,049,573	3,548,527	1,994,660	33,097	561,767	308,361
2008	19,385,858	11,895,045	37,977	11,933,022	1,402,039	2,760,106	13,291,089	3,734,193	2,360,576	33,595	577,040	309,968
2009	18,902,159	11,524,244	28,123	11,552,367	1,369,317	2,705,123	12,888,173	3,427,381	2,586,605	32,104	588,773	301,210
2010	19,376,004	11,725,620	38,517	11,764,137	1,385,082	2,765,444	13,144,499	3,343,675	2,887,830	32,306	599,756	297,159
2011	20,675,199	12,244,041	78,695	12,322,736	1,304,301	2,996,285	14,014,720	3,683,758	2,976,721	34,137	605,652	304,022
2012	21,767,680	12,926,662	66,585	12,993,247	1,350,863	3,229,462	14,871,846	3,933,062	2,962,772	35,550	612,307	308,441
2013	22,152,926	13,286,542	94,449	13,380,991	1,575,328	3,396,108	15,201,771	3,909,263	3,041,892	35,650	621,396	315,443
2014	23,349,843	13,994,345	104,490	14,098,835	1,658,403	3,484,396	15,924,828	4,261,381	3,163,634	36,884	633,070	324,254
2015	24,824,666	14,872,173	80,792	14,952,965	1,731,250	3,666,199	16,887,914	4,568,345	3,368,407	38,594	643,219	335,517
2016	26,196,048	15,672,853	51,951	15,724,804	1,821,275	3,917,541	17,821,070	4,864,171	3,510,807	39,938	655,918	346,464
2017	27,501,874	16,534,933	58,592	16,593,525	1,925,168	3,991,257	18,659,614	5,243,938	3,598,322	41,178	667,881	357,796
2018	29,206,748	17,624,304	34,638	17,658,942	2,015,153	4,288,446	19,932,235	5,455,628	3,818,885	43,098	677,677	369,527
2019	31,108,124	18,635,321	64,340	18,699,661	2,120,491	4,609,665	21,188,835	5,777,546	4,141,743	45,219	687,948	374,306
2020	33,800,744	20,004,723	74,020	20,078,743	2,290,206	4,753,283	22,541,820	5,918,628	5,340,296	48,521	696,620	380,088
2021	36,963,553	21,132,641	37,752	21,170,393	2,401,335	5,692,080	24,461,138	6,173,808	6,328,607	52,305	706,696	391,587

Personal Income and Employment by Area: Oklahoma City, OK

(Thousands of dollars, except as noted.)

Year	Personal income, total	Earnings by place of work			Less: Contributions for government social insurance	Plus: Adjustment for residence	Equals: Net earnings by place of residence	Plus: Dividends, interest, and rent	Plus: Personal current transfer receipts	Per capita personal income (dollars)	Population (persons)	Total employment
		Nonfarm	Farm	Total								
1970	3,017,627	2,484,654	27,488	2,512,142	143,758	-51,610	2,316,774	464,939	235,914	4,144	728,165	354,356
1971	3,364,882	2,741,764	26,904	2,768,668	164,431	-50,514	2,553,723	534,130	277,029	4,479	751,178	364,970
1972	3,694,011	3,051,263	24,884	3,076,147	194,150	-70,361	2,811,636	572,407	309,968	4,796	770,165	385,385
1973	4,089,347	3,349,156	61,343	3,410,499	249,832	-77,259	3,083,408	649,403	356,536	5,210	784,927	398,352
1974	4,571,230	3,727,100	40,620	3,767,720	288,038	-76,960	3,402,722	746,500	422,008	5,766	792,748	407,075
1975	5,025,160	4,021,527	34,624	4,056,151	309,340	-64,598	3,682,213	811,597	531,350	6,296	798,210	406,103
1976	5,510,871	4,415,814	30,336	4,446,150	347,102	-60,130	4,038,918	890,986	580,967	6,818	808,238	411,197
1977	6,194,095	5,057,117	17,862	5,074,979	398,459	-95,441	4,581,079	1,004,204	608,812	7,547	820,775	432,760
1978	7,111,495	5,879,414	13,197	5,892,611	480,958	-126,266	5,285,387	1,173,766	652,342	8,495	837,101	465,144
1979	8,191,439	6,780,232	37,811	6,818,043	580,145	-146,557	6,091,341	1,350,876	749,222	9,615	851,930	488,083
1980	9,603,583	7,950,111	23,121	7,973,232	688,884	-183,866	7,100,482	1,639,324	863,777	10,946	877,354	513,837
1981	11,191,572	9,218,441	5,797	9,224,238	861,510	-181,364	8,181,364	2,032,778	977,430	12,467	897,677	543,150
1982	12,613,485	10,246,235	16,888	10,263,123	981,046	-173,809	9,108,268	2,413,691	1,091,526	13,457	937,318	568,698
1983	13,051,527	10,446,756	4,078	10,450,834	1,000,019	-203,821	9,246,994	2,616,315	1,188,218	13,428	971,970	562,358
1984	14,018,964	11,171,586	10,990	11,182,576	1,089,785	-213,296	9,879,495	2,901,319	1,238,150	14,252	983,657	574,026
1985	14,536,744	11,400,213	26,215	11,426,428	1,130,774	-200,088	10,095,566	3,094,470	1,346,708	14,715	987,888	562,905
1986	14,538,004	11,313,973	49,383	11,363,356	1,144,357	-185,922	10,033,077	3,056,356	1,448,571	14,774	983,997	542,698
1987	14,551,571	11,325,693	42,464	11,368,157	1,153,140	-171,629	10,043,388	2,987,537	1,520,646	15,002	970,003	543,299
1988	15,220,534	11,850,729	57,831	11,908,560	1,271,501	-181,277	10,455,782	3,127,521	1,637,231	15,749	966,423	549,865
1989	16,348,811	12,568,148	64,905	12,633,053	1,357,679	-166,664	11,108,710	3,496,439	1,743,662	16,855	969,976	557,627
1990	17,025,368	13,126,286	51,645	13,177,931	1,467,296	-181,919	11,528,716	3,604,672	1,891,980	17,507	972,512	567,554
1991	17,567,437	13,569,205	41,302	13,610,507	1,554,084	-183,099	11,873,324	3,604,553	2,089,560	17,854	983,942	568,264
1992	18,687,635	14,426,436	61,647	14,488,083	1,644,894	-197,307	12,645,882	3,680,751	2,361,002	18,717	998,407	574,498
1993	19,594,349	15,197,954	54,227	15,252,181	1,749,775	-212,283	13,290,123	3,839,193	2,465,033	19,305	1,014,998	586,259
1994	20,579,604	15,830,712	63,012	15,893,724	1,853,382	-225,995	13,814,347	4,103,365	2,661,892	19,993	1,029,338	599,649
1995	21,552,827	16,526,980	7,759	16,534,739	1,943,716	-242,302	14,348,721	4,329,708	2,874,398	20,737	1,039,343	621,260
1996	22,910,729	17,561,956	19,233	17,581,189	2,028,027	-240,728	15,312,434	4,583,465	3,014,830	21,781	1,051,886	640,572
1997	23,928,988	18,386,764	27,930	18,414,694	2,099,330	-250,415	16,064,949	4,745,099	3,118,940	22,462	1,065,333	652,676
1998	25,481,629	19,522,769	13,887	19,536,656	2,209,087	-258,424	17,069,145	5,173,713	3,238,771	23,699	1,075,233	667,154
1999	26,525,277	20,350,961	36,648	20,387,609	2,314,528	-300,054	17,773,027	5,338,608	3,413,642	24,372	1,088,347	679,360
2000	29,292,576	22,374,597	34,232	22,408,829	2,498,503	-343,523	19,566,803	6,008,644	3,717,129	26,675	1,098,132	698,058
2001	31,630,385	24,231,233	42,071	24,273,304	2,660,654	-344,329	21,268,321	6,209,348	4,152,716	28,525	1,108,860	707,782
2002	32,523,795	25,068,072	60,875	25,128,947	2,769,050	-356,670	22,003,227	6,270,349	4,250,219	28,981	1,122,241	703,510
2003	34,712,755	26,967,698	48,043	27,015,741	2,912,457	-359,100	23,744,184	6,429,249	4,539,322	30,600	1,134,419	703,638
2004	36,757,520	28,437,526	86,110	28,523,636	3,090,463	-395,445	25,037,728	6,950,481	4,769,311	32,088	1,145,524	718,972
2005	40,088,183	30,630,618	97,620	30,728,238	3,217,045	-397,590	27,113,603	7,716,137	5,258,443	34,520	1,161,308	733,082
2006	44,034,453	33,159,799	44,091	33,203,890	3,428,080	-412,303	29,363,507	8,889,438	5,781,508	37,233	1,182,668	749,113
2007	45,308,104	33,347,154	57,505	33,404,659	3,580,531	-353,910	29,470,218	9,607,303	6,230,583	37,767	1,199,665	764,900
2008	49,936,660	36,812,820	66,739	36,879,559	3,760,016	-375,380	32,744,163	10,079,950	7,112,547	41,045	1,216,645	780,121
2009	47,749,077	35,071,389	-10,308	35,061,081	3,746,802	-386,149	30,928,130	9,119,720	7,701,227	38,576	1,237,780	766,965
2010	49,678,417	36,108,497	30,220	36,138,717	3,845,149	-413,153	31,880,415	9,494,156	8,303,846	39,496	1,257,804	771,479
2011	53,094,525	38,215,970	66,960	38,282,930	3,708,646	-466,318	34,107,966	10,523,428	8,463,131	41,572	1,277,178	790,633
2012	56,065,876	40,360,747	108,355	40,469,102	3,928,284	-482,158	36,058,660	11,328,055	8,679,161	43,193	1,298,039	814,008
2013	57,846,936	42,432,516	57,313	42,489,829	4,552,915	-513,647	37,423,267	11,453,880	8,969,789	43,810	1,320,416	832,875
2014	61,483,959	44,739,117	96,946	44,836,063	4,693,614	-497,251	39,645,198	12,530,647	9,308,114	45,955	1,337,930	846,322
2015	62,484,997	45,696,702	35,896	45,732,598	4,795,105	-521,564	40,415,929	12,385,171	9,683,897	45,972	1,359,199	857,636
2016	61,991,912	44,832,749	-18,683	44,814,066	4,775,754	-515,635	39,522,677	12,457,409	10,011,826	45,068	1,375,508	862,819
2017	64,530,002	46,760,905	-22,096	46,738,809	4,987,016	-593,721	41,158,072	12,963,712	10,408,218	46,617	1,384,267	868,919
2018	67,247,517	48,784,944	-33,251	48,751,693	5,264,074	-680,286	42,807,333	13,594,126	10,846,058	48,132	1,397,154	883,677
2019	72,992,979	53,082,230	-30,519	53,051,711	5,522,397	-680,489	46,848,825	14,563,406	11,580,748	51,658	1,413,004	886,142
2020	76,730,279	53,423,911	-30,125	53,393,786	5,614,204	-602,357	47,177,225	14,497,482	15,055,572	53,706	1,428,709	870,863
2021	82,390,048	56,815,719	-3,776	56,811,943	5,877,784	-623,163	50,310,996	15,098,322	16,980,730	57,150	1,441,647	888,577

Personal Income and Employment by Area: Olympia-Lacey-Tumwater, WA

(Thousands of dollars, except as noted.)

Year	Personal income, total	Earnings by place of work			Less: Contributions for government social insurance	Plus: Adjustment for residence	Equals: Net earnings by place of residence	Plus: Dividends, interest, and rent	Plus: Personal current transfer receipts	Per capita personal income (dollars)	Population (persons)	Total employment
		Nonfarm	Farm	Total								
1970	357,422	257,443	5,347	262,790	19,590	9,066	252,266	74,654	30,502	4,612	77,498	34,767
1971	395,612	282,099	4,690	286,789	22,570	12,001	276,220	82,623	36,769	4,950	79,920	35,873
1972	427,521	302,358	6,506	308,864	25,336	12,561	296,089	89,073	42,359	5,216	81,970	36,700
1973	487,701	336,283	15,247	351,530	32,489	19,457	338,498	100,428	48,775	5,742	84,930	37,999
1974	554,735	378,724	14,107	392,831	38,280	24,275	378,826	116,368	59,541	6,201	89,466	39,450
1975	633,132	428,183	11,846	440,029	42,959	27,113	424,183	135,535	73,414	6,753	93,760	41,096
1976	726,738	494,329	12,270	506,599	50,440	35,592	491,751	152,802	82,185	7,431	97,798	43,594
1977	823,320	558,826	11,627	570,453	57,128	46,068	559,393	175,852	88,075	7,729	106,529	45,440
1978	981,445	671,900	17,035	688,935	71,083	57,249	675,101	208,296	98,048	8,702	112,782	49,562
1979	1,128,038	756,875	18,956	775,831	81,440	76,925	771,316	244,725	111,997	9,465	119,176	53,380
1980	1,300,439	833,419	19,121	852,540	92,880	103,080	862,740	294,814	142,885	10,377	125,325	55,242
1981	1,467,770	904,824	19,848	924,672	108,596	134,400	950,476	351,806	165,488	11,349	129,326	55,939
1982	1,553,849	916,616	21,445	938,061	112,255	151,499	977,305	392,764	183,780	11,762	132,109	55,768
1983	1,681,245	1,000,683	19,571	1,020,254	124,859	140,246	1,035,641	443,697	201,907	12,556	133,899	58,575
1984	1,845,594	1,123,256	17,246	1,140,502	142,948	139,820	1,137,374	493,966	214,254	13,598	135,721	61,228
1985	2,024,542	1,231,413	17,362	1,248,775	158,993	155,616	1,245,398	540,737	238,407	14,604	138,632	63,934
1986	2,190,308	1,339,786	16,932	1,356,718	176,564	173,805	1,353,959	575,460	260,889	15,425	141,998	67,550
1987	2,335,758	1,445,632	12,531	1,458,163	189,590	195,022	1,463,595	592,468	279,695	16,019	145,813	71,492
1988	2,543,013	1,575,925	12,051	1,587,976	215,743	225,336	1,597,569	637,126	308,318	16,904	150,439	75,337
1989	2,851,672	1,742,739	19,838	1,762,577	236,833	241,308	1,767,052	737,489	347,131	18,355	155,365	79,332
1990	3,160,408	1,961,185	19,785	1,980,970	265,618	309,793	2,025,145	758,094	377,169	19,387	163,014	83,933
1991	3,511,663	2,215,612	21,606	2,237,218	299,051	325,281	2,263,448	818,916	429,299	20,731	169,388	87,571
1992	3,866,667	2,449,048	25,923	2,474,971	326,309	380,674	2,529,336	851,708	485,623	21,919	176,407	90,233
1993	4,143,497	2,635,703	26,964	2,662,667	348,416	395,367	2,709,618	907,201	526,678	22,635	183,054	92,374
1994	4,347,026	2,745,385	28,357	2,773,742	368,276	415,392	2,820,858	967,420	558,748	23,247	186,997	96,701
1995	4,593,766	2,864,437	26,118	2,890,555	384,235	448,991	2,955,311	1,030,561	607,894	23,924	192,013	97,945
1996	4,856,469	2,986,163	28,790	3,014,953	386,722	490,570	3,118,801	1,098,341	639,327	24,747	196,247	101,394
1997	5,193,718	3,172,363	29,377	3,201,740	394,405	591,031	3,398,366	1,136,127	659,225	26,032	199,512	103,918
1998	5,552,457	3,437,166	34,681	3,471,847	428,253	620,857	3,664,451	1,198,209	689,797	27,481	202,050	106,533
1999	5,774,240	3,694,592	33,051	3,727,643	447,239	588,434	3,868,838	1,167,130	738,272	28,184	204,873	108,667
2000	6,389,115	4,017,070	22,702	4,039,772	489,668	784,277	4,334,381	1,251,928	802,806	30,675	208,287	110,972
2001	6,789,948	4,335,305	24,902	4,360,207	510,946	769,992	4,619,253	1,274,327	896,368	31,965	212,421	111,844
2002	6,974,398	4,576,859	19,012	4,595,871	544,573	756,964	4,808,262	1,213,019	953,117	32,242	216,313	114,979
2003	7,289,014	4,775,666	33,291	4,808,957	573,100	729,508	4,965,365	1,316,991	1,006,658	33,208	219,499	118,075
2004	7,676,812	4,974,487	29,611	5,004,098	601,519	785,674	5,188,253	1,436,154	1,052,405	34,427	222,985	120,654
2005	8,068,622	5,266,694	22,280	5,288,974	642,786	803,618	5,449,806	1,490,004	1,128,812	35,541	227,023	124,210
2006	8,666,557	5,602,447	22,701	5,625,148	684,382	820,973	5,761,739	1,671,973	1,232,845	37,245	232,688	128,590
2007	9,398,686	6,012,698	23,627	6,036,325	729,321	844,135	6,151,139	1,900,665	1,346,882	39,528	237,772	133,305
2008	10,090,243	6,290,955	37,515	6,328,470	751,939	840,703	6,417,234	2,121,762	1,551,247	41,297	244,332	134,597
2009	9,982,452	6,173,095	40,584	6,213,679	763,813	813,915	6,263,781	1,978,506	1,740,165	39,940	249,936	130,603
2010	10,243,664	6,277,337	41,160	6,318,497	770,699	759,175	6,306,973	2,003,838	1,932,853	40,487	253,011	128,661
2011	10,503,146	6,264,223	45,170	6,309,393	702,658	767,333	6,374,068	2,170,887	1,958,191	40,958	256,439	128,331
2012	10,973,733	6,543,531	55,841	6,599,372	709,557	806,559	6,696,374	2,307,570	1,969,789	42,433	258,613	130,341
2013	11,105,402	6,869,626	61,725	6,931,351	834,435	691,369	6,788,285	2,280,989	2,036,128	42,391	261,976	133,679
2014	11,627,441	7,128,422	69,815	7,198,237	877,074	647,761	6,968,924	2,439,928	2,218,589	43,758	265,722	137,128
2015	12,144,196	7,356,079	117,446	7,473,525	915,401	694,649	7,252,773	2,586,368	2,305,055	45,148	268,989	140,196
2016	12,811,070	7,801,380	75,333	7,876,713	963,368	743,897	7,657,242	2,709,345	2,444,483	46,616	274,820	144,624
2017	13,458,789	8,366,018	77,197	8,443,215	1,051,376	636,105	8,027,944	2,879,052	2,551,793	47,822	281,435	149,907
2018	14,133,881	9,087,063	62,853	9,149,916	1,129,190	422,647	8,443,373	2,989,448	2,701,060	49,240	287,041	154,777
2019	15,229,670	9,609,675	78,513	9,688,188	1,169,455	481,776	9,000,509	3,324,343	2,904,818	52,297	291,214	155,982
2020	16,716,772	10,001,795	87,200	10,088,995	1,243,111	682,509	9,528,393	3,338,620	3,849,759	56,527	295,729	151,512
2021	18,195,215	10,833,806	58,718	10,892,524	1,325,552	941,426	10,508,398	3,445,898	4,240,919	61,062	297,977	156,405

Personal Income and Employment by Area: Omaha-Council Bluffs, NE-IA

(Thousands of dollars, except as noted.)

Year	Personal income, total	Earnings by place of work			Less: Contributions for government social insurance	Plus: Adjustment for residence	Equals: Net earnings by place of residence	Plus: Dividends, interest, and rent	Plus: Personal current transfer receipts	Per capita personal income (dollars)	Population (persons)	Total employment
		Nonfarm	Farm	Total								
1970	2,658,127	2,116,323	83,142	2,199,465	148,476	-19,851	2,031,138	421,134	205,855	4,275	621,778	297,197
1971	2,865,198	2,278,984	85,385	2,364,369	165,260	-20,673	2,178,436	452,896	233,866	4,521	633,774	301,792
1972	3,145,062	2,492,519	111,595	2,604,114	188,058	-20,522	2,395,534	491,936	257,592	4,886	643,739	308,000
1973	3,540,683	2,757,779	180,756	2,938,535	237,937	-19,679	2,680,919	551,880	307,884	5,461	648,329	318,343
1974	3,807,732	3,019,017	96,778	3,115,795	270,557	-15,226	2,830,012	622,810	354,910	5,832	652,850	324,237
1975	4,208,664	3,248,219	128,980	3,377,199	285,951	-9,372	3,081,876	680,934	445,854	6,484	649,131	321,665
1976	4,587,524	3,627,621	80,493	3,708,114	324,424	-5,899	3,377,791	735,142	474,591	6,989	656,376	330,324
1977	5,033,558	3,976,861	103,766	4,080,627	355,442	-3,453	3,721,732	816,588	495,238	7,683	655,126	339,330
1978	5,651,599	4,422,594	172,349	4,594,943	405,439	1,217	4,190,721	910,036	550,842	8,584	658,391	350,508
1979	6,191,919	4,917,955	97,417	5,015,372	469,203	3,890	4,550,059	1,023,908	617,952	9,414	657,736	359,581
1980	6,836,142	5,344,448	41,975	5,386,423	507,665	12,439	4,891,197	1,221,998	722,947	10,437	654,969	356,972
1981	7,651,517	5,791,831	125,271	5,917,102	586,703	-5,105	5,325,294	1,502,898	823,325	11,636	657,562	357,821
1982	8,299,628	6,153,201	105,617	6,258,818	635,310	-10,353	5,613,155	1,785,367	901,106	12,561	660,724	356,924
1983	8,698,224	6,553,252	44,620	6,597,872	685,649	-13,209	5,899,014	1,830,985	968,225	13,108	663,573	363,321
1984	9,612,823	7,210,488	122,261	7,332,749	774,541	-16,021	6,542,187	2,045,923	1,024,713	14,377	668,605	375,618
1985	10,246,847	7,681,521	209,689	7,891,210	844,222	-17,304	7,029,684	2,123,578	1,093,585	15,264	671,289	386,904
1986	10,667,961	8,085,405	163,430	8,248,835	913,550	-19,646	7,315,639	2,208,245	1,144,077	15,865	672,408	392,455
1987	11,206,099	8,573,341	156,780	8,730,121	961,734	-18,557	7,749,830	2,279,801	1,176,468	16,663	672,505	405,568
1988	11,895,105	9,150,158	145,083	9,295,241	1,067,328	-20,736	8,207,177	2,450,364	1,237,564	17,570	677,009	416,931
1989	12,670,227	9,747,638	149,828	9,897,466	1,136,374	-23,078	8,738,014	2,613,737	1,318,476	18,608	680,885	428,864
1990	13,701,977	10,481,838	161,014	10,642,852	1,272,819	-24,871	9,345,162	2,912,137	1,444,678	19,918	687,913	439,366
1991	14,311,637	10,972,034	159,207	11,131,241	1,344,446	-31,476	9,755,319	2,985,473	1,570,845	20,550	696,443	440,334
1992	15,219,607	11,682,087	200,167	11,882,254	1,412,508	-38,352	10,431,394	3,077,640	1,710,573	21,608	704,360	442,339
1993	15,732,403	12,162,962	87,622	12,250,584	1,473,216	-39,351	10,738,017	3,173,526	1,820,860	22,218	708,077	450,793
1994	16,888,275	13,022,545	185,663	13,208,208	1,581,812	-45,886	11,580,510	3,395,545	1,912,220	23,616	715,120	466,628
1995	18,195,224	14,101,757	62,935	14,164,692	1,687,153	-60,089	12,417,450	3,750,268	2,027,506	25,101	724,894	477,507
1996	19,651,089	15,125,447	249,890	15,375,337	1,798,568	-77,564	13,499,205	4,010,272	2,141,612	26,666	736,937	491,378
1997	20,730,341	16,040,743	188,442	16,229,185	1,935,009	-96,453	14,197,723	4,304,942	2,227,676	27,775	746,356	499,983
1998	22,251,170	17,165,317	127,937	17,293,254	2,053,627	-107,923	15,131,704	4,787,987	2,331,479	29,517	753,844	516,047
1999	23,683,038	18,473,195	120,821	18,594,016	2,193,107	-131,089	16,269,820	4,943,045	2,470,173	31,096	761,603	527,810
2000	25,305,781	19,566,422	151,266	19,717,688	2,296,117	-148,151	17,273,420	5,425,985	2,606,376	32,895	769,291	538,603
2001	26,280,689	20,350,850	154,642	20,505,492	2,366,596	-154,841	17,984,055	5,437,131	2,859,503	33,860	776,165	538,485
2002	27,124,151	21,112,244	110,763	21,223,007	2,448,152	-170,235	18,604,620	5,437,945	3,081,586	34,616	783,567	534,297
2003	28,100,373	21,876,681	172,768	22,049,449	2,554,928	-186,294	19,308,227	5,583,582	3,208,564	35,476	792,086	536,725
2004	30,201,028	23,444,927	325,872	23,770,799	2,689,023	-198,348	20,883,428	5,956,142	3,361,458	37,600	803,214	544,747
2005	31,326,254	23,975,309	248,743	24,224,052	2,834,357	-222,915	21,166,780	6,559,093	3,600,381	38,470	814,309	552,642
2006	33,721,173	25,803,315	154,060	25,957,375	3,071,262	-259,635	22,626,478	7,184,393	3,910,302	40,876	824,961	564,063
2007	35,636,066	26,674,043	226,543	26,900,586	3,151,848	-270,182	23,478,556	8,008,322	4,149,188	42,701	834,554	574,920
2008	37,622,400	27,894,336	319,062	28,213,398	3,278,580	-271,504	24,663,314	8,196,525	4,762,561	44,517	845,119	580,743
2009	37,107,320	28,122,045	374,835	28,496,880	3,284,992	-222,943	24,988,945	7,129,536	4,988,839	43,338	856,233	572,076
2010	39,352,277	29,558,213	291,421	29,849,634	3,386,299	-163,131	26,300,204	7,630,797	5,421,276	45,352	867,705	568,925
2011	42,956,747	32,199,498	524,073	32,723,571	3,115,419	-131,817	29,476,335	7,899,026	5,581,386	49,028	876,169	574,938
2012	44,913,582	33,383,704	379,111	33,762,815	3,209,086	-81,681	30,472,048	8,826,995	5,614,539	50,761	884,797	583,893
2013	43,877,258	32,914,446	460,157	33,374,603	3,667,182	-41,240	29,666,181	8,484,259	5,726,818	49,069	894,201	592,998
2014	47,444,000	35,753,912	230,730	35,984,642	3,837,692	-22,933	32,124,017	9,325,035	5,994,948	52,165	909,504	603,939
2015	49,511,895	37,227,447	233,349	37,460,796	4,026,632	-32,329	33,401,835	9,784,631	6,325,429	53,771	920,790	615,879
2016	49,279,550	36,911,394	123,300	37,034,694	4,141,650	-25,678	32,867,366	9,893,131	6,519,053	52,843	932,571	623,085
2017	51,313,192	38,609,309	119,275	38,728,584	4,329,470	-3,112	34,396,002	10,206,945	6,710,245	54,429	942,758	631,288
2018	53,895,052	40,227,059	118,530	40,345,589	4,490,200	21,893	35,877,282	10,865,742	7,152,028	56,556	952,958	639,419
2019	56,170,136	40,961,763	197,228	41,158,991	4,684,008	5,156	36,480,139	12,132,804	7,557,193	58,393	961,926	642,128
2020	58,545,119	41,241,259	232,031	41,473,290	4,880,595	59,010	36,651,705	12,248,857	9,644,557	60,450	968,493	629,223
2021	62,407,156	43,537,463	420,586	43,958,049	5,053,010	50,584	38,955,623	12,565,517	10,886,016	64,229	971,637	642,041

Personal Income and Employment by Area: Orlando-Kissimmee-Sanford, FL

(Thousands of dollars, except as noted.)

Year	Personal income, total	Earnings by place of work			Less: Contributions for government social insurance	Plus: Adjustment for residence	Equals: Net earnings by place of residence	Plus: Dividends, interest, and rent	Plus: Personal current transfer receipts	Per capita personal income (dollars)	Population (persons)	Total employment
		Nonfarm	Farm	Total								
1970	2,090,897	1,475,800	96,216	1,572,016	95,062	21,012	1,497,966	409,705	183,226	3,959	528,201	232,835
1971	2,437,079	1,741,054	108,392	1,849,446	117,558	18,945	1,750,833	464,677	221,569	4,362	558,715	252,062
1972	2,891,041	2,104,942	129,052	2,233,994	149,361	18,016	2,102,649	534,268	254,124	4,820	599,794	289,075
1973	3,413,913	2,562,815	130,585	2,693,400	208,780	12,732	2,497,352	613,688	302,873	5,300	644,122	323,363
1974	3,739,141	2,759,499	128,252	2,887,751	233,515	11,735	2,665,971	705,075	368,095	5,495	680,514	326,248
1975	4,010,805	2,825,531	150,953	2,976,484	235,913	6,317	2,746,888	771,442	492,475	5,816	689,597	315,687
1976	4,430,995	3,137,586	168,736	3,306,322	268,006	-2,942	3,035,374	849,409	546,212	6,286	704,932	327,025
1977	4,932,360	3,498,088	193,055	3,691,143	301,156	-6,855	3,383,132	958,454	590,774	6,797	725,644	344,104
1978	5,766,388	4,115,821	248,997	4,364,818	363,424	-17,613	3,983,781	1,132,571	650,036	7,698	749,095	375,240
1979	6,652,604	4,784,260	244,634	5,028,894	441,872	-25,285	4,561,737	1,328,287	762,580	8,519	780,907	396,668
1980	7,919,092	5,556,322	327,856	5,884,178	516,163	-37,826	5,330,189	1,669,404	919,499	9,738	813,225	418,551
1981	9,161,188	6,441,513	237,729	6,679,242	640,439	-53,329	5,985,474	2,096,766	1,078,948	10,835	845,498	441,015
1982	10,207,566	7,244,703	280,905	7,525,608	736,135	-95,159	6,694,314	2,288,017	1,225,235	11,635	877,348	463,274
1983	11,470,503	8,263,247	351,236	8,614,483	845,668	-136,517	7,632,298	2,500,647	1,337,558	12,520	916,199	494,692
1984	12,908,737	9,562,360	229,751	9,792,111	1,004,967	-189,229	8,597,915	2,891,393	1,419,429	13,480	957,644	537,857
1985	14,299,095	10,763,771	210,047	10,973,818	1,151,298	-247,651	9,574,869	3,183,673	1,540,553	14,352	996,347	573,928
1986	15,736,018	12,065,859	202,627	12,268,486	1,323,854	-324,095	10,620,537	3,454,366	1,661,115	15,153	1,038,445	615,381
1987	17,148,572	13,361,815	188,910	13,550,725	1,451,403	-416,091	11,683,231	3,695,828	1,769,513	15,847	1,082,164	636,135
1988	19,132,731	15,031,321	217,068	15,248,389	1,671,735	-502,114	13,074,540	4,096,041	1,962,150	17,083	1,119,977	672,874
1989	21,334,241	16,525,533	193,250	16,718,783	1,850,633	-604,232	14,263,918	4,815,612	2,254,711	18,212	1,171,413	713,886
1990	23,034,557	17,978,789	163,502	18,142,291	2,002,469	-715,400	15,424,422	5,092,778	2,517,357	18,565	1,240,724	739,630
1991	24,088,713	18,653,927	199,941	18,853,868	2,093,957	-655,956	16,103,955	5,128,714	2,856,044	18,771	1,283,301	737,044
1992	25,678,596	20,103,559	184,609	20,288,168	2,247,476	-718,926	17,321,766	5,012,544	3,344,286	19,470	1,318,902	755,421
1993	27,385,805	21,526,255	184,234	21,710,489	2,389,448	-795,098	18,525,943	5,196,230	3,663,632	20,180	1,357,101	788,146
1994	28,895,407	22,778,146	164,982	22,943,128	2,568,550	-881,051	19,493,527	5,465,882	3,935,998	20,724	1,394,315	813,296
1995	31,064,780	24,346,099	177,566	24,523,665	2,723,278	-924,260	20,876,127	5,917,631	4,271,022	21,748	1,428,415	840,455
1996	33,510,459	26,340,074	159,583	26,499,657	2,922,086	-1,002,497	22,575,074	6,370,388	4,564,997	22,802	1,469,619	885,718
1997	36,086,442	28,601,905	186,603	28,788,508	3,176,978	-1,156,342	24,455,188	6,834,139	4,797,115	23,739	1,520,145	935,200
1998	39,456,914	31,675,530	197,641	31,873,171	3,493,768	-1,353,022	27,026,381	7,497,900	4,932,633	25,165	1,567,910	987,408
1999	42,246,177	34,580,251	197,969	34,778,220	3,771,177	-1,523,649	29,483,394	7,625,434	5,137,349	26,273	1,607,993	1,032,530
2000	45,896,013	37,588,649	197,064	37,785,713	4,065,800	-1,766,325	31,953,588	8,388,710	5,553,715	27,700	1,656,890	1,071,873
2001	47,220,007	38,554,189	195,950	38,750,139	4,293,386	-1,885,195	32,571,558	8,491,820	6,156,629	27,608	1,710,359	1,083,195
2002	49,065,558	40,201,120	181,033	40,382,153	4,453,669	-1,991,426	33,937,058	8,298,503	6,829,997	27,873	1,760,345	1,082,826
2003	52,128,687	42,778,661	151,529	42,930,190	4,725,893	-2,128,007	36,076,290	8,648,735	7,403,662	28,776	1,811,544	1,121,204
2004	56,697,193	47,016,314	173,809	47,190,123	5,204,583	-2,405,502	39,580,038	9,108,762	8,008,393	30,189	1,878,077	1,179,837
2005	62,139,849	51,836,608	191,197	52,027,805	5,774,167	-2,824,754	43,428,884	10,053,475	8,657,490	31,772	1,955,794	1,250,750
2006	67,699,385	55,671,850	186,890	55,858,740	6,273,737	-3,067,033	46,517,970	11,848,084	9,333,331	33,514	2,020,057	1,303,562
2007	70,943,286	57,477,171	172,312	57,649,483	6,518,866	-3,228,492	47,902,125	13,016,262	10,024,899	34,474	2,057,865	1,340,657
2008	71,794,999	56,531,706	169,764	56,701,470	6,575,649	-3,254,856	46,870,965	13,296,400	11,627,634	34,393	2,087,489	1,316,027
2009	68,306,126	52,734,142	191,230	52,925,372	6,239,517	-2,975,078	43,710,777	11,730,519	12,864,830	32,343	2,111,917	1,253,746
2010	72,042,945	54,077,079	207,722	54,284,801	6,308,005	-2,970,898	45,005,898	12,510,648	14,526,399	33,677	2,139,227	1,254,307
2011	76,201,079	55,722,084	191,600	55,913,684	5,793,966	-3,008,672	47,111,046	13,804,071	15,285,962	35,014	2,176,297	1,295,438
2012	79,452,252	59,334,127	241,425	59,575,552	6,176,484	-3,339,394	50,059,674	14,208,971	15,183,607	35,692	2,226,080	1,335,426
2013	81,668,700	62,286,964	198,275	62,485,239	7,274,954	-3,478,671	51,731,614	14,207,546	15,729,540	35,965	2,270,811	1,374,925
2014	87,506,545	66,656,558	200,555	66,857,113	7,738,809	-3,622,609	55,495,695	15,207,982	16,802,868	37,408	2,339,238	1,438,203
2015	94,473,021	71,790,176	269,854	72,060,030	8,239,358	-3,887,225	59,933,447	16,667,156	17,872,418	39,243	2,407,405	1,504,935
2016	98,913,545	76,342,146	213,446	76,555,592	8,697,704	-4,406,183	63,451,705	16,821,597	18,640,243	39,895	2,479,365	1,567,869
2017	106,570,220	81,225,127	240,389	81,465,516	9,218,840	-4,754,236	67,492,440	19,243,923	19,833,857	41,856	2,546,121	1,645,510
2018	113,366,110	87,361,949	183,263	87,545,212	9,963,909	-5,154,413	72,426,890	20,067,572	20,871,648	43,487	2,606,900	1,728,099
2019	120,432,099	92,158,811	209,860	92,368,671	10,695,579	-5,699,026	75,974,066	22,270,691	22,187,342	45,562	2,643,259	1,772,671
2020	128,957,121	91,850,405	206,637	92,057,042	10,671,603	-5,059,441	76,325,998	22,663,186	29,967,937	48,160	2,677,687	1,704,398
2021	142,946,634	103,648,896	201,681	103,850,577	11,735,445	-6,258,647	85,856,485	23,430,348	33,659,801	53,102	2,691,925	1,790,594

Personal Income and Employment by Area: Oshkosh-Neenah, WI

(Thousands of dollars, except as noted.)

Year	Personal income, total	Earnings by place of work			Less: Contributions for government social insurance	Plus: Adjustment for residence	Equals: Net earnings by place of residence	Plus: Dividends, interest, and rent	Plus: Personal current transfer receipts	Per capita personal income (dollars)	Population (persons)	Total employment
		Nonfarm	Farm	Total								
1970	507,667	426,630	8,094	434,724	31,107	-23,835	379,782	86,312	41,573	3,899	130,213	58,052
1971	532,948	441,404	8,734	450,138	33,318	-24,933	391,887	91,773	49,288	4,061	131,228	57,187
1972	575,795	483,646	9,278	492,924	38,654	-29,932	424,338	97,177	54,280	4,375	131,616	58,727
1973	639,027	543,038	10,572	553,610	50,124	-34,170	469,316	106,937	62,774	4,896	130,530	61,323
1974	705,292	592,502	11,118	603,620	56,715	-38,572	508,333	120,816	76,143	5,462	129,132	62,563
1975	778,467	645,338	11,649	656,987	60,727	-44,291	551,969	131,687	94,811	5,969	130,425	62,538
1976	856,350	723,404	8,554	731,958	69,024	-50,845	612,089	141,797	102,464	6,559	130,569	64,799
1977	959,040	814,165	15,525	829,690	76,947	-59,724	693,019	157,453	108,568	7,342	130,632	66,556
1978	1,064,165	917,622	12,376	929,998	89,300	-69,056	771,642	173,338	119,185	8,190	129,936	68,792
1979	1,189,621	1,022,195	16,827	1,039,022	103,272	-74,109	861,641	193,782	134,198	9,092	130,845	71,146
1980	1,310,233	1,082,976	17,305	1,100,281	109,167	-77,430	913,684	233,378	163,171	9,945	131,746	69,583
1981	1,429,996	1,157,088	12,466	1,169,554	124,390	-83,999	961,165	286,401	182,430	10,888	131,335	68,777
1982	1,521,673	1,206,581	10,160	1,216,741	131,822	-88,737	996,182	319,574	205,917	11,587	131,330	68,279
1983	1,632,491	1,303,772	1,762	1,305,534	142,548	-99,589	1,063,397	346,379	222,715	12,411	131,539	68,795
1984	1,790,336	1,441,315	8,571	1,449,886	161,739	-112,060	1,176,087	386,301	227,948	13,450	133,106	72,636
1985	1,903,171	1,541,980	7,785	1,549,765	174,897	-120,610	1,254,258	408,876	240,037	14,180	134,219	74,641
1986	2,006,905	1,642,673	9,520	1,652,193	186,159	-131,553	1,334,481	425,127	247,297	14,825	135,372	76,626
1987	2,120,623	1,763,203	11,760	1,774,963	197,085	-142,325	1,435,553	431,070	254,000	15,556	136,319	78,525
1988	2,251,572	1,896,669	5,323	1,901,992	218,356	-153,409	1,530,227	456,815	264,530	16,297	138,161	80,578
1989	2,451,696	1,990,637	14,624	2,005,261	228,125	-145,417	1,631,719	534,137	285,840	17,638	139,004	81,836
1990	2,634,503	2,184,047	12,963	2,197,010	261,182	-166,885	1,768,943	558,232	307,328	18,702	140,871	86,195
1991	2,754,628	2,332,957	9,998	2,342,955	280,841	-194,163	1,867,951	556,143	330,534	19,228	143,263	88,504
1992	3,001,652	2,579,159	13,232	2,592,391	306,477	-233,981	2,051,933	591,435	358,284	20,637	145,449	90,993
1993	3,105,381	2,706,721	5,775	2,712,496	323,819	-260,812	2,127,865	603,017	374,499	20,978	148,031	92,431
1994	3,316,816	2,856,093	15,263	2,871,356	343,770	-266,661	2,260,925	666,747	389,144	22,280	148,867	94,352
1995	3,517,557	3,058,483	6,186	3,064,669	367,889	-301,646	2,395,134	710,844	411,579	23,338	150,725	97,363
1996	3,688,179	3,156,890	12,232	3,169,122	377,150	-290,469	2,501,503	761,112	425,564	24,231	152,206	98,410
1997	3,865,559	3,337,565	7,138	3,344,703	396,056	-317,706	2,630,941	795,319	439,299	25,179	153,525	99,045
1998	4,149,206	3,639,227	12,837	3,652,064	429,602	-409,274	2,813,188	886,959	449,059	26,865	154,444	101,732
1999	4,296,194	3,890,440	12,225	3,902,665	455,407	-478,738	2,968,520	863,496	464,178	27,575	155,801	103,893
2000	4,556,401	4,120,342	7,322	4,127,664	478,865	-475,679	3,173,120	885,615	497,666	29,003	157,103	106,300
2001	4,722,900	4,253,394	6,496	4,259,890	493,270	-493,772	3,272,848	899,777	550,275	29,861	158,163	106,369
2002	4,829,600	4,403,250	8,767	4,412,017	506,592	-551,264	3,354,161	879,952	595,487	30,349	159,134	107,051
2003	4,992,497	4,497,772	15,809	4,513,581	517,225	-572,458	3,423,898	959,319	609,280	31,313	159,440	106,191
2004	5,288,030	4,765,542	16,172	4,781,714	546,676	-526,104	3,708,934	950,697	628,399	33,023	160,130	107,034
2005	5,446,647	4,907,219	17,172	4,924,391	566,068	-562,694	3,795,629	978,705	672,313	33,736	161,451	108,304
2006	5,796,545	5,057,303	12,050	5,069,353	587,797	-583,094	3,898,462	1,179,150	718,933	35,621	162,727	109,149
2007	6,012,860	5,274,139	21,646	5,295,785	608,388	-612,950	4,074,447	1,167,476	770,937	36,656	164,037	110,165
2008	6,190,639	5,431,020	27,861	5,458,881	634,769	-686,083	4,138,029	1,169,234	883,376	37,540	164,910	111,420
2009	6,004,938	5,240,799	8,860	5,249,659	615,821	-690,048	3,943,790	1,042,154	1,018,994	36,081	166,429	107,969
2010	6,247,113	5,461,114	14,407	5,475,521	648,600	-737,987	4,088,934	1,072,143	1,086,036	37,376	167,144	108,916
2011	6,610,276	5,674,155	28,849	5,703,004	598,929	-814,861	4,289,214	1,265,608	1,055,454	39,446	167,579	111,014
2012	6,767,589	5,827,332	26,624	5,853,956	609,455	-798,697	4,445,804	1,253,818	1,067,967	40,134	168,623	110,642
2013	6,736,159	5,995,907	27,161	6,023,068	709,621	-884,994	4,428,453	1,208,523	1,099,183	39,768	169,388	111,756
2014	7,045,157	6,149,667	26,696	6,176,363	723,927	-871,278	4,581,158	1,322,011	1,141,988	41,568	169,486	112,446
2015	7,345,235	6,357,872	26,520	6,384,392	745,527	-881,069	4,757,796	1,385,532	1,201,907	43,352	169,433	113,078
2016	7,575,056	6,558,134	15,733	6,573,867	765,997	-934,327	4,873,543	1,485,322	1,216,191	44,594	169,866	115,452
2017	7,797,896	6,774,109	16,810	6,790,919	802,053	-985,249	5,003,617	1,512,579	1,281,700	45,700	170,632	116,130
2018	8,153,804	6,975,756	14,251	6,990,007	808,728	-972,581	5,208,698	1,586,991	1,358,115	47,717	170,879	116,233
2019	8,446,761	7,224,463	19,668	7,244,131	845,724	-994,344	5,404,063	1,617,693	1,425,005	49,145	171,875	115,558
2020	8,882,829	7,204,216	30,544	7,234,760	843,152	-942,842	5,448,766	1,616,951	1,817,112	51,751	171,646	112,242
2021	9,473,946	7,582,746	34,136	7,616,882	872,337	-966,732	5,777,813	1,661,803	2,034,330	55,202	171,623	114,335

Personal Income and Employment by Area: Owensboro, KY

(Thousands of dollars, except as noted.)

Year	Personal income, total	Earnings by place of work			Less: Contributions for government social insurance	Plus: Adjustment for residence	Equals: Net earnings by place of residence	Plus: Dividends, interest, and rent	Plus: Personal current transfer receipts	Per capita personal income (dollars)	Population (persons)	Total employment
		Nonfarm	Farm	Total								
1970	320,584	255,753	11,629	267,382	17,575	-1,232	248,575	41,388	30,621	3,348	95,768	42,800
1971	346,680	270,549	12,931	283,480	19,049	751	265,182	45,118	36,380	3,575	96,960	42,627
1972	385,742	296,311	15,826	312,137	22,120	6,029	296,046	49,231	40,465	3,968	97,215	43,642
1973	428,085	325,627	25,247	350,874	28,023	3,235	326,086	54,150	47,849	4,364	98,090	45,008
1974	476,524	359,775	24,164	383,939	32,271	3,164	354,832	62,435	59,257	4,814	98,996	46,164
1975	518,329	385,142	16,717	401,859	34,050	5,519	373,328	70,276	74,725	5,193	99,816	44,188
1976	577,142	433,257	18,542	451,799	38,732	8,008	421,075	77,790	78,277	5,749	100,389	45,399
1977	648,219	481,530	26,841	508,371	42,776	13,433	479,028	88,556	80,635	6,433	100,759	46,935
1978	726,593	560,633	15,482	576,115	51,356	14,556	539,315	101,407	85,871	7,125	101,985	49,522
1979	822,467	625,831	19,612	645,443	59,521	21,366	607,288	116,545	98,634	7,969	103,209	49,610
1980	913,637	691,076	3,400	694,476	66,050	19,807	648,233	148,122	117,282	8,791	103,927	49,868
1981	1,026,691	748,621	22,733	771,354	76,964	15,095	709,485	183,996	133,210	9,849	104,247	49,877
1982	1,081,238	764,057	15,520	779,577	79,631	19,445	719,391	215,285	146,562	10,324	104,731	49,194
1983	1,122,302	830,883	-22,117	808,766	86,159	17,917	740,524	224,725	157,053	10,646	105,422	50,297
1984	1,254,372	876,692	34,038	910,730	93,698	20,473	837,505	248,390	168,477	11,775	106,527	51,708
1985	1,284,177	897,363	21,806	919,169	97,176	20,509	842,502	262,378	179,297	12,092	106,197	51,751
1986	1,310,777	923,335	17,374	940,709	103,153	16,489	854,045	266,964	189,768	12,396	105,746	52,395
1987	1,352,898	963,108	15,413	978,521	106,507	15,735	887,749	268,309	196,840	12,878	105,054	52,141
1988	1,448,635	1,047,980	17,796	1,065,776	116,803	14,206	963,179	276,846	208,610	13,859	104,527	52,711
1989	1,567,523	1,095,825	47,480	1,143,305	124,637	14,288	1,032,956	303,753	230,814	14,992	104,559	54,131
1990	1,650,826	1,158,564	42,261	1,200,825	136,171	14,063	1,078,717	321,599	250,510	15,765	104,716	54,954
1991	1,713,422	1,198,480	33,325	1,231,805	142,422	11,556	1,100,939	329,770	282,713	16,288	105,194	54,878
1992	1,837,714	1,278,481	56,361	1,334,842	149,956	7,763	1,192,649	337,646	307,419	17,334	106,017	55,861
1993	1,901,877	1,355,874	45,428	1,401,302	162,107	4,918	1,244,113	343,251	314,513	17,834	106,646	57,276
1994	2,025,354	1,444,381	53,978	1,498,359	176,059	1,540	1,323,840	368,425	333,089	18,834	107,539	59,266
1995	2,093,512	1,502,993	31,868	1,534,861	184,350	-1,103	1,349,408	385,892	358,212	19,342	108,234	60,800
1996	2,197,463	1,534,198	64,763	1,598,961	187,131	-1,830	1,410,000	410,924	376,539	20,239	108,573	60,962
1997	2,338,396	1,673,182	43,614	1,716,796	202,595	-10,643	1,503,558	436,786	398,052	21,483	108,851	62,246
1998	2,413,298	1,740,643	29,201	1,769,844	211,952	-7,994	1,549,898	456,442	406,958	22,125	109,075	62,960
1999	2,495,273	1,836,875	26,715	1,863,590	222,740	-6,958	1,633,892	434,886	426,495	22,781	109,533	63,701
2000	2,683,021	1,923,184	62,272	1,985,456	226,118	-9,334	1,750,004	477,613	455,404	24,377	110,064	64,172
2001	2,749,405	1,962,014	63,219	2,025,233	229,522	-7,224	1,788,487	465,839	495,079	24,997	109,991	62,827
2002	2,828,773	2,037,694	19,607	2,057,301	236,200	3,721	1,824,822	470,733	533,218	25,672	110,190	62,105
2003	2,928,173	2,090,266	36,108	2,126,374	240,168	11,658	1,897,864	482,450	547,859	26,443	110,735	62,423
2004	3,104,044	2,194,609	81,850	2,276,459	247,387	19,432	2,048,504	467,415	588,125	27,965	110,999	62,784
2005	3,268,234	2,276,443	111,209	2,387,652	257,871	24,801	2,154,582	483,802	629,850	29,320	111,469	62,984
2006	3,485,882	2,426,690	88,584	2,515,274	274,462	28,796	2,269,608	532,436	683,838	31,082	112,152	64,127
2007	3,723,491	2,585,815	67,477	2,653,292	291,722	37,128	2,398,698	585,459	739,334	32,980	112,900	65,389
2008	4,142,629	2,849,689	81,031	2,930,720	316,142	37,696	2,652,274	654,455	835,900	36,450	113,651	65,107
2009	3,980,096	2,626,638	110,232	2,736,870	304,199	18,574	2,451,245	602,644	926,207	34,796	114,385	63,026
2010	4,055,929	2,711,610	62,628	2,774,238	308,368	10,889	2,476,759	595,283	983,887	35,338	114,775	63,217
2011	4,215,232	2,710,574	121,282	2,831,856	279,257	-4,234	2,548,365	671,084	995,783	36,568	115,272	64,634
2012	4,250,905	2,772,574	95,223	2,867,797	293,757	-42,535	2,531,505	729,130	990,270	36,648	115,994	66,237
2013	4,361,510	2,840,277	219,954	3,060,231	340,569	-62,665	2,656,997	691,531	1,012,982	37,468	116,407	66,028
2014	4,532,656	2,936,868	144,960	3,081,828	354,042	-60,209	2,667,577	759,684	1,105,395	38,651	117,270	66,085
2015	4,695,257	3,077,768	88,472	3,166,240	371,632	-81,259	2,713,349	809,262	1,172,646	39,639	118,451	67,080
2016	4,626,449	3,038,527	56,984	3,095,511	375,214	-79,713	2,640,584	804,723	1,181,142	38,812	119,201	67,736
2017	4,772,173	3,074,893	91,600	3,166,493	381,566	-67,969	2,716,958	838,925	1,216,290	39,862	119,716	67,816
2018	4,854,295	3,180,671	72,993	3,253,664	394,502	-73,108	2,786,054	814,780	1,253,461	40,362	120,268	67,867
2019	5,114,332	3,331,540	80,003	3,411,543	405,669	-84,948	2,920,926	882,083	1,311,323	42,264	121,008	67,405
2020	5,561,207	3,405,626	73,637	3,479,263	423,404	-87,859	2,968,000	881,767	1,711,440	45,772	121,497	65,129
2021	6,044,239	3,615,974	144,152	3,760,126	446,503	-92,111	3,221,512	898,469	1,924,258	49,859	121,227	66,909

Personal Income and Employment by Area: Oxnard-Thousand Oaks-Ventura, CA

(Thousands of dollars, except as noted.)

Year	Personal income, total	Earnings by place of work Nonfarm	Farm	Total	Less: Contributions for government social insurance	Plus: Adjustment for residence	Equals: Net earnings by place of residence	Plus: Dividends, interest, and rent	Plus: Personal current transfer receipts	Per capita personal income (dollars)	Population (persons)	Total employment
1970	1,675,029	993,450	70,144	1,063,594	59,659	266,591	1,270,526	276,675	127,828	4,394	381,174	135,394
1971	1,846,661	1,087,352	77,954	1,165,306	66,834	287,697	1,386,169	309,432	151,060	4,667	395,691	140,085
1972	2,086,155	1,221,184	91,278	1,312,462	79,079	340,746	1,574,129	342,236	169,790	5,107	408,523	147,656
1973	2,368,468	1,352,274	129,273	1,481,547	99,113	401,405	1,783,839	391,554	193,075	5,646	419,461	155,861
1974	2,697,313	1,508,134	139,016	1,647,150	114,703	473,033	2,005,480	454,295	237,538	6,217	433,885	164,301
1975	3,067,325	1,696,502	143,245	1,839,747	128,038	534,204	2,245,913	512,953	308,459	6,833	448,918	171,738
1976	3,415,649	1,894,313	110,060	2,004,373	145,545	635,485	2,494,313	565,057	356,279	7,418	460,485	176,285
1977	3,925,078	2,169,151	148,233	2,317,384	171,933	764,228	2,909,679	637,153	378,246	8,200	478,695	188,053
1978	4,631,103	2,530,991	191,946	2,722,937	206,263	940,953	3,457,627	755,761	417,715	9,373	494,086	202,771
1979	5,233,301	2,859,840	153,355	3,013,195	245,491	1,153,980	3,921,684	847,914	463,703	10,218	512,189	213,342
1980	6,075,966	3,212,435	161,842	3,374,277	270,790	1,379,112	4,482,599	1,045,953	547,414	11,403	532,827	221,151
1981	6,889,811	3,585,011	155,419	3,740,430	327,718	1,547,680	4,960,392	1,278,549	650,870	12,610	546,389	225,479
1982	7,502,143	3,908,134	206,124	4,114,258	366,910	1,616,401	5,363,749	1,420,477	717,917	13,346	562,142	229,893
1983	8,134,982	4,256,520	213,837	4,470,357	413,523	1,741,025	5,797,859	1,578,228	758,895	14,133	575,586	237,557
1984	9,076,701	4,810,054	238,127	5,048,181	488,379	1,915,735	6,475,537	1,793,120	808,044	15,416	588,790	248,225
1985	9,880,063	5,326,172	217,602	5,543,774	551,106	2,083,634	7,076,302	1,922,421	881,340	16,390	602,819	260,105
1986	10,817,704	5,881,893	317,243	6,199,136	616,305	2,255,143	7,837,974	2,027,747	951,983	17,578	615,422	270,559
1987	11,796,155	6,527,630	387,110	6,914,740	694,225	2,491,653	8,712,168	2,097,563	986,424	18,663	632,062	287,425
1988	12,944,377	7,317,836	445,607	7,763,443	804,748	2,646,744	9,605,439	2,282,859	1,056,079	19,888	650,851	305,846
1989	13,967,127	7,805,015	427,647	8,232,662	870,346	2,809,535	10,171,851	2,646,108	1,149,168	21,013	664,692	317,976
1990	14,970,554	8,453,809	465,101	8,918,910	938,783	3,079,208	11,059,335	2,664,566	1,246,653	22,340	670,117	327,267
1991	15,621,492	8,925,682	438,537	9,364,219	993,420	3,157,377	11,528,176	2,696,861	1,396,455	23,119	675,706	332,915
1992	16,207,128	9,482,041	285,341	9,767,382	1,048,851	3,190,239	11,908,770	2,707,122	1,591,236	23,690	684,143	332,193
1993	16,983,115	9,803,744	414,090	10,217,834	1,084,064	3,310,079	12,443,849	2,855,184	1,684,082	24,615	689,943	335,316
1994	17,665,815	10,297,146	358,400	10,655,546	1,145,221	3,373,256	12,883,581	3,070,044	1,712,190	25,291	698,509	344,984
1995	18,835,782	10,587,326	441,879	11,029,205	1,164,919	3,642,324	13,506,610	3,526,477	1,802,695	26,775	703,486	352,089
1996	19,600,729	11,124,804	332,740	11,457,544	1,195,213	3,721,707	13,984,038	3,712,716	1,903,975	27,598	710,215	358,399
1997	21,018,291	11,784,445	413,120	12,197,565	1,254,224	4,153,317	15,096,658	3,977,527	1,944,106	29,147	721,107	357,142
1998	21,993,732	12,631,099	406,776	13,037,875	1,339,466	4,085,732	15,784,141	4,165,147	2,044,444	30,096	730,779	371,587
1999	23,665,634	13,854,545	461,734	14,316,279	1,451,002	4,191,007	17,056,284	4,448,740	2,160,610	31,836	743,357	385,759
2000	25,841,629	15,580,589	424,619	16,005,208	1,609,561	4,375,904	18,771,551	4,784,393	2,285,685	34,159	756,506	395,387
2001	27,370,512	17,130,336	305,730	17,436,066	1,802,749	4,511,675	20,144,992	4,689,383	2,536,137	35,700	766,689	407,454
2002	28,126,558	17,881,679	370,082	18,251,761	1,906,699	4,557,627	20,902,689	4,502,516	2,721,353	36,083	779,489	415,664
2003	29,743,502	19,211,972	366,181	19,578,153	2,070,441	4,495,294	22,003,006	4,846,185	2,894,311	37,742	788,070	422,993
2004	31,773,526	20,618,575	523,310	21,141,885	2,296,975	4,832,256	23,677,166	5,084,119	3,012,241	40,017	793,994	428,584
2005	32,987,191	21,517,750	509,087	22,026,837	2,412,869	4,686,667	24,300,635	5,502,593	3,183,963	41,535	794,197	435,416
2006	35,353,194	22,294,218	648,561	22,942,779	2,451,966	4,999,418	25,490,231	6,434,810	3,428,153	44,292	798,183	441,017
2007	36,810,102	22,953,655	623,321	23,576,976	2,477,629	4,986,481	26,085,818	7,074,388	3,649,896	46,011	800,027	447,553
2008	37,041,305	22,245,760	666,983	22,912,743	2,459,404	5,216,431	25,669,770	7,153,036	4,218,499	45,937	806,353	441,320
2009	36,167,195	22,053,638	848,207	22,901,845	2,449,366	4,578,077	25,030,556	6,449,488	4,687,151	44,370	815,130	427,303
2010	37,837,831	23,195,123	930,847	24,125,970	2,463,452	4,584,226	26,246,744	6,384,019	5,207,068	45,856	825,144	424,867
2011	39,777,071	23,979,345	824,639	24,803,984	2,298,787	4,728,110	27,233,307	7,273,932	5,269,832	47,929	829,908	430,069
2012	41,563,660	24,457,367	1,054,142	25,511,509	2,329,430	5,283,274	28,465,353	7,816,252	5,282,055	49,879	833,287	438,470
2013	42,045,001	24,859,934	1,205,206	26,065,140	2,669,764	5,267,556	28,662,932	7,894,212	5,487,857	50,189	837,729	446,574
2014	44,276,206	25,776,102	1,201,458	26,977,560	2,768,261	5,573,378	29,782,677	8,651,452	5,842,077	52,544	842,648	456,374
2015	46,403,702	26,703,380	1,229,275	27,932,655	2,845,178	6,188,729	31,276,206	8,848,404	6,279,092	54,834	846,263	460,902
2016	47,773,595	27,114,675	1,086,178	28,200,853	2,913,837	6,425,578	31,712,594	9,534,740	6,526,261	56,356	847,718	464,957
2017	49,206,168	27,879,899	1,148,173	29,028,072	3,009,671	6,418,390	32,436,791	10,192,040	6,577,337	57,944	849,196	467,771
2018	51,073,359	28,475,419	901,923	29,377,342	3,116,335	7,138,565	33,399,572	10,747,804	6,925,983	60,207	848,290	474,428
2019	53,964,282	29,976,178	1,031,748	31,007,926	3,302,549	7,307,981	35,013,358	11,487,599	7,463,325	63,833	845,396	475,232
2020	57,863,763	30,990,420	1,027,943	32,018,363	3,379,482	6,920,586	35,559,467	11,475,204	10,829,092	68,647	842,921	457,685
2021	61,619,080	32,744,087	787,272	33,531,359	3,555,338	8,576,077	38,552,098	11,683,153	11,383,829	73,375	839,784	468,549

Personal Income and Employment by Area: Palm Bay-Melbourne-Titusville, FL

(Thousands of dollars, except as noted.)

Year	Personal income, total	Nonfarm	Farm	Total	Less: Contributions for government social insurance	Plus: Adjustment for residence	Equals: Net earnings by place of residence	Plus: Dividends, interest, and rent	Plus: Personal current transfer receipts	Per capita personal income (dollars)	Population (persons)	Total employment
		Earnings by place of work										
1970	960,656	824,515	3,649	828,164	48,418	-25,113	754,633	150,345	55,678	4,183	229,660	96,024
1971	997,539	816,909	5,158	822,067	49,360	-19,279	753,428	173,574	70,537	4,305	231,701	92,542
1972	1,098,130	882,554	7,339	889,893	56,797	-17,371	815,725	196,562	85,843	4,764	230,503	95,402
1973	1,214,884	957,791	9,272	967,063	71,295	-13,390	882,378	228,012	104,494	5,100	238,222	101,054
1974	1,288,875	973,540	8,879	982,419	75,325	-11,004	896,090	263,759	129,026	5,405	238,464	99,316
1975	1,425,801	1,047,870	6,844	1,054,714	80,238	-13,507	960,969	297,553	167,279	5,910	241,241	97,287
1976	1,545,551	1,120,597	6,191	1,126,788	87,661	-10,513	1,028,614	331,243	185,694	6,419	240,791	98,836
1977	1,722,462	1,250,238	6,385	1,256,623	100,298	-9,675	1,146,650	375,662	200,150	7,134	241,451	103,907
1978	2,011,797	1,458,540	7,983	1,466,523	120,935	-9,244	1,336,344	450,487	224,966	8,014	251,031	113,104
1979	2,362,778	1,724,273	10,283	1,734,556	150,984	-10,221	1,573,351	528,441	260,986	8,983	263,038	121,837
1980	2,823,655	2,014,927	13,200	2,028,127	178,073	-8,382	1,841,672	669,611	312,372	10,243	275,664	129,188
1981	3,259,509	2,273,293	9,240	2,282,533	216,346	-8,218	2,057,969	830,821	370,719	11,398	285,963	133,908
1982	3,581,183	2,479,572	12,079	2,491,651	243,013	-9,954	2,238,684	918,016	424,483	11,973	299,098	138,412
1983	3,982,208	2,772,922	13,416	2,786,338	277,932	-13,214	2,495,192	1,018,054	468,962	12,846	310,006	147,424
1984	4,530,774	3,187,974	10,245	3,198,219	330,120	-16,119	2,851,980	1,168,255	510,539	14,037	322,780	159,722
1985	5,015,727	3,545,117	10,256	3,555,373	375,182	-15,706	3,164,485	1,289,170	562,072	14,886	336,935	170,814
1986	5,347,897	3,734,718	9,107	3,743,825	407,335	-9,341	3,327,149	1,398,322	622,426	15,315	349,183	175,694
1987	5,767,566	4,048,894	9,653	4,058,547	437,498	-5,669	3,615,380	1,483,410	668,776	16,038	359,628	176,540
1988	6,370,868	4,501,813	15,615	4,517,428	500,038	-4,057	4,013,333	1,616,634	740,901	17,147	371,547	187,777
1989	7,150,560	4,916,005	14,347	4,930,352	551,202	-599	4,378,551	1,914,197	857,812	18,601	384,423	196,440
1990	7,626,357	5,236,681	14,051	5,250,732	585,860	749	4,665,621	1,995,220	965,516	18,914	403,209	202,232
1991	8,022,074	5,533,472	16,213	5,549,685	624,172	-2,683	4,922,830	1,996,133	1,103,111	19,306	415,512	203,022
1992	8,561,401	5,919,345	14,610	5,933,955	666,016	5,229	5,273,168	2,006,707	1,281,526	20,117	425,584	203,939
1993	8,923,620	6,109,457	13,347	6,122,804	685,358	23,368	5,460,814	2,077,915	1,384,891	20,454	436,282	206,630
1994	9,295,180	6,252,356	12,453	6,264,809	725,784	44,783	5,583,808	2,208,483	1,502,889	20,926	444,198	209,999
1995	9,788,712	6,407,829	11,076	6,418,905	745,828	68,157	5,741,234	2,417,623	1,629,855	21,690	451,310	211,373
1996	10,219,494	6,551,493	8,958	6,560,451	766,054	98,717	5,893,114	2,578,897	1,747,483	22,417	455,889	215,068
1997	10,930,629	6,982,652	10,210	6,992,862	816,791	123,097	6,299,168	2,788,663	1,842,798	23,675	461,686	223,138
1998	11,570,967	7,393,662	14,001	7,407,663	859,734	163,082	6,711,011	2,950,600	1,909,356	24,744	467,624	230,763
1999	12,028,632	7,753,218	15,783	7,769,001	894,939	205,353	7,079,415	2,930,057	2,019,160	25,477	472,138	234,135
2000	13,266,871	8,632,969	16,542	8,649,511	983,084	232,838	7,899,265	3,215,323	2,152,283	27,765	477,819	242,259
2001	13,867,605	8,990,141	16,267	9,006,408	1,008,906	244,642	8,242,144	3,262,152	2,363,309	28,509	486,429	244,989
2002	14,320,645	9,349,789	17,682	9,367,471	1,046,382	260,098	8,581,187	3,178,261	2,561,197	28,906	495,425	244,592
2003	15,254,889	9,983,007	14,820	9,997,827	1,121,554	280,756	9,157,029	3,346,119	2,751,741	30,217	504,847	252,217
2004	16,409,429	10,963,742	14,119	10,977,861	1,236,580	302,271	10,043,552	3,366,912	2,998,965	31,634	518,722	261,987
2005	17,626,566	11,895,394	18,427	11,913,821	1,342,369	332,231	10,903,683	3,541,130	3,181,753	33,264	529,907	272,273
2006	18,867,161	12,542,757	16,275	12,559,032	1,437,776	374,129	11,495,385	3,941,009	3,430,767	35,257	535,138	278,457
2007	19,627,336	12,590,196	11,583	12,601,779	1,460,937	430,799	11,571,641	4,403,683	3,652,012	36,366	539,719	277,306
2008	20,195,820	12,571,473	9,069	12,580,542	1,483,129	446,931	11,544,344	4,528,146	4,123,330	37,236	542,378	269,411
2009	19,380,205	12,116,437	9,963	12,126,400	1,454,584	388,127	11,059,943	3,901,692	4,418,570	35,750	542,109	258,623
2010	20,197,931	12,470,738	16,955	12,487,693	1,477,339	374,803	11,385,157	4,065,740	4,747,034	37,129	544,000	256,563
2011	20,972,616	12,526,890	15,487	12,542,377	1,337,808	379,112	11,583,681	4,415,868	4,973,067	38,521	544,442	257,435
2012	21,028,676	12,499,163	23,138	12,522,301	1,355,247	416,931	11,583,985	4,455,528	4,989,163	38,435	547,119	258,429
2013	21,016,076	12,484,141	15,642	12,499,783	1,527,213	430,715	11,403,285	4,480,310	5,132,481	38,178	550,478	260,571
2014	21,905,106	12,666,374	17,061	12,683,435	1,552,594	479,665	11,610,506	4,885,576	5,409,024	39,416	555,747	265,366
2015	23,302,452	13,389,544	24,634	13,414,178	1,625,811	499,295	12,287,662	5,259,920	5,754,870	41,169	566,018	272,815
2016	24,236,432	13,996,426	17,632	14,014,058	1,699,663	525,969	12,840,364	5,398,690	5,997,378	41,987	577,242	279,765
2017	25,789,638	14,972,847	18,311	14,991,158	1,810,258	561,587	13,742,487	5,790,666	6,256,485	43,860	588,002	291,661
2018	27,396,517	15,977,733	12,147	15,989,880	1,941,749	610,357	14,658,488	6,222,450	6,515,579	46,061	594,787	303,834
2019	29,275,434	17,179,356	11,724	17,191,080	2,110,691	609,963	15,690,352	6,637,707	6,947,375	48,725	600,836	310,807
2020	31,476,172	17,868,710	10,110	17,878,820	2,207,215	566,774	16,238,379	6,743,712	8,494,081	51,769	608,007	310,581
2021	34,208,428	19,419,064	13,715	19,432,779	2,340,238	656,450	17,748,991	6,940,517	9,518,920	55,477	616,628	323,190

Personal Income and Employment by Area: Panama City, FL

(Thousands of dollars, except as noted.)

| Year | Personal income, total | Earnings by place of work | | | Less: Contributions for government social insurance | Plus: Adjustment for residence | Equals: Net earnings by place of residence | Plus: Dividends, interest, and rent | Plus: Personal current transfer receipts | Per capita personal income (dollars) | Population (persons) | Total employment |
		Nonfarm	Farm	Total								
1970	295,964	238,906	174	239,080	14,055	-1,960	223,065	50,356	22,543	3,450	85,792	35,240
1971	323,060	256,606	210	256,816	15,682	-1,926	239,208	57,039	26,813	3,659	88,300	35,430
1972	358,760	283,390	210	283,600	18,042	-2,102	263,456	63,199	32,105	4,003	89,621	36,514
1973	411,431	324,755	439	325,194	23,516	-2,673	299,005	73,167	39,259	4,485	91,744	39,716
1974	470,682	368,908	796	369,704	28,237	-3,757	337,710	85,311	47,661	4,868	96,694	42,168
1975	527,353	402,200	793	402,993	30,812	-4,703	367,478	97,201	62,674	5,299	99,527	42,716
1976	596,019	459,916	656	460,572	36,025	-7,145	417,402	108,418	70,199	5,825	102,320	45,048
1977	644,969	491,314	448	491,762	38,689	-7,051	446,022	121,499	77,448	6,205	103,944	46,176
1978	740,384	560,790	341	561,131	44,703	-8,585	507,843	147,486	85,055	7,035	105,250	48,370
1979	818,099	611,933	277	612,210	51,796	-10,624	549,790	170,495	97,814	7,572	108,048	49,098
1980	930,336	674,518	301	674,819	57,183	-9,282	608,354	205,110	116,872	8,538	108,965	50,033
1981	1,064,830	767,481	170	767,651	70,068	-10,389	687,194	242,336	135,300	9,591	111,027	51,966
1982	1,168,232	826,531	304	826,835	76,994	-12,482	737,359	275,842	155,031	10,187	114,679	53,880
1983	1,281,370	909,719	275	909,994	86,226	-13,872	809,896	300,923	170,551	10,964	116,871	56,082
1984	1,444,872	1,039,607	321	1,039,928	101,135	-17,861	920,932	341,323	182,617	12,020	120,204	60,969
1985	1,574,306	1,136,205	375	1,136,580	113,154	-19,154	1,004,272	372,831	197,203	12,605	124,892	65,284
1986	1,702,034	1,225,373	537	1,225,910	125,384	-19,352	1,081,174	407,338	213,522	13,153	129,400	67,908
1987	1,780,431	1,279,057	621	1,279,678	129,866	-18,300	1,131,512	421,750	227,169	13,412	132,748	67,445
1988	1,929,509	1,387,241	565	1,387,806	145,912	-17,557	1,224,337	456,052	249,120	14,257	135,342	69,027
1989	2,086,314	1,446,472	279	1,446,751	154,759	-16,512	1,275,480	522,751	288,083	15,202	137,241	70,569
1990	2,262,923	1,569,300	138	1,569,438	168,708	-18,841	1,381,889	559,897	321,137	16,302	138,809	73,233
1991	2,432,462	1,696,540	-25	1,696,515	183,471	-22,112	1,490,932	576,921	364,609	17,200	141,422	74,997
1992	2,600,719	1,805,051	-263	1,804,788	196,082	-25,506	1,583,200	602,194	415,325	17,957	144,829	76,244
1993	2,786,071	1,917,383	-32	1,917,351	208,335	-28,973	1,680,043	659,091	446,937	18,669	149,232	78,539
1994	2,901,686	1,999,541	372	1,999,913	219,331	-31,371	1,749,211	668,922	483,553	19,053	152,295	79,835
1995	3,142,205	2,115,487	653	2,116,140	229,649	-33,393	1,853,098	747,651	541,456	20,285	154,905	81,750
1996	3,308,369	2,239,376	1,170	2,240,546	241,829	-37,568	1,961,149	796,173	551,047	20,981	157,681	84,598
1997	3,470,376	2,350,753	1,766	2,352,519	254,651	-40,080	2,057,788	834,409	578,179	21,769	159,420	85,586
1998	3,388,156	2,326,446	1,461	2,327,907	252,707	-52,204	2,022,996	836,123	529,037	23,047	147,011	82,258
1999	3,503,525	2,425,229	1,359	2,426,588	261,453	-56,781	2,108,354	833,509	561,662	23,649	148,149	82,839
2000	3,653,563	2,472,597	1,070	2,473,667	266,155	-57,835	2,149,677	898,873	605,013	24,621	148,393	83,228
2001	4,015,740	2,766,561	1,064	2,767,625	295,457	-65,096	2,407,072	937,698	670,970	26,735	150,207	84,003
2002	4,246,402	2,997,677	861	2,998,538	317,505	-73,651	2,607,382	899,204	739,816	27,801	152,741	85,801
2003	4,550,373	3,238,785	584	3,239,369	342,592	-76,911	2,819,866	936,257	794,250	29,349	155,044	87,915
2004	4,895,854	3,496,666	724	3,497,390	374,688	-89,424	3,033,278	1,012,599	849,977	30,830	158,804	93,082
2005	5,307,800	3,833,597	822	3,834,419	413,816	-111,359	3,309,244	1,088,352	910,204	32,580	162,917	97,038
2006	5,693,338	4,117,278	753	4,118,031	452,542	-111,884	3,553,605	1,178,351	961,382	34,371	165,644	100,143
2007	5,931,960	4,086,162	688	4,086,850	456,394	-101,875	3,528,581	1,385,856	1,017,523	35,876	165,345	100,794
2008	6,124,102	4,103,379	651	4,104,030	465,292	-95,472	3,543,266	1,421,616	1,159,220	36,833	166,267	99,109
2009	5,953,010	3,977,982	576	3,978,558	463,140	-91,147	3,424,271	1,265,317	1,263,422	35,548	167,464	96,101
2010	6,279,820	4,103,998	640	4,104,638	473,832	-98,629	3,532,177	1,322,725	1,424,918	37,113	169,209	95,619
2011	6,444,207	4,078,311	771	4,079,082	427,390	-81,748	3,569,944	1,401,188	1,473,075	37,999	169,587	96,586
2012	6,511,329	4,130,278	741	4,131,019	438,579	-68,057	3,624,383	1,444,978	1,441,968	37,897	171,818	96,974
2013	6,601,025	4,228,663	897	4,229,560	502,425	-46,903	3,680,232	1,435,670	1,485,123	37,784	174,704	98,845
2014	6,966,345	4,487,032	1,000	4,488,032	532,668	-61,651	3,893,713	1,514,377	1,558,255	38,743	179,809	102,760
2015	7,380,417	4,724,215	879	4,725,094	554,354	-69,863	4,100,877	1,652,474	1,627,066	40,240	183,408	105,232
2016	7,588,404	4,886,246	1,139	4,887,385	570,612	-101,815	4,214,958	1,675,969	1,697,477	40,831	185,851	107,227
2017	7,699,559	4,951,093	2,216	4,953,309	578,877	-102,508	4,271,924	1,636,171	1,791,464	41,113	187,276	108,558
2018	8,004,612	5,126,236	803	5,127,039	603,992	-135,021	4,388,026	1,720,314	1,896,272	42,273	189,354	109,955
2019	8,214,021	5,242,357	1,045	5,243,402	624,236	-112,083	4,507,083	1,844,550	1,862,388	46,452	176,830	104,669
2020	8,791,753	5,360,348	1,227	5,361,575	638,249	-94,833	4,628,493	1,872,502	2,290,758	50,394	174,461	105,066
2021	9,671,542	5,937,062	3,984	5,941,046	688,579	-116,797	5,135,670	1,927,003	2,608,869	53,980	179,168	110,152

Personal Income and Employment by Area: Parkersburg-Vienna, WV

(Thousands of dollars, except as noted.)

Year	Personal income, total	Earnings by place of work			Less: Contributions for government social insurance	Plus: Adjustment for residence	Equals: Net earnings by place of residence	Plus: Dividends, interest, and rent	Plus: Personal current transfer receipts	Per capita personal income (dollars)	Population (persons)	Total employment
		Nonfarm	Farm	Total								
1970	318,216	265,753	716	266,469	20,162	1,957	248,264	39,781	30,171	3,509	90,698	37,759
1971	337,191	281,115	831	281,946	22,081	-935	258,930	42,875	35,386	3,742	90,111	38,352
1972	369,651	314,547	1,037	315,584	26,269	-5,806	283,509	46,904	39,238	4,062	91,003	39,746
1973	406,901	349,601	1,456	351,057	33,776	-7,880	309,401	52,316	45,184	4,429	91,866	42,037
1974	463,093	397,299	819	398,118	40,232	-10,347	347,539	60,887	54,667	5,024	92,182	43,648
1975	495,791	401,490	280	401,770	39,454	-7,941	354,375	68,177	73,239	5,322	93,160	41,134
1976	547,765	449,447	-144	449,303	44,953	-8,070	396,280	73,983	77,502	5,820	94,121	42,127
1977	622,084	514,767	-243	514,524	51,319	-8,240	454,965	82,680	84,439	6,551	94,964	44,102
1978	701,671	585,813	151	585,964	60,451	-5,687	519,826	91,768	90,077	7,255	96,719	46,028
1979	772,357	648,676	219	648,895	69,301	-14,120	565,474	103,962	102,921	7,928	97,422	46,895
1980	849,513	696,324	344	696,668	75,171	-22,970	598,527	125,863	125,123	8,620	98,551	46,059
1981	931,764	757,522	-821	756,701	87,222	-31,702	637,777	153,807	140,180	9,461	98,486	45,220
1982	966,490	776,733	-1,633	775,100	91,943	-41,391	641,766	169,896	154,828	9,913	97,500	44,032
1983	1,023,366	814,630	-1,352	813,278	97,825	-47,167	668,286	186,640	168,440	10,510	97,368	44,220
1984	1,105,997	880,315	-197	880,118	108,095	-48,810	723,213	207,160	175,624	11,407	96,959	45,190
1985	1,171,487	930,261	103	930,364	115,381	-53,259	761,724	220,432	189,331	12,149	96,427	45,545
1986	1,200,824	953,390	-393	952,997	122,683	-55,034	775,280	224,256	201,288	12,515	95,949	45,461
1987	1,238,924	998,037	-848	997,189	130,717	-66,039	800,433	228,566	209,925	13,113	94,480	47,158
1988	1,342,717	1,101,076	-690	1,100,386	147,160	-76,351	876,875	241,124	224,718	14,301	93,892	47,850
1989	1,409,867	1,123,379	-473	1,122,906	152,118	-70,857	899,931	270,823	239,113	15,216	92,654	48,408
1990	1,495,189	1,183,029	109	1,183,138	162,087	-77,527	943,524	292,215	259,450	16,225	92,156	48,937
1991	1,538,877	1,208,214	-631	1,207,583	170,145	-81,763	955,675	291,791	291,411	16,628	92,547	48,290
1992	1,646,844	1,299,458	-114	1,299,344	183,199	-86,378	1,029,767	281,206	335,871	17,680	93,148	49,325
1993	1,722,038	1,359,514	-88	1,359,426	195,216	-89,645	1,074,565	287,566	359,907	18,365	93,766	50,279
1994	1,780,961	1,412,973	48	1,413,021	201,174	-91,617	1,120,230	299,876	360,855	18,908	94,190	51,179
1995	1,847,871	1,457,850	-335	1,457,515	208,383	-95,613	1,153,519	322,559	371,793	19,569	94,428	51,896
1996	1,922,582	1,525,764	-135	1,525,629	218,300	-116,681	1,190,648	335,978	395,956	20,386	94,308	52,966
1997	1,989,927	1,583,280	-543	1,582,737	224,583	-118,738	1,239,416	342,477	408,034	21,118	94,229	53,811
1998	2,046,990	1,601,616	-1,698	1,599,918	228,663	-104,996	1,266,259	358,893	421,838	21,768	94,035	53,323
1999	2,130,947	1,665,102	-2,112	1,662,990	235,228	-112,907	1,314,855	384,941	431,151	22,680	93,958	53,370
2000	2,221,092	1,761,423	-1,867	1,759,556	255,487	-133,765	1,370,304	396,118	454,670	23,702	93,711	54,205
2001	2,295,828	1,774,623	-2,470	1,772,153	249,284	-108,907	1,413,962	378,301	503,565	24,545	93,536	53,714
2002	2,394,754	1,798,856	-3,628	1,795,228	248,655	-78,922	1,467,651	376,218	550,885	25,633	93,424	52,634
2003	2,423,030	1,814,758	-2,598	1,812,160	255,810	-76,294	1,480,056	380,523	562,451	26,061	92,974	52,167
2004	2,495,422	1,901,234	-2,116	1,899,118	264,543	-99,186	1,535,389	398,465	561,568	26,918	92,705	52,520
2005	2,517,230	1,904,309	-2,953	1,901,356	262,512	-90,906	1,547,938	378,573	590,719	27,168	92,655	52,249
2006	2,696,252	2,016,089	-4,152	2,011,937	265,674	-97,569	1,648,694	410,796	636,762	29,198	92,343	52,837
2007	2,817,196	2,009,265	-5,183	2,004,082	253,597	-65,659	1,684,826	454,069	678,301	30,524	92,295	52,695
2008	2,955,625	2,023,897	-3,775	2,020,122	247,241	-50,636	1,722,245	480,525	752,855	31,943	92,528	51,861
2009	2,957,145	1,994,318	-4,162	1,990,156	247,270	-72,474	1,670,412	454,694	832,039	31,954	92,544	50,384
2010	3,032,862	2,037,973	-4,198	2,033,775	250,143	-86,561	1,697,071	457,334	878,457	32,718	92,697	50,082
2011	3,188,779	2,122,035	-3,067	2,118,968	231,803	-90,326	1,796,839	497,946	893,994	34,412	92,664	50,711
2012	3,305,352	2,207,702	-3,561	2,204,141	238,844	-91,914	1,873,383	530,473	901,496	35,763	92,425	51,018
2013	3,307,207	2,214,031	-2,414	2,211,617	268,328	-52,521	1,890,768	500,219	916,220	35,788	92,411	50,539
2014	3,505,734	2,280,040	-3,917	2,276,123	278,734	-2,809	1,994,580	547,442	963,712	37,876	92,559	50,441
2015	3,547,654	2,272,782	-4,123	2,268,659	281,716	-7,486	1,979,457	557,266	1,010,931	38,350	92,507	49,803
2016	3,485,747	2,170,502	-5,598	2,164,904	278,017	19,783	1,906,670	554,648	1,024,429	37,913	91,940	48,583
2017	3,570,351	2,243,172	-6,259	2,236,913	286,868	8,956	1,959,001	566,687	1,044,663	39,082	91,355	47,469
2018	3,915,929	2,413,797	-7,210	2,406,587	298,064	114,766	2,223,289	623,953	1,068,687	43,223	90,599	46,814
2019	4,137,198	2,667,491	-5,995	2,661,496	313,711	42,798	2,390,583	641,685	1,104,930	45,987	89,964	46,555
2020	4,244,807	2,582,100	-6,805	2,575,295	316,742	-1,634	2,256,919	627,590	1,360,298	47,599	89,179	44,112
2021	4,582,796	2,804,500	-7,710	2,796,790	335,018	-26,188	2,435,584	645,932	1,501,280	51,674	88,687	45,453

Personal Income and Employment by Area: Pensacola-Ferry Pass-Brent, FL

(Thousands of dollars, except as noted.)

Year	Personal income, total	Earnings by place of work			Less: Contributions for government social insurance	Plus: Adjustment for residence	Equals: Net earnings by place of residence	Plus: Dividends, interest, and rent	Plus: Personal current transfer receipts	Per capita personal income (dollars)	Population (persons)	Total employment
		Nonfarm	Farm	Total								
1970	972,357	794,688	3,947	798,635	44,344	-2,881	751,410	162,500	58,447	3,983	244,134	104,526
1971	1,100,934	895,132	5,392	900,524	52,591	-2,529	845,404	187,255	68,275	4,384	251,153	107,815
1972	1,233,579	1,002,625	5,444	1,008,069	61,568	-186	946,315	207,360	79,904	4,725	261,051	111,779
1973	1,323,451	1,059,444	12,847	1,072,291	73,602	1,476	1,000,165	225,422	97,864	5,005	264,441	114,005
1974	1,479,983	1,172,003	15,565	1,187,568	85,207	857	1,103,218	259,423	117,342	5,532	267,551	117,846
1975	1,639,777	1,275,812	16,176	1,291,988	93,858	702	1,198,832	288,913	152,032	5,948	275,666	119,341
1976	1,738,312	1,347,341	9,495	1,356,836	101,929	7,883	1,262,790	303,945	171,577	6,158	282,287	118,547
1977	1,897,906	1,467,712	5,051	1,472,763	111,237	10,067	1,371,593	341,027	185,286	6,650	285,381	121,814
1978	2,131,332	1,618,448	11,976	1,630,424	124,900	13,710	1,519,234	405,824	206,274	7,441	286,428	126,124
1979	2,378,340	1,802,495	9,538	1,812,033	146,096	14,948	1,680,885	459,220	238,235	8,225	289,161	128,844
1980	2,628,307	1,944,806	2,698	1,947,504	160,743	22,367	1,809,128	538,028	281,151	9,006	291,830	131,667
1981	3,010,209	2,213,251	4,358	2,217,609	195,341	26,237	2,048,505	633,233	328,471	10,052	299,477	135,907
1982	3,275,608	2,386,495	3,212	2,389,707	215,098	32,554	2,207,163	702,945	365,500	10,778	303,905	136,941
1983	3,552,331	2,586,381	3,495	2,589,876	241,151	32,475	2,381,200	769,782	401,349	11,375	312,280	140,353
1984	3,898,962	2,813,639	9,967	2,823,606	269,943	38,773	2,592,436	876,086	430,440	12,368	315,257	148,279
1985	4,151,703	2,978,060	8,145	2,986,205	292,900	41,407	2,734,712	953,014	463,977	12,944	320,743	154,423
1986	4,441,997	3,180,697	7,457	3,188,154	322,615	48,517	2,914,056	1,032,161	495,780	13,562	327,528	161,370
1987	4,701,642	3,356,802	12,090	3,368,892	338,530	56,194	3,086,556	1,088,069	527,017	14,040	334,873	161,606
1988	5,017,997	3,554,814	15,904	3,570,718	373,388	76,587	3,273,917	1,169,458	574,622	15,028	333,905	162,727
1989	5,431,454	3,740,755	13,018	3,753,773	399,157	81,778	3,436,394	1,329,245	665,815	15,898	341,654	165,545
1990	5,771,141	3,979,135	16,662	3,995,797	426,961	50,140	3,618,976	1,418,903	733,262	16,694	345,706	167,249
1991	6,083,425	4,156,584	17,949	4,174,533	451,021	82,930	3,806,442	1,447,026	829,957	17,234	352,981	168,899
1992	6,484,828	4,476,474	22,207	4,498,681	489,554	55,126	4,064,253	1,468,710	951,865	17,915	361,975	172,885
1993	6,770,377	4,613,137	23,817	4,636,954	505,620	94,647	4,225,981	1,526,153	1,018,243	18,413	367,689	174,170
1994	7,079,281	4,786,058	21,746	4,807,804	529,859	108,091	4,386,036	1,603,811	1,089,434	18,939	373,790	178,056
1995	7,523,876	4,946,295	12,332	4,958,627	546,166	189,476	4,601,937	1,738,239	1,183,700	19,789	380,205	183,511
1996	8,116,714	5,302,499	21,581	5,324,080	579,626	234,978	4,979,432	1,897,777	1,239,505	20,894	388,477	190,014
1997	8,598,097	5,629,591	15,609	5,645,200	616,172	238,705	5,267,733	2,034,927	1,295,437	21,499	399,925	198,535
1998	9,150,816	5,959,463	10,244	5,969,707	647,224	298,998	5,621,481	2,227,010	1,302,325	22,377	408,930	204,939
1999	9,488,692	6,192,478	16,158	6,208,636	670,496	311,066	5,849,206	2,250,663	1,388,823	23,142	410,026	207,920
2000	10,138,268	6,519,689	21,790	6,541,479	704,176	387,591	6,224,894	2,409,215	1,504,159	24,543	413,085	212,573
2001	10,905,012	7,031,146	16,454	7,047,600	756,938	399,008	6,689,670	2,530,835	1,684,507	26,024	419,037	209,983
2002	11,250,660	7,227,765	13,087	7,240,852	778,728	448,499	6,910,623	2,492,532	1,847,505	26,472	425,006	209,430
2003	11,833,747	7,635,700	23,844	7,659,544	820,420	498,373	7,337,497	2,490,529	2,005,721	27,645	428,066	213,127
2004	12,575,215	8,159,147	15,793	8,174,940	888,254	548,044	7,834,730	2,537,763	2,202,722	28,878	435,466	219,672
2005	13,310,865	8,696,029	18,089	8,714,118	951,780	596,544	8,358,882	2,669,932	2,282,051	30,288	439,471	223,707
2006	14,288,987	9,291,236	24,151	9,315,387	1,043,899	632,524	8,904,012	2,955,087	2,429,888	32,228	443,378	229,442
2007	14,946,020	9,446,042	9,982	9,456,024	1,068,131	691,800	9,079,693	3,253,875	2,612,452	33,696	443,551	232,026
2008	15,305,494	9,385,936	10,663	9,396,599	1,078,753	726,277	9,044,123	3,286,564	2,974,807	34,364	445,392	225,906
2009	15,144,421	9,226,486	1,191	9,227,677	1,079,489	722,179	8,870,367	3,046,757	3,227,297	33,914	446,559	217,869
2010	15,877,135	9,503,240	8,477	9,511,717	1,098,278	746,687	9,160,126	3,162,642	3,554,367	35,205	450,993	217,732
2011	16,700,746	9,799,304	19,992	9,819,296	1,027,465	792,749	9,584,580	3,415,188	3,700,978	36,683	455,274	220,462
2012	17,163,285	10,121,864	893	10,122,757	1,068,082	873,168	9,927,843	3,577,063	3,658,379	37,163	461,841	221,297
2013	17,174,801	10,173,377	22,146	10,195,523	1,206,127	903,805	9,893,201	3,503,077	3,778,523	36,746	467,398	225,222
2014	17,933,628	10,512,646	-3,109	10,509,537	1,245,251	949,396	10,213,682	3,750,256	3,969,690	38,065	471,131	229,456
2015	18,779,176	11,016,307	14,981	11,031,288	1,298,511	962,213	10,694,990	3,895,829	4,188,357	39,436	476,193	233,478
2016	19,715,298	11,711,441	10,800	11,722,241	1,370,967	961,135	11,312,409	4,052,799	4,350,090	40,875	482,334	243,667
2017	20,888,719	12,446,624	18,348	12,464,972	1,456,318	968,174	11,976,828	4,292,544	4,619,347	42,765	488,453	253,344
2018	21,632,453	12,839,292	13,384	12,852,676	1,513,084	1,030,963	12,370,555	4,409,015	4,852,883	43,648	495,610	257,461
2019	23,064,129	13,692,227	17,228	13,709,455	1,630,336	1,130,546	13,209,665	4,721,080	5,133,384	45,744	504,196	261,870
2020	24,883,642	14,235,697	12,540	14,248,237	1,700,715	1,197,985	13,745,507	4,751,034	6,387,101	48,643	511,557	263,004
2021	27,135,217	15,522,191	16,603	15,538,794	1,808,706	1,287,652	15,017,740	4,834,475	7,283,002	52,548	516,388	271,481

Personal Income and Employment by Area: Peoria, IL

(Thousands of dollars, except as noted.)

					Derivation of personal income							
		Earnings by place of work			Less: Contributions for government social insurance	Plus: Adjustment for residence	Equals: Net earnings by place of residence	Plus: Dividends, interest, and rent	Plus: Personal current transfer receipts	Per capita personal income (dollars)	Population (persons)	Total employment
Year	Personal income, total	Nonfarm	Farm	Total								
1970	1,566,479	1,311,884	39,905	1,351,789	88,889	-35,925	1,226,975	224,479	115,025	4,304	363,968	164,383
1971	1,708,997	1,425,476	45,525	1,471,001	99,872	-38,738	1,332,391	240,697	135,909	4,627	369,391	164,742
1972	1,838,676	1,537,555	39,836	1,577,391	113,722	-41,394	1,422,275	262,222	154,179	4,922	373,551	165,245
1973	2,121,271	1,753,150	88,311	1,841,461	151,297	-50,287	1,639,877	301,331	180,063	5,666	374,401	175,153
1974	2,383,613	1,991,148	89,396	2,080,544	178,108	-62,688	1,839,748	343,264	200,601	6,336	376,199	181,638
1975	2,721,430	2,213,786	132,393	2,346,179	193,838	-74,379	2,077,962	389,931	253,537	7,195	378,257	186,144
1976	2,932,753	2,429,021	103,506	2,532,527	217,688	-82,740	2,232,099	416,448	284,206	7,691	381,346	190,624
1977	3,189,400	2,658,038	97,330	2,755,368	237,167	-95,924	2,422,277	464,767	302,356	8,347	382,124	191,841
1978	3,555,865	3,043,587	78,840	3,122,427	281,109	-122,735	2,718,583	513,432	323,850	9,271	383,538	197,934
1979	3,811,586	3,206,616	92,214	3,298,830	306,869	-127,977	2,863,984	581,760	365,842	9,926	384,001	194,459
1980	4,152,487	3,495,257	12,668	3,507,925	335,921	-159,488	3,012,516	692,834	447,137	10,708	387,782	192,228
1981	4,590,050	3,663,265	105,728	3,768,993	378,117	-160,475	3,230,401	841,253	518,396	11,851	387,307	188,890
1982	4,648,202	3,458,035	75,482	3,533,517	360,299	-127,828	3,045,390	993,201	609,611	12,118	383,564	175,891
1983	4,475,914	3,218,657	-30,363	3,188,294	334,538	-89,466	2,764,290	1,036,069	675,555	11,830	378,344	166,495
1984	4,904,749	3,513,964	74,008	3,587,972	379,187	-97,346	3,111,439	1,146,516	646,794	13,190	371,853	172,623
1985	5,048,977	3,593,985	117,205	3,711,190	391,886	-91,840	3,227,464	1,149,571	671,942	13,853	364,457	171,203
1986	5,183,687	3,708,276	85,667	3,793,943	404,254	-97,582	3,292,107	1,187,035	704,545	14,486	357,835	172,056
1987	5,379,524	3,933,749	71,899	4,005,648	421,471	-104,884	3,479,293	1,171,204	729,027	15,156	354,936	174,514
1988	5,828,808	4,435,594	30,787	4,466,381	488,524	-123,582	3,854,275	1,216,444	758,089	16,433	354,697	181,969
1989	6,319,323	4,743,202	73,465	4,816,667	524,846	-121,533	4,170,288	1,338,123	810,912	17,689	357,249	187,671
1990	6,678,156	5,027,591	78,385	5,105,976	541,467	-109,815	4,454,694	1,348,129	875,333	18,588	359,269	191,515
1991	6,703,395	5,012,644	51,657	5,064,301	554,846	-99,052	4,410,403	1,356,859	936,133	18,543	361,500	191,716
1992	7,135,289	5,254,481	101,801	5,356,282	569,526	-98,213	4,688,543	1,385,121	1,061,625	19,699	362,223	190,752
1993	7,443,162	5,580,805	77,400	5,658,205	616,566	-122,822	4,918,817	1,429,844	1,094,501	20,533	362,492	194,442
1994	7,902,183	5,934,012	128,785	6,062,797	660,417	-115,865	5,286,515	1,495,052	1,120,616	21,779	362,843	199,927
1995	8,143,940	6,057,979	33,904	6,091,883	672,712	-96,944	5,322,227	1,626,668	1,195,045	22,228	366,385	202,647
1996	8,693,351	6,391,537	149,453	6,540,990	708,637	-125,173	5,707,180	1,722,951	1,263,220	23,719	366,521	210,524
1997	9,166,699	6,775,842	125,888	6,901,730	748,438	-141,771	6,011,521	1,873,010	1,282,168	25,003	366,624	214,200
1998	10,458,503	7,538,734	99,435	7,638,169	822,976	67,361	6,882,554	2,117,107	1,458,842	25,795	405,451	232,754
1999	10,741,943	7,884,931	67,967	7,952,898	844,021	90,459	7,199,336	2,057,178	1,485,429	26,457	406,015	232,531
2000	11,220,254	8,066,933	115,678	8,182,611	853,250	108,844	7,438,205	2,217,349	1,564,700	27,713	404,875	234,823
2001	11,540,100	8,380,599	98,862	8,479,461	893,222	122,553	7,708,792	2,165,924	1,665,384	28,601	403,480	230,044
2002	11,665,994	8,627,992	60,827	8,688,819	914,190	135,143	7,909,772	1,969,043	1,787,179	28,883	403,899	225,385
2003	12,028,592	8,803,923	120,575	8,924,498	937,340	134,113	8,121,271	2,043,514	1,863,807	29,777	403,961	222,766
2004	12,750,094	9,409,807	228,521	9,638,328	1,024,107	111,563	8,725,784	2,084,706	1,939,604	31,436	405,592	226,357
2005	13,348,197	10,161,705	91,015	10,252,720	1,117,688	71,524	9,206,556	2,043,350	2,098,291	32,779	407,224	229,721
2006	14,443,470	11,075,846	98,622	11,174,468	1,196,509	49,485	10,027,444	2,252,102	2,163,924	35,308	409,074	235,298
2007	15,277,436	11,535,460	217,564	11,753,024	1,248,968	30,155	10,534,211	2,378,045	2,365,180	37,131	411,451	239,851
2008	16,111,240	11,878,988	330,318	12,209,306	1,297,764	32,137	10,943,679	2,576,620	2,590,941	38,991	413,206	240,765
2009	15,851,002	11,437,787	204,075	11,641,862	1,249,119	39,400	10,432,143	2,507,737	2,911,122	38,061	416,463	229,705
2010	16,270,750	11,773,300	141,143	11,914,443	1,287,270	15,501	10,642,674	2,492,585	3,135,491	39,107	416,056	229,879
2011	17,691,552	12,919,673	350,466	13,270,139	1,257,938	-66,256	11,945,945	2,731,381	3,014,226	42,454	416,727	234,161
2012	18,292,043	13,669,874	191,900	13,861,774	1,337,767	-128,015	12,395,992	2,892,884	3,003,167	43,872	416,937	237,196
2013	17,960,738	12,934,273	551,460	13,485,733	1,447,538	-92,346	11,945,849	2,863,622	3,151,267	42,949	418,183	231,850
2014	18,199,074	13,068,812	271,756	13,340,568	1,453,968	-87,512	11,799,088	3,209,886	3,190,100	43,584	417,561	231,284
2015	18,706,186	13,395,138	35,590	13,430,728	1,473,782	-31,186	11,925,760	3,394,113	3,386,313	45,031	415,407	230,866
2016	18,651,629	13,198,721	183,916	13,382,637	1,460,561	-48,391	11,873,685	3,341,602	3,436,342	45,072	413,818	226,952
2017	18,646,841	12,993,853	129,593	13,123,446	1,448,208	-19,661	11,655,577	3,440,343	3,550,921	45,441	410,356	224,508
2018	19,391,975	13,659,911	182,728	13,842,639	1,513,929	-21,324	12,307,386	3,412,827	3,671,762	47,644	407,021	224,370
2019	19,649,345	13,661,917	101,248	13,763,165	1,519,612	-6,874	12,236,679	3,583,681	3,828,985	48,555	404,683	221,752
2020	21,095,434	13,649,482	239,769	13,889,251	1,521,482	25,473	12,393,242	3,557,053	5,145,139	52,586	401,160	212,344
2021	22,214,722	14,021,722	469,079	14,490,801	1,545,498	32,088	12,977,391	3,578,984	5,658,347	55,784	398,224	216,209

Personal Income and Employment by Area: Philadelphia-Camden-Wilmington, PA-NJ-DE-MD

(Thousands of dollars, except as noted.)

Year	Personal income, total	Earnings by place of work			Less: Contributions for government social insurance	Plus: Adjustment for residence	Equals: Net earnings by place of residence	Plus: Dividends, interest, and rent	Plus: Personal current transfer receipts	Per capita personal income (dollars)	Population (persons)	Total employment
		Nonfarm	Farm	Total								
1970	24,520,198	20,039,390	94,448	20,133,838	1,436,557	52,200	18,749,481	3,683,033	2,087,684	4,599	5,331,133	2,424,294
1971	26,125,091	21,114,400	99,205	21,213,605	1,571,650	73,436	19,715,391	3,944,720	2,464,980	4,872	5,362,194	2,392,220
1972	28,339,983	22,923,197	91,533	23,014,730	1,793,297	124,808	21,346,241	4,212,154	2,781,588	5,293	5,353,850	2,424,493
1973	30,621,832	24,856,753	135,537	24,992,290	2,243,235	189,927	22,938,982	4,588,136	3,094,714	5,758	5,317,951	2,467,445
1974	33,305,265	26,643,145	135,103	26,778,248	2,492,914	247,132	24,532,466	5,113,733	3,659,066	6,289	5,295,959	2,453,221
1975	35,981,127	28,016,022	110,152	28,126,174	2,557,693	280,537	25,849,018	5,441,504	4,690,605	6,804	5,288,609	2,376,788
1976	39,176,435	30,459,484	139,511	30,598,995	2,831,890	360,665	28,127,770	5,850,128	5,198,537	7,418	5,280,969	2,398,310
1977	42,605,446	33,095,270	132,403	33,227,673	3,069,436	435,113	30,593,350	6,433,671	5,578,425	8,093	5,264,778	2,415,937
1978	46,787,916	36,643,060	134,332	36,777,392	3,490,984	514,103	33,800,511	7,055,916	5,931,489	8,916	5,247,420	2,480,533
1979	51,530,923	40,225,755	136,126	40,361,881	3,982,608	594,235	36,973,508	7,892,111	6,665,304	9,819	5,248,348	2,531,977
1980	57,084,565	43,529,772	89,436	43,619,208	4,330,334	732,389	40,021,263	9,498,434	7,564,868	10,886	5,244,018	2,533,311
1981	63,222,516	47,034,778	127,745	47,162,523	5,003,327	845,587	43,004,783	11,695,986	8,521,747	12,042	5,250,278	2,530,893
1982	68,344,102	49,701,183	151,116	49,852,299	5,378,387	904,056	45,377,968	13,480,270	9,485,864	13,001	5,257,004	2,524,306
1983	72,951,858	53,427,724	143,538	53,571,262	5,875,092	979,185	48,675,355	14,095,860	10,180,643	13,865	5,261,664	2,558,593
1984	79,503,431	58,523,873	202,459	58,726,332	6,681,102	1,101,664	53,146,894	15,860,311	10,496,226	15,060	5,279,124	2,645,844
1985	85,574,904	63,363,634	225,204	63,588,838	7,331,153	1,180,665	57,438,350	17,070,567	11,065,987	16,163	5,294,461	2,722,101
1986	90,999,442	67,783,561	214,907	67,998,468	7,908,084	1,311,575	61,401,959	17,920,683	11,676,800	17,056	5,335,416	2,785,227
1987	97,572,391	73,863,745	199,920	74,063,665	8,538,491	1,444,385	66,969,559	18,606,829	11,996,003	18,125	5,383,434	2,876,967
1988	105,911,474	80,579,558	182,308	80,761,866	9,540,574	1,573,396	72,794,688	20,379,331	12,737,455	19,536	5,421,382	2,951,624
1989	114,591,373	85,840,356	185,138	86,025,494	10,048,583	1,639,604	77,616,515	23,228,385	13,746,473	21,086	5,434,490	2,987,983
1990	121,241,003	90,232,511	213,732	90,446,243	10,567,223	1,710,198	81,589,218	24,843,271	14,808,514	22,266	5,445,186	2,986,306
1991	125,340,682	92,022,458	204,036	92,226,494	10,899,355	1,907,443	83,234,582	24,893,484	17,212,616	22,873	5,479,918	2,912,895
1992	132,190,614	97,329,071	225,644	97,554,715	11,453,320	1,999,852	88,101,247	25,309,965	18,779,402	24,019	5,503,640	2,891,738
1993	136,875,461	100,649,048	239,650	100,888,698	11,911,185	2,122,342	91,099,855	26,034,028	19,741,578	24,738	5,533,081	2,910,168
1994	141,508,926	104,213,364	244,090	104,457,454	12,570,444	2,228,945	94,115,955	27,147,808	20,245,163	25,441	5,562,336	2,922,050
1995	148,930,267	108,636,644	233,869	108,870,513	13,031,443	2,405,513	98,244,583	29,377,217	21,308,467	26,660	5,586,177	2,963,541
1996	156,972,264	114,018,430	281,357	114,299,787	13,469,802	2,372,665	103,202,650	31,188,508	22,581,106	28,020	5,602,154	2,998,593
1997	165,382,500	120,802,405	273,455	121,075,860	14,146,652	2,637,368	109,566,576	32,861,578	22,954,346	29,451	5,615,600	3,061,561
1998	177,336,592	130,407,357	277,968	130,685,325	15,018,450	2,650,191	118,317,066	35,681,167	23,338,359	31,443	5,640,015	3,127,485
1999	185,613,140	138,410,317	259,226	138,669,543	15,724,565	2,663,679	125,608,657	35,726,762	24,277,721	32,764	5,665,210	3,179,438
2000	200,930,868	149,121,941	306,785	149,428,726	16,672,815	2,996,110	135,752,021	39,028,306	26,150,541	35,301	5,691,968	3,250,559
2001	210,127,445	157,464,714	269,347	157,734,061	17,235,301	3,121,758	143,620,518	38,646,721	28,460,206	36,774	5,713,954	3,267,912
2002	214,563,340	162,058,357	265,988	162,324,345	17,825,404	3,214,533	147,713,474	36,984,281	29,865,585	37,358	5,743,383	3,266,732
2003	222,691,768	168,575,831	272,878	168,848,709	18,446,925	3,306,371	153,708,155	38,063,003	30,920,610	38,569	5,773,864	3,280,167
2004	235,630,508	179,781,765	318,460	180,100,225	19,507,061	3,571,846	164,165,010	39,896,642	31,568,856	40,594	5,804,535	3,324,106
2005	244,828,486	185,144,008	298,643	185,442,651	20,359,515	3,757,312	168,840,448	42,047,350	33,940,688	42,001	5,829,139	3,384,631
2006	260,002,107	193,459,221	285,452	193,744,673	21,467,374	4,054,352	176,331,651	48,072,240	35,598,216	44,398	5,856,125	3,436,677
2007	275,588,250	203,007,495	149,947	203,157,442	22,486,817	4,456,079	185,126,704	52,317,653	38,143,893	46,852	5,882,126	3,488,513
2008	281,971,729	203,664,107	174,115	203,838,222	23,235,707	4,840,798	185,443,313	53,907,305	42,621,111	47,736	5,906,917	3,501,145
2009	275,926,071	200,242,229	232,819	200,475,048	22,880,607	4,663,730	182,258,171	47,156,795	46,511,105	46,440	5,941,539	3,415,648
2010	288,338,273	207,664,270	226,959	207,891,229	23,217,669	5,040,567	189,714,127	47,599,354	51,024,792	48,288	5,971,202	3,410,339
2011	304,159,901	216,889,628	254,741	217,144,369	21,306,009	5,309,989	201,148,349	51,419,544	51,592,008	50,719	5,996,995	3,451,664
2012	319,131,065	226,399,854	359,273	226,759,127	21,941,710	5,840,881	210,658,298	56,814,361	51,658,406	53,031	6,017,788	3,476,792
2013	322,284,363	234,391,311	523,822	234,915,133	25,493,595	5,996,995	215,418,533	54,260,074	52,605,756	53,431	6,031,789	3,525,836
2014	337,201,427	242,501,585	529,994	243,031,579	26,391,583	6,503,210	223,143,206	59,135,318	54,922,903	55,222	6,106,258	3,585,839
2015	351,598,288	251,873,472	492,028	252,365,500	27,443,016	6,609,654	231,532,138	62,299,076	57,767,074	57,357	6,129,946	3,646,425
2016	364,743,219	260,774,405	431,444	261,205,849	28,079,637	6,888,022	240,014,234	64,035,443	60,693,542	59,274	6,153,468	3,728,526
2017	370,794,771	265,141,403	492,757	265,634,160	29,361,198	6,839,864	243,112,826	66,098,728	61,583,217	60,006	6,179,246	3,784,081
2018	389,692,639	274,427,471	370,806	274,798,277	30,318,230	7,477,778	251,957,825	71,938,552	65,796,262	62,779	6,207,400	3,848,475
2019	403,161,214	281,686,994	465,804	282,152,798	31,458,713	7,886,068	258,580,153	76,160,545	68,420,516	64,723	6,229,011	3,870,856
2020	425,703,285	282,003,972	432,089	282,436,061	31,492,095	7,645,904	258,589,870	75,862,857	91,250,558	68,200	6,241,983	3,709,988
2021	450,818,306	300,248,681	395,256	300,643,937	33,021,964	8,391,290	276,013,263	77,999,944	96,805,099	72,379	6,228,601	3,836,431

Personal Income and Employment by Area: Phoenix-Mesa-Chandler, AZ

(Thousands of dollars, except as noted.)

Year	Personal income, total	Earnings by place of work			Less: Contributions for government social insurance	Plus: Adjustment for residence	Equals: Net earnings by place of residence	Plus: Dividends, interest, and rent	Plus: Personal current transfer receipts	Per capita personal income (dollars)	Population (persons)	Total employment
		Nonfarm	Farm	Total								
1970	4,435,397	3,376,315	105,153	3,481,468	230,632	-21,339	3,229,497	869,987	335,913	4,225	1,049,680	456,574
1971	5,038,059	3,818,694	120,929	3,939,623	272,161	-21,368	3,646,094	991,866	400,099	4,579	1,100,219	478,419
1972	5,785,408	4,458,900	98,528	4,557,428	335,218	-14,476	4,207,734	1,117,667	460,007	4,970	1,163,970	522,280
1973	6,707,040	5,203,336	106,777	5,310,113	448,512	-11,443	4,850,158	1,298,017	558,865	5,419	1,237,668	574,470
1974	7,613,878	5,681,015	247,112	5,928,127	506,663	-19,760	5,401,704	1,525,580	686,594	5,848	1,301,957	592,448
1975	8,141,145	5,864,612	94,831	5,959,443	515,861	-28,218	5,415,364	1,737,879	987,902	6,086	1,337,680	573,360
1976	9,126,107	6,605,949	206,113	6,812,062	585,353	-38,357	6,188,352	1,876,238	1,061,517	6,679	1,366,423	603,064
1977	10,352,142	7,674,347	159,414	7,833,761	686,978	-39,000	7,107,783	2,119,572	1,124,787	7,306	1,416,931	654,968
1978	12,273,363	9,255,747	162,453	9,418,200	851,039	-36,532	8,530,629	2,482,221	1,260,513	8,313	1,476,485	728,998
1979	14,595,699	11,111,150	246,899	11,358,049	1,067,111	-42,081	10,248,857	2,910,022	1,436,820	9,439	1,546,348	792,672
1980	16,893,996	12,533,395	296,437	12,829,832	1,214,376	-54,931	11,560,525	3,599,788	1,733,683	10,479	1,612,182	820,853
1981	19,335,537	14,067,071	256,213	14,323,284	1,466,097	-51,903	12,805,284	4,484,477	2,045,776	11,655	1,658,988	843,575
1982	20,654,673	14,737,498	222,721	14,960,219	1,559,860	-42,589	13,357,770	5,025,307	2,271,596	12,088	1,708,649	847,957
1983	22,914,802	16,351,347	175,169	16,526,516	1,751,677	-30,908	14,743,931	5,687,902	2,482,969	13,006	1,761,819	895,053
1984	26,163,791	18,829,845	320,170	19,150,015	2,069,986	-33,099	17,046,930	6,438,186	2,678,675	14,239	1,837,457	988,892
1985	29,431,887	21,334,931	288,071	21,623,002	2,383,883	-41,013	19,198,106	7,307,865	2,925,916	15,234	1,931,978	1,074,363
1986	32,324,473	23,604,280	286,319	23,890,599	2,650,089	-44,240	21,196,270	7,889,458	3,238,745	16,055	2,013,320	1,130,847
1987	34,961,445	25,591,638	356,798	25,948,436	2,847,742	-36,320	23,064,374	8,363,994	3,533,077	16,628	2,102,571	1,175,415
1988	37,813,719	27,914,751	389,911	28,304,662	3,196,896	-50,403	25,057,363	8,877,549	3,878,807	17,485	2,162,647	1,224,682
1989	40,573,599	29,020,120	423,994	29,444,114	3,409,779	-15,279	26,019,056	10,083,185	4,471,358	18,297	2,217,530	1,247,064
1990	42,474,931	30,593,481	384,406	30,977,887	3,695,289	-12,219	27,270,379	10,282,503	4,922,049	18,885	2,249,116	1,266,338
1991	44,433,254	32,272,730	443,627	32,716,357	3,916,461	-4,641	28,795,255	10,153,980	5,484,019	19,159	2,319,206	1,263,249
1992	47,360,604	34,772,605	386,057	35,158,662	4,180,070	2,848	30,981,440	10,150,719	6,228,445	19,744	2,398,760	1,271,798
1993	50,723,694	37,487,249	422,391	37,909,640	4,508,566	13,764	33,414,838	10,611,833	6,697,023	20,356	2,491,818	1,328,795
1994	55,941,697	41,527,630	367,401	41,895,031	4,998,511	11,949	36,908,469	11,896,110	7,137,118	21,405	2,613,502	1,416,403
1995	61,693,123	45,740,134	406,849	46,146,983	5,289,086	-22,678	40,835,219	13,222,803	7,635,101	22,483	2,744,046	1,508,585
1996	67,546,444	50,860,346	443,806	51,304,152	5,996,757	-56,114	45,251,281	14,178,482	8,116,681	23,653	2,855,711	1,614,248
1997	73,890,376	55,763,048	422,315	56,185,363	6,482,785	-38,212	49,664,366	15,758,527	8,467,483	24,932	2,963,714	1,702,231
1998	81,340,335	62,364,632	455,635	62,820,267	7,128,742	-33,934	55,657,591	16,961,302	8,721,442	26,456	3,074,532	1,791,395
1999	86,774,105	67,092,192	443,376	67,535,568	7,661,580	-15,848	59,858,140	17,628,525	9,287,440	27,302	3,178,349	1,857,012
2000	95,078,427	74,076,763	361,990	74,438,753	8,419,870	-2,490	66,016,393	19,204,730	9,857,304	29,045	3,273,477	1,929,164
2001	98,008,205	76,025,167	348,160	76,373,327	8,754,785	75,431	67,693,973	19,144,858	11,169,374	29,137	3,363,736	1,952,759
2002	101,552,863	78,149,230	332,554	78,481,784	8,988,529	120,150	69,613,405	19,465,982	12,473,476	29,415	3,452,470	1,963,854
2003	107,373,806	81,805,251	374,421	82,179,672	9,285,771	173,784	73,067,685	20,686,055	13,620,066	30,363	3,536,388	2,015,185
2004	118,217,025	90,591,327	534,923	91,126,250	10,128,473	225,973	81,223,750	21,958,236	15,035,039	32,501	3,637,332	2,104,069
2005	131,673,467	100,891,507	474,740	101,366,247	11,172,214	260,135	90,454,168	24,544,881	16,674,418	34,883	3,774,696	2,245,171
2006	147,209,055	112,864,316	382,042	113,246,358	12,293,605	303,548	101,256,301	27,716,289	18,236,465	37,609	3,914,212	2,363,627
2007	155,155,902	117,290,930	424,484	117,715,414	12,966,264	398,191	105,147,341	30,184,932	19,823,629	38,614	4,018,128	2,425,683
2008	154,735,108	114,030,300	361,377	114,391,677	12,968,481	526,137	101,949,333	29,476,430	23,309,345	37,682	4,106,372	2,378,751
2009	144,849,828	104,559,444	214,934	104,774,378	12,243,537	507,303	93,038,144	25,652,022	26,159,662	34,873	4,153,609	2,246,716
2010	147,896,661	104,753,834	260,588	105,014,422	12,358,976	535,458	93,190,904	25,875,733	28,830,024	35,178	4,204,289	2,209,907
2011	155,942,475	109,546,401	488,444	110,034,845	11,481,464	562,182	99,115,563	28,004,612	28,822,300	36,662	4,253,485	2,264,667
2012	164,667,784	115,915,133	444,948	116,360,081	11,956,991	592,572	104,995,662	30,796,249	28,875,873	38,025	4,330,536	2,311,182
2013	169,063,978	121,625,266	602,187	122,227,453	14,077,657	631,877	108,781,673	30,352,127	29,930,178	38,387	4,404,231	2,375,850
2014	179,475,002	128,035,776	566,489	128,602,265	14,653,854	655,930	114,604,341	33,086,719	31,783,942	40,628	4,417,491	2,441,648
2015	190,025,974	135,346,979	627,560	135,974,539	15,535,779	656,676	121,095,436	36,107,303	32,823,235	42,335	4,488,678	2,529,473
2016	198,803,908	141,963,972	698,566	142,662,538	16,230,827	641,899	127,073,610	37,733,385	33,996,913	43,557	4,564,173	2,612,738
2017	210,755,996	150,185,299	641,877	150,827,176	17,184,644	662,623	134,305,155	39,822,910	36,627,931	45,523	4,629,645	2,693,905
2018	224,584,765	161,296,939	468,510	161,765,449	18,528,113	694,624	143,931,960	42,228,879	38,423,926	47,783	4,700,060	2,791,264
2019	242,642,465	172,380,365	583,636	172,964,001	19,871,881	722,213	153,814,333	47,601,490	41,226,642	50,757	4,780,473	2,859,330
2020	267,281,852	182,110,306	397,716	182,508,022	21,086,206	643,241	162,065,057	48,374,963	56,841,832	54,907	4,867,925	2,861,048
2021	288,401,314	197,772,336	369,113	198,141,449	22,486,910	647,252	176,301,791	50,211,134	61,888,389	58,308	4,946,145	2,970,634

Personal Income and Employment by Area: Pine Bluff, AR

(Thousands of dollars, except as noted.)

| Year | Personal income, total | Derivation of personal income | | | | | | | | Per capita personal income (dollars) | Population (persons) | Total employment |
| | | Earnings by place of work | | | Less: Contributions for government social insurance | Plus: Adjustment for residence | Equals: Net earnings by place of residence | Plus: Dividends, interest, and rent | Plus: Personal current transfer receipts | | | |
		Nonfarm	Farm	Total								
1970	290,916	216,093	19,611	235,704	16,562	1,788	220,930	35,845	34,141	2,784	104,477	38,872
1971	320,454	233,791	24,064	257,855	18,270	1,696	241,281	39,906	39,267	3,090	103,719	39,197
1972	347,493	255,891	24,640	280,531	21,138	1,531	260,924	43,541	43,028	3,313	104,888	39,993
1973	405,124	285,991	44,097	330,088	27,314	1,070	303,844	49,656	51,624	3,887	104,231	41,117
1974	434,033	316,994	27,289	344,283	31,299	113	313,097	58,518	62,418	4,124	105,251	42,161
1975	476,783	332,287	34,207	366,494	31,913	-1,420	333,161	64,977	78,645	4,526	105,335	40,227
1976	535,406	374,787	39,947	414,734	36,522	-1,184	377,028	71,360	87,018	5,047	106,074	40,529
1977	592,237	423,222	39,313	462,535	41,774	-1,271	419,490	80,641	92,106	5,555	106,613	42,336
1978	679,727	504,132	48,248	552,380	50,778	-11,840	489,762	89,213	100,752	6,264	108,520	45,097
1979	758,571	587,653	44,581	632,234	61,539	-24,914	545,781	99,879	112,911	6,861	110,555	46,194
1980	825,794	657,337	14,601	671,938	68,113	-33,603	570,222	123,430	132,142	7,374	111,988	46,894
1981	908,859	661,580	39,133	700,713	73,591	-22,534	604,588	151,669	152,602	8,123	111,883	44,628
1982	919,753	646,749	23,206	669,955	74,269	-14,987	580,699	175,109	163,945	8,321	110,538	42,054
1983	964,914	691,675	11,379	703,054	80,028	-15,621	607,405	180,666	176,843	8,776	109,954	42,484
1984	1,051,281	745,001	28,861	773,862	89,511	-16,917	667,434	201,445	182,402	9,595	109,561	42,993
1985	1,100,703	783,931	26,203	810,134	95,465	-19,881	694,788	214,862	191,053	10,108	108,892	43,590
1986	1,183,695	882,991	23,889	906,880	108,926	-37,279	760,675	223,358	199,662	10,916	108,437	45,357
1987	1,209,269	872,370	39,024	911,394	105,889	-24,161	781,344	221,166	206,759	11,130	108,653	44,835
1988	1,309,406	933,750	66,385	1,000,135	119,358	-26,497	854,280	240,320	214,806	12,061	108,561	46,386
1989	1,365,021	968,517	42,115	1,010,632	125,893	-28,507	856,232	269,303	239,486	12,641	107,985	47,039
1990	1,426,971	1,038,584	34,870	1,073,454	137,678	-35,547	900,229	268,526	258,216	13,341	106,958	47,603
1991	1,463,798	1,027,682	46,134	1,073,816	132,871	-22,336	918,609	263,139	282,050	13,646	107,267	47,185
1992	1,575,596	1,099,015	66,146	1,165,161	139,970	-21,556	1,003,635	258,144	313,817	14,644	107,590	47,356
1993	1,638,622	1,146,494	52,152	1,198,646	146,765	-20,790	1,031,091	280,574	326,957	15,274	107,282	48,353
1994	1,711,484	1,174,682	83,601	1,258,283	150,940	-15,787	1,091,556	275,762	344,166	15,878	107,791	47,473
1995	1,772,981	1,227,698	54,941	1,282,639	157,250	-14,774	1,110,615	293,907	368,459	16,460	107,714	48,926
1996	1,859,345	1,254,948	94,248	1,349,196	159,871	-11,388	1,177,937	304,141	377,267	17,263	107,707	49,406
1997	1,903,658	1,300,372	83,386	1,383,758	165,901	-9,281	1,208,576	303,791	391,291	17,672	107,720	49,381
1998	1,984,217	1,366,548	76,277	1,442,825	172,916	-8,088	1,261,821	316,210	406,186	18,468	107,440	49,260
1999	2,020,265	1,410,344	84,910	1,495,254	177,056	-7,323	1,310,875	303,828	405,562	18,839	107,241	49,241
2000	2,105,749	1,487,956	73,583	1,561,539	184,671	-8,032	1,368,836	310,683	426,230	19,646	107,184	49,436
2001	2,194,069	1,520,876	86,656	1,607,532	188,925	-3,058	1,415,549	311,808	466,712	20,609	106,464	49,489
2002	2,249,764	1,566,447	52,075	1,618,522	192,930	-1,520	1,424,072	316,918	508,774	21,231	105,965	48,574
2003	2,382,648	1,635,962	114,982	1,750,944	199,549	-7,801	1,543,594	309,828	529,226	22,592	105,465	48,948
2004	2,501,581	1,736,018	131,864	1,867,882	210,283	-37,539	1,620,060	314,712	566,809	23,901	104,665	49,671
2005	2,523,604	1,776,328	94,666	1,870,994	214,380	-55,904	1,600,710	329,467	593,427	24,285	103,917	49,426
2006	2,566,673	1,834,126	67,729	1,901,855	225,650	-83,207	1,592,998	331,977	641,698	24,890	103,121	49,191
2007	2,691,159	1,826,126	93,705	1,919,831	226,999	-51,499	1,641,333	365,813	684,013	26,404	101,921	48,352
2008	2,743,537	1,836,522	88,118	1,924,640	232,793	-75,810	1,616,037	376,136	751,364	27,082	101,305	47,892
2009	2,747,282	1,848,708	58,638	1,907,346	236,993	-98,273	1,572,080	361,399	813,803	27,311	100,593	47,573
2010	2,798,586	1,914,182	47,601	1,961,783	244,581	-128,584	1,588,618	348,959	861,009	27,958	100,099	47,239
2011	2,866,769	1,924,163	55,028	1,979,191	221,774	-120,900	1,636,517	368,923	861,329	28,941	99,056	47,240
2012	2,914,912	1,964,684	95,159	2,059,843	223,074	-167,863	1,668,906	386,292	859,714	29,911	97,454	46,585
2013	2,961,976	1,889,242	192,918	2,082,160	241,202	-110,666	1,730,292	363,949	867,735	30,912	95,820	45,148
2014	2,965,622	1,877,856	124,022	2,001,878	243,623	-88,721	1,669,534	386,255	909,833	31,089	95,390	43,947
2015	2,979,179	1,847,126	110,627	1,957,753	240,937	-76,768	1,640,048	390,576	948,555	31,482	94,630	43,835
2016	2,972,777	1,858,766	106,556	1,965,322	241,583	-111,187	1,612,552	380,017	980,208	31,916	93,144	43,551
2017	3,007,430	1,891,413	92,399	1,983,812	247,350	-107,828	1,628,634	387,688	991,108	32,786	91,730	42,939
2018	3,024,216	1,917,075	75,936	1,993,011	250,972	-119,520	1,622,519	386,137	1,015,560	33,509	90,251	42,834
2019	3,054,298	1,916,413	59,544	1,975,957	255,154	-137,422	1,583,381	414,678	1,056,239	34,327	88,976	42,283
2020	3,279,731	1,965,292	75,746	2,041,038	264,313	-175,141	1,601,584	421,375	1,256,772	37,597	87,234	41,357
2021	3,578,873	2,060,798	142,187	2,202,985	271,605	-164,790	1,766,590	435,919	1,376,364	41,416	86,412	41,086

Personal Income and Employment by Area: Pittsburgh, PA

(Thousands of dollars, except as noted.)

Year	Personal income, total	Earnings by place of work			Less: Contributions for government social insurance	Plus: Adjustment for residence	Equals: Net earnings by place of residence	Plus: Dividends, interest, and rent	Plus: Personal current transfer receipts	Per capita personal income (dollars)	Population (persons)	Total employment
		Nonfarm	Farm	Total								
1970	11,286,375	9,279,300	33,266	9,312,566	683,635	-29,634	8,599,297	1,521,282	1,165,796	4,091	2,758,743	1,132,359
1971	11,887,371	9,662,772	35,548	9,698,320	738,906	-37,685	8,921,729	1,598,328	1,367,314	4,306	2,760,937	1,113,813
1972	12,858,851	10,479,485	41,854	10,521,339	840,895	-45,876	9,634,568	1,688,684	1,535,599	4,673	2,751,873	1,124,028
1973	14,023,848	11,530,303	40,406	11,570,709	1,065,963	-57,855	10,446,891	1,859,448	1,717,509	5,137	2,730,057	1,154,111
1974	15,575,362	12,762,748	43,833	12,806,581	1,226,950	-85,046	11,494,585	2,108,740	1,972,037	5,762	2,703,028	1,167,040
1975	17,206,793	13,822,385	46,381	13,868,766	1,299,014	-100,947	12,468,805	2,289,266	2,448,722	6,371	2,700,715	1,159,949
1976	18,750,712	15,035,208	57,588	15,092,796	1,434,009	-105,426	13,553,361	2,459,345	2,738,006	6,960	2,693,955	1,169,981
1977	20,644,417	16,679,938	59,236	16,739,174	1,585,810	-128,573	15,024,791	2,723,794	2,895,832	7,693	2,683,597	1,185,498
1978	22,691,978	18,459,573	53,682	18,513,255	1,802,874	-153,678	16,556,703	3,008,296	3,126,979	8,484	2,674,747	1,210,116
1979	25,139,310	20,459,137	59,775	20,518,912	2,070,691	-183,553	18,264,668	3,384,715	3,489,927	9,452	2,659,625	1,231,366
1980	27,592,002	21,660,418	42,172	21,702,590	2,199,143	-191,313	19,312,134	4,215,001	4,064,867	10,426	2,646,406	1,214,171
1981	30,417,265	23,249,238	62,251	23,311,489	2,531,332	-204,533	20,575,624	5,278,652	4,562,989	11,562	2,630,712	1,200,978
1982	32,030,452	23,083,568	55,200	23,138,768	2,558,140	-97,502	20,483,126	6,153,783	5,393,543	12,224	2,620,312	1,156,673
1983	32,710,924	23,151,437	34,791	23,186,228	2,589,793	-43,873	20,552,562	6,320,839	5,837,523	12,548	2,606,777	1,121,342
1984	34,750,629	24,628,553	66,774	24,695,327	2,854,867	-26,397	21,814,063	7,066,504	5,870,062	13,459	2,581,947	1,133,457
1985	36,109,709	25,570,865	63,081	25,633,946	3,002,045	-8,046	22,623,855	7,455,062	6,030,792	14,201	2,542,677	1,144,718
1986	37,211,076	26,206,318	54,693	26,261,011	3,099,254	2,867	23,164,624	7,669,258	6,377,194	14,786	2,516,600	1,149,933
1987	38,725,790	27,752,365	50,953	27,803,318	3,232,771	10,858	24,581,405	7,618,145	6,526,240	15,522	2,494,837	1,176,201
1988	41,950,618	30,422,119	44,317	30,466,436	3,578,101	14,111	26,902,446	8,234,881	6,813,291	16,917	2,479,863	1,207,101
1989	44,984,999	32,247,720	56,804	32,304,524	3,754,299	16,778	28,567,003	9,293,963	7,124,033	18,213	2,469,921	1,228,910
1990	48,111,189	34,315,014	85,280	34,400,294	4,036,295	-5,653	30,358,346	9,876,141	7,876,702	19,481	2,469,681	1,257,869
1991	50,328,425	35,744,233	64,794	35,809,027	4,255,383	-36,916	31,516,728	9,819,260	8,992,437	20,318	2,476,980	1,250,192
1992	52,948,437	38,344,335	79,522	38,423,857	4,546,032	-84,786	33,793,039	9,705,879	9,449,519	21,298	2,486,034	1,259,326
1993	54,739,112	39,813,557	61,947	39,875,504	4,796,859	-121,255	34,957,390	9,778,151	10,003,571	21,975	2,490,949	1,267,305
1994	56,480,779	41,306,138	39,116	41,345,254	5,068,509	-138,297	36,138,448	10,094,525	10,247,806	22,711	2,486,989	1,282,644
1995	58,677,747	42,510,302	23,790	42,534,092	5,224,775	-159,045	37,150,272	10,849,943	10,677,532	23,659	2,480,098	1,296,271
1996	61,306,402	43,998,179	42,879	44,041,058	5,299,995	-184,908	38,556,155	11,512,353	11,237,894	24,808	2,471,209	1,303,923
1997	64,561,216	46,611,419	11,972	46,623,391	5,543,863	-214,747	40,864,781	12,255,503	11,440,932	26,242	2,460,208	1,320,252
1998	67,060,561	48,872,672	20,934	48,893,606	5,728,629	-243,632	42,921,345	12,673,402	11,465,814	27,374	2,449,747	1,332,351
1999	70,365,708	52,483,838	18,895	52,502,733	6,057,608	-311,466	46,133,659	12,339,234	11,892,815	28,856	2,438,518	1,354,381
2000	74,667,859	55,449,575	44,158	55,493,733	6,299,083	-353,546	48,841,104	13,409,396	12,417,359	30,749	2,428,303	1,380,946
2001	76,814,434	57,173,836	21,415	57,195,251	6,521,994	-432,315	50,240,942	13,388,865	13,184,627	31,775	2,417,480	1,386,079
2002	77,692,770	58,181,701	23,048	58,204,749	6,653,141	-476,062	51,075,546	12,786,716	13,830,508	32,260	2,408,348	1,377,923
2003	79,375,729	59,105,899	55,197	59,161,096	6,721,072	-480,320	51,959,704	13,034,609	14,381,416	33,057	2,401,168	1,364,807
2004	82,497,974	61,968,166	53,471	62,021,637	6,990,966	-527,129	54,503,542	13,141,354	14,853,078	34,531	2,389,107	1,372,751
2005	85,491,944	64,106,761	36,997	64,143,758	7,311,757	-541,763	56,290,238	13,261,249	15,940,457	36,004	2,374,483	1,378,023
2006	90,629,317	66,863,213	50,046	66,913,259	7,674,059	-628,346	58,610,854	15,195,355	16,823,108	38,337	2,364,039	1,389,178
2007	95,436,911	69,387,049	35,495	69,422,544	7,940,319	-611,918	60,870,307	16,678,841	17,887,763	40,458	2,358,914	1,409,989
2008	99,764,638	72,028,146	34,357	72,062,503	8,236,487	-614,098	63,211,918	17,035,101	19,517,619	42,331	2,356,802	1,414,771
2009	97,158,572	69,917,097	30,205	69,947,302	8,146,996	-470,461	61,329,845	15,219,863	20,608,864	41,249	2,355,432	1,385,475
2010	101,385,867	73,253,124	46,650	73,299,774	8,444,413	-501,570	64,353,791	15,153,424	21,878,652	43,013	2,357,121	1,390,551
2011	106,572,413	76,817,410	59,771	76,877,181	7,929,716	-582,395	68,365,070	16,473,381	21,733,962	45,144	2,360,741	1,413,965
2012	110,294,726	78,980,848	85,730	79,066,578	8,134,731	-532,803	70,399,044	18,174,651	21,721,031	46,717	2,360,917	1,432,340
2013	111,245,928	82,177,007	65,009	82,242,016	9,436,858	-534,640	72,270,518	17,172,954	21,802,456	47,130	2,360,416	1,440,803
2014	115,533,441	84,791,168	73,582	84,864,750	9,689,859	-549,244	74,625,647	18,537,628	22,370,166	48,505	2,381,872	1,449,347
2015	119,920,253	88,438,810	33,493	88,472,303	10,077,633	-702,685	77,691,985	19,106,890	23,121,378	50,399	2,379,439	1,458,998
2016	121,019,480	88,062,365	15,973	88,078,338	10,111,141	-736,733	77,230,464	19,625,099	24,163,917	50,895	2,377,835	1,463,734
2017	126,311,619	93,114,137	51,172	93,165,309	10,739,278	-864,055	81,561,976	20,566,231	24,183,412	53,247	2,372,173	1,477,150
2018	134,267,445	98,748,301	10,892	98,759,193	11,201,179	-912,157	86,645,857	21,929,489	25,692,099	56,611	2,371,737	1,496,347
2019	138,491,331	100,752,887	54,255	100,807,142	11,578,826	-996,266	88,232,050	23,663,997	26,595,284	58,396	2,371,584	1,494,157
2020	147,014,914	99,019,571	35,359	99,054,930	11,300,333	-1,049,887	86,704,710	23,557,969	36,752,235	62,103	2,367,293	1,415,739
2021	154,698,269	105,356,075	52,012	105,408,087	11,772,150	-1,304,060	92,331,877	24,139,918	38,226,474	65,730	2,353,538	1,443,840

Personal Income and Employment by Area: Pittsfield, MA

(Thousands of dollars, except as noted.)

Year	Personal income, total	Earnings by place of work			Less: Contributions for government social insurance	Plus: Adjustment for residence	Equals: Net earnings by place of residence	Plus: Dividends, interest, and rent	Plus: Personal current transfer receipts	Per capita personal income (dollars)	Population (persons)	Total employment
		Nonfarm	Farm	Total								
1970	617,044	483,166	3,850	487,016	32,373	-3,355	451,288	97,099	68,657	4,117	149,893	66,119
1971	657,388	510,589	3,674	514,263	35,381	-2,942	475,940	102,987	78,461	4,354	150,987	65,091
1972	706,423	550,362	3,487	553,849	40,377	-2,114	511,358	110,296	84,769	4,745	148,869	65,585
1973	779,029	615,450	3,547	618,997	52,376	-1,649	564,972	118,250	95,807	5,208	149,573	69,449
1974	845,894	665,072	3,067	668,139	58,309	-613	609,217	128,383	108,294	5,653	149,649	70,334
1975	906,579	678,703	3,696	682,399	57,405	2,048	627,042	133,712	145,825	6,093	148,788	67,804
1976	958,249	716,704	3,568	720,272	61,743	5,004	663,533	141,123	153,593	6,547	146,360	66,846
1977	1,018,502	758,234	3,476	761,710	65,540	8,290	704,460	154,669	159,373	7,033	144,826	67,029
1978	1,119,412	840,858	4,563	845,421	75,018	11,558	781,961	168,554	168,897	7,649	146,354	68,925
1979	1,235,616	919,454	4,285	923,739	85,047	16,074	854,766	188,675	192,175	8,496	145,437	71,249
1980	1,378,108	993,177	4,098	997,275	91,459	20,510	926,326	232,303	219,479	9,499	145,081	71,264
1981	1,521,777	1,071,558	3,527	1,075,085	106,361	17,275	985,999	286,264	249,514	10,522	144,629	70,426
1982	1,651,218	1,132,450	4,247	1,136,697	114,762	12,738	1,034,673	342,402	274,143	11,615	142,162	69,487
1983	1,757,622	1,214,423	5,004	1,219,427	124,006	8,175	1,103,596	358,900	295,126	12,380	141,969	69,795
1984	1,949,744	1,360,789	6,718	1,367,507	142,937	2,695	1,227,265	411,455	311,024	13,753	141,767	72,759
1985	2,067,119	1,468,209	6,393	1,474,602	154,863	-4,547	1,315,192	427,554	324,373	14,667	140,938	74,546
1986	2,208,129	1,583,822	7,153	1,590,975	169,895	-11,783	1,409,297	459,513	339,319	15,728	140,396	77,067
1987	2,328,491	1,691,754	5,607	1,697,361	178,957	-19,259	1,499,145	479,190	350,156	16,600	140,268	76,319
1988	2,510,104	1,823,597	4,308	1,827,905	196,152	-28,564	1,603,189	528,072	378,843	17,957	139,787	78,504
1989	2,697,840	1,921,883	4,253	1,926,136	207,654	-41,245	1,677,237	601,804	418,799	19,299	139,790	79,087
1990	2,773,638	1,952,357	4,723	1,957,080	206,803	-50,866	1,699,411	613,381	460,846	19,894	139,423	77,748
1991	2,796,745	1,884,720	4,606	1,889,326	203,878	-44,005	1,641,443	627,253	528,049	20,170	138,661	73,552
1992	2,827,965	1,947,641	6,006	1,953,647	208,414	-38,662	1,706,571	574,541	546,853	20,521	137,809	73,706
1993	2,940,269	1,999,234	3,839	2,003,073	216,245	-35,854	1,750,974	625,470	563,825	21,440	137,139	75,102
1994	3,042,065	2,051,924	3,836	2,055,760	222,327	-31,104	1,802,329	643,287	596,449	22,176	137,176	75,643
1995	3,168,181	2,126,956	2,251	2,129,207	231,994	-29,002	1,868,211	673,304	626,666	23,145	136,885	75,632
1996	3,351,222	2,241,361	3,080	2,244,441	239,526	-25,780	1,979,135	728,478	643,609	24,523	136,657	76,886
1997	3,522,742	2,372,122	3,455	2,375,577	251,705	-24,135	2,099,737	756,965	666,040	25,788	136,602	77,231
1998	3,679,048	2,485,609	3,980	2,489,589	262,025	-18,764	2,208,800	814,264	655,984	27,099	135,763	78,323
1999	3,851,748	2,648,390	4,693	2,653,083	272,067	-13,474	2,367,542	804,923	679,283	28,484	135,227	79,056
2000	4,110,829	2,804,649	4,787	2,809,436	284,489	-3,008	2,521,939	881,625	707,265	30,503	134,769	79,393
2001	4,218,753	2,842,878	3,854	2,846,732	296,753	-8,362	2,541,617	908,659	768,477	31,500	133,928	79,964
2002	4,279,269	2,986,149	3,471	2,989,620	314,155	-24,203	2,651,262	801,651	826,356	32,047	133,529	80,215
2003	4,286,730	2,971,324	3,381	2,974,705	312,289	-25,989	2,636,427	769,509	880,794	32,129	133,423	79,900
2004	4,588,782	3,163,035	5,350	3,168,385	342,234	-32,553	2,793,598	874,470	920,714	34,482	133,076	80,034
2005	4,739,911	3,300,047	3,717	3,303,764	365,101	-40,943	2,897,720	851,379	990,812	35,756	132,563	81,565
2006	4,953,811	3,427,231	1,414	3,428,645	374,614	-48,329	3,005,702	904,068	1,044,041	37,535	131,977	82,231
2007	5,159,185	3,499,055	834	3,499,889	384,327	-53,995	3,061,567	1,015,515	1,082,103	39,119	131,883	83,314
2008	5,377,984	3,530,569	1,899	3,532,468	391,823	-62,948	3,077,697	1,084,594	1,215,693	40,937	131,372	83,438
2009	5,285,703	3,433,695	2,765	3,436,460	381,616	-67,432	2,987,412	982,131	1,316,160	40,268	131,264	81,386
2010	5,423,594	3,523,765	3,650	3,527,415	379,031	-65,822	3,082,562	956,728	1,384,304	41,301	131,318	80,930
2011	5,678,947	3,635,313	3,520	3,638,833	355,174	-70,417	3,213,242	1,063,872	1,401,833	43,495	130,565	81,165
2012	5,870,573	3,727,286	7,898	3,735,184	361,226	-72,986	3,300,972	1,135,705	1,433,896	45,047	130,321	82,425
2013	5,884,673	3,770,318	7,197	3,777,515	408,622	-73,562	3,295,331	1,145,100	1,444,242	45,427	129,542	83,432
2014	6,173,591	3,888,918	1,174	3,890,092	423,355	-69,432	3,397,305	1,285,839	1,490,447	47,214	130,759	83,999
2015	6,510,088	4,057,757	-1,223	4,056,534	434,462	-69,218	3,552,854	1,357,583	1,599,651	50,001	130,199	86,252
2016	6,668,456	4,174,337	-3,919	4,170,418	448,779	-73,719	3,647,920	1,362,811	1,657,725	51,355	129,850	85,652
2017	6,814,773	4,257,464	-2,209	4,255,255	460,960	-67,349	3,726,946	1,400,095	1,687,732	52,583	129,601	85,820
2018	7,078,517	4,397,730	-3,468	4,394,262	477,843	-70,203	3,846,216	1,467,505	1,764,796	54,598	129,648	85,840
2019	7,341,816	4,476,635	189	4,476,824	488,321	-58,904	3,929,599	1,601,284	1,810,933	56,861	129,119	84,838
2020	7,929,627	4,446,072	-1,809	4,444,263	484,401	-52,927	3,906,935	1,585,371	2,437,321	61,586	128,758	78,368
2021	8,369,201	4,707,505	-1,304	4,706,201	513,390	-49,684	4,143,127	1,627,340	2,598,734	65,050	128,657	81,153

Personal Income and Employment by Area: Pocatello, ID

(Thousands of dollars, except as noted.)

Year	Personal income, total	Earnings by place of work			Less: Contributions for government social insurance	Plus: Adjustment for residence	Equals: Net earnings by place of residence	Plus: Dividends, interest, and rent	Plus: Personal current transfer receipts	Per capita personal income (dollars)	Population (persons)	Total employment
		Nonfarm	Farm	Total								
1970	180,403	133,357	3,631	136,988	11,199	12,441	138,230	25,631	16,542	3,449	52,301	21,284
1971	197,548	145,649	3,624	149,273	12,336	11,737	148,674	29,185	19,689	3,711	53,234	21,673
1972	221,291	163,697	4,820	168,517	14,415	13,033	167,135	31,959	22,197	4,079	54,256	22,338
1973	245,415	188,273	1,123	189,396	19,082	14,360	184,674	35,639	25,102	4,493	54,619	23,949
1974	288,684	218,585	7,129	225,714	22,900	15,586	218,400	41,295	28,989	5,136	56,204	25,253
1975	332,065	251,085	3,668	254,753	25,495	17,814	247,072	48,818	36,175	5,818	57,076	26,556
1976	389,601	305,171	4,574	309,745	31,431	18,696	297,010	52,799	39,792	6,488	60,045	28,815
1977	428,435	335,614	2,607	338,221	34,826	22,721	326,116	59,545	42,774	6,868	62,378	30,488
1978	484,031	379,983	3,615	383,598	39,846	24,299	368,051	68,215	47,765	7,584	63,821	31,826
1979	533,850	421,919	2,156	424,075	46,323	23,402	401,154	77,567	55,129	8,229	64,871	32,145
1980	578,044	444,269	4,848	449,117	49,240	26,114	425,991	86,005	66,048	8,805	65,650	30,930
1981	625,003	468,157	5,630	473,787	55,897	33,272	451,162	100,041	73,800	9,401	66,486	30,178
1982	665,608	481,563	5,353	486,916	59,787	37,468	464,597	118,138	82,873	9,922	67,081	29,433
1983	709,757	501,745	6,435	508,180	62,289	46,608	492,499	128,757	88,501	10,545	67,307	29,207
1984	744,846	525,044	3,059	528,103	68,115	53,527	513,515	139,326	92,005	11,098	67,114	29,669
1985	804,872	565,893	4,749	570,642	74,743	57,555	553,454	152,717	98,701	12,004	67,051	30,216
1986	800,033	546,567	5,512	552,079	73,232	62,558	541,405	155,761	102,867	11,933	67,043	28,847
1987	816,251	552,322	3,786	556,108	71,438	74,937	559,607	151,050	105,594	12,341	66,140	28,462
1988	850,233	580,138	2,416	582,554	80,078	81,132	583,608	154,657	111,968	12,963	65,588	29,680
1989	911,170	616,344	5,353	621,697	86,943	84,433	619,187	169,817	122,166	13,833	65,869	30,423
1990	959,674	652,753	7,369	660,122	95,648	90,773	655,247	172,360	132,067	14,484	66,258	30,888
1991	1,025,897	685,579	6,828	692,407	100,821	109,375	700,961	177,746	147,190	15,235	67,338	31,624
1992	1,114,719	750,325	10,965	761,290	106,527	107,164	761,927	185,081	167,711	16,115	69,173	32,944
1993	1,199,290	813,472	10,158	823,630	115,189	109,709	818,150	202,267	178,873	16,946	70,770	34,329
1994	1,261,196	857,730	6,749	864,479	120,591	111,904	855,792	216,800	188,604	17,403	72,468	35,875
1995	1,326,803	886,314	9,322	895,636	125,308	111,926	882,254	240,448	204,101	18,026	73,603	36,418
1996	1,394,924	947,208	8,287	955,495	131,525	105,758	929,728	250,699	214,497	18,844	74,026	38,085
1997	1,454,686	987,733	4,435	992,168	135,579	111,733	968,322	264,540	221,824	19,491	74,635	38,859
1998	1,681,622	1,206,136	33,213	1,239,349	159,450	66,116	1,146,015	292,014	243,593	20,348	82,642	45,342
1999	1,735,311	1,266,425	46,713	1,313,138	163,775	49,167	1,198,530	283,104	253,677	20,870	83,150	46,228
2000	1,812,248	1,323,110	51,085	1,374,195	170,225	47,363	1,251,333	291,740	269,175	21,779	83,212	47,657
2001	1,886,091	1,351,902	35,714	1,387,616	173,600	66,025	1,280,041	301,993	304,057	22,529	83,718	47,949
2002	1,943,303	1,350,041	53,321	1,403,362	172,442	70,189	1,301,109	309,067	333,127	23,174	83,858	47,257
2003	2,003,709	1,402,343	33,764	1,436,107	178,097	68,306	1,326,316	329,654	347,739	23,966	83,605	47,934
2004	2,144,938	1,506,571	50,898	1,557,469	191,432	65,871	1,431,908	337,074	375,956	25,454	84,266	49,500
2005	2,229,091	1,578,703	42,079	1,620,782	203,568	66,925	1,484,139	346,226	398,726	26,273	84,845	50,751
2006	2,385,418	1,651,384	52,468	1,703,852	215,105	80,012	1,568,759	383,579	433,080	27,720	86,055	51,729
2007	2,512,902	1,713,874	67,678	1,781,552	223,087	83,786	1,642,251	406,746	463,905	28,927	86,870	52,537
2008	2,594,819	1,744,922	53,544	1,798,466	227,832	88,833	1,659,467	403,892	531,460	29,429	88,173	51,219
2009	2,566,317	1,672,828	49,119	1,721,947	223,309	108,736	1,607,374	386,045	572,898	28,635	89,622	49,341
2010	2,645,554	1,693,103	53,856	1,746,959	233,820	121,042	1,634,181	378,434	632,939	29,104	90,899	48,343
2011	2,783,713	1,719,727	81,893	1,801,620	214,568	137,297	1,724,349	414,922	644,442	30,443	91,440	48,696
2012	2,864,799	1,757,140	80,291	1,837,431	216,925	149,949	1,770,455	443,971	650,373	31,270	91,614	48,567
2013	2,891,870	1,805,040	66,904	1,871,944	240,144	161,971	1,793,771	436,466	661,633	31,679	91,288	49,033
2014	2,984,873	1,866,054	42,042	1,908,096	249,300	159,806	1,818,602	483,112	683,159	32,873	90,801	49,808
2015	3,147,325	1,949,719	52,851	2,002,570	256,096	166,326	1,912,800	516,047	718,478	34,470	91,306	50,668
2016	3,216,822	1,997,989	40,918	2,038,907	264,143	184,793	1,959,557	514,357	742,908	35,106	91,632	51,088
2017	3,387,640	2,097,308	29,000	2,126,308	277,955	206,937	2,055,290	558,540	773,810	36,728	92,237	52,005
2018	3,502,486	2,174,351	43,703	2,218,054	285,829	217,452	2,149,677	540,652	812,157	37,517	93,357	52,654
2019	3,715,154	2,261,535	63,338	2,324,873	295,288	233,872	2,263,457	589,716	861,981	39,418	94,251	53,552
2020	4,061,916	2,385,221	78,711	2,463,932	316,270	250,293	2,397,955	603,771	1,060,190	42,732	95,056	53,098
2021	4,353,075	2,521,383	42,124	2,563,507	327,608	266,378	2,502,277	620,821	1,229,977	45,244	96,213	54,530

Personal Income and Employment by Area: Portland-South Portland, ME

(Thousands of dollars, except as noted.)

Year	Personal income, total	Earnings by place of work Nonfarm	Farm	Total	Less: Contributions for government social insurance	Plus: Adjustment for residence	Equals: Net earnings by place of residence	Plus: Dividends, interest, and rent	Plus: Personal current transfer receipts	Per capita personal income (dollars)	Population (persons)	Total employment
1970	1,309,394	1,052,479	7,804	1,060,283	71,698	-38,473	950,112	239,994	119,288	3,985	328,590	156,769
1971	1,412,610	1,119,076	7,885	1,126,961	78,837	-36,951	1,011,173	260,636	140,801	4,202	336,169	155,953
1972	1,564,546	1,247,512	8,971	1,256,483	92,402	-42,343	1,121,738	284,116	158,692	4,562	342,955	160,994
1973	1,715,429	1,352,873	14,673	1,367,546	114,173	-39,605	1,213,768	312,092	189,569	4,908	349,490	165,759
1974	1,876,732	1,458,545	12,171	1,470,716	127,325	-50,650	1,292,741	353,833	230,158	5,270	356,106	169,317
1975	2,075,896	1,583,433	10,744	1,594,177	135,312	-66,038	1,392,827	387,620	295,449	5,752	360,891	170,259
1976	2,336,245	1,809,000	17,917	1,826,917	157,854	-75,808	1,593,255	419,222	323,768	6,397	365,186	177,404
1977	2,572,894	2,004,274	8,929	2,013,203	175,222	-84,894	1,753,087	474,479	345,328	6,906	372,562	184,124
1978	2,882,269	2,264,861	10,650	2,275,511	204,215	-95,892	1,975,404	536,078	370,787	7,628	377,860	193,643
1979	3,193,454	2,515,682	6,276	2,521,958	234,416	-104,731	2,182,811	592,287	418,356	8,335	383,159	200,253
1980	3,620,239	2,807,558	4,152	2,811,710	260,393	-117,323	2,433,994	701,123	485,122	9,385	385,753	204,838
1981	4,021,609	3,087,550	6,089	3,093,639	305,905	-169,384	2,618,350	847,736	555,523	10,284	391,072	207,150
1982	4,443,130	3,355,873	8,144	3,364,017	338,426	-192,715	2,832,876	1,004,799	605,455	11,266	394,395	210,235
1983	4,812,060	3,656,001	2,920	3,658,921	377,092	-191,734	3,090,095	1,069,537	652,428	12,052	399,275	217,658
1984	5,390,352	4,093,914	9,110	4,103,024	438,249	-191,245	3,473,530	1,227,545	689,277	13,294	405,463	228,798
1985	5,920,385	4,507,243	6,880	4,514,123	484,748	-170,169	3,859,206	1,325,572	735,607	14,377	411,789	239,590
1986	6,533,722	5,016,674	9,923	5,026,597	547,026	-164,003	4,315,568	1,450,286	767,868	15,631	417,991	254,199
1987	7,150,723	5,565,047	8,278	5,573,325	606,622	-161,697	4,805,006	1,555,960	789,757	16,832	424,840	265,537
1988	7,965,763	6,252,052	7,575	6,259,627	694,910	-183,844	5,380,873	1,745,449	839,441	18,370	433,634	281,206
1989	8,627,292	6,711,790	5,378	6,717,168	738,713	-212,618	5,765,837	1,958,625	902,830	19,663	438,759	287,046
1990	9,007,684	6,951,046	13,093	6,964,139	807,287	-223,226	5,933,626	2,067,306	1,006,752	20,343	442,790	285,041
1991	9,111,913	6,885,007	10,943	6,895,950	807,394	-180,000	5,908,556	2,046,643	1,156,714	20,457	445,414	273,772
1992	9,561,977	7,195,091	15,223	7,210,314	854,237	-153,002	6,203,075	2,085,985	1,272,917	21,396	446,901	274,413
1993	9,907,560	7,382,640	12,704	7,395,344	895,274	-95,209	6,404,861	2,160,766	1,341,933	22,034	449,643	276,688
1994	10,397,073	7,727,257	10,031	7,737,288	956,241	-48,463	6,732,584	2,262,296	1,402,193	22,916	453,695	283,211
1995	10,991,776	8,008,107	11,513	8,019,620	997,819	6,300	7,028,101	2,479,954	1,483,721	24,025	457,522	285,360
1996	11,705,993	8,405,806	10,943	8,416,749	1,035,159	59,434	7,441,024	2,674,795	1,590,174	25,235	463,883	290,659
1997	12,502,054	9,010,082	9,895	9,019,977	1,106,313	89,294	8,002,958	2,832,264	1,666,832	26,591	470,167	299,375
1998	13,488,803	9,724,590	11,029	9,735,619	1,179,976	145,922	8,701,565	3,077,914	1,709,324	28,371	475,444	307,580
1999	14,229,154	10,519,756	11,685	10,531,441	1,256,114	192,173	9,467,500	2,992,919	1,768,735	29,523	481,966	313,419
2000	15,370,081	11,227,090	15,799	11,242,889	1,315,947	302,248	10,229,190	3,242,545	1,898,346	31,420	489,179	323,073
2001	16,285,559	11,969,046	14,888	11,983,934	1,376,874	286,447	10,893,507	3,341,146	2,050,906	32,902	494,975	329,579
2002	16,719,039	12,444,606	14,484	12,459,090	1,384,245	258,697	11,333,542	3,197,599	2,187,898	33,426	500,178	330,414
2003	17,660,395	13,070,823	14,401	13,085,224	1,437,165	197,454	11,845,513	3,444,379	2,370,503	34,981	504,858	335,323
2004	18,814,183	13,955,232	14,523	13,969,755	1,530,513	169,725	12,608,967	3,683,760	2,521,456	37,005	508,428	343,215
2005	19,235,358	14,124,194	11,028	14,135,222	1,562,846	186,006	12,758,382	3,743,501	2,733,475	37,695	510,287	343,183
2006	20,444,297	14,931,892	10,704	14,942,596	1,673,043	204,307	13,473,860	4,172,690	2,797,747	40,039	510,614	348,308
2007	21,210,308	15,365,666	9,300	15,374,966	1,753,098	190,927	13,812,795	4,395,869	3,001,644	41,405	512,265	353,971
2008	22,019,153	15,671,941	19,729	15,691,670	1,806,137	180,772	14,066,305	4,455,404	3,497,444	42,823	514,191	353,530
2009	21,709,447	15,429,899	23,744	15,453,643	1,767,911	214,475	13,900,207	4,025,234	3,784,006	42,177	514,728	343,960
2010	22,388,846	15,933,761	32,781	15,966,542	1,818,282	300,728	14,448,988	4,060,392	3,879,466	43,564	513,925	342,237
2011	23,534,635	16,260,514	29,569	16,290,083	1,667,495	391,131	15,013,719	4,497,391	4,023,525	45,596	516,159	345,578
2012	24,268,116	16,694,539	32,327	16,726,866	1,723,810	445,410	15,448,466	4,798,631	4,021,019	46,866	517,816	347,932
2013	24,387,170	16,953,350	24,119	16,977,469	2,010,591	516,366	15,483,244	4,758,454	4,145,472	46,876	520,251	351,294
2014	25,546,700	17,566,929	22,117	17,589,046	2,059,574	599,685	16,129,157	5,126,251	4,291,292	48,379	528,051	355,934
2015	26,832,024	18,411,755	18,093	18,429,848	2,186,318	612,291	16,855,821	5,498,791	4,477,412	50,546	530,845	362,236
2016	27,953,598	19,163,454	17,331	19,180,785	2,268,755	636,464	17,548,494	5,801,691	4,603,413	52,252	534,979	369,476
2017	29,360,437	20,136,947	18,125	20,155,072	2,369,332	644,067	18,429,807	6,155,281	4,775,349	54,475	538,968	376,356
2018	30,848,491	21,181,380	13,977	21,195,357	2,512,025	669,721	19,353,053	6,417,871	5,077,567	56,752	543,562	382,994
2019	32,912,488	22,179,432	19,275	22,198,707	2,628,709	718,418	20,288,416	7,236,689	5,387,383	60,019	548,370	384,182
2020	35,502,827	23,071,320	16,451	23,087,771	2,736,630	746,015	21,097,156	7,239,368	7,166,303	64,306	552,089	369,919
2021	38,177,675	25,290,366	12,447	25,302,813	2,969,483	848,519	23,181,849	7,432,725	7,563,101	68,555	556,893	385,526

Personal Income and Employment by Area: Portland-Vancouver-Hillsboro, OR-WA

(Thousands of dollars, except as noted.)

Year	Personal income, total	Earnings by place of work Nonfarm	Farm	Total	Less: Contributions for government social insurance	Plus: Adjustment for residence	Equals: Net earnings by place of residence	Plus: Dividends, interest, and rent	Plus: Personal current transfer receipts	Per capita personal income (dollars)	Population (persons)	Total employment
1970	4,839,750	3,841,363	48,010	3,889,373	294,374	9,352	3,604,351	807,901	427,498	4,460	1,085,025	497,091
1971	5,289,170	4,160,169	44,528	4,204,697	328,026	23,091	3,899,762	892,268	497,140	4,785	1,105,374	506,310
1972	5,892,337	4,690,577	48,379	4,738,956	392,279	37,872	4,384,549	968,100	539,688	5,195	1,134,259	535,293
1973	6,599,173	5,270,140	83,122	5,353,262	510,759	47,463	4,889,966	1,075,874	633,333	5,700	1,157,768	564,082
1974	7,470,277	5,904,154	79,239	5,983,393	586,768	58,077	5,454,702	1,248,745	766,830	6,359	1,174,809	583,002
1975	8,291,936	6,364,377	72,248	6,436,625	616,976	99,017	5,918,666	1,397,285	975,985	6,953	1,192,510	587,075
1976	9,287,115	7,220,112	70,781	7,290,893	712,908	125,697	6,703,682	1,518,155	1,065,278	7,656	1,213,090	609,841
1977	10,335,263	8,167,539	71,689	8,239,228	813,974	78,467	7,503,721	1,698,889	1,132,653	8,319	1,242,430	640,432
1978	11,888,345	9,536,300	69,748	9,606,048	977,647	48,857	8,677,258	1,979,454	1,231,633	9,322	1,275,246	683,210
1979	13,497,187	10,906,532	82,997	10,989,529	1,162,884	14,792	9,841,437	2,285,654	1,370,096	10,285	1,312,315	719,013
1980	15,113,387	11,935,285	81,851	12,017,136	1,272,567	3,955	10,748,524	2,756,416	1,608,447	11,222	1,346,705	728,447
1981	16,542,871	12,643,346	83,103	12,726,449	1,436,597	14,146	11,303,998	3,377,901	1,860,972	12,124	1,364,523	717,025
1982	17,183,283	12,717,462	69,321	12,786,783	1,470,701	40,716	11,356,798	3,709,743	2,116,742	12,512	1,373,347	694,891
1983	18,134,873	13,260,740	74,090	13,334,830	1,550,685	61,243	11,845,388	3,990,696	2,298,789	13,227	1,371,007	703,207
1984	19,798,807	14,616,848	109,744	14,726,592	1,768,828	58,169	13,015,933	4,419,867	2,363,007	14,343	1,380,339	734,223
1985	20,856,719	15,482,959	109,246	15,592,205	1,885,163	50,850	13,757,892	4,646,372	2,452,455	14,989	1,391,424	754,432
1986	22,119,353	16,557,928	158,946	16,716,874	2,010,221	51,015	14,757,668	4,848,796	2,512,889	15,690	1,409,733	775,492
1987	23,367,978	17,724,844	150,209	17,875,053	2,121,464	49,291	15,802,880	4,962,510	2,602,588	16,419	1,423,238	803,521
1988	25,621,787	19,732,690	182,506	19,915,196	2,435,516	49,649	17,529,329	5,342,723	2,749,735	17,620	1,454,141	845,832
1989	28,352,210	21,597,097	187,842	21,784,939	2,663,638	57,593	19,178,894	6,154,949	3,018,367	19,064	1,487,217	883,562
1990	31,092,474	23,954,711	240,900	24,195,611	3,033,477	55,643	21,217,777	6,605,003	3,269,694	20,243	1,535,965	918,239
1991	32,816,993	25,387,312	267,345	25,654,657	3,253,596	64,719	22,465,780	6,718,655	3,632,558	20,708	1,584,767	929,685
1992	35,246,718	27,456,074	246,867	27,702,941	3,492,382	59,318	24,269,877	6,941,302	4,035,539	21,680	1,625,751	941,423
1993	37,848,194	29,485,790	249,269	29,735,059	3,752,649	49,986	26,032,396	7,508,121	4,307,677	22,668	1,669,701	969,806
1994	40,815,645	31,747,442	230,689	31,978,131	4,077,627	42,763	27,943,267	8,424,925	4,447,453	23,894	1,708,216	1,022,108
1995	44,305,203	34,294,787	238,680	34,533,467	4,428,385	5,812	30,110,894	9,311,202	4,883,107	25,328	1,749,224	1,065,398
1996	48,349,768	37,666,234	268,174	37,934,408	4,895,457	-31,434	33,007,517	10,126,701	5,215,550	26,905	1,797,066	1,112,001
1997	52,050,493	40,966,216	318,191	41,284,407	5,236,441	-68,052	35,979,914	10,711,969	5,358,610	28,290	1,839,867	1,160,405
1998	55,255,221	43,727,458	319,646	44,047,104	5,546,839	-74,085	38,426,180	11,399,186	5,429,855	29,464	1,875,365	1,188,161
1999	57,312,968	46,061,977	327,765	46,389,742	5,773,690	-75,570	40,540,482	10,902,402	5,870,084	30,066	1,906,262	1,203,732
2000	62,819,773	50,806,441	298,757	51,105,198	6,332,901	-126,097	44,646,200	11,833,026	6,340,547	32,468	1,934,792	1,230,760
2001	63,705,489	51,119,521	327,285	51,446,806	6,315,077	-93,420	45,038,309	11,513,462	7,153,718	32,319	1,971,152	1,230,201
2002	63,854,621	51,055,621	320,698	51,376,319	6,309,234	-56,242	45,010,843	10,970,819	7,872,959	31,881	2,002,918	1,213,408
2003	66,036,055	52,474,216	405,955	52,880,171	6,481,393	-8,121	46,390,657	11,588,635	8,056,763	32,625	2,024,115	1,216,494
2004	70,128,913	56,050,146	423,329	56,473,475	6,968,444	6,278	49,511,309	12,396,440	8,221,164	34,389	2,039,297	1,248,863
2005	74,273,238	59,226,008	432,555	59,658,563	7,316,915	-8,986	52,332,662	13,283,157	8,657,419	35,927	2,067,325	1,289,785
2006	81,269,551	64,043,533	488,079	64,531,612	7,863,814	-35,885	56,631,913	15,335,034	9,302,604	38,642	2,103,164	1,330,456
2007	86,029,744	67,088,308	474,614	67,562,922	8,223,900	684	59,339,706	16,617,851	10,072,187	40,242	2,137,828	1,368,280
2008	90,566,661	68,154,997	515,105	68,670,102	8,352,696	133,765	60,451,171	18,271,135	11,844,355	41,681	2,172,853	1,367,770
2009	86,361,861	64,269,554	466,236	64,735,790	8,031,351	294,058	56,998,497	15,772,208	13,591,156	39,136	2,206,737	1,310,373
2010	88,699,882	65,633,990	407,628	66,041,618	8,285,248	465,165	58,221,535	15,633,977	14,844,370	39,735	2,232,270	1,306,785
2011	94,440,960	69,028,828	467,981	69,496,809	7,734,541	377,714	62,139,982	17,371,450	14,929,528	41,728	2,263,267	1,333,678
2012	100,972,545	73,929,644	531,356	74,461,000	8,140,359	331,388	66,652,029	19,436,523	14,883,993	44,108	2,289,205	1,358,131
2013	102,397,921	76,819,728	499,111	77,318,839	9,584,922	326,328	68,060,245	18,952,153	15,385,523	44,288	2,312,095	1,389,540
2014	109,804,273	81,130,928	411,800	81,542,728	10,149,033	423,621	71,817,316	21,228,950	16,758,007	46,775	2,347,475	1,433,716
2015	118,134,203	86,860,554	506,054	87,366,608	10,759,420	430,134	77,037,322	23,487,939	17,608,942	49,510	2,386,057	1,481,578
2016	123,959,838	91,335,005	465,948	91,800,953	11,217,666	298,944	80,882,231	24,848,298	18,229,309	50,972	2,431,944	1,524,211
2017	131,421,020	97,415,235	391,738	97,806,973	12,056,947	209,615	85,959,641	26,783,143	18,678,236	53,396	2,461,234	1,570,641
2018	140,542,607	103,815,488	390,895	104,206,383	12,586,145	299,770	91,920,008	28,896,298	19,726,301	56,673	2,479,889	1,606,079
2019	147,841,973	109,067,471	357,040	109,424,511	13,243,580	267,883	96,448,814	30,438,079	20,955,080	59,189	2,497,793	1,617,571
2020	159,166,530	111,930,261	392,811	112,323,072	13,497,232	505,819	99,331,659	30,702,991	29,131,880	63,256	2,516,230	1,552,461
2021	171,728,750	121,756,586	426,477	122,183,063	14,439,638	260,163	108,003,588	31,717,978	32,007,184	68,374	2,511,612	1,593,052

Personal Income and Employment by Area: Poughkeepsie-Newburgh-Middletown, NY

(Thousands of dollars, except as noted.)

Year	Personal income, total	Earnings by place of work			Less: Contributions for government social insurance	Plus: Adjustment for residence	Equals: Net earnings by place of residence	Plus: Dividends, interest, and rent	Plus: Personal current transfer receipts	Per capita personal income (dollars)	Population (persons)	Total employment
		Nonfarm	Farm	Total								
1970	1,928,321	1,905,425	22,896	1,509,513	111,073	64,522	1,462,962	309,887	155,472	4,319	446,438	186,898
1971	2,134,783	2,113,367	21,416	1,639,510	124,703	91,649	1,606,456	340,092	188,235	4,672	456,961	189,327
1972	2,357,479	2,339,576	17,903	1,793,401	143,246	122,935	1,773,090	374,687	209,702	5,130	459,527	192,493
1973	2,610,794	2,587,484	23,310	1,965,250	180,420	164,138	1,948,968	415,400	246,426	5,570	468,716	201,165
1974	2,872,515	2,851,400	21,115	2,111,175	199,764	204,484	2,115,895	463,282	293,338	6,043	475,356	203,257
1975	3,165,617	3,140,932	24,685	2,227,161	207,727	251,725	2,271,159	505,336	389,122	6,550	483,292	199,854
1976	3,397,625	3,373,601	24,024	2,350,271	224,775	304,987	2,430,483	528,605	438,537	7,026	483,589	199,394
1977	3,705,209	3,678,748	26,461	2,549,206	243,325	360,164	2,666,045	573,952	465,212	7,564	489,832	203,486
1978	4,119,419	4,092,673	26,746	2,840,325	277,283	435,227	2,998,269	622,850	498,300	8,306	495,984	212,224
1979	4,623,555	4,589,988	33,567	3,176,483	320,495	511,560	3,367,548	716,209	539,798	9,209	502,051	221,762
1980	5,208,461	5,170,852	37,609	3,448,452	345,202	623,051	3,726,301	853,256	628,904	10,296	505,849	222,410
1981	5,914,329	5,880,993	33,336	3,831,059	407,158	727,497	4,151,398	1,036,763	726,168	11,604	509,660	225,577
1982	6,574,113	6,544,067	30,046	4,238,267	453,901	789,831	4,574,197	1,198,967	800,949	12,796	513,751	230,042
1983	7,118,887	7,099,422	19,465	4,609,171	499,453	863,291	4,973,009	1,293,204	852,674	13,710	519,246	233,972
1984	7,969,083	7,940,672	28,411	5,218,644	576,101	962,456	5,604,999	1,480,817	883,267	15,147	526,116	244,050
1985	8,612,665	8,584,859	27,806	5,688,903	637,186	1,058,279	6,109,996	1,574,588	928,081	16,193	531,875	254,676
1986	9,256,140	9,224,690	31,450	6,122,576	694,576	1,176,496	6,604,496	1,662,352	989,292	17,195	538,304	261,524
1987	9,852,451	9,813,365	39,086	6,560,340	735,400	1,272,072	7,097,012	1,746,773	1,008,666	17,984	547,857	264,793
1988	10,647,116	10,609,163	37,953	7,117,616	820,862	1,399,174	7,695,928	1,867,905	1,083,283	19,092	557,662	275,305
1989	11,593,991	11,550,197	43,794	7,609,508	864,832	1,432,133	8,176,809	2,212,576	1,204,606	20,618	562,322	278,982
1990	12,231,579	12,194,781	36,798	8,004,625	876,976	1,570,627	8,698,276	2,216,581	1,316,722	21,495	569,041	279,509
1991	12,591,290	12,549,622	41,668	8,124,661	908,731	1,658,055	8,873,985	2,258,960	1,458,345	21,936	573,990	273,759
1992	13,109,160	13,076,512	32,648	8,388,603	925,403	1,735,858	9,199,058	2,238,017	1,672,085	22,586	580,407	273,282
1993	13,298,761	13,246,478	52,283	8,333,717	921,386	1,899,743	9,312,074	2,222,387	1,764,300	22,749	584,584	269,630
1994	13,513,941	13,477,320	36,621	8,235,150	922,593	2,051,293	9,363,850	2,297,945	1,852,146	23,077	585,604	272,756
1995	14,178,331	14,147,320	31,011	8,484,600	949,931	2,185,870	9,720,539	2,486,943	1,970,849	24,032	589,989	270,432
1996	14,849,290	14,823,541	25,749	8,795,353	971,608	2,375,895	10,199,640	2,582,688	2,066,962	24,957	594,986	274,599
1997	15,670,427	15,653,061	17,366	9,063,722	986,979	2,798,718	10,875,461	2,685,239	2,109,727	26,126	599,795	277,738
1998	16,577,255	9,608,351	34,191	9,642,542	1,044,416	2,867,628	11,465,754	2,797,406	2,314,095	27,356	605,983	282,874
1999	17,681,670	10,562,886	45,595	10,608,481	1,105,679	2,981,416	12,484,218	2,812,253	2,385,199	28,787	614,216	293,769
2000	19,025,358	11,217,283	56,059	11,273,342	1,177,748	3,406,863	13,502,457	3,017,655	2,505,246	30,499	623,806	301,872
2001	20,000,611	11,863,871	53,380	11,917,251	1,275,439	3,599,254	14,241,066	3,065,150	2,694,395	31,627	632,386	303,862
2002	20,317,742	12,277,338	32,880	12,310,218	1,336,694	3,675,651	14,649,175	2,750,328	2,918,239	31,713	640,675	308,074
2003	21,295,430	12,885,667	34,707	12,920,374	1,413,899	3,779,699	15,286,174	2,974,217	3,035,039	32,787	649,508	313,034
2004	22,453,069	13,519,998	34,523	13,554,521	1,490,200	3,989,446	16,053,767	3,075,447	3,323,855	34,238	655,793	320,334
2005	23,399,594	14,045,555	34,048	14,079,603	1,560,870	4,171,966	16,690,699	3,310,947	3,397,948	35,514	658,884	325,155
2006	24,824,042	14,630,155	34,915	14,665,070	1,627,978	4,591,863	17,628,955	3,595,059	3,600,028	37,520	661,620	327,925
2007	26,345,220	15,145,349	29,007	15,174,356	1,664,645	5,013,751	18,523,462	3,999,942	3,821,816	39,690	663,783	331,551
2008	27,442,380	15,541,192	51,778	15,592,970	1,736,445	4,978,377	18,834,902	4,301,465	4,306,013	41,176	666,468	332,459
2009	27,007,105	15,678,175	46,814	15,724,989	1,741,503	4,272,542	18,256,028	3,983,586	4,767,491	40,371	668,966	325,667
2010	27,684,466	16,141,817	58,425	16,200,242	1,770,234	4,138,680	18,568,688	3,976,762	5,139,016	41,248	671,172	323,882
2011	28,878,496	16,485,608	52,986	16,538,594	1,628,442	4,393,527	19,303,679	4,309,030	5,265,787	42,954	672,312	328,527
2012	29,955,708	17,000,063	68,737	17,068,800	1,649,486	4,633,561	20,052,875	4,569,808	5,333,025	44,655	670,823	328,574
2013	30,400,947	17,295,262	65,103	17,360,365	1,891,091	4,829,554	20,298,828	4,690,745	5,411,374	45,327	670,709	332,270
2014	31,167,764	17,512,817	52,614	17,565,431	1,957,925	4,896,315	20,503,821	4,985,363	5,678,580	45,982	677,831	336,416
2015	32,549,435	18,065,241	43,203	18,108,444	2,036,450	5,148,532	21,220,526	5,314,984	6,013,925	47,898	679,560	342,370
2016	33,321,757	18,424,064	42,816	18,466,880	2,078,721	5,288,119	21,676,278	5,487,231	6,158,248	48,832	682,370	343,386
2017	34,899,460	19,293,060	51,360	19,344,420	2,184,719	5,293,400	22,453,101	5,861,695	6,584,664	50,820	686,729	347,990
2018	35,934,808	20,167,103	42,414	20,209,517	2,252,147	5,664,024	23,621,394	5,808,006	6,505,408	51,966	691,510	354,612
2019	38,371,380	21,027,452	57,514	21,084,966	2,351,873	6,203,112	24,936,205	6,406,294	7,028,881	55,119	696,160	358,226
2020	40,942,663	21,043,283	51,968	21,095,251	2,361,205	6,126,400	24,860,446	6,367,388	9,714,829	58,736	697,064	340,012
2021	43,802,109	22,651,849	51,378	22,703,227	2,547,038	7,222,547	27,378,736	6,488,251	9,935,122	62,428	701,637	350,884

Personal Income and Employment by Area: Port St. Lucie, FL

(Thousands of dollars, except as noted.)

Year	Personal income, total	Derivation of personal income									Per capita personal income (dollars)	Population (persons)	Total employment
		Earnings by place of work			Less: Contributions for government social insurance	Plus: Adjustment for residence	Equals: Net earnings by place of residence	Plus: Dividends, interest, and rent	Plus: Personal current transfer receipts				
		Nonfarm	Farm	Total									
1970	314,908	185,400	23,641	209,041	12,412	309	196,938	82,937	35,033		3,949	79,741	33,285
1971	365,479	209,249	28,337	237,586	14,601	2,417	225,402	96,936	43,141		4,321	84,589	35,253
1972	441,651	257,116	34,881	291,997	18,903	2,425	275,519	113,292	52,840		4,901	90,118	39,752
1973	539,533	318,856	34,460	353,316	26,816	3,947	330,447	141,545	67,541		5,239	102,977	44,659
1974	618,281	355,871	35,234	391,105	31,474	4,798	364,429	171,150	82,702		5,482	112,792	46,293
1975	692,720	380,117	38,997	419,114	33,146	5,579	391,547	194,063	107,110		5,883	117,754	46,049
1976	790,994	434,172	46,111	480,283	37,833	7,740	450,190	219,681	121,123		6,482	122,024	48,072
1977	910,728	489,023	58,524	547,547	43,123	11,867	516,291	257,575	136,862		7,175	126,939	51,647
1978	1,086,736	579,065	77,889	656,954	51,937	16,306	621,323	310,262	155,151		8,113	133,944	56,962
1979	1,304,264	704,186	80,958	785,144	66,063	17,067	736,148	381,803	186,313		9,108	143,206	62,851
1980	1,663,682	882,979	122,384	1,005,363	83,903	2,941	924,401	511,443	227,838		10,819	153,770	68,854
1981	1,933,556	979,152	85,659	1,064,811	99,992	20,592	985,411	678,023	270,122		11,806	163,782	71,320
1982	2,143,899	1,051,361	98,310	1,149,671	111,108	31,735	1,070,298	756,970	316,631		12,350	173,600	74,297
1983	2,409,474	1,140,439	154,046	1,294,485	119,742	56,745	1,231,488	823,248	354,738		13,282	181,413	77,623
1984	2,638,384	1,236,869	101,719	1,338,588	132,984	90,490	1,296,094	955,144	387,146		13,895	189,879	81,858
1985	2,950,357	1,345,705	110,120	1,455,825	148,160	118,861	1,426,526	1,090,650	433,181		14,917	197,784	86,119
1986	3,274,971	1,508,008	110,034	1,618,042	170,297	139,868	1,587,613	1,206,032	481,326		15,824	206,964	90,815
1987	3,647,109	1,724,234	135,300	1,859,534	192,185	159,502	1,826,851	1,296,794	523,464		16,742	217,839	93,920
1988	4,258,597	1,941,389	220,566	2,161,955	223,813	187,039	2,125,181	1,541,257	592,159		18,708	227,640	101,218
1989	4,874,855	2,141,027	167,524	2,308,551	252,123	208,584	2,265,012	1,921,420	688,423		20,377	239,233	107,262
1990	5,337,847	2,277,859	124,563	2,402,422	264,565	237,932	2,375,789	2,189,201	772,857		20,957	254,702	109,748
1991	5,540,206	2,342,531	149,173	2,491,704	273,643	248,702	2,466,763	2,185,934	887,509		21,054	263,143	108,584
1992	5,829,248	2,530,054	106,874	2,636,928	292,540	267,351	2,611,739	2,183,318	1,034,191		21,613	269,716	108,447
1993	6,178,666	2,685,556	103,939	2,789,495	308,989	280,618	2,761,124	2,297,835	1,119,707		22,287	277,235	111,244
1994	6,509,197	2,805,913	88,625	2,894,538	330,635	304,064	2,867,967	2,433,697	1,207,533		22,839	285,006	113,621
1995	7,144,672	2,959,179	97,094	3,056,273	349,116	324,949	3,032,106	2,803,206	1,309,360		24,592	290,527	117,523
1996	7,648,009	3,141,218	59,515	3,200,733	365,916	363,205	3,198,022	3,047,073	1,402,914		25,669	297,947	122,505
1997	8,149,594	3,307,848	61,224	3,369,072	386,018	394,662	3,377,716	3,286,499	1,485,379		26,728	304,912	126,227
1998	8,823,912	3,523,315	105,598	3,628,913	407,982	446,781	3,667,712	3,608,128	1,548,072		28,356	311,185	133,060
1999	9,251,367	3,777,610	89,817	3,867,427	430,797	496,449	3,933,079	3,708,354	1,609,934		29,247	316,323	136,633
2000	9,950,708	4,024,672	83,733	4,108,405	458,233	567,652	4,217,824	4,012,078	1,720,806		31,017	320,819	141,761
2001	10,755,247	4,525,801	67,306	4,593,107	507,141	725,168	4,811,134	4,093,960	1,850,153		32,759	328,315	143,578
2002	11,075,523	4,915,101	66,535	4,981,636	545,876	883,507	5,319,267	3,774,562	1,981,694		32,696	338,741	148,128
2003	11,878,067	5,265,221	51,771	5,316,992	588,229	1,080,239	5,809,002	3,961,147	2,107,918		33,790	351,522	155,145
2004	13,454,397	5,909,236	64,093	5,973,329	663,328	1,196,364	6,506,365	4,644,997	2,303,035		36,533	368,277	166,986
2005	14,972,063	6,553,542	102,016	6,655,558	746,806	1,515,109	7,423,861	5,162,657	2,385,545		39,002	383,877	179,580
2006	16,461,999	6,955,788	95,861	7,051,649	819,006	1,665,396	7,898,039	5,996,384	2,567,576		41,460	397,053	187,529
2007	17,292,782	7,121,674	68,162	7,189,836	858,233	1,794,828	8,126,431	6,416,700	2,749,651		42,136	410,402	189,637
2008	17,502,332	6,699,225	62,694	6,761,919	846,043	1,899,021	7,814,897	6,562,755	3,124,680		41,920	417,520	183,487
2009	16,115,740	6,443,445	62,799	6,506,244	816,720	1,775,016	7,464,540	5,234,177	3,417,023		38,385	419,850	175,818
2010	16,662,934	6,710,438	69,968	6,780,406	820,553	1,498,057	7,457,910	5,497,714	3,707,310		39,188	425,202	176,756
2011	17,724,833	6,840,565	81,518	6,922,083	754,986	1,622,430	7,789,527	6,069,663	3,865,643		41,376	428,385	179,263
2012	19,480,100	7,122,779	106,253	7,229,032	787,212	2,186,419	8,628,239	7,006,931	3,844,930		45,085	432,074	181,956
2013	19,103,561	7,239,318	97,577	7,336,895	900,839	2,293,798	8,729,854	6,370,322	4,003,385		43,752	436,634	185,834
2014	20,928,393	7,668,541	96,696	7,765,237	949,982	2,372,736	9,187,991	7,504,281	4,236,121		47,568	439,965	194,076
2015	22,207,006	8,194,167	123,998	8,318,165	1,004,610	2,463,337	9,776,892	7,924,616	4,505,498		49,483	448,782	202,465
2016	23,774,700	8,531,559	90,622	8,622,181	1,053,130	2,961,770	10,530,821	8,478,797	4,765,082		51,809	458,889	210,064
2017	25,300,245	8,951,606	110,952	9,062,558	1,107,078	3,133,403	11,088,883	9,162,473	5,048,889		54,216	466,658	217,812
2018	26,501,965	9,481,939	65,140	9,547,079	1,187,297	3,218,968	11,578,750	9,638,534	5,284,681		55,940	473,761	226,375
2019	28,581,443	10,041,723	79,942	10,121,665	1,279,706	3,542,004	12,383,963	10,550,399	5,647,081		59,414	481,058	230,517
2020	30,223,723	10,520,292	63,137	10,583,429	1,345,420	3,480,767	12,718,776	10,587,194	6,917,753		61,706	489,804	235,796
2021	33,549,849	11,608,369	38,749	11,647,118	1,452,705	4,545,132	14,739,545	10,985,355	7,824,949		66,630	503,521	244,373

Personal Income and Employment by Area: Prescott Valley-Prescott, AZ

(Thousands of dollars, except as noted.)

Year	Personal income, total	Earnings by place of work			Less: Contributions for government social insurance	Plus: Adjustment for residence	Equals: Net earnings by place of residence	Plus: Dividends, interest, and rent	Plus: Personal current transfer receipts	Per capita personal income (dollars)	Population (persons)	Total employment
		Nonfarm	Farm	Total								
1970	144,363	80,740	2,618	83,358	5,139	2,433	80,652	44,292	19,419	3,843	37,570	12,550
1971	171,295	95,709	3,448	99,157	6,313	4,200	97,044	50,845	23,406	4,240	40,403	13,909
1972	203,467	114,316	5,913	120,229	7,929	6,226	118,526	57,461	27,480	4,535	44,864	15,086
1973	241,208	134,784	8,017	142,801	10,487	8,490	140,804	68,156	32,248	5,030	47,951	16,708
1974	263,506	148,131	552	148,683	12,164	8,397	144,916	80,726	37,864	5,246	50,233	17,382
1975	299,669	159,161	7,979	167,140	12,876	8,034	162,298	89,212	48,159	5,970	50,194	17,370
1976	332,974	184,318	2,119	186,437	14,689	7,212	178,960	98,264	55,750	5,973	55,746	18,441
1977	384,717	212,962	4,211	217,173	17,527	8,112	207,758	114,748	62,211	6,440	59,742	20,271
1978	449,804	238,570	7,945	246,515	19,845	14,422	241,092	137,416	71,296	7,211	62,377	21,755
1979	517,155	276,862	1,932	278,794	24,174	17,305	271,925	163,633	81,597	7,854	65,842	23,433
1980	617,566	313,072	5,298	318,370	28,012	19,000	309,358	207,521	100,687	8,989	68,705	24,767
1981	713,095	344,130	1,853	345,983	33,682	21,001	333,302	259,296	120,497	10,060	70,883	25,230
1982	760,465	347,549	3,847	351,396	35,049	22,031	338,378	284,117	137,970	10,275	74,009	25,227
1983	840,906	384,232	4,085	388,317	39,454	26,930	375,793	314,582	150,531	10,954	76,769	26,696
1984	948,174	420,851	6,213	427,064	44,122	35,143	418,085	365,638	164,451	11,907	79,633	28,552
1985	1,067,781	476,148	1,593	477,741	51,314	41,622	468,049	419,193	180,539	12,921	82,642	31,802
1986	1,187,527	533,455	3,059	536,514	57,507	49,878	528,885	459,869	198,773	13,339	89,025	34,400
1987	1,275,393	583,022	2,537	585,559	62,972	55,901	578,488	475,623	221,282	13,595	93,811	36,621
1988	1,410,400	640,432	327	640,759	72,277	63,402	631,884	530,068	248,448	14,176	99,493	38,956
1989	1,546,082	671,762	3,236	674,998	81,399	69,192	662,791	603,571	279,720	14,916	103,651	40,422
1990	1,658,590	728,783	5,446	734,229	89,827	77,789	722,191	622,271	314,128	15,242	108,818	42,267
1991	1,772,412	806,902	5,430	812,332	98,982	82,414	795,764	624,351	352,297	15,669	113,119	44,202
1992	1,918,275	902,200	6,620	908,820	110,219	91,511	890,112	630,173	397,990	16,198	118,427	46,644
1993	2,084,370	1,003,163	2,783	1,005,946	123,138	99,291	982,099	673,103	429,168	16,653	125,164	49,463
1994	2,374,726	1,158,743	-296	1,158,447	141,596	109,155	1,126,006	782,188	466,532	17,992	131,986	55,718
1995	2,533,393	1,227,366	-765	1,226,601	145,686	122,775	1,203,690	821,025	508,678	18,108	139,901	57,666
1996	2,752,664	1,318,743	4,724	1,323,467	158,302	136,751	1,301,916	901,199	549,549	18,801	146,414	60,672
1997	2,995,160	1,470,415	6,124	1,476,539	171,423	150,082	1,455,198	962,967	576,995	19,715	151,924	64,787
1998	3,259,551	1,570,217	12,707	1,582,924	182,163	168,148	1,568,909	1,063,448	627,194	20,671	157,686	67,473
1999	3,437,951	1,671,013	24,213	1,695,226	193,466	184,979	1,686,739	1,088,769	662,443	21,099	162,943	66,576
2000	3,686,986	1,769,977	17,673	1,787,650	206,659	206,654	1,787,645	1,178,638	720,703	21,867	168,608	69,991
2001	3,907,509	1,905,268	23,894	1,929,162	223,293	210,728	1,916,597	1,193,344	797,568	22,634	172,636	76,403
2002	4,052,318	2,054,057	10,577	2,064,634	241,534	209,287	2,032,387	1,136,922	883,009	22,848	177,362	78,539
2003	4,316,988	2,209,410	14,393	2,223,803	257,168	213,578	2,180,213	1,186,566	950,209	23,708	182,090	80,739
2004	4,796,483	2,417,503	16,076	2,433,579	281,922	225,180	2,376,837	1,353,571	1,066,075	25,537	187,822	84,763
2005	5,371,371	2,696,065	16,577	2,712,642	318,061	239,453	2,634,034	1,565,100	1,172,237	27,486	195,424	90,797
2006	5,901,870	3,017,430	11,775	3,029,205	359,867	255,819	2,925,157	1,658,729	1,317,984	28,919	204,082	95,889
2007	6,367,042	3,148,514	9,802	3,158,316	382,800	268,160	3,043,676	1,885,805	1,437,561	30,497	208,773	98,495
2008	6,542,105	3,147,369	8,090	3,155,459	391,420	263,872	3,027,911	1,889,892	1,624,302	30,974	211,211	95,085
2009	6,218,391	2,915,656	2,022	2,917,678	374,256	233,650	2,777,072	1,627,772	1,813,547	29,447	211,172	89,442
2010	6,185,892	2,803,537	2,550	2,806,087	369,687	224,810	2,661,210	1,581,653	1,943,029	29,318	210,990	87,118
2011	6,426,393	2,775,698	7,590	2,783,288	337,779	229,630	2,675,139	1,743,387	2,007,867	30,445	211,081	87,057
2012	6,615,897	2,871,337	7,126	2,878,463	347,191	228,396	2,759,668	1,784,740	2,071,489	31,197	212,065	88,290
2013	6,956,439	3,057,309	7,547	3,064,856	404,635	220,082	2,880,303	1,884,268	2,191,868	32,425	214,539	90,098
2014	7,548,122	3,300,473	7,348	3,307,821	426,041	224,232	3,106,012	2,113,580	2,328,530	34,851	216,582	92,459
2015	7,923,856	3,493,390	9,022	3,502,412	450,652	235,601	3,287,361	2,180,957	2,455,538	36,117	219,393	94,894
2016	8,318,748	3,717,588	12,047	3,729,635	482,669	239,250	3,486,216	2,254,991	2,577,541	37,326	222,867	97,393
2017	8,926,016	3,955,553	10,389	3,965,942	516,400	256,976	3,706,518	2,427,822	2,791,676	39,478	226,100	99,068
2018	9,410,073	4,173,832	10,324	4,184,156	560,436	273,520	3,897,240	2,543,391	2,969,442	40,945	229,820	102,180
2019	10,092,937	4,268,903	8,637	4,277,540	586,589	287,737	3,978,688	2,908,039	3,206,210	43,306	233,062	102,171
2020	11,190,206	4,556,021	14,933	4,570,954	633,515	290,004	4,227,443	2,933,875	4,028,888	47,203	237,067	102,656
2021	11,884,929	4,865,520	14,636	4,880,156	670,182	319,430	4,529,404	3,029,783	4,325,742	49,060	242,253	106,125

Personal Income and Employment by Area: Providence-Warwick, RI-MA

(Thousands of dollars, except as noted.)

Year	Personal income, total	Earnings by place of work			Less: Contributions for government social insurance	Plus: Adjustment for residence	Equals: Net earnings by place of residence	Plus: Dividends, interest, and rent	Plus: Personal current transfer receipts	Per capita personal income (dollars)	Population (persons)	Total employment
		Nonfarm	Farm	Total								
1970	5,814,992	4,387,300	16,934	4,404,234	328,715	188,818	4,264,337	921,850	628,805	4,165	1,396,129	629,664
1971	6,202,171	4,612,057	15,023	4,627,080	358,216	211,732	4,480,596	979,264	742,311	4,389	1,413,149	623,177
1972	6,770,032	5,073,636	14,154	5,087,790	411,755	235,873	4,911,908	1,046,956	811,168	4,734	1,430,040	639,853
1973	7,284,619	5,452,140	12,997	5,465,137	514,209	271,749	5,222,677	1,142,054	919,888	5,068	1,437,274	652,677
1974	7,710,883	5,598,805	13,930	5,612,735	553,187	319,367	5,378,915	1,247,976	1,083,992	5,459	1,412,609	640,670
1975	8,369,663	5,793,686	14,558	5,808,244	556,877	350,698	5,602,065	1,334,317	1,433,281	5,952	1,406,082	615,617
1976	9,182,532	6,499,990	15,516	6,515,506	636,881	392,095	6,270,720	1,427,191	1,484,621	6,486	1,415,810	641,578
1977	10,070,327	7,158,790	14,737	7,173,527	701,293	456,438	6,928,672	1,587,021	1,554,634	7,082	1,422,032	665,492
1978	11,091,486	7,962,515	19,317	7,981,832	803,514	526,850	7,705,168	1,734,397	1,651,921	7,780	1,425,662	687,471
1979	12,330,433	8,834,566	17,291	8,851,857	921,195	611,522	8,542,184	1,939,167	1,849,082	8,622	1,430,055	699,681
1980	13,796,860	9,541,656	18,875	9,560,531	996,188	720,575	9,284,918	2,373,232	2,138,710	9,688	1,424,092	699,678
1981	15,287,047	10,257,155	23,193	10,280,348	1,140,405	803,131	9,943,074	2,907,291	2,436,682	10,691	1,429,942	696,826
1982	16,522,724	10,809,823	42,156	10,851,979	1,215,934	881,739	10,517,784	3,339,083	2,665,857	11,544	1,431,288	687,087
1983	17,877,820	11,763,581	54,607	11,818,188	1,337,787	988,956	11,469,357	3,576,713	2,831,750	12,465	1,434,222	697,303
1984	19,714,204	13,050,642	54,689	13,105,331	1,540,711	1,143,170	12,707,790	4,077,253	2,929,161	13,673	1,441,812	730,198
1985	21,238,561	14,203,849	60,588	14,264,437	1,660,354	1,250,734	13,854,817	4,277,502	3,106,242	14,630	1,451,669	752,699
1986	22,775,483	15,389,867	65,343	15,455,210	1,810,674	1,337,555	14,982,091	4,539,208	3,254,184	15,573	1,462,482	774,732
1987	24,381,511	16,656,773	60,720	16,717,493	1,943,190	1,514,026	16,288,329	4,735,649	3,357,533	16,485	1,478,976	783,574
1988	26,808,521	18,364,247	60,575	18,424,822	2,170,331	1,679,706	17,934,197	5,263,120	3,611,204	17,949	1,493,594	804,366
1989	28,931,015	19,391,205	50,346	19,441,551	2,266,866	1,764,485	18,939,170	5,999,583	3,992,262	19,239	1,503,781	805,887
1990	29,813,538	19,749,929	47,613	19,797,542	2,389,123	1,874,500	19,282,919	6,077,820	4,452,799	19,702	1,513,216	786,517
1991	30,160,084	19,451,557	50,386	19,501,943	2,411,286	1,865,165	18,955,822	5,877,131	5,327,131	19,852	1,519,234	749,079
1992	31,581,582	20,678,158	45,545	20,723,703	2,560,911	1,936,178	20,098,970	5,915,004	5,567,608	20,745	1,522,392	760,306
1993	32,903,703	21,616,178	46,008	21,662,186	2,707,000	1,976,073	20,931,259	6,062,672	5,909,772	21,532	1,528,117	772,176
1994	34,122,785	22,536,267	40,456	22,576,723	2,849,013	2,135,055	21,862,765	6,248,699	6,011,321	22,272	1,532,065	778,499
1995	35,896,275	23,541,977	40,440	23,582,417	2,957,763	2,220,465	22,845,119	6,709,312	6,341,844	23,373	1,535,833	784,811
1996	37,277,821	24,425,830	44,400	24,470,230	3,032,165	2,315,182	23,753,247	7,039,344	6,485,230	24,180	1,541,702	791,039
1997	39,465,746	25,725,074	35,823	25,760,897	3,177,135	2,607,517	25,191,279	7,451,928	6,822,539	25,480	1,548,897	802,598
1998	41,825,831	27,522,364	30,321	27,552,685	3,349,029	2,886,316	27,089,972	7,835,834	6,900,025	26,840	1,558,350	815,590
1999	43,892,715	29,390,292	31,357	29,421,649	3,514,350	3,148,297	29,055,596	7,672,387	7,164,732	27,929	1,571,610	832,845
2000	47,374,267	31,618,439	35,429	31,653,868	3,732,495	3,665,617	31,586,990	8,317,853	7,469,424	29,869	1,586,085	855,161
2001	50,123,137	33,350,990	35,881	33,386,871	3,911,308	3,849,012	33,324,575	8,503,105	8,295,457	31,417	1,595,424	855,796
2002	51,941,634	34,940,473	43,677	34,984,150	4,040,819	3,815,990	34,759,321	8,378,306	8,804,007	32,288	1,608,716	859,087
2003	54,265,939	36,658,678	43,247	36,701,925	4,229,572	3,868,244	36,340,597	8,792,033	9,133,309	33,547	1,617,623	865,534
2004	56,756,026	38,552,441	46,633	38,599,074	4,495,357	4,225,194	38,328,911	8,777,691	9,649,424	35,022	1,620,567	877,834
2005	58,348,161	39,700,952	41,878	39,742,830	4,684,909	4,194,178	39,252,099	8,929,522	10,166,540	36,166	1,613,353	883,474
2006	61,586,053	41,752,397	43,371	41,795,768	4,919,800	4,366,591	41,242,559	9,758,447	10,585,047	38,310	1,607,583	889,734
2007	64,162,562	42,484,854	40,844	42,525,698	5,060,242	4,595,815	42,061,271	10,729,480	11,371,811	40,036	1,602,603	898,480
2008	66,044,276	42,818,738	49,885	42,868,623	5,151,085	4,414,987	42,132,525	11,126,944	12,784,807	41,240	1,601,459	886,236
2009	64,263,127	41,085,810	47,608	41,133,418	5,043,299	4,078,232	40,168,351	10,105,749	13,989,027	40,140	1,600,970	855,319
2010	67,423,009	43,600,660	44,943	43,645,603	5,160,892	3,910,275	42,394,986	10,199,406	14,828,617	42,056	1,603,169	852,089
2011	69,931,894	44,678,092	34,352	44,712,444	4,808,107	4,176,492	44,080,829	10,923,786	14,927,279	43,621	1,603,184	860,585
2012	72,518,331	46,529,399	41,118	46,570,517	4,926,023	4,441,388	46,085,882	11,561,566	14,870,883	45,152	1,606,097	865,547
2013	72,911,684	47,579,413	39,628	47,619,041	5,642,596	4,474,546	46,450,991	11,395,371	15,065,322	45,342	1,608,055	881,148
2014	75,969,846	49,361,949	37,608	49,399,557	5,888,912	4,338,869	47,849,514	12,211,725	15,908,607	46,508	1,633,482	898,598
2015	79,156,160	51,313,359	35,534	51,348,893	6,129,863	4,557,420	49,776,450	12,798,722	16,580,988	48,238	1,640,944	919,849
2016	80,704,360	51,974,681	24,345	51,999,026	6,297,077	5,019,486	50,721,435	13,097,611	16,885,314	48,958	1,648,427	930,499
2017	84,031,273	54,090,334	33,043	54,123,377	6,544,763	5,401,238	52,979,852	13,703,741	17,347,680	50,761	1,655,425	940,820
2018	87,480,545	56,175,027	23,273	56,198,300	6,799,598	5,930,406	55,329,108	14,211,288	17,940,149	52,481	1,666,909	955,583
2019	92,854,799	58,293,768	23,626	58,317,394	7,028,733	7,263,475	58,552,136	15,618,637	18,684,026	55,560	1,671,265	957,229
2020	101,105,603	58,876,879	21,717	58,898,596	7,046,788	7,960,520	59,812,328	15,655,789	25,637,486	60,347	1,675,401	905,533
2021	108,198,058	63,083,134	22,506	63,105,640	7,517,440	9,626,071	65,214,271	16,025,605	26,958,182	64,566	1,675,774	940,124

Personal Income and Employment by Area: Provo-Orem, UT

(Thousands of dollars, except as noted.)

Year	Personal income, total	Earnings by place of work			Less: Contributions for government social insurance	Plus: Adjustment for residence	Equals: Net earnings by place of residence	Plus: Dividends, interest, and rent	Plus: Personal current transfer receipts	Per capita personal income (dollars)	Population (persons)	Total employment
		Nonfarm	Farm	Total								
1970	398,439	296,737	9,575	306,312	20,247	24,775	310,840	52,323	35,276	2,774	143,630	52,365
1971	442,217	324,740	9,460	334,200	22,891	28,744	340,053	59,468	42,696	2,936	150,643	54,182
1972	512,139	381,335	7,560	388,895	28,013	34,594	395,476	67,824	48,839	3,204	159,828	58,707
1973	589,542	435,843	17,429	453,272	37,403	39,989	455,858	75,966	57,718	3,523	167,341	63,657
1974	663,155	490,487	12,655	503,142	43,894	46,645	505,893	89,473	67,789	3,802	174,411	66,614
1975	737,418	536,507	8,587	545,094	47,786	54,792	552,100	99,527	85,791	4,112	179,319	66,238
1976	859,244	630,401	10,408	640,809	55,472	68,045	653,382	112,959	92,903	4,639	185,213	70,264
1977	992,780	735,778	8,495	744,273	64,506	81,958	761,725	130,406	100,649	5,060	196,202	75,348
1978	1,147,489	854,554	6,739	861,293	77,072	92,833	877,054	155,641	114,794	5,610	204,554	80,873
1979	1,317,997	986,055	10,277	996,332	94,196	101,583	1,003,719	182,810	131,468	6,110	215,721	84,123
1980	1,467,753	1,071,011	7,749	1,078,760	102,125	113,441	1,090,076	219,479	158,198	6,511	225,440	83,779
1981	1,645,443	1,190,030	6,033	1,196,063	122,784	128,500	1,201,779	260,207	183,457	7,088	232,150	84,370
1982	1,732,578	1,188,833	7,346	1,196,179	122,681	144,660	1,218,158	296,981	217,439	7,268	238,395	85,064
1983	1,848,030	1,251,552	8,125	1,259,677	128,847	153,627	1,284,457	329,349	234,224	7,592	243,424	87,034
1984	2,050,889	1,404,257	9,736	1,413,993	147,731	171,106	1,437,368	370,909	242,612	8,301	247,068	92,533
1985	2,192,544	1,500,322	10,980	1,511,302	160,485	185,636	1,536,453	397,736	258,355	8,743	250,774	95,049
1986	2,317,461	1,591,324	9,930	1,601,254	170,807	182,401	1,612,848	420,107	284,506	9,151	253,249	97,302
1987	2,452,731	1,656,233	14,360	1,670,593	177,161	180,691	1,674,123	436,928	341,680	9,574	256,199	101,692
1988	2,699,332	1,892,175	22,414	1,914,589	214,749	178,669	1,878,509	467,392	353,431	10,381	260,016	110,799
1989	2,962,413	2,084,605	21,389	2,105,994	241,905	186,129	2,050,218	522,410	389,785	11,130	266,166	117,040
1990	3,276,112	2,390,593	23,080	2,413,673	285,763	191,350	2,319,260	531,844	425,008	12,102	270,713	125,706
1991	3,604,614	2,664,385	28,856	2,693,241	324,901	199,076	2,567,416	567,115	470,083	12,922	278,950	131,672
1992	3,920,647	2,915,232	31,985	2,947,217	351,576	220,403	2,816,044	582,916	521,687	13,522	289,947	133,739
1993	4,265,447	3,161,303	27,338	3,188,641	381,571	240,549	3,047,619	648,668	569,160	14,124	302,004	138,561
1994	4,680,990	3,505,538	23,570	3,529,108	427,534	263,012	3,364,586	732,890	583,514	14,864	314,918	151,987
1995	5,164,548	3,889,150	19,596	3,908,746	480,668	279,192	3,707,270	830,576	626,702	15,881	325,204	161,158
1996	5,671,772	4,250,640	23,519	4,274,159	512,061	312,503	4,074,601	931,912	665,259	16,797	337,667	172,108
1997	6,033,550	4,517,010	25,750	4,542,760	537,910	354,429	4,359,279	992,580	681,691	17,344	347,876	180,366
1998	6,629,835	4,990,322	33,302	5,023,624	587,400	383,775	4,819,999	1,092,274	717,562	18,355	361,197	188,543
1999	7,051,409	5,354,072	26,234	5,380,306	627,607	411,993	5,164,692	1,128,180	758,537	19,073	369,707	195,570
2000	7,630,636	5,732,323	29,655	5,761,978	674,154	447,895	5,535,719	1,274,590	820,327	20,076	380,079	203,516
2001	8,006,761	5,957,027	27,541	5,984,568	700,341	505,179	5,789,406	1,302,176	915,179	20,319	394,059	207,244
2002	8,259,757	6,044,110	19,923	6,064,033	709,273	544,578	5,899,338	1,343,451	1,016,968	20,361	405,672	208,369
2003	8,670,503	6,281,510	29,499	6,311,009	744,754	585,564	6,151,819	1,431,730	1,086,954	20,904	414,780	211,327
2004	9,407,019	6,963,870	43,390	7,007,260	822,951	692,587	6,876,896	1,375,126	1,154,997	22,133	425,023	222,605
2005	10,569,594	7,577,751	44,372	7,622,123	897,055	827,516	7,552,584	1,750,630	1,266,380	24,042	439,623	236,232
2006	11,911,059	8,514,085	24,526	8,538,611	995,544	1,065,487	8,608,554	1,939,246	1,363,259	26,037	457,471	250,781
2007	13,372,589	9,248,152	46,905	9,295,057	1,084,134	1,284,606	9,495,529	2,375,491	1,501,569	27,907	479,181	268,048
2008	14,326,432	9,390,668	30,210	9,420,878	1,105,773	1,499,766	9,814,871	2,708,472	1,803,089	28,789	497,639	268,390
2009	13,632,324	8,851,828	28,695	8,880,523	1,059,396	1,513,305	9,334,432	2,307,276	1,990,616	26,470	515,010	262,149
2010	13,986,159	8,875,420	46,201	8,921,621	1,067,189	1,634,743	9,489,175	2,263,930	2,233,054	26,374	530,296	259,785
2011	15,146,155	9,462,975	71,179	9,534,154	1,019,828	1,734,079	10,248,405	2,592,456	2,305,294	27,988	541,161	269,378
2012	16,499,828	10,431,190	79,457	10,510,647	1,096,362	1,870,827	11,285,112	2,937,043	2,277,673	29,985	550,270	278,458
2013	17,377,919	11,443,532	84,184	11,527,716	1,335,980	1,831,907	12,023,643	3,005,657	2,348,619	30,924	561,958	289,890
2014	18,886,222	12,410,400	89,463	12,499,863	1,426,120	2,004,975	13,078,718	3,402,509	2,404,995	32,797	575,858	301,334
2015	20,727,605	13,757,185	73,179	13,830,364	1,538,102	2,041,888	14,334,150	3,839,775	2,553,680	35,177	589,239	317,112
2016	22,341,825	14,782,659	43,800	14,826,459	1,646,010	2,282,473	15,462,922	4,200,485	2,678,418	36,701	608,760	334,959
2017	23,772,640	15,812,911	32,198	15,845,109	1,778,919	2,487,871	16,554,061	4,471,262	2,747,317	37,927	626,808	351,358
2018	25,749,888	17,561,012	42,785	17,603,797	1,930,381	2,431,866	18,105,282	4,718,619	2,925,987	40,052	642,919	371,491
2019	28,960,033	19,698,048	34,195	19,732,243	2,090,327	2,797,897	20,439,813	5,317,694	3,202,526	43,996	658,240	379,326
2020	31,836,000	21,310,035	38,553	21,348,588	2,287,069	3,044,961	22,106,480	5,511,504	4,218,016	47,167	674,967	393,211
2021	35,286,303	23,362,395	59,417	23,421,812	2,490,463	3,385,735	24,317,084	5,785,054	5,184,165	50,616	697,141	416,654

Personal Income and Employment by Area: Pueblo, CO

(Thousands of dollars, except as noted.)

Year	Personal income, total	Earnings by place of work			Less: Contributions for government social insurance	Plus: Adjustment for residence	Equals: Net earnings by place of residence	Plus: Dividends, interest, and rent	Plus: Personal current transfer receipts	Per capita personal income (dollars)	Population (persons)	Total employment
		Nonfarm	Farm	Total								
1970	417,116	326,012	2,799	328,811	18,433	-8,376	302,002	66,804	48,310	3,518	118,574	46,458
1971	460,152	355,264	2,040	357,304	20,388	-8,401	328,515	74,775	56,862	3,811	120,746	46,902
1972	510,393	397,917	3,621	401,538	24,406	-8,818	368,314	80,827	61,252	4,182	122,032	49,018
1973	579,201	456,895	3,679	460,574	33,443	-11,671	415,460	92,241	71,500	4,646	124,680	51,840
1974	647,868	507,264	3,556	510,820	38,730	-13,356	458,734	107,065	82,069	5,199	124,611	52,526
1975	715,356	542,635	5,049	547,684	41,357	-12,245	494,082	121,682	99,592	5,649	126,644	51,414
1976	775,126	588,483	5,562	594,045	46,026	-12,147	535,872	128,438	110,816	6,168	125,675	52,192
1977	830,738	630,970	3,157	634,127	50,559	-11,326	572,242	138,996	119,500	6,665	124,638	51,961
1978	920,575	702,864	2,408	705,272	58,442	-12,419	634,411	155,054	131,110	7,426	123,963	53,178
1979	1,027,687	788,450	2,784	791,234	68,723	-14,219	708,292	173,498	145,897	8,164	125,884	54,608
1980	1,125,975	828,401	3,717	832,118	72,490	-13,702	745,926	207,750	172,299	8,935	126,012	53,070
1981	1,250,489	892,401	6,589	898,990	83,788	-13,956	801,246	245,776	203,467	9,935	125,863	51,665
1982	1,281,596	853,858	4,088	857,946	81,074	-10,318	766,554	276,883	238,159	10,228	125,299	49,099
1983	1,302,162	806,536	6,344	812,880	76,284	-4,752	731,844	302,290	268,028	10,356	125,737	47,022
1984	1,381,429	847,337	6,076	853,413	83,176	-2,331	767,906	336,873	276,650	11,124	124,183	47,903
1985	1,455,503	894,266	4,593	898,859	89,995	-305	808,559	365,513	281,431	11,752	123,851	48,921
1986	1,516,899	922,944	6,196	929,140	93,809	1,317	836,648	381,858	298,393	12,222	124,111	49,175
1987	1,539,556	922,410	7,908	930,318	92,412	2,829	840,735	381,747	317,074	12,385	124,312	48,884
1988	1,625,495	990,693	8,405	999,098	105,236	3,311	897,173	389,205	339,117	13,136	123,745	51,235
1989	1,741,207	1,066,164	7,117	1,073,281	117,186	1,438	957,533	414,197	369,477	14,083	123,639	52,619
1990	1,822,794	1,135,879	5,452	1,141,331	126,029	887	1,016,189	413,401	393,204	14,803	123,134	55,119
1991	1,909,055	1,180,490	4,628	1,185,118	135,039	3,787	1,053,866	406,597	448,592	15,465	123,447	54,874
1992	2,031,755	1,254,031	5,394	1,259,425	141,534	9,535	1,127,426	398,616	505,713	16,334	124,387	55,461
1993	2,151,753	1,329,059	7,188	1,336,247	153,975	13,802	1,196,074	412,052	543,627	16,991	126,644	56,530
1994	2,308,666	1,451,207	2,425	1,453,632	168,608	17,458	1,302,482	434,053	572,131	17,926	128,787	59,435
1995	2,522,345	1,541,813	-547	1,541,266	178,535	21,745	1,384,476	479,356	658,513	19,274	130,865	61,533
1996	2,638,546	1,618,536	186	1,618,722	187,794	28,498	1,459,426	517,434	661,686	19,886	132,686	64,066
1997	2,828,144	1,770,986	-37	1,770,949	201,946	32,531	1,601,534	545,881	680,729	20,982	134,792	66,762
1998	3,004,308	1,892,900	-404	1,892,496	200,751	41,659	1,733,404	574,627	696,277	21,819	137,690	69,410
1999	3,162,906	2,012,041	-716	2,011,325	207,082	52,081	1,856,324	555,810	750,772	22,563	140,184	70,034
2000	3,362,673	2,136,113	1,152	2,137,265	215,151	68,075	1,990,189	585,089	787,395	23,714	141,800	70,788
2001	3,496,894	2,192,809	5,526	2,198,335	232,050	68,325	2,034,610	609,202	853,082	24,282	144,014	71,286
2002	3,613,210	2,264,757	-2,720	2,262,037	249,019	62,929	2,075,947	596,870	940,393	24,657	146,537	70,850
2003	3,748,427	2,329,929	495	2,330,424	255,164	61,587	2,136,847	632,905	978,675	25,343	147,907	70,865
2004	3,868,406	2,487,244	10,088	2,497,332	276,430	57,530	2,278,432	567,140	1,022,834	26,023	148,654	70,866
2005	3,975,732	2,525,092	7,649	2,532,741	285,099	67,940	2,315,582	560,946	1,099,204	26,536	149,825	71,955
2006	4,161,775	2,649,713	4,128	2,653,841	300,326	73,383	2,426,898	580,430	1,154,447	27,375	152,026	73,457
2007	4,490,185	2,806,233	9,821	2,816,054	322,429	60,471	2,554,096	716,232	1,219,857	28,946	155,121	75,882
2008	4,493,800	2,864,272	2,592	2,866,864	334,562	54,494	2,586,796	780,611	1,126,393	28,669	156,748	76,134
2009	4,517,735	2,848,106	2,661	2,850,767	332,283	29,707	2,548,191	735,713	1,233,831	28,621	157,846	74,761
2010	4,687,242	2,909,926	6,386	2,916,312	338,241	24,332	2,602,403	718,499	1,366,340	29,405	159,401	74,419
2011	4,879,025	3,019,557	13,596	3,033,153	323,829	7,192	2,716,516	752,241	1,410,268	30,454	160,208	75,213
2012	5,007,408	3,114,592	6,343	3,120,935	333,424	-1,303	2,786,208	792,899	1,428,301	31,148	160,763	75,114
2013	5,107,917	3,164,510	7,767	3,172,277	368,986	13,264	2,816,555	813,614	1,477,748	31,707	161,096	75,144
2014	5,383,944	3,337,048	6,699	3,343,747	393,055	-49	2,950,643	843,419	1,589,882	33,467	160,872	76,203
2015	5,667,672	3,461,153	9,746	3,470,899	412,943	-1,273	3,056,683	894,630	1,716,359	34,899	162,401	77,382
2016	5,823,657	3,560,835	5,163	3,565,998	426,584	-1,508	3,137,906	914,813	1,770,938	35,501	164,042	78,680
2017	6,019,901	3,725,339	4,311	3,729,650	447,354	-9,711	3,272,585	957,491	1,789,825	36,399	165,387	80,213
2018	6,351,413	3,910,665	5,775	3,916,440	471,398	-8,562	3,436,480	977,294	1,937,639	38,158	166,450	81,115
2019	6,661,970	4,099,504	6,174	4,105,678	497,502	-16,079	3,592,097	1,046,535	2,023,338	39,857	167,146	81,741
2020	7,330,467	4,288,338	6,197	4,294,535	523,457	-5,309	3,765,769	1,053,731	2,510,967	43,513	168,467	81,556
2021	7,959,927	4,459,894	13,361	4,473,255	535,344	2,966	3,940,877	1,095,620	2,923,430	46,927	169,622	82,704

Personal Income and Employment by Area: Punta Gorda, FL

(Thousands of dollars, except as noted.)

Year	Personal income, total	Earnings by place of work			Less: Contributions for government social insurance	Plus: Adjustment for residence	Equals: Net earnings by place of residence	Plus: Dividends, interest, and rent	Plus: Personal current transfer receipts	Per capita personal income (dollars)	Population (persons)	Total employment
		Nonfarm	Farm	Total								
1970	104,816	49,972	1,445	51,417	3,282	620	48,755	36,936	19,125	3,747	27,977	8,072
1971	123,756	58,030	1,667	59,697	4,050	515	56,162	44,343	23,251	4,119	30,046	8,996
1972	154,008	77,599	1,915	79,514	5,624	111	74,001	51,720	28,287	4,759	32,364	10,711
1973	187,787	92,696	1,975	94,671	7,591	1,067	88,147	64,473	35,167	5,107	36,771	12,355
1974	215,874	99,322	2,118	101,440	8,688	1,889	94,641	79,150	42,083	5,206	41,468	12,512
1975	241,617	101,005	2,556	103,561	8,787	2,458	97,232	92,273	52,112	5,517	43,796	12,707
1976	278,804	118,785	3,428	122,213	10,214	2,477	114,476	105,099	59,229	6,294	44,299	13,487
1977	330,545	142,985	3,963	146,948	12,511	2,404	136,841	124,680	69,024	7,024	47,062	15,343
1978	400,771	176,874	5,226	182,100	15,797	2,346	168,649	152,129	79,993	7,867	50,945	17,656
1979	470,130	196,875	6,258	203,133	18,416	4,865	189,582	184,396	96,152	8,502	55,299	18,195
1980	579,716	232,381	8,615	240,996	22,005	6,091	225,082	233,650	120,984	9,748	59,472	19,577
1981	695,885	269,592	4,781	274,373	27,682	8,673	255,364	292,266	148,255	10,974	63,412	21,295
1982	749,629	271,497	6,998	278,495	29,458	13,486	262,523	312,823	174,283	11,030	67,961	21,403
1983	845,399	307,113	9,099	316,212	33,087	17,190	300,315	354,923	190,161	11,820	71,524	22,702
1984	986,678	343,816	6,478	350,294	37,893	23,147	335,548	444,565	206,565	12,951	76,183	24,000
1985	1,117,862	384,272	6,489	390,761	43,555	28,703	375,909	511,744	230,209	13,820	80,886	26,318
1986	1,244,686	435,209	6,475	441,684	50,794	32,368	423,258	567,189	254,239	14,460	86,079	28,995
1987	1,379,140	502,491	6,934	509,425	57,694	39,263	490,994	612,737	275,409	15,032	91,745	30,055
1988	1,576,533	588,677	12,578	601,255	69,739	44,164	575,680	691,921	308,932	16,212	97,247	32,981
1989	1,874,843	666,924	10,764	677,688	81,958	49,725	645,455	866,821	362,567	18,019	104,050	36,229
1990	2,022,784	725,921	10,902	736,823	87,588	57,216	706,451	909,954	406,379	17,929	112,821	38,654
1991	2,092,792	756,163	16,356	772,519	92,120	63,282	743,681	888,604	460,507	17,764	117,813	39,216
1992	2,224,363	825,403	13,367	838,770	100,349	67,226	805,647	890,049	528,667	18,404	120,861	39,827
1993	2,347,470	879,405	13,998	893,403	106,622	74,031	860,812	912,655	574,003	18,911	124,134	41,205
1994	2,528,248	938,938	11,591	950,529	116,547	80,676	914,658	981,472	632,118	19,840	127,434	43,349
1995	2,707,341	990,033	11,731	1,001,764	123,536	92,570	970,798	1,054,324	682,219	20,709	130,731	44,270
1996	2,882,374	1,067,133	8,462	1,075,595	130,437	95,327	1,040,485	1,120,161	721,728	21,739	132,587	46,679
1997	3,083,185	1,110,758	10,933	1,121,691	135,545	110,127	1,096,273	1,234,146	752,766	22,845	134,959	48,085
1998	3,316,445	1,217,075	15,711	1,232,786	145,467	122,938	1,210,257	1,315,591	790,597	24,102	137,598	51,813
1999	3,461,850	1,340,430	13,276	1,353,706	156,780	135,489	1,332,415	1,309,084	820,351	24,685	140,240	54,226
2000	3,743,220	1,464,363	13,559	1,477,922	168,378	152,818	1,462,362	1,410,168	870,690	26,311	142,266	56,385
2001	3,914,291	1,616,115	8,565	1,624,680	186,097	177,542	1,616,125	1,354,924	943,242	26,753	146,311	55,287
2002	3,964,448	1,693,746	10,724	1,704,470	195,026	228,898	1,738,342	1,231,334	994,772	26,408	150,123	54,855
2003	4,156,776	1,767,572	11,914	1,779,486	203,715	282,725	1,858,496	1,252,310	1,045,970	27,127	153,235	55,225
2004	4,541,111	1,898,390	13,732	1,912,122	224,996	278,950	1,966,076	1,406,728	1,168,307	28,786	157,755	57,451
2005	4,833,408	2,052,046	23,393	2,075,439	247,338	356,169	2,184,270	1,492,202	1,156,936	31,131	155,262	59,929
2006	5,195,950	2,219,346	30,769	2,250,115	281,411	388,396	2,357,100	1,585,745	1,253,105	33,074	157,099	64,678
2007	5,424,827	2,173,910	21,552	2,195,462	281,190	394,386	2,308,658	1,780,731	1,335,438	33,960	159,742	64,346
2008	5,368,028	2,062,729	24,513	2,087,242	277,660	302,428	2,112,010	1,758,631	1,497,387	33,453	160,467	61,774
2009	5,074,994	1,945,124	32,596	1,977,720	269,733	263,690	1,971,677	1,470,204	1,633,113	31,792	159,629	59,476
2010	5,223,491	2,024,418	42,947	2,067,365	277,021	192,136	1,982,480	1,489,997	1,751,014	32,668	159,897	59,627
2011	5,418,356	2,084,695	44,142	2,128,837	260,828	152,524	2,020,533	1,592,751	1,805,072	33,880	159,926	60,926
2012	5,695,259	2,184,303	63,328	2,247,631	273,916	156,698	2,130,413	1,710,888	1,853,958	34,975	162,840	61,871
2013	5,810,650	2,258,188	49,222	2,307,410	316,131	180,848	2,172,127	1,718,874	1,919,649	35,259	164,801	63,459
2014	6,235,391	2,349,851	43,220	2,393,071	328,486	211,187	2,275,772	1,920,613	2,039,006	37,610	165,789	65,560
2015	6,681,627	2,520,206	47,119	2,567,325	346,091	240,032	2,461,266	2,035,534	2,184,827	39,409	169,546	68,119
2016	7,088,057	2,658,056	33,759	2,691,815	366,757	285,319	2,610,377	2,167,772	2,309,908	40,667	174,293	69,740
2017	7,426,686	2,782,502	37,786	2,820,288	388,137	247,845	2,679,996	2,311,191	2,435,499	41,827	177,556	71,331
2018	7,818,874	2,932,637	21,949	2,954,586	418,737	312,425	2,848,274	2,399,521	2,571,079	43,422	180,069	73,788
2019	8,584,349	3,122,053	21,594	3,143,647	453,184	393,897	3,084,360	2,720,231	2,779,758	46,707	183,791	75,078
2020	9,219,838	3,239,961	19,674	3,259,635	478,482	382,676	3,163,829	2,762,554	3,293,455	49,052	187,960	76,304
2021	10,068,892	3,648,096	11,820	3,659,916	523,124	437,242	3,574,034	2,841,576	3,653,282	51,677	194,843	78,968

Personal Income and Employment by Area: Racine, WI

(Thousands of dollars, except as noted.)

Year	Personal income, total	Earnings by place of work			Less: Contributions for government social insurance	Plus: Adjustment for residence	Equals: Net earnings by place of residence	Plus: Dividends, interest, and rent	Plus: Personal current transfer receipts	Per capita personal income (dollars)	Population (persons)	Total employment
		Nonfarm	Farm	Total								
1970	704,171	506,929	8,788	515,717	36,912	60,994	539,799	105,212	59,160	4,121	170,861	65,523
1971	745,366	529,734	10,607	540,341	40,077	62,059	562,323	111,939	71,104	4,375	170,371	64,391
1972	825,049	594,902	9,099	604,001	47,589	68,011	624,423	118,702	81,924	4,845	170,296	67,536
1973	922,302	676,807	12,091	688,898	62,908	74,842	700,832	129,699	91,771	5,405	170,642	72,370
1974	1,030,446	757,626	9,860	767,486	73,325	81,340	775,501	146,323	108,622	6,001	171,715	74,830
1975	1,137,080	821,882	17,565	839,447	77,691	77,814	839,570	163,119	134,391	6,539	173,903	74,659
1976	1,243,957	919,871	14,053	933,924	88,352	80,262	925,834	172,374	145,749	7,221	172,264	76,731
1977	1,373,950	1,021,698	24,379	1,046,077	97,927	86,166	1,034,316	186,725	152,909	8,009	171,543	78,866
1978	1,546,280	1,163,971	18,325	1,182,296	115,034	102,986	1,170,248	208,053	167,979	9,002	171,762	81,566
1979	1,733,512	1,302,854	17,773	1,320,627	133,883	126,128	1,312,872	231,239	189,401	10,063	172,266	84,225
1980	1,887,080	1,353,485	16,142	1,369,627	138,305	142,501	1,373,823	280,845	232,412	10,909	172,979	81,694
1981	2,049,865	1,424,138	16,407	1,440,545	156,343	148,378	1,432,580	349,590	267,695	11,921	171,952	79,864
1982	2,099,884	1,379,544	9,325	1,388,869	152,944	167,329	1,403,254	388,329	308,301	12,274	171,080	76,027
1983	2,191,594	1,428,010	-897	1,427,113	157,879	175,635	1,444,869	417,178	329,547	12,911	169,741	75,330
1984	2,414,377	1,590,188	11,588	1,601,776	180,511	191,179	1,612,444	472,818	329,115	14,234	169,619	79,329
1985	2,500,324	1,634,236	11,683	1,645,919	186,383	202,396	1,661,932	488,624	349,768	14,684	170,270	78,935
1986	2,631,436	1,754,803	13,822	1,768,625	199,841	199,294	1,768,078	499,775	363,583	15,511	169,655	80,809
1987	2,788,794	1,867,970	17,342	1,885,312	208,179	230,885	1,908,018	511,945	368,831	16,387	170,181	82,839
1988	3,014,421	2,021,541	15,401	2,036,942	233,497	265,388	2,068,833	565,639	379,949	17,532	171,934	85,849
1989	3,241,385	2,193,274	14,220	2,207,494	253,176	265,602	2,219,920	610,677	410,788	18,665	173,657	87,306
1990	3,452,812	2,342,401	11,249	2,353,650	281,741	296,198	2,368,107	643,817	440,888	19,672	175,518	89,786
1991	3,620,822	2,443,140	12,447	2,455,587	296,607	304,695	2,463,675	676,324	480,823	20,355	177,885	89,881
1992	3,806,979	2,558,130	26,826	2,584,956	306,654	356,286	2,634,588	655,692	516,699	21,120	180,251	89,115
1993	4,004,447	2,680,610	22,638	2,703,248	322,586	409,737	2,790,399	684,863	529,185	22,030	181,776	90,045
1994	4,240,801	2,807,911	23,509	2,831,420	342,972	462,697	2,951,145	752,110	537,546	23,131	183,338	91,293
1995	4,435,200	2,856,324	21,941	2,878,265	351,129	514,228	3,041,364	828,225	565,611	23,999	184,808	93,148
1996	4,660,527	2,989,572	19,427	3,008,999	363,022	537,673	3,183,650	892,355	584,522	25,103	185,658	94,284
1997	4,973,349	3,246,982	16,886	3,263,868	389,886	572,974	3,446,956	926,844	599,549	26,649	186,621	94,788
1998	5,213,549	3,376,647	15,408	3,392,055	404,201	620,311	3,608,165	998,941	606,443	27,778	187,689	95,393
1999	5,271,907	3,510,978	15,001	3,525,979	422,203	574,742	3,678,518	962,554	630,835	27,988	188,361	94,131
2000	5,550,848	3,543,314	15,088	3,558,402	420,600	704,630	3,842,432	1,019,467	688,949	29,384	188,904	94,602
2001	5,865,683	3,716,244	18,496	3,734,740	427,265	756,319	4,063,794	1,035,030	766,859	31,028	189,047	95,781
2002	6,015,292	3,829,632	17,449	3,847,081	436,099	778,715	4,189,697	1,006,226	819,369	31,687	189,833	94,908
2003	6,209,862	3,935,890	24,694	3,960,584	450,844	799,492	4,309,232	1,054,675	845,955	32,539	190,845	94,955
2004	6,498,015	4,106,028	25,366	4,131,394	471,771	842,777	4,502,400	1,138,760	856,855	33,878	191,808	96,430
2005	6,609,069	4,186,205	19,095	4,205,300	484,666	886,199	4,606,833	1,078,635	923,601	34,199	193,251	97,069
2006	6,992,847	4,312,681	26,281	4,338,962	505,067	964,809	4,798,704	1,218,515	975,628	36,061	193,915	97,225
2007	7,274,968	4,436,524	28,288	4,464,812	518,112	989,655	4,936,355	1,280,685	1,057,928	37,424	194,395	97,383
2008	7,709,937	4,475,277	24,621	4,499,898	527,760	1,057,648	5,029,786	1,484,557	1,195,594	39,593	194,730	96,571
2009	7,348,056	4,261,155	23,388	4,284,543	505,263	967,891	4,747,171	1,190,652	1,410,233	37,657	195,130	92,186
2010	7,439,880	4,354,457	19,248	4,373,705	516,805	883,969	4,740,869	1,193,752	1,505,259	38,074	195,407	91,779
2011	7,793,905	4,575,848	24,537	4,600,385	486,426	919,083	5,033,042	1,305,383	1,455,480	39,987	194,910	93,336
2012	8,121,696	4,754,782	19,663	4,774,445	502,940	860,948	5,132,453	1,504,729	1,484,514	41,735	194,602	94,216
2013	7,955,714	4,750,081	19,019	4,769,100	567,904	907,075	5,108,271	1,324,4J5	1,523,008	40,863	194,694	93,412
2014	8,294,135	4,901,719	10,606	4,912,325	583,690	885,863	5,214,498	1,498,737	1,580,900	42,418	195,535	94,841
2015	8,750,060	4,994,236	12,246	5,006,482	595,147	995,331	5,406,666	1,698,194	1,645,200	44,733	195,606	95,298
2016	8,780,394	4,990,071	10,736	5,000,807	599,883	1,041,594	5,442,518	1,662,516	1,675,360	44,806	195,963	94,621
2017	9,247,846	5,149,619	9,850	5,159,469	626,974	1,094,349	5,626,844	1,867,262	1,753,740	46,885	197,245	95,108
2018	9,662,730	5,414,764	10,496	5,425,260	650,449	1,096,336	5,871,147	1,950,293	1,841,290	48,867	197,734	96,766
2019	9,941,859	5,510,476	11,302	5,521,778	667,730	1,151,515	6,005,563	2,030,690	1,905,606	50,274	197,753	96,329
2020	10,465,282	5,582,574	18,503	5,601,077	684,033	1,114,117	6,031,161	2,037,733	2,396,388	53,005	197,440	92,138
2021	11,200,309	5,876,672	22,326	5,898,998	707,127	1,219,027	6,410,898	2,088,627	2,700,784	56,884	196,896	94,532

Personal Income and Employment by Area: Raleigh-Cary, NC

(Thousands of dollars, except as noted.)

Year	Personal income, total	Earnings by place of work			Less: Contributions for government social insurance	Plus: Adjustment for residence	Equals: Net earnings by place of residence	Plus: Dividends, interest, and rent	Plus: Personal current transfer receipts	Per capita personal income (dollars)	Population (persons)	Total employment
		Nonfarm	Farm	Total								
1970	1,196,842	956,524	50,778	1,007,302	63,442	18,228	962,088	156,372	78,382	3,750	319,135	165,563
1971	1,319,245	1,047,907	48,736	1,096,643	71,831	26,250	1,051,062	175,796	92,387	4,014	328,641	168,259
1972	1,494,638	1,190,116	59,681	1,249,797	86,153	30,301	1,193,945	197,306	103,387	4,425	337,793	177,550
1973	1,701,509	1,363,857	71,393	1,435,250	114,504	33,354	1,354,100	227,690	119,719	4,904	346,989	188,533
1974	1,932,923	1,524,338	86,463	1,610,801	133,023	40,186	1,517,964	266,592	148,367	5,419	356,680	195,217
1975	2,156,884	1,647,284	95,251	1,742,535	142,702	54,489	1,654,322	299,696	202,866	5,945	362,809	190,837
1976	2,383,131	1,834,193	89,164	1,923,357	162,059	64,763	1,826,061	331,124	225,946	6,461	368,858	197,595
1977	2,638,378	2,062,310	64,738	2,127,048	180,758	79,323	2,025,613	374,585	238,180	6,994	377,230	205,674
1978	3,014,777	2,361,147	92,034	2,453,181	214,033	90,108	2,329,256	426,671	258,850	7,830	385,013	214,810
1979	3,417,079	2,755,899	40,794	2,796,693	260,627	94,582	2,630,648	489,039	297,392	8,686	393,407	229,255
1980	3,892,536	3,074,966	45,642	3,120,608	293,787	104,576	2,931,397	604,729	356,410	9,628	404,305	233,851
1981	4,391,883	3,345,694	75,283	3,420,977	344,406	146,172	3,222,743	752,037	417,103	10,660	411,982	236,605
1982	4,815,126	3,628,274	74,247	3,702,521	380,184	178,684	3,501,021	856,717	457,388	11,470	419,800	239,666
1983	5,413,843	4,145,100	47,984	4,193,084	438,319	201,859	3,956,624	957,815	499,404	12,550	431,398	252,652
1984	6,360,203	4,872,431	81,770	4,954,201	523,564	248,566	4,679,203	1,146,131	534,869	14,193	448,113	273,343
1985	7,278,175	5,655,921	82,595	5,738,516	616,390	295,483	5,417,609	1,284,090	576,476	15,561	467,729	294,465
1986	7,977,405	6,235,133	49,645	6,284,778	691,844	346,665	5,939,599	1,419,449	618,357	16,510	483,172	307,223
1987	8,704,245	6,770,978	69,832	6,840,810	736,800	433,633	6,537,643	1,517,654	648,948	17,602	494,491	320,160
1988	9,662,714	7,441,720	96,170	7,537,890	834,329	490,429	7,193,990	1,758,616	710,108	18,902	511,200	336,952
1989	10,704,458	8,061,082	107,346	8,168,428	901,823	591,684	7,858,289	2,039,866	806,303	20,299	527,344	350,715
1990	11,576,807	8,706,809	137,296	8,844,105	998,559	672,128	8,517,674	2,159,395	899,738	21,092	548,874	361,542
1991	12,297,883	9,065,403	151,425	9,216,828	1,054,473	863,943	9,026,298	2,243,955	1,027,630	21,647	568,119	361,975
1992	13,607,161	10,090,907	154,988	10,245,895	1,153,124	1,002,967	10,095,738	2,356,255	1,155,168	23,112	588,751	373,756
1993	14,820,083	10,998,081	162,058	11,160,139	1,253,742	1,067,189	10,973,586	2,560,952	1,285,545	24,193	612,576	394,846
1994	16,037,524	11,932,341	160,415	12,092,756	1,380,843	1,131,981	11,843,894	2,847,672	1,345,958	25,132	638,140	413,368
1995	17,535,413	12,882,755	140,888	13,023,643	1,491,560	1,294,903	12,826,986	3,183,977	1,524,450	26,317	666,317	433,235
1996	19,205,602	14,087,067	148,754	14,235,821	1,623,545	1,405,852	14,018,128	3,551,047	1,636,427	27,654	694,496	456,366
1997	21,345,498	15,545,165	197,289	15,742,454	1,794,732	1,653,957	15,601,679	4,010,736	1,733,083	29,584	721,528	484,256
1998	23,420,086	17,204,704	166,502	17,371,206	1,986,008	1,827,947	17,213,145	4,389,341	1,817,600	31,223	750,079	512,369
1999	25,085,129	18,540,217	160,949	18,701,166	2,154,115	2,114,083	18,661,134	4,503,147	1,920,848	32,293	776,786	520,966
2000	27,668,059	20,275,147	209,874	20,485,021	2,356,853	2,645,880	20,774,048	4,826,355	2,067,656	34,406	804,157	539,376
2001	29,608,807	22,063,839	191,043	22,254,882	2,512,142	2,667,455	22,410,195	4,823,717	2,374,895	35,541	833,100	548,246
2002	30,239,267	22,561,609	77,004	22,638,613	2,552,641	2,814,423	22,900,395	4,691,187	2,647,685	35,198	859,117	551,503
2003	31,531,704	23,222,989	67,838	23,290,827	2,685,284	3,103,941	23,709,484	4,995,925	2,826,295	35,696	883,333	559,703
2004	33,750,629	24,671,322	113,599	24,784,921	2,826,632	3,234,542	25,192,831	5,523,375	3,034,423	37,109	909,510	578,156
2005	36,717,516	26,070,699	112,573	26,183,272	3,027,212	3,602,430	26,758,490	6,570,396	3,388,630	38,866	944,725	605,919
2006	41,204,943	28,838,626	96,574	28,935,200	3,308,405	4,239,047	29,865,842	7,595,575	3,743,526	41,654	989,219	640,331
2007	44,869,162	30,767,080	87,940	30,855,020	3,571,527	5,076,891	32,360,384	8,411,108	4,097,670	43,374	1,034,476	677,941
2008	48,134,355	32,317,239	122,045	32,439,284	3,694,208	5,432,269	34,177,345	9,093,431	4,863,579	44,686	1,077,163	684,070
2009	46,559,072	30,773,816	131,376	30,905,192	3,590,316	5,813,492	33,128,368	7,891,136	5,539,568	41,943	1,110,061	665,891
2010	49,038,491	32,304,902	101,708	32,406,610	3,714,879	6,208,676	34,900,407	8,057,987	6,080,097	43,115	1,137,386	666,828
2011	51,140,700	33,605,538	105,709	33,711,247	3,513,233	5,641,080	35,839,094	8,993,845	6,307,761	43,999	1,162,307	688,337
2012	54,574,968	36,065,865	135,177	36,201,042	3,679,854	5,914,313	38,435,501	9,717,521	6,421,946	45,936	1,188,058	708,499
2013	55,318,268	37,572,231	138,947	37,711,178	4,399,571	5,705,862	39,017,469	9,732,745	6,568,054	45,573	1,213,826	728,481
2014	59,470,819	40,353,545	164,110	40,517,655	4,704,577	5,823,611	41,636,689	10,938,578	6,895,552	47,890	1,241,826	757,589
2015	63,933,371	43,661,193	132,813	43,794,006	5,074,677	5,563,739	44,283,068	12,196,869	7,453,434	50,269	1,271,821	792,599
2016	67,012,772	46,396,420	126,274	46,522,694	5,329,481	5,470,736	46,663,949	12,502,154	7,846,669	51,365	1,304,639	819,531
2017	70,336,478	48,985,948	149,856	49,135,804	5,591,389	5,634,441	49,178,856	12,916,835	8,240,787	52,680	1,335,169	845,490
2018	76,418,678	53,419,228	83,398	53,502,626	5,988,207	5,810,103	53,324,522	14,356,879	8,737,277	56,077	1,362,754	876,623
2019	81,134,511	56,944,260	95,837	57,040,097	6,404,920	5,963,600	56,598,777	15,252,736	9,282,998	58,285	1,392,028	898,122
2020	87,662,078	58,991,505	89,007	59,080,512	6,652,935	7,314,428	59,742,005	15,409,488	12,510,585	61,724	1,420,225	888,896
2021	96,214,366	65,897,076	92,704	65,989,780	7,284,060	7,489,837	66,195,557	15,819,531	14,199,278	66,428	1,448,411	935,265

Personal Income and Employment by Area: Rapid City, SD

(Thousands of dollars, except as noted.)

Year	Personal income, total	Earnings by place of work			Less: Contributions for government social insurance	Plus: Adjustment for residence	Equals: Net earnings by place of residence	Plus: Dividends, interest, and rent	Plus: Personal current transfer receipts	Per capita personal income (dollars)	Population (persons)	Total employment
		Nonfarm	Farm	Total								
1970	321,371	237,753	12,570	250,323	15,427	4,031	238,927	58,276	24,168	3,935	81,667	37,761
1971	362,172	272,160	13,455	285,615	18,244	2,298	269,669	64,790	27,713	4,279	84,645	39,342
1972	416,104	313,888	18,840	332,728	21,475	2,425	313,678	71,802	30,624	4,720	88,158	41,056
1973	474,757	349,942	32,633	382,575	27,099	2,269	357,745	82,979	34,033	5,396	87,982	43,482
1974	505,322	380,719	14,705	395,424	30,697	3,244	367,971	96,993	40,358	5,658	89,308	43,651
1975	563,501	414,847	19,374	434,221	34,279	4,760	404,702	108,992	49,807	6,279	89,744	44,004
1976	619,358	465,223	11,385	476,608	38,464	6,232	444,376	119,766	55,216	6,607	93,739	45,978
1977	685,169	513,094	10,741	523,835	40,910	8,081	491,006	136,310	57,853	7,092	96,608	48,360
1978	793,371	589,590	18,138	607,728	47,425	10,535	570,838	160,088	62,445	8,041	98,670	51,590
1979	885,017	650,920	22,537	673,457	55,530	13,347	631,274	180,989	72,754	8,848	100,024	52,967
1980	939,925	669,346	14,881	684,227	57,159	15,699	642,767	211,238	85,920	9,667	97,234	51,844
1981	1,031,689	709,810	16,466	726,276	64,237	15,827	677,866	251,502	102,321	10,566	97,645	50,991
1982	1,111,070	756,721	13,588	770,309	69,082	12,661	713,888	281,481	115,701	11,237	98,875	51,796
1983	1,186,853	827,982	12,515	840,497	77,075	10,720	774,142	285,852	126,859	11,827	100,353	54,204
1984	1,313,093	922,447	19,837	942,284	87,847	8,792	863,229	315,120	134,744	12,709	103,323	58,045
1985	1,360,335	964,840	6,798	971,638	94,902	7,386	884,122	331,281	144,932	12,935	105,166	58,311
1986	1,437,281	1,016,545	15,237	1,031,782	103,590	5,803	933,995	348,395	154,891	13,503	106,441	59,737
1987	1,525,536	1,094,269	11,223	1,105,492	113,141	4,145	996,496	367,598	161,442	14,024	108,783	63,586
1988	1,606,114	1,164,917	6,051	1,170,968	124,709	2,161	1,048,420	387,090	170,604	14,687	109,358	62,921
1989	1,724,166	1,236,415	10,028	1,246,443	134,164	1,168	1,113,447	420,455	190,264	15,861	108,707	64,630
1990	1,861,069	1,346,699	15,712	1,362,411	153,789	-8,895	1,199,727	455,065	206,277	16,946	109,825	67,637
1991	1,969,908	1,430,796	7,924	1,438,720	165,032	-8,025	1,265,663	480,431	223,814	17,510	112,499	69,532
1992	2,120,623	1,527,924	14,180	1,542,104	175,285	-5,160	1,361,659	512,410	246,554	18,483	114,732	70,921
1993	2,232,143	1,606,477	20,354	1,626,831	183,490	-3,775	1,439,566	526,501	266,076	19,215	116,165	72,557
1994	2,319,720	1,662,486	5,715	1,668,201	191,339	333	1,477,195	553,639	288,886	19,823	117,020	75,111
1995	2,453,052	1,715,315	14,584	1,729,899	196,496	910	1,534,313	603,846	314,893	20,789	117,995	75,455
1996	2,525,880	1,741,434	2,759	1,744,193	200,527	2,618	1,546,284	643,418	336,178	21,429	117,871	75,634
1997	2,635,140	1,808,684	7,235	1,815,919	208,796	1,385	1,608,508	683,438	343,194	22,372	117,790	76,299
1998	2,699,708	1,879,063	14,471	1,893,534	215,096	-18,786	1,659,652	706,489	333,567	24,271	111,230	74,810
1999	2,854,316	1,990,365	27,707	2,018,072	231,146	-24,085	1,762,841	740,872	350,603	25,476	112,041	77,340
2000	3,018,211	2,078,958	28,449	2,107,407	243,466	-26,858	1,837,083	801,374	379,754	26,681	113,124	79,582
2001	3,254,577	2,275,022	30,571	2,305,593	259,876	-31,796	2,013,921	818,848	421,808	28,468	114,324	78,241
2002	3,395,355	2,424,225	13,416	2,437,641	275,118	-36,898	2,125,625	817,394	452,336	29,442	115,323	78,759
2003	3,602,889	2,554,530	42,824	2,597,354	289,491	-40,784	2,267,079	864,061	471,749	31,143	115,690	79,275
2004	3,904,965	2,730,756	35,384	2,766,140	304,762	-44,380	2,416,998	982,239	505,728	33,199	117,624	80,886
2005	4,117,547	2,842,816	48,921	2,891,737	313,497	-38,791	2,539,449	1,034,921	543,177	34,839	118,188	81,783
2006	4,308,083	2,936,936	8,906	2,945,842	330,018	-39,151	2,576,673	1,141,833	589,577	36,057	119,479	82,808
2007	4,586,651	3,039,935	18,421	3,058,356	345,273	-38,469	2,674,614	1,268,200	643,837	37,941	120,890	84,457
2008	4,827,783	3,158,800	35,035	3,193,835	362,157	-45,528	2,786,150	1,292,400	749,233	39,231	123,059	85,759
2009	4,820,436	3,207,048	5,922	3,212,970	367,359	-54,954	2,790,657	1,229,958	799,821	38,514	125,159	85,075
2010	5,119,589	3,372,510	13,232	3,385,742	383,853	-48,497	2,953,392	1,271,321	894,876	40,397	126,731	84,935
2011	5,349,979	3,492,571	48,366	3,540,937	354,972	-68,554	3,117,411	1,308,227	924,341	41,814	127,947	86,445
2012	5,696,203	3,657,237	38,008	3,695,245	368,626	-64,002	3,262,617	1,496,974	936,612	43,769	130,142	87,171
2013	5,660,959	3,753,505	34,254	3,787,759	425,728	-59,434	3,302,597	1,386,084	972,278	42,750	132,420	88,259
2014	6,150,180	3,963,678	52,180	4,015,858	446,479	-47,651	3,521,728	1,600,797	1,027,655	46,459	132,379	89,551
2015	6,317,324	4,086,450	32,655	4,119,105	459,255	-60,500	3,599,350	1,626,812	1,091,162	47,655	132,563	89,692
2016	6,483,826	4,175,322	16,890	4,192,212	473,449	-92,201	3,626,562	1,707,494	1,149,770	48,500	133,687	90,709
2017	6,704,231	4,318,515	14,564	4,333,079	496,218	-87,363	3,749,498	1,746,885	1,207,848	49,564	135,263	92,377
2018	7,000,556	4,471,580	20,433	4,492,013	514,726	-77,123	3,900,164	1,820,225	1,280,167	51,245	136,609	93,632
2019	7,479,686	4,731,748	-18,333	4,713,415	545,586	-61,753	4,106,076	1,992,276	1,381,334	54,068	138,339	93,857
2020	8,142,621	5,061,128	35,009	5,096,137	590,336	-92,337	4,413,464	1,995,059	1,734,098	58,442	139,328	93,242
2021	8,697,471	5,464,496	22,887	5,487,383	633,768	-95,927	4,757,688	2,001,315	1,938,468	61,259	141,979	97,112

Personal Income and Employment by Area: Reading, PA

(Thousands of dollars, except as noted.)

Year	Personal income, total	Earnings by place of work			Less: Contributions for government social insurance	Plus: Adjustment for residence	Equals: Net earnings by place of residence	Plus: Dividends, interest, and rent	Plus: Personal current transfer receipts	Per capita personal income (dollars)	Population (persons)	Total employment
		Nonfarm	Farm	Total								
1970	1,252,791	1,027,771	18,618	1,046,389	79,002	4,950	972,337	165,861	114,593	4,221	296,772	146,430
1971	1,332,288	1,086,941	13,346	1,100,287	86,780	9,547	1,023,054	176,031	133,203	4,449	299,474	145,699
1972	1,478,467	1,201,563	20,067	1,221,630	100,840	18,095	1,138,885	189,007	150,575	4,914	300,891	148,292
1973	1,645,877	1,340,100	23,025	1,363,125	129,077	29,047	1,263,095	213,654	169,128	5,396	305,011	154,355
1974	1,811,050	1,442,564	21,103	1,463,667	143,747	42,512	1,362,432	243,787	204,831	5,924	305,720	155,151
1975	1,956,345	1,485,548	19,342	1,504,890	144,415	56,246	1,416,721	268,965	270,659	6,375	306,891	149,308
1976	2,169,731	1,654,554	25,018	1,679,572	163,067	66,675	1,583,180	293,008	293,543	7,034	308,452	153,056
1977	2,415,498	1,852,844	23,147	1,875,991	181,730	81,997	1,776,258	331,538	307,702	7,877	306,642	156,627
1978	2,698,350	2,080,827	22,645	2,103,472	209,603	104,298	1,998,167	367,848	332,335	8,729	309,110	161,553
1979	3,024,076	2,320,728	25,717	2,346,445	241,628	129,276	2,234,093	420,005	369,978	9,691	312,055	164,360
1980	3,366,073	2,493,025	23,303	2,516,328	260,503	156,543	2,412,368	520,983	432,722	10,754	313,016	165,898
1981	3,729,154	2,713,378	34,842	2,748,220	303,546	153,436	2,598,110	643,184	487,860	11,861	314,414	165,448
1982	3,980,903	2,809,421	34,229	2,843,650	319,571	154,913	2,678,992	740,376	561,535	12,654	314,597	163,637
1983	4,282,832	3,041,658	40,381	3,082,039	349,732	147,328	2,879,635	797,115	606,082	13,588	315,184	164,855
1984	4,670,276	3,374,686	62,824	3,437,510	405,486	142,924	3,174,948	890,388	604,940	14,700	317,711	171,552
1985	4,903,232	3,520,221	53,764	3,573,985	427,431	151,455	3,298,009	957,669	647,554	15,414	318,105	172,691
1986	5,151,473	3,706,100	51,486	3,757,586	449,792	153,178	3,460,972	1,004,629	685,872	16,079	320,394	173,929
1987	5,468,098	4,002,755	60,684	4,063,439	479,089	153,774	3,738,124	1,027,773	702,201	16,884	323,871	179,717
1988	5,915,967	4,387,905	48,387	4,436,292	534,326	152,741	4,054,707	1,116,921	744,339	18,038	327,977	184,644
1989	6,538,477	4,830,076	63,531	4,893,607	575,104	130,818	4,449,321	1,294,207	794,949	19,580	333,938	189,338
1990	6,746,828	4,984,826	68,319	5,053,145	597,324	127,069	4,582,890	1,288,258	875,680	19,972	337,812	190,057
1991	6,993,289	5,060,132	63,660	5,123,792	610,832	153,938	4,666,898	1,305,758	1,020,633	20,410	342,637	185,735
1992	7,504,851	5,488,015	84,278	5,572,293	654,974	170,897	5,088,216	1,321,296	1,095,339	21,687	346,050	186,648
1993	7,861,371	5,786,372	72,384	5,858,756	704,888	194,990	5,348,858	1,372,445	1,140,068	22,449	350,186	188,584
1994	8,243,934	6,126,077	81,336	6,207,413	753,245	209,160	5,663,328	1,414,862	1,165,744	23,282	354,092	190,821
1995	8,607,203	6,304,713	60,382	6,365,095	772,717	246,626	5,839,004	1,546,362	1,221,837	24,097	357,193	194,899
1996	9,043,801	6,505,984	69,451	6,575,435	777,716	301,052	6,098,771	1,642,545	1,302,485	25,095	360,380	197,093
1997	9,458,239	6,777,448	61,859	6,839,307	808,392	358,448	6,389,363	1,732,423	1,336,453	26,003	363,739	202,003
1998	9,890,549	6,994,905	67,093	7,061,998	828,932	438,373	6,671,439	1,846,573	1,372,537	26,944	367,082	206,229
1999	10,327,994	7,300,423	65,566	7,365,989	848,998	519,846	7,036,837	1,837,790	1,453,367	27,843	370,942	211,470
2000	11,074,494	7,700,150	87,715	7,787,865	884,909	611,914	7,514,870	2,004,387	1,555,237	29,568	374,546	215,764
2001	11,556,034	7,982,919	90,747	8,073,666	917,155	687,551	7,844,062	2,002,238	1,709,734	30,613	377,487	207,227
2002	11,885,110	8,191,034	65,369	8,256,403	934,076	736,965	8,059,292	1,970,609	1,855,209	31,167	381,338	204,712
2003	12,278,032	8,316,600	88,151	8,404,751	940,383	871,974	8,336,342	2,020,598	1,921,092	31,821	385,846	202,718
2004	12,728,182	8,629,336	104,833	8,734,169	974,133	952,068	8,712,104	1,997,576	2,018,502	32,566	390,848	206,368
2005	13,405,676	9,015,691	92,141	9,107,832	1,025,204	1,086,392	9,169,020	2,026,495	2,210,161	33,858	395,933	210,061
2006	14,306,497	9,610,398	68,349	9,678,747	1,104,508	1,049,134	9,623,373	2,315,805	2,367,319	35,603	401,834	216,496
2007	14,954,772	9,957,695	42,472	10,000,167	1,138,799	1,064,344	9,925,712	2,548,417	2,480,643	36,905	405,223	219,162
2008	15,453,610	9,964,232	55,440	10,019,672	1,153,976	1,090,015	9,955,711	2,681,378	2,816,521	37,901	407,737	217,938
2009	15,040,076	9,596,817	43,223	9,640,040	1,126,608	997,777	9,511,209	2,359,348	3,169,519	36,692	409,904	210,367
2010	15,801,278	10,031,751	63,409	10,095,160	1,164,143	1,101,947	10,032,964	2,350,972	3,417,342	38,349	412,041	211,636
2011	16,607,393	10,480,336	82,398	10,562,734	1,088,004	1,124,460	10,599,190	2,569,535	3,438,668	40,209	413,027	214,240
2012	17,278,838	10,716,749	103,247	10,819,996	1,109,921	1,122,123	10,832,198	2,978,145	3,468,495	41,782	413,552	215,262
2013	17,120,097	10,896,172	171,253	11,067,425	1,269,835	1,135,044	10,932,634	2,667,918	3,519,545	41,355	413,975	216,789
2014	17,873,915	11,329,024	191,317	11,520,341	1,325,673	1,143,206	11,337,874	2,915,807	3,620,234	42,776	417,854	219,852
2015	18,753,204	11,988,675	156,978	12,145,653	1,393,404	1,148,825	11,901,074	3,046,184	3,805,946	44,735	419,206	222,716
2016	19,220,073	12,297,114	101,052	12,398,166	1,425,739	1,135,107	12,107,534	3,094,597	4,017,942	45,689	420,670	224,682
2017	19,870,872	12,712,222	141,943	12,854,165	1,490,354	1,222,067	12,585,878	3,218,072	4,066,922	46,960	423,146	225,489
2018	20,800,895	13,295,588	109,119	13,404,707	1,547,443	1,263,927	13,121,191	3,334,185	4,345,519	48,741	426,762	228,794
2019	21,655,645	13,747,648	123,283	13,870,931	1,604,584	1,359,163	13,625,510	3,526,225	4,503,910	50,657	427,498	230,210
2020	23,597,379	13,698,218	104,573	13,802,791	1,577,856	1,536,252	13,761,187	3,490,459	6,345,733	55,045	428,694	216,755
2021	24,888,804	14,365,451	133,453	14,498,904	1,625,083	1,843,481	14,717,302	3,527,239	6,644,263	57,970	429,342	221,592

Personal Income and Employment by Area: Redding, CA

(Thousands of dollars, except as noted.)

Year	Personal income, total	Derivation of personal income									Per capita personal income (dollars)	Population (persons)	Total employment
		Earnings by place of work			Less: Contributions for government social insurance	Plus: Adjustment for residence	Equals: Net earnings by place of residence	Plus: Dividends, interest, and rent	Plus: Personal current transfer receipts				
		Nonfarm	Farm	Total									
1970	315,205	230,080	2,632	232,712	14,211	4,024	222,525	47,107	45,573		4,042	77,980	29,369
1971	348,129	254,054	2,018	256,072	16,311	3,852	243,613	52,903	51,613		4,383	79,434	30,699
1972	382,075	282,111	664	282,775	19,267	4,031	267,539	58,831	55,705		4,737	80,656	32,031
1973	434,362	320,437	4,603	325,040	25,065	3,584	303,559	69,563	61,240		5,156	84,249	34,817
1974	497,975	353,208	7,558	360,766	28,046	2,681	335,401	83,022	79,552		5,747	86,651	35,762
1975	562,845	393,190	6,204	399,394	30,253	2,038	371,179	95,312	96,354		6,112	92,082	37,593
1976	646,233	464,503	5,855	470,358	36,409	1,569	435,518	106,639	104,076		6,809	94,909	40,685
1977	728,667	524,941	6,150	531,091	42,076	823	489,838	123,464	115,365		7,275	100,157	43,503
1978	851,500	619,697	7,998	627,695	50,726	-681	576,288	147,668	127,544		8,221	103,572	47,369
1979	974,419	700,816	9,184	710,000	60,515	-2,305	647,180	174,743	152,496		8,685	112,199	49,477
1980	1,083,423	738,493	12,312	750,805	63,131	-3,551	684,123	212,327	186,973		9,293	116,590	50,551
1981	1,179,141	760,374	11,264	771,638	70,663	-2,386	698,589	253,461	227,091		9,804	120,270	50,078
1982	1,260,842	795,568	12,814	808,382	75,412	-2,303	730,667	280,679	249,496		10,376	121,513	49,830
1983	1,371,034	863,849	10,392	874,241	83,221	-417	790,603	317,541	262,890		11,164	122,807	51,243
1984	1,513,727	964,903	10,951	975,854	97,058	-521	878,275	352,570	282,882		12,079	125,322	53,517
1985	1,615,823	1,016,394	10,711	1,027,105	104,331	1,614	924,388	381,998	309,437		12,578	128,461	54,432
1986	1,744,320	1,109,173	8,259	1,117,432	115,821	1,880	1,003,491	404,732	336,097		13,406	130,119	56,501
1987	1,897,407	1,253,978	8,784	1,262,762	132,282	152	1,130,632	410,304	356,471		14,271	132,958	60,612
1988	2,093,170	1,409,168	9,280	1,418,448	153,691	-2,794	1,261,963	443,310	387,897		15,320	136,627	64,192
1989	2,323,011	1,545,319	10,319	1,555,638	170,893	-4,557	1,380,188	513,663	429,160		16,476	140,997	66,910
1990	2,541,648	1,695,634	10,535	1,706,169	185,725	-6,500	1,513,944	552,545	475,159		17,103	148,606	71,727
1991	2,713,034	1,813,165	9,100	1,822,265	198,716	-6,704	1,616,845	565,958	530,231		17,646	153,746	73,820
1992	2,896,498	1,914,669	9,719	1,924,388	208,119	-2,451	1,713,818	570,315	612,365		18,473	156,800	73,116
1993	3,010,702	1,978,490	10,573	1,989,063	215,942	-28	1,773,093	588,392	649,217		19,087	157,735	73,197
1994	3,135,342	2,090,798	12,873	2,103,671	226,616	3,511	1,880,566	600,728	654,048		19,766	158,621	75,586
1995	3,249,393	2,142,199	8,563	2,150,762	229,121	10,097	1,931,738	627,324	690,331		20,411	159,198	75,741
1996	3,378,817	2,205,640	9,557	2,215,197	228,109	15,230	2,002,318	646,450	730,049		21,152	159,737	77,057
1997	3,562,687	2,334,825	13,056	2,347,881	238,471	19,667	2,129,077	692,978	740,632		22,161	160,761	78,613
1998	3,751,246	2,427,596	11,137	2,438,733	243,353	26,986	2,222,366	713,515	815,365		23,151	162,034	79,004
1999	3,939,606	2,566,345	12,442	2,578,787	256,958	34,949	2,356,778	722,310	860,518		24,321	161,987	81,009
2000	4,185,219	2,725,458	12,445	2,737,903	273,177	43,121	2,507,847	764,729	912,643		25,580	163,615	83,530
2001	4,587,877	3,023,982	14,316	3,038,298	313,532	39,583	2,764,349	798,911	1,024,617		27,570	166,408	85,889
2002	4,758,695	3,258,778	14,988	3,273,766	345,404	32,869	2,961,231	704,265	1,093,199		27,960	170,198	88,589
2003	4,914,549	3,406,718	17,639	3,424,357	367,155	25,023	3,082,225	720,180	1,112,144		28,375	173,202	89,688
2004	5,062,595	3,490,757	17,943	3,508,700	395,733	-12,790	3,100,177	797,110	1,165,308		28,951	174,867	90,490
2005	5,172,670	3,570,588	17,833	3,588,421	415,443	-31,710	3,141,268	806,714	1,224,688		29,455	175,615	91,346
2006	5,540,605	3,753,356	11,632	3,764,988	423,978	-57,063	3,283,947	919,307	1,337,351		31,451	176,166	93,130
2007	5,782,966	3,851,701	7,753	3,859,454	429,052	-97,864	3,332,538	1,025,086	1,425,342		32,756	176,548	94,482
2008	5,811,619	3,683,594	18,798	3,702,392	420,971	-93,457	3,187,964	1,036,878	1,586,777		32,788	177,247	90,773
2009	5,853,713	3,548,384	26,500	3,574,884	410,202	-77,408	3,087,274	1,015,217	1,751,222		33,020	177,279	86,195
2010	6,100,254	3,643,651	36,861	3,680,512	406,157	-57,836	3,216,519	986,277	1,897,458		34,411	177,277	84,019
2011	6,243,585	3,680,197	36,496	3,716,693	378,740	-61,569	3,276,384	1,058,406	1,908,795		35,153	177,613	84,116
2012	6,370,270	3,695,595	50,347	3,745,942	379,742	-45,591	3,320,609	1,092,798	1,956,863		35,807	177,908	84,888
2013	6,472,904	3,758,937	41,350	3,800,287	426,667	5,061	3,378,681	1,061,307	2,032,916		36,274	178,447	85,738
2014	6,899,870	3,958,461	45,831	4,004,292	448,615	7,200	3,562,877	1,172,763	2,164,230		38,319	180,064	87,994
2015	7,313,862	4,186,096	46,510	4,232,606	470,401	6,753	3,768,958	1,219,656	2,325,248		40,674	179,816	89,872
2016	7,527,423	4,339,851	37,952	4,377,803	492,733	25,280	3,910,350	1,223,338	2,393,735		41,750	180,299	90,411
2017	7,797,350	4,531,228	45,301	4,576,529	518,048	33,622	4,092,103	1,348,424	2,356,823		42,985	181,395	90,813
2018	8,023,590	4,748,808	38,508	4,787,316	549,926	22,295	4,259,685	1,305,837	2,458,068		44,100	181,939	92,260
2019	8,401,549	4,963,676	44,233	5,007,909	581,184	22,154	4,448,879	1,358,678	2,593,992		46,113	182,196	92,627
2020	9,370,094	5,221,461	42,069	5,263,530	607,104	37,277	4,693,703	1,372,295	3,304,096		51,514	181,893	90,782
2021	10,012,526	5,574,501	47,250	5,621,751	641,404	49,197	5,029,544	1,374,365	3,608,617		54,972	182,139	92,780

Personal Income and Employment by Area: Reno, NV

(Thousands of dollars, except as noted.)

		Derivation of personal income										
		Earnings by place of work			Less: Contributions for government social insurance	Plus: Adjustment for residence	Equals: Net earnings by place of residence	Plus: Dividends, interest, and rent	Plus: Personal current transfer receipts	Per capita personal income (dollars)	Population (persons)	Total employment
Year	Personal income, total	Nonfarm	Farm	Total								
1970	672,283	537,954	1,110	539,064	36,240	-5,370	497,454	132,957	41,872	5,473	122,838	68,813
1971	759,099	610,678	1,099	611,777	42,479	-9,815	559,483	148,904	50,712	5,874	129,234	73,393
1972	851,823	689,353	1,411	690,764	51,278	-13,413	626,073	166,438	59,312	6,257	136,146	77,256
1973	960,495	785,071	1,992	787,063	67,580	-18,402	701,081	192,086	67,328	6,772	141,828	83,477
1974	1,059,905	847,665	896	848,561	74,021	-20,648	753,892	224,170	81,843	7,147	148,306	85,698
1975	1,205,657	951,412	1,284	952,696	80,698	-24,514	847,484	245,010	113,163	7,875	153,109	89,100
1976	1,393,220	1,124,512	1,588	1,126,100	98,386	-31,633	996,081	274,585	122,554	8,726	159,670	96,622
1977	1,644,823	1,364,377	1,022	1,365,399	122,155	-42,058	1,201,186	309,839	133,798	9,745	168,795	108,044
1978	2,037,436	1,712,238	773	1,713,011	159,462	-48,413	1,505,136	380,896	151,404	11,402	178,694	124,884
1979	2,366,064	1,994,605	-679	1,993,926	196,099	-57,946	1,739,881	451,717	174,466	12,551	188,511	134,856
1980	2,658,764	2,194,200	3,015	2,197,215	215,531	-64,293	1,917,391	535,755	205,618	13,503	196,906	135,996
1981	2,961,553	2,370,660	2,127	2,372,787	247,641	-60,469	2,064,677	651,233	245,643	14,539	203,693	136,031
1982	3,140,573	2,426,863	2,459	2,429,322	253,427	-58,788	2,117,107	750,552	272,914	14,929	210,363	133,990
1983	3,338,389	2,556,233	1,746	2,557,979	276,750	-51,492	2,229,737	804,199	304,453	15,676	212,962	133,936
1984	3,654,583	2,809,526	1,057	2,810,583	317,274	-54,312	2,438,997	893,749	321,837	16,748	218,215	141,249
1985	3,939,588	3,008,364	333	3,008,697	346,641	-53,726	2,608,330	983,941	347,317	17,611	223,695	145,142
1986	4,216,417	3,248,279	86	3,248,365	385,249	-55,724	2,807,392	1,029,507	379,518	18,318	230,182	151,010
1987	4,549,692	3,538,196	1,571	3,539,767	420,097	-60,711	3,058,959	1,093,052	397,681	19,177	237,251	160,239
1988	4,992,050	3,925,748	1,742	3,927,490	467,724	-68,414	3,391,352	1,178,505	422,193	20,426	244,395	167,081
1989	5,402,955	4,165,551	1,999	4,167,550	501,844	-65,580	3,600,126	1,320,350	482,479	21,550	250,718	170,932
1990	5,965,065	4,556,301	1,341	4,557,642	570,290	-101,097	3,886,255	1,540,999	537,811	23,015	259,178	175,220
1991	6,454,376	4,833,979	1,789	4,835,768	598,456	-96,722	4,140,590	1,660,907	652,879	24,205	266,660	174,711
1992	7,085,632	5,293,466	591	5,294,057	647,724	-108,673	4,537,660	1,824,424	723,548	25,902	273,556	175,503
1993	7,373,493	5,545,640	9,233	5,554,873	687,324	-102,243	4,765,306	1,870,304	737,883	26,213	281,288	182,728
1994	7,993,228	5,963,949	3,433	5,967,382	743,289	-110,487	5,113,606	2,146,221	733,401	27,445	291,248	192,012
1995	8,680,469	6,414,679	3,957	6,418,636	799,510	-118,493	5,500,633	2,379,749	800,087	28,911	300,246	200,861
1996	9,372,446	6,916,145	5,137	6,921,282	838,500	-125,501	5,957,281	2,575,799	839,366	30,217	310,169	209,606
1997	9,976,725	7,421,169	3,325	7,424,494	872,068	-123,824	6,428,602	2,674,738	873,385	31,233	319,425	218,118
1998	10,940,195	8,176,640	4,103	8,180,743	915,475	-148,577	7,116,691	2,919,452	904,052	33,356	327,980	225,042
1999	11,795,839	8,899,423	4,195	8,903,618	954,952	-140,517	7,808,149	3,066,216	921,474	35,083	336,225	227,450
2000	13,010,656	9,621,386	5,650	9,627,036	938,083	-143,067	8,545,886	3,482,622	982,148	37,736	344,782	237,815
2001	14,086,786	10,519,129	4,324	10,523,453	1,013,371	-171,872	9,338,210	3,649,909	1,098,667	39,643	355,341	242,495
2002	14,128,790	10,552,808	3,827	10,556,635	1,023,671	-159,109	9,373,855	3,537,071	1,217,864	38,634	365,706	243,158
2003	14,915,432	11,080,875	3,484	11,084,359	1,046,458	-170,740	9,867,161	3,756,608	1,291,663	39,699	375,713	248,625
2004	16,215,690	11,858,467	4,868	11,863,335	1,105,125	-170,722	10,587,488	4,232,204	1,395,998	41,976	386,308	259,523
2005	17,443,911	12,636,900	4,537	12,641,437	1,168,449	-193,541	11,279,447	4,671,836	1,492,628	43,990	396,546	269,843
2006	18,394,618	13,371,288	6,239	13,377,527	1,307,355	-213,056	11,857,116	4,925,243	1,612,259	45,490	404,366	278,718
2007	18,711,013	13,258,238	2,892	13,261,130	1,350,587	-166,875	11,743,668	5,209,862	1,757,483	45,335	412,724	286,859
2008	18,175,427	12,254,884	5,604	12,260,488	1,250,837	-91,598	10,918,053	5,187,357	2,070,017	43,389	418,892	278,417
2009	17,455,143	11,781,736	8,282	11,790,018	1,218,365	-30,707	10,540,946	4,532,494	2,381,703	41,384	421,787	259,859
2010	18,665,085	12,819,352	8,446	12,827,798	1,219,626	56,082	11,664,254	4,377,918	2,622,913	43,818	425,966	253,315
2011	19,497,366	12,687,517	10,910	12,698,427	1,140,429	120,640	11,678,638	5,134,490	2,684,238	45,558	427,971	255,352
2012	18,917,243	12,115,939	10,797	12,126,736	1,180,338	135,893	11,082,291	5,131,972	2,702,980	43,858	431,328	255,675
2013	19,166,802	12,064,176	7,905	12,072,081	1,309,926	197,676	10,959,831	5,413,518	2,793,453	44,057	435,050	263,928
2014	20,402,538	12,583,271	11,809	12,595,080	1,444,402	222,693	11,373,371	5,960,041	3,069,126	45,940	444,112	268,654
2015	22,653,480	14,024,498	11,983	14,036,481	1,551,230	183,522	12,668,773	6,645,141	3,339,566	50,199	451,276	278,591
2016	23,896,474	14,803,180	7,327	14,810,507	1,656,746	125,585	13,279,346	7,132,047	3,485,081	51,972	459,795	290,017
2017	25,987,666	16,431,939	6,761	16,438,700	1,789,053	137,475	14,787,122	7,572,292	3,628,252	55,563	467,714	302,519
2018	28,581,191	18,054,346	9,077	18,063,423	1,944,156	70,148	16,189,415	8,547,308	3,844,468	59,975	476,551	316,304
2019	30,158,200	19,000,138	9,053	19,009,191	2,101,074	66,882	16,974,999	9,089,808	4,093,393	62,103	485,618	318,914
2020	32,293,825	19,680,588	10,699	19,691,287	2,178,881	12,745	17,525,151	9,185,645	5,583,029	65,705	491,494	311,652
2021	35,568,402	22,229,922	14,358	22,244,280	2,400,225	-158,786	19,685,269	9,666,978	6,216,155	71,489	497,535	326,230

Personal Income and Employment by Area: Richmond, VA

(Thousands of dollars, except as noted.)

Year	Personal income, total	Earnings by place of work			Less: Contributions for government social insurance	Plus: Adjustment for residence	Equals: Net earnings by place of residence	Plus: Dividends, interest, and rent	Plus: Personal current transfer receipts	Per capita personal income (dollars)	Population (persons)	Total employment
		Nonfarm	Farm	Total								
1970	2,889,290	2,489,464	16,378	2,505,842	157,625	-85,357	2,262,860	430,650	195,780	4,028	717,320	363,604
1971	3,189,968	2,713,033	15,031	2,728,064	178,873	-70,217	2,478,974	474,541	236,453	4,376	729,032	368,947
1972	3,503,510	2,988,003	19,800	3,007,803	206,223	-90,730	2,710,850	517,069	275,591	4,787	731,939	378,331
1973	3,924,521	3,361,068	30,585	3,391,653	267,295	-113,722	3,010,636	589,474	324,411	5,294	741,343	401,104
1974	4,406,894	3,755,135	30,463	3,785,598	308,978	-131,389	3,345,231	683,197	378,466	5,892	747,915	417,651
1975	4,914,915	4,073,624	24,993	4,098,617	329,345	-84,551	3,684,721	747,404	482,790	6,477	758,781	413,944
1976	5,412,019	4,505,538	21,381	4,526,919	372,334	-91,831	4,062,754	815,697	533,568	7,006	772,532	424,700
1977	6,008,192	5,019,395	9,842	5,029,237	413,127	-89,895	4,526,215	910,414	571,563	7,636	786,806	438,435
1978	6,809,525	5,691,929	27,261	5,719,190	476,683	-106,208	5,136,299	1,045,524	627,702	8,568	794,750	457,990
1979	7,691,213	6,390,017	574	6,390,591	559,694	-76,486	5,754,411	1,218,808	717,994	9,568	803,835	471,434
1980	8,646,386	7,043,315	-9,013	7,034,302	620,379	-105,486	6,308,437	1,480,082	857,867	10,673	810,116	472,830
1981	9,714,915	7,717,858	25,268	7,743,126	728,564	-117,420	6,897,142	1,825,426	992,347	11,880	817,739	470,744
1982	10,489,952	8,231,154	9,663	8,240,817	787,999	-118,119	7,334,699	2,068,008	1,087,245	12,735	823,713	469,070
1983	11,273,448	8,857,329	-5,256	8,852,073	865,206	-110,959	7,875,908	2,225,562	1,171,978	13,581	830,095	475,270
1984	12,414,800	9,678,885	38,965	9,717,850	971,997	-106,587	8,639,266	2,532,240	1,243,294	14,840	836,596	489,234
1985	13,388,204	10,524,074	21,982	10,546,056	1,084,788	-111,042	9,350,226	2,706,614	1,331,364	15,832	845,645	509,452
1986	14,396,285	11,358,169	23,463	11,381,632	1,210,734	-112,456	10,058,442	2,919,897	1,417,946	16,790	857,407	529,695
1987	15,745,663	12,587,692	27,226	12,614,918	1,330,296	-130,021	11,154,601	3,112,096	1,478,966	18,032	873,222	556,131
1988	17,319,415	13,855,985	45,223	13,901,208	1,506,070	-147,108	12,248,030	3,482,317	1,589,068	19,485	888,857	568,478
1989	18,938,800	14,912,495	54,279	14,966,774	1,629,292	-157,335	13,180,147	4,020,958	1,737,695	20,968	903,206	583,119
1990	19,903,032	15,560,480	59,009	15,619,489	1,716,924	-166,416	13,736,149	4,296,202	1,870,681	21,640	919,735	589,433
1991	20,366,986	15,963,431	46,424	16,009,855	1,780,784	-187,892	14,041,179	4,264,430	2,061,377	21,810	933,839	578,586
1992	21,591,753	16,895,312	51,478	16,946,790	1,872,196	-214,790	14,859,804	4,412,597	2,319,352	22,706	950,908	579,119
1993	22,636,372	17,649,270	37,840	17,687,110	1,961,632	-246,377	15,479,101	4,675,804	2,481,467	23,443	965,604	587,075
1994	23,945,230	18,693,416	57,663	18,751,079	2,067,567	-287,981	16,395,531	4,972,752	2,576,947	24,458	979,035	605,263
1995	25,149,932	19,601,189	54,871	19,656,060	2,164,345	-326,899	17,164,816	5,191,148	2,793,968	25,354	991,943	621,056
1996	26,400,160	20,575,645	73,411	20,649,056	2,256,604	-362,426	18,030,026	5,421,897	2,948,237	26,292	1,004,116	632,125
1997	28,149,889	22,189,575	44,214	22,233,789	2,414,993	-433,157	19,385,639	5,722,594	3,041,656	27,652	1,017,990	650,624
1998	29,744,456	23,670,440	26,423	23,696,863	2,539,594	-575,205	20,582,064	6,090,664	3,071,728	29,277	1,015,983	656,552
1999	31,251,220	25,250,131	25,712	25,275,843	2,715,142	-631,587	21,929,114	6,106,553	3,215,553	30,331	1,030,337	672,006
2000	33,740,151	27,153,665	44,582	27,198,247	2,872,468	-699,321	23,626,458	6,676,646	3,437,047	32,335	1,043,450	688,877
2001	36,145,498	29,180,787	26,268	29,207,055	3,095,473	-708,777	25,402,805	6,929,480	3,813,213	34,253	1,055,256	693,624
2002	36,979,363	29,805,016	24,925	29,829,941	3,191,068	-674,480	25,964,393	7,023,636	3,991,334	34,612	1,068,409	694,968
2003	38,862,669	30,895,314	28,860	30,924,174	3,295,780	-631,432	26,996,962	7,602,780	4,262,927	35,916	1,082,054	696,698
2004	41,215,118	33,024,935	38,849	33,063,784	3,564,435	-648,804	28,850,545	7,907,436	4,457,137	37,512	1,098,719	711,903
2005	44,065,963	35,208,137	33,932	35,242,069	3,818,179	-662,812	30,761,078	8,447,444	4,857,441	39,472	1,116,391	730,868
2006	47,231,703	36,900,612	20,098	36,920,710	4,046,799	-614,683	32,259,228	9,653,832	5,318,643	41,523	1,137,479	746,208
2007	49,775,513	38,812,079	19,692	38,831,771	4,253,858	-598,836	33,979,077	10,088,030	5,708,406	43,144	1,153,700	764,549
2008	51,540,489	39,295,247	37,332	39,332,579	4,360,343	-529,800	34,442,436	10,515,596	6,582,457	44,126	1,168,018	764,229
2009	49,223,506	37,609,751	40,019	37,649,770	4,229,172	-484,226	32,936,372	9,104,060	7,183,074	41,738	1,179,342	741,657
2010	50,950,554	38,888,731	24,092	38,912,823	4,325,064	-450,529	34,137,230	9,010,988	7,802,336	42,872	1,188,423	737,786
2011	54,077,524	40,484,671	72,656	40,557,327	4,006,230	-455,742	36,095,355	9,893,933	8,088,236	45,165	1,197,332	750,925
2012	57,582,186	42,624,134	82,043	42,706,177	4,164,678	-475,142	38,066,357	11,343,414	8,172,415	47,534	1,211,395	763,931
2013	57,913,324	44,149,786	91,572	44,241,358	4,913,065	-468,344	38,859,949	10,527,608	8,525,767	47,351	1,223,065	776,183
2014	60,920,750	46,160,485	46,464	46,206,949	5,089,271	-497,611	40,620,067	11,380,491	8,920,192	49,101	1,240,714	789,685
2015	64,442,490	48,790,724	23,903	48,814,627	5,381,590	-623,523	42,809,514	12,269,427	9,363,549	51,399	1,253,770	814,600
2016	66,355,653	49,836,283	11,426	49,847,709	5,497,149	-564,819	43,785,741	12,843,446	9,726,466	52,368	1,267,111	831,786
2017	69,443,187	52,111,122	29,935	52,141,057	5,784,083	-594,432	45,762,542	13,509,239	10,171,406	54,269	1,279,604	848,497
2018	71,740,240	53,455,099	11,019	53,466,118	5,963,391	-574,824	46,927,903	14,114,070	10,698,267	55,499	1,292,638	861,920
2019	76,845,962	56,115,365	29,945	56,145,310	6,246,822	-604,306	49,294,182	16,190,301	11,361,479	58,865	1,305,456	871,882
2020	81,424,338	56,958,724	22,397	56,981,121	6,386,880	-638,406	49,955,835	16,115,102	15,353,401	61,885	1,315,734	854,987
2021	87,167,944	60,943,277	55,502	60,998,779	6,746,871	-677,520	53,574,388	16,569,929	17,023,627	65,834	1,324,062	875,494

Personal Income and Employment by Area: Riverside-San Bernardino-Ontario, CA

(Thousands of dollars, except as noted.)

Year	Personal income, total	Earnings by place of work			Less: Contributions for government social insurance	Plus: Adjustment for residence	Equals: Net earnings by place of residence	Plus: Dividends, interest, and rent	Plus: Personal current transfer receipts	Per capita personal income (dollars)	Population (persons)	Total employment
		Nonfarm	Farm	Total								
1970	4,910,718	3,135,466	112,771	3,248,237	204,697	439,194	3,482,734	856,272	571,712	4,294	1,143,539	418,790
1971	5,326,325	3,341,866	94,990	3,436,856	225,316	540,962	3,752,502	927,001	646,822	4,548	1,171,161	422,980
1972	5,948,005	3,683,519	144,267	3,827,786	260,583	672,950	4,240,153	1,006,723	701,129	5,001	1,189,476	436,775
1973	6,614,417	4,046,761	168,227	4,214,988	323,838	809,591	4,700,741	1,123,933	789,743	5,502	1,202,185	458,353
1974	7,425,733	4,414,477	167,136	4,581,613	364,732	958,866	5,175,747	1,286,663	963,323	6,038	1,229,743	468,665
1975	8,414,136	4,779,190	224,490	5,003,680	389,832	1,129,521	5,743,369	1,445,689	1,225,078	6,739	1,248,571	473,347
1976	9,506,530	5,383,473	257,788	5,641,261	442,192	1,334,345	6,533,414	1,589,439	1,383,677	7,412	1,282,517	491,513
1977	10,697,117	6,088,613	259,954	6,348,567	510,694	1,568,986	7,406,859	1,783,419	1,506,839	7,938	1,347,627	524,096
1978	12,367,023	7,121,761	255,381	7,377,142	610,948	1,870,814	8,637,008	2,077,828	1,652,187	8,614	1,435,733	566,072
1979	14,020,247	8,080,842	197,276	8,278,118	725,753	2,197,277	9,749,642	2,412,501	1,858,104	9,367	1,496,847	596,581
1980	16,168,124	8,889,079	263,796	9,152,875	780,376	2,592,939	10,965,438	2,967,331	2,235,355	10,282	1,572,429	609,845
1981	18,559,946	9,768,364	284,213	10,052,577	929,185	3,121,272	12,244,664	3,606,111	2,709,171	11,413	1,626,183	618,273
1982	20,053,701	10,207,063	335,822	10,542,885	992,886	3,488,818	13,038,817	4,022,272	2,992,612	11,890	1,686,602	618,248
1983	22,048,306	11,154,689	389,914	11,544,603	1,111,544	3,966,401	14,399,460	4,454,987	3,193,859	12,646	1,743,463	645,466
1984	24,849,226	12,688,834	434,226	13,123,060	1,310,782	4,639,709	16,451,987	5,005,730	3,391,509	13,721	1,811,019	685,286
1985	27,754,307	14,311,988	459,539	14,771,527	1,503,117	5,346,532	18,614,942	5,414,795	3,724,570	14,623	1,897,927	736,046
1986	30,855,008	16,059,254	519,696	16,578,950	1,708,433	6,067,605	20,938,122	5,838,247	4,078,639	15,463	1,995,378	781,634
1987	34,194,067	18,165,339	513,690	18,679,029	1,935,780	6,976,851	23,720,100	6,123,890	4,350,077	16,112	2,122,256	829,482
1988	38,084,692	20,304,888	586,423	20,891,311	2,242,076	7,903,555	26,552,790	6,717,965	4,813,937	16,798	2,267,166	889,223
1989	42,656,093	22,371,229	558,642	22,929,871	2,509,048	8,860,607	29,281,430	8,013,026	5,361,637	17,500	2,437,479	947,954
1990	47,168,306	24,489,966	610,184	25,100,150	2,724,088	10,424,343	32,800,405	8,356,588	6,011,313	17,932	2,630,471	1,003,046
1991	48,901,773	25,989,035	527,988	26,517,023	2,894,892	9,989,314	33,611,445	8,464,754	6,825,574	17,853	2,739,150	1,037,939
1992	51,266,697	27,686,170	530,221	28,216,391	3,054,213	9,716,436	34,878,614	8,476,718	7,911,365	18,171	2,821,341	1,035,249
1993	52,632,062	28,276,224	516,656	28,792,880	3,138,414	9,773,034	35,427,500	8,697,854	8,506,708	18,374	2,864,517	1,039,281
1994	54,106,404	29,562,571	562,443	30,125,014	3,293,135	9,565,778	36,397,657	8,976,703	8,732,044	18,622	2,905,505	1,065,322
1995	56,101,159	30,907,941	550,028	31,457,969	3,397,410	9,400,045	37,460,604	9,428,308	9,212,247	19,019	2,949,807	1,099,819
1996	58,776,228	32,522,674	668,841	33,191,515	3,466,710	9,275,386	39,000,191	10,038,252	9,737,785	19,656	2,990,316	1,132,225
1997	62,292,447	34,886,249	558,232	35,444,481	3,667,079	10,054,415	41,831,817	10,614,506	9,846,124	20,475	3,042,372	1,168,111
1998	67,490,863	38,830,759	741,612	39,572,371	4,005,391	10,395,776	45,962,756	11,099,270	10,428,837	21,714	3,108,220	1,244,588
1999	71,740,208	42,456,017	697,651	43,153,668	4,384,883	10,516,676	49,285,461	11,490,643	10,964,104	22,493	3,189,513	1,311,728
2000	77,121,223	46,390,367	449,493	46,839,860	4,760,005	11,266,356	53,346,211	12,263,143	11,511,869	23,534	3,277,022	1,355,540
2001	83,108,508	49,756,930	584,207	50,341,137	5,368,291	11,956,884	56,929,730	13,402,468	12,776,310	24,607	3,377,365	1,402,821
2002	87,735,624	53,811,820	502,793	54,314,613	5,904,099	12,453,465	60,863,979	13,126,019	13,745,626	25,161	3,486,938	1,458,784
2003	94,639,446	58,481,718	616,242	59,097,960	6,503,460	13,188,151	65,782,651	14,086,936	14,769,859	26,160	3,617,771	1,517,838
2004	102,580,511	65,629,651	743,363	66,373,014	7,554,519	14,016,711	72,835,206	14,068,107	15,677,198	27,314	3,755,607	1,611,428
2005	110,296,722	71,433,127	655,895	72,089,022	8,200,388	14,865,199	78,753,833	14,894,073	16,648,816	28,458	3,875,709	1,698,878
2006	119,259,903	76,883,156	465,486	77,348,642	8,506,433	15,998,708	84,840,917	16,335,921	18,083,065	29,916	3,986,510	1,766,253
2007	125,255,295	78,249,349	713,119	78,962,468	8,456,163	16,838,485	87,344,790	18,436,016	19,474,489	30,795	4,067,344	1,799,604
2008	126,950,603	75,977,213	611,879	76,589,092	8,355,041	16,442,876	84,676,927	19,791,667	22,482,009	30,862	4,113,447	1,747,886
2009	123,931,601	71,769,075	391,568	72,160,643	8,006,199	16,024,519	80,178,963	18,771,629	24,981,009	29,786	4,160,685	1,665,991
2010	128,074,670	73,371,907	480,372	73,852,279	7,949,392	15,706,641	81,609,528	18,656,103	27,809,039	30,189	4,242,365	1,638,713
2011	135,529,409	77,617,868	682,551	78,300,419	7,573,961	16,779,648	87,506,106	19,941,026	28,082,277	31,559	4,294,436	1,678,261
2012	139,024,404	80,091,067	600,426	80,691,493	7,745,084	17,199,623	90,146,032	20,465,835	28,412,537	32,079	4,333,851	1,727,702
2013	143,051,092	83,444,029	629,819	84,073,848	8,978,806	17,480,451	92,575,493	21,048,709	29,426,890	32,748	4,368,188	1,788,301
2014	150,644,684	88,284,496	803,305	89,087,801	9,568,685	17,465,979	96,985,095	22,447,624	31,211,965	34,357	4,384,684	1,868,308
2015	160,089,121	95,462,426	745,088	96,207,514	10,312,688	16,911,615	102,806,441	23,727,394	33,555,286	36,195	4,422,911	1,944,593
2016	167,438,528	99,726,290	634,900	100,361,190	10,771,856	18,776,737	108,366,071	24,326,481	34,745,976	37,496	4,465,521	1,993,216
2017	173,557,832	105,095,128	702,234	105,797,362	11,384,726	19,272,960	113,685,596	25,361,970	34,510,266	38,467	4,511,846	2,052,340
2018	181,409,114	110,774,311	536,583	111,310,894	12,191,513	20,356,656	119,476,037	25,706,898	36,226,179	39,869	4,550,170	2,121,969
2019	193,709,372	117,301,109	598,910	117,900,019	13,064,963	22,323,799	127,158,855	27,724,939	38,825,578	42,326	4,576,562	2,169,264
2020	214,883,630	121,843,727	626,798	122,470,525	13,704,444	20,137,328	128,903,409	27,989,926	57,990,295	46,658	4,605,504	2,150,133
2021	234,444,352	133,405,566	496,778	133,902,344	14,915,318	23,624,117	142,611,143	28,368,365	63,464,844	50,384	4,653,105	2,249,178

Personal Income and Employment by Area: Roanoke, VA

(Thousands of dollars, except as noted.)

Year	Personal income, total	Derivation of personal income									Per capita personal income (dollars)	Population (persons)	Total employment
		Earnings by place of work			Less: Contributions for government social insurance	Plus: Adjustment for residence	Equals: Net earnings by place of residence	Plus: Dividends, interest, and rent	Plus: Personal current transfer receipts			
		Nonfarm	Farm	Total								
1970	858,818	730,643	5,166	735,809	51,639	-17,093	667,077	114,101	77,640	3,708	231,596	113,547
1971	938,685	794,236	5,124	799,360	57,676	-19,726	721,958	126,245	90,482	3,938	238,357	115,420
1972	1,036,415	884,884	6,865	891,749	67,325	-28,058	796,366	138,359	101,690	4,257	243,439	120,323
1973	1,166,816	1,001,613	8,755	1,010,368	86,635	-34,251	889,482	158,871	118,463	4,702	248,131	128,106
1974	1,295,167	1,094,586	10,001	1,104,587	97,675	-37,637	969,275	185,867	140,025	5,153	251,318	131,119
1975	1,423,222	1,160,547	7,237	1,167,784	100,252	-27,964	1,039,568	202,276	181,378	5,616	253,423	128,335
1976	1,582,041	1,297,444	6,213	1,303,657	114,726	-25,349	1,163,582	219,675	198,784	6,190	255,587	131,459
1977	1,735,818	1,426,642	5,681	1,432,323	127,564	-22,541	1,282,218	239,864	213,736	6,711	258,644	135,493
1978	1,970,463	1,610,288	7,666	1,617,954	145,076	-9,154	1,463,724	268,415	238,324	7,578	260,021	140,517
1979	2,152,211	1,764,198	6,158	1,770,356	165,451	-27,549	1,577,356	308,356	266,499	8,219	261,869	141,562
1980	2,370,883	1,901,839	148	1,901,987	178,693	-46,885	1,676,409	381,926	312,548	9,101	260,501	140,251
1981	2,618,711	2,047,711	3,461	2,051,172	207,136	-51,690	1,792,346	470,983	355,382	10,007	261,693	138,411
1982	2,780,681	2,126,898	1,017	2,127,915	220,821	-57,125	1,849,969	544,808	385,904	10,623	261,751	138,094
1983	3,019,996	2,330,508	4,006	2,334,514	245,691	-62,051	2,026,772	578,670	414,554	11,541	261,672	140,118
1984	3,389,261	2,621,925	7,535	2,629,460	286,004	-73,820	2,269,636	686,962	432,663	12,904	262,643	146,364
1985	3,653,313	2,858,005	8,502	2,866,507	317,600	-85,205	2,463,702	726,862	462,749	13,880	263,208	152,702
1986	3,876,557	3,038,603	10,437	3,049,040	348,615	-90,241	2,610,184	773,877	492,496	14,704	263,645	155,869
1987	4,135,333	3,278,186	12,646	3,290,832	371,674	-98,532	2,820,626	801,213	513,494	15,603	265,026	160,150
1988	4,374,680	3,434,023	15,906	3,449,929	399,155	-106,690	2,944,084	894,919	535,677	16,458	265,805	159,825
1989	4,755,538	3,664,584	21,315	3,685,899	425,194	-121,032	3,139,673	1,032,903	582,962	17,828	266,749	164,203
1990	5,025,194	3,904,116	25,411	3,929,527	457,682	-140,300	3,331,545	1,066,956	626,693	18,651	269,440	166,966
1991	5,161,248	4,008,534	22,642	4,031,176	474,463	-151,806	3,404,907	1,073,299	683,042	18,912	272,906	164,617
1992	5,450,633	4,287,022	22,515	4,309,537	499,944	-174,329	3,635,264	1,061,382	753,987	19,896	273,951	166,401
1993	5,736,462	4,549,155	17,606	4,566,761	530,207	-198,509	3,838,045	1,106,195	792,222	20,736	276,643	169,750
1994	6,018,218	4,758,678	18,740	4,777,418	551,815	-221,263	4,004,340	1,164,712	849,166	21,557	279,176	175,063
1995	6,330,237	4,994,027	14,725	5,008,752	582,236	-247,484	4,179,032	1,248,448	902,757	22,533	280,938	179,737
1996	6,638,372	5,196,877	12,302	5,209,179	601,512	-268,955	4,338,712	1,357,391	942,269	23,464	282,915	183,486
1997	6,909,629	5,426,825	6,988	5,433,813	625,354	-288,335	4,520,124	1,418,453	971,052	24,279	284,593	183,985
1998	7,364,946	5,873,925	9,714	5,883,639	664,502	-329,381	4,889,756	1,466,558	1,008,632	25,773	285,762	191,061
1999	7,633,222	6,136,355	4,443	6,140,798	693,661	-357,139	5,089,998	1,490,737	1,052,487	26,579	287,193	190,906
2000	8,021,738	6,391,352	9,930	6,401,282	713,014	-395,257	5,293,011	1,610,907	1,117,820	27,786	288,699	194,558
2001	8,514,584	6,754,335	7,297	6,761,632	756,393	-410,301	5,594,938	1,691,377	1,228,269	29,407	289,547	191,045
2002	8,780,674	6,975,774	2,424	6,978,198	783,767	-423,350	5,771,081	1,701,840	1,307,753	30,230	290,466	188,705
2003	9,022,184	7,137,330	-3,557	7,133,773	799,103	-433,924	5,900,746	1,726,927	1,394,511	30,889	292,082	187,372
2004	9,478,463	7,518,435	9,460	7,527,895	849,728	-464,950	6,213,217	1,785,444	1,479,802	32,268	293,745	190,307
2005	9,824,918	7,802,613	9,866	7,812,479	893,853	-491,503	6,427,123	1,795,048	1,602,747	33,147	296,405	194,972
2006	10,322,713	8,143,446	33	8,143,479	951,045	-519,783	6,672,651	1,899,513	1,750,549	34,417	299,930	200,015
2007	11,018,848	8,532,735	3,361	8,536,096	993,885	-548,218	6,993,993	2,149,666	1,875,189	36,383	302,858	202,744
2008	11,522,504	8,781,705	7,424	8,789,129	1,028,990	-577,482	7,182,657	2,236,814	2,103,033	37,705	305,596	201,279
2009	11,314,056	8,637,433	4,361	8,641,794	1,018,593	-567,705	7,055,496	1,974,911	2,283,649	36,756	307,816	193,947
2010	11,570,330	8,679,843	8,027	8,687,870	1,018,177	-551,994	7,117,699	2,002,152	2,450,479	37,493	308,602	190,548
2011	11,995,705	8,888,892	18,566	8,907,458	941,373	-580,019	7,386,066	2,117,133	2,492,506	38,799	309,172	192,046
2012	12,702,760	9,246,345	19,748	9,266,093	970,726	-598,024	7,697,343	2,452,413	2,553,004	40,904	310,548	193,632
2013	12,493,194	9,335,938	14,961	9,350,899	1,112,343	-595,189	7,643,367	2,220,807	2,629,020	40,046	311,973	194,154
2014	12,939,387	9,503,458	17,316	9,520,774	1,130,954	-608,085	7,781,735	2,412,388	2,745,264	41,282	313,438	195,888
2015	13,602,207	10,004,458	3,840	10,008,298	1,181,214	-655,326	8,171,758	2,571,886	2,858,563	43,316	314,023	196,537
2016	13,675,550	9,898,076	-4,924	9,893,152	1,177,500	-628,738	8,086,914	2,629,274	2,959,362	43,606	313,616	197,116
2017	13,935,919	9,957,916	178	9,958,094	1,196,609	-619,574	8,141,911	2,735,279	3,058,729	44,382	314,002	196,759
2018	14,388,575	10,236,968	-8,883	10,228,085	1,235,170	-638,770	8,354,145	2,848,412	3,186,018	45,774	314,339	198,385
2019	14,794,003	10,407,078	-2,480	10,404,598	1,267,328	-655,517	8,481,753	2,957,248	3,355,002	46,975	314,933	198,296
2020	15,877,032	10,625,570	-4,254	10,621,316	1,295,625	-671,651	8,654,040	2,944,634	4,278,358	50,394	315,057	193,385
2021	16,963,669	11,256,235	-2,302	11,253,933	1,358,869	-703,388	9,191,676	3,002,587	4,769,406	53,939	314,496	196,635

Personal Income and Employment by Area: Rochester, MN

(Thousands of dollars, except as noted.)

Year	Personal income, total	Earnings by place of work			Less: Contributions for government social insurance	Plus: Adjustment for residence	Equals: Net earnings by place of residence	Plus: Dividends, interest, and rent	Plus: Personal current transfer receipts	Per capita personal income (dollars)	Population (persons)	Total employment
		Nonfarm	Farm	Total								
1970	531,247	386,908	54,160	441,068	26,598	-3,571	410,899	79,110	41,238	3,888	136,645	61,810
1971	566,507	415,324	51,141	466,465	29,647	-4,464	432,354	86,631	47,522	4,105	138,020	62,584
1972	625,050	457,361	61,672	519,033	34,157	-5,673	479,203	93,502	52,345	4,478	139,574	66,413
1973	741,615	516,543	108,372	624,915	44,716	-7,622	572,577	107,062	61,976	5,288	140,244	70,682
1974	782,079	562,304	81,076	643,380	50,508	-8,512	584,360	123,485	74,234	5,529	141,439	72,619
1975	865,503	633,726	68,272	701,998	55,511	-11,901	634,586	142,159	88,758	6,088	142,168	73,701
1976	944,395	719,060	52,250	771,310	64,229	-14,830	692,251	154,826	97,318	6,563	143,886	76,699
1977	1,098,729	802,415	106,467	908,882	71,851	-18,514	818,517	176,384	103,828	7,551	145,499	78,691
1978	1,238,530	929,187	112,323	1,041,510	86,719	-25,225	929,566	195,132	113,832	8,484	145,983	81,851
1979	1,331,857	1,037,311	72,670	1,109,981	100,475	-28,452	981,054	221,003	129,800	9,017	147,713	84,728
1980	1,487,851	1,142,203	64,120	1,206,323	110,485	-32,394	1,063,444	268,928	155,479	10,022	148,456	86,430
1981	1,654,915	1,237,975	70,431	1,308,406	128,063	-33,592	1,146,751	327,141	181,023	11,049	149,775	86,334
1982	1,834,583	1,343,421	74,810	1,418,231	143,134	-38,412	1,236,685	396,519	201,379	12,196	150,427	86,370
1983	1,889,385	1,449,568	-5,787	1,443,781	156,269	-42,342	1,245,170	422,567	221,648	12,437	151,922	88,143
1984	2,200,996	1,637,710	89,078	1,726,788	181,227	-50,056	1,495,505	466,819	238,672	14,374	153,128	91,755
1985	2,307,593	1,735,272	77,798	1,813,070	195,256	-54,814	1,563,000	490,741	253,852	14,918	154,688	92,865
1986	2,426,063	1,816,262	107,005	1,923,267	209,000	-57,444	1,656,823	503,224	266,016	15,673	154,797	92,206
1987	2,575,865	1,934,281	146,085	2,080,366	220,219	-64,215	1,795,932	504,411	275,522	16,568	155,475	94,618
1988	2,677,274	2,102,498	87,019	2,189,517	247,634	-72,277	1,869,606	515,320	292,348	16,854	158,849	98,326
1989	2,992,209	2,292,336	135,285	2,427,621	269,737	-81,994	2,075,890	594,514	321,805	18,586	160,993	101,567
1990	3,192,837	2,506,340	126,270	2,632,610	296,815	-93,328	2,242,467	608,476	341,894	19,537	163,427	104,645
1991	3,316,577	2,650,254	96,584	2,746,838	318,121	-96,462	2,332,255	619,461	364,861	19,959	166,169	106,918
1992	3,530,002	2,838,454	76,200	2,914,654	337,124	-99,931	2,477,599	657,451	394,952	20,992	168,159	108,570
1993	3,585,134	2,959,484	41,748	3,001,232	352,450	-102,613	2,546,169	627,419	411,546	20,925	171,334	110,560
1994	3,758,141	3,023,006	101,797	3,124,803	364,228	-100,983	2,659,592	658,938	439,611	21,791	172,466	110,937
1995	3,900,797	3,114,067	49,006	3,163,073	375,712	-100,557	2,686,804	741,500	472,493	22,582	172,741	113,113
1996	4,237,574	3,346,391	107,306	3,453,697	400,010	-107,489	2,946,198	791,197	500,179	24,331	174,161	114,704
1997	4,436,559	3,569,824	68,056	3,637,880	426,904	-118,813	3,092,163	834,307	510,089	25,172	176,251	118,626
1998	4,909,139	3,982,545	100,032	4,082,577	470,099	-137,135	3,475,343	913,754	520,042	27,351	179,488	123,856
1999	5,238,025	4,325,049	77,950	4,402,999	510,888	-154,195	3,737,916	941,502	558,607	28,702	182,498	127,906
2000	5,580,711	4,585,413	57,502	4,642,915	539,296	-163,877	3,939,742	1,036,034	604,935	30,073	185,573	131,560
2001	6,041,535	5,004,801	40,062	5,044,863	573,397	-178,629	4,292,837	1,069,407	679,291	32,170	187,803	132,985
2002	6,293,646	5,284,584	20,489	5,305,073	604,079	-187,517	4,513,477	1,035,289	744,880	33,012	190,646	134,146
2003	6,729,182	5,653,561	52,125	5,705,686	650,274	-210,094	4,845,318	1,085,197	798,667	34,854	193,067	136,828
2004	7,007,522	5,933,557	116,898	6,050,455	679,451	-211,892	5,159,112	1,003,694	844,716	35,881	195,300	138,421
2005	7,074,199	5,976,409	143,913	6,120,322	697,207	-212,263	5,210,852	985,626	877,721	35,875	197,188	139,865
2006	7,479,052	6,214,741	101,987	6,316,728	733,906	-201,234	5,381,588	1,141,133	956,331	37,440	199,763	141,771
2007	7,948,511	6,496,341	121,448	6,617,789	766,853	-197,129	5,653,807	1,258,786	1,035,918	39,392	201,782	143,695
2008	8,355,746	6,664,079	157,882	6,821,961	792,032	-186,646	5,843,283	1,351,558	1,160,905	40,923	204,181	142,489
2009	8,298,677	6,676,547	69,550	6,746,097	799,929	-215,876	5,730,292	1,292,531	1,275,854	40,266	206,097	139,773
2010	8,871,533	7,111,674	136,567	7,248,241	830,188	-186,486	6,231,567	1,253,408	1,386,558	42,810	207,228	138,061
2011	9,218,875	7,053,967	249,585	7,303,552	734,741	-180,362	6,388,449	1,434,489	1,395,937	44,216	208,498	139,594
2012	9,725,975	7,414,603	306,119	7,720,722	764,247	-186,206	6,770,269	1,558,183	1,397,523	46,404	209,592	142,449
2013	9,862,768	7,617,243	339,529	7,956,772	900,848	-201,460	6,854,464	1,565,619	1,442,685	46,617	211,572	144,445
2014	10,180,348	7,833,265	194,441	8,027,706	918,330	-203,019	6,906,357	1,739,431	1,534,560	47,546	214,116	145,269
2015	10,619,194	8,184,052	145,742	8,329,794	952,602	-227,100	7,150,092	1,848,116	1,620,986	49,221	215,745	147,852
2016	10,887,210	8,498,953	39,596	8,538,549	992,006	-239,478	7,307,065	1,893,833	1,686,312	49,844	218,425	149,372
2017	11,407,565	8,887,840	92,743	8,980,583	1,040,502	-280,149	7,659,932	2,009,618	1,738,015	51,716	220,579	150,520
2018	12,012,887	9,553,883	49,795	9,603,678	1,128,869	-349,019	8,125,790	2,034,663	1,852,434	53,955	222,645	153,023
2019	12,469,507	9,845,520	25,883	9,871,403	1,162,736	-373,013	8,335,654	2,182,202	1,951,651	55,431	224,956	154,321
2020	13,461,441	10,039,199	178,467	10,217,666	1,188,080	-395,563	8,634,023	2,201,492	2,625,926	59,428	226,515	150,188
2021	14,322,227	10,676,765	194,184	10,870,949	1,234,202	-446,897	9,189,850	2,238,688	2,893,689	63,052	227,151	154,225

Personal Income and Employment by Area: Rochester, NY

(Thousands of dollars, except as noted.)

Year	Personal income, total	Earnings by place of work			Less: Contributions for government social insurance	Plus: Adjustment for residence	Equals: Net earnings by place of residence	Plus: Dividends, interest, and rent	Plus: Personal current transfer receipts	Per capita personal income (dollars)	Population (persons)	Total employment
		Nonfarm	Farm	Total								
1970	4,543,716	3,774,719	64,553	3,839,272	276,964	-46,065	3,516,243	656,574	370,899	4,623	982,845	439,999
1971	4,870,129	4,012,962	61,581	4,074,543	304,319	-49,932	3,720,292	695,348	454,489	4,927	988,371	440,497
1972	5,244,349	4,371,248	41,128	4,412,376	352,229	-51,695	4,008,452	741,030	494,867	5,292	991,017	447,820
1973	5,757,009	4,798,117	72,803	4,870,920	448,781	-54,291	4,367,848	832,100	557,061	5,808	991,293	464,379
1974	6,304,031	5,220,989	84,056	5,305,045	507,725	-58,456	4,738,864	941,762	623,405	6,373	989,197	475,220
1975	6,814,001	5,484,338	65,112	5,549,450	521,206	-61,152	4,967,092	1,008,879	838,030	6,839	996,288	464,343
1976	7,260,204	5,896,373	57,078	5,953,451	572,254	-61,683	5,319,514	1,061,870	878,820	7,280	997,313	468,201
1977	7,870,948	6,424,789	60,062	6,484,851	622,054	-71,141	5,791,656	1,162,967	916,325	7,874	999,583	477,239
1978	8,531,744	7,045,322	66,337	7,111,659	698,906	-75,168	6,337,585	1,224,560	969,599	8,569	995,677	489,129
1979	9,465,090	7,842,783	80,471	7,923,254	805,638	-81,155	7,036,461	1,385,622	1,043,007	9,501	996,204	501,248
1980	10,647,796	8,648,149	68,504	8,716,653	886,640	-88,518	7,741,495	1,673,854	1,232,447	10,710	994,186	499,705
1981	11,953,264	9,561,796	83,508	9,645,304	1,041,775	-96,816	8,506,713	2,061,846	1,384,705	11,974	998,299	504,102
1982	13,021,657	10,302,710	71,042	10,373,752	1,137,881	-124,035	9,111,836	2,375,837	1,533,984	12,970	1,003,975	508,477
1983	13,611,691	10,651,487	35,353	10,686,840	1,181,442	-130,530	9,374,868	2,553,694	1,683,129	13,518	1,006,962	504,266
1984	14,916,845	11,624,049	57,621	11,681,670	1,312,840	-149,789	10,219,041	2,908,837	1,788,967	14,875	1,002,789	522,629
1985	15,997,616	12,620,376	69,579	12,689,955	1,444,272	-183,241	11,062,442	3,040,201	1,894,973	15,956	1,002,633	541,363
1986	16,847,852	13,303,278	83,299	13,386,577	1,549,087	-201,120	11,636,370	3,166,703	2,044,779	16,793	1,003,295	549,723
1987	17,474,726	13,877,368	100,828	13,978,196	1,589,925	-224,320	12,163,951	3,214,982	2,095,793	17,421	1,003,095	552,418
1988	18,953,572	15,185,577	102,315	15,287,892	1,774,322	-256,855	13,256,715	3,421,915	2,274,942	18,770	1,009,766	575,050
1989	20,782,822	16,269,777	107,259	16,377,036	1,881,934	-288,626	14,206,476	4,107,984	2,468,362	20,382	1,019,683	585,517
1990	21,598,616	16,873,844	103,722	16,977,566	1,870,985	-344,381	14,762,200	4,127,258	2,709,158	21,013	1,027,880	589,401
1991	22,464,069	17,603,528	92,143	17,695,671	1,998,597	-364,028	15,333,046	4,114,549	3,016,474	21,678	1,036,248	591,189
1992	23,555,008	18,490,932	101,400	18,592,332	2,061,092	-376,912	16,154,328	4,017,109	3,383,571	22,477	1,047,976	592,760
1993	24,178,184	19,004,638	110,352	19,114,990	2,131,981	-401,766	16,581,243	4,004,825	3,592,116	22,913	1,055,228	601,469
1994	24,867,803	19,484,024	91,886	19,575,910	2,216,694	-416,834	16,942,382	4,091,797	3,833,624	23,518	1,057,376	607,597
1995	26,005,032	20,253,521	73,772	20,327,293	2,297,160	-449,681	17,580,452	4,384,955	4,039,625	24,581	1,057,933	606,742
1996	26,944,000	20,802,572	92,886	20,895,458	2,341,806	-416,963	18,136,689	4,591,152	4,216,159	25,426	1,059,684	607,448
1997	28,029,188	21,652,744	89,680	21,742,424	2,402,551	-429,860	18,910,013	4,880,852	4,238,323	26,443	1,060,003	611,491
1998	29,286,379	22,507,752	98,589	22,606,341	2,452,560	-467,404	19,686,377	5,102,281	4,497,721	27,635	1,059,773	617,789
1999	30,386,228	23,653,099	128,573	23,781,672	2,509,413	-466,870	20,805,389	4,900,659	4,680,180	28,658	1,060,310	627,638
2000	31,990,639	24,824,504	131,775	24,956,279	2,603,917	-460,815	21,891,547	5,179,865	4,919,227	29,996	1,066,482	637,905
2001	32,754,274	25,305,511	150,023	25,455,534	2,730,345	-482,769	22,242,420	5,283,815	5,228,039	30,663	1,068,215	629,922
2002	32,999,153	25,516,306	114,681	25,630,987	2,782,890	-481,883	22,366,214	4,984,060	5,648,879	30,830	1,070,355	618,390
2003	33,624,242	26,193,807	144,017	26,337,824	2,865,708	-480,832	22,991,284	4,825,007	5,807,951	31,368	1,071,918	618,045
2004	34,901,061	27,035,670	151,554	27,187,224	2,977,687	-456,889	23,752,648	4,937,042	6,211,371	32,542	1,072,494	622,352
2005	35,444,267	27,522,025	121,160	27,643,185	3,094,180	-454,110	24,094,895	4,965,398	6,383,974	33,113	1,070,418	628,582
2006	36,870,277	28,442,351	132,263	28,574,614	3,200,414	-403,258	24,970,942	5,147,240	6,752,095	34,446	1,070,370	627,477
2007	38,838,291	29,518,349	248,587	29,766,936	3,291,034	-372,989	26,102,913	5,638,229	7,097,149	36,228	1,072,040	634,312
2008	41,022,725	30,224,495	291,941	30,516,436	3,402,391	-369,457	26,744,588	6,297,936	7,980,201	38,150	1,075,302	636,153
2009	41,147,711	30,273,897	164,295	30,438,192	3,362,951	-390,978	26,684,263	5,763,306	8,700,142	38,173	1,077,941	622,597
2010	42,900,552	31,579,932	271,013	31,850,945	3,430,814	-361,813	28,058,318	5,584,785	9,257,449	39,724	1,079,975	620,717
2011	44,809,806	32,551,865	301,580	32,853,445	3,191,440	-376,337	29,285,668	6,138,689	9,385,449	41,428	1,081,635	629,224
2012	46,900,851	33,832,132	306,379	34,138,511	3,254,592	-341,334	30,542,585	6,915,042	9,443,224	43,360	1,081,664	632,101
2013	46,619,093	34,200,677	347,866	34,548,543	3,738,271	-313,489	30,496,783	6,554,419	9,567,891	43,088	1,081,961	634,870
2014	47,522,530	34,152,056	302,607	34,454,663	3,844,159	-233,738	30,376,766	7,221,152	9,924,612	43,611	1,089,687	638,612
2015	49,799,304	35,733,225	196,261	35,929,486	4,023,944	-244,885	31,660,657	7,696,526	10,442,121	45,734	1,088,882	644,265
2016	50,458,476	35,995,492	190,029	36,185,521	4,075,523	-273,395	31,836,603	7,964,232	10,657,641	46,366	1,088,253	648,594
2017	52,883,484	37,257,692	253,530	37,511,222	4,217,108	-257,436	33,036,678	8,474,300	11,372,506	48,575	1,088,691	651,027
2018	54,126,130	38,347,108	141,442	38,488,550	4,299,047	-240,688	33,948,815	8,986,606	11,190,709	49,601	1,091,227	658,659
2019	56,427,418	39,275,314	220,522	39,495,836	4,426,139	-188,480	34,881,217	9,451,519	12,094,682	51,735	1,090,696	658,244
2020	60,747,303	39,307,220	250,370	39,557,590	4,435,444	-211,932	34,910,214	9,336,421	16,500,668	55,794	1,088,776	618,600
2021	63,471,203	41,594,071	259,189	41,853,260	4,710,367	-179,911	36,962,982	9,484,226	17,023,995	58,500	1,084,973	632,354

Personal Income and Employment by Area: Rockford, IL

(Thousands of dollars, except as noted.)

Year	Personal income, total	Earnings by place of work			Less: Contributions for government social insurance	Plus: Adjustment for residence	Equals: Net earnings by place of residence	Plus: Dividends, interest, and rent	Plus: Personal current transfer receipts	Per capita personal income (dollars)	Population (persons)	Total employment
		Nonfarm	Farm	Total								
1970	1,156,998	1,035,712	7,477	1,043,189	70,694	-47,053	925,442	150,923	80,633	4,259	271,661	127,617
1971	1,222,779	1,076,529	10,151	1,086,680	75,477	-49,191	962,012	160,534	100,233	4,510	271,149	123,947
1972	1,345,050	1,195,710	10,445	1,206,155	89,405	-54,089	1,062,661	172,444	109,945	4,961	271,136	129,119
1973	1,512,261	1,355,735	17,225	1,372,960	117,718	-61,946	1,193,296	193,662	125,303	5,535	273,201	137,581
1974	1,646,252	1,469,984	7,638	1,477,622	132,750	-64,978	1,279,894	220,675	145,683	5,992	274,734	139,257
1975	1,767,024	1,503,986	20,025	1,524,011	130,653	-64,179	1,329,179	244,670	193,175	6,443	274,255	133,933
1976	1,951,534	1,678,631	14,558	1,693,189	148,983	-67,732	1,476,474	262,294	212,766	7,132	273,627	136,512
1977	2,143,587	1,865,124	12,755	1,877,879	167,649	-73,687	1,636,543	288,163	218,881	7,831	273,731	140,705
1978	2,407,127	2,148,911	12,304	2,161,215	200,479	-97,243	1,863,493	321,729	221,905	8,719	276,063	147,308
1979	2,666,729	2,377,406	18,108	2,395,514	228,962	-107,646	2,058,906	361,673	246,150	9,629	276,951	150,437
1980	2,874,426	2,457,490	-577	2,456,913	233,655	-111,107	2,112,151	448,106	314,169	10,272	279,829	144,840
1981	3,194,602	2,645,891	16,659	2,662,550	268,965	-115,980	2,277,605	557,030	359,967	11,385	280,591	144,654
1982	3,295,387	2,565,655	12,458	2,578,113	262,571	-91,201	2,224,341	646,725	424,321	11,815	278,911	137,928
1983	3,408,355	2,657,579	-11,555	2,646,024	274,372	-90,827	2,280,825	682,678	444,852	12,289	277,354	136,046
1984	3,814,562	3,013,873	24,062	3,037,935	324,914	-112,051	2,600,970	782,837	430,755	13,770	277,028	143,578
1985	4,033,822	3,215,941	40,072	3,256,013	353,131	-125,638	2,777,244	801,484	455,094	14,478	278,623	147,717
1986	4,259,643	3,440,924	30,056	3,470,980	377,817	-144,736	2,948,427	830,303	480,913	15,287	278,638	151,509
1987	4,480,571	3,651,401	27,066	3,678,467	393,105	-148,015	3,137,347	838,118	505,106	16,056	279,051	154,960
1988	4,888,050	4,080,969	15,656	4,096,625	449,313	-169,655	3,477,657	883,657	526,736	17,472	279,763	161,185
1989	5,228,103	4,249,693	28,887	4,278,580	468,941	-162,768	3,646,871	1,014,445	566,787	18,568	281,563	163,402
1990	5,406,988	4,428,040	30,072	4,458,112	476,477	-165,565	3,816,070	973,457	617,461	18,992	284,702	167,347
1991	5,497,536	4,449,379	12,533	4,461,912	489,174	-128,105	3,844,633	973,997	678,906	18,964	289,895	165,457
1992	5,934,172	4,692,422	21,945	4,714,367	506,653	-108,370	4,099,344	1,045,977	788,851	20,164	294,298	165,482
1993	6,169,996	4,892,878	12,180	4,905,058	536,299	-100,567	4,268,192	1,072,386	829,418	20,664	298,582	168,660
1994	6,641,656	5,368,671	27,611	5,396,282	594,036	-123,354	4,678,892	1,128,461	834,303	21,980	302,172	175,923
1995	7,105,540	5,736,995	18,000	5,754,995	632,099	-119,336	5,003,560	1,206,442	895,538	23,246	305,671	184,417
1996	7,456,330	5,931,013	42,600	5,973,613	646,241	-115,225	5,212,147	1,301,033	943,150	24,080	309,644	186,765
1997	7,786,871	6,155,794	28,260	6,184,054	666,793	-99,952	5,417,309	1,398,331	971,231	24,931	312,342	188,652
1998	8,180,825	6,476,377	27,894	6,504,271	694,598	-107,003	5,702,670	1,459,746	1,018,409	25,969	315,025	191,098
1999	8,487,569	6,770,719	20,107	6,790,826	714,536	-76,077	6,000,213	1,445,392	1,041,964	26,724	317,596	192,185
2000	8,872,137	6,994,786	23,148	7,017,934	726,990	-66,529	6,224,415	1,541,730	1,105,992	27,636	321,033	194,248
2001	9,013,987	7,022,150	18,446	7,040,596	744,069	-12,509	6,284,018	1,491,341	1,238,628	27,887	323,229	190,203
2002	9,245,983	7,223,105	10,301	7,233,406	761,026	14,363	6,486,743	1,407,338	1,351,902	28,384	325,747	188,465
2003	9,526,450	7,308,989	10,102	7,319,091	775,629	58,552	6,602,014	1,496,157	1,428,279	28,914	329,472	187,307
2004	9,776,073	7,502,155	27,058	7,529,213	811,121	122,611	6,840,703	1,435,086	1,500,284	29,426	332,230	189,270
2005	10,197,539	7,803,106	10,541	7,813,647	872,262	190,862	7,132,247	1,422,241	1,643,051	30,359	335,903	189,252
2006	11,028,795	8,310,280	9,331	8,319,611	921,579	282,744	7,680,776	1,615,042	1,732,977	32,323	341,202	192,536
2007	11,690,041	8,633,913	34,035	8,667,948	954,330	357,241	8,070,859	1,698,055	1,921,127	33,640	347,503	196,276
2008	11,942,964	8,585,976	31,970	8,617,946	950,494	395,579	8,063,031	1,717,048	2,162,885	34,129	349,937	193,038
2009	11,561,763	7,929,107	2,585	7,931,692	875,266	353,079	7,409,505	1,659,456	2,492,802	33,056	349,766	180,372
2010	11,829,766	8,056,170	5,123	8,061,293	894,266	301,571	7,468,598	1,655,926	2,705,242	33,878	349,184	178,730
2011	12,255,563	8,439,284	58,460	8,497,744	854,915	277,430	7,920,259	1,766,509	2,568,795	35,238	347,790	182,051
2012	12,548,520	8,730,857	14,684	8,745,541	895,130	259,589	8,110,000	1,879,999	2,558,521	36,282	345,857	183,925
2013	12,841,954	8,866,561	84,217	8,950,778	1,012,450	310,899	8,249,227	1,907,975	2,684,752	37,251	344,743	183,163
2014	13,163,594	9,211,565	21,500	9,233,065	1,034,568	262,798	8,461,295	2,000,297	2,702,002	38,236	344,269	186,119
2015	13,690,638	9,564,695	-13,484	9,551,211	1,051,458	271,604	8,771,357	2,030,966	2,888,315	39,913	343,015	187,486
2016	13,744,257	9,536,705	39,439	9,576,144	1,062,500	274,009	8,787,653	2,038,496	2,918,108	40,147	342,349	186,261
2017	14,245,335	9,845,993	6,364	9,852,357	1,096,741	315,268	9,070,884	2,159,634	3,014,817	41,755	341,163	183,476
2018	14,792,240	10,418,021	10,313	10,428,334	1,169,217	257,945	9,517,062	2,177,725	3,097,453	43,457	340,385	187,417
2019	15,017,806	10,457,777	-178	10,457,599	1,180,208	272,875	9,550,266	2,266,328	3,201,212	44,225	339,575	185,109
2020	16,114,299	10,050,587	17,190	10,067,777	1,138,557	436,903	9,366,123	2,267,048	4,481,128	47,650	338,184	173,667
2021	17,197,161	10,524,834	50,678	10,575,512	1,169,475	487,681	9,893,718	2,287,185	5,016,258	51,140	336,278	175,502

Personal Income and Employment by Area: Rocky Mount, NC

(Thousands of dollars, except as noted.)

Year	Personal income, total	Earnings by place of work			Less: Contributions for government social insurance	Plus: Adjustment for residence	Equals: Net earnings by place of residence	Plus: Dividends, interest, and rent	Plus: Personal current transfer receipts	Per capita personal income (dollars)	Population (persons)	Total employment
		Nonfarm	Farm	Total								
1970	333,106	242,455	32,529	274,984	17,855	4,101	261,230	39,404	32,472	2,986	111,571	53,924
1971	364,218	272,178	28,080	300,258	20,676	4,257	283,839	43,190	37,189	3,243	112,296	54,910
1972	421,041	317,025	36,223	353,248	25,068	3,000	331,180	48,555	41,306	3,707	113,571	58,004
1973	492,168	369,709	52,346	422,055	33,369	582	389,268	55,678	47,222	4,278	115,045	61,874
1974	553,096	414,334	56,786	471,120	39,137	359	432,342	63,533	57,221	4,752	116,381	63,125
1975	595,696	434,918	53,180	488,098	40,477	125	447,746	70,136	77,814	5,040	118,189	60,327
1976	673,334	500,034	61,036	561,070	47,479	-2,738	510,853	77,751	84,730	5,629	119,609	62,983
1977	715,562	554,134	37,517	591,651	52,255	-4,172	535,224	88,615	91,723	5,894	121,414	64,333
1978	808,523	623,600	53,060	676,660	60,064	-7,143	609,453	99,633	99,437	6,605	122,406	65,387
1979	855,459	689,839	13,722	703,561	68,664	-7,809	627,088	113,155	115,216	6,941	123,247	66,769
1980	948,514	740,481	15,654	756,135	73,744	-8,992	673,399	138,051	137,064	7,683	123,463	65,511
1981	1,106,869	829,235	51,760	880,995	88,646	-13,378	778,971	170,280	157,618	8,899	124,388	66,742
1982	1,183,916	864,496	57,823	922,319	93,013	-14,710	814,596	194,130	175,190	9,432	125,524	64,937
1983	1,260,798	955,638	34,109	989,747	103,210	-18,240	868,297	203,957	188,544	9,969	126,478	66,048
1984	1,422,878	1,064,211	66,167	1,130,378	118,052	-24,708	987,618	235,952	199,308	11,194	127,115	68,538
1985	1,516,599	1,145,223	62,735	1,207,958	129,135	-28,253	1,050,570	253,437	212,592	11,775	128,799	69,053
1986	1,607,566	1,256,602	47,421	1,304,023	144,462	-39,821	1,119,740	266,015	221,811	12,382	129,830	71,452
1987	1,717,662	1,357,616	60,304	1,417,920	153,734	-51,489	1,212,697	275,404	229,561	13,100	131,116	71,862
1988	1,894,660	1,501,142	81,572	1,582,714	174,782	-63,524	1,344,408	303,914	246,338	14,372	131,826	75,005
1989	2,041,531	1,582,409	82,267	1,664,676	184,173	-71,766	1,408,737	360,785	272,009	15,424	132,358	76,775
1990	2,125,903	1,645,906	96,111	1,742,017	196,221	-90,294	1,455,502	366,181	304,220	15,904	133,668	76,391
1991	2,210,385	1,719,375	96,229	1,815,604	207,524	-111,281	1,496,799	367,380	346,206	16,396	134,810	76,478
1992	2,351,824	1,829,863	90,608	1,920,471	218,040	-110,446	1,591,985	375,431	384,408	17,306	135,899	77,279
1993	2,485,837	1,909,455	94,901	2,004,356	228,571	-103,069	1,672,716	395,752	417,369	18,111	137,253	77,560
1994	2,605,480	1,997,106	109,109	2,106,215	241,277	-102,528	1,762,410	411,687	431,383	18,746	138,990	77,617
1995	2,766,386	2,106,980	112,631	2,219,611	254,933	-127,072	1,837,606	444,905	483,875	19,688	140,508	80,590
1996	2,985,395	2,185,720	117,978	2,303,698	261,394	-77,236	1,965,068	490,661	529,666	21,088	141,570	81,061
1997	3,195,701	2,282,622	148,423	2,431,045	270,265	-36,202	2,124,578	520,654	550,469	22,378	142,807	79,237
1998	3,288,080	2,357,162	127,184	2,484,346	279,931	-35,943	2,168,472	552,162	567,446	23,009	142,903	78,718
1999	3,348,879	2,439,149	70,097	2,509,246	290,405	-28,264	2,190,577	539,582	618,720	23,364	143,333	78,734
2000	3,511,477	2,529,017	122,546	2,651,563	301,371	-37,893	2,312,299	570,341	628,837	24,532	143,139	79,541
2001	3,682,887	2,636,071	112,087	2,748,158	310,330	-26,009	2,411,819	578,832	692,236	25,570	144,034	78,749
2002	3,661,912	2,631,103	48,510	2,679,613	308,748	-8,698	2,362,167	547,772	751,973	25,307	144,698	77,715
2003	3,768,097	2,690,441	50,122	2,740,563	321,482	7,745	2,426,826	560,945	780,326	25,900	145,487	76,799
2004	3,968,147	2,803,954	77,509	2,881,463	331,359	150	2,550,254	589,281	828,612	27,119	146,326	77,368
2005	4,120,573	2,847,525	107,448	2,954,973	341,731	13,771	2,627,013	594,536	899,024	28,026	147,027	77,492
2006	4,327,201	2,975,226	82,469	3,057,695	357,337	22,253	2,722,611	635,251	969,339	29,187	148,256	79,869
2007	4,559,152	3,063,648	63,414	3,127,062	372,658	56,213	2,810,617	722,754	1,025,781	30,467	149,644	81,585
2008	4,813,988	3,082,915	79,840	3,162,755	376,997	66,832	2,852,590	788,409	1,172,989	31,852	151,138	80,079
2009	4,798,420	2,976,789	89,868	3,066,657	366,331	52,424	2,752,750	752,532	1,293,138	31,625	151,729	76,106
2010	4,858,922	3,032,674	70,673	3,103,347	367,378	83,450	2,819,419	683,619	1,355,884	31,880	152,414	74,961
2011	4,954,017	3,007,748	69,333	3,077,081	335,585	80,220	2,821,716	749,411	1,382,890	32,632	151,816	76,701
2012	5,112,784	3,108,733	75,642	3,184,375	340,317	67,848	2,911,906	774,028	1,426,850	33,884	150,892	74,498
2013	5,000,882	3,026,105	82,781	3,108,886	378,871	52,141	2,782,156	785,743	1,432,983	33,365	149,882	73,881
2014	5,201,466	3,101,738	92,663	3,194,401	387,254	69,121	2,876,268	841,858	1,483,340	35,086	148,247	73,845
2015	5,320,921	3,204,101	80,370	3,284,471	401,477	51,220	2,934,214	879,429	1,507,278	36,311	146,536	74,081
2016	5,356,608	3,178,917	80,173	3,259,090	397,366	83,356	2,945,080	880,450	1,531,078	36,667	146,089	74,139
2017	5,503,209	3,191,351	107,564	3,298,915	399,268	116,076	3,015,723	920,456	1,567,030	37,839	145,439	73,596
2018	5,697,383	3,350,269	51,600	3,401,869	412,586	125,920	3,115,203	958,708	1,623,472	39,416	144,544	74,465
2019	6,012,671	3,472,189	72,103	3,544,292	427,399	140,948	3,257,841	1,071,768	1,683,062	41,793	143,867	74,439
2020	6,439,992	3,487,229	66,402	3,553,631	435,140	171,744	3,290,235	1,069,873	2,079,884	44,808	143,724	71,849
2021	7,006,203	3,770,565	85,715	3,856,280	463,515	115,531	3,508,296	1,097,961	2,399,946	48,812	143,535	73,618

Personal Income and Employment by Area: Rome, GA

(Thousands of dollars, except as noted.)

Year	Personal income, total	Earnings by place of work			Less: Contributions for government social insurance	Plus: Adjustment for residence	Equals: Net earnings by place of residence	Plus: Dividends, interest, and rent	Plus: Personal current transfer receipts	Per capita personal income (dollars)	Population (persons)	Total employment
		Nonfarm	Farm	Total								
1970	249,840	213,913	1,300	215,213	14,268	-1,910	199,035	28,791	22,014	3,374	74,051	34,937
1971	272,366	231,703	1,480	233,183	16,110	-2,657	214,416	32,193	25,757	3,596	75,747	35,869
1972	304,137	261,379	1,752	263,131	19,108	-4,167	239,856	35,731	28,550	3,988	76,267	37,626
1973	343,221	296,170	2,816	298,986	24,839	-4,241	269,906	40,048	33,267	4,448	77,161	39,299
1974	378,749	322,845	1,544	324,389	28,021	-5,082	291,286	45,896	41,567	4,857	77,988	39,874
1975	403,089	325,740	1,467	327,207	27,711	-5,296	294,200	51,935	56,954	5,108	78,917	37,308
1976	447,558	367,645	1,443	369,088	31,912	-6,161	331,015	56,565	59,978	5,630	79,499	38,135
1977	489,905	404,988	1,192	406,180	35,013	-6,494	364,673	62,561	62,671	6,084	80,526	38,921
1978	533,718	441,624	1,222	442,846	39,348	-5,707	397,791	68,932	66,995	6,655	80,194	39,774
1979	592,760	488,966	3,957	492,923	45,262	-7,307	440,354	77,597	74,809	7,450	79,565	40,267
1980	654,346	521,924	925	522,849	48,203	-6,347	468,299	96,455	89,592	8,194	79,860	39,476
1981	718,459	555,272	2,734	558,006	54,995	-6,744	496,267	118,916	103,276	8,987	79,948	39,772
1982	747,798	563,932	4,178	568,110	56,719	-10,482	500,909	132,261	114,628	9,360	79,897	38,189
1983	800,844	604,816	1,948	606,764	61,168	-12,451	533,145	144,665	123,034	10,116	79,163	37,795
1984	869,932	655,564	2,528	658,092	68,094	-11,108	578,890	160,885	130,157	10,981	79,223	39,730
1985	925,102	700,726	1,250	701,976	74,220	-10,795	616,961	169,026	139,115	11,634	79,520	40,092
1986	1,000,069	761,145	583	761,728	81,288	-12,066	668,374	184,185	147,510	12,532	79,804	41,120
1987	1,076,317	828,892	-317	828,575	87,534	-13,544	727,497	194,587	154,233	13,407	80,281	42,515
1988	1,158,233	888,941	2,433	891,374	96,776	-14,024	780,574	207,733	169,926	14,291	81,046	43,653
1989	1,241,132	937,347	3,481	940,828	102,938	-15,783	822,107	238,611	180,414	15,268	81,290	44,055
1990	1,329,271	1,009,357	3,517	1,012,874	110,076	-23,092	879,706	250,317	199,248	16,313	81,483	44,628
1991	1,405,143	1,070,441	4,878	1,075,319	118,413	-33,187	923,719	255,408	226,016	17,079	82,274	44,515
1992	1,511,817	1,165,599	6,001	1,171,600	126,865	-42,110	1,002,625	259,181	250,011	18,193	83,100	45,569
1993	1,569,706	1,206,685	5,358	1,212,043	131,717	-43,000	1,037,326	265,297	267,083	18,666	84,094	47,211
1994	1,671,089	1,293,448	6,647	1,300,095	142,393	-51,271	1,106,431	282,337	282,321	19,680	84,911	49,360
1995	1,728,012	1,301,422	5,181	1,306,603	143,174	-43,610	1,119,819	305,360	302,833	20,078	86,063	49,299
1996	1,840,615	1,378,724	7,193	1,385,917	149,583	-49,917	1,186,417	333,993	320,205	21,142	87,061	49,613
1997	1,909,106	1,420,160	6,980	1,427,140	151,216	-47,639	1,228,285	352,578	328,243	21,697	87,991	50,251
1998	1,981,571	1,467,168	7,916	1,475,084	156,805	-40,163	1,278,116	363,808	339,647	22,307	88,833	49,963
1999	2,079,292	1,569,848	7,629	1,577,477	164,849	-41,232	1,371,396	345,007	362,889	23,191	89,659	49,836
2000	2,171,212	1,598,953	6,026	1,604,979	168,078	-34,627	1,402,274	384,041	384,897	23,902	90,837	50,348
2001	2,296,918	1,705,546	9,422	1,714,968	179,471	-62,607	1,472,890	398,959	425,069	25,191	91,181	50,251
2002	2,386,026	1,786,759	4,626	1,791,385	187,416	-82,816	1,521,153	388,796	476,077	25,768	92,597	50,114
2003	2,475,527	1,866,190	6,325	1,872,515	193,893	-99,458	1,579,164	420,637	475,726	26,465	93,539	50,560
2004	2,613,417	2,012,541	10,612	2,023,153	215,246	-125,780	1,682,127	401,866	529,424	27,798	94,014	51,690
2005	2,635,816	1,929,912	11,973	1,941,885	208,442	-103,210	1,630,233	434,696	570,887	27,942	94,332	51,414
2006	2,727,096	2,038,418	5,496	2,043,914	221,141	-138,420	1,684,353	448,204	594,539	28,657	95,165	52,717
2007	2,820,950	2,033,082	10,244	2,043,326	219,276	-135,280	1,688,770	510,054	622,126	29,598	95,308	52,357
2008	2,878,791	2,055,635	11,410	2,067,045	234,015	-148,396	1,684,634	521,105	673,052	30,012	95,922	51,533
2009	2,835,700	2,047,078	9,894	2,056,972	230,775	-190,307	1,635,890	456,507	743,303	29,421	96,383	49,708
2010	2,927,792	2,087,623	6,918	2,094,541	236,264	-206,658	1,651,619	464,123	812,050	30,360	96,436	49,387
2011	3,009,899	2,106,859	4,130	2,110,989	211,589	-222,246	1,677,154	479,056	853,689	31,296	96,174	49,159
2012	3,047,663	2,170,371	16,427	2,186,798	218,350	-235,565	1,732,883	476,329	838,451	31,765	95,944	49,239
2013	3,075,873	2,220,967	19,029	2,239,996	250,638	-233,899	1,755,459	467,181	853,233	32,073	95,901	49,427
2014	3,236,718	2,321,238	21,294	2,342,532	258,763	-231,497	1,852,272	498,733	885,713	33,751	95,900	50,610
2015	3,381,440	2,415,607	21,398	2,437,005	267,868	-233,715	1,935,422	539,385	906,633	35,145	96,214	51,189
2016	3,472,506	2,453,818	11,695	2,465,513	273,734	-232,616	1,959,163	583,999	929,344	35,898	96,732	51,873
2017	3,555,683	2,517,246	13,740	2,530,986	280,409	-213,464	2,037,113	569,544	949,026	36,483	97,461	52,969
2018	3,685,342	2,594,937	7,695	2,602,632	293,150	-199,315	2,110,167	581,037	994,138	37,640	97,909	53,230
2019	3,835,433	2,627,830	8,196	2,636,026	301,480	-189,261	2,145,285	647,758	1,042,390	39,008	98,324	53,268
2020	4,082,846	2,613,553	4,550	2,618,103	303,405	-211,005	2,103,693	645,994	1,333,159	41,411	98,593	51,966
2021	4,425,204	2,847,283	8,820	2,856,103	328,583	-233,583	2,293,937	664,142	1,467,125	44,803	98,771	53,562

Personal Income and Employment by Area: Sacramento-Roseville-Folsom, CA

(Thousands of dollars, except as noted.)

Year	Personal income, total	Earnings by place of work			Less: Contributions for government social insurance	Plus: Adjustment for residence	Equals: Net earnings by place of residence	Plus: Dividends, interest, and rent	Plus: Personal current transfer receipts	Per capita personal income (dollars)	Population (persons)	Total employment
		Nonfarm	Farm	Total								
1970	4,056,127	3,019,145	78,526	3,097,671	167,543	46,767	2,976,895	667,330	411,902	4,761	852,036	360,459
1971	4,462,068	3,312,958	79,496	3,392,454	189,765	46,656	3,249,345	745,796	466,927	5,093	876,053	368,520
1972	4,928,736	3,674,421	99,494	3,773,915	223,152	48,815	3,599,578	824,161	504,997	5,460	902,647	385,583
1973	5,445,749	4,031,560	137,550	4,169,110	277,364	53,004	3,944,750	942,008	558,991	6,012	905,830	400,639
1974	6,137,885	4,441,915	192,552	4,634,467	315,137	59,040	4,378,370	1,092,913	666,602	6,619	927,304	417,125
1975	6,886,120	4,928,191	162,706	5,090,897	347,042	73,596	4,817,451	1,233,363	835,306	7,257	948,850	431,998
1976	7,619,961	5,541,048	109,773	5,650,821	401,160	77,921	5,327,582	1,358,501	933,878	7,847	971,060	450,281
1977	8,521,066	6,224,320	134,273	6,358,593	461,389	86,478	5,983,682	1,527,523	1,009,861	8,521	1,000,056	471,705
1978	9,760,416	7,156,718	141,698	7,298,416	547,397	103,593	6,854,612	1,785,780	1,120,024	9,378	1,040,724	504,114
1979	11,064,177	8,108,914	160,588	8,269,502	656,579	107,234	7,720,157	2,060,878	1,283,142	10,326	1,071,481	532,619
1980	12,427,490	8,744,342	214,973	8,959,315	690,972	132,075	8,400,418	2,486,906	1,540,166	11,227	1,106,955	544,041
1981	13,762,492	9,487,978	150,893	9,638,871	817,934	117,513	8,938,450	2,970,629	1,853,413	12,143	1,133,346	557,728
1982	14,772,197	10,104,581	117,568	10,222,149	889,275	124,855	9,457,729	3,287,053	2,027,415	12,642	1,168,540	565,530
1983	15,968,174	10,974,796	70,342	11,045,138	1,005,026	131,656	10,171,768	3,646,950	2,149,456	13,374	1,193,993	586,240
1984	17,914,310	12,445,247	159,386	12,604,633	1,184,438	135,814	11,556,009	4,085,170	2,273,131	14,703	1,218,388	613,520
1985	19,823,351	13,983,584	158,081	14,141,665	1,353,674	131,066	12,919,057	4,426,572	2,477,722	15,849	1,250,764	649,028
1986	21,645,699	15,511,373	154,651	15,666,024	1,529,413	132,797	14,269,408	4,691,999	2,684,292	16,844	1,285,092	678,664
1987	23,462,946	17,127,656	194,126	17,321,782	1,701,695	130,664	15,750,751	4,871,151	2,841,044	17,625	1,331,264	718,562
1988	25,581,391	18,839,745	194,123	19,033,868	1,947,474	140,321	17,226,715	5,257,135	3,097,541	18,552	1,378,887	756,390
1989	28,335,790	20,683,946	199,257	20,883,203	2,153,381	123,653	18,853,475	6,054,295	3,428,020	19,836	1,428,491	791,265
1990	31,027,352	22,952,847	219,420	23,172,267	2,372,660	117,914	20,917,521	6,279,222	3,830,609	20,393	1,521,462	837,598
1991	32,889,865	24,411,529	189,703	24,601,232	2,541,216	75,526	22,135,542	6,477,264	4,277,059	20,989	1,566,994	846,203
1992	34,867,420	25,780,556	192,455	25,973,011	2,668,907	20,321	23,324,425	6,572,785	4,970,210	21,910	1,591,373	838,258
1993	35,759,371	26,310,906	236,163	26,547,069	2,739,299	38,692	23,846,462	6,694,507	5,218,402	22,237	1,608,074	837,172
1994	37,791,252	28,056,083	232,174	28,288,257	2,921,374	-8,253	25,358,630	7,120,544	5,312,078	23,307	1,621,444	870,499
1995	40,329,219	29,820,984	215,440	30,036,424	3,057,859	-79,255	26,899,310	7,822,312	5,607,597	24,515	1,645,098	886,610
1996	42,252,093	31,183,514	236,265	31,419,779	3,130,865	-98,637	28,190,277	8,150,930	5,910,886	25,262	1,672,583	914,825
1997	45,030,721	33,521,185	224,093	33,745,278	3,325,745	-160,274	30,259,259	8,813,320	5,958,142	26,481	1,700,488	938,908
1998	48,467,457	36,574,979	198,079	36,773,058	3,593,508	-187,080	32,992,470	9,154,268	6,320,719	27,986	1,731,847	973,971
1999	52,270,354	39,828,950	273,415	40,102,365	3,921,445	-166,246	36,014,674	9,574,693	6,680,987	29,577	1,767,237	1,017,726
2000	56,988,800	44,126,618	233,133	44,359,751	4,286,203	-145,306	39,928,242	10,072,410	6,988,148	31,521	1,807,949	1,041,891
2001	62,230,223	48,812,679	203,317	49,015,996	4,839,635	-176,967	43,999,394	10,425,574	7,805,255	33,344	1,866,310	1,084,938
2002	64,729,815	51,459,767	202,967	51,662,734	5,162,239	-193,945	46,306,550	10,117,741	8,305,524	33,652	1,923,508	1,099,722
2003	68,622,200	54,378,964	218,002	54,596,966	5,525,135	-187,992	48,883,839	10,953,079	8,785,282	34,824	1,970,542	1,124,044
2004	72,756,729	57,972,715	253,363	58,226,078	6,059,543	-292,307	51,874,228	11,548,922	9,333,579	36,221	2,008,663	1,157,385
2005	76,015,669	61,023,372	233,954	61,257,326	6,413,768	-382,290	54,461,268	11,669,689	9,884,712	37,357	2,034,850	1,191,410
2006	80,935,289	64,201,333	214,515	64,415,848	6,547,339	-368,764	57,499,745	12,623,229	10,812,315	39,329	2,057,885	1,214,206
2007	84,610,648	65,680,356	318,775	65,999,131	6,549,561	-333,427	59,116,143	13,920,425	11,574,080	40,635	2,082,217	1,232,558
2008	87,418,629	65,743,061	339,258	66,082,319	6,639,581	-288,976	59,153,762	15,108,606	13,156,261	41,464	2,108,310	1,209,043
2009	85,624,717	63,114,944	402,534	63,517,478	6,434,870	-159,773	56,922,835	14,063,678	14,638,204	40,149	2,132,657	1,162,375
2010	88,002,266	63,767,081	299,667	64,066,748	6,350,936	-36,426	57,679,386	13,944,553	16,378,327	40,863	2,153,610	1,136,573
2011	92,628,645	66,428,184	340,643	66,768,827	5,959,493	16,413	60,825,747	15,271,088	16,531,810	42,628	2,172,929	1,139,388
2012	96,635,870	69,138,651	443,717	69,582,368	6,161,265	179,451	63,600,554	16,233,754	16,801,562	44,121	2,190,259	1,176,096
2013	99,926,263	72,259,016	477,232	72,736,248	7,143,480	205,151	65,797,919	16,482,981	17,645,363	45,205	2,210,494	1,211,648
2014	105,918,106	75,836,106	460,919	76,297,025	7,508,661	209,997	68,998,361	17,893,074	19,026,671	47,182	2,244,867	1,241,767
2015	113,228,396	80,778,136	476,873	81,255,009	7,943,472	392,329	73,703,866	18,849,289	20,675,241	49,778	2,274,649	1,278,950
2016	117,819,184	83,959,511	419,337	84,378,848	8,309,150	512,183	76,581,881	19,628,215	21,609,088	51,091	2,306,062	1,309,331
2017	122,651,976	87,963,445	420,001	88,383,446	8,734,613	671,960	80,320,793	20,784,895	21,546,288	52,481	2,337,065	1,337,172
2018	128,522,500	92,523,534	343,111	92,866,645	9,306,744	684,119	84,244,020	21,565,213	22,713,267	54,407	2,362,237	1,378,655
2019	136,311,491	97,251,243	311,756	97,562,999	9,878,938	604,015	88,288,076	23,835,175	24,188,240	57,151	2,385,124	1,395,547
2020	149,158,465	100,668,614	334,298	101,002,912	10,282,551	647,430	91,367,791	24,051,830	33,738,844	62,166	2,399,351	1,364,288
2021	159,087,879	108,012,897	276,506	108,289,403	10,927,009	675,927	98,038,321	24,700,734	36,348,824	65,972	2,411,428	1,411,813

Personal Income and Employment by Area: Saginaw, MI

(Thousands of dollars, except as noted.)

Year	Personal income, total	Earnings by place of work			Less: Contributions for government social insurance	Plus: Adjustment for residence	Equals: Net earnings by place of residence	Plus: Dividends, interest, and rent	Plus: Personal current transfer receipts	Per capita personal income (dollars)	Population (persons)	Total employment
		Nonfarm	Farm	Total								
1970	833,147	725,462	9,119	734,581	51,926	-38,394	644,261	112,392	76,494	3,781	220,370	84,309
1971	967,531	865,612	7,978	873,590	63,632	-52,762	757,196	120,325	90,010	4,335	223,170	89,057
1972	1,073,395	964,157	11,033	975,190	75,246	-58,727	841,217	129,388	102,790	4,790	224,074	92,541
1973	1,201,599	1,086,788	19,860	1,106,648	98,608	-66,015	942,025	141,516	118,058	5,336	225,199	96,459
1974	1,268,242	1,084,061	39,378	1,123,439	101,700	-56,915	964,824	159,063	144,355	5,614	225,920	95,113
1975	1,373,369	1,157,164	19,777	1,176,941	106,544	-58,140	1,012,257	177,262	183,850	6,084	225,723	92,153
1976	1,569,810	1,393,476	13,623	1,407,099	130,291	-84,150	1,192,658	190,532	186,620	6,942	226,118	96,864
1977	1,756,811	1,595,456	14,954	1,610,410	148,983	-110,293	1,351,134	213,583	192,094	7,744	226,861	100,874
1978	1,949,817	1,794,530	14,664	1,809,194	172,866	-129,099	1,507,229	232,162	210,426	8,585	227,115	104,515
1979	2,106,754	1,915,839	16,481	1,932,320	190,933	-140,635	1,600,752	259,852	246,150	9,292	226,732	105,175
1980	2,229,860	1,868,510	19,111	1,887,621	183,724	-133,175	1,570,722	308,356	350,782	9,807	227,373	98,304
1981	2,375,494	2,017,804	14,596	2,032,400	214,908	-156,920	1,660,572	368,161	346,761	10,599	224,132	98,329
1982	2,375,661	1,902,316	3,440	1,905,756	205,352	-137,680	1,562,724	418,210	394,727	10,753	220,925	91,223
1983	2,529,764	2,058,947	-1,869	2,057,078	227,716	-162,989	1,666,373	450,756	412,635	11,616	217,784	91,228
1984	2,758,499	2,273,797	10,295	2,284,092	260,828	-199,036	1,824,228	508,736	425,535	12,729	216,710	94,924
1985	2,939,403	2,492,114	8,707	2,500,821	291,692	-243,514	1,965,615	536,252	437,536	13,669	215,040	98,880
1986	3,019,514	2,556,163	2,888	2,559,051	300,357	-256,911	2,001,783	556,742	460,989	14,046	214,972	99,967
1987	3,082,536	2,634,909	16,687	2,651,596	304,617	-292,725	2,054,254	556,365	471,917	14,398	214,098	103,044
1988	3,227,836	2,801,764	13,870	2,815,634	332,057	-329,793	2,153,784	581,928	492,124	15,117	213,522	105,620
1989	3,422,445	2,910,020	23,482	2,933,502	345,747	-357,693	2,230,062	655,736	536,647	16,121	212,303	107,071
1990	3,522,299	2,976,864	15,114	2,991,978	358,915	-352,085	2,280,978	655,820	585,501	16,609	212,071	106,622
1991	3,621,768	3,057,343	14,911	3,072,254	373,654	-368,169	2,330,431	644,447	646,890	17,053	212,384	105,668
1992	3,799,081	3,233,318	13,108	3,246,426	388,938	-394,114	2,463,374	654,486	681,221	17,885	212,421	107,274
1993	3,991,889	3,377,601	16,127	3,393,728	412,583	-407,990	2,573,155	688,362	730,372	18,815	212,165	107,006
1994	4,230,696	3,624,150	1,699	3,625,849	446,685	-445,374	2,733,790	753,479	743,427	19,931	212,262	109,557
1995	4,412,972	3,737,765	11,843	3,749,608	460,296	-432,932	2,856,380	790,809	765,783	20,808	212,076	112,965
1996	4,612,938	3,901,180	7,989	3,909,169	466,412	-439,928	3,002,829	822,060	788,049	21,767	211,927	115,285
1997	4,844,658	4,059,224	6,680	4,065,904	481,095	-441,197	3,143,612	851,159	849,887	22,916	211,406	116,361
1998	4,944,371	4,223,787	2,212	4,225,999	491,016	-492,135	3,242,848	850,856	850,667	23,451	210,839	114,873
1999	5,174,032	4,510,783	19,876	4,530,659	518,341	-572,911	3,439,407	805,177	929,448	24,591	210,400	116,817
2000	5,416,010	4,680,876	8,449	4,689,325	530,035	-550,231	3,609,059	841,306	965,645	25,803	209,899	118,358
2001	5,387,282	4,595,219	-1,232	4,593,987	540,393	-559,351	3,494,243	832,296	1,060,743	25,720	209,460	117,341
2002	5,297,727	4,537,002	14,350	4,551,352	533,237	-549,067	3,469,048	730,470	1,098,209	25,309	209,323	114,780
2003	5,397,367	4,637,530	12,267	4,649,797	541,051	-580,000	3,528,746	717,597	1,151,024	25,855	208,755	114,389
2004	5,588,735	4,654,030	18,459	4,672,489	549,110	-525,058	3,598,321	794,914	1,195,500	26,806	208,489	113,429
2005	5,617,400	4,623,695	17,680	4,641,375	551,201	-549,674	3,540,500	813,546	1,263,354	27,089	207,368	112,826
2006	5,719,069	4,725,583	23,581	4,749,164	577,488	-570,402	3,601,274	796,500	1,321,295	27,786	205,822	111,712
2007	5,846,610	4,617,266	28,002	4,645,268	567,053	-546,865	3,531,350	872,971	1,442,289	28,781	203,144	110,931
2008	5,978,401	4,442,442	34,967	4,477,409	551,425	-497,012	3,428,972	933,394	1,616,035	29,601	201,966	106,908
2009	5,904,081	4,351,939	12,035	4,363,974	544,337	-543,823	3,275,814	857,511	1,770,756	29,398	200,835	103,080
2010	6,125,456	4,484,996	14,060	4,499,056	548,664	-546,451	3,403,941	827,109	1,894,406	30,647	199,871	102,853
2011	6,364,183	4,683,316	44,170	4,727,486	509,909	-632,376	3,585,201	904,384	1,874,598	31,992	198,929	106,093
2012	6,437,074	4,756,187	46,152	4,802,339	518,920	-647,619	3,635,800	930,631	1,870,643	32,443	198,409	106,832
2013	6,524,704	4,815,337	52,994	4,868,331	593,390	-644,312	3,630,629	962,443	1,931,632	33,144	196,859	107,260
2014	6,672,721	4,920,088	11,816	4,931,904	606,509	-685,360	3,640,035	1,033,870	1,998,816	34,164	195,317	107,377
2015	6,933,173	5,032,887	12,305	5,045,192	617,642	-683,639	3,743,911	1,066,760	2,122,502	35,852	193,385	107,880
2016	7,035,907	5,183,637	-580	5,183,057	634,572	-735,809	3,812,676	1,064,511	2,158,720	36,524	192,638	108,045
2017	7,120,402	5,298,333	4,028	5,302,361	649,279	-794,719	3,858,363	1,102,116	2,159,923	37,084	192,006	107,487
2018	7,511,528	5,519,769	1,737	5,521,506	685,457	-701,463	4,134,586	1,123,788	2,253,154	39,360	190,844	108,141
2019	8,022,129	5,917,449	3,638	5,921,087	711,748	-699,594	4,509,745	1,149,851	2,362,533	42,114	190,488	107,217
2020	8,811,841	5,844,293	38,828	5,883,121	704,616	-652,001	4,526,504	1,149,846	3,135,491	46,419	189,831	99,697
2021	9,341,904	6,245,692	51,400	6,297,092	741,264	-717,068	4,838,760	1,156,640	3,346,504	49,274	189,591	102,066

Personal Income and Employment by Area: St. Cloud, MN

(Thousands of dollars, except as noted.)

		Earnings by place of work			Less: Contributions for government social insurance	Plus: Adjustment for residence	Equals: Net earnings by place of residence	Plus: Dividends, interest, and rent	Plus: Personal current transfer receipts	Per capita personal income (dollars)	Population (persons)	Total employment
Year	Personal income, total	Nonfarm	Farm	Total								
1970	357,436	258,985	33,599	292,584	17,712	-2,265	272,607	50,671	34,158	3,061	116,762	45,611
1971	386,589	281,632	29,727	311,359	19,811	-900	290,648	55,791	40,150	3,249	118,978	46,936
1972	426,393	309,563	34,216	343,779	22,669	883	321,993	60,241	44,159	3,563	119,660	49,580
1973	503,680	351,670	60,194	411,864	29,713	1,753	383,904	68,432	51,344	4,130	121,957	53,110
1974	556,113	402,792	48,200	450,992	35,883	894	416,003	79,044	61,066	4,497	123,661	55,774
1975	609,861	447,005	35,997	483,002	38,868	-169	443,965	90,991	74,905	4,829	126,283	56,483
1976	671,498	498,887	29,564	528,451	44,340	553	484,664	100,148	86,686	5,268	127,477	57,890
1977	763,536	549,214	54,897	604,111	48,945	1,835	557,001	115,303	91,232	5,874	129,994	59,900
1978	852,919	632,903	48,700	681,603	58,620	1,617	624,600	130,054	98,265	6,504	131,145	62,454
1979	961,603	730,534	42,507	773,041	70,525	-575	701,941	148,882	110,780	7,262	132,420	66,254
1980	1,065,857	797,952	29,890	827,842	76,943	-2,327	748,572	183,939	133,346	7,967	133,782	67,330
1981	1,201,287	882,347	42,718	925,065	91,716	-10,459	822,890	224,004	154,393	8,885	135,211	67,644
1982	1,300,980	926,627	45,042	971,669	98,108	-14,993	858,568	268,456	173,956	9,558	136,115	67,216
1983	1,354,161	987,690	6,554	994,244	105,252	-17,157	871,835	292,813	189,513	9,881	137,048	68,777
1984	1,534,274	1,093,977	49,024	1,143,001	118,888	-16,492	1,007,621	325,392	201,261	11,115	138,037	71,557
1985	1,628,625	1,156,771	58,156	1,214,927	127,546	-16,302	1,071,079	344,888	212,658	11,684	139,387	73,891
1986	1,753,669	1,263,620	69,841	1,333,461	142,823	-22,147	1,168,491	365,177	220,001	12,447	140,892	77,336
1987	1,863,932	1,373,562	70,479	1,444,041	155,225	-28,693	1,260,123	375,928	227,881	13,097	142,314	81,199
1988	1,981,998	1,520,001	46,186	1,566,187	178,235	-39,393	1,348,559	394,048	239,391	13,681	144,873	85,778
1989	2,198,078	1,656,907	89,932	1,746,839	194,523	-48,594	1,503,722	429,925	264,431	14,944	147,087	89,177
1990	2,329,886	1,764,780	86,059	1,850,839	208,383	-57,778	1,584,678	464,090	281,118	15,525	150,078	90,903
1991	2,414,386	1,866,203	54,334	1,920,537	223,180	-62,850	1,634,507	474,475	305,404	15,904	151,812	93,550
1992	2,608,717	2,039,064	64,252	2,103,316	240,982	-65,160	1,797,174	481,860	329,683	17,003	153,430	95,350
1993	2,716,359	2,168,034	43,475	2,211,509	258,124	-72,862	1,880,523	490,547	345,289	17,469	155,495	97,771
1994	2,873,286	2,296,169	59,763	2,355,932	276,656	-72,780	2,006,496	505,859	360,931	18,270	157,264	100,598
1995	3,014,647	2,416,425	24,637	2,441,062	290,978	-80,986	2,069,098	559,687	385,862	18,933	159,224	105,687
1996	3,273,661	2,579,640	80,604	2,660,244	306,917	-84,797	2,268,530	594,334	410,797	20,389	160,563	108,022
1997	3,386,964	2,704,388	40,355	2,744,743	321,415	-88,058	2,335,270	631,329	420,365	20,877	162,234	107,758
1998	3,786,151	3,054,756	88,684	3,143,440	361,069	-121,432	2,660,939	684,903	440,309	23,178	163,352	110,718
1999	3,967,376	3,181,294	86,353	3,267,647	375,872	-82,309	2,809,466	694,753	463,157	23,977	165,463	112,488
2000	4,260,831	3,400,899	69,031	3,469,930	398,395	-75,326	2,996,209	764,207	500,415	25,341	168,139	115,436
2001	4,594,228	3,648,912	67,566	3,716,478	422,741	-58,756	3,234,981	795,732	563,515	26,932	170,587	119,810
2002	4,820,367	3,864,304	64,211	3,928,515	446,856	-61,192	3,420,467	781,012	618,888	27,844	173,123	121,271
2003	5,060,433	3,986,479	103,589	4,090,068	465,032	-58,501	3,566,535	838,147	655,751	28,890	175,161	120,862
2004	5,332,008	4,228,422	150,726	4,379,148	493,983	-32,306	3,852,859	782,911	696,238	30,148	176,860	123,417
2005	5,482,721	4,352,964	150,900	4,503,864	514,182	-41,254	3,948,428	793,377	740,916	30,592	179,222	125,143
2006	5,771,109	4,533,327	138,561	4,671,888	546,799	-71,822	4,053,267	891,046	826,796	31,732	181,873	127,619
2007	6,130,835	4,756,275	136,040	4,892,315	573,390	-122,931	4,195,994	1,013,498	921,343	33,212	184,598	130,268
2008	6,474,035	4,862,534	226,249	5,088,783	590,080	-158,481	4,340,222	1,053,486	1,080,327	34,712	186,507	129,574
2009	6,280,710	4,793,954	112,482	4,906,436	585,162	-265,051	4,056,223	1,029,196	1,195,291	33,388	188,114	126,361
2010	6,524,750	4,887,575	171,209	5,058,784	589,580	-245,449	4,223,755	970,176	1,330,819	34,480	189,233	126,070
2011	7,054,228	5,170,656	212,514	5,383,170	556,404	-268,453	4,558,313	1,131,974	1,363,941	37,106	190,110	128,919
2012	7,389,319	5,419,029	291,203	5,710,232	582,463	-272,305	4,855,464	1,192,765	1,341,090	38,769	190,597	130,849
2013	7,636,122	5,664,581	275,836	5,940,417	688,081	-262,314	4,990,022	1,255,930	1,390,170	39,855	191,597	132,710
2014	8,081,720	6,039,068	298,673	6,337,741	711,760	-318,951	5,307,030	1,300,967	1,473,723	42,117	191,888	134,282
2015	8,322,094	6,280,579	234,690	6,515,269	738,189	-392,910	5,384,170	1,406,830	1,531,094	42,921	193,894	136,345
2016	8,393,549	6,437,103	127,725	6,564,828	763,577	-437,637	5,363,614	1,430,908	1,599,027	43,033	195,051	137,169
2017	8,832,840	6,739,715	154,685	6,894,400	798,762	-454,301	5,641,337	1,531,794	1,659,709	44,955	196,484	137,970
2018	9,186,884	7,010,533	119,471	7,130,004	834,340	-462,049	5,833,615	1,578,500	1,774,769	46,393	198,025	138,442
2019	9,607,933	7,275,991	89,502	7,365,493	864,334	-493,958	6,007,201	1,747,241	1,853,491	48,254	199,111	139,213
2020	10,469,898	7,493,077	195,745	7,688,822	887,323	-603,323	6,198,176	1,777,745	2,493,977	52,432	199,687	133,370
2020	11,220,149	7,971,844	190,424	8,162,268	916,854	-616,554	6,628,860	1,820,570	2,770,719	55,987	200,406	135,191

Personal Income and Employment by Area: St. George, UT

(Thousands of dollars, except as noted.)

Year	Personal income, total	Earnings by place of work			Less: Contributions for government social insurance	Plus: Adjustment for residence	Equals: Net earnings by place of residence	Plus: Dividends, interest, and rent	Plus: Personal current transfer receipts	Per capita personal income (dollars)	Population (persons)	Total employment
		Nonfarm	Farm	Total								
1970	40,890	27,300	2,048	29,348	1,684	869	28,533	7,736	4,621	2,940	13,907	4,819
1971	45,422	29,763	1,736	31,499	1,903	1,201	30,797	9,085	5,540	3,021	15,037	5,015
1972	52,409	34,658	1,700	36,358	2,345	1,355	35,368	10,605	6,436	3,376	15,526	5,512
1973	60,744	39,214	2,851	42,065	3,041	1,644	40,668	12,223	7,853	3,709	16,379	5,916
1974	66,587	42,128	1,988	44,116	3,364	2,033	42,785	14,497	9,305	3,680	18,092	5,985
1975	77,215	47,779	1,533	49,312	3,693	2,425	48,044	17,358	11,813	4,173	18,504	6,192
1976	92,191	58,536	1,635	60,171	4,506	2,859	58,524	20,139	13,528	4,645	19,846	6,898
1977	107,325	67,768	1,709	69,477	5,261	3,545	67,761	24,032	15,532	5,141	20,877	7,443
1978	129,654	80,468	1,976	82,444	6,373	4,487	80,558	30,826	18,270	5,805	22,335	8,170
1979	155,888	98,170	2,130	100,300	8,500	5,158	96,958	37,310	21,620	6,490	24,019	9,054
1980	178,589	106,873	1,285	108,158	9,509	6,030	104,679	47,391	26,519	6,745	26,478	9,442
1981	198,424	113,099	611	113,710	11,006	6,553	109,257	56,312	32,855	7,069	28,070	9,582
1982	215,582	119,667	250	119,917	11,822	6,654	114,749	63,156	37,677	7,315	29,472	9,772
1983	242,970	136,435	-19	136,416	13,208	6,853	130,061	70,020	42,889	7,847	30,963	10,358
1984	296,237	173,570	228	173,798	16,853	6,874	163,819	84,734	47,684	9,027	32,816	11,851
1985	341,552	206,233	321	206,554	20,649	6,329	192,234	94,686	54,632	9,551	35,761	13,471
1986	392,178	239,819	578	240,397	24,226	5,958	222,129	107,621	62,428	9,928	39,503	14,907
1987	433,803	260,181	51	260,232	26,301	6,592	240,523	120,607	72,673	10,140	42,781	16,230
1988	474,564	281,832	811	282,643	30,569	7,710	259,784	134,246	80,534	10,634	44,627	17,503
1989	535,760	311,485	1,128	312,613	35,775	8,658	285,496	158,870	91,394	11,462	46,744	18,975
1990	614,437	377,613	1,938	379,551	43,608	8,727	344,670	164,331	105,436	12,493	49,183	21,258
1991	699,822	441,530	638	442,168	51,360	7,258	398,066	177,236	124,520	13,251	52,811	22,774
1992	778,219	488,031	1,521	489,552	56,973	8,970	441,549	193,219	143,451	13,811	56,349	24,084
1993	909,186	574,127	1,774	575,901	67,564	9,462	517,799	223,796	167,591	14,989	60,656	27,249
1994	1,053,848	697,198	203	697,401	83,211	7,888	622,078	250,440	181,330	15,849	66,493	33,162
1995	1,170,382	773,408	-872	772,536	93,859	9,211	687,888	275,806	206,688	16,197	72,261	35,711
1996	1,304,781	853,687	-1,000	852,687	101,009	12,264	763,942	310,138	230,701	16,804	77,647	38,801
1997	1,415,135	914,889	-480	914,409	106,487	15,588	823,510	339,029	252,596	17,359	81,520	40,701
1998	1,536,865	990,887	-318	990,569	115,943	17,986	892,612	375,716	268,537	18,116	84,837	42,689
1999	1,632,503	1,055,570	-688	1,054,882	123,208	21,451	953,125	391,978	287,400	18,541	88,049	44,820
2000	1,749,022	1,100,294	-631	1,099,663	131,496	24,824	992,991	435,357	320,674	19,177	91,206	47,299
2001	1,915,348	1,225,603	713	1,226,316	145,862	24,976	1,105,430	453,925	355,993	20,266	94,512	50,066
2002	2,010,406	1,327,386	-2,018	1,325,368	159,947	24,722	1,190,143	427,763	392,500	20,251	99,274	52,665
2003	2,191,092	1,457,597	61	1,457,658	177,298	25,605	1,305,965	456,673	428,454	21,030	104,188	55,712
2004	2,478,520	1,674,105	1,123	1,675,228	206,538	26,260	1,494,950	497,422	486,148	22,490	110,207	61,676
2005	2,866,890	1,933,330	882	1,934,212	240,398	26,431	1,720,245	605,827	540,818	24,092	119,000	67,944
2006	3,230,621	2,239,229	-1,593	2,237,636	274,617	25,802	1,988,821	651,168	590,632	25,479	126,796	73,427
2007	3,507,925	2,317,283	-4,421	2,312,862	288,266	26,418	2,051,014	799,575	657,336	26,520	132,277	77,265
2008	3,610,502	2,207,692	-4,292	2,203,400	281,333	30,316	1,952,383	896,974	761,145	26,636	135,552	75,466
2009	3,499,504	2,008,015	-3,104	2,004,911	263,436	33,931	1,775,406	858,975	865,123	25,527	137,088	71,644
2010	3,623,234	2,006,110	-2,757	2,003,353	261,467	37,210	1,779,096	897,275	946,863	26,180	138,397	70,275
2011	3,807,795	2,099,310	-206	2,099,104	249,739	41,264	1,890,629	941,557	975,609	26,951	141,288	72,101
2012	4,071,950	2,254,945	-516	2,254,429	262,306	48,854	2,040,977	1,036,022	994,951	28,235	144,216	74,752
2013	4,348,366	2,482,282	2,489	2,484,771	314,672	53,500	2,223,599	1,084,549	1,040,218	29,561	147,099	77,943
2014	4,725,578	2,708,065	2,040	2,710,105	340,014	51,370	2,421,461	1,205,833	1,098,284	31,455	150,235	82,068
2015	5,147,456	2,927,860	2,093	2,929,953	357,275	50,713	2,623,391	1,339,126	1,184,939	33,517	153,578	85,546
2016	5,599,973	3,229,433	-228	3,229,205	394,311	46,317	2,881,211	1,456,518	1,262,244	35,446	157,988	90,724
2017	6,171,276	3,534,834	-1,924	3,532,910	427,302	42,709	3,148,317	1,692,049	1,330,910	37,556	164,324	94,685
2018	6,835,761	4,009,785	-1,932	4,007,853	470,572	32,676	3,569,957	1,818,892	1,446,912	40,246	169,851	100,840
2019	7,494,858	4,330,118	-1,031	4,329,087	501,128	35,525	3,863,484	2,031,627	1,599,747	42,732	175,393	103,394
2020	8,218,873	4,668,463	-256	4,668,207	552,803	32,936	4,148,340	2,101,435	1,969,098	45,178	181,924	108,400
2021	9,018,584	5,082,658	2,218	5,084,876	603,048	32,857	4,514,685	2,206,523	2,297,376	47,162	191,226	115,079

Personal Income and Employment by Area: St. Joseph, MO-KS

(Thousands of dollars, except as noted.)

Year	Personal income, total	Earnings by place of work			Less: Contributions for government social insurance	Plus: Adjustment for residence	Equals: Net earnings by place of residence	Plus: Dividends, interest, and rent	Plus: Personal current transfer receipts	Per capita personal income (dollars)	Population (persons)	Total employment
		Nonfarm	Farm	Total								
1970	413,434	288,499	28,192	316,691	19,881	3,501	300,311	65,563	47,560	3,581	115,462	49,904
1971	446,250	310,367	27,784	338,151	22,133	4,880	320,898	70,775	54,577	3,812	117,065	50,202
1972	488,578	333,766	37,538	371,304	24,893	6,155	352,566	76,404	59,608	4,122	118,538	50,712
1973	543,724	359,429	53,986	413,415	31,136	7,793	390,072	84,689	68,963	4,597	118,278	51,864
1974	569,972	390,077	31,642	421,719	35,070	8,081	394,730	96,190	79,052	4,827	118,091	52,490
1975	625,486	419,929	30,026	449,955	36,835	11,366	424,486	105,131	95,869	5,259	118,925	52,020
1976	676,430	475,341	15,865	491,206	42,255	12,388	461,339	111,996	103,095	5,645	119,830	53,138
1977	747,067	518,123	25,614	543,737	46,062	15,909	513,584	124,890	108,593	6,221	120,097	53,528
1978	825,459	568,154	35,404	603,558	52,061	20,676	572,173	137,472	115,814	6,880	119,976	54,529
1979	923,074	624,010	45,851	669,861	59,164	25,409	636,106	155,967	131,001	7,718	119,604	55,845
1980	1,000,651	683,798	7,578	691,376	64,792	25,566	652,150	192,119	156,382	8,391	119,251	56,082
1981	1,135,885	729,394	37,359	766,753	74,086	27,895	720,562	236,329	178,994	9,579	118,583	55,596
1982	1,216,697	772,982	20,054	793,036	80,240	25,565	738,361	283,589	194,747	10,325	117,842	55,548
1983	1,255,123	804,379	-5,093	799,286	83,608	26,891	742,569	303,831	208,723	10,674	117,584	56,265
1984	1,370,360	871,392	9,717	881,109	92,793	26,492	814,808	335,702	219,850	11,677	117,358	57,192
1985	1,459,619	908,627	47,897	956,524	98,336	27,991	886,179	343,486	229,954	12,502	116,748	57,089
1986	1,497,233	939,828	34,300	974,128	101,853	28,907	901,182	352,346	243,705	12,852	116,500	56,485
1987	1,535,306	987,650	30,352	1,018,002	106,092	28,768	940,678	347,790	246,838	13,221	116,125	56,308
1988	1,603,664	1,071,267	16,741	1,088,008	119,703	26,188	994,493	357,909	251,262	13,910	115,289	57,352
1989	1,739,065	1,156,207	19,612	1,175,819	130,067	22,633	1,068,385	394,219	276,461	15,003	115,917	59,405
1990	1,778,507	1,203,202	25,060	1,228,262	137,542	16,373	1,107,093	381,892	289,522	15,331	116,008	60,198
1991	1,870,030	1,249,225	22,232	1,271,457	145,062	16,440	1,142,835	392,344	334,851	16,047	116,534	59,704
1992	1,977,413	1,306,180	38,199	1,344,379	149,136	22,601	1,217,844	403,589	355,980	16,847	117,377	59,547
1993	2,031,490	1,358,948	15,992	1,374,940	156,546	22,107	1,240,501	408,289	382,700	17,194	118,153	60,305
1994	2,150,095	1,433,949	41,352	1,475,301	166,286	27,220	1,336,235	416,388	397,472	18,203	118,119	60,738
1995	2,209,207	1,507,543	9,551	1,517,094	174,647	28,859	1,371,306	420,265	417,636	18,578	118,915	62,607
1996	2,351,240	1,541,726	62,340	1,604,066	176,031	35,364	1,463,399	450,696	437,145	19,727	119,187	62,179
1997	2,488,193	1,662,989	55,857	1,718,846	187,013	35,586	1,567,419	483,235	437,539	20,733	120,013	63,975
1998	2,577,409	1,774,970	35,275	1,810,245	198,625	36,940	1,648,560	479,881	448,968	21,302	120,992	65,446
1999	2,707,873	1,914,542	15,250	1,929,792	211,669	39,721	1,757,844	472,292	477,737	22,267	121,611	67,135
2000	2,910,834	2,048,987	26,881	2,075,868	224,002	43,873	1,895,739	501,524	513,571	23,457	124,091	68,339
2001	2,964,903	2,056,804	19,830	2,076,634	229,766	51,586	1,898,454	505,957	560,492	23,923	123,936	68,251
2002	3,023,387	2,141,143	-1,702	2,139,441	237,457	50,023	1,952,007	474,830	596,550	24,403	123,894	67,734
2003	3,107,779	2,189,041	11,348	2,200,389	243,650	45,643	2,002,382	489,913	615,484	25,078	123,923	68,092
2004	3,315,414	2,346,109	70,649	2,416,758	257,647	39,877	2,198,988	468,308	648,118	26,875	123,366	69,045
2005	3,406,746	2,434,178	44,856	2,479,034	271,801	30,902	2,238,135	474,976	693,635	27,589	123,484	69,535
2006	3,584,681	2,623,875	30,964	2,654,839	296,877	-3,971	2,353,991	498,375	732,315	28,857	124,222	71,478
2007	3,774,258	2,722,821	60,450	2,783,271	315,532	-32,560	2,435,179	563,960	775,119	30,078	125,483	74,526
2008	4,025,836	2,845,157	66,114	2,911,271	329,247	-58,502	2,523,522	636,307	866,007	31,932	126,077	75,019
2009	3,996,619	2,808,713	77,526	2,886,239	325,199	-124,208	2,436,832	615,427	944,360	31,469	127,001	73,068
2010	3,989,822	2,841,319	36,286	2,877,605	323,966	-125,157	2,428,482	565,558	995,782	31,348	127,274	70,878
2011	4,242,987	2,917,338	84,316	3,001,654	299,499	-104,457	2,597,698	632,759	1,012,530	33,220	127,725	70,968
2012	4,377,377	3,135,365	44,680	3,180,045	311,803	-175,994	2,692,248	661,722	1,023,407	34,212	127,947	71,403
2013	4,472,004	3,213,676	117,471	3,331,147	359,455	-186,040	2,785,652	666,405	1,019,947	35,022	127,691	72,282
2014	4,524,433	3,258,204	77,667	3,335,871	368,493	-197,248	2,770,130	706,961	1,047,342	35,699	126,740	71,977
2015	4,581,720	3,320,263	14,087	3,334,350	383,287	-203,120	2,747,943	735,326	1,098,451	36,340	126,078	72,703
2016	4,618,549	3,366,234	32,892	3,399,126	389,537	-231,645	2,777,944	736,291	1,104,314	36,715	125,795	73,332
2017	4,752,417	3,491,782	39,610	3,531,392	403,875	-267,797	2,859,720	748,155	1,144,542	37,911	125,357	72,846
2018	4,782,922	3,559,981	20,690	3,580,671	413,279	-254,962	2,912,430	689,052	1,181,440	38,337	124,760	72,697
2019	4,990,002	3,664,021	57,578	3,721,599	433,178	-276,199	3,012,222	741,049	1,236,731	40,884	122,054	72,210
2020	5,294,235	3,754,651	78,441	3,833,092	452,399	-327,488	3,053,205	742,819	1,498,211	43,689	121,181	70,755
2021	5,590,022	3,871,696	83,712	3,955,408	453,001	-314,557	3,187,850	741,839	1,660,333	46,420	120,424	70,914

Personal Income and Employment by Area: St. Louis, MO-IL

(Thousands of dollars, except as noted.)

Year	Personal income, total	Earnings by place of work			Less: Contributions for government social insurance	Plus: Adjustment for residence	Equals: Net earnings by place of residence	Plus: Dividends, interest, and rent	Plus: Personal current transfer receipts	Per capita personal income (dollars)	Population (persons)	Total employment
		Nonfarm	Farm	Total								
1970	11,000,702	9,006,214	63,227	9,069,441	597,235	-15,927	8,456,279	1,662,650	881,773	4,365	2,520,475	1,119,503
1971	11,736,076	9,519,993	68,615	9,588,608	652,043	-17,253	8,919,312	1,772,811	1,043,953	4,668	2,514,268	1,108,632
1972	12,587,409	10,229,514	82,504	10,312,018	737,233	-19,706	9,555,079	1,899,282	1,133,048	5,023	2,506,053	1,120,309
1973	13,688,693	11,063,790	167,605	11,231,395	922,267	-42,015	10,267,113	2,095,321	1,326,259	5,489	2,493,703	1,155,750
1974	14,864,310	11,889,861	139,496	12,029,357	1,025,821	-65,160	10,938,376	2,385,057	1,540,877	5,986	2,483,293	1,165,071
1975	16,147,882	12,567,195	174,401	12,741,596	1,065,530	-78,602	11,597,464	2,586,215	1,964,203	6,503	2,483,274	1,144,591
1976	17,633,355	13,984,487	114,400	14,098,887	1,205,364	-129,380	12,764,143	2,777,740	2,091,472	7,101	2,483,161	1,174,761
1977	19,445,715	15,599,210	117,394	15,716,604	1,348,283	-177,931	14,190,390	3,089,157	2,166,168	7,852	2,476,457	1,208,780
1978	21,572,058	17,457,800	120,904	17,578,704	1,558,154	-230,083	15,790,467	3,432,529	2,349,062	8,699	2,479,899	1,251,667
1979	23,848,861	19,248,226	155,522	19,403,748	1,777,353	-285,212	17,341,183	3,872,768	2,634,910	9,599	2,484,555	1,285,355
1980	26,137,634	20,404,036	27,574	20,431,610	1,870,047	-315,297	18,246,266	4,661,425	3,229,943	10,510	2,486,989	1,260,871
1981	29,034,514	22,140,569	109,614	22,250,183	2,175,703	-385,480	19,689,000	5,791,552	3,553,962	11,673	2,487,360	1,257,134
1982	31,261,136	23,225,143	44,461	23,269,604	2,326,902	-374,710	20,567,992	6,834,650	3,858,494	12,598	2,481,504	1,247,588
1983	33,506,155	24,998,758	-17,801	24,980,957	2,531,847	-367,839	22,081,271	7,265,416	4,159,468	13,485	2,484,786	1,260,590
1984	36,970,323	27,687,282	77,105	27,764,387	2,894,145	-391,324	24,478,918	8,161,579	4,329,826	14,806	2,496,966	1,314,730
1985	39,370,361	29,680,497	26,835	29,707,332	3,167,919	-393,375	26,146,038	8,666,055	4,558,268	15,661	2,513,864	1,347,519
1986	41,603,025	31,499,199	67,476	31,566,675	3,395,482	-398,472	27,772,721	9,098,792	4,731,512	16,450	2,529,039	1,385,583
1987	43,924,851	33,522,476	101,578	33,624,054	3,567,501	-390,140	29,666,413	9,389,500	4,868,938	17,268	2,543,754	1,403,758
1988	46,887,898	35,977,104	77,380	36,054,484	3,937,046	-386,681	31,730,757	10,051,400	5,105,741	18,367	2,552,771	1,427,738
1989	50,139,906	38,095,922	207,195	38,303,117	4,186,353	-389,975	33,726,789	10,882,008	5,531,109	19,625	2,554,879	1,452,169
1990	52,807,581	39,840,607	125,746	39,966,353	4,493,631	-371,476	35,101,246	11,700,813	6,005,522	20,588	2,565,020	1,464,298
1991	54,053,990	40,335,399	77,097	40,412,496	4,633,512	-368,334	35,410,650	11,815,333	6,828,007	20,956	2,579,363	1,442,695
1992	57,183,643	42,531,335	181,608	42,712,943	4,825,152	-374,638	37,513,153	12,283,165	7,387,325	22,075	2,590,410	1,439,015
1993	59,539,972	44,105,797	130,440	44,236,237	5,027,815	-386,503	38,821,919	12,889,873	7,828,180	22,848	2,605,968	1,468,529
1994	62,724,268	46,599,541	147,419	46,746,960	5,400,715	-422,911	40,923,334	13,656,805	8,144,129	23,970	2,616,756	1,496,005
1995	66,484,767	49,464,297	47,068	49,511,365	5,725,922	-455,454	43,329,989	14,535,648	8,619,130	25,285	2,629,433	1,529,685
1996	69,654,390	51,836,192	178,404	52,014,596	5,942,880	-492,103	45,579,613	15,230,695	8,844,082	26,383	2,640,161	1,555,249
1997	73,913,556	55,200,184	166,447	55,366,631	6,303,331	-532,696	48,530,604	16,210,545	9,172,407	27,880	2,651,165	1,579,818
1998	77,746,789	58,030,430	135,961	58,166,391	6,597,976	-555,125	51,013,290	17,268,133	9,465,366	29,261	2,657,031	1,603,406
1999	80,414,174	61,207,796	103,792	61,311,588	6,892,404	-603,846	53,815,338	16,781,548	9,817,288	30,158	2,666,413	1,620,760
2000	85,686,462	64,946,486	150,002	65,096,488	7,250,091	-652,147	57,194,250	18,077,233	10,414,979	31,987	2,678,822	1,642,704
2001	88,233,394	67,091,732	155,461	67,247,193	7,427,797	-667,647	59,151,749	17,727,859	11,353,786	32,799	2,690,131	1,641,921
2002	90,644,521	69,379,548	71,296	69,450,844	7,621,908	-684,702	61,144,234	17,503,125	11,997,162	33,571	2,700,121	1,638,359
2003	93,797,431	71,173,934	187,941	71,361,875	7,853,140	-702,579	62,806,156	18,551,131	12,440,144	34,598	2,711,031	1,641,157
2004	97,699,083	73,992,093	355,535	74,347,628	8,098,003	-700,014	65,549,611	19,156,425	12,993,047	35,894	2,721,868	1,648,824
2005	102,143,454	76,837,669	178,865	77,016,534	8,475,005	-707,874	67,833,655	20,344,516	13,965,283	37,411	2,730,316	1,669,564
2006	108,939,665	80,699,238	175,935	80,875,173	8,962,956	-706,814	71,205,403	22,987,111	14,747,151	39,697	2,744,265	1,690,675
2007	113,162,006	83,119,481	184,380	83,303,861	9,349,247	-664,688	73,289,926	24,006,680	15,865,400	41,066	2,755,581	1,714,159
2008	119,181,566	86,909,181	307,660	87,216,841	9,789,557	-694,553	76,732,731	24,745,807	17,703,028	43,060	2,767,776	1,714,077
2009	114,752,555	84,126,634	218,500	84,345,134	9,378,055	-482,007	74,485,072	21,067,183	19,200,300	41,287	2,779,404	1,660,457
2010	119,280,685	85,736,860	263,482	86,000,342	9,394,663	-263,988	76,341,691	22,377,721	20,561,273	42,751	2,790,104	1,644,561
2011	123,418,128	88,003,107	388,961	88,392,068	8,676,396	-240,060	79,475,612	23,310,002	20,632,514	44,148	2,795,528	1,664,110
2012	131,183,527	91,500,542	209,754	91,710,296	8,905,081	-342,203	82,463,012	27,916,491	20,804,024	46,896	2,797,309	1,667,792
2013	130,403,593	93,684,334	440,724	94,125,058	10,326,379	-345,193	83,453,486	25,536,801	21,413,306	46,567	2,800,314	1,686,298
2014	135,378,628	95,368,485	181,361	95,549,846	10,601,975	-373,064	84,574,807	28,733,392	22,070,429	48,172	2,810,317	1,702,979
2015	140,242,929	98,541,053	-39,897	98,501,156	11,103,622	-388,646	87,008,888	29,810,608	23,423,433	49,803	2,815,929	1,733,560
2016	145,000,546	100,793,280	116,488	100,909,768	11,304,593	-417,803	89,187,372	31,868,590	23,944,584	51,499	2,815,619	1,755,649
2017	146,884,796	104,189,783	102,399	104,292,182	11,686,162	-433,478	92,172,542	30,190,105	24,522,149	52,138	2,817,214	1,772,483
2018	155,241,233	108,281,883	126,095	108,407,978	12,206,872	-490,523	95,710,583	34,106,333	25,424,317	55,116	2,816,606	1,792,279
2019	162,354,986	112,571,065	82,389	112,653,454	12,717,422	-577,772	99,358,260	36,465,872	26,530,854	57,622	2,817,594	1,790,878
2020	171,770,406	114,878,778	189,879	115,068,657	13,079,569	-585,022	101,404,066	36,350,259	34,016,081	60,949	2,818,267	1,736,806
2021	181,956,040	121,706,422	400,340	122,106,762	13,480,695	-668,917	107,957,150	36,943,451	37,055,439	64,769	2,809,299	1,779,166

Personal Income and Employment by Area: Salem, OR

(Thousands of dollars, except as noted.)

Year	Personal income, total	Nonfarm	Farm	Total	Less: Contributions for government social insurance	Plus: Adjustment for residence	Equals: Net earnings by place of residence	Plus: Dividends, interest, and rent	Plus: Personal current transfer receipts	Per capita personal income (dollars)	Population (persons)	Total employment
		Earnings by place of work			Derivation of personal income							
1970	707,190	497,430	23,467	520,897	36,554	8,890	493,233	138,172	75,785	3,769	187,645	76,935
1971	783,788	551,053	23,671	574,724	42,020	11,900	544,604	152,032	87,152	4,058	193,158	78,983
1972	875,726	623,246	21,463	644,709	50,028	16,462	611,143	167,036	97,547	4,445	197,027	82,993
1973	1,010,102	700,872	48,661	749,533	64,980	22,016	706,569	189,186	114,347	5,061	199,576	88,074
1974	1,156,016	786,042	55,197	841,239	75,685	28,500	794,054	220,482	141,480	5,590	206,796	91,136
1975	1,293,023	869,591	43,561	913,152	81,630	33,280	864,802	254,670	173,551	6,115	211,453	93,710
1976	1,486,085	1,014,105	49,548	1,063,653	95,898	42,857	1,010,612	282,866	192,607	6,796	218,659	99,232
1977	1,674,490	1,154,268	43,377	1,197,645	110,810	53,904	1,140,739	325,096	208,655	7,330	228,455	106,818
1978	1,914,276	1,329,344	38,807	1,368,151	131,790	71,191	1,307,552	376,137	230,587	8,075	237,065	113,216
1979	2,193,942	1,498,602	43,798	1,542,400	154,503	113,832	1,501,729	431,433	260,780	9,006	243,606	118,107
1980	2,452,241	1,579,499	60,347	1,639,846	164,441	143,393	1,618,798	519,896	313,547	9,776	250,849	117,287
1981	2,631,835	1,663,400	54,163	1,717,563	185,419	110,829	1,642,973	626,323	362,539	10,355	254,150	115,262
1982	2,710,730	1,646,286	49,451	1,695,737	185,816	105,304	1,615,225	690,736	404,769	10,637	254,850	111,166
1983	2,868,017	1,727,168	43,087	1,770,255	194,488	104,292	1,680,059	751,649	436,309	11,230	255,400	113,893
1984	3,078,392	1,872,442	53,676	1,926,118	216,849	104,844	1,814,113	813,410	450,869	12,000	256,540	117,372
1985	3,263,800	2,011,294	58,153	2,069,447	235,002	97,362	1,931,807	853,345	478,648	12,638	258,250	121,772
1986	3,446,279	2,134,365	88,334	2,222,699	249,493	93,138	2,066,344	883,071	496,864	13,233	260,438	125,261
1987	3,637,644	2,320,091	88,904	2,408,995	267,136	86,404	2,228,263	890,274	519,107	13,829	263,037	132,049
1988	3,980,311	2,561,451	142,866	2,704,317	310,080	88,211	2,482,448	940,907	556,956	14,839	268,239	137,126
1989	4,380,607	2,830,347	126,180	2,956,527	343,335	85,297	2,698,489	1,065,533	616,585	16,011	273,600	141,107
1990	4,737,469	3,135,137	141,187	3,276,324	386,738	75,760	2,965,346	1,098,870	673,253	16,928	279,862	146,094
1991	5,049,509	3,357,825	156,888	3,514,713	418,866	75,571	3,171,418	1,140,066	738,025	17,582	287,202	147,147
1992	5,404,705	3,631,579	167,302	3,798,881	448,813	81,060	3,431,128	1,158,711	814,866	18,319	295,039	149,319
1993	5,772,272	3,884,549	165,973	4,050,522	478,794	91,775	3,663,503	1,228,881	879,888	19,038	303,205	154,522
1994	6,202,984	4,240,353	167,168	4,407,521	525,098	105,599	3,988,022	1,304,003	910,959	19,969	310,626	161,451
1995	6,624,550	4,446,719	145,375	4,592,094	555,452	133,999	4,170,641	1,438,859	1,015,050	20,856	317,638	165,842
1996	7,134,004	4,769,686	195,494	4,965,180	600,873	166,841	4,531,148	1,520,990	1,081,866	21,988	324,457	172,393
1997	7,438,303	4,934,337	208,048	5,142,385	622,115	199,517	4,719,787	1,600,740	1,117,776	22,426	331,688	176,546
1998	7,863,259	5,285,780	203,888	5,489,668	661,176	215,218	5,043,710	1,619,224	1,200,325	23,246	338,269	178,362
1999	8,237,119	5,641,810	226,326	5,868,136	697,332	221,906	5,392,710	1,520,977	1,323,432	23,946	343,985	181,037
2000	8,630,025	5,955,241	179,144	6,134,385	733,103	269,546	5,670,828	1,618,587	1,340,610	24,798	348,007	183,466
2001	8,733,942	5,918,597	202,573	6,121,170	722,960	242,202	5,640,412	1,595,414	1,498,116	24,842	351,581	182,319
2002	8,838,836	6,187,320	179,206	6,366,526	760,527	179,488	5,785,487	1,480,794	1,572,555	24,782	356,668	184,073
2003	9,235,103	6,425,471	236,602	6,662,073	792,642	113,687	5,983,118	1,617,968	1,634,017	25,626	360,377	187,787
2004	9,602,232	6,678,260	248,585	6,926,845	837,289	104,151	6,193,707	1,695,746	1,712,779	26,401	363,708	192,318
2005	10,155,663	7,119,875	257,363	7,377,238	895,410	84,509	6,566,337	1,752,810	1,836,516	27,593	368,046	197,802
2006	11,176,300	7,765,817	316,086	8,081,903	973,152	68,595	7,177,346	2,015,664	1,983,290	29,858	374,317	202,453
2007	11,615,976	7,964,555	299,765	8,264,320	1,014,511	31,906	7,281,715	2,178,777	2,155,484	30,588	379,755	207,319
2008	12,251,356	8,208,399	303,331	8,511,730	1,044,239	-73,684	7,393,807	2,300,386	2,557,163	31,898	384,075	205,685
2009	12,044,916	7,957,532	268,293	8,225,825	1,016,369	-182,714	7,026,742	2,138,813	2,879,361	31,018	388,323	198,184
2010	12,310,728	8,142,866	257,947	8,400,813	1,032,969	-301,570	7,066,274	2,098,171	3,146,283	31,446	391,488	195,920
2011	12,692,723	8,204,543	266,975	8,471,518	920,320	-252,852	7,298,346	2,169,357	3,225,020	32,215	393,995	194,633
2012	13,132,832	8,472,082	295,778	8,767,860	947,860	-190,764	7,629,236	2,310,963	3,192,633	33,156	396,092	194,151
2013	13,379,744	8,814,149	313,913	9,128,062	1,115,089	-214,445	7,798,528	2,272,229	3,308,987	33,612	398,059	197,390
2014	14,355,269	9,399,385	264,789	9,664,174	1,199,688	-283,732	8,180,754	2,480,780	3,693,735	35,796	401,032	204,243
2015	15,420,752	10,063,952	318,429	10,382,381	1,266,503	-281,389	8,834,489	2,634,453	3,951,810	37,918	406,691	209,748
2016	16,229,394	10,761,789	316,873	11,078,662	1,340,067	-301,954	9,436,641	2,751,622	4,041,131	39,073	415,364	214,945
2017	17,115,654	11,510,548	261,160	11,771,708	1,448,260	-292,704	10,030,744	2,950,864	4,134,046	40,507	422,531	221,658
2018	18,122,081	12,422,117	262,745	12,684,862	1,527,360	-417,931	10,739,571	2,996,571	4,385,939	42,337	428,043	227,842
2019	19,187,541	13,185,294	245,449	13,430,743	1,613,666	-461,594	11,355,483	3,198,210	4,633,848	44,540	430,794	228,406
2020	20,998,575	13,924,826	259,139	14,183,965	1,704,606	-721,591	11,757,768	3,253,043	5,987,764	48,377	434,065	225,255
2021	23,110,360	15,059,015	277,406	15,336,421	1,831,526	-672,549	12,832,346	3,351,254	6,926,760	52,971	436,283	233,457

Personal Income and Employment by Area: Salinas, CA

(Thousands of dollars, except as noted.)

					Derivation of personal income							
		Earnings by place of work			Less: Contributions for government social insurance	Plus: Adjustment for residence	Equals: Net earnings by place of residence	Plus: Dividends, interest, and rent	Plus: Personal current transfer receipts	Per capita personal income (dollars)	Population (persons)	Total employment
Year	Personal income, total	Nonfarm	Farm	Total								
1970	1,364,273	908,393	109,573	1,017,966	59,309	-5,039	953,618	318,375	92,280	5,496	248,235	134,519
1971	1,537,357	1,026,264	131,596	1,157,860	70,447	-6,561	1,080,852	350,977	105,528	6,083	252,730	140,268
1972	1,643,539	1,078,857	166,158	1,245,015	76,423	-7,441	1,161,151	366,542	115,846	6,467	254,140	136,674
1973	1,839,849	1,205,691	195,923	1,401,614	94,561	-9,913	1,297,140	412,540	130,169	7,208	255,261	144,582
1974	2,050,129	1,301,198	253,541	1,554,739	106,099	-12,791	1,435,849	460,329	153,951	7,779	263,534	147,280
1975	2,188,715	1,419,258	209,655	1,628,913	117,505	-15,952	1,495,456	495,044	198,215	8,077	270,976	150,780
1976	2,290,452	1,493,285	201,272	1,694,557	125,970	-15,459	1,553,128	519,021	218,303	8,300	275,942	148,250
1977	2,521,308	1,652,411	220,800	1,873,211	140,822	-16,524	1,715,865	576,585	228,858	8,955	281,545	154,161
1978	2,899,743	1,857,164	299,584	2,156,748	158,856	-15,010	1,982,882	666,541	250,320	10,206	284,129	158,622
1979	3,121,866	2,016,145	273,706	2,289,851	179,633	-17,501	2,092,717	752,302	276,847	10,882	286,882	162,099
1980	3,501,254	2,145,504	343,054	2,488,558	186,003	-12,708	2,289,847	877,336	334,071	11,974	292,406	160,320
1981	4,033,236	2,365,806	427,400	2,793,206	221,643	-2,554	2,569,009	1,076,644	387,583	13,459	299,677	161,159
1982	4,272,966	2,537,836	432,145	2,969,981	239,698	-4,451	2,725,832	1,146,642	400,492	13,953	306,241	161,196
1983	4,758,124	2,720,079	634,627	3,354,706	264,688	1,956	3,091,974	1,231,943	434,207	15,168	313,698	164,668
1984	5,114,759	3,006,222	558,396	3,564,618	304,397	5,627	3,265,848	1,394,145	454,766	15,911	321,458	170,038
1985	5,407,320	3,306,951	482,151	3,789,102	338,804	102	3,450,400	1,466,090	490,830	16,481	328,102	175,384
1986	5,844,931	3,586,025	572,946	4,158,971	371,761	1,492	3,788,702	1,526,682	529,547	17,403	335,849	176,778
1987	6,250,071	3,910,850	614,300	4,525,150	409,511	4,394	4,120,033	1,585,503	544,535	18,314	341,268	183,254
1988	6,594,700	4,202,186	558,487	4,760,673	460,039	13,453	4,314,087	1,692,935	587,678	19,063	345,947	190,927
1989	6,966,343	4,411,361	490,591	4,901,952	489,844	21,186	4,433,294	1,886,993	646,056	19,911	349,872	194,992
1990	7,392,202	4,715,713	541,806	5,257,519	529,597	24,555	4,752,477	1,920,821	718,904	20,675	357,535	200,058
1991	7,561,106	4,952,300	414,620	5,366,920	561,913	29,166	4,834,173	1,926,851	800,082	20,726	364,805	200,838
1992	8,218,602	5,274,926	607,943	5,882,869	598,204	31,581	5,316,246	1,978,495	923,861	22,101	371,860	195,598
1993	8,362,212	5,137,732	779,971	5,917,703	582,567	51,624	5,386,760	2,000,616	974,836	22,540	371,002	191,239
1994	8,382,230	5,092,900	765,365	5,858,265	572,436	73,055	5,358,884	2,037,825	985,521	23,789	352,363	183,917
1995	8,927,730	5,298,408	888,082	6,186,490	585,085	99,359	5,700,764	2,192,815	1,034,151	25,114	355,486	187,617
1996	9,262,660	5,615,374	717,944	6,333,318	598,841	120,498	5,854,975	2,320,897	1,086,788	25,572	362,215	195,179
1997	10,006,265	5,939,085	980,677	6,919,762	622,192	149,070	6,446,640	2,452,090	1,107,535	26,556	376,794	197,557
1998	10,873,191	6,463,260	1,063,161	7,526,421	659,478	178,068	7,045,011	2,653,243	1,174,937	28,032	387,889	208,782
1999	11,647,384	7,069,718	1,111,316	8,181,034	722,519	221,690	7,680,205	2,727,696	1,239,483	29,393	396,267	218,234
2000	12,812,956	7,660,250	1,377,199	9,037,449	776,463	360,279	8,621,265	2,906,808	1,284,883	31,795	402,990	218,487
2001	12,917,703	8,100,201	1,101,554	9,201,755	876,017	262,067	8,587,805	2,924,567	1,405,331	31,732	407,082	217,510
2002	13,033,532	8,491,992	1,206,888	9,698,880	931,657	192,870	8,960,093	2,560,543	1,512,896	31,869	408,977	221,129
2003	13,657,901	8,924,459	1,335,424	10,259,883	998,374	160,161	9,421,670	2,652,620	1,583,611	33,334	409,725	223,693
2004	14,053,421	9,151,144	1,102,867	10,254,011	1,076,381	156,293	9,333,923	3,068,677	1,650,821	34,383	408,731	222,456
2005	14,581,522	9,491,733	1,182,711	10,674,444	1,106,011	130,296	9,698,729	3,160,030	1,722,763	35,991	405,139	221,519
2006	15,813,411	10,059,586	1,213,936	11,273,522	1,127,782	162,089	10,307,829	3,658,845	1,846,737	39,353	401,831	219,477
2007	16,465,641	10,465,288	1,115,577	11,580,865	1,147,486	173,220	10,606,599	3,920,635	1,938,407	40,921	402,376	224,438
2008	16,479,129	10,570,986	963,235	11,534,221	1,180,782	91,771	10,445,210	3,840,968	2,192,951	40,587	406,022	223,750
2009	16,424,781	10,358,460	1,484,466	11,842,926	1,172,207	14,871	10,685,590	3,331,761	2,407,430	40,035	410,263	217,029
2010	17,060,716	10,901,009	1,337,955	12,238,964	1,180,070	-23,064	11,035,830	3,361,848	2,663,038	40,976	416,358	220,156
2011	17,489,872	11,165,586	1,139,941	12,305,527	1,099,407	-34,647	11,171,473	3,617,172	2,701,227	41,605	420,379	221,085
2012	18,348,248	11,515,948	1,374,087	12,890,035	1,135,055	-97,301	11,657,679	3,972,608	2,717,961	43,252	424,222	225,859
2013	19,140,149	11,747,399	2,114,262	13,861,661	1,297,716	-131,685	12,432,260	3,876,131	2,831,758	44,913	426,163	230,852
2014	20,283,412	12,359,022	2,156,889	14,515,911	1,351,059	-120,217	13,044,635	4,238,770	3,000,007	47,056	431,044	238,929
2015	21,926,157	13,215,191	2,593,341	15,808,532	1,416,613	-129,381	14,262,538	4,464,265	3,199,354	50,524	433,979	244,409
2016	22,602,564	13,901,115	2,179,387	16,080,502	1,501,093	-107,065	14,472,344	4,799,087	3,331,133	51,604	438,004	248,811
2017	23,097,874	14,531,267	2,191,446	16,722,713	1,574,928	-88,360	15,059,425	4,706,505	3,331,944	52,601	439,112	250,549
2018	23,317,005	15,125,794	1,577,874	16,703,668	1,641,038	-101,591	14,961,039	4,852,590	3,503,376	53,065	439,404	257,156
2019	24,787,069	15,883,636	1,702,417	17,586,053	1,734,060	-13,075	15,838,918	5,204,771	3,743,380	56,313	440,163	258,358
2020	26,794,525	15,841,670	1,703,821	17,545,491	1,720,572	-17,276	15,807,643	5,222,586	5,764,296	61,105	438,500	246,111
2021	27,747,802	16,753,431	1,247,039	18,000,470	1,837,457	69,033	16,232,046	5,361,251	6,154,505	63,449	437,325	252,436

Personal Income and Employment by Area: Salisbury, MD-DE

(Thousands of dollars, except as noted.)

Year	Personal income, total	Earnings by place of work			Less: Contributions for government social insurance	Plus: Adjustment for residence	Equals: Net earnings by place of residence	Plus: Dividends, interest, and rent	Plus: Personal current transfer receipts	Per capita personal income (dollars)	Population (persons)	Total employment
		Nonfarm	Farm	Total								
1970	658,152	486,145	39,134	525,279	33,261	7,876	499,894	95,352	62,906	3,681	178,804	92,457
1971	711,893	526,723	34,025	560,748	37,313	9,158	532,593	105,311	73,989	3,858	184,503	94,642
1972	806,771	594,576	50,343	644,919	44,245	8,497	609,171	116,941	80,659	4,316	186,939	99,270
1973	954,731	665,628	108,938	774,566	57,552	7,754	724,768	136,066	93,897	4,998	191,029	102,800
1974	986,538	718,379	51,919	770,298	64,473	8,269	714,094	158,241	114,203	5,034	195,957	101,927
1975	1,127,097	762,703	102,351	865,054	67,220	8,557	806,391	172,061	148,645	5,637	199,933	99,153
1976	1,214,565	846,600	83,284	929,884	75,284	9,219	863,819	188,973	161,773	5,961	203,759	100,183
1977	1,284,161	910,541	55,376	965,917	81,243	10,762	895,436	212,180	176,545	6,210	206,805	101,923
1978	1,431,621	1,036,920	55,028	1,091,948	94,793	5,284	1,002,439	236,443	192,739	6,846	209,113	107,617
1979	1,549,797	1,119,731	42,052	1,161,783	107,333	1,835	1,056,285	270,081	223,431	7,310	212,004	108,124
1980	1,685,752	1,189,237	2,748	1,191,985	114,582	-2,116	1,075,287	339,495	270,970	7,923	212,780	106,381
1981	1,900,453	1,265,302	39,464	1,304,766	131,338	-3,226	1,170,202	415,923	314,328	8,923	212,984	107,068
1982	2,101,050	1,351,180	71,747	1,422,927	142,762	-4,274	1,275,891	483,343	341,816	9,842	213,485	108,398
1983	2,297,712	1,524,082	62,937	1,587,019	162,602	-9,357	1,415,060	513,204	369,448	10,637	216,011	116,348
1984	2,615,628	1,710,511	128,482	1,838,993	187,167	-7,875	1,643,951	578,964	392,713	11,869	220,383	121,778
1985	2,866,288	1,898,715	135,396	2,034,111	210,083	-8,010	1,816,018	625,504	424,766	12,735	225,063	127,936
1986	3,195,261	2,083,972	213,375	2,297,347	232,978	-1,797	2,062,572	683,353	449,336	13,918	229,583	132,093
1987	3,439,578	2,303,173	168,265	2,471,438	253,922	5,930	2,223,446	729,510	486,622	14,758	233,065	137,270
1988	3,783,146	2,493,068	239,183	2,732,251	284,727	17,149	2,464,673	788,307	530,166	15,862	238,509	141,970
1989	4,114,163	2,640,770	261,186	2,901,956	304,720	29,539	2,626,775	911,154	576,234	16,959	242,598	143,143
1990	4,290,855	2,848,500	168,364	3,016,864	326,820	42,834	2,732,878	913,988	643,989	17,327	247,645	146,525
1991	4,549,706	2,965,262	157,351	3,122,613	343,089	58,931	2,838,455	984,261	726,990	17,895	254,246	145,358
1992	4,778,332	3,115,036	134,066	3,249,102	356,748	75,917	2,968,271	1,002,392	807,669	18,327	260,733	145,227
1993	4,973,953	3,243,376	135,303	3,378,679	375,201	92,658	3,096,136	1,014,358	863,459	18,570	267,853	147,101
1994	5,326,648	3,437,550	144,446	3,581,996	402,858	112,107	3,291,245	1,105,982	929,421	19,397	274,618	150,301
1995	5,676,887	3,614,769	113,580	3,728,349	423,941	133,694	3,438,102	1,215,308	1,023,477	20,171	281,441	157,221
1996	6,135,543	3,780,624	166,396	3,947,020	437,628	156,437	3,665,829	1,328,534	1,141,180	21,262	288,563	160,039
1997	6,499,903	4,025,886	135,267	4,161,153	460,761	174,254	3,874,646	1,446,075	1,179,182	22,051	294,772	164,110
1998	7,036,611	4,384,856	176,501	4,561,357	487,942	204,393	4,277,808	1,484,607	1,274,196	23,352	301,328	166,774
1999	7,575,618	4,795,480	179,994	4,975,474	514,594	237,388	4,698,268	1,516,787	1,360,563	24,637	307,487	171,319
2000	8,196,245	5,181,591	170,416	5,352,007	540,312	273,448	5,085,143	1,655,177	1,455,925	26,124	313,744	176,762
2001	8,913,546	5,565,061	261,579	5,826,640	577,153	307,465	5,556,952	1,737,910	1,618,684	27,931	319,128	179,323
2002	9,169,712	5,845,312	90,620	5,935,932	610,928	344,187	5,669,191	1,755,169	1,745,352	28,209	325,063	182,888
2003	9,865,630	6,267,003	204,688	6,471,691	650,030	378,553	6,200,214	1,782,870	1,882,546	29,702	332,157	184,905
2004	10,966,781	6,951,648	305,439	7,257,087	717,144	423,285	6,963,228	1,977,717	2,025,836	32,395	338,528	191,815
2005	11,526,619	7,256,435	321,271	7,577,706	776,317	469,174	7,270,563	2,045,640	2,210,416	33,342	345,704	197,589
2006	12,163,606	7,649,210	227,080	7,876,290	834,141	508,821	7,550,970	2,250,090	2,362,546	34,377	353,828	203,079
2007	12,840,574	7,722,737	230,370	7,953,107	869,763	558,034	7,641,378	2,621,460	2,577,736	35,578	360,918	205,892
2008	13,552,279	7,733,308	275,173	8,008,481	888,804	589,706	7,709,383	2,888,791	2,954,105	36,950	366,772	203,789
2009	13,298,614	7,411,032	292,806	7,703,838	877,825	589,346	7,415,359	2,654,085	3,229,170	35,888	370,558	198,311
2010	13,634,045	7,575,350	261,360	7,836,710	905,564	592,160	7,523,306	2,622,296	3,488,443	36,375	374,821	197,126
2011	14,360,183	7,764,306	230,493	7,994,799	815,731	623,732	7,802,800	2,945,818	3,611,565	37,964	378,256	196,549
2012	14,952,060	8,119,102	285,322	8,404,424	849,043	645,758	8,201,139	3,035,414	3,715,507	39,212	381,310	199,150
2013	15,674,319	8,623,983	503,439	9,127,422	982,694	643,071	8,787,799	3,004,744	3,881,776	40,743	384,713	201,900
2014	16,610,734	9,026,554	530,428	9,556,982	1,034,582	659,310	9,181,710	3,295,845	4,133,179	42,871	387,460	206,027
2015	17,927,605	9,970,059	490,558	10,460,617	1,108,789	674,420	10,026,248	3,524,008	4,377,349	45,744	391,913	210,655
2016	18,175,099	10,035,071	358,105	10,393,176	1,141,185	678,296	9,930,287	3,648,292	4,596,520	45,787	396,952	215,337
2017	18,979,707	10,152,948	542,721	10,695,669	1,184,987	696,101	10,206,783	3,921,731	4,851,193	47,201	402,105	219,462
2018	19,754,379	10,690,022	385,432	11,075,454	1,252,129	724,007	10,547,332	4,046,030	5,161,017	48,428	407,913	224,146
2019	20,806,812	11,051,663	361,636	11,413,299	1,308,996	749,127	10,853,430	4,454,522	5,498,860	50,308	413,585	225,422
2020	22,036,636	11,238,352	102,319	11,340,671	1,354,517	779,208	10,765,362	4,469,181	6,802,093	52,544	419,397	218,961
2021	23,906,703	12,274,043	344,168	12,618,211	1,490,984	785,533	11,912,760	4,534,642	7,459,301	55,698	429,223	229,329

Personal Income and Employment by Area: Salt Lake City, UT

(Thousands of dollars, except as noted.)

Year	Personal income, total	Earnings by place of work			Less: Contributions for government social insurance	Plus: Adjustment for residence	Equals: Net earnings by place of residence	Plus: Dividends, interest, and rent	Plus: Personal current transfer receipts	Per capita personal income (dollars)	Population (persons)	Total employment
		Nonfarm	Farm	Total								
1970	1,887,139	1,625,670	6,530	1,632,200	109,178	-61,575	1,461,447	282,894	142,798	3,908	482,939	228,004
1971	2,096,973	1,785,767	6,465	1,792,232	124,888	-54,279	1,613,065	317,060	166,848	4,203	498,890	235,582
1972	2,340,137	2,008,657	8,087	2,016,744	147,664	-73,160	1,795,920	353,522	190,695	4,585	510,409	248,748
1973	2,596,645	2,259,655	11,838	2,271,493	192,936	-88,875	1,989,682	386,153	220,810	4,955	524,033	265,327
1974	2,930,323	2,561,674	7,010	2,568,684	225,365	-108,929	2,234,390	446,637	249,296	5,463	536,395	278,466
1975	3,277,475	2,825,191	5,609	2,830,800	244,183	-119,688	2,466,929	492,684	317,862	5,942	551,569	282,198
1976	3,687,002	3,212,485	6,480	3,218,965	282,242	-137,783	2,798,940	544,888	343,174	6,471	569,758	295,659
1977	4,174,375	3,682,801	4,582	3,687,383	323,489	-167,761	3,196,133	610,506	367,736	7,115	586,735	312,954
1978	4,790,945	4,255,876	4,779	4,260,655	381,656	-207,657	3,671,342	713,905	405,698	7,906	605,964	333,838
1979	5,366,122	4,790,583	5,104	4,795,687	452,551	-245,076	4,098,060	809,542	458,520	8,574	625,894	346,245
1980	6,010,564	5,311,974	3,846	5,315,820	505,939	-295,099	4,514,782	956,891	538,891	9,244	650,232	350,072
1981	6,786,354	5,926,180	3,152	5,929,332	608,290	-323,929	4,997,113	1,156,489	632,752	10,141	669,210	353,355
1982	7,377,345	6,341,284	-435	6,340,849	662,047	-354,269	5,324,533	1,326,210	726,602	10,773	684,802	359,618
1983	7,938,532	6,850,557	3,928	6,854,485	720,356	-436,077	5,698,052	1,457,690	782,790	11,334	700,444	367,055
1984	8,749,272	7,590,719	4,728	7,595,447	819,857	-485,244	6,290,346	1,651,742	807,184	12,272	712,930	388,686
1985	9,326,090	8,078,911	4,001	8,082,912	883,267	-521,418	6,678,227	1,768,486	879,377	12,937	720,877	403,373
1986	9,778,716	8,452,917	4,672	8,457,589	928,001	-557,301	6,972,287	1,858,594	947,835	13,396	729,985	409,417
1987	10,253,312	8,920,379	3,937	8,924,316	972,698	-633,092	7,318,526	1,946,270	988,516	13,932	735,973	423,933
1988	10,856,706	9,483,961	9,538	9,493,499	1,079,208	-678,064	7,736,227	2,086,810	1,033,669	14,642	741,463	438,149
1989	11,553,943	10,081,428	9,004	10,090,432	1,166,002	-728,361	8,196,069	2,212,979	1,144,895	15,494	745,687	451,777
1990	12,463,161	10,985,013	12,261	10,997,274	1,314,893	-881,417	8,800,964	2,406,452	1,255,745	16,472	756,611	470,479
1991	13,277,724	11,829,034	8,911	11,837,945	1,434,865	-999,305	9,403,775	2,484,278	1,389,671	17,060	778,307	481,251
1992	14,300,298	12,948,213	11,970	12,960,183	1,557,242	-1,188,871	10,214,070	2,564,901	1,521,327	17,825	802,260	489,997
1993	15,339,419	14,057,428	14,575	14,072,003	1,697,018	-1,348,789	11,026,196	2,690,359	1,622,864	18,557	826,621	518,184
1994	16,634,537	15,340,434	9,681	15,350,115	1,863,865	-1,494,530	11,991,720	2,992,243	1,650,574	19,602	848,617	547,370
1995	18,166,502	16,617,738	8,896	16,626,634	2,023,177	-1,641,756	12,961,701	3,425,198	1,779,603	20,969	866,353	571,123
1996	19,820,021	18,097,994	6,920	18,104,914	2,154,586	-1,848,172	14,102,156	3,846,942	1,870,923	22,410	884,440	602,150
1997	21,523,760	19,840,938	6,029	19,846,967	2,331,286	-2,093,772	15,421,909	4,166,408	1,935,443	23,793	904,628	624,849
1998	22,893,228	21,294,628	5,275	21,299,903	2,485,051	-2,325,586	16,489,266	4,398,995	2,004,967	24,960	917,191	645,322
1999	24,241,112	22,929,698	8,830	22,938,528	2,633,050	-2,563,981	17,741,497	4,390,284	2,109,331	26,088	929,195	656,570
2000	26,038,090	24,534,035	7,820	24,541,855	2,823,963	-2,756,536	18,961,356	4,812,839	2,263,895	27,626	942,537	677,903
2001	26,503,921	24,901,793	10,222	24,912,015	2,922,942	-2,901,974	19,087,099	4,943,772	2,473,050	27,780	954,081	680,542
2002	27,171,470	25,186,236	4,000	25,190,236	2,959,451	-2,933,696	19,297,089	5,170,092	2,704,289	28,211	963,150	674,074
2003	27,854,926	25,631,619	4,572	25,636,191	3,035,689	-2,965,694	19,634,808	5,363,342	2,856,776	28,673	971,454	671,950
2004	29,490,166	27,422,989	5,526	27,428,515	3,267,302	-3,258,686	20,902,527	5,581,738	3,005,901	30,030	982,034	685,605
2005	32,390,412	29,809,732	5,217	29,814,949	3,542,607	-3,603,624	22,668,718	6,447,875	3,273,819	32,481	997,221	712,951
2006	36,303,791	33,444,689	7,883	33,452,572	3,867,470	-4,114,909	25,470,193	7,242,858	3,590,740	35,652	1,018,281	745,183
2007	38,852,081	36,067,143	6,125	36,073,268	4,170,145	-4,751,856	27,151,267	7,829,131	3,871,683	37,446	1,037,540	781,703
2008	40,207,404	36,662,264	6,977	36,669,241	4,253,775	-5,022,842	27,392,624	8,319,944	4,494,836	38,095	1,055,462	787,814
2009	38,178,199	35,203,945	9,043	35,212,988	4,138,456	-5,104,555	25,969,977	7,218,609	4,989,613	35,547	1,074,013	761,073
2010	39,309,884	35,909,933	10,016	35,919,949	4,187,366	-5,324,758	26,407,825	7,382,768	5,519,291	36,015	1,091,499	756,966
2011	42,353,076	38,188,928	13,809	38,202,737	3,971,256	-5,729,995	28,501,486	8,111,676	5,739,914	38,263	1,106,900	776,331
2012	45,398,314	41,534,191	13,567	41,547,758	4,208,808	-6,310,624	31,028,326	8,710,435	5,659,553	40,392	1,123,950	797,545
2013	46,609,000	43,393,580	14,989	43,408,569	4,984,807	-6,527,045	31,896,717	8,844,719	5,867,564	40,874	1,140,316	820,440
2014	49,100,505	45,398,507	13,074	45,411,581	5,217,888	-6,707,542	33,486,151	9,580,994	6,033,360	42,344	1,159,550	839,590
2015	52,886,539	48,354,654	23,614	48,378,268	5,454,170	-7,124,382	35,799,716	10,717,536	6,369,287	45,009	1,175,028	866,877
2016	55,438,318	50,964,732	9,864	50,974,596	5,723,420	-7,758,091	37,493,085	11,327,965	6,617,268	46,312	1,197,061	897,509
2017	58,208,670	53,388,055	7,570	53,395,625	6,034,801	-8,245,749	39,115,075	12,342,533	6,751,062	47,771	1,218,488	920,695
2018	61,979,387	56,931,400	5,965	56,937,365	6,290,844	-8,737,686	41,908,835	12,936,077	7,134,475	50,199	1,234,679	949,118
2019	65,742,185	60,806,597	4,498	60,811,095	6,684,518	-9,883,383	44,243,194	13,757,124	7,741,867	52,655	1,248,555	963,218
2020	71,936,640	65,381,005	7,040	65,388,045	7,161,038	-10,589,542	47,637,465	14,192,753	10,106,422	57,114	1,259,517	967,938
2021	77,742,971	70,849,397	9,340	70,858,737	7,675,179	-12,118,611	51,064,947	14,913,311	11,764,713	61,551	1,263,061	1,006,934

Personal Income and Employment by Area: San Angelo, TX

(Thousands of dollars, except as noted.)

Year	Personal income, total	Earnings by place of work			Less: Contributions for government social insurance	Plus: Adjustment for residence	Equals: Net earnings by place of residence	Plus: Dividends, interest, and rent	Plus: Personal current transfer receipts	Per capita personal income (dollars)	Population (persons)	Total employment
		Nonfarm	Farm	Total								
1970	274,804	200,845	11,960	212,805	12,175	-94	200,536	50,442	23,826	3,797	72,383	33,632
1971	295,431	221,069	7,648	228,717	13,922	-597	214,198	53,903	27,330	3,979	74,244	34,481
1972	325,078	242,286	9,757	252,043	15,884	-1,022	235,137	59,636	30,305	4,415	73,632	35,458
1973	364,407	272,260	10,577	282,837	20,456	-1,595	260,786	67,532	36,089	4,799	75,927	37,376
1974	400,364	300,193	6,631	306,824	23,377	-2,089	281,358	76,814	42,192	5,204	76,932	38,027
1975	458,843	339,823	7,359	347,182	26,122	-874	320,186	88,024	50,633	5,831	78,694	39,156
1976	520,931	386,881	14,493	401,374	30,055	-3,325	367,994	96,928	56,009	6,521	79,880	40,777
1977	574,895	435,151	7,780	442,931	34,248	-4,698	403,985	111,059	59,851	7,137	80,554	43,162
1978	659,714	506,560	5,521	512,081	40,621	-5,442	466,018	127,224	66,472	8,046	81,991	45,910
1979	728,495	564,323	2,204	566,527	47,902	-6,486	512,139	140,857	75,499	8,647	84,252	46,828
1980	835,588	639,423	-4,482	634,941	54,785	-8,351	571,805	176,953	86,830	9,635	86,724	48,508
1981	1,008,691	733,106	20,265	753,371	67,730	-7,551	678,090	232,060	98,541	11,373	88,690	50,976
1982	1,131,947	812,924	16,104	829,028	77,391	-7,104	744,533	276,856	110,558	12,246	92,432	53,252
1983	1,218,655	858,708	21,544	880,252	81,255	-7,444	791,553	304,214	122,888	12,671	96,176	53,418
1984	1,305,164	902,172	22,545	924,717	87,329	-4,926	832,462	340,087	132,615	13,326	97,944	54,135
1985	1,330,473	927,533	-13,455	914,078	91,362	-3,077	819,639	366,551	144,283	13,543	98,243	54,124
1986	1,367,478	942,635	2,047	944,682	92,510	-4,088	848,084	362,410	156,984	13,808	99,036	52,823
1987	1,392,153	954,221	12,341	966,562	93,117	-3,104	870,341	356,408	165,404	14,026	99,256	54,435
1988	1,467,300	1,003,300	9,633	1,012,933	100,836	-681	911,416	375,191	180,693	14,642	100,211	55,049
1989	1,558,304	1,022,367	8,076	1,030,443	104,775	1,493	927,161	430,120	201,023	15,378	101,335	54,853
1990	1,616,148	1,073,970	17,952	1,091,922	108,624	5,729	989,027	410,439	216,682	16,174	99,924	54,813
1991	1,671,451	1,139,415	9,223	1,148,638	118,242	5,826	1,036,222	404,375	230,854	16,762	99,719	55,746
1992	1,771,929	1,204,794	13,004	1,217,798	124,399	5,743	1,099,142	406,353	266,434	17,525	101,111	55,914
1993	1,870,317	1,285,193	14,606	1,299,799	132,702	5,071	1,172,168	417,373	280,776	18,364	101,848	57,157
1994	1,939,695	1,317,899	17,100	1,334,999	137,890	5,368	1,202,477	442,908	294,310	18,802	103,167	58,121
1995	2,068,811	1,398,587	11,466	1,410,053	146,192	4,253	1,268,114	476,806	323,891	19,962	103,639	60,203
1996	2,146,922	1,439,705	7,661	1,447,366	149,427	4,443	1,302,382	497,528	347,012	20,530	104,574	61,413
1997	2,262,222	1,523,799	11,208	1,535,007	155,652	8,014	1,387,369	510,590	364,263	21,492	105,261	61,580
1998	2,420,324	1,675,155	3,384	1,678,539	168,264	5,101	1,515,376	531,886	373,062	22,564	107,267	63,494
1999	2,487,313	1,706,082	17,906	1,723,988	171,868	5,044	1,557,164	541,943	388,206	23,227	107,089	63,302
2000	2,614,108	1,762,090	12,771	1,774,861	176,810	7,374	1,605,425	604,545	404,138	24,386	107,199	64,431
2001	2,889,999	1,986,411	34,840	2,021,251	192,506	5,028	1,833,773	620,475	435,751	27,025	106,937	64,719
2002	2,936,735	2,046,139	22,159	2,068,298	197,998	-803	1,869,497	592,304	474,934	27,431	107,058	64,742
2003	3,084,908	2,110,007	37,751	2,147,758	208,761	-136	1,938,861	638,968	507,079	28,754	107,287	64,428
2004	3,144,165	2,156,504	34,323	2,190,827	217,735	-597	1,972,495	640,775	530,895	29,212	107,634	63,655
2005	3,385,459	2,269,791	38,419	2,308,210	225,796	3,392	2,085,806	722,432	577,221	31,409	107,785	64,073
2006	3,551,212	2,427,211	18,216	2,445,427	232,505	10,289	2,223,211	718,895	609,106	32,610	108,898	65,265
2007	3,738,811	2,462,007	33,247	2,495,254	241,459	22,158	2,275,953	793,439	669,419	34,163	109,441	65,959
2008	4,330,793	2,772,882	-1,226	2,771,656	261,045	38,834	2,549,445	1,048,256	733,092	39,236	110,379	66,893
2009	4,012,539	2,641,190	14,334	2,655,524	263,277	17,027	2,409,274	814,572	788,693	35,946	111,626	66,937
2010	4,286,540	2,775,789	34,573	2,810,362	275,186	10,305	2,545,481	877,912	863,147	37,791	113,427	67,506
2011	4,543,005	2,837,944	33,589	2,871,533	255,940	30,285	2,645,878	1,010,664	886,463	39,666	114,532	68,274
2012	4,837,917	3,033,956	15,669	3,049,625	270,218	13,439	2,792,846	1,168,989	876,082	41,672	116,096	70,394
2013	5,031,783	3,145,816	57,079	3,202,895	315,252	7,664	2,895,307	1,232,941	903,535	42,803	117,557	72,401
2014	5,530,590	3,455,919	37,107	3,493,026	337,649	9,611	3,164,988	1,425,690	939,912	46,341	119,346	73,663
2015	5,308,693	3,337,487	44,730	3,382,217	339,890	3,552	3,045,879	1,257,608	1,005,206	44,046	120,527	74,399
2016	5,124,696	3,213,629	17,231	3,230,860	336,560	-15,158	2,879,142	1,173,662	1,071,892	42,447	120,733	73,694
2017	5,411,375	3,378,428	13,340	3,391,768	353,313	-9,369	3,029,086	1,286,550	1,095,739	44,855	120,641	73,433
2018	5,927,320	3,665,940	15,687	3,681,627	377,012	-1,349	3,303,266	1,476,466	1,147,588	48,887	121,245	74,440
2019	6,412,159	4,048,472	21,441	4,069,913	399,849	4,136	3,674,200	1,550,839	1,187,120	52,389	122,395	74,259
2020	6,910,265	4,278,811	32,074	4,310,885	412,282	3,201	3,901,804	1,504,152	1,504,309	56,176	123,010	72,827
2021	7,363,552	4,405,358	24,660	4,430,018	424,487	302	4,005,833	1,650,779	1,706,940	60,187	122,344	73,956

Personal Income and Employment by Area: San Antonio-New Braunfels, TX

(Thousands of dollars, except as noted.)

Year	Personal income, total	Earnings by place of work			Less: Contributions for government social insurance	Plus: Adjustment for residence	Equals: Net earnings by place of residence	Plus: Dividends, interest, and rent	Plus: Personal current transfer receipts	Per capita personal income (dollars)	Population (persons)	Total employment
		Nonfarm	Farm	Total								
1970	3,684,643	2,808,085	33,294	2,841,379	159,637	-2,265	2,679,477	731,642	273,524	3,847	957,715	421,654
1971	4,105,585	3,137,631	20,888	3,158,519	186,884	-3,174	2,968,461	817,555	319,569	4,157	987,523	433,674
1972	4,520,504	3,451,810	35,480	3,487,290	213,133	-5,444	3,268,713	891,805	359,986	4,481	1,008,844	443,581
1973	5,041,111	3,811,954	64,331	3,876,285	266,226	-7,895	3,602,164	1,001,863	437,084	4,852	1,038,887	462,283
1974	5,562,333	4,159,699	47,989	4,207,688	302,457	-2,549	3,902,682	1,133,577	526,074	5,271	1,055,225	467,397
1975	6,080,004	4,450,355	47,328	4,497,683	326,809	11,658	4,182,532	1,229,972	667,500	5,712	1,064,486	461,538
1976	6,675,840	4,925,366	40,937	4,966,303	369,354	22,298	4,619,247	1,328,332	728,261	6,161	1,083,489	475,281
1977	7,294,609	5,433,993	20,951	5,454,944	409,680	3,287	5,048,551	1,476,700	769,358	6,598	1,105,551	493,057
1978	8,225,297	6,147,597	12,971	6,160,568	475,334	-3,858	5,681,376	1,695,356	848,565	7,319	1,123,898	515,788
1979	9,307,841	6,954,727	18,472	6,973,199	566,623	2,683	6,409,259	1,920,480	978,102	8,174	1,138,722	535,097
1980	10,651,527	7,921,124	-20,539	7,900,585	654,032	7,779	7,254,332	2,265,769	1,131,426	9,167	1,161,968	557,276
1981	12,197,582	9,017,941	12,971	9,030,912	797,533	22,431	8,255,810	2,669,754	1,272,018	10,275	1,187,117	575,836
1982	13,487,947	9,808,557	11,466	9,820,023	881,171	17,696	8,956,548	3,120,992	1,410,407	11,036	1,222,136	594,500
1983	14,773,312	10,655,606	39,080	10,694,686	976,871	13,015	9,730,830	3,499,009	1,543,473	11,781	1,254,044	611,333
1984	16,570,645	11,970,928	45,086	12,016,014	1,122,939	9,729	10,902,804	3,989,121	1,678,720	12,906	1,283,925	646,427
1985	18,205,892	13,143,116	6,805	13,149,921	1,253,018	11,498	11,908,401	4,506,136	1,791,355	13,819	1,317,439	676,534
1986	19,211,657	13,868,942	12,769	13,881,711	1,318,806	6,446	12,569,351	4,706,010	1,936,296	14,161	1,356,676	685,123
1987	19,644,068	14,195,585	12,077	14,207,662	1,340,468	4,256	12,871,450	4,703,536	2,069,082	14,153	1,387,997	702,912
1988	20,828,129	15,147,620	4,503	15,152,123	1,479,625	3,852	13,676,350	4,941,439	2,210,340	14,936	1,394,458	706,182
1989	22,074,120	15,717,375	31,683	15,749,058	1,567,485	6,649	14,188,222	5,366,478	2,519,420	15,753	1,401,286	713,903
1990	23,224,842	16,526,592	49,940	16,576,532	1,641,022	11,226	14,946,736	5,433,198	2,844,908	16,461	1,410,902	723,234
1991	24,416,180	17,484,395	47,919	17,532,314	1,782,766	15,707	15,765,255	5,526,800	3,124,125	17,026	1,434,060	736,292
1992	26,616,269	19,065,737	71,050	19,136,787	1,937,420	24,978	17,224,345	5,740,114	3,651,810	18,164	1,465,365	752,583
1993	28,290,688	20,432,597	84,225	20,516,822	2,082,417	34,023	18,468,428	5,987,500	3,834,760	18,882	1,498,269	780,913
1994	30,307,687	21,965,642	70,316	22,035,958	2,252,551	38,147	19,821,554	6,353,107	4,133,026	19,742	1,535,185	813,191
1995	32,571,622	23,445,175	61,379	23,506,554	2,412,350	47,951	21,142,155	6,925,206	4,504,261	20,745	1,570,083	847,156
1996	34,380,363	24,775,742	31,257	24,806,999	2,528,201	70,634	22,349,432	7,186,809	4,844,122	21,495	1,599,427	872,230
1997	36,929,120	26,490,210	69,316	26,559,526	2,710,987	91,674	23,940,213	7,895,387	5,093,520	22,674	1,628,676	908,164
1998	39,856,149	28,941,233	60,288	29,001,521	2,918,263	133,187	26,216,445	8,398,856	5,240,848	24,012	1,659,847	931,942
1999	42,435,887	31,240,513	76,901	31,317,414	3,125,547	164,899	28,356,766	8,687,377	5,391,744	25,125	1,689,009	954,739
2000	46,509,866	34,520,529	62,957	34,583,486	3,353,732	212,225	31,441,979	9,359,766	5,708,121	27,041	1,720,003	980,454
2001	48,870,775	36,502,963	71,646	36,574,609	3,536,335	264,991	33,303,265	9,322,164	6,245,346	27,956	1,748,123	993,949
2002	50,403,789	37,763,276	101,298	37,864,574	3,672,280	282,954	34,475,248	9,147,566	6,780,975	28,251	1,784,153	1,004,351
2003	53,445,721	39,856,262	115,110	39,971,372	3,923,100	364,449	36,412,721	9,671,187	7,361,813	29,433	1,815,846	1,010,902
2004	56,069,991	41,781,281	111,531	41,892,812	4,156,254	498,474	38,235,032	9,995,305	7,839,654	30,184	1,857,602	1,028,529
2005	60,247,602	44,057,714	93,905	44,151,619	4,392,382	568,083	40,327,320	11,183,032	8,737,250	31,771	1,896,328	1,064,972
2006	65,890,383	48,043,599	58,826	48,102,425	4,702,399	775,063	44,175,089	12,244,888	9,470,406	33,680	1,956,361	1,110,198
2007	70,211,067	50,137,096	54,549	50,191,645	4,992,629	972,458	46,171,474	13,552,460	10,487,133	34,904	2,011,543	1,153,153
2008	75,745,258	52,743,996	-15,995	52,728,001	5,199,967	1,222,057	48,750,091	15,062,232	11,932,935	36,747	2,061,275	1,178,789
2009	73,831,727	51,583,381	-18,228	51,565,153	5,306,376	1,039,011	47,297,788	13,435,609	13,098,330	35,063	2,105,672	1,171,263
2010	78,869,933	54,219,435	-2,183	54,217,252	5,573,113	921,228	49,565,367	14,697,002	14,607,564	36,632	2,153,021	1,179,723
2011	85,906,155	57,578,291	-636	57,577,655	5,210,341	901,494	53,268,808	17,398,491	15,238,856	39,156	2,193,950	1,205,858
2012	89,335,943	60,575,864	16,727	60,592,591	5,467,347	960,106	56,085,350	17,977,649	15,272,944	39,934	2,237,076	1,236,539
2013	93,522,639	64,460,693	77,521	64,538,214	6,445,941	865,089	58,957,362	18,754,489	15,810,788	41,017	2,280,116	1,270,478
2014	101,618,081	70,233,679	35,742	70,269,421	6,874,883	1,001,661	64,396,199	20,522,453	16,699,429	43,798	2,320,172	1,312,846
2015	105,045,224	71,839,343	88,023	71,927,366	7,299,348	966,026	65,594,044	21,582,881	17,868,299	44,356	2,368,219	1,356,211
2016	107,063,484	74,839,552	-384	74,839,168	7,701,520	893,841	68,031,489	20,393,427	18,638,568	44,379	2,412,468	1,407,425
2017	113,453,527	79,458,572	-12,466	79,446,106	8,161,311	952,118	72,236,913	22,033,637	19,182,977	46,204	2,455,494	1,451,717
2018	120,949,573	84,468,746	-28,223	84,440,523	8,518,241	1,060,438	76,982,720	23,752,268	20,214,585	48,500	2,493,824	1,491,393
2019	123,450,340	84,445,523	-38,715	84,406,808	8,826,187	1,099,212	76,679,833	25,341,254	21,429,253	48,819	2,528,761	1,513,010
2020	128,884,188	83,544,069	-25,475	83,518,594	8,992,214	1,040,864	75,567,244	24,871,951	28,444,993	50,214	2,566,683	1,487,063
2021	139,579,662	89,372,280	-20,652	89,351,628	9,582,598	1,075,815	80,844,845	26,128,910	32,605,907	53,648	2,601,788	1,533,409

Personal Income and Employment by Area: San Diego-Chula Vista-Carlsbad, CA

(Thousands of dollars, except as noted.)

Year	Personal income, total	Earnings by place of work			Less: Contributions for government social insurance	Plus: Adjustment for residence	Equals: Net earnings by place of residence	Plus: Dividends, interest, and rent	Plus: Personal current transfer receipts	Per capita personal income (dollars)	Population (persons)	Total employment
		Nonfarm	Farm	Total								
1970	7,021,079	5,197,882	55,543	5,253,425	330,158	-31,761	4,891,506	1,593,087	536,486	5,140	1,365,976	647,900
1971	7,542,007	5,552,875	53,571	5,606,446	366,432	-34,848	5,205,166	1,712,595	624,246	5,418	1,391,925	649,466
1972	8,389,601	6,185,140	66,676	6,251,816	421,658	-39,672	5,790,486	1,901,618	697,497	5,854	1,433,126	672,285
1973	9,259,626	6,782,180	93,067	6,875,247	513,822	-42,635	6,318,790	2,140,191	800,645	6,175	1,499,594	707,773
1974	10,346,671	7,432,299	90,285	7,522,584	582,505	-36,744	6,903,335	2,458,996	984,340	6,716	1,540,667	738,023
1975	11,572,053	8,121,710	127,474	8,249,184	641,270	-28,094	7,579,820	2,721,783	1,270,450	7,157	1,616,907	755,698
1976	12,917,968	9,111,012	140,674	9,251,686	733,932	-11,769	8,505,985	2,970,690	1,441,293	7,863	1,642,781	786,899
1977	14,430,966	10,243,704	145,540	10,389,244	841,360	-24,610	9,523,274	3,350,314	1,557,378	8,412	1,715,527	837,772
1978	16,558,724	11,843,665	121,391	11,965,056	989,270	-15,953	10,959,833	3,898,085	1,700,806	9,327	1,775,410	901,275
1979	18,772,293	13,466,406	115,005	13,581,411	1,184,792	6,180	12,402,799	4,456,856	1,912,638	10,272	1,827,602	951,199
1980	21,673,970	15,231,915	130,630	15,362,545	1,306,937	12,741	14,068,349	5,345,045	2,260,576	11,556	1,875,620	988,237
1981	24,710,161	16,898,694	136,921	17,035,615	1,565,281	138,157	15,608,491	6,394,583	2,707,087	12,823	1,927,018	994,581
1982	26,771,408	18,157,216	146,039	18,303,255	1,707,103	146,070	16,742,222	7,037,567	2,991,619	13,573	1,972,354	1,001,945
1983	28,899,057	19,592,410	152,031	19,744,441	1,907,010	174,796	18,012,227	7,674,025	3,212,805	14,320	2,018,133	1,036,404
1984	32,418,187	22,291,784	166,620	22,458,404	2,257,329	179,666	20,380,741	8,652,472	3,384,974	15,688	2,066,419	1,099,543
1985	35,569,628	24,746,996	197,066	24,944,062	2,543,992	198,416	22,598,486	9,304,937	3,666,205	16,730	2,126,090	1,160,801
1986	38,773,644	27,301,007	230,526	27,531,533	2,850,882	225,645	24,906,296	9,879,126	3,988,222	17,650	2,196,834	1,215,030
1987	41,871,173	30,029,243	212,305	30,241,548	3,155,298	262,122	27,348,372	10,287,290	4,235,511	18,402	2,275,309	1,277,030
1988	46,018,825	33,402,677	182,362	33,585,039	3,636,499	291,390	30,239,930	11,176,389	4,602,506	19,464	2,364,284	1,349,526
1989	50,000,601	35,620,581	230,526	35,851,107	3,928,187	333,883	32,256,803	12,702,625	5,041,173	20,455	2,444,380	1,396,314
1990	52,763,858	37,736,038	298,772	38,034,810	4,155,899	377,878	34,256,789	12,955,258	5,551,811	21,002	2,512,365	1,426,402
1991	55,032,226	39,699,075	241,204	39,940,279	4,392,161	334,774	35,882,892	12,991,145	6,158,189	21,555	2,553,122	1,436,665
1992	57,832,374	41,538,542	197,911	41,736,453	4,583,742	328,248	37,480,959	13,361,265	6,990,150	22,302	2,593,126	1,406,200
1993	59,175,096	42,104,423	211,031	42,315,454	4,665,573	312,453	37,962,334	13,825,830	7,386,932	22,762	2,599,776	1,402,948
1994	60,899,000	43,361,620	224,569	43,586,189	4,840,970	288,938	39,034,157	14,305,363	7,559,480	23,291	2,614,685	1,408,463
1995	63,689,849	44,858,354	246,325	45,104,679	4,934,866	281,857	40,451,670	15,277,759	7,960,420	24,275	2,623,697	1,440,496
1996	67,919,229	48,108,712	281,483	48,390,195	5,143,278	269,236	43,516,153	16,062,608	8,340,468	25,615	2,651,549	1,479,423
1997	72,640,103	52,055,833	320,278	52,376,111	5,532,467	249,861	47,093,505	17,082,524	8,464,074	26,978	2,692,600	1,521,768
1998	80,340,377	58,525,799	352,838	58,878,637	6,097,149	241,128	53,022,616	18,519,043	8,798,718	29,356	2,736,720	1,608,669
1999	87,435,203	65,104,996	360,400	65,465,396	6,743,671	182,201	58,903,926	19,265,718	9,265,559	31,343	2,789,593	1,656,003
2000	95,759,629	72,297,291	359,299	72,656,590	7,495,956	138,277	65,298,911	20,777,861	9,682,857	33,869	2,827,366	1,696,594
2001	98,500,708	74,783,608	347,415	75,131,023	7,944,179	-75,720	67,111,124	20,741,397	10,648,187	34,325	2,869,672	1,713,767
2002	102,424,167	79,031,111	362,119	79,393,230	8,474,995	-320,939	70,597,296	20,584,212	11,242,659	35,314	2,900,355	1,749,463
2003	108,072,559	84,394,532	400,847	84,795,379	9,096,337	-535,389	75,163,653	21,063,666	11,845,240	37,078	2,914,702	1,782,103
2004	116,712,463	92,149,911	446,449	92,596,360	10,097,202	-765,967	81,733,191	22,555,131	12,424,141	39,834	2,930,007	1,812,986
2005	122,069,367	96,631,938	465,618	97,097,556	10,555,955	-948,877	85,592,724	23,402,330	13,074,313	41,543	2,938,375	1,837,287
2006	128,619,711	101,188,657	418,804	101,607,461	10,803,629	-1,176,916	89,626,916	24,936,621	14,056,174	43,640	2,947,289	1,861,439
2007	132,558,872	102,231,468	401,462	102,632,930	10,867,329	-1,492,316	90,273,285	27,382,074	14,903,513	44,546	2,975,742	1,890,307
2008	135,573,433	101,931,305	460,295	102,391,600	11,158,296	-1,908,296	89,325,008	29,223,238	17,025,187	44,860	3,022,116	1,882,625
2009	130,932,057	98,337,506	532,785	98,870,291	10,939,103	-1,974,541	85,956,647	26,224,911	18,750,499	42,771	3,061,203	1,821,926
2010	135,927,888	101,230,863	587,227	101,818,090	11,086,243	-2,053,304	88,678,543	26,296,396	20,952,949	43,802	3,103,260	1,804,107
2011	144,239,664	105,786,678	510,655	106,297,333	10,441,514	-2,167,842	93,687,977	29,250,770	21,300,917	45,977	3,137,236	1,828,222
2012	151,467,749	111,586,952	626,989	112,213,941	10,833,798	-2,226,207	99,153,936	30,852,188	21,461,625	47,704	3,175,148	1,877,293
2013	156,734,939	116,817,984	511,177	117,329,161	12,571,922	-2,217,467	102,539,772	31,760,515	22,434,652	48,815	3,210,788	1,920,959
2014	166,466,694	122,718,721	542,689	123,261,410	13,183,791	-2,251,085	107,826,534	34,646,873	23,993,287	51,463	3,234,658	1,973,042
2015	176,125,940	129,141,195	612,807	129,754,002	13,794,021	-2,299,072	113,660,909	36,659,092	25,805,939	53,984	3,262,566	2,029,956
2016	181,952,012	133,302,254	528,197	133,830,451	14,197,881	-2,346,585	117,285,985	38,047,298	26,618,729	55,413	3,283,586	2,083,414
2017	189,127,670	139,869,183	563,689	140,432,872	14,905,203	-2,465,958	123,061,711	39,605,930	26,460,029	57,423	3,293,575	2,118,970
2018	196,316,898	145,425,994	431,212	145,857,206	15,630,089	-2,527,487	127,699,630	40,775,775	27,841,493	59,428	3,303,463	2,148,559
2019	206,231,115	150,155,679	497,849	150,653,528	16,359,719	-2,575,652	131,718,157	44,745,563	29,767,395	62,533	3,297,959	2,158,174
2020	223,652,407	153,561,302	478,483	154,039,785	16,709,340	-2,643,144	134,687,301	44,958,268	44,006,838	67,830	3,297,252	2,054,042
2021	238,691,713	167,167,238	396,710	167,563,948	18,015,946	-2,913,934	146,634,068	46,040,893	46,016,752	72,637	3,286,069	2,131,117

Personal Income and Employment by Area: San Francisco-Oakland-Berkeley, CA

(Thousands of dollars, except as noted.)

Year	Personal income, total	Earnings by place of work			Less: Contributions for government social insurance	Plus: Adjustment for residence	Equals: Net earnings by place of residence	Plus: Dividends, interest, and rent	Plus: Personal current transfer receipts	Per capita personal income (dollars)	Population (persons)	Total employment
		Nonfarm	Farm	Total								
1970	17,758,252	14,344,577	54,040	14,398,617	916,727	-490,495	12,991,395	3,279,499	1,487,358	5,713	3,108,460	1,559,634
1971	18,922,324	15,107,827	50,566	15,158,393	993,263	-478,952	13,686,178	3,531,384	1,704,762	6,066	3,119,247	1,528,383
1972	20,547,981	16,463,802	63,355	16,527,157	1,140,417	-500,443	14,886,297	3,835,355	1,826,329	6,555	3,134,632	1,561,571
1973	22,058,296	17,686,918	67,268	17,754,186	1,417,530	-524,958	15,811,698	4,234,443	2,012,155	7,011	3,146,217	1,614,085
1974	24,304,358	19,257,861	72,533	19,330,394	1,598,743	-570,040	17,161,611	4,810,231	2,332,516	7,710	3,152,349	1,648,391
1975	26,876,119	21,067,667	78,432	21,146,099	1,712,018	-633,633	18,800,448	5,188,400	2,887,271	8,510	3,158,346	1,670,337
1976	29,450,851	23,293,131	72,610	23,365,741	1,922,349	-729,849	20,713,543	5,577,687	3,159,621	9,241	3,187,017	1,693,226
1977	32,224,427	25,722,822	63,551	25,786,373	2,145,087	-877,371	22,763,915	6,141,226	3,319,286	10,072	3,199,300	1,733,826
1978	36,044,414	29,064,238	78,859	29,143,097	2,482,258	-1,037,572	25,623,267	6,906,482	3,514,665	11,216	3,213,638	1,817,444
1979	40,234,936	32,491,677	103,502	32,595,179	2,914,715	-1,162,758	28,517,706	7,859,777	3,857,453	12,470	3,226,421	1,895,178
1980	45,536,329	36,128,140	116,289	36,244,429	3,211,117	-1,360,286	31,673,026	9,490,730	4,372,573	13,964	3,260,930	1,955,758
1981	51,417,855	39,683,581	110,412	39,793,993	3,831,802	-1,415,484	34,546,707	11,850,527	5,020,621	15,601	3,295,803	1,971,802
1982	55,089,850	42,154,077	116,698	42,270,775	4,167,479	-1,377,655	36,725,641	12,916,948	5,447,261	16,524	3,333,995	1,960,504
1983	59,916,850	45,840,294	118,991	45,959,285	4,611,921	-1,304,199	40,043,165	14,070,916	5,802,769	17,695	3,386,080	1,996,122
1984	66,381,238	50,547,490	117,042	50,664,532	5,280,746	-1,296,720	44,087,066	16,292,810	6,001,362	19,364	3,428,080	2,066,961
1985	71,115,447	54,432,869	123,645	54,556,514	5,767,651	-1,292,156	47,496,707	17,227,865	6,390,875	20,439	3,479,465	2,120,828
1986	75,679,506	58,894,918	129,897	59,024,815	6,313,809	-1,542,347	51,168,659	17,710,919	6,799,928	21,476	3,523,866	2,168,002
1987	79,968,993	62,997,206	135,832	63,133,038	6,741,661	-1,517,760	54,873,617	18,034,249	7,061,127	22,470	3,558,999	2,224,223
1988	87,495,963	69,140,538	133,159	69,273,697	7,561,469	-1,496,250	60,215,978	19,749,693	7,530,292	24,281	3,603,440	2,310,192
1989	93,615,657	72,588,296	136,327	72,724,623	8,042,499	-1,647,205	63,034,919	22,298,220	8,282,518	25,599	3,656,981	2,351,774
1990	99,034,323	76,827,714	145,811	76,973,525	8,475,271	-1,647,022	66,851,232	23,168,925	9,014,166	26,624	3,719,675	2,399,266
1991	103,542,135	81,079,411	114,587	81,193,998	8,973,128	-1,772,324	70,448,546	23,306,974	9,786,615	27,535	3,760,370	2,388,786
1992	109,633,758	85,745,583	130,332	85,875,915	9,415,352	-1,628,458	74,832,105	23,671,595	11,130,058	28,809	3,805,588	2,347,136
1993	113,895,634	88,617,212	133,073	88,750,285	9,715,926	-1,592,355	77,442,004	24,809,821	11,643,809	29,663	3,839,619	2,358,677
1994	118,135,753	91,758,127	141,876	91,900,003	10,124,732	-1,545,241	80,230,030	26,094,009	11,811,714	30,606	3,859,905	2,385,264
1995	126,463,480	97,177,962	120,170	97,298,132	10,561,012	-1,293,394	85,443,726	28,658,956	12,360,798	32,561	3,883,894	2,436,826
1996	136,900,716	104,260,168	128,917	104,389,085	11,038,955	-186,488	93,163,642	30,914,496	12,822,578	34,895	3,923,208	2,492,590
1997	146,246,324	112,099,461	192,729	112,292,190	11,815,241	284,037	100,760,986	32,613,479	12,871,859	36,693	3,985,694	2,550,128
1998	162,494,632	124,195,303	181,331	124,376,634	12,843,879	874,651	112,407,406	36,540,487	13,546,739	40,170	4,045,185	2,639,817
1999	178,817,595	137,455,287	193,137	137,648,424	14,147,782	2,761,491	126,262,133	38,513,947	14,041,515	43,725	4,089,620	2,697,881
2000	205,264,266	160,621,125	207,119	160,828,244	16,333,959	3,790,105	148,284,390	42,431,222	14,548,654	49,630	4,135,875	2,770,316
2001	207,536,424	165,694,576	218,358	165,912,934	16,944,742	892,730	149,860,922	41,711,568	15,963,934	49,712	4,174,788	2,747,283
2002	201,142,728	161,500,778	208,288	161,709,066	16,718,368	-530,321	144,460,377	39,258,610	17,423,741	48,369	4,158,544	2,679,890
2003	203,848,916	163,459,706	230,808	163,690,514	17,030,698	-1,068,468	145,591,348	40,097,847	18,159,721	49,168	4,145,965	2,653,534
2004	215,055,207	171,161,545	190,013	171,351,558	18,185,450	-1,085,899	152,080,209	44,104,462	18,870,536	52,029	4,133,400	2,659,356
2005	228,854,477	179,562,232	178,991	179,741,223	18,862,141	-1,884,774	158,994,308	50,115,959	19,744,210	55,307	4,137,858	2,682,602
2006	250,178,913	190,428,689	177,038	190,605,727	19,407,582	-1,781,739	169,416,406	59,584,992	21,177,515	60,303	4,148,724	2,728,960
2007	262,004,923	197,767,931	166,139	197,934,070	19,945,631	-991,895	176,996,544	62,691,819	22,316,560	62,626	4,183,637	2,785,090
2008	266,289,723	198,276,430	162,474	198,438,904	20,584,543	-506,141	177,348,220	63,807,732	25,133,771	62,746	4,243,932	2,785,616
2009	253,552,649	192,400,365	162,878	192,563,243	19,970,857	-759,376	171,833,010	53,886,843	27,832,796	58,927	4,302,830	2,687,707
2010	263,524,412	198,611,192	163,014	198,774,206	19,940,246	1,368,042	180,202,002	52,696,644	30,625,766	60,666	4,343,886	2,663,490
2011	284,360,419	209,392,915	180,481	209,573,396	18,695,662	2,958,213	193,835,947	59,990,664	30,533,808	64,682	4,396,273	2,715,302
2012	310,036,366	232,838,802	194,365	233,033,167	20,167,025	-2,242,789	210,623,353	68,781,463	30,631,550	69,579	4,455,918	2,836,176
2013	317,919,435	242,920,075	195,272	243,115,347	24,147,580	-293,234	218,674,533	67,360,885	31,884,017	70,336	4,520,028	2,943,003
2014	344,433,038	258,248,182	225,812	258,473,994	25,825,571	2,898,645	235,547,068	74,840,821	34,045,149	74,845	4,601,942	3,059,380
2015	377,677,732	278,610,529	219,267	278,829,796	27,716,184	4,392,004	255,505,616	85,508,432	36,663,684	80,890	4,669,035	3,184,062
2016	401,626,627	299,011,399	191,415	299,202,814	29,379,187	1,122,477	270,946,104	92,549,976	38,130,547	85,214	4,713,129	3,278,552
2017	429,666,010	321,175,418	223,182	321,398,600	31,411,182	1,093,505	291,080,923	100,556,840	38,028,247	90,630	4,740,862	3,340,151
2018	461,409,833	343,270,988	157,880	343,428,868	33,653,069	1,750,936	311,526,735	109,873,768	40,009,330	96,952	4,759,142	3,408,613
2019	483,631,903	365,837,505	203,064	366,040,569	35,988,622	392,139	330,444,086	110,706,545	42,481,272	101,569	4,761,624	3,408,973
2020	522,980,548	381,134,839	237,138	381,371,977	36,848,846	3,583,358	348,106,489	110,763,827	64,110,232	110,342	4,739,649	3,192,316
2021	571,947,556	432,890,789	214,506	433,105,295	40,495,890	757,548	393,366,953	114,338,988	64,241,615	123,711	4,623,264	3,277,533

Personal Income and Employment by Area: San Jose-Sunnyvale-Santa Clara, CA

(Thousands of dollars, except as noted.)

Year	Personal income, total	Earnings by place of work			Less: Contributions for government social insurance	Plus: Adjustment for residence	Equals: Net earnings by place of residence	Plus: Dividends, interest, and rent	Plus: Personal current transfer receipts	Per capita personal income (dollars)	Population (persons)	Total employment
		Nonfarm	Farm	Total								
1970	5,534,127	4,215,123	48,867	4,263,990	284,661	369,993	4,349,322	778,460	406,345	5,079	1,089,674	465,696
1971	5,956,579	4,512,419	51,593	4,564,012	314,276	359,172	4,608,908	865,550	482,121	5,322	1,119,155	468,263
1972	6,610,349	5,105,259	57,898	5,163,157	377,334	345,027	5,130,850	958,148	521,351	5,709	1,157,841	500,625
1973	7,382,556	5,842,144	78,728	5,920,872	500,555	312,063	5,732,380	1,077,020	573,156	6,238	1,183,576	544,854
1974	8,276,698	6,583,684	81,853	6,665,537	579,590	275,225	6,361,172	1,242,730	672,796	6,986	1,184,823	576,125
1975	9,188,573	7,128,079	82,909	7,210,988	611,469	307,357	6,906,876	1,385,904	895,793	7,571	1,213,688	578,145
1976	10,249,199	8,144,218	68,233	8,212,451	715,209	283,406	7,780,648	1,501,242	967,309	8,342	1,228,572	616,284
1977	11,480,890	9,395,211	82,006	9,477,217	844,061	198,177	8,831,333	1,654,395	995,162	9,153	1,254,396	654,919
1978	13,179,444	11,023,393	83,357	11,106,750	1,020,884	120,313	10,206,179	1,909,494	1,063,771	10,264	1,284,003	708,398
1979	15,251,451	13,075,768	94,626	13,170,394	1,267,871	-7,988	11,894,535	2,216,740	1,140,176	11,771	1,295,698	770,291
1980	17,602,148	14,989,183	104,694	15,093,877	1,427,082	-122,071	13,544,724	2,734,551	1,322,873	13,268	1,326,709	814,696
1981	19,988,425	16,953,841	84,949	17,038,790	1,745,222	-297,037	14,996,531	3,439,545	1,552,349	14,799	1,350,627	832,437
1982	21,901,335	18,880,173	95,526	18,975,699	1,986,212	-553,198	16,436,289	3,798,939	1,666,107	15,964	1,371,955	848,645
1983	24,162,929	21,260,706	99,450	21,360,156	2,288,892	-899,858	18,171,406	4,206,123	1,785,400	17,237	1,401,776	879,267
1984	27,008,475	24,142,733	118,983	24,261,716	2,709,798	-1,290,765	20,261,153	4,928,494	1,818,828	18,951	1,425,185	936,276
1985	28,687,588	25,858,401	125,325	25,983,726	2,923,564	-1,628,498	21,431,664	5,283,407	1,972,517	19,786	1,449,912	949,532
1986	29,803,632	26,940,110	141,408	27,081,518	3,055,230	-1,756,278	22,270,010	5,406,699	2,126,923	20,391	1,461,582	947,268
1987	31,654,585	29,223,076	148,800	29,371,876	3,286,046	-2,187,548	23,898,282	5,543,602	2,212,701	21,380	1,480,543	978,952
1988	34,665,513	32,562,121	141,139	32,703,260	3,759,631	-2,680,069	26,263,560	6,031,959	2,369,994	23,009	1,506,608	1,023,025
1989	37,225,649	34,670,071	138,039	34,808,110	3,986,593	-3,006,249	27,815,268	6,785,190	2,625,191	24,263	1,534,258	1,036,067
1990	39,066,135	36,884,217	126,958	37,011,175	4,221,001	-3,843,936	28,946,238	7,234,820	2,885,077	25,448	1,535,142	1,052,577
1991	40,673,301	38,446,217	112,918	38,559,135	4,432,029	-3,919,521	30,207,585	7,290,649	3,175,067	26,233	1,550,447	1,040,251
1992	43,751,012	41,359,128	120,834	41,479,962	4,679,201	-4,238,479	32,562,282	7,483,879	3,704,851	27,863	1,570,207	1,017,714
1993	44,617,672	42,028,294	155,773	42,184,067	4,811,069	-4,526,487	32,846,511	7,882,502	3,888,659	28,085	1,588,680	1,023,035
1994	46,467,773	43,900,717	169,310	44,070,027	5,087,957	-4,941,200	34,040,870	8,511,997	3,914,906	29,003	1,602,152	1,036,627
1995	51,206,472	48,574,157	197,267	48,771,424	5,549,180	-5,606,237	37,616,007	9,493,318	4,097,147	31,559	1,622,579	1,075,809
1996	55,716,545	54,086,068	178,138	54,264,206	6,102,632	-7,212,730	40,948,844	10,463,513	4,304,188	33,709	1,652,864	1,131,518
1997	61,817,008	61,240,640	193,098	61,433,738	6,802,807	-8,603,956	46,026,975	11,480,361	4,309,672	36,706	1,684,121	1,175,557
1998	66,942,253	66,855,801	197,634	67,053,435	7,335,512	-9,951,158	49,766,765	12,655,689	4,519,799	39,193	1,708,031	1,221,008
1999	75,411,322	78,376,188	222,136	78,598,324	8,430,548	-12,965,383	57,202,393	13,482,931	4,725,998	43,768	1,722,965	1,226,104
2000	93,802,941	100,391,771	323,462	100,715,233	10,304,020	-16,684,824	73,726,389	15,141,131	4,935,421	53,949	1,738,728	1,283,119
2001	88,428,603	90,192,228	249,237	90,441,465	9,439,742	-13,060,106	67,941,617	15,032,077	5,454,909	50,742	1,742,726	1,245,499
2002	82,792,506	81,390,844	221,752	81,612,596	8,583,901	-10,860,634	62,168,061	14,360,329	6,264,116	48,012	1,724,404	1,151,605
2003	83,424,925	80,492,685	229,494	80,722,179	8,520,856	-10,313,102	61,888,221	15,009,303	6,527,401	48,537	1,718,790	1,111,274
2004	85,950,369	83,344,479	242,543	83,587,022	9,016,307	-10,728,414	63,842,301	15,557,057	6,551,011	50,029	1,718,016	1,110,182
2005	90,895,677	85,947,093	230,637	86,177,730	9,230,775	-10,456,823	66,490,132	17,551,090	6,854,455	52,542	1,729,959	1,120,373
2006	100,126,224	93,074,697	224,689	93,299,386	9,686,061	-11,365,850	72,247,475	20,452,740	7,426,009	57,370	1,745,283	1,146,729
2007	108,688,678	100,438,524	203,451	100,641,975	10,203,086	-12,762,078	77,676,811	23,110,352	7,901,515	61,542	1,766,098	1,183,453
2008	108,580,685	99,703,319	175,512	99,878,831	10,498,778	-12,418,334	76,961,719	22,536,427	9,082,539	60,483	1,795,231	1,186,385
2009	102,214,950	94,416,797	241,383	94,658,180	10,086,317	-11,075,614	73,496,249	18,452,978	10,265,723	56,175	1,819,573	1,130,469
2010	110,981,123	103,246,559	229,946	103,476,505	10,533,755	-12,578,492	80,364,258	19,286,024	11,330,841	60,265	1,841,545	1,126,570
2011	121,424,899	112,512,237	196,440	112,708,677	10,001,877	-14,898,051	87,808,749	22,371,713	11,244,437	65,003	1,867,985	1,159,903
2012	135,029,206	118,466,828	246,329	118,713,157	10,451,716	-10,482,534	97,778,907	26,048,434	11,201,865	71,282	1,894,309	1,206,137
2013	137,464,211	125,761,793	286,244	126,048,037	12,881,768	-13,397,407	99,768,862	26,143,346	11,552,003	71,470	1,923,370	1,254,612
2014	150,604,609	137,919,125	302,779	138,221,904	14,041,872	-16,626,906	107,553,126	30,740,272	12,311,211	76,889	1,958,735	1,300,033
2015	166,082,310	153,480,137	354,567	153,834,704	15,357,669	-19,883,843	118,593,192	34,252,679	13,236,439	83,628	1,985,975	1,358,652
2016	179,830,458	163,346,281	288,672	163,634,953	16,096,338	-18,320,872	129,217,743	36,955,549	13,657,166	89,835	2,001,778	1,395,012
2017	194,763,258	177,909,080	286,933	178,196,013	17,393,783	-19,732,939	141,069,291	40,169,375	13,524,592	96,938	2,009,163	1,424,940
2018	212,286,315	195,212,351	225,561	195,437,912	18,841,453	-21,376,166	155,220,293	42,924,707	14,141,315	105,486	2,012,463	1,459,429
2019	224,377,528	204,051,152	212,645	204,263,797	19,746,892	-22,638,774	161,878,131	47,515,304	14,984,093	111,825	2,006,501	1,466,990
2020	241,019,138	221,194,740	217,212	221,411,952	20,866,724	-29,916,790	170,628,438	47,714,345	22,676,355	120,805	1,995,105	1,399,472
2021	266,156,519	254,030,556	176,763	254,207,319	23,113,007	-37,194,171	193,900,141	49,288,813	22,967,565	136,338	1,952,185	1,432,964

Personal Income and Employment by Area: San Luis Obispo-Paso Robles, CA

(Thousands of dollars, except as noted.)

| Year | Personal income, total | Earnings by place of work | | | Less: Contributions for government social insurance | Plus: Adjustment for residence | Equals: Net earnings by place of residence | Plus: Dividends, interest, and rent | Plus: Personal current transfer receipts | Per capita personal income (dollars) | Population (persons) | Total employment |
		Nonfarm	Farm	Total								
1970	410,874	250,223	17,638	267,861	14,935	13,385	266,311	88,796	55,767	3,866	106,280	38,922
1971	455,874	282,363	17,908	300,271	17,428	13,938	296,781	98,500	60,593	4,171	109,301	40,811
1972	513,809	321,221	23,147	344,368	21,113	14,896	338,151	110,387	65,271	4,449	115,484	43,478
1973	581,196	358,830	27,270	386,100	26,863	17,791	377,028	130,047	74,121	4,850	119,843	45,667
1974	673,901	399,905	40,083	439,988	31,041	21,526	430,473	152,011	91,417	5,368	125,535	48,387
1975	767,457	451,386	33,698	485,084	34,418	27,141	477,807	176,413	113,237	6,069	126,456	50,574
1976	874,841	522,678	33,850	556,528	40,031	32,959	549,456	195,569	129,816	6,516	134,260	53,644
1977	975,928	585,484	27,105	612,589	45,708	41,666	608,547	225,112	142,269	7,040	138,635	56,552
1978	1,152,991	695,073	44,864	739,937	55,958	47,902	731,881	264,676	156,434	7,902	145,914	60,728
1979	1,312,402	792,040	41,414	833,454	67,457	59,134	825,131	311,928	175,343	8,700	150,850	65,290
1980	1,486,564	843,427	45,673	889,100	70,113	72,362	891,349	388,567	206,648	9,481	156,786	66,956
1981	1,672,093	925,234	49,536	974,770	85,267	66,813	956,316	472,008	243,769	10,329	161,886	68,339
1982	1,796,170	958,879	62,286	1,021,165	90,931	74,490	1,004,724	526,235	265,211	10,784	166,563	68,574
1983	2,166,411	1,280,798	68,083	1,348,881	127,760	49,927	1,271,048	613,373	281,990	12,642	171,365	75,005
1984	2,382,952	1,412,144	53,564	1,465,708	144,599	68,057	1,389,166	688,539	305,247	13,420	177,566	79,834
1985	2,551,924	1,480,246	53,258	1,533,504	149,855	88,468	1,472,117	746,023	333,784	13,776	185,248	84,089
1986	2,778,742	1,626,663	72,418	1,699,081	165,384	94,957	1,628,654	790,888	359,200	14,435	192,497	87,984
1987	3,019,418	1,829,764	84,857	1,914,621	186,139	93,763	1,822,245	819,199	377,974	15,147	199,345	92,685
1988	3,313,775	2,022,158	88,696	2,110,854	212,600	102,754	2,001,008	906,757	406,010	16,223	204,261	98,930
1989	3,667,188	2,181,670	91,975	2,273,645	234,621	107,789	2,146,813	1,074,119	446,256	17,192	213,314	103,273
1990	3,833,545	2,346,773	72,761	2,419,534	250,092	111,320	2,280,762	1,069,765	483,018	17,563	218,276	106,051
1991	4,009,496	2,489,432	47,156	2,536,588	264,916	123,747	2,395,419	1,086,865	527,212	18,234	219,895	110,470
1992	4,249,317	2,637,813	63,697	2,701,510	279,130	129,695	2,552,075	1,100,167	597,075	19,154	221,848	110,178
1993	4,403,078	2,697,296	77,927	2,775,223	284,869	134,940	2,625,294	1,141,854	635,930	19,712	223,370	109,848
1994	4,571,999	2,795,346	70,575	2,865,921	297,402	142,581	2,711,100	1,202,877	658,022	20,210	226,228	112,959
1995	4,835,554	2,974,326	74,240	3,048,566	311,092	150,667	2,888,141	1,257,428	689,985	21,082	229,370	116,952
1996	5,211,367	3,215,172	76,942	3,292,114	324,625	159,140	3,126,629	1,353,854	730,884	22,369	232,976	120,730
1997	5,670,563	3,501,976	125,149	3,627,125	348,348	173,190	3,451,967	1,469,847	748,749	23,967	236,601	125,634
1998	6,066,905	3,822,562	101,266	3,923,828	374,399	189,506	3,738,935	1,542,628	785,342	25,277	240,020	131,952
1999	6,468,199	4,105,521	108,469	4,213,990	403,465	209,896	4,020,421	1,631,358	816,420	26,566	243,480	137,881
2000	7,011,298	4,388,050	165,767	4,553,817	432,236	249,840	4,371,421	1,774,690	865,187	28,290	247,839	138,477
2001	7,659,871	4,903,034	130,152	5,033,186	490,281	266,238	4,809,143	1,900,088	950,640	30,461	251,462	140,627
2002	7,939,655	5,251,897	131,548	5,383,445	531,550	278,630	5,130,525	1,806,935	1,002,195	31,372	253,083	144,119
2003	8,266,467	5,484,445	132,924	5,617,369	561,091	316,541	5,372,819	1,854,515	1,039,133	32,459	254,674	144,119
2004	8,801,774	5,880,755	122,345	6,003,100	621,243	351,923	5,733,780	1,990,775	1,077,219	34,269	256,842	146,485
2005	9,183,021	6,085,618	124,991	6,210,609	652,301	395,798	5,954,106	2,080,866	1,148,049	35,508	258,615	149,346
2006	9,918,182	6,422,519	123,622	6,546,141	666,938	434,208	6,313,411	2,368,699	1,236,072	38,074	260,498	152,479
2007	10,517,099	6,587,739	123,087	6,710,826	675,502	489,421	6,524,745	2,685,827	1,306,527	40,024	262,770	156,737
2008	10,572,271	6,589,361	81,883	6,671,244	692,649	525,299	6,503,894	2,572,867	1,495,510	39,692	266,358	154,624
2009	10,444,391	6,426,909	136,217	6,563,126	681,664	499,524	6,380,986	2,429,565	1,633,840	38,951	268,145	149,202
2010	10,803,268	6,631,090	167,783	6,798,873	680,795	499,020	6,617,098	2,393,989	1,792,181	40,042	269,800	147,777
2011	11,463,052	6,969,948	161,326	7,131,274	648,330	511,807	6,994,751	2,658,325	1,809,976	42,290	271,056	151,009
2012	12,082,424	7,283,761	275,411	7,559,172	666,511	533,437	7,426,098	2,825,431	1,830,895	44,068	274,174	155,745
2013	12,477,912	7,639,943	304,728	7,944,671	775,482	532,904	7,702,093	2,874,097	1,901,722	45,257	275,713	159,400
2014	13,297,837	7,997,184	291,433	8,288,617	818,208	563,221	8,033,630	3,212,621	2,051,586	47,794	278,231	164,661
2015	14,202,463	8,533,087	302,288	8,835,375	867,588	595,967	8,563,754	3,442,823	2,195,886	50,707	280,088	169,374
2016	14,591,004	8,772,232	245,478	9,017,710	892,740	600,392	8,725,362	3,574,596	2,291,046	51,773	281,825	169,798
2017	15,331,154	9,248,082	227,833	9,475,915	944,675	639,674	9,170,914	3,825,889	2,334,351	54,288	282,406	172,944
2018	15,851,762	9,756,035	188,943	9,944,978	1,008,835	654,859	9,591,002	3,800,978	2,459,782	55,978	283,176	175,368
2019	16,904,030	10,270,970	161,556	10,432,526	1,074,840	672,886	10,030,572	4,237,169	2,636,289	59,806	282,646	175,124
2020	17,964,706	10,243,722	170,348	10,414,070	1,072,912	721,021	10,062,179	4,269,404	3,633,123	63,652	282,231	165,661
2021	18,863,123	10,961,571	123,410	11,084,981	1,146,755	763,954	10,702,180	4,358,027	3,802,916	66,617	283,159	172,325

Personal Income and Employment by Area: Santa Cruz-Watsonville, CA

(Thousands of dollars, except as noted.)

Year	Personal income, total	Earnings by place of work Nonfarm	Farm	Total	Less: Contributions for government social insurance	Plus: Adjustment for residence	Equals: Net earnings by place of residence	Plus: Dividends, interest, and rent	Plus: Personal current transfer receipts	Per capita personal income (dollars)	Population (persons)	Total employment
1970	558,375	311,740	19,379	331,119	20,780	47,906	358,245	129,153	70,977	4,475	124,788	49,358
1971	623,329	338,430	21,178	359,608	23,013	59,872	396,467	143,587	83,275	4,799	129,886	50,838
1972	707,795	384,651	24,048	408,699	27,479	74,952	456,172	159,149	92,474	4,989	141,878	55,131
1973	820,147	435,469	35,687	471,156	35,479	94,099	529,776	180,893	109,478	5,643	145,347	58,086
1974	937,464	484,551	35,625	520,176	40,742	117,270	596,704	210,309	130,451	6,257	149,828	61,601
1975	1,063,053	531,506	31,297	562,803	43,402	146,286	665,687	236,587	160,779	6,702	158,622	64,137
1976	1,217,157	622,603	36,258	658,861	50,905	174,909	782,865	259,135	175,157	7,244	168,026	68,940
1977	1,397,624	724,164	43,947	768,111	61,098	211,965	918,978	293,199	185,447	7,980	175,132	73,750
1978	1,611,473	839,356	50,910	890,266	72,490	256,893	1,074,669	336,234	200,570	9,216	174,865	77,918
1979	1,837,404	929,807	62,176	991,983	84,499	323,095	1,230,579	388,844	217,981	9,984	184,041	81,923
1980	2,135,900	1,036,844	65,159	1,102,003	92,240	392,587	1,402,350	480,840	252,710	11,283	189,305	84,798
1981	2,424,888	1,146,481	77,394	1,223,875	111,055	427,150	1,539,970	596,637	288,281	12,526	193,590	87,088
1982	2,594,812	1,215,440	80,138	1,295,578	120,503	465,163	1,640,238	648,461	306,113	13,148	197,353	87,797
1983	2,917,647	1,383,343	127,879	1,511,222	138,701	503,257	1,875,778	714,829	327,040	14,449	201,921	93,297
1984	3,238,443	1,570,778	129,453	1,700,231	164,062	556,295	2,092,464	806,842	339,137	15,723	205,964	97,417
1985	3,433,684	1,696,925	98,634	1,795,559	180,272	590,728	2,206,015	861,651	366,018	16,186	212,143	102,627
1986	3,683,657	1,850,595	135,321	1,985,916	198,743	605,165	2,392,338	901,146	390,173	17,002	216,661	103,042
1987	3,951,216	2,063,958	152,067	2,216,025	222,579	640,708	2,634,154	915,085	401,977	17,862	221,202	108,605
1988	4,325,897	2,334,269	160,563	2,494,832	261,690	685,327	2,918,469	984,514	422,914	19,167	225,700	117,109
1989	4,591,240	2,431,467	154,686	2,586,153	278,669	722,516	3,030,000	1,080,275	480,965	19,836	231,463	119,693
1990	4,982,518	2,736,409	187,277	2,923,686	309,712	748,190	3,362,164	1,109,924	510,430	21,699	229,616	125,068
1991	5,180,197	2,935,028	174,555	3,109,583	337,218	772,217	3,544,582	1,106,664	528,951	22,529	229,935	129,334
1992	5,538,322	3,121,225	214,771	3,335,996	357,756	822,740	3,800,980	1,128,475	608,867	23,779	232,912	126,162
1993	5,753,255	3,185,084	225,216	3,410,300	363,592	852,348	3,899,056	1,206,085	648,114	24,442	235,386	128,059
1994	5,977,393	3,308,486	211,314	3,519,800	377,774	889,950	4,031,976	1,298,688	646,729	25,145	237,714	129,313
1995	6,380,484	3,519,154	214,646	3,733,800	395,564	988,306	4,326,542	1,379,597	674,345	26,660	239,324	133,854
1996	6,871,429	3,761,809	227,894	3,989,703	406,366	1,110,516	4,693,853	1,483,544	694,032	28,492	241,168	136,690
1997	7,418,152	4,000,069	239,582	4,239,651	423,064	1,285,058	5,101,645	1,612,971	703,536	30,236	245,344	136,897
1998	7,994,273	4,395,922	215,350	4,611,272	453,680	1,423,765	5,581,357	1,696,404	716,512	31,864	250,889	145,249
1999	8,842,512	4,687,851	372,744	5,060,595	486,462	1,732,596	6,306,729	1,790,199	745,584	34,859	253,667	146,085
2000	10,224,645	5,491,706	294,745	5,786,451	554,320	2,267,192	7,499,323	1,959,766	765,556	39,966	255,835	145,981
2001	10,171,400	5,878,369	263,618	6,141,987	597,266	1,903,049	7,447,770	1,879,800	843,830	39,725	256,045	145,357
2002	9,946,642	5,921,052	241,747	6,162,799	596,148	1,620,000	7,186,651	1,845,750	914,241	39,078	254,531	143,460
2003	10,037,173	5,919,255	290,371	6,209,626	602,844	1,573,253	7,180,035	1,894,160	962,978	39,669	253,021	141,691
2004	10,401,614	5,963,331	309,417	6,272,748	635,418	1,652,710	7,290,040	2,122,439	989,135	41,218	252,356	141,559
2005	10,466,734	6,031,797	289,589	6,321,386	651,418	1,629,677	7,299,645	2,125,002	1,042,087	41,638	251,377	140,941
2006	11,070,833	6,320,069	248,399	6,568,468	665,307	1,610,090	7,513,251	2,441,209	1,116,373	43,999	251,616	142,051
2007	11,676,346	6,400,816	275,200	6,676,016	666,715	1,663,386	7,672,687	2,805,163	1,198,496	46,096	253,304	145,223
2008	12,033,140	6,405,635	281,663	6,687,298	677,216	1,661,784	7,671,866	2,987,112	1,374,162	46,909	256,520	142,699
2009	11,727,141	6,597,242	377,622	6,974,864	686,795	1,545,634	7,833,703	2,351,147	1,542,291	45,103	260,009	139,005
2010	12,679,406	7,439,480	398,675	7,838,155	697,465	1,615,215	8,755,905	2,215,617	1,707,884	48,179	263,174	138,372
2011	13,136,782	7,395,286	359,485	7,754,771	642,276	1,773,106	8,885,601	2,546,129	1,705,052	49,586	264,927	138,208
2012	13,968,199	7,445,582	413,740	7,859,322	639,597	2,055,692	9,275,417	2,966,104	1,726,678	52,435	266,391	140,225
2013	14,312,814	7,849,602	441,417	8,291,019	752,213	2,136,099	9,674,905	2,835,199	1,802,710	53,240	268,836	144,624
2014	15,003,954	8,211,927	445,345	8,657,272	792,630	2,085,783	9,950,425	3,104,803	1,948,726	55,363	271,009	149,207
2015	15,861,194	8,355,971	437,423	8,793,394	823,965	2,473,046	10,442,475	3,311,136	2,107,583	57,956	273,677	153,529
2016	16,331,057	8,497,681	402,468	8,900,149	862,400	2,549,540	10,587,289	3,556,019	2,187,749	59,452	274,694	154,847
2017	17,272,036	8,798,929	409,891	9,208,820	900,022	2,930,581	11,239,379	3,843,154	2,189,503	62,780	275,121	155,362
2018	18,003,333	9,204,394	328,569	9,532,963	943,965	3,201,028	11,790,026	3,899,893	2,313,414	65,704	274,005	156,800
2019	19,159,038	9,796,197	361,618	10,157,815	1,006,019	3,216,515	12,368,311	4,337,475	2,453,252	70,129	273,196	155,653
2020	20,866,180	9,615,296	369,287	9,984,583	1,006,253	3,837,436	12,815,766	4,356,570	3,693,844	77,181	270,353	146,488
2021	22,910,773	10,178,461	301,088	10,479,549	1,067,818	5,241,984	14,653,715	4,462,452	3,794,606	85,554	267,792	149,859

Personal Income and Employment by Area: Santa Fe, NM

(Thousands of dollars, except as noted.)

Year	Personal income, total	Derivation of personal income									Per capita personal income (dollars)	Population (persons)	Total employment
		Earnings by place of work			Less: Contributions for government social insurance	Plus: Adjustment for residence	Equals: Net earnings by place of residence	Plus: Dividends, interest, and rent	Plus: Personal current transfer receipts				
		Nonfarm	Farm	Total									
1970	206,513	138,862	1,931	140,793	7,853	11,240	144,180	43,510	18,823	3,753	55,026	22,514
1971	230,769	157,567	1,472	159,039	9,362	10,996	160,673	48,906	21,190	4,058	56,874	24,070
1972	263,733	181,577	1,202	182,779	11,241	13,834	185,372	55,306	23,055	4,452	59,243	26,263
1973	298,254	206,172	2,590	208,762	14,970	15,722	209,514	62,235	26,505	4,870	61,246	28,068
1974	342,090	233,644	3,170	236,814	17,567	17,806	237,053	72,880	32,157	5,406	63,278	29,166
1975	384,068	259,740	2,160	261,900	19,143	21,688	264,445	79,169	40,454	5,825	65,930	29,184
1976	435,599	294,860	1,583	296,443	21,533	26,792	301,702	89,860	44,037	6,305	69,090	30,690
1977	493,716	338,586	1,087	339,673	25,169	31,800	346,304	101,742	45,670	6,895	71,604	33,009
1978	575,018	393,001	2,639	395,640	30,115	36,578	402,103	121,592	51,323	7,913	72,669	35,227
1979	642,811	432,145	2,461	434,606	34,969	41,637	441,274	142,400	59,137	8,531	75,353	36,981
1980	725,023	478,778	533	479,311	39,903	45,468	484,876	169,115	71,032	9,556	75,872	37,378
1981	836,968	532,646	557	533,203	47,544	54,661	540,320	216,360	80,288	10,838	77,222	38,104
1982	945,909	584,071	1,011	585,082	53,555	62,007	593,534	266,449	85,926	11,806	80,118	40,035
1983	1,041,065	657,184	-385	656,799	60,722	68,843	664,920	285,662	90,483	12,657	82,250	42,732
1984	1,162,144	731,894	1,292	733,186	68,491	81,771	746,466	318,674	97,004	13,818	84,106	44,481
1985	1,289,046	797,634	3,175	800,809	76,060	96,780	821,529	362,336	105,181	15,046	85,676	46,724
1986	1,405,171	887,304	1,874	889,178	85,081	100,773	904,870	386,682	113,619	15,765	89,134	48,864
1987	1,484,602	928,245	1,061	929,306	88,325	118,810	959,791	402,236	122,575	16,081	92,323	50,998
1988	1,597,071	995,549	2,567	998,116	101,408	118,115	1,014,823	449,391	132,857	16,899	94,507	54,052
1989	1,754,997	1,096,266	1,094	1,097,360	113,377	128,567	1,112,550	491,998	150,449	18,100	96,962	56,683
1990	1,901,683	1,207,432	2,134	1,209,566	132,417	131,170	1,208,319	529,732	163,632	19,096	99,587	58,372
1991	2,059,287	1,349,144	4,009	1,353,153	149,872	115,583	1,318,864	560,738	179,685	20,084	102,536	63,309
1992	2,264,977	1,482,232	3,207	1,485,439	162,909	138,794	1,461,324	602,190	201,463	21,362	106,030	65,129
1993	2,488,321	1,653,323	2,611	1,655,934	180,393	121,509	1,597,050	667,816	223,455	22,636	109,927	68,364
1994	2,696,822	1,763,895	3,931	1,767,826	197,198	131,254	1,701,882	756,046	238,894	23,668	113,944	70,827
1995	2,996,553	1,910,188	2,885	1,913,073	214,154	133,337	1,832,256	896,305	267,992	25,295	118,462	75,227
1996	3,150,699	1,949,078	3,345	1,952,423	219,167	131,795	1,865,051	990,572	295,076	26,032	121,031	75,777
1997	3,345,694	2,085,409	2,042	2,087,451	231,305	128,474	1,984,620	1,052,396	308,678	26,944	124,172	77,163
1998	3,617,010	2,221,322	3,024	2,224,346	247,340	160,937	2,137,943	1,155,524	323,543	28,716	125,956	78,737
1999	3,693,734	2,273,784	6,992	2,280,776	257,759	181,995	2,205,012	1,136,413	352,309	28,865	127,966	79,221
2000	4,129,864	2,530,467	5,937	2,536,404	274,923	210,149	2,471,630	1,278,956	379,278	31,838	129,713	81,236
2001	4,385,298	2,740,275	7,524	2,747,799	297,072	214,435	2,665,162	1,302,191	417,945	33,461	131,057	84,055
2002	4,559,892	2,952,840	6,378	2,959,218	317,647	227,048	2,868,619	1,228,956	462,317	34,142	133,555	85,360
2003	4,699,162	3,008,976	4,901	3,013,877	327,268	260,452	2,947,061	1,258,450	493,651	34,754	135,213	87,912
2004	4,980,037	3,138,913	4,454	3,143,367	342,702	240,138	3,040,803	1,406,856	532,378	36,513	136,391	90,099
2005	5,363,956	3,321,402	5,147	3,326,549	362,227	224,682	3,189,004	1,597,834	577,118	38,979	137,610	93,143
2006	5,900,010	3,595,250	9,255	3,604,505	397,226	194,030	3,401,309	1,864,238	634,463	42,512	138,786	94,699
2007	6,252,956	3,851,284	3,213	3,854,497	430,067	111,255	3,535,685	2,019,325	697,946	44,597	140,210	98,058
2008	6,486,578	3,965,833	6,592	3,972,425	450,882	69,872	3,591,415	2,076,290	818,873	45,776	141,704	98,098
2009	6,268,567	3,786,745	4,198	3,790,943	431,988	128,458	3,487,413	1,869,806	911,348	43,773	143,205	93,942
2010	6,341,489	3,805,422	2,045	3,807,467	430,968	167,419	3,543,918	1,788,685	1,008,886	43,878	144,526	92,489
2011	6,679,521	3,855,017	1,837	3,856,854	388,564	179,610	3,647,900	1,997,359	1,034,262	45,789	145,876	92,417
2012	7,017,479	3,919,788	781	3,920,569	394,044	248,185	3,774,710	2,191,214	1,051,555	47,811	146,774	91,816
2013	7,026,112	4,018,870	-10	4,018,860	460,875	222,510	3,780,495	2,145,302	1,100,315	47,620	147,545	92,782
2014	7,666,471	4,063,079	48	4,063,127	469,910	252,268	3,845,485	2,609,909	1,211,077	51,416	149,108	93,277
2015	7,775,740	4,152,540	1,595	4,154,135	498,556	245,550	3,901,129	2,576,706	1,297,905	51,935	149,720	94,419
2016	8,222,168	4,140,828	1,749	4,142,577	499,710	375,787	4,018,654	2,845,166	1,358,348	54,557	150,708	94,539
2017	8,332,005	4,145,766	-933	4,144,833	503,451	426,867	4,068,249	2,871,848	1,391,908	54,880	151,821	93,633
2018	8,836,749	4,288,297	-1,825	4,286,472	521,524	461,806	4,226,754	3,113,034	1,496,961	57,922	152,563	94,225
2019	9,510,296	4,494,675	-897	4,493,778	546,056	505,827	4,453,549	3,469,266	1,587,481	61,879	153,693	94,325
2020	10,079,938	4,424,716	-2,407	4,422,309	550,121	674,979	4,547,167	3,421,956	2,110,815	65,042	154,977	88,034
2021	10,790,792	4,894,697	-2,473	4,892,224	602,394	609,973	4,899,803	3,550,928	2,340,061	69,528	155,201	90,633

Personal Income and Employment by Area: Santa Maria-Santa Barbara, CA

(Thousands of dollars, except as noted.)

Year	Personal income, total	Earnings by place of work			Less: Contributions for government social insurance	Plus: Adjustment for residence	Equals: Net earnings by place of residence	Plus: Dividends, interest, and rent	Plus: Personal current transfer receipts	Per capita personal income (dollars)	Population (persons)	Total employment
		Nonfarm	Farm	Total								
1970	1,338,257	919,747	35,407	955,154	57,246	-5,141	892,767	338,219	107,271	5,044	265,291	116,626
1971	1,429,790	971,262	38,675	1,009,937	62,188	-4,287	943,462	364,294	122,034	5,297	269,930	117,818
1972	1,570,222	1,058,954	53,455	1,112,409	70,796	-3,337	1,038,276	396,865	135,081	5,670	276,957	121,263
1973	1,743,627	1,173,238	66,679	1,239,917	89,602	-4,758	1,145,557	445,275	152,795	6,285	277,414	129,723
1974	1,920,803	1,274,843	69,400	1,344,243	100,943	-6,187	1,237,113	503,815	179,875	6,899	278,431	134,399
1975	2,119,517	1,404,119	68,732	1,472,851	109,221	-8,321	1,355,309	542,625	221,583	7,499	282,626	138,012
1976	2,347,422	1,584,603	68,134	1,652,737	124,281	-11,050	1,517,406	585,336	244,680	8,206	286,075	141,699
1977	2,583,164	1,757,286	74,682	1,831,968	142,677	-16,131	1,673,160	651,148	258,856	8,896	290,381	149,056
1978	2,951,811	2,036,819	80,906	2,117,725	169,472	-20,552	1,927,701	748,797	275,313	9,993	295,397	160,992
1979	3,314,174	2,277,681	94,856	2,372,537	201,658	-26,716	2,144,163	866,477	303,534	11,218	295,423	168,561
1980	3,773,852	2,499,834	132,061	2,631,895	218,153	-35,381	2,378,361	1,044,032	351,459	12,572	300,191	168,218
1981	4,302,836	2,748,752	123,347	2,872,099	261,865	-40,516	2,569,718	1,315,651	417,467	14,081	305,588	171,396
1982	4,651,106	2,946,588	149,116	3,095,704	288,350	-51,437	2,755,917	1,443,696	451,493	14,856	313,073	172,644
1983	5,036,726	3,205,696	170,756	3,376,452	318,987	-48,541	3,008,924	1,546,947	480,855	15,628	322,294	176,829
1984	5,669,668	3,725,344	133,162	3,858,506	386,737	-76,545	3,395,224	1,771,327	503,117	17,226	329,133	185,802
1985	6,103,760	4,089,207	134,969	4,224,176	429,226	-95,055	3,699,895	1,864,780	539,085	18,028	338,569	192,555
1986	6,499,147	4,405,664	154,335	4,559,999	465,482	-103,463	3,991,054	1,930,766	577,327	18,803	345,651	197,339
1987	6,868,749	4,688,973	180,566	4,869,539	492,097	-99,101	4,278,341	1,987,910	602,498	19,512	352,021	200,745
1988	7,424,092	5,060,178	204,678	5,264,856	545,355	-108,219	4,611,282	2,168,512	644,298	20,865	355,810	207,750
1989	8,026,689	5,397,950	217,498	5,615,448	589,949	-124,673	4,900,826	2,420,244	705,619	21,949	365,695	212,536
1990	8,303,443	5,604,470	239,916	5,844,386	616,109	-136,186	5,092,091	2,435,076	776,276	22,408	370,565	214,939
1991	8,770,037	6,032,922	205,414	6,238,336	661,552	-152,820	5,423,964	2,489,356	856,717	23,392	374,910	220,855
1992	9,134,464	6,224,176	170,978	6,395,154	675,919	-158,000	5,561,235	2,609,488	963,741	24,165	378,003	214,252
1993	9,333,973	6,252,664	239,029	6,491,693	679,767	-160,829	5,651,097	2,660,184	1,022,692	24,559	380,064	215,117
1994	9,654,421	6,250,292	219,509	6,469,801	690,897	-169,619	5,609,285	3,004,409	1,040,727	25,127	384,226	216,284
1995	9,863,506	6,376,221	276,876	6,653,097	699,213	-182,304	5,771,580	2,998,942	1,092,984	25,647	384,582	221,933
1996	10,319,542	6,622,239	281,121	6,903,360	707,206	-194,728	6,001,426	3,174,001	1,144,115	26,727	386,108	225,153
1997	10,720,989	6,948,609	330,822	7,279,431	737,196	-219,875	6,322,360	3,233,741	1,164,888	27,399	391,290	226,970
1998	11,637,434	7,535,112	317,224	7,852,336	782,421	-241,034	6,828,881	3,600,725	1,207,828	29,481	394,738	235,910
1999	12,375,897	7,934,433	350,133	8,284,566	828,788	-267,400	7,188,378	3,924,295	1,263,224	31,181	396,906	239,821
2000	13,452,206	8,820,933	388,110	9,209,043	925,442	-324,259	7,959,342	4,163,090	1,329,774	33,631	399,990	244,170
2001	13,712,910	9,276,103	303,980	9,580,083	984,906	-353,493	8,241,684	4,028,075	1,443,151	34,013	403,164	243,235
2002	13,646,282	9,638,099	346,251	9,984,350	1,035,512	-376,053	8,572,785	3,556,024	1,517,473	33,680	405,178	244,532
2003	14,366,153	10,243,927	381,318	10,625,245	1,116,233	-431,734	9,077,278	3,705,848	1,583,027	35,314	406,810	248,298
2004	16,035,779	11,167,310	376,225	11,543,535	1,238,443	-485,955	9,819,137	4,568,994	1,647,648	39,372	407,284	250,723
2005	16,951,642	11,727,565	411,762	12,139,327	1,294,775	-547,026	10,297,526	4,925,791	1,728,325	41,540	408,079	253,193
2006	18,293,482	12,033,899	405,404	12,439,303	1,290,371	-582,193	10,566,739	5,864,514	1,862,229	44,828	408,085	253,267
2007	18,830,753	12,396,493	395,172	12,791,665	1,312,651	-646,127	10,832,887	6,037,672	1,960,194	45,790	411,243	258,250
2008	18,849,505	12,590,920	399,573	12,990,493	1,359,075	-693,353	10,938,065	5,692,132	2,219,308	45,327	415,859	258,059
2009	18,457,537	12,511,866	663,647	13,175,513	1,356,505	-667,281	11,151,727	4,896,234	2,409,576	43,909	420,356	249,731
2010	19,169,008	12,984,126	577,467	13,561,593	1,344,424	-662,774	11,554,395	4,981,587	2,633,026	45,187	424,218	245,732
2011	20,436,051	13,571,564	501,863	14,073,427	1,274,280	-697,296	12,101,851	5,667,678	2,666,522	48,039	425,404	250,715
2012	21,686,257	14,189,115	639,033	14,828,148	1,323,156	-740,048	12,764,944	6,246,015	2,675,298	50,476	429,635	256,831
2013	21,700,940	14,384,242	781,012	15,165,254	1,499,303	-722,932	12,943,019	5,976,271	2,781,650	49,944	434,503	260,896
2014	23,104,961	15,009,463	833,175	15,842,638	1,571,298	-755,143	13,516,197	6,616,247	2,972,517	52,484	440,227	269,481
2015	24,594,404	15,916,516	935,643	16,852,159	1,649,528	-824,633	14,377,998	7,043,238	3,173,168	55,433	443,677	273,816
2016	24,971,653	16,130,786	825,945	16,956,731	1,683,451	-801,909	14,471,371	7,214,063	3,286,219	55,983	446,061	274,776
2017	25,867,804	16,927,720	891,943	17,819,663	1,766,356	-851,173	15,202,134	7,361,202	3,304,468	57,835	447,267	276,226
2018	27,067,132	17,905,912	699,145	18,605,057	1,857,803	-882,400	15,864,854	7,760,170	3,442,108	60,455	447,724	281,483
2019	28,509,928	18,365,050	755,669	19,120,719	1,945,041	-911,364	16,264,314	8,553,627	3,691,987	63,586	448,368	284,698
2020	31,123,329	19,371,098	823,693	20,194,791	2,045,325	-959,282	17,190,184	8,549,514	5,383,631	69,457	448,096	283,119
2021	33,037,087	20,964,592	693,929	21,658,521	2,210,019	-1,003,442	18,445,060	8,818,091	5,773,936	73,995	446,475	292,080

Personal Income and Employment by Area: Santa Rosa-Petaluma, CA

(Thousands of dollars, except as noted.)

Year	Personal income, total	Earnings by place of work			Less: Contributions for government social insurance	Plus: Adjustment for residence	Equals: Net earnings by place of residence	Plus: Dividends, interest, and rent	Plus: Personal current transfer receipts	Per capita personal income (dollars)	Population (persons)	Total employment
		Nonfarm	Farm	Total								
1970	957,026	508,418	24,485	532,903	32,136	136,914	637,681	203,063	116,282	4,646	206,003	74,003
1971	1,063,234	564,137	18,145	582,282	37,082	160,204	705,404	226,888	130,942	5,006	212,402	76,798
1972	1,205,719	643,504	25,319	668,823	44,342	186,463	810,944	254,154	140,621	5,380	224,091	82,982
1973	1,370,646	730,719	33,869	764,588	57,607	212,227	919,208	292,662	158,776	5,760	237,957	88,869
1974	1,552,265	813,707	27,524	841,231	66,380	246,577	1,021,428	339,694	191,143	6,387	243,028	93,352
1975	1,773,564	899,385	29,681	929,066	71,589	286,827	1,144,304	384,132	245,128	7,003	253,255	96,964
1976	2,023,175	1,053,365	33,457	1,086,822	84,482	323,872	1,326,212	423,641	273,322	7,703	262,654	103,354
1977	2,289,555	1,196,930	41,600	1,238,530	97,929	371,928	1,512,529	482,121	294,905	8,381	273,175	109,903
1978	2,664,526	1,421,880	46,255	1,468,135	119,024	436,620	1,785,731	559,454	319,341	9,467	281,442	118,796
1979	3,043,203	1,639,325	45,489	1,684,814	145,084	493,544	2,033,274	649,894	360,035	10,427	291,859	127,676
1980	3,477,261	1,798,627	39,817	1,838,444	156,982	579,299	2,260,761	797,080	419,420	11,530	301,586	133,637
1981	3,965,958	1,980,612	67,446	2,048,058	188,696	640,176	2,499,538	972,384	494,036	12,851	308,609	137,159
1982	4,236,873	2,100,006	57,548	2,157,554	204,122	690,400	2,643,832	1,063,534	529,507	13,466	314,636	138,573
1983	4,650,295	2,343,445	42,214	2,385,659	231,616	741,749	2,895,792	1,196,838	557,665	14,461	321,580	145,902
1984	5,220,940	2,725,524	54,957	2,780,481	280,949	804,132	3,303,664	1,337,185	580,091	15,973	326,863	155,144
1985	5,668,660	2,997,409	58,263	3,055,672	313,966	853,688	3,595,394	1,449,710	623,556	16,903	335,355	161,324
1986	6,130,011	3,292,610	60,464	3,353,074	347,162	918,852	3,924,764	1,532,792	672,455	17,754	345,270	166,384
1987	6,575,465	3,629,302	72,134	3,701,436	384,317	966,815	4,283,934	1,588,220	703,311	18,465	356,111	174,046
1988	7,211,764	4,032,568	81,747	4,114,315	439,938	1,039,378	4,713,755	1,740,998	757,011	19,603	367,893	186,395
1989	8,058,225	4,410,114	110,172	4,520,286	489,567	1,115,310	5,146,029	2,074,167	838,029	21,171	380,633	193,548
1990	8,677,571	4,841,062	101,673	4,942,735	535,389	1,261,228	5,668,574	2,103,478	905,519	22,222	390,495	204,435
1991	9,067,260	5,140,837	117,482	5,258,319	575,025	1,239,784	5,923,078	2,144,425	999,757	22,786	397,937	207,198
1992	9,587,374	5,475,542	112,314	5,587,856	604,671	1,250,062	6,233,247	2,217,461	1,136,666	23,664	405,151	207,086
1993	10,061,979	5,751,934	93,382	5,845,316	633,729	1,312,207	6,523,794	2,344,986	1,193,199	24,500	410,687	210,765
1994	10,550,598	6,079,918	93,567	6,173,485	668,508	1,356,787	6,861,764	2,457,091	1,231,743	25,353	416,152	218,474
1995	11,021,041	6,280,805	82,049	6,362,854	687,577	1,384,980	7,060,257	2,667,312	1,293,472	26,099	422,286	221,033
1996	11,878,837	6,840,345	108,322	6,948,667	722,347	1,392,784	7,619,104	2,901,663	1,358,070	27,728	428,399	232,015
1997	12,984,551	7,621,946	168,525	7,790,471	796,448	1,508,679	8,502,702	3,104,575	1,377,274	29,703	437,141	242,030
1998	14,021,391	8,588,576	132,986	8,721,562	877,951	1,525,461	9,369,072	3,219,799	1,432,520	31,445	445,901	254,209
1999	14,938,217	9,331,035	123,983	9,455,018	956,400	1,543,551	10,042,169	3,409,791	1,486,257	32,946	453,421	263,310
2000	16,990,757	10,601,529	191,064	10,792,593	1,089,290	2,008,982	11,712,285	3,723,003	1,555,469	36,903	460,421	267,725
2001	17,790,249	11,566,905	176,014	11,742,919	1,194,289	1,855,405	12,404,035	3,674,123	1,712,091	38,235	465,293	272,782
2002	17,774,429	11,889,753	166,697	12,056,450	1,231,870	1,702,837	12,527,417	3,427,003	1,820,009	38,200	465,298	272,287
2003	18,015,377	11,915,181	113,682	12,028,863	1.254,207	1,699,028	12,473,684	3,614,785	1,926,908	38,619	466,489	268,461
2004	18,194,304	12,216,862	136,566	12,353,428	1,346,584	1,549,909	12,556,753	3,641,042	1,996,509	38,976	466,809	271,429
2005	18,748,317	12,475,593	199,841	12,675,434	1,390,771	1,514,195	12,798,858	3,843,525	2,105,934	40,238	465,938	271,468
2006	20,065,258	13,020,091	118,571	13,138,662	1,407,076	1,490,771	13,222,357	4,544,373	2,298,528	43,134	465,188	274,369
2007	20,781,276	13,227,076	136,977	13,364,053	1,415,605	1,492,477	13,440,925	4,902,869	2,437,482	44,466	467,356	279,979
2008	20,546,186	13,050,659	103,548	13,154,207	1,434,715	1,244,346	12,963,838	4,810,785	2,771,563	43,430	473,091	276,221
2009	19,908,814	12,468,829	188,744	12,657,573	1,366,304	1,397,031	12,688,300	4,147,426	3,073,088	41,522	479,479	262,782
2010	20,706,909	13,162,783	132,423	13,295,206	1,379,832	1,167,173	13,082,547	4,221,917	3,402,445	42,723	484,675	260,148
2011	21,721,132	13,645,327	120,471	13,765,798	1,294,000	1,171,205	13,643,003	4,653,186	3,424,943	44,581	487,231	263,452
2012	22,800,347	13,734,992	318,031	14,053,023	1,286,393	1,552,054	14,318,684	5,016,854	3,464,809	46,552	489,784	267,006
2013	23,703,525	14,411,607	321,483	14,733,090	1,514,049	1,763,109	14,982,150	5,147,215	3,574,160	47,995	493,870	277,118
2014	25,181,887	15,393,409	360,055	15,753,464	1,615,590	1,443,787	15,581,661	5,710,729	3,889,497	50,603	497,635	288,662
2015	27,173,178	16,654,009	278,072	16,932,081	1,739,374	1,597,915	16,790,622	6,176,155	4,206,401	54,373	499,752	296,758
2016	28,233,501	17,305,741	219,192	17,524,933	1,812,447	1,698,964	17,411,450	6,422,954	4,399,097	56,305	501,437	299,274
2017	29,310,761	17,944,610	231,342	18,175,952	1,896,792	1,707,148	17,986,308	6,901,234	4,423,219	58,500	501,038	303,618
2018	30,589,076	18,980,207	199,985	19,180,192	2,037,800	1,493,446	18,635,838	7,335,038	4,618,200	61,682	495,914	309,068
2019	32,748,038	19,874,991	173,790	20,048,781	2,152,419	1,997,982	19,894,344	7,943,695	4,909,999	66,715	490,867	305,036
2020	35,905,845	20,063,313	195,053	20,258,366	2,167,425	2,890,845	20,981,786	7,922,645	7,001,414	73,526	488,345	289,682
2021	39,359,689	21,671,581	180,326	21,851,907	2,303,841	4,466,176	24,014,242	8,103,544	7,241,903	81,006	485,887	296,622

Personal Income and Employment by Area: Savannah, GA

(Thousands of dollars, except as noted.)

| Year | Personal income, total | Derivation of personal income | | | | | | | | Per capita personal income (dollars) | Population (persons) | Total employment |
| | | Earnings by place of work | | | Less: Contributions for government social insurance | Plus: Adjustment for residence | Equals: Net earnings by place of residence | Plus: Dividends, interest, and rent | Plus: Personal current transfer receipts | | | |
		Nonfarm	Farm	Total								
1970	745,764	614,061	3,000	617,061	39,518	-8,341	569,202	107,281	69,281	3,608	206,709	96,506
1971	790,868	638,493	3,745	642,238	42,696	-6,742	592,800	113,677	84,391	3,891	203,279	94,486
1972	844,303	684,288	3,687	687,975	48,026	-5,898	634,051	115,795	94,457	4,133	204,260	93,250
1973	923,475	748,569	5,257	753,826	60,968	-3,909	688,949	124,682	109,844	4,509	204,809	96,053
1974	1,020,920	812,730	5,277	818,007	68,884	-2,323	746,800	141,300	132,820	4,982	204,936	96,696
1975	1,192,441	931,552	4,551	936,103	76,871	-6,142	853,090	173,038	166,313	5,612	212,479	100,738
1976	1,356,515	1,039,889	3,848	1,043,737	87,331	32,875	989,281	186,220	181,014	6,204	218,664	103,097
1977	1,512,469	1,149,844	2,004	1,151,848	96,166	61,432	1,117,114	206,717	188,638	6,730	224,727	104,468
1978	1,713,715	1,300,239	6,907	1,307,146	111,123	77,737	1,273,760	235,764	204,191	7,580	226,093	108,230
1979	1,871,658	1,407,150	8,823	1,415,973	125,085	90,134	1,381,022	261,677	228,959	8,158	229,430	108,522
1980	2,108,663	1,553,612	2,042	1,555,654	138,005	95,705	1,513,354	324,155	271,154	9,101	231,691	109,966
1981	2,418,147	1,723,166	8,243	1,731,409	164,800	138,435	1,705,044	403,949	309,154	10,286	235,102	112,942
1982	2,618,390	1,853,501	10,972	1,864,473	182,852	142,180	1,823,801	459,064	335,525	10,950	239,114	114,351
1983	2,791,993	1,976,952	9,157	1,986,109	197,362	133,255	1,922,002	499,944	370,047	11,616	240,354	114,335
1984	3,050,478	2,169,922	7,643	2,177,565	223,190	132,201	2,086,576	571,272	392,630	12,581	242,463	118,390
1985	3,283,995	2,358,033	5,621	2,363,654	247,098	133,296	2,249,852	616,664	417,479	13,426	244,606	122,010
1986	3,545,327	2,614,577	4,027	2,618,604	277,737	100,385	2,441,252	661,033	443,042	14,332	247,365	126,772
1987	3,773,609	2,785,345	4,794	2,790,139	292,431	107,918	2,605,626	701,354	466,629	15,021	251,216	130,214
1988	4,039,638	2,982,046	5,151	2,987,197	323,056	100,449	2,764,590	780,940	494,108	15,900	254,061	134,151
1989	4,385,120	3,181,316	6,282	3,187,598	347,578	76,530	2,916,550	920,705	547,865	17,165	255,475	137,367
1990	4,650,792	3,488,236	4,147	3,492,383	380,909	-32,187	3,079,287	969,543	601,962	17,946	259,160	142,254
1991	4,858,666	3,532,700	5,417	3,538,117	388,471	25,720	3,175,366	1,007,337	675,963	18,496	262,690	138,590
1992	5,288,764	3,831,893	6,243	3,838,136	414,262	93,096	3,516,970	1,027,361	744,433	19,745	267,853	143,404
1993	5,501,003	4,014,389	3,211	4,017,600	433,637	34,611	3,618,574	1,080,783	801,646	20,159	272,886	145,860
1994	5,849,796	4,219,185	5,350	4,224,535	463,607	22,443	3,783,371	1,206,304	860,121	21,074	277,581	150,429
1995	6,193,056	4,448,800	2,922	4,451,722	487,444	29,381	3,993,659	1,280,609	918,788	22,029	281,126	155,080
1996	6,572,324	4,747,715	3,820	4,751,535	518,847	-10,484	4,222,204	1,384,018	966,102	23,184	283,480	158,374
1997	6,802,210	4,867,313	3,409	4,870,722	531,790	-17,129	4,321,803	1,500,321	980,086	23,726	286,697	162,397
1998	7,363,931	5,308,230	1,265	5,309,495	576,323	-15,775	4,717,397	1,661,402	985,132	25,530	288,441	164,741
1999	7,656,892	5,634,636	4,163	5,638,799	606,506	-50,602	4,981,691	1,636,564	1,038,637	26,257	291,618	167,970
2000	8,090,272	5,886,203	4,140	5,890,343	630,315	-22,750	5,237,278	1,750,640	1,102,354	27,544	293,721	172,243
2001	8,303,073	6,035,552	6,424	6,041,976	642,025	-8,315	5,391,636	1,722,741	1,188,696	27,944	297,133	172,488
2002	8,647,811	6,233,004	4,950	6,237,954	663,427	20,436	5,594,963	1,708,630	1,344,218	28,669	301,644	173,541
2003	9,198,705	6,614,535	6,940	6,621,475	696,077	72,026	5,997,424	1,850,728	1,350,553	30,201	304,585	177,613
2004	9,809,320	7,127,020	7,311	7,134,331	768,944	73,841	6,439,228	1,941,531	1,428,561	31,587	310,553	183,261
2005	10,500,957	7,576,606	8,603	7,585,209	813,638	192,223	6,963,794	2,011,923	1,525,240	33,386	314,528	190,505
2006	11,368,177	8,211,978	9,412	8,221,390	885,612	183,137	7,518,915	2,231,558	1,617,704	35,298	322,065	198,121
2007	12,198,787	8,624,522	8,668	8,633,190	924,969	258,186	7,966,407	2,501,694	1,730,686	36,972	329,943	207,508
2008	12,719,079	8,766,346	7,902	8,774,248	979,887	401,130	8,195,491	2,536,842	1,986,746	37,946	335,185	205,696
2009	12,671,007	8,703,483	7,039	8,710,522	968,504	361,027	8,103,045	2,390,293	2,177,669	36,833	344,017	198,549
2010	13,236,370	8,848,332	7,677	8,856,009	984,032	512,491	8,384,468	2,423,649	2,428,253	37,962	348,672	196,887
2011	14,210,144	9,188,179	6,492	9,194,671	909,711	541,324	8,826,284	2,814,952	2,568,908	39,953	355,674	200,445
2012	14,499,748	9,571,726	10,334	9,582,060	947,486	493,418	9,127,992	2,865,819	2,505,937	40,066	361,896	203,237
2013	14,719,308	9,955,796	9,596	9,965,392	1,109,055	448,692	9,305,029	2,826,035	2,588,244	40,291	365,328	208,599
2014	15,489,226	10,495,247	6,491	10,501,738	1,158,765	346,386	9,689,359	3,055,608	2,744,259	41,305	374,999	214,866
2015	16,350,226	11,180,576	12,712	11,193,288	1,232,424	284,741	10,245,605	3,244,439	2,860,182	42,740	382,547	223,257
2016	16,661,449	11,401,818	12,454	11,414,272	1,252,903	204,899	10,366,268	3,338,425	2,956,756	42,841	388,917	227,864
2017	17,496,960	11,935,363	15,245	11,950,608	1,309,361	192,171	10,833,418	3,612,994	3,050,548	44,503	393,161	234,223
2018	18,329,220	12,799,992	9,820	12,809,812	1,416,323	64,661	11,458,150	3,675,055	3,196,015	46,133	397,311	242,056
2019	18,928,654	13,090,709	10,646	13,101,355	1,462,007	61,230	11,700,578	3,838,624	3,389,452	47,046	402,340	246,838
2020	20,427,612	13,252,879	14,747	13,267,626	1,482,417	122,569	11,907,778	3,853,254	4,666,580	50,432	405,053	243,493
2021	21,964,121	14,568,336	14,965	14,583,301	1,624,662	30,832	12,989,471	3,953,752	5,020,898	53,570	410,008	255,641

Personal Income and Employment by Area: Scranton—Wilkes-Barre, PA

(Thousands of dollars, except as noted.)

Year	Personal income, total	Earnings by place of work			Less: Contributions for government social insurance	Plus: Adjustment for residence	Equals: Net earnings by place of residence	Plus: Dividends, interest, and rent	Plus: Personal current transfer receipts	Per capita personal income (dollars)	Population (persons)	Total employment
		Nonfarm	Farm	Total								
1970	2,147,763	1,639,360	5,903	1,645,263	123,705	45,680	1,567,238	275,347	305,178	3,602	596,204	255,288
1971	2,344,677	1,753,755	6,397	1,760,152	137,169	44,112	1,667,095	299,011	378,571	3,901	601,087	253,153
1972	2,590,425	1,930,929	5,327	1,936,256	156,322	42,974	1,822,908	324,211	443,306	4,272	606,331	258,007
1973	2,870,429	2,132,743	6,904	2,139,647	197,262	42,932	1,985,317	370,410	514,702	4,737	605,941	266,382
1974	3,082,235	2,229,467	6,496	2,235,963	213,816	44,955	2,067,102	424,184	590,949	5,083	606,407	260,623
1975	3,361,969	2,349,313	10,455	2,359,768	218,479	40,726	2,182,015	458,819	721,135	5,529	608,007	251,998
1976	3,649,913	2,567,537	10,704	2,578,241	243,952	37,345	2,371,634	489,134	789,145	6,045	603,751	251,764
1977	3,986,753	2,831,788	14,436	2,846,224	267,387	34,840	2,613,677	544,290	828,786	6,598	604,269	254,824
1978	4,399,963	3,175,778	11,739	3,187,517	306,458	36,478	2,917,537	597,577	884,849	7,290	603,524	261,329
1979	4,857,926	3,441,042	15,603	3,456,645	342,349	32,312	3,146,608	663,218	1,048,100	8,074	601,656	265,502
1980	5,242,373	3,561,643	14,502	3,576,145	360,355	32,482	3,248,272	818,118	1,175,983	8,781	597,021	259,934
1981	5,737,807	3,790,638	16,908	3,807,546	411,740	34,446	3,430,252	1,007,268	1,300,287	9,656	594,227	257,840
1982	6,207,667	3,957,695	13,128	3,970,823	435,352	32,154	3,567,625	1,204,378	1,435,664	10,502	591,104	252,572
1983	6,593,764	4,191,476	12,266	4,203,742	464,791	34,712	3,773,663	1,269,782	1,550,319	11,218	587,760	252,296
1984	6,970,919	4,439,219	19,731	4,458,950	509,762	51,157	4,000,345	1,403,446	1,567,128	11,933	584,185	254,756
1985	7,395,405	4,733,455	20,804	4,754,259	550,505	49,125	4,252,879	1,535,823	1,606,703	12,756	579,742	259,357
1986	7,756,387	5,005,375	18,539	5,023,914	585,002	40,548	4,479,460	1,606,822	1,670,105	13,409	578,457	263,798
1987	8,121,953	5,380,313	17,082	5,397,395	622,977	46,287	4,820,705	1,610,273	1,690,975	14,099	576,085	269,274
1988	8,716,038	5,874,494	12,117	5,886,611	695,418	34,776	5,225,969	1,727,240	1,762,829	15,134	575,917	278,326
1989	9,466,942	6,351,552	17,620	6,369,172	742,280	25,387	5,652,279	1,982,492	1,832,171	16,439	575,871	283,746
1990	9,948,061	6,709,686	19,382	6,729,068	785,703	27,539	5,970,904	2,012,671	1,964,486	17,268	576,090	288,238
1991	10,350,677	6,884,143	14,794	6,898,937	818,685	6,901	6,087,153	2,010,100	2,253,424	17,901	578,212	284,245
1992	10,848,943	7,361,071	24,814	7,385,885	874,744	-44,622	6,466,519	2,000,867	2,381,557	18,718	579,606	285,358
1993	11,168,065	7,672,302	19,231	7,691,533	930,333	-80,230	6,680,970	1,990,269	2,496,826	19,244	580,330	286,290
1994	11,571,051	8,015,042	15,462	8,030,504	986,339	-72,646	6,971,519	2,074,780	2,524,752	19,992	578,788	289,245
1995	12,076,971	8,343,793	8,860	8,352,653	1,025,320	-92,245	7,235,088	2,242,002	2,599,881	20,931	576,980	293,803
1996	12,585,597	8,551,079	14,813	8,565,892	1,026,042	-68,427	7,471,423	2,387,019	2,727,155	21,930	573,886	294,639
1997	13,127,841	8,982,449	10,638	8,993,087	1,064,932	-76,031	7,852,124	2,498,761	2,776,956	23,056	569,384	297,412
1998	13,589,580	9,296,379	13,069	9,309,448	1,088,726	-60,332	8,160,390	2,632,268	2,796,922	24,001	566,216	296,660
1999	14,092,967	9,804,808	11,454	9,816,262	1,128,448	-62,592	8,625,222	2,567,866	2,899,879	25,025	563,157	300,626
2000	15,034,679	10,501,260	19,556	10,520,816	1,187,472	-52,929	9,280,415	2,759,032	2,995,232	26,853	559,879	308,211
2001	15,605,453	10,948,909	12,887	10,961,796	1,243,868	-49,040	9,668,888	2,747,444	3,189,121	27,993	557,476	306,843
2002	15,806,599	11,121,351	11,892	11,133,243	1,263,368	-3,173	9,866,702	2,596,472	3,343,425	28,444	555,702	301,409
2003	16,183,976	11,367,410	19,604	11,387,014	1,288,912	22,567	10,120,669	2,625,072	3,438,235	29,135	555,483	301,889
2004	16,916,530	11,902,505	16,163	11,918,668	1,351,274	66,908	10,634,302	2,658,549	3,623,679	30,453	555,495	304,761
2005	17,433,696	12,247,535	13,293	12,260,828	1,427,984	119,783	10,952,627	2,630,227	3,850,842	31,319	556,652	308,372
2006	18,160,778	12,592,480	15,535	12,608,015	1,481,284	174,037	11,300,768	2,797,987	4,062,023	32,568	557,626	311,527
2007	19,178,619	12,987,520	11,445	12,998,965	1,528,983	234,398	11,704,380	3,176,875	4,297,364	34,246	560,032	316,218
2008	20,027,951	13,153,078	14,663	13,167,741	1,561,283	280,527	11,886,985	3,373,488	4,767,478	35,666	561,548	316,876
2009	19,932,996	12,948,693	16,697	12,965,390	1,556,278	269,030	11,678,142	3,083,876	5,170,978	35,409	562,933	309,015
2010	20,552,619	13,379,820	18,916	13,398,736	1,594,706	270,962	12,074,992	3,026,391	5,451,236	36,454	563,790	308,777
2011	21,227,926	13,772,969	19,351	13,792,320	1,484,197	247,691	12,555,814	3,170,091	5,502,021	37,652	563,792	311,684
2012	21,663,449	13,983,254	32,444	14,015,698	1,499,745	215,432	12,731,385	3,473,801	5,458,263	38,420	563,855	312,973
2013	21,524,554	14,322,364	22,316	14,344,680	1,718,252	153,345	12,779,773	3,303,221	5,441,560	38,322	561,678	315,611
2014	22,255,959	14,808,468	19,607	14,828,075	1,779,143	139,616	13,188,548	3,511,936	5,555,475	39,298	566,341	319,392
2015	23,080,029	15,345,353	5,185	15,350,538	1,840,430	131,685	13,641,793	3,643,805	5,794,431	40,824	565,361	321,126
2016	23,667,011	15,600,003	602	15,600,605	1,880,855	124,461	13,844,211	3,790,643	6,032,157	41,918	564,606	323,573
2017	24,160,265	16,075,810	2,475	16,078,285	1,970,394	127,133	14,235,024	3,817,862	6,107,379	42,670	566,208	324,402
2018	25,229,725	16,641,048	-4,265	16,636,783	2,026,714	135,241	14,745,310	3,994,690	6,489,725	44,493	567,044	325,904
2019	26,134,296	16,961,980	1,907	16,963,887	2,076,537	177,305	15,064,655	4,318,463	6,751,178	46,092	567,002	324,752
2020	28,436,403	17,021,248	-1,835	17,019,413	2,075,266	169,667	15,113,814	4,270,477	9,052,112	50,190	566,574	310,759
2021	30,235,864	18,098,156	1,473	18,099,629	2,169,128	143,998	16,074,499	4,349,686	9,811,679	53,256	567,750	317,871

Personal Income and Employment by Area: Seattle-Tacoma-Bellevue, WA

(Thousands of dollars, except as noted.)

Year	Personal income, total	Earnings by place of work			Less: Contributions for government social insurance	Plus: Adjustment for residence	Equals: Net earnings by place of residence	Plus: Dividends, interest, and rent	Plus: Personal current transfer receipts	Per capita personal income (dollars)	Population (persons)	Total employment
		Nonfarm	Farm	Total								
1970	8,731,054	7,010,889	26,946	7,037,835	559,723	18,717	6,496,829	1,472,418	761,807	4,758	1,834,990	824,119
1971	8,942,817	7,011,821	28,446	7,040,267	580,348	14,736	6,474,655	1,569,989	898,173	4,873	1,835,190	786,245
1972	9,425,134	7,460,267	33,366	7,493,633	653,159	9,385	6,849,859	1,637,838	937,437	5,219	1,806,099	789,860
1973	10,474,443	8,405,539	49,155	8,454,694	840,240	386	7,614,840	1,814,212	1,045,391	5,816	1,800,981	834,401
1974	11,829,739	9,434,527	47,977	9,482,504	969,872	19,750	8,532,382	2,095,568	1,201,789	6,450	1,833,981	869,673
1975	13,418,533	10,562,573	50,176	10,612,749	1,076,303	64,080	9,600,526	2,324,517	1,493,490	7,190	1,866,276	887,648
1976	14,884,770	11,826,526	51,174	11,877,700	1,233,342	99,984	10,744,342	2,517,491	1,622,937	7,891	1,886,242	919,384
1977	16,563,011	13,425,500	54,295	13,479,795	1,428,946	51,537	12,102,386	2,796,774	1,663,851	8,641	1,916,683	968,408
1978	19,374,731	16,003,912	49,467	16,053,379	1,756,897	29,335	14,325,817	3,250,009	1,798,905	9,829	1,971,129	1,046,539
1979	22,582,576	18,823,493	56,541	18,880,034	2,138,583	110,838	16,852,289	3,760,509	1,969,778	11,113	2,032,131	1,123,231
1980	25,831,708	21,064,163	44,721	21,108,884	2,359,828	106,492	18,855,548	4,580,204	2,395,956	12,267	2,105,824	1,159,283
1981	28,854,599	23,169,342	55,977	23,225,319	2,781,762	-30,272	20,413,285	5,622,808	2,818,506	13,410	2,151,691	1,167,540
1982	30,910,389	24,269,417	47,955	24,317,372	2,960,991	-15,123	21,341,258	6,408,799	3,160,332	14,193	2,177,909	1,160,929
1983	32,566,753	25,224,672	54,058	25,278,730	3,113,281	-18,794	22,146,655	6,928,901	3,491,197	14,884	2,188,099	1,179,085
1984	35,133,760	27,286,909	55,652	27,342,561	3,469,223	-65,902	23,807,436	7,706,293	3,620,031	15,854	2,216,022	1,236,653
1985	38,025,357	29,686,537	62,125	29,748,662	3,803,822	-116,746	25,828,094	8,320,911	3,876,352	16,840	2,258,026	1,290,615
1986	40,973,901	32,448,010	70,168	32,518,178	4,169,389	-193,404	28,155,385	8,690,212	4,128,304	17,807	2,301,024	1,346,586
1987	43,772,479	35,065,262	75,522	35,140,784	4,481,173	-265,029	30,394,582	9,016,249	4,361,648	18,577	2,356,263	1,422,816
1988	48,226,800	38,848,802	77,155	38,925,957	5,073,601	-299,246	33,553,110	9,841,474	4,832,216	19,876	2,426,393	1,505,432
1989	53,437,443	42,791,792	91,413	42,883,205	5,572,026	-361,987	36,949,192	11,164,024	5,324,227	21,433	2,493,214	1,587,002
1990	58,868,037	47,565,802	94,275	47,660,077	6,338,120	-580,054	40,741,903	12,275,373	5,850,761	22,828	2,578,807	1,653,020
1991	62,573,349	50,799,730	89,714	50,889,444	6,838,633	-638,777	43,412,034	12,600,877	6,560,438	23,786	2,630,705	1,661,101
1992	67,420,070	55,510,917	117,051	55,627,968	7,472,266	-799,040	47,356,662	12,896,430	7,166,978	25,055	2,690,858	1,669,827
1993	70,062,830	57,287,857	110,486	57,398,343	7,697,910	-969,695	48,730,738	13,677,645	7,654,447	25,567	2,740,325	1,687,223
1994	73,519,995	59,550,610	105,935	59,656,545	8,113,599	-1,029,263	50,513,683	14,972,153	8,034,159	26,502	2,774,159	1,728,057
1995	78,008,350	62,510,103	95,132	62,605,235	8,532,251	-1,110,019	52,962,965	16,499,296	8,546,089	27,715	2,814,630	1,750,246
1996	84,207,951	67,638,554	100,263	67,738,817	9,072,702	-1,231,685	57,434,430	17,868,613	8,904,908	29,476	2,856,795	1,807,825
1997	91,931,211	74,960,322	91,990	75,052,312	9,785,287	-1,661,519	63,605,506	19,100,603	9,225,102	31,504	2,918,071	1,887,996
1998	102,977,538	85,258,298	116,424	85,374,722	10,957,785	-2,005,132	72,411,805	21,011,982	9,553,751	34,571	2,978,761	1,957,069
1999	111,495,111	94,339,843	121,948	94,461,791	11,578,130	-2,152,778	80,730,883	20,680,176	10,084,052	36,923	3,019,651	1,997,050
2000	118,781,793	100,503,322	91,384	100,594,706	12,561,324	-2,602,948	85,430,434	22,752,437	10,598,922	38,917	3,052,187	2,050,200
2001	120,437,567	101,280,065	107,779	101,387,844	12,097,161	-2,664,862	86,625,821	21,870,426	11,941,320	38,940	3,092,927	2,040,022
2002	121,584,212	101,766,329	91,796	101,858,125	12,190,110	-2,663,787	87,004,228	21,693,354	12,886,630	38,991	3,118,302	1,999,926
2003	125,210,978	103,915,450	132,567	104,048,017	12,636,559	-2,708,706	88,702,752	23,139,846	13,368,380	39,965	3,133,021	2,002,177
2004	135,785,912	108,827,979	113,454	108,941,433	13,372,332	-2,817,407	92,751,694	29,768,572	13,265,646	42,984	3,158,967	2,040,998
2005	140,583,902	115,210,552	104,813	115,315,365	14,180,061	-2,990,999	98,144,305	28,550,635	13,888,962	43,956	3,198,265	2,099,077
2006	155,176,105	125,068,026	92,010	125,160,036	15,123,126	-3,142,280	106,894,630	33,491,032	14,790,443	47,643	3,257,081	2,169,876
2007	168,439,918	134,266,754	90,724	134,357,478	15,992,032	-3,520,692	114,844,754	37,633,064	15,962,100	50,973	3,304,467	2,252,591
2008	174,483,785	137,118,369	107,756	137,226,125	16,322,453	-3,577,579	117,326,093	38,667,873	18,489,819	52,006	3,355,042	2,272,430
2009	162,975,097	128,897,511	113,942	129,011,453	15,956,705	-3,434,337	109,620,411	32,238,808	21,115,878	47,726	3,414,797	2,182,713
2010	167,010,125	131,330,913	108,842	131,439,755	16,362,537	-3,212,668	111,864,550	31,695,629	23,449,946	48,418	3,449,355	2,154,810
2011	178,136,969	139,046,427	120,353	139,166,780	15,450,355	-3,175,668	120,540,757	34,480,746	23,115,466	50,833	3,504,376	2,190,360
2012	196,782,680	151,786,088	125,862	151,911,950	16,079,948	-3,210,931	132,621,071	41,184,598	22,977,011	55,280	3,559,719	2,258,786
2013	202,785,728	160,560,624	133,444	160,694,068	19,015,885	-3,171,971	138,506,212	40,866,298	23,413,218	56,117	3,613,596	2,313,257
2014	221,416,651	170,644,478	149,735	170,794,213	20,043,398	-3,244,168	147,506,647	48,541,858	25,368,146	60,175	3,679,543	2,380,336
2015	235,512,933	179,563,265	214,326	179,777,591	21,235,951	-3,400,197	155,141,443	54,524,990	25,846,500	62,884	3,745,182	2,454,112
2016	250,100,599	190,569,634	142,752	190,712,386	22,265,179	-3,616,700	164,830,507	58,066,707	27,203,385	65,403	3,824,014	2,526,951
2017	267,247,709	205,400,730	152,885	205,553,615	24,019,386	-3,793,269	177,740,960	61,675,713	27,831,036	68,633	3,893,869	2,602,436
2018	286,503,043	224,346,513	119,386	224,465,899	25,564,421	-4,162,825	194,738,653	62,839,376	28,925,014	72,654	3,943,414	2,666,906
2019	309,937,564	238,521,502	157,060	238,678,562	26,733,527	-4,959,747	206,985,288	72,197,779	30,754,497	77,788	3,984,400	2,701,611
2020	331,406,319	248,764,836	191,233	248,956,069	28,041,573	-5,514,094	215,400,402	72,087,013	43,918,904	82,342	4,024,730	2,598,354
2021	358,128,607	272,542,458	183,356	272,725,814	29,656,370	-6,985,488	236,083,956	74,528,012	47,516,639	89,274	4,011,553	2,657,505

Personal Income and Employment by Area: Sebastian-Vero Beach, FL

(Thousands of dollars, except as noted.)

Year	Personal income, total	Earnings by place of work			Less: Contributions for government social insurance	Plus: Adjustment for residence	Equals: Net earnings by place of residence	Plus: Dividends, interest, and rent	Plus: Personal current transfer receipts	Per capita personal income (dollars)	Population (persons)	Total employment
		Nonfarm	Farm	Total								
1970	147,387	85,590	5,816	91,406	5,485	-396	85,525	44,173	17,689	4,072	36,192	15,206
1971	173,674	100,446	8,454	108,900	6,783	-1,543	100,574	51,617	21,483	4,617	37,617	16,339
1972	209,071	123,376	12,145	135,521	8,814	-2,677	124,030	59,839	25,202	5,153	40,570	18,541
1973	250,946	151,902	12,463	164,365	12,477	-4,264	147,624	73,026	30,296	5,747	43,668	21,051
1974	281,597	162,102	14,098	176,200	14,028	-4,152	158,020	87,514	36,063	6,146	45,818	21,271
1975	304,978	169,386	12,033	181,419	14,352	-4,354	162,713	96,337	45,928	6,453	47,259	21,020
1976	350,589	196,505	12,234	208,739	16,601	-5,952	186,186	112,204	52,199	7,277	48,176	22,091
1977	404,668	221,991	15,598	237,589	19,349	-6,589	211,651	134,092	58,925	8,016	50,485	23,515
1978	486,509	264,691	20,580	285,271	23,668	-8,358	253,245	166,600	66,664	9,126	53,309	25,884
1979	576,112	304,667	21,828	326,495	28,335	-7,975	290,185	204,766	81,161	9,948	57,912	27,380
1980	698,671	335,779	34,903	370,682	30,950	-4,152	335,580	262,803	100,288	11,505	60,728	28,130
1981	848,789	396,955	24,184	421,139	39,720	-8,402	373,017	354,669	121,103	13,274	63,946	29,823
1982	890,445	388,328	26,785	415,113	40,811	-2,699	371,603	369,442	149,400	13,192	67,499	30,005
1983	994,919	416,631	47,608	464,239	43,849	-1,117	419,273	408,709	166,937	14,129	70,419	31,067
1984	1,142,565	480,384	43,885	524,269	51,911	-5,586	466,772	494,497	181,296	15,484	73,792	33,139
1985	1,296,847	534,884	55,544	590,428	59,593	-7,141	523,694	573,522	199,631	17,091	75,879	35,176
1986	1,433,307	610,458	56,815	667,273	69,320	-7,272	590,681	621,808	220,818	18,195	78,776	37,595
1987	1,606,315	683,276	74,750	758,026	76,745	-5,526	675,755	691,989	238,571	19,789	81,171	37,686
1988	1,859,059	769,114	113,426	882,540	89,616	-8,204	784,720	816,564	257,775	22,162	83,885	41,082
1989	2,081,819	885,334	88,911	974,245	105,386	-14,947	853,912	932,252	295,655	23,781	87,542	43,275
1990	2,296,583	943,785	63,267	1,007,052	109,888	-14,212	882,952	1,091,809	321,822	25,205	91,115	44,005
1991	2,425,511	921,811	75,091	996,902	109,894	-3,166	883,842	1,188,854	352,815	25,916	93,593	43,445
1992	2,563,399	987,513	61,340	1,048,853	116,950	1,397	933,300	1,224,762	405,337	26,696	96,023	42,812
1993	2,665,024	1,041,154	54,148	1,095,302	122,579	4,788	977,511	1,258,392	429,121	27,315	97,566	43,672
1994	2,852,067	1,118,441	49,310	1,167,751	133,668	2,018	1,036,101	1,350,106	465,860	28,561	99,858	45,180
1995	3,146,915	1,193,591	46,581	1,240,172	142,418	2,726	1,100,480	1,552,159	494,276	30,874	101,929	47,392
1996	3,380,726	1,304,404	32,527	1,336,931	152,074	-2,054	1,182,803	1,671,033	526,890	32,638	103,583	49,354
1997	3,628,890	1,373,159	30,739	1,403,898	160,700	-836	1,242,362	1,832,826	553,702	34,141	106,291	51,903
1998	3,924,387	1,476,135	48,551	1,524,686	170,949	-1,541	1,352,196	1,994,087	578,104	36,016	108,961	53,805
1999	4,115,149	1,633,856	39,142	1,672,998	185,502	-5,614	1,481,882	2,037,630	595,637	36,975	111,294	54,638
2000	4,420,215	1,729,519	42,819	1,772,338	194,832	3,310	1,580,816	2,204,081	635,318	39,005	113,323	55,510
2001	4,892,997	1,910,348	35,762	1,946,110	210,965	69,343	1,804,488	2,402,462	686,047	42,380	115,456	58,381
2002	5,019,373	1,993,985	41,096	2,035,081	219,549	123,367	1,938,899	2,343,371	737,103	42,485	118,144	59,597
2003	5,321,585	2,173,523	35,791	2,209,314	241,693	154,578	2,122,199	2,421,374	778,012	44,181	120,450	63,547
2004	6,184,044	2,308,609	41,961	2,350,570	261,718	236,063	2,324,915	3,010,357	848,772	49,472	125,001	65,719
2005	6,939,024	2,498,051	59,615	2,557,666	285,443	372,385	2,644,608	3,432,496	861,920	54,230	127,955	68,831
2006	7,978,622	2,742,009	60,917	2,802,926	318,605	480,266	2,964,587	4,089,516	924,519	60,691	131,463	72,591
2007	8,314,573	2,851,469	42,217	2,893,686	335,634	487,267	3,045,319	4,279,937	989,317	61,789	134,564	73,481
2008	8,417,750	2,783,178	36,215	2,819,393	338,870	521,389	3,001,912	4,297,156	1,118,682	61,769	136,277	71,663
2009	7,138,809	2,539,838	43,683	2,583,521	319,541	475,209	2,739,189	3,164,000	1,235,620	52,102	137,016	68,431
2010	7,377,267	2,527,230	48,723	2,575,953	312,140	372,375	2,636,188	3,408,569	1,332,510	53,351	138,277	67,970
2011	8,073,896	2,567,747	52,450	2,620,197	287,946	489,605	2,821,856	3,865,164	1,386,876	58,035	139,122	69,292
2012	8,623,571	2,750,313	61,931	2,812,244	306,815	563,472	3,068,901	4,151,823	1,402,847	61,371	140,515	70,303
2013	8,662,422	2,770,865	67,135	2,838,000	348,242	713,265	3,203,023	4,015,458	1,443,941	61,020	141,961	71,334
2014	9,616,304	3,029,163	68,601	3,097,764	375,122	705,125	3,427,767	4,653,341	1,535,196	66,896	143,749	73,883
2015	10,175,050	3,223,225	79,076	3,302,301	394,074	778,595	3,686,822	4,825,622	1,662,606	69,426	146,560	76,313
2016	10,862,468	3,346,207	62,111	3,408,318	406,486	949,704	3,951,536	5,147,728	1,763,204	72,380	150,076	77,698
2017	11,592,016	3,498,047	71,487	3,569,534	427,000	937,799	4,080,333	5,640,688	1,870,995	75,846	152,836	80,372
2018	12,595,513	3,675,329	37,245	3,712,574	461,002	1,109,845	4,361,417	6,243,242	1,990,854	81,066	155,374	83,127
2019	13,711,728	3,960,369	51,456	4,011,825	499,696	1,126,019	4,638,148	6,920,546	2,153,034	86,856	157,868	83,630
2020	14,317,852	4,156,746	39,452	4,196,198	523,668	1,147,002	4,819,532	6,906,598	2,591,722	89,294	160,345	83,572
2021	15,565,785	4,562,578	23,671	4,586,249	564,539	1,471,887	5,493,597	7,184,072	2,888,116	95,109	163,662	86,111

Personal Income and Employment by Area: Sebring-Avon Park, FL

(Thousands of dollars, except as noted.)

Year	Personal income, total	Earnings by place of work			Less: Contributions for government social insurance	Plus: Adjustment for residence	Equals: Net earnings by place of residence	Plus: Dividends, interest, and rent	Plus: Personal current transfer receipts	Per capita personal income (dollars)	Population (persons)	Total employment
		Nonfarm	Farm	Total								
1970	103,745	51,193	14,987	66,180	3,500	859	63,539	25,359	14,847	3,470	29,898	10,437
1971	117,865	57,785	16,873	74,658	4,108	828	71,378	28,555	17,932	3,691	31,931	10,970
1972	132,818	63,355	19,949	83,304	4,775	747	79,276	32,241	21,301	3,917	33,912	11,766
1973	155,727	75,313	20,943	96,256	6,415	408	90,249	39,105	26,373	4,333	35,937	12,899
1974	174,908	86,401	19,001	105,402	7,790	40	97,652	45,967	31,289	4,370	40,025	13,681
1975	198,890	93,321	21,470	114,791	8,307	156	106,640	52,585	39,665	4,843	41,070	13,811
1976	221,719	102,630	25,706	128,336	9,181	-203	118,952	57,953	44,814	5,332	41,584	13,930
1977	253,442	114,837	32,067	146,904	10,338	-742	135,824	67,448	50,170	6,040	41,962	14,676
1978	304,020	135,417	43,977	179,394	12,224	-1,582	165,588	81,705	56,727	6,975	43,588	16,021
1979	348,484	153,261	45,732	198,993	14,574	-2,589	181,830	98,686	67,968	7,604	45,828	16,722
1980	421,175	172,302	61,071	233,373	16,722	-3,072	213,579	124,883	82,713	8,756	48,102	17,930
1981	458,704	191,640	41,125	232,765	20,064	-6,964	205,737	153,653	99,314	9,117	50,315	18,584
1982	513,806	198,387	45,893	244,280	21,532	-6,801	215,947	181,334	116,525	9,827	52,286	19,097
1983	581,960	223,785	66,188	289,973	24,163	-7,743	258,067	197,299	126,594	10,843	53,670	20,205
1984	638,800	255,553	48,537	304,090	28,196	-8,196	267,698	234,487	136,615	11,482	55,636	21,386
1985	717,314	288,219	54,179	342,398	32,660	-9,160	300,578	264,035	152,701	12,473	57,508	22,542
1986	792,242	320,022	55,851	375,873	37,136	-9,564	329,173	294,117	168,952	13,343	59,375	23,609
1987	853,488	348,498	62,912	411,410	39,969	-7,259	364,182	306,238	183,068	13,740	62,119	23,712
1988	966,416	383,325	100,182	483,507	46,334	-6,786	430,387	334,813	201,216	15,024	64,325	24,811
1989	1,068,549	419,852	75,559	495,411	52,743	-5,239	437,429	397,428	233,692	16,109	66,334	25,945
1990	1,127,130	452,357	65,763	518,120	55,550	-3,616	458,954	408,671	259,505	16,279	69,238	27,382
1991	1,179,693	479,665	78,212	557,877	59,257	-4,010	494,610	396,876	288,207	16,473	71,614	28,117
1992	1,238,380	512,127	67,731	579,858	63,165	-3,217	513,476	394,034	330,870	16,782	73,790	28,451
1993	1,302,405	543,816	70,537	614,353	67,327	-3,109	543,917	400,841	357,647	17,069	76,301	28,985
1994	1,384,708	583,705	65,487	649,192	73,382	-2,252	573,558	415,772	395,378	17,589	78,724	30,386
1995	1,468,514	606,837	70,553	677,390	76,868	-177	600,345	447,433	420,736	18,176	80,792	30,952
1996	1,529,380	625,373	54,005	679,378	77,797	2,639	604,220	479,864	445,296	18,490	82,713	31,677
1997	1,598,139	659,145	55,855	715,000	81,298	5,128	638,830	496,671	462,638	18,950	84,334	32,801
1998	1,687,243	669,075	97,468	766,543	82,955	8,590	692,178	514,425	480,640	19,722	85,551	34,156
1999	1,719,946	702,483	98,878	801,361	85,495	10,967	726,833	494,102	499,011	19,860	86,604	35,518
2000	1,793,710	730,839	75,426	806,265	87,531	16,817	735,551	530,508	527,651	20,519	87,417	32,853
2001	1,902,087	809,782	56,153	865,935	99,525	20,202	786,612	542,751	572,724	21,490	88,510	32,571
2002	1,999,527	885,152	61,361	946,513	108,644	20,910	858,779	530,807	609,941	22,232	89,939	34,134
2003	2,084,326	950,288	50,744	1,001,032	116,209	23,543	908,366	536,781	639,179	22,919	90,943	35,970
2004	2,201,342	1,030,319	55,630	1,085,949	127,157	33,100	991,892	523,394	686,056	23,650	93,079	36,151
2005	2,369,801	1,099,998	79,797	1,179,795	139,574	41,735	1,081,956	555,168	732,677	24,785	95,614	37,340
2006	2,572,708	1,174,660	103,238	1,277,898	153,696	51,395	1,175,597	614,655	782,456	26,309	97,788	38,629
2007	2,723,991	1,198,152	77,063	1,275,215	160,996	56,171	1,170,390	724,942	828,659	27,509	99,023	40,082
2008	2,770,320	1,151,275	79,835	1,231,110	159,967	63,310	1,134,453	726,222	909,645	27,823	99,568	38,869
2009	2,744,090	1,146,708	94,739	1,241,447	161,749	55,667	1,135,365	621,197	987,528	27,730	98,956	37,758
2010	2,870,330	1,170,604	100,272	1,270,876	163,196	58,933	1,166,613	655,138	1,048,579	29,100	98,637	37,513
2011	2,933,941	1,192,099	96,300	1,288,399	152,478	59,091	1,195,012	666,831	1,072,098	29,788	98,493	37,769
2012	2,984,417	1,206,297	127,803	1,334,100	154,973	64,601	1,243,728	665,101	1,075,588	30,378	98,244	38,022
2013	2,929,161	1,211,095	104,707	1,315,802	172,450	66,679	1,210,031	621,489	1,097,641	29,853	98,118	37,520
2014	3,027,985	1,221,119	107,812	1,328,931	174,602	71,017	1,225,346	660,240	1,142,399	31,365	96,541	38,221
2015	3,169,640	1,276,790	121,425	1,398,215	180,771	73,623	1,291,067	672,417	1,206,156	32,482	97,582	38,834
2016	3,262,575	1,336,816	83,213	1,420,029	190,851	78,168	1,307,346	713,154	1,242,075	32,993	98,886	39,584
2017	3,416,070	1,398,977	92,154	1,491,131	199,939	83,923	1,375,115	743,121	1,297,834	34,129	100,094	40,536
2018	3,442,686	1,446,321	57,998	1,504,319	210,422	92,301	1,386,198	709,147	1,347,341	34,362	100,189	40,766
2019	3,669,412	1,504,173	70,781	1,574,954	222,704	100,739	1,452,989	805,310	1,411,113	36,309	101,061	40,949
2020	3,964,116	1,534,563	59,266	1,593,829	230,389	110,340	1,473,780	813,424	1,676,912	39,163	101,222	40,230
2021	4,293,843	1,637,573	48,609	1,686,182	243,360	119,358	1,562,180	832,608	1,899,055	41,568	103,296	39,573

Personal Income and Employment by Area: Sheboygan, WI

(Thousands of dollars, except as noted.)

Year	Personal income, total	Earnings by place of work			Less: Contributions for government social insurance	Plus: Adjustment for residence	Equals: Net earnings by place of residence	Plus: Dividends, interest, and rent	Plus: Personal current transfer receipts	Per capita personal income (dollars)	Population (persons)	Total employment
		Nonfarm	Farm	Total								
1970	381,796	297,865	11,237	309,102	22,448	-363	286,291	63,572	31,933	3,947	96,726	44,180
1971	406,232	312,983	11,680	324,663	24,438	908	301,133	68,592	36,507	4,184	97,081	44,145
1972	450,864	350,540	12,363	362,903	28,890	2,693	336,706	73,776	40,382	4,622	97,541	45,544
1973	498,159	387,255	14,081	401,336	36,779	5,105	369,662	82,037	46,460	5,042	98,803	47,761
1974	550,696	423,289	13,011	436,300	42,015	7,650	401,935	93,348	55,413	5,509	99,963	48,662
1975	596,734	437,391	17,304	454,695	42,067	9,005	421,633	102,789	72,312	5,945	100,372	47,393
1976	670,106	503,690	17,416	521,106	49,220	11,811	483,697	109,892	76,517	6,711	99,858	49,028
1977	755,393	572,442	22,151	594,593	55,830	14,434	553,197	122,138	80,058	7,517	100,495	51,286
1978	848,398	654,404	18,225	672,629	65,778	18,432	625,283	134,477	88,638	8,460	100,282	53,344
1979	960,559	739,436	22,579	762,015	77,325	23,533	708,223	150,465	101,871	9,536	100,727	55,367
1980	1,053,121	774,657	22,940	797,597	80,593	24,894	741,898	184,302	126,921	10,437	100,907	54,206
1981	1,153,895	837,311	16,912	854,223	93,101	20,687	781,809	228,497	143,589	11,475	100,554	54,019
1982	1,188,391	837,283	14,448	851,731	93,595	18,039	776,175	247,213	165,003	11,793	100,770	52,305
1983	1,239,568	883,067	2,021	885,088	98,920	14,921	801,089	263,032	175,447	12,323	100,592	51,763
1984	1,373,210	994,065	9,803	1,003,868	114,462	10,049	899,455	295,978	177,777	13,588	101,060	54,410
1985	1,423,695	1,025,862	12,451	1,038,313	118,610	7,287	926,990	309,043	187,662	14,092	101,028	54,488
1986	1,497,511	1,089,659	17,831	1,107,490	125,483	2,563	984,570	320,018	192,923	14,828	100,995	54,967
1987	1,576,558	1,165,242	21,558	1,186,800	131,329	-284	1,055,187	325,434	195,937	15,556	101,347	56,142
1988	1,692,951	1,281,860	10,271	1,292,131	148,829	-8,487	1,134,815	352,838	205,298	16,595	102,018	58,606
1989	1,852,265	1,386,232	28,321	1,414,553	160,340	-17,981	1,236,232	392,284	223,749	17,978	103,032	60,778
1990	1,920,385	1,442,748	22,717	1,465,465	172,766	-22,067	1,270,632	407,612	242,141	18,441	104,137	62,116
1991	1,974,006	1,490,765	17,541	1,508,306	180,485	-21,099	1,306,722	403,996	263,288	18,851	104,714	62,581
1992	2,145,138	1,626,472	22,572	1,649,044	194,812	-23,077	1,431,155	433,174	280,809	20,309	105,627	63,543
1993	2,282,740	1,766,222	16,296	1,782,518	213,150	-27,446	1,541,922	452,596	288,222	21,388	106,729	65,899
1994	2,444,121	1,909,135	20,155	1,929,290	232,315	-27,939	1,669,036	484,529	290,556	22,611	108,093	68,711
1995	2,579,717	1,983,885	15,082	1,998,967	242,258	-27,598	1,729,111	542,316	308,290	23,522	109,672	70,153
1996	2,690,924	2,051,025	25,566	2,076,591	249,267	-24,007	1,803,317	564,053	323,554	24,300	110,737	69,931
1997	2,791,720	2,149,203	18,727	2,167,930	259,090	-19,296	1,889,544	572,534	329,642	25,030	111,536	70,790
1998	3,001,972	2,302,110	29,778	2,331,888	276,405	-19,762	2,035,721	626,321	339,930	26,810	111,973	72,156
1999	3,136,323	2,491,032	29,928	2,520,960	299,463	-27,958	2,193,539	593,094	349,690	27,981	112,088	74,285
2000	3,340,768	2,653,717	21,716	2,675,433	314,356	-30,651	2,330,426	640,538	369,804	29,633	112,739	76,014
2001	3,443,604	2,713,160	29,747	2,742,907	315,950	-29,111	2,397,846	637,707	408,051	30,468	113,023	72,890
2002	3,576,322	2,856,885	28,949	2,885,834	324,776	-32,910	2,528,148	608,045	440,129	31,579	113,251	71,835
2003	3,644,127	2,911,613	33,783	2,945,396	334,449	-36,333	2,574,614	616,876	452,637	32,126	113,433	71,910
2004	3,856,111	3,121,461	33,762	3,155,223	359,193	-34,788	2,761,242	630,641	464,228	33,875	113,832	72,930
2005	3,922,379	3,147,572	28,221	3,175,793	367,761	-40,450	2,767,582	658,831	495,966	34,270	114,454	75,062
2006	4,093,355	3,234,902	24,592	3,259,494	381,209	-32,770	2,845,515	718,985	528,855	35,664	114,775	75,474
2007	4,307,941	3,341,763	43,446	3,385,209	392,887	-36,987	2,955,335	779,494	573,112	37,402	115,178	75,974
2008	4,602,668	3,446,080	48,966	3,495,046	404,880	-28,455	3,061,711	894,548	646,409	39,798	115,652	75,544
2009	4,490,465	3,364,839	31,368	3,396,207	393,795	-40,983	2,961,429	765,605	763,431	38,858	115,562	71,260
2010	4,501,186	3,343,147	45,786	3,388,933	395,970	-44,508	2,948,455	743,855	808,876	38,965	115,520	69,978
2011	4,731,192	3,399,856	68,745	3,468,601	363,765	-43,664	3,061,172	896,547	773,473	41,066	115,209	69,971
2012	5,047,133	3,595,995	73,575	3,669,570	377,923	-64,328	3,227,319	1,045,758	774,056	43,976	114,770	70,308
2013	4,966,437	3,685,036	74,334	3,759,370	436,119	-87,945	3,235,306	943,301	787,830	43,299	114,702	71,764
2014	5,213,321	3,834,491	80,279	3,914,770	453,097	-98,117	3,363,556	1,030,377	819,388	44,894	116,126	73,191
2015	5,438,982	4,008,524	63,258	4,071,782	464,825	-96,394	3,510,563	1,066,959	861,460	46,642	116,611	73,434
2016	5,532,642	4,189,857	45,226	4,235,083	482,736	-115,167	3,637,180	1,015,813	879,649	47,405	116,710	73,748
2017	5,826,643	4,390,343	39,447	4,429,790	504,633	-123,718	3,801,439	1,102,057	923,147	49,792	117,019	74,506
2018	6,108,041	4,606,729	34,353	4,641,082	525,950	-136,366	3,978,766	1,145,806	983,469	52,044	117,363	75,357
2019	6,202,453	4,577,951	37,262	4,615,213	536,502	-137,503	3,941,208	1,232,136	1,029,109	52,696	117,703	75,354
2020	6,519,746	4,604,316	52,058	4,656,374	544,333	-141,478	3,970,563	1,238,736	1,310,447	55,282	117,937	72,215
2021	6,879,349	4,776,809	49,067	4,825,876	555,179	-133,918	4,136,779	1,272,218	1,470,352	58,425	117,747	73,434

Personal Income and Employment by Area: Sherman-Denison, TX

(Thousands of dollars, except as noted.)

Year	Personal income, total	Earnings by place of work Nonfarm	Earnings by place of work Farm	Earnings by place of work Total	Less: Contributions for government social insurance	Plus: Adjustment for residence	Equals: Net earnings by place of residence	Plus: Dividends, interest, and rent	Plus: Personal current transfer receipts	Per capita personal income (dollars)	Population (persons)	Total employment
1970	287,412	230,159	1,806	231,965	15,720	-4,417	211,828	45,942	29,642	3,478	82,644	38,706
1971	281,123	218,099	2,094	220,193	15,732	-2,774	201,687	44,657	34,779	3,482	80,725	35,761
1972	309,089	240,745	4,397	245,142	18,457	-3,840	222,845	48,338	37,906	4,015	76,977	36,851
1973	350,654	266,832	9,335	276,167	23,650	-3,723	248,794	56,489	45,371	4,544	77,168	37,720
1974	388,371	299,154	-1,537	297,617	27,275	-3,273	267,069	67,981	53,321	4,905	79,176	38,648
1975	423,246	307,599	-1,624	305,975	27,180	-667	278,128	75,740	69,378	5,146	82,243	36,797
1976	475,796	345,489	7,204	352,693	30,962	-343	321,388	80,472	73,936	5,658	84,093	37,567
1977	529,118	397,084	-981	396,103	35,971	-643	359,489	89,133	80,496	6,292	84,089	39,578
1978	622,806	479,226	2,139	481,365	44,532	-2,783	434,050	99,349	89,407	7,346	84,776	42,554
1979	730,686	574,360	6,745	581,105	55,802	-4,159	521,144	111,066	98,476	8,351	87,500	45,113
1980	822,433	627,836	1,175	629,011	61,252	-1,051	566,708	140,597	115,128	9,126	90,118	44,931
1981	917,831	683,663	798	684,461	71,476	-80	612,905	171,575	133,351	10,071	91,140	45,027
1982	996,473	698,393	2,306	700,699	74,483	4,055	630,271	214,350	151,852	10,848	91,857	44,236
1983	1,086,038	752,624	5,191	757,815	79,010	4,385	683,190	237,172	165,676	11,733	92,562	44,445
1984	1,194,496	828,377	6,602	834,979	89,718	6,753	752,014	268,765	173,717	12,745	93,722	45,965
1985	1,293,339	885,112	9,291	894,403	96,420	8,897	806,880	302,164	184,295	13,639	94,827	47,323
1986	1,344,696	931,768	561	932,329	101,066	6,687	837,950	309,403	197,343	13,893	96,787	47,263
1987	1,359,328	948,109	-1,165	946,944	102,795	6,101	850,250	302,644	206,434	14,202	95,717	48,538
1988	1,416,400	1,008,909	-1,424	1,007,485	112,486	4,602	899,601	302,810	213,989	14,871	95,246	48,810
1989	1,468,209	1,022,459	-1,238	1,021,221	114,886	6,441	912,776	329,432	226,001	15,374	95,499	48,602
1990	1,532,353	1,083,358	919	1,084,277	118,312	6,552	972,517	310,714	249,122	16,110	95,120	49,556
1991	1,577,346	1,118,317	2,127	1,120,444	124,164	5,175	1,001,455	307,089	268,802	16,400	96,178	49,176
1992	1,636,028	1,141,896	6,504	1,148,400	125,335	9,429	1,032,494	298,040	305,494	16,977	96,370	48,581
1993	1,686,429	1,184,670	1,366	1,186,036	131,527	11,957	1,066,466	296,846	323,117	17,301	97,474	48,917
1994	1,768,372	1,237,192	5,219	1,242,411	138,242	13,164	1,117,333	310,599	340,440	17,888	98,857	50,201
1995	1,877,209	1,305,599	-1,279	1,304,320	146,903	14,440	1,171,857	333,587	371,765	18,708	100,342	52,249
1996	2,009,744	1,390,397	1,164	1,391,561	155,227	19,235	1,255,569	357,825	396,350	19,513	102,993	53,694
1997	2,160,449	1,507,357	2,126	1,509,483	164,401	26,088	1,371,170	374,794	414,485	20,552	105,122	56,132
1998	2,283,278	1,602,126	784	1,602,910	173,428	36,867	1,466,349	389,398	427,531	21,335	107,020	55,290
1999	2,411,999	1,702,202	6,374	1,708,576	183,024	39,696	1,565,248	403,271	443,480	22,093	109,173	56,291
2000	2,615,466	1,842,324	1,090	1,843,414	194,649	47,105	1,695,870	448,958	470,638	23,576	110,939	57,537
2001	2,726,465	1,856,417	-563	1,855,854	197,317	90,182	1,748,719	465,627	512,119	24,272	112,330	59,963
2002	2,785,444	1,846,339	4,953	1,851,292	195,224	120,379	1,776,447	452,811	556,186	24,598	113,239	59,732
2003	2,901,313	1,892,488	10,437	1,902,925	204,892	133,309	1,831,342	478,437	591,534	25,356	114,421	60,176
2004	3,052,372	1,937,979	13,290	1,951,269	212,166	203,533	1,942,636	493,389	616,347	26,543	114,998	60,290
2005	3,213,670	2,001,152	6,251	2,007,403	220,425	244,549	2,031,527	508,856	673,287	27,784	115,666	61,002
2006	3,481,778	2,141,270	4,242	2,145,512	227,862	303,982	2,221,632	539,519	720,627	29,715	117,174	62,162
2007	3,749,867	2,186,149	8,327	2,194,476	234,135	364,264	2,324,605	639,206	786,056	31,690	118,331	63,164
2008	4,012,774	2,219,858	-903	2,218,955	239,152	415,996	2,395,799	747,407	869,568	33,768	118,834	63,208
2009	3,869,289	2,181,417	-7,045	2,174,372	241,599	320,992	2,253,765	666,301	949,223	32,226	120,069	62,365
2010	4,003,612	2,269,210	-3,893	2,265,317	252,000	285,630	2,298,947	670,994	1,033,671	33,080	121,029	61,568
2011	4,214,606	2,365,936	2,810	2,368,746	232,167	300,552	2,437,131	713,386	1,064,089	34,708	121,429	62,940
2012	4,421,721	2,463,104	6,206	2,469,310	238,293	358,442	2,589,459	767,992	1,064,270	36,283	121,866	63,217
2013	4,519,297	2,570,130	9,998	2,580,128	280,489	334,745	2,634,384	766,569	1,118,344	36,927	122,385	64,729
2014	4,786,810	2,620,535	-4,445	2,616,090	287,130	439,082	2,768,042	842,947	1,175,821	38,988	122,778	66,166
2015	4,951,574	2,672,431	7,615	2,680,046	297,087	489,945	2,872,904	840,474	1,238,196	39,739	124,603	67,266
2016	5,220,294	2,716,863	-8,368	2,708,495	307,877	594,370	2,994,988	925,181	1,300,125	41,102	127,007	68,025
2017	5,419,633	2,877,862	-19,871	2,857,991	326,927	653,032	3,184,096	908,424	1,327,113	41,837	129,542	69,639
2018	5,762,135	3,039,537	-28,288	3,011,249	341,905	714,955	3,384,299	976,448	1,401,388	43,657	131,987	71,618
2019	6,137,645	3,157,721	-18,213	3,139,508	354,669	866,109	3,650,948	1,006,911	1,479,786	45,771	134,094	72,151
2020	6,563,975	3,297,755	-16,264	3,281,491	377,268	821,796	3,726,019	987,047	1,850,909	48,260	136,014	72,937
2021	7,253,087	3,593,424	-15,494	3,577,930	408,053	961,767	4,131,644	1,017,890	2,103,553	52,055	139,336	74,829

Personal Income and Employment by Area: Shreveport-Bossier City, LA

(Thousands of dollars, except as noted.)

Year	Personal income, total	Earnings by place of work			Less: Contributions for government social insurance	Plus: Adjustment for residence	Equals: Net earnings by place of residence	Plus: Dividends, interest, and rent	Plus: Personal current transfer receipts	Per capita personal income (dollars)	Population (persons)	Total employment
		Nonfarm	Farm	Total								
1970	1,254,974	998,298	20,875	1,019,173	64,683	-24,388	930,102	204,148	120,724	3,500	358,599	156,510
1971	1,355,283	1,067,545	24,297	1,091,842	70,745	-25,045	996,052	218,523	140,708	3,732	363,150	156,487
1972	1,470,474	1,160,349	28,537	1,188,886	80,267	-27,428	1,081,191	234,425	154,858	4,002	367,392	158,719
1973	1,626,009	1,286,557	33,249	1,319,806	101,687	-32,155	1,185,964	264,720	175,325	4,397	369,828	166,046
1974	1,838,298	1,452,681	17,995	1,470,676	118,454	-36,213	1,316,009	319,578	202,711	4,930	372,886	171,606
1975	2,060,643	1,610,754	16,932	1,627,686	129,900	-39,572	1,458,214	353,695	248,734	5,408	381,019	174,633
1976	2,273,754	1,789,322	26,541	1,815,863	147,346	-44,284	1,624,233	375,745	273,776	5,877	386,919	178,905
1977	2,526,869	2,011,351	27,547	2,038,898	163,843	-48,961	1,826,094	411,151	289,624	6,481	389,881	184,422
1978	2,851,164	2,281,377	24,296	2,305,673	189,172	-58,899	2,057,602	476,208	317,354	7,242	393,685	189,618
1979	3,196,279	2,550,354	36,753	2,587,107	220,088	-67,453	2,299,566	536,407	360,306	8,032	397,929	192,590
1980	3,641,883	2,852,213	14,678	2,866,891	245,946	-77,955	2,542,990	667,154	431,739	9,019	403,812	197,589
1981	4,187,148	3,289,408	16,314	3,305,722	303,614	-130,166	2,871,942	831,578	483,628	10,256	408,275	205,422
1982	4,524,825	3,422,564	9,175	3,431,739	321,100	-90,400	3,020,239	950,422	554,164	10,915	414,540	206,376
1983	4,811,341	3,559,962	13,518	3,573,480	333,114	-92,610	3,147,756	1,053,096	610,489	11,508	418,102	204,949
1984	5,214,317	3,875,564	16,055	3,891,619	375,108	-100,975	3,415,536	1,160,890	637,891	12,411	420,125	211,853
1985	5,500,871	4,015,985	17,067	4,033,052	392,953	-98,228	3,541,871	1,260,432	698,568	12,995	423,310	212,767
1986	5,547,118	3,943,917	22,942	3,966,859	380,780	-85,995	3,500,084	1,277,520	769,514	13,035	425,565	201,775
1987	5,629,095	4,027,837	30,791	4,058,628	381,700	-78,828	3,598,100	1,251,114	779,881	13,388	420,448	198,273
1988	5,836,284	4,173,960	31,384	4,205,344	412,351	-76,472	3,716,521	1,297,706	822,057	14,110	413,628	197,372
1989	6,090,108	4,298,815	26,206	4,325,021	427,416	-63,215	3,834,390	1,359,085	896,633	14,903	408,649	195,216
1990	6,467,303	4,520,746	21,652	4,542,398	460,476	-52,627	4,029,295	1,460,591	977,417	16,118	401,238	196,252
1991	6,694,776	4,645,364	15,054	4,660,418	487,952	-55,654	4,116,812	1,463,349	1,114,615	16,731	400,139	196,602
1992	7,202,886	5,002,578	16,400	5,018,978	520,688	-70,617	4,427,673	1,504,815	1,270,398	17,884	402,750	198,843
1993	7,652,877	5,275,071	15,535	5,290,606	553,633	-85,802	4,651,171	1,574,784	1,426,922	18,853	405,929	204,276
1994	8,053,205	5,577,889	18,448	5,596,337	595,227	-97,577	4,903,533	1,637,705	1,511,967	19,727	408,225	207,412
1995	8,353,506	5,805,944	13,126	5,819,070	620,327	-124,853	5,073,890	1,755,378	1,524,238	20,303	411,451	214,651
1996	8,637,192	6,009,804	17,880	6,027,684	638,629	-122,334	5,266,721	1,828,457	1,542,014	20,897	413,330	217,592
1997	9,022,761	6,308,082	12,491	6,320,573	666,706	-138,400	5,515,467	1,931,269	1,576,025	21,687	416,050	221,717
1998	8,582,616	6,180,383	6,030	6,186,413	655,405	-281,098	5,249,910	1,910,278	1,422,428	23,014	372,924	207,956
1999	8,831,126	6,449,530	16,648	6,466,178	675,044	-287,202	5,503,932	1,847,463	1,479,731	23,574	374,607	210,083
2000	9,376,583	6,854,220	14,104	6,868,324	703,129	-298,218	5,866,977	1,992,330	1,517,276	24,928	376,150	211,708
2001	10,354,404	7,715,095	16,531	7,731,626	756,503	-316,731	6,658,392	1,976,306	1,719,706	27,520	376,250	211,573
2002	10,616,059	7,970,769	12,676	7,983,445	775,662	-323,565	6,884,218	1,899,860	1,831,981	28,191	376,578	208,938
2003	10,956,123	8,192,355	21,276	8,213,631	800,882	-345,630	7,067,119	2,010,818	1,878,186	29,053	377,109	211,970
2004	11,329,317	8,382,765	25,532	8,408,297	837,034	-384,582	7,186,681	2,068,092	2,074,544	29,771	380,550	216,233
2005	12,454,205	9,012,073	16,482	9,028,555	876,049	-402,951	7,749,555	2,489,662	2,214,988	32,509	383,099	223,295
2006	13,372,283	9,651,432	20,481	9,671,913	941,443	-439,783	8,290,687	2,731,938	2,349,658	34,330	389,521	228,148
2007	13,694,092	9,786,294	18,707	9,805,001	970,634	-444,263	8,390,104	2,823,551	2,480,437	35,093	390,221	233,290
2008	15,703,530	11,068,117	-14,809	11,053,308	1,045,690	-460,662	9,546,956	3,340,626	2,815,948	40,023	392,367	237,256
2009	14,971,745	10,449,782	-118	10,449,664	1,025,030	-413,968	9,010,666	2,980,492	2,980,587	37,918	394,845	234,079
2010	16,046,249	11,270,362	3,484	11,273,846	1,081,951	-416,420	9,775,475	3,123,161	3,147,613	40,120	399,959	237,007
2011	16,479,290	11,062,905	4,191	11,067,096	994,844	-439,581	9,632,671	3,667,856	3,178,763	40,794	403,962	242,545
2012	16,951,955	11,169,323	12,786	11,182,109	994,168	-372,949	9,814,992	3,873,764	3,263,199	41,593	407,572	243,195
2013	17,293,784	11,810,359	20,294	11,830,653	1,131,562	-305,907	10,393,184	3,520,772	3,379,828	42,554	406,393	240,766
2014	18,568,478	13,009,087	-2,042	13,007,045	1,191,754	-296,125	11,519,166	3,675,305	3,374,007	45,868	404,826	241,596
2015	18,195,464	12,203,079	-1,838	12,201,241	1,189,722	-305,583	10,705,936	3,718,774	3,770,754	44,998	404,366	242,794
2016	17,526,750	11,525,190	-8,628	11,516,562	1,175,291	-312,040	10,029,231	3,496,984	4,000,535	43,567	402,296	241,743
2017	17,606,459	11,536,720	-9,982	11,526,738	1,193,601	-345,035	9,988,102	3,516,993	4,101,364	43,948	400,620	238,443
2018	18,619,242	12,023,247	-15,328	12,007,919	1,253,168	-345,185	10,409,566	3,954,149	4,255,527	46,800	397,844	239,013
2019	18,887,215	12,172,294	-12,384	12,159,910	1,267,351	-335,916	10,556,643	3,920,226	4,410,346	47,762	395,441	237,586
2020	20,121,692	12,212,418	-15,483	12,196,935	1,293,507	-332,510	10,570,918	3,887,262	5,663,512	51,262	392,525	228,291
2021	21,480,549	12,880,924	-16,961	12,863,963	1,347,659	-375,964	11,140,340	4,027,644	6,312,565	55,198	389,155	232,140

Personal Income and Employment by Area: Sierra Vista-Douglas, AZ

(Thousands of dollars, except as noted.)

Year	Personal income, total	Earnings by place of work			Less: Contributions for government social insurance	Plus: Adjustment for residence	Equals: Net earnings by place of residence	Plus: Dividends, interest, and rent	Plus: Personal current transfer receipts	Per capita personal income (dollars)	Population (persons)	Total employment
		Nonfarm	Farm	Total								
1970	258,346	203,119	6,493	209,612	11,329	-5,870	192,413	49,208	16,725	4,116	62,770	26,150
1971	310,805	244,189	9,400	253,589	14,297	-7,278	232,014	59,060	19,731	4,629	67,149	28,259
1972	350,963	271,112	11,193	282,305	16,344	-6,178	259,783	68,456	22,724	4,947	70,938	29,255
1973	393,750	297,934	14,483	312,417	19,246	-5,914	287,257	78,582	27,911	5,281	74,558	30,088
1974	422,424	317,600	13,649	331,249	21,768	-6,334	303,147	85,896	33,381	5,546	76,165	30,429
1975	444,691	322,041	13,448	335,489	22,551	-6,672	306,266	91,726	46,699	5,781	76,922	29,245
1976	486,415	344,990	21,298	366,288	24,075	-6,629	335,584	98,275	52,556	6,161	78,946	29,568
1977	527,949	381,694	11,603	393,297	26,597	-7,110	359,590	112,587	55,772	6,543	80,688	30,807
1978	598,871	426,557	16,333	442,890	30,254	-7,242	405,394	131,060	62,417	7,201	83,160	32,605
1979	644,379	453,440	10,252	463,692	33,640	-3,221	426,831	146,184	71,364	7,470	86,268	32,952
1980	729,673	506,074	8,623	514,697	38,656	-997	475,044	171,504	83,125	8,468	86,172	34,124
1981	811,048	551,094	11,386	562,480	45,082	-1,438	515,960	196,227	98,861	9,213	88,036	33,576
1982	859,250	566,938	13,785	580,723	46,391	-1,852	532,480	216,803	109,967	9,723	88,373	33,110
1983	937,995	612,771	18,706	631,477	52,544	-2,729	576,204	240,927	120,864	10,554	88,872	33,925
1984	1,033,492	683,141	14,677	697,818	59,650	-4,676	633,492	268,507	131,493	11,365	90,937	35,381
1985	1,085,132	712,871	10,723	723,594	65,788	-4,600	653,206	292,271	139,655	11,899	91,192	36,956
1986	1,152,180	748,877	16,665	765,542	70,853	-4,564	690,125	312,951	149,104	12,245	94,093	38,102
1987	1,227,098	799,353	18,986	818,339	75,676	-7,681	734,982	329,131	162,985	12,691	96,690	38,917
1988	1,294,453	830,427	30,623	861,050	83,964	-7,841	769,245	347,465	177,743	13,440	96,316	39,320
1989	1,358,577	858,318	19,773	878,091	91,079	-8,955	778,057	375,639	204,881	13,927	97,551	39,979
1990	1,439,562	921,108	18,913	940,021	100,320	-13,217	826,484	386,800	226,278	14,702	97,918	40,361
1991	1,527,274	977,710	19,896	997,606	107,427	-13,326	876,853	394,491	255,930	15,418	99,058	39,034
1992	1,654,714	1,057,205	28,782	1,085,987	118,798	-13,602	953,587	408,982	292,145	16,310	101,453	40,872
1993	1,719,311	1,079,140	26,738	1,105,878	123,757	-10,149	971,972	431,244	316,095	16,468	104,403	42,304
1994	1,814,646	1,138,452	9,385	1,147,837	130,616	-7,220	1,010,001	467,343	337,302	16,599	109,323	44,449
1995	1,886,593	1,156,136	6,900	1,163,036	129,596	-4,111	1,029,329	498,374	358,890	16,773	112,480	44,987
1996	1,986,665	1,192,173	23,873	1,216,046	136,244	-1,090	1,078,712	527,644	380,309	17,600	112,880	46,281
1997	2,068,792	1,245,208	30,516	1,275,724	141,091	644	1,135,277	532,443	401,072	18,004	114,907	47,434
1998	2,202,354	1,318,984	27,370	1,346,354	148,438	3,413	1,201,329	581,113	419,912	18,971	116,091	47,790
1999	2,285,577	1,352,495	34,101	1,386,596	152,316	8,593	1,242,873	595,580	447,124	19,614	116,530	48,312
2000	2,446,821	1,467,725	38,279	1,506,004	164,773	9,765	1,350,996	633,038	462,787	20,713	118,132	50,495
2001	2,641,805	1,586,948	46,986	1,633,934	176,006	-242	1,457,686	656,369	527,750	22,238	118,798	50,753
2002	2,774,825	1,707,269	33,459	1,740,728	190,031	-4,794	1,545,903	638,901	590,021	23,153	119,847	50,600
2003	3,021,406	1,904,894	34,941	1,939,835	207,520	-8,629	1,723,686	644,516	653,204	25,045	120,638	52,389
2004	3,244,742	1,994,347	42,930	2,037,277	223,076	-11,086	1,803,115	717,471	724,156	26,330	123,234	53,549
2005	3,514,017	2,173,709	68,506	2,242,215	245,388	-17,372	1,979,455	735,519	799,043	27,936	125,786	55,625
2006	3,729,670	2,329,209	34,821	2,364,030	262,463	-14,701	2,086,866	767,220	875,584	29,312	127,241	56,566
2007	4,021,309	2,473,657	46,176	2,519,833	282,288	-15,798	2,221,747	847,654	951,908	31,366	128,206	58,186
2008	4,262,581	2,615,371	23,613	2,638,984	303,764	-20,432	2,314,788	864,311	1,083,482	33,037	129,023	57,354
2009	4,435,945	2,714,177	27,653	2,741,830	318,508	-41,651	2,381,671	811,668	1,242,606	34,101	130,081	56,700
2010	4,558,412	2,823,679	31,677	2,855,356	333,490	-59,536	2,462,330	798,723	1,297,359	34,580	131,823	56,554
2011	4,690,461	2,849,267	54,486	2,903,753	305,686	-71,474	2,526,593	879,950	1,283,918	35,234	133,124	56,143
2012	4,537,419	2,732,283	40,414	2,772,697	296,824	-75,799	2,400,074	875,761	1,261,584	34,352	132,085	54,888
2013	4,459,163	2,607,504	75,937	2,683,441	318,979	-74,419	2,290,043	868,037	1,301,083	34,390	129,664	53,145
2014	4,515,201	2,571,543	46,845	2,618,388	312,962	-68,413	2,237,013	881,703	1,396,485	35,688	126,519	52,287
2015	4,632,805	2,596,240	65,482	2,661,722	317,716	-66,287	2,277,719	915,382	1,439,704	36,924	125,470	51,796
2016	4,661,736	2,604,655	59,515	2,664,170	317,511	-69,072	2,277,587	895,667	1,488,482	37,426	124,559	51,220
2017	4,825,289	2,699,261	19,303	2,718,564	329,810	-68,454	2,320,300	909,985	1,595,004	39,062	123,528	51,107
2018	4,947,502	2,754,209	12,883	2,767,092	341,851	-66,751	2,358,490	917,572	1,671,440	39,631	124,838	51,342
2019	5,206,793	2,840,583	31,809	2,872,392	357,713	-67,160	2,447,519	968,500	1,790,774	41,557	125,292	51,663
2020	5,882,308	3,151,707	25,502	3,177,209	397,162	-90,258	2,689,789	968,775	2,223,744	46,909	125,398	52,695
2021	6,188,571	3,141,760	22,781	3,164,541	395,700	-71,652	2,697,189	976,120	2,515,262	49,096	126,050	52,429

Personal Income and Employment by Area: Sioux City, IA-NE-SD

(Thousands of dollars, except as noted.)

Year	Personal income, total	Earnings by place of work			Less: Contributions for government social insurance	Plus: Adjustment for residence	Equals: Net earnings by place of residence	Plus: Dividends, interest, and rent	Plus: Personal current transfer receipts	Per capita personal income (dollars)	Population (persons)	Total employment
		Nonfarm	Farm	Total								
1970	595,480	423,596	48,259	471,855	31,052	1,783	442,586	93,075	59,819	3,772	157,876	72,833
1971	641,193	455,503	50,410	505,913	34,480	1,858	473,291	101,857	66,045	4,017	159,627	73,517
1972	728,675	497,777	85,119	582,896	39,538	1,465	544,823	112,097	71,755	4,561	159,765	75,422
1973	870,085	557,264	151,976	709,240	51,321	1,403	659,322	128,205	82,558	5,434	160,131	79,574
1974	879,866	628,764	69,123	697,887	60,531	-757	636,599	146,810	96,457	5,488	160,327	82,025
1975	999,517	701,743	83,071	784,814	66,143	-2,682	715,989	165,735	117,793	6,174	161,899	82,537
1976	1,054,368	794,915	29,894	824,809	74,913	-4,226	745,670	179,231	129,467	6,438	163,760	84,198
1977	1,170,067	844,291	66,679	910,970	78,691	-3,956	828,323	202,354	139,390	7,099	164,822	83,528
1978	1,329,850	932,203	117,995	1,050,198	89,994	-7,482	952,722	219,098	158,030	8,166	162,857	84,631
1979	1,386,120	994,978	79,542	1,074,520	100,511	-6,339	967,670	241,373	177,077	8,574	161,674	84,150
1980	1,442,107	1,060,544	364	1,060,908	106,764	-6,856	947,288	292,240	202,579	8,985	160,495	82,883
1981	1,704,006	1,160,244	88,028	1,248,272	124,067	-11,400	1,112,805	364,014	227,187	10,583	161,009	82,444
1982	1,725,922	1,154,268	36,541	1,190,809	125,121	-9,889	1,055,799	417,256	252,867	10,806	159,718	79,728
1983	1,752,372	1,218,700	-22,461	1,196,239	131,102	-9,631	1,055,506	426,465	270,401	11,042	158,696	80,852
1984	1,929,198	1,280,698	56,366	1,337,064	140,345	-8,323	1,188,396	458,078	282,724	12,190	158,265	83,017
1985	2,030,281	1,328,920	86,220	1,415,140	149,234	-8,712	1,257,194	470,214	302,873	12,964	156,606	82,318
1986	2,078,239	1,375,170	84,161	1,459,331	158,678	-9,310	1,291,343	471,825	315,071	13,420	154,861	82,879
1987	2,229,851	1,493,058	132,283	1,625,341	173,110	-11,021	1,441,210	466,247	322,394	14,523	153,535	84,732
1988	2,304,788	1,589,597	95,614	1,685,211	189,691	-10,028	1,485,492	482,754	336,542	14,912	154,564	86,760
1989	2,487,085	1,711,916	129,645	1,841,561	204,508	-10,700	1,626,353	509,975	350,757	16,124	154,246	90,853
1990	2,652,770	1,812,322	141,578	1,953,900	222,806	-12,885	1,718,209	557,595	376,966	17,109	155,053	93,372
1991	2,739,976	1,889,282	126,810	2,016,092	235,119	-16,506	1,764,467	569,520	405,989	17,499	156,583	92,809
1992	2,996,327	2,084,099	169,772	2,253,871	256,338	-21,400	1,976,133	585,480	434,714	18,938	158,214	94,798
1993	3,071,296	2,217,802	113,321	2,331,123	273,320	-23,602	2,034,201	588,883	448,212	19,151	160,369	98,232
1994	3,299,239	2,398,790	161,436	2,560,226	298,459	-28,000	2,233,767	599,586	465,886	20,331	162,280	101,761
1995	3,515,048	2,599,306	108,218	2,707,524	323,906	-35,977	2,347,641	678,966	488,441	21,426	164,052	105,716
1996	3,888,198	2,776,245	234,945	3,011,190	331,923	-41,166	2,638,101	739,891	510,206	23,443	165,859	107,604
1997	3,957,039	2,881,866	176,123	3,057,989	352,899	-41,382	2,663,708	774,211	519,120	23,818	166,138	108,743
1998	3,569,883	2,791,950	84,484	2,876,434	336,991	-129,103	2,410,340	707,915	451,628	25,143	141,981	94,340
1999	3,636,541	2,886,420	69,368	2,955,788	345,615	-133,246	2,476,927	689,456	470,158	25,452	142,877	94,810
2000	3,808,148	2,999,534	65,544	3,065,078	356,081	-138,648	2,570,349	732,345	505,454	26,651	142,892	94,186
2001	3,922,211	3,032,657	70,160	3,102,817	359,372	-130,790	2,612,655	772,511	537,045	27,584	142,193	94,796
2002	3,975,526	3,035,078	61,354	3,096,432	357,964	-113,456	2,625,012	757,984	592,530	28,033	141,815	92,185
2003	4,100,472	3,118,669	95,372	3,214,041	367,917	-105,627	2,740,497	773,206	586,769	29,004	141,374	90,929
2004	4,436,083	3,410,240	141,488	3,551,728	387,244	-112,677	3,051,807	779,414	604,862	31,431	141,136	89,779
2005	4,772,853	3,676,685	130,444	3,807,129	411,113	-97,161	3,298,855	826,516	647,482	34,126	139,860	90,203
2006	5,039,821	3,888,448	65,604	3,954,052	426,776	-80,220	3,447,056	882,952	709,813	35,906	140,363	91,233
2007	5,616,242	4,267,789	115,480	4,383,269	462,803	-81,013	3,839,453	1,026,802	749,987	39,910	140,721	94,073
2008	6,127,334	4,647,603	177,682	4,825,285	501,364	-83,859	4,240,062	1,040,665	846,607	43,365	141,298	95,334
2009	5,665,390	4,234,673	140,642	4,375,315	478,569	-49,750	3,846,996	930,036	888,358	39,717	142,645	93,617
2010	5,895,083	4,364,189	141,588	4,505,777	480,517	-49,258	3,976,002	960,418	958,663	40,966	143,902	92,744
2011	5,821,258	4,089,970	245,111	4,335,081	422,655	-33,813	3,878,613	977,155	965,490	40,373	144,188	92,769
2012	5,989,215	4,145,084	169,094	4,314,178	422,566	-19,920	3,871,692	1,147,312	970,211	41,664	143,751	93,335
2013	5,907,565	4,236,476	199,549	4,436,025	494,002	-38,270	3,903,753	1,011,434	992,378	41,124	143,652	95,071
2014	6,207,641	4,495,566	102,053	4,597,619	519,830	-66,697	4,011,092	1,157,544	1,039,005	42,635	145,600	96,622
2015	6,571,052	4,823,310	97,492	4,920,802	551,135	-94,769	4,274,898	1,197,675	1,098,479	44,939	146,222	97,693
2016	6,706,361	5,017,982	56,908	5,074,890	587,964	-137,730	4,349,196	1,219,757	1,137,408	45,692	146,772	96,970
2017	6,804,683	4,860,033	72,333	4,932,366	559,983	-28,523	4,343,860	1,335,495	1,125,328	46,421	146,587	94,845
2018	7,251,345	5,094,369	87,917	5,182,286	585,173	-34,311	4,562,802	1,465,417	1,223,126	49,112	147,648	96,184
2019	7,756,631	5,351,538	89,447	5,440,985	615,686	-8,745	4,816,554	1,646,531	1,293,546	51,981	149,220	95,755
2020	8,315,831	5,517,814	139,385	5,657,199	656,512	-9,969	4,990,718	1,680,380	1,644,733	55,534	149,743	92,947
2021	8,954,839	5,860,963	243,569	6,104,532	685,609	-34,769	5,384,154	1,737,678	1,833,007	59,993	149,265	94,890

Personal Income and Employment by Area: Sioux Falls, SD

(Thousands of dollars, except as noted.)

Year	Personal income, total	Earnings by place of work			Less: Contributions for government social insurance	Plus: Adjustment for residence	Equals: Net earnings by place of residence	Plus: Dividends, interest, and rent	Plus: Personal current transfer receipts	Per capita personal income (dollars)	Population (persons)	Total employment
		Nonfarm	Farm	Total								
1970	464,373	345,033	37,216	382,249	23,339	-3,952	354,958	68,819	40,596	3,740	124,171	60,271
1971	508,717	372,189	44,678	416,867	25,680	-3,979	387,208	74,776	46,733	4,067	125,075	60,995
1972	576,394	406,967	68,995	475,962	29,026	-4,130	442,806	81,583	52,005	4,571	126,094	61,395
1973	690,876	470,628	110,766	581,394	39,254	-4,514	537,626	92,948	60,302	5,443	126,920	65,595
1974	748,516	533,493	84,047	617,540	45,948	-4,921	566,671	110,909	70,936	5,847	128,011	67,350
1975	834,582	587,571	91,591	679,162	49,977	-4,611	624,574	124,846	85,162	6,468	129,032	68,274
1976	879,337	677,670	34,355	712,025	57,694	-4,679	649,652	136,837	92,848	6,710	131,050	71,764
1977	1,003,511	762,078	55,482	817,560	63,196	-5,282	749,082	156,347	98,082	7,550	132,916	75,138
1978	1,175,124	886,224	86,077	972,301	75,500	-5,994	890,807	177,855	106,462	8,804	133,481	79,276
1979	1,294,634	979,601	89,002	1,068,603	89,215	-5,635	973,753	200,590	120,291	9,568	135,312	80,201
1980	1,359,268	1,045,472	22,147	1,067,619	95,428	-5,236	966,955	251,262	141,051	9,766	139,185	79,520
1981	1,573,555	1,123,309	81,250	1,204,559	109,346	-7,776	1,087,437	320,173	165,945	11,309	139,142	78,983
1982	1,640,084	1,177,308	36,974	1,214,282	116,631	-9,103	1,088,548	366,536	185,000	11,653	140,747	79,169
1983	1,739,611	1,287,535	19,856	1,307,391	128,284	-11,861	1,167,246	373,474	198,891	12,162	143,042	82,261
1984	1,935,290	1,408,896	55,064	1,463,960	143,639	-14,298	1,306,023	418,660	210,607	13,248	146,081	86,170
1985	2,051,370	1,480,644	82,031	1,562,675	155,526	-16,146	1,391,003	433,759	226,608	13,867	147,929	88,138
1986	2,145,550	1,568,979	73,364	1,642,343	169,658	-18,092	1,454,593	451,362	239,595	14,517	147,796	89,382
1987	2,277,497	1,660,434	111,179	1,771,613	181,315	-20,091	1,570,207	458,792	248,498	15,319	148,672	93,682
1988	2,470,026	1,816,639	121,128	1,937,767	203,012	-23,973	1,710,782	494,384	264,860	16,308	151,460	97,090
1989	2,660,528	1,986,552	86,492	2,073,044	223,377	-26,575	1,823,092	552,526	284,910	17,476	152,240	100,812
1990	2,934,681	2,220,258	102,230	2,322,488	263,350	-30,347	2,028,791	601,426	304,464	19,038	154,148	105,115
1991	3,109,908	2,393,099	100,859	2,493,958	286,243	-32,946	2,174,769	608,275	326,864	19,817	156,928	109,696
1992	3,370,262	2,593,646	139,119	2,732,765	305,621	-37,754	2,389,390	626,714	354,158	20,965	160,753	113,135
1993	3,507,369	2,752,666	71,005	2,823,671	322,597	-42,413	2,458,661	676,625	372,083	21,375	164,088	116,256
1994	3,890,048	2,995,324	189,709	3,185,033	353,167	-48,651	2,783,215	715,467	391,366	23,157	167,987	122,281
1995	4,044,494	3,169,342	66,490	3,235,832	372,509	-53,059	2,810,264	811,142	423,088	23,694	170,698	125,850
1996	4,444,635	3,347,992	222,166	3,570,158	392,470	-59,131	3,118,557	875,952	450,126	25,550	173,960	129,330
1997	4,612,824	3,560,297	147,579	3,707,876	417,714	-69,368	3,220,794	922,838	469,192	26,246	175,756	132,805
1998	5,039,669	3,917,372	150,347	4,067,719	454,263	-82,034	3,531,422	1,021,559	486,688	28,160	178,964	136,890
1999	5,378,088	4,287,949	98,540	4,386,489	499,913	-96,576	3,790,000	1,078,225	509,863	29,366	183,138	142,582
2000	5,805,074	4,577,829	121,896	4,699,725	535,022	-111,921	4,052,782	1,196,892	555,400	30,827	188,310	147,233
2001	5,982,536	4,727,662	87,506	4,815,168	552,358	-118,847	4,143,963	1,236,235	602,338	31,209	191,693	148,941
2002	6,209,012	5,006,591	58,991	5,065,582	581,992	-129,244	4,354,346	1,202,113	652,553	31,932	194,442	150,765
2003	6,584,308	5,262,827	118,971	5,381,798	613,631	-133,877	4,634,290	1,271,475	678,543	33,286	197,813	152,571
2004	7,146,410	5,633,606	183,062	5,816,668	646,333	-141,006	5,029,329	1,385,918	731,163	35,321	202,328	155,870
2005	7,831,348	6,130,035	117,698	6,247,733	684,361	-150,473	5,412,899	1,611,024	807,425	37,905	206,605	160,492
2006	8,767,944	6,841,319	104,951	6,946,270	750,703	-155,641	6,039,926	1,832,838	895,180	41,441	211,576	165,729
2007	9,619,507	7,388,283	165,928	7,554,211	809,424	-156,665	6,588,122	2,075,010	956,375	44,341	216,943	171,417
2008	10,313,262	7,726,043	214,429	7,940,472	850,913	-164,531	6,925,028	2,269,660	1,118,574	46,480	221,887	175,343
2009	10,120,886	7,731,775	259,236	7,991,011	849,098	-159,396	6,982,517	1,957,022	1,181,347	44,800	225,913	173,762
2010	10,671,653	8,061,124	228,128	8,289,252	871,305	-151,366	7,266,581	2,116,990	1,288,082	46,579	229,110	174,143
2011	11,050,427	8,048,347	429,030	8,477,377	790,612	-160,947	7,525,818	2,206,045	1,318,564	47,593	232,185	177,722
2012	11,832,574	8,892,779	201,443	9,094,222	849,800	-165,548	8,078,874	2,425,377	1,328,323	49,904	237,105	181,848
2013	11,727,737	8,917,254	216,936	9,134,190	985,381	-157,318	7,991,491	2,348,706	1,387,540	48,485	241,883	185,908
2014	12,833,136	9,861,433	78,106	9,939,539	1,061,526	-159,350	8,718,663	2,628,415	1,486,058	51,794	247,771	190,947
2015	13,889,116	10,623,657	59,340	10,682,997	1,118,616	-178,391	9,385,990	2,927,980	1,575,146	55,101	252,066	194,266
2016	14,417,244	10,960,858	69,142	11,030,000	1,159,146	-183,207	9,687,647	3,088,912	1,640,685	56,057	257,191	197,472
2017	15,042,057	11,405,856	81,463	11,487,319	1,217,408	-196,207	10,073,704	3,239,854	1,728,499	57,179	263,071	200,615
2018	15,771,534	11,999,542	139,992	12,139,534	1,271,626	-210,693	10,657,215	3,274,532	1,839,787	59,014	267,250	205,476
2019	17,379,148	13,237,297	179,071	13,416,368	1,383,830	-235,122	11,797,416	3,606,172	1,975,560	63,690	272,871	208,473
2020	18,780,890	14,017,614	256,030	14,273,644	1,494,843	-265,876	12,512,925	3,670,632	2,597,333	67,689	277,458	207,500
2021	20,179,679	14,989,065	374,943	15,364,008	1,576,998	-286,063	13,500,947	3,771,197	2,907,535	71,570	281,958	214,084

Personal Income and Employment by Area: South Bend-Mishawaka, IN-MI

(Thousands of dollars, except as noted.)

Year	Personal income, total	Earnings by place of work			Less: Contributions for government social insurance	Plus: Adjustment for residence	Equals: Net earnings by place of residence	Plus: Dividends, interest, and rent	Plus: Personal current transfer receipts	Per capita personal income (dollars)	Population (persons)	Total employment
		Nonfarm	Farm	Total								
1970	1,110,466	852,197	7,575	859,772	57,910	62,403	864,265	156,667	89,534	3,855	288,051	115,959
1971	1,185,112	883,810	9,614	893,424	62,256	73,020	904,188	169,200	111,724	4,122	287,489	113,550
1972	1,320,268	993,533	13,150	1,006,683	74,400	90,577	1,022,860	180,535	116,873	4,558	289,656	118,965
1973	1,473,106	1,104,983	23,862	1,128,845	95,536	102,991	1,136,300	200,717	136,089	5,089	289,459	125,314
1974	1,585,458	1,189,067	15,973	1,205,040	106,729	96,462	1,194,773	229,099	161,586	5,496	288,497	126,842
1975	1,714,007	1,236,664	32,921	1,269,585	109,135	95,523	1,255,973	255,539	202,495	5,945	288,309	123,186
1976	1,879,499	1,370,286	25,181	1,395,467	122,910	124,590	1,397,147	270,170	212,182	6,546	287,124	125,452
1977	2,070,331	1,522,377	14,792	1,537,169	137,336	150,918	1,550,751	297,846	221,734	7,188	288,007	129,758
1978	2,311,819	1,699,477	23,147	1,722,624	158,574	176,095	1,740,145	331,025	240,649	7,967	290,181	134,190
1979	2,527,132	1,861,451	19,796	1,881,247	179,831	181,961	1,883,377	368,595	275,160	8,665	291,639	135,847
1980	2,732,474	1,931,582	5,766	1,937,348	184,702	174,208	1,926,854	460,088	345,532	9,390	290,984	130,558
1981	3,001,856	2,069,665	8,387	2,078,052	213,252	176,335	2,041,135	571,334	389,387	10,358	289,810	129,347
1982	3,134,345	2,122,056	8,766	2,130,822	222,222	177,371	2,085,971	617,413	430,961	10,893	287,735	126,263
1983	3,337,791	2,236,100	2,936	2,239,036	235,260	215,140	2,218,916	657,767	461,108	11,645	286,626	127,770
1984	3,695,626	2,501,646	20,435	2,522,081	269,474	233,466	2,486,073	733,306	476,247	12,822	288,222	135,669
1985	3,873,265	2,630,419	14,099	2,644,518	288,088	238,778	2,595,208	774,118	503,939	13,385	289,373	137,736
1986	4,111,016	2,800,494	24,678	2,825,172	307,980	259,326	2,776,518	801,391	533,107	14,205	289,411	141,018
1987	4,376,395	3,036,124	36,483	3,072,607	329,889	274,517	3,017,235	813,875	545,285	15,042	290,952	146,392
1988	4,643,820	3,254,332	19,540	3,273,872	365,772	282,831	3,190,931	872,266	580,623	15,862	292,757	149,826
1989	4,946,490	3,407,194	41,183	3,448,377	384,834	276,024	3,339,567	980,345	626,578	16,740	295,488	151,731
1990	5,136,215	3,556,091	42,019	3,598,110	413,197	250,927	3,435,840	1,015,200	685,175	17,283	297,187	153,679
1991	5,267,245	3,665,861	25,953	3,691,814	432,885	244,338	3,503,267	1,007,968	756,010	17,633	298,719	153,036
1992	5,674,845	3,938,136	35,995	3,974,131	461,097	281,559	3,794,593	1,027,850	852,402	18,859	300,909	155,304
1993	6,029,051	4,202,048	30,101	4,232,149	494,335	294,547	4,032,361	1,102,700	893,990	19,787	304,704	158,330
1994	6,409,497	4,475,499	29,192	4,504,691	537,634	335,861	4,302,918	1,174,187	932,392	20,863	307,216	163,946
1995	6,721,909	4,722,084	18,038	4,740,122	571,582	334,369	4,502,909	1,268,423	950,577	21,679	310,072	168,659
1996	7,021,997	4,893,172	29,566	4,922,738	584,743	332,780	4,670,775	1,351,203	1,000,019	22,498	312,119	169,345
1997	7,373,806	5,130,739	31,633	5,162,372	613,749	328,736	4,877,359	1,462,661	1,033,786	23,515	313,574	172,747
1998	7,955,053	5,581,979	18,760	5,600,739	649,269	331,248	5,282,718	1,627,525	1,044,810	25,290	314,556	175,639
1999	8,276,095	5,928,923	10,354	5,939,277	680,285	369,586	5,628,578	1,547,865	1,099,652	26,206	315,804	175,066
2000	8,634,513	6,141,967	22,101	6,164,068	698,806	362,941	5,828,203	1,645,235	1,161,075	27,239	316,991	177,109
2001	8,869,752	6,285,732	24,146	6,309,878	702,018	319,976	5,927,836	1,660,160	1,281,756	27,989	316,897	174,081
2002	9,102,379	6,465,796	10,590	6,476,386	721,112	365,908	6,121,182	1,636,179	1,345,018	28,743	316,678	172,073
2003	9,269,931	6,627,443	28,580	6,656,023	747,872	389,114	6,297,265	1,580,091	1,392,575	29,285	316,545	171,686
2004	9,785,922	6,964,915	58,013	7,022,928	787,935	527,256	6,762,249	1,562,874	1,460,799	30,887	316,831	173,844
2005	10,139,235	7,084,079	36,731	7,120,810	813,660	620,263	6,927,413	1,641,497	1,570,325	31,963	317,221	174,433
2006	10,742,162	7,373,751	32,196	7,405,947	849,529	687,084	7,243,502	1,807,967	1,690,693	33,804	317,778	175,052
2007	11,117,985	7,508,979	39,863	7,548,842	874,206	710,168	7,384,804	1,955,058	1,778,123	34,889	318,668	176,316
2008	11,317,926	7,595,316	30,214	7,625,530	898,799	566,967	7,293,698	1,978,787	2,045,441	35,372	319,966	173,666
2009	10,613,668	7,080,213	23,718	7,103,931	847,931	328,977	6,584,977	1,779,247	2,249,444	33,252	319,189	164,720
2010	10,970,629	7,166,455	42,822	7,209,277	842,191	403,898	6,770,984	1,805,206	2,394,439	34,386	319,044	163,945
2011	11,618,836	7,548,404	103,575	7,651,979	777,055	382,678	7,257,602	1,984,900	2,376,334	36,430	318,936	166,847
2012	12,148,958	7,852,092	55,853	7,907,945	797,400	449,071	7,559,616	2,161,954	2,427,388	38,157	318,391	165,809
2013	12,371,055	8,019,887	102,884	8,122,771	911,070	618,873	7,830,574	2,096,611	2,443,870	38,806	318,789	165,630
2014	13,015,291	8,416,715	38,087	8,454,802	946,781	704,259	8,212,280	2,221,832	2,581,179	40,659	320,108	168,229
2015	13,807,265	8,898,507	3,620	8,902,127	996,528	799,814	8,705,413	2,414,025	2,687,827	43,073	320,556	171,836
2016	13,930,699	9,023,940	10,440	9,034,380	1,018,737	771,131	8,786,774	2,399,286	2,744,639	43,248	322,111	175,379
2017	14,554,378	9,299,403	13,341	9,312,744	1,049,478	1,077,282	9,340,548	2,408,978	2,804,852	45,114	322,611	176,637
2018	15,192,457	9,643,891	10,833	9,654,724	1,092,931	1,094,308	9,656,101	2,623,378	2,912,978	46,933	323,707	179,111
2019	15,427,748	9,910,827	2,245	9,913,072	1,138,226	826,028	9,600,874	2,717,002	3,109,872	47,524	324,629	179,641
2020	16,426,199	9,764,479	48,328	9,812,807	1,158,259	923,022	9,577,570	2,748,135	4,100,494	50,681	324,112	169,239
2021	18,162,235	10,370,682	73,938	10,444,620	1,215,359	1,512,920	10,742,181	2,812,905	4,607,149	56,109	323,695	171,164

Personal Income and Employment by Area: Spartanburg, SC

(Thousands of dollars, except as noted.)

Year	Personal income, total	Earnings by place of work			Less: Contributions for government social insurance	Plus: Adjustment for residence	Equals: Net earnings by place of residence	Plus: Dividends, interest, and rent	Plus: Personal current transfer receipts	Per capita personal income (dollars)	Population (persons)	Total employment
		Nonfarm	Farm	Total								
1970	647,309	580,899	7,033	587,932	42,161	-22,232	523,539	65,956	57,814	3,179	203,598	95,324
1971	709,991	635,744	8,587	644,331	47,844	-24,279	572,208	73,146	64,637	3,418	207,746	97,322
1972	793,946	717,621	4,674	722,295	56,420	-25,175	640,700	81,250	71,996	3,695	214,876	102,291
1973	906,158	817,382	9,843	827,225	73,332	-26,814	727,079	93,747	85,332	4,156	218,059	108,377
1974	1,002,081	887,826	8,428	896,254	82,767	-26,329	787,158	108,478	106,445	4,541	220,651	109,521
1975	1,088,851	923,592	13,616	937,208	83,413	-34,317	819,478	119,620	149,753	4,898	222,317	104,514
1976	1,227,461	1,076,300	6,180	1,082,480	99,800	-38,651	944,029	130,791	152,641	5,544	221,399	112,098
1977	1,327,798	1,161,159	4,676	1,165,835	107,962	-37,427	1,020,446	146,472	160,880	5,861	226,538	112,592
1978	1,498,157	1,317,978	6,481	1,324,459	126,129	-40,197	1,158,133	165,648	174,376	6,555	228,545	116,562
1979	1,672,526	1,459,039	7,135	1,466,174	143,708	-38,733	1,283,733	187,533	201,260	7,251	230,660	118,727
1980	1,886,083	1,607,515	3,485	1,611,000	157,816	-43,939	1,409,245	233,673	243,165	8,040	234,585	119,546
1981	2,099,054	1,741,510	5,909	1,747,419	182,659	-43,528	1,521,232	292,052	285,770	8,856	237,011	119,197
1982	2,191,017	1,753,894	166	1,754,060	186,510	-40,464	1,527,086	340,229	323,702	9,190	238,425	115,589
1983	2,372,532	1,899,113	850	1,899,963	205,296	-40,205	1,654,462	378,338	339,732	9,902	239,608	116,366
1984	2,646,242	2,133,726	11,636	2,145,362	238,004	-44,269	1,863,089	430,461	352,692	10,909	242,564	121,852
1985	2,814,057	2,267,837	-2,360	2,265,477	256,019	-37,154	1,972,304	462,666	379,087	11,463	245,495	123,771
1986	2,992,450	2,406,564	516	2,407,080	278,219	-25,467	2,103,394	491,609	397,447	12,141	246,475	125,105
1987	3,226,898	2,625,978	6,225	2,632,203	298,691	-24,192	2,309,320	511,633	405,945	12,986	248,494	128,824
1988	3,529,801	2,884,362	10,271	2,894,633	337,264	-17,964	2,539,405	559,601	430,795	14,044	251,333	134,930
1989	3,804,630	3,071,664	8,263	3,079,927	363,431	-12,462	2,704,034	617,925	482,671	14,908	255,211	140,069
1990	4,076,249	3,247,909	5,417	3,253,326	391,774	2,393	2,863,945	678,267	534,037	15,806	257,888	141,738
1991	4,245,422	3,343,650	9,759	3,353,409	408,489	-11,517	2,933,403	699,654	612,365	16,255	261,183	138,353
1992	4,494,572	3,643,511	9,165	3,652,676	440,454	-107,789	3,104,433	717,714	672,425	17,049	263,625	141,135
1993	4,797,199	3,879,885	10,793	3,890,678	474,297	-88,023	3,328,358	754,650	714,191	18,058	265,660	144,593
1994	5,068,300	4,113,805	9,902	4,123,707	509,446	-123,864	3,490,397	811,660	766,243	18,876	268,510	150,032
1995	5,380,897	4,386,208	7,790	4,393,998	544,512	-148,785	3,700,701	856,949	823,247	19,808	271,652	154,425
1996	5,675,220	4,555,652	3,877	4,559,529	555,383	-133,876	3,870,270	921,804	883,146	20,664	274,644	156,444
1997	5,983,091	4,800,357	5,730	4,806,087	582,935	-156,043	4,067,109	996,405	919,577	21,592	277,093	159,044
1998	5,675,738	4,713,178	5,988	4,719,166	573,159	-279,881	3,866,126	975,554	834,058	22,773	249,231	147,172
1999	5,994,078	4,949,475	8,195	4,957,670	593,562	-226,639	4,137,469	964,420	892,189	23,797	251,886	146,993
2000	6,405,458	5,187,313	8,739	5,196,052	619,130	-216,327	4,360,595	1,079,186	965,677	25,174	254,443	148,302
2001	6,577,215	5,276,675	6,017	5,282,692	642,025	-219,775	4,420,892	1,072,220	1,084,103	25,645	256,469	146,802
2002	6,788,732	5,437,154	5,374	5,442,528	658,028	-252,094	4,532,406	1,080,651	1,175,675	26,265	258,467	144,905
2003	6,915,535	5,577,476	9,305	5,586,781	673,879	-246,435	4,666,467	1,019,380	1,229,688	26,575	260,223	145,121
2004	7,316,844	5,896,533	64	5,896,597	703,504	-348,363	4,844,730	1,159,054	1,313,060	27,945	261,828	145,439
2005	7,746,026	6,075,139	7,550	6,082,689	725,963	-347,483	5,009,243	1,323,793	1,412,990	29,288	264,481	146,721
2006	8,360,317	6,522,176	8,093	6,530,269	793,784	-433,150	5,303,335	1,523,488	1,533,494	31,091	268,898	150,509
2007	8,898,418	6,821,870	10,576	6,832,446	824,272	-497,282	5,510,892	1,751,232	1,636,294	32,451	274,215	154,687
2008	9,427,863	6,969,582	16,860	6,986,442	856,079	-476,653	5,653,710	1,894,586	1,879,567	33,710	279,673	154,897
2009	8,874,935	6,427,273	20,784	6,448,057	809,921	-418,246	5,219,890	1,555,043	2,100,002	31,323	283,335	145,020
2010	9,153,582	6,675,870	23,600	6,699,470	821,441	-476,885	5,401,144	1,513,612	2,238,826	32,144	284,769	143,688
2011	9,710,963	6,900,826	11,795	6,912,621	766,639	-494,601	5,651,381	1,835,021	2,224,561	33,933	286,180	148,560
2012	10,435,899	7,321,575	9,471	7,331,046	788,812	-550,040	5,992,194	2,198,401	2,245,304	36,200	288,283	151,298
2013	10,215,275	7,620,119	8,376	7,628,495	922,077	-669,958	6,036,460	1,893,458	2,285,357	35,159	290,545	157,117
2014	11,165,013	8,093,361	2,310	8,095,671	968,353	-708,799	6,418,519	2,313,520	2,432,974	37,946	294,238	161,712
2015	11,762,936	8,575,244	2,667	8,577,911	1,018,874	-706,198	6,852,839	2,349,189	2,560,908	39,458	298,115	165,643
2016	12,345,118	8,968,242	-487	8,967,755	1,068,492	-727,339	7,171,924	2,545,444	2,627,750	40,784	302,696	171,770
2017	12,776,255	9,518,894	-138	9,518,756	1,136,419	-814,914	7,567,423	2,504,234	2,704,598	41,352	308,960	180,042
2018	13,350,410	9,895,590	380	9,895,970	1,191,838	-753,062	7,951,070	2,561,803	2,837,537	42,141	316,801	186,943
2019	14,533,789	10,616,815	1,886	10,618,701	1,283,896	-936,965	8,397,840	3,135,992	2,999,957	45,010	322,898	193,546
2020	15,691,214	10,949,282	3,981	10,953,263	1,307,245	-950,698	8,695,320	3,154,834	3,841,060	47,641	329,364	193,670
2021	16,993,490	11,668,398	4,028	11,672,426	1,372,693	-873,515	9,426,218	3,267,851	4,299,421	50,596	335,864	197,673

Personal Income and Employment by Area: Spokane-Spokane Valley, WA

(Thousands of dollars, except as noted.)

Year	Personal income, total	Earnings by place of work			Less: Contributions for government social insurance	Plus: Adjustment for residence	Equals: Net earnings by place of residence	Plus: Dividends, interest, and rent	Plus: Personal current transfer receipts	Per capita personal income (dollars)	Population (persons)	Total employment
		Nonfarm	Farm	Total								
1970	1,204,080	907,081	23,387	930,468	73,775	-16,053	840,640	219,368	144,072	3,851	312,662	129,507
1971	1,316,565	985,526	23,187	1,008,713	83,296	-13,715	911,702	240,949	163,914	4,105	320,760	130,877
1972	1,454,773	1,091,713	31,408	1,123,121	96,852	-12,838	1,013,431	261,651	179,691	4,482	324,588	135,558
1973	1,608,272	1,205,850	44,486	1,250,336	123,183	-16,438	1,110,715	292,514	205,043	4,864	330,672	140,777
1974	1,843,346	1,360,492	69,245	1,429,737	142,743	-19,832	1,267,162	337,007	239,177	5,456	337,833	147,280
1975	2,039,739	1,479,525	61,514	1,541,039	152,627	-19,213	1,369,199	381,059	289,481	5,986	340,737	145,992
1976	2,281,143	1,706,727	45,867	1,752,594	179,804	-20,113	1,552,677	411,250	317,216	6,574	346,996	154,184
1977	2,529,255	1,921,192	35,768	1,956,960	203,587	-20,152	1,733,221	463,002	333,032	7,170	352,737	160,857
1978	2,888,804	2,232,348	35,661	2,268,009	242,846	-23,099	2,002,064	528,315	358,425	7,978	362,077	171,110
1979	3,268,176	2,500,904	49,342	2,550,246	281,438	-6,327	2,262,481	599,512	406,183	8,826	370,294	176,121
1980	3,658,198	2,716,350	41,158	2,757,508	305,563	-8,927	2,443,018	720,199	494,981	9,609	380,713	177,638
1981	4,010,103	2,930,967	44,896	2,975,863	353,372	-40,019	2,582,472	864,856	562,775	10,409	385,240	176,434
1982	4,207,167	2,968,379	34,231	3,002,610	363,285	-46,466	2,592,859	983,928	630,380	10,896	386,115	173,325
1983	4,546,102	3,186,841	53,286	3,240,127	396,794	-52,345	2,790,988	1,083,489	671,625	11,732	387,506	178,995
1984	4,850,285	3,424,052	38,570	3,462,622	443,708	-62,362	2,956,552	1,189,213	704,520	12,350	392,732	185,944
1985	5,033,674	3,505,860	29,999	3,535,859	458,758	-63,400	3,013,701	1,258,833	761,140	12,741	395,083	187,899
1986	5,242,537	3,650,089	46,683	3,696,772	482,390	-69,667	3,144,715	1,296,214	801,608	13,311	393,851	191,101
1987	5,431,263	3,850,142	18,018	3,868,160	503,753	-75,868	3,288,539	1,300,367	842,357	13,820	393,013	196,927
1988	5,757,028	4,110,721	32,933	4,143,654	555,532	-86,889	3,501,233	1,341,024	914,771	14,652	392,929	201,707
1989	6,259,058	4,365,692	37,217	4,402,909	589,948	-94,505	3,718,456	1,546,040	994,562	15,824	395,554	205,459
1990	6,716,147	4,804,803	30,216	4,835,019	655,351	-101,701	4,077,967	1,541,024	1,097,156	16,663	403,054	213,149
1991	7,295,392	5,220,565	23,257	5,243,822	713,976	-106,234	4,423,612	1,613,563	1,258,217	17,635	413,678	219,425
1992	7,901,004	5,717,126	31,939	5,749,065	777,561	-120,740	4,850,764	1,666,274	1,383,966	18,553	425,854	224,934
1993	8,402,002	6,122,581	38,158	6,160,739	838,582	-130,654	5,191,503	1,747,069	1,463,430	19,207	437,440	229,463
1994	8,894,319	6,519,901	23,304	6,543,205	897,617	-147,248	5,498,340	1,879,622	1,516,357	19,981	445,129	242,655
1995	9,268,137	6,722,454	33,186	6,755,640	927,247	-160,592	5,667,801	1,992,973	1,607,363	20,468	452,821	245,905
1996	9,741,788	7,035,557	34,719	7,070,276	945,082	-178,410	5,946,784	2,124,432	1,670,572	21,287	457,647	250,642
1997	10,298,882	7,450,070	26,485	7,476,555	961,232	-196,844	6,318,479	2,247,038	1,733,365	22,369	460,412	254,871
1998	10,686,784	7,920,493	24,148	7,944,641	1,003,519	-245,488	6,695,634	2,257,426	1,733,724	23,610	452,646	254,209
1999	11,079,629	8,346,376	19,788	8,366,164	1,020,137	-268,480	7,077,547	2,144,817	1,857,265	24,354	454,950	256,620
2000	11,962,371	9,052,245	25,967	9,078,212	1,118,101	-247,239	7,712,872	2,293,627	1,955,872	26,061	459,013	263,728
2001	12,099,539	8,969,493	22,667	8,992,160	1,130,481	-235,798	7,625,881	2,297,513	2,176,145	26,126	463,126	264,211
2002	12,359,449	9,173,036	32,099	9,205,135	1,156,123	-231,624	7,817,388	2,252,538	2,289,523	26,441	467,441	262,251
2003	12,827,532	9,513,297	48,388	9,561,685	1,210,501	-241,394	8,109,790	2,325,172	2,392,570	27,217	471,299	266,191
2004	13,501,461	10,105,818	32,731	10,138,549	1,296,419	-246,882	8,595,248	2,446,012	2,460,201	28,347	476,290	271,440
2005	14,069,882	10,692,048	21,784	10,713,832	1,388,110	-234,633	9,091,089	2,337,550	2,641,243	29,188	482,051	279,167
2006	15,179,369	11,399,241	14,877	11,414,118	1,468,467	-207,585	9,738,066	2,589,430	2,851,873	30,986	489,883	289,106
2007	16,433,037	12,071,237	19,484	12,090,721	1,535,688	-214,662	10,340,371	2,996,806	3,095,860	32,918	499,209	298,270
2008	17,565,279	12,457,212	11,637	12,468,849	1,568,499	-236,348	10,664,002	3,374,366	3,526,911	34,737	505,661	298,281
2009	17,243,443	12,012,204	19,467	12,031,671	1,566,288	-274,854	10,190,529	3,114,888	3,938,026	33,693	511,783	287,157
2010	17,685,501	12,221,180	33,192	12,254,372	1,587,127	-288,527	10,378,718	2,986,343	4,320,440	34,303	515,574	281,118
2011	18,381,247	12,552,989	43,213	12,596,202	1,483,452	-336,801	10,775,949	3,297,780	4,307,518	35,556	516,973	282,166
2012	19,162,641	13,180,966	32,837	13,213,803	1,512,061	-436,744	11,264,998	3,574,026	4,323,617	36,915	519,099	287,325
2013	19,358,773	13,591,345	50,003	13,641,348	1,746,466	-405,426	11,489,456	3,482,648	4,386,669	37,097	521,840	291,935
2014	20,470,892	14,070,669	23,096	14,093,765	1,812,284	-423,196	11,858,285	3,770,342	4,842,265	38,516	531,493	297,137
2015	21,391,833	14,730,604	72,948	14,803,552	1,900,238	-421,245	12,482,069	3,977,130	4,932,634	39,717	538,609	301,621
2016	22,302,406	15,389,860	45,270	15,435,130	1,958,413	-472,817	13,003,900	4,077,875	5,220,631	40,646	548,704	308,128
2017	23,478,042	16,261,518	53,823	16,315,341	2,092,692	-473,124	13,749,525	4,325,845	5,402,672	41,995	559,074	314,798
2018	24,940,494	17,336,476	39,265	17,375,741	2,192,913	-519,884	14,662,944	4,598,090	5,679,460	43,843	568,856	323,216
2019	26,455,451	18,313,096	60,215	18,373,311	2,264,934	-634,023	15,474,354	4,904,690	6,076,407	45,651	579,510	327,984
2020	28,865,711	19,033,962	91,008	19,124,970	2,396,739	-618,448	16,109,783	4,898,066	7,857,862	49,153	587,266	321,135
2021	31,618,724	20,909,388	84,008	20,993,396	2,583,484	-724,959	17,684,953	5,021,508	8,912,263	53,278	593,466	335,331

Personal Income and Employment by Area: Springfield, IL

(Thousands of dollars, except as noted.)

Year	Personal income, total	Earnings by place of work			Less: Contributions for government social insurance	Plus: Adjustment for residence	Equals: Net earnings by place of residence	Plus: Dividends, interest, and rent	Plus: Personal current transfer receipts	Per capita personal income (dollars)	Population (persons)	Total employment
		Nonfarm	Farm	Total								
1970	793,627	656,376	24,255	680,631	38,683	-26,656	615,292	119,402	58,933	4,619	171,806	90,195
1971	888,773	736,448	30,181	766,629	44,476	-32,655	689,498	130,509	68,766	5,064	175,525	92,866
1972	966,057	793,177	34,982	828,159	49,801	-35,992	742,366	145,256	78,435	5,472	176,557	93,833
1973	1,076,590	856,215	58,475	914,690	61,209	-39,450	814,031	167,768	94,791	6,028	178,605	96,418
1974	1,199,367	953,354	61,155	1,014,509	70,797	-46,115	897,597	192,624	109,146	6,681	179,531	99,017
1975	1,350,941	1,045,381	80,270	1,125,651	77,368	-51,543	996,740	213,598	140,603	7,344	183,947	100,341
1976	1,444,065	1,140,058	59,592	1,199,650	86,496	-53,686	1,059,468	228,825	155,772	7,707	187,362	101,727
1977	1,550,499	1,219,356	65,617	1,284,973	93,099	-56,355	1,135,519	252,450	162,530	8,229	188,410	103,960
1978	1,706,750	1,367,710	50,614	1,418,324	107,116	-64,825	1,246,383	283,411	176,956	9,086	187,846	107,229
1979	1,826,772	1,435,609	54,873	1,490,482	116,210	-66,032	1,308,240	322,610	195,922	9,744	187,471	106,604
1980	1,965,909	1,517,872	23,097	1,540,969	119,965	-73,244	1,347,760	382,365	235,784	10,469	187,780	103,610
1981	2,194,208	1,626,163	60,846	1,687,009	138,179	-85,139	1,463,691	455,746	274,771	11,703	187,489	102,830
1982	2,372,886	1,725,218	39,850	1,765,068	147,959	-90,741	1,526,368	549,120	297,398	12,700	186,844	103,591
1983	2,457,447	1,817,016	-1,026	1,815,990	156,440	-96,226	1,563,324	576,238	317,885	13,099	187,611	104,656
1984	2,688,967	1,957,808	42,698	2,000,506	173,027	-103,870	1,723,609	633,819	331,539	14,322	187,747	106,763
1985	2,824,113	2,079,115	44,712	2,123,827	188,037	-114,270	1,821,520	653,795	348,798	15,014	188,104	110,181
1986	3,028,221	2,287,758	38,283	2,326,041	208,804	-134,868	1,982,369	684,499	361,353	16,166	187,316	115,910
1987	3,228,427	2,502,139	43,335	2,545,474	228,130	-154,131	2,163,213	691,606	373,608	17,210	187,591	117,958
1988	3,411,382	2,711,348	13,684	2,725,032	256,930	-171,380	2,296,722	724,334	390,326	18,096	188,519	120,710
1989	3,726,487	2,857,275	57,818	2,915,093	272,203	-174,211	2,468,679	842,493	415,315	19,722	188,954	122,213
1990	3,943,407	3,139,570	43,726	3,183,296	295,291	-196,675	2,691,330	800,699	451,378	20,775	189,818	125,747
1991	4,061,743	3,245,981	26,475	3,272,456	314,841	-210,657	2,746,958	830,542	484,243	21,095	192,544	125,206
1992	4,351,038	3,481,695	54,624	3,536,319	335,406	-239,654	2,961,259	846,661	543,118	22,245	195,599	126,634
1993	4,502,212	3,628,128	31,549	3,659,677	352,480	-253,649	3,053,548	884,116	564,548	22,679	198,516	125,314
1994	4,768,786	3,843,519	62,712	3,906,231	381,047	-268,845	3,256,339	934,046	578,401	23,710	201,132	128,409
1995	4,968,596	3,984,542	11,303	3,995,845	395,248	-278,543	3,322,054	1,022,890	623,652	24,646	201,598	130,309
1996	5,269,183	4,162,744	74,866	4,237,610	411,567	-296,002	3,530,041	1,087,205	651,937	26,069	202,123	131,736
1997	5,430,507	4,258,226	69,524	4,327,750	419,173	-309,533	3,599,044	1,161,719	669,744	26,899	201,884	131,819
1998	5,677,429	4,527,711	42,744	4,570,455	443,131	-333,563	3,793,761	1,211,436	672,232	28,145	201,722	133,299
1999	5,861,882	4,766,846	31,247	4,798,093	456,392	-355,477	3,986,224	1,194,929	680,729	29,113	201,347	134,275
2000	6,245,228	5,049,641	57,576	5,107,217	471,726	-380,836	4,254,655	1,263,069	727,504	30,974	201,628	137,874
2001	6,494,661	5,319,527	60,375	5,379,902	489,799	-430,041	4,460,062	1,257,136	777,463	32,084	202,427	137,075
2002	6,629,352	5,500,073	43,683	5,543,756	509,532	-450,336	4,583,888	1,220,180	825,284	32,612	203,281	134,989
2003	6,657,128	5,373,036	73,460	5,446,496	506,316	-426,307	4,513,873	1,276,559	866,696	32,649	203,901	131,001
2004	6,750,493	5,434,190	127,750	5,561,940	518,006	-424,103	4,619,831	1,221,570	909,092	33,006	204,526	130,500
2005	6,844,623	5,577,072	61,896	5,638,968	549,264	-426,588	4,663,116	1,195,518	985,989	33,390	204,988	130,874
2006	7,060,538	5,667,995	78,718	5,746,713	557,800	-410,884	4,778,029	1,264,386	1,018,123	34,293	205,887	130,286
2007	7,383,528	5,766,672	139,130	5,905,802	577,494	-381,649	4,946,659	1,319,704	1,117,165	35,709	206,771	130,144
2008	7,710,027	5,873,651	173,661	6,047,312	596,670	-361,174	5,089,468	1,383,462	1,237,097	37,090	207,874	128,936
2009	7,877,148	5,977,082	110,419	6,087,501	604,147	-368,354	5,115,000	1,398,084	1,364,064	37,708	208,900	127,554
2010	8,265,389	6,316,338	81,971	6,398,309	630,524	-390,254	5,377,531	1,387,090	1,500,768	39,272	210,465	127,802
2011	8,604,966	6,437,463	166,105	6,603,568	581,916	-377,801	5,643,851	1,490,899	1,470,216	40,637	211,752	129,076
2012	8,641,970	6,426,613	73,600	6,500,213	587,130	-381,600	5,531,483	1,624,628	1,485,859	40,740	212,123	127,805
2013	8,913,599	6,509,254	251,472	6,760,726	657,629	-364,276	5,738,821	1,632,222	1,542,556	42,092	211,766	126,347
2014	9,155,534	6,765,625	111,249	6,876,874	684,038	-391,816	5,801,020	1,756,668	1,597,846	43,027	212,788	128,098
2015	9,328,814	7,014,593	5,682	7,020,275	709,547	-478,286	5,832,442	1,787,105	1,709,267	43,880	212,596	129,810
2016	9,435,958	6,943,122	64,577	7,007,699	715,166	-473,486	5,819,047	1,885,802	1,731,109	44,507	212,010	129,809
2017	9,636,926	7,061,329	66,743	7,128,072	731,497	-482,164	5,914,411	1,921,134	1,801,381	45,630	211,199	128,822
2018	9,914,991	7,330,221	90,423	7,420,644	765,909	-506,818	6,147,917	1,892,574	1,874,500	47,203	210,048	128,812
2019	10,311,330	7,543,778	42,181	7,585,959	783,281	-499,686	6,302,992	2,042,795	1,965,543	49,276	209,255	127,067
2020	11,018,671	7,506,040	103,493	7,609,533	782,437	-460,709	6,366,387	2,016,884	2,635,400	52,904	208,277	119,533
2021	11,819,191	8,026,141	216,249	8,242,390	826,654	-543,617	6,872,119	2,031,328	2,915,744	57,126	206,898	123,409

Personal Income and Employment by Area: Springfield, MA

(Thousands of dollars, except as noted.)

Year	Personal income, total	Earnings by place of work			Less: Contributions for government social insurance	Plus: Adjustment for residence	Equals: Net earnings by place of residence	Plus: Dividends, interest, and rent	Plus: Personal current transfer receipts	Per capita personal income (dollars)	Population (persons)	Total employment
		Nonfarm	Farm	Total								
1970	2,369,382	1,798,520	13,029	1,811,549	113,961	53,790	1,751,378	369,756	248,248	4,057	584,006	249,926
1971	2,511,903	1,886,518	11,044	1,897,562	123,208	52,009	1,826,363	389,227	296,313	4,292	585,290	247,098
1972	2,707,309	2,040,540	9,290	2,049,830	139,561	61,306	1,971,575	410,895	324,839	4,569	592,484	250,911
1973	2,960,932	2,236,239	12,735	2,248,974	175,238	74,355	2,148,091	445,940	366,901	4,978	594,809	259,342
1974	3,181,882	2,347,932	16,997	2,364,929	190,893	91,654	2,265,690	482,233	433,959	5,361	593,517	260,953
1975	3,468,645	2,418,427	12,688	2,431,115	189,414	102,632	2,344,333	510,249	614,063	5,856	592,358	250,085
1976	3,693,009	2,633,762	14,052	2,647,814	210,688	114,009	2,551,135	539,271	602,603	6,258	590,171	251,721
1977	4,036,798	2,909,334	14,935	2,924,269	233,761	131,280	2,821,788	590,613	624,397	6,879	586,804	259,644
1978	4,461,089	3,248,547	17,019	3,265,566	269,317	160,096	3,156,345	644,424	660,320	7,646	583,481	270,979
1979	4,977,340	3,607,782	13,837	3,621,619	311,234	199,567	3,509,952	723,560	743,828	8,544	582,523	278,090
1980	5,571,209	3,903,596	17,596	3,921,192	336,772	243,957	3,828,377	892,305	850,527	9,561	582,692	281,837
1981	6,123,437	4,177,851	17,961	4,195,812	386,304	267,378	4,076,886	1,081,797	964,754	10,471	584,790	278,651
1982	6,629,919	4,376,474	14,274	4,390,748	410,648	280,074	4,260,174	1,302,473	1,067,272	11,417	580,705	274,230
1983	7,074,439	4,734,913	17,120	4,752,033	450,363	288,137	4,589,807	1,337,336	1,147,296	12,160	581,778	278,420
1984	7,836,604	5,259,331	23,012	5,282,343	517,994	321,412	5,085,761	1,541,031	1,209,812	13,444	582,893	290,483
1985	8,374,821	5,679,189	22,469	5,701,658	561,195	347,191	5,487,654	1,614,461	1,272,706	14,366	582,962	298,323
1986	8,967,507	6,129,694	24,049	6,153,743	618,070	381,502	5,917,175	1,701,809	1,348,523	15,370	583,433	306,741
1987	9,735,390	6,778,098	27,143	6,805,241	674,299	409,591	6,540,533	1,793,229	1,401,628	16,498	590,082	311,695
1988	10,627,333	7,446,664	34,057	7,480,721	756,074	436,884	7,161,531	1,955,075	1,510,727	17,802	596,967	320,757
1989	11,515,045	7,799,744	28,154	7,827,898	791,005	456,490	7,493,383	2,285,744	1,735,918	19,121	602,229	319,997
1990	11,641,632	7,869,130	30,490	7,899,620	789,881	473,984	7,583,723	2,137,440	1,920,469	19,282	603,765	313,127
1991	11,863,531	7,787,551	27,645	7,815,196	796,793	476,905	7,495,308	2,096,641	2,271,582	19,678	602,886	298,962
1992	12,189,895	8,133,746	23,653	8,157,399	823,940	481,607	7,815,066	2,046,464	2,328,365	20,234	602,439	301,351
1993	12,499,739	8,378,061	21,645	8,399,706	853,670	467,785	8,013,821	2,099,525	2,386,393	20,730	602,990	302,284
1994	13,038,427	8,707,582	21,970	8,729,552	890,633	484,916	8,323,835	2,171,390	2,543,202	21,582	604,128	304,888
1995	13,599,043	8,920,143	21,449	8,941,592	923,241	477,129	8,495,480	2,426,677	2,676,886	22,518	603,922	305,322
1996	14,170,010	9,341,399	22,172	9,363,571	949,610	501,635	8,915,596	2,530,105	2,724,309	23,486	603,331	308,475
1997	14,836,951	9,798,384	21,429	9,819,813	996,891	522,926	9,345,848	2,657,972	2,833,131	24,537	604,675	312,467
1998	17,217,596	11,236,000	22,297	11,258,297	1,136,991	858,066	10,979,372	3,062,792	3,175,432	25,430	677,062	353,947
1999	17,931,137	11,854,074	25,137	11,879,211	1,178,393	915,954	11,616,772	3,013,024	3,301,341	26,424	678,597	359,754
2000	19,125,013	12,648,890	32,579	12,681,469	1,243,174	1,021,022	12,459,317	3,184,716	3,480,980	28,110	680,368	368,019
2001	20,257,199	13,569,032	26,043	13,595,075	1,341,297	1,016,622	13,270,400	3,175,773	3,811,026	29,762	680,632	370,842
2002	20,744,955	14,040,657	27,531	14,068,188	1,388,351	963,556	13,643,393	2,937,893	4,163,669	30,329	684,002	368,549
2003	21,382,059	14,449,803	25,857	14,475,660	1,424,209	948,525	13,999,976	2,935,128	4,446,955	31,118	687,131	366,378
2004	22,185,510	15,112,651	30,641	15,143,292	1,525,537	997,414	14,615,169	2,897,212	4,673,129	32,259	687,735	369,100
2005	23,008,614	15,541,581	31,382	15,572,963	1,612,736	1,017,503	14,977,730	2,911,501	5,119,383	33,423	688,409	369,614
2006	24,041,390	16,024,149	26,099	16,050,248	1,645,616	1,022,335	15,426,967	3,278,329	5,336,094	34,879	689,284	370,142
2007	25,209,966	16,515,438	26,350	16,541,788	1,696,111	1,086,669	15,932,346	3,752,507	5,525,113	36,544	689,853	375,639
2008	26,376,447	16,943,067	23,348	16,966,415	1,755,177	1,032,005	16,243,243	3,848,161	6,285,043	38,158	691,239	375,403
2009	26,536,435	16,719,420	22,113	16,741,533	1,738,891	1,020,716	16,023,358	3,645,502	6,867,575	38,343	692,079	365,042
2010	27,359,792	17,240,812	24,699	17,265,511	1,748,064	1,109,338	16,626,785	3,558,417	7,174,590	39,369	694,951	364,519
2011	28,629,602	17,805,271	13,088	17,818,359	1,642,433	1,246,243	17,422,169	3,941,011	7,266,422	41,011	698,094	367,456
2012	30,078,376	18,779,138	22,053	18,801,191	1,710,808	1,318,841	18,409,224	4,270,811	7,398,341	43,017	699,220	378,277
2013	30,413,328	19,140,929	27,765	19,168,694	1,942,853	1,381,391	18,607,232	4,345,502	7,460,594	43,435	700,196	383,472
2014	31,509,545	19,687,116	8,577	19,695,693	2,017,555	1,402,894	19,081,032	4,700,361	7,728,152	44,808	703,209	387,035
2015	33,294,800	20,488,658	7,989	20,496,647	2,060,603	1,482,101	19,918,145	5,015,386	8,361,269	47,389	702,585	399,360
2016	34,013,721	20,897,939	-1,289	20,896,650	2,119,263	1,461,800	20,239,187	5,084,801	8,689,733	48,451	702,030	404,494
2017	34,846,895	21,549,589	5,827	21,555,416	2,199,815	1,499,503	20,855,104	5,233,430	8,758,361	49,680	701,422	407,914
2018	36,241,202	22,348,478	7,445	22,355,923	2,299,469	1,585,347	21,641,801	5,412,555	9,186,846	51,601	702,334	410,755
2019	37,709,102	23,226,293	18,326	23,244,619	2,382,674	1,614,024	22,475,969	5,865,668	9,367,465	53,846	700,308	411,759
2020	40,699,220	22,844,731	11,784	22,856,515	2,376,073	1,627,161	22,107,603	5,795,010	12,796,607	58,312	697,960	387,017
2021	42,777,546	24,094,113	18,596	24,112,709	2,509,803	1,694,657	23,297,563	5,891,062	13,588,921	61,523	695,305	401,912

Personal Income and Employment by Area: Springfield, MO

(Thousands of dollars, except as noted.)

Year	Personal income, total	Earnings by place of work			Less: Contributions for government social insurance	Plus: Adjustment for residence	Equals: Net earnings by place of residence	Plus: Dividends, interest, and rent	Plus: Personal current transfer receipts	Per capita personal income (dollars)	Population (persons)	Total employment
		Nonfarm	Farm	Total								
1970	701,954	555,435	16,899	572,334	38,236	-15,082	519,016	105,513	77,425	3,332	210,653	97,284
1971	769,880	606,699	17,126	623,825	42,946	-15,894	564,985	117,001	87,894	3,531	218,024	100,075
1972	865,244	684,061	22,901	706,962	50,738	-17,390	638,834	129,024	97,386	3,832	225,777	105,645
1973	977,830	766,252	35,536	801,788	65,543	-19,137	717,108	146,627	114,095	4,227	231,356	110,471
1974	1,062,911	825,668	21,499	847,167	72,837	-19,867	754,463	171,956	136,492	4,513	235,542	109,821
1975	1,175,914	875,606	25,039	900,645	75,374	-20,151	805,120	193,452	177,342	4,971	236,572	107,489
1976	1,332,580	1,014,050	30,991	1,045,041	88,263	-23,170	933,608	212,752	186,220	5,527	241,105	113,331
1977	1,480,066	1,142,472	24,874	1,167,346	99,859	-25,850	1,041,637	243,208	195,221	5,988	247,152	119,130
1978	1,692,043	1,313,407	35,266	1,348,673	118,477	-29,785	1,200,411	276,568	215,064	6,689	252,970	125,953
1979	1,890,888	1,468,989	27,809	1,496,798	137,093	-33,317	1,326,388	319,680	244,820	7,385	256,053	130,864
1980	2,141,112	1,604,901	29,827	1,634,728	149,283	-39,351	1,446,094	398,397	296,621	8,249	259,555	131,378
1981	2,397,773	1,742,939	47,968	1,790,907	174,136	-44,574	1,572,197	485,429	340,147	9,184	261,087	132,649
1982	2,589,950	1,859,877	21,229	1,881,106	189,951	-46,624	1,644,531	578,187	367,232	9,874	262,312	134,650
1983	2,808,534	2,024,641	14,861	2,039,502	206,065	-50,694	1,782,743	627,433	398,358	10,522	266,915	139,611
1984	3,130,280	2,264,931	19,031	2,283,962	236,219	-58,790	1,988,953	726,469	414,858	11,524	271,631	147,471
1985	3,346,403	2,430,795	19,928	2,450,723	258,740	-64,467	2,127,516	771,993	446,894	12,086	276,883	153,042
1986	3,595,922	2,633,717	21,354	2,655,071	282,259	-70,456	2,302,356	814,736	478,830	12,783	281,312	158,763
1987	3,797,339	2,821,909	18,293	2,840,202	297,371	-73,435	2,469,396	826,297	501,646	13,229	287,040	161,311
1988	4,067,099	3,034,576	21,912	3,056,488	329,702	-78,990	2,647,796	886,556	532,747	13,948	291,591	168,214
1989	4,425,129	3,268,638	40,960	3,309,598	357,176	-84,973	2,867,449	973,290	584,390	15,009	294,823	172,646
1990	4,674,543	3,465,471	33,517	3,498,988	390,862	-92,317	3,015,809	1,012,521	646,213	15,563	300,354	177,682
1991	5,035,969	3,716,714	24,062	3,740,776	422,924	-104,684	3,213,168	1,067,984	754,817	16,400	307,066	179,784
1992	5,495,411	4,082,276	19,502	4,101,778	459,246	-118,839	3,523,693	1,154,147	817,571	17,469	314,578	184,602
1993	5,923,210	4,414,247	16,398	4,430,645	497,638	-120,786	3,812,221	1,214,889	896,100	18,312	323,461	194,731
1994	6,397,830	4,794,406	2,814	4,797,220	545,151	-124,912	4,127,157	1,338,861	931,812	19,218	332,908	204,646
1995	6,771,444	5,101,160	76	5,101,236	578,148	-135,449	4,387,639	1,374,379	1,009,426	19,860	340,951	211,443
1996	7,169,472	5,380,337	700	5,381,037	601,224	-147,850	4,631,963	1,456,476	1,081,033	20,702	346,324	215,750
1997	7,599,491	5,660,716	3,120	5,663,836	628,278	-161,621	4,873,937	1,572,649	1,152,905	21,546	352,705	221,150
1998	8,104,008	6,080,850	7,992	6,088,842	668,763	-161,160	5,258,919	1,661,040	1,184,049	22,608	358,461	224,809
1999	8,491,190	6,541,190	-3,519	6,537,671	711,621	-169,978	5,656,072	1,599,059	1,236,059	23,335	363,882	229,377
2000	8,945,967	6,790,875	-2,352	6,788,523	739,911	-180,791	5,867,821	1,736,398	1,341,748	24,184	369,920	234,283
2001	9,713,245	7,387,151	8,422	7,395,573	789,160	-173,953	6,432,460	1,767,177	1,513,608	25,887	375,215	235,317
2002	10,099,789	7,766,416	7,153	7,773,569	820,368	-165,954	6,787,247	1,663,679	1,648,863	26,541	380,529	237,008
2003	10,729,576	8,208,270	20,469	8,228,739	867,432	-161,372	7,199,935	1,776,556	1,753,085	27,722	387,040	241,499
2004	11,457,347	8,823,930	64,496	8,888,426	922,253	-181,429	7,784,744	1,774,421	1,898,182	29,031	394,660	246,956
2005	12,116,527	9,357,180	48,475	9,405,655	991,576	-188,358	8,225,721	1,841,730	2,049,076	30,075	402,883	256,341
2006	12,782,878	9,731,290	22,636	9,753,926	1,052,971	-191,039	8,509,916	2,084,586	2,188,376	30,894	413,765	263,627
2007	13,474,216	9,992,734	6,244	9,998,978	1,110,453	-183,522	8,705,003	2,409,398	2,359,815	31,844	423,127	270,226
2008	14,271,578	10,033,944	14,151	10,048,095	1,137,215	-156,934	8,753,946	2,825,469	2,692,163	33,245	429,289	267,387
2009	13,942,382	9,907,962	-15,238	9,892,724	1,106,472	-197,723	8,588,529	2,407,725	2,946,128	32,109	434,220	258,981
2010	14,105,754	9,908,708	558	9,909,266	1,098,058	-165,028	8,646,180	2,315,186	3,144,388	32,252	437,362	254,756
2011	14,610,496	10,020,354	21,644	10,041,998	1,017,589	-166,257	8,858,152	2,484,793	3,267,551	33,167	440,517	258,567
2012	15,399,116	10,565,813	-4,235	10,561,578	1,055,006	-183,721	9,322,851	2,719,718	3,356,547	34,645	444,487	263,488
2013	15,562,457	10,905,002	12,785	10,917,787	1,224,857	-193,862	9,499,068	2,632,585	3,430,804	34,687	448,649	266,173
2014	16,357,216	11,382,250	69,690	11,451,940	1,283,502	-209,231	9,959,207	2,841,192	3,556,817	36,164	452,305	271,200
2015	17,303,606	12,080,749	30,907	12,111,656	1,369,203	-228,253	10,514,200	3,063,468	3,725,938	37,904	456,506	276,353
2016	17,672,619	12,329,670	219	12,329,889	1,397,100	-256,314	10,676,475	3,156,600	3,839,544	38,501	459,020	278,732
2017	18,507,446	12,901,280	-4,265	12,897,015	1,454,680	-254,582	11,187,753	3,353,166	3,966,527	39,940	463,387	282,965
2018	19,271,374	13,530,404	4,071	13,534,475	1,537,884	-286,932	11,709,659	3,430,211	4,131,504	41,200	467,748	288,334
2019	20,464,668	14,325,539	-2,401	14,323,138	1,628,774	-372,387	12,321,977	3,802,014	4,340,677	43,345	472,138	290,540
2020	21,731,399	14,679,607	5,532	14,685,139	1,706,436	-472,930	12,505,773	3,814,885	5,410,741	45,642	476,128	288,695
2021	23,430,738	15,851,723	-2,240	15,849,483	1,796,411	-474,021	13,579,051	3,849,653	6,002,034	48,664	481,483	297,457

Personal Income and Employment by Area: Springfield, OH

(Thousands of dollars, except as noted.)

Year	Personal income, total	Earnings by place of work			Less: Contributions for government social insurance	Plus: Adjustment for residence	Equals: Net earnings by place of residence	Plus: Dividends, interest, and rent	Plus: Personal current transfer receipts	Per capita personal income (dollars)	Population (persons)	Total employment
		Nonfarm	Farm	Total								
1970	624,985	400,905	8,847	409,752	26,066	109,962	493,648	84,677	46,660	3,965	157,639	55,081
1971	701,759	462,524	8,279	470,803	31,270	111,595	551,128	94,620	56,011	4,386	160,007	57,561
1972	735,920	484,167	7,107	491,274	34,671	116,064	572,667	100,481	62,772	4,661	157,903	57,769
1973	802,916	530,319	13,268	543,587	43,832	120,777	620,532	109,245	73,139	5,102	157,377	59,907
1974	860,916	553,163	17,001	570,164	47,645	127,197	649,716	121,058	90,142	5,525	155,828	59,056
1975	916,174	554,517	23,663	578,180	46,403	134,405	666,182	134,128	115,864	5,924	154,645	55,640
1976	989,647	605,349	18,344	623,693	51,447	143,196	715,442	142,575	131,630	6,522	151,748	56,507
1977	1,079,820	680,408	13,125	693,533	58,395	154,529	789,667	158,063	132,090	7,163	150,753	58,103
1978	1,192,800	768,492	13,498	781,990	68,507	165,316	878,799	175,560	138,441	7,916	150,681	60,630
1979	1,306,649	836,865	17,051	853,916	77,425	178,009	954,500	195,135	157,014	8,665	150,789	61,472
1980	1,415,166	864,123	12,589	876,712	78,966	196,323	994,069	229,570	191,527	9,425	150,149	59,719
1981	1,480,026	888,972	946	889,918	86,067	182,324	986,175	269,707	224,144	9,902	149,463	58,312
1982	1,525,851	856,688	3,414	860,102	83,835	188,219	964,486	298,015	263,350	10,322	147,821	54,398
1983	1,612,044	927,370	-3,750	923,620	92,758	189,132	1,019,994	312,430	279,620	10,956	147,142	54,481
1984	1,800,730	1,077,698	12,321	1,090,019	110,922	195,511	1,174,608	344,457	281,665	12,242	147,100	57,693
1985	1,903,421	1,143,469	17,380	1,160,849	120,282	199,632	1,240,199	362,558	300,664	12,942	147,075	59,175
1986	2,002,549	1,227,097	12,845	1,239,942	132,919	198,814	1,305,837	377,513	319,199	13,586	147,403	60,508
1987	2,074,743	1,299,395	16,410	1,315,805	142,395	194,092	1,367,502	378,368	328,873	14,065	147,514	62,208
1988	2,260,471	1,455,756	23,751	1,479,507	165,889	195,611	1,509,229	401,702	349,540	15,274	147,992	63,505
1989	2,386,486	1,498,221	28,153	1,526,374	173,317	205,501	1,558,558	456,893	371,035	16,155	147,720	65,358
1990	2,520,855	1,534,793	26,221	1,561,014	180,739	249,723	1,629,998	474,340	416,517	17,079	147,596	65,336
1991	2,596,523	1,574,084	13,086	1,587,170	190,487	260,969	1,657,652	489,879	448,992	17,574	147,747	64,309
1992	2,749,563	1,708,571	32,470	1,741,041	206,264	240,157	1,774,934	484,224	490,405	18,630	147,584	64,709
1993	2,838,718	1,757,296	20,648	1,777,944	214,469	281,668	1,845,143	485,357	508,218	19,253	147,442	64,554
1994	2,976,943	1,840,584	21,952	1,862,536	225,275	309,166	1,946,427	507,183	523,333	20,203	147,355	65,631
1995	3,129,076	1,916,494	25,776	1,942,270	236,632	339,080	2,044,718	536,652	547,706	21,244	147,289	67,425
1996	3,231,731	1,942,099	23,535	1,965,634	234,640	363,133	2,094,127	563,077	574,527	21,967	147,116	67,183
1997	3,416,525	2,039,770	32,666	2,072,436	238,006	392,247	2,226,677	596,712	593,136	23,358	146,268	67,932
1998	3,584,912	2,242,249	17,576	2,259,825	249,202	338,266	2,348,889	625,000	611,023	24,598	145,742	70,742
1999	3,655,945	2,340,199	10,372	2,350,571	258,742	335,583	2,427,412	608,130	620,403	25,186	145,159	71,410
2000	3,790,831	2,360,232	15,167	2,375,399	252,890	390,869	2,513,378	612,226	665,227	26,215	144,605	72,418
2001	3,845,111	2,362,953	22,811	2,385,764	263,449	394,476	2,516,791	608,715	719,605	26,739	143,803	68,606
2002	3,825,805	2,285,094	16,517	2,301,611	248,056	429,698	2,483,253	581,007	761,545	26,711	143,229	66,993
2003	3,894,043	2,260,975	20,271	2,281,246	248,885	461,420	2,493,781	594,215	806,047	27,470	141,758	66,257
2004	3,968,490	2,289,763	38,501	2,328,264	259,281	500,208	2,569,191	559,220	840,079	28,070	141,380	65,548
2005	4,048,269	2,325,152	34,950	2,360,102	266,294	524,075	2,617,883	550,453	879,933	28,637	141,367	65,001
2006	4,202,355	2,439,313	37,045	2,476,358	281,999	515,400	2,709,759	579,317	913,279	29,874	140,668	65,338
2007	4,317,994	2,435,530	36,426	2,471,956	282,438	519,462	2,708,980	635,975	973,039	30,881	139,829	65,336
2008	4,438,436	2,500,236	27,867	2,528,103	295,994	463,537	2,695,646	665,286	1,077,504	31,839	139,404	64,851
2009	4,404,166	2,432,091	30,216	2,462,307	293,382	416,154	2,585,079	633,249	1,185,838	31,735	138,778	62,359
2010	4,469,136	2,429,812	24,434	2,454,246	286,650	422,391	2,589,987	628,656	1,250,493	32,321	138,272	61,102
2011	4,683,057	2,541,051	34,616	2,575,667	272,546	401,701	2,704,822	681,027	1,297,208	33,979	137,823	62,236
2012	4,731,435	2,610,868	17,285	2,628,153	276,302	422,194	2,774,045	688,432	1,268,958	34,486	137,198	62,301
2013	4,794,546	2,669,582	35,083	2,704,665	304,554	393,479	2,793,590	694,683	1,306,273	35,078	136,682	62,740
2014	4,917,219	2,711,824	12,052	2,723,876	308,800	416,370	2,831,446	725,728	1,360,045	35,819	137,279	63,205
2015	5,039,056	2,741,727	-2,077	2,739,650	312,169	457,554	2,885,035	755,302	1,398,719	36,798	136,937	62,537
2016	5,113,931	2,773,820	3,339	2,777,159	322,931	467,003	2,921,231	769,375	1,423,325	37,564	136,140	61,679
2017	5,276,399	2,904,714	12,389	2,917,103	346,735	478,899	3,049,267	774,568	1,452,564	38,744	136,185	62,102
2018	5,413,669	2,972,362	17,491	2,989,853	350,098	490,417	3,130,172	797,687	1,485,810	39,672	136,462	62,096
2019	5,610,843	3,033,457	1,494	3,034,951	361,947	551,638	3,224,642	839,150	1,547,051	41,168	136,290	61,902
2020	6,105,932	3,030,736	36,509	3,067,245	367,218	591,729	3,291,756	827,620	1,986,556	44,990	135,719	59,433
2021	6,500,706	3,262,970	45,362	3,308,332	387,339	576,145	3,497,138	838,823	2,164,745	47,929	135,633	60,902

Personal Income and Employment by Area: State College, PA

(Thousands of dollars, except as noted.)

Year	Personal income, total	Earnings by place of work			Less: Contributions for government social insurance	Plus: Adjustment for residence	Equals: Net earnings by place of residence	Plus: Dividends, interest, and rent	Plus: Personal current transfer receipts	Per capita personal income (dollars)	Population (persons)	Total employment
		Nonfarm	Farm	Total								
1970	311,381	273,733	3,052	276,785	18,156	-16,982	241,647	44,711	25,023	3,130	99,495	40,640
1971	338,460	298,151	2,130	300,281	20,603	-19,595	260,083	49,439	28,938	3,342	101,263	41,670
1972	377,376	328,554	2,779	331,333	23,205	-19,625	288,503	55,616	33,257	3,630	103,971	43,904
1973	428,240	368,886	4,835	373,721	29,201	-19,128	325,392	64,283	38,565	4,077	105,034	46,470
1974	475,413	406,481	5,993	412,474	33,778	-22,228	356,468	73,036	45,909	4,404	107,957	47,629
1975	530,466	437,745	4,983	442,728	35,719	-22,626	384,383	83,170	62,913	4,933	107,533	47,752
1976	591,914	490,628	6,455	497,083	41,155	-25,474	430,454	91,650	69,810	5,379	110,048	50,025
1977	658,606	551,484	5,645	557,129	46,198	-29,616	481,315	103,454	73,837	5,832	112,939	51,750
1978	725,643	610,308	3,635	613,943	52,860	-31,860	529,223	116,136	80,284	6,519	111,315	53,267
1979	819,564	683,709	8,034	691,743	61,587	-36,696	593,460	133,084	93,020	7,288	112,459	55,133
1980	909,436	736,592	8,177	744,769	67,291	-41,526	635,952	161,053	112,431	8,039	113,131	56,510
1981	993,763	784,453	9,782	794,235	77,473	-38,351	678,411	193,640	121,712	8,687	114,390	55,794
1982	1,077,007	839,029	7,119	846,148	83,543	-43,274	719,331	223,181	134,495	9,389	114,706	55,674
1983	1,170,705	908,436	3,508	911,944	91,290	-50,043	770,611	248,141	151,953	10,075	116,203	56,956
1984	1,276,452	1,006,173	10,481	1,016,654	105,992	-58,040	852,622	274,333	149,497	11,062	115,390	59,461
1985	1,350,471	1,063,136	9,944	1,073,080	114,232	-60,784	898,064	293,311	159,096	11,585	116,567	60,583
1986	1,434,656	1,140,065	7,686	1,147,751	124,853	-65,640	957,258	314,989	162,409	12,189	117,697	63,132
1987	1,556,360	1,258,169	9,246	1,267,415	136,804	-77,711	1,052,900	329,393	174,067	13,027	119,468	66,110
1988	1,724,182	1,406,658	13,392	1,420,050	159,195	-88,348	1,172,507	361,808	189,867	14,312	120,473	68,862
1989	1,933,517	1,577,695	16,006	1,593,701	174,932	-110,922	1,307,847	421,938	203,732	15,842	122,049	71,931
1990	2,049,768	1,688,862	12,166	1,701,028	188,123	-121,009	1,391,896	433,680	224,192	16,368	125,231	74,221
1991	2,186,645	1,807,604	5,159	1,812,763	203,344	-133,048	1,476,371	456,486	253,788	17,283	126,518	75,902
1992	2,325,635	1,918,670	16,831	1,935,501	213,881	-138,637	1,582,983	468,442	274,210	18,186	127,881	76,642
1993	2,397,361	1,988,224	9,622	1,997,846	223,710	-143,493	1,630,643	479,493	287,225	18,451	129,930	78,826
1994	2,528,888	2,106,336	11,365	2,117,701	238,159	-148,807	1,730,735	515,876	282,277	19,327	130,847	80,708
1995	2,653,619	2,202,699	4,197	2,206,896	249,105	-162,343	1,795,448	557,325	300,846	20,111	131,951	84,000
1996	2,812,860	2,307,483	15,646	2,323,129	254,588	-176,022	1,892,519	595,894	324,447	20,976	134,102	85,877
1997	2,980,772	2,467,545	8,575	2,476,120	271,755	-194,192	2,010,173	629,958	340,641	22,105	134,849	87,914
1998	3,125,823	2,592,692	16,798	2,609,490	278,451	-208,142	2,122,897	643,665	359,261	23,213	134,657	90,593
1999	3,295,011	2,751,243	12,424	2,763,667	291,205	-229,928	2,242,534	686,197	366,280	24,351	135,315	93,184
2000	3,463,552	2,919,438	18,923	2,938,361	306,020	-256,951	2,375,390	692,645	395,517	25,474	135,965	95,959
2001	3,662,327	3,121,884	13,825	3,135,709	318,608	-294,912	2,522,189	694,459	445,679	26,612	137,620	97,495
2002	3,842,808	3,362,720	8,285	3,371,005	339,953	-343,580	2,687,472	674,240	481,096	27,289	140,821	100,705
2003	4,018,055	3,476,205	16,072	3,492,277	344,282	-364,358	2,783,637	736,517	497,901	28,113	142,926	100,925
2004	4,301,416	3,737,121	20,947	3,758,068	365,491	-423,963	2,968,614	810,559	522,243	29,822	144,238	103,041
2005	4,563,874	4,047,109	15,575	4,062,684	394,061	-476,672	3,191,951	819,966	551,957	31,358	145,543	104,606
2006	4,725,491	4,205,817	13,000	4,218,817	411,042	-540,388	3,267,387	862,678	595,426	31,771	148,734	106,074
2007	4,928,195	4,334,637	17,653	4,352,290	426,270	-600,270	3,325,750	955,276	647,169	32,965	149,498	107,699
2008	5,227,294	4,533,865	10,686	4,544,551	444,398	-646,344	3,453,809	1,019,181	754,304	34,471	151,645	108,962
2009	5,245,227	4,502,449	3,845	4,506,294	449,197	-632,163	3,424,934	1,006,543	813,750	34,271	153,052	108,969
2010	5,567,230	4,753,478	16,091	4,769,569	467,331	-669,251	3,632,987	1,047,641	886,602	36,094	154,242	108,939
2011	5,854,364	4,934,557	24,893	4,959,450	434,028	-708,268	3,817,154	1,132,856	904,354	37,744	155,107	111,163
2012	6,131,139	5,088,068	29,699	5,117,767	441,725	-710,018	3,966,024	1,275,707	889,408	39,326	155,905	111,266
2013	6,357,690	5,419,705	30,849	5,450,554	518,117	-738,489	4,193,948	1,242,561	921,181	40,152	158,342	113,141
2014	6,639,851	5,677,368	38,471	5,715,839	546,286	-784,876	4,384,677	1,293,828	961,346	41,928	158,365	114,258
2015	6,730,022	5,740,657	18,066	5,758,723	563,179	-810,765	4,384,779	1,340,375	1,004,868	42,364	158,863	115,403
2016	6,970,288	5,916,612	12,838	5,929,450	576,786	-854,828	4,497,836	1,425,430	1,047,022	43,524	160,149	117,483
2017	7,283,957	6,203,241	27,997	6,231,238	614,317	-887,434	4,729,487	1,487,668	1,066,802	45,506	160,067	118,804
2018	7,499,932	6,339,750	13,831	6,353,581	626,930	-911,297	4,815,354	1,546,843	1,137,735	46,855	160,067	116,456
2019	7,821,644	6,460,840	29,543	6,490,383	648,459	-879,869	4,962,055	1,652,109	1,207,480	49,211	158,940	114,769
2020	8,322,652	6,612,073	24,935	6,637,008	659,918	-932,864	5,044,226	1,660,590	1,617,836	52,699	157,929	112,453
2021	8,663,114	6,897,097	31,271	6,928,368	674,930	-969,197	5,284,241	1,651,229	1,727,644	54,994	157,527	113,882

Personal Income and Employment by Area: Staunton, VA

(Thousands of dollars, except as noted.)

Year	Personal income, total	Earnings by place of work Nonfarm	Earnings by place of work Farm	Earnings by place of work Total	Less: Contributions for government social insurance	Plus: Adjustment for residence	Equals: Net earnings by place of residence	Plus: Dividends, interest, and rent	Plus: Personal current transfer receipts	Per capita personal income (dollars)	Population (persons)	Total employment
1970	298,781	258,450	6,640	265,090	16,761	-8,534	239,795	38,419	20,567	3,488	85,665	41,054
1971	315,732	268,852	6,450	275,302	18,116	-8,684	248,502	42,696	24,534	3,600	87,707	40,415
1972	346,385	294,291	8,144	302,435	21,001	-10,247	271,187	47,384	27,814	3,916	88,454	41,457
1973	392,997	331,105	13,216	344,321	27,310	-11,942	305,069	54,404	33,524	4,461	88,087	43,253
1974	434,939	369,435	9,811	379,246	31,707	-14,974	332,565	62,467	39,907	4,890	88,941	45,156
1975	468,654	378,060	9,283	387,343	31,546	-12,881	342,916	69,658	56,080	5,200	90,122	42,447
1976	519,353	427,717	7,125	434,842	36,294	-14,820	383,728	76,531	59,094	5,750	90,316	44,035
1977	571,105	475,350	1,262	476,612	40,483	-16,042	420,087	85,705	65,313	6,308	90,541	45,245
1978	629,926	522,859	1,061	523,920	45,569	-15,611	462,740	96,678	70,508	6,949	90,646	46,008
1979	698,779	572,543	2,405	574,948	51,953	-11,666	511,329	105,967	81,483	7,689	90,886	46,584
1980	774,955	637,445	971	638,416	58,333	-26,470	553,613	124,748	96,594	8,513	91,031	47,059
1981	858,637	684,397	-160	684,237	67,467	-27,600	589,170	155,417	114,050	9,404	91,309	47,007
1982	911,676	689,957	161	690,118	69,050	-17,642	603,426	180,983	127,267	9,942	91,701	45,701
1983	983,143	731,014	1,047	732,061	73,617	-9,640	648,804	196,087	138,252	10,706	91,828	45,092
1984	1,106,492	807,518	12,191	819,709	83,645	-9,462	726,602	234,409	145,481	12,058	91,764	46,741
1985	1,169,839	842,040	14,542	856,582	88,637	-5,221	762,724	250,295	156,820	12,737	91,846	47,500
1986	1,255,038	894,406	19,478	913,884	96,820	2,176	819,240	268,838	166,960	13,602	92,272	48,454
1987	1,350,162	980,786	17,277	998,063	105,404	5,919	898,578	278,346	173,238	14,404	93,737	51,201
1988	1,471,085	1,073,224	23,989	1,097,213	118,561	12,056	990,708	299,892	180,485	15,483	95,015	52,603
1989	1,609,297	1,135,215	32,172	1,167,387	126,230	22,545	1,063,702	351,784	193,811	16,672	96,527	53,093
1990	1,707,685	1,196,910	35,524	1,232,434	135,108	31,047	1,128,373	370,694	208,618	17,408	98,096	54,582
1991	1,736,283	1,203,780	32,799	1,236,579	136,997	37,309	1,136,891	368,895	230,497	17,519	99,110	53,191
1992	1,828,832	1,261,113	35,482	1,296,595	142,180	44,043	1,198,458	369,954	260,420	18,276	100,067	52,582
1993	1,912,124	1,325,462	32,834	1,358,296	149,081	50,017	1,259,232	379,880	273,012	18,901	101,163	53,648
1994	2,005,090	1,387,261	36,185	1,423,446	155,086	54,859	1,323,219	395,002	286,869	19,607	102,263	54,075
1995	2,098,439	1,421,494	32,039	1,453,533	158,982	59,518	1,354,069	433,583	310,787	20,236	103,697	54,791
1996	2,205,714	1,490,984	32,012	1,522,996	165,164	61,534	1,419,366	460,166	326,182	21,008	104,994	56,133
1997	2,333,443	1,615,870	15,239	1,631,109	177,963	63,009	1,516,155	479,485	337,803	22,016	105,988	58,271
1998	2,497,123	1,742,386	20,070	1,762,456	186,774	73,082	1,648,764	496,945	351,414	23,364	106,879	59,935
1999	2,545,798	1,770,773	16,349	1,787,122	191,532	85,112	1,680,702	495,334	369,762	23,540	108,150	60,837
2000	2,716,112	1,860,722	26,909	1,887,631	198,440	95,503	1,784,694	535,588	395,830	24,889	109,129	61,784
2001	2,780,510	1,844,689	35,872	1,880,561	210,409	118,321	1,788,473	548,568	443,469	25,369	109,602	60,313
2002	2,846,456	1,905,562	20,867	1,926,429	216,341	143,644	1,853,732	518,908	473,816	25,775	110,436	59,698
2003	3,006,111	1,983,307	8,114	1,991,421	222,686	174,762	1,943,497	556,336	506,278	26,949	111,549	59,782
2004	3,319,872	2,227,530	30,201	2,257,731	242,202	175,687	2,191,216	593,000	535,656	29,444	112,751	61,591
2005	3,428,972	2,270,937	39,723	2,310,660	256,183	199,113	2,253,590	588,103	587,279	30,056	114,085	63,083
2006	3,586,598	2,295,444	16,250	2,311,694	264,541	249,854	2,297,007	640,517	649,074	30,849	116,262	63,738
2007	3,965,599	2,517,875	21,765	2,539,640	282,031	284,109	2,541,718	737,965	685,916	33,690	117,708	64,894
2008	4,182,345	2,634,503	16,129	2,650,632	296,172	293,924	2,648,384	765,048	768,913	35,318	118,420	64,776
2009	4,156,901	2,578,696	13,580	2,592,276	292,604	307,086	2,606,758	713,753	836,390	35,052	118,593	62,262
2010	4,240,243	2,618,630	26,670	2,645,300	292,741	309,388	2,661,947	687,639	890,657	35,837	118,320	61,243
2011	4,330,071	2,550,275	43,242	2,593,517	266,482	337,016	2,664,051	743,697	922,323	36,455	118,778	61,537
2012	4,405,011	2,555,633	34,363	2,589,996	268,674	353,127	2,674,449	813,023	917,539	37,182	118,472	61,959
2013	4,469,271	2,616,233	50,513	2,666,746	312,098	354,883	2,709,531	811,047	948,693	37,517	119,126	62,619
2014	4,670,247	2,725,403	62,489	2,787,892	322,913	348,144	2,813,123	858,628	998,496	38,928	119,971	63,206
2015	4,821,565	2,813,240	54,085	2,867,325	332,552	357,430	2,892,203	888,720	1,040,642	39,966	120,642	64,144
2016	4,941,421	2,868,241	27,139	2,895,380	341,495	374,139	2,928,024	939,864	1,073,533	40,653	121,550	65,224
2017	5,144,851	2,957,162	40,241	2,997,403	357,059	389,472	3,029,816	997,953	1,117,082	41,921	122,727	65,058
2018	5,318,421	3,100,029	26,436	3,126,465	373,801	404,736	3,157,400	990,382	1,170,639	42,956	123,812	65,862
2019	5,632,192	3,191,226	22,860	3,214,086	389,216	459,640	3,284,510	1,101,846	1,245,836	45,236	124,506	66,500
2020	6,053,996	3,279,057	1,424	3,280,481	403,390	503,820	3,380,911	1,100,604	1,572,481	48,204	125,591	65,244
2021	6,535,799	3,466,874	57,716	3,524,590	422,529	523,187	3,625,248	1,118,994	1,791,557	51,965	125,774	66,112

Personal Income and Employment by Area: Stockton, CA

(Thousands of dollars, except as noted.)

Year	Personal income, total	Earnings by place of work			Less: Contributions for government social insurance	Plus: Adjustment for residence	Equals: Net earnings by place of residence	Plus: Dividends, interest, and rent	Plus: Personal current transfer receipts	Per capita personal income (dollars)	Population (persons)	Total employment
		Nonfarm	Farm	Total								
1970	1,278,250	900,345	103,228	1,003,573	56,978	-12,632	933,963	192,386	151,901	4,385	291,488	125,639
1971	1,390,528	983,384	104,415	1,087,799	64,433	-12,392	1,010,974	211,696	167,858	4,695	296,167	127,686
1972	1,528,236	1,075,883	123,592	1,199,475	74,314	-10,252	1,114,909	231,936	181,391	5,090	300,221	132,230
1973	1,704,543	1,175,239	167,599	1,342,838	93,705	-9,771	1,239,362	263,967	201,214	5,609	303,896	135,549
1974	1,936,888	1,307,453	209,817	1,517,270	108,102	-10,577	1,398,591	301,505	236,792	6,316	306,658	139,715
1975	2,130,146	1,419,692	190,228	1,609,920	114,391	-12,728	1,482,801	341,834	305,511	6,877	309,750	141,773
1976	2,320,183	1,578,559	171,009	1,749,568	130,539	-10,572	1,608,457	365,596	346,130	7,304	317,671	144,612
1977	2,556,555	1,742,951	186,272	1,929,223	147,382	-8,841	1,773,000	406,789	376,766	7,968	320,840	147,548
1978	2,868,968	1,993,874	171,395	2,165,269	171,671	-5,743	1,987,855	465,357	415,756	8,624	332,685	153,412
1979	3,245,393	2,235,724	212,841	2,448,565	203,261	-6,497	2,238,807	536,233	470,353	9,591	338,384	162,770
1980	3,690,850	2,398,775	287,853	2,686,628	215,941	-840	2,469,847	659,293	561,710	10,536	350,304	165,174
1981	4,075,817	2,624,958	212,959	2,837,917	257,384	18,131	2,598,664	810,227	666,926	11,276	361,462	167,276
1982	4,347,135	2,755,500	187,057	2,942,557	275,474	35,927	2,703,010	893,149	750,976	11,640	373,479	167,744
1983	4,579,513	2,892,580	123,438	3,016,018	293,830	67,792	2,789,980	974,631	814,902	11,873	385,721	169,304
1984	5,152,677	3,239,905	201,377	3,441,282	341,175	97,843	3,197,950	1,093,271	861,456	12,923	398,731	176,594
1985	5,582,735	3,526,682	203,962	3,730,644	375,824	130,603	3,485,423	1,163,001	934,311	13,419	416,042	181,855
1986	6,027,045	3,857,793	197,371	4,055,164	415,127	161,831	3,801,868	1,225,135	1,000,042	13,991	430,786	186,320
1987	6,557,228	4,226,092	297,989	4,524,081	455,068	198,732	4,267,745	1,244,470	1,045,013	14,711	445,726	195,501
1988	7,080,526	4,552,682	347,160	4,899,842	510,396	246,418	4,635,864	1,313,957	1,130,705	15,489	457,138	205,322
1989	7,667,579	4,871,224	317,769	5,188,993	549,747	302,129	4,941,375	1,490,859	1,235,345	16,424	466,863	209,243
1990	8,146,661	5,199,586	297,728	5,497,314	583,569	356,913	5,270,658	1,506,922	1,369,081	16,827	484,131	214,261
1991	8,542,060	5,477,326	261,403	5,738,729	622,224	376,352	5,492,857	1,521,913	1,527,290	17,337	492,694	216,618
1992	9,149,223	5,723,020	327,706	6,050,726	642,485	424,885	5,833,126	1,526,125	1,789,972	18,288	500,278	212,460
1993	9,543,968	5,943,726	374,500	6,318,226	668,946	452,432	6,101,712	1,573,831	1,868,425	18,847	506,385	214,476
1994	9,904,668	6,198,071	377,300	6,575,371	697,511	474,603	6,352,463	1,659,827	1,892,378	19,337	512,212	220,269
1995	10,231,273	6,312,788	351,001	6,663,789	704,740	546,338	6,505,387	1,748,653	1,977,233	19,754	517,923	224,933
1996	10,809,337	6,546,643	421,581	6,968,224	708,979	624,645	6,883,890	1,848,538	2,076,909	20,603	524,657	228,643
1997	11,536,532	7,121,856	449,033	7,570,889	759,186	700,851	7,512,554	1,956,082	2,067,896	21,689	531,908	233,118
1998	12,235,426	7,604,021	375,012	7,979,033	791,859	833,945	8,021,119	1,996,924	2,217,383	22,647	540,257	238,983
1999	13,093,852	8,134,641	406,711	8,541,352	851,232	990,100	8,680,220	2,089,356	2,324,276	23,703	552,424	249,510
2000	14,255,445	8,887,001	382,967	9,269,968	919,591	1,284,022	9,634,399	2,224,304	2,396,742	25,103	567,885	254,521
2001	15,555,713	9,894,834	423,307	10,318,141	1,061,648	1,305,521	10,562,014	2,279,158	2,714,541	26,312	591,207	260,519
2002	16,248,804	10,526,474	417,848	10,944,322	1,145,359	1,333,945	11,132,908	2,205,232	2,910,664	26,679	609,041	266,758
2003	17,343,135	11,267,519	505,507	11,773,026	1,243,209	1,413,713	11,943,530	2,284,101	3,115,504	27,670	626,778	274,428
2004	18,490,766	12,058,522	572,193	12,630,715	1,371,078	1,593,796	12,853,433	2,346,697	3,290,636	28,762	642,898	279,725
2005	19,562,448	12,726,472	582,890	13,309,362	1,438,041	1,837,998	13,709,319	2,407,731	3,445,398	29,776	656,985	283,427
2006	20,684,485	13,242,706	441,107	13,683,813	1,450,929	2,038,144	14,271,028	2,698,384	3,715,073	31,207	662,812	287,112
2007	21,458,733	13,175,390	597,740	13,773,130	1,448,365	2,105,141	14,429,906	3,065,734	3,963,093	32,120	668,080	293,377
2008	21,548,167	12,922,478	533,806	13,456,284	1,461,477	1,953,257	13,948,064	3,151,605	4,448,498	32,080	671,692	287,022
2009	21,601,380	12,827,444	564,508	13,391,952	1,446,057	1,830,667	13,776,562	2,891,820	4,932,998	31,873	677,736	275,719
2010	22,288,884	13,270,968	453,809	13,724,777	1,424,413	1,656,031	13,956,395	2,790,111	5,542,378	32,438	687,115	268,668
2011	22,958,164	13,344,555	561,767	13,906,322	1,317,574	1,762,963	14,351,711	3,037,301	5,569,152	33,068	694,265	269,966
2012	23,706,455	13,531,332	929,233	14,460,565	1,337,265	1,692,063	14,815,363	3,216,283	5,674,809	33,893	699,444	276,843
2013	24,670,582	13,983,059	1,042,106	15,025,165	1,540,966	2,057,699	15,541,898	3,248,889	5,879,795	35,152	701,831	285,334
2014	26,193,811	14,520,116	1,156,797	15,676,913	1,603,979	2,135,433	16,208,367	3,615,762	6,369,682	36,583	716,006	294,230
2015	28,223,664	15,931,967	983,423	16,915,390	1,738,301	2,147,309	17,324,398	3,917,835	6,981,431	38,778	727,828	310,238
2016	29,646,061	16,682,084	871,677	17,553,761	1,835,244	2,723,793	18,442,310	4,024,414	7,179,337	40,072	739,814	319,425
2017	30,921,359	17,767,634	891,271	18,658,905	1,949,799	3,002,338	19,711,444	4,194,487	7,015,428	41,134	751,714	330,710
2018	32,456,416	18,735,351	741,081	19,476,432	2,072,071	3,439,511	20,843,872	4,213,302	7,399,242	42,576	762,314	339,843
2019	35,189,770	19,738,385	733,463	20,471,848	2,208,536	4,333,018	22,596,330	4,625,425	7,968,015	45,547	772,611	345,677
2020	40,404,026	20,930,936	712,633	21,643,569	2,354,211	4,934,701	24,224,059	4,698,858	11,481,109	51,766	780,517	346,639
2021	45,614,264	22,691,215	585,868	23,277,083	2,556,937	7,478,742	28,198,888	4,844,323	12,571,053	57,783	789,410	360,664

Personal Income and Employment by Area: Sumter, SC

(Thousands of dollars, except as noted.)

Year	Personal income, total	Earnings by place of work			Less: Contributions for government social insurance	Plus: Adjustment for residence	Equals: Net earnings by place of residence	Plus: Dividends, interest, and rent	Plus: Personal current transfer receipts	Per capita personal income (dollars)	Population (persons)	Total employment
		Nonfarm	Farm	Total								
1970	236,568	197,814	8,070	205,884	12,920	-16,679	176,285	41,765	18,518	2,967	79,727	36,298
1971	257,261	215,608	7,350	222,958	14,916	-16,603	191,439	43,965	21,857	3,142	81,867	36,617
1972	288,789	240,828	9,756	250,584	17,055	-17,870	215,659	48,408	24,722	3,427	84,259	37,059
1973	313,671	260,350	8,984	269,334	20,429	-18,361	230,544	53,417	29,710	3,772	83,151	37,868
1974	348,497	276,618	14,233	290,851	22,726	-16,841	251,284	59,237	37,976	4,183	83,313	37,426
1975	382,668	300,154	9,449	309,603	24,951	-18,576	266,076	66,588	50,004	4,482	85,380	37,204
1976	419,381	333,267	8,919	342,186	28,667	-19,299	294,220	71,008	54,153	4,920	85,241	37,621
1977	455,349	363,469	7,882	371,351	31,105	-20,287	319,959	79,569	55,821	5,259	86,589	38,477
1978	514,153	410,972	6,443	417,415	35,512	-22,485	359,418	93,003	61,732	5,922	86,824	39,864
1979	564,290	446,299	9,548	455,847	40,200	-23,490	392,157	101,433	70,700	6,445	87,556	40,248
1980	620,161	485,622	555	486,177	43,263	-24,468	418,446	115,532	86,183	6,989	88,736	40,098
1981	685,923	525,064	4,277	529,341	50,062	-23,649	455,630	131,772	98,521	7,586	90,420	40,072
1982	744,160	568,062	2,676	570,738	53,926	-27,702	489,110	148,998	106,052	8,102	91,845	39,657
1983	804,042	615,574	113	615,687	60,094	-27,684	527,909	161,714	114,419	8,677	92,663	40,634
1984	908,566	680,992	20,031	701,023	68,582	-28,687	603,754	183,526	121,286	9,599	94,657	42,253
1985	973,153	735,743	13,053	748,796	75,166	-31,498	642,132	199,030	131,991	10,099	96,362	43,248
1986	1,026,048	778,971	8,303	787,274	81,799	-29,645	675,830	211,670	138,548	10,461	98,084	43,739
1987	1,098,950	834,731	13,242	847,973	87,275	-29,463	731,235	226,238	141,477	11,054	99,420	44,627
1988	1,179,160	901,610	16,398	918,008	98,520	-31,821	787,667	241,424	150,069	11,818	99,777	45,935
1989	1,284,777	950,253	18,564	968,817	106,153	-29,830	832,834	275,457	176,486	12,604	101,933	46,844
1990	1,416,072	1,026,547	16,575	1,043,122	117,376	10,053	935,799	288,681	191,592	13,983	101,271	48,598
1991	1,461,353	1,055,017	20,191	1,075,208	122,604	-14,669	937,935	298,559	224,859	14,239	102,630	47,713
1992	1,555,887	1,108,309	18,333	1,126,642	129,044	-983	996,615	308,383	250,889	15,079	103,179	48,403
1993	1,621,011	1,185,646	12,573	1,198,219	139,899	-36,502	1,021,818	333,978	265,215	15,405	105,224	50,751
1994	1,719,270	1,231,928	16,496	1,248,424	145,939	-26,636	1,075,849	350,496	292,925	16,290	105,542	51,597
1995	1,794,871	1,299,557	7,866	1,307,423	153,397	-38,000	1,116,026	369,625	309,220	16,956	105,852	53,220
1996	1,883,985	1,345,977	22,158	1,368,135	157,072	-42,290	1,168,773	385,687	329,525	17,784	105,938	53,549
1997	1,975,098	1,424,360	13,541	1,437,901	165,684	-50,094	1,222,123	406,048	346,927	18,726	105,475	54,482
1998	2,595,534	1,732,622	17,562	1,750,184	203,929	25,635	1,571,890	522,661	500,983	18,894	137,375	66,005
1999	2,701,609	1,793,258	23,129	1,816,387	209,343	53,319	1,660,363	514,874	526,372	19,709	137,074	66,359
2000	2,842,092	1,893,833	30,833	1,924,666	220,620	34,414	1,738,460	542,841	560,791	20,695	137,330	67,459
2001	2,939,114	1,906,551	49,985	1,956,536	226,029	44,034	1,774,541	543,708	620,865	21,373	137,516	65,436
2002	3,051,268	1,994,660	12,566	2,007,226	235,062	46,311	1,818,475	553,186	679,607	22,035	138,474	65,233
2003	3,188,478	2,095,495	30,570	2,126,065	245,694	51,342	1,931,713	546,579	710,186	23,035	138,417	64,933
2004	3,393,227	2,210,080	46,053	2,256,133	260,363	59,351	2,055,121	560,898	777,208	24,286	139,721	66,039
2005	3,512,096	2,269,142	43,408	2,312,550	267,324	72,849	2,118,075	562,007	832,014	25,099	139,929	66,575
2006	3,698,396	2,364,629	28,162	2,392,791	286,750	87,756	2,193,797	616,545	888,054	26,408	140,047	66,592
2007	3,862,842	2,430,018	26,924	2,456,942	294,180	102,372	2,265,134	657,389	940,319	27,540	140,264	66,986
2008	4,009,894	2,402,476	23,001	2,425,477	294,479	112,789	2,243,787	700,855	1,065,252	28,371	141,338	65,292
2009	3,952,315	2,329,886	20,677	2,350,563	289,322	94,311	2,155,552	645,831	1,150,932	27,844	141,946	62,300
2010	4,088,382	2,417,685	19,681	2,437,366	298,760	63,277	2,201,883	645,791	1,240,708	28,679	142,557	62,161
2011	4,306,199	2,551,829	21,785	2,573,614	285,212	40,139	2,328,541	731,021	1,246,637	30,320	142,027	64,228
2012	4,543,879	2,805,810	49,113	2,854,923	307,855	-5,210	2,541,858	747,056	1,254,965	31,938	142,273	65,017
2013	4,591,268	2,834,451	81,707	2,916,158	346,149	-12,388	2,557,621	740,552	1,293,095	32,309	142,107	65,035
2014	4,714,741	2,915,327	14,144	2,929,471	354,192	-9,989	2,565,290	791,331	1,358,120	33,542	140,564	65,660
2015	4,828,663	2,947,052	17,768	2,964,820	359,967	2,187	2,607,040	797,458	1,424,165	34,585	139,619	66,231
2016	4,950,290	3,000,223	17,079	3,017,302	365,601	3,712	2,655,413	836,141	1,458,736	35,502	139,438	65,587
2017	5,073,513	3,130,974	23,496	3,154,470	383,722	1,990	2,772,738	819,145	1,481,630	36,700	138,244	66,390
2018	5,237,786	3,262,314	6,828	3,269,142	401,739	-1,776	2,865,627	829,023	1,543,136	38,074	137,567	67,621
2019	5,406,899	3,348,963	4,346	3,353,309	412,683	7,963	2,948,589	840,588	1,617,722	39,354	137,393	67,287
2020	5,797,182	3,418,691	10,519	3,429,210	420,993	-6,183	3,002,034	828,444	1,966,704	42,467	136,510	66,659
2021	6,320,653	3,684,694	47,673	3,732,367	446,037	-2,671	3,283,659	822,180	2,214,814	46,550	135,782	67,776

Personal Income and Employment by Area: Syracuse, NY

(Thousands of dollars, except as noted.)

Year	Personal income, total	Derivation of personal income								Per capita personal income (dollars)	Population (persons)	Total employment
		Earnings by place of work			Less: Contributions for government social insurance	Plus: Adjustment for residence	Equals: Net earnings by place of residence	Plus: Dividends, interest, and rent	Plus: Personal current transfer receipts			
		Nonfarm	Farm	Total								
1970	2,562,246	2,134,132	25,826	2,159,958	159,044	-33,036	1,967,878	340,052	254,316	4,019	637,540	270,461
1971	2,778,329	2,306,288	24,874	2,331,162	177,611	-38,056	2,115,495	363,062	299,772	4,341	640,019	274,853
1972	2,988,887	2,511,740	22,314	2,534,054	203,519	-42,388	2,288,147	387,583	313,157	4,657	641,826	278,450
1973	3,249,712	2,745,827	28,770	2,774,597	257,308	-45,379	2,471,910	429,851	347,951	5,059	642,407	289,236
1974	3,554,107	2,981,044	26,392	3,007,436	287,568	-51,434	2,668,434	483,366	402,307	5,527	642,995	294,880
1975	3,809,864	3,033,376	21,614	3,054,990	287,290	-49,100	2,718,600	530,198	561,066	5,897	646,105	283,301
1976	4,082,945	3,304,762	22,888	3,327,650	320,529	-54,277	2,952,844	555,628	574,473	6,305	647,543	286,493
1977	4,481,088	3,685,085	16,810	3,701,895	355,778	-64,346	3,281,771	609,125	590,192	6,924	647,200	295,258
1978	4,896,592	4,067,724	24,111	4,091,835	402,548	-69,348	3,619,939	645,953	630,700	7,570	646,806	304,167
1979	5,464,280	4,573,614	31,021	4,604,635	468,697	-82,013	4,053,925	727,557	682,798	8,476	644,646	311,104
1980	6,097,030	4,961,922	31,312	4,993,234	507,669	-88,758	4,396,807	894,498	805,725	9,486	642,764	307,311
1981	6,713,000	5,373,948	35,167	5,409,115	586,156	-106,136	4,716,823	1,089,539	906,638	10,477	640,720	308,076
1982	7,334,814	5,798,723	28,946	5,827,669	637,151	-127,880	5,062,638	1,253,475	1,018,701	11,453	640,442	308,937
1983	7,943,906	6,324,443	21,258	6,345,701	698,934	-151,038	5,495,729	1,372,833	1,075,344	12,355	642,984	314,098
1984	8,865,683	7,123,028	30,728	7,153,756	805,381	-177,606	6,170,769	1,553,423	1,141,491	13,714	646,469	327,908
1985	9,448,823	7,686,438	34,666	7,721,104	878,188	-200,342	6,642,574	1,601,715	1,204,534	14,528	650,383	340,140
1986	9,968,180	8,096,865	40,575	8,137,440	935,677	-208,608	6,993,155	1,688,512	1,286,513	15,368	648,635	346,353
1987	10,271,856	8,367,092	43,463	8,410,555	957,853	-210,060	7,242,642	1,716,933	1,312,281	15,883	646,725	348,298
1988	11,025,902	9,056,761	33,579	9,090,340	1,056,380	-228,915	7,805,045	1,822,040	1,398,817	16,980	649,352	359,990
1989	12,115,751	9,786,475	46,201	9,832,676	1,126,183	-257,955	8,448,538	2,147,651	1,519,562	18,502	654,842	367,410
1990	12,789,116	10,350,434	47,141	10,397,575	1,142,373	-297,707	8,957,495	2,173,676	1,657,945	19,333	661,505	374,714
1991	13,058,689	10,456,521	39,919	10,496,440	1,182,353	-302,545	9,011,542	2,201,779	1,845,368	19,619	665,618	368,948
1992	13,797,739	11,070,719	38,854	11,109,573	1,228,735	-324,647	9,556,191	2,178,239	2,063,309	20,640	668,488	367,160
1993	14,078,481	11,240,892	49,706	11,290,598	1,254,904	-333,319	9,702,375	2,217,476	2,158,630	21,003	670,309	367,707
1994	14,410,697	11,466,575	39,718	11,506,293	1,295,586	-342,938	9,867,769	2,265,703	2,277,225	21,589	667,499	369,006
1995	14,863,453	11,663,818	27,362	11,691,180	1,319,060	-359,649	10,012,471	2,425,544	2,425,438	22,372	664,389	365,912
1996	15,192,888	11,828,229	41,231	11,869,460	1,316,544	-391,843	10,161,073	2,502,805	2,529,010	23,006	660,384	367,025
1997	15,707,277	12,292,180	24,415	12,316,595	1,350,626	-389,595	10,576,374	2,599,743	2,531,160	23,972	655,229	366,983
1998	16,432,394	12,783,876	47,366	12,831,242	1,386,050	-366,844	11,078,348	2,662,625	2,691,421	25,222	651,499	366,462
1999	17,163,384	13,574,521	54,396	13,628,917	1,431,954	-385,205	11,811,758	2,628,887	2,722,739	26,393	650,297	374,195
2000	18,118,421	14,260,420	59,220	14,319,640	1,496,406	-362,613	12,460,621	2,785,070	2,872,730	27,876	649,961	378,485
2001	18,321,151	14,330,667	72,027	14,402,694	1,565,740	-371,287	12,465,667	2,778,351	3,077,133	28,156	650,697	376,302
2002	18,754,096	14,831,163	48,830	14,879,993	1,640,854	-394,255	12,844,884	2,617,782	3,291,430	28,753	652,241	371,452
2003	19,495,036	15,316,832	54,638	15,371,470	1,698,398	-399,304	13,273,768	2,770,022	3,451,246	29,759	655,091	372,360
2004	20,368,947	16,100,150	68,326	16,168,476	1,772,947	-367,136	14,028,393	2,690,408	3,650,146	31,043	656,149	375,373
2005	20,865,227	16,487,709	66,203	16,553,912	1,845,025	-389,479	14,319,408	2,760,393	3,785,426	31,854	655,021	379,598
2006	21,858,920	17,217,647	52,102	17,269,749	1,911,833	-416,774	14,941,142	2,922,998	3,994,780	33,356	655,321	380,463
2007	23,190,642	18,054,740	89,678	18,144,418	1,985,199	-428,372	15,730,847	3,292,354	4,167,441	35,340	656,209	386,623
2008	24,174,482	18,294,915	92,099	18,387,014	2,047,108	-404,339	15,935,567	3,598,706	4,640,209	36,688	658,913	386,944
2009	24,395,132	18,315,950	46,807	18,362,757	2,028,805	-374,859	15,959,093	3,314,210	5,121,829	36,914	660,857	377,832
2010	25,235,620	18,834,047	82,648	18,916,695	2,052,361	-324,844	16,539,490	3,206,821	5,489,309	38,055	663,132	373,991
2011	26,116,502	19,110,921	103,986	19,214,907	1,879,432	-332,628	17,002,847	3,493,858	5,619,797	39,417	662,564	377,100
2012	27,072,167	19,825,842	95,274	19,921,116	1,921,942	-322,542	17,676,632	3,763,620	5,631,915	40,954	661,045	379,080
2013	27,188,972	20,142,254	123,024	20,265,278	2,201,634	-295,711	17,767,933	3,701,010	5,720,029	41,072	661,979	380,090
2014	27,959,086	20,489,615	137,025	20,626,640	2,279,362	-280,295	18,066,983	3,993,048	5,899,055	41,930	666,806	381,201
2015	29,239,405	21,225,477	79,487	21,304,964	2,366,971	-285,115	18,652,878	4,351,234	6,235,293	43,914	665,829	382,312
2016	29,601,929	21,525,475	60,396	21,585,871	2,408,039	-298,919	18,878,913	4,399,346	6,323,670	44,587	663,914	383,337
2017	31,038,918	22,467,695	94,241	22,561,936	2,509,243	-346,624	19,706,069	4,607,075	6,725,774	46,872	662,203	382,387
2018	32,060,059	23,539,408	66,547	23,605,955	2,584,874	-361,387	20,659,694	4,766,906	6,633,459	48,353	663,047	387,256
2019	33,438,256	24,116,037	116,707	24,232,744	2,657,160	-370,348	21,205,236	5,115,898	7,117,122	50,461	662,656	388,299
2020	36,366,931	24,468,755	104,244	24,572,999	2,666,066	-353,108	21,553,825	5,042,613	9,770,493	55,027	660,894	365,306
2021	38,270,807	26,150,790	122,404	26,273,194	2,862,962	-348,548	23,061,684	5,171,712	10,037,411	58,137	658,281	372,602

Personal Income and Employment by Area: Tallahassee, FL

(Thousands of dollars, except as noted.)

Year	Personal income, total	Earnings by place of work			Less: Contributions for government social insurance	Plus: Adjustment for residence	Equals: Net earnings by place of residence	Plus: Dividends, interest, and rent	Plus: Personal current transfer receipts	Per capita personal income (dollars)	Population (persons)	Total employment
		Nonfarm	Farm	Total								
1970	491,814	399,417	18,424	417,841	23,566	-13,928	380,347	75,481	35,986	3,107	158,300	68,040
1971	567,235	463,338	17,662	481,000	28,966	-15,277	436,757	87,983	42,495	3,438	165,004	71,779
1972	669,418	551,421	16,968	568,389	35,850	-17,809	514,730	103,944	50,744	3,855	173,644	77,730
1973	785,602	645,787	20,466	666,253	48,662	-19,745	597,846	125,713	62,043	4,329	181,470	83,485
1974	884,309	717,696	18,682	736,378	56,903	-20,902	658,573	149,911	75,825	4,673	189,245	86,579
1975	977,884	779,457	17,403	796,860	62,054	-21,220	713,586	166,058	98,240	5,229	186,999	87,284
1976	1,063,676	845,362	18,407	863,769	70,559	-21,125	772,085	181,158	110,433	5,612	189,529	88,025
1977	1,160,438	924,104	12,405	936,509	78,583	-20,235	837,691	200,799	121,948	5,960	194,690	90,724
1978	1,304,352	1,037,771	16,526	1,054,297	92,922	-21,553	939,822	230,728	133,802	6,519	200,091	94,497
1979	1,485,497	1,178,811	20,378	1,199,189	111,764	-23,534	1,063,891	265,915	155,691	7,278	204,111	99,612
1980	1,704,539	1,322,513	19,914	1,342,427	122,191	-24,934	1,195,302	322,578	186,659	7,996	213,167	104,810
1981	1,932,538	1,482,934	15,531	1,498,465	148,207	-26,752	1,323,506	395,100	213,932	8,874	217,765	107,359
1982	2,107,823	1,593,554	23,265	1,616,819	162,314	-30,299	1,424,206	449,757	233,860	9,513	221,584	108,947
1983	2,328,388	1,755,153	24,597	1,779,750	177,507	-32,848	1,569,395	501,653	257,340	10,340	225,185	112,794
1984	2,553,190	1,928,535	26,125	1,954,660	198,603	-34,805	1,721,252	556,913	275,025	11,130	229,399	117,358
1985	2,771,177	2,104,870	26,093	2,130,963	219,344	-38,678	1,872,941	600,144	298,092	11,888	233,106	123,662
1986	3,077,005	2,365,868	29,076	2,394,944	250,568	-43,390	2,100,986	660,104	315,915	13,047	235,840	131,759
1987	3,362,973	2,614,843	29,532	2,644,375	270,086	-50,974	2,323,315	704,069	335,589	13,953	241,026	135,906
1988	3,736,245	2,933,807	34,484	2,968,291	316,602	-55,746	2,595,943	772,235	368,067	15,141	246,756	143,371
1989	4,168,470	3,211,390	39,370	3,250,760	345,898	-62,431	2,842,431	901,442	424,597	16,429	253,724	150,382
1990	4,540,385	3,523,250	37,538	3,560,788	374,654	-68,203	3,117,931	956,164	466,290	17,383	261,192	156,015
1991	4,830,859	3,762,671	47,278	3,809,949	401,890	-75,814	3,332,245	970,241	528,373	17,793	271,509	158,565
1992	5,132,150	4,020,962	47,474	4,068,436	429,303	-81,776	3,557,357	971,361	603,432	18,593	276,025	161,167
1993	5,472,834	4,295,830	47,845	4,343,675	453,609	-88,104	3,801,962	1,029,920	640,952	19,242	284,421	166,471
1994	5,833,475	4,590,133	45,320	4,635,453	489,181	-98,756	4,047,516	1,105,761	680,198	19,929	292,713	172,345
1995	6,336,012	4,924,978	46,894	4,971,872	523,726	-107,498	4,340,648	1,254,435	740,929	21,222	298,563	179,081
1996	6,676,310	5,211,643	44,556	5,256,199	551,491	-117,510	4,587,198	1,317,545	771,567	22,038	302,943	181,936
1997	7,021,126	5,495,050	53,182	5,548,232	583,043	-127,289	4,837,900	1,378,126	805,100	22,765	308,414	188,091
1998	7,544,733	5,948,879	54,853	6,003,732	629,147	-144,063	5,230,522	1,476,272	837,939	24,129	312,685	191,646
1999	7,983,366	6,376,036	58,579	6,434,615	673,917	-159,105	5,601,593	1,501,738	880,035	25,198	316,825	195,883
2000	8,413,447	6,705,268	55,660	6,760,928	707,286	-169,503	5,884,139	1,593,282	936,026	26,183	321,336	201,044
2001	9,028,595	7,226,567	59,649	7,286,216	755,723	-184,527	6,345,966	1,645,458	1,037,171	27,833	324,386	204,473
2002	9,287,858	7,459,730	53,594	7,513,324	778,121	-195,449	6,539,754	1,610,188	1,137,916	28,322	327,940	198,342
2003	9,705,526	7,705,643	44,772	7,750,415	802,743	-207,051	6,740,621	1,743,721	1,221,184	29,033	334,289	200,990
2004	10,319,882	8,137,193	48,904	8,186,097	851,600	-215,436	7,119,061	1,926,395	1,274,426	30,426	339,179	205,899
2005	10,970,998	8,542,478	48,919	8,591,397	899,608	-231,918	7,459,871	2,117,977	1,393,150	31,869	344,257	212,085
2006	11,510,531	8,922,143	49,515	8,971,658	953,571	-250,910	7,767,177	2,289,965	1,453,389	32,833	350,580	216,913
2007	12,074,826	9,294,872	38,400	9,333,272	999,718	-267,379	8,066,175	2,433,336	1,575,315	33,789	357,357	220,398
2008	12,331,303	9,327,997	44,874	9,372,871	1,014,242	-287,348	8,071,281	2,436,361	1,823,661	34,136	361,238	217,761
2009	12,142,939	9,104,793	39,166	9,143,959	999,014	-261,028	7,883,917	2,304,735	1,954,287	33,297	364,690	210,705
2010	12,826,675	9,281,682	45,117	9,326,799	1,001,496	-265,073	8,060,230	2,583,720	2,182,725	34,728	369,351	209,441
2011	13,509,714	9,315,534	39,298	9,354,832	893,020	-251,127	8,210,685	3,006,427	2,292,602	36,385	371,296	211,131
2012	13,445,534	9,649,035	55,299	9,704,334	918,130	-242,980	8,543,224	2,669,914	2,232,396	35,821	375,356	210,402
2013	13,148,227	9,541,867	51,726	9,593,593	1,041,482	-229,346	8,322,765	2,510,686	2,314,776	35,221	373,311	211,730
2014	13,834,098	9,930,865	57,672	9,988,537	1,090,857	-234,484	8,663,196	2,708,894	2,462,008	37,037	373,517	217,288
2015	14,309,505	10,187,582	69,510	10,257,092	1,117,065	-240,936	8,899,091	2,815,646	2,594,768	38,126	375,326	219,430
2016	14,851,969	10,538,289	53,396	10,591,685	1,156,408	-248,836	9,186,441	2,967,545	2,697,983	39,505	375,951	223,614
2017	15,555,245	11,028,318	60,423	11,088,741	1,216,529	-258,373	9,613,839	3,109,094	2,832,312	40,942	379,935	227,669
2018	16,317,018	11,541,544	55,675	11,597,219	1,280,307	-286,494	10,030,418	3,228,546	3,058,054	42,869	380,627	235,294
2019	17,219,274	12,058,060	87,752	12,145,812	1,356,567	-304,401	10,484,844	3,524,338	3,210,092	44,955	383,035	238,215
2020	18,412,659	12,366,565	134,632	12,501,197	1,403,980	-317,562	10,779,655	3,542,168	4,090,836	47,882	384,546	235,048
2021	20,167,871	13,419,513	321,816	13,741,329	1,510,199	-354,550	11,876,580	3,596,877	4,694,414	52,279	385,776	242,558

Personal Income and Employment by Area: Tampa-St. Petersburg-Clearwater, FL

(Thousands of dollars, except as noted.)

Year	Personal income, total	Earnings by place of work Nonfarm	Earnings by place of work Farm	Earnings by place of work Total	Less: Contributions for government social insurance	Plus: Adjustment for residence	Equals: Net earnings by place of residence	Plus: Dividends, interest, and rent	Plus: Personal current transfer receipts	Per capita personal income (dollars)	Population (persons)	Total employment
1970	4,329,776	2,829,055	43,720	2,872,775	186,697	25,929	2,712,007	1,063,264	554,505	3,875	1,117,227	439,739
1971	4,872,882	3,171,668	50,731	3,222,399	217,856	28,540	3,033,083	1,184,145	655,654	4,127	1,180,716	460,528
1972	5,671,208	3,768,453	64,599	3,833,052	271,412	32,708	3,594,348	1,316,842	760,018	4,530	1,251,917	509,052
1973	6,638,176	4,446,246	72,983	4,519,229	369,372	42,299	4,192,156	1,525,278	920,742	4,978	1,333,538	565,986
1974	7,488,493	4,931,707	65,798	4,997,505	427,349	48,861	4,619,017	1,786,106	1,083,370	5,370	1,394,490	581,774
1975	8,233,437	5,176,323	78,963	5,255,286	438,549	52,743	4,869,480	1,986,268	1,377,689	5,774	1,425,848	564,107
1976	8,950,891	5,602,729	84,829	5,687,558	481,335	55,520	5,261,743	2,169,230	1,519,918	6,163	1,452,426	567,011
1977	10,169,956	6,410,543	91,282	6,501,825	544,288	65,375	6,022,912	2,478,619	1,668,425	6,880	1,478,254	597,815
1978	11,705,963	7,455,204	102,214	7,557,418	649,760	74,814	6,982,472	2,871,616	1,851,875	7,713	1,517,764	644,879
1979	13,479,977	8,565,514	103,451	8,668,965	783,780	86,492	7,971,677	3,374,301	2,133,999	8,568	1,573,352	679,429
1980	15,913,401	9,767,227	137,091	9,904,318	903,469	97,561	9,098,410	4,280,111	2,534,880	9,781	1,626,975	717,538
1981	18,423,485	11,000,672	113,744	11,114,416	1,099,800	92,195	10,106,811	5,361,318	2,955,356	10,983	1,677,405	753,441
1982	20,022,699	11,799,994	159,858	11,959,852	1,223,135	70,923	10,807,640	5,871,460	3,343,599	11,623	1,722,726	776,167
1983	22,282,228	13,342,460	199,741	13,542,201	1,389,413	44,329	12,197,117	6,450,776	3,634,335	12,558	1,774,374	821,026
1984	24,870,472	15,127,525	161,407	15,288,932	1,623,627	19,202	13,684,507	7,390,732	3,795,233	13,622	1,825,777	883,678
1985	27,136,994	16,665,179	152,397	16,817,576	1,820,009	-1,719	14,995,848	8,060,397	4,080,749	14,458	1,877,018	932,733
1986	29,234,365	18,123,147	159,092	18,282,239	2,026,789	-29,924	16,225,526	8,624,099	4,384,740	15,198	1,923,591	969,125
1987	31,157,648	19,790,203	152,513	19,942,716	2,189,286	-56,128	17,697,302	8,834,597	4,625,749	15,839	1,967,197	983,589
1988	33,848,439	21,736,261	191,645	21,927,906	2,476,426	-89,113	19,362,367	9,482,869	5,003,203	16,877	2,005,545	1,029,281
1989	37,628,205	23,331,506	194,477	23,525,983	2,694,959	-109,553	20,721,471	11,301,445	5,605,289	18,451	2,039,321	1,052,726
1990	39,444,797	24,859,946	174,027	25,033,973	2,834,593	-158,490	22,040,890	11,357,244	6,046,663	18,983	2,077,857	1,074,649
1991	40,554,113	25,780,658	196,034	25,976,692	2,967,958	-172,166	22,836,568	11,045,508	6,672,037	19,211	2,110,974	1,060,636
1992	42,692,004	27,741,661	198,060	27,939,721	3,181,097	-233,452	24,525,172	10,652,425	7,514,407	19,994	2,135,204	1,062,769
1993	45,371,607	29,507,125	193,303	29,700,428	3,365,923	-211,116	26,123,389	11,200,820	8,047,398	20,967	2,163,912	1,093,939
1994	47,604,258	31,624,671	175,092	31,799,763	3,642,029	-241,576	27,916,158	11,149,385	8,538,715	21,695	2,194,294	1,137,326
1995	51,264,737	33,788,107	184,475	33,972,582	3,880,883	-170,942	29,920,757	12,251,351	9,092,629	23,030	2,226,036	1,178,494
1996	54,399,379	36,349,360	169,905	36,519,265	4,126,779	-424,151	31,968,335	12,895,745	9,535,299	24,108	2,256,460	1,230,493
1997	57,872,609	38,881,308	192,798	39,074,106	4,419,311	-540,281	34,114,514	13,930,415	9,827,680	25,192	2,297,251	1,275,654
1998	62,003,821	42,638,751	242,665	42,881,416	4,787,704	-770,629	37,323,083	14,750,757	9,929,981	26,533	2,336,822	1,341,749
1999	64,828,682	46,213,437	235,916	46,449,353	5,155,467	-1,131,354	40,162,532	14,470,042	10,196,108	27,364	2,369,105	1,396,874
2000	70,276,542	50,083,888	238,821	50,322,709	5,519,213	-1,000,016	43,803,480	15,772,359	10,700,703	29,233	2,404,013	1,447,354
2001	72,758,474	51,638,492	258,564	51,897,056	5,747,132	-876,395	45,273,529	15,917,816	11,567,129	29,770	2,444,015	1,413,290
2002	75,341,199	54,203,076	261,524	54,464,600	6,006,482	-762,585	47,695,533	15,284,135	12,361,531	30,289	2,487,445	1,442,072
2003	79,457,480	56,952,278	227,948	57,180,226	6,280,112	-614,511	50,285,603	16,099,041	13,072,836	31,410	2,529,652	1,453,478
2004	85,387,065	61,418,769	235,820	61,654,589	6,788,877	-457,071	54,408,641	16,996,829	13,981,595	32,996	2,587,771	1,507,186
2005	92,114,234	65,819,016	272,654	66,091,670	7,305,033	-240,759	58,545,878	18,517,832	15,050,524	34,739	2,651,580	1,557,459
2006	98,483,744	69,204,910	277,779	69,482,689	7,832,700	-8,329	61,641,660	20,626,382	16,215,702	36,476	2,699,935	1,591,049
2007	102,633,755	70,674,861	244,229	70,919,090	8,070,516	199,461	63,048,035	22,256,535	17,329,185	37,639	2,726,780	1,608,915
2008	103,980,246	69,682,627	243,198	69,925,825	8,092,368	409,757	62,243,214	22,231,968	19,505,064	37,853	2,746,981	1,553,818
2009	101,152,735	67,201,466	248,459	67,449,925	7,931,532	407,341	59,925,734	20,069,797	21,157,204	36,597	2,763,937	1,484,482
2010	108,243,977	69,159,552	233,770	69,393,322	7,985,136	449,752	61,857,938	23,172,594	23,213,445	38,819	2,788,433	1,464,392
2011	115,422,321	71,239,892	200,025	71,439,917	7,366,566	497,592	64,570,943	26,659,756	24,191,622	41,023	2,813,619	1,485,034
2012	115,154,245	74,544,553	230,179	74,774,732	7,765,779	518,994	67,527,947	23,865,431	23,760,867	40,487	2,844,256	1,516,827
2013	115,189,521	76,389,386	230,959	76,620,345	9,000,650	569,367	68,189,062	22,536,712	24,463,747	39,976	2,881,451	1,558,599
2014	122,066,831	79,943,218	237,664	80,180,882	9,389,589	608,823	71,400,116	24,826,784	25,839,931	42,003	2,906,119	1,604,864
2015	129,024,558	84,604,689	296,217	84,900,906	9,864,092	630,230	75,667,044	26,115,268	27,242,246	43,631	2,957,181	1,664,585
2016	133,638,665	88,178,235	253,873	88,432,108	10,287,168	665,451	78,810,391	26,640,482	28,187,792	44,292	3,017,229	1,709,387
2017	141,519,467	92,011,552	274,183	92,285,735	10,711,847	753,933	82,327,821	29,589,552	29,602,094	46,102	3,069,701	1,773,447
2018	149,228,639	97,590,781	179,239	97,770,020	11,408,336	872,789	87,234,473	31,136,234	30,857,932	47,955	3,111,847	1,836,492
2019	159,404,810	103,369,509	210,870	103,580,379	12,242,526	819,625	92,157,478	34,530,387	32,716,945	50,650	3,147,199	1,875,209
2020	171,415,286	107,354,331	226,716	107,581,047	12,789,795	794,312	95,585,564	34,876,518	40,953,204	53,847	3,183,385	1,878,654
2021	187,745,719	118,485,895	188,339	118,674,234	13,705,351	895,730	105,864,613	35,838,976	46,042,130	58,315	3,219,514	1,949,487

Personal Income and Employment by Area: Terre Haute, IN

(Thousands of dollars, except as noted.)

Year	Personal income, total	Earnings by place of work			Less: Contributions for government social insurance	Plus: Adjustment for residence	Equals: Net earnings by place of residence	Plus: Dividends, interest, and rent	Plus: Personal current transfer receipts	Per capita personal income (dollars)	Population (persons)	Total employment
		Nonfarm	Farm	Total								
1970	603,941	483,409	10,413	493,822	33,374	-6,706	453,742	85,712	64,487	3,441	175,500	72,023
1971	647,877	496,848	19,716	516,564	35,422	-3,421	477,721	93,900	76,256	3,659	177,082	71,460
1972	689,170	525,299	16,170	541,469	39,329	580	502,720	100,672	85,778	3,902	176,637	71,698
1973	792,760	582,778	39,723	622,501	49,979	-43	572,479	114,952	105,329	4,516	175,537	73,710
1974	850,208	633,933	23,053	656,986	57,249	-1,227	598,510	132,142	119,556	4,920	172,796	74,911
1975	945,926	678,164	37,641	715,805	60,382	-2,026	653,397	150,212	142,317	5,470	172,939	73,605
1976	1,038,257	757,027	36,068	793,095	68,053	-1,494	723,548	162,155	152,554	5,978	173,680	74,743
1977	1,137,631	846,890	26,421	873,311	75,704	-3,207	794,400	183,000	160,231	6,518	174,548	76,933
1978	1,263,000	957,166	25,441	982,607	87,664	-7,761	887,182	203,169	172,649	7,234	174,590	79,642
1979	1,400,392	1,074,224	20,467	1,094,691	101,665	-16,832	976,194	227,102	197,096	8,029	174,406	82,452
1980	1,533,824	1,143,790	14,757	1,158,547	108,436	-25,407	1,024,704	277,003	232,117	8,695	176,395	81,575
1981	1,648,564	1,186,811	8,823	1,195,634	121,289	-24,507	1,049,838	336,035	262,691	9,407	175,255	78,331
1982	1,722,246	1,194,644	9,136	1,203,780	124,639	-25,896	1,053,245	379,032	289,969	9,854	174,781	75,509
1983	1,773,126	1,219,551	-11,604	1,207,947	126,947	-21,772	1,059,228	400,892	313,006	10,212	173,625	74,293
1984	1,923,321	1,308,374	19,567	1,327,941	139,476	-20,686	1,167,779	432,771	322,771	11,137	172,695	75,547
1985	2,005,549	1,363,066	18,956	1,382,022	148,066	-17,202	1,216,754	452,533	336,262	11,660	172,000	76,009
1986	2,092,656	1,429,253	17,126	1,446,379	155,779	-14,341	1,276,259	467,731	348,666	12,268	170,581	76,417
1987	2,154,513	1,493,607	15,205	1,508,812	160,498	-12,668	1,335,646	464,779	354,088	12,733	169,209	77,280
1988	2,240,616	1,560,768	8,188	1,568,956	174,291	-10,298	1,384,367	488,083	368,166	13,322	168,190	78,360
1989	2,450,012	1,665,379	25,585	1,690,964	187,756	-10,755	1,492,453	555,803	401,756	14,649	167,248	80,505
1990	2,564,412	1,781,005	17,295	1,798,300	205,465	-15,365	1,577,470	561,276	425,666	15,392	166,606	82,626
1991	2,677,949	1,902,001	-555	1,901,446	222,827	-26,533	1,652,086	567,634	458,229	16,041	166,943	83,969
1992	2,892,934	2,054,193	32,077	2,086,270	238,136	-30,494	1,817,640	559,126	516,168	17,207	168,127	86,041
1993	3,006,738	2,145,643	28,252	2,173,895	250,731	-37,063	1,886,101	574,697	545,940	17,731	169,575	87,972
1994	3,135,063	2,231,284	28,139	2,259,423	264,485	-34,645	1,960,293	601,909	572,861	18,444	169,975	89,740
1995	3,243,009	2,307,640	12,029	2,319,669	275,892	-39,453	2,004,324	658,955	579,730	18,974	170,921	91,712
1996	3,338,059	2,323,150	27,565	2,350,715	275,538	-38,877	2,036,300	690,747	611,012	19,443	171,682	90,589
1997	3,422,138	2,373,689	26,266	2,399,955	281,254	-42,091	2,076,610	716,710	628,818	19,935	171,665	89,365
1998	3,966,257	2,653,325	15,904	2,669,229	306,919	68,211	2,430,521	820,208	715,528	21,067	188,270	94,792
1999	4,094,655	2,797,743	22,088	2,819,831	319,911	68,665	2,568,585	771,162	754,908	21,724	188,488	95,514
2000	4,290,318	2,890,175	35,436	2,925,611	327,745	72,570	2,670,436	829,315	790,567	22,817	188,034	96,655
2001	4,470,237	2,998,160	39,895	3,038,055	334,255	71,178	2,774,978	825,150	870,109	23,816	187,699	94,380
2002	4,550,315	3,122,748	12,367	3,135,115	348,038	64,685	2,851,762	783,101	915,452	24,290	187,329	93,392
2003	4,738,483	3,246,087	49,757	3,295,844	366,408	57,660	2,987,096	806,821	944,566	25,211	187,953	94,156
2004	4,901,761	3,347,741	76,261	3,424,002	380,541	60,064	3,103,525	800,353	997,883	26,148	187,461	94,531
2005	4,952,409	3,411,788	39,843	3,451,631	396,872	60,696	3,115,455	755,968	1,080,986	26,338	188,030	94,317
2006	5,165,938	3,549,042	22,416	3,571,458	413,188	57,655	3,215,925	793,329	1,156,684	27,318	189,106	94,767
2007	5,339,233	3,616,841	57,524	3,674,365	428,338	51,512	3,297,539	846,226	1,195,468	28,185	189,436	95,641
2008	5,678,784	3,721,229	65,968	3,787,197	441,342	40,700	3,386,555	931,350	1,360,879	29,974	189,455	94,346
2009	5,606,549	3,608,204	56,269	3,664,473	433,790	32,088	3,262,771	873,018	1,470,760	29,584	189,516	92,008
2010	5,841,818	3,761,483	72,101	3,833,584	442,345	15,937	3,407,176	875,117	1,559,525	30,822	189,537	91,522
2011	6,006,837	3,787,205	111,028	3,898,233	397,156	24,020	3,525,097	916,597	1,565,143	31,687	189,567	91,646
2012	6,147,444	3,895,916	52,134	3,948,050	408,590	23,940	3,563,400	964,407	1,619,637	32,423	189,601	92,178
2013	6,200,365	3,902,472	174,967	4,077,439	465,303	29,182	3,641,318	944,095	1,614,952	32,781	189,147	91,984
2014	6,347,882	3,984,993	47,580	4,032,573	473,296	37,200	3,596,477	1,019,527	1,731,878	33,764	188,007	92,013
2015	6,417,776	4,008,919	-11,212	3,997,707	479,806	61,445	3,579,346	1,044,245	1,794,185	34,304	187,085	91,548
2016	6,563,313	4,034,207	26,954	4,061,161	483,322	82,471	3,660,310	1,038,184	1,864,819	35,125	186,855	91,896
2017	6,801,853	4,151,213	20,999	4,172,212	499,752	81,635	3,754,095	1,137,846	1,909,912	36,492	186,395	91,882
2018	6,946,667	4,234,514	24,319	4,258,833	511,501	94,855	3,842,187	1,118,096	1,986,384	37,311	186,185	91,766
2019	7,148,204	4,368,762	12,150	4,380,912	531,528	82,291	3,931,675	1,128,700	2,087,829	38,520	185,570	90,885
2020	7,766,272	4,435,663	77,667	4,513,330	551,353	88,464	4,050,441	1,129,174	2,586,657	42,029	184,784	87,394
2021	8,420,168	4,648,860	121,415	4,770,275	567,374	104,585	4,307,486	1,141,032	2,971,650	45,537	184,910	88,523

Personal Income and Employment by Area: Texarkana, TX-AR

(Thousands of dollars, except as noted.)

Year	Personal income, total	Earnings by place of work			Less: Contributions for government social insurance	Plus: Adjustment for residence	Equals: Net earnings by place of residence	Plus: Dividends, interest, and rent	Plus: Personal current transfer receipts	Per capita personal income (dollars)	Population (persons)	Total employment
		Nonfarm	Farm	Total								
1970	376,236	324,456	11,436	335,892	18,697	-30,211	286,984	51,358	37,894	3,317	113,411	51,614
1971	401,204	335,787	9,817	345,604	19,670	-25,701	300,233	57,175	43,796	3,480	115,276	49,646
1972	451,345	374,221	13,100	387,321	22,977	-24,287	340,057	62,409	48,879	3,912	115,364	50,603
1973	500,642	405,085	17,198	422,283	28,914	-23,440	369,929	72,073	58,640	4,343	115,273	51,600
1974	557,896	441,474	16,765	458,239	32,689	-24,158	401,392	85,270	71,234	4,789	116,487	51,969
1975	612,547	469,308	10,204	479,512	33,445	-22,501	423,566	99,646	89,335	5,088	120,390	50,601
1976	688,992	528,222	11,390	539,612	38,716	-21,025	479,871	111,578	97,543	5,657	121,802	52,595
1977	758,960	583,833	9,404	593,237	43,510	-20,212	529,515	126,787	102,658	6,177	122,871	54,507
1978	853,414	659,800	10,235	670,035	51,017	-19,814	599,204	141,250	112,960	6,903	123,622	56,842
1979	975,042	770,277	21,406	791,683	63,966	-38,888	688,829	157,670	128,543	7,698	126,658	59,580
1980	1,060,243	799,347	6,746	806,093	64,733	-21,466	719,894	190,984	149,365	8,325	127,351	57,931
1981	1,189,283	876,037	11,872	887,909	75,730	-22,120	790,059	229,663	169,561	9,266	128,345	57,646
1982	1,280,745	937,625	10,523	948,148	82,646	-29,627	835,875	260,720	184,150	9,903	129,332	58,212
1983	1,374,736	1,003,663	7,881	1,011,544	92,070	-32,327	887,147	286,193	201,396	10,457	131,460	59,156
1984	1,524,552	1,110,664	21,099	1,131,763	105,168	-34,762	991,833	321,056	211,663	11,532	132,198	61,554
1985	1,617,159	1,172,824	16,009	1,188,833	114,106	-36,865	1,037,862	353,411	225,886	12,133	133,288	62,566
1986	1,666,693	1,203,071	21,265	1,224,336	118,805	-37,898	1,067,633	362,072	236,988	12,472	133,636	61,580
1987	1,705,511	1,242,492	19,495	1,261,987	122,375	-39,534	1,100,078	359,892	245,541	12,738	133,889	62,892
1988	1,780,082	1,290,326	31,411	1,321,737	133,327	-37,107	1,151,303	368,700	260,079	13,221	134,645	62,821
1989	1,906,304	1,373,138	34,858	1,407,996	144,821	-44,990	1,218,185	404,017	284,102	14,248	133,795	64,410
1990	2,016,915	1,487,624	29,284	1,516,908	161,228	-60,790	1,294,890	406,190	315,835	14,996	134,497	67,025
1991	2,104,913	1,533,055	32,544	1,565,599	168,451	-35,251	1,361,897	393,750	349,266	15,563	135,250	66,542
1992	2,218,602	1,577,584	32,928	1,610,512	173,066	-21,248	1,416,198	400,343	402,061	16,294	136,162	65,220
1993	2,296,434	1,634,262	32,845	1,667,107	179,675	-16,031	1,471,401	408,483	416,550	16,689	137,598	66,853
1994	2,408,242	1,689,673	36,552	1,726,225	188,344	-10,861	1,527,020	431,784	449,438	17,325	139,004	67,344
1995	2,542,984	1,767,390	32,753	1,800,143	196,884	-4,707	1,598,552	462,961	481,471	18,183	139,853	69,282
1996	2,678,317	1,844,765	40,961	1,885,726	202,969	-100	1,682,657	491,978	503,682	18,948	141,353	70,753
1997	2,831,747	1,960,556	49,125	2,009,681	213,779	5,639	1,801,541	505,038	525,168	19,957	141,893	71,877
1998	2,910,903	2,013,867	38,110	2,051,977	217,318	15,959	1,850,618	525,883	534,402	20,453	142,322	71,041
1999	3,044,591	2,128,799	51,551	2,180,350	228,119	9,228	1,961,459	544,518	538,614	21,283	143,051	72,551
2000	3,199,636	2,221,786	44,351	2,266,137	237,032	9,507	2,038,612	600,611	560,413	22,343	143,205	73,713
2001	3,394,744	2,330,750	51,415	2,382,165	245,137	6,839	2,143,867	636,204	614,673	23,759	142,882	73,705
2002	3,480,651	2,433,140	39,633	2,472,773	255,409	-4,740	2,212,624	608,504	659,523	24,315	143,149	73,435
2003	3,570,070	2,533,016	54,742	2,587,758	269,938	-12,809	2,305,011	565,965	699,094	24,864	143,582	73,161
2004	3,790,696	2,648,946	68,917	2,717,863	284,772	-23,883	2,409,208	637,036	744,452	26,325	143,996	73,880
2005	3,951,091	2,799,784	38,868	2,838,652	300,509	-35,284	2,502,859	643,812	804,420	27,337	144,534	75,734
2006	4,136,396	2,941,285	26,621	2,967,906	316,119	-43,774	2,608,013	662,354	866,029	28,322	146,051	76,838
2007	4,410,686	3,051,673	43,531	3,095,204	335,185	-60,203	2,699,816	768,766	942,104	30,154	146,273	78,664
2008	4,624,542	3,187,262	11,864	3,199,126	355,961	-96,008	2,747,157	826,871	1,050,514	31,354	147,495	80,187
2009	4,623,327	3,196,865	868	3,197,733	361,236	-114,038	2,722,459	777,050	1,123,818	31,083	148,743	78,630
2010	4,827,842	3,286,692	9,109	3,295,801	368,463	-81,156	2,846,182	764,008	1,217,652	32,327	149,346	77,899
2011	5,032,023	3,356,284	9,979	3,366,263	336,099	-81,516	2,948,648	849,413	1,233,962	33,646	149,558	79,003
2012	5,126,048	3,382,837	19,952	3,402,789	338,049	-92,854	2,971,886	921,752	1,232,410	34,247	149,680	78,650
2013	4,986,692	3,237,766	43,336	3,281,102	365,844	-76,954	2,838,304	874,335	1,274,053	33,302	149,607	77,539
2014	5,103,799	3,261,449	42,401	3,303,850	370,613	-73,382	2,859,855	910,742	1,333,202	34,313	148,741	77,436
2015	5,294,661	3,396,641	43,061	3,439,702	389,007	-90,376	2,960,319	937,926	1,396,416	35,618	148,650	78,456
2016	5,397,341	3,473,899	23,433	3,497,332	399,548	-95,903	3,001,881	941,360	1,454,100	36,257	148,864	79,251
2017	5,521,970	3,549,512	24,128	3,573,640	408,718	-91,436	3,073,486	966,185	1,482,299	37,121	148,756	78,805
2018	5,626,186	3,592,295	18,159	3,610,454	414,336	-91,692	3,104,426	980,690	1,541,070	37,889	148,491	79,160
2019	5,780,189	3,679,305	17,165	3,696,470	426,263	-98,884	3,171,323	1,003,787	1,605,079	39,088	147,875	79,492
2020	6,196,009	3,715,560	25,160	3,740,720	438,992	-89,150	3,212,578	984,793	1,998,638	42,054	147,333	77,431
2021	6,631,374	3,883,364	33,780	3,917,144	453,730	-84,026	3,379,388	1,007,528	2,244,458	45,058	147,174	78,783

Personal Income and Employment by Area: The Villages, FL

(Thousands of dollars, except as noted.)

Year	Personal income, total	Earnings by place of work			Less: Contributions for government social insurance	Plus: Adjustment for residence	Equals: Net earnings by place of residence	Plus: Dividends, interest, and rent	Plus: Personal current transfer receipts	Per capita personal income (dollars)	Population (persons)	Total employment
		Nonfarm	Farm	Total								
1970	39,947	25,114	3,231	28,345	2,089	1,295	27,551	6,161	6,235	2,669	14,967	4,545
1971	45,938	27,459	4,346	31,805	2,296	2,017	31,526	7,111	7,301	2,908	15,797	4,724
1972	54,241	30,437	5,783	36,220	2,573	3,120	36,767	8,313	9,161	3,051	17,780	5,092
1973	65,269	34,882	7,313	42,195	3,208	4,628	43,615	10,346	11,308	3,410	19,143	5,413
1974	72,053	37,386	6,521	43,907	3,671	5,946	46,182	12,183	13,688	3,523	20,453	5,460
1975	82,166	40,682	7,113	47,795	3,978	6,857	50,674	13,848	17,644	3,913	20,999	5,497
1976	90,468	43,529	7,752	51,281	4,320	8,259	55,220	14,984	20,264	4,102	22,056	5,668
1977	100,157	47,597	7,901	55,498	4,774	10,174	60,898	16,960	22,299	4,487	22,324	5,961
1978	118,028	55,776	9,951	65,727	5,571	12,393	72,549	21,504	23,975	5,169	22,835	6,565
1979	139,092	62,836	12,223	75,059	6,433	14,668	83,294	26,771	29,027	5,965	23,318	6,841
1980	160,289	68,177	10,541	78,718	7,014	18,367	90,071	35,085	35,133	6,559	24,439	6,802
1981	178,038	74,787	7,351	82,138	8,335	19,519	93,322	43,390	41,326	7,104	25,063	6,847
1982	197,747	82,967	9,983	92,950	9,516	19,660	103,094	47,707	46,946	7,658	25,822	6,869
1983	221,897	93,219	11,107	104,326	10,554	20,701	114,473	55,216	52,208	8,349	26,577	7,337
1984	244,871	103,933	9,452	113,385	12,037	23,965	125,313	63,653	55,905	8,949	27,362	7,732
1985	266,999	115,350	7,785	123,135	13,666	26,096	135,565	69,784	61,650	9,430	28,313	8,285
1986	288,735	121,570	8,230	129,800	14,984	29,877	144,693	76,318	67,724	9,882	29,217	8,497
1987	311,323	129,283	6,940	136,223	15,473	35,048	155,798	79,931	75,594	10,457	29,771	8,769
1988	340,492	140,682	9,304	149,986	17,524	39,445	171,907	83,386	85,199	11,289	30,161	9,022
1989	374,445	150,876	11,156	162,032	18,905	43,411	186,538	98,852	89,055	12,083	30,990	9,138
1990	391,807	152,270	10,551	162,821	18,910	46,841	190,752	102,657	98,398	12,289	31,882	9,144
1991	412,782	157,377	14,012	171,389	19,854	45,923	197,458	104,605	110,719	12,561	32,863	9,069
1992	447,580	169,549	16,043	185,592	21,429	48,245	212,408	104,485	130,687	13,240	33,804	9,142
1993	469,677	178,680	14,259	192,939	22,370	51,166	221,735	105,602	142,340	13,510	34,764	9,427
1994	502,119	190,402	11,644	202,046	24,207	53,339	231,178	112,996	157,945	13,890	36,149	9,665
1995	549,588	217,251	8,772	226,023	26,926	50,469	249,566	122,887	177,135	14,297	38,441	10,357
1996	611,563	256,038	7,118	263,156	30,351	45,150	277,955	137,397	196,211	14,265	42,871	11,189
1997	661,289	277,926	9,589	287,515	32,739	45,362	300,138	146,742	214,409	14,187	46,611	11,587
1998	709,925	293,558	9,831	303,389	34,565	49,007	317,831	159,236	232,858	14,557	48,767	12,004
1999	775,018	320,990	13,398	334,388	37,458	49,039	345,969	160,345	268,704	14,983	51,725	12,199
2000	830,686	339,359	13,361	352,720	39,668	49,136	362,188	168,238	300,260	15,458	53,738	12,646
2001	973,608	420,278	14,965	435,243	47,494	52,539	440,288	170,007	363,313	17,450	55,793	14,060
2002	1,082,004	464,906	9,671	474,577	51,828	52,205	474,954	196,812	410,238	18,173	59,539	15,461
2003	1,230,183	577,800	11,124	588,924	63,445	33,001	558,480	226,449	445,254	19,863	61,934	18,140
2004	1,435,652	620,485	11,472	631,957	69,595	88,742	651,104	285,045	499,503	22,273	64,456	20,022
2005	1,693,071	764,488	13,757	778,245	85,706	96,404	788,943	319,662	584,466	24,445	69,261	24,039
2006	1,991,434	896,780	13,215	909,995	121,823	98,047	886,219	389,552	715,663	26,134	76,202	26,589
2007	2,155,195	958,723	10,101	968,824	133,500	46,198	881,522	448,917	824,756	26,251	82,101	27,723
2008	2,396,276	973,083	8,629	981,712	144,535	45,880	883,057	512,721	1,000,498	27,724	86,433	28,378
2009	2,590,806	1,031,251	8,228	1,039,479	156,699	16,874	899,654	506,929	1,184,223	28,583	90,643	29,325
2010	2,859,564	1,114,648	9,278	1,123,926	168,160	-23,070	932,696	612,052	1,314,816	30,329	94,286	30,827
2011	3,327,597	1,243,050	7,604	1,250,654	171,660	-30,090	1,048,904	813,689	1,465,004	33,951	98,011	32,744
2012	3,852,308	1,316,449	16,299	1,332,748	183,956	43,656	1,192,448	1,094,687	1,565,173	37,869	101,727	34,451
2013	4,141,542	1,418,291	10,472	1,428,763	220,138	40,299	1,248,924	1,230,487	1,662,131	38,713	106,980	37,048
2014	4,455,369	1,464,056	17,481	1,481,537	231,857	-42,277	1,207,403	1,416,091	1,831,875	40,651	109,601	39,036
2015	4,846,375	1,516,337	26,310	1,542,647	245,063	-63,367	1,234,217	1,603,947	2,008,211	42,628	113,691	40,399
2016	5,354,778	1,620,199	13,007	1,633,206	265,805	11,278	1,378,679	1,815,585	2,160,514	45,430	117,868	41,571
2017	5,770,565	1,768,889	16,858	1,785,747	291,521	-12,984	1,481,242	2,035,482	2,253,841	48,046	120,106	42,976
2018	6,311,583	1,929,619	16,978	1,946,597	324,696	-44,860	1,577,041	2,323,156	2,411,386	51,202	123,269	45,177
2019	7,504,448	2,545,255	11,436	2,556,691	386,148	-48,465	2,122,078	2,764,487	2,617,883	59,209	126,746	47,297
2020	7,971,565	2,746,955	12,862	2,759,817	418,406	-147,815	2,193,596	2,800,983	2,976,986	60,900	130,897	49,116
2021	8,719,140	3,139,338	12,390	3,151,728	462,575	-178,354	2,510,799	2,944,016	3,264,325	64,282	135,638	51,945

Personal Income and Employment by Area: Toledo, OH

(Thousands of dollars, except as noted.)

| Year | Personal income, total | Derivation of personal income | | | | | | | | | Per capita personal income (dollars) | Population (persons) | Total employment |
| | | Earnings by place of work | | | Less: Contributions for government social insurance | Plus: Adjustment for residence | Equals: Net earnings by place of residence | Plus: Dividends, interest, and rent | Plus: Personal current transfer receipts | | | |
		Nonfarm	Farm	Total								
1970	2,609,375	2,239,321	25,167	2,264,488	149,493	-85,418	2,029,577	368,524	211,274	4,295	607,493	277,346
1971	2,803,026	2,392,796	23,873	2,416,669	164,761	-84,540	2,167,368	393,992	241,666	4,567	613,790	277,628
1972	3,064,197	2,632,595	29,887	2,662,482	191,302	-92,016	2,379,164	420,258	264,775	4,956	618,239	283,180
1973	3,400,864	2,932,533	42,449	2,974,982	247,426	-102,961	2,624,595	468,538	307,731	5,474	621,256	295,425
1974	3,684,598	3,118,131	46,183	3,164,314	273,112	-110,320	2,780,882	531,446	372,270	5,915	622,934	294,935
1975	3,964,502	3,242,241	52,973	3,295,214	276,446	-112,416	2,906,352	565,961	492,189	6,387	620,746	285,579
1976	4,383,306	3,675,087	43,836	3,718,923	321,732	-138,952	3,258,239	604,680	520,387	7,126	615,085	292,558
1977	4,794,445	4,072,055	31,635	4,103,690	359,684	-169,198	3,574,808	666,973	552,664	7,811	613,830	299,282
1978	5,248,147	4,509,983	23,588	4,533,571	410,320	-198,514	3,924,737	737,816	585,594	8,588	611,100	307,404
1979	5,756,965	4,892,156	35,520	4,927,676	459,250	-223,401	4,245,025	836,143	675,797	9,357	615,273	312,170
1980	6,284,574	5,050,914	45,147	5,096,061	467,971	-228,093	4,399,997	1,000,701	883,876	10,183	617,164	301,227
1981	6,797,402	5,405,937	8,078	5,414,015	535,686	-240,371	4,637,958	1,207,116	952,328	11,017	616,977	298,217
1982	7,144,585	5,530,732	13,079	5,543,811	555,664	-240,536	4,747,611	1,335,511	1,061,463	11,617	614,991	289,638
1983	7,603,984	5,925,201	-8,666	5,916,535	605,550	-272,796	5,038,189	1,440,182	1,125,613	12,426	611,930	291,994
1984	8,427,894	6,638,133	52,912	6,691,045	695,246	-334,222	5,661,577	1,604,346	1,161,971	13,803	610,582	305,313
1985	8,975,065	7,174,063	40,848	7,214,911	764,196	-375,915	6,074,800	1,675,850	1,224,415	14,710	610,137	312,850
1986	9,363,799	7,481,854	33,956	7,515,810	818,123	-372,360	6,325,327	1,736,497	1,301,975	15,299	612,073	321,095
1987	9,794,601	7,864,800	40,103	7,904,903	856,486	-387,847	6,660,570	1,778,325	1,355,706	15,976	613,093	328,662
1988	10,415,640	8,432,431	51,846	8,484,277	948,668	-420,595	7,115,014	1,883,254	1,417,372	16,882	616,985	338,504
1989	11,132,878	8,882,634	65,124	8,947,758	1,003,998	-445,794	7,497,966	2,133,283	1,501,629	18,086	615,560	342,926
1990	11,563,741	9,110,989	84,577	9,195,566	1,042,495	-411,320	7,741,751	2,148,067	1,673,923	18,814	614,637	340,445
1991	11,654,052	9,118,531	72,457	9,190,988	1,072,860	-403,044	7,715,084	2,116,797	1,822,171	18,962	614,606	334,188
1992	12,445,740	9,835,035	77,652	9,912,687	1,151,810	-476,030	8,284,847	2,168,089	1,992,804	20,212	615,755	336,874
1993	12,921,719	10,323,544	68,729	10,392,273	1,219,926	-559,961	8,612,386	2,246,261	2,063,072	20,989	615,629	344,665
1994	13,571,163	11,023,593	76,590	11,100,183	1,318,078	-691,357	9,090,748	2,336,370	2,144,045	22,037	615,841	359,308
1995	14,201,141	11,430,907	62,893	11,493,800	1,377,179	-722,562	9,394,059	2,525,452	2,281,630	23,042	616,304	364,582
1996	14,708,355	11,793,924	85,339	11,879,263	1,410,732	-781,178	9,687,353	2,688,126	2,332,876	23,859	616,468	370,314
1997	15,451,299	12,373,944	106,693	12,480,637	1,438,837	-826,583	10,215,217	2,851,431	2,384,651	25,008	617,850	374,438
1998	17,181,172	13,541,745	80,836	13,622,581	1,520,381	-681,201	11,420,999	3,179,140	2,581,033	26,056	659,390	398,139
1999	17,682,497	14,317,351	54,677	14,372,028	1,602,041	-749,441	12,020,546	3,025,833	2,636,118	26,817	659,388	404,460
2000	18,397,408	14,747,853	72,482	14,820,335	1,593,538	-752,620	12,474,177	3,152,180	2,771,051	27,909	659,190	409,267
2001	19,034,716	15,270,832	59,514	15,330,346	1,658,263	-764,144	12,907,939	3,139,619	2,987,158	28,838	660,052	407,705
2002	19,369,229	15,565,073	28,287	15,593,360	1,658,305	-745,474	13,189,581	2,973,723	3,205,925	29,358	659,750	398,940
2003	19,951,444	16,002,160	53,803	16,055,963	1,725,518	-753,148	13,577,297	3,038,911	3,335,236	30,214	660,335	395,985
2004	20,382,014	16,391,550	94,331	16,485,881	1,803,928	-754,577	13,927,376	2,969,795	3,484,843	30,894	659,745	399,056
2005	20,866,922	16,652,551	91,602	16,744,153	1,845,108	-759,251	14,139,794	3,022,486	3,704,642	31,691	658,448	399,734
2006	21,987,771	17,363,235	92,167	17,455,402	1,921,284	-782,137	14,751,981	3,328,767	3,907,023	33,507	656,222	402,035
2007	22,865,127	17,720,117	83,296	17,803,413	1,954,003	-774,679	15,074,731	3,642,653	4,147,743	34,895	655,257	401,827
2008	23,298,052	17,587,951	72,157	17,660,108	1,963,770	-721,751	14,974,587	3,672,770	4,650,695	35,650	653,518	392,088
2009	22,639,998	16,632,483	99,934	16,732,417	1,877,055	-673,575	14,181,787	3,314,669	5,143,542	34,712	652,232	371,451
2010	23,380,958	17,111,701	78,841	17,190,542	1,889,862	-689,855	14,610,825	3,375,194	5,394,939	35,894	651,392	369,934
2011	24,582,283	17,824,341	155,040	17,979,381	1,791,274	-763,229	15,424,878	3,645,783	5,511,622	37,805	650,245	376,375
2012	25,192,981	18,449,728	120,943	18,570,671	1,842,376	-809,627	15,918,668	3,913,390	5,360,923	38,825	648,893	379,204
2013	25,513,820	18,993,742	168,464	19,162,206	2,040,611	-803,164	16,318,431	3,728,550	5,466,839	39,338	648,582	382,433
2014	26,706,206	19,834,931	80,076	19,915,007	2,128,926	-865,139	16,920,942	4,049,993	5,735,271	41,129	649,325	387,695
2015	27,817,509	20,664,079	31,383	20,695,462	2,201,139	-927,429	17,566,894	4,299,542	5,951,073	42,890	648,575	393,383
2016	28,391,767	21,213,715	31,983	21,245,698	2,308,574	-964,584	17,972,540	4,381,541	6,037,686	43,772	648,629	397,036
2017	28,866,464	21,458,611	30,796	21,489,407	2,388,451	-930,613	18,170,343	4,521,422	6,174,699	44,544	648,038	395,247
2018	30,062,793	22,506,066	56,324	22,562,390	2,459,701	-987,812	19,114,877	4,621,689	6,326,227	46,441	647,337	399,039
2019	31,146,790	23,080,418	48,770	23,129,188	2,562,306	-1,037,132	19,529,750	4,986,618	6,630,422	48,157	646,770	398,690
2020	33,215,855	22,777,098	83,215	22,860,313	2,539,982	-966,815	19,353,516	4,979,312	8,883,027	51,432	645,819	378,305
2021	35,060,467	24,072,210	122,759	24,194,969	2,631,736	-1,009,697	20,553,536	5,080,205	9,426,726	54,423	644,217	387,063

Personal Income and Employment by Area: Topeka, KS

(Thousands of dollars, except as noted.)

		Derivation of personal income										
		Earnings by place of work			Less: Contributions for government social insurance	Plus: Adjustment for residence	Equals: Net earnings by place of residence	Plus: Dividends, interest, and rent	Plus: Personal current transfer receipts	Per capita personal income (dollars)	Population (persons)	Total employment
Year	Personal income, total	Nonfarm	Farm	Total								
1970	802,172	641,190	11,624	652,814	48,295	-8,105	596,414	133,384	72,374	4,058	197,701	95,350
1971	886,240	700,964	17,642	718,606	54,401	-7,652	656,553	145,447	84,240	4,459	198,772	96,314
1972	984,741	776,891	26,766	803,657	63,058	-8,167	732,432	159,529	92,780	4,855	202,849	98,653
1973	1,089,232	858,242	32,617	890,859	79,969	-5,194	805,696	175,202	108,334	5,378	202,528	102,182
1974	1,139,465	883,697	24,742	908,439	86,911	-1,049	820,479	193,419	125,567	5,869	194,147	100,477
1975	1,246,682	951,373	16,367	967,740	91,905	1,275	877,110	213,133	156,439	6,389	195,125	100,810
1976	1,368,024	1,054,648	7,967	1,062,615	103,140	5,138	964,613	229,716	173,695	6,921	197,659	102,988
1977	1,541,924	1,187,906	17,253	1,205,159	115,875	10,168	1,099,452	255,591	186,881	7,748	199,010	106,791
1978	1,718,465	1,334,487	8,779	1,343,266	133,652	16,830	1,226,444	285,700	206,321	8,577	200,351	110,694
1979	1,888,977	1,471,723	3,293	1,475,016	153,257	19,644	1,341,403	321,259	226,315	9,368	201,651	112,914
1980	2,097,532	1,588,924	-23,286	1,565,638	165,791	24,637	1,424,484	399,084	273,964	10,277	204,099	113,888
1981	2,383,769	1,719,443	14,567	1,734,010	192,745	22,485	1,563,750	506,255	313,764	11,662	204,404	113,415
1982	2,548,515	1,798,372	7,732	1,806,104	207,240	21,900	1,620,764	588,939	338,812	12,440	204,869	111,566
1983	2,664,391	1,914,482	-10,998	1,903,484	219,580	17,381	1,701,285	605,111	357,995	12,959	205,608	112,196
1984	2,901,972	2,096,098	4,394	2,100,492	245,738	15,547	1,870,301	667,178	364,493	14,087	206,005	116,313
1985	3,095,928	2,206,756	52,017	2,258,773	262,712	4,519	2,000,580	708,374	386,974	15,079	205,319	116,597
1986	3,220,458	2,330,572	24,206	2,354,778	277,956	-515	2,076,307	746,303	397,848	15,648	205,805	117,515
1987	3,348,520	2,451,489	19,201	2,470,690	287,955	-1,702	2,181,033	760,514	406,973	16,150	207,337	123,311
1988	3,559,539	2,630,043	10,724	2,640,767	321,777	-4,298	2,314,692	813,335	431,512	16,930	210,255	125,741
1989	3,728,296	2,760,234	11,434	2,771,668	338,488	-9,774	2,423,406	835,625	469,265	17,771	209,794	127,498
1990	3,892,288	2,885,320	27,169	2,912,489	366,941	-11,625	2,533,923	851,838	506,527	18,482	210,598	128,053
1991	4,000,153	2,972,900	8,296	2,981,196	380,200	-11,591	2,589,405	865,378	545,370	18,826	212,479	127,916
1992	4,259,396	3,140,681	50,149	3,190,830	397,766	-11,515	2,781,549	872,449	605,398	19,902	214,014	128,684
1993	4,448,500	3,332,287	9,926	3,342,213	422,498	-15,385	2,904,330	902,059	642,111	20,571	216,252	131,257
1994	4,693,229	3,519,283	25,671	3,544,954	450,037	-15,459	3,079,458	952,683	661,088	21,470	218,593	133,525
1995	4,881,315	3,645,931	321	3,646,252	458,509	-16,570	3,171,173	1,009,525	700,617	22,184	220,036	137,625
1996	5,154,841	3,788,233	54,404	3,842,637	471,844	-15,567	3,355,226	1,070,835	728,780	23,299	221,246	139,732
1997	5,326,760	3,905,728	24,545	3,930,273	486,893	-5,402	3,437,978	1,118,303	770,479	23,960	222,316	139,357
1998	5,642,607	4,172,144	8,265	4,180,409	514,282	-8,139	3,657,988	1,190,836	793,783	25,240	223,555	142,312
1999	5,799,967	4,349,440	-5,895	4,343,545	534,266	-3,881	3,805,398	1,158,988	835,581	25,919	223,772	142,676
2000	6,145,973	4,560,052	-11,832	4,548,220	558,151	1,377	3,991,446	1,256,209	898,318	27,333	224,859	145,358
2001	6,517,115	4,871,643	13,557	4,885,200	592,396	-52	4,292,752	1,237,250	987,113	28,953	225,090	147,052
2002	6,638,961	4,955,379	-9,387	4,945,992	600,631	8,554	4,353,915	1,215,998	1,069,048	29,460	225,355	144,100
2003	6,757,082	4,937,088	10,880	4,947,968	603,294	18,990	4,363,664	1,270,603	1,122,815	29,878	226,153	142,484
2004	6,962,035	5,119,503	46,668	5,166,171	623,003	27,490	4,570,658	1,213,687	1,177,690	30,649	227,155	141,376
2005	7,158,710	5,258,342	16,704	5,275,046	643,478	37,934	4,669,502	1,254,382	1,234,826	31,369	228,208	141,136
2006	7,512,910	5,384,854	-4,772	5,380,082	657,699	63,889	4,786,272	1,410,108	1,316,530	32,833	228,825	140,007
2007	8,045,839	5,693,542	14,095	5,707,637	687,576	68,785	5,088,846	1,535,164	1,421,829	34,978	230,025	143,461
2008	8,507,128	5,932,665	18,923	5,951,588	709,103	84,680	5,327,165	1,600,660	1,579,303	36,784	231,272	144,190
2009	8,524,305	5,949,831	36,769	5,986,600	715,237	20,238	5,291,601	1,516,358	1,716,346	36,656	232,548	141,300
2010	8,632,471	6,070,964	-26	6,070,938	730,154	-26,112	5,314,672	1,495,677	1,822,122	36,849	234,267	141,073
2011	9,066,961	6,266,709	49,399	6,316,108	663,174	-73,333	5,579,601	1,594,395	1,892,965	38,629	234,716	142,102
2012	9,207,204	6,451,455	39,820	6,491,275	680,171	-123,596	5,687,508	1,626,952	1,892,744	39,272	234,445	142,185
2013	9,224,411	6,593,625	70,452	6,664,077	784,065	-166,445	5,713,567	1,584,543	1,926,301	39,437	233,901	143,444
2014	9,549,381	6,838,615	17,515	6,856,130	810,213	-166,894	5,879,023	1,679,648	1,990,710	40,703	234,613	145,206
2015	9,757,483	6,989,606	7,744	6,997,350	832,183	-181,857	5,983,310	1,715,097	2,059,076	41,588	234,623	144,932
2016	10,008,687	7,162,975	16,214	7,179,189	844,478	-191,182	6,143,529	1,753,333	2,111,825	42,692	234,442	145,279
2017	10,206,464	7,283,672	9,450	7,293,122	862,199	-183,528	6,247,395	1,765,092	2,193,977	43,534	234,449	144,370
2018	10,695,584	7,618,334	39,968	7,658,302	908,358	-194,711	6,555,233	1,859,503	2,280,848	45,744	233,814	144,381
2019	10,987,216	7,681,223	41,772	7,722,995	925,306	-161,349	6,636,340	1,945,278	2,405,598	47,024	233,650	142,992
2020	11,772,694	7,916,933	88,934	8,005,867	966,978	-172,151	6,866,738	1,938,563	2,967,393	50,582	232,747	139,539
2021	12,483,967	8,340,737	103,250	8,443,987	998,791	-187,095	7,258,101	1,972,236	3,253,630	53,655	232,670	142,572

Personal Income and Employment by Area: Trenton-Princeton, NJ

(Thousands of dollars, except as noted.)

		Derivation of personal income										
		Earnings by place of work			Less: Contributions for government social insurance	Plus: Adjustment for residence	Equals: Net earnings by place of residence	Plus: Dividends, interest, and rent	Plus: Personal current transfer receipts	Per capita personal income (dollars)	Population (persons)	Total employment
Year	Personal income, total	Nonfarm	Farm	Total								
1970	1,502,265	1,256,172	2,577	1,258,749	92,246	-13,057	1,153,446	237,973	110,846	4,924	305,091	153,757
1971	1,651,657	1,381,007	2,044	1,383,051	104,148	-22,573	1,256,330	261,181	134,146	5,351	308,680	153,733
1972	1,837,479	1,559,066	1,821	1,560,887	122,826	-37,860	1,400,201	287,152	150,126	5,842	314,505	161,814
1973	2,029,946	1,736,255	3,496	1,739,751	157,306	-39,270	1,543,175	314,842	171,929	6,440	315,209	166,704
1974	2,223,435	1,880,696	4,524	1,885,220	175,024	-39,310	1,670,886	350,596	201,953	7,011	317,113	169,496
1975	2,382,116	1,951,765	2,056	1,953,821	178,513	-26,107	1,749,201	368,233	264,682	7,550	315,506	163,246
1976	2,597,306	2,141,369	2,226	2,143,595	198,903	-34,758	1,909,934	398,059	289,313	8,298	313,004	166,848
1977	2,825,891	2,351,959	3,160	2,355,119	218,087	-60,324	2,076,708	440,765	308,418	9,074	311,427	169,701
1978	3,093,629	2,612,657	2,722	2,615,379	250,069	-92,598	2,272,712	486,366	334,551	9,923	311,764	175,837
1979	3,378,784	2,858,924	2,358	2,861,282	283,633	-121,920	2,455,729	546,419	376,636	10,899	309,998	180,281
1980	3,746,850	3,117,300	1,841	3,119,141	305,453	-165,310	2,648,378	660,015	438,457	12,173	307,796	182,263
1981	4,147,565	3,400,388	3,817	3,404,205	355,908	-206,494	2,841,803	824,520	481,242	13,512	306,944	182,845
1982	4,513,014	3,608,605	2,934	3,611,539	377,898	-229,663	3,003,978	974,129	534,907	14,658	307,882	181,854
1983	4,825,373	3,946,798	4,158	3,950,956	426,389	-279,165	3,245,402	1,007,204	572,767	15,513	311,052	185,431
1984	5,346,405	4,422,836	5,850	4,428,686	499,334	-337,844	3,591,508	1,157,736	597,161	17,187	311,067	194,000
1985	5,761,857	4,832,232	6,502	4,838,734	551,095	-388,126	3,899,513	1,232,156	630,188	18,342	314,133	199,290
1986	6,206,379	5,306,210	6,626	5,312,836	613,135	-449,881	4,249,820	1,296,824	659,735	19,483	318,557	207,145
1987	6,729,160	5,830,784	7,909	5,838,693	667,363	-506,716	4,664,614	1,380,045	684,501	20,880	322,280	212,933
1988	7,487,965	6,530,639	7,184	6,537,823	764,226	-580,149	5,193,448	1,567,650	726,867	22,958	326,162	218,832
1989	8,156,106	6,914,960	6,396	6,921,356	800,305	-663,732	5,457,319	1,914,511	784,276	25,000	326,246	219,559
1990	8,697,032	7,384,609	4,926	7,389,535	829,957	-711,777	5,847,801	1,988,896	860,335	26,639	326,477	219,736
1991	8,868,792	7,666,994	3,058	7,670,052	880,122	-912,431	5,877,499	2,005,533	985,760	26,982	328,694	216,604
1992	9,517,817	8,180,550	1,990	8,182,540	931,848	-866,984	6,383,708	2,005,288	1,128,821	28,783	330,674	217,454
1993	9,693,836	8,403,830	2,576	8,406,406	953,228	-945,918	6,507,260	1,987,130	1,199,446	29,085	333,292	219,615
1994	10,025,467	8,722,040	3,174	8,725,214	1,006,864	-1,012,916	6,705,434	2,109,274	1,210,759	29,906	335,229	220,293
1995	10,504,224	8,990,131	1,973	8,992,104	1,044,279	-1,052,076	6,895,749	2,315,835	1,292,640	31,126	337,476	222,501
1996	11,045,714	9,214,761	2,899	9,217,660	1,070,017	-866,524	7,281,119	2,437,355	1,327,240	32,569	339,146	220,840
1997	11,650,321	9,970,281	1,436	9,971,717	1,145,286	-1,110,449	7,715,982	2,576,622	1,357,717	34,190	340,755	224,588
1998	12,452,994	10,435,513	1,245	10,436,758	1,186,776	-965,290	8,284,692	2,804,540	1,363,762	36,199	344,013	225,414
1999	13,054,934	10,986,530	1,293	10,987,823	1,245,560	-912,577	8,829,686	2,807,838	1,417,410	37,467	348,435	228,946
2000	14,425,893	12,190,977	3,850	12,194,827	1,363,901	-1,016,691	9,814,235	3,094,102	1,517,556	41,045	351,465	242,173
2001	15,842,725	13,660,988	2,799	13,663,787	1,480,163	-1,126,802	11,056,822	3,087,460	1,698,443	44,777	353,816	247,570
2002	16,345,592	14,226,117	3,857	14,229,974	1,535,204	-1,295,738	11,399,032	3,065,968	1,880,592	45,923	355,935	249,453
2003	16,828,665	14,724,077	4,108	14,728,185	1,575,654	-1,307,075	11,845,456	3,154,206	1,829,003	46,913	358,724	252,631
2004	17,071,208	15,333,351	5,913	15,339,264	1,639,299	-1,524,663	12,175,302	3,085,852	1,810,054	47,256	361,248	257,984
2005	17,513,312	15,607,227	4,952	15,612,179	1,707,564	-1,522,180	12,382,435	3,215,054	1,915,823	48,377	362,015	259,714
2006	18,761,110	16,421,082	5,219	16,426,301	1,799,389	-1,613,423	13,013,489	3,653,579	2,094,042	51,706	362,840	265,427
2007	19,735,514	16,835,197	4,756	16,839,953	1,883,460	-1,283,313	13,673,180	3,859,725	2,202,609	54,355	363,088	264,782
2008	20,306,954	17,780,073	3,814	17,783,887	1,991,709	-1,889,990	13,902,188	3,915,275	2,489,491	55,770	364,119	265,799
2009	19,028,940	17,124,088	3,338	17,127,426	1,922,922	-2,312,246	12,892,258	3,395,256	2,741,426	52,079	365,388	259,117
2010	19,464,859	17,655,172	3,355	17,658,527	1,983,227	-2,536,981	13,138,319	3,358,586	2,967,954	52,934	367,717	260,107
2011	20,555,289	18,235,231	6,590	18,241,821	1,835,082	-2,559,461	13,847,278	3,702,937	3,005,074	55,947	367,407	262,910
2012	21,639,086	19,030,866	8,144	19,039,010	1,894,800	-2,581,017	14,563,193	4,107,659	2,968,234	58,702	368,628	263,963
2013	21,249,404	19,845,025	8,001	19,853,026	2,220,623	-3,249,034	14,383,369	3,841,067	3,024,968	57,503	369,534	267,421
2014	22,692,372	20,458,613	4,441	20,463,054	2,287,289	-3,005,617	15,170,148	4,378,149	3,144,075	60,154	377,236	272,638
2015	23,116,728	20,792,337	5,332	20,797,669	2,337,929	-3,184,088	15,275,652	4,606,806	3,234,270	61,091	378,400	276,248
2016	23,505,369	21,490,512	3,623	21,494,135	2,397,155	-3,722,970	15,374,010	4,817,127	3,314,232	61,855	380,010	282,907
2017	24,070,276	21,695,371	4,333	21,699,704	2,474,219	-3,433,466	15,792,019	4,926,433	3,351,824	62,920	382,551	283,644
2018	25,154,573	22,876,444	3,399	22,879,843	2,561,317	-3,768,292	16,550,234	5,123,123	3,481,216	65,376	384,767	290,225
2019	26,529,544	24,700,031	8,095	24,708,126	2,735,500	-4,788,916	17,183,710	5,674,884	3,670,950	68,721	386,045	296,456
2020	27,842,874	25,416,022	5,555	25,421,577	2,819,106	-5,275,944	17,326,527	5,632,817	4,883,530	71,990	386,759	286,629
2021	30,065,659	27,211,571	6,545	27,218,116	3,009,324	-5,319,085	18,889,707	5,793,400	5,382,552	77,911	385,898	294,963

Personal Income and Employment by Area: Tucson, AZ

(Thousands of dollars, except as noted.)

Year	Personal income, total	Earnings by place of work			Less: Contributions for government social insurance	Plus: Adjustment for residence	Equals: Net earnings by place of residence	Plus: Dividends, interest, and rent	Plus: Personal current transfer receipts	Per capita personal income (dollars)	Population (persons)	Total employment
		Nonfarm	Farm	Total								
1970	1,450,771	1,025,196	9,121	1,034,317	69,598	14,248	978,967	344,831	126,973	4,076	355,962	144,257
1971	1,674,034	1,188,318	8,350	1,196,668	83,587	16,944	1,130,025	391,000	153,009	4,402	380,255	153,910
1972	1,905,022	1,363,766	12,649	1,376,415	100,346	15,682	1,291,751	437,269	176,002	4,675	407,515	165,820
1973	2,167,818	1,551,236	21,896	1,573,132	129,373	23,267	1,467,026	490,888	209,904	5,058	428,558	177,412
1974	2,420,702	1,708,320	16,922	1,725,242	148,097	26,991	1,604,136	566,011	250,555	5,455	443,741	181,576
1975	2,651,180	1,800,181	14,095	1,814,276	156,145	26,964	1,685,095	630,129	335,956	5,767	459,738	180,791
1976	2,900,858	1,967,561	18,384	1,985,945	171,550	32,580	1,846,975	675,058	378,825	6,151	471,596	185,903
1977	3,209,600	2,195,387	11,834	2,207,221	191,389	35,536	2,051,368	756,391	401,841	6,638	483,484	193,919
1978	3,687,707	2,514,099	15,924	2,530,023	223,517	33,891	2,340,397	887,159	460,151	7,410	497,687	206,946
1979	4,323,806	3,005,810	16,282	3,022,092	280,713	43,094	2,784,473	1,029,904	509,429	8,262	523,341	224,813
1980	4,977,858	3,390,573	16,831	3,407,404	322,646	38,753	3,123,511	1,251,260	603,087	9,291	535,780	234,354
1981	5,783,187	3,836,259	14,326	3,850,585	392,153	78,362	3,536,794	1,540,944	705,449	10,465	552,627	240,604
1982	6,171,947	4,024,506	13,593	4,038,099	419,400	59,936	3,678,635	1,710,961	782,351	10,866	568,004	245,297
1983	6,720,540	4,366,338	14,128	4,380,466	462,151	45,170	3,963,485	1,907,118	849,937	11,544	582,172	253,316
1984	7,387,659	4,842,774	33,960	4,876,734	529,159	45,672	4,393,247	2,094,922	899,490	12,477	592,087	271,828
1985	8,089,874	5,325,158	25,642	5,350,800	589,883	48,139	4,809,056	2,315,886	964,932	13,424	602,647	291,177
1986	8,778,098	5,818,120	29,159	5,847,279	646,842	57,629	5,258,066	2,474,335	1,045,697	14,122	621,586	302,631
1987	9,288,965	6,169,748	27,872	6,197,620	679,503	63,858	5,581,975	2,562,568	1,144,422	14,505	640,419	308,273
1988	9,934,583	6,559,895	31,163	6,591,058	749,448	95,324	5,936,934	2,746,074	1,251,575	15,127	656,727	318,154
1989	10,668,032	6,717,781	24,366	6,742,147	789,961	90,360	6,042,546	3,184,808	1,440,678	16,061	664,200	318,020
1990	10,999,408	6,884,706	26,634	6,911,340	830,958	116,028	6,196,410	3,201,929	1,601,069	16,445	668,844	318,925
1991	11,640,270	7,437,719	23,808	7,461,527	906,588	110,716	6,665,655	3,204,771	1,769,844	17,123	679,813	323,434
1992	12,330,393	7,956,384	20,226	7,976,610	964,708	114,383	7,126,285	3,210,371	1,993,737	17,663	698,091	328,018
1993	13,445,904	8,653,599	28,241	8,681,840	1,044,439	105,292	7,742,693	3,544,127	2,159,084	18,685	719,598	343,969
1994	14,548,118	9,548,676	14,876	9,563,552	1,160,188	93,514	8,496,878	3,753,927	2,297,313	19,525	745,112	367,152
1995	15,521,408	10,082,827	12,521	10,095,348	1,180,975	108,447	9,022,820	4,058,346	2,440,242	20,205	768,212	381,587
1996	16,516,732	10,657,629	18,087	10,675,716	1,278,928	135,529	9,532,317	4,395,447	2,588,968	21,076	783,685	389,883
1997	17,418,989	11,332,721	18,217	11,350,938	1,338,365	116,161	10,128,734	4,590,829	2,699,426	21,814	798,521	399,857
1998	18,806,789	12,335,536	14,682	12,350,218	1,440,035	108,184	11,018,367	5,013,873	2,774,549	23,122	813,386	416,075
1999	19,862,890	13,201,066	21,400	13,222,466	1,551,573	96,845	11,767,738	5,151,801	2,943,351	23,963	828,905	425,172
2000	21,186,614	14,173,700	14,964	14,188,664	1,651,400	89,262	12,626,526	5,468,128	3,091,960	24,984	848,019	441,662
2001	22,985,831	15,572,638	10,975	15,583,613	1,737,877	82,066	13,927,802	5,557,413	3,500,616	26,750	859,280	436,864
2002	23,474,832	16,242,706	17,307	16,260,013	1,809,144	45,951	14,496,820	5,078,296	3,899,716	26,851	874,267	437,057
2003	24,739,950	17,119,782	22,216	17,141,998	1,880,224	19,680	15,281,454	5,211,349	4,247,147	27,927	885,893	441,824
2004	26,240,516	17,811,966	29,526	17,841,492	1,984,458	-12,219	15,844,815	5,784,014	4,611,687	29,113	901,342	458,654
2005	28,452,247	18,887,794	32,638	18,920,432	2,127,994	-24,715	16,767,723	6,622,710	5,061,814	30,916	920,298	473,271
2006	31,192,461	20,696,205	27,530	20,723,735	2,306,062	-72,275	18,345,398	7,330,559	5,516,504	33,151	940,930	491,400
2007	33,007,635	21,833,120	16,820	21,849,940	2,450,099	-91,073	19,308,768	7,737,363	5,961,504	34,532	955,869	504,656
2008	34,978,389	22,340,868	18,751	22,359,619	2,557,452	-92,109	19,710,058	8,373,041	6,895,290	36,143	967,778	500,711
2009	33,100,540	21,384,806	36,380	21,421,186	2,489,975	-53,881	18,877,330	6,675,951	7,547,259	33,929	975,580	481,987
2010	33,557,989	21,524,972	39,220	21,564,192	2,513,414	-31,208	19,019,570	6,436,908	8,101,511	34,185	981,649	476,945
2011	34,898,653	21,791,077	57,634	21,848,711	2,302,657	12,955	19,559,009	7,287,460	8,052,184	35,305	988,500	477,616
2012	36,172,149	22,721,650	51,453	22,773,103	2,349,909	42,611	20,465,805	7,668,452	8,037,892	36,419	993,231	484,507
2013	36,577,421	23,266,854	46,339	23,313,193	2,686,475	100,446	20,727,164	7,556,553	8,293,704	36,674	997,374	489,813
2014	37,965,814	23,493,821	39,055	23,532,876	2,721,208	118,438	20,930,106	8,143,501	8,892,207	38,046	997,883	495,725
2015	39,186,801	23,816,205	44,455	23,860,660	2,776,611	129,063	21,213,112	8,710,732	9,262,957	39,137	1,001,271	500,002
2016	40,340,692	24,551,338	45,640	24,596,978	2,864,562	111,655	21,844,071	8,849,335	9,647,286	40,050	1,007,258	507,155
2017	42,857,047	26,166,701	39,079	26,205,780	3,042,587	101,905	23,265,098	9,247,558	10,344,391	42,196	1,015,666	517,564
2018	44,873,632	27,447,221	30,194	27,477,415	3,230,964	123,311	24,369,762	9,667,527	10,836,343	43,794	1,024,650	524,890
2019	47,581,859	28,736,210	31,731	28,767,941	3,413,510	95,383	25,449,814	10,542,587	11,589,458	45,996	1,034,482	530,649
2020	52,416,791	30,086,470	31,153	30,117,623	3,601,633	146,683	26,662,673	10,584,259	15,169,859	50,131	1,045,599	523,240
2021	55,696,681	31,701,476	30,186	31,731,662	3,727,532	153,507	28,157,637	10,900,557	16,638,487	52,942	1,052,030	534,770

Personal Income and Employment by Area: Tulsa, OK

(Thousands of dollars, except as noted.)

Year	Personal income, total	Earnings by place of work — Nonfarm	Earnings by place of work — Farm	Earnings by place of work — Total	Less: Contributions for government social insurance	Plus: Adjustment for residence	Equals: Net earnings by place of residence	Plus: Dividends, interest, and rent	Plus: Personal current transfer receipts	Per capita personal income (dollars)	Population (persons)	Total employment
1970	2,244,876	1,803,417	17,819	1,821,236	118,059	-13,643	1,689,534	344,994	210,348	3,916	573,235	253,693
1971	2,423,024	1,923,488	15,964	1,939,452	129,622	-11,000	1,798,830	380,481	243,713	4,162	582,203	255,389
1972	2,660,683	2,136,833	21,145	2,157,978	151,577	-12,550	1,993,851	400,704	266,128	4,494	592,055	270,578
1973	3,010,374	2,427,869	25,672	2,453,541	201,071	-12,440	2,240,030	465,639	304,705	5,000	602,108	286,825
1974	3,535,154	2,854,603	28,731	2,883,334	242,127	-8,842	2,632,365	545,238	357,551	5,777	611,968	301,297
1975	4,037,412	3,226,449	26,245	3,252,694	267,329	10,306	2,995,671	600,416	441,325	6,457	625,290	309,562
1976	4,496,483	3,619,842	27,581	3,647,423	307,343	19,613	3,359,693	651,137	485,653	7,043	638,395	324,739
1977	5,048,189	4,114,867	17,591	4,132,458	347,292	18,843	3,804,009	723,181	520,999	7,746	651,741	336,418
1978	5,741,100	4,735,201	5,321	4,740,522	412,300	16,667	4,344,889	837,483	558,728	8,645	664,120	356,285
1979	6,570,626	5,463,555	16,969	5,480,524	494,812	-27,859	4,957,853	969,043	643,730	9,522	690,017	372,697
1980	7,754,003	6,414,764	11,648	6,426,412	582,946	-43,751	5,799,715	1,207,172	747,116	10,834	715,729	396,414
1981	9,020,964	7,407,097	22,929	7,430,026	724,104	-57,943	6,647,979	1,521,306	851,679	12,345	730,726	416,102
1982	9,865,263	7,928,027	16,706	7,944,733	799,460	-57,708	7,087,565	1,796,927	980,771	13,070	754,809	420,399
1983	10,028,274	7,890,947	14,600	7,905,547	792,124	-47,832	7,065,591	1,877,904	1,084,779	12,977	772,780	406,405
1984	10,745,623	8,413,935	12,368	8,426,303	856,524	-36,843	7,532,936	2,096,210	1,116,477	13,874	774,500	416,659
1985	11,350,185	8,838,843	10,333	8,849,176	913,651	-45,139	7,890,386	2,270,928	1,188,871	14,679	773,203	421,361
1986	11,535,530	8,970,166	21,113	8,991,279	946,414	-49,220	7,995,645	2,265,666	1,274,219	14,869	775,798	409,752
1987	11,579,981	8,981,797	16,105	8,997,902	945,958	-44,968	8,006,976	2,241,869	1,331,136	15,025	770,713	411,356
1988	12,138,355	9,463,547	26,063	9,489,610	1,040,902	-51,303	8,397,405	2,334,196	1,406,754	16,000	758,652	413,701
1989	12,976,626	10,149,835	29,269	10,179,104	1,117,270	-79,229	8,982,605	2,483,922	1,510,099	17,134	757,345	418,975
1990	13,917,909	10,829,567	13,894	10,843,461	1,237,234	-48,716	9,557,511	2,736,295	1,624,103	18,238	763,119	430,763
1991	14,433,922	11,276,525	30,254	11,306,779	1,316,608	-50,808	9,939,363	2,721,628	1,772,931	18,630	774,765	437,718
1992	15,240,048	11,861,419	31,082	11,892,501	1,371,429	-67,034	10,454,038	2,802,560	1,983,450	19,395	785,755	438,214
1993	15,822,834	12,381,108	29,253	12,410,361	1,438,718	-88,452	10,883,191	2,822,969	2,116,674	19,899	795,139	444,889
1994	16,532,367	12,845,782	35,297	12,881,079	1,515,283	-101,367	11,264,429	3,042,329	2,225,609	20,653	800,473	453,942
1995	17,471,159	13,413,972	9,776	13,423,748	1,580,280	-111,073	11,732,395	3,321,052	2,417,712	21,684	805,725	466,011
1996	18,657,703	14,313,567	13,657	14,327,224	1,654,860	-125,433	12,546,931	3,561,314	2,549,458	22,857	816,284	481,882
1997	19,979,614	15,542,980	16,410	15,559,390	1,772,424	-167,194	13,619,772	3,662,496	2,697,346	24,089	829,391	499,806
1998	21,561,537	16,834,592	-13,913	16,820,679	1,913,669	-194,604	14,712,406	4,112,823	2,736,308	25,575	843,057	523,100
1999	21,889,008	16,922,920	7,294	16,930,214	1,948,747	-176,024	14,805,443	4,217,538	2,866,027	25,612	854,631	522,394
2000	23,777,612	18,137,745	119	18,137,864	2,060,399	-205,246	15,872,219	4,887,950	3,017,443	27,609	861,237	533,529
2001	24,062,730	18,244,880	5,015	18,249,895	2,166,703	-250,250	15,832,942	4,928,077	3,301,711	27,735	867,602	537,484
2002	24,361,262	18,376,323	29,055	18,405,378	2,194,956	-264,144	15,946,278	4,905,639	3,509,345	27,846	874,844	530,126
2003	24,958,872	18,589,816	-72	18,589,744	2,174,120	-232,034	16,183,590	5,007,028	3,768,254	28,441	877,577	516,720
2004	28,419,103	21,643,863	38,102	21,681,965	2,368,691	-240,282	19,072,992	5,378,618	3,967,493	32,368	878,004	520,154
2005	32,152,843	24,355,045	53,824	24,408,869	2,545,651	-267,564	21,595,654	6,266,401	4,290,788	36,419	882,861	535,329
2006	36,861,801	27,994,685	26,381	28,021,066	2,741,575	-343,308	24,936,183	7,216,848	4,708,770	41,232	894,011	552,670
2007	37,952,433	27,910,069	32,734	27,942,803	2,872,346	-324,077	24,746,380	8,132,191	5,073,862	41,870	906,441	567,239
2008	43,362,200	32,103,601	8,374	32,111,975	2,999,508	-297,821	28,814,646	8,826,906	5,720,648	47,312	916,525	577,748
2009	37,761,510	27,173,394	-7,233	27,166,161	2,864,605	-244,174	24,057,382	7,568,916	6,135,212	40,611	929,824	559,559
2010	39,579,578	28,268,338	18,337	28,286,675	2,886,792	-86,926	25,312,957	7,650,560	6,616,061	42,112	939,868	550,837
2011	44,246,003	31,757,640	41,425	31,799,065	2,824,469	-57,708	28,916,888	8,644,380	6,684,735	46,778	945,873	556,518
2012	49,251,724	35,358,253	70,617	35,428,870	3,031,063	-3,033	32,394,774	10,013,292	6,843,658	51,697	952,694	570,545
2013	54,445,729	41,346,408	38,324	41,384,732	3,523,865	30,986	37,891,853	9,583,826	6,970,050	56,584	962,210	578,957
2014	58,545,704	44,523,975	120,297	44,644,272	3,625,099	47,674	41,066,847	10,233,737	7,245,120	60,109	973,986	587,990
2015	53,887,185	39,694,051	33,426	39,727,477	3,623,684	41,631	36,145,424	10,224,001	7,517,760	54,621	986,572	597,009
2016	47,978,879	33,877,950	-3,486	33,874,464	3,479,919	22,844	30,417,389	9,741,782	7,819,708	48,202	995,361	598,977
2017	51,333,746	36,556,734	-19,640	36,537,094	3,628,746	25,121	32,933,469	10,287,343	8,112,934	51,385	998,996	601,774
2018	54,959,046	39,236,137	-26,933	39,209,204	3,867,369	-46,706	35,295,129	11,257,271	8,406,646	54,837	1,002,232	609,624
2019	56,820,274	39,949,030	-34,257	39,914,773	3,994,275	-18,557	35,901,941	11,900,424	9,017,909	56,341	1,008,509	610,565
2020	57,649,032	38,062,484	-33,129	38,029,355	3,994,228	101,829	34,136,956	12,012,398	11,499,678	56,708	1,016,589	597,050
2021	61,378,802	39,889,513	-20,554	39,868,959	4,122,805	112,425	35,858,579	12,618,081	12,902,142	59,941	1,023,988	603,882

Personal Income and Employment by Area: Tuscaloosa, AL

(Thousands of dollars, except as noted.)

Year	Personal income, total	Earnings by place of work			Less: Contributions for government social insurance	Plus: Adjustment for residence	Equals: Net earnings by place of residence	Plus: Dividends, interest, and rent	Plus: Personal current transfer receipts	Per capita personal income (dollars)	Population (persons)	Total employment
		Nonfarm	Farm	Total								
1970	421,024	327,971	8,305	336,276	24,205	5,543	317,614	52,181	51,229	2,760	152,542	57,595
1971	477,791	370,233	11,259	381,492	28,071	6,114	359,535	59,828	58,428	3,072	155,545	59,464
1972	532,848	414,748	12,425	427,173	33,056	6,949	401,066	66,929	64,853	3,356	158,760	62,219
1973	597,587	464,592	17,845	482,437	42,654	8,638	448,421	75,759	73,407	3,712	160,974	64,792
1974	670,897	521,898	11,386	533,284	49,216	10,546	494,614	88,919	87,364	4,109	163,262	65,272
1975	754,936	568,090	12,707	580,797	53,304	12,159	539,652	102,804	112,480	4,594	164,319	64,783
1976	828,130	629,200	12,343	641,543	60,305	13,250	594,488	112,340	121,302	4,973	166,525	66,406
1977	942,678	732,568	9,710	742,278	68,752	13,626	687,152	126,212	129,314	5,599	168,371	68,549
1978	1,056,880	809,188	16,161	825,349	76,359	18,058	767,048	147,319	142,513	6,148	171,898	68,430
1979	1,173,059	891,927	15,288	907,215	86,998	20,618	840,835	168,910	163,314	6,767	173,338	69,758
1980	1,254,670	928,704	2,427	931,131	93,515	20,427	858,043	202,684	193,943	7,170	174,982	69,209
1981	1,402,575	1,010,964	7,528	1,018,492	110,261	27,908	936,139	246,412	220,024	7,965	176,099	69,349
1982	1,500,180	1,067,772	3,663	1,071,435	119,399	24,976	977,012	278,967	244,201	8,590	174,646	68,387
1983	1,611,324	1,137,285	-850	1,136,435	126,028	34,618	1,045,025	299,974	266,325	9,200	175,147	68,723
1984	1,786,750	1,268,023	8,273	1,276,296	142,022	33,042	1,167,316	336,413	283,021	10,156	175,924	71,003
1985	1,937,109	1,370,063	11,303	1,381,366	153,294	33,882	1,261,954	366,788	308,367	10,882	178,012	72,404
1986	2,031,265	1,433,360	14,355	1,447,715	162,051	39,354	1,325,018	382,488	323,759	11,262	180,361	75,044
1987	2,188,710	1,576,096	14,976	1,591,072	173,297	47,278	1,465,053	393,390	330,267	11,994	182,481	78,163
1988	2,329,599	1,667,807	21,864	1,689,671	193,321	61,694	1,558,044	426,617	344,938	12,678	183,746	81,570
1989	2,581,097	1,798,129	22,661	1,820,790	207,102	69,786	1,683,474	502,265	395,358	13,932	185,270	83,909
1990	2,814,979	1,985,493	27,036	2,012,529	230,606	66,744	1,848,667	521,705	444,607	15,028	187,311	87,832
1991	2,957,443	2,069,579	33,430	2,103,009	240,550	67,775	1,930,234	539,215	487,994	15,566	189,990	87,718
1992	3,187,706	2,206,396	36,488	2,242,884	251,662	84,438	2,075,660	550,009	562,037	16,708	190,785	88,695
1993	3,371,503	2,355,708	38,419	2,394,127	271,523	79,834	2,202,438	571,042	598,023	17,508	192,574	92,593
1994	3,583,329	2,495,967	28,915	2,524,882	289,967	77,589	2,312,504	623,529	647,296	18,445	194,272	94,585
1995	3,792,597	2,626,327	21,336	2,647,663	306,908	70,259	2,411,014	684,474	697,109	19,196	197,577	96,915
1996	3,932,597	2,714,169	27,038	2,741,207	316,023	67,100	2,492,284	707,467	732,846	19,866	197,955	99,421
1997	4,146,730	2,883,207	32,316	2,915,523	336,479	52,148	2,631,192	742,850	772,688	20,762	199,727	102,688
1998	4,567,934	3,156,754	52,379	3,209,133	363,825	71,085	2,916,393	823,631	827,910	21,611	211,366	108,113
1999	4,814,516	3,365,817	74,616	3,440,433	386,079	63,632	3,117,986	824,602	871,928	22,664	212,433	108,935
2000	4,997,160	3,450,213	55,390	3,505,603	395,865	60,875	3,170,613	896,146	930,401	23,309	214,391	109,643
2001	5,153,312	3,597,841	64,051	3,661,892	415,376	47,279	3,293,795	899,104	960,413	23,907	215,558	110,885
2002	5,319,716	3,734,935	54,648	3,789,583	431,040	31,713	3,390,256	895,884	1,033,576	24,599	216,258	111,524
2003	5,560,404	3,872,897	76,670	3,949,567	445,412	15,844	3,519,999	964,532	1,075,873	25,604	217,173	112,064
2004	5,879,325	4,113,967	92,283	4,206,250	468,645	7,583	3,745,188	998,893	1,135,244	26,872	218,791	114,914
2005	6,359,923	4,501,651	91,987	4,593,638	513,411	-70,093	4,010,134	1,134,138	1,215,651	28,620	222,220	118,558
2006	6,757,341	4,838,145	67,092	4,905,237	551,705	-132,165	4,221,367	1,246,879	1,289,095	29,729	227,299	123,813
2007	7,125,964	5,010,558	57,956	5,068,514	578,158	-167,973	4,322,383	1,381,087	1,422,494	30,963	230,142	127,135
2008	7,391,697	5,089,395	50,294	5,139,689	600,175	-224,583	4,314,931	1,496,390	1,580,376	31,634	233,663	126,968
2009	7,381,124	4,948,401	54,879	5,003,280	582,387	-223,404	4,197,489	1,453,239	1,730,396	31,038	237,813	122,019
2010	7,605,537	5,181,865	49,563	5,231,428	612,085	-290,032	4,329,311	1,397,957	1,878,269	31,757	239,492	121,790
2011	7,873,908	5,423,217	29,932	5,453,149	567,172	-300,689	4,585,288	1,402,750	1,885,870	32,752	240,408	123,857
2012	8,162,295	5,600,624	40,679	5,641,303	584,223	-308,501	4,748,579	1,557,145	1,856,571	33,671	242,413	126,988
2013	8,290,861	5,753,538	123,577	5,877,115	678,485	-285,436	4,913,194	1,481,805	1,895,862	33,910	244,499	128,365
2014	8,578,094	5,991,838	70,592	6,062,430	703,909	-330,449	5,028,072	1,577,991	1,972,031	33,872	253,251	132,774
2015	8,845,917	6,122,096	76,076	6,198,172	720,627	-365,777	5,111,768	1,622,705	2,111,444	34,434	256,895	136,443
2016	8,938,837	6,151,188	55,826	6,207,014	720,096	-328,127	5,158,791	1,632,305	2,147,741	34,432	259,612	137,224
2017	9,263,564	6,381,525	64,174	6,445,699	753,508	-374,539	5,317,652	1,767,088	2,178,824	35,360	261,980	139,632
2018	9,562,108	6,690,540	38,539	6,729,079	798,331	-388,764	5,541,984	1,766,801	2,253,323	36,232	263,910	142,401
2019	10,044,340	7,036,688	33,663	7,070,351	837,380	-451,316	5,781,655	1,901,325	2,361,360	37,609	267,072	145,579
2020	10,812,526	7,074,803	30,707	7,105,510	852,620	-333,381	5,919,509	1,939,429	2,953,588	40,238	268,711	139,871
2021	11,629,336	7,427,613	49,093	7,476,706	882,948	-232,934	6,360,824	1,986,857	3,281,655	43,362	268,191	141,057

Personal Income and Employment by Area: Twin Falls, ID

(Thousands of dollars, except as noted.)

Year	Personal income, total	Earnings by place of work			Less: Contributions for government social insurance	Plus: Adjustment for residence	Equals: Net earnings by place of residence	Plus: Dividends, interest, and rent	Plus: Personal current transfer receipts	Per capita personal income (dollars)	Population (persons)	Total employment
		Nonfarm	Farm	Total								
1970	193,857	115,179	34,956	150,135	8,618	749	142,266	32,921	18,670	3,692	52,509	25,303
1971	211,160	129,014	31,599	160,613	9,944	503	151,172	38,242	21,746	3,858	54,740	26,097
1972	244,241	143,728	44,508	188,236	11,512	819	177,543	41,913	24,785	4,305	56,740	26,921
1973	294,627	165,615	66,283	231,898	15,569	675	217,004	50,013	27,610	5,083	57,963	28,605
1974	360,419	195,209	92,805	288,014	18,974	195	269,235	58,740	32,444	6,030	59,768	30,370
1975	362,205	220,594	51,866	272,460	21,121	304	251,643	71,284	39,278	5,836	62,064	30,726
1976	383,853	249,634	41,282	290,916	24,143	255	267,028	73,680	43,145	6,122	62,700	32,480
1977	396,498	269,712	23,877	293,589	26,075	10	267,524	82,134	46,840	6,181	64,150	32,734
1978	450,350	308,982	28,809	337,791	30,090	-232	307,469	91,448	51,433	6,974	64,574	34,350
1979	498,926	349,981	23,720	373,701	36,079	-533	337,089	102,577	59,260	7,541	66,164	35,211
1980	584,032	371,461	52,978	424,439	38,634	251	386,056	127,299	70,677	8,591	67,983	34,801
1981	631,945	397,495	43,280	440,775	44,291	-2,075	394,409	155,972	81,564	9,189	68,769	34,410
1982	671,469	407,721	33,756	441,477	46,503	-2,588	392,386	187,158	91,925	9,640	69,657	33,845
1983	731,044	422,340	62,983	485,323	47,872	-2,292	435,159	196,534	99,351	10,315	70,873	34,040
1984	776,008	451,752	68,248	520,000	53,109	-2,610	464,281	208,112	103,615	10,978	70,686	34,048
1985	803,623	468,455	61,441	529,896	56,154	-3,281	470,461	222,236	110,926	11,484	69,977	33,630
1986	822,928	473,307	74,412	547,719	57,528	-2,942	487,249	219,319	116,360	11,869	69,333	33,517
1987	860,941	498,344	91,852	590,196	59,632	-2,383	528,181	212,946	119,814	12,571	68,487	34,073
1988	920,206	542,806	100,834	643,640	67,509	-1,125	575,006	215,885	129,315	13,455	68,393	35,116
1989	1,011,907	583,130	125,034	708,164	73,652	-497	634,015	239,658	138,234	14,815	68,305	35,955
1990	1,077,392	652,200	123,022	775,222	86,797	-1,520	686,905	242,550	147,937	15,607	69,033	38,157
1991	1,111,836	690,400	107,339	797,739	93,621	-789	703,329	246,680	161,827	15,752	70,584	38,905
1992	1,194,008	741,576	120,756	862,332	98,571	5	763,766	248,571	181,671	16,596	71,944	39,444
1993	1,307,901	799,106	163,535	962,641	106,760	959	856,840	260,286	190,775	17,818	73,402	40,806
1994	1,375,580	879,124	134,369	1,013,493	117,827	1,139	896,805	275,233	203,542	18,252	75,368	42,697
1995	1,479,017	925,342	148,083	1,073,425	124,249	1,672	950,848	305,790	222,379	19,311	76,590	44,397
1996	1,602,165	990,257	176,995	1,167,252	129,090	1,985	1,040,147	325,264	236,754	20,464	78,292	45,773
1997	1,650,079	1,027,697	161,088	1,188,785	133,314	2,615	1,058,086	345,450	246,543	20,705	79,696	47,072
1998	1,775,173	1,095,773	201,757	1,297,530	139,914	3,354	1,160,970	362,027	252,176	21,928	80,953	48,520
1999	1,814,762	1,153,765	192,924	1,346,689	144,148	5,521	1,208,062	341,718	264,982	22,152	81,923	48,686
2000	1,886,009	1,196,888	176,775	1,373,663	149,785	7,448	1,231,326	368,799	285,884	22,763	82,853	50,294
2001	2,013,686	1,233,672	223,721	1,457,393	154,733	6,684	1,309,344	385,868	318,474	24,222	83,135	50,131
2002	2,029,016	1,322,549	182,174	1,504,723	166,052	2,284	1,340,955	345,469	342,592	24,097	84,203	51,764
2003	2,089,079	1,370,263	162,569	1,532,832	175,088	-747	1,356,997	374,092	357,990	24,274	86,063	52,234
2004	2,289,379	1,432,111	267,508	1,699,619	182,858	643	1,517,404	389,769	382,206	26,123	87,640	52,721
2005	2,404,899	1,524,088	243,493	1,767,581	197,046	-386	1,570,149	423,170	411,580	26,874	89,487	54,863
2006	2,566,010	1,683,430	201,261	1,884,691	219,544	-4,526	1,660,621	452,642	452,747	27,866	92,085	56,593
2007	2,804,779	1,739,982	331,289	2,071,271	231,974	-5,792	1,833,505	485,887	485,387	29,740	94,310	57,877
2008	2,906,562	1,769,125	292,872	2,061,997	241,152	-10,835	1,810,010	531,144	565,408	30,164	96,360	58,300
2009	2,776,234	1,771,323	151,682	1,923,005	241,511	-13,873	1,667,621	495,651	612,962	28,240	98,310	56,659
2010	2,968,086	1,801,937	249,825	2,051,762	251,385	-13,265	1,787,112	491,045	689,929	29,685	99,985	55,501
2011	3,151,550	1,827,761	330,001	2,157,762	228,487	-11,423	1,917,852	538,541	695,157	31,320	100,624	56,044
2012	3,312,276	1,938,261	367,749	2,306,010	238,895	-13,018	2,054,097	567,741	690,438	32,751	101,136	56,340
2013	3,496,913	2,083,971	419,921	2,503,892	275,565	-12,871	2,215,456	582,706	698,751	34,057	102,678	58,153
2014	3,719,834	2,177,778	504,121	2,681,899	287,825	-19,282	2,374,792	607,416	737,626	35,589	104,523	60,201
2015	3,854,042	2,335,483	418,234	2,753,717	299,524	-28,120	2,426,073	662,907	765,062	36,363	105,988	61,325
2016	3,955,477	2,423,210	414,185	2,837,395	313,255	-26,261	2,497,879	678,979	778,619	36,566	108,175	62,382
2017	4,109,877	2,593,851	360,299	2,954,150	333,629	-27,352	2,593,169	713,050	803,658	37,267	110,282	64,399
2018	4,260,255	2,731,355	320,087	3,051,442	347,066	-36,228	2,668,148	738,098	854,009	38,223	111,458	65,277
2019	4,509,155	2,831,024	406,125	3,237,149	357,364	-45,903	2,833,882	754,088	921,185	39,910	112,983	66,137
2020	4,929,448	2,996,691	435,765	3,432,456	384,388	-42,163	3,005,905	764,920	1,158,623	43,052	114,501	66,102
2021	5,253,340	3,228,092	326,653	3,554,745	411,660	-51,021	3,092,064	782,062	1,379,214	44,937	116,905	68,301

Personal Income and Employment by Area: Tyler, TX

(Thousands of dollars, except as noted.)

Year	Personal income, total	Earnings by place of work			Less: Contributions for government social insurance	Plus: Adjustment for residence	Equals: Net earnings by place of residence	Plus: Dividends, interest, and rent	Plus: Personal current transfer receipts	Per capita personal income (dollars)	Population (persons)	Total employment
		Nonfarm	Farm	Total								
1970	351,219	290,251	2,119	292,370	19,129	-11,052	262,189	57,001	32,029	3,606	97,390	46,609
1971	386,169	316,918	3,785	320,703	21,431	-11,836	287,436	62,202	36,531	3,868	99,839	47,754
1972	438,298	367,053	3,343	370,396	26,074	-15,331	328,991	68,563	40,744	4,223	103,794	51,083
1973	500,311	415,053	8,045	423,098	34,373	-17,516	371,209	79,832	49,270	4,731	105,758	53,832
1974	570,348	464,251	8,027	472,278	39,172	-19,167	413,939	96,360	60,049	5,244	108,766	54,925
1975	637,891	506,514	3,205	509,719	41,468	-19,647	448,604	112,470	76,817	5,713	111,662	55,398
1976	733,407	589,520	7,480	597,000	48,693	-21,915	526,392	123,450	83,565	6,419	114,264	57,952
1977	841,790	694,847	5,332	700,179	57,449	-29,051	613,679	139,771	88,340	7,187	117,127	62,480
1978	973,776	810,559	3,889	814,448	68,508	-34,505	711,435	163,351	98,990	8,070	120,667	66,707
1979	1,127,369	936,018	10,433	946,451	83,063	-41,602	821,786	192,656	112,927	8,954	125,905	70,277
1980	1,283,749	1,027,624	10,260	1,037,884	91,630	-42,998	903,256	244,928	135,565	9,927	129,316	71,788
1981	1,495,480	1,178,122	11,480	1,189,602	113,283	-47,603	1,028,716	315,176	151,588	11,267	132,734	75,129
1982	1,704,299	1,303,250	17,550	1,320,800	128,982	-54,379	1,137,439	395,028	171,832	12,409	137,348	79,688
1983	1,856,465	1,411,313	23,739	1,435,052	139,100	-60,783	1,235,169	429,691	191,605	13,144	141,243	81,358
1984	2,035,226	1,567,583	21,554	1,589,137	160,465	-70,804	1,357,868	473,449	203,909	14,033	145,030	85,052
1985	2,151,033	1,629,148	8,798	1,637,946	169,055	-69,845	1,399,046	528,105	223,882	14,439	148,975	85,608
1986	2,221,483	1,657,042	18,574	1,675,616	170,825	-69,145	1,435,646	534,991	250,846	14,658	151,554	82,811
1987	2,239,646	1,657,258	18,204	1,675,462	168,973	-70,102	1,436,387	532,838	270,421	14,697	152,388	84,446
1988	2,335,766	1,707,916	12,720	1,720,636	179,711	-67,633	1,473,292	574,181	288,293	15,350	152,164	84,113
1989	2,470,890	1,764,444	16,008	1,780,452	187,529	-70,734	1,522,189	636,454	312,247	16,377	150,876	84,412
1990	2,606,041	1,876,359	14,867	1,891,226	195,386	-73,280	1,622,560	634,766	348,715	17,196	151,550	85,724
1991	2,708,520	1,970,747	12,758	1,983,505	211,493	-86,143	1,685,869	641,133	381,518	17,622	153,705	87,981
1992	2,882,811	2,131,086	13,160	2,144,246	225,167	-99,811	1,819,268	622,735	440,808	18,559	155,336	88,955
1993	3,045,388	2,274,492	14,024	2,288,516	240,888	-115,983	1,931,645	644,188	469,555	19,188	158,717	91,518
1994	3,192,026	2,379,674	13,799	2,393,473	254,151	-125,837	2,013,485	677,852	500,689	19,839	160,898	94,519
1995	3,408,371	2,507,993	14,219	2,522,212	267,755	-134,456	2,120,001	747,377	540,993	20,854	163,440	97,351
1996	3,631,056	2,693,197	12,463	2,705,660	283,333	-148,191	2,274,136	769,086	587,834	21,862	166,087	99,975
1997	3,899,334	2,959,420	22,403	2,981,823	305,022	-166,899	2,509,902	771,200	618,232	23,137	168,531	104,160
1998	4,210,290	3,200,704	27,999	3,228,703	328,140	-194,383	2,706,180	861,535	642,575	24,617	171,033	105,989
1999	4,389,629	3,368,536	34,136	3,402,672	342,995	-215,012	2,844,665	888,900	656,064	25,409	172,758	107,091
2000	4,805,894	3,693,998	28,594	3,722,592	365,009	-242,641	3,114,942	992,436	698,516	27,359	175,658	110,519
2001	5,077,082	3,931,127	35,625	3,966,752	387,295	-241,597	3,337,860	974,568	764,654	28,549	177,836	112,428
2002	5,248,223	4,070,184	38,184	4,108,368	400,139	-246,589	3,461,640	954,481	832,102	28,979	181,107	113,276
2003	5,538,401	4,250,597	34,177	4,284,774	426,463	-248,760	3,609,551	1,025,811	903,039	30,059	184,254	115,187
2004	5,901,722	4,646,169	30,755	4,676,924	465,835	-295,775	3,915,314	1,038,561	947,847	31,509	187,300	118,641
2005	6,634,878	5,177,114	32,763	5,209,877	502,092	-334,619	4,373,166	1,215,748	1,045,964	34,672	191,362	123,110
2006	7,314,655	5,712,486	25,925	5,738,411	532,215	-352,468	4,853,728	1,343,876	1,117,051	37,296	196,124	127,125
2007	7,475,726	5,686,609	19,517	5,706,126	551,409	-317,733	4,836,984	1,414,637	1,224,105	37,387	199,953	130,700
2008	8,869,848	6,718,435	15,480	6,733,915	601,304	-323,984	5,808,627	1,684,604	1,376,617	43,637	203,263	134,234
2009	8,192,431	6,116,204	19,146	6,135,350	590,870	-297,294	5,247,186	1,448,195	1,497,050	39,556	207,111	131,425
2010	9,092,441	6,787,163	21,318	6,808,481	619,764	-288,964	5,899,753	1,571,126	1,621,562	43,214	210,407	132,288
2011	10,282,913	7,732,725	17,299	7,750,024	577,574	-259,784	6,912,666	1,695,151	1,675,096	48,329	212,770	133,589
2012	10,450,466	7,833,363	27,128	7,860,491	587,854	-254,891	7,017,746	1,762,128	1,670,592	48,647	214,824	136,174
2013	10,830,421	8,209,902	22,556	8,232,458	683,602	-254,188	7,294,668	1,783,662	1,752,091	50,026	216,498	139,345
2014	11,462,702	8,673,167	16,018	8,689,185	712,544	-277,307	7,699,334	1,928,872	1,834,496	52,337	219,016	141,723
2015	10,714,581	7,822,302	18,218	7,840,520	721,619	-301,641	6,817,260	1,971,982	1,925,339	48,347	221,620	145,253
2016	10,589,210	7,669,927	12,157	7,682,084	739,573	-343,000	6,599,511	1,968,009	2,021,690	47,236	224,176	148,204
2017	12,061,487	8,999,914	9,645	9,009,559	797,260	-359,061	7,853,238	2,149,338	2,058,911	53,375	225,978	149,722
2018	12,914,436	9,724,357	8,660	9,733,017	833,064	-369,535	8,530,418	2,212,893	2,171,125	56,519	228,497	151,035
2019	13,103,925	9,768,743	3,486	9,772,229	863,824	-410,905	8,497,500	2,310,433	2,295,992	56,639	231,360	151,596
2020	13,068,217	9,141,760	9,555	9,151,315	865,336	-456,608	7,829,371	2,302,301	2,936,545	55,832	234,063	152,013
2021	14,298,554	10,008,959	6,773	10,015,732	925,317	-526,946	8,563,469	2,416,177	3,318,908	60,284	237,186	155,924

Personal Income and Employment by Area: Urban Honolulu, HI

(Thousands of dollars, except as noted.)

Year	Personal income, total	Derivation of personal income									Per capita personal income (dollars)	Population (persons)	Total employment
		Earnings by place of work			Less: Contributions for government social insurance	Plus: Adjustment for residence	Equals: Net earnings by place of residence	Plus: Dividends, interest, and rent	Plus: Personal current transfer receipts				
		Nonfarm	Farm	Total									
1970	3,634,964	2,958,005	33,864	2,991,869	183,236	4,733	2,813,366	661,296	160,302	5,828	623,756	366,968
1971	3,926,337	3,153,668	32,321	3,185,989	203,001	5,034	2,988,022	728,002	210,313	6,202	633,043	367,494
1972	4,327,655	3,480,364	32,143	3,512,507	236,141	4,610	3,280,976	797,331	249,348	6,509	664,830	381,276
1973	4,791,314	3,870,404	31,032	3,901,436	300,444	4,394	3,605,386	905,061	280,867	7,007	683,772	398,757
1974	5,274,604	4,217,804	39,362	4,257,166	343,985	4,307	3,917,488	1,024,565	332,551	7,556	698,033	407,738
1975	5,821,193	4,616,636	40,096	4,656,732	380,298	6,294	4,282,728	1,105,665	432,800	8,224	707,866	415,990
1976	6,281,530	4,969,816	41,097	5,010,913	413,473	6,456	4,603,896	1,168,788	508,846	8,762	716,911	417,620
1977	6,771,327	5,354,178	47,097	5,401,275	442,424	6,313	4,965,164	1,270,914	535,249	9,213	734,962	418,536
1978	7,496,119	5,921,228	40,954	5,962,182	502,998	5,023	5,464,207	1,460,740	571,172	10,123	740,505	431,484
1979	8,372,875	6,641,373	43,531	6,684,904	589,044	4,651	6,100,511	1,643,308	629,056	11,113	753,428	454,142
1980	9,422,314	7,372,805	63,826	7,436,631	653,607	4,972	6,787,996	1,915,931	718,387	12,336	763,820	467,461
1981	10,313,480	7,950,314	45,816	7,996,130	750,841	4,969	7,250,258	2,222,532	840,690	13,436	767,573	461,302
1982	10,892,215	8,445,216	50,452	8,495,668	787,253	4,615	7,713,030	2,274,583	904,602	14,035	776,075	457,679
1983	11,852,319	9,068,558	72,563	9,141,121	865,649	4,652	8,280,124	2,582,378	989,817	15,020	789,097	463,241
1984	12,755,379	9,716,997	51,884	9,768,881	946,084	3,616	8,826,413	2,880,632	1,048,334	15,988	797,791	467,189
1985	13,549,475	10,353,793	55,720	10,409,513	1,027,509	4,982	9,386,986	3,054,689	1,107,800	16,846	804,294	477,011
1986	14,298,161	11,032,179	59,639	11,091,818	1,119,586	5,650	9,977,882	3,171,978	1,148,301	17,642	810,444	486,861
1987	15,228,178	11,922,435	58,526	11,980,961	1,220,266	6,027	10,766,722	3,272,209	1,189,247	18,606	818,447	509,161
1988	16,651,964	13,159,375	75,279	13,234,654	1,393,147	6,226	11,847,733	3,529,307	1,274,924	20,207	824,072	525,017
1989	18,429,324	14,449,342	68,648	14,517,990	1,530,993	10,499	12,997,496	4,018,982	1,412,846	22,168	831,337	540,855
1990	20,038,505	15,941,554	76,424	16,017,978	1,760,667	12,384	14,269,695	4,243,614	1,525,196	23,897	838,534	558,346
1991	21,105,032	16,853,115	67,200	16,920,315	1,883,622	10,653	15,047,346	4,394,601	1,663,085	24,815	850,510	569,711
1992	22,665,937	18,039,436	52,140	18,091,576	2,010,280	6,749	16,088,045	4,700,806	1,877,086	26,235	863,959	570,015
1993	23,390,411	18,380,701	76,253	18,456,954	2,044,634	5,563	16,417,883	4,904,373	2,068,155	26,875	870,348	566,606
1994	23,857,762	18,465,352	64,023	18,529,375	2,070,316	1,789	16,460,848	5,154,695	2,242,219	27,155	878,591	560,810
1995	24,342,583	18,404,319	71,016	18,475,335	2,060,576	-2,183	16,412,576	5,400,427	2,529,580	27,618	881,399	556,670
1996	24,282,200	18,332,011	66,664	18,398,675	2,055,206	-4,021	16,339,448	5,358,327	2,584,425	27,486	883,443	553,469
1997	25,101,536	18,850,953	66,597	18,917,550	2,085,664	-7,107	16,824,779	5,663,439	2,613,318	28,309	886,711	550,825
1998	25,421,927	19,029,970	71,789	19,101,759	2,108,546	-9,105	16,984,108	5,795,803	2,642,016	28,664	886,909	551,211
1999	26,099,952	19,589,857	90,061	19,679,918	2,144,039	-9,383	17,526,496	5,828,212	2,745,244	29,696	878,906	546,376
2000	27,515,821	20,687,415	83,373	20,770,788	2,249,280	-11,563	18,509,945	6,088,224	2,917,652	31,388	876,629	552,871
2001	28,541,660	21,777,581	78,931	21,856,512	2,372,021	-12,269	19,472,222	5,915,661	3,153,777	32,332	882,755	549,294
2002	29,765,716	23,083,897	87,049	23,170,946	2,516,001	-12,346	20,642,599	5,729,493	3,393,624	33,427	890,473	551,443
2003	31,070,400	24,445,346	89,139	24,534,485	2,697,166	-12,801	21,824,518	5,752,804	3,493,078	34,742	894,311	561,524
2004	33,151,860	26,090,365	74,937	26,165,302	2,829,704	-13,432	23,322,166	6,125,662	3,704,032	36,511	907,997	575,830
2005	35,540,543	27,819,048	68,106	27,887,154	3,010,547	-11,568	24,865,039	6,675,896	3,999,608	38,708	918,181	587,533
2006	38,035,708	29,390,591	66,160	29,456,751	3,240,728	-10,527	26,205,496	7,608,980	4,221,232	41,033	926,954	602,446
2007	40,054,918	30,387,458	66,109	30,453,567	3,382,606	-8,539	27,062,422	8,377,856	4,614,640	43,287	925,335	614,645
2008	41,991,801	31,183,638	91,710	31,275,348	3,467,235	-8,651	27,799,462	8,845,553	5,346,786	44,975	933,680	613,203
2009	42,110,349	31,146,190	112,486	31,258,676	3,473,792	-16,761	27,768,123	8,688,351	5,653,875	44,647	943,177	598,479
2010	43,057,340	31,895,061	107,836	32,002,897	3,659,540	-21,646	28,321,711	8,424,135	6,311,494	45,024	956,320	595,786
2011	45,039,612	33,113,013	111,092	33,224,105	3,485,142	-30,546	29,708,417	8,781,173	6,550,022	46,552	967,510	603,599
2012	46,559,802	34,584,969	111,359	34,696,328	3,603,904	-35,922	31,056,502	9,035,020	6,468,280	47,593	978,295	613,464
2013	47,265,815	35,639,933	99,012	35,738,945	4,195,207	-42,059	31,501,679	9,066,247	6,697,889	47,913	986,494	625,448
2014	49,771,299	36,975,238	83,389	37,058,627	4,227,321	-44,992	32,786,314	9,798,911	7,186,074	49,343	1,008,682	634,651
2015	51,812,228	38,673,538	87,893	38,761,431	4,412,748	-47,653	34,301,030	10,060,187	7,451,011	50,923	1,017,472	648,006
2016	53,542,985	39,806,663	78,504	39,885,167	4,493,800	-50,702	35,340,665	10,495,304	7,707,016	52,296	1,023,837	657,768
2017	55,508,669	41,296,292	86,206	41,382,498	4,658,810	-51,335	36,672,353	10,835,055	8,001,261	54,279	1,022,650	659,037
2018	56,408,435	42,318,081	73,936	42,392,017	4,782,074	-50,764	37,559,179	10,715,524	8,133,732	55,214	1,021,634	658,372
2019	58,640,919	43,360,685	63,507	43,424,192	4,941,233	-50,353	38,432,606	11,710,526	8,497,787	57,560	1,018,784	644,878
2020	60,909,073	41,467,843	67,635	41,535,478	4,782,144	-53,326	36,700,008	11,559,660	12,649,405	60,114	1,013,227	584,185
2021	63,968,618	43,871,799	69,570	43,941,369	5,038,981	-49,308	38,853,080	11,740,242	13,375,296	63,912	1,000,890	600,617

Personal Income and Employment by Area: Utica-Rome, NY

(Thousands of dollars, except as noted.)

Year	Personal income, total	Earnings by place of work			Less: Contributions for government social insurance	Plus: Adjustment for residence	Equals: Net earnings by place of residence	Plus: Dividends, interest, and rent	Plus: Personal current transfer receipts	Per capita personal income (dollars)	Population (persons)	Total employment
		Nonfarm	Farm	Total								
1970	1,324,477	1,060,561	20,517	1,081,078	77,266	-17,388	986,424	197,977	140,076	3,880	341,324	144,349
1971	1,413,713	1,110,302	20,540	1,130,842	83,159	-14,307	1,033,376	212,658	167,679	4,110	343,966	142,378
1972	1,494,219	1,165,518	19,851	1,185,369	91,493	-11,875	1,082,001	226,384	185,834	4,340	344,262	140,209
1973	1,617,724	1,262,975	22,213	1,285,188	113,937	-10,573	1,160,678	250,631	206,415	4,775	338,821	143,694
1974	1,736,217	1,333,690	18,273	1,351,963	124,340	-7,833	1,219,790	279,230	237,197	5,185	334,835	143,415
1975	1,880,517	1,387,031	14,400	1,401,431	127,841	-6,472	1,267,118	304,745	308,654	5,645	333,120	138,881
1976	1,992,681	1,471,966	16,023	1,487,989	138,815	-4,516	1,344,658	322,204	325,819	6,040	329,897	137,590
1977	2,119,146	1,562,799	10,130	1,572,929	147,764	-832	1,424,333	353,200	341,613	6,482	326,942	137,404
1978	2,301,630	1,719,066	14,066	1,733,132	166,510	797	1,567,419	377,472	356,739	7,070	325,540	141,015
1979	2,512,461	1,869,017	18,552	1,887,569	187,576	4,447	1,704,440	421,200	386,821	7,762	323,689	143,203
1980	2,801,291	2,016,424	18,482	2,034,906	201,409	7,642	1,841,139	510,294	449,858	8,748	320,223	142,202
1981	3,102,660	2,182,220	18,208	2,200,428	230,838	9,522	1,979,112	610,678	512,870	9,702	319,790	141,590
1982	3,377,079	2,310,389	18,059	2,328,448	243,903	9,457	2,094,002	703,139	579,938	10,560	319,788	140,336
1983	3,571,056	2,435,840	14,724	2,450,564	259,401	11,393	2,202,556	740,821	627,679	11,147	320,361	139,924
1984	3,927,276	2,705,873	19,088	2,724,961	294,788	8,611	2,438,784	835,714	652,778	12,269	320,097	144,968
1985	4,122,627	2,841,386	24,378	2,865,764	315,513	10,654	2,560,905	871,251	690,471	12,909	319,368	145,991
1986	4,318,788	2,983,477	29,378	3,012,855	336,839	9,648	2,685,664	905,821	727,303	13,626	316,950	148,023
1987	4,507,390	3,158,965	32,302	3,191,267	351,925	8,327	2,847,669	919,382	740,339	14,254	316,211	147,894
1988	4,789,374	3,419,559	25,449	3,445,008	389,858	5,051	3,060,201	942,428	786,745	15,188	315,341	152,786
1989	5,154,461	3,587,671	34,895	3,622,566	407,575	3,896	3,218,887	1,096,372	839,202	16,307	316,088	154,516
1990	5,437,480	3,799,410	35,831	3,835,241	414,060	1,375	3,422,556	1,110,793	904,131	17,149	317,074	156,491
1991	5,559,245	3,854,658	25,501	3,880,159	431,328	7,682	3,456,513	1,111,645	991,087	17,405	319,408	153,350
1992	5,888,314	4,080,340	32,105	4,112,445	449,332	6,365	3,669,478	1,107,459	1,111,377	18,377	320,421	154,175
1993	6,037,983	4,174,443	31,784	4,206,227	464,490	8,887	3,750,624	1,128,287	1,159,072	18,892	319,608	154,382
1994	6,177,547	4,263,976	31,234	4,295,210	481,799	9,837	3,823,248	1,132,104	1,222,195	19,426	318,002	156,706
1995	6,272,749	4,271,405	22,195	4,293,600	486,686	17,729	3,824,643	1,164,304	1,283,802	20,141	311,447	154,290
1996	6,332,442	4,270,347	37,531	4,307,878	480,426	22,893	3,850,345	1,172,302	1,309,795	20,715	305,700	151,768
1997	6,560,324	4,455,754	15,591	4,471,345	494,000	22,983	4,000,328	1,230,563	1,329,433	21,674	302,681	151,824
1998	6,833,883	4,609,564	35,382	4,644,946	504,636	24,773	4,165,083	1,233,634	1,435,166	22,733	300,619	153,524
1999	7,155,083	4,961,830	40,618	5,002,448	526,643	26,403	4,502,208	1,214,018	1,438,857	23,860	299,874	157,955
2000	7,488,163	5,229,804	36,211	5,266,015	553,834	22,753	4,734,934	1,262,562	1,490,667	24,994	299,597	160,777
2001	7,574,724	5,181,478	60,450	5,241,928	574,142	27,091	4,694,877	1,280,924	1,598,923	25,374	298,521	157,591
2002	7,615,536	5,301,858	44,138	5,345,996	594,568	34,837	4,786,265	1,130,079	1,699,192	25,551	298,049	156,713
2003	7,863,984	5,479,401	50,818	5,530,219	614,890	34,142	4,949,471	1,131,924	1,782,589	26,361	298,323	156,381
2004	8,284,627	5,732,006	61,490	5,793,496	644,365	37,720	5,186,851	1,206,239	1,891,537	27,709	298,986	157,189
2005	8,465,428	5,890,978	61,122	5,952,100	671,239	40,356	5,321,217	1,178,707	1,965,504	28,353	298,574	157,620
2006	8,896,279	6,287,598	47,565	6,335,163	713,591	39,707	5,661,279	1,171,954	2,063,046	29,827	298,258	158,777
2007	9,491,485	6,659,855	44,743	6,704,598	743,320	37,537	5,998,815	1,343,201	2,149,469	31,762	298,831	160,027
2008	9,965,220	6,756,696	47,668	6,804,364	765,360	39,089	6,078,093	1,490,566	2,396,561	33,341	298,886	160,584
2009	10,185,702	6,852,029	23,935	6,875,964	764,934	52,528	6,163,558	1,399,281	2,622,863	34,066	299,000	157,597
2010	10,584,310	7,059,473	45,638	7,105,111	777,724	75,644	6,403,031	1,383,273	2,798,006	35,373	299,222	156,996
2011	10,830,596	7,055,767	64,769	7,120,536	707,828	100,629	6,513,337	1,469,181	2,848,078	36,270	298,614	155,898
2012	11,072,194	7,157,658	58,444	7,216,102	711,773	128,465	6,632,794	1,591,226	2,848,174	37,154	298,010	154,968
2013	11,151,621	7,311,974	76,300	7,388,274	817,136	155,446	6,726,584	1,542,166	2,882,871	37,515	297,258	154,538
2014	11,224,931	7,219,799	78,290	7,298,089	825,455	171,237	6,643,871	1,641,651	2,939,409	37,720	297,583	154,464
2015	11,546,631	7,385,394	37,136	7,422,530	848,441	177,285	6,751,374	1,699,991	3,095,266	39,025	295,877	154,361
2016	11,729,745	7,525,698	32,204	7,557,902	868,218	173,079	6,862,763	1,733,048	3,133,934	39,754	295,057	155,366
2017	12,315,648	7,858,516	44,416	7,902,932	906,731	183,110	7,179,311	1,802,253	3,334,084	41,779	294,784	155,808
2018	12,573,586	8,171,444	32,662	8,204,106	930,092	193,821	7,467,835	1,851,355	3,254,396	42,743	294,167	156,388
2019	13,365,935	8,595,133	54,841	8,649,974	970,321	200,349	7,880,002	1,996,388	3,489,545	45,629	292,926	156,281
2020	14,436,137	8,596,557	56,761	8,653,318	974,957	207,259	7,885,620	1,959,090	4,591,427	49,489	291,702	146,568
2021	15,357,603	9,281,725	67,650	9,349,375	1,049,702	215,091	8,514,764	2,018,407	4,824,432	52,919	290,211	149,138

Personal Income and Employment by Area: Valdosta, GA

(Thousands of dollars, except as noted.)

					Derivation of personal income							
		Earnings by place of work			Less: Contributions for government social insurance	Plus: Adjustment for residence	Equals: Net earnings by place of residence	Plus: Dividends, interest, and rent	Plus: Personal current transfer receipts	Per capita personal income (dollars)	Population (persons)	Total employment
Year	Personal income, total	Nonfarm	Farm	Total								
1970	245,043	179,555	19,547	199,102	11,387	-1,267	186,448	35,476	23,119	3,210	76,347	33,764
1971	271,673	197,873	21,745	219,618	13,112	-1,302	205,204	38,712	27,757	3,427	79,276	34,576
1972	304,782	223,945	23,089	247,034	15,309	-1,041	230,684	43,079	31,019	3,710	82,156	35,735
1973	336,050	244,220	27,018	271,238	18,758	-545	251,935	49,130	34,985	4,008	83,842	36,556
1974	374,522	263,142	32,732	295,874	21,127	-196	274,551	55,542	44,429	4,385	85,407	36,861
1975	389,535	267,730	25,892	293,622	21,582	711	272,751	61,894	54,890	4,555	85,511	35,575
1976	435,959	310,168	22,508	332,676	25,533	688	307,831	68,346	59,782	5,013	86,971	37,112
1977	464,895	345,112	6,920	352,032	28,215	1,545	325,362	76,658	62,875	5,242	88,679	38,149
1978	544,037	396,919	19,856	416,775	32,940	1,966	385,801	89,972	68,264	6,147	88,498	39,447
1979	600,913	440,089	16,711	456,800	38,008	2,005	420,797	101,181	78,935	6,641	90,486	40,040
1980	643,914	463,966	7,118	471,084	40,379	2,458	433,163	116,892	93,859	7,045	91,402	39,351
1981	731,592	510,249	16,829	527,078	47,574	1,699	481,203	139,466	110,923	7,941	92,131	40,149
1982	802,259	547,477	28,295	575,772	51,781	384	524,375	161,254	116,630	8,643	92,821	40,795
1983	853,320	594,023	15,095	609,118	56,949	1,019	553,188	173,641	126,491	9,051	94,274	42,007
1984	949,258	657,591	25,259	682,850	64,715	2,242	620,377	190,783	138,098	9,942	95,477	43,709
1985	1,019,389	711,373	25,615	736,988	71,622	1,608	666,974	203,746	148,669	10,604	96,133	44,826
1986	1,066,549	752,303	19,569	771,872	77,044	2,038	696,866	210,992	158,691	10,989	97,055	45,440
1987	1,150,168	799,885	32,496	832,381	81,333	4,833	755,881	224,802	169,485	11,753	97,863	46,586
1988	1,245,473	873,399	36,353	909,752	92,507	4,044	821,289	242,543	181,641	12,743	97,741	48,109
1989	1,358,741	945,522	37,295	982,817	100,863	-1,799	880,155	276,849	201,737	13,790	98,530	49,838
1990	1,428,007	989,328	37,252	1,026,580	106,271	-3,936	916,373	288,327	223,307	14,323	99,699	50,334
1991	1,517,159	1,039,801	45,082	1,084,883	113,106	-7,760	964,017	298,024	255,118	14,977	101,299	50,477
1992	1,627,552	1,118,863	48,259	1,167,122	120,951	-8,310	1,037,861	308,317	281,374	15,813	102,922	51,055
1993	1,722,639	1,187,933	40,102	1,228,035	129,100	-9,363	1,089,572	334,998	298,069	16,118	106,877	53,803
1994	1,847,255	1,260,115	52,868	1,312,983	137,631	-8,475	1,166,877	359,738	320,640	16,906	109,267	54,857
1995	2,011,392	1,368,451	59,701	1,428,152	147,906	-8,883	1,271,363	398,741	341,288	18,059	111,381	57,874
1996	2,121,489	1,454,549	49,757	1,504,306	155,630	-9,563	1,339,113	425,557	356,819	18,689	113,514	59,607
1997	2,249,466	1,553,060	49,694	1,602,754	164,051	-11,524	1,427,179	456,605	365,682	19,492	115,406	60,998
1998	2,382,959	1,678,265	37,090	1,715,355	174,843	-13,551	1,526,961	477,210	378,788	20,386	116,892	62,374
1999	2,487,231	1,749,804	55,911	1,805,715	180,918	-12,963	1,611,834	469,685	405,712	20,976	118,574	63,144
2000	2,607,358	1,797,444	57,645	1,855,089	185,144	-14,860	1,655,085	517,310	434,963	21,777	119,729	63,736
2001	2,721,434	1,875,355	56,674	1,932,029	193,453	-20,987	1,717,589	533,817	470,028	22,729	119,736	64,125
2002	2,872,185	2,022,883	46,192	2,069,075	208,548	-34,549	1,825,978	513,455	532,752	23,677	121,305	65,780
2003	3,007,150	2,145,532	68,695	2,214,227	218,162	-42,184	1,953,881	520,918	532,351	24,679	121,850	66,974
2004	3,140,106	2,245,924	55,037	2,300,961	236,633	-42,822	2,021,506	540,901	577,699	25,245	124,387	69,016
2005	3,335,593	2,384,000	65,486	2,449,486	249,001	-48,357	2,152,128	562,411	621,054	26,387	126,411	70,739
2006	3,453,541	2,465,930	51,267	2,517,197	264,660	-54,560	2,197,977	590,231	665,333	26,705	129,323	72,165
2007	3,655,837	2,546,257	50,252	2,596,509	270,835	-68,244	2,257,430	685,833	712,574	27,899	131,036	74,153
2008	3,863,717	2,639,300	59,804	2,699,104	297,767	-78,942	2,322,395	736,872	804,450	28,640	134,907	74,899
2009	3,905,722	2,617,913	55,121	2,673,034	295,647	-93,581	2,283,806	737,822	884,094	28,348	137,780	72,871
2010	4,083,308	2,684,231	35,893	2,720,124	300,785	-89,221	2,330,118	785,893	967,297	29,153	140,067	72,144
2011	4,281,185	2,692,936	64,012	2,756,948	271,005	-88,179	2,397,764	866,872	1,016,549	30,140	142,045	70,953
2012	4,287,856	2,800,056	49,296	2,849,352	282,378	-99,688	2,467,286	814,754	1,005,816	29,739	144,184	72,151
2013	4,345,375	2,921,489	44,158	2,965,647	321,608	-97,467	2,546,572	768,458	1,030,345	30,381	143,030	73,397
2014	4,543,562	3,048,128	25,308	3,073,436	334,160	-94,038	2,645,238	818,689	1,079,635	31,669	143,470	74,797
2015	4,718,625	3,135,950	41,825	3,177,775	341,837	-93,356	2,742,582	859,223	1,116,820	32,910	143,380	76,010
2016	4,865,786	3,204,746	38,432	3,243,178	349,120	-100,317	2,793,741	922,859	1,149,186	33,680	144,470	76,537
2017	5,034,952	3,342,289	40,140	3,382,429	363,077	-104,161	2,915,191	937,743	1,182,018	34,636	145,368	77,678
2018	5,257,064	3,546,586	22,777	3,569,363	390,514	-114,091	3,064,758	947,949	1,244,357	35,982	146,103	78,423
2019	5,465,205	3,648,632	32,513	3,681,145	406,057	-117,463	3,157,625	994,289	1,313,291	37,050	147,507	79,295
2020	5,939,845	3,690,415	52,221	3,742,636	417,317	-95,210	3,230,109	985,821	1,723,915	40,091	148,160	78,971
2021	6,351,649	3,897,597	39,467	3,937,064	436,642	-94,408	3,406,014	999,920	1,945,715	42,585	149,152	79,867

Personal Income and Employment by Area: Vallejo, CA

(Thousands of dollars, except as noted.)

Year	Personal income, total	Earnings by place of work			Less: Contributions for government social insurance	Plus: Adjustment for residence	Equals: Net earnings by place of residence	Plus: Dividends, interest, and rent	Plus: Personal current transfer receipts	Per capita personal income (dollars)	Population (persons)	Total employment
		Nonfarm	Farm	Total								
1970	786,126	668,126	24,217	692,343	33,888	-113,252	545,203	173,084	67,839	4,538	173,238	77,595
1971	873,836	725,687	25,921	751,608	39,139	-108,009	604,460	191,340	78,036	4,896	178,481	77,695
1972	959,760	763,445	32,944	796,389	43,222	-84,029	669,138	206,576	84,046	5,295	181,259	76,710
1973	1,061,626	809,775	44,398	854,173	50,016	-64,012	740,145	227,516	93,965	5,794	183,223	77,022
1974	1,215,018	900,535	62,197	962,732	56,781	-57,824	848,127	254,051	112,840	6,482	187,439	80,026
1975	1,381,732	1,031,723	47,257	1,078,980	66,472	-60,827	951,681	290,793	139,258	7,214	191,535	83,585
1976	1,522,717	1,131,899	34,330	1,166,229	74,662	-40,221	1,051,346	314,590	156,781	7,692	197,971	85,184
1977	1,709,435	1,249,162	38,937	1,288,099	83,672	-13,849	1,190,578	346,660	172,197	8,350	204,713	87,746
1978	1,964,146	1,419,020	36,523	1,455,543	96,036	10,729	1,370,236	403,397	190,513	9,195	213,619	91,583
1979	2,210,169	1,530,739	41,130	1,571,869	111,544	82,226	1,542,551	449,014	218,604	9,847	224,455	94,584
1980	2,529,292	1,610,260	77,487	1,687,747	118,844	184,347	1,753,250	515,975	260,067	10,652	237,456	98,216
1981	2,844,830	1,796,582	41,290	1,837,872	142,319	234,035	1,929,588	605,745	309,497	11,564	246,003	100,008
1982	3,126,582	1,971,178	25,536	1,996,714	157,831	278,444	2,117,327	671,555	337,700	12,293	254,348	101,168
1983	3,450,873	2,176,364	21,415	2,197,779	184,630	331,938	2,345,087	747,452	358,334	13,253	260,386	103,847
1984	3,832,150	2,377,463	37,790	2,415,253	210,800	437,176	2,641,629	813,795	376,726	14,493	264,416	107,070
1985	4,257,748	2,630,390	42,855	2,673,245	241,095	524,413	2,956,563	884,982	416,203	15,675	271,634	111,397
1986	4,653,790	2,831,161	34,113	2,865,274	267,820	666,890	3,264,344	934,929	454,517	16,409	283,617	115,639
1987	5,037,305	3,009,140	50,884	3,060,024	288,555	817,772	3,589,241	966,941	481,123	16,970	296,835	119,521
1988	5,505,874	3,248,685	53,296	3,301,981	326,793	948,077	3,923,265	1,054,540	528,069	17,758	310,048	125,976
1989	6,104,537	3,518,273	67,131	3,585,404	361,330	1,098,706	4,322,780	1,196,235	585,522	18,721	326,074	131,381
1990	6,823,378	3,796,702	48,216	3,844,918	394,409	1,486,615	4,937,124	1,233,058	653,196	19,866	343,463	136,860
1991	7,095,025	3,888,819	49,734	3,938,553	412,107	1,591,718	5,118,164	1,243,500	733,361	20,037	354,104	137,031
1992	7,490,595	4,184,805	41,478	4,226,283	444,779	1,593,732	5,375,236	1,270,735	844,624	20,812	359,919	137,870
1993	7,767,482	4,338,413	44,964	4,383,377	463,885	1,638,898	5,558,390	1,329,583	879,509	21,325	364,251	139,183
1994	7,796,480	4,153,291	52,911	4,206,202	456,410	1,785,206	5,534,998	1,369,938	891,544	21,298	366,072	141,061
1995	8,006,341	4,156,411	29,342	4,185,753	450,192	1,872,123	5,607,684	1,456,622	942,035	21,911	365,395	139,996
1996	8,331,433	4,246,464	55,611	4,302,075	449,134	1,946,414	5,799,355	1,538,722	993,356	22,664	367,608	141,128
1997	8,865,485	4,483,694	36,132	4,519,826	468,093	2,207,501	6,259,234	1,603,740	1,002,511	23,840	371,881	143,144
1998	9,490,504	4,810,758	34,332	4,845,090	497,230	2,388,106	6,735,966	1,692,074	1,062,464	25,064	378,657	146,801
1999	10,186,952	5,231,496	46,471	5,277,967	539,582	2,546,205	7,284,590	1,754,831	1,147,531	26,278	387,657	152,966
2000	11,274,240	5,902,411	39,735	5,942,146	606,221	2,909,957	8,245,882	1,834,697	1,193,661	28,400	396,974	157,624
2001	12,238,527	6,711,916	47,541	6,759,457	703,326	2,946,240	9,002,371	1,920,322	1,315,834	30,278	404,209	167,983
2002	12,633,770	7,119,584	62,943	7,182,527	754,627	2,888,712	9,316,612	1,889,708	1,427,450	30,948	408,226	172,005
2003	13,106,360	7,530,859	63,035	7,593,894	815,167	2,814,281	9,593,008	1,983,289	1,530,063	32,091	408,409	175,902
2004	13,485,746	7,844,205	66,226	7,910,431	888,104	2,877,648	9,899,975	1,968,731	1,617,040	32,948	409,301	177,452
2005	13,876,899	8,119,323	80,881	8,200,204	928,905	2,876,256	10,147,555	1,993,052	1,736,292	33,997	408,181	179,244
2006	14,626,319	8,502,068	75,857	8,577,925	943,717	3,011,150	10,645,358	2,072,116	1,908,845	35,814	408,402	180,477
2007	15,305,329	8,772,392	95,876	8,868,268	944,328	3,031,131	10,955,071	2,319,793	2,030,465	37,491	408,243	181,321
2008	15,553,067	9,022,686	121,778	9,144,464	981,201	2,602,330	10,765,593	2,462,858	2,324,616	38,030	408,972	178,995
2009	15,336,377	9,194,619	101,686	9,296,305	1,000,538	2,096,316	10,392,083	2,345,869	2,598,425	37,379	410,290	174,328
2010	15,523,758	9,372,251	83,409	9,455,660	1,001,891	1,866,020	10,319,789	2,295,722	2,908,247	37,500	413,963	172,004
2011	16,105,941	9,491,520	99,393	9,590,913	925,721	2,027,027	10,692,219	2,473,064	2,940,658	38,686	416,325	169,810
2012	16,427,187	9,840,213	138,277	9,978,490	953,511	1,880,854	10,905,833	2,563,561	2,957,793	39,145	419,645	173,409
2013	17,081,978	10,309,744	143,262	10,453,006	1,109,834	1,985,910	11,329,082	2,633,499	3,119,397	40,322	423,634	178,390
2014	17,874,569	10,709,942	151,044	10,860,986	1,158,512	1,988,748	11,691,222	2,846,145	3,337,202	41,431	431,431	182,201
2015	19,130,096	11,182,094	157,196	11,339,290	1,216,949	2,389,314	12,511,655	2,974,769	3,643,672	43,831	436,450	187,963
2016	20,203,007	11,816,138	126,564	11,942,702	1,284,756	2,593,999	13,251,945	3,104,520	3,846,542	45,652	442,544	194,197
2017	20,991,558	12,408,097	108,589	12,516,686	1,352,424	2,708,493	13,872,755	3,245,634	3,873,169	46,866	447,909	198,856
2018	21,996,412	13,118,566	104,802	13,223,368	1,446,858	2,791,962	14,568,472	3,350,408	4,077,532	48,781	450,921	204,004
2019	23,476,546	13,832,159	81,033	13,913,192	1,534,218	3,176,075	15,555,049	3,538,520	4,382,977	51,819	453,051	204,654
2020	26,474,031	13,931,488	79,077	14,010,565	1,540,560	4,094,393	16,564,398	3,576,575	6,333,058	58,406	453,274	196,403
2021	29,563,967	13,883,243	80,302	13,963,545	1,549,409	6,808,929	19,223,065	3,600,169	6,740,733	65,448	451,716	198,220

Personal Income and Employment by Area: Victoria, TX

(Thousands of dollars, except as noted.)

Year	Personal income, total	Earnings by place of work			Less: Contributions for government social insurance	Plus: Adjustment for residence	Equals: Net earnings by place of residence	Plus: Dividends, interest, and rent	Plus: Personal current transfer receipts	Per capita personal income (dollars)	Population (persons)	Total employment
		Nonfarm	Farm	Total								
1970	192,895	137,332	5,536	142,868	8,455	14,345	148,758	29,456	14,681	3,286	58,707	22,879
1971	212,966	154,479	2,694	157,173	9,867	15,898	163,204	32,801	16,961	3,570	59,656	24,144
1972	244,654	178,442	6,459	184,901	12,060	16,009	188,850	36,717	19,087	4,075	60,041	25,600
1973	272,284	193,907	10,068	203,975	15,270	18,287	206,992	41,829	23,463	4,422	61,570	26,406
1974	317,507	225,297	8,577	233,874	18,457	23,422	238,839	49,890	28,778	5,088	62,400	27,270
1975	370,669	264,375	6,762	271,137	21,345	27,103	276,895	57,988	35,786	5,789	64,032	28,572
1976	420,630	307,943	3,980	311,923	24,951	31,407	318,379	63,089	39,162	6,429	65,422	30,041
1977	469,067	347,441	-664	346,777	28,383	36,532	354,926	71,154	42,987	7,040	66,629	31,787
1978	549,409	414,129	-118	414,011	34,835	40,646	419,822	81,190	48,397	7,976	68,884	34,333
1979	643,009	471,868	10,476	482,344	41,645	53,094	493,793	93,851	55,365	8,966	71,718	35,474
1980	745,451	551,285	-5,627	545,658	49,406	61,193	557,445	121,439	66,567	9,993	74,599	37,678
1981	912,962	690,581	4,127	694,708	66,595	47,037	675,150	161,016	76,796	11,891	76,778	42,135
1982	1,002,672	731,251	-1,881	729,370	72,563	51,840	708,647	206,501	87,524	12,578	79,719	42,578
1983	1,007,915	702,531	-1,652	700,879	68,468	56,873	689,284	219,193	99,438	12,457	80,912	40,499
1984	1,082,268	749,603	-1,332	748,271	75,429	54,728	727,570	251,854	102,844	13,313	81,297	41,815
1985	1,135,975	772,260	-3,108	769,152	79,155	60,693	750,690	276,394	108,891	13,905	81,693	42,553
1986	1,115,631	725,579	-1,442	724,137	73,158	67,330	718,309	274,277	123,045	13,547	82,351	40,072
1987	1,111,571	711,764	1,204	712,968	70,983	67,750	709,735	270,834	131,002	13,704	81,112	40,743
1988	1,150,373	740,005	-1,215	738,790	76,486	70,353	732,657	280,567	137,149	14,349	80,171	40,664
1989	1,239,786	773,116	999	774,115	80,873	81,445	774,687	313,124	151,975	15,581	79,568	40,838
1990	1,355,036	838,447	3,144	841,591	85,927	93,017	848,681	341,307	165,048	16,820	80,560	41,598
1991	1,433,791	907,566	8,144	915,710	95,634	87,571	907,647	339,140	187,004	17,530	81,791	43,505
1992	1,539,494	954,385	5,790	960,175	99,325	105,461	966,311	353,943	219,240	18,480	83,304	43,216
1993	1,615,431	996,377	5,748	1,002,125	103,446	112,899	1,011,578	372,156	231,697	19,092	84,614	44,707
1994	1,667,090	1,062,588	11,512	1,074,100	111,089	116,730	1,079,741	335,675	251,674	19,408	85,899	45,882
1995	1,779,911	1,104,289	8,849	1,113,138	115,541	133,223	1,130,820	375,796	273,295	20,505	86,805	46,454
1996	1,890,636	1,176,643	-8,717	1,167,926	121,381	154,777	1,201,322	397,654	291,660	21,511	87,891	47,280
1997	1,974,213	1,252,358	1,174	1,253,532	128,314	131,455	1,256,673	413,549	303,991	22,276	88,626	48,767
1998	2,142,869	1,382,813	-8,938	1,373,875	138,921	146,342	1,381,296	454,786	306,787	23,809	90,004	49,732
1999	2,224,438	1,411,915	13,270	1,425,185	141,770	150,462	1,433,877	467,023	323,538	24,505	90,775	49,907
2000	2,420,600	1,574,579	5,872	1,580,451	154,011	161,108	1,587,548	493,763	339,289	26,616	90,944	51,226
2001	2,598,933	1,732,070	2,103	1,734,173	166,877	142,688	1,709,984	519,340	369,609	28,400	91,511	51,590
2002	2,606,966	1,771,258	2,542	1,773,800	170,843	122,319	1,725,276	482,909	398,781	28,453	91,624	51,457
2003	2,661,832	1,750,288	18,578	1,768,866	173,945	107,226	1,702,147	530,314	429,371	28,993	91,809	50,721
2004	2,773,383	1,829,171	19,596	1,848,767	182,530	97,744	1,763,981	558,658	450,744	30,215	91,789	50,878
2005	2,999,064	2,000,031	16,971	2,017,002	196,313	94,629	1,915,318	595,025	488,721	32,768	91,523	52,340
2006	3,251,127	2,254,366	13,467	2,267,833	212,540	66,821	2,122,114	608,779	520,234	35,474	91,649	54,220
2007	3,325,618	2,247,186	3,736	2,250,922	220,032	69,331	2,100,221	655,490	569,907	35,990	92,403	55,480
2008	3,615,565	2,485,517	-22,047	2,463,470	233,430	50,983	2,281,023	705,376	629,166	38,908	92,926	56,275
2009	3,269,221	2,191,291	-23,729	2,167,562	220,328	46,733	1,993,967	589,023	686,231	34,856	93,792	53,860
2010	3,488,953	2,359,256	-13,501	2,345,755	233,812	52,052	2,163,995	582,037	742,921	37,076	94,102	53,878
2011	3,777,199	2,530,737	-16,040	2,514,697	220,913	44,399	2,338,183	666,365	772,651	39,857	94,768	54,885
2012	4,139,520	2,799,571	-13,489	2,786,082	240,611	2,528	2,547,999	824,960	766,561	42,917	96,453	57,444
2013	4,373,731	3,002,734	5,618	3,008,352	289,604	-23,887	2,694,861	893,021	785,849	44,845	97,529	59,159
2014	4,698,261	3,137,332	-1,024	3,136,308	301,157	-23,020	2,812,131	1,056,375	829,755	47,939	98,004	59,764
2015	4,569,391	2,943,135	1,756	2,944,891	296,879	26,449	2,674,461	998,559	896,371	46,169	98,972	59,892
2016	4,248,827	2,642,262	-6,996	2,635,266	279,137	75,678	2,431,807	872,417	944,603	42,859	99,135	57,433
2017	4,459,831	2,660,652	-6,568	2,654,084	285,099	80,798	2,449,783	1,040,501	969,547	45,215	98,636	57,585
2018	4,732,964	2,801,252	-9,950	2,791,302	298,135	110,002	2,603,169	1,121,440	1,008,355	48,124	98,350	58,369
2019	5,219,882	3,153,992	-3,404	3,150,588	314,331	167,773	3,004,030	1,165,642	1,050,210	53,029	98,434	57,856
2020	5,311,571	2,898,471	-2,360	2,896,111	297,228	248,645	2,847,528	1,121,335	1,342,708	54,067	98,241	55,064
2021	5,720,257	3,061,336	1,646	3,062,982	309,517	247,294	3,000,759	1,200,103	1,519,395	58,294	98,127	55,783

Personal Income and Employment by Area: Vineland-Bridgeton, NJ

(Thousands of dollars, except as noted.)

Year	Personal income, total	Earnings by place of work — Nonfarm	Farm	Total	Less: Contributions for government social insurance	Plus: Adjustment for residence	Equals: Net earnings by place of residence	Plus: Dividends, interest, and rent	Plus: Personal current transfer receipts	Per capita personal income (dollars)	Population (persons)	Total employment
1970	484,498	403,917	13,534	417,451	32,316	-7,091	378,044	54,022	52,432	3,961	122,309	58,153
1971	525,214	436,580	11,888	448,468	36,077	-9,770	402,621	59,956	62,637	4,143	126,773	58,260
1972	577,162	483,794	11,364	495,158	41,580	-15,010	438,568	66,635	71,959	4,473	129,031	60,730
1973	639,905	539,214	15,511	554,725	52,807	-19,435	482,483	76,995	80,427	4,894	130,746	62,667
1974	693,446	569,549	16,967	586,516	58,025	-22,032	506,459	87,503	99,484	5,202	133,306	61,865
1975	741,572	588,557	12,184	600,741	57,976	-27,571	515,194	93,345	133,033	5,520	134,350	58,858
1976	814,288	656,021	13,483	669,504	65,587	-34,083	569,834	100,486	143,968	6,016	135,359	60,950
1977	883,666	721,598	10,309	731,907	72,390	-37,815	621,702	111,782	150,182	6,537	135,184	61,741
1978	974,644	797,603	16,199	813,802	82,460	-37,034	694,308	120,413	159,923	7,240	134,615	62,802
1979	1,053,511	859,076	14,331	873,407	91,655	-39,914	741,838	132,006	179,667	7,864	133,966	63,029
1980	1,159,936	930,866	10,718	941,584	99,041	-48,923	793,620	161,323	204,993	8,716	133,088	64,876
1981	1,286,517	987,809	15,914	1,003,723	112,078	-40,414	851,231	197,953	237,333	9,621	133,726	63,534
1982	1,388,387	1,018,669	18,554	1,037,223	115,731	-21,940	899,552	226,777	262,058	10,400	133,494	61,162
1983	1,482,063	1,067,533	21,825	1,089,358	124,197	-13,436	951,725	247,902	282,436	11,186	132,497	61,559
1984	1,591,639	1,127,441	20,777	1,148,218	136,595	4,636	1,016,259	275,117	300,263	11,866	134,138	60,966
1985	1,692,975	1,196,725	22,782	1,219,507	144,627	17,146	1,092,026	291,934	309,015	12,533	135,083	61,704
1986	1,809,164	1,314,468	23,603	1,338,071	160,475	-4,859	1,172,737	312,042	324,385	13,332	135,700	63,622
1987	1,929,349	1,436,793	26,414	1,463,207	174,087	-19,104	1,270,016	324,086	335,247	14,187	135,995	65,766
1988	2,108,069	1,580,646	29,398	1,610,044	195,349	-14,684	1,400,011	348,696	359,362	15,436	136,569	67,638
1989	2,310,681	1,684,014	30,139	1,714,153	205,544	-15,063	1,493,546	425,260	391,875	16,759	137,881	68,023
1990	2,471,644	1,766,771	32,104	1,798,875	208,842	5,960	1,595,993	443,790	431,861	17,863	138,366	68,415
1991	2,554,847	1,799,297	33,009	1,832,306	217,177	-8,213	1,606,916	447,010	500,921	18,184	140,503	66,700
1992	2,740,973	1,902,369	38,743	1,941,112	227,537	2,177	1,715,752	438,789	586,432	19,313	141,921	67,268
1993	2,817,022	1,948,757	45,932	1,994,689	232,762	9,289	1,771,216	444,673	601,133	19,654	143,334	65,632
1994	2,879,171	2,035,465	50,870	2,086,335	245,727	-3,880	1,836,728	445,873	596,570	19,919	144,544	66,357
1995	2,961,425	2,121,108	49,193	2,170,301	255,416	-59,915	1,854,970	481,087	625,368	20,448	144,829	67,555
1996	3,036,571	2,194,100	49,380	2,243,480	263,686	-75,045	1,904,749	496,901	634,921	20,880	145,430	68,018
1997	3,193,119	2,321,683	44,188	2,365,871	272,780	-70,490	2,022,601	528,136	642,382	21,899	145,811	68,540
1998	3,262,540	2,397,366	50,612	2,447,978	278,371	-81,618	2,087,989	536,508	638,043	22,358	145,924	68,962
1999	3,348,910	2,459,441	34,542	2,493,983	281,849	-46,881	2,165,253	520,805	662,852	22,892	146,293	69,065
2000	3,476,178	2,565,271	52,183	2,617,454	296,482	-72,413	2,248,559	534,155	693,464	23,767	146,263	70,953
2001	3,686,857	2,709,981	43,670	2,753,651	312,103	-65,386	2,376,162	547,403	763,292	25,175	146,451	71,167
2002	3,887,567	2,821,686	47,241	2,868,927	321,545	-78,563	2,468,819	549,979	868,769	26,393	147,294	71,224
2003	4,012,112	2,978,433	48,464	3,026,897	334,284	-107,824	2,584,789	566,819	860,504	27,029	148,437	72,417
2004	4,117,994	3,174,412	51,537	3,225,949	360,163	-135,988	2,729,798	541,491	846,705	27,483	149,837	74,740
2005	4,273,201	3,313,415	52,635	3,366,050	384,995	-157,448	2,823,607	515,847	933,747	28,109	152,022	77,027
2006	4,500,710	3,401,093	70,231	3,471,324	395,545	-109,403	2,966,376	513,140	1,021,194	29,345	153,371	76,975
2007	4,678,668	3,473,912	78,791	3,552,703	417,027	-117,641	3,018,035	593,366	1,067,267	30,285	154,489	76,637
2008	4,919,808	3,548,420	73,969	3,622,389	431,345	-137,452	3,053,592	675,180	1,191,036	31,590	155,738	76,080
2009	5,045,718	3,558,578	71,277	3,629,855	431,173	-156,439	3,042,243	662,222	1,341,253	32,235	156,531	74,699
2010	5,202,228	3,589,921	67,512	3,657,433	434,002	-146,341	3,077,090	654,309	1,470,829	33,206	156,667	73,816
2011	5,340,097	3,606,085	61,844	3,667,929	398,126	-142,339	3,127,464	710,702	1,501,931	34,007	157,028	73,477
2012	5,298,878	3,672,664	75,686	3,748,350	400,911	-237,083	3,110,356	712,872	1,475,650	33,781	156,862	73,239
2013	5,297,812	3,700,111	67,482	3,767,593	449,890	-198,989	3,118,714	694,662	1,484,436	33,980	155,912	73,794
2014	5,450,247	3,871,817	65,732	3,937,549	466,554	-279,600	3,191,395	709,565	1,549,287	34,292	158,937	74,280
2015	5,611,940	3,964,650	85,643	4,050,293	478,923	-292,787	3,278,583	741,104	1,592,253	35,447	158,321	74,531
2016	5,673,418	4,057,695	87,474	4,145,169	488,536	-371,820	3,284,813	753,783	1,634,822	36,040	157,420	75,672
2017	5,799,281	4,111,312	80,502	4,191,814	500,981	-332,267	3,358,566	773,920	1,666,795	37,123	156,217	75,496
2018	5,938,092	4,223,832	72,309	4,296,141	510,686	-362,850	3,422,605	800,497	1,714,990	38,060	156,020	75,696
2019	6,217,937	4,366,856	101,693	4,468,549	525,603	-334,516	3,608,430	846,651	1,762,856	40,014	155,394	76,018
2020	6,745,296	4,470,327	93,058	4,563,385	542,184	-431,992	3,589,209	850,197	2,305,890	43,844	153,848	73,399
2021	7,306,345	4,707,692	87,643	4,795,335	574,681	-423,797	3,796,857	867,287	2,642,201	47,559	153,627	76,174

Personal Income and Employment by Area: Virginia Beach-Norfolk-Newport News, VA-NC

(Thousands of dollars, except as noted.)

Year	Personal income, total	Derivation of personal income								Per capita personal income (dollars)	Population (persons)	Total employment
		Earnings by place of work			Less: Contributions for government social insurance	Plus: Adjustment for residence	Equals: Net earnings by place of residence	Plus: Dividends, interest, and rent	Plus: Personal current transfer receipts			
		Nonfarm	Farm	Total								
1970	4,631,568	3,765,653	21,017	3,786,670	217,484	-34,970	3,534,216	841,903	255,449	4,211	1,099,964	535,553
1971	5,070,040	4,122,410	13,745	4,136,155	250,128	-44,665	3,841,362	916,802	311,876	4,554	1,113,297	536,524
1972	5,602,009	4,582,873	28,147	4,611,020	289,659	-86,292	4,235,069	1,002,748	364,192	5,024	1,114,977	549,094
1973	6,221,222	5,076,358	42,099	5,118,457	355,467	-98,188	4,664,802	1,127,750	428,670	5,468	1,137,655	573,774
1974	6,916,687	5,608,583	31,439	5,640,022	410,330	-113,318	5,116,374	1,292,501	507,812	5,973	1,157,946	590,240
1975	7,430,141	5,919,741	35,620	5,955,361	443,770	-94,139	5,417,452	1,380,705	631,984	6,371	1,166,228	578,056
1976	8,067,566	6,450,780	31,692	6,482,472	495,932	-113,858	5,872,682	1,493,043	701,841	6,843	1,178,977	588,816
1977	8,898,113	7,129,921	14,563	7,144,484	551,779	-122,601	6,470,104	1,679,667	748,342	7,430	1,197,552	610,259
1978	10,045,421	7,989,913	22,154	8,012,067	618,009	-135,923	7,258,135	1,966,582	820,704	8,302	1,209,942	637,636
1979	11,022,930	8,696,173	-626	8,695,547	702,054	-93,955	7,899,538	2,184,368	939,024	9,115	1,209,282	645,753
1980	12,481,756	9,690,704	-131	9,690,573	773,379	-115,906	8,801,288	2,553,233	1,127,235	10,259	1,216,639	656,174
1981	14,208,440	10,933,720	31,032	10,964,752	928,769	-122,904	9,913,079	3,002,500	1,292,861	11,446	1,241,360	663,306
1982	15,539,134	11,935,088	15,869	11,950,957	1,015,746	-145,433	10,789,778	3,365,104	1,384,252	12,436	1,249,538	669,437
1983	16,758,217	12,958,037	-2,463	12,955,574	1,156,992	-146,867	11,651,715	3,615,308	1,491,194	13,084	1,280,795	689,339
1984	18,481,594	14,279,452	32,938	14,312,390	1,318,729	-149,142	12,844,519	4,056,608	1,580,467	14,130	1,307,970	721,529
1985	19,896,728	15,500,393	23,121	15,523,514	1,477,408	-148,996	13,897,110	4,319,070	1,680,548	15,068	1,320,458	753,916
1986	21,389,038	16,729,048	32,703	16,761,751	1,654,924	-146,468	14,960,359	4,649,763	1,778,916	15,803	1,353,468	782,672
1987	22,843,422	17,966,930	37,185	18,004,115	1,788,218	-146,358	16,069,539	4,920,394	1,853,489	16,400	1,392,921	817,041
1988	24,520,501	19,195,737	51,267	19,247,004	1,987,597	-129,439	17,129,968	5,404,773	1,985,760	17,271	1,419,734	833,888
1989	26,185,314	20,094,442	54,124	20,148,566	2,112,351	-110,005	17,926,210	6,009,519	2,249,585	18,227	1,436,650	848,379
1990	27,468,768	21,150,271	68,270	21,218,541	2,260,118	-110,888	18,847,535	6,184,250	2,436,983	18,811	1,460,246	860,162
1991	28,771,977	22,101,438	58,239	22,159,677	2,392,283	-113,677	19,653,717	6,375,784	2,742,476	19,535	1,472,822	849,974
1992	30,524,355	23,358,188	64,619	23,422,807	2,534,931	-113,236	20,774,640	6,682,514	3,067,201	20,273	1,505,656	854,326
1993	31,780,342	24,088,657	55,054	24,143,711	2,632,264	-107,017	21,404,430	7,088,441	3,287,471	20,813	1,526,947	862,226
1994	32,968,610	24,798,281	71,222	24,869,503	2,735,453	-100,591	22,033,459	7,426,358	3,508,793	21,453	1,536,791	865,351
1995	34,232,622	25,388,033	59,147	25,447,180	2,787,760	-93,195	22,566,225	7,873,491	3,792,906	22,169	1,544,193	880,792
1996	35,707,978	26,347,512	70,365	26,417,877	2,893,712	-80,463	23,443,702	8,229,948	4,034,328	23,016	1,551,433	896,189
1997	37,463,915	27,715,639	47,100	27,762,739	3,041,480	-64,216	24,657,043	8,657,295	4,149,577	24,067	1,556,639	910,489
1998	40,320,284	29,768,442	49,787	29,818,229	3,234,876	113,798	26,697,151	9,261,516	4,361,617	25,351	1,590,459	936,593
1999	42,257,570	31,420,208	31,975	31,452,183	3,413,083	137,681	28,176,781	9,457,512	4,623,277	26,391	1,601,182	946,312
2000	45,235,512	33,520,125	64,045	33,584,170	3,588,064	168,550	30,164,656	10,150,329	4,920,527	27,966	1,617,490	966,195
2001	47,589,076	35,558,479	54,599	35,613,078	3,814,926	149,408	31,947,560	10,191,885	5,449,631	29,263	1,626,238	969,615
2002	49,852,428	37,767,106	62,434	37,829,540	4,056,238	115,524	33,888,826	10,191,970	5,771,632	30,376	1,641,177	980,621
2003	53,382,005	40,617,222	89,745	40,706,967	4,327,692	42,133	36,421,408	10,726,583	6,234,014	32,358	1,649,748	991,565
2004	57,003,855	43,863,196	86,894	43,950,090	4,680,112	56,188	39,326,166	11,069,979	6,607,710	33,996	1,676,784	1,012,270
2005	59,734,976	45,871,515	122,776	45,994,291	4,935,984	40,217	41,098,524	11,376,712	7,259,740	35,470	1,684,092	1,027,668
2006	63,691,199	48,322,644	101,524	48,424,168	5,282,291	27,411	43,169,288	12,640,195	7,881,716	37,430	1,701,595	1,040,751
2007	66,673,175	50,187,007	77,364	50,264,371	5,488,719	-15,766	44,759,886	13,561,565	8,351,724	39,212	1,700,315	1,056,031
2008	68,289,907	50,351,417	79,757	50,431,174	5,598,544	-13,822	44,818,808	13,967,913	9,503,186	40,181	1,699,574	1,048,115
2009	67,296,678	49,474,041	78,263	49,552,304	5,582,225	-51,562	43,918,517	13,170,615	10,207,546	39,460	1,705,438	1,014,458
2010	69,243,605	50,378,286	36,215	50,414,501	5,681,577	-23,300	44,709,624	13,239,691	11,294,290	40,326	1,717,110	1,004,002
2011	71,995,096	51,082,462	91,987	51,174,449	5,209,946	4,909	45,969,412	14,242,229	11,783,455	41,771	1,723,560	1,005,801
2012	74,520,773	52,689,808	99,270	52,789,078	5,372,913	-10,270	47,405,895	15,198,185	11,916,693	42,957	1,734,772	1,009,951
2013	74,535,530	53,156,782	94,754	53,251,536	6,113,888	-44,302	47,093,346	15,042,084	12,400,100	42,780	1,742,287	1,017,874
2014	77,302,345	54,886,936	40,871	54,927,807	6,294,985	-29,906	48,602,916	15,782,029	12,917,400	43,904	1,760,700	1,025,950
2015	80,471,034	56,983,034	9,697	56,992,731	6,570,197	3,248	50,425,782	16,502,918	13,542,334	45,505	1,768,411	1,043,348
2016	82,435,844	58,055,592	12,639	58,068,231	6,674,639	-102,713	51,290,879	17,125,031	14,019,934	46,478	1,773,651	1,068,493
2017	84,734,581	59,450,037	60,387	59,510,424	6,912,330	-91,946	52,506,148	17,688,365	14,540,068	47,653	1,778,159	1,080,299
2018	85,233,899	59,444,592	34,485	59,479,077	6,937,107	-10,179	52,531,791	17,427,641	15,274,467	47,782	1,783,825	1,075,615
2019	88,826,123	61,317,835	74,783	61,392,618	7,181,041	-61,844	54,149,733	18,445,664	16,230,726	49,553	1,792,551	1,073,921
2020	95,214,995	62,711,062	51,826	62,762,888	7,367,011	-49,405	55,346,472	18,287,832	21,580,691	52,895	1,800,081	1,052,236
2021	102,277,363	67,219,759	92,108	67,311,867	7,779,829	-57,774	59,474,264	18,524,827	24,278,272	56,716	1,803,328	1,078,444

Personal Income and Employment by Area: Visalia, CA

(Thousands of dollars, except as noted.)

Year	Personal income, total	Earnings by place of work			Less: Contributions for government social insurance	Plus: Adjustment for residence	Equals: Net earnings by place of residence	Plus: Dividends, interest, and rent	Plus: Personal current transfer receipts	Per capita personal income (dollars)	Population (persons)	Total employment
		Nonfarm	Farm	Total								
1970	699,055	410,591	113,102	523,693	27,938	1,858	497,613	97,445	103,997	3,695	189,191	81,225
1971	759,398	446,047	118,462	564,509	31,161	4,700	538,048	106,076	115,274	3,912	194,103	83,183
1972	861,181	505,311	143,143	648,454	37,201	7,775	619,028	118,886	123,267	4,357	197,643	89,111
1973	1,020,924	566,337	211,175	777,512	47,547	11,363	741,328	140,922	138,674	5,059	201,805	91,598
1974	1,185,031	648,329	253,948	902,277	56,373	14,459	860,363	160,357	164,311	5,736	206,589	97,440
1975	1,262,161	714,896	194,072	908,968	59,288	21,780	871,460	183,453	207,248	5,922	213,115	99,934
1976	1,413,389	824,027	204,721	1,028,748	69,111	26,081	985,718	197,010	230,661	6,450	219,123	102,675
1977	1,555,218	915,051	222,287	1,137,338	78,662	32,469	1,091,145	220,503	243,570	6,884	225,906	106,394
1978	1,774,904	1,052,271	246,952	1,299,223	91,196	38,648	1,246,675	255,512	272,717	7,610	233,220	109,228
1979	2,100,902	1,204,960	351,225	1,556,185	108,994	50,324	1,497,515	301,669	301,718	8,751	240,074	117,964
1980	2,324,712	1,285,930	361,928	1,647,858	115,101	60,098	1,592,855	372,398	359,459	9,396	247,426	119,326
1981	2,447,435	1,375,354	265,166	1,640,520	136,230	61,089	1,565,379	451,566	430,490	9,647	253,694	119,692
1982	2,638,801	1,425,669	327,810	1,753,479	143,597	63,921	1,673,803	505,769	459,229	10,159	259,759	117,129
1983	2,712,227	1,552,814	208,208	1,761,022	159,089	64,313	1,666,246	556,934	489,047	10,157	267,034	121,911
1984	2,983,245	1,681,661	259,756	1,941,417	177,839	70,674	1,834,252	619,016	529,977	10,917	273,255	120,368
1985	3,151,598	1,786,509	249,829	2,036,338	190,837	73,833	1,919,334	640,221	592,043	11,256	280,000	122,160
1986	3,369,613	1,949,924	260,994	2,210,918	212,024	74,431	2,073,325	657,563	638,725	11,791	285,767	125,690
1987	3,721,174	2,106,553	422,426	2,528,979	228,316	83,172	2,383,835	678,098	659,241	12,755	291,752	128,885
1988	3,978,308	2,259,473	433,579	2,693,052	254,392	99,515	2,538,175	731,215	708,918	13,347	298,075	133,959
1989	4,240,546	2,433,210	375,302	2,808,512	278,996	115,458	2,644,974	814,547	781,025	13,929	304,451	137,419
1990	4,685,596	2,717,905	437,819	3,155,724	306,040	125,083	2,974,767	836,994	873,835	14,919	314,062	140,864
1991	4,808,049	2,837,075	311,785	3,148,860	319,523	135,047	2,964,384	851,136	992,529	14,853	323,705	141,436
1992	5,357,044	3,097,244	510,977	3,608,221	350,019	125,590	3,383,792	833,147	1,140,105	16,138	331,956	146,844
1993	5,506,271	3,194,774	458,402	3,653,176	360,441	133,508	3,426,243	880,502	1,199,526	16,231	339,253	150,060
1994	5,771,675	3,386,870	495,073	3,881,943	377,809	134,560	3,638,694	913,908	1,219,073	16,697	345,668	153,457
1995	5,895,436	3,523,729	413,330	3,937,059	386,456	138,778	3,689,381	941,219	1,264,836	16,935	348,127	155,994
1996	6,353,185	3,669,333	628,641	4,297,974	385,374	141,640	4,054,240	975,818	1,323,127	18,114	350,732	158,687
1997	6,476,071	3,747,098	654,039	4,401,137	391,212	141,737	4,151,662	1,017,745	1,306,664	18,245	354,946	158,454
1998	6,901,222	4,109,319	656,977	4,766,296	414,688	140,557	4,492,165	1,028,821	1,380,236	19,178	359,854	165,685
1999	7,175,557	4,313,745	642,330	4,956,075	437,788	143,212	4,661,499	1,041,785	1,472,273	19,675	364,708	169,627
2000	7,377,639	4,601,963	528,037	5,130,000	470,265	151,558	4,811,293	1,074,594	1,491,752	20,014	368,627	172,135
2001	8,082,021	4,890,120	742,896	5,633,016	534,088	194,836	5,293,764	1,118,216	1,670,041	21,658	373,171	168,668
2002	8,307,379	5,249,121	497,990	5,747,111	585,513	255,171	5,416,769	1,103,444	1,787,166	21,886	379,568	175,312
2003	9,006,153	5,595,007	597,167	6,192,174	629,385	329,044	5,891,833	1,191,744	1,922,576	23,167	388,743	174,975
2004	9,940,211	5,871,948	1,092,667	6,964,615	685,657	406,348	6,685,306	1,207,790	2,047,115	24,961	398,226	173,719
2005	10,473,140	6,202,000	1,206,896	7,408,896	734,983	456,394	7,130,307	1,209,081	2,133,752	25,671	407,970	177,770
2006	10,820,149	6,862,367	561,261	7,423,628	772,820	508,976	7,159,784	1,357,348	2,303,017	26,078	414,921	182,695
2007	12,323,476	7,182,636	1,252,488	8,435,124	790,614	593,914	8,238,424	1,591,877	2,493,175	29,193	422,140	189,082
2008	12,323,825	7,190,001	916,530	8,106,531	814,165	680,792	7,973,158	1,582,223	2,768,444	28,708	429,283	188,438
2009	12,112,142	7,106,171	570,876	7,677,047	807,308	641,443	7,511,182	1,544,573	3,056,387	27,717	436,987	182,825
2010	13,310,629	7,603,832	904,940	8,508,772	808,099	656,486	8,357,159	1,549,051	3,404,419	30,050	442,953	183,319
2011	14,150,421	7,841,638	1,312,638	9,154,276	761,987	681,383	9,073,672	1,663,629	3,413,120	31,677	446,709	184,762
2012	14,225,218	7,611,123	1,347,840	8,958,963	752,619	706,934	8,913,278	1,851,632	3,460,308	31,638	449,625	183,669
2013	14,557,034	7,880,429	1,463,603	9,344,032	863,889	680,321	9,160,464	1,791,379	3,605,191	32,187	452,259	190,415
2014	16,039,135	8,213,060	2,182,428	10,395,488	894,153	724,950	10,226,285	1,959,840	3,853,010	35,110	456,831	192,830
2015	16,456,292	8,823,543	1,523,316	10,346,859	949,849	697,498	10,094,508	2,145,708	4,216,076	35,834	459,243	200,368
2016	17,254,966	9,492,810	1,434,116	10,926,926	1,032,392	765,106	10,659,640	2,239,221	4,356,105	37,354	461,926	205,208
2017	17,787,787	9,728,809	1,767,438	11,496,247	1,065,702	863,400	11,293,945	2,256,145	4,237,697	38,212	465,503	207,008
2018	17,930,743	10,052,922	1,448,201	11,501,123	1,108,649	835,566	11,228,040	2,272,525	4,430,178	38,297	468,208	210,316
2019	18,835,476	10,456,702	1,481,048	11,937,750	1,176,608	918,104	11,679,246	2,421,601	4,734,629	40,061	470,173	212,280
2020	21,581,526	10,939,053	1,618,787	12,557,840	1,228,976	992,209	12,321,073	2,444,564	6,815,889	45,556	473,736	206,345
2021	22,891,980	11,590,984	1,302,927	12,893,911	1,316,573	1,023,583	12,600,921	2,515,383	7,775,676	47,986	477,054	213,428

Personal Income and Employment by Area: Waco, TX

(Thousands of dollars, except as noted.)

Year	Personal income, total	Earnings by place of work Nonfarm	Earnings by place of work Farm	Earnings by place of work Total	Less: Contributions for government social insurance	Plus: Adjustment for residence	Equals: Net earnings by place of residence	Plus: Dividends, interest, and rent	Plus: Personal current transfer receipts	Per capita personal income (dollars)	Population (persons)	Total employment
1970	556,788	421,624	11,223	432,847	26,930	1,428	407,345	86,733	62,710	3,374	165,008	72,540
1971	604,157	455,737	9,907	465,644	29,812	1,120	436,952	95,878	71,327	3,608	167,456	73,644
1972	668,055	507,739	9,600	517,339	34,736	907	483,510	105,689	78,856	3,907	170,979	77,099
1973	761,836	563,169	28,280	591,449	44,501	489	547,437	120,794	93,605	4,380	173,928	79,469
1974	828,262	617,405	6,428	623,833	50,124	185	573,894	141,911	112,457	4,678	177,057	80,372
1975	934,111	669,292	12,442	681,734	52,795	310	629,249	164,773	140,089	5,302	176,185	79,429
1976	1,049,382	773,660	12,136	785,796	61,837	-972	722,987	177,920	148,475	5,834	179,868	83,034
1977	1,133,212	847,726	194	847,920	68,812	-1,575	777,533	198,232	157,447	6,250	181,301	85,832
1978	1,284,680	970,655	2,092	972,747	80,694	-2,014	890,039	221,252	173,389	7,000	183,520	88,769
1979	1,431,169	1,085,036	2,361	1,087,397	95,001	-4,345	988,051	247,705	195,413	7,672	186,539	90,348
1980	1,617,123	1,195,746	-661	1,195,085	105,683	-5,599	1,083,803	307,123	226,197	8,537	189,416	92,112
1981	1,818,774	1,317,972	12,322	1,330,294	126,025	-9,249	1,195,020	370,701	253,053	9,487	191,717	93,873
1982	2,003,861	1,407,335	6,866	1,414,201	135,902	-7,916	1,270,383	456,893	276,585	10,331	193,961	94,587
1983	2,193,890	1,539,032	7,796	1,546,828	148,539	-6,674	1,391,615	502,779	299,496	11,099	197,671	96,325
1984	2,409,574	1,690,499	22,318	1,712,817	167,904	-9,820	1,535,093	561,664	312,817	12,059	199,820	100,053
1985	2,576,494	1,783,022	29,299	1,812,321	179,818	-12,354	1,620,149	621,703	334,642	12,805	201,204	101,927
1986	2,654,560	1,824,159	25,818	1,849,977	182,776	-17,300	1,649,901	642,681	361,978	12,976	204,568	100,542
1987	2,651,786	1,792,364	30,248	1,822,612	178,822	-18,166	1,625,624	644,389	381,773	12,966	204,519	101,805
1988	2,749,355	1,893,556	27,381	1,920,937	195,827	-19,777	1,705,333	641,034	402,988	13,454	204,348	103,130
1989	2,897,045	1,958,589	33,052	1,991,641	206,703	-21,540	1,763,398	701,713	431,934	14,096	205,516	103,364
1990	3,049,548	2,098,466	24,028	2,122,494	216,081	-19,173	1,887,240	685,999	476,309	14,698	207,477	104,832
1991	3,225,341	2,236,682	36,439	2,273,121	235,256	-23,614	2,014,251	689,207	521,883	15,393	209,531	107,920
1992	3,402,219	2,394,686	33,751	2,428,437	250,109	-29,044	2,149,284	662,451	590,484	16,103	211,278	109,069
1993	3,611,902	2,581,587	40,623	2,622,210	269,179	-31,655	2,321,376	668,242	622,284	16,847	214,400	112,112
1994	3,861,905	2,796,847	46,152	2,842,999	295,041	-33,603	2,514,355	687,755	659,795	17,644	218,877	115,322
1995	4,135,452	3,013,308	30,004	3,043,312	319,809	-38,197	2,685,306	749,402	700,744	18,702	221,128	119,892
1996	4,312,932	3,147,003	6,873	3,153,876	331,015	-36,693	2,786,168	789,059	737,705	19,212	224,497	121,857
1997	4,568,589	3,371,454	27,792	3,399,246	350,842	-38,400	3,010,004	794,315	764,270	20,165	226,561	124,685
1998	4,817,562	3,592,665	6,001	3,598,666	371,044	-41,010	3,186,612	853,261	777,689	21,088	228,450	126,949
1999	5,068,431	3,819,677	22,805	3,842,482	394,309	-43,412	3,404,761	863,903	799,767	22,025	230,120	129,275
2000	5,273,679	3,907,251	14,886	3,922,137	399,654	-37,797	3,484,686	937,880	851,113	22,684	232,489	130,926
2001	5,525,371	4,075,820	4,333	4,080,153	414,449	-58,924	3,606,780	989,601	928,990	23,676	233,379	130,991
2002	5,691,372	4,253,113	17,972	4,271,085	432,736	-82,698	3,755,651	922,937	1,012,784	24,254	234,661	131,509
2003	6,048,929	4,535,858	34,529	4,570,387	469,662	-115,422	3,985,303	979,447	1,084,179	25,541	236,830	133,443
2004	6,240,849	4,738,597	41,396	4,779,993	489,904	-130,409	4,159,680	953,060	1,128,109	26,067	239,419	135,175
2005	6,574,146	4,930,807	32,276	4,963,083	513,706	-154,656	4,294,721	1,050,600	1,228,825	27,303	240,784	137,127
2006	6,866,951	5,133,679	22,651	5,156,330	526,320	-173,285	4,456,725	1,109,092	1,301,134	28,329	242,397	138,958
2007	7,194,066	5,283,593	22,215	5,305,808	550,436	-190,457	4,564,915	1,206,337	1,422,814	29,429	244,453	141,938
2008	7,531,117	5,400,050	-1,076	5,398,974	566,342	-207,913	4,624,719	1,316,707	1,589,691	30,523	246,735	142,371
2009	7,585,375	5,466,666	-16,101	5,450,565	586,036	-215,316	4,649,213	1,225,626	1,710,536	30,409	249,441	141,710
2010	8,041,379	5,743,728	10,026	5,753,754	613,119	-220,631	4,920,004	1,249,708	1,871,667	31,684	253,799	141,538
2011	8,409,440	5,861,075	5,549	5,866,624	552,580	-217,992	5,096,052	1,386,076	1,927,312	32,888	255,700	142,734
2012	8,764,409	6,124,162	19,283	6,143,445	573,231	-225,155	5,345,059	1,503,632	1,915,718	34,111	256,941	144,437
2013	8,930,668	6,313,158	33,853	6,347,011	665,104	-221,253	5,460,654	1,511,195	1,958,819	34,523	258,691	147,085
2014	9,381,546	6,627,212	17,013	6,644,225	692,244	-210,163	5,741,818	1,597,527	2,042,201	35,975	260,780	149,882
2015	9,895,302	6,935,082	56,731	6,991,813	732,937	-219,731	6,039,145	1,675,950	2,180,207	37,601	263,166	152,210
2016	10,165,447	7,245,820	12,475	7,258,295	779,348	-251,725	6,227,222	1,659,339	2,278,886	38,299	265,424	156,954
2017	10,679,869	7,620,456	-5,787	7,614,669	823,770	-262,345	6,528,554	1,814,951	2,336,364	39,606	269,651	160,315
2018	11,185,460	8,013,194	-16,856	7,996,338	856,372	-277,858	6,862,108	1,874,222	2,449,130	41,093	272,201	163,190
2019	11,624,428	8,260,299	-11,807	8,248,492	876,120	-265,751	7,106,621	1,960,383	2,557,424	42,235	275,230	163,070
2020	12,641,900	8,654,603	-2,790	8,651,813	923,846	-288,203	7,439,764	1,940,933	3,261,203	45,477	277,984	162,181
2021	13,783,247	9,343,660	9,353	9,353,013	999,401	-320,491	8,033,121	2,026,884	3,723,242	49,151	280,428	169,780

Personal Income and Employment by Area: Walla Walla, WA

(Thousands of dollars, except as noted.)

Year	Personal income, total	Earnings by place of work			Less: Contributions for government social insurance	Plus: Adjustment for residence	Equals: Net earnings by place of residence	Plus: Dividends, interest, and rent	Plus: Personal current transfer receipts	Per capita personal income (dollars)	Population (persons)	Total employment
		Nonfarm	Farm	Total								
1970	190,553	122,938	24,354	147,292	9,432	-6,062	131,798	37,377	21,378	4,092	46,570	21,692
1971	201,097	131,729	21,337	153,066	10,491	-6,483	136,092	41,263	23,742	4,325	46,500	21,679
1972	231,438	143,852	34,890	178,742	12,046	-6,484	160,212	45,536	25,690	4,917	47,071	22,024
1973	283,216	155,778	66,895	222,673	15,114	-6,305	201,254	52,910	29,052	6,034	46,936	22,869
1974	300,911	174,294	58,480	232,774	17,652	-7,056	208,066	58,724	34,121	6,379	47,175	24,001
1975	334,380	195,750	58,327	254,077	19,834	-7,280	226,963	66,254	41,163	6,874	48,641	24,622
1976	360,085	229,818	49,542	279,360	23,958	-10,582	244,820	70,742	44,523	7,329	49,130	25,952
1977	378,174	250,902	34,556	285,458	26,377	-9,890	249,191	81,491	47,492	7,668	49,317	25,164
1978	431,213	290,543	42,100	332,643	31,794	-12,000	288,849	90,556	51,808	8,752	49,269	26,012
1979	486,594	354,177	37,504	391,681	40,942	-25,313	325,426	102,239	58,929	9,683	50,254	28,027
1980	554,630	377,239	54,672	431,911	43,582	-25,621	362,708	122,236	69,686	10,751	51,590	27,566
1981	603,113	391,147	52,133	443,280	48,085	-15,597	379,598	146,883	76,632	11,623	51,889	27,391
1982	615,887	398,711	38,482	437,193	49,100	-18,508	369,585	163,264	83,038	11,669	52,781	26,940
1983	685,863	421,205	73,447	494,652	52,897	-23,797	417,958	178,627	89,278	12,913	53,114	27,297
1984	703,053	451,013	57,500	508,513	58,895	-31,524	418,094	190,331	94,628	13,305	52,843	27,723
1985	699,352	451,512	37,594	489,106	59,562	-32,401	397,143	199,228	102,981	13,322	52,495	27,577
1986	720,538	450,531	56,754	507,285	60,087	-33,827	413,371	199,088	108,079	13,799	52,215	27,147
1987	712,423	455,621	49,384	505,005	60,730	-35,496	408,779	191,179	112,465	13,792	51,656	26,419
1988	732,799	485,852	46,905	532,757	67,137	-41,104	424,516	188,770	119,513	14,270	51,354	26,831
1989	782,321	517,682	38,851	556,533	71,142	-46,787	438,604	215,518	128,199	14,980	52,223	27,198
1990	827,292	547,234	58,122	605,356	77,088	-50,163	478,105	211,218	137,969	15,742	52,554	28,459
1991	870,339	584,204	46,526	630,730	82,212	-53,073	495,445	217,090	157,804	16,105	54,041	28,184
1992	943,078	643,429	48,250	691,679	90,070	-57,042	544,567	224,322	174,189	17,165	54,941	28,961
1993	1,018,390	682,540	77,839	760,379	96,268	-58,258	605,853	230,204	182,333	18,063	56,381	29,896
1994	1,042,115	728,767	51,427	780,194	102,548	-58,005	619,641	235,355	187,119	18,186	57,303	31,079
1995	1,089,502	747,274	55,885	803,159	106,284	-59,426	637,449	254,092	197,961	18,819	57,895	31,720
1996	1,194,761	774,112	106,840	880,952	107,087	-61,188	712,677	272,219	209,865	20,498	58,287	31,769
1997	1,198,235	799,912	69,057	868,969	106,719	-60,656	701,594	283,372	213,269	20,477	58,515	32,279
1998	1,175,207	798,648	78,191	876,839	104,784	-64,377	707,678	259,044	208,485	21,537	54,566	30,029
1999	1,201,201	825,604	80,504	906,108	105,861	-64,447	735,800	245,995	219,406	21,917	54,806	30,136
2000	1,324,609	874,076	138,254	1,012,330	114,259	-69,042	829,029	261,036	234,544	24,006	55,178	30,960
2001	1,383,119	924,245	131,367	1,055,612	120,929	-74,690	859,993	270,660	252,466	25,115	55,072	31,490
2002	1,368,965	966,155	102,900	1,069,055	125,961	-75,404	867,690	238,581	262,694	24,592	55,666	31,744
2003	1,451,276	1,012,923	134,541	1,147,464	132,774	-82,265	932,425	245,797	273,054	25,866	56,108	32,161
2004	1,515,117	1,067,272	112,397	1,179,669	139,540	-78,754	961,375	266,888	286,854	26,744	56,652	32,019
2005	1,560,399	1,106,125	102,880	1,209,005	142,573	-77,071	989,361	266,869	304,169	27,584	56,569	31,930
2006	1,633,673	1,144,068	101,833	1,245,901	148,713	-78,807	1,018,381	290,193	325,099	28,810	56,705	32,237
2007	1,787,886	1,204,705	109,447	1,314,152	157,052	-75,078	1,082,022	355,352	350,512	31,455	56,840	32,619
2008	1,962,209	1,270,768	127,853	1,398,621	167,486	-76,358	1,154,777	414,435	392,997	34,236	57,315	33,951
2009	1,944,266	1,290,191	125,217	1,415,408	173,792	-86,817	1,154,799	364,075	425,392	33,462	58,103	33,663
2010	2,020,837	1,345,306	136,910	1,482,216	180,904	-99,818	1,201,494	353,005	466,338	34,301	58,915	33,864
2011	2,115,236	1,358,218	162,714	1,520,932	165,891	-102,898	1,252,143	394,407	468,686	35,579	59,452	33,717
2012	2,197,982	1,405,153	186,003	1,591,156	167,399	-123,848	1,299,909	424,682	473,391	37,039	59,342	34,107
2013	2,247,457	1,442,212	189,261	1,631,473	188,215	-137,708	1,305,550	458,359	483,548	37,844	59,387	34,752
2014	2,320,940	1,491,092	151,454	1,642,546	198,429	-145,525	1,298,592	488,364	533,984	38,638	60,069	35,334
2015	2,436,156	1,513,657	229,211	1,742,868	202,332	-139,360	1,401,176	494,661	540,319	40,188	60,619	35,106
2016	2,482,373	1,581,497	192,022	1,773,519	209,916	-153,647	1,409,956	505,250	567,167	40,769	60,888	35,499
2017	2,601,221	1,643,689	183,165	1,826,854	221,839	-152,132	1,452,883	564,736	583,602	42,233	61,592	35,671
2018	2,700,687	1,738,201	137,511	1,875,712	229,120	-164,776	1,481,816	600,907	617,964	43,690	61,815	36,395
2019	2,892,687	1,808,617	167,039	1,975,656	233,365	-164,362	1,577,929	652,291	662,467	46,483	62,231	36,814
2020	3,161,236	1,918,735	207,808	2,126,543	252,224	-185,263	1,689,056	652,546	819,634	50,520	62,574	36,523
2021	3,375,142	2,039,262	164,108	2,203,370	269,711	-179,111	1,754,548	668,554	952,040	53,845	62,682	37,606

Personal Income and Employment by Area: Warner Robins, GA

(Thousands of dollars, except as noted.)

Year	Personal income, total	Earnings by place of work			Less: Contributions for government social insurance	Plus: Adjustment for residence	Equals: Net earnings by place of residence	Plus: Dividends, interest, and rent	Plus: Personal current transfer receipts	Per capita personal income (dollars)	Population (persons)	Total employment
		Nonfarm	Farm	Total								
1970	366,122	409,513	8,740	418,253	13,918	-123,053	281,282	65,626	19,214	4,174	87,709	50,074
1971	408,075	447,605	12,977	460,582	15,605	-133,940	311,037	73,889	23,149	4,492	90,839	49,359
1972	436,008	472,844	12,390	485,234	17,126	-135,975	332,133	77,782	26,093	4,688	93,008	48,562
1973	487,062	503,763	22,145	525,908	20,801	-134,696	370,411	86,724	29,927	5,180	94,022	49,211
1974	540,715	548,797	19,024	567,821	24,984	-137,744	405,093	98,137	37,485	5,611	96,373	50,280
1975	586,437	587,044	13,946	600,990	28,511	-143,165	429,314	108,059	49,064	5,969	98,251	49,765
1976	626,424	616,336	15,433	631,769	31,081	-143,918	456,770	113,595	56,059	6,290	99,591	49,403
1977	690,363	691,461	9,667	701,128	34,496	-161,994	504,638	127,969	57,756	6,849	100,792	50,158
1978	761,719	735,658	13,054	748,712	37,615	-160,494	550,603	148,260	62,856	7,434	102,471	51,101
1979	830,324	780,301	16,258	796,559	42,341	-158,126	596,092	162,078	72,154	7,953	104,400	50,783
1980	901,792	817,438	3,229	820,667	46,563	-144,870	629,234	186,377	86,181	8,499	106,108	51,799
1981	1,029,848	928,540	12,003	940,543	54,760	-175,152	710,631	219,784	99,433	9,578	107,518	51,524
1982	1,133,328	1,001,297	17,051	1,018,348	59,939	-182,945	775,464	250,936	106,928	10,486	108,084	52,289
1983	1,228,269	1,073,660	9,749	1,083,409	73,789	-175,622	833,998	275,708	118,563	11,266	109,024	53,163
1984	1,347,051	1,142,036	21,412	1,163,448	80,165	-169,354	913,929	304,661	128,461	12,321	109,327	54,057
1985	1,446,030	1,219,061	18,046	1,237,107	92,824	-163,325	980,958	324,480	140,592	13,052	110,786	56,151
1986	1,537,551	1,258,975	14,747	1,273,722	101,092	-130,378	1,042,252	345,939	149,360	13,695	112,267	58,757
1987	1,617,734	1,277,400	16,142	1,293,542	106,204	-92,016	1,095,322	365,072	157,340	14,207	113,865	59,213
1988	1,754,762	1,364,897	22,354	1,387,251	120,056	-80,847	1,186,348	396,666	171,748	15,104	116,176	60,188
1989	1,904,642	1,468,685	17,675	1,486,360	133,814	-81,057	1,271,489	444,358	188,795	16,208	117,510	62,194
1990	2,052,215	1,548,193	18,200	1,566,393	145,230	-34,293	1,386,870	454,541	210,804	17,236	119,068	62,862
1991	2,151,765	1,582,829	31,245	1,614,074	152,283	-11,055	1,450,736	459,141	241,888	17,806	120,842	61,259
1992	2,308,851	1,714,958	31,823	1,746,781	165,576	-19,025	1,562,180	472,845	273,826	18,706	123,430	63,510
1993	2,425,955	1,769,513	30,667	1,800,180	174,589	2,472	1,628,063	506,663	291,229	19,236	126,114	65,146
1994	2,534,774	1,817,581	36,603	1,854,184	182,434	32,092	1,703,842	521,466	309,466	19,582	129,441	67,590
1995	2,712,195	1,934,818	30,847	1,965,665	194,686	33,385	1,804,364	575,773	332,058	20,709	130,968	69,161
1996	2,852,993	2,100,951	32,238	2,133,189	211,457	-40,015	1,881,717	610,598	360,678	21,375	133,473	70,825
1997	3,036,095	2,169,042	36,736	2,205,778	219,440	28,464	2,014,802	649,560	371,733	22,203	136,742	70,836
1998	3,000,418	2,219,785	16,665	2,236,450	221,200	-11,532	2,003,718	643,556	353,144	23,063	130,098	66,900
1999	3,202,709	2,381,998	30,381	2,412,379	236,659	-8,958	2,166,762	656,382	379,565	24,160	132,564	69,607
2000	3,382,088	2,549,062	23,349	2,572,411	253,750	-49,834	2,268,827	704,766	408,495	25,022	135,165	71,651
2001	3,634,430	2,652,388	22,203	2,674,591	269,898	-65,406	2,339,287	835,161	459,982	26,433	137,495	72,479
2002	3,892,126	2,904,376	13,002	2,917,378	296,135	-105,683	2,515,560	856,918	519,648	27,651	140,759	74,711
2003	4,156,751	3,113,010	22,264	3,135,274	314,537	-127,461	2,693,276	921,343	542,132	28,868	143,991	76,633
2004	4,339,678	3,293,988	23,995	3,317,983	341,478	-101,324	2,875,181	864,698	599,799	29,215	148,541	78,887
2005	4,635,536	3,530,232	30,846	3,561,078	363,895	-149,173	3,048,010	909,950	677,576	30,708	150,957	81,310
2006	4,936,905	3,759,170	29,327	3,788,497	394,438	-143,897	3,250,162	948,663	738,080	31,957	154,488	84,881
2007	5,230,716	3,923,646	36,726	3,960,372	410,974	-210,079	3,339,319	1,073,666	817,731	32,931	158,840	87,884
2008	5,482,795	3,995,986	25,258	4,021,244	439,280	-181,376	3,400,588	1,125,405	956,802	33,814	162,144	87,686
2009	5,623,295	4,104,401	15,187	4,119,588	453,177	-167,917	3,498,494	1,089,009	1,035,792	34,103	164,890	87,915
2010	5,855,681	4,256,456	15,431	4,271,887	470,440	-199,537	3,601,910	1,103,035	1,150,736	34,748	168,518	88,120
2011	6,201,421	4,373,531	27,696	4,401,227	430,299	-206,150	3,764,778	1,228,094	1,208,549	36,141	171,588	89,964
2012	6,293,136	4,426,878	23,907	4,450,785	439,727	-150,122	3,860,936	1,214,977	1,217,223	36,242	173,642	90,144
2013	6,347,098	4,436,004	28,734	4,464,738	494,342	-91,425	3,878,971	1,210,467	1,257,660	36,318	174,763	90,844
2014	6,596,515	4,543,863	27,487	4,571,350	504,659	-46,542	4,020,149	1,250,353	1,326,013	37,174	177,448	91,015
2015	6,912,407	4,648,573	33,284	4,681,857	513,680	32,238	4,200,415	1,315,272	1,396,720	38,740	178,433	92,171
2016	7,060,900	4,770,244	35,852	4,806,096	523,233	-11,892	4,270,971	1,345,574	1,444,355	39,046	180,835	93,176
2017	7,345,284	4,936,192	33,546	4,969,738	540,191	9,675	4,439,222	1,407,825	1,498,237	40,184	182,792	95,920
2018	7,637,963	5,163,784	10,900	5,174,684	573,859	10,614	4,611,439	1,439,745	1,586,779	41,092	185,876	98,954
2019	8,019,431	5,447,632	23,376	5,471,008	613,393	-30,185	4,827,430	1,505,727	1,686,274	42,458	188,877	102,460
2020	8,634,761	5,579,688	28,217	5,607,905	633,196	-25,113	4,949,596	1,478,631	2,206,534	44,908	192,277	102,604
2021	9,402,997	5,925,008	16,529	5,941,537	667,738	45,124	5,318,923	1,499,306	2,584,768	48,160	195,246	104,991

Personal Income and Employment by Area: Washington-Arlington-Alexandria, DC-VA-MD-WV

(Thousands of dollars, except as noted.)

		Derivation of personal income										
		Earnings by place of work			Less: Contributions for government social insurance	Plus: Adjustment for residence	Equals: Net earnings by place of residence	Plus: Dividends, interest, and rent	Plus: Personal current transfer receipts	Per capita personal income (dollars)	Population (persons)	Total employment
Year	Personal income, total	Nonfarm	Farm	Total								
1970	18,456,145	15,141,213	52,568	15,193,781	704,394	-28,237	14,461,150	3,246,936	748,059	5,813	3,174,781	1,635,996
1971	20,676,146	16,912,680	49,559	16,962,239	808,830	-163,226	15,990,183	3,772,386	913,577	6,404	3,228,473	1,676,874
1972	22,662,316	18,630,071	58,485	18,688,556	947,358	-271,953	17,469,245	4,126,351	1,066,720	6,872	3,297,994	1,728,072
1973	24,725,061	20,419,543	73,303	20,492,846	1,196,263	-380,342	18,916,241	4,554,701	1,254,119	7,453	3,317,553	1,785,895
1974	26,831,815	22,060,989	67,726	22,128,715	1,351,827	-511,475	20,265,413	5,077,117	1,489,285	8,060	3,329,115	1,820,202
1975	29,317,020	24,086,863	68,138	24,155,001	1,487,015	-688,584	21,979,402	5,476,024	1,861,594	8,738	3,354,959	1,837,675
1976	31,917,402	26,449,003	60,804	26,509,807	1,662,192	-851,275	23,996,340	5,927,432	1,993,630	9,459	3,374,253	1,868,791
1977	34,718,667	28,857,657	51,386	28,909,043	1,803,153	-1,027,224	26,078,666	6,540,710	2,099,291	10,265	3,382,257	1,919,713
1978	38,518,855	31,979,266	76,692	32,055,958	2,036,249	-1,283,659	28,736,050	7,515,406	2,267,399	11,291	3,411,506	2,000,343
1979	42,282,522	35,313,258	66,343	35,379,601	2,375,856	-1,649,706	31,354,039	8,364,883	2,563,600	12,368	3,418,637	2,061,280
1980	47,261,506	39,172,468	35,403	39,207,871	2,686,930	-1,989,981	34,530,960	9,754,485	2,976,061	13,727	3,442,968	2,096,829
1981	52,603,506	43,047,241	47,051	43,094,292	3,213,061	-2,175,626	37,705,605	11,459,972	3,437,929	15,024	3,501,294	2,118,775
1982	57,215,050	46,163,891	47,919	46,211,810	3,515,595	-2,242,044	40,454,171	12,922,283	3,838,596	16,146	3,543,649	2,120,432
1983	61,618,257	50,304,496	31,998	50,336,494	4,169,707	-2,316,507	43,850,280	13,631,361	4,136,616	17,136	3,595,901	2,185,742
1984	68,928,319	56,424,173	56,621	56,480,794	4,861,572	-2,558,620	49,060,602	15,408,629	4,459,088	18,769	3,672,371	2,319,314
1985	75,265,030	62,386,684	60,316	62,447,000	5,659,496	-2,787,613	53,999,891	16,597,282	4,667,857	20,056	3,752,795	2,449,391
1986	81,771,968	68,264,256	48,469	68,312,725	6,454,387	-2,812,904	59,045,434	17,805,898	4,920,636	21,259	3,846,429	2,578,468
1987	88,812,637	74,888,210	89,065	74,977,275	7,153,219	-3,037,137	64,786,919	18,869,833	5,155,885	22,497	3,947,690	2,713,726
1988	98,431,905	83,495,150	94,210	83,589,360	8,218,254	-3,330,391	72,040,715	20,842,337	5,548,853	24,330	4,045,716	2,823,319
1989	106,704,485	89,630,618	102,175	89,732,793	9,009,577	-3,543,839	77,179,377	23,592,716	5,932,392	25,889	4,121,547	2,898,376
1990	112,607,747	94,300,436	131,341	94,431,777	9,662,767	-3,611,204	81,157,806	24,950,082	6,499,859	26,983	4,173,328	2,930,896
1991	117,535,609	97,939,651	113,861	98,053,512	10,123,347	-3,579,333	84,350,832	25,920,639	7,264,138	27,753	4,235,129	2,864,621
1992	124,539,864	103,909,280	123,863	104,033,143	10,726,831	-3,756,515	89,549,797	26,766,598	8,223,469	28,962	4,300,061	2,851,903
1993	130,881,356	108,784,282	106,267	108,890,549	11,272,824	-3,996,860	93,620,865	28,488,669	8,771,822	30,005	4,362,043	2,898,087
1994	137,436,260	113,878,182	98,371	113,976,553	12,021,474	-4,250,159	97,704,920	30,509,855	9,221,485	31,080	4,422,005	2,933,968
1995	143,635,847	118,192,157	67,105	118,259,262	12,527,592	-4,305,816	101,425,854	32,507,071	9,702,922	32,089	4,476,203	2,984,951
1996	150,790,779	123,797,951	99,792	123,897,743	13,123,240	-4,598,986	106,175,517	34,190,675	10,424,587	33,236	4,536,908	3,030,891
1997	160,279,601	132,208,230	65,157	132,273,387	14,084,603	-5,055,591	113,133,193	36,471,637	10,674,771	34,828	4,602,056	3,098,310
1998	174,162,029	144,571,029	75,296	144,646,325	15,113,473	-5,299,571	124,233,281	38,517,099	11,411,649	37,176	4,684,826	3,176,675
1999	188,372,210	157,849,275	58,800	157,908,075	16,430,681	-5,003,730	136,473,664	39,892,185	12,006,361	39,441	4,776,083	3,262,572
2000	207,729,994	175,137,624	103,556	175,241,180	17,971,619	-5,824,200	151,445,361	43,425,234	12,859,399	42,603	4,875,923	3,409,145
2001	218,472,698	186,652,055	60,643	186,712,698	19,321,639	-6,363,499	161,027,560	43,341,352	14,103,786	43,844	4,982,993	3,471,970
2002	224,129,710	192,862,288	55,331	192,917,619	20,081,714	-6,778,600	166,057,305	42,763,783	15,308,622	44,219	5,068,667	3,508,592
2003	236,017,477	203,968,010	39,810	204,007,820	21,127,541	-7,575,748	175,304,531	44,415,523	16,297,423	45,940	5,137,498	3,562,232
2004	254,557,270	222,655,411	52,952	222,708,363	23,008,104	-8,526,258	191,174,001	46,300,927	17,082,342	48,833	5,212,772	3,659,629
2005	272,261,197	236,737,541	35,103	236,772,644	24,454,549	-9,846,962	202,471,133	51,298,035	18,492,029	51,499	5,286,683	3,745,027
2006	288,469,574	246,930,676	-4,428	246,926,248	25,950,559	-10,146,602	210,829,087	58,104,734	19,535,753	54,100	5,332,180	3,810,723
2007	302,920,911	256,397,289	-11,948	256,385,341	27,134,618	-10,957,737	218,292,986	63,481,455	21,146,470	56,239	5,386,334	3,884,536
2008	316,569,975	265,103,766	36,093	265,139,859	28,516,051	-10,809,018	225,814,790	66,026,100	24,729,085	57,997	5,458,415	3,901,443
2009	313,976,183	267,995,292	46,486	268,041,778	29,037,745	-10,231,123	228,772,910	58,770,258	26,433,015	56,458	5,561,253	3,861,064
2010	331,887,262	283,431,097	39,187	283,470,284	30,342,194	-10,322,957	242,805,133	59,376,996	29,705,133	58,444	5,678,733	3,878,945
2011	354,736,151	296,511,147	74,771	296,585,918	27,914,015	-10,017,511	258,654,392	64,995,356	31,086,403	61,333	5,783,752	3,946,247
2012	368,914,542	304,475,892	130,913	304,606,805	28,712,130	-9,027,489	266,867,186	70,828,104	31,219,252	62,726	5,881,329	3,996,916
2013	365,075,657	304,463,447	139,668	304,603,115	33,056,083	-8,358,642	263,188,390	69,202,951	32,684,316	61,187	5,966,559	4,052,929
2014	380,636,065	313,394,569	84,960	313,479,529	33,923,436	-8,085,867	271,470,226	74,798,496	34,367,343	62,788	6,062,230	4,106,510
2015	400,559,152	328,922,944	28,758	328,951,702	35,494,311	-8,118,805	285,338,586	78,859,822	36,360,744	65,331	6,131,237	4,198,656
2016	416,127,318	341,238,925	29,897	341,268,822	36,447,045	-8,326,497	296,495,280	81,310,042	38,321,996	67,186	6,193,671	4,288,812
2017	430,437,049	352,333,076	80,952	352,414,028	38,053,235	-8,710,807	305,649,986	85,252,392	39,534,671	68,734	6,262,402	4,353,044
2018	447,533,616	365,133,133	35,868	365,169,001	39,796,194	-9,007,978	316,364,829	89,467,103	41,701,684	70,956	6,307,186	4,436,454
2019	463,844,190	375,163,682	121,192	375,284,874	41,185,958	-10,278,162	323,820,754	95,692,230	44,331,206	72,992	6,354,713	4,455,262
2020	486,013,570	380,539,634	69,938	380,609,572	41,845,241	-10,588,936	328,175,395	94,721,342	63,116,833	76,110	6,385,714	4,329,721
2021	513,737,735	405,168,548	68,549	405,237,097	43,939,641	-12,418,811	348,878,645	97,041,091	67,817,999	80,822	6,356,434	4,422,856

Personal Income and Employment by Area: Waterloo-Cedar Falls, IA

(Thousands of dollars, except as noted.)

Year	Personal income, total	Earnings by place of work — Nonfarm	Earnings by place of work — Farm	Earnings by place of work — Total	Less: Contributions for government social insurance	Plus: Adjustment for residence	Equals: Net earnings by place of residence	Plus: Dividends, interest, and rent	Plus: Personal current transfer receipts	Per capita personal income (dollars)	Population (persons)	Total employment
1970	631,415	496,061	35,859	531,920	37,991	-21,117	472,812	100,737	57,866	3,717	169,857	76,398
1971	669,022	528,899	31,473	560,372	42,010	-23,504	494,858	109,180	64,984	3,929	170,283	75,817
1972	750,312	598,609	41,420	640,029	50,161	-27,391	562,477	118,889	68,946	4,424	169,595	77,925
1973	875,548	686,373	75,857	762,230	66,689	-33,698	661,843	134,288	79,417	5,146	170,158	83,267
1974	962,897	778,027	57,856	835,883	78,109	-39,889	717,885	152,724	92,288	5,658	170,178	85,777
1975	1,071,099	848,307	57,985	906,292	83,427	-43,798	779,067	172,278	119,754	6,264	170,987	85,435
1976	1,145,694	931,895	30,969	962,864	93,158	-47,159	822,547	188,543	134,604	6,660	172,038	86,484
1977	1,324,233	1,095,686	43,267	1,138,953	109,026	-60,399	969,528	214,651	140,054	7,664	172,797	91,066
1978	1,465,258	1,196,354	63,010	1,259,364	123,198	-67,283	1,068,883	240,315	156,060	8,401	174,425	92,582
1979	1,631,641	1,367,338	44,440	1,411,778	146,711	-82,044	1,183,023	273,851	174,767	9,329	174,893	95,443
1980	1,797,821	1,482,169	25,363	1,507,532	157,952	-91,002	1,258,578	331,689	207,554	10,147	177,172	95,288
1981	1,991,937	1,591,253	43,789	1,635,042	180,524	-98,235	1,356,283	404,391	231,263	11,262	176,866	93,456
1982	2,010,653	1,526,437	21,280	1,547,717	175,724	-89,730	1,282,263	452,358	276,032	11,460	175,444	88,697
1983	2,022,857	1,495,488	7,816	1,503,304	172,475	-82,639	1,248,190	474,244	300,423	11,633	173,893	86,524
1984	2,134,211	1,537,846	43,108	1,580,954	182,588	-83,309	1,315,057	519,539	299,615	12,438	171,586	85,792
1985	2,122,895	1,487,405	54,212	1,541,617	177,760	-75,214	1,288,643	518,556	315,696	12,709	167,036	82,930
1986	2,104,171	1,435,407	64,674	1,500,081	174,139	-65,159	1,260,783	514,864	328,524	12,970	162,232	80,235
1987	2,214,195	1,583,943	73,411	1,657,354	189,558	-80,814	1,386,982	499,498	327,715	13,930	158,953	82,491
1988	2,312,787	1,734,101	37,231	1,771,332	214,527	-94,259	1,462,546	511,388	338,853	14,709	157,238	85,872
1989	2,513,231	1,862,570	49,619	1,912,189	228,634	-104,546	1,579,009	569,322	364,900	15,899	158,077	88,775
1990	2,656,280	1,975,942	77,466	2,053,408	247,888	-113,194	1,692,326	569,837	394,117	16,703	159,026	91,900
1991	2,731,177	2,049,012	60,370	2,109,382	258,477	-114,774	1,736,131	573,253	421,793	17,018	160,489	93,283
1992	2,936,419	2,207,451	97,406	2,304,857	276,257	-125,233	1,903,367	577,140	455,912	18,209	161,261	94,400
1993	2,985,513	2,304,823	37,991	2,342,814	290,568	-129,605	1,922,641	578,883	483,989	18,406	162,204	95,937
1994	3,200,337	2,436,477	101,977	2,538,454	310,239	-134,712	2,093,503	602,316	504,518	19,707	162,400	96,870
1995	3,358,848	2,514,548	96,559	2,611,107	321,199	-136,956	2,152,952	673,743	532,153	20,687	162,363	99,104
1996	3,545,672	2,590,608	137,663	2,728,271	314,415	-142,065	2,271,791	717,462	556,419	21,751	163,010	100,755
1997	3,767,333	2,800,781	133,009	2,933,790	351,772	-156,766	2,425,252	774,639	567,442	23,126	162,902	103,664
1998	3,891,395	2,923,632	94,253	3,017,885	362,878	-159,969	2,495,038	801,624	594,733	23,824	163,342	105,588
1999	3,883,883	2,929,520	68,012	2,997,532	360,657	-155,316	2,481,559	787,046	615,278	23,752	163,516	104,942
2000	4,142,510	3,113,872	79,850	3,193,722	379,427	-172,992	2,641,303	851,781	649,426	25,306	163,699	106,241
2001	4,248,493	3,222,353	71,601	3,293,954	391,863	-187,299	2,714,792	822,327	711,374	25,970	163,590	104,894
2002	4,403,313	3,324,902	69,946	3,394,848	402,805	-200,665	2,791,378	833,872	778,063	27,075	162,634	104,571
2003	4,486,758	3,434,290	48,325	3,482,615	421,569	-212,256	2,848,790	857,007	780,961	27,630	162,388	104,473
2004	4,843,570	3,729,062	134,205	3,863,267	450,396	-232,538	3,180,333	855,513	807,724	29,753	162,793	106,240
2005	4,994,261	3,872,173	115,908	3,988,081	468,528	-249,057	3,270,496	872,199	851,566	30,591	163,260	107,311
2006	5,265,743	4,041,154	78,427	4,119,581	485,519	-265,211	3,368,851	968,691	928,201	32,113	163,976	108,753
2007	5,579,030	4,250,996	109,346	4,360,342	512,911	-290,868	3,556,563	1,048,081	974,386	33,954	164,310	110,709
2008	5,918,490	4,467,086	106,624	4,573,710	543,435	-305,329	3,724,946	1,112,119	1,081,425	35,713	165,724	111,092
2009	5,902,540	4,502,955	69,260	4,572,215	548,073	-318,822	3,705,320	1,051,531	1,145,689	35,297	167,225	110,044
2010	6,062,114	4,604,270	89,541	4,693,811	562,605	-331,530	3,799,676	1,041,781	1,220,657	36,100	167,924	109,771
2011	6,507,802	4,771,931	220,905	4,992,836	529,388	-361,314	4,102,134	1,144,952	1,260,716	38,631	168,459	111,902
2012	6,826,769	5,093,980	178,682	5,272,662	552,887	-394,889	4,324,886	1,257,305	1,244,578	40,433	168,840	113,816
2013	6,796,072	5,152,193	202,513	5,354,706	626,996	-402,901	4,324,809	1,200,536	1,270,727	40,003	169,891	114,449
2014	7,012,355	5,318,089	108,673	5,426,762	635,818	-397,202	4,393,742	1,281,002	1,337,611	41,122	170,526	114,668
2015	7,159,405	5,329,662	74,309	5,403,971	627,778	-400,297	4,375,896	1,374,394	1,409,115	41,879	170,956	113,809
2016	7,153,216	5,347,754	36,144	5,383,898	648,362	-391,890	4,343,646	1,366,900	1,442,670	42,008	170,282	113,024
2017	7,346,637	5,518,556	54,740	5,573,296	673,978	-409,049	4,490,269	1,422,552	1,433,816	43,348	169,479	112,676
2018	7,764,474	5,767,887	64,234	5,832,121	712,731	-431,003	4,688,387	1,519,644	1,556,443	45,915	169,107	114,083
2019	7,896,733	5,805,242	57,123	5,862,365	725,070	-428,395	4,708,900	1,552,980	1,634,853	46,856	168,532	112,834
2020	8,451,642	5,909,141	67,906	5,977,047	753,047	-423,038	4,800,962	1,563,282	2,087,398	50,228	168,266	108,962
2021	8,991,122	6,227,612	203,139	6,430,751	783,122	-447,669	5,199,960	1,588,853	2,202,309	53,584	167,796	110,878

Personal Income and Employment by Area: Watertown-Fort Drum, NY

(Thousands of dollars, except as noted.)

Year	Personal income, total	Earnings by place of work			Less: Contributions for government social insurance	Plus: Adjustment for residence	Equals: Net earnings by place of residence	Plus: Dividends, interest, and rent	Plus: Personal current transfer receipts	Per capita personal income (dollars)	Population (persons)	Total employment
		Nonfarm	Farm	Total								
1970	313,911	233,051	13,226	246,277	17,886	1,332	229,723	45,347	38,841	3,535	88,789	36,388
1971	337,120	246,280	12,704	258,984	19,170	1,792	241,606	48,706	46,808	3,758	89,719	36,058
1972	354,161	258,045	12,596	270,641	21,020	1,164	250,785	52,350	51,026	3,902	90,773	36,058
1973	380,658	276,641	13,293	289,934	25,710	778	265,002	59,177	56,479	4,215	90,310	37,049
1974	412,204	297,281	10,516	307,797	28,471	-117	279,209	65,940	67,055	4,606	89,485	36,947
1975	450,975	315,477	7,626	323,103	29,592	-2,074	291,437	71,618	87,920	4,998	90,235	36,272
1976	480,436	336,374	10,448	346,822	32,046	-2,902	311,874	74,391	94,171	5,309	90,488	35,746
1977	507,630	360,887	5,744	366,631	34,443	-3,299	328,889	82,069	96,672	5,635	90,089	36,188
1978	560,769	406,740	10,688	417,428	39,685	-4,915	372,828	86,264	101,677	6,255	89,651	37,470
1979	617,790	453,821	11,220	465,041	45,747	-7,239	412,055	98,175	107,560	6,929	89,161	38,283
1980	686,675	493,802	8,382	502,184	49,402	-9,568	443,214	117,560	125,901	7,797	88,071	37,483
1981	749,470	527,057	7,048	534,105	55,388	-10,967	467,750	139,585	142,135	8,557	87,585	36,896
1982	824,343	555,255	9,497	564,752	58,787	-11,729	494,236	167,111	162,996	9,442	87,302	36,595
1983	880,079	597,922	7,740	605,662	63,922	-12,830	528,910	172,056	179,113	10,062	87,465	37,306
1984	976,056	674,029	9,639	683,668	73,089	-15,071	595,508	192,473	188,075	11,080	88,094	38,570
1985	1,058,050	741,730	12,640	754,370	81,387	-19,426	653,557	206,491	198,002	11,894	88,954	40,370
1986	1,168,512	841,825	15,534	857,359	92,370	-27,313	737,676	227,723	203,113	12,836	91,032	43,661
1987	1,374,848	1,059,911	17,406	1,077,317	114,820	-50,359	912,138	260,732	201,978	14,268	96,360	49,930
1988	1,581,005	1,280,260	12,875	1,293,135	143,014	-73,745	1,076,376	292,457	212,172	15,237	103,758	56,273
1989	1,787,872	1,422,493	19,483	1,441,976	156,679	-79,354	1,205,943	350,529	231,400	16,323	109,534	60,292
1990	1,852,405	1,457,107	20,830	1,477,937	156,051	-78,196	1,243,690	357,585	251,130	16,606	111,549	59,814
1991	1,946,410	1,515,191	13,645	1,528,836	165,526	-73,752	1,289,558	372,622	284,230	17,238	112,911	58,880
1992	2,055,931	1,573,569	18,860	1,592,429	172,555	-71,297	1,348,577	383,050	324,304	17,962	114,463	58,311
1993	2,059,712	1,555,290	17,626	1,572,916	173,235	-66,142	1,333,539	384,708	341,465	17,930	114,874	57,273
1994	2,119,244	1,599,431	15,834	1,615,265	177,783	-65,807	1,371,675	394,786	352,783	18,124	116,932	58,543
1995	2,201,951	1,643,327	9,650	1,652,977	180,459	-65,656	1,406,862	423,973	371,116	19,087	115,361	58,586
1996	2,261,624	1,672,858	20,720	1,693,578	182,095	-63,452	1,448,031	430,890	382,703	19,738	114,585	58,639
1997	2,318,594	1,733,861	8,033	1,741,894	186,017	-61,775	1,494,102	437,185	387,307	20,509	113,055	58,879
1998	2,433,724	1,813,967	8,916	1,822,883	193,052	-62,540	1,567,291	462,628	403,805	21,624	112,546	59,089
1999	2,545,912	1,904,832	8,920	1,913,752	197,763	-60,417	1,655,572	466,542	423,798	22,715	112,081	60,291
2000	2,692,906	2,010,563	7,663	2,018,226	207,851	-60,007	1,750,368	498,765	443,773	24,089	111,790	61,119
2001	2,717,494	2,014,208	11,694	2,025,902	217,321	-69,501	1,739,080	502,813	475,601	24,389	111,422	60,488
2002	2,855,393	2,122,015	15,459	2,137,474	230,596	-76,765	1,830,113	510,738	514,542	25,698	111,112	60,316
2003	3,039,411	2,279,687	24,788	2,304,475	245,508	-99,264	1,959,703	546,334	533,374	27,569	110,246	60,812
2004	3,239,066	2,451,609	37,821	2,489,430	267,055	-119,485	2,102,890	569,701	566,475	29,466	109,924	62,675
2005	3,514,919	2,779,078	38,357	2,817,435	302,268	-169,285	2,345,882	578,516	590,521	30,972	113,486	65,950
2006	3,809,325	3,151,982	26,096	3,178,078	343,212	-260,129	2,574,737	620,553	614,035	33,518	113,650	69,033
2007	4,070,704	3,312,916	39,747	3,352,663	357,326	-264,207	2,731,130	694,667	644,907	35,379	115,059	69,725
2008	4,353,877	3,518,761	42,701	3,561,462	382,812	-316,483	2,862,167	768,988	722,722	37,849	115,033	71,126
2009	4,544,418	3,679,478	20,789	3,700,267	401,460	-334,829	2,963,978	790,865	789,575	39,509	115,023	70,866
2010	4,837,158	3,923,471	43,370	3,966,841	428,610	-339,382	3,198,849	786,078	852,231	41,482	116,609	72,440
2011	5,050,177	4,025,162	66,913	4,092,075	404,189	-393,754	3,294,132	876,423	879,622	42,867	117,809	72,646
2012	5,105,199	3,966,860	57,278	4,024,138	399,622	-352,964	3,271,552	958,701	874,946	42,425	120,335	71,377
2013	5,011,485	3,888,942	79,907	3,968,849	432,652	-344,409	3,191,788	913,095	906,602	42,249	118,617	70,584
2014	5,044,288	3,853,911	91,696	3,945,607	435,925	-315,646	3,194,036	923,645	926,607	41,436	121,738	69,585
2015	5,046,308	3,846,158	53,297	3,899,455	437,530	-317,645	3,144,280	915,883	986,145	41,720	120,958	68,751
2016	4,975,630	3,768,505	48,002	3,816,507	425,905	-306,710	3,083,892	877,907	1,013,831	42,020	118,410	67,180
2017	5,147,259	3,838,540	59,505	3,898,045	436,190	-298,471	3,163,384	903,115	1,080,760	43,084	119,470	67,361
2018	5,203,358	3,922,588	46,741	3,969,329	440,595	-306,784	3,221,950	911,407	1,070,001	43,716	119,026	67,617
2019	5,398,665	4,026,684	66,175	4,092,859	452,361	-324,206	3,316,292	924,274	1,158,099	45,905	117,606	67,209
2020	5,849,400	4,093,843	73,272	4,167,115	459,272	-333,590	3,374,253	894,662	1,580,485	50,368	116,134	64,453
2021	6,178,742	4,394,048	82,634	4,476,682	491,416	-356,089	3,629,177	875,917	1,673,648	53,130	116,295	66,671

Personal Income and Employment by Area: Wausau-Weston, WI

(Thousands of dollars, except as noted.)

Year	Personal income, total	Earnings by place of work			Less: Contributions for government social insurance	Plus: Adjustment for residence	Equals: Net earnings by place of residence	Plus: Dividends, interest, and rent	Plus: Personal current transfer receipts	Per capita personal income (dollars)	Population (persons)	Total employment
		Nonfarm	Farm	Total								
1970	336,776	255,420	21,015	276,435	18,854	499	258,080	48,532	30,164	3,445	97,762	42,507
1971	364,714	275,088	21,010	296,098	21,036	1,009	276,071	53,374	35,269	3,678	99,164	42,664
1972	407,458	311,537	22,947	334,484	25,095	744	310,133	58,314	39,011	4,069	100,135	44,356
1973	461,198	356,405	27,446	383,851	32,904	512	351,459	65,565	44,174	4,534	101,722	46,586
1974	503,186	389,538	22,355	411,893	37,292	1,431	376,032	74,315	52,839	4,876	103,197	47,168
1975	565,233	428,179	25,566	453,745	40,005	1,149	414,889	83,428	66,916	5,395	104,779	48,012
1976	639,843	493,124	28,919	522,043	46,867	1,483	476,659	89,550	73,634	6,087	105,124	50,209
1977	736,095	573,300	39,645	612,945	54,446	665	559,164	99,555	77,376	6,876	107,054	53,684
1978	830,191	647,041	45,564	692,605	63,114	1,432	630,923	112,715	86,553	7,643	108,618	55,887
1979	925,333	707,553	56,237	763,790	71,903	2,247	694,134	128,913	102,286	8,368	110,574	56,769
1980	1,011,574	742,949	54,780	797,729	75,229	3,934	726,434	158,056	127,084	9,093	111,246	55,624
1981	1,092,193	795,894	46,290	842,184	86,030	3,874	760,028	193,551	138,614	9,850	110,887	55,453
1982	1,144,982	808,437	41,897	850,334	88,085	8,374	770,623	218,252	156,107	10,313	111,023	54,768
1983	1,199,293	869,107	21,343	890,450	94,425	10,774	806,799	224,839	167,655	10,809	110,953	55,723
1984	1,308,795	929,349	37,255	966,604	102,992	14,553	878,165	257,784	172,846	11,765	111,241	56,858
1985	1,392,973	997,293	36,975	1,034,268	111,513	13,963	936,718	273,212	183,043	12,520	111,260	57,757
1986	1,477,942	1,064,671	41,993	1,106,664	118,954	15,450	1,003,160	289,957	184,825	13,260	111,458	59,211
1987	1,569,556	1,153,438	51,154	1,204,592	127,228	15,968	1,093,332	289,214	187,010	14,007	112,058	61,043
1988	1,667,958	1,260,525	39,761	1,300,286	144,204	16,383	1,172,465	303,036	192,457	14,734	113,201	62,564
1989	1,855,697	1,360,382	76,151	1,436,533	156,596	15,391	1,295,328	346,812	213,557	16,233	114,318	64,559
1990	1,981,850	1,478,178	69,842	1,548,020	177,127	19,246	1,390,139	362,251	229,460	17,123	115,743	66,554
1991	2,068,665	1,571,719	47,284	1,619,003	189,912	16,506	1,445,597	368,767	254,301	17,685	116,972	68,392
1992	2,235,885	1,708,379	54,597	1,762,976	203,981	17,356	1,576,351	384,378	275,156	18,881	118,417	69,877
1993	2,348,607	1,810,486	42,451	1,852,937	216,374	16,017	1,652,580	405,417	290,610	19,565	120,044	70,906
1994	2,482,296	1,925,746	49,367	1,975,113	232,626	14,532	1,757,019	423,506	301,771	20,556	120,760	72,786
1995	2,605,618	2,028,304	31,637	2,059,941	245,485	8,973	1,823,429	460,354	321,835	21,419	121,649	74,772
1996	2,779,602	2,138,436	52,741	2,191,177	256,810	4,056	1,938,423	506,089	335,090	22,680	122,560	76,066
1997	2,953,168	2,317,566	27,508	2,345,074	276,444	-5,664	2,062,966	542,918	347,284	23,896	123,583	78,232
1998	3,811,847	2,875,876	54,511	2,930,387	339,900	35,163	2,625,650	722,099	464,098	24,783	153,809	97,397
1999	3,968,614	3,063,866	49,157	3,113,023	362,009	34,361	2,785,375	700,569	482,670	25,638	154,797	99,768
2000	4,234,714	3,273,967	29,690	3,303,657	380,668	31,207	2,954,196	762,384	518,134	27,204	155,665	101,578
2001	4,461,302	3,450,502	51,446	3,501,948	395,734	10,137	3,116,351	767,606	577,345	28,597	156,007	102,152
2002	4,615,911	3,630,887	42,586	3,673,473	411,842	495	3,262,126	732,088	621,697	29,491	156,521	102,916
2003	4,791,852	3,752,322	61,974	3,814,296	426,599	16,404	3,404,101	753,127	634,624	30,535	156,932	102,825
2004	4,986,411	3,959,561	70,587	4,030,148	451,885	-2,915	3,575,348	746,865	664,198	31,656	157,521	104,620
2005	5,215,897	4,158,132	57,779	4,215,911	477,619	-8,210	3,730,082	770,939	714,876	32,895	158,560	106,902
2006	5,446,907	4,323,165	41,914	4,365,079	502,028	-14,410	3,848,641	836,583	761,683	34,049	159,973	107,432
2007	5,720,589	4,451,769	71,552	4,523,321	520,000	-39,611	3,963,710	929,926	826,953	35,522	161,045	108,693
2008	5,991,406	4,531,481	65,750	4,597,231	534,075	-11,202	4,051,954	990,027	949,425	36,954	162,130	107,701
2009	6,019,708	4,366,361	24,042	4,390,403	516,052	108,587	3,982,938	936,091	1,100,679	37,016	162,626	102,886
2010	6,049,914	4,367,433	63,433	4,430,866	516,289	28,287	3,942,864	925,781	1,181,269	37,152	162,841	100,806
2011	6,372,389	4,541,462	110,667	4,652,129	480,998	65,678	4,236,809	996,866	1,138,714	39,128	162,858	101,771
2012	6,674,820	4,748,744	110,749	4,859,493	498,055	106,426	4,467,864	1,052,366	1,154,590	40,977	162,892	101,486
2013	6,723,621	4,856,106	123,648	4,979,754	574,425	88,138	4,493,467	1,070,855	1,159,299	41,195	163,213	103,028
2014	7,061,712	5,064,176	158,605	5,222,781	596,585	85,861	4,712,057	1,144,618	1,205,037	42,897	164,622	104,995
2015	7,318,135	5,239,534	121,162	5,360,696	615,055	78,516	4,824,157	1,225,202	1,268,776	44,384	164,883	106,069
2016	7,487,043	5,317,869	90,401	5,408,270	620,934	162,337	4,949,673	1,251,364	1,286,006	45,390	164,948	106,038
2017	7,744,887	5,520,669	97,533	5,618,202	647,693	129,269	5,099,778	1,301,985	1,343,124	46,780	165,559	106,559
2018	8,094,329	5,814,327	78,390	5,892,717	672,070	138,701	5,359,348	1,320,955	1,414,026	48,830	165,764	107,465
2019	8,475,629	5,995,033	103,740	6,098,773	696,313	171,664	5,574,124	1,410,016	1,491,489	50,993	166,210	107,326
2020	8,988,155	6,085,177	141,495	6,226,672	709,795	161,723	5,678,600	1,425,271	1,884,284	54,039	166,328	103,677
2021	9,463,953	6,373,028	122,869	6,495,897	733,130	135,100	5,897,867	1,444,790	2,121,296	56,947	166,189	105,801

Personal Income and Employment by Area: Weirton-Steubenville, WV-OH

(Thousands of dollars, except as noted.)

Year	Personal income, total	Earnings by place of work			Less: Contributions for government social insurance	Plus: Adjustment for residence	Equals: Net earnings by place of residence	Plus: Dividends, interest, and rent	Plus: Personal current transfer receipts	Per capita personal income (dollars)	Population (persons)	Total employment
		Nonfarm	Farm	Total								
1970	603,659	559,411	947	560,358	41,075	-43,339	475,944	69,924	57,791	3,626	166,471	67,336
1971	655,277	607,649	1,121	608,770	46,459	-50,591	511,720	75,349	68,208	3,920	167,161	68,528
1972	714,183	665,855	1,194	667,049	53,066	-56,403	557,580	80,090	76,513	4,301	166,032	68,997
1973	767,566	710,436	1,697	712,133	66,289	-58,488	587,356	89,130	91,080	4,622	166,066	70,056
1974	879,832	820,599	1,973	822,572	79,983	-71,107	671,482	103,506	104,844	5,346	164,593	71,072
1975	961,462	872,396	1,547	873,943	85,142	-72,638	716,163	117,557	127,742	5,793	165,977	69,428
1976	1,080,647	1,004,027	1,375	1,005,402	98,476	-92,584	814,342	126,079	140,226	6,563	164,666	71,679
1977	1,179,504	1,088,456	1,262	1,089,718	106,240	-96,473	887,005	139,717	152,782	7,202	163,770	71,144
1978	1,271,763	1,161,052	1,474	1,162,526	116,877	-98,125	947,524	152,799	171,440	7,857	161,867	70,906
1979	1,419,618	1,302,284	1,753	1,304,037	135,487	-113,633	1,054,917	171,395	193,306	8,785	161,602	72,151
1980	1,527,137	1,334,690	1,901	1,336,591	139,169	-121,663	1,075,759	213,100	238,278	9,349	163,345	68,618
1981	1,644,418	1,380,663	1,807	1,382,470	154,031	-110,106	1,118,333	259,194	266,891	10,181	161,525	66,467
1982	1,639,708	1,292,762	2,234	1,294,996	148,079	-104,287	1,042,630	289,163	307,915	10,217	160,486	60,765
1983	1,617,420	1,222,736	717	1,223,453	141,218	-95,555	986,680	306,337	324,403	10,307	156,918	57,943
1984	1,713,492	1,278,264	438	1,278,702	151,493	-101,123	1,026,086	347,218	340,188	11,080	154,644	58,635
1985	1,733,479	1,267,767	1,224	1,268,991	151,475	-92,300	1,025,216	349,521	358,742	11,406	151,981	57,275
1986	1,821,619	1,357,102	375	1,357,477	167,499	-101,260	1,088,718	362,089	370,812	12,215	149,132	58,845
1987	1,863,147	1,399,105	324	1,399,429	170,958	-100,782	1,127,689	353,311	382,147	12,694	146,776	59,897
1988	1,956,394	1,500,832	-1,417	1,499,415	190,199	-112,010	1,197,206	362,168	397,020	13,473	145,205	60,005
1989	2,100,860	1,618,251	748	1,618,999	207,340	-124,689	1,286,970	402,900	410,990	14,602	143,873	61,112
1990	2,224,855	1,681,031	757	1,681,788	218,628	-112,185	1,350,975	427,101	446,779	15,638	142,270	62,123
1991	2,220,048	1,619,569	-1,147	1,618,422	214,424	-71,622	1,332,376	401,801	485,871	15,651	141,845	60,857
1992	2,342,245	1,729,900	2,438	1,732,338	223,164	-102,326	1,406,848	400,438	534,959	16,610	141,012	60,156
1993	2,402,267	1,752,906	1,689	1,754,595	238,794	-72,376	1,443,425	393,462	565,380	17,073	140,704	59,913
1994	2,501,287	1,814,775	2,781	1,817,556	245,634	-69,362	1,502,560	405,609	593,118	17,866	140,001	60,141
1995	2,550,358	1,796,315	1,328	1,797,643	249,019	-33,271	1,515,353	418,123	616,882	18,276	139,547	60,826
1996	2,635,974	1,829,905	449	1,830,354	252,899	-36,657	1,540,798	446,185	648,991	19,063	138,275	60,868
1997	2,649,444	1,746,627	1,456	1,748,083	236,953	-4,439	1,506,691	474,983	667,770	19,393	136,619	59,452
1998	2,792,459	1,875,068	1,891	1,876,959	254,449	-9,807	1,612,703	502,637	677,119	20,735	134,675	61,710
1999	2,827,329	1,879,832	2,141	1,881,973	251,557	17,306	1,647,722	480,344	699,263	21,214	133,276	60,934
2000	2,980,654	1,984,652	3,796	1,988,448	268,538	23,208	1,743,118	509,185	728,351	22,635	131,681	60,717
2001	3,159,333	2,049,360	4,316	2,053,676	268,160	62,751	1,848,267	514,984	796,082	24,172	130,701	60,250
2002	3,239,821	2,122,575	4,485	2,127,060	271,581	67,697	1,923,176	480,867	835,778	24,970	129,750	60,337
2003	3,253,185	2,119,135	3,564	2,122,699	276,505	83,391	1,929,585	464,432	859,168	25,191	129,141	59,545
2004	3,353,624	2,111,816	3,125	2,114,941	276,045	146,778	1,985,674	494,555	873,395	26,151	128,241	58,166
2005	3,372,236	2,117,694	1,994	2,119,688	279,266	182,018	2,022,440	456,966	892,830	26,456	127,464	58,048
2006	3,538,680	2,163,103	1,664	2,164,767	273,860	242,297	2,133,204	458,457	947,019	28,013	126,321	57,500
2007	3,699,127	2,227,208	1,180	2,228,388	275,221	237,833	2,191,000	528,317	979,810	29,537	125,236	57,963
2008	3,886,209	2,390,148	-1,069	2,389,079	294,695	160,864	2,255,248	552,561	1,078,400	31,100	124,959	58,237
2009	3,785,086	2,180,342	-156	2,180,186	274,513	202,490	2,108,163	506,564	1,170,359	30,345	124,734	54,820
2010	3,867,706	2,105,165	-390	2,104,775	261,635	304,861	2,148,001	499,035	1,220,670	31,109	124,328	52,804
2011	4,075,075	2,188,084	-171	2,187,913	244,968	362,781	2,305,726	543,443	1,225,906	32,995	123,504	52,893
2012	4,160,873	2,228,094	171	2,228,265	246,316	388,071	2,370,020	571,565	1,219,288	33,907	122,714	52,494
2013	4,189,430	2,210,690	-752	2,209,938	268,642	443,528	2,384,824	556,306	1,248,300	34,282	122,204	52,094
2014	4,326,726	2,242,535	-3,165	2,239,370	275,705	461,562	2,425,227	590,658	1,310,841	35,399	122,228	51,807
2015	4,446,447	2,257,008	-4,061	2,252,947	277,416	484,331	2,459,862	619,634	1,366,951	36,580	121,555	51,328
2016	4,382,706	2,254,251	-4,116	2,250,135	283,739	425,026	2,391,422	601,331	1,389,953	36,442	120,265	50,333
2017	4,549,001	2,321,769	-5,794	2,315,975	295,343	484,632	2,505,264	634,129	1,409,608	38,140	119,271	49,553
2018	4,731,216	2,405,800	-5,550	2,400,250	303,353	512,711	2,609,608	673,276	1,448,332	39,991	118,307	49,626
2019	4,911,162	2,478,355	-5,883	2,472,472	311,067	527,216	2,688,621	724,315	1,498,226	41,769	117,578	49,601
2020	5,272,129	2,420,201	-4,738	2,415,463	308,903	535,491	2,642,051	733,395	1,896,683	45,217	116,595	47,411
2021	5,612,587	2,536,157	-4,704	2,531,453	319,047	586,583	2,798,989	764,073	2,049,525	48,558	115,585	48,484

Personal Income and Employment by Area: Wenatchee, WA

(Thousands of dollars, except as noted.)

| Year | Personal income, total | Derivation of personal income | | | | | | | | Per capita personal income (dollars) | Population (persons) | Total employment |
| | | Earnings by place of work | | | Less: Contributions for government social insurance | Plus: Adjustment for residence | Equals: Net earnings by place of residence | Plus: Dividends, interest, and rent | Plus: Personal current transfer receipts | | | |
		Nonfarm	Farm	Total								
1970	233,154	158,823	19,635	178,458	12,977	-166	165,315	41,612	26,227	4,026	57,905	28,819
1971	266,510	170,446	36,117	206,563	14,632	-175	191,756	45,048	29,706	4,581	58,182	28,335
1972	284,714	182,550	37,258	219,808	16,352	298	203,754	48,961	31,999	4,906	58,036	28,518
1973	329,056	202,945	53,433	256,378	21,005	1,100	236,473	56,723	35,860	5,642	58,318	29,659
1974	369,509	228,690	57,772	286,462	24,447	1,148	263,163	64,136	42,210	6,207	59,531	31,056
1975	432,793	260,413	72,111	332,524	27,982	1,110	305,652	75,039	52,102	7,122	60,767	32,893
1976	464,732	308,579	52,827	361,406	33,902	-102	327,402	80,329	57,001	7,442	62,443	35,350
1977	522,482	353,189	54,629	407,818	39,188	-206	368,424	91,784	62,274	8,121	64,337	36,078
1978	580,874	387,544	59,826	447,370	43,600	3,773	407,543	105,791	67,540	8,857	65,586	36,913
1979	630,407	423,119	52,683	475,802	48,920	4,434	431,316	122,256	76,835	9,512	66,273	38,625
1980	707,702	442,319	67,814	510,133	51,477	5,284	463,940	148,941	94,821	10,470	67,591	38,992
1981	762,803	473,188	59,802	532,990	58,946	5,318	479,362	179,278	104,163	11,054	69,004	39,690
1982	814,883	488,827	62,204	551,031	62,109	5,850	494,772	202,136	117,975	11,704	69,622	39,743
1983	894,276	530,011	72,443	602,454	68,509	6,583	540,528	226,230	127,518	12,598	70,983	41,521
1984	963,699	578,274	72,225	650,499	77,530	5,218	578,187	249,804	135,708	13,306	72,428	42,260
1985	990,285	609,131	47,732	656,863	82,939	5,973	579,897	262,761	147,627	13,458	73,586	42,158
1986	1,059,312	629,815	84,637	714,452	85,979	8,430	636,903	266,508	155,901	14,342	73,859	41,969
1987	1,150,789	667,198	133,123	800,321	90,570	9,218	718,969	269,315	162,505	15,502	74,236	43,915
1988	1,135,140	716,588	59,442	776,030	99,539	10,850	687,341	275,309	172,490	14,935	76,006	44,589
1989	1,251,178	760,485	87,670	848,155	107,927	12,672	752,900	309,590	188,688	16,143	77,504	45,586
1990	1,332,739	824,485	84,403	908,888	119,201	16,328	806,015	318,061	208,663	16,899	78,865	48,257
1991	1,486,806	908,940	125,219	1,034,159	131,365	17,755	920,549	332,030	234,227	18,306	81,220	48,854
1992	1,629,985	990,816	154,948	1,145,764	142,013	20,502	1,024,253	344,939	260,793	19,504	83,570	48,476
1993	1,728,341	1,069,658	142,267	1,211,925	153,062	22,937	1,081,800	370,368	276,173	20,091	86,027	49,733
1994	1,807,351	1,144,770	114,513	1,259,283	164,070	24,287	1,119,500	393,048	294,803	20,363	88,755	52,796
1995	1,881,852	1,165,647	113,796	1,279,443	167,817	26,691	1,138,317	433,035	310,500	20,527	91,676	53,327
1996	2,042,695	1,225,759	166,444	1,392,203	170,726	29,290	1,250,767	461,277	330,651	21,850	93,486	53,993
1997	2,138,037	1,318,402	121,829	1,440,231	174,799	32,519	1,297,951	499,839	340,247	22,478	95,118	54,720
1998	2,243,291	1,405,478	128,181	1,533,659	182,381	37,588	1,388,866	493,063	361,362	23,170	96,819	55,168
1999	2,268,607	1,464,189	106,281	1,570,470	186,028	41,421	1,425,863	459,432	383,312	23,070	98,336	56,072
2000	2,417,155	1,525,601	131,549	1,657,150	198,835	43,132	1,501,447	495,341	420,367	24,337	99,322	56,928
2001	2,496,790	1,603,814	101,423	1,705,237	207,156	42,775	1,540,856	490,770	465,164	25,128	99,361	56,354
2002	2,547,273	1,682,906	120,857	1,803,763	218,174	39,977	1,625,566	439,653	482,054	25,527	99,786	56,612
2003	2,670,310	1,730,079	148,603	1,878,682	225,850	39,033	1,691,865	468,542	509,903	26,530	100,654	57,198
2004	2,820,912	1,827,218	170,496	1,997,714	242,472	38,562	1,793,804	504,173	522,935	27,665	101,968	58,759
2005	2,917,457	1,928,484	136,618	2,065,102	259,877	38,721	1,843,946	510,861	562,650	28,224	103,369	60,974
2006	3,108,865	2,045,386	135,491	2,180,877	274,750	37,895	1,944,022	557,931	606,912	29,582	105,094	62,332
2007	3,372,587	2,155,874	134,537	2,290,411	289,008	39,931	2,041,334	673,923	657,330	31,603	106,717	63,792
2008	3,692,003	2,233,640	157,992	2,391,632	301,628	43,165	2,133,169	814,702	744,132	34,176	108,029	64,605
2009	3,659,340	2,187,039	171,172	2,358,211	308,105	48,506	2,098,612	738,289	822,439	33,384	109,614	63,716
2010	3,760,342	2,212,570	185,020	2,397,590	311,351	54,448	2,140,687	720,529	899,126	33,798	111,260	62,778
2011	3,979,436	2,251,998	237,082	2,489,080	293,622	63,206	2,258,664	815,070	905,702	35,571	111,873	63,191
2012	4,329,429	2,418,175	269,865	2,688,040	300,379	78,041	2,465,702	945,642	918,085	38,428	112,663	64,483
2013	4,392,560	2,568,464	239,455	2,807,919	347,436	88,051	2,548,534	909,723	934,303	38,837	113,102	65,699
2014	4,707,993	2,715,774	214,851	2,930,625	372,492	95,398	2,653,531	1,024,182	1,030,280	41,187	114,307	67,538
2015	4,986,498	2,866,225	292,940	3,159,165	391,581	99,315	2,866,899	1,074,769	1,044,830	42,952	116,094	69,039
2016	5,252,941	2,947,231	292,860	3,240,091	399,482	106,274	2,946,883	1,196,588	1,109,470	44,602	117,774	69,820
2017	5,516,706	3,165,382	285,005	3,450,387	432,704	113,053	3,130,736	1,253,889	1,132,081	46,383	118,937	71,207
2018	5,726,051	3,343,412	198,752	3,542,164	445,437	123,899	3,220,626	1,322,299	1,183,126	47,718	119,998	73,075
2019	6,041,966	3,538,551	198,687	3,737,238	451,416	132,125	3,417,947	1,350,018	1,274,001	49,820	121,276	73,206
2020	6,652,011	3,670,684	278,667	3,949,351	475,865	144,992	3,618,478	1,361,954	1,671,579	54,443	122,183	69,729
2021	7,154,911	3,956,752	209,673	4,166,425	517,273	154,421	3,803,573	1,416,812	1,934,526	58,009	123,342	72,286

Personal Income and Employment by Area: Wheeling, WV-OH

(Thousands of dollars, except as noted.)

Year	Personal income, total	Earnings by place of work			Less: Contributions for government social insurance	Plus: Adjustment for residence	Equals: Net earnings by place of residence	Plus: Dividends, interest, and rent	Plus: Personal current transfer receipts	Per capita personal income (dollars)	Population (persons)	Total employment
		Nonfarm	Farm	Total								
1970	644,855	513,841	1,901	515,742	38,769	7,056	484,029	91,851	68,975	3,532	182,552	74,553
1971	688,713	541,975	2,345	544,320	42,239	7,153	509,234	98,826	80,653	3,699	186,174	74,644
1972	748,314	588,226	2,802	591,028	47,447	7,826	551,407	106,257	90,650	4,027	185,831	74,658
1973	817,931	641,793	3,185	644,978	60,044	7,197	592,131	118,050	107,750	4,416	185,230	76,692
1974	893,606	689,250	1,677	690,927	67,207	9,685	633,405	135,031	125,170	4,851	184,209	77,111
1975	992,231	756,596	2,702	759,298	71,683	4,363	691,978	147,633	152,620	5,360	185,114	76,968
1976	1,112,204	857,184	2,585	859,769	82,833	4,085	781,021	161,441	169,742	5,966	186,432	78,256
1977	1,232,362	957,365	1,932	959,297	92,719	2,979	869,557	180,780	182,025	6,637	185,683	79,725
1978	1,348,998	1,051,647	1,367	1,053,014	104,981	-842	947,191	197,318	204,489	7,282	185,256	81,408
1979	1,499,362	1,153,813	1,076	1,154,889	118,437	8,055	1,044,507	218,935	235,920	8,041	186,463	81,667
1980	1,620,122	1,175,054	732	1,175,786	121,537	16,009	1,070,258	274,588	275,276	8,741	185,340	78,635
1981	1,768,266	1,244,445	385	1,244,830	137,959	10,742	1,117,613	344,057	306,596	9,602	184,158	76,299
1982	1,850,522	1,255,148	-252	1,254,896	142,592	2,643	1,114,947	388,273	347,302	10,149	182,331	74,012
1983	1,882,262	1,218,777	-1,025	1,217,752	139,547	8,871	1,087,076	415,872	379,314	10,454	180,057	71,069
1984	1,985,983	1,275,937	501	1,276,438	148,814	14,913	1,142,537	455,364	388,082	11,234	176,777	70,504
1985	2,025,382	1,282,802	2,314	1,285,116	150,783	9,515	1,143,848	472,958	408,576	11,702	173,087	69,315
1986	2,066,117	1,296,187	1,747	1,297,934	156,896	7,945	1,148,983	491,249	425,885	12,246	168,724	68,607
1987	2,139,364	1,380,057	1,010	1,381,067	167,850	6,938	1,220,155	485,462	433,747	12,875	166,158	70,059
1988	2,223,793	1,456,222	-1,577	1,454,645	183,796	-7,541	1,263,308	505,751	454,734	13,581	163,741	71,434
1989	2,378,281	1,533,260	1,392	1,534,652	195,465	-7,099	1,332,088	567,464	478,729	14,711	161,663	71,939
1990	2,495,498	1,618,363	1,314	1,619,677	208,013	-2,194	1,409,470	578,010	508,018	15,699	158,961	72,385
1991	2,568,572	1,662,334	-2,791	1,659,543	219,889	-8,943	1,430,711	583,575	554,286	16,228	158,283	72,525
1992	2,730,575	1,731,967	2,101	1,734,068	230,546	20,565	1,524,087	587,680	618,808	17,225	158,525	71,690
1993	2,784,668	1,783,497	1,332	1,784,829	245,159	7,187	1,546,857	586,642	651,169	17,575	158,445	72,312
1994	2,905,485	1,887,290	1,625	1,888,915	258,848	3,300	1,633,367	605,120	666,998	18,396	157,944	74,195
1995	2,978,757	1,926,768	557	1,927,325	266,974	-9,016	1,651,335	639,718	687,704	19,033	156,502	75,761
1996	3,124,422	1,991,736	-1,726	1,990,010	274,725	8,480	1,723,765	675,457	725,200	19,856	157,354	76,900
1997	3,233,433	2,073,520	-1,875	2,071,645	279,854	1,465	1,793,256	698,360	741,817	20,714	156,100	77,888
1998	3,440,355	2,185,962	-531	2,185,431	293,377	12,240	1,904,294	744,787	791,274	22,116	155,562	79,973
1999	3,492,549	2,276,282	-490	2,275,792	303,703	9,921	1,982,010	709,596	800,943	22,645	154,230	79,789
2000	3,609,199	2,337,320	4,851	2,342,171	315,287	9,341	2,036,225	749,982	822,992	23,603	152,914	80,874
2001	3,995,463	2,657,847	4,463	2,662,310	325,937	5,833	2,342,206	750,451	902,806	26,333	151,728	79,685
2002	4,097,655	2,747,352	2,062	2,749,414	329,769	10,486	2,430,131	711,767	955,757	27,058	151,442	79,961
2003	4,175,061	2,837,003	190	2,837,193	347,751	7,468	2,496,910	702,250	975,901	27,711	150,666	79,043
2004	4,308,599	2,972,202	7,657	2,979,859	361,772	-38	2,618,049	693,047	997,503	28,688	150,186	80,122
2005	4,427,518	3,107,805	5,921	3,113,726	378,631	-9,563	2,725,532	682,879	1,019,107	29,628	149,438	81,069
2006	4,668,694	3,257,166	543	3,257,709	383,249	-11,446	2,863,014	730,578	1,075,102	31,290	149,208	81,521
2007	4,887,919	3,364,331	-3,484	3,360,847	381,011	3,014	2,982,850	784,356	1,120,713	32,865	148,727	81,881
2008	5,147,992	3,480,530	-6,871	3,473,659	390,501	11,522	3,094,680	844,619	1,208,693	34,767	148,073	81,915
2009	4,913,967	3,290,100	-7,715	3,282,385	386,043	-42,964	2,853,378	757,577	1,303,012	33,223	147,910	80,143
2010	4,893,661	3,235,238	-7,428	3,227,810	381,619	-73,859	2,772,332	764,316	1,357,013	33,087	147,905	80,099
2011	5,115,643	3,339,622	-5,132	3,334,490	351,774	-81,919	2,900,797	857,635	1,357,211	34,733	147,283	80,520
2012	5,301,525	3,528,683	-7,999	3,520,684	368,407	-123,155	3,029,122	902,933	1,369,470	36,170	146,572	81,080
2013	5,417,805	3,760,694	-4,565	3,756,129	433,190	-182,913	3,140,026	899,891	1,377,888	37,108	146,002	82,092
2014	5,717,645	3,948,154	-7,493	3,940,661	459,323	-207,244	3,274,094	990,120	1,453,431	39,212	145,814	82,776
2015	5,872,770	3,936,617	-7,101	3,929,516	457,259	-198,812	3,273,445	1,090,315	1,509,010	40,446	145,202	81,542
2016	5,927,350	3,948,259	-8,948	3,939,311	464,931	-199,067	3,275,313	1,094,043	1,557,994	41,117	144,158	80,447
2017	6,460,075	4,561,152	-13,137	4,548,015	529,231	-248,000	3,770,784	1,105,393	1,583,898	45,273	142,691	81,593
2018	6,846,625	5,002,065	-12,865	4,989,200	576,017	-355,709	4,057,474	1,178,534	1,610,617	48,341	141,633	83,130
2019	6,687,889	4,547,195	-13,988	4,533,207	540,161	-284,821	3,708,225	1,309,724	1,669,940	47,503	140,788	80,316
2020	6,566,095	3,846,854	-12,761	3,834,093	495,423	-195,894	3,142,776	1,308,829	2,114,490	47,257	138,943	73,951
2021	6,985,686	4,037,790	-12,889	4,024,901	506,661	-191,666	3,326,574	1,381,471	2,277,641	50,716	137,740	75,387

Personal Income and Employment by Area: Wichita, KS

(Thousands of dollars, except as noted.)

Year	Personal income, total	Earnings by place of work			Less: Contributions for government social insurance	Plus: Adjustment for residence	Equals: Net earnings by place of residence	Plus: Dividends, interest, and rent	Plus: Personal current transfer receipts	Per capita personal income (dollars)	Population (persons)	Total employment
		Nonfarm	Farm	Total								
1970	1,806,083	1,465,274	38,013	1,503,287	104,731	-14,008	1,384,548	255,444	166,091	4,038	447,283	210,746
1971	1,909,086	1,514,053	53,110	1,567,163	111,656	-14,399	1,441,108	276,796	191,182	4,320	441,929	205,860
1972	2,118,795	1,708,974	70,116	1,779,090	133,326	-18,883	1,626,881	298,740	193,174	4,847	437,170	216,199
1973	2,372,250	1,902,244	112,894	2,015,138	170,583	-22,036	1,822,519	329,582	220,149	5,408	438,655	227,741
1974	2,668,634	2,172,920	84,732	2,257,652	201,772	-27,764	2,028,116	391,666	248,852	5,990	445,506	238,535
1975	3,008,477	2,440,177	69,542	2,509,719	222,988	-29,545	2,257,186	444,905	306,386	6,682	450,230	241,789
1976	3,299,765	2,726,922	37,217	2,764,139	253,687	-35,991	2,474,461	479,899	345,405	7,216	457,265	250,873
1977	3,558,749	2,947,938	28,271	2,976,209	278,608	-38,860	2,658,741	529,766	370,242	7,735	460,059	254,590
1978	4,047,572	3,404,419	18,230	3,422,649	333,735	-47,554	3,041,360	606,582	399,630	8,728	463,740	267,224
1979	4,673,210	3,977,304	39,032	4,016,336	405,815	-61,039	3,549,482	687,620	436,108	9,918	471,185	282,468
1980	5,291,799	4,446,923	-3,519	4,443,404	441,881	-72,425	3,929,098	843,086	519,615	11,063	478,352	287,480
1981	5,995,338	4,914,776	6,350	4,921,126	520,677	-74,734	4,325,715	1,060,654	608,969	12,344	485,677	291,074
1982	6,408,344	4,971,980	53,353	5,025,333	539,381	-71,422	4,414,530	1,267,538	726,276	13,081	489,883	279,479
1983	6,568,763	5,093,624	20,837	5,114,461	552,892	-67,779	4,493,790	1,303,230	771,743	13,414	489,678	280,797
1984	7,191,364	5,616,795	41,780	5,658,575	626,164	-73,793	4,958,618	1,449,117	783,629	14,597	492,652	291,814
1985	7,484,936	5,836,181	11,388	5,847,569	660,583	-72,513	5,114,473	1,548,201	822,262	15,085	496,168	292,297
1986	7,980,322	6,235,768	64,481	6,300,249	704,738	-78,846	5,516,665	1,596,585	867,072	16,012	498,385	292,210
1987	8,337,822	6,598,624	61,968	6,660,592	735,034	-79,741	5,845,817	1,600,124	891,881	16,546	503,923	302,541
1988	8,870,295	6,990,836	72,104	7,062,940	805,481	-82,296	6,175,163	1,743,965	951,167	17,413	509,395	307,398
1989	9,437,042	7,424,776	50,847	7,475,623	850,684	-84,649	6,540,290	1,842,881	1,053,871	18,281	516,224	314,218
1990	10,055,953	7,897,061	65,913	7,962,974	957,321	-85,402	6,920,251	1,985,430	1,150,272	19,321	520,465	320,176
1991	10,588,514	8,261,416	47,959	8,309,375	1,017,595	-93,303	7,198,477	2,126,779	1,263,258	20,059	527,868	325,468
1992	11,355,526	8,938,946	83,115	9,022,061	1,090,884	-104,078	7,827,099	2,132,634	1,395,793	21,108	537,981	327,396
1993	11,797,706	9,188,157	71,012	9,259,169	1,116,201	-104,649	8,038,319	2,266,941	1,492,446	21,661	544,645	329,318
1994	12,069,154	9,403,740	81,079	9,484,819	1,179,481	-106,526	8,198,812	2,323,438	1,546,904	22,015	548,229	332,894
1995	12,812,617	9,956,995	31,207	9,988,202	1,245,267	-114,780	8,628,155	2,557,377	1,627,085	23,217	551,873	339,959
1996	13,789,567	10,705,838	74,450	10,780,288	1,346,719	-125,686	9,307,883	2,799,331	1,682,353	24,736	557,473	349,157
1997	14,990,176	11,680,601	120,596	11,801,197	1,473,465	-144,678	10,183,054	3,043,197	1,763,925	26,538	564,862	361,796
1998	15,688,303	12,448,474	40,711	12,489,185	1,575,659	-196,240	10,717,286	3,255,895	1,715,122	27,722	565,914	367,762
1999	15,823,908	12,571,991	46,311	12,618,302	1,589,165	-198,121	10,831,016	3,210,717	1,782,175	27,764	569,949	365,827
2000	16,539,272	12,910,660	35,725	12,946,385	1,624,039	-200,352	11,121,994	3,439,152	1,978,126	28,903	572,226	365,971
2001	17,637,059	13,782,017	3,329	13,785,346	1,602,388	-221,405	11,961,553	3,490,191	2,185,315	30,649	575,446	370,228
2002	17,688,886	13,828,763	12,717	13,841,480	1,609,025	-226,129	12,006,326	3,294,953	2,387,607	30,485	580,247	364,260
2003	17,787,498	13,688,261	87,093	13,775,354	1,612,142	-229,864	11,933,348	3,326,497	2,527,653	30,554	582,168	359,035
2004	18,644,132	14,204,265	135,513	14,339,778	1,702,242	-237,779	12,399,757	3,663,227	2,581,148	31,894	584,565	361,989
2005	19,515,638	14,497,257	114,052	14,611,309	1,805,734	-258,738	12,546,837	4,258,309	2,710,492	33,189	588,021	366,848
2006	22,031,832	15,920,117	143,781	16,063,898	1,942,017	-280,032	13,841,849	5,292,722	2,897,261	37,129	593,382	374,661
2007	23,254,007	16,540,143	100,123	16,640,266	2,009,028	-291,095	14,340,143	5,797,773	3,116,091	38,705	600,805	385,608
2008	25,814,246	18,071,239	169,552	18,240,791	2,100,488	-322,247	15,818,056	6,449,179	3,547,011	42,371	609,250	392,697
2009	24,453,834	17,026,911	137,761	17,164,672	2,002,912	-280,193	14,881,567	5,588,301	3,983,966	39,484	619,330	379,218
2010	24,433,144	17,770,640	139,622	17,910,262	2,027,841	-236,766	15,645,655	4,543,842	4,243,647	39,162	623,898	371,922
2011	27,310,153	19,299,478	108,508	19,407,986	1,879,672	-223,916	17,304,398	5,730,875	4,274,880	43,669	625,391	372,719
2012	28,867,715	19,892,665	174,269	20,066,934	1,914,988	-175,471	17,976,475	6,724,154	4,167,086	45,948	628,264	376,545
2013	29,353,870	20,705,325	197,953	20,903,278	2,231,660	-148,499	18,523,119	6,601,615	4,229,136	46,555	630,518	382,408
2014	30,930,461	21,135,208	89,983	21,225,191	2,292,688	-123,158	18,809,345	7,743,466	4,377,650	48,730	634,729	387,001
2015	30,138,586	21,233,279	41,879	21,275,158	2,376,761	-128,569	18,769,828	6,842,536	4,526,222	47,244	637,932	392,293
2016	29,713,652	21,032,832	41,637	21,074,469	2,349,390	-114,884	18,610,195	6,413,628	4,689,829	46,384	640,603	394,734
2017	31,027,500	21,802,716	22,302	21,825,018	2,400,650	-101,279	19,323,089	6,881,576	4,822,835	48,412	640,908	392,398
2018	31,977,357	21,952,317	44,070	21,996,387	2,489,801	-102,652	19,403,934	7,513,327	5,060,096	49,849	641,487	396,361
2019	33,398,836	23,318,068	64,890	23,382,958	2,630,759	-157,189	20,595,010	7,418,932	5,384,894	51,801	644,752	401,672
2020	34,875,378	22,930,000	138,357	23,068,357	2,624,350	-89,302	20,354,705	7,377,368	7,143,305	53,827	647,921	388,146
2021	36,505,805	23,842,515	167,849	24,010,364	2,695,289	-110,187	21,204,888	7,564,175	7,736,742	56,343	647,919	396,660

Personal Income and Employment by Area: Wichita Falls, TX

(Thousands of dollars, except as noted.)

Year	Personal income, total	Earnings by place of work			Less: Contributions for government social insurance	Plus: Adjustment for residence	Equals: Net earnings by place of residence	Plus: Dividends, interest, and rent	Plus: Personal current transfer receipts	Per capita personal income (dollars)	Population (persons)	Total employment
		Nonfarm	Farm	Total								
1970	574,667	443,324	4,504	447,828	25,967	-1,777	420,084	114,736	39,847	4,271	134,547	68,460
1971	645,432	500,386	5,309	505,695	30,869	-2,709	472,117	127,973	45,342	4,749	135,914	71,202
1972	674,171	521,053	5,494	526,547	32,823	-3,506	490,218	133,516	50,437	5,023	134,213	69,547
1973	750,253	570,747	12,043	582,790	40,178	-4,519	538,093	151,913	60,247	5,651	132,776	72,373
1974	842,465	639,305	17,915	657,220	47,369	-7,062	602,789	169,968	69,708	6,207	135,739	74,009
1975	906,418	683,863	13,239	697,102	51,542	-7,940	637,620	184,172	84,626	6,662	136,058	73,601
1976	1,004,485	773,977	11,610	785,587	59,718	-10,336	715,533	197,127	91,825	7,226	139,008	76,059
1977	1,068,280	829,237	6,475	835,712	64,364	-12,142	759,206	211,847	97,227	7,719	138,389	77,471
1978	1,196,734	936,713	2,831	939,544	73,381	-15,515	850,648	239,678	106,408	8,724	137,175	79,811
1979	1,343,033	1,047,148	9,006	1,056,154	86,157	-18,588	951,409	271,829	119,795	9,776	137,384	82,264
1980	1,481,526	1,150,728	-1,816	1,148,912	96,220	-23,307	1,029,385	316,740	135,401	10,698	138,486	84,353
1981	1,734,448	1,331,489	11,081	1,342,570	119,850	-26,159	1,196,561	386,493	151,394	12,362	140,309	88,921
1982	1,833,997	1,366,420	13,655	1,380,075	126,246	-24,315	1,229,514	433,966	170,517	12,840	142,833	88,337
1983	1,906,966	1,379,536	19,283	1,398,819	127,419	-22,135	1,249,265	469,620	188,081	13,232	144,114	85,451
1984	2,049,189	1,469,723	25,273	1,494,996	140,483	-22,099	1,332,414	518,607	198,168	14,210	144,209	86,935
1985	2,113,275	1,507,748	12,272	1,520,020	146,573	-21,035	1,352,412	550,939	209,924	14,628	144,471	87,027
1986	2,121,704	1,481,865	22,374	1,504,239	144,488	-19,074	1,340,677	549,287	231,740	14,648	144,842	82,505
1987	2,121,141	1,475,651	23,056	1,498,707	142,864	-17,068	1,338,775	539,723	242,643	14,892	142,433	81,957
1988	2,214,492	1,531,750	28,040	1,559,790	155,736	-16,545	1,387,509	568,215	258,768	15,663	141,380	81,928
1989	2,293,376	1,593,471	23,736	1,617,207	163,580	-14,779	1,438,848	578,552	275,976	16,271	140,953	81,822
1990	2,415,383	1,657,109	42,191	1,699,300	167,912	-22,164	1,509,224	606,776	299,383	17,215	140,303	81,730
1991	2,401,746	1,625,834	30,069	1,655,903	170,542	-20,373	1,464,988	608,661	328,097	17,270	139,070	79,063
1992	2,526,742	1,711,388	37,065	1,748,453	177,837	-20,887	1,549,729	599,438	377,575	18,206	138,786	78,932
1993	2,654,738	1,830,116	24,050	1,854,166	190,835	-23,536	1,639,795	616,685	398,258	18,774	141,403	82,583
1994	2,781,329	1,908,678	24,431	1,933,109	199,539	-25,947	1,707,623	651,893	421,813	19,317	143,986	84,658
1995	2,989,143	2,043,573	21,702	2,065,275	213,215	-29,808	1,822,252	714,053	452,838	20,232	147,740	87,085
1996	3,121,792	2,135,914	21,286	2,157,200	219,448	-30,997	1,906,755	735,203	479,834	20,651	151,170	88,384
1997	3,300,975	2,307,832	22,113	2,329,945	230,927	-31,631	2,067,387	732,135	501,453	21,791	151,480	89,491
1998	3,445,760	2,392,894	33,661	2,426,555	236,405	-30,952	2,159,198	783,999	502,563	22,789	151,206	89,655
1999	3,596,082	2,478,662	43,077	2,521,739	245,182	-30,721	2,245,836	830,875	519,371	23,756	151,374	88,964
2000	3,767,975	2,599,690	34,176	2,633,866	254,535	-32,188	2,347,143	872,466	548,366	24,814	151,847	90,930
2001	4,031,615	2,798,140	41,788	2,839,928	271,760	-30,946	2,537,222	900,475	593,918	26,740	150,770	90,627
2002	4,194,974	2,941,725	41,821	2,983,546	284,088	-28,177	2,671,281	883,984	639,709	27,782	150,995	89,770
2003	4,359,971	3,030,881	50,286	3,081,167	296,643	-22,197	2,762,327	915,239	682,405	28,933	150,694	89,026
2004	4,413,847	3,090,582	48,280	3,138,862	305,059	-15,656	2,818,147	873,061	722,639	29,032	152,033	87,369
2005	4,656,089	3,264,611	33,878	3,298,489	316,049	-6,014	2,976,426	907,808	771,855	30,804	151,152	85,765
2006	5,194,196	3,672,978	17,472	3,690,450	343,367	6,785	3,353,868	1,025,033	815,295	34,263	151,596	90,069
2007	5,291,243	3,651,018	12,758	3,663,776	353,989	18,372	3,328,159	1,072,220	890,864	35,125	150,641	90,385
2008	6,109,317	4,312,532	10,811	4,323,343	384,683	32,053	3,970,713	1,158,860	979,744	40,651	150,287	91,461
2009	5,535,334	3,779,174	-9,787	3,769,387	369,947	24,345	3,423,785	1,043,519	1,068,030	36,714	150,768	89,312
2010	5,793,445	3,954,581	-4,814	3,949,767	378,198	24,407	3,595,976	1,041,125	1,156,344	38,201	151,657	88,561
2011	6,423,833	4,404,504	2,058	4,406,562	350,351	21,726	4,077,937	1,160,447	1,185,449	42,731	150,333	87,265
2012	6,466,048	4,344,980	9,927	4,354,907	353,368	17,164	4,018,703	1,262,027	1,185,318	42,798	151,082	89,244
2013	6,572,460	4,494,289	31,689	4,525,978	399,938	14,190	4,140,230	1,200,240	1,231,990	43,379	151,512	89,005
2014	6,558,826	4,333,380	43,012	4,376,392	397,732	19,443	3,998,103	1,269,589	1,291,134	43,658	150,231	87,732
2015	6,181,088	3,932,337	35,743	3,968,080	393,068	16,050	3,591,062	1,230,263	1,359,763	41,740	148,086	88,215
2016	6,069,422	3,817,235	11,991	3,829,226	398,296	8,169	3,439,099	1,202,624	1,427,699	41,027	147,939	89,018
2017	6,289,408	3,858,460	5,158	3,863,618	410,796	11,864	3,464,686	1,368,413	1,456,309	42,443	148,185	89,520
2018	6,544,049	4,019,542	4,424	4,023,966	427,404	18,504	3,615,066	1,406,155	1,522,828	44,230	147,955	89,515
2019	6,752,625	4,156,494	6,732	4,163,226	445,394	14,775	3,732,607	1,426,456	1,593,562	45,697	147,771	88,962
2020	7,097,432	4,114,030	27,339	4,141,369	446,142	9,893	3,705,120	1,401,200	1,991,112	47,843	148,348	86,370
2021	7,585,540	4,312,869	13,759	4,326,628	465,754	5,217	3,866,091	1,462,869	2,256,580	50,905	149,013	87,061

Personal Income and Employment by Area: Williamsport, PA

(Thousands of dollars, except as noted.)

Year	Personal income, total	Nonfarm	Farm	Total	Less: Contributions for government social insurance	Plus: Adjustment for residence	Equals: Net earnings by place of residence	Plus: Dividends, interest, and rent	Plus: Personal current transfer receipts	Per capita personal income (dollars)	Population (persons)	Total employment
1970	411,949	351,224	3,655	354,879	26,745	-13,976	314,158	52,234	45,557	3,628	113,547	53,041
1971	436,332	367,561	2,763	370,324	28,974	-13,610	327,740	55,742	52,850	3,780	115,429	52,143
1972	480,933	406,612	2,080	408,692	33,627	-14,728	360,337	60,870	59,726	4,166	115,443	53,343
1973	538,407	459,906	5,231	465,137	43,423	-16,014	405,700	66,742	65,965	4,620	116,542	56,253
1974	592,531	497,016	6,364	503,380	48,661	-16,777	437,942	74,980	79,609	5,049	117,354	56,294
1975	644,690	521,412	5,317	526,729	49,365	-18,253	459,111	81,543	104,036	5,464	117,985	54,271
1976	709,786	577,654	6,010	583,664	55,905	-19,285	508,474	88,387	112,925	5,980	118,684	55,204
1977	776,113	634,961	5,930	640,891	61,927	-21,450	557,514	98,915	119,684	6,581	117,927	55,790
1978	865,105	719,522	4,877	724,399	71,902	-23,586	628,911	108,817	127,377	7,314	118,274	58,649
1979	947,090	779,232	8,306	787,538	80,034	-24,934	682,570	120,361	144,159	7,920	119,588	58,472
1980	1,026,380	808,711	6,340	815,051	82,731	-25,952	706,368	148,380	171,632	8,678	118,271	56,384
1981	1,126,684	862,723	10,760	873,483	94,270	-28,932	750,281	184,049	192,354	9,592	117,455	55,670
1982	1,187,939	882,320	9,655	891,975	98,007	-31,737	762,231	209,984	215,724	10,123	117,354	54,240
1983	1,226,835	889,632	1,486	891,118	99,398	-29,676	762,044	227,616	237,175	10,478	117,083	52,384
1984	1,325,397	974,344	9,562	983,906	113,145	-34,373	836,388	257,070	231,939	11,364	116,627	54,551
1985	1,394,043	1,029,434	9,553	1,038,987	120,571	-39,253	879,163	273,853	241,027	12,040	115,787	54,780
1986	1,482,767	1,109,139	7,883	1,117,022	130,133	-43,541	943,348	285,755	253,664	12,825	115,613	56,188
1987	1,593,793	1,222,379	7,793	1,230,172	141,692	-51,736	1,036,744	298,177	258,872	13,651	116,750	59,376
1988	1,723,399	1,343,730	8,936	1,352,666	158,859	-56,349	1,137,458	311,463	274,478	14,635	117,756	61,254
1989	1,864,425	1,415,164	11,994	1,427,158	164,131	-60,026	1,203,001	367,053	294,371	15,711	118,673	61,947
1990	1,918,569	1,444,061	12,709	1,456,770	169,624	-64,469	1,222,677	373,405	322,487	16,139	118,876	62,293
1991	1,999,795	1,482,365	6,141	1,488,506	175,516	-62,223	1,250,767	380,841	368,187	16,656	120,068	61,029
1992	2,107,315	1,562,554	17,758	1,580,312	184,990	-61,199	1,334,123	380,656	392,536	17,372	121,303	61,727
1993	2,188,316	1,610,893	17,926	1,628,819	194,211	-55,592	1,379,016	395,259	414,041	17,916	122,141	61,763
1994	2,228,055	1,649,704	15,949	1,665,653	203,888	-52,708	1,409,057	403,522	415,476	18,222	122,273	62,543
1995	2,318,213	1,714,145	7,926	1,722,071	209,749	-51,247	1,461,075	421,732	435,406	19,029	121,825	63,196
1996	2,422,144	1,771,052	15,708	1,786,760	212,016	-52,855	1,521,889	442,024	458,231	19,963	121,333	64,164
1997	2,526,395	1,848,837	6,787	1,855,624	218,869	-50,187	1,586,568	469,549	470,278	20,882	120,983	64,890
1998	2,622,948	1,930,779	8,671	1,939,450	225,633	-49,482	1,664,335	495,109	463,504	21,751	120,590	64,892
1999	2,675,144	2,000,829	6,927	2,007,756	232,440	-49,405	1,725,911	472,373	476,860	22,259	120,182	65,414
2000	2,822,453	2,103,358	11,429	2,114,787	242,868	-52,915	1,819,004	500,047	503,402	23,550	119,851	67,284
2001	2,990,958	2,240,528	9,165	2,249,693	254,040	-56,614	1,939,039	509,480	542,439	25,149	118,930	68,014
2002	3,064,739	2,246,152	6,740	2,252,892	252,835	-46,749	1,953,308	532,283	579,148	25,897	118,344	66,927
2003	3,167,742	2,303,449	15,160	2,318,609	258,133	-42,823	2,017,653	543,773	606,316	26,821	118,108	66,630
2004	3,277,338	2,419,883	22,634	2,442,517	270,746	-47,776	2,123,995	519,993	633,350	27,795	117,911	67,246
2005	3,339,075	2,491,320	19,168	2,510,488	283,129	-51,622	2,175,737	486,885	676,453	28,410	117,530	67,180
2006	3,431,790	2,524,998	16,436	2,541,434	290,503	-50,828	2,200,103	523,826	707,861	29,336	116,983	67,406
2007	3,601,761	2,600,322	14,914	2,615,236	298,593	-51,299	2,265,344	579,040	757,377	30,910	116,524	67,921
2008	3,764,067	2,622,705	10,253	2,632,958	304,550	-42,897	2,285,511	630,226	848,330	32,408	116,147	67,884
2009	3,777,095	2,568,715	6,603	2,575,318	303,381	-39,345	2,232,592	609,252	935,251	32,538	116,081	66,144
2010	3,963,678	2,755,527	11,481	2,767,008	322,320	-48,466	2,396,222	586,527	980,929	34,106	116,215	67,169
2011	4,314,690	3,062,614	16,724	3,079,338	320,134	-91,670	2,667,534	666,095	981,061	36,958	116,747	69,897
2012	4,432,110	3,200,981	20,234	3,221,215	332,299	-136,565	2,752,351	690,968	988,791	37,805	117,237	71,051
2013	4,451,643	3,240,812	19,618	3,260,430	375,347	-134,768	2,750,315	689,917	1,011,411	38,170	116,626	70,499
2014	4,600,920	3,343,046	22,391	3,365,437	391,855	-157,584	2,815,998	735,813	1,049,109	39,429	116,688	71,300
2015	4,673,450	3,373,073	11,191	3,384,264	397,758	-155,410	2,831,096	735,254	1,107,100	40,260	116,083	70,731
2016	4,584,205	3,156,935	7,925	3,164,860	376,276	-75,614	2,712,970	713,085	1,158,150	39,698	115,476	68,118
2017	4,714,865	3,277,263	18,489	3,295,752	397,408	-95,740	2,802,604	748,300	1,163,961	41,091	114,742	68,123
2018	4,902,333	3,395,459	10,888	3,406,347	411,062	-96,693	2,898,592	767,157	1,236,584	42,684	114,853	68,401
2019	5,075,801	3,462,002	20,991	3,482,993	419,046	-86,880	2,977,067	811,691	1,287,043	44,394	114,336	67,718
2020	5,479,618	3,407,265	14,879	3,422,144	413,027	-92,207	2,916,910	808,259	1,754,449	48,075	113,980	64,380
2021	5,732,928	3,520,596	20,730	3,541,326	421,245	-113,860	3,006,221	820,291	1,906,416	50,464	113,605	64,989

Personal Income and Employment by Area: Wilmington, NC

(Thousands of dollars, except as noted.)

Year	Personal income, total	Earnings by place of work			Less: Contributions for government social insurance	Plus: Adjustment for residence	Equals: Net earnings by place of residence	Plus: Dividends, interest, and rent	Plus: Personal current transfer receipts	Per capita personal income (dollars)	Population (persons)	Total employment
		Nonfarm	Farm	Total								
1970	327,087	262,927	10,504	273,431	18,307	-1,770	253,354	45,048	28,685	3,212	101,837	47,452
1971	358,922	289,002	9,525	298,527	20,660	-4,025	273,842	50,661	34,419	3,400	105,562	47,676
1972	417,525	339,820	9,578	349,398	25,410	-2,614	321,374	57,205	38,946	3,795	110,029	50,224
1973	479,995	394,734	11,934	406,668	34,045	-3,468	369,155	65,634	45,206	4,220	113,741	54,092
1974	530,365	424,060	10,382	434,442	38,188	1,414	397,668	76,758	55,939	4,552	116,500	54,463
1975	583,584	448,144	8,833	456,977	39,491	4,698	422,184	85,565	75,835	4,912	118,805	52,367
1976	652,765	501,693	8,679	510,372	44,899	7,349	472,822	94,667	85,276	5,414	120,568	54,105
1977	722,594	553,591	8,893	562,484	49,170	11,104	524,418	107,027	91,149	5,891	122,652	55,642
1978	811,457	624,292	10,567	634,859	56,948	12,665	590,576	123,819	97,062	6,645	122,115	57,773
1979	925,923	704,492	12,207	716,699	66,690	16,143	666,152	146,656	113,115	7,510	123,292	60,898
1980	1,051,344	778,317	13,609	791,926	73,770	18,189	736,345	179,868	135,131	8,328	126,245	61,704
1981	1,157,575	831,804	16,534	848,338	84,945	16,815	780,208	219,905	157,462	9,049	127,918	61,913
1982	1,231,636	868,767	12,260	881,027	90,921	20,893	810,999	243,571	177,066	9,446	130,392	61,420
1983	1,341,434	944,746	5,842	950,588	98,899	26,108	877,797	269,133	194,504	10,176	131,827	62,633
1984	1,494,919	1,050,486	10,013	1,060,499	111,780	25,947	974,666	315,750	204,503	11,164	133,911	66,887
1985	1,643,436	1,168,555	5,880	1,174,435	126,377	20,784	1,068,842	353,237	221,357	12,048	136,404	70,397
1986	1,826,460	1,328,929	5,593	1,334,522	146,475	5,907	1,193,954	389,464	243,042	13,096	139,471	74,836
1987	1,965,609	1,413,855	13,524	1,427,379	153,212	1,410	1,275,577	428,788	261,244	13,827	142,160	75,940
1988	2,164,239	1,558,529	12,586	1,571,115	174,670	-6,021	1,390,424	486,819	286,996	15,033	143,969	79,824
1989	2,355,383	1,703,585	13,925	1,717,510	191,848	-18,390	1,507,272	523,321	324,790	16,108	146,223	82,275
1990	2,577,345	1,828,866	18,259	1,847,125	211,041	-31,033	1,605,051	614,771	357,523	17,156	150,226	85,684
1991	2,784,739	1,937,471	27,367	1,964,838	226,428	-7,093	1,731,317	642,294	411,128	17,900	155,570	86,116
1992	3,022,479	2,122,050	30,177	2,152,227	244,476	-12,896	1,894,855	666,351	461,273	18,902	159,904	88,808
1993	3,273,164	2,274,752	32,573	2,307,325	262,179	-3,556	2,041,590	719,814	511,760	19,730	165,895	91,851
1994	3,586,727	2,477,209	32,810	2,510,019	290,621	2,373	2,221,771	833,960	530,996	20,825	172,233	96,120
1995	3,914,515	2,672,866	33,719	2,706,585	314,665	-1,584	2,390,336	922,530	601,649	21,851	179,144	101,327
1996	4,258,679	2,907,650	42,791	2,950,441	340,402	-23,304	2,586,735	1,018,291	653,653	22,958	185,496	106,945
1997	4,591,549	3,111,332	47,948	3,159,280	365,011	-39,774	2,754,495	1,151,565	685,489	24,021	191,148	113,067
1998	4,904,073	3,396,446	17,142	3,413,588	397,169	-66,585	2,949,834	1,233,204	721,035	24,953	196,533	116,103
1999	5,197,638	3,700,005	13,963	3,713,968	434,866	-90,038	3,189,064	1,244,387	764,187	26,078	199,312	119,821
2000	5,560,166	3,912,102	31,963	3,944,065	455,695	-93,222	3,395,148	1,350,143	814,875	27,512	202,099	121,732
2001	5,822,874	4,102,376	38,975	4,141,351	467,159	-83,662	3,590,530	1,317,669	914,675	28,267	205,996	125,064
2002	5,925,416	4,197,395	17,323	4,214,718	475,576	-90,652	3,648,490	1,277,500	999,426	28,141	210,563	127,090
2003	6,251,359	4,385,556	11,742	4,397,298	506,643	-57,589	3,833,066	1,371,782	1,046,511	29,093	214,877	130,232
2004	6,901,455	4,796,118	29,561	4,825,679	546,230	-50,696	4,228,753	1,545,240	1,127,462	31,018	222,498	136,557
2005	7,596,281	5,309,739	42,782	5,352,521	610,593	-78,762	4,663,166	1,717,637	1,215,478	32,899	230,897	144,084
2006	8,295,711	5,826,219	28,277	5,854,496	661,570	-148,571	5,044,355	1,940,022	1,311,334	34,816	238,272	150,847
2007	8,745,129	6,155,814	41,230	6,197,044	711,297	-235,290	5,250,457	2,089,642	1,405,030	35,911	243,520	158,078
2008	9,046,842	6,144,651	52,179	6,196,830	716,790	-190,391	5,289,649	2,170,063	1,587,130	36,441	248,260	156,516
2009	8,658,251	5,847,667	52,020	5,899,687	697,479	-257,354	4,944,854	1,939,138	1,774,259	34,384	251,814	149,467
2010	8,842,357	5,882,939	58,578	5,941,517	698,618	-219,279	5,023,620	1,920,997	1,897,740	34,580	255,710	147,606
2011	9,240,955	5,948,992	43,211	5,992,203	651,643	-185,604	5,154,956	2,112,323	1,973,676	35,654	259,186	151,006
2012	9,494,429	5,972,084	48,752	6,020,836	653,547	-133,528	5,233,761	2,234,922	2,025,746	36,121	262,848	152,682
2013	9,816,606	6,274,317	66,367	6,340,684	777,390	-132,277	5,431,017	2,287,051	2,098,538	36,651	267,837	156,292
2014	10,638,048	6,776,218	75,970	6,852,188	831,691	-105,477	5,915,020	2,527,964	2,195,064	39,910	266,550	161,788
2015	11,242,196	7,143,119	71,469	7,214,588	873,461	-168,529	6,172,598	2,726,994	2,342,604	41,612	270,164	166,308
2016	11,728,662	7,645,229	64,231	7,709,460	918,315	-355,212	6,435,933	2,859,675	2,433,054	42,602	275,310	172,691
2017	12,173,056	8,031,176	79,756	8,110,932	954,780	-374,113	6,782,039	2,843,487	2,547,530	43,530	279,645	174,070
2018	13,048,959	8,500,820	45,512	8,546,332	999,107	-436,090	7,111,135	3,234,566	2,703,258	46,093	283,102	182,181
2019	14,004,178	9,147,353	56,087	9,203,440	1,066,954	-560,642	7,575,844	3,559,449	2,868,885	49,275	284,206	187,487
2020	15,043,590	9,781,640	51,418	9,833,058	1,143,290	-846,329	7,843,439	3,594,111	3,606,040	52,486	286,623	185,732
2021	16,269,692	10,824,341	54,170	10,878,511	1,251,855	-976,329	8,650,327	3,611,391	4,007,974	55,750	291,833	194,388

Personal Income and Employment by Area: Winchester, VA-WV

(Thousands of dollars, except as noted.)

Year	Personal income, total	Earnings by place of work Nonfarm	Earnings by place of work Farm	Earnings by place of work Total	Less: Contributions for government social insurance	Plus: Adjustment for residence	Equals: Net earnings by place of residence	Plus: Dividends, interest, and rent	Plus: Personal current transfer receipts	Per capita personal income (dollars)	Population (persons)	Total employment
1970	180,907	142,653	2,873	145,526	9,607	4,385	140,304	24,386	16,217	3,255	55,578	27,231
1971	201,808	159,930	3,377	163,307	11,196	3,162	155,273	27,556	18,979	3,497	57,715	28,508
1972	223,153	177,058	4,151	181,209	13,030	3,024	171,203	30,811	21,139	3,835	58,191	29,150
1973	257,504	205,821	7,724	213,545	17,494	671	196,722	36,443	24,339	4,335	59,398	30,736
1974	291,957	234,272	9,152	243,424	20,715	-2,491	220,218	42,880	28,859	4,742	61,566	31,775
1975	308,011	245,694	6,299	251,993	21,065	-8,880	222,048	47,421	38,542	4,890	62,987	30,639
1976	346,187	284,745	4,398	289,143	24,797	-12,325	252,021	52,561	41,605	5,408	64,015	32,116
1977	386,363	321,706	4,078	325,784	28,167	-15,916	281,701	60,186	44,476	5,867	65,849	33,218
1978	445,347	370,638	12,744	383,382	33,036	-21,491	328,855	68,272	48,220	6,557	67,918	35,126
1979	487,659	406,503	13,121	419,624	37,630	-26,975	355,019	76,667	55,973	7,055	69,124	35,530
1980	530,210	438,929	3,881	442,810	40,757	-28,961	373,092	90,354	66,764	7,636	69,435	35,358
1981	599,318	478,298	5,750	484,048	47,696	-26,003	410,349	112,141	76,828	8,546	70,125	35,469
1982	644,532	499,261	5,584	504,845	50,636	-24,221	429,988	127,984	86,560	9,092	70,891	34,837
1983	700,421	541,218	3,724	544,942	55,310	-22,554	467,078	140,289	93,054	9,829	71,263	35,582
1984	794,716	608,208	7,330	615,538	63,192	-19,880	532,466	164,562	97,688	11,054	71,897	36,973
1985	874,059	672,410	4,858	677,268	71,095	-16,887	589,286	180,160	104,613	12,046	72,562	38,962
1986	978,945	761,663	11,008	772,671	82,865	-17,291	672,515	195,502	110,928	13,260	73,828	41,228
1987	1,085,096	856,376	12,518	868,894	92,881	-14,353	761,660	208,215	115,221	14,257	76,112	44,617
1988	1,206,529	945,609	10,723	956,332	104,281	-5,150	846,901	233,391	126,237	15,327	78,717	46,300
1989	1,338,592	1,019,989	8,936	1,028,925	114,052	7,307	922,180	277,925	138,487	16,433	81,456	48,563
1990	1,424,329	1,062,092	9,248	1,071,340	121,434	28,167	978,073	292,872	153,384	16,764	84,964	50,045
1991	1,456,973	1,073,662	12,241	1,085,903	124,789	25,577	986,691	297,331	172,951	16,750	86,981	49,180
1992	1,560,417	1,163,882	11,307	1,175,189	134,340	16,407	1,057,256	303,402	199,759	17,601	88,657	50,686
1993	1,662,582	1,250,540	9,805	1,260,345	144,157	15,888	1,132,076	322,371	208,135	18,340	90,652	52,047
1994	1,784,025	1,348,831	9,572	1,358,403	154,482	15,929	1,219,850	343,248	220,927	19,214	92,848	53,821
1995	1,912,081	1,421,658	12,342	1,434,000	162,475	17,048	1,288,573	383,153	240,355	20,191	94,698	55,672
1996	2,045,056	1,528,577	6,923	1,535,500	172,339	19,457	1,382,618	404,602	257,836	21,197	96,479	57,680
1997	2,144,365	1,607,588	5,293	1,612,881	180,788	29,352	1,461,445	413,766	269,154	21,836	98,202	58,997
1998	2,351,314	1,751,439	4,980	1,756,419	193,755	58,628	1,621,292	447,597	282,425	23,525	99,949	61,402
1999	2,494,894	1,870,105	5,780	1,875,885	206,152	80,868	1,750,601	446,727	297,566	24,597	101,429	62,096
2000	2,744,571	2,040,046	3,974	2,044,020	221,530	101,987	1,924,477	496,088	324,006	26,485	103,626	64,579
2001	2,960,979	2,136,668	6,181	2,142,849	238,480	160,566	2,064,935	530,143	365,901	27,868	106,252	65,186
2002	3,064,535	2,268,171	-2,326	2,265,845	253,841	152,626	2,164,630	504,514	395,391	28,129	108,945	66,069
2003	3,270,736	2,372,069	-3,110	2,368,959	264,067	212,162	2,317,054	530,817	422,865	29,343	111,464	66,412
2004	3,585,172	2,570,214	5,019	2,575,233	285,037	281,292	2,571,488	571,364	442,320	31,344	114,383	68,919
2005	3,915,700	2,822,515	-996	2,821,519	314,242	336,011	2,843,288	589,212	483,200	33,227	117,847	72,146
2006	4,250,155	2,977,121	-10,067	2,967,054	335,518	410,194	3,041,730	675,590	532,835	35,059	121,229	74,460
2007	4,425,026	3,011,422	-14,389	2,997,033	340,586	436,784	3,093,231	767,098	564,697	35,725	123,863	75,098
2008	4,635,921	2,971,484	-4,033	2,967,451	342,469	505,036	3,130,018	834,761	671,142	36,873	125,728	73,713
2009	4,528,290	2,908,104	-3,189	2,904,915	338,907	482,259	3,048,267	750,701	729,322	35,563	127,333	70,838
2010	4,735,507	3,030,441	-2,107	3,028,334	351,199	496,030	3,173,165	768,213	794,129	36,812	128,640	70,846
2011	5,013,350	3,176,664	1,925	3,178,589	328,482	519,807	3,369,914	838,122	805,314	38,577	129,957	73,097
2012	5,260,804	3,322,807	10,583	3,333,390	339,394	516,439	3,510,435	924,346	826,023	40,181	130,927	73,900
2013	5,281,241	3,434,008	546	3,434,554	399,958	463,065	3,497,661	919,145	864,435	39,918	132,301	75,338
2014	5,494,595	3,607,081	-1,771	3,605,310	415,346	420,311	3,610,275	969,558	914,762	41,034	133,905	77,856
2015	5,817,772	3,791,437	-6,905	3,784,532	435,725	459,063	3,807,870	1,035,634	974,268	43,169	134,766	79,117
2016	6,134,840	3,910,351	-7,217	3,903,134	450,769	552,552	4,004,917	1,110,599	1,019,324	44,988	136,366	80,217
2017	6,422,421	4,116,714	788	4,117,502	477,357	562,118	4,202,263	1,152,229	1,067,929	46,295	138,728	81,760
2018	6,670,650	4,299,311	-10,063	4,289,248	498,169	579,893	4,370,972	1,171,940	1,127,738	47,527	140,355	83,271
2019	7,093,687	4,534,263	-8,000	4,526,263	527,291	623,463	4,622,435	1,263,226	1,208,026	50,120	141,533	83,930
2020	7,576,342	4,803,015	-7,993	4,795,022	563,306	506,717	4,738,433	1,265,243	1,572,666	53,040	142,841	84,939
2021	8,207,684	5,154,492	-7,478	5,147,014	599,345	574,046	5,121,715	1,291,177	1,794,792	56,544	145,155	87,300

Personal Income and Employment by Area: Winston-Salem, NC

(Thousands of dollars, except as noted.)

Year	Personal income, total	Earnings by place of work			Less: Contributions for government social insurance	Plus: Adjustment for residence	Equals: Net earnings by place of residence	Plus: Dividends, interest, and rent	Plus: Personal current transfer receipts	Per capita personal income (dollars)	Population (persons)	Total employment
		Nonfarm	Farm	Total								
1970	1,446,372	1,148,746	28,572	1,177,318	80,499	61,225	1,158,044	184,906	103,422	3,814	379,270	176,320
1971	1,574,441	1,243,206	30,541	1,273,747	90,286	67,666	1,251,127	200,669	122,645	4,055	388,244	178,777
1972	1,762,561	1,409,698	29,508	1,439,206	107,273	73,272	1,405,205	219,881	137,475	4,436	397,369	186,455
1973	1,992,434	1,604,394	45,796	1,650,190	140,746	75,694	1,585,138	248,772	158,524	4,947	402,778	197,084
1974	2,206,700	1,762,240	47,581	1,809,821	160,546	79,911	1,729,186	286,528	190,986	5,417	407,337	199,954
1975	2,410,149	1,880,544	43,895	1,924,439	168,190	78,456	1,834,705	310,567	264,877	5,855	411,650	193,474
1976	2,694,649	2,135,171	46,596	2,181,767	194,757	83,590	2,070,600	344,257	279,792	6,469	416,569	201,477
1977	2,991,631	2,398,943	40,238	2,439,181	217,575	87,865	2,309,471	388,543	293,617	7,085	422,231	210,239
1978	3,342,886	2,680,546	49,795	2,730,341	250,523	109,931	2,589,749	438,791	314,346	7,773	430,074	217,753
1979	3,701,489	2,983,833	33,880	3,017,713	290,181	120,419	2,847,951	494,103	359,435	8,453	437,876	224,330
1980	4,147,750	3,268,258	28,126	3,296,384	318,797	133,703	3,111,290	610,723	425,737	9,331	444,515	224,907
1981	4,698,878	3,605,381	54,839	3,660,220	377,432	154,884	3,437,672	773,049	488,157	10,459	449,284	228,321
1982	5,003,261	3,751,384	43,157	3,794,541	394,636	172,720	3,572,625	885,319	545,317	11,025	453,824	225,398
1983	5,414,802	4,073,725	24,697	4,098,422	430,034	208,519	3,876,907	949,708	588,187	11,839	457,356	229,151
1984	6,097,018	4,550,799	40,275	4,591,074	492,124	250,576	4,349,526	1,129,317	618,175	13,190	462,248	242,002
1985	6,615,240	4,961,656	40,881	5,002,537	543,113	268,365	4,727,789	1,223,298	664,153	14,131	468,149	251,201
1986	7,092,801	5,309,801	19,179	5,328,980	592,672	303,357	5,039,665	1,321,378	731,758	15,040	471,586	258,786
1987	7,706,261	5,820,736	22,124	5,842,860	637,994	352,325	5,557,191	1,411,355	737,715	16,083	479,157	268,061
1988	8,511,129	6,406,198	35,284	6,441,482	723,843	392,089	6,109,728	1,604,607	796,794	17,648	482,283	278,597
1989	9,200,503	6,772,581	42,576	6,815,157	763,721	440,164	6,491,600	1,821,116	887,787	18,955	485,397	281,675
1990	9,614,655	6,841,277	60,153	6,901,430	795,950	481,702	6,587,182	2,056,276	971,197	19,620	490,034	288,314
1991	9,836,797	6,995,841	70,763	7,066,604	823,929	464,187	6,706,862	2,029,327	1,100,608	19,814	496,463	283,093
1992	10,490,757	7,530,157	72,156	7,602,313	876,944	497,022	7,222,391	2,058,828	1,209,538	20,851	503,138	286,803
1993	11,077,410	7,896,906	63,196	7,960,102	931,081	570,766	7,599,787	2,151,707	1,325,916	21,633	512,062	294,537
1994	11,706,256	8,417,939	64,387	8,482,326	998,429	585,080	8,068,977	2,255,977	1,381,302	22,433	521,836	300,829
1995	12,584,951	8,883,846	48,271	8,932,117	1,057,656	679,315	8,553,776	2,486,379	1,544,796	23,714	530,693	308,135
1996	13,325,335	9,223,572	65,218	9,288,790	1,091,949	750,008	8,946,849	2,700,627	1,677,859	24,644	540,712	314,617
1997	14,155,489	9,876,386	56,926	9,933,312	1,158,296	771,186	9,546,202	2,857,503	1,751,784	25,757	549,576	320,761
1998	15,077,409	10,484,897	63,776	10,548,673	1,231,355	768,032	10,085,350	3,183,309	1,808,750	27,049	557,410	326,706
1999	15,552,467	10,892,914	69,651	10,962,565	1,278,363	827,643	10,511,845	3,130,938	1,909,684	27,579	563,928	330,837
2000	16,467,536	11,525,513	63,207	11,588,720	1,351,416	827,812	11,065,116	3,335,694	2,066,726	28,829	571,210	336,834
2001	16,864,664	11,790,250	61,806	11,852,056	1,371,367	853,007	11,333,696	3,241,407	2,289,561	29,168	578,186	328,671
2002	17,120,289	11,962,068	29,792	11,991,860	1,378,125	879,830	11,493,565	3,148,320	2,478,404	29,299	584,321	324,828
2003	17,754,493	12,330,437	36,492	12,366,929	1,444,619	923,096	11,845,406	3,289,574	2,619,513	30,145	588,964	323,784
2004	19,025,807	12,998,745	63,455	13,062,200	1,496,592	1,011,439	12,577,047	3,599,928	2,848,832	31,989	594,765	327,520
2005	19,830,661	13,430,615	70,567	13,501,182	1,572,676	1,097,799	13,026,305	3,727,116	3,077,240	32,897	602,805	334,166
2006	21,176,680	14,151,195	60,864	14,212,059	1,634,240	1,158,441	13,736,260	4,043,256	3,397,164	34,518	613,494	340,048
2007	22,170,579	14,512,145	58,802	14,570,947	1,694,133	1,238,978	14,115,792	4,389,391	3,665,396	35,583	623,068	345,798
2008	23,087,236	14,796,126	66,071	14,862,197	1,718,672	1,262,961	14,406,486	4,555,104	4,125,646	36,520	632,186	342,342
2009	22,158,242	14,176,029	57,912	14,233,941	1,675,872	1,112,725	13,670,794	3,871,973	4,615,475	34,748	637,688	329,508
2010	22,921,464	14,897,959	52,139	14,950,098	1,719,546	1,105,035	14,335,587	3,696,231	4,889,646	35,746	641,236	325,618
2011	23,254,213	14,585,537	37,533	14,623,070	1,578,811	1,118,235	14,162,494	4,098,760	4,992,959	36,093	644,284	328,719
2012	24,176,933	15,283,749	65,499	15,349,248	1,620,963	1,264,324	14,992,609	4,160,442	5,023,882	37,376	646,858	332,566
2013	24,032,628	15,278,191	77,310	15,355,501	1,870,223	1,386,744	14,872,022	4,025,491	5,135,115	36,972	650,027	335,631
2014	25,766,542	16,416,621	93,316	16,509,937	1,998,334	1,320,753	15,832,356	4,579,727	5,354,459	39,508	652,182	341,321
2015	26,867,017	17,063,125	87,446	17,150,571	2,074,776	1,351,649	16,427,444	4,795,091	5,644,482	41,024	654,916	346,907
2016	27,470,131	17,361,637	65,007	17,426,644	2,098,801	1,484,045	16,811,888	4,854,974	5,803,269	41,655	659,470	351,981
2017	28,826,674	18,320,564	71,879	18,392,443	2,186,726	1,533,016	17,738,733	5,082,259	6,005,682	43,369	664,684	354,533
2018	29,459,293	18,729,541	24,338	18,753,879	2,228,134	1,526,331	18,052,076	5,091,193	6,316,024	44,058	668,646	360,889
2019	31,113,761	19,628,054	31,974	19,660,028	2,344,048	1,516,913	18,832,893	5,642,116	6,638,752	46,218	673,189	365,789
2020	33,172,146	19,978,606	24,054	20,002,660	2,403,368	1,537,560	19,136,852	5,664,837	8,370,457	49,044	676,369	356,659
2021	36,220,999	21,813,552	52,252	21,865,804	2,575,242	1,568,742	20,859,304	5,789,359	9,572,336	53,154	681,438	367,970

Personal Income and Employment by Area: Worcester, MA-CT

(Thousands of dollars, except as noted.)

Year	Personal income, total	Earnings by place of work			Less: Contributions for government social insurance	Plus: Adjustment for residence	Equals: Net earnings by place of residence	Plus: Dividends, interest, and rent	Plus: Personal current transfer receipts	Per capita personal income (dollars)	Population (persons)	Total employment
		Nonfarm	Farm	Total								
1970	2,936,952	2,187,578	17,410	2,204,988	144,579	166,498	2,226,907	413,891	296,154	4,059	723,625	303,453
1971	3,122,407	2,276,258	17,035	2,293,293	155,062	192,965	2,331,196	435,877	355,334	4,280	729,613	299,766
1972	3,394,252	2,470,779	18,892	2,489,671	177,513	229,145	2,541,303	460,909	392,040	4,646	730,558	305,815
1973	3,761,499	2,759,923	23,340	2,783,263	228,772	266,797	2,821,288	503,462	436,749	5,113	735,701	320,736
1974	4,086,860	2,952,112	15,189	2,967,301	253,560	307,987	3,021,728	557,552	507,580	5,562	734,725	323,556
1975	4,428,904	3,016,742	15,877	3,032,619	249,893	341,857	3,124,583	588,729	715,592	6,040	733,288	309,349
1976	4,814,796	3,343,304	18,528	3,361,832	284,544	389,465	3,466,753	626,623	721,420	6,588	730,817	317,500
1977	5,248,947	3,632,445	16,555	3,649,000	311,374	478,967	3,816,593	688,081	744,273	7,184	730,608	324,246
1978	5,857,676	4,072,032	24,527	4,096,559	359,606	568,781	4,305,734	744,637	807,305	7,918	739,765	337,775
1979	6,536,437	4,515,531	20,310	4,535,841	417,250	681,121	4,799,712	825,565	911,160	8,816	741,446	348,159
1980	7,370,455	4,900,305	16,516	4,916,821	452,368	828,289	5,292,742	1,018,871	1,058,842	9,967	739,491	348,593
1981	8,215,810	5,360,624	20,046	5,380,670	523,478	906,595	5,763,787	1,247,419	1,204,604	11,086	741,103	347,686
1982	8,888,343	5,596,273	31,330	5,627,603	554,140	1,011,321	6,084,784	1,492,426	1,311,133	11,973	742,351	341,024
1983	9,507,163	5,944,602	27,918	5,972,520	596,891	1,147,366	6,522,995	1,610,405	1,373,763	12,822	741,465	343,763
1984	10,726,435	6,776,412	34,314	6,810,726	701,484	1,306,531	7,415,773	1,876,762	1,433,900	14,313	749,409	361,994
1985	11,569,696	7,403,902	29,516	7,433,418	772,509	1,433,828	8,094,737	1,965,862	1,509,097	15,270	757,692	374,819
1986	12,557,204	8,173,489	34,556	8,208,045	863,506	1,502,969	8,847,508	2,114,755	1,594,941	16,398	765,781	390,359
1987	13,678,868	9,132,808	29,315	9,162,123	950,689	1,593,017	9,804,451	2,228,574	1,645,843	17,580	778,071	397,657
1988	15,001,480	10,123,267	26,989	10,150,256	1,070,261	1,722,078	10,802,073	2,449,923	1,749,484	18,916	793,074	413,617
1989	15,957,729	10,582,805	25,262	10,608,067	1,110,465	1,769,635	11,267,237	2,714,797	1,975,695	19,744	808,224	410,592
1990	16,452,448	10,644,295	32,529	10,676,824	1,100,796	1,879,490	11,455,518	2,769,502	2,227,428	20,227	813,391	400,251
1991	16,563,540	10,577,781	32,476	10,610,257	1,110,664	1,805,909	11,305,502	2,725,437	2,532,601	20,386	812,492	382,147
1992	17,312,304	11,250,624	39,186	11,289,810	1,166,011	1,830,541	11,954,340	2,679,633	2,678,331	21,291	813,137	391,834
1993	17,924,129	11,880,588	36,463	11,917,051	1,240,207	1,730,714	12,407,558	2,762,183	2,754,388	21,923	817,597	401,887
1994	18,880,607	12,630,125	33,435	12,663,560	1,323,092	1,768,404	13,108,872	2,856,837	2,914,898	22,949	822,735	411,296
1995	19,755,621	12,978,514	23,408	13,001,922	1,367,829	1,980,201	13,614,294	3,053,282	3,088,045	23,927	825,647	415,200
1996	20,902,087	13,722,182	31,154	13,753,336	1,426,927	2,099,020	14,425,429	3,289,926	3,186,732	25,179	830,128	420,409
1997	22,445,708	14,575,797	31,150	14,606,947	1,506,638	2,548,721	15,649,030	3,506,377	3,290,301	26,824	836,766	429,799
1998	23,684,086	15,576,351	28,875	15,605,226	1,598,779	2,729,868	16,736,315	3,619,460	3,328,311	28,049	844,368	437,985
1999	25,044,942	16,376,252	37,620	16,413,872	1,661,956	3,259,443	18,011,359	3,606,365	3,427,218	29,350	853,319	442,402
2000	27,875,086	18,438,815	39,066	18,477,881	1,857,030	3,704,862	20,325,713	3,920,185	3,629,188	32,349	861,697	454,078
2001	28,909,746	18,979,911	30,865	19,010,776	1,926,871	3,869,118	20,953,023	4,011,110	3,945,613	33,188	871,081	457,330
2002	28,951,739	19,211,722	26,613	19,238,335	1,949,215	3,801,124	21,090,244	3,555,524	4,305,971	32,916	879,568	455,348
2003	30,008,594	19,926,839	28,808	19,955,647	2,008,939	3,877,346	21,824,054	3,641,359	4,543,181	33,827	887,129	457,339
2004	31,627,527	20,881,134	33,100	20,914,234	2,167,520	4,335,577	23,082,291	3,814,755	4,730,481	35,450	892,171	463,766
2005	32,859,688	21,359,256	26,614	21,385,870	2,265,370	4,809,996	23,930,496	3,884,752	5,044,440	36,637	896,901	467,587
2006	34,954,044	22,297,258	20,230	22,317,488	2,333,687	5,262,875	25,246,676	4,390,866	5,316,502	38,746	902,123	472,689
2007	36,903,434	22,965,199	21,099	22,986,298	2,396,603	5,748,021	26,337,716	4,966,675	5,599,043	40,754	905,524	478,942
2008	38,452,195	23,348,692	36,034	23,384,726	2,450,401	5,895,123	26,829,448	5,235,276	6,387,471	42,314	908,735	477,372
2009	37,831,749	22,734,028	29,377	22,763,405	2,396,435	5,605,946	25,972,916	4,804,452	7,054,381	41,420	913,363	464,206
2010	39,351,405	23,819,734	34,175	23,853,909	2,433,523	5,715,542	27,135,928	4,747,738	7,467,739	42,822	918,947	461,436
2011	41,213,525	25,043,922	34,388	25,078,310	2,312,544	5,779,215	28,544,981	5,203,385	7,465,159	44,679	922,436	469,335
2012	42,916,845	25,876,962	41,085	25,918,047	2,359,130	6,141,280	29,700,197	5,685,270	7,531,378	46,397	924,992	473,664
2013	42,892,375	26,495,143	36,764	26,531,907	2,727,776	5,754,527	29,558,658	5,751,918	7,581,799	46,193	928,545	485,078
2014	44,543,796	27,252,850	15,191	27,268,041	2,836,692	6,070,997	30,502,346	6,204,022	7,837,428	47,099	945,756	493,007
2015	46,784,953	28,348,718	10,642	28,359,360	2,905,466	6,366,207	31,820,101	6,569,113	8,395,739	49,172	951,448	509,495
2016	48,173,164	29,247,776	2,080	29,249,856	3,007,583	6,679,563	32,921,836	6,567,278	8,684,050	50,374	956,319	515,870
2017	49,796,830	30,583,005	9,148	30,592,153	3,155,390	6,571,115	34,007,878	6,969,988	8,818,964	51,595	965,148	524,643
2018	51,696,624	31,718,605	3,588	31,722,193	3,281,591	6,863,131	35,303,733	7,130,464	9,262,427	53,178	972,147	531,626
2019	54,323,264	32,932,135	22,029	32,954,164	3,400,396	7,528,661	37,082,429	7,658,647	9,582,188	55,671	975,790	531,268
2020	59,017,932	33,377,785	9,160	33,386,945	3,457,583	7,596,523	37,525,885	7,655,637	13,836,410	60,364	977,701	507,721
2021	63,148,967	35,595,940	9,311	35,605,251	3,712,736	8,997,644	40,890,159	7,802,472	14,456,336	64,540	978,447	525,591

Personal Income and Employment by Area: Yakima, WA

(Thousands of dollars, except as noted.)

Year	Personal income, total	Earnings by place of work			Less: Contributions for government social insurance	Plus: Adjustment for residence	Equals: Net earnings by place of residence	Plus: Dividends, interest, and rent	Plus: Personal current transfer receipts	Per capita personal income (dollars)	Population (persons)	Total employment
		Nonfarm	Farm	Total								
1970	514,992	329,853	45,375	375,228	27,791	8,438	355,875	83,553	75,564	3,537	145,600	63,707
1971	569,171	354,361	64,535	418,896	31,102	7,792	395,586	90,713	82,872	3,845	148,017	62,448
1972	629,237	389,841	76,739	466,580	35,780	8,699	439,499	98,973	90,765	4,180	150,541	64,284
1973	731,091	436,456	114,457	550,913	46,136	10,848	515,625	115,668	99,798	4,845	150,902	67,149
1974	839,680	494,599	137,963	632,562	53,685	13,765	592,642	131,246	115,792	5,409	155,229	69,450
1975	970,992	564,133	151,451	715,584	60,611	20,803	675,776	155,746	139,470	6,099	159,209	72,488
1976	1,016,332	647,718	101,320	749,038	72,029	23,159	700,168	165,139	151,025	6,271	162,074	77,178
1977	1,096,377	710,924	80,806	791,730	79,686	34,101	746,145	188,106	162,126	6,677	164,202	76,262
1978	1,291,969	814,489	134,548	949,037	92,894	44,234	900,377	215,769	175,823	7,763	166,436	78,991
1979	1,436,395	916,956	117,398	1,034,354	107,704	56,288	982,938	249,840	203,617	8,500	168,987	82,216
1980	1,572,482	973,163	116,390	1,089,553	114,788	58,548	1,033,313	295,439	243,730	9,083	173,118	82,688
1981	1,736,534	1,038,836	125,848	1,164,684	131,870	79,250	1,112,064	353,726	270,744	9,911	175,218	82,751
1982	1,828,637	1,057,033	133,228	1,190,261	135,778	69,674	1,124,157	399,479	305,001	10,342	176,825	81,334
1983	1,937,270	1,125,227	141,956	1,267,183	146,168	59,628	1,180,643	431,500	325,127	10,808	179,248	84,131
1984	2,082,747	1,194,894	177,018	1,371,912	161,293	48,837	1,259,456	474,247	349,044	11,557	180,209	84,048
1985	2,118,521	1,226,055	129,882	1,355,937	168,027	52,015	1,239,925	498,628	379,968	11,684	181,321	83,388
1986	2,254,408	1,271,311	195,348	1,466,659	175,992	53,260	1,343,927	513,104	397,377	12,458	180,961	84,095
1987	2,413,624	1,369,906	254,204	1,624,110	190,656	52,657	1,486,111	514,730	412,783	13,283	181,707	92,689
1988	2,485,110	1,469,506	211,266	1,680,772	210,961	55,506	1,525,317	518,897	440,896	13,400	185,454	96,178
1989	2,771,691	1,582,525	285,068	1,867,593	229,564	56,452	1,694,481	589,379	487,831	14,777	187,574	99,415
1990	3,031,486	1,747,375	266,181	2,013,556	257,487	63,279	1,819,348	667,692	544,446	16,001	189,454	101,956
1991	3,234,151	1,888,794	356,699	2,245,493	280,226	40,239	2,005,506	616,402	612,243	16,679	193,904	101,599
1992	3,523,192	2,072,349	382,568	2,454,917	307,326	40,115	2,187,706	644,709	690,777	17,706	198,983	102,197
1993	3,716,883	2,190,600	395,175	2,585,775	323,782	41,249	2,303,242	676,430	737,211	18,196	204,266	103,901
1994	3,873,016	2,333,425	358,599	2,692,024	341,767	42,844	2,393,101	724,559	755,356	18,534	208,963	108,409
1995	4,003,289	2,378,550	352,389	2,730,939	351,871	37,895	2,416,963	762,551	823,775	18,830	212,601	109,268
1996	4,271,553	2,472,624	427,577	2,900,201	352,463	33,638	2,581,376	826,859	863,318	19,872	214,951	111,266
1997	4,409,115	2,621,429	352,730	2,974,159	357,630	30,979	2,647,508	879,354	882,253	20,300	217,201	112,404
1998	4,646,721	2,819,617	407,412	3,227,029	376,463	25,926	2,876,492	875,278	894,951	21,146	219,748	112,073
1999	4,696,711	2,918,366	338,218	3,256,584	382,616	23,479	2,897,447	848,280	950,984	21,197	221,573	112,619
2000	4,966,040	3,037,836	409,241	3,447,077	405,275	19,221	3,061,023	890,854	1,014,163	22,308	222,615	112,920
2001	5,076,949	3,138,952	342,906	3,481,858	420,188	21,241	3,082,911	869,240	1,124,798	22,791	222,757	112,685
2002	5,137,862	3,253,223	366,692	3,619,915	435,840	23,881	3,207,956	779,768	1,150,138	22,998	223,402	112,734
2003	5,496,975	3,411,487	447,849	3,859,336	456,305	22,112	3,425,143	856,402	1,215,430	24,414	225,161	114,189
2004	5,757,660	3,560,481	520,944	4,081,425	480,912	22,187	3,622,700	883,593	1,251,367	25,333	227,280	113,223
2005	5,852,899	3,683,183	449,586	4,132,769	509,296	20,025	3,643,498	879,923	1,329,478	25,607	228,570	114,927
2006	6,119,601	3,860,306	412,924	4,273,230	531,502	13,599	3,755,327	951,344	1,412,930	26,536	230,617	117,779
2007	6,720,381	4,064,040	536,815	4,600,855	555,371	13,457	4,058,941	1,131,570	1,529,870	28,876	232,733	118,536
2008	7,301,125	4,281,593	548,973	4,830,566	593,618	8,990	4,245,938	1,316,237	1,738,950	31,033	235,272	121,722
2009	7,271,292	4,318,647	503,729	4,822,376	614,888	13,687	4,221,175	1,148,999	1,901,118	30,347	239,604	120,007
2010	7,748,493	4,475,432	613,090	5,088,522	631,559	20,411	4,477,374	1,163,710	2,107,409	31,724	244,249	119,123
2011	8,183,555	4,540,347	787,672	5,328,019	589,671	29,345	4,767,693	1,288,913	2,126,949	33,280	245,899	120,041
2012	8,683,466	4,817,007	851,399	5,668,406	610,036	14,082	5,072,452	1,478,324	2,132,690	35,289	246,064	124,847
2013	8,733,443	4,902,924	866,170	5,769,094	683,098	10,104	5,096,100	1,507,920	2,129,423	35,445	246,395	125,387
2014	9,230,415	5,046,822	943,901	5,990,723	720,916	9,814	5,279,621	1,546,874	2,403,920	37,121	248,660	127,305
2015	9,529,470	5,176,384	1,087,887	6,264,271	743,691	17,640	5,538,220	1,638,852	2,352,398	38,115	250,020	128,600
2016	9,750,235	5,391,561	1,046,606	6,438,167	764,188	18,527	5,692,506	1,548,596	2,509,133	38,664	252,180	130,545
2017	10,074,531	5,740,725	1,022,798	6,763,523	824,339	22,282	5,961,466	1,587,957	2,525,108	39,794	253,166	132,628
2018	10,426,221	6,116,728	768,166	6,884,894	846,303	23,211	6,061,802	1,740,001	2,624,418	40,980	254,420	135,025
2019	11,053,209	6,332,376	924,583	7,256,959	850,473	31,676	6,438,162	1,832,939	2,782,108	43,208	255,815	136,742
2020	12,137,974	6,579,203	1,053,025	7,632,228	912,977	33,248	6,752,499	1,831,600	3,553,875	47,315	256,533	132,504
2021	13,025,027	6,843,130	844,288	7,687,418	979,457	37,576	6,745,537	1,889,979	4,389,511	50,872	256,035	136,027

Personal Income and Employment by Area: York-Hanover, PA

(Thousands of dollars, except as noted.)

Year	Personal income, total	Earnings by place of work			Less: Contributions for government social insurance	Plus: Adjustment for residence	Equals: Net earnings by place of residence	Plus: Dividends, interest, and rent	Plus: Personal current transfer receipts	Per capita personal income (dollars)	Population (persons)	Total employment
		Nonfarm	Farm	Total								
1970	1,206,079	1,063,173	9,208	1,072,381	78,376	-31,911	962,094	153,738	90,247	4,411	273,427	139,933
1971	1,279,619	1,100,094	2,949	1,103,043	83,738	-12,199	1,007,106	168,431	104,082	4,587	278,991	137,875
1972	1,425,322	1,215,586	5,097	1,220,683	98,313	4,561	1,126,931	183,687	114,704	5,043	282,646	142,624
1973	1,589,893	1,330,118	14,619	1,344,737	123,335	29,057	1,250,459	209,367	130,067	5,557	286,122	147,199
1974	1,742,726	1,402,195	15,927	1,418,122	133,836	63,257	1,347,543	239,490	155,693	6,036	288,739	146,547
1975	1,899,048	1,455,589	13,416	1,469,005	133,920	88,997	1,424,082	267,599	207,367	6,486	292,808	140,987
1976	2,116,001	1,616,229	19,089	1,635,318	152,229	122,404	1,605,493	285,542	224,966	7,123	297,047	144,496
1977	2,360,782	1,804,018	15,226	1,819,244	170,638	160,373	1,808,979	317,269	234,534	7,852	300,642	148,395
1978	2,683,469	2,069,032	11,914	2,080,946	201,666	204,194	2,083,474	351,589	248,406	8,783	305,545	154,993
1979	3,034,776	2,313,487	22,491	2,335,978	233,864	253,654	2,355,768	400,633	278,375	9,780	310,297	160,882
1980	3,395,023	2,500,700	10,514	2,511,214	254,619	316,783	2,573,378	493,747	327,898	10,826	313,599	161,194
1981	3,726,704	2,693,415	19,911	2,713,326	293,384	323,098	2,743,040	604,794	378,870	11,821	315,266	159,431
1982	3,941,551	2,740,164	16,675	2,756,839	300,531	321,702	2,778,010	712,502	451,039	12,474	315,972	155,440
1983	4,121,294	2,843,039	2,225	2,845,264	317,874	349,470	2,876,860	757,994	486,440	13,037	316,125	154,109
1984	4,524,698	3,161,299	24,713	3,186,012	370,748	376,851	3,192,115	853,818	478,765	14,158	319,582	161,378
1985	4,828,656	3,384,335	20,956	3,405,291	400,799	388,545	3,393,037	924,947	510,672	15,082	320,150	165,404
1986	5,114,408	3,560,217	19,619	3,579,836	422,196	429,750	3,587,390	983,759	543,259	15,881	322,055	169,374
1987	5,461,816	3,888,224	19,581	3,907,805	455,349	439,617	3,892,073	1,010,477	559,266	16,758	325,922	176,386
1988	5,946,635	4,312,767	8,427	4,321,194	513,368	458,476	4,266,302	1,078,546	601,787	17,969	330,944	184,414
1989	6,456,078	4,585,005	20,529	4,605,534	535,964	473,422	4,542,992	1,258,989	654,097	19,211	336,068	188,133
1990	6,771,767	4,843,410	26,711	4,870,121	568,238	486,389	4,788,272	1,263,509	719,986	19,870	340,810	191,073
1991	7,078,679	5,018,191	13,380	5,031,571	594,222	520,292	4,957,641	1,296,188	824,850	20,446	346,209	188,389
1992	7,519,043	5,315,529	37,621	5,353,150	626,641	584,710	5,311,219	1,316,714	891,110	21,419	351,046	188,825
1993	7,911,940	5,519,147	24,733	5,543,880	665,167	639,199	5,517,912	1,461,353	932,675	22,215	356,156	190,523
1994	8,118,686	5,734,614	23,343	5,757,957	706,628	713,539	5,764,868	1,401,464	952,354	22,484	361,092	193,790
1995	8,560,821	6,020,193	11,880	6,032,073	739,982	770,955	6,063,046	1,488,587	1,009,188	23,390	365,997	198,685
1996	9,012,837	6,245,612	35,026	6,280,638	751,965	832,075	6,360,748	1,566,630	1,085,459	24,373	369,781	201,286
1997	9,477,674	6,592,550	12,813	6,605,363	783,392	866,812	6,688,783	1,663,830	1,125,061	25,429	372,706	204,054
1998	9,970,633	6,814,862	16,013	6,830,875	804,427	997,092	7,023,540	1,765,884	1,181,209	26,531	375,810	200,364
1999	10,367,765	7,116,768	9,134	7,125,902	833,167	1,093,718	7,386,453	1,733,730	1,247,582	27,362	378,905	204,405
2000	11,163,228	7,608,911	35,757	7,644,668	878,531	1,141,244	7,907,381	1,909,087	1,346,760	29,166	382,743	210,164
2001	11,540,266	7,800,016	26,391	7,826,407	894,576	1,222,233	8,154,064	1,886,357	1,499,845	29,915	385,773	211,514
2002	11,812,578	7,997,278	10,855	8,008,133	913,868	1,354,373	8,448,638	1,736,066	1,627,874	30,313	389,692	211,138
2003	12,512,475	8,381,488	65,403	8,446,891	946,759	1,446,316	8,946,448	1,829,322	1,736,705	31,670	395,093	211,658
2004	13,806,584	9,250,801	64,880	9,315,681	1,015,615	1,693,996	9,994,062	2,000,687	1,811,835	34,396	401,403	217,006
2005	14,832,287	10,064,916	44,220	10,109,136	1,111,218	1,822,760	10,820,678	2,011,142	2,000,467	36,259	409,066	223,488
2006	15,265,534	9,871,010	27,044	9,898,054	1,127,762	2,104,341	10,874,633	2,225,483	2,165,418	36,517	418,043	226,836
2007	16,706,908	10,675,869	39,815	10,715,684	1,179,812	2,282,372	11,818,244	2,574,275	2,314,389	39,318	424,919	231,790
2008	18,075,800	11,449,478	42,940	11,492,418	1,227,422	2,402,635	12,667,631	2,737,167	2,671,002	42,096	429,399	232,142
2009	17,466,956	10,584,795	30,101	10,614,896	1,184,654	2,429,951	11,860,193	2,607,615	2,999,148	40,337	433,022	223,008
2010	17,728,800	10,745,530	32,063	10,777,593	1,215,354	2,336,839	11,899,078	2,579,550	3,250,172	40,717	435,420	221,987
2011	18,187,806	10,851,737	36,219	10,887,956	1,130,539	2,391,291	12,148,708	2,765,430	3,273,668	41,644	436,749	224,717
2012	18,432,317	10,804,100	51,479	10,855,579	1,130,848	2,362,744	12,087,475	3,026,142	3,318,700	42,126	437,551	225,936
2013	18,521,213	10,983,660	55,157	11,038,817	1,298,367	2,402,844	12,143,294	2,959,567	3,418,352	42,186	439,041	227,264
2014	19,049,849	11,214,050	45,448	11,259,498	1,327,174	2,460,206	12,392,530	3,099,568	3,557,751	42,990	443,127	229,563
2015	19,869,897	11,727,644	17,181	11,744,825	1,384,045	2,590,930	12,951,710	3,153,577	3,764,610	44,649	445,022	231,735
2016	20,591,132	12,130,749	-2,334	12,128,415	1,437,504	2,689,462	13,380,373	3,209,060	4,001,699	45,990	447,735	235,663
2017	21,448,897	12,794,163	23,776	12,817,939	1,528,908	2,748,279	14,037,310	3,346,628	4,064,959	47,637	450,261	237,734
2018	22,434,412	13,276,373	1,438	13,277,811	1,577,189	2,852,745	14,553,367	3,513,663	4,367,382	49,483	453,380	240,499
2019	23,334,786	13,639,431	29,028	13,668,459	1,627,695	3,025,938	15,066,702	3,693,086	4,574,998	51,295	454,912	240,701
2020	25,013,876	13,495,239	10,379	13,505,618	1,600,750	3,145,408	15,050,276	3,679,293	6,284,307	54,808	456,389	230,125
2021	26,544,888	14,462,411	51,104	14,513,515	1,690,621	3,231,669	16,054,563	3,739,183	6,751,142	57,870	458,696	237,934

Personal Income and Employment by Area: Youngstown-Warren-Boardman, OH-PA

(Thousands of dollars, except as noted.)

Year	Personal income, total	Earnings by place of work			Less: Contributions for government social insurance	Plus: Adjustment for residence	Equals: Net earnings by place of residence	Plus: Dividends, interest, and rent	Plus: Personal current transfer receipts	Per capita personal income (dollars)	Population (persons)	Total employment
		Nonfarm	Farm	Total								
1970	2,586,501	2,238,856	8,172	2,247,028	154,468	-36,575	2,055,985	302,231	228,285	3,886	665,569	279,196
1971	2,757,559	2,363,330	7,656	2,370,986	167,755	-39,449	2,163,782	325,056	268,721	4,111	670,741	276,899
1972	3,046,740	2,635,873	8,730	2,644,603	197,250	-46,526	2,400,827	345,972	299,941	4,472	681,278	282,795
1973	3,438,961	3,016,279	14,941	3,031,220	263,301	-55,104	2,712,815	385,235	340,911	5,143	668,722	296,124
1974	3,758,820	3,251,298	15,570	3,266,868	294,955	-62,409	2,909,504	439,851	409,465	5,569	675,013	299,829
1975	3,976,949	3,292,945	17,575	3,310,520	292,039	-59,492	2,958,989	479,999	537,961	6,005	662,274	285,651
1976	4,373,755	3,629,637	20,754	3,650,391	325,744	-68,030	3,256,617	516,562	600,576	6,560	666,754	288,266
1977	4,840,148	4,063,895	17,270	4,081,165	366,240	-76,033	3,638,892	574,078	627,178	7,252	667,417	294,002
1978	5,315,357	4,472,435	12,833	4,485,268	416,924	-76,424	3,991,920	637,191	686,246	7,994	664,956	298,304
1979	5,857,395	4,905,322	13,963	4,919,285	474,007	-79,687	4,365,591	717,975	773,829	8,899	658,231	301,663
1980	6,365,198	5,035,540	8,081	5,043,621	481,906	-76,512	4,485,203	908,296	971,699	9,665	658,600	291,643
1981	6,947,526	5,379,300	12,046	5,391,346	552,630	-84,079	4,754,637	1,123,210	1,069,679	10,640	652,946	286,983
1982	6,934,357	4,925,211	9,375	4,934,586	509,401	-37,514	4,387,671	1,249,465	1,297,221	10,676	649,503	264,325
1983	7,237,696	5,124,635	1,050	5,125,685	538,677	-37,507	4,549,501	1,332,335	1,355,860	11,229	644,566	259,259
1984	7,866,481	5,649,422	17,182	5,666,604	611,158	-40,685	5,014,761	1,499,026	1,352,694	12,344	637,279	267,611
1985	8,216,618	5,885,405	19,729	5,905,134	645,437	-38,678	5,221,019	1,573,157	1,422,442	13,012	631,445	270,681
1986	8,452,983	5,982,789	16,567	5,999,356	667,063	-23,532	5,308,761	1,629,076	1,515,146	13,520	625,219	275,735
1987	8,642,591	6,135,992	22,379	6,158,371	684,228	-15,349	5,458,794	1,602,806	1,580,991	13,957	619,212	280,875
1988	9,360,441	6,773,995	29,579	6,803,574	774,133	-33,250	5,996,191	1,718,182	1,646,068	15,202	615,749	288,063
1989	10,059,013	7,234,872	35,429	7,270,301	835,787	-37,698	6,396,816	1,904,884	1,757,313	16,355	615,048	293,661
1990	10,431,129	7,383,589	33,616	7,417,205	870,440	-28,187	6,518,578	1,919,800	1,992,751	16,989	613,980	294,927
1991	10,700,232	7,555,122	19,772	7,574,894	915,359	-39,668	6,619,867	1,952,970	2,127,395	17,386	615,462	294,326
1992	11,275,211	7,973,450	38,592	8,012,042	955,716	-39,863	7,016,463	1,955,837	2,302,911	18,254	617,681	292,356
1993	11,611,003	8,251,065	25,312	8,276,377	1,010,518	-25,296	7,240,563	1,974,584	2,395,856	18,778	618,328	293,654
1994	12,191,023	8,745,285	26,268	8,771,553	1,081,259	-24,416	7,665,878	2,061,466	2,463,679	19,750	617,253	299,990
1995	12,704,098	8,991,516	21,431	9,012,947	1,121,229	4,143	7,895,861	2,221,992	2,586,245	20,637	615,595	309,477
1996	13,124,480	9,181,409	29,310	9,210,719	1,129,411	35,741	8,117,049	2,324,892	2,682,539	21,363	614,369	311,996
1997	13,706,351	9,564,928	22,530	9,587,458	1,139,754	42,072	8,489,776	2,469,263	2,747,312	22,400	611,902	315,429
1998	14,111,745	9,764,781	24,828	9,789,609	1,133,977	85,026	8,740,658	2,582,902	2,788,185	23,161	609,286	315,929
1999	14,431,489	10,137,844	21,532	10,159,376	1,166,572	91,035	9,083,839	2,488,640	2,859,010	23,815	605,978	317,483
2000	14,951,519	10,362,565	25,020	10,387,585	1,155,371	115,228	9,347,442	2,575,906	3,028,171	24,827	602,227	318,418
2001	15,523,760	10,683,630	18,625	10,702,255	1,190,590	158,201	9,669,866	2,580,167	3,273,727	25,911	599,116	311,150
2002	15,745,732	10,927,480	9,881	10,937,361	1,193,976	169,076	9,912,461	2,401,772	3,431,499	26,465	594,958	305,452
2003	16,301,179	11,309,812	17,732	11,327,544	1,244,562	191,066	10,274,048	2,461,533	3,565,598	27,535	592,016	302,591
2004	16,738,292	11,636,756	25,413	11,662,169	1,301,806	238,063	10,598,426	2,446,352	3,693,514	28,443	588,478	301,803
2005	17,212,008	11,904,728	18,231	11,922,959	1,348,413	261,790	10,836,336	2,470,311	3,905,361	29,461	584,222	303,520
2006	18,140,759	12,559,328	15,097	12,574,425	1,424,440	262,046	11,412,031	2,669,951	4,058,777	31,255	580,420	302,814
2007	18,592,975	12,382,431	30,345	12,412,776	1,414,585	310,985	11,309,176	3,019,839	4,263,960	32,305	575,543	301,433
2008	19,088,275	12,203,707	17,892	12,221,599	1,412,426	362,149	11,171,322	3,158,871	4,758,082	33,432	570,952	295,953
2009	18,144,795	11,079,743	11,652	11,091,395	1,317,140	376,897	10,151,152	2,777,723	5,215,920	31,936	568,156	280,869
2010	18,719,541	11,554,839	25,746	11,580,585	1,349,339	343,013	10,574,259	2,780,342	5,364,940	33,146	564,760	280,982
2011	19,846,393	12,319,379	53,122	12,372,501	1,290,793	347,938	11,429,646	2,971,944	5,444,803	35,293	562,339	285,225
2012	20,234,142	12,599,645	43,137	12,642,782	1,305,705	382,568	11,719,645	3,160,261	5,354,236	36,223	558,594	287,302
2013	20,297,659	12,642,090	52,924	12,695,014	1,426,425	437,781	11,706,370	3,106,566	5,484,723	36,507	555,998	287,503
2014	20,892,452	12,832,017	44,006	12,876,023	1,452,493	479,450	11,902,980	3,288,793	5,700,679	37,515	556,915	287,915
2015	21,425,360	13,136,963	10,734	13,147,697	1,486,922	486,783	12,147,558	3,392,688	5,885,114	38,703	553,591	287,937
2016	21,564,914	13,072,518	-1,805	13,070,713	1,511,318	477,208	12,036,603	3,479,667	6,048,644	39,204	550,063	288,173
2017	21,953,984	13,225,337	11,998	13,237,335	1,558,517	511,345	12,190,163	3,639,002	6,124,819	40,099	547,497	284,325
2018	22,591,657	13,585,807	11,568	13,597,375	1,592,218	566,748	12,571,905	3,693,427	6,326,325	41,450	545,030	284,880
2019	23,032,361	13,482,195	9,046	13,491,241	1,605,855	658,927	12,544,313	3,914,921	6,573,127	42,450	542,582	280,234
2020	24,830,397	13,315,564	17,655	13,333,219	1,593,784	682,643	12,422,078	3,914,586	8,493,733	46,009	539,686	266,565
2021	26,313,563	14,099,572	38,870	14,138,442	1,654,938	740,689	13,224,193	3,980,765	9,108,605	48,904	538,069	271,861

Personal Income and Employment by Area: Yuba City, CA

(Thousands of dollars, except as noted.)

Year	Personal income, total	Earnings by place of work			Less: Contributions for government social insurance	Plus: Adjustment for residence	Equals: Net earnings by place of residence	Plus: Dividends, interest, and rent	Plus: Personal current transfer receipts	Per capita personal income (dollars)	Population (persons)	Total employment
		Nonfarm	Farm	Total								
1970	381,992	247,601	45,848	293,449	17,043	-1,081	275,325	67,151	39,516	4,385	87,104	38,704
1971	416,455	269,274	52,357	321,631	19,232	-1,053	301,346	71,329	43,780	4,714	88,345	39,301
1972	453,626	290,533	63,161	353,694	21,250	-1,525	330,919	76,324	46,383	5,184	87,505	39,903
1973	511,582	304,200	96,542	400,742	24,323	-2,038	374,381	85,213	51,988	5,686	89,980	39,333
1974	589,712	336,569	125,115	461,684	27,903	-3,630	430,151	95,524	64,037	6,455	91,363	40,753
1975	639,526	374,793	111,918	486,711	31,194	-4,492	451,025	110,054	78,447	6,889	92,830	42,061
1976	647,325	410,241	71,770	482,011	35,046	-5,656	441,309	116,543	89,473	6,744	95,979	42,261
1977	729,495	447,835	99,000	546,835	38,607	-6,366	501,862	128,930	98,703	7,524	96,962	42,971
1978	800,278	504,366	85,799	590,165	43,672	-6,830	539,663	149,769	110,846	8,139	98,325	44,298
1979	894,183	559,315	95,175	654,490	49,749	-6,324	598,417	170,628	125,138	8,888	100,611	45,882
1980	1,012,341	601,249	121,553	722,802	52,199	-7,344	663,259	197,953	151,129	9,887	102,388	45,871
1981	1,101,199	641,567	119,557	761,124	60,425	-8,748	691,951	231,541	177,707	10,606	103,831	45,667
1982	1,118,935	665,971	75,625	741,596	62,819	-6,008	672,769	251,352	194,814	10,516	106,405	45,349
1983	1,151,034	691,779	41,179	732,958	66,645	692	667,005	270,596	213,433	10,610	108,483	45,038
1984	1,307,254	741,008	100,198	841,206	73,967	10,438	777,677	300,839	228,738	11,987	109,052	45,505
1985	1,412,011	779,330	127,016	906,346	79,025	22,850	850,171	314,183	247,657	12,729	110,929	46,019
1986	1,472,359	842,915	94,718	937,633	86,561	32,406	883,478	324,136	264,745	13,116	112,256	46,253
1987	1,582,880	899,183	123,432	1,022,615	93,710	44,673	973,578	334,836	274,466	13,818	114,554	48,049
1988	1,684,424	979,189	106,519	1,085,708	106,289	55,869	1,035,288	351,552	297,584	14,407	116,916	50,737
1989	1,844,201	1,056,469	105,023	1,161,492	116,786	69,504	1,114,210	400,703	329,288	15,405	119,714	53,653
1990	1,937,776	1,120,634	79,553	1,200,187	123,512	89,210	1,165,885	406,105	365,786	15,691	123,499	54,925
1991	2,111,973	1,191,846	121,389	1,313,235	133,488	89,124	1,268,871	429,192	413,910	16,672	126,677	56,571
1992	2,260,180	1,246,224	135,722	1,381,946	139,558	93,742	1,336,130	443,911	480,139	17,401	129,886	56,076
1993	2,329,892	1,271,636	151,036	1,422,672	142,812	96,344	1,376,204	449,940	503,748	17,657	131,950	56,416
1994	2,430,384	1,325,659	173,133	1,498,792	147,653	105,572	1,456,711	465,993	507,680	18,067	134,518	57,920
1995	2,524,598	1,380,505	160,978	1,541,483	151,059	115,902	1,506,326	486,488	531,784	18,656	135,323	59,036
1996	2,621,575	1,422,083	160,395	1,582,478	151,366	126,390	1,557,502	509,258	554,815	19,254	136,160	60,320
1997	2,732,275	1,527,763	139,784	1,667,547	157,720	142,043	1,651,870	524,956	555,449	20,028	136,425	60,517
1998	2,876,502	1,647,110	101,503	1,748,613	164,775	161,126	1,744,964	537,394	594,144	20,994	137,016	61,798
1999	3,132,338	1,759,555	199,079	1,958,634	177,675	182,379	1,963,338	535,708	633,292	22,682	138,097	63,347
2000	3,263,431	1,863,093	169,554	2,032,647	187,549	212,581	2,057,679	558,159	647,593	23,383	139,564	63,301
2001	3,375,608	1,984,893	125,132	2,110,025	212,204	222,767	2,120,588	538,544	716,476	23,875	141,387	61,499
2002	3,541,209	2,117,430	116,146	2,233,576	228,961	251,446	2,256,061	516,285	768,863	24,547	144,262	62,404
2003	3,804,270	2,262,049	152,882	2,414,931	245,998	282,847	2,451,780	530,546	821,944	25,808	147,404	62,573
2004	4,090,908	2,392,703	158,332	2,551,035	269,310	372,466	2,654,191	581,850	854,867	27,232	150,226	63,898
2005	4,337,785	2,496,039	121,052	2,617,091	281,570	508,040	2,843,561	613,890	880,334	27,977	155,049	64,648
2006	4,742,914	2,674,224	139,515	2,813,739	292,823	607,197	3,128,113	659,199	955,602	29,572	160,384	66,167
2007	5,134,442	2,809,052	160,200	2,969,252	300,487	672,571	3,341,336	767,855	1,025,251	31,361	163,720	67,736
2008	5,417,032	2,793,418	262,138	3,055,556	304,945	723,917	3,474,528	785,213	1,157,291	32,706	165,628	65,442
2009	5,446,689	2,802,294	353,535	3,155,829	310,255	582,729	3,428,303	751,802	1,266,584	32,817	165,973	63,426
2010	5,524,565	2,898,307	275,591	3,173,898	308,127	539,133	3,404,904	718,811	1,400,850	33,064	167,087	62,526
2011	5,708,358	2,958,370	288,913	3,247,283	290,405	548,621	3,505,499	773,455	1,429,404	34,193	166,946	62,563
2012	5,715,872	3,027,936	231,056	3,258,992	299,536	510,369	3,469,825	804,081	1,441,966	34,243	166,923	63,966
2013	5,964,527	3,116,124	311,468	3,427,592	341,214	554,889	3,621,267	847,940	1,495,320	35,601	167,539	65,465
2014	6,110,566	3,275,029	168,314	3,443,343	356,390	540,800	3,627,753	879,016	1,603,797	35,914	170,146	66,816
2015	6,586,420	3,458,352	200,625	3,658,977	372,684	612,661	3,898,954	943,329	1,744,137	38,377	171,626	68,645
2016	6,804,613	3,617,973	231,827	3,849,800	391,954	579,029	4,036,875	956,736	1,811,002	39,213	173,529	69,835
2017	6,951,901	3,797,302	229,655	4,026,957	413,297	599,274	4,212,934	962,554	1,776,413	39,484	176,069	71,448
2018	7,307,447	3,980,034	211,856	4,191,890	435,587	687,998	4,444,301	995,352	1,867,794	41,149	177,586	73,172
2019	7,726,896	4,185,977	173,502	4,359,479	463,209	751,285	4,647,555	1,055,002	2,024,339	42,979	179,785	74,956
2020	8,698,071	4,430,533	209,152	4,639,685	492,565	702,052	4,849,172	1,073,672	2,775,227	47,947	181,412	75,348
2021	9,338,369	4,717,719	154,349	4,872,068	522,666	793,336	5,142,738	1,095,842	3,099,789	51,174	182,484	76,860

Personal Income and Employment by Area: Yuma, AZ

(Thousands of dollars, except as noted.)

| Year | Personal income, total | Derivation of personal income | | | | | | | | | Per capita personal income (dollars) | Population (persons) | Total employment |
| | | Earnings by place of work | | | Less: Contributions for government social insurance | Plus: Adjustment for residence | Equals: Net earnings by place of residence | Plus: Dividends, interest, and rent | Plus: Personal current transfer receipts | | | |
		Nonfarm	Farm	Total								
1970	235,094	166,029	29,515	195,544	11,394	-7,832	176,318	42,539	16,237	3,828	61,415	29,730
1971	272,044	197,321	27,253	224,574	14,114	-8,281	202,179	50,514	19,351	4,195	64,853	31,172
1972	296,854	210,699	34,364	245,063	15,579	-9,060	220,424	54,072	22,358	4,421	67,150	31,018
1973	323,703	231,159	30,905	262,064	18,851	-9,420	233,793	62,827	27,083	4,713	68,685	31,328
1974	414,496	261,191	82,162	343,353	22,284	-11,295	309,774	72,681	32,041	5,806	71,396	32,675
1975	432,086	297,812	49,068	346,880	25,142	-14,734	307,004	82,298	42,784	6,223	69,434	33,614
1976	485,479	335,643	57,368	393,011	28,944	-16,513	347,554	88,321	49,604	6,348	76,476	35,033
1977	520,645	362,899	61,665	424,564	31,563	-20,921	372,080	96,629	51,936	6,553	79,454	36,573
1978	580,758	410,261	64,781	475,042	36,149	-28,224	410,669	112,713	57,376	7,198	80,680	38,692
1979	703,048	474,938	105,570	580,508	44,524	-33,164	502,820	131,658	68,570	8,419	83,512	39,541
1980	791,920	520,044	117,724	637,768	49,114	-37,484	551,170	155,490	85,260	8,665	91,393	40,634
1981	863,428	555,336	106,873	662,209	56,585	-22,536	583,088	178,186	102,154	9,402	91,834	40,844
1982	903,925	563,940	104,043	667,983	57,259	-20,977	589,747	202,453	111,725	9,629	93,878	40,449
1983	865,388	554,421	68,863	623,284	57,148	-17,587	548,549	207,200	109,639	10,299	84,027	38,578
1984	978,765	627,396	88,653	716,049	66,181	-18,540	631,328	235,898	111,539	11,465	85,373	40,324
1985	1,084,486	668,738	130,208	798,946	71,816	-17,213	709,917	260,738	113,831	12,384	87,572	41,031
1986	1,144,579	737,509	88,883	826,392	80,405	-14,977	731,010	284,635	128,934	12,647	90,505	42,571
1987	1,294,495	800,117	163,863	963,980	87,571	-12,610	863,799	289,346	141,350	13,967	92,684	45,954
1988	1,436,977	864,850	236,865	1,101,715	98,423	-8,111	995,181	288,803	152,993	14,804	97,064	48,117
1989	1,473,542	918,771	160,598	1,079,369	109,005	-988	969,376	312,368	191,798	14,254	103,380	50,231
1990	1,533,564	971,705	137,633	1,109,338	118,748	2,223	992,813	323,245	217,506	14,191	108,063	50,626
1991	1,688,767	1,070,171	171,190	1,241,361	130,802	-7,047	1,103,512	333,826	251,429	15,083	111,967	53,294
1992	1,818,271	1,151,568	162,719	1,314,287	141,263	-4,433	1,168,591	342,483	307,197	15,323	118,660	54,781
1993	1,979,645	1,201,331	245,996	1,447,327	148,331	-5,198	1,293,798	351,600	334,247	15,851	124,892	55,460
1994	2,014,037	1,284,795	153,413	1,438,208	157,771	-8,876	1,271,561	386,184	356,292	15,738	127,975	57,080
1995	2,355,018	1,355,256	376,898	1,732,154	158,176	-11,050	1,562,928	413,608	378,482	17,871	131,776	59,415
1996	2,273,318	1,421,267	196,477	1,617,744	169,677	-12,589	1,435,478	438,473	399,367	16,564	137,248	63,061
1997	2,454,744	1,546,450	216,401	1,762,851	179,788	-16,118	1,566,945	471,186	416,613	17,059	143,896	63,462
1998	2,674,837	1,633,708	324,637	1,958,345	187,860	-15,317	1,755,168	476,107	443,562	17,944	149,065	66,554
1999	2,707,199	1,692,126	258,433	1,950,559	194,492	-12,692	1,743,375	485,899	477,925	17,391	155,665	66,938
2000	2,873,314	1,772,768	307,903	2,080,671	202,805	-12,719	1,865,147	515,555	492,612	17,894	160,576	67,936
2001	3,059,482	1,935,107	237,813	2,172,920	226,046	-826	1,946,048	551,902	561,532	18,784	162,873	70,656
2002	3,338,272	2,071,415	324,370	2,395,785	246,650	832	2,149,967	561,067	627,238	20,183	165,398	72,784
2003	3,612,220	2,376,946	217,181	2,594,127	271,686	3,016	2,325,457	600,393	686,370	21,501	168,003	74,549
2004	4,060,614	2,644,438	324,288	2,968,726	301,169	2,594	2,670,151	653,478	736,985	23,496	172,824	78,518
2005	4,330,635	2,810,279	319,080	3,129,359	324,237	6,493	2,811,615	712,449	806,571	24,218	178,816	80,808
2006	4,585,650	3,083,977	225,494	3,309,471	351,815	11,363	2,969,019	743,623	873,008	24,943	183,848	83,776
2007	4,930,766	3,219,653	293,505	3,513,158	379,060	14,305	3,148,403	835,246	947,117	26,317	187,357	85,115
2008	5,105,880	3,297,855	187,889	3,485,744	396,181	19,539	3,109,102	877,810	1,118,968	26,704	191,202	83,665
2009	5,195,269	3,208,666	188,849	3,397,515	391,913	16,419	3,022,021	904,811	1,268,437	26,819	193,714	79,960
2010	5,447,386	3,273,668	311,060	3,584,728	400,555	21,984	3,206,157	847,494	1,393,735	27,631	197,148	79,901
2011	5,749,007	3,365,075	457,085	3,822,160	369,652	25,829	3,478,337	892,877	1,377,793	28,337	202,881	80,988
2012	5,670,567	3,454,632	270,773	3,725,405	378,927	33,448	3,379,926	930,558	1,360,083	28,000	202,520	82,389
2013	5,979,268	3,522,224	472,829	3,995,053	430,418	41,524	3,606,159	983,847	1,389,262	29,535	202,447	83,070
2014	6,041,347	3,643,369	339,459	3,982,828	439,722	44,260	3,587,366	988,700	1,465,281	30,409	198,670	83,664
2015	6,466,569	3,816,940	566,752	4,383,692	459,973	51,269	3,974,988	980,728	1,510,853	32,576	198,510	85,800
2016	6,622,756	3,882,402	588,163	4,470,565	472,828	51,270	4,049,007	1,003,974	1,569,775	33,253	199,165	88,201
2017	7,117,783	4,209,284	612,109	4,821,393	513,463	53,177	4,361,107	1,077,842	1,678,834	35,604	199,915	87,430
2018	7,155,092	4,404,019	399,516	4,803,535	545,661	52,018	4,309,892	1,081,496	1,763,704	35,673	200,572	89,420
2019	7,603,746	4,500,725	578,416	5,079,141	564,152	53,816	4,568,805	1,120,307	1,914,634	37,624	202,099	90,291
2020	8,735,911	4,833,440	343,071	5,176,511	610,063	58,316	4,624,764	1,131,102	2,980,045	42,732	204,437	89,418
2021	9,169,548	5,188,165	284,696	5,472,861	660,548	62,967	4,875,280	1,137,536	3,156,732	44,299	206,990	91,280

PART B

GROSS DOMESTIC PRODUCT (GDP) BY REGION, STATE, AND AREA

PART B: GROSS DOMESTIC PRODUCT (GDP) BY REGION, STATE, AND AREA

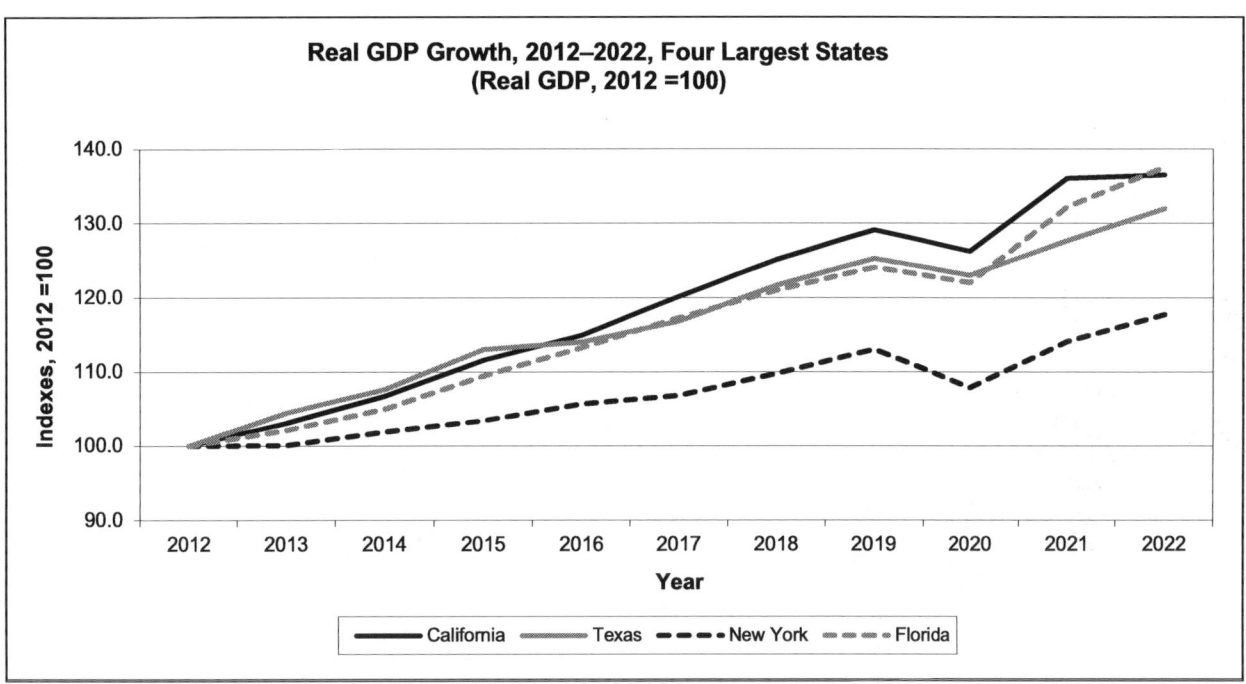

Real GDP Growth, 2012–2022, Four Largest States
(Real GDP, 2012 =100)

HIGHLIGHTS

- GDP increased in all states in 2021, after decreasing in all states in 2020. The nationwide GDP rose 5.7 percent in 2021. Tennessee had the largest increase in GDP of 8.6 percent, followed by New Hampshire (8.5 percent) and California (7.8 percent). The states with the smallest increase were Alaska (0.3 percent), Wyoming (1.1 percent), and North Dakota (2.1 percent).

- The three states with the largest GDP in 2021 were California ($2.9 trillion), Texas ($1.8 trillion), and New York ($1.5 trillion). Together, those three states produced 31.9 percent of the total U.S. GDP in 2021. The states with the lowest GDP were Vermont ($29.7 billion), Wyoming ($36.7 billion), and Montana ($49.0 billion).

- GDP fell in all but 33 metropolitan statistical areas (MSAs) in 2020. Sierra Vista-Douglas, AZ, experienced the largest growth in GDP among all MSAs from 2019 to 2020 at 5.2 percent. Kahului-Wailuku-Lahaina, HI, experienced the largest decline in GDP from 2019 to 2020, at −20.4 percent.

- New York-Newark-Jersey City, NY-NJ-PA, which had the largest GDP among all MSAs, comprised 9.2 percent of the total U.S. metropolitan portion of GDP in 2020, followed by Los Angeles-Long Beach-Anaheim, CA, with 5.4 percent of the total GDP from all MSAs.

PART B NOTES AND DEFINITIONS: GROSS DOMESTIC PRODUCT BY REGION, STATE, AND AREA

Source: U.S. Department of Commerce, Bureau of Economic Analysis (BEA), https://www.bea.gov.

The following definitions are from the BEA. In a following section, further detail and explanation of the concepts is provided.

BEA Definitions

Definitions. GDP by state is the state counterpart of the nation's gross domestic product (GDP), the BEA's featured and most comprehensive measure of U.S. economic activity. GDP by state is derived as the sum of the GDP originating in all the industries in a state.

The statistics of real GDP by state are prepared in chained (1997 or 2012) dollars. Real GDP by state is an inflation-adjusted measure of each state's gross product that is based on national prices for the goods and services produced within that state. The statistics of real GDP by state and of quantity indexes with a reference year of 2012 were derived by applying national chain-type price indexes to the current-dollar values of GDP by state for the 64 detailed NAICS-based industries for 1997 forward.

The chain-type index formula that is used in the national accounts is then used to calculate the values of total real GDP by state and of real GDP by state at more aggregated industry levels. Real GDP by state may reflect a substantial volume of output that is sold to other states and countries. To the extent that a state's output is produced and sold in national markets at relatively uniform prices (or sold locally at national prices), real GDP by state captures the differences across states that reflect the relative differences in the mix of goods and services that the states produce. However, real GDP by state does not capture geographic differences in the prices of goods and services that are produced and sold locally.

Relation of GDP by state to U.S. Gross Domestic Product (GDP). An industry's GDP by state, or its value added, in practice, is calculated as the sum of incomes earned by labor and capital and the costs incurred in the production of goods and services. That is, it includes the wages and salaries that workers earn, the income earned by individual or joint entrepreneurs as well as by corporations, and business taxes such as sales, property, and federal excise taxes, which count as a business expense.

GDP is calculated as the sum of what consumers, businesses, and government spend on final goods and services, plus investment and net foreign trade. In theory, incomes earned should equal what is spent, but due to different data sources, income earned, usually referred to as gross domestic income (GDI), does not always equal what is spent (GDP). The difference is referred to as the "statistical discrepancy."

Starting with the 2004 comprehensive revision, BEA's annual industry accounts and its GDP-by-state accounts allocate the statistical discrepancy across all private-sector industries. Therefore, the GDP-by-state statistics are now conceptually more similar to the GDP statistics in the national accounts than they had been in the past.

U.S. real GDP by state for the advance year, 2020, may differ from the Annual Industry Accounts' GDP by industry and, hence NIPA (national income and product accounts) GDP, because of different sources and vintages of data used to estimate GDP by state and NIPA GDP. For the revised years of 1997–2019, U.S. GDP by state is nearly identical to GDP by industry except for small differences resulting from GDP by state's exclusion of overseas Federal military and civilian activity (because it cannot be attributed to a particular state). The statistics of GDP by industry are from the 2020 annual update of the NIPAs, released in July 2020. However, because of revisions since July 2020, GDP in the NIPAs may differ from U.S. GDP by state.

BEA's national, international, regional, and industry statistics; the Survey of Current Business; and BEA news releases are available without charge on BEA's Web site at www.bea.gov. By visiting the site, you can also subscribe to receive free e-mail summaries of BEA releases and announcements.

Further Notes

The value of an industry's GDP is equal to the market value of its gross output (which consists of sales or receipts and other operating income, taxes on production and imports, and inventory change) minus the value of its intermediate inputs (which consist of energy, raw materials, semifinished goods, and services that are purchased from domestic industries or foreign sources). In concept, this definition is equal to the sum of labor and property-type income earned in that industry in the production of GDP, plus commodity taxes. Property-type income is the sum of corporate profits, proprietors' income, rental income of persons, net interest, capital consumption allowances, business transfer payments, and the current surplus of government enterprises less subsidies.

In practice, GDP by state, like GDP by industry, is measured using the incomes data rather than data on gross output and intermediate inputs, which are not available on a sufficiently detailed and timely basis.

Therefore, the *value* of *GDP by state* is defined as the sum of labor and property-type incomes originating in each of 63 industries in that state, plus commodity taxes, and plus the allocated value of the statistical discrepancy between national GDP and national gross national income.

Chained-dollar estimates. The effect of the "chained-dollar" deflation procedure that BEA uses is to combine the real, inflation-adjusted, quantity changes in output between two adjacent time periods for individual products and industries using, as weights for the individual products, their average prices in those two periods. The estimates for successive time periods are then "chained" each to the previous one to provide a continuous index of real quantities that is not distorted by using prices from a single base year.

GDP by state is now calculated on a North American Industry Classification System (NAICS) basis back through 1997. Data for earlier years, beginning with 1977, were calculated on the Standard Industrial Classification (SIC) basis. According to BEA (in a "Cautionary note" on the Web site, dated June 7, 2007), "There is a discontinuity in the GDP by state time series at 1997, where the data change from SIC industry definitions to NAICS industry definitions. This discontinuity results from many sources, including differences in source data and different estimation methodologies. In addition, the NAICS-based GDP by state estimates are consistent with U.S. gross domestic product (GDP) while the SIC-based GDP by state estimates are consistent with U.S. gross domestic income (GDI). This data discontinuity may affect both the levels and the growth rates of the GDP by state estimates. Users of the GDP by state estimates are strongly cautioned against appending the two data series in an attempt to construct a single time series of GDP by state estimates for 1963 to 2006."

Patterns of Economic Change nevertheless provides SIC-based data for 1980–1997 for those who require information about states' economic growth before 1997.

Gross Domestic Product by Region and State

(Millions of chained 1997 or 2012 dollars; index numbers)

Year	United States	New England	Mideast	Great Lakes	Plains	Southeast	Southwest	Rocky Mountain	Far West	Alabama	Alaska	Arizona	Arkansas
VALUE													
Chained 1997 Dollars													
1980............................	4,908,867	1,012,776	854,483	344,295	976,312	481,736	143,449	824,862	64,582	22,440	55,561	34,773	599,507
1981............................	5,042,118	1,028,056	861,593	355,679	1,008,512	508,762	148,620	851,427	65,771	25,866	57,106	36,018	619,243
1982............................	4,977,350	1,020,670	822,244	346,904	997,979	510,378	147,222	849,741	64,134	26,543	55,763	35,055	619,420
1983............................	5,120,074	1,055,252	849,428	349,664	1,037,194	509,902	148,939	874,727	67,305	25,822	58,950	36,179	641,585
1984............................	5,485,271	1,120,588	916,372	376,210	1,116,483	541,315	156,456	936,298	70,481	26,854	65,288	39,015	693,095
1985............................	5,704,145	1,158,560	946,668	386,662	1,166,972	564,578	160,383	979,706	73,801	29,834	69,447	39,403	728,599
1986............................	5,826,832	1,192,646	962,229	388,432	1,203,514	555,866	158,252	1,010,168	74,558	24,957	73,546	40,177	756,166
1987............................	6,076,695	1,253,511	988,285	401,771	1,265,154	556,371	160,106	1,071,727	78,659	29,525	76,600	41,566	802,816
1988............................	6,398,624	1,327,678	1,035,997	416,799	1,330,988	586,844	166,009	1,131,172	82,508	27,843	80,258	43,158	848,273
1989............................	6,540,047	1,340,174	1,057,952	427,444	1,361,603	598,852	169,205	1,177,017	82,408	28,986	80,971	44,012	880,307
1990............................	6,638,210	1,351,182	1,062,296	433,341	1,382,836	614,113	174,758	1,218,168	83,766	28,772	81,606	44,496	906,103
1991............................	6,627,809	1,330,568	1,057,697	438,079	1,397,392	625,303	179,276	1,207,739	86,116	25,821	81,946	46,498	893,112
1992............................	6,828,525	1,353,418	1,106,985	457,254	1,449,519	654,652	189,490	1,218,219	89,814	26,151	90,282	49,260	891,631
1993............................	6,967,716	1,366,936	1,133,832	459,352	1,498,996	681,390	201,103	1,225,572	91,168	26,048	94,916	50,756	888,070
1994............................	7,288,327	1,395,466	1,207,063	490,357	1,587,062	723,716	214,348	1,255,607	94,803	26,188	104,104	53,641	904,778
1995............................	7,539,096	1,426,803	1,235,447	505,631	1,651,779	759,372	226,604	1,300,697	98,024	27,609	112,020	55,836	940,599
1996............................	7,871,721	1,475,796	1,283,159	532,340	1,720,686	805,125	239,357	1,363,152	101,379	27,271	120,869	58,346	978,300
1997............................	8,284,432	1,535,947	1,345,334	558,791	1,802,254	866,050	253,743	1,443,206	104,805	27,581	129,279	60,333	1,037,091
Chained 2012 Dollars													
1997[1]........................	11,529,157	644,304	2,247,518	1,886,638	775,779	2,559,825	1,219,650	355,338	1,952,513	144,501	42,211	168,409	82,571
1998[1]........................	12,045,824	669,385	2,303,815	1,952,414	799,886	2,679,378	1,291,419	380,836	2,068,915	149,568	41,096	183,061	84,571
1999[1]........................	12,623,361	698,205	2,404,258	2,028,189	823,041	2,805,799	1,349,498	404,324	2,204,996	154,900	40,591	198,700	89,115
2000[1]........................	13,138,035	747,745	2,495,475	2,086,428	859,199	2,875,573	1,399,178	430,731	2,346,005	157,221	39,407	208,440	89,872
2001[1]........................	13,263,417	757,420	2,545,358	2,066,244	858,190	2,915,810	1,433,412	435,651	2,335,553	156,853	40,959	213,166	89,789
2002[1]........................	13,488,357	761,438	2,564,150	2,103,977	878,909	2,988,954	1,468,710	440,386	2,379,319	160,422	42,979	220,697	92,951
2003[1]........................	13,865,519	776,352	2,602,140	2,147,347	908,826	3,095,288	1,494,711	448,010	2,465,193	165,135	42,355	234,066	96,945
2004[1]........................	14,399,696	808,409	2,674,645	2,203,913	943,499	3,238,847	1,574,754	462,706	2,557,366	176,625	44,055	244,317	101,734
2005[1]........................	14,901,269	823,541	2,732,263	2,245,204	973,678	3,393,498	1,631,071	488,570	2,675,247	184,370	45,657	262,326	105,980
2006[1]........................	15,315,943	845,679	2,779,648	2,264,732	987,473	3,478,442	1,741,494	509,836	2,782,330	187,271	49,190	274,179	108,461
2007[1]........................	15,623,871	864,737	2,816,894	2,280,391	1,007,712	3,491,403	1,812,223	530,342	2,848,735	189,003	51,721	283,251	107,606
2008[1]........................	15,642,962	871,392	2,834,463	2,232,291	1,018,608	3,465,267	1,812,205	538,772	2,877,635	186,947	51,252	280,810	106,537
2009[1]........................	15,236,262	847,918	2,826,401	2,120,547	994,034	3,344,254	1,783,064	524,741	2,783,389	180,707	56,215	257,499	102,997
2010[1]........................	15,648,991	871,287	2,915,024	2,190,695	1,019,544	3,406,995	1,818,424	530,904	2,840,235	184,702	54,602	260,307	105,662
2011[1]........................	15,891,534	874,676	2,931,298	2,239,180	1,042,277	3,429,359	1,873,580	539,570	2,881,974	187,606	55,280	266,102	107,933
2012[1]........................	16,253,970	886,831	3,000,390	2,272,451	1,068,680	3,463,375	1,955,420	545,856	2,947,740	189,246	58,284	271,440	108,492
2013[1]........................	16,553,348	883,832	3,015,840	2,296,353	1,082,005	3,504,568	2,022,738	561,828	3,024,136	191,370	55,354	273,482	110,752
2014[1]........................	16,932,051	892,794	3,064,347	2,350,413	1,112,701	3,566,659	2,084,949	581,511	3,120,257	189,886	54,188	276,949	111,735
2015[1]........................	17,390,295	919,158	3,117,788	2,377,290	1,131,523	3,659,520	2,175,132	603,077	3,256,305	191,335	54,741	282,577	112,351
2016[1]........................	17,680,274	930,060	3,169,515	2,397,150	1,139,111	3,731,746	2,194,018	615,453	3,356,107	194,284	54,247	291,275	112,798
2017[1]........................	18,076,651	942,450	3,199,015	2,421,179	1,149,399	3,825,002	2,247,198	635,757	3,504,872	196,975	54,279	303,606	113,850
2018[1]........................	18,609,078	966,287	3,266,142	2,471,548	1,172,804	3,907,658	2,332,746	663,719	3,658,195	200,373	53,327	314,828	115,885
2019[1]........................	19,036,052	985,447	3,333,589	2,497,887	1,186,500	3,995,899	2,402,683	690,940	3,772,219	203,433	53,434	325,395	117,126
2020[1]........................	18,509,143	951,602	3,187,182	2,397,206	1,159,977	3,903,180	2,362,144	687,772	3,689,413	199,881	50,705	327,178	117,268
2021[1]........................	19,609,812	1,011,338	3,354,244	2,543,643	1,209,836	4,158,108	2,452,810	727,705	3,963,354	209,979	50,869	347,656	123,347
2022[1]........................	20,014,128	1,030,930	3,436,608	2,591,533	1,219,712	4,268,053	2,521,769	749,335	3,993,762	213,265	49,634	356,417	126,532

Gross Domestic Product by Region and State—*Continued*

(Millions of chained 1997 or 2012 dollars; index numbers)

Year	United States	New England	Mideast	Great Lakes	Plains	Southeast	Southwest	Rocky Mountain	Far West	Alabama	Alaska	Arizona	Arkansas
QUANTITY INDEX													
1997=100													
1980.............................	59.3	56.6	65.9	63.5	61.6	54.2	55.6	56.5	57.2	61.6	81.4	43.0	57.6
1981.............................	60.9	58.0	66.9	64.0	63.7	56.0	58.7	58.6	59.0	62.8	93.8	44.2	59.7
1982.............................	60.1	58.6	66.5	61.1	62.1	55.4	58.9	58.0	58.9	61.2	96.2	43.1	58.1
1983.............................	61.8	61.7	68.7	63.1	62.6	57.6	58.9	58.7	60.6	64.2	93.6	45.6	60.0
1984.............................	66.2	67.3	73.0	68.1	67.3	61.9	62.5	61.7	64.9	67.3	97.4	50.5	64.7
1985.............................	68.9	71.2	75.4	70.4	69.2	64.8	65.2	63.2	67.9	70.4	108.2	53.7	65.3
1986.............................	70.3	74.7	77.6	71.5	69.5	66.8	64.2	62.4	70.0	71.1	90.5	56.9	66.6
1987.............................	73.4	80.0	81.6	73.5	71.9	70.2	64.2	63.1	74.3	75.1	107.0	59.3	68.9
1988.............................	77.2	85.0	86.4	77.0	74.6	73.9	67.8	65.4	78.4	78.7	101.0	62.1	71.5
1989.............................	78.9	85.9	87.3	78.6	76.5	75.6	69.1	66.7	81.6	78.6	105.1	62.6	72.9
1990.............................	80.1	84.5	88.0	79.0	77.6	76.7	70.9	68.9	84.4	79.9	104.3	63.1	73.8
1991.............................	80.0	82.3	86.6	78.6	78.4	77.5	72.2	70.7	83.7	82.2	93.6	63.4	77.1
1992.............................	82.4	83.7	88.1	82.3	81.8	80.4	75.6	74.7	84.4	85.7	94.8	69.8	81.6
1993.............................	84.1	83.8	89.0	84.3	82.2	83.2	78.7	79.3	84.9	87.0	94.4	73.4	84.1
1994.............................	88.0	86.8	90.9	89.7	87.8	88.1	83.6	84.5	87.0	90.5	94.9	80.5	88.9
1995.............................	91.0	90.5	92.9	91.8	90.5	91.7	87.7	89.3	90.1	93.5	100.1	86.6	92.5
1996.............................	95.0	94.4	96.1	95.4	95.3	95.5	93.0	94.3	94.5	96.7	98.9	93.5	96.7
1997.............................	100.0	100.0	100.0	100.0	100.0	100.0	100.0	100.0	100.0	100.0	100.0	100.0	100.0
2012 = 100													
1997[1]	70.9	72.7	74.9	83.0	72.6	73.9	62.4	65.1	66.2	76.4	72.4	62.0	76.1
1998[1]	74.1	75.5	76.8	85.9	74.8	77.4	66.0	69.8	70.2	79.0	70.5	67.4	78.0
1999[1]	77.7	78.7	80.1	89.3	77.0	81.0	69.0	74.1	74.8	81.9	69.6	73.2	82.1
2000[1]	80.8	84.3	83.2	91.8	80.4	83.0	71.6	78.9	79.6	83.1	67.6	76.8	82.8
2001[1]	81.6	85.4	84.8	90.9	80.3	84.2	73.3	79.8	79.2	82.9	70.3	78.5	82.8
2002[1]	83.0	85.9	85.5	92.6	82.2	86.3	75.1	80.7	80.7	84.8	73.7	81.3	85.7
2003[1]	85.3	87.5	86.7	94.5	85.0	89.4	76.4	82.1	83.6	87.3	72.7	86.2	89.4
2004[1]	88.6	91.2	89.1	97.0	88.3	93.5	80.5	84.8	86.8	93.3	75.6	90.0	93.8
2005[1]	91.7	92.9	91.1	98.8	91.1	98.0	83.4	89.5	90.8	97.4	78.3	96.6	97.7
2006[1]	94.2	95.4	92.6	99.7	92.4	100.4	89.1	93.4	94.4	99.0	84.4	101.0	100.0
2007[1]	96.1	97.5	93.9	100.3	94.3	100.8	92.7	97.2	96.6	99.9	88.7	104.4	99.2
2008[1]	96.2	98.3	94.5	98.2	95.3	100.1	92.7	98.7	97.6	98.8	87.9	103.5	98.2
2009[1]	93.7	95.6	94.2	93.3	93.0	96.6	91.2	96.1	94.4	95.5	96.5	94.9	94.9
2010[1]	96.3	98.2	97.2	96.4	95.4	98.4	93.0	97.3	96.4	97.6	93.7	95.9	97.4
2011[1]	97.8	98.6	97.7	98.5	97.5	99.0	95.8	98.8	97.8	99.1	94.8	98.0	99.5
2012[1]	100.0	100.0	100.0	100.0	100.0	100.0	100.0	100.0	100.0	100.0	100.0	100.0	100.0
2013[1]	101.8	99.7	100.5	101.1	101.2	101.2	103.4	102.9	102.6	101.1	95.0	100.8	102.1
2014[1]	104.2	100.7	102.1	103.4	104.1	103.0	106.6	106.5	105.9	100.3	93.0	102.0	103.0
2015[1]	107.0	103.6	103.9	104.6	105.9	105.7	111.2	110.5	110.5	101.1	93.9	104.1	103.6
2016[1]	108.8	104.9	105.6	105.5	106.6	107.7	112.2	112.8	113.9	102.7	93.1	107.3	104.0
2017[1]	111.2	106.3	106.6	106.5	107.6	110.4	114.9	116.5	118.9	104.1	93.1	111.9	104.9
2018[1]	114.5	109.0	108.9	108.8	109.7	112.8	119.3	121.6	124.1	105.9	91.5	116.0	106.8
2019[1]	117.1	111.1	111.1	109.9	111.0	115.4	122.9	126.6	128.0	107.5	91.7	119.9	108.0
2020[1]	113.9	107.3	106.2	105.5	108.5	112.7	120.8	126.0	125.2	105.6	87.0	120.5	108.1
2021[1]	120.6	114.0	111.8	111.9	113.2	120.1	125.4	133.3	134.5	111.0	87.3	128.1	113.7
2022[1]	123.1	116.2	114.5	114.0	114.1	123.2	129.0	137.3	135.5	112.7	85.2	131.3	116.6

1 = NAICS basis, not continuous with previous years, which are based on the SIC.

Gross Domestic Product by Region and State—*Continued*

(Millions of chained 1997 or 2012 dollars; index numbers)

Year	California	Colorado	Connecticut	Delaware	District of Columbia	Florida	Georgia	Hawaii	Idaho	Illinois	Indiana	Iowa	Kansas	Kentucky
VALUE														
Chained 1997 Dollars														
1980	70,410	78,644	16,126	45,655	186,914	102,952	26,760	16,415	258,832	102,247	56,387	49,642	63,053	98,826
1981	73,467	80,480	16,456	44,856	195,993	107,314	26,654	16,493	262,248	103,494	58,097	51,081	64,756	101,477
1982	74,962	82,538	16,640	43,539	200,772	108,942	26,867	15,824	253,052	97,816	54,248	50,638	62,456	97,626
1983	75,947	86,663	17,959	43,965	212,495	116,030	27,932	16,597	255,786	100,129	52,043	50,956	62,542	96,515
1984	80,299	94,619	19,290	44,880	230,407	127,323	28,979	16,892	274,171	109,229	54,893	53,241	67,270	102,251
1985	82,357	99,671	20,492	45,563	242,870	136,869	29,973	17,274	282,224	111,327	56,009	55,267	69,294	104,078
1986	81,845	104,258	21,068	45,848	253,651	144,853	30,989	16,937	288,439	113,098	55,262	55,466	68,323	103,870
1987	83,322	112,210	22,563	47,149	270,018	152,163	32,376	17,350	297,698	117,397	56,536	57,350	70,822	104,284
1988	85,880	119,047	23,599	49,206	286,786	158,946	34,587	18,284	314,485	123,242	59,479	58,843	75,562	108,142
1989	86,898	120,607	25,312	50,146	297,215	162,167	36,643	19,453	320,572	127,701	61,636	59,286	77,233	108,117
1990	88,933	121,176	25,887	51,175	304,324	165,062	39,176	20,161	324,012	128,197	63,460	60,672	78,206	110,272
1991	90,780	118,216	26,930	50,241	305,979	167,209	39,756	20,593	323,641	128,215	63,818	61,275	78,908	110,055
1992	97,058	119,832	27,178	50,598	317,416	176,731	40,834	22,022	336,296	136,439	66,862	63,062	83,288	102,935
1993	103,457	118,315	26,946	51,310	329,410	184,789	40,152	23,940	343,470	140,645	66,913	63,516	85,810	105,296
1994	110,529	121,002	28,750	51,290	345,550	198,125	40,062	25,845	364,916	149,157	72,503	66,732	91,063	114,156
1995	116,821	128,538	29,941	49,889	358,419	209,292	39,552	27,996	374,858	153,785	74,568	67,531	94,259	120,333
1996	123,144	131,913	30,503	49,232	376,851	223,307	39,132	28,927	389,704	160,020	78,834	70,361	97,781	121,489
1997	133,204	140,280	31,450	49,702	393,075	235,200	39,064	30,312	408,048	167,366	83,113	74,147	103,621	126,003
Chained 2012 Dollars														
1997[1]	1,378,277	184,185	190,519	45,980	79,828	559,805	328,119	55,804	36,997	576,730	231,714	113,290	104,575	146,523
1998[1]	1,468,731	200,680	196,391	50,434	81,214	587,971	352,472	54,405	38,795	595,616	245,676	114,087	108,184	150,774
1999[1]	1,574,306	215,295	202,352	54,237	84,756	615,238	377,127	54,852	42,510	618,148	254,089	116,523	111,006	155,612
2000[1]	1,696,172	231,590	216,158	56,550	85,356	642,708	389,727	55,891	47,295	640,723	264,122	121,924	114,031	151,495
2001[1]	1,692,324	234,979	218,135	58,373	88,441	660,660	394,317	55,679	46,085	642,293	259,475	120,450	114,328	151,834
2002[1]	1,722,522	235,417	216,678	56,535	91,142	689,974	399,413	56,991	47,057	647,518	265,345	123,298	116,195	155,644
2003[1]	1,789,999	237,782	219,186	57,300	92,921	722,375	411,686	59,979	48,594	658,317	277,152	128,962	118,193	159,991
2004[1]	1,850,905	240,748	233,427	60,070	97,464	769,141	428,555	63,318	51,815	676,806	287,656	139,978	119,392	164,650
2005[1]	1,926,842	251,558	238,550	59,335	99,481	815,756	447,153	67,124	56,043	687,707	290,328	144,577	123,950	171,180
2006[1]	2,002,437	257,430	248,234	60,624	99,806	839,964	453,032	68,759	57,614	704,828	296,113	146,555	130,365	175,658
2007[1]	2,041,192	266,888	257,953	60,478	102,739	850,049	455,904	70,080	58,671	712,620	304,086	152,862	137,094	174,407
2008[1]	2,061,639	270,981	257,756	58,656	106,769	816,070	445,765	70,461	60,310	706,617	300,963	149,881	139,537	173,810
2009[1]	1,995,440	264,966	244,895	61,518	105,894	769,061	428,741	67,928	57,328	688,161	279,521	146,183	134,227	166,704
2010[1]	2,036,015	267,859	244,355	60,577	109,987	775,040	433,727	69,628	58,282	698,180	297,517	150,148	135,723	173,780
2011[1]	2,063,828	271,701	238,542	62,919	111,647	772,021	441,627	70,647	58,226	711,283	299,065	152,435	139,579	175,745
2012[1]	2,113,096	276,823	240,912	62,355	112,157	778,545	447,765	71,905	58,324	726,399	300,514	158,538	141,818	178,144
2013[1]	2,179,229	286,259	236,051	60,236	112,332	794,842	454,909	73,063	60,631	726,125	307,279	158,481	141,723	181,506
2014[1]	2,256,055	298,655	235,781	64,940	114,554	817,234	470,010	73,512	62,454	741,194	316,783	166,619	145,344	181,472
2015[1]	2,357,453	312,410	242,707	66,794	116,808	852,242	489,182	75,870	63,081	751,755	313,751	171,127	148,811	182,916
2016[1]	2,427,895	318,953	243,287	63,001	119,644	881,539	506,816	77,304	65,479	749,334	319,602	170,389	153,695	184,115
2017[1]	2,538,204	329,913	247,036	60,358	120,759	912,687	523,805	78,947	66,941	753,027	324,998	170,888	155,515	185,921
2018[1]	2,644,061	342,733	249,075	61,425	123,681	941,627	538,605	79,845	70,857	771,696	336,327	173,548	158,734	187,927
2019[1]	2,729,226	358,439	251,568	64,144	124,597	965,673	557,364	79,213	74,163	775,998	337,902	173,722	159,826	192,972
2020[1]	2,667,221	353,345	235,235	62,282	122,485	950,164	537,616	70,109	75,146	734,385	327,278	170,957	158,348	188,396
2021[1]	2,874,731	373,763	246,556	64,405	126,983	1,029,576	575,292	74,547	80,094	780,061	346,241	179,753	162,291	197,818
2022[1]	2,885,627	385,835	252,533	65,755	129,268	1,070,930	591,257	75,418	84,003	797,969	352,956	177,090	164,939	201,375

Gross Domestic Product by Region and State—*Continued*

(Millions of chained 1997 or 2012 dollars; index numbers)

Year	California	Colorado	Connecticut	Delaware	District of Columbia	Florida	Georgia	Hawaii	Idaho	Illinois	Indiana	Iowa	Kansas	Kentucky
QUANTITY INDEX														
1997=100														
1980	57.8	52.9	56.1	51.3	91.9	47.6	43.8	68.5	54.2	63.4	61.1	67.8	67.0	60.8
1981	59.7	55.2	57.4	52.3	90.3	49.9	45.6	68.2	54.4	64.3	61.8	69.9	68.9	62.5
1982	59.7	56.3	58.8	52.9	87.6	51.1	46.3	68.8	52.2	62.0	58.4	65.3	68.3	60.3
1983	61.9	57.0	61.8	57.1	88.5	54.1	49.3	71.5	54.8	62.7	59.8	62.6	68.7	60.4
1984	66.8	60.3	67.5	61.3	90.3	58.6	54.1	74.2	55.7	67.2	65.3	66.0	71.8	64.9
1985	70.3	61.8	71.1	65.2	91.7	61.8	58.2	76.7	57.0	69.2	66.5	67.4	74.5	66.9
1986	72.9	61.4	74.3	67.0	92.2	64.5	61.6	79.3	55.9	70.7	67.6	66.5	74.8	65.9
1987	77.4	62.6	80.0	71.7	94.9	68.7	64.7	82.9	57.2	73.0	70.1	68.0	77.3	68.3
1988	81.8	64.5	84.9	75.0	99.0	73.0	67.6	88.5	60.3	77.1	73.6	71.6	79.4	72.9
1989	84.9	65.2	86.0	80.5	100.9	75.6	68.9	93.8	64.2	78.6	76.3	74.2	80.0	74.5
1990	87.4	66.8	86.4	82.3	103.0	77.4	70.2	100.3	66.5	79.4	76.6	76.4	81.8	75.5
1991	86.1	68.2	84.3	85.6	101.1	77.8	71.1	101.8	67.9	79.3	76.6	76.8	82.6	76.2
1992	86.0	72.9	85.4	86.4	101.8	80.8	75.1	104.5	72.7	82.4	81.5	80.4	85.1	80.4
1993	85.6	77.7	84.3	85.7	103.2	83.8	78.6	102.8	79.0	84.2	84.0	80.5	85.7	82.8
1994	87.2	83.0	86.3	91.4	103.2	87.9	84.2	102.6	85.3	89.4	89.1	87.2	90.0	87.9
1995	90.7	87.7	91.6	95.2	100.4	91.2	89.0	101.2	92.4	91.9	91.9	89.7	91.1	91.0
1996	94.3	92.4	94.0	97.0	99.1	95.9	94.9	100.2	95.4	95.5	95.6	94.9	94.9	94.4
1997	100.0	100.0	100.0	100.0	100.0	100.0	100.0	100.0	100.0	100.0	100.0	100.0	100.0	100.0
2012 = 100														
1997[1]	65.2	66.5	79.1	73.7	71.2	71.9	73.3	77.6	63.4	79.4	77.1	71.5	73.7	82.3
1998[1]	69.5	72.5	81.5	80.9	72.4	75.5	78.7	75.7	66.5	82.0	81.8	72.0	76.3	84.6
1999[1]	74.5	77.8	84.0	87.0	75.6	79.0	84.2	76.3	72.9	85.1	84.6	73.5	78.3	87.4
2000[1]	80.3	83.7	89.7	90.7	76.1	82.6	87.0	77.7	81.1	88.2	87.9	76.9	80.4	85.0
2001[1]	80.1	84.9	90.5	93.6	78.9	84.9	88.1	77.4	79.0	88.4	86.3	76.0	80.6	85.2
2002[1]	81.5	85.0	89.9	90.7	81.3	88.6	89.2	79.3	80.7	89.1	88.3	77.8	81.9	87.4
2003[1]	84.7	85.9	91.0	91.9	82.8	92.8	91.9	83.4	83.3	90.6	92.2	81.3	83.3	89.8
2004[1]	87.6	87.0	96.9	96.3	86.9	98.8	95.7	88.1	88.8	93.2	95.7	88.3	84.2	92.4
2005[1]	91.2	90.9	99.0	95.2	88.7	104.8	99.9	93.4	96.1	94.7	96.6	91.2	87.4	96.1
2006[1]	94.8	93.0	103.0	97.2	89.0	107.9	101.2	95.6	98.8	97.0	98.5	92.4	91.9	98.6
2007[1]	96.6	96.4	107.1	97.0	91.6	109.2	101.8	97.5	100.6	98.1	101.2	96.4	96.7	97.9
2008[1]	97.6	97.9	107.0	94.1	95.2	104.8	99.6	98.0	103.4	97.3	100.1	94.5	98.4	97.6
2009[1]	94.4	95.7	101.7	98.7	94.4	98.8	95.8	94.5	98.3	94.7	93.0	92.2	94.6	93.6
2010[1]	96.4	96.8	101.4	97.1	98.1	99.6	96.9	96.8	99.9	96.1	99.0	94.7	95.7	97.6
2011[1]	97.7	98.2	99.0	100.9	99.5	99.2	98.6	98.3	99.8	97.9	99.5	96.2	98.4	98.7
2012[1]	100.0	100.0	100.0	100.0	100.0	100.0	100.0	100.0	100.0	100.0	100.0	100.0	100.0	100.0
2013[1]	103.1	103.4	98.0	96.6	100.2	102.1	101.6	101.6	104.0	100.0	102.3	100.0	99.9	101.9
2014[1]	106.8	107.9	97.9	104.1	102.1	105.0	105.0	102.2	107.1	102.0	105.4	105.1	102.5	101.9
2015[1]	111.6	112.9	100.7	107.1	104.1	109.5	109.3	105.5	108.2	103.5	104.4	107.9	104.9	102.7
2016[1]	114.9	115.2	101.0	101.0	106.7	113.2	113.2	107.5	112.3	103.2	106.4	107.5	108.4	103.4
2017[1]	120.1	119.2	102.5	96.8	107.7	117.2	117.0	109.8	114.8	103.7	108.1	107.8	109.7	104.4
2018[1]	125.1	123.8	103.4	98.5	110.3	120.9	120.3	111.0	121.5	106.2	111.9	109.5	111.9	105.5
2019[1]	129.2	129.5	104.4	102.9	111.1	124.0	124.5	110.2	127.2	106.8	112.4	109.6	112.7	108.3
2020[1]	126.2	127.6	97.6	99.9	109.2	122.0	120.1	97.5	128.8	101.1	108.9	107.8	111.7	105.8
2021[1]	136.0	135.0	102.3	103.3	113.2	132.2	128.5	103.7	137.3	107.4	115.2	113.4	114.4	111.0
2022[1]	136.6	139.4	104.8	105.5	115.3	137.6	132.0	104.9	144.0	109.9	117.5	111.7	116.3	113.0

1 = NAICS basis, not continuous with previous years, which are based on the SIC.

Gross Domestic Product by Region and State—*Continued*

(Millions of chained 1997 or 2012 dollars; index numbers)

Year	Louisiana	Maine	Maryland	Massachusetts	Michigan	Minnesota	Mississippi	Missouri	Montana	Nebraska	Nevada	New Hampshire	New Jersey
VALUE													
Chained 1997 Dollars													
1980	19,252	93,518	130,465	190,628	87,377	36,032	95,522	15,018	31,159	22,324	16,236	165,044	24,597
1981	19,384	95,346	133,647	190,543	89,820	37,270	96,740	15,606	32,929	23,256	16,905	169,389	24,949
1982	19,610	94,470	134,243	178,645	88,444	36,090	95,532	14,916	32,135	22,994	17,246	169,773	24,540
1983	20,471	99,052	142,103	190,879	91,405	36,857	98,611	14,932	31,360	23,738	18,344	181,669	24,951
1984	21,917	105,743	155,335	206,385	100,958	39,379	107,071	15,023	33,716	24,833	20,558	196,143	26,158
1985	22,858	111,803	164,593	215,019	104,958	40,474	108,667	14,635	34,881	25,888	22,435	206,429	27,135
1986	23,880	117,037	172,628	218,860	105,789	40,569	111,652	14,521	34,264	27,351	23,933	216,138	26,881
1987	25,426	123,260	183,712	221,362	110,916	43,229	116,060	14,624	34,351	29,144	26,669	230,997	26,932
1988	27,344	131,777	194,619	230,563	115,398	44,252	121,171	14,497	36,304	31,701	28,319	248,031	27,464
1989	27,882	134,612	195,609	234,224	118,868	44,669	123,688	15,089	37,389	34,125	28,278	251,515	28,056
1990	27,644	136,165	189,730	229,534	120,078	44,853	122,285	15,355	39,011	36,891	27,259	253,360	28,714
1991	26,836	133,662	183,996	225,576	120,067	45,841	124,167	15,739	40,250	37,713	27,411	252,718	31,980
1992	27,176	134,748	186,430	235,241	126,777	48,317	127,857	16,566	42,242	40,564	28,486	256,965	33,855
1993	27,337	137,003	187,751	242,175	127,068	50,440	128,278	17,285	42,385	43,994	28,832	259,805	37,463
1994	28,058	142,086	196,432	263,500	134,715	53,852	137,379	17,932	45,807	48,267	30,113	265,388	42,030
1995	28,769	144,424	203,189	264,125	138,724	56,528	144,371	18,036	46,556	51,081	32,379	271,764	42,733
1996	29,627	147,889	214,299	273,563	147,643	58,230	150,268	18,342	49,276	55,725	34,858	283,608	44,605
1997	30,775	154,783	226,880	286,408	156,650	59,875	158,308	18,932	50,308	59,467	36,935	292,671	48,683
Chained 2012 Dollars													
1997[1]	200,863	42,942	221,212	302,724	396,975	212,378	83,153	227,797	29,047	70,413	89,895	48,360	426,003
1998[1]	207,612	44,140	231,806	315,040	406,052	223,655	85,194	231,693	30,342	72,090	94,673	51,539	433,564
1999[1]	211,953	46,351	240,946	331,602	429,936	232,068	87,638	238,452	30,461	73,626	101,395	53,085	447,872
2000[1]	205,723	48,490	250,772	358,122	438,464	247,803	88,078	244,706	31,241	76,368	105,635	56,779	471,427
2001[1]	208,618	49,471	261,533	362,664	425,103	247,599	87,310	243,060	31,533	78,181	106,635	57,633	476,617
2002[1]	213,079	50,910	270,468	362,582	436,802	253,478	88,569	247,437	32,504	79,180	110,449	59,475	484,657
2003[1]	221,774	52,210	278,332	369,007	443,652	264,166	92,355	252,677	33,811	83,773	115,275	61,893	494,704
2004[1]	232,713	54,256	290,285	379,086	448,888	275,560	94,483	259,741	35,529	85,987	127,326	64,409	498,245
2005[1]	247,773	54,927	301,661	386,804	457,138	284,637	96,821	265,735	37,374	89,309	137,509	65,034	507,895
2006[1]	245,500	55,448	305,794	395,536	449,854	284,382	99,006	267,221	38,578	91,833	142,967	66,628	516,681
2007[1]	230,368	55,360	306,756	406,421	446,943	286,299	100,212	267,691	40,438	93,911	144,107	66,854	520,898
2008[1]	232,151	54,654	314,758	414,920	420,974	288,421	101,778	273,436	40,471	93,841	139,954	65,854	534,501
2009[1]	236,411	53,630	311,342	407,220	383,140	277,494	98,001	266,835	39,513	93,978	128,241	65,023	506,851
2010[1]	246,836	54,305	325,370	425,793	404,217	287,140	98,601	270,733	40,794	97,466	129,828	67,126	513,918
2011[1]	234,976	53,789	332,437	434,495	414,834	293,783	98,516	268,534	41,876	102,587	130,698	67,559	507,604
2012[1]	235,385	53,680	332,524	442,917	422,691	298,328	100,448	271,535	42,341	102,726	129,313	68,498	517,196
2013[1]	228,453	53,239	334,269	444,874	428,738	305,486	100,331	274,599	42,968	104,680	129,721	69,080	523,726
2014[1]	235,355	54,038	339,605	451,569	434,313	314,091	100,284	276,081	43,829	107,937	130,897	70,214	522,166
2015[1]	233,016	54,426	348,152	468,061	443,831	318,913	100,482	279,021	45,396	111,402	136,347	72,042	529,954
2016[1]	228,429	55,565	360,082	475,349	452,325	324,030	101,255	279,109	44,437	112,612	140,081	73,572	535,055
2017[1]	233,352	56,469	366,204	482,808	457,614	327,483	101,245	281,253	45,974	114,144	145,486	73,973	537,579
2018[1]	237,298	58,100	367,977	501,542	466,559	336,892	100,873	284,540	46,584	116,793	150,448	75,433	550,060
2019[1]	237,045	59,553	368,056	514,171	467,107	340,557	100,983	290,620	46,886	118,604	156,959	76,819	559,649
2020[1]	218,422	59,881	352,384	500,001	448,455	328,490	100,527	282,754	46,750	118,142	146,493	75,928	535,324
2021[1]	221,153	63,595	368,571	533,102	481,778	346,204	104,354	295,687	48,976	122,136	159,567	82,986	566,893
2022[1]	217,156	64,766	368,680	543,872	490,318	350,315	104,535	300,676	49,752	123,540	165,455	83,004	581,704

Gross Domestic Product by Region and State—*Continued*

(Millions of chained 1997 or 2012 dollars; index numbers)

Year	Louisiana	Maine	Maryland	Massachusetts	Michigan	Minnesota	Mississippi	Missouri	Montana	Nebraska	Nevada	New Hampshire	New Jersey
QUANTITY INDEX													
1997=100													
1980	78.4	62.6	60.4	57.5	66.6	55.8	60.2	60.3	79.3	61.9	37.5	44.0	56.4
1981	80.5	63.0	61.6	58.9	66.5	57.3	62.2	61.1	82.4	65.5	39.1	45.8	57.9
1982	77.5	63.7	61.0	59.2	62.4	56.5	60.3	60.3	78.8	63.9	38.7	46.7	58.0
1983	76.6	66.5	64.0	62.6	66.6	58.4	61.6	62.3	78.9	62.3	39.9	49.7	62.1
1984	81.1	71.2	68.3	68.5	72.1	64.4	65.8	67.6	79.4	67.0	41.8	55.7	67.0
1985	82.6	74.3	72.2	72.5	75.1	67.0	67.6	68.6	77.3	69.3	43.5	60.7	70.5
1986	82.4	77.6	75.6	76.1	76.4	67.5	67.8	70.5	76.7	68.1	46.0	64.8	73.9
1987	82.8	82.6	79.6	81.0	77.3	70.8	72.2	73.3	77.2	68.3	49.0	72.2	78.9
1988	85.8	88.9	85.1	85.8	80.5	73.7	73.9	76.5	76.6	72.2	53.3	76.7	84.7
1989	85.8	90.6	87.0	86.2	81.8	75.9	74.6	78.1	79.7	74.3	57.4	76.6	85.9
1990	87.5	89.8	88.0	83.6	80.1	76.7	74.9	77.2	81.1	77.5	62.0	73.8	86.6
1991	87.3	87.2	86.4	81.1	78.8	76.6	76.6	78.4	83.1	80.0	63.4	74.2	86.3
1992	81.7	88.3	87.1	82.2	82.1	80.9	80.7	80.8	87.5	84.0	68.2	77.1	87.8
1993	83.6	88.8	88.5	82.8	84.6	81.1	84.2	81.0	91.3	84.3	74.0	78.1	88.8
1994	90.6	91.2	91.8	86.6	92.0	86.0	89.9	86.8	94.7	91.1	81.2	81.5	90.7
1995	95.5	93.5	93.3	89.6	92.2	88.6	94.4	91.2	95.3	92.5	85.9	87.7	92.9
1996	96.4	96.3	95.5	94.5	95.5	94.3	97.3	94.9	96.9	97.9	93.7	94.4	96.9
1997	100.0	100.0	100.0	100.0	100.0	100.0	100.0	100.0	100.0	100.0	100.0	100.0	100.0
2012 = 100													
1997[1]	85.3	80.0	66.5	68.3	93.9	71.2	82.8	83.9	68.6	68.5	69.5	70.6	82.4
1998[1]	88.2	82.2	69.7	71.1	96.1	75.0	84.8	85.3	71.7	70.2	73.2	75.2	83.8
1999[1]	90.0	86.3	72.5	74.9	101.7	77.8	87.2	87.8	71.9	71.7	78.4	77.5	86.6
2000[1]	87.4	90.3	75.4	80.9	103.7	83.1	87.7	90.1	73.8	74.3	81.7	82.9	91.2
2001[1]	88.6	92.2	78.7	81.9	100.6	83.0	86.9	89.5	74.5	76.1	82.5	84.1	92.2
2002[1]	90.5	94.8	81.3	81.9	103.3	85.0	88.2	91.1	76.8	77.1	85.4	86.8	93.7
2003[1]	94.2	97.3	83.7	83.3	105.0	88.5	91.9	93.1	79.9	81.6	89.1	90.4	95.7
2004[1]	98.9	101.1	87.3	85.6	106.2	92.4	94.1	95.7	83.9	83.7	98.5	94.0	96.3
2005[1]	105.3	102.3	90.7	87.3	108.1	95.4	96.4	97.9	88.3	86.9	106.3	94.9	98.2
2006[1]	104.3	103.3	92.0	89.3	106.4	95.3	98.6	98.4	91.1	89.4	110.6	97.3	99.9
2007[1]	97.9	103.1	92.3	91.8	105.7	96.0	99.8	98.6	95.5	91.4	111.4	97.6	100.7
2008[1]	98.6	101.8	94.7	93.7	99.6	96.7	101.3	100.7	95.6	91.4	108.2	96.1	103.3
2009[1]	100.4	99.9	93.6	91.9	90.6	93.0	97.6	98.3	93.3	91.5	99.2	94.9	98.0
2010[1]	104.9	101.2	97.8	96.1	95.6	96.3	98.2	99.7	96.3	94.9	100.4	98.0	99.4
2011[1]	99.8	100.2	100.0	98.1	98.1	98.5	98.1	98.9	98.9	99.9	101.1	98.6	98.1
2012[1]	100.0	100.0	100.0	100.0	100.0	100.0	100.0	100.0	100.0	100.0	100.0	100.0	100.0
2013[1]	97.1	99.2	100.5	100.4	101.4	102.4	99.9	101.1	101.5	101.9	100.3	100.9	101.3
2014[1]	100.0	100.7	102.1	102.0	102.8	105.3	99.8	101.7	103.5	105.1	101.2	102.5	101.0
2015[1]	99.0	101.4	104.7	105.7	105.0	106.9	100.0	102.8	107.2	108.4	105.4	105.2	102.5
2016[1]	97.0	103.5	108.3	107.3	107.0	108.6	100.8	102.8	105.0	109.6	108.3	107.4	103.5
2017[1]	99.1	105.2	110.1	109.0	108.3	109.8	100.8	103.6	108.6	111.1	112.5	108.0	103.9
2018[1]	100.8	108.2	110.7	113.2	110.4	112.9	100.4	104.8	110.0	113.7	116.3	110.1	106.4
2019[1]	100.7	110.9	110.7	116.1	110.5	114.2	100.5	107.0	110.7	115.5	121.4	112.1	108.2
2020[1]	92.8	111.6	106.0	112.9	106.1	110.1	100.1	104.1	110.4	115.0	113.3	110.8	103.5
2021[1]	94.0	118.5	110.8	120.4	114.0	116.0	103.9	108.9	115.7	118.9	123.4	121.2	109.6
2022[1]	92.3	120.7	110.9	122.8	116.0	117.4	104.1	110.7	117.5	120.3	127.9	121.2	112.5

1 = NAICS basis, not continuous with previous years, which are based on the SIC.

Gross Domestic Product by Region and State—*Continued*

(Millions of chained 1997 or 2012 dollars; index numbers)

Year	New Mexico	New York	North Carolina	North Dakota	Ohio	Oklahoma	Oregon	Pennsylvania	Rhode Island	South Carolina	South Dakota	Tennessee
VALUE												
Chained 1997 Dollars												
1980	461,419	110,120	12,243	211,743	61,673	53,343	231,709	18,167	48,649	11,511	80,420	339,794
1981	469,897	113,991	14,085	213,962	65,276	51,928	232,708	18,609	50,326	12,201	82,680	361,250
1982	473,335	111,615	13,545	203,226	67,173	49,176	223,811	18,553	49,457	11,849	80,817	362,556
1983	483,340	117,269	13,282	211,442	63,976	49,722	229,968	19,086	52,632	11,778	85,226	362,005
1984	512,501	127,347	13,588	229,868	66,997	52,794	242,572	20,422	57,695	12,694	91,426	383,084
1985	526,285	135,374	13,668	238,150	68,101	54,080	248,495	21,754	59,771	13,174	94,918	400,230
1986	539,859	140,634	12,743	240,299	64,580	55,144	253,122	22,862	62,607	13,346	97,962	391,309
1987	562,846	147,274	13,074	247,287	63,487	56,988	266,991	23,871	67,198	13,623	104,884	389,772
1988	595,326	155,811	12,023	256,727	66,540	60,568	279,975	25,528	70,664	13,733	109,796	413,114
1989	594,267	160,953	12,733	262,187	66,722	62,292	284,585	26,214	72,984	13,961	110,896	423,660
1990	595,908	161,998	13,161	264,948	67,083	64,881	288,955	25,937	75,344	14,696	110,321	437,292
1991	577,446	162,239	13,118	263,064	67,424	65,969	289,708	25,005	76,010	15,411	114,266	444,358
1992	585,395	171,223	14,176	275,324	69,025	68,519	298,366	25,370	78,505	16,279	123,167	461,816
1993	588,213	176,678	13,987	277,702	70,761	72,548	303,021	25,653	81,301	17,208	128,543	478,420
1994	596,435	189,755	15,045	294,384	72,406	76,924	311,576	25,882	85,856	18,141	136,301	505,162
1995	608,937	199,056	15,325	304,834	73,889	81,919	321,832	26,552	89,046	18,520	140,814	530,666
1996	634,107	206,757	16,508	315,189	77,538	93,489	330,321	27,006	91,716	19,410	145,391	562,108
1997	664,679	221,259	16,501	332,476	81,106	100,363	342,662	28,717	96,465	19,765	152,687	606,982
Chained 2012 Dollars												
1997[1]	67,285	977,798	315,648	22,413	471,451	115,089	118,360	496,659	40,146	134,608	24,951	210,637
1998[1]	66,944	997,252	326,786	23,675	487,533	117,596	123,995	509,551	41,913	139,526	26,440	223,711
1999[1]	70,488	1,051,338	345,458	23,771	499,293	119,685	126,739	524,961	43,145	146,104	27,463	230,896
2000[1]	71,653	1,092,188	356,913	24,706	509,949	124,228	137,401	538,790	45,179	150,156	29,386	233,732
2001[1]	71,731	1,112,794	359,617	24,910	502,968	128,891	136,166	547,261	45,750	151,016	29,455	233,363
2002[1]	73,910	1,106,151	364,870	26,291	513,216	131,293	138,933	555,056	47,225	155,275	32,785	240,972
2003[1]	76,768	1,110,613	373,988	27,870	519,939	133,417	144,803	568,242	48,571	161,269	32,979	248,994
2004[1]	83,039	1,144,125	389,210	28,284	534,065	138,097	152,001	584,328	50,514	164,083	34,270	260,554
2005[1]	84,034	1,168,891	409,004	29,345	545,969	143,471	158,163	594,855	51,370	169,489	35,842	268,392
2006[1]	86,058	1,199,277	434,209	30,590	545,504	152,858	166,107	597,219	52,900	173,371	36,351	274,879
2007[1]	86,739	1,208,565	438,960	32,022	546,729	156,220	168,975	617,310	51,469	178,475	37,756	273,224
2008[1]	86,965	1,190,081	450,538	34,256	537,124	162,387	173,599	629,808	50,575	176,568	39,081	274,571
2009[1]	88,070	1,230,672	431,955	35,244	511,077	160,092	165,527	610,148	50,004	168,852	39,987	264,737
2010[1]	87,610	1,277,467	437,837	37,917	523,979	160,564	169,234	627,726	51,333	172,131	40,370	268,450
2011[1]	87,593	1,279,527	443,289	42,341	541,180	166,327	173,832	637,114	51,280	176,083	43,050	276,898
2012[1]	87,925	1,328,234	445,095	51,833	545,740	174,874	174,611	647,926	51,583	177,618	43,902	286,342
2013[1]	86,857	1,329,376	452,056	52,892	556,211	177,699	175,934	655,929	51,911	180,882	44,147	289,795
2014[1]	88,991	1,353,410	462,253	57,790	574,178	189,360	181,221	669,643	52,293	185,987	44,847	294,130
2015[1]	89,701	1,373,643	475,097	56,542	578,852	197,072	189,947	682,466	52,819	192,020	45,665	304,484
2016[1]	89,151	1,403,231	482,969	52,975	583,946	193,025	198,079	688,359	52,903	198,006	46,076	310,143
2017[1]	88,963	1,419,112	495,221	54,187	593,636	194,017	205,524	694,867	52,692	202,512	45,776	318,964
2018[1]	90,934	1,458,382	501,565	55,914	597,926	197,453	214,903	704,028	52,553	207,101	46,300	323,542
2019[1]	94,897	1,500,833	512,835	56,385	613,251	201,162	219,588	715,061	53,411	213,238	46,651	331,177
2020[1]	92,496	1,432,507	506,658	53,654	594,144	192,486	215,744	680,957	51,516	208,234	47,402	323,454
2021[1]	93,625	1,514,779	541,934	53,804	629,287	193,230	227,979	710,973	54,606	221,045	49,558	352,461
2022[1]	94,663	1,563,044	559,510	53,125	638,910	191,388	234,806	726,036	55,413	226,420	49,809	367,776

Gross Domestic Product by Region and State—*Continued*

(Millions of chained 1997 or 2012 dollars; index numbers)

Year	New Mexico	New York	North Carolina	North Dakota	Ohio	Oklahoma	Oregon	Pennsylvania	Rhode Island	South Carolina	South Dakota	Tennessee
QUANTITY INDEX												
1997=100												
1980	50.5	69.4	49.8	74.2	63.7	76.0	53.2	67.6	63.3	50.4	58.2	52.7
1981	51.2	70.7	51.5	85.4	64.4	80.5	51.7	67.9	64.8	52.2	61.7	54.2
1982	50.4	71.2	50.4	82.1	61.1	82.8	49.0	65.3	64.6	51.3	60.0	52.9
1983	51.3	72.7	53.0	80.5	63.6	78.9	49.5	67.1	66.5	54.6	59.6	55.8
1984	53.7	77.1	57.6	82.3	69.1	82.6	52.6	70.8	71.1	59.8	64.2	59.9
1985	55.7	79.2	61.2	82.8	71.6	84.0	53.9	72.5	75.8	62.0	66.7	62.2
1986	55.2	81.2	63.6	77.2	72.3	79.6	54.9	73.9	79.6	64.9	67.5	64.2
1987	55.3	84.7	66.6	79.2	74.4	78.3	56.8	77.9	83.1	69.7	68.9	68.7
1988	56.4	89.6	70.4	72.9	77.2	82.0	60.3	81.7	88.9	73.3	69.5	71.9
1989	57.6	89.4	72.7	77.2	78.9	82.3	62.1	83.1	91.3	75.7	70.6	72.6
1990	59.0	89.7	73.2	79.8	79.7	82.7	64.6	84.3	90.3	78.1	74.4	72.3
1991	65.7	86.9	73.3	79.5	79.1	83.1	65.7	84.5	87.1	78.8	78.0	74.8
1992	69.5	88.1	77.4	85.9	82.8	85.1	68.3	87.1	88.3	81.4	82.4	80.7
1993	77.0	88.5	79.9	84.8	83.5	87.2	72.3	88.4	89.3	84.3	87.1	84.2
1994	86.3	89.7	85.8	91.2	88.5	89.3	76.6	90.9	90.1	89.0	91.8	89.3
1995	87.8	91.6	90.0	92.9	91.7	91.1	81.6	93.9	92.5	92.3	93.7	92.2
1996	91.6	95.4	93.4	100.0	94.8	95.6	93.2	96.4	94.0	95.1	98.2	95.2
1997	100.0	100.0	100.0	100.0	100.0	100.0	100.0	100.0	100.0	100.0	100.0	100.0
2012 = 100												
1997[1]	76.5	73.6	70.9	43.2	86.4	65.8	67.8	76.7	77.8	75.8	56.8	73.6
1998[1]	76.1	75.1	73.4	45.7	89.3	67.2	71.0	78.6	81.3	78.6	60.2	78.1
1999[1]	80.2	79.2	77.6	45.9	91.5	68.4	72.6	81.0	83.6	82.3	62.6	80.6
2000[1]	81.5	82.2	80.2	47.7	93.4	71.0	78.7	83.2	87.6	84.5	66.9	81.6
2001[1]	81.6	83.8	80.8	48.1	92.2	73.7	78.0	84.5	88.7	85.0	67.1	81.5
2002[1]	84.1	83.3	82.0	50.7	94.0	75.1	79.6	85.7	91.6	87.4	74.7	84.2
2003[1]	87.3	83.6	84.0	53.8	95.3	76.3	82.9	87.7	94.2	90.8	75.1	87.0
2004[1]	94.4	86.1	87.4	54.6	97.9	79.0	87.1	90.2	97.9	92.4	78.1	91.0
2005[1]	95.6	88.0	91.9	56.6	100.0	82.0	90.6	91.8	99.6	95.4	81.6	93.7
2006[1]	97.9	90.3	97.6	59.0	100.0	87.4	95.1	92.2	102.6	97.6	82.8	96.0
2007[1]	98.7	91.0	98.6	61.8	100.2	89.3	96.8	95.3	99.8	100.5	86.0	95.4
2008[1]	98.9	89.6	101.2	66.1	98.4	92.9	99.4	97.2	98.0	99.4	89.0	95.9
2009[1]	100.2	92.7	97.0	68.0	93.6	91.5	94.8	94.2	96.9	95.1	91.1	92.5
2010[1]	99.6	96.2	98.4	73.2	96.0	91.8	96.9	96.9	99.5	96.9	92.0	93.8
2011[1]	99.6	96.3	99.6	81.7	99.2	95.1	99.6	98.3	99.4	99.1	98.1	96.7
2012[1]	100.0	100.0	100.0	100.0	100.0	100.0	100.0	100.0	100.0	100.0	100.0	100.0
2013[1]	98.8	100.1	101.6	102.0	101.9	101.6	100.8	101.2	100.6	101.8	100.6	101.2
2014[1]	101.2	101.9	103.9	111.5	105.2	108.3	103.8	103.4	101.4	104.7	102.2	102.7
2015[1]	102.0	103.4	106.7	109.1	106.1	112.7	108.8	105.3	102.4	108.1	104.0	106.3
2016[1]	101.4	105.6	108.5	102.2	107.0	110.4	113.4	106.2	102.6	111.5	105.0	108.3
2017[1]	101.2	106.8	111.3	104.5	108.8	110.9	117.7	107.2	102.2	114.0	104.3	111.4
2018[1]	103.4	109.8	112.7	107.9	109.6	112.9	123.1	108.7	101.9	116.6	105.5	113.0
2019[1]	107.9	113.0	115.2	108.8	112.4	115.0	125.8	110.4	103.5	120.1	106.3	115.7
2020[1]	105.2	107.9	113.8	103.5	108.9	110.1	123.6	105.1	99.9	117.2	108.0	113.0
2021[1]	106.5	114.0	121.8	103.8	115.3	110.5	130.6	109.7	105.9	124.5	112.9	123.1
2022[1]	107.7	117.7	125.7	102.5	117.1	109.4	134.5	112.1	107.4	127.5	113.5	128.4

1 = NAICS basis, not continuous with previous years, which are based on the SIC.

Gross Domestic Product by Region and State—*Continued*

(Millions of chained 1997 or 2012 dollars; index numbers)

Year	Texas	Utah	Vermont	Virginia	Washington	West Virginia	Wisconsin	Wyoming
VALUE								
Chained 1997 Dollars								
1980	27,127	8,540	115,633	100,522	29,233	91,254	13,547	271,111
1981	28,129	8,814	119,300	103,616	28,878	91,533	14,013	277,668
1982	27,956	8,777	119,714	103,652	28,069	89,641	13,124	280,768
1983	28,917	9,130	125,223	105,339	27,319	91,390	12,431	295,605
1984	31,159	9,590	133,820	109,176	28,766	96,922	13,028	322,249
1985	32,938	10,153	140,418	110,215	29,085	100,204	13,191	341,303
1986	32,467	10,597	147,618	115,190	28,673	101,810	12,581	358,010
1987	32,682	11,522	156,426	120,393	28,734	104,770	12,272	383,298
1988	34,413	12,521	164,558	127,672	30,865	111,180	13,050	407,276
1989	34,827	13,091	170,267	134,180	30,816	113,430	13,019	411,580
1990	36,697	13,313	173,022	141,946	31,349	115,638	13,673	404,914
1991	38,105	12,952	172,407	145,050	31,986	117,167	14,118	394,303
1992	39,564	13,562	175,795	150,245	32,880	123,617	14,327	400,774
1993	41,509	13,755	180,782	154,090	33,836	128,390	14,785	401,601
1994	44,958	14,178	188,082	159,470	35,963	135,190	15,105	415,642
1995	48,212	14,211	193,402	160,183	36,902	138,010	15,539	433,600
1996	52,980	14,839	201,703	169,162	37,750	144,558	15,968	452,476
1997	55,212	15,521	210,361	179,640	38,570	151,035	16,084	479,107
Chained 2012 Dollars								
1997[1]	870,724	80,659	20,049	298,922	271,271	58,934	209,112	24,960
1998[1]	925,557	85,725	20,678	315,091	288,207	59,847	216,956	25,530
1999[1]	961,513	89,282	21,830	332,373	308,950	61,784	225,784	26,598
2000[1]	995,661	92,498	23,017	348,327	311,210	61,666	232,412	27,435
2001[1]	1,020,538	93,557	23,752	360,601	303,674	61,819	236,089	29,131
2002[1]	1,043,567	95,383	24,570	364,932	307,583	62,834	240,543	29,777
2003[1]	1,050,609	97,017	25,465	377,724	312,556	63,146	247,766	30,673
2004[1]	1,109,477	102,847	26,855	392,941	319,849	64,160	256,167	31,696
2005[1]	1,141,374	110,046	26,996	412,085	340,428	65,678	263,699	33,484
2006[1]	1,228,547	118,482	27,129	419,871	353,264	66,861	268,246	37,813
2007[1]	1,286,193	123,835	26,887	424,940	373,181	67,119	269,934	40,632
2008[1]	1,282,089	124,226	27,758	431,217	381,290	68,484	266,627	42,868
2009[1]	1,277,295	121,431	27,222	427,649	370,137	68,192	258,761	41,546
2010[1]	1,309,962	123,902	28,404	441,242	380,990	69,154	266,831	40,057
2011[1]	1,353,600	127,993	29,014	444,288	387,745	70,361	272,813	39,768
2012[1]	1,421,180	129,513	29,241	445,974	400,531	70,322	277,107	38,855
2013[1]	1,484,700	133,113	28,682	449,064	410,874	70,550	278,015	38,850
2014[1]	1,529,617	136,994	28,912	447,678	424,468	70,533	283,981	39,559
2015[1]	1,605,902	141,721	29,119	455,162	441,952	70,663	289,077	40,418
2016[1]	1,619,954	147,962	29,408	459,966	458,264	70,011	291,920	38,189
2017[1]	1,659,453	154,758	29,491	467,362	482,007	71,426	291,923	37,522
2018[1]	1,728,304	164,622	29,602	477,915	515,029	73,170	299,063	38,080
2019[1]	1,779,781	172,038	29,941	489,199	533,150	72,633	303,669	38,447
2020[1]	1,747,562	174,955	29,065	478,909	538,856	70,444	293,105	36,269
2021[1]	1,815,064	186,910	30,547	505,351	575,129	71,343	306,467	36,400
2022[1]	1,876,328	191,965	31,395	512,946	582,172	71,652	311,702	36,346

Gross Domestic Product by Region and State—*Continued*

(Millions of chained 1997 or 2012 dollars; index numbers)

Year	Texas	Utah	Vermont	Virginia	Washington	West Virginia	Wisconsin	Wyoming
QUANTITY INDEX								
1997=100								
1980	56.0	49.1	55.0	55.0	56.0	75.8	60.4	84.2
1981	59.5	50.9	56.8	56.7	57.7	74.9	60.6	87.1
1982	59.7	50.6	56.6	56.9	57.7	72.8	59.4	81.6
1983	59.6	52.4	58.8	59.5	58.6	70.8	60.5	77.3
1984	63.1	56.4	61.8	63.6	60.8	74.6	64.2	81.0
1985	65.9	59.7	65.4	66.8	61.4	75.4	66.3	82.0
1986	64.5	58.8	68.3	70.2	64.1	74.3	67.4	78.2
1987	64.2	59.2	74.2	74.4	67.0	74.5	69.4	76.3
1988	68.1	62.3	80.7	78.2	71.1	80.0	73.6	81.1
1989	69.8	63.1	84.3	80.9	74.7	79.9	75.1	80.9
1990	72.0	66.5	85.8	82.3	79.0	81.3	76.6	85.0
1991	73.2	69.0	83.5	82.0	80.7	82.9	77.6	87.8
1992	76.1	71.7	87.4	83.6	83.6	85.2	81.8	89.1
1993	78.8	75.2	88.6	85.9	85.8	87.7	85.0	91.9
1994	83.2	81.4	91.3	89.4	88.8	93.2	89.5	93.9
1995	87.4	87.3	91.6	91.9	89.2	95.7	91.4	96.6
1996	92.6	96.0	95.6	95.9	94.2	97.9	95.7	99.3
1997	100.0	100.0	100.0	100.0	100.0	100.0	100.0	100.0
2012 = 100								
1997[1]	61.3	62.3	68.6	67.0	67.7	83.8	75.5	64.2
1998[1]	65.1	66.2	70.7	70.7	72.0	85.1	78.3	65.7
1999[1]	67.7	68.9	74.7	74.5	77.1	87.9	81.5	68.5
2000[1]	70.1	71.4	78.7	78.1	77.7	87.7	83.9	70.6
2001[1]	71.8	72.2	81.2	80.9	75.8	87.9	85.2	75.0
2002[1]	73.4	73.6	84.0	81.8	76.8	89.4	86.8	76.6
2003[1]	73.9	74.9	87.1	84.7	78.0	89.8	89.4	78.9
2004[1]	78.1	79.4	91.8	88.1	79.9	91.2	92.4	81.6
2005[1]	80.3	85.0	92.3	92.4	85.0	93.4	95.2	86.2
2006[1]	86.4	91.5	92.8	94.1	88.2	95.1	96.8	97.3
2007[1]	90.5	95.6	91.9	95.3	93.2	95.4	97.4	104.6
2008[1]	90.2	95.9	94.9	96.7	95.2	97.4	96.2	110.3
2009[1]	89.9	93.8	93.1	95.9	92.4	97.0	93.4	106.9
2010[1]	92.2	95.7	97.1	98.9	95.1	98.3	96.3	103.1
2011[1]	95.2	98.8	99.2	99.6	96.8	100.1	98.5	102.3
2012[1]	100.0	100.0	100.0	100.0	100.0	100.0	100.0	100.0
2013[1]	104.5	102.8	98.1	100.7	102.6	100.3	100.3	100.0
2014[1]	107.6	105.8	98.9	100.4	106.0	100.3	102.5	101.8
2015[1]	113.0	109.4	99.6	102.1	110.3	100.5	104.3	104.0
2016[1]	114.0	114.2	100.6	103.1	114.4	99.6	105.3	98.3
2017[1]	116.8	119.5	100.9	104.8	120.3	101.6	105.3	96.6
2018[1]	121.6	127.1	101.2	107.2	128.6	104.1	107.9	98.0
2019[1]	125.2	132.8	102.4	109.7	133.1	103.3	109.6	98.9
2020[1]	123.0	135.1	99.4	107.4	134.5	100.2	105.8	93.3
2021[1]	127.7	144.3	104.5	113.3	143.6	101.5	110.6	93.7
2022[1]	132.0	148.2	107.4	115.0	145.4	101.9	112.5	93.5

1 = NAICS basis, not continuous with previous years, which are based on the SIC.

Gross Domestic Product by Metropolitan Statistical Area

(Millions of chained 2012 dollars.)

Metropolitan Statistical Area	2001	2002	2003	2004	2005	2006	2007	2008	2009	2010
Abilene, TX	4,923	4,979	5,059	5,175	5,295	5,724	5,898	5,973	5,822	6,011
Akron, OH	28,478	29,606	30,443	31,100	31,921	31,637	32,169	31,729	29,801	30,542
Albany, GA	5,500	5,563	5,593	5,616	5,731	5,580	5,425	5,326	5,240	5,079
Albany-Lebanon, OR	3,403	3,607	3,463	3,712	3,819	4,060	3,781	3,729	3,646	3,598
Albany-Schenectady-Troy, NY	43,695	44,491	45,807	46,952	46,941	47,304	47,365	48,190	49,013	49,358
Albuquerque, NM	30,106	30,593	33,336	38,033	37,981	38,544	38,163	38,027	38,941	38,202
Alexandria, LA	4,710	4,887	4,950	5,191	5,525	5,545	5,274	5,265	5,421	5,514
Allentown-Bethlehem-Easton, PA-NJ	42,736	42,712	38,962	36,037	36,269	35,860	37,500	37,845	36,660	37,549
Altoona, PA	4,668	4,666	4,783	4,982	5,138	5,225	5,158	5,160	5,151	5,223
Amarillo, TX	9,749	9,944	10,065	10,188	10,260	10,790	11,054	11,146	11,101	11,503
Ames, IA	4,025	4,186	4,391	4,577	4,700	4,806	4,909	5,033	4,952	5,004
Anchorage, AK	17,737	18,066	18,509	18,970	19,794	19,879	20,193	20,999	21,976	22,872
Ann Arbor, MI	18,822	19,988	20,335	20,248	20,739	20,608	20,947	19,661	18,105	18,709
Anniston-Oxford, AL	3,487	3,585	3,716	4,033	4,275	4,285	4,400	4,439	4,198	4,367
Appleton, WI	9,575	9,596	9,904	10,205	10,496	10,705	10,770	10,639	10,281	10,493
Asheville, NC	13,426	13,812	14,070	14,535	15,015	15,558	15,269	15,434	14,785	15,402
Athens-Clarke County, GA	6,633	6,711	7,077	7,224	7,363	7,377	7,471	7,482	7,414	7,405
Atlanta-Sandy Springs-Alpharetta, GA	254,140	257,216	265,981	278,370	292,429	297,391	299,889	291,267	277,827	281,781
Atlantic City-Hammonton, NJ	13,586	13,969	14,057	14,092	14,630	15,315	15,398	15,647	13,650	13,308
Auburn-Opelika, AL	2,960	3,114	3,312	3,714	3,914	4,039	4,172	4,234	4,166	4,292
Augusta-Richmond County, GA-SC	19,673	19,913	20,659	21,051	21,138	20,976	21,818	22,085	21,705	22,145
Austin-Round Rock-Georgetown, TX	61,469	63,385	65,154	68,521	74,249	83,401	87,066	90,385	88,157	93,428
Bakersfield, CA	27,652	31,075	30,773	33,320	35,506	40,305	44,041	42,722	45,552	43,467
Baltimore-Columbia-Towson, MD	131,684	135,284	138,046	142,658	148,647	151,931	152,507	154,761	153,026	158,941
Bangor, ME	5,628	5,796	5,792	5,991	6,085	6,050	6,048	5,879	5,872	5,848
Barnstable Town, MA	11,079	11,185	11,200	11,503	11,326	10,825	10,864	11,316	10,779	11,066
Baton Rouge, LA	37,594	40,289	42,084	46,638	51,413	50,286	45,792	44,654	44,868	47,302
Battle Creek, MI	5,635	5,734	5,790	5,939	6,076	6,142	6,144	5,972	5,480	5,608
Bay City, MI	3,595	3,608	3,643	3,654	3,691	3,683	3,649	3,501	3,451	3,558
Beaumont-Port Arthur, TX	23,701	22,677	23,156	27,604	24,791	24,464	26,421	25,400	24,991	26,978
Beckley, WV	3,761	3,816	3,759	3,860	4,031	4,055	4,093	4,305	4,188	4,353
Bellingham, WA	8,005	8,536	8,686	8,825	10,807	9,727	9,898	9,798	10,057	10,478
Bend, OR	4,594	4,798	5,031	5,235	5,757	6,158	6,363	6,245	5,676	5,494
Billings, MT	6,940	7,038	7,545	7,960	7,933	8,222	9,048	8,691	8,088	8,405
Binghamton, NY	8,416	8,393	8,384	8,455	8,528	8,869	9,214	9,853	9,833	10,398
Birmingham-Hoover, AL	46,046	47,575	48,323	50,873	52,739	52,563	53,239	53,030	50,517	50,791
Bismarck, ND	4,134	4,248	4,549	4,756	4,862	4,985	5,009	5,135	5,291	5,436
Blacksburg-Christiansburg, VA	5,418	5,473	5,772	5,790	6,106	6,304	6,500	6,112	5,707	5,791
Bloomington, IL	8,681	8,924	9,230	9,610	9,696	10,429	10,384	10,113	10,206	10,583
Bloomington, IN	4,919	5,049	5,246	5,428	5,693	5,866	5,740	5,680	5,655	5,728
Bloomsburg-Berwick, PA	3,183	3,367	3,369	3,563	3,625	3,802	3,742	3,784	3,775	3,942
Boise City, ID	18,509	18,973	20,207	21,833	24,160	24,333	24,595	25,379	24,169	24,411
Boston-Cambridge-Newton, MA-NH	284,104	283,248	288,879	298,678	306,067	314,625	325,031	329,980	325,924	342,090
Boulder, CO	18,077	16,864	17,120	17,609	17,995	18,493	19,668	20,593	20,213	20,673
Bowling Green, KY	4,489	4,641	4,845	5,085	5,407	5,694	5,672	5,677	5,267	5,776
Bremerton-Silverdale-Port Orchard, WA	8,478	8,933	9,101	9,531	9,897	9,874	9,931	10,469	10,202	10,211
Bridgeport-Stamford-Norwalk, CT	76,534	76,661	76,222	80,392	82,968	86,202	89,983	91,869	86,819	85,096
Brownsville-Harlingen, TX	7,387	7,747	7,870	7,991	8,190	8,626	8,566	8,625	8,598	8,974
Brunswick, GA	3,414	3,497	3,675	3,911	4,014	4,185	4,148	3,978	3,896	3,949
Buffalo-Cheektowaga, NY	49,408	50,709	51,255	52,835	52,516	53,568	54,061	54,639	54,753	56,297
Burlington, NC	4,644	4,891	4,885	5,145	5,208	5,373	5,292	5,219	4,833	5,027
Burlington-South Burlington, VT	8,848	9,129	9,759	10,462	10,501	10,692	10,464	11,143	11,032	11,561
California-Lexington Park, MD	4,067	4,339	4,608	4,802	4,925	5,084	5,251	5,358	5,481	5,920
Canton-Massillon, OH	14,910	15,153	15,156	15,442	15,727	15,205	15,003	14,764	13,857	14,603
Cape Coral-Fort Myers, FL	17,209	18,639	20,556	23,332	25,529	27,436	27,513	25,137	22,800	22,394
Cape Girardeau, MO-IL	3,315	3,426	3,457	3,613	3,784	3,832	3,893	3,945	3,884	3,820
Carbondale-Marion, IL	4,396	4,599	4,637	4,703	4,847	4,930	4,861	5,114	5,141	5,318
Carson City, NV	2,899	2,940	2,982	3,029	3,098	3,193	3,273	3,296	3,227	3,402
Casper, WY	3,142	3,226	3,322	3,558	3,848	4,393	4,475	4,610	4,262	4,490
Cedar Rapids, IA	10,521	10,405	11,216	12,285	12,872	12,984	14,233	14,068	14,257	15,070
Chambersburg-Waynesboro, PA	4,071	3,997	4,285	4,644	5,066	5,375	5,655	5,615	5,250	5,220
Champaign-Urbana, IL	8,500	8,942	8,978	9,166	9,129	9,312	9,500	9,923	9,813	10,194
Charleston, WV	13,536	13,610	13,607	13,542	13,902	14,164	14,173	14,060	14,037	13,715
Charleston-North Charleston, SC	21,756	22,752	24,081	25,582	27,238	28,129	29,359	29,140	28,122	29,371
Charlotte-Concord-Gastonia, NC-SC	91,493	93,890	97,664	103,670	111,445	119,228	121,062	129,500	120,805	116,605
Charlottesville, VA	8,065	8,156	8,458	8,820	9,265	9,643	9,933	10,320	10,221	10,787
Chattanooga, TN-GA	20,285	20,659	21,283	22,186	22,769	23,031	23,243	23,151	22,279	22,727
Cheyenne, WY	3,621	3,771	3,966	4,168	4,249	4,473	4,972	5,459	4,688	4,748
Chicago-Naperville-Elgin, IL-IN-WI	513,555	516,783	525,123	539,222	550,328	563,768	572,141	560,759	540,793	547,912
Chico, CA	6,436	6,869	7,144	7,238	7,395	7,651	7,524	7,351	7,548	7,576
Cincinnati, OH-KY-IN	101,429	103,717	105,562	107,535	110,431	110,954	111,556	110,918	106,733	110,202
Clarksville, TN-KY	7,692	8,326	8,584	9,263	10,179	10,676	10,474	10,677	10,645	11,058

Gross Domestic Product by Metropolitan Statistical Area—*Continued*

(Millions of chained 2012 dollars.)

Metropolitan Statistical Area	2011	2012	2013	2014	2015	2016	2017	2018	2019	2020	2021
Abilene, TX	6,061	6,222	6,254	6,336	6,216	6,114	6,254	6,556	6,795	7,069	7,312
Akron, OH	30,658	30,948	31,395	32,018	32,175	32,247	32,750	33,233	33,844	32,181	34,041
Albany, GA	5,183	5,239	5,216	5,108	5,073	5,138	5,108	5,093	5,225	5,134	5,210
Albany-Lebanon, OR	3,630	3,670	3,724	3,808	3,979	4,202	4,172	4,441	4,495	4,384	4,523
Albany-Schenectady-Troy, NY	49,585	49,696	50,249	50,851	52,150	53,455	54,668	54,897	58,056	56,189	60,213
Albuquerque, NM	37,723	37,345	36,487	37,116	37,462	37,989	37,912	38,682	39,842	39,180	41,184
Alexandria, LA	5,553	5,566	5,517	5,504	5,395	5,471	5,485	5,545	5,528	5,408	5,547
Allentown-Bethlehem-Easton, PA-NJ	37,837	38,024	38,162	38,710	39,435	40,294	40,686	41,085	42,608	40,407	42,807
Altoona, PA	5,215	5,165	5,174	5,186	5,249	5,299	5,412	5,447	5,562	5,371	5,586
Amarillo, TX	11,589	11,481	11,719	12,000	12,405	12,306	12,260	12,655	12,977	13,133	13,706
Ames, IA	5,164	5,324	5,645	5,778	5,797	5,655	5,844	5,903	5,973	5,901	6,166
Anchorage, AK	23,298	23,337	22,730	22,815	23,823	23,938	23,518	23,724	23,696	22,746	23,107
Ann Arbor, MI	18,841	19,390	19,528	19,826	20,618	21,118	21,788	22,319	22,967	22,506	23,860
Anniston-Oxford, AL	4,161	4,156	4,027	3,863	3,806	3,845	3,895	3,949	4,139	4,027	4,245
Appleton, WI	10,848	11,264	11,093	11,514	12,070	12,392	12,578	13,058	13,391	12,831	13,476
Asheville, NC	15,684	15,399	15,754	16,330	16,573	17,092	17,997	18,664	19,352	18,487	19,899
Athens-Clarke County, GA	7,345	7,709	7,817	7,971	8,319	8,486	8,918	9,171	9,267	8,888	9,381
Atlanta-Sandy Springs-Alpharetta, GA	287,933	292,331	299,097	312,364	327,440	343,398	356,812	370,215	385,448	369,428	399,130
Atlantic City-Hammonton, NJ	13,688	13,391	13,326	13,124	12,766	12,315	12,141	12,115	12,451	11,403	12,407
Auburn-Opelika, AL	4,618	4,849	4,877	4,935	5,120	5,267	5,435	5,379	5,600	5,605	5,898
Augusta-Richmond County, GA-SC	22,511	22,576	22,605	22,728	23,607	23,915	24,348	24,610	25,186	24,703	25,479
Austin-Round Rock-Georgetown, TX	97,421	100,427	105,495	111,176	120,013	126,238	131,820	139,619	146,516	149,801	165,604
Bakersfield, CA	42,644	46,566	45,535	45,616	45,836	45,928	46,642	46,683	47,994	48,039	47,529
Baltimore-Columbia-Towson, MD	161,984	163,424	166,049	168,708	172,797	178,332	181,493	183,778	185,632	177,312	185,182
Bangor, ME	5,709	5,619	5,585	5,611	5,600	5,693	5,758	5,886	6,021	6,015	6,309
Barnstable Town, MA	11,273	11,181	11,240	11,473	11,567	11,555	11,486	11,753	12,089	11,317	12,084
Baton Rouge, LA	52,370	52,352	52,310	57,884	57,579	55,232	52,192	54,790	53,732	48,950	49,408
Battle Creek, MI	5,454	5,417	5,514	5,547	5,697	5,812	5,799	5,848	5,853	5,828	6,495
Bay City, MI	3,557	3,553	3,554	3,378	3,361	3,365	3,279	3,326	3,253	3,190	3,427
Beaumont-Port Arthur, TX	27,335	28,583	28,685	23,579	23,388	24,203	25,156	26,055	25,666	21,933	21,221
Beckley, WV	4,443	4,317	4,124	3,912	3,768	3,583	3,748	3,816	3,907	3,710	3,838
Bellingham, WA	9,686	9,650	9,576	9,681	10,013	10,655	11,411	12,429	13,229	12,222	13,143
Bend, OR	5,557	5,694	6,063	6,635	7,135	7,793	8,461	8,816	9,338	9,385	10,243
Billings, MT	8,856	8,929	9,112	9,609	10,115	9,414	10,206	10,293	9,744	9,491	9,970
Binghamton, NY	10,291	10,391	10,380	10,263	10,229	9,950	9,903	10,084	10,266	9,781	10,285
Birmingham-Hoover, AL	52,072	53,135	52,814	52,644	53,310	53,839	54,592	55,645	56,168	55,066	58,051
Bismarck, ND	5,725	6,468	6,579	7,134	7,380	7,020	6,970	6,801	6,716	6,476	6,715
Blacksburg-Christiansburg, VA	5,982	5,885	5,923	5,951	6,133	6,128	6,267	6,584	6,488	6,253	6,784
Bloomington, IL	10,583	10,841	10,745	11,903	12,831	13,221	13,035	13,504	13,518	12,412	12,925
Bloomington, IN	5,787	5,778	5,865	6,183	6,117	6,279	6,550	6,764	6,738	6,498	6,740
Bloomsburg-Berwick, PA	4,050	4,040	4,114	4,044	4,104	4,065	4,099	4,065	4,147	3,942	4,186
Boise City, ID	24,401	24,537	25,574	26,678	27,001	28,128	29,211	31,503	32,870	33,306	36,295
Boston-Cambridge-Newton, MA-NH	348,885	357,088	358,707	364,733	379,370	386,932	394,470	411,807	424,318	414,213	444,403
Boulder, CO	20,817	20,899	21,534	22,180	23,062	23,747	25,117	25,875	27,672	27,025	29,155
Bowling Green, KY	5,683	5,901	6,013	6,108	6,110	6,250	6,469	6,356	6,696	6,608	6,989
Bremerton-Silverdale-Port Orchard, WA	10,161	10,030	9,931	9,954	10,247	10,716	10,771	11,015	11,142	11,408	11,742
Bridgeport-Stamford-Norwalk, CT	80,039	82,579	80,027	79,635	80,578	80,078	80,537	81,862	82,355	75,389	79,182
Brownsville-Harlingen, TX	9,232	9,327	9,440	9,443	9,454	9,689	9,661	9,824	10,073	10,130	10,741
Brunswick, GA	3,834	3,763	3,758	3,754	3,941	3,878	3,977	4,070	4,004	3,878	4,054
Buffalo-Cheektowaga, NY	55,716	56,950	56,708	57,989	58,791	59,452	59,113	59,766	61,297	59,203	62,336
Burlington, NC	5,153	5,116	5,320	5,410	5,377	5,577	5,504	5,531	5,699	5,629	6,083
Burlington-South Burlington, VT	11,864	11,981	11,809	11,964	12,068	12,393	12,453	12,575	12,795	12,449	13,103
California-Lexington Park, MD	6,233	6,238	6,187	6,271	6,434	6,602	6,732	6,778	6,902	7,037	7,168
Canton-Massillon, OH	15,655	15,337	16,362	17,397	17,481	17,226	17,380	17,208	17,361	16,324	17,157
Cape Coral-Fort Myers, FL	22,203	22,669	23,151	24,280	25,739	27,624	28,253	29,155	29,515	29,571	32,192
Cape Girardeau, MO-IL	3,794	3,828	3,835	3,854	3,956	4,007	4,013	4,063	4,032	3,895	3,996
Carbondale-Marion, IL	5,500	5,498	5,315	5,190	5,160	5,117	5,129	5,275	5,272	4,983	5,151
Carson City, NV	3,125	3,085	3,065	2,907	2,931	2,916	3,099	3,216	3,411	3,310	3,446
Casper, WY	4,755	5,349	5,486	5,866	5,784	5,253	5,171	5,648	5,518	4,899	4,818
Cedar Rapids, IA	15,459	15,577	15,308	15,934	16,497	16,864	16,719	17,160	16,721	16,384	16,854
Chambersburg-Waynesboro, PA	5,246	5,201	5,311	5,418	5,554	5,395	5,838	5,810	5,761	5,444	5,657
Champaign-Urbana, IL	10,293	10,298	10,725	10,915	10,904	10,635	10,573	10,457	10,496	10,387	10,799
Charleston, WV	13,746	13,231	12,797	12,536	12,187	12,033	11,777	12,408	11,765	11,041	11,349
Charleston-North Charleston, SC	30,801	32,514	32,399	33,259	34,735	36,548	37,190	38,332	40,077	38,678	41,626
Charlotte-Concord-Gastonia, NC-SC	123,247	130,054	129,316	133,022	138,394	142,319	149,263	151,036	154,912	156,867	167,253
Charlottesville, VA	10,790	10,901	10,954	11,010	11,336	11,530	12,120	12,424	12,525	12,035	12,816
Chattanooga, TN-GA	23,491	24,388	24,696	24,582	25,257	25,686	26,414	26,638	27,202	26,474	28,336
Cheyenne, WY	4,918	5,048	4,955	5,003	5,197	5,031	5,035	5,311	5,517	5,261	5,508
Chicago-Naperville-Elgin, IL-IN-WI	556,699	570,955	571,812	585,491	598,224	600,346	605,948	622,008	626,389	592,461	630,126
Chico, CA	7,509	7,363	7,413	7,310	7,601	8,085	8,415	8,513	8,658	8,083	8,095
Cincinnati, OH-KY-IN	113,936	114,926	115,881	119,162	122,081	126,814	129,571	130,388	136,730	133,563	141,604
Clarksville, TN-KY	11,654	11,715	11,441	11,283	11,326	11,136	11,072	11,162	11,348	11,369	11,956

Gross Domestic Product by Metropolitan Statistical Area—*Continued*

(Millions of chained 2012 dollars.)

Metropolitan Statistical Area	2001	2002	2003	2004	2005	2006	2007	2008	2009	2010
Cleveland, TN	3,348	3,505	3,533	3,754	3,784	3,727	3,745	3,782	3,705	3,861
Cleveland-Elyria, OH	106,396	107,794	109,582	112,172	115,183	115,199	115,243	114,119	106,621	107,682
Coeur d'Alene, ID	3,457	3,529	3,683	3,979	4,366	4,565	4,774	4,786	4,418	4,616
College Station-Bryan, TX	7,042	7,383	7,660	7,804	8,452	9,180	9,971	10,412	11,254	10,681
Colorado Springs, CO	24,619	24,675	24,970	25,389	26,678	27,073	27,789	27,820	27,900	28,570
Columbia, MO	6,816	6,940	7,123	7,389	7,572	7,676	7,636	7,766	7,735	7,862
Columbia, SC	28,055	28,552	29,515	30,864	31,742	32,980	33,924	33,870	32,995	33,115
Columbus, GA-AL	11,131	11,448	11,451	11,618	11,893	12,155	12,543	12,549	12,656	12,871
Columbus, IN	3,592	3,488	3,659	3,935	4,179	4,549	5,093	5,332	4,384	5,287
Columbus, OH	84,664	85,964	87,652	91,000	94,237	94,568	95,866	94,646	91,720	94,509
Corpus Christi, TX	18,033	17,927	18,556	19,877	18,843	19,435	20,734	19,773	19,443	20,668
Corvallis, OR	2,658	2,687	2,733	2,858	3,043	3,308	3,565	3,762	3,669	3,812
Crestview-Fort Walton Beach-Destin, FL	8,704	9,404	10,210	11,301	12,099	12,101	12,004	11,362	10,896	10,715
Cumberland, MD-WV	3,231	3,264	3,229	3,209	3,185	3,161	3,134	3,240	3,229	3,443
Dallas-Fort Worth-Arlington, TX	273,532	281,691	285,518	302,019	317,441	342,706	354,614	357,232	346,156	352,861
Dalton, GA	5,779	6,041	6,117	6,812	7,115	7,038	6,991	6,641	5,987	5,721
Danville, IL	2,831	2,929	3,050	3,186	3,120	3,246	3,212	3,231	3,038	3,035
Daphne-Fairhope-Foley, AL	4,008	4,193	4,426	4,912	5,503	5,674	5,852	5,570	5,329	5,382
Davenport-Moline-Rock Island, IA-IL	16,882	16,804	17,284	18,335	18,767	18,828	19,036	19,510	18,638	19,257
Dayton-Kettering, OH	35,306	36,172	36,772	37,762	38,164	38,021	37,173	36,197	34,208	35,095
Decatur, AL	4,866	4,807	5,193	5,879	5,552	5,635	5,816	5,618	5,503	5,566
Decatur, IL	5,572	5,574	5,657	5,837	5,922	5,973	6,132	6,465	6,428	6,493
Deltona-Daytona Beach-Ormond Beach, FL	13,431	14,518	15,703	17,112	17,705	18,271	18,611	17,494	16,290	16,179
Denver-Aurora-Lakewood, CO	134,532	134,766	135,055	135,615	141,128	143,494	149,694	149,718	145,070	147,944
Des Moines-West Des Moines, IA	28,302	28,637	31,022	34,070	36,677	36,291	40,100	36,021	35,561	36,152
Detroit-Warren-Dearborn, MI	220,103	225,105	229,157	230,222	234,960	228,600	226,462	210,963	187,252	199,338
Dothan, AL	4,593	4,809	4,870	5,050	5,178	5,281	5,277	5,101	4,947	4,929
Dover, DE	5,752	5,893	6,083	6,714	6,699	6,834	6,857	6,868	7,170	6,974
Dubuque, IA	3,607	3,772	3,943	4,387	4,688	4,808	5,028	4,791	4,493	4,840
Duluth, MN-WI	11,720	12,183	12,301	12,976	13,243	12,978	12,677	12,989	12,325	13,609
Durham-Chapel Hill, NC	27,360	28,596	30,201	30,828	33,065	39,865	42,495	43,637	40,077	43,526
East Stroudsburg, PA	4,635	4,813	4,914	5,379	5,769	6,072	6,429	6,479	6,261	6,335
Eau Claire, WI	5,296	5,541	5,806	6,125	6,565	6,659	6,836	6,698	6,665	7,009
El Centro, CA	5,056	6,085	5,657	5,429	5,903	6,314	6,083	7,093	6,844	6,783
Elizabethtown-Fort Knox, KY	4,190	4,231	4,378	4,544	4,676	4,845	4,867	5,136	5,140	5,718
Elkhart-Goshen, IN	7,794	8,460	9,299	9,929	10,704	11,412	11,410	9,873	7,254	9,625
Elmira, NY	3,115	3,136	3,175	3,210	3,257	3,218	3,302	3,504	3,475	3,668
El Paso, TX	20,084	20,931	20,948	22,207	22,704	23,345	23,758	23,102	23,453	25,309
Enid, OK	1,980	2,020	2,112	2,183	2,268	2,373	2,535	2,784	2,870	2,964
Erie, PA	10,409	10,318	10,411	10,734	11,214	11,410	11,779	12,327	11,239	11,497
Eugene-Springfield, OR	11,078	11,307	11,519	12,021	12,659	13,057	13,283	13,193	12,323	12,474
Evansville, IN-KY	14,865	15,649	16,285	17,298	16,844	15,966	15,709	16,282	15,653	16,079
Fairbanks, AK	5,789	5,061	5,128	5,170	5,658	5,900	5,970	6,412	6,285	6,340
Fargo, ND-MN	7,708	8,207	8,628	8,985	9,318	9,802	10,150	10,393	10,124	10,501
Farmington, NM	6,556	6,574	6,461	6,633	6,659	6,809	7,008	6,938	6,998	6,542
Fayetteville, NC	14,606	15,314	15,753	16,644	17,686	18,019	17,806	18,485	19,070	19,592
Fayetteville-Springdale-Rogers, AR	13,374	14,453	15,353	16,775	17,954	18,331	17,968	17,526	16,755	17,704
Flagstaff, AZ	4,908	4,986	5,051	5,266	5,519	5,708	6,224	6,114	5,803	6,124
Flint, MI	14,104	14,883	15,128	15,137	15,345	15,134	14,766	13,415	12,130	12,773
Florence, SC	7,204	7,268	7,467	7,635	7,793	7,870	7,899	7,742	7,450	7,306
Florence-Muscle Shoals, AL	4,169	4,155	4,346	4,605	4,754	4,791	4,769	4,742	4,479	4,715
Fond du Lac, WI	3,672	3,627	3,766	3,971	4,060	4,100	4,136	4,198	3,913	4,100
Fort Collins, CO	10,453	11,111	11,213	11,422	11,715	11,972	12,344	12,693	12,531	12,881
Fort Smith, AR-OK	7,857	8,098	8,482	8,972	9,279	9,716	9,387	9,147	8,455	8,722
Fort Wayne, IN	15,439	15,849	16,592	17,001	17,477	18,078	18,462	17,441	16,110	16,578
Fresno, CA	28,185	30,398	32,093	32,709	33,944	35,837	34,880	33,768	34,242	34,497
Gadsden, AL	2,639	2,677	2,719	2,884	2,926	2,836	2,819	2,783	2,758	2,771
Gainesville, FL	10,103	10,412	10,525	11,429	11,720	11,903	12,525	12,361	12,047	11,945
Gainesville, GA	6,202	6,271	6,564	6,779	7,029	7,068	7,305	7,275	6,840	6,952
Gettysburg, PA	2,683	2,891	2,883	2,931	3,057	3,192	3,179	3,255	3,307	3,244
Glens Falls, NY	4,376	4,491	4,669	4,989	4,889	4,917	4,895	5,198	5,441	5,517
Goldsboro, NC	4,347	4,179	4,076	4,287	4,347	4,487	4,489	4,569	4,469	4,574
Grand Forks, ND-MN	3,506	3,683	3,955	3,843	3,975	4,201	4,193	4,417	4,254	4,360
Grand Island, NE	2,643	2,716	2,891	2,956	3,179	3,314	3,308	3,383	3,415	3,546
Grand Junction, CO	4,384	4,505	4,641	4,777	5,076	5,401	6,004	6,560	6,027	5,695
Grand Rapids-Kentwood, MI	43,121	44,428	45,410	46,822	48,095	47,842	47,787	46,170	42,925	44,566
Grants Pass, OR	1,762	1,850	1,933	2,026	2,147	2,150	2,155	2,096	2,028	2,028
Great Falls, MT	2,761	2,844	2,853	2,984	3,201	3,166	3,232	3,170	3,161	3,255
Greeley, CO	7,583	7,508	7,805	8,375	9,047	9,273	9,663	10,264	10,399	10,755
Green Bay, WI	13,900	14,233	14,687	15,156	15,497	15,745	15,872	15,824	15,292	16,029

Gross Domestic Product by Metropolitan Statistical Area—*Continued*

(Millions of chained 2012 dollars.)

Metropolitan Statistical Area	2011	2012	2013	2014	2015	2016	2017	2018	2019	2020	2021
Cleveland, TN	3,907	4,370	4,441	4,367	4,431	4,272	4,289	4,277	4,303	4,282	4,464
Cleveland-Elyria, OH	109,634	110,449	110,726	112,901	113,216	113,545	115,177	117,067	119,911	114,787	122,275
Coeur d'Alene, ID	4,476	4,550	4,934	5,033	5,066	5,294	5,455	5,754	5,875	6,043	6,553
College Station-Bryan, TX	10,473	10,589	11,349	12,081	12,846	12,906	13,213	13,742	14,300	14,318	14,696
Colorado Springs, CO	29,300	29,544	29,951	30,159	30,399	30,823	31,877	32,949	34,094	34,594	36,364
Columbia, MO	8,025	8,257	8,509	8,526	8,698	8,757	8,931	8,992	9,373	9,354	9,849
Columbia, SC	33,158	33,021	33,843	35,029	35,976	36,925	37,294	37,694	38,403	37,832	39,506
Columbus, GA-AL	13,073	13,223	12,981	12,946	13,008	12,809	12,901	12,890	13,131	13,066	13,379
Columbus, IN	5,438	5,945	6,234	5,945	5,755	5,652	5,629	6,066	6,042	5,590	6,068
Columbus, OH	98,191	101,853	104,567	107,732	109,401	111,826	115,372	116,736	120,326	118,636	127,767
Corpus Christi, TX	21,317	21,256	21,611	20,229	20,199	19,797	20,560	21,532	21,710	20,710	21,097
Corvallis, OR	3,943	3,895	3,741	3,719	3,751	3,873	4,004	4,221	4,270	4,230	4,433
Crestview-Fort Walton Beach-Destin, FL	10,784	11,360	11,640	11,815	12,090	12,566	12,969	13,344	14,090	14,314	15,554
Cumberland, MD-WV	3,427	3,404	3,313	3,304	3,358	3,505	3,458	3,504	3,493	3,264	3,284
Dallas-Fort Worth-Arlington, TX	365,601	377,846	388,536	402,788	422,048	435,498	450,467	469,741	486,572	480,618	513,979
Dalton, GA	5,773	5,975	5,902	6,059	6,247	6,478	6,485	6,406	6,417	6,257	6,689
Danville, IL	3,072	3,131	3,154	3,100	3,027	2,976	3,014	3,006	3,006	2,925	3,025
Daphne-Fairhope-Foley, AL	5,372	5,427	5,679	5,776	5,993	6,266	6,430	6,787	7,132	7,142	7,830
Davenport-Moline-Rock Island, IA-IL	19,909	20,552	19,918	19,955	19,594	19,325	19,534	19,483	19,677	19,457	20,300
Dayton-Kettering, OH	36,091	35,902	35,994	36,360	36,693	37,233	38,384	39,177	40,258	39,373	41,277
Decatur, AL	5,364	5,371	5,389	5,444	5,335	5,429	5,494	5,583	5,628	5,689	5,855
Decatur, IL	6,613	6,476	6,955	7,176	7,356	6,874	6,131	6,032	5,954	5,914	6,366
Deltona-Daytona Beach-Ormond Beach, FL	16,015	16,343	16,367	16,838	17,245	17,956	18,552	19,064	19,359	19,297	20,633
Denver-Aurora-Lakewood, CO	150,563	154,899	161,007	167,765	176,211	180,036	185,671	193,776	202,973	200,471	214,521
Des Moines-West Des Moines, IA	36,230	38,521	37,500	41,897	45,259	46,488	45,836	46,362	47,444	47,819	50,800
Detroit-Warren-Dearborn, MI	207,488	214,466	218,446	221,200	224,592	228,599	230,337	234,506	233,889	222,348	241,603
Dothan, AL	4,943	5,017	5,226	5,287	5,378	5,625	5,745	5,764	5,876	5,820	6,056
Dover, DE	6,893	6,537	6,501	6,662	6,773	6,834	6,804	7,121	7,672	7,668	8,130
Dubuque, IA	4,815	5,480	5,161	5,608	5,706	5,511	5,825	5,839	6,075	6,104	6,428
Duluth, MN-WI	14,001	13,411	13,765	13,697	12,415	12,753	12,764	13,123	13,318	12,713	13,239
Durham-Chapel Hill, NC	44,100	44,461	45,116	44,321	43,549	43,213	42,819	44,651	46,578	47,012	50,698
East Stroudsburg, PA	6,251	6,122	6,147	6,194	6,419	6,484	6,859	6,651	6,839	6,538	6,787
Eau Claire, WI	7,198	7,450	7,426	8,006	8,176	8,091	8,143	8,397	8,626	8,264	8,652
El Centro, CA	7,039	6,640	7,021	7,437	8,043	8,170	8,142	8,134	8,320	8,443	8,412
Elizabethtown-Fort Knox, KY	6,034	5,719	5,625	5,450	5,170	5,263	5,330	5,259	5,449	5,399	5,662
Elkhart-Goshen, IN	9,495	9,694	10,489	11,382	12,270	13,341	14,792	14,831	14,377	13,985	17,529
Elmira, NY	3,740	3,743	3,750	3,738	3,606	3,522	3,441	3,489	3,487	3,328	3,492
El Paso, TX	26,559	27,326	26,973	26,505	26,851	27,152	27,754	28,696	30,024	29,726	30,825
Enid, OK	3,044	3,512	3,622	4,242	4,259	4,600	3,209	3,181	3,149	2,999	3,169
Erie, PA	12,004	11,687	11,762	11,151	11,143	10,807	10,523	10,614	10,734	10,074	10,415
Eugene-Springfield, OR	12,515	12,596	12,631	12,750	13,355	13,720	14,172	14,569	14,567	14,350	15,113
Evansville, IN-KY	16,245	15,840	15,126	14,919	15,014	15,308	16,238	16,966	17,689	16,947	17,508
Fairbanks, AK	5,901	5,589	5,488	5,418	5,375	5,379	5,329	5,274	5,221	5,135	5,286
Fargo, ND-MN	11,088	12,075	11,961	12,794	13,173	13,045	13,261	13,445	13,774	13,550	14,487
Farmington, NM	6,494	6,469	6,350	6,550	6,648	6,095	5,919	5,576	5,664	5,358	5,140
Fayetteville, NC	19,705	19,200	19,134	19,130	19,351	19,342	18,495	18,635	19,054	18,845	19,840
Fayetteville-Springdale-Rogers, AR	18,052	18,730	19,934	20,812	21,858	22,300	23,507	24,276	24,961	25,850	28,042
Flagstaff, AZ	6,540	6,303	6,541	6,416	6,509	6,528	7,152	7,094	6,938	6,541	6,855
Flint, MI	12,989	13,090	13,401	13,302	13,920	14,243	14,421	14,771	14,976	13,854	14,846
Florence, SC	7,610	7,720	8,034	8,354	8,561	8,713	8,794	8,724	8,944	8,678	9,066
Florence-Muscle Shoals, AL	4,853	4,901	5,167	4,968	4,848	4,702	4,631	4,721	4,708	4,686	4,888
Fond du Lac, WI	4,286	4,546	4,574	4,680	4,641	4,616	4,712	4,769	4,847	4,629	4,835
Fort Collins, CO	12,913	13,408	13,927	14,608	15,291	15,860	17,063	17,851	18,829	19,021	20,345
Fort Smith, AR-OK	8,937	8,799	8,608	8,551	8,419	8,376	8,424	8,622	8,750	8,587	9,011
Fort Wayne, IN	16,763	17,455	17,281	18,489	19,216	19,774	20,345	21,195	21,216	20,043	21,269
Fresno, CA	34,810	33,632	34,890	35,928	37,348	38,649	39,794	40,879	41,883	41,329	41,821
Gadsden, AL	2,802	2,718	2,761	2,741	2,809	2,805	2,804	2,834	2,766	2,558	2,597
Gainesville, FL	11,756	11,704	11,799	12,177	12,394	12,652	13,115	13,524	13,800	14,098	14,953
Gainesville, GA	7,491	7,430	7,573	7,995	8,355	8,658	9,334	9,749	10,115	10,103	10,988
Gettysburg, PA	3,313	3,413	3,416	3,413	3,499	3,540	3,700	3,597	3,531	3,334	3,504
Glens Falls, NY	5,414	5,484	5,436	5,465	5,559	5,522	5,687	5,712	6,014	5,721	6,089
Goldsboro, NC	4,361	4,370	4,487	4,368	4,413	4,396	4,480	4,490	4,536	4,451	4,704
Grand Forks, ND-MN	4,407	4,680	4,742	4,687	4,753	4,837	4,862	4,801	4,927	4,843	4,981
Grand Island, NE	3,599	3,705	3,904	3,873	3,872	3,912	3,801	3,789	3,858	3,819	3,991
Grand Junction, CO	5,757	5,677	5,578	5,647	5,575	5,461	5,730	5,968	6,067	5,921	6,142
Grand Rapids-Kentwood, MI	45,538	46,665	47,617	49,176	51,248	52,581	53,546	54,932	55,127	53,502	57,145
Grants Pass, OR	2,029	2,043	2,065	2,091	2,229	2,244	2,398	2,506	2,677	2,727	2,955
Great Falls, MT	3,284	3,289	3,208	3,179	3,275	3,251	3,428	3,437	3,365	3,277	3,376
Greeley, CO	11,153	12,261	13,751	16,631	18,787	19,696	21,120	23,082	24,310	22,716	21,188
Green Bay, WI	16,380	16,829	16,767	17,699	18,141	18,298	18,146	18,728	18,831	17,961	18,482

Gross Domestic Product by Metropolitan Statistical Area—*Continued*

(Millions of chained 2012 dollars.)

Metropolitan Statistical Area	2001	2002	2003	2004	2005	2006	2007	2008	2009	2010
Greensboro-High Point, NC	34,569	35,491	35,410	35,177	36,132	37,600	37,540	37,967	37,111	37,461
Greenville, NC	5,609	5,566	5,542	5,734	6,196	6,712	6,969	6,986	7,230	7,416
Greenville-Anderson, SC	32,086	33,592	34,734	31,903	32,326	32,251	33,476	33,120	31,241	32,219
Gulfport-Biloxi, MS	14,599	14,679	15,810	15,826	16,367	16,930	20,872	18,787	17,722	17,553
Hagerstown-Martinsburg, MD-WV	7,696	7,900	8,073	8,501	8,754	9,140	9,137	9,116	8,793	8,938
Hammond, LA	2,457	2,558	2,782	3,049	3,388	3,928	3,691	3,794	3,605	3,819
Hanford-Corcoran, CA	4,350	4,591	5,040	5,268	5,501	5,121	5,932	5,311	4,816	4,926
Harrisburg-Carlisle, PA	27,536	28,251	29,215	30,391	30,856	31,324	31,964	31,941	30,890	31,361
Harrisonburg, VA	7,068	6,161	6,074	6,196	6,549	6,635	6,652	6,659	6,965	7,409
Hartford-East Hartford-Middletown, CT	74,350	70,882	72,814	78,431	79,769	83,691	88,618	87,813	86,004	86,187
Hattiesburg, MS	4,385	4,554	4,753	4,974	5,180	5,488	5,331	5,491	5,434	5,568
Hickory-Lenoir-Morganton, NC	13,584	13,613	13,297	13,786	13,878	14,210	13,721	13,270	12,585	13,056
Hilton Head Island-Bluffton, SC	5,852	5,961	6,345	6,811	7,200	7,550	7,724	7,456	7,170	7,032
Hinesville, GA	2,407	2,491	2,725	2,857	3,065	3,066	3,176	3,449	3,487	3,707
Homosassa Springs, FL	3,461	3,583	3,718	3,945	4,111	4,419	4,563	4,327	4,078	3,828
Hot Springs, AR	2,537	2,642	2,718	2,782	2,889	2,904	2,869	2,757	2,715	2,804
Houma-Thibodaux, LA	10,288	9,925	9,496	9,360	9,638	11,251	11,327	11,114	11,200	10,977
Houston-The Woodlands-Sugar Land, TX	294,041	293,513	294,404	320,585	325,736	353,055	380,410	371,347	367,676	383,630
Huntington-Ashland, WV-KY-OH	12,373	12,624	12,840	13,278	13,398	13,647	13,441	14,087	14,128	13,857
Huntsville, AL	15,279	15,868	16,813	18,155	19,231	19,992	20,672	21,292	21,466	22,639
Idaho Falls, ID	4,167	4,421	4,442	4,650	4,835	5,240	5,360	5,432	5,466	5,447
Indianapolis-Carmel-Anderson, IN	94,753	95,730	99,224	104,578	105,882	109,127	113,144	115,237	111,549	115,316
Iowa City, IA	6,433	6,648	6,814	7,134	7,263	7,584	7,611	7,950	7,867	8,092
Ithaca, NY	4,566	4,745	4,959	5,082	5,009	4,996	5,020	5,242	5,382	5,581
Jackson, MI	4,992	5,146	5,110	5,289	5,420	5,360	5,282	5,100	4,640	4,809
Jackson, MS	21,034	21,509	22,422	23,174	23,754	24,115	23,349	23,853	23,114	23,609
Jackson, TN	6,460	6,422	6,583	6,752	6,923	7,068	6,889	7,013	7,079	7,514
Jacksonville, FL	53,489	55,204	57,935	60,773	63,448	65,647	66,860	64,385	61,103	60,794
Jacksonville, NC	5,288	5,138	5,384	5,889	6,303	6,373	6,863	7,621	8,064	8,430
Janesville-Beloit, WI	5,423	6,017	6,136	6,279	6,243	6,551	6,480	6,148	5,694	5,856
Jefferson City, MO	5,830	5,858	5,987	6,219	6,324	6,415	6,396	6,607	6,496	6,626
Johnson City, TN	5,267	5,385	5,649	6,043	6,221	6,326	6,406	6,591	6,353	6,205
Johnstown, PA	4,477	4,443	4,510	4,569	4,650	4,570	4,596	4,717	4,616	4,724
Jonesboro, AR	3,350	3,492	3,784	3,959	4,115	4,174	3,974	4,040	4,033	4,233
Joplin, MO	6,040	6,075	6,168	6,402	6,549	6,593	6,537	6,721	6,438	6,573
Kahului-Wailuku-Lahaina, HI	5,878	6,100	6,515	6,961	7,583	8,121	8,259	7,828	7,045	7,242
Kalamazoo-Portage, MI	10,741	11,413	11,233	11,399	11,308	11,233	11,461	11,079	10,784	10,952
Kankakee, IL	3,580	3,696	3,733	3,814	3,788	3,922	3,935	4,050	4,082	4,120
Kansas City, MO-KS	92,174	94,867	96,395	98,560	101,599	104,960	107,940	110,528	106,751	106,378
Kennewick-Richland, WA	9,017	9,670	9,731	9,945	10,494	10,832	10,908	11,197	11,696	12,904
Killeen-Temple, TX	11,098	11,532	12,074	12,601	13,585	14,770	15,389	16,273	16,390	16,310
Kingsport-Bristol, TN-VA	10,542	10,563	10,765	11,491	11,266	11,795	11,875	11,822	11,668	11,617
Kingston, NY	5,390	5,574	5,815	6,083	6,054	6,131	6,120	6,400	6,325	6,455
Knoxville, TN	28,408	29,880	31,112	32,625	33,887	34,656	34,635	34,930	33,259	33,632
Kokomo, IN	3,366	3,727	4,323	4,121	4,038	4,152	4,374	3,825	2,586	4,106
La Crosse-Onalaska, WI-MN	5,108	5,181	5,376	5,545	5,720	5,763	5,845	5,951	5,977	6,207
Lafayette, LA	19,955	18,816	18,658	19,050	19,618	22,405	21,983	22,446	22,158	22,471
Lafayette-West Lafayette, IN	7,028	7,196	7,512	7,755	7,955	8,327	8,613	8,431	7,714	8,270
Lake Charles, LA	14,683	15,698	18,810	20,521	24,367	20,689	17,117	14,836	12,436	11,248
Lake Havasu City-Kingman, AZ	3,796	4,181	4,284	4,635	4,869	4,893	5,009	4,908	4,630	4,628
Lakeland-Winter Haven, FL	17,187	17,775	18,354	19,252	20,400	21,070	21,578	21,032	19,764	19,843
Lancaster, PA	21,484	21,899	22,789	23,204	23,788	23,822	23,720	23,623	22,680	23,476
Lansing-East Lansing, MI	21,106	21,824	22,045	22,221	22,629	22,917	22,980	21,617	20,176	21,747
Laredo, TX	8,058	8,250	8,136	7,877	8,166	8,282	8,147	7,768	7,827	7,928
Las Cruces, NM	4,902	5,109	5,488	5,908	6,398	6,408	6,452	6,497	6,741	7,048
Las Vegas-Henderson-Paradise, NV	72,916	76,231	79,958	89,395	97,900	102,438	103,794	100,444	90,714	89,957
Lawrence, KS	3,700	3,806	3,783	3,862	3,871	3,848	3,933	4,030	4,002	3,938
Lawton, OK	3,736	3,855	4,147	4,333	4,262	4,440	4,512	4,670	4,816	5,038
Lebanon, PA	3,927	4,042	4,264	4,491	4,548	4,638	4,793	4,786	4,769	4,950
Lewiston, ID-WA	2,045	2,074	2,102	2,154	2,193	2,206	2,218	2,291	2,247	2,341
Lewiston-Auburn, ME	3,455	3,718	3,834	3,925	3,923	3,981	4,107	4,169	4,003	3,947
Lexington-Fayette, KY	19,384	20,303	20,760	21,549	22,627	23,548	23,781	23,241	21,515	22,343
Lima, OH	5,716	5,922	5,817	5,951	5,986	6,117	6,043	6,062	7,496	7,822
Lincoln, NE	13,323	13,377	13,875	14,117	14,764	15,112	15,378	14,809	14,440	14,867
Little Rock-North Little Rock-Conway, AR	26,490	27,334	28,655	29,718	31,492	32,437	33,337	32,719	31,772	31,689
Logan, UT-ID	2,944	2,940	3,121	3,284	3,341	3,447	3,654	3,857	3,935	4,257
Longview, TX	12,561	13,002	12,854	13,148	13,968	15,163	16,549	17,560	18,453	17,226
Longview, WA	3,310	3,213	3,334	3,401	3,563	3,680	3,902	3,807	3,733	4,032
Los Angeles-Long Beach-Anaheim, CA	632,418	645,850	673,627	696,494	717,803	746,823	754,276	762,205	729,623	750,124
Louisville/Jefferson County, KY-IN	51,068	51,298	52,762	54,549	56,364	58,303	58,534	57,245	54,115	56,593

Gross Domestic Product by Metropolitan Statistical Area—*Continued*

(Millions of chained 2012 dollars.)

Metropolitan Statistical Area	2011	2012	2013	2014	2015	2016	2017	2018	2019	2020	2021
Greensboro-High Point, NC	38,157	36,212	36,950	36,769	37,566	37,050	37,226	37,142	37,072	35,625	37,467
Greenville, NC	7,492	7,145	7,546	7,758	8,424	8,423	8,674	8,444	8,461	8,313	8,795
Greenville-Anderson, SC	33,607	33,978	34,982	36,174	37,611	38,602	39,594	40,767	41,604	40,400	43,081
Gulfport-Biloxi, MS	16,683	17,103	15,675	16,565	16,102	16,497	16,555	16,176	16,385	16,596	17,663
Hagerstown-Martinsburg, MD-WV	9,164	9,330	9,360	9,442	9,524	9,918	10,151	10,392	10,206	9,755	10,282
Hammond, LA	4,291	3,879	3,603	3,587	3,398	3,510	3,798	3,831	3,924	3,943	4,043
Hanford-Corcoran, CA	5,626	5,097	5,102	5,508	5,419	5,688	6,065	5,957	6,096	6,135	6,074
Harrisburg-Carlisle, PA	32,114	32,678	33,228	34,206	35,034	35,022	34,955	35,694	36,735	35,103	36,687
Harrisonburg, VA	7,449	7,533	7,702	7,346	7,118	6,851	6,995	7,154	7,389	7,387	7,973
Hartford-East Hartford-Middletown, CT	85,715	85,826	82,876	84,484	89,538	89,923	92,189	91,832	92,668	86,379	90,664
Hattiesburg, MS	5,537	5,640	5,682	5,632	5,709	5,616	5,687	5,649	5,582	5,570	5,859
Hickory-Lenoir-Morganton, NC	13,036	12,642	12,715	12,780	13,059	13,353	13,873	13,660	13,450	12,983	13,820
Hilton Head Island-Bluffton, SC	6,952	6,997	7,275	7,481	7,589	7,746	7,836	8,138	8,466	8,531	9,212
Hinesville, GA	3,889	3,751	3,659	3,515	3,463	3,407	3,384	3,423	3,463	3,426	3,608
Homosassa Springs, FL	3,694	3,615	3,587	3,461	3,400	3,466	3,385	3,522	3,853	3,857	4,152
Hot Springs, AR	3,006	2,948	2,904	2,912	2,913	2,929	2,994	3,052	3,065	3,047	3,164
Houma-Thibodaux, LA	10,553	10,865	11,229	11,293	10,345	8,997	8,650	8,916	8,852	8,192	7,913
Houston-The Woodlands-Sugar Land, TX	392,977	406,973	424,880	430,368	455,910	449,875	455,494	470,350	465,337	454,644	463,233
Huntington-Ashland, WV-KY-OH	13,839	14,553	15,574	14,813	14,752	14,294	14,220	14,991	15,063	13,914	14,339
Huntsville, AL	23,065	23,116	23,419	23,453	23,769	24,449	25,146	26,076	27,313	27,443	29,065
Idaho Falls, ID	5,354	5,400	5,469	5,518	5,838	6,081	6,391	6,774	7,594	7,793	8,183
Indianapolis-Carmel-Anderson, IN	115,407	114,570	117,819	120,224	117,112	119,615	120,594	125,704	129,069	126,788	133,188
Iowa City, IA	8,473	8,622	8,975	9,256	9,038	9,125	9,610	9,710	9,741	9,321	9,615
Ithaca, NY	5,526	5,556	5,431	5,354	5,464	5,492	5,537	5,627	5,692	5,357	5,736
Jackson, MI	5,025	5,091	5,150	5,111	5,158	5,379	5,423	5,778	6,036	5,816	6,338
Jackson, MS	24,046	24,259	24,793	25,107	25,270	25,102	24,929	24,745	24,721	24,502	25,415
Jackson, TN	8,083	7,149	7,089	7,026	7,105	7,220	7,566	7,602	7,617	7,465	8,042
Jacksonville, FL	60,281	60,830	62,480	63,913	66,523	69,010	71,854	74,270	77,188	77,702	82,963
Jacksonville, NC	8,558	8,262	8,043	7,945	7,792	7,139	7,479	7,520	7,623	7,614	8,131
Janesville-Beloit, WI	5,927	6,085	6,251	6,209	6,225	6,321	6,194	6,543	6,837	6,715	6,991
Jefferson City, MO	6,655	6,676	6,775	6,873	7,079	7,036	6,886	6,967	7,319	7,218	7,281
Johnson City, TN	6,432	6,564	6,461	6,348	6,604	6,402	6,603	6,671	6,862	6,926	7,509
Johnstown, PA	4,739	4,704	4,585	4,568	4,441	4,360	4,379	4,373	4,342	4,256	4,275
Jonesboro, AR	4,334	4,307	4,456	4,334	4,397	4,428	4,606	4,715	4,883	4,975	5,244
Joplin, MO	6,623	6,602	6,690	6,707	6,982	6,907	6,946	7,054	6,940	6,603	6,856
Kahului-Wailuku-Lahaina, HI	7,346	7,612	7,800	7,829	8,256	8,519	8,642	9,103	9,209	7,348	8,340
Kalamazoo-Portage, MI	10,916	11,019	11,137	11,057	11,396	11,785	12,349	12,626	12,782	12,332	13,094
Kankakee, IL	4,135	4,407	4,317	4,497	4,583	4,967	5,445	5,673	5,802	5,623	5,885
Kansas City, MO-KS	106,482	110,105	111,477	114,543	118,234	118,350	121,387	124,012	127,200	124,788	130,199
Kennewick-Richland, WA	12,708	12,189	12,114	12,432	13,030	13,587	13,734	14,114	14,672	14,301	14,718
Killeen-Temple, TX	16,625	16,597	16,146	16,032	16,617	16,245	16,585	16,749	17,035	17,400	18,026
Kingsport-Bristol, TN-VA	11,896	11,972	11,717	11,311	11,501	11,634	12,072	12,159	11,980	11,626	12,280
Kingston, NY	6,384	6,440	6,450	6,414	6,345	6,341	6,456	6,591	6,760	6,516	6,902
Knoxville, TN	34,683	35,322	35,361	35,752	36,414	37,600	38,625	39,434	40,413	40,194	43,595
Kokomo, IN	4,232	4,443	4,489	4,300	3,996	3,876	3,771	3,848	3,844	3,660	4,045
La Crosse-Onalaska, WI-MN	6,358	6,465	6,451	6,742	6,874	6,980	7,134	7,277	7,379	7,206	7,568
Lafayette, LA	22,904	23,738	23,375	23,488	21,857	19,881	19,696	20,404	20,257	19,318	19,592
Lafayette-West Lafayette, IN	8,465	8,465	8,807	9,048	9,099	9,535	9,916	10,484	10,559	10,065	10,527
Lake Charles, LA	14,009	13,632	12,016	12,596	13,217	14,326	16,776	16,505	16,643	13,353	13,550
Lake Havasu City-Kingman, AZ	4,608	4,566	4,783	4,788	4,751	4,965	4,841	4,917	5,096	5,242	5,634
Lakeland-Winter Haven, FL	19,750	20,020	20,524	20,466	21,532	22,171	23,407	23,945	24,742	25,553	26,955
Lancaster, PA	23,298	23,366	23,854	24,404	25,457	25,542	26,686	27,021	27,197	25,973	27,184
Lansing-East Lansing, MI	21,178	20,705	20,538	21,002	21,702	22,593	22,978	23,365	23,535	23,042	24,604
Laredo, TX	8,761	9,354	9,990	11,501	12,788	12,709	12,678	12,067	12,692	12,829	12,833
Las Cruces, NM	6,764	6,397	6,342	6,388	6,436	6,560	6,634	6,757	6,938	6,651	6,847
Las Vegas-Henderson-Paradise, NV	91,092	89,890	91,080	92,764	97,006	99,491	102,088	107,751	112,654	101,884	111,289
Lawrence, KS	4,038	4,019	4,058	4,130	4,153	4,354	4,439	4,562	4,579	4,397	4,520
Lawton, OK	4,916	4,705	4,768	4,710	4,846	4,801	4,689	4,649	4,692	4,592	4,657
Lebanon, PA	5,056	5,174	5,135	5,273	5,366	5,269	5,436	5,606	5,645	5,447	5,775
Lewiston, ID-WA	2,295	2,266	2,336	2,331	2,389	2,473	2,444	2,428	2,530	2,538	2,677
Lewiston-Auburn, ME	3,905	4,033	3,952	4,000	4,072	4,133	4,085	4,236	4,349	4,416	4,616
Lexington-Fayette, KY	22,651	23,094	23,965	24,603	25,441	26,005	26,281	26,832	27,413	26,562	27,667
Lima, OH	7,931	7,279	6,917	7,597	7,366	7,660	7,544	7,598	7,558	7,253	7,605
Lincoln, NE	14,897	15,091	15,332	15,912	16,475	16,663	17,488	17,942	18,205	17,911	18,458
Little Rock-North Little Rock-Conway, AR	32,283	32,311	32,380	32,617	33,181	33,306	33,060	33,578	34,095	33,852	35,159
Logan, UT-ID	4,397	4,272	4,331	4,479	4,642	4,803	5,064	5,386	5,643	5,699	6,162
Longview, TX	16,407	16,420	16,264	16,192	15,461	14,691	14,811	15,325	15,312	14,648	14,901
Longview, WA	3,935	4,026	4,078	4,064	4,141	4,196	4,170	4,370	4,643	4,679	4,823
Los Angeles-Long Beach-Anaheim, CA	759,139	770,616	784,821	803,961	835,964	851,204	880,169	908,730	930,863	882,790	950,158
Louisville/Jefferson County, KY-IN	57,468	59,622	59,762	60,416	61,676	62,685	63,200	64,158	66,144	64,910	68,748

Gross Domestic Product by Metropolitan Statistical Area—*Continued*

(Millions of chained 2012 dollars.)

Metropolitan Statistical Area	2001	2002	2003	2004	2005	2006	2007	2008	2009	2010
Lubbock, TX	9,289	9,514	9,760	9,970	10,391	10,773	10,861	10,762	10,738	11,242
Lynchburg, VA	8,326	8,507	8,911	9,084	9,176	9,468	9,336	9,435	9,253	9,693
Macon-Bibb County, GA	10,088	10,035	9,834	10,083	10,009	9,882	9,689	9,791	9,425	9,477
Madera, CA	3,296	3,686	3,806	4,335	4,638	4,819	4,813	4,738	4,205	4,883
Madison, WI	29,519	30,557	31,660	33,222	34,801	35,226	36,067	35,471	35,014	36,052
Manchester-Nashua, NH	17,378	18,040	19,454	20,341	20,667	21,327	21,545	21,522	21,166	21,369
Manhattan, KS	4,671	4,711	4,904	5,131	5,292	5,757	6,216	6,516	6,471	6,824
Mankato, MN	3,722	3,895	3,870	4,135	4,313	4,634	4,536	4,577	4,375	4,624
Mansfield, OH	4,494	4,693	4,707	4,913	5,010	4,921	4,702	4,546	3,864	4,086
McAllen-Edinburg-Mission, TX	14,476	15,421	15,727	15,879	16,285	17,027	17,722	17,384	17,291	17,181
Medford, OR	6,047	6,380	6,731	6,989	7,194	7,321	7,338	7,273	6,861	6,986
Memphis, TN-MS-AR	61,987	62,878	63,999	65,169	66,549	67,640	66,304	64,932	62,054	62,158
Merced, CA	5,920	6,244	6,774	7,387	7,706	7,547	8,412	7,401	7,114	7,257
Miami-Fort Lauderdale-Pompano Beach, FL	227,290	236,275	245,315	258,885	273,957	281,130	282,649	270,626	252,921	260,032
Michigan City-La Porte, IN	3,918	3,908	3,940	4,096	4,058	4,076	4,112	4,117	3,767	3,909
Midland, MI	4,662	4,802	4,547	4,796	4,313	4,328	4,368	4,197	3,965	4,096
Midland, TX	6,832	6,950	6,676	7,012	7,393	8,661	9,553	10,575	11,378	12,454
Milwaukee-Waukesha, WI	78,439	78,153	80,274	81,757	84,693	86,826	87,479	85,930	83,070	85,055
Minneapolis-St. Paul-Bloomington, MN-WI	176,319	178,865	187,900	196,167	203,483	202,171	204,976	204,506	196,281	201,984
Missoula, MT	3,605	3,773	3,906	4,051	4,162	4,271	4,357	4,462	4,413	4,359
Mobile, AL	15,334	15,388	15,630	16,186	16,909	18,085	18,155	18,189	18,108	18,249
Modesto, CA	15,758	16,344	16,885	17,801	18,455	18,817	18,560	17,973	17,822	17,932
Monroe, LA	6,400	6,872	7,041	7,388	7,709	7,798	6,972	6,634	6,864	7,014
Monroe, MI	5,412	5,673	5,820	5,762	5,787	5,916	5,862	5,551	5,179	5,453
Montgomery, AL	13,448	13,708	14,136	14,924	15,584	16,004	16,085	15,725	15,250	15,614
Morgantown, WV	4,547	4,703	4,792	5,056	5,311	5,412	5,411	5,567	5,784	6,268
Morristown, TN	3,775	3,770	3,799	3,957	4,008	4,112	4,149	4,013	3,683	3,995
Mount Vernon-Anacortes, WA	5,280	6,281	5,999	5,642	6,830	6,333	6,481	6,719	6,909	7,033
Muncie, IN	4,193	4,184	4,368	4,298	4,237	4,231	4,030	3,944	3,769	3,989
Muskegon, MI	5,441	5,517	5,486	5,597	5,715	5,628	5,570	5,390	5,164	5,324
Myrtle Beach-Conway-North Myrtle Beach, SC-NC	10,676	10,843	11,465	12,409	13,404	13,875	14,141	13,467	12,991	12,985
Napa, CA	7,233	7,613	7,666	7,579	7,945	7,939	8,095	8,169	7,981	7,851
Naples-Marco Island, FL	12,281	13,043	13,771	14,431	15,774	15,966	15,835	14,698	13,390	13,491
Nashville-Davidson--Murfreesboro--Franklin, TN	67,338	70,077	73,774	78,303	81,546	85,045	85,453	88,293	86,065	87,444
New Bern, NC	4,355	4,269	4,462	4,668	5,009	5,074	5,198	5,095	4,940	5,077
New Haven-Milford, CT	41,110	41,974	42,223	44,899	45,388	46,510	46,846	46,844	43,802	44,351
New Orleans-Metairie, LA	73,442	75,329	78,919	81,334	84,319	79,450	77,914	83,434	84,652	92,142
New York-Newark-Jersey City, NY-NJ-PA	1,197,117	1,191,033	1,194,011	1,221,677	1,253,179	1,288,491	1,299,235	1,281,766	1,303,016	1,346,449
Niles, MI	6,331	6,453	6,514	6,731	6,612	6,821	7,081	6,543	5,736	6,326
North Port-Sarasota-Bradenton, FL	21,929	23,835	25,112	27,640	30,220	31,039	30,163	27,538	26,063	24,942
Norwich-New London, CT	14,449	15,169	15,902	17,689	18,253	19,204	20,490	19,178	16,682	16,557
Ocala, FL	6,554	6,896	7,370	7,852	8,490	9,132	9,362	9,222	8,385	8,220
Ocean City, NJ	4,503	4,671	4,803	4,912	5,104	5,025	4,984	5,023	4,536	4,934
Odessa, TX	5,660	6,106	5,828	6,068	6,239	7,264	7,991	8,656	8,842	9,319
Ogden-Clearfield, UT	16,691	17,122	17,594	18,064	19,245	20,576	21,183	21,149	21,008	21,282
Oklahoma City, OK	45,379	46,368	47,640	49,666	51,765	55,767	56,309	60,039	61,152	61,144
Olympia-Lacey-Tumwater, WA	8,522	8,622	8,768	8,927	9,293	9,542	10,056	10,601	10,250	10,360
Omaha-Council Bluffs, NE-IA	38,441	39,476	41,288	43,332	44,548	46,139	47,376	46,956	47,062	48,420
Orlando-Kissimmee-Sanford, FL	80,634	83,708	88,106	94,517	101,918	105,178	107,714	104,287	97,035	97,770
Oshkosh-Neenah, WI	7,957	8,558	8,620	8,802	8,976	9,132	8,958	8,817	8,541	8,834
Owensboro, KY	4,230	4,461	4,679	4,701	4,730	4,959	4,776	4,961	4,845	5,059
Oxnard-Thousand Oaks-Ventura, CA	37,003	38,017	40,367	44,219	46,386	51,531	55,457	50,733	50,424	50,250
Palm Bay-Melbourne-Titusville, FL	15,344	15,936	17,102	18,632	19,967	20,795	21,954	21,979	20,590	20,650
Panama City, FL	5,654	6,046	6,328	6,900	7,362	7,569	7,640	7,534	7,245	7,185
Parkersburg-Vienna, WV	3,457	3,591	3,592	3,599	3,543	3,735	3,561	3,699	3,999	3,921
Pensacola-Ferry Pass-Brent, FL	14,430	14,695	15,168	15,789	16,336	16,771	16,900	16,369	15,810	15,968
Peoria, IL	17,371	17,262	17,594	18,226	19,070	20,176	21,239	21,700	21,098	22,998
Philadelphia-Camden-Wilmington, PA-NJ-DE-MD	307,312	310,762	322,657	335,040	338,417	342,294	354,733	363,761	350,995	357,335
Phoenix-Mesa-Chandler, AZ	150,333	156,247	166,666	175,453	189,540	199,474	205,315	202,383	183,713	184,554
Pine Bluff, AR	3,553	3,518	3,673	3,833	3,852	3,861	3,676	3,681	3,568	3,667
Pittsburgh, PA	106,602	108,500	111,215	113,664	114,408	113,494	115,946	118,190	116,521	121,141
Pittsfield, MA	5,778	5,933	5,797	5,964	6,124	6,058	6,073	6,256	6,073	6,200
Pocatello, ID	2,679	2,546	2,584	2,795	2,967	2,979	2,977	3,102	2,920	2,871
Portland-South Portland, ME	22,546	22,967	23,975	25,141	25,433	25,773	25,788	25,629	25,354	25,621
Portland-Vancouver-Hillsboro, OR-WA	87,061	87,782	92,978	98,756	103,201	108,637	111,607	117,136	110,754	113,740
Port St. Lucie, FL	10,997	11,629	12,113	13,368	14,576	15,644	15,744	14,930	14,257	14,055

Gross Domestic Product by Metropolitan Statistical Area—*Continued*

(Millions of chained 2012 dollars.)

Metropolitan Statistical Area	2011	2012	2013	2014	2015	2016	2017	2018	2019	2020	2021
Lubbock, TX	11,008	11,517	12,015	11,927	12,272	12,462	12,532	12,871	13,121	13,128	13,509
Lynchburg, VA	9,492	9,227	9,228	9,129	9,150	9,042	9,151	9,579	9,563	9,069	9,352
Macon-Bibb County, GA	9,652	9,740	9,708	9,770	9,864	9,771	9,804	9,972	9,789	9,130	9,672
Madera, CA	4,901	5,077	5,137	5,520	5,226	5,766	5,995	5,958	6,152	6,125	5,949
Madison, WI	37,031	38,003	38,615	40,244	41,700	43,032	43,161	44,857	46,148	45,344	47,922
Manchester-Nashua, NH	21,924	22,064	22,310	22,759	23,442	23,914	23,865	24,698	25,148	25,277	27,575
Manhattan, KS	7,088	7,033	6,813	6,589	6,632	6,486	6,410	6,370	6,167	6,171	6,347
Mankato, MN	4,692	4,912	5,002	5,152	5,217	5,144	5,222	5,251	5,260	5,132	5,159
Mansfield, OH	4,215	4,284	4,196	4,305	4,239	4,187	4,219	4,285	4,254	4,115	4,355
McAllen-Edinburg-Mission, TX	17,451	17,704	18,375	18,594	18,783	18,828	18,994	19,445	19,934	19,980	20,878
Medford, OR	6,895	6,738	7,051	7,158	7,435	7,720	8,074	8,193	8,376	8,256	8,762
Memphis, TN-MS-AR	62,672	64,481	65,114	64,749	65,978	66,456	66,936	67,024	67,782	66,027	69,923
Merced, CA	7,459	7,303	7,569	8,310	8,437	8,463	8,968	8,967	9,095	9,072	8,987
Miami-Fort Lauderdale-Pompano Beach, FL	260,331	261,235	268,003	276,767	288,628	297,645	309,184	319,778	324,371	312,032	341,292
Michigan City-La Porte, IN	3,881	3,871	3,924	3,988	3,820	3,860	3,811	3,963	3,826	3,658	3,754
Midland, MI	4,167	4,278	4,189	4,759	5,142	4,824	4,958	5,051	4,779	4,779	4,807
Midland, TX	14,541	18,277	19,034	20,620	23,013	23,856	28,141	34,590	42,692	40,926	39,498
Milwaukee-Waukesha, WI	86,897	87,427	87,394	87,567	88,533	88,972	89,083	91,170	92,518	88,460	92,835
Minneapolis-St. Paul-Bloomington, MN-WI	207,107	210,305	215,994	224,533	228,528	232,500	235,720	243,386	246,061	236,073	249,963
Missoula, MT	4,410	4,367	4,375	4,452	4,592	4,624	4,894	4,934	5,069	5,064	5,477
Mobile, AL	18,685	18,542	18,708	18,683	18,556	18,887	18,915	19,136	19,434	19,099	19,637
Modesto, CA	17,858	17,532	17,659	18,740	19,372	19,623	20,558	21,173	21,574	21,179	21,954
Monroe, LA	6,828	7,043	7,623	7,629	7,777	7,783	7,655	7,782	7,510	7,250	7,262
Monroe, MI	5,486	5,305	5,465	5,468	5,469	5,450	5,455	5,360	5,423	5,048	5,393
Montgomery, AL	15,764	15,983	15,858	15,668	15,924	16,348	16,317	16,305	16,348	16,022	16,686
Morgantown, WV	6,299	6,340	6,779	6,731	6,964	6,891	7,043	6,974	6,870	6,753	6,874
Morristown, TN	4,129	4,204	4,208	4,300	4,376	4,404	4,547	4,523	4,667	4,667	5,049
Mount Vernon-Anacortes, WA	5,808	5,683	5,989	6,110	7,147	7,059	6,942	7,075	7,036	6,514	6,766
Muncie, IN	4,336	3,557	3,643	3,619	3,592	3,552	3,628	3,652	3,678	3,601	3,667
Muskegon, MI	5,477	5,556	5,684	5,774	5,838	5,706	5,619	5,663	5,699	5,425	5,726
Myrtle Beach-Conway-North Myrtle Beach, SC-NC	13,212	13,177	13,526	14,176	14,577	15,201	15,891	16,100	16,427	16,069	17,437
Napa, CA	7,727	8,195	8,549	9,117	9,517	9,692	9,833	9,856	9,987	9,471	10,063
Naples-Marco Island, FL	13,234	13,416	13,859	14,601	15,509	16,478	16,685	17,601	17,849	17,734	19,299
Nashville-Davidson--Murfreesboro--Franklin, TN	90,813	95,678	97,796	102,215	108,994	112,541	117,112	120,073	124,740	121,665	136,285
New Bern, NC	4,973	4,975	5,219	5,366	5,331	4,803	4,921	4,815	5,022	4,975	5,262
New Haven-Milford, CT	43,971	43,956	44,205	43,997	44,497	45,211	45,371	46,236	46,951	45,728	47,715
New Orleans-Metairie, LA	70,705	72,043	69,331	70,313	70,756	71,093	75,820	75,547	76,035	69,154	69,658
New York-Newark-Jersey City, NY-NJ-PA	1,346,879	1,400,779	1,408,541	1,429,380	1,453,551	1,486,750	1,502,226	1,548,722	1,585,494	1,510,364	1,598,388
Niles, MI	6,443	6,345	6,471	6,517	6,634	6,930	7,091	6,945	6,791	6,765	6,917
North Port-Sarasota-Bradenton, FL	25,060	24,785	25,674	27,003	28,766	29,673	31,089	32,569	33,624	33,590	36,458
Norwich-New London, CT	16,419	16,304	16,716	15,771	16,200	16,313	17,204	17,439	17,522	16,143	17,009
Ocala, FL	8,143	7,899	7,990	7,999	8,179	8,739	8,883	9,164	9,379	9,711	10,436
Ocean City, NJ	4,844	4,674	4,764	4,928	4,771	4,732	4,907	4,929	4,981	4,719	5,021
Odessa, TX	10,941	12,954	13,296	13,342	11,962	10,386	11,152	12,898	13,457	11,433	11,098
Ogden-Clearfield, UT	21,441	21,335	22,164	22,617	22,984	23,721	25,025	26,243	27,189	27,984	29,258
Oklahoma City, OK	63,468	67,598	69,543	73,572	79,155	78,725	79,300	80,906	81,980	78,626	79,334
Olympia-Lacey-Tumwater, WA	10,299	10,361	10,431	10,567	10,600	11,143	11,539	12,280	12,479	12,336	13,055
Omaha-Council Bluffs, NE-IA	50,911	51,722	50,855	53,487	55,158	55,203	57,401	58,788	59,677	58,614	60,955
Orlando-Kissimmee-Sanford, FL	97,781	99,955	102,766	106,558	112,244	116,537	121,842	125,979	130,109	124,633	138,271
Oshkosh-Neenah, WI	8,956	8,959	8,886	9,056	8,944	9,316	9,213	9,497	9,776	9,444	9,967
Owensboro, KY	5,132	5,172	5,408	5,304	5,336	5,371	5,384	5,271	5,344	5,168	5,345
Oxnard-Thousand Oaks-Ventura, CA	47,397	46,388	46,808	46,461	46,506	46,203	46,594	46,724	47,847	47,211	48,642
Palm Bay-Melbourne-Titusville, FL	19,893	19,338	19,483	19,966	20,872	21,397	22,582	23,561	24,352	24,460	26,063
Panama City, FL	6,992	6,967	7,014	7,183	7,396	7,530	7,532	7,625	7,713	7,764	8,292
Parkersburg-Vienna, WV	3,799	3,541	3,405	3,388	3,339	3,252	3,266	3,265	3,188	3,102	3,241
Pensacola-Ferry Pass-Brent, FL	16,191	16,080	16,249	16,401	16,985	17,581	18,221	18,291	18,667	18,674	19,763
Peoria, IL	25,909	28,863	24,722	24,232	22,159	20,768	19,737	20,266	19,456	18,361	19,223
Philadelphia-Camden-Wilmington, PA-NJ-DE-MD	359,489	367,779	370,229	379,988	385,500	388,217	385,595	391,655	397,486	381,417	399,782
Phoenix-Mesa-Chandler, AZ	189,684	195,823	197,408	201,270	207,171	214,025	222,960	232,915	242,939	244,883	261,707
Pine Bluff, AR	3,611	3,647	3,742	3,548	3,379	3,302	3,194	3,138	3,105	2,994	3,238
Pittsburgh, PA	123,875	125,989	127,479	129,697	133,408	133,033	136,758	140,739	143,057	135,324	141,317
Pittsfield, MA	6,268	6,541	6,551	6,585	6,610	6,550	6,341	6,453	6,291	5,958	6,184
Pocatello, ID	2,864	2,939	2,842	2,828	2,833	2,837	2,895	2,915	2,993	2,987	3,068
Portland-South Portland, ME	25,597	25,853	25,679	26,189	26,441	27,288	28,010	29,034	29,816	29,991	32,276
Portland-Vancouver-Hillsboro, OR-WA	117,932	119,707	120,207	123,909	130,843	136,712	142,294	149,894	153,194	149,949	159,208
Port St. Lucie, FL	13,801	13,906	13,951	14,203	14,603	14,949	15,205	15,703	15,820	15,972	16,700

Gross Domestic Product by Metropolitan Statistical Area—*Continued*

(Millions of chained 2012 dollars.)

Metropolitan Statistical Area	2001	2002	2003	2004	2005	2006	2007	2008	2009	2010
Poughkeepsie-Newburgh-Middletown, NY	22,352	22,890	24,254	25,334	25,534	25,245	25,742	26,899	26,960	27,900
Prescott Valley-Prescott, AZ	4,684	4,877	5,147	5,524	6,014	6,334	6,285	6,441	5,892	5,691
Providence-Warwick, RI-MA	65,771	67,495	69,095	71,018	71,920	74,067	72,471	72,480	70,765	72,668
Provo-Orem, UT	11,182	11,337	11,792	12,629	13,598	14,688	15,993	16,334	16,428	16,802
Pueblo, CO	4,530	4,572	4,678	4,913	4,624	4,764	4,757	5,032	5,032	5,120
Punta Gorda, FL	3,671	3,921	4,103	4,402	4,825	4,748	4,695	4,249	4,085	4,018
Racine, WI	7,958	8,018	8,208	8,433	8,378	8,531	8,328	8,061	7,752	8,166
Raleigh-Cary, NC	41,840	43,093	44,560	46,745	49,547	52,906	55,365	56,444	53,848	57,159
Rapid City, SD	4,326	4,936	4,944	4,813	4,995	4,810	4,965	5,000	4,908	5,089
Reading, PA	14,978	15,206	15,486	15,763	16,120	16,854	16,683	16,785	16,130	16,484
Redding, CA	6,169	6,829	6,990	6,835	6,673	6,945	6,711	6,483	6,401	6,604
Reno, NV	19,834	20,093	20,648	22,246	23,222	23,271	23,108	22,046	20,723	21,592
Richmond, VA	61,163	59,999	61,039	61,566	64,433	64,673	65,586	65,429	63,908	65,538
Riverside-San Bernardino-Ontario, CA	101,691	106,817	114,051	122,088	129,833	135,298	137,393	134,032	126,966	129,376
Roanoke, VA	13,492	13,278	13,489	13,429	13,945	14,342	14,667	14,671	14,124	14,346
Rochester, MN	7,929	8,493	9,122	9,586	9,769	9,972	9,983	10,304	10,221	10,684
Rochester, NY	52,379	52,629	53,338	53,522	52,964	53,338	53,826	54,732	54,787	56,347
Rockford, IL	13,117	13,369	13,623	13,946	14,192	14,656	14,878	14,676	13,486	13,562
Rocky Mount, NC	6,006	5,879	5,947	5,967	6,094	6,297	6,278	6,299	7,580	6,856
Rome, GA	4,115	3,666	3,695	3,834	3,734	3,767	3,807	3,776	3,643	3,684
Sacramento-Roseville-Folsom, CA	87,620	90,481	94,761	98,310	102,921	105,844	106,847	106,070	102,443	100,862
Saginaw, MI	7,690	7,876	8,167	8,094	8,265	8,069	7,793	7,278	6,877	7,227
St. Cloud, MN	7,312	7,520	7,594	7,950	8,096	8,268	8,254	8,351	8,138	8,158
St. George, UT	2,574	2,697	2,894	3,161	3,533	3,904	4,041	3,893	3,522	3,504
St. Joseph, MO-KS	4,387	4,508	4,552	4,837	4,856	4,924	4,987	5,131	5,052	5,048
St. Louis, MO-IL	132,417	134,411	138,190	140,814	143,509	143,390	144,124	147,409	143,701	145,825
Salem, OR	11,436	11,666	12,034	12,216	12,835	13,663	13,500	13,669	13,104	13,198
Salinas, CA	21,016	22,188	22,131	19,859	20,306	21,770	20,775	20,448	21,834	21,336
Salisbury, MD-DE	14,513	14,101	14,580	15,379	16,224	16,707	16,859	17,063	16,844	16,320
Salt Lake City, UT	50,133	51,231	51,480	54,962	58,366	62,756	65,443	65,152	63,007	64,519
San Angelo, TX	4,350	4,303	4,242	4,244	4,274	4,372	4,504	4,747	5,070	5,362
San Antonio-New Braunfels, TX	67,691	69,586	72,145	74,706	77,715	82,295	84,368	85,072	83,216	86,359
San Diego-Chula Vista-Carlsbad, CA	142,064	148,244	155,871	164,695	173,137	177,089	179,913	178,718	171,103	173,540
San Francisco-Oakland-Berkeley, CA	308,081	301,359	305,362	309,303	322,146	331,141	332,995	349,237	335,822	335,782
San Jose-Sunnyvale-Santa Clara, CA	115,771	110,593	117,127	121,706	129,351	139,185	152,613	161,546	158,676	172,968
San Luis Obispo-Paso Robles, CA	10,996	12,163	12,420	12,490	12,899	13,148	13,051	12,574	12,427	13,053
Santa Cruz-Watsonville, CA	11,107	11,060	11,296	10,968	10,970	10,903	10,880	10,946	11,212	12,109
Santa Fe, NM	5,369	5,771	5,593	5,842	6,031	6,390	6,622	6,918	6,379	6,401
Santa Maria-Santa Barbara, CA	17,976	18,691	19,398	20,026	20,830	21,164	21,555	22,046	22,574	22,376
Santa Rosa-Petaluma, CA	20,913	21,717	21,512	21,456	21,822	22,033	22,409	22,251	21,430	22,072
Savannah, GA	12,584	12,839	13,209	13,846	14,737	15,430	15,753	15,511	15,390	15,692
Scranton--Wilkes-Barre, PA	20,606	20,573	20,941	21,424	21,660	21,859	22,381	22,737	22,499	22,948
Seattle-Tacoma-Bellevue, WA	197,752	197,811	200,489	205,096	219,008	229,388	245,639	251,340	241,681	248,596
Sebastian-Vero Beach, FL	3,979	4,261	4,556	4,860	5,267	5,291	5,461	5,123	4,795	4,612
Sebring-Avon Park, FL	1,868	2,020	2,088	2,219	2,369	2,574	2,561	2,411	2,425	2,340
Sheboygan, WI	5,594	5,694	5,830	6,210	6,081	6,041	6,203	6,090	5,791	5,881
Sherman-Denison, TX	3,128	3,208	3,262	3,474	3,508	3,807	3,747	3,788	3,788	3,883
Shreveport-Bossier City, LA	15,298	15,404	16,091	16,978	17,993	18,654	17,196	17,295	19,843	20,989
Sierra Vista-Douglas, AZ	3,382	3,422	3,663	3,789	3,981	4,050	4,319	4,411	4,422	4,580
Sioux City, IA-NE-SD	7,585	6,839	6,740	7,170	7,481	7,623	7,805	8,171	7,661	7,839
Sioux Falls, SD	8,863	10,431	10,197	12,029	12,949	14,147	14,290	14,699	15,521	14,970
South Bend-Mishawaka, IN-MI	11,679	11,940	12,582	12,991	13,068	13,331	13,398	12,843	11,544	12,141
Spartanburg, SC	10,016	10,328	10,779	11,388	11,779	12,399	12,291	11,977	10,850	11,267
Spokane-Spokane Valley, WA	17,471	17,501	17,788	18,464	19,268	19,906	20,625	21,018	20,240	20,354
Springfield, IL	9,979	10,165	9,920	9,908	9,860	9,915	9,820	9,959	9,939	10,177
Springfield, MA	26,428	26,650	27,023	27,344	27,460	27,361	27,378	27,869	27,164	28,121
Springfield, MO	14,071	14,448	15,118	15,780	16,516	16,663	16,719	16,855	16,467	16,407
Springfield, OH	4,381	4,409	4,322	4,521	4,528	4,581	4,359	4,230	4,017	4,025
State College, PA	5,419	5,666	5,859	6,193	6,584	6,386	6,516	6,721	6,678	7,043
Staunton, VA	4,538	4,305	4,252	4,429	4,563	4,428	4,615	4,784	4,820	4,898
Stockton, CA	20,846	21,746	22,713	23,637	24,941	24,375	24,328	23,588	23,369	22,784
Sumter, SC	3,621	3,673	3,808	3,913	3,982	4,109	4,144	4,040	3,885	3,996
Syracuse, NY	30,269	30,620	31,734	32,348	32,574	32,374	32,976	32,944	32,678	34,078
Tallahassee, FL	13,835	14,222	14,513	15,009	15,050	15,030	15,604	15,319	14,839	14,714
Tampa-St. Petersburg-Clearwater, FL	100,297	104,806	109,967	116,955	123,106	126,088	127,286	123,388	118,861	119,868
Terre Haute, IN	6,225	6,398	6,715	6,883	6,872	7,002	7,055	7,036	6,722	7,061
Texarkana, TX-AR	4,524	4,701	4,750	5,002	5,133	5,249	5,285	5,326	5,252	5,268
The Villages, FL	960	1,059	1,238	1,304	1,499	1,652	1,801	1,764	1,804	1,892
Toledo, OH	31,399	31,776	31,973	32,573	33,660	33,900	33,425	31,367	29,703	30,757
Topeka, KS	9,187	9,324	9,353	9,590	9,522	9,182	9,619	9,752	9,618	9,582
Trenton-Princeton, NJ	24,716	25,203	25,703	25,821	26,447	26,606	26,289	27,408	26,170	26,519
Tucson, AZ	31,708	31,836	33,626	33,324	34,930	35,599	37,047	37,628	35,148	36,033

Gross Domestic Product by Metropolitan Statistical Area—*Continued*

(Millions of chained 2012 dollars.)

Metropolitan Statistical Area	2011	2012	2013	2014	2015	2016	2017	2018	2019	2020	2021
Poughkeepsie-Newburgh-Middletown, NY	27,732	27,801	27,897	27,710	28,270	28,284	28,879	29,611	30,930	30,199	32,002
Prescott Valley-Prescott, AZ	5,608	5,551	5,810	6,059	6,039	6,224	6,646	6,687	6,736	6,797	7,193
Providence-Warwick, RI-MA	72,863	73,068	73,688	74,620	76,198	76,197	76,237	76,314	77,574	75,102	79,398
Provo-Orem, UT	17,338	17,508	18,317	19,059	20,560	21,932	23,033	25,304	27,513	28,748	31,136
Pueblo, CO	5,273	5,393	5,337	5,215	5,325	5,456	5,442	5,618	5,851	5,639	6,009
Punta Gorda, FL	3,916	4,083	4,065	4,142	4,363	4,530	4,756	4,923	5,112	5,201	5,607
Racine, WI	8,106	8,110	7,860	7,932	7,853	7,678	7,281	7,392	7,330	7,177	7,413
Raleigh-Cary, NC	57,548	58,953	62,543	66,170	70,991	75,324	78,507	83,027	85,781	84,380	91,958
Rapid City, SD	5,176	5,370	5,271	5,411	5,518	5,531	5,557	5,670	5,783	5,833	6,123
Reading, PA	16,998	17,099	17,273	17,586	18,309	18,542	18,669	18,762	18,780	18,094	18,519
Redding, CA	6,742	6,460	6,434	6,530	6,622	6,931	7,425	7,218	7,583	7,378	7,496
Reno, NV	21,250	21,768	21,491	21,694	23,427	24,269	25,901	25,282	26,248	26,194	28,502
Richmond, VA	67,155	68,389	69,938	70,524	73,064	74,104	75,453	76,885	78,897	77,032	80,910
Riverside-San Bernardino-Ontario, CA	131,676	131,713	135,932	139,961	145,728	148,897	153,123	158,608	163,952	161,465	171,400
Roanoke, VA	14,287	14,215	14,473	14,670	14,950	14,694	14,547	14,735	14,569	14,326	15,012
Rochester, MN	10,816	11,062	11,300	11,454	11,755	11,895	12,328	12,798	13,034	12,793	13,390
Rochester, NY	54,871	54,978	54,435	53,925	54,924	54,930	55,045	55,551	57,479	54,633	57,285
Rockford, IL	14,013	14,077	13,831	13,912	14,122	14,047	14,210	14,649	14,540	13,275	14,008
Rocky Mount, NC	6,285	5,491	5,557	6,919	7,705	7,673	6,384	5,957	5,783	5,800	6,269
Rome, GA	3,671	3,579	3,474	3,626	3,734	3,880	3,752	3,715	3,674	3,504	3,719
Sacramento-Roseville-Folsom, CA	102,507	103,254	106,019	108,471	112,728	114,782	117,889	122,722	126,455	123,604	130,674
Saginaw, MI	7,368	7,358	7,384	7,219	7,228	7,392	7,359	7,572	7,745	7,400	7,884
St. Cloud, MN	8,478	8,483	8,773	9,135	9,203	9,526	9,746	9,811	9,842	9,645	10,077
St. George, UT	3,544	3,808	4,128	4,269	4,527	4,942	5,431	5,822	6,042	6,256	6,730
St. Joseph, MO-KS	5,096	5,468	5,601	5,386	5,219	5,245	5,478	5,337	5,505	5,310	5,419
St. Louis, MO-IL	145,854	147,315	148,338	150,687	151,539	151,409	150,314	152,771	155,221	149,412	156,926
Salem, OR	12,906	12,997	12,973	13,346	14,050	14,739	15,400	16,184	16,624	16,439	17,338
Salinas, CA	20,089	20,854	22,081	22,453	24,189	24,814	25,093	25,931	26,427	25,646	26,112
Salisbury, MD-DE	16,462	16,537	17,328	18,270	19,696	19,482	19,151	19,460	20,157	19,379	20,598
Salt Lake City, UT	67,537	69,166	70,185	71,983	74,487	77,979	80,877	86,132	89,433	90,392	96,833
San Angelo, TX	5,571	6,040	6,832	7,454	7,676	7,203	7,264	7,584	8,279	8,418	8,300
San Antonio-New Braunfels, TX	90,113	92,575	96,611	101,556	107,313	108,986	109,386	114,629	117,689	116,002	122,836
San Diego-Chula Vista-Carlsbad, CA	176,547	178,241	184,863	189,967	195,600	197,160	204,289	209,678	213,886	208,634	224,954
San Francisco-Oakland-Berkeley, CA	337,525	363,996	377,150	399,520	422,319	447,060	482,611	512,110	534,564	524,209	577,348
San Jose-Sunnyvale-Santa Clara, CA	186,416	193,663	211,714	227,291	248,011	263,976	285,712	309,686	324,595	339,613	384,702
San Luis Obispo-Paso Robles, CA	13,263	13,544	14,002	14,214	14,946	15,195	15,423	15,797	15,841	15,360	15,900
Santa Cruz-Watsonville, CA	11,923	11,705	12,049	12,299	12,361	12,597	12,769	13,246	14,128	14,003	14,951
Santa Fe, NM	6,277	6,163	6,203	6,334	6,169	6,182	6,123	6,240	6,240	5,719	6,083
Santa Maria-Santa Barbara, CA	22,434	22,960	23,302	23,807	24,987	25,172	25,825	26,917	27,069	27,086	28,531
Santa Rosa-Petaluma, CA	22,434	22,780	23,247	24,075	25,156	25,745	26,260	27,527	27,622	26,626	28,339
Savannah, GA	16,064	16,579	16,549	17,247	17,731	18,403	18,997	19,116	19,804	18,981	20,661
Scranton--Wilkes-Barre, PA	23,130	23,254	23,316	23,782	24,471	24,776	24,716	24,835	25,221	23,944	24,881
Seattle-Tacoma-Bellevue, WA	256,700	269,459	279,660	291,561	303,614	315,434	335,074	361,522	375,997	384,268	413,817
Sebastian-Vero Beach, FL	4,654	4,758	4,832	5,016	5,379	5,823	5,900	6,019	6,233	6,202	6,558
Sebring-Avon Park, FL	2,256	2,344	2,202	2,204	2,246	2,317	2,364	2,272	2,416	2,393	2,429
Sheboygan, WI	5,987	6,036	6,051	6,141	6,282	6,506	6,485	6,587	6,459	6,223	6,470
Sherman-Denison, TX	4,078	4,193	4,227	4,283	4,416	4,508	4,494	4,730	4,761	4,751	4,988
Shreveport-Bossier City, LA	22,174	21,049	19,423	19,368	19,977	19,835	20,309	20,925	21,390	20,144	20,905
Sierra Vista-Douglas, AZ	4,611	4,429	4,288	4,148	4,223	4,288	4,225	4,257	4,310	4,519	4,488
Sioux City, IA-NE-SD	7,527	7,192	7,064	7,062	7,293	7,375	7,218	7,585	7,629	7,695	8,192
Sioux Falls, SD	15,965	17,428	16,859	17,642	17,861	18,147	17,919	17,874	18,681	18,657	19,752
South Bend-Mishawaka, IN-MI	12,279	12,397	12,536	12,977	13,188	13,173	13,234	13,820	14,151	13,221	14,070
Spartanburg, SC	11,442	11,270	11,375	11,596	12,028	12,688	13,262	13,590	14,341	14,021	14,975
Spokane-Spokane Valley, WA	20,378	20,639	20,875	21,232	21,733	22,269	22,927	24,115	24,687	24,593	26,236
Springfield, IL	10,171	10,094	10,087	10,277	10,287	10,316	10,259	10,585	10,577	9,985	10,683
Springfield, MA	28,513	28,771	28,887	28,874	29,696	29,798	29,888	30,120	30,418	29,042	30,271
Springfield, MO	16,191	16,393	16,295	16,820	17,338	17,340	17,576	17,955	18,661	18,294	19,491
Springfield, OH	4,139	4,100	4,130	4,165	4,181	4,134	4,149	4,154	4,195	3,973	4,255
State College, PA	7,241	7,576	7,546	7,581	7,666	7,904	8,051	8,054	8,100	7,788	7,957
Staunton, VA	4,742	4,535	4,672	4,624	4,615	4,590	4,616	4,656	4,713	4,554	4,784
Stockton, CA	22,580	22,741	23,523	24,175	25,315	25,837	26,716	27,757	28,576	28,432	30,175
Sumter, SC	4,080	4,155	4,164	4,071	4,065	4,133	4,248	4,285	4,339	4,246	4,537
Syracuse, NY	33,627	34,566	34,782	35,271	36,322	35,918	36,104	36,324	37,177	35,799	37,718
Tallahassee, FL	14,601	14,678	14,291	14,535	14,658	15,017	15,527	15,481	15,725	15,675	16,386
Tampa-St. Petersburg-Clearwater, FL	119,579	121,305	123,613	126,024	130,999	135,194	138,121	142,356	146,965	146,674	158,130
Terre Haute, IN	7,070	6,963	7,728	7,695	7,170	7,091	6,967	6,947	6,917	6,758	7,093
Texarkana, TX-AR	5,321	5,276	5,067	4,973	4,991	5,013	4,939	4,902	4,906	4,865	4,928
The Villages, FL	1,982	2,348	2,595	2,522	2,655	2,723	2,864	3,097	3,725	3,964	4,376
Toledo, OH	32,258	31,882	32,696	34,731	33,018	32,994	33,217	33,996	34,826	32,547	34,716
Topeka, KS	9,950	10,063	9,805	10,033	10,122	10,328	10,387	10,778	10,543	10,586	10,885
Trenton-Princeton, NJ	26,553	28,169	28,141	28,057	28,219	29,297	29,204	29,907	33,159	33,685	35,953
Tucson, AZ	35,862	36,733	36,231	36,350	36,113	37,220	37,888	38,683	39,612	40,384	41,618

Gross Domestic Product by Metropolitan Statistical Area—*Continued*

(Millions of chained 2012 dollars.)

Metropolitan Statistical Area	2001	2002	2003	2004	2005	2006	2007	2008	2009	2010
Tulsa, OK	37,802	37,850	37,718	38,958	41,083	44,996	45,287	46,534	43,987	43,361
Tuscaloosa, AL	8,158	8,610	9,202	9,919	10,498	10,520	10,930	10,465	9,647	9,961
Twin Falls, ID	2,992	3,011	3,037	3,220	3,425	3,597	3,756	3,736	3,388	3,560
Tyler, TX	7,438	7,486	7,694	8,595	8,986	9,543	9,515	9,368	9,266	9,563
Urban Honolulu, HI	42,313	43,210	45,241	47,591	49,948	50,785	51,815	52,658	51,771	52,902
Utica-Rome, NY	10,443	10,704	10,823	10,964	10,866	10,947	11,240	11,261	11,354	11,635
Valdosta, GA	3,958	4,112	4,263	4,327	4,484	4,556	4,620	4,746	4,619	4,652
Vallejo, CA	15,162	15,192	15,822	15,935	16,460	16,685	17,314	18,808	18,152	18,160
Victoria, TX	4,442	4,313	4,337	4,612	4,837	5,137	4,885	4,783	4,389	4,421
Vineland-Bridgeton, NJ	5,377	5,422	5,676	5,876	6,010	5,931	5,887	6,066	5,877	5,801
Virginia Beach-Norfolk-Newport News, VA-NC	73,393	74,864	78,165	81,228	84,303	85,081	86,173	86,640	85,019	85,326
Visalia, CA	11,404	10,612	11,131	12,305	13,481	12,736	14,167	13,386	12,302	13,545
Waco, TX	8,066	8,120	8,420	8,749	8,922	9,149	9,162	9,077	8,938	9,301
Walla Walla, WA	2,404	2,235	2,335	2,275	2,349	2,621	2,448	2,535	2,631	2,588
Warner Robins, GA	5,373	5,573	5,768	5,876	6,123	6,291	6,370	6,375	6,357	6,436
Washington-Arlington-Alexandria, DC-VA-MD-WV	332,261	344,597	357,410	378,459	395,402	400,417	406,868	420,661	418,828	438,471
Waterloo-Cedar Falls, IA	6,508	6,791	6,738	7,640	7,942	7,992	8,168	8,046	7,929	8,383
Watertown-Fort Drum, NY	4,624	4,668	4,875	5,149	5,587	5,890	5,996	6,308	6,498	6,784
Wausau-Weston, WI	6,780	6,956	7,290	7,599	7,893	7,989	8,033	7,877	7,602	7,792
Weirton-Steubenville, WV-OH	5,361	5,612	5,452	5,248	5,247	4,903	5,133	5,540	5,046	5,042
Wenatchee, WA	3,917	4,329	4,306	4,328	4,062	4,495	4,486	4,458	4,522	4,727
Wheeling, WV-OH	6,054	6,092	6,128	6,142	6,260	6,225	6,375	6,501	6,303	6,365
Wichita, KS	26,091	25,892	25,381	25,341	25,600	28,341	30,215	29,968	26,793	28,050
Wichita Falls, TX	5,460	5,573	5,501	5,459	5,452	5,756	5,704	5,788	5,675	5,700
Williamsport, PA	4,153	4,087	4,205	4,326	4,420	4,383	4,405	4,425	4,359	4,626
Wilmington, NC	8,801	9,013	9,333	9,676	10,434	11,041	11,559	11,629	11,169	11,370
Winchester, VA-WV	4,786	4,863	4,950	5,103	5,437	5,571	5,509	5,361	5,484	5,680
Winston-Salem, NC	26,978	26,929	27,614	28,849	29,558	30,489	29,860	30,491	29,192	29,243
Worcester, MA-CT	34,857	35,720	36,911	37,583	38,094	39,005	39,240	39,955	38,414	39,987
Yakima, WA	6,801	7,064	7,327	7,635	7,826	7,889	8,318	8,134	8,008	8,474
York-Hanover, PA	15,080	15,427	16,196	17,200	18,132	17,794	18,730	19,298	18,183	18,622
Youngstown-Warren-Boardman, OH-PA	20,468	21,071	21,185	21,837	22,301	22,251	21,824	21,198	19,134	19,694
Yuba City, CA	4,521	5,167	5,273	5,315	5,218	5,527	5,543	6,007	6,278	6,004
Yuma, AZ	4,812	5,572	5,424	6,027	6,436	6,581	6,952	6,447	6,336	6,628

Gross Domestic Product by Metropolitan Statistical Area—*Continued*

(Millions of chained 2012 dollars.)

Metropolitan Statistical Area	2011	2012	2013	2014	2015	2016	2017	2018	2019	2020	2021
Tulsa, OK	45,639	48,085	48,621	52,470	53,795	50,782	52,087	53,766	54,653	52,131	52,270
Tuscaloosa, AL	10,869	10,357	10,567	10,264	10,064	10,348	10,685	10,765	11,258	10,716	11,139
Twin Falls, ID	3,552	3,712	3,860	4,103	4,126	4,362	4,482	4,683	4,802	4,859	4,987
Tyler, TX	9,663	9,792	9,875	9,721	9,998	10,020	10,024	10,519	10,851	10,841	11,131
Urban Honolulu, HI	53,974	54,584	55,329	55,680	57,194	58,096	59,174	59,318	58,464	52,577	55,363
Utica-Rome, NY	11,448	11,485	11,328	11,296	11,222	11,362	11,367	11,569	12,013	11,474	11,996
Valdosta, GA	4,595	4,598	4,595	4,651	4,684	4,759	4,818	4,885	5,074	5,088	5,213
Vallejo, CA	17,507	18,974	19,881	20,029	20,203	20,619	20,925	22,185	25,816	26,244	26,796
Victoria, TX	4,582	4,884	5,007	5,067	4,692	4,329	4,275	4,478	4,421	4,176	4,285
Vineland-Bridgeton, NJ	5,695	5,727	5,669	5,647	5,730	5,847	5,727	5,936	5,889	5,728	5,948
Virginia Beach-Norfolk-Newport News, VA-NC	84,794	83,770	84,359	83,221	84,393	84,916	84,887	83,807	85,010	82,921	88,176
Visalia, CA	13,997	13,290	13,590	15,191	15,188	16,101	16,776	16,986	17,687	17,426	17,361
Waco, TX	9,444	9,795	10,580	11,005	10,832	10,993	11,636	12,072	12,198	11,776	12,429
Walla Walla, WA	2,705	2,699	2,673	2,729	2,938	3,108	3,241	3,277	3,255	2,974	2,997
Warner Robins, GA	6,511	6,570	6,517	6,498	6,608	6,685	6,853	6,949	7,213	7,114	7,377
Washington-Arlington-Alexandria, DC-VA-MD-WV	446,255	448,273	447,824	452,421	461,637	473,528	482,039	492,263	499,120	486,968	511,254
Waterloo-Cedar Falls, IA	8,324	10,081	8,881	9,941	9,329	8,371	8,447	8,621	8,551	8,493	9,089
Watertown-Fort Drum, NY	6,938	6,733	6,524	6,350	6,118	5,969	5,799	5,770	5,744	5,496	5,685
Wausau-Weston, WI	7,999	8,122	8,160	8,613	8,894	9,166	8,883	9,043	9,386	8,918	9,322
Weirton-Steubenville, WV-OH	4,908	4,931	5,571	6,300	6,374	5,162	5,250	5,132	5,484	5,686	5,625
Wenatchee, WA	5,235	5,330	5,174	5,196	5,471	5,600	5,783	5,885	5,838	5,728	5,970
Wheeling, WV-OH	6,414	6,428	7,032	7,936	8,729	9,261	10,001	10,015	10,003	10,191	9,505
Wichita, KS	28,751	28,592	26,942	28,709	30,222	32,725	33,428	33,146	33,668	33,135	34,060
Wichita Falls, TX	5,621	5,843	5,858	5,829	5,668	5,638	5,711	5,838	6,070	5,965	6,103
Williamsport, PA	5,242	5,768	5,786	6,261	6,143	5,806	5,909	5,821	5,856	5,711	5,781
Wilmington, NC	11,368	10,921	11,451	11,887	12,017	12,582	12,711	13,028	13,644	13,740	14,829
Winchester, VA-WV	5,697	5,691	5,853	5,810	6,046	6,147	6,145	6,288	6,447	6,534	6,839
Winston-Salem, NC	28,304	28,286	28,839	29,452	29,632	29,971	31,154	30,402	31,160	28,854	31,082
Worcester, MA-CT	41,262	41,507	41,936	42,094	42,994	43,226	43,359	44,260	44,528	43,141	45,232
Yakima, WA	8,366	8,428	8,463	8,952	8,933	9,304	9,452	9,945	10,092	9,997	9,978
York-Hanover, PA	18,462	18,085	18,437	18,463	18,571	18,853	19,267	19,085	19,452	18,325	19,257
Youngstown-Warren-Boardman, OH-PA	20,294	20,070	20,052	19,791	19,555	19,314	19,122	19,080	19,375	18,376	19,164
Yuba City, CA	5,861	5,675	5,890	5,596	5,727	5,859	6,017	6,287	6,356	6,372	6,618
Yuma, AZ	6,461	6,032	6,419	6,297	6,684	6,985	7,294	7,362	7,461	7,551	7,521

Quantity Indexes for Real GDP by Metropolitan Area

(2012 = 100.0)

Metropolitan Statistical Area	2001	2002	2003	2004	2005	2006	2007	2008	2009	2010
Abilene, TX	79.1	80.0	81.3	83.2	85.1	92.0	94.8	96.0	93.6	96.6
Akron, OH	92.0	95.7	98.4	100.5	103.1	102.2	103.9	102.5	96.3	98.7
Albany, GA	105.0	106.2	106.8	107.2	109.4	106.5	103.6	101.7	100.0	97.0
Albany-Lebanon, OR	92.7	98.3	94.4	101.2	104.1	110.6	103.0	101.6	99.4	98.0
Albany-Schenectady-Troy, NY	87.9	89.5	92.2	94.5	94.5	95.2	95.3	97.0	98.6	99.3
Albuquerque, NM	80.6	81.9	89.3	101.8	101.7	103.2	102.2	101.8	104.3	102.3
Alexandria, LA	84.6	87.8	88.9	93.3	99.3	99.6	94.7	94.6	97.4	99.1
Allentown-Bethlehem-Easton, PA-NJ	112.4	112.3	102.5	94.8	95.4	94.3	98.6	99.5	96.4	98.8
Altoona, PA	90.4	90.4	92.6	96.5	99.5	101.2	99.9	99.9	99.7	101.1
Amarillo, TX	84.9	86.6	87.7	88.7	89.4	94.0	96.3	97.1	96.7	100.2
Ames, IA	75.6	78.6	82.5	86.0	88.3	90.3	92.2	94.5	93.0	94.0
Anchorage, AK	76.0	77.4	79.3	81.3	84.8	85.2	86.5	90.0	94.2	98.0
Ann Arbor, MI	97.1	103.1	104.9	104.4	107.0	106.3	108.0	101.4	93.4	96.5
Anniston-Oxford, AL	83.9	86.3	89.4	97.0	102.9	103.1	105.9	106.8	101.0	105.1
Appleton, WI	85.0	85.2	87.9	90.6	93.2	95.0	95.6	94.4	91.3	93.2
Asheville, NC	87.2	89.7	91.4	94.4	97.5	101.0	99.2	100.2	96.0	100.0
Athens-Clarke County, GA	86.0	87.1	91.8	93.7	95.5	95.7	96.9	97.1	96.2	96.1
Atlanta-Sandy Springs-Alpharetta, GA	86.9	88.0	91.0	95.2	100.0	101.7	102.6	99.6	95.0	96.4
Atlantic City-Hammonton, NJ	101.5	104.3	105.0	105.2	109.3	114.4	115.0	116.8	101.9	99.4
Auburn-Opelika, AL	61.0	64.2	68.3	76.6	80.7	83.3	86.0	87.3	85.9	88.5
Augusta-Richmond County, GA-SC	87.1	88.2	91.5	93.2	93.6	92.9	96.6	97.8	96.1	98.1
Austin-Round Rock-Georgetown, TX	61.2	63.1	64.9	68.2	73.9	83.0	86.7	90.0	87.8	93.0
Bakersfield, CA	59.4	66.7	66.1	71.6	76.2	86.6	94.6	91.7	97.8	93.3
Baltimore-Columbia-Towson, MD	80.6	82.8	84.5	87.3	91.0	93.0	93.3	94.7	93.6	97.3
Bangor, ME	100.2	103.1	103.1	106.6	108.3	107.7	107.6	104.6	104.5	104.1
Barnstable Town, MA	99.1	100.0	100.2	102.9	101.3	96.8	97.2	101.2	96.4	99.0
Baton Rouge, LA	71.8	77.0	80.4	89.1	98.2	96.1	87.5	85.3	85.7	90.4
Battle Creek, MI	104.0	105.9	106.9	109.6	112.2	113.4	113.4	110.3	101.2	103.5
Bay City, MI	101.2	101.6	102.5	102.9	103.9	103.7	102.7	98.6	97.1	100.2
Beaumont-Port Arthur, TX	82.9	79.3	81.0	96.6	86.7	85.6	92.4	88.9	87.4	94.4
Beckley, WV	87.1	88.4	87.1	89.4	93.4	93.9	94.8	99.7	97.0	100.8
Bellingham, WA	83.0	88.5	90.0	91.5	112.0	100.8	102.6	101.5	104.2	108.6
Bend, OR	80.7	84.3	88.4	91.9	101.1	108.2	111.8	109.7	99.7	96.5
Billings, MT	77.7	78.8	84.5	89.2	88.8	92.1	101.3	97.3	90.6	94.1
Binghamton, NY	81.0	80.8	80.7	81.4	82.1	85.4	88.7	94.8	94.6	100.1
Birmingham-Hoover, AL	86.7	89.5	90.9	95.7	99.3	98.9	100.2	99.8	95.1	95.6
Bismarck, ND	63.9	65.7	70.3	73.5	75.2	77.1	77.4	79.4	81.8	84.0
Blacksburg-Christiansburg, VA	92.1	93.0	98.1	98.4	103.8	107.1	110.5	103.9	97.0	98.4
Bloomington, IL	80.1	82.3	85.1	88.6	89.4	96.2	95.8	93.3	94.1	97.6
Bloomington, IN	85.1	87.4	90.8	93.9	98.5	101.5	99.3	98.3	97.9	99.1
Bloomsburg-Berwick, PA	78.8	83.4	83.4	88.2	89.7	94.1	92.6	93.7	93.5	97.6
Boise City, ID	75.4	77.3	82.4	89.0	98.5	99.2	100.2	103.4	98.5	99.5
Boston-Cambridge-Newton, MA-NH	79.6	79.3	80.9	83.6	85.7	88.1	91.0	92.4	91.3	95.8
Boulder, CO	86.5	80.7	81.9	84.3	86.1	88.5	94.1	98.5	96.7	98.9
Bowling Green, KY	76.1	78.7	82.1	86.2	91.6	96.5	96.1	96.2	89.3	97.9
Bremerton-Silverdale-Port Orchard, WA	84.5	89.1	90.7	95.0	98.7	98.4	99.0	104.4	101.7	101.8
Bridgeport-Stamford-Norwalk, CT	92.7	92.8	92.3	97.4	100.5	104.4	109.0	111.2	105.1	103.0
Brownsville-Harlingen, TX	79.2	83.1	84.4	85.7	87.8	92.5	91.8	92.5	92.2	96.2
Brunswick, GA	90.7	92.9	97.7	103.9	106.7	111.2	110.2	105.7	103.5	104.9
Buffalo-Cheektowaga, NY	86.8	89.0	90.0	92.8	92.2	94.1	94.9	95.9	96.1	98.9
Burlington, NC	90.8	95.6	95.5	100.6	101.8	105.0	103.4	102.0	94.5	98.3
Burlington-South Burlington, VT	73.8	76.2	81.5	87.3	87.7	89.2	87.3	93.0	92.1	96.5
California-Lexington Park, MD	65.2	69.6	73.9	77.0	78.9	81.5	84.2	85.9	87.9	94.9
Canton-Massillon, OH	97.2	98.8	98.8	100.7	102.5	99.1	97.8	96.3	90.4	95.2
Cape Coral-Fort Myers, FL	75.9	82.2	90.7	102.9	112.6	121.0	121.4	110.9	100.6	98.8
Cape Girardeau, MO-IL	86.6	89.5	90.3	94.4	98.8	100.1	101.7	103.1	101.5	99.8
Carbondale-Marion, IL	80.0	83.6	84.3	85.5	88.2	89.7	88.4	93.0	93.5	96.7
Carson City, NV	94.0	95.3	96.7	98.2	100.4	103.5	106.1	106.8	104.6	110.3
Casper, WY	58.7	60.3	62.1	66.5	71.9	82.1	83.7	86.2	79.7	83.9
Cedar Rapids, IA	67.5	66.8	72.0	78.9	82.6	83.4	91.4	90.3	91.5	96.7
Chambersburg-Waynesboro, PA	78.3	76.9	82.4	89.3	97.4	103.4	108.7	108.0	100.9	100.4
Champaign-Urbana, IL	82.5	86.8	87.2	89.0	88.6	90.4	92.3	96.4	95.3	99.0
Charleston, WV	102.3	102.9	102.8	102.4	105.1	107.1	107.1	106.3	106.1	103.7
Charleston-North Charleston, SC	66.9	70.0	74.1	78.7	83.8	86.5	90.3	89.6	86.5	90.3
Charlotte-Concord-Gastonia, NC-SC	70.4	72.2	75.1	79.7	85.7	91.7	93.1	99.6	92.9	89.7
Charlottesville, VA	74.0	74.8	77.6	80.9	85.0	88.5	91.1	94.7	93.8	99.0
Chattanooga, TN-GA	83.2	84.7	87.3	91.0	93.4	94.4	95.3	94.9	91.3	93.2
Cheyenne, WY	71.7	74.7	78.6	82.6	84.2	88.6	98.5	108.1	92.9	94.1
Chicago-Naperville-Elgin, IL-IN-WI	89.9	90.5	92.0	94.4	96.4	98.7	100.2	98.2	94.7	96.0
Chico, CA	87.4	93.3	97.0	98.3	100.4	103.9	102.2	99.8	102.5	102.9
Cincinnati, OH-KY-IN	88.3	90.2	91.9	93.6	96.1	96.5	97.1	96.5	92.9	95.9
Clarksville, TN-KY	65.7	71.1	73.3	79.1	86.9	91.1	89.4	91.1	90.9	94.4
Cleveland, TN	76.6	80.2	80.8	85.9	86.6	85.3	85.7	86.5	84.8	88.3

Quantity Indexes for Real GDP by Metropolitan Area—*Continued*

(2012 = 100.0)

Metropolitan Statistical Area	2011	2012	2013	2014	2015	2016	2017	2018	2019	2020	2021
Abilene, TX	97.4	100.0	100.5	101.8	99.9	98.3	100.5	105.4	109.2	113.6	117.5
Akron, OH	99.1	100.0	101.4	103.5	104.0	104.2	105.8	107.4	109.4	104.0	110.0
Albany, GA	98.9	100.0	99.6	97.5	96.8	98.1	97.5	97.2	99.7	98.0	99.5
Albany-Lebanon, OR	98.9	100.0	101.5	103.8	108.4	114.5	113.7	121.0	122.5	119.5	123.3
Albany-Schenectady-Troy, NY	99.8	100.0	101.1	102.3	104.9	107.6	110.0	110.5	116.8	113.1	121.2
Albuquerque, NM	101.0	100.0	97.7	99.4	100.3	101.7	101.5	103.6	106.7	104.9	110.3
Alexandria, LA	99.8	100.0	99.1	98.9	96.9	98.3	98.5	99.6	99.3	97.2	99.7
Allentown-Bethlehem-Easton, PA-NJ	99.5	100.0	100.4	101.8	103.7	106.0	107.0	108.0	112.1	106.3	112.6
Altoona, PA	101.0	100.0	100.2	100.4	101.6	102.6	104.8	105.5	107.7	104.0	108.2
Amarillo, TX	100.9	100.0	102.1	104.5	108.0	107.2	106.8	110.2	113.0	114.4	119.4
Ames, IA	97.0	100.0	106.0	108.5	108.9	106.2	109.8	110.9	112.2	110.8	115.8
Anchorage, AK	99.8	100.0	97.4	97.8	102.1	102.6	100.8	101.7	101.5	97.5	99.0
Ann Arbor, MI	97.2	100.0	100.7	102.3	106.3	108.9	112.4	115.1	118.5	116.1	123.1
Anniston-Oxford, AL	100.1	100.0	96.9	93.0	91.6	92.5	93.7	95.0	99.6	96.9	102.2
Appleton, WI	96.3	100.0	98.5	102.2	107.2	110.0	111.7	115.9	118.9	113.9	119.6
Asheville, NC	101.8	100.0	102.3	106.0	107.6	111.0	116.9	121.2	125.7	120.1	129.2
Athens-Clarke County, GA	95.3	100.0	101.4	103.4	107.9	110.1	115.7	119.0	120.2	115.3	121.7
Atlanta-Sandy Springs-Alpharetta, GA	98.5	100.0	102.3	106.9	112.0	117.5	122.1	126.6	131.9	126.4	136.5
Atlantic City-Hammonton, NJ	102.2	100.0	99.5	98.0	95.3	92.0	90.7	90.5	93.0	85.2	92.7
Auburn-Opelika, AL	95.3	100.0	100.6	101.8	105.6	108.6	112.1	110.9	115.5	115.6	121.7
Augusta-Richmond County, GA-SC	99.7	100.0	100.1	100.7	104.6	105.9	107.8	109.0	111.6	109.4	112.9
Austin-Round Rock-Georgetown, TX	97.0	100.0	105.0	110.7	119.5	125.7	131.3	139.0	145.9	149.2	164.9
Bakersfield, CA	91.6	100.0	97.8	98.0	98.4	98.6	100.2	100.3	103.1	103.2	102.1
Baltimore-Columbia-Towson, MD	99.1	100.0	101.6	103.2	105.7	109.1	111.1	112.5	113.6	108.5	113.3
Bangor, ME	101.6	100.0	99.4	99.8	99.7	101.3	102.5	104.8	107.2	107.0	112.3
Barnstable Town, MA	100.8	100.0	100.5	102.6	103.4	103.3	102.7	105.1	108.1	101.2	108.1
Baton Rouge, LA	100.0	100.0	99.9	110.6	110.0	105.5	99.7	104.7	102.6	93.5	94.4
Battle Creek, MI	100.7	100.0	101.8	102.4	105.2	107.3	107.1	108.0	108.0	107.6	119.9
Bay City, MI	100.1	100.0	100.1	95.1	94.6	94.7	92.3	93.6	91.6	89.8	96.5
Beaumont-Port Arthur, TX	95.6	100.0	100.4	82.5	81.8	84.7	88.0	91.2	89.8	76.7	74.2
Beckley, WV	102.9	100.0	95.5	90.6	87.3	83.0	86.8	88.4	90.5	85.9	88.9
Bellingham, WA	100.4	100.0	99.2	100.3	103.8	110.4	118.3	128.8	137.1	126.7	136.2
Bend, OR	97.6	100.0	106.5	116.5	125.3	136.9	148.6	154.8	164.0	164.8	179.9
Billings, MT	99.2	100.0	102.1	107.6	113.3	105.4	114.3	115.3	109.1	106.3	111.7
Binghamton, NY	99.0	100.0	99.9	98.8	98.4	95.8	95.3	97.0	98.8	94.1	99.0
Birmingham-Hoover, AL	98.0	100.0	99.4	99.1	100.3	101.3	102.7	104.7	105.7	103.6	109.3
Bismarck, ND	88.5	100.0	101.7	110.3	114.1	108.5	107.8	105.1	103.8	100.1	103.8
Blacksburg-Christiansburg, VA	101.7	100.0	100.6	101.1	104.2	104.1	106.5	111.9	110.2	106.3	115.3
Bloomington, IL	97.6	100.0	99.1	109.8	118.4	122.0	120.2	124.6	124.7	114.5	119.2
Bloomington, IN	100.2	100.0	101.5	107.0	105.9	108.7	113.4	117.1	116.6	112.5	116.6
Bloomsburg-Berwick, PA	100.3	100.0	101.8	100.1	101.6	100.6	101.5	100.6	102.6	97.6	103.6
Boise City, ID	99.4	100.0	104.2	108.7	110.0	114.6	119.1	128.4	134.0	135.7	147.9
Boston-Cambridge-Newton, MA-NH	97.7	100.0	100.5	102.1	106.2	108.4	110.5	115.3	118.8	116.0	124.5
Boulder, CO	99.6	100.0	103.0	106.1	110.4	113.6	120.2	123.8	132.4	129.3	139.5
Bowling Green, KY	96.3	100.0	101.9	103.5	103.5	105.9	109.6	107.7	113.5	112.0	118.4
Bremerton-Silverdale-Port Orchard, WA	101.3	100.0	99.0	99.2	102.2	106.8	107.4	109.8	111.1	113.7	117.1
Bridgeport-Stamford-Norwalk, CT	96.9	100.0	96.9	96.4	97.6	97.0	97.5	99.1	99.7	91.3	95.9
Brownsville-Harlingen, TX	99.0	100.0	101.2	101.2	101.4	103.9	103.6	105.3	108.0	108.6	115.2
Brunswick, GA	101.9	100.0	99.9	99.8	104.7	103.1	105.7	108.2	106.4	103.1	107.7
Buffalo-Cheektowaga, NY	97.8	100.0	99.6	101.8	103.2	104.4	103.8	104.9	107.6	104.0	109.5
Burlington, NC	100.7	100.0	104.0	105.8	105.1	109.0	107.6	108.1	111.4	110.0	118.9
Burlington-South Burlington, VT	99.0	100.0	98.6	99.9	100.7	103.4	103.9	105.0	106.8	103.9	109.4
California-Lexington Park, MD	99.9	100.0	99.2	100.5	103.1	105.8	107.9	108.6	110.6	112.8	114.9
Canton-Massillon, OH	102.1	100.0	106.7	113.4	114.0	112.3	113.3	112.2	113.2	106.4	111.9
Cape Coral-Fort Myers, FL	97.9	100.0	102.1	107.1	113.5	121.9	124.6	128.6	130.2	130.5	142.0
Cape Girardeau, MO-IL	99.1	100.0	100.2	100.7	103.3	104.7	104.8	106.1	105.3	101.7	104.4
Carbondale-Marion, IL	100.0	100.0	96.7	94.4	93.8	93.1	93.3	95.9	95.9	90.6	93.7
Carson City, NV	101.3	100.0	99.3	94.2	95.0	94.5	100.4	104.2	110.6	107.3	111.7
Casper, WY	88.9	100.0	102.6	109.7	108.1	98.2	96.7	105.6	103.2	91.6	90.1
Cedar Rapids, IA	99.2	100.0	98.3	102.3	105.9	108.3	107.3	110.2	107.3	105.2	108.2
Chambersburg-Waynesboro, PA	100.9	100.0	102.1	104.2	106.8	103.7	112.3	111.7	110.8	104.7	108.8
Champaign-Urbana, IL	99.9	100.0	104.1	106.0	105.9	103.3	102.7	101.5	101.9	100.9	104.9
Charleston, WV	103.9	100.0	96.7	94.7	92.1	90.9	89.0	93.8	88.9	83.5	85.8
Charleston-North Charleston, SC	94.7	100.0	99.6	102.3	106.8	112.4	114.4	117.9	123.3	119.0	128.0
Charlotte-Concord-Gastonia, NC-SC	94.8	100.0	99.4	102.3	106.4	109.4	114.8	116.1	119.1	120.6	128.6
Charlottesville, VA	99.0	100.0	100.5	101.0	104.0	105.8	111.2	114.0	114.9	110.4	117.6
Chattanooga, TN-GA	96.3	100.0	101.3	100.8	103.6	105.3	108.3	109.2	111.5	108.6	116.2
Cheyenne, WY	97.4	100.0	98.1	99.1	103.0	99.7	99.7	105.2	109.3	104.2	109.1
Chicago-Naperville-Elgin, IL-IN-WI	97.5	100.0	100.2	102.5	104.8	105.1	106.1	108.9	109.7	103.8	110.4
Chico, CA	102.0	100.0	100.7	99.3	103.2	109.8	114.3	115.6	117.6	109.8	109.9
Cincinnati, OH-KY-IN	99.1	100.0	100.8	103.7	106.2	110.3	112.7	113.5	119.0	116.2	123.2
Clarksville, TN-KY	99.5	100.0	97.7	96.3	96.7	95.1	94.5	95.3	96.9	97.0	102.1
Cleveland, TN	89.4	100.0	101.6	99.9	101.4	97.7	98.2	97.9	98.5	98.0	102.1

Quantity Indexes for Real GDP by Metropolitan Area—*Continued*

(2012 = 100.0)

Metropolitan Statistical Area	2001	2002	2003	2004	2005	2006	2007	2008	2009	2010
Cleveland-Elyria, OH	96.3	97.6	99.2	101.6	104.3	104.3	104.3	103.3	96.5	97.5
Coeur d'Alene, ID	76.0	77.6	81.0	87.5	96.0	100.3	104.9	105.2	97.1	101.4
College Station-Bryan, TX	66.5	69.7	72.3	73.7	79.8	86.7	94.2	98.3	106.3	100.9
Colorado Springs, CO	83.3	83.5	84.5	85.9	90.3	91.6	94.1	94.2	94.4	96.7
Columbia, MO	82.5	84.1	86.3	89.5	91.7	93.0	92.5	94.0	93.7	95.2
Columbia, SC	85.0	86.5	89.4	93.5	96.1	99.9	102.7	102.6	99.9	100.3
Columbus, GA-AL	84.2	86.6	86.6	87.9	89.9	91.9	94.9	94.9	95.7	97.3
Columbus, IN	60.4	58.7	61.5	66.2	70.3	76.5	85.7	89.7	73.7	88.9
Columbus, OH	83.1	84.4	86.1	89.3	92.5	92.8	94.1	92.9	90.1	92.8
Corpus Christi, TX	84.8	84.3	87.3	93.5	88.6	91.4	97.5	93.0	91.5	97.2
Corvallis, OR	68.2	69.0	70.2	73.4	78.1	84.9	91.5	96.6	94.2	97.9
Crestview-Fort Walton Beach-Destin, FL	76.6	82.8	89.9	99.5	106.5	106.5	105.7	100.0	95.9	94.3
Cumberland, MD-WV	94.9	95.9	94.9	94.3	93.6	92.9	92.1	95.2	94.9	101.1
Dallas-Fort Worth-Arlington, TX	72.4	74.6	75.6	79.9	84.0	90.7	93.9	94.5	91.6	93.4
Dalton, GA	96.7	101.1	102.4	114.0	119.1	117.8	117.0	111.2	100.2	95.8
Danville, IL	90.4	93.5	97.4	101.7	99.6	103.7	102.6	103.2	97.0	96.9
Daphne-Fairhope-Foley, AL	73.9	77.3	81.6	90.5	101.4	104.6	107.8	102.6	98.2	99.2
Davenport-Moline-Rock Island, IA-IL	82.1	81.8	84.1	89.2	91.3	91.6	92.6	94.9	90.7	93.7
Dayton-Kettering, OH	98.3	100.8	102.4	105.2	106.3	105.9	103.5	100.8	95.3	97.8
Decatur, AL	90.6	89.5	96.7	109.4	103.4	104.9	108.3	104.6	102.5	103.6
Decatur, IL	86.0	86.1	87.4	90.1	91.4	92.2	94.7	99.8	99.3	100.3
Deltona-Daytona Beach-Ormond Beach, FL	82.2	88.8	96.1	104.7	108.3	111.8	113.9	107.0	99.7	99.0
Denver-Aurora-Lakewood, CO	86.9	87.0	87.2	87.6	91.1	92.6	96.6	96.7	93.7	95.5
Des Moines-West Des Moines, IA	73.5	74.3	80.5	88.4	95.2	94.2	104.1	93.5	92.3	93.8
Detroit-Warren-Dearborn, MI	102.6	105.0	106.9	107.3	109.6	106.6	105.6	98.4	87.3	92.9
Dothan, AL	91.5	95.8	97.1	100.6	103.2	105.3	105.2	101.7	98.6	98.2
Dover, DE	88.0	90.1	93.1	102.7	102.5	104.5	104.9	105.1	109.7	106.7
Dubuque, IA	65.8	68.8	71.9	80.0	85.5	87.7	91.7	87.4	82.0	88.3
Duluth, MN-WI	87.4	90.8	91.7	96.8	98.7	96.8	94.5	96.9	91.9	101.5
Durham-Chapel Hill, NC	61.5	64.3	67.9	69.3	74.4	89.7	95.6	98.1	90.1	97.9
East Stroudsburg, PA	75.7	78.6	80.3	87.9	94.2	99.2	105.0	105.8	102.3	103.5
Eau Claire, WI	71.1	74.4	77.9	82.2	88.1	89.4	91.8	89.9	89.5	94.1
El Centro, CA	76.1	91.6	85.2	81.8	88.9	95.1	91.6	106.8	103.1	102.1
Elizabethtown-Fort Knox, KY	73.3	74.0	76.5	79.5	81.8	84.7	85.1	89.8	89.9	100.0
Elkhart-Goshen, IN	80.4	87.3	95.9	102.4	110.4	117.7	117.7	101.8	74.8	99.3
Elmira, NY	83.2	83.8	84.8	85.8	87.0	86.0	88.2	93.6	92.9	98.0
El Paso, TX	73.5	76.6	76.7	81.3	83.1	85.4	86.9	84.5	85.8	92.6
Enid, OK	56.4	57.5	60.1	62.2	64.6	67.6	72.2	79.2	81.7	84.4
Erie, PA	89.1	88.3	89.1	91.8	96.0	97.6	100.8	105.5	96.2	98.4
Eugene-Springfield, OR	87.9	89.8	91.5	95.4	100.5	103.7	105.5	104.7	97.8	99.0
Evansville, IN-KY	93.8	98.8	102.8	109.2	106.3	100.8	99.2	102.8	98.8	101.5
Fairbanks, AK	103.6	90.6	91.7	92.5	101.2	105.6	106.8	114.7	112.4	113.4
Fargo, ND-MN	63.8	68.0	71.5	74.4	77.2	81.2	84.1	86.1	83.8	87.0
Farmington, NM	101.3	101.6	99.9	102.5	102.9	105.3	108.3	107.2	108.2	101.1
Fayetteville, NC	76.1	79.8	82.0	86.7	92.1	93.9	92.7	96.3	99.3	102.0
Fayetteville-Springdale-Rogers, AR	71.4	77.2	82.0	89.6	95.9	97.9	95.9	93.6	89.5	94.5
Flagstaff, AZ	77.9	79.1	80.1	83.5	87.6	90.6	98.7	97.0	92.1	97.2
Flint, MI	107.7	113.7	115.6	115.6	117.2	115.6	112.8	102.5	92.7	97.6
Florence, SC	93.3	94.1	96.7	98.9	100.9	101.9	102.3	100.3	96.5	94.6
Florence-Muscle Shoals, AL	85.1	84.8	88.7	94.0	97.0	97.8	97.3	96.8	91.4	96.2
Fond du Lac, WI	80.8	79.8	82.9	87.3	89.3	90.2	91.0	92.3	86.1	90.2
Fort Collins, CO	78.0	82.9	83.6	85.2	87.4	89.3	92.1	94.7	93.5	96.1
Fort Smith, AR-OK	89.3	92.0	96.4	102.0	105.5	110.4	106.7	104.0	96.1	99.1
Fort Wayne, IN	88.4	90.8	95.1	97.4	100.1	103.6	105.8	99.9	92.3	95.0
Fresno, CA	83.8	90.4	95.4	97.3	100.9	106.6	103.7	100.4	101.8	102.6
Gadsden, AL	97.1	98.5	100.0	106.1	107.6	104.3	103.7	102.4	101.5	102.0
Gainesville, FL	86.3	89.0	89.9	97.6	100.1	101.7	107.0	105.6	102.9	102.1
Gainesville, GA	83.5	84.4	88.4	91.2	94.6	95.1	98.3	97.9	92.1	93.6
Gettysburg, PA	78.6	84.7	84.5	85.9	89.6	93.5	93.2	95.4	96.9	95.0
Glens Falls, NY	79.8	81.9	85.1	91.0	89.2	89.7	89.3	94.8	99.2	100.6
Goldsboro, NC	99.5	95.6	93.3	98.1	99.5	102.7	102.7	104.6	102.3	104.7
Grand Forks, ND-MN	74.9	78.7	84.5	82.1	85.0	89.8	89.6	94.4	90.9	93.2
Grand Island, NE	71.3	73.3	78.0	79.8	85.8	89.4	89.3	91.3	92.2	95.7
Grand Junction, CO	77.2	79.4	81.8	84.2	89.4	95.1	105.8	115.6	106.2	100.3
Grand Rapids-Kentwood, MI	92.4	95.2	97.3	100.3	103.1	102.5	102.4	98.9	92.0	95.5
Grants Pass, OR	86.2	90.6	94.6	99.2	105.1	105.2	105.5	102.6	99.3	99.3
Great Falls, MT	83.9	86.5	86.7	90.7	97.3	96.3	98.3	96.4	96.1	99.0
Greeley, CO	61.8	61.2	63.7	68.3	73.8	75.6	78.8	83.7	84.8	87.7
Green Bay, WI	82.6	84.6	87.3	90.1	92.1	93.6	94.3	94.0	90.9	95.2
Greensboro-High Point, NC	95.5	98.0	97.8	97.1	99.8	103.8	103.7	104.8	102.5	103.5
Greenville, NC	78.5	77.9	77.6	80.3	86.7	93.9	97.5	97.8	101.2	103.8
Greenville-Anderson, SC	94.4	98.9	102.2	93.9	95.1	94.9	98.5	97.5	91.9	94.8

Quantity Indexes for Real GDP by Metropolitan Area—*Continued*

(2012 = 100.0)

Metropolitan Statistical Area	2011	2012	2013	2014	2015	2016	2017	2018	2019	2020	2021
Cleveland-Elyria, OH	99.3	100.0	100.3	102.2	102.5	102.8	104.3	106.0	108.6	103.9	110.7
Coeur d'Alene, ID	98.4	100.0	108.5	110.6	111.3	116.4	119.9	126.5	129.1	132.8	144.0
College Station-Bryan, TX	98.9	100.0	107.2	114.1	121.3	121.9	124.8	129.8	135.0	135.2	138.8
Colorado Springs, CO	99.2	100.0	101.4	102.1	102.9	104.3	107.9	111.5	115.4	117.1	123.1
Columbia, MO	97.2	100.0	103.0	103.3	105.3	106.0	108.2	108.9	113.5	113.3	119.3
Columbia, SC	100.4	100.0	102.5	106.1	109.0	111.8	112.9	114.2	116.3	114.6	119.6
Columbus, GA-AL	98.9	100.0	98.2	97.9	98.4	96.9	97.6	97.5	99.3	98.8	101.2
Columbus, IN	91.5	100.0	104.9	100.0	96.8	95.1	94.7	102.0	101.6	94.0	102.1
Columbus, OH	96.4	100.0	102.7	105.8	107.4	109.8	113.3	114.6	118.1	116.5	125.4
Corpus Christi, TX	100.3	100.0	101.7	95.2	95.0	93.1	96.7	101.3	102.1	97.4	99.2
Corvallis, OR	101.2	100.0	96.0	95.5	96.3	99.4	102.8	108.4	109.6	108.6	113.8
Crestview-Fort Walton Beach-Destin, FL	94.9	100.0	102.5	104.0	106.4	110.6	114.2	117.5	124.0	126.0	136.9
Cumberland, MD-WV	100.7	100.0	97.3	97.1	98.6	103.0	101.6	102.9	102.6	95.9	96.5
Dallas-Fort Worth-Arlington, TX	96.8	100.0	102.8	106.6	111.7	115.3	119.2	124.3	128.8	127.2	136.0
Dalton, GA	96.6	100.0	98.8	101.4	104.6	108.4	108.6	107.2	107.4	104.7	112.0
Danville, IL	98.1	100.0	100.7	99.0	96.7	95.1	96.3	96.0	96.0	93.4	96.6
Daphne-Fairhope-Foley, AL	99.0	100.0	104.7	106.4	110.4	115.5	118.5	125.1	131.4	131.6	144.3
Davenport-Moline-Rock Island, IA-IL	96.9	100.0	96.9	97.1	95.3	94.0	95.0	94.8	95.7	94.7	98.8
Dayton-Kettering, OH	100.5	100.0	100.3	101.3	102.2	103.7	106.9	109.1	112.1	109.7	115.0
Decatur, AL	99.9	100.0	100.3	101.4	99.3	101.1	102.3	103.9	104.8	105.9	109.0
Decatur, IL	102.1	100.0	107.4	110.8	113.6	106.1	94.7	93.1	91.9	91.3	98.3
Deltona-Daytona Beach-Ormond Beach, FL	98.0	100.0	100.1	103.0	105.5	109.9	113.5	116.6	118.5	118.1	126.3
Denver-Aurora-Lakewood, CO	97.2	100.0	103.9	108.3	113.8	116.2	119.9	125.1	131.0	129.4	138.5
Des Moines-West Des Moines, IA	94.1	100.0	97.4	108.8	117.5	120.7	119.0	120.4	123.2	124.1	131.9
Detroit-Warren-Dearborn, MI	96.7	100.0	101.9	103.1	104.7	106.6	107.4	109.3	109.1	103.7	112.7
Dothan, AL	98.5	100.0	104.2	105.4	107.2	112.1	114.5	114.9	117.1	116.0	120.7
Dover, DE	105.4	100.0	99.4	101.9	103.6	104.5	104.1	108.9	117.4	117.3	124.4
Dubuque, IA	87.9	100.0	94.2	102.3	104.1	100.6	106.3	106.6	110.9	111.4	117.3
Duluth, MN-WI	104.4	100.0	102.6	102.1	92.6	95.1	95.2	97.9	99.3	94.8	98.7
Durham-Chapel Hill, NC	99.2	100.0	101.5	99.7	97.9	97.2	96.3	100.4	104.8	105.7	114.0
East Stroudsburg, PA	102.1	100.0	100.4	101.2	104.8	105.9	112.0	108.6	111.7	106.8	110.9
Eau Claire, WI	96.6	100.0	99.7	107.5	109.7	108.6	109.3	112.7	115.8	110.9	116.1
El Centro, CA	106.0	100.0	105.7	112.0	121.1	123.0	122.6	122.5	125.3	127.1	126.7
Elizabethtown-Fort Knox, KY	105.5	100.0	98.4	95.3	90.4	92.0	93.2	92.0	95.3	94.4	99.0
Elkhart-Goshen, IN	98.0	100.0	108.2	117.4	126.6	137.6	152.6	153.0	148.3	144.3	180.8
Elmira, NY	99.9	100.0	100.2	99.9	96.4	94.1	91.9	93.2	93.2	88.9	93.3
El Paso, TX	97.2	100.0	98.7	97.0	98.3	99.4	101.6	105.0	109.9	108.8	112.8
Enid, OK	86.7	100.0	103.1	120.8	121.2	131.0	91.4	90.6	89.7	85.4	90.2
Erie, PA	102.7	100.0	100.6	95.4	95.4	92.5	90.0	90.8	91.8	86.2	89.1
Eugene-Springfield, OR	99.4	100.0	100.3	101.2	106.0	108.9	112.5	115.7	115.6	113.9	120.0
Evansville, IN-KY	102.6	100.0	95.5	94.2	94.8	96.6	102.5	107.1	111.7	107.0	110.5
Fairbanks, AK	105.6	100.0	98.2	96.9	96.2	96.2	95.3	94.4	93.4	91.9	94.6
Fargo, ND-MN	91.8	100.0	99.1	106.0	109.1	108.0	109.8	111.3	114.1	112.2	120.0
Farmington, NM	100.4	100.0	98.2	101.3	102.8	94.2	91.5	86.2	87.5	82.8	79.5
Fayetteville, NC	102.6	100.0	99.7	99.6	100.8	100.7	96.3	97.1	99.2	98.2	103.3
Fayetteville-Springdale-Rogers, AR	96.4	100.0	106.4	111.1	116.7	119.1	125.5	129.6	133.3	138.0	149.7
Flagstaff, AZ	103.8	100.0	103.8	101.8	103.3	103.6	113.5	112.5	110.1	103.8	108.8
Flint, MI	99.2	100.0	102.4	101.6	106.3	108.8	110.2	112.8	114.4	105.8	113.4
Florence, SC	98.6	100.0	104.1	108.2	110.9	112.9	113.9	113.0	115.9	112.4	117.4
Florence-Muscle Shoals, AL	99.0	100.0	105.4	101.4	98.9	96.0	94.5	96.3	96.1	95.6	99.7
Fond du Lac, WI	94.3	100.0	100.6	102.9	102.1	101.5	103.6	104.9	106.6	101.8	106.3
Fort Collins, CO	96.3	100.0	103.9	109.0	114.0	118.3	127.3	133.1	140.4	141.9	151.7
Fort Smith, AR-OK	101.6	100.0	97.8	97.2	95.7	95.2	95.7	98.0	99.4	97.6	102.4
Fort Wayne, IN	96.0	100.0	99.0	105.9	110.1	113.3	116.6	121.4	121.6	114.8	121.8
Fresno, CA	103.5	100.0	103.7	106.8	111.0	114.9	118.3	121.5	124.5	122.9	124.3
Gadsden, AL	103.1	100.0	101.6	100.8	103.3	103.2	103.2	104.3	101.8	94.1	95.5
Gainesville, FL	100.4	100.0	100.8	104.0	105.9	108.1	112.1	115.5	117.9	120.4	127.8
Gainesville, GA	100.8	100.0	101.9	107.6	112.5	116.5	125.6	131.2	136.1	136.0	147.9
Gettysburg, PA	97.1	100.0	100.1	100.0	102.5	103.7	108.4	105.4	103.4	97.7	102.7
Glens Falls, NY	98.7	100.0	99.1	99.7	101.4	100.7	103.7	104.2	109.7	104.3	111.0
Goldsboro, NC	99.8	100.0	102.7	99.9	101.0	100.6	102.5	102.8	103.8	101.9	107.7
Grand Forks, ND-MN	94.2	100.0	101.3	100.1	101.6	103.4	103.9	102.6	105.3	103.5	106.4
Grand Island, NE	97.1	100.0	105.4	104.5	104.5	105.6	102.6	102.3	104.1	103.1	107.7
Grand Junction, CO	101.4	100.0	98.3	99.5	98.2	96.2	100.9	105.1	106.9	104.3	108.2
Grand Rapids-Kentwood, MI	97.6	100.0	102.0	105.4	109.8	112.7	114.7	117.7	118.1	114.7	122.5
Grants Pass, OR	99.3	100.0	101.1	102.4	109.1	109.8	117.4	122.7	131.1	133.5	144.6
Great Falls, MT	99.8	100.0	97.5	96.7	99.6	98.8	104.2	104.5	102.3	99.6	102.7
Greeley, CO	91.0	100.0	112.2	135.6	153.2	160.6	172.3	188.3	198.3	185.3	172.8
Green Bay, WI	97.3	100.0	99.6	105.2	107.8	108.7	107.8	111.3	111.9	106.7	109.8
Greensboro-High Point, NC	105.4	100.0	102.0	101.5	103.7	102.3	102.8	102.6	102.4	98.4	103.5
Greenville, NC	104.9	100.0	105.6	108.6	117.9	117.9	121.4	118.2	118.4	116.3	123.1
Greenville-Anderson, SC	98.9	100.0	103.0	106.5	110.7	113.6	116.5	120.0	122.4	118.9	126.8

Quantity Indexes for Real GDP by Metropolitan Area—*Continued*

(2012 = 100.0)

Metropolitan Statistical Area	2001	2002	2003	2004	2005	2006	2007	2008	2009	2010
Gulfport-Biloxi, MS	85.4	85.8	92.4	92.5	95.7	99.0	122.0	109.8	103.6	102.6
Hagerstown-Martinsburg, MD-WV	82.5	84.7	86.5	91.1	93.8	98.0	97.9	97.7	94.2	95.8
Hammond, LA	63.3	65.9	71.7	78.6	87.3	101.2	95.1	97.8	92.9	98.4
Hanford-Corcoran, CA	85.3	90.1	98.9	103.3	107.9	100.5	116.4	104.2	94.5	96.6
Harrisburg-Carlisle, PA	84.3	86.5	89.4	93.0	94.4	95.9	97.8	97.7	94.5	96.0
Harrisonburg, VA	93.8	81.8	80.6	82.2	86.9	88.1	88.3	88.4	92.5	98.3
Hartford-East Hartford-Middletown, CT	86.6	82.6	84.8	91.4	92.9	97.5	103.3	102.3	100.2	100.4
Hattiesburg, MS	77.7	80.7	84.3	88.2	91.8	97.3	94.5	97.3	96.3	98.7
Hickory-Lenoir-Morganton, NC	107.5	107.7	105.2	109.0	109.8	112.4	108.5	105.0	99.6	103.3
Hilton Head Island-Bluffton, SC	83.6	85.2	90.7	97.4	102.9	107.9	110.4	106.6	102.5	100.5
Hinesville, GA	64.2	66.4	72.6	76.2	81.7	81.7	84.7	91.9	93.0	98.8
Homosassa Springs, FL	95.7	99.1	102.8	109.1	113.7	122.2	126.2	119.7	112.8	105.9
Hot Springs, AR	86.0	89.6	92.2	94.4	98.0	98.5	97.3	93.5	92.1	95.1
Houma-Thibodaux, LA	94.7	91.3	87.4	86.1	88.7	103.6	104.2	102.3	103.1	101.0
Houston-The Woodlands-Sugar Land, TX.	72.3	72.1	72.3	78.8	80.0	86.8	93.5	91.2	90.3	94.3
Huntington-Ashland, WV-KY-OH	85.0	86.7	88.2	91.2	92.1	93.8	92.4	96.8	97.1	95.2
Huntsville, AL	66.1	68.6	72.7	78.5	83.2	86.5	89.4	92.1	92.9	97.9
Idaho Falls, ID	77.2	81.9	82.3	86.1	89.6	97.0	99.3	100.6	101.2	100.9
Indianapolis-Carmel-Anderson, IN	82.7	83.6	86.6	91.3	92.4	95.3	98.8	100.6	97.4	100.7
Iowa City, IA	74.6	77.1	79.0	82.7	84.2	88.0	88.3	92.2	91.2	93.8
Ithaca, NY	82.2	85.4	89.2	91.5	90.2	89.9	90.4	94.3	96.9	100.5
Jackson, MI	98.1	101.1	100.4	103.9	106.5	105.3	103.8	100.2	91.1	94.5
Jackson, MS	86.7	88.7	92.4	95.5	97.9	99.4	96.2	98.3	95.3	97.3
Jackson, TN	90.4	89.8	92.1	94.4	96.8	98.9	96.4	98.1	99.0	105.1
Jacksonville, FL	87.9	90.8	95.2	99.9	104.3	107.9	109.9	105.8	100.4	99.9
Jacksonville, NC	64.0	62.2	65.2	71.3	76.3	77.1	83.1	92.2	97.6	102.0
Janesville-Beloit, WI	89.1	98.9	100.8	103.2	102.6	107.7	106.5	101.0	93.6	96.2
Jefferson City, MO	87.3	87.8	89.7	93.2	94.7	96.1	95.8	99.0	97.3	99.3
Johnson City, TN	80.2	82.0	86.1	92.1	94.8	96.4	97.6	100.4	96.8	94.5
Johnstown, PA	95.2	94.5	95.9	97.1	98.9	97.1	97.7	100.3	98.1	100.4
Jonesboro, AR	77.8	81.1	87.8	91.9	95.5	96.9	92.3	93.8	93.6	98.3
Joplin, MO	91.5	92.0	93.4	97.0	99.2	99.9	99.0	101.8	97.5	99.6
Kahului-Wailuku-Lahaina, HI	77.2	80.1	85.6	91.4	99.6	106.7	108.5	102.8	92.6	95.1
Kalamazoo-Portage, MI	97.5	103.6	101.9	103.5	102.6	101.9	104.0	100.5	97.9	99.4
Kankakee, IL	81.2	83.9	84.7	86.5	85.9	89.0	89.3	91.9	92.6	93.5
Kansas City, MO-KS	83.7	86.2	87.5	89.5	92.3	95.3	98.0	100.4	97.0	96.6
Kennewick-Richland, WA	74.0	79.3	79.8	81.6	86.1	88.9	89.5	91.9	96.0	105.9
Killeen-Temple, TX	66.9	69.5	72.7	75.9	81.9	89.0	92.7	98.1	98.8	98.3
Kingsport-Bristol, TN-VA	88.1	88.2	89.9	96.0	94.1	98.5	99.2	98.7	97.5	97.0
Kingston, NY	83.7	86.6	90.3	94.5	94.0	95.2	95.0	99.4	98.2	100.2
Knoxville, TN	80.4	84.6	88.1	92.4	95.9	98.1	98.1	98.9	94.2	95.2
Kokomo, IN	75.8	83.9	97.3	92.8	90.9	93.5	98.4	86.1	58.2	92.4
La Crosse-Onalaska, WI-MN	79.0	80.1	83.1	85.8	88.5	89.1	90.4	92.0	92.5	96.0
Lafayette, LA	84.1	79.3	78.6	80.3	82.6	94.4	92.6	94.6	93.3	94.7
Lafayette-West Lafayette, IN	83.0	85.0	88.7	91.6	94.0	98.4	101.7	99.6	91.1	97.7
Lake Charles, LA	107.7	115.2	138.0	150.5	178.7	151.8	125.6	108.8	91.2	82.5
Lake Havasu City-Kingman, AZ	83.1	91.6	93.8	101.5	106.7	107.2	109.7	107.5	101.4	101.4
Lakeland-Winter Haven, FL	85.8	88.8	91.7	96.2	101.9	105.2	107.8	105.1	98.7	99.1
Lancaster, PA	91.9	93.7	97.5	99.3	101.8	102.0	101.5	101.1	97.1	100.5
Lansing-East Lansing, MI	101.9	105.4	106.5	107.3	109.3	110.7	111.0	104.4	97.4	105.0
Laredo, TX	86.2	88.2	87.0	84.2	87.3	88.5	87.1	83.0	83.7	84.8
Las Cruces, NM	76.6	79.9	85.8	92.4	100.0	100.2	100.9	101.6	105.4	110.2
Las Vegas-Henderson-Paradise, NV	81.1	84.8	89.0	99.4	108.9	114.0	115.5	111.7	100.9	100.1
Lawrence, KS	92.1	94.7	94.1	96.1	96.3	95.7	97.9	100.3	99.6	98.0
Lawton, OK	79.4	81.9	88.1	92.1	90.6	94.4	95.9	99.3	102.4	107.1
Lebanon, PA	75.9	78.1	82.4	86.8	87.9	89.6	92.6	92.5	92.2	95.7
Lewiston, ID-WA	90.2	91.5	92.8	95.1	96.8	97.3	97.8	101.1	99.1	103.3
Lewiston-Auburn, ME	85.7	92.2	95.1	97.3	97.3	98.7	101.8	103.4	99.3	97.9
Lexington-Fayette, KY	83.9	87.9	89.9	93.3	98.0	102.0	103.0	100.6	93.2	96.7
Lima, OH	78.5	81.4	79.9	81.8	82.2	84.0	83.0	83.3	103.0	107.5
Lincoln, NE	88.3	88.6	91.9	93.6	97.8	100.1	101.9	98.1	95.7	98.5
Little Rock-North Little Rock-Conway, AR.	82.0	84.6	88.7	92.0	97.5	100.4	103.2	101.3	98.3	98.1
Logan, UT-ID	68.9	68.8	73.1	76.9	78.2	80.7	85.5	90.3	92.1	99.6
Longview, TX	76.5	79.2	78.3	80.1	85.1	92.3	100.8	106.9	112.4	104.9
Longview, WA	82.2	79.8	82.8	84.5	88.5	91.4	96.9	94.6	92.7	100.1
Los Angeles-Long Beach-Anaheim, CA	82.1	83.8	87.4	90.4	93.1	96.9	97.9	98.9	94.7	97.3
Louisville/Jefferson County, KY-IN	85.7	86.0	88.5	91.5	94.5	97.8	98.2	96.0	90.8	94.9
Lubbock, TX	80.7	82.6	84.7	86.6	90.2	93.5	94.3	93.4	93.2	97.6
Lynchburg, VA	90.2	92.2	96.6	98.5	99.5	102.6	101.2	102.3	100.3	105.0
Macon-Bibb County, GA	103.6	103.0	101.0	103.5	102.8	101.5	99.5	100.5	96.8	97.3
Madera, CA	64.9	72.6	75.0	85.4	91.3	94.9	94.8	93.3	82.8	96.2
Madison, WI	77.7	80.4	83.3	87.4	91.6	92.7	94.9	93.3	92.1	94.9
Manchester-Nashua, NH	78.8	81.8	88.2	92.2	93.7	96.7	97.6	97.5	95.9	96.9

Quantity Indexes for Real GDP by Metropolitan Area—*Continued*

(2012 = 100.0)

Metropolitan Statistical Area	2011	2012	2013	2014	2015	2016	2017	2018	2019	2020	2021
Gulfport-Biloxi, MS	97.5	100.0	91.7	96.9	94.1	96.5	96.8	94.6	95.8	97.0	103.3
Hagerstown-Martinsburg, MD-WV	98.2	100.0	100.3	101.2	102.1	106.3	108.8	111.4	109.4	104.6	110.2
Hammond, LA	110.6	100.0	92.9	92.5	87.6	90.5	97.9	98.7	101.2	101.7	104.2
Hanford-Corcoran, CA	110.4	100.0	100.1	108.1	106.3	111.6	119.0	116.9	119.6	120.4	119.2
Harrisburg-Carlisle, PA	98.3	100.0	101.7	104.7	107.2	107.2	107.0	109.2	112.4	107.4	112.3
Harrisonburg, VA	98.9	100.0	102.2	97.5	94.5	90.9	92.9	95.0	98.1	98.1	105.8
Hartford-East Hartford-Middletown, CT	99.9	100.0	96.6	98.4	104.3	104.8	107.4	107.0	108.0	100.6	105.6
Hattiesburg, MS	98.2	100.0	100.7	99.8	101.2	99.6	100.8	100.2	99.0	98.8	103.9
Hickory-Lenoir-Morganton, NC	103.1	100.0	100.6	101.1	103.3	105.6	109.7	108.1	106.4	102.7	109.3
Hilton Head Island-Bluffton, SC	99.4	100.0	104.0	106.9	108.5	110.7	112.0	116.3	121.0	121.9	131.7
Hinesville, GA	103.7	100.0	97.5	93.7	92.3	90.8	90.2	91.2	92.3	91.3	96.2
Homosassa Springs, FL	102.2	100.0	99.2	95.7	94.1	95.9	93.6	97.4	106.6	106.7	114.8
Hot Springs, AR	102.0	100.0	98.5	98.8	98.8	99.3	101.5	103.5	104.0	103.4	107.3
Houma-Thibodaux, LA	97.1	100.0	103.4	103.9	95.2	82.8	79.6	82.1	81.5	75.4	72.8
Houston-The Woodlands-Sugar Land, TX	96.6	100.0	104.4	105.7	112.0	110.5	111.9	115.6	114.3	111.7	113.8
Huntington-Ashland, WV-KY-OH	95.1	100.0	107.0	101.8	101.4	98.2	97.7	103.0	103.5	95.6	98.5
Huntsville, AL	99.8	100.0	101.3	101.5	102.8	105.8	108.8	112.8	118.2	118.7	125.7
Idaho Falls, ID	99.2	100.0	101.3	102.2	108.1	112.6	118.4	125.5	140.6	144.3	151.5
Indianapolis-Carmel-Anderson, IN	100.7	100.0	102.8	104.9	102.2	104.4	105.3	109.7	112.7	110.7	116.3
Iowa City, IA	98.3	100.0	104.1	107.4	104.8	105.8	111.5	112.6	113.0	108.1	111.5
Ithaca, NY	99.5	100.0	97.7	96.4	98.3	98.8	99.6	101.3	102.4	96.4	103.2
Jackson, MI	98.7	100.0	101.2	100.4	101.3	105.7	106.5	113.5	118.6	114.2	124.5
Jackson, MS	99.1	100.0	102.2	103.5	104.2	103.5	102.8	102.0	101.9	101.0	104.8
Jackson, TN	113.1	100.0	99.2	98.3	99.4	101.0	105.8	106.3	106.6	104.4	112.5
Jacksonville, FL	99.1	100.0	102.7	105.1	109.4	113.4	118.1	122.1	126.9	127.7	136.4
Jacksonville, NC	103.6	100.0	97.4	96.2	94.3	86.4	90.5	91.0	92.3	92.2	98.4
Janesville-Beloit, WI	97.4	100.0	102.7	102.0	102.3	103.9	101.8	107.5	112.4	110.4	114.9
Jefferson City, MO	99.7	100.0	101.5	103.0	106.0	105.4	103.2	104.4	109.6	108.1	109.1
Johnson City, TN	98.0	100.0	98.4	96.7	100.6	97.5	100.6	101.6	104.5	105.5	114.4
Johnstown, PA	100.8	100.0	97.5	97.1	94.4	92.7	93.1	93.0	92.3	90.5	90.9
Jonesboro, AR	100.6	100.0	103.5	100.6	102.1	102.8	106.9	109.5	113.4	115.5	121.7
Joplin, MO	100.3	100.0	101.3	101.6	105.8	104.6	105.2	106.8	105.1	100.0	103.8
Kahului-Wailuku-Lahaina, HI	96.5	100.0	102.5	102.9	108.5	111.9	113.5	119.6	121.0	96.5	109.6
Kalamazoo-Portage, MI	99.1	100.0	101.1	100.3	103.4	106.9	112.1	114.6	116.0	111.9	118.8
Kankakee, IL	93.8	100.0	98.0	102.0	104.0	112.7	123.5	128.7	131.6	127.6	133.5
Kansas City, MO-KS	96.7	100.0	101.2	104.0	107.4	107.5	110.2	112.6	115.5	113.3	118.3
Kennewick-Richland, WA	104.3	100.0	99.9	102.0	106.9	111.5	112.7	115.8	120.4	117.3	120.8
Killeen-Temple, TX	100.2	100.0	97.3	96.6	100.1	97.9	99.9	100.9	102.6	104.8	108.6
Kingsport-Bristol, TN-VA	99.4	100.0	97.9	94.5	96.1	97.2	100.8	101.6	100.1	97.1	102.6
Kingston, NY	99.1	100.0	100.2	99.6	98.5	98.5	100.2	102.4	105.0	101.2	107.2
Knoxville, TN	98.2	100.0	100.1	101.2	103.1	106.4	109.4	111.6	114.4	113.8	123.4
Kokomo, IN	95.2	100.0	101.0	96.8	89.9	87.2	84.9	86.6	86.5	82.4	91.0
La Crosse-Onalaska, WI-MN	98.3	100.0	99.8	104.3	106.3	108.0	110.3	112.6	114.1	111.5	117.1
Lafayette, LA	96.5	100.0	98.5	98.9	92.1	83.8	83.0	86.0	85.3	81.4	82.5
Lafayette-West Lafayette, IN	100.0	100.0	104.0	106.9	107.5	112.6	117.1	123.8	124.7	118.9	124.4
Lake Charles, LA	102.8	100.0	88.1	92.4	97.0	105.1	123.1	121.1	122.1	98.0	99.4
Lake Havasu City-Kingman, AZ	100.9	100.0	104.8	104.9	104.1	108.7	106.0	107.7	111.6	114.8	123.4
Lakeland-Winter Haven, FL	98.7	100.0	102.5	102.2	107.6	110.7	116.9	119.6	123.6	127.6	134.6
Lancaster, PA	99.7	100.0	102.1	104.4	108.9	109.3	114.2	115.6	116.4	111.2	116.3
Lansing-East Lansing, MI	102.3	100.0	99.2	101.4	104.8	109.1	111.0	112.9	113.7	111.3	118.8
Laredo, TX	93.7	100.0	106.8	123.0	136.7	135.9	135.5	129.0	135.7	137.2	137.2
Las Cruces, NM	105.7	100.0	99.1	99.9	100.6	102.5	103.7	105.6	108.5	104.0	107.0
Las Vegas-Henderson-Paradise, NV	101.3	100.0	101.3	103.2	107.9	110.7	113.6	119.9	125.3	113.3	123.8
Lawrence, KS	100.5	100.0	101.0	102.8	103.3	108.3	110.5	113.5	113.9	109.4	112.5
Lawton, OK	104.5	100.0	101.4	100.1	103.0	102.0	99.7	98.8	99.7	97.6	99.0
Lebanon, PA	97.7	100.0	99.2	101.9	103.7	101.8	105.1	108.3	109.1	105.3	111.6
Lewiston, ID-WA	101.3	100.0	103.1	102.8	105.4	109.1	107.9	107.1	111.6	112.0	118.1
Lewiston-Auburn, ME	96.8	100.0	98.0	99.2	101.0	102.5	101.3	105.0	107.9	109.5	114.5
Lexington-Fayette, KY	98.1	100.0	103.8	106.5	110.2	112.6	113.8	116.2	118.7	115.0	119.8
Lima, OH	109.0	100.0	95.0	104.4	101.2	105.2	103.6	104.4	103.8	99.7	104.5
Lincoln, NE	98.7	100.0	101.6	105.4	109.2	110.4	115.9	118.9	120.6	118.7	122.3
Little Rock-North Little Rock-Conway, AR	99.9	100.0	100.2	100.9	102.7	103.1	102.3	103.9	105.5	104.8	108.8
Logan, UT-ID	102.9	100.0	101.4	104.8	108.7	112.4	118.5	126.1	132.1	133.4	144.2
Longview, TX	99.9	100.0	99.0	98.6	94.2	89.5	90.2	93.3	93.3	89.2	90.7
Longview, WA	97.7	100.0	101.3	101.0	102.9	104.2	103.6	108.5	115.3	116.2	119.8
Los Angeles-Long Beach-Anaheim, CA	98.5	100.0	101.8	104.3	108.5	110.5	114.2	117.9	120.8	114.6	123.3
Louisville/Jefferson County, KY-IN	96.4	100.0	100.2	101.3	103.4	105.1	106.0	107.6	110.9	108.9	115.3
Lubbock, TX	95.6	100.0	104.3	103.6	106.6	108.2	108.8	111.8	113.9	114.0	117.3
Lynchburg, VA	102.9	100.0	100.0	98.9	99.2	98.0	99.2	103.8	103.6	98.3	101.4
Macon-Bibb County, GA	99.1	100.0	99.7	100.3	101.3	100.3	100.7	102.4	100.5	93.7	99.3
Madera, CA	96.5	100.0	101.2	108.7	102.9	113.6	118.1	117.3	121.2	120.6	117.2
Madison, WI	97.4	100.0	101.6	105.9	109.7	113.2	113.6	118.0	121.4	119.3	126.1
Manchester-Nashua, NH	99.4	100.0	101.1	103.2	106.3	108.4	108.2	111.9	114.0	114.6	125.0

Quantity Indexes for Real GDP by Metropolitan Area—*Continued*

(2012 = 100.0)

Metropolitan Statistical Area	2001	2002	2003	2004	2005	2006	2007	2008	2009	2010
Manhattan, KS	66.4	67.0	69.7	73.0	75.3	81.9	88.4	92.7	92.0	97.0
Mankato, MN	75.8	79.3	78.8	84.2	87.8	94.3	92.3	93.2	89.1	94.1
Mansfield, OH	104.9	109.6	109.9	114.7	117.0	114.9	109.8	106.1	90.2	95.4
McAllen-Edinburg-Mission, TX	81.8	87.1	88.8	89.7	92.0	96.2	100.1	98.2	97.7	97.0
Medford, OR	89.7	94.7	99.9	103.7	106.8	108.6	108.9	107.9	101.8	103.7
Memphis, TN-MS-AR	96.1	97.5	99.3	101.1	103.2	104.9	102.8	100.7	96.2	96.4
Merced, CA	81.1	85.5	92.8	101.2	105.5	103.4	115.2	101.4	97.4	99.4
Miami-Fort Lauderdale-Pompano Beach, FL	87.0	90.4	93.9	99.1	104.9	107.6	108.2	103.6	96.8	99.5
Michigan City-La Porte, IN	101.2	100.9	101.8	105.8	104.8	105.3	106.2	106.3	97.3	101.0
Midland, MI	109.0	112.2	106.3	112.1	100.8	101.2	102.1	98.1	92.7	95.8
Midland, TX	37.4	38.0	36.5	38.4	40.4	47.4	52.3	57.9	62.3	68.1
Milwaukee-Waukesha, WI	89.7	89.4	91.8	93.5	96.9	99.3	100.1	98.3	95.0	97.3
Minneapolis-St. Paul-Bloomington, MN-WI	83.8	85.1	89.3	93.3	96.8	96.1	97.5	97.2	93.3	96.0
Missoula, MT	82.5	86.4	89.4	92.8	95.3	97.8	99.8	102.2	101.0	99.8
Mobile, AL	82.7	83.0	84.3	87.3	91.2	97.5	97.9	98.1	97.7	98.4
Modesto, CA	89.9	93.2	96.3	101.5	105.3	107.3	105.9	102.5	101.7	102.3
Monroe, LA	90.9	97.6	100.0	104.9	109.5	110.7	99.0	94.2	97.5	99.6
Monroe, MI	102.0	106.9	109.7	108.6	109.1	111.5	110.5	104.6	97.6	102.8
Montgomery, AL	84.1	85.8	88.4	93.4	97.5	100.1	100.6	98.4	95.4	97.7
Morgantown, WV	71.7	74.2	75.6	79.8	83.8	85.4	85.4	87.8	91.2	98.9
Morristown, TN	89.8	89.7	90.4	94.1	95.4	97.8	98.7	95.5	87.6	95.0
Mount Vernon-Anacortes, WA	92.9	110.5	105.6	99.3	120.2	111.4	114.1	118.2	121.6	123.8
Muncie, IN	117.9	117.6	122.8	120.8	119.1	118.9	113.3	110.9	106.0	112.1
Muskegon, MI	97.9	99.3	98.7	100.7	102.9	101.3	100.3	97.0	92.9	95.8
Myrtle Beach-Conway-North Myrtle Beach, SC-NC	81.0	82.3	87.0	94.2	101.7	105.3	107.3	102.2	98.6	98.5
Napa, CA	88.3	92.9	93.5	92.5	97.0	96.9	98.8	99.7	97.4	95.8
Naples-Marco Island, FL	91.5	97.2	102.6	107.6	117.6	119.0	118.0	109.6	99.8	100.6
Nashville-Davidson--Murfreesboro--Franklin, TN	70.4	73.2	77.1	81.8	85.2	88.9	89.3	92.3	90.0	91.4
New Bern, NC	87.5	85.8	89.7	93.8	100.7	102.0	104.5	102.4	99.3	102.0
New Haven-Milford, CT	93.5	95.5	96.1	102.1	103.3	105.8	106.6	106.6	99.7	100.9
New Orleans-Metairie, LA	101.9	104.6	109.5	112.9	117.0	110.3	108.1	115.8	117.5	127.9
New York-Newark-Jersey City, NY-NJ-PA	85.5	85.0	85.2	87.2	89.5	92.0	92.8	91.5	93.0	96.1
Niles, MI	99.8	101.7	102.7	106.1	104.2	107.5	111.6	103.1	90.4	99.7
North Port-Sarasota-Bradenton, FL	88.5	96.2	101.3	111.5	121.9	125.2	121.7	111.1	105.2	100.6
Norwich-New London, CT	88.6	93.0	97.5	108.5	112.0	117.8	125.7	117.6	102.3	101.6
Ocala, FL	83.0	87.3	93.3	99.4	107.5	115.6	118.5	116.8	106.2	104.1
Ocean City, NJ	96.3	99.9	102.8	105.1	109.2	107.5	106.6	107.5	97.0	105.6
Odessa, TX	43.7	47.1	45.0	46.8	48.2	56.1	61.7	66.8	68.3	71.9
Ogden-Clearfield, UT	78.2	80.3	82.5	84.7	90.2	96.4	99.3	99.1	98.5	99.8
Oklahoma City, OK	67.1	68.6	70.5	73.5	76.6	82.5	83.3	88.8	90.5	90.5
Olympia-Lacey-Tumwater, WA	82.2	83.2	84.6	86.2	89.7	92.1	97.1	102.3	98.9	100.0
Omaha-Council Bluffs, NE-IA	74.3	76.3	79.8	83.8	86.1	89.2	91.6	90.8	91.0	93.6
Orlando-Kissimmee-Sanford, FL	80.7	83.7	88.1	94.6	102.0	105.2	107.8	104.3	97.1	97.8
Oshkosh-Neenah, WI	88.8	95.5	96.2	98.2	100.2	101.9	100.0	98.4	95.3	98.6
Owensboro, KY	81.8	86.3	90.5	90.9	91.5	95.9	92.4	95.9	93.7	97.8
Oxnard-Thousand Oaks-Ventura, CA	79.8	82.0	87.0	95.3	100.0	111.1	119.6	109.4	108.7	108.3
Palm Bay-Melbourne-Titusville, FL	79.3	82.4	88.4	96.4	103.3	107.5	113.5	113.7	106.5	106.8
Panama City, FL	81.1	86.8	90.8	99.0	105.7	108.6	109.7	108.1	104.0	103.1
Parkersburg-Vienna, WV	97.6	101.4	101.4	101.6	100.1	105.5	100.6	104.4	112.9	110.7
Pensacola-Ferry Pass-Brent, FL	89.7	91.4	94.3	98.2	101.6	104.3	105.1	101.8	98.3	99.3
Peoria, IL	60.2	59.8	61.0	63.1	66.1	69.9	73.6	75.2	73.1	79.7
Philadelphia-Camden-Wilmington, PA-NJ-DE-MD	83.6	84.5	87.7	91.1	92.0	93.1	96.5	98.9	95.4	97.2
Phoenix-Mesa-Chandler, AZ	76.8	79.8	85.1	89.6	96.8	101.9	104.8	103.4	93.8	94.2
Pine Bluff, AR	97.4	96.5	100.7	105.1	105.6	105.9	100.8	100.9	97.8	100.5
Pittsburgh, PA	84.6	86.1	88.3	90.2	90.8	90.1	92.0	93.8	92.5	96.2
Pittsfield, MA	88.3	90.7	88.6	91.2	93.6	92.6	92.8	95.6	92.8	94.8
Pocatello, ID	91.2	86.6	87.9	95.1	101.0	101.4	101.3	105.6	99.3	97.7
Portland-South Portland, ME	87.2	88.8	92.7	97.2	98.4	99.7	99.7	99.1	98.1	99.1
Portland-Vancouver-Hillsboro, OR-WA	72.7	73.3	77.7	82.5	86.2	90.8	93.2	97.9	92.5	95.0
Port St. Lucie, FL	79.1	83.6	87.1	96.1	104.8	112.5	113.2	107.4	102.5	101.1
Poughkeepsie-Newburgh-Middletown, NY.	80.4	82.3	87.2	91.1	91.8	90.8	92.6	96.8	97.0	100.4
Prescott Valley-Prescott, AZ	84.4	87.9	92.7	99.5	108.4	114.1	113.2	116.0	106.1	102.5
Providence-Warwick, RI-MA	90.0	92.4	94.6	97.2	98.4	101.4	99.2	99.2	96.8	99.5
Provo-Orem, UT	63.9	64.8	67.4	72.1	77.7	83.9	91.4	93.3	93.8	96.0
Pueblo, CO	84.0	84.8	86.7	91.1	85.7	88.3	88.2	93.3	93.3	94.9
Punta Gorda, FL	89.9	96.0	100.5	107.8	118.2	116.3	115.0	104.1	100.1	98.4
Racine, WI	98.1	98.9	101.2	104.0	103.3	105.2	102.7	99.4	95.6	100.7
Raleigh-Cary, NC	71.0	73.1	75.6	79.3	84.0	89.7	93.9	95.7	91.3	97.0

Quantity Indexes for Real GDP by Metropolitan Area—*Continued*

(2012 = 100.0)

Metropolitan Statistical Area	2011	2012	2013	2014	2015	2016	2017	2018	2019	2020	2021
Manhattan, KS	100.8	100.0	96.9	93.7	94.3	92.2	91.1	90.6	87.7	87.7	90.3
Mankato, MN	95.5	100.0	101.8	104.9	106.2	104.7	106.3	106.9	107.1	104.5	105.0
Mansfield, OH	98.4	100.0	98.0	100.5	99.0	97.8	98.5	100.0	99.3	96.1	101.7
McAllen-Edinburg-Mission, TX	98.6	100.0	103.8	105.0	106.1	106.4	107.3	109.8	112.6	112.9	117.9
Medford, OR	102.3	100.0	104.6	106.2	110.3	114.6	119.8	121.6	124.3	122.5	130.0
Memphis, TN-MS-AR	97.2	100.0	101.0	100.4	102.3	103.1	103.8	103.9	105.1	102.4	108.4
Merced, CA	102.1	100.0	103.7	113.8	115.5	115.9	122.8	122.8	124.5	124.2	123.1
Miami-Fort Lauderdale-Pompano Beach, FL	99.7	100.0	102.6	105.9	110.5	113.9	118.4	122.4	124.2	119.4	130.6
Michigan City-La Porte, IN	100.3	100.0	101.4	103.0	98.7	99.7	98.4	102.4	98.8	94.5	97.0
Midland, MI	97.4	100.0	97.9	111.2	120.2	112.8	115.9	118.1	111.7	111.7	112.4
Midland, TX	79.6	100.0	104.1	112.8	125.9	130.5	154.0	189.3	233.6	223.9	216.1
Milwaukee-Waukesha, WI	99.4	100.0	100.0	100.2	101.3	101.8	101.9	104.3	105.8	101.2	106.2
Minneapolis-St. Paul-Bloomington, MN-WI	98.5	100.0	102.7	106.8	108.7	110.6	112.1	115.7	117.0	112.3	118.9
Missoula, MT	101.0	100.0	100.2	101.9	105.2	105.9	112.1	113.0	116.1	116.0	125.4
Mobile, AL	100.8	100.0	100.9	100.8	100.1	101.9	102.0	103.2	104.8	103.0	105.9
Modesto, CA	101.9	100.0	100.7	106.9	110.5	111.9	117.3	120.8	123.1	120.8	125.2
Monroe, LA	97.0	100.0	108.2	108.3	110.4	110.5	108.7	110.5	106.6	102.9	103.1
Monroe, MI	103.4	100.0	103.0	103.1	103.1	102.7	102.8	101.0	102.2	95.2	101.7
Montgomery, AL	98.6	100.0	99.2	98.0	99.6	102.3	102.1	102.0	102.3	100.2	104.4
Morgantown, WV	99.4	100.0	106.9	106.2	109.9	108.7	111.1	110.0	108.4	106.5	108.4
Morristown, TN	98.2	100.0	100.1	102.3	104.1	104.8	108.2	107.6	111.0	111.0	120.1
Mount Vernon-Anacortes, WA	102.2	100.0	105.4	107.5	125.8	124.2	122.2	124.5	123.8	114.6	119.1
Muncie, IN	121.9	100.0	102.4	101.7	101.0	99.8	102.0	102.7	103.4	101.2	103.1
Muskegon, MI	98.6	100.0	102.3	103.9	105.1	102.7	101.1	101.9	102.6	97.6	103.0
Myrtle Beach-Conway-North Myrtle Beach, SC-NC	100.3	100.0	102.7	107.6	110.6	115.4	120.6	122.2	124.7	122.0	132.3
Napa, CA	94.3	100.0	104.3	111.3	116.1	118.3	120.0	120.3	121.9	115.6	122.8
Naples-Marco Island, FL	98.6	100.0	103.3	108.8	115.6	122.8	124.4	131.2	133.0	132.2	143.8
Nashville-Davidson--Murfreesboro--Franklin, TN	94.9	100.0	102.2	106.8	113.9	117.6	122.4	125.5	130.4	127.2	142.4
New Bern, NC	99.9	100.0	104.9	107.9	107.1	96.5	98.9	96.8	100.9	100.0	105.8
New Haven-Milford, CT	100.0	100.0	100.6	100.1	101.2	102.9	103.2	105.2	106.8	104.0	108.6
New Orleans-Metairie, LA	98.1	100.0	96.2	97.6	98.2	98.7	105.2	104.9	105.5	96.0	96.7
New York-Newark-Jersey City, NY-NJ-PA	96.2	100.0	100.6	102.0	103.8	106.1	107.2	110.6	113.2	107.8	114.1
Niles, MI	101.6	100.0	102.0	102.7	104.6	109.2	111.8	109.5	107.0	106.6	109.0
North Port-Sarasota-Bradenton, FL	101.1	100.0	103.6	109.0	116.1	119.7	125.4	131.4	135.7	135.5	147.1
Norwich-New London, CT	100.7	100.0	102.5	96.7	99.4	100.1	105.5	107.0	107.5	99.0	104.3
Ocala, FL	103.1	100.0	101.2	101.3	103.5	110.6	112.5	116.0	118.7	122.9	132.1
Ocean City, NJ	103.6	100.0	101.9	105.4	102.1	101.2	105.0	105.5	106.6	101.0	107.4
Odessa, TX	84.5	100.0	102.6	103.0	92.3	80.2	86.1	99.6	103.9	88.3	85.7
Ogden-Clearfield, UT	100.5	100.0	103.9	106.0	107.7	111.2	117.3	123.0	127.4	131.2	137.1
Oklahoma City, OK	93.9	100.0	102.9	108.8	117.1	116.5	117.3	119.7	121.3	116.3	117.4
Olympia-Lacey-Tumwater, WA	99.4	100.0	100.7	102.0	102.3	107.5	111.4	118.5	120.4	119.1	126.0
Omaha-Council Bluffs, NE-IA	98.4	100.0	98.3	103.4	106.6	106.7	111.0	113.7	115.4	113.3	117.9
Orlando-Kissimmee-Sanford, FL	97.8	100.0	102.8	106.6	112.3	116.6	121.9	126.0	130.2	124.7	138.3
Oshkosh-Neenah, WI	100.0	100.0	99.2	101.1	99.8	104.0	102.8	106.0	109.1	105.4	111.2
Owensboro, KY	99.2	100.0	104.6	102.6	103.2	103.8	104.1	101.9	103.3	99.9	103.3
Oxnard-Thousand Oaks-Ventura, CA	102.2	100.0	100.9	100.2	100.3	99.6	100.4	100.7	103.1	101.8	104.9
Palm Bay-Melbourne-Titusville, FL	102.9	100.0	100.8	103.2	107.9	110.6	116.8	121.8	125.9	126.5	134.8
Panama City, FL	100.4	100.0	100.7	103.1	106.2	108.1	108.1	109.4	110.7	111.4	119.0
Parkersburg-Vienna, WV	107.3	100.0	96.2	95.7	94.3	91.8	92.2	92.2	90.0	87.6	91.5
Pensacola-Ferry Pass-Brent, FL	100.7	100.0	101.1	102.0	105.6	109.3	113.3	113.7	116.1	116.1	122.9
Peoria, IL	89.8	100.0	85.7	84.0	76.8	72.0	68.4	70.2	67.4	63.6	66.6
Philadelphia-Camden-Wilmington, PA-NJ-DE-MD	97.7	100.0	100.7	103.3	104.8	105.6	104.8	106.5	108.1	103.7	108.7
Phoenix-Mesa-Chandler, AZ	96.9	100.0	100.8	102.8	105.8	109.3	113.9	118.9	124.1	125.1	133.6
Pine Bluff, AR	99.0	100.0	102.6	97.3	92.6	90.5	87.6	86.1	85.1	82.1	88.8
Pittsburgh, PA	98.3	100.0	101.2	102.9	105.9	105.6	108.5	111.7	113.5	107.4	112.2
Pittsfield, MA	95.8	100.0	100.1	100.7	101.1	100.1	96.9	98.7	96.2	91.1	94.5
Pocatello, ID	97.4	100.0	96.7	96.2	96.4	96.5	98.5	99.2	101.9	101.6	104.4
Portland-South Portland, ME	99.0	100.0	99.3	101.3	102.3	105.6	108.3	112.3	115.3	116.0	124.8
Portland-Vancouver-Hillsboro, OR-WA	98.5	100.0	100.4	103.5	109.3	114.2	118.9	125.2	128.0	125.3	133.0
Port St. Lucie, FL	99.2	100.0	100.3	102.1	105.0	107.5	109.3	112.9	113.8	114.9	120.1
Poughkeepsie-Newburgh-Middletown, NY.	99.8	100.0	100.3	99.7	101.7	101.7	103.9	106.5	111.3	108.6	115.1
Prescott Valley-Prescott, AZ	101.0	100.0	104.7	109.2	108.8	112.1	119.7	120.5	121.3	122.4	129.6
Providence-Warwick, RI-MA	99.7	100.0	100.8	102.1	104.3	104.3	104.3	104.4	106.2	102.8	108.7
Provo-Orem, UT	99.0	100.0	104.6	108.9	117.4	125.3	131.6	144.5	157.1	164.2	177.8
Pueblo, CO	97.8	100.0	99.0	96.7	98.7	101.2	100.9	104.2	108.5	104.6	111.4
Punta Gorda, FL	95.9	100.0	99.6	101.4	106.9	110.9	116.5	120.6	125.2	127.4	137.3
Racine, WI	100.0	100.0	96.9	97.8	96.8	94.7	89.8	91.2	90.4	88.5	91.4
Raleigh-Cary, NC	97.6	100.0	106.1	112.2	120.4	127.8	133.2	140.8	145.5	143.1	156.0

Quantity Indexes for Real GDP by Metropolitan Area—*Continued*

(2012 = 100.0)

Metropolitan Statistical Area	2001	2002	2003	2004	2005	2006	2007	2008	2009	2010
Rapid City, SD	80.6	91.9	92.1	89.6	93.0	89.6	92.5	93.1	91.4	94.8
Reading, PA	87.6	88.9	90.6	92.2	94.3	98.6	97.6	98.2	94.3	96.4
Redding, CA	95.5	105.7	108.2	105.8	103.3	107.5	103.9	100.4	99.1	102.2
Reno, NV	91.1	92.3	94.9	102.2	106.7	106.9	106.2	101.3	95.2	99.2
Richmond, VA	89.4	87.7	89.3	90.0	94.2	94.6	95.9	95.7	93.4	95.8
Riverside-San Bernardino-Ontario, CA	77.2	81.1	86.6	92.7	98.6	102.7	104.3	101.8	96.4	98.2
Roanoke, VA	94.9	94.1	94.9	94.5	98.1	100.9	103.2	103.2	99.4	100.9
Rochester, MN	71.7	76.8	82.5	86.7	88.3	90.1	90.2	93.2	92.4	96.6
Rochester, NY	95.3	95.7	97.0	97.4	96.3	97.0	97.9	99.6	99.7	102.5
Rockford, IL	93.2	95.0	96.8	99.1	100.8	104.1	105.7	104.3	95.8	96.3
Rocky Mount, NC	109.4	107.1	108.3	108.7	111.0	114.7	114.3	114.7	138.0	124.8
Rome, GA	115.0	102.4	103.3	107.1	104.3	105.3	106.4	105.5	101.8	102.9
Sacramento-Roseville-Folsom, CA	84.9	87.6	91.8	95.2	99.7	102.5	103.5	102.7	99.2	97.7
Saginaw, MI	104.5	107.0	111.0	110.0	112.3	109.7	105.9	98.9	93.5	98.2
St. Cloud, MN	86.2	88.6	89.5	93.7	95.4	97.5	97.3	98.4	95.9	96.2
St. George, UT	67.6	70.8	76.0	83.0	92.8	102.5	106.1	102.2	92.5	92.0
St. Joseph, MO-KS	80.2	82.4	83.2	88.5	88.8	90.0	91.2	93.8	92.4	92.3
St. Louis, MO-IL	89.9	91.2	93.8	95.6	97.4	97.3	97.8	100.1	97.5	99.0
Salem, OR	88.0	89.8	92.6	94.0	98.8	105.1	103.9	105.2	100.8	101.5
Salinas, CA	100.8	106.4	106.1	95.2	97.4	104.4	99.6	98.1	104.7	102.3
Salisbury, MD-DE	87.8	85.3	88.2	93.0	98.1	101.0	101.9	103.2	101.9	98.7
Salt Lake City, UT	72.5	74.1	74.4	79.5	84.4	90.7	94.6	94.2	91.1	93.3
San Angelo, TX	72.0	71.3	70.2	70.3	70.8	72.4	74.6	78.6	84.0	88.8
San Antonio-New Braunfels, TX	73.1	75.2	77.9	80.7	83.9	88.9	91.1	91.9	89.9	93.3
San Diego-Chula Vista-Carlsbad, CA	79.7	83.2	87.4	92.4	97.1	99.4	100.9	100.3	96.0	97.4
San Francisco-Oakland-Berkeley, CA	84.6	82.8	83.9	85.0	88.5	91.0	91.5	95.9	92.3	92.2
San Jose-Sunnyvale-Santa Clara, CA	59.8	57.1	60.5	62.8	66.8	71.9	78.8	83.4	81.9	89.3
San Luis Obispo-Paso Robles, CA	81.2	89.8	91.7	92.2	95.2	97.1	96.4	92.8	91.8	96.4
Santa Cruz-Watsonville, CA	94.9	94.5	96.5	93.7	93.7	93.2	92.9	93.5	95.8	103.4
Santa Fe, NM	87.1	93.6	90.8	94.8	97.9	103.7	107.5	112.2	103.5	103.9
Santa Maria-Santa Barbara, CA	78.3	81.4	84.5	87.2	90.7	92.2	93.9	96.0	98.3	97.5
Santa Rosa-Petaluma, CA	91.8	95.3	94.4	94.2	95.8	96.7	98.4	97.7	94.1	96.9
Savannah, GA	75.9	77.4	79.7	83.5	88.9	93.1	95.0	93.6	92.8	94.6
Scranton--Wilkes-Barre, PA	88.6	88.5	90.1	92.1	93.1	94.0	96.2	97.8	96.8	98.7
Seattle-Tacoma-Bellevue, WA	73.4	73.4	74.4	76.1	81.3	85.1	91.2	93.3	89.7	92.3
Sebastian-Vero Beach, FL	83.6	89.5	95.7	102.1	110.7	111.2	114.8	107.7	100.8	96.9
Sebring-Avon Park, FL	79.7	86.2	89.1	94.7	101.1	109.8	109.3	102.9	103.5	99.8
Sheboygan, WI	92.7	94.3	96.6	102.9	100.7	100.1	102.8	100.9	95.9	97.4
Sherman-Denison, TX	74.6	76.5	77.8	82.8	83.7	90.8	89.4	90.3	90.4	92.6
Shreveport-Bossier City, LA	72.7	73.2	76.4	80.7	85.5	88.6	81.7	82.2	94.3	99.7
Sierra Vista-Douglas, AZ	76.4	77.3	82.7	85.5	89.9	91.4	97.5	99.6	99.8	103.4
Sioux City, IA-NE-SD	105.5	95.1	93.7	99.7	104.0	106.0	108.5	113.6	106.5	109.0
Sioux Falls, SD	50.9	59.9	58.5	69.0	74.3	81.2	82.0	84.3	89.1	85.9
South Bend-Mishawaka, IN-MI	94.2	96.3	101.5	104.8	105.4	107.5	108.1	103.6	93.1	97.9
Spartanburg, SC	88.9	91.6	95.6	101.0	104.5	110.0	109.1	106.3	96.3	100.0
Spokane-Spokane Valley, WA	84.7	84.8	86.2	89.5	93.4	96.5	99.9	101.8	98.1	98.6
Springfield, IL	98.9	100.7	98.3	98.2	97.7	98.2	97.3	98.7	98.5	100.8
Springfield, MA	91.9	92.6	93.9	95.0	95.4	95.1	95.2	96.9	94.4	97.7
Springfield, MO	85.8	88.1	92.2	96.3	100.8	101.6	102.0	102.8	100.5	100.1
Springfield, OH	106.9	107.6	105.4	110.3	110.5	111.7	106.3	103.2	98.0	98.2
State College, PA	71.5	74.8	77.3	81.7	86.9	84.3	86.0	88.7	88.2	93.0
Staunton, VA	100.1	94.9	93.7	97.7	100.6	97.6	101.8	105.5	106.3	108.0
Stockton, CA	91.7	95.6	99.9	103.9	109.7	107.2	107.0	103.7	102.8	100.2
Sumter, SC	87.2	88.4	91.7	94.2	95.8	98.9	99.7	97.2	93.5	96.2
Syracuse, NY	87.6	88.6	91.8	93.6	94.2	93.7	95.4	95.3	94.5	98.6
Tallahassee, FL	94.3	96.9	98.9	102.3	102.5	102.4	106.3	104.4	101.1	100.3
Tampa-St. Petersburg-Clearwater, FL	82.7	86.4	90.7	96.4	101.5	103.9	104.9	101.7	98.0	98.8
Terre Haute, IN	89.4	91.9	96.4	98.9	98.7	100.6	101.3	101.0	96.5	101.4
Texarkana, TX-AR	85.8	89.1	90.0	94.8	97.3	99.5	100.2	101.0	99.6	99.8
The Villages, FL	40.9	45.1	52.7	55.5	63.8	70.4	76.7	75.1	76.9	80.6
Toledo, OH	98.5	99.7	100.3	102.2	105.6	106.3	104.8	98.4	93.2	96.5
Topeka, KS	91.3	92.7	92.9	95.3	94.6	91.3	95.6	96.9	95.6	95.2
Trenton-Princeton, NJ	87.7	89.5	91.2	91.7	93.9	94.5	93.3	97.3	92.9	94.1
Tucson, AZ	86.3	86.7	91.5	90.7	95.1	96.9	100.9	102.4	95.7	98.1
Tulsa, OK	78.6	78.7	78.4	81.0	85.4	93.6	94.2	96.8	91.5	90.2
Tuscaloosa, AL	78.8	83.1	88.8	95.8	101.4	101.6	105.5	101.0	93.1	96.2
Twin Falls, ID	80.6	81.1	81.8	86.8	92.3	96.9	101.2	100.7	91.3	95.9
Tyler, TX	76.0	76.5	78.6	87.8	91.8	97.5	97.2	95.7	94.6	97.7
Urban Honolulu, HI	77.5	79.2	82.9	87.2	91.5	93.0	94.9	96.5	94.8	96.9
Utica-Rome, NY	90.9	93.2	94.2	95.5	94.6	95.3	97.9	98.1	98.9	101.3
Valdosta, GA	86.1	89.4	92.7	94.1	97.5	99.1	100.5	103.2	100.5	101.2

Quantity Indexes for Real GDP by Metropolitan Area—*Continued*

(2012 = 100.0)

Metropolitan Statistical Area	2011	2012	2013	2014	2015	2016	2017	2018	2019	2020	2021
Rapid City, SD	96.4	100.0	98.2	100.8	102.8	103.0	103.5	105.6	107.7	108.6	114.0
Reading, PA	99.4	100.0	101.0	102.8	107.1	108.4	109.2	109.7	109.8	105.8	108.3
Redding, CA	104.4	100.0	99.6	101.1	102.5	107.3	114.9	111.7	117.4	114.2	116.0
Reno, NV	97.6	100.0	98.7	99.7	107.6	111.5	119.0	116.1	120.6	120.3	130.9
Richmond, VA	98.2	100.0	102.3	103.1	106.8	108.4	110.3	112.4	115.4	112.6	118.3
Riverside-San Bernardino-Ontario, CA	100.0	100.0	103.2	106.3	110.6	113.0	116.3	120.4	124.5	122.6	130.1
Roanoke, VA	100.5	100.0	101.8	103.2	105.2	103.4	102.3	103.7	102.5	100.8	105.6
Rochester, MN	97.8	100.0	102.2	103.5	106.3	107.5	111.4	115.7	117.8	115.7	121.1
Rochester, NY	99.8	100.0	99.0	98.1	99.9	99.9	100.1	101.0	104.5	99.4	104.2
Rockford, IL	99.5	100.0	98.2	98.8	100.3	99.8	100.9	104.1	103.3	94.3	99.5
Rocky Mount, NC	114.5	100.0	101.2	126.0	140.3	139.7	116.3	108.5	105.3	105.6	114.2
Rome, GA	102.6	100.0	97.1	101.3	104.3	108.4	104.8	103.8	102.7	97.9	103.9
Sacramento-Roseville-Folsom, CA	99.3	100.0	102.7	105.1	109.2	111.2	114.2	118.9	122.5	119.7	126.6
Saginaw, MI	100.1	100.0	100.4	98.1	98.2	100.5	100.0	102.9	105.3	100.6	107.1
St. Cloud, MN	99.9	100.0	103.4	107.7	108.5	112.3	114.9	115.7	116.0	113.7	118.8
St. George, UT	93.1	100.0	108.4	112.1	118.9	129.8	142.6	152.9	158.7	164.3	176.8
St. Joseph, MO-KS	93.2	100.0	102.4	98.5	95.4	95.9	100.2	97.6	100.7	97.1	99.1
St. Louis, MO-IL	99.0	100.0	100.7	102.3	102.9	102.8	102.0	103.7	105.4	101.4	106.5
Salem, OR	99.3	100.0	99.8	102.7	108.1	113.4	118.5	124.5	127.9	126.5	133.4
Salinas, CA	96.3	100.0	105.9	107.7	116.0	119.0	120.3	124.3	126.7	123.0	125.2
Salisbury, MD-DE	99.5	100.0	104.8	110.5	119.1	117.8	115.8	117.7	121.9	117.2	124.6
Salt Lake City, UT	97.6	100.0	101.5	104.1	107.7	112.7	116.9	124.5	129.3	130.7	140.0
San Angelo, TX	92.2	100.0	113.1	123.4	127.1	119.3	120.3	125.6	137.1	139.4	137.4
San Antonio-New Braunfels, TX	97.3	100.0	104.4	109.7	115.9	117.7	118.2	123.8	127.1	125.3	132.7
San Diego-Chula Vista-Carlsbad, CA	99.0	100.0	103.7	106.6	109.7	110.6	114.6	117.6	120.0	117.1	126.2
San Francisco-Oakland-Berkeley, CA	92.7	100.0	103.6	109.8	116.0	122.8	132.6	140.7	146.9	144.0	158.6
San Jose-Sunnyvale-Santa Clara, CA	96.3	100.0	109.3	117.4	128.1	136.3	147.5	159.9	167.6	175.4	198.6
San Luis Obispo-Paso Robles, CA	97.9	100.0	103.4	104.9	110.4	112.2	113.9	116.6	117.0	113.4	117.4
Santa Cruz-Watsonville, CA	101.9	100.0	102.9	105.1	105.6	107.6	109.1	113.2	120.7	119.6	127.7
Santa Fe, NM	101.8	100.0	100.7	102.8	100.1	100.3	99.4	101.2	101.3	92.8	98.7
Santa Maria-Santa Barbara, CA	97.7	100.0	101.5	103.7	108.8	109.6	112.5	117.2	117.9	118.0	124.3
Santa Rosa-Petaluma, CA	98.5	100.0	102.1	105.7	110.4	113.0	115.3	120.8	121.3	116.9	124.4
Savannah, GA	96.9	100.0	99.8	104.0	107.0	111.0	114.6	115.3	119.5	114.5	124.6
Scranton--Wilkes-Barre, PA	99.5	100.0	100.3	102.3	105.2	106.5	106.3	106.8	108.5	103.0	107.0
Seattle-Tacoma-Bellevue, WA	95.3	100.0	103.8	108.2	112.7	117.1	124.4	134.2	139.5	142.6	153.6
Sebastian-Vero Beach, FL	97.8	100.0	101.5	105.4	113.0	122.4	124.0	126.5	131.0	130.3	137.8
Sebring-Avon Park, FL	96.2	100.0	94.0	94.0	95.8	98.9	100.9	97.0	103.1	102.1	103.6
Sheboygan, WI	99.2	100.0	100.2	101.7	104.1	107.8	107.4	109.1	107.0	103.1	107.2
Sherman-Denison, TX	97.3	100.0	100.8	102.1	105.3	107.5	107.2	112.8	113.6	113.3	119.0
Shreveport-Bossier City, LA	105.3	100.0	92.3	92.0	94.9	94.2	96.5	99.4	101.6	95.7	99.3
Sierra Vista-Douglas, AZ	104.1	100.0	96.8	93.6	95.3	96.8	95.4	96.1	97.3	102.0	101.3
Sioux City, IA-NE-SD	104.7	100.0	98.2	98.2	101.4	102.6	100.4	105.5	106.1	107.0	113.9
Sioux Falls, SD	91.6	100.0	96.7	101.2	102.5	104.1	102.8	102.6	107.2	107.1	113.3
South Bend-Mishawaka, IN-MI	99.1	100.0	101.1	104.7	106.4	106.3	106.8	111.5	114.2	106.7	113.5
Spartanburg, SC	101.5	100.0	100.9	102.9	106.7	112.6	117.7	120.6	127.2	124.4	132.9
Spokane-Spokane Valley, WA	98.7	100.0	101.1	102.9	105.3	107.9	111.1	116.8	119.6	119.2	127.1
Springfield, IL	100.8	100.0	99.9	101.8	101.9	102.2	101.6	104.9	104.8	98.9	105.8
Springfield, MA	99.1	100.0	100.4	100.4	103.2	103.6	103.9	104.7	105.7	100.9	105.2
Springfield, MO	98.8	100.0	99.4	102.6	105.8	105.8	107.2	109.5	113.8	111.6	118.9
Springfield, OH	101.0	100.0	100.7	101.6	102.0	100.8	101.2	101.3	102.3	96.9	103.8
State College, PA	95.6	100.0	99.6	100.1	101.2	104.3	106.3	106.3	106.9	102.8	105.0
Staunton, VA	104.6	100.0	103.0	101.9	101.8	101.2	101.8	102.7	103.9	100.4	105.5
Stockton, CA	99.3	100.0	103.4	106.3	111.3	113.6	117.5	122.1	125.7	125.0	132.7
Sumter, SC	98.2	100.0	100.2	98.0	97.8	99.5	102.3	103.1	104.4	102.2	109.2
Syracuse, NY	97.3	100.0	100.6	102.0	105.1	103.9	104.4	105.1	107.6	103.6	109.1
Tallahassee, FL	99.5	100.0	97.4	99.0	99.9	102.3	105.8	105.5	107.1	106.8	111.6
Tampa-St. Petersburg-Clearwater, FL	98.6	100.0	101.9	103.9	108.0	111.5	113.9	117.4	121.2	120.9	130.4
Terre Haute, IN	101.5	100.0	111.0	110.5	103.0	101.8	100.1	99.8	99.3	97.1	101.9
Texarkana, TX-AR	100.9	100.0	96.0	94.3	94.6	95.0	93.6	92.9	93.0	92.2	93.4
The Villages, FL	84.4	100.0	110.5	107.4	113.1	116.0	122.0	131.9	158.6	168.8	186.4
Toledo, OH	101.2	100.0	102.6	108.9	103.6	103.5	104.2	106.6	109.2	102.1	108.9
Topeka, KS	98.9	100.0	97.4	99.7	100.6	102.6	103.2	107.1	104.8	105.2	108.2
Trenton-Princeton, NJ	94.3	100.0	99.9	99.6	100.2	104.0	103.7	106.2	117.7	119.6	127.6
Tucson, AZ	97.6	100.0	98.6	99.0	98.3	101.3	105.3	107.8	109.9	108.6	113.3
Tulsa, OK	94.9	100.0	101.1	109.1	111.9	105.6	108.3	111.8	113.7	108.4	108.7
Tuscaloosa, AL	104.9	100.0	102.0	99.1	97.2	99.9	103.2	103.9	108.7	103.5	107.6
Twin Falls, ID	95.7	100.0	104.0	110.5	111.2	117.5	120.7	126.2	129.4	130.9	134.4
Tyler, TX	98.7	100.0	100.9	99.3	102.1	102.3	102.4	107.4	110.8	110.7	113.7
Urban Honolulu, HI	98.9	100.0	101.4	102.0	104.8	106.4	108.4	108.7	107.1	96.3	101.4
Utica-Rome, NY	99.7	100.0	98.6	98.4	97.7	98.9	99.0	100.7	104.6	99.9	104.5
Valdosta, GA	99.9	100.0	99.9	101.1	101.9	103.5	104.8	106.2	110.4	110.7	113.4

Quantity Indexes for Real GDP by Metropolitan Area—*Continued*

(2012 = 100.0)

Metropolitan Statistical Area	2001	2002	2003	2004	2005	2006	2007	2008	2009	2010
Vallejo, CA	79.9	80.1	83.4	84.0	86.7	87.9	91.3	99.1	95.7	95.7
Victoria, TX	91.0	88.3	88.8	94.4	99.0	105.2	100.0	97.9	89.9	90.5
Vineland-Bridgeton, NJ	93.9	94.7	99.1	102.6	104.9	103.6	102.8	105.9	102.6	101.3
Virginia Beach-Norfolk-Newport News, VA-NC	87.6	89.4	93.3	97.0	100.6	101.6	102.9	103.4	101.5	101.9
Visalia, CA	85.8	79.9	83.8	92.6	101.4	95.8	106.6	100.7	92.6	101.9
Waco, TX	82.3	82.9	86.0	89.3	91.1	93.4	93.5	92.7	91.2	95.0
Walla Walla, WA	89.0	82.8	86.5	84.3	87.0	97.1	90.7	93.9	97.5	95.9
Warner Robins, GA	81.8	84.8	87.8	89.4	93.2	95.7	97.0	97.0	96.7	97.9
Washington-Arlington-Alexandria, DC-VA-MD-WV	74.1	76.9	79.7	84.4	88.2	89.3	90.8	93.8	93.4	97.8
Waterloo-Cedar Falls, IA	64.6	67.4	66.8	75.8	78.8	79.3	81.0	79.8	78.7	83.2
Watertown-Fort Drum, NY	68.7	69.3	72.4	76.5	83.0	87.5	89.1	93.7	96.5	100.8
Wausau-Weston, WI	83.5	85.6	89.8	93.6	97.2	98.4	98.9	97.0	93.6	95.9
Weirton-Steubenville, WV-OH	108.7	113.8	110.6	106.4	106.4	99.4	104.1	112.3	102.3	102.2
Wenatchee, WA	73.5	81.2	80.8	81.2	76.2	84.3	84.2	83.6	84.8	88.7
Wheeling, WV-OH	94.2	94.8	95.3	95.6	97.4	96.8	99.2	101.1	98.1	99.0
Wichita, KS	91.3	90.6	88.8	88.6	89.5	99.1	105.7	104.8	93.7	98.1
Wichita Falls, TX	93.4	95.4	94.1	93.4	93.3	98.5	97.6	99.0	97.1	97.5
Williamsport, PA	72.0	70.9	72.9	75.0	76.6	76.0	76.4	76.7	75.6	80.2
Wilmington, NC	80.6	82.5	85.5	88.6	95.5	101.1	105.8	106.5	102.3	104.1
Winchester, VA-WV	84.1	85.4	87.0	89.7	95.5	97.9	96.8	94.2	96.4	99.8
Winston-Salem, NC	95.4	95.2	97.6	102.0	104.5	107.8	105.6	107.8	103.2	103.4
Worcester, MA-CT	84.0	86.1	88.9	90.5	91.8	94.0	94.5	96.3	92.5	96.3
Yakima, WA	80.7	83.8	86.9	90.6	92.9	93.6	98.7	96.5	95.0	100.5
York-Hanover, PA	83.4	85.3	89.6	95.1	100.3	98.4	103.6	106.7	100.5	103.0
Youngstown-Warren-Boardman, OH-PA	102.0	105.0	105.6	108.8	111.1	110.9	108.7	105.6	95.3	98.1
Yuba City, CA	79.7	91.0	92.9	93.7	91.9	97.4	97.7	105.8	110.6	105.8
Yuma, AZ	79.8	92.4	89.9	99.9	106.7	109.1	115.3	106.9	105.0	109.9

Quantity Indexes for Real GDP by Metropolitan Area—*Continued*

(2012 = 100.0)

Metropolitan Statistical Area	2011	2012	2013	2014	2015	2016	2017	2018	2019	2020	2021
Vallejo, CA	92.3	100.0	104.8	105.6	106.5	108.7	110.3	116.9	136.1	138.3	141.2
Victoria, TX	93.8	100.0	102.5	103.8	96.1	88.6	87.5	91.7	90.5	85.5	87.7
Vineland-Bridgeton, NJ	99.4	100.0	99.0	98.6	100.0	102.1	100.0	103.6	102.8	100.0	103.8
Virginia Beach-Norfolk-Newport News, VA-NC	101.2	100.0	100.7	99.3	100.7	101.4	101.3	100.0	101.5	99.0	105.3
Visalia, CA	105.3	100.0	102.3	114.3	114.3	121.2	126.2	127.8	133.1	131.1	130.6
Waco, TX	96.4	100.0	108.0	112.4	110.6	112.2	118.8	123.2	124.5	120.2	126.9
Walla Walla, WA	100.2	100.0	99.0	101.1	108.9	115.1	120.1	121.4	120.6	110.2	111.0
Warner Robins, GA	99.1	100.0	99.2	98.9	100.6	101.7	104.3	105.8	109.8	108.3	112.3
Washington-Arlington-Alexandria, DC-VA-MD-WV	99.6	100.0	99.9	100.9	103.0	105.6	107.5	109.8	111.3	108.6	114.1
Waterloo-Cedar Falls, IA	82.6	100.0	88.1	98.6	92.5	83.0	83.8	85.5	84.8	84.2	90.2
Watertown-Fort Drum, NY	103.0	100.0	96.9	94.3	90.9	88.6	86.1	85.7	85.3	81.6	84.4
Wausau-Weston, WI	98.5	100.0	100.5	106.0	109.5	112.9	109.4	111.3	115.6	109.8	114.8
Weirton-Steubenville, WV-OH	99.5	100.0	113.0	127.8	129.3	104.7	106.5	104.1	111.2	115.3	114.1
Wenatchee, WA	98.2	100.0	97.1	97.5	102.6	105.1	108.5	110.4	109.5	107.5	112.0
Wheeling, WV-OH	99.8	100.0	109.4	123.5	135.8	144.1	155.6	155.8	155.6	158.5	147.9
Wichita, KS	100.6	100.0	94.2	100.4	105.7	114.5	116.9	115.9	117.8	115.9	119.1
Wichita Falls, TX	96.2	100.0	100.3	99.8	97.0	96.5	97.7	99.9	103.9	102.1	104.4
Williamsport, PA	90.9	100.0	100.3	108.5	106.5	100.7	102.4	100.9	101.5	99.0	100.2
Wilmington, NC	104.1	100.0	104.9	108.9	110.0	115.2	116.4	119.3	124.9	125.8	135.8
Winchester, VA-WV	100.1	100.0	102.8	102.1	106.2	108.0	108.0	110.5	113.3	114.8	120.2
Winston-Salem, NC	100.1	100.0	102.0	104.1	104.8	106.0	110.1	107.5	110.2	102.0	109.9
Worcester, MA-CT	99.4	100.0	101.0	101.4	103.6	104.1	104.5	106.6	107.3	103.9	109.0
Yakima, WA	99.3	100.0	100.4	106.2	106.0	110.4	112.2	118.0	119.7	118.6	118.4
York-Hanover, PA	102.1	100.0	101.9	102.1	102.7	104.2	106.5	105.5	107.6	101.3	106.5
Youngstown-Warren-Boardman, OH-PA	101.1	100.0	99.9	98.6	97.4	96.2	95.3	95.1	96.5	91.6	95.5
Yuba City, CA	103.3	100.0	103.8	98.6	100.9	103.2	106.0	110.8	112.0	112.3	116.6
Yuma, AZ	107.1	100.0	106.4	104.4	110.8	115.8	120.9	122.1	123.7	125.2	124.7

PART C
INCOME AND POVERTY BY STATE

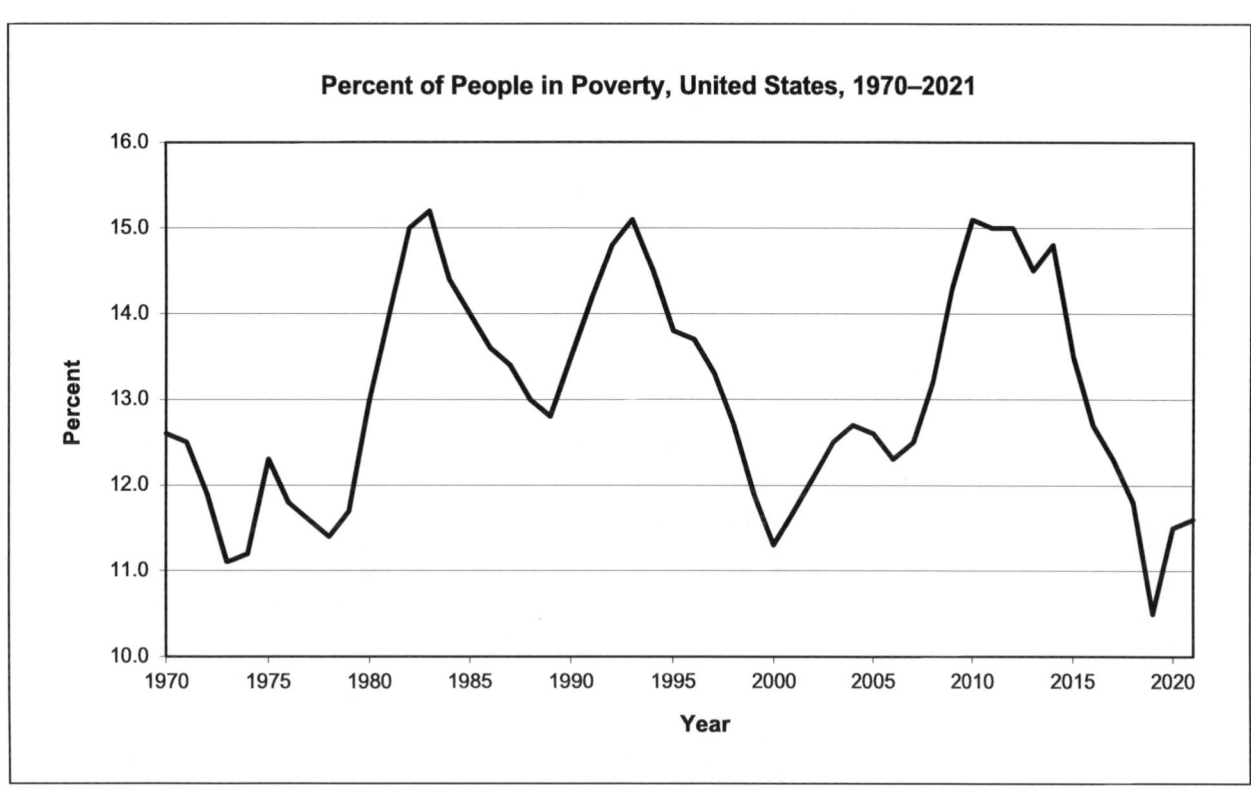

Percent of People in Poverty, United States, 1970–2021

HIGHLIGHTS

- The percent of people in poverty in the United States increased slightly from 11.5 percent in 2020 to 11.6 percent in 2021.

- The median household income in the United States decreased 0.6 percent to $70,784 in 2021. This was the second year in a row that median household income declined.

- In 2021, Maryland had the highest median household income at $97,332 (in 2021 dollars), followed by the District of Columbia ($90,640), New Hampshire ($88,841), New Jersey ($88,559), and Utah ($87,649). Mississippi and West Virginia had the lowest median household incomes at $46,637 and $46,836, respectively.

- The South was the region with the highest poverty rate among U.S. regions, with 13.2 percent of the population living in poverty in 2021, followed by the West at 12.7 percent, Northeast at 11.0. percent, and Midwest at 9.8 percent.

PART C NOTES AND DEFINITIONS: MEDIAN HOUSEHOLD INCOME AND POVERTY

Source: U.S. Department of Commerce, Bureau of the Census, https://www.census.gov.

These data are derived from the Current Population Survey (CPS), which is also the source of the widely followed monthly report on the civilian labor force, employment, and unemployment. In March of each year (with some data also collected in February and April), the households in this survey are asked additional questions concerning earnings and other income in the previous year. This additional information, informally known as the "March Supplement," is now formally known as the Current Population Survey Annual Social and Economic Supplement (CPS-ASEC). It was previously called the Annual Demographic Supplement.

The population represented by the income and poverty survey is the civilian noninstitutional population of the United States. It includes members of the armed forces in the United States living off post or with their families on post but excludes all other members of the armed forces. This is slightly different from the population base for the civilian employment and unemployment data, which excludes all armed forces households. As it is a survey of households, homeless persons are not included.

Definitions

A *household* consists of all persons who occupy a housing unit. A household includes the related family members and all the unrelated persons, if any (such as lodgers, foster children, wards, or employees), who share the housing unit. A person living alone in a housing unit or a group of unrelated persons sharing a housing unit as partners is also counted as a household. The count of households excludes group quarters.

Earnings includes all income from work, including wages, salaries, armed forces pay, commissions, tips, piece-rate payments, and cash bonuses, before deductions such as taxes, bonds, pensions, and union dues. This category also includes net income from farm and nonfarm self-employment. Wage and salary supplements that are paid directly by the employer, such as the employer share of Social Security taxes and the cost of employer-provided health insurance, are not included.

Income, in the official definition used in the survey, is money income, including *earnings* from work as defined above; unemployment compensation; workers' compensation; Social Security; Supplemental Security Income; cash public assistance (welfare payments); veterans' payments; survivor benefits; disability benefits; pension or retirement income; interest income; dividends (but not capital gains); rents, royalties, and payments from estates or trusts; educational assistance, such as scholarships or grants; child support; alimony; financial assistance from outside of the household; and other cash income regularly received, such as foster child payments, military family allotments, and foreign government pensions. Receipts not counted as income include capital gains or losses, withdrawals of bank deposits, money borrowed, tax refunds, gifts, and lump-sum inheritances or insurance payments.

Median income is the amount of income that divides a ranked income distribution into two equal groups, with half of the households having incomes above the median, and half having incomes below the median.

Historical income figures are shown in constant *2021 dollars*. All constant-dollar figures are converted from current-dollar values using the *CPI-U-RS* (the Consumer Price Index, All Urban, Research Series), compiled by the Bureau of Labor Statistics, which measures changes in prices for past periods using the methodologies of the current CPI-U.

The *number of people below poverty level*, or the number of poor people, is the number of people with family or individual incomes below a specified level representing the estimated cost of a minimum standard of living. These minimum levels vary by size and composition of family and are known as poverty thresholds. These *poverty thresholds* have been adjusted each year for price increases, using the percent change in the Consumer Price Index for All Urban Consumers (CPI-U).

The *poverty rate* for a demographic group is the number of poor people in that group expressed as a percentage of the total number of people in the group.

The data in this chapter were derived from the "Historical Income Tables" and "Historical Poverty Tables," which are available on the Census website.

A different set of estimates of median household income and poverty for states and smaller geographic units is also available. It is based on a different, more comprehensive Census survey, the American Community Survey (ACS); it is more precise but less timely, and it does not provide the historical record that is available in the CPS-ASEC data presented here. (The median household income data by state are available even farther back than shown here; they begin in 1984.) Further information on ACS and small-area statistics and on other research in measuring poverty can be found in the report referenced above and other reports posted on the Census website, under the subjects "Income" and "Poverty."

Median Household Income by State

(2021 CPI-U-RS adjusted dollars)

State	1990	1991	1992	1993	1994	1995	1996	1997	1998	1999	2000	2001	2002	2003	2004	2005	2006
United States	60,370	58,607	58,153	57,843	58,515	60,348	61,225	62,484	64,781	66,385	66,248	64,779	64,047	63,967	63,745	64,427	64,930
Alabama	47,092	47,363	48,989	46,440	49,324	46,029	52,272	53,930	60,418	59,134	55,888	53,936	56,789	55,014	52,667	51,666	51,124
Alaska	79,231	79,006	79,348	79,487	82,279	84,925	91,045	81,039	84,451	83,839	83,377	87,996	79,700	76,547	79,172	77,729	75,999
Arizona	58,921	59,796	55,727	56,490	56,754	54,658	54,575	55,283	61,791	60,348	62,766	65,509	60,007	60,789	63,043	62,924	62,850
Arkansas	45,940	45,590	45,333	42,657	46,366	45,716	46,788	44,175	46,089	48,418	46,853	51,143	48,911	47,257	50,301	50,981	49,918
California	67,118	65,490	66,253	63,086	64,078	65,542	66,952	67,025	68,195	71,169	73,862	72,501	71,640	72,801	70,773	71,977	74,518
Colorado	61,963	61,278	61,661	63,855	68,615	72,089	70,640	73,000	77,633	78,588	76,108	75,776	72,935	73,746	73,166	70,161	75,027
Connecticut	78,369	82,006	77,524	73,164	74,535	71,269	72,657	74,270	77,481	82,529	79,156	81,836	80,626	81,166	79,225	79,042	84,062
Delaware	62,106	63,391	67,724	66,773	65,061	61,857	67,809	72,663	69,068	76,061	79,461	76,091	74,982	72,386	69,087	71,254	70,637
District of Columbia	55,227	58,138	57,415	50,554	54,619	54,454	55,142	53,797	55,698	63,080	65,036	63,154	59,004	66,516	62,475	62,573	65,302
Florida	53,801	53,016	51,914	52,861	53,129	52,678	52,857	54,801	58,157	58,449	61,303	55,871	57,425	57,549	58,283	59,787	61,528
Georgia	55,568	52,938	54,662	58,624	57,070	60,388	56,057	61,907	64,415	64,311	66,107	65,313	64,847	62,668	58,928	63,871	66,469
Hawaii	78,471	72,458	79,939	78,989	76,635	75,888	72,058	69,118	68,017	72,596	81,324	72,773	71,438	76,542	80,867	82,868	81,457
Idaho	51,019	50,806	52,588	57,415	57,195	57,868	59,874	56,404	61,108	58,398	59,339	58,663	56,958	62,570	63,780	61,437	62,252
Illinois	65,610	62,027	59,890	60,835	63,624	67,423	68,232	69,708	71,933	75,575	72,675	70,827	64,501	66,677	66,251	67,308	65,563
Indiana	54,291	52,699	54,155	54,573	50,524	59,124	60,630	65,665	66,191	66,616	64,473	61,942	61,990	62,648	60,862	59,018	61,166
Iowa	55,017	55,547	54,560	53,070	59,993	62,903	57,287	57,044	61,673	67,040	64,671	62,858	61,993	61,111	62,389	64,669	64,829
Kansas	60,318	56,990	57,603	55,119	51,366	53,733	56,210	61,582	61,159	60,923	64,779	63,532	64,364	65,317	59,046	58,448	61,361
Kentucky	49,961	46,230	44,579	45,132	48,234	52,793	55,913	56,485	60,395	55,035	57,215	58,963	55,519	54,543	51,201	51,038	53,189
Louisiana	45,172	49,216	48,288	48,717	46,567	49,497	52,203	56,161	52,870	53,266	48,464	51,117	51,360	49,479	52,379	51,785	49,152
Maine	55,372	54,214	56,219	50,802	54,982	59,962	59,852	55,337	59,375	63,393	58,795	56,164	55,656	54,804	59,424	61,085	61,483
Maryland	78,342	71,886	70,618	73,947	71,091	72,682	75,889	78,829	83,325	85,159	86,040	82,116	85,187	77,251	82,105	84,156	85,765
Massachusetts	73,080	69,478	69,016	68,624	73,452	68,313	68,128	70,957	70,546	71,782	73,762	80,157	75,292	75,244	74,795	77,904	74,533
Michigan	60,358	62,480	61,249	60,474	63,992	64,509	67,664	65,417	69,673	75,182	71,804	69,103	64,509	66,483	60,757	63,880	65,531
Minnesota	63,439	57,348	58,808	62,362	61,018	67,178	70,711	71,871	79,843	76,730	85,592	80,814	82,491	78,003	80,668	75,398	75,720
Mississippi	40,682	37,887	39,046	41,087	46,066	46,998	46,019	48,121	48,513	52,979	54,113	46,268	46,639	48,329	49,972	45,720	46,788
Missouri	55,106	54,327	51,936	53,105	54,754	61,674	59,108	61,721	66,974	67,505	71,149	63,415	64,601	64,623	60,586	59,782	60,051
Montana	47,128	48,298	50,350	49,009	50,113	49,157	49,481	49,325	52,606	50,630	51,712	49,282	52,608	50,367	48,823	51,892	55,371
Nebraska	55,408	57,484	57,037	57,412	57,663	58,316	58,675	58,579	60,663	63,008	65,869	66,900	64,631	64,936	62,957	66,648	64,854
Nevada	64,564	64,075	60,568	66,310	65,057	63,904	66,483	65,606	66,232	67,633	72,192	69,649	67,896	66,722	67,872	67,046	70,427
New Hampshire	82,270	70,096	74,857	70,291	63,922	69,371	67,978	69,226	74,899	75,127	80,346	78,743	83,547	82,055	81,691	79,249	83,477
New Jersey	78,094	77,911	74,029	74,986	76,681	77,788	81,884	81,085	83,009	81,128	79,524	79,418	82,410	82,761	79,476	88,128	91,680
New Mexico	50,483	51,631	49,087	49,543	48,796	46,029	43,274	50,801	52,550	53,136	55,366	50,813	53,548	51,839	56,884	54,165	53,920
New York	63,693	61,852	58,941	58,687	57,853	58,492	61,083	60,446	62,297	65,231	64,282	64,604	63,378	63,184	64,198	65,609	64,958
North Carolina	53,084	52,240	52,715	53,360	54,616	56,634	61,413	60,517	59,705	60,770	60,453	58,541	55,146	55,049	57,856	58,488	53,609
North Dakota	50,937	50,370	51,173	52,061	51,286	51,516	54,287	53,461	50,486	53,281	56,791	54,907	54,670	59,673	56,392	58,678	55,293
Ohio	60,511	57,953	59,611	57,924	57,773	61,880	58,772	61,013	64,848	64,416	67,781	64,099	64,462	64,265	61,906	61,474	61,830
Oklahoma	49,162	49,534	47,994	48,621	48,952	46,596	47,330	52,937	56,188	53,314	51,168	54,625	55,060	53,016	56,959	52,354	52,317
Oregon	59,035	58,731	60,604	61,355	57,050	64,417	61,225	62,893	65,084	66,259	67,051	63,314	63,130	61,486	58,943	61,413	63,435
Pennsylvania	58,479	59,076	56,722	57,387	58,156	61,141	60,202	63,349	64,998	61,592	66,541	66,729	64,181	63,398	63,417	64,391	65,302
Rhode Island	64,453	59,988	57,766	62,042	57,906	62,620	63,802	58,756	67,782	69,685	66,574	70,140	64,059	66,024	68,923	68,819	72,386
South Carolina	57,935	53,426	52,348	48,237	54,130	51,484	59,798	57,852	55,422	59,478	59,274	57,888	57,104	56,821	55,631	55,949	53,367
South Dakota	49,539	47,933	49,845	51,355	53,925	52,382	50,933	50,139	54,621	58,444	57,547	60,856	57,197	58,362	59,105	60,011	61,193
Tennessee	45,549	47,571	46,160	46,477	51,941	51,385	53,114	51,730	56,795	59,576	53,793	54,892	55,923	55,410	54,741	54,803	54,816
Texas	56,912	53,952	53,060	53,188	55,778	56,740	57,050	59,225	59,613	63,109	60,913	62,680	60,634	57,991	59,522	57,607	58,337
Utah	60,771	54,502	65,015	66,258	64,776	64,605	63,892	72,227	73,801	75,118	75,020	72,624	72,281	72,764	73,144	76,230	73,587
Vermont	62,699	56,718	62,175	57,517	64,932	59,901	55,819	59,188	65,593	67,833	62,467	62,579	64,938	63,883	68,051	70,515	70,022
Virginia	70,713	70,301	72,507	67,456	68,278	64,148	67,640	72,534	72,226	74,536	74,409	77,071	74,954	80,897	73,532	72,198	76,943
Washington	64,743	66,085	64,349	66,016	60,817	62,990	63,267	75,244	79,002	74,177	67,092	65,181	68,236	70,154	71,780	70,435	73,715
West Virginia	44,632	45,030	38,478	41,513	42,737	44,062	43,552	46,414	44,488	47,790	46,402	45,519	44,339	48,381	47,985	50,685	51,753
Wisconsin	61,919	60,566	63,225	58,815	64,181	72,530	69,003	66,857	68,850	74,494	71,135	69,562	69,324	68,325	65,755	62,096	69,632
Wyoming	59,396	56,514	57,342	54,512	60,104	55,837	53,395	56,436	58,725	60,760	62,523	60,930	60,051	62,840	65,274	62,191	63,367

Median Household Income by State—*Continued*

(2021 CPI-U-RS adjusted dollars)

State	2007	2008	2009[1]	2010	2011	2012	2013[2]	2013[3]	2014	2015	2016	2017	2017[4]	2018	2019	2020	2021
United States	65,801	63,455	63,011	61,364	60,428	60,313	60,507	62,425	61,468	64,631	66,657	67,832	67,571	68,168	72,808	71,186	70,784
Alabama	55,294	56,105	50,609	50,975	51,417	51,384	48,207	55,126	48,432	50,900	53,314	56,493	56,219	53,879	59,558	57,243	56,929
Alaska	82,515	80,720	77,982	72,039	69,334	75,246	71,222	84,427	77,473	85,898	85,494	79,834	86,196	74,161	83,079	78,236	81,133
Arizona	61,848	59,180	57,899	58,400	58,698	55,616	58,949	61,290	56,424	59,751	64,468	67,559	65,984	67,201	74,897	70,220	70,821
Arkansas	53,438	49,936	46,252	48,053	49,862	46,128	46,504	45,872	51,461	48,944	51,830	53,969	54,988	53,712	57,799	53,148	50,784
California	73,007	71,921	71,058	67,600	64,428	67,410	67,018	70,823	69,292	72,774	75,235	77,102	77,410	76,055	82,772	81,278	81,575
Colorado	80,089	76,877	70,800	75,009	70,781	67,688	73,825	79,115	69,811	76,159	79,671	81,980	82,877	78,801	76,832	87,689	84,954
Connecticut	84,019	81,594	82,092	82,189	78,973	75,954	78,962	80,721	80,374	83,355	85,720	80,441	82,125	78,561	92,507	83,141	80,958
Delaware	71,507	63,959	65,969	68,759	65,989	57,896	60,833	63,014	65,895	66,049	65,536	68,878	71,799	70,145	78,628	73,292	68,687
District of Columbia	66,521	70,125	67,269	70,893	66,702	77,135	70,684	69,964	78,216	80,133	80,141	92,159	89,838	92,521	98,675	92,337	90,640
Florida	59,986	56,585	57,763	54,876	54,454	54,466	55,785	56,538	52,856	55,836	57,779	59,332	58,674	58,959	61,856	60,460	59,734
Georgia	63,716	58,314	54,862	54,940	55,501	56,890	55,265	54,744	56,768	58,058	60,434	63,018	64,089	60,229	60,012	62,033	61,497
Hawaii	83,863	77,606	70,444	74,145	71,285	66,515	71,538	74,831	81,591	73,778	81,440	81,320	81,346	86,433	93,265	84,600	82,199
Idaho	64,427	59,818	59,215	58,592	57,295	56,654	60,307	56,462	61,217	59,037	63,863	66,546	65,760	63,365	69,932	69,841	76,918
Illinois	68,778	67,178	66,926	63,173	61,132	61,166	66,631	62,835	62,910	69,088	69,307	71,410	72,913	75,684	78,845	77,805	79,253
Indiana	62,159	58,683	56,084	57,458	53,657	54,569	58,892	57,613	55,056	59,447	63,332	65,070	64,953	64,621	70,679	69,925	70,190
Iowa	64,065	63,252	64,206	61,041	60,627	63,180	63,904	70,080	66,225	69,593	66,719	70,163	70,148	74,144	70,002	72,030	72,429
Kansas	63,527	60,395	56,606	57,352	55,712	59,115	59,978	55,709	61,224	62,743	64,140	63,964	62,889	68,987	77,523	76,495	75,979
Kentucky	51,679	51,907	54,007	51,188	48,117	48,573	49,113	52,282	49,014	48,474	51,223	56,753	54,901	58,863	58,989	59,405	55,629
Louisiana	54,117	49,907	57,512	48,941	49,085	46,207	46,158	54,083	48,579	52,516	47,641	48,524	48,151	53,919	54,797	53,576	57,206
Maine	62,737	59,576	60,131	59,689	59,992	58,116	58,389	64,023	59,237	58,044	57,418	57,102	58,928	63,295	70,523	66,667	71,139
Maryland	85,970	80,369	81,251	79,951	83,151	84,926	76,028	80,794	87,252	84,162	83,277	89,619	90,734	93,031	101,283	99,215	97,332
Massachusetts	76,582	76,091	75,158	75,882	76,435	75,256	73,350	72,844	72,344	77,605	81,591	80,935	84,269	93,163	92,949	91,912	86,566
Michigan	64,670	62,806	58,222	57,628	59,010	59,129	56,851	65,898	59,575	61,986	64,458	63,774	62,342	65,222	67,951	67,399	64,488
Minnesota	76,051	69,286	71,002	65,156	69,804	73,055	70,954	74,935	77,032	78,599	79,278	79,491	77,341	77,488	86,292	82,431	80,441
Mississippi	48,832	45,975	44,404	47,521	49,606	43,318	47,589	37,673	40,692	45,786	46,402	48,014	47,837	46,159	47,463	47,242	46,637
Missouri	60,263	58,075	61,735	57,057	55,261	58,832	58,610	53,941	64,873	67,696	62,115	62,873	62,481	66,600	64,218	65,081	63,594
Montana	57,184	54,117	51,188	51,407	48,625	53,304	51,412	50,328	58,541	58,775	64,440	65,307	63,450	62,233	63,792	59,390	64,999
Nebraska	64,414	63,991	62,780	65,384	67,143	61,707	62,645	67,129	65,148	69,158	67,035	65,895	65,855	72,911	77,437	75,622	78,109
Nevada	70,811	69,057	65,108	63,760	56,793	55,958	52,853	60,399	57,135	59,476	62,583	62,503	64,151	66,749	75,143	64,020	64,340
New Hampshire	88,519	83,478	81,181	82,979	79,534	80,177	83,088	80,498	84,081	86,541	86,100	82,675	83,591	87,769	92,093	93,045	88,841
New Jersey	79,260	82,381	81,999	78,415	75,258	78,845	71,974	74,271	74,740	78,173	77,303	80,681	78,739	80,033	92,969	89,543	88,559
New Mexico	58,103	53,110	55,118	56,206	50,683	51,337	49,076	46,792	53,482	51,598	54,703	52,892	50,401	52,096	56,287	53,283	53,463
New York	64,112	63,655	63,567	61,993	61,131	56,368	62,725	58,209	62,216	66,334	69,364	69,020	68,021	72,586	76,149	71,865	72,920
North Carolina	56,998	54,155	53,047	54,582	54,575	49,125	48,006	53,981	53,594	58,091	60,701	55,642	54,762	57,583	64,814	63,252	62,891
North Dakota	61,835	62,608	63,388	63,519	68,042	65,928	61,613	68,910	69,570	65,659	67,950	66,190	66,500	71,756	74,216	67,109	68,882
Ohio	64,315	59,205	58,077	57,143	53,902	52,461	54,052	59,120	56,870	60,955	60,951	66,059	67,076	66,500	68,527	63,198	62,689
Oklahoma	56,609	58,167	58,075	53,677	58,498	57,228	50,999	53,777	54,069	53,837	57,516	60,796	57,343	58,732	62,946	54,921	60,096
Oregon	65,805	65,252	62,151	63,016	62,205	61,210	65,596	57,082	67,445	69,569	66,765	71,411	69,077	74,626	78,860	80,443	81,855
Pennsylvania	63,448	64,842	60,979	60,166	60,254	61,362	62,852	64,255	63,204	69,061	68,847	69,823	67,736	69,619	74,800	74,094	72,627
Rhode Island	71,010	67,161	65,362	64,287	59,196	66,281	67,349	65,614	67,168	63,699	69,467	73,378	72,285	67,183	74,344	83,918	74,982
South Carolina	57,915	53,177	52,028	51,927	48,392	52,492	50,966	50,749	51,469	53,017	61,347	60,757	60,278	61,980	65,735	63,159	62,542
South Dakota	60,804	65,091	58,009	56,478	57,011	58,420	63,436	62,224	60,776	62,972	64,863	62,883	62,905	64,158	68,095	73,467	73,893
Tennessee	53,962	50,083	51,289	48,058	51,042	50,830	49,510	50,514	50,079	54,126	57,969	61,055	61,128	60,487	60,011	57,542	62,166
Texas	60,325	58,645	60,097	58,861	59,213	61,388	61,775	59,886	61,717	64,582	65,649	65,537	66,417	64,506	71,474	71,599	67,404
Utah	70,118	78,888	74,042	70,611	66,995	68,972	73,354	71,118	72,609	75,772	76,188	78,826	77,135	83,152	89,574	87,915	87,649
Vermont	62,077	63,964	66,227	69,648	62,611	65,710	63,889	76,320	69,545	68,037	68,687	70,521	70,385	75,599	78,746	70,398	76,079
Virginia	77,496	78,192	76,586	75,176	75,594	76,409	78,775	76,779	75,785	70,315	75,025	78,798	78,265	83,243	86,172	86,053	80,268
Washington	76,080	71,438	76,448	69,941	68,633	73,519	70,021	74,467	67,666	76,899	79,382	83,357	79,071	86,021	87,381	85,157	87,648
West Virginia	55,136	47,928	51,255	53,271	50,489	51,489	46,879	50,174	45,309	48,973	50,077	50,170	51,900	54,566	56,916	54,396	46,836
Wisconsin	67,168	64,587	64,859	62,703	62,848	62,751	64,374	60,259	66,534	63,384	67,535	70,130	70,164	67,574	71,380	70,553	69,943
Wyoming	63,850	67,283	66,420	65,007	65,807	67,992	64,888	78,566	63,796	69,673	65,291	63,925	65,803	67,477	69,027	68,506	71,052

[1] Beginning with 2009 income data, the Census Bureau expanded the upper income interval used to calculate medians and Gini indexes to $250,000 or more. Medians falling in the upper open-ended interval are plugged with "$250,000." Before 2009, the upper open-ended interval was $100,000 and a plug of "$100,000" was used.

[2] The 2014 CPS ASEC included redesigned questions for income and health insurance coverage. All of the approximately 98,000 addresses were eligible to receive the redesigned set of health insurance coverage questions. The redesigned income questions were implemented to a subsample of the 98,000 addresses using a probability split panel design. Approximately 68,000 addresses were eligible to receive a set of income questions similar to those used in the 2013 CPS ASEC and the remaining 30,000 addresses were eligible to receive the redesigned income questions. The source of these 2013 estimates is the portion of the CPS ASEC sample which received the income questions consistent with the 2013 CPS ASEC, approximately 68,000 addresses.

[3] The source of these 2013 estimates is the portion of the CPS ASEC sample which received the redesigned income questions, approximately 30,000 addresses.

[4] Estimates reflect the implementation of an updated data processing system, allowing users to evaluate the impact, and should be used to make comparisons to 2018 and subsequent years.

Historical Poverty Rates by State

(Percent of population.)

State	2000	2001	2002	2003	2004	2005	2006	2007	2008	2009	2010	2011	2012	2013[1]	2013[2]	2014	2015	2016	2017	2017[3]	2018	2019	2020	2021
United States	11.3	11.7	12.1	12.5	12.7	12.6	12.3	12.5	13.2	14.3	15.1	15.0	15.0	14.5	14.8	14.8	13.5	12.7	12.3	12.3	11.8	10.5	11.5	11.6
Alabama	13.3	15.9	14.5	15.0	16.9	16.7	14.3	14.5	14.3	16.6	17.2	15.4	16.2	16.7	18.5	17.8	16.3	16.2	15.0	15.3	16.0	12.9	14.9	15.9
Alaska	7.6	8.5	8.8	9.6	9.1	10.0	8.9	7.6	8.2	11.7	12.5	11.7	10.0	10.9	9.7	11.9	9.2	12.6	14.4	12.1	13.1	10.2	13.4	11.4
Arizona	11.7	14.6	13.5	13.5	14.4	15.2	14.4	14.3	18.0	21.2	18.8	17.2	19.0	20.2	17.8	21.2	17.2	16.1	13.2	13.6	12.8	9.9	10.9	12.6
Arkansas	16.5	17.8	19.8	17.8	15.1	13.8	17.7	13.8	15.3	18.9	15.3	18.7	20.1	17.1	13.9	18.4	16.1	16.0	14.8	14.9	15.9	14.1	14.1	16.8
California	12.7	12.6	13.1	13.1	13.2	13.2	12.2	12.7	14.6	15.3	16.3	16.9	15.9	14.9	15.1	15.8	13.9	13.9	12.4	12.1	11.9	10.1	11.1	11.9
Colorado	9.8	8.7	9.8	9.7	10.0	11.4	9.7	9.8	11.0	12.3	12.3	13.2	11.9	10.6	10.7	12.3	9.9	8.5	7.7	8.9	9.1	9.3	9.5	7.9
Connecticut	7.7	7.3	8.3	8.1	10.1	9.3	8.0	8.9	8.1	8.4	8.6	10.1	10.3	11.3	10.9	8.6	9.1	9.8	10.9	10.6	10.2	8.3	11.2	8.0
Delaware	8.4	6.7	9.1	7.3	9.0	9.2	9.3	9.3	9.6	12.3	12.2	13.7	13.5	14.0	11.2	11.0	11.1	11.6	9.2	8.8	7.4	6.5	10.5	11.7
D.C.	15.2	18.2	17.0	16.8	17.0	21.3	18.3	18.0	16.5	17.9	19.5	19.9	18.4	21.3	23.2	19.0	16.6	16.3	13.6	13.9	14.7	12.5	16.8	14.0
Florida	11.0	12.7	12.6	12.7	11.6	11.1	11.5	12.5	13.1	14.6	16.0	14.9	15.3	14.9	14.8	16.7	16.2	13.0	13.7	13.4	13.7	11.5	13.3	12.6
Georgia	12.1	12.9	11.2	11.9	13.0	14.4	12.6	13.6	15.5	18.4	18.8	18.4	18.1	16.3	18.5	16.8	18.1	15.4	13.3	13.1	14.8	12.1	13.3	14.0
Hawaii	8.9	11.4	11.3	9.3	8.6	8.6	9.2	7.5	9.9	12.5	12.4	12.1	13.8	11.1	10.6	10.8	10.9	9.3	10.3	10.6	9.2	8.4	10.9	10.9
Idaho	12.5	11.5	11.3	10.2	9.9	9.9	9.5	9.9	12.2	13.7	13.8	15.7	14.4	12.9	12.4	12.4	12.3	11.1	11.7	11.5	11.5	7.1	9.1	9.3
Illinois	10.7	10.1	12.8	12.6	12.3	11.5	10.6	10.0	12.3	13.2	14.1	14.2	12.6	13.3	13.6	13.7	10.9	12.1	10.9	11.5	10.3	9.3	8.0	10.7
Indiana	8.5	8.5	9.1	9.9	11.6	12.6	10.6	11.8	14.3	16.1	16.3	15.6	15.2	11.6	16.5	14.6	13.5	11.8	11.4	11.7	11.6	10.1	12.1	10.4
Iowa	8.3	7.4	9.2	8.9	10.9	11.3	10.3	8.9	9.5	10.7	10.3	10.4	10.3	10.8	13.2	10.3	10.4	9.8	9.1	7.5	8.9	9.5	9.2	9.7
Kansas	8.0	10.1	10.1	10.8	11.4	12.5	12.8	11.7	12.7	13.7	14.5	14.3	14.0	13.2	11.4	12.1	14.2	11.2	14.7	14.3	7.5	9.5	9.3	7.1
Kentucky	12.6	12.6	14.2	14.4	17.8	14.8	16.8	15.5	17.1	17.0	17.7	16.0	17.9	20.0	22.0	20.0	19.5	15.2	14.4	13.5	15.7	13.6	13.9	16.2
Louisiana	17.2	16.2	17.5	17.0	16.8	18.3	17.0	16.1	18.2	14.3	21.5	21.1	21.1	19.2	21.2	23.1	18.6	20.2	21.4	20.5	19.0	17.9	15.5	18.4
Maine	10.1	10.3	13.4	11.6	11.6	12.6	10.2	10.9	12.0	11.4	12.6	13.4	12.8	12.3	11.4	14.6	12.3	12.7	12.0	12.4	11.6	10.4	8.0	9.1
Maryland	7.4	7.2	7.4	8.6	9.9	9.7	8.4	8.8	8.7	9.6	10.9	9.3	9.9	10.3	10.5	9.8	9.6	7.1	7.8	7.6	8.0	7.0	9.4	7.7
Massachusetts	9.8	8.9	10.0	10.3	9.3	10.1	12.0	11.2	11.3	10.8	10.9	10.6	11.3	11.9	12.1	13.6	11.5	9.6	10.6	11.2	8.7	7.5	8.4	7.6
Michigan	9.9	9.4	11.6	11.4	13.3	12.0	13.3	10.8	13.0	14.0	15.7	15.0	13.7	14.5	12.7	14.8	12.8	11.1	12.7	11.5	10.5	10.2	11.2	11.7
Minnesota	5.7	7.4	6.5	7.4	7.0	8.1	8.2	9.3	9.9	11.1	10.8	10.0	10.0	12.0	11.0	8.3	7.8	8.7	9.2	8.5	7.9	5.7	8.5	6.9
Mississippi	14.9	19.3	18.4	16.0	18.7	20.1	20.6	22.6	18.1	23.1	22.5	17.4	22.0	22.5	19.1	22.1	19.1	21.1	18.3	18.5	19.6	19.2	17.6	17.4
Missouri	9.2	9.7	9.9	10.7	12.2	11.6	11.4	12.8	13.3	15.5	15.0	15.4	15.2	13.7	17.5	10.4	9.8	13.0	11.1	11.4	12.4	9.4	10.7	12.3
Montana	14.1	13.3	13.5	15.1	14.2	13.8	13.5	13.0	12.9	13.5	14.5	16.5	13.4	14.5	10.5	12.0	11.9	11.7	9.7	10.3	10.3	9.7	10.9	10.7
Nebraska	8.6	9.4	10.6	9.8	9.5	9.5	10.2	9.9	10.6	9.9	10.2	10.2	12.2	11.0	10.5	11.8	10.3	9.6	10.4	11.5	10.5	8.7	8.3	8.1
Nevada	8.8	7.1	8.9	10.9	10.9	10.6	9.5	9.7	10.8	13.0	16.6	15.5	15.8	17.4	14.5	17.0	13.0	10.1	13.7	13.2	13.0	10.4	12.9	12.8
New Hampshire	4.5	6.5	5.8	5.8	5.5	5.6	5.4	5.8	7.0	7.8	6.5	7.6	8.1	9.0	5.5	7.2	7.3	6.4	6.6	7.2	6.1	3.7	6.2	6.9
New Jersey	7.3	8.1	7.9	8.6	8.0	6.8	8.8	8.7	9.2	9.3	11.1	11.4	9.3	11.1	9.9	11.3	11.2	9.4	8.6	9.9	8.2	6.3	8.2	7.6
New Mexico	17.5	18.0	17.9	18.1	16.5	17.9	16.9	14.0	19.3	19.3	18.3	22.2	20.4	21.7	25.8	20.0	19.7	17.8	18.6	19.7	16.6	15.3	16.6	18.0
New York	13.9	14.2	14.0	14.3	15.0	14.5	14.0	14.5	14.2	15.8	16.0	16.0	17.2	14.5	17.3	14.0	14.2	11.9	13.4	12.7	11.1	12.5	11.8	12.5
North Carolina	12.5	12.5	14.3	15.7	14.6	13.1	13.8	15.5	13.9	16.9	17.4	15.4	17.2	18.6	14.7	17.1	15.3	13.6	14.5	15.2	13.1	12.7	13.8	11.8
North Dakota	10.4	13.8	11.6	9.7	9.7	11.2	11.4	9.3	11.8	10.9	12.6	9.9	11.4	9.9	13.2	9.7	10.7	11.1	11.3	12.4	9.7	8.1	10.7	8.5
Ohio	10.0	10.5	9.8	10.9	11.6	12.3	12.1	12.8	13.7	13.3	15.4	15.1	15.4	13.7	14.9	15.6	13.6	13.7	12.7	12.9	11.9	12.4	12.7	11.6
Oklahoma	14.9	15.1	14.1	12.8	10.8	15.6	15.2	13.4	13.6	12.9	16.3	13.9	18.0	14.0	21.2	17.3	14.2	14.6	12.6	12.8	13.4	10.8	15.5	15.1
Oregon	10.9	11.8	10.9	12.5	11.8	12.0	11.8	12.8	10.6	13.4	14.3	14.4	13.5	15.1	14.0	14.4	11.9	11.8	10.2	11.5	9.7	8.1	9.4	9.2
Pennsylvania	8.6	9.6	9.5	10.5	11.4	11.2	11.3	10.4	11.0	11.1	12.2	12.6	13.9	12.4	11.2	12.5	12.3	11.1	11.2	10.9	11.8	8.7	10.7	10.8
Rhode Island	10.2	9.6	11.0	11.5	11.5	12.1	10.5	9.5	12.7	13.0	14.0	13.4	13.6	13.5	9.3	11.3	11.8	11.4	12.2	11.3	8.9	9.2	8.5	9.4
South Carolina	11.1	15.1	14.3	12.7	14.9	15.0	11.2	14.1	14.0	13.7	16.9	19.0	16.7	15.9	19.3	16.5	14.3	14.1	15.6	15.2	12.8	15.1	13.4	13.7
South Dakota	10.7	8.4	11.5	12.7	13.5	11.8	10.7	9.4	13.1	14.1	13.6	14.5	12.8	10.3	13.3	12.8	13.9	14.5	10.4	10.7	10.6	10.6	11.6	8.4
Tennessee	13.5	14.1	14.8	14.0	15.9	14.9	14.9	14.8	15.0	16.5	16.7	16.3	18.6	18.1	15.5	17.3	14.7	14.9	11.5	11.3	12.0	13.1	13.1	10.6
Texas	15.5	14.9	15.6	17.0	16.5	16.2	16.4	16.5	15.9	17.3	18.4	17.4	17.0	16.8	16.9	16.4	14.7	13.8	13.4	13.2	13.7	11.1	14.0	13.5
Utah	7.6	10.5	9.9	9.1	10.1	9.2	9.3	9.6	7.6	9.7	10.0	11.0	11.0	8.3	12.2	10.2	9.3	8.6	8.6	8.7	6.9	7.3	7.4	7.9
Vermont	10.0	9.7	9.9	8.5	7.8	7.6	7.8	9.9	9.0	9.4	10.8	11.6	11.2	8.7	6.8	9.3	10.7	9.6	10.2	8.6	9.7	8.6	8.6	7.5
Virginia	8.3	8.0	9.9	10.0	9.4	9.2	8.6	8.6	10.3	10.7	10.7	11.4	10.6	10.4	9.8	10.2	10.9	11.4	10.3	10.5	9.8	8.8	7.8	9.8
Washington	10.8	10.7	11.0	12.6	11.4	10.2	8.0	10.2	10.4	11.7	11.6	12.5	11.6	12.0	12.2	12.0	11.4	11.0	9.9	10.9	8.6	7.0	8.2	7.7
West Virginia	14.7	16.4	16.8	17.4	14.2	15.4	15.3	14.8	14.5	15.8	16.8	17.5	16.7	17.3	19.8	20.6	14.5	18.0	17.3	17.1	15.9	13.9	14.2	16.9
Wisconsin	9.3	7.9	8.6	9.8	12.4	10.2	10.1	11.0	9.8	10.8	10.1	13.1	11.4	11.0	13.5	10.9	11.4	10.7	9.5	9.2	8.6	8.4	8.0	9.3
Wyoming	10.8	8.7	9.0	8.8	10.0	10.6	10.0	10.9	10.1	9.2	9.6	10.7	9.6	11.8	11.4	9.7	9.8	10.9	12.4	13.0	9.5	9.2	9.7	9.4

[1]The source of these 2013 estimates is the portion of the CPS ASEC sample that received the income questions consistent with the 2013 CPS ASEC, approximately 68,000 addresses.
[2]The 2014 CPS ASEC included redesigned questions for income and health insurance coverage. All of the approximately 98,000 addresses were eligible to receive the redesigned set of health insurance coverage questions. The redesigned income questions were implemented to a subsample of the 98,000 addresses using a probability split panel design. Approximately 68,000 addresses were eligible to receive a set of income questions similar to those used in the 2013 CPS ASEC, and the remaining 30,000 addresses were eligible to receive the redesigned income questions. The source of these 2013 estimates is the portion of the CPS ASEC sample that received the redesigned income questions, approximately 30,000 addresses.
[3]Estimates reflect the implementation of an updated processing system and should be used to make comparisons to 2018 and subsequent years.

Historical Poverty Rates by Region

(Numbers in thousands, percent.)

Year	All Regions Below Poverty		Northeast Below Poverty		Midwest Below Poverty		South Below Poverty		West Below Poverty	
	Number	Percent	Number	Percent	Number	Percent	Number	Percent	Number	Percent
1959	39,490	22.4	...	...	...	...	19,116	35.4	...	...
1960	39,851	22.2	...	...	...	...	...	...	...	...
1969	24,147	12.1	4,108	8.6	5,424	9.6	11,090	17.9	3,525	10.4
1970	25,420	12.6	...	...	...	...	11,480	18.5	...	...
1971	25,559	12.5	4,512	9.3	5,764	10.3	11,182	17.5	4,101	11.4
1972	24,460	11.9	4,266	8.7	5,258	9.3	10,928	16.9	4,008	11.1
1973	22,973	11.1	4,207	8.6	4,864	8.6	10,061	15.3	3,841	10.5
1974	23,370	11.2	4,473	9.3	4,990	8.8	10,761	16.1	4,036	10.7
1975	25,877	12.3	4,904	10.2	5,459	9.7	11,059	16.2	4,454	11.7
1976	24,975	11.8	4,949	10.2	5,657	9.9	10,354	15.2	4,015	10.5
1977	24,720	11.6	4,956	10.2	5,589	9.8	10,249	14.8	3,927	10.1
1978	24,497	11.4	5,050	10.4	5,192	9.1	10,255	14.7	4,000	10.0
1979	26,072	11.7	5,029	10.4	5,594	9.7	10,627	15.0	4,095	10.0
1980	29,272	13.0	5,369	11.1	6,592	11.4	12,363	16.5	4,958	11.4
1981	31,822	14.0	5,815	11.9	7,142	12.3	13,256	17.4	5,609	12.7
1982	34,398	15.0	6,364	13.0	7,772	13.3	13,967	18.1	6,296	14.1
1983	35,303	15.2	6,561	13.4	8,536	14.6	13,484	17.2	6,684	14.7
1984	33,700	14.4	6,531	13.2	8,303	14.1	12,792	16.2	6,074	13.1
1985	33,064	14.0	5,751	11.6	8,191	13.9	12,921	16.0	6,201	13.0
1986	32,370	13.6	5,211	10.5	7,641	13.0	13,106	16.1	6,412	13.2
1987	32,221	13.4	5,476	11.0	7,499	12.7	13,287	16.1	6,285	12.6
1988	31,745	13.0	5,089	10.1	6,804	11.4	13,530	16.1	6,322	12.7
1989	31,528	12.8	5,061	10.0	7,043	11.9	12,943	15.4	6,481	12.5
1990	33,585	13.5	5,794	11.4	7,458	12.4	13,456	15.8	6,877	13.0
1991	35,708	14.2	6,177	12.2	7,989	13.2	13,783	16.0	7,759	14.3
1992	38,014	14.8	6,414	12.6	8,060	13.3	15,198	17.1	8,343	14.8
1993	39,265	15.1	6,839	13.3	8,172	13.4	15,375	17.1	8,879	15.6
1994	38,059	14.5	6,597	12.9	7,965	13.0	14,729	16.1	8,768	15.3
1995	36,425	13.8	6,445	12.5	6,785	11.0	14,458	15.7	8,736	14.9
1996	36,529	13.7	6,558	12.7	6,654	10.7	14,098	15.1	9,219	15.4
1997	35,574	13.3	6,474	12.6	6,493	10.4	13,748	14.6	8,858	14.6
1998	34,476	12.7	6,357	12.3	6,501	10.3	12,992	13.7	8,625	14.0
1999	32,791	11.9	5,814	11.0	6,250	9.8	12,744	13.2	7,982	12.7
2000	31,581	11.3	5,474	10.3	5,916	9.3	12,705	12.8	7,485	11.8
2001	32,907	11.7	5,687	10.7	5,966	9.4	13,515	13.5	7,739	12.1
2002	34,570	12.1	5,871	10.9	6,616	10.3	14,019	13.8	8,064	12.4
2003	35,861	12.5	6,052	11.3	6,932	10.7	14,548	14.1	8,329	12.6
2004	37,040	12.7	6,260	11.6	7,545	11.7	14,817	14.1	8,419	12.5
2005	36,950	12.6	6,103	11.3	7,419	11.4	14,854	14.0	8,573	12.6
2006	36,460	12.3	6,222	11.5	7,324	11.2	14,882	13.8	8,032	11.6
2007	37,276	12.5	6,166	11.4	7,237	11.1	15,501	14.2	8,372	12.0
2008	39,829	13.2	6,295	11.6	8,120	12.4	15,862	14.3	9,552	13.5
2009	43,569	14.3	6,650	12.2	8,768	13.3	17,609	15.7	10,542	14.8
2010	46,343	15.1	7,038	12.9	9,216	14.0	19,123	16.8	10,966	15.3
2011	46,247	15.0	7,208	13.1	9,221	14.0	18,380	16.0	11,437	15.8
2012	46,496	15.0	7,490	13.6	8,851	13.3	19,106	16.5	11,049	15.1
2013	45,318	14.5	7,046	12.7	8,590	12.9	18,870	16.1	10,812	14.7
2014	46,657	14.8	7,020	12.6	8,714	13.0	19,531	16.5	11,391	15.2
2015	43,123	13.5	6,891	12.4	7,849	11.7	18,305	15.3	10,079	13.3
2016	40,616	12.7	5,969	10.8	7,809	11.7	17,028	14.1	9,810	12.8
2017	39,564	12.3	6,347	11.3	7,571	11.2	16,474	13.5	9,172	11.9
2018	38,146	11.8	5,682	10.3	7,005	10.4	16,757	13.6	8,701	11.2
2019	33,984	10.5	5,177	9.4	6,518	9.7	14,845	12.0	7,443	9.5
2020	37,548	11.5	5,734	10.2	6,906	10.1	16,653	13.3	8,254	10.6
2021	37,933	11.6	5,664	10.1	7,043	10.4	16,634	13.2	8,592	11.0

PART D

CONSUMER SPENDING AND PRICES BY REGION, STATE, AND AREA

PART D: CONSUMER SPENDING AND PRICES BY REGION, STATE, AND AREA

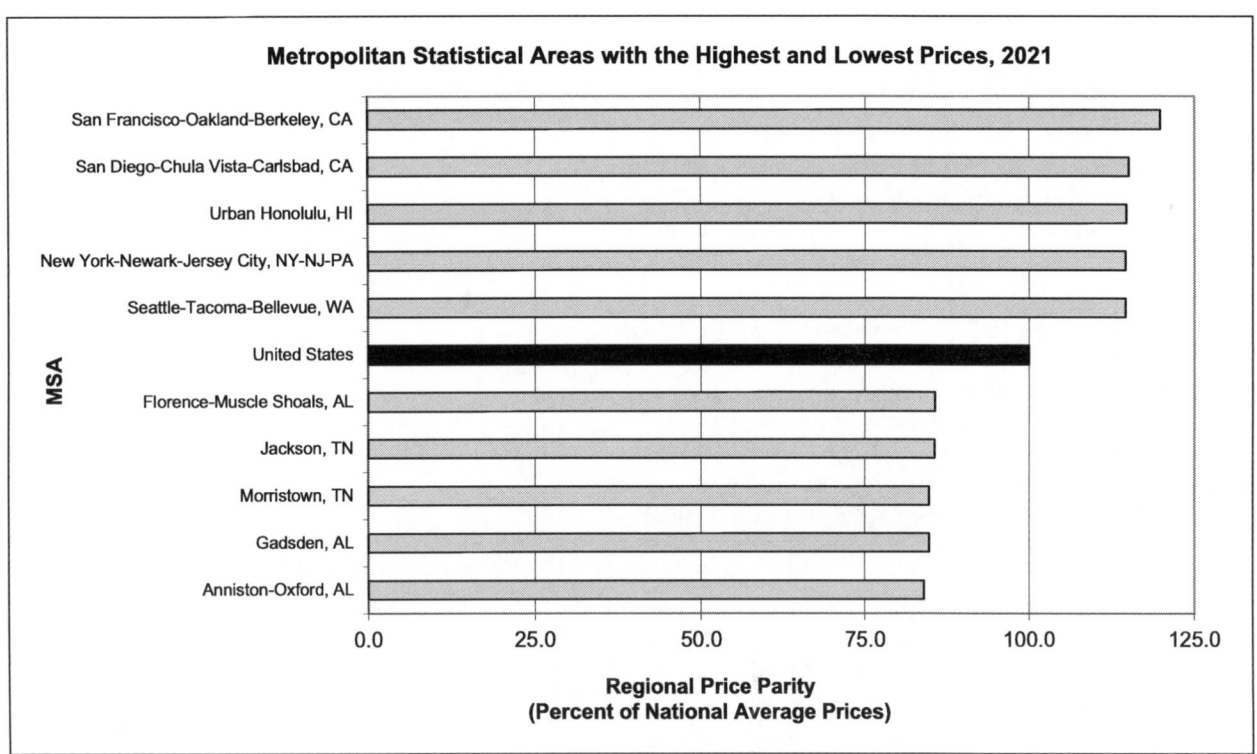

HIGHLIGHTS

- The MSAs with the highest regional price parities (RPP) in 2021 were: San Francisco-Oakland-Berkeley, CA (119.8), San Diego-Chula Vista-Carlsbad, CA (115.2), Urban Honolulu, HI (114.7), New York-Newark-Jersey City, NY-NJ-PA (114.6), and Seattle-Tacoma-Bellevue, WA (114.6). The MSAs with the lowest RPPs were: Anniston-Oxford, AL (83.8), Gadsden, AL (84.6), Morristown, TN (84.6), Jackson, TN (85.5), and Florence-Muscle Shoals, AL (85.5).

- New England was the region with the highest total per capita consumption expenditure in 2021 ($55,813), and the Southwest had the lowest per capita consumption expenditure ($44,222).

- Among all the states, Washington, D.C., had the highest total per capita consumption expenditure ($78,809). It also had the highest per capita expenditures on groceries ($3,908), housing and utilities ($12,593), and health care ($12,201). The national averages were $47,915 total, $3,631 on groceries, $8,362 on housing and utilities, and $7,784 on health care.

- Residents of Hawaii spent the second most on groceries ($4,647) and housing and utilities ($10,724) in 2021. Residents of Oklahoma spent the least on groceries ($2,756) and housing/utilities ($5,817).

- Per person health care spending was second highest in South Dakota ($11,493) and was lowest in Utah ($5,735) in 2021.

- We see the impact of post-pandemic inflation on grocery prices reflected in the increase in per capita spending on groceries from 2019 to 2021. U.S. per capita spending on groceries increased 16.3 percent from 2019 to 2021.

PART D NOTES AND DEFINITIONS: CONSUMER SPENDING AND PRICES BY REGION, STATE, AND AREA

Source: U.S. Department of Commerce, Bureau of Economic Analysis (BEA), https://www.bea.gov.

BEA Definitions

Personal Consumption Expenditures (PCE) includes a measure of consumer spending on goods and services among households in the U.S. The PCE is used as a mechanism to gauge how much earned income of households is being spent on current consumption for various goods and services.

Data are sourced from several statistical reports. These reports come from various government agencies, administrative and regulatory agencies, and other private organizations. PCE utilizes data sourced for other agencies and organizations that measure the goods and services purchased by households and nonprofit institutions serving households (NPISHs) who are resident in the United States.

PCE estimates are not derived from a dedicated sample, but rather are based on statistical reports from various government agencies, administrative and regulatory agency reports, and reports from private organizations, such as trade associations. The sample represents households and nonprofit institutions serving households. The sample also includes expenditures of the institutionalized population, domestic military personnel living on post, federal military and civilian personnel stationed abroad regardless of the length of their assignments, and US citizens who are employees of US businesses working abroad for less than one year and whose usual residence is in the United States. Also included are expenditures by those who died during the year.

Excluded from PCE are expenditures of students, temporary workers, and foreign nationals residing in the United States who are employees of international organizations and other countries.

Regional price parities (RPPs) are price indexes that measure geographic price level differences for one period in time within the United States. For example, if the RPP for Washington, DC, is 120, prices in Washington are on average 20 percent higher than the U.S. average. An RPP is a weighted average of the price level of goods and services for the average consumer in one geographic region compared to all other regions in the United States. The U.S. Bureau of Economic Analysis (BEA) estimates of real personal consumption and real personal income consist of their respective current-dollar estimates adjusted by the RPPs and converted to constant dollars using the U.S. personal consumption expenditures (PCE) price index.

Limitations

The RPPs use mainly price- and expenditure-related survey data that are collected or published by U.S. federal agencies. These include the Consumer Price Index (CPI) survey data from the U.S. Bureau of Labor Statistics (BLS) and the Public Use Microdata Sample (PUMS) from the American Community Survey (ACS) published by the U.S. Census Bureau. As of 2021, they also include BEA's PCE by state series. These distinct data sources are estimated at different geographic scales and must be reconciled to a common unit. We allocate each series down to the county level using either housing unit or income shares as the distributional assumption.

The CPI survey was not designed for place-to-place comparisons, which can lead to volatility in the results, especially across areas that have few observations or where sampling sizes are unevenly distributed. In past estimates, the CPI results were averaged over 5 years, but as of 2021, the RPPs use annual results. Regional price levels for selected CPI items with extreme volatility, particularly in medical and education services, will be substituted with national price levels. Both BEA and BLS are looking for alternative data sources for these categories.

Per Capita Personal Consumption Expenditures by Region and State: Total

(Dollars.)

State	2000	2001	2002	2003	2004	2005	2006	2007	2008	2009	2010
United States	23,983	24,823	25,550	26,682	28,114	29,674	31,092	32,356	33,049	32,243	33,164
New England	28,433	29,701	30,757	32,380	34,237	36,143	37,809	39,071	40,049	39,305	40,364
Mideast	25,732	26,773	27,734	29,195	30,859	32,684	34,334	35,835	36,872	36,291	37,419
Great Lakes	23,461	24,250	24,968	25,991	27,234	28,537	29,644	30,732	31,426	30,866	31,858
Plains	23,824	24,717	25,489	26,638	28,000	29,261	30,384	31,561	32,510	31,954	32,889
Southeast	22,569	23,280	23,898	24,912	26,278	27,761	29,197	30,286	30,720	29,922	30,806
Southwest	22,225	23,032	23,516	24,389	25,588	27,139	28,342	29,477	30,090	29,344	30,233
Rocky Mountain	23,565	24,319	24,865	25,840	27,242	28,667	30,100	31,434	31,956	30,860	31,431
Far West	24,774	25,559	26,329	27,479	29,071	30,842	32,551	34,165	34,867	33,535	34,352
Alabama	20,199	20,912	21,745	22,719	23,980	25,355	26,312	27,290	27,658	27,044	27,769
Alaska	27,199	28,551	30,198	31,649	33,081	34,956	36,276	38,108	39,547	39,219	40,051
Arizona	23,507	24,112	24,748	25,903	27,463	29,091	30,543	31,554	31,375	30,081	30,688
Arkansas	18,936	19,677	20,332	21,276	22,361	23,646	24,593	25,555	26,219	25,824	26,615
California	24,661	25,528	26,326	27,466	29,071	30,892	32,680	34,419	35,148	33,695	34,573
Colorado	26,946	27,754	28,126	29,120	30,585	32,006	33,336	34,682	35,273	34,219	34,812
Connecticut	29,557	30,645	31,635	33,003	34,895	36,880	38,604	40,101	40,946	39,730	40,745
Delaware	27,049	28,209	29,299	30,760	32,405	34,126	35,303	36,804	37,287	36,401	37,541
D.C.	39,154	40,272	42,115	44,734	47,942	50,683	52,795	55,240	56,910	54,734	56,040
Florida	25,696	26,460	26,845	27,884	29,493	31,232	33,104	34,345	34,548	33,333	34,194
Georgia	22,935	23,598	24,123	25,125	26,254	27,684	28,633	29,507	29,589	28,475	29,189
Hawaii	25,083	25,801	26,446	27,901	29,357	31,370	33,062	34,375	35,182	34,562	35,140
Idaho	20,072	20,658	21,162	22,113	23,254	24,646	26,073	27,106	27,265	26,173	26,797
Illinois	25,035	25,778	26,440	27,510	28,859	30,426	31,898	33,304	33,992	33,182	34,160
Indiana	21,936	22,633	23,293	24,237	25,676	26,977	27,862	28,697	29,272	28,764	29,452
Iowa	21,720	22,436	22,961	24,114	25,510	26,774	27,974	29,071	30,022	29,738	30,680
Kansas	22,798	23,611	24,119	25,214	26,583	27,938	29,515	30,919	31,665	30,726	31,242
Kentucky	20,684	21,318	22,018	22,934	24,134	25,350	26,454	27,107	27,816	27,642	28,460
Louisiana	19,591	20,371	21,050	22,145	23,250	24,190	27,330	28,407	29,153	28,669	29,545
Maine	24,405	25,620	26,885	28,201	29,715	31,274	32,565	33,702	34,596	34,505	35,635
Maryland	26,292	27,419	28,281	29,546	31,226	33,143	34,923	36,336	37,169	36,483	37,328
Massachusetts	29,712	31,112	32,122	33,918	35,945	37,934	39,730	40,889	41,955	41,107	42,172
Michigan	23,084	23,819	24,547	25,399	26,492	27,552	28,459	29,362	30,333	29,985	31,200
Minnesota	27,055	28,019	28,967	30,223	31,800	32,915	33,931	34,936	35,774	35,042	36,097
Mississippi	17,703	18,509	19,320	20,225	21,317	22,443	23,916	24,772	25,521	25,084	26,015
Missouri	23,596	24,500	25,358	26,380	27,438	28,643	29,480	30,623	31,691	31,181	32,028
Montana	21,539	22,567	23,709	24,942	26,446	28,094	29,821	31,514	32,634	31,705	32,796
Nebraska	22,682	23,536	24,116	25,331	26,913	28,330	29,587	30,930	31,869	31,186	32,352
Nevada	25,070	25,619	26,253	27,255	28,885	30,648	32,010	32,975	32,945	31,048	31,529
New Hampshire	27,894	29,152	30,338	32,149	33,912	35,750	37,213	38,526	39,547	39,218	40,513
New Jersey	28,089	29,355	30,595	32,220	33,956	35,815	37,629	39,062	39,992	39,056	39,894
New Mexico	20,024	20,760	21,369	22,353	23,597	25,090	26,365	27,503	28,424	27,705	28,392
New York	24,595	25,483	26,345	27,719	29,416	31,401	33,175	34,862	35,982	35,576	36,768
North Carolina	22,491	22,980	23,331	24,202	25,436	26,862	27,895	29,017	29,352	28,532	29,424
North Dakota	21,761	23,043	24,157	25,461	26,833	28,447	29,861	31,444	32,837	33,409	34,946
Ohio	22,970	23,856	24,614	25,673	26,750	27,968	28,853	29,939	30,412	29,885	30,898
Oklahoma	19,583	20,408	20,871	21,886	22,928	24,475	25,815	26,932	27,949	27,143	28,064
Oregon	23,590	24,194	24,830	25,793	27,433	28,955	30,346	31,545	31,860	30,905	31,682
Pennsylvania	24,923	25,986	26,895	28,407	29,886	31,357	32,648	33,907	34,990	34,512	35,845
Rhode Island	24,132	25,199	26,328	27,983	29,386	31,120	32,589	33,801	34,439	34,159	34,773
South Carolina	21,375	22,020	22,668	23,607	24,989	26,451	27,559	28,714	29,288	28,556	29,654
South Dakota	20,577	21,491	22,379	23,613	25,115	26,735	28,214	29,536	30,692	30,617	31,869
Tennessee	22,127	22,604	23,228	24,047	25,245	26,532	27,636	28,759	29,083	28,403	29,379
Texas	22,536	23,387	23,819	24,582	25,703	27,228	28,329	29,493	30,219	29,620	30,592
Utah	19,969	20,525	21,161	21,962	23,333	24,666	26,098	27,385	27,738	26,631	26,892
Vermont	25,735	27,142	28,280	29,814	31,537	33,312	34,851	36,004	37,352	37,157	38,362
Virginia	24,737	25,652	26,708	28,076	29,850	31,725	33,209	34,585	35,511	34,807	35,817
Washington	25,689	26,144	26,811	28,087	29,606	31,176	32,802	34,270	35,251	34,350	35,012
West Virginia	19,492	20,307	21,102	21,953	23,208	24,380	25,356	26,355	27,395	27,731	28,759
Wisconsin	23,284	24,176	24,992	26,239	27,642	28,967	30,316	31,297	32,080	31,567	32,497
Wyoming	23,182	24,086	24,841	26,250	28,003	29,929	32,043	33,960	34,788	33,135	34,016

Per Capita Personal Consumption Expenditures by Region and State: Total—*Continued*

(Dollars.)

State	2011	2012	2013	2014	2015	2016	2017	2018	2019	2020	2021
United States..................	34,309	35,144	35,877	37,109	38,106	39,132	40,516	42,323	43,584	42,583	47,915
New England	41,479	42,212	42,980	44,366	45,559	46,713	48,183	49,907	51,211	49,555	55,813
Mideast	38,578	39,382	40,142	41,437	42,453	43,501	44,905	47,017	48,415	46,714	52,160
Great Lakes	33,012	33,876	34,596	35,753	36,679	37,743	39,054	40,705	41,673	40,881	45,811
Plains	34,179	35,030	35,673	36,668	37,383	38,166	39,421	40,946	41,846	40,864	45,556
Southeast	31,875	32,592	33,251	34,405	35,333	36,237	37,404	39,027	40,155	39,607	44,881
Southwest	31,448	32,333	33,141	34,416	35,213	36,014	37,222	38,821	39,863	39,317	44,222
Rocky Mountain	32,456	33,214	34,100	35,408	36,596	37,784	39,314	41,016	42,387	42,174	47,800
Far West	35,499	36,548	37,353	38,733	40,081	41,475	43,380	45,597	47,471	45,954	51,959
Alabama	28,542	29,002	29,609	30,427	31,123	31,866	32,977	34,321	35,458	35,244	39,657
Alaska	41,747	42,634	42,963	44,495	45,319	46,029	47,486	49,666	51,364	48,921	54,331
Arizona...........................	31,542	32,229	32,907	34,074	34,980	35,935	37,567	39,220	40,630	40,237	44,875
Arkansas	27,648	28,329	28,866	29,848	30,755	31,668	32,732	33,928	34,670	34,786	39,044
California........................	35,741	36,896	37,687	39,116	40,584	42,099	44,094	46,385	48,478	46,802	53,082
Colorado	35,909	36,502	37,581	39,149	40,643	42,226	44,024	45,758	47,559	47,072	53,374
Connecticut	41,895	42,757	43,524	44,956	45,966	47,095	48,502	50,248	51,243	50,018	55,803
Delaware	38,684	39,273	39,904	40,815	41,816	42,558	43,536	45,398	46,607	45,481	51,113
D.C.................................	57,399	58,208	59,395	60,979	62,416	64,021	66,116	69,463	71,454	69,170	78,809
Florida............................	35,454	36,334	37,042	38,529	39,862	40,728	41,883	43,862	45,155	44,269	50,689
Georgia	30,231	30,926	31,784	33,089	34,040	35,075	36,462	38,032	39,055	38,253	43,482
Hawaii	36,072	36,902	37,641	38,770	39,445	40,346	41,955	44,193	45,954	44,102	49,155
Idaho..............................	27,614	28,234	28,963	29,890	30,724	31,664	33,051	34,699	35,364	35,232	39,739
Illinois............................	35,266	36,007	36,640	37,936	38,919	40,056	41,434	43,382	44,598	43,510	49,558
Indiana	30,509	31,472	32,062	32,964	33,629	34,594	36,226	37,720	38,412	38,113	42,697
Iowa...............................	31,952	32,680	33,189	34,109	34,610	35,383	36,422	37,631	38,214	37,419	41,758
Kansas	32,195	32,728	33,171	34,139	34,840	35,457	36,582	38,006	39,038	38,651	43,147
Kentucky	29,469	29,943	30,391	31,355	32,259	33,327	34,431	35,822	36,633	36,444	40,816
Louisiana	30,577	31,232	31,891	32,950	33,688	34,270	35,335	36,705	37,735	37,388	42,294
Maine	36,742	37,102	37,757	38,868	39,934	40,926	42,811	44,474	45,686	45,050	50,559
Maryland.........................	38,406	39,028	39,491	40,428	41,162	42,018	43,153	44,599	45,443	43,658	48,650
Massachusetts	43,267	44,045	44,775	46,281	47,657	48,923	50,391	52,093	53,622	51,342	58,532
Michigan	32,473	33,467	34,362	35,698	36,758	37,965	39,224	40,885	41,895	40,922	45,591
Minnesota	37,475	38,192	38,947	40,061	40,777	41,693	43,280	45,125	46,007	44,170	48,615
Mississippi.....................	26,905	27,494	28,020	28,753	29,372	29,967	30,649	31,855	32,497	32,577	36,445
Missouri..........................	33,234	34,202	34,753	35,580	36,365	37,186	38,450	39,931	40,955	40,131	44,990
Montana	34,113	35,097	35,801	36,757	37,655	38,195	39,483	41,239	42,304	42,370	47,887
Nebraska	33,723	34,593	35,222	36,190	36,944	37,876	39,015	40,406	41,213	40,816	46,190
Nevada	32,629	33,281	33,970	35,039	35,934	36,783	38,263	39,879	40,966	39,829	44,831
New Hampshire...............	41,538	42,272	43,259	44,414	45,795	47,136	48,901	50,916	52,399	51,625	56,727
New Jersey	40,751	41,667	42,315	43,410	44,232	45,222	46,135	48,080	49,386	48,244	54,700
New Mexico	29,213	29,791	30,368	31,430	32,254	32,904	33,912	35,443	35,940	35,129	40,028
New York.........................	38,048	38,923	39,878	41,592	42,777	44,048	45,826	48,246	49,963	47,930	53,255
North Carolina.................	30,442	31,288	32,050	33,143	33,909	34,092	36,118	37,788	39,244	38,979	43,959
North Dakota...................	37,561	40,175	41,820	43,556	43,524	42,959	43,066	44,210	44,800	43,417	48,182
Ohio	32,069	33,110	33,876	34,958	35,922	36,874	38,015	39,377	40,261	39,666	44,089
Oklahoma.......................	29,266	30,038	30,573	31,516	31,791	32,241	33,048	34,613	35,199	34,832	38,650
Oregon	32,592	33,143	33,968	35,256	36,523	37,567	39,369	41,331	42,766	42,232	47,779
Pennsylvania..................	37,043	37,741	38,384	39,336	40,318	41,131	42,411	44,425	45,640	44,088	49,040
Rhode Island..................	35,656	35,897	36,682	37,775	38,716	39,485	40,614	42,036	42,976	41,548	46,909
South Carolina	30,630	31,170	32,065	33,194	34,009	34,984	36,093	37,546	38,665	38,355	43,305
South Dakota..................	33,073	33,883	34,619	35,659	37,108	38,118	39,532	41,258	42,486	42,246	47,740
Tennessee	30,493	31,104	31,437	32,509	33,252	34,249	35,416	36,805	37,910	37,481	42,469
Texas..............................	31,929	32,899	33,792	35,151	35,984	36,798	37,965	39,553	40,600	40,003	45,114
Utah	27,691	28,664	29,377	30,561	31,585	32,658	34,003	35,744	37,034	37,320	42,653
Vermont	39,950	40,945	41,754	43,048	43,506	44,127	44,964	46,846	47,860	46,205	50,761
Virginia...........................	36,762	37,430	37,910	38,801	39,392	40,263	41,257	42,883	43,822	42,831	48,249
Washington.....................	36,170	37,139	38,121	39,446	40,584	41,939	43,739	45,989	47,385	46,198	51,751
West Virginia...................	30,016	30,852	31,415	32,144	32,997	33,949	35,022	36,770	37,764	37,176	41,153
Wisconsin	33,621	34,071	34,749	35,739	36,549	37,565	38,822	40,599	41,482	40,726	45,165
Wyoming	35,596	36,747	37,539	38,822	39,446	39,662	40,890	42,372	43,115	42,556	47,832

Per Capita Personal Consumption Expenditures by Region and State: Groceries

(Dollars.)

State	2000	2001	2002	2003	2004	2005	2006	2007	2008	2009	2010
United States	1,916	1,979	1,999	2,067	2,160	2,261	2,347	2,448	2,529	2,520	2,543
New England	2,184	2,285	2,337	2,384	2,523	2,623	2,719	2,825	2,917	2,920	2,956
Mideast	1,872	1,944	1,979	2,070	2,152	2,272	2,359	2,456	2,551	2,546	2,598
Great Lakes	1,877	1,934	1,959	2,020	2,107	2,169	2,239	2,328	2,399	2,400	2,418
Plains	1,887	1,952	1,988	2,042	2,124	2,212	2,262	2,352	2,451	2,481	2,504
Southeast	1,949	1,996	1,990	2,041	2,135	2,236	2,317	2,401	2,490	2,506	2,527
Southwest	1,778	1,835	1,825	1,891	2,001	2,116	2,202	2,292	2,373	2,363	2,383
Rocky Mountain	1,967	2,034	2,023	2,119	2,234	2,346	2,436	2,580	2,651	2,634	2,606
Far West	1,961	2,038	2,088	2,170	2,259	2,372	2,489	2,631	2,691	2,613	2,631
Alabama	1,872	1,968	2,019	2,074	2,138	2,196	2,216	2,262	2,336	2,348	2,352
Alaska	2,606	2,666	2,766	2,922	3,048	3,202	3,338	3,523	3,717	3,693	3,712
Arizona	1,829	1,887	1,910	2,004	2,175	2,329	2,456	2,564	2,616	2,544	2,551
Arkansas	1,610	1,649	1,644	1,696	1,751	1,809	1,835	1,917	1,993	2,060	2,091
California	1,875	1,959	2,014	2,086	2,152	2,256	2,362	2,512	2,564	2,472	2,495
Colorado	2,063	2,162	2,128	2,221	2,326	2,455	2,476	2,598	2,705	2,715	2,695
Connecticut	2,120	2,234	2,299	2,360	2,463	2,573	2,667	2,781	2,840	2,807	2,852
Delaware	2,164	2,262	2,335	2,425	2,528	2,622	2,730	2,815	2,883	2,862	2,881
D.C.	2,965	3,140	3,184	3,427	3,673	3,753	3,946	4,046	4,302	4,373	4,479
Florida	2,144	2,206	2,136	2,201	2,332	2,449	2,542	2,616	2,694	2,679	2,681
Georgia	1,926	1,963	1,975	2,019	2,108	2,200	2,255	2,331	2,384	2,417	2,449
Hawaii	2,356	2,423	2,427	2,465	2,582	2,748	2,877	3,010	3,125	3,253	3,282
Idaho	1,968	2,010	2,007	2,134	2,220	2,318	2,470	2,605	2,583	2,553	2,498
Illinois	1,765	1,819	1,848	1,934	2,052	2,138	2,264	2,378	2,399	2,354	2,355
Indiana	1,910	1,932	1,936	1,993	2,117	2,216	2,271	2,322	2,408	2,419	2,409
Iowa	1,776	1,832	1,847	1,907	2,013	2,105	2,199	2,310	2,412	2,436	2,466
Kansas	1,960	2,013	2,010	2,109	2,183	2,363	2,461	2,596	2,671	2,644	2,640
Kentucky	1,921	1,970	1,993	2,067	2,196	2,285	2,353	2,441	2,566	2,650	2,668
Louisiana	1,851	1,881	1,881	1,961	2,022	2,064	2,304	2,375	2,454	2,487	2,458
Maine	2,188	2,279	2,317	2,377	2,472	2,594	2,689	2,791	2,900	3,000	3,046
Maryland	1,992	2,056	2,055	2,114	2,204	2,300	2,400	2,495	2,556	2,551	2,595
Massachusetts	2,211	2,310	2,361	2,388	2,563	2,660	2,761	2,864	2,957	2,950	2,974
Michigan	1,982	2,050	2,071	2,105	2,188	2,200	2,224	2,292	2,370	2,417	2,455
Minnesota	2,071	2,172	2,221	2,244	2,274	2,306	2,321	2,352	2,450	2,478	2,513
Mississippi	1,717	1,767	1,769	1,839	1,937	2,038	2,169	2,172	2,276	2,331	2,367
Missouri	1,789	1,830	1,889	1,939	2,031	2,129	2,151	2,252	2,364	2,429	2,465
Montana	1,984	2,020	2,106	2,234	2,347	2,465	2,634	2,842	2,954	2,950	2,935
Nebraska	1,840	1,893	1,899	1,947	2,095	2,166	2,236	2,374	2,470	2,457	2,440
Nevada	2,145	2,200	2,168	2,266	2,409	2,463	2,612	2,711	2,754	2,669	2,634
New Hampshire	2,423	2,512	2,553	2,630	2,787	2,825	2,896	2,981	3,100	3,111	3,172
New Jersey	2,174	2,279	2,333	2,426	2,548	2,643	2,724	2,839	2,916	2,873	2,915
New Mexico	1,768	1,790	1,775	1,864	1,956	2,073	2,215	2,346	2,445	2,443	2,424
New York	1,626	1,699	1,738	1,799	1,887	2,047	2,121	2,201	2,287	2,301	2,377
North Carolina	1,991	2,018	2,015	2,029	2,076	2,192	2,223	2,343	2,421	2,369	2,388
North Dakota	1,840	1,911	1,984	2,074	2,181	2,239	2,331	2,389	2,489	2,554	2,566
Ohio	1,844	1,922	1,974	2,055	2,077	2,118	2,144	2,238	2,355	2,363	2,411
Oklahoma	1,540	1,565	1,544	1,590	1,645	1,736	1,799	1,884	1,973	2,006	2,019
Oregon	2,102	2,182	2,237	2,338	2,525	2,628	2,793	2,936	2,987	2,921	2,937
Pennsylvania	1,923	1,968	1,994	2,137	2,166	2,258	2,351	2,465	2,596	2,586	2,606
Rhode Island	1,904	1,991	2,030	2,083	2,169	2,282	2,382	2,501	2,554	2,544	2,566
South Carolina	1,959	1,989	1,961	1,984	2,120	2,283	2,318	2,398	2,540	2,574	2,624
South Dakota	1,731	1,827	1,873	1,946	2,075	2,179	2,245	2,317	2,402	2,464	2,489
Tennessee	1,808	1,849	1,847	1,887	1,955	2,040	2,135	2,284	2,394	2,482	2,528
Texas	1,806	1,870	1,853	1,913	2,017	2,124	2,198	2,279	2,365	2,364	2,391
Utah	1,755	1,789	1,774	1,847	2,003	2,081	2,217	2,370	2,409	2,351	2,325
Vermont	2,257	2,373	2,434	2,514	2,627	2,747	2,851	2,980	3,195	3,313	3,387
Virginia	1,979	2,024	2,077	2,128	2,215	2,329	2,431	2,518	2,619	2,614	2,654
Washington	2,160	2,207	2,259	2,383	2,519	2,689	2,813	2,918	3,010	2,954	2,964
West Virginia	1,811	1,822	1,842	1,879	1,975	2,056	2,155	2,253	2,401	2,478	2,524
Wisconsin	1,973	2,009	2,002	2,023	2,140	2,233	2,372	2,471	2,529	2,527	2,523
Wyoming	2,064	2,115	2,119	2,226	2,331	2,481	2,673	2,896	3,007	2,955	2,901

Per Capita Personal Consumption Expenditures by Region and State: Groceries—*Continued*

(Dollars.)

State	2011	2012	2013	2014	2015	2016	2017	2018	2019	2020	2021
United States..................	2,628	2,692	2,728	2,809	2,862	2,900	2,979	3,043	3,121	3,397	3,631
New England..................	3,064	3,146	3,187	3,281	3,326	3,383	3,505	3,554	3,638	3,919	4,191
Mideast.......................	2,667	2,718	2,754	2,816	2,858	2,884	2,952	3,024	3,118	3,354	3,610
Great Lakes..................	2,505	2,565	2,599	2,671	2,739	2,803	2,921	2,979	3,049	3,296	3,516
Plains........................	2,594	2,661	2,667	2,722	2,757	2,792	2,838	2,889	2,926	3,155	3,359
Southeast....................	2,606	2,671	2,705	2,781	2,833	2,869	2,942	3,009	3,093	3,374	3,606
Southwest...................	2,474	2,549	2,581	2,677	2,713	2,735	2,804	2,858	2,894	3,193	3,384
Rocky Mountain............	2,678	2,758	2,793	2,913	2,986	3,057	3,141	3,196	3,274	3,538	3,705
Far West.....................	2,726	2,787	2,839	2,942	3,009	3,039	3,112	3,190	3,298	3,629	3,908
Alabama......................	2,419	2,447	2,444	2,500	2,541	2,584	2,626	2,698	2,768	3,007	3,261
Alaska........................	3,834	3,860	3,818	3,815	3,752	3,661	3,650	3,716	3,781	3,963	4,120
Arizona.......................	2,573	2,589	2,599	2,715	2,761	2,800	2,908	2,940	2,940	3,213	3,346
Arkansas.....................	2,186	2,240	2,274	2,351	2,426	2,498	2,539	2,562	2,573	2,838	3,126
California.....................	2,590	2,659	2,711	2,826	2,909	2,959	3,039	3,113	3,231	3,553	3,865
Colorado......................	2,782	2,886	2,939	3,088	3,194	3,314	3,441	3,489	3,598	3,925	4,098
Connecticut..................	2,960	3,029	3,076	3,180	3,242	3,273	3,360	3,343	3,374	3,658	4,005
Delaware.....................	2,905	2,914	2,985	3,045	3,055	3,027	3,067	3,152	3,163	3,464	3,645
D.C...........................	4,582	4,724	4,817	5,009	5,176	5,164	5,330	5,403	5,543	5,826	6,241
Florida........................	2,762	2,809	2,877	2,975	3,063	3,099	3,172	3,273	3,392	3,655	3,886
Georgia.......................	2,560	2,644	2,699	2,825	2,869	2,871	3,012	3,067	3,133	3,415	3,699
Hawaii........................	3,382	3,363	3,414	3,451	3,456	3,500	3,634	3,796	3,967	4,336	4,647
Idaho.........................	2,560	2,670	2,738	2,798	2,861	2,870	2,929	2,944	2,965	3,149	3,296
Illinois........................	2,429	2,445	2,472	2,532	2,593	2,629	2,724	2,802	2,913	3,168	3,451
Indiana........................	2,472	2,522	2,574	2,644	2,740	2,827	2,925	2,944	2,981	3,209	3,424
Iowa..........................	2,574	2,660	2,663	2,728	2,773	2,819	2,845	2,854	2,819	3,050	3,255
Kansas........................	2,746	2,780	2,810	2,896	2,978	3,045	3,133	3,197	3,280	3,579	3,833
Kentucky.....................	2,753	2,825	2,812	2,902	2,993	3,084	3,200	3,229	3,243	3,495	3,703
Louisiana.....................	2,534	2,598	2,633	2,698	2,777	2,808	2,853	2,896	2,939	3,179	3,486
Maine.........................	3,089	3,175	3,229	3,349	3,364	3,426	3,556	3,678	3,835	4,213	4,499
Maryland......................	2,669	2,671	2,676	2,724	2,715	2,720	2,767	2,797	2,820	3,035	3,265
Massachusetts...............	3,101	3,188	3,215	3,308	3,356	3,421	3,568	3,612	3,709	3,961	4,221
Michigan......................	2,532	2,602	2,618	2,703	2,765	2,865	3,005	3,072	3,157	3,433	3,634
Minnesota....................	2,619	2,716	2,703	2,731	2,745	2,741	2,775	2,845	2,873	3,063	3,214
Mississippi...................	2,445	2,490	2,519	2,589	2,643	2,672	2,732	2,802	2,882	3,163	3,296
Missouri......................	2,528	2,569	2,563	2,602	2,623	2,672	2,737	2,790	2,848	3,078	3,293
Montana......................	3,048	3,146	3,152	3,272	3,312	3,299	3,325	3,435	3,497	3,727	3,971
Nebraska.....................	2,493	2,545	2,563	2,689	2,761	2,821	2,872	2,928	2,993	3,247	3,477
Nevada........................	2,708	2,751	2,811	2,945	3,038	3,070	3,159	3,217	3,290	3,558	3,784
New Hampshire..............	3,279	3,386	3,467	3,513	3,510	3,599	3,737	3,809	3,913	4,245	4,402
New Jersey...................	2,973	2,987	3,016	3,068	3,106	3,105	3,162	3,205	3,317	3,577	3,840
New Mexico	2,513	2,553	2,596	2,698	2,796	2,837	2,877	2,927	2,954	3,213	3,468
New York......................	2,467	2,539	2,597	2,667	2,723	2,756	2,853	2,968	3,095	3,344	3,597
North Carolina...............	2,414	2,571	2,641	2,714	2,763	2,788	2,857	2,930	3,080	3,455	3,630
North Dakota.................	2,689	2,885	3,007	3,027	2,996	2,987	2,936	2,947	2,939	3,105	3,353
Ohio..........................	2,537	2,642	2,703	2,800	2,890	2,955	3,104	3,152	3,199	3,448	3,651
Oklahoma....................	2,088	2,121	2,147	2,201	2,224	2,238	2,288	2,345	2,394	2,610	2,756
Oregon........................	3,026	3,089	3,139	3,241	3,304	3,247	3,299	3,386	3,494	3,857	4,104
Pennsylvania.................	2,651	2,715	2,731	2,785	2,826	2,876	2,913	2,953	3,021	3,222	3,491
Rhode Island.................	2,618	2,667	2,739	2,851	2,928	3,013	3,119	3,225	3,295	3,554	3,803
South Carolina	2,669	2,677	2,759	2,869	2,899	2,967	2,969	3,058	3,124	3,433	3,629
South Dakota	2,603	2,639	2,640	2,705	2,754	2,782	2,765	2,815	2,865	3,102	3,301
Tennessee	2,653	2,675	2,604	2,598	2,525	2,493	2,480	2,525	2,581	2,840	3,016
Texas.........................	2,504	2,601	2,639	2,735	2,764	2,782	2,844	2,903	2,947	3,266	3,471
Utah..........................	2,369	2,391	2,387	2,494	2,526	2,577	2,621	2,689	2,748	2,956	3,112
Vermont......................	3,508	3,596	3,618	3,665	3,692	3,664	3,693	3,852	3,923	4,210	4,443
Virginia.......................	2,735	2,809	2,797	2,830	2,879	2,949	3,068	3,112	3,179	3,459	3,729
Washington...................	3,062	3,107	3,167	3,207	3,209	3,182	3,224	3,301	3,370	3,756	3,914
West Virginia.................	2,607	2,624	2,664	2,693	2,717	2,809	2,872	2,901	2,994	3,253	3,496
Wisconsin.....................	2,606	2,666	2,670	2,701	2,716	2,752	2,836	2,901	2,940	3,131	3,288
Wyoming	2,950	2,990	3,026	3,126	3,185	3,237	3,350	3,438	3,550	3,848	4,022

Per Capita Personal Consumption Expenditures by Region and State: Housing and Utilities

(Dollars.)

State	2000	2001	2002	2003	2004	2005	2006	2007	2008	2009	2010
United States	4,248	4,518	4,622	4,795	5,009	5,347	5,583	5,841	6,158	6,194	6,296
New England	4,700	5,015	5,151	5,366	5,623	6,032	6,355	6,585	6,962	7,013	7,125
Mideast	4,540	4,846	4,984	5,194	5,443	5,834	6,065	6,358	6,766	6,873	6,981
Great Lakes	3,978	4,257	4,356	4,556	4,753	5,102	5,255	5,462	5,689	5,706	5,785
Plains	3,876	4,142	4,199	4,374	4,581	4,900	5,074	5,265	5,529	5,515	5,614
Southeast	4,127	4,383	4,485	4,637	4,834	5,139	5,414	5,698	5,949	5,954	6,069
Southwest	3,972	4,203	4,266	4,408	4,586	4,881	5,113	5,314	5,548	5,554	5,716
Rocky Mountain	4,278	4,528	4,638	4,779	5,010	5,320	5,529	5,688	5,996	6,034	6,084
Far West	4,591	4,858	4,977	5,132	5,369	5,725	5,998	6,335	6,816	6,884	6,953
Alabama	3,476	3,713	3,824	3,939	4,132	4,399	4,640	4,920	5,118	5,148	5,277
Alaska	4,499	4,770	4,937	5,104	5,324	5,674	5,877	6,294	6,622	6,699	6,758
Arizona	4,706	4,962	5,117	5,232	5,411	5,666	5,878	6,134	6,335	6,319	6,390
Arkansas	3,293	3,516	3,581	3,719	3,850	4,130	4,339	4,504	4,720	4,717	4,834
California	4,617	4,888	4,995	5,155	5,400	5,775	6,053	6,386	6,914	6,971	7,059
Colorado	4,828	5,089	5,197	5,380	5,661	6,007	6,239	6,396	6,806	6,866	6,938
Connecticut	4,734	5,052	5,184	5,396	5,641	6,019	6,292	6,606	7,043	7,101	7,282
Delaware	4,619	4,912	5,067	5,216	5,418	5,768	6,093	6,559	6,738	6,741	6,857
D.C.	5,102	5,439	5,579	5,841	6,174	6,576	6,953	7,438	7,999	8,020	8,511
Florida	5,272	5,557	5,692	5,838	6,041	6,393	6,852	7,279	7,550	7,442	7,462
Georgia	4,102	4,347	4,417	4,583	4,763	5,069	5,205	5,332	5,546	5,499	5,636
Hawaii	4,910	5,195	5,323	5,477	5,672	6,078	6,413	6,788	7,144	7,276	7,412
Idaho	3,907	4,129	4,253	4,324	4,501	4,763	4,963	5,091	5,282	5,302	5,375
Illinois	4,188	4,484	4,525	4,754	4,956	5,318	5,464	5,749	6,005	6,074	6,163
Indiana	3,779	4,034	4,127	4,299	4,475	4,820	4,921	5,072	5,342	5,360	5,344
Iowa	3,686	3,939	3,965	4,164	4,362	4,651	4,803	4,972	5,146	5,175	5,304
Kansas	3,677	3,930	3,985	4,115	4,322	4,622	4,781	4,936	5,255	5,230	5,301
Kentucky	3,334	3,559	3,655	3,775	3,972	4,248	4,350	4,473	4,758	4,831	4,951
Louisiana	3,298	3,523	3,523	3,667	3,813	4,037	4,493	4,722	5,012	4,992	5,144
Maine	4,344	4,632	4,800	4,949	5,181	5,568	5,754	6,012	6,269	6,437	6,528
Maryland	4,913	5,216	5,312	5,525	5,755	6,172	6,559	6,940	7,456	7,595	7,559
Massachusetts	4,819	5,142	5,276	5,506	5,781	6,200	6,590	6,740	7,139	7,137	7,200
Michigan	4,033	4,318	4,499	4,698	4,921	5,280	5,398	5,647	5,882	5,887	6,005
Minnesota	4,505	4,804	4,879	5,114	5,366	5,762	5,955	6,156	6,433	6,363	6,426
Mississippi	3,157	3,380	3,457	3,590	3,764	4,017	4,261	4,432	4,683	4,684	4,763
Missouri	3,744	4,001	4,047	4,200	4,378	4,662	4,833	5,038	5,314	5,313	5,429
Montana	3,548	3,795	3,902	4,019	4,233	4,584	4,894	5,051	5,214	5,199	5,352
Nebraska	3,562	3,811	3,888	4,022	4,210	4,513	4,690	4,860	5,062	5,061	5,193
Nevada	4,981	5,195	5,333	5,461	5,635	6,020	6,282	6,776	6,983	6,948	6,860
New Hampshire	4,837	5,143	5,277	5,495	5,746	6,210	6,393	6,709	7,066	7,076	7,332
New Jersey	5,124	5,463	5,623	5,880	6,177	6,598	6,856	7,168	7,671	7,734	7,783
New Mexico	3,638	3,884	3,971	4,106	4,282	4,571	4,784	4,961	5,165	5,119	5,242
New York	4,449	4,748	4,886	5,090	5,340	5,762	5,981	6,287	6,686	6,846	6,936
North Carolina	3,901	4,135	4,213	4,365	4,569	4,853	5,020	5,244	5,466	5,546	5,717
North Dakota	3,450	3,695	3,770	3,911	4,109	4,428	4,517	4,830	5,157	5,324	5,411
Ohio	3,778	4,044	4,128	4,314	4,500	4,824	5,016	5,158	5,330	5,305	5,393
Oklahoma	3,415	3,649	3,709	3,864	4,032	4,328	4,579	4,696	4,874	4,886	5,103
Oregon	4,221	4,475	4,632	4,772	5,021	5,275	5,437	5,747	6,020	6,166	6,244
Pennsylvania	4,086	4,379	4,514	4,701	4,918	5,233	5,381	5,582	5,896	5,947	6,168
Rhode Island	4,153	4,434	4,550	4,787	4,999	5,412	5,841	6,055	6,293	6,535	6,554
South Carolina	3,825	4,066	4,174	4,307	4,517	4,787	4,930	5,202	5,438	5,559	5,799
South Dakota	3,279	3,505	3,578	3,705	3,900	4,202	4,472	4,636	4,963	4,919	5,062
Tennessee	3,712	3,951	4,032	4,161	4,326	4,590	4,810	5,132	5,302	5,371	5,445
Texas	3,913	4,132	4,170	4,315	4,491	4,792	5,025	5,226	5,478	5,494	5,676
Utah	3,752	3,977	4,082	4,194	4,374	4,623	4,763	4,936	5,190	5,239	5,199
Vermont	4,693	5,014	5,173	5,372	5,655	6,055	6,363	6,720	7,046	7,122	7,229
Virginia	4,669	4,956	5,091	5,290	5,526	5,870	6,144	6,558	6,928	7,020	7,201
Washington	4,470	4,734	4,876	5,023	5,231	5,511	5,828	6,123	6,616	6,727	6,736
West Virginia	3,149	3,379	3,520	3,667	3,867	4,157	4,281	4,489	4,744	4,807	4,893
Wisconsin	4,044	4,322	4,438	4,639	4,825	5,180	5,391	5,550	5,761	5,766	5,848
Wyoming	4,170	4,467	4,585	4,728	4,968	5,353	5,571	5,816	6,081	6,002	6,062

Per Capita Personal Consumption Expenditures by Region and State: Housing and Utilities—*Continued*

(Dollars.)

State	2011	2012	2013	2014	2015	2016	2017	2018	2019	2020	2021
United States.................	6,360	6,409	6,578	6,738	6,857	7,032	7,237	7,528	7,791	8,044	8,362
New England..............	7,209	7,283	7,442	7,660	7,810	7,980	8,189	8,560	8,866	9,183	9,598
Mideast......................	7,070	7,169	7,344	7,509	7,604	7,732	7,924	8,246	8,487	8,748	9,124
Great Lakes...............	5,814	5,884	6,044	6,213	6,263	6,434	6,600	6,854	6,981	7,138	7,363
Plains.......................	5,731	5,800	6,045	6,203	6,284	6,385	6,577	6,814	7,013	7,192	7,437
Southeast..................	6,130	6,139	6,279	6,416	6,539	6,692	6,843	7,110	7,379	7,612	7,893
Southwest..................	5,784	5,771	5,953	6,132	6,273	6,435	6,563	6,817	7,069	7,255	7,503
Rocky Mountain...........	6,250	6,292	6,513	6,631	6,892	7,111	7,388	7,653	8,069	8,397	8,766
Far West....................	6,976	7,056	7,222	7,388	7,541	7,825	8,202	8,569	8,949	9,360	9,824
Alabama....................	5,306	5,303	5,401	5,448	5,520	5,650	5,765	6,011	6,219	6,397	6,683
Alaska......................	7,091	7,213	7,243	7,425	7,517	7,653	7,876	8,134	8,344	8,511	8,696
Arizona.....................	6,411	6,487	6,539	6,586	6,694	6,936	7,122	7,368	7,678	7,901	8,184
Arkansas...................	4,912	4,906	5,005	5,207	5,334	5,402	5,482	5,628	5,696	5,776	5,928
California....................	7,051	7,149	7,322	7,493	7,653	7,942	8,313	8,690	9,089	9,504	9,972
Colorado....................	7,184	7,175	7,469	7,611	8,047	8,364	8,692	8,911	9,527	9,948	10,447
Connecticut.................	7,366	7,570	7,645	7,816	7,900	8,061	8,136	8,551	8,786	9,018	9,342
Delaware...................	6,998	7,049	7,211	7,308	7,427	7,521	7,707	8,159	8,488	8,817	9,270
D.C...........................	8,803	8,843	9,233	9,646	9,755	9,894	10,328	10,814	11,225	11,726	12,593
Florida......................	7,532	7,515	7,592	7,719	7,904	8,105	8,310	8,641	8,995	9,320	9,656
Georgia.....................	5,664	5,699	5,793	5,882	5,993	6,208	6,356	6,610	6,930	7,176	7,495
Hawaii......................	7,508	7,721	8,118	8,300	8,412	8,588	8,865	9,131	9,564	10,077	10,724
Idaho.......................	5,411	5,426	5,581	5,643	5,689	5,836	5,986	6,364	6,571	6,827	7,109
Illinois......................	6,196	6,271	6,389	6,613	6,671	6,860	7,046	7,330	7,466	7,631	7,884
Indiana.....................	5,397	5,419	5,640	5,815	5,855	5,906	6,139	6,476	6,482	6,654	6,865
Iowa........................	5,484	5,560	5,727	5,870	5,964	6,057	6,208	6,458	6,687	6,841	7,041
Kansas.....................	5,379	5,403	5,581	5,756	5,817	5,973	6,212	6,439	6,619	6,766	6,986
Kentucky...................	5,029	5,013	5,188	5,327	5,369	5,501	5,627	5,880	6,014	6,196	6,436
Louisiana..................	5,227	5,247	5,421	5,606	5,680	5,811	5,923	6,182	6,407	6,626	6,914
Maine.......................	6,636	6,676	6,839	6,989	7,232	7,291	7,666	7,946	8,151	8,460	8,760
Maryland...................	7,741	7,749	8,016	8,115	8,164	8,303	8,420	8,700	8,897	9,110	9,378
Massachusetts..............	7,280	7,305	7,511	7,791	7,949	8,180	8,415	8,847	9,254	9,641	10,178
Michigan....................	5,977	6,095	6,290	6,423	6,434	6,663	6,830	7,045	7,257	7,437	7,697
Minnesota..................	6,485	6,561	6,846	7,036	7,026	7,215	7,482	7,701	7,980	8,233	8,555
Mississippi..................	4,787	4,790	4,965	5,106	5,204	5,294	5,367	5,566	5,585	5,677	5,817
Missouri....................	5,538	5,599	5,847	5,924	6,044	6,070	6,220	6,499	6,664	6,833	7,061
Montana....................	5,532	5,567	5,799	5,945	6,130	6,240	6,658	6,951	7,234	7,557	7,708
Nebraska...................	5,364	5,398	5,670	5,872	6,028	6,119	6,358	6,613	6,808	7,019	7,347
Nevada.....................	6,778	6,728	6,703	6,657	6,729	6,812	7,183	7,448	7,886	8,300	8,772
New Hampshire.............	7,378	7,392	7,558	7,682	7,954	8,103	8,506	8,647	8,892	9,148	9,367
New Jersey	7,786	7,964	8,084	8,176	8,202	8,426	8,528	8,891	9,095	9,332	9,722
New Mexico	5,273	5,353	5,501	5,652	5,774	5,886	6,131	6,231	6,452	6,633	6,883
New York....................	7,056	7,141	7,296	7,565	7,613	7,774	8,001	8,331	8,657	8,978	9,450
North Carolina..............	5,797	5,760	5,938	6,134	6,233	6,298	6,455	6,706	6,948	7,157	7,350
North Dakota................	5,778	6,031	6,436	6,848	7,013	7,023	6,887	6,833	6,693	6,626	6,662
Ohio	5,411	5,488	5,645	5,774	5,860	6,039	6,140	6,363	6,484	6,604	6,797
Oklahoma..................	5,214	5,242	5,387	5,612	5,545	5,651	5,756	6,060	6,087	6,177	6,314
Oregon.....................	6,321	6,350	6,530	6,646	6,863	7,121	7,522	7,805	8,167	8,537	8,924
Pennsylvania...............	6,209	6,318	6,504	6,577	6,807	6,813	7,031	7,311	7,448	7,640	7,886
Rhode Island................	6,632	6,608	6,812	6,947	7,013	7,060	7,207	7,406	7,530	7,768	8,120
South Carolina	5,878	5,965	6,145	6,328	6,536	6,710	6,820	7,039	7,391	7,616	7,904
South Dakota	5,175	5,303	5,565	5,761	5,902	5,877	6,032	6,269	6,438	6,535	6,668
Tennessee	5,567	5,597	5,690	5,803	5,928	6,081	6,223	6,390	6,784	7,018	7,303
Texas.......................	5,753	5,703	5,926	6,133	6,311	6,465	6,571	6,830	7,099	7,287	7,540
Utah	5,289	5,408	5,534	5,614	5,732	5,873	6,077	6,358	6,635	6,915	7,278
Vermont....................	7,385	7,607	7,639	7,944	8,051	8,121	8,134	8,556	8,806	9,126	9,544
Virginia.....................	7,180	7,188	7,459	7,587	7,621	7,705	7,822	8,121	8,296	8,489	8,774
Washington.................	6,888	6,922	7,082	7,329	7,461	7,856	8,301	8,743	9,020	9,447	9,930
West Virginia...............	4,978	5,051	5,207	5,277	5,370	5,587	5,708	6,038	6,126	6,197	6,388
Wisconsin..................	5,960	5,974	6,109	6,296	6,337	6,492	6,669	6,898	7,020	7,180	7,379
Wyoming	6,216	6,398	6,594	6,778	6,851	7,005	7,380	7,656	7,853	7,876	7,941

Per Capita Personal Consumption Expenditures by Region and State: Health Care

(Dollars.)

State	2000	2001	2002	2003	2004	2005	2006	2007	2008	2009	2010
United States	3,255	3,497	3,765	3,978	4,231	4,469	4,665	4,907	5,115	5,322	5,493
New England	4,062	4,369	4,710	5,020	5,345	5,642	5,958	6,319	6,628	6,906	7,122
Mideast	3,727	3,991	4,292	4,554	4,846	5,090	5,322	5,581	5,793	6,007	6,205
Great Lakes	3,259	3,510	3,788	4,008	4,294	4,568	4,801	5,069	5,256	5,491	5,717
Plains	3,432	3,715	4,003	4,214	4,454	4,707	4,871	5,166	5,407	5,605	5,776
Southeast	3,116	3,352	3,602	3,783	4,017	4,222	4,401	4,596	4,738	4,919	5,049
Southwest	2,835	3,086	3,354	3,529	3,723	3,955	4,069	4,254	4,475	4,672	4,833
Rocky Mountain	2,761	3,011	3,280	3,455	3,710	3,882	4,042	4,285	4,467	4,656	4,800
Far West	3,059	3,243	3,473	3,693	3,941	4,195	4,408	4,685	4,970	5,195	5,364
Alabama	3,078	3,270	3,543	3,690	3,902	4,162	4,279	4,414	4,499	4,625	4,712
Alaska	3,716	4,308	4,798	5,089	5,342	5,789	6,023	6,521	6,972	7,288	7,632
Arizona	2,683	2,872	3,137	3,404	3,618	3,905	4,016	4,185	4,390	4,564	4,737
Arkansas	2,882	3,150	3,409	3,579	3,778	4,009	4,110	4,306	4,473	4,609	4,679
California	3,039	3,191	3,405	3,629	3,873	4,127	4,355	4,615	4,906	5,134	5,310
Colorado	3,006	3,294	3,603	3,784	4,081	4,178	4,331	4,604	4,778	4,972	5,101
Connecticut	4,019	4,314	4,630	4,829	5,128	5,355	5,518	5,760	6,061	6,325	6,528
Delaware	3,488	3,815	4,137	4,503	4,870	5,233	5,421	5,747	6,065	6,276	6,667
D.C.	5,727	5,980	6,505	6,798	7,281	7,764	7,998	8,346	8,725	8,981	9,185
Florida	3,388	3,649	3,936	4,107	4,332	4,509	4,720	4,949	5,127	5,335	5,490
Georgia	3,010	3,164	3,360	3,535	3,731	3,925	4,012	4,139	4,184	4,319	4,386
Hawaii	3,349	3,540	3,667	3,870	4,066	4,379	4,531	4,787	5,020	5,180	5,175
Idaho	2,522	2,747	2,992	3,141	3,295	3,507	3,710	3,982	4,091	4,284	4,456
Illinois	3,260	3,496	3,742	3,927	4,158	4,420	4,641	4,961	5,116	5,301	5,532
Indiana	3,138	3,367	3,645	3,876	4,212	4,432	4,675	4,972	5,087	5,419	5,578
Iowa	3,172	3,406	3,649	3,815	4,035	4,275	4,465	4,681	4,881	5,039	5,211
Kansas	3,164	3,452	3,651	3,838	4,088	4,325	4,527	4,811	5,027	5,179	5,298
Kentucky	3,173	3,445	3,716	3,853	4,064	4,322	4,511	4,670	4,775	4,997	5,126
Louisiana	3,024	3,269	3,532	3,728	3,975	4,110	4,456	4,664	4,857	5,079	5,200
Maine	3,548	3,828	4,144	4,378	4,738	5,039	5,303	5,609	5,881	6,103	6,324
Maryland	3,422	3,718	4,010	4,258	4,559	4,831	5,053	5,346	5,629	5,845	6,019
Massachusetts	4,425	4,758	5,119	5,503	5,841	6,161	6,557	7,001	7,321	7,587	7,793
Michigan	3,138	3,296	3,520	3,724	3,990	4,277	4,532	4,806	5,032	5,234	5,490
Minnesota	3,981	4,230	4,610	4,812	5,083	5,329	5,540	5,802	5,938	6,191	6,384
Mississippi	2,850	3,091	3,360	3,550	3,853	3,995	4,270	4,578	4,772	4,867	5,043
Missouri	3,309	3,621	3,887	4,133	4,333	4,549	4,575	4,967	5,304	5,469	5,603
Montana	3,018	3,301	3,565	3,751	3,962	4,281	4,450	4,664	4,915	5,193	5,451
Nebraska	3,188	3,504	3,772	3,992	4,268	4,605	4,883	5,106	5,364	5,513	5,736
Nevada	2,609	2,849	3,117	3,258	3,497	3,645	3,778	4,042	4,219	4,275	4,363
New Hampshire	3,432	3,716	4,089	4,429	4,783	5,149	5,565	5,982	6,315	6,741	7,030
New Jersey	3,551	3,758	4,107	4,358	4,606	4,821	5,008	5,277	5,532	5,727	5,814
New Mexico	2,630	2,815	3,007	3,129	3,379	3,722	3,832	4,087	4,453	4,722	4,916
New York	3,923	4,187	4,482	4,769	5,061	5,262	5,508	5,745	5,894	6,156	6,338
North Carolina	3,066	3,315	3,508	3,719	3,972	4,154	4,351	4,476	4,600	4,785	4,914
North Dakota	3,382	3,745	4,033	4,233	4,509	4,803	5,032	5,347	5,665	6,070	6,304
Ohio	3,334	3,669	3,980	4,209	4,519	4,829	5,028	5,207	5,393	5,640	5,849
Oklahoma	2,848	3,071	3,298	3,612	3,798	4,108	4,267	4,495	4,740	4,789	4,918
Oregon	2,947	3,214	3,476	3,651	3,959	4,236	4,450	4,733	4,918	5,116	5,318
Pennsylvania	3,597	3,887	4,158	4,391	4,695	4,998	5,247	5,509	5,739	5,887	6,182
Rhode Island	3,733	3,976	4,256	4,507	4,834	5,114	5,393	5,680	5,962	6,190	6,379
South Carolina	2,901	3,171	3,404	3,554	3,765	3,978	4,144	4,345	4,535	4,691	4,862
South Dakota	3,314	3,609	3,977	4,234	4,496	4,931	5,259	5,535	5,893	6,209	6,524
Tennessee	3,267	3,506	3,737	3,916	4,198	4,450	4,597	4,781	4,846	4,990	5,152
Texas	2,888	3,165	3,447	3,581	3,767	3,964	4,072	4,249	4,459	4,678	4,838
Utah	2,299	2,472	2,685	2,858	3,110	3,325	3,461	3,630	3,845	4,003	4,081
Vermont	3,440	3,766	4,155	4,556	4,792	5,122	5,466	5,760	6,052	6,388	6,629
Virginia	2,836	3,049	3,313	3,530	3,775	4,018	4,182	4,453	4,682	4,901	5,033
Washington	3,261	3,522	3,809	4,058	4,319	4,567	4,739	5,091	5,440	5,729	5,889
West Virginia	3,460	3,734	4,003	4,214	4,501	4,762	4,899	5,161	5,364	5,702	5,832
Wisconsin	3,455	3,767	4,144	4,446	4,782	5,047	5,322	5,608	5,881	6,148	6,417
Wyoming	2,867	3,138	3,413	3,596	3,865	4,192	4,428	4,767	4,972	5,126	5,454

Per Capita Personal Consumption Expenditures by Region and State: Health Care—*Continued*

(Dollars.)

State	2011	2012	2013	2014	2015	2016	2017	2018	2019	2020	2021
United States..................	5,635	5,794	5,867	6,078	6,393	6,657	6,851	7,117	7,458	7,056	7,784
New England...............	7,255	7,355	7,406	7,617	7,920	8,186	8,280	8,426	8,761	8,265	9,245
Mideast........................	6,342	6,461	6,529	6,759	7,093	7,397	7,622	7,976	8,361	7,967	8,674
Great Lakes.................	5,884	6,094	6,171	6,383	6,650	6,915	7,065	7,317	7,625	7,198	7,900
Plains..........................	5,943	6,120	6,195	6,401	6,735	7,024	7,238	7,505	7,850	7,394	8,151
Southeast.....................	5,161	5,327	5,372	5,561	5,861	6,107	6,263	6,499	6,809	6,449	7,198
Southwest.....................	4,944	5,080	5,119	5,301	5,587	5,806	5,959	6,148	6,436	6,034	6,695
Rocky Mountain............	4,921	5,047	5,154	5,376	5,714	6,037	6,180	6,359	6,618	6,280	6,929
Far West......................	5,554	5,736	5,879	6,135	6,518	6,799	7,127	7,485	7,932	7,533	8,280
Alabama......................	4,785	4,963	5,050	5,166	5,401	5,558	5,706	5,884	6,195	5,862	6,545
Alaska.........................	7,978	8,232	8,360	8,854	9,244	9,641	10,045	10,850	11,522	10,591	11,473
Arizona........................	4,816	4,942	5,018	5,183	5,492	5,739	5,978	6,237	6,615	6,337	6,828
Arkansas......................	4,769	4,922	4,939	5,094	5,437	5,743	6,040	6,298	6,606	6,318	6,943
California.....................	5,520	5,706	5,884	6,141	6,537	6,834	7,209	7,581	8,046	7,697	8,501
Colorado......................	5,158	5,241	5,346	5,629	6,014	6,458	6,576	6,708	6,980	6,656	7,364
Connecticut..................	6,710	6,840	6,927	7,096	7,234	7,498	7,618	7,792	8,160	7,795	8,606
Delaware......................	6,939	7,087	7,210	7,492	7,899	8,157	8,305	8,538	8,859	8,260	9,064
D.C.............................	9,531	9,622	9,673	9,962	10,444	10,751	10,985	11,173	11,535	10,771	12,201
Florida.........................	5,581	5,769	5,751	5,984	6,316	6,507	6,579	6,835	7,199	6,814	7,676
Georgia.......................	4,476	4,670	4,820	5,015	5,391	5,745	5,913	6,194	6,405	5,985	6,595
Hawaii.........................	5,227	5,289	5,381	5,588	5,883	6,071	6,327	6,699	7,137	6,864	7,449
Idaho..........................	4,702	4,862	4,960	5,198	5,582	5,872	6,093	6,406	6,654	6,191	6,714
Illinois........................	5,668	5,801	5,889	6,156	6,307	6,547	6,691	6,972	7,248	6,864	7,449
Indiana........................	5,788	6,209	6,229	6,367	6,615	6,961	7,304	7,556	7,935	7,580	8,494
Iowa............................	5,352	5,469	5,533	5,786	6,020	6,263	6,352	6,472	6,656	6,159	6,894
Kansas........................	5,461	5,671	5,734	5,890	6,146	6,312	6,463	6,665	7,026	6,753	7,495
Kentucky	5,275	5,356	5,452	5,663	6,038	6,395	6,525	6,683	6,954	6,613	7,430
Louisiana.....................	5,280	5,329	5,411	5,692	6,038	6,276	6,430	6,577	7,007	6,826	7,679
Maine..........................	6,592	6,672	6,740	6,969	7,411	7,659	7,893	8,030	8,244	7,879	8,670
Maryland......................	6,180	6,251	6,242	6,461	6,790	7,008	7,178	7,316	7,601	7,146	7,846
Massachusetts...............	7,851	7,941	7,941	8,170	8,525	8,799	8,826	8,925	9,235	8,653	9,876
Michigan	5,683	5,848	5,890	6,049	6,352	6,581	6,666	6,899	7,161	6,677	7,325
Minnesota	6,534	6,658	6,773	6,995	7,344	7,652	7,905	8,308	8,622	8,052	8,687
Mississippi...................	5,190	5,360	5,336	5,455	5,704	5,863	5,926	6,217	6,489	6,173	6,794
Missouri.......................	5,766	6,015	6,032	6,183	6,510	6,785	6,974	7,210	7,615	7,177	7,892
Montana.......................	5,645	5,861	6,116	6,267	6,691	6,973	7,220	7,518	7,887	7,634	8,289
Nebraska......................	5,880	6,017	6,051	6,253	6,643	6,997	7,238	7,447	7,719	7,381	8,193
Nevada........................	4,511	4,636	4,665	4,885	5,069	5,218	5,371	5,673	5,907	5,603	5,976
New Hampshire...............	7,189	7,241	7,350	7,619	8,027	8,337	8,558	8,879	9,352	8,809	9,526
New Jersey	5,875	6,127	6,197	6,446	6,797	7,096	7,299	7,570	7,949	7,589	8,266
New Mexico	5,009	5,143	5,251	5,474	5,803	6,029	6,162	6,451	6,784	6,473	7,311
New York......................	6,423	6,483	6,580	6,800	7,108	7,469	7,750	8,221	8,693	8,344	9,006
North Carolina...............	5,074	5,274	5,272	5,382	5,532	5,781	6,130	6,438	6,823	6,428	7,179
North Dakota.................	6,678	6,798	7,140	7,593	7,955	8,370	8,702	8,955	9,481	8,966	9,947
Ohio	6,007	6,310	6,448	6,717	7,060	7,340	7,458	7,650	7,988	7,550	8,326
Oklahoma.....................	5,101	5,242	5,290	5,460	5,745	5,956	6,091	6,376	6,671	6,238	6,878
Oregon	5,443	5,552	5,663	6,016	6,434	6,723	6,981	7,216	7,629	7,219	7,956
Pennsylvania.................	6,418	6,556	6,609	6,838	7,187	7,450	7,633	7,984	8,291	7,871	8,641
Rhode Island.................	6,523	6,545	6,561	6,709	6,999	7,160	7,248	7,316	7,623	7,077	7,916
South Carolina	4,942	4,979	5,014	5,193	5,409	5,562	5,653	5,823	5,985	5,626	6,429
South Dakota	6,807	7,020	7,154	7,438	8,172	8,722	9,342	9,790	10,417	9,872	11,493
Tennessee	5,242	5,407	5,488	5,640	5,923	6,151	6,260	6,412	6,586	6,347	6,946
Texas..........................	4,947	5,085	5,109	5,293	5,572	5,784	5,921	6,072	6,335	5,900	6,593
Utah	4,214	4,358	4,429	4,552	4,761	4,948	5,048	5,171	5,379	5,080	5,735
Vermont.......................	6,851	7,125	7,367	7,552	7,693	7,961	8,040	8,325	8,734	8,350	8,859
Virginia........................	5,199	5,378	5,416	5,611	5,912	6,190	6,345	6,555	6,879	6,421	7,178
Washington...................	6,029	6,269	6,293	6,492	6,884	7,139	7,333	7,681	8,131	7,481	8,126
West Virginia.................	6,002	6,352	6,514	6,821	7,287	7,697	8,032	8,485	9,034	8,747	9,552
Wisconsin	6,586	6,615	6,667	6,814	7,146	7,403	7,514	7,852	8,162	7,673	8,313
Wyoming	5,643	5,815	5,906	6,173	6,469	6,570	6,811	7,198	7,477	7,064	7,562

Regional Price Parities by Metropolitan Statistical Area

(Percent of U.S. Price Level; U.S. Average Price = 100.0)

Metropolitan Statistical Area	2008	2009	2010	2011	2012	2013	2014	2015	2016	2017	2018	2019	2020	2021
United States	100.0	100.0	100.0	100.0	100.0	100.0	100.0	100.0	100.0	100.0	100.0	100.0	100.0	100.0
United States (Nonmetropolitan Portion)	87.1	87.4	89.2	89.0	89.1	89.4	89.3	89.1	88.2	87.6	89.2	89.3	88.3	89.0
Abilene, TX	93.5	91.1	94.9	93.8	94.4	92.3	95.5	94.2	94.9	93.9	92.4	92.5	90.5	92.0
Akron, OH	92.3	95.3	94.1	94.2	96.0	96.0	96.1	95.3	95.0	95.4	94.3	94.7	93.7	93.7
Albany, GA	87.2	87.5	88.6	89.0	88.6	89.1	89.2	89.4	90.2	87.3	86.4	84.1	83.8	89.4
Albany-Lebanon, OR	100.2	100.1	95.9	96.3	97.2	97.8	98.7	99.3	99.5	98.9	103.2	103.1	102.7	101.8
Albany-Schenectady-Troy, NY	101.8	101.1	100.0	100.1	99.7	100.5	98.7	101.3	100.6	100.7	99.8	99.8	99.3	99.2
Albuquerque, NM	96.7	99.1	97.1	99.8	99.5	98.1	98.2	96.1	96.1	98.1	93.9	94.8	94.0	92.3
Alexandria, LA	91.2	88.8	91.1	89.2	92.7	93.0	92.6	92.7	93.9	90.4	87.3	89.1	86.9	89.1
Allentown-Bethlehem-Easton, PA-NJ	101.1	102.1	100.0	99.5	100.3	101.2	99.3	101.0	101.1	101.7	99.3	99.4	100.0	98.3
Altoona, PA	91.9	91.3	94.0	92.7	92.1	92.1	88.8	90.1	92.0	91.0	91.3	90.8	90.0	89.6
Amarillo, TX	96.2	94.4	95.2	97.0	96.9	97.1	96.9	97.3	97.5	96.2	93.3	94.2	94.6	93.8
Ames, IA	85.0	90.3	94.1	92.6	92.9	94.5	93.6	91.9	91.1	90.0	93.9	96.0	93.0	91.3
Anchorage, AK	108.2	111.7	106.3	107.7	107.5	105.1	105.2	105.8	108.2	108.0	106.4	104.6	102.7	106.3
Ann Arbor, MI	102.4	101.3	100.3	100.4	100.6	100.3	101.5	99.4	98.3	98.4	99.4	100.8	98.7	99.8
Anniston-Oxford, AL	87.7	84.5	88.9	89.3	91.1	89.5	87.6	90.5	91.7	88.4	84.8	87.6	85.6	83.8
Appleton, WI	96.4	94.4	94.8	94.1	94.5	94.3	94.7	93.7	93.0	92.1	93.5	93.7	92.3	93.5
Asheville, NC	93.7	92.7	93.6	94.5	94.6	94.8	94.7	93.7	95.3	93.9	93.0	94.1	93.2	94.7
Athens-Clarke County, GA	95.2	94.1	94.8	94.6	93.5	93.5	93.7	92.9	94.2	93.9	90.6	90.7	90.3	94.4
Atlanta-Sandy Springs-Alpharetta, GA	98.4	95.3	98.6	96.6	99.5	98.6	98.8	98.3	98.8	99.4	98.1	98.0	98.7	99.1
Atlantic City-Hammonton, NJ	109.2	107.0	106.3	106.0	105.2	102.1	102.5	103.5	102.4	97.8	99.9	97.3	100.9	97.2
Auburn-Opelika, AL	92.0	90.4	91.8	93.3	91.5	92.8	92.2	89.4	90.9	89.5	88.8	90.7	89.1	89.7
Augusta-Richmond County, GA-SC	91.3	90.8	92.8	93.7	94.0	94.2	92.9	94.0	94.4	92.5	91.4	90.3	89.7	92.0
Austin-Round Rock-Georgetown, TX	100.1	99.4	100.4	100.8	101.3	101.4	101.8	102.2	103.0	101.9	99.2	99.5	101.1	100.0
Bakersfield, CA	96.4	99.4	97.2	99.0	99.6	98.5	97.7	96.7	95.7	98.6	102.0	101.4	100.6	100.9
Baltimore-Columbia-Towson, MD	106.0	109.1	106.0	108.9	106.3	106.5	105.7	106.0	106.0	107.6	105.2	104.0	105.3	105.0
Bangor, ME	96.2	95.1	95.1	95.3	95.2	97.3	92.7	95.1	92.9	94.4	93.7	96.0	97.2	96.7
Barnstable Town, MA	106.9	104.6	103.9	103.5	103.0	103.5	103.6	104.6	105.9	105.9	101.2	105.0	101.1	101.1
Baton Rouge, LA	94.6	93.9	95.2	96.1	95.8	95.6	96.1	95.9	96.4	94.0	92.8	92.9	93.1	93.2
Battle Creek, MI	95.3	94.2	93.2	91.8	93.4	94.1	94.5	92.2	93.4	91.0	91.9	91.8	90.8	90.6
Bay City, MI	94.4	94.1	92.5	93.1	93.3	92.9	93.4	90.5	91.6	89.3	92.7	92.4	88.9	91.7
Beaumont-Port Arthur, TX	93.8	92.7	93.6	95.4	93.8	94.3	94.3	94.0	95.0	92.5	91.7	92.4	90.3	93.3
Beckley, WV	84.7	78.9	85.1	83.4	83.7	87.6	87.7	87.7	84.6	84.5	85.9	86.0	83.6	89.0
Bellingham, WA	96.8	101.7	99.5	103.3	101.1	99.6	101.3	100.1	99.5	100.9	104.4	104.3	103.6	104.7
Bend, OR	100.3	99.5	97.0	96.5	96.6	96.8	98.7	101.0	101.8	102.6	103.5	104.0	104.6	102.7
Billings, MT	95.6	96.7	94.3	97.9	97.6	96.4	96.9	97.8	94.6	97.2	94.1	95.7	91.9	92.5
Binghamton, NY	97.3	97.1	96.7	96.6	95.4	96.4	94.4	97.3	97.0	97.9	96.0	94.0	97.2	94.6
Birmingham-Hoover, AL	93.7	93.0	94.7	95.3	95.0	95.0	95.1	94.1	95.3	93.3	90.3	91.3	91.8	90.9
Bismarck, ND	92.2	93.6	92.1	91.0	95.8	97.1	97.4	96.6	96.3	91.0	91.5	94.3	93.1	94.2
Blacksburg-Christiansburg, VA	90.7	89.2	91.8	92.4	91.1	93.2	92.7	93.0	91.0	89.1	91.7	91.0	91.0	92.2
Bloomington, IL	96.8	96.9	97.0	95.1	96.0	95.4	96.6	95.7	95.0	92.9	94.4	95.1	92.9	93.1
Bloomington, IN	94.7	96.7	95.5	96.2	95.3	95.4	96.1	94.6	93.9	93.8	93.8	94.6	93.5	94.1
Bloomsburg-Berwick, PA	94.4	94.2	93.8	92.7	93.2	94.6	92.1	94.3	93.4	93.8	93.2	91.6	91.6	89.8
Boise City, ID	94.7	97.9	95.6	97.0	96.6	95.4	96.1	94.7	93.4	95.9	93.5	95.7	93.6	93.9
Boston-Cambridge-Newton, MA-NH	107.2	105.8	105.8	105.8	105.1	103.5	105.7	105.7	109.3	109.0	110.6	110.3	112.6	109.7
Boulder, CO	107.5	105.4	103.7	106.1	107.2	106.8	105.7	106.3	105.0	105.3	101.5	105.4	101.9	101.3
Bowling Green, KY	86.7	85.6	89.4	87.9	88.3	90.7	89.4	89.3	87.5	87.8	87.8	88.8	89.4	88.4
Bremerton-Silverdale-Port Orchard, WA	106.1	105.6	103.0	103.8	103.6	102.7	104.2	103.9	107.1	107.9	107.3	105.8	105.5	103.7
Bridgeport-Stamford-Norwalk, CT	115.0	115.9	111.4	113.6	112.6	113.0	113.6	111.9	112.1	111.6	107.5	106.0	108.4	105.8
Brownsville-Harlingen, TX	87.0	86.4	89.1	90.1	89.8	89.0	89.7	89.7	90.3	88.0	85.2	87.8	85.3	88.4
Brunswick, GA	89.7	88.0	91.7	90.4	90.5	90.9	91.1	90.7	90.1	89.4	91.8	86.7	89.0	90.1
Buffalo-Cheektowaga, NY	97.4	97.6	95.5	96.0	95.9	96.6	95.3	97.6	97.4	97.3	95.5	94.7	94.5	95.1
Burlington, NC	93.0	92.4	92.9	94.2	93.5	94.2	93.2	92.7	93.3	92.3	91.3	90.5	89.8	89.6
Burlington-South Burlington, VT	103.0	103.9	100.6	100.9	101.3	102.8	101.1	101.8	102.2	103.9	102.2	104.5	104.8	102.6
California-Lexington Park, MD	97.6	96.4	97.7	99.6	99.4	99.0	99.3	98.8	98.9	94.8	98.1	96.3	98.2	96.4
Canton-Massillon, OH	93.2	92.3	92.5	91.0	91.8	91.8	91.9	91.3	91.0	90.2	90.8	91.0	89.0	90.0
Cape Coral-Fort Myers, FL	101.6	99.0	98.8	99.1	99.0	98.9	99.3	100.7	102.3	99.5	99.3	97.9	98.1	100.0
Cape Girardeau, MO-IL	81.1	83.2	88.4	87.8	89.6	89.2	89.4	86.7	86.8	85.3	87.8	90.1	88.9	88.6
Carbondale-Marion, IL	81.0	84.5	85.9	88.6	88.0	86.5	86.6	86.5	84.4	82.8	87.8	88.7	87.7	86.8
Carson City, NV	102.4	99.5	98.7	98.1	96.3	96.5	97.0	99.8	96.4	97.7	94.7	98.5	94.7	94.2
Casper, WY	92.9	97.3	95.9	98.6	99.2	98.8	98.6	96.5	96.4	98.2	95.2	93.0	93.2	91.3
Cedar Rapids, IA	93.4	93.6	94.1	92.9	93.7	91.2	93.9	92.0	91.4	91.7	92.4	92.0	90.9	91.8
Chambersburg-Waynesboro, PA	97.3	97.2	95.8	94.9	96.2	97.3	94.6	97.1	95.4	98.0	96.2	94.7	94.5	95.2
Champaign-Urbana, IL	97.2	96.6	96.4	95.5	95.0	95.7	95.6	95.1	94.5	92.8	93.4	94.3	92.3	93.5
Charleston, WV	90.2	89.4	91.4	92.7	92.8	91.0	92.3	91.7	92.2	89.3	90.1	88.9	86.8	90.7
Charleston-North Charleston, SC	97.6	97.7	98.7	99.6	99.7	99.7	100.0	99.7	100.6	99.4	98.4	98.3	98.2	99.1
Charlotte-Concord-Gastonia, NC-SC	95.7	94.4	96.0	96.2	96.2	96.4	96.8	96.4	97.4	96.3	95.5	94.5	94.2	96.6
Charlottesville, VA	100.7	99.1	101.3	101.9	99.2	101.5	99.8	100.4	100.3	100.0	98.2	95.9	98.3	100.3
Chattanooga, TN-GA	92.8	91.8	94.0	94.3	95.1	94.0	93.7	93.8	94.6	94.2	89.3	91.2	90.1	90.2
Cheyenne, WY	94.0	98.1	96.6	99.9	98.5	97.7	98.4	97.0	96.3	98.7	93.5	96.2	91.4	92.9
Chicago-Naperville-Elgin, IL-IN-WI	105.4	106.8	106.1	107.0	105.6	104.8	103.5	102.8	104.2	104.2	105.4	104.4	102.8	104.7	105.4
Chico, CA	98.2	101.5	99.6	100.7	102.3	99.2	98.7	97.3	96.8	100.9	104.4	102.5	102.0	102.5
Cincinnati, OH-KY-IN	97.1	96.7	94.9	93.3	92.6	92.9	92.5	91.8	93.7	93.6	94.3	94.9	94.0	94.3
Clarksville, TN-KY	90.4	91.3	92.8	94.5	94.2	94.6	93.6	93.8	94.2	92.1	88.5	89.4	88.8	90.6

Regional Price Parities by Metropolitan Statistical Area—*Continued*

(Percent of U.S. Price Level; U.S. Average Price = 100.0)

Metropolitan Statistical Area	2008	2009	2010	2011	2012	2013	2014	2015	2016	2017	2018	2019	2020	2021
Cleveland, TN	88.5	86.7	88.1	87.8	89.0	90.2	89.7	88.8	88.5	85.1	88.1	86.6	86.7	88.0
Cleveland-Elyria, OH	93.0	96.2	95.1	95.8	96.3	96.8	96.7	96.0	96.2	95.5	94.7	94.4	93.7	94.2
Coeur d'Alene, ID	97.8	95.0	92.6	94.3	94.3	96.3	97.2	97.5	96.0	97.6	94.0	90.6	93.0	93.8
College Station-Bryan, TX	95.3	94.9	96.5	96.5	96.9	96.4	96.1	96.6	96.6	96.8	94.7	94.7	95.2	95.1
Colorado Springs, CO	98.1	101.4	99.1	102.1	101.8	101.1	101.0	99.3	98.9	102.1	97.8	100.3	98.7	96.8
Columbia, MO	94.2	94.0	94.1	93.0	94.0	93.6	93.8	92.7	91.8	91.1	91.7	92.5	91.2	89.5
Columbia, SC	94.1	93.0	95.0	95.8	94.9	95.6	94.7	95.6	95.9	93.7	92.3	91.1	90.0	93.3
Columbus, GA-AL	89.2	88.9	90.8	91.8	90.9	91.5	92.5	91.7	91.8	89.6	88.2	87.8	86.2	89.0
Columbus, IN	85.6	86.1	91.5	90.2	92.1	90.3	91.7	88.2	88.5	87.6	94.0	93.8	91.5	92.0
Columbus, OH	96.2	95.8	95.8	94.3	95.3	95.4	95.4	94.7	94.7	93.7	95.3	95.7	94.6	95.0
Corpus Christi, TX	96.6	94.2	96.3	95.6	96.5	97.7	97.0	97.4	98.2	96.9	94.0	95.1	95.0	94.8
Corvallis, OR	100.2	100.1	95.9	96.3	97.2	97.8	98.7	99.3	99.5	98.9	103.2	103.1	102.7	101.8
Crestview-Fort Walton Beach-Destin, FL	95.9	95.0	96.1	97.4	97.9	97.6	97.9	97.2	97.8	95.6	96.2	95.9	95.0	96.9
Cumberland, MD-WV	91.4	90.2	90.7	92.5	93.3	90.5	92.2	91.2	92.4	89.9	88.9	89.0	88.2	91.2
Dallas-Fort Worth-Arlington, TX	101.4	101.8	101.5	100.5	101.2	101.1	100.5	99.6	98.3	99.6	101.4	103.6	104.3	103.9
Dalton, GA	90.4	87.4	90.7	89.1	89.5	89.2	90.1	89.7	88.2	85.4	88.8	87.6	84.3	90.8
Danville, IL	82.0	83.3	88.2	85.9	87.5	87.3	87.7	86.6	83.5	84.0	87.8	86.9	86.8	88.3
Daphne-Fairhope-Foley, AL	96.3	95.7	97.3	96.5	96.6	95.2	95.3	94.5	96.9	95.6	91.4	94.7	90.7	92.1
Davenport-Moline-Rock Island, IA-IL	94.8	93.4	93.6	92.9	93.9	93.9	93.2	91.9	91.3	91.1	92.0	92.0	91.7	91.4
Dayton-Kettering, OH	95.9	94.7	94.4	92.9	92.8	93.8	93.5	92.4	92.9	91.9	92.8	92.4	92.0	92.5
Decatur, AL	90.7	87.5	89.7	92.1	90.3	92.7	91.4	87.9	85.6	88.7	87.0	84.3	87.0	86.3
Decatur, IL	92.9	92.4	90.7	92.2	91.7	91.6	89.8	89.3	88.5	85.9	89.8	89.5	88.5	89.8
Deltona-Daytona Beach-Ormond Beach, FL	98.8	97.1	96.8	98.6	98.4	97.9	98.7	98.7	99.0	98.3	97.1	95.8	96.7	97.8
Denver-Aurora-Lakewood, CO	105.4	103.0	101.4	103.9	104.7	105.0	103.9	104.6	104.4	104.3	102.3	104.3	109.5	109.2
Des Moines-West Des Moines, IA	96.1	96.9	96.3	95.1	95.0	96.1	96.9	96.9	95.6	95.2	94.0	95.7	93.7	93.3
Detroit-Warren-Dearborn, MI	99.9	99.8	98.5	98.1	97.4	98.0	98.6	96.7	96.0	95.6	97.1	98.3	98.4	96.1
Dothan, AL	87.7	86.7	88.6	89.2	89.0	90.3	89.2	88.5	89.0	86.1	84.7	85.8	86.4	86.2
Dover, DE	97.1	97.1	98.0	99.5	97.5	96.5	98.4	98.4	100.0	96.8	94.9	95.2	93.8	95.9
Dubuque, IA	94.1	91.9	91.3	91.3	93.5	92.6	93.6	86.7	91.9	91.5	90.4	89.7	89.3	87.9
Duluth, MN-WI	91.7	93.4	91.4	89.9	91.7	90.0	90.1	88.6	89.3	86.0	90.6	90.1	82.4	88.8
Durham-Chapel Hill, NC	96.4	95.4	96.9	97.4	96.4	96.9	97.2	97.2	97.1	96.4	95.3	94.4	94.4	96.0
East Stroudsburg, PA	102.1	99.3	99.1	98.7	97.4	100.5	99.2	99.9	97.9	101.5	98.4	100.7	98.7	97.9
Eau Claire, WI	95.9	93.8	94.0	93.5	94.1	93.6	94.1	92.3	92.9	91.1	93.1	92.8	92.2	91.9
El Centro, CA	95.7	95.2	94.3	93.4	92.3	93.1	92.2	93.0	92.7	96.1	93.1	96.7	97.1	95.7
Elizabethtown-Fort Knox, KY	90.3	88.5	91.5	92.6	89.5	89.9	90.6	89.9	88.7	87.2	87.2	88.9	87.9	87.4
Elkhart-Goshen, IN	97.1	94.9	94.4	93.2	93.6	93.3	93.0	93.3	92.1	91.0	92.4	91.4	91.2	87.9
Elmira, NY	95.5	96.3	95.4	96.1	94.8	96.9	97.0	95.9	96.6	97.8	96.1	95.9	95.6	94.9
El Paso, TX	93.5	92.8	94.7	96.0	95.7	95.1	94.6	94.6	95.4	94.8	91.5	91.7	92.8	93.1
Enid, OK	NA	NA	NA	NA	NA	90.8	90.5	91.7	92.6	91.6	88.1	86.2	86.9	87.5
Erie, PA	95.7	94.8	95.5	94.8	94.9	96.7	94.1	95.3	94.7	96.5	94.6	94.0	93.0	92.2
Eugene-Springfield, OR	95.4	99.9	97.8	100.1	99.6	98.1	98.1	97.6	97.4	99.8	102.1	101.6	100.7	100.6
Evansville, IN-KY	94.9	94.8	94.2	93.0	92.4	92.7	92.3	91.2	91.5	90.4	89.7	91.2	89.6	90.3
Fairbanks, AK	106.5	104.5	103.0	104.2	100.1	101.0	102.5	104.6	102.0	103.9	104.5	102.7	98.4	103.9
Fargo, ND-MN	95.9	95.0	94.9	93.7	95.3	95.5	94.8	94.7	94.6	94.6	93.2	95.1	92.6	92.6
Farmington, NM	96.9	92.6	92.3	91.9	93.5	91.2	95.0	95.5	94.3	97.1	92.1	91.8	89.1	89.5
Fayetteville, NC	92.0	90.4	92.9	93.7	93.3	93.4	93.6	92.6	92.3	90.4	90.7	89.1	88.9	91.7
Fayetteville-Springdale-Rogers, AR	93.4	92.6	93.8	95.0	94.9	94.7	94.3	94.6	95.0	93.2	90.8	91.7	92.8	93.3
Flagstaff, AZ	101.3	101.3	98.9	98.9	99.1	100.8	99.1	103.0	97.1	100.9	97.4	99.4	97.0	95.6
Flint, MI	95.7	94.4	94.0	93.0	92.6	93.7	93.6	91.1	90.7	89.2	91.6	92.1	89.9	89.2
Florence, SC	86.4	86.1	88.3	88.4	89.4	89.7	89.4	90.0	91.2	88.6	88.1	87.7	86.4	90.6
Florence-Muscle Shoals, AL	84.8	85.8	89.0	87.1	88.5	84.6	87.9	88.3	87.0	86.4	83.7	81.9	82.7	85.5
Fond du Lac, WI	84.1	85.8	89.7	88.3	90.8	92.0	91.3	90.1	88.3	87.2	92.2	92.9	91.2	92.2
Fort Collins, CO	97.5	101.1	100.9	102.8	103.8	102.1	101.7	101.2	100.7	100.7	104.5	100.7	102.2	98.0
Fort Smith, AR-OK	90.3	88.6	89.3	89.8	90.2	90.0	91.2	88.3	89.9	88.3	86.0	87.0	87.0	88.0
Fort Wayne, IN	95.0	93.5	94.1	92.7	93.0	91.7	93.1	92.2	92.8	90.7	91.7	92.3	90.1	92.1
Fresno, CA	96.2	100.1	97.4	100.0	99.6	98.2	97.2	96.6	95.7	98.4	102.8	102.8	101.5	101.6
Gadsden, AL	88.8	88.6	89.2	88.3	88.3	89.1	90.4	88.2	87.8	87.0	85.7	86.2	85.0	84.6
Gainesville, FL	97.6	97.6	97.1	97.5	96.1	96.6	97.2	96.4	96.8	96.2	96.0	94.0	92.8	95.9
Gainesville, GA	93.6	89.9	94.2	94.1	92.8	93.4	93.6	92.7	92.2	92.1	94.5	92.4	94.6	94.0
Gettysburg, PA	96.9	97.9	96.9	96.3	95.4	97.1	94.8	96.6	97.1	98.0	96.7	96.7	96.8	95.6
Glens Falls, NY	99.5	99.5	98.6	97.4	98.2	99.1	95.2	97.1	97.9	97.8	95.5	95.8	95.3	95.7
Goldsboro, NC	89.4	88.9	91.1	91.0	88.3	93.5	91.3	93.0	94.0	91.4	90.4	89.6	85.7	90.1
Grand Forks, ND-MN	94.5	93.9	93.6	92.5	92.7	94.8	94.4	94.7	93.2	90.9	91.8	94.2	91.4	90.1
Grand Island, NE	83.7	82.7	89.1	90.1	88.9	89.4	87.0	88.3	87.2	83.1	87.9	89.7	90.1	88.9
Grand Junction, CO	101.6	99.4	95.6	97.4	95.2	96.0	97.4	98.2	97.0	99.5	93.9	98.5	95.2	92.5
Grand Rapids-Kentwood, MI	96.2	96.2	95.5	94.6	95.0	95.5	95.3	94.5	95.3	92.4	94.1	95.9	94.7	96.7
Grants Pass, OR	96.7	95.1	94.1	94.9	94.2	94.7	94.5	95.9	94.7	96.1	99.9	100.3	95.1	98.6
Great Falls, MT	89.3	92.8	89.6	93.3	94.6	93.4	91.9	91.5	90.2	90.0	91.8	88.7	86.4	87.2
Greeley, CO	102.0	98.6	96.1	98.5	100.6	100.6	100.5	100.6	100.2	99.7	97.8	100.7	97.4	95.5
Green Bay, WI	94.5	94.2	94.3	93.9	94.1	93.9	93.3	93.3	92.3	92.0	91.4	93.3	92.4	92.4
Greensboro-High Point, NC	93.2	91.4	92.9	93.9	93.6	93.3	94.3	94.2	93.5	92.5	92.1	90.3	89.5	92.8
Greenville, NC	91.5	90.9	93.5	93.1	93.0	93.2	92.5	91.8	93.3	91.1	87.7	89.4	87.6	89.6
Greenville-Anderson, SC	92.2	91.7	93.4	94.2	93.3	93.6	93.1	93.7	94.5	93.0	91.7	90.8	90.5	93.5

Regional Price Parities by Metropolitan Statistical Area—*Continued*

(Percent of U.S. Price Level; U.S. Average Price = 100.0)

Metropolitan Statistical Area	2008	2009	2010	2011	2012	2013	2014	2015	2016	2017	2018	2019	2020	2021
Gulfport-Biloxi, MS	96.2	93.6	94.7	95.2	95.2	94.2	94.9	93.6	94.0	91.8	87.3	89.1	89.4	89.2
Hagerstown-Martinsburg, MD-WV	100.7	100.9	98.9	100.6	99.5	99.8	99.3	100.4	99.5	98.7	94.0	93.3	93.1	95.3
Hammond, LA	90.2	87.3	91.6	90.9	88.9	89.6	88.7	89.9	89.2	87.7	88.6	89.2	86.6	88.5
Hanford-Corcoran, CA	100.4	96.6	95.5	97.3	94.3	94.3	93.2	97.0	95.5	96.1	101.9	98.4	100.1	98.6
Harrisburg-Carlisle, PA	99.3	99.5	97.4	97.5	97.1	98.5	96.5	98.4	98.5	99.4	97.8	96.9	96.3	97.5
Harrisonburg, VA	92.9	92.1	93.3	93.5	94.4	94.9	93.2	92.7	91.9	90.6	93.5	92.7	90.5	94.1
Hartford-East Hartford-Middletown, CT	103.9	103.8	102.1	101.9	101.5	102.1	101.2	102.5	102.3	103.7	102.5	102.7	103.8	101.7
Hattiesburg, MS	90.0	86.7	90.0	90.7	88.9	90.0	89.9	88.3	88.6	87.9	88.3	87.8	85.4	88.6
Hickory-Lenoir-Morganton, NC	90.8	90.8	91.8	92.6	91.1	91.0	91.1	89.7	91.7	90.9	88.5	87.0	87.1	89.3
Hilton Head Island-Bluffton, SC	96.7	94.9	96.3	94.0	95.2	96.4	96.3	95.7	96.6	92.2	95.9	97.8	93.7	99.1
Hinesville, GA	92.1	88.2	93.9	92.9	93.5	93.7	94.1	92.3	93.6	90.1	93.7	93.4	89.7	93.6
Homosassa Springs, FL	90.7	91.8	92.7	91.1	92.9	93.3	92.2	91.3	91.9	88.5	93.9	90.9	90.1	93.8
Hot Springs, AR	87.8	86.0	86.6	88.1	88.3	88.1	86.5	86.9	88.3	85.4	85.8	86.2	87.4	89.2
Houma-Thibodaux, LA	92.3	91.5	95.5	96.5	96.8	97.0	95.2	96.0	96.1	93.9	89.8	90.9	92.0	88.1
Houston-The Woodlands-Sugar Land, TX	99.9	101.1	101.2	99.0	100.2	101.3	102.2	103.7	102.5	99.8	101.6	101.2	99.9	99.7
Huntington-Ashland, WV-KY-OH	88.3	87.7	88.5	91.1	90.0	88.7	89.9	90.6	90.7	88.6	88.2	87.0	86.8	88.5
Huntsville, AL	93.0	92.8	93.7	95.0	94.9	94.6	93.3	93.6	94.6	93.9	89.7	91.2	90.6	91.5
Idaho Falls, ID	96.1	94.6	91.9	93.1	92.9	93.1	90.2	96.1	94.8	95.4	90.8	92.0	90.9	90.6
Indianapolis-Carmel-Anderson, IN	97.0	96.5	96.4	95.0	95.0	96.0	95.6	95.0	95.1	93.3	94.8	95.3	93.8	95.0
Iowa City, IA	97.1	95.5	96.8	96.4	97.2	97.3	97.8	94.4	95.4	94.8	94.9	95.8	95.6	92.8
Ithaca, NY	101.9	103.4	102.4	102.4	104.8	101.5	100.9	104.9	104.8	105.1	101.6	104.2	101.5	102.4
Jackson, MI	96.4	94.1	91.1	93.7	93.6	92.6	90.2	91.5	92.0	91.3	92.9	93.3	92.2	93.8
Jackson, MS	93.0	92.4	94.8	95.1	94.0	94.2	93.9	93.3	94.5	92.9	89.0	88.7	89.1	89.0
Jackson, TN	87.3	83.2	86.5	86.4	87.8	85.4	87.4	87.2	85.7	85.9	84.1	84.1	83.7	85.5
Jacksonville, FL	99.8	97.9	98.9	99.5	99.2	98.7	99.4	99.4	99.9	98.8	97.0	96.0	96.4	98.7
Jacksonville, NC	95.4	95.3	97.2	98.3	96.7	95.0	95.6	94.0	95.0	92.9	90.7	90.2	88.4	89.7
Janesville-Beloit, WI	95.1	95.5	94.5	93.7	94.0	93.4	95.6	93.0	93.3	92.5	94.0	94.1	91.5	93.1
Jefferson City, MO	81.5	84.4	87.6	87.7	90.0	89.8	88.1	87.7	86.2	82.5	89.3	91.2	89.1	88.2
Johnson City, TN	92.0	88.6	91.4	91.8	93.6	90.5	92.5	91.9	91.4	90.0	86.3	89.1	88.5	87.3
Johnstown, PA	84.0	90.5	89.7	88.4	86.3	86.6	87.8	87.9	89.4	90.6	89.3	87.0	87.8	86.6
Jonesboro, AR	85.3	83.4	85.4	86.7	86.0	86.4	86.9	86.3	86.4	85.1	84.7	85.4	85.6	87.3
Joplin, MO	92.1	88.5	90.4	90.8	89.6	91.3	91.2	90.6	90.0	87.9	87.8	89.6	88.2	88.0
Kahului-Wailuku-Lahaina, HI	109.6	105.7	105.5	105.1	104.5	105.8	103.9	109.1	104.6	104.9	109.0	109.0	110.9	112.0
Kalamazoo-Portage, MI	96.7	95.9	96.1	94.5	95.0	96.3	95.7	94.2	94.0	93.4	94.9	94.1	95.5	93.2
Kankakee, IL	99.0	99.4	99.0	99.3	99.6	98.6	98.1	96.6	96.1	98.5	93.5	94.4	90.7	92.2
Kansas City, MO-KS	93.6	95.2	96.2	97.1	97.6	96.6	98.1	98.7	97.6	96.9	94.3	95.1	95.1	93.7
Kennewick-Richland, WA	95.0	99.4	96.4	101.2	99.8	99.1	99.6	96.4	97.4	98.7	101.2	102.6	100.0	100.5
Killeen-Temple, TX	95.5	93.6	95.5	96.3	95.5	96.2	96.3	95.2	95.5	94.2	92.0	92.0	92.0	93.6
Kingsport-Bristol, TN-VA	89.8	88.6	88.6	90.1	90.6	89.5	87.2	89.3	90.1	88.8	85.1	86.5	83.4	85.9
Kingston, NY	104.8	104.4	102.9	102.0	101.4	103.0	100.9	102.7	101.6	103.1	100.9	102.0	101.8	100.1
Knoxville, TN	92.3	91.9	93.3	94.2	95.2	94.0	93.4	92.6	94.2	93.4	88.9	90.8	89.5	90.4
Kokomo, IN	87.5	90.9	91.9	87.8	89.4	91.7	88.3	88.6	88.5	87.5	89.1	90.2	88.6	90.8
La Crosse-Onalaska, WI-MN	95.1	95.3	95.6	93.6	94.6	94.2	95.8	95.3	93.7	93.1	94.7	93.9	89.3	94.9
Lafayette, LA	90.1	91.0	91.1	92.4	93.3	93.0	94.2	93.2	93.3	91.8	90.3	90.0	90.0	90.7
Lafayette-West Lafayette, IN	93.1	94.1	94.2	93.7	94.5	95.1	94.3	93.8	92.6	91.3	92.5	93.1	90.9	92.5
Lake Charles, LA	92.3	90.1	92.2	93.1	92.9	93.3	91.5	92.6	92.6	92.3	89.3	90.0	91.1	90.2
Lake Havasu City-Kingman, AZ	94.7	98.0	94.5	95.4	95.0	95.6	93.1	91.9	93.1	93.8	89.9	88.3	87.8	89.6
Lakeland-Winter Haven, FL	97.4	95.9	96.1	97.4	96.7	95.7	96.6	96.9	97.4	96.0	94.5	93.6	93.3	96.2
Lancaster, PA	100.1	100.1	98.7	98.1	98.7	99.9	97.7	100.0	99.8	101.1	98.3	97.2	98.1	97.1
Lansing-East Lansing, MI	96.5	96.3	97.2	94.7	95.6	96.4	95.9	93.8	94.5	93.3	94.2	94.8	93.7	94.1
Laredo, TX	93.3	92.7	93.4	94.6	93.6	92.8	94.6	95.2	95.4	90.7	90.7	90.8	91.8	89.9
Las Cruces, NM	92.4	93.1	94.0	96.1	95.4	92.6	93.3	90.7	91.0	92.7	87.8	91.1	87.1	86.1
Las Vegas-Henderson-Paradise, NV	101.8	104.4	101.4	102.8	102.4	100.3	99.5	98.7	97.7	100.3	96.3	99.0	97.7	95.5
Lawrence, KS	98.8	98.2	97.9	96.3	96.6	97.3	96.3	94.3	95.5	94.3	94.4	92.2	93.9	92.7
Lawton, OK	88.8	88.9	90.8	93.6	92.5	93.6	93.4	92.2	93.8	89.7	87.2	87.4	85.7	87.5
Lebanon, PA	98.2	98.4	96.2	95.9	96.1	96.4	96.0	98.3	96.0	98.0	96.7	94.7	95.1	96.1
Lewiston, ID-WA	96.4	95.1	94.4	95.1	90.8	91.6	92.9	93.6	91.0	89.8	87.8	89.7	86.1	87.2
Lewiston-Auburn, ME	97.4	98.1	94.9	94.8	96.3	96.7	93.4	95.2	94.0	95.3	99.3	95.6	99.5	94.0
Lexington-Fayette, KY	95.0	94.3	94.0	95.7	96.4	95.7	95.3	95.3	94.8	94.7	91.2	92.5	91.6	92.0
Lima, OH	92.8	89.4	91.8	89.1	91.9	91.8	91.9	90.0	87.5	87.3	88.9	89.7	89.5	89.0
Lincoln, NE	96.2	95.8	95.7	93.7	94.5	95.8	95.8	94.6	94.4	93.6	94.5	95.1	94.9	93.1
Little Rock-North Little Rock-Conway, AR	94.1	92.8	94.6	95.1	94.8	94.8	94.3	94.8	94.8	93.2	90.4	90.5	90.7	92.0
Logan, UT-ID	96.7	94.5	93.5	93.0	93.9	94.0	95.2	98.0	96.1	95.3	91.8	92.2	91.1	92.0
Longview, TX	92.9	92.2	93.6	94.3	94.8	94.3	93.8	94.5	94.8	92.2	90.9	92.2	92.5	92.7
Longview, WA	98.2	96.0	94.8	95.2	93.6	95.0	96.2	97.2	96.3	97.3	99.5	98.7	100.2	98.8
Los Angeles-Long Beach-Anaheim, CA	112.0	110.7	111.1	110.2	110.9	111.1	110.7	112.1	110.1	110.0	111.0	110.6	113.6	113.8
Louisville/Jefferson County, KY-IN	93.9	92.6	94.6	95.1	95.7	95.8	96.0	95.3	95.3	94.8	91.8	91.4	91.8	91.8
Lubbock, TX	96.8	95.0	97.0	96.9	96.8	97.1	96.9	97.7	97.3	95.5	92.5	93.4	94.7	93.9
Lynchburg, VA	92.1	89.9	91.7	94.2	92.1	93.5	92.6	93.5	91.2	91.7	89.6	89.0	88.1	91.3
Macon-Bibb County, GA	92.1	89.8	90.9	92.1	91.5	91.1	89.2	89.5	90.3	89.8	88.6	87.0	85.1	87.4
Madera, CA	97.0	99.3	95.2	97.1	98.6	95.6	96.0	95.4	93.8	97.7	100.9	98.4	94.6	100.1
Madison, WI	98.3	98.2	98.7	97.3	97.7	98.1	98.1	96.3	97.0	95.7	98.3	98.2	96.0	96.7
Manchester-Nashua, NH	107.5	104.0	103.2	103.6	102.3	101.5	103.2	103.7	106.4	107.1	103.5	104.1	104.8	102.2

Regional Price Parities by Metropolitan Statistical Area—*Continued*

(Percent of U.S. Price Level; U.S. Average Price = 100.0)

Metropolitan Statistical Area	2008	2009	2010	2011	2012	2013	2014	2015	2016	2017	2018	2019	2020	2021
Manhattan, KS	87.3	90.3	94.5	93.9	95.5	96.0	96.0	92.9	90.8	91.0	93.8	93.0	91.7	90.6
Mankato, MN	85.1	88.8	94.1	90.0	93.7	90.1	90.0	91.8	90.2	89.5	95.0	95.0	91.1	88.3
Mansfield, OH	92.2	90.4	91.3	90.5	90.9	87.6	89.0	88.9	89.3	87.6	85.6	89.1	89.0	88.6
McAllen-Edinburg-Mission, TX	87.3	87.6	88.6	88.6	90.0	89.5	90.1	90.3	90.3	89.3	86.9	86.9	88.3	87.8
Medford, OR	96.9	99.9	99.2	100.9	99.6	98.4	98.1	97.3	97.3	100.2	102.6	100.0	102.1	102.1
Memphis, TN-MS-AR	94.9	93.7	95.5	96.2	95.9	95.5	95.5	94.8	96.3	94.3	89.6	91.3	90.5	90.6
Merced, CA	94.3	98.3	96.3	97.9	97.7	96.4	95.7	94.3	94.3	98.3	101.4	101.5	99.0	100.3
Miami-Fort Lauderdale-Pompano Beach, FL	106.0	106.2	105.4	106.7	107.3	106.8	105.8	107.1	107.9	108.5	110.1	109.3	109.9	109.9
Michigan City-La Porte, IN	84.7	86.3	90.9	89.1	90.1	91.5	90.3	87.5	87.9	84.7	91.6	89.9	92.0	90.9
Midland, MI	94.4	94.1	92.5	93.1	93.3	92.9	93.4	90.5	91.6	89.3	92.7	92.4	88.9	91.7
Midland, TX	97.3	96.6	99.5	101.6	101.5	101.7	104.2	104.3	103.0	100.7	99.9	100.6	95.9	97.9
Milwaukee-Waukesha, WI	98.2	98.9	97.6	96.5	97.1	96.7	97.2	97.5	98.9	100.8	95.9	97.6	95.9	95.6
Minneapolis-St. Paul-Bloomington, MN-WI	102.3	104.3	102.5	102.6	101.4	102.4	103.6	102.3	102.1	102.3	104.8	103.0	102.6	103.6
Missoula, MT	99.9	97.1	96.9	98.4	94.4	94.4	96.4	97.5	95.1	97.8	92.6	95.7	93.6	94.7
Mobile, AL	91.3	90.7	91.7	93.0	93.4	93.2	92.6	92.0	92.7	91.7	87.3	88.1	86.9	87.8
Modesto, CA	98.0	101.7	99.1	100.4	101.0	99.6	98.1	97.7	96.8	99.9	104.7	104.8	103.5	103.0
Monroe, LA	88.9	86.3	91.0	89.9	88.7	89.4	89.6	87.0	88.3	87.3	86.6	86.0	82.8	86.4
Monroe, MI	96.0	96.7	96.7	97.1	93.5	94.4	96.5	94.4	91.9	93.2	95.3	93.6	93.7	92.2
Montgomery, AL	92.7	92.4	93.9	92.8	95.4	92.8	92.3	92.5	94.7	92.7	88.2	88.7	87.4	88.6
Morgantown, WV	89.9	88.0	93.8	93.9	90.6	93.1	91.9	97.1	94.6	92.1	90.1	93.9	91.4	91.8	95.6
Morristown, TN	86.7	84.2	86.4	88.7	87.6	87.9	86.9	87.5	85.8	86.6	85.8	86.7	83.9	84.6
Mount Vernon-Anacortes, WA	103.1	101.2	99.1	99.7	99.1	99.3	97.9	101.2	100.6	101.8	104.1	102.0	102.3	100.4
Muncie, IN	93.4	92.7	91.9	92.3	91.2	92.8	91.6	89.0	89.5	89.0	90.9	88.4	87.3	89.1
Muskegon, MI	93.2	91.4	92.3	91.3	90.2	90.5	92.5	87.8	90.4	89.8	91.7	93.4	93.6	92.1
Myrtle Beach-Conway-North Myrtle Beach, SC-NC	95.6	95.4	95.5	96.4	96.2	94.5	95.1	94.8	95.7	93.5	92.1	92.3	92.7	94.8
Napa, CA	116.6	112.9	112.2	110.7	109.8	111.6	113.6	112.2	113.6	121.4	115.9	112.7	112.2	112.1
Naples-Marco Island, FL	104.9	103.0	102.9	101.1	102.7	102.7	102.2	103.3	105.8	104.5	100.8	100.7	99.1	102.2
Nashville-Davidson--Murfreesboro--Franklin, TN	96.2	95.5	97.2	97.5	98.0	98.0	97.7	98.0	99.8	98.7	94.0	95.8	96.1	95.5
New Bern, NC	87.7	87.2	88.2	89.7	90.3	92.4	90.0	91.7	89.3	85.9	89.0	89.1	88.3	91.2
New Haven-Milford, CT	112.5	111.4	108.3	109.8	108.7	108.9	109.1	107.6	108.5	108.6	103.2	103.0	103.5	101.3
New Orleans-Metairie, LA	99.2	97.6	98.7	98.5	99.0	98.8	98.5	98.2	99.1	97.1	93.9	95.1	95.8	94.4
New York-Newark-Jersey City, NY-NJ-PA	112.9	114.4	112.9	114.3	113.7	113.2	113.1	113.2	113.4	113.4	114.6	115.0	115.4	114.6
Niles, MI	93.8	91.6	92.4	91.3	90.0	92.2	92.1	91.1	91.1	89.6	89.0	87.3	90.4	92.1
North Port-Sarasota-Bradenton, FL	102.0	101.8	100.5	101.4	101.5	100.6	101.6	102.0	102.5	102.3	101.0	100.1	99.6	99.3
Norwich-New London, CT	104.0	103.2	101.6	100.6	101.0	100.5	98.0	101.5	101.9	102.7	102.1	102.7	102.4	100.0
Ocala, FL	96.0	95.5	95.2	95.5	95.0	94.0	93.9	94.3	95.0	94.4	93.3	91.9	91.4	94.0
Ocean City, NJ	105.8	106.1	110.2	110.9	103.5	100.6	105.7	104.3	103.5	107.0	102.6	98.4	102.3	94.5
Odessa, TX	96.3	95.0	95.9	98.1	98.5	100.7	101.3	100.3	99.2	98.5	97.0	98.2	99.2	96.5
Ogden-Clearfield, UT	95.8	98.7	97.7	99.5	99.5	97.7	97.6	95.8	95.4	97.6	95.6	97.6	95.3	93.6
Oklahoma City, OK	94.2	93.1	95.0	95.6	96.4	95.8	96.1	95.3	95.4	94.4	92.3	92.2	92.8	92.8
Olympia-Lacey-Tumwater, WA	105.9	104.9	101.1	103.9	101.4	101.8	104.2	103.0	105.7	107.5	105.0	104.7	102.1	103.6
Omaha-Council Bluffs, NE-IA	97.2	96.9	96.4	95.2	95.9	95.5	96.4	95.2	95.5	94.2	94.2	94.9	94.7	93.6
Orlando-Kissimmee-Sanford, FL	101.5	99.7	100.1	100.8	100.0	99.8	100.3	100.6	101.2	100.7	98.9	98.3	98.5	99.8
Oshkosh-Neenah, WI	96.4	94.4	94.8	94.1	93.5	93.0	94.3	92.6	93.2	92.0	92.2	92.5	92.6	92.6
Owensboro, KY	89.3	88.0	90.6	92.0	93.0	92.7	92.6	91.9	92.1	93.3	87.9	89.2	89.0	87.4
Oxnard-Thousand Oaks-Ventura, CA	108.2	108.8	107.8	107.6	108.9	108.8	110.7	111.3	109.1	107.7	114.1	112.6	111.6	111.4
Palm Bay-Melbourne-Titusville, FL	100.1	97.6	98.9	98.8	98.5	97.4	98.8	99.4	99.3	99.5	98.4	96.7	96.8	99.0
Panama City, FL	98.5	96.6	98.0	98.6	97.0	95.6	96.4	96.5	97.1	94.6	94.3	94.7	94.7	96.8
Parkersburg-Vienna, WV	88.0	86.3	87.9	88.8	89.7	91.4	90.7	92.9	93.0	91.0	89.5	87.8	86.2	89.5
Pensacola-Ferry Pass-Brent, FL	97.2	95.7	96.6	99.0	97.9	96.7	96.8	97.2	97.1	96.7	95.3	94.0	93.4	95.8
Peoria, IL	93.0	93.8	93.1	91.8	92.5	92.6	93.6	92.3	90.6	89.2	91.5	92.0	90.1	90.5
Philadelphia-Camden-Wilmington, PA-NJ-DE-MD	107.0	107.6	106.6	105.1	103.7	101.8	102.5	102.4	102.8	104.0	103.1	103.7	102.1	99.2
Phoenix-Mesa-Chandler, AZ	105.8	106.2	102.8	100.3	99.1	99.8	99.2	98.8	100.8	98.7	99.8	100.2	102.9	99.2
Pine Bluff, AR	87.0	86.5	88.2	88.1	89.1	88.2	87.7	86.5	88.0	84.0	82.9	84.4	84.2	87.9
Pittsburgh, PA	91.7	92.5	94.5	94.8	95.6	94.4	94.8	95.3	94.1	95.0	95.7	95.7	95.9	95.2
Pittsfield, MA	99.0	99.1	97.8	97.1	96.8	97.8	93.5	98.7	99.5	100.9	100.5	99.0	99.3	95.9
Pocatello, ID	94.3	91.8	89.3	90.5	91.8	89.9	91.2	94.5	90.4	91.9	89.0	88.0	88.9	88.8
Portland-South Portland, ME	101.7	101.6	98.5	98.8	100.4	100.6	96.6	99.8	99.5	102.2	102.1	97.0	102.6	101.7
Portland-Vancouver-Hillsboro, OR-WA	98.3	101.6	100.7	101.4	103.7	102.8	101.4	102.5	101.0	103.7	107.2	106.6	106.1	105.4
Port St. Lucie, FL	102.0	98.7	98.9	99.1	99.1	98.1	100.0	99.7	101.5	99.4	99.1	94.4	98.6	98.5
Poughkeepsie-Newburgh-Middletown, NY	NA	NA	NA	NA	NA	NA	NA	NA	109.3	109.3	110.6	111.9	109.5	110.1
Prescott Valley-Prescott, AZ	102.1	98.7	97.1	97.3	96.5	96.5	96.8	99.3	98.9	99.5	93.7	95.9	93.3	94.0
Providence-Warwick, RI-MA	102.3	102.5	100.8	100.7	99.6	101.0	99.8	101.2	101.4	103.1	101.6	101.8	101.7	101.2
Provo-Orem, UT	96.9	101.5	98.1	100.5	100.5	99.3	97.6	97.2	96.8	99.3	96.5	98.1	94.7	95.8
Pueblo, CO	89.9	95.1	92.9	96.5	94.4	93.5	92.0	91.7	92.9	94.4	90.9	92.6	90.0	90.9
Punta Gorda, FL	98.3	96.8	98.8	98.1	98.7	96.6	97.8	98.8	98.2	98.9	97.2	95.7	98.9	96.3
Racine, WI	96.0	96.4	94.8	94.2	94.3	94.8	94.1	96.4	96.1	98.4	93.6	94.2	93.9	92.2
Raleigh-Cary, NC	97.2	96.3	97.6	98.4	98.4	98.4	98.8	98.7	99.8	98.5	96.8	95.6	95.5	97.6
Rapid City, SD	91.1	90.6	91.5	87.9	95.2	91.9	93.0	91.7	91.4	89.8	92.2	92.4	93.6	91.9
Reading, PA	99.5	99.8	98.5	99.0	98.4	99.3	97.6	98.3	99.0	99.0	98.5	97.6	96.3	96.3
Redding, CA	96.5	99.5	97.7	100.7	100.2	97.3	98.7	96.5	95.9	99.1	102.9	102.5	99.9	99.4
Reno, NV	101.5	103.9	101.5	102.9	102.9	100.8	100.2	99.1	98.3	101.0	97.8	100.3	98.5	97.4

Regional Price Parities by Metropolitan Statistical Area—*Continued*

(Percent of U.S. Price Level; U.S. Average Price = 100.0)

Metropolitan Statistical Area	2008	2009	2010	2011	2012	2013	2014	2015	2016	2017	2018	2019	2020	2021
Richmond, VA	98.5	97.9	99.2	99.8	99.2	98.8	98.9	99.3	99.9	97.9	97.2	95.3	96.0	97.9
Riverside-San Bernardino-Ontario, CA	104.8	104.6	103.5	102.7	103.1	103.9	105.0	105.4	103.8	102.5	106.0	105.5	104.5	105.5
Roanoke, VA	92.6	92.0	95.1	92.7	93.5	93.0	94.2	93.7	93.3	91.3	91.9	91.1	90.3	93.8
Rochester, MN	94.7	96.2	92.9	93.6	94.3	93.8	95.8	93.5	93.3	92.9	93.3	94.9	96.9	91.9
Rochester, NY	100.6	100.3	99.1	98.3	98.4	99.4	97.8	99.4	99.3	101.0	98.9	98.0	97.6	97.7
Rockford, IL	96.9	96.2	93.7	94.1	93.8	93.1	93.5	92.9	93.1	91.0	91.0	92.8	91.9	93.4
Rocky Mount, NC	89.4	88.9	90.3	91.2	89.5	89.8	89.4	89.0	87.5	89.9	86.1	84.0	84.0	87.8
Rome, GA	87.3	86.1	89.2	86.1	86.0	87.9	88.4	88.0	87.9	85.9	88.7	87.8	86.3	90.9
Sacramento-Roseville-Folsom, CA	100.8	104.4	101.9	104.0	104.2	102.4	102.0	100.3	100.1	103.5	109.1	107.6	107.2	106.3
Saginaw, MI	93.8	92.3	91.2	92.3	91.3	92.0	91.2	90.6	90.7	89.4	90.8	90.1	89.0	91.1
St. Cloud, MN	96.5	95.1	92.1	95.7	95.3	95.2	95.5	92.5	94.0	90.6	93.2	94.8	91.3	87.5
St. George, UT	97.8	94.5	93.7	93.1	95.2	95.4	94.3	98.8	98.9	99.1	94.6	95.3	95.8	94.2
St. Joseph, MO-KS	93.1	91.6	90.4	90.8	91.4	92.3	90.6	90.5	89.0	88.1	89.7	88.7	87.8	88.9
St. Louis, MO-IL	92.3	94.0	97.3	96.3	94.7	96.3	97.7	95.2	95.6	95.9	94.7	95.1	95.2	96.2
Salem, OR	94.4	98.4	98.7	98.0	99.6	96.8	96.4	98.1	97.1	99.0	102.4	101.9	101.1	101.8
Salinas, CA	103.3	107.1	105.8	108.0	108.5	107.2	105.7	104.8	103.8	107.7	112.3	111.7	110.6	109.3
Salisbury, MD-DE	91.1	91.2	93.1	93.0	92.2	94.4	94.6	94.0	90.6	90.3	95.0	92.3	90.6	94.0
Salt Lake City, UT	98.7	102.1	99.7	102.3	101.9	101.0	99.7	98.8	97.8	100.6	97.7	99.5	97.3	96.2
San Angelo, TX	93.6	95.1	93.9	94.6	96.2	97.1	96.8	98.0	97.0	95.2	94.2	93.8	95.0	92.1
San Antonio-New Braunfels, TX	96.4	95.7	96.9	97.3	97.9	98.2	98.2	98.2	98.9	97.3	95.6	95.8	96.8	96.4
San Diego-Chula Vista-Carlsbad, CA	112.1	112.1	110.8	112.0	111.1	109.8	108.8	110.8	112.0	112.1	112.6	113.3	115.2	115.1
San Francisco-Oakland-Berkeley, CA	117.8	113.9	112.6	111.1	111.7	111.7	112.6	114.3	114.9	121.6	122.1	119.2	119.2	119.8
San Jose-Sunnyvale-Santa Clara, CA	117.7	113.6	112.4	111.0	112.0	112.6	113.8	115.1	115.8	122.8	114.6	113.1	113.7	111.6
San Luis Obispo-Paso Robles, CA	104.2	108.2	105.7	107.5	106.8	105.4	105.0	103.9	102.9	108.1	111.5	110.4	111.4	108.6
Santa Cruz-Watsonville, CA	117.2	111.9	112.0	110.8	111.2	110.4	111.8	113.5	113.6	120.8	111.4	110.9	111.9	109.1
Santa Fe, NM	97.2	101.3	99.4	102.2	101.7	100.0	101.7	97.8	98.2	98.8	96.2	96.7	96.4	93.4
Santa Maria-Santa Barbara, CA	106.3	110.5	107.2	108.7	109.1	107.4	106.8	105.3	106.6	108.7	112.9	111.1	112.2	111.8
Santa Rosa-Petaluma, CA	115.8	112.2	111.6	109.1	110.8	109.8	110.7	111.8	113.1	120.3	113.2	111.7	111.8	109.8
Savannah, GA	97.1	95.0	97.8	98.7	98.4	97.2	96.8	96.7	98.3	96.4	95.2	94.2	92.4	95.4
Scranton--Wilkes-Barre, PA	95.2	95.4	94.2	94.0	93.8	95.1	92.0	95.6	94.5	95.1	92.8	93.0	93.3	93.4
Seattle-Tacoma-Bellevue, WA	108.2	108.1	105.6	105.2	105.0	104.6	106.5	106.7	109.1	112.7	110.4	112.3	112.9	114.6
Sebastian-Vero Beach, FL	94.0	92.0	96.0	93.5	93.8	95.7	94.9	93.7	96.0	92.1	94.1	94.3	95.3	98.2
Sebring-Avon Park, FL	90.2	88.8	91.1	89.7	89.7	89.7	89.1	89.9	89.0	88.3	90.1	90.0	88.4	90.0
Sheboygan, WI	96.0	95.5	92.6	94.9	93.0	94.3	92.7	92.3	94.3	93.1	92.0	92.6	93.2	93.3
Sherman-Denison, TX	93.0	92.0	95.4	94.5	95.0	93.7	94.6	93.4	95.0	95.4	92.7	92.5	92.5	93.2
Shreveport-Bossier City, LA	92.4	92.1	93.0	94.9	94.9	93.4	95.0	94.4	93.6	90.5	89.9	89.8	88.5	90.3
Sierra Vista-Douglas, AZ	95.3	93.8	92.2	92.1	92.5	92.9	91.6	93.9	93.4	93.8	89.6	91.0	88.7	88.1
Sioux City, IA-NE-SD	91.8	91.4	92.4	90.9	91.2	91.2	91.3	89.5	90.3	89.4	91.3	92.1	90.0	90.0
Sioux Falls, SD	95.9	95.1	95.5	94.2	95.6	94.5	96.2	93.8	94.6	91.9	95.3	95.5	93.4	93.0
South Bend-Mishawaka, IN-MI	93.5	93.0	93.8	92.7	91.5	92.8	92.6	91.2	91.7	88.5	91.8	92.1	91.7	91.9
Spartanburg, SC	92.9	91.4	91.2	93.7	92.3	91.9	92.9	93.4	94.2	93.1	90.1	90.0	89.3	92.7
Spokane-Spokane Valley, WA	94.9	98.4	96.6	98.3	98.7	97.0	96.8	95.4	96.0	97.2	100.4	99.7	98.8	98.7
Springfield, IL	96.0	94.5	93.9	92.5	93.9	93.9	93.7	91.3	93.0	90.7	93.0	91.7	91.1	91.9
Springfield, MA	100.1	100.5	99.1	98.2	97.6	99.9	98.1	100.2	99.7	100.2	98.6	97.5	100.0	97.8
Springfield, MO	92.9	92.8	92.7	91.2	91.5	91.9	90.8	90.9	90.2	88.2	89.8	90.2	88.5	89.1
Springfield, OH	92.4	92.5	91.4	91.2	91.2	90.8	90.8	91.0	91.1	88.9	90.4	91.5	89.4	87.2
State College, PA	100.8	101.2	100.4	99.9	102.0	101.7	100.1	102.2	102.8	102.1	98.1	97.1	98.2	95.8
Staunton, VA	90.7	87.3	89.6	88.7	91.2	91.6	92.5	90.8	85.5	89.3	92.5	89.6	87.7	92.9
Stockton, CA	99.1	103.4	100.0	102.2	102.0	100.9	100.6	98.9	98.7	101.7	106.2	106.0	105.5	104.6
Sumter, SC	89.3	88.2	89.7	92.6	89.2	90.1	88.7	88.9	87.1	89.0	87.5	85.9	81.6	86.6
Syracuse, NY	98.4	98.2	97.8	96.9	96.4	97.3	95.8	98.6	98.7	98.9	97.6	95.3	96.3	96.5
Tallahassee, FL	96.1	94.4	96.0	97.5	97.6	96.4	96.3	96.5	97.1	97.1	93.9	93.2	91.2	95.0
Tampa-St. Petersburg-Clearwater, FL	103.4	103.4	101.8	100.5	100.7	101.2	101.2	101.2	97.3	96.7	95.2	96.3	101.2	99.0
Terre Haute, IN	89.1	89.2	91.6	89.8	88.9	88.5	90.2	88.1	86.5	87.1	89.3	89.3	87.3	87.4
Texarkana, TX-AR	89.0	88.3	89.5	91.3	89.7	88.9	90.3	90.2	91.3	88.3	87.2	87.8	87.8	88.4
The Villages, FL	90.7	91.8	92.7	91.1	93.6	94.2	94.0	93.7	94.3	91.4	93.3	94.3	92.3	96.1
Toledo, OH	94.4	92.9	93.7	92.6	92.7	92.6	93.0	92.4	92.1	91.3	92.4	92.6	90.8	90.5
Topeka, KS	92.8	92.4	93.9	92.7	92.7	92.5	92.2	91.8	90.0	89.2	91.7	90.8	90.1	89.2
Trenton-Princeton, NJ	104.3	109.6	106.2	107.6	108.0	107.7	108.4	108.6	108.0	109.9	104.0	104.5	104.4	101.9
Tucson, AZ	97.7	101.0	99.0	100.5	100.8	99.2	98.5	97.7	96.9	97.7	94.9	95.3	94.0	92.9
Tulsa, OK	93.6	93.1	94.1	94.5	94.2	94.6	94.9	94.7	94.9	93.7	91.4	91.4	91.8	92.0
Tuscaloosa, AL	90.4	89.7	91.3	90.5	91.2	90.2	92.2	89.5	91.3	92.3	85.5	88.5	86.9	88.1
Twin Falls, ID	NA	NA	NA	NA	NA	NA	NA	93.6	93.1	94.7	89.3	90.4	87.9	90.0
Tyler, TX	97.1	96.3	98.4	98.8	97.1	98.1	96.1	98.4	98.3	95.3	93.5	94.6	95.4	94.8
Urban Honolulu, HI	110.7	115.7	112.6	113.1	112.4	115.2	114.6	113.6	113.9	113.5	112.8	113.1	115.2	114.7
Utica-Rome, NY	94.8	95.1	94.7	94.1	93.4	95.5	93.9	95.8	95.1	95.4	94.9	93.0	93.8	92.8
Valdosta, GA	90.3	87.3	90.3	88.2	89.1	86.4	89.0	87.6	88.0	85.9	86.9	87.3	84.9	88.3
Vallejo, CA	114.9	111.0	109.8	107.9	108.5	108.2	108.7	110.5	110.6	117.6	110.6	109.4	110.8	109.4
Victoria, TX	94.8	92.8	92.4	96.5	95.6	96.1	97.2	96.8	98.5	94.9	93.7	93.6	95.4	92.1
Vineland-Bridgeton, NJ	103.2	104.7	103.6	102.8	101.7	99.6	99.2	98.5	99.3	96.2	98.3	98.3	96.9	96.8
Virginia Beach-Norfolk-Newport News, VA-NC	99.6	99.1	101.1	101.1	100.3	100.0	99.9	100.2	101.0	99.1	97.9	95.6	95.6	97.8
Visalia, CA	94.2	97.1	95.4	97.3	97.7	95.8	95.4	94.6	93.7	96.6	100.7	99.9	99.1	99.0
Waco, TX	94.6	93.4	94.9	95.5	96.2	93.8	95.4	96.7	95.7	94.0	92.3	92.6	93.7	94.7

Regional Price Parities by Metropolitan Statistical Area—*Continued*

(Percent of U.S. Price Level; U.S. Average Price = 100.0)

Metropolitan Statistical Area	2008	2009	2010	2011	2012	2013	2014	2015	2016	2017	2018	2019	2020	2021
Walla Walla, WA	97.7	97.3	95.1	95.9	94.3	95.5	97.4	97.7	95.7	99.8	99.7	101.0	95.4	99.2
Warner Robins, GA	93.6	92.3	92.2	94.4	95.5	94.9	94.0	93.6	93.4	93.6	92.5	89.9	92.0	92.0
Washington-Arlington-Alexandria, DC-VA-MD-WV	114.2	114.2	113.9	112.8	111.1	113.3	113.4	113.3	111.5	109.9	111.4	109.8	111.5	111.3
Waterloo-Cedar Falls, IA	91.7	90.5	93.2	91.3	92.2	92.3	92.7	91.2	91.1	90.2	91.1	92.8	90.6	88.9
Watertown-Fort Drum, NY	94.3	97.9	97.2	98.3	97.6	98.0	96.2	97.1	97.3	98.5	96.7	95.2	91.1	94.0
Wausau-Weston, WI	93.0	92.7	93.5	92.9	92.6	91.1	91.1	91.5	90.6	89.8	91.1	91.8	89.3	90.0
Weirton-Steubenville, WV-OH	87.5	87.2	88.3	86.0	88.5	88.6	88.3	87.8	87.3	86.0	86.7	87.4	86.7	89.2
Wenatchee, WA	96.8	98.4	95.0	95.6	97.1	96.7	97.2	98.2	96.2	101.3	102.2	104.3	102.6	103.1
Wheeling, WV-OH	87.0	86.5	89.0	88.2	90.3	90.0	90.2	90.1	90.1	89.2	86.9	87.5	86.9	89.3
Wichita, KS	94.7	94.0	94.1	93.0	93.4	94.1	93.5	92.4	93.2	91.1	91.0	92.3	92.0	90.8
Wichita Falls, TX	94.4	91.2	93.1	94.4	94.4	93.6	94.6	93.3	94.2	91.9	88.6	89.8	92.6	91.1
Williamsport, PA	95.4	92.2	91.9	94.3	93.5	94.9	93.9	94.8	92.3	96.0	94.6	92.4	93.8	91.8
Wilmington, NC	94.3	93.9	95.6	95.9	98.2	97.2	97.5	96.1	96.3	95.7	95.9	95.2	94.3	97.6
Winchester, VA-WV	92.5	91.0	94.4	94.4	95.2	96.0	94.7	95.6	95.5	93.0	95.9	94.6	94.4	97.3
Winston-Salem, NC	92.2	91.4	93.0	94.1	92.9	92.6	93.3	93.3	93.7	91.7	90.7	89.4	89.6	91.7
Worcester, MA-CT	103.5	102.3	101.9	102.0	101.3	100.0	101.7	102.0	104.3	104.1	101.0	100.6	101.2	100.0
Yakima, WA	92.3	96.1	95.9	96.6	96.5	96.3	95.8	93.4	94.0	94.9	97.5	97.2	96.5	97.7
York-Hanover, PA	99.3	99.1	97.8	96.2	96.9	98.9	97.3	98.2	97.8	100.2	97.8	96.8	97.9	96.9
Youngstown-Warren-Boardman, OH-PA	91.9	91.0	91.0	89.6	91.5	90.8	90.7	89.5	90.2	88.0	88.5	89.2	86.1	87.4
Yuba City, CA	96.7	99.7	96.8	100.6	100.8	99.4	97.4	97.1	95.9	98.1	103.7	103.0	102.2	101.5
Yuma, AZ	92.0	99.3	94.2	96.2	95.6	95.1	94.4	93.3	91.1	93.3	90.3	90.3	88.9	89.5

NOTE: Regional Price Parities are not available for Enid, OK prior to 2013, Twin Falls, ID prior to 2015, and Poughkeepsie-Newburgh-Middletown, NY prior to 2016.
NA = Not available

Metropolitan Statistical Areas, Metropolitan Divisions, and Components

Core based statistical area (CBSA)	State/ County FIPS code	Title and Geographic Components	Core based statistical area (CBSA)	State/ County FIPS code	Title and Geographic Components
10180		Abilene, TX	12060	13063	Clayton County
10180	48059	Callahan County	12060	13067	Cobb County
10180	48253	Jones County	12060	13077	Coweta County
10180	48441	Taylor County	12060	13085	Dawson County
10420		Akron, OH	12060	13089	DeKalb County
10420	39133	Portage County	12060	13097	Douglas County
10420	39153	Summit County	12060	13113	Fayette County
10500		Albany, GA	12060	13117	Forsyth County
10500	13095	Dougherty County	12060	13121	Fulton County
10500	13177	Lee County	12060	13135	Gwinnett County
10500	13273	Terrell County	12060	13143	Haralson County
10500	13321	Worth County	12060	13149	Heard County
10540		Albany-Lebanon, OR	12060	13151	Henry County
10540	41043	Linn County	12060	13159	Jasper County
10580		Albany-Schenectady-Troy, NY	12060	13171	Lamar County
10580	36001	Albany County	12060	13199	Meriwether County
10580	36083	Rensselaer County	12060	13211	Morgan County
10580	36091	Saratoga County	12060	13217	Newton County
10580	36093	Schenectady County	12060	13223	Paulding County
10580	36095	Schoharie County	12060	13227	Pickens County
10740		Albuquerque, NM	12060	13231	Pike County
10740	35001	Bernalillo County	12060	13247	Rockdale County
10740	35043	Sandoval County	12060	13255	Spalding County
10740	35057	Torrance County	12060	13297	Walton County
10740	35061	Valencia County	12100		Atlantic City-Hammonton, NJ
10780		Alexandria, LA	12100	34001	Atlantic County
10780	22043	Grant Parish	12220		Auburn-Opelika, AL
10780	22079	Rapides Parish	12220	01081	Lee County
10900		Allentown-Bethlehem-Easton, PA-NJ	12260		Augusta-Richmond County, GA-SC
10900	34041	Warren County, NJ	12260	13033	Burke County
10900	42025	Carbon County, PA	12260	13073	Columbia County
10900	42077	Lehigh County, PA	12260	13181	Lincoln County
10900	42095	Northampton County, PA	12260	13189	McDuffie County
11020		Altoona, PA	12260	13245	Richmond County
11020	42013	Blair County	12260	45003	Aiken County
11100		Amarillo, TX	12260	45037	Edgefield County
11100	48011	Armstrong County	12420		Austin-Round Rock-Georgetown, TX
11100	48065	Carson County	12420	48021	Bastrop County
11100	48359	Oldham County	12420	48055	Caldwell County
11100	48375	Potter County	12420	48209	Hays County
11100	48381	Randall County	12420	48453	Travis County
11180		Ames, IA	12420	48491	Williamson County
11180	19015	Boone County	12540		Bakersfield, CA
11180	19169	Story County	12540	06029	Kern County
11260		Anchorage, AK	12580		Baltimore-Columbia-Towson, MD
11260	02020	Anchorage Municipality	12580	24003	Anne Arundel County
11260	02170	Matanuska-Susitna Borough	12580	24005	Baltimore County
11460		Ann Arbor, MI	12580	24013	Carroll County
11460	26161	Washtenaw County	12580	24025	Harford County
11500		Anniston-Oxford, AL	12580	24027	Howard County
11500	01015	Calhoun County	12580	24035	Queen Anne's County
11540		Appleton, WI	12580	24510	Baltimore city
11540	55015	Calumet County	12620		Bangor, ME
11540	55087	Outagamie County	12620	23019	Penobscot County
11700		Asheville, NC	12700		Barnstable Town, MA
11700	37021	Buncombe County	12700	25001	Barnstable County
11700	37087	Haywood County	12940		Baton Rouge, LA
11700	37089	Henderson County	12940	22005	Ascension Parish
11700	37115	Madison County	12940	22007	Assumption Parish
12020		Athens-Clarke County, GA	12940	22033	East Baton Rouge Parish
12020	13059	Clarke County	12940	22037	East Feliciana Parish
12020	13195	Madison County	12940	22047	Iberville Parish
12020	13219	Oconee County	12940	22063	Livingston Parish
12020	13221	Oglethorpe County	12940	22077	Pointe Coupee Parish
12060		Atlanta-Sandy Springs-Alpharetta, GA	12940	22091	St. Helena Parish
12060	13013	Barrow County	12940	22121	West Baton Rouge Parish
12060	13015	Bartow County	12940	22125	West Feliciana Parish
12060	13035	Butts County	12980		Battle Creek, MI
12060	13045	Carroll County	12980	26025	Calhoun County
12060	13057	Cherokee County	13020		Bay City, MI

Metropolitan Statistical Areas, Metropolitan Divisions, and Components—*Continued*

Core based statistical area (CBSA)	State/ County FIPS code	Title and Geographic Components
13020	26017	Bay County
13140		Beaumont-Port Arthur, TX
13140	48199	Hardin County
13140	48245	Jefferson County
13140	48361	Orange County
13220		Beckley, WV
13220	54019	Fayette County
13220	54081	Raleigh County
13380		Bellingham, WA
13380	53073	Whatcom County
13460		Bend, OR
13460	41017	Deschutes County
13740		Billings, MT
13740	30009	Carbon County
13740	30095	Stillwater County
13740	30111	Yellowstone County
13780		Binghamton, NY
13780	36007	Broome County
13780	36107	Tioga County
13820		Birmingham-Hoover, AL
13820	01007	Bibb County
13820	01009	Blount County
13820	01021	Chilton County
13820	01073	Jefferson County
13820	01115	St. Clair County
13820	01117	Shelby County
13900		Bismarck, ND
13900	38015	Burleigh County
13900	38059	Morton County
13900	38065	Oliver County
13980		Blacksburg-Christiansburg, VA
13980	51071	Giles County
13980	51155	Pulaski County
13980	51933	Montgomery + Radford
14010		Bloomington, IL
14010	17113	McLean County
14020		Bloomington, IN
14020	18105	Monroe County
14020	18119	Owen County
14100		Bloomsburg-Berwick, PA
14100	42037	Columbia County
14100	42093	Montour County
14260		Boise City, ID
14260	16001	Ada County
14260	16015	Boise County
14260	16027	Canyon County
14260	16045	Gem County
14260	16073	Owyhee County
14460		Boston-Cambridge-Newton, MA-NH
14460		Boston, MA Div 14454
14460	25021	Norfolk County
14460	25023	Plymouth County
14460	25025	Suffolk County
14460		Cambridge-Newton-Framingham, MA Div 15764
14460	25009	Essex County
14460	25017	Middlesex County
14460		Rockingham County-Strafford County, NH Div 40484
14460	33015	Rockingham County
14460	33017	Strafford County
14500		Boulder, CO
14500	08013	Boulder County
14540		Bowling Green, KY
14540	21003	Allen County
14540	21031	Butler County
14540	21061	Edmonson County
14540	21227	Warren County
14740		Bremerton-Silverdale-Port Orchard, WA
14740	53035	Kitsap County
14860		Bridgeport-Stamford-Norwalk, CT
14860	09001	Fairfield County
15180		Brownsville-Harlingen, TX
15180	48061	Cameron County
15260		Brunswick, GA
15260	13025	Brantley County
15260	13127	Glynn County
15260	13191	McIntosh County
15380		Buffalo-Cheektowaga, NY
15380	36029	Erie County
15380	36063	Niagara County
15500		Burlington, NC
15500	37001	Alamance County
15540		Burlington-South Burlington, VT
15540	50007	Chittenden County
15540	50011	Franklin County
15540	50013	Grand Isle County
15680		California-Lexington Park, MD
15680	24037	St. Mary's County
15940		Canton-Massillon, OH
15940	39019	Carroll County
15940	39151	Stark County
15980		Cape Coral-Fort Myers, FL
15980	12071	Lee County
16020		Cape Girardeau, MO-IL
16020	17003	Alexander County, IL
16020	29017	Bollinger County, MO
16020	29031	Cape Girardeau County, MO
16060		Carbondale-Marion, IL
16060	17077	Jackson County
16060	17087	Johnson County
16060	17199	Williamson County
16180		Carson City, NV
16180	32510	Carson City
16220		Casper, WY
16220	56025	Natrona County
16300		Cedar Rapids, IA
16300	19011	Benton County
16300	19105	Jones County
16300	19113	Linn County
16540		Chambersburg-Waynesboro, PA
16540	42055	Franklin County
16580		Champaign-Urbana, IL
16580	17019	Champaign County
16580	17147	Piatt County
16620		Charleston, WV
16620	54005	Boone County
16620	54015	Clay County
16620	54035	Jackson County
16620	54039	Kanawha County
16620	54043	Lincoln County
16700		Charleston-North Charleston, SC
16700	45015	Berkeley County
16700	45019	Charleston County
16700	45035	Dorchester County
16740		Charlotte-Concord-Gastonia, NC-SC
16740	37007	Anson County, NC
16740	37025	Cabarrus County, NC
16740	37071	Gaston County, NC
16740	37097	Iredell County, NC
16740	37109	Lincoln County, NC
16740	37119	Mecklenburg County, NC
16740	37159	Rowan County, NC
16740	37179	Union County, NC
16740	45023	Chester County, SC
16740	45057	Lancaster County, SC
16740	45091	York County, SC
16820		Charlottesville, VA
16820	51065	Fluvanna County
16820	51079	Greene County
16820	51125	Nelson County
16820	51901	Albemarle + Charlottesville
16860		Chattanooga, TN-GA
16860	13047	Catoosa County, GA
16860	13083	Dade County, GA
16860	13295	Walker County, GA
16860	47065	Hamilton County, TN
16860	47115	Marion County, TN
16860	47153	Sequatchie County, TN
16940		Cheyenne, WY
16940	56021	Laramie County
16980		Chicago-Naperville-Elgin, IL-IN-WI
16980		Chicago-Naperville-Evanston, IL Div 16984
16980	17031	Cook County
16980	17043	DuPage County
16980	17063	Grundy County
16980	17111	McHenry County
16980	17197	Will County
16980		Elgin, IL Div 20994
16980	17037	DeKalb County
16980	17089	Kane County
16980	17093	Kendall County
16980		Gary, IN Div 23844
16980	18073	Jasper County
16980	18089	Lake County
16980	18111	Newton County
16980	18127	Porter County
16980		Lake County-Kenosha County, IL-WI Div 29404

Metropolitan Statistical Areas, Metropolitan Divisions, and Components—*Continued*

Core based statistical area (CBSA)	State/ County FIPS code	Title and Geographic Components	Core based statistical area (CBSA)	State/ County FIPS code	Title and Geographic Components
16980	17097	Lake County, IL	18880	12131	Walton County
16980	55059	Kenosha County, WI	19060		Cumberland, MD-WV
17020		Chico, CA	19060	24001	Allegany County, MD
17020	06007	Butte County	19060	54057	Mineral County, WV
17140		Cincinnati, OH-KY-IN	19100		Dallas-Fort Worth-Arlington, TX
17140	18029	Dearborn County, IN	19100		Dallas-Plano-Irving, TX Div 19124
17140	18047	Franklin County, IN	19100	48085	Collin County
17140	18115	Ohio County, IN	19100	48113	Dallas County
17140	18161	Union County, IN	19100	48121	Denton County
17140	21015	Boone County, KY	19100	48139	Ellis County
17140	21023	Bracken County, KY	19100	48231	Hunt County
17140	21037	Campbell County, KY	19100	48257	Kaufman County
17140	21077	Gallatin County, KY	19100	48397	Rockwall County
17140	21081	Grant County, KY	19100		Fort Worth-Arlington-Grapevine, TX Div 23104
17140	21117	Kenton County, KY	19100	48251	Johnson County
17140	21191	Pendleton County, KY	19100	48367	Parker County
17140	39015	Brown County, OH	19100	48439	Tarrant County
17140	39017	Butler County, OH	19100	48497	Wise County
17140	39025	Clermont County, OH	19140		Dalton, GA
17140	39061	Hamilton County, OH	19140	13213	Murray County
17140	39165	Warren County, OH	19140	13313	Whitfield County
17300		Clarksville, TN-KY	19180		Danville, IL
17300	21047	Christian County, KY	19180	17183	Vermilion County
17300	21221	Trigg County, KY	19300		Daphne-Fairhope-Foley, AL
17300	47125	Montgomery County, TN	19300	01003	Baldwin County
17300	47161	Stewart County, TN	19340		Davenport-Moline-Rock Island, IA-IL
17420		Cleveland, TN	19340	17073	Henry County, IL
17420	47011	Bradley County	19340	17131	Mercer County, IL
17420	47139	Polk County	19340	17161	Rock Island County, IL
17460		Cleveland-Elyria, OH	19340	19163	Scott County, IA
17460	39035	Cuyahoga County	19380		Dayton-Kettering, OH
17460	39055	Geauga County	19380	39057	Greene County
17460	39085	Lake County	19380	39109	Miami County
17460	39093	Lorain County	19380	39113	Montgomery County
17460	39103	Medina County	19460		Decatur, AL
17660		Coeur d'Alene, ID	19460	01079	Lawrence County
17660	16055	Kootenai County	19460	01103	Morgan County
17780		College Station-Bryan, TX	19500		Decatur, IL
17780	48041	Brazos County	19500	17115	Macon County
17780	48051	Burleson County	19660		Deltona-Daytona Beach-Ormond Beach, FL
17780	48395	Robertson County	19660	12035	Flagler County
17820		Colorado Springs, CO	19660	12127	Volusia County
17820	08041	El Paso County	19740		Denver-Aurora-Lakewood, CO
17820	08119	Teller County	19740	08001	Adams County
17860		Columbia, MO	19740	08005	Arapahoe County
17860	29019	Boone County	19740	08014	Broomfield County
17860	29053	Cooper County	19740	08019	Clear Creek County
17860	29089	Howard County	19740	08031	Denver County
17900		Columbia, SC	19740	08035	Douglas County
17900	45017	Calhoun County	19740	08039	Elbert County
17900	45039	Fairfield County	19740	08047	Gilpin County
17900	45055	Kershaw County	19740	08059	Jefferson County
17900	45063	Lexington County	19740	08093	Park County
17900	45079	Richland County	19780		Des Moines-West Des Moines, IA
17900	45081	Saluda County	19780	19049	Dallas County
17980		Columbus, GA-AL	19780	19077	Guthrie County
17980	01113	Russell County, AL	19780	19099	Jasper County
17980	13053	Chattahoochee County, GA	19780	19121	Madison County
17980	13145	Harris County, GA	19780	19153	Polk County
17980	13197	Marion County, GA	19780	19181	Warren County
17980	13215	Muscogee County, GA	19820		Detroit-Warren-Dearborn, MI
17980	13259	Stewart County, GA	19820		Detroit-Dearborn-Livonia, MI Div 19804
17980	13263	Talbot County, GA	19820	26163	Wayne County
18020		Columbus, IN	19820		Warren-Troy-Farmington Hills, MI 47664
18020	18005	Bartholomew County	19820	26087	Lapeer County
18140		Columbus, OH	19820	26093	Livingston County
18140	39041	Delaware County	19820	26099	Macomb County
18140	39045	Fairfield County	19820	26125	Oakland County
18140	39049	Franklin County	19820	26147	St. Clair County
18140	39073	Hocking County	20020		Dothan, AL
18140	39089	Licking County	20020	01061	Geneva County
18140	39097	Madison County	20020	01067	Henry County
18140	39117	Morrow County	20020	01069	Houston County
18140	39127	Perry County	20100		Dover, DE
18140	39129	Pickaway County	20100	10001	Kent County
18140	39159	Union County	20220		Dubuque, IA
18580		Corpus Christi, TX	20220	19061	Dubuque County
18580	48355	Nueces County	20260		Duluth, MN-WI
18580	48409	San Patricio County	20260	27017	Carlton County, MN
18700		Corvallis, OR	20260	27075	Lake County, MN
18700	41003	Benton County	20260	27137	St. Louis County, MN
18880		Crestview-Fort Walton Beach-Destin, FL	20260	55031	Douglas County, WI
18880	12091	Okaloosa County	20500		Durham-Chapel Hill, NC

Metropolitan Statistical Areas, Metropolitan Divisions, and Components—*Continued*

Core based statistical area (CBSA)	State/ County FIPS code	Title and Geographic Components	Core based statistical area (CBSA)	State/ County FIPS code	Title and Geographic Components
20500	37037	Chatham County	24020		Glens Falls, NY
20500	37063	Durham County	24020	36113	Warren County
20500	37077	Granville County	24020	36115	Washington County
20500	37135	Orange County	24140		Goldsboro, NC
20500	37145	Person County	24140	37191	Wayne County
20700		East Stroudsburg, PA	24220		Grand Forks, ND-MN
20700	42089	Monroe County	24220	27119	Polk County, MN
20740		Eau Claire, WI	24220	38035	Grand Forks County, ND
20740	55017	Chippewa County	24260		Grand Island, NE
20740	55035	Eau Claire County	24260	31079	Hall County
20940		El Centro, CA	24260	31093	Howard County
20940	06025	Imperial County	24260	31121	Merrick County
21060		Elizabethtown-Fort Knox, KY	24300		Grand Junction, CO
21060	21093	Hardin County	24300	08077	Mesa County
21060	21123	Larue County	24340		Grand Rapids-Kentwood, MI
21060	21163	Meade County	24340	26067	Ionia County
21140		Elkhart-Goshen, IN	24340	26081	Kent County
21140	18039	Elkhart County	24340	26117	Montcalm County
21300		Elmira, NY	24340	26139	Ottawa County
21300	36015	Chemung County	24420		Grants Pass, OR
21340		El Paso, TX	24420	41033	Josephine County
21340	48141	El Paso County	24500		Great Falls, MT
21340	48229	Hudspeth County	24500	30013	Cascade County
21420		Enid, OK	24540		Greeley, CO
21420	40047	Garfield County	24540	08123	Weld County
21500		Erie, PA	24580		Green Bay, WI
21500	42049	Erie County	24580	55009	Brown County
21660		Eugene-Springfield, OR	24580	55061	Kewaunee County
21660	41039	Lane County	24580	55083	Oconto County
21780		Evansville, IN-KY	24660		Greensboro-High Point, NC
21780	18129	Posey County, IN	24660	37081	Guilford County
21780	18163	Vanderburgh County, IN	24660	37151	Randolph County
21780	18173	Warrick County, IN	24660	37157	Rockingham County
21780	21101	Henderson County, KY	24780		Greenville, NC
21820		Fairbanks, AK	24780	37147	Pitt County
21820	02090	Fairbanks North Star Borough	24860		Greenville-Anderson, SC
22020		Fargo, ND-MN	24860	45007	Anderson County
22020	27027	Clay County, MN	24860	45045	Greenville County
22020	38017	Cass County, ND	24860	45059	Laurens County
22140		Farmington, NM	24860	45077	Pickens County
22140	35045	San Juan County	25060		Gulfport-Biloxi, MS
22180		Fayetteville, NC	25060	28045	Hancock County
22180	37051	Cumberland County	25060	28047	Harrison County
22180	37085	Harnett County	25060	28059	Jackson County
22180	37093	Hoke County	25060	28131	Stone County
22220		Fayetteville-Springdale-Rogers, AR-MO	25180		Hagerstown-Martinsburg, MD-WV
22220	05007	Benton County, AR	25180	24043	Washington County, MD
22220	05087	Madison County, AR	25180	54003	Berkeley County, WV
22220	05143	Washington County, AR	25180	54065	Morgan County, WV
22380		Flagstaff, AZ	25220		Hammond, LA
22380	04005	Coconino County	25220	22105	Tangipahoa Parish
22420		Flint, MI	25260		Hanford-Corcoran, CA
22420	26049	Genesee County	25260	06031	Kings County
22500		Florence, SC	25420		Harrisburg-Carlisle, PA
22500	45031	Darlington County	25420	42041	Cumberland County
22500	45041	Florence County	25420	42043	Dauphin County
22520		Florence-Muscle Shoals, AL	25420	42099	Perry County
22520	01033	Colbert County	25500		Harrisonburg, VA
22520	01077	Lauderdale County	25500	51947	Rockingham + Harrisonburg, VA
22540		Fond du Lac, WI	25540		Hartford-East Hartford-Middletown, CT
22540	55039	Fond du Lac County	25540	09003	Hartford County
22660		Fort Collins, CO	25540	09007	Middlesex County
22660	08069	Larimer County	25540	09013	Tolland County
22900		Fort Smith, AR-OK	25620		Hattiesburg, MS
22900	05033	Crawford County, AR	25620	28031	Covington County
22900	05047	Franklin County, AR	25620	28035	Forrest County
22900	05131	Sebastian County, AR	25620	28073	Lamar County
22900	40135	Sequoyah County, OK	25620	28111	Perry County
23060		Fort Wayne, IN	25860		Hickory-Lenoir-Morganton, NC
23060	18003	Allen County	25860	37003	Alexander County
23060	18183	Whitley County	25860	37023	Burke County
23420		Fresno, CA	25860	37027	Caldwell County
23420	06019	Fresno County	25860	37035	Catawba County
23460		Gadsden, AL	25940		Hilton Head Island-Bluffton, SC
23460	01055	Etowah County	25940	45013	Beaufort County
23540		Gainesville, FL	25940	45053	Jasper County
23540	12001	Alachua County	25980		Hinesville, GA
23540	12041	Gilchrist County	25980	13179	Liberty County
23540	12075	Levy County	25980	13183	Long County
23580		Gainesville, GA	26140		Homosassa Springs, FL
23580	13139	Hall County	26140	12017	Citrus County
23900		Gettysburg, PA	26300		Hot Springs, AR
23900	42001	Adams County	26300	05051	Garland County

Metropolitan Statistical Areas, Metropolitan Divisions, and Components—*Continued*

Core based statistical area (CBSA)	State/County FIPS code	Title and Geographic Components
26380		Houma-Thibodaux, LA
26380	22057	Lafourche Parish
26380	22109	Terrebonne Parish
26420		Houston-The Woodlands-Sugar Land, TX
26420	48015	Austin County
26420	48039	Brazoria County
26420	48071	Chambers County
26420	48157	Fort Bend County
26420	48167	Galveston County
26420	48201	Harris County
26420	48291	Liberty County
26420	48339	Montgomery County
26420	48473	Waller County
26580		Huntington-Ashland, WV-KY-OH
26580	21019	Boyd County, KY
26580	21043	Carter County, KY
26580	21089	Greenup County, KY
26580	39087	Lawrence County, OH
26580	54011	Cabell County, WV
26580	54079	Putnam County, WV
26580	54099	Wayne County, WV
26620		Huntsville, AL
26620	01083	Limestone County
26620	01089	Madison County
26820		Idaho Falls, ID
26820	16019	Bonneville County
26820	16023	Butte County
26820	16051	Jefferson County
26900		Indianapolis-Carmel-Anderson, IN
26900	18011	Boone County
26900	18013	Brown County
26900	18057	Hamilton County
26900	18059	Hancock County
26900	18063	Hendricks County
26900	18081	Johnson County
26900	18095	Madison County
26900	18097	Marion County
26900	18109	Morgan County
26900	18133	Putnam County
26900	18145	Shelby County
26980		Iowa City, IA
26980	19103	Johnson County
26980	19183	Washington County
27060		Ithaca, NY
27060	36109	Tompkins County
27100		Jackson, MI
27100	26075	Jackson County
27140		Jackson, MS
27140	28029	Copiah County
27140	28049	Hinds County
27140	28051	Holmes County
27140	28089	Madison County
27140	28121	Rankin County
27140	28127	Simpson County
27140	28163	Yazoo County
27180		Jackson, TN
27180	47023	Chester County
27180	47033	Crockett County
27180	47053	Gibson County
27180	47113	Madison County
27260		Jacksonville, FL
27260	12003	Baker County
27260	12019	Clay County
27260	12031	Duval County
27260	12089	Nassau County
27260	12109	St. Johns County
27340		Jacksonville, NC
27340	37133	Onslow County
27500		Janesville-Beloit, WI
27500	55105	Rock County
27620		Jefferson City, MO
27620	29027	Callaway County
27620	29051	Cole County
27620	29135	Moniteau County
27620	29151	Osage County
27740		Johnson City, TN
27740	47019	Carter County
27740	47171	Unicoi County
27740	47179	Washington County
27780		Johnstown, PA
27780	42021	Cambria County
27860		Jonesboro, AR
27860	05031	Craighead County
27860	05111	Poinsett County
27900		Joplin, MO
27900	29097	Jasper County
27900	29145	Newton County
27980		Kahului-Wailuku-Lahaina, HI
27980	15009	Maui County
28020		Kalamazoo-Portage, MI
28020	26077	Kalamazoo County
28100		Kankakee, IL
28100	17091	Kankakee County
28140		Kansas City, MO-KS
28140	20091	Johnson County, KS
28140	20103	Leavenworth County, KS
28140	20107	Linn County, KS
28140	20121	Miami County, KS
28140	20209	Wyandotte County, KS
28140	29013	Bates County, MO
28140	29025	Caldwell County, MO
28140	29037	Cass County, MO
28140	29047	Clay County, MO
28140	29049	Clinton County, MO
28140	29095	Jackson County, MO
28140	29107	Lafayette County, MO
28140	29165	Platte County, MO
28140	29177	Ray County, MO
28420		Kennewick-Richland, WA
28420	53005	Benton County
28420	53021	Franklin County
28660		Killeen-Temple, TX
28660	48027	Bell County
28660	48099	Coryell County
28660	48281	Lampasas County
28700		Kingsport-Bristol, TN-VA
28700	47073	Hawkins County, TN
28700	47163	Sullivan County, TN
28700	51169	Scott County, VA
28700	51953	Washington + Bristol, VA
28740		Kingston, NY
28740	36111	Ulster County
28940		Knoxville, TN
28940	47001	Anderson County
28940	47009	Blount County
28940	47013	Campbell County
28940	47093	Knox County
28940	47105	Loudon County
28940	47129	Morgan County
28940	47145	Roane County
28940	47173	Union County
29020		Kokomo, IN
29020	18067	Howard County
29100		La Crosse-Onalaska, WI-MN
29100	27055	Houston County, MN
29100	55063	La Crosse County, WI
29180		Lafayette, LA
29180	22001	Acadia Parish
29180	22045	Iberia Parish
29180	22055	Lafayette Parish
29180	22099	St. Martin Parish
29180	22113	Vermilion Parish
29200		Lafayette-West Lafayette, IN
29200	18007	Benton County
29200	18015	Carroll County
29200	18157	Tippecanoe County
29200	18171	Warren County
29340		Lake Charles, LA
29340	22019	Calcasieu Parish
29340	22023	Cameron Parish
29420		Lake Havasu City-Kingman, AZ
29420	04015	Mohave County
29460		Lakeland-Winter Haven, FL
29460	12105	Polk County
29540		Lancaster, PA
29540	42071	Lancaster County
29620		Lansing-East Lansing, MI
29620	26037	Clinton County
29620	26045	Eaton County
29620	26065	Ingham County
29620	26155	Shiawassee County
29700		Laredo, TX
29700	48479	Webb County
29740		Las Cruces, NM
29740	35013	Doña Ana County
29820		Las Vegas-Henderson-Paradise, NV

Metropolitan Statistical Areas, Metropolitan Divisions, and Components—*Continued*

Core based statistical area (CBSA)	State/ County FIPS code	Title and Geographic Components	Core based statistical area (CBSA)	State/ County FIPS code	Title and Geographic Components
29820	32003	Clark County	31740	20061	Geary County
29940		Lawrence, KS	31740	20149	Pottawatomie County
29940	20045	Douglas County	31740	20161	Riley County
30020		Lawton, OK	31860		Mankato, MN
30020	40031	Comanche County	31860	27013	Blue Earth County
30020	40033	Cotton County	31860	27103	Nicollet County
30140		Lebanon, PA	31900		Mansfield, OH
30140	42075	Lebanon County	31900	39139	Richland County
30300		Lewiston, ID-WA	32580		McAllen-Edinburg-Mission, TX
30300	16069	Nez Perce County, ID	32580	48215	Hidalgo County
30300	53003	Asotin County, WA	32780		Medford, OR
30340		Lewiston-Auburn, ME	32780	41029	Jackson County
30340	23001	Androscoggin County	32820		Memphis, TN-MS-AR
30460		Lexington-Fayette, KY	32820	05035	Crittenden County, AR
30460	21017	Bourbon County	32820	28033	DeSoto County, MS
30460	21049	Clark County	32820	28093	Marshall County, MS
30460	21067	Fayette County	32820	28137	Tate County, MS
30460	21113	Jessamine County	32820	28143	Tunica County, MS
30460	21209	Scott County	32820	47047	Fayette County, TN
30460	21239	Woodford County	32820	47157	Shelby County, TN
30620		Lima, OH	32820	47167	Tipton County, TN
30620	39003	Allen County	32900		Merced, CA
30700		Lincoln, NE	32900	06047	Merced County
30700	31109	Lancaster County	33100		Miami-Fort Lauderdale-Pompano Beach, FL
30700	31159	Seward County	33100		Fort Lauderdale-Pompano Beach-Sunrise, FL Div 22744
30780		Little Rock-North Little Rock-Conway, AR	33100	12011	Broward County
30780	05045	Faulkner County	33100		Miami-Miami Beach-Kendall, FL Div 33124
30780	05053	Grant County	33100	12086	Miami-Dade County
30780	05085	Lonoke County	33100		West Palm Beach-Boca Raton-Boynton Beach, FL Div 48424
30780	05105	Perry County	33100	12099	Palm Beach County
30780	05119	Pulaski County	33140		Michigan City-La Porte, IN
30780	05125	Saline County	33140	18091	LaPorte County
30860		Logan, UT-ID	33220		Midland, MI
30860	16041	Franklin County, ID	33220	26111	Midland County
30860	49005	Cache County, UT	33260		Midland, TX
30980		Longview, TX	33260	48317	Martin County
30980	48183	Gregg County	33260	48329	Midland County
30980	48203	Harrison County	33340		Milwaukee-Waukesha, WI
30980	48401	Rusk County	33340	55079	Milwaukee County
30980	48459	Upshur County	33340	55089	Ozaukee County
31020		Longview, WA	33340	55131	Washington County
31020	53015	Cowlitz County	33340	55133	Waukesha County
31080		Los Angeles-Long Beach-Anaheim, CA	33460		Minneapolis-St. Paul-Bloomington, MN-WI
31080		Anaheim-Santa Ana-Irvine, CA Div 11244	33460	27003	Anoka County, MN
31080	06059	Orange County	33460	27019	Carver County, MN
31080		Los Angeles-Long Beach-Glendale, CA Div 31084	33460	27025	Chisago County, MN
31080	06037	Los Angeles County	33460	27037	Dakota County, MN
31140		Louisville/Jefferson County, KY-IN	33460	27053	Hennepin County, MN
31140	18019	Clark County, IN	33460	27059	Isanti County, MN
31140	18043	Floyd County, IN	33460	27079	Le Sueur County, MN
31140	18061	Harrison County, IN	33460	27095	Mille Lacs County, MN
31140	18175	Washington County, IN	33460	27123	Ramsey County, MN
31140	21029	Bullitt County, KY	33460	27139	Scott County, MN
31140	21103	Henry County, KY	33460	27141	Sherburne County, MN
31140	21111	Jefferson County, KY	33460	27163	Washington County, MN
31140	21185	Oldham County, KY	33460	27171	Wright County, MN
31140	21211	Shelby County, KY	33460	55093	Pierce County, WI
31140	21215	Spencer County, KY	33460	55109	St. Croix County, WI
31180		Lubbock, TX	33540		Missoula, MT
31180	48107	Crosby County	33540	30063	Missoula County
31180	48303	Lubbock County	33660		Mobile, AL
31180	48305	Lynn County	33660	01097	Mobile County
31340		Lynchburg, VA	33660	01129	Washington County
31340	51009	Amherst County	33700		Modesto, CA
31340	51011	Appomattox County	33700	06099	Stanislaus County
31340	51909	Bedford County	33740		Monroe, LA
31340	51911	Campbell + Lynchburg, VA	33740	22067	Morehouse Parish
31420		Macon-Bibb County, GA	33740	22073	Ouachita Parish
31420	13021	Bibb County	33740	22111	Union Parish
31420	13079	Crawford County	33780		Monroe, MI
31420	13169	Jones County	33780	26115	Monroe County
31420	13207	Monroe County	33860		Montgomery, AL
31420	13289	Twiggs County	33860	01001	Autauga County
31460		Madera, CA	33860	01051	Elmore County
31460	06039	Madera County	33860	01085	Lowndes County
31540		Madison, WI	33860	01101	Montgomery County
31540	55021	Columbia County	34060		Morgantown, WV
31540	55025	Dane County	34060	54061	Monongalia County
31540	55045	Green County	34060	54077	Preston County
31540	55049	Iowa County	34100		Morristown, TN
31700		Manchester-Nashua, NH	34100	47057	Grainger County
31700	33011	Hillsborough County	34100	47063	Hamblen County
31740		Manhattan, KS	34100	47089	Jefferson County

Metropolitan Statistical Areas, Metropolitan Divisions, and Components—*Continued*

Core based statistical area (CBSA)	State/ County FIPS code	Title and Geographic Components	Core based statistical area (CBSA)	State/ County FIPS code	Title and Geographic Components
34580		Mount Vernon-Anacortes, WA	36260		Ogden-Clearfield, UT
34580	53057	Skagit County	36260	49003	Box Elder County
34620		Muncie, IN	36260	49011	Davis County
34620	18035	Delaware County	36260	49029	Morgan County
34740		Muskegon, MI	36260	49057	Weber County
34740	26121	Muskegon County	36420		Oklahoma City, OK
34820		Myrtle Beach-Conway-North Myrtle Beach, SC-NC	36420	40017	Canadian County
34820	37019	Brunswick County, NC	36420	40027	Cleveland County
34820	45051	Horry County, SC	36420	40051	Grady County
34900		Napa, CA	36420	40081	Lincoln County
34900	06055	Napa County	36420	40083	Logan County
34940		Naples-Marco Island, FL	36420	40087	McClain County
34940	12021	Collier County	36420	40109	Oklahoma County
34980		Nashville-Davidson—Murfreesboro—Franklin, TN	36500		Olympia-Lacey-Tumwater, WA
34980	47015	Cannon County	36500	53067	Thurston County
34980	47021	Cheatham County	36540		Omaha-Council Bluffs, NE-IA
34980	47037	Davidson County	36540	19085	Harrison County, IA
34980	47043	Dickson County	36540	19129	Mills County, IA
34980	47111	Macon County	36540	19155	Pottawattamie County, IA
34980	47119	Maury County	36540	31025	Cass County, NE
34980	47147	Robertson County	36540	31055	Douglas County, NE
34980	47149	Rutherford County	36540	31153	Sarpy County, NE
34980	47159	Smith County	36540	31155	Saunders County, NE
34980	47165	Sumner County	36540	31177	Washington County, NE
34980	47169	Trousdale County	36740		Orlando-Kissimmee-Sanford, FL
34980	47187	Williamson County	36740	12069	Lake County
34980	47189	Wilson County	36740	12095	Orange County
35100		New Bern, NC	36740	12097	Osceola County
35100	37049	Craven County	36740	12117	Seminole County
35100	37103	Jones County	36780		Oshkosh-Neenah, WI
35100	37137	Pamlico County	36780	55139	Winnebago County
35300		New Haven-Milford, CT	36980		Owensboro, KY
35300	09009	New Haven County	36980	21059	Daviess County
35380		New Orleans-Metairie, LA	36980	21091	Hancock County
35380	22051	Jefferson Parish	36980	21149	McLean County
35380	22071	Orleans Parish	37100		Oxnard-Thousand Oaks-Ventura, CA
35380	22075	Plaquemines Parish	37100	06111	Ventura County
35380	22087	St. Bernard Parish	37340		Palm Bay-Melbourne-Titusville, FL
35380	22089	St. Charles Parish	37340	12009	Brevard County
35380	22093	St. James Parish	37460		Panama City, FL
35380	22095	St. John the Baptist Parish	37460	12005	Bay County
35380	22103	St. Tammany Parish	37620		Parkersburg-Vienna, WV
35620		New York-Newark-Jersey City, NY-NJ-PA	37620	54105	Wirt County
35620		Nassau County-Suffolk County, NY Div 35004	37620	54107	Wood County
35620	36059	Nassau County	37860		Pensacola-Ferry Pass-Brent, FL
35620	36103	Suffolk County	37860	12033	Escambia County
35620		Newark, NJ-PA Div 35084	37860	12113	Santa Rosa County
35620	34013	Essex County, NJ	37900		Peoria, IL
35620	34019	Hunterdon County, NJ	37900	17057	Fulton County
35620	34027	Morris County, NJ	37900	17123	Marshall County
35620	34037	Sussex County, NJ	37900	17143	Peoria County
35620	34039	Union County, NJ	37900	17175	Stark County
35620	42103	Pike County, PA	37900	17179	Tazewell County
35620		New Brunswick-Lakewood, NJ Div 35154	37900	17203	Woodford County
35620	34023	Middlesex County	37980		Philadelphia-Camden-Wilmington, PA-NJ-DE-MD
35620	34025	Monmouth County	37980		Camden, NJ Div 15804
35620	34029	Ocean County	37980	34005	Burlington County, NJ
35620	34035	Somerset County	37980	34007	Camden County, NJ
35620		New York-Jersey City-White Plains, NY-NJ Div 35614	37980	34015	Gloucester County, NJ
35620	34003	Bergen County, NJ	37980		Montgomery County-Bucks County-Chester County, PA Div 33874
35620	34017	Hudson County, NJ	37980	42017	Bucks County, PA
35620	34031	Passaic County, NJ	37980	42029	Chester County, PA
35620	36005	Bronx County, NY	37980	42091	Montgomery County, PA
35620	36047	Kings County, NY	37980		Philadelphia, PA Div 37964
35620	36061	New York County, NY	37980	42045	Delaware County, PA
35620	36079	Putnam County, NY	37980	42101	Philadelphia County, PA
35620	36081	Queens County, NY	37980		Wilmington, DE-MD-NJ Div 48864
35620	36085	Richmond County, NY	37980	10003	New Castle County, DE
35620	36087	Rockland County, NY	37980	24015	Cecil County, MD
35620	36119	Westchester County, NY	37980	34033	Salem County, NJ
35660		Niles-Benton Harbor, MI	38060		Phoenix-Mesa-Chandler, AZ
35660	26021	Berrien County	38060	04013	Maricopa County
35840		North Port-Sarasota-Bradenton, FL	38060	04021	Pinal County
35840	12081	Manatee County	38220		Pine Bluff, AR
35840	12115	Sarasota County	38220	05025	Cleveland County
35980		Norwich-New London, CT	38220	05069	Jefferson County
35980	09011	New London County	38220	05079	Lincoln County
36100		Ocala, FL	38300		Pittsburgh, PA
36100	12083	Marion County	38300	42003	Allegheny County
36140		Ocean City, NJ	38300	42005	Armstrong County
36140	34009	Cape May County	38300	42007	Beaver County
36220		Odessa, TX	38300	42019	Butler County
36220	48135	Ector County	38300	42051	Fayette County

Metropolitan Statistical Areas, Metropolitan Divisions, and Components—*Continued*

Core based statistical area (CBSA)	State/ County FIPS code	Title and Geographic Components	Core based statistical area (CBSA)	State/ County FIPS code	Title and Geographic Components
38300	42125	Washington County	40340	27045	Fillmore County
38300	42129	Westmoreland County	40340	27109	Olmsted County
38340		Pittsfield, MA	40340	27157	Wabasha County
38340	25003	Berkshire County	40380		Rochester, NY
38540		Pocatello, ID	40380	36051	Livingston County
38540	16005	Bannock County	40380	36055	Monroe County
38540	16077	Power County	40380	36069	Ontario County
38860		Portland-South Portland, ME	40380	36073	Orleans County
38860	23005	Cumberland County	40380	36117	Wayne County
38860	23023	Sagadahoc County	40380	36123	Yates County
38860	23031	York County	40420		Rockford, IL
38900		Portland-Vancouver-Hillsboro, OR-WA	40420	17007	Boone County
38900	41005	Clackamas County, OR	40420	17201	Winnebago County
38900	41009	Columbia County, OR	40580		Rocky Mount, NC
38900	41051	Multnomah County, OR	40580	37065	Edgecombe County
38900	41067	Washington County, OR	40580	37127	Nash County
38900	41071	Yamhill County, OR	40660		Rome, GA
38900	53011	Clark County, WA	40660	13115	Floyd County
38900	53059	Skamania County, WA	40900		Sacramento—Roseville—Folsom, CA
38940		Port St. Lucie, FL	40900	06017	El Dorado County
38940	12085	Martin County	40900	06061	Placer County
38940	12111	St. Lucie County	40900	06067	Sacramento County
39100		Poughkeepsie-Newburgh-Middletown, NY	40900	06113	Yolo County
39100	36027	Dutchess County	40980		Saginaw, MI
39100	36071	Orange County	40980	26145	Saginaw County
39140		Prescott Valley-Prescott, AZ	41060		St. Cloud, MN
39140	04025	Yavapai County	41060	27009	Benton County
39300		Providence-Warwick, RI-MA	41060	27145	Stearns County
39300	25005	Bristol County, MA	41100		St. George, UT
39300	44001	Bristol County, RI	41100	49053	Washington County
39300	44003	Kent County, RI	41140		St. Joseph, MO-KS
39300	44005	Newport County, RI	41140	20043	Doniphan County, KS
39300	44007	Providence County, RI	41140	29003	Andrew County, MO
39300	44009	Washington County, RI	41140	29021	Buchanan County, MO
39340		Provo-Orem, UT	41140	29063	DeKalb County, MO
39340	49023	Juab County	41180		St. Louis, MO-IL
39340	49049	Utah County	41180	17005	Bond County, IL
39380		Pueblo, CO	41180	17013	Calhoun County, IL
39380	08101	Pueblo County	41180	17027	Clinton County, IL
39460		Punta Gorda, FL	41180	17083	Jersey County, IL
39460	12015	Charlotte County	41180	17117	Macoupin County, IL
39540		Racine, WI	41180	17119	Madison County, IL
39540	55101	Racine County	41180	17133	Monroe County, IL
39580		Raleigh-Cary, NC	41180	17163	St. Clair County, IL
39580	37069	Franklin County	41180	29055	Crawford County + Sullivan, MO
39580	37101	Johnston County	41180	29071	Franklin County, MO
39580	37183	Wake County	41180	29099	Jefferson County, MO
39660		Rapid City, SD	41180	29113	Lincoln County, MO
39660	46093	Meade County	41180	29183	St. Charles County, MO
39660	46103	Pennington County	41180	29189	St. Louis County, MO
39740		Reading, PA	41180	29219	Warren County, MO
39740	42011	Berks County	41180	29510	St. Louis city, MO
39820		Redding, CA	41420		Salem, OR
39820	06089	Shasta County	41420	41047	Marion County
39900		Reno, NV	41420	41053	Polk County
39900	32029	Storey County	41500		Salinas, CA
39900	32031	Washoe County	41500	06053	Monterey County
40060		Richmond, VA	41540		Salisbury, MD-DE
40060	51007	Amelia County	41540	10005	Sussex County, DE
40060	51036	Charles City County	41540	24039	Somerset County, MD
40060	51041	Chesterfield County	41540	24045	Wicomico County, MD
40060	51075	Goochland County	41540	24047	Worcester County, MD
40060	51085	Hanover County	41620		Salt Lake City, UT
40060	51087	Henrico County	41620	49035	Salt Lake County
40060	51097	King and Queen County	41620	49045	Tooele County
40060	51101	King William County	41660		San Angelo, TX
40060	51127	New Kent County	41660	48235	Irion County
40060	51145	Powhatan County	41660	48431	Sterling County
40060	51183	Sussex County	41660	48451	Tom Green County
40060	51760	Richmond city	41700		San Antonio-New Braunfels, TX
40060	51918	Dinwiddie, Colonial Heights + Petersburg, VA	41700	48013	Atascosa County
40060	51941	Prince George + Hopewell, VA	41700	48019	Bandera County
40140		Riverside-San Bernardino-Ontario, CA	41700	48029	Bexar County
40140	06065	Riverside County	41700	48091	Comal County
40140	06071	San Bernardino County	41700	48187	Guadalupe County
40220		Roanoke, VA	41700	48259	Kendall County
40220	51023	Botetourt County	41700	48325	Medina County
40220	51045	Craig County	41700	48493	Wilson County
40220	51067	Franklin County	41740		San Diego-Chula Vista-Carlsbad, CA
40220	51770	Roanoke city	41740	06073	San Diego County
40220	51944	Roanoke + Salem, VA	41860		San Francisco-Oakland-Berkeley, CA
40340		Rochester, MN	41860		Oakland-Berkeley-Livermore, CA Div 36084
40340	27039	Dodge County	41860	06001	Alameda County

Metropolitan Statistical Areas, Metropolitan Divisions, and Components—*Continued*

Core based statistical area (CBSA)	State/County FIPS code	Title and Geographic Components
41860	06013	Contra Costa County
41860		San Francisco-San Mateo-Redwood City, CA Div 41884
41860	06075	San Francisco County
41860	06081	San Mateo County
41860		San Rafael, CA Div 42034
41860	06041	Marin County
41940		San Jose-Sunnyvale-Santa Clara, CA
41940	06069	San Benito County
41940	06085	Santa Clara County
42020		San Luis Obispo-Paso Robles, CA
42020	06079	San Luis Obispo County
42100		Santa Cruz-Watsonville, CA
42100	06087	Santa Cruz County
42140		Santa Fe, NM
42140	35049	Santa Fe County
42200		Santa Maria-Santa Barbara, CA
42200	06083	Santa Barbara County
42220		Santa Rosa-Petaluma, CA
42220	06097	Sonoma County
42340		Savannah, GA
42340	13029	Bryan County
42340	13051	Chatham County
42340	13103	Effingham County
42540		Scranton—Wilkes-Barre, PA
42540	42069	Lackawanna County
42540	42079	Luzerne County
42540	42131	Wyoming County
42660		Seattle-Tacoma-Bellevue, WA
42660		Seattle-Bellevue-Kent, WA Div 42644
42660	53033	King County
42660	53061	Snohomish County
42660		Tacoma-Lakewood, WA Div 45104
42660	53053	Pierce County
42680		Sebastian-Vero Beach, FL
42680	12061	Indian River County
42700		Sebring-Avon Park, FL
42700	12055	Highlands County
43100		Sheboygan, WI
43100	55117	Sheboygan County
43300		Sherman-Denison, TX
43300	48181	Grayson County
43340		Shreveport-Bossier City, LA
43340	22015	Bossier Parish
43340	22017	Caddo Parish
43340	22031	De Soto Parish
43420		Sierra Vista-Douglas, AZ
43420	04003	Cochise County
43580		Sioux City, IA-NE-SD
43580	19193	Woodbury County, IA
43580	31043	Dakota County, NE
43580	31051	Dixon County, NE
43580	46127	Union County, SD
43620		Sioux Falls, SD
43620	46083	Lincoln County
43620	46087	McCook County
43620	46099	Minnehaha County
43620	46125	Turner County
43780		South Bend-Mishawaka, IN-MI
43780	18141	St. Joseph County, IN
43780	26027	Cass County, MI
43900		Spartanburg, SC
43900	45083	Spartanburg County
44060		Spokane-Spokane Valley, WA
44060	53063	Spokane County
44060	53065	Stevens County
44100		Springfield, IL
44100	17129	Menard County
44100	17167	Sangamon County
44140		Springfield, MA
44140	25011	Franklin County
44140	25013	Hampden County
44140	25015	Hampshire County
44180		Springfield, MO
44180	29043	Christian County
44180	29059	Dallas County
44180	29077	Greene County
44180	29167	Polk County
44180	29225	Webster County
44220		Springfield, OH
44220	39023	Clark County
44300		State College, PA
44300	42027	Centre County
44420		Staunton, VA
44420	51907	Augusta County + Staunton + Waynesboro, VA
44700		Stockton, CA
44700	06077	San Joaquin County
44940		Sumter, SC
44940	45027	Clarendon County
44940	45085	Sumter County
45060		Syracuse, NY
45060	36053	Madison County
45060	36067	Onondaga County
45060	36075	Oswego County
45220		Tallahassee, FL
45220	12039	Gadsden County
45220	12065	Jefferson County
45220	12073	Leon County
45220	12129	Wakulla County
45300		Tampa-St. Petersburg-Clearwater, FL
45300	12053	Hernando County
45300	12057	Hillsborough County
45300	12101	Pasco County
45300	12103	Pinellas County
45460		Terre Haute, IN
45460	18021	Clay County
45460	18121	Parke County
45460	18153	Sullivan County
45460	18165	Vermillion County
45460	18167	Vigo County
45500		Texarkana, TX-AR
45500	05081	Little River County, AR
45500	05091	Miller County, AR
45500	48037	Bowie County, TX
45540		The Villages, FL
45540	12119	Sumter County
45780		Toledo, OH
45780	39051	Fulton County
45780	39095	Lucas County
45780	39123	Ottawa County
45780	39173	Wood County
45820		Topeka, KS
45820	20085	Jackson County
45820	20087	Jefferson County
45820	20139	Osage County
45820	20177	Shawnee County
45820	20197	Wabaunsee County
45940		Trenton-Princeton, NJ
45940	34021	Mercer County
46060		Tucson, AZ
46060	04019	Pima County
46140		Tulsa, OK
46140	40037	Creek County
46140	40111	Okmulgee County
46140	40113	Osage County
46140	40117	Pawnee County
46140	40131	Rogers County
46140	40143	Tulsa County
46140	40145	Wagoner County
46220		Tuscaloosa, AL
46220	01063	Greene County
46220	01065	Hale County
46220	01107	Pickens County
46220	01125	Tuscaloosa County
46300		Twin Falls, ID
46300	16053	Jerome County
46300	16083	Twin Falls County
46340		Tyler, TX
46340	48423	Smith County
46520		Urban Honolulu, HI
46520	15003	Honolulu County
46540		Utica-Rome, NY
46540	36043	Herkimer County
46540	36065	Oneida County
46660		Valdosta, GA
46660	13027	Brooks County
46660	13101	Echols County
46660	13173	Lanier County
46660	13185	Lowndes County
46700		Vallejo, CA
46700	06095	Solano County
47020		Victoria, TX
47020	48175	Goliad County
47020	48469	Victoria County
47220		Vineland-Bridgeton, NJ
47220	34011	Cumberland County
47260		Virginia Beach-Norfolk-Newport News, VA-NC

Metropolitan Statistical Areas, Metropolitan Divisions, and Components—*Continued*

Core based statistical area (CBSA)	State/ County FIPS code	Title and Geographic Components	Core based statistical area (CBSA)	State/ County FIPS code	Title and Geographic Components
47260	37029	Camden County, NC	48060	36045	Jefferson County
47260	37053	Currituck County, NC	48140		Wausau-Weston, WI
47260	37073	Gates County, NC	48140	55069	Lincoln County
47260	51073	Gloucester County, VA	48140	55073	Marathon County
47260	51093	Isle of Wight County, VA	48260		Weirton-Steubenville, WV-OH
47260	51115	Mathews County, VA	48260	39081	Jefferson County, OH
47260	51175	Southampton County, VA	48260	54009	Brooke County, WV
47260	51550	Chesapeake city, VA	48260	54029	Hancock County, WV
47260	51650	Hampton city, VA	48300		Wenatchee, WA
47260	51700	Newport News city, VA	48300	53007	Chelan County
47260	51710	Norfolk city, VA	48300	53017	Douglas County
47260	51735	Poquoson city, VA	48540		Wheeling, WV-OH
47260	51740	Portsmouth city, VA	48540	39013	Belmont County, OH
47260	51800	Suffolk city, VA	48540	54051	Marshall County, WV
47260	51810	Virginia Beach city, VA	48540	54069	Ohio County, WV
47260	51931	James City County + Williamsburg, VA	48620		Wichita, KS
47300		Visalia, CA	48620	20015	Butler County
47300	06107	Tulare County	48620	20079	Harvey County
47380		Waco, TX	48620	20173	Sedgwick County
47380	48145	Falls County	48620	20191	Sumner County
47380	48309	McLennan County	48660		Wichita Falls, TX
47460		Walla Walla, WA	48660	48009	Archer County
47460	53071	Walla Walla County	48660	48077	Clay County
47580		Warner Robins, GA	48660	48485	Wichita County
47580	13153	Houston County	48700		Williamsport, PA
47580	13225	Peach County	48700	42081	Lycoming County
47900		Washington-Arlington-Alexandria, DC-VA-MD-WV	48900		Wilmington, NC
47900		Frederick-Gaithersburg-Rockville, MD Div 23224	48900	37129	New Hanover County
47900	24021	Frederick County, MD	48900	37141	Pender County
47900	24031	Montgomery County, MD	49020		Winchester, VA-WV
47900		Washington-Arlington-Alexandria, DC-VA-MD-WV Div 47894	49020	51921	Frederick County + Winchester, VA
47900	11001	District of Columbia, DC	49020	54027	Hampshire County, WV
47900	24009	Calvert County, MD	49180		Winston-Salem, NC
47900	24017	Charles County, MD	49180	37057	Davidson County
47900	24033	Prince George's County, MD	49180	37059	Davie County
47900	51013	Arlington County, VA	49180	37067	Forsyth County
47900	51043	Clarke County, VA	49180	37169	Stokes County
47900	51047	Culpeper County, VA	49180	37197	Yadkin County
47900	51061	Fauquier County, VA	49340		Worcester, MA-CT
47900	51107	Loudoun County, VA	49340	09015	Windham County, CT
47900	51113	Madison County, VA	49340	25027	Worcester County, MA
47900	51157	Rappahannock County, VA	49420		Yakima, WA
47900	51179	Stafford County, VA	49420	53077	Yakima County
47900	51187	Warren County, VA	49620		York-Hanover, PA
47900	51510	Alexandria city, VA	49620	42133	York County
47900	51919	Fairfax County + Fairfax + Falls Church, VA	49660		Youngstown-Warren-Boardman, OH-PA
47900	51942	Prince William County + Manassas + Manassas Park, VA	49660	39099	Mahoning County, OH
47900	51951	Spotsylvania County + Fredericksburg, VA	49660	39155	Trumbull County, OH
47900	54037	Jefferson County, WV	49660	42085	Mercer County, PA
47940		Waterloo-Cedar Falls, IA	49700		Yuba City, CA
47940	19013	Black Hawk County	49700	06101	Sutter County
47940	19017	Bremer County	49700	06115	Yuba County
47940	19075	Grundy County	49740		Yuma, AZ
48060		Watertown-Fort Drum, NY	49740	04027	Yuma County